EMPLOYMENT, HOURS, AND EARNINGS

STATES AND AREAS

11th Edition
2016

EMPLOYMENT, HOURS, AND EARNINGS

STATES AND AREAS

11th Edition
2016

Edited by Mary Meghan Ryan

Lanham, MD

Published in the United States of America
by Bernan Press, a wholly owned subsidiary of
The Rowman & Littlefield Publishing Group, Inc.
4501 Forbes Boulevard, Suite 200
Lanham, Maryland 20706

Bernan Press
800-462-6420
www.rowman.com

Copyright © 2017 by Bernan Press

ISBN-13: 978-1-59888-867-6
e-ISBN-13: 978-1-59888-868-3

∞™ The paper used in this publication meets the minimum requirements of
American National Standard for Information Sciences—Permanence of
Paper for Printed Library Materials, ANSI/NISO Z39.48-1992.
Manufactured in the United States of America.

CONTENTS

PART B: METROPOLITAN STATISTICAL AREA (MSA) DATA

PART B: METROPOLITAN STATISTICAL AREA (MSA) DATA—*Continued*

APPENDIX

Bernan Press proudly presents the 11th edition of *Employment, Hours, and Earnings: States and Areas, 2016*. A special addition to Bernan Press's *Handbook of U.S. Labor Statistics: Employment, Earnings, Prices, Productivity, and Other Labor Data*, this reference is a consolidated wealth of employment information, providing monthly and annual data on hours worked and earnings made by industry across America for the years 2005 through 2015, including figures and summary information spanning years the same time period. These data, compiled by the Bureau of Labor Statistics, are presented for states and metropolitan statistical areas.

This edition features:

- Nearly 300 tables with data on employment for each state, the District of Columbia, and the nation's 75 largest metropolitan statistical areas (MSAs)

- Detailed, non-seasonally adjusted, industry data organized by month and year

- Hours and earnings data for each state, by industry

- An introduction for each state and the District of Columbia that denotes salient data and noteworthy trends, including changes in population and the civilian labor force, industry increases and declines, employment and unemployment statistics, and a chart detailing employment percentages, by industry

- Ranking of the 75 largest MSAs, including Census population estimates for 2015, unemployment rates for 2005, 2010, and 2015, and the percent change in total nonfarm employment from 2005 through 2015

- Concise technical notes that explain pertinent facts about the data, including sources, definitions, and significant changes; and provides references for further guidance

- A comprehensive appendix that details the geographical components of the 75 largest MSAs

The employment, hours, and earnings data in this publication provide a detailed and timely picture of the 50 states, the District of Columbia, and the nation's 75 largest MSAs. These data can be used to analyze key factors affecting state and local economies and to compare national cyclical trends to local-level economic activity.

This reference is an excellent source of information for analysts in both the public and private sectors. Readers who are involved in public policy can use these data to determine the health of the economy, to clearly identify which sectors are growing and which are declining, and to determine the need for federal assistance. State and local jurisdictions can use the data to determine the need for services, including training and unemployment assistance, and for planning and budgetary purposes. In addition, the data can be used to forecast tax revenue. In private industry, the data can be used by business owners to compare their business to the economy as a whole; and to identify suitable areas when making decisions about plant locations, wholesale and retail trade outlets, and for locating a particular sector base.

In this 11th edition, *Employment, Hours, and Earnings: States and Areas* presents monthly and annual average data on employment for each state, the District of Columbia, and the nation's 75 largest metropolitan statistical areas (MSAs). In addition, hours and earnings data are provided, where available, for each state. The industry data are based on the North American Industry Classification System (NAICS), which is discussed in greater detail later in these notes. The employment data are presented on a monthly and annual basis for 2005 through 2015. The hours and earnings data are available from 2011 through 2015.

The Bureau of Labor Statistics (BLS), the statistical agency within the U.S. Department of Labor, conducts the Current Employment Statistics (CES) survey to provide industry data on the employment, hours, and earnings of workers on nonfarm payrolls. The unemployment data and the civilian labor force estimates in this publication were obtained from the Local Area Unemployment Statistics (LAUS) program, which provides monthly employment and unemployment data for approximately 7,500 geographic areas including Census regions and divisions, states, counties, metropolitan areas, and many cities and towns.

The data from both the CES and LAUS are derived from federal and state cooperative collection efforts in which state employment security agencies prepare data using concepts, definitions, and technical procedures prescribed by the BLS. Although the estimation of the two data sets are based on differing methodologies (described in more detail later in this section), their inclusion together in this reference is intended to provide a broad overview of state and local labor market conditions.

THE CURRENT EMPLOYMENT STATISTICS (CES) SURVEY—EMPLOYMENT, HOURS, AND EARNINGS DATA

The CES survey is a monthly survey commonly referred to as the establishment or payroll survey that provides estimates of employment, hours, and earnings data by industry. Its estimates are derived from a sample of about 146,000 private nonfarm businesses and federal, state, and local government entities, which cover approximately 623,000 individual worksites in all 50 states, the District of Columbia, Puerto Rico, the U.S. Virgin Islands, and about 450 metropolitan areas and divisions. These establishments are classified on the basis of their primary activity by major industry groupings in accordance with NAICS. For an establishment engaging in more than one activity, the entire establishment is included under the industry indicated as the principal activity.

All establishments with 1,000 employees or more are asked to participate in the survey, along with a representative sample of smaller businesses. The BLS Regional Data Collection Centers gather the data every month. Each firm is initially enrolled by telephone and the data is then collected for several months by a process called Computer Assisted Telephone Interviewing (CATI). Whenever possible, respondents are transferred to a self-reporting mode such as Touchtone Data Entry (TDE), fax, or Internet collection. Gathering data via the Internet is one of the fastest growing forms of data collection, but still remains a relatively small percentage of the total data collected each month. Electronic Data Interchange (EDI), in which each firm provides the BLS with an electronic file in a prescribed format, remains the most popular method for collecting data.

State estimation procedures are designed to produce accurate data for each individual state. The BLS independently develops the national series and does not force state estimates to sum to the national total. Because each state series is subject to larger sampling and nonsampling errors than the national series, summing them cumulates individual state level errors and can cause significant distortions at an aggregate level. As a result of these statistical limitations, the BLS does not compile a "sum of states" employment series, and cautions users that doing so may result in a series with a relatively large and volatile error structure.

More information on the exact methodology used to obtain data for employment, hours, and earnings was originally detailed in the *BLS Handbook of Methods*. The *Handbook* is updated online and can be found at www.bls.gov/opub/hom. Information on the CES survey can also be found on the BLS website at www.bls.gov/ces/cesprog.htm.

CONCEPTS

Employment is the total number of persons employed either full or part-time in nonfarm business establishments during a specific payroll period. Temporary employees are included as well as civilian government employees. Unpaid family members working in a family-owned business, domestic workers in private homes, farm employees, and self-employed persons are excluded from the CES, as well as military personnel and employees of the Central Intelligence Agency, the National Security Agency, the National Imagery and Mapping Agency, and the Defense Intelligence Agency. In addition, employees on layoff, on leave without pay, on strike for the entire pay period, or who had been hired but did not start work during the pay period are also excluded.

The reference period includes all persons who worked during or received pay for any part of the pay period that includes the 12th of the month, a standard for all federal agencies collecting employment data from business xii EMPLOYMENT, HOURS, AND EARNINGS: STATES AND AREAS (BERNAN PRESS)

establishments. Workers who are on paid sick leave (when pay is received directly from the employer) or paid holiday or vacation, or who worked during only part of the specified pay period (because of unemployment or strike during the rest of the pay period) are counted as employed. Employees on the payroll of more than one establishment during the pay period are counted in each establishment that reports them, whether the duplication is due to turnover or dual jobholding.

Nonfarm employment includes employment in all goods-producing and service-providing industries. The goods-producing sector includes mining and logging, construction, and manufacturing, the last of which is made up of durable and nondurable goods (these breakdowns are not provided in this publication). The service-providing sector includes both private service-providing and government employment. Private service sector employment includes trade, transportation, and utilities (which is comprised of wholesale trade, retail trade, and transportation and utilities); information; financial activities; professional and business services; educational and health services; leisure and hospitality; and other services. Government employment encompasses federal-, state-, and local-level civilian employees. Subcategories of these industries are available on the BLS website at www.bls.gov/sae.

Unemployment consists of those who were not employed during the reference week but were available for work, except for temporary illness, and had made specific efforts to find employment some time during the 4-week period ending with the reference week. Persons who were waiting to be recalled to a job from which they had been laid off are classified as unemployed even if they have not been looking for another job.

The *unemployment rate* is the number of unemployed persons as a percent of the civilian labor force.

The *civilian labor force* consists of all persons classified as employed or unemployed as described above.

Hours and earnings data for each state are based on reports from industry payrolls and the corresponding hours paid for construction workers, production workers, and nonsupervisory workers. The data include workers who received pay for any part of the pay period that includes the 12th day of the month. Because not all sample respondents report production worker hours and earnings data, insufficient sample sizes preclude hours and earnings data from many sectors in many states. Therefore, the data available, and thus published, vary from state to state.

The payroll for these workers is reported before deductions of any kind, including Social Security, unemployment insurance, group health insurance, withholding taxes, retirement plans, or union dues.

Included in the payroll report of earnings is pay for all hours worked, including overtime, shift premiums, vacations, holiday, and sick-leave pay. Bonuses and commissions are excluded unless they are earned and paid regularly each pay period. Benefits, such as health insurance and contribution to a retirement fund, are also excluded.

Hours include all hours worked (including overtime hours) and hours paid for holidays, vacations, and sick leave during the pay period that includes the 12th day of the month. Average weekly hours differ from the concept of scheduled hours worked because of factors such as unpaid absenteeism, labor turnover, part-time work, and strikes, as well as fluctuations in work schedules. Average weekly hours are typically lower than scheduled hours of work.

Average hourly earnings are derived by dividing gross payrolls by total hours, reflecting the actual earnings of workers (including premium pay). They differ from wage rates, which are the amounts stipulated for a given unit of work or time. Average hourly earnings do not represent total labor costs per hour because they exclude retroactive payments and irregular bonuses, employee benefits, and the employer's share of payroll taxes. Earnings for employees not included in the production worker or nonsupervisory categories are not reflected in the estimates in this publication.

Average weekly earnings are derived by multiplying average weekly hours by average hourly earnings.

Users should note that in the context of historical data, long-term trends in hours and earnings data also reflect structural changes, such as the changing mixes of full-time and part-time employees and highly paid and lower-wage workers within businesses and across industries.

METROPOLITAN STATISTICAL AREAS (MSAs) AND NEW ENGLAND CITY AND TOWN AREAS (NECTAs)

A metropolitan statistical area (MSA) is a core area with a large population nucleus, combined with adjacent communities that have high degrees of economic and social integration with the core area. The standard definition of a MSA is determined by the Office of Management and Budget (OMB), which updates the definition based on the decennial census and updated information provided by the Census Bureau between the censuses. Each MSA must have at least one urbanized area of 50,000 inhabitants or more.

New England city and town areas (NECTAs) are similar to MSAs, but are defined using cities and towns instead of counties in the six New England states. BLS only provides employment data on NECTAs in the New England region. Employment and Unemployment data are provided for the following NECTAs in this publication: Boston–Cambridge–Newton, MA–NH; Bridgeport–Stamford–Norwalk, CT; Hartford–West Hartford–East Hartford, CT; New Haven, CT; Providence–Warwick, RI–MA; and Worcester, MA–CT. All other areas are MSAs.

The appendix details the geographic components for each MSA and NECTA.

REVISIONS TO THE DATA

North American Industry Classification System (NAICS)

The most far-reaching revision of the CES data occurred when the industrial classification system was changed from the 60-year-old Standard Industrial Classification (SIC) system to the North American Industry Classification System (NAICS) in January 2003. The revision changed the way establishments were classified into industries in order to more accurately reflect the current composition of U.S. businesses. In March 2008, the CES state and area nonfarm payroll series was converted to the 2007 NAICS series. This resulted in relatively minor changes. In February 2012, CES updated the national payroll series to NAICS 2012 from NAICS 2007. This resulted in minor content changes within the Manufacturing and Retail trade sectors as well as minor coding changes within the Utilities and Leisure and hospitality sectors. Several industry titles and descriptions were updated as well. More information on the NAICS conversion can be found at www.bls.gov/ces/cesnaics12.htm.

NAICS was adopted as the standard measure of industry classification by statistical agencies in the United States, Canada, and Mexico to enhance the comparability of economic data across the North American Free Trade Association (NAFTA) trade area. Comparison between the NAICS and the old SIC are limited, however, the historical industry series from April 1995 through 2001 are available on both SIC and NAICS bases. The BLS has not updated the SIC data nor (for the most part) linked the historical SIC data with the current NAICS data.

Benchmark Revisions

Employment estimates are adjusted annually to a complete count of jobs—called benchmarks—which are primarily derived from tax reports submitted by employers covered by state unemployment laws (which cover most establishments). In this re-anchoring of sample-based employment estimates to full population counts, the original sample-based estimates are replaced with the benchmark data from the previous year. The benchmark information is used to adjust monthly estimates between the new benchmark and the preceding benchmark, thereby preserving the continuity of the series and establishing the level of employment for the new benchmark month.

Seasonal Adjustment

Over the course of a year, the size of a state's employment level undergoes sharp fluctuations because of changes in the weather, reduced or expanded production, harvests, major holidays, and the like. Because these seasonal events follow a more or less regular pattern each year, adjusting the data on a month-to-month basis may eliminate their influence on data trends. These adjustments make it easier for users to observe the cyclical and other nonseasonal movements in the data series, but it must be noted that the seasonally adjusted series are only an approximation based on past experience. The seasonally adjusted data have a broader margin of error than the unadjusted data because they are subject to both sampling and other errors in the seasonal adjustment process. The data presented in this publication are not seasonally adjusted; therefore, the month-to-month variations in the data contain seasonal variations that may distort month-to-month comparisons. Data for the MSAs are also not seasonally adjusted, as the sample sizes do not allow for reliable estimates for seasonal adjustment factors.

THE LOCAL AREA UNEMPLOYMENT STATISTICS (LAUS) PROGRAM

The Local Area Unemployment Statistics (LAUS) program provides monthly and annual estimates on several labor force concepts, including employment, unemployment, labor force totals, and the employment-population ratio. The unemployment data as well as the civilian labor force estimates presented in this publication are from the LAUS program. The unemployment rate is shown for each state in 2005, 2010, and 2015 along with the rank for each state. The rankings are from highest to lowest—a change from earlier editions of *Employment, Hours, and Earnings* but consistent with the 10th edition which was published last year. In 2015, unemployment ranged from a high of 6.9 percent in the District of Columbia, to a low of 2.7 percent in North Dakota. Therefore, North Dakota is ranked last and the District of Columbia is ranked first. Unemployment data are not available by industry.

The concepts and definitions underlying the LAUS program come from the Current Population Survey (CPS), the household survey conducted by the Census Bureau for the BLS. The LAUS models combine current and historical data from the CPS, Current Employment Statistics (CES), and the State Unemployment Insurance (UI) Systems. Numerous conceptual and technical differences exist between the household and establishment surveys, and estimates of monthly employment changes from these two surveys usually do not match in size or even direction. As a result, the unemployment data and the civilian labor force estimates on each state header page presented in this edition are not directly comparable to the employment data. However, this publication includes this information to provide complementary information on labor market conditions in each state and the District of Columbia. Monthly and annual data are available from the BLS on their website at www.bls.gov/lau. More information on the differences between the surveys, as well as guidance on the complex methods used to obtain the LAUS data, is provided on the BLS website at www.bls.gov/lau/laufaq.htm.

PART A

STATE DATA

ALABAMA
At a Glance

Population:
  2005 estimate: 4,569,805
  2010 census: 4,779,736
  2015 estimate: 4,858,979

Percent change in population:
  2005–2015: 6.3%
  2010–2015: 1.7%

Percent change in total nonfarm employment:
  2005–2015: 0.1%

Industry with the largest growth in employment, 2005–2015 (thousands):
  Education and health services, 27.7

Industry with the largest decline or smallest growth in employment, 2005–2015 (thousands):
  Manufacturing, –41.2

Civilian labor force:
  2005: 2,146,025
  2010: 2,196,042
  2015: 2,146,157

Unemployment rate and rank among states (highest to lowest):
  2005: 4.5%, 32nd
  2010: 10.5%, 9th
  2015: 6.1%, 9th

Over-the-year change in unemployment rates:
  2012–2013: –0.8%
  2013–2014: –0.4%
  2014–2015: –0.7%

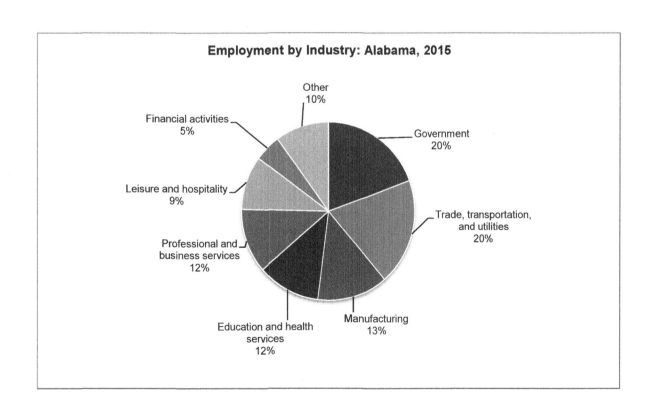

Employment by Industry: Alabama, 2015

Other 10%
Government 20%
Trade, transportation, and utilities 20%
Manufacturing 13%
Education and health services 12%
Professional and business services 12%
Leisure and hospitality 9%
Financial activities 5%

1. Employment by Industry: Alabama, 2005–2015

(Numbers in thousands, not seasonally adjusted)

Industry and year	January	February	March	April	May	June	July	August	September	October	November	December	Annual average
Total Nonfarm													
2005	1,899.8	1,910.5	1,925.1	1,943.1	1,948.2	1,951.4	1,939.6	1,947.9	1,958.2	1,961.9	1,974.2	1,979.2	1,944.9
2006	1,944.9	1,956.1	1,974.5	1,978.5	1,984.2	1,994.6	1,972.0	1,981.0	1,990.4	1,984.2	1,994.6	2,000.1	1,979.6
2007	1,974.9	1,987.3	2,004.4	2,000.9	2,009.4	2,018.4	1,994.0	2,004.4	2,013.3	2,012.4	2,022.0	2,026.7	2,005.7
2008	1,986.0	1,994.5	2,002.7	2,008.7	2,012.5	2,012.1	1,989.0	1,991.1	1,992.2	1,981.3	1,970.9	1,964.4	1,992.1
2009	1,905.6	1,899.9	1,900.1	1,900.1	1,899.7	1,895.5	1,873.5	1,870.8	1,872.6	1,868.4	1,875.8	1,876.0	1,886.5
2010	1,840.1	1,844.6	1,860.7	1,872.1	1,888.2	1,889.3	1,870.4	1,868.7	1,872.3	1,877.1	1,883.4	1,882.4	1,870.8
2011	1,839.4	1,853.3	1,865.6	1,875.0	1,877.8	1,878.2	1,863.2	1,868.3	1,879.6	1,873.5	1,883.6	1,882.7	1,870.0
2012	1,850.5	1,862.1	1,880.4	1,889.1	1,892.9	1,897.2	1,874.0	1,884.2	1,890.6	1,892.5	1,904.7	1,903.0	1,885.1
2013	1,865.7	1,881.2	1,896.3	9.0	1,912.5	1,914.8	1,895.9	1,903.5	1,905.8	1,907.4	1,919.3	1,923.7	1,902.6
2014	1,885.4	1,893.0	1,908.2	1,922.1	1,929.4	1,932.4	1,914.2	1,925.2	1,931.2	1,935.9	1,943.7	1,950.1	1,922.6
2015	1,911.5	1,922.2	1,931.6	1,945.9	1,956.3	1,957.5	1,945.3	1,951.2	1,951.9	1,957.9	1,971.2	1,965.0	1,947.3
Total Private													
2005	1,539.7	1,547.5	1,561.6	1,578.3	1,582.7	1,587.2	1,587.2	1,592.8	1,595.3	1,594.5	1,606.1	1,611.4	1,582.0
2006	1,578.2	1,587.1	1,603.9	1,606.4	1,611.2	1,622.4	1,612.0	1,618.4	1,618.8	1,610.3	1,619.8	1,624.8	1,609.4
2007	1,600.7	1,610.7	1,626.5	1,622.5	1,630.1	1,639.3	1,629.4	1,635.8	1,635.5	1,632.0	1,640.1	1,644.9	1,629.0
2008	1,605.7	1,610.4	1,617.4	1,622.1	1,624.4	1,624.2	1,616.8	1,616.1	1,609.1	1,593.7	1,583.7	1,576.6	1,608.4
2009	1,522.5	1,514.7	1,514.0	1,511.6	1,510.9	1,507.9	1,502.3	1,497.6	1,490.6	1,481.6	1,488.5	1,488.0	1,502.5
2010	1,456.0	1,458.0	1,471.1	1,480.9	1,487.9	1,494.7	1,494.2	1,492.6	1,488.4	1,490.1	1,495.2	1,494.3	1,483.6
2011	1,455.2	1,466.6	1,477.8	1,487.2	1,490.4	1,494.0	1,491.6	1,497.0	1,499.4	1,491.7	1,500.3	1,501.8	1,487.8
2012	1,472.4	1,480.7	1,496.9	1,506.4	1,510.9	1,517.8	1,508.2	1,517.8	1,516.0	1,512.8	1,523.7	1,522.8	1,507.2
2013	1,489.3	1,501.0	1,513.9	1,523.0	1,530.8	1,536.6	1,526.7	1,534.2	1,531.1	1,528.7	1,539.1	1,545.0	1,525.0
2014	1,509.3	1,514.1	1,527.9	1,540.7	1,546.6	1,551.6	1,546.8	1,555.4	1,553.6	1,555.4	1,562.1	1,568.5	1,544.3
2015	1,535.6	1,544.0	1,552.5	1,565.3	1,574.1	1,577.3	1,577.0	1,580.4	1,575.4	1,579.1	1,592.3	1,587.4	1,570.0
Goods-Producing													
2005	405.6	406.8	411.0	416.8	417.5	417.5	418.0	419.6	421.3	422.2	424.6	425.4	417.2
2006	421.6	423.7	427.6	427.9	428.0	430.5	427.7	427.2	426.6	423.3	422.3	422.6	425.8
2007	420.1	421.6	423.9	420.9	421.3	423.9	421.0	421.8	423.2	423.0	421.0	420.6	421.9
2008	413.2	412.5	412.1	411.1	411.2	411.1	409.0	406.0	404.6	397.1	389.8	386.1	405.3
2009	369.7	363.7	360.9	356.0	352.9	348.9	347.3	344.3	342.3	339.5	339.2	339.1	350.3
2010	332.1	331.5	334.3	336.6	338.3	339.4	338.6	337.4	336.8	335.3	333.9	331.9	335.5
2011	322.5	326.3	329.0	330.0	331.5	332.5	331.2	332.6	332.7	331.4	332.4	333.8	330.5
2012	328.5	329.9	333.3	335.1	335.5	336.9	336.7	338.2	337.9	339.0	339.0	339.6	335.8
2013	334.7	336.1	340.5	341.0	340.9	342.6	340.7	342.2	341.6	341.9	341.7	343.2	340.6
2014	338.5	339.2	341.7	342.5	344.0	345.5	345.1	346.6	347.5	348.6	348.4	349.5	344.8
2015	345.5	346.8	347.5	348.5	349.8	351.3	351.2	351.5	351.6	350.4	350.6	349.4	349.5
Service-Providing													
2005	1,494.2	1,503.7	1,514.1	1,526.3	1,530.7	1,533.9	1,521.6	1,528.3	1,536.9	1,539.7	1,549.6	1,553.8	1,527.7
2006	1,523.3	1,532.4	1,546.9	1,550.6	1,556.2	1,564.1	1,544.3	1,553.8	1,563.8	1,560.9	1,572.3	1,577.5	1,553.8
2007	1,554.8	1,565.7	1,580.5	1,580.0	1,588.1	1,594.5	1,573.0	1,582.6	1,590.1	1,589.4	1,601.0	1,606.1	1,583.8
2008	1,572.8	1,582.0	1,590.6	1,597.6	1,601.3	1,601.0	1,580.0	1,585.1	1,587.6	1,584.2	1,581.1	1,578.3	1,586.8
2009	1,535.9	1,536.2	1,539.2	1,544.1	1,546.8	1,546.6	1,526.2	1,526.5	1,530.3	1,528.9	1,536.6	1,536.9	1,536.2
2010	1,508.0	1,513.1	1,526.4	1,535.5	1,549.9	1,549.9	1,531.8	1,531.3	1,535.5	1,541.8	1,549.5	1,550.5	1,535.3
2011	1,516.9	1,527.0	1,536.6	1,545.0	1,546.3	1,545.7	1,532.0	1,535.7	1,546.9	1,542.1	1,551.2	1,548.9	1,539.5
2012	1,522.0	1,532.2	1,547.1	1,554.0	1,557.4	1,560.3	1,537.3	1,546.0	1,552.7	1,553.5	1,565.7	1,563.4	1,549.3
2013	1,531.0	1,545.1	1,555.8	1,564.3	1,571.6	1,572.2	1,555.2	1,561.3	1,564.2	1,565.5	1,577.6	1,580.5	1,562.0
2014	1,546.9	1,553.8	1,566.5	1,579.6	1,585.4	1,586.9	1,569.1	1,578.6	1,583.7	1,587.3	1,595.3	1,600.6	1,577.8
2015	1,566.0	1,575.4	1,584.1	1,597.4	1,606.5	1,606.2	1,594.1	1,599.7	1,600.3	1,607.5	1,620.6	1,615.6	1,597.8
Mining and Logging													
2005	12.7	12.7	12.7	12.8	13.0	13.0	13.1	13.0	13.2	13.0	13.1	13.1	13.0
2006	13.0	13.1	13.1	13.0	13.0	13.2	13.1	13.1	13.2	12.9	13.0	13.1	13.1
2007	12.9	13.0	13.1	12.8	12.9	12.9	12.8	12.9	12.8	12.8	12.7	12.8	12.9
2008	12.5	12.6	12.6	12.6	12.4	12.5	12.6	12.6	12.7	12.6	12.5	12.5	12.6
2009	12.2	12.2	11.9	11.8	11.7	11.8	11.8	11.6	11.7	11.7	11.7	11.6	11.8
2010	11.7	11.7	11.7	11.9	12.0	12.0	12.1	12.2	12.1	12.3	12.2	12.2	12.0
2011	12.1	12.1	12.1	12.3	12.4	12.5	12.3	12.5	12.6	12.5	12.5	12.6	12.4
2012	12.7	12.6	12.5	12.5	12.5	12.6	12.8	12.8	12.7	12.6	12.6	12.6	12.6
2013	12.3	12.3	12.4	12.1	12.2	12.3	11.9	12.0	12.0	11.9	11.9	11.9	12.1
2014	11.8	11.6	11.7	11.7	11.6	11.7	11.8	11.8	11.8	11.7	11.6	11.5	11.7
2015	11.5	11.4	11.3	11.2	11.2	11.2	11.1	11.0	10.8	10.9	10.8	10.7	11.1

1. Employment by Industry: Alabama, 2005–2015—*Continued*

(Numbers in thousands, not seasonally adjusted)

Industry and year	January	February	March	April	May	June	July	August	September	October	November	December	Annual average
Construction													
2005	100.6	101.6	104.2	106.2	105.4	105.2	105.2	106.2	107.0	108.6	108.6	107.5	105.5
2006	105.1	106.2	109.5	110.2	110.2	111.1	110.4	111.0	111.7	111.1	111.0	110.2	109.8
2007	109.4	110.7	113.2	112.0	112.3	113.1	112.0	113.2	114.7	114.9	113.6	113.1	112.7
2008	109.5	110.0	110.4	110.3	110.9	110.7	110.1	109.0	108.8	105.9	103.8	102.3	108.5
2009	94.8	93.6	94.3	92.9	93.3	92.9	92.0	90.5	89.7	88.5	89.0	89.3	91.7
2010	85.4	85.4	87.4	88.2	89.1	90.2	89.3	88.2	87.8	86.8	85.1	83.5	87.2
2011	77.2	79.2	81.1	80.8	82.0	81.8	81.2	81.1	81.9	81.0	80.7	80.6	80.7
2012	76.7	77.7	79.9	80.3	79.9	80.0	79.7	80.2	80.2	80.7	80.0	79.3	79.6
2013	76.5	76.9	79.9	80.4	79.9	80.1	79.5	80.1	79.4	80.0	78.7	79.3	79.2
2014	76.2	77.4	79.0	79.4	79.9	80.3	80.3	80.9	81.1	82.0	81.1	81.0	79.9
2015	78.5	79.1	79.6	80.6	81.0	81.9	81.8	82.0	82.1	82.1	81.6	81.0	80.9
Manufacturing													
2005	292.3	292.5	294.1	297.8	299.1	299.3	299.7	300.4	301.1	300.6	302.9	304.8	298.7
2006	303.5	304.4	305.0	304.7	304.8	306.2	304.2	303.1	301.7	299.3	298.3	299.3	302.9
2007	297.8	297.9	297.6	296.1	296.1	297.9	296.2	295.7	295.7	295.3	294.7	294.7	296.3
2008	291.2	289.9	289.1	288.2	287.9	287.9	286.3	284.4	283.1	278.6	273.5	271.3	284.3
2009	262.7	257.9	254.7	251.3	247.9	244.2	243.5	242.2	240.9	239.3	238.5	238.2	246.8
2010	235.0	234.4	235.2	236.5	237.2	237.2	237.2	237.0	236.9	236.2	236.6	236.2	236.3
2011	233.2	235.0	235.8	236.9	237.1	238.2	237.7	239.0	238.2	237.9	239.2	240.6	237.4
2012	239.1	239.6	240.9	242.3	243.1	244.3	244.2	245.2	245.0	245.7	246.4	247.7	243.6
2013	245.9	246.9	248.2	248.5	248.8	250.2	249.3	250.1	250.2	250.0	251.1	252.0	249.3
2014	250.5	250.2	251.0	251.4	252.5	253.5	253.0	253.9	254.6	254.9	255.7	257.0	253.2
2015	255.5	256.3	256.6	256.7	257.6	258.2	258.3	258.5	258.7	257.4	258.2	257.7	257.5
Trade, Transportation, and Utilities													
2005	376.6	376.0	378.3	380.5	381.6	382.9	382.4	382.8	382.5	383.3	391.2	396.3	382.9
2006	382.6	381.5	385.4	384.1	385.2	387.4	386.3	387.3	388.1	388.9	396.8	401.7	387.9
2007	387.8	387.5	391.8	390.8	394.4	396.2	395.2	394.8	395.1	394.9	402.6	406.0	394.8
2008	390.7	388.8	391.1	389.6	390.2	390.4	389.6	389.8	388.4	385.9	389.0	390.2	389.5
2009													
	371.3	367.5	366.8	364.9	366.0	366.0	364.4	363.2	363.0	361.1	366.8	368.7	365.8
2010	356.7	355.7	358.6	359.1	360.7	361.2	360.7	360.8	359.9	363.1	368.8	372.0	361.4
2011	358.8	358.8	360.7	362.0	362.5	364.0	364.2	364.9	364.1	365.1	371.5	374.3	364.2
2012	361.9	360.3	363.5	363.8	365.5	366.4	364.3	364.7	364.4	366.2	374.9	376.7	366.1
2013	361.7	362.1	364.2	365.0	367.2	369.0	368.4	369.2	367.9	369.1	377.2	381.6	368.6
2014	367.3	366.1	369.1	370.3	371.1	372.4	372.6	372.3	371.9	373.2	382.1	385.8	372.9
2015	371.2	370.3	373.1	375.1	377.3	378.0	378.1	378.2	377.0	378.8	388.5	390.7	378.0
Wholesale Trade													
2005	78.1	78.4	78.8	79.3	79.3	79.5	79.8	79.7	80.0	79.9	80.0	80.5	79.4
2006	79.9	80.3	81.0	81.0	81.5	81.9	81.9	82.0	82.1	81.9	82.1	82.5	81.5
2007	81.3	81.6	82.1	81.9	82.3	82.8	82.2	82.2	82.4	82.5	82.3	82.4	82.2
2008	80.8	80.8	81.0	81.0	81.3	81.3	80.9	80.8	80.7	80.4	79.5	79.1	80.6
2009	77.0	76.3	75.9	75.0	74.8	74.4	73.6	73.6	73.3	73.3	73.2	72.9	74.4
2010	71.7	71.5	71.5	71.8	72.1	71.9	72.0	71.9	71.6	72.1	71.9	71.8	71.8
2011	70.9	71.3	71.5	71.8	71.9	71.9	72.3	72.5	72.4	72.9	72.7	72.9	72.1
2012	71.9	72.0	72.5	72.6	72.9	73.0	72.6	72.6	72.6	73.0	72.9	73.0	72.6
2013	72.0	72.4	72.5	72.8	73.1	72.9	73.1	73.1	73.0	73.2	73.3	73.3	72.9
2014	72.2	72.4	72.5	72.8	73.2	73.2	73.3	73.4	73.4	73.6	73.9	74.0	73.2
2015	72.8	73.0	73.3	73.7	74.0	73.8	74.0	73.9	73.8	74.7	74.5	74.6	73.8
Retail Trade													
2005	232.7	231.5	233.1	234.3	234.9	235.4	234.6	235.2	234.3	234.7	242.4	246.3	235.8
2006	234.2	232.7	235.2	233.6	233.9	234.9	234.0	234.6	234.9	236.2	243.5	247.1	236.2
2007	236.4	235.7	238.9	238.5	240.8	241.7	241.5	241.0	240.7	240.7	248.0	250.5	241.2
2008	239.1	237.5	239.7	237.7	237.8	238.2	237.2	237.2	236.0	234.6	239.0	240.6	237.9
2009	227.5	224.7	224.7	224.0	224.8	225.1	224.4	223.0	223.2	221.8	227.5	229.0	225.0
2010	220.0	219.2	221.9	221.5	222.4	222.9	222.0	222.1	221.2	224.1	229.8	232.3	223.3
2011	221.5	220.7	222.1	223.3	223.3	224.5	224.4	224.5	223.7	224.6	231.1	232.9	224.7
2012	222.5	220.2	222.2	222.3	223.6	224.0	222.6	222.5	222.0	223.5	232.0	232.9	224.2
2013	219.6	219.4	221.1	221.8	223.3	224.9	224.4	225.0	223.7	224.6	232.2	235.4	224.6
2014	223.5	222.4	224.6	225.5	225.9	226.8	226.9	226.4	225.8	227.2	235.3	237.7	227.3
2015	225.3	225.0	227.0	228.5	230.0	230.8	230.8	230.8	230.0	231.2	240.5	240.7	230.9

1. Employment by Industry: Alabama, 2005–2015—*Continued*

(Numbers in thousands, not seasonally adjusted)

Industry and year	January	February	March	April	May	June	July	August	September	October	November	December	Annual average
Transportation and Utilities													
2005	65.8	66.1	66.4	66.9	67.4	68.0	68.0	67.9	68.2	68.7	68.8	69.5	67.6
2006	68.5	68.5	69.2	69.5	69.8	70.6	70.4	70.7	71.1	70.8	71.2	72.1	70.2
2007	70.1	70.2	70.8	70.4	71.3	71.7	71.5	71.6	72.0	71.7	72.3	73.1	71.4
2008	70.8	70.5	70.4	70.9	71.1	70.9	71.5	71.8	71.7	70.9	70.5	70.5	71.0
2009	66.8	66.5	66.2	65.9	66.4	66.5	66.4	66.6	66.5	66.0	66.1	66.8	66.4
2010	65.0	65.0	65.2	65.8	66.2	66.4	66.7	66.8	67.1	66.9	67.1	67.9	66.3
2011	66.4	66.8	67.1	66.9	67.3	67.6	67.5	67.9	68.0	67.6	67.7	68.5	67.4
2012	67.5	68.1	68.8	68.9	69.0	69.4	69.1	69.6	69.8	69.7	70.0	70.8	69.2
2013	70.1	70.3	70.6	70.4	70.8	71.2	70.9	71.1	71.2	71.3	71.7	72.9	71.0
2014	71.6	71.3	72.0	72.0	72.0	72.4	72.4	72.5	72.7	72.4	72.9	74.1	72.4
2015	73.1	72.3	72.8	72.9	73.3	73.4	73.3	73.5	73.2	72.9	73.5	75.4	73.3
Information													
2005	29.3	29.3	29.3	29.4	29.3	29.3	29.3	29.3	29.0	28.9	29.0	29.1	29.2
2006	28.7	28.7	28.8	28.7	28.8	28.8	28.5	28.4	28.2	28.1	28.2	28.3	28.5
2007	27.9	28.1	28.2	28.2	28.4	28.4	28.0	27.9	27.7	27.7	27.9	27.9	28.0
2008	27.4	27.3	27.3	27.3	27.3	27.1	26.9	26.8	26.4	26.2	26.2	26.3	26.9
2009	25.8	25.6	25.5	25.3	25.3	25.4	24.9	24.8	24.7	24.6	24.7	24.8	25.1
2010	24.5	24.4	24.3	24.1	24.2	24.2	24.0	23.9	23.7	23.7	23.7	23.6	24.0
2011	23.5	23.4	23.2	23.1	23.3	23.3	23.2	23.1	23.1	22.7	22.8	22.8	23.1
2012	22.9	22.9	22.9	22.8	22.8	22.8	22.7	22.6	22.5	22.2	22.4	22.4	22.7
2013	22.4	22.3	22.3	22.4	22.8	22.8	22.8	22.7	22.5	22.6	22.8	22.9	22.6
2014	22.2	22.1	22.1	22.1	22.1	22.0	22.0	21.9	21.7	21.7	21.9	21.9	22.0
2015	21.6	21.8	21.8	21.5	22.0	21.5	21.6	21.3	21.0	21.0	21.3	21.1	21.5
Financial Activities													
2005	96.2	96.8	97.3	97.6	97.6	98.2	98.4	98.1	98.5	101.2	99.9	100.1	98.3
2006	97.1	98.3	98.5	98.4	98.8	99.4	99.1	99.1	98.9	98.8	99.1	99.7	98.8
2007	99.0	99.1	99.7	99.2	99.7	100.6	100.3	100.2	100.1	99.8	100.0	100.2	99.8
2008	98.8	99.2	99.2	99.2	99.2	99.6	99.8	99.7	99.2	99.0	98.4	98.2	99.1
2009	96.9	96.6	96.6	96.6	96.9	96.9	96.4	95.8	95.0	94.3	93.7	93.6	95.8
2010	92.1	92.0	92.4	92.3	92.5	92.7	92.2	91.8	91.2	91.7	91.7	91.9	92.0
2011	91.1	91.5	91.6	92.4	93.8	93.0	93.2	92.5	93.3	92.1	92.0	91.8	92.4
2012	90.6	91.1	91.5	91.7	92.2	92.7	93.5	93.4	93.6	93.5	94.0	93.9	92.6
2013	93.2	93.3	93.8	93.7	94.0	94.5	94.7	94.9	94.2	94.6	94.8	95.0	94.2
2014	93.8	93.9	94.2	94.6	95.1	95.5	95.4	95.4	94.4	94.7	94.8	95.2	94.8
2015	94.2	94.3	94.8	95.2	95.8	96.1	96.3	96.0	95.3	94.9	95.9	96.3	95.4
Professional and Business Services													
2005	200.1	202.9	204.2	206.8	206.3	207.8	209.7	212.0	213.5	214.7	215.4	214.9	209.0
2006	208.8	211.4	213.5	213.7	213.7	216.7	214.2	217.1	217.8	216.7	217.0	217.1	214.8
2007	215.4	218.1	221.1	219.8	219.9	221.7	218.8	221.8	222.4	222.2	223.7	224.8	220.8
2008	220.1	221.5	222.2	223.8	222.1	222.1	220.0	220.5	220.1	219.7	216.8	214.1	220.3
2009	205.6	205.3	204.7	205.5	203.4	205.0	205.0	205.0	202.9	202.6	203.8	203.3	204.3
2010	200.3	201.5	203.4	206.1	207.0	210.9	212.9	212.0	212.2	212.8	213.8	213.9	208.9
2011	208.2	211.1	211.9	212.8	212.2	213.1	212.4	214.6	216.8	215.4	215.3	215.6	213.3
2012	210.3	213.7	215.9	217.3	218.2	219.5	217.3	221.6	220.9	219.5	219.8	218.2	217.7
2013	212.7	216.2	218.2	219.6	219.6	221.0	218.5	220.1	218.9	219.4	219.2	220.8	218.7
2014	215.9	216.7	218.6	221.8	222.6	223.6	223.5	226.7	226.1	227.6	227.4	227.8	223.2
2015	221.8	223.5	224.9	226.9	227.9	228.0	228.5	230.2	229.4	232.4	232.9	228.9	227.9
Education and Health Services													
2005	196.0	197.3	198.2	199.4	200.1	199.1	199.2	200.3	202.6	200.7	202.2	201.8	199.7
2006	199.6	200.4	202.1	203.2	203.8	203.1	202.0	203.9	205.3	205.5	207.5	206.5	203.6
2007	204.8	206.6	207.5	207.8	208.3	207.8	207.3	209.8	210.1	210.5	211.4	212.1	208.7
2008	208.2	210.1	210.7	211.1	211.8	210.4	210.0	211.6	212.3	212.8	212.3	211.8	211.1
2009													
	209.2	209.8	209.9	210.7	211.3	209.3	209.7	211.0	211.7	212.3	214.1	212.7	211.0
2010	210.9	212.4	212.4	213.4	213.7	212.5	214.0	215.4	216.1	216.7	217.3	216.2	214.3
2011	213.2	214.3	215.7	215.8	215.7	213.9	214.0	215.3	217.8	217.3	218.7	217.6	215.8
2012	216.0	216.7	218.1	218.9	217.8	217.3	214.9	218.0	220.2	219.6	221.6	221.8	218.4
2013	218.0	221.6	220.3	221.1	222.9	220.6	217.8	220.9	223.6	222.8	225.2	225.5	221.7
2014	219.8	222.2	221.7	223.6	223.2	221.3	219.4	222.6	225.1	226.4	225.8	227.6	223.2
2015	223.3	225.9	224.5	226.5	226.4	225.7	225.7	227.8	228.9	229.8	232.4	231.9	227.4

1. Employment by Industry: Alabama, 2005–2015—*Continued*

(Numbers in thousands, not seasonally adjusted)

Industry and year	January	February	March	April	May	June	July	August	September	October	November	December	Annual average
Leisure and Hospitality													
2005	155.1	157.5	162.0	166.4	168.5	170.4	168.7	169.6	167.2	163.6	163.9	163.6	164.7
2006	160.3	163.3	167.6	170.1	172.6	174.9	173.5	174.8	173.4	169.0	168.8	168.7	169.8
2007	165.8	169.2	172.9	174.6	176.7	178.9	177.6	178.5	176.1	172.9	172.3	171.9	174.0
2008	166.3	169.2	172.7	177.8	180.3	181.2	179.3	179.9	176.6	171.8	170.3	169.3	174.6
2009	163.8	166.0	169.2	172.3	174.6	175.7	174.0	173.4	171.5	167.5	166.9	166.4	170.1
2010	160.3	161.0	165.9	169.5	171.4	173.0	170.9	171.0	168.8	166.5	166.5	165.5	167.5
2011	159.5	162.3	166.5	171.5	171.8	174.1	173.7	174.7	172.4	168.5	168.0	166.7	169.1
2012	163.1	166.3	170.9	176.1	178.2	180.6	177.7	178.8	176.6	172.7	172.7	171.0	173.7
2013	167.9	170.4	174.8	180.3	183.4	185.4	183.6	184.0	182.5	178.7	179.0	176.8	178.9
2014	173.1	174.8	180.4	185.6	187.9	190.4	188.3	189.6	187.0	183.6	182.3	181.4	183.7
2015	178.8	182.1	186.0	191.0	193.7	195.2	194.6	194.6	191.5	190.6	190.3	188.3	189.7
Other Services													
2005	80.8	80.9	81.3	81.4	81.8	82.0	81.5	81.1	80.7	79.9	79.9	80.2	81.0
2006	79.5	79.8	80.4	80.3	80.3	81.6	80.7	80.6	80.5	80.0	80.1	80.2	80.3
2007	79.9	80.5	81.4	81.2	81.4	81.8	81.2	81.0	80.8	81.0	81.2	81.4	81.1
2008	81.0	81.8	82.1	82.2	82.3	82.3	82.2	81.8	81.5	81.2	80.9	80.6	81.7
2009	80.2	80.2	80.4	80.3	80.5	80.7	80.6	80.1	79.5	79.7	79.3	79.4	80.1
2010	79.1	79.5	79.8	79.8	80.1	80.8	80.9	80.3	79.7	80.3	79.5	79.3	79.9
2011	78.4	78.9	79.2	79.6	79.6	80.1	79.7	79.3	79.2	79.2	79.6	79.2	79.3
2012	79.1	79.8	80.8	80.7	80.7	81.6	81.1	80.5	79.9	80.1	79.3	79.2	80.2
2013	78.7	79.0	79.8	79.9	80.0	80.7	80.2	80.2	79.9	79.6	79.2	79.2	79.7
2014	78.7	79.1	80.1	80.2	80.6	80.9	80.5	80.3	79.9	79.6	79.4	79.3	79.9
2015	79.2	79.3	79.9	80.6	81.2	81.5	81.0	80.8	80.7	81.2	80.4	80.8	80.6
Government													
2005	360.1	363.0	363.5	364.8	365.5	364.2	352.4	355.1	362.9	367.4	368.1	367.8	362.9
2006	366.7	369.0	370.6	372.1	373.0	372.2	360.0	362.6	371.6	373.9	374.8	375.3	370.2
2007	374.2	376.6	377.9	378.4	379.3	379.1	364.6	368.6	377.8	380.4	381.9	381.8	376.7
2008	380.3	384.1	385.3	386.6	388.1	387.9	372.2	375.0	383.1	387.6	387.2	387.8	383.8
2009	383.1	385.2	386.1	388.5	388.8	387.6	371.2	373.2	382.0	386.8	387.3	388.0	384.0
2010	384.1	386.6	389.6	391.2	400.3	394.6	376.2	376.1	383.9	387.0	388.2	388.1	387.2
2011	384.2	386.7	387.8	387.8	387.4	384.2	371.6	371.3	380.2	381.8	383.3	380.9	382.3
2012	378.1	381.4	383.5	382.7	382.0	379.4	365.8	366.4	374.6	379.7	381.0	380.2	377.9
2013	376.4	380.2	382.4	382.3	381.7	378.2	369.2	369.3	374.7	378.7	380.2	378.7	377.7
2014	376.1	378.9	380.3	381.4	382.8	380.8	367.4	369.8	377.6	380.5	381.6	381.6	378.2
2015	375.9	378.2	379.1	380.6	382.2	380.2	368.3	370.8	376.5	378.8	378.9	377.6	377.3

2. Average Weekly Hours by Selected Industry: Alabama, 2011–2015

(Not seasonally adjusted)

Industry and year	January	February	March	April	May	June	July	August	September	October	November	December	Annual average
Total Private													
2011	34.8	35.0	35.0	34.9	35.2	35.0	35.2	35.6	35.7	35.7	35.3	35.7	35.3
2012	35.5	35.9	35.7	36.2	35.6	35.8	35.9	36.0	36.4	36.1	36.1	36.6	36.0
2013	35.5	35.8	36.0	36.0	35.8	36.6	36.0	36.1	36.6	36.1	36.2	36.3	36.1
2014	35.0	35.2	36.0	35.6	35.5	35.9	35.4	35.7	35.5	35.2	35.6	35.5	35.5
2015	34.9	35.5	35.4	35.2	35.5	35.5	35.5	35.9	35.4	35.8	35.9	35.6	35.5
Goods-Producing													
2011	39.9	40.1	40.2	39.7	40.5	40.4	39.8	41.2	41.8	41.0	41.0	41.5	40.6
2012	41.2	41.8	41.8	42.3	42.0	42.1	41.5	42.7	42.9	42.8	43.2	43.2	42.3
2013	42.3	42.9	42.9	42.8	42.7	43.0	42.4	43.1	43.2	43.4	43.4	43.0	42.9
2014	41.4	40.2	42.6	41.9	41.9	42.0	41.8	42.5	42.4	41.8	41.7	42.1	41.9
2015	41.2	41.2	41.3	41.2	41.7	41.7	41.6	41.9	40.8	42.2	41.7	42.2	41.6
Construction													
2011	42.3	42.4	42.2	41.6	42.7	42.5	42.8	43.3	43.4	42.3	41.4	42.0	42.4
2012	39.0	40.7	41.1	42.1	41.3	40.8	40.1	40.9	40.2	40.2	39.7	39.3	40.4
2013	37.5	38.7	40.4	41.7	41.9	40.9	40.9	41.8	42.9	41.9	41.1	41.0	40.9
2014	39.5	37.7	40.1	39.8	40.6	40.8	41.3	42.3	42.2	40.3	41.4	40.9	40.6
2015	38.6	39.7	39.6	39.5	41.4	41.5	41.7	41.6	40.1	41.8	41.7	42.4	40.8
Manufacturing													
2011	41.0	41.2	41.2	40.4	40.8	40.6	40.3	41.2	41.5	40.6	40.7	41.2	40.9
2012	41.7	42.0	42.1	42.2	42.1	42.3	41.8	42.4	42.9	42.8	42.4	42.6	42.3
2013	41.8	42.5	42.3	41.9	41.7	42.3	41.7	42.4	42.3	42.9	43.1	42.7	42.3
2014	41.1	40.3	42.1	41.4	41.3	41.4	41.1	41.9	41.7	41.7	41.3	42.1	41.5
2015	41.8	41.6	41.7	41.7	41.4	41.4	41.2	41.8	41.4	42.4	41.8	42.0	41.7
Trade, Transportation, and Utilities													
2011	36.5	36.6	36.5	36.5	36.1	35.5	36.2	35.9	35.7	35.6	35.3	35.8	36.0
2012	35.7	36.1	35.3	36.1	35.3	35.9	35.6	35.1	36.2	35.8	36.2	36.0	35.8
2013	35.7	36.0	36.1	36.3	35.8	36.6	35.9	36.2	36.7	35.9	36.0	36.2	36.1
2014	35.1	35.4	35.8	35.9	35.6	35.6	35.4	35.2	35.1	34.8	34.9	35.2	35.3
2015	34.2	34.6	34.3	34.5	34.6	34.7	34.7	34.9	34.4	34.5	34.5	34.4	34.5
Financial Activities													
2011	36.4	36.3	35.9	36.0	37.2	36.2	36.4	36.8	36.4	37.8	37.2	37.1	36.6
2012	38.1	37.0	36.9	37.9	37.2	37.3	38.6	37.8	37.9	36.8	37.0	38.1	37.6
2013	37.3	37.3	36.9	37.1	37.3	38.6	37.1	36.9	38.1	36.8	37.0	37.5	37.3
2014	35.7	36.7	36.7	36.0	36.2	37.1	36.4	36.5	36.4	36.4	37.9	36.8	36.6
2015	37.0	38.1	38.4	36.8	37.2	37.2	36.9	38.3	37.2	36.9	38.6	37.3	37.5
Professional and Business Services													
2011	36.6	36.7	36.9	37.3	37.5	36.8	36.8	37.1	37.1	37.5	36.3	36.8	37.0
2012	36.1	36.6	36.2	36.9	36.7	36.6	36.7	36.8	37.0	36.5	36.1	36.4	36.5
2013	35.6	36.0	36.7	36.9	36.4	37.5	36.8	36.9	38.0	37.3	37.4	37.3	36.9
2014	35.8	36.3	36.8	36.3	36.5	37.1	36.6	37.2	36.6	36.9	37.6	37.3	36.8
2015	36.3	37.0	36.7	36.5	36.7	36.6	36.7	37.3	36.7	36.7	36.9	36.0	36.7
Education and Health Services													
2011	35.1	35.3	34.9	34.4	35.1	34.7	35.1	35.0	35.3	35.1	34.5	34.7	34.9
2012	34.6	34.4	34.6	34.8	34.1	34.0	34.5	34.1	34.7	34.0	34.0	34.4	34.3
2013	33.9	33.9	33.8	33.4	33.4	34.2	33.5	33.6	33.9	33.1	33.5	33.9	33.7
2014	33.1	33.1	33.3	32.8	32.7	33.2	32.8	33.0	32.6	32.4	33.4	32.4	32.9
2015	32.5	33.4	33.2	33.1	33.3	33.3	33.3	33.8	33.4	33.8	34.6	33.3	33.4
Leisure and Hospitality													
2011	26.4	26.5	26.5	26.5	26.4	27.1	27.1	27.1	26.7	27.4	27.0	27.5	26.9
2012	26.5	27.3	27.3	27.1	26.5	26.7	27.2	27.1	26.0	26.3	25.8	26.4	26.7
2013	25.5	26.2	26.6	26.3	26.3	27.0	26.8	26.9	26.4	26.5	26.3	26.5	26.4
2014	25.4	25.9	26.7	26.5	26.5	26.9	26.5	26.3	26.2	25.7	26.3	26.3	26.3
2015	25.7	26.5	26.6	26.9	26.9	27.3	27.1	26.7	26.0	26.2	25.8	26.1	26.5
Other Services													
2011	30.4	30.4	30.5	30.9	31.7	31.6	31.9	32.5	32.1	32.6	31.4	31.2	31.4
2012	29.8	31.6	31.9	32.1	30.7	32.0	32.2	32.4	33.5	34.2	33.0	33.4	32.2
2013	31.8	30.9	32.2	32.8	32.5	35.2	33.0	32.7	34.9	33.7	33.4	33.9	33.1
2014	31.6	31.9	32.7	32.2	31.1	32.1	30.0	30.2	32.8	32.8	32.6	31.5	31.8
2015	32.0	32.9	33.5	33.1	33.9	33.2	32.1	33.6	32.6	33.8	34.5	34.5	33.3

3. Average Hourly Earnings by Selected Industry: Alabama, 2011–2015

(Dollars, not seasonally adjusted)

Industry and year	January	February	March	April	May	June	July	August	September	October	November	December	Annual average
Total Private													
2011	19.97	19.95	19.85	20.04	20.24	20.20	20.19	20.20	20.34	20.43	20.20	20.08	20.14
2012	20.41	20.30	20.31	20.38	20.09	20.21	20.14	19.94	20.18	20.04	20.16	20.40	20.21
2013	20.26	20.27	20.24	20.11	19.97	20.09	20.03	20.12	20.35	20.18	20.10	20.47	20.18
2014	20.51	20.87	20.73	20.62	20.61	20.85	20.67	20.69	20.73	20.76	20.96	20.79	20.73
2015	21.01	21.41	21.30	20.64	20.62	20.73	20.79	21.00	21.01	21.10	21.31	21.35	21.02
Goods-Producing													
2011	21.77	21.54	21.53	21.36	21.56	21.66	22.18	21.93	22.13	22.08	21.87	21.57	21.77
2012	21.83	21.64	21.72	21.99	21.47	21.72	21.74	21.60	21.44	21.39	21.68	22.09	21.69
2013	21.93	22.05	22.25	22.01	21.75	21.92	22.00	21.84	21.96	21.98	21.96	22.37	22.00
2014	22.29	22.89	22.50	22.46	22.30	22.50	22.39	22.29	22.28	22.51	22.64	22.59	22.47
2015	22.55	22.78	22.60	22.58	22.44	22.46	22.47	22.61	22.90	22.86	23.14	23.12	22.71
Construction													
2011	18.41	18.50	18.69	18.38	19.46	19.59	19.68	19.46	19.60	19.68	19.85	19.07	19.21
2012	19.61	19.49	19.80	19.49	19.81	20.34	20.29	20.51	20.36	20.60	20.95	20.38	20.14
2013	20.16	20.60	21.27	20.63	20.45	21.08	20.99	20.79	21.23	21.57	21.33	23.05	21.11
2014	23.11	23.26	22.37	22.66	22.56	22.41	22.23	22.50	22.31	22.57	22.64	22.93	22.62
2015	23.05	22.82	22.55	22.51	22.06	22.22	22.11	22.32	22.70	22.97	23.08	22.86	22.60
Manufacturing													
2011	20.51	20.62	20.52	20.67	20.56	20.83	21.06	20.97	21.00	21.28	20.97	20.96	20.83
2012	21.21	21.13	21.00	21.70	20.99	21.22	21.33	21.11	21.07	20.99	20.83	20.93	21.12
2013	20.92	21.13	21.36	21.33	21.18	21.35	21.58	21.49	21.62	21.60	21.68	21.97	21.44
2014	22.03	22.38	22.20	22.14	22.00	22.34	22.35	22.12	22.24	22.49	22.67	22.56	22.29
2015	22.36	22.74	22.60	22.53	22.56	22.57	22.62	22.72	23.00	22.85	23.19	23.29	22.75
Trade, Transportation, and Utilities													
2011	17.25	17.31	17.34	17.66	18.71	18.48	18.54	18.62	18.87	18.93	18.41	18.44	18.21
2012	18.68	18.60	18.38	18.47	18.23	18.65	18.54	18.01	18.28	18.32	17.99	18.20	18.34
2013	18.16	18.27	18.23	17.80	17.92	18.03	17.81	17.83	18.11	18.04	17.80	18.18	18.01
2014	18.34	18.69	18.76	18.76	18.71	18.94	18.96	18.85	18.91	18.81	18.74	18.31	18.73
2015	18.92	19.09	18.99	19.13	19.04	18.88	18.99	19.16	19.32	19.17	19.17	18.87	19.06
Financial Activities													
2011	20.57	20.54	20.76	21.23	21.53	21.19	20.98	20.95	21.12	21.54	20.59	20.58	20.97
2012	21.20	21.03	21.12	21.36	21.51	21.21	21.21	20.62	20.95	20.93	20.94	21.41	21.12
2013	21.03	21.32	21.57	21.49	21.66	21.47	21.47	21.51	21.78	21.04	20.85	21.33	21.38
2014	21.01	21.57	22.02	21.74	22.16	22.10	21.89	21.77	21.86	21.89	21.92	21.59	21.80
2015	21.67	22.12	22.14	22.45	22.23	22.89	23.00	22.65	23.08	23.59	23.64	24.14	22.80
Professional and Business Services													
2011	24.34	24.40	24.38	24.39	24.25	23.89	23.75	23.45	23.43	23.31	23.04	22.65	23.77
2012	23.51	23.23	23.29	23.28	22.95	22.65	22.90	22.90	22.99	22.66	22.73	22.75	22.98
2013	23.01	23.28	23.06	23.31	23.02	23.00	23.03	23.17	23.37	22.82	22.82	23.62	23.13
2014	23.72	24.33	24.12	23.94	23.91	24.35	23.95	23.94	24.06	23.89	24.60	24.41	24.11
2015	24.74	26.08	26.09	23.40	23.62	24.17	23.99	24.65	24.70	24.70	25.06	25.38	24.71
Education and Health Services													
2011	19.70	19.71	19.52	20.11	19.69	20.26	20.22	20.40	20.38	20.73	20.65	20.70	20.17
2012	20.64	20.69	20.53	20.64	20.44	20.80	20.78	20.88	21.14	20.78	21.23	21.39	20.83
2013	20.87	20.95	20.97	20.91	20.65	20.94	20.81	20.99	21.07	21.00	20.93	20.96	20.92
2014	21.09	21.57	21.58	21.59	21.51	21.83	21.49	21.52	21.74	21.70	22.11	21.84	21.63
2015	22.16	22.14	21.83	22.04	21.91	22.06	22.17	22.16	22.19	22.49	22.69	22.88	22.23
Leisure and Hospitality													
2011	10.74	10.70	10.62	10.67	10.71	10.57	10.53	10.62	10.53	10.58	10.65	10.90	10.65
2012	10.85	10.93	10.87	10.92	10.94	10.90	10.89	10.80	11.02	11.02	11.09	11.23	10.95
2013	11.19	11.15	11.10	11.00	10.98	10.88	10.88	10.84	10.84	10.87	10.82	11.05	10.96
2014	10.99	11.09	10.94	10.91	10.85	10.86	10.75	11.00	10.79	10.86	10.90	11.03	10.91
2015	10.93	11.16	11.05	11.04	11.00	10.88	10.84	10.97	11.03	10.99	11.08	11.28	11.02
Other Services													
2011	16.10	16.19	16.32	16.78	17.41	17.75	17.45	17.51	17.17	17.34	18.19	18.87	17.27
2012	19.21	18.38	18.73	19.10	18.63	19.59	18.79	19.03	19.61	19.81	19.69	20.08	19.23
2013	19.95	19.92	19.79	19.83	19.99	20.55	19.89	20.60	20.27	20.13	20.15	20.18	20.11
2014	20.55	20.58	20.65	20.11	21.13	21.90	21.76	22.15	21.86	21.49	21.22	21.54	21.24
2015	20.87	21.18	21.52	19.99	20.06	20.23	20.05	20.28	19.72	19.54	19.25	19.12	20.14

4. Average Weekly Earnings by Selected Industry: Alabama, 2011–2015

(Dollars, not seasonally adjusted)

Industry and year	January	February	March	April	May	June	July	August	September	October	November	December	Annual average
Total Private													
2011	694.96	698.25	694.75	699.40	712.45	707.00	710.69	719.12	726.14	729.35	713.06	716.86	710.94
2012	724.56	728.77	725.07	737.76	715.20	723.52	723.03	717.84	734.55	723.44	727.78	746.64	727.56
2013	719.23	725.67	728.64	723.96	714.93	735.29	721.08	726.33	744.81	728.50	727.62	743.06	728.50
2014	717.85	734.62	746.28	734.07	731.66	748.52	731.72	738.63	735.92	730.75	746.18	738.05	735.92
2015	733.25	760.06	754.02	726.53	732.01	735.92	738.05	753.90	743.75	755.38	765.03	760.06	746.21
Goods-Producing													
2011	868.62	863.75	865.51	847.99	873.18	875.06	882.76	903.52	925.03	905.28	896.67	895.16	883.86
2012	899.40	904.55	907.90	930.18	901.74	914.41	902.21	922.32	919.78	915.49	936.58	954.29	917.49
2013	927.64	945.95	954.53	942.03	928.73	942.56	932.80	941.30	948.67	953.93	953.06	961.91	943.80
2014	922.81	920.18	958.50	941.07	934.37	945.00	935.90	947.33	944.67	940.92	944.09	951.04	941.49
2015	929.06	938.54	933.38	930.30	935.75	936.58	934.75	947.36	934.32	964.69	964.94	975.66	944.74
Construction													
2011	778.74	784.40	788.72	764.61	830.94	832.58	842.30	842.62	850.64	832.46	821.79	800.94	814.50
2012	764.79	793.24	813.78	820.53	818.15	829.87	813.63	838.86	818.47	828.12	831.72	800.93	813.66
2013	756.00	797.22	859.31	860.27	856.86	862.17	858.49	869.02	910.77	903.78	876.66	945.05	863.40
2014	912.85	876.90	897.04	901.87	915.94	914.33	918.10	951.75	941.48	909.57	937.30	937.84	918.37
2015	889.73	905.95	892.98	889.15	913.28	922.13	921.99	928.51	910.27	960.15	962.44	969.26	922.08
Manufacturing													
2011	840.91	849.54	845.42	835.07	838.85	845.70	848.72	863.96	871.50	863.97	853.48	863.55	851.95
2012	884.46	887.46	884.10	915.74	883.68	897.61	891.59	895.06	903.90	898.37	883.19	891.62	893.38
2013	874.46	898.03	903.53	893.73	883.21	903.11	899.89	911.18	914.53	926.64	934.41	938.12	906.91
2014	905.43	901.91	934.62	916.60	908.60	924.88	918.59	926.83	927.41	937.83	936.27	949.78	925.04
2015	934.65	945.98	942.42	939.50	933.98	934.40	931.94	949.70	952.20	968.84	969.34	978.18	948.68
Trade, Transportation, and Utilities													
2011	629.63	633.55	632.91	644.59	675.43	656.04	671.15	668.46	673.66	673.91	649.87	660.15	655.56
2012	666.88	671.46	648.81	666.77	643.52	669.54	650.77	632.15	661.74	655.86	651.24	655.20	656.57
2013	648.31	657.72	658.10	646.14	641.54	659.90	639.38	645.45	664.64	647.64	640.80	658.12	650.16
2014	643.73	661.63	671.61	673.48	666.08	674.26	671.18	663.52	663.74	654.59	654.03	644.51	661.17
2015	647.06	660.51	651.36	659.99	658.78	655.14	658.95	668.68	664.61	661.37	661.37	649.13	657.57
Financial Activities													
2011	748.75	745.60	745.28	764.28	800.92	767.08	763.67	770.96	768.77	814.21	765.95	763.52	767.50
2012	807.72	778.11	779.33	809.54	800.17	791.13	818.71	779.44	794.01	770.22	774.78	815.72	794.11
2013	784.42	795.24	795.93	797.28	807.92	828.74	796.54	793.72	829.82	774.27	771.45	799.88	797.47
2014	750.06	791.62	808.13	782.64	802.19	819.91	796.80	794.61	795.70	796.80	830.77	794.51	797.88
2015	801.79	842.77	850.18	826.16	826.96	851.51	848.70	867.50	858.58	870.47	912.50	900.42	855.00
Professional and Business Services													
2011	890.84	895.48	899.62	909.75	909.38	879.15	874.00	870.00	869.25	874.13	836.35	833.52	879.49
2012	848.71	850.22	843.10	859.03	842.27	828.99	840.43	842.72	850.63	827.09	820.55	828.10	838.77
2013	819.16	838.08	846.30	860.14	837.93	862.50	847.50	854.97	888.06	851.19	853.47	881.03	853.50
2014	849.18	883.18	887.62	869.02	872.72	903.39	876.57	890.57	880.60	881.54	924.96	910.49	887.25
2015	898.06	964.96	957.50	854.10	866.85	884.62	880.43	919.45	906.49	906.49	924.71	913.68	906.86
Education and Health Services													
2011	691.47	695.76	681.25	691.78	691.12	703.02	709.72	714.00	719.41	727.62	712.43	718.29	703.93
2012	714.14	711.74	710.34	718.27	697.00	707.20	716.91	712.01	733.56	706.52	721.82	735.82	714.47
2013	707.49	710.21	708.79	698.39	689.71	716.15	697.14	705.26	714.27	695.10	701.16	710.54	705.00
2014	698.08	713.97	718.61	708.15	703.38	724.76	704.87	710.16	708.72	703.08	738.47	707.62	711.63
2015	720.20	739.48	724.76	729.52	729.60	734.60	738.26	749.01	741.15	760.16	785.07	761.90	742.48
Leisure and Hospitality													
2011	283.54	283.55	281.43	282.76	282.74	286.45	285.36	287.80	281.15	289.89	287.55	299.75	286.49
2012	287.53	298.39	296.75	295.93	289.91	291.03	296.21	292.68	286.52	289.83	286.12	296.47	292.37
2013	285.35	292.13	295.26	289.30	288.77	293.76	291.58	291.60	286.18	288.06	284.57	292.83	289.34
2014	279.15	287.23	292.10	289.12	287.53	292.13	284.88	289.30	282.70	279.10	286.67	290.09	286.93
2015	280.90	295.74	293.93	296.98	295.90	297.02	293.76	292.90	286.78	287.94	285.86	294.41	292.03
Other Services													
2011	489.44	492.18	497.76	518.50	551.90	560.90	556.66	569.08	551.16	565.28	571.17	588.74	542.28
2012	572.46	580.81	597.49	613.11	571.94	626.88	605.04	616.57	656.94	677.50	649.77	670.67	619.21
2013	634.41	615.53	637.24	650.42	649.68	723.36	656.37	673.62	707.42	678.38	673.01	684.10	665.64
2014	649.38	656.50	675.26	647.54	657.14	702.99	652.80	668.93	717.01	704.87	691.77	678.51	675.43
2015	667.84	696.82	720.92	661.67	680.03	671.64	643.61	681.41	642.87	660.45	664.13	659.64	670.66

ALASKA
At a Glance

Population:
  2005 Population: 666,946
  2010 census: 710,231
  2015 estimate: 738,432

Percent change in population:
  2005–2015: 10.7%
  2010–2015: 4.0%

Percent change in total nonfarm employment:
  2005–2015: 9.9%

Industry with the largest growth in employment, 2005–2015 (thousands):
  Education and health services, 10.9

Industry with the largest decline or smallest growth in employment, 2005–2015 (thousands):
  Construction, –1.5

Civilian labor force:
  2005: 344,559
  2010: 361,913
  2015: 363,822

Unemployment rate and rank among states (highest to lowest):
  2005: 6.9%, 3rd
  2010: 7.9%, 36th
  2015: 6.5%, 5th

Over-the-year change in unemployment rates:
  2012–2013: –0.2%
  2013–2014: 0.0%
  2014–2015: –0.4%

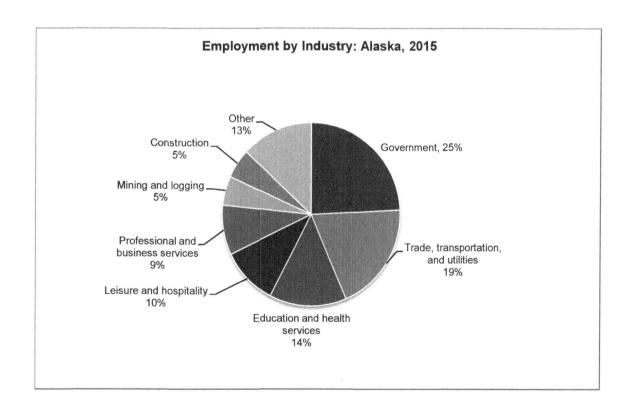

Employment by Industry: Alaska, 2015

Other 13%
Construction 5%
Mining and logging 5%
Professional and business services 9%
Leisure and hospitality 10%
Education and health services 14%
Government, 25%
Trade, transportation, and utilities 19%

1. Employment by Industry: Alaska, 2005–2015

(Numbers in thousands, not seasonally adjusted)

Industry and year	January	February	March	April	May	June	July	August	September	October	November	December	Annual average
Total Nonfarm													
2005	287.7	292.0	295.3	300.3	312.5	324.5	332.4	332.1	324.6	307.7	300.2	296.1	308.8
2006	290.4	297.0	301.4	306.4	318.8	335.8	336.7	336.3	329.1	310.2	303.9	300.7	313.9
2007	295.3	302.0	304.9	308.9	321.1	335.6	338.8	339.5	331.2	314.3	307.1	303.7	316.9
2008	299.3	305.1	307.5	312.1	326.3	340.1	345.4	344.6	336.4	318.1	310.7	308.2	321.2
2009	301.7	306.7	308.0	312.8	322.1	337.2	343.0	341.7	333.1	316.8	309.5	306.3	319.9
2010	301.9	306.1	308.7	314.6	324.9	342.9	348.7	347.1	340.5	323.9	316.6	313.4	324.1
2011	307.9	313.4	315.7	320.4	329.8	348.1	353.3	351.9	346.5	328.4	320.6	317.4	329.5
2012	312.1	319.4	322.2	326.2	337.2	354.1	357.3	356.5	348.6	336.0	324.8	321.3	334.6
2013	314.3	321.9	324.3	328.8	339.7	354.9	359.6	359.5	350.7	332.8	324.3	321.5	336.0
2014	318.1	322.4	324.9	330.9	343.6	356.2	361.9	359.6	350.2	334.7	325.9	323.7	337.7
2015	321.6	325.6	328.1	333.2	345.4	358.2	364.7	360.3	351.8	332.9	325.2	324.6	339.3
Total Private													
2005	207.8	210.4	213.2	217.4	229.6	244.6	256.6	255.3	243.3	225.5	218.1	214.4	228.0
2006	211.8	215.3	219.0	223.2	235.5	253.8	260.8	259.1	247.1	228.1	222.1	219.1	232.9
2007	216.4	220.1	222.3	225.8	238.0	255.1	263.1	262.6	249.2	231.1	224.4	221.2	235.8
2008	218.9	222.7	224.8	228.1	243.4	258.0	268.1	265.9	252.9	234.1	226.9	224.9	239.1
2009	220.1	223.1	224.4	227.1	238.7	252.9	263.6	261.4	248.2	230.8	224.0	220.8	236.3
2010	218.8	220.9	223.0	227.5	239.1	256.1	267.6	265.1	253.2	236.5	229.8	226.7	238.7
2011	223.7	227.6	230.2	233.8	244.9	262.4	273.4	271.8	260.3	241.8	234.7	231.5	244.7
2012	230.1	234.1	236.4	240.3	252.4	269.8	278.3	276.1	263.0	250.3	239.6	236.3	250.6
2013	233.1	237.8	240.0	243.9	255.4	271.3	281.7	280.7	267.3	249.6	241.0	238.6	253.4
2014	236.7	239.6	241.9	246.9	259.6	273.5	284.1	281.0	267.2	251.8	242.7	240.6	255.5
2015	240.0	242.9	245.1	249.2	261.5	275.7	287.0	282.1	269.0	250.2	242.5	241.8	257.3
Goods-Producing													
2005	35.4	36.6	37.6	37.7	39.8	46.2	54.7	53.5	48.0	42.1	37.4	34.1	41.9
2006	36.3	38.2	39.3	40.1	41.7	50.5	56.5	54.6	49.1	43.4	39.1	35.7	43.7
2007	38.0	39.7	40.1	40.6	42.1	50.0	57.3	56.3	50.5	44.8	40.1	36.8	44.7
2008	38.5	40.7	41.2	41.2	43.8	51.3	58.6	57.2	51.4	45.1	40.1	37.8	45.6
2009	38.9	40.6	41.0	41.1	42.6	50.2	58.3	55.7	48.2	42.1	38.0	35.0	44.3
2010	37.3	38.5	39.5	39.8	41.9	49.9	58.7	56.3	50.1	43.6	39.3	36.2	44.3
2011	37.7	39.9	40.8	41.0	42.7	51.5	59.9	58.2	52.4	45.3	40.4	37.0	45.6
2012	39.6	42.1	43.3	43.5	45.5	54.1	61.2	59.2	52.2	47.3	42.0	38.6	47.4
2013	40.3	43.1	44.3	44.6	45.8	54.0	62.2	60.3	54.5	47.2	42.4	40.2	48.2
2014	42.9	44.7	45.6	47.2	47.6	55.8	63.7	60.6	53.7	47.6	43.6	41.4	49.5
2015	44.0	45.8	46.8	47.2	47.7	55.2	63.6	60.0	52.9	45.4	41.0	39.0	49.1
Service-Providing													
2005	252.3	255.4	257.7	262.6	272.7	278.3	277.7	278.6	276.6	265.6	262.8	262.0	266.9
2006	254.1	258.8	262.1	266.3	277.1	285.3	280.2	281.7	280.0	266.8	264.8	265.0	270.2
2007	257.3	262.3	264.8	268.3	279.0	285.6	281.5	283.2	280.7	269.5	267.0	266.9	272.2
2008	260.8	264.4	266.3	270.9	282.5	288.8	286.8	287.4	285.0	273.0	270.6	270.4	275.6
2009	262.8	266.1	267.0	271.7	279.5	287.0	284.7	286.0	284.9	274.7	271.5	271.3	275.6
2010	264.6	267.6	269.2	274.8	283.0	293.0	290.0	290.8	290.4	280.3	277.3	277.2	279.9
2011	270.2	273.5	274.9	279.4	287.1	296.6	293.4	293.7	294.1	283.1	280.2	280.4	283.9
2012	272.5	277.3	278.9	282.7	291.7	300.0	296.1	297.3	296.4	288.7	282.8	282.7	287.3
2013	274.0	278.8	280.0	284.2	293.9	300.9	297.4	299.2	296.2	285.6	281.9	281.3	287.8
2014	275.2	277.7	279.3	283.7	296.0	300.4	298.2	299.0	296.5	287.1	282.3	282.3	288.1
2015	277.6	279.8	281.3	286.0	297.7	303.0	301.1	300.3	298.9	287.5	284.2	285.6	290.3
Mining and Logging													
2005	9.5	9.9	10.0	10.0	10.1	10.2	10.6	10.6	10.7	10.8	10.7	10.8	10.3
2006	10.5	10.9	11.0	11.6	11.9	12.3	12.1	12.3	12.4	12.2	12.3	12.4	11.8
2007	12.5	13.0	13.1	13.3	13.4	13.9	14.2	14.4	14.4	14.3	14.1	14.2	13.7
2008	14.1	14.4	14.6	14.7	14.9	15.3	15.5	15.8	15.8	15.7	15.5	15.8	15.2
2009	15.2	15.3	15.2	15.1	15.2	15.4	15.1	15.1	14.8	14.3	14.1	14.1	14.9
2010	13.8	13.8	14.1	14.4	14.9	15.5	15.9	16.0	15.7	15.3	15.0	15.0	15.0
2011	14.4	14.6	14.8	15.0	15.2	15.8	16.2	16.2	16.1	15.9	15.6	15.8	15.5
2012	15.1	15.3	15.5	16.0	16.4	16.9	17.2	17.4	16.9	16.7	16.4	16.2	16.3
2013	15.8	16.3	16.7	16.6	16.8	17.3	17.3	17.4	17.1	16.5	16.4	16.5	16.7
2014	16.2	16.5	16.7	17.1	17.2	17.6	17.9	17.9	17.7	17.6	17.7	17.8	17.3
2015	17.5	17.5	17.7	17.8	17.6	17.8	17.8	17.7	17.5	17.0	16.4	16.1	17.4

1. Employment by Industry: Alaska, 2005–2015—*Continued*

(Numbers in thousands, not seasonally adjusted)

Industry and year	January	February	March	April	May	June	July	August	September	October	November	December	Annual average
Construction													
2005	15.0	15.1	15.8	17.5	19.4	21.7	22.8	23.4	22.2	20.7	18.2	16.8	19.1
2006	15.0	15.2	15.8	17.1	19.3	21.5	22.0	22.1	21.5	20.4	17.9	16.6	18.7
2007	14.7	15.0	15.1	16.3	18.2	20.4	20.9	21.3	20.4	19.3	16.8	15.6	17.8
2008	13.8	14.2	14.6	15.8	18.0	20.1	20.9	21.4	20.3	18.9	15.9	15.0	17.4
2009	13.2	13.5	13.9	14.7	17.0	19.0	19.8	20.1	19.0	17.9	15.6	14.6	16.5
2010	13.0	13.1	13.4	14.4	16.7	19.1	20.1	20.4	19.6	18.5	15.8	14.7	16.6
2011	12.8	13.0	13.2	14.5	16.6	18.8	19.5	19.9	19.2	18.2	15.7	14.5	16.3
2012	13.5	13.7	14.1	15.0	17.1	19.6	20.5	21.0	20.0	19.1	16.2	15.1	17.1
2013	13.4	13.9	14.5	15.1	16.9	19.5	20.4	21.4	20.4	18.9	16.6	15.8	17.2
2014	14.5	14.8	15.4	16.1	18.2	20.2	20.9	21.6	20.6	18.7	16.6	15.8	17.8
2015	14.9	15.3	15.9	16.9	18.5	20.2	21.0	20.8	19.5	17.4	15.6	15.4	17.6
Manufacturing													
2005	10.9	11.6	11.8	10.2	10.3	14.3	21.3	19.5	15.1	10.6	8.5	6.5	12.6
2006	10.8	12.1	12.5	11.4	10.5	16.7	22.4	20.2	15.2	10.8	8.9	6.7	13.2
2007	10.8	11.7	11.9	11.0	10.5	15.7	22.2	20.6	15.7	11.2	9.2	7.0	13.1
2008	10.6	12.1	12.0	10.7	10.9	15.9	22.2	20.0	15.3	10.5	8.7	7.0	13.0
2009	10.5	11.8	11.9	11.3	10.4	15.8	23.4	20.5	14.4	9.9	8.3	6.3	12.9
2010	10.5	11.6	12.0	11.0	10.3	15.3	22.7	19.9	14.8	9.8	8.5	6.5	12.7
2011	10.5	12.3	12.8	11.5	10.9	16.9	24.2	22.1	17.1	11.2	9.1	6.7	13.8
2012	11.0	13.1	13.7	12.5	12.0	17.6	23.5	20.8	15.3	11.5	9.4	7.3	14.0
2013	11.1	12.9	13.1	12.9	12.1	17.2	24.5	21.5	17.0	11.8	9.4	7.9	14.3
2014	12.2	13.4	13.5	14.0	12.2	18.0	24.9	21.1	15.4	11.3	9.3	7.8	14.4
2015	11.6	13.0	13.2	12.5	11.6	17.2	24.8	21.5	15.9	11.0	9.0	7.5	14.1
Trade, Transportation, and Utilities													
2005	58.3	58.4	59.0	60.7	64.8	66.9	68.5	68.5	66.3	62.6	61.4	61.0	63.0
2006	59.4	58.9	60.0	61.6	65.8	68.6	69.0	69.0	66.5	62.2	61.8	61.9	63.7
2007	59.9	59.8	60.4	61.8	65.9	68.7	69.3	69.5	67.0	63.0	62.1	62.4	64.2
2008	60.8	60.6	61.3	62.5	66.9	69.0	69.8	69.5	67.2	63.0	62.3	62.5	64.6
2009	60.0	59.5	60.0	61.4	64.9	66.8	67.7	68.0	66.0	61.7	61.3	61.1	63.2
2010	58.9	58.6	59.0	60.6	64.2	66.9	67.7	67.8	65.2	61.7	61.0	61.3	62.7
2011	58.9	58.9	59.8	60.9	64.9	67.3	68.3	68.6	66.5	62.4	61.7	61.6	63.3
2012	59.8	59.6	59.8	61.5	65.3	67.7	68.5	68.6	66.9	64.1	62.0	62.2	63.8
2013	60.1	59.8	60.1	61.5	65.8	67.9	68.6	69.4	67.3	63.3	62.4	62.5	64.1
2014	60.2	60.5	60.5	62.3	67.2	68.6	69.7	70.0	67.7	64.4	63.0	63.2	64.8
2015	61.3	61.3	61.7	63.4	67.7	69.5	70.6	70.9	69.0	66.1	65.1	65.7	66.0
Wholesale Trade													
2005	5.9	6.0	6.0	6.1	6.4	6.5	6.8	6.7	6.5	6.3	6.2	6.2	6.3
2006	6.2	6.2	6.3	6.3	6.6	6.8	7.0	7.0	6.8	6.5	6.3	6.4	6.5
2007	6.3	6.3	6.4	6.5	6.6	6.9	6.9	7.0	6.7	6.5	6.4	6.4	6.6
2008	6.3	6.3	6.3	6.4	6.6	6.8	7.0	6.9	6.6	6.3	6.2	6.2	6.5
2009													
	6.2	6.1	6.2	6.2	6.4	6.6	6.7	6.6	6.4	6.0	6.0	6.0	6.3
2010	5.9	5.9	6.0	6.1	6.3	6.5	6.8	6.8	6.4	6.2	6.1	6.2	6.3
2011	6.0	6.1	6.1	6.1	6.3	6.5	6.8	6.7	6.4	6.3	6.1	6.1	6.3
2012	6.0	6.0	6.0	6.2	6.3	6.5	6.6	6.6	6.6	6.4	6.4	6.5	6.3
2013	6.4	6.4	6.5	6.5	6.7	6.8	6.8	6.8	6.6	6.6	6.5	6.5	6.6
2014	6.4	6.4	6.4	6.4	6.6	6.7	6.7	6.7	6.6	6.4	6.4	6.5	6.5
2015	6.4	6.4	6.5	6.5	6.6	6.7	6.7	6.7	6.6	6.5	6.4	6.4	6.5
Retail Trade													
2005	33.8	33.7	33.9	34.8	36.3	37.7	38.0	37.9	37.0	35.8	35.7	35.8	35.9
2006	34.3	33.6	34.0	34.9	36.5	37.9	37.8	37.5	36.5	35.4	35.5	35.7	35.8
2007	34.3	33.8	34.2	34.9	36.5	37.8	38.2	37.9	36.8	35.7	35.8	36.2	36.0
2008	35.0	34.3	34.6	35.3	36.7	37.9	38.1	37.6	36.8	36.0	35.9	36.0	36.2
2009	34.2	33.6	33.8	34.7	36.1	37.0	37.3	37.3	36.6	35.4	35.6	35.5	35.6
2010	34.0	33.7	33.7	34.7	35.9	37.2	37.4	37.1	36.0	35.2	35.4	35.5	35.5
2011	34.0	33.6	33.9	34.5	36.0	37.2	37.5	37.5	36.7	35.7	35.9	35.9	35.7
2012	34.5	34.0	34.0	34.7	36.2	37.3	37.4	37.3	36.5	35.8	35.7	35.7	35.8
2013	34.3	33.8	33.9	34.6	36.1	37.3	37.6	38.0	37.2	36.1	36.2	36.3	36.0
2014	34.8	34.7	34.7	35.6	37.3	38.3	38.8	38.8	37.7	36.9	37.0	37.0	36.8
2015	35.6	35.3	35.5	36.3	37.8	38.9	39.4	39.4	38.6	38.3	38.9	38.8	37.7

1. Employment by Industry: Alaska, 2005–2015—*Continued*

(Numbers in thousands, not seasonally adjusted)

Industry and year	January	February	March	April	May	June	July	August	September	October	November	December	Annual average
Transportation and Utilities													
2005	18.6	18.7	19.1	19.8	22.1	22.7	23.7	23.9	22.8	20.5	19.5	19.0	20.9
2006	18.9	19.1	19.7	20.4	22.7	23.9	24.2	24.5	23.2	20.3	20.0	19.8	21.4
2007	19.3	19.7	19.8	20.4	22.8	24.0	24.2	24.6	23.5	20.8	19.9	19.8	21.6
2009	19.5	20.0	20.4	20.8	23.6	24.3	24.7	25.0	23.8	20.7	20.2	20.3	21.9
2010	19.6	19.8	20.0	20.5	22.4	23.2	23.7	24.1	23.0	20.3	19.7	19.6	21.3
2011	19.0	19.0	19.3	19.8	22.0	23.2	23.5	23.9	22.8	20.3	19.5	19.6	21.0
2012	18.9	19.2	19.8	20.3	22.6	23.6	24.0	24.4	23.4	20.4	19.7	19.6	21.3
2013	19.3	19.6	19.8	20.6	22.8	23.9	24.5	24.7	23.8	21.9	19.9	20.0	21.7
2014	19.4	19.6	19.7	20.4	23.0	23.8	24.2	24.6	23.5	20.6	19.7	19.7	21.5
2015	19.0	19.4	19.4	20.3	23.3	23.6	24.2	24.5	23.4	21.1	19.6	19.7	21.5
	19.3	19.6	19.7	20.6	23.3	23.9	24.5	24.8	23.8	21.3	19.8	20.5	21.8
Information													
2005	6.8	6.9	6.9	6.9	7.0	7.0	7.0	7.0	7.0	6.9	7.0	7.0	7.0
2006	6.9	7.0	7.0	6.9	7.0	7.1	7.0	7.1	7.0	7.0	7.0	7.0	7.0
2007	6.9	6.9	6.9	6.8	6.9	7.0	7.0	7.0	7.0	6.9	6.9	6.9	6.9
2008	6.8	6.9	6.9	6.9	7.1	7.1	7.1	7.1	7.1	7.0	7.0	7.0	7.0
2009	6.7	6.8	6.7	6.6	6.5	6.6	6.6	6.5	6.5	6.5	6.4	6.4	6.6
2010	6.3	6.3	6.3	6.3	6.3	6.5	6.6	6.5	6.7	7.0	6.9	6.6	6.5
2011	6.3	6.3	6.4	6.4	6.3	6.4	6.4	6.3	6.2	6.3	6.3	6.3	6.3
2012	6.2	6.2	6.2	6.2	6.3	6.3	6.3	6.2	6.1	6.2	6.1	6.2	6.2
2013	6.0	6.0	6.0	6.1	6.2	6.2	6.2	6.2	6.2	6.2	6.3	6.3	6.2
2014	6.2	6.2	6.2	6.2	6.3	6.2	6.3	6.3	6.2	6.3	6.3	6.3	6.3
2015	6.3	6.3	6.4	6.3	6.3	6.3	6.3	6.3	6.3	6.2	6.1	6.2	6.3
Financial Activities													
2005	12.1	12.0	12.0	12.2	12.4	12.8	13.0	12.9	12.9	12.8	12.7	12.5	12.5
2006	12.2	12.2	12.3	12.4	12.7	13.0	13.0	13.1	12.8	12.5	12.4	12.4	12.6
2007	12.0	12.2	12.3	12.3	12.6	13.0	12.9	13.1	12.7	12.5	12.3	12.3	12.5
2008	11.9	12.0	12.1	12.1	12.5	12.5	12.7	12.6	12.4	12.0	11.9	11.9	12.2
2009	11.8	11.8	11.8	11.9	12.1	12.4	12.6	12.6	12.2	12.3	12.2	12.1	12.2
2010	11.9	11.8	11.8	12.0	12.2	12.6	12.7	12.7	12.4	12.4	12.2	11.9	12.2
2011	11.9	12.0	12.0	12.0	12.1	12.5	12.7	12.7	12.3	12.1	12.0	11.9	12.2
2012	11.9	11.9	11.8	11.9	12.2	12.5	12.7	12.7	12.2	12.3	12.1	12.1	12.2
2013	11.8	11.9	11.8	12.0	12.1	12.7	12.9	12.8	12.2	12.2	12.0	12.0	12.2
2014	11.9	11.9	11.8	11.9	12.2	12.6	12.7	12.5	12.1	12.0	11.8	11.8	12.1
2015	11.6	11.6	11.6	11.8	12.1	12.8	13.1	12.7	12.3	12.3	12.1	12.0	12.2
Professional and Business Services													
2005	23.1	23.6	23.5	24.2	25.5	26.9	27.0	27.3	26.3	24.7	24.3	24.3	25.1
2006	23.5	24.2	24.6	25.1	26.3	27.5	27.4	27.4	27.0	25.4	24.9	25.1	25.7
2007	24.6	25.1	25.3	25.9	27.3	28.3	28.1	28.2	27.7	26.3	26.1	25.9	26.6
2008	25.6	26.1	26.2	27.1	28.6	29.6	29.8	29.8	29.1	27.9	27.4	27.5	27.9
2009	26.6	27.0	27.1	27.1	28.3	29.1	29.1	29.1	28.6	27.4	26.7	26.7	27.7
2010	26.3	26.7	26.8	27.0	28.1	29.5	29.5	29.6	29.3	28.2	27.5	27.3	28.0
2011	26.9	27.5	27.4	28.1	29.0	30.3	30.1	29.8	29.9	28.9	28.6	28.6	28.8
2012	28.0	28.6	28.8	29.1	30.2	31.4	31.5	31.4	31.2	30.1	29.3	29.2	29.9
2013	28.6	29.4	29.3	29.8	30.6	31.5	31.6	32.1	30.9	29.7	29.5	29.5	30.2
2014	28.7	28.6	29.2	29.4	30.6	31.2	31.4	31.5	30.9	30.2	29.1	29.3	30.0
2015	29.0	29.2	29.2	29.8	30.8	31.5	31.5	31.3	30.7	29.6	28.0	28.0	29.9
Education and Health Services													
2005	35.5	35.8	36.3	36.2	36.5	36.8	36.4	36.5	36.5	36.6	36.8	37.1	36.4
2006	36.8	37.3	37.4	37.6	37.9	38.0	37.7	37.7	37.6	37.2	37.4	37.5	37.5
2007	37.1	37.7	37.9	37.9	37.9	37.7	37.3	37.5	37.1	37.3	37.4	37.6	37.5
2008	37.4	37.9	38.1	38.1	38.3	38.1	38.3	38.3	38.1	38.4	38.6	38.9	38.2
2009	38.5	39.0	39.1	39.5	39.6	39.7	39.9	40.0	40.0	40.6	40.5	40.9	39.8
2010	40.8	41.2	41.3	41.9	42.1	42.2	42.4	42.3	42.6	43.1	43.2	43.5	42.2
2011	43.5	43.9	44.0	44.4	44.6	44.6	44.7	45.0	45.0	45.1	45.3	45.8	44.7
2012	45.4	46.0	46.0	46.2	46.4	46.5	45.6	45.7	45.5	46.6	46.8	46.9	46.1
2013	46.5	47.0	47.1	47.4	47.4	47.1	47.1	47.1	47.0	47.0	47.1	47.1	47.1
2014	46.5	46.8	46.9	47.1	47.0	46.8	46.7	46.7	46.6	46.8	46.7	46.8	46.8
2015	46.7	47.1	47.1	47.3	47.3	47.3	47.4	47.2	47.0	47.2	47.3	48.2	47.3

1. Employment by Industry: Alaska, 2005–2015—*Continued*

(Numbers in thousands, not seasonally adjusted)

Industry and year	January	February	March	April	May	June	July	August	September	October	November	December	Annual average
Leisure and Hospitality													
2005	25.8	26.1	26.8	28.3	32.4	36.7	38.6	38.3	35.1	28.6	27.3	27.3	30.9
2006	25.8	26.5	27.2	28.5	32.9	37.9	38.8	38.9	35.7	29.0	28.1	28.2	31.5
2007	26.8	27.3	27.9	29.3	33.8	39.0	39.8	39.6	35.9	29.1	28.3	28.1	32.1
2008	27.0	27.4	27.8	29.0	34.8	38.9	40.3	39.9	36.2	29.2	28.3	28.1	32.2
2009	26.5	27.1	27.5	28.1	33.1	36.5	37.7	37.8	35.1	29.0	27.7	27.5	31.1
2010	26.4	26.9	27.2	28.6	32.9	36.9	38.4	38.4	35.5	29.2	28.5	28.8	31.5
2011	27.5	28.0	28.6	29.7	33.9	38.3	39.8	39.7	36.5	30.2	29.0	28.9	32.5
2012	27.9	28.4	29.1	30.4	34.7	39.4	40.7	40.5	37.2	32.1	29.7	29.6	33.3
2013	28.4	29.1	29.8	30.8	35.6	39.9	41.2	41.0	37.5	32.4	29.7	29.5	33.7
2014	28.8	29.4	30.3	31.1	36.8	40.3	41.5	41.4	38.1	32.4	30.3	30.3	34.2
2015	29.7	30.2	30.8	31.7	37.6	41.1	42.7	42.1	39.2	31.7	31.2	30.9	34.9
Other Services													
2005	10.8	11.0	11.1	11.2	11.2	11.3	11.4	11.3	11.2	11.2	11.2	11.1	11.2
2006	10.9	11.0	11.2	11.0	11.2	11.2	11.4	11.3	11.4	11.4	11.4	11.3	11.2
2007	11.1	11.4	11.5	11.2	11.5	11.4	11.4	11.4	11.3	11.2	11.2	11.2	11.3
2008	10.9	11.1	11.2	11.2	11.4	11.5	11.5	11.5	11.4	11.5	11.3	11.2	11.3
2009													
	11.1	11.3	11.2	11.4	11.6	11.6	11.7	11.7	11.6	11.2	11.2	11.1	11.4
2010	10.9	10.9	11.1	11.3	11.4	11.6	11.6	11.5	11.4	11.3	11.2	11.1	11.3
2011	11.0	11.1	11.2	11.3	11.4	11.5	11.5	11.5	11.5	11.5	11.4	11.4	11.4
2012	11.3	11.3	11.4	11.5	11.8	11.9	11.8	11.8	11.7	11.6	11.6	11.5	11.6
2013	11.4	11.5	11.6	11.7	11.9	12.0	11.9	11.8	11.7	11.6	11.6	11.5	11.7
2014	11.5	11.5	11.4	11.7	11.9	12.0	12.1	12.0	11.9	12.1	11.9	11.5	11.8
2015	11.4	11.4	11.5	11.7	12.0	12.0	11.8	11.6	11.6	11.7	11.7	11.8	11.7
Government													
2005	79.9	81.6	82.1	82.9	82.9	79.9	75.8	76.8	81.3	82.2	82.1	81.7	80.8
2006	78.6	81.7	82.4	83.2	83.3	82.0	75.9	77.2	82.0	82.1	81.8	81.6	81.0
2007	78.9	81.9	82.6	83.1	83.1	80.5	75.7	76.9	82.0	83.2	82.7	82.5	81.1
2008	80.4	82.4	82.7	84.0	82.9	82.1	77.3	78.7	83.5	84.0	83.8	83.3	82.1
2009	81.6	83.6	83.6	85.7	83.4	84.3	79.4	80.3	84.9	86.0	85.5	85.5	83.7
2010	83.1	85.2	85.7	87.1	85.8	86.8	81.1	82.0	87.3	87.4	86.8	86.7	85.4
2011	84.2	85.8	85.5	86.6	84.9	85.7	79.9	80.1	86.2	86.6	85.9	85.9	84.8
2012	82.0	85.3	85.8	85.9	84.8	84.3	79.0	80.4	85.6	85.7	85.2	85.0	84.1
2013	81.2	84.1	84.3	84.9	84.3	83.6	77.9	78.8	83.4	83.2	83.3	82.9	82.7
2014	81.4	82.8	83.0	84.0	84.0	82.7	77.8	78.6	83.0	82.9	83.2	83.1	82.2
2015	81.6	82.7	83.0	84.0	83.9	82.5	77.7	78.2	82.8	82.7	82.7	82.8	82.1

2. Average Weekly Hours by Selected Industry: Alaska, 2011–2015

(Not seasonally adjusted)

Industry and year	January	February	March	April	May	June	July	August	September	October	November	December	Annual average
Total Private													
2011	36.5	36.4	35.8	35.0	35.5	36.1	36.8	36.4	35.7	36.2	34.5	34.2	35.8
2012	34.6	34.7	34.5	34.6	34.5	35.7	37.2	36.9	36.4	35.3	34.6	34.7	35.4
2013	33.7	35.5	35.2	34.3	34.5	36.3	36.6	36.5	35.9	34.6	34.1	34.5	35.2
2014	33.5	34.5	34.6	33.9	34.1	35.3	35.8	35.3	34.9	34.5	34.3	33.7	34.6
2015	34.1	35.0	35.0	34.0	34.7	35.2	35.8	36.1	34.7	34.2	34.1	33.4	34.7
Goods-Producing													
2011	42.6	42.3	42.7	38.0	38.7	40.6	44.1	42.5	40.7	42.4	38.0	37.5	41.0
2012	36.4	38.1	37.7	35.5	37.5	39.4	43.4	43.9	42.3	40.5	38.3	39.3	39.7
2013	37.3	42.8	42.9	38.6	39.8	42.8	45.1	45.0	42.0	39.2	38.5	39.4	41.4
2014	37.9	39.1	40.1	37.1	37.3	37.6	41.8	40.1	39.5	38.9	36.0	37.2	38.7
2015	38.3	39.0	39.7	35.0	37.9	37.8	39.2	39.5	35.6	35.7	34.0	34.5	37.3
Construction													
2011	35.5	36.7	37.1	38.3	39.0	40.1	40.6	41.4	41.4	40.6	36.2	34.2	38.8
2012	34.5	35.2	34.3	34.7	37.4	39.5	40.6	40.6	40.8	39.4	36.6	38.5	38.0
2013	38.0	38.8	38.4	39.2	38.7	41.0	42.4	42.7	41.6	40.0	38.8	40.0	40.2
2014	39.7	39.7	39.2	39.8	37.3	39.1	39.1	40.1	39.3	39.7	35.4	37.1	38.8
2015	36.2	35.5	35.7	38.0	38.4	40.5	40.2	40.4	36.4	38.1	35.5	35.2	37.7
Manufacturing													
2011	40.0	47.3	47.7	41.0	40.4	44.7	52.2	47.0	40.3	45.6	38.7	40.7	44.8
2012	36.3	49.7	48.7	39.7	39.9	42.4	52.1	53.6	46.0	42.4	38.2	38.2	45.4
2013	36.0	53.0	52.7	37.6	40.8	44.6	50.3	49.7	40.7	33.8	33.1	32.7	43.7
2014	31.0	35.8	40.3	37.0	40.2	38.0	47.5	39.1	38.5	35.7	34.7	34.8	38.7
2015	41.0	44.5	45.8	35.0	44.3	37.3	47.1	45.0	38.2	34.0	31.5	31.8	40.8
Trade, Transportation, and Utilities													
2011	36.5	36.1	34.9	34.8	35.5	36.0	35.9	35.3	34.7	35.4	34.6	34.2	35.3
2012	34.4	34.5	34.2	34.6	34.3	35.6	36.1	35.2	34.8	33.5	33.8	33.3	34.6
2013	32.4	33.5	33.4	33.1	33.8	36.1	36.4	36.0	36.3	34.3	34.0	34.4	34.5
2014	33.8	34.0	34.4	33.8	34.2	35.9	35.3	35.2	34.8	34.0	34.4	33.3	34.5
2015	33.0	34.1	34.0	33.7	34.4	34.9	35.3	35.5	35.0	33.3	34.1	33.4	34.2
Professional and Business Services													
2011	40.2	39.3	38.6	38.1	38.3	38.8	38.3	38.6	38.3	38.6	37.0	37.0	38.4
2012	38.6	37.1	36.8	37.5	37.1	37.2	38.0	37.5	37.4	37.7	36.9	36.4	37.3
2013	35.4	36.6	35.9	35.9	35.5	36.8	36.6	36.9	36.5	36.5	35.7	36.1	36.2
2014	34.9	36.0	36.0	35.4	36.3	37.8	37.6	38.2	37.2	36.3	36.2	35.3	36.5
2015	34.8	36.6	36.9	36.9	36.6	37.9	37.8	38.7	37.6	37.6	37.3	35.0	37.0
Leisure and Hospitality													
2011	23.6	23.5	23.0	23.5	24.8	25.0	25.9	26.3	25.2	25.4	24.8	24.4	24.7
2012	25.2	25.7	26.2	26.8	26.1	28.2	30.0	29.1	29.3	28.2	27.0	27.8	27.6
2013	26.4	26.7	27.6	27.2	26.9	28.5	28.1	28.5	28.2	27.1	26.5	27.2	27.5
2014	25.7	27.4	27.6	26.7	26.4	28.7	28.9	28.8	27.7	27.2	27.4	26.5	27.5
2015	26.8	27.3	27.6	27.3	27.4	28.6	29.0	29.7	28.5	26.9	26.6	25.9	27.8

3. Average Hourly Earnings by Selected Industry: Alaska, 2011–2015

(Dollars, not seasonally adjusted)

Industry and year	January	February	March	April	May	June	July	August	September	October	November	December	Annual average
Total Private													
2011	23.61	23.55	23.82	24.68	24.46	24.24	24.20	24.32	25.39	25.27	25.23	25.36	24.51
2012	25.27	24.72	24.70	25.45	25.54	25.37	25.26	25.26	25.94	26.43	26.45	26.75	25.59
2013	26.43	26.05	26.07	26.56	26.43	26.30	26.50	26.79	27.40	27.50	27.43	27.52	26.74
2014	27.10	27.35	26.99	27.19	27.07	26.86	26.66	26.95	27.22	27.75	27.39	27.46	27.15
2015	26.93	27.02	27.41	28.10	27.86	27.74	27.83	28.07	27.90	28.46	28.63	28.58	27.88
Goods-Producing													
2011	32.83	31.94	31.59	35.93	35.36	34.10	30.82	31.33	34.91	33.94	35.24	35.63	33.42
2012	33.07	30.41	30.01	33.30	34.38	33.33	30.98	30.97	33.19	34.63	35.50	36.10	32.83
2013	33.35	31.55	30.62	33.80	34.18	32.94	32.27	33.24	35.41	36.15	36.75	36.45	33.76
2014	34.49	34.51	33.39	35.62	36.56	36.07	33.24	34.21	34.48	36.15	35.38	35.66	34.89
2015	30.93	30.60	31.60	36.26	35.57	35.51	34.62	35.39	35.55	36.91	38.16	38.18	34.81
Construction													
2011	35.38	36.10	35.73	36.49	35.51	36.98	36.94	36.47	37.25	35.61	34.46	35.79	36.16
2012	35.21	35.25	34.74	35.85	36.58	37.95	37.54	37.59	37.69	37.71	37.20	37.31	36.93
2013	35.89	37.18	36.07	36.63	36.27	36.91	37.74	38.22	37.91	37.58	37.53	36.76	37.17
2014	36.13	37.06	36.41	37.28	38.17	38.46	38.96	38.44	38.42	38.41	36.25	35.73	37.62
2015	35.94	36.05	37.31	38.72	38.34	39.44	39.05	39.07	38.19	37.49	37.25	37.06	38.00
Manufacturing													
2011	20.80	17.57	17.56	22.47	22.90	19.28	16.42	16.77	19.44	19.32	23.75	24.31	19.08
2012	19.98	16.80	17.08	21.13	22.95	18.89	16.81	16.71	18.52	21.08	23.65	24.98	18.91
2013	20.46	17.31	16.29	20.22	21.44	18.92	16.79	16.97	19.49	22.25	22.19	24.10	18.78
2014	21.34	19.88	18.11	20.34	22.20	19.59	17.19	17.39	18.36	21.09	21.97	23.66	19.40
2015	17.54	16.30	17.24	20.08	20.58	19.21	17.18	19.41	20.32	23.66	25.93	26.96	19.40
Trade, Transportation, and Utilities													
2011	20.71	20.68	20.49	20.75	20.55	19.78	20.08	19.97	20.34	20.66	20.64	20.60	20.42
2012	20.81	20.60	20.50	20.73	20.30	19.94	20.17	20.11	20.66	20.95	21.00	21.06	20.55
2013	21.16	20.91	21.59	21.45	20.75	20.50	20.77	21.00	21.58	21.93	21.86	22.32	21.30
2014	22.15	22.34	22.67	22.52	21.93	21.55	21.76	22.00	22.41	22.85	22.81	22.93	22.31
2015	23.19	22.97	23.27	22.85	22.63	22.26	22.51	22.64	22.60	23.41	23.16	23.42	22.89
Professional and Business Services													
2011	33.79	34.48	34.05	34.19	33.27	32.71	32.69	32.62	33.14	33.32	33.05	33.34	33.37
2012	32.91	31.75	32.38	33.00	32.47	32.62	33.09	32.95	33.06	33.17	33.40	34.34	32.93
2013	34.64	34.22	34.25	34.48	34.79	34.82	34.81	35.34	35.33	35.19	35.28	35.25	34.87
2014	34.64	35.00	34.40	34.64	34.52	33.89	33.80	34.30	34.73	35.47	35.49	33.97	34.56
2015	34.16	33.82	33.95	34.08	34.26	33.57	33.65	34.34	33.60	34.01	34.33	34.26	33.99
Leisure and Hospitality													
2011	13.84	14.03	14.29	14.21	13.96	13.60	13.90	13.69	14.18	14.13	14.02	14.17	13.98
2012	14.19	14.52	14.40	14.35	14.45	14.17	14.20	14.35	14.48	14.75	15.13	15.07	14.48
2013	14.93	15.14	15.05	15.12	15.31	15.05	15.31	15.45	15.71	15.73	16.02	16.00	15.40
2014	16.21	16.96	16.33	16.64	16.52	16.03	16.42	16.48	16.95	16.94	16.98	17.48	16.64
2015	16.96	17.15	17.13	17.19	17.01	16.81	16.79	16.80	16.87	17.58	17.60	18.04	17.11

4. Average Weekly Earnings by Selected Industry: Alaska, 2011–2015

(Dollars, not seasonally adjusted)

Industry and year	January	February	March	April	May	June	July	August	September	October	November	December	Annual average
Total Private													
2011	861.77	857.22	852.76	863.80	868.33	875.06	890.56	885.25	906.42	914.77	870.44	867.31	877.46
2012	874.34	857.78	852.15	880.57	881.13	905.71	939.67	932.09	944.22	932.98	915.17	928.23	905.89
2013	890.69	924.78	917.66	911.01	911.84	954.69	969.90	977.84	983.66	951.50	935.36	949.44	941.25
2014	907.85	943.58	933.85	921.74	923.09	948.16	954.43	951.34	949.98	957.38	939.48	925.40	939.39
2015	918.31	945.70	959.35	955.40	966.74	976.45	996.31	1,013.33	968.13	973.33	976.28	954.57	967.44
Goods-Producing													
2011	1,398.56	1,351.06	1,348.89	1,365.34	1,368.43	1,384.46	1,359.16	1,331.53	1,420.84	1,439.06	1,339.12	1,336.13	1,370.22
2012	1,203.75	1,158.62	1,131.38	1,182.15	1,289.25	1,313.20	1,344.53	1,359.58	1,403.94	1,402.52	1,359.65	1,418.73	1,303.35
2013	1,243.96	1,350.34	1,313.60	1,304.68	1,360.36	1,409.83	1,455.38	1,495.80	1,487.22	1,417.08	1,414.88	1,436.13	1,397.66
2014	1,307.17	1,349.34	1,338.94	1,321.50	1,363.69	1,356.23	1,389.43	1,371.82	1,361.96	1,406.24	1,273.68	1,326.55	1,350.24
2015	1,184.62	1,193.40	1,254.52	1,269.10	1,348.10	1,342.28	1,357.10	1,397.91	1,265.58	1,317.69	1,297.44	1,317.21	1,298.41
Construction													
2011	1,255.99	1,324.87	1,325.58	1,397.57	1,384.89	1,482.90	1,499.76	1,509.86	1,542.15	1,445.77	1,247.45	1,224.02	1,403.01
2012	1,214.75	1,240.80	1,191.58	1,244.00	1,368.09	1,499.03	1,524.12	1,526.15	1,537.75	1,485.77	1,361.52	1,436.44	1,403.34
2013	1,363.82	1,442.58	1,385.09	1,435.90	1,403.65	1,513.31	1,600.18	1,631.99	1,577.06	1,503.20	1,456.16	1,470.40	1,494.23
2014	1,434.36	1,471.28	1,427.27	1,483.74	1,423.74	1,503.79	1,523.34	1,541.44	1,509.91	1,524.88	1,283.25	1,325.58	1,459.66
2015	1,301.03	1,279.78	1,331.97	1,471.36	1,472.26	1,597.32	1,569.81	1,578.43	1,390.12	1,428.37	1,322.38	1,304.51	1,432.60
Manufacturing													
2011	832.00	831.06	837.61	921.27	925.16	861.82	857.12	788.19	783.43	880.99	919.13	989.42	854.78
2012	725.27	834.96	831.80	838.86	915.71	800.94	875.80	895.66	851.92	893.79	903.43	954.24	858.51
2013	736.56	917.43	858.48	760.27	874.75	843.83	844.54	843.41	793.24	752.05	734.49	788.07	820.69
2014	661.54	711.70	729.83	752.58	892.44	744.42	816.53	679.95	706.86	752.91	762.36	823.37	750.78
2015	719.14	725.35	789.59	702.80	911.69	716.53	809.18	873.45	776.22	804.44	816.80	857.33	791.52
Trade, Transportation, and Utilities													
2011	755.92	746.55	715.10	722.10	729.53	712.08	720.87	704.94	705.80	731.36	714.14	704.52	720.83
2012	715.86	710.70	701.10	717.26	696.29	709.86	728.14	707.87	718.97	701.83	709.80	701.30	711.03
2013	685.58	700.49	721.11	710.00	701.35	740.05	756.03	756.00	783.35	752.20	743.24	767.81	734.85
2014	748.67	759.56	779.85	761.18	750.01	773.65	768.13	774.40	779.87	776.90	784.66	763.57	769.70
2015	765.27	783.28	791.18	770.05	778.47	776.87	794.60	803.72	791.00	779.55	789.76	782.23	782.84
Professional and Business Services													
2011	1,358.36	1,355.06	1,314.33	1,302.64	1,274.24	1,269.15	1,252.03	1,259.13	1,269.26	1,286.15	1,222.85	1,233.58	1,281.41
2012	1,270.33	1,177.93	1,191.58	1,237.50	1,204.64	1,213.46	1,257.42	1,235.63	1,236.44	1,250.51	1,232.46	1,249.98	1,228.29
2013	1,226.26	1,252.45	1,229.58	1,237.83	1,235.05	1,281.38	1,274.05	1,304.05	1,289.55	1,284.44	1,259.50	1,272.53	1,262.29
2014	1,208.94	1,260.00	1,238.40	1,226.26	1,253.08	1,281.04	1,270.88	1,310.26	1,291.96	1,287.56	1,284.74	1,199.14	1,261.44
2015	1,188.77	1,237.81	1,252.76	1,257.55	1,253.92	1,272.30	1,271.97	1,328.96	1,263.36	1,278.78	1,280.51	1,199.10	1,257.63
Leisure and Hospitality													
2011	326.62	329.71	328.67	333.94	346.21	340.00	360.01	360.05	357.34	358.90	347.70	345.75	345.31
2012	357.59	373.16	377.28	384.58	377.15	399.59	426.00	417.59	424.26	415.95	408.51	418.95	399.65
2013	394.15	404.24	415.38	411.26	411.84	428.93	430.21	440.33	443.02	426.28	424.53	435.20	423.50
2014	416.60	464.70	450.71	444.29	436.13	460.06	474.54	474.62	469.52	460.77	465.25	463.22	457.60
2015	454.53	468.20	472.79	469.29	466.07	480.77	486.91	498.96	480.80	472.90	468.16	467.24	475.66

ARIZONA
At a Glance

Population:
  2005 estimate: 5,839,077
  2010 census: 6,392,017
  2015 estimate: 6,828,065

Percent change in population:
  2005–2015: 16.9%
  2010–2015: 6.8%

Percent change in total nonfarm employment:
  2005–2015: 4.9%

Industry with the largest growth in employment, 2005–2015 (thousands):
  Education and health services, 119.7

Industry with the largest decline or smallest growth in employment, 2005–2015 (thousands):
  Construction, –91.8

Civilian labor force:
  2005: 2,883,226
  2010: 3,089,705
  2015: 3,152,708

Unemployment rate and rank among states (highest to lowest):
  2005: 4.7%, 30th
  2010: 10.4%, 11th
  2015: 6.1%, 9th

Over-the-year change in unemployment rates:
  2012–2013: –0.6%
  2013–2014: –0.9%
  2014–2015: –0.7%

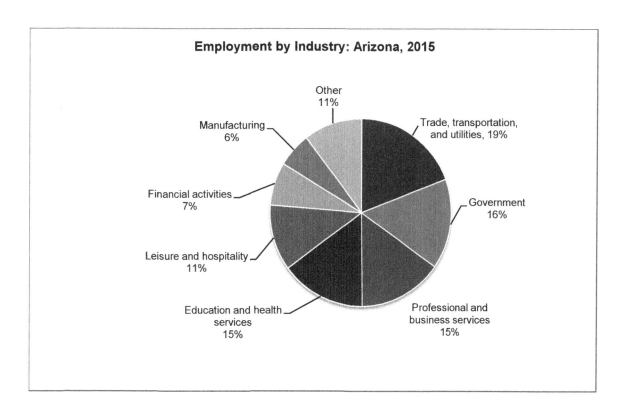

Employment by Industry: Arizona, 2015

Other 11%
Manufacturing 6%
Financial activities 7%
Leisure and hospitality 11%
Education and health services 15%
Trade, transportation, and utilities, 19%
Government 16%
Professional and business services 15%

1. Employment by Industry: Arizona, 2005–2015

(Numbers in thousands, not seasonally adjusted)

Industry and year	January	February	March	April	May	June	July	August	September	October	November	December	Annual average
Total Nonfarm													
2005	2,416.7	2,458.2	2,477.4	2,509.8	2,511.6	2,485.0	2,472.0	2,511.3	2,549.7	2,562.1	2,589.5	2,608.6	2,512.7
2006	2,566.2	2,610.6	2,633.4	2,639.0	2,648.1	2,620.7	2,592.4	2,629.7	2,661.3	2,674.1	2,692.4	2,703.7	2,639.3
2007	2,636.3	2,674.2	2,692.1	2,682.1	2,687.1	2,655.7	2,629.4	2,668.1	2,688.7	2,701.3	2,718.4	2,719.7	2,679.4
2008	2,650.5	2,673.2	2,672.3	2,661.9	2,655.0	2,605.5	2,563.4	2,601.6	2,607.4	2,600.4	2,597.0	2,581.8	2,622.5
2009	2,498.6	2,493.7	2,485.3	2,467.5	2,451.7	2,391.6	2,363.6	2,387.5	2,400.6	2,407.4	2,421.7	2,422.1	2,432.6
2010	2,366.3	2,385.2	2,396.9	2,407.1	2,414.0	2,351.9	2,326.5	2,357.3	2,373.8	2,402.2	2,423.1	2,429.7	2,386.2
2011	2,380.7	2,403.0	2,415.9	2,427.3	2,426.8	2,362.4	2,338.4	2,393.4	2,423.2	2,441.2	2,465.0	2,468.3	2,412.1
2012	2,426.0	2,449.0	2,466.8	2,468.5	2,464.5	2,423.0	2,390.3	2,448.4	2,475.6	2,494.6	2,523.3	2,531.6	2,463.5
2013	2,479.0	2,505.5	2,518.3	2,527.1	2,524.6	2,474.3	2,450.3	2,504.6	2,531.0	2,554.0	2,586.4	2,592.5	2,520.6
2014	2,536.5	2,558.6	2,567.0	2,578.0	2,565.3	2,521.7	2,497.1	2,549.9	2,575.4	2,608.8	2,638.4	2,648.2	2,570.4
2015	2,596.0	2,620.9	2,628.3	2,637.1	2,627.7	2,575.2	2,564.7	2,617.4	2,646.4	2,683.8	2,717.0	2,722.7	2,636.4
Total Private													
2005	2,021.1	2,043.6	2,065.5	2,097.3	2,101.8	2,106.4	2,106.6	2,122.3	2,138.6	2,147.2	2,173.1	2,193.3	2,109.7
2006	2,165.8	2,194.3	2,217.1	2,222.8	2,230.4	2,238.2	2,221.9	2,235.6	2,244.6	2,249.2	2,266.9	2,282.6	2,230.8
2007	2,226.5	2,248.6	2,265.2	2,255.6	2,261.2	2,264.1	2,244.3	2,256.1	2,255.6	2,264.5	2,278.5	2,280.5	2,258.4
2008	2,220.6	2,230.6	2,230.7	2,219.1	2,213.1	2,199.1	2,172.3	2,179.4	2,168.6	2,157.7	2,151.8	2,139.2	2,190.2
2009	2,068.5	2,054.1	2,047.4	2,027.3	2,018.0	1,999.8	1,981.7	1,982.5	1,973.6	1,976.8	1,990.4	1,994.9	2,009.6
2010	1,947.9	1,955.6	1,968.8	1,975.6	1,973.5	1,964.5	1,950.5	1,958.5	1,954.6	1,980.5	1,998.6	2,009.9	1,969.9
2011	1,968.9	1,980.3	1,993.9	2,003.8	2,005.0	1,993.1	1,984.1	1,998.1	2,005.8	2,020.3	2,042.6	2,052.6	2,004.0
2012	2,017.0	2,027.7	2,045.0	2,045.9	2,048.7	2,044.0	2,029.7	2,048.5	2,054.8	2,072.3	2,099.1	2,109.7	2,053.5
2013	2,066.4	2,082.4	2,096.2	2,103.7	2,105.8	2,099.0	2,090.6	2,108.8	2,111.7	2,131.1	2,163.0	2,172.4	2,110.9
2014	2,122.8	2,135.9	2,145.8	2,155.4	2,154.4	2,144.4	2,133.1	2,152.9	2,155.0	2,183.7	2,211.8	2,226.2	2,160.1
2015	2,184.2	2,197.0	2,205.1	2,213.8	2,213.2	2,204.2	2,205.9	2,223.5	2,227.5	2,261.5	2,292.3	2,303.9	2,227.7
Goods-Producing													
2005	386.3	391.5	396.6	403.1	406.2	412.9	415.4	417.9	419.6	420.4	423.8	428.1	410.2
2006	423.6	430.3	434.9	437.8	440.3	444.9	443.4	442.5	439.7	434.5	430.0	428.4	435.9
2007	418.7	421.8	422.6	419.0	420.2	425.1	423.0	423.6	418.7	413.9	408.0	402.1	418.1
2008	391.4	388.8	386.7	383.0	381.5	380.1	376.1	373.4	367.0	357.7	347.2	338.5	372.6
2009	322.0	311.9	306.5	298.7	295.4	294.4	291.0	287.5	283.2	280.0	277.0	274.4	293.5
2010	267.6	267.7	268.5	270.9	271.0	272.6	272.8	272.2	270.4	272.4	271.8	271.2	270.8
2011	266.2	266.1	268.0	269.6	271.6	274.4	275.8	276.4	276.4	276.5	275.9	276.3	272.8
2012	273.5	274.7	278.3	279.3	281.5	285.5	286.8	288.7	288.5	288.9	288.8	288.5	283.6
2013	283.7	285.6	288.0	288.8	291.4	295.3	296.1	296.4	294.6	295.6	295.1	294.5	292.1
2014	292.2	294.2	294.2	295.1	295.4	296.3	295.6	295.7	293.5	295.4	295.0	295.4	294.8
2015	291.2	293.1	293.8	295.4	296.7	299.0	301.4	301.8	299.9	300.4	304.2	302.5	298.3
Service-Providing													
2005	2,030.4	2,066.7	2,080.8	2,106.7	2,105.4	2,072.1	2,056.6	2,093.4	2,130.1	2,141.7	2,165.7	2,180.5	2,102.5
2006	2,142.6	2,180.3	2,198.5	2,201.2	2,207.8	2,175.8	2,149.0	2,187.2	2,221.6	2,239.6	2,262.4	2,275.3	2,203.4
2007	2,217.6	2,252.4	2,269.5	2,263.1	2,266.9	2,230.6	2,206.4	2,244.5	2,270.0	2,287.4	2,310.4	2,317.6	2,261.4
2008	2,259.1	2,284.4	2,285.6	2,278.9	2,273.5	2,225.4	2,187.3	2,228.2	2,240.4	2,242.7	2,249.8	2,243.3	2,249.9
2009	2,176.6	2,181.8	2,178.8	2,168.8	2,156.3	2,097.2	2,072.6	2,100.0	2,117.4	2,127.4	2,144.7	2,147.7	2,139.1
2010	2,098.7	2,117.5	2,128.4	2,136.2	2,143.0	2,079.3	2,053.7	2,085.1	2,103.4	2,129.8	2,151.3	2,158.5	2,115.4
2011	2,114.5	2,136.9	2,147.9	2,157.7	2,155.2	2,088.0	2,062.6	2,117.0	2,146.8	2,164.7	2,189.1	2,192.0	2,139.4
2012	2,152.5	2,174.3	2,188.5	2,189.2	2,183.0	2,137.5	2,103.5	2,159.7	2,187.1	2,205.7	2,234.5	2,243.1	2,179.9
2013	2,195.3	2,219.9	2,230.3	2,238.3	2,233.2	2,179.0	2,154.2	2,208.2	2,236.4	2,258.4	2,291.3	2,298.0	2,228.5
2014	2,244.3	2,264.4	2,272.8	2,282.9	2,269.9	2,225.4	2,201.5	2,254.2	2,281.9	2,313.4	2,343.4	2,352.8	2,275.6
2015	2,304.8	2,327.8	2,334.5	2,341.7	2,331.0	2,276.2	2,263.3	2,315.6	2,346.5	2,383.4	2,412.8	2,420.2	2,338.2
Mining and Logging													
2005	8.6	8.7	8.8	9.0	9.1	9.3	8.1	8.0	8.0	8.0	8.4	9.0	8.6
2006	9.0	9.1	9.2	9.5	9.7	10.1	10.2	10.3	10.4	10.4	10.5	10.5	9.9
2007	10.5	10.5	10.7	10.7	10.9	11.2	11.8	12.1	12.1	12.3	12.4	12.5	11.5
2008	12.7	12.7	12.9	13.0	13.3	13.7	14.0	14.2	14.4	14.0	13.8	13.8	13.5
2009	12.6	12.1	12.1	10.9	10.6	10.7	10.7	10.8	10.7	10.8	10.8	10.8	11.1
2010	10.8	10.9	10.8	10.9	11.0	11.0	10.8	10.8	10.7	11.0	11.1	11.2	10.9
2011	11.3	11.4	11.5	11.2	11.4	11.6	11.2	11.3	11.4	12.1	12.1	12.2	11.6
2012	12.2	12.3	12.4	12.5	12.6	12.7	12.9	12.9	12.9	12.8	12.9	13.0	12.7
2013	13.0	13.1	13.1	13.3	13.3	13.6	13.6	13.5	13.2	13.2	13.0	13.0	13.2
2014	13.0	13.0	13.0	13.1	13.0	13.3	13.3	13.2	13.1	13.2	13.2	13.2	13.1
2015	12.6	12.7	12.6	12.5	12.6	12.9	12.9	12.8	12.5	12.0	11.9	11.9	12.5

1. Employment by Industry: Arizona, 2005–2015—*Continued*

(Numbers in thousands, not seasonally adjusted)

Industry and year	January	February	March	April	May	June	July	August	September	October	November	December	Annual average
Construction													
2005	199.2	203.3	207.9	213.7	215.9	220.8	224.1	226.0	228.2	228.8	231.6	233.3	219.4
2006	229.7	234.4	238.7	241.1	244.0	247.5	246.1	245.6	243.8	240.0	237.8	235.4	240.3
2007	226.7	227.6	228.5	226.4	227.6	231.7	228.7	229.1	225.9	221.4	215.7	210.0	224.9
2008	200.7	198.8	198.2	195.1	193.6	192.0	188.6	186.3	181.1	173.9	165.8	158.8	186.1
2009	147.3	140.4	137.4	132.7	131.0	130.8	128.2	125.3	122.0	119.3	116.5	114.0	128.7
2010	109.0	109.0	109.9	111.8	111.6	113.0	113.3	113.0	111.8	113.1	112.0	110.7	111.5
2011	106.6	106.4	107.9	109.4	110.1	112.4	113.7	113.9	113.9	113.1	112.1	111.2	110.9
2012	108.8	109.3	112.0	112.6	114.1	117.0	118.1	119.8	120.1	120.7	120.5	119.5	116.0
2013	116.2	117.6	120.0	120.9	123.1	126.1	126.5	127.4	126.4	127.2	126.9	125.9	123.7
2014	123.7	124.8	124.8	125.9	125.8	125.8	125.4	125.4	124.1	125.9	125.2	124.4	125.1
2015	122.5	123.8	124.7	126.3	127.0	127.9	129.1	129.5	128.8	129.1	131.9	130.0	127.6
Manufacturing													
2005	178.5	179.5	179.9	180.4	181.2	182.8	183.2	183.9	183.4	183.6	183.8	185.8	182.2
2006	184.9	186.8	187.0	187.2	186.6	187.3	187.1	186.6	185.5	184.1	181.7	182.5	185.6
2007	181.5	183.7	183.4	181.9	181.7	182.2	182.5	182.4	180.7	180.2	179.9	179.6	181.6
2008	178.0	177.3	175.6	174.9	174.6	174.4	173.5	172.9	171.5	169.8	167.6	165.9	173.0
2009	162.1	159.4	157.0	155.1	153.8	152.9	152.1	151.4	150.5	149.9	149.7	149.6	153.6
2010	147.8	147.8	147.8	148.2	148.4	148.6	148.7	148.4	147.9	148.3	148.7	149.3	148.3
2011	148.3	148.3	148.6	149.0	150.1	150.4	150.9	151.2	151.1	151.3	151.7	152.9	150.3
2012	152.5	153.1	153.9	154.2	154.8	155.8	155.8	156.0	155.5	155.4	155.4	156.0	154.9
2013	154.5	154.9	154.9	154.6	155.0	155.6	156.0	155.5	155.0	155.2	155.2	155.6	155.2
2014	155.5	156.4	156.4	156.1	156.6	157.2	156.9	157.1	156.3	156.3	156.6	157.8	156.6
2015	156.1	156.6	156.5	156.6	157.1	158.2	159.4	159.5	158.6	159.3	160.4	160.6	158.2
Trade, Transportation, and Utilities													
2005	476.8	477.8	479.9	481.8	482.3	482.3	485.8	487.2	490.1	494.4	507.7	516.8	488.6
2006	502.1	501.6	505.9	505.7	506.4	506.4	507.8	509.8	510.9	517.9	531.3	540.4	512.2
2007	522.0	520.8	523.2	522.7	524.0	523.8	524.2	525.2	526.0	528.8	542.4	549.2	527.7
2008	527.9	525.2	524.2	518.7	519.2	517.8	510.4	511.4	507.5	508.6	514.8	515.3	516.8
2009	495.5	487.1	484.9	479.3	478.0	474.4	471.7	471.1	469.1	468.9	478.2	482.9	478.4
2010	467.9	466.7	467.2	467.6	467.7	465.6	463.1	463.0	459.9	465.7	476.6	482.8	467.8
2011	468.0	467.5	468.9	470.7	470.7	469.8	468.3	469.4	468.3	474.6	487.9	491.3	473.0
2012	475.9	472.6	474.2	473.1	473.6	472.3	470.3	470.6	471.2	476.4	491.4	495.7	476.4
2013	475.2	473.5	473.6	474.9	476.2	476.1	476.3	478.4	479.3	484.6	499.5	506.7	481.2
2014	488.7	487.1	487.6	487.9	487.8	488.0	486.8	489.3	489.3	495.8	510.0	517.5	493.0
2015	499.0	497.9	498.7	499.2	499.9	500.6	501.3	504.3	506.0	514.1	527.3	531.2	506.6
Wholesale Trade													
2005	97.6	98.6	99.2	99.3	99.3	99.6	100.0	99.9	100.2	100.8	102.1	104.0	100.1
2006	103.4	104.2	104.7	104.5	104.6	105.2	105.5	105.8	106.2	106.8	107.9	109.4	105.7
2007	107.7	108.3	108.9	108.1	108.2	108.9	108.9	108.6	108.4	108.8	109.8	110.6	108.8
2008	108.9	109.3	109.3	108.0	108.1	107.6	106.7	106.7	106.4	106.5	106.5	106.2	107.5
2009	103.9	102.8	101.7	100.0	99.0	98.0	97.5	97.1	96.2	96.5	96.5	96.7	98.8
2010	95.2	95.5	95.6	95.5	95.4	95.0	94.5	93.9	93.1	93.5	93.9	94.2	94.6
2011	93.3	94.0	94.1	94.4	94.4	94.3	93.6	93.2	93.0	93.4	93.8	93.9	93.8
2012	93.0	93.4	93.9	93.7	93.7	93.9	93.6	93.4	93.5	93.8	94.2	94.5	93.7
2013	93.1	93.8	93.8	93.9	93.5	93.8	93.2	93.2	93.0	93.9	94.3	94.8	93.7
2014	93.3	93.7	93.9	93.5	93.7	93.3	93.1	93.1	93.0	93.0	93.2	94.1	93.4
2015	92.6	92.8	92.8	93.0	93.3	93.4	93.1	93.3	93.5	94.5	95.3	94.8	93.5
Retail Trade													
2005	299.5	299.1	300.6	302.7	302.3	302.0	305.0	305.8	307.8	311.6	322.5	328.2	307.3
2006	316.1	314.9	318.3	317.9	318.3	317.7	318.3	319.2	319.1	325.7	337.4	343.1	322.2
2007	328.5	326.6	328.5	328.4	329.0	327.7	328.6	329.4	330.1	332.9	344.9	348.7	331.9
2008	332.3	328.8	328.0	324.0	324.3	323.6	317.8	318.4	315.3	316.6	322.0	321.9	322.8
2009	306.9	300.3	299.4	297.3	297.0	294.8	293.1	292.7	292.1	292.2	301.5	304.5	297.7
2010	293.1	291.6	292.1	292.4	292.4	290.5	288.8	288.7	286.3	291.0	300.9	304.2	292.7
2011	292.9	291.4	292.4	293.7	293.3	292.1	291.9	293.2	292.3	297.4	309.6	311.1	295.9
2012	299.0	295.3	296.1	295.6	296.4	294.8	293.1	293.4	294.1	298.8	312.9	315.0	298.7
2013	297.6	295.1	295.9	297.8	298.6	298.4	299.5	301.4	302.4	305.9	319.3	324.1	303.0
2014	309.3	307.5	307.4	309.0	308.2	308.5	308.1	309.9	309.8	314.9	327.6	331.9	312.7
2015	316.5	314.7	315.3	316.8	316.9	317.6	318.4	320.9	322.1	328.1	338.6	340.9	322.2

1. Employment by Industry: Arizona, 2005–2015—*Continued*

(Numbers in thousands, not seasonally adjusted)

Industry and year	January	February	March	April	May	June	July	August	September	October	November	December	Annual average
Transportation and Utilities													
2005	79.7	80.1	80.1	79.8	80.7	80.7	80.8	81.5	82.1	82.0	83.1	84.6	81.3
2006	82.6	82.5	82.9	83.3	83.5	83.5	84.0	84.8	85.6	85.4	86.0	87.9	84.3
2007	85.8	85.9	85.8	86.2	86.8	87.2	86.7	87.2	87.5	87.1	87.7	89.9	87.0
2009	86.7	87.1	86.9	86.7	86.8	86.6	85.9	86.3	85.8	85.5	86.3	87.2	86.5
2010	84.7	84.0	83.8	82.0	82.0	81.6	81.1	81.3	80.8	80.2	80.2	81.7	82.0
2011	79.6	79.6	79.5	79.7	79.9	80.1	79.8	80.4	80.5	81.2	81.8	84.4	80.5
2012	81.8	82.1	82.4	82.6	83.0	83.4	82.8	83.0	83.0	83.8	84.5	86.3	83.2
2013	83.9	83.9	84.2	83.8	83.5	83.6	83.6	83.8	83.6	83.8	84.3	86.2	84.0
2014	84.5	84.6	83.9	83.2	84.1	83.9	83.6	83.8	83.9	84.8	85.9	87.8	84.5
2015	86.1	85.9	86.3	85.4	85.9	86.2	85.6	86.3	86.5	87.9	89.2	91.5	86.9
	89.9	90.4	90.6	89.4	89.7	89.6	89.8	90.1	90.4	91.5	93.4	95.5	90.9
Information													
2005	43.7	44.3	44.6	45.4	45.6	45.2	44.8	44.6	44.1	44.4	45.0	45.6	44.8
2006	44.9	45.0	45.0	44.0	44.1	44.0	43.2	43.1	42.2	41.8	42.4	42.5	43.5
2007	40.7	41.6	41.5	41.8	42.4	42.2	41.9	41.6	41.2	40.9	41.8	41.4	41.6
2008	40.7	41.6	42.0	41.1	42.2	41.8	40.6	40.3	40.7	39.8	40.3	40.5	41.0
2009	39.2	39.6	39.0	38.9	39.2	38.4	38.1	37.7	37.1	36.5	37.0	37.0	38.1
2010	36.5	36.7	37.0	37.0	36.9	37.3	36.4	36.2	36.0	35.7	36.3	36.7	36.6
2011	36.4	36.4	36.5	36.8	37.0	37.1	37.5	37.5	37.3	37.7	38.6	38.6	37.3
2012	38.4	38.9	39.1	39.4	40.0	39.9	40.0	40.3	39.7	39.8	40.9	41.1	39.8
2013	40.8	41.4	41.6	41.7	42.6	42.0	42.2	42.4	41.7	41.9	42.8	42.6	42.0
2014	42.5	42.5	42.9	43.3	43.8	44.0	44.4	44.2	43.3	43.7	44.0	44.4	43.6
2015	44.1	45.4	44.4	45.0	45.5	45.3	45.4	44.9	44.3	45.7	46.5	47.4	45.3
Financial Activities													
2005	169.1	170.6	171.3	174.0	174.4	175.4	176.9	178.6	179.6	181.1	181.9	183.3	176.4
2006	180.7	182.1	183.1	183.6	184.5	185.0	185.1	185.9	186.4	187.5	187.8	189.7	185.1
2007	186.8	188.4	189.1	189.1	188.9	188.6	187.9	185.6	184.5	183.3	183.1	183.8	186.6
2008	179.3	180.6	180.5	180.1	180.0	179.5	178.1	177.9	177.1	176.4	175.4	175.3	178.4
2009	171.6	171.5	171.3	170.9	171.0	170.4	170.0	170.0	168.7	168.5	168.3	169.2	170.1
2010	166.6	167.1	167.7	166.2	166.5	166.6	167.0	167.4	166.6	169.0	169.5	170.9	167.6
2011	168.3	169.2	169.8	170.5	170.4	171.0	171.5	172.0	172.0	172.7	173.3	175.3	171.3
2012	173.5	175.3	175.6	175.3	175.4	175.5	175.7	176.4	176.8	178.9	180.1	181.3	176.7
2013	179.5	182.2	182.2	183.3	183.9	184.6	184.7	185.3	185.5	188.0	189.4	190.1	184.9
2014	187.1	188.1	187.7	189.9	190.0	189.6	189.4	189.7	189.4	191.4	192.4	192.7	189.8
2015	190.7	191.7	192.0	192.5	193.2	193.6	194.6	195.6	195.7	197.8	198.0	201.0	194.7
Professional and Business Services													
2005	346.6	352.1	356.7	364.2	363.8	367.1	368.3	372.0	375.4	374.8	377.8	380.3	366.6
2006	374.6	383.3	387.2	390.2	392.5	397.2	395.4	399.6	403.1	404.3	405.7	408.1	395.1
2007	395.4	400.2	404.8	402.7	402.9	405.5	402.8	406.4	405.1	408.5	409.8	407.6	404.3
2008	395.1	398.1	396.1	393.9	390.5	387.3	383.7	385.8	382.5	380.8	376.9	374.0	387.1
2009	359.2	356.2	353.4	349.5	345.3	342.7	341.0	338.8	337.6	342.1	345.0	345.4	346.4
2010	335.0	336.4	340.1	342.5	340.5	339.3	337.1	337.9	336.8	344.3	345.7	350.4	340.5
2011	341.1	344.4	346.4	347.8	344.2	343.1	343.2	344.9	346.6	351.0	353.8	358.6	347.1
2012	348.6	350.5	353.5	354.0	353.4	355.5	354.4	358.0	358.3	363.6	369.8	373.1	357.7
2013	367.1	367.2	370.3	372.4	371.9	373.3	371.7	373.8	373.4	379.3	388.8	390.5	375.0
2014	374.3	374.2	376.2	379.1	379.3	379.7	378.6	382.8	383.6	391.8	399.2	402.9	383.5
2015	391.4	391.0	390.5	392.9	391.5	391.0	393.1	395.6	397.0	407.1	414.4	419.5	397.9
Education and Health Services													
2005	268.0	270.2	273.2	277.5	278.6	275.7	273.4	278.9	281.6	282.9	284.8	286.2	277.6
2006	284.5	288.2	290.9	291.4	292.6	291.5	289.8	295.6	298.2	299.8	301.9	305.0	294.1
2007	299.7	304.3	306.0	304.2	305.7	305.2	302.5	308.0	310.7	315.5	316.4	318.2	308.0
2008	314.0	318.6	320.1	322.1	323.5	320.9	319.5	325.1	327.8	329.8	331.9	333.6	323.9
2009	328.0	330.4	331.1	331.1	332.1	329.3	327.7	333.8	335.6	339.4	342.0	343.7	333.7
2010	339.2	340.7	342.2	342.0	343.1	339.8	337.8	344.6	346.3	351.8	353.3	353.2	344.5
2011	348.9	351.2	352.1	353.9	357.2	349.5	347.2	355.2	359.2	361.4	363.8	365.0	355.4
2012	362.0	365.1	365.9	366.1	366.3	361.6	357.1	365.4	368.5	370.7	372.9	374.4	366.3
2013	367.8	371.2	373.7	374.1	373.0	366.7	364.3	372.9	375.5	376.2	379.2	379.7	372.9
2014	374.9	377.6	378.0	379.5	379.7	374.5	372.9	381.5	384.0	389.0	391.7	393.9	381.4
2015	388.5	392.4	393.4	395.2	395.2	389.8	389.6	397.9	399.7	405.9	409.4	411.0	397.3

1. Employment by Industry: Arizona, 2005–2015—*Continued*

(Numbers in thousands, not seasonally adjusted)

Industry and year	January	February	March	April	May	June	July	August	September	October	November	December	Annual average
Leisure and Hospitality													
2005	242.5	248.1	252.9	259.9	259.0	255.7	250.6	251.8	256.1	256.6	258.8	259.4	254.3
2006	258.1	264.2	268.9	271.6	270.1	267.6	261.3	262.6	266.6	267.5	271.0	271.1	266.7
2007	266.8	272.9	278.4	278.1	277.9	273.0	264.0	267.7	269.9	273.9	276.2	276.9	273.0
2008	272.0	276.3	279.1	279.2	275.1	270.3	263.2	265.3	266.0	265.6	266.2	263.8	270.2
2009	257.5	261.2	264.9	264.6	262.7	255.9	249.1	250.9	250.2	250.6	252.2	251.8	256.0
2010	247.3	251.7	257.1	261.2	259.1	254.2	248.3	249.8	251.4	253.8	257.1	256.2	253.9
2011	252.1	256.5	263.0	265.3	264.6	259.0	252.7	255.5	259.2	259.8	262.7	261.5	259.3
2012	259.9	265.0	272.2	272.6	271.8	266.5	259.4	263.5	266.0	267.8	268.4	268.8	266.8
2013	266.7	273.6	279.4	280.9	279.2	273.4	268.6	273.3	275.3	278.3	280.7	280.8	275.9
2014	277.0	285.0	291.4	292.6	290.5	284.4	278.3	282.9	284.9	288.6	291.2	291.1	286.5
2015	292.1	297.2	303.6	305.2	302.2	296.1	292.4	295.8	297.1	301.3	303.8	302.4	299.1
Other Services													
2005	88.1	89.0	90.3	91.4	91.9	92.1	91.4	91.3	92.1	92.6	93.3	93.6	91.4
2006	97.3	99.6	101.2	98.5	99.9	101.6	95.9	96.5	97.5	95.9	96.8	97.4	98.2
2007	96.4	98.6	99.6	98.0	99.2	100.7	98.0	98.0	99.5	99.7	100.8	101.3	99.2
2008	100.2	101.4	102.0	101.0	101.1	101.4	100.7	100.2	100.0	99.0	99.1	98.2	100.4
2009	95.5	96.2	96.3	94.3	94.3	94.3	93.1	92.7	92.1	90.8	90.7	90.5	93.4
2010	87.8	88.6	89.0	88.2	88.7	89.1	88.0	87.4	87.2	87.8	88.3	88.5	88.2
2011	87.9	89.0	89.2	89.2	89.3	89.2	87.9	87.2	86.8	86.6	86.6	86.0	87.9
2012	85.2	85.6	86.2	86.1	86.7	87.2	86.0	85.6	85.8	86.2	86.8	86.8	86.2
2013	85.6	87.7	87.4	87.6	87.6	87.6	86.7	86.3	86.4	87.2	87.5	87.5	87.1
2014	86.1	87.2	87.8	88.0	87.9	87.9	87.1	86.8	87.0	88.0	88.3	88.3	87.5
2015	87.2	88.3	88.7	88.4	89.0	88.8	88.1	87.6	87.8	89.2	88.7	88.9	88.4
Government													
2005	395.6	414.6	411.9	412.5	409.8	378.6	365.4	389.0	411.1	414.9	416.4	415.3	402.9
2006	400.4	416.3	416.3	416.2	417.7	382.5	370.5	394.1	416.7	424.9	425.5	421.1	408.5
2007	409.8	425.6	426.9	426.5	425.9	391.6	385.1	412.0	433.1	436.8	439.9	439.2	421.0
2008	429.9	442.6	441.6	442.8	441.9	406.4	391.1	422.2	438.8	442.7	445.2	442.6	432.3
2009	430.1	439.6	437.9	440.2	433.7	391.8	381.9	405.0	427.0	430.6	431.3	427.2	423.0
2010	418.4	429.6	428.1	431.5	440.5	387.4	376.0	398.8	419.2	421.7	424.5	419.8	416.3
2011	411.8	422.7	422.0	423.5	421.8	369.3	354.3	395.3	417.4	420.9	422.4	415.7	408.1
2012	409.0	421.3	421.8	422.6	415.8	379.0	360.6	399.9	420.8	422.3	424.2	421.9	409.9
2013	412.6	423.1	422.1	423.4	418.8	375.3	359.7	395.8	419.3	422.9	423.4	420.1	409.7
2014	413.7	422.7	421.2	422.6	410.9	377.3	364.0	397.0	420.4	425.1	426.6	422.0	410.3
2015	411.8	423.9	423.2	423.3	414.5	371.0	358.8	393.9	418.9	422.3	424.7	418.8	408.8

2. Average Weekly Hours by Selected Industry: Arizona, 2011–2015

(Not seasonally adjusted)

Industry and year	January	February	March	April	May	June	July	August	September	October	November	December	Annual average
Total Private													
2011	35.2	35.0	35.1	35.1	35.1	35.0	34.9	35.0	34.9	35.4	34.8	34.7	35.0
2012	35.0	34.6	34.8	35.1	34.8	35.0	35.3	34.8	35.3	34.9	35.0	35.2	35.0
2013	34.6	34.8	34.9	34.8	34.7	35.4	34.5	34.7	34.9	34.6	34.5	35.2	34.8
2014	34.5	35.2	35.2	34.4	34.3	35.0	34.2	34.3	33.9	34.1	34.8	34.6	34.5
2015	34.4	35.1	34.9	34.7	34.6	34.8	34.6	35.1	34.4	34.4	34.6	34.3	34.7
Goods-Producing													
2011	38.1	38.1	38.0	38.3	37.8	38.9	37.4	38.5	38.3	38.1	38.2	37.4	38.1
2012	37.7	37.2	37.7	38.1	38.7	39.3	38.4	38.8	38.8	38.8	38.5	38.7	38.4
2013	38.5	38.7	38.8	39.1	39.2	39.9	39.3	39.7	38.5	39.1	39.0	39.5	39.1
2014	39.3	39.1	39.5	39.1	39.0	39.0	38.9	38.4	37.8	37.8	38.4	38.3	38.7
2015	37.8	38.1	38.2	38.6	38.7	39.2	38.6	38.5	37.9	38.2	38.2	38.3	38.4
Construction													
2011	36.7	36.8	36.3	36.5	35.7	37.4	35.8	37.1	36.8	36.6	36.2	34.6	36.4
2012	36.1	35.3	36.4	36.5	37.0	37.7	36.6	37.2	37.5	37.6	36.7	36.8	36.8
2013	37.4	37.5	37.6	37.7	38.2	39.5	38.5	38.7	37.4	38.4	38.3	38.3	38.1
2014	38.6	38.2	38.1	37.7	37.5	37.8	37.5	36.6	35.6	36.1	37.0	36.4	37.3
2015	35.9	36.6	37.0	37.7	38.0	38.2	37.8	37.2	35.9	37.1	36.9	36.8	37.1
Manufacturing													
2011	39.2	39.2	39.5	39.9	39.8	40.4	39.1	39.9	40.0	39.7	40.4	40.9	39.8
2012	39.7	39.5	39.5	39.8	40.3	40.8	40.2	40.4	40.1	39.9	40.2	40.4	40.1
2013	39.5	39.6	39.7	40.3	40.1	40.2	40.0	40.6	39.4	39.6	39.5	40.4	39.9
2014	39.8	39.7	40.5	40.2	40.2	40.0	40.0	40.4	40.2	39.6	39.8	40.2	40.0
2015	39.7	39.3	39.2	39.5	39.4	40.4	39.5	39.7	39.9	39.4	39.4	39.6	39.6
Trade, Transportation, and Utilities													
2011	36.3	35.9	35.9	36.1	36.1	36.0	36.2	36.1	35.8	36.4	35.5	35.8	36.0
2012	35.7	35.7	35.8	36.1	35.8	36.3	36.5	35.7	36.2	36.0	36.0	36.3	36.0
2013	35.6	35.6	35.8	35.4	35.3	36.3	35.2	35.3	35.8	35.2	34.8	35.7	35.5
2014	34.2	35.2	35.2	34.8	34.6	35.0	34.4	34.5	34.6	34.7	35.2	35.1	34.8
2015	34.9	35.4	35.3	35.4	35.3	35.3	35.4	35.5	35.3	35.0	34.7	34.0	35.1
Financial Activities													
2011	39.5	38.9	38.7	38.8	39.5	39.2	39.7	39.0	39.5	39.9	39.2	38.6	39.2
2012	39.4	38.8	38.7	38.9	38.6	38.5	39.3	38.7	39.3	38.7	38.9	39.2	38.9
2013	38.6	38.4	38.2	38.5	38.3	38.6	37.6	38.5	38.4	38.2	38.2	39.0	38.4
2014	38.1	38.7	38.3	38.1	37.8	38.6	38.4	38.8	38.4	38.4	38.8	38.5	38.4
2015	38.7	39.1	39.0	38.9	38.6	38.8	38.8	40.0	39.2	38.9	39.4	39.2	39.1
Professional and Business Services													
2011	34.6	34.6	34.7	34.8	35.3	34.9	35.1	35.3	34.8	35.8	35.3	36.0	35.1
2012	35.9	35.6	35.3	36.2	36.0	36.4	36.9	36.7	36.9	36.1	36.3	36.8	36.3
2013	35.9	36.3	36.4	36.3	36.1	36.5	35.9	36.1	36.6	36.3	36.2	36.8	36.3
2014	35.9	36.8	36.6	35.7	35.5	36.1	35.4	35.5	35.2	35.7	36.3	36.3	35.9
2015	35.7	36.4	36.4	35.9	35.8	36.1	35.9	37.2	36.0	35.9	36.4	36.5	36.2
Education and Health Services													
2011	34.7	33.7	34.1	33.9	34.0	33.6	33.4	33.4	33.4	33.9	33.3	33.2	33.7
2012	33.5	33.0	33.3	33.5	33.2	33.0	33.6	33.5	33.9	33.6	33.5	33.9	33.5
2013	33.3	33.6	33.8	33.7	33.6	34.0	32.9	32.8	33.7	33.1	33.0	33.6	33.4
2014	33.4	34.0	33.9	33.3	33.3	34.2	33.7	33.6	33.5	33.6	34.4	33.7	33.7
2015	33.8	34.4	34.1	33.9	33.8	33.6	33.7	33.9	33.7	33.5	33.8	33.3	33.8
Leisure and Hospitality													
2011	27.1	27.5	27.1	27.1	26.6	26.0	25.9	26.0	26.6	27.0	26.6	26.2	26.6
2012	27.2	27.0	27.8	27.5	26.8	26.5	26.9	25.6	26.3	26.1	26.6	26.7	26.8
2013	25.9	26.3	26.8	26.3	26.2	26.9	26.0	25.7	26.1	26.0	26.2	26.6	26.3
2014	26.3	27.1	27.8	26.3	26.2	26.7	25.4	26.0	25.9	26.3	27.7	26.8	26.5
2015	27.1	28.2	28.2	27.2	27.2	26.9	26.4	26.6	26.0	26.2	26.5	26.2	26.9
Other Services													
2011	33.4	34.2	34.2	33.6	34.1	32.8	32.7	32.6	32.6	32.4	31.4	31.6	33.0
2012	32.9	32.5	32.8	32.1	31.6	31.7	31.8	31.4	32.0	31.2	31.5	31.4	31.9
2013	30.8	31.1	31.5	31.1	30.7	32.1	30.8	31.2	31.7	31.5	31.6	32.4	31.4
2014	31.8	33.4	33.1	32.3	31.2	32.6	31.3	31.7	31.0	31.2	30.7	30.4	31.7
2015	30.9	32.7	31.8	32.5	31.6	32.8	32.1	33.4	31.5	32.2	32.8	32.6	32.2

3. Average Hourly Earnings by Selected Industry: Arizona, 2011–2015

(Not seasonally adjusted)

Industry and year	January	February	March	April	May	June	July	August	September	October	November	December	Annual average
Total Private													
2011	22.57	22.59	22.59	22.75	22.73	22.40	22.61	22.40	22.53	22.61	22.41	22.54	22.56
2012	22.77	22.53	22.43	22.66	22.45	22.51	22.69	22.49	22.70	22.63	22.52	22.83	22.60
2013	22.74	22.73	22.57	22.85	22.79	23.05	23.01	23.17	23.45	23.08	23.22	23.29	23.00
2014	23.25	23.24	23.10	22.98	22.87	22.91	22.86	22.76	22.81	22.74	22.80	22.49	22.90
2015	22.91	23.01	23.00	23.05	22.96	22.95	23.02	23.36	23.25	23.31	23.48	23.25	23.13
Goods-Producing													
2011	22.43	22.84	23.20	23.24	23.24	22.88	23.06	23.03	23.12	23.29	23.42	24.08	23.15
2012	24.04	23.85	23.60	23.89	23.80	23.70	23.74	23.68	24.07	23.91	23.82	24.01	23.84
2013	23.90	23.81	23.78	23.71	23.63	23.72	23.82	23.85	24.08	24.02	24.23	24.38	23.91
2014	24.52	24.71	24.67	24.73	24.51	24.59	24.43	24.49	24.35	24.09	24.36	24.23	24.48
2015	24.12	23.94	23.92	24.15	23.61	23.42	23.72	23.73	23.73	23.81	24.28	24.15	23.88
Construction													
2011	22.25	22.57	22.89	22.52	22.08	21.66	21.53	21.91	21.87	21.85	21.79	22.39	22.10
2012	22.39	22.30	21.99	22.59	22.75	22.57	22.19	22.50	23.00	22.93	22.78	22.83	22.58
2013	22.69	22.52	22.62	22.40	22.54	22.70	22.96	23.45	23.42	23.47	23.53	23.61	23.00
2014	24.09	24.23	24.22	24.46	24.33	24.04	24.05	24.18	23.91	23.58	24.04	23.94	24.09
2015	23.67	23.14	23.14	23.49	22.64	22.69	22.94	22.89	23.17	23.01	23.45	23.86	23.17
Manufacturing													
2011	22.56	23.09	23.41	23.89	24.37	24.17	24.78	24.28	24.56	24.85	24.83	25.56	24.21
2012	25.45	25.13	25.00	25.02	24.71	24.69	25.12	24.70	24.98	24.70	24.63	24.96	24.92
2013	24.96	24.92	24.82	24.88	24.63	24.67	24.54	24.10	24.57	24.39	24.83	25.03	24.69
2014	24.85	25.10	25.01	24.85	24.57	24.77	24.45	24.44	24.43	24.43	24.49	24.34	24.64
2015	24.38	24.62	24.60	24.67	24.59	24.13	24.50	24.57	24.28	24.57	25.06	24.38	24.53
Trade, Transportation, and Utilities													
2011	20.14	20.15	20.15	20.25	20.25	19.96	20.29	19.90	20.37	20.80	20.56	20.51	20.28
2012	21.20	20.60	20.58	21.19	20.68	21.14	21.46	20.92	21.22	21.00	20.68	21.18	20.99
2013	21.30	21.20	21.05	21.27	21.06	21.06	20.97	20.83	21.11	20.68	20.63	20.38	20.96
2014	20.61	20.79	20.87	20.49	20.58	20.66	20.66	20.53	20.69	20.68	20.47	20.25	20.60
2015	20.79	20.90	20.41	20.63	20.82	20.54	20.51	20.81	20.69	20.85	21.30	21.57	20.82
Financial Activities													
2011	23.23	23.04	23.13	23.62	23.24	23.15	23.61	23.73	23.78	23.66	23.71	23.79	23.48
2012	23.97	23.65	24.32	24.70	24.28	24.34	24.28	24.02	24.31	24.30	24.43	24.84	24.29
2013	24.14	24.64	24.81	25.19	25.79	26.64	26.52	27.51	27.94	26.39	26.84	27.38	26.16
2014	26.92	26.73	26.92	26.51	26.56	26.33	26.14	25.95	26.12	25.95	26.08	25.91	26.34
2015	25.81	26.17	26.56	26.40	26.37	26.71	26.74	27.35	26.99	27.22	27.28	27.09	26.73
Professional and Business Services													
2011	28.02	28.16	27.93	28.11	27.82	27.31	27.26	26.99	27.15	26.90	26.40	25.94	27.32
2012	26.57	26.58	26.66	26.46	26.02	25.91	26.18	25.87	26.04	26.05	25.77	26.14	26.18
2013	26.05	26.03	25.73	25.61	25.64	25.84	25.48	25.30	25.58	25.50	25.74	25.50	25.66
2014	25.10	25.35	25.19	25.16	24.99	25.28	24.94	25.06	25.18	25.29	25.52	24.04	25.09
2015	25.89	26.30	26.66	26.53	26.30	26.40	26.15	26.67	26.53	26.53	26.23	25.05	26.26
Education and Health Services													
2011	23.53	23.88	23.89	23.85	23.92	23.46	23.65	23.53	23.56	23.17	23.29	23.56	23.61
2012	23.51	23.74	23.45	23.53	23.66	23.62	23.84	23.72	23.75	23.77	23.99	24.07	23.72
2013	24.26	24.09	24.03	24.42	23.97	24.31	24.48	24.26	24.53	24.62	24.77	25.20	24.41
2014	25.08	24.90	24.61	24.88	24.64	24.33	24.65	24.47	24.57	24.48	24.67	24.98	24.69
2015	24.79	24.83	24.80	24.68	24.60	24.72	24.83	25.03	25.14	25.12	25.29	25.22	24.92
Leisure and Hospitality													
2011	13.26	13.24	13.16	13.54	13.99	13.67	13.73	13.46	13.53	13.71	13.89	13.83	13.58
2012	13.91	13.81	13.73	13.56	13.54	13.40	13.31	13.33	13.40	13.60	13.58	13.56	13.56
2013	13.54	13.51	13.46	13.43	13.50	13.33	13.36	13.38	13.65	13.52	13.52	13.64	13.49
2014	13.66	13.70	13.70	13.62	13.57	13.40	13.46	13.41	13.57	13.83	13.77	13.77	13.62
2015	14.01	14.07	13.95	13.97	14.03	13.83	13.94	14.02	14.10	14.15	14.30	14.33	14.06
Other Services													
2011	16.12	16.29	16.49	16.89	16.83	16.71	17.15	16.88	16.92	16.89	17.30	17.40	16.81
2012	17.72	17.59	17.90	17.89	18.02	18.11	18.71	18.91	19.17	18.99	19.26	19.74	18.49
2013	19.35	19.35	19.24	20.07	19.79	19.84	19.83	19.98	20.54	20.25	20.46	20.45	19.93
2014	20.87	21.11	20.20	19.70	19.29	20.14	19.72	20.09	19.23	19.02	19.40	18.92	19.82
2015	19.23	19.58	19.67	19.69	20.29	20.15	20.87	21.36	21.27	21.19	21.21	21.12	20.48

4. Average Weekly Earnings by Selected Industry: Arizona, 2011–2015

(Dollars, not seasonally adjusted)

	January	February	March	April	May	June	July	August	September	October	November	December	Annual average
Total Private													
2011	794.46	790.65	792.91	798.53	797.82	784.00	789.09	784.00	786.30	800.39	779.87	782.14	789.60
2012	796.95	779.54	780.56	795.37	781.26	787.85	800.96	782.65	801.31	789.79	788.20	803.62	791.00
2013	786.80	791.00	787.69	795.18	790.81	815.97	793.85	804.00	818.41	798.57	801.09	819.81	800.40
2014	802.13	818.05	813.12	790.51	784.44	801.85	781.81	780.67	773.26	775.43	793.44	778.15	790.05
2015	788.10	807.65	802.70	799.84	794.42	798.66	796.49	819.94	799.80	801.86	812.41	797.48	802.61
Goods-Producing													
2011	854.58	870.20	881.60	890.09	878.47	890.03	862.44	886.66	885.50	887.35	894.64	900.59	882.02
2012	906.31	887.22	889.72	910.21	921.06	931.41	911.62	918.78	933.92	927.71	917.07	929.19	915.46
2013	920.15	921.45	922.66	927.06	926.30	946.43	936.13	946.85	927.08	939.18	944.97	963.01	934.88
2014	963.64	966.16	974.47	966.94	955.89	959.01	950.33	940.42	920.43	910.60	935.42	928.01	947.38
2015	911.74	912.11	913.74	932.19	913.71	918.06	915.59	913.61	899.37	909.54	927.50	924.95	916.99
Construction													
2011	816.58	830.58	830.91	821.98	788.26	810.08	770.77	812.86	804.82	799.71	788.80	774.69	804.44
2012	808.28	787.19	800.44	824.54	841.75	850.89	812.15	837.00	862.50	862.17	836.03	840.14	830.94
2013	848.61	844.50	850.51	844.48	861.03	896.65	883.96	907.52	875.91	901.25	901.20	904.26	876.30
2014	929.87	925.59	922.78	922.14	912.38	908.71	901.88	884.99	851.20	851.24	889.48	871.42	898.56
2015	849.75	846.92	856.18	885.57	860.32	866.76	867.13	851.51	831.80	853.67	865.31	878.05	859.61
Manufacturing													
2011	884.35	905.13	924.70	953.21	969.93	976.47	968.90	968.77	982.40	986.55	1,003.13	1,045.40	963.56
2012	1,010.37	992.64	987.50	995.80	995.81	1,007.35	1,009.82	997.88	1,001.70	985.53	990.13	1,008.38	999.29
2013	985.92	986.83	985.35	1,002.66	987.66	991.73	981.60	978.46	968.06	965.84	980.79	1,011.21	985.13
2014	989.03	996.47	1,012.91	998.97	987.71	990.80	978.00	987.38	982.09	967.43	974.70	978.47	985.60
2015	967.89	967.57	964.32	974.47	968.85	974.85	967.75	975.43	968.77	968.06	987.36	965.45	971.39
Trade, Transportation, and Utilities													
2011	731.08	723.39	723.39	731.03	731.03	718.56	734.50	718.39	729.25	757.12	729.88	734.26	730.08
2012	756.84	735.42	736.76	764.96	740.34	767.38	783.29	746.84	768.16	756.00	744.48	768.83	755.64
2013	758.28	754.72	753.59	752.96	743.42	764.48	738.14	735.30	755.74	727.94	717.92	727.57	744.08
2014	704.86	731.81	734.62	713.05	712.07	723.10	710.70	708.29	715.87	717.60	720.54	710.78	716.88
2015	725.57	739.86	720.47	730.30	734.95	725.06	726.05	738.76	730.36	729.75	739.11	733.38	730.78
Financial Activities													
2011	917.59	896.26	895.13	916.46	917.98	907.48	937.32	925.47	939.31	944.03	929.43	918.29	920.42
2012	944.42	917.62	941.18	960.83	937.21	937.09	954.20	950.33	929.57	955.38	940.41	973.73	944.88
2013	931.80	946.18	947.74	969.82	987.76	1,028.30	997.15	1,059.14	1,072.90	1,008.10	1,025.29	1,067.82	1,004.54
2014	1,025.65	1,034.45	1,031.04	1,010.03	1,003.97	1,016.34	1,003.78	1,006.86	1,003.01	996.48	1,011.90	997.54	1,011.46
2015	998.85	1,023.25	1,035.84	1,026.96	1,017.88	1,036.35	1,037.51	1,094.00	1,058.01	1,058.86	1,074.83	1,061.93	1,045.14
Professional and Business Services													
2011	969.49	974.34	969.17	978.23	982.05	953.12	956.83	952.75	944.82	963.02	931.92	933.84	958.93
2012	953.86	946.25	941.10	957.85	936.72	943.12	966.04	949.43	960.88	940.41	935.45	961.95	950.33
2013	935.20	944.89	936.57	929.64	925.60	943.16	914.73	913.33	936.23	925.65	931.79	938.40	931.46
2014	901.09	932.88	921.95	898.21	887.15	912.61	882.88	889.63	886.34	902.85	926.38	872.65	900.73
2015	924.27	957.32	970.42	952.43	941.54	953.04	938.79	992.12	955.08	952.43	954.77	914.33	950.61
Education and Health Services													
2011	816.49	804.76	814.65	808.52	813.28	788.26	789.91	785.90	786.90	785.46	775.56	782.19	795.66
2012	787.59	783.42	780.89	788.26	785.51	779.46	801.02	794.62	805.13	798.67	803.67	815.97	794.62
2013	807.86	809.42	812.21	822.95	805.39	826.54	805.39	795.73	826.66	814.92	817.41	846.72	815.29
2014	837.67	846.60	834.28	828.50	820.51	832.09	830.71	822.19	823.10	822.53	848.65	841.83	832.05
2015	837.90	854.15	845.68	836.65	831.48	830.59	836.77	848.52	847.22	841.52	854.80	839.83	842.30
Leisure and Hospitality													
2011	359.35	364.10	356.64	366.93	372.13	355.42	355.61	349.96	359.90	370.17	369.47	362.35	361.23
2012	378.35	372.87	381.69	372.90	362.87	355.10	358.04	341.25	352.42	354.96	361.23	362.05	363.41
2013	350.69	355.31	360.73	353.21	353.70	358.58	347.36	343.87	356.27	351.52	354.22	362.82	354.79
2014	359.26	371.27	380.86	358.21	355.53	357.78	341.88	348.66	351.46	363.73	381.43	369.04	360.93
2015	379.67	396.77	393.39	379.98	381.62	372.03	368.02	372.93	366.60	370.73	378.95	375.45	378.21
Other Services													
2011	538.41	557.12	563.96	567.50	573.90	548.09	560.81	550.29	551.59	547.24	543.22	549.84	554.73
2012	582.99	571.68	587.12	574.27	569.43	574.09	594.98	593.77	613.44	592.49	606.69	619.84	589.83
2013	595.98	601.79	606.06	624.18	607.55	636.86	610.76	623.38	651.12	637.88	646.54	662.58	625.80
2014	663.67	705.07	668.62	636.31	601.85	656.56	617.24	636.85	596.13	593.42	595.58	575.17	628.29
2015	594.21	640.27	625.51	639.93	641.16	660.92	669.93	713.42	670.01	682.32	695.69	688.51	659.46

ARKANSAS
At a Glance

Population:
  2005 estimate: 2,781,097
  2010 census: 2,915,918
  2015 estimate: 2,978,204

Percent change in population:
  2005–2015: 7.1%
  2010–2015: 2.1%

Percent change in total nonfarm employment:
  2005–2015: 2.6%

Industry with the largest growth in employment, 2005–2015 (thousands):
  Education and health services, 28.9

Industry with the largest decline or smallest growth in employment, 2005–2015 (thousands):
  Manufacturing, –47.0

Civilian labor force:
  2005: 1,345,913
  2010: 1,353,338
  2015: 1,330,099

Unemployment rate and rank among states (highest to lowest):
  2005: 5.2%, 18th
  2010: 8.2%, 31st
  2015: 5.2%, 25th

Over-the-year change in unemployment rates:
  2012–2013: –0.3%
  2013–2014: –1.2%
  2014–2015: –0.9%

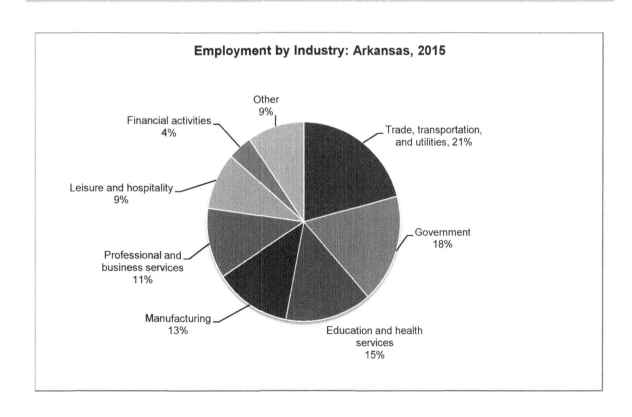

Employment by Industry: Arkansas, 2015

Other 9%
Financial activities 4%
Trade, transportation, and utilities, 21%
Leisure and hospitality 9%
Government 18%
Professional and business services 11%
Manufacturing 13%
Education and health services 15%

1. Employment by Industry: Arkansas, 2005–2015

(Numbers in thousands, not seasonally adjusted)

Industry and year	January	February	March	April	May	June	July	August	September	October	November	December	Annual average
Total Nonfarm													
2005	1,151.0	1,162.1	1,173.0	1,178.4	1,182.2	1,180.9	1,165.3	1,172.0	1,192.7	1,189.1	1,193.1	1,194.7	1,177.9
2006	1,178.2	1,186.6	1,198.5	1,203.8	1,206.7	1,205.3	1,184.1	1,193.2	1,208.6	1,205.5	1,205.7	1,207.3	1,198.6
2007	1,184.9	1,193.3	1,207.8	1,207.4	1,211.2	1,209.7	1,188.1	1,200.1	1,213.2	1,211.2	1,213.0	1,214.2	1,204.5
2008	1,190.8	1,200.0	1,207.9	1,207.9	1,212.6	1,208.4	1,189.8	1,198.4	1,211.8	1,205.4	1,200.8	1,195.9	1,202.5
2009	1,166.4	1,169.2	1,174.2	1,175.0	1,171.0	1,164.0	1,150.7	1,153.3	1,165.4	1,162.5	1,164.3	1,163.2	1,164.9
2010	1,134.9	1,138.6	1,155.1	1,164.0	1,175.0	1,177.3	1,158.2	1,162.8	1,172.6	1,171.7	1,172.4	1,173.5	1,163.0
2011	1,146.7	1,149.0	1,163.2	1,179.5	1,174.6	1,167.9	1,160.3	1,166.2	1,179.2	1,184.7	1,185.6	1,184.2	1,170.1
2012	1,158.5	1,166.8	1,178.7	1,183.2	1,186.5	1,181.8	1,160.9	1,168.6	1,181.1	1,182.0	1,183.9	1,185.6	1,176.5
2013	1,159.1	1,169.3	1,176.6	1,182.6	1,184.6	1,176.3	1,161.4	1,166.8	1,182.3	1,184.9	1,188.3	1,182.7	1,176.2
2014	1,160.9	1,171.3	1,180.5	1,189.0	1,195.1	1,188.1	1,171.3	1,180.3	1,197.5	1,201.0	1,206.5	1,208.6	1,187.5
2015	1,181.4	1,193.3	1,195.0	1,206.7	1,213.5	1,207.3	1,193.7	1,203.1	1,221.4	1,226.1	1,228.2	1,232.7	1,208.5
Total Private													
2005	950.1	956.1	966.6	970.5	975.6	979.5	976.9	979.4	985.2	980.2	983.7	986.3	974.2
2006	972.6	976.6	987.3	992.0	996.1	1001.2	992.3	996.2	997.8	993.2	992.1	995.0	991.0
2007	976.8	979.7	993.2	992.9	998.0	1001.1	994.4	1000.0	999.3	995.3	996.0	998.1	993.7
2008	979.8	983.6	990.6	990.5	995.0	996.6	992.3	996.0	995.3	986.8	981.4	977.3	988.8
2009	952.2	949.8	953.7	953.5	950.6	949.2	948.1	947.0	948.3	940.7	941.7	940.9	948.0
2010	920.6	920.5	934.1	941.9	947.5	956.4	951.9	954.9	954.4	951.1	951.1	952.8	944.8
2011	931.6	929.5	942.0	956.8	953.0	952.5	960.7	960.5	961.6	963.1	963.1	963.6	953.2
2012	944.5	946.9	957.6	962.5	966.4	967.1	960.0	964.9	964.2	961.8	962.3	965.0	960.3
2013	945.0	950.0	956.5	962.0	965.4	963.1	961.1	963.7	966.1	967.3	970.2	965.6	961.3
2014	949.7	954.8	963.1	971.3	977.8	976.5	972.3	978.4	982.5	984.4	987.9	991.4	974.2
2015	970.2	977.5	978.6	990.0	997.6	996.7	995.0	1001.2	1006.3	1009.0	1009.7	1015.2	995.6
Goods-Producing													
2005	258.7	259.2	261.3	261.9	264.0	265.2	264.4	265.4	266.7	265.2	265.5	265.6	263.6
2006	262.8	263.7	263.6	265.4	266.3	268.7	266.1	266.9	265.9	262.5	259.2	259.9	264.3
2007	256.2	255.1	258.1	257.5	258.2	258.5	257.1	257.1	256.4	254.6	253.1	253.5	256.3
2008	249.7	249.5	251.2	251.0	252.2	253.2	253.1	253.4	253.1	250.5	246.4	243.8	250.6
2009	235.9	232.5	230.3	227.0	224.9	224.0	224.5	225.2	224.6	220.1	219.1	218.3	225.5
2010	213.5	212.4	216.6	219.0	220.8	224.8	223.5	223.4	222.1	220.2	219.3	219.3	219.6
2011	214.0	213.9	216.5	218.5	218.1	217.9	220.3	219.1	219.3	217.6	216.7	216.1	217.3
2012	212.7	212.7	214.9	214.7	216.1	216.6	214.9	214.8	213.9	211.2	209.7	210.0	213.5
2013	206.7	206.9	207.9	207.3	208.6	208.9	208.5	208.6	208.4	207.8	207.3	206.0	207.7
2014	205.0	204.4	205.3	207.2	209.0	209.9	210.7	211.3	212.0	212.2	211.3	212.5	209.2
2015	210.5	210.5	209.6	210.2	210.8	212.3	213.7	213.9	214.8	214.3	210.9	212.1	212.0
Service-Providing													
2005	892.3	902.9	911.7	916.5	918.2	915.7	900.9	906.6	926.0	923.9	927.6	929.1	914.3
2006	915.4	922.9	934.9	938.4	940.4	936.6	918.0	926.3	942.7	943.0	946.5	947.4	934.4
2007	928.7	938.2	949.7	949.9	953.0	951.2	931.0	943.0	956.8	956.6	959.9	960.7	948.2
2008	941.1	950.5	956.7	956.9	960.4	955.2	936.7	945.0	958.7	954.9	954.4	952.1	951.9
2009	930.5	936.7	943.9	948.0	946.1	940.0	926.2	928.1	940.8	942.4	945.2	944.9	939.4
2010	921.4	926.2	938.5	945.0	954.2	952.5	934.7	939.4	950.5	951.5	953.1	954.2	943.4
2011	932.7	935.1	946.7	961.0	956.5	950.0	940.0	947.1	959.9	967.1	968.9	968.1	952.8
2012	945.8	954.1	963.8	968.5	970.4	965.2	946.0	953.8	967.2	970.8	974.2	975.6	963.0
2013	952.4	962.4	968.7	975.3	976.0	967.4	952.9	958.2	973.9	977.1	981.0	976.7	968.5
2014	955.9	966.9	975.2	981.8	986.1	978.2	960.6	969.0	985.5	988.8	995.2	996.1	978.3
2015	970.9	982.8	985.4	996.5	1002.7	995.0	980.0	989.2	1006.6	1011.8	1017.3	1020.6	996.6
Mining and Logging													
2005	6.5	6.6	6.7	6.9	7.0	7.2	7.2	7.3	7.3	7.2	7.2	7.3	7.0
2006	6.8	6.8	6.9	7.4	7.6	7.8	7.7	7.8	8.1	8.0	8.1	8.2	7.6
2007	8.4	8.7	9.0	9.0	9.3	9.6	9.6	9.9	10.0	9.8	9.8	9.9	9.4
2008	9.9	9.8	10.0	10.2	10.6	10.8	11.0	11.0	11.1	11.3	11.4	11.2	10.7
2009	10.6	10.5	10.5	10.3	10.1	10.2	10.4	10.4	10.3	9.9	10.0	10.0	10.3
2010	9.9	9.8	10.2	10.6	10.8	11.0	10.8	10.9	10.9	10.9	10.9	11.0	10.6
2011	10.6	10.6	10.7	10.9	10.8	11.0	11.5	11.4	11.5	11.6	11.6	11.5	11.1
2012	11.3	11.2	11.3	11.1	11.1	11.0	10.7	10.5	10.3	10.1	10.1	10.0	10.7
2013	9.6	9.6	9.6	9.5	9.6	9.6	9.7	9.6	9.5	9.3	9.2	9.0	9.5
2014	8.7	8.7	8.7	8.8	8.9	8.9	8.9	9.0	9.1	9.0	9.1	9.1	8.9
2015	8.7	8.7	8.4	8.3	8.1	8.0	7.9	7.8	7.7	7.7	7.6	7.5	8.0

1. Employment by Industry: Arkansas, 2005–2015—*Continued*

(Numbers in thousands, not seasonally adjusted)

Industry and year	January	February	March	April	May	June	July	August	September	October	November	December	Annual average
Construction													
2005	50.3	50.9	52.5	53.8	55.3	55.7	56.0	56.5	56.8	55.9	55.9	56.2	54.7
2006	54.0	55.0	54.8	56.6	57.9	58.9	57.8	58.4	59.0	57.3	56.1	56.4	56.9
2007	53.9	53.6	56.4	56.7	57.4	58.0	57.1	57.5	57.2	56.3	56.0	55.5	56.3
2008	53.4	53.8	55.1	55.7	56.6	57.3	57.8	58.5	58.2	57.4	56.0	55.0	56.2
2009	52.1	51.9	51.6	51.0	50.7	51.7	53.2	53.6	53.3	50.5	49.9	49.2	51.6
2010	46.0	45.0	47.3	48.8	49.7	51.3	51.1	50.8	50.0	48.9	47.8	47.5	48.7
2011	43.6	43.6	45.5	47.3	47.2	48.3	49.3	48.8	49.2	48.6	48.1	47.8	47.3
2012	45.6	46.1	47.5	47.6	48.6	49.4	47.7	48.3	48.5	47.3	46.1	46.0	47.4
2013	43.9	44.4	45.3	45.4	46.4	46.5	46.3	46.3	46.0	45.4	45.2	44.3	45.5
2014	43.9	43.2	43.7	45.0	46.1	46.5	46.8	47.2	47.6	47.6	47.4	47.7	46.1
2015	45.9	46.2	46.0	47.2	48.4	49.4	50.8	51.3	52.3	51.4	49.5	49.5	49.0
Manufacturing													
2005	201.9	201.7	202.1	201.2	201.7	202.3	201.2	201.6	202.6	202.1	202.4	202.1	201.9
2006	202.0	201.9	201.9	201.4	200.8	202.0	200.6	200.7	198.8	197.2	195.0	195.3	199.8
2007	193.9	192.8	192.7	191.8	191.5	190.9	190.4	189.7	189.2	188.5	187.3	188.1	190.6
2008	186.4	185.9	186.1	185.1	185.0	185.1	184.3	183.9	183.8	181.8	179.0	177.6	183.7
2009	173.2	170.1	168.2	165.7	164.1	162.1	160.9	161.2	161.0	159.7	159.2	159.1	163.7
2010	157.6	157.6	159.1	159.6	160.3	162.5	161.6	161.7	161.2	160.4	160.6	160.8	160.3
2011	159.8	159.7	160.3	160.3	160.1	158.6	159.5	158.9	158.6	157.4	157.0	156.8	158.9
2012	155.8	155.4	156.1	156.0	156.4	156.2	156.5	156.0	155.1	153.8	153.5	154.0	155.4
2013	153.2	152.9	153.0	152.4	152.6	152.8	152.5	152.7	152.9	153.1	152.9	152.7	152.8
2014	152.4	152.5	152.9	153.4	154.0	154.5	155.0	155.1	155.3	155.6	154.8	155.7	154.3
2015	155.9	155.6	155.2	154.7	154.3	154.9	155.0	154.8	154.8	155.2	153.8	155.1	154.9
Trade, Transportation, and Utilities													
2005	241.1	240.6	242.7	244.2	244.9	246.0	245.7	245.4	247.2	246.4	249.7	252.0	245.5
2006	244.8	244.4	247.8	247.3	248.8	248.8	247.7	248.3	249.2	249.6	252.5	254.6	248.7
2007	246.2	245.9	250.3	248.2	250.2	250.8	249.7	250.4	250.4	249.8	253.5	255.2	250.1
2008	247.2	246.4	248.2	247.2	248.3	248.7	247.1	247.2	246.4	244.2	245.9	246.3	246.9
2009	237.3	235.2	236.8	236.3	235.9	235.3	235.4	234.0	234.2	233.3	235.9	237.0	235.6
2010	229.7	228.7	231.6	231.9	233.6	235.7	235.6	236.1	234.8	236.6	239.6	241.4	234.6
2011	233.7	231.3	233.9	238.0	237.0	237.8	239.6	239.0	238.7	240.3	243.1	245.3	238.1
2012	238.2	237.0	239.5	240.7	241.7	242.4	241.4	241.7	241.5	241.4	245.0	246.5	241.4
2013	238.1	238.0	239.7	239.9	239.9	240.2	241.2	241.8	241.1	242.6	246.0	246.7	241.3
2014	239.2	238.6	240.6	242.7	243.7	244.8	244.5	245.7	245.9	247.1	251.6	253.7	244.8
2015	245.8	245.5	246.7	249.5	251.7	252.9	251.9	253.4	252.7	254.3	258.6	262.4	252.1
Wholesale Trade													
2005	46.5	46.8	47.3	47.5	47.8	48.0	47.8	47.6	47.6	47.2	47.1	47.5	47.4
2006	46.9	47.1	47.5	47.9	48.2	48.5	48.1	48.1	48.2	47.9	47.9	48.2	47.9
2007	47.2	47.4	48.0	48.1	48.3	48.6	48.2	48.1	47.9	48.0	48.0	48.3	48.0
2008	47.8	48.1	48.4	48.6	48.9	49.0	48.9	48.8	48.8	48.4	48.2	48.1	48.5
2009	47.0	47.0	47.2	47.2	47.3	47.2	47.0	46.7	46.3	46.2	46.1	46.1	46.8
2010	45.3	45.4	46.0	46.4	46.6	47.0	46.6	46.4	46.0	46.5	46.3	46.3	46.2
2011	45.5	45.4	45.8	46.8	46.5	46.6	47.3	47.0	46.9	47.1	46.9	47.1	46.6
2012	46.5	46.6	47.1	47.9	48.0	48.2	47.4	47.4	47.1	46.9	46.7	46.9	47.2
2013	46.5	46.7	47.1	47.2	47.2	47.1	46.9	46.7	46.4	46.6	45.8	45.7	46.7
2014	45.6	45.9	46.2	46.4	46.7	46.9	46.7	46.8	46.7	46.8	46.8	46.8	46.5
2015	46.4	46.6	46.8	47.1	47.4	47.6	47.6	47.6	47.3	47.0	47.2	48.1	47.2
Retail Trade													
2005	129.9	128.8	130.2	131.3	131.5	132.1	131.6	131.4	131.9	132.2	135.5	136.9	131.9
2006	131.8	130.9	133.5	132.6	133.6	132.9	132.2	132.7	132.6	133.2	136.0	137.5	133.3
2007	132.3	131.4	134.6	132.9	134.2	134.3	134.0	134.1	134.3	133.9	137.7	139.4	134.4
2008	133.7	132.6	133.9	132.8	133.6	134.2	133.4	133.7	132.9	131.6	133.9	135.1	133.5
2009	129.2	128.0	129.6	129.6	130.0	129.7	129.2	129.2	129.3	129.0	131.6	132.7	129.8
2010	126.7	125.6	127.5	127.7	128.9	130.1	129.8	130.1	128.9	130.4	133.5	134.8	129.5
2011	129.4	127.4	129.1	131.3	130.5	130.8	131.6	131.2	130.2	131.9	134.9	136.0	131.2
2012	130.9	129.8	131.2	131.9	132.5	132.6	132.5	132.3	132.3	132.3	136.0	136.6	132.6
2013	130.5	130.2	131.4	131.7	131.7	131.7	133.3	133.7	133.2	134.5	138.4	139.0	133.3
2014	133.1	132.2	133.4	135.2	135.5	136.3	136.0	136.6	136.2	137.4	141.4	142.4	136.3
2015	136.6	136.3	137.0	139.1	140.7	141.1	140.4	141.6	140.8	142.7	145.5	146.7	140.7

1. Employment by Industry: Arkansas, 2005–2015—*Continued*

(Numbers in thousands, not seasonally adjusted)

Industry and year	January	February	March	April	May	June	July	August	September	October	November	December	Annual average
Transportation and Utilities													
2005	64.7	65.0	65.2	65.4	65.6	65.9	66.3	66.4	67.7	67.0	67.1	67.6	66.2
2006	66.1	66.4	66.8	66.8	67.0	67.4	67.4	67.5	68.4	68.5	68.6	68.9	67.5
2007	66.7	67.1	67.7	67.2	67.7	67.9	67.5	68.2	68.2	67.9	67.8	67.5	67.6
2008	65.7	65.7	65.9	65.8	65.8	65.5	64.8	64.7	64.7	64.2	63.8	63.1	65.0
2009	61.1	60.2	60.0	59.5	58.6	58.4	59.2	58.1	58.6	58.1	58.2	58.2	59.0
2010	57.7	57.7	58.1	57.8	58.1	58.6	59.2	59.6	59.9	59.7	59.8	60.3	58.9
2011	58.8	58.5	59.0	59.9	60.0	60.4	60.7	60.8	61.6	61.3	61.3	62.2	60.4
2012	60.8	60.6	61.2	60.9	61.2	61.6	61.5	62.0	62.1	62.2	62.3	63.0	61.6
2013	61.1	61.1	61.2	61.0	61.0	61.4	61.0	61.4	61.5	61.5	61.8	62.0	61.3
2014	60.5	60.5	61.0	61.1	61.5	61.6	61.8	62.3	63.0	62.9	63.4	64.5	62.0
2015	62.8	62.6	62.9	63.3	63.6	64.2	63.9	64.2	64.6	64.6	65.9	67.6	64.2
Information													
2005	19.6	19.8	19.7	19.4	19.4	19.3	19.2	19.3	19.0	19.0	19.0	19.0	19.3
2006	18.8	18.8	18.8	18.8	18.7	18.6	18.6	18.7	18.6	18.3	18.3	18.3	18.6
2007	18.4	18.4	18.4	18.4	18.4	18.2	18.1	18.1	18.0	17.8	17.8	17.8	18.2
2008	17.6	17.7	17.6	17.8	17.5	17.6	17.5	17.5	17.2	17.0	16.9	16.9	17.4
2009	16.5	16.4	16.4	16.4	16.5	16.5	16.4	16.2	16.0	15.8	15.7	15.7	16.2
2010	15.3	15.4	15.5	15.4	15.5	15.8	15.3	15.2	15.2	15.1	15.1	15.1	15.3
2011	15.0	15.0	14.9	14.9	14.9	14.9	14.9	14.9	14.7	14.7	14.7	14.7	14.9
2012	14.6	14.6	14.5	14.5	14.6	14.5	14.4	14.4	14.4	14.4	14.4	14.5	14.5
2013	14.2	14.2	14.2	14.1	14.2	14.3	14.2	14.2	14.0	14.0	14.1	14.1	14.2
2014	13.8	13.8	13.7	13.7	13.7	13.6	13.7	13.6	13.3	13.3	13.4	13.4	13.6
2015	13.2	13.2	13.1	13.2	13.2	13.3	13.7	13.4	13.4	13.5	13.8	13.8	13.4
Financial Activities													
2005	50.8	50.7	50.9	50.7	51.0	51.6	51.8	51.8	51.8	51.7	51.8	52.5	51.4
2006	51.8	51.8	52.0	52.2	52.5	52.9	52.9	53.1	53.0	52.7	52.9	53.2	52.6
2007	52.4	52.4	52.6	53.1	53.3	53.7	53.7	53.6	53.4	53.2	53.1	53.3	53.2
2008	52.6	52.6	52.7	52.5	52.7	52.7	52.5	52.5	52.3	51.6	51.5	52.0	52.4
2009	51.0	50.7	50.8	50.8	50.9	51.0	50.5	50.3	50.1	49.7	49.6	49.8	50.4
2010	48.7	48.6	48.5	48.8	48.7	49.1	48.9	48.9	48.7	48.8	48.8	49.1	48.8
2011	48.2	48.0	48.2	48.7	48.4	48.6	49.0	48.7	48.3	48.7	48.7	49.0	48.5
2012	48.5	48.6	48.7	48.8	49.1	49.4	49.2	49.4	49.1	49.1	49.2	49.4	49.0
2013	48.9	49.0	49.1	49.3	49.6	49.8	49.7	50.0	49.6	49.9	49.9	49.9	49.6
2014	49.1	49.3	49.3	49.3	49.6	49.7	49.5	49.5	48.9	49.2	49.2	49.3	49.3
2015	48.8	48.7	48.7	49.0	49.3	49.4	49.6	49.7	49.3	49.5	49.7	49.6	49.3
Professional and Business Services													
2005	107.1	108.8	110.5	110.6	110.7	111.5	111.8	112.8	113.2	113.1	113.1	113.3	111.4
2006	111.5	112.9	115.1	114.5	114.9	115.6	114.0	114.6	115.6	115.1	114.7	114.6	114.4
2007	114.0	115.1	116.6	116.5	116.8	117.4	116.2	118.8	119.2	118.5	117.8	117.7	117.1
2008	115.0	117.2	117.3	117.0	117.8	117.2	116.4	117.9	118.1	117.9	116.3	115.5	117.0
2009	112.7	113.3	113.5	113.5	112.2	111.7	112.1	113.0	113.5	114.1	115.2	115.8	113.4
2010	114.1	115.0	117.3	118.6	118.5	119.4	119.5	120.2	120.5	120.1	119.5	120.1	118.6
2011	118.7	119.5	121.5	123.6	122.1	122.7	124.7	125.3	124.8	125.7	124.6	124.5	123.1
2012	121.6	122.7	124.2	125.9	125.7	125.2	125.4	125.7	125.6	126.7	126.0	126.6	125.1
2013	124.9	127.2	128.2	129.7	129.6	127.5	127.0	127.1	130.2	132.4	132.7	130.7	128.9
2014	128.0	132.3	133.8	133.8	134.3	131.9	130.7	132.3	135.3	137.6	137.8	138.0	133.8
2015	131.9	137.2	136.1	138.6	139.1	136.6	136.2	137.5	140.6	141.3	140.7	140.7	138.0
Education and Health Services													
2005	144.1	145.4	145.8	146.0	146.0	144.1	143.6	144.9	148.1	149.1	148.9	148.6	146.2
2006	148.4	149.7	150.7	151.2	150.9	150.0	148.2	149.8	152.5	152.7	152.8	153.0	150.8
2007	150.8	153.0	153.9	154.2	154.4	153.6	152.2	154.3	156.0	156.3	156.7	157.0	154.4
2008	156.8	157.7	158.5	157.5	157.6	156.3	155.3	156.9	159.3	160.0	160.0	159.7	158.0
2009	158.2	160.2	161.6	163.5	162.6	161.2	161.0	161.6	165.0	165.8	165.9	166.0	162.7
2010	163.7	164.5	165.2	165.4	165.7	164.6	163.6	165.4	168.2	168.2	168.4	168.5	166.0
2011	165.4	165.2	166.5	168.0	167.0	163.5	164.2	166.2	170.0	171.1	171.7	171.3	167.5
2012	169.5	170.0	170.8	170.3	170.1	167.4	165.6	169.5	172.0	173.5	173.5	173.4	170.5
2013	170.4	171.6	171.5	172.4	172.5	169.2	168.2	170.3	172.8	172.9	173.6	172.9	171.5
2014	170.7	171.3	171.9	172.3	172.9	169.5	168.4	170.4	173.1	173.8	174.1	174.7	171.9
2015	172.8	173.3	173.5	174.6	175.0	172.2	171.9	174.2	177.3	178.5	178.8	179.4	175.1

1. Employment by Industry: Arkansas, 2005–2015—*Continued*

(Numbers in thousands, not seasonally adjusted)

Industry and year	January	February	March	April	May	June	July	August	September	October	November	December	Annual average
Leisure and Hospitality													
2005	87.5	90.1	93.5	94.9	96.6	98.3	97.1	96.8	96.2	93.4	93.3	92.7	94.2
2006	92.0	92.7	96.2	99.0	99.8	101.7	99.8	99.7	98.0	97.5	96.7	96.1	97.4
2007	94.0	94.9	97.8	99.7	101.3	102.8	101.8	102.1	100.6	99.9	98.8	98.2	99.3
2008	95.9	97.3	99.5	101.7	102.9	104.4	104.0	104.3	102.7	99.9	99.0	97.5	100.8
2009	95.6	96.5	99.1	100.9	102.6	104.1	103.1	102.1	100.7	98.3	97.0	95.2	99.6
2010	93.0	93.5	96.6	99.7	101.4	103.0	101.9	102.3	101.6	99.0	97.4	96.5	98.8
2011	93.8	94.0	97.3	101.3	102.1	103.3	103.7	103.7	102.4	101.4	100.1	99.1	100.2
2012	96.6	98.3	101.6	104.0	105.3	107.1	105.4	105.9	104.3	102.2	101.3	101.4	102.8
2013	99.1	100.3	102.9	106.0	107.6	109.4	108.6	108.3	106.7	104.5	103.6	102.3	104.9
2014	101.1	102.2	105.3	108.6	110.7	112.5	110.4	111.1	109.9	107.6	106.9	106.4	107.7
2015	104.4	106.1	107.9	111.6	114.9	115.8	113.7	115.1	114.5	112.9	112.8	112.2	111.8
Other Services													
2005	41.2	41.5	42.2	42.8	43.0	43.5	43.3	43.0	43.0	42.3	42.4	42.6	42.6
2006	42.5	42.6	43.1	43.6	44.2	44.9	45.0	45.1	45.0	44.8	45.0	45.3	44.3
2007	44.8	44.9	45.5	45.3	45.4	46.1	45.6	45.6	45.3	45.2	45.2	45.4	45.4
2008	45.0	45.2	45.6	45.8	46.0	46.5	46.4	46.3	46.2	45.7	45.4	45.6	45.8
2009	45.0	45.0	45.2	45.1	45.0	45.4	45.1	44.6	44.2	43.6	43.3	43.1	44.6
2010	42.6	42.4	42.8	43.1	43.3	44.0	43.6	43.4	43.3	43.1	43.0	42.8	43.1
2011	42.8	42.6	43.2	43.8	43.4	43.8	44.3	43.6	43.4	43.6	43.5	43.6	43.5
2012	42.8	43.0	43.4	43.6	43.8	44.5	43.7	43.5	43.4	43.3	43.2	43.2	43.5
2013	42.7	42.8	43.0	43.3	43.4	43.8	43.7	43.4	43.3	43.2	43.0	43.0	43.2
2014	42.8	42.9	43.2	43.7	43.9	44.6	44.4	44.5	44.1	43.6	43.6	43.4	43.7
2015	42.8	43.0	43.0	43.3	43.6	44.2	44.3	44.0	43.7	44.7	44.4	45.0	43.8
Government													
2005	200.9	206.0	206.4	207.9	206.6	201.4	188.4	192.6	207.5	208.9	209.4	208.4	203.7
2006	205.6	210.0	211.2	211.8	210.6	204.1	191.8	197.0	210.8	212.3	213.6	212.3	207.6
2007	208.1	213.6	214.6	214.5	213.2	208.6	193.7	200.1	213.9	215.9	217.0	216.1	210.8
2008	211.0	216.4	217.3	217.4	217.6	211.8	197.5	202.4	216.5	218.6	219.4	218.6	213.7
2009	214.2	219.4	220.5	221.5	220.4	214.8	202.6	206.3	217.1	221.8	222.6	222.3	217.0
2010	214.3	218.1	221.0	222.1	227.5	220.9	206.3	207.9	218.2	220.6	221.3	220.7	218.2
2011	215.1	219.5	221.2	222.7	221.6	215.4	199.6	205.7	217.6	221.6	222.5	220.6	216.9
2012	214.0	219.9	221.1	220.7	220.1	214.7	200.9	203.7	216.9	220.2	221.6	220.6	216.2
2013	214.1	219.3	220.1	220.6	219.2	213.2	200.3	203.1	216.2	217.6	218.1	217.1	214.9
2014	211.2	216.5	217.4	217.7	217.3	211.6	199.0	201.9	215.0	216.6	218.6	217.2	213.3
2015	211.2	215.8	216.4	216.7	215.9	210.6	198.7	201.9	215.1	217.1	218.5	217.5	213.0

2. Average Weekly Hours by Selected Industry: Arkansas, 2011–2015

(Not seasonally adjusted)

Industry and year	January	February	March	April	May	June	July	August	September	October	November	December	Annual average
Total Private													
2011	34.1	33.1	35.0	35.0	35.5	35.4	35.3	35.1	35.3	36.0	35.1	35.3	35.0
2012	35.2	34.5	34.8	35.1	34.7	34.9	35.2	35.0	35.2	34.6	34.7	35.2	34.9
2013	34.0	34.4	34.6	34.5	34.7	35.7	35.0	35.2	35.7	34.8	34.9	34.9	34.9
2014	34.8	35.0	35.3	35.0	34.8	35.3	34.7	34.9	34.8	34.8	34.9	34.8	34.9
2015	34.6	34.7	34.5	34.6	34.3	34.3	34.4	34.9	34.3	34.5	34.8	34.3	34.5
Goods-Producing													
2011	36.2	35.3	39.2	38.4	39.0	39.3	39.7	39.4	40.5	40.9	39.8	41.1	39.1
2012	40.2	40.0	40.4	41.1	40.6	41.1	40.9	41.1	41.8	41.2	41.2	41.8	40.9
2013	39.7	40.7	40.5	40.5	40.5	41.9	41.3	41.6	41.5	40.7	41.2	41.2	40.9
2014	40.8	41.1	41.7	41.7	40.9	41.5	39.8	41.3	41.1	41.2	40.8	41.6	41.1
2015	41.0	40.5	39.9	40.5	40.0	40.4	40.1	41.2	39.6	41.1	40.7	40.1	40.4
Construction													
2011	31.0	32.0	37.6	36.0	36.9	38.1	38.0	37.6	38.7	38.4	37.6	38.0	36.7
2012	36.7	36.2	38.2	38.4	38.8	39.0	39.1	38.7	38.8	38.3	38.2	39.4	38.3
2013	38.3	39.5	40.3	38.9	39.8	41.1	40.8	41.2	41.1	39.7	41.2	41.3	40.3
2014	39.9	40.5	42.4	40.5	39.5	40.0	41.1	42.7	39.9	40.1	39.4	40.9	40.6
2015	38.9	36.7	35.6	37.9	37.3	39.3	37.7	38.5	35.4	37.3	37.3	35.7	37.3
Manufacturing													
2011	38.3	36.9	39.4	39.3	39.7	39.7	40.3	40.3	41.1	41.8	40.7	41.9	39.9
2012	41.2	41.2	41.0	41.8	41.1	41.8	41.4	41.8	42.7	42.1	42.1	42.5	41.7
2013	39.9	40.9	40.5	41.0	40.6	42.0	41.4	41.7	41.5	41.1	41.2	41.0	41.1
2014	41.0	41.0	41.3	41.9	41.3	41.7	39.2	40.7	41.4	41.5	40.9	41.8	41.1
2015	41.4	41.4	41.1	40.8	40.6	40.4	40.6	41.6	40.9	41.2	40.8	40.8	41.0
Trade, Transportation, and Utilities													
2011	36.3	35.3	36.6	37.0	37.3	37.5	37.2	36.7	36.3	37.1	35.6	35.1	36.5
2012	34.6	34.6	35.1	36.0	35.5	35.5	35.4	35.3	35.6	35.4	34.3	34.9	35.2
2013	34.0	34.6	35.3	35.2	34.8	36.0	36.2	36.1	36.6	36.0	35.9	35.9	35.6
2014	35.8	35.8	36.8	36.2	36.1	36.5	36.2	36.1	36.1	36.0	35.8	35.9	36.1
2015	35.8	35.9	36.0	35.8	35.3	35.0	34.9	35.6	35.1	34.6	35.0	34.6	35.3
Financial Activities													
2011	38.0	36.4	38.0	37.2	38.0	37.5	37.6	37.8	37.2	38.7	37.4	37.5	37.6
2012	39.0	36.8	36.6	37.5	37.3	36.5	37.6	36.7	35.5	35.2	35.4	36.8	36.7
2013	34.7	35.4	35.0	35.1	35.3	36.6	34.4	35.5	36.2	34.8	35.5	36.5	35.4
2014	35.4	36.4	36.9	36.0	37.5	37.8	36.5	35.5	35.6	35.2	36.8	35.8	36.3
2015	36.7	37.0	37.2	35.7	35.9	35.9	36.0	36.3	35.7	35.7	37.0	36.3	36.3
Professional and Business Services													
2011	32.2	32.3	33.8	34.6	35.9	34.6	34.8	34.9	35.3	35.9	35.6	35.3	34.6
2012	35.6	34.7	35.4	36.4	35.7	35.5	36.2	36.4	35.9	35.2	36.1	35.7	35.7
2013	34.5	35.5	35.4	35.4	36.7	37.4	35.7	36.4	37.8	36.7	36.4	36.7	36.2
2014	36.3	36.2	36.3	36.2	36.1	36.5	35.9	36.4	36.4	36.3	36.7	35.6	36.2
2015	34.9	35.8	35.7	36.2	35.7	35.8	36.1	36.1	36.3	36.1	36.7	35.8	35.9
Education and Health Services													
2011	32.2	31.2	32.4	32.6	32.7	32.6	32.5	32.4	32.2	32.9	32.5	32.6	32.4
2012	32.9	32.0	32.7	33.6	33.0	33.1	33.4	33.0	33.7	33.2	33.3	33.9	33.2
2013	33.5	33.2	33.1	33.2	33.7	34.4	33.5	33.2	33.8	33.0	33.3	33.4	33.4
2014	33.1	33.2	32.8	32.9	32.9	33.3	33.4	33.5	33.5	33.4	33.5	33.5	33.2
2015	33.3	33.6	33.1	33.5	33.4	33.3	33.5	33.7	33.3	33.3	34.2	33.9	33.5
Leisure and Hospitality													
2011	25.7	25.0	26.1	25.6	25.9	26.2	25.9	25.9	25.9	26.3	25.6	25.5	25.8
2012	25.6	25.5	25.5	26.7	26.6	27.1	27.1	26.7	26.3	25.7	25.9	26.2	26.3
2013	25.1	25.7	26.4	26.3	25.6	26.9	26.4	26.3	26.3	25.7	25.3	24.1	25.9
2014	25.1	26.1	26.7	25.9	25.7	26.4	26.3	25.9	25.2	25.6	25.5	25.4	25.8
2015	25.1	25.0	24.9	24.7	25.1	25.3	25.8	25.7	25.0	25.1	25.0	25.1	25.1

3. Average Hourly Earnings by Selected Industry: Arkansas, 2011–2015

(Dollars, not seasonally adjusted)

Industry and year	January	February	March	April	May	June	July	August	September	October	November	December	Annual average
Total Private													
2011	18.58	18.62	18.26	18.21	18.38	18.12	18.16	18.13	18.42	18.54	18.40	18.52	18.36
2012	18.84	18.83	18.61	18.05	17.89	17.92	18.45	18.29	18.78	18.92	19.05	19.21	18.57
2013	19.11	19.03	19.01	19.07	19.02	19.13	19.23	19.22	19.61	19.41	19.54	19.92	19.28
2014	19.55	19.70	19.81	19.47	19.48	19.67	19.53	19.39	19.52	19.40	19.61	19.40	19.54
2015	19.39	19.44	19.61	19.38	19.44	19.29	19.40	19.61	19.51	19.59	19.72	19.69	19.51
Goods-Producing													
2011	18.26	18.39	18.02	18.03	18.28	17.93	17.91	18.09	18.21	18.25	18.29	18.62	18.19
2012	18.59	18.82	18.45	18.49	18.35	18.52	18.59	18.39	18.58	18.71	18.58	18.49	18.55
2013	18.92	18.41	18.63	18.58	18.81	18.94	18.95	18.89	19.34	19.40	19.61	19.73	19.02
2014	19.45	19.47	19.62	19.15	19.36	19.50	19.75	19.55	19.62	19.59	19.93	19.66	19.55
2015	19.66	19.82	20.17	20.10	20.15	19.93	20.04	20.28	20.27	20.50	20.32	20.30	20.13
Construction													
2011	19.30	19.01	18.23	18.08	18.15	17.58	17.69	17.87	18.08	18.56	18.33	18.33	18.23
2012	18.19	18.86	17.93	17.89	17.79	17.67	17.87	17.56	17.80	17.97	18.26	18.00	17.97
2013	17.18	17.41	17.64	17.69	18.13	18.21	18.51	18.42	19.09	19.78	20.24	21.29	18.65
2014	20.35	20.35	20.08	20.15	20.61	20.68	20.46	20.14	20.22	20.39	20.66	20.33	20.37
2015	20.33	20.58	21.12	20.94	20.96	20.70	20.76	21.12	21.20	21.88	21.40	21.28	21.03
Manufacturing													
2011	17.06	17.26	17.14	17.30	17.70	17.55	17.50	17.68	17.78	17.78	17.96	18.44	17.60
2012	18.46	18.56	18.38	18.42	18.28	18.56	18.63	18.48	18.63	18.76	18.52	18.50	18.52
2013	19.33	18.60	18.80	18.71	18.87	18.99	18.88	18.83	19.28	19.19	19.31	19.13	18.99
2014	18.97	19.07	19.32	18.70	18.86	18.98	19.34	19.15	19.22	19.09	19.45	19.14	19.11
2015	19.20	19.36	19.76	19.67	19.64	19.45	19.57	19.66	19.56	19.51	19.54	19.66	19.55
Trade, Transportation, and Utilities													
2011	18.87	18.94	18.79	19.08	19.15	18.83	19.05	18.43	18.83	18.70	18.31	18.66	18.80
2012	18.79	18.76	18.61	18.54	18.18	18.58	18.64	18.48	18.98	18.68	18.73	19.06	18.67
2013	18.76	18.82	18.84	18.92	18.66	18.70	19.53	19.66	19.99	19.58	19.69	20.13	19.29
2014	19.86	19.69	20.04	19.40	19.50	19.80	19.62	19.45	19.53	19.46	19.50	18.92	19.56
2015	19.09	19.37	19.77	19.24	19.22	19.18	19.31	19.52	19.32	19.42	19.60	19.44	19.37
Financial Activities													
2011	23.53	23.26	22.71	22.48	22.19	21.65	21.45	21.59	21.59	23.37	22.60	22.54	22.41
2012	24.12	24.35	24.04	24.86	24.63	23.65	25.77	24.63	25.06	26.28	26.31	25.45	24.92
2013	23.04	23.84	23.09	23.29	23.15	23.94	23.20	22.47	22.57	21.91	23.05	24.39	23.17
2014	22.86	23.71	23.41	22.66	22.27	23.30	22.86	23.08	22.90	22.78	22.92	23.00	22.98
2015	23.30	23.18	22.82	23.62	23.68	22.60	23.08	23.06	22.95	22.72	23.49	24.02	23.21
Professional and Business Services													
2011	20.65	20.78	20.04	19.96	20.72	20.49	20.83	20.80	21.22	21.45	21.95	21.61	20.89
2012	22.60	22.26	22.54	22.62	22.13	22.28	22.56	21.95	21.91	22.49	22.79	23.55	22.47
2013	24.59	23.75	23.46	23.99	23.13	23.04	23.09	22.20	22.73	22.61	22.41	22.82	23.13
2014	22.32	22.61	22.76	22.24	22.12	22.57	21.93	21.92	21.87	21.88	22.09	22.27	22.21
2015	21.60	21.06	21.30	20.82	20.93	21.15	21.06	21.32	20.83	20.99	21.18	21.02	21.10
Education and Health Services													
2011	16.52	16.87	16.88	16.69	16.80	16.99	17.22	17.30	17.40	17.58	17.45	17.51	17.11
2012	17.91	18.00	17.91	18.06	17.93	17.97	18.81	18.90	19.24	19.00	19.52	19.74	18.59
2013	19.35	19.70	19.78	19.79	19.99	20.38	19.95	20.71	20.92	20.60	20.60	20.67	20.22
2014	20.74	21.28	21.58	21.80	21.72	21.75	21.63	21.37	21.68	21.17	21.51	21.21	21.45
2015	21.09	21.12	21.09	20.66	21.01	20.85	20.91	20.91	20.78	20.81	20.75	20.72	20.89
Leisure and Hospitality													
2011	10.33	10.49	10.41	10.32	10.44	10.31	10.28	10.34	10.34	10.65	10.74	10.77	10.45
2012	10.81	10.66	10.48	9.68	9.71	9.64	9.73	9.86	9.92	9.98	9.98	10.03	10.02
2013	10.24	10.26	10.29	10.27	10.33	10.20	10.34	10.40	10.49	10.42	10.60	10.90	10.39
2014	10.76	10.84	10.50	10.46	10.54	10.58	10.57	10.69	10.75	10.90	10.68	10.91	10.68
2015	10.92	11.02	11.21	11.15	11.05	10.92	10.92	11.26	11.50	11.42	11.60	11.69	11.22

4. Average Weekly Earnings by Selected Industry: Arkansas, 2011–2015

(Dollars, not seasonally adjusted)

Industry and year	January	February	March	April	May	June	July	August	September	October	November	December	Annual average
Total Private													
2011	633.58	616.32	639.10	637.35	652.49	641.45	641.05	636.36	650.23	667.44	645.84	653.76	642.60
2012	663.17	649.64	647.63	633.56	620.78	625.41	649.44	640.15	661.06	654.63	661.04	676.19	648.09
2013	649.74	654.63	657.75	657.92	659.99	682.94	673.05	676.54	700.08	675.47	681.95	695.21	672.87
2014	680.34	689.50	699.29	681.45	677.90	694.35	677.69	676.71	679.30	675.12	684.39	675.12	681.95
2015	670.89	674.57	676.55	670.55	666.79	661.65	667.36	684.39	669.19	675.86	686.26	675.37	673.10
Goods-Producing													
2011	661.01	649.17	706.38	692.35	712.92	704.65	711.03	712.75	737.51	746.43	727.94	765.28	711.23
2012	747.32	752.80	745.38	759.94	745.01	761.17	760.33	755.83	776.64	770.85	765.50	772.88	758.70
2013	751.12	749.29	754.52	752.49	761.81	793.59	782.64	785.82	802.61	789.58	807.93	812.88	777.92
2014	793.56	800.22	818.15	798.56	791.82	809.25	786.05	807.42	806.38	807.11	813.14	817.86	803.51
2015	806.06	802.71	804.78	814.05	806.00	805.17	803.60	835.54	802.69	842.55	827.02	814.03	813.25
Construction													
2011	598.30	608.32	685.45	650.88	669.74	669.80	672.22	671.91	699.70	712.70	689.21	696.54	669.04
2012	667.57	682.73	684.93	686.98	690.25	689.13	698.72	679.57	690.64	688.25	697.53	709.20	688.25
2013	657.99	687.70	710.89	688.14	721.57	748.43	755.21	758.90	784.60	785.27	833.89	879.28	751.60
2014	811.97	824.18	851.39	816.08	814.10	827.20	840.91	859.98	806.78	817.64	814.00	831.50	827.02
2015	790.84	755.29	751.87	793.63	781.81	813.51	782.65	813.12	750.48	816.12	798.22	759.70	784.42
Manufacturing													
2011	653.40	636.89	675.32	679.89	702.69	696.74	705.25	712.50	730.76	743.20	730.97	772.64	702.24
2012	760.55	764.67	753.58	769.96	751.31	775.81	771.28	772.46	795.50	789.80	779.69	786.25	772.28
2013	771.27	760.74	761.40	767.11	766.12	797.58	781.63	785.21	800.12	788.71	795.57	784.33	780.49
2014	777.77	781.87	797.92	783.53	778.92	791.47	758.13	779.41	795.71	792.24	795.51	800.05	785.42
2015	794.88	801.50	812.14	802.54	797.38	785.78	794.54	817.86	800.00	803.81	797.23	802.13	801.55
Trade, Transportation, and Utilities													
2011	684.98	668.58	687.71	705.96	714.30	706.13	708.66	676.38	683.53	693.77	651.84	654.97	686.20
2012	650.13	649.10	653.21	667.44	645.39	659.59	659.86	652.34	675.69	661.27	642.44	665.19	657.18
2013	637.84	651.17	665.05	665.98	649.37	673.20	706.99	709.73	731.63	704.88	706.87	722.67	686.72
2014	710.99	704.90	737.47	702.28	703.95	722.70	710.24	702.15	705.03	700.56	698.10	679.23	706.12
2015	683.42	695.38	711.72	688.79	678.47	671.30	673.92	694.91	678.13	671.93	686.00	672.62	683.76
Financial Activities													
2011	894.14	846.66	862.98	836.26	843.22	811.88	806.52	816.10	803.15	904.42	845.24	845.25	842.62
2012	940.68	896.08	879.86	932.25	918.70	863.23	968.95	903.92	889.63	925.06	931.37	936.56	914.56
2013	799.49	843.94	808.15	817.48	817.20	876.20	798.08	797.69	817.03	762.47	818.28	890.24	820.22
2014	809.24	863.04	863.83	815.76	835.13	880.74	834.39	819.34	815.24	801.86	843.46	823.40	834.17
2015	855.11	857.66	848.90	843.23	850.11	811.34	830.88	837.08	819.32	811.10	869.13	871.93	842.52
Professional and Business Services													
2011	664.93	671.19	677.35	690.62	743.85	708.95	724.88	725.92	749.07	770.06	781.42	762.83	722.79
2012	804.56	772.42	797.92	823.37	790.04	790.94	816.67	798.98	786.57	791.65	822.72	840.74	802.18
2013	848.36	843.13	830.48	849.25	848.87	861.70	824.31	808.08	859.19	829.79	815.72	837.49	837.31
2014	810.22	818.48	826.19	805.09	798.53	823.81	787.29	797.89	796.07	794.24	810.70	792.81	804.00
2015	753.84	753.95	760.41	753.68	747.20	757.17	760.27	769.65	756.13	757.74	777.31	752.52	757.49
Education and Health Services													
2011	531.94	526.34	546.91	544.09	549.36	553.87	559.65	560.52	560.28	578.38	567.13	570.83	554.36
2012	589.24	576.00	585.66	606.82	591.69	594.81	628.25	623.70	648.39	630.80	650.02	669.19	617.19
2013	648.23	654.04	654.72	657.03	673.66	701.07	668.33	687.57	707.10	685.74	685.98	690.38	675.35
2014	686.49	706.50	707.82	717.22	714.59	724.28	722.44	715.90	726.28	707.08	720.59	710.54	712.14
2015	702.30	709.63	698.08	692.11	701.73	694.31	700.49	704.67	691.97	692.97	709.65	702.41	699.82
Leisure and Hospitality													
2011	265.48	262.25	271.70	264.19	270.40	270.12	266.25	267.81	267.81	280.10	274.94	274.64	269.61
2012	276.74	271.83	267.24	258.46	258.29	261.24	263.68	263.26	260.90	256.49	258.48	262.79	263.53
2013	257.02	263.68	271.66	270.10	264.45	274.38	272.98	273.52	275.89	267.79	268.18	262.69	269.10
2014	270.08	282.92	280.35	270.91	270.88	279.31	277.99	276.87	270.90	279.04	272.34	277.11	275.54
2015	274.09	275.50	279.13	275.41	277.36	276.28	281.74	289.38	287.50	286.64	290.00	293.42	281.62

CALIFORNIA
At a Glance

Population:
  2005 estimate: 35,827,943
  2010 census: 37,253,956
  2015 estimate: 39,144,818

Percent change in population:
  2005–2015: 9.3%
  2010–2015: 5.1%

Percent change in total nonfarm employment:
  2005–2015: 6.7%

Industry with the largest growth in employment, 2005–2015 (thousands):
  Education and health services, 621.3

Industry with the largest decline or smallest growth in employment, 2005–2015 (thousands):
  Manufacturing, –213.3

Civilian labor force:
  2005: 17,530,064
  2010: 18,336,271
  2015: 18,981,770

Unemployment rate and rank among states (highest to lowest):
  2005: 5.4%, 14th
  2010: 12.2%, 3rd
  2015: 6.2%, 8th

Over-the-year change in unemployment rates:
  2012–2013: –1.5%
  2013–2014: –1.4%
  2014–2015: –1.3%

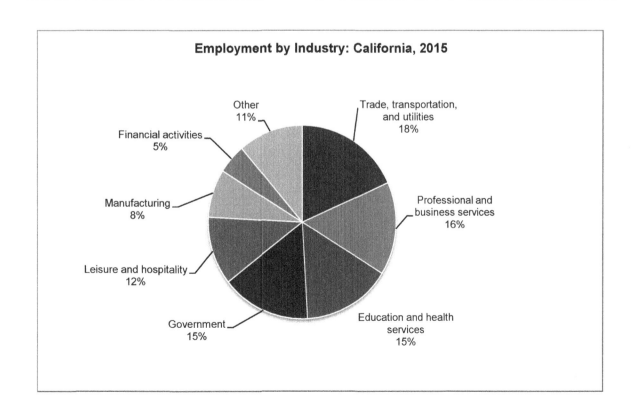

Employment by Industry: California, 2015

Other 11%
Financial activities 5%
Manufacturing 8%
Leisure and hospitality 12%
Government 15%
Trade, transportation, and utilities 18%
Professional and business services 16%
Education and health services 15%

1. Employment by Industry: California, 2005–2015

(Numbers in thousands, not seasonally adjusted)

Industry and year	January	February	March	April	May	June	July	August	September	October	November	December	Annual average
Total Nonfarm													
2005	14,685.2	14,802.5	14,906.9	14,964.9	15,022.7	15,094.3	14,984.0	15,044.1	15,158.8	15,207.3	15,299.5	15,372.4	15,045.2
2006	15,018.2	15,144.7	15,229.5	15,233.1	15,345.5	15,434.7	15,265.5	15,319.4	15,407.7	15,443.8	15,509.5	15,555.0	15,325.6
2007	15,214.7	15,326.4	15,433.0	15,385.4	15,477.1	15,551.5	15,423.5	15,433.8	15,495.3	15,535.5	15,604.2	15,647.6	15,460.7
2008	15,242.2	15,334.7	15,387.7	15,399.2	15,435.4	15,461.8	15,252.1	15,239.5	15,267.6	15,240.1	15,181.0	15,142.2	15,298.6
2009	14,687.0	14,622.4	14,600.8	14,535.1	14,543.9	14,513.0	14,222.4	14,201.9	14,219.8	14,351.8	14,373.3	14,382.2	14,437.8
2010	14,047.6	14,088.7	14,157.6	14,289.4	14,381.7	14,394.9	14,186.4	14,208.6	14,265.4	14,412.2	14,463.5	14,493.7	14,282.5
2011	14,196.8	14,279.6	14,338.9	14,404.3	14,451.1	14,470.1	14,322.8	14,369.6	14,466.4	14,574.3	14,654.7	14,677.4	14,433.8
2012	14,435.2	14,532.2	14,626.2	14,663.6	14,762.1	14,829.5	14,658.1	14,736.9	14,802.7	14,944.6	15,061.4	15,084.4	14,761.4
2013	14,796.8	14,923.4	15,001.2	15,066.8	15,149.9	15,181.4	15,035.4	15,149.9	15,205.1	15,349.3	15,487.9	15,504.9	15,154.3
2014	15,236.5	15,334.8	15,419.0	15,485.9	15,572.5	15,604.3	15,445.9	15,583.3	15,656.3	15,811.9	15,926.2	15,951.1	15,585.6
2015	15,675.6	15,770.9	15,860.2	15,938.4	16,017.8	16,039.0	15,995.6	16,095.2	16,151.0	16,290.8	16,376.2	16,407.8	16,051.5
Total Private													
2005	12,281.5	12,372.7	12,460.8	12,513.0	12,563.4	12,640.6	12,652.1	12,717.3	12,768.3	12,767.5	12,840.4	12,923.0	12,625.1
2006	12,587.0	12,687.8	12,756.1	12,786.2	12,859.9	12,950.6	12,898.0	12,965.7	12,985.9	12,962.5	13,007.3	13,062.6	12,873.3
2007	12,739.6	12,827.6	12,911.8	12,860.5	12,941.7	13,017.0	13,016.2	13,040.7	13,033.4	13,021.1	13,067.5	13,116.1	12,966.1
2008	12,731.0	12,797.5	12,833.4	12,837.0	12,863.6	12,888.4	12,827.5	12,825.7	12,792.7	12,710.7	12,638.0	12,611.1	12,779.7
2009	12,173.0	12,089.4	12,049.6	11,971.8	11,986.1	11,970.0	11,865.0	11,863.0	11,839.2	11,878.8	11,892.9	11,919.6	11,958.2
2010	11,603.4	11,628.7	11,677.4	11,763.1	11,809.6	11,863.5	11,856.2	11,898.0	11,894.9	11,964.6	11,998.3	12,051.0	11,834.1
2011	11,772.5	11,834.0	11,869.7	11,934.7	11,981.3	12,012.6	12,044.5	12,097.0	12,130.0	12,166.4	12,228.7	12,275.8	12,028.9
2012	12,052.8	12,123.9	12,198.1	12,237.9	12,328.5	12,403.7	12,406.4	12,479.5	12,485.2	12,558.8	12,654.7	12,692.3	12,385.2
2013	12,433.5	12,532.0	12,588.5	12,654.5	12,727.0	12,768.0	12,796.5	12,878.1	12,869.4	12,950.1	13,064.1	13,098.7	12,780.0
2014	12,843.6	12,919.8	12,979.1	13,034.4	13,109.9	13,152.8	13,166.7	13,274.2	13,275.3	13,361.1	13,452.3	13,490.8	13,171.7
2015	13,229.4	13,304.9	13,374.6	13,446.0	13,520.0	13,543.5	13,669.7	13,737.0	13,719.7	13,793.9	13,863.6	13,910.1	13,592.7
Goods-Producing													
2005	2,336.6	2,363.7	2,384.9	2,403.8	2,420.0	2,449.3	2,473.1	2,491.0	2,494.0	2,473.7	2,460.8	2,457.2	2,434.0
2006	2,405.5	2,428.0	2,431.3	2,418.0	2,457.4	2,484.6	2,480.3	2,497.0	2,495.0	2,458.2	2,429.6	2,410.7	2,449.6
2007	2,357.2	2,369.1	2,386.1	2,372.9	2,391.0	2,419.0	2,425.8	2,430.0	2,411.3	2,377.7	2,348.7	2,326.9	2,384.6
2008	2,262.4	2,266.9	2,266.1	2,258.1	2,267.0	2,275.4	2,275.6	2,277.8	2,259.1	2,215.3	2,165.0	2,128.9	2,243.1
2009	2,043.8	1,995.3	1,979.3	1,947.4	1,946.4	1,942.6	1,923.1	1,921.5	1,904.1	1,883.8	1,864.7	1,841.5	1,932.8
2010	1,804.7	1,797.1	1,808.7	1,812.9	1,829.4	1,844.6	1,853.9	1,865.4	1,854.1	1,848.4	1,831.5	1,816.8	1,830.6
2011	1,789.6	1,796.4	1,799.1	1,815.4	1,831.5	1,847.7	1,869.5	1,883.9	1,882.3	1,869.8	1,853.9	1,843.0	1,840.2
2012	1,821.6	1,825.1	1,833.5	1,834.4	1,861.7	1,888.5	1,905.0	1,920.4	1,917.4	1,909.0	1,897.2	1,887.6	1,875.1
2013	1,862.8	1,877.2	1,885.1	1,890.8	1,906.7	1,928.7	1,950.1	1,969.8	1,964.1	1,959.8	1,952.7	1,943.1	1,924.2
2014	1,917.0	1,931.5	1,940.6	1,945.4	1,964.0	1,983.6	2,003.6	2,027.3	2,025.2	2,016.9	2,008.2	1,995.2	1,979.9
2015	1,982.6	1,993.7	2,008.0	2,017.4	2,036.1	2,056.5	2,087.8	2,105.2	2,095.8	2,078.7	2,062.7	2,055.2	2,048.3
Service-Providing													
2005	12,348.6	12,438.8	12,522.0	12,561.1	12,602.7	12,645.0	12,510.9	12,553.1	12,664.8	12,733.6	12,838.7	12,915.2	12,611.2
2006	12,612.7	12,716.7	12,798.2	12,815.1	12,888.1	12,950.1	12,785.2	12,822.4	12,912.7	12,985.6	13,079.9	13,144.3	12,875.9
2007	12,857.5	12,957.3	13,046.9	13,012.5	13,086.1	13,132.5	12,997.7	13,003.8	13,084.0	13,157.8	13,255.5	13,320.7	13,076.0
2008	12,979.8	13,067.8	13,121.6	13,141.1	13,168.4	13,186.4	12,976.5	12,961.7	13,008.5	13,024.8	13,016.0	13,013.3	13,055.5
2009	12,643.2	12,627.1	12,621.5	12,587.7	12,597.5	12,570.4	12,299.3	12,280.4	12,315.7	12,468.0	12,508.6	12,540.7	12,505.0
2010	12,242.9	12,291.6	12,348.9	12,476.5	12,552.3	12,550.3	12,332.5	12,343.2	12,411.3	12,563.8	12,632.0	12,676.9	12,451.9
2011	12,407.2	12,483.2	12,539.8	12,588.9	12,619.6	12,622.4	12,453.3	12,485.7	12,584.1	12,704.5	12,800.8	12,834.4	12,593.7
2012	12,613.6	12,707.1	12,792.7	12,829.2	12,900.4	12,941.0	12,753.1	12,816.5	12,885.3	13,035.6	13,164.2	13,196.8	12,886.3
2013	12,934.0	13,046.2	13,116.1	13,176.0	13,243.2	13,252.7	13,085.3	13,180.1	13,241.0	13,389.5	13,535.2	13,561.8	13,230.1
2014	13,319.5	13,403.3	13,478.4	13,540.5	13,608.5	13,620.7	13,442.3	13,556.0	13,631.1	13,795.0	13,918.0	13,955.9	13,605.8
2015	13,693.0	13,777.2	13,852.2	13,921.0	13,981.7	13,982.5	13,907.8	13,990.0	14,055.2	14,212.1	14,313.5	14,352.6	14,003.2
Mining and Logging													
2005	21.7	21.9	22.0	22.4	23.0	23.8	24.5	24.7	24.8	24.9	24.6	24.3	23.6
2006	23.0	23.4	23.3	23.4	24.8	25.7	26.2	26.6	26.7	26.4	25.9	25.2	25.1
2007	24.6	24.8	24.6	25.3	26.3	27.0	27.7	28.0	28.0	28.2	28.0	27.5	26.7
2008	26.6	27.0	27.0	27.9	28.6	29.2	29.9	30.0	29.9	30.2	29.5	28.7	28.7
2009	27.1	26.5	26.0	25.4	25.5	26.1	26.4	26.3	26.2	26.3	25.8	25.2	26.1
2010	25.0	24.6	25.1	25.4	27.0	27.5	28.1	28.2	28.2	28.1	27.7	27.0	26.8
2011	26.7	27.0	26.9	27.7	28.3	28.9	29.9	30.2	30.2	30.3	30.1	29.7	28.8
2012	29.3	29.0	29.0	29.2	30.3	31.0	31.8	32.0	31.6	31.4	31.1	30.4	30.5
2013	29.6	29.7	29.6	30.0	30.8	31.3	31.5	31.5	31.2	31.3	30.8	30.3	30.6
2014	30.1	30.2	30.2	30.7	31.5	31.9	32.5	32.6	32.7	32.6	32.4	31.7	31.6
2015	30.4	29.0	28.9	29.5	29.4	29.4	29.6	29.2	28.8	29.0	28.2	27.3	29.1

1. Employment by Industry: California, 2005–2015—*Continued*

(Numbers in thousands, not seasonally adjusted)

Industry and year	January	February	March	April	May	June	July	August	September	October	November	December	Annual average
Construction													
2005	823.8	844.8	862.3	880.4	895.0	915.7	931.5	942.8	947.4	944.2	940.1	935.6	905.3
2006	903.9	916.0	914.6	908.8	940.9	959.0	957.9	966.3	962.7	941.3	923.8	908.8	933.7
2007	874.6	879.9	894.0	890.6	903.5	917.8	918.7	919.8	905.3	886.9	868.9	850.8	892.6
2008	803.3	804.8	803.7	800.3	803.6	805.9	803.2	802.4	788.4	769.6	744.2	723.5	787.7
2009	674.4	644.7	644.1	630.4	632.2	632.3	621.7	619.6	607.6	600.2	594.2	576.2	623.1
2010	550.6	542.7	549.3	553.9	562.2	568.8	572.4	574.8	566.9	566.5	560.4	549.6	559.8
2011	532.7	535.1	534.3	545.8	554.4	562.8	578.6	584.6	584.0	580.6	575.5	567.3	561.3
2012	556.2	556.0	559.1	560.9	579.0	595.2	605.8	612.1	613.1	616.7	615.2	609.7	589.9
2013	597.6	606.5	612.6	617.7	627.9	639.8	652.4	661.5	657.9	662.0	660.1	651.8	637.3
2014	637.9	645.2	651.4	655.7	667.3	675.9	685.9	697.5	696.8	697.1	696.1	682.4	674.1
2015	681.1	687.6	698.2	706.1	719.0	730.0	748.3	758.1	754.1	753.9	748.4	743.6	727.4
Manufacturing													
2005	1,491.1	1,497.0	1,500.6	1,501.0	1,502.0	1,509.8	1,517.1	1,523.5	1,521.8	1,504.6	1,496.1	1,497.3	1,505.2
2006	1,478.6	1,488.6	1,493.4	1,485.8	1,491.7	1,499.9	1,496.2	1,504.1	1,505.6	1,490.5	1,479.9	1,476.7	1,490.9
2007	1,458.0	1,464.4	1,467.5	1,457.0	1,461.2	1,474.2	1,479.4	1,482.2	1,478.0	1,462.6	1,451.8	1,448.6	1,465.4
2008	1,432.5	1,435.1	1,435.4	1,429.9	1,434.8	1,440.3	1,442.5	1,445.4	1,440.8	1,415.5	1,391.3	1,376.7	1,426.7
2009	1,342.3	1,324.0	1,309.2	1,291.6	1,288.7	1,284.2	1,275.0	1,275.6	1,270.3	1,257.3	1,244.7	1,240.1	1,283.6
2010	1,229.1	1,229.7	1,234.3	1,233.6	1,240.2	1,248.4	1,253.4	1,262.3	1,259.0	1,253.8	1,243.5	1,240.2	1,244.0
2011	1,230.2	1,234.4	1,238.0	1,242.0	1,248.8	1,256.0	1,261.1	1,269.2	1,268.1	1,259.0	1,248.3	1,246.0	1,250.1
2012	1,236.1	1,240.1	1,245.3	1,244.2	1,252.4	1,262.3	1,267.5	1,276.3	1,272.7	1,260.8	1,250.9	1,247.6	1,254.7
2013	1,235.7	1,241.1	1,242.9	1,243.0	1,248.0	1,257.6	1,266.2	1,276.8	1,274.9	1,266.6	1,261.8	1,261.0	1,256.3
2014	1,249.0	1,256.1	1,259.1	1,259.0	1,265.2	1,275.8	1,285.2	1,297.2	1,295.7	1,287.2	1,279.7	1,281.1	1,274.2
2015	1,271.1	1,277.1	1,280.9	1,281.8	1,287.7	1,297.1	1,309.9	1,317.9	1,312.9	1,295.8	1,286.1	1,284.3	1,291.9
Trade, Transportation, and Utilities													
2005	2,776.8	2,759.9	2,766.9	2,768.0	2,782.9	2,796.9	2,807.9	2,820.8	2,835.4	2,849.9	2,909.7	2,964.3	2,820.0
2006	2,829.8	2,814.2	2,827.2	2,826.7	2,846.4	2,866.4	2,866.2	2,879.9	2,888.5	2,899.7	2,964.8	3,006.9	2,876.4
2007	2,895.8	2,871.4	2,878.2	2,864.2	2,881.3	2,892.0	2,907.1	2,911.1	2,912.5	2,923.2	2,987.1	3,031.3	2,912.9
2008	2,894.3	2,867.6	2,863.2	2,848.2	2,852.0	2,853.7	2,843.1	2,836.3	2,827.8	2,818.4	2,837.5	2,850.1	2,849.4
2009	2,713.1	2,669.3	2,647.7	2,621.6	2,629.2	2,625.5	2,604.0	2,603.4	2,610.1	2,621.6	2,665.6	2,696.8	2,642.3
2010	2,598.0	2,578.3	2,578.0	2,590.2	2,604.7	2,613.5	2,616.5	2,628.1	2,627.8	2,650.8	2,706.5	2,742.3	2,627.9
2011	2,641.4	2,625.2	2,624.4	2,641.4	2,653.3	2,660.4	2,669.2	2,682.4	2,683.1	2,702.3	2,766.8	2,794.6	2,678.7
2012	2,704.2	2,673.5	2,677.2	2,684.8	2,703.2	2,716.0	2,722.8	2,733.2	2,735.9	2,754.6	2,839.4	2,859.4	2,733.7
2013	2,753.0	2,737.6	2,735.4	2,740.3	2,759.5	2,772.3	2,782.2	2,795.4	2,789.3	2,814.1	2,900.9	2,932.4	2,792.7
2014	2,823.2	2,805.2	2,804.3	2,812.9	2,828.6	2,840.7	2,847.0	2,866.9	2,866.1	2,887.4	2,968.5	3,002.9	2,862.8
2015	2,895.5	2,874.1	2,879.0	2,884.4	2,902.0	2,905.3	2,934.3	2,951.1	2,949.4	2,970.8	3,043.6	3,070.2	2,938.3
Wholesale Trade													
2005	658.0	660.6	664.3	669.7	673.0	675.7	676.5	677.8	679.5	681.5	682.2	684.7	673.6
2006	681.4	688.0	692.2	695.0	699.1	704.9	704.2	705.7	708.3	706.6	707.4	710.2	700.3
2007	702.5	706.9	711.5	710.5	714.1	716.9	719.7	718.8	719.0	720.8	720.2	722.4	715.3
2008	710.6	711.8	713.7	710.4	710.0	709.1	705.4	703.1	699.5	696.0	688.9	684.0	703.5
2009	665.6	660.5	654.6	649.3	648.1	646.9	640.7	637.3	634.8	637.1	634.9	634.2	645.3
2010	629.8	631.1	632.8	641.8	645.3	647.2	648.4	649.1	648.6	650.8	651.1	651.9	644.0
2011	645.7	648.7	649.2	656.0	657.8	659.0	661.1	663.1	663.0	663.2	663.6	664.7	657.9
2012	659.5	662.9	665.6	669.1	674.3	677.2	678.7	681.8	681.2	684.0	685.6	686.4	675.5
2013	679.6	683.0	685.2	688.4	692.7	695.7	696.9	698.9	698.0	699.0	702.6	705.6	693.8
2014	699.9	704.6	706.2	706.3	709.3	711.0	710.7	713.4	712.8	712.5	715.7	717.6	710.0
2015	708.3	711.5	711.6	716.0	719.3	719.3	724.3	726.5	726.0	729.3	730.7	731.6	721.2
Retail Trade													
2005	1,638.6	1,618.0	1,622.0	1,615.6	1,624.5	1,634.8	1,643.5	1,654.7	1,664.1	1,676.5	1,735.0	1,783.8	1,659.3
2006	1,663.6	1,640.6	1,646.5	1,644.3	1,654.1	1,663.5	1,666.2	1,676.0	1,677.0	1,690.6	1,752.6	1,785.9	1,680.1
2007	1,695.5	1,666.1	1,669.7	1,653.8	1,663.1	1,668.0	1,676.5	1,682.2	1,678.1	1,687.9	1,751.3	1,787.1	1,689.9
2008	1,682.1	1,649.1	1,646.8	1,635.1	1,633.1	1,635.7	1,633.0	1,627.6	1,619.9	1,618.7	1,647.5	1,662.5	1,640.9
2009	1,562.3	1,528.5	1,514.8	1,498.9	1,505.9	1,504.0	1,494.2	1,496.9	1,502.5	1,512.5	1,560.6	1,589.0	1,522.5
2010	1,507.7	1,487.3	1,486.1	1,489.3	1,496.3	1,500.7	1,502.4	1,510.8	1,509.0	1,528.0	1,582.6	1,611.6	1,517.7
2011	1,531.8	1,512.5	1,510.1	1,515.4	1,521.9	1,527.0	1,533.6	1,541.0	1,540.8	1,558.2	1,621.8	1,644.3	1,546.5
2012	1,570.6	1,537.8	1,536.4	1,537.4	1,546.2	1,549.9	1,553.9	1,559.0	1,559.1	1,575.2	1,656.4	1,668.4	1,570.9
2013	1,581.5	1,560.8	1,557.2	1,558.6	1,569.1	1,577.2	1,582.1	1,589.2	1,583.6	1,605.0	1,683.1	1,705.9	1,596.1
2014	1,616.5	1,592.8	1,592.3	1,596.9	1,601.9	1,609.2	1,614.5	1,625.4	1,620.2	1,638.1	1,710.2	1,733.3	1,629.3
2015	1,649.6	1,628.3	1,627.3	1,628.4	1,638.1	1,638.3	1,652.5	1,661.1	1,657.2	1,674.0	1,742.1	1,760.8	1,663.1

1. Employment by Industry: California, 2005–2015—*Continued*

(Numbers in thousands, not seasonally adjusted)

Industry and year	January	February	March	April	May	June	July	August	September	October	November	December	Annual average
Transportation and Utilities													
2005	480.2	481.3	480.6	482.7	485.4	486.4	487.9	488.3	491.8	491.9	492.5	495.8	487.1
2006	484.8	485.6	488.5	487.4	493.2	498.0	495.8	498.2	503.2	502.5	504.8	510.8	496.1
2007	497.8	498.4	497.0	499.9	504.1	507.1	510.9	510.1	515.4	514.5	515.6	521.8	507.7
2008	501.6	506.7	502.7	502.7	508.9	508.9	504.7	505.6	508.4	503.7	501.1	503.6	504.9
2009	485.2	480.3	478.3	473.4	475.2	474.6	469.1	469.2	472.8	472.0	470.1	473.6	474.5
2010	460.5	459.9	459.1	459.1	463.1	465.6	465.7	468.2	470.2	472.0	472.8	478.8	466.3
2011	463.9	464.0	465.1	470.0	473.6	474.4	474.5	478.3	479.3	480.9	481.4	485.6	474.3
2012	474.1	472.8	475.2	478.3	482.7	488.9	490.2	492.4	495.6	495.4	497.4	504.6	487.3
2013	491.9	493.8	493.0	493.3	497.7	499.4	503.2	507.3	507.7	510.1	515.2	520.9	502.8
2014	506.8	507.8	505.8	509.7	517.4	520.5	521.8	528.1	533.1	536.8	542.6	552.0	523.5
2015	537.6	534.3	540.1	540.0	544.6	547.7	557.5	563.5	566.2	567.5	570.8	577.8	554.0
Information													
2005	473.1	477.0	480.7	470.3	469.9	470.3	466.9	473.2	472.5	471.4	480.2	478.0	473.6
2006	468.3	476.4	475.6	467.8	468.7	470.8	464.9	465.0	459.5	456.2	456.7	463.6	466.1
2007	463.5	471.4	473.7	464.8	470.3	473.8	471.7	476.0	474.7	464.5	470.7	478.3	471.1
2008	459.6	469.9	478.2	477.6	482.7	486.3	478.9	479.8	481.6	474.6	471.5	472.2	476.1
2009	450.9	452.0	454.3	442.8	440.8	442.8	438.0	437.5	438.0	428.9	431.3	438.3	441.3
2010	425.5	425.6	428.7	420.7	422.4	429.2	429.7	434.1	433.6	427.9	432.0	439.1	429.0
2011	430.9	431.3	432.8	428.1	427.7	429.7	431.2	433.0	429.2	431.1	429.2	433.2	430.6
2012	426.4	427.4	430.3	431.8	430.7	431.1	436.3	438.5	434.1	439.1	445.6	449.7	435.1
2013	438.7	442.1	443.9	444.8	444.7	449.4	447.5	451.0	450.9	454.4	461.2	460.7	449.1
2014	454.2	454.1	457.2	460.8	458.1	459.9	461.7	467.8	466.9	471.1	470.7	473.1	463.0
2015	466.3	475.6	479.4	480.0	480.3	484.2	484.5	488.8	488.7	488.2	489.5	490.8	483.0
Financial Activities													
2005	901.4	905.5	910.4	911.5	914.9	918.8	923.3	926.7	927.6	930.3	931.1	938.0	920.0
2006	926.6	929.4	932.5	931.5	935.3	934.5	927.9	927.5	924.8	920.0	918.3	920.7	927.4
2007	906.0	912.2	913.9	905.1	904.2	903.6	899.1	895.5	886.2	879.3	875.1	874.3	896.2
2008	856.1	857.1	855.5	848.9	847.3	845.4	843.0	839.7	832.5	827.8	822.5	821.8	841.5
2009	805.4	801.7	798.5	790.9	786.4	784.6	778.1	774.0	766.4	770.0	767.2	768.2	782.6
2010	756.2	757.3	758.9	758.3	758.3	760.7	760.5	760.4	758.5	762.2	760.7	764.8	759.7
2011	757.8	759.6	760.5	758.4	759.2	762.1	762.4	762.7	761.4	762.8	762.9	767.0	761.4
2012	760.8	764.6	768.2	766.7	769.9	773.7	776.7	777.4	774.7	778.7	779.5	783.5	772.9
2013	774.3	777.7	778.3	780.5	783.3	784.7	786.9	786.4	780.8	784.1	783.5	784.2	782.1
2014	774.4	775.3	775.3	776.7	780.3	783.3	784.3	785.2	781.3	785.2	787.4	790.3	781.6
2015	783.5	786.5	787.4	792.3	796.4	797.3	806.4	806.4	801.9	801.3	802.4	806.8	797.4
Professional and Business Services													
2005	2,096.3	2,123.1	2,138.6	2,145.2	2,142.0	2,159.0	2,164.6	2,181.2	2,191.5	2,189.8	2,199.8	2,212.7	2,162.0
2006	2,167.3	2,195.2	2,212.0	2,218.2	2,228.3	2,253.9	2,251.0	2,270.2	2,275.9	2,283.2	2,286.9	2,292.8	2,244.6
2007	2,215.9	2,243.7	2,259.4	2,247.1	2,254.5	2,272.6	2,269.9	2,280.0	2,279.5	2,294.8	2,296.3	2,300.2	2,267.8
2008	2,228.9	2,250.6	2,256.3	2,258.9	2,250.5	2,257.1	2,248.8	2,254.2	2,245.7	2,233.3	2,210.4	2,196.2	2,240.9
2009	2,113.9	2,097.8	2,081.7	2,061.1	2,051.0	2,048.3	2,035.5	2,041.6	2,031.8	2,063.7	2,068.7	2,069.7	2,063.7
2010	2,008.5	2,030.1	2,040.0	2,060.3	2,060.6	2,079.2	2,082.8	2,095.6	2,090.8	2,125.7	2,124.1	2,125.1	2,076.9
2011	2,069.9	2,093.0	2,099.8	2,107.7	2,109.9	2,119.5	2,139.4	2,153.3	2,164.5	2,179.4	2,185.7	2,191.9	2,134.5
2012	2,157.7	2,190.1	2,205.4	2,210.4	2,220.3	2,241.9	2,243.6	2,262.8	2,265.4	2,295.1	2,306.8	2,308.6	2,242.3
2013	2,259.5	2,289.7	2,301.6	2,316.6	2,321.1	2,328.3	2,347.2	2,371.1	2,369.5	2,388.1	2,401.1	2,400.4	2,341.2
2014	2,354.4	2,374.4	2,386.6	2,395.0	2,404.0	2,411.0	2,416.9	2,441.9	2,441.6	2,477.2	2,490.6	2,495.5	2,424.1
2015	2,427.6	2,440.9	2,455.1	2,463.8	2,465.1	2,473.7	2,506.5	2,523.8	2,514.1	2,540.0	2,550.6	2,564.3	2,493.8
Education and Health Services													
2005	1,793.0	1,816.6	1,826.0	1,836.3	1,840.3	1,830.4	1,806.5	1,810.8	1,843.4	1,864.8	1,875.1	1,875.9	1,834.9
2006	1,845.5	1,872.5	1,883.2	1,883.6	1,887.0	1,877.6	1,852.3	1,858.1	1,889.6	1,908.1	1,917.4	1,921.9	1,883.1
2007	1,905.9	1,939.9	1,956.5	1,951.1	1,959.8	1,948.7	1,934.7	1,937.8	1,971.9	1,997.0	2,010.4	2,016.6	1,960.9
2008	1,994.3	2,028.5	2,036.0	2,050.4	2,052.5	2,040.2	2,011.1	2,019.0	2,050.2	2,073.6	2,084.5	2,098.0	2,044.9
2009	2,068.5	2,093.7	2,105.0	2,112.0	2,117.1	2,104.1	2,076.0	2,079.8	2,103.7	2,134.5	2,136.8	2,143.4	2,106.2
2010	2,094.5	2,112.2	2,118.8	2,139.1	2,136.5	2,119.2	2,090.8	2,093.0	2,121.1	2,143.7	2,151.0	2,160.4	2,123.4
2011	2,126.1	2,152.1	2,160.0	2,165.2	2,163.0	2,142.7	2,110.3	2,115.7	2,150.1	2,174.7	2,187.7	2,201.6	2,154.1
2012	2,172.0	2,208.9	2,226.5	2,223.6	2,228.3	2,213.4	2,181.0	2,197.0	2,222.1	2,254.8	2,265.8	2,279.0	2,222.7
2013	2,254.2	2,287.2	2,299.0	2,307.8	2,309.4	2,280.2	2,253.9	2,269.5	2,293.1	2,327.2	2,342.6	2,348.2	2,297.7
2014	2,321.1	2,351.5	2,362.8	2,361.9	2,364.8	2,343.3	2,322.8	2,344.9	2,372.6	2,405.3	2,416.0	2,420.3	2,365.6
2015	2,396.4	2,426.8	2,436.9	2,448.3	2,453.1	2,428.1	2,429.9	2,441.5	2,468.0	2,508.2	2,515.5	2,521.3	2,456.2

1. Employment by Industry: California, 2005–2015—*Continued*

(Numbers in thousands, not seasonally adjusted)

Industry and year	January	February	March	April	May	June	July	August	September	October	November	December	Annual average
Leisure and Hospitality													
2005	1,408.5	1,424.5	1,446.1	1,468.6	1,483.0	1,502.3	1,504.9	1,509.6	1,497.4	1,483.1	1,480.9	1,492.9	1,475.2
2006	1,451.1	1,472.8	1,491.8	1,506.5	1,526.6	1,548.3	1,548.4	1,556.2	1,540.4	1,526.8	1,523.6	1,535.9	1,519.0
2007	1,496.8	1,514.2	1,534.7	1,548.1	1,569.4	1,590.5	1,593.5	1,595.5	1,580.0	1,567.2	1,562.8	1,571.7	1,560.4
2008	1,529.7	1,545.4	1,563.1	1,578.5	1,593.0	1,609.9	1,611.7	1,607.5	1,585.8	1,559.2	1,543.7	1,544.1	1,572.6
2009	1,489.9	1,491.6	1,494.3	1,504.2	1,522.4	1,529.3	1,526.5	1,522.7	1,504.9	1,491.8	1,477.0	1,482.3	1,503.1
2010	1,440.8	1,450.0	1,463.0	1,497.2	1,510.0	1,526.8	1,533.9	1,536.0	1,523.1	1,515.9	1,505.0	1,517.3	1,501.6
2011	1,476.8	1,491.1	1,506.6	1,524.8	1,541.0	1,554.4	1,565.1	1,569.6	1,561.3	1,547.0	1,544.7	1,546.7	1,535.8
2012	1,520.0	1,538.3	1,558.0	1,583.6	1,606.1	1,627.1	1,633.8	1,643.2	1,627.5	1,616.9	1,612.1	1,617.3	1,598.7
2013	1,590.1	1,612.5	1,634.8	1,658.6	1,684.5	1,704.2	1,710.7	1,715.8	1,702.3	1,699.2	1,697.6	1,706.9	1,676.4
2014	1,678.1	1,700.2	1,721.7	1,744.8	1,769.7	1,788.7	1,792.9	1,801.5	1,782.5	1,776.7	1,770.7	1,775.4	1,758.6
2015	1,746.2	1,770.5	1,789.7	1,815.2	1,838.5	1,850.2	1,867.7	1,869.5	1,851.7	1,855.4	1,849.0	1,856.1	1,830.0
Other Services													
2005	495.8	502.4	507.2	509.3	510.4	513.6	504.9	504.0	506.5	504.5	502.8	504.0	505.5
2006	492.9	499.3	502.5	503.9	510.2	514.5	507.0	511.8	512.2	510.3	510.0	510.1	507.1
2007	498.5	505.7	509.3	507.2	511.2	516.8	514.4	514.8	517.3	517.4	516.4	516.8	512.2
2008	505.7	511.5	515.0	516.4	518.6	520.4	515.3	511.4	510.0	508.5	502.9	499.8	511.3
2009	487.5	488.0	488.8	491.8	492.8	492.8	483.8	482.5	480.2	484.5	481.6	479.4	486.1
2010	475.2	478.1	481.3	484.4	487.7	490.3	488.1	485.4	485.9	490.0	487.5	485.2	484.9
2011	480.0	485.3	486.5	493.7	495.7	496.1	497.4	496.4	498.1	499.3	497.8	497.8	493.7
2012	490.1	496.0	499.0	502.6	508.3	512.0	507.2	507.0	508.1	510.6	508.3	507.2	504.7
2013	500.9	508.0	510.4	515.1	517.8	520.2	518.0	519.1	519.4	523.2	524.5	522.8	516.6
2014	521.2	527.6	530.6	536.9	540.4	542.3	537.5	538.7	539.1	541.3	540.2	538.1	536.2
2015	531.3	536.8	539.1	544.6	548.5	548.2	552.6	550.7	550.1	551.3	550.3	545.4	545.7
Government													
2005	2,403.7	2,429.8	2,446.1	2,451.9	2,459.3	2,453.7	2,331.9	2,326.8	2,390.5	2,439.8	2,459.1	2,449.4	2,420.2
2006	2,431.2	2,456.9	2,473.4	2,476.9	2,485.6	2,484.1	2,367.5	2,353.7	2,421.8	2,481.3	2,502.2	2,492.4	2,452.3
2007	2,475.1	2,498.8	2,521.2	2,524.9	2,535.4	2,534.5	2,407.3	2,393.1	2,461.9	2,514.4	2,536.7	2,531.5	2,494.6
2008	2,511.2	2,537.2	2,554.3	2,562.2	2,571.8	2,573.4	2,424.6	2,413.8	2,474.9	2,529.4	2,543.0	2,531.1	2,518.9
2009	2,514.0	2,533.0	2,551.2	2,563.3	2,557.8	2,543.0	2,357.4	2,338.9	2,380.6	2,473.0	2,480.4	2,462.6	2,479.6
2010	2,444.2	2,460.0	2,480.2	2,526.3	2,572.1	2,531.4	2,330.2	2,310.6	2,370.5	2,447.6	2,465.2	2,442.7	2,448.4
2011	2,424.3	2,445.6	2,469.2	2,469.6	2,469.8	2,457.5	2,278.3	2,272.6	2,336.4	2,407.9	2,426.0	2,401.6	2,404.9
2012	2,382.4	2,408.3	2,428.1	2,425.7	2,433.6	2,425.8	2,251.7	2,257.4	2,317.5	2,385.8	2,406.7	2,392.1	2,376.3
2013	2,363.3	2,391.4	2,412.7	2,412.3	2,422.9	2,413.4	2,238.9	2,271.8	2,335.7	2,399.2	2,423.8	2,406.2	2,374.3
2014	2,392.9	2,415.0	2,439.9	2,451.5	2,462.6	2,451.5	2,279.2	2,309.1	2,381.0	2,450.8	2,473.9	2,460.3	2,414.0
2015	2,446.2	2,466.0	2,485.6	2,492.4	2,497.8	2,495.5	2,325.9	2,358.2	2,431.3	2,496.9	2,512.6	2,497.7	2,458.8

2. Average Weekly Hours by Selected Industry: California, 2011–2015

(Not seasonally adjusted)

Industry and year	January	February	March	April	May	June	July	August	September	October	November	December	Annual average
Total Private													
2011	34.6	34.1	34.1	34.1	34.8	34.1	34.3	34.4	34.3	35.0	34.1	34.3	34.4
2012	34.7	34.0	34.0	34.5	34.1	34.3	35.0	34.4	34.9	34.1	34.0	34.8	34.4
2013	33.8	34.0	34.1	34.2	34.2	35.1	34.2	34.4	35.0	34.2	34.2	35.2	34.4
2014	33.9	34.9	34.8	34.2	34.2	35.0	34.2	34.5	34.3	34.3	35.0	34.2	34.5
2015	34.1	34.9	35.0	34.4	34.3	34.5	34.5	35.4	34.4	34.5	35.1	34.5	34.6
Goods-Producing													
2011	39.0	38.6	38.5	38.5	39.1	38.9	38.7	39.0	38.8	39.1	38.4	38.4	38.7
2012	38.5	38.1	38.1	37.6	38.3	38.6	38.7	38.7	39.0	38.9	38.4	39.0	38.5
2013	38.2	38.5	38.9	38.7	38.6	39.1	38.6	38.9	39.0	39.0	38.7	39.5	38.8
2014	38.2	38.6	38.9	38.6	38.9	38.9	38.3	38.9	38.8	38.8	39.0	38.1	38.7
2015	38.5	38.8	39.1	38.8	38.6	38.9	38.9	39.6	38.2	39.3	39.2	39.3	38.9
Construction													
2011	34.7	34.6	34.5	35.1	35.7	35.6	35.5	35.9	35.4	35.8	34.6	35.1	35.2
2012	35.8	35.1	35.2	34.0	36.4	36.7	36.3	36.5	36.7	36.8	35.9	36.5	36.0
2013	35.9	36.0	36.4	37.0	36.6	37.1	36.7	37.1	36.8	36.8	36.3	37.1	36.7
2014	35.8	36.0	36.5	36.2	36.9	36.7	36.2	36.9	36.5	36.7	36.2	34.9	36.3
2015	36.5	36.6	37.1	36.9	36.5	37.2	37.1	37.7	35.0	37.8	36.9	37.2	36.9
Manufacturing													
2011	39.7	39.2	39.2	39.1	39.7	39.5	38.8	39.1	39.1	39.5	39.2	39.1	39.3
2012	39.0	38.9	38.9	38.8	38.8	39.1	39.5	39.3	39.7	39.6	39.4	40.0	39.3
2013	39.1	39.5	39.9	39.6	39.7	40.2	39.6	39.9	40.2	40.3	40.1	40.9	39.9
2014	39.5	40.1	40.2	40.0	40.2	40.3	39.7	40.2	40.3	40.2	40.8	40.4	40.2
2015	40.0	40.4	40.5	40.2	40.2	40.1	40.2	40.9	40.3	40.3	40.7	40.7	40.4
Trade, Transportation, and Utilities													
2011	34.5	34.0	34.5	34.8	35.3	34.8	34.9	35.1	35.0	35.6	34.6	35.1	34.9
2012	34.8	34.4	34.5	35.0	34.6	34.8	35.4	34.9	35.3	34.3	34.4	35.1	34.8
2013	33.6	34.1	34.4	34.6	34.9	35.7	35.0	35.2	35.6	34.7	34.5	36.3	34.9
2014	34.3	35.3	35.3	35.1	35.2	35.9	35.2	35.6	35.3	34.8	35.2	35.3	35.2
2015	34.4	35.4	35.7	35.2	35.2	35.4	35.5	36.2	35.9	35.3	35.7	35.3	35.4
Information													
2011	37.0	36.5	36.9	36.8	37.8	36.3	36.7	36.6	37.1	38.6	37.4	37.4	37.1
2012	37.4	36.9	36.7	37.8	37.1	36.9	37.7	37.7	38.2	37.4	37.4	38.2	37.5
2013	36.7	36.9	37.1	38.2	37.5	38.5	37.2	37.5	38.5	37.6	37.3	38.9	37.7
2014	37.5	38.9	38.6	37.5	37.0	38.2	36.7	36.8	36.7	36.7	37.8	37.1	37.5
2015	37.2	38.0	37.4	36.7	36.4	36.7	37.3	37.8	36.9	36.9	37.7	36.9	37.2
Financial Activities													
2011	37.2	36.0	35.7	36.0	37.1	36.5	36.7	36.3	36.8	38.1	36.7	36.5	36.6
2012	37.6	36.1	36.2	36.8	36.1	36.3	37.5	36.6	37.6	36.6	36.4	37.7	36.8
2013	36.0	36.1	36.3	36.2	36.3	37.6	36.3	36.4	37.3	36.4	36.5	38.0	36.6
2014	36.3	37.4	37.5	36.4	36.5	37.6	36.5	36.7	36.8	37.0	38.0	37.0	37.0
2015	36.8	37.8	37.8	36.9	36.9	37.0	36.8	38.0	37.0	36.8	37.8	37.0	37.2
Professional and Business Services													
2011	36.4	35.7	35.6	36.0	36.9	36.1	35.9	36.2	36.1	37.0	36.0	35.8	36.1
2012	36.3	35.6	35.6	36.4	35.7	35.7	36.4	35.8	36.6	35.5	35.4	36.5	36.0
2013	35.4	35.6	35.6	35.8	35.6	36.6	35.5	35.8	36.6	35.8	35.8	36.5	35.9
2014	35.4	36.6	36.5	35.7	35.5	36.8	35.8	36.2	35.8	36.0	37.0	35.6	36.1
2015	35.7	36.4	36.9	36.0	35.9	36.2	35.9	37.2	35.8	36.2	37.2	36.2	36.3
Education and Health Services													
2011	34.0	33.6	33.5	32.4	33.3	31.5	32.9	32.7	32.9	33.5	33.0	33.2	33.0
2012	34.2	33.2	33.2	33.9	33.1	33.4	34.1	33.2	34.1	33.3	33.4	34.1	33.6
2013	33.5	33.6	33.4	33.4	33.5	34.3	33.5	33.4	34.4	33.4	33.5	34.2	33.7
2014	33.4	34.1	33.9	33.3	33.1	33.7	33.1	33.0	33.2	33.2	34.0	33.2	33.4
2015	33.3	34.1	33.9	33.1	33.1	33.1	33.1	33.9	33.1	32.8	33.8	32.8	33.3
Leisure and Hospitality													
2011	26.6	26.6	26.4	26.5	27.2	26.5	26.6	26.7	26.0	26.9	26.0	26.1	26.5
2012	27.0	26.2	26.1	27.2	26.4	26.7	27.8	27.0	27.2	26.3	26.1	26.8	26.7
2013	25.9	26.2	26.2	26.2	26.3	27.2	26.4	26.6	26.9	26.1	26.0	26.9	26.4
2014	26.0	27.2	27.3	26.5	26.6	27.6	26.7	27.1	26.5	26.6	27.3	26.3	26.8
2015	26.3	27.4	27.4	26.7	26.7	27.0	27.0	28.0	26.8	26.8	27.3	26.6	27.0
Other Services													
2011	32.5	31.5	31.4	31.7	32.2	32.3	32.3	32.5	31.7	32.6	31.1	31.3	31.9
2012	32.3	31.3	31.3	31.6	31.2	31.3	32.5	31.9	32.1	30.6	30.2	31.4	31.5
2013	30.8	30.8	31.1	31.2	30.9	32.3	31.7	31.3	31.7	30.7	31.0	31.7	31.3
2014	30.9	31.7	31.6	31.0	30.8	31.6	31.2	31.0	31.0	31.2	31.6	30.7	31.2
2015	31.0	32.2	32.4	31.5	31.5	31.6	32.1	33.3	31.6	31.8	32.1	31.6	31.9

3. Average Hourly Earnings by Selected Industry: California, 2011–2015

(Dollars, not seasonally adjusted)

Industry and year	January	February	March	April	May	June	July	August	September	October	November	December	Annual average
Total Private													
2011	26.85	27.05	27.13	26.98	27.15	26.65	26.87	26.62	26.78	26.99	26.86	26.81	26.89
2012	27.23	26.97	26.90	27.09	26.81	26.76	26.80	26.49	26.89	26.72	26.76	27.15	26.88
2013	27.02	26.99	26.86	27.31	27.24	27.46	27.23	27.14	27.52	27.26	27.27	27.42	27.23
2014	27.41	27.58	27.52	27.31	27.22	27.40	27.46	27.29	27.51	27.62	27.99	27.75	27.51
2015	28.02	28.10	28.02	27.94	27.99	27.89	27.93	28.09	27.92	28.12	28.34	28.11	28.04
Goods-Producing													
2011	28.52	28.16	28.30	28.44	28.25	28.03	28.41	28.39	28.45	28.54	28.59	28.92	28.42
2012	28.72	28.50	28.64	28.94	28.61	28.49	28.35	28.18	28.55	28.46	28.64	28.98	28.59
2013	29.08	29.10	28.83	29.05	29.17	29.16	29.24	28.98	29.18	29.09	29.14	29.50	29.13
2014	29.54	29.49	29.49	29.46	29.29	29.41	29.69	29.37	29.50	29.53	29.65	29.98	29.53
2015	29.78	29.52	29.53	29.55	29.56	29.52	29.60	29.52	29.57	29.83	29.90	30.01	29.66
Construction													
2011	27.59	26.21	26.69	26.80	26.90	27.33	27.68	28.30	28.63	28.67	28.88	29.73	27.81
2012	28.98	29.26	29.38	29.63	29.59	29.52	29.77	29.83	30.06	30.15	30.38	30.89	29.81
2013	30.91	30.70	30.57	30.50	30.56	30.75	31.14	31.03	31.28	31.26	31.21	31.63	30.97
2014	31.21	31.30	31.37	31.40	31.22	31.17	31.50	31.23	31.42	31.08	31.08	31.65	31.30
2015	31.09	30.81	30.96	31.06	30.74	30.98	31.27	31.32	31.40	31.39	31.59	31.70	31.20
Manufacturing													
2011	27.07	26.72	26.96	27.28	27.14	26.80	27.02	26.92	27.03	27.27	27.40	27.56	27.10
2012	27.72	27.32	27.56	27.99	27.52	27.40	27.15	26.89	27.40	27.27	27.47	27.77	27.45
2013	27.92	28.05	27.85	28.16	28.33	28.20	28.13	27.77	27.96	27.84	27.94	28.28	28.04
2014	28.60	28.45	28.38	28.35	28.18	28.40	28.64	28.23	28.36	28.59	28.76	29.02	28.50
2015	28.94	28.68	28.60	28.60	28.78	28.57	28.50	28.35	28.44	28.77	28.75	28.87	28.65
Trade, Transportation, and Utilities													
2011	23.10	23.20	24.23	23.97	23.65	23.22	23.09	22.65	22.63	22.69	22.46	22.02	23.06
2012	22.54	22.33	22.06	22.28	21.82	21.78	21.75	21.35	21.80	21.57	21.50	21.96	21.89
2013	21.82	21.85	21.87	21.79	21.74	22.15	21.73	21.57	21.98	21.55	21.44	21.20	21.72
2014	21.70	21.80	21.73	21.49	21.38	21.53	21.54	21.52	21.85	21.94	22.18	21.45	21.68
2015	22.54	22.47	22.13	22.26	22.48	22.33	22.36	22.63	22.42	22.67	22.80	22.54	22.47
Information													
2011	39.05	40.09	39.73	39.80	40.34	39.64	40.23	40.49	40.33	40.58	42.02	40.95	40.28
2012	43.52	42.48	42.12	42.09	42.12	41.54	42.00	40.77	40.89	40.63	40.08	40.11	41.51
2013	39.76	39.75	39.99	40.30	40.39	40.30	39.77	39.87	40.79	40.71	40.45	40.97	40.26
2014	40.79	41.06	41.02	40.61	40.31	40.69	40.77	40.66	40.50	41.17	41.44	40.82	40.82
2015	41.02	41.90	41.99	42.24	42.32	41.62	41.34	42.11	41.50	41.36	41.60	41.11	41.68
Financial Activities													
2011	31.14	31.17	30.59	30.25	30.66	29.78	29.71	30.04	30.16	30.37	30.12	29.89	30.32
2012	30.35	29.94	30.37	30.63	30.70	30.53	30.62	30.10	30.64	30.54	30.55	30.70	30.47
2013	30.77	30.82	30.79	31.47	31.31	31.54	31.51	31.72	31.95	31.61	31.76	32.22	31.46
2014	32.27	32.95	33.07	32.83	32.72	33.39	33.69	33.04	33.10	33.45	34.00	33.47	33.17
2015	33.90	34.09	34.28	33.52	33.44	33.28	33.09	33.31	33.17	33.40	34.15	33.68	33.61
Professional and Business Services													
2011	33.86	34.81	34.35	34.23	34.86	34.07	34.36	33.80	33.93	34.42	33.80	33.90	34.20
2012	34.55	33.87	33.76	34.19	33.71	33.79	34.18	33.49	34.10	33.51	33.79	34.59	33.96
2013	34.12	33.76	33.53	35.37	35.31	35.90	35.13	34.74	35.28	34.70	34.78	35.21	34.83
2014	34.59	35.12	35.09	34.59	34.65	35.02	34.88	34.48	34.72	34.53	35.49	35.29	34.88
2015	35.16	35.80	35.85	35.55	35.75	35.62	35.90	36.05	35.56	35.57	36.20	35.29	35.70
Education and Health Services													
2011	26.03	26.22	26.14	25.85	26.32	25.82	26.56	26.05	26.41	26.71	26.87	27.26	26.36
2012	27.55	27.45	27.35	27.50	27.47	27.59	27.59	27.61	27.75	27.59	27.61	27.86	27.58
2013	27.65	27.72	27.53	27.63	27.51	27.66	27.86	27.92	28.12	28.01	28.07	28.36	27.84
2014	28.05	28.07	27.94	27.88	27.90	27.89	27.90	27.94	28.04	28.16	28.39	28.45	28.05
2015	28.40	28.32	28.07	28.11	28.00	28.05	28.16	28.23	28.10	28.41	28.35	28.63	28.24
Leisure and Hospitality													
2011	14.90	15.00	14.91	14.76	14.89	14.72	14.71	14.71	14.79	14.76	14.61	14.65	14.78
2012	14.73	14.75	14.71	14.76	14.73	14.71	14.54	14.54	14.57	14.61	14.64	14.72	14.67
2013	14.66	14.86	14.73	14.79	14.87	14.85	14.83	14.88	15.05	14.97	15.14	15.20	14.91
2014	15.18	15.25	15.20	15.19	15.35	15.29	15.42	15.49	15.64	15.69	15.88	15.95	15.46
2015	15.92	16.05	16.06	16.15	16.20	16.13	16.03	16.10	16.24	16.28	16.33	16.43	16.16
Other Services													
2011	21.20	21.04	20.95	21.10	21.44	20.85	20.79	20.83	21.11	21.23	20.96	20.84	21.03
2012	21.23	21.34	21.20	21.37	20.78	20.78	21.01	20.70	21.36	21.29	21.45	21.88	21.20
2013	21.82	21.51	21.73	21.74	21.71	21.70	21.48	21.84	22.23	21.83	21.95	22.50	21.84
2014	22.35	22.27	22.28	22.41	22.07	22.45	22.51	22.57	22.85	22.97	23.25	23.26	22.60
2015	23.28	23.37	23.52	23.16	23.47	23.33	22.96	23.32	23.66	23.49	23.59	23.30	23.37

4. Average Weekly Earnings by Selected Industry: California, 2011–2015

(Dollars, not seasonally adjusted)

Industry and year	January	February	March	April	May	June	July	August	September	October	November	December	Annual average
Total Private													
2011	929.01	922.41	925.13	920.02	944.82	908.77	921.64	915.73	918.55	944.65	915.93	919.58	925.02
2012	944.88	916.98	914.60	934.61	914.22	917.87	938.00	911.26	938.46	911.15	909.84	944.82	924.67
2013	913.28	917.66	915.93	934.00	931.61	963.85	931.27	933.62	963.20	932.29	932.63	965.18	936.71
2014	929.20	962.54	957.70	934.00	930.92	959.00	939.13	941.51	943.59	947.37	979.65	949.05	949.10
2015	955.48	980.69	980.70	961.14	960.06	962.21	963.59	994.39	960.45	970.14	994.73	969.80	970.18
Goods-Producing													
2011	1,112.28	1,086.98	1,089.55	1,094.94	1,104.58	1,090.37	1,099.47	1,107.21	1,103.86	1,115.91	1,097.86	1,110.53	1,099.85
2012	1,105.72	1,085.85	1,091.18	1,088.14	1,095.76	1,099.71	1,097.15	1,090.57	1,113.45	1,107.09	1,099.78	1,130.22	1,100.72
2013	1,110.86	1,120.35	1,121.49	1,124.24	1,125.96	1,140.16	1,128.66	1,127.32	1,138.02	1,134.51	1,127.72	1,165.25	1,130.24
2014	1,128.43	1,138.31	1,147.16	1,137.16	1,139.38	1,144.05	1,137.13	1,142.49	1,144.60	1,145.76	1,156.35	1,142.24	1,142.81
2015	1,146.53	1,145.38	1,154.62	1,146.54	1,141.02	1,148.33	1,151.44	1,168.99	1,129.57	1,172.32	1,172.08	1,179.39	1,153.77
Construction													
2011	957.37	906.87	920.81	940.68	960.33	972.95	982.64	1,015.97	1,013.50	1,026.39	999.25	1,043.52	978.91
2012	1,037.48	1,027.03	1,034.18	1,007.42	1,077.08	1,083.38	1,080.65	1,088.80	1,103.20	1,109.52	1,090.64	1,127.49	1,073.16
2013	1,109.67	1,105.20	1,112.75	1,128.50	1,118.50	1,140.83	1,142.84	1,151.21	1,151.10	1,150.37	1,132.92	1,173.47	1,136.60
2014	1,117.32	1,126.80	1,145.01	1,136.68	1,152.02	1,143.94	1,140.30	1,152.39	1,146.83	1,140.64	1,125.10	1,104.59	1,136.19
2015	1,134.79	1,127.65	1,148.62	1,146.11	1,122.01	1,152.46	1,160.12	1,180.76	1,099.00	1,186.54	1,165.67	1,179.24	1,151.28
Manufacturing													
2011	1,074.68	1,047.42	1,056.83	1,066.65	1,077.46	1,058.60	1,048.38	1,052.57	1,056.87	1,077.17	1,074.08	1,077.60	1,065.03
2012	1,081.08	1,062.75	1,072.08	1,086.01	1,067.78	1,071.34	1,072.43	1,056.78	1,087.78	1,079.89	1,082.32	1,110.80	1,078.79
2013	1,091.67	1,107.98	1,111.22	1,115.14	1,124.70	1,133.64	1,113.95	1,108.02	1,123.99	1,121.95	1,120.39	1,156.65	1,118.80
2014	1,129.70	1,140.85	1,140.88	1,134.00	1,132.84	1,144.52	1,137.01	1,134.85	1,142.91	1,149.32	1,173.41	1,172.41	1,145.70
2015	1,157.60	1,158.67	1,158.30	1,149.72	1,156.96	1,145.66	1,145.70	1,159.52	1,146.13	1,159.43	1,170.13	1,175.01	1,157.46
Trade, Transportation, and Utilities													
2011	796.95	788.80	835.94	834.16	834.85	808.06	805.84	795.02	792.05	807.76	777.12	772.90	804.79
2012	784.39	768.15	761.07	779.80	754.97	757.94	769.95	745.12	769.54	739.85	739.60	770.80	761.77
2013	733.15	745.09	752.33	753.93	758.73	790.76	760.55	759.26	782.49	747.79	739.68	769.56	758.03
2014	744.31	769.54	767.07	754.30	752.58	772.93	758.21	766.11	771.31	763.51	780.74	757.19	763.14
2015	775.38	795.44	790.04	783.55	791.30	790.48	793.78	819.21	804.88	800.25	813.96	795.66	795.44
Information													
2011	1,444.85	1,463.29	1,466.04	1,464.64	1,524.85	1,438.93	1,476.44	1,481.93	1,496.24	1,566.39	1,571.55	1,531.53	1,494.39
2012	1,627.65	1,567.51	1,545.80	1,591.00	1,562.65	1,532.83	1,583.40	1,537.03	1,562.00	1,519.56	1,498.99	1,532.20	1,556.63
2013	1,459.19	1,466.78	1,483.63	1,539.46	1,514.63	1,551.55	1,479.44	1,495.13	1,570.42	1,530.70	1,508.79	1,593.73	1,517.80
2014	1,529.63	1,597.23	1,583.37	1,522.88	1,491.47	1,554.36	1,496.26	1,496.29	1,486.35	1,510.94	1,566.43	1,514.42	1,530.75
2015	1,525.94	1,592.20	1,570.43	1,550.21	1,540.45	1,527.45	1,541.98	1,591.76	1,531.35	1,526.18	1,568.32	1,516.96	1,550.50
Financial Activities													
2011	1,158.41	1,122.12	1,092.06	1,089.00	1,137.49	1,086.97	1,090.36	1,090.45	1,109.89	1,157.10	1,105.40	1,090.99	1,109.71
2012	1,141.16	1,080.83	1,099.39	1,127.18	1,108.27	1,108.24	1,148.25	1,101.66	1,152.06	1,117.76	1,112.02	1,157.39	1,121.30
2013	1,107.72	1,112.60	1,117.68	1,139.21	1,136.55	1,185.90	1,143.81	1,154.61	1,191.74	1,150.60	1,159.24	1,224.36	1,151.44
2014	1,171.40	1,232.33	1,240.13	1,195.01	1,194.28	1,255.46	1,229.69	1,212.57	1,218.08	1,237.65	1,292.00	1,238.39	1,227.29
2015	1,247.52	1,288.60	1,295.78	1,236.89	1,233.94	1,231.36	1,217.71	1,265.78	1,227.29	1,229.12	1,290.87	1,246.16	1,250.29
Professional and Business Services													
2011	1,232.50	1,242.72	1,222.86	1,232.28	1,286.33	1,229.93	1,233.52	1,223.56	1,224.87	1,273.54	1,216.80	1,213.62	1,234.62
2012	1,254.17	1,205.77	1,201.86	1,244.52	1,203.45	1,206.30	1,244.15	1,198.94	1,248.06	1,189.61	1,196.17	1,262.54	1,222.56
2013	1,207.85	1,201.86	1,193.67	1,266.25	1,257.04	1,313.94	1,247.12	1,243.69	1,291.25	1,242.26	1,245.12	1,285.17	1,250.40
2014	1,224.49	1,285.39	1,280.79	1,234.86	1,230.08	1,288.74	1,248.70	1,248.18	1,242.98	1,243.08	1,313.13	1,256.32	1,259.17
2015	1,255.21	1,303.12	1,322.87	1,279.80	1,283.43	1,289.44	1,288.81	1,341.06	1,273.05	1,287.63	1,346.64	1,277.50	1,295.91
Education and Health Services													
2011	885.02	880.99	875.69	837.54	876.46	813.33	873.82	851.84	868.89	894.79	886.71	905.03	869.88
2012	942.21	911.34	908.02	932.25	909.26	921.51	940.82	916.65	946.28	918.75	922.17	950.03	926.69
2013	926.28	931.39	919.50	922.84	921.59	948.74	933.31	932.53	967.33	935.53	940.35	969.91	938.21
2014	936.87	957.19	947.17	928.40	923.49	939.89	923.49	922.02	930.93	934.91	965.26	944.54	936.87
2015	945.72	965.71	951.57	930.44	926.80	928.46	932.10	957.00	930.11	931.85	958.23	939.06	940.39
Leisure and Hospitality													
2011	396.34	399.00	393.62	391.14	405.01	390.08	391.29	392.76	384.54	397.04	379.86	382.37	391.67
2012	397.71	386.45	383.93	401.47	388.87	392.76	404.21	392.58	396.30	384.24	382.10	394.50	391.69
2013	379.69	389.33	385.93	387.50	391.08	403.92	391.51	395.81	404.85	390.72	393.64	408.88	393.62
2014	394.68	414.80	414.96	402.54	408.31	422.00	411.71	419.78	414.46	417.35	433.52	419.49	414.33
2015	418.70	439.77	440.04	431.21	432.54	435.51	432.81	450.80	435.23	436.30	445.81	437.04	436.32
Other Services													
2011	689.00	662.76	657.83	668.87	690.37	673.46	671.52	676.98	669.19	692.10	651.86	652.29	670.86
2012	685.73	667.94	663.56	675.29	648.34	650.41	682.83	660.33	685.66	651.47	647.79	687.03	667.80
2013	672.06	662.51	675.80	678.29	670.84	700.91	680.92	683.59	704.69	670.18	680.45	713.25	683.59
2014	690.62	705.96	704.05	694.71	679.76	709.42	702.31	699.67	708.35	716.66	734.70	714.08	705.12
2015	721.68	752.51	762.05	729.54	739.31	737.23	737.02	776.56	747.66	746.98	757.24	736.28	745.50

COLORADO
At a Glance

Population:
  2005 estimate: 4,631,888
  2010 census: 5,029,196
  2015 estimate: 5,456,574

Percent change in population:
  2005–2015: 17.8%
  2010–2015: 8.5%

Percent change in total nonfarm employment:
  2005–2015: 14.2%

Industry with the largest growth in employment, 2005–2015 (thousands):
  Construction, –10.5

Industry with the largest decline or smallest growth in employment, 2005–2015 (thousands):
  Education and health services, 88.3

Civilian labor force:
  2005: 2,563,900
  2010: 2,724,417
  2015: 2,828,529

Unemployment rate and rank among states (highest to lowest):
  2005: 5.0%, 22nd
  2010: 8.7%, 24th
  2015: 3.9%, 42nd

Over-the-year change in unemployment rates:
  2012–2013: –1.1%
  2013–2014: –1.8%
  2014–2015: –1.1%

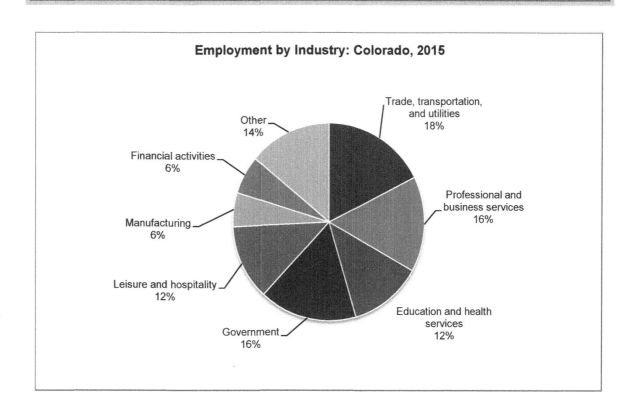

Employment by Industry: Colorado, 2015

- Trade, transportation, and utilities 18%
- Professional and business services 16%
- Education and health services 12%
- Government 16%
- Leisure and hospitality 12%
- Manufacturing 6%
- Financial activities 6%
- Other 14%

1. Employment by Industry: Colorado, 2005–2015

(Numbers in thousands, not seasonally adjusted)

Industry and year	January	February	March	April	May	June	July	August	September	October	November	December	Annual average
Total Nonfarm													
2005	2,163.5	2,181.9	2,199.1	2,207.3	2,215.8	2,244.6	2,238.4	2,241.4	2,247.7	2,244.0	2,251.3	2,276.6	2,226.0
2006	2,220.1	2,235.2	2,255.0	2,259.9	2,274.3	2,307.4	2,286.4	2,294.1	2,295.1	2,293.3	2,303.0	2,325.8	2,279.1
2007	2,262.6	2,280.5	2,306.4	2,313.1	2,327.7	2,358.3	2,342.1	2,350.4	2,352.3	2,350.5	2,359.1	2,372.9	2,331.3
2008	2,314.5	2,330.9	2,343.6	2,349.0	2,359.8	2,379.0	2,363.3	2,369.4	2,361.0	2,351.9	2,341.0	2,340.5	2,350.3
2009	2,271.2	2,261.9	2,257.9	2,248.2	2,250.9	2,258.8	2,238.1	2,235.5	2,231.9	2,231.3	2,227.0	2,234.7	2,245.6
2010	2,174.8	2,188.5	2,201.2	2,211.8	2,225.6	2,241.0	2,231.5	2,234.2	2,228.7	2,236.5	2,238.5	2,254.8	2,222.3
2011	2,202.9	2,213.5	2,229.0	2,248.1	2,252.7	2,274.7	2,263.5	2,274.3	2,280.2	2,277.6	2,285.0	2,301.7	2,258.6
2012	2,249.6	2,263.2	2,282.6	2,292.6	2,303.1	2,330.8	2,319.3	2,329.0	2,330.4	2,341.1	2,351.1	2,363.6	2,313.0
2013	2,311.0	2,332.3	2,349.9	2,358.7	2,371.2	2,396.6	2,389.5	2,403.5	2,403.4	2,409.7	2,421.6	2,435.0	2,381.9
2014	2,391.2	2,406.6	2,423.1	2,440.1	2,454.0	2,479.3	2,471.9	2,488.1	2,489.1	2,501.4	2,506.1	2,528.4	2,464.9
2015	2,482.4	2,499.1	2,509.4	2,521.8	2,530.3	2,554.9	2,550.3	2,555.3	2,558.0	2,564.5	2,570.3	2,598.1	2,541.2
Total Private													
2005	1,810.7	1,817.2	1,833.2	1,839.8	1,845.1	1,881.6	1,893.2	1,896.3	1,882.7	1,873.1	1,880.6	1,906.9	1,863.4
2006	1,863.3	1,866.8	1,883.4	1,889.1	1,899.8	1,939.3	1,937.6	1,942.7	1,925.3	1,918.1	1,927.0	1,950.5	1,911.9
2007	1,902.3	1,905.8	1,928.4	1,934.6	1,945.7	1,983.7	1,986.6	1,991.1	1,972.8	1,966.4	1,973.5	1,988.9	1,956.7
2008	1,943.8	1,947.6	1,957.3	1,962.1	1,967.2	1,997.0	1,998.7	1,999.5	1,972.5	1,956.4	1,945.0	1,947.2	1,966.2
2009	1,888.7	1,869.8	1,863.2	1,851.6	1,849.4	1,868.9	1,869.0	1,864.5	1,839.4	1,831.2	1,827.8	1,837.8	1,855.1
2010	1,792.4	1,792.5	1,801.4	1,811.7	1,814.0	1,846.5	1,857.0	1,860.2	1,835.8	1,836.2	1,837.1	1,856.3	1,828.4
2011	1,819.5	1,817.6	1,830.6	1,847.7	1,849.4	1,882.4	1,891.9	1,902.0	1,884.8	1,876.4	1,883.1	1,903.0	1,865.7
2012	1,865.8	1,866.8	1,883.0	1,891.8	1,898.7	1,936.8	1,946.2	1,951.4	1,932.2	1,937.8	1,945.9	1,961.9	1,918.2
2013	1,919.2	1,926.8	1,942.1	1,950.1	1,958.3	1,995.9	2,008.9	2,018.0	1,995.3	1,994.7	2,005.4	2,023.5	1,978.2
2014	1,992.1	1,997.1	2,011.0	2,026.7	2,035.7	2,072.4	2,087.1	2,099.0	2,078.5	2,081.5	2,084.0	2,111.7	2,056.4
2015	2,076.0	2,082.4	2,090.5	2,100.2	2,103.6	2,140.4	2,156.9	2,158.8	2,138.4	2,135.7	2,139.8	2,171.4	2,124.5
Goods-Producing													
2005	307.4	310.0	314.3	317.3	322.1	330.5	335.3	336.6	334.9	333.8	333.0	331.3	325.5
2006	323.1	324.3	328.8	331.5	337.4	345.1	344.3	344.5	342.0	340.3	336.9	334.7	336.1
2007	321.2	321.8	328.7	332.4	339.7	347.4	348.5	348.5	344.6	345.3	342.6	337.0	338.1
2008	326.2	326.0	328.4	330.7	336.6	342.3	341.7	341.4	336.6	334.2	328.0	318.7	332.6
2009	300.9	293.9	289.9	284.9	285.1	287.0	285.5	282.9	278.6	276.1	272.1	265.7	283.6
2010	255.0	253.5	254.9	259.2	262.8	268.6	270.7	270.1	268.2	269.2	266.9	265.0	263.7
2011	254.8	253.6	257.4	263.8	266.3	272.6	275.5	277.4	276.0	276.8	275.2	273.1	268.5
2012	265.0	264.4	266.9	270.9	275.8	281.4	283.3	284.2	282.4	284.8	283.3	281.4	277.0
2013	273.5	275.1	278.8	281.8	288.1	294.9	297.6	300.2	298.1	300.8	301.2	299.8	290.8
2014	294.9	295.5	299.1	304.9	311.0	316.9	321.0	322.4	321.5	323.0	322.1	322.0	312.9
2015	314.0	314.1	314.4	317.0	320.0	324.3	326.5	325.3	323.5	328.2	328.1	328.2	322.0
Service-Providing													
2005	1,856.1	1,871.9	1,884.8	1,890.0	1,893.7	1,914.1	1,903.1	1,904.8	1,912.8	1,910.2	1,918.3	1,945.3	1,900.4
2006	1,897.0	1,910.9	1,926.2	1,928.4	1,936.9	1,962.3	1,942.1	1,949.6	1,953.1	1,953.0	1,966.1	1,991.1	1,943.1
2007	1,941.4	1,958.7	1,977.7	1,980.7	1,988.0	2,010.9	1,993.6	2,001.9	2,007.7	2,005.2	2,016.5	2,035.9	1,993.2
2008	1,988.3	2,004.9	2,015.2	2,018.3	2,023.2	2,036.7	2,021.6	2,028.0	2,024.4	2,017.7	2,013.0	2,021.8	2,017.8
2009	1,970.3	1,968.0	1,968.0	1,963.3	1,965.8	1,971.8	1,952.6	1,952.6	1,953.3	1,955.2	1,954.9	1,969.0	1,962.1
2010	1,919.8	1,935.0	1,946.3	1,952.6	1,962.8	1,972.4	1,960.8	1,964.1	1,960.5	1,967.3	1,971.6	1,989.8	1,958.6
2011	1,948.1	1,959.9	1,971.6	1,984.3	1,986.4	2,002.1	1,988.0	1,996.9	2,004.2	2,000.8	2,009.8	2,028.6	1,990.1
2012	1,984.6	1,998.8	2,015.7	2,021.7	2,027.3	2,049.4	2,036.0	2,044.8	2,048.0	2,056.3	2,067.8	2,082.2	2,036.1
2013	2,037.5	2,057.2	2,071.1	2,076.9	2,083.1	2,101.7	2,091.9	2,103.3	2,105.3	2,108.9	2,120.4	2,135.2	2,091.0
2014	2,096.3	2,111.1	2,124.0	2,135.2	2,143.0	2,162.4	2,150.9	2,165.7	2,167.6	2,178.4	2,184.0	2,206.4	2,152.1
2015	2,168.4	2,185.0	2,195.0	2,204.8	2,210.3	2,230.6	2,223.8	2,230.0	2,234.5	2,236.3	2,242.2	2,269.9	2,219.2
Mining and Logging													
2005	15.4	15.8	16.1	16.2	16.5	17.2	17.7	18.1	18.1	18.2	18.5	18.7	17.2
2006	18.7	19.1	19.6	19.7	20.3	21.1	21.6	22.2	22.2	22.7	22.8	23.3	21.1
2007	23.1	23.6	23.9	24.5	25.2	25.9	25.9	26.2	25.8	25.9	26.2	26.2	25.2
2008	26.4	26.7	26.8	27.5	28.0	28.6	28.9	29.2	29.2	30.0	30.2	29.9	28.5
2009	28.4	27.0	26.0	24.2	23.9	23.6	23.1	23.0	22.9	22.8	22.7	22.8	24.2
2010	22.5	22.8	23.0	23.5	23.9	24.4	25.0	25.2	25.1	25.4	25.5	26.0	24.4
2011	25.7	25.9	26.3	26.8	27.2	27.9	28.5	28.9	28.7	29.5	29.8	30.1	27.9
2012	30.0	30.2	30.3	30.2	30.4	30.7	30.7	30.6	30.1	30.1	29.9	29.9	30.3
2013	29.5	29.6	29.6	29.6	30.0	30.5	30.8	31.2	31.1	31.4	31.6	31.8	30.6
2014	31.8	32.1	32.3	32.7	33.2	33.7	34.5	35.0	35.2	35.8	36.1	36.4	34.1
2015	35.6	34.5	33.1	31.7	31.1	30.6	30.3	29.7	29.1	29.2	29.0	29.0	31.1

1. Employment by Industry: Colorado, 2005–2015—*Continued*

(Numbers in thousands, not seasonally adjusted)

Industry and year	January	February	March	April	May	June	July	August	September	October	November	December	Annual average
Construction													
2005	144.7	146.3	150.1	153.3	157.7	164.6	168.1	169.3	168.3	167.2	166.0	164.2	160.0
2006	157.7	158.3	161.9	164.7	169.7	175.7	174.6	174.4	172.6	170.7	167.6	165.3	167.8
2007	154.0	154.4	160.5	164.1	169.8	175.7	176.9	176.7	173.1	173.1	170.1	164.7	167.8
2008	155.4	155.6	157.9	160.0	165.0	169.6	169.5	169.2	166.0	163.4	158.5	151.3	161.8
2009	138.4	134.8	133.3	131.4	132.7	135.5	135.0	133.2	130.0	127.9	124.6	118.9	131.3
2010	110.3	108.6	109.6	112.9	115.3	119.3	120.6	119.6	118.2	118.3	115.8	113.1	115.1
2011	104.3	102.7	105.3	110.1	111.6	116.0	117.5	118.6	117.5	117.5	115.7	113.0	112.5
2012	106.5	105.4	107.4	111.0	115.1	119.2	120.5	121.4	120.5	122.4	121.1	119.4	115.8
2013	113.4	114.4	117.5	120.3	125.8	131.1	133.2	135.1	133.7	135.8	135.7	134.0	127.5
2014	130.0	130.0	133.0	137.5	142.2	146.3	148.8	149.3	148.0	148.7	146.8	146.1	142.2
2015	139.8	140.6	141.9	145.6	148.4	151.8	154.0	153.5	152.5	156.0	155.4	154.4	149.5
Manufacturing													
2005	147.3	147.9	148.1	147.8	147.9	148.7	149.5	149.2	148.5	148.4	148.5	148.4	148.4
2006	146.7	146.9	147.3	147.1	147.4	148.3	148.1	147.9	147.2	146.9	146.5	146.1	147.2
2007	144.1	143.8	144.3	143.8	144.7	145.8	145.7	145.6	145.7	146.3	146.3	146.1	145.2
2008	144.4	143.7	143.7	143.2	143.6	144.1	143.3	143.0	141.4	140.8	139.3	137.5	142.3
2009	134.1	132.1	130.6	129.3	128.5	127.9	127.4	126.7	125.7	125.4	124.8	124.0	128.0
2010	122.2	122.1	122.3	122.8	123.6	124.9	125.1	125.3	124.9	125.5	125.6	125.9	124.2
2011	124.8	125.0	125.8	126.9	127.5	128.7	129.5	129.9	129.8	129.8	129.7	130.0	128.1
2012	128.5	128.8	129.2	129.7	130.3	131.5	132.1	132.2	131.8	132.3	132.3	132.1	130.9
2013	130.6	131.1	131.7	131.9	132.3	133.3	133.6	133.9	133.3	133.6	133.9	134.0	132.8
2014	133.1	133.4	133.8	134.7	135.6	136.9	137.7	138.1	138.3	138.5	139.2	139.5	136.6
2015	138.6	139.0	139.4	139.7	140.5	141.9	142.2	142.1	141.9	143.0	143.7	144.8	141.4
Trade, Transportation, and Utilities													
2005	405.8	403.7	406.1	405.9	407.4	411.7	413.7	413.3	414.3	416.7	425.1	431.8	413.0
2006	414.2	409.5	411.9	413.3	414.8	419.6	418.9	419.6	418.7	421.9	431.2	438.3	419.3
2007	424.2	419.7	422.3	422.7	424.4	428.9	430.5	430.8	429.7	431.6	440.1	445.3	429.2
2008	430.9	426.6	428.2	427.7	427.8	431.5	431.8	431.7	427.8	426.1	428.8	432.1	429.3
2009	413.4	406.4	403.2	400.7	401.5	404.0	402.7	402.1	399.4	399.9	404.2	408.4	403.8
2010	393.0	391.0	391.6	392.7	394.6	398.6	400.0	400.4	396.5	398.8	404.5	409.6	397.6
2011	395.1	392.6	393.8	397.2	398.9	402.6	403.9	404.8	401.8	403.6	410.9	415.6	401.7
2012	402.5	399.2	401.1	402.6	405.3	409.9	411.3	411.4	409.8	413.5	422.5	427.1	409.7
2013	412.6	410.7	412.0	413.1	415.6	420.0	421.5	423.4	420.8	423.1	432.2	437.8	420.2
2014	424.1	422.4	423.4	425.5	428.0	433.6	434.5	435.7	433.4	436.5	444.8	452.6	432.9
2015	438.7	436.8	437.6	439.6	441.2	446.6	449.5	449.6	446.8	445.6	452.9	458.8	445.3
Wholesale Trade													
2005	91.7	92.1	92.6	92.9	93.2	93.7	94.2	94.4	94.4	94.2	94.3	94.7	93.5
2006	93.9	94.3	94.9	95.4	96.1	97.2	97.0	97.4	97.2	97.5	97.9	98.5	96.4
2007	97.2	97.7	98.4	98.7	99.2	100.0	99.9	100.0	99.6	100.2	100.3	100.5	99.3
2008	99.5	99.8	100.1	100.4	100.7	101.0	101.0	100.7	100.2	99.7	99.0	98.8	100.1
2009	96.7	95.7	94.7	93.8	93.6	93.4	92.8	92.4	91.7	91.7	91.3	91.4	93.3
2010	90.1	89.9	90.0	90.4	90.6	91.1	91.3	91.3	90.9	91.3	91.2	91.4	90.8
2011	90.5	90.6	91.0	91.6	91.9	92.3	92.6	92.8	92.5	92.4	92.5	92.6	91.9
2012	91.7	92.1	92.7	93.3	93.8	94.5	94.9	95.0	94.8	95.3	95.3	95.8	94.1
2013	94.6	95.1	95.5	95.9	96.2	96.9	97.0	97.2	96.8	97.2	97.5	97.7	96.5
2014	97.2	97.8	98.1	98.8	99.3	100.0	100.5	100.9	100.6	101.2	101.6	102.4	99.9
2015	101.6	102.0	102.1	102.6	103.0	103.5	104.0	103.9	103.5	102.9	103.1	103.1	102.9
Retail Trade													
2005	240.9	238.3	240.3	240.1	241.9	244.8	245.7	245.1	246.2	248.4	256.4	261.0	245.8
2006	246.3	241.4	243.0	244.2	245.0	247.4	247.3	247.5	246.8	250.0	258.4	262.5	248.3
2007	251.1	246.7	248.4	248.3	249.6	252.6	254.3	254.4	253.8	254.7	262.2	265.4	253.5
2008	254.0	250.3	251.4	250.7	250.6	253.5	253.7	254.1	251.7	251.3	254.3	256.1	252.6
2009	242.9	237.9	236.3	234.3	236.0	238.2	237.8	237.6	236.2	236.7	241.6	244.0	238.3
2010	232.9	230.8	231.5	233.1	234.8	237.9	239.3	239.4	236.2	237.6	243.0	245.9	236.9
2011	235.0	233.0	233.7	236.5	237.9	240.5	241.1	242.0	239.6	241.1	247.6	250.4	239.9
2012	240.1	236.4	237.8	238.8	240.8	243.9	244.6	244.5	243.3	245.1	253.2	255.8	243.7
2013	244.2	241.8	242.9	243.9	245.8	249.1	250.3	251.5	249.4	250.6	258.3	261.7	249.1
2014	250.4	248.2	249.2	250.5	251.9	256.0	256.3	256.7	254.9	257.1	264.0	268.3	255.3
2015	256.6	254.9	256.4	258.0	259.6	263.7	265.3	265.8	263.7	263.6	269.9	273.4	262.6

1. Employment by Industry: Colorado, 2005–2015—*Continued*

(Numbers in thousands, not seasonally adjusted)

Industry and year	January	February	March	April	May	June	July	August	September	October	November	December	Annual average
Transportation and Utilities													
2005..............	73.2	73.3	73.2	72.9	72.3	73.2	73.8	73.8	73.7	74.1	74.4	76.1	73.7
2006..............	74.0	73.8	74.0	73.7	73.7	75.0	74.6	74.7	74.7	74.4	74.9	77.3	74.6
2007..............	75.9	75.3	75.5	75.7	75.6	76.3	76.3	76.4	76.3	76.7	77.6	79.4	76.4
2008..............	77.4	76.5	76.7	76.6	76.5	77.0	77.1	76.9	75.9	75.1	75.5	77.2	76.5
2009..............	73.8	72.8	72.2	72.6	71.9	72.4	72.1	72.1	71.5	71.5	71.3	73.0	72.3
2010..............	70.0	70.3	70.1	69.2	69.2	69.6	69.4	69.7	69.4	69.9	70.3	72.3	70.0
2011..............	69.6	69.0	69.1	69.1	69.1	69.8	70.2	70.0	69.7	70.1	70.8	72.6	69.9
2012..............	70.7	70.7	70.6	70.5	70.7	71.5	71.8	71.9	71.7	73.1	74.0	75.5	71.9
2013..............	73.8	73.8	73.6	73.3	73.6	74.0	74.2	74.7	74.6	75.3	76.4	78.4	74.6
2014..............	76.5	76.4	76.1	76.2	76.8	77.6	77.7	78.1	77.9	78.2	79.2	81.9	77.7
2015..............	80.5	79.9	79.1	79.0	78.6	79.4	80.2	79.9	79.6	79.1	79.9	82.3	79.8
Information													
2005..............	78.3	77.9	77.8	77.1	77.1	77.1	76.8	76.4	76.0	75.8	76.0	76.2	76.9
2006..............	75.8	75.6	75.8	75.4	75.7	75.7	75.3	75.2	74.7	75.0	75.4	75.5	75.4
2007..............	74.9	75.0	75.0	75.8	76.2	77.0	76.7	76.8	76.3	77.3	77.6	77.9	76.4
2008..............	77.4	77.6	77.4	77.2	77.0	77.2	77.0	76.8	76.3	76.1	76.0	76.1	76.8
2009..............	76.7	76.2	76.0	75.4	75.0	74.8	74.5	73.9	73.5	73.5	73.6	72.9	74.7
2010..............	72.2	71.9	72.0	71.7	71.8	72.3	71.8	72.0	71.5	71.9	72.5	72.5	72.0
2011..............	72.3	72.2	71.8	71.8	71.6	71.5	71.2	71.1	70.9	70.7	70.8	70.5	71.4
2012..............	70.2	70.2	70.3	69.7	69.8	70.0	69.6	69.5	69.2	69.4	69.7	69.9	69.8
2013..............	69.5	69.7	69.7	69.4	69.6	70.2	70.3	70.3	69.7	69.5	70.1	70.1	69.8
2014..............	70.1	70.2	70.1	69.6	69.8	70.5	71.0	71.2	70.0	70.2	70.5	70.7	70.3
2015..............	70.3	70.6	70.4	70.1	70.3	70.9	71.2	71.5	70.7	70.5	70.9	71.5	70.7
Financial Activities													
2005..............	155.2	156.0	157.0	157.2	157.1	158.7	159.6	160.0	159.9	159.3	159.9	162.4	158.5
2006..............	159.3	159.8	160.2	160.0	160.0	161.3	161.0	161.1	160.3	159.8	160.1	162.3	160.4
2007..............	159.6	160.1	160.4	159.9	159.2	160.5	160.3	160.0	158.7	157.8	157.9	159.2	159.5
2008..............	157.0	157.4	157.7	156.9	156.0	156.6	156.6	155.7	154.0	153.2	152.5	153.7	155.6
2009..............	150.5	149.8	149.1	148.7	147.9	148.3	147.9	147.7	146.1	146.1	145.9	147.4	148.0
2010..............	144.9	144.6	144.7	144.2	143.2	144.2	144.7	144.7	143.6	143.7	143.6	145.7	144.3
2011..............	143.6	143.4	143.5	143.3	142.8	144.0	144.1	144.4	143.7	143.3	144.3	146.2	143.9
2012..............	144.3	144.7	145.4	145.3	145.2	146.8	147.3	147.7	146.8	147.8	148.3	150.3	146.7
2013..............	148.6	149.4	150.3	150.0	149.7	151.3	152.0	152.2	151.3	151.5	151.9	153.4	151.0
2014..............	151.5	152.0	152.2	152.5	152.4	153.6	154.7	155.1	154.1	155.0	155.7	157.8	153.9
2015..............	156.2	156.9	157.3	157.5	157.5	159.2	160.4	160.7	159.7	161.8	161.6	165.1	159.5
Professional and Business Services													
2005..............	304.7	305.8	308.5	316.2	318.0	322.7	325.0	326.1	324.9	324.6	323.6	326.6	318.9
2006..............	316.7	320.4	323.6	329.3	333.7	340.4	339.7	341.9	340.0	339.4	338.9	341.0	333.8
2007..............	333.9	335.8	340.7	346.0	350.7	356.9	356.5	358.3	357.1	355.1	352.7	353.2	349.7
2008..............	344.2	347.0	348.4	354.7	356.2	360.4	359.9	361.3	357.6	355.7	350.5	348.2	353.7
2009..............	335.8	331.9	330.9	331.8	332.6	334.3	333.5	332.4	329.4	330.2	329.5	328.9	331.8
2010..............	319.4	321.1	323.8	329.4	331.4	335.6	337.1	337.4	332.8	334.8	333.6	332.6	330.8
2011..............	328.5	330.0	330.8	338.7	341.4	344.8	346.4	348.8	346.6	346.6	347.1	347.8	341.5
2012..............	340.3	342.2	345.0	351.7	355.7	360.8	362.9	365.1	362.7	367.5	365.0	363.6	356.9
2013..............	356.3	359.5	362.8	368.0	371.5	376.6	378.7	381.2	378.1	380.4	379.2	378.5	372.6
2014..............	370.1	372.1	374.1	380.9	384.4	389.9	391.4	396.7	393.5	397.0	393.3	394.7	386.5
2015..............	386.7	388.6	389.9	394.9	397.6	401.8	404.6	405.7	402.9	403.5	399.1	398.8	397.8
Education and Health Services													
2005..............	220.3	223.0	223.5	224.0	225.0	225.3	223.6	224.6	225.2	225.5	226.9	228.0	224.6
2006..............	225.9	228.5	229.3	230.0	231.1	231.2	229.4	230.8	232.1	233.9	235.3	236.5	231.2
2007..............	233.7	236.8	238.4	238.8	239.9	240.1	238.7	240.5	241.7	243.8	245.7	247.1	240.4
2008..............	244.5	247.6	248.0	248.8	250.2	249.3	248.9	250.6	251.6	254.2	256.1	256.1	250.5
2009..............	254.1	255.8	256.0	256.5	257.2	256.4	256.1	256.8	256.9	259.5	260.4	261.2	257.2
2010..............	258.9	261.3	262.1	263.5	264.4	263.8	263.6	265.0	265.3	268.6	269.3	270.3	264.7
2011..............	268.0	270.0	271.4	272.5	273.1	272.3	271.9	274.2	275.6	277.1	277.8	280.2	273.7
2012..............	277.4	280.1	281.0	281.2	281.5	281.4	280.7	282.3	283.4	285.9	287.1	288.9	282.6
2013..............	281.2	283.5	284.3	285.6	285.9	284.5	284.7	287.0	287.7	290.5	292.4	293.5	286.7
2014..............	291.2	294.0	295.2	297.5	298.4	297.1	296.8	299.7	300.7	304.2	305.4	306.5	298.9
2015..............	305.6	308.4	309.7	311.5	312.2	311.8	312.3	314.0	314.5	317.0	318.0	319.5	312.9

1. Employment by Industry: Colorado, 2005–2015—*Continued*

(Numbers in thousands, not seasonally adjusted)

Industry and year	January	February	March	April	May	June	July	August	September	October	November	December	Annual average
Leisure and Hospitality													
2005	250.8	252.7	257.5	253.7	250.0	266.0	269.7	270.0	259.1	249.5	248.6	262.5	257.5
2006	258.5	259.0	263.3	259.2	256.5	273.7	277.2	277.9	266.7	257.4	258.7	271.0	264.9
2007	263.4	264.7	270.0	266.5	263.0	278.6	281.9	282.6	271.7	262.5	264.1	275.7	270.4
2008	269.7	271.1	274.5	271.7	268.7	283.7	286.4	285.9	273.3	262.3	259.1	268.7	272.9
2009	262.2	261.3	263.5	260.2	256.6	269.4	274.5	274.7	262.6	253.3	250.0	260.7	262.4
2010	256.7	257.0	259.9	259.3	253.7	270.1	275.7	277.2	265.6	257.4	255.0	268.6	263.0
2011	265.4	264.1	269.4	267.0	261.6	279.5	284.1	286.0	275.8	264.6	263.4	275.4	271.4
2012	272.0	271.5	278.1	275.0	269.8	289.3	293.7	294.0	281.6	272.5	274.0	284.3	279.7
2013	281.2	282.6	287.4	285.3	280.3	299.6	305.1	304.7	291.7	281.4	280.7	292.4	289.4
2014	291.7	292.4	297.9	296.3	291.8	309.3	315.3	315.4	304.2	294.0	291.0	305.5	300.4
2015	303.0	305.4	309.2	307.4	302.5	321.9	327.9	327.6	316.9	305.7	306.4	325.3	313.3
Other Services													
2005	88.2	88.1	88.5	88.4	88.4	89.6	89.5	89.3	88.4	87.9	87.5	88.1	88.5
2006	89.8	89.7	90.5	90.4	90.6	92.3	91.8	91.7	90.8	90.4	90.5	91.2	90.8
2007	91.4	91.9	92.9	92.5	92.6	94.3	93.5	93.6	93.0	93.0	92.8	93.5	92.9
2008	93.9	94.3	94.7	94.4	94.7	96.0	96.4	96.1	95.3	94.6	94.0	93.6	94.8
2009	95.1	94.5	94.6	93.4	93.5	94.7	94.3	94.0	92.9	92.6	92.1	92.6	93.7
2010	92.3	92.1	92.4	91.7	92.1	93.3	93.4	93.4	92.3	91.8	91.7	92.0	92.4
2011	91.8	91.7	92.5	93.4	93.7	95.1	94.8	95.3	94.4	93.7	93.6	94.2	93.7
2012	94.1	94.5	95.2	95.4	95.6	97.2	97.4	97.2	96.3	96.4	96.0	96.4	96.0
2013	96.3	96.3	96.8	96.9	97.6	98.8	99.0	99.0	97.9	97.5	97.7	98.0	97.7
2014	98.5	98.5	99.0	99.5	99.9	101.5	102.4	102.8	101.1	101.6	101.2	101.9	100.7
2015	101.5	101.6	102.0	102.2	102.3	103.9	104.5	104.4	103.4	103.4	102.8	104.2	103.0
Government													
2005	352.8	364.7	365.9	367.5	370.7	363.0	345.2	345.1	365.0	370.9	370.7	369.7	362.6
2006	356.8	368.4	371.6	370.8	374.5	368.1	348.8	351.4	369.8	375.2	376.0	375.3	367.2
2007	360.3	374.7	378.0	378.5	382.0	374.6	355.5	359.3	379.5	384.1	385.6	384.0	374.7
2008	370.7	383.3	386.3	386.9	392.6	382.0	364.6	369.9	388.5	395.5	396.0	393.3	384.1
2009	382.5	392.1	394.7	396.6	401.5	389.9	369.1	371.0	392.5	400.1	399.2	396.9	390.5
2010	382.4	396.0	399.8	400.1	411.6	394.5	374.5	374.0	392.9	400.3	401.4	398.5	393.8
2011	383.4	395.9	398.4	400.4	403.3	392.3	371.6	372.3	395.4	401.2	401.9	398.7	392.9
2012	383.8	396.4	399.6	400.8	404.4	394.0	373.1	377.6	398.2	403.3	405.2	401.7	394.8
2013	391.8	405.5	407.8	408.6	412.9	400.7	380.6	385.5	408.1	415.0	416.2	411.5	403.7
2014	399.1	409.5	412.1	413.4	418.3	406.9	384.8	389.1	410.6	419.9	422.1	416.7	408.5
2015	406.4	416.7	418.9	421.6	426.7	414.5	393.4	396.5	419.6	428.8	430.5	426.7	416.7

2. Average Weekly Hours by Selected Industry: Colorado, 2011–2015

(Not seasonally adjusted)

Industry and year	January	February	March	April	May	June	July	August	September	October	November	December	Annual average
Total Private													
2011	34.3	33.9	33.9	34.2	35.1	34.5	34.7	34.5	34.6	35.4	34.7	34.6	34.5
2012	35.0	34.4	34.3	35.1	34.6	34.9	35.6	35.0	35.5	35.0	34.7	35.4	35.0
2013	34.3	34.5	34.7	34.4	34.6	35.6	34.8	34.9	35.2	34.6	34.8	35.1	34.8
2014	34.2	35.0	34.9	34.1	34.1	35.2	34.5	34.5	34.3	34.4	34.4	34.1	34.5
2015	33.6	34.4	34.4	33.6	33.7	34.0	34.1	34.8	33.9	33.9	34.0	33.2	34.0
Goods-Producing													
2011	36.5	37.0	37.5	38.5	39.1	38.9	39.2	38.9	39.4	39.5	39.2	38.7	38.6
2012	37.4	37.1	37.9	38.1	38.5	39.0	39.4	39.1	39.2	39.8	39.1	38.5	38.6
2013	37.5	37.6	38.0	37.7	38.6	39.6	39.1	40.0	39.2	39.4	39.1	39.6	38.8
2014	38.4	39.3	38.9	38.9	38.8	40.0	39.7	40.3	40.0	40.7	38.9	40.5	39.5
2015	39.3	40.1	40.3	39.4	39.0	40.0	40.0	40.8	39.8	40.2	40.1	40.0	39.9
Construction													
2011	35.3	35.8	36.6	37.6	38.2	38.0	38.7	38.4	38.2	38.4	37.4	36.8	37.5
2012	36.3	35.6	36.7	36.6	36.7	37.9	38.8	37.9	37.4	39.3	38.3	37.8	37.5
2013	36.8	37.0	37.6	36.7	37.7	38.9	38.7	39.6	39.0	39.3	38.9	38.4	38.3
2014	37.7	37.9	38.1	38.5	37.5	39.4	39.8	40.4	39.9	40.9	38.4	40.0	39.1
2015	37.8	38.7	39.0	38.7	37.6	39.4	39.8	40.9	39.0	40.3	39.5	39.9	39.2
Manufacturing													
2011	37.9	38.2	38.5	39.2	39.6	39.5	39.5	39.1	39.8	40.0	39.9	40.2	39.3
2012	37.8	37.9	38.5	39.1	39.6	39.8	39.4	40.1	40.5	40.0	39.7	38.9	39.3
2013	38.1	38.6	38.3	38.7	39.1	40.0	39.1	40.2	39.6	39.6	39.2	39.8	39.2
2014	39.5	40.5	39.5	39.2	40.0	40.3	39.2	39.8	39.8	40.1	40.0	39.5	39.8
2015	39.3	40.3	40.4	39.2	39.7	40.1	39.9	40.2	40.1	39.8	40.0	39.6	39.9
Trade, Transportation, and Utilities													
2011	35.7	35.0	35.0	35.2	36.0	35.8	36.2	36.0	36.3	36.8	36.2	36.3	35.9
2012	36.9	36.2	35.8	36.5	35.4	35.7	36.4	35.6	36.2	35.4	35.2	36.2	36.0
2013	34.8	35.2	35.4	35.0	35.2	36.3	35.8	35.7	35.9	35.0	35.1	35.8	35.4
2014	34.7	35.4	35.1	34.3	34.2	35.1	34.4	34.4	34.4	34.5	34.6	34.6	34.6
2015	33.7	34.6	34.5	33.4	34.0	34.2	34.5	34.7	34.5	34.2	34.3	34.0	34.2
Financial Activities													
2011	37.1	36.6	36.7	36.9	38.4	36.4	36.9	36.8	37.0	37.8	36.8	36.3	37.0
2012	38.6	36.9	36.4	37.5	36.7	36.9	38.6	37.3	38.2	37.2	37.4	38.5	37.5
2013	37.7	37.2	37.3	37.5	36.9	38.4	37.3	37.0	37.8	36.7	36.6	37.5	37.3
2014	36.6	37.2	37.5	36.3	36.2	38.3	37.1	37.0	36.9	37.1	38.6	36.9	37.1
2015	36.8	37.7	37.5	36.5	36.4	36.0	36.1	37.4	36.3	36.1	37.6	36.2	36.7
Professional and Business Services													
2011	36.9	36.7	36.2	36.6	37.2	36.6	36.5	36.3	36.2	37.3	36.5	36.7	36.6
2012	37.3	37.0	36.7	38.0	37.2	37.4	37.7	37.4	38.2	37.5	37.0	38.6	37.5
2013	36.9	37.2	37.1	36.8	37.2	38.3	36.9	37.3	37.6	37.2	37.4	37.6	37.3
2014	36.7	37.8	37.5	37.2	36.8	37.8	36.4	36.6	36.7	36.8	36.8	36.2	36.9
2015	36.2	37.0	37.2	36.5	36.6	36.6	36.6	37.2	36.2	36.2	36.2	35.1	36.5
Education and Health Services													
2011	33.5	33.5	33.0	33.3	33.4	33.0	33.0	32.7	33.0	34.1	33.2	33.4	33.3
2012	33.3	32.7	31.9	32.8	32.5	32.8	33.1	32.8	33.2	32.6	32.8	33.4	32.8
2013	32.4	32.5	32.2	32.3	32.0	32.6	31.8	31.8	32.3	31.8	32.1	32.1	32.2
2014	31.4	31.8	32.0	31.2	31.4	32.1	31.6	31.4	31.3	31.4	32.2	31.6	31.6
2015	31.3	32.0	31.9	31.1	31.1	30.9	30.6	31.4	30.7	30.6	31.4	30.5	31.1
Leisure and Hospitality													
2011	25.4	25.4	26.3	25.7	26.8	26.9	27.1	26.8	26.3	27.1	26.2	26.2	26.4
2012	27.0	26.7	27.3	27.2	26.9	27.6	28.2	27.8	28.1	27.3	26.8	27.5	27.4
2013	27.1	27.7	28.0	27.0	27.5	28.6	28.1	28.1	27.7	26.8	27.0	26.7	27.5
2014	26.6	27.3	28.1	26.1	26.5	27.9	27.9	27.9	26.8	26.4	26.0	25.7	26.9
2015	25.9	26.7	26.9	26.0	26.1	26.6	26.8	27.6	26.1	26.2	25.2	25.0	26.3
Other Services													
2011	33.3	31.6	31.1	31.0	33.2	32.6	32.1	32.4	32.6	34.0	32.6	33.3	32.5
2012	35.1	33.9	33.4	35.0	33.9	34.1	35.6	35.6	34.6	34.1	34.8	35.3	34.6
2013	34.5	34.3	34.4	33.9	33.9	34.9	33.3	33.5	34.1	33.4	33.9	34.6	34.1
2014	34.3	34.7	34.0	33.6	33.3	34.4	33.0	34.1	33.7	32.4	32.3	31.0	33.4
2015	29.8	31.0	31.1	30.1	30.4	32.2	32.3	33.6	32.5	32.7	34.2	32.8	31.9

3. Average Hourly Earnings by Selected Industry: Colorado, 2011–2015

(Dollars, not seasonally adjusted)

Industry and year	January	February	March	April	May	June	July	August	September	October	November	December	Annual average
Total Private													
2011	24.11	24.09	23.87	24.02	23.90	23.53	23.75	23.65	23.86	24.31	24.11	24.20	23.95
2012	24.54	24.00	24.22	24.87	24.48	24.49	24.72	24.43	24.89	24.61	24.77	25.18	24.61
2013	25.11	25.31	25.26	25.49	25.47	25.77	25.54	25.51	26.17	25.80	25.98	26.22	25.64
2014	26.04	26.20	26.39	26.35	26.24	26.39	26.10	26.02	26.34	26.34	26.66	26.44	26.29
2015	26.64	26.74	26.81	26.85	26.82	26.41	26.76	27.00	26.81	27.07	27.27	27.03	26.85
Goods-Producing													
2011	26.39	26.19	25.97	26.08	25.63	25.70	25.30	25.20	25.53	25.40	25.27	25.70	25.68
2012	25.91	25.68	25.43	25.59	25.41	25.70	25.50	25.57	25.86	25.70	25.93	26.70	25.75
2013	26.79	27.08	27.11	27.10	27.04	27.27	27.18	27.00	27.65	27.56	27.71	28.03	27.31
2014	27.88	27.78	28.25	28.18	28.02	28.29	28.33	28.10	28.60	28.57	28.74	28.79	28.31
2015	29.10	29.28	29.42	29.57	29.54	29.43	29.88	30.08	29.96	29.96	30.19	30.13	29.72
Construction													
2011	23.89	24.02	24.07	24.58	24.08	23.97	23.58	23.55	23.52	23.57	23.77	23.95	23.87
2012	23.55	23.49	23.62	23.34	23.50	22.53	22.90	23.44	23.50	23.36	23.59	24.29	23.42
2013	24.60	25.02	24.97	24.77	25.34	25.18	25.07	25.02	25.65	26.28	26.18	26.66	25.43
2014	26.64	27.04	27.21	26.98	26.90	27.04	27.75	27.53	28.15	28.02	28.43	28.27	27.53
2015	28.06	28.64	28.22	28.44	28.21	27.83	28.04	27.75	27.61	27.78	27.73	27.41	27.96
Manufacturing													
2011	27.51	27.26	27.01	26.87	26.57	26.67	26.20	26.18	26.91	26.57	26.10	26.29	26.67
2012	26.99	26.83	26.28	26.63	26.37	27.28	26.56	26.15	26.56	26.41	26.59	27.26	26.66
2013	27.30	27.47	27.40	27.53	26.69	26.89	26.92	26.61	27.54	26.70	27.31	27.29	27.13
2014	27.42	27.28	27.68	27.42	27.35	27.84	27.20	26.73	27.18	27.27	27.23	27.60	27.35
2015	28.40	28.31	29.19	29.66	29.61	29.76	30.63	30.83	30.50	30.69	31.14	31.49	30.03
Trade, Transportation, and Utilities													
2011	19.77	19.69	19.39	19.46	19.96	19.67	20.04	20.12	20.58	21.05	21.22	21.11	20.19
2012	21.92	21.25	21.62	22.52	22.00	22.09	22.42	22.34	23.03	22.22	22.22	23.02	22.23
2013	22.81	22.57	22.46	22.71	22.87	23.23	22.80	22.71	23.48	22.72	22.96	22.93	22.86
2014	22.96	22.74	23.02	22.94	22.63	23.04	22.50	22.61	22.66	22.92	23.19	22.28	22.79
2015	22.87	22.93	23.08	23.07	22.97	22.65	22.98	23.21	23.02	23.06	22.88	22.65	22.95
Financial Activities													
2011	22.57	22.52	22.64	23.17	23.94	23.61	24.06	23.95	23.88	24.97	24.32	24.35	23.67
2012	24.52	25.45	25.55	26.08	25.55	26.07	27.22	26.32	27.16	27.10	26.89	27.05	26.26
2013	27.07	27.70	27.79	28.13	28.68	28.91	29.05	29.70	30.38	29.61	30.22	30.53	28.99
2014	29.87	31.02	31.20	30.82	31.40	31.81	31.30	31.15	30.87	30.60	30.94	30.37	30.95
2015	30.77	30.85	31.23	31.59	31.57	30.63	31.35	31.94	31.38	31.64	31.63	30.86	31.29
Professional and Business Services													
2011	30.21	29.92	29.71	29.84	29.63	29.06	29.52	29.26	29.27	30.42	29.64	29.94	29.70
2012	30.42	29.33	29.77	30.60	29.88	29.75	29.97	29.48	29.66	29.22	29.54	30.29	29.82
2013	30.60	30.99	30.94	31.14	31.04	32.01	31.82	31.50	32.07	31.57	31.61	32.40	31.49
2014	32.41	32.42	32.62	32.37	32.04	31.94	31.66	31.32	31.48	31.67	32.36	32.03	32.02
2015	32.56	32.48	32.30	32.13	31.86	31.45	32.05	32.43	32.18	32.44	33.32	33.26	32.37
Education and Health Services													
2011	23.86	24.20	24.23	24.33	24.40	24.37	24.30	24.51	24.39	24.42	24.65	24.49	24.35
2012	24.62	24.39	24.88	24.91	24.69	24.81	24.88	24.36	24.77	24.44	24.68	24.37	24.65
2013	24.12	24.14	23.94	24.00	23.73	23.75	23.73	23.70	23.70	23.60	23.60	23.63	23.80
2014	23.76	23.89	24.08	23.97	23.89	24.14	24.45	24.69	25.10	24.63	25.20	25.22	24.43
2015	24.87	25.31	25.30	25.24	25.46	25.81	26.09	25.83	25.99	26.19	26.49	26.43	25.75
Leisure and Hospitality													
2011	14.27	14.51	14.51	14.43	14.24	13.94	14.14	14.08	14.34	14.34	14.45	14.36	14.30
2012	14.59	14.48	14.69	15.16	14.85	14.72	14.62	14.49	14.78	14.95	15.11	15.22	14.80
2013	15.33	15.33	15.35	15.43	15.29	14.90	14.98	15.12	15.32	15.39	15.32	15.25	15.24
2014	15.37	15.35	15.30	15.30	15.13	14.86	14.72	14.79	15.27	15.31	15.30	15.64	15.18
2015	15.82	15.70	16.04	15.89	15.80	15.36	15.43	15.64	15.20	15.65	15.43	15.92	15.65
Other Services													
2011	20.95	21.01	21.07	21.10	21.30	20.94	21.88	21.13	21.60	21.24	21.35	21.60	21.27
2012	21.04	21.19	21.61	21.57	21.45	21.60	22.11	21.44	21.98	21.73	21.44	21.97	21.60
2013	21.21	21.80	22.10	22.19	21.79	22.02	21.52	21.42	22.18	22.55	22.96	22.78	22.04
2014	22.52	23.50	23.88	23.97	23.79	25.26	25.03	24.68	25.06	24.25	23.79	24.19	24.17
2015	23.03	23.24	23.44	23.27	23.32	22.68	23.03	23.63	23.66	24.3	24.23	23.52	23.46

4. Average Weekly Earnings by Selected Industry: Colorado, 2011–2015

(Dollars, not seasonally adjusted)

Industry and year	January	February	March	April	May	June	July	August	September	October	November	December	Annual average
Total Private													
2011	826.97	816.65	809.19	821.48	838.89	811.79	824.13	815.93	825.56	860.57	836.62	837.32	826.28
2012	858.90	825.60	830.75	872.94	847.01	854.70	880.03	855.05	883.60	861.35	859.52	891.37	861.35
2013	861.27	873.20	876.52	876.86	881.26	917.41	888.79	890.30	921.18	892.68	904.10	920.32	892.27
2014	890.57	917.00	921.01	898.54	894.78	928.93	900.45	897.69	903.46	906.10	917.10	901.60	907.01
2015	895.10	919.86	922.26	902.16	903.83	897.94	912.52	939.60	908.86	917.67	927.18	897.40	912.90
Goods-Producing													
2011	963.24	969.03	973.88	1,004.08	1,002.13	999.73	991.76	980.28	1,005.88	1,003.30	990.58	994.59	991.25
2012	969.03	952.73	963.80	974.98	978.29	1,002.30	1,004.70	999.79	1,013.71	1,022.86	1,013.86	1,027.95	993.95
2013	1,004.63	1,018.21	1,030.18	1,021.67	1,043.74	1,079.89	1,062.74	1,080.00	1,083.88	1,085.86	1,083.46	1,109.99	1,059.63
2014	1,070.59	1,091.75	1,098.93	1,096.20	1,087.18	1,131.60	1,124.70	1,132.43	1,144.00	1,162.80	1,117.99	1,166.00	1,118.25
2015	1,143.63	1,174.13	1,185.63	1,165.06	1,152.06	1,177.20	1,195.20	1,227.26	1,192.41	1,204.39	1,210.62	1,205.20	1,185.83
Construction													
2011	843.32	859.92	880.96	924.21	919.86	910.86	912.55	904.32	898.46	905.09	889.00	881.36	895.13
2012	854.87	836.24	866.85	854.24	862.45	853.89	888.52	888.38	878.90	918.05	903.50	918.16	878.25
2013	905.28	925.74	938.87	909.06	955.32	979.50	970.21	990.79	1,000.35	1,032.80	1,018.40	1,023.74	973.97
2014	1,004.33	1,024.82	1,036.70	1,038.73	1,008.75	1,065.38	1,104.45	1,112.21	1,123.19	1,146.02	1,091.71	1,130.80	1,076.42
2015	1,060.67	1,108.37	1,100.58	1,100.63	1,060.70	1,096.50	1,115.99	1,134.98	1,076.79	1,119.53	1,095.34	1,093.66	1,096.03
Manufacturing													
2011	1,042.63	1,041.33	1,039.89	1,053.30	1,052.17	1,053.47	1,034.90	1,023.64	1,071.02	1,062.80	1,041.39	1,056.86	1,048.13
2012	1,020.22	1,016.86	1,011.78	1,041.23	1,044.25	1,085.74	1,046.46	1,048.62	1,075.68	1,056.40	1,055.62	1,060.41	1,047.74
2013	1,040.13	1,060.34	1,049.42	1,065.41	1,043.58	1,075.60	1,052.57	1,069.72	1,090.58	1,057.32	1,070.55	1,086.14	1,063.50
2014	1,083.09	1,104.84	1,093.36	1,074.86	1,094.00	1,121.95	1,066.24	1,063.85	1,081.76	1,093.53	1,089.20	1,090.20	1,088.53
2015	1,116.12	1,140.89	1,179.28	1,162.67	1,175.52	1,193.38	1,222.14	1,239.37	1,223.05	1,221.46	1,245.60	1,247.00	1,198.20
Trade, Transportation, and Utilities													
2011	705.79	689.15	678.65	684.99	718.56	704.19	725.45	724.32	747.05	774.64	768.16	766.29	724.82
2012	808.85	769.25	774.00	821.98	778.80	788.61	816.09	795.30	833.69	786.59	782.14	833.32	800.28
2013	793.79	794.46	795.08	794.85	805.02	843.25	816.24	810.75	842.93	795.20	805.90	820.89	809.24
2014	796.71	805.00	808.00	786.84	773.95	808.70	774.00	777.78	779.50	790.74	802.37	770.89	788.53
2015	770.72	793.38	796.26	770.54	780.98	774.63	792.81	805.39	794.19	788.65	784.78	770.10	784.89
Financial Activities													
2011	837.35	824.23	830.89	854.97	919.30	859.40	887.81	881.36	883.56	943.87	894.98	883.91	875.79
2012	946.47	939.11	930.02	978.00	937.69	961.98	1,050.69	981.74	1,037.51	1,008.12	1,005.69	1,041.43	984.75
2013	1,020.54	1,030.44	1,036.57	1,054.88	1,058.29	1,110.14	1,083.57	1,098.90	1,148.36	1,086.69	1,106.05	1,144.88	1,081.33
2014	1,093.24	1,153.94	1,170.00	1,118.77	1,136.68	1,218.32	1,161.23	1,152.55	1,139.10	1,135.26	1,194.28	1,120.65	1,148.25
2015	1,132.34	1,163.05	1,171.13	1,153.04	1,149.15	1,102.68	1,131.74	1,194.56	1,139.09	1,142.20	1,189.29	1,117.13	1,148.34
Professional and Business Services													
2011	1,114.75	1,098.06	1,075.50	1,092.14	1,102.24	1,063.60	1,077.48	1,062.14	1,059.57	1,134.67	1,081.86	1,098.80	1,087.02
2012	1,134.67	1,085.21	1,092.56	1,162.80	1,111.54	1,112.65	1,129.87	1,102.55	1,133.01	1,095.75	1,092.98	1,169.19	1,118.25
2013	1,129.14	1,152.83	1,147.87	1,145.95	1,154.69	1,225.98	1,174.16	1,174.95	1,205.83	1,174.40	1,182.21	1,218.24	1,174.58
2014	1,189.45	1,225.48	1,223.25	1,204.16	1,179.07	1,207.33	1,152.42	1,146.31	1,155.32	1,165.46	1,190.85	1,159.49	1,181.54
2015	1,178.67	1,201.76	1,201.56	1,172.75	1,166.08	1,151.07	1,173.03	1,206.40	1,164.92	1,174.33	1,206.18	1,167.43	1,181.51
Education and Health Services													
2011	799.31	810.70	799.59	810.19	814.96	804.21	801.90	801.48	804.87	832.72	818.38	817.97	810.86
2012	819.85	797.55	793.67	817.05	802.43	813.77	823.53	799.01	822.36	796.74	809.50	813.96	808.52
2013	781.49	784.55	770.87	775.20	759.36	774.25	754.61	753.66	765.51	750.48	757.56	758.52	766.36
2014	746.06	759.70	770.56	747.86	750.15	774.89	772.62	775.27	785.63	773.38	811.44	796.95	771.99
2015	778.43	809.92	807.07	784.96	791.81	797.53	798.35	811.06	797.89	801.41	831.79	806.12	800.83
Leisure and Hospitality													
2011	362.46	368.55	381.61	370.85	381.63	374.99	383.19	377.34	377.14	388.61	378.59	376.23	377.52
2012	393.93	386.62	401.04	412.35	399.47	406.27	412.28	402.82	415.32	408.14	404.95	418.55	405.52
2013	415.44	424.64	429.80	416.61	420.48	426.14	420.94	424.87	424.36	412.45	413.64	407.18	419.10
2014	408.84	419.06	429.93	399.33	400.95	414.59	410.69	412.64	409.24	404.18	397.80	401.95	408.34
2015	409.74	419.19	431.48	413.14	412.38	408.58	413.52	431.66	396.72	410.03	388.84	398.00	411.60
Other Services													
2011	697.64	663.92	655.28	654.10	707.16	682.64	702.35	684.61	704.16	722.16	696.01	719.28	691.28
2012	738.50	718.34	721.77	754.95	727.16	736.56	787.12	763.26	760.51	740.99	746.11	775.54	747.36
2013	731.75	747.74	760.24	752.24	738.68	768.50	716.62	717.57	756.34	753.17	778.34	788.19	751.56
2014	772.44	815.45	811.92	805.39	792.21	868.94	825.99	841.59	844.52	785.70	768.42	749.89	807.28
2015	686.29	720.44	728.98	700.43	708.93	730.30	743.87	793.97	768.95	794.61	828.67	771.46	748.37

CONNECTICUT
At a Glance

Population:
  2005 estimate: 3,506,956
  2010 census: 3,574,097
  2015 estimate: 3,590,886

Percent change in population:
  2005–2015: 2.4%
  2010–2015: 0.5%

Percent change in total nonfarm employment:
  2005–2015: 0.7%

Industry with the largest growth in employment, 2005–2015 (thousands):
  Education and health services, 53.3

Industry with the largest decline or smallest growth in employment, 2005–2015 (thousands):
  Manufacturing, –35.8

Civilian labor force:
  2005: 1,796,976
  2010: 1,911,712
  2015: 1,888,001

Unemployment rate and rank among states (highest to lowest):
  2005: 4.9%, 27th
  2010: 9.1%, 22nd
  2015: 5.6%, 19th

Over-the-year change in unemployment rates:
  2012–2013: –0.5%
  2013–2014: –1.2%
  2014–2015: –1.0%

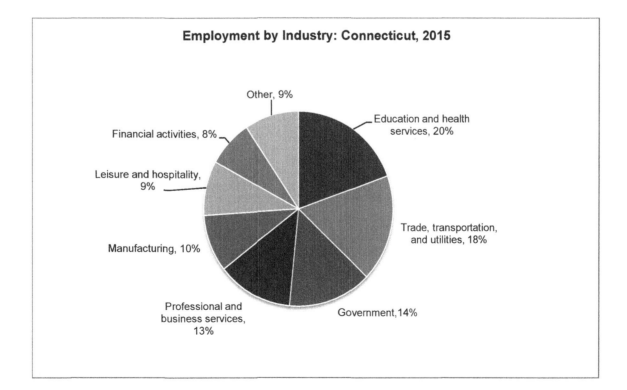

Employment by Industry: Connecticut, 2015

Other, 9%
Education and health services, 20%
Financial activities, 8%
Leisure and hospitality, 9%
Trade, transportation, and utilities, 18%
Manufacturing, 10%
Professional and business services, 13%
Government, 14%

1. Employment by Industry: Connecticut, 2005–2015

(Numbers in thousands, not seasonally adjusted)

Industry and year	January	February	March	April	May	June	July	August	September	October	November	December	Annual average
Total Nonfarm													
2005	1,630.4	1,636.1	1,639.7	1,663.6	1,670.5	1,681.8	1,654.0	1,651.1	1,668.1	1,673.4	1,684.0	1,692.9	1,662.1
2006	1,648.6	1,650.8	1,656.1	1,678.5	1,687.4	1,698.6	1,672.6	1,673.8	1,685.4	1,694.6	1,705.0	1,716.7	1,680.7
2007	1,666.6	1,668.5	1,672.0	1,689.9	1,705.7	1,720.5	1,691.5	1,690.6	1,704.4	1,714.3	1,724.3	1,731.0	1,698.3
2008	1,685.4	1,687.9	1,692.6	1,705.7	1,717.8	1,724.6	1,690.5	1,686.8	1,697.3	1,701.0	1,701.5	1,698.1	1,699.1
2009	1,639.2	1,634.8	1,626.9	1,626.8	1,639.7	1,640.7	1,608.4	1,602.6	1,617.4	1,623.1	1,628.5	1,631.5	1,626.6
2010	1,569.1	1,571.8	1,575.1	1,600.3	1,622.4	1,625.0	1,607.3	1,604.2	1,616.8	1,629.0	1,635.4	1,639.2	1,608.0
2011	1,591.4	1,597.7	1,599.8	1,627.1	1,634.0	1,637.2	1,621.4	1,615.3	1,631.3	1,636.6	1,644.6	1,650.4	1,623.9
2012	1,606.8	1,612.8	1,620.2	1,631.6	1,644.6	1,652.6	1,631.4	1,627.4	1,642.4	1,652.3	1,661.8	1,666.5	1,637.5
2013	1,617.6	1,615.9	1,626.5	1,648.8	1,661.9	1,675.0	1,653.0	1,645.9	1,653.2	1,660.8	1,672.1	1,670.1	1,650.1
2014	1,627.7	1,625.1	1,633.8	1,659.6	1,674.0	1,683.2	1,659.2	1,656.3	1,666.2	1,676.4	1,686.5	1,689.5	1,661.5
2015	1,645.7	1,641.9	1,648.8	1,668.5	1,687.7	1,698.7	1,670.0	1,664.7	1,674.0	1,687.7	1,700.2	1,700.3	1,674.0
Total Private													
2005	1,386.5	1,386.8	1,390.9	1,412.6	1,420.3	1,434.8	1,426.5	1,420.3	1,422.5	1,421.8	1,429.8	1,438.6	1,416.0
2006	1,400.6	1,399.0	1,404.5	1,425.9	1,435.2	1,451.4	1,442.1	1,438.6	1,439.1	1,442.0	1,449.5	1,460.8	1,432.4
2007	1,416.7	1,413.7	1,417.8	1,435.2	1,451.3	1,469.6	1,458.2	1,454.0	1,453.8	1,455.9	1,463.2	1,470.6	1,446.7
2008	1,430.4	1,427.8	1,433.5	1,446.3	1,457.8	1,469.9	1,454.3	1,448.1	1,444.8	1,441.1	1,439.3	1,437.6	1,444.2
2009	1,385.2	1,376.8	1,369.5	1,369.6	1,382.4	1,390.0	1,377.0	1,370.0	1,370.9	1,370.6	1,373.0	1,377.4	1,376.0
2010	1,320.9	1,319.7	1,324.9	1,350.6	1,366.0	1,378.7	1,377.1	1,372.8	1,374.0	1,379.3	1,384.2	1,388.9	1,361.4
2011	1,348.0	1,350.2	1,352.3	1,377.4	1,386.7	1,398.0	1,394.4	1,389.5	1,390.3	1,389.8	1,396.4	1,402.2	1,381.3
2012	1,366.0	1,366.1	1,373.8	1,386.4	1,400.9	1,414.5	1,406.0	1,401.8	1,402.7	1,407.9	1,414.5	1,418.8	1,396.6
2013	1,375.0	1,372.2	1,382.1	1,403.6	1,416.3	1,430.1	1,422.7	1,420.0	1,416.9	1,419.7	1,428.0	1,426.8	1,409.5
2014	1,388.3	1,383.3	1,390.6	1,414.6	1,428.3	1,440.0	1,433.3	1,429.0	1,427.9	1,433.8	1,440.9	1,445.0	1,421.3
2015	1,405.7	1,400.2	1,406.3	1,425.1	1,443.2	1,457.5	1,445.5	1,439.1	1,437.1	1,446.1	1,455.9	1,456.8	1,434.9
Goods-Producing													
2005	257.6	255.5	256.7	261.3	263.4	266.6	265.2	264.8	263.2	262.0	261.5	259.8	261.5
2006	255.0	254.4	253.1	260.6	262.3	266.0	265.3	265.2	263.4	262.4	261.8	261.2	260.9
2007	254.6	252.5	254.3	257.9	260.5	264.6	263.7	264.0	262.1	261.2	260.8	258.7	259.6
2008	251.9	249.8	250.8	254.3	256.3	258.4	256.6	256.3	254.2	251.8	248.4	244.0	252.7
2009	233.3	228.6	226.8	226.7	227.7	229.1	226.1	225.0	224.3	222.0	220.5	218.5	225.7
2010	208.4	206.3	207.4	213.2	216.0	219.2	219.8	219.7	219.5	218.9	218.6	217.2	215.4
2011	210.6	210.2	211.4	215.5	218.0	221.3	221.8	222.0	220.7	219.8	219.7	217.9	217.4
2012	211.8	211.0	211.7	214.3	216.1	219.0	219.2	219.2	217.5	217.8	216.9	216.4	215.9
2013	210.9	210.1	211.1	215.0	217.9	220.4	221.0	220.5	219.0	218.2	217.1	215.3	216.4
2014	209.2	208.2	208.8	213.7	216.1	218.6	220.0	220.1	218.5	218.9	217.6	216.3	215.5
2015	210.7	209.2	210.4	215.2	218.6	221.6	221.2	221.5	220.2	219.8	219.2	216.0	217.0
Service-Providing													
2005	1,372.8	1,380.6	1,383.0	1,402.3	1,407.1	1,415.2	1,388.8	1,386.3	1,404.9	1,411.4	1,422.5	1,433.1	1,400.7
2006	1,393.6	1,396.4	1,403.0	1,417.9	1,425.1	1,432.6	1,407.3	1,408.6	1,422.0	1,432.2	1,443.2	1,455.5	1,419.8
2007	1,412.0	1,416.0	1,417.7	1,432.0	1,445.2	1,455.9	1,427.8	1,426.6	1,442.3	1,453.1	1,463.5	1,472.3	1,438.7
2008	1,433.5	1,438.1	1,441.8	1,451.4	1,461.5	1,466.2	1,433.9	1,430.5	1,443.1	1,449.2	1,453.1	1,454.1	1,446.4
2009	1,405.9	1,406.2	1,400.1	1,400.1	1,412.0	1,411.6	1,382.3	1,377.6	1,393.1	1,401.1	1,408.0	1,413.0	1,400.9
2010	1,360.7	1,365.5	1,367.7	1,387.1	1,406.4	1,405.8	1,387.5	1,384.5	1,397.3	1,410.1	1,416.8	1,422.0	1,392.6
2011	1,380.8	1,387.5	1,388.4	1,411.6	1,416.0	1,415.9	1,399.6	1,393.3	1,410.6	1,416.8	1,424.9	1,432.5	1,406.5
2012	1,395.0	1,401.8	1,408.5	1,417.3	1,428.5	1,433.6	1,412.2	1,408.2	1,424.9	1,434.5	1,444.9	1,450.1	1,421.6
2013	1,406.7	1,405.8	1,415.4	1,433.8	1,444.0	1,454.6	1,432.0	1,425.4	1,434.2	1,442.6	1,455.0	1,454.8	1,433.7
2014	1,418.5	1,416.9	1,425.0	1,445.9	1,457.9	1,464.6	1,439.2	1,436.2	1,447.7	1,457.5	1,468.9	1,473.2	1,446.0
2015	1,435.0	1,432.7	1,438.4	1,453.3	1,469.1	1,477.1	1,448.8	1,443.2	1,453.8	1,467.9	1,481.0	1,484.3	1,457.1
Mining and Logging													
2005	0.7	0.6	0.6	0.7	0.8	0.8	0.8	0.8	0.8	0.8	0.8	0.7	0.7
2006	0.7	0.7	0.7	0.8	0.8	0.8	0.8	0.8	0.8	0.8	0.8	0.7	0.8
2007	0.7	0.6	0.6	0.7	0.7	0.8	0.8	0.8	0.8	0.8	0.8	0.7	0.7
2008	0.7	0.6	0.7	0.7	0.8	0.8	0.8	0.8	0.8	0.8	0.8	0.7	0.8
2009	0.6	0.6	0.6	0.6	0.7	0.7	0.7	0.7	0.7	0.6	0.6	0.6	0.6
2010	0.5	0.5	0.5	0.6	0.6	0.6	0.6	0.6	0.6	0.6	0.6	0.6	0.6
2011	0.5	0.5	0.5	0.5	0.6	0.6	0.6	0.6	0.6	0.6	0.6	0.6	0.6
2012	0.5	0.5	0.5	0.6	0.6	0.6	0.6	0.6	0.6	0.6	0.6	0.5	0.6
2013	0.5	0.5	0.5	0.5	0.6	0.6	0.6	0.6	0.6	0.6	0.6	0.6	0.6
2014	0.5	0.4	0.4	0.5	0.6	0.6	0.6	0.6	0.6	0.6	0.6	0.6	0.6
2015	0.5	0.5	0.5	0.5	0.6	0.6	0.6	0.6	0.6	0.6	0.6	0.6	0.6

1. Employment by Industry: Connecticut, 2005–2015—*Continued*

(Numbers in thousands, not seasonally adjusted)

Industry and year	January	February	March	April	May	June	July	August	September	October	November	December	Annual average
Construction													
2005	60.9	59.6	60.5	65.2	67.1	69.0	70.0	70.1	68.9	67.7	67.2	65.1	65.9
2006	60.9	60.4	61.9	66.0	67.8	69.8	70.9	71.3	70.2	69.8	68.9	67.6	67.1
2007	62.6	60.7	62.4	67.1	69.7	71.9	72.7	72.9	71.9	71.7	71.0	68.8	68.6
2008	63.0	61.9	62.9	66.2	67.5	68.4	68.6	68.4	67.1	65.8	63.5	60.5	65.3
2009	53.8	52.0	51.8	53.7	55.5	56.7	56.8	56.6	56.1	55.2	54.2	52.2	54.6
2010	44.3	42.9	43.6	49.1	50.9	52.3	53.3	53.7	53.1	52.9	52.6	50.9	50.0
2011	45.6	45.2	45.9	50.1	52.1	53.8	54.7	55.0	54.5	54.1	54.2	52.0	51.4
2012	47.1	46.2	47.1	50.0	51.3	52.8	53.9	54.1	53.8	54.2	53.4	52.4	51.4
2013	47.7	46.9	48.0	52.0	54.5	55.7	56.8	57.1	56.7	56.2	55.7	53.5	53.4
2014	48.6	48.0	48.8	53.9	56.5	57.9	59.4	59.7	59.2	59.4	58.3	56.7	55.5
2015	52.0	50.7	51.5	56.3	59.2	60.5	60.6	61.1	60.5	60.4	59.7	56.8	57.4
Manufacturing													
2005	196.0	195.3	195.6	195.4	195.5	196.8	194.4	193.9	193.5	193.5	193.5	194.0	194.8
2006	193.4	193.3	190.5	193.8	193.7	195.4	193.6	193.1	192.4	191.8	192.1	192.9	193.0
2007	191.3	191.2	191.3	190.1	190.1	191.9	190.2	190.3	189.4	188.7	189.0	189.2	190.2
2008	188.2	187.3	187.2	187.4	188.0	189.2	187.2	187.1	186.3	185.2	184.1	182.8	186.7
2009	178.9	176.0	174.4	172.4	171.5	171.7	168.6	167.7	167.5	166.2	165.7	165.7	170.5
2010	163.6	162.9	163.3	163.5	164.5	166.3	165.9	165.4	165.8	165.4	165.4	165.7	164.8
2011	164.5	164.5	165.0	164.9	165.3	166.9	166.5	166.4	165.6	165.1	164.9	165.3	165.4
2012	164.2	164.3	164.1	163.7	164.2	165.6	164.7	164.5	163.1	163.0	162.9	163.5	164.0
2013	162.7	162.7	162.6	162.5	162.8	164.1	163.6	162.8	161.7	161.4	160.8	161.2	162.4
2014	160.1	159.8	159.6	159.3	159.0	160.1	160.0	159.8	158.7	158.9	158.7	159.0	159.4
2015	158.2	158.0	158.4	158.4	158.8	160.5	160.0	159.8	159.1	158.8	158.9	158.6	159.0
Trade, Transportation, and Utilities													
2005	306.2	302.4	302.7	304.5	306.1	308.5	302.3	301.0	305.3	306.3	313.6	320.6	306.6
2006	307.8	301.5	303.4	304.8	306.5	309.3	302.4	301.2	304.6	307.4	315.0	321.3	307.1
2007	307.4	301.5	302.8	302.5	307.6	311.1	304.4	302.9	306.6	308.8	316.4	323.1	307.9
2008	310.5	303.9	304.7	304.0	306.7	308.8	301.9	300.4	303.4	303.7	308.2	312.2	305.7
2009	296.1	290.1	288.1	283.4	288.9	291.1	283.6	282.5	285.8	287.5	293.0	297.6	289.0
2010	283.3	278.3	279.1	279.3	285.3	289.1	284.0	283.3	284.9	288.4	294.6	300.3	285.8
2011	286.5	283.0	283.2	287.0	288.9	291.6	285.9	285.3	287.5	289.2	295.3	301.5	288.7
2012	290.4	285.2	287.0	286.3	291.0	293.7	287.2	286.7	289.9	293.1	300.7	304.1	291.3
2013	291.4	285.6	288.3	290.7	293.5	296.6	290.6	290.7	292.9	295.9	303.1	307.5	293.9
2014	294.5	289.6	290.9	292.8	295.6	298.1	292.0	291.2	294.1	297.2	304.1	309.0	295.8
2015	295.6	290.1	291.3	292.0	297.0	300.2	292.7	291.8	295.6	298.3	306.1	311.6	296.9
Wholesale Trade													
2005	65.7	65.4	65.6	65.9	66.3	66.7	66.8	66.8	66.9	66.9	67.1	67.5	66.5
2006	66.9	66.8	67.1	67.5	67.7	68.1	67.7	67.6	67.3	67.7	67.7	67.9	67.5
2007	67.5	67.5	67.5	67.7	67.9	68.6	68.5	68.6	68.7	68.7	68.7	69.5	68.3
2008	69.2	69.1	69.5	69.4	69.8	70.0	69.4	69.1	68.9	68.7	68.6	68.4	69.2
2009	67.2	66.5	65.9	65.2	65.1	65.1	64.6	64.4	64.2	63.7	63.4	63.6	64.9
2010	61.9	61.6	61.9	62.3	62.7	63.3	63.1	63.2	62.8	62.7	63.1	63.4	62.7
2011	62.2	62.3	62.4	63.0	63.2	63.7	63.5	63.4	63.1	62.9	62.8	63.1	63.0
2012	62.5	62.5	62.7	63.0	63.3	63.7	63.3	63.1	62.8	63.3	63.1	63.1	63.0
2013	62.3	62.2	62.6	62.8	63.0	63.4	63.3	63.1	62.9	63.0	63.0	63.2	62.9
2014	62.3	62.1	62.3	62.7	63.0	63.3	63.1	62.9	62.6	62.6	62.5	62.8	62.7
2015	62.1	62.0	62.2	62.5	62.9	63.2	62.8	62.6	62.4	62.5	62.8	63.6	62.6
Retail Trade													
2005	193.0	189.3	189.1	190.1	191.0	192.4	190.2	189.8	189.2	190.4	196.7	202.2	192.0
2006	192.3	186.4	187.8	188.7	189.8	191.9	189.6	189.4	188.4	190.5	197.8	202.4	191.3
2007	191.1	185.5	186.7	186.4	190.6	192.9	190.4	190.0	188.7	190.7	198.0	202.7	191.1
2008	192.9	186.5	186.8	185.8	187.9	189.5	186.7	186.8	185.1	185.6	190.1	193.3	188.1
2009	181.2	176.3	175.2	173.9	177.1	179.5	176.5	176.8	175.9	178.0	183.7	186.9	178.4
2010	176.6	172.0	172.5	173.6	177.0	179.8	178.7	178.3	176.2	179.6	184.9	188.9	178.2
2011	179.1	175.4	175.3	178.0	179.2	180.9	179.1	179.5	177.9	179.8	185.7	190.3	180.0
2012	181.8	176.7	178.0	177.9	180.9	182.8	180.5	180.5	179.1	181.7	189.0	191.3	181.7
2013	181.8	177.1	178.0	179.8	181.9	184.1	182.4	183.2	181.0	183.8	190.4	193.4	183.1
2014	183.9	179.4	180.2	181.6	183.5	185.5	183.6	183.3	181.7	184.4	190.6	193.6	184.3
2015	184.2	179.4	180.1	180.4	184.0	186.4	183.3	183.6	182.1	184.3	191.0	193.3	184.3

1. Employment by Industry: Connecticut, 2005–2015—*Continued*

(Numbers in thousands, not seasonally adjusted)

Industry and year	January	February	March	April	May	June	July	August	September	October	November	December	Annual average
Transportation and Utilities													
2005	47.5	47.7	48.0	48.5	48.8	49.4	45.3	44.4	49.2	49.0	49.8	50.9	48.2
2006	48.6	48.3	48.5	48.6	49.0	49.3	45.1	44.2	48.9	49.2	49.5	51.0	48.4
2007	48.8	48.5	48.6	48.4	49.1	49.6	45.5	44.3	49.2	49.4	49.7	50.9	48.5
2008	48.4	48.3	48.4	48.8	49.0	49.3	45.8	44.5	49.4	49.4	49.5	50.5	48.4
2009	47.7	47.3	47.0	44.3	46.7	46.5	42.5	41.3	45.7	45.8	45.9	47.1	45.7
2010	44.8	44.7	44.7	43.4	45.6	46.0	42.2	41.8	45.9	46.1	46.6	48.0	45.0
2011	45.2	45.3	45.5	46.0	46.5	47.0	43.3	42.4	46.5	46.5	46.8	48.1	45.8
2012	46.1	46.0	46.3	45.4	46.8	47.2	43.4	43.1	48.0	48.1	48.6	49.7	46.6
2013	47.3	46.3	47.7	48.1	48.6	49.1	44.9	44.4	49.0	49.1	49.7	50.9	47.9
2014	48.3	48.1	48.4	48.5	49.1	49.3	45.3	45.0	49.8	50.2	51.0	52.6	48.8
2015	49.3	48.7	49.0	49.1	50.1	50.6	46.6	45.6	51.1	51.5	52.3	54.7	49.9
Information													
2005	38.5	38.6	38.3	38.2	38.2	38.5	38.2	38.0	37.6	37.5	37.7	37.8	38.1
2006	37.9	37.9	37.9	37.7	37.8	37.9	38.0	38.0	37.7	37.8	38.1	38.3	37.9
2007	37.5	37.9	37.7	38.0	39.0	38.6	38.8	38.9	39.2	39.0	38.1	38.2	38.4
2008	37.9	38.2	37.9	38.5	38.6	38.6	37.9	38.1	37.1	36.9	36.9	37.0	37.8
2009	36.4	36.3	35.5	35.1	34.6	34.5	34.3	34.0	33.3	32.7	32.8	32.3	34.3
2010	31.8	31.7	31.6	31.5	31.7	31.6	31.6	32.0	31.8	31.6	31.7	31.8	31.7
2011	31.5	31.5	31.5	31.4	31.2	31.3	31.4	31.4	31.1	31.0	31.3	31.1	31.3
2012	31.3	31.5	30.9	30.9	31.2	31.0	31.2	31.6	31.4	31.4	31.9	31.4	31.3
2013	31.5	32.3	32.0	31.6	32.2	32.3	32.4	32.4	31.8	31.8	32.1	32.1	32.0
2014	31.9	31.8	32.0	32.0	32.0	32.0	32.2	32.4	31.7	31.4	32.6	32.5	32.0
2015	32.1	32.1	32.2	32.4	32.5	32.6	32.4	32.7	32.2	32.8	32.6	32.8	32.5
Financial Activities													
2005	140.5	140.5	140.5	141.6	141.5	143.4	144.2	144.0	142.7	142.4	142.6	143.5	142.3
2006	143.0	142.7	142.9	142.9	143.4	145.1	145.6	145.8	144.5	144.6	145.1	145.6	144.3
2007	144.9	144.4	144.1	144.1	144.4	146.3	146.2	145.7	144.0	143.6	143.5	144.1	144.6
2008	143.0	143.3	144.0	143.2	143.5	145.3	144.8	144.9	142.8	142.0	142.1	142.0	143.4
2009	139.7	139.3	139.4	137.7	137.5	138.5	138.2	137.6	135.8	135.9	135.9	136.0	137.6
2010	134.1	134.1	134.4	133.9	134.3	136.2	136.7	137.0	135.2	135.1	135.6	135.8	135.2
2011	135.3	135.2	135.2	134.9	134.9	135.5	136.6	136.3	134.4	133.8	133.9	134.0	135.0
2012	132.9	132.7	133.0	132.7	133.0	134.7	134.8	134.1	132.6	132.5	132.2	132.1	133.1
2013	131.6	131.1	130.8	130.4	130.2	132.0	132.2	131.5	129.5	129.0	129.0	129.2	130.5
2014	128.1	127.7	127.4	127.4	128.3	129.7	130.3	130.0	128.7	128.8	129.1	129.3	128.7
2015	128.9	128.7	129.0	129.4	129.8	131.4	131.7	131.4	129.5	129.8	130.3	130.5	130.0
Professional and Business Services													
2005	194.0	195.2	197.3	201.1	201.2	205.1	204.4	204.3	205.3	204.2	205.1	206.0	201.9
2006	198.0	200.5	202.8	206.5	206.7	210.9	207.0	208.2	208.8	207.7	208.3	210.3	206.3
2007	201.4	202.4	203.6	208.1	209.7	213.4	209.4	210.3	209.9	210.4	210.9	212.6	208.5
2008	206.1	205.8	207.5	210.4	210.1	212.8	209.5	208.8	207.3	205.1	203.4	202.4	207.4
2009	195.0	192.4	191.1	193.0	192.4	193.4	190.5	191.1	190.5	191.4	191.6	192.7	192.1
2010	181.8	184.0	185.1	193.2	193.5	195.9	195.5	195.2	194.9	196.1	195.7	196.1	192.3
2011	190.4	192.3	191.9	199.0	198.7	200.9	200.2	199.9	200.3	201.2	202.9	203.2	198.4
2012	196.7	197.2	200.7	205.2	205.2	207.3	206.6	206.5	206.4	206.5	207.0	206.4	204.3
2013	198.7	200.8	201.3	206.8	207.8	210.3	209.8	211.3	210.2	210.8	211.3	210.4	207.5
2014	203.8	205.0	205.9	212.7	214.5	216.0	214.7	214.5	213.5	214.9	215.6	215.8	212.2
2015	209.9	211.4	211.9	216.8	218.2	220.6	218.5	217.9	217.2	218.1	219.1	218.3	216.5
Education and Health Services													
2005	269.0	273.4	271.8	275.6	274.0	270.1	268.6	265.9	273.1	278.3	279.7	279.8	273.3
2006	274.7	278.4	277.2	280.9	279.5	276.1	275.8	273.7	280.6	284.8	286.4	287.2	279.6
2007	282.1	286.6	285.2	289.3	287.5	285.9	283.8	281.3	288.5	293.0	294.7	295.4	287.8
2008	290.7	295.8	295.3	297.9	296.2	294.4	292.2	289.8	296.8	302.2	304.6	304.7	296.7
2009	299.1	304.3	301.6	302.8	301.9	299.0	298.4	296.3	302.3	306.7	307.5	308.4	302.4
2010	301.8	304.9	304.4	308.8	307.3	304.1	302.9	300.6	308.0	312.8	313.9	313.8	306.9
2011	310.1	313.0	312.5	315.8	314.7	310.9	308.8	306.7	314.0	315.8	316.9	317.2	313.0
2012	312.6	317.5	316.6	317.8	317.9	314.9	311.9	310.1	317.9	321.2	322.3	324.1	317.1
2013	315.9	318.8	319.8	323.0	321.1	318.6	315.4	314.4	321.5	324.7	327.1	324.5	320.4
2014	319.7	321.1	321.5	326.2	324.9	322.2	319.5	318.5	325.8	328.9	330.6	330.7	324.1
2015	324.8	326.2	325.3	327.8	327.1	325.1	322.0	319.8	325.2	330.4	333.0	331.9	326.6

1. Employment by Industry: Connecticut, 2005–2015—*Continued*

(Numbers in thousands, not seasonally adjusted)

Industry and year	January	February	March	April	May	June	July	August	September	October	November	December	Annual average
Leisure and Hospitality													
2005	119.1	119.5	121.5	127.6	133.0	138.5	139.5	138.8	132.8	128.6	126.9	127.7	129.5
2006	122.1	121.8	124.8	129.3	135.2	141.6	142.8	141.7	135.7	133.1	130.6	132.3	132.6
2007	125.4	125.2	126.5	131.4	138.5	144.4	146.4	146.0	139.5	136.1	135.0	134.5	135.7
2008	127.5	128.3	130.3	134.8	142.7	147.1	147.4	146.1	140.7	136.8	133.3	133.0	137.3
2009	124.2	124.9	125.9	129.9	138.1	142.2	143.8	141.9	137.8	133.7	131.0	130.9	133.7
2010	120.3	121.3	123.3	130.8	137.4	141.0	144.4	143.1	139.1	135.8	133.6	133.3	133.6
2011	124.3	125.7	127.1	133.6	139.7	144.8	147.9	146.4	142.3	139.5	136.6	137.1	137.1
2012	130.4	131.0	133.8	138.6	145.4	151.6	152.1	150.9	145.3	143.3	141.2	142.3	142.2
2013	134.3	132.7	137.4	144.5	151.4	156.8	157.9	156.2	150.2	147.8	146.6	145.8	146.8
2014	139.8	138.7	142.3	147.4	154.0	159.4	160.1	158.1	152.5	150.4	148.1	148.0	149.9
2015	141.1	140.0	143.1	148.1	155.7	160.9	161.5	158.5	153.3	153.3	151.7	150.8	151.5
Other Services													
2005	61.6	61.7	62.1	62.7	62.9	64.1	64.1	63.5	62.5	62.5	62.7	63.4	62.8
2006	62.1	61.8	62.4	63.2	63.8	64.5	65.2	64.8	63.8	64.2	64.2	64.6	63.7
2007	63.4	63.2	63.6	63.9	64.1	65.3	65.5	64.9	64.0	63.8	63.8	64.0	64.1
2008	62.8	62.7	63.0	63.2	63.7	64.5	64.0	63.7	62.5	62.6	62.4	62.3	63.1
2009	61.4	60.9	61.1	61.0	61.3	62.2	62.1	61.6	61.1	60.7	60.7	61.0	61.3
2010	59.4	59.1	59.6	59.9	60.5	61.6	62.2	61.9	60.6	60.6	60.5	60.6	60.5
2011	59.3	59.3	59.5	60.2	60.6	61.7	61.8	61.5	60.0	59.5	59.8	60.2	60.3
2012	59.9	60.0	60.1	60.6	61.1	62.3	63.0	62.7	61.7	62.1	62.3	62.0	61.5
2013	60.7	60.8	61.4	61.6	62.2	63.1	63.4	63.0	61.8	61.5	61.7	62.0	61.9
2014	61.3	61.2	61.8	62.4	62.9	64.0	64.5	64.2	63.1	63.3	63.2	63.4	62.9
2015	62.6	62.5	63.1	63.4	64.3	65.1	65.5	65.5	63.9	63.6	63.9	64.9	64.0
Government													
2005	243.9	249.3	248.8	251.0	250.2	247.0	227.5	230.8	245.6	251.6	254.2	254.3	246.2
2006	248.0	251.8	251.6	252.6	252.2	247.2	230.5	235.2	246.3	252.6	255.5	255.9	248.3
2007	249.9	254.8	254.2	254.7	254.4	250.9	233.3	236.6	250.6	258.4	261.1	260.4	251.6
2008	255.0	260.1	259.1	259.4	260.0	254.7	236.2	238.7	252.5	259.9	262.2	260.5	254.9
2009	254.0	258.0	257.4	257.2	257.3	250.7	231.4	232.6	246.5	252.5	255.5	254.1	250.6
2010	248.2	252.1	250.2	249.7	256.4	246.3	230.2	231.4	242.8	249.7	251.2	250.3	246.5
2011	243.4	247.5	247.5	249.7	247.3	239.2	227.0	225.8	241.0	246.8	248.2	248.2	242.6
2012	240.8	246.7	246.4	245.2	243.7	238.1	225.4	225.6	239.7	244.4	247.3	247.7	240.9
2013	242.6	243.7	244.4	245.2	245.6	244.9	230.3	225.9	236.3	241.1	244.1	243.3	240.6
2014	239.4	241.8	243.2	245.0	245.7	243.2	225.9	227.3	238.3	242.6	245.6	244.5	240.2
2015	240.0	241.7	242.5	243.4	244.5	241.2	224.5	225.6	236.9	241.6	244.3	243.5	239.1

2. Average Weekly Hours by Selected Industry: Connecticut, 2011–2015

(Not seasonally adjusted)

Industry and year	January	February	March	April	May	June	July	August	September	October	November	December	Annual average
Total Private													
2011	33.2	33.6	33.7	33.7	34.0	33.8	33.9	34.1	34.1	34.4	34.1	34.2	33.9
2012	34.2	33.8	33.9	34.3	33.7	33.8	34.0	33.9	34.3	34.0	34.0	34.2	34.0
2013	33.2	33.0	33.2	33.6	33.6	34.0	33.6	33.6	34.1	33.7	33.6	33.6	33.6
2014	33.2	32.8	33.6	33.6	33.5	33.8	33.7	33.8	33.9	33.9	34.2	33.8	33.7
2015	33.5	33.4	33.6	33.5	33.3	33.3	33.4	34.0	33.4	33.7	33.8	33.6	33.5
Goods-Producing													
2011	36.8	38.1	38.5	38.5	38.6	38.7	38.8	39.1	39.0	39.0	39.2	39.4	38.6
2012	39.0	39.2	39.2	39.6	38.8	39.3	38.8	39.0	39.5	39.3	39.4	40.0	39.3
2013	39.5	38.6	39.6	39.7	39.6	40.0	39.4	40.3	40.4	39.8	39.7	39.6	39.7
2014	39.3	37.8	39.7	39.2	39.4	39.8	39.5	39.3	39.6	39.7	40.5	39.8	39.5
2015	39.6	38.9	39.9	39.4	39.2	39.1	39.1	39.9	39.2	39.7	40.2	40.2	39.5
Construction													
2011	34.0	35.4	35.9	35.9	36.5	36.8	36.9	37.8	37.2	36.6	36.3	37.1	36.4
2012	35.9	36.5	36.7	37.6	37.4	37.5	37.4	37.6	38.7	38.2	38.5	38.7	37.6
2013	38.7	37.6	38.7	38.8	39.1	37.9	38.6	39.8	39.4	37.7	37.7	35.9	38.3
2014	36.7	34.5	36.2	36.5	37.4	37.6	38.0	38.1	38.8	38.5	39.1	37.9	37.5
2015	38.2	36.3	38.6	39.0	39.7	38.8	39.6	39.7	38.6	40.2	39.2	39.8	39.0
Manufacturing													
2011	38.2	39.3	39.5	39.5	39.5	39.6	39.7	39.8	39.9	40.1	40.4	40.4	39.7
2012	40.1	40.1	40.0	40.3	39.4	40.0	39.4	39.6	39.9	39.8	39.9	40.6	39.9
2013	39.8	38.9	39.9	40.0	39.8	40.6	39.6	40.4	40.7	40.4	40.4	40.9	40.1
2014	40.3	39.0	40.4	39.7	39.8	40.3	39.8	39.6	39.8	40.1	41.0	40.5	40.0
2015	40.1	40.0	40.6	39.8	39.1	39.3	38.9	40.0	39.6	40.2	41.3	41.0	40.0
Trade, Transportation, and Utilities													
2011	33.9	34.5	34.4	34.5	34.7	34.3	34.2	34.4	34.8	35.1	35.0	35.3	34.6
2012	34.8	34.6	34.7	34.9	34.8	34.4	34.8	34.2	34.9	34.6	34.8	34.7	34.7
2013	33.7	33.5	33.8	34.0	34.0	34.0	33.7	33.6	33.8	33.4	33.4	33.9	33.7
2014	33.1	32.2	33.0	32.9	33.0	33.2	33.5	33.5	33.7	33.1	33.3	33.5	33.2
2015	32.6	32.4	32.7	33.0	32.9	32.8	33.1	33.4	33.6	33.4	32.8	33.1	33.0
Financial Activities													
2011	37.3	37.0	37.1	36.8	37.4	36.8	36.8	36.8	37.0	37.7	37.0	37.0	37.1
2012	37.9	36.6	36.7	37.4	36.6	36.9	38.1	37.1	37.7	36.9	37.1	37.9	37.2
2013	36.6	37.3	37.2	37.1	36.9	37.7	36.5	36.7	37.9	37.1	37.2	37.9	37.2
2014	37.3	38.2	38.3	37.2	37.5	38.2	37.4	37.8	38.0	38.3	38.9	38.3	38.0
2015	38.2	39.1	39.0	38.2	38.1	38.1	37.9	39.0	37.9	38.1	39.4	37.5	38.4
Professional and Business Services													
2011	33.7	33.8	34.0	34.0	35.2	35.1	35.0	34.8	35.0	34.9	34.4	34.4	34.5
2012	34.7	33.8	34.3	35.0	34.8	35.2	35.4	35.0	35.7	34.7	34.9	35.3	34.9
2013	33.7	33.7	34.1	35.0	35.0	35.8	34.7	34.2	35.7	35.0	34.5	34.7	34.7
2014	33.7	34.2	35.0	36.0	35.5	35.9	35.8	35.4	36.0	36.3	36.4	35.5	35.5
2015	34.8	34.9	35.1	34.7	34.7	34.8	34.6	35.2	34.2	34.7	35.2	35.0	34.8
Education and Health Services													
2011	30.2	30.6	30.7	30.9	30.9	30.8	31.0	31.2	31.0	31.1	30.9	31.3	30.9
2012	31.4	31.0	31.0	31.3	31.0	30.9	31.0	31.2	30.9	31.2	31.0	31.4	31.1
2013	31.2	31.2	31.2	31.3	31.1	31.4	31.3	31.2	31.4	31.2	31.2	31.0	31.2
2014	31.3	30.9	31.2	31.2	31.2	31.3	31.4	31.7	31.4	31.4	31.4	31.2	31.3
2015	31.4	31.1	31.2	31.2	31.0	31.2	31.4	31.7	31.3	31.5	31.5	31.1	31.3
Leisure and Hospitality													
2011	25.0	26.4	26.2	26.4	26.6	26.7	27.0	26.8	26.7	27.0	27.1	26.9	26.6
2012	26.0	26.1	26.1	26.3	25.8	26.0	26.5	26.8	26.4	26.0	25.5	26.1	26.1
2013	24.5	24.4	24.9	26.0	26.2	26.3	26.8	26.8	26.7	26.1	25.7	24.8	25.8
2014	24.6	24.1	25.0	25.6	25.6	25.2	25.7	26.2	26.1	26.0	26.2	25.7	25.5
2015	25.3	25.0	25.5	26.1	26.0	25.8	26.0	26.5	25.6	26.0	25.8	25.7	25.8
Other Services													
2011	29.4	29.9	29.2	29.9	30.8	30.5	31.8	32.0	31.0	32.1	31.1	31.2	30.7
2012	31.9	31.7	31.8	32.0	30.8	31.2	31.3	32.1	31.6	31.2	31.0	30.7	31.4
2013	30.5	30.2	30.0	29.8	30.5	31.1	31.7	31.7	31.6	31.3	31.7	30.7	30.9
2014	31.0	30.0	31.0	30.7	30.9	31.2	30.5	30.5	30.2	28.9	30.2	29.9	30.4
2015	29.2	29.2	28.9	29.0	28.8	28.9	29.8	29.5	29.5	30.4	30.6	31.1	29.6

3. Average Hourly Earnings by Selected Industry: Connecticut, 2011–2015

(Dollars, not seasonally adjusted)

Industry and year	January	February	March	April	May	June	July	August	September	October	November	December	Annual average
Total Private													
2011	28.39	28.35	28.29	28.21	28.24	27.88	28.15	28.06	28.14	28.47	28.37	28.32	28.24
2012	28.72	28.33	28.24	28.50	27.96	27.77	27.91	27.72	28.10	27.93	28.22	28.31	28.14
2013	28.33	28.32	28.01	28.08	27.89	28.08	27.82	27.79	27.93	27.72	27.60	28.02	27.96
2014	27.84	28.40	28.15	27.98	27.82	28.13	27.90	27.99	28.26	28.33	28.67	28.47	28.16
2015	28.54	29.14	29.04	28.73	28.68	28.75	28.80	29.35	29.49	29.49	29.89	29.80	29.15
Goods-Producing													
2011	30.44	30.32	30.43	30.26	29.85	30.27	30.13	30.22	30.26	30.41	30.15	30.75	30.29
2012	30.87	30.31	30.53	30.73	30.33	29.93	30.16	30.03	30.15	30.06	30.06	30.20	30.28
2013	30.50	30.22	29.95	29.68	29.93	29.97	30.09	29.91	30.18	29.96	30.18	30.31	30.07
2014	30.27	30.41	30.02	30.05	30.14	30.53	30.38	30.35	30.47	30.47	30.82	30.91	30.41
2015	31.01	30.88	30.84	30.74	30.52	30.27	30.61	31.00	31.25	31.39	31.55	31.67	30.98
Construction													
2011	29.64	29.54	29.69	28.92	28.35	28.50	29.14	28.79	29.08	29.12	29.33	29.15	29.08
2012	28.31	28.42	28.77	28.64	28.60	28.46	28.70	28.55	28.75	29.14	29.71	29.58	28.82
2013	29.63	29.72	29.34	28.88	29.47	29.25	29.29	29.61	30.08	29.71	29.65	30.39	29.58
2014	29.95	30.87	30.20	30.13	30.34	30.25	31.06	31.24	30.67	31.11	30.72	31.30	30.68
2015	31.28	30.72	31.84	31.31	31.05	30.76	31.19	30.78	30.95	31.37	31.07	30.93	31.10
Manufacturing													
2011	30.60	30.47	30.58	30.61	30.29	30.80	30.42	30.47	30.41	30.64	30.26	31.02	30.55
2012	31.39	30.66	30.86	31.14	30.68	30.22	30.47	30.36	30.47	30.24	30.05	30.32	30.57
2013	30.70	30.32	30.07	29.87	30.01	30.10	30.26	29.93	30.15	29.99	30.32	30.25	30.16
2014	30.36	30.27	29.92	30.01	30.04	30.59	30.06	29.95	30.34	30.18	30.88	30.80	30.29
2015	30.93	31.23	30.60	30.67	30.32	30.09	30.38	30.92	31.23	31.28	31.60	31.81	30.93
Trade, Transportation, and Utilities													
2011	24.25	24.73	24.46	24.89	25.38	25.06	25.49	25.18	25.74	25.69	26.06	25.11	25.18
2012	25.40	25.30	25.14	25.65	25.00	24.88	25.32	25.33	25.59	24.97	25.35	24.97	25.24
2013	25.31	25.06	24.32	24.59	24.22	24.41	24.25	24.11	24.21	24.02	23.39	23.67	24.29
2014	23.52	23.89	23.41	24.03	23.70	23.84	23.88	23.64	24.12	24.15	24.21	23.85	23.86
2015	24.45	25.08	24.57	24.30	24.53	24.23	24.18	24.23	24.89	25.01	25.29	25.17	24.67
Financial Activities													
2011	43.10	42.87	42.82	42.75	43.56	42.39	42.18	42.58	40.61	42.77	41.54	41.60	42.40
2012	41.80	40.80	41.01	42.25	40.99	41.46	42.28	41.26	41.70	40.79	41.65	41.70	41.48
2013	40.95	40.74	41.71	43.33	42.66	44.08	43.50	43.44	44.62	43.44	43.17	43.93	42.97
2014	43.82	44.36	44.95	44.20	43.89	45.07	43.84	43.29	43.24	43.00	44.21	42.56	43.87
2015	42.42	43.82	44.04	43.07	43.31	43.61	44.33	46.01	44.45	44.49	44.79	44.95	44.11
Professional and Business Services													
2011	31.44	30.97	30.68	30.55	30.12	29.45	29.99	29.99	30.11	30.39	30.35	30.48	30.36
2012	31.19	30.92	30.58	30.54	30.28	29.77	29.88	29.73	30.51	29.84	30.00	30.40	30.29
2013	30.82	31.00	30.82	30.45	30.47	30.33	30.10	30.40	30.48	30.39	30.56	30.98	30.56
2014	31.42	32.51	32.25	30.98	31.10	31.61	31.20	31.77	32.23	32.33	32.22	32.52	31.84
2015	32.07	32.67	33.10	33.11	32.76	33.84	33.97	34.71	34.50	33.96	34.46	33.95	33.60
Education and Health Services													
2011	26.95	26.27	26.17	26.19	26.18	26.27	26.78	26.34	26.41	26.47	26.56	26.59	26.43
2012	26.87	26.44	26.41	26.27	26.10	26.00	26.06	26.04	26.14	25.93	26.09	26.17	26.21
2013	25.89	25.74	25.24	25.31	25.15	25.01	24.98	25.03	25.03	25.02	24.91	25.38	25.22
2014	24.73	25.07	24.86	25.01	24.84	24.84	25.08	25.31	25.25	25.37	25.59	25.91	25.16
2015	25.72	26.12	25.94	26.05	26.06	26.18	26.05	26.06	26.45	26.39	26.67	27.10	26.24
Leisure and Hospitality													
2011	15.55	15.46	15.49	15.42	15.38	14.96	15.02	14.90	15.21	15.03	15.11	15.17	15.21
2012	14.98	15.18	15.00	15.26	15.18	15.06	14.93	14.85	15.16	15.20	15.29	15.52	15.13
2013	15.59	15.70	15.59	15.41	15.37	14.99	14.89	14.74	15.13	15.15	15.15	15.32	15.23
2014	15.07	15.45	15.34	15.45	15.36	15.37	15.31	15.42	15.62	15.98	16.07	16.10	15.55
2015	16.13	16.49	16.30	16.44	16.37	16.02	15.81	15.89	15.93	16.33	16.60	16.63	16.24
Other Services													
2011	22.60	21.56	21.22	21.03	20.83	20.57	19.61	19.25	19.88	19.30	19.38	19.12	20.33
2012	19.89	20.14	19.87	19.56	20.08	20.00	19.78	19.93	20.17	20.48	20.10	21.00	20.08
2013	21.42	21.93	21.28	21.48	21.72	21.29	20.81	21.03	21.42	21.64	21.66	21.97	21.47
2014	21.97	22.56	23.32	22.72	23.01	22.37	22.17	22.15	22.49	22.14	22.51	22.46	22.49
2015	22.27	22.66	22.19	21.68	22.23	21.98	20.95	21.13	21.58	22.24	22.34	22.08	21.94

4. Average Weekly Earnings by Selected Industry: Connecticut, 2011–2015

(Dollars, not seasonally adjusted)

Industry and year	January	February	March	April	May	June	July	August	September	October	November	December	Annual average
Total Private													
2011	942.55	952.56	953.37	950.68	960.16	942.34	954.29	956.85	959.57	979.37	967.42	968.54	957.34
2012	982.22	957.55	957.34	977.55	942.25	938.63	948.94	939.71	963.83	949.62	959.48	968.20	956.76
2013	940.56	934.56	929.93	943.49	937.10	954.72	934.75	933.74	952.41	934.16	927.36	941.47	939.46
2014	924.29	931.52	945.84	940.13	931.97	950.79	940.23	946.06	958.01	960.39	980.51	962.29	948.99
2015	956.09	973.28	975.74	962.46	955.04	957.38	961.92	997.90	984.97	993.81	1,010.28	1,001.28	976.53
Goods-Producing													
2011	1,120.19	1,155.19	1,171.56	1,165.01	1,152.21	1,171.45	1,169.04	1,181.60	1,180.14	1,185.99	1,181.88	1,211.55	1,169.19
2012	1,203.93	1,188.15	1,196.78	1,216.91	1,176.80	1,176.25	1,170.21	1,171.17	1,190.93	1,181.36	1,184.36	1,208.00	1,190.00
2013	1,204.75	1,166.49	1,186.02	1,178.30	1,185.23	1,198.80	1,185.55	1,205.37	1,219.27	1,192.41	1,198.15	1,200.28	1,193.78
2014	1,189.61	1,149.50	1,191.79	1,177.96	1,187.52	1,215.09	1,200.01	1,192.76	1,206.61	1,209.66	1,248.21	1,230.22	1,201.20
2015	1,228.00	1,201.23	1,230.52	1,211.16	1,196.38	1,183.56	1,196.85	1,236.90	1,225.00	1,246.18	1,268.31	1,273.13	1,223.71
Construction													
2011	1,007.76	1,045.72	1,065.87	1,038.23	1,034.78	1,048.80	1,075.27	1,088.26	1,081.78	1,065.79	1,064.68	1,081.47	1,058.51
2012	1,016.33	1,037.33	1,055.86	1,076.86	1,069.64	1,067.25	1,073.38	1,073.48	1,112.63	1,113.15	1,143.84	1,144.75	1,083.63
2013	1,146.68	1,117.47	1,135.46	1,120.54	1,152.28	1,108.58	1,130.59	1,178.48	1,185.15	1,120.07	1,117.81	1,091.00	1,132.91
2014	1,099.17	1,065.02	1,093.24	1,099.75	1,134.72	1,137.40	1,180.28	1,190.24	1,190.00	1,197.74	1,201.15	1,186.27	1,150.50
2015	1,194.90	1,115.14	1,229.02	1,221.09	1,232.69	1,193.49	1,235.12	1,221.97	1,194.67	1,261.07	1,217.94	1,231.01	1,212.90
Manufacturing													
2011	1,168.92	1,197.47	1,207.91	1,209.10	1,196.46	1,219.68	1,207.67	1,212.71	1,213.36	1,228.66	1,222.50	1,253.21	1,212.84
2012	1,258.74	1,229.47	1,234.40	1,254.94	1,208.79	1,208.80	1,200.52	1,202.26	1,215.75	1,203.55	1,199.00	1,230.99	1,219.74
2013	1,221.86	1,179.45	1,199.79	1,194.80	1,194.40	1,222.06	1,198.30	1,209.17	1,227.11	1,211.60	1,224.93	1,237.23	1,209.42
2014	1,223.51	1,180.53	1,208.77	1,191.40	1,195.59	1,232.78	1,196.39	1,186.02	1,207.53	1,210.22	1,266.08	1,247.40	1,211.60
2015	1,240.29	1,249.20	1,242.36	1,220.67	1,185.51	1,182.54	1,181.78	1,236.80	1,236.71	1,257.46	1,305.08	1,304.21	1,237.20
Trade, Transportation, and Utilities													
2011	822.08	853.19	841.42	858.71	880.69	859.56	871.76	866.19	895.75	901.72	912.10	886.38	871.23
2012	883.92	875.38	872.36	895.19	870.00	855.87	881.14	866.29	893.09	863.96	882.18	866.46	875.83
2013	852.95	839.51	822.02	836.06	823.48	829.94	817.23	810.10	818.30	802.27	781.23	802.41	818.57
2014	778.51	769.26	772.53	790.59	782.10	791.49	799.98	791.94	812.84	799.37	806.19	798.98	792.15
2015	797.07	812.59	803.44	801.90	807.04	794.74	800.36	809.28	836.30	835.33	829.51	833.13	814.11
Financial Activities													
2011	1,607.63	1,586.19	1,588.62	1,573.20	1,629.14	1,559.95	1,552.22	1,566.94	1,502.57	1,612.43	1,536.98	1,539.20	1,573.04
2012	1,584.22	1,493.28	1,505.07	1,580.15	1,500.23	1,529.87	1,610.87	1,530.75	1,572.09	1,505.15	1,545.22	1,580.43	1,543.06
2013	1,498.77	1,519.60	1,551.61	1,607.54	1,574.15	1,661.82	1,587.75	1,594.25	1,691.10	1,611.62	1,605.92	1,664.95	1,598.48
2014	1,634.49	1,694.55	1,721.59	1,644.24	1,645.88	1,721.67	1,639.62	1,636.36	1,643.12	1,646.90	1,719.77	1,630.05	1,667.06
2015	1,620.44	1,713.36	1,717.56	1,645.27	1,650.11	1,661.54	1,680.11	1,794.39	1,684.66	1,695.07	1,764.73	1,685.63	1,693.82
Professional and Business Services													
2011	1,059.53	1,046.79	1,043.12	1,038.70	1,060.22	1,033.70	1,049.65	1,043.65	1,053.85	1,060.61	1,044.04	1,048.51	1,047.42
2012	1,082.29	1,045.10	1,048.89	1,068.90	1,053.74	1,047.90	1,057.75	1,040.55	1,089.21	1,035.45	1,047.00	1,073.12	1,057.12
2013	1,038.63	1,044.70	1,050.96	1,065.75	1,066.45	1,085.81	1,044.47	1,039.68	1,088.14	1,063.65	1,054.32	1,075.01	1,060.43
2014	1,058.85	1,111.84	1,128.75	1,115.28	1,104.05	1,134.80	1,116.96	1,124.66	1,160.28	1,173.58	1,172.81	1,154.46	1,130.32
2015	1,116.04	1,140.18	1,161.81	1,148.92	1,136.77	1,177.63	1,175.36	1,221.79	1,179.90	1,178.41	1,212.99	1,188.25	1,169.28
Education and Health Services													
2011	813.89	803.86	803.42	809.27	808.96	809.12	830.18	821.81	818.71	823.22	820.70	832.27	816.69
2012	843.72	819.64	818.71	822.25	809.10	803.40	807.86	812.45	807.73	809.02	808.79	821.74	815.13
2013	807.77	803.09	787.49	792.20	782.17	785.31	781.87	780.94	785.94	780.62	777.19	786.78	786.86
2014	774.05	774.66	775.63	780.31	775.01	777.49	787.51	802.33	792.85	796.62	803.53	808.39	787.51
2015	807.61	812.33	809.33	812.76	807.86	816.82	817.97	826.10	827.89	831.29	840.11	842.81	821.31
Leisure and Hospitality													
2011	388.75	408.14	405.84	407.09	409.11	399.43	405.54	399.32	406.11	405.81	409.48	408.07	404.59
2012	389.48	396.20	391.50	401.34	391.64	391.56	395.65	397.98	400.22	395.20	389.90	405.07	394.89
2013	381.96	383.08	388.19	400.66	402.69	394.24	399.05	395.03	403.97	395.42	389.36	379.94	392.93
2014	370.72	372.35	383.50	395.52	393.22	387.32	393.47	404.00	407.68	415.48	421.03	413.77	396.53
2015	408.09	412.25	415.65	429.08	425.62	413.32	411.06	421.09	407.81	424.58	428.28	427.39	418.99
Other Services													
2011	664.44	644.64	619.62	628.80	641.56	627.39	623.60	616.00	616.28	619.53	602.72	596.54	624.13
2012	634.49	638.44	631.87	625.92	618.46	624.00	619.11	639.75	637.37	638.98	623.10	644.70	630.51
2013	653.31	662.29	638.40	640.10	662.46	662.12	659.68	666.65	676.87	677.33	686.62	674.48	663.42
2014	681.07	676.80	722.92	697.50	711.01	697.94	676.19	675.58	679.20	639.85	679.80	671.55	683.70
2015	650.28	661.67	641.29	628.72	640.22	635.22	624.31	623.34	636.61	676.10	683.60	686.69	649.42

DELAWARE
At a Glance

Population:
  2005 estimate: 845,150
  2010 census: 897,934
  2015 estimate: 945,934

Percent change in population:
  2005–2015: 11.9%
  2010–2015: 5.3%

Percent change in total nonfarm employment:
  2005–2015: 3.7%

Industry with the largest growth in employment, 2005–2015 (thousands):
  Education and health services, 19.8

Industry with the largest decline or smallest growth in employment, 2005–2015 (thousands):
  Mining, logging, and construction: –6.9

Civilian labor force:
  2005: 432,409
  2010: 434,419
  2015: 467,472

Unemployment rate and rank among states (highest to lowest):
  2005: 4.1%, 37th
  2010: 8.4%, 29th
  2015: 4.9%, 30th

Over-the-year change in unemployment rates:
  2012–2013: –0.5%
  2013–2014: –1.0%
  2014–2015: –0.8%

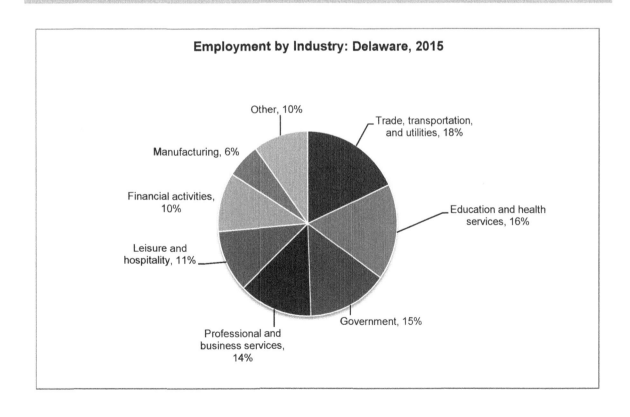

Employment by Industry: Delaware, 2015

Other, 10%
Trade, transportation, and utilities, 18%
Manufacturing, 6%
Financial activities, 10%
Education and health services, 16%
Leisure and hospitality, 11%
Government, 15%
Professional and business services, 14%

1. Employment by Industry: Delaware, 2005–2015

(Numbers in thousands, not seasonally adjusted)

Industry and year	January	February	March	April	May	June	July	August	September	October	November	December	Annual average
Total Nonfarm													
2005	418.6	419.5	424.4	430.6	434.9	436.3	436.0	436.2	437.4	437.6	442.5	441.3	432.9
2006	427.5	428.0	432.5	436.3	441.6	444.3	439.6	439.2	439.9	441.0	442.9	444.8	438.1
2007	428.7	427.6	432.8	436.7	442.3	445.8	441.7	441.1	440.2	440.5	444.3	445.7	439.0
2008	430.7	431.8	434.9	439.7	441.8	443.7	439.7	438.2	436.3	435.4	435.9	433.4	436.8
2009	415.6	414.1	415.0	416.9	422.1	421.5	416.7	415.6	414.9	416.1	415.7	414.8	416.6
2010	400.0	397.2	403.9	411.4	417.2	419.8	420.2	419.0	419.3	418.0	419.2	420.3	413.8
2011	406.7	407.7	411.6	419.5	420.1	421.5	420.5	418.5	419.6	418.3	420.0	420.8	417.1
2012	406.7	407.6	412.4	416.6	422.2	423.4	422.8	421.9	421.8	423.6	426.9	427.3	419.4
2013	412.8	414.9	419.4	425.0	430.0	432.4	432.5	433.0	432.4	434.7	439.1	436.9	428.6
2014	424.4	423.8	428.5	434.3	441.2	443.3	442.5	441.3	441.3	443.7	448.7	449.5	438.5
2015	434.6	434.5	439.2	442.5	451.0	453.5	454.8	451.1	450.9	454.4	458.6	460.2	448.8
Total Private													
2005	360.6	360.6	364.3	370.0	374.1	378.2	378.5	379.8	377.5	375.9	380.6	379.7	373.3
2006	367.6	366.9	370.1	373.8	378.3	384.7	381.2	382.1	379.5	378.8	380.3	382.3	377.1
2007	368.1	365.9	369.9	373.5	378.8	385.1	382.2	382.5	378.7	376.9	380.4	382.0	377.0
2008	368.6	369.0	370.9	375.2	377.2	382.2	379.4	378.6	373.6	371.2	371.9	369.6	374.0
2009	353.5	350.5	349.9	351.7	357.0	359.6	357.2	356.3	352.3	350.8	350.4	350.1	353.3
2010	338.0	334.2	339.2	346.1	350.8	356.4	358.7	358.7	355.6	353.2	353.8	355.1	350.0
2011	344.0	344.0	346.7	353.2	355.1	359.2	359.8	358.4	356.0	353.2	354.8	355.8	353.4
2012	344.5	343.7	347.3	351.6	356.8	360.9	362.0	362.1	358.4	358.7	361.8	362.2	355.8
2013	351.4	350.9	354.0	359.4	364.3	369.3	371.3	372.8	368.5	369.3	373.2	371.3	364.6
2014	359.9	358.2	362.2	368.3	374.9	379.9	380.6	380.9	376.7	377.7	382.6	383.3	373.8
2015	370.4	369.7	371.5	376.4	384.0	388.9	392.0	390.0	385.7	387.5	391.2	393.3	383.4
Goods-Producing													
2005	58.1	59.0	60.0	61.2	61.9	61.1	61.1	62.4	62.3	61.9	64.2	61.2	61.2
2006	61.7	61.3	62.0	62.7	63.1	64.1	63.0	63.7	63.8	63.7	63.2	62.8	62.9
2007	60.3	59.0	60.1	60.6	61.5	61.9	60.9	61.4	60.5	59.9	61.0	60.4	60.6
2008	57.3	58.1	58.0	58.6	57.6	58.6	56.9	56.8	55.5	54.7	55.4	53.9	56.8
2009	50.5	48.9	48.3	48.2	48.5	48.5	47.8	47.7	46.9	47.2	46.8	46.1	48.0
2010	44.4	42.9	43.9	45.4	45.5	46.3	45.9	46.1	45.8	45.8	45.6	45.5	45.3
2011	44.0	43.9	44.7	45.8	46.0	45.8	45.7	45.0	45.0	45.2	44.7	44.5	45.0
2012	43.0	42.7	42.9	43.7	44.3	44.5	45.2	45.0	44.9	44.7	44.8	44.6	44.2
2013	43.9	43.5	43.7	44.5	44.8	45.3	45.6	46.0	45.8	46.7	46.0	45.1	45.1
2014	44.1	44.1	45.0	45.8	46.6	47.4	47.6	47.7	47.5	47.7	47.8	47.6	46.6
2015	46.2	46.2	46.3	47.5	48.3	48.6	49.0	49.1	49.2	49.8	49.2	49.8	48.3
Service-Providing													
2005	360.5	360.5	364.4	369.4	373.0	375.2	374.9	373.8	375.1	375.7	378.3	380.1	371.7
2006	365.8	366.7	370.5	373.6	378.5	380.2	376.6	375.5	376.1	377.3	379.7	382.0	375.2
2007	368.4	368.6	372.7	376.1	380.8	383.9	380.8	379.7	379.7	380.6	383.3	385.3	378.3
2008	373.4	373.7	376.9	381.1	384.2	385.1	382.8	381.4	380.8	380.7	380.5	379.5	380.0
2009	365.1	365.2	366.7	368.7	373.6	373.0	368.9	367.9	368.0	368.9	368.9	368.7	368.6
2010	355.6	354.3	360.0	366.0	371.7	373.5	374.3	372.9	373.5	372.2	373.6	374.8	368.5
2011	362.7	363.8	366.9	373.7	374.1	375.7	374.8	373.5	374.6	373.1	375.3	376.3	372.0
2012	363.7	364.9	369.5	372.9	377.9	378.9	377.6	376.9	376.9	378.9	382.1	382.7	375.2
2013	368.9	371.4	375.7	380.5	385.2	387.1	386.9	387.0	386.6	388.0	393.1	391.8	383.5
2014	380.3	379.7	383.5	388.5	394.6	395.9	394.9	393.6	393.8	396.0	400.9	401.9	392.0
2015	388.4	388.3	392.9	395.0	402.7	404.9	405.8	402.0	401.7	404.6	409.4	410.4	400.5
Mining, Logging, and Construction													
2005	25.9	25.5	26.3	27.5	27.9	28.5	28.7	28.5	28.4	29.6	30.4	28.9	28.0
2006	28.0	27.8	28.3	29.3	29.6	30.5	30.1	30.2	30.1	30.1	29.5	29.1	29.4
2007	27.2	26.0	26.8	27.4	28.0	28.2	28.1	28.0	28.0	27.3	27.5	26.9	27.5
2008	25.7	25.1	25.3	26.3	26.1	26.1	25.8	25.6	24.7	23.8	23.6	22.7	25.1
2009	20.7	19.9	20.1	20.0	20.4	20.6	20.4	20.3	19.6	19.8	19.5	19.1	20.0
2010	18.0	17.1	18.0	19.3	19.6	20.1	19.9	20.1	19.8	20.0	20.0	19.9	19.3
2011	18.7	18.6	19.3	20.2	20.1	19.9	19.6	19.1	19.2	19.3	18.9	18.8	19.3
2012	17.7	17.3	17.4	18.1	18.5	18.7	19.1	19.1	19.0	19.1	19.3	19.2	18.5
2013	18.5	18.3	18.6	19.2	19.6	19.9	20.2	20.5	20.3	20.8	20.3	19.6	19.7
2014	18.9	18.7	19.4	20.0	20.7	21.2	21.4	21.3	21.0	21.0	21.0	20.8	20.5
2015	19.4	19.4	19.5	20.5	21.2	21.2	21.7	21.7	21.9	22.4	21.6	22.1	21.1

1. Employment by Industry: Delaware, 2005–2015—*Continued*

(Numbers in thousands, not seasonally adjusted)

Industry and year	January	February	March	April	May	June	July	August	September	October	November	December	Annual average
Manufacturing													
2005	32.2	33.5	33.7	33.7	34.0	32.6	32.4	33.9	33.9	32.3	33.8	32.3	33.2
2006	33.7	33.5	33.7	33.4	33.5	33.6	32.9	33.5	33.7	33.6	33.7	33.7	33.5
2007	33.1	33.0	33.3	33.2	33.5	33.7	32.8	33.4	32.5	32.6	33.5	33.5	33.2
2008	31.6	33.0	32.7	32.3	31.5	32.5	31.1	31.2	30.8	30.9	31.8	31.2	31.7
2009	29.8	29.0	28.2	28.2	28.1	27.9	27.4	27.4	27.3	27.4	27.3	27.0	27.9
2010	26.4	25.8	25.9	26.1	25.9	26.2	26.0	26.0	26.0	25.8	25.6	25.6	25.9
2011	25.3	25.3	25.4	25.6	25.9	25.9	26.1	25.9	25.8	25.9	25.8	25.7	25.7
2012	25.3	25.4	25.5	25.6	25.8	25.8	26.1	25.9	25.9	25.6	25.5	25.4	25.7
2013	25.4	25.2	25.1	25.3	25.2	25.4	25.4	25.5	25.5	25.9	25.7	25.5	25.4
2014	25.2	25.4	25.6	25.8	25.9	26.2	26.2	26.4	26.5	26.7	26.8	26.8	26.1
2015	26.8	26.8	26.8	27.0	27.1	27.4	27.3	27.4	27.3	27.4	27.6	27.7	27.2
Trade, Transportation, and Utilities													
2005	79.9	78.9	79.8	80.3	81.1	81.8	82.1	82.1	81.7	82.5	84.5	86.1	81.7
2006	81.1	80.1	80.9	81.7	82.8	83.5	83.0	82.4	81.9	82.5	84.7	85.6	82.5
2007	81.9	80.6	81.1	81.3	82.9	83.9	83.8	83.7	83.2	82.8	85.2	86.1	83.0
2008	81.5	80.4	80.9	80.4	81.3	81.9	81.3	80.9	80.3	80.7	81.7	82.6	81.2
2009	76.3	74.9	74.7	74.3	75.1	75.5	75.0	74.9	74.9	74.8	76.3	76.8	75.3
2010	72.6	71.2	72.2	73.2	74.5	75.2	75.0	74.8	74.8	75.1	77.1	78.0	74.5
2011	74.0	73.4	73.7	75.1	75.3	76.1	75.6	75.5	75.4	75.3	77.7	78.5	75.5
2012	74.4	73.4	74.3	74.6	75.9	76.1	75.8	75.7	75.3	76.2	79.1	79.4	75.9
2013	75.0	74.4	75.2	76.0	76.8	77.5	77.5	78.0	78.1	79.0	81.6	82.3	77.6
2014	77.7	76.8	77.3	78.1	78.9	79.8	79.9	80.4	79.9	80.4	82.7	84.0	79.7
2015	79.2	78.8	79.1	79.8	80.6	81.2	81.7	81.8	81.4	81.7	84.1	85.5	81.2
Wholesale Trade													
2005	14.8	14.8	14.9	14.9	14.9	14.8	14.8	14.9	14.8	15.0	15.1	15.3	14.9
2006	14.9	15.0	15.0	15.2	15.3	15.3	15.3	15.2	15.1	15.0	14.9	15.2	15.1
2007	14.8	14.7	14.7	14.9	15.0	15.1	15.2	15.2	15.0	14.8	14.9	14.9	14.9
2008	14.7	14.7	14.8	14.6	14.8	14.7	14.7	14.5	14.4	14.5	14.4	14.2	14.6
2009	13.7	13.6	13.5	13.5	13.4	13.2	13.2	13.1	12.9	12.9	12.8	12.7	13.2
2010	12.4	12.5	12.5	12.6	12.6	12.5	12.6	12.5	12.6	12.4	12.4	12.4	12.5
2011	12.5	12.6	12.5	12.6	12.5	12.6	12.6	12.6	12.5	12.5	12.5	12.5	12.5
2012	12.4	12.4	12.6	12.6	12.5	12.5	12.5	12.4	12.3	12.3	12.3	12.3	12.4
2013	12.0	12.1	12.2	12.2	12.3	12.3	12.2	12.2	12.2	12.0	12.1	12.2	12.2
2014	11.9	11.8	11.9	12.0	12.1	12.2	12.0	12.0	11.9	11.9	11.9	12.0	12.0
2015	11.7	11.7	11.8	11.8	11.9	12.0	11.9	11.9	11.8	11.7	11.8	11.8	11.8
Retail Trade													
2005	52.0	51.1	51.6	52.3	53.1	53.8	54.4	54.4	53.4	53.7	55.6	57.0	53.5
2006	52.9	51.7	52.4	52.9	53.6	54.2	54.3	53.9	52.8	53.2	55.7	56.1	53.6
2007	53.1	52.1	52.7	52.8	53.9	54.9	55.1	54.9	54.2	54.1	56.5	57.2	54.3
2008	53.4	52.2	52.5	52.2	52.8	53.6	53.2	53.1	52.2	52.4	53.5	54.3	53.0
2009	49.9	48.6	48.6	48.4	49.2	49.9	50.2	50.1	49.5	49.4	51.0	51.6	49.7
2010	48.0	46.7	47.6	48.5	49.6	50.5	50.9	50.8	49.9	50.3	52.3	53.0	49.8
2011	49.2	48.5	48.9	50.1	50.3	51.1	51.3	51.4	50.4	50.2	52.5	53.1	50.6
2012	49.6	48.6	49.2	49.9	50.7	51.2	51.2	51.1	50.0	50.4	53.0	53.1	50.7
2013	49.4	48.9	49.5	50.2	50.9	51.7	52.1	52.5	51.5	52.1	54.4	54.8	51.5
2014	50.9	50.2	50.6	51.4	52.1	53.2	53.3	53.2	52.2	52.5	54.5	55.2	52.4
2015	51.5	50.9	51.1	51.8	52.5	53.3	53.6	53.4	52.5	52.5	54.3	55.2	52.7
Transportation and Utilities													
2005	13.1	13.0	13.3	13.1	13.1	13.2	12.9	12.8	13.5	13.8	13.8	13.8	13.3
2006	13.3	13.4	13.5	13.6	13.9	14.0	13.4	13.3	14.0	14.3	14.1	14.3	13.8
2007	14.0	13.8	13.7	13.6	14.0	13.9	13.5	13.6	14.0	13.9	13.8	14.0	13.8
2009	13.4	13.5	13.6	13.6	13.7	13.6	13.4	13.3	13.7	13.8	13.8	14.1	13.6
2010	12.7	12.7	12.6	12.4	12.5	12.4	11.6	11.7	12.5	12.5	12.5	12.5	12.4
2011	12.2	12.0	12.1	12.1	12.3	12.2	11.5	11.5	12.3	12.4	12.4	12.6	12.1
2012	12.3	12.3	12.3	12.4	12.5	12.4	11.7	11.5	12.5	12.6	12.7	12.9	12.3
2013	12.4	12.4	12.5	12.1	12.7	12.4	12.1	12.2	13.0	13.5	13.8	14.0	12.8
2014	13.6	13.4	13.5	13.6	13.6	13.5	13.2	13.3	14.4	14.9	15.1	15.3	14.0
2015	14.9	14.8	14.8	14.7	14.7	14.4	14.6	15.2	15.8	16.0	16.3	16.8	15.3

1. Employment by Industry: Delaware, 2005–2015—*Continued*

(Numbers in thousands, not seasonally adjusted)

Industry and year	January	February	March	April	May	June	July	August	September	October	November	December	Annual average
Information													
2005	6.4	6.4	6.5	6.7	6.8	6.8	6.8	6.7	6.7	6.8	6.8	6.8	6.7
2006	6.7	6.7	6.6	6.6	6.6	6.7	6.7	6.8	6.7	6.7	6.8	6.8	6.7
2007	6.8	6.8	6.8	6.8	6.8	6.9	7.0	7.0	7.0	7.1	7.1	7.1	6.9
2008	7.0	7.1	7.1	7.1	7.1	7.2	7.0	7.1	7.0	7.0	6.9	6.8	7.0
2009	6.8	6.7	6.7	6.6	6.6	6.5	6.5	6.4	6.3	6.4	6.2	6.1	6.5
2010	5.9	5.9	6.0	6.1	6.0	6.0	6.0	5.9	6.0	5.9	5.9	5.8	6.0
2011	5.8	5.8	5.8	5.8	5.6	5.8	5.7	5.2	5.7	5.5	5.6	5.7	5.7
2012	5.6	5.6	5.6	5.5	5.5	5.5	5.4	5.5	5.3	5.3	5.3	5.3	5.5
2013	5.3	5.4	5.3	5.3	5.2	5.2	5.2	5.2	5.1	5.0	5.1	5.0	5.2
2014	5.1	4.9	4.9	4.9	5.0	4.9	4.9	5.0	4.8	4.9	4.9	4.8	4.9
2015	4.8	4.7	4.7	4.7	4.8	4.7	4.7	4.7	4.6	4.7	4.8	4.8	4.7
Financial Activities													
2005	45.1	45.1	44.9	44.8	45.0	45.3	45.9	45.8	45.3	45.1	45.2	45.2	45.2
2006	44.5	44.4	44.2	44.5	44.4	44.6	44.7	45.3	45.0	44.9	45.0	45.2	44.7
2007	44.8	44.9	44.9	45.1	45.3	45.8	45.8	45.6	45.2	45.3	45.2	45.2	45.3
2008	45.0	45.0	45.2	45.5	45.7	46.3	46.5	46.2	45.5	45.3	45.0	44.6	45.5
2009	44.3	44.0	43.9	43.9	44.2	44.5	44.6	44.2	43.9	43.3	43.1	43.0	43.9
2010	42.4	42.4	42.6	42.5	42.5	43.1	43.4	43.4	43.0	42.3	42.2	42.8	42.7
2011	42.3	42.4	42.3	42.3	42.2	42.8	43.1	42.8	42.3	41.4	41.3	41.6	42.2
2012	41.3	41.3	41.5	41.5	42.0	42.7	43.3	43.4	42.7	42.8	42.9	43.3	42.4
2013	42.9	43.2	43.2	43.2	43.4	44.1	44.7	44.8	44.1	44.0	44.2	44.5	43.9
2014	44.1	44.1	44.1	44.3	44.7	45.3	45.6	45.7	45.3	45.4	45.7	46.1	45.0
2015	45.8	46.0	46.1	46.2	46.3	46.6	47.0	47.3	47.1	47.0	47.0	47.3	46.6
Professional and Business Services													
2005	60.8	60.7	61.2	62.6	62.7	63.1	62.7	62.7	62.7	62.7	63.3	64.3	62.5
2006	60.8	61.0	61.5	61.3	61.4	61.2	60.7	61.0	60.7	60.7	60.9	62.6	61.2
2007	58.3	58.5	59.4	60.2	60.5	61.0	60.3	60.3	60.2	60.6	61.5	62.7	60.3
2008	59.6	59.4	59.4	60.3	59.9	60.0	59.6	59.4	59.0	59.0	59.5	59.5	59.6
2009	56.0	55.9	55.7	55.8	56.2	56.1	55.1	54.9	54.5	55.0	55.3	56.2	55.6
2010	53.2	53.3	53.5	54.1	54.7	55.0	55.7	55.5	55.2	55.7	55.5	56.7	54.8
2011	53.9	54.2	54.1	55.8	55.3	55.6	55.7	55.8	55.6	56.0	57.1	57.5	55.6
2012	54.8	54.5	55.1	56.0	55.8	55.8	55.9	56.0	55.9	56.9	58.3	58.5	56.1
2013	55.8	55.4	55.4	57.4	57.6	57.9	58.5	59.0	58.6	59.1	61.8	60.3	58.1
2014	57.6	56.5	57.2	58.4	59.2	59.4	59.3	59.0	58.9	59.9	63.4	62.8	59.3
2015	59.0	57.9	58.1	57.8	59.0	59.5	60.4	59.1	58.4	60.3	63.4	63.5	59.7
Education and Health Services													
2005	54.7	54.9	55.3	55.6	55.8	55.9	55.0	55.1	55.9	56.1	56.4	56.6	55.6
2006	56.5	56.7	57.0	57.4	57.7	57.9	58.0	57.9	58.3	58.6	59.1	59.2	57.9
2007	58.9	59.0	59.3	59.6	59.9	59.8	59.5	59.6	60.5	60.8	61.0	61.4	59.9
2008	61.4	62.0	61.9	62.6	62.8	62.7	62.1	62.4	62.9	63.0	63.4	63.4	62.6
2009	63.3	63.4	63.4	63.6	63.8	63.5	63.3	63.4	63.5	64.1	64.3	64.2	63.7
2010	63.7	63.6	64.2	64.8	64.9	64.5	65.1	65.4	65.2	65.3	65.5	65.5	64.8
2011	65.4	65.6	66.2	66.7	66.5	66.2	66.3	66.4	66.8	67.3	67.4	68.0	66.6
2012	67.3	67.4	67.8	68.1	68.4	68.5	68.3	68.4	69.0	69.5	69.7	70.0	68.5
2013	69.3	69.6	69.8	69.8	70.0	69.8	69.9	70.3	70.5	70.9	71.6	71.9	70.3
2014	71.4	71.6	72.1	72.4	72.8	72.4	72.3	72.5	73.0	73.6	74.1	74.3	72.7
2015	74.1	74.4	74.4	75.0	75.4	75.7	75.6	75.0	75.4	76.3	76.8	76.5	75.4
Leisure and Hospitality													
2005	37.4	37.5	38.3	40.4	42.3	45.5	46.0	46.0	44.2	41.8	41.1	40.3	41.7
2006	37.5	37.8	38.8	40.4	43.2	47.2	45.7	45.7	44.2	42.4	41.1	40.4	42.0
2007	38.0	38.2	39.2	40.8	42.9	46.4	45.8	46.0	43.3	41.5	40.5	40.1	41.9
2008	38.0	38.2	39.6	41.6	43.8	46.3	46.8	46.7	44.6	42.7	41.2	40.1	42.5
2009	37.9	38.3	38.8	40.9	43.9	46.3	46.4	46.3	44.0	41.9	40.3	39.6	42.1
2010	37.8	37.2	38.8	41.8	44.4	47.6	49.1	49.0	47.2	44.8	43.8	42.6	43.7
2011	40.5	40.6	41.8	43.6	46.0	48.5	49.3	49.3	47.0	44.4	43.0	42.0	44.7
2012	40.2	40.8	42.0	44.0	46.6	49.3	49.6	49.5	47.0	44.9	43.3	42.7	45.0
2013	41.0	41.2	42.2	44.7	48.0	50.8	51.2	50.8	47.9	46.2	44.4	43.7	46.0
2014	41.7	41.9	43.2	45.8	49.0	51.9	52.3	51.8	48.8	47.2	45.3	45.0	47.0
2015	43.0	43.3	44.5	46.8	50.8	53.6	54.7	54.2	51.0	49.3	47.3	47.6	48.8

1. Employment by Industry: Delaware, 2005–2015—*Continued*

(Numbers in thousands, not seasonally adjusted)

Industry and year	January	February	March	April	May	June	July	August	September	October	November	December	Annual average
Other Services													
2005	18.2	18.1	18.3	18.4	18.5	18.7	18.9	19.0	18.7	19.0	19.1	19.2	18.7
2006	18.8	18.9	19.1	19.2	19.1	19.5	19.4	19.3	18.9	19.3	19.5	19.7	19.2
2007	19.1	18.9	19.1	19.1	19.0	19.4	19.1	18.9	18.8	18.9	18.9	19.0	19.0
2008	18.8	18.8	18.8	19.1	19.0	19.2	19.2	19.1	18.8	18.8	18.8	18.7	18.9
2009	18.4	18.4	18.4	18.4	18.7	18.7	18.5	18.5	18.3	18.1	18.1	18.1	18.4
2010	18.0	17.7	18.0	18.2	18.3	18.7	18.5	18.6	18.4	18.3	18.2	18.2	18.3
2011	18.1	18.1	18.1	18.1	18.2	18.4	18.4	18.4	18.2	18.1	18.0	18.0	18.2
2012	17.9	18.0	18.1	18.2	18.3	18.5	18.5	18.6	18.3	18.4	18.4	18.4	18.3
2013	18.2	18.2	18.3	18.5	18.5	18.7	18.7	18.7	18.4	18.4	18.5	18.5	18.5
2014	18.2	18.3	18.4	18.6	18.7	18.8	18.7	18.8	18.5	18.6	18.7	18.7	18.6
2015	18.3	18.4	18.3	18.6	18.8	19.0	18.9	18.8	18.6	18.4	18.6	18.3	18.6
Government													
2005	58.0	58.9	60.1	60.6	60.8	58.1	57.5	56.4	59.9	61.7	61.9	61.6	59.6
2006	59.9	61.1	62.4	62.5	63.3	59.6	58.4	57.1	60.4	62.2	62.6	62.5	61.0
2007	60.6	61.7	62.9	63.2	63.5	60.7	59.5	58.6	61.5	63.6	63.9	63.7	62.0
2008	62.1	62.8	64.0	64.5	64.6	61.5	60.3	59.6	62.7	64.2	64.0	63.8	62.8
2009	62.1	63.6	65.1	65.2	65.1	61.9	59.5	59.3	62.6	65.3	65.3	64.7	63.3
2010	62.0	63.0	64.7	65.3	66.4	63.4	61.5	60.3	63.7	64.8	65.4	65.2	63.8
2011	62.7	63.7	64.9	66.3	65.0	62.3	60.7	60.1	63.6	65.1	65.2	65.0	63.7
2012	62.2	63.9	65.1	65.0	65.4	62.5	60.8	59.8	63.4	64.9	65.1	65.1	63.6
2013	61.4	64.0	65.4	65.6	65.7	63.1	61.2	60.2	63.9	65.4	65.9	65.6	64.0
2014	64.5	65.6	66.3	66.0	66.3	63.4	61.9	60.4	64.6	66.0	66.1	66.2	64.8
2015	64.2	64.8	67.7	66.1	67.0	64.6	62.8	61.1	65.2	66.9	67.4	66.9	65.4

2. Average Weekly Hours by Selected Industry: Delaware, 2011–2015

(Not seasonally adjusted)

Industry and year	January	February	March	April	May	June	July	August	September	October	November	December	Annual average
Total Private													
2011............	32.8	32.8	32.6	32.8	33.2	33.0	33.4	33.3	33.3	33.6	33.1	33.3	33.1
2012............	33.1	33.0	33.0	33.3	32.8	33.0	33.2	33.3	32.7	32.5	32.8	33.3	33.0
2013............	32.0	32.4	32.7	32.4	32.4	32.9	32.5	32.9	33.0	32.2	32.4	32.8	32.5
2014............	31.9	32.0	32.6	32.6	32.7	32.9	33.1	33.5	33.0	32.9	33.5	33.8	32.9
2015............	33.1	33.3	33.3	33.3	33.4	33.0	33.4	33.5	33.2	32.6	32.4	33.6	33.2
Goods-Producing													
2011............	36.9	37.3	37.1	37.3	38.7	38.3	38.9	38.8	39.7	38.7	38.5	39.4	38.3
2012............	38.7	38.4	37.9	37.9	38.0	37.7	37.0	37.6	37.5	36.8	37.0	38.0	37.7
2013............	37.1	37.5	37.7	37.3	37.9	37.9	37.1	38.1	38.5	38.2	38.7	38.5	37.9
2014............	38.7	38.1	38.8	38.7	39.3	39.9	40.4	40.7	40.2	39.4	38.0	38.5	39.2
2015............	39.0	38.0	37.9	39.4	39.3	38.9	38.8	39.1	38.9	38.5	36.9	38.5	38.6
Mining, Logging, and Construction													
2011............	35.2	35.7	35.4	36.1	36.6	37.1	37.7	37.6	39.1	36.9	38.0	38.0	36.9
2012............	37.4	37.9	37.0	37.3	37.7	37.7	37.5	37.9	38.8	38.0	37.4	37.9	37.7
2013............	37.6	37.6	37.8	36.8	38.1	36.5	35.7	37.2	37.9	37.2	38.5	37.5	37.4
2014............	37.4	36.9	38.3	38.4	38.4	40.1	40.5	41.4	39.3	39.0	37.1	37.3	38.7
2015............	36.9	36.3	36.8	38.4	36.7	37.6	36.4	37.0	36.4	36.1	34.5	37.3	36.7
Manufacturing													
2011............	38.3	38.5	38.5	38.3	40.4	39.2	40.0	39.7	40.0	40.0	38.8	40.6	39.3
2012............	39.6	38.7	38.5	38.3	38.3	37.7	36.7	37.2	36.7	36.0	36.7	38.0	37.7
2013............	36.8	37.4	37.5	37.8	37.7	39.0	38.4	38.9	38.9	39.1	38.6	39.2	38.3
2014............	39.7	38.9	39.3	39.1	40.0	39.7	40.3	40.2	40.9	39.7	38.8	39.4	39.7
2015............	40.6	39.3	38.7	40.2	41.4	40.0	40.9	40.9	40.8	40.4	38.9	39.5	40.1
Trade, Transportation, and Utilities													
2011............	33.3	33.0	33.2	33.0	33.8	33.4	33.7	33.4	33.5	33.4	33.4	33.1	33.4
2012............	32.9	32.8	33.3	33.6	32.9	33.0	33.4	33.5	32.6	32.7	33.1	33.3	33.1
2013............	31.6	32.2	32.8	32.6	32.4	32.6	32.9	32.8	32.5	32.1	32.4	33.6	32.6
2014............	31.2	31.4	32.3	32.1	32.3	32.3	32.8	33.6	32.8	32.7	33.7	34.5	32.7
2015............	32.4	32.7	32.9	33.2	34.2	34.0	34.1	34.2	34.6	33.1	33.4	35.2	33.7
Financial Activities													
2011............	37.2	37.1	37.3	37.3	38.0	37.9	38.3	37.9	38.1	38.9	37.8	37.1	37.7
2012............	37.8	36.7	37.2	36.8	36.9	36.0	36.4	36.2	36.8	35.8	35.9	36.4	36.6
2013............	35.5	35.4	35.9	36.1	36.2	37.1	36.3	36.3	37.7	36.2	36.4	36.4	36.3
2014............	36.1	35.8	36.2	36.1	36.4	36.7	36.3	36.7	36.7	36.9	37.8	37.8	36.6
2015............	37.5	38.5	38.3	38.2	38.2	38.4	38.6	38.8	38.4	38.3	38.8	38.5	38.4
Professional and Business Services													
2011............	33.9	33.7	33.1	33.8	34.5	33.8	33.3	34.4	34.3	35.6	34.0	34.7	34.1
2012............	34.6	33.5	34.8	35.1	35.4	36.0	36.3	36.5	37.4	37.2	36.2	37.8	35.9
2013............	34.2	35.0	35.7	35.3	35.4	36.0	33.8	35.3	36.2	34.5	34.2	35.5	35.1
2014............	34.4	35.5	35.8	36.4	36.0	35.3	34.7	34.9	34.4	34.7	36.2	36.5	35.4
2015............	35.8	36.8	36.9	37.1	36.4	35.2	35.1	35.3	33.7	32.9	32.5	36.0	35.3
Education and Health Services													
2011............	33.7	33.3	33.4	33.5	33.8	33.5	33.7	33.2	33.4	33.3	33.1	33.5	33.5
2012............	33.2	34.6	33.5	33.5	33.2	33.3	33.2	33.0	31.7	31.4	32.6	32.4	33.0
2013............	32.3	32.1	32.1	32.0	31.8	32.5	31.8	32.1	32.6	31.9	31.9	31.5	32.1
2014............	31.6	31.1	31.2	31.8	32.2	32.3	32.3	32.8	32.9	32.8	33.0	32.8	32.2
2015............	32.6	32.5	32.1	31.7	31.9	32.3	32.3	32.0	32.1	31.7	32.0	32.4	32.1
Leisure and Hospitality													
2011............	23.7	24.0	24.0	24.6	24.2	24.7	25.6	25.9	24.4	24.8	24.4	24.5	24.6
2012............	23.9	24.4	24.7	24.8	24.9	25.7	26.9	26.8	25.0	25.5	24.9	25.6	25.3
2013............	24.3	25.0	25.4	24.9	25.0	26.0	26.7	27.2	25.4	24.1	24.4	24.5	25.3
2014............	24.1	24.1	24.7	24.8	24.5	25.2	26.2	26.2	24.9	24.4	24.8	24.9	24.9
2015............	24.3	24.4	24.6	24.5	24.9	24.5	26.0	26.3	25.0	24.3	23.8	23.5	24.7

3. Average Hourly Earnings by Selected Industry: Delaware, 2011–2015

(Dollars, not seasonally adjusted)

Industry and year	January	February	March	April	May	June	July	August	September	October	November	December	Annual average
Total Private													
2011	22.85	22.58	22.40	22.45	22.25	21.87	21.81	22.00	22.39	22.42	22.26	22.54	22.32
2012	22.47	21.95	21.97	22.06	21.61	21.47	21.75	21.51	22.28	22.30	22.12	22.66	22.01
2013	22.72	22.77	22.67	22.53	22.23	21.97	21.59	21.51	22.06	21.96	21.79	21.82	22.12
2014	21.95	22.17	21.92	21.61	21.73	21.81	21.37	21.31	21.69	21.75	21.70	21.50	21.70
2015	22.07	22.53	22.56	22.27	22.12	22.09	22.12	22.67	22.87	23.36	23.63	23.28	22.63
Goods-Producing													
2011	24.12	24.13	23.98	23.98	23.44	23.66	23.44	23.37	23.75	23.50	23.61	23.60	23.71
2012	23.61	23.34	23.51	23.77	24.15	23.96	24.21	24.12	24.49	24.95	24.60	24.95	24.14
2013	24.71	25.07	25.17	24.90	25.15	25.07	25.07	24.93	25.11	25.11	24.81	24.10	24.93
2014	23.93	24.24	24.45	24.14	24.61	25.03	24.73	24.99	24.89	24.83	25.33	24.95	24.69
2015	24.64	25.09	24.99	24.36	24.37	24.79	24.93	25.42	25.33	25.18	25.30	25.24	24.97
Mining, Logging, and Construction													
2011	28.35	28.20	27.79	27.51	27.24	27.37	27.15	27.24	27.86	27.59	27.63	27.40	27.60
2012	27.33	27.11	27.31	27.28	28.50	28.40	28.45	28.70	28.88	29.48	28.39	29.24	28.29
2013	29.13	29.89	29.89	29.13	29.34	29.44	29.69	28.86	29.09	29.00	28.24	26.68	29.02
2014	26.88	27.03	27.44	27.06	28.11	28.20	27.83	27.40	27.64	27.77	28.19	28.09	27.65
2015	28.19	28.67	28.51	27.70	28.27	28.35	28.60	28.86	28.07	28.05	27.83	28.02	28.26
Manufacturing													
2011	21.25	21.34	21.30	21.37	20.76	20.96	20.81	20.66	20.76	20.68	20.72	21.00	20.96
2012	21.14	20.82	21.00	21.35	21.07	20.75	21.02	20.67	21.08	21.39	21.68	21.73	21.14
2013	21.40	21.55	21.66	21.76	21.86	21.87	21.65	21.91	22.01	22.13	22.11	22.20	21.85
2014	21.85	22.30	22.25	21.92	21.92	22.45	22.18	23.00	22.79	22.55	23.18	22.64	22.43
2015	22.30	22.70	22.56	21.93	21.66	22.21	22.33	22.96	23.37	23.09	23.54	23.14	22.65
Trade, Transportation, and Utilities													
2011	19.41	19.09	19.23	19.68	19.57	19.29	19.32	19.40	19.35	19.47	19.25	19.66	19.39
2012	19.56	19.50	19.39	19.31	18.87	18.83	19.16	18.87	19.21	19.01	18.71	19.08	19.12
2013	19.18	19.23	18.94	19.25	18.88	19.00	18.74	18.58	19.00	18.88	18.45	18.49	18.88
2014	18.69	18.81	18.71	18.21	18.14	18.52	18.15	18.05	18.08	17.95	18.07	18.10	18.28
2015	19.01	18.97	18.95	18.66	18.44	18.67	18.55	18.90	18.76	19.11	19.03	19.02	18.84
Financial Activities													
2011	28.21	27.38	27.40	27.79	27.32	26.21	25.92	26.58	26.68	27.35	25.99	26.12	26.91
2012	26.99	26.67	26.06	27.36	26.25	26.19	28.04	26.32	27.23	26.46	26.31	27.60	26.79
2013	27.59	27.40	27.63	26.84	25.92	26.18	25.96	25.68	25.43	23.09	23.46	23.56	25.70
2014	23.49	23.74	23.29	22.62	23.37	24.71	24.29	24.62	25.15	25.68	27.13	26.12	24.55
2015	25.93	27.28	27.76	26.91	27.21	27.68	28.22	29.60	29.17	29.63	31.14	30.42	28.44
Professional and Business Services													
2011	27.82	27.28	26.96	26.68	26.88	26.10	26.01	26.51	26.48	26.50	26.81	26.90	26.74
2012	26.70	26.00	25.51	25.42	24.56	24.53	24.87	24.90	25.20	24.73	25.17	25.21	25.22
2013	26.49	26.84	27.07	27.31	27.26	27.12	26.52	26.81	27.64	27.51	27.75	28.13	27.22
2014	28.24	28.27	27.45	27.33	27.69	26.73	26.25	26.13	26.46	25.68	23.39	22.89	26.31
2015	24.53	24.74	24.57	24.94	24.90	24.27	24.68	26.25	26.86	26.59	25.71	23.76	25.12
Education and Health Services													
2011	21.69	21.84	21.70	22.02	21.83	22.13	22.43	22.06	22.67	22.61	22.53	23.09	22.22
2012	23.31	22.34	23.26	22.63	22.70	22.82	22.87	23.14	24.55	24.82	24.01	24.87	23.43
2013	24.03	23.94	23.82	23.48	23.11	22.88	22.95	22.78	22.94	23.28	23.14	23.22	23.30
2014	23.10	23.35	23.20	23.21	23.01	23.03	23.24	22.54	22.88	23.35	22.99	23.57	23.12
2015	23.81	23.87	24.11	24.42	24.27	24.12	24.79	24.84	25.37	26.40	25.98	26.16	24.85
Leisure and Hospitality													
2011	13.40	13.23	13.34	12.87	12.93	12.73	12.85	12.82	13.25	13.33	13.47	13.74	13.14
2012	13.94	13.67	13.68	13.60	13.44	12.99	12.93	12.70	12.69	12.81	13.39	13.72	13.26
2013	13.99	13.72	13.54	13.41	13.34	12.81	12.58	12.56	12.94	13.01	12.88	13.02	13.11
2014	13.11	13.37	13.20	13.01	13.05	13.02	12.91	13.09	13.19	13.36	13.16	13.21	13.13
2015	12.94	13.13	13.08	13.08	13.22	13.02	12.93	12.91	13.19	13.35	13.70	13.88	13.19

4. Average Weekly Earnings by Selected Industry: Delaware, 2011–2015

(Dollars, not seasonally adjusted)

Industry and year	January	February	March	April	May	June	July	August	September	October	November	December	Annual average
Total Private													
2011	749.48	740.62	730.24	736.36	738.70	721.71	728.45	732.60	745.59	753.31	736.81	750.58	738.79
2012	743.76	724.35	725.01	734.60	708.81	708.51	722.10	716.28	728.56	724.75	725.54	754.58	726.33
2013	727.04	737.75	741.31	729.97	720.25	722.81	701.68	707.68	727.98	707.11	706.00	715.70	718.90
2014	700.21	709.44	714.59	704.49	710.57	717.55	707.35	713.89	715.77	715.58	726.95	726.70	713.93
2015	730.52	750.25	751.25	741.59	738.81	728.97	738.81	759.45	759.28	761.54	765.61	782.21	751.32
Goods-Producing													
2011	890.03	900.05	889.66	894.45	907.13	906.18	911.82	906.76	942.88	909.45	908.99	929.84	908.09
2012	913.71	896.26	891.03	900.88	917.70	903.29	895.77	906.91	918.38	918.16	910.20	948.10	910.08
2013	916.74	940.13	948.91	928.77	953.19	950.15	930.10	949.83	966.74	959.20	960.15	927.85	944.85
2014	926.09	923.54	948.66	934.22	967.17	998.70	999.09	1,017.09	1,000.58	978.30	962.54	960.58	967.85
2015	960.96	953.42	947.12	959.78	957.74	964.33	967.28	993.92	985.34	969.43	933.57	971.74	963.84
Mining, Logging, and Construction													
2011	997.92	1,006.74	983.77	993.11	996.98	1,015.43	1,023.56	1,024.22	1,089.33	1,018.07	1,049.94	1,041.20	1,018.44
2012	1,022.14	1,027.47	1,010.47	1,017.54	1,074.45	1,070.68	1,066.88	1,087.73	1,120.54	1,120.24	1,061.79	1,108.20	1,066.53
2013	1,095.29	1,123.86	1,129.84	1,071.98	1,117.85	1,074.56	1,059.93	1,073.59	1,102.51	1,078.80	1,087.24	1,000.50	1,085.35
2014	1,005.31	997.41	1,050.95	1,039.10	1,079.42	1,130.82	1,127.12	1,134.36	1,086.25	1,083.03	1,045.85	1,047.76	1,070.06
2015	1,040.21	1,040.72	1,049.17	1,063.68	1,037.51	1,065.96	1,041.04	1,067.82	1,021.75	1,012.61	960.14	1,045.15	1,037.14
Manufacturing													
2011	813.88	821.59	820.05	818.47	838.70	821.63	832.40	820.20	830.40	827.20	803.94	852.60	823.73
2012	837.14	805.73	808.50	817.71	806.98	782.28	771.43	768.92	773.64	770.04	795.66	825.74	796.98
2013	787.52	805.97	812.25	822.53	824.12	852.93	831.36	852.30	856.19	865.28	853.45	870.24	836.86
2014	867.45	867.47	874.43	857.07	876.80	891.27	893.85	924.60	932.11	895.24	899.38	892.02	890.47
2015	905.38	892.11	873.07	881.59	896.72	888.40	913.30	939.06	953.50	932.84	915.71	914.03	908.27
Trade, Transportation, and Utilities													
2011	646.35	629.97	638.44	649.44	661.47	644.29	651.08	647.96	648.23	650.30	642.95	650.75	647.63
2012	643.52	639.60	645.69	648.82	620.82	621.39	639.94	632.15	626.25	621.63	619.30	635.36	632.87
2013	606.09	619.21	621.23	627.55	611.71	619.40	616.55	609.42	617.50	606.05	597.78	621.26	615.49
2014	583.13	590.63	604.33	584.54	585.92	598.20	595.32	606.48	593.02	586.97	608.96	624.45	597.76
2015	615.92	620.32	623.46	619.51	630.65	634.78	632.56	646.38	649.10	632.54	635.60	669.50	634.91
Financial Activities													
2011	1,049.41	1,015.80	1,022.02	1,036.57	1,038.16	993.36	992.74	1,007.38	1,016.51	1,063.92	982.42	969.05	1,014.51
2012	1,020.22	978.79	969.43	1,006.85	968.63	942.84	1,020.66	952.78	1,002.06	947.27	944.53	1,004.64	980.51
2013	979.45	969.96	991.92	968.92	938.30	971.28	942.35	932.18	958.71	835.86	853.94	857.58	932.91
2014	847.99	849.89	843.10	816.58	850.67	906.86	881.73	903.55	923.01	947.59	1,025.51	987.34	898.53
2015	972.38	1,050.28	1,063.21	1,027.96	1,039.42	1,062.91	1,089.29	1,148.48	1,120.13	1,134.83	1,208.23	1,171.17	1,092.10
Professional and Business Services													
2011	943.10	919.34	892.38	901.78	927.36	882.18	866.13	911.94	908.26	943.40	911.54	933.43	911.83
2012	923.82	871.00	887.75	892.24	869.42	883.08	902.78	908.85	942.48	919.96	911.15	952.94	905.40
2013	905.96	939.40	966.40	964.04	965.00	976.32	896.38	946.39	1,000.57	949.10	949.05	998.62	955.42
2014	971.46	1,003.59	982.71	994.81	996.84	943.57	910.88	911.94	910.22	891.10	846.72	835.49	931.37
2015	878.17	910.43	906.63	925.27	906.36	854.30	866.27	926.63	905.18	874.81	835.58	855.36	886.74
Education and Health Services													
2011	730.95	727.27	724.78	737.67	737.85	741.36	755.89	732.39	757.18	752.91	745.74	773.52	744.37
2012	773.89	772.96	779.21	758.11	753.64	759.91	759.28	763.62	778.24	779.35	782.73	805.79	773.19
2013	776.17	768.47	764.62	751.36	734.90	743.60	729.81	731.24	747.84	742.63	738.17	731.43	747.93
2014	729.96	726.19	723.84	738.08	740.92	743.87	750.65	739.31	752.75	765.88	758.67	773.10	744.46
2015	776.21	775.78	773.93	774.11	774.21	779.08	800.72	794.88	814.38	836.88	831.36	847.58	797.69
Leisure and Hospitality													
2011	317.58	317.52	320.16	316.60	312.91	314.43	328.96	332.04	323.30	330.58	328.67	336.63	323.24
2012	333.17	333.55	337.90	337.28	334.66	333.84	347.82	340.36	317.25	326.66	333.41	351.23	335.48
2013	339.96	343.00	343.92	333.91	333.50	333.06	335.89	341.63	328.68	313.54	314.27	318.99	331.68
2014	315.95	322.22	326.04	322.65	319.73	328.10	338.24	342.96	328.43	325.98	326.37	328.93	326.94
2015	314.44	320.37	321.77	320.46	329.18	318.99	336.18	339.53	329.75	324.41	326.06	326.18	325.79

DISTRICT OF COLUMBIA
At a Glance

Population:
  2005 estimate: 567,136
  2010 census: 601,723
  2015 estimate: 672,228

Percent change in population:
  2005–2015: 18.5%
  2010–2015: 11.7%

Percent change in total nonfarm employment:
  2005–2015: 12.3%

Industry with the largest growth in employment, 2005–2015 (thousands):
  Education and health services, 35.7

Industry with the largest decline or smallest growth in employment, 2005–2015 (thousands):
  Information, –5.6

Civilian labor force:
  2005: 315,616
  2010: 346,065
  2015: 388,388

Unemployment rate and rank among states (highest to lowest):
  2005: 6.4%, 6th
  2010: 9.4%, 21st
  2015: 6.9%, 1st

Over-the-year change in unemployment rates:
  2012–2013: –0.5%
  2013–2014: –0.7%
  2014–2015: –0.9%

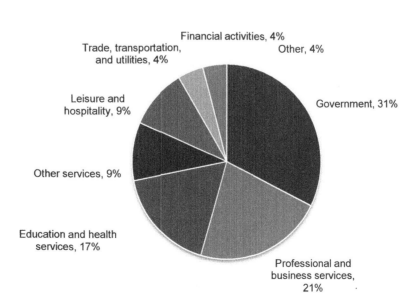

Employment by Industry: District of Columbia, 2015

Financial activities, 4%
Other, 4%
Trade, transportation, and utilities, 4%
Leisure and hospitality, 9%
Government, 31%
Other services, 9%
Education and health services, 17%
Professional and business services, 21%

1. Employment by Industry: District of Columbia, 2005–2015

(Numbers in thousands, not seasonally adjusted)

Industry and year	January	February	March	April	May	June	July	August	September	October	November	December	Annual average
Total Nonfarm													
2005	670.3	676.0	679.3	681.9	681.6	683.3	688.1	684.8	679.7	684.2	688.5	688.7	682.2
2006	675.4	681.8	686.2	685.3	684.6	689.4	695.5	689.8	685.3	691.4	693.6	693.4	687.6
2007	680.7	689.2	692.0	692.1	689.6	691.3	701.4	695.5	690.3	700.0	701.1	701.8	693.8
2008	689.0	693.6	698.2	701.2	702.7	704.1	720.0	715.9	705.1	705.9	706.0	704.5	703.9
2009	697.8	697.4	697.2	696.5	697.3	698.1	718.1	706.6	694.2	703.8	706.8	705.6	701.6
2010	698.2	695.5	703.4	713.6	715.5	715.6	732.1	707.7	711.1	717.2	718.4	717.3	712.1
2011	713.9	716.9	721.4	727.8	723.8	726.3	740.8	724.7	730.3	729.8	729.7	729.1	726.2
2012	721.9	725.1	729.9	730.9	733.9	732.9	743.1	729.0	736.1	744.0	745.8	744.8	734.8
2013	733.6	738.4	741.5	748.5	749.4	743.9	757.8	743.9	752.9	754.4	758.5	756.7	748.3
2014	739.2	743.9	747.6	752.9	754.9	749.6	760.1	745.1	759.2	762.5	764.0	763.8	753.6
2015	755.8	759.8	762.2	767.3	770.0	764.3	775.6	759.1	766.6	772.0	773.3	771.2	766.4
Total Private													
2005	438.6	444.8	448.1	450.1	449.7	448.6	446.1	443.4	448.8	452.0	455.5	456.1	448.5
2006	443.6	450.4	454.8	455.3	453.9	455.9	452.7	449.4	454.6	460.2	462.4	462.0	454.6
2007	453.8	461.4	464.9	465.2	462.3	461.3	459.8	456.9	461.6	467.3	469.0	469.5	462.8
2008	458.1	463.0	467.1	471.4	471.8	470.1	471.5	469.5	472.6	471.7	471.7	469.6	469.0
2009	463.7	463.4	463.3	462.0	462.0	459.3	458.3	454.4	455.9	463.3	465.5	465.2	461.4
2010	456.9	454.8	462.5	471.5	470.7	468.1	464.2	461.4	465.1	468.4	469.4	469.5	465.2
2011	467.0	470.5	474.6	481.7	477.3	477.8	480.1	478.1	483.6	486.1	486.5	486.1	479.1
2012	479.5	483.8	488.0	490.1	492.6	489.3	488.3	486.9	494.5	501.3	503.2	502.8	491.7
2013	493.4	498.8	501.6	509.1	509.9	503.9	507.7	506.1	513.5	514.8	519.0	517.0	507.9
2014	506.6	510.9	514.3	520.5	522.0	515.7	513.5	511.8	523.6	526.1	528.1	527.4	518.4
2015	520.3	523.8	526.1	531.3	533.4	527.1	525.3	523.0	529.4	534.1	534.9	532.6	528.4
Goods-Producing													
2005	14.5	14.8	14.8	15.1	15.2	15.2	14.8	14.9	14.5	14.3	14.4	14.4	14.7
2006	13.7	14.0	14.2	14.1	14.3	14.5	14.7	14.8	14.6	14.2	14.0	13.8	14.2
2007	13.9	13.7	13.8	13.9	14.3	14.5	14.6	15.0	14.9	14.8	14.7	14.2	14.4
2008	14.4	14.5	14.5	14.1	14.5	14.6	14.6	15.0	14.5	14.6	14.5	14.2	14.5
2009	14.0	14.0	13.5	13.4	13.4	13.3	12.8	12.7	12.4	11.9	11.7	11.6	12.9
2010	11.3	10.4	11.2	11.8	11.8	11.8	12.2	12.0	11.8	12.1	12.0	12.0	11.7
2011	12.1	12.1	12.3	12.8	13.0	13.2	14.1	14.1	13.8	13.6	13.5	13.6	13.2
2012	13.5	13.8	14.1	14.5	14.7	14.9	15.0	15.0	14.9	15.2	14.9	14.8	14.6
2013	14.5	14.6	14.7	14.5	14.9	15.1	15.7	15.8	15.3	15.1	15.1	15.0	15.0
2014	14.8	14.7	14.9	15.0	15.2	15.5	15.9	15.9	15.6	15.7	15.5	15.3	15.3
2015	14.6	14.5	14.7	15.2	15.5	15.7	15.9	16.1	15.8	15.6	15.4	15.3	15.4
Service-Providing													
2005	655.8	661.2	664.5	666.8	666.4	668.1	673.3	669.9	665.2	669.9	674.1	674.3	667.5
2006	661.7	667.8	672.0	671.2	670.3	674.9	680.8	675.0	670.7	677.2	679.6	679.6	673.4
2007	666.8	675.5	678.2	678.2	675.3	676.8	686.8	680.5	675.4	685.2	686.4	687.6	679.4
2008	674.6	679.1	683.7	687.1	688.2	689.5	705.4	700.9	690.6	691.3	691.5	690.3	689.4
2009	683.8	683.4	683.7	683.1	683.9	684.8	705.3	693.9	681.8	691.9	695.1	694.0	688.7
2010	686.9	685.1	692.2	701.8	703.7	703.8	719.9	695.7	699.3	705.1	706.4	705.3	700.4
2011	701.8	704.8	709.1	715.0	710.8	713.1	726.7	710.6	716.5	716.2	716.2	715.5	713.0
2012	708.4	711.3	715.8	716.4	719.2	718.0	728.1	714.0	721.2	728.8	730.9	730.0	720.2
2013	719.1	723.8	726.8	734.0	734.5	728.8	742.1	728.1	737.6	739.3	743.4	741.7	733.3
2014	724.4	729.2	732.7	737.9	739.7	734.1	744.2	729.2	743.6	746.8	748.5	748.5	738.2
2015	741.2	745.3	747.5	752.1	754.5	748.6	759.7	743.0	750.8	756.4	757.9	755.9	751.1
Mining, Logging, and Construction													
2005	12.3	12.6	12.6	12.9	13.0	13.0	12.7	12.8	12.5	12.4	12.5	12.4	12.6
2006	11.9	12.2	12.4	12.3	12.5	12.7	13.0	13.1	12.9	12.5	12.3	12.1	12.5
2007	12.2	12.0	12.1	12.2	12.6	12.8	12.9	13.4	13.2	13.1	13.0	12.5	12.7
2008	12.7	12.8	12.8	12.6	12.9	13.0	13.1	13.5	13.1	13.2	13.1	12.8	13.0
2009	12.6	12.6	12.2	12.1	12.1	12.0	11.5	11.4	11.2	10.7	10.5	10.4	11.6
2010	10.1	9.2	10.1	10.7	10.7	10.7	11.1	11.0	10.7	11.0	11.0	11.0	10.6
2011	11.0	11.1	11.2	11.7	11.9	12.1	13.0	13.1	12.8	12.6	12.5	12.6	12.1
2012	12.5	12.8	13.0	13.5	13.7	13.9	14.0	14.0	13.9	14.2	13.9	13.8	13.6
2013	13.5	13.6	13.7	13.5	13.9	14.1	14.7	14.8	14.3	14.1	14.1	14.0	14.0
2014	13.8	13.7	13.9	14.0	14.2	14.5	14.9	14.9	14.6	14.6	14.4	14.2	14.3
2015	13.6	13.5	13.6	14.1	14.4	14.6	14.8	15.0	14.6	14.5	14.3	14.2	14.3

1. Employment by Industry: District of Columbia, 2005–2015—*Continued*

(Numbers in thousands, not seasonally adjusted)

Industry and year	January	February	March	April	May	June	July	August	September	October	November	December	Annual average
Manufacturing													
2005	2.2	2.2	2.2	2.2	2.2	2.2	2.1	2.1	2.0	1.9	1.9	2.0	2.1
2006	1.8	1.8	1.8	1.8	1.8	1.8	1.7	1.7	1.7	1.7	1.7	1.7	1.8
2007	1.7	1.7	1.7	1.7	1.7	1.7	1.7	1.6	1.7	1.7	1.7	1.7	1.7
2008	1.7	1.7	1.7	1.5	1.6	1.6	1.5	1.5	1.4	1.4	1.4	1.4	1.5
2009	1.4	1.4	1.3	1.3	1.3	1.3	1.3	1.3	1.2	1.2	1.2	1.2	1.3
2010	1.2	1.2	1.1	1.1	1.1	1.1	1.1	1.0	1.1	1.1	1.0	1.0	1.1
2011	1.1	1.0	1.1	1.1	1.1	1.1	1.1	1.0	1.0	1.0	1.0	1.0	1.1
2012	1.0	1.0	1.1	1.0	1.0	1.0	1.0	1.0	1.0	1.0	1.0	1.0	1.0
2013	1.0	1.0	1.0	1.0	1.0	1.0	1.0	1.0	1.0	1.0	1.0	1.0	1.0
2014	1.0	1.0	1.0	1.0	1.0	1.0	1.0	1.0	1.0	1.1	1.1	1.1	1.0
2015	1.0	1.0	1.1	1.1	1.1	1.1	1.1	1.1	1.2	1.1	1.1	1.1	1.1
Trade, Transportation, and Utilities													
2005	27.3	27.1	27.6	27.4	27.5	27.6	27.8	27.5	27.6	28.2	28.4	29.3	27.8
2006	28.1	27.9	27.8	27.5	27.6	27.9	27.7	27.6	27.8	27.9	28.2	28.6	27.9
2007	27.5	27.2	27.4	27.8	27.9	27.9	27.7	27.5	27.6	27.6	28.1	28.4	27.7
2008	27.4	27.5	27.4	27.9	27.9	28.2	28.3	27.9	28.0	27.6	28.3	28.5	27.9
2009	27.3	26.8	26.7	26.8	26.6	26.5	26.5	26.4	26.5	27.0	27.5	27.5	26.8
2010	26.9	26.1	26.9	27.4	27.4	27.6	27.4	27.2	27.2	27.6	28.1	28.2	27.3
2011	27.3	27.1	27.1	27.5	27.3	27.2	27.1	27.1	27.3	27.9	28.1	28.3	27.4
2012	27.4	27.4	27.5	27.7	28.0	28.2	28.0	28.0	28.2	28.3	29.1	29.4	28.1
2013	28.5	28.6	28.6	28.6	28.7	28.7	28.7	28.7	29.1	29.4	30.5	30.7	29.1
2014	29.5	29.5	29.8	30.5	30.5	30.7	30.3	30.5	30.7	31.2	32.1	32.1	30.6
2015	31.4	31.3	31.3	31.4	31.5	31.9	32.1	32.0	32.5	33.0	33.9	34.4	32.2
Wholesale Trade													
2005	4.6	4.6	4.6	4.6	4.6	4.7	4.6	4.6	4.6	4.6	4.5	4.6	4.6
2006	4.7	4.7	4.6	4.6	4.6	4.6	4.7	4.7	4.7	4.7	4.7	4.8	4.7
2007	4.8	4.8	4.8	4.8	4.8	4.8	4.8	4.8	4.8	4.8	4.8	4.8	4.8
2008	4.7	4.8	4.7	4.7	4.7	4.9	5.0	4.9	4.8	4.8	4.7	4.7	4.8
2009	4.7	4.6	4.6	4.6	4.6	4.6	4.6	4.5	4.5	4.6	4.6	4.6	4.6
2010	4.6	4.6	4.6	4.7	4.7	4.8	4.7	4.6	4.6	4.7	4.7	4.7	4.7
2011	4.6	4.6	4.6	4.6	4.6	4.5	4.5	4.7	4.6	4.8	4.8	4.8	4.6
2012	4.8	4.9	4.9	4.9	5.0	5.1	5.0	5.1	5.1	5.0	5.0	5.0	5.0
2013	4.9	5.0	4.9	4.8	4.8	4.8	4.9	4.8	4.9	4.8	4.9	4.9	4.9
2014	4.8	4.8	4.9	4.9	4.9	4.9	5.0	4.9	4.9	5.0	5.0	5.0	4.9
2015	5.0	5.0	5.0	4.8	4.9	4.9	4.8	4.8	4.9	4.9	4.9	4.9	4.9
Retail Trade													
2005	17.4	17.1	17.5	17.3	17.4	17.4	17.6	17.4	17.5	17.9	18.2	18.9	17.6
2006	18.0	17.9	17.8	17.5	17.5	17.9	17.8	17.7	18.0	18.2	18.5	18.8	18.0
2007	18.0	17.8	17.8	18.2	18.2	18.3	18.1	17.9	18.0	18.2	18.6	18.9	18.2
2008	18.1	18.2	18.2	18.6	18.5	18.6	18.5	18.3	18.5	18.1	18.9	19.0	18.5
2009	18.0	17.6	17.5	17.5	17.3	17.3	17.3	17.4	17.6	18.1	18.7	18.8	17.8
2010	18.3	17.5	18.1	18.4	18.4	18.5	18.4	18.3	18.3	18.6	19.1	19.3	18.4
2011	18.6	18.4	18.3	18.6	18.5	18.4	18.3	18.1	18.5	18.9	19.2	19.5	18.6
2012	18.6	18.5	18.5	18.6	18.8	18.8	18.8	18.7	18.9	19.1	20.0	20.3	19.0
2013	19.5	19.5	19.5	19.6	19.7	19.6	19.6	19.8	20.1	20.5	21.5	21.7	20.1
2014	20.7	20.6	20.7	21.3	21.2	21.3	20.9	21.1	21.4	21.7	22.6	22.7	21.4
2015	22.0	21.8	21.8	21.9	21.8	22.1	22.3	22.2	22.6	23.2	24.2	24.6	22.5
Transportation and Utilities													
2005	5.3	5.4	5.5	5.5	5.5	5.5	5.6	5.5	5.5	5.7	5.7	5.8	5.5
2006	5.4	5.3	5.4	5.4	5.5	5.4	5.2	5.2	5.1	5.0	5.0	5.0	5.2
2007	4.7	4.6	4.8	4.8	4.9	4.8	4.8	4.8	4.8	4.6	4.7	4.7	4.8
2009	4.6	4.5	4.5	4.6	4.7	4.7	4.8	4.7	4.7	4.7	4.7	4.8	4.7
	4.6	4.6	4.6	4.7	4.7	4.6	4.6	4.5	4.4	4.3	4.2	4.1	4.5
2010	4.0	4.0	4.2	4.3	4.3	4.3	4.3	4.3	4.3	4.3	4.3	4.2	4.2
2011	4.1	4.1	4.2	4.3	4.2	4.3	4.3	4.3	4.2	4.2	4.1	4.0	4.2
2012	4.0	4.0	4.1	4.2	4.2	4.3	4.2	4.2	4.2	4.2	4.1	4.1	4.2
2013	4.1	4.1	4.2	4.2	4.2	4.3	4.2	4.1	4.1	4.1	4.1	4.1	4.2
2014	4.0	4.1	4.2	4.3	4.4	4.5	4.4	4.5	4.4	4.5	4.5	4.4	4.4
2015	4.4	4.5	4.5	4.7	4.8	4.9	5.0	5.0	5.0	4.9	4.8	4.9	4.8

1. Employment by Industry: District of Columbia, 2005–2015—*Continued*

(Numbers in thousands, not seasonally adjusted)

Industry and year	January	February	March	April	May	June	July	August	September	October	November	December	Annual average
Information													
2005	22.8	23.0	22.8	22.6	22.4	22.6	22.7	22.5	22.4	22.2	22.3	22.3	22.6
2006	22.0	21.9	22.2	22.1	22.1	22.4	22.4	22.2	22.3	22.0	22.1	22.1	22.2
2007	22.4	22.5	22.4	21.8	21.8	22.2	22.5	22.3	21.4	21.3	21.3	21.3	21.9
2008	21.1	21.2	21.3	20.9	21.0	20.9	21.0	21.0	20.8	20.6	20.6	20.4	20.9
2009	19.8	19.7	19.0	19.4	19.3	19.4	19.1	18.8	18.6	18.6	18.5	18.5	19.1
2010	18.5	18.4	18.5	18.7	18.6	18.9	19.0	18.7	18.8	18.7	18.5	18.7	18.7
2011	18.3	18.5	18.6	18.8	18.5	18.7	18.4	17.9	18.2	18.0	18.0	18.2	18.3
2012	17.5	17.7	17.6	17.3	17.4	17.7	17.4	17.7	17.3	17.3	17.6	17.4	17.5
2013	17.1	17.2	17.2	16.9	17.1	17.1	17.3	17.4	16.9	16.6	16.9	16.7	17.0
2014	17.1	17.1	17.1	17.2	17.3	17.4	17.6	17.3	17.2	17.1	17.1	17.1	17.2
2015	16.6	16.7	16.7	17.0	17.2	17.3	17.3	17.2	17.1	17.0	17.1	17.0	17.0
Financial Activities													
2005	29.9	30.1	29.8	30.6	30.7	30.5	30.3	30.2	30.3	30.1	30.0	30.4	30.2
2006	29.5	29.7	29.9	29.2	29.3	29.4	29.6	29.6	29.5	29.3	29.1	29.2	29.4
2007	29.5	29.7	29.7	29.3	29.0	29.1	29.3	29.1	28.9	28.9	29.0	28.9	29.2
2008	28.3	28.4	28.3	28.4	28.3	28.4	28.2	28.2	28.2	27.8	27.8	27.6	28.2
2009	27.2	26.9	26.8	26.6	26.6	26.9	26.8	26.8	26.9	27.0	27.1	27.2	26.9
2010	26.8	26.7	27.0	27.1	27.1	27.3	26.6	26.5	26.1	27.0	27.2	27.2	26.9
2011	27.1	27.0	27.2	27.5	27.5	27.4	27.7	27.9	27.9	27.9	28.0	28.1	27.6
2012	28.1	28.1	28.2	28.2	28.1	28.4	28.2	28.1	28.0	28.3	28.4	28.3	28.2
2013	28.2	28.4	28.6	28.8	28.6	29.1	29.1	29.1	29.0	29.5	29.6	29.8	29.0
2014	29.7	29.8	30.0	29.8	30.0	30.2	30.5	30.4	30.2	30.3	30.3	30.3	30.1
2015	30.2	30.4	30.5	30.0	30.1	30.3	30.6	30.4	30.1	30.3	30.2	30.6	30.3
Professional and Business Services													
2005	144.2	145.5	147.0	147.4	147.8	150.3	150.3	149.5	149.4	149.5	149.6	150.1	148.4
2006	147.4	149.2	150.5	151.4	152.1	155.8	153.7	152.5	152.3	153.4	153.5	153.5	152.1
2007	150.7	152.3	152.8	152.6	153.5	155.4	153.1	152.7	151.7	152.3	152.9	153.3	152.8
2008	150.5	152.0	153.3	153.6	153.6	155.0	153.6	152.9	151.9	151.8	150.6	150.1	152.4
2009	149.2	148.9	148.5	146.1	146.4	148.4	148.7	147.1	145.4	147.1	147.7	148.0	147.6
2010	145.8	145.8	147.3	148.7	148.6	150.0	149.1	148.2	146.8	147.2	147.2	147.4	147.7
2011	146.7	147.4	148.4	150.4	150.5	151.8	152.7	152.1	150.2	151.8	151.5	151.0	150.4
2012	150.7	151.5	152.7	152.6	152.9	154.4	155.6	154.9	153.7	156.2	156.9	156.5	154.1
2013	153.3	154.6	154.9	155.0	154.9	156.1	157.8	157.5	156.0	156.5	157.7	156.6	155.9
2014	153.7	154.6	155.2	155.9	156.3	158.4	159.1	158.1	158.2	159.1	159.3	159.4	157.3
2015	158.2	159.3	159.5	160.8	161.7	163.6	163.0	162.6	161.6	162.9	163.5	162.0	161.6
Education and Health Services													
2005	91.6	94.7	94.6	93.8	91.5	87.4	86.5	86.0	91.3	94.6	97.4	96.4	92.2
2006	92.6	96.0	96.4	96.6	93.1	88.8	88.3	87.5	92.6	97.1	99.4	98.8	93.9
2007	97.3	101.6	102.4	101.3	96.9	92.1	92.3	91.5	97.5	102.9	103.0	103.2	98.5
2008	99.4	100.8	101.5	102.6	102.2	97.8	99.7	99.7	103.8	104.8	105.9	106.2	102.0
2009	104.9	106.0	106.6	106.8	105.3	100.3	100.9	100.2	103.4	107.9	109.1	108.9	105.0
2010	107.4	107.2	108.4	111.3	110.4	104.7	103.1	103.5	109.6	109.1	109.9	109.9	107.9
2011	112.7	113.6	114.1	114.3	110.3	108.5	109.4	108.6	115.6	115.5	115.9	116.0	112.9
2012	114.6	115.2	115.5	116.3	116.2	109.9	107.7	108.7	118.0	121.1	122.3	122.8	115.7
2013	120.5	122.3	122.7	127.1	126.6	117.9	119.7	119.4	128.3	130.3	131.3	131.2	124.8
2014	127.4	129.0	129.3	130.3	129.9	120.4	118.1	117.8	129.6	130.5	131.4	132.2	127.2
2015	129.0	130.6	130.9	132.1	131.3	121.5	121.0	119.9	128.0	130.4	131.0	128.9	127.9
Leisure and Hospitality													
2005	50.5	51.5	52.8	54.2	55.4	55.1	54.1	53.4	54.4	54.4	54.3	53.8	53.7
2006	51.7	52.7	54.3	54.6	55.3	55.8	54.5	53.9	54.5	54.9	54.3	53.6	54.2
2007	51.5	52.8	54.5	56.3	56.3	56.4	56.4	55.7	56.5	56.4	56.6	56.3	55.5
2008	53.9	55.2	56.4	59.1	59.2	59.0	59.1	58.6	59.4	58.9	58.1	56.6	57.8
2009	56.0	56.0	57.4	58.4	59.8	59.1	58.5	57.8	58.6	59.2	59.1	58.4	58.2
2010	56.1	56.1	58.6	61.7	61.4	61.4	60.5	59.6	59.6	60.9	60.4	59.7	59.7
2011	57.2	58.5	60.1	63.9	63.5	63.5	62.6	63.0	63.8	64.3	64.2	63.2	62.3
2012	60.7	62.5	64.4	66.3	67.7	67.4	66.7	66.0	66.3	66.6	65.4	64.7	65.4
2013	63.1	64.6	66.3	69.3	69.9	69.9	69.2	68.6	69.4	68.2	68.5	67.5	67.9
2014	65.4	66.5	68.3	71.6	72.4	71.7	70.5	70.6	71.2	71.4	71.4	70.2	70.1
2015	70.1	70.4	71.8	74.0	75.0	74.7	73.4	73.7	73.3	73.8	73.1	73.8	73.1

1. Employment by Industry: District of Columbia, 2005–2015—*Continued*

(Numbers in thousands, not seasonally adjusted)

Industry and year	January	February	March	April	May	June	July	August	September	October	November	December	Annual average
Other Services													
2005	57.8	58.1	58.7	59.0	59.2	59.9	59.6	59.4	58.9	58.7	59.1	59.4	59.0
2006	58.6	59.0	59.5	59.8	60.1	61.3	61.8	61.3	61.0	61.4	61.8	62.4	60.7
2007	61.0	61.6	61.9	62.2	62.6	63.7	63.9	63.1	63.1	63.1	63.4	63.9	62.8
2008	63.1	63.4	64.4	64.8	65.1	66.2	67.0	66.2	66.0	65.6	65.9	66.0	65.3
2009	65.3	65.1	64.8	64.5	64.6	65.4	65.0	64.6	64.1	64.6	64.8	65.1	64.8
2010	64.1	64.1	64.6	64.8	65.4	66.4	66.3	65.7	65.2	65.8	66.1	66.4	65.4
2011	65.6	66.3	66.8	66.5	66.7	67.5	68.1	67.4	66.8	67.1	67.3	67.7	67.0
2012	67.0	67.6	68.0	67.2	67.6	68.4	69.7	68.5	68.1	68.3	68.6	68.9	68.2
2013	68.2	68.5	68.6	68.9	69.2	70.0	70.2	69.6	69.5	69.2	69.4	69.5	69.2
2014	69.0	69.7	69.7	70.2	70.4	71.4	71.5	71.2	70.9	70.8	71.0	70.8	70.6
2015	70.2	70.6	70.7	70.8	71.1	72.1	72.0	71.1	71.0	71.1	70.7	70.6	71.0
Government													
2005	231.7	231.2	231.2	231.8	231.9	234.7	242.0	241.4	230.9	232.2	233.0	232.6	233.7
2006	231.8	231.4	231.4	230.0	230.7	233.5	242.8	240.4	230.7	231.2	231.2	231.4	233.0
2007	226.9	227.8	227.1	226.9	227.3	230.0	241.6	238.6	228.7	232.7	232.1	232.3	231.0
2008	230.9	230.6	231.1	229.8	230.9	234.0	248.5	246.4	232.5	234.2	234.3	234.9	234.8
2009	234.1	234.0	233.9	234.5	235.3	238.8	259.8	252.2	238.3	240.5	241.3	240.4	240.3
2010	241.3	240.7	240.9	242.1	244.8	247.5	267.9	246.3	246.0	248.8	249.0	247.8	246.9
2011	246.9	246.4	246.8	246.1	246.5	248.5	260.7	246.6	246.7	243.7	243.2	243.0	247.1
2012	242.4	241.3	241.9	240.8	241.3	243.6	254.8	242.1	241.6	242.7	242.6	242.0	243.1
2013	240.2	239.6	239.9	239.4	239.5	240.0	250.1	237.8	239.4	239.6	239.5	239.7	240.4
2014	232.6	233.0	233.3	232.4	232.9	233.9	246.6	233.3	235.6	236.4	235.9	236.4	235.2
2015	235.5	236.0	236.1	236.0	236.6	237.2	250.3	236.1	237.2	237.9	238.4	238.6	238.0

2. Average Weekly Hours by Selected Industry: District of Columbia, 2011–2015

(Not seasonally adjusted)

Industry and year	January	February	March	April	May	June	July	August	September	October	November	December	Annual average
Total Private													
2011	36.3	35.7	35.0	35.3	35.9	35.3	35.3	35.3	35.2	36.2	35.1	35.0	35.5
2012	35.7	35.0	35.3	36.1	35.5	35.6	36.5	35.4	36.4	35.6	35.8	36.4	35.8
2013	35.6	36.0	35.7	35.6	35.7	36.7	35.5	35.7	36.5	35.8	36.0	36.6	36.0
2014	35.8	36.7	36.7	36.0	36.0	36.6	36.0	36.0	35.7	35.8	36.9	35.5	36.1
2015	35.3	36.8	36.4	35.5	35.8	35.5	35.0	35.9	35.0	35.3	36.0	35.2	35.6
Goods-Producing													
2011	34.5	35.7	36.7	36.3	37.0	38.2	36.7	37.6	38.7	38.1	36.4	36.3	36.9
2012	36.6	35.9	37.6	38.8	37.4	36.2	38.2	37.0	37.5	35.3	36.0	36.7	36.9
2013	37.3	37.3	38.1	36.2	38.0	37.4	37.7	38.9	40.7	37.2	37.2	38.4	37.9
2014	39.7	37.6	40.4	39.8	38.9	39.9	41.6	38.6	40.5	38.3	37.8	40.0	39.4
2015	38.3	40.1	40.4	39.0	40.5	40.6	39.0	39.7	38.2	40.6	37.7	40.9	39.6
Trade, Transportation, and Utilities													
2011	35.3	35.3	35.3	35.3	34.8	35.3	35.9	36.3	35.7	36.8	36.2	36.5	35.7
2012	37.9	37.0	38.3	39.2	38.6	38.8	40.3	39.1	38.7	38.6	38.7	37.6	38.5
2013	37.9	36.9	36.9	37.8	37.6	37.3	36.9	36.0	36.7	36.1	35.9	36.0	36.8
2014	35.2	35.6	36.7	36.4	36.8	35.8	35.9	35.5	36.5	35.3	36.5	36.3	36.0
2015	35.4	36.6	35.9	35.7	36.0	35.7	35.3	35.1	37.3	35.9	36.2	36.3	36.0
Professional and Business Services													
2011	34.5	33.7	32.9	33.8	34.6	33.9	33.6	34.2	34.3	35.6	34.7	34.6	34.2
2012	35.5	35.1	34.8	36.0	35.1	35.5	36.3	35.4	36.3	35.1	35.4	36.3	35.6
2013	35.3	36.2	35.5	35.4	35.7	37.7	35.9	36.4	37.5	36.0	36.8	37.5	36.3
2014	37.0	38.3	38.2	37.2	37.3	37.8	36.6	37.1	36.5	36.7	37.9	36.0	37.2
2015	36.0	37.8	37.5	36.2	36.3	36.3	35.4	37.4	35.7	36.1	37.1	36.1	36.5
Leisure and Hospitality													
2011	30.3	31.6	32.3	32.6	32.5	31.6	31.6	30.6	31.2	30.5	30.2	29.4	31.2
2012	29.6	29.6	29.3	29.6	29.9	30.2	30.4	29.3	30.7	30.6	30.2	30.7	30.0
2013	30.6	31.8	31.4	31.6	30.9	30.1	30.1	29.8	30.7	30.1	30.0	29.9	30.6
2014	28.6	29.3	29.7	30.3	30.5	30.7	30.2	29.7	29.6	30.1	30.1	29.7	29.9
2015	28.2	29.1	29.9	30.2	30.7	30.0	29.0	28.7	28.2	28.8	29.0	28.5	29.2
Other Services													
2011	36.7	35.8	35.3	35.1	35.9	35.3	35.6	35.2	34.7	35.5	34.7	34.9	35.4
2012	35.4	34.6	34.9	35.5	35.1	35.3	35.7	35.4	36.3	35.6	35.9	36.3	35.5
2013	35.2	35.9	35.9	35.7	35.9	36.9	35.2	35.9	36.3	36.0	35.7	36.4	35.9
2014	35.1	36.2	36.2	35.2	35.2	36.2	35.7	35.7	35.2	35.7	37.6	35.8	35.8
2015	35.7	37.2	36.1	34.9	35.4	34.8	35.1	36.2	35.5	35.6	36.8	35.2	35.7

3. Average Hourly Earnings by Selected Industry: District of Columbia, 2011–2015

(Dollars, not seasonally adjusted)

Industry and year	January	February	March	April	May	June	July	August	September	October	November	December	Annual average
Total Private													
2011	35.63	34.72	35.24	35.12	35.58	34.86	35.18	34.98	35.59	36.23	35.68	36.46	35.44
2012	37.11	36.38	36.36	37.06	36.03	36.24	37.30	36.65	37.32	36.95	36.87	37.72	36.84
2013	37.36	38.21	37.85	37.93	37.93	38.68	37.83	37.92	38.80	38.45	38.82	39.76	38.31
2014	38.93	39.67	39.22	38.36	38.54	39.14	38.25	38.32	38.87	38.55	39.55	39.27	38.89
2015	39.61	40.49	40.52	38.94	38.19	38.30	37.65	37.97	37.38	36.08	37.38	36.90	38.29
Goods-Producing													
2011	30.76	30.33	29.21	29.21	29.01	28.91	29.00	29.30	28.96	28.40	29.14	31.09	29.41
2012	34.12	32.30	32.22	31.08	31.45	31.55	32.10	32.28	32.46	32.76	33.18	34.18	32.45
2013	33.55	34.05	33.93	32.60	32.20	31.82	32.38	32.86	32.22	32.84	33.22	33.15	32.89
2014	30.77	30.58	29.39	29.12	28.35	28.43	27.34	27.54	27.13	27.33	27.69	28.55	28.49
2015	27.87	27.93	28.78	28.09	28.01	28.19	27.61	28.60	30.33	29.24	30.66	30.33	28.81
Trade, Transportation, and Utilities													
2011	23.55	23.19	22.82	22.98	23.12	22.53	22.66	23.37	24.20	25.26	24.43	23.47	23.48
2012	24.96	24.58	25.44	26.45	25.25	25.94	27.15	26.50	26.24	25.70	24.96	24.97	25.69
2013	24.39	25.46	25.25	25.12	24.81	24.61	23.57	24.11	24.07	25.00	24.47	24.87	24.65
2014	25.72	24.76	24.06	24.19	23.57	23.42	23.15	23.10	23.11	23.58	23.75	23.53	23.81
2015	24.18	24.74	24.88	24.46	24.54	24.63	25.01	26.11	25.43	25.82	26.63	25.68	25.20
Professional and Business Services													
2011	39.51	38.52	39.23	39.46	40.49	40.05	40.84	40.00	41.16	42.30	41.77	43.18	40.57
2012	44.61	43.60	43.42	44.15	43.51	43.79	44.90	43.64	45.36	44.55	44.40	46.01	44.34
2013	45.76	47.03	46.87	46.51	46.41	47.43	46.74	46.34	48.10	47.45	48.06	49.33	47.19
2014	47.85	49.44	49.01	48.06	48.45	49.35	47.62	47.84	48.22	47.66	49.21	48.63	48.45
2015	48.54	49.33	48.95	47.45	47.73	47.54	46.49	47.38	46.84	46.49	47.75	47.30	47.65
Leisure and Hospitality													
2011	17.82	17.83	18.17	18.18	18.46	17.95	17.57	17.24	17.86	18.10	17.76	18.09	17.92
2012	17.14	17.44	17.34	17.37	17.57	17.39	17.22	17.10	17.55	18.18	17.91	17.89	17.51
2013	17.87	18.63	17.83	18.03	17.92	17.70	17.16	17.34	17.44	17.90	16.90	17.67	17.70
2014	17.83	17.44	17.38	17.15	16.69	16.98	17.06	17.35	17.74	18.09	17.80	18.26	17.47
2015	18.08	17.97	18.49	18.07	17.94	17.71	17.64	17.67	17.79	17.85	17.86	17.70	17.90
Other Services													
2011	41.60	40.23	41.61	40.62	40.67	39.61	39.36	39.60	40.68	40.00	39.88	40.36	40.35
2012	41.29	39.52	38.93	40.26	39.44	39.21	40.21	39.98	40.70	40.36	40.12	41.10	40.10
2013	40.49	40.70	40.05	41.32	41.53	41.45	40.37	40.74	41.49	40.49	41.21	42.57	41.04
2014	41.87	42.71	41.75	41.97	42.79	42.96	43.15	43.07	44.61	44.24	44.92	45.05	43.27
2015	45.35	46.56	46.83	45.39	45.09	45.26	44.73	46.26	45.50	44.42	45.68	45.38	45.54

4. Average Weekly Earnings by Selected Industry: District of Columbia, 2011–2015

(Dollars, not seasonally adjusted)

Industry and year	January	February	March	April	May	June	July	August	September	October	November	December	Annual average
Total Private													
2011	1,293.37	1,239.50	1,233.40	1,239.74	1,277.32	1,230.56	1,241.85	1,234.79	1,252.77	1,311.53	1,252.37	1,276.10	1,258.12
2012	1,324.83	1,273.30	1,283.51	1,337.87	1,279.07	1,290.14	1,361.45	1,297.41	1,358.45	1,315.42	1,319.95	1,373.01	1,318.87
2013	1,330.02	1,375.56	1,351.25	1,350.31	1,354.10	1,419.56	1,342.97	1,353.74	1,416.20	1,376.51	1,397.52	1,455.22	1,379.16
2014	1,393.69	1,455.89	1,439.37	1,380.96	1,387.44	1,432.52	1,377.00	1,379.52	1,387.66	1,380.09	1,459.40	1,394.09	1,403.93
2015	1,398.23	1,490.03	1,474.93	1,382.37	1,367.20	1,359.65	1,317.75	1,363.12	1,308.30	1,273.62	1,345.68	1,298.88	1,363.12
Goods-Producing													
2011	1,061.22	1,082.78	1,072.01	1,060.32	1,073.37	1,104.36	1,064.30	1,101.68	1,120.75	1,082.04	1,060.70	1,128.57	1,085.23
2012	1,248.79	1,159.57	1,211.47	1,205.90	1,176.23	1,142.11	1,226.22	1,194.36	1,217.25	1,156.43	1,194.48	1,254.41	1,197.41
2013	1,251.42	1,270.07	1,292.73	1,180.12	1,223.60	1,190.07	1,220.73	1,278.25	1,311.35	1,221.65	1,235.78	1,272.96	1,246.53
2014	1,221.57	1,149.81	1,187.36	1,158.98	1,102.82	1,134.36	1,137.34	1,063.04	1,098.77	1,046.74	1,046.68	1,142.00	1,122.51
2015	1,067.42	1,119.99	1,162.71	1,095.51	1,134.41	1,144.51	1,076.79	1,135.42	1,158.61	1,187.14	1,155.88	1,240.50	1,140.88
Trade, Transportation, and Utilities													
2011	831.32	818.61	805.55	811.19	804.58	795.31	813.49	848.33	863.94	929.57	884.37	856.66	838.24
2012	945.98	909.46	974.35	1,036.84	974.65	1,006.47	1,094.15	1,036.15	1,015.49	992.02	965.95	938.87	989.07
2013	924.38	939.47	931.73	949.54	932.86	917.95	869.73	867.96	883.37	902.50	878.47	895.32	907.12
2014	905.34	881.46	883.00	880.52	867.38	838.44	831.09	820.05	843.52	832.37	866.88	854.14	857.16
2015	855.97	905.48	893.19	873.22	883.44	879.29	882.85	916.46	948.54	926.94	964.01	932.18	906.84
Professional and Business Services													
2011	1,363.10	1,298.12	1,290.67	1,333.75	1,400.95	1,357.70	1,372.22	1,368.00	1,411.79	1,505.88	1,449.42	1,494.03	1,387.49
2012	1,583.66	1,530.36	1,511.02	1,589.40	1,527.20	1,554.55	1,629.87	1,544.86	1,646.57	1,563.71	1,571.76	1,670.16	1,578.50
2013	1,615.33	1,702.49	1,663.89	1,646.45	1,656.84	1,788.11	1,677.97	1,686.78	1,803.75	1,708.20	1,768.61	1,849.88	1,713.00
2014	1,770.45	1,893.55	1,872.18	1,787.83	1,807.19	1,865.43	1,742.89	1,774.86	1,760.03	1,749.12	1,865.06	1,750.68	1,802.34
2015	1,747.44	1,864.67	1,835.63	1,717.69	1,732.60	1,725.70	1,645.75	1,772.01	1,672.19	1,678.29	1,771.53	1,707.53	1,739.23
Leisure and Hospitality													
2011	539.95	563.43	586.89	592.67	599.95	567.22	555.21	527.54	557.23	552.05	536.35	531.85	559.10
2012	507.34	516.22	508.06	514.15	525.34	525.18	523.49	501.03	538.79	556.31	540.88	549.22	525.30
2013	546.82	592.43	559.86	569.75	553.73	532.77	516.52	516.73	535.41	538.79	507.00	528.33	541.62
2014	509.94	510.99	516.19	519.65	509.05	521.29	515.21	515.30	525.10	544.51	535.78	542.32	522.35
2015	509.86	522.93	552.85	545.71	550.76	531.30	511.56	507.13	501.68	514.08	517.94	504.45	522.68
Other Services													
2011	1,526.72	1,440.23	1,468.83	1,425.76	1,460.05	1,398.23	1,401.22	1,393.92	1,411.60	1,420.00	1,383.84	1,408.56	1,428.39
2012	1,461.67	1,367.39	1,358.66	1,429.23	1,384.34	1,384.11	1,435.50	1,415.29	1,477.41	1,436.82	1,440.31	1,491.93	1,423.55
2013	1,425.25	1,461.13	1,437.80	1,475.12	1,490.93	1,529.51	1,421.02	1,462.57	1,506.09	1,457.64	1,471.20	1,549.55	1,473.34
2014	1,469.64	1,546.10	1,511.35	1,477.34	1,506.21	1,555.15	1,540.46	1,537.60	1,570.27	1,579.37	1,688.99	1,612.79	1,549.07
2015	1,619.00	1,732.03	1,690.56	1,584.11	1,596.19	1,575.05	1,570.02	1,674.61	1,615.25	1,581.35	1,681.02	1,597.38	1,625.78

FLORIDA
At a Glance

Population:
  2005 estimate: 17,842,038
  2010 census: 18,801,310
  2015 estimate: 20,271,272

Percent change in population:
  2005–2015: 13.6%
  2010–2015: 7.8%

Percent change in total nonfarm employment:
  2005–2015: 4.0%

Industry with the largest growth in employment, 2005–2015 (thousands):
  Education and health services, 239.2

Industry with the largest decline or smallest growth in employment, 2005–2015 (thousands):
  Construction, –208.2

Civilian labor force:
  2005: 8,720,970
  2010: 9,212,066
  2015: 9,675,328

Unemployment rate and rank among states (highest to lowest):
  2005: 3.7%, 45th
  2010: 11.1%, 6th
  2015: 5.4%, 21st

Over-the-year change in unemployment rates:
  2012–2013: –1.2%
  2013–2014: –1.0%
  2014–2015: –0.9%

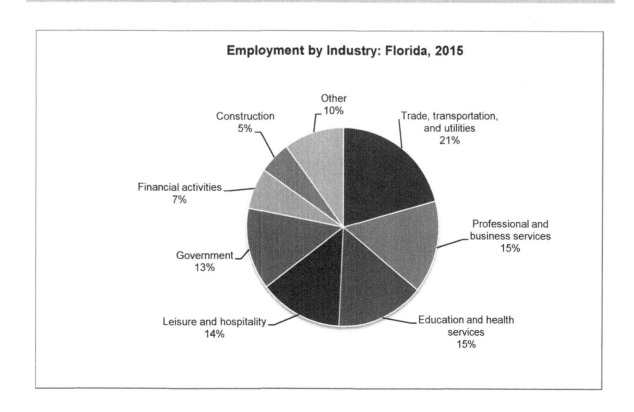

Employment by Industry: Florida, 2015

Other 10%
Construction 5%
Trade, transportation, and utilities 21%
Financial activities 7%
Professional and business services 15%
Government 13%
Leisure and hospitality 14%
Education and health services 15%

1. Employment by Industry: Florida, 2005–2015

(Numbers in thousands, not seasonally adjusted)

Industry and year	January	February	March	April	May	June	July	August	September	October	November	December	Annual average
Total Nonfarm													
2005	7,603.4	7,686.3	7,732.9	7,775.6	7,793.6	7,699.6	7,679.2	7,796.1	7,841.0	7,847.8	7,922.1	7,995.5	7,781.1
2006	7,863.4	7,938.0	8,018.5	7,998.8	8,016.4	7,931.8	7,858.6	7,975.2	7,991.3	7,993.2	8,076.6	8,133.4	7,982.9
2007	7,992.0	8,058.7	8,122.9	8,074.9	8,069.5	7,960.9	7,851.9	7,951.3	7,937.8	7,927.0	7,999.8	8,032.7	7,998.3
2008	7,851.4	7,907.3	7,928.8	7,845.1	7,813.7	7,672.5	7,562.4	7,636.9	7,608.3	7,579.6	7,586.9	7,586.1	7,714.9
2009	7,377.7	7,377.1	7,372.3	7,324.4	7,284.4	7,152.3	7,063.8	7,131.1	7,125.5	7,150.8	7,204.6	7,224.0	7,232.3
2010	7,095.1	7,145.5	7,192.7	7,213.1	7,236.4	7,115.1	7,057.8	7,143.5	7,133.2	7,196.8	7,258.1	7,286.9	7,172.9
2011	7,173.5	7,224.0	7,270.9	7,307.9	7,277.6	7,163.9	7,126.6	7,212.5	7,238.8	7,280.9	7,356.7	7,389.6	7,251.9
2012	7,283.5	7,344.9	7,404.9	7,424.1	7,414.6	7,320.8	7,266.2	7,364.8	7,379.9	7,452.3	7,540.7	7,565.9	7,396.9
2013	7,444.3	7,520.1	7,573.9	7,583.9	7,585.4	7,495.4	7,458.7	7,567.7	7,579.5	7,647.5	7,751.4	7,781.8	7,582.5
2014	7,663.4	7,735.1	7,791.4	7,820.8	7,827.6	7,728.7	7,699.4	7,812.2	7,830.3	7,918.1	8,014.2	8,057.0	7,824.9
2015	7,940.7	8,013.6	8,064.7	8,088.6	8,093.5	7,998.8	7,981.9	8,086.6	8,100.7	8,182.0	8,268.1	8,302.1	8,093.4
Total Private													
2005	6,522.3	6,592.8	6,637.1	6,680.1	6,694.9	6,700.4	6,678.5	6,713.0	6,743.1	6,739.7	6,811.2	6,885.9	6,699.9
2006	6,763.1	6,827.1	6,903.8	6,887.4	6,908.5	6,917.7	6,843.8	6,872.3	6,876.2	6,864.3	6,939.9	7,000.0	6,883.7
2007	6,868.2	6,923.6	6,982.3	6,935.7	6,933.9	6,919.9	6,810.8	6,821.2	6,799.6	6,781.4	6,848.5	6,883.3	6,875.7
2008	6,711.1	6,755.5	6,779.6	6,698.2	6,672.8	6,627.8	6,518.6	6,503.8	6,466.1	6,433.7	6,442.1	6,446.6	6,588.0
2009	6,244.6	6,237.9	6,235.4	6,181.8	6,153.9	6,116.9	6,029.6	6,017.4	6,001.6	6,022.2	6,072.8	6,098.7	6,117.7
2010	5,973.2	6,017.5	6,064.3	6,079.0	6,074.7	6,067.1	6,024.5	6,031.4	6,017.9	6,074.5	6,132.7	6,169.9	6,060.6
2011	6,058.9	6,099.7	6,148.2	6,185.1	6,167.0	6,145.5	6,114.7	6,128.9	6,146.9	6,173.7	6,249.3	6,287.8	6,158.8
2012	6,188.8	6,238.4	6,299.2	6,324.0	6,325.1	6,315.6	6,267.0	6,289.8	6,294.9	6,354.6	6,440.2	6,471.4	6,317.4
2013	6,354.1	6,420.0	6,472.5	6,484.7	6,496.3	6,492.6	6,465.0	6,496.3	6,497.7	6,554.1	6,652.8	6,689.4	6,506.3
2014	6,578.2	6,640.9	6,693.1	6,725.7	6,740.3	6,729.7	6,703.3	6,742.1	6,750.0	6,823.7	6,916.5	6,962.4	6,750.5
2015	6,853.9	6,915.2	6,963.1	6,987.5	7,000.2	6,994.4	6,979.2	7,008.1	7,012.6	7,077.1	7,161.1	7,197.8	7,012.5
Goods-Producing													
2005	1,013.8	1,024.5	1,032.5	1,043.4	1,052.2	1,061.6	1,066.1	1,072.9	1,081.5	1,082.6	1,089.7	1,098.8	1,060.0
2006	1,085.7	1,099.2	1,111.6	1,110.2	1,117.3	1,123.6	1,110.2	1,112.0	1,109.5	1,098.3	1,093.7	1,091.4	1,105.2
2007	1,063.3	1,064.8	1,068.6	1,048.1	1,047.2	1,048.8	1,022.7	1,019.2	1,009.5	990.8	983.6	977.1	1,028.6
2008	945.2	944.0	938.8	915.5	911.9	908.8	886.6	880.1	872.7	852.8	838.1	823.5	893.2
2009	784.9	771.5	762.4	741.3	734.7	730.6	714.5	708.3	701.9	693.2	687.4	683.2	726.2
2010	660.6	662.1	664.5	668.6	669.1	672.4	673.1	670.7	666.2	661.3	658.4	657.0	665.3
2011	643.0	645.6	648.4	651.4	652.9	655.3	656.0	657.5	659.6	656.9	658.1	658.4	653.6
2012	649.1	651.9	657.8	657.1	661.9	667.1	665.3	670.5	672.0	673.8	677.5	677.1	665.1
2013	666.1	672.3	678.7	682.8	689.8	695.2	696.9	703.8	706.2	708.0	713.0	715.1	694.0
2014	706.1	713.3	717.0	722.5	731.0	736.5	739.0	744.4	747.1	752.4	754.0	755.8	734.9
2015	747.9	754.9	761.0	766.0	773.3	781.0	784.2	787.7	791.3	790.1	797.9	799.5	777.9
Service-Providing													
2005	6,589.6	6,661.8	6,700.4	6,732.2	6,741.4	6,638.0	6,613.1	6,723.2	6,759.5	6,765.2	6,832.4	6,896.7	6,721.1
2006	6,777.7	6,838.8	6,906.9	6,888.6	6,899.1	6,808.2	6,748.4	6,863.2	6,881.8	6,894.9	6,982.9	7,042.0	6,877.7
2007	6,928.7	6,993.9	7,054.3	7,026.8	7,022.3	6,912.1	6,829.2	6,932.1	6,928.3	6,936.2	7,016.2	7,055.6	6,969.6
2008	6,906.2	6,963.3	6,990.0	6,929.6	6,901.8	6,763.7	6,675.8	6,756.8	6,735.6	6,726.8	6,748.8	6,762.6	6,821.8
2009	6,592.8	6,605.6	6,609.9	6,583.1	6,549.7	6,421.7	6,349.3	6,422.8	6,423.6	6,457.6	6,517.2	6,540.8	6,506.2
2010	6,434.5	6,483.4	6,528.2	6,544.5	6,567.3	6,442.7	6,384.7	6,472.8	6,467.0	6,535.5	6,599.7	6,629.9	6,507.5
2011	6,530.5	6,578.4	6,622.5	6,656.5	6,624.7	6,508.6	6,470.6	6,555.0	6,579.2	6,624.0	6,698.6	6,731.2	6,598.3
2012	6,634.4	6,693.0	6,747.1	6,767.0	6,752.7	6,653.7	6,600.9	6,694.3	6,707.9	6,778.5	6,863.2	6,888.8	6,731.8
2013	6,778.2	6,847.8	6,895.2	6,901.1	6,895.6	6,800.2	6,761.8	6,863.9	6,873.3	6,939.5	7,038.4	7,066.7	6,888.5
2014	6,957.3	7,021.8	7,074.4	7,098.3	7,096.6	6,992.2	6,960.4	7,067.8	7,083.2	7,165.7	7,260.2	7,301.2	7,089.9
2015	7,192.8	7,258.7	7,303.7	7,322.6	7,320.2	7,217.8	7,197.7	7,298.9	7,309.4	7,391.9	7,470.2	7,502.6	7,315.5
Mining and Logging													
2005	7.1	7.1	7.1	7.2	7.2	7.2	7.2	7.2	7.0	6.8	6.8	6.9	7.1
2006	6.6	6.6	6.7	6.7	6.7	6.8	6.6	6.4	6.5	6.5	6.6	6.6	6.6
2007	6.7	6.8	6.7	6.8	6.8	6.9	6.6	6.7	6.6	6.6	6.7	6.7	6.7
2008	6.6	6.6	6.5	6.4	6.3	6.2	6.1	6.1	6.0	5.9	5.8	5.8	6.2
2009	5.7	5.6	5.5	5.5	5.5	5.5	5.4	5.4	5.4	5.4	5.4	5.4	5.5
2010	5.3	5.3	5.2	5.3	5.3	5.4	5.4	5.5	5.6	5.6	5.7	5.7	5.4
2011	5.7	5.7	5.7	5.7	5.7	5.7	5.6	5.6	5.6	5.6	5.6	5.6	5.7
2012	5.6	5.6	5.6	5.6	5.7	5.7	5.6	5.6	5.6	5.6	5.7	5.7	5.6
2013	5.7	5.7	5.7	5.6	5.6	5.6	5.6	5.7	5.6	5.6	5.7	5.8	5.7
2014	5.6	5.7	5.7	5.7	5.8	5.8	5.7	5.7	5.7	5.7	5.7	5.7	5.7
2015	5.7	5.8	5.8	5.8	5.9	5.9	5.9	5.8	5.8	5.8	5.9	5.8	5.8

1. Employment by Industry: Florida, 2005–2015—*Continued*

(Numbers in thousands, not seasonally adjusted)

Industry and year	January	February	March	April	May	June	July	August	September	October	November	December	Annual average
Construction													
2005	597.3	605.8	612.3	621.9	629.1	636.9	643.2	649.1	656.8	659.0	665.7	672.3	637.5
2006	661.7	673.4	684.3	685.1	690.9	696.1	687.9	690.0	688.1	680.4	676.3	672.6	682.2
2007	650.0	651.0	655.1	637.3	636.9	639.0	619.0	616.2	608.6	593.2	587.2	581.2	622.9
2008	554.4	553.6	550.6	531.1	528.8	527.1	511.1	506.0	501.0	486.4	475.4	465.3	515.9
2009	434.1	426.2	421.4	407.0	402.8	400.6	390.8	386.0	381.6	374.7	368.9	365.4	396.6
2010	347.5	349.2	351.5	355.1	353.8	356.1	357.8	355.7	351.6	347.3	343.3	340.4	350.8
2011	328.5	330.3	332.6	334.3	334.8	336.1	337.4	338.1	340.5	337.5	338.1	337.6	335.5
2012	328.8	330.9	335.1	334.9	338.4	343.1	342.6	347.0	349.2	350.4	352.8	352.1	342.1
2013	344.4	348.5	353.6	356.8	362.0	365.9	369.0	374.8	376.6	378.0	380.7	381.4	366.0
2014	373.7	379.4	383.1	387.6	393.9	398.7	401.5	405.8	407.9	411.3	412.1	412.7	397.3
2015	407.1	412.4	416.6	420.6	425.8	431.3	434.4	437.2	440.0	439.1	443.7	443.4	429.3
Manufacturing													
2005	409.4	411.6	413.1	414.3	415.9	417.5	415.7	416.6	417.7	416.8	417.2	419.6	415.5
2006	417.4	419.2	420.6	418.4	419.7	420.7	415.7	415.6	414.9	411.4	410.8	412.2	416.4
2007	406.6	407.0	406.8	404.0	403.5	402.9	397.1	396.3	394.3	391.0	389.7	389.2	399.0
2008	384.2	383.8	381.7	378.0	376.8	375.5	369.4	368.0	365.7	360.5	356.9	352.4	371.1
2009	345.1	339.7	335.5	328.8	326.4	324.5	318.3	316.9	314.9	313.1	313.1	312.4	324.1
2010	307.8	307.6	307.8	308.2	310.0	310.9	309.9	309.5	309.0	308.4	309.4	310.9	309.1
2011	308.8	309.6	310.1	311.4	312.4	313.5	313.0	313.8	313.5	313.8	314.4	315.2	312.5
2012	314.7	315.4	317.1	316.6	317.8	318.3	317.1	317.9	317.2	317.8	319.0	319.3	317.4
2013	316.0	318.1	319.4	320.4	322.2	323.7	322.3	323.3	324.0	324.4	326.6	327.9	322.4
2014	326.8	328.2	328.2	329.2	331.3	332.0	331.8	332.9	333.5	335.4	336.2	337.4	331.9
2015	335.1	336.7	338.6	339.6	341.6	343.8	343.9	344.7	345.5	345.2	348.3	350.3	342.8
Trade, Transportation, and Utilities													
2005	1,566.1	1,569.2	1,576.0	1,586.7	1,591.8	1,590.4	1,591.0	1,596.7	1,600.6	1,608.1	1,636.8	1,668.3	1,598.5
2006	1,618.5	1,617.6	1,629.0	1,625.2	1,628.0	1,625.9	1,615.2	1,619.6	1,619.2	1,626.5	1,663.5	1,693.0	1,631.8
2007	1,639.8	1,636.6	1,645.5	1,639.6	1,644.3	1,639.1	1,623.2	1,624.9	1,624.8	1,628.1	1,668.1	1,688.8	1,641.9
2008	1,632.7	1,628.0	1,628.8	1,610.0	1,606.7	1,595.0	1,576.9	1,574.6	1,565.6	1,562.8	1,579.8	1,594.2	1,596.3
2009	1,527.6	1,514.4	1,505.7	1,489.6	1,486.5	1,477.9	1,461.3	1,459.8	1,456.9	1,462.6	1,492.5	1,510.8	1,487.1
2010	1,464.4	1,462.9	1,467.7	1,468.8	1,470.6	1,468.9	1,457.9	1,461.3	1,456.4	1,474.0	1,508.4	1,531.0	1,474.4
2011	1,484.4	1,482.4	1,487.3	1,495.5	1,494.0	1,491.4	1,489.5	1,493.9	1,495.1	1,506.9	1,546.7	1,566.0	1,502.8
2012	1,523.0	1,520.4	1,526.8	1,527.2	1,531.6	1,528.2	1,520.1	1,522.9	1,524.6	1,537.8	1,582.4	1,599.1	1,537.0
2013	1,550.9	1,550.7	1,554.8	1,555.7	1,559.8	1,562.1	1,557.2	1,562.8	1,562.7	1,580.4	1,629.8	1,652.4	1,573.3
2014	1,597.2	1,600.0	1,604.7	1,608.8	1,611.1	1,610.3	1,605.8	1,614.6	1,615.8	1,636.4	1,688.6	1,715.4	1,625.7
2015	1,661.2	1,661.0	1,664.9	1,666.7	1,669.2	1,672.5	1,666.6	1,674.3	1,670.8	1,685.7	1,723.2	1,743.3	1,680.0
Wholesale Trade													
2005	338.2	340.5	341.3	344.4	346.4	346.4	346.1	346.9	348.1	348.4	350.0	353.6	345.9
2006	349.3	352.0	354.0	354.9	356.6	357.1	355.2	356.1	356.6	357.4	359.0	361.8	355.8
2007	360.2	362.7	363.8	362.4	363.3	363.1	359.2	359.1	358.9	359.4	360.4	362.0	361.2
2008	356.4	358.0	357.5	353.7	354.0	352.3	347.9	346.9	346.0	344.2	342.7	342.5	350.2
2009	333.5	332.3	329.3	325.7	324.8	322.2	317.9	317.0	315.5	316.2	316.9	318.3	322.5
2010	311.8	312.8	313.4	313.4	315.0	313.8	311.4	311.7	311.1	313.2	314.3	316.6	313.2
2011	309.8	311.2	312.0	313.0	312.5	311.8	310.7	310.8	311.2	312.3	313.7	316.7	312.1
2012	312.8	314.8	316.4	317.6	318.6	317.8	316.7	317.2	317.6	319.6	321.8	323.1	317.8
2013	318.3	320.1	321.2	320.5	321.5	320.7	318.6	319.4	319.9	321.4	324.0	325.4	320.9
2014	322.2	324.6	324.8	325.6	327.2	326.2	325.6	327.5	327.7	329.9	333.1	335.1	327.5
2015	331.8	332.9	333.6	333.3	334.6	334.0	333.7	334.5	334.9	335.5	338.1	338.8	334.6
Retail Trade													
2005	982.5	982.2	987.0	993.1	995.2	995.7	996.7	1,001.2	1,002.5	1,009.9	1,033.6	1,056.0	1,003.0
2006	1,017.3	1,013.5	1,021.3	1,017.0	1,017.9	1,016.3	1,010.2	1,011.7	1,010.0	1,017.4	1,050.3	1,069.4	1,022.7
2007	1,027.6	1,022.3	1,028.8	1,023.0	1,027.5	1,023.0	1,013.2	1,014.5	1,013.9	1,016.2	1,051.6	1,065.5	1,027.3
2008	1,023.8	1,016.9	1,017.8	1,005.1	1,002.2	995.2	984.2	982.8	976.6	975.3	992.6	1,001.4	997.8
2009	953.5	943.8	939.5	929.9	929.0	924.8	915.4	915.6	915.0	919.9	947.7	959.2	932.8
2010	926.6	923.2	926.8	928.4	929.1	929.2	921.6	924.7	921.0	934.5	964.9	979.1	934.1
2011	943.8	939.5	942.2	947.8	947.0	945.1	944.0	948.3	948.6	958.5	993.9	1,004.6	955.3
2012	972.4	966.6	970.7	970.4	973.5	970.4	964.4	966.7	967.8	977.4	1,016.6	1,026.0	978.6
2013	989.3	986.1	988.0	989.0	991.9	994.9	993.9	997.7	996.6	1,011.3	1,054.6	1,069.6	1,005.2
2014	1,025.5	1,024.5	1,027.5	1,030.6	1,030.8	1,031.1	1,027.6	1,033.2	1,033.7	1,050.1	1,094.5	1,110.7	1,043.3
2015	1,067.8	1,067.4	1,069.3	1,070.7	1,071.4	1,074.9	1,069.1	1,074.9	1,070.1	1,082.4	1,112.8	1,124.2	1,079.6

1. Employment by Industry: Florida, 2005–2015—*Continued*

(Numbers in thousands, not seasonally adjusted)

Industry and year	January	February	March	April	May	June	July	August	September	October	November	December	Annual average
Transportation and Utilities													
2005	245.4	246.5	247.7	249.2	250.2	248.3	248.2	248.6	250.0	249.8	253.2	258.7	249.7
2006	251.9	252.1	253.7	253.3	253.5	252.5	249.8	251.8	252.6	251.7	254.2	261.8	253.2
2007	252.0	251.6	252.9	254.2	253.5	253.0	250.8	251.3	252.0	252.5	256.1	261.3	253.4
2008	252.5	253.1	253.5	251.2	250.5	247.5	244.8	244.9	243.0	243.3	244.5	250.3	248.3
2009	240.6	238.3	236.9	234.0	232.7	230.9	228.0	227.2	226.4	226.5	227.9	233.3	231.9
2010	226.0	226.9	227.5	227.0	226.5	225.9	224.9	224.9	224.3	226.3	229.2	235.3	227.1
2011	230.8	231.7	233.1	234.7	234.5	234.5	234.8	234.8	235.3	236.1	239.1	244.7	235.3
2012	237.8	239.0	239.7	239.2	239.5	240.0	239.0	239.0	239.2	240.8	244.0	250.0	240.6
2013	243.3	244.5	245.6	246.2	246.4	246.5	244.7	245.7	246.2	247.7	251.2	257.4	247.1
2014	249.5	250.9	252.4	252.6	253.1	253.0	252.6	253.9	254.4	256.4	261.0	269.6	255.0
2015	261.6	260.7	262.0	262.7	263.2	263.6	263.8	264.9	265.8	267.8	272.3	280.3	265.7
Information													
2005	163.3	164.1	164.3	163.5	165.2	165.3	164.9	164.9	165.4	164.0	165.0	165.4	164.6
2006	161.9	162.7	162.9	162.6	163.7	164.4	164.1	163.4	162.4	162.2	163.2	164.0	163.1
2007	161.6	162.6	163.2	163.8	164.5	164.8	163.1	162.8	161.4	161.2	161.2	161.7	162.7
2008	160.1	160.6	160.4	159.1	159.3	158.8	157.9	156.6	154.3	153.8	153.4	152.4	157.2
2009	149.3	148.9	147.9	146.3	145.5	145.1	142.9	141.7	139.8	139.3	139.2	139.3	143.8
2010	137.7	137.4	138.2	137.2	137.0	137.1	136.8	136.9	136.0	136.6	137.1	136.7	137.1
2011	136.2	136.3	136.2	135.8	135.9	135.8	135.7	135.4	135.2	135.0	135.6	135.4	135.7
2012	134.1	134.0	133.9	133.8	133.6	133.4	133.4	133.0	132.0	133.9	133.9	134.0	133.6
2013	132.8	133.1	133.7	133.5	133.5	134.3	134.5	134.6	133.9	134.6	135.3	135.9	134.1
2014	135.6	136.1	136.0	136.2	136.2	137.1	136.7	135.8	135.0	135.6	136.9	136.7	136.2
2015	135.7	135.8	135.7	135.6	136.4	136.1	136.5	136.5	135.6	135.7	135.9	135.2	135.9
Financial Activities													
2005	522.3	526.2	528.1	533.6	536.3	540.2	542.6	544.3	545.5	548.5	552.0	558.2	539.8
2006	548.3	552.5	556.0	556.7	558.7	560.2	556.9	557.6	555.6	556.9	557.9	562.3	556.6
2007	550.7	554.3	556.3	554.0	554.5	555.7	552.2	550.5	547.3	545.1	546.0	547.7	551.2
2008	537.4	538.2	538.2	532.5	531.8	529.7	524.9	522.4	517.9	513.9	511.6	512.1	525.9
2009	497.7	495.7	493.9	491.3	490.6	490.0	485.7	483.7	479.3	479.6	480.0	481.2	487.4
2010	473.1	474.3	476.0	475.6	476.9	478.7	478.5	478.7	475.9	480.4	482.4	485.5	478.0
2011	478.9	480.7	483.3	484.3	484.4	484.9	487.0	488.2	489.3	490.4	491.4	495.0	486.5
2012	488.8	491.7	494.4	496.5	497.9	500.1	500.2	501.2	500.4	504.8	507.2	509.7	499.4
2013	503.2	506.0	508.7	510.0	511.1	513.8	514.1	515.1	513.9	516.7	518.9	521.0	512.7
2014	512.6	514.4	516.9	518.3	520.3	521.2	522.4	523.0	522.0	525.9	527.8	530.2	521.3
2015	525.3	527.1	529.5	530.6	532.4	534.2	537.4	538.6	537.3	539.6	542.7	543.0	534.8
Professional and Business Services													
2005	1,059.2	1,080.6	1,087.4	1,097.0	1,096.9	1,098.4	1,096.1	1,106.0	1,115.3	1,107.7	1,121.6	1,132.1	1,099.9
2006	1,111.5	1,126.6	1,146.7	1,143.3	1,149.7	1,156.4	1,143.2	1,152.9	1,158.2	1,150.1	1,163.1	1,174.3	1,148.0
2007	1,155.5	1,170.9	1,182.0	1,170.3	1,166.3	1,164.1	1,143.5	1,147.1	1,140.4	1,139.7	1,145.1	1,148.9	1,156.2
2008	1,102.2	1,117.3	1,121.4	1,104.1	1,095.9	1,088.7	1,067.6	1,066.5	1,063.5	1,059.7	1,053.6	1,052.5	1,082.8
2009	1,009.1	1,009.9	1,007.2	998.6	993.4	991.5	977.1	977.6	978.3	987.5	996.2	999.1	993.8
2010	977.9	990.0	998.0	1,000.5	1,000.5	1,005.2	1,001.7	1,007.4	1,007.7	1,022.5	1,027.3	1,033.9	1,006.1
2011	1,014.9	1,028.6	1,035.9	1,043.8	1,036.6	1,034.7	1,027.7	1,030.2	1,033.7	1,039.9	1,049.8	1,056.9	1,036.1
2012	1,034.6	1,050.4	1,061.5	1,074.8	1,073.2	1,072.9	1,065.4	1,071.8	1,072.6	1,093.8	1,105.7	1,108.6	1,073.8
2013	1,082.1	1,099.9	1,108.4	1,110.1	1,114.6	1,113.9	1,111.0	1,118.6	1,119.1	1,133.8	1,146.4	1,148.7	1,117.2
2014	1,127.8	1,140.4	1,146.5	1,155.3	1,162.2	1,158.6	1,156.9	1,168.3	1,169.6	1,188.2	1,199.9	1,205.3	1,164.9
2015	1,184.6	1,197.6	1,202.2	1,213.3	1,218.0	1,214.9	1,219.3	1,223.8	1,224.3	1,248.1	1,262.5	1,266.8	1,223.0
Education and Health Services													
2005	942.7	951.5	954.6	959.3	960.7	955.3	950.7	959.8	967.5	969.4	972.8	978.3	960.2
2006	967.0	975.4	982.0	982.2	986.1	983.5	974.5	985.3	992.7	994.6	1,001.2	1,007.0	986.0
2007	996.9	1,007.9	1,013.2	1,015.2	1,017.6	1,015.5	1,002.3	1,014.0	1,021.9	1,025.2	1,031.7	1,036.5	1,016.5
2008	1,026.7	1,036.3	1,040.8	1,038.5	1,041.2	1,034.3	1,022.7	1,030.5	1,036.8	1,042.9	1,049.9	1,054.4	1,037.9
2009	1,037.4	1,044.2	1,048.3	1,048.1	1,051.1	1,044.8	1,036.2	1,043.1	1,051.1	1,064.8	1,071.3	1,073.7	1,051.2
2010	1,059.3	1,066.7	1,071.5	1,072.8	1,074.2	1,066.5	1,057.2	1,061.3	1,066.9	1,081.0	1,086.6	1,086.2	1,070.9
2011	1,077.4	1,085.1	1,087.5	1,096.2	1,094.8	1,083.9	1,075.1	1,082.4	1,094.2	1,100.2	1,107.1	1,108.5	1,091.0
2012	1,093.8	1,101.9	1,106.3	1,112.0	1,113.0	1,104.3	1,091.8	1,103.6	1,113.0	1,119.9	1,125.0	1,126.7	1,109.3
2013	1,115.0	1,125.9	1,129.6	1,131.7	1,131.3	1,120.3	1,108.0	1,121.1	1,128.3	1,137.7	1,145.1	1,145.6	1,128.3
2014	1,134.4	1,145.3	1,148.8	1,158.4	1,159.8	1,149.6	1,140.9	1,157.2	1,166.4	1,177.9	1,184.6	1,188.1	1,159.3
2015	1,176.4	1,186.8	1,191.2	1,196.1	1,199.9	1,190.0	1,180.5	1,193.5	1,204.8	1,218.8	1,226.3	1,228.4	1,199.4

1. Employment by Industry: Florida, 2005–2015—*Continued*

(Numbers in thousands, not seasonally adjusted)

Industry and year	January	February	March	April	May	June	July	August	September	October	November	December	Annual average
Leisure and Hospitality													
2005	931.7	951.2	967.6	969.0	963.7	961.0	941.5	943.6	940.7	936.3	949.2	959.3	951.2
2006	949.1	968.4	987.6	980.4	976.1	971.9	952.9	954.3	949.7	946.4	965.5	974.2	964.7
2007	966.8	989.2	1,011.8	1,006.9	1,001.6	993.2	972.1	971.5	963.4	959.9	978.8	986.3	983.5
2008	973.9	995.7	1,013.7	1,005.5	993.9	982.5	959.0	951.8	938.8	934.5	945.1	949.0	970.3
2009	933.9	948.5	964.4	961.4	947.7	934.1	913.3	905.7	897.8	897.4	908.1	912.8	927.1
2010	904.2	926.1	948.7	955.0	946.8	939.1	923.0	920.1	914.9	922.2	935.4	942.6	931.5
2011	931.5	946.5	973.0	979.6	970.5	963.1	948.9	947.1	945.4	949.0	964.1	970.5	957.4
2012	967.9	988.7	1,016.9	1,019.0	1,010.8	1,006.2	990.7	987.0	980.0	988.4	1,005.0	1,011.6	997.7
2013	1,001.8	1,027.3	1,052.1	1,052.3	1,047.2	1,043.7	1,035.5	1,031.5	1,024.0	1,030.8	1,049.1	1,054.2	1,037.5
2014	1,047.5	1,070.9	1,100.0	1,102.6	1,096.1	1,093.5	1,080.3	1,076.4	1,071.3	1,081.8	1,097.5	1,102.8	1,085.1
2015	1,096.7	1,123.3	1,147.8	1,147.6	1,139.4	1,134.0	1,125.1	1,123.8	1,118.4	1,126.4	1,136.2	1,145.7	1,130.4
Other Services													
2005	323.2	325.5	326.6	327.6	328.1	328.2	325.6	324.8	326.6	323.1	324.1	325.5	325.7
2006	321.1	324.7	328.0	326.8	328.9	331.8	326.8	327.2	328.9	329.3	331.8	333.8	328.3
2007	333.6	337.3	341.7	337.8	337.9	338.7	331.7	331.2	330.9	331.4	334.0	336.3	335.2
2008	332.9	335.4	337.5	333.0	332.1	330.0	323.0	321.3	316.5	313.3	310.6	308.5	324.5
2009	304.7	304.8	305.6	305.2	304.4	302.9	298.6	297.5	296.5	297.8	298.1	298.6	301.2
2010	296.0	298.0	299.7	300.5	299.6	299.2	296.3	295.0	293.9	296.5	297.1	297.0	297.4
2011	292.6	294.5	296.6	298.5	297.9	296.4	294.8	294.2	294.4	295.4	296.5	297.1	295.7
2012	297.5	299.4	301.6	303.6	303.1	303.4	300.1	299.8	300.3	302.2	303.5	304.6	301.6
2013	302.2	304.8	306.5	308.6	309.0	309.3	307.8	308.8	309.6	312.1	315.2	316.5	309.2
2014	317.0	320.5	323.2	323.6	323.6	322.9	321.3	322.4	322.8	325.5	327.2	328.1	323.2
2015	326.1	328.7	330.8	331.6	331.6	331.7	329.6	329.9	330.1	332.7	336.4	335.9	331.3
Government													
2005	1,081.1	1,093.5	1,095.8	1,095.5	1,098.7	999.2	1,000.7	1,083.1	1,097.9	1,108.1	1,110.9	1,109.6	1,081.2
2006	1,100.3	1,110.9	1,114.7	1,111.4	1,107.9	1,014.1	1,014.8	1,102.9	1,115.1	1,128.9	1,136.7	1,133.4	1,099.3
2007	1,123.8	1,135.1	1,140.6	1,139.2	1,135.6	1,041.0	1,041.1	1,130.1	1,138.2	1,145.6	1,151.3	1,149.4	1,122.6
2008	1,140.3	1,151.8	1,149.2	1,146.9	1,140.9	1,044.7	1,043.8	1,133.1	1,142.2	1,145.9	1,144.8	1,139.5	1,126.9
2009	1,133.1	1,139.2	1,136.9	1,142.6	1,130.5	1,035.4	1,034.2	1,113.7	1,123.9	1,128.6	1,131.8	1,125.3	1,114.6
2010	1,121.9	1,128.0	1,128.4	1,134.1	1,161.7	1,048.0	1,033.3	1,112.1	1,115.3	1,122.3	1,125.4	1,117.0	1,112.3
2011	1,114.6	1,124.3	1,122.7	1,122.8	1,110.6	1,018.4	1,011.9	1,083.6	1,091.9	1,107.2	1,107.4	1,101.8	1,093.1
2012	1,094.7	1,106.5	1,105.7	1,100.1	1,089.5	1,005.2	999.2	1,075.0	1,085.0	1,097.7	1,100.5	1,094.5	1,079.5
2013	1,090.2	1,100.1	1,101.4	1,099.2	1,089.1	1,002.8	993.7	1,071.4	1,081.8	1,093.4	1,098.6	1,092.4	1,076.2
2014	1,085.2	1,094.2	1,098.3	1,095.1	1,087.3	999.0	996.1	1,070.1	1,080.3	1,094.4	1,097.7	1,094.6	1,074.4
2015	1,086.8	1,098.4	1,101.6	1,101.1	1,093.3	1,004.4	1,002.7	1,078.5	1,088.1	1,104.9	1,107.0	1,104.3	1,080.9

2. Average Weekly Hours by Selected Industry: Florida, 2011–2015

(Not seasonally adjusted)

Industry and year	January	February	March	April	May	June	July	August	September	October	November	December	Annual average
Total Private													
2011	35.4	35.2	35.1	35.2	35.0	34.7	34.7	34.5	34.4	34.7	34.5	34.6	34.8
2012	34.5	34.4	34.5	34.4	34.1	34.1	34.5	34.2	34.3	34.1	34.2	34.6	34.3
2013	34.1	34.5	34.5	34.3	34.2	34.5	34.2	34.4	34.5	34.2	34.3	34.6	34.4
2014	34.2	34.6	34.6	34.4	34.2	34.5	34.3	34.4	34.3	34.2	34.6	34.4	34.4
2015	34.1	34.7	34.7	34.3	34.2	34.1	34.2	34.5	33.9	34.1	34.5	34.3	34.3
Goods-Producing													
2011	39.4	39.2	39.5	40.1	40.0	40.2	39.8	39.6	40.2	40.1	40.2	40.4	39.9
2012	40.2	39.8	40.1	40.5	40.4	40.3	40.1	40.2	40.4	40.4	40.4	40.3	40.3
2013	39.6	40.1	40.3	40.1	40.1	40.2	39.6	39.9	40.2	39.9	40.1	40.7	40.1
2014	39.2	39.6	40.0	39.9	40.0	40.2	39.9	40.2	40.3	40.0	40.6	40.5	40.0
2015	39.4	39.6	40.2	39.8	39.9	40.1	39.9	40.1	38.7	40.1	40.5	40.4	39.9
Construction													
2011	39.5	39.1	39.5	40.4	40.3	40.7	40.2	40.0	40.4	40.7	40.6	40.4	40.2
2012	40.0	39.5	39.7	40.4	40.3	39.9	39.7	40.1	40.0	40.3	40.2	39.9	40.0
2013	39.1	39.0	39.6	39.5	39.3	39.3	38.9	39.3	39.4	39.2	39.2	39.6	39.3
2014	38.0	38.4	38.9	38.5	39.2	39.2	38.9	39.4	39.5	39.5	39.4	39.7	39.1
2015	38.1	38.6	39.4	38.8	39.2	39.4	39.2	39.6	38.0	40.1	40.2	40.2	39.2
Manufacturing													
2011	38.9	39.0	39.0	39.3	39.3	39.2	38.9	38.8	39.7	39.2	39.5	40.2	39.3
2012	40.2	39.9	40.3	40.3	40.2	40.3	40.2	39.9	40.5	40.1	40.2	40.4	40.2
2013	39.8	40.9	40.8	40.5	40.8	41.1	40.4	40.5	40.9	40.5	40.9	41.8	40.7
2014	40.5	40.9	41.0	41.2	40.6	41.0	40.7	40.8	41.0	40.2	41.8	41.1	40.9
2015	40.7	40.5	40.9	40.7	40.4	40.7	40.5	40.6	39.6	40.2	40.9	40.8	40.5
Trade, Transportation, and Utilities													
2011	35.3	35.7	35.5	35.4	35.0	34.6	34.6	34.1	33.9	33.8	33.7	34.1	34.6
2012	33.5	33.7	33.5	32.9	32.9	32.7	32.8	32.7	33.1	32.8	33.1	33.3	33.1
2013	32.8	33.2	33.2	32.8	33.0	33.1	32.9	32.8	32.9	32.6	32.7	33.1	32.9
2014	32.6	32.9	33.0	33.2	32.8	32.9	33.0	33.2	33.1	33.3	33.6	33.8	33.1
2015	33.2	33.8	33.6	33.5	33.5	33.2	33.2	33.3	33.4	33.3	33.4	33.5	33.4
Financial Activities													
2011	37.5	37.1	36.9	37.0	37.5	36.9	37.7	36.5	37.2	37.9	37.0	37.0	37.2
2012	37.7	37.0	36.8	37.3	36.4	36.8	37.6	36.8	37.6	37.0	37.5	39.1	37.3
2013	37.9	38.1	37.8	37.9	37.8	38.4	37.5	38.0	38.2	37.7	38.0	37.9	37.9
2014	37.4	37.5	37.6	37.0	37.2	37.9	37.2	37.1	37.6	37.4	38.4	37.7	37.5
2015	37.7	38.7	38.6	37.9	37.7	37.7	37.9	38.6	37.9	37.9	38.6	38.1	38.1
Professional and Business Services													
2011	36.7	36.8	36.6	36.9	37.1	36.7	36.3	36.5	36.3	37.0	36.6	36.7	36.7
2012	36.5	36.0	36.3	36.7	36.2	36.1	36.7	36.5	36.7	36.1	36.4	36.7	36.4
2013	35.8	36.0	36.0	36.2	35.9	36.7	36.6	36.8	37.2	36.6	36.4	36.8	36.4
2014	35.9	36.5	36.4	35.5	35.6	36.3	35.8	36.0	35.7	35.8	36.2	35.6	35.9
2015	35.0	36.0	35.8	35.6	35.7	35.7	35.6	36.3	35.4	35.6	36.0	35.6	35.7
Education and Health Services													
2011	35.3	35.0	34.8	34.8	34.5	34.1	34.2	34.1	34.1	34.5	34.0	34.1	34.5
2012	34.2	34.3	34.0	34.2	34.0	34.4	34.7	34.5	34.4	34.4	34.3	34.8	34.3
2013	34.7	34.9	34.8	34.7	34.7	34.8	34.6	34.6	34.9	34.8	35.0	34.8	34.8
2014	34.9	35.2	35.0	35.0	34.9	34.9	34.9	35.0	35.0	34.9	35.3	34.8	35.0
2015	35.1	35.1	35.2	34.8	34.8	34.7	34.8	34.9	34.6	34.5	34.9	34.5	34.8
Leisure and Hospitality													
2011	28.6	28.8	29.0	28.5	27.8	27.4	27.7	27.6	26.5	27.5	27.7	27.2	27.9
2012	27.8	28.2	28.7	28.1	27.4	27.1	27.9	27.1	26.8	27.0	27.4	27.3	27.6
2013	27.5	28.1	28.3	27.8	27.3	27.6	27.5	27.4	26.8	26.9	27.3	27.9	27.5
2014	28.1	28.9	29.3	28.7	28.2	28.4	28.4	28.2	27.5	27.6	28.2	28.1	28.3
2015	28.4	29.1	29.2	28.4	27.8	27.7	27.8	28.0	27.0	27.1	27.7	27.5	28.0
Other Services													
2011	35.4	34.9	34.7	34.7	35.2	33.9	34.2	34.5	34.1	34.4	33.7	33.4	34.4
2012	32.7	32.8	32.9	33.2	32.8	32.6	33.7	33.6	33.2	32.7	33.0	33.8	33.1
2013	33.4	33.4	33.7	33.9	33.3	33.9	33.3	33.4	33.1	32.8	32.7	33.0	33.3
2014	32.7	33.2	33.1	32.5	32.7	32.5	31.9	33.0	32.2	32.4	32.6	33.2	32.7
2015	32.7	32.7	33.1	32.4	31.9	32.5	32.4	33.0	32.7	33.2	33.3	33.4	32.8

3. Average Hourly Earnings by Selected Industry: Florida, 2011–2015

(Dollars, not seasonally adjusted)

Industry and year	January	February	March	April	May	June	July	August	September	October	November	December	Annual average
Total Private													
2011	21.66	21.62	21.43	21.46	21.50	21.36	21.34	21.26	21.46	21.59	21.42	21.41	21.46
2012	21.67	21.46	21.40	21.81	21.44	21.55	21.57	21.41	21.79	21.77	21.65	21.93	21.62
2013	21.89	21.81	21.75	21.92	21.89	22.06	21.93	21.85	22.11	22.01	22.01	22.21	21.95
2014	22.14	22.18	22.09	22.26	22.12	22.22	22.22	22.27	22.22	22.17	22.28	22.13	22.19
2015	22.32	22.53	22.45	22.42	22.51	22.41	22.55	22.80	22.80	22.81	22.98	22.88	22.63
Goods-Producing													
2011	22.48	22.67	22.53	22.54	22.54	22.39	22.33	22.54	22.42	22.54	22.31	22.37	22.47
2012	22.50	22.48	22.78	22.75	22.61	22.74	22.78	22.95	22.94	22.88	22.94	22.95	22.78
2013	23.27	22.93	22.95	23.02	22.95	22.94	23.11	23.05	23.01	22.90	22.65	22.94	22.97
2014	22.96	22.96	22.76	22.52	22.34	22.45	22.69	22.71	22.61	22.59	22.52	22.62	22.64
2015	23.01	22.92	22.95	22.93	23.03	22.90	23.12	23.43	23.36	23.23	23.41	23.18	23.13
Construction													
2011	22.16	22.19	22.20	22.21	21.92	21.74	21.46	21.62	21.31	21.27	21.09	21.10	21.68
2012	20.97	21.31	21.65	21.71	21.68	21.69	21.76	21.91	22.09	22.07	22.13	22.20	21.77
2013	22.68	22.48	22.37	22.41	22.41	22.26	22.52	22.45	22.13	22.15	21.75	22.09	22.30
2014	22.24	22.22	22.16	22.08	21.88	21.97	22.35	22.28	22.21	22.31	22.39	22.13	22.19
2015	22.44	22.41	22.48	22.68	22.66	22.64	22.75	23.07	22.93	22.89	23.31	23.33	22.81
Manufacturing													
2011	23.13	23.45	23.15	23.13	23.45	23.34	23.56	23.79	23.83	24.16	23.87	23.90	23.57
2012	24.25	23.83	24.07	24.00	23.74	23.96	23.95	24.13	23.87	23.77	23.82	23.74	23.93
2013	23.92	23.37	23.58	23.74	23.62	23.78	23.87	23.83	24.09	23.85	23.71	23.89	23.77
2014	23.78	23.81	23.44	23.03	22.92	23.06	23.17	23.29	23.15	23.02	22.69	23.30	23.22
2015	23.74	23.57	23.58	23.29	23.56	23.27	23.62	23.93	23.97	23.72	23.57	24.06	23.66
Trade, Transportation, and Utilities													
2011	18.74	18.86	18.41	18.46	18.30	18.06	17.78	17.65	18.06	18.10	18.03	18.18	18.22
2012	18.18	17.91	18.02	18.76	18.31	18.33	18.35	18.18	18.52	18.58	18.31	18.83	18.36
2013	18.83	18.75	18.81	18.93	18.78	18.88	18.87	18.74	19.16	19.09	19.18	19.17	18.93
2014	19.37	19.57	19.49	19.38	18.97	19.07	19.29	19.36	19.21	19.10	19.23	19.03	19.25
2015	19.58	19.82	19.55	19.68	20.12	20.02	20.28	20.44	20.58	20.05	20.08	20.45	20.06
Financial Activities													
2011	25.82	25.59	25.74	25.66	26.16	25.81	25.22	25.06	24.90	25.46	25.40	25.10	25.49
2012	25.46	25.16	25.66	25.94	25.32	25.60	25.45	25.26	25.77	25.47	25.28	25.16	25.46
2013	24.67	25.13	25.07	25.36	25.21	25.78	25.76	25.62	26.16	26.04	26.39	26.90	25.68
2014	26.40	26.32	26.60	26.27	26.03	26.54	26.32	26.41	26.06	26.21	26.43	26.26	26.32
2015	26.34	27.22	28.07	27.22	27.14	27.09	27.04	27.87	27.30	27.17	28.03	27.74	27.36
Professional and Business Services													
2011	25.26	24.75	24.61	24.73	24.88	24.78	25.08	25.01	25.16	25.45	25.16	25.46	25.03
2012	25.90	25.64	25.07	25.59	24.95	25.16	25.27	24.61	25.41	25.24	25.09	25.57	25.29
2013	25.32	25.48	25.43	25.56	25.48	25.85	25.18	24.92	25.33	25.07	25.13	25.60	25.36
2014	25.41	25.45	25.38	25.65	25.80	25.94	25.79	25.75	25.92	25.76	26.03	25.75	25.72
2015	25.90	26.05	26.03	25.94	25.74	25.63	25.84	26.12	26.22	26.30	26.69	26.39	26.08
Education and Health Services													
2011	23.56	23.14	23.20	23.25	23.26	23.39	23.57	23.45	23.74	23.77	23.79	23.79	23.49
2012	24.21	23.98	24.08	24.30	23.99	24.12	24.16	24.01	24.30	24.60	24.59	24.88	24.27
2013	24.85	24.63	24.57	24.83	24.90	24.99	24.90	25.01	24.89	24.82	24.68	24.88	24.83
2014	24.69	24.60	24.44	24.38	24.19	24.08	24.00	23.97	24.08	24.11	24.06	24.32	24.24
2015	24.01	24.27	24.31	24.38	24.19	24.11	24.18	24.23	24.44	24.70	24.61	24.38	24.32
Leisure and Hospitality													
2011	13.75	13.89	13.88	13.78	13.68	13.29	13.29	13.12	13.46	13.44	13.41	13.38	13.54
2012	13.61	13.81	13.87	13.89	13.70	13.49	13.37	13.49	13.50	13.49	13.64	13.51	13.62
2013	13.69	13.59	13.53	13.44	13.45	13.33	13.30	13.26	13.22	13.46	13.45	13.51	13.44
2014	13.60	13.75	13.75	13.69	13.69	13.67	13.65	13.85	13.84	14.03	14.19	14.15	13.82
2015	14.48	14.53	14.33	14.27	14.36	14.06	14.20	14.14	14.22	14.55	14.65	14.68	14.37
Other Services													
2011	19.35	19.13	19.07	18.69	18.99	19.06	18.85	18.80	18.48	18.40	18.70	18.49	18.84
2012	18.83	18.69	18.83	18.73	18.64	18.54	18.51	18.40	18.84	18.64	18.83	18.84	18.69
2013	18.67	18.73	18.53	18.80	18.80	18.99	18.94	18.83	19.03	18.86	19.18	19.33	18.89
2014	19.11	19.06	19.09	19.25	19.37	19.55	19.37	19.75	19.60	19.26	19.62	19.49	19.38
2015	19.54	19.76	19.74	19.69	19.97	20.22	20.46	20.55	20.26	20.35	20.79	20.57	20.16

4. Average Weekly Earnings by Selected Industry: Florida, 2011–2015

(Dollars, not seasonally adjusted)

Industry and year	January	February	March	April	May	June	July	August	September	October	November	December	Annual average
Total Private													
2011	766.76	761.02	752.19	755.39	752.50	741.19	740.50	733.47	738.22	749.17	738.99	740.79	746.81
2012	747.62	738.22	738.30	750.26	731.10	734.86	744.17	732.22	747.40	742.36	740.43	758.78	741.57
2013	746.45	752.45	750.38	751.86	748.64	761.07	750.01	751.64	762.80	752.74	754.94	768.47	755.08
2014	757.19	767.43	764.31	765.74	756.50	766.59	762.15	766.09	762.15	758.21	770.89	761.27	763.34
2015	761.11	781.79	779.02	769.01	769.84	764.18	771.21	786.60	772.92	777.82	792.81	784.78	776.21
Goods-Producing													
2011	885.71	888.66	889.94	903.85	901.60	900.08	888.73	892.58	901.28	903.85	896.86	903.75	896.55
2012	904.50	894.70	913.48	921.38	913.44	916.42	913.48	922.59	926.78	924.35	926.78	924.89	918.03
2013	921.49	919.49	924.89	923.10	920.30	922.19	915.16	919.70	925.00	913.71	908.27	933.66	921.10
2014	900.03	909.22	910.40	898.55	893.60	902.49	905.33	912.94	911.18	903.60	914.31	916.11	905.60
2015	906.59	907.63	922.59	912.61	918.90	918.29	922.49	939.54	904.03	931.52	948.11	936.47	922.89
Construction													
2011	875.32	867.63	876.90	897.28	883.38	884.82	862.69	864.80	860.92	865.69	856.25	852.44	871.54
2012	838.80	841.75	859.51	877.08	873.70	865.43	863.87	878.59	883.60	889.42	889.63	885.78	870.80
2013	886.79	876.72	885.85	885.20	880.71	874.82	876.03	882.29	871.92	868.28	852.60	874.76	876.39
2014	845.12	853.25	862.02	850.08	857.70	861.22	869.42	877.83	877.30	881.25	882.17	878.56	867.63
2015	854.96	865.03	885.71	879.98	888.27	892.02	891.80	913.57	871.34	917.89	937.06	937.87	894.15
Manufacturing													
2011	899.76	914.55	902.85	909.01	921.59	914.93	916.48	923.05	946.05	947.07	942.87	960.78	926.30
2012	974.85	950.82	970.02	967.20	954.35	965.59	962.79	962.79	966.74	953.18	957.56	959.10	961.99
2013	952.02	955.83	962.06	961.47	963.70	977.36	964.35	965.12	985.28	965.93	969.74	998.60	967.44
2014	963.09	973.83	961.04	948.84	930.55	945.46	943.02	950.23	949.15	925.40	948.44	957.63	949.70
2015	966.22	954.59	964.42	947.90	951.82	947.09	956.61	971.56	949.21	953.54	964.01	981.65	958.23
Trade, Transportation, and Utilities													
2011	661.52	673.30	653.56	653.48	640.50	624.88	615.19	601.87	612.23	611.78	607.61	619.94	630.41
2012	609.03	603.57	603.67	617.20	602.40	599.39	601.88	594.49	613.01	609.42	606.06	627.04	607.72
2013	617.62	622.50	624.49	620.90	619.74	624.93	620.82	614.67	630.36	622.33	627.19	634.53	622.80
2014	631.46	643.85	643.17	643.42	622.22	627.40	636.57	642.75	635.85	636.03	646.13	643.21	637.18
2015	650.06	669.92	656.88	659.28	674.02	664.66	673.30	680.65	687.37	667.67	670.67	685.08	670.00
Financial Activities													
2011	968.25	949.39	949.81	949.42	981.00	952.39	950.79	914.69	926.28	964.93	939.80	928.70	948.23
2012	959.84	930.92	944.29	967.56	921.65	942.08	956.92	929.57	968.95	942.39	948.00	983.76	949.66
2013	934.99	957.45	947.65	961.14	952.94	989.95	966.00	973.56	999.31	981.71	1,002.82	1,019.51	973.27
2014	987.36	987.00	1,000.16	971.99	968.32	1,005.87	979.10	979.81	979.86	980.25	1,014.91	990.00	987.00
2015	993.02	1,053.41	1,083.50	1,031.64	1,023.18	1,021.29	1,024.82	1,075.78	1,034.67	1,029.74	1,081.96	1,056.89	1,042.42
Professional and Business Services													
2011	927.04	910.80	900.73	912.54	923.05	909.43	910.40	912.87	913.31	941.65	920.86	934.38	918.60
2012	945.35	923.04	910.04	939.15	903.19	908.28	927.41	898.27	932.55	911.16	913.28	938.42	920.56
2013	906.46	917.28	915.48	925.27	914.73	948.70	921.59	917.06	942.28	917.56	914.73	942.08	923.10
2014	912.22	928.93	923.83	910.58	918.48	941.62	923.28	927.00	925.34	922.21	942.29	916.70	923.35
2015	906.50	937.80	931.87	923.46	918.92	914.99	919.90	948.16	928.19	936.28	960.84	939.48	931.06
Education and Health Services													
2011	831.67	809.90	807.36	809.10	802.47	797.60	806.09	799.65	809.53	820.07	808.86	811.24	810.41
2012	827.98	822.51	818.72	831.06	815.66	829.73	838.35	828.35	835.92	846.24	843.44	865.82	832.46
2013	862.30	859.59	855.04	861.60	864.03	869.65	861.54	865.35	868.66	863.74	863.80	865.82	864.08
2014	861.68	865.92	855.40	853.30	844.23	840.39	837.60	838.95	842.80	841.44	849.32	846.34	848.40
2015	842.75	851.88	855.71	848.42	841.81	836.62	841.46	845.63	845.62	852.15	858.89	841.11	846.34
Leisure and Hospitality													
2011	393.25	400.03	402.52	392.73	380.30	364.15	368.13	362.11	356.69	369.60	371.46	363.94	377.77
2012	378.36	389.44	398.07	390.31	375.38	365.58	373.02	365.58	361.80	364.23	373.74	368.82	375.91
2013	376.48	381.88	382.90	373.63	367.19	367.91	365.75	363.32	354.30	362.07	367.19	376.93	369.60
2014	382.16	397.38	402.88	392.90	386.06	388.23	387.66	390.57	380.60	387.23	400.16	397.62	391.11
2015	411.23	422.82	418.44	405.27	399.21	389.46	394.76	395.92	383.94	394.31	405.81	403.70	402.36
Other Services													
2011	684.99	667.64	661.73	648.54	668.45	646.13	644.67	648.60	630.17	632.96	630.19	617.57	648.10
2012	615.74	613.03	619.51	621.84	611.39	604.40	623.79	618.24	625.49	609.53	621.39	636.79	618.64
2013	623.58	625.58	624.46	637.32	626.04	643.76	630.70	628.92	629.89	618.61	627.19	637.89	629.04
2014	624.90	632.79	631.88	625.63	633.40	635.38	617.90	651.75	631.12	624.02	639.61	647.07	633.73
2015	638.96	646.15	653.39	637.96	637.04	657.15	662.90	678.15	662.50	675.62	692.31	687.04	661.25

GEORGIA
At a Glance

Population:
2005 estimate: 8,925,922
2010 census: 9,687,653
2015 estimate: 10,214,860

Percent change in population:
2005–2015: 14.4%
2010–2015: 5.4%

Percent change in total nonfarm employment:
2005–2015: 6.0%

Industry with the largest growth in employment, 2005–2015 (thousands):
Education and health services, 120.7

Industry with the largest decline or smallest growth in employment, 2005–2015 (thousands):
Manufacturing, –70.3

Civilian labor force:
2005: 4,586,420
2010: 4,696,676
2015: 4,770,873

Unemployment rate and rank among states (highest to lowest):
2005: 5.3%, 17th
2010: 10.5%, 9th
2015: 5.9%, 13th

Over-the-year change in unemployment rates:
2012–2013: –1.0%
2013–2014: –1.1%
2014–2015: –1.2%

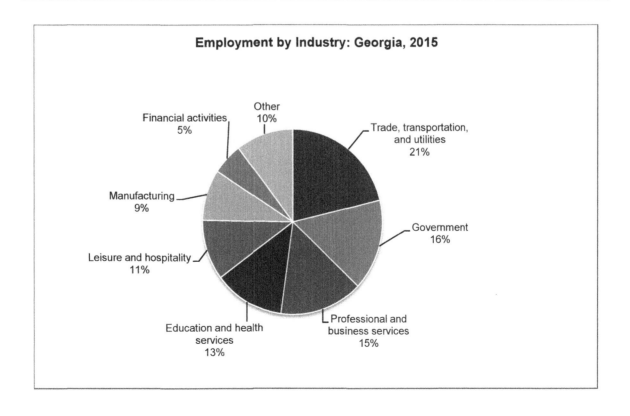

Employment by Industry: Georgia, 2015

Other 10%
Financial activities 5%
Trade, transportation, and utilities 21%
Manufacturing 9%
Government 16%
Leisure and hospitality 11%
Professional and business services 15%
Education and health services 13%

1. Employment by Industry: Georgia, 2005–2015

(Numbers in thousands, not seasonally adjusted)

Industry and year	January	February	March	April	May	June	July	August	September	October	November	December	Annual average
Total Nonfarm													
2005	3,932.4	3,952.7	3,960.2	4,016.3	4,034.2	4,019.7	4,006.6	4,055.9	4,054.4	4,067.3	4,094.4	4,098.8	4,024.4
2006	4,038.3	4,059.5	4,078.4	4,104.5	4,120.4	4,113.4	4,080.7	4,122.4	4,118.6	4,149.3	4,171.9	4,174.8	4,111.0
2007	4,115.8	4,136.1	4,151.9	4,161.0	4,179.7	4,168.7	4,137.6	4,181.3	4,174.8	4,184.1	4,204.8	4,201.3	4,166.4
2008	4,131.4	4,150.6	4,151.8	4,157.3	4,168.4	4,141.1	4,100.8	4,128.0	4,104.1	4,094.2	4,081.3	4,059.0	4,122.3
2009	3,954.2	3,943.3	3,929.4	3,931.7	3,930.5	3,898.5	3,859.2	3,870.8	3,860.1	3,868.9	3,881.8	3,872.2	3,900.1
2010	3,795.1	3,807.6	3,827.3	3,859.4	3,891.4	3,867.4	3,852.6	3,868.6	3,859.7	3,893.0	3,905.8	3,896.7	3,860.4
2011	3,804.8	3,856.1	3,876.9	3,917.0	3,926.5	3,904.7	3,885.6	3,910.6	3,910.0	3,929.4	3,948.9	3,935.4	3,900.5
2012	3,876.6	3,898.1	3,921.5	3,955.1	3,972.0	3,957.4	3,926.3	3,961.3	3,955.1	3,992.2	4,022.7	4,009.7	3,954.0
2013	3,950.0	3,977.9	3,993.3	4,026.7	4,039.9	4,023.6	4,005.7	4,044.2	4,043.5	4,078.5	4,107.5	4,101.6	4,032.7
2014	4,036.1	4,046.0	4,087.3	4,129.3	4,153.2	4,139.2	4,130.2	4,174.4	4,172.1	4,199.4	4,233.2	4,242.4	4,145.2
2015	4,161.8	4,188.1	4,208.8	4,241.8	4,267.2	4,268.5	4,248.6	4,281.9	4,284.1	4,334.4	4,362.4	4,360.3	4,267.3
Total Private													
2005	3,272.3	3,285.2	3,291.3	3,347.3	3,365.6	3,364.0	3,369.9	3,388.4	3,380.4	3,390.0	3,414.9	3,420.2	3,357.5
2006	3,364.9	3,378.5	3,395.3	3,423.4	3,439.7	3,441.5	3,433.2	3,447.0	3,433.0	3,458.6	3,477.4	3,481.2	3,431.1
2007	3,428.7	3,440.1	3,454.3	3,465.4	3,484.2	3,484.7	3,478.1	3,495.4	3,478.7	3,480.6	3,497.8	3,495.3	3,473.6
2008	3,426.8	3,436.0	3,435.6	3,442.7	3,453.3	3,438.2	3,419.5	3,422.5	3,394.0	3,374.0	3,356.3	3,337.3	3,411.4
2009	3,238.3	3,221.5	3,207.0	3,209.5	3,212.4	3,195.7	3,181.3	3,176.9	3,152.5	3,161.6	3,173.5	3,166.6	3,191.4
2010	3,093.5	3,101.5	3,118.7	3,150.7	3,169.2	3,164.1	3,174.1	3,182.4	3,169.7	3,197.9	3,208.4	3,202.4	3,161.1
2011	3,116.3	3,160.9	3,179.7	3,223.8	3,231.5	3,222.1	3,223.2	3,236.0	3,224.4	3,238.9	3,255.4	3,244.9	3,213.1
2012	3,193.0	3,209.5	3,227.7	3,261.2	3,280.2	3,274.4	3,269.6	3,287.1	3,270.5	3,301.4	3,325.8	3,318.6	3,268.3
2013	3,264.9	3,287.2	3,301.4	3,334.9	3,352.9	3,351.2	3,354.2	3,376.1	3,364.1	3,392.7	3,418.4	3,415.6	3,351.1
2014	3,362.4	3,367.6	3,406.0	3,445.7	3,468.4	3,468.2	3,479.1	3,501.6	3,491.3	3,514.1	3,543.1	3,557.3	3,467.1
2015	3,484.5	3,505.3	3,525.1	3,557.9	3,585.7	3,596.7	3,597.1	3,610.4	3,604.0	3,645.5	3,672.0	3,673.9	3,588.2
Goods-Producing													
2005	657.0	659.3	658.6	667.8	671.9	673.3	673.7	678.1	677.8	674.0	677.9	677.0	670.5
2006	671.8	674.6	675.9	678.8	681.7	684.8	681.5	684.5	681.8	678.6	674.2	671.5	678.3
2007	667.4	668.3	667.6	667.1	668.8	669.0	666.0	667.0	662.1	657.5	657.1	653.8	664.3
2008	643.6	642.1	638.5	634.2	633.5	630.8	625.8	623.3	616.8	608.7	596.7	586.7	623.4
2009	567.1	558.4	551.7	543.8	540.7	533.8	525.5	522.3	518.2	514.4	511.9	508.1	533.0
2010	499.8	498.9	499.9	501.7	505.2	504.9	507.4	507.7	506.4	506.1	505.3	502.0	503.8
2011	491.0	500.2	503.5	507.6	508.7	509.5	510.2	510.3	507.6	506.5	505.3	502.9	505.3
2012	498.0	499.5	500.8	502.9	504.4	505.1	506.0	507.2	506.5	508.0	509.0	506.4	504.5
2013	502.2	504.6	507.4	507.5	510.2	511.7	514.0	516.1	515.5	517.5	519.7	519.1	512.1
2014	516.5	519.2	523.7	526.9	530.5	533.6	537.1	540.4	540.9	542.9	543.2	544.9	533.3
2015	541.2	545.1	545.8	549.6	552.8	555.5	556.5	557.3	558.0	563.2	565.7	567.6	554.9
Service-Providing													
2005	3,275.4	3,293.4	3,301.6	3,348.5	3,362.3	3,346.4	3,332.9	3,377.8	3,376.6	3,393.3	3,416.5	3,421.8	3,353.9
2006	3,366.5	3,384.9	3,402.5	3,425.7	3,438.7	3,428.6	3,399.2	3,437.9	3,436.8	3,470.7	3,497.7	3,503.3	3,432.7
2007	3,448.4	3,467.8	3,484.3	3,493.9	3,510.9	3,499.7	3,471.6	3,514.3	3,512.7	3,526.6	3,547.7	3,547.5	3,502.1
2008	3,487.8	3,508.5	3,513.3	3,523.1	3,534.9	3,510.3	3,475.0	3,504.7	3,487.3	3,485.5	3,484.6	3,472.3	3,498.9
2009	3,387.1	3,384.9	3,377.7	3,387.9	3,389.8	3,364.7	3,333.7	3,348.5	3,341.9	3,354.5	3,369.9	3,364.1	3,367.1
2010	3,295.3	3,308.7	3,327.4	3,357.7	3,386.2	3,362.5	3,345.2	3,360.9	3,353.3	3,386.9	3,400.5	3,394.7	3,356.6
2011	3,313.8	3,355.9	3,373.4	3,409.4	3,417.8	3,395.2	3,375.4	3,400.3	3,402.4	3,422.9	3,443.6	3,432.5	3,395.2
2012	3,378.6	3,398.6	3,420.7	3,452.2	3,467.6	3,452.3	3,420.3	3,454.1	3,448.6	3,484.2	3,513.7	3,503.3	3,449.5
2013	3,447.8	3,473.3	3,485.9	3,519.2	3,529.7	3,511.9	3,491.7	3,528.1	3,528.0	3,561.0	3,587.8	3,582.5	3,520.6
2014	3,519.6	3,526.8	3,563.6	3,602.4	3,622.7	3,605.6	3,593.1	3,634.0	3,631.2	3,656.5	3,690.0	3,697.5	3,611.9
2015	3,620.6	3,643.0	3,663.0	3,692.2	3,714.4	3,713.0	3,692.1	3,724.6	3,726.1	3,771.2	3,796.7	3,792.7	3,712.5
Mining and Logging													
2005	11.8	11.9	11.9	12.1	12.2	12.2	12.3	12.3	12.2	12.1	12.1	12.1	12.1
2006	12.4	12.1	12.1	12.3	12.3	12.3	12.3	12.3	12.1	12.2	12.1	12.1	12.2
2007	12.1	12.1	12.1	12.0	12.0	11.9	11.9	11.9	11.8	11.7	11.6	11.4	11.9
2008	10.8	10.6	10.5	10.5	10.4	10.3	10.3	10.3	10.3	10.3	10.2	10.1	10.4
2009	9.7	9.5	9.3	9.4	9.4	9.4	9.3	9.4	9.2	9.3	9.3	9.2	9.4
2010	9.3	9.2	9.2	9.2	9.2	9.2	9.3	9.3	9.3	9.3	9.3	9.1	9.2
2011	9.0	9.1	9.0	9.0	9.0	9.0	9.1	9.1	9.0	8.9	8.8	8.7	9.0
2012	8.6	8.7	8.5	8.6	8.6	8.6	8.7	8.7	8.5	8.7	8.7	8.6	8.6
2013	8.7	8.7	8.7	8.9	8.9	8.8	8.9	8.9	8.9	9.0	9.1	9.0	8.9
2014	9.0	8.9	9.0	8.8	8.9	8.8	9.0	9.0	9.0	9.0	9.1	9.1	9.0
2015	9.0	9.0	9.0	9.0	9.0	9.0	9.1	9.2	9.1	9.2	9.1	9.0	9.1

1. Employment by Industry: Georgia, 2005–2015—*Continued*

(Numbers in thousands, not seasonally adjusted)

Industry and year	January	February	March	April	May	June	July	August	September	October	November	December	Annual average
Construction													
2005	199.8	200.6	200.0	206.3	209.1	210.0	212.2	213.9	213.4	213.4	214.6	212.7	208.8
2006	209.2	211.0	212.5	215.4	217.9	220.6	223.0	224.5	223.7	223.6	222.9	221.4	218.8
2007	218.6	220.2	221.3	221.7	223.2	224.1	223.0	224.1	221.7	220.7	219.5	216.6	221.2
2008	211.1	211.4	209.9	208.7	209.5	208.1	206.9	204.5	201.2	197.4	193.0	187.7	204.1
2009	177.8	175.9	172.9	170.4	170.1	167.9	164.5	162.0	159.3	158.3	157.0	153.9	165.8
2010	148.1	148.4	148.9	150.1	151.0	150.6	152.0	151.6	150.7	150.3	149.5	145.6	149.7
2011	137.9	143.6	146.3	148.2	147.8	148.2	148.5	148.2	147.4	146.8	145.0	142.7	145.9
2012	138.3	139.3	139.9	140.9	140.9	141.2	142.7	143.5	142.7	143.6	143.5	141.3	141.5
2013	138.6	140.0	142.2	142.7	145.2	146.2	147.8	149.1	149.0	150.0	151.0	149.3	145.9
2014	147.4	149.1	151.2	153.5	155.5	157.1	159.4	160.6	160.9	162.7	161.8	162.1	156.8
2015	159.1	161.3	161.1	164.5	165.6	167.6	167.9	168.3	168.5	171.0	171.2	172.3	166.5
Manufacturing													
2005	445.4	446.8	446.7	449.4	450.6	451.1	449.2	451.9	452.2	448.5	451.2	452.2	449.6
2006	450.2	451.5	451.3	451.1	451.5	451.9	446.2	447.7	446.0	442.8	439.2	438.0	447.3
2007	436.7	436.0	434.2	433.4	433.6	433.0	431.1	431.0	428.6	425.1	426.0	425.8	431.2
2008	421.7	420.1	418.1	415.0	413.6	412.4	408.6	408.5	405.3	401.0	393.5	388.9	408.9
2009	379.6	373.0	369.5	364.0	361.2	356.5	351.7	350.9	349.7	346.8	345.6	345.0	357.8
2010	342.4	341.3	341.8	342.4	345.0	345.1	346.1	346.8	346.4	346.5	346.5	347.3	344.8
2011	344.1	347.5	348.2	350.4	351.9	352.3	352.6	353.0	351.2	350.8	351.5	351.5	350.4
2012	351.1	351.5	352.4	353.4	354.9	355.3	354.6	355.0	355.3	355.7	356.8	356.5	354.4
2013	354.9	355.9	356.5	355.9	356.1	356.7	357.3	358.1	357.6	358.5	359.6	360.8	357.3
2014	360.1	361.2	363.5	364.6	366.1	367.7	368.7	370.8	371.0	371.2	372.3	373.7	367.6
2015	373.1	374.8	375.7	376.1	378.2	378.9	379.5	379.8	380.4	383.0	385.4	386.3	379.3
Trade, Transportation, and Utilities													
2005	837.7	836.3	838.0	851.1	854.9	853.3	861.2	860.1	858.2	866.3	883.8	892.7	857.8
2006	861.6	858.6	862.7	870.5	875.9	874.6	870.8	872.9	872.6	885.9	904.4	912.1	876.9
2007	886.6	880.6	882.9	884.3	890.0	890.5	890.9	891.4	890.6	895.7	912.4	916.0	892.7
2008	889.3	885.0	886.0	882.3	883.5	879.8	878.9	878.2	873.5	870.3	874.6	875.6	879.8
2009	839.5	828.5	824.4	821.1	823.4	819.7	818.6	818.4	813.6	816.3	828.1	831.5	823.6
2010	804.1	801.6	803.1	807.0	811.8	811.1	813.5	814.8	810.5	823.7	834.8	839.5	814.6
2011	809.0	813.5	816.2	823.1	826.5	824.7	825.2	826.9	823.3	832.8	847.0	849.3	826.5
2012	827.9	824.9	827.1	832.7	837.9	834.8	835.1	836.2	832.7	843.1	861.8	863.0	838.1
2013	836.6	834.7	835.2	839.7	844.3	844.7	848.8	852.7	849.1	858.9	876.5	883.3	850.4
2014	858.4	853.6	859.0	867.6	871.9	871.8	875.0	877.6	875.8	888.8	909.5	920.2	877.4
2015	887.2	884.1	888.4	894.2	899.2	902.6	903.2	906.1	905.9	918.1	935.8	940.4	905.4
Wholesale Trade													
2005	208.1	209.2	209.3	211.7	212.0	212.0	212.9	213.6	213.8	213.7	213.9	214.4	212.1
2006	212.0	212.8	213.2	214.4	216.0	215.6	216.4	216.5	216.7	219.4	218.4	218.6	215.8
2007	216.9	217.6	217.7	219.0	219.3	219.0	219.6	219.7	219.2	220.0	220.2	219.8	219.0
2008	218.2	219.0	218.4	219.2	219.2	218.2	217.9	218.1	217.2	216.4	214.0	211.8	217.3
2009	207.0	205.0	202.3	201.4	200.4	198.6	198.4	197.7	196.1	197.3	197.3	196.4	199.8
2010	194.4	194.7	194.6	195.9	196.6	196.0	196.6	196.6	195.2	197.4	197.2	196.0	195.9
2011	194.4	195.5	195.4	197.6	198.7	197.7	198.8	199.5	198.5	200.0	200.3	199.3	198.0
2012	198.3	199.5	199.5	201.1	202.5	201.7	202.8	203.3	202.2	204.6	205.0	204.5	202.1
2013	202.4	203.4	203.1	204.3	204.9	204.7	205.1	205.3	204.1	206.6	207.6	207.1	204.9
2014	206.0	206.7	206.9	208.1	209.1	209.3	210.2	210.8	210.4	212.3	213.9	214.4	209.8
2015	212.0	213.2	214.0	214.8	216.4	217.0	217.5	218.4	218.3	219.5	219.3	217.3	216.5
Retail Trade													
2005	452.8	448.9	450.1	460.3	463.0	462.0	466.2	464.9	461.8	469.7	484.8	491.6	464.7
2006	470.2	466.2	468.7	474.0	476.6	474.7	470.1	471.5	469.8	480.4	499.2	503.9	477.1
2007	485.7	478.6	480.3	479.7	482.8	481.0	482.2	481.5	480.2	484.3	500.6	502.7	485.0
2008	480.9	475.5	476.7	473.0	473.4	470.4	470.4	470.0	466.4	465.5	472.6	474.1	472.4
2009	448.5	441.4	440.4	440.5	443.2	441.1	440.6	441.5	438.6	439.7	451.3	454.1	443.4
2010	433.8	430.9	432.2	435.0	437.7	437.1	438.2	438.9	435.4	444.2	455.2	458.5	439.8
2011	436.6	437.9	439.5	444.1	445.4	443.8	443.8	444.0	441.1	448.4	461.1	462.3	445.7
2012	445.7	441.7	443.4	446.3	449.2	447.0	447.1	447.4	445.1	452.6	469.6	469.0	450.3
2013	448.0	446.7	447.7	450.9	453.8	454.6	458.0	460.9	459.0	465.5	480.2	484.8	459.2
2014	463.4	459.3	462.5	466.5	468.8	468.4	470.0	470.7	469.4	476.3	494.0	499.3	472.4
2015	472.6	470.9	474.2	478.8	480.8	482.9	481.8	483.4	483.4	492.1	507.4	510.8	484.9

1. Employment by Industry: Georgia, 2005–2015—*Continued*

(Numbers in thousands, not seasonally adjusted)

Industry and year	January	February	March	April	May	June	July	August	September	October	November	December	Annual average
Transportation and Utilities													
2005	176.8	178.2	178.6	179.1	179.9	179.3	182.1	181.6	182.6	182.9	185.1	186.7	181.1
2006	179.4	179.6	180.8	182.1	183.3	184.3	184.3	184.9	186.1	186.1	186.8	189.6	183.9
2007	184.0	184.4	184.9	185.6	187.9	190.5	189.1	190.2	191.2	191.4	191.6	193.5	188.7
2008	190.2	190.5	190.9	190.1	190.9	191.2	190.6	190.1	189.9	188.4	188.0	189.7	190.0
2009	184.0	182.1	181.7	179.2	179.8	180.0	179.6	179.2	178.9	179.3	179.5	181.0	180.4
2010	175.9	176.0	176.3	176.1	177.5	178.0	178.7	179.3	179.9	182.1	182.4	185.0	178.9
2011	178.0	180.1	181.3	181.4	182.4	183.2	182.6	183.4	183.7	184.4	185.6	187.7	182.8
2012	183.9	183.7	184.2	185.3	186.2	186.1	185.2	185.5	185.4	185.9	187.2	189.5	185.7
2013	186.2	184.6	184.4	184.5	185.6	185.4	185.7	186.5	186.0	186.8	188.7	191.4	186.3
2014	189.0	187.6	189.6	193.0	194.0	194.1	194.8	196.1	196.0	200.2	201.6	206.5	195.2
2015	202.6	200.0	200.2	200.6	202.0	202.7	203.9	204.3	204.2	206.5	209.1	212.3	204.0
Information													
2005	107.1	107.4	107.8	107.6	106.9	108.2	107.6	106.2	106.3	106.8	107.6	108.1	107.3
2006	106.1	106.4	107.2	106.0	106.5	106.0	104.5	104.6	104.5	105.0	106.0	106.4	105.8
2007	106.9	106.7	106.7	105.2	105.8	105.9	105.5	105.6	105.5	104.6	105.1	105.1	105.7
2008	102.9	103.8	103.9	103.7	104.2	104.6	103.4	103.1	102.4	101.4	101.7	101.7	103.1
2009	102.3	102.1	101.5	101.3	101.1	100.8	99.5	99.0	98.6	97.5	97.6	98.2	100.0
2010	96.3	96.3	96.5	96.7	96.9	96.4	95.2	95.0	94.7	93.1	93.8	94.2	95.4
2011	93.4	94.1	94.0	94.8	94.6	94.0	94.7	94.9	94.5	94.8	96.3	94.4	94.5
2012	94.3	95.5	95.4	95.1	96.1	95.9	96.6	96.8	96.5	97.8	98.3	98.3	96.4
2013	96.0	97.0	97.2	98.2	99.0	98.1	98.7	99.1	99.0	100.8	100.7	100.9	98.7
2014	100.8	101.6	102.2	103.0	103.7	105.0	105.1	104.4	104.0	105.9	106.5	106.6	104.1
2015	103.3	104.1	104.2	105.0	107.9	107.3	111.6	108.1	105.2	106.1	105.8	104.2	106.1
Financial Activities													
2005	234.1	235.1	234.8	235.7	236.9	237.1	236.5	237.5	237.1	239.8	240.0	241.4	237.2
2006	237.8	239.2	239.6	241.4	242.5	242.4	243.0	244.1	243.5	245.3	245.3	245.9	242.5
2007	242.3	243.9	243.8	243.4	243.5	243.4	243.9	243.8	242.0	242.3	242.2	241.8	243.0
2008	238.1	238.9	237.9	238.1	238.4	237.3	237.4	236.3	233.8	234.3	231.6	230.8	236.1
2009	228.0	226.9	225.4	224.9	225.0	224.4	223.9	222.7	220.6	220.5	220.0	219.9	223.5
2010	216.4	216.2	216.1	216.4	217.7	218.0	218.1	218.9	218.2	220.4	221.1	221.7	218.3
2011	219.0	219.6	219.7	222.5	223.1	223.4	223.8	224.8	224.7	225.9	226.1	226.3	223.2
2012	225.0	225.5	225.9	225.7	225.9	226.1	226.9	227.2	226.0	227.8	228.9	228.6	226.6
2013	226.4	227.3	227.6	228.5	228.9	228.9	229.4	230.0	228.4	230.3	231.5	230.8	229.0
2014	229.2	229.5	229.8	230.5	231.3	231.4	231.9	232.5	230.9	232.7	233.0	233.1	231.3
2015	231.2	231.7	232.2	233.8	234.6	235.4	236.0	235.8	234.9	239.2	240.1	238.5	235.3
Professional and Business Services													
2005	518.8	523.9	524.2	530.7	532.1	533.4	536.1	544.2	545.4	547.2	548.0	546.1	535.8
2006	539.5	543.2	545.9	551.0	549.7	553.0	553.6	556.5	553.5	555.7	556.0	557.2	551.2
2007	549.6	554.8	560.3	558.6	561.5	563.3	562.1	569.4	567.4	568.9	569.4	574.4	563.3
2008	558.7	561.7	559.4	565.5	564.8	565.6	555.9	557.8	553.0	549.8	544.5	540.6	556.4
2009	515.9	513.9	509.3	507.7	505.1	507.7	507.6	506.7	504.6	515.4	518.6	519.0	511.0
2010	504.6	509.2	514.3	522.8	524.2	526.3	529.4	530.9	530.8	539.6	540.0	539.0	525.9
2011	518.6	531.8	535.6	546.3	544.4	545.0	544.9	549.3	550.1	551.2	553.4	552.2	543.6
2012	538.5	545.8	550.4	557.8	560.9	564.8	561.1	566.5	563.3	570.0	574.0	573.1	560.5
2013	563.2	573.3	576.6	582.1	584.2	587.1	586.2	591.7	591.8	598.7	602.6	599.5	586.4
2014	589.9	592.4	605.6	609.1	614.7	616.5	620.4	626.1	626.0	628.1	633.1	632.4	616.2
2015	617.8	625.3	629.7	631.3	639.0	643.4	640.7	645.3	646.1	657.7	660.5	660.8	641.5
Education and Health Services													
2005	410.6	412.2	409.3	417.9	419.5	414.6	417.1	421.3	422.2	426.0	427.3	426.9	418.7
2006	427.2	429.7	429.0	431.3	432.5	427.2	429.0	432.8	432.6	442.7	443.7	442.8	433.4
2007	439.8	443.7	442.6	446.7	447.6	443.4	444.2	450.7	452.2	455.8	457.2	454.8	448.2
2008	451.6	456.6	455.9	457.4	459.2	452.0	453.4	459.7	458.9	463.5	464.8	463.9	458.1
2009	461.3	463.4	461.3	464.3	466.4	459.0	459.7	465.0	462.7	469.5	471.0	469.7	464.4
2010	466.4	469.9	470.8	473.4	475.8	469.4	471.8	477.9	477.7	484.8	485.0	482.9	475.5
2011	476.0	482.9	482.6	487.2	486.4	478.3	478.5	484.9	486.1	492.0	492.2	489.8	484.7
2012	486.2	490.9	491.2	495.5	496.3	488.8	487.6	497.1	497.8	503.7	505.2	503.4	495.3
2013	501.1	505.9	506.0	510.7	511.7	504.3	501.5	510.5	511.9	517.2	520.6	518.4	510.0
2014	513.3	515.4	518.3	521.8	523.3	516.7	516.5	527.1	528.5	530.0	532.4	534.3	523.1
2015	529.4	533.3	534.4	536.3	538.2	533.8	533.0	541.4	543.9	549.0	550.2	549.7	539.4

1. Employment by Industry: Georgia, 2005–2015—*Continued*

(Numbers in thousands, not seasonally adjusted)

Industry and year	January	February	March	April	May	June	July	August	September	October	November	December	Annual average
Leisure and Hospitality													
2005	352.1	355.2	362.7	378.3	384.2	384.7	377.4	379.8	374.4	371.7	371.7	369.7	371.8
2006	364.0	369.4	377.5	385.1	390.4	392.4	389.5	391.1	385.4	386.1	388.3	386.8	383.8
2007	378.0	383.5	391.4	399.5	405.4	406.7	403.0	405.2	398.4	395.0	393.9	390.4	395.9
2008	383.1	387.0	393.2	400.0	407.0	404.9	402.2	402.1	395.2	386.4	383.1	379.7	393.7
2009	367.2	370.7	376.5	388.5	392.1	391.7	387.8	385.9	379.0	373.5	372.1	367.4	379.4
2010	355.0	357.9	366.2	379.0	382.7	383.4	382.8	382.6	377.7	375.7	373.9	370.5	374.0
2011	358.5	365.8	375.0	387.7	392.4	391.3	390.4	390.8	385.0	382.7	382.3	378.7	381.7
2012	372.6	375.9	385.5	398.4	404.8	404.2	401.2	402.1	395.1	397.0	394.9	393.6	393.8
2013	387.9	392.0	399.3	414.6	420.3	421.6	420.8	422.1	415.5	416.2	414.0	412.0	411.4
2014	403.6	404.7	416.1	433.1	438.4	437.7	437.3	438.5	431.5	432.1	431.6	432.1	428.1
2015	422.0	428.1	436.5	452.0	457.2	460.6	457.4	458.9	453.3	456.0	456.4	454.0	449.4
Other Services													
2005	154.9	155.8	155.9	158.2	159.2	159.4	160.3	161.2	159.0	158.2	158.6	158.3	158.3
2006	156.9	157.4	157.5	159.3	160.5	161.1	161.3	160.5	159.1	159.3	159.5	158.5	159.2
2007	158.1	158.6	159.0	160.6	161.6	162.5	162.5	162.3	160.5	160.8	160.5	159.0	160.5
2008	159.5	160.9	160.8	161.5	162.7	163.2	162.5	162.0	160.4	159.6	159.3	158.3	160.9
2009	157.0	157.6	156.9	157.9	158.6	158.6	158.7	156.9	155.2	154.5	154.2	152.8	156.6
2010	150.9	151.5	151.8	153.7	154.9	154.6	155.9	154.6	153.7	154.5	154.5	152.6	153.6
2011	150.8	153.0	153.1	154.6	155.4	155.9	155.5	154.1	153.1	153.0	152.8	151.3	153.6
2012	150.5	151.5	151.4	153.1	153.9	154.7	155.1	154.0	152.6	154.0	153.7	152.2	153.1
2013	151.5	152.4	152.1	153.6	154.3	154.8	154.8	153.9	152.9	153.1	152.8	151.6	153.2
2014	150.7	151.2	151.3	153.7	154.6	155.5	155.8	155.0	153.7	153.6	153.8	153.7	153.6
2015	152.4	153.6	153.9	155.7	156.8	158.1	158.7	157.5	156.7	156.2	157.5	158.7	156.3
Government													
2005	660.1	667.5	668.9	669.0	668.6	655.7	636.7	667.5	674.0	677.3	679.5	678.6	667.0
2006	673.4	681.0	683.1	681.1	680.7	671.9	647.5	675.4	685.6	690.7	694.5	693.6	679.9
2007	687.1	696.0	697.6	695.6	695.5	684.0	659.5	685.9	696.1	703.5	707.0	706.0	692.8
2008	704.6	714.6	716.2	714.6	715.1	702.9	681.3	705.5	710.1	720.2	725.0	721.7	711.0
2009	715.9	721.8	722.4	722.2	718.1	702.8	677.9	693.9	707.6	707.3	708.3	705.6	708.7
2010	701.6	706.1	708.6	708.7	722.2	703.3	678.5	686.2	690.0	695.1	697.4	694.3	699.3
2011	688.5	695.2	697.2	693.2	695.0	682.6	662.4	674.6	685.6	690.5	693.5	690.5	687.4
2012	683.6	688.6	693.8	693.9	691.8	683.0	656.7	674.2	684.6	690.8	696.9	691.1	685.8
2013	685.1	690.7	691.9	691.8	687.0	672.4	651.5	668.1	679.4	685.8	689.1	686.0	681.6
2014	673.7	678.4	681.3	683.6	684.8	671.0	651.1	672.8	680.8	685.3	690.1	685.1	678.2
2015	677.3	682.8	683.7	683.9	681.5	671.8	651.5	671.5	680.1	688.9	690.4	686.4	679.2

2. Average Weekly Hours by Selected Industry: Georgia, 2011–2015

(Not seasonally adjusted)

Industry and year	January	February	March	April	May	June	July	August	September	October	November	December	Annual average
Total Private													
2011	33.5	34.6	34.7	34.7	35.1	34.7	34.8	34.7	34.6	35.1	34.8	34.8	34.7
2012	35.0	34.8	34.8	35.2	34.8	34.9	35.2	35.0	35.6	34.9	34.9	35.5	35.0
2013	34.8	34.9	35.2	35.1	34.9	35.6	35.0	35.0	35.6	35.0	35.2	35.5	35.2
2014	34.6	34.0	35.8	35.2	35.2	35.8	35.2	35.4	35.3	35.1	35.6	35.2	35.2
2015	34.8	35.3	35.3	34.8	35.1	35.1	35.1	35.6	34.8	34.8	35.1	34.8	35.1
Goods-Producing													
2011	35.9	39.1	39.2	39.4	39.6	39.2	39.5	39.9	39.7	39.7	40.1	40.4	39.3
2012	39.1	39.4	39.6	39.9	39.7	40.1	39.4	39.7	40.2	40.1	40.3	40.8	39.9
2013	40.4	40.1	41.0	40.9	41.3	42.0	41.4	41.4	42.2	41.5	41.7	41.7	41.3
2014	40.2	37.4	42.1	41.3	41.3	42.0	41.8	41.9	42.0	41.4	41.9	42.2	41.3
2015	40.7	40.4	40.6	40.5	41.4	41.4	41.7	42.3	40.8	41.6	41.0	41.9	41.2
Construction													
2011	34.0	38.7	37.9	39.3	39.7	39.3	39.1	39.3	39.5	38.7	39.1	38.5	38.6
2012	37.3	38.5	38.5	39.8	39.0	39.1	40.1	39.6	40.1	39.9	40.5	39.7	39.3
2013	39.1	38.0	40.4	40.3	41.2	41.5	40.9	40.2	41.6	40.6	40.8	40.1	40.4
2014	38.6	34.9	41.6	41.6	41.8	41.9	43.0	42.7	42.6	40.9	42.2	42.4	41.2
2015	40.0	39.5	39.8	39.7	42.2	42.0	42.3	42.3	40.4	42.5	41.2	42.4	41.2
Manufacturing													
2011	36.8	39.3	39.9	39.4	39.5	39.3	39.9	40.4	40.0	40.2	40.6	41.5	39.7
2012	40.2	40.0	40.3	39.9	40.1	40.6	39.1	39.8	40.2	40.2	40.3	41.4	40.2
2013	41.2	41.2	41.2	41.2	41.3	42.2	41.6	42.1	42.4	41.9	42.2	42.5	41.8
2014	41.1	38.8	42.4	41.1	41.0	42.0	41.0	41.3	41.5	41.7	41.7	42.1	41.3
2015	41.3	41.0	41.1	41.0	40.8	40.9	41.2	42.2	40.9	40.9	40.7	41.4	41.1
Trade, Transportation, and Utilities													
2011	33.7	34.6	34.7	34.6	35.0	34.7	34.8	34.5	34.7	35.0	34.7	35.0	34.7
2012	34.9	34.9	34.7	34.7	34.6	34.5	34.8	34.4	34.6	34.3	34.6	35.0	34.7
2013	34.1	34.5	34.5	34.5	34.4	34.9	34.5	34.7	35.1	34.6	34.9	35.2	34.7
2014	34.3	33.8	35.4	35.1	35.0	35.4	35.0	35.4	35.3	34.9	35.5	35.2	35.0
2015	34.7	35.4	35.3	35.0	35.2	34.9	34.8	35.1	34.3	34.5	34.7	34.6	34.9
Financial Activities													
2011	36.3	35.0	35.5	35.1	36.5	35.6	35.9	35.4	35.6	37.2	35.9	35.8	35.8
2012	37.3	36.3	36.1	37.4	35.9	36.2	38.2	36.5	37.8	36.8	37.0	38.2	37.0
2013	36.8	36.9	36.7	36.9	36.9	38.1	37.0	37.1	38.2	36.6	36.7	38.0	37.2
2014	36.7	37.7	38.0	37.0	37.3	38.1	36.4	36.5	36.2	36.4	38.0	36.7	37.1
2015	36.6	38.1	38.1	36.9	36.9	37.3	37.1	38.6	37.4	37.1	38.9	37.6	37.6
Professional and Business Services													
2011	34.2	35.2	35.1	35.5	36.1	36.3	35.9	35.6	35.5	36.6	35.9	35.9	35.7
2012	36.4	36.2	36.4	37.6	36.9	36.8	37.4	38.3	38.9	37.5	37.0	38.3	37.3
2013	37.0	37.5	37.3	37.4	37.2	38.1	36.8	37.0	37.7	36.6	37.0	37.4	37.2
2014	35.8	36.2	37.8	36.8	36.4	37.4	36.1	36.6	36.3	36.3	37.1	36.0	36.6
2015	35.9	36.5	36.4	35.4	35.6	35.9	35.4	36.0	35.1	34.3	34.8	34.2	35.4
Education and Health Services													
2011	34.9	35.4	35.5	35.5	35.6	35.3	35.3	35.1	35.2	35.5	35.1	34.9	35.3
2012	35.6	34.6	34.6	34.7	34.6	34.4	34.8	34.5	35.1	34.5	34.2	34.9	34.7
2013	34.5	34.2	34.3	34.2	34.2	34.8	34.2	34.7	34.9	34.4	34.5	35.0	34.5
2014	34.9	34.5	35.3	34.7	34.8	35.4	34.9	35.1	35.2	35.2	35.6	34.9	35.0
2015	34.9	35.2	35.3	34.7	34.8	34.7	34.9	35.3	34.9	35.1	35.6	35.1	35.0
Leisure and Hospitality													
2011	25.3	26.9	27.0	27.0	27.2	26.7	26.9	26.8	26.2	26.5	26.3	26.3	26.6
2012	26.3	26.5	26.6	26.6	26.6	26.8	26.9	26.4	26.4	26.3	26.0	26.2	26.5
2013	25.6	26.2	26.6	26.6	26.4	26.9	26.3	26.0	26.1	26.1	26.2	26.4	26.3
2014	25.9	25.5	27.5	27.0	27.3	27.4	27.0	26.8	26.5	26.5	26.7	26.6	26.7
2015	26.2	26.8	26.7	26.8	26.8	26.7	26.5	27.0	26.4	26.7	26.6	26.4	26.6
Other Services													
2011	31.8	33.3	32.8	32.9	32.7	32.3	31.6	31.8	31.1	31.5	31.3	29.9	31.9
2012	30.4	30.3	30.8	30.7	29.4	30.2	30.4	30.7	31.4	30.2	30.2	31.1	30.5
2013	30.1	30.4	30.8	29.2	29.1	29.7	29.6	30.3	31.9	31.2	31.9	32.1	30.5
2014	31.7	31.7	32.9	32.6	32.9	34.4	34.2	33.9	33.7	32.9	33.8	33.6	33.2
2015	33.1	33.7	34.6	33.9	34.2	34.1	34.6	35.1	34.7	34.3	34.4	33.9	34.2

3. Average Hourly Earnings by Selected Industry: Georgia, 2011–2015

(Dollars, not seasonally adjusted)

Industry and year	January	February	March	April	May	June	July	August	September	October	November	December	Annual average
Total Private													
2011	22.40	21.77	21.61	21.83	21.77	21.72	21.78	21.75	21.80	21.98	21.83	21.78	21.83
2012	21.98	21.59	21.57	21.77	21.35	21.43	21.90	21.59	21.92	21.77	21.90	22.21	21.75
2013	22.21	22.40	22.15	22.26	22.18	22.44	22.34	22.45	22.77	22.61	22.71	23.06	22.47
2014	23.07	23.64	23.10	22.95	22.90	23.32	23.19	23.46	23.39	23.49	23.90	23.62	23.34
2015	23.86	24.06	23.92	23.65	23.50	23.39	23.55	23.84	23.71	24.11	24.28	24.13	23.84
Goods-Producing													
2011	21.84	21.21	20.99	21.31	21.47	21.94	21.82	21.63	21.87	22.10	21.88	22.14	21.68
2012	22.05	21.80	21.80	22.03	21.70	21.67	21.89	21.51	21.47	21.40	21.93	22.09	21.78
2013	21.86	22.16	22.00	22.08	22.22	22.53	22.47	22.42	22.51	22.39	22.50	22.85	22.34
2014	22.94	23.55	22.84	22.73	22.99	23.22	23.17	23.16	22.98	23.06	23.34	23.28	23.10
2015	23.30	23.47	23.19	23.20	23.12	23.26	23.48	23.89	23.99	24.09	24.34	24.73	23.68
Construction													
2011	22.29	21.18	21.02	21.39	21.39	21.66	21.48	21.53	21.78	22.17	21.93	22.34	21.67
2012	22.42	21.99	22.15	21.83	21.59	21.77	22.16	21.65	21.70	21.60	22.98	22.79	22.05
2013	22.47	22.91	22.39	22.21	22.49	22.54	22.48	22.59	22.91	22.51	22.46	22.88	22.57
2014	23.00	23.58	22.67	22.30	22.52	22.76	22.73	22.67	22.36	22.56	22.75	22.55	22.68
2015	22.88	23.19	23.09	23.26	23.18	22.87	23.10	23.30	23.36	23.51	24.14	23.85	23.32
Manufacturing													
2011	20.79	20.51	20.33	20.69	21.00	21.73	21.60	21.37	21.60	21.96	21.74	21.94	21.28
2012	21.80	21.62	21.58	22.07	21.71	21.58	21.69	21.49	21.35	21.32	21.45	21.78	21.62
2013	21.60	21.83	21.82	22.02	22.09	22.52	22.47	22.32	22.27	22.30	22.47	22.78	22.21
2014	22.86	23.46	22.87	22.91	23.21	23.45	23.41	23.44	23.37	23.35	23.70	23.77	23.32
2015	23.60	23.66	23.27	23.30	23.16	23.55	23.77	24.30	24.42	24.51	24.51	25.33	23.96
Trade, Transportation, and Utilities													
2011	20.19	20.04	20.11	20.16	20.20	20.08	20.22	20.21	20.16	20.26	19.92	20.07	20.13
2012	20.59	19.99	20.09	20.48	19.96	20.12	20.87	20.39	20.81	20.69	20.49	20.61	20.43
2013	20.47	20.64	20.13	20.12	20.24	20.54	20.39	20.37	20.59	20.48	20.46	20.76	20.44
2014	21.00	21.59	21.21	21.22	21.23	21.51	21.42	21.75	21.75	21.79	22.02	21.72	21.52
2015	22.44	22.26	22.25	21.94	21.68	21.43	21.56	21.48	21.49	21.58	21.33	21.30	21.72
Financial Activities													
2011	24.71	24.50	24.36	24.64	24.81	24.29	24.71	24.43	24.46	24.68	24.45	24.20	24.52
2012	24.81	25.18	25.50	26.39	26.59	27.09	27.10	27.29	28.55	27.92	27.04	28.78	26.87
2013	28.58	28.84	29.18	29.60	29.67	30.08	30.08	30.38	30.95	31.34	30.61	31.20	30.05
2014	30.71	31.89	30.69	30.78	30.56	31.07	30.90	30.46	30.17	30.14	30.54	29.72	30.64
2015	29.47	29.98	30.16	29.33	29.46	29.03	29.06	29.32	29.13	29.09	28.95	28.45	29.28
Professional and Business Services													
2011	27.57	26.41	26.35	26.56	26.60	26.70	26.81	26.81	26.84	27.02	27.20	27.23	26.84
2012	27.01	26.32	26.02	25.55	25.12	25.24	25.72	24.78	25.00	24.71	25.04	25.14	25.45
2013	25.47	25.63	25.16	25.52	25.28	25.66	25.53	25.69	26.09	25.55	26.18	26.64	25.71
2014	26.86	27.28	26.73	26.31	26.41	27.06	26.85	27.17	27.20	27.30	28.12	27.80	27.10
2015	28.29	28.97	28.63	28.06	28.02	27.76	28.16	29.01	28.56	29.18	30.09	29.60	28.70
Education and Health Services													
2011	22.60	22.11	21.87	22.19	21.83	21.86	22.25	21.94	21.91	22.22	22.24	22.01	22.08
2012	22.14	22.18	22.15	22.46	22.04	22.32	22.58	22.88	22.52	22.88	22.94	23.18	22.52
2013	23.34	23.88	23.89	23.73	23.50	23.57	23.79	24.00	24.10	24.09	24.10	23.94	23.83
2014	24.21	24.38	24.08	24.17	23.92	24.61	24.32	25.18	24.90	25.08	25.34	25.29	24.63
2015	24.94	25.05	24.90	25.14	24.83	24.98	24.91	25.02	25.06	25.86	25.52	25.50	25.15
Leisure and Hospitality													
2011	12.40	12.15	12.04	12.22	12.25	12.05	12.04	12.12	12.29	12.46	12.37	12.46	12.23
2012	12.29	12.36	12.22	12.25	12.21	12.08	12.26	12.07	12.15	12.11	12.10	12.17	12.19
2013	12.16	12.10	12.02	12.00	12.01	11.85	11.79	11.98	12.09	12.10	12.13	12.25	12.04
2014	12.02	12.11	12.08	11.94	11.95	11.73	11.74	11.91	11.96	12.05	12.42	12.37	12.02
2015	12.47	12.48	12.57	12.47	12.58	12.38	12.47	12.58	12.58	12.59	12.70	12.74	12.55
Other Services													
2011	18.74	18.12	17.77	18.12	17.81	17.72	17.74	17.39	17.66	17.89	17.55	18.02	17.88
2012	18.18	18.09	17.84	18.25	17.77	17.13	17.41	17.68	18.03	17.77	18.14	18.08	17.86
2013	18.07	18.55	18.66	19.22	19.20	18.93	18.46	18.74	18.93	19.71	19.38	19.64	18.96
2014	19.26	19.72	19.91	20.57	19.66	19.91	20.45	20.40	20.45	20.55	20.35	20.81	20.18
2015	20.76	20.86	20.58	21.14	20.99	21.03	20.91	22.00	21.56	21.61	21.60	21.59	21.23

4. Average Weekly Earnings by Selected Industry: Georgia, 2011–2015

(Dollars, not seasonally adjusted)

Industry and year	January	February	March	April	May	June	July	August	September	October	November	December	Annual average
Total Private													
2011	750.40	753.24	749.87	757.50	764.13	753.68	757.94	754.73	754.28	771.50	759.68	757.94	757.50
2012	769.30	751.33	750.64	766.30	742.98	747.91	770.88	755.65	780.35	759.77	764.31	788.46	761.25
2013	772.91	781.76	779.68	781.33	774.08	798.86	781.90	785.75	810.61	791.35	799.39	818.63	790.94
2014	798.22	803.76	826.98	807.84	806.08	834.86	816.29	830.48	825.67	824.50	850.84	831.42	821.57
2015	830.33	849.32	844.38	823.02	824.85	820.99	826.61	848.70	825.11	839.03	852.23	839.72	836.78
Goods-Producing													
2011	784.06	829.31	822.81	839.61	850.21	860.05	861.89	863.04	868.24	877.37	877.39	894.46	852.02
2012	862.16	858.92	863.28	879.00	861.49	868.97	862.47	853.95	863.09	858.14	883.78	901.27	869.02
2013	883.14	888.62	902.00	903.07	917.69	946.26	930.26	928.19	949.92	929.19	938.25	952.85	922.64
2014	922.19	880.77	961.56	938.75	949.49	975.24	968.51	970.40	965.16	954.68	977.95	982.42	954.03
2015	948.31	948.19	941.51	939.60	957.17	962.96	979.12	1,010.55	978.79	1,002.14	997.94	1,036.19	975.62
Construction													
2011	757.86	819.67	796.66	840.63	849.18	851.24	839.87	846.13	860.31	857.98	857.46	860.09	836.46
2012	836.27	846.62	852.78	868.83	842.01	851.21	888.62	857.34	870.17	861.84	930.69	904.76	866.57
2013	878.58	870.58	904.56	895.06	926.59	935.41	919.43	908.12	953.06	913.91	916.37	917.49	911.83
2014	887.80	822.94	943.07	927.68	941.34	953.64	977.39	968.01	952.54	922.70	960.05	956.12	934.42
2015	915.20	916.01	918.98	923.42	978.20	960.54	977.13	985.59	943.74	999.18	994.57	1,011.24	960.78
Manufacturing													
2011	765.07	806.04	811.17	815.19	829.50	853.99	861.84	863.35	864.00	882.79	882.64	910.51	844.82
2012	876.36	864.80	869.67	880.59	870.57	876.15	848.08	855.30	858.27	857.06	864.44	901.69	869.12
2013	889.92	899.40	898.98	907.22	912.32	950.34	934.75	939.67	944.25	934.37	948.23	968.15	928.38
2014	939.55	910.25	969.69	941.60	951.61	984.90	959.81	968.07	969.86	973.70	988.29	1,000.72	963.12
2015	974.68	970.06	956.40	955.30	944.93	963.20	979.32	1,025.46	998.78	1,002.46	997.56	1,048.66	984.76
Trade, Transportation, and Utilities													
2011	680.40	693.38	697.82	697.54	707.00	696.78	703.66	697.25	699.55	709.10	691.22	702.45	698.51
2012	718.59	697.65	697.12	710.66	690.62	694.14	726.28	701.42	720.03	709.67	708.95	721.35	708.92
2013	698.03	712.08	694.49	694.14	696.26	716.85	703.46	706.84	722.71	708.61	714.05	730.75	709.27
2014	720.30	729.74	750.83	744.82	743.05	761.45	749.70	769.95	767.78	760.47	781.71	764.54	753.20
2015	778.67	788.00	785.43	767.90	763.14	747.91	750.29	753.95	737.11	744.51	740.15	736.98	758.03
Financial Activities													
2011	896.97	857.50	864.78	864.86	905.57	864.72	887.09	864.82	870.78	918.10	877.76	866.36	877.82
2012	925.41	914.03	920.55	986.99	954.58	980.66	1,035.22	996.09	1,079.19	1,027.46	1,000.48	1,099.40	994.19
2013	1,051.74	1,064.20	1,070.91	1,092.24	1,094.82	1,146.05	1,112.96	1,127.10	1,182.29	1,147.04	1,123.39	1,185.60	1,117.86
2014	1,127.06	1,202.25	1,166.22	1,138.86	1,139.89	1,183.77	1,124.76	1,111.79	1,092.15	1,097.10	1,160.52	1,090.72	1,136.74
2015	1,078.60	1,142.24	1,149.10	1,082.28	1,087.07	1,082.82	1,078.13	1,131.75	1,089.46	1,079.24	1,126.16	1,069.72	1,100.93
Professional and Business Services													
2011	942.89	929.63	924.89	942.88	960.26	969.21	962.48	954.44	952.82	988.93	976.48	977.56	958.19
2012	983.16	952.78	947.13	960.68	926.93	928.83	961.93	949.07	972.50	926.63	926.48	962.86	949.29
2013	942.39	961.13	938.47	954.45	940.42	977.65	939.50	950.53	983.59	935.13	968.66	996.34	956.41
2014	961.59	987.54	1,010.39	968.21	961.32	1,012.04	969.29	994.42	987.36	990.99	1,043.25	1,000.80	991.86
2015	1,015.61	1,057.41	1,042.13	993.32	997.51	996.58	996.86	1,044.36	1,002.46	1,000.87	1,047.13	1,012.32	1,015.98
Education and Health Services													
2011	788.74	782.69	776.39	787.75	777.15	771.66	785.43	770.09	771.23	788.81	780.62	768.15	779.42
2012	788.18	767.43	766.39	779.36	762.58	767.81	785.78	789.36	790.45	789.36	784.55	808.98	781.44
2013	805.23	816.70	819.43	811.57	803.70	820.24	813.62	832.80	841.09	828.70	831.45	837.90	822.14
2014	844.93	841.11	850.02	838.70	832.42	871.19	848.77	883.82	876.48	882.82	902.10	882.62	862.05
2015	870.41	881.76	878.97	872.36	864.08	866.81	869.36	883.21	874.59	907.69	908.51	895.05	880.25
Leisure and Hospitality													
2011	313.72	326.84	325.08	329.94	333.20	321.74	323.88	324.82	322.00	330.19	325.33	327.70	325.32
2012	323.23	327.54	325.05	325.85	324.79	323.74	329.79	318.65	320.76	318.49	314.60	318.85	323.04
2013	311.30	317.02	319.73	319.20	317.06	318.77	310.08	311.48	315.55	315.81	317.81	323.40	316.65
2014	311.32	308.81	332.20	322.38	326.24	321.40	316.98	319.19	316.94	319.33	331.61	329.04	320.93
2015	326.71	334.46	335.62	334.20	337.14	330.55	330.46	339.66	332.11	336.15	337.82	336.34	333.83
Other Services													
2011	595.93	603.40	582.86	596.15	582.39	572.36	560.58	553.00	549.23	563.54	549.32	538.80	570.37
2012	552.67	548.13	549.47	560.28	522.44	517.33	529.26	542.78	566.14	536.65	547.83	562.29	544.73
2013	543.91	563.92	574.73	561.22	558.72	562.22	546.42	567.82	603.87	614.95	618.22	630.44	578.28
2014	610.54	625.12	655.04	670.58	646.81	684.90	699.39	691.56	689.17	676.10	687.83	699.22	669.98
2015	687.16	702.98	712.07	716.65	717.86	717.12	723.49	772.20	748.13	741.22	743.04	731.90	726.07

HAWAII
At a Glance

Population:
  2005 estimate: 1,292,729
  2010 census: 1,360,301
  2015 estimate: 1,431,603

Percent change in population:
  2005–2015: 10.7%
  2010–2015: 5.2%

Percent change in total nonfarm employment:
  2005–2015: 5.9%

Industry with the largest growth in employment, 2005–2015 (thousands):
  Education and health services, 11.4

Industry with the largest decline or smallest growth in employment, 2005–2015 (thousands):
  Information, –2.3

Civilian labor force:
  2005: 626,912
  2010: 647,249
  2015: 677,439

Unemployment rate and rank among states (highest to lowest):
  2005: 2.9%, 51st
  2010: 6.9%, 43rd
  2015: 3.6%, 46th

Over-the-year change in unemployment rates:
  2012–2013: –1.1%
  2013–2014: –0.5%
  2014–2015: –0.8%

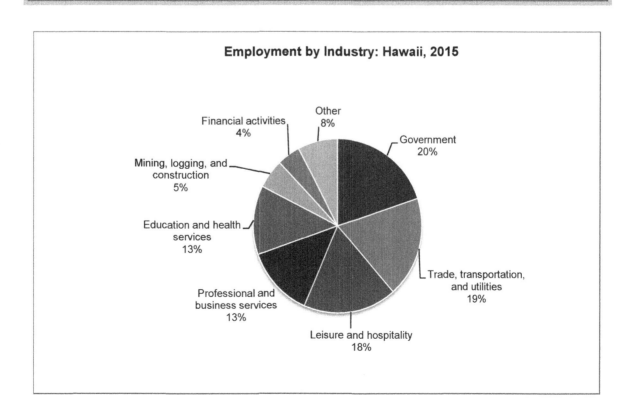

Employment by Industry: Hawaii, 2015

- Financial activities 4%
- Other 8%
- Government 20%
- Mining, logging, and construction 5%
- Education and health services 13%
- Trade, transportation, and utilities 19%
- Professional and business services 13%
- Leisure and hospitality 18%

1. Employment by Industry: Hawaii, 2005–2015

(Numbers in thousands, not seasonally adjusted)

Industry and year	January	February	March	April	May	June	July	August	September	October	November	December	Annual average
Total Nonfarm													
2005	585.0	593.1	597.4	598.5	602.0	604.4	597.3	601.3	604.2	605.8	611.8	618.9	601.6
2006	600.2	611.0	615.2	612.5	617.9	621.0	610.6	615.7	620.4	618.2	630.3	632.3	617.1
2007	615.0	622.9	626.5	618.5	627.1	630.5	618.0	619.7	624.6	626.4	632.3	637.0	624.9
2008	619.9	626.6	629.4	620.5	626.6	624.4	612.6	613.4	613.0	611.5	618.1	614.8	619.2
2009	597.6	599.3	600.6	594.8	595.0	594.3	583.0	580.8	584.3	587.1	588.6	592.5	591.5
2010	578.9	583.9	587.6	586.7	589.9	586.2	581.1	577.7	584.8	589.6	597.3	599.2	586.9
2011	580.7	592.1	595.8	592.7	593.4	591.2	587.5	584.8	593.9	597.1	603.1	608.4	593.4
2012	584.7	600.3	602.9	604.2	607.4	606.1	599.2	605.6	607.5	611.7	623.1	622.7	606.3
2013	600.1	615.8	618.7	615.7	620.6	617.5	613.7	611.6	619.7	624.1	631.0	634.4	618.6
2014	618.7	623.4	627.1	625.5	628.9	624.9	619.2	622.2	627.9	630.9	639.5	638.5	627.2
2015	627.9	633.4	637.0	634.9	637.0	635.4	629.3	632.5	635.5	642.5	645.9	651.1	636.9
Total Private													
2005	468.8	472.1	475.2	477.1	479.3	482.9	483.3	485.6	487.7	485.7	490.0	496.3	482.0
2006	484.5	489.1	492.3	490.3	494.0	498.7	496.1	499.7	500.4	495.9	502.1	507.0	495.8
2007	495.1	498.7	501.6	498.6	501.8	507.0	502.6	504.3	503.7	502.7	506.8	510.4	502.8
2008	498.5	501.4	502.4	498.7	498.7	498.5	494.2	493.1	489.7	484.5	485.1	485.9	494.2
2009	472.5	472.2	471.6	465.8	464.8	466.3	462.8	462.0	461.9	461.7	462.4	465.5	465.8
2010	456.6	458.5	460.0	459.1	460.1	460.1	460.1	461.2	462.5	464.3	466.6	471.6	461.7
2011	460.5	465.2	468.1	465.5	465.2	465.8	467.9	469.3	471.4	471.2	475.7	480.3	468.8
2012	469.6	472.8	474.6	475.8	478.4	480.2	480.5	483.1	483.8	485.2	491.1	493.8	480.7
2013	484.5	487.8	490.3	490.3	491.4	492.6	494.9	495.7	495.9	497.1	503.0	505.7	494.1
2014	494.0	495.1	498.5	497.6	499.3	498.8	499.9	501.4	503.1	503.8	508.0	512.2	501.0
2015	503.0	505.1	508.3	506.1	507.6	509.1	510.4	510.9	510.9	514.4	516.9	520.9	510.3
Goods-Producing													
2005	45.9	46.3	47.0	47.5	48.1	48.7	49.1	49.7	50.2	49.9	50.1	50.6	48.6
2006	49.5	49.8	50.1	50.1	50.9	51.7	52.0	52.8	53.5	53.1	53.9	54.6	51.8
2007	52.8	53.2	53.4	53.5	54.0	54.9	54.7	55.1	55.3	55.1	55.3	55.2	54.4
2008	53.9	54.1	54.0	53.7	53.2	53.3	53.0	52.9	52.4	51.4	50.8	50.1	52.7
2009	48.0	47.1	46.6	45.5	45.4	45.3	44.9	44.3	44.1	43.6	43.2	43.1	45.1
2010	42.2	41.9	42.0	41.7	41.7	41.5	41.7	41.6	41.7	42.1	42.2	42.4	41.9
2011	40.6	41.2	41.3	41.6	41.6	42.2	42.7	42.7	43.1	42.6	42.6	42.8	42.1
2012	41.7	41.8	41.8	41.7	41.9	42.6	42.7	43.1	43.6	43.8	44.1	44.1	42.7
2013	43.2	43.5	44.0	44.0	44.6	44.5	45.0	45.1	45.2	45.0	45.5	45.5	44.6
2014	44.1	44.4	44.8	44.7	45.4	45.8	46.5	46.9	47.1	47.3	47.3	47.3	46.0
2015	46.0	46.4	47.0	47.0	47.8	48.5	49.5	49.5	49.6	51.2	51.6	52.1	48.9
Service-Providing													
2005	539.1	546.8	550.4	551.0	553.9	555.7	548.2	551.6	554.0	555.9	561.7	568.3	553.1
2006	550.7	561.2	565.1	562.4	567.0	569.3	558.6	562.9	566.9	565.1	576.4	577.7	565.3
2007	562.2	569.7	573.1	565.0	573.1	575.6	563.3	564.6	569.3	571.3	577.0	581.8	570.5
2008	566.0	572.5	575.4	566.8	573.4	571.1	559.6	560.5	560.6	560.1	567.3	564.7	566.5
2009	549.6	552.2	554.0	549.3	549.6	549.0	538.1	536.5	540.2	543.5	545.4	549.4	546.4
2010	536.7	542.0	545.6	545.0	548.2	544.7	539.4	536.1	543.1	547.5	555.1	556.8	545.0
2011	540.1	550.9	554.5	551.1	551.8	549.0	544.8	542.1	550.8	554.5	560.5	565.6	551.3
2012	543.0	558.5	561.1	562.5	565.5	563.5	556.5	562.5	563.9	567.9	579.0	578.6	563.5
2013	556.9	572.3	574.7	571.7	576.0	573.0	568.7	566.5	574.5	579.1	585.5	588.9	574.0
2014	574.6	579.0	582.3	580.8	583.5	579.1	572.7	575.3	580.8	583.6	592.2	591.2	581.3
2015	581.9	587.0	590.0	587.9	589.2	586.9	579.8	583.0	585.9	591.3	594.3	599.0	588.0
Mining, Logging, and Construction													
2005	30.8	31.1	31.8	32.4	33.0	33.6	34.0	34.4	34.9	34.7	34.9	35.3	33.4
2006	34.5	34.7	34.9	35.0	35.7	36.4	36.7	37.3	37.9	37.8	38.4	39.0	36.5
2007	37.5	37.9	38.1	38.3	38.7	39.5	39.5	39.8	40.0	40.0	40.1	39.9	39.1
2008	38.9	39.0	38.9	38.6	38.1	38.2	38.1	37.9	37.7	37.0	36.3	35.6	37.9
2009	33.9	33.2	32.7	31.8	31.7	31.7	31.4	30.7	30.4	30.1	29.7	29.6	31.4
2010	29.0	28.8	28.9	28.8	28.8	28.7	28.9	28.7	28.8	29.1	29.1	29.2	28.9
2011	27.6	28.0	28.1	28.4	28.4	29.0	29.5	29.4	29.6	29.2	29.1	29.3	28.8
2012	28.4	28.4	28.5	28.5	28.8	29.4	29.5	29.8	30.2	30.4	30.5	30.5	29.4
2013	29.8	30.1	30.5	30.7	31.2	31.0	31.4	31.5	31.5	31.3	31.6	31.7	31.0
2014	30.6	30.9	31.1	31.1	31.8	32.0	32.5	32.7	33.1	33.3	33.2	33.1	32.1
2015	32.0	32.3	33.0	33.2	33.8	34.5	35.4	35.5	35.7	37.2	37.7	38.2	34.9

1. Employment by Industry: Hawaii, 2005–2015—*Continued*

(Numbers in thousands, not seasonally adjusted)

Industry and year	January	February	March	April	May	June	July	August	September	October	November	December	Annual average
Manufacturing													
2005	15.1	15.2	15.2	15.1	15.1	15.1	15.1	15.3	15.3	15.2	15.2	15.3	15.2
2006	15.0	15.1	15.2	15.1	15.2	15.3	15.3	15.5	15.6	15.3	15.5	15.6	15.3
2007	15.3	15.3	15.3	15.2	15.3	15.4	15.2	15.3	15.3	15.1	15.2	15.3	15.3
2008	15.0	15.1	15.1	15.1	15.1	15.1	14.9	15.0	14.7	14.4	14.5	14.5	14.9
2009	14.1	13.9	13.9	13.7	13.7	13.6	13.5	13.6	13.7	13.5	13.5	13.5	13.7
2010	13.2	13.1	13.1	12.9	12.9	12.8	12.8	12.9	12.9	13.0	13.1	13.2	13.0
2011	13.0	13.2	13.2	13.2	13.2	13.2	13.2	13.3	13.5	13.4	13.5	13.5	13.3
2012	13.3	13.4	13.3	13.2	13.1	13.2	13.2	13.3	13.4	13.4	13.6	13.6	13.3
2013	13.4	13.4	13.5	13.3	13.4	13.5	13.6	13.6	13.7	13.7	13.9	13.8	13.6
2014	13.5	13.5	13.7	13.6	13.6	13.8	14.0	14.2	14.0	14.0	14.1	14.2	13.9
2015	14.0	14.1	14.0	13.8	14.0	14.0	14.1	14.0	13.9	14.0	13.9	13.9	14.0
Trade, Transportation, and Utilities													
2005	114.9	114.9	115.2	115.5	116.4	117.3	118.2	118.7	119.1	118.9	120.7	122.9	117.7
2006	119.2	118.9	119.8	119.5	120.0	121.3	120.7	121.7	121.7	120.6	123.2	125.0	121.0
2007	121.6	120.3	121.4	120.3	120.8	121.6	121.3	121.4	121.2	121.5	124.5	126.4	121.9
2008	122.1	120.7	120.9	118.9	118.6	118.2	117.2	117.1	116.1	115.0	115.8	116.5	118.1
2009	113.4	112.3	111.7	110.3	110.0	110.5	110.2	109.8	110.1	110.0	111.4	112.8	111.0
2010	109.7	109.1	109.0	109.2	108.9	109.3	109.7	110.2	109.8	110.4	112.1	114.0	110.1
2011	110.8	110.3	110.5	110.1	110.0	110.3	111.0	111.2	111.2	112.3	114.4	116.1	111.5
2012	113.4	112.7	113.3	113.0	113.5	114.2	114.5	114.8	114.9	115.3	118.7	119.7	114.8
2013	115.9	115.6	116.0	115.6	115.8	116.3	116.5	116.8	116.9	116.9	119.5	121.1	116.9
2014	117.1	116.2	116.5	116.3	116.5	116.8	117.4	117.1	117.2	117.9	120.5	122.7	117.7
2015	119.3	118.6	118.9	118.5	118.5	118.9	119.1	119.1	119.0	118.7	119.4	120.8	119.1
Wholesale Trade													
2005	17.1	17.3	17.4	17.4	17.5	17.6	17.7	17.8	17.9	17.9	17.9	18.1	17.6
2006	17.7	17.7	17.7	17.8	17.9	18.1	18.0	18.2	18.2	18.2	18.4	18.5	18.0
2007	18.2	18.2	18.4	18.3	18.4	18.6	18.6	18.7	18.8	18.8	19.0	19.1	18.6
2008	18.7	18.8	18.9	18.8	18.9	18.9	18.9	18.8	18.8	18.7	18.6	18.6	18.8
2009	18.2	18.1	18.0	17.9	17.8	17.8	17.8	17.7	17.8	17.7	17.7	17.8	.17.9
2010	17.5	17.5	17.6	17.6	17.6	17.6	17.7	17.7	17.6	17.7	17.7	17.8	17.6
2011	17.4	17.3	17.3	17.4	17.4	17.4	17.5	17.5	17.5	17.6	17.6	17.8	17.5
2012	17.5	17.5	17.6	17.5	17.5	17.7	17.7	17.8	17.8	17.8	17.9	17.9	17.7
2013	17.7	17.7	17.8	17.7	17.7	17.7	17.7	17.7	17.7	17.6	17.7	17.7	17.7
2014	17.6	17.6	17.7	17.6	17.6	17.7	17.7	17.7	17.7	17.8	17.9	18.2	17.7
2015	17.9	17.9	17.9	17.9	17.9	18.0	18.0	18.0	18.0	18.0	18.0	18.0	18.0
Retail Trade													
2005	68.5	68.1	68.2	67.8	68.0	68.3	69.1	69.3	69.3	69.7	71.3	73.3	69.2
2006	70.0	69.5	69.8	69.1	69.2	69.8	69.4	69.7	69.4	69.5	71.7	73.1	70.0
2007	70.4	69.4	70.1	69.3	69.6	70.1	69.9	69.8	69.6	69.8	72.4	73.8	70.4
2008	70.6	69.9	70.7	69.7	69.6	70.1	70.0	69.8	69.2	68.5	69.5	70.3	69.8
2009	67.9	67.0	66.6	65.6	65.3	65.8	65.7	65.5	65.9	66.0	67.5	68.6	66.5
2010	66.0	65.4	65.3	65.3	65.0	65.5	65.7	65.8	65.5	65.8	67.5	68.9	66.0
2011	66.6	66.0	66.2	65.9	65.8	66.1	66.5	66.6	66.7	67.3	69.3	70.5	67.0
2012	68.3	67.7	67.8	67.6	68.0	68.3	68.4	68.4	68.4	68.8	71.7	72.6	68.8
2013	69.4	68.8	69.1	68.7	68.8	69.1	69.3	69.4	69.4	69.4	71.9	73.1	69.7
2014	69.6	68.7	68.8	68.7	68.8	69.3	69.7	69.4	69.6	69.9	72.1	73.6	69.9
2015	70.7	70.0	70.3	69.9	69.8	70.0	70.2	70.3	70.3	70.0	70.5	71.7	70.3
Transportation and Utilities													
2005	29.3	29.5	29.6	30.3	30.9	31.4	31.4	31.6	31.9	31.3	31.5	31.5	30.9
2006	31.5	31.7	32.3	32.6	32.9	33.4	33.3	33.8	34.1	32.9	33.1	33.4	32.9
2007	33.0	32.7	32.9	32.7	32.8	32.9	32.8	32.9	32.8	32.9	33.1	33.5	32.9
2008	32.8	32.0	31.3	30.4	30.1	29.2	28.3	28.5	28.1	27.8	27.7	27.6	29.5
2009	27.3	27.2	27.1	26.8	26.9	26.9	26.7	26.6	26.4	26.3	26.2	26.4	26.7
2010	26.2	26.2	26.1	26.3	26.3	26.2	26.3	26.7	26.7	26.9	26.9	27.3	26.5
2011	26.8	27.0	27.0	26.8	26.8	26.8	27.0	27.1	27.0	27.4	27.5	27.8	27.1
2012	27.6	27.5	27.9	27.9	28.0	28.2	28.4	28.6	28.7	28.7	29.1	29.2	28.3
2013	28.8	29.1	29.1	29.2	29.3	29.5	29.5	29.7	29.8	29.9	29.9	30.3	29.5
2014	29.9	29.9	30.0	30.0	30.1	29.8	30.0	30.0	29.9	30.2	30.5	30.9	30.1
2015	30.7	30.7	30.7	30.7	30.8	30.9	30.9	30.8	30.7	30.7	30.9	31.1	30.8

1. Employment by Industry: Hawaii, 2005–2015—*Continued*

(Numbers in thousands, not seasonally adjusted)

Industry and year	January	February	March	April	May	June	July	August	September	October	November	December	Annual average
Information													
2005	10.4	10.6	10.4	10.7	10.9	10.5	10.5	10.9	11.0	10.9	11.1	11.6	10.8
2006	10.8	11.1	10.9	10.2	11.0	10.8	10.3	10.5	11.0	10.3	10.8	10.9	10.7
2007	10.4	11.0	10.9	10.5	11.1	11.1	10.3	10.8	10.4	10.2	10.3	10.4	10.6
2008	9.6	10.1	10.4	10.4	10.7	11.1	9.9	9.6	9.6	9.4	9.8	10.0	10.1
2009	9.1	9.6	9.4	9.4	9.1	9.1	8.7	8.8	9.0	9.2	9.0	9.0	9.1
2010	8.9	9.7	9.9	9.5	10.7	10.0	8.8	9.4	11.1	9.8	9.4	10.3	9.8
2011	8.5	9.4	10.2	8.1	8.0	7.8	8.3	8.3	8.2	8.3	8.6	8.7	8.5
2012	8.3	8.4	8.5	8.4	8.4	7.8	8.1	8.3	8.4	8.6	9.2	8.9	8.4
2013	8.3	8.4	8.5	8.4	8.0	7.9	9.6	8.4	8.8	9.4	9.6	9.9	8.8
2014	8.3	8.4	8.5	8.3	8.8	8.1	8.2	8.7	8.8	8.5	8.7	8.7	8.5
2015	8.5	8.6	8.6	8.4	8.3	8.2	8.6	8.6	8.5	8.5	8.7	8.8	8.5
Financial Activities													
2005	28.7	29.0	29.0	28.9	29.1	29.2	29.4	29.5	29.5	29.5	29.7	29.9	29.3
2006	29.5	29.6	29.9	29.9	30.0	30.2	30.1	30.2	30.0	29.9	30.1	30.3	30.0
2007	29.9	30.0	30.2	29.9	30.0	30.2	30.2	30.1	29.9	30.0	29.9	30.1	30.0
2008	29.4	29.7	29.6	29.7	29.8	29.7	29.6	29.5	29.2	28.7	28.9	28.8	29.4
2009	27.9	27.9	27.8	27.8	27.8	27.8	27.6	27.6	27.5	27.5	27.4	27.5	27.7
2010	27.1	27.0	27.1	26.9	26.9	26.8	27.0	26.9	26.8	26.9	26.9	26.9	26.9
2011	26.5	26.5	26.6	26.6	26.5	26.5	26.7	26.7	26.6	26.5	26.8	26.8	26.6
2012	26.3	26.5	26.6	26.5	26.6	26.8	26.8	26.8	26.8	26.9	27.0	27.0	26.7
2013	26.7	26.8	27.0	27.1	27.2	27.2	27.3	27.2	27.3	27.2	27.3	27.5	27.2
2014	27.1	27.2	27.4	27.4	27.5	27.7	27.8	27.8	27.7	27.7	27.8	28.1	27.6
2015	27.7	27.9	28.1	28.1	28.2	28.4	28.3	28.3	28.1	27.8	28.2	28.1	28.1
Professional and Business Services													
2005	71.9	72.5	73.1	73.6	73.0	74.0	74.2	74.9	74.8	75.1	76.1	77.3	74.2
2006	75.3	76.8	77.2	76.7	76.6	77.6	77.5	77.7	77.2	75.6	76.1	77.2	76.8
2007	75.1	75.7	76.0	75.0	75.3	77.1	76.4	76.6	76.8	77.1	77.2	78.1	76.4
2008	75.8	76.1	76.3	76.1	75.8	75.5	75.4	75.6	75.1	74.7	74.5	75.4	75.5
2009	73.1	72.9	72.9	71.5	71.0	71.1	70.5	70.4	70.0	71.2	70.8	71.6	71.4
2010	70.2	70.6	70.9	70.9	70.8	71.2	71.9	71.8	71.9	72.5	72.8	73.5	71.6
2011	73.2	74.3	75.0	75.2	74.7	75.0	74.7	75.5	75.8	75.8	76.5	77.6	75.3
2012	75.0	75.7	76.0	76.8	77.1	77.3	76.9	77.8	77.2	77.9	78.7	79.1	77.1
2013	78.0	78.9	79.4	79.4	79.1	79.2	79.7	80.3	80.0	81.2	82.0	82.1	79.9
2014	81.2	81.4	82.1	82.3	82.0	82.1	81.7	82.3	82.6	82.6	83.2	83.9	82.3
2015	82.6	83.0	83.5	83.2	83.1	83.3	83.5	83.1	83.1	84.2	83.7	84.5	83.4
Education and Health Services													
2005	68.7	69.5	69.9	69.9	70.2	70.3	69.5	69.0	70.2	69.9	70.4	70.8	69.9
2006	68.9	70.1	70.7	70.7	71.4	71.8	70.6	71.2	71.7	71.8	72.6	73.0	71.2
2007	71.1	72.7	72.9	72.9	73.4	73.8	72.6	72.4	73.2	73.3	73.6	73.8	73.0
2008	72.5	73.7	73.9	73.8	74.2	74.7	74.0	73.8	74.4	74.7	75.2	75.5	74.2
2009	73.8	74.8	75.0	74.5	74.6	75.1	74.1	73.7	74.3	74.5	75.0	75.4	74.6
2010	74.5	75.2	75.6	75.2	75.6	75.3	74.9	74.6	74.6	75.9	75.9	76.3	75.3
2011	73.9	75.8	75.9	75.7	76.0	75.2	75.6	75.1	76.2	76.3	77.0	77.5	75.9
2012	75.0	76.4	76.1	76.7	77.4	76.8	76.7	77.2	77.9	78.1	78.3	79.1	77.1
2013	77.5	78.7	79.0	79.0	79.0	79.2	78.3	78.7	79.2	78.7	80.0	79.6	78.9
2014	77.8	78.4	79.0	79.0	79.0	78.3	78.3	78.4	79.4	79.7	80.2	80.8	79.0
2015	79.7	80.8	81.5	81.3	81.2	80.7	80.1	80.2	81.3	82.4	83.0	83.4	81.3
Leisure and Hospitality													
2005	103.8	104.7	105.9	105.9	106.2	107.5	107.2	107.5	107.4	106.1	106.4	107.4	106.3
2006	105.9	107.1	107.8	107.3	107.9	109.1	108.9	109.3	109.0	108.2	108.9	109.5	108.2
2007	108.4	109.6	110.4	110.2	110.7	111.7	110.5	111.1	110.0	108.5	108.9	109.4	110.0
2008	108.5	109.7	109.8	108.6	108.7	108.7	108.1	107.5	105.8	103.6	103.1	102.7	107.1
2009	101.2	101.4	101.8	100.9	101.0	101.5	101.0	101.5	100.8	99.7	99.6	100.2	100.9
2010	98.8	99.4	99.8	99.7	99.4	100.0	100.2	100.8	100.7	100.7	101.4	102.3	100.3
2011	101.5	101.9	102.9	102.4	102.5	102.9	103.0	103.8	104.1	103.2	103.7	104.7	103.1
2012	104.3	105.4	106.3	106.5	107.1	108.3	108.6	108.7	108.4	108.1	108.5	109.5	107.5
2013	108.6	109.5	110.0	110.3	111.1	111.8	111.9	112.5	111.7	111.9	112.4	113.2	111.2
2014	112.0	112.6	113.5	113.2	113.6	113.4	113.5	113.6	113.6	113.4	113.5	113.7	113.3
2015	112.8	113.2	113.8	113.1	113.8	114.2	114.7	115.5	114.5	114.7	115.3	116.2	114.3

1. Employment by Industry: Hawaii, 2005–2015—*Continued*

(Numbers in thousands, not seasonally adjusted)

Industry and year	January	February	March	April	May	June	July	August	September	October	November	December	Annual average
Other Services													
2005	24.5	24.6	24.7	25.1	25.4	25.4	25.2	25.4	25.5	25.4	25.5	25.8	25.2
2006	25.4	25.7	25.9	25.9	26.2	26.2	26.0	26.3	26.3	26.4	26.5	26.5	26.1
2007	25.8	26.2	26.4	26.3	26.5	26.6	26.6	26.8	26.9	27.0	27.1	27.0	26.6
2008	26.7	27.3	27.5	27.5	27.7	27.3	27.0	27.1	27.1	27.0	27.0	26.9	27.2
2009	26.0	26.2	26.4	25.9	25.9	25.9	25.8	25.9	26.1	26.0	26.0	25.9	26.0
2010	25.2	25.6	25.7	26.0	26.1	26.0	25.9	25.9	25.9	26.0	25.9	25.9	25.8
2011	25.5	25.8	25.7	25.8	25.9	25.9	25.9	26.0	26.2	26.2	26.1	26.1	25.9
2012	25.6	25.9	26.0	26.2	26.4	26.4	26.2	26.4	26.6	26.5	26.6	26.4	26.3
2013	26.3	26.4	26.4	26.5	26.6	26.5	26.6	26.7	26.8	26.8	26.7	26.8	26.6
2014	26.4	26.5	26.7	26.4	26.5	26.6	26.5	26.6	26.7	26.7	26.8	27.0	26.6
2015	26.4	26.6	26.9	26.5	26.7	26.9	26.6	26.6	26.8	26.9	27.0	27.0	26.7
Government													
2005	116.2	121.0	122.2	121.4	122.7	121.5	114.0	115.7	116.5	120.1	121.8	122.6	119.6
2006	115.7	121.9	122.9	122.2	123.9	122.3	114.5	116.0	120.0	122.3	128.2	125.3	121.3
2007	119.9	124.2	124.9	119.9	125.3	123.5	115.4	115.4	120.9	123.7	125.5	126.6	122.1
2008	121.4	125.2	127.0	121.8	127.9	125.9	118.4	120.3	123.3	127.0	133.0	128.9	125.0
2009	125.1	127.1	129.0	129.0	130.2	128.0	120.2	118.8	122.4	125.4	126.2	127.0	125.7
2010	122.3	125.4	127.6	127.6	129.8	126.1	121.0	116.5	122.3	125.3	130.7	127.6	125.2
2011	120.2	126.9	127.7	127.2	128.2	125.4	119.6	115.5	122.5	125.9	127.4	128.1	124.6
2012	115.1	127.5	128.3	128.4	129.0	125.9	118.7	122.5	123.7	126.5	132.0	128.9	125.5
2013	115.6	128.0	128.4	125.4	129.2	124.9	118.8	115.9	123.8	127.0	128.0	128.7	124.5
2014	124.7	128.3	128.6	127.9	129.6	126.1	119.3	120.8	124.8	127.1	131.5	126.3	126.3
2015	124.9	128.3	128.7	128.8	129.4	126.3	118.9	121.6	124.6	128.1	129.0	130.2	126.6

2. Average Weekly Hours by Selected Industry: Hawaii, 2011–2015

(Not seasonally adjusted)

Industry and year	January	February	March	April	May	June	July	August	September	October	November	December	Annual average
Total Private													
2011	34.1	33.3	33.0	33.4	34.1	33.4	33.2	33.1	33.1	34.0	32.7	32.6	33.4
2012	33.9	33.2	33.1	34.6	34.1	34.1	34.0	33.5	34.6	33.6	33.7	34.2	33.9
2013	33.0	33.1	33.1	33.2	32.9	34.1	33.2	33.0	33.8	32.9	32.6	33.7	33.2
2014	33.2	34.2	34.2	33.4	33.1	34.3	33.6	33.6	33.5	33.0	33.9	33.5	33.6
2015	33.2	34.1	34.1	33.0	33.0	32.9	33.3	34.0	32.6	32.6	33.5	33.0	33.3
Goods-Producing													
2011	36.3	37.7	36.6	37.9	37.2	36.8	36.8	36.4	36.6	35.1	33.7	35.7	36.4
2012	35.6	35.1	35.1	36.7	37.6	34.8	37.2	36.1	37.6	35.3	35.9	37.6	36.2
2013	35.3	35.2	35.7	36.3	36.4	34.8	37.3	36.5	37.1	37.3	34.5	37.2	36.2
2014	36.4	36.6	36.7	37.0	37.1	35.9	37.5	36.3	37.0	35.3	36.2	37.3	36.6
2015	36.6	36.5	36.9	37.4	37.7	34.9	36.7	36.5	34.4	36.6	35.9	38.5	36.6
Mining, Logging, and Construction													
2011	36.3	38.7	37.4	38.9	37.3	36.9	37.1	37.3	37.3	34.8	34.1	36.4	36.9
2012	36.5	36.2	35.5	37.7	38.3	35.1	37.8	35.9	37.9	35.1	36.4	37.8	36.7
2013	35.9	35.6	36.6	37.0	36.8	34.4	38.4	36.8	37.4	38.3	34.3	37.1	36.5
2014	37.0	36.8	37.1	37.5	38.3	35.8	37.9	36.5	37.1	34.2	35.0	36.8	36.7
2015	36.2	36.3	37.1	37.6	37.6	34.3	36.1	35.7	33.4	35.9	35.3	38.2	36.1
Manufacturing													
2011	36.3	35.8	34.9	35.5	36.8	36.6	35.9	34.2	35.0	35.5	32.9	34.1	35.4
2012	33.5	33.0	34.5	34.4	35.8	34.3	35.5	36.2	36.9	35.9	35.0	37.1	35.2
2013	34.1	34.4	33.8	34.6	35.6	35.6	35.2	35.9	36.5	35.0	35.4	37.4	35.3
2014	35.1	35.9	35.9	35.7	34.4	36.0	36.4	35.8	36.8	37.9	39.2	38.2	36.5
2015	37.6	37.2	36.6	36.8	38.3	36.6	38.5	38.7	36.6	38.5	37.5	39.2	37.7
Trade, Transportation, and Utilities													
2011	35.1	34.1	34.0	34.1	35.3	34.4	34.4	34.2	34.4	35.1	34.0	34.1	34.4
2012	35.0	33.8	33.4	34.2	33.5	33.9	34.3	33.2	34.2	32.9	33.0	34.5	33.8
2013	33.6	33.5	33.3	33.1	33.0	34.8	33.6	33.4	34.1	33.1	32.9	34.0	33.5
2014	33.3	34.4	34.3	33.5	33.2	34.4	33.7	33.8	33.3	33.4	34.3	34.2	33.8
2015	33.7	34.7	34.7	33.5	33.4	34.2	34.0	34.6	34.3	33.8	34.4	33.8	34.1
Professional and Business Services													
2011	35.1	35.6	35.2	35.9	34.8	34.6	33.8	33.2	33.0	34.6	33.9	34.5	34.5
2012	35.7	37.3	37.5	39.8	41.6	40.9	35.5	37.3	39.7	38.9	38.7	34.6	38.1
2013	33.8	34.5	34.1	34.7	34.4	35.5	34.1	34.0	35.5	35.1	34.5	35.5	34.7
2014	34.8	35.9	35.7	34.5	34.2	35.0	34.5	35.3	34.9	33.6	33.8	34.6	34.7
2015	34.2	34.6	34.8	34.3	33.8	33.3	33.7	34.1	33.0	33.4	35.0	34.6	34.1
Education and Health Services													
2011	32.4	31.7	31.2	31.3	32.8	31.5	31.2	31.6	31.8	33.2	32.0	31.8	31.9
2012	32.8	32.2	32.1	33.6	32.7	32.6	33.4	32.7	33.3	33.0	32.8	34.3	32.9
2013	33.4	33.1	33.3	33.5	33.3	34.4	33.8	33.3	34.2	33.3	32.9	33.0	33.5
2014	32.6	33.1	33.2	32.3	32.5	33.9	32.6	32.3	32.6	32.6	33.5	32.9	32.8
2015	31.9	32.7	31.7	31.5	31.2	31.6	31.7	32.9	31.6	31.2	32.1	31.6	31.8
Leisure and Hospitality													
2011	30.4	29.5	28.9	29.1	30.0	29.0	29.7	29.6	29.2	30.0	28.9	28.4	29.4
2012	30.1	29.0	28.8	30.1	29.1	30.0	30.9	29.9	30.4	29.5	30.0	30.8	29.9
2013	29.6	29.6	29.5	29.5	28.9	30.6	29.5	29.8	30.1	28.7	29.0	29.6	29.5
2014	30.4	31.7	31.6	30.3	29.7	31.6	30.5	30.3	29.9	29.6	31.2	29.1	30.5
2015	29.6	31.1	31.0	29.2	29.6	29.6	30.0	31.0	28.8	28.7	30.3	28.5	29.8

3. Average Hourly Earnings by Selected Industry: Hawaii, 2011–2015

(Dollars, not seasonally adjusted)

Industry and year	January	February	March	April	May	June	July	August	September	October	November	December	Annual average
Total Private													
2011	22.46	22.23	22.16	22.12	22.23	22.14	22.16	22.06	22.04	22.08	22.00	22.22	22.16
2012	22.39	22.35	22.54	22.49	22.40	22.45	23.01	22.77	23.08	22.84	22.99	23.23	22.72
2013	23.31	23.48	23.73	23.79	23.85	23.71	23.77	23.60	23.85	23.87	23.83	24.01	23.74
2014	23.98	24.02	24.13	24.08	24.29	24.34	24.42	24.51	24.61	24.57	24.60	24.39	24.33
2015	24.51	24.61	24.62	24.59	24.61	24.45	24.45	24.52	24.47	24.73	24.87	25.10	24.63
Goods-Producing													
2011	30.21	30.22	30.55	30.51	30.41	30.21	30.53	30.38	30.40	29.85	29.67	29.89	30.24
2012	30.21	30.89	30.17	30.73	30.80	30.16	30.78	30.31	30.64	30.34	31.61	30.91	30.64
2013	30.45	30.96	31.28	30.79	30.81	30.46	31.40	30.62	31.52	31.79	31.62	31.90	31.14
2014	31.59	31.68	31.82	32.25	32.78	32.10	32.76	33.49	34.26	33.13	33.13	33.25	32.71
2015	33.54	32.75	33.15	33.53	33.27	32.60	32.29	32.43	32.79	33.22	32.60	33.26	32.95
Mining, Logging, and Construction													
2011	34.50	34.32	34.80	34.69	34.81	34.67	34.98	34.54	34.81	34.56	33.93	34.07	34.56
2012	34.44	35.26	34.63	35.07	35.15	34.32	35.02	34.58	35.01	34.89	36.40	35.70	35.05
2013	35.13	35.64	35.83	35.22	35.32	35.36	35.73	35.02	35.92	36.20	36.87	36.92	35.77
2014	36.31	36.67	36.86	37.30	37.77	37.54	38.36	39.54	40.47	39.86	39.92	39.85	38.39
2015	40.19	38.91	38.97	39.11	38.98	38.11	37.23	37.43	38.14	38.41	37.28	37.98	38.37
Manufacturing													
2011	21.10	20.82	20.93	20.66	20.81	20.32	20.33	20.41	20.13	19.81	20.19	20.26	20.48
2012	20.41	20.67	20.28	20.44	20.57	20.66	20.70	20.88	20.53	20.28	20.41	19.97	20.48
2013	19.49	20.11	20.09	19.87	19.92	19.58	20.45	20.21	21.17	20.78	19.99	20.46	20.19
2014	20.30	20.00	20.00	20.10	19.83	19.55	19.26	19.23	19.47	18.77	18.89	18.47	19.46
2015	18.89	18.92	19.24	19.86	19.69	19.90	20.62	20.74	20.29	20.35	20.66	20.63	19.99
Trade, Transportation, and Utilities													
2011	20.24	19.66	19.48	19.53	19.61	19.29	20.12	19.49	19.54	19.73	19.98	20.28	19.75
2012	20.55	20.68	20.88	20.92	20.48	20.85	21.26	21.06	21.61	21.33	21.28	21.53	21.04
2013	21.68	21.87	22.25	22.43	22.60	22.36	22.31	22.50	22.92	22.70	22.71	22.86	22.44
2014	23.06	23.24	23.17	23.20	23.53	23.44	23.41	23.53	23.30	23.68	24.26	23.40	23.44
2015	23.92	24.46	24.34	24.44	24.10	23.70	23.63	24.02	23.70	23.77	24.15	24.12	24.03
Professional and Business Services													
2011	23.91	23.78	23.76	23.40	24.68	24.05	23.81	24.08	24.20	24.25	24.15	24.01	24.00
2012	24.30	23.69	23.72	23.41	22.78	23.08	23.72	23.32	23.30	22.98	23.22	24.22	23.45
2013	23.87	23.84	23.96	23.73	23.74	23.91	23.70	23.51	23.83	23.62	23.80	23.73	23.77
2014	23.75	24.00	24.52	24.32	24.35	24.74	24.47	24.70	24.76	24.25	24.01	23.44	24.28
2015	23.34	23.46	23.40	23.14	23.46	23.49	23.35	23.30	23.20	23.85	24.23	23.65	23.49
Education and Health Services													
2011	22.54	22.40	22.73	22.83	23.07	22.83	23.39	23.38	23.65	23.92	24.35	24.64	23.32
2012	24.93	24.77	25.68	24.99	25.33	25.81	26.46	26.41	26.60	26.62	26.55	26.61	25.91
2013	26.96	27.14	27.60	27.89	27.72	27.89	27.52	27.44	26.83	27.15	26.67	26.64	27.29
2014	26.11	26.04	26.11	25.64	26.01	26.27	26.54	26.54	26.67	27.01	26.98	26.95	26.41
2015	26.98	27.18	26.52	25.97	26.32	26.69	26.84	26.64	26.87	27.52	27.26	27.72	26.88
Leisure and Hospitality													
2011	16.49	16.56	16.76	16.81	16.62	16.72	16.82	16.89	16.85	16.72	16.01	16.03	16.61
2012	16.37	16.35	16.45	16.69	16.62	16.93	17.13	17.23	17.73	17.25	17.37	17.64	16.99
2013	18.04	18.15	18.15	18.19	18.20	18.05	18.08	17.76	17.96	17.87	18.05	18.54	18.09
2014	18.78	18.68	18.59	18.44	18.34	18.78	18.86	18.64	18.92	18.96	18.60	18.78	18.70
2015	19.25	19.15	19.17	18.93	19.20	19.44	19.73	19.45	19.38	19.13	19.63	19.51	19.33

4. Average Weekly Earnings by Selected Industry: Hawaii, 2011–2015

(Dollars, not seasonally adjusted)

Industry and year	January	February	March	April	May	June	July	August	September	October	November	December	Annual average
Total Private													
2011	765.89	740.26	731.28	738.81	758.04	739.48	735.71	730.19	729.52	750.72	719.40	724.37	740.14
2012	759.02	742.02	746.07	778.15	763.84	765.55	782.34	762.80	798.57	767.42	774.76	794.47	770.21
2013	769.23	777.19	785.46	789.83	784.67	808.51	789.16	778.80	806.13	785.32	776.86	809.14	788.17
2014	796.14	821.48	825.25	804.27	804.00	834.86	820.51	823.54	824.44	810.81	833.94	817.07	817.49
2015	813.73	839.20	839.54	811.47	812.13	804.41	814.19	833.68	797.72	806.20	833.15	828.30	820.18
Goods-Producing													
2011	1,096.62	1,139.29	1,118.13	1,156.33	1,131.25	1,111.73	1,123.50	1,105.83	1,112.64	1,047.74	999.88	1,067.07	1,100.74
2012	1,075.48	1,084.24	1,058.97	1,127.79	1,158.08	1,049.57	1,145.02	1,094.19	1,152.06	1,071.00	1,134.80	1,162.22	1,109.17
2013	1,074.89	1,089.79	1,116.70	1,117.68	1,121.48	1,060.01	1,171.22	1,117.63	1,169.39	1,185.77	1,090.89	1,186.68	1,127.27
2014	1,149.88	1,159.49	1,167.79	1,193.25	1,216.14	1,152.39	1,228.50	1,215.69	1,267.62	1,169.49	1,199.31	1,240.23	1,197.19
2015	1,227.56	1,195.38	1,223.24	1,254.02	1,254.28	1,137.74	1,185.04	1,183.70	1,127.98	1,215.85	1,170.34	1,280.51	1,205.97
Mining, Logging, and Construction													
2011	1,252.35	1,328.18	1,301.52	1,349.44	1,298.41	1,279.32	1,297.76	1,288.34	1,298.41	1,202.69	1,157.01	1,240.15	1,275.26
2012	1,257.06	1,276.41	1,229.37	1,322.14	1,346.25	1,204.63	1,323.76	1,241.42	1,326.88	1,224.64	1,324.96	1,349.46	1,286.34
2013	1,261.17	1,268.78	1,311.38	1,303.14	1,299.78	1,216.38	1,372.03	1,288.74	1,343.41	1,386.46	1,264.64	1,369.73	1,305.61
2014	1,343.47	1,349.46	1,367.51	1,398.75	1,446.59	1,343.93	1,453.84	1,443.21	1,501.44	1,363.21	1,397.20	1,466.48	1,408.91
2015	1,454.88	1,412.43	1,445.79	1,470.54	1,465.65	1,307.17	1,344.00	1,336.25	1,273.88	1,378.92	1,315.98	1,450.84	1,385.16
Manufacturing													
2011	765.93	745.36	730.46	733.43	765.81	743.71	729.85	698.02	704.55	703.26	664.25	690.87	724.99
2012	683.74	682.11	699.66	703.14	736.41	708.64	734.85	755.86	757.56	728.05	714.35	740.89	720.90
2013	664.61	691.78	679.04	687.50	709.15	697.05	719.84	725.54	772.71	727.30	707.65	765.20	712.71
2014	712.53	718.00	718.00	717.57	682.15	703.80	701.06	688.43	716.50	711.38	740.49	705.55	710.29
2015	710.26	703.82	704.18	730.85	754.13	728.34	793.87	802.64	742.61	783.48	774.75	808.70	753.62
Trade, Transportation, and Utilities													
2011	710.42	670.41	662.32	665.97	692.23	663.58	692.13	666.56	672.18	692.52	679.32	691.55	679.40
2012	719.25	698.98	697.39	715.46	686.08	706.82	729.22	699.19	739.06	701.76	702.24	742.79	711.15
2013	728.45	732.65	740.93	742.43	745.80	778.13	749.62	751.50	781.57	751.37	747.16	777.24	751.74
2014	767.90	799.46	794.73	777.20	781.20	806.34	788.92	795.31	775.89	790.91	832.12	800.28	792.27
2015	806.10	848.76	844.60	818.74	804.94	810.54	803.42	831.09	812.91	803.43	830.76	815.26	819.42
Professional and Business Services													
2011	839.24	846.57	836.35	840.06	858.86	832.13	804.78	799.46	798.60	839.05	818.69	828.35	828.00
2012	867.51	883.64	889.50	931.72	947.65	943.97	842.06	869.84	925.01	893.92	898.61	838.01	893.45
2013	806.81	822.48	817.04	823.43	816.66	848.81	808.17	799.34	845.97	829.06	821.10	842.42	824.82
2014	826.50	861.60	875.36	839.04	832.77	865.90	844.22	871.91	864.12	814.80	811.54	811.02	842.52
2015	798.23	811.72	814.32	793.70	792.95	782.22	786.90	794.53	765.60	796.59	848.05	818.29	801.01
Education and Health Services													
2011	730.30	710.08	709.18	714.58	756.70	719.15	729.77	738.81	752.07	794.14	779.20	783.55	743.91
2012	817.70	797.59	824.33	839.66	828.29	841.41	883.76	863.61	885.78	878.46	870.84	912.72	852.44
2013	900.46	898.33	919.08	934.32	923.08	959.42	930.18	913.75	917.59	904.10	877.44	879.12	914.22
2014	851.19	861.92	866.85	828.17	845.33	890.55	865.20	857.24	869.44	880.53	903.83	886.66	866.25
2015	860.66	888.79	840.68	818.06	821.18	843.40	850.83	876.46	849.09	858.62	875.05	875.95	854.78
Leisure and Hospitality													
2011	501.30	488.52	484.36	489.17	498.60	484.88	499.55	499.94	492.02	501.60	462.69	455.25	488.33
2012	492.74	474.15	473.76	502.37	483.64	507.90	529.32	515.18	538.99	508.88	521.10	543.31	508.00
2013	533.98	537.24	535.43	536.61	525.98	552.33	533.36	529.25	540.60	512.87	523.45	548.78	533.66
2014	570.91	592.16	587.44	558.73	544.70	593.45	575.23	564.79	565.71	561.22	580.32	546.50	570.35
2015	569.80	595.57	594.27	552.76	568.32	575.42	591.90	602.95	558.14	549.03	594.79	556.04	576.03

IDAHO
At a Glance

Population:
  2005 estimate: 1,428,241
  2010 census: 1,567,582
  2015 estimate: 1,654,930

Percent change in population:
  2005–2015: 15.9%
  2010–2015: 5.6%

Percent change in total nonfarm employment:
  2005–2015: 10.2%

Industry with the largest growth in employment, 2005–2015 (thousands):
  Education and health services, 29.8

Industry with the largest decline or smallest growth in employment, 2005–2015 (thousands):
  Construction, –6.5

Civilian labor force:
  2005: 731,670
  2010: 761,056
  2015: 797,475

Unemployment rate and rank among states (highest to lowest):
  2005: 4.0%, 42nd
  2010: 9.0%, 23rd
  2015: 4.1%, 40th

Over-the-year change in unemployment rates:
  2012–2013: –1.0%
  2013–2014: –1.4%
  2014–2015: –0.7%

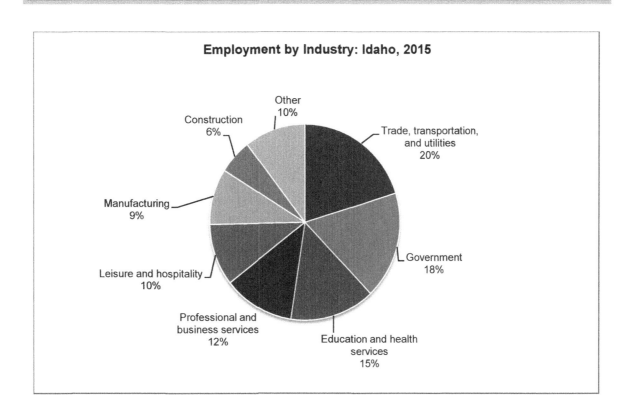

Employment by Industry: Idaho, 2015

Other 10%
Construction 6%
Trade, transportation, and utilities 20%
Manufacturing 9%
Leisure and hospitality 10%
Government 18%
Professional and business services 12%
Education and health services 15%

1. Employment by Industry: Idaho, 2005–2015

(Numbers in thousands, not seasonally adjusted)

Industry and year	January	February	March	April	May	June	July	August	September	October	November	December	Annual average
Total Nonfarm													
2005	581.5	588.5	594.4	603.2	609.5	617.9	617.5	621.1	628.4	624.0	624.6	625.0	611.3
2006	607.9	615.0	622.6	631.7	640.4	649.7	645.7	649.2	654.0	649.0	648.6	647.4	638.4
2007	628.2	635.5	642.3	649.8	659.6	668.7	661.6	665.3	666.9	661.6	661.3	658.3	654.9
2008	633.3	639.4	643.6	649.3	657.7	663.0	659.6	659.4	659.0	648.7	639.1	633.6	648.8
2009	606.7	605.5	604.1	607.8	612.8	618.1	610.9	611.0	614.2	612.9	608.7	605.5	609.9
2010	581.7	587.3	591.9	600.6	610.1	610.5	608.9	610.2	612.6	613.4	610.1	606.1	603.6
2011	585.9	592.6	595.2	605.8	612.6	616.1	616.8	618.3	624.0	621.9	621.1	618.9	610.8
2012	596.8	603.0	608.3	613.8	624.7	628.5	626.8	628.8	634.7	635.7	634.7	631.5	622.3
2013	612.5	620.1	626.1	631.0	641.5	645.1	642.3	643.1	646.4	651.4	649.4	646.2	637.9
2014	631.2	638.3	643.5	650.2	657.4	662.4	659.9	659.8	662.3	664.7	662.6	661.3	654.5
2015	646.8	652.6	659.9	666.9	675.9	680.7	680.0	677.1	683.0	689.5	687.4	686.6	673.9
Total Private													
2005	469.4	472.6	477.8	486.4	492.1	501.8	508.4	512.3	511.7	505.9	506.8	508.5	496.1
2006	493.9	497.6	504.8	513.1	521.1	532.4	535.7	539.6	537.6	530.6	530.8	530.9	522.3
2007	515.1	518.7	525.1	531.6	540.4	550.8	551.0	553.5	547.8	542.1	542.3	539.6	538.2
2008	517.9	519.9	523.5	528.9	536.0	542.8	545.8	545.2	538.4	527.2	517.6	512.5	529.6
2009	489.0	485.9	483.0	484.3	489.9	496.2	498.4	498.1	495.6	491.5	487.7	485.0	490.4
2010	466.8	467.6	471.2	478.5	484.5	490.3	496.5	497.7	494.4	493.7	491.4	487.5	485.0
2011	472.8	473.9	476.0	485.8	491.4	498.9	505.7	507.1	506.4	502.7	502.3	500.1	493.6
2012	483.5	485.2	490.1	494.6	503.9	511.5	516.4	518.0	516.2	514.7	514.5	511.7	505.0
2013	496.9	500.3	506.0	511.5	520.4	527.7	532.4	533.5	528.8	531.0	529.8	527.7	520.5
2014	516.0	518.9	523.1	529.8	536.3	544.3	548.2	548.3	543.7	543.2	541.7	541.7	536.3
2015	530.8	532.7	539.1	545.8	553.0	561.4	567.2	565.7	563.0	565.4	564.1	564.2	554.4
Goods-Producing													
2005	103.1	103.7	105.7	108.5	110.9	114.5	116.9	118.3	118.5	118.2	117.2	116.9	112.7
2006	112.4	113.5	115.9	118.8	122.4	127.1	128.1	128.4	127.8	126.0	124.5	122.6	122.3
2007	117.3	118.0	119.4	121.4	124.7	127.7	128.1	127.6	125.4	122.9	121.2	118.5	122.7
2008	111.6	110.2	110.7	112.0	114.6	116.7	117.2	116.5	114.8	111.8	106.5	102.9	112.1
2009	94.1	90.9	89.7	89.8	91.8	94.0	95.1	95.1	94.4	93.8	91.1	88.1	92.3
2010	83.3	82.6	83.4	85.4	87.6	89.9	91.3	92.2	91.6	91.6	89.7	86.2	87.9
2011	82.3	82.5	83.3	85.9	88.3	90.9	92.4	93.2	92.8	93.5	92.7	90.2	89.0
2012	86.4	86.2	86.9	88.6	91.8	94.6	96.0	96.6	95.8	96.4	95.4	93.9	92.4
2013	90.6	91.4	92.9	94.1	97.4	99.7	100.7	101.3	100.4	100.8	99.4	97.4	97.2
2014	94.8	94.6	95.3	97.2	99.5	102.1	103.4	103.6	103.3	103.4	102.0	100.8	100.0
2015	97.9	98.4	100.1	102.4	104.2	106.7	107.2	107.7	107.1	108.3	107.5	106.4	104.5
Service-Providing													
2005	478.4	484.8	488.7	494.7	498.6	503.4	500.6	502.8	509.9	505.8	507.4	508.1	498.6
2006	495.5	501.5	506.7	512.9	518.0	522.6	517.6	520.8	526.2	523.0	524.1	524.8	516.1
2007	510.9	517.5	522.9	528.4	534.9	541.0	533.5	537.7	541.5	538.7	540.1	539.8	532.2
2008	521.7	529.2	532.9	537.3	543.1	546.3	542.4	542.9	544.2	536.9	532.6	530.7	536.7
2009	512.6	514.6	514.4	518.0	521.0	524.1	515.8	515.9	519.8	519.1	517.6	517.4	517.5
2010	498.4	504.7	508.5	515.2	522.5	520.6	517.6	518.0	521.0	521.8	520.4	519.9	515.7
2011	503.6	510.1	511.9	519.9	524.3	525.2	524.4	525.1	531.2	528.4	528.4	528.7	521.8
2012	510.4	516.8	521.4	525.2	532.9	533.9	530.8	532.2	538.9	539.3	539.3	537.6	529.9
2013	521.9	528.7	533.2	536.9	544.1	545.4	541.6	541.8	546.0	550.6	550.0	548.8	540.8
2014	536.4	543.7	548.2	553.0	557.9	560.3	556.5	556.2	559.0	561.3	560.6	560.5	554.5
2015	548.9	554.2	559.8	564.5	571.7	574.0	572.8	569.4	575.9	581.2	579.9	580.2	569.4
Mining and Logging													
2005	3.8	3.6	3.5	3.4	3.8	4.3	4.5	4.7	4.7	4.6	4.3	4.2	4.1
2006	3.8	3.7	3.7	3.5	4.0	4.6	4.7	4.7	4.8	4.5	4.3	4.3	4.2
2007	4.0	4.0	3.8	3.6	4.3	4.8	4.9	5.0	4.9	4.7	4.6	4.4	4.4
2008	4.1	4.1	3.7	3.5	4.0	4.5	4.8	4.8	4.6	4.4	4.1	3.9	4.2
2009	3.4	3.2	2.7	2.5	2.7	3.2	3.6	3.7	3.7	3.6	3.4	3.2	3.2
2010	3.0	2.9	2.8	2.8	3.2	3.7	3.9	4.1	4.1	4.1	3.8	3.5	3.5
2011	3.4	3.4	3.3	3.1	3.3	3.9	4.3	4.4	4.4	4.4	4.3	4.1	3.9
2012	3.9	3.8	3.4	3.2	3.7	4.3	4.5	4.5	4.4	4.2	4.0	4.0	4.0
2013	3.8	3.7	3.6	3.4	3.9	4.2	4.3	4.3	4.2	4.2	4.1	3.9	4.0
2014	3.8	3.7	3.3	3.2	3.6	4.0	4.2	4.2	4.1	4.1	3.9	3.8	3.8
2015	3.6	3.5	3.4	3.5	3.8	4.1	4.2	4.1	4.1	4.0	3.8	3.6	3.8

1. Employment by Industry: Idaho, 2005–2015—*Continued*

(Numbers in thousands, not seasonally adjusted)

Industry and year	January	February	March	April	May	June	July	August	September	October	November	December	Annual average
Construction													
2005	37.7	38.2	40.0	42.8	44.3	46.9	48.4	49.1	49.0	48.3	48.5	47.2	45.0
2006	44.4	45.4	47.4	50.1	52.8	55.9	56.2	56.5	55.6	54.3	53.5	51.4	52.0
2007	47.4	47.8	49.4	51.4	53.6	55.6	55.8	56.1	54.4	52.5	51.0	48.9	52.0
2008	43.3	42.1	43.2	44.8	46.9	48.2	48.5	48.2	47.1	45.0	42.2	39.8	44.9
2009	33.7	31.9	31.8	32.8	34.6	36.0	36.8	36.9	36.3	35.5	33.9	31.7	34.3
2010	28.1	27.6	28.6	30.2	31.8	32.9	33.9	34.2	33.7	32.9	31.8	29.4	31.3
2011	25.7	25.6	26.2	28.5	30.3	32.1	33.2	33.5	32.9	32.9	32.7	30.8	30.4
2012	27.5	27.3	28.0	29.4	31.3	32.8	33.9	34.2	33.8	33.8	32.9	31.8	31.4
2013	28.8	29.4	30.5	31.7	33.8	35.3	36.1	36.6	36.2	36.1	35.2	33.6	33.6
2014	31.7	31.4	32.4	34.1	35.8	37.4	38.2	38.8	38.5	38.0	37.3	36.3	35.8
2015	34.0	34.5	36.0	37.8	38.9	40.3	40.5	40.8	40.0	40.4	40.2	39.1	38.5
Manufacturing													
2005	61.6	61.9	62.2	62.3	62.8	63.3	64.0	64.5	64.8	65.3	64.4	65.5	63.6
2006	64.2	64.4	64.8	65.2	65.6	66.6	67.2	67.2	67.4	67.2	66.7	66.9	66.1
2007	65.9	66.2	66.2	66.4	66.8	67.3	67.4	66.5	66.1	65.7	65.6	65.2	66.3
2008	64.2	64.0	63.8	63.7	63.7	64.0	63.9	63.5	63.1	62.4	60.2	59.2	63.0
2009	57.0	55.8	55.2	54.5	54.5	54.8	54.7	54.5	54.4	54.7	53.8	53.2	54.8
2010	52.2	52.1	52.0	52.4	52.6	53.3	53.5	53.9	53.8	54.6	54.1	53.3	53.2
2011	53.2	53.5	53.8	54.3	54.7	54.9	54.9	55.3	55.5	56.2	55.7	55.3	54.8
2012	55.0	55.1	55.5	56.0	56.8	57.5	57.6	57.9	57.6	58.4	58.5	58.1	57.0
2013	58.0	58.3	58.8	59.0	59.7	60.2	60.3	60.4	60.0	60.5	60.1	59.9	59.6
2014	59.3	59.5	59.6	59.9	60.1	60.7	61.0	60.6	60.7	61.3	60.8	60.7	60.4
2015	60.3	60.4	60.7	61.1	61.5	62.3	62.5	62.8	63.0	63.9	63.5	63.7	62.1
Trade, Transportation, and Utilities													
2005	118.4	118.4	119.6	121.0	122.0	123.4	124.5	125.2	125.5	125.2	127.4	128.5	123.3
2006	123.6	123.3	124.4	126.0	127.3	129.0	128.8	129.8	130.2	130.3	132.6	133.6	128.2
2007	129.5	129.3	130.8	131.4	132.4	133.6	133.7	134.2	133.8	134.2	136.6	136.9	133.0
2008	131.4	130.6	131.1	131.6	132.6	133.3	133.9	133.7	132.3	131.6	132.0	131.8	132.2
2009	124.1	122.6	122.2	122.0	123.0	123.1	123.0	123.1	122.8	122.5	123.6	123.3	122.9
2010	119.1	118.0	118.6	120.0	121.2	121.8	122.5	123.5	122.2	122.9	124.2	124.3	121.5
2011	119.2	118.6	119.2	121.1	122.1	122.4	124.2	124.9	125.2	125.3	127.3	127.4	123.1
2012	123.1	122.3	123.4	123.8	125.6	126.5	127.6	127.9	128.0	128.6	130.4	130.2	126.5
2013	125.3	125.1	125.8	127.0	128.3	128.9	130.1	130.5	130.3	130.7	132.1	132.5	128.9
2014	128.6	127.8	128.7	130.3	131.3	132.3	133.1	133.4	132.8	133.6	135.4	136.1	132.0
2015	132.1	131.7	133.1	134.6	135.9	136.5	137.8	137.7	137.5	138.1	139.2	139.2	136.1
Wholesale Trade													
2005	25.7	25.9	26.4	26.6	26.6	26.6	26.8	26.7	27.0	26.7	26.8	26.8	26.6
2006	26.1	26.4	26.7	27.0	27.1	27.3	27.1	27.1	27.3	27.1	27.4	27.4	27.0
2007	27.2	27.5	27.7	27.8	28.0	28.3	28.3	28.3	28.4	28.1	28.1	28.1	28.0
2008	27.6	27.7	27.9	27.8	28.0	28.1	28.3	28.0	28.1	27.8	27.5	27.3	27.8
2009	26.4	26.3	26.3	26.1	26.1	26.1	26.2	25.7	25.9	25.7	25.6	25.4	26.0
2010	25.2	25.2	25.5	25.9	26.1	26.2	26.5	26.5	26.2	26.4	26.2	26.1	26.0
2011	25.6	25.7	26.0	26.5	26.7	26.6	27.2	27.1	27.2	27.3	27.2	27.1	26.7
2012	26.7	26.9	27.4	27.6	27.9	27.9	28.5	28.1	28.2	28.4	28.1	28.1	27.8
2013	27.9	28.2	28.4	28.6	28.6	28.7	29.4	28.7	28.9	28.9	28.6	28.7	28.6
2014	28.5	28.5	28.9	29.1	29.1	29.2	29.7	29.0	28.8	28.9	28.8	28.9	29.0
2015	28.5	28.7	28.8	28.9	29.0	29.1	29.6	29.2	29.1	29.2	29.3	28.9	29.0
Retail Trade													
2005	73.4	73.0	73.8	74.9	75.9	76.9	77.5	78.1	78.0	77.9	80.0	80.8	76.7
2006	77.3	76.6	77.5	78.5	79.7	80.7	80.9	81.6	81.7	82.0	83.9	84.5	80.4
2007	81.1	80.6	82.1	82.4	83.1	83.7	84.0	84.1	83.5	83.9	86.3	86.5	83.4
2008	82.4	81.5	82.0	82.4	83.1	83.4	83.8	83.6	82.2	81.7	82.6	82.4	82.6
2009	76.5	75.4	75.5	75.5	76.5	76.8	76.8	76.8	76.0	75.6	76.9	76.9	76.3
2010	73.4	72.4	73.1	74.0	74.9	75.2	75.5	76.0	74.9	75.3	76.7	76.6	74.8
2011	72.8	72.1	72.4	73.7	74.7	75.1	76.0	76.3	76.2	76.4	78.5	78.3	75.2
2012	75.0	74.2	74.8	75.3	76.7	77.5	78.0	78.0	77.7	78.1	80.3	79.9	77.1
2013	75.9	75.4	75.9	77.4	78.6	79.2	79.8	80.3	79.7	79.8	81.5	81.4	78.7
2014	78.0	77.3	78.0	79.3	80.4	81.4	81.5	81.7	80.9	81.5	83.4	83.5	80.6
2015	80.3	80.0	81.1	82.5	83.7	84.6	85.1	85.1	84.6	85.1	85.9	85.7	83.6

1. Employment by Industry: Idaho, 2005–2015—*Continued*

(Numbers in thousands, not seasonally adjusted)

Industry and year	January	February	March	April	May	June	July	August	September	October	November	December	Annual average
Transportation and Utilities													
2005	19.3	19.5	19.4	19.5	19.5	19.9	20.2	20.4	20.5	20.6	20.6	20.9	20.0
2006	20.2	20.3	20.2	20.5	20.5	21.0	20.8	21.1	21.2	21.2	21.3	21.7	20.8
2007	21.2	21.2	21.0	21.2	21.3	21.6	21.4	21.8	21.9	22.2	22.2	22.3	21.6
2008	21.4	21.4	21.2	21.4	21.5	21.8	21.8	22.1	22.0	22.1	21.9	22.1	21.7
2009	21.2	20.9	20.4	20.4	20.4	20.2	20.0	20.6	20.9	21.2	21.1	21.0	20.7
2010	20.5	20.4	20.0	20.1	20.2	20.4	20.5	21.0	21.1	21.2	21.3	21.6	20.7
2011	20.8	20.8	20.8	20.9	20.7	20.7	21.0	21.5	21.8	21.6	21.6	22.0	21.2
2012	21.4	21.2	21.2	20.9	21.0	21.1	21.1	21.8	22.1	22.1	22.0	22.2	21.5
2013	21.5	21.5	21.5	21.0	21.1	21.0	20.9	21.5	21.7	22.0	22.0	22.4	21.5
2014	22.1	22.0	21.8	21.9	21.8	21.7	21.9	22.7	23.1	23.2	23.2	23.7	22.4
2015	23.3	23.0	23.2	23.2	23.2	22.8	23.1	23.4	23.8	23.8	24.0	24.6	23.5
Information													
2005	10.0	10.1	10.1	10.3	10.4	10.4	10.5	10.3	10.3	10.5	10.4	10.6	10.3
2006	10.3	10.3	10.3	10.5	10.6	10.8	10.8	10.8	10.7	10.6	10.7	10.8	10.6
2007	10.6	10.6	10.7	10.8	10.9	11.0	10.9	11.0	10.8	10.9	11.0	11.0	10.9
2008	11.0	11.1	11.3	10.9	11.1	11.1	11.2	11.5	11.1	10.7	10.7	10.6	11.0
2009	10.4	10.5	10.3	10.0	10.0	10.1	10.0	9.8	9.7	9.7	9.8	9.8	10.0
2010	9.8	9.7	9.7	9.6	9.7	9.7	9.7	9.7	9.5	9.4	9.5	9.5	9.6
2011	9.4	9.3	9.3	9.5	9.6	9.6	9.6	9.6	9.4	9.4	9.4	9.5	9.5
2012	9.4	9.4	9.4	9.3	9.4	9.4	9.5	9.5	9.2	9.3	9.3	9.3	9.4
2013	9.1	9.1	9.3	9.4	9.4	9.4	9.4	9.4	9.1	9.2	9.4	9.3	9.3
2014	9.1	9.2	9.2	9.3	9.4	9.4	9.4	9.5	9.1	9.3	9.5	9.5	9.3
2015	9.1	9.2	9.2	9.3	9.3	9.3	9.4	9.3	9.2	9.2	9.2	9.3	9.3
Financial Activities													
2005	28.3	28.5	28.4	28.8	29.1	29.6	30.2	30.4	30.5	30.5	30.7	30.8	29.7
2006	30.5	30.7	31.1	31.4	31.6	31.9	32.2	32.4	32.3	32.0	32.0	32.3	31.7
2007	31.8	31.9	32.0	32.3	32.7	32.7	33.0	32.8	32.4	32.3	32.5	32.4	32.4
2008	31.6	31.6	31.6	31.8	31.9	32.1	32.2	32.0	31.8	31.3	30.9	31.1	31.7
2009	30.1	30.0	29.8	29.8	29.7	29.7	29.7	29.5	29.2	29.3	29.2	29.4	29.6
	28.7	28.6	28.7	28.9	29.1	29.2	29.7	29.5	29.2	29.4	29.4	29.6	29.2
2010													
2011	29.2	29.2	29.2	29.5	29.7	29.9	30.4	30.3	30.3	30.2	30.2	30.3	29.9
2012	29.5	29.5	29.6	30.1	30.3	30.5	30.8	30.8	30.5	30.7	30.7	30.9	30.3
2013	30.4	30.6	30.7	30.8	31.1	31.3	31.4	31.6	31.3	31.5	31.5	31.9	31.2
2014	31.8	32.2	32.4	32.5	32.7	32.8	33.4	33.1	32.9	32.7	32.8	32.8	32.7
2015	32.7	32.7	32.9	33.2	33.3	33.7	33.9	33.6	33.2	33.7	33.8	33.6	33.4
Professional and Business Services													
2005	70.8	72.6	73.8	76.3	77.3	78.4	79.1	80.0	79.9	78.2	78.6	78.1	76.9
2006	75.3	76.6	78.1	80.2	81.9	83.2	82.6	83.6	83.1	81.2	81.2	80.3	80.6
2007	76.8	78.1	79.5	82.2	83.5	85.3	84.5	85.7	85.1	83.9	83.2	82.4	82.5
2008	76.4	78.0	78.8	81.7	82.7	83.3	83.3	84.0	82.5	80.4	78.3	77.3	80.6
2009	73.8	73.5	72.8	73.7	74.5	75.3	75.4	75.9	76.0	75.5	74.9	74.6	74.7
2010	70.0	70.4	71.4	73.3	74.1	74.3	75.6	76.2	75.4	76.0	75.8	75.0	74.0
2011	72.2	72.3	72.6	74.2	74.8	75.9	76.9	77.8	77.5	76.5	76.0	75.1	75.2
2012	71.2	71.8	73.3	74.1	75.2	76.6	77.0	78.1	77.4	77.2	77.7	75.9	75.5
2013	72.6	73.3	74.9	75.5	77.1	78.7	78.9	79.9	79.1	80.2	80.2	79.7	77.5
2014	76.2	77.6	78.5	79.8	79.8	80.8	80.2	81.1	80.8	80.5	80.4	79.9	79.6
2015	77.8	77.9	78.8	80.5	81.2	82.2	83.5	84.1	83.5	83.0	82.3	82.5	81.4
Education and Health Services													
2005	66.9	67.5	67.4	67.8	67.0	67.1	66.6	67.1	68.4	68.3	68.6	68.6	67.6
2006	67.8	68.5	69.2	69.2	68.8	68.8	69.9	70.4	71.8	72.1	72.7	72.7	70.2
2007	71.7	72.5	72.8	72.9	73.3	73.8	73.3	73.8	74.4	75.8	76.7	76.7	74.0
2008	75.9	77.0	77.5	77.5	77.3	77.5	77.6	76.3	78.0	79.2	79.3	79.6	77.7
2009	78.7	80.2	80.2	80.7	80.6	80.8	80.5	79.6	81.6	82.8	83.0	83.2	81.0
2010	80.9	83.0	83.5	83.8	84.0	83.6	83.6	81.9	84.3	85.7	85.9	85.7	83.8
2011	85.4	86.2	86.2	86.6	86.9	86.9	85.9	84.4	86.7	87.6	87.6	88.1	86.5
2012	86.8	87.7	88.1	88.1	88.7	88.4	87.5	86.3	88.8	89.8	89.9	90.1	88.4
2013	88.9	90.3	90.6	91.2	91.2	90.6	90.7	89.4	90.0	92.8	93.1	93.1	91.0
2014	92.8	93.8	93.8	94.4	94.4	93.8	93.8	92.4	93.7	95.5	95.6	96.0	94.2
2015	95.2	96.2	96.9	97.2	97.1	97.2	97.1	95.1	97.2	99.7	99.6	99.8	97.4

1. Employment by Industry: Idaho, 2005–2015—*Continued*

(Numbers in thousands, not seasonally adjusted)

Industry and year	January	February	March	April	May	June	July	August	September	October	November	December	Annual average
Leisure and Hospitality													
2005	54.0	53.7	54.7	55.4	57.0	59.8	61.5	62.0	60.1	56.5	55.4	56.6	57.2
2006	55.7	56.2	57.2	58.2	59.6	62.3	63.6	64.5	62.5	59.4	58.2	59.6	59.8
2007	58.7	59.4	60.7	61.3	63.4	66.9	67.6	68.3	66.3	62.7	61.8	62.3	63.3
2008	60.5	61.3	61.9	62.1	64.3	66.8	68.2	68.9	66.1	61.2	59.1	58.4	63.2
2009	56.7	56.9	56.8	57.1	58.9	61.5	63.0	63.3	60.8	57.3	55.6	56.1	58.7
2010	54.2	54.3	54.9	56.6	57.8	60.6	62.3	63.2	61.2	57.8	56.1	56.5	58.0
2011	54.6	55.2	55.7	58.0	58.8	61.9	64.3	65.2	63.1	59.0	57.8	58.1	59.3
2012	56.1	57.2	58.2	59.4	61.4	63.7	65.8	66.7	64.8	61.0	59.7	60.0	61.2
2013	58.8	59.1	60.3	61.9	64.0	66.8	68.5	68.5	66.1	63.9	62.1	61.9	63.5
2014	61.0	61.8	63.0	64.0	66.6	70.1	71.4	71.7	68.0	65.5	63.5	64.1	65.9
2015	63.3	63.8	65.1	65.4	68.4	71.8	74.1	74.3	71.7	69.6	69.0	70.0	68.9
Other Services													
2005	17.9	18.1	18.1	18.3	18.4	18.6	19.1	19.0	18.5	18.5	18.5	18.4	18.5
2006	18.3	18.5	18.6	18.8	18.9	19.3	19.7	19.7	19.2	19.0	18.9	19.0	19.0
2007	18.7	18.9	19.2	19.3	19.5	19.8	19.9	20.1	19.6	19.4	19.3	19.4	19.4
2008	19.5	20.1	20.6	21.3	21.5	22.0	22.2	22.3	21.8	21.0	20.8	20.8	21.2
2009	21.1	21.3	21.2	21.2	21.4	21.7	21.7	21.8	21.1	20.6	20.5	20.5	21.2
2010	20.8	21.0	21.0	20.9	21.0	21.2	21.8	21.5	21.0	20.9	20.8	20.7	21.1
2011	20.5	20.6	20.5	21.0	21.2	21.4	22.0	21.7	21.4	21.2	21.3	21.4	21.2
2012	21.0	21.1	21.2	21.2	21.5	21.8	22.2	22.1	21.7	21.7	21.4	21.4	21.5
2013	21.2	21.4	21.5	21.6	21.9	22.3	22.7	22.9	22.5	21.9	22.0	21.9	22.0
2014	21.7	21.9	22.2	22.3	22.6	23.0	23.5	23.5	23.1	22.7	22.5	22.5	22.6
2015	22.7	22.8	23.0	23.2	23.6	24.0	24.2	23.9	23.6	23.8	23.5	23.4	23.5
Government													
2005	112.1	115.9	116.6	116.8	117.4	116.1	109.1	108.8	116.7	118.1	117.8	116.5	115.2
2006	114.0	117.4	117.8	118.6	119.3	117.3	110.0	109.6	116.4	118.4	117.8	116.5	116.1
2007	113.1	116.8	117.2	118.2	119.2	117.9	110.6	111.8	119.1	119.5	119.0	118.7	116.8
2008	115.4	119.5	120.1	120.4	121.7	120.2	113.8	114.2	120.6	121.5	121.5	121.1	119.2
2009	117.7	119.6	121.1	123.5	122.9	121.9	112.5	112.9	118.6	121.4	121.0	120.5	119.5
2010	114.9	119.7	120.7	122.1	125.6	120.2	112.4	112.5	118.2	119.7	118.7	118.6	118.6
2011	113.1	118.7	119.2	120.0	121.2	117.2	111.1	111.2	117.6	119.2	118.8	118.8	117.2
2012	113.3	117.8	118.2	119.2	120.8	117.0	110.4	110.8	118.5	121.0	120.2	119.8	117.3
2013	115.6	119.8	120.1	119.5	121.1	117.4	109.9	109.6	117.6	120.4	119.6	118.5	117.4
2014	115.2	119.4	120.4	120.4	121.1	118.1	111.7	111.5	118.6	121.5	120.9	119.6	118.2
2015	116.0	119.9	120.8	121.1	122.9	119.3	112.8	111.4	120.0	124.1	123.3	122.4	119.5

2. Average Weekly Hours by Selected Industry: Idaho, 2011–2015

(Not seasonally adjusted)

Industry and year	January	February	March	April	May	June	July	August	September	October	November	December	Annual average
Total Private													
2011	34.1	33.3	33.0	33.7	34.2	34.1	34.0	33.9	33.7	34.6	33.8	33.8	33.9
2012	33.9	33.3	33.0	34.0	33.1	33.6	34.0	33.7	34.2	33.4	32.9	33.8	33.6
2013	32.3	32.9	33.2	33.2	33.3	34.3	33.7	33.8	34.1	33.5	33.3	33.5	33.4
2014	32.5	33.5	33.5	33.0	33.0	34.1	33.3	33.9	33.5	33.3	34.0	33.3	33.4
2015	32.6	33.7	33.7	33.3	33.4	33.6	33.9	34.5	33.2	33.2	33.5	32.7	33.4
Goods-Producing													
2011	40.9	40.0	39.8	40.3	40.4	40.3	39.6	40.1	39.8	40.4	39.2	39.7	40.0
2012	39.7	38.9	38.2	39.3	38.8	39.3	39.1	39.2	39.6	38.7	37.6	38.5	38.9
2013	37.1	37.6	37.9	38.2	38.8	39.4	39.2	39.7	39.8	39.6	38.7	37.8	38.7
2014	37.6	38.9	38.7	39.3	37.9	39.0	39.0	40.0	40.1	39.4	39.2	38.8	39.0
2015	38.5	39.2	39.4	39.4	39.4	39.5	39.5	39.8	37.7	38.5	38.2	37.4	38.9
Construction													
2011	34.4	34.0	33.9	36.0	35.2	36.7	35.6	37.5	36.9	38.3	35.3	35.9	35.9
2012	34.3	33.9	31.2	33.7	35.2	37.6	37.5	37.2	37.0	36.5	33.4	33.8	35.2
2013	31.7	33.0	32.8	33.9	35.5	36.8	35.4	36.8	36.5	37.1	34.9	31.9	34.8
2014	31.7	31.2	33.0	35.3	36.0	37.0	37.5	38.4	37.8	38.2	36.8	36.1	35.9
2015	35.3	36.3	36.6	37.8	38.6	38.8	37.7	38.3	35.7	36.4	35.8	34.8	36.9
Manufacturing													
2011	40.6	39.5	39.6	39.9	40.6	40.0	39.4	39.3	39.4	40.0	39.4	40.0	39.8
2012	40.6	39.8	39.7	40.6	39.4	39.4	39.1	39.3	40.2	39.1	39.0	40.1	39.7
2013	38.9	39.4	40.0	40.0	40.1	40.4	40.6	40.8	41.1	40.9	40.7	40.3	40.3
2014	40.1	41.6	40.9	41.0	39.0	40.4	40.2	41.2	41.5	40.3	40.4	40.0	40.5
2015	39.9	40.2	40.4	39.8	39.5	39.4	40.0	40.3	38.8	39.7	39.6	39.0	39.7
Trade, Transportation, and Utilities													
2011	34.0	33.2	33.4	34.5	34.6	35.1	34.9	34.6	34.5	35.1	34.6	34.7	34.4
2012	33.6	33.8	33.7	34.2	33.6	34.3	34.4	34.3	34.0	34.2	34.0	34.6	34.1
2013	32.9	33.9	34.4	34.1	34.4	34.8	34.5	34.0	33.8	33.8	33.0	32.7	33.9
2014	32.0	32.5	32.7	32.9	33.3	34.1	33.8	34.5	34.1	34.0	34.5	33.8	33.5
2015	33.0	33.7	33.9	33.4	33.9	34.0	34.3	34.6	33.8	33.2	33.4	33.5	33.7
Financial Activities													
2011	36.5	36.3	35.7	36.2	37.1	36.3	36.4	36.5	36.5	37.6	36.1	35.9	36.4
2012	38.5	35.9	35.9	37.6	33.8	34.2	35.5	34.8	36.2	34.3	34.9	36.1	35.6
2013	34.3	35.1	34.9	35.1	34.8	36.6	34.8	35.4	37.1	35.0	36.2	38.0	35.6
2014	36.0	38.1	37.1	34.9	35.6	37.5	35.3	36.3	36.3	36.1	38.6	36.9	36.5
2015	37.2	39.6	38.4	38.6	38.1	37.9	37.8	38.8	37.1	37.6	38.8	36.9	38.1
Professional and Business Services													
2011	33.3	33.8	33.5	34.6	35.0	35.1	34.7	34.4	34.7	35.2	34.4	34.0	34.4
2012	33.5	33.8	33.3	34.7	35.0	35.3	36.2	35.5	37.1	35.4	34.0	35.2	34.9
2013	33.7	34.2	34.9	34.1	34.6	35.6	34.6	35.0	35.3	34.4	34.3	35.4	34.7
2014	34.3	35.7	35.7	35.1	35.6	36.9	35.7	36.5	36.0	36.1	37.3	36.3	35.9
2015	35.8	37.0	36.9	36.4	36.0	36.3	36.0	37.3	36.1	36.0	36.5	35.5	36.3
Education and Health Services													
2011	32.8	32.0	31.5	32.0	32.5	32.1	32.0	31.4	31.3	32.3	32.1	32.0	32.0
2012	32.4	31.9	31.5	32.3	31.5	31.3	31.7	31.6	32.6	31.6	31.6	32.2	31.8
2013	30.8	31.3	31.2	31.4	31.2	31.8	31.0	30.6	31.4	30.7	31.1	31.5	31.2
2014	30.5	31.0	31.0	30.3	30.1	31.1	29.9	30.0	29.7	29.5	30.7	30.2	30.3
2015	29.2	30.1	30.0	29.7	29.4	29.7	29.8	30.5	29.6	29.3	30.2	29.2	29.7
Leisure and Hospitality													
2011	22.1	21.6	21.0	21.2	22.4	21.8	23.1	23.0	22.0	23.6	22.3	21.9	22.2
2012	22.5	21.9	22.0	22.8	22.3	23.7	24.8	24.3	23.5	22.7	22.0	23.2	23.0
2013	21.8	22.9	23.5	23.6	23.3	25.8	25.8	26.1	26.2	24.7	24.4	25.6	24.5
2014	24.3	25.7	25.8	25.0	24.8	26.3	25.5	26.0	24.4	24.5	24.6	23.8	25.1
2015	23.1	24.6	24.7	23.4	24.0	24.7	26.2	26.6	24.7	24.6	24.8	23.9	24.6

3. Average Hourly Earnings by Selected Industry: Idaho, 2011–2015

(Dollars, not seasonally adjusted)

Industry and year	January	February	March	April	May	June	July	August	September	October	November	December	Annual average
Total Private													
2011	21.09	21.16	21.03	20.79	20.64	20.43	20.79	20.50	20.81	20.81	20.70	20.76	20.79
2012	20.81	21.10	20.96	21.18	21.01	20.94	20.94	20.85	21.17	21.09	21.10	21.27	21.04
2013	21.46	21.40	21.28	21.24	21.09	21.00	20.91	20.94	21.20	21.14	21.25	21.54	21.20
2014	21.10	21.32	21.24	21.21	21.24	21.09	21.19	21.30	21.53	21.68	21.78	21.71	21.37
2015	22.01	22.10	21.85	22.03	22.01	21.89	21.83	22.20	22.06	22.25	22.34	22.39	22.08
Goods-Producing													
2011	23.48	23.64	23.74	23.53	23.16	23.14	23.15	23.28	23.54	23.42	23.43	23.78	23.44
2012	23.81	23.75	23.79	23.93	24.17	23.95	24.20	23.87	24.19	23.78	24.03	23.97	23.96
2013	24.53	24.23	23.83	23.64	23.59	23.51	23.64	23.70	23.86	23.49	23.85	24.32	23.84
2014	22.84	22.88	22.44	22.41	22.63	22.38	23.04	22.47	22.80	22.92	23.05	23.04	22.74
2015	23.32	23.58	23.59	23.94	23.86	24.03	23.81	23.82	23.58	23.34	23.01	23.87	23.65
Construction													
2011	21.64	21.46	21.55	21.82	20.96	21.22	20.92	21.29	21.45	21.28	20.76	21.85	21.33
2012	21.68	21.13	21.12	21.02	21.41	20.65	20.88	20.46	20.53	19.77	20.26	20.13	20.71
2013	20.82	20.73	20.67	20.32	20.20	20.17	20.35	20.52	20.49	20.10	20.25	21.32	20.47
2014	20.60	21.07	20.28	19.83	20.00	20.05	19.88	19.92	20.26	20.81	21.30	21.54	20.45
2015	21.12	21.25	21.40	21.10	21.16	21.10	20.42	20.77	20.96	21.00	21.20	21.75	21.09
Manufacturing													
2011	25.16	25.13	25.19	24.91	24.50	24.42	24.64	24.65	24.89	24.71	24.79	24.79	24.81
2012	24.75	24.63	24.64	24.66	24.85	24.93	25.28	25.04	25.31	24.98	25.05	24.89	24.92
2013	25.30	24.99	24.64	24.56	24.52	24.56	24.68	24.73	24.99	24.62	24.99	25.09	24.80
2014	23.45	23.40	23.00	23.04	23.22	22.86	23.69	23.00	23.31	23.33	23.31	23.27	23.24
2015	23.72	24.06	24.11	25.00	24.93	25.31	25.41	25.30	24.90	24.49	24.17	25.07	24.71
Trade, Transportation, and Utilities													
2011	17.65	17.61	17.64	17.63	17.48	17.18	17.67	17.19	17.38	17.60	17.20	17.23	17.45
2012	17.79	17.42	17.48	17.65	17.38	17.36	17.45	17.69	18.00	17.37	17.36	17.38	17.53
2013	17.42	17.48	17.64	17.68	17.69	17.71	17.52	17.88	17.73	17.79	17.73	18.17	17.70
2014	18.16	18.49	18.88	18.35	18.81	18.65	18.46	18.57	19.05	19.48	19.23	19.32	18.80
2015	19.84	19.47	19.24	18.95	19.16	19.07	19.36	19.89	19.69	19.87	20.05	19.64	19.52
Financial Activities													
2011	20.78	20.31	20.60	20.41	20.84	20.39	20.73	20.26	20.77	20.87	20.78	20.62	20.62
2012	19.37	20.48	19.91	20.51	20.50	20.64	20.63	20.46	20.57	20.76	20.84	21.32	20.50
2013	21.02	21.32	21.14	20.97	21.04	21.04	20.95	20.83	20.48	20.34	20.70	21.22	20.92
2014	20.59	20.82	21.16	21.87	21.73	22.30	22.37	23.93	22.82	23.70	24.71	24.25	22.54
2015	25.11	26.15	25.86	26.14	26.77	25.62	25.85	27.61	25.63	25.67	26.65	25.80	26.08
Professional and Business Services													
2011	28.12	28.33	27.77	27.11	26.74	26.43	27.10	27.18	28.18	27.80	27.97	27.54	27.51
2012	27.65	28.43	28.06	28.00	27.87	27.71	27.49	26.95	26.94	27.31	27.09	26.98	27.52
2013	27.25	27.24	27.25	26.96	26.43	26.62	26.98	26.60	27.39	27.63	27.09	27.27	27.06
2014	27.24	27.90	28.13	28.96	28.64	28.50	28.47	28.70	28.71	28.52	28.47	28.44	28.40
2015	28.72	29.17	28.60	29.03	28.97	28.85	28.84	29.15	29.74	30.09	29.91	29.68	29.23
Education and Health Services													
2011	20.38	20.72	20.31	19.83	19.86	19.98	20.26	19.48	19.94	19.83	19.88	20.22	20.06
2012	19.92	20.27	20.31	20.91	20.31	20.68	20.69	20.51	20.71	21.02	21.04	20.93	20.61
2013	21.41	21.24	21.21	21.13	20.94	21.23	21.17	21.07	21.35	21.08	21.48	21.56	21.24
2014	21.42	21.82	21.30	21.22	21.18	21.40	21.99	22.06	22.17	22.03	22.17	22.65	21.78
2015	22.39	22.11	21.73	21.92	21.52	21.50	21.44	21.46	21.49	21.50	21.53	21.79	21.70
Leisure and Hospitality													
2011	11.37	11.41	11.47	11.38	11.46	11.07	11.48	11.43	11.44	11.53	11.61	11.77	11.45
2012	11.99	11.97	11.88	11.73	11.62	11.29	11.33	11.41	11.63	11.64	11.75	11.57	11.63
2013	11.44	11.46	11.51	11.51	11.74	11.34	11.31	11.26	11.72	11.76	12.03	12.28	11.61
2014	12.19	12.15	12.12	11.96	12.00	11.82	11.87	11.89	11.86	11.80	11.91	12.01	11.96
2015	12.08	12.15	12.13	12.17	11.97	11.86	11.83	11.96	11.97	11.85	11.83	12.15	11.99

4. Average Weekly Earnings by Selected Industry: Idaho, 2011–2015

(Dollars, not seasonally adjusted)

Industry and year	January	February	March	April	May	June	July	August	September	October	November	December	Annual average
Total Private													
2011	719.17	704.63	693.99	700.62	705.89	696.66	706.86	694.95	701.30	720.03	699.66	701.69	704.78
2012	705.46	702.63	691.68	720.12	695.43	703.58	711.96	702.65	724.01	704.41	694.19	718.93	706.94
2013	693.16	704.06	706.50	705.17	702.30	720.30	704.67	707.77	722.92	708.19	707.63	721.59	708.08
2014	685.75	714.22	711.54	699.93	700.92	719.17	705.63	722.07	721.26	721.94	740.52	722.94	713.76
2015	717.53	744.77	736.35	733.60	735.13	735.50	740.04	765.90	732.39	738.70	748.39	732.15	737.47
Goods-Producing													
2011	960.33	945.60	944.85	948.26	935.66	932.54	916.74	933.53	936.89	946.17	918.46	944.07	937.60
2012	945.26	923.88	908.78	940.45	937.80	941.24	946.22	935.70	957.92	920.29	903.53	922.85	932.04
2013	910.06	911.05	903.16	903.05	915.29	926.29	926.69	940.89	949.63	930.20	923.00	919.30	922.61
2014	858.78	890.03	868.43	880.71	857.68	872.82	898.56	898.80	914.28	903.05	903.56	893.95	886.86
2015	897.82	924.34	929.45	943.24	940.08	949.19	940.50	948.04	888.97	898.59	878.98	892.74	919.99
Construction													
2011	744.42	729.64	730.55	785.52	737.79	778.77	744.75	798.38	791.51	815.02	732.83	784.42	765.75
2012	743.62	716.31	658.94	708.37	753.63	776.44	783.00	761.11	759.61	721.61	676.68	680.39	728.99
2013	659.99	684.09	677.98	688.85	717.10	742.26	720.39	755.14	747.89	745.71	706.73	680.11	712.36
2014	653.02	657.38	669.24	700.00	720.00	741.85	745.50	764.93	765.83	794.94	783.84	777.59	734.16
2015	745.54	771.38	783.24	797.58	816.78	818.68	769.83	795.49	748.27	764.40	758.96	756.90	778.22
Manufacturing													
2011	1021.50	992.64	997.52	993.91	994.70	976.80	970.82	968.75	980.67	988.40	976.73	991.60	987.44
2012	1004.85	980.27	978.21	1001.20	979.09	982.24	988.45	984.07	1017.46	976.72	976.95	998.09	989.32
2013	984.17	984.61	985.60	982.40	983.25	992.22	1002.01	1008.98	1027.09	1006.96	1017.09	1011.13	999.44
2014	940.35	973.44	940.70	944.64	905.58	923.54	952.34	947.60	967.37	940.20	941.72	930.80	941.22
2015	946.43	967.21	974.04	995.00	984.74	997.21	1016.40	1019.59	966.12	972.25	957.13	977.73	980.99
Trade, Transportation, and Utilities													
2011	600.10	584.65	589.18	608.24	604.81	603.02	616.68	594.77	599.61	617.76	595.12	597.88	600.28
2012	597.74	588.80	589.08	603.63	583.97	595.45	600.28	606.77	612.00	594.05	590.24	601.35	597.77
2013	573.12	592.57	606.82	602.89	608.54	616.31	604.44	607.92	599.27	601.30	585.09	594.16	600.03
2014	581.12	600.93	617.38	603.72	626.37	635.97	623.95	640.67	649.61	662.32	663.44	653.02	629.80
2015	654.72	656.14	652.24	632.93	649.52	648.38	664.05	688.19	665.52	659.68	669.67	657.94	657.82
Financial Activities													
2011	758.47	737.25	735.42	738.84	773.16	740.16	754.57	739.49	758.11	784.71	750.16	740.26	750.57
2012	745.75	735.23	714.77	771.18	692.90	705.89	732.37	712.01	744.63	712.07	727.32	769.65	729.80
2013	720.99	748.33	737.79	736.05	732.19	770.06	729.06	737.38	759.81	711.90	749.34	806.36	744.75
2014	741.24	793.24	785.04	763.26	773.59	836.25	789.66	868.66	828.37	855.57	953.81	894.83	822.71
2015	934.09	1035.54	993.02	1009.00	1019.94	971.00	977.13	1071.27	950.87	965.19	1034.02	952.02	993.65
Professional and Business Services													
2011	936.40	957.55	930.30	938.01	935.90	927.69	940.37	934.99	977.85	978.56	962.17	936.36	946.34
2012	926.28	960.93	934.40	971.60	975.45	978.16	995.14	956.73	999.47	966.77	921.06	949.70	960.45
2013	918.33	931.61	951.03	919.34	914.48	947.67	933.51	931.00	966.87	950.47	929.19	965.36	938.98
2014	934.33	996.03	1004.24	1016.50	1019.58	1051.65	1016.38	1047.55	1033.56	1029.57	1061.93	1032.37	1019.56
2015	1028.18	1079.29	1055.34	1056.69	1042.92	1047.26	1038.24	1087.30	1073.61	1083.24	1091.72	1053.64	1061.05
Education and Health Services													
2011	668.46	663.04	639.77	634.56	645.45	641.36	648.32	611.67	624.12	640.51	638.15	647.04	641.92
2012	645.41	646.61	639.77	675.39	639.77	647.28	655.87	648.12	675.15	664.23	664.86	673.95	655.40
2013	659.43	664.81	661.75	663.48	653.33	675.11	656.27	644.74	670.39	647.16	668.03	679.14	662.69
2014	653.31	676.42	660.30	642.97	637.52	665.54	657.50	661.80	658.45	649.89	680.62	684.03	659.93
2015	653.79	665.51	651.90	651.02	632.69	638.55	638.91	654.53	636.10	629.95	650.21	636.27	644.49
Leisure and Hospitality													
2011	251.28	246.46	240.87	241.26	256.70	241.33	265.19	262.89	251.68	272.11	258.90	257.76	254.19
2012	269.78	262.14	261.36	267.44	259.13	267.57	280.98	277.26	273.31	264.23	258.50	268.42	267.49
2013	249.39	262.43	270.49	271.64	273.54	292.57	291.80	293.89	307.06	290.47	293.53	314.37	284.45
2014	296.22	312.26	312.70	299.00	297.60	310.87	302.69	309.14	289.38	289.10	292.99	285.84	300.20
2015	279.05	298.89	299.61	284.78	287.28	292.94	309.95	318.14	295.66	291.51	293.38	290.39	294.95

ILLINOIS
At a Glance

Population:
  2005 estimate: 12,609,903
  2010 census: 12,830,632
  2015 estimate: 12,859,995

Percent change in population:
  2005–2015: 2.0%
  2010–2015: 0.2%

Percent change in total nonfarm employment:
  2005–2015: 1.7%

Industry with the largest growth in employment, 2005–2015 (thousands):
  Education and health services, 154.3

Industry with the largest decline or smallest growth in employment, 2005–2015 (thousands):
  Manufacturing, –106.8

Civilian labor force:
  2005: 6,397,808
  2010: 6,625,321
  2015: 6,512,386

Unemployment rate and rank among states (highest to lowest):
  2005: 5.7%, 10th
  2010: 10.4%, 11th
  2015: 5.9%, 13th

Over-the-year change in unemployment rates:
  2012–2013: 0.1%
  2013–2014: –2.0%
  2014–2015: –1.2%

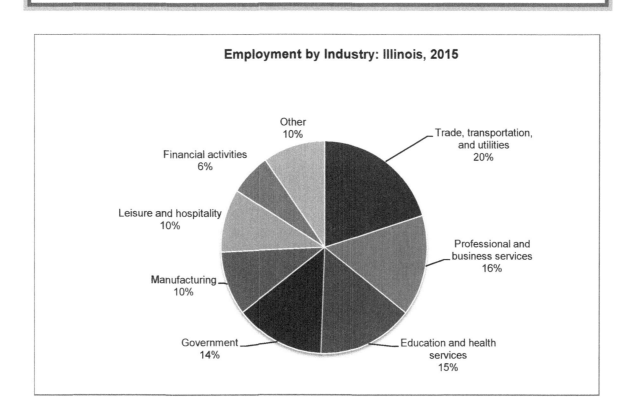

Employment by Industry: Illinois, 2015

- Other 10%
- Trade, transportation, and utilities 20%
- Financial activities 6%
- Professional and business services 16%
- Leisure and hospitality 10%
- Manufacturing 10%
- Government 14%
- Education and health services 15%

1. Employment by Industry: Illinois, 2005–2015

(Numbers in thousands, not seasonally adjusted)

Industry and year	January	February	March	April	May	June	July	August	September	October	November	December	Annual average
Total Nonfarm													
2005	5,700.6	5,717.6	5,758.2	5,845.8	5,886.7	5,903.5	5,901.8	5,903.7	5,919.5	5,922.4	5,938.1	5,936.6	5,861.2
2006	5,773.1	5,798.4	5,845.2	5,903.7	5,951.7	5,999.8	5,961.6	5,967.9	5,980.0	5,982.5	5,999.2	6,000.0	5,930.3
2007	5,841.6	5,844.1	5,902.0	5,957.9	6,016.3	6,045.9	6,005.6	6,007.8	6,017.4	6,022.6	6,043.2	6,034.2	5,978.2
2008	5,867.7	5,874.9	5,904.2	5,960.9	6,009.9	6,018.6	5,980.5	5,977.9	5,969.6	5,966.2	5,939.6	5,897.8	5,947.3
2009	5,677.4	5,659.0	5,653.1	5,670.0	5,697.6	5,690.1	5,638.0	5,622.0	5,637.5	5,646.9	5,648.3	5,628.0	5,655.7
2010	5,461.2	5,483.5	5,516.5	5,594.5	5,654.0	5,659.3	5,606.6	5,630.0	5,650.2	5,685.5	5,697.0	5,686.1	5,610.4
2011	5,525.4	5,545.6	5,590.1	5,666.7	5,701.5	5,719.2	5,691.8	5,702.1	5,727.1	5,740.8	5,750.9	5,745.8	5,675.6
2012	5,595.0	5,619.2	5,672.3	5,730.8	5,774.9	5,797.0	5,758.4	5,775.3	5,807.0	5,814.7	5,835.3	5,823.3	5,750.3
2013	5,657.2	5,688.2	5,722.3	5,770.8	5,832.0	5,849.6	5,815.4	5,832.5	5,854.3	5,866.5	5,883.5	5,880.0	5,804.4
2014	5,711.0	5,733.8	5,777.1	5,853.7	5,914.8	5,932.6	5,894.4	5,907.2	5,928.0	5,961.0	5,971.4	5,969.2	5,879.5
2015	5,790.0	5,819.9	5,853.2	5,935.4	6,001.9	6,016.6	5,986.8	5,985.6	6,008.9	6,059.3	6,052.9	6,017.0	5,960.6
Total Private													
2005	4,867.6	4,866.5	4,902.1	4,991.6	5,029.5	5,066.4	5,075.4	5,082.5	5,074.6	5,066.9	5,078.6	5,082.2	5,015.3
2006	4,940.8	4,945.0	4,988.5	5,049.0	5,093.7	5,154.8	5,141.5	5,152.8	5,134.3	5,128.7	5,141.3	5,147.2	5,084.8
2007	5,006.6	4,987.3	5,042.6	5,095.9	5,152.8	5,201.0	5,186.1	5,193.2	5,166.3	5,161.6	5,178.4	5,175.6	5,129.0
2008	5,026.1	5,010.6	5,039.2	5,093.2	5,138.7	5,167.9	5,154.3	5,159.3	5,114.5	5,096.2	5,069.3	5,031.3	5,091.7
2009	4,833.0	4,794.5	4,787.2	4,793.8	4,821.3	4,837.0	4,809.5	4,806.3	4,778.8	4,776.4	4,775.8	4,763.0	4,798.1
2010	4,617.0	4,617.1	4,650.4	4,722.7	4,768.0	4,805.1	4,788.3	4,812.6	4,800.6	4,827.0	4,837.2	4,833.4	4,756.6
2011	4,696.2	4,695.4	4,739.0	4,810.5	4,847.2	4,885.9	4,881.5	4,901.4	4,891.5	4,896.6	4,903.7	4,903.6	4,837.7
2012	4,775.8	4,779.3	4,829.3	4,884.0	4,928.3	4,970.9	4,959.7	4,981.1	4,969.9	4,968.9	4,987.1	4,980.1	4,917.9
2013	4,836.9	4,846.8	4,880.5	4,926.8	4,984.9	5,024.1	5,016.3	5,040.3	5,019.7	5,030.0	5,043.9	5,043.0	4,974.4
2014	4,900.5	4,904.9	4,945.8	5,013.5	5,072.1	5,109.6	5,096.0	5,115.1	5,092.3	5,118.5	5,129.3	5,127.7	5,052.1
2015	4,976.3	4,984.8	5,016.8	5,094.1	5,159.7	5,193.5	5,187.5	5,192.8	5,172.2	5,210.9	5,203.4	5,171.9	5,130.3
Goods-Producing													
2005	931.9	931.2	940.0	963.7	974.0	984.9	984.1	985.2	984.0	980.1	976.5	963.5	966.6
2006	935.7	935.2	942.7	964.8	973.9	991.2	987.9	988.5	985.5	981.3	975.7	964.0	968.9
2007	931.2	918.6	936.6	953.0	967.3	980.6	975.6	975.8	970.8	963.8	961.1	947.5	956.8
2008	913.1	904.6	912.8	927.3	939.1	948.0	947.2	947.2	939.8	929.0	912.5	884.5	925.4
2009	831.9	818.0	813.3	807.3	805.8	808.8	804.7	804.6	800.9	793.8	783.3	766.9	803.3
2010	731.1	729.6	739.9	761.0	770.9	782.7	778.7	789.9	787.9	791.4	786.1	771.3	768.4
2011	743.6	742.6	755.1	773.2	784.1	796.7	799.5	802.2	796.1	793.4	787.9	776.7	779.3
2012	749.5	749.1	761.3	775.4	784.1	796.5	800.8	801.7	799.1	797.4	790.6	781.2	782.2
2013	752.8	753.2	759.2	768.0	783.0	794.3	796.6	798.5	794.7	793.6	791.1	778.4	780.3
2014	752.6	752.7	764.5	780.0	794.1	806.4	809.7	812.3	809.4	812.1	807.6	799.8	791.8
2015	771.2	771.3	780.4	798.3	811.0	821.3	822.5	821.7	819.4	820.2	810.3	799.2	803.9
Service-Providing													
2005	4,768.7	4,786.4	4,818.2	4,882.1	4,912.7	4,918.6	4,917.7	4,918.5	4,935.5	4,942.3	4,961.6	4,973.1	4,894.6
2006	4,837.4	4,863.2	4,902.5	4,938.9	4,977.8	5,008.6	4,973.7	4,979.4	4,994.5	5,001.2	5,023.5	5,036.0	4,961.4
2007	4,910.4	4,925.5	4,965.4	5,004.9	5,049.0	5,065.3	5,030.0	5,032.0	5,046.6	5,058.8	5,082.1	5,086.7	5,021.4
2008	4,954.6	4,970.3	4,991.4	5,033.6	5,070.8	5,070.6	5,033.3	5,030.7	5,029.8	5,037.2	5,027.1	5,013.3	5,021.9
2009	4,845.5	4,841.0	4,839.8	4,862.7	4,891.8	4,881.3	4,833.3	4,817.4	4,836.6	4,853.1	4,865.0	4,861.1	4,852.4
2010	4,730.1	4,753.9	4,776.6	4,833.5	4,883.1	4,876.6	4,827.9	4,840.1	4,862.3	4,894.1	4,910.9	4,914.8	4,842.0
2011	4,781.8	4,803.0	4,835.0	4,893.5	4,917.4	4,922.5	4,892.3	4,899.9	4,931.0	4,947.4	4,963.0	4,969.1	4,896.3
2012	4,845.5	4,870.1	4,911.0	4,955.4	4,990.8	5,000.5	4,957.6	4,973.6	5,007.9	5,017.3	5,044.7	5,042.1	4,968.0
2013	4,904.4	4,935.0	4,963.1	5,002.8	5,049.0	5,055.3	5,018.8	5,034.0	5,059.6	5,072.9	5,092.4	5,101.6	5,024.1
2014	4,958.4	4,981.1	5,012.6	5,073.7	5,120.7	5,126.2	5,084.7	5,094.9	5,118.6	5,148.9	5,163.8	5,169.4	5,087.8
2015	5,018.8	5,048.6	5,072.8	5,137.1	5,190.9	5,195.3	5,164.3	5,163.9	5,189.5	5,239.1	5,242.6	5,217.8	5,156.7
Mining and Logging													
2005	8.8	8.9	9.2	9.6	9.8	10.1	10.2	10.2	10.3	10.4	10.4	10.4	9.9
2006	10.0	9.9	10.0	10.1	10.4	10.6	10.5	10.3	10.3	10.4	10.3	10.2	10.3
2007	9.7	9.7	10.0	10.2	10.5	10.7	10.5	10.3	10.0	10.1	10.1	9.7	10.1
2008	9.3	9.3	9.6	9.5	9.9	9.9	9.9	10.1	10.0	10.0	9.9	9.8	9.8
2009	9.2	9.3	9.4	9.6	9.5	9.7	9.5	9.3	9.4	9.1	9.1	8.9	9.3
2010	8.4	8.4	8.5	9.0	9.1	9.3	9.5	9.4	9.6	9.6	9.5	9.4	9.1
2011	9.0	8.8	9.0	9.3	9.5	9.7	10.0	10.1	10.1	10.1	10.1	9.8	9.6
2012	9.6	9.6	9.9	10.3	10.3	10.4	10.6	10.6	10.4	10.2	10.2	10.0	10.2
2013	9.6	9.5	9.3	9.4	9.7	9.9	10.0	9.9	9.8	9.8	9.8	9.6	9.7
2014	9.4	9.2	9.5	9.7	10.1	10.2	10.1	10.2	10.3	10.2	10.2	10.2	9.9
2015	9.6	9.4	9.4	9.4	9.6	9.7	9.5	9.6	9.5	9.5	9.5	9.3	9.5

1. Employment by Industry: Illinois, 2005–2015—*Continued*

(Numbers in thousands, not seasonally adjusted)

Industry and year	January	February	March	April	May	June	July	August	September	October	November	December	Annual average
Construction													
2005	236.7	235.7	243.1	263.5	273.8	281.6	285.0	285.8	285.6	284.8	280.5	266.4	268.5
2006	245.2	244.7	252.9	272.5	281.8	292.3	292.1	293.6	289.9	287.9	281.7	269.0	275.3
2007	244.5	233.6	249.8	266.5	279.8	288.9	289.4	290.1	287.2	284.3	278.9	263.8	271.4
2008	236.3	231.2	239.2	255.3	266.9	273.2	277.3	278.8	274.7	269.7	257.8	239.1	258.3
2009	205.8	201.9	206.1	214.1	221.8	227.7	231.2	231.0	227.8	224.2	215.3	199.7	217.2
2010	172.5	169.9	178.9	196.6	203.5	210.9	206.6	215.1	213.4	213.9	207.1	190.6	198.3
2011	168.9	167.7	177.2	192.3	201.7	209.5	212.4	214.0	210.2	206.3	200.0	188.7	195.7
2012	166.0	163.9	173.0	185.0	191.8	199.2	202.5	203.1	201.7	202.1	194.8	186.0	189.1
2013	164.4	164.6	170.1	180.6	194.1	201.3	207.1	208.2	207.4	206.8	202.0	189.8	191.4
2014	168.8	168.4	177.2	192.8	204.2	212.4	217.6	219.4	218.8	220.4	215.0	205.4	201.7
2015	182.2	181.8	190.0	209.0	219.0	225.3	228.0	229.5	229.2	231.0	220.6	210.7	213.0
Manufacturing													
2005	686.4	686.6	687.7	690.6	690.4	693.2	688.9	689.2	688.1	684.9	685.6	686.7	688.2
2006	680.5	680.6	679.8	682.2	681.7	688.3	685.3	684.6	685.3	683.0	683.7	684.8	683.3
2007	677.0	675.3	676.8	676.3	677.0	681.0	675.7	675.4	673.6	669.4	672.1	674.0	675.3
2008	667.5	664.1	664.0	662.5	662.3	664.9	660.0	658.3	655.1	649.3	644.8	635.6	657.4
2009	616.9	606.8	597.8	583.6	574.5	571.4	564.0	564.3	563.7	560.5	558.9	558.3	576.7
2010	550.2	551.3	552.5	555.4	558.3	562.5	562.6	565.4	564.9	567.9	569.5	571.3	561.0
2011	565.7	566.1	568.9	571.6	572.9	577.5	577.1	578.1	575.8	577.0	577.8	578.2	573.9
2012	573.9	575.6	578.4	580.1	582.0	586.9	587.7	588.0	587.0	585.1	585.6	585.2	583.0
2013	578.8	579.1	579.8	578.0	579.2	583.1	579.5	580.4	577.5	577.0	579.3	579.0	579.2
2014	574.4	575.1	577.8	577.5	579.8	583.8	582.0	582.7	580.3	581.5	582.4	584.2	580.1
2015	579.4	580.1	581.0	579.9	582.4	586.3	585.0	582.6	580.7	579.7	580.2	579.2	581.4
Trade, Transportation, and Utilities													
2005	1,170.9	1,159.2	1,166.4	1,176.0	1,184.5	1,188.6	1,184.2	1,187.0	1,188.4	1,193.0	1,213.1	1,230.2	1,186.8
2006	1,182.0	1,171.7	1,179.7	1,185.1	1,195.2	1,203.4	1,195.6	1,197.5	1,197.8	1,203.0	1,226.4	1,242.2	1,198.3
2007	1,201.3	1,185.7	1,196.3	1,195.8	1,209.8	1,217.5	1,210.4	1,210.1	1,211.1	1,214.5	1,240.7	1,254.6	1,212.3
2008	1,210.4	1,194.0	1,199.0	1,200.1	1,209.1	1,212.2	1,203.4	1,203.1	1,198.4	1,200.2	1,210.9	1,216.9	1,204.8
2009	1,161.9	1,143.9	1,138.2	1,134.0	1,140.7	1,141.7	1,128.8	1,129.4	1,127.1	1,129.9	1,145.2	1,153.2	1,139.5
2010	1,109.4	1,099.7	1,104.1	1,113.9	1,123.5	1,128.7	1,124.1	1,127.9	1,124.7	1,133.9	1,151.9	1,165.4	1,125.6
2011	1,126.0	1,116.8	1,122.2	1,133.2	1,140.1	1,145.4	1,141.7	1,145.9	1,145.4	1,152.3	1,171.4	1,185.3	1,143.8
2012	1,141.4	1,130.5	1,138.7	1,143.4	1,152.3	1,156.1	1,153.7	1,157.0	1,155.7	1,163.2	1,188.8	1,195.1	1,156.3
2013	1,148.0	1,138.9	1,143.1	1,149.4	1,159.7	1,166.6	1,163.7	1,168.4	1,165.4	1,171.3	1,192.9	1,205.9	1,164.4
2014	1,158.8	1,147.7	1,154.6	1,163.3	1,175.8	1,183.2	1,179.0	1,183.7	1,181.8	1,190.4	1,212.9	1,225.5	1,179.7
2015	1,177.4	1,169.3	1,174.9	1,186.0	1,198.8	1,206.7	1,202.0	1,205.2	1,202.9	1,216.4	1,231.4	1,234.9	1,200.5
Wholesale Trade													
2005	296.7	296.9	299.5	302.0	303.1	305.2	305.2	304.7	304.7	304.7	305.4	306.6	302.9
2006	303.2	303.3	305.2	306.7	308.4	311.2	309.7	308.9	308.3	308.8	308.8	310.0	307.7
2007	305.9	305.5	307.6	308.8	310.7	313.8	312.8	312.1	311.7	312.9	312.9	313.8	310.7
2008	309.0	308.2	309.5	310.7	312.8	314.1	312.3	311.4	309.7	309.9	308.8	307.4	310.3
2009	299.2	296.7	295.6	293.8	293.2	293.2	290.4	289.1	287.1	287.9	287.6	287.5	291.8
2010	281.8	280.9	282.7	285.1	286.6	288.2	287.7	287.6	286.5	287.4	287.0	287.2	285.7
2011	284.3	284.3	285.9	288.6	289.7	292.0	292.2	291.8	290.8	291.5	291.2	292.1	289.5
2012	289.0	289.4	292.3	293.7	295.2	297.8	296.3	296.1	295.4	295.9	296.3	296.6	294.5
2013	293.9	294.0	295.7	297.2	299.0	301.8	300.7	299.6	298.9	299.3	299.8	300.1	298.3
2014	296.4	296.5	297.6	298.0	300.0	301.7	300.8	300.1	298.7	300.6	301.4	301.1	299.4
2015	296.9	296.2	297.8	300.7	303.3	305.6	304.8	303.7	302.3	304.8	302.8	300.1	301.6
Retail Trade													
2005	619.9	608.1	611.4	617.0	623.2	626.6	625.8	627.4	624.1	627.3	645.4	659.3	626.3
2006	622.6	611.8	615.8	618.2	624.2	630.8	627.3	628.5	622.8	628.5	650.8	661.7	628.6
2007	632.8	618.0	624.5	623.3	632.6	638.2	635.6	634.1	630.3	632.4	657.1	667.1	635.5
2008	635.6	620.4	623.0	623.4	628.0	632.2	628.8	626.7	620.4	621.9	633.7	639.1	627.8
2009	604.1	590.7	587.6	588.6	594.8	597.9	593.2	592.9	588.5	590.4	605.6	611.4	595.5
2010	580.8	572.0	574.4	579.1	585.6	591.1	589.9	590.2	583.5	590.2	607.1	617.1	588.4
2011	587.0	577.5	580.2	586.8	591.2	595.7	594.6	597.1	592.3	598.1	616.3	625.8	595.2
2012	593.0	581.9	585.4	587.0	592.3	596.7	596.2	595.7	591.5	598.4	622.1	624.8	597.1
2013	592.0	582.8	584.6	586.8	593.7	601.0	599.9	600.8	596.5	601.9	620.5	629.6	599.2
2014	594.6	584.0	587.6	594.7	601.7	608.7	607.1	607.4	603.4	609.7	628.5	636.1	605.3
2015	602.5	595.3	598.7	604.4	611.3	617.9	616.6	617.7	614.2	623.2	638.6	642.4	615.2

1. Employment by Industry: Illinois, 2005–2015—*Continued*

(Numbers in thousands, not seasonally adjusted)

Industry and year	January	February	March	April	May	June	July	August	September	October	November	December	Annual average
Transportation and Utilities													
2005	254.3	254.2	255.5	257.0	258.2	256.8	253.2	254.9	259.6	261.0	262.3	264.3	257.6
2006	256.2	256.6	258.7	260.2	262.6	261.4	258.6	260.1	266.7	265.7	266.8	270.5	262.0
2007	262.6	262.2	264.2	263.7	266.5	265.5	262.0	263.9	269.1	269.2	270.7	273.7	266.1
2008	265.8	265.4	266.5	266.0	268.3	265.9	262.3	265.0	268.3	268.4	268.4	270.4	266.7
2009	258.6	256.5	255.0	251.6	252.7	250.6	245.2	247.4	251.5	251.6	252.0	254.3	252.3
2010	246.8	246.8	247.0	249.7	251.3	249.4	246.5	250.1	254.7	256.3	257.8	261.1	251.5
2011	254.7	255.0	256.1	257.8	259.2	257.7	254.9	257.0	262.3	262.7	263.9	267.4	259.1
2012	259.4	259.2	261.0	262.7	264.8	261.6	261.2	265.2	268.8	268.9	270.4	273.7	264.7
2013	262.1	262.1	262.8	265.4	267.0	263.8	263.1	268.0	270.0	270.1	272.6	276.2	266.9
2014	267.8	267.2	269.4	270.6	274.1	272.8	271.1	276.2	279.7	280.1	283.0	288.3	275.0
2015	278.0	277.8	278.4	280.9	284.2	283.2	280.6	283.8	286.4	288.4	290.0	292.4	283.7
Information													
2005	118.8	118.3	118.4	119.0	119.0	119.4	119.3	118.4	117.3	116.6	116.7	117.0	118.2
2006	116.4	116.0	116.2	116.9	117.1	117.4	117.1	116.3	115.1	115.3	115.3	115.9	116.3
2007	115.3	115.7	115.7	115.7	116.2	116.9	116.9	116.8	115.6	115.5	115.7	116.0	116.0
2008	115.4	115.4	115.9	115.6	115.9	115.8	115.5	115.0	113.0	112.1	111.7	111.6	114.4
2009	109.9	108.9	108.2	107.4	107.0	106.7	105.7	105.4	104.5	104.2	103.8	104.8	106.4
2010	103.3	102.3	102.3	102.1	102.1	102.4	101.8	101.9	100.6	100.9	100.9	101.1	101.8
2011	100.6	99.9	100.1	100.4	101.0	101.3	101.6	101.4	99.8	99.8	100.4	100.5	100.6
2012	100.2	99.8	100.1	100.4	101.1	100.5	100.5	100.2	99.1	99.9	99.8	100.0	100.1
2013	99.0	98.5	98.5	99.4	100.2	100.4	99.8	99.3	98.0	97.6	98.2	98.6	99.0
2014	97.3	97.4	98.4	99.3	99.3	100.3	100.2	100.3	98.4	99.0	99.1	99.9	99.1
2015	99.5	99.5	99.6	100.5	102.2	101.3	101.9	102.1	100.7	100.7	101.4	100.1	100.8
Financial Activities													
2005	403.7	403.4	404.2	407.2	408.5	411.7	414.2	414.2	411.6	411.5	411.4	414.0	409.6
2006	408.7	408.9	410.2	411.0	412.3	416.1	416.6	416.7	413.5	413.9	413.6	415.2	413.1
2007	411.2	410.7	410.8	411.2	412.3	415.3	414.4	412.8	408.2	407.2	406.7	407.3	410.7
2008	401.4	401.4	401.5	401.3	402.1	404.1	402.4	401.9	396.7	395.6	393.7	393.8	399.7
2009	386.5	384.4	382.8	381.9	381.7	382.9	381.0	379.8	375.7	374.7	374.1	374.7	380.0
2010	369.2	368.7	368.8	370.2	371.2	373.9	373.6	373.9	370.7	372.6	372.5	373.9	371.6
2011	368.8	368.6	368.4	369.1	369.8	372.4	374.1	374.1	371.3	373.2	371.9	372.8	371.2
2012	368.8	369.3	370.1	371.8	373.4	377.2	378.0	378.6	376.1	375.6	375.4	377.1	374.3
2013	373.7	374.1	374.3	376.7	377.3	381.1	380.9	380.3	377.9	378.1	377.4	378.0	377.5
2014	373.8	373.3	373.5	373.8	375.5	378.6	379.7	380.7	376.5	377.6	376.8	378.0	376.5
2015	375.0	374.9	375.0	377.5	379.8	383.4	384.4	384.4	379.8	380.8	381.1	381.1	379.8
Professional and Business Services													
2005	779.1	783.3	790.2	812.4	814.0	824.3	830.7	835.3	837.3	842.6	840.9	836.6	818.9
2006	807.5	811.3	822.2	839.5	844.6	858.4	858.5	865.1	862.7	867.0	862.3	857.3	846.4
2007	827.3	829.6	839.2	858.5	864.5	874.8	877.0	881.8	876.8	878.6	874.4	871.0	862.8
2008	838.9	841.0	842.7	858.1	861.7	865.9	864.4	866.8	856.9	852.9	842.6	830.7	851.9
2009	789.2	779.9	772.0	777.4	779.6	781.7	779.6	780.7	775.1	781.3	782.2	778.0	779.7
2010	754.1	758.2	760.9	787.3	791.8	801.7	805.1	810.6	807.7	817.2	817.2	815.3	793.9
2011	787.1	790.5	796.6	817.8	818.0	829.2	834.9	840.2	840.4	844.4	843.6	839.2	823.5
2012	816.8	819.5	829.3	848.6	855.1	868.0	867.5	875.1	875.3	874.9	878.5	872.7	856.8
2013	839.0	846.9	853.2	868.9	879.7	890.8	893.1	902.0	898.4	908.6	909.7	906.9	883.1
2014	871.5	877.3	882.4	901.8	911.2	920.5	919.2	926.3	922.6	929.4	930.0	922.1	909.5
2015	886.4	891.4	893.2	912.6	921.8	930.3	934.1	934.8	930.4	935.0	928.9	916.0	917.9
Education and Health Services													
2005	734.4	739.6	741.5	746.4	747.3	740.3	737.5	737.4	747.0	752.2	754.5	755.4	744.5
2006	746.3	755.2	758.9	758.1	760.0	756.6	751.5	754.7	765.0	766.0	771.5	773.5	759.8
2007	764.3	772.4	776.2	777.1	778.0	774.1	768.6	770.2	779.2	787.0	791.8	792.9	777.7
2008	784.1	792.0	793.9	797.4	799.2	794.1	791.2	794.6	803.6	810.6	815.2	815.2	799.3
2009	804.7	812.4	816.2	814.3	816.1	811.2	806.6	805.1	813.4	822.3	826.3	826.8	814.6
2010	816.7	824.4	828.9	829.8	832.6	827.3	820.0	820.9	832.0	842.4	847.3	847.5	830.8
2011	836.5	844.0	849.2	847.9	848.7	843.4	834.8	836.6	850.0	856.3	859.6	862.9	847.5
2012	851.6	860.9	864.9	863.4	863.1	860.2	849.9	853.4	865.6	869.0	872.4	873.4	862.3
2013	865.5	875.3	880.2	875.2	875.6	868.1	858.1	865.2	875.3	881.5	885.6	886.9	874.4
2014	874.9	883.7	887.7	889.1	889.1	880.2	871.1	874.5	883.2	892.8	896.7	898.7	885.1
2015	884.9	891.3	895.4	898.0	902.3	892.7	886.9	887.4	897.2	916.2	918.7	914.0	898.8

1. Employment by Industry: Illinois, 2005–2015—*Continued*

(Numbers in thousands, not seasonally adjusted)

Industry and year	January	February	March	April	May	June	July	August	September	October	November	December	Annual average
Leisure and Hospitality													
2005	476.4	478.5	487.0	511.0	525.4	534.8	537.8	537.7	530.9	514.3	508.4	506.4	512.4
2006	487.5	491.0	500.7	517.9	533.4	548.1	547.9	547.4	537.1	524.3	518.6	518.9	522.7
2007	500.7	499.2	509.4	526.6	544.6	555.9	553.7	556.0	544.6	534.9	527.6	524.7	531.5
2008	504.7	503.5	513.1	532.8	548.8	559.7	556.7	557.6	543.9	533.3	521.1	517.0	532.7
2009	493.4	491.4	499.5	515.1	532.4	541.3	538.0	537.1	527.9	514.9	506.0	502.7	516.6
2010	482.1	483.2	492.6	511.5	527.8	538.5	536.4	538.9	530.0	520.2	513.1	509.9	515.4
2011	488.4	487.5	500.0	519.5	534.1	543.8	542.2	549.0	538.2	527.6	520.5	516.0	522.2
2012	501.0	502.9	515.8	532.4	548.4	558.3	557.1	564.0	549.3	540.1	532.7	531.3	536.1
2013	513.2	513.3	524.0	540.9	559.3	570.4	570.8	573.0	559.0	549.6	539.8	538.0	545.9
2014	524.1	524.4	534.1	554.6	572.9	583.2	580.7	583.2	569.2	565.0	554.8	551.9	558.2
2015	533.6	537.7	547.0	569.1	590.4	601.5	600.5	602.8	589.8	586.9	576.9	573.1	575.8
Other Services													
2005	252.4	253.0	254.4	255.9	256.8	262.4	267.6	267.3	258.1	256.6	257.1	259.1	258.4
2006	256.7	255.7	257.9	255.7	257.2	263.6	266.4	266.6	257.6	257.9	257.9	260.2	259.5
2007	255.3	255.4	258.4	258.0	260.1	265.9	269.5	269.7	260.0	260.1	260.4	261.6	261.2
2008	258.1	258.7	260.3	260.6	262.8	268.1	273.5	273.1	262.2	262.5	261.6	261.6	263.6
2009	255.5	255.6	257.0	256.4	258.0	262.7	265.1	264.2	254.2	255.3	254.9	255.9	257.9
2010	251.1	251.0	252.9	246.9	248.1	249.9	248.6	248.6	247.0	248.4	248.2	249.0	249.1
2011	245.2	245.5	247.4	249.4	251.4	253.7	252.7	252.0	250.3	249.6	248.4	250.2	249.7
2012	246.5	247.3	249.1	248.6	250.8	254.1	252.2	251.1	249.7	248.8	248.9	249.3	249.7
2013	245.7	246.6	248.0	248.3	250.1	252.4	253.3	253.6	251.0	249.7	249.2	250.3	249.9
2014	247.5	248.4	250.6	251.6	254.2	257.2	256.4	254.1	251.2	252.2	251.4	251.8	252.2
2015	248.3	249.4	251.3	252.1	253.4	256.3	255.2	254.4	252.0	254.7	254.7	253.5	252.9
Government													
2005	833.0	851.1	856.1	854.2	857.2	837.1	826.4	821.2	844.9	855.5	859.5	854.4	845.9
2006	832.3	853.4	856.7	854.7	858.0	845.0	820.1	815.1	845.7	853.8	857.9	852.8	845.5
2007	835.0	856.8	859.4	862.0	863.5	844.9	819.5	814.6	851.1	861.0	864.8	858.6	849.3
2008	841.6	864.3	865.0	867.7	871.2	850.7	826.2	818.6	855.1	870.0	870.3	866.5	855.6
2009	844.4	864.5	865.9	876.2	876.3	853.1	828.5	815.7	858.7	870.5	872.5	865.0	857.6
2010	844.2	866.4	866.1	871.8	886.0	854.2	818.3	817.4	849.6	858.5	859.8	852.7	853.8
2011	829.2	850.2	851.1	856.2	854.3	833.3	810.3	800.7	835.6	844.2	847.2	842.2	837.9
2012	819.2	839.9	843.0	846.8	846.6	826.1	798.7	794.2	837.1	845.8	848.2	843.2	832.4
2013	820.3	841.4	841.8	844.0	847.1	825.5	799.1	792.2	834.6	836.5	839.6	837.0	829.9
2014	810.5	828.9	831.3	840.2	842.7	823.0	798.4	792.1	835.7	842.5	842.1	841.5	827.4
2015	813.7	835.1	836.4	841.3	842.2	823.1	799.3	792.8	836.7	848.4	849.5	845.1	830.3

2. Average Weekly Hours by Selected Industry: Illinois, 2011–2015

(Not seasonally adjusted)

Industry and year	January	February	March	April	May	June	July	August	September	October	November	December	Annual average
Total Private													
2011	34.3	34.3	34.4	34.5	34.7	34.5	34.5	34.5	34.6	35.0	34.6	34.7	34.6
2012	34.7	34.5	34.5	34.9	34.6	34.8	35.1	34.6	35.2	34.6	34.4	34.9	34.7
2013	33.9	34.2	34.3	34.3	34.3	34.8	34.3	34.5	34.9	34.6	34.6	35.0	34.5
2014	34.0	34.6	34.6	34.3	34.3	34.8	34.2	34.4	34.3	34.4	34.9	34.3	34.4
2015	33.9	34.5	34.4	34.1	34.2	34.3	34.2	34.8	34.2	34.4	34.7	34.3	34.3
Goods-Producing													
2011	39.3	39.2	39.5	39.5	40.1	39.6	39.2	39.9	39.8	40.0	39.5	39.9	39.6
2012	39.8	39.6	39.6	39.9	39.7	40.0	39.7	39.6	40.2	39.8	39.5	39.9	39.8
2013	38.9	38.9	39.4	39.3	39.3	39.9	39.6	40.3	40.4	40.2	39.9	40.5	39.7
2014	39.4	39.5	39.2	39.5	39.5	39.9	39.8	40.0	39.6	39.8	40.2	40.2	39.7
2015	39.5	39.6	39.7	39.7	39.9	39.8	39.5	40.1	39.0	39.4	39.5	39.8	39.6
Construction													
2011	37.4	37.3	37.6	37.9	38.6	38.3	39.4	39.6	39.2	39.0	37.5	37.8	38.4
2012	36.9	37.2	37.3	37.6	38.0	38.8	38.6	38.2	38.5	38.7	37.7	36.8	37.9
2013	36.0	35.7	35.9	35.4	37.6	37.8	37.2	37.9	38.0	37.9	36.8	36.8	37.0
2014	35.4	36.8	36.5	37.5	37.0	38.1	38.7	38.5	37.0	37.5	37.9	37.6	37.4
2015	36.6	36.2	36.6	37.0	37.1	37.7	37.5	38.5	35.6	36.4	35.3	35.6	36.7
Manufacturing													
2011	40.8	40.7	40.9	40.8	41.1	40.7	39.7	40.6	40.6	41.0	40.8	41.1	40.7
2012	41.0	40.6	40.5	40.7	40.7	40.7	40.4	40.4	41.0	40.4	40.4	41.2	40.7
2013	40.1	40.1	40.7	40.7	40.5	41.0	40.8	41.4	41.4	41.2	41.2	41.9	40.9
2014	40.9	41.3	41.0	41.0	41.1	41.1	40.6	40.9	40.9	40.9	41.3	41.3	41.0
2015	40.6	40.8	40.9	40.8	41.1	40.8	40.4	40.8	40.6	39.5	40.2	40.6	40.6
Trade, Transportation, and Utilities													
2011	34.6	34.5	34.5	34.7	35.0	35.0	35.1	35.0	35.2	35.5	35.2	35.2	35.0
2012	34.8	34.9	35.1	35.4	35.2	35.4	35.7	35.2	35.8	35.2	34.8	35.4	35.2
2013	34.3	34.7	35.0	34.8	35.2	35.2	35.0	35.0	35.4	35.3	34.9	35.6	35.0
2014	34.4	35.0	35.1	35.0	34.9	35.4	35.0	35.0	35.1	34.9	35.3	35.1	35.0
2015	34.3	34.8	34.5	34.2	34.4	34.4	34.5	34.8	34.7	34.8	35.0	34.7	34.6
Information													
2011	38.4	38.4	37.0	36.5	36.9	36.9	36.4	36.3	36.4	37.8	37.4	37.7	37.2
2012	37.8	37.1	37.0	37.4	36.7	36.5	37.1	36.7	37.9	36.5	36.9	37.3	37.1
2013	36.6	36.7	36.8	37.0	36.9	37.5	37.4	37.2	37.7	36.6	36.5	37.2	37.0
2014	36.9	37.6	37.7	36.6	36.3	36.9	36.4	36.0	36.5	36.2	36.9	36.0	36.7
2015	36.2	36.7	36.6	36.1	35.8	36.4	36.4	36.6	35.9	35.6	36.3	35.5	36.2
Financial Activities													
2011	36.4	36.6	36.6	36.6	36.7	36.3	36.6	36.3	36.6	37.8	37.7	37.3	36.8
2012	38.4	37.9	37.7	39.0	37.3	37.7	38.4	37.2	38.3	36.4	36.3	37.5	37.7
2013	35.9	36.5	36.5	36.6	36.2	37.1	35.6	35.7	37.3	36.1	36.1	37.1	36.4
2014	36.3	37.4	37.2	36.1	36.2	37.1	35.1	35.5	35.5	35.7	36.0	34.6	36.1
2015	35.1	36.4	36.3	35.4	35.6	35.8	35.7	36.9	36.0	35.9	36.3	35.4	35.9
Professional and Business Services													
2011	36.0	36.1	36.1	36.3	36.7	36.1	35.8	35.8	35.9	36.4	35.7	35.6	36.0
2012	35.9	35.6	35.7	36.4	36.3	36.5	36.4	36.1	37.0	36.3	36.1	36.7	36.3
2013	35.7	36.0	36.0	35.9	35.7	36.5	35.6	35.8	36.4	36.1	36.2	36.6	36.0
2014	35.6	36.6	36.4	36.0	35.9	36.6	35.8	36.0	35.7	36.0	36.7	35.5	36.1
2015	35.3	36.4	35.9	35.7	35.7	36.1	35.9	36.9	35.6	36.8	37.3	36.4	36.2
Education and Health Services													
2011	32.9	32.8	32.9	33.0	33.2	32.9	33.4	33.1	33.2	33.5	33.2	33.1	33.1
2012	33.7	33.1	32.8	33.1	32.8	32.9	33.4	32.9	33.3	32.6	33.0	33.0	33.0
2013	32.7	32.7	32.6	32.5	32.6	33.1	32.9	32.6	33.0	32.6	33.0	32.8	32.8
2014	32.5	32.8	32.7	32.3	32.4	32.8	32.6	32.5	32.4	32.4	33.1	32.5	32.6
2015	32.4	32.4	32.5	32.3	32.3	32.3	32.3	32.6	32.4	32.2	32.6	32.3	32.4
Leisure and Hospitality													
2011	24.6	24.5	25.2	25.2	25.0	25.3	25.2	25.2	25.1	25.4	25.2	25.5	25.1
2012	24.7	25.1	25.4	25.3	25.8	26.1	26.3	25.8	25.7	25.7	25.3	25.8	25.6
2013	24.5	24.9	25.4	25.4	25.8	26.3	25.7	26.0	25.9	26.0	25.8	25.9	25.6
2014	24.5	25.5	25.9	25.7	26.0	25.8	25.5	25.7	25.7	25.6	25.9	25.7	25.6
2015	24.6	25.6	25.9	25.6	26.0	26.1	26.1	26.4	26.2	26.1	25.8	25.8	25.9
Other Services													
2011	32.3	32.2	32.0	32.2	32.6	32.3	32.9	32.5	32.5	32.9	31.9	32.1	32.4
2012	32.7	31.6	31.5	32.0	31.6	31.5	32.2	31.3	31.8	31.4	31.2	32.2	31.7
2013	30.8	31.0	30.8	31.3	31.4	32.4	31.7	31.9	32.2	31.4	31.7	32.5	31.6
2014	30.8	31.3	31.4	31.0	31.4	31.9	31.0	31.4	31.6	31.9	32.5	31.7	31.5
2015	32.1	32.8	33.3	32.5	32.3	32.2	32.4	33.3	32.7	32.7	33.7	32.5	32.7

3. Average Hourly Earnings by Selected Industry: Illinois, 2011–2015

(Dollars, not seasonally adjusted)

Industry and year	January	February	March	April	May	June	July	August	September	October	November	December	Annual average
Total Private													
2011	23.45	23.37	23.15	23.36	23.55	23.38	23.60	23.54	23.70	23.98	23.83	23.95	23.58
2012	24.20	24.03	24.02	24.54	24.22	24.16	24.51	24.23	24.48	24.27	24.47	24.64	24.32
2013	24.69	24.74	24.67	24.77	24.72	24.85	24.82	24.73	25.05	24.80	24.92	25.07	24.82
2014	25.05	25.33	25.41	25.24	25.25	25.33	25.25	25.42	25.47	25.51	25.89	25.64	25.40
2015	25.74	26.12	25.98	25.77	25.71	25.62	25.76	26.02	25.95	26.23	26.54	26.30	25.98
Goods-Producing													
2011	25.31	25.24	25.23	25.50	25.67	25.62	26.04	25.94	25.91	26.29	26.13	26.17	25.76
2012	25.72	25.63	25.82	26.19	26.16	26.12	26.55	26.52	26.58	26.61	26.76	26.67	26.29
2013	26.34	26.44	26.32	26.23	26.55	26.72	26.82	26.74	26.87	26.87	27.06	26.79	26.65
2014	26.44	26.48	26.53	26.72	27.05	27.34	27.62	27.86	27.91	28.11	28.08	27.99	27.36
2015	27.79	27.96	27.95	27.86	28.08	28.25	28.72	28.88	28.59	29.74	29.83	29.72	28.62
Construction													
2011	33.22	33.24	32.91	33.15	33.18	33.23	33.20	33.32	32.98	33.50	33.66	33.89	33.29
2012	33.22	33.32	33.68	33.61	33.60	33.58	34.07	34.19	34.16	33.96	34.46	34.44	33.88
2013	33.81	34.46	34.02	33.82	33.49	33.73	34.45	34.11	34.23	34.32	34.63	34.15	34.11
2014	33.66	34.27	33.98	33.87	34.03	34.32	34.50	34.80	35.56	35.54	35.57	35.90	34.72
2015	35.05	36.03	36.21	35.96	36.15	36.19	36.69	36.90	36.33	36.30	37.06	37.47	36.39
Manufacturing													
2011	23.90	23.99	23.89	23.93	24.08	23.89	24.16	23.93	24.02	24.23	24.05	24.29	24.03
2012	24.13	23.94	23.91	24.21	24.01	23.81	24.12	24.02	24.15	24.14	24.36	24.71	24.13
2013	24.60	24.52	24.42	24.28	24.47	24.47	24.28	24.23	24.41	24.38	24.65	24.68	24.45
2014	24.56	24.40	24.49	24.53	24.83	24.90	25.04	25.25	25.16	25.38	25.35	25.28	24.93
2015	25.52	25.50	25.31	25.06	25.15	25.23	25.59	25.59	25.60	26.52	26.55	26.38	25.66
Trade, Transportation, and Utilities													
2011	23.90	23.99	23.89	23.93	24.08	23.89	24.16	23.93	24.02	24.23	24.05	24.29	24.03
2012	24.13	23.94	23.91	24.21	24.01	23.81	24.12	24.02	24.15	24.14	24.36	24.71	24.13
2013	24.60	24.52	24.42	24.28	24.47	24.47	24.28	24.23	24.41	24.38	24.65	24.68	24.45
2014	24.56	24.40	24.49	24.53	24.83	24.90	25.04	25.25	25.16	25.38	25.35	25.28	24.93
2015	25.52	25.50	25.31	25.06	25.15	25.23	25.59	25.59	25.60	26.52	26.55	26.38	25.66
Information													
2011	26.83	26.82	27.21	27.29	27.21	26.63	27.19	27.00	27.77	26.91	27.26	26.15	27.02
2012	26.68	26.78	27.04	27.91	27.80	27.64	27.74	27.49	28.11	28.09	28.12	28.85	27.69
2013	28.45	28.73	28.84	29.45	29.58	30.38	29.84	29.93	30.51	30.50	30.74	30.47	29.79
2014	29.77	31.32	31.81	31.59	31.42	31.69	31.63	31.61	31.60	31.63	32.15	31.42	31.47
2015	31.23	31.92	32.24	31.57	31.80	31.38	31.63	32.46	31.68	31.93	32.31	31.93	31.84
Financial Activities													
2011	28.22	28.29	28.10	28.53	29.00	28.28	28.22	28.61	28.65	29.28	29.13	29.36	28.64
2012	30.06	29.98	29.76	30.44	29.93	29.39	29.88	29.56	30.07	30.02	30.61	30.30	30.00
2013	29.97	30.67	30.15	30.46	30.49	30.22	30.47	30.70	31.08	30.64	31.38	31.55	30.65
2014	31.73	32.63	32.47	32.38	32.42	31.84	32.02	33.09	33.29	33.14	34.67	34.16	32.81
2015	34.01	35.34	35.67	34.95	34.25	33.61	33.71	34.32	34.56	34.81	35.54	34.88	34.64
Professional and Business Services													
2011	28.26	28.22	27.80	27.71	28.07	27.92	28.06	27.86	27.69	28.10	27.83	28.15	27.97
2012	28.83	28.26	28.44	28.75	28.20	28.15	28.69	27.83	28.21	27.67	27.94	28.65	28.30
2013	28.74	28.80	28.65	28.42	28.53	28.72	28.34	28.08	28.70	27.77	28.31	28.61	28.47
2014	28.66	29.21	29.39	28.57	28.63	28.86	28.48	28.31	28.51	28.34	29.22	28.68	28.74
2015	28.98	29.91	29.49	28.91	28.79	28.60	28.70	28.89	28.91	28.59	29.27	28.94	28.99
Education and Health Services													
2011	22.47	22.47	22.34	22.45	22.64	22.85	22.89	23.03	23.22	23.42	23.30	23.41	22.88
2012	23.33	23.57	23.72	23.89	24.03	24.14	24.17	24.09	24.09	24.13	24.39	24.27	23.99
2013	24.50	24.44	24.59	24.68	24.61	24.81	24.97	24.84	25.00	25.04	25.10	25.26	24.82
2014	24.97	24.78	24.97	25.16	24.89	24.84	24.83	25.03	24.63	24.68	24.61	24.88	24.85
2015	24.61	24.63	24.64	24.52	24.61	24.61	24.54	24.57	24.76	25.64	25.65	25.56	24.87
Leisure and Hospitality													
2011	13.16	13.23	13.12	13.29	12.65	12.47	12.48	12.65	12.96	12.40	12.59	12.80	12.81
2012	12.90	12.89	12.98	14.34	13.54	13.53	13.62	13.57	13.35	12.15	12.15	12.71	13.16
2013	12.60	12.51	12.63	12.72	12.79	12.61	12.53	13.02	13.14	12.43	11.97	12.55	12.63
2014	12.58	12.82	12.77	12.88	13.02	13.18	13.27	13.38	13.54	13.73	13.94	14.09	13.28
2015	13.93	14.03	13.85	13.94	13.99	13.97	14.11	14.13	14.18	14.24	14.35	14.51	14.11
Other Services													
2011	22.21	21.21	21.31	21.27	21.68	21.72	21.49	21.45	21.88	21.97	21.78	22.31	21.69
2012	22.59	22.35	22.64	22.98	22.78	22.53	23.10	22.93	23.10	23.17	23.37	23.83	22.95
2013	23.83	23.76	23.77	23.56	23.43	23.69	23.58	23.57	24.36	24.02	23.52	24.00	23.76
2014	24.15	24.57	24.48	24.42	24.39	24.61	24.38	24.81	25.10	25.20	25.50	25.39	24.75
2015	25.35	25.64	25.15	25.06	25.22	25.09	25.04	25.64	25.40	25.85	25.97	26.48	25.49

4. Average Weekly Earnings by Selected Industry: Illinois, 2011–2015

(Dollars, not seasonally adjusted)

Industry and year	January	February	March	April	May	June	July	August	September	October	November	December	Annual average
Total Private													
2011	804.34	801.59	796.36	805.92	817.19	806.61	814.20	812.13	820.02	839.30	824.52	831.07	815.87
2012	839.74	829.04	828.69	856.45	838.01	840.77	860.30	838.36	861.70	839.74	841.77	859.94	843.90
2013	836.99	846.11	846.18	849.61	847.90	864.78	851.33	853.19	874.25	858.08	862.23	877.45	856.29
2014	851.70	876.42	879.19	865.73	866.08	881.48	863.55	874.45	873.62	877.54	903.56	879.45	873.76
2015	872.59	901.14	893.71	878.76	879.28	878.77	880.99	905.50	887.49	902.31	920.94	902.09	891.11
Goods-Producing													
2011	994.68	989.41	996.59	1,007.25	1,029.37	1,014.55	1,020.77	1,035.01	1,031.22	1,051.60	1,032.14	1,044.18	1,020.10
2012	1,023.66	1,014.95	1,022.47	1,044.98	1,038.55	1,044.80	1,054.04	1,050.19	1,068.52	1,059.08	1,057.02	1,064.13	1,046.34
2013	1,024.63	1,028.52	1,037.01	1,030.84	1,043.42	1,066.13	1,062.07	1,077.62	1,085.55	1,080.17	1,079.69	1,085.00	1,058.01
2014	1,041.74	1,045.96	1,039.98	1,055.44	1,068.48	1,090.87	1,099.28	1,114.40	1,105.24	1,118.78	1,128.82	1,125.20	1,086.19
2015	1,097.71	1,107.22	1,109.62	1,106.04	1,120.39	1,124.35	1,134.44	1,158.09	1,115.01	1,171.76	1,178.29	1,182.86	1,133.35
Construction													
2011	1,242.43	1,239.85	1,237.42	1,256.39	1,280.75	1,272.71	1,308.08	1,319.47	1,292.82	1,306.50	1,262.25	1,281.04	1,278.34
2012	1,225.82	1,239.50	1,256.26	1,263.74	1,276.80	1,302.90	1,315.10	1,306.06	1,315.16	1,314.25	1,299.14	1,267.39	1,284.05
2013	1,217.16	1,230.22	1,221.32	1,197.23	1,259.22	1,274.99	1,281.54	1,292.77	1,300.74	1,300.73	1,274.38	1,256.72	1,262.07
2014	1,191.56	1,261.14	1,240.27	1,270.13	1,259.11	1,307.59	1,335.15	1,339.80	1,315.72	1,332.75	1,348.10	1,349.84	1,298.53
2015	1,282.83	1,304.29	1,325.29	1,330.52	1,341.17	1,364.36	1,375.88	1,420.65	1,293.35	1,321.32	1,308.22	1,333.93	1,335.51
Manufacturing													
2011	975.12	976.39	977.10	976.34	989.69	972.32	959.15	971.56	975.21	993.43	981.24	998.32	978.02
2012	989.33	971.96	968.36	985.35	977.21	969.07	974.45	970.41	990.15	975.26	984.14	1,018.05	982.09
2013	986.46	983.25	993.89	988.20	991.04	1,003.27	990.62	1,003.12	1,010.57	1,004.46	1,015.58	1,034.09	1,000.01
2014	1,004.50	1,007.72	1,004.09	1,005.73	1,020.51	1,023.39	1,016.62	1,032.73	1,029.04	1,038.04	1,046.96	1,044.06	1,022.13
2015	1,036.11	1,040.40	1,035.18	1,022.45	1,033.67	1,029.38	1,033.84	1,044.07	1,039.36	1,047.54	1,067.31	1,071.03	1,041.80
Trade, Transportation, and Utilities													
2011	975.12	976.39	977.10	976.34	989.69	972.32	959.15	971.56	975.21	993.43	981.24	998.32	978.02
2012	989.33	971.96	968.36	985.35	977.21	969.07	974.45	970.41	990.15	975.26	984.14	1,018.05	982.09
2013	986.46	983.25	993.89	988.20	991.04	1,003.27	990.62	1,003.12	1,010.57	1,004.46	1,015.58	1,034.09	1,000.01
2014	1,004.50	1,007.72	1,004.09	1,005.73	1,020.51	1,023.39	1,016.62	1,032.73	1,029.04	1,038.04	1,046.96	1,044.06	1,022.13
2015	1,036.11	1,040.40	1,035.18	1,022.45	1,033.67	1,029.38	1,033.84	1,044.07	1,039.36	1,047.54	1,067.31	1,071.03	1,041.80
Information													
2011	1,030.27	1,029.89	1,006.77	996.09	1,004.05	982.65	989.72	980.10	1,010.83	1,017.20	1,019.52	985.86	1,005.14
2012	1,008.50	993.54	1,000.48	1,043.83	1,020.26	1,008.86	1,029.15	1,008.88	1,065.37	1,025.29	1,037.63	1,076.11	1,027.30
2013	1,041.27	1,054.39	1,061.31	1,089.65	1,091.50	1,139.25	1,116.02	1,113.40	1,150.23	1,116.30	1,122.01	1,133.48	1,102.23
2014	1,098.51	1,177.63	1,199.24	1,156.19	1,140.55	1,169.36	1,151.33	1,137.96	1,153.40	1,145.01	1,186.34	1,131.12	1,154.95
2015	1,130.53	1,171.46	1,179.98	1,139.68	1,138.44	1,142.23	1,151.33	1,188.04	1,137.31	1,136.71	1,172.85	1,133.52	1,152.61
Financial Activities													
2011	1,027.21	1,035.41	1,028.46	1,044.20	1,064.30	1,026.56	1,032.85	1,038.54	1,048.59	1,106.78	1,098.20	1,095.13	1,053.95
2012	1,154.30	1,136.24	1,121.95	1,187.16	1,116.39	1,108.00	1,147.39	1,099.63	1,151.68	1,092.73	1,111.14	1,136.25	1,131.00
2013	1,075.92	1,119.46	1,100.48	1,114.84	1,103.74	1,121.16	1,084.73	1,095.99	1,159.28	1,106.10	1,132.82	1,170.51	1,115.66
2014	1,151.80	1,220.36	1,207.88	1,168.92	1,173.60	1,181.26	1,123.90	1,174.70	1,181.80	1,183.10	1,248.12	1,181.94	1,184.44
2015	1,193.75	1,286.38	1,294.82	1,237.23	1,219.30	1,203.24	1,203.45	1,266.41	1,244.16	1,249.68	1,290.10	1,234.75	1,243.58
Professional and Business Services													
2011	1,017.36	1,018.74	1,003.58	1,005.87	1,030.17	1,007.91	1,004.55	997.39	994.07	1,022.84	993.53	1,002.14	1,006.92
2012	1,035.00	1,006.06	1,015.31	1,046.50	1,023.66	1,027.48	1,044.32	1,004.66	1,043.77	1,004.42	1,008.63	1,051.46	1,027.29
2013	1,026.02	1,036.80	1,031.40	1,020.28	1,018.52	1,048.28	1,008.90	1,005.26	1,044.68	1,002.50	1,024.82	1,047.13	1,024.92
2014	1,020.30	1,069.09	1,069.80	1,028.52	1,027.82	1,056.28	1,019.58	1,019.16	1,017.81	1,020.24	1,072.37	1,018.14	1,037.51
2015	1,022.99	1,088.72	1,058.69	1,032.09	1,027.80	1,032.46	1,030.33	1,066.04	1,029.20	1,052.11	1,091.77	1,053.42	1,049.44
Education and Health Services													
2011	739.26	737.02	734.99	740.85	751.65	751.77	764.53	762.29	770.90	784.57	773.56	774.87	757.33
2012	786.22	780.17	778.02	790.76	788.18	794.21	807.28	792.56	802.20	786.64	804.87	800.91	791.67
2013	801.15	799.19	801.63	802.10	802.29	821.21	821.51	809.78	825.00	816.30	828.30	828.53	814.10
2014	811.53	812.78	816.52	812.67	806.44	814.75	809.46	813.48	798.01	799.63	814.59	808.60	810.11
2015	797.36	798.01	800.80	792.00	794.90	794.90	792.64	800.98	802.22	825.61	836.19	825.59	805.79
Leisure and Hospitality													
2011	323.74	324.14	330.62	334.91	316.25	315.49	314.50	318.78	325.30	314.96	317.27	326.40	321.53
2012	318.63	323.54	329.69	362.80	349.33	353.13	358.21	350.11	343.10	312.26	307.40	327.92	336.90
2013	308.70	311.50	320.80	323.09	329.98	331.64	322.02	338.52	340.33	323.18	308.83	325.05	323.33
2014	308.21	326.91	330.74	331.02	338.52	340.04	338.39	343.87	347.98	351.49	361.05	362.11	339.97
2015	342.68	359.17	358.72	356.86	363.74	364.62	368.27	373.03	371.52	371.66	370.23	374.36	365.45
Other Services													
2011	717.38	682.96	681.92	684.89	706.77	701.56	707.02	697.13	711.10	722.81	694.78	716.15	702.76
2012	738.69	706.26	713.16	735.36	719.85	709.70	743.82	717.71	734.58	727.54	729.14	767.33	727.52
2013	733.96	736.56	732.12	737.43	735.70	767.56	747.49	751.88	784.39	754.23	745.58	780.00	750.82
2014	743.82	769.04	768.67	757.02	765.85	785.06	755.78	779.03	793.16	803.88	828.75	804.86	779.63
2015	813.74	840.99	837.50	814.45	814.61	807.90	811.30	853.81	830.58	845.30	875.19	860.60	833.52

INDIANA
At a Glance

Population:
  2005 estimate: 6,278,616
  2010 census: 6,483,802
  2015 estimate: 6,619,680

Percent change in population:
  2005–2015: 5.4%
  2010–2015: 2.1%

Percent change in total nonfarm employment:
  2005–2015: 2.5%

Industry with the largest growth in employment, 2005–2015 (thousands):
  Education and health services, 73.7

Industry with the largest decline or smallest growth in employment, 2005–2015 (thousands):
  Manufacturing, –52.0

Civilian labor force:
  2005: 3,205,436
  2010: 3,175,192
  2015: 3,265,761

Unemployment rate and rank among states (highest to lowest):
  2005: 5.5%, 13th
  2010: 10.4%, 11th
  2015: 4.8%, 32nd

Over-the-year change in unemployment rates:
  2012–2013: –0.6%
  2013–2014: –1.8%
  2014–2015: –1.1%

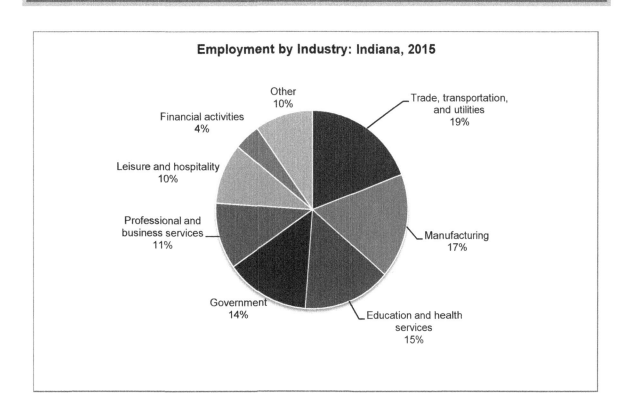

Employment by Industry: Indiana, 2015

Other 10%
Financial activities 4%
Leisure and hospitality 10%
Professional and business services 11%
Government 14%
Trade, transportation, and utilities 19%
Manufacturing 17%
Education and health services 15%

1. Employment by Industry: Indiana, 2005–2015

(Numbers in thousands, not seasonally adjusted)

Industry and year	January	February	March	April	May	June	July	August	September	October	November	December	Annual average
Total Nonfarm													
2005	2,887.2	2,905.6	2,928.1	2,968.8	2,979.6	2,961.3	2,930.4	2,945.8	3,003.1	3,005.2	3,008.9	2,999.3	2,960.3
2006	2,916.4	2,933.1	2,963.3	2,984.6	2,998.6	2,989.6	2,939.5	2,963.7	3,011.6	3,014.9	3,017.9	3,016.9	2,979.2
2007	2,927.2	2,930.3	2,971.1	2,995.0	3,016.3	3,006.5	2,955.5	2,990.5	3,024.2	3,027.8	3,032.5	3,021.6	2,991.5
2008	2,931.3	2,942.2	2,956.0	2,981.7	3,010.4	2,986.8	2,930.6	2,967.8	2,986.6	2,978.5	2,956.3	2,925.1	2,962.8
2009	2,800.1	2,792.1	2,798.1	2,805.5	2,814.7	2,772.7	2,717.9	2,761.7	2,804.4	2,812.8	2,812.9	2,804.3	2,791.4
2010	2,721.9	2,729.8	2,761.7	2,805.3	2,833.2	2,803.7	2,775.2	2,806.5	2,829.3	2,841.6	2,841.0	2,833.7	2,798.6
2011	2,765.2	2,776.4	2,808.5	2,849.4	2,873.4	2,838.0	2,808.2	2,844.4	2,889.5	2,892.2	2,893.6	2,895.7	2,844.5
2012	2,826.1	2,846.4	2,874.7	2,901.2	2,924.4	2,903.0	2,849.6	2,910.6	2,943.0	2,944.5	2,950.0	2,945.4	2,901.6
2013	2,859.7	2,887.7	2,907.4	2,934.6	2,947.6	2,932.2	2,880.6	2,950.5	2,970.7	2,978.7	3,002.6	2,997.6	2,937.5
2014	2,885.8	2,913.6	2,942.4	2,979.1	3,007.2	2,989.6	2,933.7	2,988.0	3,009.8	3,023.8	3,041.3	3,045.1	2,980.0
2015	2,956.4	2,973.2	2,995.9	3,030.4	3,057.5	3,034.4	3,001.4	3,043.8	3,068.7	3,082.2	3,086.8	3,080.9	3,034.3
Total Private													
2005	2,458.4	2,466.4	2,489.1	2,529.8	2,543.6	2,558.4	2,550.4	2,559.0	2,564.0	2,562.3	2,568.1	2,561.6	2,534.3
2006	2,490.7	2,495.6	2,524.7	2,547.5	2,562.5	2,585.4	2,563.5	2,573.0	2,573.1	2,572.2	2,574.3	2,573.0	2,553.0
2007	2,499.2	2,489.7	2,527.1	2,553.8	2,578.6	2,596.5	2,575.6	2,582.1	2,581.0	2,581.1	2,585.3	2,575.0	2,560.4
2008	2,496.5	2,493.2	2,504.5	2,531.8	2,558.5	2,564.0	2,536.0	2,544.8	2,537.9	2,524.3	2,502.0	2,474.3	2,522.3
2009	2,360.5	2,344.3	2,346.6	2,355.0	2,360.3	2,354.5	2,339.4	2,354.2	2,357.3	2,355.1	2,360.2	2,352.5	2,353.3
2010	2,281.8	2,280.6	2,312.5	2,351.7	2,372.8	2,379.3	2,382.5	2,395.0	2,389.5	2,397.8	2,398.0	2,395.6	2,361.4
2011	2,335.8	2,339.2	2,369.6	2,407.0	2,427.0	2,427.2	2,425.2	2,442.1	2,449.7	2,450.4	2,450.2	2,452.2	2,414.6
2012	2,392.6	2,406.6	2,432.6	2,461.7	2,487.7	2,495.5	2,482.9	2,497.2	2,504.3	2,503.1	2,508.8	2,509.3	2,473.5
2013	2,435.1	2,449.8	2,468.8	2,495.6	2,522.4	2,530.8	2,518.5	2,537.2	2,538.3	2,540.9	2,560.8	2,557.2	2,513.0
2014	2,468.9	2,478.1	2,504.6	2,542.0	2,574.3	2,580.2	2,562.2	2,577.6	2,577.5	2,586.3	2,602.0	2,604.5	2,554.9
2015	2,528.2	2,538.1	2,560.5	2,594.5	2,624.0	2,630.1	2,621.8	2,632.2	2,632.1	2,645.8	2,646.8	2,641.8	2,608.0
Goods-Producing													
2005	707.5	707.2	713.2	725.7	729.8	736.0	731.4	737.1	735.3	733.3	730.9	726.8	726.2
2006	710.2	707.8	715.8	723.6	728.1	738.2	729.9	734.1	727.9	724.3	718.9	716.1	722.9
2007	695.2	688.2	700.4	706.5	714.9	722.3	718.5	719.5	715.3	710.5	707.8	701.0	708.3
2008	679.2	676.7	675.7	681.2	689.2	692.9	676.7	682.0	673.0	663.1	649.0	628.8	672.3
2009	589.0	578.7	571.7	570.5	562.9	563.2	562.8	568.7	567.2	565.0	564.1	559.2	568.6
2010	540.7	538.7	548.8	564.7	572.1	579.1	585.0	586.2	582.4	583.3	578.1	574.9	569.5
2011	562.5	562.5	572.8	584.3	591.1	599.4	599.8	604.8	604.8	606.3	600.1	599.3	590.6
2012	588.4	590.1	598.6	608.2	616.1	626.3	626.5	627.7	624.0	623.4	618.7	617.3	613.8
2013	601.4	605.7	610.3	617.5	623.8	632.5	628.6	632.8	629.0	630.3	630.1	626.3	622.4
2014	610.4	612.3	621.6	630.5	638.6	649.3	646.3	650.8	647.2	648.6	648.8	647.7	637.7
2015	632.8	632.6	639.0	646.9	654.9	663.3	662.6	664.1	660.1	664.4	661.2	655.2	653.1
Service-Providing													
2005	2,179.7	2,198.4	2,214.9	2,243.1	2,249.8	2,225.3	2,199.0	2,208.7	2,267.8	2,271.9	2,278.0	2,272.5	2,234.1
2006	2,206.2	2,225.3	2,247.5	2,261.0	2,270.5	2,251.4	2,209.6	2,229.6	2,283.7	2,290.6	2,299.0	2,300.8	2,256.3
2007	2,232.0	2,242.1	2,270.7	2,288.5	2,301.4	2,284.2	2,237.0	2,271.0	2,308.9	2,317.3	2,324.7	2,320.6	2,283.2
2008	2,252.1	2,265.5	2,280.3	2,300.5	2,321.2	2,293.9	2,253.9	2,285.8	2,313.6	2,315.4	2,307.3	2,296.3	2,290.5
2009	2,211.1	2,213.4	2,226.4	2,235.0	2,251.8	2,209.5	2,155.1	2,193.0	2,237.2	2,247.8	2,248.8	2,245.1	2,222.9
2010	2,181.2	2,191.1	2,212.9	2,240.6	2,261.1	2,224.6	2,190.2	2,220.3	2,246.9	2,258.3	2,262.9	2,258.8	2,229.1
2011	2,202.7	2,213.9	2,235.7	2,265.1	2,282.3	2,238.6	2,208.4	2,239.6	2,284.7	2,285.9	2,293.5	2,296.4	2,253.9
2012	2,237.7	2,256.3	2,276.1	2,293.0	2,308.3	2,276.7	2,223.1	2,282.9	2,319.0	2,321.1	2,331.3	2,328.1	2,287.8
2013	2,258.3	2,282.0	2,297.1	2,317.1	2,323.8	2,299.7	2,252.0	2,317.7	2,341.7	2,348.4	2,372.5	2,371.3	2,315.1
2014	2,275.4	2,301.3	2,320.8	2,348.6	2,368.6	2,340.3	2,287.4	2,337.2	2,362.6	2,375.2	2,392.5	2,397.4	2,342.3
2015	2,323.6	2,340.6	2,356.9	2,383.5	2,402.6	2,371.1	2,338.8	2,379.7	2,408.6	2,417.8	2,425.6	2,425.7	2,381.2
Mining and Logging													
2005	6.7	6.7	6.8	7.0	7.0	7.1	7.0	7.0	6.9	6.9	6.9	6.8	6.9
2006	6.5	6.5	6.6	7.0	7.1	7.2	7.2	7.1	7.1	7.1	7.0	7.0	7.0
2007	6.8	6.7	6.9	7.0	7.1	7.1	7.1	7.1	7.1	7.0	6.9	6.8	7.0
2008	6.4	6.4	6.5	6.7	6.8	6.9	6.8	6.9	6.9	6.9	6.8	6.7	6.7
2009	6.3	6.3	6.5	6.6	6.7	6.8	6.8	6.8	6.8	6.7	6.7	6.5	6.6
2010	6.2	6.2	6.4	6.6	6.6	6.6	6.7	6.7	6.8	6.7	6.7	6.6	6.6
2011	6.3	6.4	6.6	6.7	6.8	6.9	6.9	7.0	6.9	7.0	7.0	6.9	6.8
2012	6.8	6.8	6.9	7.0	7.1	7.1	7.1	7.1	7.0	7.0	6.9	6.8	7.0
2013	6.7	6.7	6.7	6.9	7.0	7.1	7.1	7.1	7.2	7.1	7.1	7.1	7.0
2014	6.7	6.6	6.9	7.2	7.3	7.5	7.4	7.4	7.3	7.1	7.2	7.2	7.2
2015	6.9	6.7	6.8	6.9	7.0	7.0	7.0	6.9	6.7	6.7	6.6	6.4	6.8

1. Employment by Industry: Indiana, 2005–2015—*Continued*

(Numbers in thousands, not seasonally adjusted)

Industry and year	January	February	March	April	May	June	July	August	September	October	November	December	Annual average
Construction													
2005........................	132.4	132.1	136.8	147.7	150.2	154.1	156.6	156.8	155.5	155.1	153.2	148.2	148.2
2006........................	136.9	136.1	140.9	148.0	153.4	157.1	157.3	157.8	156.2	156.4	154.3	152.0	150.5
2007........................	138.9	132.4	142.1	149.0	155.6	159.2	159.4	159.5	157.6	156.9	155.7	149.1	151.3
2008........................	135.5	133.2	137.6	143.6	148.7	151.8	153.2	152.0	150.0	149.2	143.3	133.7	144.3
2009........................	115.9	113.2	116.6	120.2	123.5	125.6	125.9	124.7	122.9	122.4	120.0	113.5	120.4
2010........................	100.3	98.3	104.5	115.0	118.3	121.1	126.1	124.7	121.9	123.0	120.9	114.0	115.7
2011........................	104.2	102.2	108.0	115.9	121.3	124.5	128.4	129.2	129.2	129.3	127.5	122.1	120.2
2012........................	112.4	111.2	116.9	123.8	127.4	130.9	131.9	132.0	131.5	130.8	127.4	123.7	125.0
2013........................	111.2	112.2	116.0	122.0	126.0	129.6	130.6	129.2	127.3	128.4	126.8	120.9	123.4
2014........................	108.2	107.4	113.3	120.2	124.7	129.7	131.6	130.3	128.8	129.5	128.1	124.0	123.0
2015........................	112.9	112.3	116.5	124.4	129.7	132.4	133.2	134.1	132.6	135.0	134.2	129.2	127.2
Manufacturing													
2005........................	568.4	568.4	569.6	571.0	572.6	574.8	567.8	573.3	572.9	571.3	570.8	571.8	571.1
2006........................	566.8	565.2	568.3	568.6	567.6	573.9	565.4	569.2	564.6	560.8	557.6	557.1	565.4
2007........................	549.5	549.1	551.4	550.5	552.2	556.0	552.0	552.9	550.6	546.6	545.2	545.1	550.1
2008........................	537.3	537.1	531.6	530.9	533.7	534.2	516.7	523.1	516.1	507.0	498.9	488.4	521.3
2009........................	466.8	459.2	448.6	443.7	432.7	430.8	430.1	437.2	437.5	435.9	437.4	439.2	441.6
2010........................	434.2	434.2	437.9	443.1	447.2	451.4	452.2	454.8	453.7	453.6	450.5	454.3	447.3
2011........................	452.0	453.9	458.2	461.7	463.0	468.0	464.5	468.6	468.7	470.0	465.6	470.3	463.7
2012........................	469.2	472.1	474.8	477.4	481.6	488.3	487.5	488.6	485.5	485.6	484.4	486.8	481.8
2013........................	483.5	486.8	487.6	488.6	490.8	495.8	490.9	496.5	494.5	494.8	496.2	498.3	492.0
2014........................	495.5	498.3	501.4	503.1	506.6	512.1	507.3	513.1	511.1	512.0	513.5	516.5	507.5
2015........................	513.0	513.6	515.7	515.6	518.2	523.9	522.4	523.1	520.8	522.7	520.4	519.6	519.1
Trade, Transportation, and Utilities													
2005........................	570.1	567.6	571.7	578.4	583.6	584.0	585.2	585.4	585.0	588.0	597.7	600.9	583.1
2006........................	576.9	572.6	577.4	579.2	584.4	587.0	584.8	585.7	584.5	587.8	598.6	602.8	585.1
2007........................	578.8	572.5	579.9	582.0	588.3	592.1	588.3	587.1	585.4	587.4	599.6	602.7	587.0
2008........................	576.4	571.9	574.4	577.2	583.9	584.9	582.0	583.0	578.9	578.6	582.0	582.4	579.6
2009........................	553.1	545.7	544.5	545.6	550.3	551.6	547.9	547.1	544.6	545.9	552.8	554.4	548.6
2010........................	532.3	527.1	532.3	537.6	542.5	544.9	545.5	545.3	542.1	547.9	555.9	558.4	542.7
2011........................	539.3	536.2	539.5	546.2	551.7	553.7	553.5	554.3	552.2	556.8	565.9	569.1	551.5
2012........................	549.8	546.1	550.4	554.6	561.1	564.2	562.1	561.5	561.0	564.7	577.4	579.0	561.0
2013........................	553.8	552.3	554.7	560.1	568.1	572.0	568.9	571.0	569.6	573.1	585.8	589.0	568.2
2014........................	562.7	559.9	563.4	568.0	574.5	577.1	575.5	576.2	574.1	577.1	588.5	593.3	574.2
2015........................	569.8	567.1	570.1	574.5	582.1	586.1	584.6	586.3	584.0	587.0	596.5	605.6	582.8
Wholesale Trade													
2005........................	119.0	119.2	119.8	121.1	121.8	122.5	122.9	122.5	121.8	122.0	122.1	122.3	121.4
2006........................	121.1	121.2	122.0	122.8	123.8	125.0	124.4	123.8	123.4	123.6	123.5	123.9	123.2
2007........................	122.8	122.9	124.0	124.7	125.5	126.5	127.4	126.2	125.4	125.5	125.8	125.8	125.2
2008........................	124.0	124.1	124.6	125.3	126.2	126.4	125.9	125.2	124.2	123.7	122.6	121.7	124.5
2009........................	117.9	116.8	116.2	115.4	115.7	115.5	115.4	114.1	113.1	113.3	112.9	112.8	114.9
2010........................	111.3	111.1	112.1	113.1	113.5	113.8	114.5	113.6	113.0	113.2	112.7	112.4	112.9
2011........................	112.3	112.5	113.3	114.4	115.3	116.0	116.4	115.7	115.1	115.3	115.3	115.2	114.7
2012........................	114.2	114.3	115.2	115.9	116.9	117.8	117.8	116.8	116.4	116.3	116.0	116.1	116.1
2013........................	114.3	114.8	115.6	116.4	117.4	118.2	118.1	117.4	116.7	117.0	117.1	117.1	116.7
2014........................	115.2	115.4	116.1	117.0	118.2	119.0	119.0	118.6	117.8	117.8	118.1	118.4	117.6
2015........................	117.2	117.5	118.1	119.0	120.1	120.7	120.2	119.9	119.2	117.6	116.6	117.4	118.6
Retail Trade													
2005........................	325.4	321.8	324.5	328.1	332.0	331.5	332.5	331.9	331.3	333.7	342.4	345.7	331.7
2006........................	326.9	322.0	325.0	325.9	329.0	329.8	328.5	329.3	327.6	330.5	340.3	343.4	329.9
2007........................	325.6	319.5	324.0	324.7	329.1	330.7	327.7	326.9	325.4	327.1	338.0	340.5	328.3
2008........................	321.3	316.8	317.9	319.0	323.7	324.3	323.4	323.5	321.2	321.6	326.4	327.8	322.2
2009........................	308.4	303.0	303.1	305.6	309.4	311.0	308.4	307.8	305.8	306.3	313.5	315.4	308.1
2010........................	299.7	294.9	297.8	300.9	304.4	305.9	305.6	305.3	302.0	306.8	314.5	316.9	304.6
2011........................	302.2	298.1	300.4	304.6	307.8	308.5	307.5	308.3	306.5	310.9	319.1	321.4	307.9
2012........................	306.9	302.6	305.0	307.8	312.0	313.1	311.8	311.2	310.9	314.6	326.2	326.0	312.3
2013........................	307.6	305.0	306.1	310.3	315.7	318.2	316.0	317.5	316.1	319.3	330.0	332.3	316.2
2014........................	312.0	309.6	311.5	315.0	318.8	320.3	319.1	319.7	318.0	320.8	330.4	333.0	319.0
2015........................	315.5	312.9	314.9	318.5	323.4	325.9	325.2	326.8	325.1	328.4	335.6	340.2	324.4

1. Employment by Industry: Indiana, 2005–2015—*Continued*

(Numbers in thousands, not seasonally adjusted)

Industry and year	January	February	March	April	May	June	July	August	September	October	November	December	Annual average
Transportation and Utilities													
2005	125.7	126.6	127.4	129.2	129.8	130.0	129.8	131.0	131.9	132.3	133.2	132.9	130.0
2006	128.9	129.4	130.4	130.5	131.6	132.2	131.9	132.6	133.5	133.7	134.8	135.5	132.1
2007	130.4	130.1	131.9	132.6	133.7	134.9	133.2	134.0	134.6	134.8	135.8	136.4	133.5
2008	131.1	131.0	131.9	132.9	134.0	134.2	132.7	134.3	133.5	133.3	133.0	132.9	132.9
2009	126.8	125.9	125.2	124.6	125.2	125.1	124.1	125.2	125.7	126.3	126.4	126.2	125.6
2010	121.3	121.1	122.4	123.6	124.6	125.2	125.4	126.4	127.1	127.9	128.7	129.1	125.2
2011	124.8	125.6	125.8	127.2	128.6	129.2	129.6	130.3	130.6	130.6	131.5	132.5	128.9
2012	128.7	129.2	130.2	130.9	132.2	133.3	132.5	133.5	133.7	133.8	135.2	136.9	132.5
2013	131.9	132.5	133.0	133.4	135.0	135.6	134.8	136.1	136.8	136.8	138.7	139.6	135.4
2014	135.5	134.9	135.8	136.0	137.5	137.8	137.4	137.9	138.3	138.5	140.0	141.9	137.6
2015	137.1	136.7	137.1	137.0	138.6	139.5	139.2	139.6	139.7	141.0	144.3	148.0	139.8
Information													
2005	40.0	40.1	40.1	40.2	40.7	41.0	40.8	40.7	40.0	39.7	40.0	40.4	40.3
2006	39.5	39.8	39.8	39.9	40.2	40.6	40.3	40.1	39.5	39.3	39.6	39.8	39.9
2007	39.5	39.6	39.5	39.6	40.1	40.6	40.6	40.5	39.9	39.6	39.9	40.0	40.0
2008	39.6	39.6	39.7	39.8	40.3	40.5	40.4	40.2	39.5	39.1	39.1	39.3	39.8
2009	38.6	38.4	38.1	37.8	38.1	38.4	37.8	37.6	36.8	36.4	36.5	36.7	37.6
2010	35.9	35.7	35.7	35.7	36.1	36.4	35.8	35.6	35.0	34.9	34.9	34.9	35.6
2011	34.4	34.2	34.4	34.3	34.8	35.1	35.0	35.1	35.0	35.0	35.2	35.4	34.8
2012	35.5	35.5	35.7	35.5	35.8	36.0	35.8	35.7	35.4	35.7	35.8	35.8	35.7
2013	35.7	35.6	35.8	35.8	35.8	36.1	36.3	35.9	35.5	35.5	35.6	35.8	35.8
2014	35.3	35.3	35.5	35.3	35.5	35.8	35.8	35.4	34.8	34.4	34.4	34.4	35.2
2015	34.0	33.8	33.8	33.6	33.9	34.1	34.0	33.6	33.1	32.8	32.7	33.2	33.6
Financial Activities													
2005	137.2	137.2	137.2	138.0	138.7	139.9	140.4	140.7	139.6	139.0	138.8	139.4	138.8
2006	138.4	138.6	138.8	139.1	139.9	141.2	140.6	140.5	139.2	138.8	138.5	139.3	139.4
2007	137.5	137.8	138.1	138.4	139.1	140.3	140.1	139.6	138.5	138.2	137.7	138.0	138.6
2008	135.6	135.8	136.0	136.1	136.6	137.6	137.8	137.1	135.5	134.9	134.0	134.0	135.9
2009	132.3	131.7	131.6	131.5	132.0	132.4	132.3	131.8	130.4	130.0	129.5	129.9	131.3
2010	129.9	129.4	129.7	129.7	130.4	131.7	132.3	132.2	130.9	131.6	131.3	131.7	130.9
2011	130.9	130.9	131.3	131.0	131.9	132.5	132.6	132.0	130.9	130.7	130.3	130.5	131.3
2012	129.0	128.9	129.2	129.5	130.2	131.0	130.8	130.3	129.4	129.2	129.0	129.4	129.7
2013	127.6	127.3	127.3	127.8	128.9	129.8	130.0	129.6	128.6	128.4	128.3	128.8	128.5
2014	126.2	126.2	126.4	126.7	127.8	129.0	129.2	129.3	128.8	129.0	129.4	129.5	128.1
2015	128.3	128.6	129.0	129.2	130.4	131.7	132.0	132.3	131.5	131.8	131.2	131.7	130.6
Professional and Business Services													
2005	260.5	264.1	266.8	273.1	274.2	276.2	276.2	279.8	280.4	281.2	280.5	278.2	274.3
2006	266.5	269.5	274.7	280.0	282.6	285.5	282.8	288.9	288.2	286.5	285.8	285.0	281.3
2007	275.8	276.8	283.5	289.6	292.3	294.0	290.1	295.7	295.5	295.1	293.7	292.0	289.5
2008	280.1	279.4	282.2	287.7	287.9	289.3	286.4	290.2	289.6	288.8	282.9	276.6	285.1
2009	259.4	257.7	258.3	259.1	257.9	259.1	255.8	260.8	263.1	267.7	271.1	269.2	261.6
2010	256.9	258.4	263.0	272.7	274.5	277.3	278.5	283.1	281.9	284.4	285.1	285.8	275.1
2011	275.3	276.2	282.2	288.7	287.2	287.0	287.4	292.4	295.5	295.9	295.9	295.0	288.2
2012	282.5	288.4	293.0	297.1	299.2	303.1	300.3	304.3	305.3	305.1	304.7	302.9	298.8
2013	290.4	291.8	296.7	302.6	303.8	307.0	308.6	313.9	315.1	315.8	324.4	322.2	307.7
2014	304.5	305.5	310.4	320.0	323.7	322.7	319.1	325.3	326.0	330.3	335.6	333.9	321.4
2015	317.3	316.4	320.3	330.6	332.3	333.1	331.8	333.3	331.6	333.3	333.1	330.0	328.6
Education and Health Services													
2005	371.6	375.7	377.5	380.6	373.1	371.3	369.8	366.6	382.9	388.5	390.1	387.0	377.9
2006	381.7	386.7	389.5	389.8	382.4	380.8	377.6	374.0	390.5	396.7	397.2	394.5	386.8
2007	389.2	391.4	393.6	396.5	392.2	389.8	387.3	385.5	400.2	407.5	408.7	406.5	395.7
2008	401.1	404.2	405.4	407.2	405.7	400.7	397.6	394.4	410.2	416.3	417.6	419.0	406.6
2009	409.6	412.9	416.4	416.8	415.7	402.9	400.1	405.8	419.7	422.5	423.6	423.0	414.1
2010	417.2	421.1	425.6	423.3	421.4	408.9	406.0	411.1	422.2	425.6	427.0	425.7	419.6
2011	419.6	423.6	424.6	428.9	427.3	412.2	411.8	416.3	430.4	430.4	431.1	432.3	424.0
2012	425.6	431.9	431.3	434.5	433.1	417.9	413.7	421.6	439.8	439.9	442.0	443.0	431.2
2013	434.7	442.9	442.7	441.5	439.8	426.5	422.5	429.0	441.3	442.8	445.6	444.1	437.8
2014	433.7	439.9	440.7	443.4	444.0	431.5	424.7	428.8	441.7	445.3	447.6	448.8	439.2
2015	439.7	450.6	451.9	452.8	452.2	439.0	438.0	442.7	457.7	464.9	466.0	463.9	451.6

1. Employment by Industry: Indiana, 2005–2015—*Continued*

(Numbers in thousands, not seasonally adjusted)

Industry and year	January	February	March	April	May	June	July	August	September	October	November	December	Annual average
Leisure and Hospitality													
2005	257.5	260.0	266.9	277.2	286.2	292.0	289.2	291.4	284.4	276.8	274.6	273.0	277.4
2006	263.2	266.0	272.6	279.2	287.2	293.3	289.8	292.2	286.4	282.5	279.9	279.1	281.0
2007	268.1	268.1	275.1	283.4	292.8	297.4	291.8	296.0	288.7	285.3	280.9	277.6	283.8
2008	267.9	268.8	273.8	284.0	294.9	297.8	295.5	298.8	293.2	285.3	280.1	277.2	284.8
2009	263.6	264.5	270.4	278.2	287.5	290.1	286.8	287.6	281.8	273.8	269.2	266.5	276.7
2010	256.3	257.7	263.5	273.4	280.9	284.8	283.1	285.9	279.8	274.8	270.5	269.1	273.3
2011	259.7	261.1	268.7	277.3	286.2	289.3	287.5	289.7	284.1	278.9	275.5	274.3	277.7
2012	266.2	269.6	277.1	284.7	293.6	297.5	294.8	297.3	291.2	286.1	282.5	282.5	285.3
2013	272.8	274.6	280.5	289.0	299.7	302.6	299.7	301.2	296.4	291.8	287.6	286.8	290.2
2014	273.8	275.7	281.9	292.9	303.8	307.2	304.5	305.7	299.7	296.6	292.7	291.7	293.9
2015	282.0	284.4	290.7	300.3	310.8	314.0	310.5	312.4	307.0	304.3	299.9	297.3	301.1
Other Services													
2005	114.0	114.5	115.7	116.6	117.3	118.0	117.4	117.3	116.4	115.8	115.5	115.9	116.2
2006	114.3	114.6	116.1	116.7	117.7	118.8	117.7	117.5	116.9	116.3	115.8	116.4	116.6
2007	115.1	115.3	117.0	117.8	118.9	120.0	118.9	118.2	117.5	117.5	117.0	117.2	117.5
2008	116.6	116.8	117.3	118.6	120.0	120.3	119.6	119.1	118.0	118.2	117.3	117.0	118.2
2009	114.9	114.7	115.6	115.5	115.9	116.8	115.9	114.8	113.7	113.8	113.4	113.6	114.9
2010	112.6	112.5	113.9	114.6	114.9	116.2	116.3	115.6	115.2	115.3	115.2	115.1	114.8
2011	114.1	114.5	116.1	116.3	116.8	118.0	117.6	117.5	116.8	116.4	116.2	116.3	116.4
2012	115.6	116.1	117.3	117.6	118.6	119.5	118.9	118.8	118.2	119.0	118.7	119.4	118.1
2013	118.7	119.6	120.8	121.3	122.5	124.3	123.9	123.8	122.8	123.2	123.4	124.2	122.4
2014	122.3	123.3	124.7	125.2	126.4	127.6	127.1	126.1	125.2	125.0	125.0	125.2	125.3
2015	124.3	124.6	125.7	126.6	127.4	128.8	128.3	127.5	127.1	127.3	126.2	124.9	126.6
Government													
2005	428.8	439.2	439.0	439.0	436.0	402.9	380.0	386.8	439.1	442.9	440.8	437.7	426.0
2006	425.7	437.5	438.6	437.1	436.1	404.2	376.0	390.7	438.5	442.7	443.6	443.9	426.2
2007	428.0	440.6	444.0	441.2	437.7	410.0	379.9	408.4	443.2	446.7	447.2	446.6	431.1
2008	434.8	449.0	451.5	449.9	451.9	422.8	394.6	423.0	448.7	454.2	454.3	450.8	440.5
2009	439.6	447.8	451.5	450.5	454.4	418.2	378.5	407.5	447.1	457.7	452.7	451.8	438.1
2010	440.1	449.2	449.2	453.6	460.4	424.4	392.7	411.5	439.8	443.8	443.0	438.1	437.2
2011	429.4	437.2	438.9	442.4	446.4	410.8	383.0	402.3	439.8	441.8	443.4	443.5	429.9
2012	433.5	439.8	442.1	439.5	436.7	407.5	366.7	413.4	438.7	441.4	441.2	436.1	428.1
2013	424.6	437.9	438.6	439.0	425.2	401.4	362.1	413.3	432.4	437.8	441.8	440.4	424.5
2014	416.9	435.5	437.8	437.1	432.9	409.4	371.5	410.4	432.3	437.5	439.3	440.6	425.1
2015	428.2	435.1	435.4	435.9	433.5	404.3	379.6	411.6	436.6	436.4	440.0	439.1	426.3

2. Average Weekly Hours by Selected Industry: Indiana, 2011–2015

(Not seasonally adjusted)

Industry and year	January	February	March	April	May	June	July	August	September	October	November	December	Annual average
Total Private													
2011	35.0	34.9	35.0	34.9	35.1	35.1	34.8	35.1	35.0	35.3	34.8	34.7	35.0
2012	34.5	34.6	34.6	34.9	34.5	34.8	35.0	34.7	34.8	34.6	34.5	34.8	34.7
2013	34.4	34.6	34.6	34.7	34.5	34.9	34.4	34.5	34.8	34.7	34.6	35.0	34.6
2014	33.7	34.6	34.9	34.6	34.8	35.3	34.8	35.1	35.0	35.0	35.4	35.4	34.9
2015	34.7	35.0	35.0	34.8	35.0	34.9	34.8	35.3	34.5	34.9	35.0	35.1	34.9
Goods-Producing													
2011	41.3	41.1	41.3	40.9	41.2	40.7	40.1	41.3	41.3	41.6	40.8	41.0	41.0
2012	40.7	40.8	40.6	41.5	40.8	41.1	41.4	41.1	41.0	40.8	40.8	41.0	41.0
2013	40.9	40.9	41.0	41.2	40.3	40.9	39.6	40.4	41.3	41.0	40.9	41.6	40.8
2014	39.4	40.5	40.5	40.5	41.0	41.4	40.2	40.9	40.6	40.5	41.5	41.1	40.7
2015	40.5	40.6	40.6	40.1	40.6	40.3	39.7	40.9	39.5	40.9	41.2	41.0	40.5
Construction													
2011	37.4	36.5	37.4	37.7	39.7	38.4	38.8	39.7	38.8	39.1	37.7	38.0	38.3
2012	36.5	37.4	38.2	39.1	38.8	39.8	39.4	39.9	39.6	40.6	39.4	38.1	39.0
2013	38.4	38.5	38.2	37.7	37.7	38.8	38.5	39.3	38.9	39.4	39.3	36.8	38.5
2014	34.8	34.5	35.9	37.7	36.0	37.9	38.1	39.0	37.9	37.3	38.1	38.0	37.2
2015	36.9	36.8	36.4	37.8	38.9	39.4	38.2	39.3	35.9	38.2	37.5	37.4	37.8
Manufacturing													
2011	41.8	41.8	42.0	41.6	41.4	41.1	40.3	41.5	41.5	41.9	41.3	41.5	41.5
2012	41.5	41.4	41.1	41.9	41.1	41.3	41.7	41.2	41.1	40.5	40.8	41.4	41.2
2013	41.2	41.2	41.4	41.8	40.6	41.2	39.6	40.4	41.5	41.1	41.0	42.3	41.1
2014	40.1	41.6	41.4	40.9	42.0	41.9	40.3	40.9	40.9	40.9	42.1	41.6	41.2
2015	41.1	41.3	41.5	40.6	40.9	40.4	40.0	41.3	40.6	41.2	41.9	41.7	41.0
Trade, Transportation, and Utilities													
2011	35.0	34.6	35.0	35.2	35.3	35.7	35.3	35.2	35.1	35.2	34.3	34.3	35.0
2012	33.9	34.0	34.4	34.8	34.6	35.0	34.8	34.6	34.6	34.4	34.0	34.1	34.4
2013	33.5	33.6	33.7	33.8	34.1	34.3	34.1	34.1	34.3	34.0	33.7	34.1	33.9
2014	33.4	33.8	34.3	33.8	34.3	34.6	34.5	34.6	34.4	34.5	34.7	34.9	34.3
2015	33.7	34.5	34.7	34.5	34.9	34.5	34.9	34.8	34.7	34.4	34.4	35.0	34.6
Financial Activities													
2011	36.8	36.4	36.3	36.8	37.5	36.9	37.1	36.3	36.5	36.9	36.4	36.6	36.7
2012	36.8	36.5	36.6	36.7	36.6	36.2	36.2	36.2	37.2	36.5	37.5	37.6	36.7
2013	37.3	37.3	37.3	36.9	37.0	37.5	37.0	36.7	36.9	37.0	37.2	37.0	37.1
2014	36.5	36.7	37.0	36.5	36.9	37.3	36.4	36.6	36.4	36.4	37.2	36.6	36.7
2015	36.8	37.2	37.3	36.3	36.6	36.4	36.1	37.4	36.3	35.9	36.2	35.2	36.5
Professional and Business Services													
2011	36.0	35.8	35.5	35.5	36.2	36.0	35.1	35.4	35.7	36.1	35.4	34.9	35.6
2012	35.2	35.1	34.6	35.9	35.0	35.1	35.1	34.6	35.2	34.8	35.1	35.5	35.1
2013	34.8	35.5	35.1	35.9	36.3	36.6	35.9	35.9	35.9	35.9	35.8	35.9	35.8
2014	34.1	35.9	36.3	36.1	36.5	37.1	36.0	36.9	36.8	36.9	36.9	37.1	36.4
2015	36.2	36.3	36.2	36.0	36.2	36.0	35.7	36.4	34.7	35.4	35.3	35.5	35.8
Education and Health Services													
2011	32.1	32.1	32.4	32.3	32.6	32.4	32.5	32.5	32.6	32.7	32.7	32.7	32.5
2012	32.7	32.8	32.7	32.8	32.3	32.7	32.9	32.7	33.0	33.0	32.9	33.1	32.8
2013	33.0	32.8	32.9	32.7	32.7	32.9	32.9	32.7	33.2	32.9	33.1	33.8	33.0
2014	32.9	33.3	33.3	33.3	33.3	33.5	33.6	33.3	33.4	33.5	33.8	33.8	33.4
2015	33.5	33.7	33.7	34.0	33.9	34.0	33.9	34.1	33.9	33.7	33.9	34.0	33.9
Leisure and Hospitality													
2011	25.8	26.3	26.4	26.3	26.4	26.3	26.3	26.2	25.8	26.0	26.0	25.6	26.1
2012	25.0	25.8	25.8	25.1	25.1	25.4	25.7	25.8	25.4	25.2	24.9	25.2	25.4
2013	24.2	24.5	24.6	24.6	24.8	25.3	25.3	25.2	25.0	24.8	25.0	24.7	24.8
2014	23.3	25.0	25.2	25.2	25.2	25.8	26.0	25.9	25.5	25.4	25.4	26.1	25.4
2015	24.7	25.3	25.3	25.1	25.3	25.5	25.7	25.5	24.8	25.0	24.7	25.2	25.2
Other Services													
2011	29.1	28.7	29.1	28.8	28.0	28.6	28.6	28.6	28.7	29.2	28.7	28.4	28.7
2012	28.8	28.8	29.1	28.8	28.8	29.2	30.1	29.0	28.2	28.6	28.5	29.1	28.9
2013	28.1	28.8	28.8	28.5	28.9	29.4	29.0	29.1	28.0	28.8	28.5	28.3	28.7
2014	27.9	29.1	29.7	29.0	28.4	29.2	28.9	28.2	29.2	29.1	29.1	29.0	28.9
2015	29.2	29.1	29.8	29.6	29.5	30.5	29.8	29.7	29.5	28.6	28.9	29.6	29.5

3. Average Hourly Earnings by Selected Industry: Indiana, 2011–2015

(Dollars, not seasonally adjusted)

Industry and year	January	February	March	April	May	June	July	August	September	October	November	December	Annual average
Total Private													
2011	20.79	20.55	20.43	20.29	20.43	20.32	20.61	20.63	20.70	20.99	20.87	21.12	20.65
2012	21.22	21.12	21.17	21.26	21.06	21.04	21.43	21.28	21.64	21.57	21.61	22.17	21.38
2013	22.07	22.04	22.03	22.06	21.77	21.95	21.91	21.99	22.26	22.07	22.23	22.53	22.08
2014	22.57	22.62	22.62	22.72	22.49	22.60	22.52	22.54	22.44	22.54	22.90	22.70	22.61
2015	23.00	22.86	22.78	22.71	22.65	22.65	22.75	22.97	22.93	22.90	23.07	23.00	22.86
Goods-Producing													
2011	23.32	22.91	23.12	23.00	23.27	23.18	23.51	23.57	23.64	24.11	23.99	24.43	23.51
2012	24.42	24.30	24.28	24.61	24.59	24.34	24.87	24.60	24.84	24.42	24.44	25.16	24.58
2013	24.92	24.91	24.65	24.66	24.37	24.75	24.68	24.23	24.81	24.54	24.90	25.22	24.72
2014	24.90	25.25	25.27	25.47	25.16	25.34	25.32	25.21	25.03	25.16	25.46	25.30	25.24
2015	25.30	25.29	25.36	25.13	25.03	25.17	25.23	25.50	25.42	25.26	25.65	25.40	25.31
Construction													
2011	26.65	26.33	26.45	26.09	26.62	26.14	26.07	26.21	26.33	26.05	26.68	26.94	26.37
2012	26.51	26.45	26.59	26.55	26.68	26.76	27.34	27.41	27.79	27.02	27.19	28.12	27.06
2013	28.28	28.04	28.24	28.42	27.77	27.02	26.86	26.29	26.49	26.79	26.14	25.98	27.16
2014	25.95	27.24	26.90	26.89	26.77	27.81	27.75	26.93	26.52	27.05	27.01	26.76	26.99
2015	26.94	26.83	27.31	27.13	26.33	26.58	26.70	27.19	27.05	27.33	27.07	26.88	26.94
Manufacturing													
2011	22.49	22.13	22.33	22.20	22.33	22.32	22.70	22.71	22.81	23.38	23.08	23.64	22.68
2012	23.81	23.71	23.52	23.96	23.92	23.61	24.16	23.78	23.99	23.66	23.70	24.44	23.86
2013	24.16	24.20	23.86	23.79	23.54	24.03	23.99	23.58	24.15	23.77	24.40	24.88	24.03
2014	24.50	24.70	24.80	25.04	24.70	24.58	24.40	24.55	24.44	24.46	24.88	24.77	24.65
2015	24.79	24.84	24.82	24.52	24.64	24.74	24.79	24.99	24.99	24.65	25.26	25.01	24.84
Trade, Transportation, and Utilities													
2011	20.04	19.59	19.31	19.23	19.35	19.12	19.30	19.27	19.36	19.54	19.49	19.30	19.41
2012	19.49	19.57	19.42	19.23	18.89	18.85	19.34	19.17	19.49	19.32	19.27	19.85	19.32
2013	19.63	19.80	19.99	19.67	19.50	19.77	19.84	20.08	20.15	20.13	20.27	20.48	19.95
2014	20.69	20.63	20.77	20.79	20.57	20.70	20.52	20.57	20.29	20.36	20.80	20.47	20.60
2015	20.94	20.64	20.78	20.74	20.56	20.46	20.44	20.37	20.41	20.02	20.13	20.14	20.46
Financial Activities													
2011	24.38	23.42	23.11	22.90	22.72	22.72	22.85	23.02	22.72	23.08	22.68	21.94	22.96
2012	23.16	22.24	22.41	22.72	22.06	22.11	22.67	22.15	22.90	22.92	22.94	23.32	22.64
2013	23.74	24.00	23.99	25.05	24.87	24.79	24.44	24.82	25.34	25.29	25.01	25.23	24.71
2014	25.06	24.93	24.85	25.10	24.67	24.30	24.06	24.10	23.75	23.75	23.72	23.53	24.31
2015	23.31	23.08	23.03	23.13	23.22	22.85	23.49	23.88	24.24	24.31	24.39	24.96	23.65
Professional and Business Services													
2011	20.86	20.67	20.67	20.49	20.94	20.78	21.37	21.28	21.18	21.27	21.63	21.83	21.08
2012	22.10	22.00	21.78	21.30	20.91	21.00	21.28	20.82	21.07	20.69	20.98	21.10	21.24
2013	21.10	21.29	21.17	21.13	21.05	21.29	21.65	21.97	22.23	21.86	22.21	22.48	21.64
2014	23.51	23.80	23.94	23.68	23.74	24.14	24.28	23.84	23.93	24.13	24.63	24.66	24.04
2015	25.33	25.73	25.42	24.87	24.72	24.99	25.08	25.33	25.53	25.12	25.17	25.00	25.19
Education and Health Services													
2011	21.54	21.72	21.59	21.43	21.59	21.84	22.23	22.13	22.07	22.27	21.95	22.42	21.90
2012	21.92	22.13	22.40	22.62	22.55	22.76	23.02	23.20	23.60	23.71	23.72	24.24	23.00
2013	23.89	23.74	24.11	24.25	23.92	24.11	24.08	24.47	24.24	24.06	24.01	24.30	24.10
2014	23.99	23.63	23.75	24.03	23.86	23.89	23.89	24.04	24.21	24.17	24.54	24.28	24.03
2015	24.53	24.51	24.33	24.77	24.90	24.68	25.08	25.20	24.88	25.29	25.15	25.13	24.87
Leisure and Hospitality													
2011	12.83	12.82	12.66	12.44	12.35	12.24	12.26	12.22	12.51	12.30	12.46	12.80	12.48
2012	12.91	12.67	12.49	12.36	12.22	12.03	12.11	11.95	12.05	12.24	12.33	12.59	12.32
2013	12.40	12.46	12.36	12.21	12.23	11.84	11.71	11.87	12.12	12.01	12.15	12.30	12.13
2014	12.28	12.66	12.34	12.17	12.11	12.20	12.22	12.17	12.36	12.50	12.67	12.85	12.37
2015	12.78	12.91	12.81	12.75	12.62	12.51	12.44	12.57	12.77	13.02	13.30	13.55	12.83
Other Services													
2011	18.96	18.85	18.62	18.31	18.13	17.59	16.99	16.73	16.57	16.60	16.49	16.94	17.56
2012	17.00	16.70	17.09	17.05	16.99	17.06	17.00	17.04	17.64	17.23	17.19	17.84	17.15
2013	17.79	17.63	17.56	17.32	17.05	16.84	17.23	17.20	17.60	17.52	17.52	17.99	17.43
2014	17.85	17.57	17.18	17.61	17.66	17.47	17.47	17.99	17.77	17.66	17.84	18.09	17.68
2015	17.71	17.65	17.66	17.50	17.68	17.58	17.17	17.91	18.12	18.12	18.56	18.81	17.87

4. Average Weekly Earnings by Selected Industry: Indiana, 2011–2015

(Dollars, not seasonally adjusted)

Industry and year	January	February	March	April	May	June	July	August	September	October	November	December	Annual average
Total Private													
2011	727.65	717.20	715.05	708.12	717.09	713.23	717.23	724.11	724.50	740.95	726.28	732.86	722.75
2012	732.09	730.75	732.48	741.97	726.57	732.19	750.05	738.42	753.07	746.32	745.55	771.52	741.89
2013	759.21	762.58	762.24	765.48	751.07	766.06	753.70	758.66	774.65	765.83	769.16	788.55	763.97
2014	760.61	782.65	789.44	786.11	782.65	797.78	783.70	791.15	785.40	788.90	810.66	803.58	789.09
2015	798.10	800.10	797.30	790.31	792.75	790.49	791.70	810.84	791.09	799.21	807.45	807.30	797.81
Goods-Producing													
2011	963.12	941.60	954.86	940.70	958.72	943.43	942.75	973.44	976.33	1,002.98	978.79	1,001.63	963.91
2012	993.89	991.44	985.77	1,021.32	1,003.27	1,000.37	1,029.62	1,011.06	1,018.44	996.34	997.15	1,031.56	1,007.78
2013	1,019.23	1,018.82	1,010.65	1,015.99	982.11	1,012.28	977.33	978.89	1,024.65	1,006.14	1,018.41	1,049.15	1,008.58
2014	981.06	1,022.63	1,023.44	1,031.54	1,031.56	1,049.08	1,017.86	1,031.09	1,016.22	1,018.98	1,056.59	1,039.83	1,027.27
2015	1,024.65	1,026.77	1,029.62	1,007.71	1,016.22	1,014.35	1,001.63	1,042.95	1,004.09	1,033.13	1,056.78	1,041.40	1,025.06
Construction													
2011	996.71	961.05	989.23	983.59	1,056.81	1,003.78	1,011.52	1,040.54	1,021.60	1,018.56	1,005.84	1,023.72	1,009.97
2012	967.62	989.23	1,015.74	1,038.11	1,035.18	1,065.05	1,077.20	1,093.66	1,100.48	1,097.01	1,071.29	1,071.37	1,055.34
2013	1,085.95	1,079.54	1,078.77	1,071.43	1,046.93	1,048.38	1,034.11	1,033.20	1,030.46	1,055.53	1,027.30	956.06	1,045.66
2014	903.06	939.78	965.71	1,013.75	963.72	1,054.00	1,057.28	1,050.27	1,005.11	1,008.97	1,029.08	1,016.88	1,004.03
2015	994.09	987.34	994.08	1,025.51	1,024.24	1,047.25	1,019.94	1,068.57	971.10	1,044.01	1,015.13	1,005.31	1,018.33
Manufacturing													
2011	940.08	925.03	937.86	923.52	924.46	917.35	914.81	942.47	946.62	979.62	953.20	981.06	941.22
2012	988.12	981.59	966.67	1,003.92	983.11	975.09	1,007.47	979.74	985.99	958.23	966.96	1,011.82	983.03
2013	995.39	997.04	987.80	994.42	955.72	990.04	950.00	952.63	1,002.23	976.95	1,000.40	1,052.42	987.63
2014	982.45	1,027.52	1,026.72	1,024.14	1,037.40	1,029.90	983.32	1,004.10	999.60	1,000.41	1,047.45	1,030.43	1,015.58
2015	1,018.87	1,025.89	1,030.03	995.51	1,007.78	999.50	991.60	1,032.09	1,014.59	1,015.58	1,058.39	1,042.92	1,018.44
Trade, Transportation, and Utilities													
2011	701.40	677.81	675.85	676.90	683.06	682.58	681.29	678.30	679.54	687.81	668.51	661.99	679.35
2012	660.71	665.38	668.05	669.20	653.59	659.75	673.03	663.28	674.35	664.61	655.18	676.89	664.61
2013	657.61	665.28	673.66	664.85	664.95	678.11	676.54	684.73	691.15	684.42	683.10	698.37	676.31
2014	691.05	697.29	712.41	702.70	705.55	716.22	707.94	711.72	697.98	702.42	721.76	714.40	706.58
2015	705.68	712.08	721.07	715.53	717.54	705.87	713.36	708.88	708.23	688.69	692.47	704.90	707.92
Financial Activities													
2011	897.18	852.49	838.89	842.72	852.00	838.37	847.74	835.63	829.28	851.65	825.55	803.00	842.63
2012	852.29	811.76	820.21	833.82	807.40	800.38	820.65	801.83	851.88	836.58	860.25	876.83	830.89
2013	885.50	895.20	894.83	924.35	920.19	929.63	904.28	910.89	935.05	935.73	930.37	933.51	916.74
2014	914.69	914.93	919.45	916.15	910.32	906.39	875.78	882.06	864.50	864.50	882.38	861.20	892.18
2015	857.81	858.58	859.02	839.62	849.85	831.74	847.99	893.11	879.91	872.73	882.92	878.59	863.23
Professional and Business Services													
2011	750.96	739.99	733.79	727.40	758.03	748.08	750.09	753.31	756.13	767.85	765.70	761.87	750.45
2012	777.92	772.20	753.59	764.67	731.85	737.10	746.93	720.37	741.66	720.01	736.40	749.05	745.52
2013	734.28	755.80	743.07	758.57	764.12	779.21	777.24	788.72	798.06	784.77	795.12	807.03	774.71
2014	801.69	854.42	869.02	854.85	866.51	895.59	874.08	879.70	880.62	890.40	908.85	914.89	875.06
2015	916.95	934.00	920.20	895.32	894.86	899.64	895.36	922.01	885.89	889.25	888.50	887.50	901.80
Education and Health Services													
2011	691.43	697.21	699.52	692.19	703.83	707.62	722.48	719.23	719.48	728.23	717.77	733.13	711.75
2012	716.78	725.86	732.48	741.94	728.37	744.25	757.36	758.64	778.80	782.43	780.39	802.34	754.40
2013	788.37	778.67	793.22	792.98	782.18	793.22	792.23	800.17	804.77	791.57	794.73	821.34	795.30
2014	789.27	786.88	790.88	800.20	794.54	800.32	802.70	800.53	808.61	809.70	829.45	820.66	802.60
2015	821.76	825.99	819.92	842.18	844.11	839.12	850.21	859.32	843.43	852.27	852.59	854.42	843.09
Leisure and Hospitality													
2011	331.01	337.17	334.22	327.17	326.04	321.91	322.44	320.16	322.76	319.80	323.96	327.68	325.73
2012	322.75	326.89	322.24	310.24	306.72	305.56	311.23	308.31	306.07	308.45	307.02	317.27	312.93
2013	300.08	305.27	304.06	300.37	303.30	299.55	296.26	299.12	303.00	297.85	303.75	303.81	300.82
2014	286.12	316.50	310.97	306.68	305.17	314.76	317.72	315.20	315.18	317.50	321.82	335.39	314.20
2015	315.67	326.62	324.09	320.03	319.29	319.01	319.71	320.54	316.70	325.50	328.51	341.46	323.32
Other Services													
2011	551.74	541.00	541.84	527.33	507.64	503.07	485.91	478.48	475.56	484.72	473.26	481.10	503.97
2012	489.60	480.96	497.32	491.04	489.31	498.15	511.70	494.16	497.45	492.78	489.92	519.14	495.64
2013	499.90	507.74	505.73	493.62	492.75	495.10	499.67	500.52	492.80	504.58	499.32	509.12	500.24
2014	498.02	511.29	510.25	510.69	501.54	510.12	504.88	507.32	518.88	513.91	519.14	524.61	510.95
2015	517.13	513.62	526.27	518.00	521.56	536.19	511.67	531.93	534.54	518.23	536.38	556.78	527.17

IOWA
At a Glance

Population:
  2005 estimate: 2,964,454
  2010 census: 3,046,355
  2015 estimate: 3,123,899

Percent change in population:
  2005–2015: 5.4%
  2010–2015: 2.5%

Percent change in total nonfarm employment:
  2005–2015: 5.5%

Industry with the largest growth in employment, 2005–2015 (thousands):
  Education and health services, 30.2

Industry with the largest decline or smallest growth in employment, 2005–2015 (thousands):
  Manufacturing, –13.1

Civilian labor force:
  2005: 1,629,764
  2010: 1,678,281
  2015: 1,701,329

Unemployment rate and rank among states (highest to lowest):
  2005: 4.3%, 36th
  2010: 6.0%, 47th
  2015: 3.7%, 43rd

Over-the-year change in unemployment rates:
  2012–2013: –0.4%
  2013–2014: –0.5%
  2014–2015: –0.5%

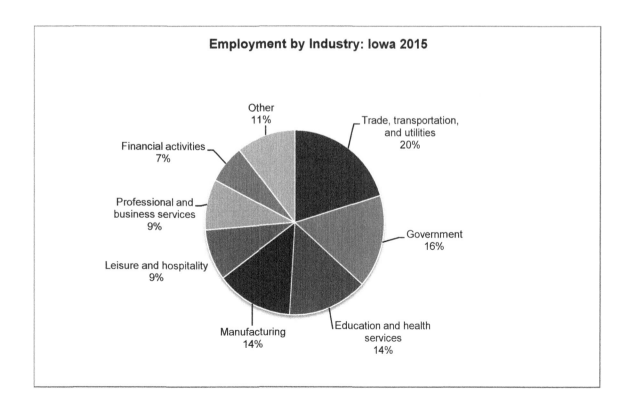

Employment by Industry: Iowa 2015

Other 11%
Trade, transportation, and utilities 20%
Financial activities 7%
Professional and business services 9%
Leisure and hospitality 9%
Government 16%
Manufacturing 14%
Education and health services 14%

1. Employment by Industry: Iowa, 2005–2015

(Numbers in thousands, not seasonally adjusted)

Industry and year	January	February	March	April	May	June	July	August	September	October	November	December	Annual average
Total Nonfarm													
2005	1,434.2	1,442.3	1,459.1	1,483.4	1,494.3	1,499.3	1,473.1	1,472.6	1,496.0	1,501.7	1,505.7	1,504.3	1,480.5
2006	1,462.9	1,471.0	1,484.8	1,506.6	1,519.6	1,527.0	1,492.6	1,492.5	1,515.6	1,523.4	1,527.6	1,527.2	1,504.2
2007	1,482.6	1,485.7	1,496.4	1,517.8	1,534.1	1,542.2	1,508.5	1,508.8	1,529.3	1,538.6	1,545.9	1,538.9	1,519.1
2008	1,496.1	1,499.9	1,509.6	1,529.6	1,546.6	1,544.7	1,515.3	1,514.8	1,534.4	1,540.8	1,535.6	1,525.3	1,524.4
2009	1,471.7	1,472.0	1,473.0	1,488.5	1,497.8	1,493.6	1,460.6	1,461.3	1,479.2	1,487.2	1,486.8	1,476.8	1,479.0
2010	1,432.2	1,437.4	1,449.8	1,477.0	1,489.0	1,486.4	1,457.4	1,455.7	1,474.3	1,490.6	1,494.0	1,487.7	1,469.3
2011	1,443.8	1,449.9	1,460.9	1,489.1	1,500.4	1,499.8	1,477.7	1,479.8	1,501.5	1,509.7	1,513.5	1,507.8	1,486.2
2012	1,467.4	1,474.6	1,488.9	1,511.0	1,524.2	1,524.1	1,500.4	1,505.3	1,519.8	1,528.8	1,533.8	1,527.4	1,508.8
2013	1,484.2	1,493.3	1,501.6	1,520.9	1,542.0	1,543.6	1,527.5	1,532.7	1,545.2	1,548.0	1,554.3	1,547.6	1,528.4
2014	1,503.9	1,512.6	1,522.7	1,548.3	1,564.3	1,564.2	1,540.4	1,545.3	1,561.6	1,565.6	1,569.7	1,564.6	1,546.9
2015	1,525.2	1,532.1	1,542.3	1,564.4	1,578.9	1,576.5	1,554.8	1,554.5	1,567.9	1,583.1	1,590.3	1,578.5	1,562.4
Total Private													
2005	1,191.8	1,194.3	1,209.7	1,233.2	1,241.8	1,250.8	1,248.9	1,248.2	1,250.5	1,249.9	1,252.6	1,251.9	1,235.3
2006	1,219.1	1,220.3	1,233.5	1,254.8	1,265.9	1,275.4	1,266.9	1,266.9	1,267.8	1,269.9	1,272.7	1,272.8	1,257.2
2007	1,235.0	1,232.0	1,242.8	1,263.8	1,277.6	1,288.7	1,279.9	1,280.3	1,279.0	1,281.7	1,287.8	1,281.8	1,269.2
2008	1,246.2	1,244.0	1,252.6	1,272.4	1,286.1	1,288.6	1,284.0	1,283.8	1,279.7	1,280.5	1,274.3	1,265.2	1,271.5
2009	1,218.6	1,213.3	1,213.3	1,227.4	1,234.7	1,235.8	1,226.3	1,227.1	1,224.8	1,226.5	1,225.4	1,217.6	1,224.2
2010	1,181.9	1,181.5	1,191.5	1,218.6	1,225.6	1,228.7	1,224.6	1,223.7	1,223.0	1,232.5	1,233.6	1,229.0	1,216.2
2011	1,194.2	1,194.4	1,204.4	1,231.2	1,241.1	1,244.5	1,241.8	1,243.6	1,247.5	1,251.8	1,254.7	1,249.5	1,233.2
2012	1,215.6	1,218.4	1,232.1	1,252.6	1,264.3	1,269.7	1,265.8	1,265.9	1,265.4	1,270.5	1,274.0	1,268.2	1,255.2
2013	1,234.0	1,236.8	1,244.6	1,263.3	1,281.3	1,287.3	1,288.8	1,290.8	1,288.3	1,288.6	1,293.4	1,287.3	1,273.7
2014	1,251.4	1,255.0	1,264.4	1,289.3	1,303.8	1,309.8	1,304.4	1,306.3	1,303.0	1,304.4	1,307.0	1,303.3	1,291.8
2015	1,270.5	1,272.6	1,283.0	1,304.6	1,317.7	1,324.2	1,320.2	1,318.1	1,312.3	1,320.9	1,326.3	1,318.3	1,307.4
Goods-Producing													
2005	285.5	284.9	290.8	300.0	304.3	311.0	312.6	312.0	309.7	308.6	307.9	303.6	302.6
2006	295.7	295.0	298.8	306.2	310.4	316.3	316.1	315.6	313.0	310.8	309.0	305.5	307.7
2007	293.6	289.3	292.9	299.5	305.2	311.5	313.1	313.3	310.8	310.2	309.9	304.7	304.5
2008	293.9	290.9	293.0	301.0	307.7	311.0	312.8	312.5	308.7	305.5	300.8	292.3	302.5
2009	274.3	268.5	266.4	270.3	272.2	274.2	272.3	273.4	271.6	268.4	266.9	260.8	269.9
2010	250.0	248.5	252.1	263.7	266.4	270.5	272.3	272.1	270.7	270.7	269.6	263.8	264.2
2011	254.0	253.4	257.5	266.8	272.1	277.3	279.6	279.7	278.6	277.3	276.0	271.0	270.3
2012	261.5	260.9	266.3	275.0	280.4	285.2	286.4	286.0	283.6	283.6	281.6	278.2	277.4
2013	268.7	268.5	270.7	278.0	285.9	291.3	293.4	294.2	291.9	292.3	291.5	286.4	284.4
2014	276.3	276.3	280.2	290.8	297.2	302.3	303.2	303.3	300.4	299.5	298.5	293.9	293.5
2015	284.8	284.0	287.3	296.1	299.1	303.9	304.3	303.3	300.2	300.5	302.3	297.1	296.9
Service-Providing													
2005	1,148.7	1,157.4	1,168.3	1,183.4	1,190.0	1,188.3	1,160.5	1,160.6	1,186.3	1,193.1	1,197.8	1,200.7	1,177.9
2006	1,167.2	1,176.0	1,186.0	1,200.4	1,209.2	1,210.7	1,176.5	1,176.9	1,202.6	1,212.6	1,218.6	1,221.7	1,196.5
2007	1,189.0	1,196.4	1,203.5	1,218.3	1,228.9	1,230.7	1,195.4	1,195.5	1,218.5	1,228.4	1,236.0	1,234.2	1,214.6
2008	1,202.2	1,209.0	1,216.6	1,228.6	1,238.9	1,233.7	1,202.5	1,202.3	1,225.7	1,235.3	1,234.8	1,233.0	1,221.9
2009	1,197.4	1,203.5	1,206.6	1,218.2	1,225.6	1,219.4	1,188.3	1,187.9	1,207.6	1,218.8	1,219.9	1,216.0	1,209.1
2010	1,182.2	1,188.9	1,197.7	1,213.3	1,222.6	1,215.9	1,185.1	1,183.6	1,203.6	1,219.9	1,224.4	1,223.9	1,205.1
2011	1,189.8	1,196.5	1,203.4	1,222.3	1,228.3	1,222.5	1,198.1	1,200.1	1,222.9	1,232.4	1,237.5	1,236.8	1,215.9
2012	1,205.9	1,213.7	1,222.6	1,236.0	1,243.8	1,238.9	1,214.0	1,219.3	1,236.2	1,245.2	1,252.2	1,249.2	1,231.4
2013	1,215.5	1,224.8	1,230.9	1,242.9	1,256.1	1,252.3	1,234.1	1,238.5	1,253.3	1,255.7	1,262.8	1,261.2	1,244.0
2014	1,227.6	1,236.3	1,242.5	1,257.5	1,267.1	1,261.9	1,237.2	1,242.0	1,261.2	1,266.1	1,271.2	1,270.7	1,253.4
2015	1,240.4	1,248.1	1,255.0	1,268.3	1,279.8	1,272.6	1,250.5	1,251.2	1,267.7	1,282.6	1,288.0	1,281.4	1,265.5
Mining and Logging													
2005	1.7	1.7	2.0	2.1	2.2	2.3	2.3	2.3	2.2	2.2	2.2	2.0	2.1
2006	1.8	1.8	1.9	2.2	2.3	2.4	2.4	2.4	2.3	2.2	2.2	2.1	2.2
2007	1.8	1.7	2.0	2.1	2.2	2.3	2.3	2.3	2.3	2.3	2.3	2.1	2.1
2008	1.7	1.8	1.9	2.2	2.3	2.3	2.3	2.4	2.3	2.3	2.3	2.1	2.2
2009	1.6	1.8	2.0	2.3	2.4	2.4	2.4	2.5	2.4	2.3	2.3	2.1	2.2
2010	1.6	1.7	1.8	2.3	2.3	2.3	2.3	2.3	2.3	2.4	2.3	2.1	2.1
2011	1.7	1.8	1.8	2.2	2.3	2.4	2.4	2.4	2.4	2.4	2.3	2.2	2.2
2012	1.8	1.9	2.1	2.2	2.4	2.4	2.4	2.4	2.4	2.3	2.3	2.2	2.2
2013	1.8	1.8	2.0	2.1	2.4	2.5	2.5	2.5	2.5	2.4	2.4	2.3	2.3
2014	1.8	1.8	1.9	2.2	2.4	2.5	2.4	2.4	2.4	2.3	2.3	2.2	2.2
2015	1.8	1.9	2.1	2.3	2.4	2.5	2.5	2.5	2.4	2.4	2.3	2.2	2.3

1. Employment by Industry: Iowa, 2005–2015—*Continued*

(Numbers in thousands, not seasonally adjusted)

Industry and year	January	February	March	April	May	June	July	August	September	October	November	December	Annual average
Construction													
2005	59.0	58.4	62.3	69.9	72.7	76.6	78.5	78.8	77.0	76.4	75.9	71.3	71.4
2006	64.9	64.6	67.1	72.8	76.3	79.7	80.8	80.7	79.7	77.8	76.2	72.4	74.4
2007	64.0	60.7	63.4	69.5	74.6	78.4	79.0	79.4	77.9	77.7	76.6	71.4	72.7
2008	63.1	60.5	62.4	70.0	75.9	78.4	81.6	81.5	79.4	78.0	75.0	69.8	73.0
2009	58.7	57.2	58.2	64.5	67.5	69.5	70.7	70.2	68.9	68.0	66.0	60.1	65.0
2010	51.6	50.3	52.3	62.2	64.7	67.2	68.1	67.2	66.1	66.0	64.5	58.8	61.6
2011	50.6	49.6	52.1	60.8	64.5	67.4	69.0	69.3	68.6	68.3	66.8	61.4	62.4
2012	54.1	52.9	56.5	63.8	67.4	69.9	70.5	70.6	69.2	69.2	67.0	63.9	64.6
2013	56.1	55.3	56.5	63.0	69.5	72.8	74.9	75.6	74.1	74.4	73.3	67.9	67.8
2014	59.9	59.5	62.4	72.0	77.0	80.3	81.3	82.2	81.2	81.1	79.7	74.9	74.3
2015	67.2	66.8	69.3	78.0	80.3	82.9	84.0	83.7	82.6	83.6	85.1	80.2	78.6
Manufacturing													
2005	224.8	224.8	226.5	228.0	229.4	232.1	231.8	230.9	230.5	230.0	229.8	230.3	229.1
2006	229.0	228.6	229.8	231.2	231.8	234.2	232.9	232.5	231.0	230.8	230.6	231.0	231.1
2007	227.8	226.9	227.5	227.9	228.4	230.8	231.8	231.6	230.6	230.2	231.0	231.2	229.6
2008	229.1	228.6	228.7	228.8	229.5	230.3	228.9	228.6	227.0	225.2	223.5	220.4	227.4
2009	214.0	209.5	206.2	203.5	202.3	202.3	199.2	200.7	200.3	198.1	198.6	198.6	202.8
2010	196.8	196.5	198.0	199.2	199.4	201.0	201.9	202.6	202.3	202.3	202.8	202.9	200.5
2011	201.7	202.0	203.6	203.8	205.3	207.5	208.2	208.0	207.6	206.6	206.9	207.4	205.7
2012	205.6	206.1	207.7	209.0	210.6	212.9	213.5	213.0	212.0	212.1	212.3	212.1	210.6
2013	210.8	211.4	212.2	212.9	214.0	216.0	216.0	216.1	215.3	215.5	215.8	216.2	214.4
2014	214.6	215.0	215.9	216.6	217.8	219.5	219.5	218.7	216.8	216.1	216.5	216.8	217.0
2015	215.8	215.3	215.9	215.8	216.4	218.5	217.8	217.1	215.2	214.5	214.9	214.7	216.0
Trade, Transportation, and Utilities													
2005	300.1	298.2	301.1	305.4	306.9	307.8	308.3	307.5	306.7	307.5	312.3	314.9	306.4
2006	303.8	301.5	303.6	308.0	309.9	311.1	309.3	308.6	307.6	309.5	314.3	316.5	308.6
2007	305.5	302.5	304.1	306.9	310.6	312.2	310.1	308.8	307.7	309.0	314.7	315.9	309.0
2008	306.6	304.1	306.0	307.5	310.6	311.2	310.6	310.5	308.7	310.4	313.2	314.3	309.5
2009	301.9	299.3	299.7	301.8	304.2	305.0	303.8	303.3	300.4	300.8	304.8	304.7	302.5
2010	294.7	291.9	293.8	298.5	300.5	302.1	301.0	300.6	297.9	301.2	305.0	306.8	299.5
2011	295.9	294.2	296.3	300.9	304.1	305.3	304.4	304.2	302.7	305.4	310.3	312.3	303.0
2012	301.4	299.3	300.7	304.2	307.3	309.0	308.5	308.1	307.3	309.1	315.1	316.1	307.2
2013	304.6	303.0	304.8	307.8	311.4	313.2	312.7	311.9	310.4	312.3	318.0	318.9	310.8
2014	307.3	305.4	306.5	310.6	312.5	314.5	312.8	312.4	310.6	313.1	318.7	321.3	312.1
2015	310.8	309.1	310.6	314.4	316.7	318.9	317.6	316.1	314.1	317.0	322.0	323.1	315.9
Wholesale Trade													
2005	65.3	65.3	66.2	67.8	67.9	68.1	68.7	68.1	67.9	68.1	67.7	67.3	67.4
2006	66.6	66.3	66.8	68.0	68.1	68.3	68.4	67.9	67.7	67.5	67.7	67.1	67.5
2007	66.2	65.9	66.5	67.8	68.4	68.6	68.8	68.2	68.3	68.9	69.0	68.4	67.9
2008	67.3	67.2	67.8	68.7	69.8	69.6	69.8	69.2	68.5	69.4	68.7	68.2	68.7
2009	66.1	66.1	66.2	67.6	67.6	67.5	67.6	66.7	66.0	66.9	66.8	66.4	66.8
2010	64.7	64.4	64.9	67.1	66.8	66.8	66.6	66.0	65.8	66.7	66.7	66.0	66.0
2011	65.0	64.8	65.5	67.0	67.5	67.6	67.6	67.1	67.2	68.4	68.7	68.1	67.0
2012	66.8	66.9	68.0	69.1	69.4	69.6	69.3	68.7	68.8	69.1	69.3	68.5	68.6
2013	67.3	67.4	67.8	69.1	70.3	70.2	69.6	69.1	68.3	69.3	69.8	69.0	68.9
2014	67.6	67.4	67.7	69.5	69.9	70.0	69.4	68.9	68.1	69.1	69.5	68.7	68.8
2015	67.1	66.8	67.2	68.7	68.7	68.8	68.1	67.7	67.1	67.7	67.7	67.4	67.8
Retail Trade													
2005	177.6	175.6	176.8	179.0	180.2	180.8	180.4	180.1	179.1	179.5	184.3	186.7	180.0
2006	177.8	176.0	176.9	179.4	180.7	181.2	179.8	178.9	177.8	179.5	183.9	186.1	179.8
2007	178.0	175.3	175.7	177.1	179.6	180.6	179.4	178.3	177.0	177.6	182.7	184.3	178.8
2008	177.4	175.2	176.3	177.1	178.2	179.1	178.5	178.4	177.1	177.9	181.3	182.5	178.3
2009	174.7	172.5	172.8	173.8	175.9	177.3	176.3	176.3	174.0	173.8	177.6	177.6	175.2
2010	171.4	169.1	170.0	171.6	173.6	174.6	173.7	173.3	170.7	172.6	176.0	177.5	172.8
2011	170.8	169.1	170.1	172.6	174.7	175.5	175.1	175.0	173.3	174.8	179.0	180.9	174.2
2012	173.5	171.3	171.2	173.1	175.3	176.1	176.1	176.0	174.8	176.3	181.8	182.6	175.7
2013	174.6	172.8	173.8	175.6	177.3	178.7	178.9	178.6	177.8	178.8	183.3	183.9	177.8
2014	176.6	175.0	175.3	176.8	178.0	179.1	178.2	177.9	176.4	177.8	182.2	183.7	178.1
2015	177.1	175.9	176.8	179.0	181.0	182.4	181.5	180.7	179.0	180.9	184.6	184.7	180.3

1. Employment by Industry: Iowa, 2005–2015—*Continued*

(Numbers in thousands, not seasonally adjusted)

Industry and year	January	February	March	April	May	June	July	August	September	October	November	December	Annual average
Transportation and Utilities													
2005	57.2	57.3	58.1	58.6	58.8	58.9	59.2	59.3	59.7	59.9	60.3	60.9	59.0
2006	59.4	59.2	59.9	60.6	61.1	61.6	61.1	61.8	62.1	62.5	62.7	63.3	61.3
2007	61.3	61.3	61.9	62.0	62.6	63.0	61.9	62.3	62.4	62.5	63.0	63.2	62.3
2008	61.9	61.7	61.9	61.7	62.6	62.5	62.3	62.9	63.1	63.1	63.2	63.6	62.5
2009	61.1	60.7	60.7	60.4	60.7	60.2	59.9	60.3	60.4	60.1	60.4	60.7	60.5
2010	58.6	58.4	58.9	59.8	60.1	60.7	60.7	61.3	61.4	61.9	62.3	63.3	60.6
2011	60.1	60.3	60.7	61.3	61.9	62.2	61.7	62.1	62.2	62.2	62.6	63.3	61.7
2012	61.1	61.1	61.5	62.0	62.6	63.3	63.1	63.4	63.7	63.7	64.0	65.0	62.9
2013	62.7	62.8	63.2	63.1	63.8	64.3	64.2	64.2	64.3	64.2	64.9	66.0	64.0
2014	63.1	63.0	63.5	64.3	64.6	65.4	65.2	65.6	66.1	66.2	67.0	68.9	65.2
2015	66.6	66.4	66.6	66.7	67.0	67.7	68.0	67.7	68.0	68.4	69.7	71.0	67.8
Information													
2005	33.4	33.3	33.5	33.3	33.2	33.1	33.1	32.6	32.5	32.4	32.5	32.7	33.0
2006	32.2	32.4	32.6	32.9	33.0	33.2	33.1	33.0	33.0	33.1	33.4	33.7	33.0
2007	33.0	33.5	33.7	34.1	34.3	34.4	33.6	33.3	33.2	33.1	33.4	33.4	33.6
2008	33.2	33.5	33.5	33.8	33.9	33.6	33.0	32.6	32.3	32.3	31.9	31.7	32.9
2009	31.3	31.4	31.4	31.0	31.1	30.6	30.0	29.5	29.2	29.3	29.3	29.4	30.3
2010	29.0	29.2	29.0	29.1	29.2	28.8	28.6	28.3	27.7	28.2	28.4	28.7	28.7
2011	28.2	28.4	28.3	28.4	28.4	28.1	28.0	27.8	27.6	27.5	27.6	27.6	28.0
2012	27.2	27.4	27.6	27.3	27.2	27.1	26.8	26.6	26.3	26.5	26.8	26.5	26.9
2013	26.1	26.5	26.6	26.4	26.6	26.3	26.2	26.1	25.7	25.6	25.6	25.8	26.1
2014	25.8	25.9	26.0	26.1	26.2	26.0	25.7	25.5	25.4	25.5	25.3	25.5	25.7
2015	25.1	25.2	25.2	25.3	25.6	25.4	24.8	24.5	24.2	23.9	23.9	23.9	24.8
Financial Activities													
2005	97.3	97.4	97.5	97.6	98.0	98.9	99.0	99.0	98.6	98.4	98.5	99.4	98.3
2006	98.8	99.0	99.7	99.8	100.4	101.6	101.5	101.3	101.2	101.1	100.9	101.8	100.6
2007	101.1	101.2	101.6	101.9	102.4	103.8	103.8	103.4	102.8	103.0	103.2	103.5	102.6
2008	102.6	102.7	102.8	102.6	102.8	103.6	103.6	103.2	102.0	101.8	101.9	102.4	102.7
2009	101.7	101.4	101.4	101.8	102.2	102.9	102.8	102.7	101.6	101.6	101.6	102.3	102.0
2010	101.2	100.9	101.2	100.8	101.2	101.9	101.7	101.6	100.8	101.1	101.1	101.7	101.3
2011	100.7	100.4	100.3	100.4	100.7	101.0	101.3	101.4	100.5	100.3	100.6	101.1	100.7
2012	100.2	100.1	100.5	101.2	101.6	102.5	102.5	102.3	101.8	102.1	102.3	103.0	101.7
2013	102.5	102.4	102.6	103.2	103.6	104.3	104.4	104.3	103.6	104.0	104.3	104.5	103.6
2014	103.5	103.3	103.5	103.6	103.7	104.8	104.5	104.8	104.0	104.2	104.2	104.7	104.1
2015	104.0	104.0	104.5	104.9	105.4	106.6	106.6	106.6	105.9	106.2	106.7	107.2	105.7
Professional and Business Services													
2005	107.0	108.4	109.8	112.6	112.5	113.9	114.6	115.1	116.1	116.7	116.3	116.2	113.3
2006	111.7	112.6	114.3	116.8	117.2	118.7	118.5	118.8	118.7	120.0	120.4	119.4	117.3
2007	116.1	117.1	117.7	121.4	120.9	123.2	123.1	124.0	122.9	123.6	123.9	123.2	121.4
2008	119.6	119.9	120.4	123.5	123.6	124.8	126.2	125.7	124.5	125.2	122.4	121.3	123.1
2009	117.1	117.3	116.1	117.3	116.8	117.6	117.2	118.0	117.2	119.0	118.5	117.9	117.5
2010	115.6	116.7	117.6	121.6	121.1	122.0	123.6	124.1	123.1	125.3	125.1	124.5	121.7
2011	121.5	121.7	121.6	125.0	124.1	124.8	127.1	127.6	128.1	129.2	129.0	127.4	125.6
2012	124.8	125.8	127.4	129.8	129.4	131.3	132.5	132.3	132.0	132.3	131.4	129.7	129.9
2013	127.0	127.7	128.4	131.2	131.4	133.4	134.0	135.0	134.2	135.3	135.6	134.8	132.3
2014	131.2	132.3	131.8	136.1	136.9	138.2	138.7	139.8	138.2	139.7	138.9	137.5	136.6
2015	134.6	135.1	135.7	139.1	139.9	141.2	141.2	142.0	139.6	143.0	141.3	138.1	139.2
Education and Health Services													
2005	193.1	195.5	196.7	197.2	196.0	191.1	186.7	186.8	195.5	199.9	200.9	201.5	195.1
2006	197.5	199.8	201.0	201.6	200.3	195.2	190.4	190.6	198.6	203.5	204.8	205.3	199.1
2007	201.2	204.1	205.5	205.7	204.1	199.2	193.7	194.7	203.1	208.2	210.1	209.8	203.3
2008	206.1	208.4	209.7	210.1	208.4	202.4	197.5	197.8	206.6	213.1	214.8	214.8	207.5
2009	210.5	212.9	213.9	214.6	212.5	206.4	201.6	202.1	211.1	218.4	219.2	219.3	211.9
2010	214.2	216.3	217.8	217.6	215.0	208.4	203.0	202.7	212.4	219.7	220.6	221.0	214.1
2011	215.6	218.0	219.1	221.5	218.6	211.3	205.6	206.0	216.6	224.0	225.0	225.2	217.2
2012	219.6	222.8	224.2	223.8	221.6	214.2	208.4	209.6	218.5	225.5	226.8	226.1	220.1
2013	221.5	223.6	224.2	223.8	223.5	215.7	214.3	215.0	223.8	225.0	225.8	226.1	221.9
2014	220.3	223.5	225.7	226.5	225.1	218.2	214.8	215.3	223.7	226.6	227.1	227.5	222.9
2015	222.4	225.0	226.7	226.8	226.6	220.0	218.3	218.2	225.8	230.3	231.4	231.5	225.3

1. Employment by Industry: Iowa, 2005–2015—*Continued*

(Numbers in thousands, not seasonally adjusted)

Industry and year	January	February	March	April	May	June	July	August	September	October	November	December	Annual average
Leisure and Hospitality													
2005	120.1	121.1	124.3	130.7	134.6	137.7	137.6	138.6	135.2	130.3	128.1	127.3	130.5
2006	123.5	124.3	127.3	132.9	137.8	141.5	140.6	141.9	138.9	135.1	132.9	133.3	134.2
2007	127.9	127.9	130.2	136.7	142.1	145.3	144.2	144.9	140.9	136.8	134.8	133.4	137.1
2008	127.1	127.7	130.0	136.2	140.9	143.3	141.9	143.4	139.1	134.0	131.2	130.4	135.4
2009	124.6	125.2	127.0	132.9	137.8	140.6	140.3	140.7	136.6	131.9	128.2	126.2	132.7
2010	120.9	121.7	123.2	130.0	134.8	137.3	137.1	137.4	133.9	129.3	127.1	125.8	129.9
2011	122.1	122.2	124.9	131.7	136.4	139.6	138.7	139.8	136.5	131.1	129.4	127.9	131.7
2012	124.0	125.4	128.3	133.7	138.8	141.9	142.5	142.6	138.2	133.3	131.8	130.8	134.3
2013	126.4	127.9	130.0	135.3	140.7	144.5	144.9	145.2	140.4	135.5	134.1	132.2	136.4
2014	128.8	130.1	132.1	136.8	142.7	145.8	144.9	145.5	141.6	136.7	135.1	134.0	137.8
2015	130.2	131.7	134.1	138.7	144.7	147.8	147.0	147.1	142.5	138.7	137.4	135.2	139.6
Other Services													
2005	55.3	55.5	56.0	56.4	56.3	57.3	57.0	56.6	56.2	56.1	56.1	56.3	56.3
2006	55.9	55.7	56.2	56.6	56.9	57.8	57.4	57.1	56.8	56.8	57.0	57.3	56.8
2007	56.6	56.4	57.1	57.6	58.0	59.1	58.3	57.9	57.6	57.8	57.8	57.9	57.7
2008	57.1	56.8	57.2	57.7	58.2	58.7	58.4	58.1	57.8	58.2	58.1	58.0	57.9
2009	57.2	57.3	57.4	57.7	57.9	58.5	58.3	57.4	57.1	57.1	56.9	57.0	57.5
2010	56.3	56.3	56.8	57.3	57.4	57.7	57.3	56.9	56.5	57.0	56.7	56.7	56.9
2011	56.2	56.1	56.4	56.5	56.7	57.1	57.1	57.1	56.9	57.0	56.8	57.0	56.7
2012	56.9	56.7	57.1	57.6	58.0	58.5	58.2	58.4	57.7	58.1	58.2	57.8	57.8
2013	57.2	57.2	57.3	57.6	58.2	58.6	58.9	59.1	58.3	58.6	58.5	58.6	58.2
2014	58.2	58.2	58.6	58.8	59.5	60.0	59.8	59.7	59.1	59.1	59.2	58.9	59.1
2015	58.6	58.5	58.9	59.3	59.7	60.4	60.4	60.3	60.0	61.3	61.3	62.2	60.1
Government													
2005	242.4	248.0	249.4	250.2	252.5	248.5	224.2	224.4	245.5	251.8	253.1	252.4	245.2
2006	243.8	250.7	251.3	251.8	253.7	251.6	225.7	225.6	247.8	253.5	254.9	254.4	247.1
2007	247.6	253.7	253.6	254.0	256.5	253.5	228.6	228.5	250.3	256.9	258.1	257.1	249.9
2008	249.9	255.9	257.0	257.2	260.5	256.1	231.3	231.0	254.7	260.3	261.3	260.1	252.9
2009	253.1	258.7	259.7	261.1	263.1	257.8	234.3	234.2	254.4	260.7	261.4	259.2	254.8
2010	250.3	255.9	258.3	258.4	263.4	257.7	232.8	232.0	251.3	258.1	260.4	258.7	253.1
2011	249.6	255.5	256.5	257.9	259.3	255.3	235.9	236.2	254.0	257.9	258.8	258.3	252.9
2012	251.8	256.2	256.8	258.4	259.9	254.4	234.6	239.4	254.4	258.3	259.8	259.2	253.6
2013	250.2	256.5	257.0	257.6	260.7	256.3	238.7	241.9	256.9	259.4	260.9	260.3	254.7
2014	252.5	257.6	258.3	259.0	260.5	254.4	236.0	239.0	258.6	261.2	262.7	261.3	255.1
2015	254.7	259.5	259.3	259.8	261.2	252.3	234.6	236.4	255.6	262.2	264.0	260.2	255.0

2. Average Weekly Hours by Selected Industry: Iowa, 2011–2015

(Not seasonsally adjusted)

Industry and year	January	February	March	April	May	June	July	August	September	October	November	December	Annual average
Total Private													
2011	33.8	33.2	33.5	33.8	34.1	34.0	33.9	34.0	34.1	34.6	34.2	34.2	34.0
2012	34.2	33.7	33.9	34.6	34.5	34.5	34.7	34.1	34.8	34.2	34.2	34.5	34.3
2013	33.7	33.9	33.8	34.0	34.4	35.1	34.5	34.7	35.1	34.7	34.7	35.0	34.5
2014	34.2	35.1	35.0	35.0	34.9	35.7	35.2	35.3	35.1	35.2	35.4	34.8	35.1
2015	34.2	34.8	34.7	34.7	34.6	34.8	34.9	35.3	34.5	34.7	34.7	34.3	34.7
Goods-Producing													
2011	39.8	38.6	39.3	39.5	40.3	40.1	40.0	40.7	40.4	41.0	40.4	40.5	40.1
2012	40.2	39.8	39.9	40.6	41.2	40.6	40.3	40.0	40.5	40.3	40.0	39.8	40.3
2013	38.9	38.8	39.4	39.7	40.7	41.1	41.0	41.2	41.4	41.6	41.2	41.1	40.5
2014	40.0	40.6	40.7	41.2	41.5	42.5	42.0	42.0	41.4	42.0	41.8	41.3	41.4
2015	40.3	40.5	40.6	41.1	40.9	41.1	41.1	41.8	40.0	41.7	41.3	41.3	41.0
Construction													
2011	39.0	37.9	38.8	39.5	41.2	41.7	40.7	41.9	41.3	41.3	39.5	38.8	40.3
2012	38.4	38.2	38.9	39.3	42.3	40.6	40.9	41.1	40.2	40.8	39.0	38.1	39.9
2013	36.5	36.9	38.0	38.2	42.0	41.2	42.7	42.6	42.9	43.6	42.0	40.6	40.9
2014	38.7	38.4	39.8	42.6	42.0	43.6	43.3	43.3	41.3	43.8	41.9	40.4	41.8
2015	38.6	38.5	38.9	40.4	40.6	41.2	41.9	42.9	38.9	42.0	41.7	41.7	40.7
Manufacturing													
2011	40.4	39.9	40.5	40.4	40.6	40.0	40.4	40.8	40.8	41.6	41.4	41.7	40.7
2012	41.4	41.0	40.8	41.6	41.2	41.1	40.5	40.0	41.1	40.4	40.6	40.6	40.9
2013	40.0	39.6	40.0	40.3	40.1	41.0	40.2	40.5	40.7	40.8	40.9	41.3	40.5
2014	40.5	41.4	41.0	40.7	41.3	42.0	41.5	41.5	41.6	41.3	41.9	41.9	41.4
2015	41.1	41.4	41.4	41.6	41.2	41.2	40.9	41.4	40.7	41.7	41.2	41.2	41.3
Trade, Transportation, and Utilities													
2011	32.3	31.9	31.8	32.6	32.9	32.7	32.7	33.0	32.9	33.0	33.0	32.7	32.6
2012	32.5	32.3	32.9	33.4	33.5	33.3	33.5	33.1	33.5	32.8	33.0	32.8	33.1
2013	32.3	32.7	32.4	32.5	33.1	33.4	32.9	33.2	33.7	33.5	33.2	33.2	33.0
2014	32.8	33.2	32.8	33.1	33.2	33.7	33.2	33.1	33.1	32.7	32.8	32.0	33.0
2015	31.7	32.2	31.8	31.9	32.1	32.5	32.5	32.8	33.0	32.5	32.1	31.8	32.2
Financial Activities													
2011	38.4	37.6	37.6	37.4	38.3	37.7	37.8	37.6	37.9	38.6	38.1	37.9	37.9
2012	38.7	38.2	38.1	39.0	38.4	38.1	38.5	37.7	38.8	38.0	38.0	38.8	38.4
2013	37.7	38.0	37.8	37.9	37.9	38.9	38.1	38.4	39.1	38.1	38.2	39.2	38.3
2014	38.4	39.1	38.8	38.3	38.2	39.2	38.5	38.7	38.7	38.7	39.6	38.8	38.7
2015	38.2	39.2	39.0	38.7	38.2	38.3	38.2	38.7	38.1	38.1	39.0	37.7	38.5
Professional and Business Services													
2011	33.3	32.8	33.7	34.3	34.7	34.7	34.2	33.8	34.3	34.9	34.5	34.0	34.1
2012	33.9	33.4	33.6	34.7	34.4	34.3	34.6	34.3	35.5	34.3	34.4	35.1	34.4
2013	33.3	33.7	33.3	33.9	34.1	35.7	33.9	34.5	34.9	34.5	34.6	35.5	34.3
2014	34.5	36.9	37.3	36.5	34.7	35.9	35.2	35.5	35.3	36.2	36.7	36.0	35.9
2015	35.0	36.2	36.3	36.0	35.9	35.9	36.4	36.8	35.2	35.7	35.9	35.6	35.9
Education and Health Services													
2011	31.2	30.8	30.9	31.2	31.3	31.3	31.1	31.1	31.1	31.4	31.2	31.4	31.2
2012	31.6	31.1	31.0	31.8	31.4	31.4	32.0	31.3	32.2	31.3	31.5	32.4	31.6
2013	32.0	31.8	31.7	31.7	31.5	32.4	31.5	31.4	32.1	31.3	31.7	31.7	31.7
2014	31.3	31.4	31.5	31.6	31.5	32.4	31.9	32.0	32.1	32.0	32.2	31.8	31.8
2015	31.8	31.9	31.7	31.6	31.6	31.9	32.3	32.5	32.1	31.9	32.3	31.7	31.9
Leisure and Hospitality													
2011	24.4	24.4	23.9	23.9	23.7	24.0	23.7	24.1	24.0	24.4	23.8	23.6	24.0
2012	23.7	23.6	23.8	23.8	23.6	24.6	24.8	24.6	24.8	24.2	24.3	24.2	24.2
2013	23.9	24.3	24.5	24.2	24.8	25.5	25.0	24.8	24.6	24.2	24.5	24.6	24.6
2014	23.7	24.8	24.9	24.6	25.1	25.7	25.6	25.4	24.8	25.0	24.7	24.7	24.9
2015	23.5	24.7	24.8	24.2	24.4	24.8	25.2	25.7	24.5	24.3	24.1	23.8	24.5
Other Services													
2011	28.5	28.3	29.1	29.1	29.4	30.1	29.6	29.0	29.0	29.7	28.3	28.3	29.0
2012	28.7	28.4	28.4	29.8	28.9	29.9	31.8	29.9	30.7	29.1	29.3	29.6	29.5
2013	29.6	29.1	28.3	28.7	28.6	29.4	29.8	29.9	29.7	28.9	27.6	29.2	29.1
2014	28.2	28.5	28.7	28.6	28.6	29.9	29.4	29.4	29.6	29.4	30.0	29.9	29.2
2015	30.0	30.5	29.4	28.7	28.7	29.2	29.6	29.4	28.5	28.3	26.9	26.9	28.8

3. Average Hourly Earnings by Selected Industry: Iowa, 2011–2015

(Dollars, not seasonally adjusted)

Industry and year	January	February	March	April	May	June	July	August	September	October	November	December	Annual average
Total Private													
2011	20.23	20.37	20.12	20.19	20.14	19.97	20.17	20.08	20.29	20.42	20.25	20.45	20.22
2012	20.64	20.60	20.54	20.83	20.69	20.54	20.87	20.70	21.11	21.10	21.22	21.52	20.87
2013	21.52	21.46	21.38	21.58	21.38	21.40	21.38	21.41	21.68	21.63	21.78	22.15	21.56
2014	21.92	21.86	21.87	21.68	21.71	21.81	21.75	21.79	21.92	22.02	22.09	22.11	21.88
2015	22.10	22.28	22.35	22.48	22.57	22.30	22.37	23.01	22.98	22.94	22.51	22.68	22.55
Goods-Producing													
2011	20.38	20.53	20.16	20.20	20.30	20.04	20.07	20.04	20.40	20.57	20.45	20.90	20.34
2012	21.02	20.85	20.94	21.39	21.58	21.22	21.58	21.62	22.03	21.73	21.84	22.51	21.54
2013	21.83	22.11	22.09	22.20	22.05	22.18	22.20	22.10	22.49	22.29	22.51	23.42	22.30
2014	22.88	22.96	23.00	23.02	22.78	23.03	22.92	23.29	23.35	23.52	23.73	24.15	23.22
2015	23.87	24.18	24.11	24.14	24.16	24.01	24.27	24.57	24.44	23.48	22.90	23.20	23.94
Construction													
2011	22.57	22.71	22.64	22.49	22.49	22.18	22.05	22.08	22.75	22.31	22.12	22.68	22.40
2012	22.94	22.95	23.03	22.96	24.10	22.54	22.23	22.86	23.31	23.13	22.91	23.80	23.06
2013	23.94	24.57	24.84	24.45	23.78	23.45	23.56	23.45	23.54	24.05	24.35	24.94	24.02
2014	25.03	24.97	24.76	24.86	24.43	24.42	24.35	24.59	24.91	25.27	25.54	26.05	24.92
2015	25.89	25.80	26.00	25.29	25.19	25.54	25.35	25.84	26.17	26.90	27.54	28.53	26.20
Manufacturing													
2011	20.28	20.40	19.87	19.83	19.83	19.51	19.59	19.50	19.70	20.11	20.00	20.43	19.92
2012	20.53	20.28	20.33	20.92	20.64	20.83	21.43	21.22	21.61	21.22	21.47	22.08	21.05
2013	21.06	21.22	21.08	21.33	21.29	21.62	21.48	21.39	21.93	21.42	21.63	22.78	21.53
2014	22.09	22.22	22.34	22.27	22.08	22.42	22.27	22.71	22.69	22.71	22.93	23.39	22.51
2015	23.17	23.61	23.47	23.64	23.70	23.33	23.79	23.98	23.69	24.90	24.15	23.72	23.76
Trade, Transportation, and Utilities													
2011	17.33	17.57	17.49	17.55	17.47	17.38	17.54	17.39	17.61	17.64	17.52	17.39	17.49
2012	17.72	17.99	17.75	18.07	17.85	17.90	17.99	17.74	17.98	17.97	17.86	17.75	17.88
2013	17.90	18.19	18.09	18.27	17.85	17.95	17.84	18.06	18.54	18.59	18.74	18.80	18.24
2014	18.81	18.76	18.88	18.81	18.79	18.79	18.94	19.23	19.36	19.15	19.45	19.15	19.01
2015	19.22	19.55	19.56	20.11	20.23	19.53	19.80	20.68	20.62	21.14	20.57	20.95	20.17
Financial Activities													
2011	25.52	25.96	25.61	25.87	26.03	25.96	25.90	25.95	25.90	26.05	25.99	26.05	25.90
2012	25.92	26.11	26.13	26.56	26.48	26.88	27.36	26.74	27.61	27.88	28.76	28.86	27.11
2013	29.30	28.57	28.18	28.34	29.46	29.22	29.09	28.79	28.91	28.81	28.97	28.80	28.87
2014	28.52	28.72	28.82	28.56	28.45	28.22	28.08	27.65	27.72	28.16	27.51	27.40	28.15
2015	27.61	27.28	27.79	28.13	28.19	27.87	27.77	28.15	28.16	28.42	28.73	28.73	28.07
Professional and Business Services													
2011	22.16	22.20	21.74	21.26	21.41	20.81	21.26	21.02	21.00	21.39	20.83	21.06	21.33
2012	21.60	20.98	20.89	20.70	20.51	19.97	20.18	20.11	20.29	20.42	20.48	20.90	20.58
2013	21.83	21.61	21.84	21.97	21.61	21.84	22.26	22.53	22.73	22.76	22.95	23.65	22.32
2014	23.45	22.86	23.02	22.37	23.59	24.29	23.84	23.79	23.94	23.66	24.14	23.99	23.58
2015	23.88	24.33	24.14	23.61	24.18	24.07	24.27	24.63	24.71	24.82	23.19	23.16	24.09
Education and Health Services													
2011	20.43	20.62	20.51	20.97	20.65	20.75	21.28	21.03	21.32	21.38	21.19	21.42	20.96
2012	21.64	21.61	21.58	21.92	21.50	21.64	22.24	22.17	22.53	22.51	22.43	22.50	22.03
2013	22.40	22.03	21.90	22.33	21.35	21.18	21.26	21.40	21.11	21.14	21.21	21.32	21.55
2014	21.13	20.80	20.77	20.53	20.62	20.54	20.61	20.19	20.33	20.16	20.14	20.21	20.50
2015	20.20	20.40	20.68	20.69	20.74	20.92	20.55	20.68	20.88	21.09	20.97	21.19	20.75
Leisure and Hospitality													
2011	11.69	11.76	11.74	11.79	11.77	11.55	11.80	11.59	11.69	11.64	11.78	11.93	11.73
2012	11.87	12.00	11.92	12.00	11.96	11.62	11.71	11.77	11.96	12.30	12.35	12.64	12.00
2013	12.44	12.36	12.30	12.30	12.19	11.95	11.99	12.15	12.23	12.38	12.42	12.70	12.27
2014	12.53	12.65	12.45	12.50	12.37	12.25	12.09	12.13	12.37	12.37	12.38	12.71	12.39
2015	12.72	12.61	12.30	12.43	12.47	12.19	12.22	12.49	12.46	12.60	12.79	12.95	12.51
Other Services													
2011	17.43	17.38	17.19	17.45	17.57	17.92	18.25	19.04	19.05	19.14	19.31	18.76	18.21
2012	18.50	18.79	18.60	18.66	18.63	18.37	19.24	19.55	19.85	19.60	19.98	20.06	19.16
2013	19.49	19.54	19.16	19.22	18.97	19.07	18.66	18.64	19.42	18.97	18.65	19.06	19.07
2014	19.36	19.52	19.54	19.70	19.49	19.13	19.56	19.69	19.24	20.07	20.21	20.06	19.63
2015	20.57	21.11	21.09	21.14	21.37	20.48	20.5	20.61	20.56	20.61	20.07	19.97	20.68

4. Average Weekly Earnings by Selected Industry: Iowa, 2011–2015

(Dollars, not seasonally adjusted)

Industry and year	January	February	March	April	May	June	July	August	September	October	November	December	Annual average
Total Private													
2011	683.77	676.28	674.02	682.42	686.77	678.98	683.76	682.72	691.89	706.53	692.55	699.39	687.48
2012	705.89	694.22	696.31	720.72	713.81	708.63	724.19	705.87	734.63	721.62	725.72	742.44	715.84
2013	725.22	727.49	722.64	733.72	735.47	751.14	737.61	742.93	760.97	750.56	755.77	775.25	743.82
2014	749.66	767.29	765.45	758.80	757.68	778.62	765.60	769.19	769.39	775.10	781.99	769.43	767.99
2015	755.82	775.34	775.55	780.06	780.92	776.04	780.71	812.25	792.81	796.02	781.10	777.92	782.49
Goods-Producing													
2011	811.12	792.46	792.29	797.90	818.09	803.60	802.80	815.63	824.16	843.37	826.18	846.45	815.63
2012	845.00	829.83	835.51	868.43	889.10	861.53	869.67	864.80	892.22	875.72	873.60	895.90	868.06
2013	849.19	857.87	870.35	881.34	897.44	911.60	910.20	910.52	931.09	927.26	927.41	962.56	903.15
2014	915.20	932.18	936.10	948.42	945.37	978.78	962.64	978.18	966.69	987.84	991.91	997.40	961.31
2015	961.96	979.29	978.87	992.15	988.14	986.81	997.50	1,027.03	977.60	979.12	945.77	958.16	981.54
Construction													
2011	880.23	860.71	878.43	888.36	926.59	924.91	897.44	925.15	939.58	921.40	873.74	879.98	902.72
2012	880.90	876.69	895.87	902.33	1,019.43	915.12	909.21	939.55	937.06	943.70	893.49	906.78	920.09
2013	873.81	906.63	943.92	933.99	998.76	966.14	1,006.01	998.97	1,009.87	1,048.58	1,022.70	1,012.56	982.42
2014	968.66	958.85	985.45	1,059.04	1,026.06	1,064.71	1,054.36	1,064.75	1,028.78	1,106.83	1,070.13	1,052.42	1,041.66
2015	999.35	993.30	1,011.40	1,021.72	1,022.71	1,052.25	1,062.17	1,108.54	1,018.01	1,129.80	1,148.42	1,189.70	1,066.34
Manufacturing													
2011	819.31	813.96	804.74	801.13	805.10	780.40	791.44	795.60	803.76	836.58	828.00	851.93	810.74
2012	849.94	831.48	829.46	870.27	850.37	856.11	867.92	848.80	888.17	857.29	871.68	896.45	860.95
2013	842.40	840.31	843.20	859.60	853.73	886.42	863.50	866.30	892.55	873.94	884.67	940.81	871.97
2014	894.65	919.91	915.94	906.39	911.90	941.64	924.21	942.47	943.90	937.92	960.77	980.04	931.91
2015	952.29	977.45	971.66	983.42	976.44	961.20	973.01	992.77	964.18	1,038.33	994.98	977.26	981.29
Trade, Transportation, and Utilities													
2011	559.76	560.48	556.18	572.13	574.76	568.33	573.56	573.87	579.37	582.12	578.16	568.65	570.17
2012	575.90	581.08	583.98	603.54	597.98	596.07	602.67	587.19	602.33	589.42	589.38	582.20	591.83
2013	578.17	594.81	586.12	593.78	590.84	599.53	586.94	599.59	624.80	622.77	622.17	624.16	601.92
2014	616.97	622.83	619.26	622.61	623.83	633.22	628.81	636.51	640.82	626.21	637.96	612.80	627.33
2015	609.27	629.51	622.01	641.51	649.38	634.73	643.50	678.30	680.46	687.05	660.30	666.21	649.47
Financial Activities													
2011	979.97	976.10	962.94	967.54	996.95	978.69	979.02	975.72	981.61	1,005.53	990.22	987.30	981.61
2012	1,003.10	997.40	995.55	1,035.84	1,016.83	1,024.13	1,053.36	1,008.10	1,071.27	1,059.44	1,092.88	1,119.77	1,041.02
2013	1,104.61	1,085.66	1,065.20	1,074.09	1,116.53	1,136.66	1,108.33	1,105.54	1,130.38	1,097.66	1,106.65	1,128.96	1,105.72
2014	1,095.17	1,122.95	1,118.22	1,093.85	1,086.79	1,106.22	1,081.08	1,070.06	1,072.76	1,089.79	1,089.40	1,063.12	1,089.41
2015	1,054.70	1,069.38	1,083.81	1,088.63	1,076.86	1,067.42	1,060.81	1,089.41	1,072.90	1,082.80	1,120.47	1,083.12	1,080.70
Professional and Business Services													
2011	737.93	728.16	732.64	729.22	742.93	722.11	727.09	710.48	720.30	746.51	718.64	716.04	727.35
2012	732.24	700.73	701.90	718.29	705.54	684.97	698.23	689.77	720.30	700.41	704.51	733.59	707.95
2013	726.94	728.26	727.27	744.78	736.90	779.69	754.61	777.29	793.28	785.22	794.07	839.58	765.58
2014	809.03	843.53	858.65	816.51	818.57	872.01	839.17	844.55	845.08	856.49	885.94	863.64	846.52
2015	835.80	880.75	876.28	849.96	868.06	864.11	883.43	906.38	869.79	886.07	832.52	824.50	864.83
Education and Health Services													
2011	637.42	635.10	633.76	654.26	646.35	649.48	661.81	654.03	663.05	671.33	661.13	672.59	653.95
2012	683.82	672.07	668.98	697.06	675.10	679.50	711.68	693.92	725.47	704.56	706.55	729.00	696.15
2013	716.80	700.55	694.23	707.86	672.53	686.23	669.69	671.96	677.63	661.68	672.36	675.84	683.14
2014	661.37	653.12	654.26	648.75	649.53	665.50	657.46	646.08	652.59	645.12	648.51	642.68	651.90
2015	642.36	650.76	655.56	653.80	655.38	667.35	663.77	672.10	670.25	672.77	677.33	671.72	661.93
Leisure and Hospitality													
2011	285.24	286.94	280.59	281.78	278.95	277.20	279.66	279.32	280.56	284.02	280.36	281.55	281.52
2012	281.32	283.20	283.70	285.60	282.26	285.85	290.41	289.54	296.61	297.66	300.11	305.89	290.40
2013	297.32	300.35	301.35	297.66	302.31	304.73	299.75	301.32	300.86	299.60	304.29	312.42	301.84
2014	296.96	313.72	310.01	307.50	310.49	314.83	309.50	308.10	306.78	309.25	305.79	313.94	308.51
2015	298.92	311.47	305.04	300.81	304.27	302.31	307.94	320.99	305.27	306.18	308.24	308.21	306.50
Other Services													
2011	496.76	491.85	500.23	507.80	516.56	539.39	540.20	552.16	552.45	568.46	546.47	530.91	528.09
2012	530.95	533.64	528.24	556.07	538.41	549.26	611.83	584.55	609.40	570.36	585.41	593.78	565.22
2013	576.90	568.61	542.23	551.61	542.54	560.66	556.07	557.34	576.77	548.23	514.74	556.55	554.94
2014	545.95	556.32	560.80	563.42	557.41	571.99	575.06	578.89	569.50	590.06	606.30	599.79	573.20
2015	617.10	643.86	620.05	606.72	613.32	598.02	606.80	605.93	585.96	583.26	539.88	537.19	595.58

KANSAS
At a Glance

Population:
  2005 estimate: 2,745,299
  2010 census: 2,853,118
  2015 estimate: 2,911,641

Percent change in population:
  2005–2015: 6.1%
  2010–2015: 2.1%

Percent change in total nonfarm employment:
  2005–2015: 5.0%

Industry with the largest growth in employment, 2005–2015 (thousands):
  Professional and business services, 42.8

Industry with the largest decline or smallest growth in employment, 2005–2015 (thousands):
  Manufacturing, –18.0

Civilian labor force:
  2005: 1,465,640
  2010: 1,500,764
  2015: 1,499,009

Unemployment rate and rank among states (highest to lowest):
  2005: 5.0%, 22nd
  2010: 7.1%, 41st
  2015: 4.2%, 37th

Over-the-year change in unemployment rates:
  2012–2013: –0.4%
  2013–2014: –0.7%
  2014–2015: –0.4%

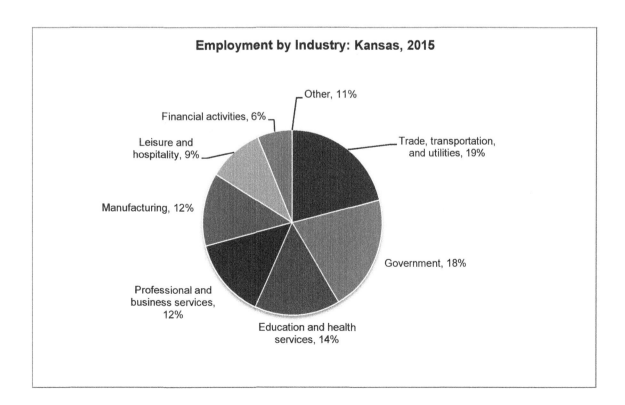

Employment by Industry: Kansas, 2015

Other, 11%
Financial activities, 6%
Leisure and hospitality, 9%
Trade, transportation, and utilities, 19%
Manufacturing, 12%
Government, 18%
Professional and business services, 12%
Education and health services, 14%

1. Employment by Industry: Kansas, 2005–2015

(Numbers in thousands, not seasonally adjusted)

Industry and year	January	February	March	April	May	June	July	August	September	October	November	December	Annual average
Total Nonfarm													
2005	1,303.0	1,315.8	1,329.8	1,338.7	1,344.9	1,350.0	1,312.4	1,312.7	1,341.9	1,345.4	1,353.0	1,356.6	1,333.7
2006	1,318.7	1,333.9	1,346.6	1,352.3	1,362.1	1,370.4	1,331.1	1,336.7	1,370.8	1,372.7	1,375.3	1,384.9	1,354.6
2007	1,342.2	1,352.8	1,373.9	1,378.7	1,388.1	1,398.6	1,370.5	1,369.2	1,392.4	1,397.9	1,405.8	1,403.2	1,381.1
2008	1,367.2	1,378.3	1,390.5	1,400.7	1,407.2	1,406.3	1,376.6	1,371.5	1,396.8	1,405.0	1,403.8	1,400.4	1,392.0
2009	1,359.6	1,357.1	1,357.4	1,357.7	1,360.8	1,350.9	1,319.8	1,314.6	1,334.7	1,340.3	1,343.3	1,339.3	1,344.6
2010	1,302.0	1,305.4	1,316.0	1,334.8	1,346.9	1,342.7	1,318.6	1,319.1	1,332.9	1,347.8	1,345.7	1,345.6	1,329.8
2011	1,315.6	1,316.9	1,326.7	1,347.4	1,353.9	1,341.0	1,325.0	1,328.4	1,348.1	1,357.5	1,359.7	1,354.9	1,339.6
2012	1,331.6	1,339.6	1,351.2	1,360.0	1,370.6	1,366.1	1,337.4	1,344.1	1,360.9	1,374.8	1,377.6	1,375.3	1,357.4
2013	1,341.8	1,353.0	1,358.9	1,375.4	1,380.7	1,374.6	1,354.0	1,359.8	1,382.6	1,391.4	1,397.4	1,395.3	1,372.1
2014	1,359.1	1,370.4	1,381.4	1,395.0	1,403.7	1,396.5	1,375.5	1,380.0	1,397.5	1,409.3	1,412.9	1,412.4	1,391.1
2015	1,374.8	1,387.8	1,393.1	1,403.9	1,411.4	1,406.3	1,385.2	1,387.3	1,404.9	1,416.8	1,415.6	1,413.2	1,400.0
Total Private													
2005	1,057.6	1,061.6	1,071.8	1,080.0	1,085.3	1,093.1	1,090.3	1,090.2	1,090.3	1,086.9	1,092.6	1,095.4	1,082.9
2006	1,070.6	1,075.7	1,085.4	1,092.5	1,098.6	1,109.9	1,105.4	1,109.2	1,113.3	1,110.0	1,111.2	1,119.7	1,100.1
2007	1,091.0	1,092.7	1,110.5	1,116.0	1,122.9	1,132.5	1,133.9	1,134.2	1,132.6	1,132.9	1,138.9	1,136.4	1,122.9
2008	1,112.9	1,115.6	1,123.9	1,134.6	1,137.0	1,145.7	1,141.7	1,136.1	1,136.1	1,137.0	1,133.9	1,129.9	1,132.0
2009	1,097.4	1,090.9	1,089.5	1,088.6	1,087.1	1,088.9	1,084.4	1,080.7	1,074.6	1,072.8	1,074.3	1,070.4	1,083.3
2010	1,042.1	1,041.9	1,048.4	1,065.9	1,070.8	1,076.0	1,076.8	1,075.8	1,070.0	1,081.2	1,081.4	1,080.7	1,067.6
2011	1,054.0	1,053.5	1,061.5	1,079.4	1,084.9	1,084.7	1,086.9	1,088.4	1,085.7	1,091.7	1,093.9	1,092.2	1,079.7
2012	1,073.9	1,076.6	1,086.7	1,095.4	1,103.0	1,110.9	1,102.8	1,104.2	1,101.9	1,108.9	1,111.3	1,111.2	1,098.9
2013	1,085.8	1,089.6	1,095.3	1,109.5	1,116.7	1,123.6	1,121.8	1,124.0	1,121.9	1,126.9	1,132.0	1,131.8	1,114.9
2014	1,104.7	1,108.2	1,118.0	1,131.4	1,140.1	1,144.4	1,141.4	1,143.6	1,138.0	1,144.5	1,147.9	1,149.0	1,134.3
2015	1,120.1	1,125.2	1,129.3	1,139.5	1,147.3	1,153.3	1,152.0	1,151.7	1,146.3	1,153.0	1,151.0	1,150.7	1,143.3
Goods-Producing													
2005	239.6	240.9	245.1	247.7	250.2	254.0	254.8	254.4	252.3	251.7	251.7	250.6	249.4
2006	246.1	247.8	250.1	251.7	253.7	258.8	259.4	259.5	258.1	256.7	255.2	255.9	254.4
2007	250.7	248.9	254.9	255.4	257.3	262.0	264.0	264.2	263.3	262.3	263.1	260.8	258.9
2008	255.4	255.0	258.3	260.4	259.7	265.3	265.9	259.7	262.6	260.5	257.5	254.4	259.6
2009	243.7	240.0	237.7	234.6	231.0	231.6	230.4	229.1	225.8	224.6	222.5	218.6	230.8
2010	212.1	211.5	213.6	219.3	220.6	223.7	225.6	225.4	224.2	224.6	222.6	220.6	220.3
2011	212.2	211.5	215.5	219.5	221.0	223.2	224.9	225.1	224.3	225.8	224.5	223.4	220.9
2012	219.8	219.4	223.6	223.7	226.3	228.4	229.0	228.6	228.2	228.0	226.7	224.5	225.5
2013	219.9	220.6	222.7	226.5	228.2	230.5	230.8	231.1	230.9	231.5	231.9	230.7	227.9
2014	225.4	227.5	230.0	232.4	234.1	237.0	235.6	235.9	234.1	234.5	233.4	232.6	232.7
2015	224.7	227.8	229.3	229.2	232.3	233.8	233.6	232.1	232.0	233.5	232.1	231.2	231.0
Service-Providing													
2005	1,063.4	1,074.9	1,084.7	1,091.0	1,094.7	1,096.0	1,057.6	1,058.3	1,089.6	1,093.7	1,101.3	1,106.0	1,084.3
2006	1,072.6	1,086.1	1,096.5	1,100.6	1,108.4	1,111.6	1,071.7	1,077.2	1,112.7	1,116.0	1,120.1	1,129.0	1,100.2
2007	1,091.5	1,103.9	1,119.0	1,123.3	1,130.8	1,136.6	1,106.5	1,105.0	1,129.1	1,135.6	1,142.7	1,142.4	1,122.2
2008	1,111.8	1,123.3	1,132.2	1,140.3	1,147.5	1,141.0	1,110.7	1,111.8	1,134.2	1,144.5	1,146.3	1,146.0	1,132.5
2009	1,115.9	1,117.1	1,119.7	1,123.1	1,129.8	1,119.3	1,089.4	1,085.5	1,108.9	1,115.7	1,120.8	1,120.7	1,113.8
2010	1,089.9	1,093.9	1,102.4	1,115.5	1,126.3	1,119.0	1,093.0	1,093.7	1,108.7	1,123.2	1,123.1	1,125.0	1,109.5
2011	1,103.4	1,105.4	1,111.2	1,127.9	1,132.9	1,117.8	1,100.1	1,103.3	1,123.8	1,131.7	1,135.2	1,131.5	1,118.7
2012	1,111.8	1,120.2	1,127.6	1,136.3	1,144.3	1,137.7	1,108.4	1,115.5	1,132.7	1,146.8	1,150.9	1,150.8	1,131.9
2013	1,121.9	1,132.4	1,136.2	1,148.9	1,152.5	1,144.1	1,123.2	1,128.7	1,151.7	1,159.9	1,165.5	1,164.6	1,144.1
2014	1,133.7	1,142.9	1,151.4	1,162.6	1,169.6	1,159.5	1,139.9	1,144.1	1,163.4	1,174.8	1,179.5	1,179.8	1,158.4
2015	1,150.1	1,160.0	1,163.8	1,174.7	1,179.1	1,172.5	1,151.6	1,155.2	1,172.9	1,183.3	1,183.5	1,182.0	1,169.1
Mining and Logging													
2005	7.2	7.3	7.3	7.4	7.5	7.6	7.6	7.7	7.7	7.9	7.9	8.0	7.6
2006	8.0	8.2	8.4	8.3	8.5	8.7	8.8	8.9	8.9	8.9	9.0	9.1	8.6
2007	8.9	8.9	9.0	9.2	9.1	9.1	9.3	9.3	9.2	9.3	9.3	9.4	9.2
2008	9.4	9.4	9.5	9.6	9.6	9.7	10.0	10.2	10.1	10.0	9.9	9.8	9.8
2009	8.7	8.3	8.1	7.8	7.7	7.8	8.0	8.0	8.0	8.1	8.0	8.1	8.1
2010	7.8	7.9	8.0	8.3	8.3	8.4	8.5	8.5	8.5	8.8	8.6	8.6	8.4
2011	8.4	8.3	8.5	8.8	8.8	9.0	9.5	9.5	9.4	9.5	9.5	9.6	9.1
2012	9.5	9.5	9.6	9.6	9.8	10.0	10.3	10.3	10.1	10.5	10.5	10.5	10.0
2013	10.1	10.1	10.1	10.4	10.5	10.5	10.7	10.6	10.5	10.6	10.7	10.8	10.5
2014	10.4	10.3	10.4	10.6	10.7	10.6	10.6	10.6	10.5	10.5	10.4	10.3	10.5
2015	9.9	9.3	8.9	8.7	8.6	8.5	8.5	8.4	8.1	8.3	8.1	8.1	8.6

1. Employment by Industry: Kansas, 2005–2015—*Continued*

(Numbers in thousands, not seasonally adjusted)

Industry and year	January	February	March	April	May	June	July	August	September	October	November	December	Annual average
Construction													
2005	55.1	56.0	59.3	61.7	63.3	65.6	66.7	66.6	65.3	64.5	63.6	61.6	62.4
2006	59.2	59.8	61.7	63.2	64.4	67.2	67.7	67.4	66.3	64.6	63.9	63.6	64.1
2007	60.6	57.8	62.5	63.6	64.8	67.8	68.5	68.6	67.8	67.3	67.0	64.4	65.1
2008	59.9	59.0	61.8	64.5	66.3	68.2	68.5	67.9	66.3	65.1	63.8	62.2	64.5
2009	56.1	55.5	56.2	57.3	58.9	60.3	61.4	60.0	58.4	57.0	55.9	53.1	57.5
2010	47.2	46.7	49.2	53.8	54.7	56.9	58.6	58.4	57.4	57.6	55.5	53.2	54.1
2011	47.1	46.8	49.9	52.6	53.9	55.2	56.0	55.8	55.6	56.3	54.7	53.1	53.1
2012	50.5	50.4	53.9	54.8	56.2	57.8	57.6	57.2	56.7	56.2	54.9	53.5	55.0
2013	50.0	50.9	52.1	55.4	56.7	59.0	59.7	60.2	59.9	60.1	59.6	57.9	56.8
2014	55.3	54.6	57.4	59.8	61.6	62.6	63.2	62.3	61.1	61.4	59.7	58.7	59.8
2015	55.1	56.1	58.3	61.6	61.9	62.7	63.9	63.3	62.6	63.8	61.7	60.0	60.9
Manufacturing													
2005	177.3	177.6	178.5	178.6	179.4	180.8	180.5	180.1	179.3	179.3	180.2	181.0	179.4
2006	178.9	179.8	180.0	180.2	180.8	182.9	182.9	183.2	182.9	183.2	182.3	183.2	181.7
2007	181.2	182.2	183.4	182.6	183.4	185.1	186.2	186.3	186.3	185.7	186.8	187.0	184.7
2008	186.1	186.6	187.0	186.3	183.8	187.4	187.4	181.6	186.2	185.4	183.8	182.4	185.3
2009	178.9	176.2	173.4	169.5	164.4	163.5	161.0	161.1	159.4	159.5	158.6	157.4	165.2
2010	157.1	156.9	156.4	157.2	157.6	158.4	158.5	158.5	158.3	158.2	158.5	158.8	157.9
2011	156.7	156.4	157.1	158.1	158.3	159.0	159.4	159.8	159.3	160.0	160.3	160.7	158.8
2012	159.8	159.5	160.1	159.3	160.3	160.6	161.1	161.1	161.4	161.3	161.3	160.5	160.5
2013	159.8	159.6	160.5	160.7	161.0	161.0	160.4	160.3	160.5	160.8	161.6	162.0	160.7
2014	159.7	162.6	162.2	162.0	161.8	163.8	161.8	163.0	162.5	162.6	163.3	163.6	162.4
2015	159.7	162.4	162.1	158.9	161.8	162.6	161.2	160.4	161.3	161.4	162.3	163.1	161.4
Trade, Transportation, and Utilities													
2005	258.2	257.1	258.1	259.3	260.6	261.3	260.0	260.3	259.9	260.0	264.4	267.0	260.5
2006	256.9	255.7	257.3	257.6	258.7	259.9	258.3	259.7	260.4	260.1	263.7	267.4	259.6
2007	258.4	257.2	261.0	260.7	262.3	263.4	262.9	263.0	262.4	263.6	268.0	269.2	262.7
2008	260.9	259.5	260.4	260.9	261.9	263.0	263.6	262.5	261.0	262.5	265.2	266.1	262.3
2009	257.4	255.1	254.8	253.8	254.1	254.8	253.3	252.3	251.2	251.9	255.0	255.8	254.1
2010	247.3	245.8	246.9	249.8	251.3	252.5	252.1	251.8	250.3	253.6	256.9	258.3	251.4
2011	250.2	248.9	248.2	253.0	254.5	254.0	253.9	253.9	253.1	255.2	259.3	260.2	253.7
2012	252.9	251.2	252.3	253.8	255.5	257.5	254.4	254.6	254.1	256.8	260.7	261.6	255.5
2013	253.8	252.7	253.1	254.5	256.2	257.5	257.2	258.3	257.4	259.7	264.4	266.1	257.6
2014	257.0	255.2	257.9	259.8	261.4	262.2	262.1	262.8	261.2	264.0	268.3	270.6	261.9
2015	261.8	259.7	260.5	262.6	265.1	266.9	266.3	266.6	265.5	268.3	270.1	272.1	265.5
Wholesale Trade													
2005	57.7	57.8	58.1	58.9	59.1	60.4	60.0	59.6	59.3	58.4	58.5	58.8	58.9
2006	58.1	58.3	58.5	57.5	57.9	59.3	59.2	58.9	58.8	58.4	58.3	58.9	58.5
2007	58.4	58.4	59.1	58.8	59.0	60.3	60.4	59.7	59.4	60.1	60.1	60.0	59.5
2008	60.2	60.0	59.9	60.2	60.5	61.3	61.9	60.9	60.3	60.5	60.4	60.1	60.5
2009	60.2	59.9	59.9	58.4	58.2	58.9	59.0	58.0	57.6	57.5	57.3	56.9	58.5
2010	56.1	56.0	56.2	57.7	57.7	58.5	58.4	57.7	57.1	57.4	56.9	56.8	57.2
2011	56.5	56.5	56.8	57.3	57.7	58.2	58.4	57.9	57.5	57.6	57.5	57.6	57.5
2012	56.9	56.9	57.2	57.1	57.5	58.8	57.8	57.5	56.9	57.2	57.0	57.1	57.3
2013	56.9	56.8	56.8	57.1	57.4	58.2	59.5	59.0	58.4	58.9	58.9	59.0	58.1
2014	58.1	57.8	58.9	59.0	59.4	60.1	60.5	59.9	59.4	59.8	59.7	59.8	59.4
2015	59.5	59.4	59.6	59.6	60.2	61.2	61.2	60.6	60.1	60.7	60.4	60.1	60.2
Retail Trade													
2005	148.1	146.8	147.3	147.9	148.9	148.8	147.7	147.3	147.1	148.2	152.1	153.7	148.7
2006	146.3	145.0	146.3	147.0	147.8	147.7	146.8	147.2	147.6	147.7	151.2	153.3	147.8
2007	146.3	145.3	147.8	147.3	148.5	148.1	148.2	148.1	147.4	148.3	152.3	153.3	148.4
2008	146.7	145.3	146.5	146.5	147.2	147.5	147.5	147.0	146.0	145.9	148.6	149.4	147.0
2009	142.2	140.5	140.7	141.6	142.4	142.4	141.5	141.3	141.1	141.7	144.5	145.4	142.1
2010	139.4	138.0	138.7	139.9	141.1	141.2	140.7	140.4	139.2	141.2	144.5	145.5	140.8
2011	139.2	138.0	139.0	141.2	142.0	141.9	141.7	141.4	140.7	142.2	146.1	146.5	141.7
2012	141.3	139.7	140.6	141.5	142.5	143.0	142.5	142.1	141.9	143.5	147.4	147.9	142.8
2013	141.3	140.4	141.0	142.1	143.0	143.8	143.8	144.4	144.1	145.3	149.3	150.6	144.1
2014	143.8	142.6	143.7	145.3	146.1	146.6	146.5	146.6	145.4	147.2	151.1	152.3	146.4
2015	145.7	144.5	145.2	147.0	148.6	149.9	149.4	149.1	148.1	150.0	151.0	151.6	148.3

1. Employment by Industry: Kansas, 2005–2015—*Continued*

(Numbers in thousands, not seasonally adjusted)

Industry and year	January	February	March	April	May	June	July	August	September	October	November	December	Annual average
Transportation and Utilities													
2005	52.4	52.5	52.7	52.5	52.6	52.1	52.3	53.4	53.5	53.4	53.8	54.5	53.0
2006	52.5	52.4	52.5	53.1	53.0	52.9	52.3	53.6	54.0	54.0	54.2	55.2	53.3
2007	53.7	53.5	54.1	54.6	54.8	55.0	54.3	55.2	55.6	55.2	55.6	55.9	54.8
2008	54.0	54.2	54.0	54.2	54.2	54.2	54.2	54.6	54.7	56.1	56.2	56.6	54.8
2009	55.0	54.7	54.2	53.8	53.5	53.5	52.8	53.0	52.5	52.7	53.2	53.5	53.5
2010	51.8	51.8	52.0	52.2	52.5	52.8	53.0	53.7	54.0	55.0	55.5	56.0	53.4
2011	54.5	54.4	52.4	54.5	54.8	53.9	53.8	54.6	54.9	55.4	55.7	56.1	54.6
2012	54.7	54.6	54.5	55.2	55.5	55.7	54.1	55.0	55.3	56.1	56.3	56.6	55.3
2013	55.6	55.5	55.3	55.3	55.8	55.5	53.9	54.9	54.9	55.5	56.2	56.5	55.4
2014	55.1	54.8	55.3	55.5	55.9	55.5	55.1	56.3	56.4	57.0	57.5	58.5	56.1
2015	56.6	55.8	55.7	56.0	56.3	55.8	55.7	56.9	57.3	57.6	58.7	60.4	56.9
Information													
2005	39.5	39.6	39.3	39.5	39.4	39.2	39.1	38.5	38.2	37.2	37.6	37.8	38.7
2006	37.5	37.4	37.8	38.9	38.8	39.2	39.1	38.9	38.7	39.1	39.2	39.4	38.7
2007	39.7	39.6	39.7	39.6	39.6	39.6	39.5	39.1	38.5	38.1	38.1	38.0	39.1
2008	37.8	37.7	37.6	37.5	37.0	37.0	36.9	36.3	35.5	35.6	35.0	34.8	36.6
2009	34.1	33.8	33.7	33.9	33.4	32.9	32.5	31.8	30.9	29.0	28.8	28.8	32.0
2010	28.2	27.9	27.7	27.7	27.4	27.1	26.7	26.3	25.8	25.6	25.5	25.5	26.8
2011	25.2	25.1	25.0	24.6	23.9	23.8	23.6	23.3	22.9	22.9	22.9	22.9	23.8
2012	23.3	23.0	23.1	23.0	23.0	23.0	22.8	22.6	22.4	22.5	22.5	22.5	22.8
2013	22.1	22.1	22.0	22.1	22.1	22.2	22.5	22.5	22.2	22.2	22.3	22.5	22.2
2014	22.4	22.2	22.1	22.1	22.1	22.1	22.1	21.9	21.5	21.6	21.6	21.6	21.9
2015	21.2	21.2	21.2	21.1	21.0	21.1	21.1	21.0	20.6	20.6	20.5	20.3	20.9
Financial Activities													
2005	69.3	69.4	69.6	70.0	70.1	70.7	71.1	71.0	70.8	71.0	71.1	71.8	70.5
2006	70.9	70.8	71.0	71.6	72.1	72.5	73.3	73.2	73.0	72.9	73.3	74.2	72.4
2007	73.2	73.3	73.9	73.7	74.1	74.7	75.1	74.9	74.5	74.1	74.1	74.5	74.2
2008	73.0	73.2	73.0	73.4	73.5	73.9	73.8	73.7	73.0	73.2	73.0	73.4	73.3
2009	72.0	72.0	71.9	71.4	71.5	72.0	72.7	72.8	71.9	72.3	72.5	72.7	72.1
2010	71.5	71.5	71.3	71.7	72.1	72.2	72.3	72.2	71.4	72.3	72.3	72.6	72.0
2011	71.5	71.3	71.5	72.2	73.3	73.5	74.0	74.1	73.6	74.2	74.2	74.6	73.2
2012	74.1	74.7	75.1	75.5	75.5	76.2	76.2	76.1	75.5	75.8	76.1	76.4	75.6
2013	75.6	75.8	75.5	76.4	77.0	77.9	78.0	77.7	77.2	77.2	77.4	77.5	76.9
2014	76.5	76.5	76.8	77.0	77.4	78.0	78.2	78.5	78.0	78.5	78.7	79.1	77.8
2015	78.4	78.7	79.0	79.2	79.4	79.9	80.5	80.3	79.5	78.8	79.5	79.2	79.4
Professional and Business Services													
2005	130.1	131.1	132.9	134.3	133.9	135.7	136.7	138.0	138.2	138.8	139.8	140.8	135.9
2006	136.7	138.8	140.8	141.4	140.7	142.8	141.7	142.4	144.1	144.4	144.5	146.1	142.0
2007	142.3	143.8	145.7	148.0	148.6	149.8	151.5	152.7	153.0	152.9	154.4	153.7	149.7
2008	149.3	150.6	152.6	154.8	154.6	156.3	155.5	156.1	155.6	156.5	156.0	154.6	154.4
2009	149.4	147.9	147.5	148.2	147.5	147.7	147.5	146.8	145.9	147.3	148.5	148.7	147.7
2010	145.3	145.3	146.8	152.6	151.8	152.6	154.7	154.6	152.6	156.1	155.8	156.1	152.0
2011	152.4	153.2	154.8	158.3	157.3	156.4	157.9	158.8	159.1	160.3	160.6	159.2	157.4
2012	157.5	158.7	160.3	163.1	163.4	165.4	164.0	164.7	164.9	168.0	167.7	168.3	163.8
2013	164.6	166.2	167.9	171.6	171.1	173.4	174.4	175.3	175.5	176.0	176.8	177.4	172.5
2014	172.8	174.0	175.6	178.3	178.4	179.9	179.3	180.1	179.4	181.2	181.6	181.8	178.5
2015	175.0	175.8	176.2	178.9	178.7	180.0	180.2	180.9	179.7	181.4	179.4	177.9	178.7
Education and Health Services													
2005	163.3	163.9	164.2	165.1	165.1	164.4	161.7	161.8	164.6	163.8	164.4	165.0	163.9
2006	163.1	164.3	165.1	165.6	166.3	166.3	164.3	164.9	168.5	169.0	169.1	169.9	166.4
2007	167.6	168.8	170.1	170.7	171.0	171.3	170.0	170.4	173.0	174.3	174.5	174.8	171.4
2008	173.4	174.9	175.6	177.0	177.2	176.6	174.2	175.5	177.6	178.6	179.2	179.2	176.6
2009	178.2	179.0	179.1	179.9	180.3	179.7	178.5	178.9	180.5	181.9	182.2	182.4	180.1
2010	179.1	180.1	180.1	179.5	180.1	179.3	178.2	178.5	179.8	182.5	183.2	183.5	180.3
2011	183.8	184.2	184.3	185.9	186.3	184.4	183.2	183.8	185.2	186.5	187.0	186.9	185.1
2012	184.4	185.2	185.5	186.2	186.9	186.2	184.3	185.2	186.7	188.2	188.9	189.5	186.4
2013	186.9	187.0	187.3	188.3	188.7	187.9	185.8	186.2	187.3	188.8	189.4	189.0	187.7
2014	187.1	187.6	187.8	189.9	191.0	190.0	188.7	189.1	190.9	192.2	193.2	193.0	190.0
2015	192.0	193.2	192.9	195.1	195.1	193.9	193.3	193.3	193.9	196.1	195.6	196.3	194.2

1. Employment by Industry: Kansas, 2005–2015—*Continued*

(Numbers in thousands, not seasonally adjusted)

Industry and year	January	February	March	April	May	June	July	August	September	October	November	December	Annual average
Leisure and Hospitality													
2005	105.5	106.8	109.2	111.3	113.3	115.2	114.8	114.5	113.9	111.7	111.1	110.3	111.5
2006	107.6	108.7	110.7	114.1	116.4	118.4	117.9	118.9	118.2	116.2	114.7	114.9	114.7
2007	108.3	109.8	113.0	115.4	117.7	119.3	118.8	117.6	115.6	114.4	113.7	112.6	114.7
2008	110.7	111.5	113.0	116.9	119.2	120.3	118.3	118.9	117.5	116.5	114.6	114.4	116.0
2009	109.9	110.1	112.0	114.1	116.6	117.8	117.4	117.2	116.3	113.5	112.5	111.4	114.1
2010	107.1	108.2	110.3	113.4	115.8	117.4	116.3	116.2	114.9	114.2	113.4	112.5	113.3
2011	108.3	108.5	111.4	115.1	117.9	119.2	118.9	119.1	117.0	115.9	114.8	114.4	115.0
2012	112.3	114.3	116.9	120.2	122.5	124.5	122.8	123.3	120.4	119.7	119.1	118.9	119.6
2013	114.9	116.4	118.2	121.1	124.6	125.6	124.7	124.4	122.7	122.4	120.5	119.6	121.3
2014	115.6	116.7	119.0	122.7	126.8	126.8	127.0	126.9	124.6	123.6	122.4	122.1	122.9
2015	119.5	120.9	122.7	125.6	127.9	129.9	129.4	129.7	127.2	126.1	125.4	125.2	125.8
Other Services													
2005	52.1	52.8	53.4	52.8	52.7	52.6	52.1	51.7	52.4	52.7	52.5	52.1	52.5
2006	51.8	52.2	52.6	51.6	51.9	52.0	51.4	51.7	52.3	51.6	51.5	51.9	51.9
2007	50.8	51.3	52.2	52.5	52.3	52.4	52.1	52.3	52.3	53.2	53.0	52.8	52.3
2008	52.4	53.2	53.4	53.7	53.9	53.3	53.5	53.4	53.3	53.6	53.4	53.0	53.3
2009	52.7	53.0	52.8	52.7	52.7	52.4	52.1	51.8	52.1	52.3	52.3	52.0	52.4
2010	51.5	51.6	51.7	51.9	51.7	51.2	50.9	50.8	51.0	52.3	51.7	51.6	51.5
2011	50.4	50.8	50.8	50.8	50.7	50.2	50.5	50.3	50.5	50.9	50.6	50.6	50.6
2012	49.6	50.1	49.9	49.9	49.9	49.7	49.3	49.1	49.7	49.9	49.6	49.5	49.7
2013	48.0	48.8	48.6	49.0	48.8	48.6	48.4	48.5	48.7	49.1	49.3	49.0	48.7
2014	47.9	48.5	48.8	49.2	48.9	48.4	48.4	48.4	48.3	48.9	48.7	48.2	48.6
2015	47.5	47.9	47.5	47.8	47.8	47.8	47.6	47.8	47.9	48.2	48.4	48.5	47.9
Government													
2005	245.4	254.2	258.0	258.7	259.6	256.9	222.1	222.5	251.6	258.5	260.4	261.2	250.8
2006	248.1	258.2	261.2	259.8	263.5	260.5	225.7	227.5	257.5	262.7	264.1	265.2	254.5
2007	251.2	260.1	263.4	262.7	265.2	266.1	236.6	235.0	259.8	265.0	266.9	266.8	258.2
2008	254.3	262.7	266.6	266.1	270.2	260.6	234.9	235.4	260.7	268.0	269.9	270.5	260.0
2009	262.2	266.2	267.9	269.1	273.7	262.0	235.4	233.9	260.1	267.5	269.0	268.9	261.3
2010	259.9	263.5	267.6	268.9	276.1	266.7	241.8	243.3	262.9	266.6	264.3	264.9	262.2
2011	261.6	263.4	265.2	268.0	269.0	256.3	238.1	240.0	262.4	265.8	265.8	262.7	259.9
2012	257.7	263.0	264.5	264.6	267.6	255.2	234.6	239.9	259.0	265.9	266.3	264.1	258.5
2013	256.0	263.4	263.6	265.9	264.0	251.0	232.2	235.8	260.7	264.5	265.4	263.5	257.2
2014	254.4	262.2	263.4	263.6	263.6	252.1	234.1	236.4	259.5	264.8	265.0	263.4	256.9
2015	254.7	262.6	263.8	264.4	264.1	253.0	233.2	235.6	258.6	263.8	264.6	262.5	256.7

2. Average Weekly Hours by Selected Industry: Kansas, 2011–2015

(Not seasonally adjusted)

Industry and year	January	February	March	April	May	June	July	August	September	October	November	December	Annual average
Total Private													
2011	33.8	33.8	34.1	34.4	34.8	34.7	34.6	34.5	34.5	35.1	34.5	34.5	34.5
2012	34.7	34.3	34.5	34.9	34.6	35.1	35.1	35.1	35.4	34.8	34.7	35.1	34.9
2013	34.3	34.3	34.5	34.5	34.3	35.3	34.6	34.5	35.0	34.5	34.4	34.8	34.6
2014	34.0	34.4	34.8	34.4	34.4	35.0	34.6	34.7	34.6	34.5	35.2	34.5	34.6
2015	34.2	34.5	34.6	34.0	34.1	34.6	34.4	35.0	34.0	34.2	34.4	33.8	34.3
Goods-Producing													
2011	39.6	40.6	41.5	41.7	42.1	42.2	41.7	41.5	42.0	42.2	41.5	40.9	41.5
2012	41.0	40.3	40.9	41.4	41.6	41.8	41.8	41.8	41.3	41.6	41.5	41.6	41.4
2013	40.4	40.4	41.2	40.9	40.5	41.6	41.5	41.5	41.7	41.9	41.6	42.0	41.3
2014	41.0	40.6	40.8	41.0	41.1	41.1	41.3	41.9	41.7	41.4	41.9	41.8	41.3
2015	40.8	40.1	40.8	40.0	39.8	40.3	40.2	40.7	39.7	40.8	40.7	40.4	40.4
Construction													
2011	36.0	36.2	38.4	39.8	41.0	40.9	40.8	39.5	41.1	40.4	38.3	38.7	39.4
2012	37.9	36.9	38.6	38.6	39.8	39.6	39.6	40.2	38.9	40.0	38.9	38.8	39.0
2013	36.7	37.6	37.4	36.9	39.2	40.1	39.4	39.2	39.5	40.3	38.9	37.9	38.6
2014	38.6	36.3	39.4	39.6	40.2	38.2	39.5	40.0	38.6	37.7	37.9	39.1	38.8
2015	38.1	37.7	39.0	36.9	36.1	37.6	37.5	40.0	36.4	38.7	38.1	36.7	37.7
Manufacturing													
2011	41.4	41.4	42.0	41.8	41.9	42.1	41.5	41.9	41.8	42.4	42.4	41.6	41.9
2012	42.0	41.4	41.5	42.5	42.1	42.6	42.5	42.2	42.1	42.1	42.6	43.0	42.2
2013	41.9	41.5	42.7	42.4	42.2	43.4	43.1	43.2	43.3	43.3	43.2	43.9	42.8
2014	41.9	42.2	42.0	42.0	42.0	43.0	42.4	43.1	43.6	43.5	44.2	43.3	42.8
2015	42.4	42.2	42.7	42.4	42.5	42.4	42.1	41.7	42.4	42.6	42.8	43.3	42.5
Trade, Transportation, and Utilities													
2011	32.5	32.1	33.0	33.5	34.0	33.9	34.1	34.0	33.7	34.2	33.8	34.7	33.6
2012	35.1	34.4	34.7	35.3	35.4	35.7	36.0	35.6	36.1	35.5	35.8	35.8	35.5
2013	34.8	34.8	34.9	34.4	34.5	35.0	34.4	34.2	34.8	34.1	34.0	34.3	34.5
2014	33.5	33.9	34.4	34.1	34.0	34.4	33.7	33.8	34.0	34.1	34.6	34.3	34.1
2015	33.4	34.5	34.5	33.9	33.8	34.2	34.4	34.8	34.2	33.8	33.9	33.4	34.1
Financial Activities													
2011	38.1	37.4	37.2	37.1	37.6	37.1	37.2	37.0	37.0	38.4	37.5	37.5	37.4
2012	37.1	36.6	36.8	37.5	35.7	36.8	36.9	36.0	37.3	35.9	36.0	37.4	36.7
2013	35.8	36.8	36.5	36.3	36.0	38.0	36.2	36.2	37.2	35.8	36.5	36.7	36.5
2014	35.5	37.0	36.9	35.9	36.2	36.4	35.8	35.5	35.3	35.0	36.7	35.3	36.0
2015	35.5	36.6	36.4	35.9	36.1	36.1	36.3	37.4	36.2	36.2	37.4	36.6	36.4
Professional and Business Services													
2011	34.9	35.2	35.0	35.6	35.7	35.8	35.7	35.4	35.3	36.3	35.6	35.4	35.5
2012	35.2	34.8	35.0	35.5	34.8	35.1	35.4	35.5	36.3	35.0	34.8	35.2	35.2
2013	34.3	35.1	34.8	35.4	35.7	37.0	35.7	36.0	36.2	36.3	36.1	36.4	35.8
2014	35.0	35.7	37.2	36.7	36.8	37.2	36.7	37.0	36.8	36.5	37.5	36.1	36.6
2015	35.9	36.4	36.8	36.3	36.5	37.0	36.3	37.0	35.8	36.2	36.1	35.6	36.3
Education and Health Services													
2011	32.3	31.8	31.3	31.6	32.3	32.1	32.2	31.9	32.0	32.3	31.5	31.7	31.9
2012	32.5	31.9	31.7	31.9	31.3	31.8	32.0	31.2	32.0	31.2	31.2	32.4	31.8
2013	31.7	31.4	31.3	31.6	31.1	32.2	31.7	31.5	32.5	31.3	31.4	32.1	31.6
2014	31.4	32.1	32.2	31.5	31.4	32.7	32.0	31.9	32.2	31.7	33.0	31.9	32.0
2015	32.4	32.7	32.5	31.9	32.1	32.4	32.4	33.1	32.4	32.2	33.0	31.7	32.4
Leisure and Hospitality													
2011	24.1	24.1	24.6	24.7	24.6	24.8	24.6	25.3	24.9	25.9	25.2	25.0	24.8
2012	25.0	25.4	25.2	25.1	25.3	26.0	25.8	25.9	25.6	25.0	24.2	24.5	25.3
2013	23.8	24.0	24.1	24.0	24.0	24.7	23.7	23.7	23.7	23.6	23.5	23.5	23.9
2014	23.0	23.3	23.6	23.3	23.6	24.5	24.1	23.6	23.3	23.4	23.2	23.2	23.5
2015	22.8	23.3	23.3	23.0	23.6	24.2	23.7	24.1	23.0	23.5	23.4	22.6	23.4
Other Services													
2011	30.9	30.1	30.6	30.8	30.7	32.3	31.9	31.1	30.0	31.1	30.6	30.8	30.9
2012	29.4	30.1	29.8	29.9	30.2	31.6	31.2	30.9	30.5	29.7	30.5	30.8	30.4
2013	31.5	29.8	29.7	29.7	29.4	31.7	31.6	31.2	31.0	29.5	29.7	30.3	30.4
2014	30.7	29.1	30.0	29.0	30.4	31.4	30.6	30.8	29.8	29.4	29.4	29.2	30.0
2015	29.6	29.2	28.2	29.3	30.2	30.6	30.5	31.3	29.2	29.7	29.5	29.3	29.7

3. Average Hourly Earnings by Selected Industry: Kansas, 2011–2015

(Dollars, not seasonally adjusted)

Industry and year	January	February	March	April	May	June	July	August	September	October	November	December	Annual average
Total Private													
2011	20.58	20.65	20.34	20.45	20.47	20.36	20.47	20.44	20.41	20.62	20.66	20.63	20.51
2012	21.09	20.98	20.91	21.12	21.01	20.82	21.11	20.84	21.06	21.09	21.00	21.26	21.02
2013	21.42	21.47	21.36	21.50	21.38	21.44	21.32	21.32	21.49	21.48	21.52	21.70	21.45
2014	21.78	22.07	22.03	21.97	21.85	21.89	21.96	22.09	22.21	22.19	22.52	22.45	22.09
2015	22.52	22.66	22.48	22.26	22.32	22.17	22.36	22.56	22.60	22.78	22.97	23.19	22.57
Goods-Producing													
2011	21.58	21.87	21.88	21.82	21.75	21.73	21.70	21.86	21.91	22.06	22.07	22.24	21.87
2012	22.10	22.28	22.18	21.79	21.80	21.63	21.80	21.94	21.92	21.89	21.87	22.10	21.94
2013	21.61	21.84	21.43	21.43	21.12	21.64	21.59	21.66	22.12	22.16	22.50	22.88	21.84
2014	22.93	23.09	23.67	23.53	23.59	23.59	23.68	23.65	24.12	24.26	24.35	24.46	23.75
2015	24.31	23.94	24.09	23.41	23.84	24.01	24.14	24.38	24.33	25.11	25.17	26.02	24.40
Construction													
2011	21.76	21.63	21.12	21.18	21.68	21.58	21.36	21.82	22.09	22.17	22.66	22.49	21.80
2012	22.35	23.43	23.21	22.61	22.60	22.06	22.49	22.80	22.96	23.17	23.30	23.66	22.88
2013	23.08	23.27	21.49	21.94	22.01	22.38	22.34	22.28	22.65	23.08	23.65	23.80	22.67
2014	23.90	24.24	24.25	24.21	24.26	23.41	23.36	23.77	23.57	24.26	24.19	24.25	23.96
2015	25.03	24.40	24.25	23.34	23.56	23.79	24.03	24.56	24.76	24.42	24.35	24.33	24.23
Manufacturing													
2011	21.66	22.09	22.25	22.12	21.92	21.76	21.81	21.87	21.80	22.00	21.78	22.17	21.94
2012	22.00	21.91	21.76	21.55	21.58	21.52	21.51	21.60	21.51	21.34	21.31	21.56	21.59
2013	21.17	21.40	21.37	21.23	21.01	21.69	21.58	21.64	21.85	21.70	22.03	22.13	21.57
2014	22.26	22.36	23.14	23.17	23.20	23.61	23.86	23.51	24.37	24.16	24.37	24.50	23.56
2015	23.88	23.61	23.92	23.26	23.80	23.97	24.07	24.08	23.92	24.19	24.44	25.97	24.10
Trade, Transportation, and Utilities													
2011	18.37	18.44	18.27	18.67	18.69	18.68	18.71	18.64	18.82	19.34	19.25	18.96	18.74
2012	19.88	19.13	19.22	19.85	19.33	19.52	19.90	19.82	20.37	20.90	20.25	20.64	19.91
2013	21.11	20.94	21.00	21.03	20.62	20.82	20.55	20.51	20.44	20.47	19.98	20.09	20.63
2014	20.28	20.46	20.30	20.67	20.51	20.22	20.16	20.48	20.74	20.66	21.12	20.75	20.53
2015	21.62	21.82	21.78	22.14	21.92	21.66	21.47	21.64	21.49	21.73	21.78	21.70	21.73
Financial Activities													
2011	23.86	23.40	23.10	23.48	23.85	23.46	23.65	23.33	23.40	23.45	23.16	22.73	23.41
2012	24.27	24.32	23.09	23.49	24.45	24.15	23.88	23.71	24.28	23.87	23.76	23.88	23.93
2013	24.54	24.80	24.52	24.47	25.41	24.91	24.92	25.56	25.38	25.65	26.06	25.70	25.16
2014	26.31	26.54	26.16	26.46	26.39	28.10	28.49	28.24	27.86	27.61	28.81	27.60	27.39
2015	28.01	28.52	26.00	25.78	26.12	25.43	26.67	27.44	27.18	27.11	27.02	26.90	26.85
Professional and Business Services													
2011	26.07	25.45	25.16	24.99	25.29	25.00	25.40	25.12	24.52	24.75	24.56	24.91	25.09
2012	25.16	24.94	24.89	25.02	24.79	24.43	24.67	23.95	23.96	23.97	23.79	24.35	24.48
2013	24.29	24.13	23.83	24.16	23.81	23.72	23.57	23.46	24.05	23.72	23.66	23.60	23.83
2014	23.80	24.23	24.11	23.65	23.29	23.30	23.25	23.27	23.34	23.69	23.83	24.15	23.65
2015	23.99	24.87	24.98	24.49	24.57	24.32	24.82	25.24	25.52	25.13	25.61	25.36	24.91
Education and Health Services													
2011	20.02	20.39	19.55	19.48	19.21	19.34	19.36	19.34	19.41	19.47	19.57	19.41	19.54
2012	19.55	19.59	19.65	19.89	19.76	19.73	19.92	20.00	19.91	19.89	19.81	19.81	19.79
2013	19.76	19.95	20.05	20.60	20.85	20.90	20.88	20.91	21.04	21.15	21.33	21.52	20.75
2014	21.64	22.00	21.82	21.78	21.72	21.68	21.78	21.99	22.19	21.96	22.09	22.26	21.91
2015	21.79	21.59	21.40	21.16	21.03	20.89	20.76	20.86	21.11	21.05	21.25	21.69	21.21
Leisure and Hospitality													
2011	10.89	11.20	11.10	11.07	11.00	10.98	11.12	11.53	11.52	11.46	11.43	11.42	11.23
2012	11.56	11.39	11.27	11.29	11.31	11.25	11.21	10.89	11.11	11.18	11.13	11.31	11.24
2013	11.30	11.29	11.30	11.38	11.35	11.01	11.18	11.24	11.37	11.25	11.26	11.40	11.28
2014	11.44	11.55	11.74	11.59	11.72	11.50	11.57	11.59	11.69	11.65	11.79	12.16	11.67
2015	11.85	11.97	11.88	11.82	11.79	11.72	11.82	11.88	12.08	11.94	12.02	12.26	11.92
Other Services													
2011	19.42	19.71	19.39	19.69	19.65	19.29	19.17	19.36	19.11	19.34	19.29	19.32	19.39
2012	20.30	19.48	19.73	19.91	19.78	19.61	20.03	20.02	20.05	19.81	19.88	19.89	19.87
2013	20.76	20.50	20.84	20.69	21.22	21.31	21.46	21.35	21.07	21.08	21.12	22.11	21.13
2014	21.38	21.98	21.53	21.51	21.35	21.95	21.72	21.78	21.97	21.57	21.72	21.48	21.66
2015	21.39	21.27	21.34	20.84	20.84	21.02	20.90	20.67	20.68	21.51	21.85	21.55	21.15

4. Average Weekly Earnings by Selected Industry: Kansas, 2011–2015

(Dollars, not seasonally adjusted)

Industry and year	January	February	March	April	May	June	July	August	September	October	November	December	Annual average
Total Private													
2011	695.60	697.97	693.59	703.48	712.36	706.49	708.26	705.18	704.15	723.76	712.77	711.74	707.60
2012	731.82	719.61	721.40	737.09	726.95	730.78	740.96	731.48	745.52	733.93	728.70	746.23	733.60
2013	734.71	736.42	736.92	741.75	733.33	756.83	737.67	735.54	752.15	741.06	740.29	755.16	742.17
2014	740.52	759.21	766.64	755.77	751.64	766.15	759.82	766.52	768.47	765.56	792.70	774.53	764.31
2015	770.18	781.77	777.81	756.84	761.11	767.08	769.18	789.60	768.40	779.08	790.17	783.82	774.15
Goods-Producing													
2011	854.57	887.92	908.02	909.89	915.68	917.01	904.89	907.19	920.22	930.93	915.91	909.62	907.61
2012	906.10	897.88	907.16	902.11	906.88	904.13	911.24	917.09	905.30	910.62	907.61	919.36	908.32
2013	873.04	882.34	882.92	876.49	855.36	900.22	895.99	898.89	922.40	928.50	936.00	960.96	901.99
2014	940.13	937.45	965.74	964.73	969.55	969.55	977.98	990.94	1,005.80	1,004.36	1,020.27	1,022.43	980.88
2015	991.85	959.99	982.87	936.40	948.83	967.60	970.43	992.27	965.90	1,024.49	1,024.42	1,051.21	985.76
Construction													
2011	783.36	783.01	811.01	842.96	888.88	882.62	871.49	861.89	907.90	895.67	867.88	870.36	858.92
2012	847.07	864.57	895.91	872.75	899.48	873.58	890.60	916.56	893.14	926.80	906.37	918.01	892.32
2013	847.04	874.95	803.73	809.59	862.79	897.44	880.20	873.38	894.68	930.12	919.99	902.02	875.06
2014	922.54	879.91	955.45	958.72	975.25	894.26	922.72	950.80	909.80	914.60	916.80	948.18	929.65
2015	953.64	919.88	945.75	861.25	850.52	894.50	901.13	982.40	901.26	945.05	927.74	892.91	913.47
Manufacturing													
2011	896.72	914.53	934.50	924.62	918.45	916.10	905.12	916.35	911.24	932.80	923.47	922.27	919.29
2012	924.00	907.07	903.04	915.88	908.52	916.75	914.18	911.52	905.57	898.41	907.81	927.08	911.10
2013	887.02	888.10	912.50	900.15	886.62	941.35	930.10	934.85	946.11	939.61	951.70	971.51	923.20
2014	932.69	943.59	971.88	973.14	974.40	1,015.23	1,011.66	1,013.28	1,062.53	1,050.96	1,077.15	1,060.85	1,008.37
2015	1,012.51	996.34	1,021.38	986.22	1,011.50	1,016.33	1,013.35	1,004.14	1,014.21	1,030.49	1,046.03	1,124.50	1,024.25
Trade, Transportation, and Utilities													
2011	597.03	591.92	602.91	625.45	635.46	633.25	638.01	633.76	634.23	661.43	650.65	657.91	629.66
2012	697.79	658.07	666.93	700.71	684.28	696.86	716.40	705.59	735.36	741.95	724.95	738.91	706.81
2013	734.63	728.71	732.90	723.43	711.39	728.70	706.92	701.44	711.31	698.03	679.32	689.09	711.74
2014	679.38	693.59	698.32	704.85	697.34	695.57	679.39	692.22	705.16	704.51	730.75	711.73	700.07
2015	722.11	752.79	751.41	750.55	740.90	740.77	738.57	753.07	734.96	734.47	738.34	724.78	740.99
Financial Activities													
2011	909.07	875.16	859.32	871.11	896.76	870.37	879.78	863.21	865.80	900.48	868.50	852.38	875.53
2012	900.42	890.11	849.71	880.88	872.87	888.72	881.17	853.56	905.64	856.93	855.36	893.11	878.23
2013	878.53	912.64	894.98	888.26	914.76	946.58	902.10	925.27	944.14	918.27	951.19	943.19	918.34
2014	934.01	981.98	965.30	949.91	955.32	1,022.84	1,019.94	1,002.52	983.46	966.35	1,057.33	974.28	986.04
2015	994.36	1,043.83	946.40	925.50	942.93	918.02	968.12	1,026.26	983.92	981.38	1,010.55	984.54	977.34
Professional and Business Services													
2011	909.84	895.84	880.60	889.64	902.85	895.00	906.78	889.25	865.56	898.43	874.34	881.81	890.70
2012	885.63	867.91	871.15	888.21	862.69	857.49	873.32	850.23	869.75	838.95	827.89	857.12	861.70
2013	833.15	846.96	829.28	855.26	850.02	877.64	841.45	844.56	870.61	861.04	854.13	859.04	853.11
2014	833.00	865.01	896.89	867.96	857.07	866.76	853.28	860.99	858.91	864.69	893.63	871.82	865.59
2015	861.24	905.27	919.26	888.99	896.81	899.84	900.97	933.88	913.62	909.71	924.52	902.82	904.23
Education and Health Services													
2011	646.65	648.40	611.92	615.57	620.48	620.81	623.39	616.95	621.12	628.88	616.46	615.30	623.33
2012	635.38	624.92	622.91	634.49	618.49	627.41	637.44	624.00	637.12	620.57	618.07	641.84	629.32
2013	626.39	626.43	627.57	650.96	648.44	672.98	661.90	658.67	683.80	662.00	669.76	690.79	655.70
2014	679.50	706.20	702.60	686.07	682.01	708.94	696.96	701.48	714.52	696.13	728.97	710.09	701.12
2015	706.00	705.99	695.50	675.00	675.06	676.84	672.62	690.47	683.96	677.81	701.25	687.57	687.20
Leisure and Hospitality													
2011	262.45	269.92	273.06	273.43	270.60	272.30	273.55	291.71	286.85	296.81	288.04	285.50	278.50
2012	289.00	289.31	284.00	283.38	286.14	292.50	289.22	282.05	284.42	279.50	269.35	277.10	284.37
2013	268.94	270.96	272.33	273.12	272.40	271.95	264.97	266.39	269.47	265.50	264.61	267.90	269.59
2014	263.12	269.12	277.06	270.05	276.59	281.75	278.84	273.52	272.38	272.61	273.53	282.11	274.25
2015	270.18	278.90	276.80	271.86	278.24	283.62	280.13	286.31	277.84	280.59	281.27	277.08	278.93
Other Services													
2011	600.08	593.27	593.33	606.45	603.26	623.07	611.52	602.10	573.30	601.47	590.27	595.06	599.15
2012	596.82	586.35	587.95	595.31	597.36	619.68	624.94	618.62	611.53	588.36	606.34	612.61	604.05
2013	653.94	610.90	618.95	614.49	623.87	675.53	678.14	666.12	653.17	621.86	627.26	669.93	642.35
2014	656.37	639.62	645.90	623.79	649.04	689.23	664.63	670.82	654.71	634.16	638.57	627.22	649.80
2015	633.14	621.08	601.79	610.61	629.37	643.21	637.45	646.97	603.86	638.85	644.58	631.42	628.16

KENTUCKY
At a Glance

Population:
  2005 estimate: 4,182,742
  2010 census: 4,339,367
  2015 estimate: 4,425,092

Percent change in population:
  2005–2015: 5.8%
  2010–2015: 2.0%

Percent change in total nonfarm employment:
  2005–2015: 3.9%

Industry with the largest growth in employment, 2005–2015 (thousands):
  Professional and business services, 41.4

Industry with the largest decline or smallest growth in employment, 2005–2015 (thousands):
  Manufacturing, –21.0

Civilian labor force:
  2005: 1,999,777
  2010: 2,054,375
  2015: 1,953,393

Unemployment rate and rank among states (highest to lowest):
  2005: 5.9%, 8th
  2010: 10.2%, 16th
  2015: 5.4%, 21st

Over-the-year change in unemployment rates:
  2012–2013: –0.1%
  2013–2014: –1.6%
  2014–2015: –1.1%

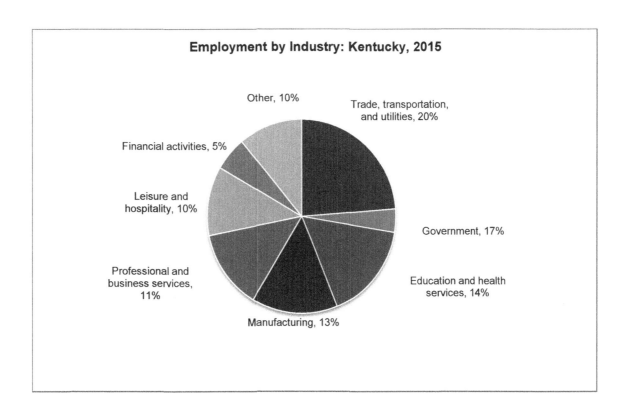

Employment by Industry: Kentucky, 2015

Other, 10%
Trade, transportation, and utilities, 20%
Financial activities, 5%
Leisure and hospitality, 10%
Government, 17%
Professional and business services, 11%
Education and health services, 14%
Manufacturing, 13%

1. Employment by Industry: Kentucky, 2005–2015

(Numbers in thousands, not seasonally adjusted)

Industry and year	January	February	March	April	May	June	July	August	September	October	November	December	Annual average
Total Nonfarm													
2005	1,768.2	1,776.6	1,790.9	1,813.0	1,823.1	1,827.2	1,806.6	1,823.7	1,831.4	1,830.0	1,839.6	1,837.9	1,814.0
2006	1,799.5	1,803.5	1,825.5	1,835.7	1,847.0	1,848.4	1,822.3	1,839.6	1,846.3	1,845.3	1,855.9	1,866.4	1,836.3
2007	1,820.1	1,820.3	1,839.3	1,855.1	1,871.8	1,875.5	1,848.9	1,858.6	1,864.6	1,865.1	1,877.7	1,877.1	1,856.2
2008	1,828.4	1,829.2	1,837.7	1,852.0	1,868.3	1,861.1	1,838.0	1,848.4	1,837.7	1,834.5	1,834.4	1,825.2	1,841.2
2009	1,754.4	1,745.8	1,751.5	1,763.9	1,768.7	1,764.6	1,747.9	1,753.2	1,757.6	1,761.7	1,769.5	1,767.3	1,758.8
2010	1,715.0	1,708.3	1,732.6	1,759.2	1,774.7	1,775.7	1,754.5	1,760.2	1,771.0	1,780.1	1,786.9	1,791.6	1,759.2
2011	1,737.9	1,743.2	1,761.3	1,782.4	1,786.2	1,791.3	1,773.3	1,791.2	1,799.7	1,800.1	1,813.5	1,814.1	1,782.9
2012	1,771.7	1,776.2	1,793.7	1,808.9	1,821.3	1,824.9	1,801.3	1,813.0	1,819.0	1,823.4	1,837.5	1,839.0	1,810.8
2013	1,790.8	1,794.4	1,809.0	1,825.1	1,837.1	1,834.7	1,816.7	1,837.6	1,842.4	1,846.0	1,863.5	1,864.8	1,830.2
2014	1,811.7	1,810.0	1,828.8	1,853.8	1,865.5	1,862.8	1,848.8	1,867.1	1,870.7	1,878.0	1,892.0	1,898.5	1,857.3
2015	1,846.8	1,843.9	1,853.5	1,875.6	1,892.7	1,892.9	1,871.7	1,887.5	1,895.9	1,908.6	1,920.4	1,924.5	1,884.5
Total Private													
2005	1,471.5	1,475.6	1,488.6	1,508.6	1,517.7	1,526.8	1,516.6	1,528.7	1,528.8	1,525.3	1,533.8	1,533.2	1,512.9
2006	1,498.6	1,498.4	1,518.9	1,527.2	1,537.5	1,546.4	1,528.7	1,540.0	1,538.9	1,536.1	1,545.7	1,556.7	1,531.1
2007	1,515.4	1,511.4	1,528.8	1,541.7	1,556.7	1,565.3	1,548.2	1,553.6	1,552.7	1,552.8	1,563.6	1,562.5	1,546.1
2008	1,519.0	1,516.3	1,523.7	1,538.5	1,553.6	1,552.5	1,540.5	1,546.3	1,531.1	1,522.4	1,521.6	1,513.3	1,531.6
2009	1,449.9	1,439.2	1,442.1	1,449.0	1,452.8	1,453.3	1,446.9	1,447.6	1,444.8	1,444.3	1,451.6	1,450.7	1,447.7
2010	1,403.6	1,393.7	1,415.0	1,438.3	1,446.4	1,453.8	1,448.9	1,454.0	1,453.4	1,459.5	1,465.2	1,471.1	1,441.9
2011	1,422.3	1,422.6	1,438.5	1,457.8	1,461.6	1,470.7	1,465.1	1,477.0	1,477.0	1,475.4	1,487.1	1,487.2	1,461.9
2012	1,449.2	1,449.2	1,464.7	1,478.1	1,491.5	1,500.9	1,492.1	1,498.6	1,495.5	1,497.4	1,510.3	1,512.0	1,486.6
2013	1,469.5	1,468.1	1,481.3	1,495.5	1,507.3	1,510.5	1,505.1	1,519.0	1,515.4	1,521.1	1,536.6	1,537.9	1,505.6
2014	1,490.6	1,487.1	1,504.1	1,525.8	1,537.5	1,540.2	1,536.5	1,546.5	1,545.0	1,552.8	1,566.1	1,574.1	1,533.9
2015	1,527.7	1,523.5	1,532.6	1,551.9	1,569.5	1,575.1	1,568.3	1,576.7	1,576.8	1,589.6	1,600.3	1,605.1	1,566.4
Goods-Producing													
2005	358.9	359.1	362.2	366.8	369.4	372.3	365.4	372.0	372.3	371.8	372.5	370.6	367.8
2006	364.3	362.6	365.6	366.7	368.6	371.3	364.4	371.1	369.8	364.1	363.8	367.7	366.7
2007	358.7	356.1	358.5	363.5	366.1	369.8	362.7	364.6	367.2	362.6	365.9	361.8	363.1
2008	353.9	352.5	353.6	355.6	362.1	360.1	354.4	357.6	353.6	349.5	348.4	340.0	353.4
2009	321.4	317.5	314.6	313.5	311.4	310.3	307.4	308.0	307.7	306.0	305.1	303.0	310.5
2010	292.1	286.1	293.2	297.9	299.3	300.8	299.7	303.6	304.6	305.0	303.4	301.8	299.0
2011	292.5	293.1	296.7	301.7	302.9	307.2	302.8	308.7	309.0	308.0	309.1	307.3	303.3
2012	302.3	300.7	305.4	308.1	311.1	315.2	314.8	315.9	315.7	315.3	315.3	313.9	311.1
2013	306.5	306.1	308.7	310.7	314.2	317.1	314.1	318.2	319.3	319.6	320.0	319.2	314.5
2014	311.2	311.7	316.5	320.4	324.5	327.0	327.6	330.2	330.1	330.7	331.9	330.4	324.4
2015	323.0	322.3	323.3	325.6	331.5	333.4	331.8	336.0	336.2	337.5	337.4	335.6	331.1
Service-Providing													
2005	1,409.3	1,417.5	1,428.7	1,446.2	1,453.7	1,454.9	1,441.2	1,451.7	1,459.1	1,458.2	1,467.1	1,467.3	1,446.2
2006	1,435.2	1,440.9	1,459.9	1,469.0	1,478.4	1,477.1	1,457.9	1,468.5	1,476.5	1,481.2	1,492.1	1,498.7	1,469.6
2007	1,461.4	1,464.2	1,480.8	1,491.6	1,505.7	1,505.7	1,486.2	1,494.0	1,497.4	1,502.5	1,511.8	1,515.3	1,493.1
2008	1,474.5	1,476.7	1,484.1	1,496.4	1,506.2	1,501.0	1,483.6	1,490.8	1,484.1	1,485.0	1,486.0	1,485.2	1,487.8
2009	1,433.0	1,428.3	1,436.9	1,450.4	1,457.3	1,454.3	1,440.5	1,445.2	1,449.9	1,455.7	1,464.4	1,464.3	1,448.4
2010	1,422.9	1,422.2	1,439.4	1,461.3	1,475.4	1,474.9	1,454.8	1,456.6	1,466.4	1,475.1	1,483.5	1,489.8	1,460.2
2011	1,445.4	1,450.1	1,464.6	1,480.7	1,483.3	1,484.1	1,470.5	1,482.5	1,490.7	1,492.1	1,504.4	1,506.8	1,479.6
2012	1,469.4	1,475.5	1,488.3	1,500.8	1,510.2	1,509.7	1,486.5	1,497.1	1,503.3	1,508.1	1,522.2	1,525.1	1,499.7
2013	1,484.3	1,488.3	1,500.3	1,514.4	1,522.9	1,517.6	1,502.6	1,519.4	1,523.1	1,526.4	1,543.5	1,545.6	1,515.7
2014	1,500.5	1,498.3	1,512.3	1,533.4	1,541.0	1,535.8	1,521.2	1,536.9	1,540.6	1,547.3	1,560.1	1,568.1	1,533.0
2015	1,523.8	1,521.6	1,530.2	1,550.0	1,561.2	1,559.5	1,539.9	1,551.5	1,559.7	1,571.1	1,583.0	1,588.9	1,553.4
Mining and Logging													
2005	20.1	20.1	20.5	20.9	21.2	21.5	21.6	21.8	22.2	22.3	22.6	22.7	21.5
2006	22.3	22.3	22.7	22.9	23.0	23.2	23.2	23.1	23.1	22.9	22.9	22.9	22.9
2007	22.2	22.2	22.4	22.1	22.0	22.2	22.0	22.1	22.1	22.1	22.1	22.2	22.1
2008	22.2	22.1	22.3	22.8	23.4	23.7	24.0	24.6	24.8	25.4	25.5	25.6	23.9
2009	25.1	25.0	25.2	24.9	24.3	24.0	23.0	22.7	22.8	22.1	22.1	22.0	23.6
2010	21.3	21.3	21.5	21.8	21.9	22.3	22.2	22.4	22.5	22.4	22.5	22.7	22.1
2011	22.0	22.1	22.3	22.7	22.9	23.2	23.4	23.5	23.4	23.2	23.2	23.3	22.9
2012	23.0	22.5	22.1	21.6	21.1	21.0	20.4	19.9	19.5	18.7	18.6	18.1	20.5
2013	17.6	17.2	17.6	17.5	17.6	17.8	17.7	17.6	17.5	17.2	17.1	16.9	17.4
2014	16.2	16.1	16.3	16.4	16.7	16.8	16.7	16.8	16.7	16.7	16.6	16.5	16.5
2015	15.3	15.1	14.6	14.5	14.5	14.4	14.2	13.8	13.6	13.6	13.5	13.1	14.2

1. Employment by Industry: Kentucky, 2005–2015—*Continued*

(Numbers in thousands, not seasonally adjusted)

Industry and year	January	February	March	April	May	June	July	August	September	October	November	December	Annual average
Construction													
2005	76.2	77.4	79.5	83.2	85.6	87.6	89.1	88.0	87.2	87.0	86.0	84.0	84.2
2006	78.8	78.2	80.2	82.1	84.3	85.5	85.8	86.0	85.2	84.4	84.0	83.1	83.1
2007	77.4	75.5	80.9	84.3	86.5	88.3	88.7	89.1	88.9	89.3	88.4	85.8	85.3
2008	79.1	77.8	79.6	84.0	87.8	88.4	88.8	88.7	87.7	86.4	83.9	81.0	84.4
2009	72.7	71.1	71.9	73.3	74.4	75.4	76.1	75.5	75.1	75.3	74.1	71.9	73.9
2010	63.6	61.5	64.7	68.2	68.7	69.2	71.1	70.6	70.1	70.6	69.3	66.7	67.9
2011	60.4	60.7	63.7	67.5	69.0	71.3	70.9	71.3	70.6	69.5	69.4	67.3	67.6
2012	62.2	62.3	64.3	66.9	68.4	69.9	70.1	70.0	69.7	69.0	68.5	66.5	67.3
2013	61.4	61.5	63.5	65.7	68.3	70.0	71.1	71.4	71.9	71.7	71.3	69.4	68.1
2014	64.1	64.1	68.4	71.3	73.8	75.3	75.9	76.1	76.7	77.2	76.8	74.4	72.8
2015	69.1	68.8	70.0	74.3	76.2	77.5	79.9	79.2	79.1	80.1	79.0	76.9	75.8
Manufacturing													
2005	262.6	261.6	262.2	262.7	262.6	263.2	254.7	262.2	262.9	262.5	263.9	263.9	262.1
2006	263.2	262.1	262.7	261.7	261.3	262.6	255.4	262.0	261.5	256.8	256.9	261.7	260.7
2007	259.1	258.4	255.2	257.1	257.6	259.3	252.0	253.4	256.2	251.2	255.4	253.8	255.7
2008	252.6	252.6	251.7	248.8	250.9	248.0	241.6	244.3	241.1	237.7	239.0	233.4	245.1
2009	223.6	221.4	217.5	215.3	212.7	210.9	208.3	209.8	209.8	208.6	208.9	209.1	213.0
2010	207.2	203.3	207.0	207.9	208.7	209.3	206.4	210.6	212.0	212.0	211.6	212.4	209.0
2011	210.1	210.3	210.7	211.5	211.0	212.7	208.5	213.9	215.0	215.3	216.5	216.7	212.7
2012	217.1	215.9	219.0	219.6	221.6	224.3	224.3	226.0	226.5	227.6	228.2	229.3	223.3
2013	227.5	227.4	227.6	227.5	228.3	229.3	225.3	229.2	229.9	230.7	231.6	232.9	228.9
2014	230.9	231.5	231.8	232.7	234.0	234.9	235.0	237.3	236.7	236.8	238.5	239.5	235.0
2015	238.6	238.4	238.7	236.8	240.8	241.5	237.7	243.0	243.5	243.8	244.9	245.6	241.1
Trade, Transportation, and Utilities													
2005	372.4	370.1	372.7	375.1	377.5	378.5	378.3	379.0	377.8	377.9	385.5	388.7	377.8
2006	374.7	371.6	376.5	377.1	380.2	381.9	378.5	379.4	379.1	381.9	389.2	394.2	380.4
2007	381.1	378.2	383.2	382.9	386.4	388.3	384.9	384.9	385.2	387.6	394.4	396.6	386.1
2008	381.1	377.7	378.8	380.4	383.1	383.4	381.2	382.1	378.0	377.5	383.0	386.2	381.0
2009	366.0	360.0	360.2	360.6	362.8	363.4	361.2	360.9	360.4	360.9	367.3	370.5	362.9
2010	354.7	352.0	355.1	357.4	359.9	361.2	360.4	361.2	359.8	363.9	370.2	375.2	360.9
2011	358.7	356.9	360.0	362.0	363.2	365.4	365.0	366.2	365.2	367.2	376.4	379.6	365.5
2012	363.9	362.0	364.9	366.4	369.2	370.5	368.6	369.3	369.1	369.1	377.0	379.7	369.1
2013	364.3	362.3	364.8	365.8	368.4	369.9	368.7	370.7	370.2	371.6	380.4	385.4	370.2
2014	368.9	366.7	369.7	371.8	375.1	376.7	375.4	378.0	377.6	380.1	388.5	395.7	377.0
2015	380.1	377.3	379.4	381.9	385.6	387.2	385.4	387.8	387.2	390.0	397.8	401.5	386.8
Wholesale Trade													
2005	74.3	74.0	74.1	74.4	74.6	74.6	74.5	74.6	74.5	74.5	74.8	75.2	74.5
2006	74.7	74.7	75.4	75.8	76.2	76.5	75.9	76.0	75.9	76.5	76.7	77.3	76.0
2007	76.6	76.6	77.2	77.2	77.2	77.6	77.0	76.9	77.0	76.8	76.9	77.2	77.0
2008	76.5	76.6	76.6	76.4	76.6	76.9	76.5	76.4	75.8	75.9	75.9	75.7	76.3
2009	73.9	72.9	72.6	72.4	72.5	72.3	72.1	71.8	71.7	71.7	72.2	72.6	72.4
2010	71.4	71.1	71.4	71.2	71.6	71.9	72.0	71.8	71.7	72.0	72.1	72.2	71.7
2011	71.0	71.4	71.7	71.4	71.6	72.0	72.5	72.6	72.5	72.4	72.5	72.8	72.0
2012	71.9	72.0	72.2	72.4	72.7	72.9	72.8	73.2	73.2	73.1	73.3	73.5	72.8
2013	73.2	73.2	73.6	73.6	73.7	74.2	74.0	74.2	74.2	73.7	73.9	74.2	73.8
2014	73.6	73.6	74.1	74.1	74.5	74.4	74.1	74.3	74.2	73.8	74.1	74.7	74.1
2015	73.9	73.7	73.8	73.9	74.8	75.1	74.8	75.0	75.1	75.8	75.7	74.9	74.7
Retail Trade													
2005	210.0	207.7	209.5	210.6	212.5	212.7	212.2	212.0	210.9	211.1	217.5	220.3	212.3
2006	209.8	207.4	210.5	210.5	212.3	212.2	210.2	210.5	209.2	211.2	217.4	220.0	211.8
2007	211.0	208.5	212.3	212.0	214.8	214.8	213.6	212.8	212.2	212.7	219.0	220.4	213.7
2008	210.4	208.1	209.8	210.1	211.5	211.8	210.9	211.2	208.7	208.3	212.6	214.0	210.6
2009	202.2	198.4	199.0	200.8	202.5	203.0	201.7	200.8	200.3	200.7	205.5	206.8	201.8
2010	197.0	195.2	197.6	199.5	201.1	200.7	200.5	200.7	198.8	201.7	205.9	207.6	200.5
2011	198.3	196.2	198.3	200.7	201.3	201.5	200.6	201.1	199.2	201.2	207.0	208.7	201.2
2012	199.8	197.3	199.7	201.3	203.5	204.1	202.8	202.4	201.8	202.8	209.0	209.6	202.8
2013	199.7	198.1	199.6	200.9	202.8	203.5	203.0	203.6	202.4	203.9	210.1	212.4	203.3
2014	200.9	199.4	200.9	203.3	204.9	205.8	204.7	205.7	204.2	205.8	212.0	215.3	205.2
2015	205.4	204.1	205.9	208.0	210.1	211.0	209.5	210.1	208.8	210.9	216.4	217.5	209.8

1. Employment by Industry: Kentucky, 2005–2015—*Continued*

(Numbers in thousands, not seasonally adjusted)

Industry and year	January	February	March	April	May	June	July	August	September	October	November	December	Annual average
Transportation and Utilities													
2005	88.1	88.4	89.1	90.1	90.4	91.2	91.6	92.4	92.4	92.3	93.2	93.2	91.0
2006	90.2	89.5	90.6	90.8	91.7	93.2	92.4	92.9	94.0	94.2	95.1	96.9	92.6
2007	93.5	93.1	93.7	93.7	94.4	95.9	94.3	95.2	96.0	98.1	98.5	99.0	95.5
2008	94.2	93.0	92.4	93.9	95.0	94.7	93.8	94.5	93.5	93.3	94.5	96.5	94.1
2009	89.9	88.7	88.6	87.4	87.8	88.1	87.4	88.3	88.4	88.5	89.6	91.1	88.7
2010	86.3	85.7	86.1	86.7	87.2	88.6	87.9	88.7	89.3	90.2	92.2	95.4	88.7
2011	89.4	89.3	90.0	89.9	90.3	91.9	91.9	92.5	93.5	93.6	96.9	98.1	92.3
2012	92.2	92.7	93.0	92.7	93.0	93.5	93.0	93.7	94.1	93.2	94.7	96.6	93.5
2013	91.4	91.0	91.6	91.3	91.9	92.2	91.7	92.9	93.6	94.0	96.4	98.8	93.1
2014	94.4	93.7	94.7	94.4	95.7	96.5	96.6	98.0	99.2	100.5	102.4	105.7	97.7
2015	100.8	99.5	99.7	100.0	100.7	101.1	101.1	102.7	103.3	103.3	105.7	109.1	102.3
Information													
2005	28.6	28.7	29.0	29.0	29.4	29.6	29.6	29.6	29.3	29.2	29.5	29.7	29.3
2006	29.4	29.5	29.5	29.4	29.6	29.7	29.5	29.4	29.2	29.5	29.6	29.7	29.5
2007	29.6	29.5	29.6	29.9	30.3	30.5	30.3	30.2	30.1	29.9	30.2	30.3	30.0
2008	29.8	29.7	29.7	29.6	29.8	30.1	29.7	29.6	29.1	28.5	28.6	28.3	29.4
2009	27.9	27.7	27.5	27.3	27.3	27.2	27.0	26.9	26.5	26.5	26.6	26.7	27.1
2010	26.2	26.1	26.2	26.2	26.4	26.5	26.1	26.2	26.1	26.2	26.7	27.4	26.4
2011	27.1	26.9	26.8	26.7	26.8	26.8	26.8	26.8	26.5	26.6	27.0	27.2	26.8
2012	26.9	26.7	26.4	26.5	26.5	26.5	26.5	26.5	26.1	26.2	26.4	26.5	26.5
2013	26.4	26.4	26.4	26.2	26.4	26.4	26.2	26.4	26.0	26.1	26.1	26.2	26.3
2014	26.4	26.2	26.2	26.0	26.1	26.2	26.0	26.1	25.8	26.0	25.8	25.7	26.0
2015	25.5	25.4	25.3	25.2	25.3	25.4	25.3	25.2	24.9	24.7	24.9	25.3	25.2
Financial Activities													
2005	84.3	84.4	84.5	85.2	85.4	86.3	86.1	86.3	86.1	86.3	86.5	87.1	85.7
2006	86.9	87.2	88.0	88.3	88.9	89.5	89.0	89.2	89.5	89.8	90.2	91.0	89.0
2007	90.2	90.2	90.3	90.8	91.1	91.8	91.9	91.8	91.2	91.4	91.5	92.1	91.2
2008	91.6	92.3	92.3	92.0	92.3	92.0	92.2	92.0	91.0	90.6	90.9	90.9	91.7
2009	89.5	88.9	88.7	88.8	89.0	88.8	88.7	88.2	87.5	87.5	87.1	87.4	88.3
2010	86.3	85.8	85.9	86.1	86.1	86.3	86.1	85.6	84.9	84.9	84.8	85.4	85.7
2011	84.2	84.4	84.6	84.1	84.2	84.8	85.1	85.4	85.5	85.3	85.3	85.9	84.9
2012	85.3	85.3	85.6	85.6	86.0	86.9	87.3	87.4	87.6	87.4	87.8	88.2	86.7
2013	87.7	87.6	88.0	88.0	88.4	88.9	89.4	89.8	89.5	89.0	89.2	89.6	88.8
2014	88.8	88.5	88.6	89.0	89.7	90.1	90.7	90.9	90.8	91.0	91.5	92.2	90.2
2015	91.1	91.1	91.3	91.1	91.8	92.5	92.7	92.8	92.6	93.8	94.2	94.5	92.5
Professional and Business Services													
2005	166.2	167.8	169.6	172.1	172.0	173.8	172.5	175.8	177.8	179.5	181.1	181.1	174.1
2006	174.2	174.5	179.1	179.2	179.5	181.7	180.1	183.0	183.5	184.7	187.1	189.5	181.3
2007	179.1	179.1	181.7	182.5	184.0	184.7	182.5	184.4	184.0	187.2	189.3	191.8	184.2
2008	182.4	181.7	182.2	184.3	184.4	185.9	183.5	184.1	182.3	181.3	179.9	180.1	182.7
2009	169.5	168.6	167.6	167.8	166.7	167.5	169.0	170.9	171.2	174.6	178.8	180.4	171.1
2010	172.6	170.5	173.0	178.3	178.6	181.4	180.9	181.3	182.0	182.9	184.8	189.6	179.7
2011	179.6	178.8	181.0	184.6	183.3	185.0	186.1	189.7	190.0	190.7	192.6	195.3	186.4
2012	186.2	185.3	186.7	189.3	190.3	192.7	191.1	194.2	193.5	196.4	200.7	203.7	192.5
2013	193.0	191.4	193.2	196.7	197.9	198.6	197.7	203.6	202.3	206.8	214.4	215.6	200.9
2014	204.1	199.8	203.5	207.6	209.5	208.2	207.8	211.0	210.1	214.7	221.9	224.4	210.2
2015	210.7	206.5	208.0	210.9	213.2	214.9	214.0	215.6	215.6	220.5	224.8	231.2	215.5
Education and Health Services													
2005	233.6	236.0	235.9	237.7	238.3	237.0	236.7	237.9	239.9	239.4	239.3	239.6	237.6
2006	237.4	238.7	239.8	240.8	240.6	240.2	238.2	238.8	241.0	242.3	242.5	242.9	240.3
2007	241.2	242.0	243.1	242.9	243.7	243.2	241.9	242.8	244.1	245.6	245.7	245.8	243.5
2008	243.6	244.0	245.0	247.5	247.7	246.2	245.5	247.1	248.3	250.0	250.3	250.2	247.1
2009	246.9	246.9	248.1	249.7	249.9	248.9	247.6	249.2	250.8	252.4	253.0	252.9	249.7
2010	249.7	250.6	252.5	253.7	254.3	253.3	253.1	253.8	255.9	257.5	258.1	258.0	254.2
2011	255.0	255.6	256.4	257.5	257.2	255.8	255.4	256.7	259.5	259.8	259.9	258.7	257.3
2012	256.9	258.7	259.6	259.4	259.7	259.6	257.9	259.2	260.5	261.7	262.4	262.4	259.8
2013	259.0	260.5	261.4	261.7	261.0	258.5	259.0	260.6	261.5	263.2	263.0	261.9	260.9
2014	258.6	260.1	259.9	261.0	259.3	258.0	256.5	258.4	261.7	263.7	261.3	263.2	260.1
2015	259.7	261.9	262.5	264.0	263.5	262.1	261.1	262.3	265.8	268.2	270.0	270.5	264.3

1. Employment by Industry: Kentucky, 2005–2015—*Continued*

(Numbers in thousands, not seasonally adjusted)

Industry and year	January	February	March	April	May	June	July	August	September	October	November	December	Annual average
Leisure and Hospitality													
2005	152.1	153.6	158.4	166.5	169.1	172.6	171.9	172.0	169.6	165.4	163.5	160.4	164.6
2006	156.6	158.8	163.9	169.8	174.0	175.5	173.3	173.9	171.7	168.8	168.4	166.4	168.4
2007	160.9	161.7	166.9	173.5	178.8	180.2	178.3	179.1	175.2	172.8	171.1	168.5	172.3
2008	162.1	163.7	166.9	174.0	178.6	179.2	179.7	179.7	175.5	171.4	167.4	165.1	171.9
2009	158.3	158.9	164.4	170.8	175.2	176.1	175.4	173.1	170.9	167.0	164.7	160.9	168.0
2010	154.2	155.2	160.5	169.7	172.7	175.0	173.4	173.4	171.6	170.0	168.4	165.0	167.4
2011	157.5	159.1	164.6	173.4	176.2	177.6	175.8	175.8	173.9	170.6	170.0	166.4	170.1
2012	161.3	164.2	169.2	176.1	182.3	182.9	179.8	180.5	177.8	176.3	175.8	172.7	174.9
2013	168.4	169.3	173.8	181.2	185.8	185.8	185.3	185.0	182.2	180.9	179.6	176.1	179.5
2014	169.8	171.0	176.0	185.9	188.9	189.8	188.6	188.0	185.1	183.5	181.3	179.3	182.3
2015	175.0	176.3	179.4	189.8	194.6	195.2	194.4	193.2	191.3	191.4	188.7	183.5	187.7
Other Services													
2005	75.4	75.9	76.3	76.2	76.6	76.7	76.1	76.1	76.0	75.8	75.9	76.0	76.1
2006	75.1	75.5	76.5	75.9	76.1	76.6	75.7	75.2	75.1	75.0	74.9	75.3	75.6
2007	74.6	74.6	75.5	75.7	76.3	76.8	75.7	75.8	75.7	75.7	75.5	75.6	75.6
2008	74.5	74.7	75.2	75.1	75.6	75.6	74.3	74.1	73.3	73.6	73.1	72.5	74.3
2009	70.4	70.7	71.0	70.5	70.5	71.1	70.6	70.4	69.8	69.4	69.0	68.9	70.2
2010	67.8	67.4	68.6	69.0	69.1	69.3	69.2	68.9	68.5	69.1	68.8	68.7	68.7
2011	67.7	67.8	68.4	67.8	67.8	68.1	68.1	67.7	67.4	67.2	66.8	66.8	67.6
2012	66.4	66.3	66.9	66.7	66.4	66.6	66.1	65.6	65.2	65.0	64.9	64.9	65.9
2013	64.2	64.5	65.0	65.2	65.2	65.3	64.7	64.7	64.4	63.9	63.9	63.9	64.6
2014	62.8	63.1	63.7	64.1	64.4	64.2	63.9	63.9	63.8	63.1	63.9	63.2	63.7
2015	62.6	62.7	63.4	63.4	64.0	64.4	63.6	63.8	63.2	63.5	62.5	63.0	63.3
Government													
2005	296.7	301.0	302.3	304.4	305.4	300.4	290.0	295.0	302.6	304.7	305.8	304.7	301.1
2006	300.9	305.1	306.6	308.5	309.5	302.0	293.6	299.6	307.4	309.2	310.2	309.7	305.2
2007	304.7	308.9	310.5	313.4	315.1	310.2	300.7	305.0	311.9	312.3	314.1	314.6	310.1
2008	309.4	312.9	314.0	313.5	314.7	308.6	297.5	302.1	306.6	312.1	312.8	311.9	309.7
2009	304.5	306.6	309.4	314.9	315.9	311.3	301.0	305.6	312.8	317.4	317.9	316.6	311.2
2010	311.4	314.6	317.6	320.9	328.3	321.9	305.6	306.2	317.6	320.6	321.7	320.5	317.2
2011	315.6	320.6	322.8	324.6	324.6	320.6	308.2	314.2	322.7	324.7	326.4	326.9	321.0
2012	322.5	327.0	329.0	330.8	329.8	324.0	309.2	314.4	323.5	326.0	327.2	327.0	324.2
2013	321.3	326.3	327.7	329.6	329.8	324.2	311.6	318.6	327.0	324.9	326.9	326.9	324.6
2014	321.1	322.9	324.7	328.0	328.0	322.6	312.3	320.6	325.7	325.2	325.9	324.4	323.5
2015	319.1	320.4	320.9	323.7	323.2	317.8	303.4	310.8	319.1	319.0	320.1	319.4	318.1

2. Average Weekly Hours by Selected Industry: Kentucky, 2011–2015

(Not seasonally adjusted)

Industry and year	January	February	March	April	May	June	July	August	September	October	November	December	Annual average
Total Private													
2011	34.6	34.6	34.8	34.9	35.2	35.2	35.1	35.2	35.0	35.4	34.9	34.8	35.0
2012	34.8	34.7	34.6	34.5	34.5	34.8	34.8	34.6	34.7	34.6	34.6	35.1	34.7
2013	34.4	34.6	34.6	34.5	34.4	34.9	34.7	34.7	34.9	34.9	34.9	35.3	34.7
2014	33.7	34.6	34.6	34.6	34.8	35.2	34.8	34.9	35.0	35.0	35.5	35.6	34.9
2015	34.9	34.4	35.0	35.0	35.2	35.4	35.4	35.7	35.3	35.5	35.7	35.8	35.3
Goods-Producing													
2011	39.6	40.0	40.8	40.3	40.5	40.8	40.5	41.7	40.7	41.1	40.0	40.2	40.5
2012	40.2	40.1	40.4	40.8	40.4	40.8	40.4	40.4	40.5	40.4	40.3	41.1	40.5
2013	40.5	40.5	40.1	40.1	40.0	40.5	40.5	40.5	40.5	40.7	40.8	40.9	40.5
2014	38.6	39.4	39.7	39.7	40.0	40.6	40.4	40.8	40.6	40.7	41.5	41.9	40.3
2015	41.1	39.8	40.5	40.9	41.4	41.6	41.0	41.8	40.8	41.2	41.2	42.0	41.1
Construction													
2011	36.2	36.1	37.8	37.3	39.6	39.8	38.9	40.8	38.4	39.2	39.1	37.7	38.5
2012	36.2	37.0	37.1	38.6	38.2	39.1	38.8	39.2	39.8	39.7	38.6	38.0	38.4
2013	36.5	36.9	36.3	37.7	36.8	37.8	39.3	39.0	38.7	39.8	39.9	38.0	38.1
2014	34.9	34.6	35.9	36.3	36.9	37.5	38.0	38.8	37.9	36.1	38.2	38.6	37.1
2015	38.1	36.7	36.9	37.8	39.6	39.8	39.8	40.4	38.1	41.1	39.7	40.5	39.1
Manufacturing													
2011	40.5	40.8	41.4	40.8	40.3	40.4	40.3	41.5	41.0	41.2	40.0	40.6	40.7
2012	40.9	40.4	41.0	40.9	40.6	40.8	40.3	39.7	39.8	39.9	39.9	41.0	40.4
2013	40.6	40.6	40.7	40.3	40.5	40.9	40.3	40.6	40.6	40.6	40.7	41.2	40.6
2014	39.8	41.1	41.0	40.8	40.9	41.6	41.1	41.3	41.3	41.8	42.3	42.6	41.3
2015	41.2	39.9	40.8	41.2	41.4	41.8	40.9	41.7	41.2	41.2	41.7	42.5	41.3
Trade, Transportation, and Utilities													
2011	34.0	33.9	34.0	34.5	34.8	35.2	35.2	34.9	35.0	35.4	35.0	35.0	34.7
2012	34.8	34.6	34.3	34.3	34.5	35.0	34.8	34.8	34.8	34.8	34.6	34.9	34.7
2013	34.6	34.8	34.9	35.0	35.1	35.2	35.2	35.5	35.5	35.3	35.2	35.6	35.2
2014	33.8	34.7	34.7	34.7	35.5	35.4	35.0	34.9	35.4	35.2	35.9	36.2	35.1
2015	34.7	34.7	35.3	35.7	35.9	36.0	35.8	36.2	36.0	35.9	36.2	36.3	35.7
Financial Activities													
2011	39.4	37.7	38.5	37.8	39.2	37.8	37.9	37.5	37.2	37.7	37.0	36.6	37.9
2012	38.5	36.4	36.4	37.2	36.0	36.3	37.2	35.9	36.9	35.8	36.0	38.2	36.7
2013	36.7	36.1	36.4	36.7	36.0	37.2	36.4	36.5	37.5	36.4	36.1	37.0	36.6
2014	36.0	37.0	36.6	36.1	36.5	37.6	36.4	36.2	36.5	36.6	37.2	36.1	36.6
2015	35.9	36.0	36.9	36.0	36.3	36.7	36.7	37.1	36.6	37.2	37.6	37.0	36.7
Professional and Business Services													
2011	35.2	35.2	35.4	35.9	35.9	35.6	35.5	36.2	35.4	36.2	35.2	35.1	35.6
2012	34.5	34.7	33.9	34.1	34.4	34.6	34.8	35.0	35.2	34.6	34.8	34.3	34.6
2013	32.9	33.8	33.9	33.4	33.3	34.7	34.2	34.0	34.1	34.8	34.5	36.4	34.2
2014	34.8	36.7	36.4	36.9	36.3	36.7	35.4	35.9	35.8	35.7	35.9	36.2	36.1
2015	35.7	35.6	35.8	36.1	36.0	36.1	36.4	36.5	35.8	36.3	36.5	36.4	36.1
Education and Health Services													
2011	34.7	34.8	34.6	34.7	35.2	35.2	35.1	34.9	34.9	34.9	34.6	34.6	34.8
2012	34.6	34.7	34.8	33.9	34.8	34.6	34.7	34.5	34.5	34.3	34.7	34.5	34.5
2013	34.0	33.8	33.9	33.9	33.8	34.2	33.9	34.1	34.3	34.3	34.5	34.4	34.1
2014	33.7	34.2	34.0	34.2	34.0	34.4	34.3	34.4	34.5	34.6	35.0	34.8	34.3
2015	34.7	34.2	34.6	34.5	34.5	34.7	35.0	35.2	35.0	34.9	35.3	34.8	34.8
Leisure and Hospitality													
2011	24.0	24.8	25.0	24.8	25.5	25.5	25.6	25.0	25.1	25.5	25.1	25.2	25.1
2012	25.1	25.8	25.9	25.6	25.6	26.0	25.8	25.4	25.0	25.1	24.6	25.6	25.5
2013	24.2	24.7	24.9	25.0	25.0	25.3	25.2	25.0	24.9	25.0	24.9	24.8	24.9
2014	24.4	25.3	25.6	25.7	25.4	26.0	25.6	25.3	25.2	25.2	25.1	25.2	25.3
2015	24.2	23.8	24.7	24.8	24.3	24.9	24.9	24.9	24.6	25.1	24.9	25.4	24.7

3. Average Hourly Earnings by Selected Industry: Kentucky, 2011–2015

(Dollars, not seasonally adjusted)

Industry and year	January	February	March	April	May	June	July	August	September	October	November	December	Annual average
Total Private													
2011	19.98	20.19	19.81	19.82	19.85	19.62	19.73	19.72	19.67	19.81	19.69	19.79	19.80
2012	20.18	20.15	19.99	20.14	19.92	19.84	20.02	19.93	20.14	20.17	20.02	20.29	20.06
2013	20.43	20.27	20.21	20.32	20.04	19.99	20.06	19.99	20.10	20.03	20.14	20.29	20.16
2014	20.36	20.60	20.63	20.40	20.23	20.32	20.46	20.50	20.35	20.51	20.87	21.13	20.53
2015	21.21	21.26	21.17	21.13	21.08	20.97	21.16	21.14	21.08	20.90	20.94	20.98	21.08
Goods-Producing													
2011	21.58	21.52	21.37	21.10	21.24	21.02	21.41	21.14	21.09	20.94	20.66	20.84	21.15
2012	21.12	21.41	21.06	21.21	21.26	21.22	21.11	21.17	21.29	21.19	21.26	21.27	21.21
2013	21.27	21.18	20.85	21.12	21.09	21.30	21.32	21.30	21.56	21.64	21.77	21.85	21.36
2014	21.33	21.35	21.33	21.55	21.29	21.36	21.51	21.72	21.88	22.10	22.34	23.43	21.78
2015	22.71	22.71	22.75	22.94	22.78	22.68	23.10	22.72	22.62	22.73	22.93	22.97	22.80
Construction													
2011	22.08	22.44	21.96	21.90	21.84	21.86	22.02	22.32	21.95	22.01	21.94	22.21	22.04
2012	22.18	22.03	22.14	22.00	22.04	22.37	22.08	22.45	22.28	22.78	22.79	22.47	22.31
2013	21.26	21.67	21.13	21.58	21.18	21.15	21.26	20.96	20.76	21.19	21.43	21.15	21.22
2014	21.33	21.08	20.74	21.08	20.85	20.70	21.55	21.99	22.12	22.63	22.77	23.31	21.72
2015	23.11	23.46	23.61	23.73	23.50	23.72	24.63	23.99	23.45	23.42	23.90	23.92	23.72
Manufacturing													
2011	21.34	21.19	20.96	20.57	20.81	20.42	20.90	20.34	20.49	20.30	19.90	20.11	20.61
2012	20.40	20.21	20.20	20.36	20.26	20.16	20.22	20.15	20.42	20.12	20.23	20.31	20.25
2013	20.40	20.29	20.08	20.24	20.34	20.67	20.63	20.69	20.92	20.94	21.10	21.24	20.63
2014	21.27	21.56	21.62	21.75	21.43	21.54	21.42	21.46	21.54	21.74	21.91	23.27	21.72
2015	22.24	22.15	22.17	22.38	22.19	21.89	22.13	21.80	21.94	21.96	22.04	22.03	22.07
Trade, Transportation, and Utilities													
2011	18.23	18.21	18.04	17.91	17.83	17.65	17.70	17.64	17.29	17.50	17.43	17.51	17.74
2012	17.85	17.62	17.77	18.06	17.82	17.57	17.76	17.62	17.59	17.45	17.36	17.47	17.66
2013	17.96	17.89	18.09	18.08	18.08	18.33	18.36	18.57	18.55	18.66	18.68	19.33	18.39
2014	19.55	19.54	19.77	19.50	19.58	19.75	19.76	19.63	19.61	19.71	19.70	19.59	19.64
2015	20.04	20.00	19.89	20.10	20.01	20.18	20.09	20.25	20.17	20.08	20.03	19.89	20.06
Financial Activities													
2011	21.57	21.84	20.81	20.89	20.72	20.57	20.22	20.84	20.30	21.06	21.09	20.97	20.91
2012	20.60	21.61	21.28	21.53	21.19	21.32	21.27	21.55	22.10	22.13	22.37	22.50	21.62
2013	22.76	22.95	22.72	22.74	22.55	22.61	22.59	22.82	22.32	22.68	22.47	22.26	22.62
2014	22.25	22.63	22.65	21.93	22.10	22.47	22.36	22.37	22.08	22.12	22.46	22.17	22.30
2015	22.31	22.68	22.44	22.92	22.25	22.34	22.69	23.16	22.86	23.11	23.07	23.14	22.75
Professional and Business Services													
2011	22.16	21.88	21.64	21.25	21.43	21.31	21.51	21.18	20.96	21.21	20.73	20.63	21.31
2012	20.58	20.23	20.45	20.36	20.45	20.61	21.15	20.70	20.79	20.81	20.36	21.02	20.63
2013	20.77	21.03	21.33	21.24	20.74	20.62	20.84	20.51	20.65	20.40	20.19	19.86	20.66
2014	20.65	20.64	21.26	20.90	20.76	20.90	20.87	20.46	20.81	20.64	20.66	20.34	20.74
2015	20.84	21.33	21.54	21.09	21.24	21.28	21.88	22.29	22.16	22.19	22.33	22.21	21.71
Education and Health Services													
2011	21.79	22.31	21.63	22.09	22.68	22.68	22.77	22.95	23.18	23.45	23.58	23.76	22.74
2012	24.91	24.69	24.34	24.73	23.96	24.05	24.67	24.60	25.46	25.83	25.14	25.73	24.84
2013	25.65	25.04	24.98	24.85	24.09	23.90	24.04	23.72	23.59	23.10	23.41	23.25	24.13
2014	23.20	23.50	23.28	23.36	22.93	22.85	23.31	23.13	23.34	23.32	23.77	24.10	23.34
2015	24.34	24.18	24.02	23.65	23.87	23.48	23.47	23.12	23.26	23.29	22.89	23.22	23.56
Leisure and Hospitality													
2011	10.77	10.83	10.74	10.74	10.60	10.66	10.54	10.72	10.65	10.77	10.82	10.87	10.72
2012	10.72	10.67	10.62	10.52	10.61	10.56	10.56	10.54	10.60	10.55	10.45	10.49	10.57
2013	10.41	10.46	10.28	10.31	10.33	10.29	10.27	10.41	10.48	10.58	10.47	10.65	10.41
2014	10.62	10.80	10.79	10.75	10.77	10.75	10.72	11.01	11.08	11.20	11.26	11.39	10.93
2015	11.37	11.55	11.36	11.41	11.33	11.19	11.31	11.44	11.34	11.47	11.51	11.58	11.40

4. Average Weekly Earnings by Selected Industry: Kentucky, 2011–2015

(Dollars, not seasonally adjusted)

Industry and year	January	February	March	April	May	June	July	August	September	October	November	December	Annual average
Total Private													
2011	691.31	698.57	689.39	691.72	698.72	690.62	692.52	694.14	688.45	701.27	687.18	688.69	693.00
2012	702.26	699.21	691.65	694.83	687.24	690.43	696.70	689.58	698.86	697.88	692.69	712.18	696.08
2013	702.79	701.34	699.27	701.04	689.38	697.65	696.08	693.65	701.49	699.05	702.89	716.24	699.55
2014	686.13	712.76	713.80	705.84	704.00	715.26	712.01	715.45	712.25	717.85	740.89	752.23	716.50
2015	740.23	731.34	740.95	739.55	742.02	742.34	749.06	754.70	744.12	741.95	747.56	751.08	744.12
Goods-Producing													
2011	854.57	860.80	871.90	850.33	860.22	857.62	867.11	881.54	858.36	860.63	826.40	837.77	856.58
2012	849.02	858.54	850.82	865.37	858.90	865.78	852.84	855.27	862.25	856.08	856.78	874.20	859.01
2013	861.44	857.79	836.09	846.91	843.60	862.65	863.46	862.65	873.18	880.75	888.22	893.67	865.08
2014	823.34	841.19	846.80	855.54	851.60	867.22	869.00	886.18	888.33	899.47	927.11	981.72	877.73
2015	933.38	903.86	921.38	938.25	943.09	943.49	947.10	949.70	922.90	936.48	944.72	964.74	937.08
Construction													
2011	799.30	810.08	830.09	816.87	864.86	870.03	856.58	910.66	842.88	862.79	857.85	837.32	848.54
2012	802.92	815.11	821.39	849.20	841.93	874.67	856.70	880.04	886.74	904.37	879.69	853.86	856.70
2013	775.99	799.62	767.02	813.57	779.42	799.47	835.52	817.44	803.41	843.36	855.06	803.70	808.48
2014	744.42	729.37	744.57	765.20	769.37	776.25	818.90	853.21	838.35	816.94	869.81	899.77	805.81
2015	880.49	860.98	871.21	896.99	930.60	944.06	980.27	969.20	893.45	962.56	948.83	968.76	927.45
Manufacturing													
2011	864.27	864.55	867.74	839.26	838.64	824.97	842.27	844.11	840.09	836.36	796.00	816.47	838.83
2012	834.36	816.48	828.20	832.72	822.56	822.53	814.87	799.96	812.72	802.79	807.18	832.71	818.10
2013	828.24	823.77	817.26	815.67	823.77	845.40	831.39	840.01	849.35	850.16	858.77	875.09	837.58
2014	846.55	886.12	886.42	887.40	876.49	896.06	880.36	886.30	889.60	908.73	926.79	991.30	897.04
2015	916.29	883.79	904.54	922.06	918.67	915.00	905.12	909.06	903.93	904.75	919.07	936.28	911.49
Trade, Transportation, and Utilities													
2011	619.82	617.32	613.36	617.90	620.48	621.28	623.04	615.64	605.15	619.50	610.05	612.85	615.58
2012	621.18	609.65	609.51	619.46	614.79	614.95	618.05	613.18	612.13	607.26	600.66	609.70	612.80
2013	621.42	622.57	631.34	632.80	634.61	645.22	646.27	659.24	658.53	658.70	657.54	688.15	647.33
2014	660.79	678.04	686.02	676.65	695.09	699.15	691.60	685.09	694.19	693.79	707.23	709.16	689.36
2015	695.39	694.00	702.12	717.57	718.36	726.48	719.22	733.05	726.12	720.87	725.09	722.01	716.14
Financial Activities													
2011	849.86	823.37	801.19	789.64	812.22	777.55	766.34	781.50	755.16	793.96	780.33	767.50	792.49
2012	793.10	786.60	774.59	800.92	762.84	773.92	791.24	773.65	815.49	792.25	805.32	859.50	793.45
2013	835.29	828.50	827.01	834.56	811.80	841.09	822.28	832.93	837.00	825.55	811.17	823.62	827.89
2014	801.00	837.31	828.99	791.67	806.65	844.87	813.90	809.79	805.92	809.59	835.51	800.34	816.18
2015	800.93	816.48	828.04	825.12	807.68	819.88	832.72	859.24	836.68	859.69	867.43	856.18	834.93
Professional and Business Services													
2011	780.03	770.18	766.06	762.88	769.34	758.64	763.61	766.72	741.98	767.80	729.70	724.11	758.64
2012	710.01	701.98	693.26	694.28	703.48	713.11	736.02	724.50	731.81	720.03	708.53	720.99	713.80
2013	683.33	710.81	723.09	709.42	690.64	715.51	712.73	697.34	704.17	709.92	696.56	722.90	706.57
2014	718.62	757.49	773.86	771.21	753.59	767.03	738.80	734.51	745.00	736.85	741.69	736.31	748.71
2015	743.99	759.35	771.13	761.35	764.64	768.21	796.43	813.59	793.33	805.50	815.05	808.44	783.73
Education and Health Services													
2011	756.11	776.39	748.40	766.52	798.34	798.34	799.23	800.96	808.98	818.41	815.87	822.10	791.35
2012	861.89	856.74	847.03	838.35	833.81	832.13	856.05	848.70	878.37	885.97	872.36	887.69	856.98
2013	872.10	846.35	846.82	842.42	814.24	817.38	814.96	808.85	809.14	792.33	807.65	799.80	822.83
2014	781.84	803.70	791.52	798.91	779.62	786.04	799.53	795.67	805.23	806.87	831.95	838.68	800.56
2015	844.60	826.96	831.09	815.93	823.52	814.76	821.45	813.82	814.10	812.82	808.02	808.06	819.89
Leisure and Hospitality													
2011	258.48	268.58	268.50	266.35	270.30	271.83	269.82	268.00	267.32	274.64	271.58	273.92	269.07
2012	269.07	275.29	275.06	269.31	271.62	274.56	272.45	267.72	265.00	264.81	257.07	268.54	269.54
2013	251.92	258.36	255.97	257.75	258.25	260.34	258.80	260.25	260.95	264.50	260.70	264.12	259.21
2014	259.13	273.24	276.22	276.28	273.56	279.50	274.43	278.55	279.22	282.24	282.63	287.03	276.53
2015	275.15	274.89	280.59	282.97	275.32	278.63	281.62	284.86	278.96	287.90	286.60	294.13	281.58

LOUISIANA
At a Glance

Population:
  2005 estimate: 4,576,628
  2010 census: 4,533,372
  2015 estimate: 4,670,724

Percent change in population:
  2005–2015: 2.1%
  2010–2015: 3.0%

Percent change in total nonfarm employment:
  2005–2015: 5.2%

Industry with the largest growth in employment, 2005–2015 (thousands):
  Education and health services, 58.7

Industry with the largest decline or smallest growth in employment, 2005–2015 (thousands):
  Manufacturing, –8.0

Civilian labor force:
  2005: 2,069,403
  2010: 2,086,076
  2015: 2,160,195

Unemployment rate and rank among states (highest to lowest):
  2005: 7.2%, 2nd
  2010: 8.0%, 35th
  2015: 6.3%, 7th

Over-the-year change in unemployment rates:
  2012–2013: –0.4%
  2013–2014: –0.3%
  2014–2015: –0.1%

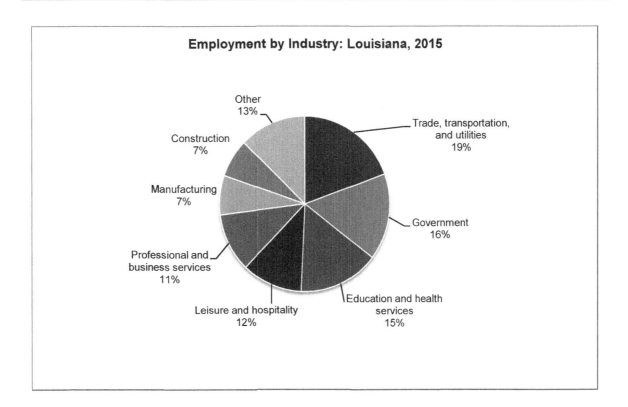

Employment by Industry: Louisiana, 2015

Other 13%
Construction 7%
Manufacturing 7%
Professional and business services 11%
Leisure and hospitality 12%
Education and health services 15%
Trade, transportation, and utilities 19%
Government 16%

1. Employment by Industry: Louisiana, 2005–2015

(Numbers in thousands, not seasonally adjusted)

Industry and year	January	February	March	April	May	June	July	August	September	October	November	December	Annual average
Total Nonfarm													
2005	1,904.9	1,913.9	1,930.8	1,948.5	1,951.8	1,953.3	1,937.6	1,941.1	1,823.8	1,776.0	1,801.9	1,817.6	1,891.8
2006	1,789.8	1,813.1	1,839.8	1,841.6	1,854.4	1,859.5	1,835.1	1,852.6	1,875.0	1,880.6	1,893.1	1,904.8	1,853.3
2007	1,876.7	1,895.6	1,915.8	1,904.8	1,911.9	1,918.0	1,894.3	1,911.6	1,922.3	1,936.9	1,947.5	1,953.9	1,915.8
2008	1,911.0	1,929.0	1,938.0	1,940.3	1,946.0	1,941.3	1,920.3	1,938.5	1,923.1	1,951.0	1,958.1	1,959.4	1,938.0
2009	1,910.8	1,918.7	1,919.0	1,910.3	1,912.7	1,897.8	1,881.7	1,886.6	1,891.5	1,895.1	1,902.2	1,896.1	1,901.9
2010	1,856.4	1,864.8	1,881.8	1,890.6	1,898.5	1,896.4	1,873.8	1,877.1	1,886.7	1,896.5	1,901.4	1,903.2	1,885.6
2011	1,872.5	1,886.7	1,898.6	1,907.5	1,909.1	1,897.3	1,888.5	1,895.7	1,910.2	1,918.3	1,925.3	1,924.6	1,902.9
2012	1,894.9	1,909.0	1,920.5	1,935.0	1,941.2	1,931.7	1,908.0	1,917.5	1,921.7	1,939.4	1,952.3	1,951.5	1,926.9
2013	1,918.4	1,937.2	1,946.0	1,953.9	1,957.1	1,953.5	1,936.3	1,950.8	1,957.2	1,974.6	1,985.4	1,977.0	1,954.0
2014	1,947.8	1,958.8	1,970.8	1,977.8	1,986.9	1,981.8	1,969.8	1,983.8	1,991.0	2,009.8	2,017.7	2,018.3	1,984.5
2015	1,982.2	1,987.9	1,989.1	1,995.0	1,999.4	1,991.4	1,978.0	1,980.8	1,983.2	1,994.3	1,998.0	1,993.8	1,989.4
Total Private													
2005	1,528.4	1,530.6	1,547.7	1,564.3	1,569.6	1,573.6	1,567.8	1,570.9	1,445.7	1,415.8	1,441.1	1,458.7	1,517.9
2006	1,446.8	1,463.6	1,488.7	1,492.3	1,504.5	1,517.9	1,501.1	1,513.4	1,522.1	1,526.9	1,537.1	1,549.2	1,505.3
2007	1,528.0	1,538.4	1,556.3	1,551.0	1,558.3	1,566.6	1,554.1	1,565.3	1,562.1	1,573.6	1,581.6	1,588.6	1,560.3
2008	1,553.8	1,563.9	1,573.6	1,573.6	1,579.2	1,580.3	1,567.0	1,579.1	1,558.1	1,579.9	1,584.5	1,588.5	1,573.5
2009	1,546.1	1,547.0	1,547.5	1,536.9	1,540.6	1,532.5	1,526.4	1,529.5	1,521.9	1,518.7	1,524.5	1,520.8	1,532.7
2010	1,489.8	1,493.5	1,508.2	1,517.5	1,520.5	1,526.2	1,521.3	1,523.8	1,525.7	1,531.4	1,535.0	1,538.6	1,519.3
2011	1,514.9	1,524.9	1,536.8	1,545.9	1,549.1	1,543.5	1,545.2	1,550.8	1,553.5	1,557.3	1,563.9	1,566.3	1,546.0
2012	1,544.9	1,554.8	1,567.1	1,580.6	1,587.9	1,584.6	1,572.3	1,580.6	1,575.7	1,588.4	1,600.5	1,600.7	1,578.2
2013	1,577.9	1,592.1	1,601.1	1,609.4	1,613.5	1,615.8	1,609.5	1,625.1	1,620.5	1,636.5	1,645.0	1,639.3	1,615.5
2014	1,618.1	1,624.7	1,637.9	1,645.2	1,654.7	1,653.9	1,654.0	1,664.9	1,660.4	1,676.2	1,682.2	1,686.0	1,654.9
2015	1,656.0	1,657.0	1,659.8	1,664.6	1,669.8	1,666.1	1,663.7	1,663.9	1,655.3	1,663.5	1,665.4	1,663.8	1,662.4
Goods-Producing													
2005	309.7	311.3	315.2	320.8	322.8	324.4	322.5	323.9	308.4	312.4	315.9	318.4	317.1
2006	321.2	323.6	328.7	330.5	332.7	337.0	328.8	333.2	337.3	338.9	339.0	341.9	332.7
2007	333.1	336.4	339.6	341.0	343.5	345.7	343.1	345.1	344.4	346.6	345.9	344.7	342.4
2008	337.8	339.2	340.0	341.2	344.1	345.8	344.0	345.6	342.0	347.8	346.0	345.2	343.2
2009	336.2	333.4	331.3	326.9	327.5	325.2	323.5	321.7	318.7	317.9	316.1	312.2	324.2
2010	306.4	305.9	309.4	310.5	311.5	314.9	315.1	315.0	314.3	315.4	312.7	312.4	312.0
2011	307.6	310.5	313.8	316.6	316.4	316.3	319.4	319.1	320.4	320.3	317.7	316.2	316.2
2012	315.7	319.5	322.4	323.1	325.8	327.7	323.2	325.5	326.4	328.1	327.8	325.0	324.2
2013	320.4	325.0	328.4	328.5	330.3	333.2	332.5	334.0	334.5	338.6	336.1	331.6	331.1
2014	331.4	333.7	337.7	336.5	341.8	341.6	345.5	347.4	348.0	351.7	346.1	343.7	342.1
2015	338.2	336.2	334.8	331.7	331.1	332.4	333.3	332.9	331.8	334.3	331.5	329.9	333.2
Service-Providing													
2005	1,595.2	1,602.6	1,615.6	1,627.7	1,629.0	1,628.9	1,615.1	1,617.2	1,515.4	1,463.6	1,486.0	1,499.2	1,574.6
2006	1,468.6	1,489.5	1,511.1	1,511.1	1,521.7	1,522.5	1,506.3	1,519.4	1,537.7	1,541.7	1,554.1	1,562.9	1,520.6
2007	1,543.6	1,559.2	1,576.2	1,563.8	1,568.4	1,572.3	1,551.2	1,566.5	1,577.9	1,590.3	1,601.6	1,609.2	1,573.4
2008	1,573.2	1,589.8	1,598.0	1,599.1	1,601.9	1,595.5	1,576.3	1,592.9	1,581.1	1,603.2	1,612.1	1,614.2	1,594.8
2009	1,574.6	1,585.3	1,587.7	1,583.4	1,585.2	1,572.6	1,558.2	1,564.9	1,572.8	1,577.2	1,586.1	1,583.9	1,577.7
2010	1,550.0	1,558.9	1,572.4	1,580.1	1,587.0	1,581.5	1,558.7	1,562.1	1,572.4	1,581.1	1,588.7	1,590.8	1,573.6
2011	1,564.9	1,576.2	1,584.8	1,590.9	1,592.7	1,581.0	1,569.1	1,576.6	1,589.8	1,598.0	1,607.6	1,608.4	1,586.7
2012	1,579.2	1,589.5	1,598.1	1,611.9	1,615.4	1,604.0	1,584.8	1,592.0	1,595.3	1,611.3	1,624.5	1,626.5	1,602.7
2013	1,598.0	1,612.2	1,617.6	1,625.4	1,626.8	1,620.3	1,603.8	1,616.8	1,622.7	1,636.0	1,649.3	1,645.4	1,622.9
2014	1,616.4	1,625.1	1,633.1	1,641.3	1,645.1	1,640.2	1,624.3	1,636.4	1,643.0	1,658.1	1,671.6	1,674.6	1,642.4
2015	1,644.0	1,651.7	1,654.3	1,663.3	1,668.3	1,659.0	1,644.7	1,647.9	1,651.4	1,660.0	1,666.5	1,663.9	1,656.3
Mining and Logging													
2005	44.8	45.0	45.6	46.1	46.4	46.9	46.7	46.9	46.6	46.2	45.9	46.0	46.1
2006	47.2	47.7	48.1	48.0	48.4	49.4	49.9	50.5	51.3	51.0	50.8	51.0	49.4
2007	50.5	50.7	50.9	52.0	52.5	52.9	52.8	53.8	53.2	53.3	53.7	53.6	52.5
2008	54.7	54.5	54.8	54.9	55.2	55.8	56.2	56.3	55.7	57.2	56.8	56.5	55.7
2009	55.7	54.9	54.1	52.0	52.2	52.1	50.9	50.8	50.3	50.5	50.6	51.1	52.1
2010	50.3	51.4	51.9	52.5	53.1	53.6	53.1	53.3	52.9	53.2	52.9	53.0	52.6
2011	52.4	52.9	53.1	54.1	53.9	54.6	55.6	55.8	55.8	55.7	55.7	55.9	54.6
2012	56.9	57.7	57.4	56.1	56.6	56.5	54.8	55.1	54.5	54.7	54.7	54.2	55.8
2013	54.0	54.4	54.6	55.0	55.3	55.8	56.1	56.4	56.0	56.0	55.8	55.5	55.4
2014	55.4	55.2	55.3	54.9	55.6	55.6	56.2	56.1	55.9	56.0	55.7	55.6	55.6
2015	54.5	52.4	51.0	49.0	48.7	47.6	47.7	47.4	46.3	45.5	43.7	43.2	48.1

1. Employment by Industry: Louisiana, 2005–2015—*Continued*

(Numbers in thousands, not seasonally adjusted)

Industry and year	January	February	March	April	May	June	July	August	September	October	November	December	Annual average
Construction													
2005	112.2	113.9	116.2	120.7	121.4	121.6	120.9	121.2	114.5	118.5	121.8	122.8	118.8
2006	125.7	127.3	130.8	132.4	133.3	134.9	127.3	129.0	130.3	131.8	131.6	133.3	130.6
2007	129.1	130.5	132.7	132.2	133.8	134.3	132.3	133.8	133.5	134.7	133.6	132.8	132.8
2008	129.3	131.0	132.0	133.7	135.3	136.1	134.8	136.4	135.3	138.0	137.7	137.1	134.7
2009	132.7	132.9	132.7	130.8	131.9	131.1	131.6	130.3	128.3	127.9	126.9	123.5	130.1
2010	119.5	118.7	120.6	119.5	119.7	122.5	123.9	123.6	123.4	123.5	121.8	121.1	121.5
2011	118.4	120.3	122.8	124.4	123.5	122.5	123.4	122.5	123.1	122.3	120.3	118.8	121.9
2012	119.2	122.1	124.4	125.2	126.5	127.6	125.2	127.0	128.8	130.6	130.1	127.8	126.2
2013	124.5	128.4	131.1	130.6	131.1	132.3	131.4	132.2	132.8	135.6	133.6	129.7	131.1
2014	129.7	132.8	136.6	135.4	138.8	138.2	141.2	142.9	144.2	146.8	141.8	139.6	139.0
2015	136.6	137.5	138.9	138.2	138.1	140.2	141.7	141.9	142.9	145.2	145.2	144.9	140.9
Manufacturing													
2005	152.7	152.4	153.4	154.0	155.0	155.9	154.9	155.8	147.3	147.7	148.2	149.6	152.2
2006	148.3	148.6	149.8	150.1	151.0	152.7	151.6	153.7	155.7	156.1	156.6	157.6	152.7
2007	153.5	155.2	156.0	156.8	157.2	158.5	158.0	157.5	157.7	158.6	158.6	158.3	157.2
2008	153.8	153.7	153.2	152.6	153.6	153.9	153.0	152.9	151.0	152.6	151.5	151.6	152.8
2009	147.8	145.6	144.5	144.1	143.4	142.0	141.0	140.6	140.1	139.5	138.6	137.6	142.1
2010	136.6	135.8	136.9	138.5	138.7	138.8	138.1	138.1	138.0	138.7	138.0	138.3	137.9
2011	136.8	137.3	137.9	138.1	139.0	139.2	140.4	140.8	141.5	142.3	141.7	141.5	139.7
2012	139.6	139.7	140.6	141.8	142.7	143.6	143.2	143.4	143.1	142.8	143.0	143.0	142.2
2013	141.9	142.2	142.7	142.9	143.9	145.1	145.0	145.4	145.7	147.0	146.7	146.4	144.6
2014	146.3	145.7	145.8	146.2	147.4	147.8	148.1	148.4	147.9	148.9	148.6	148.5	147.5
2015	147.1	146.3	144.9	144.5	144.3	144.6	143.9	143.6	142.6	143.6	142.6	141.8	144.2
Trade, Transportation, and Utilities													
2005	375.8	375.1	378.2	381.3	382.9	384.2	385.1	385.1	353.2	348.5	361.8	369.9	373.4
2006	361.1	362.9	369.6	368.9	371.4	374.4	373.2	374.6	375.2	377.0	382.4	388.6	373.3
2007	378.9	377.9	382.4	378.8	380.3	381.3	380.6	382.3	382.7	385.8	391.9	396.2	383.3
2008	383.5	381.9	384.7	382.9	384.0	383.8	381.9	383.8	378.1	382.2	386.9	390.5	383.7
2009	375.5	373.0	373.0	369.2	369.2	369.7	369.5	368.8	367.7	365.2	370.1	371.2	370.2
2010	359.6	358.6	361.7	364.2	365.6	366.4	365.9	366.6	366.1	370.5	376.3	379.9	366.8
2011	369.8	368.9	370.7	373.1	374.0	373.1	373.9	373.9	373.1	374.6	381.3	384.2	374.2
2012	373.6	372.1	374.7	376.3	377.6	377.3	375.6	375.9	374.8	378.7	387.6	389.5	377.8
2013	378.0	376.5	379.7	380.2	380.4	381.4	380.8	382.5	383.2	384.7	391.0	395.5	382.8
2014	383.2	381.7	384.2	385.5	387.3	388.6	388.0	389.8	389.6	391.9	399.5	405.4	389.6
2015	392.4	389.7	391.4	392.0	392.8	393.1	392.2	392.8	390.7	391.0	396.5	398.2	392.7
Wholesale Trade													
2005	73.6	73.8	74.1	75.0	75.3	75.4	76.3	76.3	71.6	71.0	71.4	71.8	73.8
2006	70.5	71.1	71.8	72.1	72.7	73.5	73.2	73.5	73.5	73.4	73.7	74.1	72.8
2007	74.9	75.2	75.8	74.9	75.3	75.9	76.4	76.8	76.3	76.6	76.6	76.9	76.0
2008	75.6	75.9	76.3	75.9	76.1	76.1	75.8	76.0	75.5	75.4	75.0	75.2	75.7
2009	73.3	73.2	72.8	72.1	72.0	71.7	71.5	71.3	71.0	70.9	70.8	70.4	71.8
2010	69.2	69.4	69.9	70.2	70.5	70.6	70.6	70.8	70.6	71.3	71.2	71.2	70.5
2011	71.6	71.8	72.1	71.5	72.0	72.0	72.5	72.5	72.4	72.6	72.7	72.8	72.2
2012	71.9	72.1	72.4	72.7	72.7	72.8	72.5	72.5	72.1	72.3	72.6	72.6	72.4
2013	72.7	72.8	73.2	73.1	73.2	73.2	73.2	73.5	73.4	73.5	73.6	73.5	73.2
2014	72.4	72.6	72.9	72.9	73.4	73.4	73.3	73.5	73.7	73.6	73.6	73.8	73.3
2015	73.0	72.8	73.0	72.7	72.7	72.7	72.6	72.6	72.1	71.9	71.8	72.2	72.5
Retail Trade													
2005	222.1	220.9	223.1	224.9	225.8	226.7	226.5	226.6	204.2	201.7	213.4	219.6	219.6
2006	213.8	214.7	219.2	218.1	219.3	220.4	219.3	219.9	219.8	222.1	226.7	230.3	220.3
2007	222.3	221.2	224.8	222.6	223.6	223.6	223.2	223.4	224.3	226.6	232.6	236.1	225.4
2008	226.6	224.5	226.6	224.6	224.9	224.9	224.0	225.0	220.6	223.5	228.5	231.4	225.4
2009	220.7	219.7	220.3	219.8	220.3	221.1	221.3	220.6	220.1	217.7	222.7	223.7	220.7
2010	215.1	214.1	216.2	216.7	217.2	217.2	216.2	216.0	215.6	218.4	224.5	226.8	217.8
2011	218.7	217.7	219.2	221.2	221.4	220.6	220.1	219.5	218.6	219.9	226.4	228.1	221.0
2012	220.4	218.8	220.4	221.2	222.0	221.7	220.9	220.3	219.5	222.9	230.6	231.8	222.5
2013	221.3	219.3	221.4	221.7	221.9	223.0	222.8	223.6	224.2	225.0	231.0	233.8	224.1
2014	223.6	222.4	223.8	224.9	225.8	227.4	226.8	227.2	226.6	228.6	235.8	239.6	227.7
2015	229.3	228.5	230.4	231.1	231.9	232.9	232.5	232.9	231.5	232.3	237.1	237.6	232.3

1. Employment by Industry: Louisiana, 2005–2015—*Continued*

(Numbers in thousands, not seasonally adjusted)

Industry and year	January	February	March	April	May	June	July	August	September	October	November	December	Annual average
Transportation and Utilities													
2005	80.1	80.4	81.0	81.4	81.8	82.1	82.3	82.2	77.4	75.8	77.0	78.5	80.0
2006	76.8	77.1	78.6	78.7	79.4	80.5	80.7	81.2	81.9	81.5	82.0	84.2	80.2
2007	81.7	81.5	81.8	81.3	81.4	81.8	81.0	82.1	82.1	82.6	82.7	83.2	81.9
2008	81.3	81.5	81.8	82.4	83.0	82.8	82.1	82.8	82.0	83.3	83.4	83.9	82.5
2009	81.5	80.1	79.9	77.3	76.9	76.9	76.7	76.9	76.6	76.6	76.6	77.1	77.8
2010	75.3	75.1	75.6	77.3	77.9	78.6	79.1	79.8	79.9	80.8	80.6	81.9	78.5
2011	79.5	79.4	79.4	80.4	80.6	80.5	81.3	81.9	82.1	82.1	82.2	83.3	81.1
2012	81.3	81.2	81.9	82.4	82.9	82.8	82.2	83.1	83.2	83.5	84.4	85.1	82.8
2013	84.0	84.4	85.1	85.4	85.3	85.2	84.8	85.4	85.6	86.2	86.4	88.2	85.5
2014	87.2	86.7	87.5	87.7	88.1	87.8	87.9	89.1	89.3	89.7	90.1	92.0	88.6
2015	90.1	88.4	88.0	88.2	88.2	87.5	87.1	87.3	87.1	86.8	87.6	88.4	87.9
Information													
2005	31.2	30.3	30.3	29.5	29.3	29.6	30.0	30.4	28.6	26.4	26.9	27.0	29.1
2006	27.2	27.3	29.2	28.2	28.3	27.6	25.9	25.8	25.7	25.8	26.4	26.6	27.0
2007	26.5	27.5	29.6	28.7	28.5	29.0	27.9	27.4	26.2	27.0	26.7	27.1	27.7
2008	26.7	28.5	30.2	30.1	30.8	31.7	26.6	28.0	27.9	26.2	27.1	27.8	28.5
2009	24.9	25.2	25.2	24.5	24.8	24.9	24.5	24.1	23.9	24.2	25.4	24.8	24.7
2010	24.4	24.8	24.5	25.3	25.8	26.4	23.4	23.5	25.6	23.6	24.0	24.7	24.7
2011	23.4	23.5	25.1	23.7	24.6	24.0	22.9	22.9	23.0	23.6	23.5	24.2	23.7
2012	23.2	23.9	23.9	27.1	28.0	25.4	24.8	24.7	24.3	23.9	25.0	25.7	25.0
2013	25.4	26.9	26.3	27.0	27.7	28.0	25.4	25.5	24.4	26.3	27.6	25.7	26.4
2014	23.6	25.0	26.0	26.3	27.8	27.0	26.6	25.3	24.3	25.4	27.4	26.8	26.0
2015	24.8	26.6	25.5	26.5	28.6	27.3	26.0	24.4	23.3	23.4	24.5	24.1	25.4
Financial Activities													
2005	98.6	98.9	99.1	98.8	98.9	99.6	100.5	100.7	95.3	96.2	96.8	97.0	98.4
2006	95.2	95.1	95.3	94.7	95.0	95.2	94.6	94.9	94.8	95.3	95.3	95.9	95.1
2007	97.3	97.6	96.7	95.9	95.7	95.9	95.8	95.4	94.8	95.1	95.1	95.1	95.9
2008	93.7	94.1	94.4	93.9	93.9	94.2	93.6	93.3	92.5	94.3	93.3	93.2	93.7
2009	91.0	90.9	91.0	91.7	91.7	91.8	91.6	91.3	90.7	90.1	90.6	91.0	91.1
2010	90.0	90.2	90.8	90.8	91.0	91.7	92.2	92.2	91.8	92.2	92.0	92.4	91.4
2011	91.9	92.3	92.3	91.8	91.9	91.6	91.6	91.3	91.7	91.9	91.7	91.7	91.8
2012	90.8	91.2	91.4	91.4	91.5	91.6	91.4	91.4	91.1	91.7	92.4	92.7	91.6
2013	91.4	91.4	91.6	91.9	92.4	92.9	92.9	93.3	93.5	93.8	93.6	93.2	92.7
2014	92.2	92.1	92.0	92.2	92.6	92.7	93.1	93.5	93.2	93.5	93.5	93.5	92.8
2015	92.3	92.0	92.1	91.8	91.8	92.0	91.9	91.9	91.1	90.1	90.1	89.9	91.4
Professional and Business Services													
2005	186.2	186.6	189.0	193.2	191.2	190.7	190.9	191.8	174.8	180.2	185.0	187.5	187.3
2006	184.9	187.7	190.6	191.6	193.0	194.8	192.5	194.7	196.0	196.2	196.2	197.2	193.0
2007	196.9	198.8	200.8	199.6	200.1	201.4	198.6	200.8	200.8	204.6	205.1	206.1	201.1
2008	200.9	203.4	203.3	203.7	204.0	203.3	201.8	203.9	202.8	205.0	205.6	205.4	203.6
2009	197.7	198.2	197.1	193.8	193.5	192.0	190.1	190.3	188.5	190.1	190.4	190.4	192.7
2010	186.7	188.3	190.1	192.0	192.6	194.6	195.7	194.9	193.6	194.3	193.7	193.5	192.5
2011	191.3	193.8	193.8	195.3	195.4	194.9	194.6	196.4	196.6	197.7	197.7	198.0	195.5
2012	195.9	198.2	199.9	204.0	204.5	203.2	202.1	202.4	201.7	204.4	204.7	203.4	202.0
2013	200.8	206.9	205.9	205.9	205.7	205.7	205.6	207.7	205.7	210.0	210.8	210.1	206.7
2014	207.7	208.7	210.5	212.1	210.0	210.5	210.2	210.7	210.3	213.9	215.1	216.6	211.4
2015	211.8	212.5	213.3	214.6	214.1	212.7	213.5	214.1	211.9	213.2	211.9	211.1	212.9
Education and Health Services													
2005	254.9	254.9	256.2	258.1	257.1	254.9	252.3	252.6	239.8	222.7	222.3	223.2	245.8
2006	225.1	226.8	228.8	232.0	233.6	233.0	232.2	234.9	238.4	240.0	242.1	241.2	234.0
2007	241.2	243.1	244.6	246.0	245.6	245.6	243.8	248.2	249.2	251.7	253.0	253.9	247.2
2008	251.2	254.2	255.2	255.9	254.9	253.8	254.4	259.1	257.3	260.7	261.8	262.1	256.7
2009	261.0	263.4	264.1	264.9	265.5	261.0	262.3	266.4	267.3	270.2	271.0	270.8	265.7
2010	267.8	268.8	270.4	272.2	270.2	267.7	268.4	270.3	272.8	274.7	275.1	275.1	271.1
2011	272.5	274.7	275.7	277.1	276.6	273.1	273.5	276.1	279.0	281.2	282.7	282.2	277.0
2012	277.8	280.1	281.6	282.5	283.1	281.4	279.3	283.1	283.4	286.7	287.2	287.2	282.8
2013	287.0	288.8	289.1	289.5	289.0	285.2	284.7	292.4	293.4	297.8	298.1	297.0	291.0
2014	295.6	296.2	296.4	297.6	297.8	294.7	294.5	300.1	301.4	303.8	303.6	303.1	298.7
2015	302.2	302.6	302.7	305.2	305.5	302.2	301.6	304.2	305.0	307.0	307.5	308.8	304.5

1. Employment by Industry: Louisiana, 2005–2015—*Continued*

(Numbers in thousands, not seasonally adjusted)

Industry and year	January	February	March	April	May	June	July	August	September	October	November	December	Annual average
Leisure and Hospitality													
2005	202.0	203.3	208.3	211.0	215.6	218.0	214.3	214.3	180.4	167.3	169.8	171.9	198.0
2006	169.7	176.6	181.8	181.6	184.8	189.5	188.0	189.0	187.6	186.5	188.2	189.9	184.4
2007	186.4	188.7	193.2	192.5	195.5	198.2	195.3	196.2	193.7	192.3	193.4	194.7	193.3
2008	191.1	193.4	196.0	198.9	200.0	200.3	198.2	198.7	191.4	194.2	194.2	194.7	195.9
2009	190.7	193.4	196.1	196.3	198.5	198.2	195.2	196.0	194.0	191.3	191.2	190.6	194.3
2010	187.9	189.6	193.6	195.9	197.1	197.7	194.8	195.3	195.7	194.5	195.3	194.7	194.3
2011	192.6	195.0	198.9	201.6	203.7	203.6	202.2	203.9	202.5	201.1	202.5	203.1	200.9
2012	201.6	203.2	205.9	208.6	209.5	209.6	208.0	209.6	206.1	206.6	207.4	208.7	207.1
2013	206.6	207.6	210.6	214.8	216.1	217.1	215.5	217.6	213.7	213.3	215.7	214.3	213.6
2014	212.4	214.9	218.4	221.9	224.0	225.2	222.7	224.7	220.5	222.5	223.8	223.6	221.2
2015	221.3	224.1	226.5	229.0	231.6	232.0	230.5	229.3	227.5	230.1	228.7	227.7	228.2
Other Services													
2005	70.0	70.2	71.4	71.6	71.8	72.2	72.2	72.1	65.2	62.1	62.6	63.8	68.8
2006	62.4	63.6	64.7	64.8	65.7	66.4	65.9	66.3	67.1	67.2	67.5	67.9	65.8
2007	67.7	68.4	69.4	68.5	69.1	69.5	69.0	69.9	70.3	70.5	70.5	70.8	69.5
2008	68.9	69.2	69.8	67.0	67.5	67.4	66.5	66.7	66.1	69.5	69.6	69.6	68.2
2009	69.1	69.5	69.7	69.6	69.9	69.7	69.7	70.9	71.1	69.7	69.7	69.8	69.9
2010	67.0	67.3	67.7	66.6	66.7	66.8	65.8	66.0	65.8	66.2	65.9	65.9	66.5
2011	65.8	66.2	66.5	66.7	66.5	66.9	67.1	67.2	67.2	66.9	66.8	66.7	66.7
2012	66.3	66.6	67.1	67.6	67.9	68.4	67.9	68.0	67.9	68.3	68.4	68.5	67.7
2013	68.3	69.0	69.5	71.6	71.9	72.3	72.1	72.1	72.1	72.0	72.1	71.9	71.2
2014	72.0	72.4	72.7	73.1	73.4	73.6	73.4	73.4	73.1	73.5	73.2	73.3	73.1
2015	73.0	73.3	73.5	73.8	74.3	74.4	74.7	74.3	74.0	74.4	74.7	74.1	74.0
Government													
2005	376.5	383.3	383.1	384.2	382.2	379.7	369.8	370.2	378.1	360.2	360.8	358.9	373.9
2006	343.0	349.5	351.1	349.3	349.9	341.6	334.0	339.2	352.9	353.7	356.0	355.6	348.0
2007	348.7	357.2	359.5	353.8	353.6	351.4	340.2	346.3	360.2	363.3	365.9	365.3	355.5
2008	357.2	365.1	364.4	366.7	366.8	361.0	353.3	359.4	365.0	371.1	373.6	370.9	364.5
2009	364.7	371.7	371.5	373.4	372.1	365.3	355.3	357.1	369.6	376.4	377.7	375.3	369.2
2010	366.6	371.3	373.6	373.1	378.0	370.2	352.5	353.3	361.0	365.1	366.4	364.6	366.3
2011	357.6	361.8	361.8	361.6	360.0	353.8	343.3	344.9	356.7	361.0	361.4	358.3	356.9
2012	350.0	354.2	353.4	354.4	353.3	347.1	335.7	336.9	346.0	351.0	351.8	350.8	348.7
2013	340.5	345.1	344.9	344.5	343.6	337.7	326.8	325.7	336.7	338.1	340.4	337.7	338.5
2014	329.7	334.1	332.9	332.6	332.2	327.9	315.8	318.9	330.6	333.6	335.5	332.3	329.7
2015	326.2	330.9	329.3	330.4	329.6	325.3	314.3	316.9	327.9	330.8	332.6	330.0	327.0

2. Average Weekly Hours by Selected Industry: Louisiana, 2011–2015

(Not seasonally adjusted)

Industry and year	January	February	March	April	May	June	July	August	September	October	November	December	Annual average
Total Private													
2011	36.5	36.2	36.0	36.4	36.7	36.4	36.3	36.2	36.1	36.8	36.1	36.1	36.3
2012	36.1	36.0	36.1	36.6	36.5	36.4	36.4	36.4	36.2	35.8	35.7	35.9	36.2
2013	35.0	35.4	36.0	35.7	35.7	36.4	35.6	35.9	36.1	35.9	35.8	36.1	35.8
2014	35.5	36.2	36.5	36.0	36.1	36.4	36.1	36.4	36.2	36.4	36.8	36.6	36.3
2015	35.9	36.4	35.9	35.7	35.8	35.9	35.9	36.3	35.4	35.9	36.0	35.8	35.9
Goods-Producing													
2011	41.8	41.4	40.9	42.0	42.3	42.0	41.6	42.1	41.6	43.0	42.5	41.9	41.9
2012	41.3	42.6	42.9	43.1	43.9	43.4	41.8	43.0	43.7	43.5	43.3	43.2	43.0
2013	41.1	41.9	42.8	43.3	43.2	43.5	42.8	43.9	44.0	44.5	43.7	44.2	43.2
2014	43.1	42.8	43.1	42.8	43.1	43.0	42.8	43.6	43.0	43.4	43.6	44.0	43.2
2015	42.2	42.1	40.6	41.0	41.5	41.3	41.3	41.8	40.3	42.5	42.3	42.4	41.6
Construction													
2011	42.0	40.8	40.2	41.9	42.4	41.9	40.7	41.8	41.6	41.8	41.3	40.6	41.4
2012	38.9	39.5	41.4	41.4	42.0	41.8	40.7	42.6	42.5	43.0	43.1	42.9	41.7
2013	38.6	41.2	42.6	42.4	42.1	43.5	41.7	43.0	43.6	44.0	41.9	42.1	42.2
2014	41.8	41.9	42.5	42.9	43.2	41.8	42.8	43.4	42.8	42.3	41.6	42.2	42.4
2015	40.3	40.6	38.6	40.0	40.9	41.5	41.4	41.5	38.6	41.8	41.5	42.3	40.7
Manufacturing													
2011	40.8	40.8	40.6	41.0	41.1	41.2	41.2	41.1	40.2	42.8	42.2	41.8	41.2
2012	42.2	44.0	42.9	43.5	44.3	43.6	41.9	42.9	44.3	43.7	43.4	43.8	43.4
2013	42.8	42.1	42.6	43.6	43.7	43.3	43.2	44.4	43.9	44.7	44.8	44.9	43.7
2014	43.3	42.3	42.6	42.2	42.8	43.1	42.3	42.6	42.5	44.6	45.4	45.7	43.3
2015	43.9	43.2	42.5	42.2	41.9	40.9	41.1	41.2	40.7	42.3	42.3	42.1	42.0
Trade, Transportation, and Utilities													
2011	37.0	36.7	36.8	36.8	37.8	37.5	37.5	36.7	36.6	37.0	36.2	36.2	36.9
2012	36.7	35.2	35.6	36.1	36.4	36.3	36.5	36.4	37.4	36.2	35.7	36.0	36.2
2013	35.8	35.9	36.7	36.3	36.7	37.2	36.4	36.2	36.2	35.4	35.1	35.1	36.1
2014	34.9	35.7	35.8	35.5	35.8	35.7	35.7	36.1	36.2	36.1	36.2	36.2	35.8
2015	35.6	35.9	36.1	36.2	36.4	36.1	36.3	36.6	35.9	35.4	35.9	36.1	36.0
Financial Activities													
2011	37.0	36.6	36.7	36.7	38.8	37.4	37.4	37.0	37.8	39.0	37.3	37.3	37.4
2012	38.1	37.7	37.4	38.2	38.1	38.3	39.7	38.5	39.3	38.9	38.7	39.6	38.5
2013	38.7	38.5	38.7	38.1	38.3	39.7	37.6	38.6	38.5	38.5	38.2	38.6	38.5
2014	38.4	39.2	39.3	38.3	38.1	38.6	37.3	37.6	37.5	37.3	39.2	37.9	38.2
2015	37.6	38.7	38.5	37.5	37.9	38.0	37.9	38.9	37.4	37.4	38.6	37.3	38.0
Professional and Business Services													
2011	41.0	39.8	39.3	39.8	39.6	39.0	38.8	38.6	38.1	39.4	38.5	38.7	39.2
2012	38.8	38.7	38.8	39.9	38.4	38.4	39.1	38.6	39.7	38.6	38.4	38.5	38.8
2013	37.1	37.0	37.9	36.0	36.0	37.1	35.5	35.9	36.4	36.2	36.7	36.6	36.5
2014	35.9	37.3	37.1	37.2	36.9	37.8	36.7	37.5	37.6	37.9	38.6	37.9	37.4
2015	37.6	38.2	37.6	37.2	36.9	36.9	37.0	37.8	36.6	37.2	37.7	37.6	37.4
Education and Health Services													
2011	33.5	33.1	32.8	33.4	33.2	32.9	33.2	33.0	33.0	33.3	33.3	33.3	33.2
2012	33.4	33.0	32.8	33.0	33.2	33.3	33.5	33.1	33.2	33.4	33.4	33.6	33.2
2013	33.0	32.8	32.9	33.3	33.0	33.4	33.3	33.2	33.1	32.9	33.0	33.3	33.1
2014	32.8	33.4	33.5	33.0	33.0	33.8	33.8	33.7	33.5	33.6	34.3	33.9	33.5
2015	33.9	33.9	33.7	33.5	33.3	33.7	34.1	34.1	33.9	34.0	34.2	34.0	33.9
Leisure and Hospitality													
2011	25.9	26.8	26.8	26.5	26.7	26.5	26.4	26.6	26.2	26.7	26.4	26.8	26.5
2012	26.7	27.1	27.4	27.1	27.2	27.1	26.9	26.8	26.7	26.9	27.1	27.6	27.0
2013	26.7	27.6	27.8	27.5	27.3	27.6	27.1	26.9	26.8	26.9	27.0	27.6	27.2
2014	26.8	27.5	28.5	27.7	27.6	27.6	27.3	27.1	26.9	27.7	28.0	27.9	27.6
2015	27.2	28.5	28.2	28.0	28.2	28.4	28.1	27.9	27.4	27.6	27.7	27.3	27.9

3. Average Hourly Earnings Selected Industry: Louisiana, 2011–2015

(Dollars, not seasonally adjusted)

Industry and year	January	February	March	April	May	June	July	August	September	October	November	December	Annual average
Total Private													
2011	20.08	20.10	20.05	20.36	20.43	20.43	20.73	20.74	21.07	21.21	21.23	21.10	20.63
2012	21.12	21.03	21.11	21.37	21.05	21.09	21.22	21.26	21.92	21.76	21.59	21.85	21.36
2013	21.81	21.95	21.90	22.00	21.83	22.15	21.95	21.67	22.19	22.00	22.00	22.23	21.98
2014	22.09	22.11	22.21	22.11	22.10	22.21	22.23	22.18	22.11	22.04	22.05	21.94	22.12
2015	22.13	22.15	22.32	22.26	21.98	21.95	21.93	22.25	22.15	22.32	22.57	22.41	22.20
Goods-Producing													
2011	23.69	23.81	23.94	24.12	24.09	24.13	24.55	24.10	24.71	24.58	24.50	24.46	24.23
2012	24.41	24.21	24.51	24.49	24.40	24.42	24.63	24.76	24.67	24.97	24.67	25.17	24.61
2013	25.86	25.80	26.03	26.09	25.72	26.02	25.90	25.14	25.70	25.27	25.51	26.27	25.77
2014	26.21	26.71	26.72	26.73	26.65	26.64	26.60	26.55	26.20	26.01	25.86	26.18	26.42
2015	26.39	26.30	26.74	26.41	26.12	25.93	26.18	26.38	26.39	26.27	26.51	26.58	26.35
Construction													
2011	21.66	21.93	22.03	22.10	22.14	22.01	22.17	22.10	22.47	22.74	22.68	22.82	22.24
2012	22.44	22.56	22.92	23.03	23.19	22.86	23.01	23.43	23.55	23.76	23.56	24.06	23.22
2013	24.74	24.20	24.66	24.39	24.01	23.45	23.56	23.13	23.27	23.77	23.60	24.47	23.92
2014	24.14	25.03	25.05	24.65	24.92	24.80	24.39	24.61	24.25	24.54	24.41	24.78	24.63
2015	25.28	25.29	25.47	25.14	24.63	24.29	24.68	24.52	24.56	25.17	25.08	25.29	24.95
Manufacturing													
2011	24.10	24.32	24.60	25.00	24.82	24.90	25.44	25.02	25.84	25.24	25.14	24.90	24.95
2012	25.18	24.55	24.92	24.86	24.76	24.98	25.34	25.18	24.83	25.26	24.83	25.32	25.00
2013	26.13	26.40	26.46	26.84	26.38	27.05	26.84	25.85	26.29	25.45	25.66	26.33	26.30
2014	26.53	26.45	26.29	26.08	25.73	26.00	26.69	26.52	26.23	25.41	25.29	25.58	26.06
2015	25.76	25.54	26.44	26.02	25.83	25.83	25.88	26.33	26.26	25.46	25.93	25.95	25.93
Trade, Transportation, and Utilities													
2011	18.01	17.56	17.80	18.41	18.62	18.34	19.19	19.16	19.27	19.66	20.16	19.77	18.83
2012	20.30	19.73	19.84	20.63	20.10	20.29	20.32	20.13	20.40	20.14	20.09	20.01	20.17
2013	19.77	19.99	19.96	20.21	20.16	20.54	20.51	20.18	20.62	20.55	20.34	20.51	20.28
2014	20.50	20.60	20.83	20.53	20.70	21.05	21.34	21.00	21.19	20.98	20.86	20.49	20.84
2015	20.62	20.61	20.86	20.86	20.62	20.89	20.50	20.94	20.76	20.78	20.50	20.79	20.73
Financial Activities													
2011	19.59	19.80	18.03	19.16	19.10	20.07	19.43	19.40	19.40	19.85	19.71	18.78	19.36
2012	18.39	18.65	19.44	19.71	19.26	19.54	19.95	19.91	20.17	20.11	19.56	20.18	19.58
2013	20.71	20.55	20.51	21.04	21.06	21.17	21.51	21.06	21.43	21.25	21.59	21.81	21.14
2014	21.88	22.03	22.16	21.99	21.92	22.41	22.17	22.70	22.92	23.35	23.50	23.07	22.51
2015	23.63	23.89	23.97	24.67	23.98	24.12	24.53	24.92	24.85	24.96	26.12	25.40	24.58
Professional and Business Services													
2011	24.39	24.54	24.81	24.34	24.93	24.63	24.54	24.65	25.18	25.33	25.01	25.20	24.79
2012	25.11	25.53	25.46	25.73	25.59	25.25	25.50	25.27	25.55	25.03	24.84	25.73	25.38
2013	25.10	25.77	25.17	25.30	24.81	25.61	25.14	25.21	26.31	25.92	25.93	25.99	25.53
2014	25.59	25.59	25.95	25.62	25.67	25.93	25.81	25.59	25.36	25.02	25.36	25.27	25.56
2015	25.70	26.16	26.21	25.90	25.52	25.59	25.56	26.00	25.60	25.75	26.26	25.50	25.82
Education and Health Services													
2011	17.31	17.68	17.76	18.24	18.30	18.52	18.71	19.00	19.39	19.52	19.63	20.00	18.68
2012	19.76	20.04	19.92	20.04	19.62	19.72	19.88	19.99	19.85	19.61	19.78	19.79	19.83
2013	19.52	19.41	19.48	19.20	19.10	19.24	19.04	19.07	19.33	19.28	19.27	19.43	19.28
2014	19.10	19.20	19.04	18.97	18.77	18.62	18.46	18.42	18.43	18.40	18.36	18.28	18.67
2015	18.33	18.40	18.65	19.04	18.91	18.58	18.50	18.78	19.00	19.49	19.98	19.98	18.98
Leisure and Hospitality													
2011	12.63	12.24	12.34	12.28	12.32	11.89	11.85	11.86	11.89	12.13	12.12	12.14	12.14
2012	12.36	12.18	12.21	12.17	12.21	11.90	11.94	11.90	12.22	12.47	12.46	12.66	12.22
2013	12.49	12.58	12.40	12.42	12.39	12.27	12.16	12.31	12.30	12.71	12.75	12.82	12.47
2014	12.53	12.70	12.79	12.62	12.65	12.37	12.65	12.69	12.87	13.13	13.13	13.28	12.79
2015	13.29	13.12	13.07	13.06	12.96	12.87	12.87	12.88	12.98	13.16	13.16	13.31	13.06

4. Average Weekly Earnings Selected Industry: Louisiana, 2011–2015

(Dollars, not seasonally adjusted)

Industry and year	January	February	March	April	May	June	July	August	September	October	November	December	Annual average
Total Private													
2011	732.92	727.62	721.80	741.10	749.78	743.65	752.50	750.79	760.63	780.53	766.40	761.71	748.87
2012	762.43	757.08	762.07	782.14	768.33	767.68	772.41	773.86	793.50	779.01	770.76	784.42	773.23
2013	763.35	777.03	788.40	785.40	779.33	806.26	781.42	777.95	801.06	789.80	787.60	802.50	786.88
2014	784.20	800.38	810.67	795.96	797.81	808.44	802.50	807.35	800.38	802.26	811.44	803.00	802.96
2015	794.47	806.26	801.29	794.68	786.88	788.01	787.29	807.68	784.11	801.29	812.52	802.28	796.98
Goods-Producing													
2011	990.24	985.73	979.15	1,013.04	1,019.01	1,013.46	1,021.28	1,014.61	1,027.94	1,056.94	1,041.25	1,024.87	1,015.24
2012	1,008.13	1,031.35	1,051.48	1,055.52	1,071.16	1,059.83	1,029.53	1,064.68	1,078.08	1,086.20	1,068.21	1,087.34	1,058.23
2013	1,062.85	1,081.02	1,114.08	1,129.70	1,111.10	1,131.87	1,108.52	1,103.65	1,130.80	1,124.52	1,114.79	1,161.13	1,113.26
2014	1,129.65	1,143.19	1,151.63	1,144.04	1,148.62	1,145.52	1,138.48	1,157.58	1,126.60	1,128.83	1,127.50	1,151.92	1,141.34
2015	1,113.66	1,107.23	1,085.64	1,082.81	1,083.98	1,070.91	1,081.23	1,102.68	1,063.52	1,116.48	1,121.37	1,126.99	1,096.16
Construction													
2011	909.72	894.74	885.61	925.99	938.74	922.22	902.32	923.78	934.75	950.53	936.68	926.49	920.74
2012	872.92	891.12	948.89	953.44	973.98	955.55	936.51	998.12	1,000.88	1,021.68	1,015.44	1,032.17	968.27
2013	954.96	997.04	1,050.52	1,034.14	1,010.82	1,020.08	982.45	994.59	1,014.57	1,045.88	988.84	1,030.19	1,009.42
2014	1,009.05	1,048.76	1,064.63	1,057.49	1,076.54	1,036.64	1,043.89	1,068.07	1,037.90	1,038.04	1,015.46	1,045.72	1,044.31
2015	1,018.78	1,026.77	983.14	1,005.60	1,007.37	1,008.04	1,021.75	1,017.58	948.02	1,052.11	1,040.82	1,069.77	1,015.47
Manufacturing													
2011	983.28	992.26	998.76	1,025.00	1,020.10	1,025.88	1,048.13	1,028.32	1,038.77	1,080.27	1,060.91	1,040.82	1,027.94
2012	1,062.60	1,080.20	1,069.07	1,081.41	1,096.87	1,089.13	1,061.75	1,080.22	1,099.97	1,103.86	1,077.62	1,109.02	1,085.00
2013	1,118.36	1,111.44	1,127.20	1,170.22	1,152.81	1,171.27	1,159.49	1,147.74	1,154.13	1,137.62	1,149.57	1,182.22	1,149.31
2014	1,148.75	1,118.84	1,119.95	1,100.58	1,101.24	1,120.60	1,128.99	1,129.75	1,114.78	1,133.29	1,148.17	1,169.01	1,128.40
2015	1,130.86	1,103.33	1,123.70	1,098.04	1,082.28	1,056.45	1,063.67	1,084.80	1,068.78	1,076.96	1,096.84	1,092.50	1,089.06
Trade, Transportation, and Utilities													
2011	666.37	644.45	655.04	677.49	703.84	687.75	719.63	703.17	705.28	727.42	729.79	715.67	694.83
2012	745.01	694.50	706.30	744.74	731.64	736.53	741.68	732.73	762.96	729.07	717.21	720.36	730.15
2013	707.77	717.64	732.53	733.62	739.87	764.09	746.56	730.52	746.44	727.47	713.93	719.90	732.11
2014	715.45	735.42	745.71	728.82	741.06	751.49	761.84	758.10	767.08	757.38	755.13	741.74	746.07
2015	734.07	739.90	753.05	755.13	750.57	754.13	744.15	766.40	745.28	735.61	735.95	750.52	746.28
Financial Activities													
2011	724.83	724.68	661.70	703.17	741.08	750.62	726.68	717.80	733.32	774.15	735.18	700.49	724.06
2012	700.66	703.11	727.06	752.92	733.81	748.38	792.02	766.54	792.68	782.28	756.97	799.13	753.83
2013	801.48	791.18	793.74	801.62	806.60	840.45	808.78	812.92	825.06	818.13	824.74	841.87	813.89
2014	840.19	863.58	870.89	842.22	835.15	865.03	826.94	853.52	859.50	870.96	921.20	874.35	859.88
2015	888.49	924.54	922.85	925.13	908.84	916.56	929.69	969.39	929.39	933.50	1,008.23	947.42	934.04
Professional and Business Services													
2011	999.99	976.69	975.03	968.73	987.23	960.57	952.15	951.49	959.36	998.00	962.89	975.24	971.77
2012	974.27	988.01	987.85	1,026.63	982.66	969.60	997.05	975.42	1,014.34	966.16	953.86	990.61	984.74
2013	931.21	953.49	953.94	910.80	893.16	950.13	892.47	905.04	957.68	938.30	951.63	951.23	931.85
2014	918.68	954.51	962.75	953.06	947.22	980.15	947.23	959.63	953.54	948.26	978.90	957.73	955.94
2015	966.32	999.31	985.50	963.48	941.69	944.27	945.72	982.80	936.96	957.90	990.00	958.80	965.29
Education and Health Services													
2011	579.89	585.21	582.53	609.22	607.56	609.31	621.17	627.00	639.87	650.02	653.68	666.00	620.18
2012	659.98	661.32	653.38	661.32	651.38	656.68	665.98	661.67	659.02	654.97	660.65	664.94	658.36
2013	644.16	636.65	640.89	639.36	630.30	642.62	634.03	633.12	639.82	634.31	635.91	647.02	638.17
2014	626.48	641.28	637.84	626.01	619.41	629.36	623.95	620.75	617.41	618.24	629.75	619.69	625.45
2015	621.39	623.76	628.51	637.84	629.70	626.15	630.85	640.40	644.10	662.66	683.32	679.32	643.42
Leisure and Hospitality													
2011	327.12	328.03	330.71	325.42	328.94	315.09	312.84	315.48	311.52	323.87	319.97	325.35	321.71
2012	330.01	330.08	334.55	329.81	332.11	322.49	321.19	318.92	326.27	335.44	337.67	349.42	329.94
2013	333.48	347.21	344.72	341.55	338.25	338.65	329.54	331.14	329.64	341.90	344.25	353.83	339.18
2014	335.80	349.25	364.52	349.57	349.14	341.41	345.35	343.90	346.20	363.70	367.64	370.51	353.00
2015	361.49	373.92	368.57	365.68	365.47	365.51	361.65	359.35	355.65	363.22	364.53	363.36	364.37

MAINE

At a Glance

Population:
  2005 estimate: 1,318,787
  2010 census: 1,328,361
  2015 estimate: 1,329,328

Percent change in population:
  2005–2015: 0.8%
  2010–2015: 0.1%

Percent change in total nonfarm employment:
  2005–2015: –0.3%

Industry with the largest growth in employment, 2005–2015 (thousands):
  Professional and Business Services, 13.6

Industry with the largest decline or smallest growth in employment, 2005–2015 (thousands):
  Manufacturing, –10.8

Civilian labor force:
  2005: 697,153
  2010: 695,182
  2015: 679,756

Unemployment rate and rank among states (highest to lowest):
  2005: 4.9%, 27th
  2010: 8.1%, 32nd
  2015: 4.4%, 35th

Over-the-year change in unemployment rates:
  2012–2013: –0.9%
  2013–2014: –1.0%
  2014–2015: –1.2%

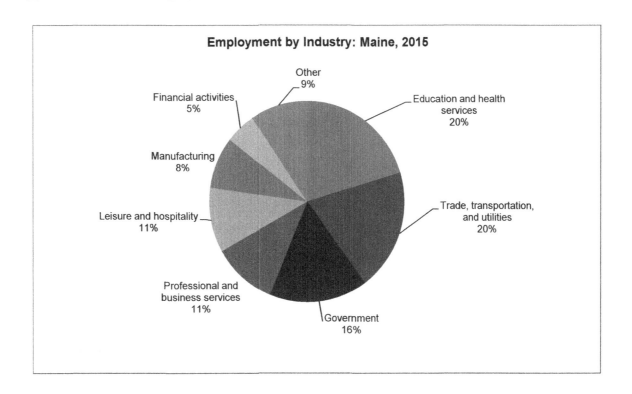

Employment by Industry: Maine, 2015

Other 9%
Financial activities 5%
Education and health services 20%
Manufacturing 8%
Leisure and hospitality 11%
Trade, transportation, and utilities 20%
Professional and business services 11%
Government 16%

1. Employment by Industry: Maine, 2005–2015

(Numbers in thousands, not seasonally adjusted)

Industry and year	January	February	March	April	May	June	July	August	September	October	November	December	Annual average
Total Nonfarm													
2005	589.5	591.3	592.1	603.0	614.6	625.6	623.2	623.2	623.1	619.2	618.2	617.8	611.7
2006	592.1	592.6	596.1	606.5	617.4	629.9	624.1	626.6	625.1	622.9	621.1	621.4	614.7
2007	596.1	596.2	599.1	604.4	618.2	632.4	629.0	629.0	628.6	627.8	626.6	625.2	617.7
2008	599.7	600.1	601.8	609.6	623.0	633.6	630.0	628.1	625.8	625.0	617.6	612.6	617.2
2009	584.1	582.5	579.9	588.4	601.9	607.6	603.9	603.9	605.3	603.8	598.6	595.8	596.3
2010	572.0	572.9	574.9	583.8	599.1	604.4	602.9	602.6	604.4	603.9	598.7	596.1	593.0
2011	572.4	574.2	575.4	582.8	594.6	605.9	608.6	608.6	608.9	606.3	601.3	597.5	594.7
2012	575.0	577.3	578.7	587.6	602.3	613.4	611.5	611.5	610.8	608.9	601.7	598.8	598.1
2013	577.8	578.1	579.8	588.9	604.5	616.2	618.0	617.1	616.4	615.0	605.4	603.3	601.7
2014	580.2	581.7	583.7	591.6	607.5	621.2	621.0	620.9	619.1	617.0	609.4	608.5	605.2
2015	586.5	585.4	588.2	597.7	613.5	625.8	627.0	626.3	623.5	620.1	612.8	611.0	609.8
Total Private													
2005	485.5	483.7	484.5	495.4	506.7	519.3	530.2	530.6	518.0	511.5	509.2	508.9	507.0
2006	487.8	485.9	488.8	499.3	509.7	525.3	532.1	533.4	520.7	514.8	512.2	512.7	510.2
2007	492.4	489.9	492.1	497.9	510.5	527.3	536.8	537.6	523.9	519.5	517.8	516.5	513.5
2008	495.8	493.6	494.4	501.9	515.1	528.4	537.9	535.8	521.4	516.8	508.8	504.1	512.8
2009	480.6	476.3	473.3	481.0	494.3	502.9	513.1	513.1	501.4	496.7	490.8	488.3	492.7
2010	468.3	466.6	467.1	476.2	489.0	499.7	511.0	511.7	501.4	497.0	491.3	488.9	489.0
2011	469.3	468.9	469.8	477.8	490.0	504.2	516.4	517.3	506.6	501.8	496.0	493.2	492.6
2012	474.0	473.5	474.5	483.8	497.4	512.4	519.6	519.5	509.2	504.4	497.3	494.5	496.7
2013	476.2	475.1	476.2	485.5	500.8	516.4	527.3	527.0	516.1	511.6	502.4	500.2	501.2
2014	480.7	480.3	481.4	489.4	505.3	520.4	530.6	530.9	518.6	513.9	506.1	505.1	505.2
2015	487.0	484.3	486.2	496.0	512.1	526.2	536.0	535.5	523.6	517.8	510.2	508.4	510.3
Goods-Producing													
2005	91.3	90.5	90.5	92.8	95.0	97.2	97.6	98.1	96.6	95.6	96.3	94.8	94.7
2006	90.7	89.8	90.3	92.3	94.7	96.8	97.1	97.8	96.1	95.1	94.5	93.3	94.0
2007	89.3	87.7	88.5	89.7	92.3	95.7	96.1	96.5	95.1	95.2	95.2	93.5	92.9
2008	89.1	87.9	87.7	88.8	91.7	94.0	94.2	93.9	92.1	91.8	90.3	87.1	90.7
2009	80.9	78.6	76.8	77.6	80.1	81.3	81.9	82.0	80.9	80.8	80.0	77.6	79.9
2010	73.9	72.9	73.2	74.8	78.0	79.4	80.0	80.9	80.3	80.3	80.0	78.1	77.7
2011	74.7	73.8	74.1	75.3	77.9	80.5	81.5	82.0	81.3	81.0	80.8	79.4	78.5
2012	75.1	74.5	74.6	76.7	79.4	81.5	82.1	82.1	81.3	80.8	79.8	77.9	78.8
2013	74.1	73.5	73.6	75.2	78.3	80.7	81.9	82.2	81.3	81.2	80.4	78.4	78.4
2014	73.9	73.7	73.7	75.1	78.7	81.2	82.0	82.3	81.3	81.1	81.3	79.7	78.7
2015	75.3	74.3	74.5	76.4	79.1	81.6	82.6	82.8	81.9	81.7	81.9	80.1	79.4
Service-Providing													
2005	498.2	500.8	501.6	510.2	519.6	528.4	525.6	525.1	526.5	523.6	521.9	523.0	517.0
2006	501.4	502.8	505.8	514.2	522.7	533.1	527.0	528.8	529.0	527.8	526.6	528.1	520.6
2007	506.8	508.5	510.6	514.7	525.9	536.7	532.9	532.5	533.5	532.6	531.4	531.7	524.8
2008	510.6	512.2	514.1	520.8	531.3	539.6	535.8	534.2	533.7	533.2	527.3	525.5	526.5
2009	503.2	503.9	503.1	510.8	521.8	526.3	522.0	521.9	524.4	523.0	518.6	518.2	516.4
2010	498.1	500.0	501.7	509.0	521.1	525.0	522.9	521.7	524.1	523.6	518.7	518.0	515.3
2011	497.7	500.4	501.3	507.5	516.7	525.4	527.1	526.6	527.6	525.3	520.5	518.1	516.2
2012	499.9	502.8	504.1	510.9	522.9	531.9	529.4	529.4	529.5	528.1	521.9	520.9	519.3
2013	503.7	504.6	506.2	513.7	526.2	535.5	536.1	534.9	535.1	533.8	525.0	524.9	523.3
2014	506.3	508.0	510.0	516.5	528.8	540.0	539.0	538.6	537.8	535.9	528.1	528.8	526.5
2015	511.2	511.1	513.7	521.3	534.4	544.2	544.4	543.5	541.6	538.4	530.9	530.9	530.5
Mining and Logging													
2005	2.9	2.9	2.8	2.2	2.0	2.5	2.8	2.8	2.8	2.8	2.9	2.9	2.7
2006	2.9	2.9	2.8	2.1	2.1	2.6	2.9	2.9	2.9	3.0	2.8	2.9	2.7
2007	2.9	2.9	2.9	2.0	1.8	2.5	2.8	2.8	2.8	2.8	2.9	2.8	2.7
2008	2.8	2.8	2.8	2.1	1.8	2.3	2.6	2.6	2.6	2.8	2.8	2.8	2.6
2009	2.8	2.8	2.6	1.5	1.5	1.9	2.4	2.6	2.6	2.7	2.8	2.7	2.4
2010	2.7	2.7	2.6	1.9	2.1	2.5	2.7	2.7	2.7	2.7	2.6	2.6	2.5
2011	2.6	2.6	2.6	1.9	1.8	2.4	2.7	2.7	2.7	2.7	2.7	2.7	2.5
2012	2.6	2.6	2.5	1.8	1.9	2.4	2.6	2.7	2.7	2.7	2.6	2.6	2.5
2013	2.6	2.6	2.4	1.8	1.9	2.3	2.5	2.6	2.6	2.6	2.6	2.6	2.4
2014	2.6	2.6	2.6	2.1	1.7	2.3	2.6	2.6	2.6	2.6	2.6	2.6	2.5
2015	2.5	2.5	2.6	2.0	1.8	2.3	2.6	2.6	2.6	2.6	2.5	2.5	2.4

1. Employment by Industry: Maine, 2005–2015—*Continued*

(Numbers in thousands, not seasonally adjusted)

Industry and year	January	February	March	April	May	June	July	August	September	October	November	December	Annual average
Construction													
2005	27.0	26.5	26.7	29.2	31.4	32.8	33.6	33.2	32.7	32.4	31.9	30.4	30.7
2006	28.3	27.5	28.0	30.3	32.3	33.7	33.9	33.9	33.1	32.6	31.6	30.6	31.3
2007	28.1	26.9	27.4	29.1	31.4	33.0	33.2	33.3	32.8	32.7	31.9	30.3	30.8
2008	27.6	26.7	26.6	28.0	30.6	31.8	31.8	31.5	30.8	30.9	29.3	27.1	29.4
2009	24.0	22.8	22.3	23.8	26.0	26.8	27.1	27.0	26.5	26.6	25.2	23.7	25.2
2010	21.3	20.6	20.6	22.8	25.0	25.7	26.2	26.5	26.6	26.6	25.9	24.4	24.4
2011	22.0	21.3	21.4	23.2	25.3	27.0	27.7	27.7	27.6	27.6	26.9	25.6	25.3
2012	22.9	22.2	22.3	24.5	26.6	27.4	27.7	27.8	27.4	27.1	26.1	24.7	25.6
2013	22.3	21.9	21.9	23.9	26.1	27.2	27.8	28.0	27.8	27.8	26.8	25.3	25.6
2014	22.7	22.5	22.5	23.9	26.7	27.7	28.3	28.4	28.0	27.9	27.2	25.8	26.0
2015	23.3	22.7	22.7	24.4	27.0	28.1	28.7	28.7	28.2	28.2	27.7	26.4	26.3
Manufacturing													
2005	61.4	61.1	61.0	61.4	61.6	61.9	61.2	62.1	61.1	60.4	61.5	61.5	61.4
2006	59.5	59.4	59.5	59.9	60.3	60.5	60.3	61.0	60.1	59.5	60.1	59.8	60.0
2007	58.3	57.9	58.2	58.6	59.1	60.2	60.1	60.4	59.5	59.7	60.4	60.4	59.4
2008	58.7	58.4	58.3	58.7	59.3	59.9	59.8	59.8	58.7	58.1	58.2	57.2	58.8
2009	54.1	53.0	51.9	52.3	52.6	52.6	52.4	52.4	51.8	51.5	52.0	51.2	52.3
2010	49.9	49.6	50.0	50.1	50.9	51.2	51.1	51.7	51.0	51.0	51.5	51.1	50.8
2011	50.1	49.9	50.1	50.2	50.8	51.1	51.1	51.6	51.0	50.7	51.2	51.1	50.7
2012	49.6	49.7	49.8	50.4	50.9	51.7	51.8	51.6	51.2	51.0	51.1	50.6	50.8
2013	49.2	49.0	49.3	49.5	50.3	51.2	51.6	51.6	50.9	50.8	51.0	50.5	50.4
2014	48.6	48.6	48.6	49.1	50.3	51.2	51.1	51.3	50.7	50.6	51.5	51.3	50.2
2015	49.5	49.1	49.2	50.0	50.3	51.2	51.3	51.5	51.1	50.9	51.7	51.2	50.6
Trade, Transportation, and Utilities													
2005	123.1	120.7	119.8	121.3	123.0	126.1	127.7	127.9	126.1	126.4	129.4	130.8	125.2
2006	123.4	119.9	120.3	121.7	123.3	126.7	127.7	128.0	126.2	127.2	131.1	132.2	125.6
2007	123.9	120.7	121.1	121.0	123.8	127.2	129.1	129.2	126.5	127.4	131.1	132.0	126.1
2008	124.7	121.1	120.8	121.7	123.9	126.4	127.7	127.6	124.8	125.3	126.9	127.0	124.8
2009	118.8	115.4	114.3	114.9	117.6	119.6	120.9	121.3	119.3	119.4	121.6	122.4	118.8
2010	114.7	112.2	111.6	112.6	115.1	118.1	119.6	120.1	117.2	118.7	120.2	121.5	116.8
2011	114.5	112.3	111.5	112.8	114.8	118.0	119.6	120.2	118.1	119.2	121.1	121.8	117.0
2012	115.2	112.9	112.3	113.1	115.8	119.1	119.9	120.3	117.9	119.4	121.6	121.8	117.4
2013	114.4	112.0	111.5	112.8	115.8	119.6	121.7	122.2	120.0	120.6	122.5	123.4	118.0
2014	115.8	114.3	113.7	114.8	117.4	120.6	122.1	122.6	120.3	121.0	122.7	123.9	119.1
2015	116.4	114.5	114.0	115.6	118.5	121.8	123.3	123.6	120.8	120.6	122.3	122.8	119.5
Wholesale Trade													
2005	20.9	20.9	20.9	21.1	21.4	21.7	21.9	21.9	21.7	21.6	21.5	21.6	21.4
2006	21.1	21.0	21.1	21.4	21.5	22.0	22.0	21.9	21.6	21.5	21.3	21.3	21.5
2007	20.8	20.7	20.9	20.9	21.2	21.4	21.6	21.5	21.2	21.1	20.9	21.0	21.1
2008	20.7	20.5	20.5	20.5	20.8	21.1	21.3	21.2	20.9	20.8	20.5	20.5	20.8
2009	19.7	19.4	19.3	19.3	19.5	19.6	19.9	19.8	19.5	19.3	19.2	19.2	19.5
2010	18.5	18.4	18.5	18.6	18.9	19.2	19.4	19.5	19.2	19.2	19.1	19.1	19.0
2011	18.7	18.6	18.5	18.7	18.9	19.3	19.7	19.7	19.5	19.3	19.2	19.3	19.1
2012	18.9	18.8	18.8	19.1	19.4	19.9	20.1	20.0	19.7	19.7	19.5	19.5	19.5
2013	18.8	18.8	18.8	19.0	19.5	20.0	20.2	20.2	20.0	19.8	19.7	19.7	19.5
2014	19.0	18.9	19.0	19.2	19.7	20.2	20.4	20.4	20.1	20.1	19.9	19.9	19.7
2015	19.4	19.3	19.3	19.5	20.0	20.4	20.6	20.6	20.3	19.7	19.5	19.5	19.8
Retail Trade													
2005	83.6	81.7	81.3	82.8	84.0	86.1	87.2	87.3	85.6	85.5	88.0	89.0	85.2
2006	83.8	80.9	81.4	82.7	83.9	86.1	87.0	87.5	85.8	86.4	89.6	90.2	85.4
2007	84.3	81.6	82.0	82.2	84.5	87.0	88.5	88.4	85.8	86.4	89.7	90.2	85.9
2008	85.4	82.5	82.3	83.4	85.1	86.9	87.9	87.9	85.4	85.8	87.2	87.1	85.6
2009	81.3	79.0	78.2	78.8	81.1	82.9	83.9	84.4	82.7	82.9	84.4	84.8	82.0
2010	79.7	77.6	77.1	77.9	79.8	82.0	83.2	83.7	81.1	82.3	83.8	84.5	81.1
2011	79.4	77.6	77.0	78.0	79.7	81.9	83.1	83.6	81.4	82.6	84.2	84.6	81.1
2012	79.7	77.7	77.4	78.0	80.0	82.3	83.1	83.5	81.1	82.3	84.4	84.2	81.1
2013	79.0	76.8	76.4	77.4	79.6	82.3	84.2	84.5	82.2	82.8	84.3	84.7	81.2
2014	79.6	78.4	77.8	78.7	80.4	82.5	83.9	84.3	82.0	82.5	83.9	84.6	81.6
2015	79.3	77.9	77.6	78.7	80.8	83.2	84.4	84.7	82.0	82.1	83.7	84.0	81.5

1. Employment by Industry: Maine, 2005–2015—*Continued*

(Numbers in thousands, not seasonally adjusted)

Industry and year	January	February	March	April	May	June	July	August	September	October	November	December	Annual average
Transportation and Utilities													
2005	18.6	18.1	17.6	17.4	17.6	18.3	18.6	18.7	18.8	19.3	19.9	20.2	18.6
2006	18.5	18.0	17.8	17.6	17.9	18.6	18.7	18.6	18.8	19.3	20.2	20.7	18.7
2007	18.8	18.4	18.2	17.9	18.1	18.8	19.0	19.3	19.5	19.9	20.5	20.8	19.1
2008	18.6	18.1	18.0	17.8	18.0	18.4	18.5	18.5	18.5	18.7	19.2	19.4	18.5
2009	17.8	17.0	16.8	16.8	17.0	17.1	17.1	17.1	17.1	17.2	18.0	18.4	17.3
2010	16.5	16.2	16.0	16.1	16.4	16.9	17.0	16.9	16.9	17.2	17.3	17.9	16.8
2011	16.4	16.1	16.0	16.1	16.2	16.8	16.8	16.9	17.2	17.3	17.7	17.9	16.8
2012	16.6	16.4	16.1	16.0	16.4	16.9	16.7	16.8	17.1	17.4	17.7	18.1	16.9
2013	16.6	16.4	16.3	16.4	16.7	17.3	17.3	17.5	17.8	18.0	18.5	19.0	17.3
2014	17.2	17.0	16.9	16.9	17.3	17.9	17.8	17.9	18.2	18.4	18.9	19.4	17.8
2015	17.7	17.3	17.1	17.4	17.7	18.2	18.3	18.3	18.5	18.8	19.1	19.3	18.1
Information													
2005	11.2	11.1	11.2	11.1	11.2	11.1	11.2	11.2	11.1	11.1	11.1	11.3	11.2
2006	11.2	11.2	11.1	11.1	11.1	11.3	11.3	11.3	11.1	11.3	11.3	11.4	11.2
2007	11.2	11.4	11.4	11.4	11.3	11.3	11.3	11.2	11.0	11.1	11.1	11.1	11.2
2008	10.9	10.9	10.8	10.7	10.6	10.7	10.6	10.4	10.1	10.2	10.0	9.9	10.5
2009	9.4	9.2	9.0	9.1	9.2	9.1	9.0	8.9	8.8	8.8	8.8	8.7	9.0
2010	8.7	8.8	8.7	8.7	8.8	8.8	8.8	8.7	8.6	8.6	8.6	8.5	8.7
2011	8.4	8.3	8.3	8.3	8.3	8.3	8.3	8.3	8.1	8.1	8.1	8.1	8.2
2012	7.9	8.0	7.9	7.9	7.9	7.9	7.9	7.9	7.8	7.7	7.8	7.8	7.9
2013	7.8	7.7	7.7	7.7	7.7	7.7	7.7	7.7	7.5	7.5	7.5	7.5	7.6
2014	7.4	7.4	7.4	7.4	7.4	7.5	7.6	7.6	7.5	7.6	7.2	7.2	7.4
2015	7.3	7.3	7.5	7.6	7.7	7.8	7.8	7.7	7.5	7.4	7.4	7.4	7.5
Financial Activities													
2005	33.6	33.5	33.6	33.4	33.6	33.8	34.3	34.1	33.5	33.7	33.5	33.6	33.7
2006	33.2	33.0	32.9	32.9	32.9	33.5	33.4	33.5	32.8	32.9	32.6	32.8	33.0
2007	32.3	32.3	32.3	32.4	32.6	33.0	33.2	33.0	32.4	32.0	31.9	32.0	32.5
2008	31.6	31.7	31.7	31.9	32.2	32.5	32.7	32.6	31.7	31.5	31.4	31.2	31.9
2009	30.9	30.9	30.9	30.9	31.3	31.7	31.8	31.6	31.0	30.9	30.7	30.7	31.1
2010	30.2	30.3	30.4	30.5	30.6	31.0	31.1	31.1	30.7	30.5	30.3	30.4	30.6
2011	30.0	30.1	30.2	30.0	30.3	30.7	31.0	31.0	30.4	30.4	30.2	30.4	30.4
2012	29.9	29.8	29.8	29.9	30.2	30.6	30.9	30.8	30.2	30.0	29.8	29.9	30.2
2013	29.8	29.7	29.9	30.0	30.4	30.8	31.2	31.1	30.6	30.4	30.4	30.4	30.4
2014	29.9	29.8	29.9	30.0	30.4	30.8	31.0	31.2	30.5	30.4	30.3	30.4	30.4
2015	30.1	30.0	30.0	30.2	30.6	30.9	31.4	31.4	30.9	30.6	30.2	30.5	30.6
Professional and Business Services													
2005	48.2	48.2	48.6	50.2	51.1	51.7	52.4	52.6	51.8	51.7	51.4	51.5	50.8
2006	49.4	50.0	50.3	52.9	53.6	54.6	54.1	54.2	53.4	52.9	53.0	53.3	52.6
2007	51.8	51.7	52.0	53.7	54.7	56.1	56.2	56.4	55.5	55.9	56.1	56.0	54.7
2008	55.0	55.3	55.8	57.1	57.9	58.9	58.9	59.0	58.0	58.1	57.3	56.9	57.4
2009	55.2	54.8	54.5	55.7	56.9	57.1	57.1	57.3	56.5	56.9	56.9	56.5	56.3
2010	55.1	54.8	55.1	56.5	57.2	57.6	58.3	58.3	57.7	57.8	57.9	57.3	57.0
2011	56.0	56.3	56.4	58.0	58.8	59.8	60.3	60.6	60.1	59.8	59.7	58.6	58.7
2012	57.3	57.2	57.3	58.9	59.6	60.9	60.7	61.0	60.6	60.7	60.3	59.8	59.5
2013	58.2	58.9	58.6	60.4	61.6	62.9	63.6	63.6	63.1	62.9	62.1	61.9	61.5
2014	59.9	60.7	61.0	62.3	64.1	65.1	65.4	65.3	64.7	64.6	63.8	63.2	63.3
2015	61.7	62.3	62.3	63.4	65.7	66.1	66.0	65.9	65.2	65.2	64.7	64.1	64.4
Education and Health Services													
2005	110.0	111.6	111.9	112.7	112.8	111.5	111.5	111.3	112.3	113.6	114.1	113.5	112.2
2006	111.6	113.6	114.2	114.4	114.1	113.0	112.9	113.3	114.4	115.5	115.9	115.9	114.1
2007	114.2	116.5	116.6	116.4	116.2	115.1	114.7	115.0	115.9	117.1	117.5	117.7	116.1
2008	115.3	117.4	117.7	117.7	117.8	116.6	116.5	116.2	117.4	119.1	119.3	119.1	117.5
2009	117.2	119.0	119.1	119.6	119.4	117.4	117.4	117.2	117.9	119.7	119.8	119.8	118.6
2010	117.5	119.3	119.3	119.8	119.6	117.5	117.2	117.0	119.3	120.3	120.3	120.2	118.9
2011	117.1	119.3	119.6	120.1	119.9	118.1	118.0	118.2	120.2	122.0	122.1	122.0	119.7
2012	119.5	121.6	121.6	121.9	122.2	119.9	119.6	119.0	121.5	123.1	122.9	122.7	121.3
2013	120.6	122.4	122.4	122.9	122.2	120.2	119.9	119.7	122.5	123.6	123.4	122.7	121.9
2014	121.7	122.4	122.6	123.0	122.0	120.8	120.1	120.1	122.7	123.6	123.8	123.1	122.2
2015	122.6	123.1	123.7	124.4	123.8	122.6	122.4	122.5	124.7	126.2	126.0	125.9	124.0

1. Employment by Industry: Maine, 2005–2015—*Continued*

(Numbers in thousands, not seasonally adjusted)

Industry and year	January	February	March	April	May	June	July	August	September	October	November	December	Annual average
Leisure and Hospitality													
2005	48.6	48.6	49.2	53.9	59.8	67.6	74.9	75.0	66.4	59.5	53.6	53.5	59.2
2006	48.9	49.0	50.2	54.5	60.3	69.4	75.3	75.2	67.1	60.2	54.1	54.0	59.9
2007	50.3	50.3	50.8	53.6	59.6	68.7	75.6	75.8	67.4	61.0	55.2	54.5	60.2
2008	49.8	49.8	50.3	54.3	61.0	69.0	76.8	76.0	67.5	60.8	53.7	53.1	60.2
2009	48.8	49.0	49.5	53.7	60.0	66.7	74.7	74.5	67.2	60.4	53.3	52.9	59.2
2010	48.9	49.0	49.5	53.8	60.0	67.4	75.6	75.5	67.7	61.1	54.3	53.4	59.7
2011	49.3	49.5	50.3	53.6	59.9	68.5	77.1	76.6	68.4	61.3	54.2	53.1	60.2
2012	49.6	50.0	51.3	55.5	62.3	72.2	77.8	77.9	69.8	62.6	55.1	54.6	61.6
2013	51.3	50.9	52.3	56.0	63.9	73.3	79.9	79.3	70.3	64.7	55.5	55.3	62.7
2014	51.7	51.7	52.7	56.2	64.3	73.0	80.6	80.1	70.4	64.3	56.0	56.6	63.1
2015	52.9	52.3	53.5	57.4	65.3	73.6	80.4	79.7	71.3	65.3	56.7	56.6	63.8
Other Services													
2005	19.5	19.5	19.7	20.0	20.2	20.3	20.6	20.4	20.2	19.9	19.8	19.9	20.0
2006	19.4	19.4	19.5	19.5	19.7	20.0	20.3	20.1	19.6	19.7	19.7	19.8	19.7
2007	19.4	19.3	19.4	19.7	20.0	20.2	20.6	20.5	20.1	19.8	19.7	19.7	19.9
2008	19.4	19.5	19.6	19.7	20.0	20.3	20.5	20.1	19.8	20.0	19.9	19.8	19.9
2009	19.4	19.4	19.2	19.5	19.8	20.0	20.3	20.3	19.8	19.8	19.7	19.7	19.7
2010	19.3	19.3	19.3	19.5	19.7	19.9	20.4	20.1	19.9	19.7	19.7	19.5	19.7
2011	19.3	19.3	19.4	19.7	20.1	20.3	20.6	20.4	20.0	20.0	19.8	19.8	19.9
2012	19.5	19.5	19.7	19.9	20.0	20.3	20.7	20.5	20.1	20.1	20.0	20.0	20.0
2013	20.0	20.0	20.2	20.5	20.9	21.2	21.4	21.2	20.8	20.7	20.6	20.6	20.7
2014	20.4	20.3	20.4	20.6	21.0	21.4	21.8	21.7	21.2	21.3	21.0	21.0	21.0
2015	20.7	20.5	20.7	21.0	21.4	21.8	22.1	21.9	21.3	20.8	21.0	21.0	21.2
Government													
2005	104.0	107.6	107.6	107.6	107.9	106.3	93.0	92.6	105.1	107.7	109.0	108.9	104.8
2006	104.3	106.7	107.3	107.2	107.7	104.6	92.0	93.2	104.4	108.1	108.9	108.7	104.4
2007	103.7	106.3	107.0	106.5	107.7	105.1	92.2	91.4	104.7	108.3	108.8	108.7	104.2
2008	103.9	106.5	107.4	107.7	107.9	105.2	92.1	92.3	104.4	108.2	108.8	108.5	104.4
2009	103.5	106.2	106.6	107.4	107.6	104.7	90.8	90.8	103.9	107.1	107.8	107.5	103.7
2010	103.7	106.3	107.8	107.6	110.1	104.7	91.9	90.9	103.0	106.9	107.4	107.2	104.0
2011	103.1	105.3	105.6	105.0	104.6	101.7	92.2	91.3	102.3	104.5	105.3	104.3	102.1
2012	101.0	103.8	104.2	103.8	104.9	101.0	91.9	92.0	101.6	104.5	104.4	104.3	101.5
2013	101.6	103.0	103.6	103.4	103.7	99.8	90.7	90.1	100.3	103.4	103.0	103.1	100.5
2014	99.5	101.4	102.3	102.2	102.2	100.8	90.4	90.0	100.5	103.1	103.3	103.4	99.9
2015	99.5	101.1	102.0	101.7	101.4	99.6	91.0	90.8	99.9	102.3	102.6	102.6	99.5

2. Average Weekly Hours by Selected Industry: Maine, 2011–2015

(Not seasonally adjusted)

Industry and year	January	February	March	April	May	June	July	August	September	October	November	December	Annual average
Total Private													
2011	33.7	33.9	33.7	33.7	33.8	34.0	34.4	34.4	34.1	34.2	33.9	34.2	34.0
2012	34.0	33.9	33.8	34.2	33.9	34.0	34.4	34.3	34.4	34.1	33.9	34.6	34.1
2013	33.5	33.7	33.9	33.9	34.1	34.0	34.2	34.6	34.2	34.0	33.8	34.4	34.0
2014	33.6	33.8	33.7	33.8	33.9	33.9	34.3	34.3	34.2	34.1	34.1	33.9	34.0
2015	33.9	34.0	34.1	33.9	34.3	34.3	34.6	34.7	34.5	34.3	34.3	34.1	34.3
Goods-Producing													
2011	39.2	39.6	38.9	38.8	39.1	40.1	40.0	39.7	40.2	40.1	39.4	39.4	39.5
2012	39.4	39.2	39.4	39.2	39.1	40.3	39.6	40.0	40.4	40.2	39.9	40.1	39.7
2013	39.5	39.6	39.8	39.7	40.1	40.1	40.0	40.6	40.1	40.5	39.6	40.7	40.0
2014	40.8	39.9	40.0	40.0	40.0	40.1	40.6	40.1	40.6	40.4	39.7	39.7	40.2
2015	40.2	39.7	40.1	40.2	41.4	41.5	41.8	41.8	40.9	41.8	41.2	41.4	41.0
Construction													
2011	36.7	37.4	37.3	37.6	38.5	39.1	39.7	39.0	40.3	39.5	40.2	38.8	38.7
2012	37.6	37.4	38.2	38.3	39.1	39.8	39.4	39.6	40.1	39.3	38.6	38.9	38.9
2013	38.1	37.8	38.4	38.4	39.4	39.0	39.0	40.3	39.0	39.4	38.7	38.4	38.9
2014	38.7	38.5	37.3	37.2	39.0	38.3	40.1	38.3	39.7	39.4	38.9	37.1	38.6
2015	37.3	37.2	37.1	38.5	40.7	41.0	41.6	40.7	39.5	40.9	40.4	40.1	39.7
Manufacturing													
2011	40.2	40.2	39.5	39.5	39.6	40.6	40.1	39.9	40.0	40.3	38.8	38.8	39.8
2012	39.1	38.8	38.9	39.0	38.4	39.6	38.8	39.2	39.7	39.6	39.6	39.7	39.2
2013	39.1	39.3	39.5	39.6	39.8	39.9	39.8	40.0	40.0	40.4	39.5	40.2	39.7
2014	40.2	39.0	39.7	40.1	39.8	40.0	39.6	40.0	39.9	39.8	38.9	39.7	39.7
2015	40.3	39.6	40.5	40.1	40.9	40.9	40.8	41.4	40.8	41.6	41.1	41.6	40.8
Trade, Transportation, and Utilities													
2011	31.5	32.5	32.4	32.3	32.2	32.8	33.4	33.2	32.3	32.2	31.8	33.5	32.5
2012	31.7	32.2	32.5	32.9	32.8	32.9	33.4	33.3	33.2	32.5	31.8	33.6	32.7
2013	31.5	32.5	32.5	32.7	32.7	33.1	33.7	34.2	33.4	33.1	32.3	33.9	33.0
2014	32.1	32.5	32.1	32.4	32.9	33.2	33.6	33.7	33.8	33.2	33.4	33.9	33.1
2015	33.1	33.8	33.4	33.1	33.7	33.4	34.3	34.2	34.8	33.7	33.5	34.1	33.8
Professional and Business Services													
2011	35.0	34.8	35.1	35.0	34.8	34.8	34.6	34.8	34.8	34.6	34.4	34.3	34.7
2012	33.7	34.0	33.9	34.7	34.2	34.1	34.4	34.2	35.1	34.6	33.7	34.2	34.2
2013	32.8	33.3	33.5	33.6	34.1	34.0	33.5	33.6	33.9	33.5	33.5	34.3	33.7
2014	32.4	33.9	33.2	33.4	33.6	33.8	33.3	33.4	33.2	33.3	33.8	33.6	33.4
2015	33.7	34.1	34.6	33.9	34.1	34.4	34.3	34.8	34.3	34.7	35.1	34.4	34.4
Education and Health Services													
2011	33.9	33.3	33.1	33.3	33.8	33.8	33.7	33.7	33.8	33.9	34.0	33.9	33.7
2012	34.9	34.3	34.2	34.4	34.0	34.1	34.3	33.8	34.0	34.0	34.2	34.6	34.2
2013	34.3	34.0	34.2	34.3	34.2	34.0	34.3	34.4	34.4	33.9	34.3	33.9	34.2
2014	34.3	33.5	33.6	33.7	33.8	33.9	34.2	34.0	34.0	33.9	34.0	33.8	33.9
2015	34.4	34.3	34.1	34.1	34.1	34.0	34.0	33.7	33.9	33.5	33.7	33.4	33.9
Leisure and Hospitality													
2011	24.0	25.0	24.6	25.0	25.2	25.4	28.0	28.8	26.5	26.5	25.9	25.1	26.0
2012	24.3	25.6	25.3	25.5	25.6	25.7	27.6	28.3	26.8	26.1	25.0	25.0	26.1
2013	25.0	25.0	25.7	25.6	25.6	25.5	27.6	28.4	26.0	26.2	25.2	24.1	26.0
2014	23.9	24.8	25.1	25.3	25.4	25.4	27.7	28.0	26.2	27.0	25.4	24.7	25.9
2015	24.5	24.3	25.1	25.2	25.6	26.2	27.3	27.9	26.4	25.8	25.3	24.4	25.8

3. Average Hourly Earnings by Selected Industry: Maine, 2011–2015

(Dollars, not seasonally adjusted)

Industry and year	January	February	March	April	May	June	July	August	September	October	November	December	Annual average
Total Private													
2011	19.95	19.78	19.91	20.01	19.89	19.67	19.57	19.58	20.04	20.28	20.33	20.49	19.96
2012	21.15	20.87	21.14	20.92	20.91	20.75	20.66	20.70	20.99	21.17	21.18	21.12	20.96
2013	21.37	21.40	21.22	21.26	20.97	20.87	20.68	20.59	20.98	20.85	21.10	20.92	21.01
2014	21.23	21.41	21.65	21.39	21.23	21.07	20.90	20.85	21.41	21.35	21.74	21.75	21.33
2015	21.93	22.00	22.11	21.94	21.67	21.46	21.42	21.54	21.82	22.01	22.20	22.24	21.85
Goods-Producing													
2011	22.29	22.33	22.43	22.33	22.26	21.92	21.77	22.07	22.34	22.51	22.92	22.72	22.32
2012	23.31	22.96	22.95	23.20	22.84	22.34	22.39	22.58	22.79	22.56	22.64	22.90	22.78
2013	23.20	23.16	22.95	22.87	22.86	22.79	22.70	22.59	23.07	22.91	23.44	23.29	22.98
2014	23.43	23.58	23.37	23.23	23.40	23.26	22.81	23.13	23.23	23.26	23.63	23.63	23.33
2015	23.64	23.35	23.13	23.18	22.89	22.80	22.93	23.37	22.85	23.22	23.26	23.68	23.19
Construction													
2011	20.93	20.98	20.93	20.90	20.81	20.71	20.41	20.87	21.47	21.87	21.68	22.54	21.19
2012	23.21	23.44	23.45	23.41	23.21	22.93	22.64	23.07	22.83	22.53	22.83	22.88	23.01
2013	23.12	22.93	22.72	22.64	22.47	22.23	21.94	21.61	21.98	21.98	21.91	22.31	22.28
2014	22.65	23.02	22.75	22.61	22.36	22.14	21.44	21.93	22.03	22.43	22.46	23.16	22.38
2015	23.30	23.27	22.67	22.81	22.44	21.98	22.24	22.71	22.31	22.44	22.74	23.07	22.63
Manufacturing													
2011	23.08	23.14	23.25	22.90	22.89	22.47	22.51	22.89	23.07	23.16	23.80	23.64	23.06
2012	24.30	23.56	23.46	23.65	23.34	23.02	23.34	23.43	24.01	23.75	23.61	23.88	23.61
2013	24.15	24.27	23.97	23.73	23.81	23.87	23.91	23.85	24.31	24.09	24.92	24.39	24.11
2014	24.47	24.53	24.36	24.11	24.32	24.16	23.93	24.17	24.32	24.16	24.75	24.31	24.30
2015	24.29	23.86	23.79	23.70	23.41	23.57	23.71	24.16	23.52	24.00	23.71	24.21	23.83
Trade, Transportation, and Utilities													
2011	17.45	17.47	17.58	17.87	18.16	17.55	17.62	17.29	17.44	17.58	17.62	17.48	17.59
2012	18.09	18.24	18.44	18.67	18.74	18.56	18.52	18.38	18.61	18.65	18.66	18.19	18.48
2013	19.02	18.78	18.64	18.80	18.70	18.60	18.43	18.53	18.94	18.69	18.88	18.47	18.70
2014	18.95	19.20	19.51	19.53	19.10	19.11	19.17	18.81	19.42	19.08	19.34	19.29	19.21
2015	19.88	19.83	19.91	19.97	20.09	20.00	20.10	20.03	20.26	20.28	20.45	20.22	20.09
Professional and Business Services													
2011	22.94	22.65	22.41	22.31	22.46	22.35	22.16	21.93	21.83	21.94	21.81	22.08	22.23
2012	23.32	23.16	23.14	22.75	23.30	23.14	22.93	23.21	22.80	22.60	23.04	23.01	23.03
2013	23.10	23.14	23.10	23.31	22.60	22.96	22.80	22.55	22.72	22.61	22.87	22.51	22.85
2014	23.60	23.83	24.27	23.80	23.41	23.40	23.66	23.53	24.15	23.99	24.15	24.26	23.84
2015	24.47	24.31	24.51	24.21	23.73	23.95	24.26	24.19	24.50	24.11	24.47	24.31	24.25
Education and Health Services													
2011	20.57	20.23	20.49	20.85	20.19	20.59	20.83	20.94	21.61	21.89	21.78	22.19	21.02
2012	22.58	22.22	22.57	21.64	21.86	22.07	22.46	22.67	22.71	22.65	22.29	22.64	22.36
2013	22.08	22.16	21.96	21.97	21.63	21.75	21.90	21.83	21.38	21.23	20.88	20.88	21.64
2014	21.32	21.43	21.90	21.28	21.34	21.22	21.55	21.43	21.86	22.12	22.23	22.36	21.67
2015	22.15	22.51	23.04	22.50	22.14	21.88	21.86	22.21	22.66	23.18	23.20	23.24	22.55
Leisure and Hospitality													
2011	12.70	12.88	12.75	12.78	12.71	12.54	12.64	12.82	12.89	12.94	12.86	13.01	12.79
2012	12.91	12.65	12.81	12.80	12.78	12.80	12.61	12.71	12.99	13.10	13.02	13.06	12.84
2013	12.94	13.15	12.98	13.12	13.15	12.73	12.73	12.88	13.26	13.43	13.36	13.40	13.07
2014	13.34	13.35	13.30	13.22	13.22	13.07	13.00	13.34	13.50	13.33	13.64	13.82	13.33
2015	13.41	13.60	13.51	13.76	13.57	13.48	13.37	13.54	13.86	14.18	14.25	14.62	13.74

4. Average Weekly Earnings by Selected Industry: Maine, 2011–2015

(Dollars, not seasonally adjusted)

Industry and year	January	February	March	April	May	June	July	August	September	October	November	December	Annual average
Total Private													
2011	672.32	670.54	670.97	674.34	672.28	668.78	673.21	673.55	683.36	693.58	689.19	700.76	678.64
2012	719.10	707.49	714.53	715.46	708.85	705.50	710.70	710.01	722.06	721.90	718.00	730.75	714.74
2013	715.90	721.18	719.36	720.71	715.08	709.58	707.26	712.41	717.52	708.90	713.18	719.65	714.34
2014	713.33	723.66	729.61	722.98	719.70	714.27	716.87	715.16	732.22	728.04	741.33	737.33	725.22
2015	743.43	748.00	753.95	743.77	743.28	736.08	741.13	747.44	752.79	754.94	761.46	758.38	749.46
Goods-Producing													
2011	873.77	884.27	872.53	866.40	870.37	878.99	870.80	876.18	898.07	902.65	903.05	895.17	881.64
2012	918.41	900.03	904.23	909.44	893.04	900.30	886.64	903.20	920.72	906.91	903.34	918.29	904.37
2013	916.40	917.14	913.41	907.94	916.69	913.88	908.00	917.15	925.11	927.86	928.22	947.90	919.20
2014	955.94	940.84	934.80	929.20	936.00	932.73	926.09	927.51	943.14	939.70	938.11	938.11	937.87
2015	950.33	927.00	927.51	931.84	947.65	946.20	958.47	976.87	934.57	970.60	958.31	980.35	950.79
Construction													
2011	768.13	784.65	780.69	785.84	801.19	809.76	810.28	813.93	865.24	863.87	871.54	874.55	820.05
2012	872.70	876.66	895.79	896.60	907.51	912.61	892.02	913.57	915.48	885.43	881.24	890.03	895.09
2013	880.87	866.75	872.45	869.38	885.32	866.97	855.66	870.88	857.22	866.01	847.92	856.70	866.69
2014	876.56	886.27	848.58	841.09	872.04	847.96	859.74	839.92	874.59	883.74	873.69	859.24	863.87
2015	869.09	865.64	841.06	878.19	913.31	901.18	925.18	924.30	881.25	917.80	918.70	925.11	898.41
Manufacturing													
2011	927.82	930.23	918.38	904.55	906.44	912.28	902.65	913.31	922.80	933.35	923.44	917.23	917.79
2012	950.13	914.13	912.59	922.35	896.26	911.59	905.59	918.46	953.20	940.50	934.96	948.04	925.51
2013	944.27	953.81	946.82	939.71	947.64	952.41	951.62	954.00	972.40	973.24	984.34	980.48	957.17
2014	983.69	956.67	967.09	966.81	967.94	966.40	947.63	966.80	970.37	961.57	962.78	965.11	964.71
2015	978.89	944.86	963.50	950.37	957.47	964.01	967.37	1,000.22	959.62	998.40	974.48	1,007.14	972.26
Trade, Transportation, and Utilities													
2011	549.68	567.78	569.59	577.20	584.75	575.64	588.51	574.03	563.31	566.08	560.32	585.58	571.68
2012	573.45	587.33	599.30	614.24	614.67	610.62	618.57	612.05	617.85	606.13	593.39	611.18	604.30
2013	599.13	610.35	605.80	614.76	611.49	615.66	621.09	633.73	632.60	618.64	609.82	626.13	617.10
2014	608.30	624.00	626.27	632.77	628.39	634.45	644.11	633.90	656.40	633.46	645.96	653.93	635.85
2015	658.03	670.25	664.99	661.01	677.03	668.00	689.43	685.03	705.05	683.44	685.08	689.50	679.04
Professional and Business Services													
2011	802.90	788.22	786.59	780.85	781.61	777.78	766.74	763.16	759.68	759.12	750.26	757.34	771.38
2012	785.88	787.44	784.45	789.43	796.86	789.07	788.79	793.78	800.28	781.96	776.45	786.94	787.63
2013	757.68	770.56	773.85	783.22	770.66	780.64	763.80	757.68	770.21	757.44	766.15	772.09	770.05
2014	764.64	807.84	805.76	794.92	786.58	790.92	787.88	785.90	801.78	798.87	816.27	815.14	796.26
2015	824.64	828.97	848.05	820.72	809.19	823.88	832.12	841.81	840.35	836.62	858.90	836.26	834.20
Education and Health Services													
2011	697.32	673.66	678.22	694.31	682.42	695.94	701.97	705.68	730.42	742.07	740.52	752.24	708.37
2012	788.04	762.15	771.89	744.42	743.24	752.59	770.38	766.25	772.14	770.10	762.32	783.34	764.71
2013	757.34	753.44	751.03	753.57	739.75	739.50	751.17	750.95	735.47	719.70	716.18	707.83	740.09
2014	731.28	717.91	735.84	717.14	721.29	719.36	737.01	728.62	743.24	749.87	755.82	755.77	734.61
2015	761.96	772.09	785.66	767.25	754.97	743.92	743.24	748.48	768.17	776.53	781.84	776.22	764.45
Leisure and Hospitality													
2011	304.80	322.00	313.65	319.50	320.29	318.52	353.92	369.22	341.59	342.91	333.07	326.55	332.54
2012	313.71	323.84	324.09	326.40	327.17	328.96	348.04	359.69	348.13	341.91	325.50	326.50	335.12
2013	323.50	328.75	333.59	335.87	336.64	324.62	351.35	365.79	344.76	351.87	336.67	322.94	339.82
2014	318.83	331.08	333.83	334.47	335.79	331.98	360.10	373.52	353.70	359.91	346.46	341.35	345.25
2015	328.55	330.48	339.10	346.75	347.39	353.18	365.00	377.77	365.90	365.84	360.53	356.73	354.49

MARYLAND
At a Glance

Population:
  2005 estimate: 5,592,379
  2010 census: 5,773,552
  2015 estimate: 6,006,401

Percent change in population:
  2005–2015: 7.4%
  2010–2015: 4.0%

Percent change in total nonfarm employment:
  2005–2015: 4.1%

Industry with the largest growth in employment, 2005–2015 (thousands):
  Education and health services, 82.6

Industry with the largest decline or smallest growth in employment, 2005–2015 (thousands):
  Manufacturing, –34.9

Civilian labor force:
  2005: 2,924,546
  2010: 3,073,826
  2015: 3,151,929

Unemployment rate and rank among states (highest to lowest):
  2005: 4.1%, 37th
  2010: 7.7%, 38th
  2015: 5.2%, 25th

Over-the-year change in unemployment rates:
  2012–2013: –0.4%
  2013–2014: –0.8%
  2014–2015: –0.6%

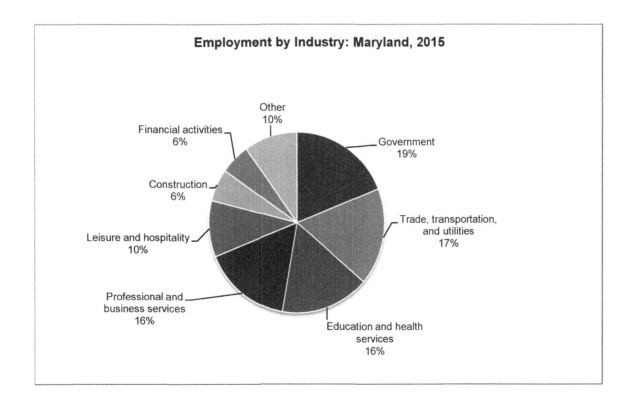

Employment by Industry: Maryland, 2015

Other 10%
Financial activities 6%
Government 19%
Construction 6%
Trade, transportation, and utilities 17%
Leisure and hospitality 10%
Professional and business services 16%
Education and health services 16%

1. Employment by Industry: Maryland, 2005–2015

(Numbers in thousands, not seasonally adjusted)

Industry and year	January	February	March	April	May	June	July	August	September	October	November	December	Annual average
Total Nonfarm													
2005	2,480.8	2,494.0	2,513.8	2,544.3	2,564.7	2,579.3	2,569.9	2,568.6	2,579.3	2,577.5	2,589.6	2,597.5	2,554.9
2006	2,522.2	2,535.7	2,568.2	2,583.7	2,601.2	2,617.3	2,595.8	2,593.5	2,598.8	2,604.6	2,614.1	2,626.7	2,588.5
2007	2,549.8	2,553.2	2,587.1	2,599.6	2,621.9	2,634.9	2,618.9	2,616.9	2,616.6	2,620.5	2,629.7	2,638.1	2,607.3
2008	2,558.1	2,569.2	2,588.9	2,610.1	2,624.5	2,626.7	2,611.3	2,605.1	2,598.1	2,602.7	2,597.1	2,592.7	2,598.7
2009	2,497.6	2,498.8	2,512.5	2,529.6	2,543.8	2,551.2	2,525.6	2,516.0	2,514.9	2,524.9	2,526.9	2,525.9	2,522.3
2010	2,445.1	2,424.1	2,480.8	2,520.6	2,542.1	2,552.8	2,532.5	2,527.2	2,528.7	2,544.5	2,548.3	2,553.2	2,516.7
2011	2,473.1	2,490.0	2,517.1	2,542.1	2,554.3	2,564.0	2,555.4	2,543.5	2,552.4	2,565.6	2,570.8	2,576.6	2,542.1
2012	2,507.2	2,522.8	2,552.5	2,567.2	2,584.4	2,596.8	2,578.8	2,577.2	2,587.9	2,597.0	2,603.2	2,609.4	2,573.7
2013	2,533.3	2,550.2	2,572.1	2,592.9	2,612.4	2,623.3	2,603.0	2,600.7	2,606.2	2,614.5	2,629.3	2,624.6	2,596.9
2014	2,544.5	2,557.3	2,580.9	2,613.8	2,639.0	2,650.7	2,622.2	2,628.3	2,636.7	2,652.6	2,662.0	2,663.1	2,620.9
2015	2,578.2	2,596.9	2,613.6	2,651.1	2,681.6	2,686.9	2,668.5	2,668.9	2,672.7	2,695.6	2,698.3	2,699.2	2,659.3
Total Private													
2005	2,023.6	2,027.8	2,045.8	2,074.6	2,092.1	2,118.0	2,120.5	2,119.6	2,113.6	2,102.3	2,109.9	2,119.6	2,089.0
2006	2,062.3	2,063.8	2,091.5	2,106.1	2,122.6	2,151.2	2,142.1	2,141.3	2,129.5	2,123.7	2,130.9	2,142.9	2,117.3
2007	2,082.4	2,074.7	2,102.9	2,116.5	2,136.0	2,161.3	2,157.0	2,155.5	2,141.6	2,133.3	2,138.1	2,146.8	2,128.8
2008	2,082.3	2,080.3	2,096.0	2,116.4	2,130.3	2,144.1	2,138.3	2,132.8	2,114.6	2,106.0	2,097.1	2,093.4	2,111.0
2009	2,016.3	2,004.9	2,013.3	2,027.3	2,041.5	2,060.9	2,046.6	2,040.4	2,027.3	2,020.3	2,020.3	2,020.7	2,028.3
2010	1,958.0	1,926.2	1,974.9	2,011.6	2,026.1	2,048.8	2,045.2	2,042.2	2,032.1	2,036.6	2,035.8	2,043.4	2,015.1
2011	1,979.8	1,981.8	2,003.0	2,028.8	2,041.8	2,061.2	2,066.2	2,060.5	2,051.7	2,051.2	2,058.7	2,064.3	2,037.4
2012	2,012.2	2,012.4	2,036.1	2,053.2	2,071.6	2,098.0	2,095.8	2,096.0	2,086.0	2,084.0	2,089.2	2,096.1	2,069.2
2013	2,038.8	2,040.8	2,059.1	2,078.8	2,098.3	2,120.3	2,120.4	2,119.2	2,105.8	2,103.8	2,114.6	2,114.2	2,092.8
2014	2,053.6	2,050.7	2,071.2	2,101.5	2,127.5	2,146.6	2,145.5	2,147.8	2,132.8	2,139.3	2,146.3	2,151.5	2,117.9
2015	2,087.0	2,089.0	2,103.1	2,138.4	2,168.2	2,183.6	2,191.0	2,189.0	2,170.7	2,183.7	2,185.9	2,189.1	2,156.6
Goods-Producing													
2005	314.6	312.7	315.7	322.4	325.1	328.9	329.7	331.0	330.6	327.2	328.4	327.9	324.5
2006	318.6	317.9	323.1	325.0	326.5	331.2	330.9	331.0	329.2	326.6	325.2	324.9	325.8
2007	316.1	312.0	318.1	320.9	323.8	328.3	328.4	328.6	325.8	323.1	320.7	318.5	322.0
2008	310.3	308.7	310.1	310.9	311.1	313.5	313.1	312.5	309.3	304.8	300.0	294.5	308.2
2009	281.0	277.1	276.0	275.3	275.4	277.3	276.7	274.6	271.8	269.3	266.8	264.3	273.8
2010	253.8	244.2	252.8	259.8	261.7	264.5	265.6	265.1	262.9	260.9	259.9	257.7	259.1
2011	250.6	249.9	252.5	257.3	258.7	261.8	263.3	262.4	259.6	258.7	257.7	256.5	257.4
2012	249.1	247.7	249.9	252.6	253.4	257.9	259.1	258.8	256.3	255.5	254.7	253.7	254.1
2013	246.8	246.2	248.2	252.4	254.4	257.3	258.4	258.9	257.0	255.1	255.2	251.8	253.5
2014	245.3	243.6	246.5	252.1	255.3	258.6	259.1	260.1	258.4	258.5	258.3	256.4	254.4
2015	248.3	248.0	249.7	255.4	258.8	262.5	264.7	265.9	264.5	267.2	268.2	265.6	259.9
Service-Providing													
2005	2,166.2	2,181.3	2,198.1	2,221.9	2,239.6	2,250.4	2,240.2	2,237.6	2,248.7	2,250.3	2,261.2	2,269.6	2,230.4
2006	2,203.6	2,217.8	2,245.1	2,258.7	2,274.7	2,286.1	2,264.9	2,262.5	2,269.6	2,278.0	2,288.9	2,301.8	2,262.6
2007	2,233.7	2,241.2	2,269.0	2,278.7	2,298.1	2,306.6	2,290.5	2,288.3	2,290.8	2,297.4	2,309.0	2,319.6	2,285.2
2008	2,247.8	2,260.5	2,278.8	2,299.2	2,313.4	2,313.2	2,298.2	2,292.6	2,288.8	2,297.9	2,297.1	2,298.2	2,290.5
2009	2,216.6	2,221.7	2,236.5	2,254.3	2,268.4	2,273.9	2,248.9	2,241.4	2,243.1	2,255.6	2,260.1	2,261.6	2,248.5
2010	2,191.3	2,179.9	2,228.0	2,260.8	2,280.4	2,288.3	2,266.9	2,262.1	2,265.8	2,283.6	2,288.4	2,295.5	2,257.6
2011	2,222.5	2,240.1	2,264.6	2,284.8	2,295.6	2,302.2	2,292.1	2,281.1	2,292.8	2,306.9	2,313.1	2,320.1	2,284.7
2012	2,258.1	2,275.1	2,302.6	2,314.6	2,331.0	2,338.9	2,319.7	2,318.4	2,331.6	2,341.5	2,348.5	2,355.7	2,319.6
2013	2,286.5	2,304.0	2,323.9	2,340.5	2,358.0	2,366.0	2,344.6	2,341.8	2,349.2	2,359.4	2,374.1	2,372.8	2,343.4
2014	2,299.2	2,313.7	2,334.4	2,361.7	2,383.7	2,392.1	2,363.1	2,368.2	2,378.3	2,394.1	2,403.7	2,406.7	2,366.6
2015	2,329.9	2,348.9	2,363.9	2,395.7	2,422.8	2,424.4	2,403.8	2,403.0	2,408.2	2,428.4	2,430.1	2,433.6	2,399.4
Mining and Logging													
2005	1.7	1.7	1.7	1.7	1.7	1.8	1.8	1.8	1.8	1.8	1.7	1.7	1.7
2006	1.7	1.7	1.7	1.7	1.8	1.8	1.8	1.8	1.8	1.8	1.7	1.6	1.7
2007	1.5	1.5	1.5	1.5	1.5	1.5	1.5	1.5	1.5	1.5	1.5	1.5	1.5
2008	1.5	1.4	1.5	1.5	1.5	1.5	1.5	1.5	1.5	1.5	1.5	1.4	1.5
2009	1.4	1.4	1.4	1.4	1.4	1.4	1.4	1.4	1.4	1.4	1.3	1.3	1.4
2010	1.3	1.2	1.3	1.4	1.4	1.4	1.4	1.4	1.4	1.4	1.4	1.4	1.4
2011	1.3	1.3	1.4	1.4	1.4	1.4	1.5	1.5	1.5	1.5	1.5	1.5	1.4
2012	1.4	1.4	1.4	1.5	1.5	1.5	1.5	1.5	1.5	1.5	1.5	1.5	1.5
2013	1.3	1.3	1.4	1.4	1.4	1.4	1.4	1.5	1.5	1.4	1.4	1.4	1.4
2014	1.3	1.3	1.3	1.4	1.4	1.4	1.5	1.5	1.5	1.5	1.5	1.4	1.4
2015	1.4	1.4	1.4	1.4	1.5	1.4	1.6	1.6	1.6	1.6	1.5	1.5	1.5

1. Employment by Industry: Maryland, 2005–2015—*Continued*

(Numbers in thousands, not seasonally adjusted)

Industry and year	January	February	March	April	May	June	July	August	September	October	November	December	Annual average
Construction													
2005	173.0	171.3	174.1	180.8	183.7	187.2	188.7	189.7	189.9	187.6	188.6	188.0	183.6
2006	181.4	180.9	185.6	187.8	189.4	193.2	193.2	193.4	192.5	190.7	189.7	189.3	188.9
2007	182.4	178.7	184.5	187.4	190.0	193.7	194.1	194.4	192.5	190.0	187.9	185.5	188.4
2008	178.9	177.5	179.2	180.6	180.9	182.8	182.7	182.2	180.1	177.0	173.1	168.6	178.6
2009	157.4	154.9	154.4	154.7	155.1	156.8	156.9	155.2	152.8	150.5	148.3	146.1	153.6
2010	137.1	129.6	136.9	143.1	145.0	147.3	148.5	148.7	147.6	146.4	146.1	144.1	143.4
2011	136.6	136.0	138.1	142.4	143.9	146.6	148.1	147.6	146.0	145.6	145.1	144.3	143.4
2012	138.0	137.2	139.2	141.5	142.3	145.8	147.1	147.4	146.9	146.7	146.1	145.1	143.6
2013	139.4	138.6	140.5	144.8	146.7	149.1	150.2	150.8	149.9	148.6	149.0	146.0	146.1
2014	141.0	139.5	142.3	147.5	150.5	153.1	153.7	154.7	153.6	153.3	152.9	151.7	149.5
2015	144.1	143.8	145.4	150.6	153.6	156.4	158.3	159.4	158.8	160.2	160.7	158.0	154.1
Manufacturing													
2005	139.9	139.7	139.9	139.9	139.7	139.9	139.2	139.5	138.9	137.8	138.1	138.2	139.2
2006	135.5	135.3	135.8	135.5	135.3	136.2	135.9	135.8	134.9	134.1	133.8	134.0	135.2
2007	132.2	131.8	132.1	132.0	132.3	133.1	132.8	132.7	131.8	131.6	131.3	131.5	132.1
2008	129.9	129.8	129.4	128.8	128.7	129.2	128.9	128.8	127.7	126.3	125.4	124.5	128.1
2009	122.2	120.8	120.2	119.2	118.9	119.1	118.4	118.0	117.6	117.4	117.2	116.9	118.8
2010	115.4	113.4	114.6	115.3	115.3	115.8	115.7	115.0	113.9	113.1	112.4	112.2	114.3
2011	112.7	112.6	113.0	113.5	113.4	113.8	113.7	113.3	112.1	111.6	111.1	110.7	112.6
2012	109.7	109.1	109.3	109.6	109.6	110.6	110.5	109.9	107.9	107.3	107.1	107.1	109.0
2013	106.1	106.3	106.3	106.2	106.3	106.8	106.8	106.6	105.6	105.1	104.8	104.4	105.9
2014	103.0	102.8	102.9	103.2	103.4	104.1	103.9	103.9	103.3	103.7	103.9	103.3	103.5
2015	102.8	102.8	102.9	103.4	103.7	104.7	104.8	104.9	104.1	105.4	106.0	106.1	104.3
Trade, Transportation, and Utilities													
2005	462.1	459.4	461.7	464.0	467.9	471.8	472.6	472.0	471.8	473.4	482.0	491.8	470.9
2006	470.6	465.1	468.9	469.8	473.5	477.6	473.9	473.7	472.6	476.4	487.5	496.0	475.5
2007	474.8	467.3	471.8	470.2	475.4	479.0	476.2	474.4	473.1	474.6	484.5	493.2	476.2
2008	469.3	462.5	464.2	463.0	465.4	468.6	465.0	464.3	461.5	461.2	465.4	470.0	465.0
2009	445.5	437.6	436.6	436.1	438.9	441.8	436.5	436.4	436.6	436.8	445.6	449.9	439.9
2010	429.5	418.8	427.8	434.4	437.9	441.5	438.8	439.1	437.2	442.5	450.7	457.5	438.0
2011	436.8	432.1	434.9	439.3	442.2	444.9	443.5	444.5	443.8	447.0	456.8	464.0	444.2
2012	444.2	439.5	444.1	445.4	448.9	451.5	448.3	448.4	449.2	451.4	462.6	468.8	450.2
2013	446.4	440.9	443.2	444.8	449.1	452.3	451.0	451.5	450.2	452.9	464.3	471.1	451.5
2014	449.4	442.4	445.6	449.3	453.0	457.1	455.5	456.6	454.7	458.7	470.1	478.3	455.9
2015	454.9	449.2	450.9	457.0	462.0	466.5	465.6	465.5	464.7	466.1	475.4	482.7	463.4
Wholesale Trade													
2005	92.6	92.9	93.1	93.8	94.4	95.0	95.2	95.1	94.6	94.4	94.4	95.0	94.2
2006	93.7	94.1	94.6	95.3	95.6	96.2	95.7	95.6	95.2	95.3	95.1	95.6	95.2
2007	94.0	94.3	94.7	95.1	95.4	95.7	95.3	95.2	94.9	94.3	94.3	94.7	94.8
2008	93.1	93.1	93.9	93.8	94.0	94.4	93.6	93.4	92.8	92.2	91.4	90.9	93.1
2009	89.2	88.7	88.2	88.2	88.0	87.9	87.2	87.2	86.7	86.3	86.0	85.8	87.5
2010	84.2	83.7	84.6	85.5	86.1	86.3	86.0	86.0	85.1	85.8	85.8	86.0	85.4
2011	84.8	84.8	85.3	85.8	86.4	86.5	86.7	86.6	86.2	86.1	85.9	86.0	85.9
2012	84.7	85.0	85.8	86.1	86.8	87.2	86.8	86.8	86.3	86.3	86.2	86.3	86.2
2013	85.0	85.0	85.3	85.6	85.8	86.1	85.7	85.6	85.1	85.0	85.1	85.2	85.4
2014	83.9	83.8	83.8	84.3	84.9	85.1	85.1	85.1	84.5	84.6	84.7	85.4	84.6
2015	84.1	84.2	84.4	85.4	85.9	86.4	86.9	86.7	86.5	85.8	86.9	86.3	85.8
Retail Trade													
2005	291.9	288.5	289.9	292.6	295.2	297.7	299.7	299.3	297.7	299.2	307.2	314.4	297.8
2006	298.2	291.8	294.5	294.8	297.5	300.1	298.8	298.5	296.2	299.9	310.7	316.2	299.8
2007	300.2	292.5	295.9	295.2	299.1	301.5	301.0	299.7	297.5	299.6	309.4	315.3	300.6
2008	297.6	290.7	292.1	291.3	292.9	294.9	293.5	292.8	289.7	289.9	294.1	297.2	293.1
2009	279.4	273.0	272.7	272.7	275.4	277.7	275.5	275.5	274.1	275.2	283.1	286.7	276.8
2010	271.7	262.7	269.3	272.7	275.7	278.4	278.0	278.4	275.6	279.6	287.2	291.8	276.8
2011	276.4	272.2	274.1	276.8	278.5	280.8	280.1	281.1	279.2	282.5	291.2	296.5	280.8
2012	281.5	276.8	280.1	280.5	282.8	284.6	283.5	283.5	282.7	285.1	295.0	298.4	284.5
2013	281.9	277.7	279.2	280.6	283.5	285.9	286.6	287.1	284.2	286.8	296.2	300.1	285.8
2014	284.6	279.4	281.5	283.9	286.0	289.4	289.9	290.4	287.0	290.3	298.5	303.1	288.7
2015	286.6	282.0	283.4	286.7	290.0	293.2	292.4	292.3	289.4	291.6	297.5	302.7	290.7

1. Employment by Industry: Maryland, 2005–2015—*Continued*

(Numbers in thousands, not seasonally adjusted)

Industry and year	January	February	March	April	May	June	July	August	September	October	November	December	Annual average
Transportation and Utilities													
2005	77.6	78.0	78.7	77.6	78.3	79.1	77.7	77.6	79.5	79.8	80.4	82.4	78.9
2006	78.7	79.2	79.8	79.7	80.4	81.3	79.4	79.6	81.2	81.2	81.7	84.2	80.5
2007	80.6	80.5	81.2	79.9	80.9	81.8	79.9	79.5	80.7	80.7	80.8	83.2	80.8
2008	78.6	78.7	78.2	77.9	78.5	79.3	77.9	78.1	79.0	79.1	79.9	81.9	78.9
2009	76.9	75.9	75.7	75.2	75.5	76.2	73.8	73.7	75.8	75.3	76.5	77.4	75.7
2010	73.6	72.4	73.9	76.2	76.1	76.8	74.8	74.7	76.5	77.1	77.7	79.7	75.8
2011	75.6	75.1	75.5	76.7	77.3	77.6	76.7	76.8	78.4	78.4	79.7	81.5	77.4
2012	78.0	77.7	78.2	78.8	79.3	79.7	78.0	78.1	80.2	80.0	81.4	84.1	79.5
2013	79.5	78.2	78.7	78.6	79.8	80.3	78.7	78.8	80.9	81.1	83.0	85.8	80.3
2014	80.9	79.2	80.3	81.1	82.1	82.6	80.5	81.1	83.2	83.8	86.9	89.8	82.6
2015	84.2	83.0	83.1	84.9	86.1	86.9	86.3	86.5	88.8	88.7	91.0	93.7	86.9
Information													
2005	48.8	49.0	49.1	49.3	49.8	50.1	51.3	51.7	51.6	51.9	51.8	51.9	50.5
2006	50.5	50.8	51.2	50.6	50.9	50.9	50.2	50.2	49.9	49.6	50.2	50.5	50.5
2007	49.3	49.7	50.5	50.5	51.0	51.8	51.4	52.1	51.5	50.0	50.8	51.4	50.8
2008	50.0	50.3	50.6	50.6	50.7	50.1	49.8	49.5	49.3	48.1	49.0	48.8	49.7
2009	46.4	46.6	47.5	46.3	46.0	46.7	45.4	45.7	44.6	43.7	44.0	44.0	45.6
2010	43.2	43.6	45.0	44.8	44.7	45.5	44.1	43.1	43.9	43.4	42.3	44.2	44.0
2011	41.3	41.9	42.1	41.4	41.2	41.1	41.2	38.1	40.2	40.2	40.9	40.7	40.9
2012	39.8	39.9	39.9	38.8	39.1	40.5	40.4	40.5	40.0	39.5	39.8	40.7	39.9
2013	39.7	39.8	40.0	39.5	39.6	39.7	39.8	39.8	39.2	39.2	39.8	39.6	39.6
2014	40.2	38.8	38.8	38.6	39.6	38.7	38.9	39.9	38.3	39.3	38.9	38.9	39.1
2015	38.8	38.3	38.4	38.9	39.0	38.1	38.7	38.2	37.5	38.6	38.6	38.1	38.4
Financial Activities													
2005	156.2	156.6	156.6	157.7	158.2	160.0	160.8	160.9	160.4	159.3	159.3	160.0	158.8
2006	158.5	159.0	159.6	159.6	159.9	161.6	161.2	161.0	159.8	159.1	159.1	160.1	159.9
2007	157.9	158.0	158.3	157.9	158.5	159.5	159.4	158.8	157.3	156.4	155.9	156.4	157.9
2008	153.5	153.9	154.1	153.8	153.9	154.6	154.1	153.6	151.8	151.5	150.4	150.7	153.0
2009	147.5	146.9	146.3	146.7	146.8	147.6	146.9	146.5	145.3	145.1	144.9	145.2	146.3
2010	142.4	141.8	142.5	142.8	143.3	144.9	145.0	144.8	143.9	144.3	144.4	145.5	143.8
2011	142.6	142.8	143.2	143.5	143.5	144.3	144.4	143.7	142.7	142.9	142.4	142.8	143.2
2012	141.8	141.7	141.8	141.6	142.4	143.9	144.4	144.4	143.8	143.9	144.3	144.7	143.2
2013	143.5	143.5	143.9	144.4	144.9	146.3	146.9	146.3	145.4	145.1	145.1	145.3	145.1
2014	143.1	143.0	142.8	143.5	144.1	145.4	145.8	145.7	144.5	144.9	145.0	145.4	144.4
2015	143.9	144.1	144.2	145.1	145.9	147.5	148.0	147.8	146.3	147.7	147.4	147.4	146.3
Professional and Business Services													
2005	373.9	377.0	382.6	388.4	390.6	393.9	393.5	394.6	394.3	392.8	391.6	391.4	388.7
2006	383.4	386.3	392.7	396.3	397.4	400.9	400.2	400.9	398.5	396.7	395.5	396.1	395.4
2007	385.5	386.9	392.6	396.9	398.2	402.0	401.3	402.9	400.8	400.6	400.5	401.1	397.4
2008	390.3	391.1	394.3	400.4	400.7	402.2	402.6	403.2	399.9	398.2	395.2	392.6	397.6
2009	380.5	378.3	380.6	384.8	384.7	388.5	386.5	387.1	383.7	384.6	383.3	382.5	383.8
2010	372.7	369.4	378.7	387.1	387.6	393.3	393.2	393.7	391.6	395.5	393.1	394.4	387.5
2011	384.4	385.5	390.1	396.9	397.2	402.6	405.9	406.8	405.5	405.9	406.9	406.6	399.5
2012	396.9	397.4	403.4	406.4	409.2	413.7	414.2	417.3	415.6	415.8	417.0	415.4	410.2
2013	406.4	408.8	414.0	415.0	416.4	420.6	420.5	423.3	421.0	419.9	421.6	418.7	417.2
2014	408.9	411.2	415.1	422.0	425.7	428.5	429.2	430.2	426.9	428.7	428.6	427.3	423.5
2015	415.4	417.0	420.2	428.1	431.1	433.5	437.3	438.3	432.1	437.0	435.8	433.7	430.0
Education and Health Services													
2005	346.3	350.1	351.4	353.6	352.9	351.2	349.9	348.7	353.3	358.9	360.5	361.8	353.2
2006	355.2	359.3	362.4	362.8	362.6	361.6	358.3	357.3	362.8	368.2	370.2	372.2	362.7
2007	365.9	369.9	372.8	373.0	372.2	370.9	368.4	367.3	372.2	376.8	378.4	380.1	372.3
2008	374.1	378.6	380.7	383.0	382.2	380.0	378.8	377.7	383.5	390.0	391.7	393.6	382.8
2009	386.6	391.1	392.8	395.0	393.2	391.8	388.0	385.9	391.1	397.3	399.0	400.4	392.7
2010	393.7	391.5	398.9	401.3	399.1	396.2	394.6	392.2	397.4	403.7	405.3	406.1	398.3
2011	399.2	404.6	406.3	406.0	403.8	400.1	399.9	398.3	404.1	410.3	411.9	412.6	404.8
2012	407.7	413.2	415.4	416.8	414.7	412.4	411.1	409.0	414.3	420.2	420.5	422.8	414.8
2013	414.2	419.6	420.9	422.4	420.2	417.1	415.6	414.0	419.6	426.6	428.0	429.0	420.6
2014	419.8	424.6	427.5	428.6	426.8	424.4	422.7	422.1	427.5	433.7	435.7	437.4	427.6
2015	429.0	434.5	436.3	437.9	439.2	433.6	432.4	430.3	435.2	439.1	440.1	441.8	435.8

1. Employment by Industry: Maryland, 2005–2015—*Continued*

(Numbers in thousands, not seasonally adjusted)

Industry and year	January	February	March	April	May	June	July	August	September	October	November	December	Annual average
Leisure and Hospitality													
2005	206.8	207.3	212.1	222.6	230.6	244.0	245.5	243.8	235.4	223.6	220.7	218.8	225.9
2006	210.7	210.2	217.4	225.3	234.6	248.8	249.2	249.3	239.5	230.5	226.4	225.6	230.6
2007	216.7	214.7	221.4	229.5	238.6	249.9	252.0	252.5	242.5	233.5	228.7	227.3	233.9
2008	218.2	218.2	224.5	236.2	247.3	254.9	255.2	253.4	241.3	234.8	228.1	225.8	236.5
2009	213.3	212.5	218.1	227.4	240.1	249.5	249.6	248.1	238.7	228.3	221.4	218.6	230.5
2010	209.2	205.0	214.8	226.8	236.6	246.8	248.1	248.8	240.7	231.9	225.6	223.5	229.8
2011	211.8	212.1	220.4	229.9	240.5	250.6	252.7	252.2	242.7	233.5	229.2	227.6	233.6
2012	220.8	221.7	229.8	239.0	251.1	264.4	264.7	264.7	254.7	246.5	239.3	238.3	244.6
2013	232.2	232.6	239.3	248.9	261.9	274.5	275.4	273.4	261.6	254.0	248.9	247.1	254.2
2014	237.0	237.4	244.2	255.6	270.4	279.8	280.2	279.7	268.9	262.5	256.0	253.9	260.5
2015	244.8	245.8	250.7	262.5	277.7	286.6	288.6	286.8	274.6	272.0	262.8	262.1	267.9
Other Services													
2005	114.9	115.7	116.6	116.6	117.0	118.1	117.2	116.9	116.2	115.2	115.6	116.0	116.3
2006	114.8	115.2	116.2	116.7	117.2	118.6	118.2	117.9	117.2	116.6	116.8	117.5	116.9
2007	116.2	116.2	117.4	117.6	118.3	119.9	119.9	118.9	118.4	118.3	118.6	118.8	118.2
2008	116.6	117.0	117.5	118.5	119.0	120.2	119.7	118.6	118.0	117.4	117.3	117.4	118.1
2009	115.5	114.8	115.4	115.7	116.4	117.7	117.0	116.1	115.5	115.2	115.3	115.8	115.9
2010	113.5	111.9	114.4	114.6	115.2	116.1	115.8	115.4	114.5	114.4	114.5	114.5	114.6
2011	113.1	112.9	113.5	114.5	114.7	115.8	115.3	114.5	113.1	112.7	112.9	113.5	113.9
2012	111.9	111.3	111.8	112.6	112.8	113.7	113.6	112.9	112.1	111.2	111.0	111.7	112.2
2013	109.6	109.4	109.6	111.4	111.8	112.5	112.8	112.0	111.8	111.0	111.7	111.6	111.3
2014	109.9	109.7	110.7	111.8	112.6	114.1	114.1	113.5	113.6	113.0	113.7	113.9	112.6
2015	111.9	112.1	112.7	113.5	114.5	115.3	115.7	116.2	115.8	116.0	117.6	117.7	114.9
Government													
2005	457.2	466.2	468.0	469.7	472.6	461.3	449.4	449.0	465.7	475.2	479.7	477.9	466.0
2006	459.9	471.9	476.7	477.6	478.6	466.1	453.7	452.2	469.3	480.9	483.2	483.8	471.2
2007	467.4	478.5	484.2	483.1	485.9	473.6	461.9	461.4	475.0	487.2	491.6	491.3	478.4
2008	475.8	488.9	492.9	493.7	494.2	482.6	473.0	472.3	483.5	496.7	500.0	499.3	487.7
2009	481.3	493.9	499.2	502.3	502.3	490.3	479.0	475.6	487.6	504.6	506.6	505.2	494.0
2010	487.1	497.9	505.9	509.0	516.0	504.0	487.3	485.0	496.6	507.9	512.5	509.8	501.6
2011	493.3	508.2	514.1	513.3	512.5	502.8	489.2	483.0	500.7	514.4	512.1	512.3	504.7
2012	495.0	510.4	516.4	514.0	512.8	498.8	483.0	481.2	501.9	513.0	514.0	513.3	504.5
2013	494.5	509.4	513.0	514.1	514.1	503.0	482.6	481.5	500.4	510.7	514.7	510.4	504.0
2014	490.9	506.6	509.7	512.3	511.5	504.1	476.7	480.5	503.9	513.3	515.7	511.6	503.1
2015	491.2	507.9	510.5	512.7	513.4	503.3	477.5	479.9	502.0	511.9	512.4	510.1	502.7

2. Average Weekly Hours by Selected Industry: Maryland, 2011–2015

(Not seasonally adjusted)

Industry and year	January	February	March	April	May	June	July	August	September	October	November	December	Annual average
Total Private													
2011	34.3	34.2	34.3	34.4	34.8	34.6	34.7	34.3	34.3	34.7	33.9	33.9	34.4
2012	33.9	33.9	33.9	34.2	33.9	34.0	34.0	33.8	34.1	33.8	33.8	34.3	34.0
2013	33.4	33.5	33.5	33.8	33.8	34.1	34.0	34.1	34.6	33.8	34.1	34.1	33.9
2014	33.8	33.6	34.4	34.1	34.1	34.6	34.3	34.3	34.2	33.9	34.5	33.7	34.1
2015	33.3	33.9	34.1	34.1	34.3	34.3	34.4	34.7	34.5	34.6	34.6	34.3	34.3
Goods-Producing													
2011	38.5	38.4	38.8	38.9	39.4	39.5	39.1	39.1	38.0	38.8	39.1	39.4	38.9
2012	38.5	38.6	38.4	38.8	38.5	38.7	38.7	38.9	39.5	39.5	39.0	39.3	38.9
2013	38.2	38.4	38.3	38.3	38.5	37.6	37.8	38.7	39.0	38.7	39.5	38.4	38.5
2014	38.5	36.3	39.2	39.6	39.6	40.4	40.4	40.1	40.0	39.1	40.0	38.8	39.3
2015	37.5	37.8	38.6	38.9	39.6	40.0	39.9	39.8	39.3	40.6	39.1	40.3	39.3
Mining, Logging, and Construction													
2011	36.6	37.0	37.2	37.4	38.3	38.9	38.5	38.4	36.7	37.5	38.5	38.6	37.8
2012	37.6	37.7	36.9	37.5	37.7	37.9	37.8	38.2	39.0	39.0	38.3	38.7	38.0
2013	37.5	37.4	36.6	37.2	37.8	36.3	37.0	38.3	38.4	37.4	38.9	37.4	37.5
2014	37.9	34.4	38.6	38.9	39.2	40.0	40.7	39.7	39.8	38.6	39.6	37.9	38.8
2015	35.9	36.7	36.9	37.8	39.2	39.5	39.4	39.0	37.6	39.9	37.7	39.9	38.3
Manufacturing													
2011	40.8	40.2	40.9	40.8	40.8	40.2	40.0	40.0	39.8	40.6	40.0	40.4	40.4
2012	39.7	39.7	40.2	40.5	39.7	39.8	39.9	39.8	40.2	40.2	39.9	40.2	40.0
2013	39.2	39.7	40.6	39.9	39.4	39.5	39.0	39.3	39.9	40.6	40.5	39.9	39.8
2014	39.3	38.9	40.0	40.6	40.3	40.9	40.1	40.6	40.3	39.8	40.5	40.0	40.1
2015	39.7	39.3	41.1	40.4	40.2	40.7	40.7	41.0	42.0	41.7	41.2	41.0	40.8
Trade, Transportation, and Utilities													
2011	33.2	33.0	33.2	33.5	33.9	33.7	33.8	33.3	33.7	33.5	33.7	33.7	33.5
2012	33.0	33.5	33.7	34.3	34.0	33.8	34.1	33.6	33.9	33.7	33.7	34.5	33.8
2013	33.2	33.3	33.5	33.2	33.5	34.1	33.9	34.0	34.0	33.0	32.8	33.0	33.5
2014	32.2	32.1	33.5	33.2	33.4	33.6	33.7	33.6	33.5	33.2	33.6	33.2	33.2
2015	32.4	32.9	33.2	33.1	33.5	33.4	34.1	33.9	34.5	33.4	33.6	33.6	33.5
Financial Activities													
2011	38.4	38.0	38.3	38.4	38.2	38.3	37.8	37.9	39.0	39.7	39.2	39.1	38.5
2012	39.4	38.6	38.9	38.4	38.2	37.5	37.9	37.3	37.6	36.8	36.8	37.2	37.9
2013	36.1	36.5	36.5	36.6	36.4	37.1	36.7	36.5	37.5	36.8	37.0	36.8	36.7
2014	37.3	37.2	37.3	36.8	36.9	37.6	37.1	37.3	37.0	37.1	37.9	37.3	37.2
2015	37.6	38.2	38.3	37.5	37.9	37.7	37.6	38.5	38.0	38.1	38.0	37.6	37.9
Professional and Business Services													
2011	37.8	37.5	37.4	37.5	38.0	37.9	37.8	37.3	37.5	38.2	37.9	37.5	37.7
2012	37.5	37.2	37.3	37.3	36.5	36.5	36.7	36.2	36.5	35.8	36.2	36.8	36.7
2013	35.4	35.3	35.3	36.3	35.7	36.1	36.3	36.6	37.1	35.8	36.3	36.5	36.1
2014	36.1	36.5	36.5	36.1	36.0	36.7	35.7	35.7	35.5	35.2	36.0	34.8	35.9
2015	34.7	35.8	35.8	35.8	35.7	35.7	35.4	36.1	35.5	36.2	36.5	35.7	35.7
Education and Health Services													
2011	32.9	32.7	32.8	32.9	33.1	32.9	33.0	33.0	32.9	33.1	32.8	32.6	32.9
2012	33.1	32.9	32.8	32.5	32.5	33.1	33.1	33.4	33.4	33.0	32.7	32.8	32.9
2013	33.0	33.3	33.0	33.3	33.3	33.9	33.3	33.1	33.5	33.2	33.2	33.1	33.3
2014	33.1	33.0	33.0	32.9	32.8	32.8	32.9	33.1	33.0	32.6	32.9	32.7	32.9
2015	32.6	33.0	32.8	32.6	32.7	32.8	33.0	32.9	32.9	33.2	33.5	32.8	32.9
Leisure and Hospitality													
2011	26.5	27.0	27.1	27.0	27.4	27.3	27.7	27.4	26.3	26.9	26.3	26.2	26.9
2012	26.5	26.8	26.6	27.0	26.9	27.3	27.4	27.4	26.9	26.6	26.5	26.5	26.9
2013	25.6	26.0	25.8	25.7	25.9	26.5	26.9	26.4	26.2	25.6	25.6	25.3	26.0
2014	24.9	24.7	25.4	25.0	25.3	25.8	26.1	26.2	25.9	25.5	25.4	25.4	25.5
2015	25.2	25.3	25.8	26.1	26.8	27.3	27.6	28.0	26.9	26.7	26.7	26.5	26.6
Other Services													
2011	32.9	33.1	33.6	33.4	33.2	34.3	33.8	33.1	33.9	34.0	34.4	34.4	33.7
2012	34.0	33.5	33.1	33.7	33.2	33.3	33.6	33.2	33.5	33.5	33.3	33.0	33.4
2013	31.8	32.4	32.5	32.8	33.3	32.5	32.5	31.8	33.5	32.2	33.1	33.4	32.7
2014	32.6	32.9	34.0	32.9	33.1	33.4	32.8	32.6	32.6	32.9	33.7	33.8	33.1
2015	32.1	33.3	33.5	33.6	34.0	33.6	33.7	32.9	32.6	32.3	32.5	32.3	33.0

3. Average Hourly Earnings by Selected Industry: Maryland, 2011–2015

(Dollars, not seasonally adjusted)

Industry and year	January	February	March	April	May	June	July	August	September	October	November	December	Annual average
Total Private													
2011	26.54	26.43	25.91	25.78	25.79	25.41	25.47	25.35	25.48	25.79	25.75	25.99	25.80
2012	26.41	26.00	25.85	25.88	25.61	25.49	25.92	25.59	26.11	25.93	26.02	26.54	25.95
2013	26.70	26.36	26.45	26.43	26.34	26.64	26.26	26.44	27.00	26.95	27.00	27.38	26.66
2014	27.42	27.82	27.41	27.28	27.09	27.29	27.15	27.19	27.46	27.19	27.51	27.45	27.35
2015	27.64	27.71	27.77	27.28	27.08	26.81	26.75	27.28	27.20	27.21	27.69	27.38	27.31
Goods-Producing													
2011	25.79	25.67	25.34	25.53	25.54	25.41	25.76	25.57	25.67	25.52	25.34	25.75	25.57
2012	25.75	25.73	25.69	25.05	24.90	24.96	24.88	24.88	24.96	24.65	24.91	24.98	25.11
2013	25.39	25.08	25.53	25.63	25.73	26.25	25.96	26.25	26.24	25.80	26.05	26.69	25.89
2014	27.03	27.16	26.33	26.34	26.19	26.43	26.14	26.20	26.13	26.43	26.74	26.60	26.46
2015	26.74	26.60	26.57	26.27	26.24	26.37	26.20	26.21	26.30	26.05	26.37	26.44	26.36
Mining, Logging, and Construction													
2011	27.83	27.71	27.34	27.43	27.51	27.09	27.54	27.25	27.40	27.30	27.18	27.39	27.41
2012	27.33	27.35	27.53	27.24	27.25	27.26	27.05	27.06	27.22	26.82	27.11	27.24	27.20
2013	26.73	26.69	27.07	27.08	27.19	27.50	27.10	26.97	26.94	27.12	27.03	27.22	27.05
2014	27.30	27.78	26.86	26.86	26.71	27.07	26.68	26.83	26.92	27.53	27.17	27.30	27.07
2015	27.62	27.31	27.17	27.07	26.87	26.91	26.85	26.51	26.49	26.34	26.26	26.66	26.82
Manufacturing													
2011	23.55	23.38	23.10	23.33	23.18	23.29	23.50	23.45	23.58	23.35	23.00	23.70	23.37
2012	23.84	23.78	23.51	22.41	21.96	22.04	22.11	22.05	21.95	21.74	22.01	22.01	22.45
2013	23.68	23.08	23.67	23.77	23.77	24.63	24.43	25.24	25.28	24.07	24.71	26.00	24.36
2014	26.66	26.40	25.62	25.63	25.44	25.50	25.32	25.28	24.95	24.84	26.11	25.61	25.61
2015	25.61	25.66	25.80	25.17	25.31	25.58	25.23	25.78	26.04	25.62	26.53	26.12	25.71
Trade, Transportation, and Utilities													
2011	19.58	19.65	19.38	19.36	19.83	19.52	19.63	19.44	19.69	19.80	19.70	19.81	19.62
2012	19.53	19.15	19.00	18.69	18.50	18.80	19.35	18.86	19.56	19.41	19.14	19.68	19.14
2013	19.84	20.16	19.89	20.28	20.29	20.33	20.15	20.12	20.13	20.42	20.26	20.11	20.17
2014	20.06	20.87	20.31	20.62	20.46	20.29	20.88	20.65	21.63	21.27	21.49	22.34	20.92
2015	22.64	22.69	22.27	22.39	22.03	21.99	22.02	22.30	22.11	22.68	22.66	22.29	22.34
Financial Activities													
2011	26.61	26.72	26.28	25.52	26.04	26.15	25.94	26.30	25.40	26.12	25.88	27.09	26.17
2012	27.65	27.41	27.35	27.10	27.29	27.82	28.62	28.42	28.91	28.91	29.76	31.04	28.35
2013	31.15	31.68	31.45	31.23	31.39	31.43	32.01	32.29	32.49	32.05	32.57	32.96	31.90
2014	32.48	32.96	32.72	32.69	32.68	32.50	32.78	33.25	33.08	33.02	33.71	34.06	33.00
2015	33.76	34.57	34.96	35.50	35.58	35.11	35.45	36.52	36.66	36.36	37.73	36.82	35.76
Professional and Business Services													
2011	35.46	34.94	34.39	34.13	33.96	33.51	33.74	33.26	33.39	34.13	33.48	34.00	34.02
2012	34.84	33.55	32.91	33.20	33.14	32.49	33.39	32.77	33.75	33.63	33.59	34.86	33.51
2013	34.60	33.86	33.87	33.19	31.29	32.42	31.46	31.84	33.06	33.15	33.34	34.26	33.02
2014	34.16	34.87	34.79	33.75	33.88	34.48	34.02	34.30	34.22	33.93	34.74	34.51	34.30
2015	34.51	34.53	34.57	33.49	33.35	33.16	33.08	34.07	33.64	33.31	34.42	34.18	33.85
Education and Health Services													
2011	25.87	26.02	25.87	26.20	26.34	26.46	26.58	26.45	26.62	26.80	26.71	26.90	26.40
2012	27.24	27.25	27.35	27.34	27.37	27.66	27.75	27.83	28.11	27.94	28.03	28.10	27.67
2013	28.32	28.05	28.27	28.27	27.95	27.72	27.72	27.79	27.82	27.82	27.61	27.71	27.92
2014	27.58	27.21	27.16	26.92	26.57	26.61	26.72	26.53	26.46	26.76	26.44	26.30	26.77
2015	26.34	26.08	26.11	25.96	25.66	25.58	25.68	25.52	26.01	25.45	25.38	25.38	25.76
Leisure and Hospitality													
2011	15.55	15.63	15.33	15.14	14.94	14.57	14.28	14.18	14.43	14.55	15.10	14.99	14.86
2012	14.69	14.67	14.62	14.63	14.34	14.07	13.82	13.53	13.98	13.99	14.08	14.22	14.20
2013	13.94	14.07	13.86	13.84	14.05	13.86	13.56	13.64	14.91	14.92	14.97	15.19	14.22
2014	14.88	14.77	14.64	15.28	14.96	14.85	14.71	14.65	15.19	14.81	15.06	14.88	14.89
2015	15.08	15.10	15.23	15.48	15.95	15.18	14.82	15.04	15.06	15.32	15.09	15.16	15.21
Other Services													
2011	22.70	22.23	22.11	21.90	21.82	20.83	20.82	21.03	20.91	20.99	19.94	20.20	21.28
2012	20.21	19.88	20.49	20.67	20.20	20.26	20.48	21.05	21.57	21.04	21.73	21.68	20.77
2013	22.02	22.53	22.49	23.04	22.64	23.92	24.08	23.78	23.62	24.14	23.75	23.65	23.31
2014	24.40	23.91	23.83	24.16	24.45	24.62	24.56	25.07	25.72	25.48	25.45	25.11	24.73
2015	26.11	26.02	26.29	25.40	25.36	25.82	26.05	27.68	27.09	27.66	27.60	27.10	26.51

4. Average Weekly Earnings by Selected Industry: Maryland, 2011–2015

(Dollars, not seasonally adjusted)

Industry and year	January	February	March	April	May	June	July	August	September	October	November	December	Annual average
Total Private													
2011	910.32	903.91	888.71	886.83	897.49	879.19	883.81	869.51	873.96	894.91	872.93	881.06	887.52
2012	895.30	881.40	876.32	885.10	868.18	866.66	881.28	864.94	890.35	876.43	879.48	910.32	882.30
2013	891.78	883.06	886.08	893.33	890.29	908.42	892.84	901.60	934.20	910.91	920.70	933.66	903.77
2014	926.80	934.75	942.90	930.25	923.77	944.23	931.25	932.62	939.13	921.74	949.10	925.07	932.64
2015	920.41	939.37	946.96	930.25	928.84	919.58	920.20	946.62	938.40	941.47	958.07	939.13	936.73
Goods-Producing													
2010	992.92	985.73	983.19	993.12	1,006.28	1,003.70	1,007.22	999.79	975.46	990.18	990.79	1,014.55	994.67
2011	991.38	993.18	986.50	971.94	958.65	965.95	962.86	967.83	985.92	973.68	971.49	981.71	976.78
2012	969.90	963.07	977.80	981.63	990.61	987.00	981.29	1,015.88	1,023.36	998.46	1,028.98	1,024.90	996.77
2013	1,040.66	985.91	1,032.14	1,043.06	1,037.12	1,067.77	1,056.06	1,050.62	1,045.20	1,033.41	1,069.60	1,032.08	1,039.88
2014	1,002.75	1,005.48	1,025.60	1,021.90	1,039.10	1,054.80	1,045.38	1,043.16	1,033.59	1,057.63	1,031.07	1,065.53	1,035.95
Mining, Logging, and Construction													
2011	1,018.58	1,025.27	1,017.05	1,025.88	1,053.63	1,053.80	1,060.29	1,046.40	1,005.58	1,023.75	1,046.43	1,057.25	1,036.10
2012	1,027.61	1,031.10	1,015.86	1,021.50	1,027.33	1,033.15	1,022.49	1,033.69	1,061.58	1,045.98	1,038.31	1,054.19	1,033.60
2013	1,002.38	998.21	990.76	1,007.38	1,027.78	998.25	1,002.70	1,032.95	1,034.50	1,014.29	1,051.47	1,018.03	1,014.38
2014	1,034.67	955.63	1,036.80	1,044.85	1,047.03	1,082.80	1,085.88	1,065.15	1,071.42	1,062.66	1,075.93	1,034.67	1,050.32
2015	991.56	1,002.28	1,002.57	1,023.25	1,053.30	1,062.95	1,057.89	1,033.89	996.02	1,050.97	990.00	1,063.73	1,027.21
Manufacturing													
2011	960.84	939.88	944.79	951.86	945.74	936.26	940.00	938.00	938.48	948.01	920.00	957.48	944.15
2012	946.45	944.07	945.10	907.61	871.81	877.19	882.19	877.59	882.39	873.95	878.20	884.80	898.00
2013	928.26	916.28	961.00	948.42	936.54	972.89	952.77	991.93	1,008.67	977.24	1,000.76	1,037.40	969.53
2014	1,047.74	1,026.96	1,024.80	1,040.58	1,025.23	1,042.95	1,015.33	1,026.37	1,005.49	988.63	1,057.46	1,024.40	1,026.96
2015	1,016.72	1,008.44	1,060.38	1,016.87	1,017.46	1,041.11	1,026.86	1,056.98	1,093.68	1,068.35	1,093.04	1,070.92	1,048.97
Trade, Transportation, and Utilities													
2011	650.06	648.45	643.42	648.56	672.24	657.82	663.49	647.35	663.55	663.30	663.89	667.60	657.27
2012	644.49	641.53	640.30	641.07	629.00	635.44	659.84	633.70	663.08	654.12	645.02	678.96	646.93
2013	658.69	671.33	666.32	673.30	679.72	693.25	683.09	684.08	684.42	673.86	664.53	663.63	675.70
2014	645.93	669.93	680.39	684.58	683.36	681.74	703.66	693.84	724.61	706.16	722.06	741.69	694.54
2015	733.54	746.50	739.36	741.11	738.01	734.47	750.88	755.97	762.80	757.51	761.38	748.94	748.39
Financial Activities													
2011	1,021.82	1,015.36	1,006.52	979.97	994.73	1,001.55	980.53	996.77	990.60	1,036.96	1,014.50	1,059.22	1,007.55
2012	1,089.41	1,058.03	1,063.92	1,040.64	1,042.48	1,043.25	1,084.70	1,060.07	1,087.02	1,063.89	1,095.17	1,154.69	1,074.47
2013	1,124.52	1,156.32	1,147.93	1,143.02	1,142.60	1,166.05	1,174.77	1,178.59	1,218.38	1,179.44	1,205.09	1,212.93	1,170.73
2014	1,211.50	1,226.11	1,220.46	1,202.99	1,205.89	1,222.00	1,216.14	1,240.23	1,223.96	1,225.04	1,277.61	1,270.44	1,227.60
2015	1,269.38	1,320.57	1,338.97	1,331.25	1,348.48	1,323.65	1,332.92	1,406.02	1,393.08	1,385.32	1,433.74	1,384.43	1,355.30
Professional and Business Services													
2011	1,340.39	1,310.25	1,286.19	1,279.88	1,290.48	1,270.03	1,275.37	1,240.60	1,252.13	1,303.77	1,268.89	1,275.00	1,282.55
2012	1,306.50	1,248.06	1,227.54	1,238.36	1,209.61	1,185.89	1,225.41	1,186.27	1,231.88	1,203.95	1,215.96	1,282.85	1,229.82
2013	1,224.84	1,195.26	1,195.61	1,204.80	1,117.05	1,170.36	1,142.00	1,165.34	1,226.53	1,186.77	1,210.24	1,250.49	1,192.02
2014	1,233.18	1,272.76	1,269.84	1,218.38	1,219.68	1,265.42	1,214.51	1,224.51	1,214.81	1,194.34	1,250.64	1,200.95	1,231.37
2015	1,197.50	1,236.17	1,237.61	1,198.94	1,190.60	1,183.81	1,171.03	1,229.93	1,194.22	1,205.82	1,256.33	1,220.23	1,208.45
Education and Health Services													
2011	851.12	850.85	848.54	861.98	871.85	870.53	877.14	872.85	875.80	887.08	876.09	876.94	868.56
2012	901.64	896.53	897.08	888.55	889.53	915.55	918.53	929.52	938.87	922.02	916.58	921.68	910.34
2013	934.56	934.07	932.91	941.39	930.74	939.71	923.08	919.85	931.97	923.62	916.65	917.20	929.74
2014	912.90	897.93	896.28	885.67	871.50	872.81	879.09	878.14	873.18	872.38	869.88	860.01	880.73
2015	858.68	860.64	856.41	846.30	839.08	839.02	847.44	839.61	855.73	844.94	850.23	832.46	847.50
Leisure and Hospitality													
2011	412.08	422.01	415.44	408.78	409.36	397.76	395.56	388.53	379.51	391.40	397.13	392.74	399.73
2012	389.29	393.16	388.89	395.01	385.75	384.11	378.67	370.72	376.06	372.13	373.12	376.83	381.98
2013	356.86	365.82	357.59	355.69	363.90	367.29	364.76	360.10	390.64	381.95	383.23	384.31	369.72
2014	370.51	364.82	371.86	382.00	378.49	383.13	383.93	383.83	393.42	377.66	382.52	377.95	379.70
2015	380.02	382.03	392.93	404.03	427.46	414.41	409.03	421.12	405.11	409.04	402.90	401.74	404.59
Other Services													
2011	746.83	735.81	742.90	731.46	724.42	714.47	703.72	696.09	708.85	713.66	685.94	694.88	717.14
2012	687.14	665.98	678.22	696.58	670.64	674.66	688.13	698.86	722.60	704.84	723.61	715.44	693.72
2013	700.24	729.97	730.93	755.71	753.91	777.40	782.60	756.20	791.27	777.31	786.13	789.91	762.24
2014	795.44	786.64	810.22	794.86	809.30	822.31	805.57	817.28	838.47	838.29	857.67	848.72	818.56
2015	838.13	866.47	880.72	853.44	862.24	867.55	877.89	910.67	883.13	893.42	897.00	875.33	874.83

MASSACHUSETTS
At a Glance

Population:
  2005 estimate: 6,403,290
  2010 census: 6,547,629
  2015 estimate: 6,794,422

Percent change in population:
  2005–2015: 6.1%
  2010–2015: 3.8%

Percent change in total nonfarm employment:
  2005–2015: 8.1%

Industry with the largest growth in employment, 2005–2015 (thousands):
  Education and health services, 156.0

Industry with the largest decline or smallest growth in employment, 2005–2015 (thousands):
  Manufacturing, –55.0

Civilian labor force:
  2005: 3,384,116
  2010: 3,480,083
  2015: 3,569,956

Unemployment rate and rank among states (highest to lowest):
  2005: 4.8%, 29th
  2010: 8.3%, 30th
  2015: 5.0%, 28th

Over-the-year change in unemployment rates:
  2012–2013: 0.0%
  2013–2014: –1.0%
  2014–2015: –0.7%

Employment by Industry: Massachusetts, 2015

- Other 11%
- Financial activities 7%
- Manufacturing 7%
- Leisure and hospitality 10%
- Government 13%
- Education and health services 22%
- Trade, transportation, and utilities 14%
- Professional and business services 16%

1. Employment by Industry: Massachusetts, 2005–2015

(Numbers in thousands, not seasonally adjusted)

Industry and year	January	February	March	April	May	June	July	August	September	October	November	December	Annual average
Total Nonfarm													
2005	3,144.2	3,161.3	3,169.6	3,224.0	3,246.6	3,268.0	3,244.1	3,234.9	3,263.3	3,264.4	3,275.1	3,278.9	3,231.2
2006	3,178.7	3,189.8	3,210.4	3,254.4	3,277.4	3,307.5	3,279.6	3,271.5	3,296.1	3,307.6	3,313.5	3,318.8	3,267.1
2007	3,221.8	3,229.7	3,244.9	3,286.9	3,321.4	3,352.0	3,319.4	3,312.7	3,331.2	3,344.2	3,351.0	3,348.4	3,305.3
2008	3,252.6	3,265.3	3,280.9	3,320.5	3,347.5	3,364.0	3,335.9	3,324.0	3,336.6	3,346.3	3,327.3	3,311.4	3,317.7
2009	3,187.9	3,187.1	3,184.0	3,215.7	3,231.7	3,238.7	3,206.6	3,191.3	3,213.1	3,228.6	3,222.2	3,224.9	3,211.0
2010	3,145.7	3,148.2	3,160.9	3,214.4	3,250.0	3,253.6	3,237.6	3,222.5	3,240.0	3,267.3	3,264.4	3,264.4	3,222.4
2011	3,166.5	3,179.1	3,194.1	3,250.8	3,271.6	3,288.9	3,283.2	3,266.9	3,294.6	3,308.0	3,305.0	3,305.4	3,259.5
2012	3,217.0	3,227.3	3,254.8	3,292.2	3,321.5	3,359.9	3,329.3	3,321.0	3,340.3	3,356.0	3,360.4	3,354.2	3,311.2
2013	3,259.7	3,274.4	3,299.6	3,354.6	3,389.0	3,418.4	3,385.1	3,379.9	3,391.3	3,414.4	3,417.9	3,415.8	3,366.7
2014	3,314.8	3,333.7	3,355.0	3,415.2	3,451.5	3,478.5	3,459.1	3,438.7	3,464.8	3,493.9	3,500.9	3,501.8	3,434.0
2015	3,386.7	3,389.7	3,420.0	3,475.2	3,519.6	3,548.3	3,533.3	3,514.5	3,514.0	3,542.8	3,539.3	3,531.7	3,492.9
Total Private													
2005	2,722.9	2,727.9	2,736.3	2,789.5	2,810.6	2,841.0	2,849.1	2,847.1	2,837.3	2,830.4	2,838.4	2,844.2	2,806.2
2006	2,753.6	2,754.0	2,773.5	2,816.4	2,837.5	2,875.2	2,880.0	2,879.7	2,866.1	2,869.6	2,872.7	2,879.6	2,838.2
2007	2,791.9	2,790.0	2,804.1	2,844.9	2,876.7	2,916.1	2,917.9	2,917.8	2,897.5	2,902.4	2,907.0	2,905.2	2,872.6
2008	2,819.3	2,820.4	2,835.3	2,873.2	2,898.8	2,925.3	2,929.5	2,924.5	2,899.0	2,899.2	2,879.1	2,864.6	2,880.7
2009	2,752.1	2,738.9	2,736.4	2,762.7	2,781.5	2,799.7	2,801.2	2,793.7	2,778.5	2,781.3	2,775.2	2,775.3	2,773.0
2010	2,707.2	2,702.0	2,713.6	2,763.0	2,789.8	2,811.6	2,831.9	2,825.0	2,803.4	2,820.5	2,813.9	2,815.2	2,783.1
2011	2,733.7	2,733.9	2,748.5	2,805.3	2,824.2	2,852.9	2,881.3	2,873.5	2,858.3	2,864.9	2,861.3	2,859.6	2,824.8
2012	2,785.3	2,783.4	2,807.8	2,845.5	2,873.2	2,921.0	2,925.6	2,923.3	2,900.1	2,909.0	2,908.8	2,904.6	2,874.0
2013	2,825.9	2,823.3	2,847.2	2,897.9	2,933.0	2,974.0	2,976.4	2,977.9	2,949.6	2,960.5	2,959.8	2,957.3	2,923.6
2014	2,870.8	2,875.6	2,896.3	2,950.7	2,988.3	3,027.6	3,042.0	3,029.5	3,010.7	3,031.1	3,031.2	3,034.4	2,982.4
2015	2,942.4	2,930.5	2,956.8	3,009.4	3,057.8	3,093.5	3,114.4	3,106.9	3,065.1	3,082.8	3,075.7	3,067.7	3,041.9
Goods-Producing													
2005	433.9	430.1	430.6	443.3	450.4	456.4	456.0	457.1	455.4	451.2	450.7	446.7	446.8
2006	431.1	428.3	430.8	441.4	446.1	452.5	451.1	451.9	449.0	445.9	442.7	439.8	442.6
2007	425.0	419.4	421.0	428.2	437.3	445.0	443.3	444.6	441.6	437.9	435.8	430.1	434.1
2008	414.3	410.0	412.4	420.0	426.3	431.1	430.7	430.6	425.8	421.6	414.6	405.1	420.2
2009	380.8	372.0	368.2	372.1	374.1	377.4	376.2	374.3	370.9	368.8	366.3	362.2	371.9
2010	348.8	343.9	346.3	355.9	362.4	368.4	371.9	371.0	368.5	368.7	366.9	362.6	361.3
2011	348.3	344.5	347.1	358.9	365.4	372.4	376.4	377.2	373.6	372.2	370.0	366.6	364.4
2012	355.3	352.0	356.1	363.6	368.2	376.5	377.7	378.1	375.1	375.7	374.3	371.1	368.6
2013	358.9	356.3	358.9	367.5	375.8	382.7	384.6	385.8	382.5	381.4	379.5	375.9	374.2
2014	365.2	361.9	363.9	373.2	381.4	387.9	390.3	390.7	387.2	388.4	388.1	385.4	380.3
2015	373.7	368.9	371.8	383.7	392.8	398.9	400.8	400.8	395.9	398.0	399.3	394.6	389.9
Service-Providing													
2005	2,710.3	2,731.2	2,739.0	2,780.7	2,796.2	2,811.6	2,788.1	2,777.8	2,807.9	2,813.2	2,824.4	2,832.2	2,784.4
2006	2,747.6	2,761.5	2,779.6	2,813.0	2,831.3	2,855.0	2,828.5	2,819.6	2,847.1	2,861.7	2,870.8	2,879.0	2,824.6
2007	2,796.8	2,810.3	2,823.9	2,858.7	2,884.1	2,907.0	2,876.1	2,868.1	2,889.6	2,906.3	2,915.2	2,918.3	2,871.2
2008	2,838.3	2,855.3	2,868.5	2,900.5	2,921.2	2,932.9	2,905.2	2,893.4	2,910.8	2,924.7	2,912.7	2,906.3	2,897.5
2009	2,807.1	2,815.1	2,815.8	2,843.6	2,857.6	2,861.3	2,830.4	2,817.0	2,842.2	2,859.8	2,855.9	2,862.7	2,839.0
2010	2,796.9	2,804.3	2,814.6	2,858.5	2,887.6	2,885.2	2,865.7	2,851.5	2,871.5	2,898.6	2,897.5	2,901.8	2,861.1
2011	2,818.2	2,834.6	2,847.0	2,891.9	2,906.2	2,916.5	2,906.8	2,889.7	2,921.0	2,935.8	2,935.0	2,938.8	2,895.1
2012	2,861.7	2,875.3	2,898.7	2,928.6	2,953.3	2,983.4	2,951.6	2,942.9	2,965.2	2,980.3	2,986.1	2,983.1	2,942.5
2013	2,900.8	2,918.1	2,940.7	2,987.1	3,013.2	3,035.7	3,000.5	2,994.1	3,008.8	3,033.0	3,038.4	3,039.9	2,992.5
2014	2,949.6	2,971.8	2,991.1	3,042.0	3,070.1	3,090.6	3,068.8	3,048.0	3,077.6	3,105.5	3,112.8	3,116.4	3,053.7
2015	3,013.0	3,020.8	3,048.2	3,091.5	3,126.8	3,149.4	3,132.5	3,113.7	3,118.1	3,144.8	3,140.0	3,137.1	3,103.0
Mining and Logging													
2005	1.8	1.7	1.7	2.0	2.1	2.1	2.1	2.1	2.1	2.0	2.0	1.8	2.0
2006	1.6	1.6	1.7	1.8	1.9	1.9	2.0	1.9	1.9	1.9	1.9	1.7	1.8
2007	1.4	1.3	1.4	1.5	1.7	1.8	1.7	1.7	1.7	1.6	1.6	1.5	1.6
2008	1.2	1.2	1.2	1.4	1.5	1.5	1.5	1.4	1.4	1.4	1.4	1.3	1.4
2009	1.1	1.1	1.1	1.3	1.4	1.4	1.4	1.4	1.4	1.4	1.4	1.3	1.3
2010	1.0	1.0	1.0	1.2	1.3	1.3	1.2	1.2	1.2	1.1	1.1	1.1	1.1
2011	0.9	0.9	0.9	1.1	1.2	1.2	1.2	1.2	1.2	1.2	1.1	1.1	1.1
2012	0.9	0.8	0.9	0.9	1.0	1.0	1.0	1.0	1.0	1.0	1.0	1.0	1.0
2013	0.8	0.8	0.9	1.0	1.0	1.0	1.0	1.1	1.1	1.1	1.0	1.0	1.0
2014	0.9	0.9	0.9	1.0	1.1	1.1	1.1	1.1	1.1	1.1	1.1	1.0	1.0
2015	0.9	0.9	0.9	1.1	1.1	1.2	1.2	1.1	1.2	1.2	1.1	1.1	1.1

1. Employment by Industry: Massachusetts, 2005–2015—*Continued*

(Numbers in thousands, not seasonally adjusted)

Industry and year	January	February	March	April	May	June	July	August	September	October	November	December	Annual average
Construction													
2005	124.5	120.7	122.3	135.3	141.9	146.4	150.3	150.7	149.3	145.8	145.8	141.4	139.5
2006	129.2	126.6	129.3	140.1	144.4	148.3	150.2	150.4	147.7	145.4	142.5	138.7	141.1
2007	126.7	121.5	123.8	131.8	140.2	145.4	147.5	147.6	145.7	143.9	141.8	135.9	137.7
2008	123.4	120.4	123.1	130.7	136.7	139.9	142.4	141.6	138.7	136.1	131.7	124.8	132.5
2009	109.0	104.3	103.6	110.1	114.0	116.8	118.1	117.2	114.6	113.1	110.4	106.0	111.4
2010	96.1	92.3	94.5	103.3	108.7	112.8	116.3	115.5	114.0	113.2	111.5	107.3	107.1
2011	96.8	94.0	95.8	105.9	111.7	116.6	120.6	121.1	119.3	117.9	116.3	112.6	110.7
2012	103.3	100.4	103.8	111.5	115.5	120.4	123.5	123.9	122.0	122.5	121.3	118.0	115.5
2013	108.8	106.7	108.6	116.8	124.2	128.5	131.8	132.3	130.2	129.5	127.5	123.2	122.3
2014	114.8	112.3	113.9	122.8	130.4	135.0	138.0	138.1	136.5	137.1	136.3	133.1	129.0
2015	123.8	119.0	121.4	132.4	140.8	144.6	147.8	148.4	145.6	147.2	148.4	143.1	138.5
Manufacturing													
2005	307.6	307.7	306.6	306.0	306.4	307.9	303.6	304.3	304.0	303.4	302.9	303.5	305.3
2006	300.3	300.1	299.8	299.5	299.8	302.3	298.9	299.6	299.4	298.6	298.3	299.4	299.7
2007	296.9	296.6	295.8	294.9	295.4	297.8	294.1	295.3	294.2	292.4	292.4	292.7	294.9
2008	289.7	288.4	288.1	287.9	288.1	289.7	286.8	287.6	285.7	284.1	281.5	279.0	286.4
2009	270.7	266.6	263.5	260.7	258.7	259.2	256.7	255.7	254.9	254.3	254.5	254.9	259.2
2010	251.7	250.6	250.8	251.4	252.4	254.3	254.4	254.3	253.3	254.4	254.3	254.2	253.0
2011	250.6	249.6	250.4	251.9	252.5	254.6	254.6	254.9	253.1	253.1	252.6	252.9	252.6
2012	251.1	250.8	251.4	251.2	251.7	255.1	253.2	253.2	252.1	252.2	252.0	252.1	252.2
2013	249.3	248.8	249.4	249.7	250.6	253.2	251.8	252.4	251.2	250.8	251.0	251.7	250.8
2014	249.5	248.7	249.1	249.4	249.9	251.8	251.2	251.5	249.6	250.2	250.7	251.3	250.2
2015	249.0	249.0	249.5	250.2	250.9	253.1	251.8	251.3	249.1	249.6	249.8	250.4	250.3
Trade, Transportation, and Utilities													
2005	565.2	559.8	559.0	563.7	568.2	575.4	569.6	569.4	568.5	570.9	579.9	590.5	570.0
2006	566.5	555.3	558.0	562.6	566.8	575.1	569.4	569.8	570.4	573.9	584.1	593.3	570.4
2007	567.3	557.2	558.8	560.7	568.5	577.5	571.1	569.3	568.9	574.1	585.7	592.2	570.9
2008	570.9	558.9	560.2	563.1	568.8	576.1	570.2	569.2	566.8	568.6	571.7	576.7	568.4
2009	547.4	536.7	533.1	533.1	539.3	547.4	539.7	538.5	539.6	543.9	550.7	556.8	542.2
2010	537.4	528.3	528.9	535.5	542.0	548.8	545.7	545.4	541.8	548.6	555.6	565.1	543.6
2011	541.7	534.6	534.6	541.0	545.1	552.0	549.6	549.5	548.4	552.6	560.2	567.7	548.1
2012	545.9	535.7	537.9	540.6	548.5	558.4	552.9	552.7	550.8	555.6	565.8	571.2	551.3
2013	548.6	539.7	541.4	547.0	554.6	564.1	558.2	558.7	556.4	559.2	568.1	576.1	556.0
2014	555.8	548.0	549.1	554.5	561.1	569.5	563.6	553.2	563.1	568.6	578.5	587.6	562.7
2015	563.9	551.3	553.6	559.1	566.8	576.0	572.7	572.2	568.2	571.3	577.3	581.9	567.9
Wholesale Trade													
2005	131.4	131.2	131.1	132.1	133.1	134.2	134.6	135.0	134.6	135.3	136.1	136.8	133.8
2006	134.9	134.5	135.0	136.2	136.6	138.1	138.3	138.7	137.9	138.1	138.2	138.8	137.1
2007	136.7	136.4	136.9	136.9	137.5	139.1	139.1	138.9	137.8	138.4	138.3	138.5	137.9
2008	137.0	135.9	136.3	136.8	137.1	138.1	137.6	136.8	135.6	134.9	134.0	133.6	136.1
2009	130.0	128.5	127.7	127.2	127.0	127.5	126.6	125.8	124.4	124.2	123.5	123.2	126.3
2010	121.4	120.8	121.0	121.5	122.5	123.3	123.7	123.5	122.1	122.9	122.7	122.7	122.3
2011	121.1	120.9	120.7	122.0	122.1	122.5	123.3	122.6	121.2	121.2	120.8	120.8	121.6
2012	119.8	119.5	120.0	121.1	121.7	122.9	123.1	123.2	121.9	122.6	122.5	122.4	121.7
2013	121.2	121.0	121.4	122.4	122.8	123.9	124.4	124.2	123.2	123.7	123.5	123.5	122.9
2014	122.2	121.9	122.1	123.3	123.8	124.7	124.9	124.6	123.5	123.7	123.8	123.9	123.5
2015	122.3	121.4	121.6	123.0	123.5	124.7	125.4	125.2	123.9	125.1	124.0	123.6	123.6
Retail Trade													
2005	352.3	347.2	346.5	349.5	352.2	357.3	355.1	355.4	351.0	353.4	361.7	370.3	354.3
2006	351.1	340.5	342.3	344.9	347.4	352.5	350.4	350.6	346.5	350.4	360.8	368.1	350.5
2007	347.3	338.1	338.8	340.3	346.2	352.0	350.2	349.3	344.8	349.5	361.7	366.8	348.8
2008	349.8	339.5	340.0	341.8	345.8	351.1	350.4	351.1	344.7	348.0	353.0	357.3	347.7
2009	335.7	327.3	324.6	325.1	330.4	336.9	334.7	335.4	332.1	336.5	344.2	348.9	334.3
2010	334.6	326.6	327.1	331.8	335.9	340.8	341.8	342.8	336.1	341.8	349.2	356.2	338.7
2011	338.7	332.0	331.9	336.1	339.0	344.0	344.9	346.5	341.7	346.2	354.3	360.4	343.0
2012	343.3	333.8	335.1	336.4	342.3	349.3	348.1	348.6	343.1	347.0	357.6	360.8	345.5
2013	343.6	334.9	336.0	339.8	345.3	351.8	349.9	351.6	345.2	347.6	356.5	362.6	347.1
2014	347.1	339.5	339.9	343.1	347.1	352.7	351.3	342.1	347.5	352.8	361.7	367.3	349.3
2015	351.3	340.4	342.2	345.0	350.5	356.8	356.6	356.9	349.3	351.4	357.9	360.7	351.6

1. Employment by Industry: Massachusetts, 2005–2015—*Continued*

(Numbers in thousands, not seasonally adjusted)

Industry and year	January	February	March	April	May	June	July	August	September	October	November	December	Annual average
Transportation and Utilities													
2005	81.5	81.4	81.4	82.1	82.9	83.9	79.9	79.0	82.9	82.2	82.1	83.4	81.9
2006	80.5	80.3	80.7	81.5	82.8	84.5	80.7	80.5	86.0	85.4	85.1	86.4	82.9
2007	83.3	82.7	83.1	83.5	84.8	86.4	81.8	81.1	86.3	86.2	85.7	86.9	84.3
2008	84.1	83.5	83.9	84.5	85.9	86.9	82.2	81.3	86.5	85.7	84.7	85.8	84.6
2009	81.7	80.9	80.8	80.8	81.9	83.0	78.4	77.3	83.1	83.2	83.0	84.7	81.6
2010	81.4	80.9	80.8	82.2	83.6	84.7	80.2	79.1	83.6	83.9	83.7	86.2	82.5
2011	81.9	81.7	82.0	82.9	84.0	85.5	81.4	80.4	85.5	85.2	85.1	86.5	83.5
2012	82.8	82.4	82.8	83.1	84.5	86.2	81.7	80.9	85.8	86.0	85.7	88.0	84.2
2013	83.8	83.8	84.0	84.8	86.5	88.4	83.9	82.9	88.0	87.9	88.1	90.0	86.0
2014	86.5	86.6	87.1	88.1	90.2	92.1	87.4	86.5	92.1	92.1	93.0	96.4	89.8
2015	90.3	89.5	89.8	91.1	92.8	94.5	90.7	90.1	95.0	94.8	95.4	97.6	92.6
Information													
2005	86.5	86.7	86.7	86.4	86.6	87.3	88.0	87.6	86.9	86.2	86.6	87.1	86.9
2006	86.5	86.5	86.5	85.9	86.4	87.3	87.1	87.5	86.5	87.0	87.4	88.0	86.9
2007	86.4	86.7	87.6	88.2	87.9	88.9	89.8	89.9	89.9	88.8	88.8	89.4	88.5
2008	87.7	88.7	89.4	90.7	90.6	90.5	89.7	89.5	88.8	87.7	87.6	87.8	89.1
2009	86.8	85.4	85.5	85.2	85.1	85.8	85.2	86.0	87.0	86.0	86.1	85.9	85.8
2010	84.8	84.8	85.0	85.2	85.7	86.7	85.8	85.4	84.7	83.6	83.8	84.3	85.0
2011	83.3	83.4	83.8	83.8	84.3	85.5	86.8	83.2	85.4	85.5	85.3	85.7	84.7
2012	85.4	85.0	85.3	85.7	86.3	88.1	89.3	88.6	86.0	86.1	85.6	85.5	86.4
2013	84.7	84.7	84.7	85.2	85.7	87.3	87.7	87.5	86.3	85.8	87.6	86.1	86.1
2014	84.6	84.8	84.8	85.5	86.3	87.6	88.0	87.6	86.5	86.6	86.8	87.2	86.4
2015	86.9	86.5	86.9	87.1	87.4	88.9	89.4	89.1	87.8	87.7	87.0	87.7	87.7
Financial Activities													
2005	222.8	222.4	223.0	223.6	225.0	228.4	231.1	231.4	229.3	227.6	228.3	230.0	226.9
2006	226.3	226.1	226.5	227.3	228.6	231.6	233.7	233.3	230.9	230.1	230.3	231.9	229.7
2007	229.9	229.9	229.9	230.0	230.7	233.5	234.1	233.8	230.0	228.7	228.1	228.9	230.6
2008	226.9	226.6	226.9	227.2	227.7	230.2	231.4	230.9	227.7	226.8	225.9	226.0	227.9
2009	223.1	221.8	221.2	220.4	220.5	222.1	222.1	221.4	217.9	216.8	216.6	217.1	220.1
2010	214.5	213.9	213.6	213.7	214.8	216.5	217.8	217.6	214.7	214.4	213.9	215.0	215.0
2011	212.4	212.1	212.1	213.0	213.4	215.6	217.6	217.7	215.0	214.3	213.5	214.0	214.2
2012	212.0	212.1	212.2	212.4	213.6	216.7	217.3	217.6	214.3	214.0	213.7	214.4	214.2
2013	212.2	212.4	213.0	213.2	214.6	217.5	218.2	218.8	215.4	215.1	215.2	215.9	215.1
2014	213.4	213.4	213.5	214.5	216.3	219.2	220.3	220.2	217.0	217.3	217.4	218.1	216.7
2015	215.9	215.5	215.6	216.5	218.1	221.1	224.3	224.5	220.6	220.4	221.6	221.7	219.7
Professional and Business Services													
2005	443.1	443.3	445.4	459.5	460.8	467.9	468.8	469.5	468.3	466.5	468.5	467.8	460.8
2006	453.0	454.7	458.4	469.1	471.8	480.4	479.3	481.0	477.5	478.2	479.0	478.2	471.7
2007	461.9	463.8	467.2	480.2	484.7	492.4	490.4	492.5	487.5	488.3	489.8	489.5	482.4
2008	475.7	477.0	478.6	488.4	491.6	497.6	496.9	496.0	491.7	490.3	485.4	480.0	487.4
2009	461.5	457.1	455.1	461.1	460.1	462.8	461.6	460.5	456.8	457.0	456.0	455.4	458.8
2010	447.4	447.4	449.5	462.3	464.2	469.1	473.5	472.6	467.2	472.5	471.2	469.8	463.9
2011	460.3	461.2	461.3	477.8	478.0	484.3	489.6	488.1	485.4	488.6	488.5	486.1	479.1
2012	472.2	472.6	478.8	490.0	492.4	501.6	502.6	502.7	498.6	501.0	501.8	497.2	492.6
2013	484.8	487.9	490.4	504.1	508.0	515.4	516.8	517.5	511.3	514.1	515.3	511.8	506.5
2014	497.6	498.5	500.2	514.9	519.0	526.9	530.2	531.2	526.4	530.1	529.3	526.5	519.2
2015	512.0	512.1	515.3	529.5	535.7	543.2	547.5	546.9	538.8	542.6	541.0	536.8	533.5
Education and Health Services													
2005	592.0	605.1	606.9	610.5	603.1	590.5	591.1	589.1	603.5	616.4	621.8	621.7	604.3
2006	606.8	619.7	624.2	625.7	619.5	609.0	609.0	606.4	621.9	634.4	639.3	640.0	621.3
2007	629.3	640.6	642.4	648.2	642.0	629.2	631.6	630.1	643.2	657.3	661.4	662.2	643.1
2008	647.0	660.6	664.6	667.5	659.7	646.9	649.9	647.8	660.1	674.4	678.3	678.9	661.3
2009	663.8	675.9	679.6	682.4	674.5	660.0	664.1	662.2	674.5	686.3	690.7	691.7	675.5
2010	680.2	691.2	694.4	693.9	688.2	671.9	675.1	673.1	686.9	699.3	703.0	702.7	688.3
2011	688.2	699.5	703.4	705.3	698.8	683.2	688.4	686.0	700.4	710.0	714.6	714.5	699.4
2012	702.0	713.6	717.8	717.1	712.3	700.1	700.1	698.6	711.8	722.7	727.1	727.4	712.6
2013	713.4	721.2	726.9	731.1	726.2	714.5	712.5	709.3	719.8	732.2	735.2	736.7	723.3
2014	717.1	732.2	737.7	746.2	741.3	730.0	733.9	731.3	740.3	755.9	761.3	761.8	740.8
2015	740.9	754.2	761.1	764.6	764.4	751.5	753.6	749.8	758.0	773.1	776.6	776.3	760.3

1. Employment by Industry: Massachusetts, 2005–2015—*Continued*

(Numbers in thousands, not seasonally adjusted)

Industry and year	January	February	March	April	May	June	July	August	September	October	November	December	Annual average
Leisure and Hospitality													
2005	265.2	265.9	269.2	285.3	298.8	314.1	322.0	321.3	307.2	294.6	285.3	282.2	292.6
2006	267.6	267.9	272.1	286.7	299.7	317.2	326.8	326.6	311.3	302.0	292.1	289.9	296.7
2007	276.2	276.0	279.8	291.1	305.6	325.4	331.7	332.2	315.6	307.4	297.1	292.4	302.5
2008	279.5	280.7	284.5	297.1	313.8	329.0	334.6	335.2	318.1	310.2	296.4	291.2	305.9
2009	272.9	274.2	276.9	290.5	308.6	321.2	327.9	327.1	313.8	304.7	291.5	288.6	299.8
2010	278.7	277.4	279.9	298.8	313.4	327.6	336.7	335.7	321.2	315.7	302.1	298.2	307.1
2011	284.1	282.8	288.7	306.2	319.0	336.4	346.5	346.2	330.0	322.0	309.6	305.1	314.7
2012	295.2	295.0	300.6	315.4	329.9	352.9	357.3	357.7	340.3	330.9	317.4	314.4	325.6
2013	302.1	299.8	308.3	324.1	340.8	360.5	364.2	366.5	349.1	344.2	330.1	325.3	334.6
2014	310.0	309.3	317.1	330.1	349.3	368.1	375.3	375.7	356.7	351.0	336.8	334.7	342.8
2015	318.8	313.4	321.4	335.8	358.0	374.7	383.8	382.5	361.2	353.5	337.5	332.7	347.8
Other Services													
2005	114.2	114.6	115.5	117.2	117.7	121.0	122.5	121.7	118.2	117.0	117.3	118.2	117.9
2006	115.8	115.5	117.0	117.7	118.6	122.1	123.6	123.2	118.6	118.1	117.8	118.5	118.9
2007	115.9	116.4	117.4	118.3	120.0	124.2	125.9	125.4	120.8	119.9	120.3	120.5	120.4
2008	117.3	117.9	118.7	119.2	120.3	123.9	126.1	125.3	120.0	119.6	119.2	118.9	120.5
2009	115.8	115.8	116.8	117.9	119.3	123.0	124.4	123.7	118.0	117.8	117.3	117.6	119.0
2010	115.4	115.1	116.0	117.7	119.1	122.6	125.4	124.2	118.4	117.7	117.4	117.5	118.9
2011	115.4	115.8	117.5	119.3	120.2	123.5	126.4	125.6	120.1	119.7	119.6	119.9	120.3
2012	117.3	117.4	119.1	120.7	122.0	126.7	128.4	127.3	123.2	123.0	123.1	123.4	122.6
2013	121.2	121.3	123.6	125.7	127.3	132.0	134.2	133.8	128.8	128.5	128.8	129.5	127.9
2014	127.1	127.5	130.0	131.8	133.6	138.4	140.4	139.6	133.5	133.2	133.0	133.1	133.4
2015	130.3	128.6	131.1	133.1	134.6	139.2	142.3	141.1	134.6	136.2	135.4	136.0	135.2
Government													
2005	421.3	433.4	433.3	434.5	436.0	427.0	395.0	387.8	426.0	434.0	436.7	434.7	425.0
2006	425.1	435.8	436.9	438.0	439.9	432.3	399.6	391.8	430.0	438.0	440.8	439.2	429.0
2007	429.9	439.7	440.8	442.0	444.7	435.9	401.5	394.9	433.7	441.8	444.0	443.2	432.7
2008	433.3	444.9	445.6	447.3	448.7	438.7	406.4	399.5	437.6	447.1	448.2	446.8	437.0
2009	435.8	448.2	447.6	453.0	450.2	439.0	405.4	397.6	434.6	447.3	447.0	449.6	437.9
2010	438.5	446.2	447.3	451.4	460.2	442.0	405.7	397.5	436.6	446.8	450.5	449.2	439.3
2011	432.8	445.2	445.6	445.5	447.4	436.0	401.9	393.4	436.3	443.1	443.7	445.8	434.7
2012	431.7	443.9	447.0	446.7	448.3	438.9	403.7	397.7	440.2	447.0	451.6	449.6	437.2
2013	433.8	451.1	452.4	456.7	456.0	444.4	408.7	402.0	441.7	453.9	458.1	458.5	443.1
2014	444.0	458.1	458.7	464.5	463.2	450.9	417.1	409.2	454.1	462.8	469.7	467.4	451.6
2015	444.3	459.2	463.2	465.8	461.8	454.8	418.9	407.6	448.9	460.0	463.6	464.0	451.0

2. Average Weekly Hours by Selected Industry: Massachusetts, 2011–2015

(Not seasonally adjusted)

Industry and year	January	February	March	April	May	June	July	August	September	October	November	December	Annual average
Total Private													
2011	32.9	32.9	33.0	33.1	33.2	33.1	33.2	33.2	33.2	33.1	33.1	33.1	33.1
2012	32.9	32.7	32.9	33.1	32.9	33.0	33.3	33.0	33.2	32.8	33.0	33.4	33.0
2013	32.8	33.0	32.9	33.0	33.1	33.3	33.3	33.5	33.7	33.3	33.2	33.6	33.2
2014	33.0	33.1	33.3	33.2	33.2	33.5	33.2	33.4	33.4	33.3	33.7	33.4	33.3
2015	33.1	33.0	33.4	33.3	33.5	33.5	33.6	33.8	33.5	33.5	33.8	33.7	33.5
Goods-Producing													
2011	38.7	39.6	40.1	39.8	40.0	40.2	39.7	39.8	39.9	39.2	39.6	40.0	39.7
2012	39.5	39.3	39.3	39.3	39.0	39.1	39.0	38.8	39.0	38.9	39.2	39.8	39.2
2013	39.3	39.2	39.3	39.3	39.5	39.6	39.2	39.8	39.8	39.9	39.4	40.0	39.5
2014	39.2	38.8	39.6	39.7	39.6	39.5	39.1	39.4	40.0	39.3	39.9	39.5	39.5
2015	39.3	38.0	39.5	39.2	39.6	39.9	39.5	39.9	38.8	39.4	39.5	40.3	39.4
Construction													
2011	34.0	33.2	34.1	34.6	35.7	36.0	36.3	36.4	36.8	35.4	36.7	37.3	35.6
2012	36.3	36.3	36.6	37.0	37.1	37.5	37.8	37.8	38.0	36.8	37.1	38.0	37.2
2013	38.0	37.1	37.3	38.0	38.6	38.2	38.0	38.9	38.3	38.2	37.3	37.7	38.0
2014	37.6	36.8	37.5	38.3	38.5	37.8	37.8	37.8	38.9	37.3	37.7	37.3	37.8
2015	37.4	35.1	37.8	37.7	38.9	39.3	38.9	39.2	37.5	38.0	37.7	39.2	38.1
Manufacturing													
2011	39.9	39.9	40.2	39.9	39.7	40.1	39.4	39.8	39.9	39.7	39.9	40.3	39.9
2012	40.1	39.9	39.9	39.8	39.5	39.4	39.3	39.1	39.3	39.8	40.0	40.5	39.7
2013	39.7	40.0	40.1	39.8	39.8	40.2	39.7	40.1	40.4	40.4	40.2	40.9	40.1
2014	39.8	39.6	40.4	40.2	40.0	40.3	39.6	40.2	40.4	40.3	41.1	40.9	40.2
2015	40.5	39.7	40.5	40.1	40.1	40.3	40.0	40.5	39.8	40.1	40.5	40.7	40.2
Trade, Transportation, and Utilities													
2011	31.6	32.1	32.5	32.5	32.3	32.3	32.4	32.6	33.0	32.4	33.1	33.0	32.5
2012	32.3	32.4	32.7	32.9	32.9	33.2	32.8	32.6	33.1	32.6	33.0	33.0	32.8
2013	32.0	32.3	32.3	32.5	32.9	32.8	33.0	33.3	33.6	33.1	32.7	33.6	32.8
2014	32.5	32.2	32.5	32.7	32.9	33.1	33.1	33.3	33.2	33.0	33.1	33.5	32.9
2015	32.4	32.1	32.7	32.9	33.1	33.3	33.5	33.1	33.1	32.9	33.3	33.6	33.0
Information													
2011	36.2	35.4	35.3	34.9	35.0	34.2	34.9	35.2	35.1	36.2	35.5	35.8	35.3
2012	36.8	35.9	36.0	37.2	35.9	35.5	37.2	36.1	37.5	36.3	36.5	37.4	36.5
2013	35.8	35.6	35.9	35.2	35.1	36.9	36.0	35.9	36.7	35.8	36.1	37.4	36.0
2014	36.4	37.1	37.5	36.2	36.3	37.7	36.5	36.7	36.7	36.7	38.1	36.4	36.9
2015	37.1	38.5	38.5	37.2	37.9	37.3	37.7	39.1	37.6	37.5	38.7	37.4	37.9
Financial Activities													
2011	36.6	35.7	35.6	35.8	36.6	36.0	35.4	35.6	36.0	36.3	35.8	35.6	35.9
2012	36.5	35.4	35.5	35.8	35.6	35.7	36.0	35.6	36.0	35.7	35.5	36.1	35.8
2013	35.4	35.9	36.0	35.9	35.8	36.8	36.1	36.2	37.1	36.2	36.2	36.9	36.2
2014	36.2	37.1	37.1	36.6	36.5	37.0	36.2	36.3	36.5	36.5	37.0	36.4	36.6
2015	36.5	37.1	37.1	36.7	36.6	36.5	36.7	37.4	36.7	36.7	37.3	36.6	36.8
Professional and Business Services													
2011	35.5	34.6	34.9	35.3	35.8	35.4	35.5	35.8	35.7	36.2	35.8	36.0	35.5
2012	35.6	35.5	35.4	36.2	35.6	35.4	36.2	35.4	35.6	34.7	34.9	35.8	35.5
2013	34.7	35.4	35.2	35.4	35.5	36.3	35.7	36.0	36.5	35.9	36.0	36.4	35.8
2014	35.8	36.3	36.3	36.0	36.1	36.6	35.9	35.8	35.8	35.8	36.8	35.6	36.1
2015	35.4	36.0	36.1	35.9	36.2	36.1	35.8	36.8	36.0	36.3	37.1	36.7	36.2
Education and Health Services													
2011	31.4	31.0	31.0	31.1	31.0	31.0	31.2	30.9	30.7	30.5	30.3	30.0	30.8
2012	30.1	30.0	30.2	30.5	30.5	30.5	30.8	31.0	31.1	31.1	31.4	31.8	30.8
2013	31.6	31.8	31.6	31.7	31.7	31.8	31.9	31.9	32.0	31.9	32.0	32.0	31.8
2014	31.8	31.8	31.6	31.6	31.5	31.8	31.6	31.6	31.8	32.0	32.0	31.9	31.8
2015	31.8	31.7	31.7	31.5	31.5	31.7	31.8	31.9	32.1	32.1	31.9	31.7	31.8
Leisure and Hospitality													
2011	24.8	25.7	25.6	26.0	26.1	25.9	26.6	26.6	26.2	26.1	25.8	25.8	26.0
2012	25.6	25.4	26.0	25.8	26.1	26.2	26.8	26.7	26.3	25.7	25.4	25.4	26.0
2013	24.8	24.6	25.1	25.4	25.6	25.5	26.4	26.3	26.0	25.4	24.8	24.4	25.4
2014	23.9	24.0	24.8	25.1	25.5	25.3	25.8	26.0	25.5	25.2	25.0	25.0	25.1
2015	24.6	24.1	25.3	25.4	26.1	25.6	26.2	26.2	25.7	25.4	25.2	25.1	25.4
Other Services													
2011	31.7	31.6	31.2	31.2	31.1	30.8	31.5	31.4	30.7	30.7	30.3	30.6	31.1
2012	30.4	30.3	30.6	30.7	30.2	30.5	31.3	31.0	30.3	29.9	29.6	29.7	30.4
2013	28.8	28.8	28.3	28.0	27.9	27.3	28.3	28.8	27.7	27.5	27.4	27.7	28.0
2014	27.4	27.9	28.3	28.3	28.2	28.0	29.3	29.7	28.9	28.9	29.1	29.0	28.6
2015	29.1	28.9	29.1	29.1	28.7	28.6	29.9	30.4	29.7	29.0	29.8	29.6	29.3

3. Average Hourly Earnings by Selected Industry: Massachusetts, 2011–2015

(Dollars, not seasonally adjusted)

Industry and year	January	February	March	April	May	June	July	August	September	October	November	December	Annual average
Total Private													
2011	27.80	27.51	27.39	27.47	27.54	27.27	27.44	27.23	27.68	28.11	28.00	28.12	27.63
2012	28.47	28.33	28.14	28.46	28.01	27.80	27.93	27.70	28.14	28.02	28.08	28.69	28.14
2013	28.74	28.96	28.87	28.79	28.61	28.83	28.58	28.63	29.19	29.08	29.24	29.49	28.92
2014	29.49	29.86	29.65	29.32	29.19	29.16	29.02	29.25	29.54	29.75	30.21	29.80	29.52
2015	30.47	30.60	30.39	30.24	30.19	29.94	29.89	30.23	30.40	30.79	31.23	30.98	30.44
Goods-Producing													
2011	29.68	29.50	29.24	29.24	29.16	28.76	29.25	29.35	29.38	29.65	29.60	29.74	29.38
2012	29.67	29.34	29.20	29.55	29.43	29.56	29.61	29.57	29.84	29.74	29.44	29.81	29.57
2013	29.45	30.00	29.90	30.08	30.15	29.94	30.15	30.24	30.18	30.13	30.42	30.57	30.11
2014	30.66	30.54	30.27	30.37	30.23	30.40	31.08	30.84	30.80	30.96	30.89	31.51	30.72
2015	31.74	31.70	31.55	31.67	31.67	31.44	31.68	32.08	31.81	32.33	32.45	32.34	31.88
Construction													
2011	33.81	33.77	33.42	33.13	32.98	32.80	33.03	33.03	33.46	33.18	33.33	33.86	33.30
2012	34.62	34.06	33.79	33.46	33.44	33.41	33.52	33.51	33.61	33.57	33.46	33.62	33.65
2013	33.01	34.02	33.67	33.62	33.45	33.35	33.25	33.60	33.44	33.17	33.98	34.43	33.58
2014	35.22	34.89	34.59	34.51	33.89	34.08	34.23	34.54	34.46	34.48	35.03	35.70	34.62
2015	36.38	36.43	36.57	36.70	36.11	35.59	35.98	36.19	35.82	36.68	36.64	37.17	36.35
Manufacturing													
2011	28.17	28.06	27.81	27.78	27.59	27.06	27.64	27.79	27.67	28.31	28.10	28.10	27.84
2012	27.80	27.59	27.46	27.82	27.59	27.72	27.73	27.66	28.03	27.96	27.61	28.11	27.76
2013	27.92	28.01	28.04	28.18	28.33	28.11	28.47	28.44	28.53	28.57	28.69	28.82	28.34
2014	28.60	28.61	28.35	28.47	28.45	28.41	29.36	28.77	28.71	29.00	28.60	29.26	28.72
2015	29.41	29.51	29.16	29.12	29.18	29.03	29.11	29.57	29.44	29.61	29.81	29.32	29.36
Trade, Transportation, and Utilities													
2011	22.77	22.42	22.46	22.50	22.50	22.39	22.43	22.26	22.44	22.47	22.38	21.65	22.38
2012	22.36	22.32	22.37	22.75	22.73	22.60	22.73	22.42	22.54	22.38	22.29	22.61	22.51
2013	23.38	23.32	23.39	23.39	23.18	23.47	23.60	23.46	23.80	24.12	24.07	24.14	23.62
2014	24.89	25.05	24.99	25.11	24.81	24.68	24.83	24.36	24.57	24.84	24.94	24.36	24.78
2015	25.20	24.72	24.82	25.08	24.78	24.47	25.02	24.61	24.73	25.45	25.32	25.18	24.95
Information													
2011	35.58	36.06	36.27	36.05	37.43	36.48	37.21	37.81	39.02	39.85	41.44	40.32	37.82
2012	41.94	41.64	41.25	41.00	39.55	40.15	40.85	40.23	41.07	41.55	41.11	42.17	41.04
2013	42.17	42.65	42.51	41.72	42.38	42.48	42.90	43.79	43.24	42.90	43.41	43.51	42.82
2014	43.62	42.96	42.16	41.26	42.59	41.94	41.49	43.07	42.18	43.28	43.71	43.20	42.62
2015	45.36	45.76	45.32	45.75	45.22	45.85	44.92	44.00	45.07	45.56	45.99	46.26	45.41
Financial Activities													
2011	33.89	33.20	33.21	33.01	32.76	33.11	33.30	33.21	33.76	34.31	34.45	35.00	33.60
2012	34.91	35.08	34.68	35.12	34.76	34.30	34.00	34.49	34.89	34.36	34.64	35.07	34.69
2013	34.66	34.95	33.65	34.19	34.00	35.02	34.14	34.38	35.35	34.67	34.00	34.24	34.44
2014	34.37	35.50	35.51	35.92	36.04	34.95	35.12	35.58	36.74	36.57	37.31	36.46	35.84
2015	37.43	37.54	38.08	37.86	37.52	37.66	37.69	38.78	38.10	38.78	39.34	38.90	38.15
Professional and Business Services													
2011	35.85	35.20	35.08	34.99	34.94	34.47	34.87	34.18	34.80	35.32	35.06	35.76	35.04
2012	36.33	36.09	35.73	36.31	35.86	35.73	36.08	35.24	35.92	35.62	35.81	36.85	35.96
2013	36.54	36.48	36.61	36.46	36.29	36.51	36.37	36.09	37.01	36.88	36.86	37.58	36.64
2014	37.16	37.71	37.94	36.60	36.63	36.81	36.49	37.28	37.44	37.66	38.32	38.08	37.34
2015	38.89	39.18	39.15	38.28	38.32	37.77	37.93	38.70	38.70	38.71	39.33	38.65	38.63
Education and Health Services													
2011	26.22	26.59	26.28	26.85	27.10	27.10	27.38	27.06	27.40	27.92	27.60	27.96	27.12
2012	27.93	27.78	27.62	27.76	27.11	27.36	27.12	27.11	27.45	27.45	27.58	28.31	27.52
2013	28.34	28.49	28.74	28.54	28.34	28.64	28.32	28.61	29.03	28.63	28.99	29.02	28.64
2014	28.46	28.91	28.55	28.35	28.16	28.40	28.11	28.54	28.62	28.76	29.34	28.66	28.58
2015	28.90	28.84	28.40	28.41	28.88	28.73	28.32	28.58	29.13	29.23	29.96	29.89	28.94
Leisure and Hospitality													
2011	15.34	15.02	15.08	15.05	15.09	14.88	14.83	14.85	15.11	15.29	15.17	15.25	15.07
2012	15.08	15.10	15.18	15.14	15.16	14.82	14.62	14.77	14.94	14.90	15.01	15.27	14.99
2013	15.21	15.38	15.39	15.45	15.32	15.21	15.12	15.13	15.44	15.55	15.49	15.73	15.36
2014	15.53	15.66	15.56	15.46	15.48	15.31	15.21	15.35	15.53	15.59	15.72	15.71	15.50
2015	15.66	15.82	15.70	15.63	15.75	15.62	15.72	15.67	15.77	15.91	15.78	15.72	15.73
Other Services													
2011	22.51	22.09	22.12	22.34	22.61	22.03	21.27	21.13	22.09	22.09	22.05	22.24	22.04
2012	22.66	22.73	22.85	22.91	22.73	22.34	21.91	21.84	22.33	22.30	22.22	22.27	22.41
2013	22.48	22.64	22.13	22.04	22.14	21.91	20.93	20.91	22.06	21.94	21.71	22.27	21.92
2014	22.38	22.78	22.62	22.61	22.66	22.71	21.92	22.08	23.33	23.38	23.52	23.71	22.80
2015	23.97	24.66	24.44	24.54	24.67	24.49	23.45	23.81	25.31	25.59	25.75	26.12	24.73

4. Average Weekly Earnings by Selected Industry: Massachusetts, 2011–2015

(Dollars, not seasonally adjusted)

Industry and year	January	February	March	April	May	June	July	August	September	October	November	December	Annual average
Total Private													
2011	914.62	905.08	903.87	909.26	914.33	902.64	911.01	904.04	918.98	930.44	926.80	930.77	914.55
2012	936.66	926.39	925.81	942.03	921.53	917.40	930.07	914.10	934.25	919.06	926.64	958.25	928.62
2013	942.67	955.68	949.82	950.07	946.99	960.04	951.71	959.11	983.70	968.36	970.77	990.86	960.14
2014	973.17	988.37	987.35	973.42	969.11	976.86	963.46	976.95	986.64	990.68	1,018.08	995.32	983.02
2015	1,008.56	1,009.80	1,015.03	1,006.99	1,011.37	1,002.99	1,004.30	1,021.77	1,018.40	1,031.47	1,055.57	1,044.03	1,019.74
Goods-Producing													
2011	1,148.62	1,168.20	1,172.52	1,163.75	1,166.40	1,156.15	1,161.23	1,168.13	1,172.26	1,162.28	1,172.16	1,189.60	1,166.39
2012	1,171.97	1,153.06	1,147.56	1,161.32	1,147.77	1,155.80	1,154.79	1,147.32	1,163.76	1,156.89	1,154.05	1,186.44	1,159.14
2013	1,157.39	1,176.00	1,175.07	1,182.14	1,190.93	1,185.62	1,181.88	1,203.55	1,201.16	1,202.19	1,198.55	1,222.80	1,189.35
2014	1,201.87	1,184.95	1,198.69	1,205.69	1,197.11	1,200.80	1,215.23	1,215.10	1,232.00	1,216.73	1,232.51	1,244.65	1,213.44
2015	1,247.38	1,204.60	1,246.23	1,241.46	1,254.13	1,254.46	1,251.36	1,279.99	1,234.23	1,273.80	1,281.78	1,303.30	1,256.07
Construction													
2011	1,149.54	1,121.16	1,139.62	1,146.30	1,177.39	1,180.80	1,198.99	1,202.29	1,231.33	1,174.57	1,223.21	1,262.98	1,185.48
2012	1,256.71	1,236.38	1,236.71	1,238.02	1,240.62	1,252.88	1,267.06	1,266.68	1,277.18	1,235.38	1,241.37	1,277.56	1,251.78
2013	1,254.38	1,262.14	1,255.89	1,277.56	1,291.17	1,273.97	1,263.50	1,307.04	1,280.75	1,267.09	1,267.45	1,298.01	1,276.04
2014	1,324.27	1,283.95	1,297.13	1,321.73	1,304.77	1,288.22	1,293.89	1,305.61	1,340.49	1,286.10	1,320.63	1,331.61	1,308.64
2015	1,360.61	1,278.69	1,382.35	1,383.59	1,404.68	1,398.69	1,399.62	1,418.65	1,343.25	1,393.84	1,381.33	1,457.06	1,384.94
Manufacturing													
2011	1,123.98	1,119.59	1,117.96	1,108.42	1,095.32	1,085.11	1,089.02	1,106.04	1,104.03	1,123.91	1,121.19	1,132.43	1,110.82
2012	1,114.78	1,100.84	1,095.65	1,107.24	1,089.81	1,092.17	1,089.79	1,081.51	1,101.58	1,112.81	1,104.40	1,138.46	1,102.07
2013	1,108.42	1,120.40	1,124.40	1,121.56	1,127.53	1,130.02	1,130.26	1,140.44	1,152.61	1,154.23	1,153.34	1,178.74	1,136.43
2014	1,138.28	1,132.96	1,145.34	1,144.49	1,138.00	1,144.92	1,162.66	1,156.55	1,159.88	1,168.70	1,175.46	1,196.73	1,154.54
2015	1,191.11	1,171.55	1,180.98	1,167.71	1,170.12	1,169.91	1,164.40	1,197.59	1,171.71	1,187.36	1,207.31	1,193.32	1,180.27
Trade, Transportation, and Utilities													
2011	719.53	719.68	729.95	731.25	726.75	723.20	726.73	725.68	740.52	728.03	740.78	714.45	727.35
2012	722.23	723.17	731.50	748.48	747.82	750.32	745.54	730.89	746.07	729.59	735.57	746.13	738.33
2013	748.16	753.24	755.50	760.18	762.62	769.82	778.80	781.22	799.68	798.37	787.09	811.10	774.74
2014	808.93	806.61	812.18	821.10	816.25	816.91	821.87	811.19	815.72	819.72	825.51	816.06	815.26
2015	816.48	793.51	811.61	825.13	820.22	814.85	838.17	814.59	818.56	837.31	843.16	846.05	823.35
Information													
2011	1,288.00	1,276.52	1,280.33	1,258.15	1,310.05	1,247.62	1,298.63	1,330.91	1,369.60	1,442.57	1,471.12	1,443.46	1,335.05
2012	1,543.39	1,494.88	1,485.00	1,525.20	1,419.85	1,425.33	1,519.62	1,452.30	1,540.13	1,508.27	1,500.52	1,577.16	1,497.96
2013	1,509.69	1,518.34	1,526.11	1,468.54	1,487.54	1,567.51	1,544.40	1,572.06	1,586.91	1,535.82	1,567.10	1,627.27	1,541.52
2014	1,587.77	1,593.82	1,581.00	1,493.61	1,546.02	1,581.14	1,514.39	1,580.67	1,548.01	1,588.38	1,665.35	1,572.48	1,572.68
2015	1,682.86	1,761.76	1,744.82	1,701.90	1,713.84	1,710.21	1,693.48	1,720.40	1,694.63	1,708.50	1,779.81	1,730.12	1,721.04
Financial Activities													
2011	1,240.37	1,185.24	1,182.28	1,181.76	1,199.02	1,191.96	1,178.82	1,182.28	1,215.36	1,245.45	1,233.31	1,246.00	1,206.24
2012	1,274.22	1,241.83	1,231.14	1,257.30	1,237.46	1,224.51	1,224.00	1,227.84	1,256.04	1,226.65	1,229.72	1,266.03	1,241.90
2013	1,226.96	1,254.71	1,211.40	1,227.42	1,217.20	1,288.74	1,232.45	1,244.56	1,311.49	1,255.05	1,230.80	1,263.46	1,246.73
2014	1,244.19	1,317.05	1,317.42	1,314.67	1,315.46	1,293.15	1,271.34	1,291.55	1,341.01	1,334.81	1,380.47	1,327.14	1,311.74
2015	1,366.20	1,392.73	1,412.77	1,389.46	1,373.23	1,374.59	1,383.22	1,450.37	1,398.27	1,423.23	1,467.38	1,423.74	1,403.92
Professional and Business Services													
2011	1,272.68	1,217.92	1,224.29	1,235.15	1,250.85	1,220.24	1,237.89	1,223.64	1,242.36	1,278.58	1,255.15	1,287.36	1,243.92
2012	1,293.35	1,281.20	1,264.84	1,314.42	1,276.62	1,264.84	1,306.10	1,247.50	1,278.75	1,236.01	1,249.77	1,319.23	1,276.58
2013	1,267.94	1,291.39	1,288.67	1,290.68	1,288.30	1,325.31	1,298.41	1,299.24	1,350.87	1,323.99	1,326.96	1,367.91	1,311.71
2014	1,330.33	1,368.87	1,377.22	1,317.60	1,322.34	1,347.25	1,309.99	1,334.62	1,340.35	1,348.23	1,410.18	1,355.65	1,347.97
2015	1,376.71	1,410.48	1,413.32	1,374.25	1,387.18	1,363.50	1,357.89	1,424.16	1,393.20	1,405.17	1,459.14	1,418.46	1,398.41
Education and Health Services													
2011	823.31	824.29	814.68	835.04	840.10	840.10	854.26	836.15	841.18	851.56	836.28	838.80	835.30
2012	840.69	833.40	834.12	846.68	826.86	821.37	835.30	840.41	853.70	853.70	866.01	900.26	847.62
2013	895.54	905.98	908.18	904.72	898.38	910.75	903.41	912.66	928.96	913.30	927.68	928.64	910.75
2014	905.03	919.34	902.18	895.86	887.04	903.12	888.28	901.86	910.12	920.32	938.88	914.25	908.84
2015	919.02	914.23	900.28	894.92	909.72	910.74	900.58	911.70	935.07	938.28	955.72	947.51	920.29
Leisure and Hospitality													
2011	380.43	386.01	386.05	391.30	393.85	385.39	394.48	395.01	395.88	399.07	391.39	393.45	391.82
2012	386.05	383.54	394.68	390.61	395.68	388.28	391.82	394.36	392.92	382.93	381.25	387.86	389.74
2013	377.21	378.35	386.29	392.43	392.19	387.86	399.17	397.92	401.44	394.97	384.15	383.81	390.14
2014	371.17	375.84	385.89	388.05	394.74	387.34	392.42	399.10	396.02	392.87	393.00	392.75	389.05
2015	385.24	381.26	397.21	397.00	411.08	399.87	411.86	410.55	405.29	404.11	397.66	394.57	399.54
Other Services													
2011	713.57	698.04	690.14	697.01	703.17	678.52	670.01	663.48	678.16	678.16	668.12	680.54	685.44
2012	688.86	688.72	699.21	703.34	686.45	681.37	685.78	677.04	676.60	666.77	657.71	661.42	681.26
2013	647.42	652.03	626.28	617.12	617.71	598.14	592.32	602.21	611.06	603.35	594.85	616.88	613.76
2014	613.21	635.56	640.15	639.86	639.01	635.88	642.26	655.78	674.24	675.68	684.43	687.59	652.08
2015	697.53	712.67	711.20	714.11	708.03	700.41	701.16	723.82	751.71	742.11	767.35	773.15	724.59

MICHIGAN
At a Glance

Population:
  2005 estimate: 10,051,137
  2010 census: 9,883,640
  2015 estimate: 9,922,576

Percent change in population:
  2005–2015: –1.3%
  2010–2015: 0.4%

Percent change in total nonfarm employment:
  2005–2015: –3.3%

Industry with the largest growth in employment, 2005–2015 (thousands):
  Education and health services, 75.9

Industry with the largest decline or smallest growth in employment, 2005–2015 (thousands):
  Manufacturing, –79.9

Civilian labor force:
  2005: 5,083,130
  2010: 4,798,954
  2015: 4,750,627

Unemployment rate and rank among states (highest to lowest):
  2005: 6.8%, 4th
  2010: 12.6%, 2nd
  2015: 5.4%, 21st

Over-the-year change in unemployment rates:
  2012–2013: –0.3%
  2013–2014: –1.5%
  2014–2015: –1.9%

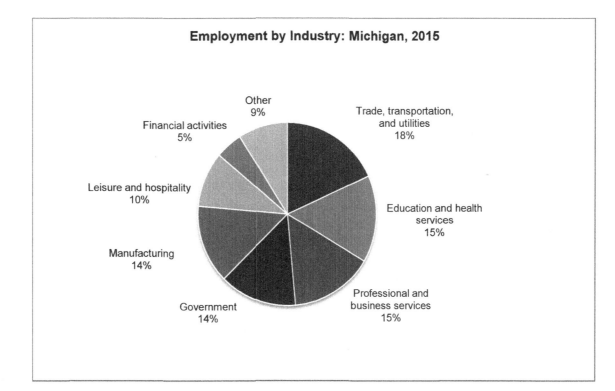

Employment by Industry: Michigan, 2015

Other
9%

Financial activities
5%

Trade, transportation,
and utilities
18%

Leisure and hospitality
10%

Education and health
services
15%

Manufacturing
14%

Professional and
business services
15%

Government
14%

1. Employment by Industry: Michigan, 2005–2015

(Numbers in thousands, not seasonally adjusted)

Industry and year	January	February	March	April	May	June	July	August	September	October	November	December	Annual average
Total Nonfarm													
2005	4,289.5	4,323.2	4,339.3	4,398.0	4,449.1	4,440.5	4,325.2	4,366.2	4,444.3	4,433.5	4,443.3	4,427.0	4,389.9
2006	4,265.7	4,280.1	4,303.3	4,341.3	4,385.5	4,394.4	4,249.6	4,295.1	4,362.0	4,344.7	4,354.2	4,345.4	4,326.8
2007	4,186.0	4,212.6	4,233.6	4,262.0	4,325.8	4,330.4	4,214.4	4,256.5	4,302.6	4,294.3	4,306.0	4,293.2	4,268.1
2008	4,145.9	4,159.1	4,159.4	4,173.1	4,225.9	4,244.1	4,112.8	4,147.9	4,180.5	4,168.9	4,139.6	4,092.4	4,162.5
2009	3,863.9	3,882.2	3,872.4	3,896.0	3,911.1	3,882.9	3,793.8	3,818.6	3,876.7	3,896.2	3,886.7	3,869.2	3,870.8
2010	3,752.1	3,768.6	3,781.2	3,838.9	3,896.2	3,908.0	3,846.1	3,851.5	3,913.6	3,941.7	3,942.6	3,922.7	3,863.6
2011	3,831.9	3,846.9	3,874.5	3,926.3	3,972.7	3,986.2	3,931.4	3,952.6	4,012.7	4,033.9	4,038.6	4,017.5	3,952.1
2012	3,929.9	3,948.8	3,976.7	4,015.8	4,061.3	4,069.1	4,007.2	4,026.8	4,076.8	4,095.3	4,103.1	4,093.2	4,033.7
2013	4,004.4	4,029.8	4,051.3	4,068.8	4,138.9	4,150.0	4,072.7	4,106.3	4,157.1	4,181.6	4,186.1	4,169.7	4,109.7
2014	4,065.4	4,099.2	4,114.8	4,136.8	4,212.2	4,243.1	4,163.5	4,180.7	4,216.0	4,245.9	4,254.3	4,251.7	4,182.0
2015	4,141.7	4,158.0	4,174.0	4,208.7	4,279.0	4,292.4	4,223.4	4,237.2	4,273.5	4,314.9	4,317.2	4,303.8	4,243.7
Total Private													
2005	3,612.0	3,625.8	3,640.4	3,700.4	3,757.2	3,777.2	3,727.8	3,767.0	3,766.5	3,738.2	3,743.3	3,734.1	3,715.8
2006	3,594.0	3,589.7	3,608.0	3,653.6	3,704.9	3,740.5	3,705.2	3,705.2	3,697.1	3,659.8	3,665.5	3,663.0	3,661.5
2007	3,525.8	3,534.7	3,550.6	3,587.7	3,652.4	3,683.6	3,623.1	3,662.4	3,647.8	3,623.0	3,633.3	3,624.8	3,612.4
2008	3,496.7	3,493.6	3,492.5	3,504.9	3,567.9	3,602.2	3,519.8	3,549.3	3,525.7	3,498.2	3,467.9	3,430.4	3,512.4
2009	3,211.2	3,217.2	3,206.4	3,226.7	3,251.2	3,243.8	3,204.2	3,229.1	3,231.0	3,232.3	3,222.3	3,213.1	3,224.0
2010	3,110.4	3,113.2	3,125.3	3,180.4	3,239.0	3,274.3	3,261.4	3,275.5	3,283.6	3,295.7	3,294.4	3,282.7	3,228.0
2011	3,206.9	3,210.7	3,236.2	3,288.7	3,349.2	3,376.8	3,366.4	3,391.0	3,393.1	3,401.9	3,403.9	3,391.5	3,334.7
2012	3,314.1	3,320.7	3,348.4	3,388.2	3,445.4	3,472.9	3,451.7	3,471.1	3,464.5	3,472.4	3,476.9	3,475.7	3,425.2
2013	3,401.3	3,413.8	3,436.3	3,453.4	3,534.6	3,564.3	3,525.7	3,561.3	3,552.3	3,564.3	3,567.6	3,559.1	3,511.2
2014	3,468.3	3,488.4	3,503.7	3,525.5	3,613.0	3,658.3	3,617.4	3,635.3	3,616.6	3,630.6	3,636.6	3,641.1	3,586.2
2015	3,547.0	3,549.7	3,564.5	3,598.1	3,677.6	3,712.1	3,678.9	3,692.9	3,678.7	3,700.1	3,701.6	3,691.4	3,649.4
Goods-Producing													
2005	842.6	849.8	848.5	861.9	879.7	884.9	850.9	877.3	878.8	874.5	872.8	858.5	865.0
2006	817.5	813.2	815.6	832.1	843.0	851.5	803.7	837.9	832.7	818.5	817.1	806.4	824.1
2007	762.0	770.2	772.9	780.1	794.3	804.6	775.6	801.2	794.6	777.7	780.8	769.6	782.0
2008	735.1	732.7	721.4	719.5	733.5	758.8	713.4	737.6	730.3	718.0	706.0	682.1	724.0
2009	588.9	599.8	594.4	593.5	583.4	578.4	577.3	594.8	596.0	597.4	588.6	580.3	589.4
2010	559.5	556.6	559.4	577.5	593.1	605.6	608.6	609.1	619.1	622.2	617.8	608.0	594.7
2011	593.0	593.5	598.8	615.1	632.9	647.2	647.2	658.1	657.3	657.9	657.3	651.1	634.1
2012	635.6	634.1	641.0	650.9	665.8	677.4	678.9	683.5	682.4	681.5	677.5	674.1	665.2
2013	657.3	658.1	663.0	666.6	688.3	700.4	694.0	708.4	707.8	709.9	707.8	696.4	688.2
2014	679.9	688.7	691.0	698.7	722.9	744.0	738.5	746.0	737.9	738.8	739.6	735.8	721.8
2015	714.5	714.1	716.0	726.3	745.1	759.2	755.8	760.6	758.3	756.9	759.6	748.0	742.9
Service-Providing													
2005	3,446.9	3,473.4	3,490.8	3,536.1	3,569.4	3,555.6	3,474.3	3,488.9	3,565.5	3,559.0	3,570.5	3,568.5	3,524.9
2006	3,448.2	3,466.9	3,487.7	3,509.2	3,542.5	3,542.9	3,445.9	3,457.2	3,529.3	3,526.2	3,537.1	3,539.0	3,502.7
2007	3,424.0	3,442.4	3,460.7	3,481.9	3,531.5	3,525.8	3,438.8	3,455.3	3,508.0	3,516.6	3,525.2	3,523.6	3,486.2
2008	3,410.8	3,426.4	3,438.0	3,453.6	3,492.4	3,485.3	3,399.4	3,410.3	3,450.2	3,450.9	3,433.6	3,410.3	3,438.4
2009	3,275.0	3,282.4	3,278.0	3,302.5	3,327.7	3,304.5	3,216.5	3,223.8	3,280.7	3,298.8	3,298.1	3,288.9	3,281.4
2010	3,192.6	3,212.0	3,221.8	3,261.4	3,303.1	3,302.4	3,237.5	3,242.4	3,294.5	3,319.5	3,324.8	3,314.7	3,268.9
2011	3,238.9	3,253.4	3,275.7	3,311.2	3,339.8	3,339.0	3,284.2	3,294.5	3,355.4	3,376.0	3,381.3	3,366.4	3,318.0
2012	3,294.3	3,314.7	3,335.7	3,364.9	3,395.5	3,391.7	3,328.3	3,343.3	3,394.4	3,413.8	3,425.6	3,419.1	3,368.4
2013	3,347.1	3,371.7	3,388.3	3,402.2	3,450.6	3,449.6	3,378.7	3,397.9	3,449.3	3,471.7	3,478.3	3,473.3	3,421.6
2014	3,385.5	3,410.5	3,423.8	3,438.1	3,489.3	3,499.1	3,425.0	3,434.7	3,478.1	3,507.1	3,514.7	3,515.9	3,460.2
2015	3,427.2	3,443.9	3,458.0	3,482.4	3,533.9	3,533.2	3,467.6	3,476.6	3,515.2	3,558.0	3,557.6	3,555.8	3,500.8
Mining and Logging													
2005	7.7	7.7	7.7	8.4	8.8	9.0	9.0	8.9	8.6	8.6	8.4	8.0	8.4
2006	7.4	7.5	7.5	7.9	8.2	8.5	8.5	8.5	8.3	8.3	8.1	7.6	8.0
2007	7.2	7.2	7.0	7.3	7.8	8.2	8.2	8.1	8.0	7.9	7.7	7.4	7.7
2008	7.1	7.1	7.1	7.5	8.0	8.2	8.4	8.4	8.3	8.2	8.1	7.8	7.9
2009	6.7	6.9	6.3	6.5	6.8	7.1	7.2	7.2	7.2	7.2	7.0	6.8	6.9
2010	6.6	6.5	6.2	6.8	7.2	7.5	7.6	7.6	7.5	7.5	7.3	7.0	7.1
2011	6.7	6.7	6.7	7.0	7.5	7.8	7.9	7.9	7.8	7.9	7.8	7.6	7.4
2012	7.4	7.5	7.3	7.7	8.0	8.0	8.0	8.1	8.2	8.1	7.9	7.7	7.8
2013	7.5	7.5	7.5	7.5	8.1	8.3	8.4	8.5	8.4	8.4	8.3	8.0	8.0
2014	7.8	7.9	7.9	7.9	8.3	8.6	8.6	8.6	8.5	8.5	8.3	8.1	8.3
2015	7.7	7.6	7.5	7.6	7.9	8.1	7.7	7.7	7.7	7.7	7.5	7.2	7.7

1. Employment by Industry: Michigan, 2005–2015—*Continued*

(Numbers in thousands, not seasonally adjusted)

Industry and year	January	February	March	April	May	June	July	August	September	October	November	December	Annual average
Construction													
2005	168.3	164.9	167.7	183.4	195.5	203.5	207.0	205.2	201.8	199.1	194.3	182.8	189.5
2006	162.9	159.1	162.1	174.9	185.8	192.9	192.9	191.6	188.1	183.9	177.4	169.1	178.4
2007	151.1	145.6	150.1	158.4	172.0	179.3	180.8	180.8	178.2	174.7	169.1	160.0	166.7
2008	143.2	138.2	139.7	146.8	160.5	166.4	166.6	166.6	163.7	159.8	151.1	138.9	153.5
2009	119.6	116.6	115.8	124.1	133.5	136.8	137.5	136.3	133.0	132.3	127.2	118.5	127.6
2010	102.8	100.0	103.4	114.5	123.7	129.1	133.6	134.5	133.8	134.5	129.4	120.4	121.6
2011	108.0	104.9	107.4	114.5	126.1	133.9	138.9	139.6	137.6	135.7	132.3	124.6	125.3
2012	113.2	110.1	114.0	122.1	129.9	135.4	137.9	138.7	138.5	137.6	133.1	127.9	128.2
2013	118.3	115.4	117.2	121.1	135.7	140.4	144.5	145.7	144.7	145.2	140.7	133.0	133.5
2014	122.8	122.2	122.8	128.9	144.0	151.5	153.6	155.5	154.9	153.7	149.4	142.4	141.8
2015	130.6	128.6	131.4	140.4	151.7	158.3	158.8	159.2	158.2	158.2	154.1	144.9	147.9
Manufacturing													
2005	666.6	677.2	673.1	670.1	675.4	672.4	634.9	663.2	668.4	666.8	670.1	667.7	667.2
2006	647.2	646.6	646.0	649.3	649.0	650.1	602.3	637.8	636.3	626.3	631.6	629.7	637.7
2007	603.7	617.4	615.8	614.4	614.5	617.1	586.6	612.3	608.4	595.1	604.0	602.2	607.6
2008	584.8	587.4	574.6	565.2	565.0	584.2	538.4	562.6	558.3	550.0	546.8	535.4	562.7
2009	462.6	476.3	472.3	462.9	443.1	434.5	432.6	451.3	455.8	457.9	454.4	455.0	454.9
2010	450.1	450.1	449.8	456.2	462.2	469.0	467.4	467.0	477.8	480.2	481.1	480.6	466.0
2011	478.3	481.9	484.7	493.6	499.3	505.5	500.4	510.6	511.9	514.3	517.2	518.9	501.4
2012	515.0	516.5	519.7	521.1	527.9	534.0	533.0	536.7	535.7	535.8	536.5	538.5	529.2
2013	531.5	535.2	538.3	538.0	544.5	551.7	541.1	554.2	554.7	556.3	558.8	555.4	546.6
2014	549.3	558.6	560.3	561.9	570.6	583.9	576.3	581.9	574.5	576.6	581.9	585.3	571.8
2015	576.2	577.9	577.1	578.3	585.5	592.8	589.3	593.7	592.4	591.0	598.0	595.9	587.3
Trade, Transportation, and Utilities													
2005	791.0	785.3	788.1	796.9	807.8	811.9	811.0	811.7	806.8	806.1	818.8	825.7	805.1
2006	784.5	776.1	780.3	787.3	797.5	803.6	796.8	798.8	795.0	795.4	809.1	816.0	795.0
2007	779.2	770.1	772.1	777.1	789.4	794.4	789.6	791.1	787.3	787.0	800.6	806.5	787.0
2008	771.9	763.7	765.8	764.6	776.1	780.6	774.1	774.1	769.4	765.2	769.2	769.2	770.3
2009	723.6	714.0	709.8	711.6	720.4	722.6	714.3	717.3	713.0	713.1	721.3	725.4	717.2
2010	695.0	687.9	690.8	699.4	710.3	716.6	717.1	716.8	711.6	719.0	729.6	733.6	710.6
2011	704.7	698.7	700.6	709.5	720.8	727.0	728.8	728.9	725.1	729.2	742.0	746.1	721.8
2012	715.6	708.4	713.0	718.1	729.7	735.5	735.3	735.0	730.7	735.1	751.9	754.2	730.2
2013	726.2	721.7	724.8	728.3	742.1	750.2	750.8	752.1	745.9	751.2	764.7	771.3	744.1
2014	740.0	736.4	737.6	744.1	758.1	765.9	762.4	763.9	759.6	765.6	780.7	787.7	758.5
2015	756.6	750.7	752.9	760.8	773.6	780.3	774.6	776.0	772.1	774.0	785.4	790.8	770.7
Wholesale Trade													
2005	167.8	168.2	169.1	170.3	172.0	172.5	172.4	172.2	171.1	171.2	170.9	171.2	170.7
2006	167.9	168.1	169.0	171.1	172.2	173.7	172.8	172.0	170.7	170.0	169.5	169.8	170.6
2007	167.2	166.8	167.2	169.0	170.4	171.4	170.5	170.1	169.0	169.1	168.6	169.0	169.0
2008	167.0	167.1	167.7	168.5	170.0	170.6	169.1	169.0	168.1	166.9	165.3	163.8	167.8
2009	158.0	156.4	155.0	154.9	154.9	153.2	150.9	151.3	150.5	150.1	149.8	150.0	152.9
2010	146.8	147.1	147.9	149.8	151.4	152.0	152.0	152.5	151.4	152.2	152.5	152.2	150.7
2011	150.8	151.1	152.1	153.6	155.4	156.5	156.7	157.2	156.4	156.5	156.9	156.9	155.0
2012	155.1	155.6	156.6	158.2	160.0	161.3	161.5	161.5	160.6	160.9	160.8	161.3	159.5
2013	160.1	160.7	161.8	162.4	164.4	165.4	165.0	165.2	164.3	164.4	164.4	165.2	163.6
2014	163.8	164.5	164.7	166.1	168.5	169.9	168.9	169.1	167.7	167.4	167.9	168.6	167.3
2015	166.4	166.7	167.4	169.3	171.1	172.4	171.6	171.8	170.3	171.6	172.9	173.5	170.4
Retail Trade													
2005	499.0	492.2	493.5	500.1	507.5	509.7	510.5	508.8	505.5	504.9	517.4	523.3	506.0
2006	490.1	481.9	484.6	488.8	496.1	499.4	497.4	497.2	494.9	496.7	510.5	514.8	496.0
2007	486.6	476.7	478.6	481.1	490.0	492.4	492.3	490.9	488.5	489.3	503.2	507.1	489.7
2008	481.0	472.2	473.5	472.4	480.5	482.3	480.7	480.0	476.3	474.8	481.1	482.3	478.1
2009	452.6	443.3	441.4	444.7	453.2	457.1	452.0	453.5	449.3	449.9	458.8	461.2	451.4
2010	437.7	431.1	432.3	438.6	446.5	450.5	451.6	450.2	445.4	450.6	460.4	463.5	446.5
2011	439.4	433.6	434.1	440.6	447.7	451.0	452.8	451.7	448.2	452.3	464.3	467.0	448.6
2012	441.8	434.2	437.4	440.9	448.6	451.7	452.2	451.2	447.5	451.2	467.4	467.6	449.3
2013	444.4	439.1	441.0	443.5	453.0	458.5	460.8	460.5	455.5	459.8	472.0	476.0	455.3
2014	449.1	445.2	446.1	451.5	460.4	465.3	463.5	464.2	460.6	467.0	480.5	482.8	461.4
2015	457.2	453.0	454.6	458.8	467.7	471.9	468.2	469.8	466.1	468.0	476.4	479.5	465.9

1. Employment by Industry: Michigan, 2005–2015—*Continued*

(Numbers in thousands, not seasonally adjusted)

Industry and year	January	February	March	April	May	June	July	August	September	October	November	December	Annual average
Transportation and Utilities													
2005	124.2	124.9	125.5	126.5	128.3	129.7	128.1	130.7	130.2	130.0	130.5	131.2	128.3
2006	126.5	126.1	126.7	127.4	129.2	130.5	126.6	129.6	129.4	128.7	129.1	131.4	128.4
2007	125.4	126.6	126.3	127.0	129.0	130.6	126.8	130.1	129.8	128.6	128.8	130.4	128.3
2008	123.9	124.4	124.6	123.7	125.6	127.7	124.3	125.1	125.0	123.5	122.8	123.1	124.5
2009	113.0	114.3	113.4	112.0	112.3	112.3	111.4	112.5	113.2	113.1	112.7	114.2	112.9
2010	110.5	109.7	110.6	111.0	112.4	114.1	113.5	114.1	114.8	116.2	116.7	117.9	113.5
2011	114.5	114.0	114.4	115.3	117.7	119.5	119.3	120.0	120.5	120.4	120.8	122.2	118.2
2012	118.7	118.6	119.0	119.0	121.1	122.5	121.6	122.3	122.6	123.0	123.7	125.3	121.5
2013	121.7	121.9	122.0	122.4	124.7	126.3	125.0	126.4	126.1	127.0	128.3	130.1	125.2
2014	127.1	126.7	126.8	126.5	129.2	130.7	130.0	130.6	131.3	131.2	132.3	136.3	129.9
2015	133.0	131.0	130.9	132.7	134.8	136.0	134.8	134.4	135.7	134.4	136.1	137.8	134.3
Information													
2005	65.5	64.9	65.0	65.0	65.4	65.6	65.3	65.0	64.2	63.9	64.6	64.8	64.9
2006	64.4	64.5	64.1	64.2	64.7	65.1	63.8	63.6	62.8	62.9	63.2	63.3	63.9
2007	63.4	63.4	63.1	63.4	64.1	64.0	63.2	62.9	62.0	61.8	62.0	62.0	62.9
2008	61.2	61.2	60.5	60.0	60.6	60.9	59.9	60.2	60.2	59.0	59.5	59.1	60.2
2009	57.8	57.7	56.7	56.8	57.0	57.0	56.2	55.6	55.0	55.0	55.6	55.7	56.3
2010	54.3	54.2	53.9	54.2	54.8	55.3	54.8	57.0	56.5	54.0	54.0	54.2	54.8
2011	53.8	53.5	53.4	52.1	52.7	52.8	53.1	53.2	52.7	53.6	53.8	53.8	53.2
2012	53.4	53.2	53.1	52.9	53.2	53.2	53.6	54.2	52.9	53.2	53.5	53.6	53.3
2013	54.0	54.2	54.4	55.0	55.4	55.9	56.0	56.1	55.3	55.3	56.0	56.1	55.3
2014	56.3	56.0	56.3	57.1	57.4	58.2	59.0	58.6	57.1	57.9	58.0	57.6	57.5
2015	56.5	56.3	56.3	56.0	56.8	57.3	57.8	56.8	56.5	57.0	56.8	56.8	56.7
Financial Activities													
2005	214.5	214.5	214.5	215.5	216.9	218.8	218.4	218.4	216.2	215.0	215.0	215.2	216.1
2006	213.4	213.3	213.0	213.5	215.2	217.3	216.0	215.9	213.2	211.6	211.2	212.0	213.8
2007	209.1	209.0	208.8	209.9	211.5	213.2	213.1	211.5	208.0	207.0	206.1	206.5	209.5
2008	204.4	204.4	203.6	203.0	205.0	205.3	203.7	203.0	199.8	198.2	196.8	196.5	202.0
2009	193.1	192.6	191.4	192.4	193.5	194.3	193.2	192.6	189.8	188.4	187.8	187.5	191.4
2010	186.2	185.8	185.0	184.7	186.7	188.9	190.0	190.7	189.2	189.3	189.6	190.7	188.1
2011	190.4	190.9	191.5	191.0	192.2	194.1	195.7	196.5	194.1	193.4	193.6	194.4	193.2
2012	192.2	192.6	193.3	194.6	196.2	198.4	199.9	200.1	197.3	197.3	197.5	198.4	196.5
2013	198.5	199.2	199.5	201.1	203.4	206.5	207.2	207.3	203.5	202.8	202.9	202.9	202.9
2014	202.3	202.1	201.9	202.2	205.0	207.3	207.5	207.5	204.4	203.3	203.5	204.3	204.3
2015	202.8	202.4	202.6	203.8	206.9	209.7	210.2	210.5	207.7	208.5	209.3	211.0	207.1
Professional and Business Services													
2005	584.0	585.0	586.6	602.1	606.9	610.1	605.5	615.3	617.9	612.2	611.1	608.3	603.8
2006	586.4	583.7	584.0	593.5	598.4	607.0	594.3	605.0	604.9	601.7	602.7	601.8	597.0
2007	575.1	577.8	578.2	587.5	594.6	598.5	585.6	596.3	595.8	599.7	602.0	598.4	590.8
2008	574.5	576.3	577.5	581.2	587.6	584.0	567.5	570.8	567.9	572.0	563.6	554.2	573.1
2009	519.0	518.2	514.0	515.1	514.8	503.7	488.4	493.6	506.0	515.2	517.3	514.4	510.0
2010	498.1	504.1	504.6	516.1	523.9	527.5	517.2	524.8	536.5	546.9	548.0	541.7	524.1
2011	536.7	542.0	548.6	560.6	569.3	564.2	552.2	561.6	575.2	585.4	584.9	575.0	563.0
2012	569.1	574.7	579.1	591.1	599.8	592.3	577.1	586.6	596.1	604.8	604.1	600.3	589.6
2013	594.2	601.1	607.0	607.9	624.0	618.7	592.7	608.2	619.5	626.9	627.5	623.5	612.6
2014	607.2	614.0	616.8	618.1	634.0	634.4	613.0	619.6	628.0	639.4	639.0	637.7	625.1
2015	623.8	627.2	628.2	636.5	648.8	646.9	628.2	633.2	639.6	655.1	653.0	646.6	638.9
Education and Health Services													
2005	564.1	572.8	576.0	576.1	577.1	570.1	566.4	566.9	579.7	583.8	588.6	588.1	575.8
2006	575.2	580.6	585.4	583.0	586.0	580.6	573.7	573.6	587.6	588.4	592.6	593.2	583.3
2007	584.9	591.3	594.2	596.0	598.4	594.8	588.6	589.3	599.4	605.2	608.6	609.2	596.7
2008	600.0	605.4	607.2	607.2	610.3	606.1	600.1	600.1	607.8	613.8	616.0	614.6	607.4
2009	602.6	609.9	611.4	611.2	613.0	609.5	600.7	600.7	605.8	614.5	616.8	614.6	609.2
2010	603.6	609.4	610.9	611.9	613.8	609.6	605.3	605.6	610.3	618.9	621.8	620.8	611.8
2011	610.8	615.1	618.0	622.0	622.1	618.6	616.0	617.1	623.8	630.4	633.1	633.2	621.7
2012	623.3	630.6	632.7	632.3	632.6	630.6	624.1	626.0	631.5	638.7	641.5	642.6	632.2
2013	630.4	636.9	639.0	640.1	640.3	638.4	632.1	633.8	639.3	645.5	649.4	648.0	639.4
2014	636.5	643.5	645.4	643.4	645.6	643.3	634.0	635.6	641.1	647.1	650.0	651.6	643.1
2015	641.7	647.3	650.5	648.8	652.0	650.3	643.3	646.6	649.1	660.7	665.8	664.3	651.7

1. Employment by Industry: Michigan, 2005–2015—*Continued*

(Numbers in thousands, not seasonally adjusted)

Industry and year	January	February	March	April	May	June	July	August	September	October	November	December	Annual average
Leisure and Hospitality													
2005	374.2	376.5	383.2	402.7	421.7	432.1	429.0	431.8	423.2	404.3	394.2	394.3	405.6
2006	377.8	382.4	388.1	402.4	421.1	434.3	429.5	431.6	423.0	405.1	393.5	393.3	406.8
2007	379.3	379.2	386.0	398.1	422.4	433.9	429.5	431.8	423.4	408.0	397.1	395.5	407.0
2008	376.3	375.7	381.3	393.4	416.7	426.9	423.6	426.1	414.2	397.1	384.1	382.8	399.9
2009	358.8	357.2	361.1	376.8	398.1	406.0	404.2	405.1	397.0	380.9	367.8	367.1	381.7
2010	349.9	350.7	355.4	371.2	389.7	402.0	400.0	403.3	393.9	379.2	367.8	367.6	377.6
2011	353.6	352.7	359.8	372.0	391.3	403.2	404.1	406.0	397.0	384.2	372.2	370.2	380.5
2012	360.0	361.5	369.2	380.0	398.2	413.2	411.3	413.7	402.7	391.8	381.3	382.7	388.8
2013	372.3	373.7	378.3	385.0	410.4	422.0	420.4	422.8	410.5	402.5	389.5	390.9	398.2
2014	377.8	378.8	385.3	393.4	419.7	433.4	431.6	433.5	419.2	409.1	397.5	398.2	406.5
2015	386.4	386.9	392.5	399.8	426.1	438.4	439.0	439.5	427.3	417.6	402.6	402.9	413.3
Other Services													
2005	176.1	177.0	178.5	180.2	181.7	183.7	181.3	180.8	179.7	178.4	178.2	179.2	179.6
2006	174.8	175.9	177.5	177.6	179.0	181.1	178.4	178.8	177.9	176.2	176.1	177.0	177.5
2007	172.8	173.7	175.3	175.6	177.7	180.2	177.9	178.3	177.3	176.6	176.1	177.1	176.6
2008	173.3	174.2	175.2	176.0	178.1	179.6	177.5	177.4	176.1	174.9	172.7	171.9	175.6
2009	167.4	167.8	167.6	169.3	171.0	172.3	169.9	169.4	168.4	167.8	167.1	168.1	168.8
2010	163.8	164.5	165.3	165.4	166.7	168.8	168.4	168.2	166.5	166.2	165.8	166.1	166.3
2011	163.9	164.3	165.5	166.4	167.9	169.7	169.3	169.6	167.9	167.8	167.0	167.7	167.3
2012	164.9	165.6	167.0	168.3	169.9	172.3	171.5	172.0	170.9	170.0	169.6	169.8	169.3
2013	168.4	168.9	170.3	169.4	170.7	172.2	172.5	172.6	170.5	170.2	169.8	170.0	170.5
2014	168.3	168.9	169.4	168.5	170.3	171.8	171.4	170.6	169.3	169.4	168.3	168.2	169.5
2015	164.7	164.8	165.5	166.1	168.3	170.0	170.0	169.7	168.1	170.3	169.1	171.0	168.1
Government													
2005	677.5	697.4	698.9	697.6	691.9	663.3	597.4	599.0	677.8	695.3	700.0	692.9	674.1
2006	671.7	690.4	695.3	687.7	680.6	653.9	593.4	589.9	664.9	684.9	688.7	682.4	665.3
2007	660.2	677.9	683.0	674.3	673.4	646.8	591.3	594.1	654.8	671.3	672.7	668.4	655.7
2008	649.2	665.5	666.9	668.2	658.0	641.9	593.0	598.6	654.8	670.7	671.7	662.0	650.0
2009	652.7	665.0	666.0	669.3	659.9	639.1	589.6	589.5	645.7	663.9	664.4	656.1	646.8
2010	641.7	655.4	655.9	658.5	657.2	633.7	584.7	576.0	630.0	646.0	648.2	640.0	635.6
2011	625.0	636.2	638.3	637.6	623.5	609.4	565.0	561.6	619.6	632.0	634.7	626.0	617.4
2012	615.8	628.1	628.3	627.6	615.9	596.2	555.5	555.7	612.3	622.9	626.2	617.5	608.5
2013	603.1	616.0	615.0	615.4	604.3	585.7	547.0	545.0	604.8	617.3	618.5	610.6	598.6
2014	597.1	610.8	611.1	611.3	599.2	584.8	546.1	545.4	599.4	615.3	617.7	610.6	595.7
2015	594.7	608.3	609.5	610.6	601.4	580.3	544.5	544.3	594.8	614.8	615.6	612.4	594.3

2. Average Weekly Hours by Selected Industry: Michigan, 2011–2015

(Not seasonally adjusted)

Industry and year	January	February	March	April	May	June	July	August	September	October	November	December	Annual average
Total Private													
2011	34.0	33.8	33.8	34.0	34.4	34.1	34.2	34.3	34.2	34.5	34.2	34.2	34.2
2012	34.1	34.1	34.0	34.2	34.0	34.3	34.4	34.3	34.4	34.0	34.0	34.4	34.2
2013	33.6	33.8	33.9	33.8	34.2	34.8	34.3	34.5	34.7	34.3	34.3	34.7	34.2
2014	33.8	34.4	34.2	34.1	34.2	34.7	34.3	34.5	34.5	34.3	34.7	34.7	34.4
2015	34.1	34.3	34.5	34.3	34.6	34.6	34.3	34.9	34.1	34.3	34.5	34.3	34.4
Goods-Producing													
2011	41.3	41.1	41.3	41.1	41.7	41.2	40.5	41.6	41.7	41.6	41.5	41.3	41.3
2012	40.9	40.7	40.3	40.7	40.4	40.8	40.4	41.1	41.3	41.3	40.9	41.8	40.9
2013	41.0	40.9	41.1	40.6	40.9	41.5	41.0	41.9	42.3	41.8	41.5	42.2	41.4
2014	40.8	41.7	41.4	41.1	41.5	41.8	40.9	41.1	41.5	41.0	41.1	42.1	41.3
2015	40.6	40.9	41.5	41.1	41.8	42.0	40.7	41.9	39.7	41.3	40.8	41.1	41.1
Construction													
2011	37.8	37.7	37.7	38.3	39.4	39.5	40.2	40.5	40.8	40.4	39.6	38.7	39.3
2012	37.9	37.7	37.0	38.0	38.8	40.0	39.1	39.4	39.6	40.1	38.8	38.8	38.8
2013	38.0	37.9	37.5	37.4	39.9	39.9	40.5	39.2	39.3	39.4	37.0	37.6	38.7
2014	36.8	37.1	36.5	37.3	37.5	39.6	38.8	38.7	39.6	38.9	37.8	38.7	38.2
2015	37.7	37.2	38.1	38.3	39.5	39.6	39.2	39.9	37.4	40.3	37.7	38.3	38.7
Manufacturing													
2011	41.6	41.4	41.6	41.3	41.8	41.3	40.2	41.3	41.4	41.4	41.5	41.5	41.4
2012	41.2	41.1	40.7	41.1	40.6	41.0	40.8	41.5	41.7	41.6	41.5	42.5	41.3
2013	41.6	41.5	41.8	41.3	41.1	41.8	41.0	42.5	43.0	42.4	42.5	43.1	42.0
2014	41.5	42.5	42.3	41.9	42.5	42.3	41.4	41.7	41.9	41.6	42.0	43.0	42.1
2015	41.3	41.8	42.3	41.8	42.4	42.7	41.1	42.5	40.4	41.7	41.8	41.9	41.8
Trade, Transportation, and Utilities													
2011	32.8	32.9	32.7	33.2	33.4	33.3	33.6	33.5	33.5	33.7	33.1	33.4	33.3
2012	32.8	33.1	33.3	33.5	33.3	33.8	33.7	33.2	33.4	32.9	33.0	33.3	33.3
2013	32.4	32.9	33.0	32.9	33.6	33.8	33.5	33.6	33.8	33.2	33.3	33.6	33.3
2014	32.9	33.2	33.2	33.2	33.3	33.8	33.8	33.9	33.7	33.5	33.8	33.8	33.5
2015	33.1	33.1	33.2	33.2	33.4	33.2	33.4	33.7	33.7	33.1	33.4	33.5	33.3
Information													
2011	35.6	34.7	35.2	34.9	36.5	35.7	36.0	35.8	35.7	36.3	36.0	36.1	35.7
2012	37.6	35.8	35.7	37.0	35.7	35.3	35.8	34.9	35.5	34.5	35.1	35.7	35.7
2013	35.1	35.6	35.0	35.4	35.8	37.3	37.5	36.7	37.9	35.9	36.0	36.6	36.2
2014	36.4	37.5	37.1	36.4	36.1	37.3	37.2	37.1	37.9	36.3	36.9	36.3	36.9
2015	36.7	36.9	37.0	36.8	36.7	37.9	37.8	37.7	37.0	35.8	36.8	36.4	37.0
Financial Activities													
2011	36.2	35.8	35.8	35.6	36.5	36.3	36.5	36.7	36.4	36.8	36.7	37.1	36.4
2012	36.9	37.2	36.7	36.9	36.4	36.9	36.6	36.7	36.3	36.1	35.9	36.2	36.6
2013	35.5	35.7	35.5	35.8	35.9	36.3	35.6	35.7	36.1	35.7	35.5	35.6	35.7
2014	35.7	36.1	36.0	35.3	35.5	36.3	35.6	35.9	35.7	36.0	36.7	35.9	35.9
2015	36.4	37.0	37.3	36.9	37.1	37.0	36.9	36.9	36.5	36.4	36.9	36.7	36.8
Professional and Business Services													
2011	35.7	35.2	35.5	35.8	36.5	35.7	35.7	35.9	35.6	36.5	36.0	35.7	35.8
2012	36.3	36.4	36.4	36.4	35.8	36.0	36.4	36.2	36.6	35.8	35.9	36.6	36.2
2013	34.9	35.5	35.6	35.9	36.2	37.8	36.6	36.4	36.8	36.4	36.4	37.1	36.3
2014	36.0	36.3	36.1	35.9	36.0	36.7	35.9	36.1	36.2	36.2	36.5	36.5	36.2
2015	35.8	36.2	36.3	35.9	36.1	36.2	35.3	36.0	35.0	35.8	36.0	35.3	35.8
Education and Health Services													
2011	32.5	32.1	32.1	32.1	32.3	32.2	32.3	32.0	32.0	32.2	32.0	31.9	32.1
2012	32.2	32.0	32.1	32.4	32.3	32.5	32.5	32.5	32.8	32.4	32.6	32.7	32.4
2013	32.4	32.4	32.3	32.1	32.2	32.7	32.3	32.4	32.7	32.3	32.6	32.9	32.4
2014	32.2	32.6	32.5	32.2	32.3	32.4	32.2	32.5	32.5	32.5	33.0	32.7	32.5
2015	32.5	32.6	32.8	32.6	32.7	32.6	32.6	32.9	32.7	32.5	33.0	32.7	32.7
Leisure and Hospitality													
2011	23.9	23.8	23.9	23.9	24.8	24.8	25.3	25.3	24.7	24.7	24.4	24.3	24.5
2012	23.8	23.9	23.8	23.7	24.0	24.5	25.0	25.0	24.2	23.6	23.4	23.6	24.1
2013	22.5	22.9	23.3	23.3	24.2	24.3	24.3	24.6	24.0	23.7	23.4	23.7	23.7
2014	22.6	23.5	23.6	23.8	23.9	24.6	24.7	24.9	24.2	23.9	23.6	23.6	23.9
2015	23.2	23.6	23.6	23.5	24.1	24.4	25.1	25.4	24.6	24.1	23.9	23.9	24.1
Other Services													
2011	31.8	32.0	31.2	31.8	32.0	32.0	31.9	31.7	31.7	31.8	31.6	31.4	31.7
2012	31.6	31.3	31.3	31.4	31.5	31.4	32.6	31.4	31.0	30.7	30.5	31.1	31.3
2013	31.0	30.8	31.1	30.9	30.9	31.2	31.0	32.2	30.8	30.1	30.2	30.4	30.9
2014	29.9	30.5	30.2	31.0	30.6	31.1	30.9	31.6	31.9	31.8	32.5	32.5	31.2
2015	32.4	32.1	32.4	31.9	32.2	32.7	32.4	33.2	32.8	32.5	32.4	31.8	32.4

3. Average Hourly Earnings by Selected Industry: Michigan, 2011–2015

(Dollars, not seasonally adjusted)

Industry and year	January	February	March	April	May	June	July	August	September	October	November	December	Annual average
Total Private													
2011...	22.85	22.66	22.36	22.43	22.53	22.04	22.21	21.98	22.12	22.45	22.28	22.36	22.35
2012...	22.75	22.41	22.39	22.63	22.18	22.07	22.46	22.18	22.59	22.48	22.46	22.85	22.45
2013...	22.95	22.86	22.84	22.85	22.65	22.99	22.89	22.68	23.22	23.01	23.05	23.29	22.94
2014...	23.52	23.70	23.84	23.70	23.46	23.50	23.30	23.29	23.58	23.61	23.86	23.64	23.58
2015...	23.88	23.97	23.95	23.86	23.70	23.61	23.92	24.28	24.26	24.41	24.47	24.35	24.06
Goods-Producing													
2011...	25.48	25.44	25.40	25.04	25.04	24.59	24.74	24.29	24.45	24.57	24.43	24.57	24.82
2012...	24.86	24.72	24.64	24.75	24.37	24.26	24.92	24.47	24.94	24.77	24.82	24.97	24.71
2013...	24.93	24.67	24.62	24.56	24.66	24.74	24.87	24.56	24.84	24.61	24.66	24.80	24.71
2014...	24.74	24.77	25.06	25.06	24.88	24.78	24.70	24.71	25.04	24.84	24.95	25.00	24.88
2015...	25.08	25.09	25.16	25.12	24.93	24.84	24.97	25.57	25.61	25.36	25.42	25.58	25.23
Construction													
2011...	26.52	26.71	26.34	26.06	25.30	25.03	25.15	25.03	25.14	25.01	25.38	25.84	25.55
2012...	25.96	26.05	25.83	25.72	25.52	24.97	25.13	25.19	25.35	25.26	25.82	26.27	25.56
2013...	26.03	25.99	26.03	26.07	25.82	25.45	26.20	26.07	26.07	25.90	26.11	26.77	26.04
2014...	25.81	25.70	26.29	26.62	25.92	25.45	25.57	25.94	26.11	25.44	25.06	25.94	25.80
2015...	25.76	25.90	26.31	26.40	26.07	25.59	25.90	26.16	26.14	26.51	26.67	27.29	26.22
Manufacturing													
2011...	25.43	25.35	25.37	24.95	25.09	24.58	24.75	24.16	24.35	24.55	24.29	24.51	24.77
2012...	24.82	24.65	24.55	24.69	24.26	24.19	24.96	24.37	24.90	24.69	24.65	24.92	24.64
2013...	24.93	24.62	24.54	24.41	24.46	24.64	24.56	24.23	24.57	24.33	24.40	24.50	24.51
2014...	24.62	24.70	24.90	24.78	24.68	24.62	24.45	24.35	24.72	24.67	24.93	24.81	24.69
2015...	24.99	25.00	24.99	24.86	24.64	24.65	24.74	25.43	25.51	25.07	24.97	25.05	24.99
Trade, Transportation, and Utilities													
2011...	20.17	20.08	19.33	19.44	19.40	19.26	19.22	19.08	19.12	19.40	19.29	19.26	19.41
2012...	19.88	19.45	19.55	20.10	19.69	19.59	19.76	19.63	19.95	19.83	19.59	19.86	19.74
2013...	20.04	20.19	20.21	20.18	19.89	20.15	20.33	20.19	20.49	20.56	20.71	20.57	20.30
2014...	20.81	20.91	21.03	20.76	20.74	20.67	20.50	20.42	20.63	20.57	20.73	20.41	20.68
2015...	20.63	20.65	20.47	20.47	20.44	20.48	20.71	20.96	20.96	20.81	20.91	20.53	20.67
Information													
2011...	32.35	31.88	31.75	32.43	32.36	31.32	31.02	30.90	30.59	31.41	31.00	30.82	31.48
2012...	30.17	29.84	29.63	30.27	29.91	29.66	29.88	29.63	29.94	29.68	29.49	29.94	29.84
2013...	29.49	29.95	29.57	29.77	29.23	29.53	29.05	29.09	29.87	29.57	29.76	30.09	29.58
2014...	29.81	29.81	30.74	31.05	30.97	31.06	30.51	30.56	30.89	31.27	31.12	31.42	30.77
2015...	30.71	30.66	31.47	31.39	31.27	31.43	31.08	31.64	31.40	31.12	31.61	31.54	31.28
Financial Activities													
2011...	24.91	24.61	23.97	24.79	24.18	23.46	24.10	23.72	23.76	24.19	24.11	23.89	24.14
2012...	24.43	24.04	23.66	23.84	23.57	23.14	23.40	22.69	22.76	22.70	22.57	22.72	23.29
2013...	22.87	22.60	22.90	23.04	22.71	22.68	22.42	22.56	22.83	23.31	23.31	23.56	22.90
2014...	23.62	24.13	24.64	24.18	24.47	25.05	25.15	25.18	26.02	25.81	26.51	26.61	25.12
2015...	26.84	27.49	27.70	27.79	27.67	27.16	27.25	27.68	27.80	27.83	28.74	28.01	27.67
Professional and Business Services													
2011...	28.41	27.85	27.41	27.54	28.57	27.32	27.96	27.45	27.48	28.03	27.50	27.96	27.79
2012...	28.18	27.46	27.58	27.86	27.04	26.87	27.86	27.31	27.77	27.42	27.42	28.69	27.62
2013...	28.69	28.36	28.50	28.39	28.16	29.45	28.78	27.78	29.13	28.40	28.09	29.37	28.60
2014...	29.99	30.72	30.90	30.65	29.84	30.21	29.67	29.47	29.30	29.52	29.95	29.17	29.94
2015...	29.79	29.88	29.95	29.14	29.07	29.06	30.31	30.78	30.28	30.19	30.22	30.49	29.93
Education and Health Services													
2011...	21.13	21.13	20.98	21.26	21.25	21.32	21.69	21.61	21.66	21.75	21.63	21.72	21.43
2012...	22.10	21.79	21.79	21.76	21.59	21.84	22.11	21.94	22.13	22.03	22.06	22.14	21.94
2013...	22.37	22.44	22.15	22.47	22.36	22.58	22.85	22.78	23.11	22.78	22.87	22.88	22.64
2014...	23.08	23.01	22.98	23.02	22.95	23.10	23.23	23.35	23.61	23.48	23.64	23.47	23.24
2015...	23.69	23.73	23.58	23.98	23.80	23.77	24.39	24.44	24.51	25.59	25.03	24.87	24.29
Leisure and Hospitality													
2011...	11.83	11.83	11.69	11.75	11.65	11.51	11.42	11.36	11.42	11.57	11.47	11.56	11.58
2012...	11.43	11.61	11.60	11.73	11.53	11.47	11.40	11.41	11.49	11.64	11.67	11.86	11.56
2013...	12.01	11.81	11.77	11.74	11.68	11.59	11.63	11.68	11.84	11.86	11.97	12.18	11.81
2014...	12.33	12.23	12.12	12.08	12.13	11.98	11.98	12.00	12.32	12.57	12.65	12.81	12.26
2015...	12.58	12.55	12.59	12.63	12.50	12.28	12.26	12.43	12.49	12.57	12.57	12.66	12.50
Other Services													
2011...	20.14	19.55	19.61	19.70	19.62	19.31	19.21	19.13	19.39	19.76	19.69	19.58	19.56
2012...	19.66	19.38	19.25	19.65	19.68	19.92	19.82	19.76	20.23	20.00	20.35	20.69	19.87
2013...	20.58	20.76	20.97	20.94	20.54	19.99	20.50	21.58	21.01	20.42	20.43	19.69	20.62
2014...	19.87	20.14	20.10	20.52	20.05	19.81	19.89	20.13	20.08	20.38	20.51	20.39	20.16
2015...	20.89	21.15	20.90	20.99	21.34	21.37	21.33	21.51	21.89	21.01	21.40	20.83	21.22

4. Average Weekly Earnings by Selected Industry: Michigan, 2011–2015

(Dollars, not seasonally adjusted)

Industry and year	January	February	March	April	May	June	July	August	September	October	November	December	Annual average
Total Private													
2011	776.90	765.91	755.77	762.62	775.03	751.56	759.58	753.91	756.50	774.53	761.98	764.71	764.37
2012	775.78	764.18	761.26	773.95	754.12	757.00	772.62	760.77	777.10	764.32	763.64	786.04	767.79
2013	771.12	772.67	774.28	772.33	774.63	800.05	785.13	782.46	805.73	789.24	790.62	808.16	784.55
2014	794.98	815.28	815.33	808.17	802.33	815.45	799.19	803.51	813.51	809.82	827.94	820.31	811.15
2015	814.31	822.17	826.28	818.40	820.02	816.91	820.46	847.37	827.27	837.26	844.22	835.21	827.66
Goods-Producing													
2011	1,052.32	1,045.58	1,049.02	1,029.14	1,044.17	1,013.11	1,001.97	1,010.46	1,019.57	1,022.11	1,013.85	1,014.74	1,025.07
2012	1,016.77	1,006.10	992.99	1,007.33	984.55	989.81	1,006.77	1,005.72	1,030.02	1,023.00	1,015.14	1,043.75	1,010.64
2013	1,022.13	1,009.00	1,011.88	997.14	1,008.59	1,026.71	1,019.67	1,029.06	1,050.73	1,028.70	1,023.39	1,046.56	1,022.99
2014	1,009.39	1,032.91	1,037.48	1,029.97	1,032.52	1,035.80	1,010.23	1,015.58	1,039.16	1,018.44	1,025.45	1,052.50	1,027.54
2015	1,018.25	1,026.18	1,044.14	1,032.43	1,042.07	1,043.28	1,016.28	1,071.38	1,016.72	1,047.37	1,037.14	1,051.34	1,036.95
Construction													
2011	1,002.46	1,006.97	993.02	998.10	996.82	988.69	1,011.03	1,013.72	1,025.71	1,010.40	1,005.05	1,000.01	1,004.12
2012	983.88	982.09	955.71	977.36	990.18	998.80	982.58	992.49	1,003.86	1,012.93	1,001.82	1,019.28	991.73
2013	989.14	985.02	976.13	975.02	1,030.22	1,015.46	1,061.10	1,021.94	1,024.55	1,020.46	966.07	1,006.55	1,007.75
2014	949.81	953.47	959.59	992.93	972.00	1,007.82	992.12	1,003.88	1,033.96	989.62	947.27	1,003.88	985.56
2015	971.15	963.48	1,002.41	1,011.12	1,029.77	1,013.36	1,015.28	1,043.78	977.64	1,068.35	1,005.46	1,045.21	1,014.71
Manufacturing													
2011	1,057.89	1,049.49	1,055.39	1,030.44	1,048.76	1,015.15	994.95	997.81	1,008.09	1,016.37	1,008.04	1,017.17	1,025.48
2012	1,022.58	1,013.12	999.19	1,014.76	984.96	991.79	1,018.37	1,011.36	1,038.33	1,027.10	1,022.98	1,059.10	1,017.63
2013	1,037.09	1,021.73	1,025.77	1,008.13	1,005.31	1,029.95	1,006.96	1,029.78	1,056.51	1,031.59	1,037.00	1,055.95	1,029.42
2014	1,021.73	1,049.75	1,053.27	1,038.28	1,048.90	1,041.43	1,012.23	1,015.40	1,035.77	1,026.27	1,047.06	1,066.83	1,039.45
2015	1,032.09	1,045.00	1,057.08	1,039.15	1,044.74	1,052.56	1,016.81	1,080.78	1,030.60	1,045.42	1,043.75	1,049.60	1,044.58
Trade, Transportation, and Utilities													
2011	661.58	660.63	632.09	645.41	647.96	641.36	645.79	639.18	640.52	653.78	638.50	643.28	646.35
2012	652.06	643.80	651.02	673.35	655.68	662.14	665.91	651.72	666.33	652.41	646.47	661.34	657.34
2013	649.30	664.25	666.93	663.92	668.30	681.07	681.06	678.38	692.56	682.59	689.64	691.15	675.99
2014	684.65	694.21	698.20	689.23	690.64	698.65	692.90	692.24	695.23	689.10	700.67	689.86	692.78
2015	682.85	683.52	679.60	679.60	682.70	679.94	691.71	706.35	706.35	688.81	698.39	687.76	688.31
Information													
2011	1,151.66	1,106.24	1,117.60	1,131.81	1,181.14	1,118.12	1,116.72	1,106.22	1,092.06	1,140.18	1,116.00	1,112.60	1,123.84
2012	1,134.39	1,068.27	1,057.79	1,119.99	1,067.79	1,047.00	1,069.70	1,034.09	1,062.87	1,023.96	1,035.10	1,068.86	1,065.29
2013	1,035.10	1,066.22	1,034.95	1,053.86	1,046.43	1,101.47	1,089.38	1,067.60	1,132.07	1,061.56	1,071.36	1,101.29	1,070.80
2014	1,085.08	1,117.88	1,140.45	1,130.22	1,118.02	1,158.54	1,134.97	1,133.78	1,170.73	1,135.10	1,148.33	1,140.55	1,135.41
2015	1,127.06	1,131.35	1,164.39	1,155.15	1,147.61	1,191.20	1,174.82	1,192.83	1,161.80	1,114.10	1,163.25	1,148.06	1,157.36
Financial Activities													
2011	901.74	881.04	858.13	882.52	882.57	851.60	879.65	870.52	864.86	890.19	884.84	886.32	878.70
2012	901.47	894.29	868.32	879.70	857.95	853.87	856.44	832.72	826.19	819.47	810.26	822.46	852.41
2013	811.89	806.82	812.95	824.83	815.29	823.28	798.15	805.39	824.16	832.17	827.51	838.74	817.53
2014	843.23	871.09	887.04	853.55	868.69	909.32	895.34	903.96	928.91	929.16	972.92	955.30	901.81
2015	976.98	1,017.13	1,033.21	1,025.45	1,026.56	1,004.92	1,005.53	1,021.39	1,014.70	1,013.01	1,060.51	1,027.97	1,018.26
Professional and Business Services													
2011	1,014.24	980.32	973.06	985.93	1,042.81	975.32	998.17	985.46	978.29	1,023.10	990.00	998.17	994.88
2012	1,022.93	999.54	1,003.91	1,014.10	968.03	967.32	1,014.10	988.62	1,016.38	981.64	984.38	1,050.05	999.84
2013	1,001.28	1,006.78	1,014.60	1,019.20	1,019.39	1,113.21	1,053.35	1,011.19	1,071.98	1,033.76	1,022.48	1,089.63	1,038.18
2014	1,079.64	1,115.14	1,115.49	1,100.34	1,074.24	1,108.71	1,065.15	1,063.87	1,060.66	1,068.62	1,093.18	1,064.71	1,083.83
2015	1,066.48	1,081.66	1,087.19	1,046.13	1,049.43	1,051.97	1,069.94	1,108.08	1,059.80	1,080.80	1,087.92	1,076.30	1,071.49
Education and Health Services													
2011	686.73	678.27	673.46	682.45	686.38	686.50	700.59	691.52	693.12	700.35	692.16	692.87	687.90
2012	711.62	697.28	699.46	705.02	697.36	709.80	718.58	713.05	725.86	713.77	719.16	723.98	710.86
2013	724.79	727.06	715.45	721.29	719.99	738.37	738.06	738.07	755.70	735.79	745.56	752.75	733.54
2014	743.18	750.13	746.85	741.24	741.29	748.44	748.01	758.88	767.33	763.10	780.12	767.47	755.30
2015	769.93	773.60	773.42	781.75	778.26	774.90	795.11	804.08	801.48	831.68	825.99	813.25	794.28
Leisure and Hospitality													
2011	282.74	281.55	279.39	280.83	288.92	285.45	288.93	287.41	282.07	285.78	279.87	280.91	283.71
2012	272.03	277.48	276.08	278.00	276.72	281.02	285.00	285.25	278.06	274.70	273.08	279.90	278.60
2013	270.23	270.45	274.24	273.54	282.66	281.64	282.61	287.33	284.16	281.08	280.10	288.67	279.90
2014	278.66	287.41	286.03	287.50	289.91	294.71	295.91	298.80	298.14	300.42	298.54	302.32	293.01
2015	291.86	296.18	297.12	296.81	301.25	299.63	307.73	315.72	307.25	302.94	300.42	302.57	301.25
Other Services													
2011	640.45	625.60	611.83	626.46	627.84	617.92	612.80	606.42	614.66	628.37	622.20	614.81	620.05
2012	621.26	606.59	602.53	617.01	619.92	625.49	646.13	620.46	627.13	614.00	620.68	643.46	621.93
2013	637.98	639.41	652.17	647.05	634.69	623.69	635.50	694.88	647.11	614.64	616.99	598.58	637.16
2014	594.11	614.27	607.02	636.12	613.53	616.09	614.60	636.11	640.55	648.08	666.58	662.68	628.99
2015	676.84	678.92	677.16	669.58	687.15	698.80	691.09	714.13	717.99	682.83	693.36	662.39	687.53

MINNESOTA
At a Glance

Population:
2005 estimate: 5,119,598
2010 census: 5,303,925
2015 estimate: 5,489,594

Percent change in population:
2005–2015: 7.2%
2010–2015: 3.5%

Percent change in total nonfarm employment:
2005–2015: 4.9%

Industry with the largest growth in employment, 2005–2015 (thousands):
Education and health services, 118.4

Industry with the largest decline or smallest growth in employment, 2005–2015 (thousands):
Manufacturing, –30.4

Civilian labor force:
2005: 2,879,760
2010: 2,938,795
2015: 3,010,367

Unemployment rate and rank among states (highest to lowest):
2005: 4.1%, 37th
2010: 7.4%, 39th
2015: 3.7%, 43rd

Over-the-year change in unemployment rates:
2012–2013: –0.7%
2013–2014: –0.7%
2014–2015: –0.5%

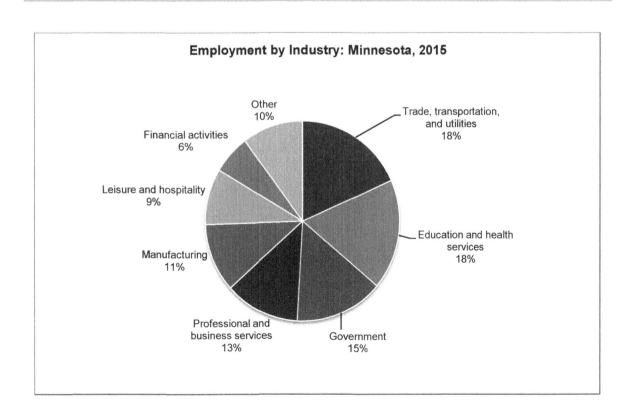

Employment by Industry: Minnesota, 2015

Other 10%
Financial activities 6%
Leisure and hospitality 9%
Manufacturing 11%
Professional and business services 13%
Government 15%
Education and health services 18%
Trade, transportation, and utilities 18%

1. Employment by Industry: Minnesota, 2005–2015

(Numbers in thousands, not seasonally adjusted)

Industry and year	January	February	March	April	May	June	July	August	September	October	November	December	Annual average
Total Nonfarm													
2005	2,629.3	2,634.4	2,648.3	2,705.1	2,746.5	2,768.3	2,737.9	2,743.8	2,757.5	2,769.6	2,769.8	2,768.9	2,723.3
2006	2,701.9	2,700.8	2,715.7	2,737.9	2,775.1	2,809.9	2,766.0	2,767.6	2,775.8	2,781.4	2,783.7	2,781.1	2,758.1
2007	2,711.4	2,711.7	2,722.0	2,745.9	2,793.7	2,823.2	2,784.1	2,786.1	2,788.1	2,798.7	2,799.4	2,788.8	2,771.1
2008	2,718.8	2,721.4	2,729.1	2,746.8	2,791.7	2,814.2	2,774.7	2,778.8	2,777.1	2,787.4	2,768.0	2,743.7	2,762.6
2009	2,653.8	2,640.1	2,631.5	2,652.6	2,682.7	2,689.8	2,649.9	2,646.4	2,638.8	2,665.3	2,657.5	2,646.5	2,654.6
2010	2,569.7	2,571.1	2,580.7	2,628.3	2,662.7	2,682.3	2,649.0	2,654.1	2,656.3	2,685.0	2,680.8	2,667.2	2,640.6
2011	2,606.6	2,613.9	2,623.2	2,672.4	2,709.3	2,729.9	2,679.4	2,709.8	2,727.9	2,733.2	2,728.2	2,719.7	2,687.8
2012	2,651.8	2,657.6	2,673.3	2,715.7	2,745.7	2,768.4	2,728.4	2,744.9	2,759.6	2,774.8	2,774.6	2,763.0	2,729.8
2013	2,701.6	2,713.6	2,721.7	2,745.0	2,792.7	2,817.4	2,772.0	2,791.8	2,806.7	2,823.6	2,818.4	2,807.6	2,776.0
2014	2,733.3	2,742.6	2,745.7	2,786.7	2,832.6	2,862.9	2,834.4	2,844.0	2,839.0	2,855.8	2,852.8	2,844.2	2,814.5
2015	2,773.8	2,785.3	2,792.3	2,843.6	2,881.0	2,906.8	2,880.6	2,883.9	2,875.5	2,891.8	2,886.6	2,874.6	2,856.3
Total Private													
2005	2,212.9	2,212.3	2,225.4	2,280.5	2,321.6	2,348.3	2,346.8	2,359.1	2,348.8	2,349.0	2,349.6	2,346.7	2,308.4
2006	2,286.7	2,279.3	2,293.2	2,314.9	2,351.6	2,374.8	2,374.8	2,381.2	2,364.9	2,359.0	2,357.9	2,354.1	2,342.2
2007	2,297.2	2,291.2	2,302.4	2,325.7	2,369.7	2,401.1	2,394.6	2,402.1	2,380.5	2,376.2	2,373.5	2,363.8	2,356.5
2008	2,301.7	2,297.5	2,304.7	2,322.9	2,363.5	2,387.7	2,382.6	2,390.2	2,363.2	2,360.1	2,337.4	2,313.7	2,343.8
2009	2,236.4	2,215.1	2,206.3	2,225.9	2,254.2	2,264.1	2,256.8	2,261.1	2,234.7	2,241.6	2,231.0	2,220.4	2,237.3
2010	2,153.0	2,147.6	2,155.3	2,202.0	2,232.1	2,256.5	2,259.7	2,270.9	2,251.5	2,262.7	2,255.0	2,242.4	2,224.1
2011	2,193.0	2,192.6	2,202.2	2,250.3	2,287.7	2,310.9	2,317.4	2,331.4	2,322.3	2,313.7	2,306.7	2,298.0	2,277.2
2012	2,241.7	2,239.4	2,254.6	2,294.7	2,325.2	2,349.6	2,350.8	2,364.0	2,351.3	2,351.9	2,347.0	2,337.5	2,317.3
2013	2,288.2	2,290.7	2,300.3	2,323.1	2,369.3	2,397.4	2,396.1	2,411.7	2,395.6	2,397.2	2,388.2	2,379.5	2,361.4
2014	2,317.2	2,316.7	2,320.0	2,358.6	2,404.6	2,435.2	2,438.1	2,450.7	2,425.6	2,426.1	2,420.4	2,413.8	2,393.9
2015	2,355.6	2,359.2	2,367.7	2,415.7	2,452.7	2,478.1	2,481.2	2,488.2	2,461.9	2,464.6	2,455.5	2,443.8	2,435.4
Goods-Producing													
2005	454.7	452.5	455.7	470.7	487.2	499.4	502.9	506.4	500.7	494.2	488.6	477.6	482.6
2006	461.5	457.6	460.7	469.3	482.6	497.6	496.8	498.5	492.1	487.4	477.0	467.7	479.1
2007	452.0	446.6	449.4	454.9	471.9	485.5	485.0	486.9	479.0	474.8	468.0	456.5	467.5
2008	440.4	436.6	437.5	442.2	458.9	470.0	471.1	472.3	463.7	459.9	445.9	429.5	452.3
2009	406.2	395.5	389.5	391.1	399.1	406.7	407.8	407.9	402.8	400.3	392.6	381.3	398.4
2010	362.9	358.3	359.7	375.3	386.4	397.5	404.3	405.8	402.5	402.0	395.1	385.0	386.2
2011	372.9	371.2	373.6	386.1	399.4	411.2	417.1	420.5	416.1	414.6	407.1	397.9	399.0
2012	383.1	381.0	386.5	398.8	409.3	421.6	424.9	427.3	422.5	420.1	412.4	404.1	407.6
2013	390.0	388.8	392.6	399.1	416.0	428.5	431.5	435.7	431.4	429.2	423.3	413.0	414.9
2014	399.6	398.7	400.8	410.9	428.3	442.1	446.7	449.8	443.7	442.4	434.9	427.8	427.1
2015	413.7	413.2	416.7	431.5	443.3	455.4	459.3	459.7	452.3	451.1	442.2	430.0	439.0
Service-Providing													
2005	2,174.6	2,181.9	2,192.6	2,234.4	2,259.3	2,268.9	2,235.0	2,237.4	2,256.8	2,275.4	2,281.2	2,291.3	2,240.7
2006	2,240.4	2,243.2	2,255.0	2,268.6	2,292.5	2,312.3	2,269.2	2,269.1	2,283.7	2,294.0	2,306.7	2,313.4	2,279.0
2007	2,259.4	2,265.1	2,272.6	2,291.0	2,321.8	2,337.7	2,299.1	2,299.2	2,309.1	2,323.9	2,331.4	2,332.3	2,303.6
2008	2,278.4	2,284.8	2,291.6	2,304.6	2,332.8	2,344.2	2,303.6	2,306.5	2,313.4	2,327.5	2,322.1	2,314.2	2,310.3
2009	2,247.6	2,244.6	2,242.0	2,261.5	2,283.6	2,283.1	2,242.1	2,238.5	2,236.0	2,265.0	2,264.9	2,265.2	2,256.2
2010	2,206.8	2,212.8	2,221.0	2,253.0	2,276.3	2,284.8	2,244.7	2,248.3	2,253.8	2,283.0	2,285.7	2,282.2	2,254.4
2011	2,233.7	2,242.7	2,249.6	2,286.3	2,309.9	2,318.7	2,262.3	2,289.3	2,311.8	2,318.6	2,321.1	2,321.8	2,288.8
2012	2,268.7	2,276.6	2,286.8	2,316.9	2,336.4	2,346.8	2,303.5	2,317.6	2,337.1	2,354.7	2,362.2	2,358.9	2,322.2
2013	2,311.6	2,324.8	2,329.1	2,345.9	2,376.7	2,388.9	2,340.5	2,356.1	2,375.3	2,394.4	2,395.1	2,394.6	2,361.1
2014	2,333.7	2,343.9	2,344.9	2,375.8	2,404.3	2,420.8	2,387.7	2,394.2	2,395.3	2,413.4	2,417.9	2,416.4	2,387.4
2015	2,360.1	2,372.1	2,375.6	2,412.1	2,437.7	2,451.4	2,421.3	2,424.2	2,423.2	2,440.7	2,444.4	2,444.6	2,417.3
Mining and Logging													
2005	5.6	5.7	5.7	5.8	6.1	6.3	6.3	6.3	6.2	6.1	6.0	5.7	6.0
2006	5.7	5.8	5.8	5.8	5.9	6.3	6.4	6.4	6.2	6.2	6.0	5.8	6.0
2007	5.6	5.6	5.6	5.6	5.9	6.1	6.3	6.4	6.2	6.2	6.2	6.0	6.0
2008	5.9	5.9	5.9	5.9	6.3	6.4	6.7	6.7	6.5	6.5	6.3	6.0	6.3
2009	5.8	5.6	5.3	5.1	4.6	4.4	5.3	5.0	4.6	5.7	5.4	5.0	5.2
2010	5.3	5.4	5.4	5.7	6.0	5.6	6.5	6.5	6.4	6.5	6.3	6.0	6.0
2011	6.0	6.2	6.1	6.1	6.5	6.8	7.0	7.1	6.9	7.0	6.9	6.6	6.6
2012	6.6	6.6	6.6	6.8	7.0	7.3	7.4	7.5	7.2	7.2	7.1	6.8	7.0
2013	6.6	6.6	6.7	6.6	6.9	7.2	7.2	7.4	7.2	7.2	7.1	6.9	7.0
2014	6.6	6.7	6.7	6.8	7.1	7.3	7.6	7.6	7.4	7.5	7.4	7.1	7.2
2015	6.8	6.9	7.0	7.1	7.3	7.4	7.6	7.2	6.9	6.8	6.7	5.8	7.0

1. Employment by Industry: Minnesota, 2005–2015—*Continued*

(Numbers in thousands, not seasonally adjusted)

Industry and year	January	February	March	April	May	June	July	August	September	October	November	December	Annual average
Construction													
2005	108.3	106.5	108.5	120.6	132.7	140.9	145.5	146.1	143.2	139.0	135.1	126.4	129.4
2006	114.6	112.8	114.2	120.8	131.6	139.7	139.7	139.3	136.7	133.7	127.7	118.8	127.5
2007	108.0	104.0	106.5	110.3	124.9	132.6	132.7	133.4	129.2	126.7	121.6	111.3	120.1
2008	100.3	97.4	98.4	102.3	115.7	122.6	123.8	123.9	119.5	116.6	107.9	97.4	110.5
2009	82.1	79.6	79.6	86.5	97.7	102.4	103.9	103.8	102.3	100.0	95.2	87.3	93.4
2010	73.3	69.5	70.2	81.9	89.4	95.6	99.2	99.8	98.0	97.9	92.8	83.4	87.6
2011	74.2	72.7	74.5	83.3	93.6	101.1	103.8	105.6	103.8	102.5	97.3	88.8	91.8
2012	77.4	75.9	79.7	90.0	98.0	104.4	106.9	108.2	105.2	104.0	98.2	91.4	94.9
2013	80.5	80.0	82.4	88.9	102.7	110.3	113.4	116.2	114.2	112.8	107.7	98.1	100.6
2014	87.9	86.7	88.9	96.5	110.6	119.3	122.1	123.4	120.4	119.0	112.3	105.2	107.7
2015	94.4	93.9	96.3	110.0	119.9	127.5	130.6	131.1	126.9	125.9	119.0	107.5	115.3
Manufacturing													
2005	340.8	340.3	341.5	344.3	348.4	352.2	351.1	354.0	351.3	349.1	347.5	345.5	347.2
2006	341.2	339.0	340.7	342.7	345.1	351.6	350.7	352.8	349.2	347.5	343.3	343.1	345.6
2007	338.4	337.0	337.3	339.0	341.1	346.8	346.0	347.1	343.6	341.9	340.2	339.2	341.5
2008	334.2	333.3	333.2	334.0	336.9	341.0	340.6	341.7	337.7	336.8	331.7	326.1	335.6
2009	318.3	310.3	304.6	299.5	296.8	299.9	298.6	299.1	295.9	294.6	292.0	289.0	299.9
2010	284.3	283.4	284.1	287.7	291.0	296.3	298.6	299.5	298.1	297.6	296.0	295.6	292.7
2011	292.7	292.3	293.0	296.7	299.3	303.3	306.3	307.8	305.4	305.1	302.9	302.5	300.6
2012	299.1	298.5	300.2	302.0	304.3	309.9	310.6	311.6	310.1	308.9	307.1	305.9	305.7
2013	302.9	302.2	303.5	303.6	306.4	311.0	310.9	312.1	310.0	309.2	308.5	308.0	307.4
2014	305.1	305.3	305.2	307.6	310.6	315.5	317.0	318.8	315.9	315.9	315.2	315.5	312.3
2015	312.5	312.4	313.4	314.4	316.1	320.5	321.1	321.4	318.5	318.4	316.5	316.7	316.8
Trade, Transportation, and Utilities													
2005	517.6	512.7	514.4	522.6	528.3	531.1	527.6	528.7	526.9	531.9	540.0	545.0	527.2
2006	525.7	519.4	520.5	523.7	529.4	534.1	527.1	527.0	526.2	527.8	538.3	541.1	528.4
2007	523.7	518.8	519.3	523.2	530.7	534.4	529.4	529.8	528.2	531.7	539.6	543.0	529.3
2008	523.6	516.8	518.2	519.9	526.7	527.2	522.4	522.2	519.0	520.7	524.1	523.7	522.0
2009	502.9	495.2	492.5	494.1	500.0	501.2	494.7	494.5	490.6	493.0	499.6	500.5	496.6
2010	482.3	476.6	477.5	486.4	491.6	496.1	491.6	491.5	489.5	494.1	500.7	503.1	490.1
2011	484.7	480.9	482.3	492.2	499.0	500.9	499.5	500.4	500.7	502.3	509.6	513.0	497.1
2012	495.4	488.6	491.4	498.4	504.9	506.9	503.4	505.1	503.4	507.8	517.1	517.5	503.3
2013	502.3	497.0	498.2	501.4	510.7	515.3	511.5	514.8	512.8	516.3	523.7	527.2	510.9
2014	506.8	502.2	503.0	510.7	517.9	521.9	519.2	520.7	515.8	520.9	528.0	533.4	516.7
2015	514.0	509.6	510.9	519.4	526.0	530.5	527.3	528.4	524.4	526.4	533.0	535.0	523.7
Wholesale Trade													
2005	127.3	127.4	127.5	131.1	131.4	133.3	132.8	133.1	132.0	132.2	132.3	132.4	131.1
2006	131.3	131.4	132.2	133.1	134.0	135.1	134.6	134.5	133.1	133.0	133.0	132.7	133.2
2007	131.1	131.0	131.6	132.9	134.5	135.5	135.2	135.2	133.2	133.6	133.7	133.6	133.4
2008	131.7	131.5	132.1	132.8	134.3	134.9	135.0	134.9	132.9	132.6	132.1	131.2	133.0
2009	128.2	127.0	126.1	127.3	127.5	127.6	127.2	126.5	124.0	123.9	124.0	123.5	126.1
2010	120.8	120.4	120.8	123.0	123.6	124.9	125.1	124.8	123.0	124.3	124.2	123.6	123.2
2011	122.1	122.3	122.8	125.4	127.0	127.2	128.0	128.0	126.6	126.7	126.6	126.4	125.8
2012	125.2	125.2	126.2	128.6	129.5	130.7	131.1	130.5	128.9	129.3	129.4	129.4	128.7
2013	127.9	127.8	128.3	129.3	131.4	132.4	132.5	132.1	130.4	130.9	131.4	130.7	130.4
2014	128.9	129.0	129.4	130.7	132.7	133.8	133.7	133.5	131.7	132.3	132.6	132.4	131.7
2015	130.4	130.2	130.6	132.7	133.3	134.5	134.7	134.2	132.2	132.0	131.8	131.3	132.3
Retail Trade													
2005	296.0	290.7	291.9	296.0	300.7	303.2	300.3	301.8	299.8	303.8	311.9	316.5	301.1
2006	300.3	294.7	294.8	297.4	301.4	305.2	301.5	302.2	298.5	300.0	309.0	312.5	301.5
2007	299.2	293.7	294.4	296.3	301.5	304.9	302.3	302.7	299.2	301.2	309.2	311.6	301.4
2008	297.2	290.2	290.9	292.1	296.4	297.5	295.4	295.5	290.7	291.7	296.1	296.1	294.2
2009	282.8	276.8	274.8	275.9	281.3	283.6	280.4	281.6	276.1	278.0	284.1	285.3	280.1
2010	272.8	267.9	268.2	273.7	277.8	281.2	279.3	280.5	276.2	278.0	283.9	286.1	277.1
2011	272.6	268.4	269.0	275.5	280.0	282.9	282.5	284.1	281.6	282.2	289.5	292.1	280.0
2012	279.3	272.7	274.4	277.7	282.3	284.9	283.0	284.6	281.6	284.6	293.4	293.5	282.7
2013	282.0	276.5	277.4	279.6	285.4	290.3	288.8	291.1	287.5	288.5	295.0	298.5	286.7
2014	283.1	278.8	279.3	283.9	288.4	292.3	292.1	293.0	287.0	289.9	296.4	300.3	288.7
2015	286.5	282.3	283.2	287.8	293.4	298.0	296.8	298.1	292.6	294.4	299.9	301.2	292.9

1. Employment by Industry: Minnesota, 2005–2015—*Continued*

(Numbers in thousands, not seasonally adjusted)

Industry and year	January	February	March	April	May	June	July	August	September	October	November	December	Annual average
Transportation and Utilities													
2005	94.3	94.6	95.0	95.5	96.2	94.6	94.5	93.8	95.1	95.9	95.8	96.1	95.1
2006	94.1	93.3	93.5	93.2	94.0	93.8	91.0	90.3	94.6	94.8	96.3	95.9	93.7
2007	93.4	94.1	93.3	94.0	94.7	94.0	91.9	91.9	95.8	96.9	96.7	97.8	94.5
2008	94.7	95.1	95.2	95.0	96.0	94.8	92.0	91.8	95.4	96.4	95.9	96.4	94.9
2009	91.9	91.4	91.6	90.9	91.2	90.0	87.1	86.4	90.5	91.1	91.5	91.7	90.4
2010	88.7	88.3	88.5	89.7	90.2	90.0	87.2	86.2	90.3	91.8	92.6	93.4	89.7
2011	90.0	90.2	90.5	91.3	92.0	90.8	89.0	88.3	92.5	93.4	93.5	94.5	91.3
2012	90.9	90.7	90.8	92.1	93.1	91.3	89.3	90.0	92.9	93.9	94.3	94.6	92.0
2013	92.4	92.7	92.5	92.5	93.9	92.6	90.2	91.6	94.9	96.9	97.3	98.0	93.8
2014	94.8	94.4	94.3	96.1	96.8	95.8	93.4	94.2	97.1	98.7	99.0	100.7	96.3
2015	97.1	97.1	97.1	98.9	99.3	98.0	95.8	96.1	99.6	100.0	101.3	102.5	98.6
Information													
2005	58.7	58.6	58.7	59.7	59.8	60.0	59.6	59.0	58.5	58.4	58.7	59.0	59.1
2006	58.3	58.1	58.4	57.8	58.3	58.7	58.2	58.3	57.5	57.3	57.7	57.8	58.0
2007	57.9	57.9	58.2	58.2	58.3	58.6	58.2	58.2	57.6	57.3	57.4	57.8	58.0
2008	57.6	57.4	57.6	57.8	57.7	57.9	58.0	58.0	57.6	57.0	57.1	56.4	57.5
2009	56.1	55.9	55.7	55.1	55.2	55.3	55.6	55.5	54.9	54.7	55.0	54.8	55.3
2010	54.4	54.4	54.3	54.1	54.0	54.2	54.4	54.4	53.7	53.8	53.9	53.7	54.1
2011	53.7	53.3	53.1	53.8	53.8	54.1	54.3	54.6	54.0	53.8	53.8	53.8	53.8
2012	52.9	53.0	53.0	53.5	53.9	54.0	54.0	54.0	53.6	53.7	53.6	53.8	53.6
2013	53.1	53.2	53.1	53.1	53.3	53.3	53.8	53.6	52.8	52.7	53.0	53.1	53.2
2014	52.6	52.5	52.2	52.2	52.4	52.8	53.1	53.1	52.1	52.2	52.0	52.4	52.5
2015	51.4	51.2	51.1	51.2	51.6	52.1	52.0	52.9	51.7	51.7	51.8	52.1	51.7
Financial Activities													
2005	175.2	175.1	175.7	179.9	180.6	182.5	181.5	182.1	180.8	180.0	180.2	181.2	179.6
2006	179.8	179.6	180.1	179.4	180.5	182.2	181.5	181.2	179.7	179.5	179.7	180.6	180.3
2007	178.2	178.7	178.8	178.4	178.3	180.5	180.2	179.9	178.2	178.1	178.1	178.6	178.8
2008	175.9	175.9	176.1	175.6	176.0	177.4	177.8	177.5	175.4	174.9	174.5	175.2	176.0
2009	172.5	172.0	171.3	171.2	171.8	172.7	173.0	172.3	171.0	171.2	170.9	171.5	171.8
2010	169.1	168.8	168.7	169.2	169.8	171.4	171.9	172.1	170.9	172.3	172.0	173.1	170.8
2011	170.8	171.0	170.9	171.1	171.7	172.5	173.5	173.7	172.1	172.2	171.9	172.4	172.0
2012	172.0	172.3	172.5	174.6	175.6	176.2	176.9	177.0	175.8	176.6	176.7	177.3	175.3
2013	176.6	176.9	177.0	177.1	178.0	179.7	180.4	180.4	178.4	178.5	178.5	178.7	178.4
2014	177.0	176.6	176.8	177.1	178.1	180.2	180.5	180.3	177.9	178.0	178.0	178.7	178.3
2015	178.6	178.7	178.6	179.9	181.2	183.0	184.7	184.7	181.8	181.2	181.1	183.2	181.4
Professional and Business Services													
2005	291.1	292.0	294.8	304.1	307.3	311.6	310.5	314.5	315.1	319.5	319.2	319.0	308.2
2006	313.2	313.6	315.4	319.9	323.0	329.1	327.1	329.7	328.3	329.8	329.7	328.9	324.0
2007	320.2	321.4	323.5	326.4	329.9	334.2	334.8	338.3	334.4	334.6	333.8	332.4	330.3
2008	323.2	324.0	323.9	326.9	330.1	333.5	334.4	336.9	333.2	333.4	329.0	325.1	329.5
2009	309.1	304.8	302.5	306.1	307.7	308.6	308.2	311.9	306.6	312.7	312.2	312.4	308.6
2010	301.1	302.0	301.9	310.8	313.2	317.0	320.6	324.8	319.4	324.0	324.3	322.7	315.2
2011	315.7	316.4	318.2	326.8	328.8	332.1	336.6	340.8	339.4	340.7	339.5	337.6	331.1
2012	326.3	326.3	328.0	335.1	336.6	340.3	343.1	346.6	343.3	346.2	344.6	344.2	338.4
2013	335.0	338.2	339.1	342.8	345.6	351.0	352.0	355.8	352.1	357.0	354.0	353.7	348.0
2014	341.6	342.2	342.0	347.1	351.2	355.9	359.1	362.3	356.8	361.2	362.4	357.5	353.3
2015	346.9	348.0	347.6	356.4	359.3	360.4	362.2	363.3	356.3	361.7	361.3	357.3	356.7
Education and Health Services													
2005	377.6	384.1	385.9	388.3	392.1	387.1	388.8	389.8	394.8	399.8	402.2	403.8	391.2
2006	399.2	402.1	404.4	407.0	408.3	406.3	407.7	407.9	411.4	415.2	419.0	420.6	409.1
2007	418.0	421.1	422.9	426.1	428.1	426.3	425.6	426.0	429.4	435.1	438.4	437.6	427.9
2008	433.0	437.8	439.8	442.9	442.4	439.6	438.6	439.8	443.2	450.5	452.7	452.9	442.8
2009	448.2	452.1	453.8	458.1	457.5	450.3	448.6	448.6	448.1	458.0	458.5	458.8	453.4
2010	451.3	456.4	458.3	460.4	460.7	456.4	451.5	454.1	457.3	464.0	466.2	464.5	458.4
2011	461.7	466.4	466.7	471.8	472.3	467.6	464.8	466.2	471.1	473.7	475.0	475.5	469.4
2012	470.1	475.5	475.9	478.2	478.1	472.1	470.0	473.1	480.4	485.4	487.5	486.7	477.8
2013	482.9	488.4	488.3	492.3	492.4	485.4	482.3	485.2	491.5	497.0	499.0	497.5	490.2
2014	491.8	497.0	496.9	500.5	500.5	494.7	493.0	495.2	501.2	504.1	506.1	505.4	498.9
2015	498.9	505.5	506.3	509.7	510.0	503.8	504.5	506.6	513.3	519.2	519.6	518.3	509.6

1. Employment by Industry: Minnesota, 2005–2015—*Continued*

(Numbers in thousands, not seasonally adjusted)

Industry and year	January	February	March	April	May	June	July	August	September	October	November	December	Annual average
Leisure and Hospitality													
2005	223.0	222.3	224.6	237.0	247.3	256.9	256.8	259.0	252.7	246.0	241.7	241.3	242.4
2006	233.5	233.5	236.4	239.8	250.9	260.3	257.7	259.8	251.4	243.4	237.7	238.1	245.2
2007	232.1	231.9	234.0	241.6	254.8	263.3	263.6	265.1	257.0	248.1	241.3	240.5	247.8
2008	232.9	232.4	234.9	239.5	253.2	261.9	260.9	263.8	253.2	245.2	236.4	234.6	245.7
2009	226.7	224.9	225.8	234.2	246.5	252.1	252.4	254.0	245.3	237.2	228.3	227.0	237.9
2010	219.5	218.5	221.3	232.1	242.3	248.5	250.2	252.6	244.5	237.7	228.8	226.4	235.2
2011	220.8	220.4	223.8	233.7	247.5	255.9	255.1	258.3	252.7	241.1	234.6	232.3	239.7
2012	227.7	228.4	232.5	240.6	251.0	260.6	261.4	263.7	256.6	246.2	239.3	238.0	245.5
2013	233.3	232.9	235.9	241.3	256.4	266.4	267.8	269.1	261.1	252.1	243.2	243.0	250.2
2014	236.7	236.9	237.5	247.7	262.6	272.6	271.7	274.5	264.7	253.7	245.9	245.6	254.2
2015	240.3	240.8	243.6	253.3	266.5	276.8	274.9	276.4	267.6	257.4	250.6	251.1	258.3
Other Services													
2005	115.0	115.0	115.6	118.2	119.0	119.7	119.1	119.6	119.3	119.2	119.0	119.8	118.2
2006	115.5	115.4	117.3	118.0	118.6	119.9	118.7	118.8	118.3	118.6	118.8	119.3	118.1
2007	115.1	114.8	116.3	116.9	117.7	118.3	117.8	117.9	116.7	116.5	116.9	117.4	116.9
2008	115.1	116.6	116.7	118.1	118.5	120.2	119.4	119.7	117.9	118.5	117.7	116.3	117.9
2009	114.7	114.7	115.2	116.0	116.4	117.2	116.5	116.4	115.4	114.5	113.9	114.1	115.4
2010	112.4	112.6	113.6	113.7	114.1	115.4	115.2	115.6	113.7	114.8	114.0	113.9	114.1
2011	112.7	113.0	113.6	114.8	115.2	116.6	116.5	116.9	116.2	115.3	115.2	115.5	115.1
2012	114.2	114.3	114.8	115.5	115.8	117.9	117.1	117.2	115.7	115.9	115.8	115.9	115.8
2013	115.0	115.3	116.1	116.0	116.9	117.8	116.8	117.1	115.5	114.4	113.5	113.3	115.6
2014	111.1	110.6	110.8	112.4	113.6	115.0	114.8	114.8	113.4	113.6	113.1	113.0	113.0
2015	111.8	112.2	112.9	114.3	114.8	116.1	116.3	116.2	114.5	115.9	115.9	116.8	114.8
Government													
2005	416.4	422.1	422.9	424.6	424.9	420.0	391.1	384.7	408.7	420.6	420.2	422.2	414.9
2006	415.2	421.5	422.5	423.0	423.5	421.7	391.2	386.4	410.9	422.4	425.8	427.0	415.9
2007	414.2	420.5	419.6	420.2	424.0	422.1	389.5	384.0	407.6	422.5	425.9	425.0	414.6
2008	417.1	423.9	424.4	423.9	428.2	426.5	392.1	388.6	413.9	427.3	430.6	430.0	418.9
2009	417.4	425.0	425.2	426.7	428.5	425.7	393.1	385.3	404.1	423.7	426.5	426.1	417.3
2010	416.7	423.5	425.4	426.3	430.6	425.8	389.3	383.2	404.8	422.3	425.8	424.8	416.5
2011	413.6	421.3	421.0	422.1	421.6	419.0	362.0	378.4	405.6	419.5	421.5	421.7	410.6
2012	410.1	418.2	418.7	421.0	420.5	418.8	377.6	380.9	408.3	422.9	427.6	425.5	412.5
2013	413.4	422.9	421.4	421.9	423.4	420.0	375.9	380.1	411.1	426.4	430.2	428.1	414.6
2014	416.1	425.9	425.7	428.1	428.0	427.7	396.3	393.3	413.4	429.7	432.4	430.4	420.6
2015	418.2	426.1	424.6	427.9	428.3	428.7	399.4	395.7	413.6	427.2	431.1	430.8	421.0

2. Average Weekly Hours by Selected Industry: Minnesota, 2011–2015

(Not seasonally adjusted)

Industry and year	January	February	March	April	May	June	July	August	September	October	November	December	Annual average
Total Private													
2011	33.3	32.9	32.9	33.1	33.4	33.1	33.2	33.3	33.5	33.8	33.3	33.5	33.3
2012	33.7	33.2	33.2	33.9	33.2	33.5	33.9	33.7	34.3	33.5	33.2	33.7	33.6
2013	33.1	33.2	33.4	33.2	33.4	34.3	33.4	33.7	34.3	33.7	33.7	34.0	33.6
2014	33.2	33.9	34.0	33.7	34.0	34.5	34.2	34.3	34.1	34.1	34.2	33.9	34.0
2015	33.5	33.9	33.9	33.6	33.8	34.1	34.2	34.8	33.9	34.0	34.2	33.7	34.0
Goods-Producing													
2011	38.0	37.9	38.3	38.7	38.8	38.9	38.8	40.0	40.8	40.4	39.4	40.0	39.2
2012	39.8	39.6	39.7	40.3	40.0	40.6	40.5	40.7	41.1	40.6	39.8	39.8	40.2
2013	39.8	39.8	40.0	40.1	40.1	41.0	40.5	41.2	41.3	41.3	40.5	40.3	40.5
2014	39.7	40.2	40.6	40.4	41.1	41.4	41.2	41.8	41.4	41.3	40.4	40.3	40.8
2015	39.2	39.3	39.2	39.1	39.7	40.1	39.6	40.4	38.9	39.5	39.3	39.1	39.5
Construction													
2011	35.6	34.6	35.6	36.6	37.4	37.3	37.5	41.1	41.5	40.3	38.5	37.8	38.1
2012	37.6	36.8	38.6	39.3	39.5	40.6	40.7	41.3	42.0	41.3	38.8	38.8	39.8
2013	38.9	38.4	38.7	38.4	39.1	41.1	40.2	41.2	41.2	41.5	39.4	37.8	39.8
2014	37.7	37.0	38.2	38.3	40.6	40.9	41.6	42.0	41.2	40.8	37.6	37.5	39.6
2015	36.3	37.0	37.0	38.2	40.2	41.6	41.2	42.1	38.6	40.3	38.8	38.1	39.3
Manufacturing													
2011	39.0	39.0	39.2	39.5	39.4	39.5	39.3	40.0	40.4	40.3	39.5	40.3	39.6
2012	40.0	39.9	39.7	40.3	39.8	40.2	40.0	40.2	40.6	40.3	40.1	40.1	40.1
2013	40.0	40.1	40.3	40.6	40.4	40.8	40.4	41.0	41.2	41.2	40.9	41.0	40.7
2014	40.2	41.0	41.1	40.7	41.0	41.3	40.6	41.4	41.3	41.3	41.3	41.0	41.0
2015	39.8	39.8	39.8	39.3	39.6	39.6	39.0	39.9	39.4	39.6	40.0	39.8	39.6
Trade, Transportation, and Utilities													
2011	31.5	31.4	31.4	31.5	32.3	32.0	32.2	31.9	32.7	33.0	32.5	32.9	32.1
2012	32.5	32.1	32.0	32.5	32.3	32.3	33.1	32.7	33.3	32.4	32.1	33.0	32.5
2013	31.9	32.3	32.6	32.4	33.2	33.6	33.2	32.9	33.6	33.0	33.0	33.7	33.0
2014	32.4	32.9	33.1	33.2	33.8	33.6	33.7	33.4	33.7	33.4	33.5	33.3	33.3
2015	32.7	33.2	32.8	32.6	32.7	33.0	33.3	33.8	33.3	32.9	33.0	32.9	33.0
Financial Activities													
2011	39.2	38.0	37.6	37.5	38.4	37.3	37.5	37.8	37.7	39.0	38.3	38.2	38.0
2012	39.8	38.1	38.0	39.1	37.5	37.5	38.8	37.5	39.0	37.4	37.6	38.7	38.2
2013	37.2	37.5	37.2	37.2	37.1	38.6	36.1	36.5	38.1	36.4	36.8	37.8	37.2
2014	37.1	37.7	37.7	36.5	36.8	37.9	36.6	37.1	36.7	36.9	37.7	36.8	37.1
2015	37.0	37.4	37.3	36.9	36.6	36.8	36.5	37.5	36.5	36.7	37.6	36.7	37.0
Professional and Business Services													
2011	36.6	36.1	35.9	35.9	36.7	36.0	35.9	35.7	35.2	36.0	34.7	35.3	35.8
2012	36.2	35.6	35.7	36.8	35.7	35.9	36.2	35.3	36.8	35.2	35.0	35.7	35.8
2013	34.8	35.4	35.5	35.1	35.0	36.5	34.3	34.8	36.3	35.1	35.3	35.7	35.3
2014	34.4	36.1	36.1	35.3	35.7	36.8	35.8	36.0	35.4	35.8	36.4	35.5	35.8
2015	35.4	36.4	36.6	35.8	36.2	36.4	36.3	37.5	35.6	36.7	37.3	35.8	36.3
Education and Health Services													
2011	30.9	30.7	30.7	30.6	30.7	30.6	30.8	30.7	30.7	31.0	31.0	30.9	30.8
2012	30.9	30.8	30.7	31.1	30.7	30.7	30.9	30.9	31.2	30.9	30.9	31.0	30.9
2013	31.1	30.9	31.0	30.8	30.8	31.2	31.0	31.2	31.3	31.1	31.1	31.3	31.1
2014	31.1	31.1	31.0	31.3	31.1	31.3	31.2	31.4	31.6	31.7	32.0	32.2	31.4
2015	32.2	32.4	32.6	32.5	32.6	32.9	33.2	33.2	33.3	33.1	33.2	33.2	32.9
Leisure and Hospitality													
2011	22.1	22.1	22.1	21.9	22.0	22.4	22.7	22.9	22.3	22.8	22.4	22.7	22.4
2012	22.3	22.5	22.8	22.8	22.8	23.5	23.7	24.0	23.5	22.9	22.4	22.7	23.0
2013	22.0	22.6	23.2	22.4	22.9	23.9	24.2	24.4	24.0	23.3	23.0	22.9	23.3
2014	22.2	23.4	23.5	23.1	23.5	24.3	24.0	24.1	23.4	23.2	23.3	22.6	23.4
2015	22.4	23.1	23.4	22.7	23.0	24.0	24.1	24.7	23.6	23.5	23.4	22.6	23.4
Other Services													
2011	27.8	27.2	27.3	28.0	29.1	29.1	29.1	28.4	28.8	29.5	29.3	29.7	28.6
2012	30.1	29.4	29.5	29.8	29.5	29.8	29.9	29.9	29.5	28.9	29.3	29.1	29.6
2013	28.4	28.7	29.5	29.2	29.5	30.1	29.1	29.5	30.0	30.2	30.5	31.5	29.7
2014	31.1	31.6	31.4	30.9	30.7	31.4	30.9	30.6	30.6	30.5	30.9	29.9	30.9
2015	30.4	31.3	30.5	30.1	30.6	30.1	31.0	31.2	29.8	29.6	30.2	29.0	30.3

3. Average Hourly Earnings by Selected Industry: Minnesota, 2011–2015

(Dollars, not seasonally adjusted)

Industry and year	January	February	March	April	May	June	July	August	September	October	November	December	Annual average
Total Private													
2011	24.45	24.33	24.55	24.58	24.59	24.17	24.31	24.31	24.61	24.90	24.74	24.89	24.54
2012	24.69	24.51	24.49	24.89	24.69	24.70	25.00	24.81	25.44	25.20	25.27	25.67	24.95
2013	25.71	25.55	25.55	25.68	25.52	25.55	25.57	25.40	25.77	25.75	25.74	25.93	25.64
2014	26.00	25.95	25.83	25.86	25.81	25.73	25.60	25.58	25.75	25.68	25.88	25.82	25.79
2015	26.08	26.08	26.32	25.98	25.79	25.71	25.80	25.98	26.00	26.39	26.32	26.36	26.06
Goods-Producing													
2011	26.09	25.61	25.75	25.79	25.58	25.36	25.42	25.45	25.81	25.79	25.76	26.17	25.71
2012	25.71	25.33	25.39	25.56	25.60	25.53	25.74	25.54	26.09	26.07	26.06	26.20	25.74
2013	26.23	26.11	26.25	26.59	26.51	26.46	26.51	26.25	26.45	26.40	26.40	26.61	26.40
2014	26.72	26.44	26.58	26.68	27.07	26.83	26.85	26.68	26.91	26.64	26.28	26.47	26.68
2015	26.72	26.42	26.38	26.57	26.44	26.35	26.58	26.58	26.37	26.74	26.29	26.26	26.48
Construction													
2011	28.49	28.19	28.64	28.56	28.02	27.49	27.24	27.86	29.00	27.93	28.05	28.57	28.14
2012	28.34	28.48	28.53	28.41	28.22	27.95	28.08	28.12	29.16	29.10	28.86	29.01	28.52
2013	29.14	28.69	29.45	29.86	28.97	28.58	28.27	28.24	28.30	28.38	28.15	28.54	28.65
2014	28.70	28.78	28.58	28.63	29.75	28.73	28.92	29.18	29.89	29.74	30.02	30.21	29.30
2015	30.49	30.73	30.78	30.36	30.73	30.31	30.27	30.60	30.68	30.84	30.19	30.48	30.53
Manufacturing													
2011	25.40	24.90	24.89	24.92	24.72	24.51	24.68	24.38	24.48	24.80	24.85	25.37	24.82
2012	25.32	24.87	24.85	25.01	25.00	24.75	25.01	24.66	24.93	24.91	25.05	25.30	24.97
2013	25.28	25.34	25.23	25.44	25.55	25.55	25.70	25.32	25.57	25.50	25.59	25.81	25.49
2014	25.93	25.57	25.76	25.83	25.87	25.90	25.80	25.38	25.39	25.08	24.69	25.06	25.52
2015	25.42	24.98	24.91	25.12	24.71	24.58	24.90	24.75	24.55	24.97	24.73	24.70	24.86
Trade, Transportation, and Utilities													
2011	22.12	21.75	21.88	21.95	21.82	21.28	21.30	21.08	21.44	21.80	21.27	21.07	21.56
2012	21.62	21.04	20.98	21.66	21.50	21.55	21.75	21.64	22.28	21.75	21.86	22.13	21.65
2013	22.39	22.49	22.40	22.57	22.32	22.56	22.50	22.46	22.94	22.73	22.75	22.34	22.54
2014	22.85	22.52	22.54	23.12	22.98	22.87	22.45	22.53	22.57	22.46	22.77	22.25	22.66
2015	22.92	22.72	22.68	22.63	22.52	22.10	22.24	22.20	22.21	22.27	22.01	22.03	22.37
Financial Activities													
2011	26.51	26.96	28.65	28.36	28.66	28.61	28.55	29.02	28.86	29.55	30.20	29.90	28.65
2012	29.80	29.61	29.63	30.21	30.31	30.65	30.99	31.62	32.09	31.39	31.94	32.40	30.89
2013	32.83	33.50	33.80	33.43	33.47	33.87	34.23	34.01	33.53	33.62	33.43	33.56	33.61
2014	33.08	33.46	33.08	32.96	32.55	32.29	31.66	31.19	31.14	31.15	31.88	31.46	32.16
2015	30.88	31.59	31.64	31.79	32.24	32.39	32.43	32.27	32.20	32.59	32.98	33.45	32.21
Professional and Business Services													
2011	31.08	30.65	30.72	30.86	31.44	30.84	31.15	30.83	30.79	30.90	30.18	30.49	30.83
2012	30.61	29.93	29.60	29.98	29.00	28.74	29.44	28.80	29.01	28.59	28.86	29.50	29.33
2013	29.04	28.84	28.91	28.52	28.39	28.36	28.37	28.05	28.40	27.94	27.95	28.70	28.45
2014	28.60	28.55	28.38	28.06	27.95	28.39	28.54	28.83	29.29	28.93	29.96	30.52	28.84
2015	30.97	30.86	31.58	30.79	31.20	31.19	31.25	31.71	32.13	32.15	32.91	32.99	31.65
Education and Health Services													
2011	23.93	24.30	24.35	24.57	24.44	24.02	24.37	24.39	24.69	25.01	24.83	25.05	24.50
2012	25.22	25.25	25.38	25.50	25.53	25.73	25.87	25.69	25.93	26.08	25.98	26.33	25.71
2013	26.16	26.10	26.07	26.23	26.24	26.26	26.27	26.06	26.41	26.61	26.48	26.64	26.28
2014	26.52	26.61	26.37	26.33	26.28	25.96	26.14	26.06	26.18	26.32	26.26	26.18	26.27
2015	26.37	26.65	27.10	26.58	26.01	26.16	26.33	26.56	26.55	27.14	26.71	26.87	26.59
Leisure and Hospitality													
2011	13.97	13.95	13.69	13.69	13.47	12.98	12.95	12.81	13.01	12.99	13.25	13.20	13.31
2012	13.19	13.25	13.16	13.15	13.06	12.81	12.86	12.70	13.01	13.24	13.28	13.51	13.09
2013	13.44	13.51	13.45	13.46	13.31	13.02	13.03	12.97	13.29	13.50	13.70	13.83	13.36
2014	13.89	13.89	13.88	13.81	13.73	13.55	13.51	13.85	14.28	14.41	14.64	14.78	14.01
2015	14.66	14.87	14.89	14.88	14.51	14.55	14.62	15.12	15.23	15.37	15.48	15.50	14.97
Other Services													
2011	19.00	19.18	19.91	19.71	19.97	20.11	20.07	20.23	19.81	19.89	19.71	20.26	19.83
2012	20.86	20.38	20.20	20.18	20.47	20.52	21.02	21.19	21.45	21.54	21.42	21.90	20.93
2013	22.48	22.20	22.39	22.59	22.84	23.20	23.57	22.97	23.37	23.10	23.04	23.93	22.98
2014	23.49	22.77	22.34	22.75	23.05	23.35	23.21	23.26	23.22	23.01	22.50	23.06	23.00
2015	22.53	22.21	22.06	22.29	22.14	21.83	21.68	22.44	22.74	23.10	22.75	22.86	22.38

4. Average Weekly Earnings by Selected Industry: Minnesota, 2011–2015

(Dollars, not seasonally adjusted)

Industry and year	January	February	March	April	May	June	July	August	September	October	November	December	Annual average
Total Private													
2011	814.19	800.46	807.70	813.60	821.31	800.03	807.09	809.52	824.44	841.62	823.84	833.82	817.18
2012	832.05	813.73	813.07	843.77	819.71	827.45	847.50	836.10	872.59	844.20	838.96	865.08	838.32
2013	851.00	848.26	853.37	852.58	852.37	876.37	854.04	855.98	883.91	867.78	867.44	881.62	861.50
2014	863.20	879.71	878.22	871.48	877.54	887.69	875.52	877.39	878.08	875.69	885.10	875.30	876.86
2015	873.68	884.11	892.25	872.93	871.70	876.71	882.36	904.10	881.40	897.26	900.14	888.33	886.04
Goods-Producing													
2011	991.42	970.62	986.23	998.07	992.50	986.50	986.30	1,018.00	1,053.05	1,041.92	1,014.94	1,046.80	1,007.83
2012	1,023.26	1,003.07	1,007.98	1,030.07	1,024.00	1,036.52	1,042.47	1,039.48	1,072.30	1,058.44	1,037.19	1,042.76	1,034.75
2013	1,043.95	1,039.18	1,050.00	1,066.26	1,063.05	1,084.86	1,073.66	1,081.50	1,092.39	1,090.32	1,069.20	1,072.38	1,069.20
2014	1,060.78	1,062.89	1,079.15	1,077.87	1,112.58	1,110.76	1,106.22	1,115.22	1,114.07	1,100.23	1,061.71	1,066.74	1,088.54
2015	1,047.42	1,038.31	1,034.10	1,038.89	1,049.67	1,056.64	1,052.57	1,073.83	1,025.79	1,056.23	1,033.20	1,026.77	1,045.96
Construction													
2011	1,014.24	975.37	1,019.58	1,045.30	1,047.95	1,025.38	1,021.50	1,145.05	1,203.50	1,125.58	1,079.93	1,079.95	1,072.13
2012	1,065.58	1,048.06	1,101.26	1,116.51	1,114.69	1,134.77	1,142.86	1,161.36	1,224.72	1,201.83	1,119.77	1,125.59	1,135.10
2013	1,133.55	1,101.70	1,139.72	1,146.62	1,132.73	1,174.64	1,136.45	1,163.49	1,165.96	1,177.77	1,109.11	1,078.81	1,140.27
2014	1,081.99	1,064.86	1,091.76	1,096.53	1,207.85	1,175.06	1,203.07	1,225.56	1,231.47	1,213.39	1,128.75	1,132.88	1,160.28
2015	1,106.79	1,137.01	1,138.86	1,159.75	1,235.35	1,260.90	1,247.12	1,288.26	1,184.25	1,242.85	1,171.37	1,161.29	1,199.83
Manufacturing													
2011	990.60	971.10	975.69	984.34	973.97	968.15	969.92	975.20	988.99	999.44	981.58	1,022.41	982.87
2012	1,012.80	992.31	986.55	1,007.90	995.00	994.95	1,000.40	991.33	1,012.16	1,003.87	1,004.51	1,014.53	1,001.30
2013	1,011.20	1,016.13	1,016.77	1,032.86	1,032.22	1,042.44	1,038.28	1,038.12	1,053.48	1,050.60	1,046.63	1,058.21	1,037.44
2014	1,042.39	1,048.37	1,058.74	1,051.28	1,060.67	1,069.67	1,047.48	1,050.73	1,048.61	1,035.80	1,019.70	1,027.46	1,046.32
2015	1,011.72	994.20	991.42	987.22	978.52	973.37	971.10	987.53	967.27	988.81	989.20	983.06	984.46
Trade, Transportation, and Utilities													
2011	696.78	682.95	687.03	691.43	704.79	680.96	685.86	672.45	701.09	719.40	691.28	693.20	692.08
2012	702.65	675.38	671.36	703.95	694.45	696.07	719.93	707.63	741.92	704.70	701.71	730.29	703.63
2013	714.24	726.43	730.24	731.27	741.02	758.02	747.00	738.93	770.78	750.09	750.75	752.86	743.82
2014	740.34	740.91	746.07	767.58	776.72	768.43	756.57	752.50	760.61	750.16	762.80	740.93	754.58
2015	749.48	754.30	743.90	737.74	736.40	729.30	740.59	750.36	739.59	732.68	726.33	724.79	738.21
Financial Activities													
2011	1,039.19	1,024.48	1,077.24	1,063.50	1,100.54	1,067.15	1,070.63	1,096.96	1,088.02	1,152.45	1,156.66	1,142.18	1,088.70
2012	1,186.04	1,128.14	1,125.94	1,181.21	1,136.63	1,149.38	1,202.41	1,185.75	1,251.51	1,173.99	1,200.94	1,253.88	1,180.00
2013	1,221.28	1,256.25	1,257.36	1,243.60	1,241.74	1,307.38	1,235.70	1,241.37	1,277.49	1,223.77	1,230.22	1,268.57	1,250.29
2014	1,227.27	1,261.44	1,247.12	1,203.04	1,197.84	1,223.79	1,158.76	1,157.15	1,142.84	1,149.44	1,201.88	1,157.73	1,193.14
2015	1,142.56	1,181.47	1,180.17	1,173.05	1,179.98	1,191.95	1,183.70	1,210.13	1,175.30	1,196.05	1,240.05	1,227.62	1,191.77
Professional and Business Services													
2011	1,137.53	1,106.47	1,102.85	1,107.87	1,153.85	1,110.24	1,118.29	1,100.63	1,083.81	1,112.40	1,047.25	1,076.30	1,103.71
2012	1,108.08	1,065.51	1,056.72	1,103.26	1,035.30	1,031.77	1,065.73	1,016.64	1,067.57	1,006.37	1,010.10	1,053.15	1,050.01
2013	1,010.59	1,020.94	1,026.31	1,001.05	993.65	1,035.14	973.09	976.14	1,030.92	980.69	986.64	1,024.59	1,004.29
2014	983.84	1,030.66	1,024.52	990.52	997.82	1,044.75	1,021.73	1,037.88	1,036.87	1,035.69	1,090.54	1,083.46	1,032.47
2015	1,096.34	1,123.30	1,155.83	1,102.28	1,129.44	1,135.32	1,134.38	1,189.13	1,143.83	1,179.91	1,227.54	1,181.04	1,148.90
Education and Health Services													
2011	739.44	746.01	747.55	751.84	750.31	735.01	750.60	748.77	757.98	775.31	769.73	774.05	754.60
2012	779.30	777.70	779.17	793.05	783.77	789.91	799.38	793.82	809.02	805.87	802.78	816.23	794.44
2013	813.58	806.49	808.17	807.88	808.19	813.07	814.37	813.07	826.63	827.57	823.53	833.83	817.31
2014	824.77	827.57	817.47	824.13	817.31	812.55	815.57	818.28	827.29	834.34	840.32	843.00	824.88
2015	849.11	863.46	883.46	863.85	847.93	860.66	874.16	881.79	884.12	898.33	886.77	892.08	874.81
Leisure and Hospitality													
2011	308.74	308.30	302.55	299.81	296.34	290.75	293.97	293.35	290.12	296.17	296.80	299.64	298.14
2012	294.14	298.13	300.05	299.82	297.77	301.04	304.78	304.80	305.74	303.20	297.47	306.68	301.07
2013	295.68	305.33	312.04	301.50	304.80	311.18	315.33	316.47	318.96	314.55	315.10	316.71	311.29
2014	308.36	325.03	326.18	319.01	322.66	329.27	324.24	333.79	334.15	334.31	341.11	334.03	327.83
2015	328.38	343.50	348.43	337.78	333.73	349.20	352.34	373.46	359.43	361.20	362.23	350.30	350.30
Other Services													
2011	528.20	521.70	543.54	551.88	581.13	585.20	584.04	574.53	570.53	586.76	577.50	601.72	567.14
2012	627.89	599.17	595.90	601.36	603.87	611.50	628.50	633.58	632.78	622.51	627.61	637.29	619.53
2013	638.43	637.14	660.51	659.63	673.78	698.32	685.89	677.62	701.10	697.62	702.72	753.80	682.51
2014	730.54	719.53	701.48	702.98	707.64	733.19	717.19	711.76	710.53	701.81	695.25	689.49	710.70
2015	684.91	695.17	672.83	670.93	677.48	657.08	672.08	700.13	677.65	683.76	687.05	662.94	678.11

MISSISSIPPI
At a Glance

Population:
  2005 Population: 2,905,943
  2010 census: 2,967,297
  2015 estimate: 2,992,333

Percent change in population:
  2005–2015: 3.0%
  2010–2015: 0.8%

Percent change in total nonfarm employment:
  2005–2015: 0.2%

Industry with the largest growth in employment, 2005–2015 (thousands):
  Education and health services, 18.4

Industry with the largest decline or smallest growth in employment, 2005–2015 (thousands):
  Manufacturing, –36.3

Civilian labor force:
  2005: 1,317,392
  2010: 1,306,608
  2015: 1,272,657

Unemployment rate and rank among states (highest to lowest):
  2005: 7.5%, 1st
  2010: 10.4%, 11th
  2015: 6.5%, 5th

Over-the-year change in unemployment rates:
  2012–2013: –0.4%
  2013–2014: –1.0%
  2014–2015: –1.1%

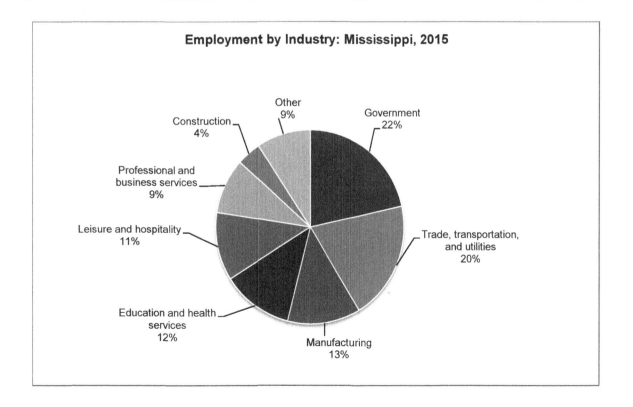

Employment by Industry: Mississippi, 2015

Other 9%
Construction 4%
Government 22%
Professional and business services 9%
Leisure and hospitality 11%
Trade, transportation, and utilities 20%
Education and health services 12%
Manufacturing 13%

1. Employment by Industry: Mississippi, 2005–2015

(Numbers in thousands, not seasonally adjusted)

Industry and year	January	February	March	April	May	June	July	August	September	October	November	December	Annual average
Total Nonfarm													
2005	1,119.7	1,127.9	1,135.9	1,140.7	1,140.0	1,134.6	1,124.4	1,135.4	1,122.0	1,127.1	1,139.7	1,133.1	1,131.7
2006	1,117.5	1,127.8	1,138.9	1,142.8	1,146.2	1,145.0	1,126.2	1,144.9	1,154.8	1,152.1	1,157.8	1,157.1	1,142.6
2007	1,139.7	1,146.3	1,150.0	1,155.5	1,157.5	1,153.9	1,138.1	1,154.9	1,163.0	1,160.4	1,166.1	1,165.3	1,154.2
2008	1,148.6	1,155.2	1,159.3	1,163.3	1,162.3	1,153.6	1,130.5	1,144.9	1,149.0	1,145.6	1,143.1	1,132.7	1,149.0
2009	1,107.9	1,107.8	1,107.0	1,105.5	1,105.6	1,097.8	1,080.6	1,088.6	1,095.5	1,091.3	1,094.1	1,090.0	1,097.6
2010	1,072.2	1,077.9	1,087.9	1,097.9	1,104.8	1,100.6	1,083.5	1,089.6	1,098.4	1,100.2	1,099.5	1,098.0	1,092.5
2011	1,078.3	1,084.0	1,094.4	1,099.9	1,100.2	1,093.6	1,078.4	1,088.8	1,099.0	1,099.0	1,101.7	1,097.6	1,092.9
2012	1,085.2	1,095.4	1,103.7	1,107.3	1,108.2	1,100.4	1,086.6	1,102.0	1,107.8	1,107.5	1,112.5	1,110.7	1,102.3
2013	1,092.7	1,104.7	1,110.1	1,114.7	1,115.1	1,110.0	1,094.2	1,108.8	1,118.5	1,118.2	1,124.9	1,123.1	1,111.3
2014	1,107.4	1,110.9	1,116.7	1,124.3	1,124.4	1,118.1	1,105.1	1,118.7	1,125.9	1,129.3	1,135.5	1,135.6	1,121.0
2015	1,114.5	1,123.3	1,125.3	1,135.6	1,139.9	1,130.5	1,123.2	1,131.7	1,140.7	1,148.2	1,148.1	1,149.6	1,134.2
Total Private													
2005	879.3	883.7	891.3	896.1	896.5	894.6	892.6	897.9	880.7	885.7	897.6	895.0	890.9
2006	879.6	886.8	897.8	901.8	906.3	907.4	898.8	908.3	911.5	909.0	914.0	916.8	903.2
2007	898.9	901.7	905.2	909.5	912.2	911.9	905.1	913.7	915.8	911.8	917.5	919.8	910.3
2008	902.8	905.8	909.5	912.5	912.9	908.1	895.6	900.7	898.8	893.5	890.6	883.3	901.2
2009	859.4	856.5	855.5	852.9	852.8	848.8	841.3	843.7	843.7	838.4	841.8	840.7	848.0
2010	823.9	826.2	834.4	845.6	849.3	849.8	844.9	847.8	850.6	849.7	850.1	849.7	843.5
2011	833.1	836.5	846.1	851.1	852.1	849.5	841.7	847.0	851.5	849.9	853.1	852.5	847.0
2012	839.8	847.0	854.5	858.5	859.6	856.6	851.3	860.3	860.8	858.6	863.6	865.0	856.3
2013	848.0	856.4	861.4	865.8	867.0	866.6	859.8	868.0	871.2	870.5	877.4	879.4	866.0
2014	864.1	864.4	869.5	876.6	877.6	875.9	870.7	878.5	879.3	881.5	888.6	892.3	876.6
2015	872.2	877.7	878.9	889.5	893.4	889.0	887.2	892.0	895.0	900.0	900.7	904.2	890.0
Goods-Producing													
2005	235.9	235.8	238.0	239.7	240.2	240.7	239.4	239.8	236.0	239.8	241.9	243.7	239.2
2006	239.5	239.5	241.7	242.8	244.6	247.1	244.0	244.0	242.8	242.3	243.0	243.1	242.9
2007	239.0	238.2	235.0	239.3	238.9	238.7	236.5	237.5	238.0	236.5	236.9	237.8	237.7
2008	234.3	233.9	234.1	236.1	236.4	235.1	228.5	227.7	225.7	224.4	221.2	217.1	229.5
2009	209.3	206.5	204.8	202.8	202.8	202.2	199.9	198.6	197.4	194.3	194.3	193.9	200.6
2010	190.1	189.5	192.0	196.5	197.0	196.7	195.8	195.5	194.8	194.6	193.8	193.4	194.1
2011	190.0	190.3	193.4	193.7	195.3	195.4	193.4	193.1	193.9	193.4	192.6	192.5	193.1
2012	191.1	193.0	194.5	195.9	195.9	195.6	194.4	195.3	195.2	195.0	194.5	194.8	194.6
2013	191.5	194.0	194.5	195.8	197.9	198.7	197.4	198.1	199.0	199.7	199.2	198.7	197.0
2014	196.9	196.7	198.7	199.3	200.1	200.4	198.0	197.7	197.1	197.4	196.5	197.0	198.0
2015	193.7	195.0	194.5	196.1	197.1	197.2	197.0	196.1	196.8	198.8	198.2	199.2	196.6
Service-Providing													
2005	883.8	892.1	897.9	901.0	899.8	893.9	885.0	895.6	886.0	887.3	897.8	889.4	892.5
2006	878.0	888.3	897.2	900.0	901.6	897.9	882.2	900.9	912.0	909.8	914.8	914.0	899.7
2007	900.7	908.1	915.0	916.2	918.6	915.2	901.6	917.4	925.0	923.9	929.2	927.5	916.5
2008	914.3	921.3	925.2	927.2	925.9	918.5	902.0	917.2	923.3	921.2	921.9	915.6	919.5
2009	898.6	901.3	902.2	902.7	902.8	895.6	880.7	890.0	898.1	897.0	899.8	896.1	897.1
2010	882.1	888.4	895.9	901.4	907.8	903.9	887.7	894.1	903.6	905.6	905.7	904.6	898.4
2011	888.3	893.7	901.0	906.2	904.9	898.2	885.0	895.7	905.1	905.6	909.1	905.1	899.8
2012	894.1	902.4	909.2	911.4	912.3	904.8	892.2	906.7	912.6	912.5	918.0	915.9	907.7
2013	901.2	910.7	915.6	918.9	917.2	911.3	896.8	910.7	919.5	918.5	925.7	924.4	914.2
2014	910.5	914.2	918.0	925.0	924.3	917.7	907.1	921.0	928.8	931.9	939.0	938.6	923.0
2015	920.8	928.3	930.8	939.5	942.8	933.3	926.2	935.6	943.9	949.4	949.9	950.4	937.6
Mining and Logging													
2005	8.5	8.4	8.6	8.8	8.8	8.8	8.8	8.9	8.8	8.9	8.9	8.9	8.8
2006	8.9	9.0	9.2	9.6	9.6	9.5	9.5	9.7	9.6	9.7	9.8	9.6	9.5
2007	9.2	9.3	9.4	9.6	9.7	9.5	9.5	9.6	9.6	9.5	9.7	9.6	9.5
2008	9.4	9.1	9.2	9.4	9.5	9.5	9.4	9.5	9.5	10.0	10.0	9.8	9.5
2009	9.2	9.0	8.8	8.5	8.4	8.3	8.3	8.2	8.2	8.1	8.1	8.1	8.4
2010	8.1	8.1	8.4	8.8	8.9	8.9	8.9	9.0	9.0	9.0	8.9	8.8	8.7
2011	8.8	8.8	9.0	9.0	9.1	9.1	9.3	9.3	9.2	9.1	9.1	9.0	9.1
2012	9.0	9.1	9.2	9.3	9.3	9.3	9.4	9.4	9.4	9.2	9.3	9.2	9.3
2013	8.9	9.0	9.0	9.1	9.2	9.2	9.3	9.3	9.2	9.1	9.1	9.1	9.1
2014	9.1	8.9	9.0	9.0	9.1	9.3	9.3	9.4	9.4	9.4	9.4	9.3	9.2
2015	8.9	8.7	8.3	8.2	8.2	8.1	7.9	7.9	7.8	7.7	7.5	7.5	8.1

1. Employment by Industry: Mississippi, 2005–2015—*Continued*

(Numbers in thousands, not seasonally adjusted)

Industry and year	January	February	March	April	May	June	July	August	September	October	November	December	Annual average
Construction													
2005	47.4	47.5	49.0	50.5	51.5	52.1	52.3	52.6	54.5	55.6	56.4	57.3	52.2
2006	54.7	54.3	55.6	56.8	58.6	60.7	58.9	59.1	58.9	58.3	58.3	58.3	57.7
2007	56.9	56.6	58.4	58.0	58.2	58.7	58.5	59.0	59.4	59.5	60.2	61.2	58.7
2008	59.7	60.0	61.0	63.5	64.5	63.9	60.8	59.4	59.1	59.3	57.3	55.8	60.4
2009	52.5	52.1	52.1	52.0	53.1	53.9	52.3	51.3	49.8	48.4	48.3	47.4	51.1
2010	45.6	45.7	47.6	50.6	50.8	50.7	50.5	50.7	50.8	50.6	50.3	49.5	49.5
2011	46.9	47.2	49.1	49.3	50.3	50.5	49.3	48.8	49.5	49.1	48.2	47.2	48.8
2012	46.0	47.6	48.8	50.0	49.8	48.9	47.9	48.4	48.7	48.4	47.9	47.6	48.3
2013	46.2	48.6	49.3	50.3	52.2	52.9	52.6	52.5	53.0	53.2	52.0	50.5	51.1
2014	48.8	48.6	50.3	50.9	51.5	51.2	50.1	49.0	48.3	47.7	46.9	46.8	49.2
2015	44.5	45.8	45.8	46.6	46.9	46.5	47.2	46.3	46.6	47.6	47.5	47.5	46.6
Manufacturing													
2005	180.0	179.9	180.4	180.4	179.9	179.8	178.3	178.3	172.7	175.3	176.6	177.5	178.3
2006	175.9	176.2	176.9	176.4	176.4	176.9	175.6	175.2	174.3	174.3	174.9	175.2	175.7
2007	172.9	172.3	167.2	171.7	171.0	170.5	168.5	168.9	169.0	167.5	167.0	167.0	169.5
2008	165.2	164.8	163.9	163.2	162.4	161.7	158.3	158.8	157.1	155.1	153.9	151.5	159.7
2009	147.6	145.4	143.9	142.3	141.3	140.0	139.3	139.1	139.4	137.8	137.9	138.4	141.0
2010	136.4	135.7	136.0	137.1	137.3	137.1	136.4	135.8	135.0	135.0	134.6	135.1	136.0
2011	134.3	134.3	135.3	135.4	135.9	135.8	134.8	135.0	135.2	135.2	135.3	136.3	135.2
2012	136.1	136.3	136.5	136.6	136.8	137.4	137.1	137.5	137.1	137.4	137.3	138.0	137.0
2013	136.4	136.4	136.2	136.4	136.5	136.6	135.5	136.3	136.8	137.4	138.1	139.1	136.8
2014	139.0	139.2	139.4	139.4	139.5	139.9	138.6	139.3	139.4	140.3	140.2	140.9	139.6
2015	140.3	140.5	140.4	141.3	142.0	142.6	141.9	141.9	142.4	143.5	143.2	144.2	142.0
Trade, Transportation, and Utilities													
2005	218.1	217.3	219.4	220.1	220.3	220.5	220.8	222.4	217.1	218.3	224.0	228.2	220.5
2006	221.3	221.5	224.7	224.7	225.8	226.1	224.8	226.1	226.2	225.7	228.7	231.8	225.6
2007	224.2	223.3	226.1	225.7	227.2	227.7	225.6	226.7	227.0	226.9	230.6	232.4	227.0
2008	225.1	224.4	226.1	224.5	224.4	224.0	222.9	224.2	223.2	221.7	224.1	225.3	224.2
2009	216.9	215.3	214.8	213.9	214.7	214.6	213.5	213.2	213.7	213.4	216.2	217.0	214.8
2010	210.3	209.6	211.3	212.9	213.8	213.5	212.7	213.3	212.8	214.3	217.3	219.8	213.5
2011	212.5	212.2	214.2	215.1	215.3	214.6	213.8	214.6	214.2	214.4	218.5	220.7	215.0
2012	213.9	213.3	214.2	214.8	215.8	215.5	215.1	215.5	215.1	214.7	219.1	220.9	215.7
2013	213.2	212.5	213.3	214.1	215.0	216.0	216.0	217.1	217.0	217.1	222.8	225.3	216.6
2014	217.2	216.7	217.5	218.2	218.7	219.6	219.5	220.6	219.9	221.7	227.1	229.8	220.5
2015	221.5	221.0	221.2	223.8	224.8	225.0	223.9	224.7	224.6	226.2	230.0	232.7	225.0
Wholesale Trade													
2005	34.6	34.7	34.9	35.2	35.4	35.5	35.6	35.9	35.3	35.2	35.3	35.8	35.3
2006	35.7	35.9	36.1	35.9	36.2	36.5	36.4	37.0	36.7	36.6	36.6	37.1	36.4
2007	36.6	36.6	36.6	36.6	36.7	36.8	36.8	37.2	37.0	36.7	36.5	37.2	36.8
2008	36.8	36.7	36.6	36.5	36.5	36.6	36.3	36.4	36.0	36.1	35.7	36.0	36.4
2009	35.5	35.4	35.1	34.8	34.7	34.7	34.6	34.7	34.4	34.3	34.1	34.5	34.7
2010	34.0	34.0	33.9	34.2	34.2	34.3	34.2	34.6	34.2	34.3	34.1	34.7	34.2
2011	34.2	34.3	34.2	34.2	34.3	34.1	34.2	34.6	34.5	34.2	34.2	34.7	34.3
2012	34.5	34.6	34.3	34.1	34.2	34.3	34.2	34.5	34.3	33.9	33.9	34.2	34.3
2013	34.3	34.2	34.0	33.9	34.1	34.1	33.9	34.3	34.2	33.8	33.8	34.3	34.1
2014	34.0	34.2	33.8	33.9	33.9	34.0	34.0	34.4	34.1	34.0	34.0	34.6	34.1
2015	34.5	34.5	34.1	34.3	34.6	34.6	34.4	34.7	34.6	34.7	34.1	34.3	34.5
Retail Trade													
2005	137.0	136.1	137.4	137.8	137.8	137.9	138.1	138.9	134.8	136.4	141.7	144.9	138.2
2006	139.1	138.8	141.5	141.5	142.0	142.0	141.2	141.4	141.3	141.0	143.9	145.9	141.6
2007	139.9	139.2	141.5	141.0	142.0	142.5	140.5	140.7	141.0	141.2	144.8	146.1	141.7
2008	140.2	139.5	141.2	140.0	139.7	139.1	138.3	138.7	138.1	137.0	139.6	140.8	139.4
2009	133.8	132.6	132.8	132.7	133.5	133.6	132.6	131.7	132.3	132.2	135.1	135.7	133.2
2010	130.3	129.7	131.3	132.1	133.0	132.6	131.9	131.7	131.2	132.2	135.4	136.9	132.4
2011	131.2	130.8	132.4	133.4	133.5	133.1	132.4	132.3	131.7	132.4	136.3	137.7	133.1
2012	132.4	131.7	132.6	133.3	133.8	133.5	133.2	132.7	132.1	132.6	136.8	137.7	133.5
2013	130.8	130.2	131.1	131.8	132.3	133.3	133.6	133.7	133.6	133.7	138.8	140.3	133.6
2014	133.7	133.3	134.4	134.8	134.9	135.6	135.3	135.4	134.9	135.8	140.4	142.0	135.9
2015	135.5	135.3	135.7	137.5	138.0	138.2	137.5	137.5	137.2	138.1	142.4	143.9	138.1

1. Employment by Industry: Mississippi, 2005–2015—*Continued*

(Numbers in thousands, not seasonally adjusted)

Industry and year	January	February	March	April	May	June	July	August	September	October	November	December	Annual average
Transportation and Utilities													
2005	46.5	46.5	47.1	47.1	47.1	47.1	47.1	47.6	47.0	46.7	47.0	47.5	47.0
2006	46.5	46.8	47.1	47.3	47.6	47.6	47.2	47.7	48.2	48.1	48.2	48.8	47.6
2007	47.7	47.5	48.0	48.1	48.5	48.4	48.3	48.8	49.0	49.0	49.3	49.1	48.5
2008	48.1	48.2	48.3	48.0	48.2	48.3	48.3	49.1	49.1	48.6	48.8	48.5	48.5
2009	47.6	47.3	46.9	46.4	46.5	46.3	46.3	46.8	47.0	46.9	47.0	46.8	46.8
2010	46.0	45.9	46.1	46.6	46.6	46.6	46.6	47.0	47.4	47.8	47.8	48.2	46.9
2011	47.1	47.1	47.6	47.5	47.5	47.4	47.2	47.7	48.0	47.8	48.0	48.3	47.6
2012	47.0	47.0	47.3	47.4	47.8	47.7	47.7	48.3	48.7	48.2	48.4	49.0	47.9
2013	48.1	48.1	48.2	48.4	48.6	48.6	48.5	49.1	49.2	49.6	50.2	50.7	48.9
2014	49.5	49.2	49.3	49.5	49.9	50.0	50.2	50.8	50.9	51.9	52.7	53.2	50.6
2015	51.5	51.2	51.4	52.0	52.2	52.2	52.0	52.5	52.8	53.4	53.5	54.5	52.4
Information													
2005	14.5	14.5	14.5	14.4	14.4	14.6	14.3	14.3	14.0	14.0	14.0	14.1	14.3
2006	14.0	13.9	13.9	13.8	13.8	13.9	13.7	13.6	13.4	13.3	13.3	13.4	13.7
2007	13.2	13.3	13.3	13.3	13.3	13.5	13.6	13.5	13.4	13.3	13.5	13.5	13.4
2008	13.4	13.5	13.5	13.5	13.5	13.6	13.6	13.5	13.4	13.2	13.4	13.4	13.5
2009	13.3	13.2	13.1	13.0	12.9	12.9	12.6	12.6	12.6	12.4	12.4	12.3	12.8
2010	12.2	12.2	12.3	12.1	12.2	12.3	12.3	12.3	12.6	12.7	12.3	12.2	12.3
2011	12.0	12.0	12.0	11.9	12.0	12.1	12.1	12.1	12.1	12.1	12.2	12.4	12.1
2012	12.5	12.5	12.5	12.5	12.5	12.5	12.6	12.4	12.4	12.4	12.7	12.7	12.5
2013	12.8	12.8	12.7	12.7	12.6	12.8	12.7	12.7	12.8	12.8	12.9	13.2	12.8
2014	13.8	13.0	13.0	12.8	12.7	12.9	13.0	13.2	13.3	13.5	13.8	13.8	13.2
2015	13.4	13.4	13.4	13.3	13.6	13.6	13.6	13.5	13.6	13.5	13.4	13.4	13.5
Financial Activities													
2005	45.4	45.4	45.6	45.5	45.7	45.8	46.2	46.1	45.3	46.1	46.3	46.4	45.8
2006	45.1	45.8	45.8	45.7	45.8	46.2	46.3	46.3	46.2	46.0	46.3	46.6	46.0
2007	46.0	46.2	46.3	46.4	46.6	46.8	46.6	46.8	46.5	46.7	46.7	46.9	46.5
2008	46.5	46.5	46.7	46.5	46.6	46.6	46.5	46.4	46.2	46.5	46.3	46.5	46.5
2009	46.0	45.7	45.6	45.4	45.6	45.4	45.0	45.0	44.9	44.8	44.8	45.0	45.3
2010	44.5	44.4	44.5	44.5	44.7	44.8	44.7	44.5	44.4	44.2	44.2	44.4	44.5
2011	43.9	44.0	44.0	44.3	44.1	44.4	44.2	44.3	44.2	44.1	44.2	44.2	44.2
2012	43.9	43.9	44.0	44.1	44.3	44.3	44.3	44.4	44.2	43.9	44.0	44.0	44.1
2013	43.6	43.8	43.9	43.9	43.8	43.9	43.7	43.8	43.6	43.8	43.9	43.9	43.8
2014	43.2	43.3	43.2	43.1	43.5	43.5	43.4	43.6	43.4	43.4	43.7	43.7	43.4
2015	43.3	43.3	43.3	43.5	43.7	43.9	43.9	43.7	43.6	43.6	43.5	43.4	43.6
Professional and Business Services													
2005	84.6	86.7	87.0	87.1	85.7	85.8	86.2	87.1	87.5	89.9	91.6	91.3	87.5
2006	90.1	92.0	93.7	94.2	94.4	93.6	91.5	92.8	92.7	92.0	92.8	92.5	92.7
2007	91.0	92.3	93.4	92.4	92.2	92.3	91.9	93.2	93.9	94.0	95.0	95.8	93.1
2008	94.5	95.4	95.5	96.3	96.1	95.7	94.1	94.6	95.2	94.6	94.1	92.2	94.9
2009	89.8	89.5	89.0	87.8	87.0	86.7	85.3	86.2	85.9	86.3	87.0	87.3	87.3
2010	85.7	87.3	87.9	90.2	92.4	95.8	95.3	93.7	95.1	94.2	93.6	93.6	92.1
2011	91.9	92.8	94.2	94.9	94.4	93.8	91.8	92.9	94.0	94.2	94.5	93.5	93.6
2012	91.9	94.3	96.3	96.3	96.5	95.8	93.9	97.2	97.7	98.1	99.0	99.1	96.3
2013	97.0	100.0	100.7	100.1	99.3	98.4	95.6	98.9	98.2	98.3	99.5	101.1	98.9
2014	99.6	99.4	99.2	101.3	100.3	99.5	98.7	101.9	102.4	103.0	104.8	106.2	101.4
2015	102.2	103.4	103.2	104.7	104.4	102.6	103.4	106.0	106.0	107.0	105.9	106.9	104.6
Education and Health Services													
2005	119.2	120.3	120.6	120.9	120.3	116.5	116.1	118.6	120.5	120.7	120.8	120.7	119.6
2006	119.8	121.2	122.1	122.3	122.3	118.2	117.9	121.2	124.8	125.1	125.6	125.1	122.1
2007	124.4	125.5	126.2	126.2	126.2	123.1	122.0	126.2	128.3	128.6	128.4	127.5	126.1
2008	125.9	127.0	126.9	126.9	125.7	123.2	122.2	125.8	128.4	129.2	128.9	128.1	126.5
2009	127.0	127.7	127.9	128.3	127.3	124.4	124.6	127.7	130.5	131.3	131.5	130.7	128.2
2010	129.6	130.3	130.7	131.1	130.0	126.8	125.9	129.1	132.7	133.6	133.6	132.4	130.5
2011	131.7	132.5	132.7	133.0	131.3	128.9	127.6	130.2	134.5	134.9	134.6	133.6	132.1
2012	132.7	134.1	134.4	134.2	132.2	129.7	129.0	132.0	134.5	135.4	135.3	134.5	133.2
2013	133.4	134.7	135.0	135.7	133.6	130.4	129.3	131.6	135.7	136.1	136.2	135.1	133.9
2014	133.7	134.5	134.6	135.5	134.2	131.3	131.7	135.0	137.3	137.7	138.3	137.6	135.1
2015	136.7	137.8	138.0	138.6	138.6	134.8	134.5	136.5	139.5	140.3	140.6	140.4	138.0

1. Employment by Industry: Mississippi, 2005–2015—*Continued*

(Numbers in thousands, not seasonally adjusted)

Industry and year	January	February	March	April	May	June	July	August	September	October	November	December	Annual average
Leisure and Hospitality													
2005	120.9	122.4	125.0	126.9	128.4	129.2	128.5	128.6	120.1	116.8	118.8	110.4	123.0
2006	109.8	112.2	115.2	117.6	118.9	121.1	119.7	123.5	124.8	124.3	124.1	124.1	119.6
2007	120.6	122.1	123.8	125.4	126.9	128.6	127.9	128.9	127.8	125.3	125.8	125.3	125.7
2008	122.6	124.2	125.5	127.5	128.7	128.6	126.9	127.7	125.8	123.4	122.6	121.0	125.4
2009	118.0	119.6	121.2	122.4	123.3	123.3	121.3	121.6	119.9	117.5	117.3	116.3	120.1
2010	113.4	114.8	117.3	119.5	120.4	121.2	119.7	121.0	119.7	117.8	117.4	116.2	118.2
2011	113.8	115.4	118.1	120.6	121.8	122.2	121.0	122.2	121.0	119.1	118.9	118.1	119.4
2012	116.3	118.4	120.8	122.7	124.2	124.7	123.5	124.9	123.1	120.8	120.6	120.5	121.7
2013	118.2	120.0	122.5	124.7	125.9	127.0	126.1	126.9	126.0	123.9	124.1	123.4	124.1
2014	121.2	122.2	124.5	127.6	129.1	129.2	127.2	127.2	126.8	125.8	125.1	124.8	125.9
2015	122.2	124.3	125.7	129.7	131.3	131.8	130.9	131.7	131.1	130.9	129.2	127.7	128.9
Other Services													
2005	40.7	41.3	41.2	41.5	41.5	41.5	41.1	41.0	40.2	40.1	40.2	40.2	40.9
2006	40.0	40.7	40.7	40.7	40.7	41.2	40.9	40.8	40.6	40.3	40.2	40.2	40.6
2007	40.5	40.8	41.1	40.8	40.9	41.2	41.0	40.9	40.9	40.5	40.6	40.6	40.8
2008	40.5	40.9	41.2	41.2	41.5	41.3	40.9	40.8	40.9	40.5	40.0	39.7	40.8
2009	39.1	39.0	39.1	39.3	39.2	39.3	39.1	38.8	38.8	38.4	38.3	38.2	38.9
2010	38.1	38.1	38.4	38.8	38.8	38.7	38.5	38.4	38.5	38.3	37.9	37.7	38.4
2011	37.3	37.3	37.5	37.6	37.9	38.1	37.8	37.6	37.6	37.7	37.6	37.5	37.6
2012	37.5	37.5	37.8	38.0	38.2	38.5	38.5	38.6	38.6	38.3	38.4	38.5	38.2
2013	38.3	38.6	38.8	38.8	38.9	39.4	39.0	38.9	38.9	38.8	38.8	38.7	38.8
2014	38.5	38.6	38.8	38.8	39.0	39.5	39.2	39.3	39.1	39.0	39.3	39.4	39.0
2015	39.2	39.5	39.6	39.8	39.9	40.1	40.0	39.8	39.8	39.7	39.9	40.5	39.8
Government													
2005	240.4	244.2	244.6	244.6	243.5	240.0	231.8	237.5	241.3	241.4	242.1	238.1	240.8
2006	237.9	241.0	241.1	241.0	239.9	237.6	227.4	236.6	243.3	243.1	243.8	240.3	239.4
2007	240.8	244.6	244.8	246.0	245.3	242.0	233.0	241.2	247.2	248.6	248.6	245.5	244.0
2008	245.8	249.4	249.8	250.8	249.4	245.5	234.9	244.2	250.2	252.1	252.5	249.4	247.8
2009	248.5	251.3	251.5	252.6	252.8	249.0	239.3	244.9	251.8	252.9	252.3	249.3	249.7
2010	248.3	251.7	253.5	252.3	255.5	250.8	238.6	241.8	247.8	250.5	249.4	248.3	249.0
2011	245.2	247.5	248.3	248.8	248.1	244.1	236.7	241.8	247.5	249.1	248.6	245.1	245.9
2012	245.4	248.4	249.2	248.8	248.6	243.8	235.3	241.7	247.0	248.9	248.9	245.7	246.0
2013	244.7	248.3	248.7	248.9	248.1	243.4	234.4	240.8	247.3	247.7	247.5	243.7	245.3
2014	243.3	246.5	247.2	247.7	246.8	242.2	234.4	240.2	246.6	247.8	246.9	243.3	244.4
2015	242.3	245.6	246.4	246.1	246.5	241.5	236.0	239.7	245.7	248.2	247.4	245.4	244.2

2. Average Weekly Hours by Selected Industry: Mississippi, 2011–2015

(Not seasonally adjusted)

Industry and year	January	February	March	April	May	June	July	August	September	October	November	December	Annual average
Total Private													
2011	35.5	35.5	35.7	36.1	36.6	36.0	36.2	36.1	36.0	36.3	35.7	35.9	36.0
2012	35.7	35.6	35.5	36.0	35.2	35.4	35.6	35.5	36.0	35.5	35.3	36.0	35.6
2013	35.0	35.2	35.4	34.9	34.7	35.5	35.1	35.5	36.2	35.7	35.6	36.1	35.4
2014	35.5	35.6	36.0	35.5	35.5	36.1	35.7	35.9	36.0	35.7	36.0	35.6	35.8
2015	35.0	35.3	35.3	34.4	34.6	34.7	34.7	35.1	34.2	34.7	35.1	34.7	34.8
Goods-Producing													
2011	39.0	39.2	39.9	40.5	41.0	40.5	40.7	41.3	41.3	41.4	40.6	41.4	40.6
2012	40.1	40.7	40.8	41.2	40.5	40.6	40.8	41.2	42.0	41.3	41.2	42.3	41.1
2013	40.7	40.4	41.6	41.1	40.3	41.4	41.0	42.0	43.1	42.2	42.2	43.3	41.6
2014	42.5	41.3	42.0	41.8	41.3	42.1	41.7	42.4	43.1	42.7	42.5	42.3	42.1
2015	41.1	40.9	41.0	39.6	40.4	40.5	40.1	41.1	39.7	41.1	41.7	41.8	40.7
Construction													
2011	38.7	39.1	39.4	40.8	41.5	41.2	41.2	41.2	39.5	39.3	37.9	38.5	39.9
2012	37.0	39.7	39.6	40.4	39.5	39.7	39.4	42.1	42.3	42.2	40.7	40.0	40.2
2013	37.4	38.3	41.5	40.6	40.1	41.2	41.0	41.3	44.6	44.9	43.2	41.1	41.3
2014	40.2	38.9	42.2	41.0	42.2	42.2	43.5	44.0	44.3	43.8	44.3	43.7	42.5
2015	40.8	40.7	40.6	36.1	38.5	37.6	38.2	38.6	36.5	40.0	40.1	40.5	39.0
Manufacturing													
2011	39.1	39.2	40.0	40.4	40.9	40.2	40.5	41.1	41.5	41.6	41.1	42.0	40.6
2012	40.8	40.4	40.6	40.9	40.2	40.4	40.8	40.5	41.6	40.5	41.0	42.6	40.9
2013	41.2	40.7	41.1	40.6	40.0	41.1	40.7	41.9	42.3	41.0	41.5	43.6	41.3
2014	42.8	41.9	42.7	42.9	41.7	42.5	41.4	42.1	42.9	42.5	42.0	42.1	42.3
2015	41.6	41.3	41.7	41.7	41.8	42.3	41.5	42.7	41.4	42.2	42.9	42.9	42.0
Trade, Transportation, and Utilities													
2011	35.8	35.9	35.7	36.4	37.0	36.5	36.4	36.3	36.4	36.3	36.1	36.3	36.3
2012	36.0	35.9	35.9	36.3	35.6	35.8	35.8	35.8	35.9	35.7	35.4	36.0	35.8
2013	34.9	35.5	35.9	35.1	35.6	36.2	36.0	36.0	36.6	35.8	35.3	35.8	35.7
2014	35.3	35.9	36.2	35.6	35.8	36.2	36.1	35.7	35.8	35.1	35.3	35.0	35.7
2015	34.3	35.1	35.2	34.5	34.9	34.7	34.6	34.7	34.2	33.9	34.1	33.7	34.5
Financial Activities													
2011	37.4	37.2	37.2	37.0	38.8	37.4	38.0	37.4	37.4	38.8	37.0	37.2	37.6
2012	39.5	37.9	38.0	39.5	37.4	37.5	40.0	38.7	40.7	38.6	37.9	40.3	38.8
2013	38.2	38.4	37.6	37.5	37.1	40.3	37.5	37.4	40.2	37.2	37.4	39.6	38.2
2014	37.8	39.2	39.2	38.3	38.1	40.0	38.5	38.6	38.2	37.3	39.2	37.4	38.5
2015	37.6	38.9	39.2	36.3	36.4	36.6	36.7	39.1	36.7	37.4	39.1	36.7	37.6
Professional and Business Services													
2011	35.0	34.7	35.8	36.2	36.5	35.9	35.8	36.1	35.1	36.3	35.2	35.5	35.7
2012	35.1	34.7	34.3	35.3	33.9	34.1	33.5	33.9	34.4	34.4	34.2	35.0	34.4
2013	34.0	34.9	35.0	33.4	33.3	34.0	33.3	34.5	34.7	34.5	35.0	35.1	34.3
2014	34.6	34.9	35.3	34.5	35.0	35.6	34.8	35.7	35.7	35.5	36.0	35.6	35.3
2015	35.1	36.3	36.2	35.3	35.4	35.6	35.6	36.7	35.1	36.1	36.1	35.8	35.8
Education and Health Services													
2011	34.3	33.5	33.2	33.8	34.2	33.7	34.0	33.8	33.8	33.9	33.8	33.5	33.8
2012	34.2	33.4	33.2	33.9	33.5	33.3	34.1	33.6	34.1	33.3	33.3	33.5	33.6
2013	33.3	33.5	32.9	33.2	33.0	33.3	33.0	33.0	33.7	33.5	33.5	33.4	33.3
2014	33.5	33.4	33.3	33.1	33.2	33.7	33.5	33.8	33.7	33.6	34.3	33.8	33.6
2015	33.7	33.9	33.5	33.6	33.3	33.1	33.4	34.1	33.6	33.7	34.0	33.5	33.6
Leisure and Hospitality													
2011	29.0	29.4	29.3	28.8	28.8	28.9	29.1	28.5	28.0	28.7	28.1	27.5	28.7
2012	27.1	27.9	28.3	28.1	27.6	27.9	28.3	27.6	27.9	27.9	27.7	28.4	27.9
2013	27.3	27.5	27.5	27.5	27.4	28.1	28.1	27.7	27.4	27.6	27.3	27.5	27.6
2014	27.0	27.5	28.3	27.5	27.6	27.6	27.5	27.4	26.9	27.3	27.1	27.3	27.4
2015	26.7	28.0	28.2	26.7	26.8	27.3	27.7	26.2	25.8	26.1	26.3	26.1	26.8

3. Average Hourly Earnings by Selected Industry: Mississippi, 2011–2015

(Dollars, not seasonally adjusted)

Industry and year	January	February	March	April	May	June	July	August	September	October	November	December	Annual average
Total Private													
2011	18.31	18.19	18.12	18.06	18.06	17.94	17.91	17.98	18.07	18.36	18.14	18.43	18.13
2012	18.33	18.75	18.80	18.86	18.63	18.67	18.89	18.80	19.12	18.90	19.03	19.20	18.83
2013	19.16	19.42	19.29	19.36	19.24	19.27	19.26	19.41	19.68	19.69	19.62	19.73	19.43
2014	19.65	19.75	19.57	19.44	19.13	19.37	19.36	19.36	19.31	19.27	19.29	19.22	19.39
2015	19.31	19.76	19.90	19.79	19.57	19.55	19.64	19.79	19.77	19.70	19.90	19.87	19.71
Goods-Producing													
2011	18.26	18.18	18.39	18.46	18.39	18.27	18.38	18.42	18.38	18.32	18.38	19.24	18.42
2012	19.41	20.55	20.97	21.00	20.73	20.52	20.68	20.67	20.86	20.53	20.62	20.82	20.62
2013	20.40	20.48	20.35	20.16	20.04	20.08	20.12	20.30	20.68	21.02	20.63	20.47	20.40
2014	20.48	20.77	20.37	20.11	19.95	20.26	20.56	20.73	20.81	20.54	20.18	20.22	20.42
2015	20.14	20.41	20.84	20.87	20.65	20.68	20.83	20.77	20.75	20.79	21.08	21.41	20.77
Construction													
2011	18.88	18.83	19.30	19.21	19.31	18.79	18.80	19.11	18.70	18.68	18.64	20.25	19.04
2012	20.53	22.00	22.81	22.42	22.41	22.05	22.00	21.41	21.22	21.30	21.12	21.16	21.71
2013	20.90	21.24	21.04	21.14	20.76	20.53	20.27	20.40	20.98	21.32	21.05	21.07	20.89
2014	21.09	21.74	21.30	20.95	20.75	20.88	21.46	21.61	21.63	21.69	21.60	21.93	21.38
2015	21.63	21.42	22.27	22.19	21.72	22.45	22.12	22.08	21.95	21.89	22.13	22.47	22.03
Manufacturing													
2011	17.37	17.38	17.51	17.66	17.53	17.59	17.74	17.75	17.90	17.82	17.95	17.96	17.68
2012	18.06	19.23	19.07	19.24	19.02	18.95	19.28	19.51	19.91	19.55	19.69	20.12	19.31
2013	19.66	19.69	19.59	19.39	19.37	19.52	19.66	19.95	20.29	20.68	20.27	20.06	19.85
2014	20.06	20.23	19.91	19.63	19.54	19.87	20.04	20.30	20.40	19.97	19.53	19.48	19.91
2015	19.48	19.91	20.14	20.23	20.16	19.90	20.23	20.17	20.22	20.34	20.70	21.04	20.22
Trade, Transportation, and Utilities													
2011	16.15	16.28	16.12	16.37	16.35	16.02	15.94	16.18	16.33	16.53	16.19	16.30	16.23
2012	15.54	15.80	15.80	16.10	16.13	16.17	16.21	16.15	16.45	16.35	16.43	16.69	16.15
2013	17.18	17.45	17.47	17.80	17.65	17.68	17.83	17.77	17.87	17.94	18.04	18.44	17.77
2014	18.86	18.60	18.52	18.68	18.35	18.77	18.61	18.67	18.43	18.55	18.47	18.27	18.56
2015	18.20	18.38	18.38	18.38	17.80	18.00	18.22	18.42	18.39	18.47	18.33	18.03	18.25
Financial Activities													
2011	20.30	20.23	20.31	20.40	20.61	20.40	20.28	20.26	20.46	20.89	20.53	20.72	20.45
2012	20.66	20.79	21.29	22.04	21.74	22.37	22.31	22.30	22.98	22.67	23.66	23.06	22.16
2013	22.84	23.54	23.48	23.25	25.05	24.18	24.06	24.97	25.20	24.93	25.63	24.85	24.33
2014	24.18	24.99	25.07	24.20	23.97	23.68	23.34	23.22	22.95	23.24	24.14	23.43	23.87
2015	23.51	25.13	25.02	24.54	24.43	24.83	24.83	25.03	25.31	25.21	26.29	26.40	25.05
Professional and Business Services													
2011	19.58	19.52	19.42	18.96	19.47	19.56	19.77	19.62	19.70	20.12	19.61	19.95	19.61
2012	19.71	20.64	20.39	20.56	20.34	20.44	21.16	20.68	21.02	20.93	20.97	21.02	20.66
2013	20.92	21.49	21.44	22.34	22.08	22.19	22.19	21.81	22.37	22.06	22.00	22.49	21.95
2014	21.81	22.09	22.12	21.99	21.79	21.92	21.84	21.60	21.30	21.35	21.86	21.70	21.78
2015	21.78	22.61	22.73	22.30	22.12	21.56	21.55	21.82	21.74	21.39	21.60	20.84	21.83
Education and Health Services													
2011	19.44	19.33	19.22	19.21	19.00	19.33	19.18	19.17	19.26	19.59	19.34	19.33	19.28
2012	19.36	19.53	19.51	19.62	19.37	19.68	19.79	19.58	19.54	19.57	19.65	19.31	19.54
2013	19.65	19.88	19.87	20.09	19.74	20.02	20.02	20.21	20.14	20.14	19.82	19.90	19.96
2014	19.82	19.75	19.72	19.77	19.44	19.50	19.52	19.49	19.58	19.57	19.37	19.57	19.59
2015	19.95	20.13	20.24	20.41	20.38	20.45	20.75	20.80	20.86	20.78	20.74	21.02	20.54
Leisure and Hospitality													
2011	12.39	12.42	12.27	12.27	12.31	12.19	12.22	12.36	12.37	12.47	12.47	12.48	12.35
2012	12.60	12.69	12.43	12.35	12.21	12.22	12.17	12.12	12.24	12.25	12.32	12.38	12.33
2013	12.48	12.62	12.29	12.04	11.96	11.89	11.95	12.13	12.07	12.07	12.06	12.15	12.14
2014	12.17	12.24	11.98	11.81	11.76	11.78	11.80	11.86	11.73	11.85	11.80	11.80	11.88
2015	11.99	11.98	12.05	11.76	11.79	11.71	11.79	11.75	11.80	11.58	11.70	11.67	11.80

4. Average Weekly Earnings by Selected Industry: Mississippi, 2011–2015

(Dollars, not seasonally adjusted)

Industry and year	January	February	March	April	May	June	July	August	September	October	November	December	Annual average
Total Private													
2011	650.01	645.75	646.88	651.97	661.00	645.84	648.34	649.08	650.52	666.47	647.60	661.64	652.68
2012	654.38	667.50	667.40	678.96	655.78	660.92	672.48	667.40	688.32	670.95	671.76	691.20	670.35
2013	670.60	683.58	682.87	675.66	667.63	684.09	676.03	689.06	712.42	702.93	698.47	712.25	687.82
2014	697.58	703.10	704.52	690.12	679.12	699.26	691.15	695.02	695.16	687.94	694.44	684.23	694.16
2015	675.85	697.53	702.47	680.78	677.12	678.39	681.51	694.63	676.13	683.59	698.49	689.49	685.91
Goods-Producing													
2011	712.14	712.66	733.76	747.63	753.99	739.94	748.07	760.75	759.09	758.45	746.23	796.54	747.85
2012	778.34	836.39	855.58	865.20	839.57	833.11	843.74	851.60	876.12	847.89	849.54	880.69	847.48
2013	830.28	827.39	846.56	828.58	807.61	831.31	824.92	852.60	891.31	887.04	870.59	886.35	848.64
2014	870.40	857.80	855.54	840.60	823.94	852.95	857.35	878.95	896.91	877.06	857.65	855.31	859.68
2015	827.75	834.77	854.44	826.45	834.26	837.54	835.28	853.65	823.78	854.47	879.04	894.94	845.34
Construction													
2011	730.66	736.25	760.42	783.77	801.37	774.15	774.56	787.33	738.65	734.12	706.46	779.63	759.70
2012	759.61	873.40	903.28	905.77	885.20	875.39	866.80	901.36	897.61	898.86	859.58	846.40	872.74
2013	781.66	813.49	873.16	858.28	832.48	845.84	831.07	842.52	935.71	957.27	909.36	865.98	862.76
2014	847.82	845.69	898.86	858.95	875.65	881.14	933.51	950.84	958.21	950.02	956.88	958.34	908.65
2015	882.50	871.79	904.16	801.06	836.22	844.12	844.98	852.29	801.18	875.60	887.41	910.04	859.17
Manufacturing													
2011	679.17	681.30	700.40	713.46	716.98	707.12	718.47	729.53	742.85	741.31	737.75	754.32	717.81
2012	736.85	776.89	774.24	786.92	764.60	765.58	786.62	790.16	828.26	791.78	807.29	857.11	789.78
2013	809.99	801.38	805.15	787.23	774.80	802.27	800.16	835.91	858.27	847.88	841.21	874.62	819.81
2014	858.57	847.64	850.16	842.13	814.82	844.48	829.66	854.63	875.16	848.73	820.26	820.11	842.19
2015	810.37	822.28	839.84	843.59	842.69	841.77	839.55	861.26	837.11	858.35	888.03	902.62	849.24
Trade, Transportation, and Utilities													
2011	578.17	584.45	575.48	595.87	604.95	584.73	580.22	587.33	594.41	600.04	584.46	591.69	589.15
2012	559.44	567.22	567.22	584.43	574.23	578.89	580.32	578.17	590.56	583.70	581.62	600.84	578.17
2013	599.58	619.48	627.17	624.78	628.34	640.02	641.88	639.72	654.04	642.25	636.81	660.15	634.39
2014	665.76	667.74	670.42	665.01	656.93	679.47	671.82	666.52	659.79	651.11	651.99	639.45	662.59
2015	624.26	645.14	646.98	634.11	621.22	624.60	630.41	639.17	628.94	626.13	625.05	607.61	629.63
Financial Activities													
2011	759.22	752.56	755.53	754.80	799.67	762.96	770.64	757.72	765.20	810.53	759.61	770.78	768.92
2012	816.07	787.94	809.02	870.58	813.08	838.88	892.40	863.01	935.29	875.06	896.71	929.32	859.81
2013	872.49	903.94	882.85	871.88	929.36	974.45	902.25	933.88	1013.04	927.40	958.56	984.06	929.41
2014	914.00	979.61	982.74	926.86	913.26	947.20	898.59	896.29	876.69	866.85	946.29	876.28	919.00
2015	883.98	977.56	980.78	890.80	889.25	908.78	911.26	978.67	928.88	942.85	1027.94	968.88	941.88
Professional and Business Services													
2011	685.30	677.34	695.24	686.35	710.66	702.20	707.77	708.28	691.47	730.36	690.27	708.23	700.08
2012	691.82	716.21	699.38	725.77	689.53	697.00	708.86	701.05	723.09	719.99	717.17	735.70	710.70
2013	711.28	750.00	750.40	746.16	735.26	754.46	738.93	752.45	776.24	761.07	770.00	789.40	752.89
2014	754.63	770.94	780.84	758.66	762.65	780.35	760.03	771.12	760.41	757.93	786.96	772.52	768.83
2015	764.48	820.74	822.83	787.19	783.05	767.54	767.18	800.79	763.07	772.18	779.76	746.07	781.51
Education and Health Services													
2011	666.79	647.56	638.10	649.30	649.80	651.42	652.12	647.95	650.99	664.10	653.69	647.56	651.66
2012	662.11	652.30	647.73	665.12	648.90	655.34	674.84	657.89	666.31	651.68	654.35	646.89	656.54
2013	654.35	665.98	653.72	666.99	651.42	666.67	660.66	666.93	678.72	674.69	663.97	664.66	664.67
2014	663.97	659.65	656.68	654.39	645.41	657.15	653.92	658.76	659.85	657.55	664.39	661.47	658.22
2015	672.32	682.41	678.04	685.78	678.65	676.90	693.05	709.28	700.90	700.29	705.16	704.17	690.14
Leisure and Hospitality													
2011	359.31	365.15	359.51	353.38	354.53	352.29	355.60	352.26	346.36	357.89	350.41	343.20	354.45
2012	341.46	354.05	351.77	347.04	337.00	340.94	344.41	334.51	341.50	341.78	341.26	351.59	344.01
2013	340.70	347.05	337.98	331.10	327.70	334.11	335.80	336.00	330.72	333.13	329.24	334.13	335.06
2014	328.59	336.60	339.03	324.78	324.58	325.13	324.50	324.96	315.54	323.51	319.78	322.14	325.51
2015	320.13	335.44	339.81	313.99	315.97	319.68	326.58	307.85	304.44	302.24	307.71	304.59	316.24

MISSOURI
At a Glance

Population:
  2005 Population: 5,790,300
  2010 census: 5,988,927
  2015 estimate: 6,083,672

Percent change in population:
  2005–2015: 5.1%
  2010–2015: 1.6%

Percent change in total nonfarm employment:
  2005–2015: 1.7%

Industry with the largest growth in employment, 2005–2015 (thousands):
  Education and health services, 76.7

Industry with the largest decline or smallest growth in employment, 2005–2015 (thousands):
  Manufacturing, –50.8

Civilian labor force:
  2005: 3,009,334
  2010: 3,056,484
  2015: 3,113,760

Unemployment rate and rank among states (highest to lowest):
  2005: 5.4%, 14th
  2010: 9.6%, 19th
  2015: 5.0%, 28th

Over-the-year change in unemployment rates:
  2012–2013: –0.3%
  2013–2014: –0.5%
  2014–2015: –1.2%

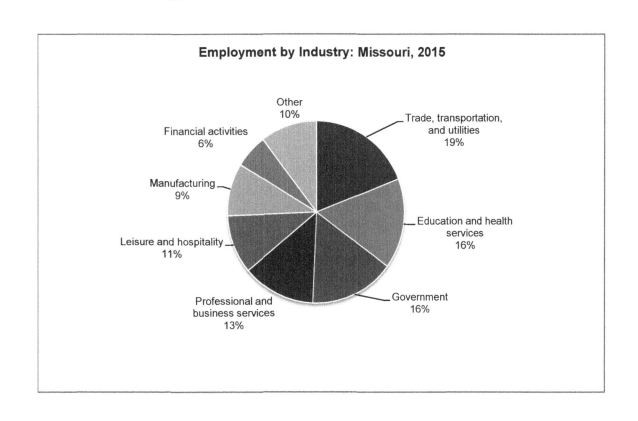

Employment by Industry: Missouri, 2015

Other 10%
Financial activities 6%
Manufacturing 9%
Leisure and hospitality 11%
Professional and business services 13%
Government 16%
Education and health services 16%
Trade, transportation, and utilities 19%

1. Employment by Industry: Missouri, 2005–2015

(Numbers in thousands, not seasonally adjusted)

Industry and year	January	February	March	April	May	June	July	August	September	October	November	December	Annual average
Total Nonfarm													
2005	2,657.8	2,673.4	2,705.2	2,751.2	2,760.2	2,766.0	2,723.5	2,737.7	2,763.0	2,765.3	2,771.0	2,773.6	2,737.3
2006	2,708.6	2,725.1	2,757.8	2,787.0	2,800.6	2,807.1	2,754.1	2,763.5	2,796.0	2,800.0	2,808.2	2,812.2	2,776.7
2007	2,731.9	2,744.6	2,788.3	2,806.5	2,827.5	2,828.7	2,771.2	2,789.1	2,818.5	2,818.7	2,825.9	2,822.3	2,797.8
2008	2,751.5	2,764.9	2,786.1	2,813.8	2,832.7	2,832.5	2,772.8	2,784.2	2,807.4	2,805.1	2,791.4	2,776.4	2,793.2
2009	2,686.0	2,684.2	2,698.0	2,714.4	2,721.7	2,714.8	2,656.0	2,664.2	2,687.7	2,687.4	2,684.0	2,678.2	2,689.7
2010	2,596.9	2,609.1	2,639.3	2,672.6	2,691.3	2,681.4	2,631.0	2,658.7	2,675.9	2,683.9	2,682.8	2,677.4	2,658.4
2011	2,606.7	2,612.3	2,646.6	2,687.0	2,698.2	2,689.4	2,646.4	2,654.3	2,685.0	2,690.2	2,692.9	2,691.3	2,666.7
2012	2,625.3	2,637.0	2,667.3	2,693.4	2,710.5	2,707.2	2,658.5	2,675.2	2,699.4	2,713.3	2,719.0	2,716.7	2,685.2
2013	2,646.5	2,664.9	2,685.4	2,720.5	2,739.7	2,733.5	2,685.0	2,703.4	2,727.6	2,742.7	2,744.4	2,738.5	2,711.0
2014	2,660.7	2,681.0	2,703.6	2,752.6	2,771.0	2,760.7	2,716.3	2,736.0	2,753.9	2,776.9	2,779.0	2,778.8	2,739.2
2015	2,717.7	2,735.5	2,754.0	2,797.0	2,817.2	2,813.1	2,775.0	2,783.4	2,804.6	2,814.8	2,809.6	2,797.6	2,785.0
Total Private													
2005	2,230.0	2,236.9	2,266.2	2,310.9	2,320.9	2,337.1	2,326.9	2,337.0	2,333.5	2,329.4	2,331.8	2,334.0	2,307.9
2006	2,276.9	2,283.6	2,313.2	2,342.1	2,354.6	2,376.2	2,358.5	2,364.5	2,360.0	2,356.6	2,361.6	2,366.0	2,342.8
2007	2,295.3	2,298.2	2,339.2	2,356.0	2,375.1	2,390.6	2,373.9	2,384.9	2,375.6	2,366.8	2,371.2	2,368.9	2,358.0
2008	2,310.0	2,311.7	2,331.6	2,356.8	2,374.1	2,385.6	2,369.9	2,372.0	2,358.5	2,345.9	2,330.7	2,316.4	2,346.9
2009	2,237.1	2,226.6	2,238.1	2,247.8	2,255.2	2,261.6	2,246.8	2,248.9	2,231.5	2,223.5	2,220.5	2,216.1	2,237.8
2010	2,147.0	2,149.8	2,176.8	2,209.6	2,220.3	2,234.8	2,232.8	2,238.6	2,227.9	2,232.5	2,230.3	2,227.4	2,210.7
2011	2,164.1	2,164.5	2,196.5	2,233.1	2,243.1	2,253.3	2,252.4	2,253.0	2,244.2	2,243.0	2,243.5	2,242.4	2,227.8
2012	2,188.4	2,189.9	2,218.0	2,241.8	2,258.4	2,272.1	2,266.3	2,270.8	2,258.1	2,264.8	2,269.5	2,268.4	2,247.2
2013	2,209.9	2,218.4	2,236.6	2,269.8	2,289.0	2,300.2	2,296.3	2,303.9	2,291.5	2,299.0	2,299.4	2,294.8	2,275.7
2014	2,229.9	2,240.2	2,261.3	2,306.5	2,323.6	2,330.2	2,329.1	2,337.6	2,319.0	2,334.8	2,336.3	2,337.8	2,307.2
2015	2,285.2	2,290.9	2,307.2	2,349.2	2,369.5	2,377.8	2,383.4	2,383.7	2,369.8	2,373.3	2,366.6	2,355.5	2,351.0
Goods-Producing													
2005	442.8	444.2	451.4	460.3	464.2	468.4	458.8	468.8	466.8	466.4	465.0	463.4	460.0
2006	452.6	453.9	460.5	464.9	466.3	473.2	467.0	468.3	465.4	462.7	461.7	460.3	463.1
2007	446.7	443.8	455.0	456.9	461.7	465.9	459.5	464.1	461.5	457.0	455.2	450.6	456.5
2008	437.2	435.9	437.8	441.6	446.5	449.5	445.0	443.2	440.3	434.2	426.1	416.8	437.8
2009	395.0	389.6	389.6	385.9	382.8	384.4	382.7	378.5	374.5	369.4	365.7	359.6	379.8
2010	344.1	342.1	349.2	355.4	356.6	362.5	361.9	363.7	361.8	362.8	360.1	357.2	356.5
2011	342.1	341.1	349.1	356.0	359.2	364.4	366.4	363.6	364.0	361.4	358.9	357.3	357.0
2012	349.9	349.1	355.6	359.1	361.6	366.7	366.9	366.7	364.2	363.2	361.0	359.4	360.3
2013	350.5	352.3	354.7	360.7	365.9	371.4	370.3	372.2	370.6	369.9	367.6	363.8	364.2
2014	352.7	355.8	362.3	367.9	372.3	376.3	377.2	378.4	376.7	377.2	376.0	375.4	370.7
2015	366.7	367.2	371.6	377.5	381.2	385.0	386.5	385.6	384.4	383.9	381.9	380.8	379.4
Service-Providing													
2005	2,215.0	2,229.2	2,253.8	2,290.9	2,296.0	2,297.6	2,264.7	2,268.9	2,296.2	2,298.9	2,306.0	2,310.2	2,277.3
2006	2,256.0	2,271.2	2,297.3	2,322.1	2,334.3	2,333.9	2,287.1	2,295.2	2,330.6	2,337.3	2,346.5	2,351.9	2,313.6
2007	2,285.2	2,300.8	2,333.3	2,349.6	2,365.8	2,362.8	2,311.7	2,325.0	2,357.0	2,361.7	2,370.7	2,371.7	2,341.3
2008	2,314.3	2,329.0	2,348.3	2,372.2	2,386.2	2,383.0	2,327.8	2,341.0	2,367.1	2,370.9	2,365.3	2,359.6	2,355.4
2009	2,291.0	2,294.6	2,308.4	2,328.5	2,338.9	2,330.4	2,273.3	2,285.7	2,313.2	2,318.0	2,318.3	2,318.6	2,309.9
2010	2,252.8	2,267.0	2,290.1	2,317.2	2,334.7	2,318.9	2,269.1	2,295.0	2,314.1	2,321.1	2,322.7	2,320.2	2,301.9
2011	2,264.6	2,271.2	2,297.5	2,331.0	2,339.0	2,325.0	2,280.0	2,290.7	2,321.0	2,328.8	2,334.0	2,334.0	2,309.7
2012	2,275.4	2,287.9	2,311.7	2,334.3	2,348.9	2,340.5	2,291.6	2,307.9	2,335.2	2,350.1	2,358.0	2,357.3	2,324.9
2013	2,296.0	2,312.6	2,330.7	2,359.8	2,373.8	2,362.1	2,314.7	2,331.2	2,357.0	2,372.8	2,376.8	2,374.7	2,346.9
2014	2,308.0	2,325.2	2,341.3	2,384.7	2,398.7	2,384.4	2,339.1	2,357.6	2,377.2	2,399.7	2,403.0	2,403.4	2,368.5
2015	2,351.0	2,368.3	2,382.4	2,419.5	2,436.0	2,428.1	2,388.5	2,397.8	2,420.2	2,430.9	2,427.7	2,416.8	2,405.6
Mining and Logging													
2005	4.9	4.9	5.1	5.3	5.4	5.5	5.5	5.5	5.4	5.4	5.4	5.4	5.3
2006	5.3	5.3	5.4	5.4	5.5	5.6	5.6	5.5	5.5	5.4	5.3	5.2	5.4
2007	5.1	5.0	5.2	5.2	5.2	5.4	5.7	6.2	6.1	6.0	6.0	5.7	5.6
2008	5.4	5.2	5.1	5.0	4.9	5.0	5.1	5.3	5.4	5.4	4.9	4.7	5.1
2009	4.4	4.3	4.3	4.3	4.2	4.3	4.3	4.4	4.3	4.3	4.2	4.1	4.3
2010	3.8	3.9	4.1	4.3	4.3	4.4	4.4	4.4	4.3	4.3	4.3	4.2	4.2
2011	3.9	3.8	4.2	4.3	4.3	4.4	4.4	4.4	4.4	4.3	4.3	4.1	4.2
2012	3.9	3.9	4.1	4.2	4.2	4.3	4.2	4.2	4.2	4.2	4.1	4.1	4.1
2013	3.8	3.9	3.9	4.1	4.2	4.2	4.3	4.3	4.2	4.1	4.1	3.9	4.1
2014	3.6	3.7	3.9	4.1	4.1	4.2	4.2	4.2	4.3	4.2	4.2	4.1	4.1
2015	4.0	4.0	4.1	4.2	4.1	4.1	4.1	4.2	4.2	4.2	4.2	4.0	4.1

1. Employment by Industry: Missouri, 2005–2015—*Continued*

(Numbers in thousands, not seasonally adjusted)

Industry and year	January	February	March	April	May	June	July	August	September	October	November	December	Annual average
Construction													
2005	126.5	127.6	133.9	142.0	145.6	148.6	150.9	151.1	149.9	148.8	147.0	144.8	143.1
2006	139.1	139.5	143.6	147.8	149.2	153.9	153.6	153.4	151.1	149.3	146.9	145.1	147.7
2007	138.2	133.1	143.4	146.4	150.7	155.2	154.7	154.9	152.0	150.2	147.7	143.0	147.5
2008	136.0	132.5	137.4	140.4	144.3	146.6	147.3	147.2	143.9	141.0	136.8	130.7	140.3
2009	117.9	116.7	119.0	119.7	121.6	123.4	124.4	121.8	119.3	116.2	114.2	108.9	118.6
2010	97.7	95.6	101.0	106.7	106.8	110.7	112.1	111.4	110.2	109.9	107.6	104.1	106.2
2011	91.6	90.5	96.9	102.8	105.2	108.4	110.4	109.7	108.6	107.3	104.9	102.8	103.3
2012	96.1	94.9	99.7	102.6	105.6	108.4	109.2	109.6	108.2	107.3	105.8	104.7	104.3
2013	96.8	97.5	99.4	104.1	108.6	112.5	114.5	113.8	113.2	113.0	110.9	107.2	107.6
2014	100.7	99.1	105.4	108.9	111.6	114.0	115.9	115.7	114.6	114.2	112.6	111.5	110.4
2015	104.1	104.1	107.5	112.8	115.2	117.2	119.1	119.4	118.5	120.2	118.1	116.4	114.4
Manufacturing													
2005	311.4	311.7	312.4	313.0	313.2	314.3	302.4	312.2	311.5	312.2	312.6	313.2	311.7
2006	308.2	309.1	311.5	311.7	311.6	313.7	307.8	309.4	308.8	308.0	309.5	310.0	309.9
2007	303.4	305.7	306.4	305.3	305.8	305.3	299.1	303.0	303.4	300.8	301.5	301.9	303.5
2008	295.8	298.2	295.3	296.2	297.3	297.9	292.6	290.7	291.0	287.8	284.4	281.4	292.4
2009	272.7	268.6	266.3	261.9	257.0	256.7	254.0	252.3	250.9	248.9	247.3	246.6	256.9
2010	242.6	242.6	244.1	244.4	245.5	247.4	245.4	247.9	247.3	248.6	248.2	248.9	246.1
2011	246.6	246.8	248.0	248.9	249.7	251.6	251.6	249.5	251.0	249.8	249.7	250.4	249.5
2012	249.9	250.3	251.8	252.3	251.8	254.0	253.5	253.5	251.8	251.7	251.1	250.6	251.9
2013	249.9	250.9	251.4	252.5	253.1	254.7	251.5	254.1	253.2	252.8	252.6	252.7	252.5
2014	248.4	253.0	253.0	254.9	256.6	258.1	257.1	258.5	257.8	258.8	259.2	259.8	256.3
2015	258.6	259.1	260.0	260.5	261.9	263.7	263.3	262.0	261.7	259.5	259.6	260.4	260.9
Trade, Transportation, and Utilities													
2005	530.4	526.0	531.2	538.0	540.8	541.5	540.4	541.2	541.0	542.8	551.9	556.3	540.1
2006	538.3	534.1	538.8	541.2	544.4	545.7	541.3	543.3	544.7	547.1	555.6	561.0	544.6
2007	542.1	538.4	546.0	546.5	550.2	549.9	545.7	546.0	547.3	548.8	559.4	562.1	548.5
2008	542.4	537.1	540.4	542.7	545.7	546.0	542.0	542.1	540.9	540.2	544.2	545.1	542.4
2009	522.6	516.9	516.8	517.9	520.0	519.8	515.8	517.1	516.7	517.4	523.4	525.2	519.1
2010	506.4	502.3	506.7	510.6	514.4	515.1	512.5	514.4	511.9	514.0	521.4	524.9	512.9
2011	506.9	503.5	507.9	515.3	516.8	516.5	513.5	514.2	513.2	514.3	522.9	526.2	514.3
2012	507.6	502.7	506.2	509.1	513.2	513.6	511.1	512.5	512.2	514.9	525.3	527.5	513.0
2013	507.1	503.0	505.3	511.5	515.3	517.0	515.5	517.8	516.3	520.3	530.5	534.8	516.2
2014	513.5	510.1	513.7	519.2	523.0	525.3	522.5	524.7	523.1	526.8	536.5	541.5	523.3
2015	522.7	519.1	521.7	527.9	532.8	534.7	533.3	534.4	532.7	533.8	539.5	540.4	531.1
Wholesale Trade													
2005	121.7	120.9	121.5	121.6	121.7	122.6	122.5	122.4	121.3	120.9	121.3	121.8	121.7
2006	120.7	120.5	121.5	122.3	123.0	124.0	123.1	123.4	123.3	123.5	123.8	124.8	122.8
2007	123.0	123.7	124.8	124.6	124.9	125.9	125.5	125.5	125.2	125.3	125.6	126.1	125.0
2008	124.7	124.6	125.2	125.6	125.7	126.3	125.9	125.7	125.0	124.5	123.6	123.4	125.0
2009	120.5	119.8	119.2	118.9	118.4	118.6	118.0	117.5	116.6	117.2	116.6	117.1	118.2
2010	115.2	115.1	115.9	116.4	116.7	116.9	116.6	116.1	115.5	115.9	115.6	116.1	116.0
2011	114.2	114.3	115.1	116.4	116.4	117.1	117.1	116.6	116.2	116.4	116.5	117.2	116.1
2012	116.0	116.2	117.0	117.5	117.9	118.6	118.2	118.2	117.8	117.6	117.7	118.0	117.6
2013	115.9	116.3	116.8	118.4	119.0	119.5	119.3	119.3	118.9	119.6	119.8	120.5	118.6
2014	118.6	119.0	119.6	120.2	120.9	121.4	121.2	121.1	120.2	120.2	120.1	120.6	120.3
2015	119.0	118.9	119.1	120.2	120.8	121.5	121.6	121.3	120.3	120.3	119.9	119.3	120.2
Retail Trade													
2005	309.2	305.7	309.5	313.8	316.0	316.3	316.8	316.4	315.3	317.5	325.8	328.7	315.9
2006	313.3	309.3	312.7	314.1	316.0	316.7	314.5	314.6	314.4	316.8	324.8	328.0	316.3
2007	312.9	308.6	314.0	315.4	317.9	318.2	315.4	314.4	314.3	315.9	325.5	327.2	316.6
2008	312.7	307.3	309.6	311.2	313.5	314.7	311.8	311.3	309.6	310.1	315.2	316.4	312.0
2009	300.5	296.3	297.4	298.6	301.1	302.6	300.3	300.9	300.6	301.1	307.8	309.3	301.4
2010	294.9	291.5	294.5	296.1	299.1	301.0	299.9	300.2	297.6	299.4	306.8	309.2	299.2
2011	295.9	292.3	295.4	300.1	301.9	302.8	301.3	301.5	300.2	301.6	310.2	312.2	301.3
2012	298.2	294.1	296.8	298.8	301.6	302.3	301.3	300.4	299.9	302.3	312.3	313.0	301.8
2013	297.3	293.2	294.6	298.1	300.9	303.1	302.0	302.5	300.8	303.9	313.0	315.7	302.1
2014	299.4	296.0	298.6	302.6	305.0	307.7	306.1	306.2	304.8	307.9	317.1	320.0	306.0
2015	304.4	301.7	304.0	308.2	311.4	313.7	312.5	312.6	310.9	312.8	318.1	318.4	310.7

1. Employment by Industry: Missouri, 2005–2015—*Continued*

(Numbers in thousands, not seasonally adjusted)

Industry and year	January	February	March	April	May	June	July	August	September	October	November	December	Annual average
Transportation and Utilities													
2005	99.5	99.4	100.2	102.6	103.1	102.6	101.1	102.4	104.4	104.4	104.8	105.8	102.5
2006	104.3	104.3	104.6	104.8	105.4	105.0	103.7	105.3	107.0	106.8	107.0	108.2	105.5
2007	106.2	106.1	107.2	106.5	107.4	105.8	104.8	106.1	107.8	107.6	108.3	108.8	106.9
2008	105.0	105.2	105.6	105.9	106.5	105.0	104.3	105.1	106.3	105.6	105.4	105.3	105.4
2009	101.6	100.8	100.2	100.4	100.5	98.6	97.5	98.7	99.5	99.1	99.0	98.8	99.6
2010	96.3	95.7	96.3	98.1	98.6	97.2	96.0	98.1	98.8	98.7	99.0	99.6	97.7
2011	96.8	96.9	97.4	98.8	98.5	96.6	95.1	96.1	96.8	96.3	96.2	96.8	96.9
2012	93.4	92.4	92.4	92.8	93.7	92.7	91.6	93.9	94.5	95.0	95.3	96.5	93.7
2013	93.9	93.5	93.9	95.0	95.4	94.4	94.2	96.0	96.6	96.8	97.7	98.6	95.5
2014	95.5	95.1	95.5	96.4	97.1	96.2	95.2	97.4	98.1	98.7	99.3	100.9	97.1
2015	99.3	98.5	98.6	99.5	100.6	99.5	99.2	100.5	101.5	100.7	101.5	102.7	100.2
Information													
2005	62.8	62.9	63.2	64.2	64.3	64.5	64.4	64.0	63.8	63.9	63.9	64.0	63.8
2006	63.0	63.0	63.2	62.9	63.0	63.4	62.9	62.8	62.8	62.7	63.1	63.5	63.0
2007	62.2	62.4	62.9	62.6	63.1	63.7	63.4	63.6	63.7	64.0	64.4	64.6	63.4
2008	64.3	64.0	64.2	63.8	64.4	64.9	64.6	64.5	64.1	64.2	64.0	64.5	64.3
2009	64.0	64.0	63.7	64.4	64.5	64.9	63.6	63.6	63.2	61.1	61.0	61.4	63.3
2010	58.9	58.6	58.8	61.3	61.0	61.4	60.5	60.5	60.3	60.2	60.1	60.0	60.1
2011	58.5	58.3	58.2	59.2	59.5	59.7	60.0	59.8	59.8	59.4	59.4	59.4	59.3
2012	58.7	58.4	58.3	58.4	58.7	58.7	59.0	58.7	58.4	58.1	58.0	58.0	58.5
2013	57.5	57.8	57.9	57.4	57.7	57.9	57.6	57.4	57.0	57.2	57.2	57.4	57.5
2014	56.5	56.5	56.7	56.6	56.6	56.8	56.6	56.1	55.5	55.0	54.9	54.8	56.1
2015	54.5	54.3	54.2	54.2	54.5	54.7	54.8	54.3	53.6	52.6	53.1	52.6	54.0
Financial Activities													
2005	160.8	161.6	162.2	162.7	162.7	164.1	165.4	165.0	164.3	163.9	163.9	164.3	163.4
2006	162.1	162.5	163.3	164.5	165.6	167.0	166.9	167.2	166.4	165.1	165.0	165.6	165.1
2007	164.5	164.9	165.6	165.3	166.2	167.6	167.8	167.6	166.2	166.2	165.6	166.0	166.1
2008	165.3	165.6	165.3	165.3	166.2	166.8	167.3	167.3	165.8	165.7	165.3	165.1	165.9
2009	163.8	163.4	163.8	163.9	164.2	164.9	163.9	163.6	161.7	162.4	161.7	161.6	163.2
2010	160.9	160.8	161.1	162.1	162.6	163.6	163.7	162.9	161.9	162.5	162.5	162.3	162.2
2011	159.8	160.1	160.3	160.8	161.1	161.4	162.3	162.6	161.7	162.7	162.9	163.0	161.6
2012	161.4	162.1	162.8	162.6	163.3	164.0	164.5	164.7	163.5	164.6	164.9	164.5	163.6
2013	161.9	162.3	162.4	164.0	164.4	165.1	166.1	165.6	164.4	164.6	164.6	164.2	164.1
2014	162.2	162.4	162.2	164.0	164.9	165.5	166.2	166.2	164.6	165.1	165.1	165.4	164.5
2015	163.9	164.1	164.3	165.0	166.3	167.4	168.4	168.0	166.3	165.7	166.3	166.4	166.0
Professional and Business Services													
2005	306.6	309.1	313.2	319.0	316.4	320.0	320.4	320.3	321.9	320.7	321.3	322.5	317.6
2006	315.8	319.3	324.3	328.7	327.6	332.5	329.8	331.5	331.3	333.7	333.9	336.2	328.7
2007	324.3	325.5	331.5	334.1	333.9	337.5	336.6	338.7	336.9	336.4	336.7	337.8	334.2
2008	331.8	333.9	337.7	343.9	340.8	342.5	340.6	341.1	339.0	335.9	332.2	329.6	337.4
2009	318.4	316.5	316.1	316.1	313.7	314.4	312.2	313.1	310.4	311.5	312.3	313.5	314.0
2010	306.5	309.4	312.4	318.9	317.0	319.3	321.6	323.0	321.0	323.4	322.6	323.6	318.2
2011	318.0	319.7	324.5	330.6	328.8	330.7	329.1	329.3	329.3	330.5	331.0	332.1	327.8
2012	325.2	326.5	331.3	335.5	335.5	338.4	336.7	337.4	336.6	339.6	341.3	341.5	335.5
2013	332.2	336.2	341.0	345.1	345.8	348.2	348.2	350.5	348.5	351.7	352.0	352.3	346.0
2014	340.8	343.9	347.0	355.2	355.3	356.7	356.0	359.2	357.6	362.2	362.9	364.2	355.1
2015	354.0	357.2	360.9	367.6	368.2	368.4	371.4	372.6	372.0	376.4	374.8	373.0	368.0
Education and Health Services													
2005	361.4	365.0	366.3	370.6	370.1	369.2	369.2	369.4	373.7	376.7	377.5	378.3	370.6
2006	371.7	376.2	377.5	379.5	379.4	378.0	376.4	376.7	382.2	384.8	387.7	386.9	379.8
2007	379.2	384.1	386.2	387.5	387.5	385.8	385.6	386.7	390.9	392.7	394.1	395.1	388.0
2008	388.5	393.6	393.8	396.2	395.7	394.7	394.7	395.8	399.4	404.1	405.5	406.2	397.4
2009	399.9	403.3	404.2	405.2	405.5	403.4	403.8	405.5	409.0	412.8	414.1	415.0	406.8
2010	406.9	411.0	412.3	414.7	414.9	412.7	412.3	413.1	417.7	422.5	424.0	424.1	415.5
2011	419.3	422.8	424.3	425.5	423.7	419.8	419.6	420.3	424.1	426.2	427.6	426.9	423.3
2012	422.2	425.9	425.9	426.3	426.0	423.0	423.4	425.4	428.4	431.9	432.5	433.4	427.0
2013	427.7	433.0	431.3	436.6	434.4	428.6	429.2	430.1	431.9	437.5	437.9	435.2	432.8
2014	429.7	435.5	432.3	440.2	437.9	431.9	434.3	435.1	436.1	443.8	444.7	441.9	437.0
2015	441.6	444.9	442.0	449.6	447.9	442.9	446.2	445.9	446.2	455.2	453.3	451.6	447.3

1. Employment by Industry: Missouri, 2005–2015—*Continued*

(Numbers in thousands, not seasonally adjusted)

Industry and year	January	February	March	April	May	June	July	August	September	October	November	December	Annual average
Leisure and Hospitality													
2005	247.2	249.7	259.9	276.2	282.6	288.3	287.6	288.0	282.5	276.0	269.8	266.2	272.8
2006	254.3	256.5	266.6	280.2	288.0	294.6	292.9	293.8	286.9	280.4	274.4	272.2	278.4
2007	257.7	260.1	271.7	282.6	291.3	298.3	293.9	297.2	288.9	281.8	276.0	272.9	281.0
2008	260.5	261.3	271.4	282.1	293.0	298.5	293.3	295.8	287.4	280.0	273.2	269.6	280.5
2009	255.2	254.6	265.1	275.6	285.4	290.1	285.4	288.9	278.4	271.6	265.3	262.8	273.2
2010	248.2	250.3	260.5	274.4	281.3	286.9	286.9	287.9	281.2	274.5	267.3	263.2	271.9
2011	248.7	248.2	260.1	271.2	279.3	285.4	286.0	288.0	277.8	274.1	266.6	263.4	270.7
2012	251.0	252.5	264.2	276.0	284.6	291.4	288.6	289.2	280.1	277.6	271.6	269.3	274.7
2013	258.7	259.0	268.7	281.3	291.8	297.3	295.1	296.0	289.6	284.9	277.1	274.7	281.2
2014	263.3	264.3	274.3	289.4	298.8	302.3	301.0	303.0	291.5	290.9	282.8	280.9	286.9
2015	269.1	270.9	278.6	292.4	303.1	308.0	306.5	307.0	299.7	290.9	283.6	275.7	290.5
Other Services													
2005	118.0	118.4	118.8	119.9	119.8	121.1	120.7	120.3	119.5	119.0	118.5	119.0	119.4
2006	119.1	118.1	119.0	120.2	120.3	121.8	121.3	120.9	120.3	120.1	120.2	120.3	120.1
2007	118.6	119.0	120.3	120.5	121.2	121.9	121.4	121.0	120.2	119.9	119.8	119.8	120.3
2008	120.0	120.3	121.0	121.2	121.8	122.7	122.4	122.2	121.6	121.6	120.2	119.5	121.2
2009	118.2	118.3	118.8	118.8	119.1	119.7	119.4	118.6	117.6	117.3	117.0	117.0	118.3
2010	115.1	115.3	115.8	112.2	112.5	113.3	113.4	113.1	112.1	112.6	112.3	112.1	113.3
2011	110.8	110.8	112.1	114.5	114.7	115.4	115.5	115.2	114.3	114.4	114.2	114.1	113.8
2012	112.4	112.7	113.7	114.8	115.5	116.3	116.1	115.6	114.7	114.9	114.9	114.8	114.7
2013	114.3	114.8	115.3	113.2	113.7	114.7	114.3	114.3	113.2	112.9	112.5	112.4	113.8
2014	111.2	111.7	112.8	114.0	114.8	115.4	115.3	114.9	113.9	113.8	113.4	113.7	113.7
2015	112.7	113.2	113.9	115.0	115.5	116.7	116.3	115.9	114.9	114.8	114.1	115.0	114.8
Government													
2005	427.8	436.5	439.0	440.3	439.3	428.9	396.6	400.7	429.5	435.9	439.2	439.6	429.4
2006	431.7	441.5	444.6	444.9	446.0	430.9	395.6	399.0	436.0	443.4	446.6	446.2	433.9
2007	436.6	446.4	449.1	450.5	452.4	438.1	397.3	404.2	442.9	451.9	454.7	453.4	439.8
2008	441.5	453.2	454.5	457.0	458.6	446.9	402.9	412.2	448.9	459.2	460.7	460.0	446.3
2009	448.9	457.6	459.9	466.6	466.5	453.2	409.2	415.3	456.2	463.9	463.5	462.1	451.9
2010	449.9	459.3	462.5	463.0	471.0	446.6	398.2	420.1	448.0	451.4	452.5	450.0	447.7
2011	442.6	447.8	450.1	453.9	455.1	436.1	394.0	401.3	440.8	447.2	449.4	448.9	438.9
2012	436.9	447.1	449.3	451.6	452.1	435.1	392.2	404.4	441.3	448.5	449.5	448.3	438.0
2013	436.6	446.5	448.8	450.7	450.7	433.3	388.7	399.5	436.1	443.7	445.0	443.7	435.3
2014	430.8	440.8	442.3	446.1	447.4	430.5	387.2	398.4	434.9	442.1	442.7	441.0	432.0
2015	432.5	444.6	446.8	447.8	447.7	435.3	391.6	399.7	434.8	441.5	443.0	442.1	434.0

2. Average Weekly Hours by Selected Industry: Missouri, 2011–2015

(Not seasonally adjusted)

Industry and year	January	February	March	April	May	June	July	August	September	October	November	December	Annual average
Total Private													
2011	34.6	34.3	34.5	34.6	35.0	34.9	34.8	34.7	34.9	35.3	34.5	34.5	34.7
2012	34.7	34.3	34.5	34.7	34.4	34.6	34.9	34.4	35.1	34.4	34.5	35.0	34.6
2013	34.1	34.3	34.3	34.2	34.3	35.2	34.4	34.6	34.9	34.2	34.1	34.4	34.4
2014	33.6	34.3	34.5	34.1	34.1	34.6	34.3	34.2	34.0	33.8	34.5	34.2	34.2
2015	33.7	34.2	34.2	34.0	33.5	33.8	33.8	34.4	33.6	33.8	34.0	33.7	33.9
Goods-Producing													
2011	37.6	38.4	38.0	38.3	38.7	39.1	39.4	39.2	39.7	39.7	38.5	38.9	38.8
2012	38.2	38.5	39.0	39.2	39.4	39.3	39.6	39.3	39.3	39.4	38.8	39.5	39.1
2013	39.0	39.4	39.7	39.1	39.4	40.2	39.3	39.5	39.9	39.7	38.7	38.6	39.4
2014	37.9	38.1	38.5	38.9	39.2	39.4	39.5	39.6	38.4	38.5	39.2	40.0	38.9
2015	38.8	39.1	38.6	39.0	39.0	39.7	39.2	40.0	38.2	39.6	38.7	39.5	39.1
Construction													
2011	34.7	35.3	35.0	35.2	36.3	36.8	37.0	37.3	37.5	37.7	35.6	36.0	36.3
2012	35.1	35.6	37.7	37.6	37.7	36.8	37.5	37.6	38.1	37.7	35.6	36.3	37.0
2013	35.9	37.1	37.7	36.2	37.2	37.9	37.0	37.8	37.8	37.5	34.9	34.4	36.8
2014	34.0	33.1	35.0	35.2	35.5	36.0	37.5	37.3	36.5	35.0	35.9	37.4	35.8
2015	36.4	35.6	36.1	36.3	35.9	37.6	36.7	38.0	34.9	38.2	35.5	38.2	36.6
Manufacturing													
2011	38.4	39.3	39.0	39.4	39.6	39.9	40.4	40.0	40.7	40.6	41.1	40.7	39.8
2012	40.1	40.2	40.2	40.4	40.6	40.7	40.8	40.3	40.1	40.4	40.2	40.8	40.4
2013	40.2	40.3	40.6	40.5	40.6	41.4	40.5	40.4	41.1	40.9	40.7	40.9	40.7
2014	39.9	40.6	40.3	40.8	41.1	41.1	40.4	40.7	39.3	40.3	40.9	41.3	40.6
2015	39.9	40.7	39.7	40.2	40.4	40.8	40.5	41.0	39.9	40.6	40.7	40.3	40.4
Trade, Transportation, and Utilities													
2011	33.8	33.9	34.3	34.7	35.3	35.3	35.2	35.4	35.6	35.7	35.0	35.6	35.0
2012	35.0	35.1	35.5	35.6	35.6	35.7	35.7	35.5	35.9	35.1	35.3	35.6	35.5
2013	34.7	34.7	34.4	34.7	34.9	35.1	34.8	34.9	34.8	34.4	34.3	34.4	34.7
2014	33.3	34.0	34.5	34.2	33.8	34.1	33.8	33.6	33.9	33.6	33.8	34.2	33.9
2015	33.1	33.6	33.5	33.6	33.4	33.9	33.8	34.2	34.1	34.1	34.2	34.2	33.8
Financial Activities													
2011	37.6	37.1	37.5	37.5	37.7	37.3	37.2	36.9	37.4	38.3	37.3	37.1	37.4
2012	38.1	37.3	37.0	37.2	36.6	36.8	37.1	36.2	37.8	36.5	37.1	37.9	37.1
2013	36.8	37.2	37.3	37.1	36.9	38.3	37.0	37.9	38.1	37.1	36.8	37.5	37.3
2014	36.8	38.0	37.8	36.8	36.7	37.1	36.0	36.1	36.0	35.9	37.6	36.5	36.8
2015	36.5	37.6	37.6	36.9	36.8	36.8	37.1	37.8	36.5	36.2	37.2	36.2	36.9
Professional and Business Services													
2011	35.8	35.0	35.2	35.4	35.9	35.6	35.1	35.1	35.1	35.8	34.7	34.7	35.3
2012	35.6	34.9	35.4	36.3	35.4	35.5	36.3	35.6	36.8	36.1	36.1	36.5	35.9
2013	35.5	36.3	35.8	36.1	35.6	37.1	35.2	36.5	37.1	35.8	35.8	36.4	36.1
2014	35.8	36.8	36.6	36.8	36.6	37.5	36.7	36.8	36.4	36.1	37.1	35.8	36.6
2015	35.8	36.7	36.5	36.1	35.5	35.6	35.4	37.0	35.7	36.2	36.3	35.4	36.0
Education and Health Services													
2011	33.8	33.1	33.5	33.4	34.1	34.1	33.9	33.9	33.8	34.3	33.8	33.7	33.8
2012	34.8	33.5	33.4	33.9	33.2	33.6	34.0	33.0	34.3	33.1	33.1	33.8	33.6
2013	32.6	32.5	32.5	32.5	32.3	33.5	32.9	32.7	33.3	32.5	32.7	32.9	32.7
2014	32.3	32.5	32.8	32.1	32.2	33.2	32.8	32.6	32.6	32.5	33.6	32.7	32.7
2015	32.8	33.1	33.1	32.8	33.0	32.3	33.0	33.5	33.2	32.3	33.9	33.0	33.0
Leisure and Hospitality													
2011	25.7	25.6	26.4	26.0	26.2	26.5	26.4	26.0	25.7	26.6	25.8	25.6	26.1
2012	24.9	25.6	25.7	25.3	25.5	25.6	25.8	25.3	25.5	25.6	25.4	25.6	25.5
2013	24.2	25.0	25.4	25.1	25.5	26.2	25.9	25.5	25.5	25.6	25.2	24.8	25.3
2014	24.0	25.0	25.4	24.9	25.1	25.8	26.1	25.9	25.5	25.5	25.6	25.5	25.4
2015	24.8	25.8	26.4	25.9	25.1	25.8	25.7	25.7	25.3	25.4	25.1	24.7	25.5

3. Average Hourly Earnings by Selected Industry: Missouri, 2011–2015

(Dollars, not seasonally adjusted)

Industry and year	January	February	March	April	May	June	July	August	September	October	November	December	Annual average
Total Private													
2011...	20.78	20.86	20.63	20.79	20.84	20.54	20.78	20.66	20.69	20.93	20.95	21.05	20.79
2012...	21.23	21.37	21.33	21.53	21.41	21.53	21.55	21.41	21.71	21.39	21.60	21.66	21.48
2013...	21.78	22.00	21.76	21.73	21.70	21.77	21.63	21.81	22.04	21.82	22.16	22.22	21.87
2014...	22.12	22.28	22.22	22.11	21.93	21.97	21.74	21.78	21.83	21.91	22.17	21.90	22.00
2015...	22.07	22.21	22.16	21.99	22.19	22.00	22.00	22.08	22.09	22.04	22.22	22.13	22.10
Goods-Producing													
2011...	24.59	24.01	23.95	23.77	23.65	22.99	23.14	22.90	22.83	22.88	23.13	22.83	23.37
2012...	22.77	22.63	23.20	23.19	23.08	23.04	23.54	23.52	23.95	23.93	23.92	23.87	23.39
2013...	24.10	24.22	24.46	24.50	24.61	24.89	25.04	25.43	25.76	25.45	26.35	26.05	25.08
2014...	25.92	25.88	25.95	25.62	25.74	25.50	25.86	25.87	25.97	26.28	26.41	26.33	25.95
2015...	26.24	25.53	25.78	25.28	25.30	25.21	25.46	25.83	26.33	25.91	26.00	26.39	25.77
Construction													
2011...	27.99	27.45	27.43	27.19	27.06	26.63	26.83	26.98	27.29	26.86	28.31	28.48	27.35
2012...	28.40	28.51	28.46	28.55	28.17	27.91	28.23	28.53	28.44	28.54	28.08	27.76	28.30
2013...	27.62	27.59	27.55	27.77	27.60	27.91	28.29	28.41	28.17	27.96	27.75	26.87	27.81
2014...	26.51	26.36	26.36	26.44	26.95	26.51	27.16	26.92	27.18	27.44	27.95	27.88	27.00
2015...	27.61	27.66	28.07	27.73	28.07	27.77	28.15	28.17	28.41	28.42	28.20	28.48	28.07
Manufacturing													
2011...	23.40	22.83	22.62	22.37	22.14	21.71	21.80	21.36	21.11	21.36	20.98	20.57	21.84
2012...	20.60	20.42	21.03	21.04	21.02	21.10	21.65	21.55	22.15	22.10	22.40	22.46	21.46
2013...	22.83	22.93	23.28	23.25	23.40	23.62	23.59	24.01	24.63	24.29	24.73	24.96	23.80
2014...	25.03	25.13	25.23	24.78	24.80	24.67	24.91	25.05	25.10	25.53	25.51	25.46	25.10
2015...	25.50	24.51	24.69	24.10	24.00	23.98	24.19	24.72	24.95	24.65	24.96	25.01	24.60
Trade, Transportation, and Utilities													
2011...	19.05	18.74	18.56	18.94	18.82	18.64	19.10	18.67	18.57	19.14	18.93	18.89	18.84
2012...	19.61	19.48	19.52	19.94	19.62	19.88	20.01	19.52	19.97	19.57	19.60	19.78	19.71
2013...	19.95	20.47	20.15	20.12	20.04	20.09	19.74	19.91	20.33	19.88	20.01	20.13	20.07
2014...	20.47	20.62	20.70	20.91	20.51	20.53	20.18	19.99	19.90	19.81	19.95	19.19	20.22
2015...	19.72	19.88	19.85	19.83	19.87	19.46	19.56	19.60	19.61	19.61	19.58	19.29	19.65
Financial Activities													
2011...	22.40	23.31	22.16	22.20	21.89	21.16	21.60	21.63	21.65	21.90	21.89	21.93	21.97
2012...	22.02	24.23	23.78	24.23	25.09	26.09	24.77	25.27	25.35	25.07	26.59	26.09	24.88
2013...	26.13	27.95	26.49	26.44	26.63	26.38	25.99	26.46	26.05	25.75	26.98	27.25	26.54
2014...	26.64	27.25	26.76	26.61	26.43	26.38	26.11	26.33	26.10	26.04	26.69	26.32	26.48
2015...	26.55	27.08	26.90	26.61	26.61	26.17	25.87	26.15	26.14	26.01	26.51	26.24	26.40
Professional and Business Services													
2011...	25.67	26.08	25.90	25.44	25.48	25.24	25.50	25.83	26.13	26.28	26.48	26.69	25.89
2012...	26.63	26.91	26.68	26.41	26.53	26.69	26.32	26.15	26.62	25.64	26.12	26.23	26.41
2013...	25.92	25.78	25.69	25.43	25.59	25.87	25.85	25.69	25.93	25.60	25.72	25.30	25.70
2014...	25.17	25.41	25.22	24.78	24.84	25.21	24.82	24.82	25.10	25.34	25.71	25.42	25.15
2015...	25.80	26.52	26.55	26.28	26.35	26.24	26.34	26.86	26.95	26.80	27.33	26.96	26.59
Education and Health Services													
2011...	21.50	21.38	21.01	21.32	21.22	21.43	21.43	21.02	20.94	21.02	20.69	21.06	21.17
2012...	20.69	20.46	20.39	20.24	20.08	19.91	19.97	20.00	19.81	19.67	19.53	19.66	20.03
2013...	19.71	19.57	19.48	19.60	19.51	19.52	19.46	19.43	19.54	19.48	19.38	19.55	19.52
2014...	19.18	19.27	19.17	19.09	18.77	18.38	18.33	18.51	18.49	18.51	18.49	18.56	18.73
2015...	18.52	18.72	18.75	18.82	18.64	18.98	18.99	18.36	18.09	18.12	18.18	18.32	18.54
Leisure and Hospitality													
2011...	11.76	11.91	11.74	11.74	11.57	11.57	11.70	11.73	11.99	11.83	12.07	12.26	11.82
2012...	12.27	12.25	12.11	12.02	12.14	11.94	11.99	12.07	12.16	12.10	12.22	12.46	12.14
2013...	12.52	12.49	12.41	12.46	12.16	11.99	12.09	12.23	12.49	12.50	12.59	12.68	12.37
2014...	12.74	12.66	12.82	12.66	12.48	12.44	12.35	12.42	12.68	12.66	12.83	13.09	12.65
2015...	12.95	13.04	12.96	12.96	13.28	13.09	13.07	13.09	13.11	13.34	13.23	13.42	13.13

4. Average Weekly Earnings by Selected Industry: Missouri, 2011–2015

(Dollars, not seasonally adjusted)

Industry and year	January	February	March	April	May	June	July	August	September	October	November	December	Annual average
Total Private													
2011	718.99	715.50	711.74	719.33	729.40	716.85	723.14	716.90	722.08	738.83	722.78	726.23	721.41
2012	736.68	732.99	735.89	747.09	736.50	744.94	752.10	736.50	762.02	735.82	745.20	758.10	743.21
2013	742.70	754.60	746.37	743.17	744.31	766.30	744.07	754.63	769.20	746.24	755.66	764.37	752.33
2014	743.23	764.20	766.59	753.95	747.81	760.16	745.68	744.88	742.22	740.56	764.87	748.98	752.40
2015	743.76	759.58	757.87	747.66	743.37	743.60	743.60	759.55	742.22	744.95	755.48	745.78	749.19
Goods-Producing													
2011	924.58	921.98	910.10	910.39	915.26	898.91	911.72	897.68	906.35	908.34	890.51	888.09	906.76
2012	869.81	871.26	904.80	909.05	909.35	905.47	932.18	924.34	941.24	942.84	928.10	942.87	914.55
2013	939.90	954.27	971.06	957.95	969.63	1,000.58	984.07	1,004.49	1,027.82	1,010.37	1,019.75	1,005.53	988.15
2014	982.37	986.03	999.08	996.62	1,009.01	1,004.70	1,021.47	1,024.45	997.25	1,011.78	1,035.27	1,053.20	1,009.46
2015	1,018.11	998.22	995.11	985.92	986.70	1,000.84	998.03	1,033.20	1,005.81	1,026.04	1,006.20	1,042.41	1,007.61
Construction													
2011	971.25	968.99	960.05	957.09	982.28	979.98	992.71	1,006.35	1,023.38	1,012.62	1,007.84	1,025.28	992.81
2012	996.84	1,014.96	1,072.94	1,073.48	1,062.01	1,027.09	1,058.63	1,072.73	1,083.56	1,075.96	999.65	1,007.69	1,047.10
2013	991.56	1,023.59	1,038.64	1,005.27	1,026.72	1,057.79	1,046.73	1,073.90	1,064.83	1,048.50	968.48	924.33	1,023.41
2014	901.34	872.52	922.60	930.69	956.73	954.36	1,018.50	1,004.12	992.07	960.40	1,003.41	1,042.71	966.60
2015	1,005.00	984.70	1,013.33	1,006.60	1,007.71	1,044.15	1,033.11	1,070.46	991.51	1,085.64	1,001.10	1,087.94	1,027.36
Manufacturing													
2011	898.56	897.22	882.18	881.38	876.74	866.23	880.72	854.40	859.18	867.22	841.30	837.20	869.23
2012	826.06	820.88	845.41	850.02	853.41	858.77	883.32	868.47	888.22	892.84	900.48	916.37	866.98
2013	917.77	924.08	945.17	941.63	950.04	977.87	955.40	970.00	1,012.29	993.46	1,006.51	1,020.86	968.66
2014	998.70	1,020.28	1,016.77	1,011.02	1,019.28	1,013.94	1,006.36	1,019.54	986.43	1,028.86	1,043.36	1,051.50	1,019.06
2015	1,017.45	997.56	980.19	968.82	969.60	978.38	979.70	1,013.52	995.51	1,000.79	1,015.87	1,007.90	993.84
Trade, Transportation, and Utilities													
2011	643.89	635.29	636.61	657.22	664.35	657.99	672.32	660.92	661.09	683.30	662.55	672.48	659.40
2012	686.35	683.75	692.96	709.86	698.47	709.72	714.36	692.96	716.92	686.91	691.88	704.17	699.71
2013	692.27	710.31	693.16	698.16	699.40	705.16	686.95	694.86	707.48	683.87	686.34	692.47	696.43
2014	681.65	701.08	714.15	715.12	693.24	700.07	682.08	671.66	674.61	665.62	674.31	656.30	685.46
2015	652.73	667.97	664.98	666.29	663.66	659.69	661.13	670.32	668.70	668.70	669.64	659.72	664.17
Financial Activities													
2011	842.24	864.80	831.00	832.50	825.25	789.27	803.52	798.15	809.71	838.77	816.50	813.60	821.68
2012	838.96	903.78	879.86	901.36	918.29	960.11	918.97	914.77	958.23	915.06	986.49	988.81	923.05
2013	961.58	1,039.74	988.08	980.92	982.65	1,010.35	961.63	1,002.83	992.51	955.33	992.86	1,021.88	989.94
2014	980.35	1,035.50	1,011.53	979.25	969.98	978.70	939.96	950.51	939.60	934.84	1,003.54	960.68	974.46
2015	969.08	1,018.21	1,011.44	981.91	979.25	963.06	959.78	988.47	954.11	941.56	986.17	949.89	974.16
Professional and Business Services													
2011	918.99	912.80	911.68	900.58	914.73	898.54	895.05	906.63	917.16	940.82	918.86	926.14	913.92
2012	948.03	939.16	944.47	958.68	939.16	947.50	955.42	930.94	979.62	925.60	942.93	957.40	948.12
2013	920.16	935.81	919.70	918.02	911.00	959.78	909.92	937.69	962.00	916.48	920.78	920.92	927.77
2014	901.09	935.09	923.05	911.90	909.14	945.38	910.89	913.38	913.64	914.77	953.84	910.04	920.49
2015	923.64	973.28	969.08	948.71	935.43	934.14	932.44	993.82	962.12	970.16	992.08	954.38	957.24
Education and Health Services													
2011	726.70	707.68	703.84	712.09	723.60	730.76	726.48	712.58	707.77	720.99	699.32	709.72	715.55
2012	720.01	685.41	681.03	686.14	666.66	668.98	678.98	660.00	679.48	651.08	646.44	664.51	673.01
2013	642.55	636.03	633.10	637.00	630.17	653.92	640.23	635.36	650.68	633.10	633.73	643.20	638.30
2014	619.51	626.28	628.78	612.79	604.39	610.22	601.22	603.43	602.77	601.58	621.26	606.91	612.47
2015	607.46	619.63	620.63	617.30	615.12	613.05	626.67	615.06	600.59	585.28	616.30	604.56	611.82
Leisure and Hospitality													
2011	302.23	304.90	309.94	305.24	303.13	306.61	308.88	304.98	308.14	314.68	311.41	313.86	308.50
2012	305.52	313.60	311.23	304.11	309.57	305.66	309.34	305.37	310.08	309.76	310.39	318.98	309.57
2013	302.98	312.25	315.21	312.75	310.08	314.14	313.13	311.87	318.50	320.00	317.27	314.46	312.96
2014	305.76	316.50	325.63	315.23	313.25	320.95	322.34	321.68	323.34	322.83	328.45	333.80	321.31
2015	321.16	336.43	342.14	335.66	333.33	337.72	335.90	336.41	331.68	338.84	332.07	331.47	334.82

MONTANA
At a Glance

Population:
  2005 estimate: 940,102
  2010 census: 989,415
  2015 estimate: 1,032,949

Percent change in population:
  2005–2015: 9.9%
  2010–2015: 4.4%

Percent change in total nonfarm employment:
  2005–2015: 9.6%

Industry with the largest growth in employment, 2005–2015 (thousands):
  Education and health services, 15.7

Industry with the largest decline or smallest growth in employment, 2005–2015 (thousands):
  Construction, –1.1

Civilian labor force:
  2005: 486,054
  2010: 500,525
  2015: 522,727

Unemployment rate and rank among states (highest to lowest):
  2005: 4.4%, 35th
  2010: 7.3%, 40th
  2015: 4.1%, 40th

Over-the-year change in unemployment rates:
  2012–2013: –0.3%
  2013–2014: –0.7%
  2014–2015: –0.6%

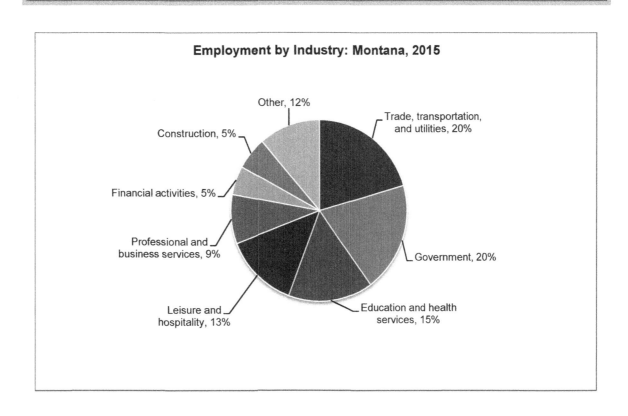

Employment by Industry: Montana, 2015

Other, 12%
Trade, transportation, and utilities, 20%
Construction, 5%
Financial activities, 5%
Professional and business services, 9%
Government, 20%
Leisure and hospitality, 13%
Education and health services, 15%

1. Employment by Industry: Montana, 2005–2015

(Numbers in thousands, not seasonally adjusted)

Industry and year	January	February	March	April	May	June	July	August	September	October	November	December	Annual average
Total Nonfarm													
2005	400.1	405.3	410.0	414.1	420.7	427.8	427.6	427.8	429.0	428.1	426.9	426.1	420.3
2006	413.9	418.4	423.2	429.0	436.9	446.5	445.9	442.3	439.8	438.4	436.9	438.4	434.1
2007	426.2	429.3	435.7	439.1	446.9	453.3	452.1	452.9	449.4	449.6	447.1	447.1	444.1
2008	432.7	435.5	439.2	441.4	449.8	454.0	452.4	453.3	450.3	447.1	442.5	439.8	444.8
2009	420.1	420.0	419.7	425.4	431.6	438.2	435.5	435.6	433.6	432.0	428.7	426.8	428.9
2010	413.3	414.0	418.6	423.8	432.2	437.4	436.7	437.5	435.6	433.0	428.0	427.4	428.1
2011	413.7	415.7	419.7	425.5	433.6	438.8	437.4	440.3	441.2	438.2	434.7	434.7	431.1
2012	422.8	424.0	427.9	434.5	443.6	448.5	448.3	450.2	449.9	447.1	443.0	443.6	440.3
2013	432.1	435.4	438.7	444.6	452.5	456.5	454.1	457.0	455.6	454.8	450.7	450.9	448.6
2014	437.7	441.3	442.6	449.1	456.3	462.0	461.4	462.4	460.3	457.3	452.5	454.5	453.1
2015	444.8	448.8	452.6	458.5	464.4	469.4	468.5	469.2	467.9	465.2	460.5	458.9	460.7
Total Private													
2005	315.3	318.1	322.4	326.5	332.4	341.6	346.3	347.6	342.9	339.8	337.9	337.7	334.0
2006	329.1	330.8	334.8	340.2	346.6	357.4	357.6	359.0	353.3	349.6	347.2	349.9	346.3
2007	340.5	341.3	346.7	351.0	357.6	366.3	368.6	370.0	363.8	359.5	357.5	358.4	356.8
2008	347.3	347.6	350.7	353.3	359.0	365.9	368.7	369.3	362.3	355.9	350.7	349.7	356.7
2009	333.3	331.1	330.1	335.2	339.5	347.9	350.1	349.7	344.5	339.2	336.1	334.5	339.3
2010	323.1	322.6	325.4	331.1	336.2	344.3	348.0	348.8	343.9	339.8	335.2	334.9	336.1
2011	324.3	324.7	327.8	333.9	340.3	347.8	352.9	354.5	350.4	347.0	343.9	344.1	341.0
2012	334.1	334.4	337.5	344.2	351.2	359.4	362.1	364.6	359.6	356.1	352.0	353.1	350.7
2013	341.9	343.9	346.8	353.1	360.4	367.4	370.3	372.2	366.3	363.1	359.6	361.1	358.8
2014	349.7	349.9	350.9	357.8	364.2	372.3	375.8	377.0	370.1	365.6	360.8	363.7	363.2
2015	356.3	357.8	360.7	366.1	371.6	379.8	383.1	383.5	377.1	372.8	368.5	367.9	370.4
Goods-Producing													
2005	48.0	49.4	50.6	52.8	54.7	56.6	58.4	59.2	58.1	58.7	57.5	55.1	54.9
2006	52.7	52.8	53.8	55.8	58.9	62.0	62.4	62.5	61.5	61.4	60.1	59.2	58.6
2007	56.1	55.8	57.8	59.8	62.2	64.4	64.3	64.9	63.2	63.0	61.8	59.8	61.1
2008	55.6	55.1	56.0	57.0	59.1	60.5	61.4	61.2	59.5	58.8	56.5	53.8	57.9
2009	47.8	46.1	45.1	47.3	48.6	50.5	50.9	51.1	50.0	49.8	48.3	45.7	48.4
2010	42.2	41.6	42.4	44.9	46.7	48.3	49.5	50.0	49.5	49.8	47.9	45.1	46.5
2011	41.6	41.6	42.5	45.4	47.3	49.3	50.9	51.7	51.4	51.5	49.9	48.1	47.6
2012	44.8	44.5	45.4	48.5	50.5	52.0	52.8	53.5	53.3	53.5	51.7	50.6	50.1
2013	46.3	46.8	47.7	50.4	53.7	54.3	54.5	55.1	54.3	54.6	53.5	51.7	51.9
2014	48.1	47.7	48.5	51.1	53.6	56.0	56.7	56.6	55.3	56.0	53.5	53.0	53.0
2015	49.8	50.0	50.7	52.4	54.6	56.3	57.1	56.9	55.5	55.8	54.2	52.7	53.8
Service-Providing													
2005	352.1	355.9	359.4	361.3	366.0	371.2	369.2	368.6	370.9	369.4	369.4	371.0	365.4
2006	361.2	365.6	369.4	373.2	378.0	384.5	383.5	379.8	378.3	377.0	376.8	379.2	375.5
2007	370.1	373.5	377.9	379.3	384.7	388.9	387.8	388.0	386.2	386.6	385.3	387.3	383.0
2008	377.1	380.4	383.2	384.4	390.7	393.5	391.0	392.1	390.8	388.3	386.0	386.0	387.0
2009	372.3	373.9	374.6	378.1	383.0	387.7	384.6	384.5	383.6	382.2	380.4	381.1	380.5
2010	371.1	372.4	376.2	378.9	385.5	389.1	387.2	387.5	386.1	383.2	380.1	382.3	381.6
2011	372.1	374.1	377.2	380.1	386.3	389.5	386.5	388.6	389.8	386.7	384.8	386.6	383.5
2012	378.0	379.5	382.5	386.0	393.1	396.5	395.5	396.7	396.6	393.6	391.3	393.0	390.2
2013	385.8	388.6	391.0	394.2	398.8	402.2	399.6	401.9	401.3	400.2	397.2	399.2	396.7
2014	389.6	393.6	394.1	398.0	402.7	406.0	404.7	405.8	405.0	401.3	399.0	401.5	400.1
2015	395.0	398.8	401.9	406.1	409.8	413.1	411.4	412.3	412.4	409.4	406.3	406.2	406.9
Mining and Logging													
2005	7.3	7.5	7.4	7.2	7.5	7.9	8.1	8.2	8.0	8.0	7.9	7.9	7.7
2006	7.8	7.8	7.9	7.8	8.2	8.6	8.7	8.6	8.4	8.4	8.4	8.3	8.2
2007	8.1	8.1	8.3	8.1	8.2	8.6	8.7	8.7	8.4	8.4	8.3	8.3	8.4
2008	7.9	7.9	7.9	7.8	8.0	8.4	8.6	8.8	8.8	8.8	8.8	8.4	8.3
2009	7.7	7.1	6.9	6.8	6.8	6.9	7.2	7.2	7.0	7.1	7.0	7.0	7.1
2010	6.9	6.9	7.0	7.1	7.3	7.5	7.7	7.9	7.8	7.8	7.7	7.5	7.4
2011	7.4	7.5	7.6	7.6	7.8	8.0	8.5	8.8	8.6	8.7	8.8	8.7	8.2
2012	8.7	8.8	8.7	8.8	9.0	9.4	9.7	9.9	9.7	9.8	9.7	9.8	9.3
2013	9.1	9.3	9.3	9.2	9.5	9.7	9.6	9.7	9.6	9.4	9.5	9.4	9.4
2014	8.9	8.8	8.7	8.7	9.0	9.2	9.4	9.5	9.4	9.5	9.3	9.2	9.1
2015	8.8	8.6	8.4	8.1	8.3	8.4	8.4	8.3	8.0	7.8	7.7	7.5	8.2

1. Employment by Industry: Montana, 2005–2015—*Continued*

(Numbers in thousands, not seasonally adjusted)

Industry and year	January	February	March	April	May	June	July	August	September	October	November	December	Annual average
Construction													
2005..........................	21.7	22.8	24.0	26.3	27.8	29.0	30.5	31.1	30.6	30.7	29.6	27.2	27.6
2006..........................	25.3	25.3	26.2	28.2	30.6	32.9	33.2	33.5	32.8	32.5	31.1	30.2	30.2
2007..........................	27.8	27.6	29.1	31.5	33.7	35.1	35.0	35.6	34.4	34.0	32.8	30.9	32.3
2008..........................	27.6	27.2	28.1	29.1	30.8	31.7	32.5	32.2	31.0	30.1	28.3	26.3	29.6
2009..........................	22.1	21.5	21.2	23.2	24.3	26.0	26.3	26.5	25.8	25.2	24.0	21.5	24.0
2010..........................	18.9	18.4	19.3	21.7	23.1	24.3	25.2	25.4	25.1	25.2	23.3	20.8	22.6
2011..........................	17.9	17.8	18.5	21.3	22.9	24.5	25.5	25.9	25.9	25.6	24.0	22.1	22.7
2012..........................	19.3	19.0	20.0	22.5	24.0	24.9	25.2	25.6	25.7	25.4	23.7	22.4	23.1
2013..........................	19.6	19.8	20.7	23.2	26.0	26.1	26.2	26.7	26.1	26.2	24.9	23.2	24.1
2014..........................	20.8	20.5	21.5	23.8	25.8	27.7	28.1	27.9	26.9	27.2	25.2	24.6	25.0
2015..........................	22.4	22.7	23.7	25.5	27.4	28.7	29.3	29.2	28.2	28.4	27.1	25.7	26.5
Manufacturing													
2005..........................	19.0	19.1	19.2	19.3	19.4	19.7	19.8	19.9	19.5	20.0	20.0	20.0	19.6
2006..........................	19.6	19.7	19.7	19.8	20.1	20.5	20.5	20.4	20.3	20.5	20.6	20.7	20.2
2007..........................	20.2	20.1	20.4	20.2	20.3	20.7	20.6	20.6	20.4	20.6	20.7	20.6	20.5
2008..........................	20.1	20.0	20.0	20.1	20.3	20.4	20.3	20.2	19.7	19.9	19.4	19.1	20.0
2009..........................	18.0	17.5	17.0	17.3	17.5	17.6	17.4	17.4	17.2	17.5	17.3	17.2	17.4
2010..........................	16.4	16.3	16.1	16.1	16.3	16.5	16.6	16.7	16.6	16.8	16.9	16.8	16.5
2011..........................	16.3	16.3	16.4	16.5	16.6	16.8	16.9	17.0	16.9	17.2	17.1	17.3	16.8
2012..........................	16.8	16.7	16.7	17.2	17.5	17.7	17.9	18.0	17.9	18.3	18.3	18.4	17.6
2013..........................	17.6	17.7	17.7	18.0	18.2	18.5	18.7	18.7	18.6	19.0	19.1	19.1	18.4
2014..........................	18.4	18.4	18.3	18.6	18.8	19.1	19.2	19.2	19.0	19.3	19.0	19.2	18.9
2015..........................	18.6	18.7	18.6	18.8	18.9	19.2	19.4	19.4	19.3	19.6	19.4	19.5	19.1
Trade, Transportation, and Utilities													
2005..........................	84.4	84.0	84.9	85.7	86.8	87.9	88.3	88.2	87.5	87.6	88.3	89.5	86.9
2006..........................	86.0	85.8	86.4	87.4	88.7	89.9	89.5	89.7	89.1	89.3	90.6	91.7	88.7
2007..........................	88.8	88.6	89.4	89.8	91.4	92.0	92.9	92.5	92.2	92.5	93.9	94.6	91.6
2008..........................	91.0	90.1	90.6	90.8	91.4	92.1	91.9	92.1	91.4	90.9	91.1	91.4	91.2
2009..........................	86.9	85.7	85.1	86.2	87.1	88.0	87.9	87.9	87.2	86.7	87.3	87.7	87.0
2010..........................	84.3	83.6	84.1	85.0	86.0	86.9	86.7	86.8	86.0	85.9	86.5	87.2	85.8
2011..........................	84.1	83.6	83.7	85.0	86.2	87.2	87.5	87.8	87.1	87.2	88.3	88.9	86.4
2012..........................	85.9	85.5	85.9	87.0	88.6	89.9	89.8	90.2	89.8	90.2	91.2	91.8	88.8
2013..........................	88.4	88.2	88.6	90.0	91.6	92.3	92.2	92.7	91.8	92.3	93.3	94.3	91.3
2014..........................	90.8	90.3	90.2	91.3	92.8	93.7	93.6	93.9	93.2	93.1	94.3	95.3	92.7
2015..........................	92.3	91.9	92.5	93.6	94.6	95.5	95.5	95.7	95.0	95.6	96.0	96.4	94.6
Wholesale Trade													
2005..........................	15.8	15.9	16.1	16.3	16.5	16.6	16.6	16.5	16.3	16.2	16.2	16.4	16.3
2006..........................	16.0	16.1	16.3	16.3	16.6	16.8	16.8	16.8	16.7	16.7	16.8	16.8	16.6
2007..........................	16.4	16.6	16.7	16.8	17.1	17.1	17.3	17.1	17.1	17.0	17.0	17.1	16.9
2008..........................	16.5	16.5	16.7	16.8	16.9	17.0	16.9	16.9	16.7	16.6	16.5	16.5	16.7
2009..........................	16.0	15.9	15.8	16.1	16.1	16.2	16.2	16.0	15.8	15.7	15.7	15.7	15.9
2010..........................	15.3	15.3	15.5	15.7	15.7	15.8	15.8	15.8	15.6	15.5	15.5	15.5	15.6
2011..........................	15.2	15.2	15.3	15.6	15.8	15.9	16.0	16.0	15.9	15.9	15.9	16.0	15.7
2012..........................	15.8	15.8	16.1	16.3	16.4	16.6	16.6	16.7	16.6	16.6	16.5	16.5	16.4
2013..........................	16.5	16.6	16.9	17.1	17.3	17.3	17.2	17.2	17.0	16.9	16.9	17.0	17.0
2014..........................	16.6	16.6	16.7	16.9	17.1	17.2	17.2	17.2	17.0	16.9	17.0	17.1	17.0
2015..........................	17.1	17.1	17.3	17.5	17.6	17.8	17.8	17.8	17.5	17.2	17.4	17.1	17.4
Retail Trade													
2005..........................	53.6	53.1	53.7	54.3	55.1	56.0	56.4	56.4	55.7	55.8	56.5	57.2	55.3
2006..........................	54.5	54.1	54.4	55.2	56.1	57.0	57.0	57.1	56.2	56.5	57.8	58.6	56.2
2007..........................	56.5	56.0	56.7	56.9	58.0	58.8	59.5	59.4	58.9	59.1	60.5	60.9	58.4
2008..........................	58.7	57.9	58.1	58.1	58.7	59.3	59.5	59.6	58.7	58.4	58.7	58.8	58.7
2009..........................	55.5	54.5	54.1	54.7	55.5	56.4	56.6	56.7	55.8	55.3	56.0	56.1	55.6
2010..........................	53.7	53.0	53.2	53.9	54.7	55.6	55.5	55.6	54.6	54.7	55.3	55.6	54.6
2011..........................	53.2	52.7	52.8	53.7	54.5	55.3	55.7	55.8	55.1	55.1	56.1	56.3	54.7
2012..........................	53.9	53.3	53.4	54.1	55.3	56.2	56.3	56.2	55.6	56.0	57.1	57.2	55.4
2013..........................	54.1	53.6	53.7	55.0	56.0	56.8	57.2	57.3	56.4	57.0	57.9	58.3	56.1
2014..........................	55.6	55.2	55.1	56.2	57.3	58.1	58.4	58.5	57.6	57.8	58.8	59.1	57.3
2015..........................	56.8	56.5	56.9	57.9	58.8	59.5	59.7	59.8	59.0	59.8	59.9	59.8	58.7

1. Employment by Industry: Montana, 2005–2015—*Continued*

(Numbers in thousands, not seasonally adjusted)

Industry and year	January	February	March	April	May	June	July	August	September	October	November	December	Annual average
Transportation and Utilities													
2005	15.0	15.0	15.1	15.1	15.2	15.3	15.3	15.3	15.5	15.6	15.6	15.9	15.3
2006	15.5	15.6	15.7	15.9	16.0	16.1	15.7	15.8	16.2	16.1	16.0	16.3	15.9
2007	15.9	16.0	16.0	16.1	16.3	16.1	16.1	16.0	16.2	16.4	16.4	16.6	16.2
2008	15.8	15.7	15.8	15.9	15.8	15.8	15.5	15.6	16.0	15.9	15.9	16.1	15.8
2009	15.4	15.3	15.2	15.4	15.5	15.4	15.1	15.2	15.6	15.7	15.6	15.9	15.4
2010	15.3	15.3	15.4	15.4	15.6	15.5	15.4	15.4	15.8	15.7	15.7	16.1	15.6
2011	15.7	15.7	15.6	15.7	15.9	16.0	15.8	16.0	16.1	16.2	16.3	16.6	16.0
2012	16.2	16.4	16.4	16.6	16.9	17.1	16.9	17.3	17.6	17.6	17.6	18.1	17.1
2013	17.8	18.0	18.0	17.9	18.3	18.2	17.8	18.2	18.4	18.4	18.5	19.0	18.2
2014	18.6	18.5	18.4	18.2	18.4	18.4	18.0	18.2	18.6	18.4	18.5	19.1	18.4
2015	18.4	18.3	18.3	18.2	18.2	18.2	18.0	18.1	18.5	18.6	18.7	19.5	18.4
Information													
2005	7.7	7.8	7.8	7.7	7.8	7.9	7.9	7.9	7.7	7.7	7.7	7.8	7.8
2006	7.7	7.8	7.7	7.7	7.8	7.9	7.8	7.8	7.7	7.6	7.6	7.7	7.7
2007	7.4	7.5	7.5	7.5	7.6	7.6	7.6	7.7	7.6	7.5	7.6	7.6	7.6
2008	7.6	7.6	7.6	7.7	7.7	7.8	7.7	7.7	7.8	7.7	7.7	7.8	7.7
2009	7.5	7.6	7.5	7.4	7.5	7.6	7.5	7.4	7.4	7.3	7.3	7.3	7.4
2010	7.3	7.4	7.4	7.3	7.3	7.5	7.4	7.3	7.2	7.2	7.2	7.2	7.3
2011	7.1	7.2	7.2	7.2	7.2	7.3	7.3	7.3	7.2	7.2	7.2	7.1	7.2
2012	6.9	7.0	6.9	6.8	6.9	6.9	6.9	7.0	6.9	6.9	7.0	7.0	6.9
2013	6.8	7.0	6.9	6.8	6.9	6.8	6.8	6.8	6.7	6.7	6.7	6.7	6.8
2014	6.5	6.5	6.4	6.4	6.4	6.4	6.4	6.4	6.4	6.3	6.3	6.3	6.4
2015	6.3	6.4	6.3	6.3	6.4	6.4	6.4	6.4	6.3	6.4	6.5	6.4	6.4
Financial Activities													
2005	20.8	20.8	20.8	21.0	21.2	21.5	21.8	21.8	21.7	21.8	21.9	22.2	21.4
2006	21.7	21.8	21.9	22.0	21.9	22.3	22.3	22.2	21.9	21.8	21.7	21.9	22.0
2007	21.4	21.4	21.6	21.5	21.7	21.9	22.0	22.1	21.8	21.9	21.8	22.2	21.8
2008	21.7	21.7	21.7	21.8	21.8	22.1	22.1	22.2	21.7	21.8	21.7	21.7	21.8
2009	21.1	21.0	21.0	21.1	21.3	21.6	21.8	21.8	21.6	21.6	21.6	22.0	21.5
2010	21.0	21.0	21.1	21.0	21.1	21.4	21.5	21.4	21.1	21.2	20.9	21.2	21.2
2011	20.7	20.7	20.8	20.7	20.8	21.2	21.4	21.3	21.2	21.6	21.6	21.9	21.2
2012	20.9	20.9	20.9	21.0	21.3	21.7	21.9	22.0	21.9	21.9	21.8	22.2	21.5
2013	21.6	21.7	21.8	22.2	22.3	22.6	23.0	23.2	22.9	23.2	23.1	23.4	22.6
2014	22.9	23.1	23.1	23.3	23.4	23.7	24.0	24.0	23.6	23.6	23.5	23.8	23.5
2015	23.4	23.4	23.5	23.5	23.7	24.1	24.2	24.2	24.0	23.8	23.8	24.1	23.8
Professional and Business Services													
2005	32.1	32.7	33.3	34.4	34.7	35.8	36.6	36.8	36.2	36.4	36.5	36.2	35.1
2006	35.5	35.9	36.6	37.5	38.2	39.6	39.4	40.2	39.2	39.0	38.5	38.6	38.2
2007	38.1	38.5	39.3	40.3	41.0	42.1	42.0	42.5	41.2	41.5	40.8	40.3	40.6
2008	39.1	39.6	39.7	40.8	41.6	41.8	42.2	42.2	40.9	40.4	39.5	39.3	40.6
2009	37.9	37.7	37.9	38.7	38.8	39.5	39.9	39.6	38.9	38.9	39.0	38.0	38.7
2010	37.1	37.4	37.7	38.9	39.2	40.0	40.6	40.6	39.8	40.5	39.7	39.7	39.3
2011	38.6	38.8	39.3	40.4	40.8	41.3	41.8	41.9	40.9	40.5	40.1	39.4	40.3
2012	38.7	38.8	39.4	40.7	41.1	41.6	41.9	41.8	40.6	40.5	39.8	39.4	40.4
2013	37.9	38.1	38.4	39.5	39.9	40.7	41.3	40.8	39.9	39.8	39.2	38.9	39.5
2014	37.5	38.0	38.1	39.1	39.7	40.4	40.9	41.2	40.2	39.5	38.5	38.4	39.3
2015	38.5	38.9	39.3	40.4	40.4	41.3	42.0	41.9	40.9	40.9	40.0	39.3	40.3
Education and Health Services													
2005	55.5	55.7	56.1	55.5	55.7	55.8	54.9	55.0	56.1	56.5	56.9	56.9	55.9
2006	56.4	56.9	57.3	57.7	57.6	57.2	56.4	56.8	57.9	58.0	58.4	58.7	57.4
2007	58.2	58.7	59.0	58.9	59.0	58.5	57.6	58.0	59.3	59.4	59.5	60.0	58.8
2008	60.0	60.6	60.9	60.9	61.0	60.3	59.6	60.2	61.3	61.7	62.0	62.5	60.9
2009	61.8	62.3	62.3	62.5	62.4	62.2	61.4	61.6	62.5	63.2	63.4	63.8	62.5
2010	63.1	63.3	63.5	63.9	63.9	63.8	63.1	63.2	64.0	64.3	64.4	64.6	63.8
2011	63.9	64.2	64.3	64.2	64.8	64.6	63.9	64.5	65.6	66.4	66.5	67.1	65.0
2012	66.8	67.3	67.3	67.5	67.8	67.3	66.6	67.2	67.7	68.2	68.4	68.8	67.6
2013	68.3	68.6	68.8	68.8	69.1	68.7	68.0	68.6	69.5	70.0	70.0	70.3	69.1
2014	69.7	70.0	70.1	70.9	70.8	70.1	69.1	69.4	70.1	70.5	70.8	71.1	70.2
2015	70.6	71.0	71.2	71.7	71.7	71.3	70.3	70.7	71.7	72.5	73.2	73.3	71.6

1. Employment by Industry: Montana, 2005–2015—*Continued*

(Numbers in thousands, not seasonally adjusted)

Industry and year	January	February	March	April	May	June	July	August	September	October	November	December	Annual average
Leisure and Hospitality													
2005	50.4	51.1	52.2	52.7	54.7	59.1	61.7	61.9	58.8	54.5	52.5	53.2	55.2
2006	52.6	53.2	54.2	55.1	56.4	61.2	62.7	62.7	58.9	55.4	53.3	55.0	56.7
2007	53.7	54.0	54.9	55.9	57.5	62.3	65.0	65.2	61.4	56.5	54.9	56.7	58.2
2008	55.2	55.6	56.6	56.7	58.8	63.5	66.1	66.1	62.2	57.0	54.7	55.9	59.0
2009	53.5	53.7	54.2	55.0	56.7	61.3	63.5	63.4	59.9	54.7	52.3	53.1	56.8
2010	51.5	51.7	52.4	53.4	55.2	59.4	62.4	62.8	59.6	54.2	52.0	53.3	55.7
2011	51.9	52.1	53.3	54.2	56.2	59.8	62.9	63.0	60.0	55.6	53.4	54.5	56.4
2012	53.4	53.5	54.7	55.4	57.5	62.3	64.6	65.2	61.7	57.1	54.6	55.9	58.0
2013	55.4	56.1	57.1	57.8	59.1	64.1	66.7	67.1	63.5	58.6	55.9	57.9	59.9
2014	56.8	56.8	57.1	58.0	59.6	64.3	67.1	67.6	63.7	58.6	56.1	58.4	60.3
2015	57.7	58.4	59.3	60.2	62.1	66.7	69.4	69.5	65.7	59.8	57.1	57.8	62.0
Other Services													
2005	16.4	16.6	16.7	16.7	16.8	17.0	16.7	16.8	16.8	16.6	16.6	16.8	16.7
2006	16.5	16.6	16.9	17.0	17.1	17.3	17.1	17.1	17.1	17.1	17.0	17.1	17.0
2007	16.8	16.8	17.2	17.3	17.2	17.5	17.2	17.1	17.1	17.2	17.2	17.2	17.2
2008	17.1	17.3	17.6	17.6	17.6	17.8	17.7	17.6	17.5	17.6	17.5	17.3	17.5
2009	16.8	17.0	17.0	17.0	17.1	17.2	17.2	16.9	17.0	17.0	16.9	16.9	17.0
2010	16.6	16.6	16.8	16.7	16.8	17.0	16.8	16.7	16.7	16.7	16.6	16.6	16.7
2011	16.4	16.5	16.7	16.8	17.0	17.1	17.2	17.0	17.0	17.0	16.9	17.1	16.9
2012	16.7	16.9	17.0	17.3	17.5	17.7	17.6	17.7	17.7	17.8	17.5	17.4	17.4
2013	17.2	17.4	17.5	17.6	17.8	17.9	17.8	17.9	17.7	17.9	17.9	17.9	17.7
2014	17.4	17.5	17.4	17.7	17.9	17.7	18.0	17.9	17.6	18.0	17.8	17.4	17.7
2015	17.7	17.8	17.9	18.0	18.1	18.2	18.2	18.2	18.0	18.0	17.7	17.9	18.0
Government													
2005	84.8	87.2	87.6	87.6	88.3	86.2	81.3	80.2	86.1	88.3	89.0	88.4	86.3
2006	84.8	87.6	88.4	88.8	90.3	89.1	88.3	83.3	86.5	88.8	89.7	88.5	87.8
2007	85.7	88.0	89.0	88.1	89.3	87.0	83.5	82.9	85.6	90.1	89.6	88.7	87.3
2008	85.4	87.9	88.5	88.1	90.8	88.1	83.7	84.0	88.0	91.2	91.8	90.1	88.1
2009	86.8	88.9	89.6	90.2	92.1	90.3	85.4	85.9	89.1	92.8	92.6	92.3	89.7
2010	90.2	91.4	93.2	92.7	96.0	93.1	88.7	88.7	91.7	93.2	92.8	92.5	92.0
2011	89.4	91.0	91.9	91.6	93.3	91.0	84.5	85.8	90.8	91.2	90.8	90.6	90.2
2012	88.7	89.6	90.4	90.3	92.4	89.1	86.2	85.6	90.3	91.0	91.0	90.5	89.6
2013	90.2	91.5	91.9	91.5	92.1	89.1	83.8	84.8	89.3	91.7	91.1	89.8	89.7
2014	88.0	91.4	91.7	91.3	92.1	89.7	85.6	85.4	90.2	91.7	91.7	90.8	90.0
2015	88.5	91.0	91.9	92.4	92.8	89.6	85.4	85.7	90.8	92.4	92.0	91.0	90.3

2. Average Weekly Hours by Selected Industry: Montana, 2011–2015

(Not seasonally adjusted)

Industry and year	January	February	March	April	May	June	July	August	September	October	November	December	Annual average
Total Private													
2011	33.0	32.7	32.6	33.1	33.6	33.1	33.1	33.2	32.9	33.4	32.4	32.3	32.9
2012	32.7	32.3	32.4	33.4	32.9	33.1	34.0	33.4	34.0	33.0	32.7	33.9	33.2
2013	32.7	33.2	33.0	33.1	33.3	34.1	33.3	33.6	33.9	33.3	33.0	33.3	33.3
2014	32.2	32.9	32.8	32.4	32.7	33.7	33.0	33.1	32.8	32.7	33.0	32.3	32.8
2015	32.1	32.7	32.5	32.0	32.5	32.7	32.9	33.5	32.7	32.5	33.0	32.3	32.6
Goods-Producing													
2011	39.8	38.7	38.7	39.9	40.0	40.1	39.9	39.9	39.0	39.4	37.6	37.7	39.2
2012	37.6	36.9	37.7	39.3	38.8	39.7	40.1	38.9	38.4	38.4	37.3	37.3	38.4
2013	36.2	37.0	37.0	37.4	38.4	39.4	38.1	38.4	38.5	38.0	37.3	37.1	37.8
2014	36.3	37.0	37.2	37.6	38.4	39.4	38.2	37.5	38.2	38.6	37.2	37.4	37.8
2015	36.1	36.8	36.8	37.1	38.2	38.5	38.0	38.2	36.8	37.3	37.7	37.7	37.4
Construction													
2011	31.6	31.3	32.4	34.8	34.9	36.2	36.7	37.1	36.3	36.6	34.4	33.2	34.9
2012	32.9	32.9	34.8	37.2	38.8	39.3	38.6	38.6	36.0	37.2	34.6	34.2	36.4
2013	32.4	34.3	35.1	35.7	37.6	39.4	37.3	38.5	38.5	38.3	36.0	35.8	36.8
2014	34.5	35.6	35.4	36.4	38.4	39.0	37.8	37.0	38.1	38.8	37.0	37.3	37.2
2015	35.5	36.0	36.5	37.4	39.1	38.8	38.1	38.4	36.8	37.4	37.3	37.8	37.5
Trade, Transportation, and Utilities													
2011	34.8	34.3	34.3	34.9	34.5	34.7	34.3	34.4	33.7	33.5	32.6	33.4	34.1
2012	33.5	33.3	33.3	33.9	33.2	32.9	33.7	33.5	34.0	32.7	32.4	35.4	33.5
2013	34.0	34.4	34.1	34.3	34.4	35.5	34.6	34.8	34.7	33.4	32.9	33.4	34.2
2014	32.3	33.1	33.0	32.5	32.9	33.6	33.5	33.4	33.2	32.9	33.2	33.0	33.1
2015	32.8	33.1	32.8	32.3	32.7	33.2	33.4	34.4	33.5	33.1	33.4	32.9	33.1
Financial Activities													
2011	37.1	36.3	36.4	36.7	37.6	36.6	36.7	36.8	37.3	38.3	36.7	35.8	36.9
2012	38.1	36.3	35.9	38.6	37.6	37.2	38.9	37.6	38.9	37.1	37.5	38.9	37.7
2013	37.3	37.7	37.6	37.6	37.6	38.9	37.3	37.8	38.6	38.2	38.3	38.8	38.0
2014	37.3	38.2	38.0	36.5	36.8	37.7	35.7	36.1	35.8	35.7	37.2	35.0	36.6
2015	35.3	36.1	36.0	34.9	35.3	35.0	35.4	36.3	35.6	35.5	36.8	35.1	35.6
Professional and Business Services													
2011	33.5	33.0	33.0	33.5	34.2	33.0	32.8	32.7	33.6	34.2	33.8	33.3	33.4
2012	32.9	33.5	33.5	33.9	34.2	34.6	34.3	34.4	35.1	34.2	33.8	34.1	34.0
2013	32.6	33.8	34.1	34.0	34.3	35.5	33.4	34.5	34.4	34.1	33.9	33.6	34.0
2014	32.7	33.8	33.6	33.5	33.6	34.9	33.1	34.4	34.6	34.1	35.0	34.3	34.0
2015	34.2	34.8	34.2	33.6	34.5	34.4	34.1	34.9	34.6	33.7	34.8	33.9	34.3
Education and Health Services													
2011	33.8	33.9	33.7	33.7	34.0	32.9	33.1	32.6	33.0	33.5	33.2	32.9	33.4
2012	33.3	32.9	33.0	33.5	33.0	33.2	34.2	33.5	34.2	33.6	33.6	34.1	33.5
2013	33.4	33.4	33.5	33.5	33.1	33.0	33.4	33.4	34.1	33.9	33.8	34.5	33.6
2014	33.7	33.8	33.6	33.2	33.3	34.0	33.6	33.6	33.3	33.3	34.0	33.5	33.6
2015	33.6	34.1	34.0	33.7	33.6	33.6	33.8	34.0	33.9	33.8	34.1	33.7	33.8
Leisure and Hospitality													
2011	21.3	21.4	21.3	21.7	22.8	22.7	24.2	24.9	23.4	23.8	22.4	22.4	22.8
2012	23.3	22.6	22.8	23.6	23.7	24.4	26.6	25.8	25.7	23.6	22.9	24.2	24.2
2013	22.7	23.7	23.2	22.7	23.4	25.1	24.8	24.8	24.5	23.5	22.9	23.2	23.8
2014	22.2	23.5	23.7	22.7	23.4	25.2	25.4	25.5	24.1	23.5	24.0	22.6	23.9
2015	22.5	23.8	23.4	22.4	23.3	24.1	25.4	25.9	24.0	23.4	23.5	22.4	23.7

3. Average Hourly Earnings by Selected Industry: Montana, 2011–2015

(Dollars, not seasonally adjusted)

Industry and year	January	February	March	April	May	June	July	August	September	October	November	December	Annual average
Total Private													
2011	20.54	20.44	20.58	20.74	20.83	20.40	20.61	20.32	20.81	21.06	21.15	20.55	20.67
2012	20.61	20.67	20.69	20.93	20.91	20.48	20.69	20.48	20.57	20.76	20.56	21.06	20.70
2013	21.20	21.37	20.87	21.02	20.79	20.82	20.86	20.63	20.99	20.95	20.98	21.16	20.96
2014	21.23	21.53	21.26	21.35	21.33	21.30	21.25	21.13	21.46	21.82	21.68	21.74	21.42
2015	21.81	22.10	21.73	21.78	21.90	21.81	21.78	22.29	22.13	22.25	22.66	22.38	22.05
Goods-Producing													
2011	24.90	24.98	25.77	24.63	24.69	24.30	24.55	23.84	24.03	24.13	24.02	23.61	24.42
2012	22.88	23.66	23.69	24.35	24.14	23.48	23.86	23.80	23.92	24.10	23.60	23.95	23.80
2013	23.83	23.87	23.04	23.70	23.83	23.93	23.21	23.16	22.88	22.78	22.97	23.20	23.36
2014	23.11	23.22	23.28	23.47	23.60	24.10	23.31	23.36	23.25	23.34	23.85	24.13	23.51
2015	23.79	23.75	23.83	24.51	24.70	24.58	24.20	24.95	25.38	25.05	24.97	24.30	24.52
Construction													
2011	24.37	24.15	23.76	24.56	24.77	24.34	24.37	24.45	24.90	24.67	23.96	24.04	24.39
2012	23.48	23.61	24.05	24.83	24.38	23.20	23.13	23.35	23.71	24.03	23.25	24.22	23.76
2013	24.33	23.58	23.49	23.84	24.52	24.75	23.67	23.66	23.46	23.55	24.07	24.32	23.94
2014	24.18	24.56	24.56	24.88	25.06	25.84	24.25	24.43	23.98	24.13	24.74	25.20	24.66
2015	24.30	24.32	24.22	24.59	25.27	24.99	24.19	25.09	25.46	25.43	25.28	25.28	24.90
Trade, Transportation, and Utilities													
2011	18.51	18.50	18.55	19.03	18.87	18.65	18.50	18.34	18.44	18.51	18.30	18.36	18.55
2012	19.17	19.11	19.36	19.84	19.43	19.53	19.38	19.13	19.41	19.13	19.06	20.78	19.46
2013	20.94	20.81	20.49	20.54	20.25	20.26	20.15	20.03	20.10	19.89	19.86	19.84	20.26
2014	19.89	19.69	20.01	19.84	20.04	19.73	19.66	19.72	19.98	19.95	20.16	19.97	19.89
2015	20.13	20.02	19.93	19.98	19.76	19.95	20.12	20.05	20.20	19.97	19.99	19.78	19.99
Financial Activities													
2011	20.52	21.09	21.12	22.00	21.77	20.96	22.00	21.86	22.92	23.48	22.50	20.44	21.74
2012	20.44	20.61	20.73	20.70	20.34	20.38	22.28	21.33	21.46	21.42	21.37	21.53	21.07
2013	22.09	22.11	22.09	21.90	21.50	21.75	21.52	21.47	21.82	22.15	22.31	22.00	21.89
2014	22.46	22.80	22.54	22.30	21.98	23.02	23.26	22.92	23.52	23.35	23.74	23.56	22.95
2015	23.20	23.38	24.10	24.08	24.23	24.29	24.27	25.07	24.98	24.98	25.34	25.12	24.43
Professional and Business Services													
2011	21.62	21.19	21.10	21.36	21.29	20.97	21.09	21.25	21.51	22.04	21.85	22.45	21.48
2012	22.93	23.23	22.85	22.87	22.36	22.29	23.31	22.70	22.77	22.68	22.49	22.95	22.78
2013	22.80	22.68	22.57	22.45	22.14	22.29	22.41	22.29	23.86	23.11	23.40	24.15	22.84
2014	23.80	23.72	23.80	23.33	23.22	23.20	23.17	22.87	23.43	23.33	23.80	23.57	23.43
2015	23.62	23.96	23.78	23.29	23.06	22.85	23.08	22.86	23.36	24.11	24.24	24.56	23.55
Education and Health Services													
2011	21.78	21.34	21.48	22.14	23.20	22.91	23.60	23.59	23.69	23.78	25.03	23.08	22.97
2012	23.14	22.53	22.62	22.61	23.59	22.43	22.16	22.58	21.90	22.33	21.72	22.05	22.47
2013	22.33	23.26	22.04	22.27	21.83	22.16	23.10	22.26	22.44	22.43	21.98	22.47	22.38
2014	22.86	24.26	22.94	23.34	23.16	23.27	24.01	23.52	23.89	23.83	23.24	23.63	23.49
2015	24.19	25.26	23.74	23.59	24.22	24.20	24.38	25.83	24.06	24.13	25.48	24.96	24.51
Leisure and Hospitality													
2011	13.35	13.48	13.31	13.06	12.86	12.59	12.54	12.28	12.52	12.45	12.45	12.63	12.76
2012	12.55	12.49	12.35	12.41	12.35	12.19	12.03	12.04	12.28	12.12	12.26	12.31	12.27
2013	12.35	12.26	12.23	12.09	12.04	11.77	11.92	11.88	12.07	12.14	12.08	12.30	12.08
2014	12.32	12.41	12.36	12.45	12.27	12.02	12.12	12.29	12.45	12.42	12.36	12.63	12.33
2015	12.79	13.00	12.97	13.03	13.14	13.02	13.01	13.13	13.22	13.41	13.43	13.44	13.13

4. Average Weekly Earnings by Selected Industry: Montana, 2011–2015

(Dollars, not seasonally adjusted)

Industry and year	January	February	March	April	May	June	July	August	September	October	November	December	Annual average
Total Private													
2011	677.82	668.39	670.91	686.49	699.89	675.24	682.19	674.62	684.65	703.40	685.26	663.77	680.04
2012	673.95	667.64	670.36	699.06	687.94	677.89	703.46	684.03	699.38	685.08	672.31	713.93	687.24
2013	693.24	709.48	688.71	695.76	692.31	709.96	694.64	693.17	711.56	697.64	692.34	704.63	697.97
2014	683.61	708.34	697.33	691.74	697.49	717.81	701.25	699.40	703.89	713.51	715.44	702.20	702.58
2015	700.10	722.67	706.23	696.96	711.75	713.19	716.56	746.72	723.65	723.13	747.78	722.87	718.83
Goods-Producing													
2011	991.02	966.73	997.30	982.74	987.60	974.43	979.55	951.22	937.17	950.72	903.15	890.10	957.26
2012	860.29	873.05	893.11	956.96	936.63	932.16	956.79	925.82	918.53	925.44	880.28	893.34	913.92
2013	862.65	883.19	852.48	886.38	915.07	942.84	884.30	889.34	880.88	865.64	856.78	860.72	883.01
2014	838.89	859.14	866.02	882.47	906.24	949.54	890.44	876.00	888.15	900.92	887.22	902.46	888.68
2015	858.82	874.00	876.94	909.32	943.54	946.33	919.60	953.09	933.98	934.37	941.37	916.11	917.05
Construction													
2011	770.09	755.90	769.82	854.69	864.47	881.11	894.38	907.10	903.87	902.92	824.22	798.13	851.21
2012	772.49	776.77	836.94	923.68	945.94	911.76	892.82	901.31	853.56	893.92	804.45	828.32	864.86
2013	788.29	808.79	824.50	851.09	921.95	975.15	882.89	910.91	903.21	901.97	866.52	870.66	880.99
2014	834.21	874.34	869.42	905.63	962.30	1,007.76	916.65	903.91	913.64	936.24	915.38	939.96	917.35
2015	862.65	875.52	884.03	919.67	988.06	969.61	921.64	963.46	936.93	951.08	942.94	955.58	933.75
Trade, Transportation, and Utilities													
2011	644.15	634.55	636.27	664.15	651.02	647.16	634.55	630.90	621.43	620.09	596.58	613.22	632.56
2012	642.20	636.36	644.69	672.58	645.08	642.54	653.11	640.86	659.94	625.55	617.54	735.61	651.91
2013	711.96	715.86	698.71	704.52	696.60	719.23	697.19	697.04	697.47	664.33	653.39	662.66	692.89
2014	642.45	651.74	660.33	644.80	659.32	662.93	658.61	658.65	663.34	656.36	669.31	659.01	658.36
2015	660.26	662.66	653.70	645.35	646.15	662.34	672.01	689.72	676.70	661.01	667.67	650.76	661.67
Financial Activities													
2011	761.29	765.57	768.77	807.40	818.55	767.14	807.40	804.45	854.92	899.28	825.75	731.75	802.21
2012	778.76	748.14	744.21	799.02	764.78	758.14	866.69	802.01	834.79	794.68	801.38	837.52	794.34
2013	823.96	833.55	830.58	823.44	808.40	846.08	802.70	811.57	842.25	846.13	854.47	853.60	831.82
2014	837.76	870.96	856.52	813.95	808.86	867.85	830.38	827.41	842.02	833.60	883.13	824.60	839.97
2015	818.96	844.02	867.60	840.39	855.32	850.15	859.16	910.04	889.29	886.79	932.51	881.71	869.71
Professional and Business Services													
2011	724.27	699.27	696.30	715.56	728.12	692.01	691.75	694.88	722.74	753.77	738.53	747.59	717.43
2012	754.40	778.21	765.48	775.29	764.71	771.23	799.53	780.88	799.23	775.66	760.16	782.60	774.52
2013	743.28	766.58	769.64	763.30	759.40	791.30	748.49	769.01	820.78	788.05	793.26	811.44	776.56
2014	778.26	801.74	799.68	781.56	780.19	809.68	766.93	786.73	810.68	795.55	833.00	808.45	796.62
2015	807.80	833.81	813.28	782.54	795.57	786.04	787.03	797.81	808.26	812.51	843.55	832.58	807.77
Education and Health Services													
2011	736.16	723.43	723.88	746.12	788.80	753.74	781.16	769.03	781.77	796.63	831.00	759.33	767.20
2012	770.56	741.24	746.46	757.44	778.47	744.68	757.87	756.43	748.98	750.29	729.79	751.91	752.75
2013	745.82	776.88	738.34	746.05	722.57	731.28	771.54	743.48	765.20	760.38	742.92	775.22	751.97
2014	770.38	819.99	770.78	774.89	771.23	791.18	806.74	790.27	795.54	793.54	790.16	791.61	789.26
2015	812.78	861.37	807.16	794.98	813.79	813.12	824.04	878.22	815.63	815.59	868.87	841.15	828.44
Leisure and Hospitality													
2011	284.36	288.47	283.50	283.40	293.21	285.79	303.47	305.77	292.97	296.31	278.88	282.91	290.93
2012	292.42	282.27	281.58	292.88	292.70	297.44	320.00	310.63	315.60	286.03	280.75	297.90	296.93
2013	280.35	290.56	283.74	274.44	281.74	295.43	295.62	294.62	295.72	285.29	276.63	285.36	287.50
2014	273.50	291.64	292.93	282.62	287.12	302.90	307.85	313.40	300.05	291.87	296.64	285.44	294.69
2015	287.78	309.40	303.50	291.87	306.16	313.78	330.45	340.07	317.28	313.79	315.61	301.06	311.18

NEBRASKA
At a Glance

Population:
  2005 estimate: 1,761,497
  2010 census: 1,826,341
  2015 estimate: 1,896,190

Percent change in population:
  2005–2015: 7.6%
  2010–2015: 3.8%

Percent change in total nonfarm employment:
  2005–2015: 7.7%

Industry with the largest growth in employment, 2005–2015 (thousands):
  Education and health services, 22.0

Industry with the largest decline or smallest growth in employment, 2005–2015 (thousands):
  Manufacturing, –4.0

Civilian labor force:
  2005: 972,992
  2010: 993,398
  2015: 1,012,973

Unemployment rate and rank among states (highest to lowest):
  2005: 3.8%, 43rd
  2010: 4.6%, 50th
  2015: 3.0%, 50th

Over-the-year change in unemployment rates:
  2012–2013: –0.2%
  2013–2014: –0.5%
  2014–2015: –0.3%

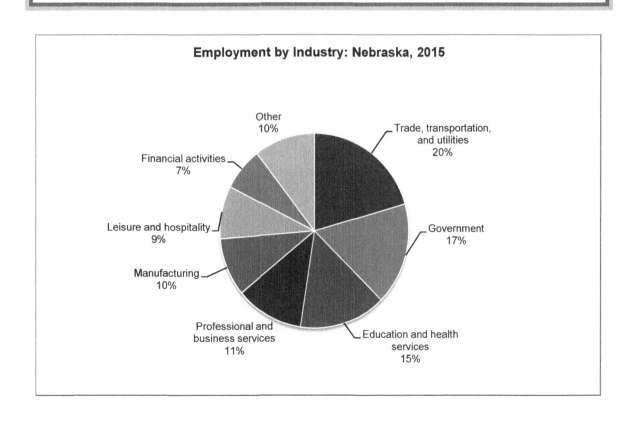

Employment by Industry: Nebraska, 2015

Other 10%
Trade, transportation, and utilities 20%
Financial activities 7%
Leisure and hospitality 9%
Government 17%
Manufacturing 10%
Professional and business services 11%
Education and health services 15%

1. Employment by Industry: Nebraska, 2005–2015

(Numbers in thousands, not seasonally adjusted)

Industry and year	January	February	March	April	May	June	July	August	September	October	November	December	Annual average
Total Nonfarm													
2005	909.3	914.4	923.0	932.8	940.7	946.1	934.6	934.5	940.2	942.4	946.1	944.4	934.0
2006	922.8	928.1	934.8	941.5	951.2	958.2	943.8	944.8	951.5	953.1	958.3	957.9	945.5
2007	936.4	939.5	946.3	956.5	968.6	974.1	961.5	965.5	970.0	972.6	975.5	973.6	961.7
2008	953.5	955.0	961.3	969.7	979.9	979.5	966.7	969.5	972.6	978.3	976.0	972.0	969.5
2009	944.8	944.0	946.4	951.5	959.6	957.6	948.5	946.7	948.8	952.0	952.1	945.8	949.8
2010	921.7	925.1	931.2	944.5	954.5	956.8	947.1	947.9	948.1	955.8	954.9	953.9	945.1
2011	928.6	931.8	939.0	953.6	960.9	959.7	950.4	953.1	957.4	964.5	966.7	965.8	952.6
2012	944.9	947.8	957.6	967.6	978.0	977.1	967.1	969.4	973.7	979.4	981.6	981.7	968.8
2013	955.7	959.8	965.8	975.9	989.3	987.2	978.2	982.5	986.6	992.8	995.8	994.8	980.4
2014	971.1	975.6	981.5	992.1	1,002.7	1,000.1	989.9	992.8	996.7	1,002.9	1,003.1	1,005.9	992.9
2015	981.0	985.9	993.2	1,004.0	1,013.2	1,013.1	1,005.1	1,008.0	1,010.4	1,022.1	1,021.3	1,017.9	1,006.3
Total Private													
2005	750.3	753.4	761.1	770.2	776.1	782.8	780.9	781.4	778.4	778.5	781.9	781.1	773.0
2006	762.3	765.6	771.5	777.7	785.2	793.0	790.1	790.7	788.8	788.6	793.1	793.6	783.4
2007	774.7	776.2	782.6	792.3	801.6	808.4	808.6	811.4	807.8	807.8	810.2	809.5	799.3
2008	790.6	791.7	797.7	804.2	811.9	813.8	811.3	813.7	808.5	810.7	808.1	804.7	805.6
2009	779.1	776.0	777.7	780.8	787.1	787.8	785.0	784.5	780.8	781.1	780.4	775.9	781.4
2010	754.7	755.6	759.8	772.5	779.2	784.7	784.7	785.4	780.3	783.9	782.9	782.7	775.5
2011	761.3	762.3	769.2	782.2	788.7	791.7	791.3	792.3	790.8	793.2	795.3	795.2	784.5
2012	777.8	778.1	787.8	796.7	804.5	810.0	807.3	808.0	805.5	808.4	810.0	811.0	800.4
2013	788.6	790.3	796.2	805.2	815.2	818.9	817.7	820.9	818.2	820.5	823.3	823.3	811.5
2014	803.0	804.7	810.6	820.9	828.4	831.5	829.6	831.0	826.5	829.6	829.8	833.3	823.2
2015	812.8	814.9	821.5	830.0	838.0	842.6	842.4	843.8	839.8	847.1	846.2	843.7	835.2
Goods-Producing													
2005	142.7	143.2	145.7	148.3	150.0	152.7	153.3	152.8	151.5	150.9	150.3	148.3	149.1
2006	144.9	145.2	146.6	148.9	150.2	153.0	153.1	152.7	152.1	151.5	150.5	149.2	149.8
2007	144.7	144.4	146.6	149.7	152.1	155.0	156.7	156.9	155.8	155.0	153.9	151.7	151.9
2008	147.4	147.2	149.0	151.9	154.1	155.2	155.2	155.2	153.2	152.6	150.1	146.6	151.5
2009	140.2	138.8	139.0	140.7	142.8	143.6	144.1	143.4	142.4	140.6	139.0	135.2	140.8
2010	128.9	128.9	129.4	133.8	135.7	138.1	138.0	137.5	136.6	136.2	135.4	133.3	134.3
2011	128.7	128.4	130.7	134.1	136.0	137.8	138.1	137.4	137.0	137.0	137.2	135.9	134.9
2012	132.5	131.6	134.1	136.5	139.0	141.4	141.3	141.4	140.8	140.9	140.5	139.7	138.3
2013	134.8	135.5	136.6	139.9	143.2	145.2	145.3	145.5	145.0	144.3	143.9	141.6	141.7
2014	138.1	138.1	139.6	144.3	146.1	148.1	148.5	148.6	147.3	147.6	146.1	145.7	144.8
2015	141.0	141.7	143.8	146.8	148.5	150.0	150.3	150.4	149.3	150.3	148.6	145.7	147.2
Service-Providing													
2005	766.6	771.2	777.3	784.5	790.7	793.4	781.3	781.7	788.7	791.5	795.8	796.1	784.9
2006	777.9	782.9	788.2	792.6	801.0	805.2	790.7	792.1	799.4	801.6	807.8	808.7	795.7
2007	791.7	795.1	799.7	806.8	816.5	819.1	804.8	808.6	814.2	817.6	821.6	821.9	809.8
2008	806.1	807.8	812.3	817.8	825.8	824.3	811.5	814.3	819.4	825.7	825.9	825.4	818.0
2009	804.6	805.2	807.4	810.8	816.8	814.0	804.4	803.3	806.4	811.4	813.1	810.6	809.0
2010	792.8	796.2	801.8	810.7	818.8	818.7	809.1	810.4	811.5	819.6	819.5	820.6	810.8
2011	799.9	803.4	808.3	819.5	824.9	821.9	812.3	815.7	820.4	827.5	829.5	829.9	817.8
2012	812.4	816.2	823.5	831.1	839.0	835.7	825.8	828.0	832.9	838.5	841.1	842.0	830.5
2013	820.9	824.3	829.2	836.0	846.1	842.5	832.9	837.0	841.6	848.5	851.9	853.2	838.7
2014	833.0	837.5	841.9	847.8	856.6	852.0	841.4	844.2	849.4	855.3	857.0	860.2	848.0
2015	840.0	844.2	849.4	857.2	864.7	863.1	854.8	857.6	861.1	871.8	872.7	872.2	859.1
Mining and Logging													
2005	1.2	1.2	1.3	1.3	1.5	1.4	1.6	1.5	1.5	1.4	1.4	1.2	1.4
2006	1.2	1.2	1.2	1.3	1.3	1.2	1.2	1.2	1.0	1.0	0.9	0.8	1.1
2007	0.8	0.7	0.9	0.9	0.9	0.9	1.1	1.0	1.0	0.9	1.1	0.9	0.9
2008	0.8	0.9	1.0	1.0	1.1	1.1	1.0	1.1	1.0	1.0	1.0	0.9	1.0
2009	0.8	0.9	0.9	1.0	1.0	1.0	1.0	1.0	1.0	1.0	1.0	0.9	1.0
2010	0.8	0.8	0.8	0.9	1.0	1.0	1.0	1.0	1.0	1.0	1.0	0.9	0.9
2011	0.9	0.9	0.9	1.0	1.1	1.1	1.1	1.1	1.1	1.1	1.1	1.0	1.0
2012	1.0	1.0	1.1	1.1	1.2	1.2	1.2	1.4	1.2	1.2	1.1	1.1	1.2
2013	0.9	1.0	1.0	1.1	1.1	1.1	1.1	1.1	1.1	1.1	1.1	1.0	1.1
2014	1.1	1.0	1.1	1.2	1.2	1.2	1.2	1.2	1.1	1.2	1.2	1.1	1.2
2015	1.0	1.0	1.1	1.1	1.1	1.1	1.1	1.1	1.1	1.1	1.1	1.0	1.1

1. Employment by Industry: Nebraska, 2005–2015—*Continued*

(Numbers in thousands, not seasonally adjusted)

Industry and year	January	February	March	April	May	June	July	August	September	October	November	December	Annual average
Construction													
2005	41.8	41.5	43.4	45.8	47.5	49.5	49.8	49.6	48.6	47.8	47.1	45.0	46.5
2006	42.2	42.3	43.7	46.1	47.9	50.0	50.1	49.9	49.8	49.1	48.5	47.2	47.2
2007	43.9	43.3	45.3	48.2	50.0	52.1	53.6	54.0	53.1	52.3	50.6	48.3	49.6
2008	44.7	44.1	45.7	48.9	50.8	52.0	52.5	52.3	51.3	50.7	48.9	47.1	49.1
2009	42.6	42.2	43.3	45.9	48.2	49.5	50.9	50.4	49.5	48.0	46.2	42.9	46.6
2010	37.6	37.3	37.7	41.5	42.9	44.9	44.8	44.5	43.6	43.2	42.0	39.8	41.7
2011	36.0	35.6	37.4	40.2	41.6	42.9	43.1	42.8	42.3	42.2	41.5	39.9	40.5
2012	37.7	36.9	38.9	41.3	43.2	44.6	44.4	44.6	44.1	44.5	43.6	42.5	42.2
2013	38.8	38.9	39.9	42.8	45.6	47.1	47.7	47.7	47.0	46.3	45.4	43.3	44.2
2014	40.4	40.1	41.7	45.8	47.6	49.2	49.7	49.3	48.5	48.9	47.2	46.6	46.3
2015	42.9	43.3	45.1	48.2	50.0	51.4	52.1	51.9	51.0	52.0	50.1	47.4	48.8
Manufacturing													
2005	99.7	100.5	101.0	101.2	101.0	101.8	101.9	101.7	101.4	101.7	101.8	102.1	101.3
2006	101.5	101.7	101.7	101.5	101.0	101.8	101.8	101.6	101.3	101.4	101.1	101.2	101.5
2007	100.0	100.4	100.4	100.6	101.2	102.0	102.0	101.9	101.7	101.8	102.2	102.5	101.4
2008	101.9	102.2	102.3	102.0	102.2	102.1	101.7	101.8	100.9	100.9	100.2	98.6	101.4
2009	96.8	95.7	94.8	93.8	93.6	93.1	92.2	92.0	91.9	91.6	91.8	91.4	93.2
2010	90.5	90.8	90.9	91.4	91.8	92.2	92.2	92.0	92.0	92.0	92.4	92.6	91.7
2011	91.8	91.9	92.4	92.9	93.3	93.8	93.9	93.5	93.6	93.7	94.6	95.0	93.4
2012	93.8	93.7	94.1	94.1	94.6	95.6	95.7	95.4	95.5	95.2	95.8	96.1	95.0
2013	95.1	95.6	95.7	96.0	96.5	97.0	96.5	96.7	96.9	96.9	97.4	97.3	96.5
2014	96.6	97.0	96.8	97.3	97.3	97.7	97.6	98.1	97.7	97.5	97.7	98.0	97.4
2015	97.1	97.4	97.6	97.5	97.4	97.5	97.1	97.4	97.2	97.2	97.4	97.3	97.3
Trade, Transportation, and Utilities													
2005	197.1	196.5	198.1	198.6	200.9	201.0	200.1	200.1	199.7	200.4	203.4	205.1	200.1
2006	196.8	196.0	197.1	197.9	200.3	200.7	200.0	200.5	200.8	202.1	206.0	208.1	200.5
2007	200.9	199.9	201.1	202.4	205.0	205.4	204.9	205.3	205.1	205.9	209.5	211.1	204.7
2008	203.9	202.2	203.7	203.3	205.4	205.5	203.9	204.4	203.5	206.4	208.6	210.0	205.1
2009	200.6	198.1	198.1	197.4	198.8	198.1	196.6	196.5	195.8	197.6	199.8	200.5	198.2
2010	192.8	191.4	192.5	194.6	196.3	196.3	195.7	195.6	194.5	197.5	200.1	202.6	195.8
2011	193.8	192.7	193.8	196.4	197.6	197.8	197.6	198.4	198.1	199.3	203.2	204.8	197.8
2012	197.2	195.2	196.5	198.4	200.0	200.2	199.3	198.9	198.9	200.7	204.8	206.8	199.7
2013	198.1	196.4	197.4	198.7	201.1	201.6	201.1	201.6	200.8	202.4	206.7	209.6	201.3
2014	201.2	199.7	200.4	202.4	204.4	204.7	203.8	204.5	203.3	205.2	209.0	212.4	204.3
2015	203.2	202.5	203.1	205.1	206.9	208.0	207.0	207.3	205.8	208.4	211.0	212.3	206.7
Wholesale Trade													
2005	40.0	40.0	40.4	40.5	40.9	41.0	41.3	40.8	40.4	40.5	40.4	40.5	40.6
2006	40.2	40.2	40.4	40.8	41.2	41.4	41.3	40.9	40.7	40.6	40.6	40.9	40.8
2007	39.9	39.8	40.2	40.8	41.2	41.7	41.7	41.2	41.2	41.5	41.6	41.8	41.1
2008	41.2	41.2	41.5	41.9	42.5	42.8	42.5	42.1	41.9	42.3	42.1	42.1	42.0
2009	41.2	40.9	41.0	41.2	41.5	41.6	41.5	41.0	40.8	41.4	41.2	41.3	41.2
2010	39.9	39.8	40.1	40.9	41.2	41.4	41.2	40.7	40.4	40.7	40.4	40.5	40.6
2011	39.8	39.8	40.1	40.7	41.1	41.3	41.3	41.0	40.9	41.1	41.2	41.3	40.8
2012	40.6	40.5	41.0	41.5	41.8	42.1	41.8	41.4	41.1	41.3	41.3	41.6	41.3
2013	40.9	40.9	41.3	41.8	42.5	42.7	42.6	42.1	41.8	42.1	42.2	42.6	42.0
2014	42.2	41.9	42.4	43.0	43.5	43.8	43.7	43.2	42.6	42.6	42.5	42.8	42.9
2015	41.8	41.7	42.0	42.5	42.9	43.1	42.9	42.4	41.9	42.4	41.8	41.3	42.2
Retail Trade													
2005	106.0	105.0	105.9	106.5	107.7	107.4	106.8	106.8	106.3	107.2	109.8	111.1	107.2
2006	105.0	103.8	104.4	104.8	106.1	106.1	105.7	105.9	105.7	107.0	110.5	111.9	106.4
2007	105.6	104.5	105.2	106.1	107.9	107.7	107.2	107.5	106.9	107.7	110.9	112.4	107.5
2008	107.3	105.7	106.5	105.9	106.8	106.9	106.0	106.1	105.4	107.1	109.5	110.9	107.0
2009	105.0	103.2	103.3	103.5	104.6	104.4	103.7	103.9	103.2	104.1	106.6	106.8	104.4
2010	102.4	101.2	101.9	102.8	104.1	104.2	103.7	103.6	102.5	104.7	107.1	108.5	103.9
2011	102.8	101.9	102.4	103.9	104.6	104.6	104.3	104.8	104.2	105.2	108.7	109.7	104.8
2012	104.1	102.4	103.1	104.2	105.2	105.3	104.9	104.7	104.6	106.3	109.8	110.5	105.4
2013	104.3	103.3	103.9	104.6	105.7	106.1	106.0	106.3	105.8	107.1	110.8	112.2	106.3
2014	106.3	105.2	105.3	106.8	108.0	108.2	108.0	108.4	107.6	109.0	111.8	113.3	108.2
2015	107.9	107.3	107.6	108.6	109.6	110.4	110.0	110.2	109.1	111.1	113.5	114.0	109.9

1. Employment by Industry: Nebraska, 2005–2015—*Continued*

(Numbers in thousands, not seasonally adjusted)

Industry and year	January	February	March	April	May	June	July	August	September	October	November	December	Annual average
Transportation and Utilities													
2005	51.1	51.5	51.8	51.6	52.3	52.6	52.0	52.5	53.0	52.7	53.2	53.5	52.3
2006	51.6	52.0	52.3	52.3	53.0	53.2	53.0	53.7	54.4	54.5	54.9	55.3	53.4
2007	55.4	55.6	55.7	55.5	55.9	56.0	56.0	56.6	57.0	56.7	57.0	56.9	56.2
2008	55.4	55.3	55.7	55.5	56.1	55.8	55.4	56.2	56.2	57.0	57.0	57.0	56.1
2009	54.4	54.0	53.8	52.7	52.7	52.1	51.4	51.6	51.8	52.1	52.0	52.4	52.6
2010	50.5	50.4	50.5	50.9	51.0	50.7	50.8	51.3	51.6	52.1	52.6	53.6	51.3
2011	51.2	51.0	51.3	51.8	51.9	51.9	52.0	52.6	53.0	53.0	53.3	53.8	52.2
2012	52.5	52.3	52.4	52.7	53.0	52.8	52.6	52.8	53.2	53.1	53.7	54.7	53.0
2013	52.9	52.2	52.2	52.3	52.9	52.8	52.5	53.2	53.2	53.2	53.7	54.8	53.0
2014	52.7	52.6	52.7	52.6	52.9	52.7	52.1	52.9	53.1	53.6	54.7	56.3	53.2
2015	53.5	53.5	53.5	54.0	54.4	54.5	54.1	54.7	54.8	54.9	55.7	57.0	54.6
Information													
2005	20.4	20.5	20.4	20.3	20.0	20.3	20.2	20.2	20.0	20.0	20.0	20.1	20.2
2006	19.7	19.6	19.6	19.6	19.5	19.7	19.6	19.5	19.3	19.1	19.2	19.3	19.5
2007	19.1	19.1	19.1	19.4	19.3	19.6	19.6	19.6	19.4	19.4	19.5	19.4	19.4
2008	19.2	19.2	19.1	19.1	18.8	18.8	18.7	18.5	18.2	18.2	18.2	18.1	18.7
2009	17.7	17.7	17.6	17.4	17.3	17.6	17.5	17.5	17.3	17.2	17.4	17.4	17.5
2010	17.2	17.1	17.0	16.9	17.0	17.1	17.0	17.0	16.9	16.9	17.0	17.1	17.0
2011	16.9	16.9	16.8	16.8	16.8	16.9	17.3	17.2	17.1	17.2	17.2	17.3	17.0
2012	17.2	17.3	17.3	17.2	17.1	17.2	17.2	17.2	17.1	17.2	17.2	17.2	17.2
2013	17.1	17.2	17.2	17.1	17.1	17.1	17.1	17.1	17.1	17.2	17.2	17.2	17.1
2014	17.2	17.0	17.0	17.0	16.9	17.0	17.1	17.1	17.1	17.1	17.3	17.4	17.1
2015	17.3	17.3	17.4	17.4	17.5	17.6	17.6	17.7	17.5	17.7	17.8	17.7	17.5
Financial Activities													
2005	63.5	63.8	63.9	64.1	64.5	64.9	64.9	65.0	64.7	64.8	64.7	65.0	64.5
2006	64.6	64.9	65.2	65.7	66.4	67.2	67.4	67.6	67.2	67.4	67.8	68.5	66.7
2007	67.7	68.2	68.4	68.4	69.1	69.4	69.4	69.1	68.7	68.6	68.6	68.8	68.7
2008	68.5	68.9	69.0	69.0	69.3	69.7	69.7	69.6	69.0	69.2	69.1	69.5	69.2
2009	68.6	68.8	68.8	68.4	68.5	68.7	68.4	68.4	67.9	68.1	68.2	68.5	68.4
2010	68.0	68.1	68.3	68.4	68.6	69.3	69.5	69.6	69.1	69.4	69.4	69.6	68.9
2011	69.3	69.2	69.4	69.9	70.1	70.4	70.4	70.4	70.3	70.4	70.6	71.0	70.1
2012	70.3	70.2	70.4	70.7	71.0	71.4	71.4	71.3	71.0	71.2	71.4	71.8	71.0
2013	71.0	71.2	71.2	71.2	71.6	72.0	72.1	72.0	71.7	71.8	72.0	72.1	71.7
2014	71.9	71.9	72.0	71.7	71.8	72.3	72.4	72.0	71.7	71.7	71.8	71.7	71.9
2015	71.1	70.9	70.9	71.1	71.6	72.1	72.3	72.3	72.0	72.1	72.7	72.7	71.8
Professional and Business Services													
2005	93.9	94.5	95.7	97.3	97.5	98.5	98.5	99.0	98.9	100.3	100.5	100.5	97.9
2006	97.9	98.7	100.4	101.2	102.3	104.4	103.8	103.4	102.9	102.5	102.5	102.1	101.8
2007	100.5	101.2	102.0	103.2	103.8	105.7	105.8	106.2	105.5	105.2	105.8	106.4	104.3
2008	103.8	104.4	105.2	106.6	106.8	107.2	106.7	106.7	106.5	106.6	105.3	104.2	105.8
2009	101.1	100.7	100.3	100.8	100.5	101.4	100.5	100.0	99.1	100.1	99.4	99.2	100.3
2010	97.5	97.7	98.0	100.6	100.7	102.0	103.0	102.7	102.7	103.3	102.5	102.8	101.1
2011	99.5	100.1	100.8	102.8	102.9	103.7	104.8	105.0	105.6	105.7	105.2	105.1	103.4
2012	103.8	104.7	105.2	106.7	107.1	109.1	109.0	108.6	108.7	108.8	108.4	108.2	107.4
2013	106.1	106.5	107.3	108.8	109.5	110.8	111.1	111.3	111.4	113.0	112.8	113.2	110.2
2014	110.0	111.2	111.9	113.3	113.7	114.4	114.5	114.2	114.0	114.4	114.3	114.5	113.4
2015	112.9	113.8	114.5	116.5	116.7	118.2	118.7	118.2	118.0	120.7	119.8	118.8	117.2
Education and Health Services													
2005	125.0	126.2	126.6	127.8	127.0	127.3	126.5	126.6	128.1	128.4	130.0	129.7	127.4
2006	127.6	129.2	129.4	129.3	129.5	129.6	128.4	129.4	130.6	130.5	132.6	131.6	129.8
2007	129.9	131.3	131.5	132.2	132.8	132.6	132.2	133.5	134.6	135.4	136.1	136.3	133.2
2008	134.7	136.5	136.6	136.7	137.3	136.0	136.2	137.7	138.5	138.8	139.8	139.7	137.4
2009	137.8	138.6	138.5	138.5	138.7	136.9	137.1	137.4	139.0	140.1	140.6	140.7	138.7
2010	138.7	140.2	140.4	140.5	140.8	140.4	140.2	140.9	140.8	141.8	141.9	142.0	140.7
2011	141.0	142.0	142.1	143.1	143.5	142.1	141.3	142.0	143.0	144.7	145.0	145.2	142.9
2012	143.1	144.5	146.1	145.9	146.0	144.9	144.3	145.6	146.6	147.9	148.0	148.2	145.9
2013	145.5	146.6	147.3	147.8	147.8	146.0	145.6	146.5	147.0	147.9	148.2	148.2	147.0
2014	145.7	147.3	148.5	148.5	148.5	146.7	146.1	147.2	148.0	149.4	149.3	149.9	147.9
2015	147.8	148.4	149.1	148.6	149.1	147.2	147.6	148.3	149.6	151.6	152.3	153.0	149.4

1. Employment by Industry: Nebraska, 2005–2015—*Continued*

(Numbers in thousands, not seasonally adjusted)

Industry and year	January	February	March	April	May	June	July	August	September	October	November	December	Annual average
Leisure and Hospitality													
2005	73.9	74.4	76.3	79.3	81.5	83.2	82.5	83.1	81.1	79.4	78.8	78.2	79.3
2006	76.8	77.8	78.7	80.5	82.5	83.6	83.0	83.3	81.6	80.9	80.0	80.4	80.8
2007	77.7	77.8	79.2	82.1	84.4	85.6	85.1	86.1	84.1	83.3	81.8	80.8	82.3
2008	78.5	78.5	80.1	82.4	84.7	85.8	85.6	86.4	84.6	83.1	81.4	80.8	82.7
2009	77.8	77.9	79.9	81.7	84.3	84.9	84.2	84.7	82.8	80.9	79.2	77.6	81.3
2010	75.3	75.8	77.3	80.7	83.0	84.3	84.1	85.1	83.1	82.2	80.1	78.7	80.8
2011	76.1	76.8	79.0	82.4	85.0	86.1	85.1	85.5	83.4	82.6	80.7	79.6	81.9
2012	77.7	78.5	81.7	84.7	87.4	88.6	87.8	88.1	85.6	85.0	83.0	82.4	84.2
2013	79.8	80.5	82.2	84.7	87.8	88.9	88.4	89.9	88.4	87.4	86.1	84.9	85.8
2014	82.7	83.2	84.8	86.8	89.9	90.8	90.1	90.6	88.4	87.3	85.1	84.8	87.0
2015	82.9	83.5	85.8	87.4	90.4	92.1	91.5	92.3	90.6	89.3	86.6	86.4	88.2
Other Services													
2005	33.8	34.3	34.4	34.5	34.7	34.9	34.9	34.6	34.4	34.3	34.2	34.2	34.4
2006	34.0	34.2	34.5	34.6	34.5	34.8	34.8	34.3	34.3	34.6	34.5	34.4	34.5
2007	34.2	34.3	34.7	34.9	35.1	35.1	34.9	34.7	34.6	35.0	35.0	35.0	34.8
2008	34.6	34.8	35.0	35.2	35.5	35.6	35.3	35.2	35.0	35.8	35.6	35.8	35.3
2009	35.3	35.4	35.5	35.9	36.2	36.6	36.6	36.6	36.5	36.5	36.8	36.8	36.2
2010	36.3	36.4	36.9	37.0	37.1	37.2	37.2	37.0	36.6	36.6	36.5	36.6	36.8
2011	36.0	36.2	36.6	36.7	36.8	36.9	36.7	36.4	36.3	36.3	36.2	36.3	36.5
2012	36.0	36.1	36.5	36.6	36.9	37.2	37.0	36.9	36.8	36.7	36.7	36.7	36.7
2013	36.2	36.4	37.0	37.0	37.1	37.3	37.0	37.0	36.8	36.5	36.4	36.5	36.8
2014	36.2	36.3	36.4	36.9	37.1	37.5	37.1	36.8	36.7	36.9	36.9	36.9	36.8
2015	36.6	36.8	36.9	37.1	37.3	37.4	37.4	37.3	37.0	37.0	37.4	37.1	37.1
Government													
2005	159.0	161.0	161.9	162.6	164.6	163.3	153.7	153.1	161.8	163.9	164.2	163.3	161.0
2006	160.5	162.5	163.3	163.8	166.0	165.2	153.7	154.1	162.7	164.5	165.2	164.3	162.2
2007	161.7	163.3	163.7	164.2	167.0	165.7	152.9	154.1	162.2	164.8	165.3	164.1	162.4
2008	162.9	163.3	163.6	165.5	168.0	165.7	155.4	155.8	164.1	167.6	167.9	167.3	163.9
2009	165.7	168.0	168.7	170.7	172.5	169.8	163.5	162.2	168.0	170.9	171.7	169.9	168.5
2010	167.0	169.5	171.4	172.0	175.3	172.1	162.4	162.5	167.8	171.9	172.0	171.2	169.6
2011	167.3	169.5	169.8	171.4	172.2	168.0	159.1	160.8	166.6	171.3	171.4	170.6	168.2
2012	167.1	169.7	169.8	170.9	173.5	167.1	159.8	161.4	168.2	171.0	171.6	170.7	168.4
2013	167.1	169.5	169.6	170.7	174.1	168.8	160.5	161.6	168.4	172.3	172.5	171.5	168.9
2014	168.1	170.9	170.9	171.2	174.3	168.6	160.3	161.8	170.2	173.3	173.3	172.6	169.6
2015	168.2	171.0	171.7	174.0	175.2	170.5	162.7	164.2	170.6	175.0	175.1	174.2	171.0

2. Average Weekly Hours by Selected Industry: Nebraska, 2011–2015

(Not seasonally adjusted)

Industry and year	January	February	March	April	May	June	July	August	September	October	November	December	Annual average
Total Private													
2011	34.0	33.8	33.9	34.0	34.5	34.3	34.2	34.1	34.0	34.7	34.0	33.8	34.1
2012	34.2	33.7	33.7	34.3	33.7	34.0	34.2	33.8	34.6	34.2	33.8	34.3	34.0
2013	33.5	33.9	33.9	33.9	34.3	35.2	34.3	34.3	34.6	34.1	33.9	34.1	34.2
2014	33.4	33.8	34.1	33.8	34.1	35.0	34.4	34.4	34.0	34.1	34.3	33.9	34.1
2015	33.6	34.3	34.2	33.8	33.9	34.5	34.3	34.9	33.9	34.3	34.2	33.8	34.1
Goods-Producing													
2011	39.5	39.7	40.2	40.4	40.3	41.0	41.1	40.8	41.2	41.1	40.4	39.9	40.5
2012	39.9	39.8	39.7	40.2	40.8	40.5	40.0	40.7	40.5	40.8	40.2	40.4	40.3
2013	39.4	39.9	39.8	39.8	40.6	41.4	40.7	40.7	40.8	40.9	40.4	40.5	40.4
2014	40.0	39.5	40.3	40.5	41.3	41.6	41.2	41.3	40.7	40.8	40.1	40.7	40.7
2015	40.0	41.0	40.4	40.5	40.9	41.2	41.3	42.3	40.4	41.8	40.3	40.4	40.9
Mining, Logging, and Construction													
2011	37.4	37.5	37.8	38.7	38.7	39.8	40.4	39.3	40.4	41.2	39.9	38.5	39.2
2012	38.8	37.5	38.9	39.2	41.6	41.0	41.5	41.9	40.4	40.1	40.3	39.9	40.1
2013	38.5	38.4	37.7	38.7	40.9	42.1	41.6	40.0	40.5	40.4	39.0	38.4	39.8
2014	37.4	36.2	39.1	40.0	41.3	42.0	41.5	41.5	40.1	41.4	38.6	39.5	40.0
2015	37.6	39.7	40.2	39.3	39.2	41.1	42.0	43.0	41.6	42.5	40.6	40.4	40.7
Manufacturing													
2011	40.4	40.6	41.2	41.2	41.0	41.6	41.4	41.5	41.6	41.0	40.6	40.5	41.1
2012	40.4	40.8	40.1	40.6	40.4	40.2	39.3	40.1	40.6	41.2	40.2	40.6	40.4
2013	39.8	40.6	40.6	40.3	40.5	41.0	40.3	41.0	40.9	41.1	41.1	41.4	40.7
2014	41.2	40.9	40.8	40.8	41.3	41.4	41.0	41.2	41.0	40.6	40.8	41.3	41.0
2015	41.1	41.6	40.5	41.1	41.8	41.2	40.9	41.9	39.7	41.4	40.1	40.4	41.0
Trade, Transportation, and Utilities													
2011	32.2	32.1	32.5	32.6	33.3	33.4	33.2	33.1	33.2	34.2	33.5	33.8	33.1
2012	33.2	33.5	33.9	34.1	33.8	33.9	33.9	33.6	34.5	33.8	33.7	34.2	33.8
2013	33.9	34.4	34.5	34.3	34.9	35.3	34.6	34.6	34.8	34.2	33.6	34.0	34.4
2014	33.4	33.7	34.1	34.2	34.5	35.1	34.8	34.3	33.8	34.1	33.8	33.9	34.1
2015	33.1	33.7	33.8	33.7	33.5	34.3	34.0	34.2	33.4	33.9	33.5	33.6	33.7
Financial Activities													
2011	39.1	37.3	36.7	37.8	38.2	36.8	37.6	38.3	36.9	39.4	36.9	36.6	37.6
2012	39.4	36.6	36.7	39.1	36.1	36.9	38.5	36.6	38.2	37.4	36.3	37.9	37.5
2013	36.6	37.0	36.8	36.9	36.9	38.6	37.1	37.5	38.4	37.0	37.7	38.6	37.4
2014	37.3	38.5	38.6	37.7	37.7	39.4	38.0	38.0	37.9	38.0	39.5	37.8	38.2
2015	38.1	39.2	38.9	38.0	37.9	38.1	38.0	39.7	38.0	38.2	39.0	38.1	38.4
Professional and Business Services													
2011	34.9	34.6	34.3	34.3	34.8	34.5	34.5	34.5	34.6	35.6	34.8	35.1	34.7
2012	35.7	35.6	35.5	35.8	35.2	35.7	35.7	35.4	36.4	36.1	35.4	35.9	35.7
2013	34.2	34.9	34.9	34.9	35.4	36.3	34.7	35.1	35.1	34.8	34.9	34.7	35.0
2014	34.0	35.1	35.1	34.5	34.9	36.4	35.5	36.1	35.6	36.2	36.5	36.3	35.5
2015	35.7	36.4	36.2	35.7	35.5	36.0	35.4	36.3	35.5	35.9	36.4	35.1	35.8
Education and Health Services													
2011	32.1	32.2	32.3	32.5	32.9	32.7	32.2	31.6	31.6	31.9	31.8	31.5	32.1
2012	31.9	31.4	31.4	32.3	31.4	31.8	32.1	31.5	31.7	31.5	31.1	31.8	31.7
2013	31.5	31.7	31.9	32.2	32.1	33.1	32.1	32.0	32.8	32.2	31.9	32.3	32.2
2014	31.6	32.0	32.0	31.8	31.8	32.9	32.5	32.4	32.3	31.9	32.6	31.7	32.1
2015	31.2	31.8	31.9	31.4	31.6	32.3	32.4	32.3	32.2	31.8	32.3	31.1	31.9
Leisure and Hospitality													
2011	21.8	22.6	22.5	22.3	22.6	22.9	22.5	22.5	22.4	22.4	22.4	22.2	22.4
2012	22.2	22.8	22.8	22.5	22.7	23.4	23.6	22.8	23.1	22.3	22.3	22.4	22.7
2013	21.7	22.2	22.2	21.5	22.0	23.4	22.7	22.7	22.3	21.9	22.1	22.0	22.2
2014	21.0	22.0	22.4	21.9	22.1	23.6	22.6	23.1	22.7	22.7	22.6	22.0	22.4
2015	22.2	22.8	23.0	22.0	22.8	23.9	23.2	23.4	22.5	22.8	22.8	22.9	22.9

3. Average Hourly Earnings by Selected Industry: Nebraska, 2011–2015

(Dollars, not seasonally adjusted)

Industry and year	January	February	March	April	May	June	July	August	September	October	November	December	Annual average
Total Private													
2011	21.08	21.06	20.82	20.70	20.74	20.55	20.55	20.66	20.90	21.10	20.84	21.13	20.84
2012	21.30	21.16	20.92	20.86	20.91	20.59	20.85	20.84	20.97	20.78	20.97	21.24	20.95
2013	21.09	21.09	21.13	21.06	20.66	20.72	20.63	20.74	20.99	20.84	21.03	21.12	20.92
2014	21.18	21.23	21.35	21.26	21.16	21.21	21.24	21.33	21.38	21.51	21.66	21.74	21.36
2015	21.98	22.03	22.08	21.85	21.91	21.72	21.93	22.50	22.60	22.35	22.65	22.51	22.18
Goods-Producing													
2011	20.04	20.08	20.12	19.76	19.64	19.51	19.58	19.61	19.65	19.83	19.74	20.08	19.80
2012	20.16	20.05	20.02	19.90	20.10	20.01	20.04	20.16	20.37	20.12	20.09	20.12	20.10
2013	20.18	20.09	20.23	20.06	19.95	19.88	20.02	20.35	20.32	20.24	20.38	20.27	20.16
2014	20.34	19.91	20.10	20.36	20.33	20.33	20.55	20.59	20.46	20.61	20.75	21.02	20.45
2015	21.10	21.13	21.03	21.05	21.30	21.22	21.44	21.86	22.44	21.68	21.75	21.33	21.45
Mining, Logging, and Construction													
2011	21.34	21.64	21.55	20.66	20.35	20.28	20.27	20.41	20.18	20.50	20.42	21.42	20.71
2012	20.95	21.54	21.50	21.06	21.58	21.34	21.37	21.52	21.82	21.35	21.21	21.65	21.41
2013	21.43	21.55	21.60	21.25	20.96	20.45	20.86	21.33	21.24	21.62	21.61	21.75	21.28
2014	21.74	22.13	22.12	22.16	21.78	21.74	21.32	21.60	21.41	21.35	21.31	21.90	21.69
2015	22.15	21.99	21.62	21.80	21.79	21.71	22.24	22.89	23.84	22.81	22.40	21.81	22.29
Manufacturing													
2011	19.56	19.51	19.57	19.39	19.34	19.16	19.27	19.25	19.41	19.52	19.44	19.53	19.41
2012	19.85	19.49	19.41	19.40	19.38	19.36	19.37	19.48	19.68	19.54	19.56	19.44	19.50
2013	19.68	19.51	19.69	19.54	19.46	19.59	19.58	19.87	19.87	19.57	19.82	19.65	19.65
2014	19.79	19.08	19.25	19.51	19.61	19.60	20.14	20.06	19.99	20.22	20.48	20.61	19.86
2015	20.67	20.75	20.75	20.69	21.06	20.96	20.99	21.29	21.65	21.04	21.41	21.09	21.03
Trade, Transportation, and Utilities													
2011	18.05	18.03	17.91	17.82	17.99	18.55	18.33	18.53	19.02	18.56	18.22	18.25	18.28
2012	18.99	18.82	18.62	18.30	18.15	18.08	18.23	18.38	18.41	18.25	18.12	18.29	18.38
2013	18.44	18.75	18.68	18.56	18.28	18.33	18.16	18.20	18.31	18.29	18.48	18.47	18.41
2014	19.13	19.17	19.51	19.37	19.37	19.24	19.36	19.81	19.65	19.82	19.91	19.50	19.49
2015	19.69	19.64	19.51	19.42	19.41	19.20	19.34	20.00	19.70	19.59	19.68	19.50	19.56
Financial Activities													
2011	26.24	26.16	25.67	26.03	26.57	25.85	25.68	25.52	26.00	26.29	26.07	26.52	26.05
2012	26.06	25.95	25.92	26.19	26.47	25.73	26.40	25.62	25.66	25.09	25.49	25.09	25.81
2013	24.51	24.85	25.07	25.19	25.50	25.83	25.23	25.46	26.04	25.63	25.75	27.02	25.52
2014	26.45	27.14	27.12	26.58	26.53	26.97	26.17	26.34	26.09	26.10	26.84	26.81	26.60
2015	26.78	27.58	27.75	27.93	27.73	27.32	27.24	28.34	28.05	28.11	29.02	28.39	27.86
Professional and Business Services													
2011	24.22	24.06	24.07	24.13	24.15	23.79	23.62	23.91	24.02	24.61	24.70	25.02	24.20
2012	25.29	25.39	25.39	25.48	25.42	25.17	25.40	25.42	25.10	25.36	25.41	26.55	25.45
2013	26.22	25.92	25.82	25.96	25.07	25.60	25.58	25.27	25.60	25.47	25.67	25.86	25.66
2014	25.04	25.21	25.46	25.45	25.45	25.61	25.62	25.62	25.70	25.72	25.98	25.99	25.58
2015	26.65	26.25	26.69	26.42	26.63	26.53	26.69	26.69	26.84	26.46	26.94	27.01	26.65
Education and Health Services													
2011	20.52	20.50	20.15	19.98	20.04	19.99	20.37	20.46	20.73	21.00	20.57	20.89	20.43
2012	20.93	20.50	20.49	20.66	20.58	20.82	21.08	21.01	21.22	20.75	20.95	21.41	20.87
2013	21.39	21.20	21.40	21.31	21.25	21.24	21.37	21.57	21.78	21.65	21.96	22.06	21.52
2014	22.36	22.01	21.89	21.93	21.70	21.58	21.79	21.64	22.07	22.07	21.68	22.08	21.90
2015	22.22	22.28	22.33	22.27	22.30	22.13	22.43	22.73	22.87	22.56	22.46	22.52	22.43
Leisure and Hospitality													
2011	11.42	11.47	11.28	11.40	11.43	11.17	11.31	11.41	11.74	11.74	11.76	12.33	11.53
2012	12.09	12.35	12.44	12.43	12.22	12.06	12.01	12.00	11.94	12.11	12.00	12.32	12.16
2013	12.00	12.03	11.98	11.98	11.80	11.61	11.46	11.48	11.70	11.63	11.66	11.65	11.74
2014	11.72	11.80	11.94	11.91	11.96	11.85	11.84	11.78	11.86	12.11	12.13	12.27	11.93
2015	12.33	12.27	12.28	12.30	12.37	12.23	12.41	12.67	12.84	12.88	13.07	13.28	12.58

4. Average Weekly Earnings by Selected Industry: Nebraska, 2011–2015

(Dollars, not seasonally adjusted)

Industry and year	January	February	March	April	May	June	July	August	September	October	November	December	Annual average
Total Private													
2011	716.72	711.83	705.80	703.80	715.53	704.87	702.81	704.51	710.60	732.17	708.56	714.19	710.64
2012	728.46	713.09	705.00	715.50	704.67	700.06	713.07	704.39	725.56	710.68	708.79	728.53	712.30
2013	706.52	714.95	716.31	713.93	708.64	729.34	707.61	711.38	726.25	710.64	712.92	720.19	715.46
2014	707.41	717.57	728.04	718.59	721.56	742.35	730.66	733.75	726.92	733.49	742.94	736.99	728.38
2015	738.53	755.63	755.14	738.53	742.75	749.34	752.20	785.25	766.14	766.61	774.63	760.84	756.34
Goods-Producing													
2011	791.58	797.18	808.82	798.30	791.49	799.91	804.74	800.09	809.58	815.01	797.50	801.19	801.90
2012	804.38	797.99	794.79	799.98	820.08	810.41	801.60	820.51	824.99	820.90	807.62	812.85	810.03
2013	795.09	801.59	805.15	798.39	809.97	823.03	814.81	828.25	829.06	827.82	823.35	820.94	814.46
2014	813.60	786.45	810.03	824.58	839.63	845.73	846.66	850.37	832.72	840.89	832.08	855.51	832.32
2015	844.00	866.33	849.61	852.53	871.17	874.26	885.47	924.68	906.58	906.22	876.53	861.73	877.31
Mining, Logging, and Construction													
2011	798.12	811.50	814.59	799.54	787.55	807.14	818.91	802.11	815.27	844.60	814.76	824.67	811.83
2012	812.86	807.75	836.35	825.55	897.73	874.94	886.86	901.69	881.53	856.14	854.76	863.84	858.54
2013	825.06	827.52	814.32	822.38	857.26	860.95	867.78	853.20	860.22	873.45	842.79	835.20	846.94
2014	813.08	801.11	864.89	886.40	899.51	913.08	884.78	896.40	858.54	883.89	822.57	865.05	867.60
2015	832.84	873.00	869.12	856.74	854.17	892.28	934.08	984.27	991.74	969.43	909.44	881.12	907.20
Manufacturing													
2011	790.22	792.11	806.28	798.87	792.94	797.06	797.78	798.88	807.46	800.32	789.26	790.97	797.75
2012	801.94	795.19	778.34	787.64	782.95	778.27	761.24	781.15	799.01	805.05	786.31	789.26	787.80
2013	783.26	792.11	799.41	787.46	788.13	803.19	789.07	814.67	812.68	804.33	814.60	813.51	799.76
2014	815.35	780.37	785.40	796.01	809.89	811.44	825.74	826.47	819.59	820.93	835.58	851.19	814.26
2015	849.54	863.20	840.38	850.36	880.31	863.55	858.49	892.05	859.51	871.06	858.54	852.04	862.23
Trade, Transportation, and Utilities													
2011	581.21	578.76	582.08	580.93	599.07	619.57	608.56	613.34	631.46	634.75	610.37	616.85	605.07
2012	630.47	630.47	631.22	624.03	613.47	612.91	618.00	617.57	635.15	616.85	610.64	625.52	621.24
2013	625.12	645.00	644.46	636.61	637.97	647.05	628.34	629.72	637.19	625.52	620.93	627.98	633.30
2014	638.94	646.03	665.29	662.45	668.27	675.32	673.73	679.48	664.17	675.86	672.96	661.05	664.61
2015	651.74	661.87	659.44	654.45	650.24	658.56	657.56	684.00	657.98	664.10	659.28	655.20	659.17
Financial Activities													
2011	1,025.98	975.77	942.09	983.93	1,014.97	951.28	965.57	977.42	959.40	1,035.83	961.98	970.63	979.48
2012	1,026.76	949.77	951.26	1,024.03	955.57	949.44	1,016.40	937.69	980.21	938.37	925.29	950.91	967.88
2013	897.07	919.45	922.58	929.51	940.95	997.04	936.03	954.75	999.94	948.31	970.78	1,042.97	954.45
2014	986.59	1,044.89	1,046.83	1,002.07	1,000.18	1,062.62	994.46	1,000.92	988.81	991.80	1,060.18	1,013.42	1,016.12
2015	1,020.32	1,081.14	1,079.48	1,061.34	1,050.97	1,040.89	1,035.12	1,125.10	1,065.90	1,073.80	1,131.78	1,081.66	1,069.82
Professional and Business Services													
2011	845.28	832.48	825.60	827.66	840.42	820.76	814.89	824.90	831.09	876.12	859.56	878.20	839.74
2012	902.85	903.88	901.35	912.18	894.78	898.57	906.78	899.87	913.64	915.50	899.51	953.15	908.57
2013	896.72	904.61	901.12	906.00	887.48	929.28	887.63	886.98	898.56	886.36	895.88	897.34	898.10
2014	851.36	884.87	893.65	878.03	888.21	932.20	909.51	924.88	914.92	931.06	948.27	943.44	908.09
2015	951.41	955.50	966.18	943.19	945.37	955.08	944.83	968.85	952.82	949.91	980.62	948.05	954.07
Education and Health Services													
2011	658.69	660.10	650.85	649.35	659.32	653.67	655.91	646.54	655.07	669.90	654.13	658.04	655.80
2012	667.67	643.70	643.39	667.32	646.21	662.08	676.67	661.82	672.67	653.63	651.55	680.84	661.58
2013	673.79	672.04	682.66	686.18	682.13	703.04	685.98	690.24	714.38	697.13	700.52	712.54	692.94
2014	706.58	704.32	700.48	697.37	690.06	709.98	708.18	701.14	712.86	704.03	706.77	699.94	702.99
2015	693.26	708.50	712.33	699.28	704.68	714.80	726.73	734.18	736.41	717.41	725.46	700.37	715.52
Leisure and Hospitality													
2011	248.96	259.22	253.80	254.22	258.32	255.79	254.48	256.73	262.98	262.98	263.42	273.73	258.27
2012	268.40	281.58	283.63	279.68	277.39	282.20	283.44	273.60	275.81	270.05	267.60	275.97	276.03
2013	260.40	267.07	265.96	257.57	259.60	271.67	260.14	260.60	260.91	254.70	257.69	256.30	260.63
2014	246.12	259.60	267.46	260.83	264.32	279.66	267.58	272.12	269.22	274.90	274.14	269.94	267.23
2015	273.73	279.76	282.44	270.60	282.04	292.30	287.91	296.48	288.90	293.66	298.00	304.11	288.08

NEVADA
At a Glance

Population:
  2005 Population: 2,432,143
  2010 census: 2,700,551
  2015 estimate: 2,890,845

Percent change in population:
  2005–2015: 18.9%
  2010–2015: 7.0%

Percent change in total nonfarm employment:
  2005–2015: 2.8%

Industry with the largest growth in employment, 2005–2015 (thousands):
  Education and health services, 36.6

Industry with the largest decline or smallest growth in employment, 2005–2015 (thousands):
  Construction, –65.1

Civilian labor force:
  2005: 1,223,831
  2010: 1,358,578
  2015: 1,425,711

Unemployment rate and rank among states (highest to lowest):
  2005: 4.1%, 37th
  2010: 13.5%, 1st
  2015: 6.7%, 2nd

Over-the-year change in unemployment rates:
  2012–2013: –1.6%
  2013–2014: –1.7%
  2014–2015: –1.2%

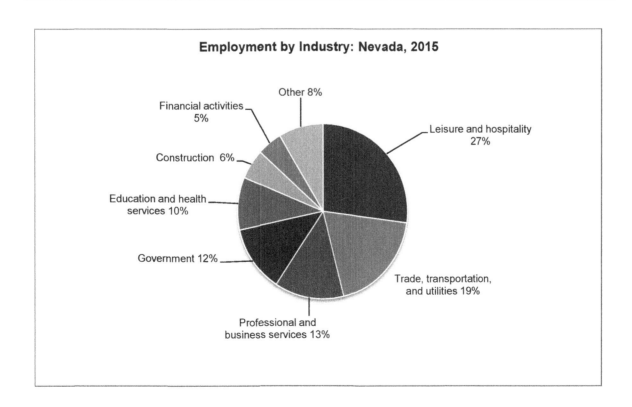

Employment by Industry: Nevada, 2015

Other 8%
Financial activities 5%
Construction 6%
Education and health services 10%
Government 12%
Professional and business services 13%
Leisure and hospitality 27%
Trade, transportation, and utilities 19%

1. Employment by Industry: Nevada, 2005–2015

(Numbers in thousands, not seasonally adjusted)

Industry and year	January	February	March	April	May	June	July	August	September	October	November	December	Annual average
Total Nonfarm													
2005	1,166.7	1,179.5	1,195.0	1,216.5	1,221.8	1,226.7	1,225.7	1,229.5	1,246.4	1,250.3	1,256.3	1,261.5	1,223.0
2006	1,239.8	1,255.0	1,268.3	1,276.3	1,286.3	1,291.2	1,279.8	1,282.9	1,292.6	1,292.0	1,294.8	1,295.6	1,279.6
2007	1,268.2	1,283.3	1,290.9	1,294.5	1,303.8	1,302.1	1,287.2	1,288.1	1,292.3	1,297.7	1,301.0	1,300.4	1,292.5
2008	1,269.1	1,272.9	1,275.8	1,281.0	1,286.2	1,279.5	1,265.2	1,260.6	1,261.7	1,252.5	1,238.1	1,221.1	1,263.6
2009	1,180.8	1,171.7	1,163.2	1,158.5	1,155.9	1,147.6	1,133.5	1,128.1	1,135.5	1,135.5	1,134.5	1,134.1	1,148.2
2010	1,104.2	1,105.7	1,108.9	1,120.9	1,128.3	1,124.0	1,116.7	1,114.0	1,116.0	1,124.0	1,125.7	1,124.7	1,117.8
2011	1,107.0	1,109.5	1,114.7	1,126.6	1,130.4	1,128.6	1,122.9	1,122.4	1,132.4	1,138.1	1,139.3	1,136.8	1,125.7
2012	1,120.3	1,123.4	1,131.1	1,139.5	1,148.1	1,150.0	1,139.5	1,145.4	1,153.7	1,160.8	1,165.6	1,160.5	1,144.8
2013	1,145.0	1,148.8	1,158.4	1,168.1	1,176.4	1,179.1	1,171.0	1,178.7	1,183.0	1,189.6	1,198.2	1,195.4	1,174.3
2014	1,180.5	1,186.8	1,198.4	1,208.9	1,219.8	1,216.8	1,209.5	1,221.1	1,230.6	1,240.6	1,244.6	1,245.0	1,216.9
2015	1,228.8	1,234.1	1,242.7	1,253.6	1,260.4	1,257.2	1,251.2	1,260.4	1,269.8	1,281.7	1,276.9	1,274.3	1,257.6
Total Private													
2005	1,028.6	1,036.3	1,049.7	1,071.3	1,075.7	1,085.2	1,090.8	1,095.7	1,102.9	1,102.1	1,107.0	1,111.9	1,079.8
2006	1,096.6	1,105.9	1,118.3	1,125.0	1,134.5	1,144.0	1,139.6	1,143.2	1,143.0	1,136.9	1,138.5	1,139.2	1,130.4
2007	1,117.8	1,126.4	1,133.4	1,135.4	1,144.2	1,147.4	1,140.0	1,142.1	1,136.8	1,137.0	1,139.4	1,138.1	1,136.5
2008	1,112.8	1,110.6	1,112.6	1,116.7	1,121.2	1,119.7	1,111.7	1,108.3	1,100.8	1,086.8	1,072.2	1,055.6	1,102.4
2009	1,022.5	1,009.5	1,001.0	996.6	994.7	991.7	983.8	979.9	979.2	977.4	976.7	976.8	990.8
2010	951.9	948.7	951.1	963.0	967.1	970.3	969.1	969.2	964.1	970.5	971.8	970.9	964.0
2011	955.9	954.9	960.3	971.9	976.1	981.0	980.6	980.0	983.8	987.5	988.5	985.1	975.5
2012	973.3	973.2	979.3	987.7	995.8	1,002.5	997.0	1,003.2	1,003.9	1,009.1	1,013.1	1,007.2	995.4
2013	995.5	996.9	1,005.3	1,015.0	1,022.8	1,029.7	1,028.5	1,033.2	1,031.9	1,036.6	1,044.0	1,040.0	1,023.3
2014	1,029.5	1,033.0	1,043.2	1,054.0	1,064.1	1,067.9	1,065.5	1,075.9	1,076.9	1,085.5	1,088.8	1,088.4	1,064.4
2015	1,076.2	1,078.6	1,085.8	1,096.8	1,103.3	1,104.8	1,104.7	1,112.7	1,113.4	1,123.2	1,117.6	1,114.5	1,102.6
Goods-Producing													
2005	176.8	181.1	185.5	190.0	191.0	193.7	197.8	199.7	201.9	201.2	200.5	201.1	193.4
2006	196.3	200.1	202.5	205.6	208.7	211.5	210.0	210.5	208.5	204.4	201.3	198.9	204.9
2007	191.9	193.5	196.9	197.1	200.2	200.8	199.7	200.5	197.1	193.9	191.1	187.8	195.9
2008	179.8	179.9	179.3	179.7	181.6	182.5	182.8	181.2	177.6	173.1	165.6	158.5	176.8
2009	149.4	144.9	141.6	138.5	134.4	133.2	131.3	129.7	127.6	126.1	122.4	117.3	133.0
2010	108.6	107.1	107.1	109.7	110.6	111.5	111.3	111.3	109.6	110.1	109.0	107.1	109.4
2011	102.7	102.7	101.3	102.7	103.8	105.4	106.4	106.8	106.4	106.5	105.2	104.0	104.5
2012	100.8	100.6	101.8	103.4	105.5	107.7	108.6	110.4	110.3	110.5	110.2	109.5	106.6
2013	106.6	107.5	108.8	110.7	111.3	113.4	114.2	116.0	115.6	116.2	116.1	114.5	112.6
2014	113.7	113.9	114.9	116.3	118.2	119.4	121.2	122.5	122.4	123.1	122.7	122.2	119.2
2015	120.9	121.6	121.8	123.2	125.3	126.5	127.2	129.2	129.2	128.9	129.3	127.9	125.9
Service-Providing													
2005	989.9	998.4	1,009.5	1,026.5	1,030.8	1,033.0	1,027.9	1,029.8	1,044.5	1,049.1	1,055.8	1,060.4	1,029.6
2006	1,043.5	1,054.9	1,065.8	1,070.7	1,077.6	1,079.7	1,069.8	1,072.4	1,084.1	1,087.6	1,093.5	1,096.7	1,074.7
2007	1,076.3	1,089.8	1,094.0	1,097.4	1,103.6	1,101.3	1,087.5	1,087.6	1,095.2	1,103.8	1,109.9	1,112.6	1,096.6
2008	1,089.3	1,093.0	1,096.5	1,101.3	1,104.6	1,097.0	1,082.4	1,079.4	1,084.1	1,079.4	1,072.5	1,062.6	1,086.8
2009	1,031.4	1,026.8	1,021.6	1,020.0	1,021.5	1,014.4	1,002.2	998.4	1,007.9	1,009.4	1,012.1	1,016.8	1,015.2
2010	995.6	998.6	1,001.8	1,011.2	1,017.7	1,012.5	1,005.4	1,002.7	1,006.4	1,013.9	1,016.7	1,017.6	1,008.3
2011	1,004.3	1,006.8	1,013.4	1,023.9	1,026.6	1,023.2	1,016.5	1,015.6	1,026.0	1,031.6	1,034.1	1,032.8	1,021.2
2012	1,019.5	1,022.8	1,029.3	1,036.1	1,042.6	1,042.3	1,030.9	1,035.0	1,043.4	1,050.3	1,055.4	1,051.0	1,038.2
2013	1,038.4	1,041.3	1,049.6	1,057.4	1,065.1	1,065.7	1,056.8	1,062.7	1,067.4	1,073.4	1,082.1	1,080.9	1,061.7
2014	1,066.8	1,072.9	1,083.5	1,092.6	1,101.6	1,097.4	1,088.3	1,098.6	1,108.2	1,117.5	1,121.9	1,122.8	1,097.7
2015	1,107.9	1,112.5	1,120.9	1,130.4	1,135.1	1,130.7	1,124.0	1,131.2	1,140.6	1,152.8	1,147.6	1,146.4	1,131.7
Mining and Logging													
2005	9.8	9.8	10.1	10.5	10.4	10.8	11.1	11.2	11.1	11.2	11.0	11.0	10.7
2006	11.0	10.9	11.1	11.3	11.5	11.7	11.9	12.0	11.9	11.8	11.8	11.8	11.6
2007	11.8	11.7	11.9	11.9	12.0	12.3	12.3	12.4	12.1	11.9	12.0	11.9	12.0
2008	11.9	11.9	11.9	11.9	12.0	12.2	12.5	12.6	12.5	12.2	12.2	12.0	12.2
2009	11.6	11.5	11.5	11.4	11.5	11.9	11.9	11.9	11.7	11.7	11.6	11.6	11.7
2010	11.5	11.5	11.7	11.7	12	12.4	12.7	12.7	12.4	12.4	12.7	12.8	12.2
2011	12.8	13.0	13.2	13.4	13.7	14.3	14.6	14.6	14.5	14.5	14.6	14.7	14.0
2012	14.4	14.6	15.0	15.2	15.4	15.8	16.1	16.1	15.9	15.7	15.6	15.6	15.5
2013	15.4	15.5	15.4	15.3	15.3	15.4	15.7	15.6	15.0	14.8	14.8	14.7	15.2
2014	14.4	14.1	14.2	14.2	14.3	14.5	14.6	14.6	14.4	14.6	14.7	14.7	14.4
2015	14.3	14.3	14.3	14.4	14.4	14.5	14.6	14.4	14.0	14.2	14.0	13.8	14.3

1. Employment by Industry: Nevada, 2005–2015—*Continued*

(Numbers in thousands, not seasonally adjusted)

Industry and year	January	February	March	April	May	June	July	August	September	October	November	December	Annual average
Construction													
2005	120.2	124.3	128.1	131.8	132.9	134.8	138.4	140.3	142.2	141.4	141.0	141.5	134.7
2006	136.9	140.2	141.9	144.2	146.7	148.8	146.9	147.3	145.3	141.9	138.8	136.3	142.9
2007	130.3	132.0	134.7	134.7	137.5	137.6	136.7	137.5	134.6	132.1	129.4	126.7	133.7
2008	118.9	119.2	118.7	119.0	120.6	121.2	121.3	119.8	117.0	113.3	107.1	101.3	116.5
2009	94.4	91.2	88.6	86.2	82.7	81.5	79.8	78.5	76.7	75.4	71.9	67.0	81.2
2010	59.3	57.9	57.7	60.0	60.6	60.9	60.5	60.6	59.2	59.9	58.5	56.4	59.3
2011	52.4	52.1	50.2	51.3	51.9	52.6	53.3	53.5	53.1	53.1	51.9	50.6	52.2
2012	48.0	47.6	48.1	49.3	51.0	52.4	52.9	54.6	54.8	55.2	55.1	54.4	52.0
2013	51.9	52.4	53.6	55.3	55.6	57.2	57.8	59.5	59.6	60.3	60.1	58.6	56.8
2014	58.1	58.6	59.5	61.0	62.5	63.3	64.9	66.3	66.4	66.9	66.3	65.8	63.3
2015	65.1	65.7	65.8	67.1	69.0	69.7	70.4	72.6	73.0	72.4	73.1	71.8	69.6
Manufacturing													
2005	46.8	47.0	47.3	47.7	47.7	48.1	48.3	48.2	48.6	48.6	48.5	48.6	48.0
2006	48.4	49.0	49.5	50.1	50.5	51.0	51.2	51.2	51.3	50.7	50.7	50.8	50.4
2007	49.8	49.8	50.3	50.5	50.7	50.9	50.7	50.6	50.4	49.9	49.7	49.2	50.2
2008	49.0	48.8	48.7	48.8	49.0	49.1	49.0	48.8	48.1	47.6	46.3	45.2	48.2
2009	43.4	42.2	41.5	40.9	40.2	39.8	39.6	39.3	39.2	39.0	38.9	38.7	40.2
2010	37.8	37.7	37.7	38.0	38.0	38.2	38.1	38.0	38.0	37.8	37.8	37.9	37.9
2011	37.5	37.6	37.9	38.0	38.2	38.5	38.5	38.7	38.8	38.9	38.7	38.7	38.3
2012	38.4	38.4	38.7	38.9	39.1	39.5	39.6	39.7	39.6	39.6	39.5	39.5	39.2
2013	39.3	39.6	39.8	40.1	40.4	40.8	40.7	40.9	41.0	41.1	41.2	41.2	40.5
2014	41.2	41.2	41.2	41.1	41.4	41.6	41.7	41.6	41.6	41.6	41.7	41.7	41.5
2015	41.5	41.6	41.7	41.7	41.9	42.3	42.2	42.2	42.2	42.3	42.2	42.3	42.0
Trade, Transportation, and Utilities													
2005	207.6	207.5	208.9	211.0	211.9	213.5	215.1	215.8	217.9	219.4	223.6	226.2	214.9
2006	220.4	220.2	222.6	223.0	224.2	225.4	225.1	226.1	226.9	228.6	233.1	235.9	226.0
2007	228.6	227.5	228.8	229.6	231.1	232.1	231.6	232.8	232.9	234.1	239.7	242.6	232.6
2008	233.7	231.3	231.8	231.3	231.3	231.6	232.2	232.3	231.2	230.2	231.2	230.1	231.5
2009	219.2	215.0	213.5	211.8	211.8	212.1	211.5	211.0	211.4	212.2	215.9	217.0	213.5
2010	208.6	206.3	206.4	207.2	208.2	209.1	209.9	210.2	209.8	211.8	216.0	217.5	210.1
2011	209.0	207.4	208.0	209.5	210.5	211.2	212.2	212.9	213.3	215.5	221.2	222.0	212.7
2012	215.0	212.7	213.9	214.9	216.1	217.1	217.1	217.7	218.4	219.9	226.8	226.7	218.0
2013	218.2	216.2	215.8	216.7	219.6	220.8	221.7	222.5	223.1	225.3	231.9	233.5	222.1
2014	225.0	223.7	225.0	226.4	227.9	228.6	229.0	230.4	231.3	234.6	240.7	242.8	230.5
2015	234.7	232.9	233.9	235.2	236.7	237.2	237.3	238.2	239.1	242.7	246.4	248.9	238.6
Wholesale Trade													
2005	36.1	36.5	36.7	37.0	37.2	37.4	37.6	37.6	37.8	37.7	37.8	38.0	37.3
2006	37.8	38.1	38.4	38.5	38.7	38.9	38.9	39.0	39.1	39.1	39.1	39.3	38.7
2007	38.9	39.1	39.3	39.3	39.4	39.6	39.5	39.6	39.5	39.4	39.4	39.4	39.4
2008	39.0	39.1	39.1	39.1	39.2	39.2	39.2	39.1	38.9	38.5	37.9	37.4	38.8
2009	36.5	36.0	35.6	35.0	34.7	34.4	34.2	34.0	33.7	33.6	33.4	33.3	34.5
2010	32.7	32.6	32.7	32.9	33.1	33.1	33.0	33.0	32.9	33.1	32.9	33.0	32.9
2011	32.5	32.6	32.7	32.7	32.8	32.9	32.9	32.8	32.7	32.7	32.7	32.7	32.7
2012	32.3	32.3	32.5	32.5	32.6	32.7	32.8	32.7	32.6	32.7	32.7	32.8	32.6
2013	32.3	32.4	32.5	32.7	32.9	33.0	33.2	33.3	33.3	33.3	33.5	33.6	33.0
2014	33.3	33.5	33.6	33.7	33.8	33.8	34.1	34.1	34.2	34.2	34.2	34.4	33.9
2015	34.1	34.1	34.3	34.3	34.4	34.5	34.6	34.6	34.7	35.2	35.1	34.9	34.6
Retail Trade													
2005	126.6	125.8	126.6	127.4	127.8	128.8	130.1	130.5	131.7	133.1	136.6	138.4	130.3
2006	133.2	132.8	134.4	134.4	135.0	135.3	134.9	135.4	135.7	137.1	140.7	142.5	136.0
2007	136.4	135.5	136.2	136.8	137.8	138.1	138.2	138.7	138.4	139.0	144.0	146.3	138.8
2008	139.4	137.3	137.7	137.3	136.9	137.2	137.4	137.4	136.8	136.5	138.2	137.9	137.5
2009	130.1	126.9	126.1	125.2	125.5	126.0	125.9	125.7	126.6	127.5	131.3	132.3	127.4
2010	125.4	123.4	123.6	124.2	124.7	125.3	126.0	126.3	126.0	127.7	131.8	132.7	126.4
2011	126.0	124.3	124.7	125.4	126.2	126.5	127.0	127.6	127.7	129.4	134.7	135.1	127.9
2012	129.7	127.7	128.6	129.1	129.9	130.5	130.2	130.7	131.2	132.3	138.9	138.4	131.4
2013	131.6	129.8	130.0	130.7	132.3	133.1	133.6	134.3	134.4	136.0	141.7	142.9	134.2
2014	135.6	133.9	134.5	135.3	136.3	136.8	137.0	138.0	138.5	141.5	146.9	148.1	138.5
2015	140.9	139.4	140.4	141.4	142.2	142.5	142.3	142.9	142.8	145.8	149.0	150.7	143.4

1. Employment by Industry: Nevada, 2005–2015—*Continued*

(Numbers in thousands, not seasonally adjusted)

Industry and year	January	February	March	April	May	June	July	August	September	October	November	December	Annual average
Transportation and Utilities													
2005	44.9	45.2	45.6	46.6	46.9	47.3	47.4	47.7	48.4	48.6	49.2	49.8	47.3
2006	49.4	49.3	49.8	50.1	50.5	51.2	51.3	51.7	52.1	52.4	53.3	54.1	51.3
2007	53.3	52.9	53.3	53.5	53.9	54.4	53.9	54.5	55.0	55.7	56.3	56.9	54.5
2008	55.3	54.9	55.0	54.9	55.2	55.2	55.6	55.8	55.5	55.2	55.1	54.8	55.2
2009	52.6	52.1	51.8	51.6	51.6	51.7	51.4	51.3	51.1	51.1	51.2	51.4	51.6
2010	50.5	50.3	50.1	50.1	50.4	50.7	50.9	50.9	50.9	51.0	51.3	51.8	50.7
2011	50.5	50.5	50.6	51.4	51.5	51.8	52.3	52.5	52.9	53.4	53.8	54.2	52.1
2012	53.0	52.7	52.8	53.3	53.6	53.9	54.1	54.3	54.6	54.9	55.2	55.5	54.0
2013	54.3	54.0	53.3	53.3	54.4	54.7	54.9	54.9	55.4	56.0	56.7	57.0	54.9
2014	56.1	56.3	56.9	57.4	57.8	58.0	57.9	58.3	58.6	58.9	59.6	60.3	58.0
2015	59.7	59.4	59.2	59.5	60.1	60.2	60.4	60.7	61.6	61.7	62.3	63.3	60.7
Information													
2005	15.0	14.4	14.4	15.0	15.4	14.7	14.5	14.4	14.2	14.7	14.6	14.5	14.7
2006	14.8	15.2	14.7	15.1	15.2	15.2	15.6	15.7	15.2	15.2	15.1	15.0	15.2
2007	15.3	15.8	15.6	15.7	16.0	15.8	15.2	15.6	15.2	15.5	15.6	15.3	15.6
2008	15.2	15.2	15.1	15.4	15.9	15.2	14.8	14.8	14.5	14.9	14.4	14.1	15.0
2009	13.5	13.6	13.6	13.0	13.2	13.1	13.1	13.2	12.8	12.8	12.9	12.9	13.1
2010	12.3	12.4	12.3	12.6	12.6	12.5	12.8	12.5	12.3	12.4	12.6	12.5	12.5
2011	12.4	12.3	12.4	12.6	12.7	12.7	12.5	12.4	12.6	13.0	12.3	12.8	12.6
2012	12.2	12.3	12.5	12.3	12.6	12.6	12.3	12.7	12.7	13.3	14.4	12.9	12.7
2013	12.0	12.3	12.5	12.7	13.0	13.9	13.1	12.9	12.9	13.0	13.3	13.1	12.9
2014	12.7	13.0	12.7	13.9	14.8	15.4	13.4	13.4	13.5	13.5	14.1	13.7	13.7
2015	13.3	13.8	13.5	13.7	13.8	14.0	13.7	13.9	13.5	14.2	14.2	14.0	13.8
Financial Activities													
2005	63.0	63.0	63.6	63.7	64.0	64.5	64.3	64.8	65.0	64.8	65.0	65.3	64.3
2006	64.2	64.2	64.8	64.8	65.2	65.7	65.7	65.8	66.1	65.5	65.8	66.2	65.3
2007	65.0	65.1	65.5	65.0	65.3	65.4	64.7	64.5	64.4	63.9	63.4	63.5	64.6
2008	62.2	62.3	62.4	62.2	62.0	61.9	61.5	61.0	60.8	60.5	59.9	59.3	61.3
2009	57.3	57.0	56.6	56.3	55.8	55.8	54.7	54.8	54.2	54.2	53.8	53.6	55.3
2010	52.9	52.5	52.5	53.3	53.0	52.9	53.0	52.7	52.5	53.1	52.8	53.0	52.9
2011	52.4	52.1	52.1	52.5	52.4	52.6	52.7	52.3	52.7	52.9	52.7	53.0	52.5
2012	52.6	52.7	53.0	53.9	54.2	54.6	54.5	54.8	54.9	55.7	55.7	55.8	54.4
2013	55.4	56.1	56.7	56.6	57.0	57.0	56.5	56.5	56.4	56.8	57.1	57.3	56.6
2014	56.1	56.2	56.3	56.3	57.0	56.9	56.7	57.2	57.4	58.1	58.3	58.5	57.1
2015	57.9	58.4	58.5	59.1	59.7	59.4	59.9	59.9	59.9	60.6	60.3	59.8	59.5
Professional and Business Services													
2005	139.4	140.1	141.9	144.4	144.4	145.4	145.5	147.8	148.9	150.9	153.4	154.3	146.4
2006	153.6	154.8	157.3	157.8	158.8	159.8	157.4	159.0	158.6	158.9	159.8	159.1	157.9
2007	158.4	161.3	159.6	160.3	160.4	159.7	156.9	158.5	156.8	159.8	159.2	157.4	159.0
2008	156.5	155.2	155.4	156.0	156.8	154.4	150.7	150.7	151.0	147.6	146.1	143.3	152.0
2009	141.7	139.3	137.1	134.9	135.3	134.1	130.7	131.4	133.8	133.9	136.1	136.6	135.4
2010	134.8	133.2	133.4	135.3	135.8	136.2	134.8	137.0	134.9	137.6	138.0	137.9	135.7
2011	138.6	137.0	137.4	138.9	138.6	139.5	138.7	139.2	141.3	142.9	142.7	141.8	139.7
2012	144.5	143.6	142.3	143.4	144.0	145.4	141.7	145.4	146.2	147.8	147.4	145.2	144.7
2013	148.8	147.1	148.7	150.2	151.2	150.2	147.7	150.7	148.8	151.5	152.7	151.4	149.9
2014	152.9	152.7	154.0	155.0	155.6	155.7	153.1	157.0	157.1	162.1	161.5	160.9	156.5
2015	163.4	161.5	162.7	165.7	165.5	164.4	163.7	167.8	167.9	173.1	169.5	168.6	166.2
Education and Health Services													
2005	82.9	83.9	84.7	85.5	85.6	85.8	85.2	85.2	85.8	85.6	86.1	86.9	85.3
2006	86.0	87.1	87.8	87.7	88.1	88.7	87.8	88.4	89.6	90.3	91.0	91.6	88.7
2007	90.7	92.2	92.6	92.2	92.9	92.9	92.6	92.9	93.4	94.2	94.5	94.2	92.9
2008	94.2	95.3	95.6	96.8	97.0	96.9	96.7	96.8	97.1	97.9	98.2	98.2	96.7
2009	97.1	97.4	97.4	97.8	98.1	98.2	98.3	98.5	98.5	100.3	100.2	100.2	98.5
2010	99.7	100.1	100.6	101.5	101.7	101.4	101.1	101.1	101.4	103.0	103.3	103.6	101.5
2011	103.1	104.0	104.7	105.3	105.3	105.5	104.9	105.4	105.9	106.5	107.1	107.5	105.4
2012	106.9	107.8	108.1	108.6	109.1	108.6	107.4	108.7	108.5	109.1	109.2	109.6	108.5
2013	108.7	110.1	110.6	111.0	111.4	111.4	111.0	111.8	112.3	113.2	113.7	113.6	111.6
2014	112.8	114.1	114.8	115.3	115.7	116.0	115.8	116.7	117.2	118.6	118.9	119.3	116.3
2015	118.0	119.2	119.9	120.8	121.1	121.7	121.8	122.8	123.6	124.9	124.1	125.0	121.9

1. Employment by Industry: Nevada, 2005–2015—*Continued*

(Numbers in thousands, not seasonally adjusted)

Industry and year	January	February	March	April	May	June	July	August	September	October	November	December	Annual average
Leisure and Hospitality													
2005	311.5	313.6	317.5	328.5	329.9	333.5	334.2	333.6	334.6	331.0	329.1	328.5	327.1
2006	327.4	330.0	333.6	336.0	338.8	341.8	342.0	341.4	341.7	337.9	336.4	336.6	337.0
2007	332.7	335.7	338.4	339.4	341.8	343.6	342.3	340.2	340.0	338.9	339.0	340.1	339.3
2008	334.6	334.9	336.2	338.7	339.4	340.0	336.1	334.4	331.6	326.1	321.0	317.0	332.5
2009	310.6	308.9	307.6	310.4	311.9	310.9	310.1	307.2	306.9	304.5	302.2	306.2	308.1
2010	302.4	304.4	305.8	310.4	312.1	313.6	312.8	311.2	310.6	309.5	307.8	307.3	309.0
2011	306.1	307.6	312.4	317.9	320.1	321.2	320.2	318.1	319.0	317.9	315.1	311.7	315.6
2012	309.2	311.3	315.1	318.2	320.8	322.6	321.6	319.6	319.0	318.5	316.3	314.7	317.2
2013	313.4	315.0	319.3	323.6	325.4	328.7	330.0	328.5	328.6	326.5	325.0	322.4	323.9
2014	322.2	325.1	330.7	335.3	338.8	339.7	340.0	342.6	341.9	339.0	336.7	335.5	335.6
2015	332.8	335.8	339.7	343.0	344.8	344.9	344.4	344.3	343.9	342.5	337.7	334.7	340.7
Other Services													
2005	32.4	32.7	33.2	33.2	33.5	34.1	34.2	34.4	34.6	34.5	34.7	35.1	33.9
2006	33.9	34.3	35.0	35.0	35.5	35.9	36.0	36.3	36.4	36.1	36.0	35.9	35.5
2007	35.2	35.3	36.0	36.1	36.5	37.1	37.0	37.1	37.0	36.7	36.9	37.2	36.5
2008	36.6	36.5	36.8	36.6	37.2	37.2	36.9	37.1	37.0	36.5	35.8	35.1	36.6
2009	33.7	33.4	33.6	33.9	34.2	34.3	34.1	34.1	34.0	33.4	33.2	33.0	33.7
2010	32.6	32.7	33.0	33.0	33.1	33.1	33.4	33.2	33.0	33.0	32.3	32.0	32.9
2011	31.6	31.8	32.0	32.5	32.7	32.9	33.0	32.9	32.6	32.3	32.2	32.3	32.4
2012	32.1	32.2	32.6	33.0	33.5	33.9	33.8	33.9	33.9	34.3	33.1	32.8	33.3
2013	32.4	32.6	32.9	33.5	33.9	34.3	34.3	34.3	34.2	34.1	34.2	34.2	33.7
2014	34.1	34.3	34.8	35.5	36.1	36.2	36.3	36.1	36.1	36.5	35.9	35.5	35.6
2015	35.2	35.4	35.8	36.1	36.4	36.7	36.7	36.6	36.3	36.3	36.1	35.6	36.1
Government													
2005	138.1	143.2	145.3	145.2	146.1	141.5	134.9	133.8	143.5	148.2	149.3	149.6	143.2
2006	143.2	149.1	150.0	151.3	151.8	147.2	140.2	139.7	149.6	155.1	156.3	156.4	149.2
2007	150.4	156.9	157.5	159.1	159.6	154.7	147.2	146.0	155.5	160.7	161.6	162.3	156.0
2008	156.3	162.3	163.2	164.3	165.0	159.8	153.5	152.3	160.9	165.7	165.9	165.5	161.2
2009	158.3	162.2	162.2	161.9	161.2	155.9	149.7	148.2	156.3	158.1	157.8	157.3	157.4
2010	152.3	157.0	157.8	157.9	161.2	153.7	147.6	144.8	151.9	153.5	153.9	153.8	153.8
2011	151.1	154.6	154.4	154.7	154.3	147.6	142.3	142.4	148.6	150.6	150.8	151.7	150.3
2012	147.0	150.2	151.8	151.8	152.3	147.5	142.5	142.2	149.8	151.7	152.5	153.3	149.4
2013	149.5	151.9	153.1	153.1	153.6	149.4	142.5	145.5	151.1	153.0	154.2	155.4	151.0
2014	151.0	153.8	155.2	154.9	155.7	148.9	144.0	145.2	153.7	155.1	155.8	156.6	152.5
2015	152.6	155.5	156.9	156.8	157.1	152.4	146.5	147.7	156.4	158.5	159.3	159.8	155.0

2. Average Weekly Hours by Selected Industry: Nevada, 2011–2015

(Not seasonally adjusted)

Industry and year	January	February	March	April	May	June	July	August	September	October	November	December	Annual average
Total Private													
2011	34.6	34.6	34.6	34.7	34.8	34.3	34.1	34.5	34.4	34.7	34.0	33.5	34.4
2012	33.8	33.6	33.7	34.0	33.8	34.0	34.4	34.1	34.5	34.2	34.1	34.0	34.0
2013	33.5	33.3	33.5	33.3	33.3	33.8	33.4	33.6	33.7	33.6	33.3	33.6	33.5
2014	33.1	33.3	33.5	33.3	33.2	33.7	33.5	33.8	33.6	33.4	33.6	33.2	33.4
2015	33.2	33.5	33.6	33.4	33.5	33.6	33.7	34.1	33.8	33.5	33.9	33.4	33.6
Goods-Producing													
2011	35.7	35.8	36.4	36.6	36.6	36.8	37.2	37.8	37.8	39.0	36.4	36.7	36.9
2012	36.2	35.5	35.6	35.9	36.5	36.3	36.5	36.9	37.1	36.5	36.1	36.4	36.3
2013	36.8	35.8	36.6	37.3	37.6	38.2	37.7	38.7	38.0	38.5	38.5	39.0	37.8
2014	39.0	38.2	38.0	37.7	37.8	38.4	38.1	38.6	38.1	38.6	37.6	38.4	38.2
2015	37.7	37.7	38.7	38.7	38.4	38.8	38.1	38.3	38.0	38.5	38.1	38.2	38.3
Construction													
2011	33.2	33.3	33.9	34.8	34.7	35.9	36.0	36.3	35.6	35.7	34.8	35.2	35.0
2012	34.5	33.9	34.6	34.9	35.0	35.2	35.1	35.5	34.9	34.5	34.3	34.7	34.8
2013	35.0	33.7	34.6	35.3	35.6	37.6	37.1	38.0	36.9	37.3	37.5	37.3	36.4
2014	36.7	36.4	36.4	35.6	35.4	36.0	36.1	36.9	36.7	37.3	36.0	36.8	36.4
2015	36.0	36.5	37.6	37.5	37.1	37.8	37.0	37.2	37.2	38.1	36.5	36.0	37.1
Trade, Transportation, and Utilities													
2011	35.5	35.3	34.7	35.9	35.4	34.9	34.6	35.3	35.2	34.6	34.4	34.3	35.0
2012	33.7	34.0	34.4	34.1	34.5	34.4	34.5	34.3	34.9	34.2	34.4	34.3	34.3
2013	33.5	33.8	34.1	33.8	34.0	34.4	34.2	34.1	34.1	33.6	33.0	33.7	33.9
2014	32.5	33.1	33.7	33.6	33.4	34.0	34.1	34.5	34.2	34.2	34.4	34.4	33.8
2015	33.9	34.5	35.5	34.6	35.2	35.4	35.6	35.9	36.3	35.7	36.6	36.0	35.4
Financial Activities													
2011	36.6	36.5	36.8	36.4	38.2	37.8	37.3	37.7	38.5	38.7	37.3	36.3	37.3
2012	36.7	36.1	36.7	37.5	37.3	37.3	37.9	36.8	39.5	39.1	39.4	40.2	37.9
2013	39.6	39.3	39.5	39.1	39.4	39.9	38.6	38.3	38.8	38.0	38.4	38.7	39.0
2014	38.4	38.5	38.7	38.1	38.1	38.6	37.9	37.5	37.0	37.3	38.6	36.9	38.0
2015	37.1	37.6	37.7	37.7	37.9	37.0	37.4	37.8	38.3	37.3	37.5	36.7	37.5
Professional and Business Services													
2011	32.4	32.2	33.0	32.9	33.0	32.2	32.3	33.5	32.9	34.0	33.4	33.7	33.0
2012	34.3	34.1	34.2	34.5	34.2	35.1	35.4	34.9	35.1	35.3	35.5	36.0	34.9
2013	34.9	34.6	34.4	34.4	34.6	35.6	34.8	35.5	36.0	35.4	35.3	35.2	35.1
2014	34.7	35.0	34.5	34.4	34.3	35.4	34.8	35.2	34.8	34.8	35.6	35.0	34.9
2015	34.9	35.2	33.9	34.3	34.1	34.3	34.6	35.8	34.0	34.1	34.2	33.9	34.4
Leisure and Hospitality													
2011	31.5	31.6	31.5	31.3	31.4	30.9	30.7	31.0	31.1	31.4	30.9	29.5	31.1
2012	29.6	29.3	29.4	29.8	29.3	29.7	29.8	30.0	30.1	30.4	30.1	30.1	29.8
2013	29.8	29.7	30.0	29.7	29.6	29.9	29.8	30.0	29.8	30.3	29.8	29.5	29.8
2014	29.9	30.2	30.6	30.2	30.0	30.5	30.3	30.6	30.4	30.1	30.1	29.3	30.2
2015	29.8	30.1	30.2	29.9	30.1	30.2	30.5	30.4	30.0	29.7	29.9	29.4	30.0

3. Average Hourly Earnings by Selected Industry: Nevada, 2011–2015

(Dollars, not seasonally adjusted)

Industry and year	January	February	March	April	May	June	July	August	September	October	November	December	Annual average
Total Private													
2011..	19.11	19.10	19.12	19.27	19.57	19.23	19.44	19.56	19.49	19.63	19.34	19.36	19.35
2012..	19.66	19.67	19.73	19.97	19.62	19.53	19.82	19.84	19.84	19.92	20.11	20.20	19.83
2013..	20.07	20.08	20.14	20.13	20.05	20.23	20.00	20.13	20.35	20.18	20.48	20.65	20.21
2014..	20.85	20.89	20.79	20.86	20.75	20.87	20.72	20.83	20.91	21.02	21.45	21.41	20.95
2015..	21.61	21.88	21.95	21.85	21.78	21.73	21.87	22.12	22.11	22.14	22.24	22.07	21.95
Goods-Producing													
2011..	23.59	23.60	23.80	24.81	24.64	24.78	25.20	25.32	25.15	25.38	24.70	23.99	24.60
2012..	24.08	24.08	24.75	24.84	24.33	24.68	25.00	24.86	24.34	24.56	24.96	25.48	24.67
2013..	23.99	24.23	24.87	24.33	24.82	24.88	25.02	24.72	25.08	24.66	25.06	25.11	24.74
2014..	25.43	25.81	25.51	25.72	25.06	25.75	25.76	25.53	25.63	25.62	25.67	26.03	25.63
2015..	26.10	26.41	26.43	26.52	26.11	26.14	26.78	26.76	27.13	27.16	26.97	27.11	26.64
Construction													
2011..	24.70	24.71	24.55	26.00	25.78	25.52	26.28	26.40	25.17	25.61	25.48	26.10	25.54
2012..	26.18	26.07	26.60	26.40	26.12	26.42	27.16	27.24	26.90	27.14	26.73	27.78	26.75
2013..	27.25	27.54	27.28	25.95	26.34	26.16	25.80	25.45	25.56	25.17	25.53	25.90	26.10
2014..	26.43	27.60	26.78	27.39	26.82	27.84	27.40	27.24	26.68	26.46	26.69	27.01	27.02
2015..	26.21	26.40	26.64	26.71	27.16	27.06	28.25	28.26	28.40	28.36	28.00	28.08	27.50
Trade, Transportation, and Utilities													
2011..	17.13	17.11	17.19	17.24	17.38	16.84	17.44	17.21	17.11	17.19	17.09	17.15	17.17
2012..	17.53	17.54	17.43	17.81	17.42	17.61	18.05	18.27	18.33	18.56	18.64	18.70	18.00
2013..	18.86	18.81	19.02	19.31	18.76	18.85	18.47	18.42	18.70	18.93	19.05	18.90	18.84
2014..	19.54	19.61	19.27	19.78	19.41	19.26	19.21	19.19	19.41	19.37	19.62	19.41	19.42
2015..	19.82	19.93	19.89	19.92	19.79	19.55	19.53	19.45	19.67	19.57	19.65	19.34	19.67
Financial Activities													
2011..	21.92	21.91	22.05	21.67	21.48	21.21	21.03	20.94	20.59	20.87	20.83	20.91	21.28
2012..	21.25	21.50	21.50	21.70	20.84	20.49	20.79	20.86	20.71	20.92	21.00	20.85	21.02
2013..	21.28	21.58	21.74	21.62	22.40	23.03	22.35	22.52	21.55	21.62	21.85	21.57	21.93
2014..	21.18	21.31	21.38	21.04	21.28	22.11	21.85	22.01	21.26	21.85	22.17	21.75	21.60
2015..	22.19	22.69	22.96	23.49	23.85	23.89	26.20	26.57	26.11	26.33	25.98	26.49	24.75
Professional and Business Services													
2011..	25.33	25.30	24.89	24.62	25.05	24.21	23.82	23.87	23.58	23.79	23.52	23.45	24.27
2012..	23.08	23.00	22.82	22.78	22.31	21.91	22.00	21.94	21.80	21.73	22.19	22.35	22.32
2013..	22.34	22.86	22.64	22.88	22.71	22.93	23.25	23.40	23.85	23.62	24.31	25.02	23.33
2014..	24.78	24.37	24.32	24.38	24.28	24.22	23.82	23.94	23.72	23.32	23.61	23.39	24.00
2015..	23.63	24.54	24.77	24.12	24.24	24.14	24.30	24.55	24.03	24.31	24.48	23.90	24.25
Leisure and Hospitality													
2011..	13.66	13.68	13.62	13.60	13.82	13.50	13.62	13.67	13.83	14.01	14.14	14.14	13.77
2012..	14.51	14.39	14.30	14.21	14.17	14.15	14.20	14.29	14.34	14.46	14.57	14.53	14.34
2013..	14.71	14.58	14.52	14.46	14.37	14.42	14.55	14.75	15.06	14.82	15.03	15.08	14.70
2014..	15.52	15.48	15.53	15.51	15.55	15.45	15.45	15.50	15.86	15.93	16.16	16.26	15.68
2015..	16.58	16.28	16.13	15.97	16.20	15.94	15.91	16.06	16.29	16.35	16.64	16.49	16.23

4. Average Weekly Earnings by Selected Industry: Nevada, 2011–2015

(Dollars, not seasonally adjusted)

Industry and year	January	February	March	April	May	June	July	August	September	October	November	December	Annual average
Total Private													
2011	661.21	660.86	661.55	668.67	681.04	659.59	662.90	674.82	670.46	681.16	657.56	648.56	665.64
2012	664.51	660.91	664.90	678.98	663.16	664.02	681.81	676.54	684.48	681.26	685.75	686.80	674.22
2013	672.35	668.66	674.69	670.33	667.67	683.77	668.00	676.37	685.80	678.05	681.98	693.84	677.04
2014	690.14	695.64	696.47	694.64	688.90	703.32	694.12	704.05	702.58	702.07	720.72	710.81	699.73
2015	717.45	732.98	737.52	729.79	729.63	730.13	737.02	754.29	747.32	741.69	753.94	737.14	737.52
Goods-Producing													
2011	842.16	844.88	866.32	908.05	901.82	911.90	937.44	957.10	950.67	989.82	899.08	880.43	907.74
2012	871.70	854.84	881.10	891.76	888.05	895.88	912.50	917.33	903.01	896.44	901.06	927.47	895.52
2013	882.83	867.43	910.24	907.51	933.23	950.42	943.25	956.66	953.04	949.41	964.81	979.29	935.17
2014	991.77	985.94	969.38	969.64	947.27	988.80	981.46	985.46	976.50	988.93	965.19	999.55	979.07
2015	983.97	995.66	1,022.84	1,026.32	1,002.62	1,014.23	1,020.32	1,024.91	1,030.94	1,045.66	1,027.56	1,035.60	1,020.31
Construction													
2011	820.04	822.84	832.25	904.80	894.57	916.17	946.08	958.32	896.05	914.28	886.70	918.72	893.90
2012	903.21	883.77	920.36	921.36	914.20	929.98	953.32	967.02	938.81	936.33	916.84	963.97	930.90
2013	953.75	928.10	943.89	916.04	937.70	983.62	957.18	967.10	943.16	938.84	957.38	966.07	950.04
2014	969.98	1,004.64	974.79	975.08	949.43	1,002.24	989.14	1,005.16	979.16	986.96	960.84	993.97	983.53
2015	943.56	963.60	1,001.66	1,001.63	1,007.64	1,022.87	1,045.25	1,051.27	1,056.48	1,080.52	1,022.00	1,010.88	1,020.25
Trade, Transportation, and Utilities													
2011	608.12	603.98	596.49	618.92	615.25	587.72	603.42	607.51	602.27	594.77	587.90	588.25	600.95
2012	590.76	596.36	599.59	607.32	600.99	605.78	622.73	626.66	639.72	634.75	641.22	641.41	617.40
2013	631.81	635.78	648.58	652.68	637.84	648.44	631.67	628.12	637.67	636.05	628.65	636.93	638.68
2014	635.05	649.09	649.40	664.61	648.29	654.84	655.06	662.06	663.82	662.45	674.93	667.70	656.40
2015	671.90	687.59	706.10	689.23	696.61	692.07	695.27	698.26	714.02	698.65	719.19	696.24	696.32
Financial Activities													
2011	802.27	799.72	811.44	788.79	820.54	801.74	784.42	789.44	792.72	807.67	776.96	759.03	793.74
2012	779.88	776.15	789.05	813.75	777.33	764.28	787.94	767.65	818.05	817.97	827.40	838.17	796.66
2013	842.69	848.09	858.73	845.34	882.56	918.90	862.71	862.52	836.14	821.56	839.04	834.76	855.27
2014	813.31	820.44	827.41	801.62	810.77	853.45	828.12	825.38	786.62	815.01	855.76	802.58	820.80
2015	823.25	853.14	865.59	885.57	903.92	883.93	979.88	1,004.35	1,000.01	982.11	974.25	972.18	928.13
Professional and Business Services													
2011	820.69	814.66	821.37	810.00	826.65	779.56	769.39	799.65	775.78	808.86	785.57	790.27	800.91
2012	791.64	784.30	780.44	785.91	763.00	769.04	778.80	765.71	765.18	767.07	787.75	804.60	778.97
2013	779.67	790.96	778.82	787.07	785.77	816.31	809.10	830.70	858.60	836.15	858.14	880.70	818.88
2014	859.87	852.95	839.04	838.67	832.80	857.39	828.94	842.69	825.46	811.54	840.52	818.65	837.60
2015	824.69	863.81	839.70	827.32	826.58	828.00	840.78	878.89	817.02	828.97	837.22	810.21	834.20
Leisure and Hospitality													
2011	430.29	432.29	429.03	425.68	433.95	417.15	418.13	423.77	430.11	439.91	436.93	417.13	428.25
2012	429.50	421.63	420.42	423.46	415.18	420.26	423.16	428.70	431.63	439.58	438.56	437.35	427.33
2013	438.36	433.03	435.60	429.46	425.35	431.16	433.59	442.50	448.79	449.05	447.89	444.86	438.06
2014	464.05	467.50	475.22	468.40	466.50	471.23	468.14	474.30	482.14	479.49	486.42	476.42	473.54
2015	494.08	490.03	487.13	477.50	487.62	481.39	485.26	488.22	488.70	485.60	497.54	484.81	486.90

NEW HAMPSHIRE
At a Glance

Population:
2005 estimate: 1,298,492
2010 census: 1,316,470
2015 estimate: 1,330,608

Percent change in population:
2005–2015: 2.5%
2010–2015: 1.1%

Percent change in total nonfarm employment:
2005–2015: 3.1%

Industry with the largest growth in employment, 2005–2015 (thousands):
Education and health services, 19.8

Industry with the largest decline or smallest growth in employment, 2005–2015 (thousands):
Manufacturing, –13.2

Civilian labor force:
2005: 725,849
2010: 738,257
2015: 741,192

Unemployment rate and rank among states (highest to lowest):
2005: 3.6%, 46th
2010: 5.8%, 48th
2015: 3.4%, 48th

Over-the-year change in unemployment rates:
2012–2013: –0.4%
2013–2014: –0.8%
2014–2015: –0.9%

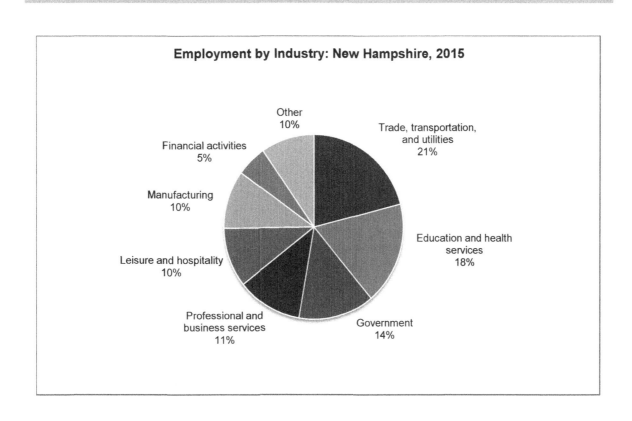

Employment by Industry: New Hampshire, 2015

Other 10%
Financial activities 5%
Manufacturing 10%
Leisure and hospitality 10%
Professional and business services 11%
Trade, transportation, and utilities 21%
Education and health services 18%
Government 14%

1. Employment by Industry: New Hampshire, 2005–2015

(Numbers in thousands, not seasonally adjusted)

Industry and year	January	February	March	April	May	June	July	August	September	October	November	December	Annual average
Total Nonfarm													
2005	621.0	620.4	622.2	631.0	638.4	643.8	640.7	639.5	645.7	642.9	643.9	649.0	636.5
2006	625.4	627.8	631.2	639.3	644.5	651.8	646.8	645.5	650.7	649.2	648.6	654.0	642.9
2007	633.1	635.6	637.5	640.5	650.6	658.1	651.9	651.2	654.3	652.9	653.8	657.8	648.1
2008	640.0	639.8	641.1	644.6	653.8	659.2	653.0	653.6	655.5	654.2	650.3	649.5	649.6
2009	628.0	625.4	622.3	624.0	633.2	635.8	624.7	625.1	630.5	631.4	628.4	631.5	628.4
2010	609.5	612.4	615.3	619.4	629.7	632.8	625.0	625.1	630.3	631.6	630.1	634.0	624.6
2011	613.6	616.7	618.8	624.4	630.7	634.4	628.1	627.3	634.5	634.7	635.3	638.0	628.0
2012	620.1	620.5	624.0	627.4	635.1	642.3	636.3	638.1	641.8	641.8	641.1	643.3	634.3
2013	624.7	627.7	628.2	633.1	642.7	647.4	640.5	642.9	643.0	647.1	646.8	650.4	639.5
2014	631.3	634.7	635.1	640.3	648.0	655.6	650.0	644.3	652.3	655.5	654.0	657.8	646.6
2015	640.1	641.0	644.2	649.2	660.0	665.4	660.6	659.5	661.1	664.0	663.3	665.9	656.2
Total Private													
2005	528.1	526.3	527.3	536.9	543.5	555.4	560.7	560.6	552.9	548.3	548.3	553.2	545.1
2006	535.2	533.0	535.8	543.9	549.2	562.8	565.3	565.8	556.1	552.8	552.1	556.7	550.7
2007	541.0	539.2	540.8	544.0	554.5	567.2	569.9	570.1	560.0	555.2	556.0	559.8	554.8
2008	546.3	542.7	542.8	546.8	556.1	566.0	569.8	569.6	557.9	554.5	549.2	548.5	554.2
2009	531.7	526.3	522.8	524.5	533.2	540.0	541.0	541.2	533.6	530.8	527.0	530.1	531.9
2010	514.3	512.1	513.8	519.2	528.1	538.1	542.1	542.7	534.4	533.4	531.0	535.1	528.7
2011	521.6	519.9	521.7	528.5	534.2	544.4	549.7	550.3	542.3	539.5	539.1	541.6	536.1
2012	528.8	526.0	528.6	532.6	540.5	554.4	556.3	558.5	548.4	546.7	545.3	546.7	542.7
2013	534.5	533.2	534.3	539.2	548.6	559.4	563.4	564.4	553.0	552.6	552.2	555.0	549.2
2014	541.7	541.0	541.0	546.2	556.0	566.9	571.0	565.3	560.2	560.7	558.4	562.1	555.9
2015	550.2	547.7	549.7	555.0	566.2	577.1	581.9	581.8	570.6	570.8	569.7	571.9	566.1
Goods-Producing													
2005	107.1	106.6	106.9	110.1	111.4	112.9	112.2	112.9	111.9	112.0	112.2	111.3	110.6
2006	106.5	105.4	106.2	108.8	109.8	111.0	110.0	111.1	110.2	109.8	108.6	107.4	108.7
2007	104.1	102.9	103.4	105.0	107.2	108.4	108.2	108.6	107.2	106.9	106.5	105.4	106.2
2008	102.2	101.3	101.6	102.6	104.0	105.2	105.2	105.5	103.8	103.2	101.6	99.2	103.0
2009	94.1	92.1	90.6	91.3	92.2	92.3	91.4	92.1	91.7	91.4	89.6	88.4	91.4
2010	84.5	83.7	84.3	86.6	88.4	89.4	90.1	90.7	90.0	90.3	89.7	89.1	88.1
2011	86.2	85.7	86.6	88.9	89.9	91.0	91.6	91.9	91.2	90.9	90.6	89.7	89.5
2012	86.7	86.0	86.7	88.6	89.4	90.6	90.7	91.0	90.6	90.5	89.5	88.7	89.1
2013	86.5	86.0	86.4	88.1	89.8	91.2	91.2	91.5	90.7	91.0	91.0	90.3	89.5
2014	87.8	87.5	87.8	89.8	91.1	92.3	92.4	92.7	91.6	91.6	91.6	91.3	90.6
2015	89.2	88.3	88.5	90.6	92.6	94.0	94.7	94.8	94.1	94.0	94.0	92.7	92.3
Service-Providing													
2005	513.9	513.8	515.3	520.9	527.0	530.9	528.5	526.6	533.8	530.9	531.7	537.7	525.9
2006	518.9	522.4	525.0	530.5	534.7	540.8	536.8	534.4	540.5	539.4	540.0	546.6	534.2
2007	529.0	532.7	534.1	535.5	543.4	549.7	543.7	542.6	547.1	546.0	547.3	552.4	542.0
2008	537.8	538.5	539.5	542.0	549.8	554.0	547.8	548.1	551.7	551.0	548.7	550.3	546.6
2009	533.9	533.3	531.7	532.7	541.0	543.5	533.3	533.0	538.8	540.0	538.8	543.1	536.9
2010	525.0	528.7	531.0	532.8	541.3	543.4	534.9	534.4	540.3	541.3	540.4	544.9	536.5
2011	527.4	531.0	532.2	535.5	540.8	543.4	536.5	535.4	543.3	543.8	544.7	548.3	538.5
2012	533.4	534.5	537.3	538.8	545.7	551.7	545.6	547.1	551.2	551.3	551.6	554.6	545.2
2013	538.2	541.7	541.8	545.0	552.9	556.2	549.3	551.4	552.3	556.1	555.8	560.1	550.1
2014	543.5	547.2	547.3	550.5	556.9	563.3	557.6	551.6	560.7	563.9	562.4	566.5	556.0
2015	550.9	552.7	555.7	558.6	567.4	571.4	565.9	564.7	567.0	570.0	569.3	573.2	563.9
Mining and Logging													
2005	0.9	0.9	1.0	1.0	1.0	1.1	1.1	1.1	1.1	1.1	1.1	1.1	1.0
2006	0.9	0.9	1.0	1.0	1.1	1.1	1.2	1.2	1.2	1.2	1.1	1.1	1.1
2007	1.0	1.0	1.0	1.1	1.1	1.2	1.2	1.2	1.2	1.2	1.2	1.1	1.1
2008	1.0	1.0	1.0	1.0	1.0	1.1	1.1	1.1	1.1	1.1	1.0	0.9	1.0
2009	0.8	0.8	0.8	0.8	0.9	1.0	1.0	1.0	1.0	1.0	1.0	0.9	0.9
2010	0.8	0.8	0.8	0.9	0.9	1.0	1.0	1.0	1.0	0.9	0.9	0.9	0.9
2011	0.8	0.8	0.8	0.8	0.9	0.9	1.0	1.0	1.0	1.0	1.0	0.9	0.9
2012	0.8	0.8	0.8	0.9	0.9	1.0	1.0	1.0	1.0	1.0	0.9	0.9	0.9
2013	0.8	0.8	0.8	0.9	0.9	1.0	1.0	1.0	1.0	1.0	1.0	1.0	0.9
2014	0.9	0.9	0.9	0.9	1.0	1.0	1.0	1.1	1.1	1.1	1.0	1.0	1.0
2015	0.9	0.9	0.9	0.9	0.9	1.0	1.0	1.0	1.0	1.0	1.0	1.0	1.0

1. Employment by Industry: New Hampshire, 2005–2015—*Continued*

(Numbers in thousands, not seasonally adjusted)

Industry and year	January	February	March	April	May	June	July	August	September	October	November	December	Annual average
Construction													
2005	26.3	25.8	26.0	28.9	30.1	31.0	31.5	31.5	30.9	30.7	30.7	29.8	29.4
2006	27.2	26.5	27.1	29.2	30.2	31.3	31.3	31.3	30.9	30.3	29.2	28.0	29.4
2007	25.6	24.6	24.8	26.2	28.4	29.1	29.5	29.4	28.7	28.2	27.8	26.6	27.4
2008	24.2	23.6	23.9	25.5	26.7	27.3	28.2	28.0	27.2	27.0	26.0	24.5	26.0
2009	21.5	20.6	20.3	21.6	22.9	23.4	23.7	23.9	24.3	24.1	22.9	21.9	22.6
2010	18.9	18.2	18.6	20.4	21.7	22.2	23.0	23.2	22.9	23.1	22.6	21.7	21.4
2011	19.6	19.1	19.7	21.7	22.5	23.1	23.6	23.6	23.5	23.5	23.2	22.4	22.1
2012	20.0	19.5	20.1	21.8	22.6	23.2	23.5	23.7	23.7	23.6	22.8	21.9	22.2
2013	20.3	19.8	20.2	21.7	23.2	23.8	23.8	23.9	23.7	23.6	23.5	22.7	22.5
2014	20.8	20.6	20.9	22.7	23.7	24.2	24.7	24.7	24.2	24.3	24.2	23.5	23.2
2015	21.8	21.1	21.2	22.9	24.5	25.2	25.7	25.8	25.9	26.2	26.6	25.6	24.4
Manufacturing													
2005	79.9	79.9	79.9	80.2	80.3	80.8	79.6	80.3	79.9	80.2	80.4	80.4	80.2
2006	78.4	78.0	78.1	78.6	78.5	78.6	77.5	78.6	78.1	78.3	78.3	78.3	78.3
2007	77.5	77.3	77.6	77.7	77.7	78.1	77.5	78.0	77.3	77.5	77.5	77.7	77.6
2008	77.0	76.7	76.7	76.1	76.3	76.8	75.9	76.4	75.5	75.1	74.6	73.8	75.9
2009	71.8	70.7	69.5	68.9	68.4	67.9	66.7	67.2	66.4	66.3	65.7	65.6	67.9
2010	64.8	64.7	64.9	65.3	65.8	66.2	66.1	66.5	66.1	66.3	66.2	66.5	65.8
2011	65.8	65.8	66.1	66.4	66.5	67.0	67.0	67.3	66.7	66.4	66.4	66.4	66.5
2012	65.9	65.7	65.8	65.9	65.9	66.4	66.2	66.3	65.9	65.9	65.8	65.9	66.0
2013	65.4	65.4	65.4	65.5	65.7	66.4	66.4	66.6	66.0	66.4	66.5	66.6	66.0
2014	66.1	66.0	66.0	66.2	66.4	67.1	66.7	66.9	66.3	66.2	66.4	66.8	66.4
2015	66.5	66.3	66.4	66.8	67.2	67.8	68.0	68.0	67.2	66.8	66.4	66.1	67.0
Trade, Transportation, and Utilities													
2005	139.2	136.7	136.6	137.8	139.5	141.8	141.5	141.7	140.2	141.7	144.2	146.8	140.6
2006	140.2	137.5	138.3	140.1	141.1	143.0	142.2	142.3	140.7	141.5	144.9	147.7	141.6
2007	141.5	138.0	138.5	138.9	140.9	142.9	142.6	142.0	139.7	140.5	144.2	146.5	141.4
2008	140.9	137.6	137.4	137.2	139.4	141.4	141.0	140.8	138.6	139.8	141.4	142.7	139.9
2009	136.1	132.8	131.6	131.7	134.0	135.4	133.6	133.2	132.5	133.2	135.5	137.3	133.9
2010	131.5	129.2	129.3	130.1	132.3	134.3	133.6	133.5	131.8	133.5	136.2	138.8	132.8
2011	132.7	130.3	130.5	131.7	133.1	135.1	134.4	134.4	133.7	134.7	137.3	140.0	134.0
2012	134.4	131.8	132.4	132.7	134.4	137.9	137.0	137.3	135.5	136.0	139.6	140.8	135.8
2013	134.8	132.5	132.9	134.3	136.3	138.2	137.6	137.6	135.8	136.3	139.4	141.7	136.5
2014	135.7	133.6	133.7	134.3	136.3	138.2	137.6	131.5	137.1	138.0	140.8	143.0	136.7
2015	136.9	134.1	134.3	135.3	137.4	139.3	138.4	138.7	137.2	137.4	141.2	143.3	137.8
Wholesale Trade													
2005	27.1	26.9	27.0	27.4	27.6	27.7	27.8	27.7	27.4	27.8	27.7	27.7	27.5
2006	27.5	27.4	27.6	27.9	28.2	28.4	28.3	28.4	28.2	28.2	28.1	28.3	28.0
2007	28.2	28.0	28.2	28.3	28.4	28.5	28.5	28.4	28.2	28.1	28.1	28.1	28.3
2008	28.0	27.9	27.9	28.1	28.3	28.4	28.4	28.3	28.0	28.0	27.8	27.6	28.1
2009	27.1	26.7	26.5	26.6	26.7	26.6	26.4	26.4	26.1	26.2	26.1	26.1	26.5
2010	25.6	25.6	25.6	25.7	25.9	26.0	26.1	26.1	25.8	26.0	26.1	26.0	25.9
2011	25.8	25.9	26.0	26.1	26.3	26.3	26.4	26.3	26.2	26.3	26.2	26.4	26.2
2012	26.3	26.2	26.3	26.5	26.6	26.9	26.9	26.9	26.8	26.7	26.7	26.7	26.6
2013	26.4	26.4	26.5	26.6	26.8	27.0	27.0	27.0	26.8	26.7	26.8	26.9	26.7
2014	26.7	26.7	26.8	26.9	27.2	27.3	27.4	27.5	27.3	27.3	27.4	27.5	27.2
2015	27.2	27.1	27.2	27.4	27.6	27.8	27.8	27.8	27.6	27.6	28.1	28.3	27.6
Retail Trade													
2005	96.6	94.4	94.2	95.0	96.3	98.1	98.3	98.6	96.9	98.1	100.7	103.0	97.5
2006	97.5	94.9	95.4	96.7	97.2	98.6	98.5	98.6	96.6	97.6	101.1	103.2	98.0
2007	98.0	94.9	95.1	95.3	97.0	98.6	98.8	98.4	95.8	96.9	100.9	102.5	97.7
2008	97.9	95.0	94.8	94.3	95.8	97.6	97.7	97.6	95.3	96.6	98.6	99.6	96.7
2009	94.4	91.6	90.7	90.8	92.7	93.9	93.4	93.2	91.7	92.3	94.8	96.1	93.0
2010	91.7	89.4	89.5	90.2	91.8	93.4	93.6	93.6	91.2	92.5	95.1	97.2	92.4
2011	92.3	90.0	90.0	90.9	91.8	93.6	93.7	93.9	92.4	93.4	96.2	98.2	93.0
2012	93.6	91.2	91.5	91.6	92.9	95.8	95.8	95.8	93.5	94.2	97.9	98.5	94.4
2013	93.7	91.5	91.7	92.9	94.4	95.9	96.1	96.0	93.7	94.5	97.4	99.1	94.7
2014	94.3	92.2	92.1	92.7	94.0	95.5	95.7	89.4	94.3	95.2	97.8	99.4	94.4
2015	94.6	92.1	92.2	93.0	94.4	95.8	95.7	95.9	93.8	94.0	97.6	98.7	94.8

1. Employment by Industry: New Hampshire, 2005–2015—*Continued*

(Numbers in thousands, not seasonally adjusted)

Industry and year	January	February	March	April	May	June	July	August	September	October	November	December	Annual average
Transportation and Utilities													
2005	15.5	15.4	15.4	15.4	15.6	16.0	15.4	15.4	15.9	15.8	15.8	16.1	15.6
2006	15.2	15.2	15.3	15.5	15.7	16.0	15.4	15.3	15.9	15.7	15.7	16.2	15.6
2007	15.3	15.1	15.2	15.3	15.5	15.8	15.3	15.2	15.7	15.5	15.2	15.9	15.4
2008	15.0	14.7	14.7	14.8	15.3	15.4	14.9	14.9	15.3	15.2	15.0	15.5	15.1
2009	14.6	14.5	14.4	14.3	14.6	14.9	13.8	13.6	14.7	14.7	14.6	15.1	14.5
2010	14.2	14.2	14.2	14.2	14.6	14.9	13.9	13.8	14.8	15.0	15.0	15.6	14.5
2011	14.6	14.4	14.5	14.7	15.0	15.2	14.3	14.2	15.1	15.0	14.9	15.4	14.8
2012	14.5	14.4	14.6	14.6	14.9	15.2	14.3	14.6	15.2	15.1	15.0	15.6	14.8
2013	14.7	14.6	14.7	14.8	15.1	15.3	14.5	14.6	15.3	15.1	15.2	15.7	15.0
2014	14.7	14.7	14.8	14.7	15.1	15.4	14.5	14.6	15.5	15.5	15.6	16.1	15.1
2015	15.1	14.9	14.9	14.9	15.4	15.7	14.9	15.0	15.8	15.8	15.5	16.3	15.4
Information													
2005	12.5	12.5	12.5	12.7	12.8	12.8	12.9	12.9	12.7	12.7	12.9	12.9	12.7
2006	12.8	12.6	12.7	12.7	12.6	12.7	12.6	12.5	12.3	12.1	12.1	12.2	12.5
2007	12.3	12.2	12.1	12.3	12.3	12.5	12.6	12.8	12.4	12.4	12.5	12.5	12.4
2008	12.7	12.6	12.5	12.6	12.6	12.8	12.8	12.8	12.5	12.5	12.5	12.5	12.6
2009	12.5	12.4	12.3	12.7	12.6	12.5	12.4	12.3	12.2	12.1	12.0	12.0	12.3
2010	11.8	11.7	11.6	11.5	11.4	11.5	11.4	11.3	11.1	11.1	11.0	11.0	11.4
2011	11.0	10.9	11.0	11.1	11.2	11.4	11.6	11.6	11.6	11.6	11.8	11.8	11.4
2012	11.8	11.8	12.0	12.0	12.1	12.1	12.2	12.2	12.0	12.0	12.0	12.1	12.0
2013	11.9	11.8	11.8	11.9	11.8	12.0	12.0	12.0	11.8	11.7	11.8	11.9	11.9
2014	12.0	12.0	12.0	12.0	12.1	12.1	12.2	12.2	12.1	12.2	11.8	11.7	12.0
2015	11.9	11.9	12.3	12.3	12.3	12.4	12.5	12.4	12.1	12.5	12.5	12.5	12.3
Financial Activities													
2005	38.2	38.1	38.3	38.9	39.1	39.8	40.3	40.4	40.0	39.7	39.6	40.0	39.4
2006	39.1	39.2	39.3	39.3	39.2	39.8	40.0	39.7	39.3	39.2	39.0	39.2	39.4
2007	38.1	38.1	38.2	38.1	38.4	38.8	39.1	39.1	38.4	38.1	38.2	38.4	38.4
2008	38.0	38.0	38.0	38.1	38.2	38.6	38.6	38.5	37.8	37.8	37.6	37.7	38.1
2009	37.3	36.9	36.7	36.7	36.8	37.2	36.9	36.5	36.1	35.9	35.8	35.8	36.6
2010	35.6	35.1	35.2	35.1	35.1	35.4	35.5	35.3	34.8	34.7	34.5	34.6	35.1
2011	34.2	34.0	34.0	34.1	34.0	34.2	34.4	34.3	34.2	34.0	34.0	34.0	34.1
2012	33.8	33.8	33.9	34.0	34.3	35.1	35.1	35.3	34.8	34.9	34.8	34.8	34.6
2013	34.5	34.6	34.6	34.7	35.0	35.5	35.7	35.8	35.2	35.2	35.1	35.2	35.1
2014	34.7	34.7	34.8	34.8	35.0	35.5	35.7	35.7	35.1	34.9	34.8	34.9	35.1
2015	34.6	34.6	34.7	34.8	35.2	35.7	36.2	36.5	36.0	35.4	35.6	36.4	35.5
Professional and Business Services													
2005	56.6	56.7	56.9	58.9	59.0	60.0	60.4	60.6	60.1	60.0	60.4	60.3	59.2
2006	58.3	58.8	58.8	61.6	61.7	63.4	63.2	63.4	63.0	63.2	63.1	63.4	61.8
2007	62.4	63.2	63.1	64.7	65.6	66.6	66.5	67.1	66.3	66.6	66.5	67.3	65.5
2008	65.4	65.0	64.8	67.3	67.7	67.9	67.3	67.5	67.0	66.4	65.8	64.6	66.4
2009	63.2	62.2	61.6	62.5	62.6	63.1	63.0	62.9	62.6	63.2	63.6	63.6	62.8
2010	61.3	61.3	61.7	64.1	64.5	64.9	65.2	65.4	64.6	65.7	65.9	65.4	64.2
2011	64.1	64.1	63.9	66.4	66.3	67.4	67.4	67.6	67.3	67.5	68.6	67.7	66.5
2012	66.0	65.4	66.0	67.7	68.3	69.1	68.8	69.7	69.1	69.5	69.8	69.1	68.2
2013	67.4	68.2	68.5	69.1	70.3	71.0	71.7	71.8	71.1	71.7	72.6	72.2	70.4
2014	71.0	71.1	70.6	72.7	73.8	74.8	75.2	75.8	74.4	75.2	75.3	75.2	73.8
2015	73.3	74.3	74.0	75.6	76.6	77.7	77.9	78.3	77.6	79.0	77.9	77.4	76.6
Education and Health Services													
2005	95.4	96.9	97.2	98.2	98.1	97.6	97.4	97.3	99.5	99.5	99.8	100.5	98.1
2006	98.9	100.3	100.7	100.9	100.9	100.7	100.1	100.1	101.9	102.5	103.1	103.9	101.2
2007	101.9	104.1	104.5	104.6	104.7	104.9	103.7	103.5	105.7	106.0	106.6	106.9	104.8
2008	105.4	106.6	107.4	107.7	108.1	107.5	107.6	107.2	109.1	109.9	110.4	111.0	108.2
2009	109.4	110.8	111.1	111.0	111.2	110.1	109.5	109.4	111.1	111.8	112.1	112.7	110.9
2010	111.0	112.2	112.8	112.5	112.6	112.0	111.1	110.8	112.7	113.1	113.5	113.9	112.4
2011	112.5	113.9	114.5	114.2	114.1	113.0	112.3	112.0	113.7	114.6	114.4	114.7	113.7
2012	113.9	114.9	115.0	114.7	114.6	114.2	113.0	113.2	114.7	115.3	115.7	116.3	114.6
2013	115.3	116.2	116.4	115.4	115.3	114.6	113.6	113.9	115.0	115.8	116.2	116.4	115.3
2014	114.6	115.9	116.0	116.1	115.7	115.5	114.6	114.4	115.7	116.9	117.3	117.5	115.9
2015	117.0	117.5	118.1	118.1	118.2	117.5	116.9	116.3	117.4	119.1	119.7	119.5	117.9

1. Employment by Industry: New Hampshire, 2005–2015—*Continued*

(Numbers in thousands, not seasonally adjusted)

Industry and year	January	February	March	April	May	June	July	August	September	October	November	December	Annual average
Leisure and Hospitality													
2005	58.5	58.2	58.1	59.0	62.3	69.0	74.3	73.1	67.0	61.6	58.1	60.1	63.3
2006	58.5	58.3	58.8	59.1	62.3	70.1	74.8	74.3	67.0	62.9	59.6	61.2	63.9
2007	59.2	59.1	59.2	58.7	63.3	70.3	74.2	74.1	67.9	62.3	59.2	60.4	64.0
2008	59.4	59.5	59.1	59.2	63.7	69.8	74.4	74.3	66.6	62.5	57.9	58.8	63.8
2009	57.5	57.5	57.3	56.9	61.8	67.2	71.9	72.3	65.6	61.4	56.7	58.4	62.0
2010	56.9	57.2	57.1	57.4	61.5	67.9	72.2	72.6	66.8	62.2	57.4	59.5	62.4
2011	58.0	58.1	58.0	58.9	62.1	68.2	73.7	74.1	66.8	62.6	58.8	60.0	63.3
2012	58.7	58.9	59.2	59.3	63.5	71.0	75.0	75.2	67.7	64.4	60.0	61.0	64.5
2013	60.4	60.3	60.6	61.6	65.8	72.2	76.7	76.8	68.9	66.5	61.8	62.8	66.2
2014	61.5	61.8	61.7	61.9	67.0	73.2	77.7	77.5	69.2	67.0	62.1	64.0	67.1
2015	62.8	62.5	63.1	63.3	68.5	74.7	79.5	79.1	70.9	67.9	63.3	64.6	68.4
Other Services													
2005	20.6	20.6	20.8	21.3	21.3	21.5	21.7	21.7	21.5	21.1	21.1	21.3	21.2
2006	20.9	20.9	21.0	21.4	21.6	22.1	22.4	22.4	21.7	21.6	21.7	21.7	21.6
2007	21.5	21.6	21.8	21.7	22.1	22.8	23.0	22.9	22.4	22.4	22.3	22.4	22.2
2008	22.3	22.1	22.0	22.1	22.4	22.8	22.9	23.0	22.5	22.4	22.0	22.0	22.4
2009	21.6	21.6	21.6	21.7	22.0	22.2	22.3	22.5	21.8	21.8	21.7	21.9	21.9
2010	21.7	21.7	21.8	21.9	22.3	22.7	23.0	23.1	22.6	22.8	22.8	22.8	22.4
2011	22.9	22.9	23.2	23.2	23.5	24.1	24.3	24.4	23.8	23.6	23.6	23.7	23.6
2012	23.5	23.4	23.4	23.6	23.9	24.4	24.5	24.6	24.0	24.1	23.9	23.9	23.9
2013	23.7	23.6	23.8	24.1	24.3	24.7	24.9	25.0	24.5	24.4	24.3	24.5	24.3
2014	24.4	24.4	24.4	24.6	25.0	25.3	25.6	25.5	25.0	24.9	24.7	24.5	24.9
2015	24.5	24.5	24.7	25.0	25.4	25.8	25.8	25.7	25.3	25.5	25.5	25.5	25.3
Government													
2005	92.9	94.1	94.9	94.1	94.9	88.4	80.0	78.9	92.8	94.6	95.6	95.8	91.4
2006	90.2	94.8	95.4	95.4	95.3	89.0	81.5	79.7	94.6	96.4	96.5	97.3	92.2
2007	92.1	96.4	96.7	96.5	96.1	90.9	82.0	81.1	94.3	97.7	97.8	98.0	93.3
2008	93.7	97.1	98.3	97.8	97.7	93.2	83.2	84.0	97.6	99.7	101.1	101.0	95.4
2009	96.3	99.1	99.5	99.5	100.0	95.8	83.7	83.9	96.9	100.6	101.4	101.4	96.5
2010	95.2	100.3	101.5	100.2	101.6	94.7	82.9	82.4	95.9	98.2	99.1	98.9	95.9
2011	92.0	96.8	97.1	95.9	96.5	90.0	78.4	77.0	92.2	95.2	96.2	96.4	92.0
2012	91.3	94.5	95.4	94.8	94.6	87.9	80.0	79.6	93.4	95.1	95.8	96.6	91.6
2013	90.2	94.5	93.9	93.9	94.1	88.0	77.1	78.5	90.0	94.5	94.6	95.4	90.4
2014	89.6	93.7	94.1	94.1	92.0	88.7	79.0	79.0	92.1	94.8	95.6	95.7	90.7
2015	89.9	93.3	94.5	94.2	93.8	88.3	78.7	77.7	90.5	93.2	93.6	94.0	90.1

2. Average Weekly Hours by Selected Industry: New Hampshire, 2011–2015

(Not seasonally adjusted)

Industry and year	January	February	March	April	May	June	July	August	September	October	November	December	Annual average
Total Private													
2011	32.8	33.0	33.1	33.2	33.2	32.9	33.3	33.6	33.3	33.4	33.2	33.2	33.2
2012	32.7	32.8	32.7	33.0	32.8	32.7	33.5	33.4	33.4	33.1	33.0	33.4	33.1
2013	32.9	33.0	33.2	33.6	33.5	33.5	33.6	33.9	33.9	33.7	33.5	33.5	33.5
2014	33.2	32.9	33.1	33.4	33.4	33.4	33.4	33.5	33.5	33.5	33.7	33.3	33.4
2015	32.9	32.9	33.5	33.6	33.7	33.5	33.9	34.1	33.7	33.8	33.9	33.7	33.6
Goods-Producing													
2011	38.8	38.3	38.6	38.8	39.0	39.1	38.9	39.3	39.5	38.2	39.9	39.6	39.0
2012	38.4	38.5	38.5	38.7	38.4	38.6	38.8	39.9	39.6	39.4	39.5	40.1	39.0
2013	39.4	39.5	39.8	39.5	39.8	39.9	39.7	40.0	40.4	40.1	39.8	40.3	39.9
2014	39.6	39.0	39.1	39.2	40.1	40.2	39.7	39.5	39.9	39.4	39.7	39.5	39.6
2015	38.9	38.7	39.4	39.1	39.2	39.2	39.5	39.5	38.5	38.9	39.5	39.6	39.2
Manufacturing													
2011	39.0	38.2	38.8	38.8	38.7	38.9	38.8	39.3	39.3	38.4	40.2	40.4	39.1
2012	39.1	39.1	39.2	39.3	39.2	39.2	39.3	40.4	40.3	40.1	40.4	40.7	39.7
2013	40.3	40.0	40.5	40.0	40.3	40.9	40.7	40.5	41.3	41.1	41.1	41.8	40.7
2014	41.1	40.7	40.8	40.5	40.9	41.3	40.5	40.2	40.9	40.4	41.0	40.9	40.8
2015	40.7	40.4	40.6	40.2	40.0	40.3	40.2	40.1	39.4	39.4	40.2	40.4	40.2
Trade, Transportation, and Utilities													
2011	32.2	33.2	33.4	33.7	34.0	33.9	34.4	34.4	34.2	35.1	34.3	34.5	34.0
2012	33.8	33.4	33.1	33.3	33.1	33.4	33.8	33.3	34.1	33.3	32.7	33.8	33.4
2013	32.7	32.7	33.1	33.3	33.5	33.3	33.7	33.8	33.9	33.4	32.4	32.8	33.2
2014	32.4	32.0	32.4	32.4	32.9	32.8	32.8	33.0	33.0	32.6	32.7	32.5	32.6
2015	31.8	32.1	32.9	33.0	33.5	33.4	33.9	34.2	34.4	33.9	33.9	34.0	33.4
Professional and Business Services													
2011	34.6	33.3	33.7	33.9	33.3	32.9	32.7	32.9	32.9	33.6	33.5	32.9	33.3
2012	32.4	32.9	33.5	33.9	33.8	33.7	34.3	34.2	34.9	34.2	35.1	35.1	34.0
2013	35.5	35.1	35.0	36.0	35.9	35.6	34.9	35.2	35.9	36.1	36.2	36.5	35.7
2014	36.4	35.6	35.9	36.5	36.2	36.1	35.9	35.8	36.0	36.2	36.4	35.8	36.1
2015	35.0	35.2	35.6	35.4	36.3	36.1	35.7	36.0	35.4	35.7	36.3	35.8	35.7
Education and Health Services													
2011	32.3	32.5	32.7	32.4	32.7	32.3	32.0	32.8	32.8	32.9	33.0	32.9	32.6
2012	32.7	33.3	32.9	32.8	32.9	32.7	33.8	33.6	33.2	33.2	32.8	32.8	33.1
2013	32.7	33.0	32.9	33.3	33.2	33.1	33.2	33.4	33.3	33.5	33.6	33.4	33.2
2014	33.0	32.6	32.6	32.5	32.8	32.9	32.6	32.8	33.0	33.0	33.0	32.5	32.8
2015	32.6	32.3	32.7	32.8	32.4	32.7	32.7	32.7	32.0	32.2	32.0	31.7	32.4
Leisure and Hospitality													
2011	23.1	23.4	23.4	23.6	23.8	23.9	26.5	26.6	24.3	24.3	22.9	22.4	24.1
2012	22.4	22.5	22.9	23.2	23.4	24.0	25.6	25.6	24.1	23.6	22.8	22.8	23.7
2013	22.3	22.6	23.1	24.0	23.1	24.2	25.2	25.8	23.4	23.3	22.6	21.9	23.5
2014	21.8	22.3	22.6	23.1	22.5	23.1	25.2	25.8	23.6	24.1	24.1	23.5	23.5
2015	22.9	22.9	23.7	24.3	24.3	23.9	25.8	26.2	25.4	25.2	24.7	24.3	24.5

3. Average Hourly Earnings by Selected Industry: New Hampshire, 2011–2015

(Dollars, not seasonally adjusted)

Industry and year	January	February	March	April	May	June	July	August	September	October	November	December	Annual average
Total Private													
2011	23.23	23.08	23.08	23.39	23.02	22.72	22.46	22.34	23.19	23.12	23.25	23.18	23.00
2012	23.57	23.65	23.66	23.82	23.71	23.57	23.47	23.27	23.86	23.80	24.11	23.99	23.70
2013	24.21	24.27	24.24	24.56	24.16	24.08	23.74	23.79	24.44	24.36	24.69	24.56	24.26
2014	24.32	24.56	24.57	24.54	24.30	24.16	23.88	23.81	24.37	24.32	24.42	24.39	24.30
2015	24.60	24.91	24.81	25.08	24.92	24.63	24.51	24.51	24.86	25.21	25.45	25.26	24.90
Goods-Producing													
2011	26.26	26.43	26.10	26.50	26.25	25.56	25.64	26.02	26.35	26.34	25.94	25.79	26.09
2012	26.12	26.60	26.07	25.97	25.90	25.80	25.76	25.42	25.59	25.34	25.77	25.62	25.82
2013	25.75	26.00	25.65	26.14	25.65	25.66	25.41	25.58	25.90	25.90	26.25	26.27	25.85
2014	26.26	26.52	26.53	26.59	26.39	26.41	26.45	26.44	26.62	26.69	26.35	26.16	26.45
2015	26.19	26.60	26.51	26.66	26.64	26.26	26.39	26.28	26.86	27.12	26.61	26.98	26.59
Manufacturing													
2011	26.93	27.08	26.66	27.30	27.01	26.12	26.28	26.51	26.95	26.89	26.43	26.09	26.68
2012	26.62	27.08	26.44	26.27	26.16	25.85	26.05	25.67	25.70	25.38	25.82	25.80	26.06
2013	25.96	25.88	25.79	26.31	25.59	25.76	25.33	25.33	25.58	25.48	25.78	25.76	25.71
2014	25.74	25.95	26.07	25.95	25.52	25.73	25.77	25.93	25.91	26.20	25.99	25.58	25.86
2015	25.75	26.18	26.02	26.40	26.33	25.98	26.01	25.74	26.58	26.65	26.24	26.77	26.22
Trade, Transportation, and Utilities													
2011	18.81	18.71	19.09	19.44	19.11	19.00	19.14	18.95	19.79	19.64	19.74	19.34	19.24
2012	20.27	20.11	20.67	21.05	21.17	20.94	20.88	20.57	21.16	21.10	21.42	20.87	20.85
2013	21.57	21.46	20.92	21.18	20.91	21.02	20.84	20.87	21.38	21.19	21.33	20.86	21.12
2014	20.86	21.26	21.62	21.29	21.09	21.22	21.00	21.16	20.98	21.14	21.39	21.52	21.21
2015	21.72	22.14	21.53	21.81	22.02	21.65	21.80	22.16	22.46	22.79	23.01	22.24	22.12
Professional and Business Services													
2011	28.37	28.17	28.37	28.53	27.69	27.75	27.26	26.87	27.22	27.07	27.13	27.44	27.65
2012	27.94	27.73	27.87	28.32	28.08	28.12	28.68	28.14	29.23	28.83	28.72	29.26	28.43
2013	29.16	28.78	29.24	29.22	28.75	28.94	28.56	28.97	28.73	28.68	28.80	29.26	28.92
2014	28.42	28.93	28.86	28.27	28.96	28.61	28.24	28.16	28.38	28.27	27.98	28.55	28.46
2015	28.99	28.54	28.55	28.40	27.91	28.08	28.31	27.29	27.61	28.30	28.47	28.28	28.22
Education and Health Services													
2011	22.98	23.18	23.34	23.73	23.83	24.29	24.67	24.10	24.74	24.91	25.01	25.18	24.17
2012	25.05	25.19	25.29	25.31	25.25	25.33	25.58	25.52	25.56	25.40	25.49	25.61	25.38
2013	25.59	25.61	26.18	26.73	26.71	26.76	26.96	27.03	27.11	27.04	26.98	26.85	26.63
2014	26.82	26.76	26.39	26.28	26.00	25.90	25.99	25.68	26.36	26.06	25.78	26.00	26.17
2015	25.91	26.34	26.51	27.49	27.64	27.22	27.31	27.16	27.73	27.77	27.74	28.19	27.25
Leisure and Hospitality													
2011	13.23	13.34	13.30	13.45	13.35	13.16	12.69	12.82	13.44	13.66	13.83	13.57	13.29
2012	13.63	13.78	13.56	13.65	13.51	13.11	12.89	13.07	13.39	13.55	13.75	13.84	13.44
2013	13.53	13.92	13.60	13.64	13.69	13.50	12.99	13.07	13.82	14.09	14.17	14.11	13.64
2014	13.74	13.92	13.74	13.94	13.83	13.40	13.07	12.83	13.78	13.86	13.69	13.96	13.61
2015	13.75	14.06	13.92	14.09	13.78	13.44	13.26	13.55	14.06	14.30	14.51	14.54	13.91

4. Average Weekly Earnings by Selected Industry: New Hampshire, 2011–2015

(Dollars, not seasonally adjusted)

Industry and year	January	February	March	April	May	June	July	August	September	October	November	December	Annual average
Total Private													
2011	761.94	761.64	763.95	776.55	764.26	747.49	747.92	750.62	772.23	772.21	771.90	769.58	763.60
2012	770.74	775.72	773.68	786.06	777.69	770.74	786.25	777.22	796.92	787.78	795.63	801.27	784.47
2013	796.51	800.91	804.77	825.22	809.36	806.68	797.66	806.48	828.52	820.93	827.12	822.76	812.71
2014	807.42	808.02	813.27	819.64	811.62	806.94	797.59	797.64	816.40	814.72	822.95	812.19	811.62
2015	809.34	819.54	831.14	842.69	839.80	825.11	830.89	835.79	837.78	852.10	862.76	851.26	836.64
Goods-Producing													
2011	1,018.89	1,012.27	1,007.46	1,028.20	1,023.75	999.40	997.40	1,022.59	1,040.83	1,006.19	1,035.01	1,021.28	1,017.51
2012	1,003.01	1,024.10	1,003.70	1,005.04	994.56	995.88	999.49	1,014.26	1,013.36	998.40	1,017.92	1,027.36	1,006.98
2013	1,014.55	1,027.00	1,020.87	1,032.53	1,020.87	1,023.83	1,008.78	1,023.20	1,046.36	1,038.59	1,044.75	1,058.68	1,031.42
2014	1,039.90	1,034.28	1,037.32	1,042.33	1,058.24	1,061.68	1,050.07	1,044.38	1,062.14	1,051.59	1,046.10	1,033.32	1,047.42
2015	1,018.79	1,029.42	1,044.49	1,042.41	1,044.29	1,029.39	1,042.41	1,038.06	1,034.11	1,054.97	1,051.10	1,068.41	1,042.33
Manufacturing													
2011	1,050.27	1,034.46	1,034.41	1,059.24	1,045.29	1,016.07	1,019.66	1,041.84	1,059.14	1,032.58	1,062.49	1,054.04	1,043.19
2012	1,040.84	1,058.83	1,036.45	1,032.41	1,025.47	1,013.32	1,023.77	1,037.07	1,035.71	1,017.74	1,043.13	1,050.06	1,034.58
2013	1,046.19	1,035.20	1,044.50	1,052.40	1,031.28	1,053.58	1,030.93	1,025.87	1,056.45	1,047.23	1,059.56	1,076.77	1,046.40
2014	1,057.91	1,056.17	1,063.66	1,050.98	1,043.77	1,062.65	1,043.69	1,042.39	1,059.72	1,058.48	1,065.59	1,046.22	1,055.09
2015	1,048.03	1,057.67	1,056.41	1,061.28	1,053.20	1,046.99	1,045.60	1,032.17	1,047.25	1,050.01	1,054.85	1,081.51	1,054.04
Trade, Transportation, and Utilities													
2011	605.68	621.17	637.61	655.13	649.74	644.10	658.42	651.88	676.82	689.36	677.08	667.23	654.16
2012	685.13	671.67	684.18	700.97	700.73	699.40	705.74	684.98	721.56	702.63	700.43	705.41	696.39
2013	705.34	701.74	692.45	705.29	700.49	699.97	702.31	705.41	724.78	707.75	691.09	684.21	701.18
2014	675.86	680.32	700.49	689.80	693.86	696.02	688.80	698.28	692.34	689.16	699.45	699.40	691.45
2015	690.70	710.69	708.34	719.73	737.67	723.11	739.02	757.87	772.62	772.58	780.04	756.16	738.81
Professional and Business Services													
2011	981.60	938.06	956.07	967.17	922.08	912.98	891.40	884.02	895.54	909.55	908.86	902.78	920.75
2012	905.26	912.32	933.65	960.05	949.10	947.64	983.72	962.39	1,020.13	985.99	1,008.07	1,027.03	966.62
2013	1,035.18	1,010.18	1,023.40	1,051.92	1,032.13	1,030.26	996.74	1,019.74	1,031.41	1,035.35	1,042.56	1,067.99	1,032.44
2014	1,034.49	1,029.91	1,036.07	1,031.86	1,048.35	1,032.82	1,013.82	1,008.13	1,021.68	1,023.37	1,018.47	1,022.09	1,027.41
2015	1,014.65	1,004.61	1,016.38	1,005.36	1,013.13	1,013.69	1,010.67	982.44	977.39	1,010.31	1,033.46	1,012.42	1,007.45
Education and Health Services													
2011	742.25	753.35	763.22	768.85	779.24	784.57	789.44	790.48	811.47	819.54	825.33	828.42	787.94
2012	819.14	838.83	832.04	830.17	830.73	828.29	864.60	857.47	848.59	843.28	836.07	840.01	840.08
2013	836.79	845.13	861.32	890.11	886.77	885.76	895.07	902.80	902.76	905.84	906.53	896.79	884.12
2014	885.06	872.38	860.31	854.10	852.80	852.11	847.27	842.30	869.88	859.98	850.74	845.00	858.38
2015	844.67	850.78	866.88	901.67	895.54	890.09	893.04	888.13	887.36	894.19	887.68	893.62	882.90
Leisure and Hospitality													
2011	305.61	312.16	311.22	317.42	317.73	314.52	336.29	341.01	326.59	331.94	316.71	303.97	320.29
2012	305.31	310.05	310.52	316.68	316.13	314.64	329.98	334.59	322.70	319.78	313.50	315.55	318.53
2013	301.72	314.59	314.16	327.36	316.24	326.70	327.35	337.21	323.39	328.30	320.24	309.01	320.54
2014	299.53	310.42	310.52	322.01	311.18	309.54	329.36	331.01	325.21	334.03	329.93	328.06	319.84
2015	314.88	321.97	329.90	342.39	334.85	321.22	342.11	355.01	357.12	360.36	358.40	353.32	340.80

NEW JERSEY
At a Glance

Population:
 2005 estimate: 8,651,974
 2010 census: 8,791,894
 2015 estimate: 8,958,013

Percent change in population:
 2005–2015: 3.5%
 2010–2015: 1.9%

Percent change in total nonfarm employment:
 2005–2015: –0.4%

Industry with the largest growth in employment, 2005–2015 (thousands):
 Education and health services, 102.8

Industry with the largest decline or smallest growth in employment, 2005–2015 (thousands):
 Manufacturing, –89.6

Civilian labor force:
 2005: 4,391,579
 2010: 4,555,330
 2015: 4,543,777

Unemployment rate and rank among states (highest to lowest):
 2005: 4.5%, 32nd
 2010: 9.5%, 20th
 2015: 5.6%, 19th

Over-the-year change in unemployment rates:
 2012–2013: –1.1%
 2013–2014: –1.5 %
 2014–2015: –1.1%

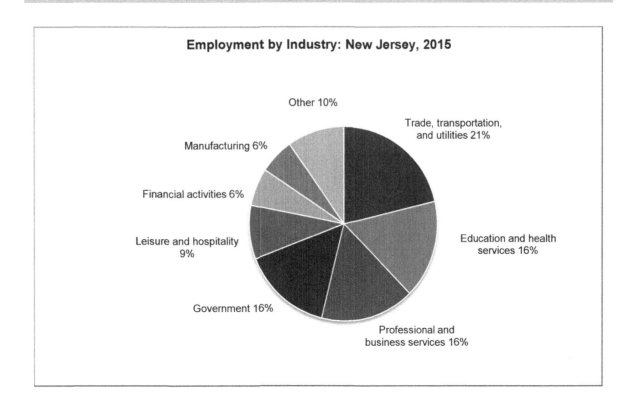

Employment by Industry: New Jersey, 2015

Other 10%

Manufacturing 6%

Financial activities 6%

Leisure and hospitality 9%

Government 16%

Trade, transportation, and utilities 21%

Education and health services 16%

Professional and business services 16%

1. Employment by Industry: New Jersey, 2005–2015

(Numbers in thousands, not seasonally adjusted)

Industry and year	January	February	March	April	May	June	July	August	September	October	November	December	Annual average
Total Nonfarm													
2005	3,943.2	3,950.2	3,974.1	4,023.6	4,058.2	4,111.4	4,065.1	4,046.9	4,054.0	4,058.6	4,081.7	4,091.5	4,038.2
2006	3,983.2	3,991.5	4,027.4	4,049.8	4,090.2	4,141.3	4,088.6	4,074.8	4,074.1	4,086.8	4,106.0	4,120.7	4,069.5
2007	3,995.9	3,991.6	4,024.5	4,052.9	4,104.1	4,156.6	4,098.5	4,083.0	4,074.2	4,100.9	4,115.4	4,125.2	4,076.9
2008	4,013.3	4,015.7	4,041.4	4,060.7	4,091.7	4,135.8	4,069.9	4,040.9	4,036.3	4,033.7	4,024.0	4,015.3	4,048.2
2009	3,880.1	3,868.6	3,874.0	3,889.6	3,928.6	3,963.2	3,892.9	3,871.7	3,877.4	3,882.5	3,894.6	3,903.1	3,893.9
2010	3,774.5	3,766.7	3,797.4	3,848.3	3,893.5	3,936.6	3,865.3	3,840.3	3,841.7	3,861.4	3,874.2	3,880.0	3,848.3
2011	3,754.0	3,763.6	3,793.2	3,836.6	3,866.3	3,916.5	3,861.9	3,838.5	3,862.8	3,876.0	3,895.1	3,902.7	3,847.3
2012	3,793.9	3,811.5	3,848.8	3,862.2	3,909.7	3,971.2	3,895.7	3,886.3	3,908.7	3,922.2	3,924.4	3,949.2	3,890.3
2013	3,836.8	3,853.6	3,886.7	3,906.7	3,948.2	4,007.9	3,945.3	3,938.8	3,952.8	3,965.0	3,989.2	3,988.5	3,935.0
2014	3,860.3	3,861.8	3,894.1	3,949.7	3,996.6	4,044.4	3,984.7	3,969.3	3,985.9	4,002.6	4,024.5	4,036.2	3,967.5
2015	3,899.0	3,906.4	3,938.8	3,993.8	4,049.5	4,099.1	4,036.8	4,024.5	4,044.2	4,074.8	4,095.4	4,106.5	4,022.4
Total Private													
2005	3,305.4	3,300.0	3,322.5	3,370.2	3,408.0	3,458.9	3,448.0	3,440.2	3,424.2	3,407.3	3,423.5	3,433.4	3,395.1
2006	3,337.7	3,333.5	3,367.4	3,389.4	3,433.1	3,482.3	3,465.4	3,462.7	3,442.3	3,430.0	3,444.5	3,459.5	3,420.7
2007	3,349.0	3,333.3	3,363.0	3,391.9	3,444.5	3,494.4	3,480.8	3,472.2	3,442.7	3,443.5	3,452.7	3,462.6	3,427.6
2008	3,362.8	3,354.4	3,377.6	3,397.8	3,428.7	3,471.8	3,444.7	3,431.6	3,402.0	3,378.0	3,363.3	3,355.0	3,397.3
2009	3,228.5	3,207.0	3,209.0	3,223.1	3,262.1	3,296.7	3,265.8	3,255.8	3,238.3	3,222.6	3,228.5	3,238.2	3,239.6
2010	3,125.1	3,110.4	3,138.0	3,187.2	3,222.3	3,270.8	3,246.1	3,242.9	3,227.6	3,228.1	3,234.3	3,244.1	3,206.4
2011	3,134.6	3,132.6	3,160.0	3,200.8	3,234.7	3,286.0	3,270.9	3,262.3	3,257.2	3,246.1	3,260.0	3,270.4	3,226.3
2012	3,178.4	3,182.7	3,215.6	3,232.7	3,283.4	3,341.0	3,308.6	3,310.6	3,304.1	3,293.4	3,294.5	3,319.2	3,272.0
2013	3,217.5	3,220.0	3,252.7	3,283.3	3,327.9	3,383.6	3,361.0	3,361.7	3,349.3	3,335.7	3,356.3	3,357.9	3,317.2
2014	3,245.2	3,234.0	3,265.3	3,312.8	3,366.0	3,414.3	3,395.6	3,390.4	3,379.7	3,376.2	3,392.2	3,406.2	3,348.2
2015	3,288.8	3,282.8	3,313.5	3,365.0	3,424.8	3,474.6	3,453.4	3,449.4	3,442.4	3,451.1	3,466.1	3,479.0	3,407.6
Goods-Producing													
2005	485.2	481.5	485.9	495.8	502.1	506.9	504.8	506.8	507.6	503.1	504.0	500.1	498.7
2006	486.9	486.1	492.2	499.3	503.3	506.6	503.9	504.3	502.6	498.4	495.9	493.1	497.7
2007	474.5	467.6	472.9	481.0	486.7	491.8	490.5	490.7	487.4	485.5	482.3	477.2	482.3
2008	460.1	456.7	460.8	466.4	469.0	472.2	468.9	468.1	464.3	458.7	451.5	441.7	461.5
2009	411.3	404.0	402.9	402.9	405.4	406.4	402.3	401.1	397.5	395.4	392.8	389.8	401.0
2010	372.3	368.3	372.5	382.0	386.5	389.9	389.6	388.9	387.8	387.7	387.4	382.7	383.0
2011	364.3	362.0	368.4	376.3	380.2	384.8	385.4	386.6	384.3	383.2	382.4	379.0	378.1
2012	365.1	363.2	366.2	369.8	372.8	376.8	375.5	376.8	376.0	376.2	376.1	376.9	372.6
2013	363.9	362.5	367.2	374.5	378.5	382.8	382.8	385.3	384.5	385.3	385.0	379.2	377.6
2014	365.5	362.1	367.6	378.6	384.7	388.1	389.6	390.6	390.5	389.7	388.6	385.8	381.8
2015	372.1	368.7	372.7	383.6	390.3	395.1	395.8	396.3	394.3	393.4	395.2	392.8	387.5
Service-Providing													
2005	3,458.0	3,468.7	3,488.2	3,527.8	3,556.1	3,604.5	3,560.3	3,540.1	3,546.4	3,555.5	3,577.7	3,591.4	3,539.6
2006	3,496.3	3,505.4	3,535.2	3,550.5	3,586.9	3,634.7	3,584.7	3,570.5	3,571.5	3,588.4	3,610.1	3,627.6	3,571.8
2007	3,521.4	3,524.0	3,551.6	3,571.9	3,617.4	3,664.8	3,608.0	3,592.3	3,586.8	3,615.4	3,633.1	3,648.0	3,594.6
2008	3,553.2	3,559.0	3,580.6	3,594.3	3,622.7	3,663.6	3,601.0	3,572.8	3,572.0	3,575.0	3,572.5	3,573.6	3,586.7
2009	3,468.8	3,464.6	3,471.1	3,486.7	3,523.2	3,556.8	3,490.6	3,470.6	3,479.9	3,487.1	3,501.8	3,513.3	3,492.9
2010	3,402.2	3,398.4	3,424.9	3,466.3	3,507.0	3,546.7	3,475.7	3,451.4	3,453.9	3,473.7	3,486.8	3,497.3	3,465.4
2011	3,389.7	3,401.6	3,424.8	3,460.3	3,486.1	3,531.7	3,476.5	3,451.9	3,478.5	3,492.8	3,512.7	3,523.7	3,469.2
2012	3,428.8	3,448.3	3,482.6	3,492.4	3,536.9	3,594.4	3,520.2	3,509.5	3,532.7	3,546.0	3,548.3	3,572.3	3,517.7
2013	3,472.9	3,491.1	3,519.5	3,532.2	3,569.7	3,625.1	3,562.5	3,553.5	3,568.3	3,579.7	3,604.2	3,609.3	3,557.3
2014	3,494.8	3,499.7	3,526.5	3,571.1	3,611.9	3,656.3	3,595.1	3,578.7	3,595.4	3,612.9	3,635.9	3,650.4	3,585.7
2015	3,526.9	3,537.7	3,566.1	3,610.2	3,659.2	3,704.0	3,641.0	3,628.2	3,649.9	3,681.4	3,700.2	3,713.7	3,634.9
Mining and Logging													
2005	1.6	1.5	1.6	1.7	1.8	1.8	1.8	1.8	1.8	1.8	1.8	1.8	1.7
2006	1.6	1.6	1.7	1.8	1.8	1.8	1.8	1.7	1.7	1.7	1.7	1.6	1.7
2007	1.6	1.5	1.6	1.7	1.7	1.7	1.7	1.7	1.7	1.7	1.7	1.7	1.7
2008	1.6	1.5	1.6	1.6	1.7	1.7	1.7	1.7	1.7	1.7	1.7	1.6	1.7
2009	1.4	1.4	1.4	1.4	1.5	1.5	1.5	1.6	1.6	1.6	1.5	1.5	1.5
2010	1.2	1.3	1.3	1.4	1.4	1.4	1.4	1.4	1.4	1.4	1.4	1.4	1.4
2011	1.2	1.2	1.2	1.3	1.3	1.4	1.3	1.3	1.3	1.3	1.3	1.3	1.3
2012	1.2	1.2	1.2	1.3	1.3	1.3	1.3	1.3	1.3	1.3	1.3	1.3	1.3
2013	1.2	1.1	1.2	1.3	1.3	1.4	1.4	1.4	1.4	1.4	1.4	1.4	1.3
2014	1.3	1.3	1.4	1.4	1.5	1.5	1.5	1.5	1.4	1.4	1.5	1.5	1.4
2015	1.4	1.4	1.3	1.4	1.4	1.4	1.4	1.4	1.4	1.4	1.4	1.4	1.4

1. Employment by Industry: New Jersey, 2005–2015—*Continued*

(Numbers in thousands, not seasonally adjusted)

Industry and year	January	February	March	April	May	June	July	August	September	October	November	December	Annual average
Construction													
2005	155.4	151.4	154.7	166.0	171.6	174.8	176.6	178.0	178.5	174.7	176.0	172.0	169.1
2006	161.5	161.2	166.5	175.4	178.8	180.9	181.0	182.2	181.1	178.3	176.7	175.2	174.9
2007	161.2	155.4	160.7	169.9	175.7	179.5	179.6	181.0	179.1	178.1	175.5	171.5	172.3
2008	158.7	156.7	160.1	165.4	168.8	171.1	171.1	170.8	168.5	166.2	161.4	154.9	164.5
2009	137.2	134.1	135.7	139.0	141.9	143.0	142.7	142.5	139.8	138.1	136.3	133.4	138.6
2010	119.8	116.7	120.8	129.2	132.4	134.2	135.2	134.8	133.7	134.2	133.9	128.8	129.5
2011	114.2	112.4	118.3	126.9	130.9	134.3	137.2	138.3	137.4	137.5	137.2	134.2	129.9
2012	123.6	122.1	123.3	127.9	129.8	132.5	133.3	134.4	133.7	134.3	134.7	135.3	130.4
2013	125.8	124.6	128.0	135.8	139.2	141.6	142.6	144.4	143.6	144.1	143.5	137.6	137.6
2014	127.6	124.4	129.2	138.1	143.3	145.3	148.1	149.2	149.8	149.6	148.7	145.7	141.6
2015	134.7	132.0	135.4	146.0	151.0	153.5	154.8	155.3	153.2	153.0	154.5	152.3	148.0
Manufacturing													
2005	328.2	328.6	329.6	328.1	328.7	330.3	326.4	327.0	327.3	326.6	326.2	326.3	327.8
2006	323.8	323.3	324.0	322.1	322.7	323.9	321.1	320.4	319.8	318.4	317.5	316.3	321.1
2007	311.7	310.7	310.6	309.4	309.3	310.6	309.2	308.0	306.6	305.7	305.1	304.0	308.4
2008	299.8	298.5	299.1	299.4	298.5	299.4	296.1	295.6	294.1	290.8	288.4	285.2	295.4
2009	272.7	268.5	265.8	262.5	262.0	261.9	258.1	257.0	256.1	255.7	255.0	254.9	260.9
2010	251.3	250.3	250.4	251.4	252.7	254.3	253.0	252.7	252.7	252.1	252.1	252.5	252.1
2011	248.9	248.4	248.9	248.1	248.0	249.1	246.9	247.0	245.6	244.4	243.9	243.5	246.9
2012	240.3	239.9	241.7	240.6	241.7	243.0	240.9	241.1	241.0	240.6	240.1	240.3	240.9
2013	236.9	236.8	238.0	237.4	238.0	239.8	238.8	239.5	239.5	239.8	240.1	240.2	238.7
2014	236.6	236.4	237.0	239.1	239.9	241.3	240.0	239.9	239.3	238.7	238.4	238.6	238.8
2015	236.0	235.3	236.0	236.2	237.9	240.2	239.6	239.6	239.7	239.0	239.3	239.1	238.2
Trade, Transportation, and Utilities													
2005	869.4	861.2	863.7	867.2	876.3	886.3	877.5	873.0	875.0	876.6	890.3	905.8	876.9
2006	870.6	857.6	862.1	861.4	871.1	879.7	870.4	867.8	869.6	876.1	892.6	907.2	873.9
2007	870.2	855.1	859.4	859.7	872.1	883.1	871.9	867.7	868.4	873.0	889.6	904.0	872.9
2008	867.1	854.7	857.3	854.7	862.7	871.0	859.6	855.5	855.1	855.2	861.4	868.4	860.2
2009	827.6	814.9	811.5	806.9	816.5	824.3	811.8	807.6	811.7	812.7	826.0	836.9	817.4
2010	799.8	788.0	790.7	798.3	805.8	816.0	807.1	806.6	806.4	813.1	825.9	839.8	808.1
2011	804.6	797.4	800.1	804.5	810.1	820.4	812.7	812.3	813.9	817.7	834.5	847.1	814.6
2012	815.5	806.2	810.9	807.7	820.9	831.5	819.2	817.0	820.0	822.9	838.4	850.3	821.7
2013	815.3	806.6	810.4	813.5	822.5	834.3	826.7	826.1	827.3	831.8	851.1	860.7	827.2
2014	824.4	814.3	819.5	824.4	834.9	845.4	838.0	837.8	838.7	843.5	863.0	876.3	838.4
2015	838.6	829.4	833.3	840.1	852.4	864.6	856.7	856.8	858.2	864.6	879.6	893.7	855.7
Wholesale Trade													
2005	231.3	232.1	232.0	232.6	234.9	236.7	235.5	234.3	233.7	232.4	232.4	232.9	233.4
2006	230.4	229.9	230.4	230.8	232.7	234.0	233.3	232.7	231.8	231.5	232.0	232.8	231.9
2007	230.8	228.7	230.7	230.8	231.7	233.6	232.4	232.0	230.9	231.3	231.0	231.4	231.3
2008	228.0	229.0	229.3	228.6	230.1	231.0	229.7	228.4	227.1	226.0	224.2	223.2	227.9
2009	219.6	219.2	217.8	217.3	217.2	217.7	215.4	214.1	213.3	213.1	213.0	213.2	215.9
2010	208.0	206.5	206.6	207.5	207.8	209.1	208.6	208.1	207.5	207.7	207.9	208.0	207.8
2011	205.4	206.8	207.9	209.2	210.2	211.7	212.1	212.3	211.0	211.0	211.4	212.9	210.2
2012	210.4	211.0	212.2	211.8	212.9	214.8	213.8	213.6	213.3	212.6	213.1	213.6	212.8
2013	210.7	210.7	211.4	211.8	212.9	214.6	214.4	214.4	213.7	213.5	213.9	214.0	213.0
2014	210.7	211.3	212.4	213.1	214.7	216.3	215.9	215.6	215.5	215.1	216.0	216.8	214.5
2015	213.4	213.2	214.1	215.0	216.4	218.5	218.5	218.7	218.4	217.3	220.1	218.3	216.8
Retail Trade													
2005	466.1	457.3	457.7	460.8	466.7	473.3	472.5	470.7	465.1	467.2	479.7	492.3	469.1
2006	465.7	452.9	456.7	456.3	462.1	469.1	466.7	465.7	459.9	466.0	481.0	491.9	466.2
2007	464.8	452.7	454.2	455.5	463.4	470.9	469.1	466.6	459.7	463.3	479.3	489.9	465.8
2008	463.7	450.0	451.3	449.7	455.3	462.5	460.5	458.3	452.2	454.5	462.4	469.5	457.5
2009	439.4	427.9	426.7	425.0	432.7	439.2	436.5	435.7	432.6	434.9	447.0	456.1	436.1
2010	430.7	421.1	423.7	427.5	434.1	441.9	440.6	441.3	434.5	440.3	451.6	461.9	437.4
2011	435.8	427.7	428.7	431.8	435.6	443.3	442.2	442.5	437.5	440.8	455.1	464.1	440.4
2012	441.3	430.9	433.8	433.3	441.0	448.3	444.7	444.2	439.6	443.0	457.3	465.3	443.6
2013	439.8	431.4	433.6	435.9	442.8	452.2	451.5	452.1	446.7	450.5	466.5	473.5	448.0
2014	446.7	438.1	441.4	444.8	451.4	459.1	459.2	459.1	452.8	456.4	471.0	480.2	455.0
2015	452.6	444.4	446.7	451.4	459.9	468.3	465.3	466.5	461.3	467.5	477.9	485.5	462.3

1. Employment by Industry: New Jersey, 2005–2015—*Continued*

(Numbers in thousands, not seasonally adjusted)

Industry and year	January	February	March	April	May	June	July	August	September	October	November	December	Annual average
Transportation and Utilities													
2005	172.0	171.8	174.0	173.8	174.7	176.3	169.5	168.0	176.2	177.0	178.2	180.6	174.3
2006	174.5	174.8	175.0	174.3	176.3	176.6	170.4	169.4	177.9	178.6	179.6	182.5	175.8
2007	174.6	173.7	174.5	173.4	177.0	178.6	170.4	169.1	177.8	178.4	179.3	182.7	175.8
2008	175.4	175.7	176.7	176.4	177.3	177.5	169.4	168.9	175.8	174.7	174.8	175.7	174.9
2009	168.6	167.8	167.0	164.6	166.6	167.4	159.9	157.8	165.8	164.7	166.0	167.6	165.3
2010	161.1	160.4	160.4	163.3	163.9	165.0	157.9	157.2	164.4	165.1	166.4	169.9	162.9
2011	163.4	162.9	163.5	163.5	164.3	165.4	158.4	157.5	165.4	165.9	168.0	170.1	164.0
2012	163.8	164.3	164.9	162.6	167.0	168.4	160.7	159.2	167.1	167.3	168.0	171.4	165.4
2013	164.8	164.5	165.4	165.8	166.8	167.5	160.8	159.6	166.9	167.8	170.7	173.2	166.2
2014	167.0	164.9	165.7	166.5	168.8	170.0	162.9	163.1	170.4	172.0	176.0	179.3	168.9
2015	172.6	171.8	172.5	173.7	176.1	177.8	172.9	171.6	178.5	179.8	181.6	189.9	176.6
Information													
2005	96.7	96.4	97.0	96.2	96.6	97.8	97.4	97.2	96.7	96.9	97.8	98.3	97.1
2006	97.4	98.1	98.2	97.0	97.4	98.3	97.6	98.0	97.8	96.3	96.1	96.4	97.4
2007	96.3	97.1	97.5	96.7	96.5	96.7	96.5	97.2	95.4	94.0	94.3	93.9	96.0
2008	93.7	94.2	94.2	92.8	92.2	92.7	91.0	90.8	89.7	88.4	88.3	87.8	91.3
2009	86.5	85.9	86.1	84.5	84.8	85.0	84.0	84.7	83.1	82.0	82.1	82.4	84.3
2010	80.4	80.3	80.5	79.5	79.4	80.3	78.7	78.8	78.7	78.4	76.6	79.0	79.2
2011	75.5	75.3	75.4	76.3	76.5	77.7	78.9	73.0	78.6	76.3	76.5	76.6	76.4
2012	76.7	77.2	77.7	76.6	76.7	77.2	77.8	77.6	77.0	76.2	76.1	76.3	76.9
2013	74.9	75.2	74.9	75.0	75.1	75.9	75.9	76.2	74.7	74.9	75.4	75.2	75.3
2014	74.4	74.3	74.6	75.4	75.8	76.0	76.0	76.0	75.2	74.6	74.0	74.6	75.1
2015	74.2	73.8	73.8	74.1	75.1	75.7	75.4	74.9	74.2	73.9	73.9	74.0	74.4
Financial Activities													
2005	275.8	275.1	275.9	277.5	278.7	281.8	284.0	284.4	281.7	279.6	280.8	281.0	279.7
2006	276.8	276.5	277.3	278.3	279.6	281.9	283.6	283.0	279.1	278.4	278.1	278.3	279.2
2007	274.9	274.3	274.3	274.8	276.1	278.7	279.9	279.0	274.7	274.0	274.0	273.9	275.7
2008	272.0	271.9	272.3	271.7	272.4	274.2	273.5	272.7	268.4	265.7	264.6	264.0	270.3
2009	258.6	257.7	256.8	257.1	257.3	258.2	257.5	256.1	253.8	252.0	251.5	251.7	255.7
2010	250.4	250.0	250.5	250.6	251.1	254.1	253.7	253.7	251.7	250.7	250.7	251.4	251.6
2011	248.6	248.4	248.9	249.0	249.7	252.6	252.0	252.2	250.0	247.3	247.4	247.9	249.5
2012	246.4	246.3	247.4	248.5	250.1	253.4	252.8	252.9	250.7	250.1	250.1	251.9	250.1
2013	253.1	253.4	253.9	253.3	253.9	256.5	256.1	255.4	252.8	250.8	249.9	249.9	253.3
2014	245.4	244.5	244.8	245.2	246.4	248.9	249.5	248.8	246.6	245.7	246.3	247.1	246.6
2015	243.8	244.0	245.1	247.4	249.7	253.2	254.0	254.6	253.4	254.3	255.2	255.1	250.8
Professional and Business Services													
2005	572.6	574.1	579.6	595.6	596.8	606.9	602.9	604.2	602.4	603.3	602.9	600.0	595.1
2006	580.4	585.9	594.9	600.8	606.5	616.3	614.5	618.7	615.8	616.9	618.4	617.9	607.3
2007	591.6	592.9	602.0	613.2	619.4	629.4	630.9	633.6	629.2	630.5	631.8	629.8	619.5
2008	609.1	610.4	616.2	622.3	623.4	629.9	628.9	629.5	623.7	618.3	614.4	608.8	619.6
2009	588.6	583.7	583.5	590.7	591.7	596.9	593.3	593.9	590.9	589.5	589.4	587.8	590.0
2010	565.2	567.6	574.9	588.1	591.7	601.7	598.3	600.8	599.4	601.2	602.3	601.6	591.1
2011	584.5	585.5	591.5	602.1	605.2	614.2	613.5	615.7	615.8	617.7	619.3	616.4	606.8
2012	595.5	599.2	607.3	614.7	620.8	630.8	625.0	631.8	633.6	631.9	636.8	637.9	622.1
2013	610.5	613.7	622.7	626.6	634.1	643.3	640.3	644.8	643.1	639.2	642.4	641.5	633.5
2014	616.1	617.2	619.4	631.1	637.3	644.0	641.4	643.5	644.5	648.8	652.8	653.6	637.5
2015	624.5	626.6	634.0	646.3	653.0	658.4	652.2	654.5	656.9	666.7	671.6	672.0	651.4
Education and Health Services													
2005	546.3	551.3	553.7	555.3	559.7	558.2	552.5	549.0	555.6	563.5	566.1	566.5	556.5
2006	558.1	561.6	565.5	564.5	569.4	568.3	560.8	560.3	565.7	571.0	574.2	577.4	566.4
2007	568.8	573.9	578.4	575.2	583.2	578.6	572.5	569.4	575.5	584.9	583.7	587.8	577.7
2008	581.0	585.9	588.7	588.5	590.2	591.0	581.8	579.7	586.0	591.2	593.3	597.8	587.9
2009	587.3	592.5	595.0	595.7	598.4	599.1	587.5	585.5	592.7	600.5	603.2	607.8	595.4
2010	596.4	597.8	601.6	601.6	602.6	600.9	589.5	586.5	594.0	603.5	605.2	604.8	598.7
2011	595.6	600.8	604.7	605.0	606.8	606.3	595.0	592.0	603.6	609.0	612.0	616.2	603.9
2012	608.1	616.5	621.3	617.9	623.3	622.2	608.2	606.3	618.3	625.7	623.7	629.5	618.4
2013	620.5	627.0	632.4	634.1	637.4	633.8	620.8	618.9	630.6	637.4	643.1	643.0	631.6
2014	630.2	633.2	640.8	644.3	649.1	647.2	636.2	632.5	645.4	652.8	656.9	660.9	644.1
2015	646.5	651.5	657.4	659.2	663.2	661.6	648.6	644.7	658.1	671.5	673.3	675.9	659.3

1. Employment by Industry: New Jersey, 2005–2015—*Continued*

(Numbers in thousands, not seasonally adjusted)

Industry and year	January	February	March	April	May	June	July	August	September	October	November	December	Annual average
Leisure and Hospitality													
2005	305.1	305.3	311.3	324.2	338.8	359.8	367.5	364.9	348.2	327.7	324.5	323.9	333.4
2006	310.7	310.8	319.0	327.5	343.7	366.5	371.5	368.7	352.7	333.2	329.2	328.1	338.5
2007	313.2	312.8	318.2	328.0	345.6	367.9	371.9	369.2	349.7	337.9	333.4	332.1	340.0
2008	317.3	317.9	325.0	336.2	352.2	371.7	373.4	368.9	351.7	337.7	327.5	324.4	342.0
2009	309.1	308.3	313.0	323.8	344.8	361.3	365.7	363.7	348.7	330.3	323.1	321.6	334.5
2010	303.4	302.0	309.6	326.7	343.4	362.7	365.7	364.5	349.7	333.1	325.9	323.5	334.2
2011	303.7	305.2	311.7	326.9	344.2	364.1	368.7	367.1	350.5	334.2	327.4	325.8	335.8
2012	311.1	314.0	323.2	334.6	353.8	379.9	382.2	381.2	363.8	346.3	329.9	331.6	346.0
2013	317.8	319.6	328.2	341.5	360.3	386.4	388.7	386.2	370.5	350.9	343.8	342.3	353.0
2014	325.7	325.0	333.4	346.9	368.8	391.9	393.2	390.7	370.8	353.6	343.1	339.8	356.9
2015	324.0	324.1	331.0	346.2	370.5	391.5	397.9	395.8	378.2	359.5	350.1	346.2	359.6
Other Services													
2005	154.3	155.1	155.4	158.4	159.0	161.2	161.4	160.7	157.0	156.6	157.1	157.8	157.8
2006	156.8	156.9	158.2	160.6	162.1	164.7	163.1	161.9	159.0	159.7	160.0	161.1	160.3
2007	159.5	159.6	160.3	163.3	164.9	168.2	166.7	165.4	162.4	163.7	163.6	163.9	163.5
2008	162.5	162.7	163.1	165.2	166.6	169.1	167.6	166.3	163.1	162.8	162.3	162.1	164.5
2009	159.5	160.0	160.2	161.5	163.2	165.5	163.7	163.2	159.9	160.2	160.4	160.2	161.5
2010	157.2	156.4	157.7	160.4	161.8	165.2	163.5	163.1	159.9	160.4	160.3	161.3	160.6
2011	157.8	158.0	159.3	160.7	162.0	165.9	164.7	163.4	160.5	160.7	160.5	161.4	161.2
2012	160.0	160.1	161.6	162.9	165.0	169.2	167.9	167.0	164.7	164.1	163.4	164.8	164.2
2013	161.5	162.0	163.0	164.8	166.1	170.6	169.7	168.8	165.8	165.4	165.6	166.1	165.8
2014	163.5	163.4	165.2	166.9	169.0	172.8	171.7	170.5	168.0	167.5	167.5	168.1	167.8
2015	165.1	164.7	166.2	168.1	170.6	174.5	172.8	171.8	169.1	167.2	167.2	169.3	168.9
Government													
2005	637.8	650.2	651.6	653.4	650.2	652.5	617.1	606.7	629.8	651.3	658.2	658.1	643.1
2006	645.5	658.0	660.0	660.4	657.1	659.0	623.2	612.1	631.8	656.8	661.5	661.2	648.9
2007	646.9	658.3	661.5	661.0	659.6	662.2	617.7	610.8	631.5	657.4	662.7	662.6	649.4
2008	650.5	661.3	663.8	662.9	663.0	664.0	625.2	609.3	634.3	655.7	660.7	660.3	650.9
2009	651.6	661.6	665.0	666.5	666.5	666.5	627.1	615.9	639.1	659.9	666.1	664.9	654.2
2010	649.4	656.3	659.4	661.1	671.2	665.8	619.2	597.4	614.1	633.3	639.9	635.9	641.9
2011	619.4	631.0	633.2	635.8	631.6	630.5	591.0	576.2	605.6	629.9	635.1	632.3	621.0
2012	615.5	628.8	633.2	629.5	626.3	630.2	587.1	575.7	604.6	628.8	629.9	630.0	618.3
2013	619.3	633.6	634.0	623.4	620.3	624.3	584.3	577.1	603.5	629.3	632.9	630.6	617.7
2014	615.1	627.8	628.8	636.9	630.6	630.1	589.1	578.9	606.2	626.4	632.3	630.0	619.4
2015	610.2	623.6	625.3	628.8	624.7	624.5	583.4	575.1	601.8	623.7	629.3	627.5	614.8

2. Average Weekly Hours by Selected Industry: New Jersey, 2011–2015

(Not seasonally adjusted)

Industry and year	January	February	March	April	May	June	July	August	September	October	November	December	Annual average
Total Private													
2011	34.3	34.4	34.2	34.4	34.6	33.5	33.6	33.5	33.5	33.8	33.5	33.7	33.9
2012	33.6	33.5	33.6	33.7	33.2	33.4	33.7	33.3	33.7	33.4	33.9	34.2	33.6
2013	33.3	33.4	33.6	33.4	33.6	33.8	33.5	33.5	34.0	33.6	33.6	33.8	33.6
2014	33.4	33.0	33.8	33.6	33.6	33.9	33.8	33.8	33.8	33.6	33.9	33.8	33.7
2015	33.2	33.5	33.7	33.7	33.7	33.7	33.9	34.2	33.8	33.9	34.0	34.0	33.8
Goods-Producing													
2011	38.3	38.6	38.5	38.4	38.7	38.9	38.5	38.5	38.5	39.1	38.7	39.4	38.7
2012	38.3	38.7	38.7	38.6	36.5	37.0	36.9	37.4	37.9	38.4	38.9	39.3	38.0
2013	38.5	38.2	38.5	38.4	38.9	38.6	38.4	38.5	38.8	38.7	39.4	39.3	38.7
2014	38.5	37.1	39.1	38.8	38.9	39.1	38.8	38.5	39.0	38.6	38.5	39.3	38.7
2015	38.3	37.9	38.8	38.6	38.7	38.9	38.6	38.6	38.1	39.0	38.6	39.1	38.6
Construction													
2011	35.2	35.5	35.9	35.4	36.0	36.3	36.1	36.3	36.2	37.0	36.3	37.4	36.2
2012	35.8	36.4	36.8	36.2	30.6	31.2	32.1	33.1	33.9	34.5	35.0	36.1	34.3
2013	35.9	35.4	35.7	35.4	36.5	35.9	36.5	36.3	36.4	36.5	37.3	36.0	36.2
2014	36.3	34.4	38.1	37.9	38.1	37.7	37.9	37.6	38.5	37.7	36.9	38.1	37.5
2015	37.1	36.6	38.1	37.8	38.5	38.3	37.9	37.6	37.1	39.1	37.2	38.1	37.8
Manufacturing													
2011	39.0	39.2	39.0	39.2	39.3	39.6	39.2	39.2	39.4	40.0	39.9	40.5	39.5
2012	39.7	39.9	39.8	40.0	39.8	40.3	39.6	39.8	40.0	40.4	40.7	40.8	40.1
2013	39.7	39.4	39.7	39.7	40.0	39.9	39.3	39.7	40.1	39.9	40.6	40.9	39.9
2014	39.6	38.5	39.7	39.3	39.3	39.9	39.3	39.0	39.3	39.3	39.4	40.0	39.4
2015	38.9	38.5	39.1	39.0	38.7	39.2	39.0	39.1	38.6	38.9	39.4	39.7	39.0
Trade, Transportation, and Utilities													
2011	33.8	34.1	34.0	34.5	34.4	34.1	34.5	34.5	34.7	34.5	34.0	34.7	34.3
2012	34.1	34.0	34.1	34.3	34.4	34.4	34.7	33.8	34.1	33.7	34.3	34.3	34.2
2013	33.3	33.6	34.0	33.9	34.1	34.2	34.3	34.0	34.6	34.0	33.8	34.2	34.0
2014	33.8	33.2	34.1	34.2	34.0	33.9	34.2	34.2	34.3	33.9	34.0	34.4	34.0
2015	33.4	33.6	33.8	34.0	34.2	34.0	34.3	34.5	34.7	34.0	34.3	34.2	34.1
Financial Activities													
2011	38.4	37.8	37.4	37.2	37.7	37.0	36.5	36.3	36.6	37.6	36.4	36.0	37.1
2012	37.3	36.6	36.3	36.9	35.8	36.0	37.2	35.8	37.2	35.8	36.0	37.1	36.5
2013	36.1	36.2	36.1	35.6	35.5	37.0	35.4	35.9	36.9	35.5	35.3	36.7	36.0
2014	35.6	37.1	36.4	36.1	36.0	37.0	35.7	36.2	36.2	36.5	37.0	36.3	36.3
2015	36.3	37.0	37.3	36.6	36.5	36.6	37.0	37.4	36.5	36.8	37.4	36.9	36.9
Professional and Business Services													
2011	35.1	35.4	35.1	35.4	36.2	35.5	35.3	35.4	35.4	35.7	35.4	35.7	35.5
2012	35.8	35.7	36.2	36.4	35.6	36.0	36.1	35.6	36.0	35.5	35.8	36.4	35.9
2013	35.2	35.9	36.3	36.1	36.2	36.8	35.8	35.9	36.7	35.9	36.2	36.0	36.1
2014	35.6	34.9	35.8	35.6	35.9	36.7	35.9	36.0	35.7	35.5	36.1	35.4	35.8
2015	35.2	36.0	35.8	35.5	35.5	35.4	35.4	35.8	35.1	35.7	35.5	35.9	35.6
Education and Health Services													
2011	32.6	32.5	32.3	32.4	32.2	31.8	31.5	31.7	31.4	31.5	31.6	31.6	31.9
2012	31.7	31.3	31.3	31.2	31.2	31.3	31.2	31.1	31.2	31.0	31.1	31.2	31.2
2013	31.2	31.2	31.0	30.6	30.7	31.0	30.9	30.6	30.8	30.6	30.7	30.5	30.8
2014	30.7	30.5	30.9	30.9	30.7	30.8	31.0	31.0	31.1	31.0	31.2	31.3	30.9
2015	31.2	31.4	31.5	31.4	31.6	31.6	31.7	31.9	31.7	31.7	31.9	31.6	31.6
Leisure and Hospitality													
2011	25.2	25.7	25.8	26.1	26.3	25.8	26.1	26.2	25.3	26.2	26.4	26.1	25.9
2012	26.1	26.1	26.1	26.3	26.1	26.2	27.0	26.9	26.3	26.0	25.9	26.3	26.3
2013	25.4	25.7	26.0	26.1	26.5	26.6	27.0	27.4	27.3	26.9	27.0	26.8	26.6
2014	26.4	26.0	27.0	26.9	27.3	27.4	28.1	28.2	27.3	27.1	26.9	26.4	27.1
2015	26.0	26.1	26.2	26.9	26.7	26.6	27.4	27.7	27.1	26.8	26.8	26.5	26.8
Other Services													
2011	32.1	31.6	31.3	31.5	32.0	31.2	31.8	31.6	31.9	31.9	31.1	31.6	31.6
2012	31.8	31.2	31.4	31.7	31.5	31.8	32.8	33.0	33.4	33.4	33.1	33.1	32.4
2013	31.8	31.1	31.8	31.3	30.7	31.2	31.2	31.9	30.7	30.1	29.7	30.2	31.0
2014	29.1	29.3	29.5	28.8	29.4	29.7	30.0	29.9	29.8	29.3	29.9	29.5	29.5
2015	29.1	29.1	29.2	28.8	29.2	29.3	30.0	30.9	29.8	30.1	30.3	30.1	29.7

3. Average Hourly Earnings by Selected Industry: New Jersey, 2011–2015

(Dollars, not seasonally adjusted)

Industry and year	January	February	March	April	May	June	July	August	September	October	November	December	Annual average
Total Private													
2011.................................	26.02	25.81	25.73	25.71	25.67	25.39	25.20	25.19	25.58	25.99	25.70	25.59	25.63
2012.................................	26.37	26.13	26.17	26.64	26.37	26.16	26.61	26.18	26.69	26.42	26.69	26.91	26.45
2013.................................	26.83	26.87	26.76	27.07	26.69	26.93	26.42	26.43	27.03	26.85	26.84	26.85	26.80
2014.................................	26.66	27.10	27.09	26.80	26.63	26.74	26.62	26.64	27.02	27.04	27.42	27.15	26.91
2015.................................	27.68	28.13	28.13	27.55	27.61	27.59	27.45	27.72	27.78	27.82	28.12	27.73	27.78
Goods-Producing													
2011.................................	28.64	28.52	28.56	28.46	28.33	28.41	28.56	28.29	28.32	28.08	28.02	28.06	28.35
2012.................................	27.80	27.93	28.14	28.57	29.59	29.69	29.68	29.88	29.51	29.07	28.98	29.44	29.02
2013.................................	28.87	28.76	28.75	29.16	28.83	28.99	28.67	28.86	28.95	28.54	28.24	27.42	28.67
2014.................................	27.60	27.62	28.21	28.49	28.49	28.86	29.32	29.29	29.65	29.49	29.86	30.05	28.93
2015.................................	29.58	29.95	30.01	29.99	30.21	29.98	30.08	29.95	29.98	30.05	30.25	30.12	30.02
Construction													
2011.................................	33.53	33.72	33.51	33.32	33.05	33.44	33.81	34.05	33.59	33.11	32.93	32.78	33.40
2012.................................	32.34	32.59	33.41	33.77	37.46	37.09	36.41	36.40	36.09	35.81	35.34	35.71	35.17
2013.................................	34.55	34.67	34.84	35.30	34.29	33.98	33.58	33.83	33.81	33.38	33.46	33.24	34.05
2014.................................	32.65	32.95	33.61	33.98	34.02	34.46	35.15	35.30	36.19	35.86	36.12	36.08	34.78
2015.................................	35.07	35.75	35.60	35.46	35.54	35.68	35.49	34.91	34.78	34.60	34.67	34.08	35.12
Manufacturing													
2011.................................	24.90	24.76	24.65	24.68	24.61	24.50	24.48	23.90	24.38	24.41	24.53	24.82	24.55
2012.................................	24.95	25.10	24.90	25.18	24.95	25.22	25.52	25.71	25.44	24.87	25.19	25.75	25.23
2013.................................	25.63	25.60	25.54	25.85	25.75	26.16	25.89	26.18	26.19	25.80	25.42	25.83	25.82
2014.................................	26.24	26.15	26.42	26.41	26.22	26.52	26.61	26.51	26.50	26.38	26.50	26.84	26.44
2015.................................	26.74	27.12	27.19	27.01	27.18	26.86	27.10	27.18	27.28	27.39	27.77	27.87	27.23
Trade, Transportation, and Utilities													
2011.................................	22.98	22.82	22.53	22.53	22.44	21.96	22.03	21.96	22.53	22.65	22.45	22.08	22.41
2012.................................	23.02	22.71	22.86	23.39	22.96	22.78	23.14	22.71	22.97	22.80	23.33	22.69	22.95
2013.................................	22.79	23.02	23.09	23.61	23.02	23.09	23.07	22.92	23.27	23.17	23.09	22.93	23.09
2014.................................	23.53	23.75	23.55	23.52	23.38	23.15	23.39	23.53	23.72	23.72	23.94	23.42	23.55
2015.................................	24.25	24.62	24.50	23.99	24.24	24.38	24.52	24.89	25.01	24.92	24.84	24.63	24.57
Financial Activities													
2011.................................	33.86	33.25	33.29	34.04	34.31	33.51	33.29	33.51	33.77	37.04	35.71	35.37	34.24
2012.................................	36.77	36.08	36.83	38.28	36.22	35.64	37.49	36.16	36.34	35.64	35.10	36.55	36.43
2013.................................	36.33	35.95	35.57	36.13	35.50	36.72	34.32	34.13	34.39	34.14	34.11	33.57	35.08
2014.................................	33.07	33.54	34.08	32.45	33.12	33.67	33.61	33.52	34.17	34.07	35.05	34.18	33.72
2015.................................	34.93	36.13	36.41	35.37	35.72	35.67	35.42	36.17	35.94	35.64	36.77	35.91	35.85
Professional and Business Services													
2011.................................	32.83	31.94	31.94	31.99	31.96	31.56	31.72	31.40	31.23	32.13	31.09	30.85	31.71
2012.................................	32.83	32.49	31.98	32.28	32.30	32.07	33.09	32.02	33.19	32.86	32.81	33.19	32.60
2013.................................	33.14	33.26	33.06	33.05	32.79	33.10	32.63	32.93	33.90	33.40	33.57	34.19	33.25
2014.................................	32.92	34.33	33.96	33.24	32.63	32.94	32.32	32.14	32.45	32.52	33.15	32.78	32.94
2015.................................	31.70	32.59	32.70	31.66	31.63	31.78	31.88	32.47	32.61	32.29	32.60	31.62	32.13
Education and Health Services													
2011.................................	24.92	24.88	24.75	24.87	24.61	24.64	24.59	24.57	24.88	24.42	24.66	24.74	24.71
2012.................................	24.79	25.04	24.98	25.10	24.81	24.84	25.37	25.14	25.26	25.00	25.56	25.82	25.14
2013.................................	25.77	25.73	25.75	26.18	25.92	26.11	25.96	25.55	25.81	25.76	25.92	26.08	25.88
2014.................................	25.37	25.44	25.32	25.46	25.67	25.83	25.89	26.08	26.24	26.03	26.23	26.31	25.83
2015.................................	26.95	27.08	27.12	27.10	27.41	27.66	27.66	27.65	27.46	27.69	27.92	28.10	27.49
Leisure and Hospitality													
2011.................................	14.71	14.47	14.52	14.35	15.18	16.34	14.28	15.98	15.27	14.26	14.33	14.32	14.86
2012.................................	14.04	14.02	14.05	13.95	14.20	13.77	13.46	13.51	13.81	13.91	14.06	14.15	13.90
2013.................................	14.00	14.12	13.91	14.10	14.18	14.15	13.96	13.97	13.99	14.18	14.19	14.54	14.11
2014.................................	14.54	14.49	14.53	14.67	14.67	14.55	14.39	14.33	14.69	14.76	14.83	15.06	14.62
2015.................................	15.01	15.10	14.93	14.91	15.05	14.89	14.71	14.65	14.86	14.89	14.90	14.98	14.90
Other Services													
2011.................................	24.23	24.05	23.89	23.34	23.16	23.01	21.97	21.84	22.20	22.29	22.66	22.45	22.92
2012.................................	21.94	21.65	21.84	21.83	22.27	21.81	21.20	21.03	21.63	21.19	21.34	22.42	21.67
2013.................................	22.26	22.71	21.76	22.17	22.58	22.38	21.61	21.61	22.78	22.76	22.46	23.22	22.35
2014.................................	23.32	23.17	23.27	23.02	22.72	22.65	22.60	22.32	23.24	23.04	22.88	22.76	22.91
2015.................................	22.61	22.34	22.47	22.48	21.72	21.71	21.12	20.99	21.77	22.02	22.61	22.56	22.02

4. Average Weekly Earnings by Selected Industry: New Jersey, 2011–2015

(Dollars, not seasonally adjusted)

Industry and year	January	February	March	April	May	June	July	August	September	October	November	December	Annual average
Total Private													
2011	892.49	887.86	879.97	884.42	888.18	850.57	846.72	843.87	856.93	878.46	860.95	862.38	868.86
2012	886.03	875.36	879.31	897.77	875.48	873.74	896.76	871.79	899.45	882.43	904.79	920.32	888.72
2013	893.44	897.46	899.14	904.14	896.78	910.23	885.07	885.41	919.02	902.16	901.82	907.53	900.48
2014	890.44	894.30	915.64	900.48	894.77	906.49	899.76	900.43	913.28	908.54	929.54	917.67	906.87
2015	918.98	942.36	947.98	928.44	930.46	929.78	930.56	948.02	938.96	943.10	956.08	942.82	938.96
Goods-Producing													
2011	1,096.91	1,100.87	1,099.56	1,092.86	1,096.37	1,105.15	1,099.56	1,089.17	1,090.32	1,097.93	1,084.37	1,105.56	1,097.15
2012	1,064.74	1,080.89	1,089.02	1,102.80	1,080.04	1,098.53	1,095.19	1,117.51	1,118.43	1,116.29	1,127.32	1,156.99	1,102.76
2013	1,111.50	1,098.63	1,106.88	1,119.74	1,121.49	1,119.01	1,100.93	1,111.11	1,123.26	1,104.50	1,112.66	1,077.61	1,109.53
2014	1,062.60	1,024.70	1,103.01	1,105.41	1,108.26	1,128.43	1,137.62	1,127.67	1,156.35	1,138.31	1,149.61	1,180.97	1,119.59
2015	1,132.91	1,135.11	1,164.39	1,157.61	1,169.13	1,166.22	1,161.09	1,156.07	1,142.24	1,171.95	1,167.65	1,177.69	1,158.77
Construction													
2011	1,180.26	1,197.06	1,203.01	1,179.53	1,189.80	1,213.87	1,220.54	1,236.02	1,215.96	1,225.07	1,195.36	1,225.97	1,209.08
2012	1,157.77	1,186.28	1,229.49	1,222.47	1,146.28	1,157.21	1,168.76	1,204.84	1,223.45	1,235.45	1,236.90	1,289.13	1,206.33
2013	1,240.35	1,230.79	1,243.79	1,249.62	1,251.59	1,219.88	1,225.67	1,228.03	1,230.68	1,218.37	1,248.06	1,196.64	1,232.61
2014	1,185.20	1,133.48	1,280.54	1,287.84	1,296.16	1,299.14	1,332.19	1,327.28	1,393.32	1,351.92	1,332.83	1,374.65	1,304.25
2015	1,301.10	1,308.45	1,356.36	1,340.39	1,368.29	1,366.54	1,345.07	1,312.62	1,290.34	1,352.86	1,289.72	1,298.45	1,327.54
Manufacturing													
2011	971.10	970.59	961.35	967.46	967.17	970.20	959.62	936.88	960.57	976.40	978.75	1,005.21	969.73
2012	990.52	1,001.49	991.02	1,007.20	993.01	1,016.37	1,010.59	1,023.26	1,017.60	1,004.75	1,025.23	1,050.60	1,011.72
2013	1,017.51	1,008.64	1,013.94	1,026.25	1,030.00	1,043.78	1,017.48	1,039.35	1,050.22	1,029.42	1,032.05	1,056.45	1,030.22
2014	1,039.10	1,006.78	1,048.87	1,037.91	1,030.45	1,058.15	1,045.77	1,033.89	1,041.45	1,036.73	1,044.10	1,073.60	1,041.74
2015	1,040.19	1,044.12	1,063.13	1,053.39	1,051.87	1,052.91	1,056.90	1,062.74	1,053.01	1,065.47	1,094.14	1,106.44	1,061.97
Trade, Transportation, and Utilities													
2011	776.72	778.16	766.02	777.29	771.94	748.84	760.04	757.62	781.79	781.43	763.30	766.18	768.66
2012	784.98	772.14	779.53	802.28	789.82	783.63	802.96	767.60	783.28	768.36	800.22	778.27	784.89
2013	758.91	773.47	785.06	800.38	784.98	789.68	791.30	779.28	805.14	787.78	780.44	784.21	785.06
2014	795.31	788.50	803.06	804.38	794.92	784.79	799.94	804.73	813.60	804.11	813.96	805.65	800.70
2015	809.95	827.23	828.10	815.66	829.01	828.92	841.04	858.71	867.85	847.28	852.01	842.35	837.84
Financial Activities													
2011	1,300.22	1,256.85	1,245.05	1,266.29	1,293.49	1,239.87	1,215.09	1,216.41	1,235.98	1,392.70	1,299.84	1,273.32	1,270.30
2012	1,371.52	1,320.53	1,336.93	1,412.53	1,296.68	1,283.04	1,394.63	1,294.53	1,351.85	1,275.91	1,263.60	1,356.01	1,329.70
2013	1,311.51	1,301.39	1,284.08	1,286.23	1,260.25	1,358.64	1,214.93	1,225.27	1,268.99	1,211.97	1,204.08	1,232.02	1,262.88
2014	1,177.29	1,244.33	1,240.51	1,171.45	1,192.32	1,245.79	1,199.88	1,213.42	1,236.95	1,243.56	1,296.85	1,240.73	1,224.04
2015	1,267.96	1,336.81	1,358.09	1,294.54	1,303.78	1,305.52	1,310.54	1,352.76	1,311.81	1,311.55	1,375.20	1,325.08	1,322.87
Professional and Business Services													
2011	1,152.33	1,130.68	1,121.09	1,132.45	1,156.95	1,120.38	1,119.72	1,111.56	1,105.54	1,147.04	1,100.59	1,101.35	1,125.71
2012	1,175.31	1,159.89	1,157.68	1,174.99	1,149.88	1,154.52	1,194.55	1,139.91	1,194.84	1,166.53	1,174.60	1,208.12	1,170.34
2013	1,166.53	1,194.03	1,200.08	1,193.11	1,187.00	1,218.08	1,168.15	1,182.19	1,244.13	1,199.06	1,215.23	1,230.84	1,200.33
2014	1,171.95	1,198.12	1,215.77	1,183.34	1,171.42	1,208.90	1,160.29	1,157.04	1,158.47	1,154.46	1,196.72	1,160.41	1,179.25
2015	1,115.84	1,173.24	1,170.66	1,123.93	1,122.87	1,125.01	1,128.55	1,162.43	1,144.61	1,152.75	1,157.30	1,135.16	1,143.83
Education and Health Services													
2011	812.39	808.60	799.43	805.79	792.44	783.55	774.59	778.87	781.23	769.23	779.26	781.78	788.25
2012	785.84	783.75	781.87	783.12	774.07	777.49	791.54	781.85	788.11	775.00	794.92	805.58	784.37
2013	804.02	802.78	798.25	801.11	795.74	809.41	802.16	781.83	794.95	788.26	795.74	795.44	797.10
2014	778.86	775.92	782.39	786.71	788.07	795.56	802.59	808.48	816.06	806.93	818.38	823.50	798.15
2015	840.84	850.31	854.28	850.94	866.16	874.06	876.82	882.04	870.48	877.77	890.65	887.96	868.68
Leisure and Hospitality													
2011	370.69	371.88	374.62	374.54	399.23	421.57	372.71	418.68	386.33	373.61	378.31	373.75	384.87
2012	366.44	365.92	366.71	366.89	370.62	360.77	363.42	363.42	363.20	361.66	364.15	372.15	365.57
2013	355.60	362.88	361.66	368.01	375.77	376.39	376.92	382.78	381.93	381.44	383.13	389.67	375.33
2014	383.86	376.74	392.31	394.62	400.49	398.67	404.36	404.11	401.04	400.00	398.93	397.58	396.20
2015	390.26	394.11	391.17	401.08	401.84	396.07	403.05	405.81	402.71	399.05	399.32	396.97	399.32
Other Services													
2011	777.78	759.98	747.76	735.21	741.12	717.91	698.65	690.14	708.18	711.05	704.73	709.42	724.27
2012	697.69	675.48	685.78	692.01	701.51	693.56	695.36	693.99	722.44	707.75	706.35	742.10	702.11
2013	707.87	706.28	691.97	693.92	693.21	698.26	674.23	689.36	699.35	685.08	667.06	701.24	692.85
2014	678.61	678.88	686.47	662.98	667.97	672.71	678.00	667.37	692.55	675.07	684.11	671.42	675.85
2015	657.95	650.09	656.12	647.42	634.22	636.10	633.60	648.59	648.75	662.80	685.08	679.06	653.99

NEW MEXICO
At a Glance

Population:
  2005 estimate: 1,932,274
  2010 census: 2,059,179
  2015 estimate: 2,085,109

Percent change in population:
  2005–2015: 7.9%
  2010–2015: 1.3%

Percent change in total nonfarm employment:
  2005–2015: 2.1%

Industry with the largest growth in employment, 2005–2015 (thousands):
  Education and health services, 27.7

Industry with the largest decline or smallest growth in employment, 2005–2015 (thousands):
  Construction, –10.9

Civilian labor force:
  2005: 918,156
  2010: 936,088
  2015: 919,889

Unemployment rate and rank among states (highest to lowest):
  2005: 5.1%, 20th
  2010: 8.1%, 32nd
  2015: 6.6%, 4th

Over-the-year change in unemployment rates:
  2012–2013: –0.1%
  2013–2014: –0.3%
  2014–2015: –0.1%

Employment by Industry: New Mexico, 2015

Other, 12%
Government, 23%
Financial activities, 4%
Construction, 5%
Leisure and hospitality, 11%
Trade, transportation, and utilities, 17%
Professional and business services, 12%
Education and health services, 16%

1. Employment by Industry: New Mexico, 2005–2015

(Numbers in thousands, not seasonally adjusted)

Industry and year	January	February	March	April	May	June	July	August	September	October	November	December	Annual average
Total Nonfarm													
2005	786.5	793.6	799.1	806.9	810.1	808.6	805.2	809.7	818.8	818.5	822.3	824.5	808.7
2006	809.2	819.7	827.1	828.6	835.2	837.3	828.0	832.0	842.5	839.5	842.9	844.3	832.2
2007	824.4	833.9	842.3	840.2	845.6	845.9	837.8	843.2	850.2	851.9	853.9	855.3	843.7
2008	834.0	843.3	847.5	848.8	852.8	850.2	841.7	846.8	854.7	852.2	847.2	842.4	846.8
2009	816.9	818.2	816.7	816.0	817.0	811.7	803.5	807.6	812.4	811.3	808.8	808.5	812.4
2010	789.4	795.8	801.1	807.1	810.5	808.2	800.9	802.7	803.7	807.9	806.3	807.2	803.4
2011	787.9	795.8	800.0	806.4	806.7	804.2	797.9	800.9	807.2	806.5	805.6	805.5	802.1
2012	786.2	795.5	800.9	803.8	806.0	803.2	795.1	800.6	807.1	818.6	818.1	815.4	804.2
2013	799.1	805.4	807.2	814.8	818.4	804.9	800.7	809.9	813.0	819.1	819.4	819.2	810.9
2014	805.0	809.1	810.7	818.0	824.5	811.2	811.0	820.4	823.3	832.2	831.9	832.2	819.1
2015	816.7	821.8	823.5	829.1	830.9	818.0	815.7	825.2	827.3	831.6	834.4	833.0	825.6
Total Private													
2005	590.3	591.5	595.7	603.2	606.0	609.1	611.4	614.9	615.4	613.9	617.3	620.1	607.4
2006	610.4	614.1	620.8	623.2	629.3	645.7	642.5	645.1	647.0	642.8	645.9	647.4	634.5
2007	633.8	637.9	644.6	643.4	648.9	653.2	651.3	655.5	653.9	653.7	654.7	655.9	648.9
2008	640.8	644.6	647.8	649.3	652.4	654.5	652.4	656.3	654.9	650.8	645.3	640.8	649.2
2009	621.2	617.3	615.0	613.4	614.8	614.3	612.5	615.6	613.4	609.7	606.8	606.7	613.4
2010	595.0	595.2	597.8	602.0	603.7	607.9	607.9	610.0	606.5	606.6	605.4	607.1	603.8
2011	595.4	597.4	600.6	607.1	608.7	611.9	613.3	614.8	613.0	610.2	609.6	608.5	607.5
2012	598.3	600.9	605.3	608.8	610.6	614.8	613.2	615.9	614.1	622.8	622.1	620.0	612.2
2013	609.7	611.0	611.8	619.0	622.0	621.0	622.9	626.7	621.6	625.7	626.3	626.3	620.3
2014	616.9	616.2	617.4	624.4	629.7	628.1	632.0	636.0	631.6	638.6	638.0	638.5	629.0
2015	628.9	629.1	629.8	635.5	637.4	635.1	639.5	640.9	635.8	638.0	640.2	639.5	635.8
Goods-Producing													
2005	101.4	101.4	103.0	104.5	105.7	107.4	109.8	110.7	111.2	111.3	111.6	111.4	107.5
2006	110.1	111.7	113.1	113.8	115.3	117.2	117.5	118.3	118.4	118.3	116.5	115.7	115.5
2007	112.5	113.1	114.4	114.5	115.9	117.6	117.2	118.1	117.0	117.1	115.8	114.9	115.7
2008	112.0	112.5	113.1	114.2	114.9	115.9	115.1	116.6	115.9	114.3	111.6	108.3	113.7
2009	102.2	99.6	97.4	95.8	95.3	95.5	95.0	95.5	93.9	93.9	92.1	90.7	95.6
2010	88.6	88.2	88.4	89.9	90.7	91.7	92.6	93.3	93.1	93.7	92.6	91.8	91.2
2011	89.5	89.3	91.1	92.4	93.1	94.2	95.1	96.0	95.7	95.4	94.4	93.3	93.3
2012	91.3	91.7	92.7	93.4	94.2	95.6	95.7	96.4	96.2	99.0	97.2	96.1	95.0
2013	94.1	94.7	95.1	96.2	96.8	97.6	98.2	99.6	98.9	100.2	99.1	97.5	97.3
2014	96.5	95.6	95.9	96.8	98.0	98.7	100.0	100.4	99.8	102.3	100.9	100.5	98.8
2015	98.9	97.6	96.7	97.2	96.8	96.8	97.5	97.1	96.1	97.7	94.9	93.8	96.8
Service-Providing													
2005	685.1	692.2	696.1	702.4	704.4	701.2	695.4	699.0	707.6	707.2	710.7	713.1	701.2
2006	699.1	708.0	714.0	714.8	719.9	720.1	710.5	713.7	724.1	721.2	726.4	728.6	716.7
2007	711.9	720.8	727.9	725.7	729.7	728.3	720.6	725.1	733.2	734.8	738.1	740.4	728.0
2008	722.0	730.8	734.4	734.6	737.9	734.3	726.6	730.2	738.8	737.9	735.6	734.1	733.1
2009	714.7	718.6	719.3	720.2	721.7	716.2	708.5	712.1	718.5	717.4	716.7	717.8	716.8
2010	700.8	707.6	712.7	717.2	719.8	716.5	708.3	709.4	710.6	714.2	713.7	715.4	712.2
2011	698.4	706.5	708.9	714.0	713.6	710.0	702.8	704.9	711.5	711.1	711.2	712.2	708.8
2012	694.9	703.8	708.2	710.4	711.8	707.6	699.4	704.2	710.9	719.6	720.9	719.3	709.3
2013	705.0	710.7	712.1	718.6	721.6	707.3	702.5	710.3	714.1	718.9	720.3	721.7	713.6
2014	708.5	713.5	714.8	721.2	726.5	712.5	711.0	720.0	723.5	729.9	731.0	731.7	720.3
2015	717.8	724.2	726.8	731.9	734.1	721.2	718.2	728.1	731.2	733.9	739.5	739.2	728.8
Mining and Logging													
2005	15.9	15.9	16.1	16.2	16.4	16.6	17.2	17.4	17.8	17.8	17.7	17.7	16.9
2006	17.8	18.0	18.1	18.3	18.5	18.8	18.8	19.1	19.1	19.2	19.1	19.2	18.7
2007	19.3	19.0	19.1	19.2	19.4	19.7	19.9	20.0	19.6	19.7	19.9	19.9	19.6
2008	19.8	19.8	20.0	20.6	21.0	21.3	21.5	22.1	22.1	22.1	21.9	21.3	21.1
2009	19.9	19.1	18.3	17.8	17.5	17.5	17.5	17.5	17.1	17.3	17.5	17.5	17.9
2010	17.4	17.6	17.6	17.9	18.3	18.7	18.9	18.9	18.8	19.2	19.3	19.6	18.5
2011	19.7	20.0	20.2	20.6	21.0	21.4	21.7	22.1	22.3	22.6	22.9	23.2	21.5
2012	23.2	23.4	23.3	23.5	23.8	24.2	24.4	24.5	24.6	25.1	24.9	24.9	24.2
2013	25.2	25.4	25.5	25.8	26.0	26.2	26.4	26.5	26.2	26.4	26.7	26.6	26.1
2014	26.8	26.9	27.2	27.6	27.7	28.0	28.2	28.1	28.2	28.9	29.0	29.0	28.0
2015	28.9	28.1	27.0	26.3	25.7	25.3	25.4	25.2	24.7	24.5	23.2	22.7	25.6

1. Employment by Industry: New Mexico, 2005–2015—*Continued*

(Numbers in thousands, not seasonally adjusted)

Industry and year	January	February	March	April	May	June	July	August	September	October	November	December	Annual average
Construction													
2005	50.2	50.3	51.6	52.8	53.7	55.0	56.5	56.6	56.5	56.4	56.9	56.8	54.4
2006	55.9	56.8	58.1	58.5	59.8	60.9	60.4	60.4	60.4	60.4	59.4	58.7	59.1
2007	56.0	56.8	58.1	58.6	59.6	60.8	60.2	60.5	59.9	60.6	59.7	59.0	59.2
2008	57.0	57.5	58.1	58.5	58.6	59.1	58.0	58.3	57.6	57.2	55.7	53.6	57.4
2009	50.7	49.6	48.9	48.1	48.1	48.1	47.7	47.9	46.9	46.6	45.4	44.0	47.7
2010	42.7	42.2	42.3	43.4	43.5	43.9	44.6	44.6	44.3	44.4	43.9	43.0	43.6
2011	40.9	40.5	41.9	42.7	43.0	43.4	43.8	43.4	42.7	42.2	41.6	40.5	42.2
2012	38.9	39.2	40.2	40.5	40.9	41.8	41.5	41.6	41.1	43.2	42.5	41.8	41.1
2013	40.1	40.5	40.9	41.6	41.8	42.2	42.6	43.2	43.0	44.2	43.8	42.4	42.2
2014	41.7	40.9	40.9	41.4	42.4	42.8	43.6	43.6	43.1	45.1	44.1	43.7	42.8
2015	42.3	42.1	42.2	43.5	43.5	43.7	44.1	43.7	43.5	45.4	44.6	43.8	43.5
Manufacturing													
2005	35.3	35.2	35.3	35.5	35.6	35.8	36.1	36.7	36.9	37.1	37.0	36.9	36.1
2006	36.4	36.9	36.9	37.0	37.0	37.5	38.3	38.8	38.9	38.7	38.0	37.8	37.7
2007	37.2	37.3	37.2	36.7	36.9	37.1	37.1	37.6	37.5	36.8	36.2	36.0	37.0
2008	35.2	35.2	35.0	35.1	35.3	35.5	35.6	36.2	36.2	35.0	34.0	33.4	35.1
2009	31.6	30.9	30.2	29.9	29.7	29.9	29.8	30.1	29.9	30.0	29.2	29.2	30.0
2010	28.5	28.4	28.5	28.6	28.9	29.1	29.1	29.8	30.0	30.1	29.4	29.2	29.1
2011	28.9	28.8	29.0	29.1	29.1	29.4	29.6	30.5	30.7	30.6	29.9	29.6	29.6
2012	29.2	29.1	29.2	29.4	29.5	29.6	29.8	30.3	30.5	30.7	29.8	29.4	29.7
2013	28.8	28.8	28.7	28.8	29.0	29.2	29.2	29.9	29.7	29.6	28.6	28.5	29.1
2014	28.0	27.8	27.8	27.8	27.9	27.9	28.2	28.7	28.5	28.3	27.8	27.8	28.0
2015	27.7	27.4	27.5	27.4	27.6	27.8	28.0	28.2	27.9	27.8	27.1	27.3	27.6
Trade, Transportation, and Utilities													
2005	137.5	136.9	137.4	138.0	139.2	138.9	139.5	140.4	140.0	140.5	143.0	144.5	139.7
2006	139.6	138.5	139.8	140.0	141.3	141.4	141.6	142.3	142.0	142.0	144.9	146.3	141.6
2007	142.3	141.8	143.2	142.4	144.1	143.8	144.3	145.2	145.0	146.3	149.1	150.5	144.8
2008	145.8	145.1	145.8	144.9	145.0	144.3	144.1	144.5	143.7	143.3	143.7	144.2	144.5
2009	138.7	136.5	136.3	134.8	135.3	135.2	134.7	135.1	135.0	134.8	135.7	136.6	135.7
2010	132.0	131.0	131.8	132.0	132.6	132.7	133.0	133.7	132.5	133.6	135.2	136.2	133.0
2011	131.9	131.0	131.3	132.7	133.5	133.4	133.1	133.6	133.6	134.8	137.0	137.6	133.6
2012	134.0	133.3	133.9	134.2	134.9	135.0	135.0	135.2	135.3	137.4	139.4	139.9	135.6
2013	135.3	134.5	134.2	135.3	136.0	136.2	137.1	137.7	136.5	138.1	140.1	141.1	136.8
2014	136.5	136.0	135.9	137.1	137.6	137.3	138.3	138.7	138.4	139.8	141.4	142.5	138.3
2015	138.5	138.0	138.2	138.7	139.3	138.5	139.2	139.3	138.6	139.4	142.4	141.7	139.3
Wholesale Trade													
2005	22.2	22.4	22.5	22.6	22.8	22.9	23.0	22.9	22.8	22.8	22.9	23.0	22.7
2006	22.6	22.7	22.9	23.1	23.3	23.6	23.7	23.7	23.6	23.5	23.5	23.5	23.3
2007	23.4	23.4	23.4	23.5	23.6	23.9	24.1	24.0	23.9	24.1	24.1	24.2	23.8
2008	23.9	23.8	23.8	23.9	23.9	23.9	23.9	23.8	23.4	23.3	23.0	22.7	23.6
2009	22.3	22.1	22.0	21.7	21.7	22.0	21.8	21.6	21.5	21.7	21.6	21.8	21.8
2010	21.5	21.5	21.6	21.7	21.7	21.9	21.8	21.6	21.2	21.2	21.0	21.0	21.5
2011	20.7	20.6	20.7	20.8	21.1	21.3	21.4	21.3	21.2	21.1	21.0	21.0	21.0
2012	20.8	21.0	21.2	21.2	21.4	21.7	21.8	21.6	21.5	21.7	21.6	21.7	21.4
2013	21.3	21.4	21.4	21.5	21.6	21.8	21.8	21.9	21.5	21.6	21.5	21.5	21.6
2014	21.3	21.5	21.4	21.5	21.7	21.7	21.8	21.9	21.8	21.8	21.6	21.7	21.6
2015	21.4	21.3	21.4	21.4	21.5	21.6	21.6	21.5	21.3	21.3	21.3	21.2	21.4
Retail Trade													
2005	92.3	91.5	91.6	92.2	93.1	93.4	93.9	94.2	93.6	94.1	96.4	97.3	93.6
2006	93.1	91.9	93.1	93.1	94.0	94.2	94.3	94.6	94.1	94.3	97.0	97.8	94.3
2007	94.2	93.6	95.0	94.2	95.6	95.7	96.2	96.3	95.8	96.6	99.3	100.2	96.1
2008	96.5	96.1	96.7	96.1	96.0	96.5	96.6	96.5	96.0	95.9	96.7	97.3	96.4
2009	92.7	90.9	91.1	90.5	90.8	91.4	91.4	91.7	91.7	91.2	92.2	92.7	91.5
2010	88.9	88.0	88.7	88.7	89.2	89.6	89.8	90.3	89.2	90.1	91.9	92.6	89.8
2011	89.0	88.1	88.5	89.6	90.0	89.9	89.6	89.9	89.8	90.8	93.1	93.4	90.1
2012	90.2	89.2	89.5	89.9	90.2	90.3	90.3	90.3	90.4	91.9	94.0	94.2	90.9
2013	90.4	89.6	89.5	90.5	90.9	91.3	92.1	92.3	91.4	92.7	94.9	95.5	91.8
2014	91.5	90.8	91.0	91.8	91.8	92.0	92.7	92.7	92.2	93.3	95.1	95.6	92.5
2015	92.5	92.0	92.1	92.9	93.4	92.9	93.5	93.6	93.2	94.2	97.6	96.5	93.7

1. Employment by Industry: New Mexico, 2005–2015—*Continued*

(Numbers in thousands, not seasonally adjusted)

Industry and year	January	February	March	April	May	June	July	August	September	October	November	December	Annual average
Transportation and Utilities													
2005	23.0	23.0	23.3	23.2	23.3	22.6	22.6	23.3	23.6	23.6	23.7	24.2	23.3
2006	23.9	23.9	23.8	23.8	24.0	23.6	23.6	24.0	24.3	24.2	24.4	25.0	24.0
2007	24.7	24.8	24.8	24.7	24.9	24.2	24.0	24.9	25.3	25.6	25.7	26.1	25.0
2008	25.4	25.2	25.3	24.9	25.1	23.9	23.6	24.2	24.3	24.1	24.0	24.2	24.5
2009	23.7	23.5	23.2	22.6	22.8	21.8	21.5	21.8	21.8	21.9	21.9	22.1	22.4
2010	21.6	21.5	21.5	21.6	21.7	21.2	21.4	21.8	22.1	22.3	22.3	22.6	21.8
2011	22.2	22.3	22.1	22.3	22.4	22.2	22.1	22.4	22.6	22.9	22.9	23.2	22.5
2012	23.0	23.1	23.2	23.1	23.3	23.0	22.9	23.3	23.4	23.8	23.8	24.0	23.3
2013	23.6	23.5	23.5	23.3	23.5	23.1	23.2	23.5	23.6	23.8	23.7	24.1	23.5
2014	23.7	23.7	23.5	23.8	24.1	23.6	23.8	24.1	24.4	24.7	24.7	25.2	24.1
2015	24.6	24.7	24.7	24.4	24.4	24.0	24.1	24.2	24.1	23.9	23.5	24.0	24.2
Information													
2005	13.9	14.1	14.1	15.3	15.1	14.7	14.8	14.8	14.5	14.9	15.0	15.4	14.7
2006	14.5	15.4	15.9	15.0	15.6	17.4	15.1	15.9	17.1	14.9	15.9	16.9	15.8
2007	14.5	15.5	15.8	14.4	14.8	16.3	15.3	16.5	17.4	16.8	17.1	17.1	16.0
2008	15.6	16.3	16.1	15.1	15.4	16.2	16.0	15.8	16.5	16.3	16.3	15.6	15.9
2009	14.0	14.4	14.3	14.5	14.8	15.1	14.6	15.0	15.5	15.0	15.0	14.4	14.7
2010	14.2	14.6	14.7	15.3	14.7	15.0	13.8	14.1	14.1	13.7	14.0	14.3	14.4
2011	13.8	13.4	13.6	14.4	14.6	14.3	13.6	13.1	12.4	12.6	13.0	12.6	13.5
2012	13.2	13.7	14.3	13.9	13.6	13.1	13.3	14.0	13.2	13.0	14.0	13.1	13.5
2013	13.1	13.6	12.9	13.6	14.2	13.6	13.2	12.8	12.3	12.4	12.6	12.3	13.1
2014	11.6	12.0	12.2	12.3	12.8	12.7	12.4	12.8	11.9	12.5	13.2	13.0	12.5
2015	11.7	12.2	12.6	13.0	13.4	12.9	13.2	13.6	12.7	12.5	13.0	12.0	12.7
Financial Activities													
2005	34.7	34.6	34.6	34.7	34.8	35.1	35.2	35.1	35.0	34.9	35.0	35.6	34.9
2006	35.2	35.2	35.2	35.1	35.2	35.3	35.2	35.1	35.0	34.9	34.9	35.3	35.1
2007	34.9	35.0	35.3	35.1	35.2	35.4	35.5	35.5	35.2	35.2	35.1	35.3	35.2
2008	34.7	34.8	34.8	34.7	34.7	34.8	34.9	34.8	34.7	34.4	34.1	34.3	34.6
2009	33.7	33.5	33.2	33.8	33.9	33.7	33.7	33.6	33.5	33.9	33.5	33.8	33.7
2010	33.3	33.1	33.3	32.9	33.7	33.0	33.0	32.9	32.6	32.7	32.7	33.0	33.0
2011	32.5	32.4	32.4	32.6	32.5	32.5	32.7	32.6	32.5	32.5	32.5	32.7	32.5
2012	32.3	32.5	32.7	32.6	32.6	32.8	32.9	32.8	32.6	33.3	33.3	33.3	32.8
2013	33.0	32.9	32.9	33.0	33.0	33.0	33.2	33.2	33.1	33.3	33.6	33.8	33.2
2014	33.1	33.1	33.2	33.2	33.2	33.2	33.4	33.3	33.0	33.3	33.3	33.4	33.2
2015	33.2	33.2	33.2	33.2	33.3	33.2	33.4	33.3	32.9	32.8	33.4	33.3	33.2
Professional and Business Services													
2005	90.2	90.5	90.7	92.8	92.4	93.3	93.2	93.6	94.0	93.5	94.3	94.3	92.7
2006	93.6	94.5	95.2	96.0	96.6	108.1	107.3	107.6	107.5	107.7	107.6	107.9	102.5
2007	106.3	107.6	108.3	108.3	108.7	109.3	109.5	110.3	109.2	108.6	108.4	108.2	108.6
2008	106.5	107.5	107.4	108.1	108.5	109.0	109.2	110.3	109.7	109.1	107.5	107.0	108.3
2009	104.1	103.4	102.4	102.4	102.0	102.4	102.8	103.5	102.7	101.8	101.1	101.1	102.5
2010	99.3	99.6	99.1	100.3	99.5	100.6	101.1	101.4	101.0	101.1	100.5	100.7	100.4
2011	98.8	101.0	99.6	100.3	99.9	100.4	101.4	101.2	101.5	99.7	99.0	98.6	100.1
2012	96.5	96.7	97.2	98.5	97.8	99.1	97.9	98.1	98.2	99.2	99.2	98.2	98.1
2013	98.0	98.3	98.1	99.5	99.3	98.9	99.7	99.9	98.8	99.3	98.8	99.0	99.0
2014	98.1	98.0	97.5	99.5	99.3	98.8	99.9	100.6	98.9	99.6	99.3	99.7	99.1
2015	98.4	98.5	98.4	99.1	98.8	99.2	100.6	100.8	99.7	100.0	100.1	100.4	99.5
Education and Health Services													
2005	104.0	104.6	105.1	105.4	105.6	102.0	101.5	102.7	106.7	107.1	107.6	107.6	105.0
2006	106.9	107.4	108.4	108.3	108.7	105.6	104.5	105.2	109.4	109.7	110.8	110.6	108.0
2007	110.1	110.9	111.8	112.4	112.8	109.2	107.9	108.6	112.0	113.2	113.8	114.2	111.4
2008	112.6	114.1	114.8	115.8	116.3	113.0	111.9	113.2	116.9	117.8	118.3	118.7	115.3
2009	117.8	118.9	119.4	119.3	119.6	115.5	114.6	115.9	119.2	119.5	120.0	120.0	118.3
2010	119.4	119.9	120.4	120.1	120.1	117.8	117.0	117.0	120.3	120.9	121.4	121.6	119.7
2011	120.5	121.0	121.6	122.2	122.2	119.4	119.3	119.8	122.9	123.1	123.1	122.6	121.5
2012	121.8	122.8	122.7	122.9	122.9	120.5	120.1	120.2	123.3	124.5	124.8	125.0	122.6
2013	123.8	124.3	124.7	125.6	125.6	121.6	119.9	121.6	124.9	125.9	126.7	126.5	124.3
2014	126.1	126.7	126.7	127.5	128.0	124.0	123.4	125.4	129.4	131.1	131.3	131.3	127.6
2015	131.0	131.9	132.1	133.1	133.6	129.3	128.6	130.2	133.9	135.1	136.2	137.0	132.7

1. Employment by Industry: New Mexico, 2005–2015—*Continued*

(Numbers in thousands, not seasonally adjusted)

Industry and year	January	February	March	April	May	June	July	August	September	October	November	December	Annual average
Leisure and Hospitality													
2005	80.6	81.1	82.5	84.1	84.6	86.7	86.3	86.7	85.2	83.3	82.3	82.7	83.8
2006	82.6	83.0	84.6	86.3	87.6	89.3	89.9	89.7	88.4	86.3	86.3	86.0	86.7
2007	84.9	85.3	86.9	87.6	88.4	90.2	90.3	90.6	89.2	87.5	86.5	86.7	87.8
2008	84.9	85.1	86.5	87.2	87.9	89.0	89.1	89.4	87.8	85.7	84.3	83.9	86.7
2009	82.4	82.5	83.5	84.5	85.4	86.2	86.5	86.8	85.3	82.9	81.5	82.1	84.1
2010	80.7	81.1	82.4	83.8	84.6	86.2	86.1	86.3	84.9	83.3	81.8	82.4	83.6
2011	81.4	82.0	83.5	84.9	85.2	86.4	86.5	87.3	86.2	84.7	83.3	83.8	84.6
2012	82.0	82.6	84.0	85.4	86.6	88.4	88.3	89.4	87.3	87.9	86.1	86.4	86.2
2013	84.9	85.1	86.2	88.1	89.1	90.0	91.4	91.9	89.3	88.8	87.8	88.6	88.4
2014	87.7	87.3	88.4	90.2	92.5	92.9	93.9	94.4	91.9	91.6	90.5	90.2	91.0
2015	89.7	89.9	90.9	93.4	94.1	94.8	96.2	96.0	93.6	92.3	92.1	93.2	93.0
Other Services													
2005	28.0	28.3	28.3	28.4	28.6	31.0	31.1	30.9	28.8	28.4	28.5	28.6	29.1
2006	27.9	28.4	28.6	28.7	29.0	31.4	31.4	31.0	29.2	29.0	29.0	28.7	29.4
2007	28.3	28.7	28.9	28.7	29.0	31.4	31.3	30.7	28.9	29.0	28.9	29.0	29.4
2008	28.7	29.2	29.3	29.3	29.7	32.3	32.1	31.7	29.7	29.9	29.5	28.8	30.0
2009	28.3	28.5	28.5	28.3	28.5	30.7	30.6	30.2	28.3	27.9	27.9	28.0	28.8
2010	27.5	27.7	27.7	27.7	27.8	30.9	31.3	31.3	28.0	27.6	27.2	27.1	28.5
2011	27.0	27.3	27.5	27.6	27.7	31.3	31.6	31.2	28.2	27.4	27.3	27.3	28.5
2012	27.2	27.6	27.8	27.9	28.0	30.3	30.0	29.8	28.0	28.5	28.1	28.0	28.4
2013	27.5	27.6	27.7	27.7	28.0	30.1	30.2	30.0	27.8	27.7	27.6	27.5	28.3
2014	27.3	27.5	27.6	27.8	28.3	30.5	30.7	30.4	28.3	28.4	28.1	27.9	28.6
2015	27.5	27.8	27.7	27.8	28.1	30.4	30.8	30.6	28.3	28.2	28.1	28.1	28.6
Government													
2005	196.2	202.1	203.4	203.7	204.1	199.5	193.8	194.8	203.4	204.6	205.0	204.4	201.3
2006	198.8	205.6	206.3	205.4	205.9	191.6	185.5	186.9	195.5	196.7	197.0	196.9	197.7
2007	190.6	196.0	197.7	196.8	196.7	192.7	186.5	187.7	196.3	198.2	199.2	199.4	194.8
2008	193.2	198.7	199.7	199.5	200.4	195.7	189.3	190.5	199.8	201.4	201.9	201.6	197.6
2009	195.7	200.9	201.7	202.6	202.2	197.4	191.0	192.0	199.0	201.6	202.0	201.8	199.0
2010	194.4	200.6	203.3	205.1	206.8	200.3	193.0	192.7	197.2	201.3	200.9	200.1	199.6
2011	192.5	198.4	199.4	199.3	198.0	192.3	184.6	186.1	194.2	196.3	196.0	197.0	194.5
2012	187.9	194.6	195.6	195.0	195.4	188.4	181.9	184.7	193.0	195.8	196.0	195.4	192.0
2013	189.4	194.4	195.4	195.8	196.4	183.9	177.8	183.2	191.4	193.4	193.1	192.9	190.6
2014	188.1	192.9	193.3	193.6	194.8	183.1	179.0	184.4	191.7	193.6	193.9	193.7	190.2
2015	187.8	192.7	193.7	193.6	193.5	182.9	176.2	184.3	191.5	193.6	194.2	193.5	189.8

2. Average Weekly Hours by Selected Industry: New Mexico, 2011–2015

(Not seasonally adjusted)

Industry and year	January	February	March	April	May	June	July	August	September	October	November	December	Annual average
Total Private													
2011	35.7	35.0	34.9	34.9	35.2	35.2	35.2	35.1	34.8	35.7	34.9	34.1	35.1
2012	34.6	34.5	34.5	34.6	34.4	34.9	35.2	35.0	35.2	34.9	34.4	34.7	34.8
2013	34.0	34.3	34.3	34.7	34.9	35.4	34.9	35.2	35.2	35.0	34.9	35.0	34.8
2014	34.4	34.7	35.1	34.7	34.8	35.2	34.7	34.7	34.5	34.5	34.9	34.6	34.7
2015	33.9	34.3	34.3	33.9	33.8	34.1	34.3	34.9	34.2	34.2	34.3	34.0	34.2
Goods-Producing													
2011	40.6	40.4	40.3	41.2	41.2	41.9	41.8	42.4	41.9	42.1	42.3	41.3	41.5
2012	41.7	42.0	42.1	42.4	42.4	42.6	42.5	43.7	42.1	42.9	41.9	41.5	42.3
2013	40.8	41.9	41.6	43.1	43.4	43.3	43.0	45.0	43.4	44.1	43.9	41.9	43.0
2014	42.2	42.1	42.9	42.9	42.1	42.2	40.9	41.2	40.2	40.6	40.5	40.2	41.5
2015	38.9	39.5	39.2	39.9	39.7	39.7	39.7	40.9	39.5	40.8	41.3	41.1	40.0
Construction													
2011	40.2	38.8	39.1	40.1	39.6	40.5	40.4	41.0	40.4	40.7	40.8	39.0	40.1
2012	39.8	40.5	41.2	40.8	41.4	41.5	40.2	41.6	38.6	39.7	38.9	37.7	40.2
2013	37.0	38.9	38.4	39.6	40.5	40.7	39.0	41.4	39.3	40.9	41.1	39.0	39.7
2014	39.0	38.4	39.4	40.0	39.9	40.7	39.1	39.6	38.1	38.5	38.5	38.1	39.1
2015	35.6	37.0	36.1	37.3	37.2	37.3	38.1	39.2	36.3	38.2	38.8	38.1	37.4
Trade, Transportation, and Utilities													
2011	35.3	33.6	34.6	34.3	34.9	34.5	34.7	34.7	34.6	35.2	33.8	32.4	34.4
2012	32.1	32.8	33.1	33.6	33.1	34.4	34.8	34.7	35.2	35.1	34.7	35.2	34.1
2013	34.8	34.8	35.0	35.6	35.5	35.6	35.1	35.0	35.1	34.9	34.3	34.8	35.0
2014	34.1	34.7	35.2	34.6	34.9	35.3	34.9	34.7	34.6	35.0	35.0	35.0	34.8
2015	34.1	34.3	34.7	34.1	34.4	34.6	34.6	35.0	34.8	34.3	33.8	34.3	34.4
Professional and Business Services													
2011	36.8	36.6	36.6	37.0	37.1	36.8	36.2	36.0	36.0	37.1	36.4	35.8	36.5
2012	36.4	36.4	36.1	36.4	35.8	36.4	36.2	36.4	36.6	35.8	36.0	36.1	36.2
2013	34.8	35.0	35.2	35.7	35.7	36.2	35.6	36.1	36.1	36.0	35.8	36.9	35.8
2014	36.2	36.6	36.5	36.3	36.5	36.6	35.5	36.2	35.9	35.6	36.7	35.7	36.2
2015	35.4	35.5	35.6	35.0	34.7	35.0	34.9	35.7	35.2	35.8	36.2	35.1	35.3
Education and Health Services													
2011	36.6	35.2	34.7	34.9	35.0	34.9	34.9	34.8	34.0	35.0	35.2	34.1	34.9
2012	34.4	34.1	33.8	33.8	33.3	33.4	33.8	33.1	34.1	33.6	33.2	33.4	33.7
2013	33.2	33.0	32.8	32.7	32.9	33.2	32.8	32.9	33.2	32.7	33.4	33.4	33.0
2014	32.9	32.7	32.9	32.4	32.9	33.2	33.7	33.3	33.5	33.4	34.0	34.6	33.3
2015	33.9	34.1	33.9	33.6	33.6	34.0	33.3	33.7	33.6	33.2	33.5	33.5	33.7
Leisure and Hospitality													
2011	25.3	25.9	25.5	25.0	25.6	26.3	26.7	26.6	25.8	26.5	25.2	25.1	25.8
2012	25.8	25.9	26.3	25.9	26.6	26.7	27.5	27.0	27.1	26.7	26.3	26.8	26.6
2013	26.3	26.4	27.2	26.8	27.3	27.8	27.6	27.1	26.8	27.4	26.9	27.1	27.1
2014	25.9	26.7	27.5	26.0	26.7	27.3	27.4	27.2	26.6	26.0	26.2	25.7	26.6
2015	25.1	26.0	26.0	25.0	25.4	26.0	26.5	26.9	26.0	26.1	25.8	25.7	25.9

3. Average Hourly Earnings by Selected Industry: New Mexico, 2011–2015

(Dollars, not seasonally adjusted)

Industry and year	January	February	March	April	May	June	July	August	September	October	November	December	Annual average
Total Private													
2011	19.96	19.84	19.79	19.74	19.82	19.65	19.78	19.44	19.69	19.47	19.50	19.78	19.70
2012	19.88	19.73	19.74	19.93	19.79	19.56	19.77	19.74	19.92	19.76	19.95	20.06	19.82
2013	19.86	19.88	19.96	20.08	19.99	20.08	19.94	20.08	20.47	20.60	20.62	20.63	20.19
2014	20.34	20.44	20.45	20.52	20.57	20.70	20.50	20.40	20.44	20.54	20.47	20.48	20.49
2015	20.62	20.65	20.67	20.48	20.52	20.21	20.23	20.32	20.48	20.46	20.57	20.40	20.47
Goods-Producing													
2011	21.78	22.25	22.30	22.15	21.96	21.80	22.01	21.90	22.23	22.40	22.17	23.69	22.22
2012	23.46	23.20	23.35	23.15	22.80	22.39	22.47	22.90	22.89	22.80	22.81	23.46	22.97
2013	23.42	22.86	22.54	22.79	22.76	22.91	22.54	22.35	22.69	23.63	24.53	24.33	23.11
2014	23.84	23.95	23.54	23.55	23.78	23.53	23.52	23.59	23.83	23.64	23.74	23.81	23.69
2015	24.03	23.89	23.89	23.42	23.93	23.50	23.89	23.88	24.11	23.63	23.82	23.62	23.80
Construction													
2011	21.18	21.67	21.77	21.80	21.36	21.07	21.07	21.19	21.45	21.42	21.26	21.06	21.36
2012	20.56	20.22	20.31	20.00	19.90	19.73	19.93	20.66	21.03	21.36	20.81	21.21	20.47
2013	21.22	20.35	20.41	20.57	20.33	20.47	20.48	20.10	20.57	20.47	20.92	21.12	20.58
2014	21.38	21.24	21.08	21.42	21.54	21.23	21.44	21.44	21.53	20.96	21.06	20.73	21.25
2015	21.14	21.14	21.29	20.94	21.38	20.68	20.60	20.94	20.98	20.67	20.74	20.86	20.94
Trade, Transportation, and Utilities													
2011	16.86	17.01	16.61	16.33	16.65	16.67	17.05	16.47	16.73	16.64	17.02	16.47	16.71
2012	17.04	17.17	17.39	17.77	17.76	18.44	18.24	18.43	18.50	18.40	18.59	18.57	18.05
2013	18.47	18.60	18.87	18.88	18.55	18.64	18.50	18.32	18.86	18.75	18.78	18.75	18.66
2014	18.77	18.66	18.57	18.35	18.32	18.23	18.24	17.89	17.73	17.58	17.46	16.94	18.05
2015	17.50	17.41	17.35	17.45	17.15	16.62	16.58	17.26	16.81	16.53	16.91	16.40	17.00
Professional and Business Services													
2011	23.92	23.82	23.79	24.10	24.65	24.59	24.94	24.01	24.43	22.95	22.95	23.65	23.99
2012	24.37	24.06	24.19	24.50	24.09	23.99	24.33	24.08	24.73	24.30	24.74	25.33	24.39
2013	25.26	25.45	25.40	25.03	25.48	25.66	25.65	25.69	26.34	25.84	25.50	26.02	25.61
2014	25.80	26.05	26.26	26.08	25.72	25.99	25.80	26.03	26.21	26.14	26.00	26.16	26.02
2015	26.26	26.47	26.38	26.29	26.58	26.31	26.18	26.30	26.27	26.46	26.32	26.59	26.37
Education and Health Services													
2011	20.23	20.21	20.07	20.02	19.86	19.94	20.01	19.95	19.89	19.73	19.61	19.74	19.94
2012	19.37	19.03	19.04	18.90	19.62	18.73	19.32	18.95	18.92	18.67	18.94	18.70	19.02
2013	18.60	18.89	19.29	19.32	19.54	19.24	19.07	20.05	20.09	20.53	20.32	20.54	19.63
2014	20.38	20.63	20.75	21.37	21.28	21.61	21.52	21.18	21.23	21.51	20.99	21.19	21.14
2015	20.79	20.88	21.01	20.44	20.33	20.13	20.45	20.53	20.74	20.67	20.65	20.59	20.60
Leisure and Hospitality													
2011	12.28	11.97	12.26	12.09	11.92	11.80	11.83	11.52	11.60	11.73	11.70	11.61	11.85
2012	11.57	11.47	11.38	11.70	11.56	11.88	12.13	11.76	11.72	11.68	11.52	11.54	11.67
2013	11.57	11.67	11.59	11.58	11.63	11.87	12.06	12.13	11.87	11.62	11.69	11.97	11.78
2014	12.13	12.06	12.11	11.97	12.04	12.38	12.63	12.52	12.14	12.38	12.43	12.59	12.29
2015	12.41	12.73	12.72	12.49	12.79	12.70	13.06	12.84	13.05	13.08	13.03	13.17	12.84

4. Average Weekly Earnings by Selected Industry: New Mexico, 2011–2015

(Dollars, not seasonally adjusted)

Industry and year	January	February	March	April	May	June	July	August	September	October	November	December	Annual average
Total Private													
2011	712.57	694.40	690.67	688.93	697.66	691.68	696.26	682.34	685.21	695.08	680.55	674.50	691.47
2012	687.85	680.69	681.03	689.58	680.78	682.64	695.90	690.90	701.18	689.62	686.28	696.08	689.74
2013	675.24	681.88	684.63	696.78	697.65	710.83	695.91	706.82	720.54	721.00	719.64	722.05	702.61
2014	699.70	709.27	717.80	712.04	715.84	728.64	711.35	707.88	705.18	708.63	714.40	708.61	711.00
2015	699.02	708.30	708.98	694.27	693.58	689.16	693.89	709.17	700.42	699.73	705.55	693.60	700.07
Goods-Producing													
2011	884.27	898.90	898.69	912.58	904.75	913.42	920.02	928.56	931.44	943.04	937.79	978.40	922.13
2012	978.28	974.40	983.04	981.56	966.72	953.81	954.98	1,000.73	963.67	978.12	955.74	973.59	971.63
2013	955.54	957.83	937.66	982.25	987.78	992.00	969.22	1,005.75	984.75	1,042.08	1,076.87	1,019.43	993.73
2014	1,006.05	1,008.30	1,009.87	1,010.30	1,001.14	992.97	961.97	971.91	957.97	959.78	961.47	957.16	983.14
2015	934.77	943.66	936.49	934.46	950.02	932.95	948.43	976.69	952.35	964.10	983.77	970.78	952.00
Construction													
2011	851.44	840.80	851.21	874.18	845.86	853.34	851.23	868.79	866.58	871.79	867.41	821.34	856.54
2012	818.29	818.91	836.77	816.00	823.86	818.80	801.19	859.46	811.76	847.99	809.51	799.62	822.89
2013	785.14	791.62	783.74	814.57	823.37	833.13	798.72	832.14	808.40	837.22	859.81	823.68	817.03
2014	833.82	815.62	830.55	856.80	859.45	864.06	838.30	849.02	820.29	806.96	810.81	789.81	830.88
2015	752.58	782.18	768.57	781.06	795.34	771.36	784.86	820.85	761.57	789.59	804.71	794.77	783.16
Trade, Transportation, and Utilities													
2011	595.16	571.54	574.71	560.12	581.09	575.12	591.64	571.51	578.86	585.73	575.28	533.63	574.82
2012	546.98	563.18	575.61	597.07	587.86	634.34	634.75	639.52	651.20	645.84	645.07	653.66	615.51
2013	642.76	647.28	660.45	672.13	658.53	663.58	649.35	641.20	661.99	654.38	644.15	652.50	653.10
2014	640.06	647.50	653.66	634.91	639.37	643.52	636.58	620.78	613.46	615.30	611.10	592.90	628.14
2015	596.75	597.16	602.05	595.05	589.96	575.05	573.67	604.10	584.99	566.98	571.56	562.52	584.80
Professional and Business Services													
2011	880.26	871.81	870.71	891.70	914.52	904.91	902.83	864.36	879.48	851.45	835.38	846.67	875.64
2012	887.07	875.78	873.26	891.80	862.42	873.24	880.75	876.51	905.12	869.94	890.64	914.41	882.92
2013	879.05	890.75	894.08	893.57	909.64	928.89	913.14	927.41	950.87	930.24	912.90	960.14	916.84
2014	933.96	953.43	958.49	946.70	938.78	951.23	915.90	942.29	940.94	930.58	954.20	933.91	941.92
2015	929.60	939.69	939.13	920.15	922.33	920.85	913.68	938.91	924.70	947.27	952.78	933.31	930.86
Education and Health Services													
2011	740.42	711.39	696.43	698.70	695.10	695.91	698.35	694.26	676.26	690.55	690.27	673.13	695.91
2012	666.33	648.92	643.55	638.82	653.35	625.58	653.02	627.25	645.17	627.31	628.81	624.58	640.97
2013	617.52	623.37	632.71	631.76	642.87	638.77	625.50	659.65	666.99	671.33	678.69	686.04	647.79
2014	670.50	674.60	682.68	692.39	700.11	717.45	725.22	705.29	711.21	718.43	713.66	733.17	703.96
2015	704.78	712.01	712.24	686.78	683.09	684.42	680.99	691.86	696.86	686.24	691.78	689.77	694.22
Leisure and Hospitality													
2011	310.68	310.02	312.63	302.25	305.15	310.34	315.86	306.43	299.28	310.85	294.84	291.41	305.73
2012	298.51	297.07	299.29	303.03	307.50	317.20	333.58	317.52	317.61	311.86	302.98	309.27	310.42
2013	304.29	308.09	315.25	310.34	317.50	329.99	332.86	328.72	318.12	318.39	314.46	324.39	319.24
2014	314.17	322.00	333.03	311.22	321.47	337.97	346.06	340.54	322.92	321.88	325.67	323.56	326.91
2015	311.49	330.98	330.72	312.25	324.87	330.20	346.09	345.40	339.30	341.39	336.17	338.47	332.56

NEW YORK
At a Glance

Population:
2005 estimate: 19,132,610
2010 census: 19,378,102
2015 estimate: 19,795,791

Percent change in population:
2005–2015: 3.5%
2010–2015: 2.2%

Percent change in total nonfarm employment:
2005–2015: 8.5%

Industry with the largest growth in employment, 2005–2015 (thousands):
Education and health services, 357.7

Industry with the largest decline or smallest growth in employment, 2005–2015 (thousands):
Manufacturing, –124.6

Civilian labor force:
2005: 9,460,866
2010: 9,595,362
2015: 9,679,321

Unemployment rate and rank among states (highest to lowest):
2005: 5.0%, 22nd
2010: 8.6%, 27th
2015: 5.3%, 24th

Over-the-year change in unemployment rates:
2012–2013: –0.8%
2013–2014: –1.4%
2014–2015: –1.0%

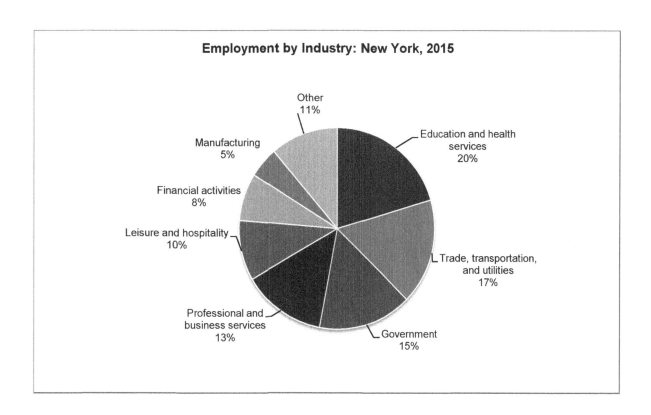

Employment by Industry: New York, 2015

Other 11%
Manufacturing 5%
Financial activities 8%
Leisure and hospitality 10%
Professional and business services 13%
Government 15%
Trade, transportation, and utilities 17%
Education and health services 20%

1. Employment by Industry: New York, 2005–2015

(Numbers in thousands, not seasonally adjusted)

Industry and year	January	February	March	April	May	June	July	August	September	October	November	December	Annual average
Total Nonfarm													
2005	8,317.7	8,357.6	8,402.6	8,497.7	8,552.4	8,602.7	8,526.2	8,511.8	8,553.9	8,599.4	8,651.7	8,695.0	8,522.4
2006	8,390.5	8,431.9	8,496.8	8,553.7	8,632.6	8,689.9	8,593.5	8,570.1	8,619.3	8,700.1	8,756.8	8,806.9	8,603.5
2007	8,517.9	8,556.5	8,612.8	8,648.5	8,745.8	8,810.7	8,717.3	8,687.1	8,724.0	8,827.3	8,872.9	8,906.2	8,718.9
2008	8,620.6	8,664.5	8,704.8	8,770.6	8,834.0	8,876.3	8,803.9	8,765.4	8,780.0	8,840.8	8,836.4	8,830.3	8,777.3
2009	8,490.3	8,507.1	8,509.4	8,515.2	8,578.2	8,587.0	8,542.2	8,494.0	8,488.8	8,569.0	8,590.6	8,608.0	8,540.0
2010	8,324.0	8,372.6	8,428.1	8,541.8	8,625.7	8,627.3	8,526.1	8,487.2	8,533.1	8,661.5	8,696.7	8,707.0	8,544.3
2011	8,440.6	8,503.3	8,548.0	8,664.4	8,695.6	8,717.7	8,669.2	8,636.7	8,690.9	8,788.4	8,827.0	8,844.5	8,668.9
2012	8,566.9	8,648.6	8,703.5	8,762.1	8,841.8	8,857.5	8,765.3	8,754.5	8,802.8	8,928.5	8,929.0	8,980.6	8,795.1
2013	8,668.4	8,744.6	8,802.7	8,897.1	8,951.9	8,974.7	8,920.8	8,897.2	8,954.5	9,081.6	9,128.6	9,137.4	8,930.0
2014	8,804.0	8,892.5	8,945.2	9,042.0	9,125.3	9,159.0	9,106.6	9,090.8	9,118.1	9,246.0	9,290.9	9,309.6	9,094.2
2015	8,989.8	9,060.8	9,106.8	9,206.8	9,300.8	9,327.3	9,283.1	9,252.4	9,263.3	9,372.8	9,398.9	9,395.1	9,246.5
Total Private													
2005	6,838.5	6,860.1	6,903.5	6,992.6	7,043.2	7,094.1	7,064.6	7,070.6	7,092.7	7,106.6	7,146.8	7,184.4	7,033.1
2006	6,915.2	6,938.7	7,001.2	7,054.9	7,128.6	7,188.8	7,141.6	7,139.7	7,161.7	7,205.3	7,250.4	7,292.4	7,118.2
2007	7,028.4	7,047.5	7,101.7	7,139.2	7,228.1	7,293.7	7,250.7	7,236.8	7,249.1	7,314.5	7,350.1	7,375.0	7,217.9
2008	7,125.2	7,148.6	7,185.0	7,240.8	7,300.4	7,342.9	7,304.6	7,294.3	7,292.3	7,314.6	7,301.3	7,291.2	7,261.8
2009	6,983.2	6,975.6	6,975.0	6,977.3	7,035.6	7,056.0	7,011.0	6,990.3	7,013.5	7,045.0	7,058.3	7,074.0	7,016.2
2010	6,823.1	6,848.0	6,898.4	7,005.7	7,048.1	7,073.2	7,053.5	7,046.3	7,070.0	7,154.8	7,180.9	7,195.1	7,033.1
2011	6,964.9	7,005.8	7,047.9	7,157.5	7,193.8	7,228.1	7,216.1	7,194.9	7,241.2	7,300.7	7,334.3	7,353.7	7,186.6
2012	7,122.3	7,171.0	7,223.0	7,281.9	7,357.7	7,386.7	7,340.1	7,347.0	7,375.7	7,461.8	7,461.7	7,507.5	7,336.4
2013	7,242.0	7,287.2	7,342.6	7,437.5	7,486.5	7,521.4	7,506.2	7,498.5	7,543.9	7,627.8	7,667.9	7,678.3	7,486.7
2014	7,396.6	7,449.8	7,498.0	7,589.9	7,672.1	7,714.5	7,698.6	7,696.2	7,707.2	7,796.7	7,833.2	7,852.8	7,658.8
2015	7,580.3	7,620.3	7,661.0	7,759.4	7,845.3	7,880.1	7,871.4	7,853.7	7,845.5	7,915.5	7,934.2	7,929.3	7,808.0
Goods-Producing													
2005	879.8	873.7	881.3	900.1	914.8	928.2	926.5	934.2	931.1	923.5	922.8	910.6	910.6
2006	874.0	870.5	879.6	899.1	915.6	930.9	925.6	932.8	929.1	927.5	921.7	913.3	910.0
2007	877.1	867.8	877.5	894.1	915.9	931.2	928.8	933.1	928.8	929.1	924.1	912.2	910.0
2008	876.4	869.9	876.3	891.0	908.4	919.2	920.7	924.7	916.4	910.0	892.8	868.0	897.8
2009	815.2	801.0	798.7	803.1	812.8	817.7	818.2	817.8	810.0	803.9	793.4	777.9	805.8
2010	737.3	729.9	739.5	762.1	773.0	783.6	789.2	793.9	789.3	786.2	779.9	764.4	769.0
2011	729.1	726.6	736.4	757.7	774.0	787.9	796.5	802.1	796.5	793.4	787.9	776.2	772.0
2012	746.5	743.1	752.7	767.4	780.2	794.3	797.9	801.1	796.6	796.1	787.2	783.8	778.9
2013	754.9	749.5	757.5	776.2	792.0	801.3	806.9	811.9	806.0	808.8	803.2	790.0	788.2
2014	757.6	751.2	762.2	784.1	804.3	818.6	826.1	830.0	824.9	827.6	822.8	812.0	801.8
2015	777.0	770.4	782.1	806.3	826.5	839.1	844.8	847.4	839.3	844.2	843.0	827.6	820.6
Service-Providing													
2005	7,437.9	7,483.9	7,521.3	7,597.6	7,637.6	7,674.5	7,599.7	7,577.6	7,622.8	7,675.9	7,728.9	7,784.4	7,611.8
2006	7,516.5	7,561.4	7,617.2	7,654.6	7,717.0	7,759.0	7,667.9	7,637.3	7,690.2	7,772.6	7,835.1	7,893.6	7,693.5
2007	7,640.8	7,688.7	7,735.3	7,754.4	7,829.9	7,879.5	7,788.5	7,754.0	7,795.2	7,898.2	7,948.8	7,994.0	7,808.9
2008	7,744.2	7,794.6	7,828.5	7,879.6	7,925.6	7,957.1	7,883.2	7,840.7	7,863.6	7,930.8	7,943.6	7,962.3	7,879.5
2009	7,675.1	7,706.1	7,710.7	7,712.1	7,765.4	7,769.3	7,724.0	7,676.2	7,678.8	7,765.1	7,797.2	7,830.1	7,734.2
2010	7,586.7	7,642.7	7,688.6	7,779.7	7,852.7	7,843.7	7,736.9	7,693.3	7,743.8	7,875.3	7,916.8	7,942.6	7,775.2
2011	7,711.5	7,776.7	7,811.6	7,906.7	7,921.6	7,929.8	7,872.7	7,834.6	7,894.4	7,995.0	8,039.1	8,068.3	7,896.8
2012	7,820.4	7,905.5	7,950.8	7,994.7	8,061.6	8,063.2	7,967.4	7,953.4	8,006.2	8,132.4	8,141.8	8,196.8	8,016.2
2013	7,913.5	7,995.1	8,045.2	8,120.9	8,159.9	8,173.4	8,113.9	8,085.3	8,148.5	8,272.8	8,325.4	8,347.4	8,141.8
2014	8,046.4	8,141.3	8,183.0	8,257.9	8,321.0	8,340.4	8,280.5	8,260.8	8,293.2	8,418.4	8,468.1	8,497.6	8,292.4
2015	8,212.8	8,290.4	8,324.7	8,400.5	8,474.3	8,488.2	8,438.3	8,405.0	8,424.0	8,528.6	8,555.9	8,567.5	8,425.9
Mining and Logging													
2005	4.9	4.8	5.0	5.7	6.0	6.3	6.4	6.5	6.4	6.4	6.2	5.9	5.9
2006	5.0	5.1	5.4	6.1	6.4	6.6	6.7	6.7	6.7	6.8	6.6	6.1	6.2
2007	5.2	5.3	5.5	5.9	6.4	6.7	6.8	6.7	6.7	6.7	6.6	6.2	6.2
2008	5.3	5.2	5.5	6.0	6.6	6.9	7.1	7.0	6.9	6.8	6.3	5.8	6.3
2009	4.8	4.8	4.9	5.2	5.6	5.8	5.9	5.8	5.7	5.7	5.6	5.2	5.4
2010	4.4	4.5	4.7	5.3	5.6	5.7	5.7	5.8	5.8	5.6	5.5	5.1	5.3
2011	4.3	4.4	4.5	5.1	5.4	5.6	5.7	5.8	5.8	5.8	5.6	5.4	5.3
2012	4.5	4.6	4.9	5.3	5.5	5.6	5.7	5.6	5.6	5.6	5.3	5.0	5.3
2013	4.3	4.3	4.5	5.0	5.4	5.3	5.3	5.3	5.4	5.5	5.3	5.0	5.1
2014	4.4	4.5	4.6	5.0	5.4	5.6	5.7	5.7	5.6	5.7	5.5	5.2	5.2
2015	4.6	4.6	4.7	5.1	5.5	5.7	5.8	5.7	5.7	5.6	5.4	5.1	5.3

1. Employment by Industry: New York, 2005–2015—*Continued*

(Numbers in thousands, not seasonally adjusted)

Industry and year	January	February	March	April	May	June	July	August	September	October	November	December	Annual average
Construction													
2005	295.0	290.1	294.8	314.6	328.6	337.8	341.7	346.8	345.1	339.4	340.0	329.1	325.3
2006	303.3	300.3	308.0	326.3	340.6	350.8	353.1	358.6	356.2	356.0	351.1	344.9	337.4
2007	318.8	310.5	318.8	336.9	355.9	367.7	370.5	374.2	371.7	373.1	369.5	358.8	352.2
2008	334.9	330.1	335.9	351.3	366.3	373.1	379.8	383.3	377.3	374.5	363.6	345.8	359.7
2009	310.8	305.3	307.9	318.0	329.7	335.7	342.3	342.6	335.5	331.3	324.5	310.5	324.5
2010	280.1	273.2	281.2	302.4	310.7	317.5	325.5	329.4	324.2	320.1	315.1	300.3	306.6
2011	273.4	270.6	278.9	296.0	310.0	319.5	329.7	333.6	328.7	325.8	321.2	310.1	308.1
2012	288.0	283.9	291.6	305.4	315.0	324.9	330.4	333.1	328.7	328.8	323.4	319.9	314.4
2013	299.0	294.3	300.6	316.4	330.0	336.2	344.1	347.4	342.7	345.5	340.3	327.5	327.0
2014	304.1	298.2	308.3	328.6	346.1	355.7	365.0	367.5	363.9	366.3	361.7	351.1	343.0
2015	323.7	316.6	326.1	348.7	366.4	374.6	380.0	382.9	376.3	380.5	381.4	369.0	360.5
Manufacturing													
2005	579.9	578.8	581.5	579.8	580.2	584.1	578.4	580.9	579.6	577.7	576.6	575.6	579.4
2006	565.7	565.1	566.2	566.7	568.6	573.5	565.8	567.5	566.2	564.7	564.0	562.3	566.4
2007	553.1	552.0	553.2	551.3	553.6	556.8	551.5	552.2	550.4	549.3	548.0	547.2	551.6
2008	536.2	534.6	534.9	533.7	535.5	539.2	533.8	534.4	532.2	528.7	522.9	516.4	531.9
2009	499.6	490.9	485.9	479.9	477.5	476.2	470.0	469.4	468.8	466.9	463.3	462.2	475.9
2010	452.8	452.2	453.6	454.4	456.7	460.4	458.0	458.7	459.3	460.5	459.3	459.0	457.1
2011	451.4	451.6	453.0	456.6	458.6	462.8	461.1	462.7	462.0	461.8	461.1	460.7	458.6
2012	454.0	454.6	456.2	456.7	459.7	463.8	461.8	462.4	462.3	461.7	458.5	458.9	459.2
2013	451.6	450.9	452.4	454.8	456.6	459.8	457.5	459.2	457.9	457.8	457.6	457.5	456.1
2014	449.1	448.5	449.3	450.5	452.8	457.3	455.4	456.8	455.4	455.6	455.6	455.7	453.5
2015	448.7	449.2	451.3	452.5	454.6	458.8	459.0	458.8	457.3	458.1	456.2	453.5	454.8
Trade, Transportation, and Utilities													
2005	1479.6	1462.4	1467.4	1478.4	1491.9	1508.5	1491.6	1493.4	1502.7	1509.8	1536.7	1567.9	1499.2
2006	1492.3	1468.9	1476.9	1482.4	1498.0	1518.9	1497.1	1495.5	1505.6	1523.1	1555.5	1582.2	1508.0
2007	1512.1	1488.4	1495.3	1493.7	1516.7	1537.5	1516.6	1509.2	1520.9	1534.7	1568.8	1592.5	1523.9
2008	1525.1	1501.1	1506.4	1507.7	1519.7	1535.7	1514.1	1511.3	1520.2	1524.9	1540.2	1555.9	1521.9
2009	1470.4	1446.7	1440.4	1432.1	1449.9	1464.3	1441.6	1440.2	1449.9	1458.9	1483.2	1503.8	1456.8
2010	1437.3	1418.2	1425.2	1441.8	1455.1	1474.3	1456.2	1457.0	1464.8	1482.2	1507.3	1527.0	1462.2
2011	1466.6	1449.4	1451.9	1463.9	1476.5	1496.0	1476.6	1480.6	1490.6	1503.1	1533.7	1556.8	1487.1
2012	1496.6	1476.5	1481.3	1483.8	1505.4	1522.6	1494.4	1499.4	1510.7	1525.6	1555.1	1576.7	1510.7
2013	1504.2	1481.1	1491.7	1502.9	1518.9	1539.6	1525.0	1522.5	1535.4	1550.2	1587.7	1606.6	1530.5
2014	1534.3	1516.3	1520.9	1532.5	1548.1	1566.4	1550.3	1550.3	1559.3	1576.9	1610.2	1630.6	1558.0
2015	1558.9	1538.9	1540.2	1548.9	1569.1	1586.0	1565.9	1564.8	1571.6	1579.2	1603.3	1620.4	1570.6
Wholesale Trade													
2005	347.3	348.1	349.1	350.5	351.9	353.6	353.6	354.5	354.1	354.3	355.4	357.7	352.5
2006	348.0	347.9	349.9	351.2	353.0	356.0	354.5	355.2	354.1	355.2	355.6	358.9	353.3
2007	352.0	351.8	353.1	353.0	354.9	358.0	356.9	355.9	354.9	357.4	357.2	358.7	355.3
2008	351.3	351.0	351.4	351.3	352.0	353.8	352.3	351.2	350.0	348.9	347.2	346.0	350.5
2009	337.4	334.1	332.3	328.9	329.0	329.7	326.7	326.2	324.8	324.6	324.5	325.3	328.6
2010	318.6	318.1	319.9	322.0	323.9	326.5	327.2	327.1	326.5	328.2	329.2	330.3	324.8
2011	324.6	324.1	325.7	328.3	330.1	332.6	332.8	333.2	331.9	332.7	332.7	334.3	330.3
2012	329.4	330.1	331.3	332.5	334.0	336.4	335.4	334.9	333.1	335.2	334.6	336.6	333.6
2013	330.9	331.0	331.8	333.6	335.1	338.5	338.5	338.0	336.6	336.8	337.8	339.1	335.6
2014	334.0	333.6	334.0	336.3	338.2	340.5	340.8	340.7	339.1	340.4	341.8	343.0	338.5
2015	337.7	337.2	338.0	339.1	341.3	343.9	344.3	343.9	341.7	338.6	340.6	342.2	340.7
Retail Trade													
2005	868.4	850.7	853.8	862.2	870.8	882.8	878.3	880.3	876.0	883.8	907.7	932.0	878.9
2006	875.6	853.2	857.8	862.4	871.5	886.0	881.3	880.5	875.8	891.8	922.1	940.4	883.2
2007	889.1	866.1	870.7	869.9	885.2	899.7	894.9	891.6	887.9	897.6	930.6	948.7	894.3
2008	899.6	876.8	880.4	879.7	888.2	899.9	896.0	895.4	891.0	897.7	914.2	926.3	895.4
2009	865.2	846.3	843.2	839.4	854.0	867.0	860.9	861.7	860.2	868.8	891.3	906.8	863.7
2010	859.5	843.2	847.4	856.5	866.0	881.0	877.3	879.1	872.2	886.6	908.4	923.3	875.0
2011	877.6	862.9	863.1	873.1	881.3	895.5	892.5	896.8	892.1	904.2	931.8	948.9	893.3
2012	905.2	885.2	887.5	890.9	904.7	916.5	911.8	912.5	908.6	921.1	949.5	961.7	912.9
2013	908.6	892.4	896.1	903.0	914.9	929.8	929.0	930.2	925.8	937.8	971.0	984.1	926.9
2014	927.3	912.1	914.2	921.1	930.7	945.2	942.6	945.0	938.7	952.6	980.4	993.5	942.0
2015	939.5	922.6	922.8	928.7	941.7	953.4	948.0	948.1	941.8	952.6	967.1	974.8	945.1

1. Employment by Industry: New York, 2005–2015—*Continued*

(Numbers in thousands, not seasonally adjusted)

Industry and year	January	February	March	April	May	June	July	August	September	October	November	December	Annual average
Transportation and Utilities													
2005	263.9	263.6	264.5	265.7	269.2	272.1	259.7	258.6	272.6	271.7	273.6	278.2	267.8
2006	268.7	267.8	269.2	268.8	273.5	276.9	261.3	259.8	275.7	276.1	277.8	282.9	271.5
2007	271.0	270.5	271.5	270.8	276.6	279.8	264.8	261.7	278.1	279.7	281.0	285.1	274.2
2008	274.2	273.3	274.6	276.7	279.5	282.0	265.8	264.7	279.2	278.3	278.8	283.6	275.9
2009	267.8	266.3	264.9	263.8	266.9	267.6	254.0	252.3	264.9	265.5	267.4	271.7	264.4
2010	259.2	256.9	257.9	263.3	265.2	266.8	251.7	250.8	266.1	267.4	269.7	273.4	262.4
2011	264.4	262.4	263.1	262.5	265.1	267.9	251.3	250.6	266.6	266.2	269.2	273.6	263.6
2012	262.0	261.2	262.5	260.4	266.7	269.7	247.2	252.0	269.0	269.3	271.0	278.4	264.1
2013	264.7	257.7	263.8	266.3	268.9	271.3	257.5	254.3	273.0	275.6	278.9	283.4	268.0
2014	273.0	270.6	272.7	275.1	279.2	280.7	266.9	264.6	281.5	283.9	288.0	294.1	277.5
2015	281.7	279.1	279.4	281.1	286.1	288.7	273.6	272.8	288.1	288.0	295.6	303.4	284.8
Information													
2005	267.1	269.3	270.2	270.6	272.4	276.6	273.9	274.9	274.6	275.5	276.7	280.0	273.5
2006	271.3	271.4	272.8	270.0	272.1	274.7	272.4	272.8	270.7	268.8	270.8	272.5	271.7
2007	265.6	267.2	267.6	267.3	270.0	272.6	271.2	271.8	270.4	268.9	271.2	272.5	269.7
2008	265.8	267.7	268.2	266.8	269.6	272.9	270.8	271.6	271.1	269.9	270.8	272.1	269.8
2009	263.3	261.2	261.8	260.5	260.9	260.8	259.5	258.4	257.1	256.1	256.6	257.3	259.5
2010	249.2	249.4	250.8	250.1	251.6	253.2	254.5	254.9	253.8	255.7	256.6	258.6	253.2
2011	251.4	252.1	253.5	255.8	256.3	257.7	258.7	243.4	258.2	257.3	258.3	259.5	255.2
2012	254.5	255.4	256.1	258.3	260.6	262.3	260.1	259.9	258.7	260.2	261.3	261.6	259.1
2013	253.6	255.1	256.8	258.7	260.5	263.0	262.7	264.1	263.4	265.5	267.3	267.9	261.6
2014	260.0	263.2	264.1	262.5	263.1	267.1	265.2	266.2	264.1	267.2	267.2	269.4	264.9
2015	261.8	263.2	263.4	263.0	263.8	265.9	267.8	266.4	266.2	269.7	268.5	269.4	265.8
Financial Activities													
2005	701.0	701.2	703.4	707.1	707.2	717.6	723.6	723.6	716.3	716.4	718.2	723.8	713.3
2006	712.8	714.7	717.8	719.4	722.6	732.5	736.7	737.3	728.6	727.7	729.8	735.1	726.3
2007	723.0	724.4	726.4	725.2	726.0	737.9	741.3	739.0	729.3	731.9	733.3	735.8	731.1
2008	723.3	723.0	723.6	720.9	720.9	728.5	730.6	729.6	715.6	711.5	708.5	708.7	720.4
2009	692.9	687.5	683.9	677.7	676.3	678.8	678.9	675.7	669.2	667.2	665.8	668.3	676.9
2010	657.1	657.9	659.8	664.8	666.0	675.3	678.7	678.7	671.5	672.2	673.9	678.4	669.5
2011	672.4	673.3	674.6	677.4	678.6	688.6	693.3	694.5	684.9	683.8	684.0	686.8	682.7
2012	677.5	679.4	679.3	679.1	679.5	689.1	691.7	690.8	680.8	683.4	683.2	688.0	683.5
2013	672.5	674.2	675.1	676.9	676.8	686.9	691.9	690.5	681.2	683.6	686.8	690.9	682.3
2014	680.8	682.5	683.9	684.8	688.6	700.6	705.3	704.9	695.1	696.6	698.1	703.6	693.7
2015	693.4	694.7	696.1	697.8	700.6	711.5	718.0	717.8	706.6	708.0	707.2	708.7	705.0
Professional and Business Services													
2005	1,044.4	1,046.0	1,052.0	1,075.3	1,076.4	1,091.2	1,094.3	1,096.6	1,095.5	1,094.9	1,101.9	1,108.7	1,081.4
2006	1,068.9	1,073.4	1,086.7	1,098.1	1,101.8	1,119.9	1,117.4	1,121.0	1,114.7	1,119.1	1,127.7	1,135.3	1,107.0
2007	1,097.5	1,102.8	1,114.5	1,122.5	1,129.7	1,149.8	1,149.8	1,152.6	1,140.1	1,152.5	1,156.7	1,162.4	1,135.9
2008	1,126.5	1,133.1	1,139.7	1,154.5	1,155.4	1,170.2	1,171.5	1,169.1	1,156.0	1,154.4	1,149.0	1,144.5	1,152.0
2009	1,096.1	1,091.8	1,091.0	1,091.6	1,089.9	1,100.1	1,095.8	1,090.7	1,084.2	1,087.5	1,090.2	1,092.2	1,091.8
2010	1,059.2	1,064.9	1,072.4	1,095.9	1,096.4	1,111.0	1,115.4	1,114.6	1,104.8	1,116.6	1,118.8	1,120.0	1,099.2
2011	1,091.9	1,097.7	1,106.1	1,129.7	1,130.1	1,148.3	1,154.2	1,152.8	1,148.4	1,149.5	1,156.0	1,156.1	1,135.1
2012	1,126.2	1,132.3	1,143.1	1,159.0	1,164.4	1,182.6	1,182.9	1,185.6	1,178.1	1,192.0	1,195.1	1,197.6	1,169.2
2013	1,160.4	1,166.9	1,175.4	1,192.6	1,196.6	1,212.7	1,218.4	1,217.3	1,207.5	1,219.5	1,222.4	1,222.6	1,201.0
2014	1,182.4	1,190.7	1,195.8	1,218.2	1,227.0	1,240.6	1,248.1	1,248.7	1,237.8	1,249.2	1,255.8	1,256.8	1,229.3
2015	1,221.0	1,227.8	1,231.5	1,255.5	1,265.8	1,282.7	1,288.0	1,285.9	1,272.9	1,278.8	1,278.5	1,278.6	1,263.9
Education and Health Services													
2005	1,499.9	1,533.2	1,542.1	1,547.4	1,538.3	1,502.9	1,482.1	1,475.7	1,525.1	1,558.4	1,568.7	1,570.4	1,528.7
2006	1,525.7	1,560.7	1,571.4	1,573.8	1,569.0	1,533.6	1,505.9	1,497.5	1,555.7	1,592.6	1,602.6	1,608.3	1,558.1
2007	1,556.2	1,589.4	1,600.3	1,597.7	1,590.3	1,557.1	1,529.4	1,521.8	1,579.0	1,621.2	1,627.8	1,631.4	1,583.5
2008	1,584.1	1,621.3	1,628.0	1,631.4	1,622.6	1,590.7	1,559.9	1,554.9	1,611.0	1,649.2	1,661.5	1,667.7	1,615.2
2009	1,621.4	1,658.5	1,663.9	1,662.4	1,653.9	1,621.2	1,593.0	1,587.1	1,640.9	1,683.0	1,694.4	1,701.0	1,648.4
2010	1,655.7	1,693.0	1,703.9	1,710.4	1,694.0	1,640.6	1,607.1	1,595.3	1,659.0	1,722.4	1,736.8	1,740.3	1,679.9
2011	1,688.8	1,731.6	1,738.4	1,752.6	1,726.4	1,667.9	1,643.7	1,633.2	1,695.5	1,755.4	1,765.5	1,770.6	1,714.1
2012	1,718.0	1,764.3	1,775.5	1,778.3	1,768.1	1,704.3	1,675.3	1,672.3	1,740.1	1,799.2	1,800.0	1,812.3	1,750.6
2013	1,758.2	1,808.3	1,819.6	1,831.6	1,801.8	1,745.1	1,718.4	1,715.5	1,799.3	1,848.7	1,861.9	1,863.1	1,797.6
2014	1,796.9	1,847.4	1,860.0	1,868.2	1,853.4	1,807.4	1,781.4	1,780.9	1,836.9	1,891.8	1,906.1	1,907.9	1,844.9
2015	1,847.1	1,894.3	1,904.5	1,915.2	1,898.5	1,850.4	1,830.2	1,824.4	1,869.7	1,921.6	1,942.3	1,938.4	1,886.4

1. Employment by Industry: New York, 2005–2015—*Continued*

(Numbers in thousands, not seasonally adjusted)

Industry and year	January	February	March	April	May	June	July	August	September	October	November	December	Annual average
Leisure and Hospitality													
2005	617.5	623.5	634.1	656.3	683.3	708.6	714.9	716.8	692.0	671.8	664.0	663.3	670.5
2006	620.7	628.4	641.7	656.6	690.7	717.5	728.6	727.1	700.3	686.7	681.6	682.4	680.2
2007	640.9	649.8	659.8	677.3	713.5	739.7	750.3	748.2	719.4	711.0	702.0	700.9	701.1
2008	662.3	669.8	678.2	701.8	733.7	754.4	767.4	765.0	734.9	724.7	708.8	704.8	717.2
2009	662.2	666.1	671.2	686.6	725.2	745.5	757.8	756.5	739.7	723.5	709.1	707.3	712.6
2010	670.4	677.4	687.3	717.8	746.5	768.6	784.3	784.9	762.6	751.1	739.1	736.9	735.6
2011	701.2	709.8	719.9	747.9	776.5	804.9	817.7	815.1	792.9	782.9	773.1	770.4	767.7
2012	731.7	747.2	759.1	778.5	817.8	846.5	856.0	858.1	830.5	821.6	797.7	803.3	804.0
2013	761.1	773.2	786.0	814.4	852.6	883.0	893.7	887.9	864.7	860.6	846.8	844.7	839.1
2014	799.4	811.0	821.8	846.3	890.1	915.3	924.1	918.5	894.1	887.9	872.3	871.1	871.0
2015	826.7	835.6	846.1	872.2	916.5	937.8	951.1	942.9	918.5	911.3	889.1	879.9	894.0
Other Services													
2005	349.2	350.8	353.0	357.4	358.9	360.5	357.7	355.4	355.4	356.3	357.8	359.7	356.0
2006	349.5	350.7	354.3	355.5	358.8	360.8	357.9	355.7	357.0	359.8	360.7	363.3	357.0
2007	356.0	357.7	360.3	361.4	366.0	367.9	363.3	361.1	361.2	365.2	366.2	367.3	362.8
2008	361.7	362.7	364.6	366.7	370.1	371.3	369.6	368.1	367.1	370.0	369.7	369.5	367.6
2009	361.7	362.8	364.1	363.3	366.7	367.6	366.2	363.9	362.5	364.9	365.6	366.2	364.6
2010	356.9	357.3	359.5	362.8	365.5	366.6	368.1	367.0	364.2	368.4	368.5	369.5	364.5
2011	363.5	365.3	367.1	372.5	375.4	376.8	375.4	373.2	374.2	375.3	375.8	377.3	372.7
2012	371.3	372.8	375.9	377.5	381.7	385.0	381.8	379.8	380.2	383.7	382.1	384.2	379.7
2013	377.1	378.9	380.5	384.2	387.3	389.8	389.2	388.8	386.4	390.9	391.8	392.5	386.5
2014	385.2	387.5	389.3	393.3	397.5	398.5	398.1	396.7	395.0	399.5	400.7	401.4	395.2
2015	394.4	395.4	397.1	400.5	404.5	406.7	405.6	404.1	400.7	402.7	402.3	406.3	401.7
Government													
2005	1,479.2	1,497.5	1,499.1	1,505.1	1,509.2	1,508.6	1,461.6	1,441.2	1,461.2	1,492.8	1,504.9	1,510.6	1,489.3
2006	1,475.3	1,493.2	1,495.6	1,498.8	1,504.0	1,501.1	1,451.9	1,430.4	1,457.6	1,494.8	1,506.4	1,514.5	1,485.3
2007	1,489.5	1,509.0	1,511.1	1,509.3	1,517.7	1,517.0	1,466.6	1,450.3	1,474.9	1,512.8	1,522.8	1,531.2	1,501.0
2008	1,495.4	1,515.9	1,519.8	1,529.8	1,533.6	1,533.4	1,499.3	1,471.1	1,487.7	1,526.2	1,535.1	1,539.1	1,515.5
2009	1,507.1	1,531.5	1,534.4	1,537.9	1,542.6	1,531.0	1,531.2	1,503.7	1,475.3	1,524.0	1,532.3	1,534.0	1,523.8
2010	1,500.9	1,524.6	1,529.7	1,536.1	1,577.6	1,554.1	1,472.6	1,440.9	1,463.1	1,506.7	1,515.8	1,511.9	1,511.2
2011	1,475.7	1,497.5	1,500.1	1,506.9	1,501.8	1,489.6	1,453.1	1,441.8	1,449.7	1,487.7	1,492.7	1,490.8	1,482.3
2012	1,444.6	1,477.6	1,480.5	1,480.2	1,484.1	1,470.8	1,425.2	1,407.5	1,427.1	1,466.7	1,467.3	1,473.1	1,458.7
2013	1,426.4	1,457.4	1,460.1	1,459.6	1,465.4	1,453.3	1,414.6	1,398.7	1,410.6	1,453.8	1,460.7	1,459.1	1,443.3
2014	1,407.4	1,442.7	1,447.2	1,452.1	1,453.2	1,444.5	1,408.0	1,394.6	1,410.9	1,449.3	1,457.7	1,456.8	1,435.4
2015	1,409.5	1,440.5	1,445.8	1,447.4	1,455.5	1,447.2	1,411.7	1,398.7	1,417.8	1,457.3	1,464.7	1,465.8	1,438.5

2. Average Weekly Hours by Selected Industry: New York, 2011–2015

(Not seasonally adjusted)

Industry and year	January	February	March	April	May	June	July	August	September	October	November	December	Annual average
Total Private													
2011	33.9	33.8	33.7	34.0	34.2	34.2	34.4	34.3	34.2	34.3	34.1	34.2	34.1
2012	34.1	33.8	33.7	33.9	33.8	34.0	34.2	34.0	34.4	33.7	33.8	34.3	34.0
2013	33.5	33.5	33.6	33.6	33.6	34.2	33.9	34.0	34.1	33.7	33.7	33.9	33.8
2014	33.4	33.6	33.8	33.6	33.6	34.0	33.8	33.9	33.8	33.6	34.0	33.7	33.7
2015	33.5	33.7	33.8	33.5	33.7	33.7	33.8	34.2	33.7	33.7	34.0	33.7	33.7
Goods-Producing													
2011	37.8	38.4	38.4	38.8	39.0	39.0	39.0	38.9	38.9	38.9	39.1	39.1	38.8
2012	38.3	38.5	38.6	38.5	38.4	38.9	38.6	38.6	39.1	38.8	38.6	39.1	38.7
2013	38.2	37.7	37.6	38.0	38.1	38.1	38.4	38.4	38.7	38.5	38.3	38.4	38.2
2014	38.1	37.4	37.9	38.3	38.7	38.6	38.7	38.9	39.1	38.7	38.8	38.9	38.5
2015	38.7	38.0	38.8	38.9	39.3	39.1	39.1	39.0	38.2	38.9	38.8	39.0	38.8
Construction													
2011	35.6	36.8	37.0	37.5	38.0	38.2	38.4	37.9	37.8	37.9	38.1	37.5	37.6
2012	36.7	37.3	37.5	37.1	36.9	37.6	37.3	37.2	37.8	37.5	37.0	37.3	37.3
2013	37.0	35.5	35.4	36.6	36.9	36.2	37.5	36.7	37.2	36.7	36.7	36.1	36.6
2014	36.0	34.7	35.4	36.2	36.6	36.3	37.0	37.3	37.5	36.6	36.7	36.5	36.5
2015	36.6	35.6	37.1	37.5	38.6	38.2	38.6	38.5	37.3	38.1	37.8	38.3	37.7
Manufacturing													
2011	39.0	39.4	39.4	39.8	39.9	39.8	39.6	39.8	39.8	39.8	39.9	40.3	39.7
2012	39.5	39.3	39.3	39.4	39.3	39.7	39.4	39.5	40.0	39.7	39.7	40.2	39.6
2013	38.8	38.8	38.8	38.6	38.7	39.2	38.7	39.3	39.5	39.4	39.2	39.6	39.1
2014	39.1	39.0	39.3	39.5	40.0	40.1	39.8	40.0	40.2	40.3	40.3	40.6	39.9
2015	40.1	39.6	39.9	39.7	39.7	39.7	39.3	39.2	38.7	39.3	39.4	39.4	39.5
Trade, Transportation, and Utilities													
2011	33.8	33.8	34.0	34.3	34.5	34.9	34.8	34.9	35.2	35.1	34.9	35.5	34.6
2012	34.9	34.6	34.6	34.6	34.8	34.9	35.1	35.0	35.2	34.4	34.8	35.3	34.9
2013	34.2	34.3	34.6	34.6	34.7	35.0	34.8	34.8	34.6	34.2	34.2	34.5	34.5
2014	33.7	33.8	34.2	34.2	34.2	34.4	34.5	34.5	34.6	34.2	34.5	34.6	34.3
2015	34.0	34.2	34.2	34.0	34.1	33.9	34.1	34.4	34.6	34.1	34.5	34.0	34.2
Information													
2011	34.4	34.4	34.2	34.6	35.3	34.9	34.9	34.9	35.0	35.3	35.3	35.0	34.9
2012	35.7	34.9	35.0	35.3	34.8	34.5	35.4	35.0	35.5	35.1	35.5	35.9	35.2
2013	35.3	35.1	34.9	35.2	34.8	35.8	34.9	35.0	35.3	34.9	34.8	35.0	35.1
2014	34.6	34.6	34.7	34.3	34.5	34.7	33.9	34.3	34.2	34.1	34.7	33.9	34.4
2015	34.6	35.0	34.8	34.3	34.4	34.3	34.8	35.4	34.9	35.1	35.5	34.8	34.8
Financial Activities													
2011	37.0	36.6	36.6	36.9	37.3	37.2	37.4	37.6	37.6	37.9	37.3	37.0	37.2
2012	37.6	36.9	36.4	37.1	36.4	36.7	37.4	36.4	37.4	36.6	37.0	37.9	37.0
2013	36.5	36.7	36.6	36.8	36.6	38.0	36.8	37.1	37.8	36.7	37.0	37.7	37.0
2014	36.8	37.9	38.0	36.9	37.0	37.8	37.0	37.0	36.7	36.8	37.9	36.8	37.2
2015	36.6	37.9	37.9	37.0	37.3	37.4	37.4	38.6	37.5	37.6	37.7	37.4	37.5
Professional and Business Services													
2011	35.3	35.0	34.8	35.1	35.4	35.0	35.0	34.9	34.8	35.5	35.0	35.1	35.1
2012	35.4	34.8	34.9	35.6	34.8	35.2	35.8	35.3	36.4	34.9	35.0	35.7	35.3
2013	34.4	34.8	34.8	34.7	34.7	35.8	35.0	35.0	35.8	34.8	34.8	35.2	35.0
2014	34.6	35.2	35.1	34.6	34.6	35.5	35.0	35.2	35.0	34.8	35.7	34.8	35.0
2015	34.7	35.5	35.4	34.5	34.7	34.8	34.4	35.3	34.4	34.8	35.6	34.8	34.9
Education and Health Services													
2011	33.1	32.8	32.8	32.9	33.0	32.8	33.1	32.8	32.7	32.8	32.6	32.6	32.8
2012	32.7	32.5	32.2	32.3	32.2	32.4	32.5	32.4	32.5	32.3	32.2	32.5	32.4
2013	32.4	32.3	32.2	32.1	32.1	32.5	32.5	32.4	32.4	32.3	32.3	32.4	32.3
2014	32.3	32.2	32.3	32.1	32.0	32.3	32.0	32.1	32.1	31.9	32.1	31.7	32.1
2015	31.8	31.8	31.8	31.8	31.9	32.0	32.2	32.3	32.1	31.9	32.0	31.9	32.0
Leisure and Hospitality													
2011	26.9	27.2	27.0	27.3	27.5	28.4	29.0	28.8	27.6	27.7	27.5	27.5	27.7
2012	26.8	26.8	27.0	27.4	27.7	27.7	28.1	28.0	27.7	27.7	27.4	27.7	27.5
2013	26.9	26.9	27.1	27.1	27.4	27.7	28.2	28.6	27.8	27.8	27.7	27.7	27.6
2014	27.0	27.4	27.6	27.9	28.2	28.1	28.4	28.5	27.8	28.0	28.1	28.1	27.9
2015	27.7	27.9	27.8	28.3	28.6	28.3	28.7	29.0	28.1	28.3	28.2	28.2	28.3
Other Services													
2011	32.6	32.6	32.3	32.6	32.8	32.2	32.3	32.1	32.0	31.9	31.7	32.0	32.3
2012	31.9	31.3	31.4	31.8	31.8	31.5	31.9	31.4	31.5	30.4	30.1	31.5	31.4
2013	31.1	31.4	31.5	31.6	31.8	32.2	31.8	32.2	32.6	31.3	31.0	31.6	31.7
2014	30.9	31.9	32.0	31.7	31.6	32.2	31.9	32.1	32.0	31.9	32.2	31.3	31.8
2015	31.2	31.7	31.4	31.2	31.5	30.8	31.4	32.0	31.2	31.1	31.3	30.9	31.3

3. Average Hourly Earnings by Selected Industry: New York, 2011–2015

(Dollars, not seasonally adjusted)

Industry and year	January	February	March	April	May	June	July	August	September	October	November	December	Annual average
Total Private													
2011..............................	26.75	26.37	26.43	26.36	26.55	26.11	26.22	26.10	26.56	26.92	26.72	26.70	26.48
2012..............................	27.38	27.09	27.08	27.46	26.88	26.81	27.11	26.77	27.33	27.15	27.28	27.80	27.18
2013..............................	27.83	27.77	27.72	27.80	27.63	27.87	27.67	27.62	28.04	27.76	27.86	28.11	27.81
2014..............................	28.02	28.29	28.26	28.09	27.94	28.28	27.87	27.83	28.08	28.23	28.63	28.34	28.16
2015..............................	28.70	29.03	28.98	28.85	28.55	28.45	28.45	28.75	28.63	28.76	29.23	29.03	28.79
Goods-Producing													
2011..............................	26.72	26.51	27.08	27.01	27.15	27.07	27.64	27.57	27.75	28.02	28.49	28.39	27.47
2012..............................	28.16	28.32	28.53	28.49	28.42	28.49	28.70	28.54	28.59	28.62	28.73	28.70	28.53
2013..............................	28.94	28.84	29.05	29.05	28.73	28.63	28.93	28.99	28.80	28.69	28.81	28.78	28.85
2014..............................	29.10	28.71	28.81	29.15	29.11	28.98	29.25	29.46	29.61	29.65	29.72	29.83	29.29
2015..............................	29.65	29.38	29.89	29.63	29.63	29.71	29.89	29.84	30.03	30.36	30.58	30.84	29.96
Construction													
2011..............................	32.71	32.11	32.75	31.89	31.43	31.27	31.65	31.70	32.02	32.18	32.69	32.74	32.07
2012..............................	32.75	32.94	33.36	33.30	33.21	33.15	33.28	33.54	33.90	34.00	34.90	34.94	33.62
2013..............................	34.67	35.30	35.27	35.01	34.66	34.35	34.53	35.00	34.50	34.16	34.68	34.94	34.74
2014..............................	35.54	35.06	35.40	35.69	35.46	34.84	34.85	35.26	35.57	35.83	35.89	35.64	35.42
2015..............................	35.76	35.19	36.15	35.58	35.12	35.79	36.04	35.92	36.09	36.73	37.16	37.89	36.14
Manufacturing													
2011..............................	23.59	23.54	23.81	23.93	24.36	24.33	25.00	24.91	25.10	25.39	25.86	25.85	24.65
2012..............................	25.73	25.87	25.95	25.90	25.79	25.85	26.07	25.64	25.57	25.59	25.42	25.40	25.73
2013..............................	25.88	25.57	25.80	25.78	25.34	25.37	25.45	25.33	25.37	25.45	25.35	25.65	25.53
2014..............................	25.83	25.86	25.64	25.67	25.63	25.81	26.04	26.00	25.88	25.78	25.87	26.39	25.87
2015..............................	26.13	26.19	26.20	25.89	25.76	25.42	25.35	25.19	25.46	25.37	25.40	25.67	25.67
Trade, Transportation, and Utilities													
2011..............................	22.12	22.01	22.04	21.96	22.02	21.59	21.62	21.55	21.93	21.91	21.66	21.51	21.82
2012..............................	21.93	21.78	21.89	22.36	21.70	21.59	21.77	21.23	21.83	21.68	21.59	22.02	21.78
2013..............................	22.30	22.20	22.21	22.35	22.18	22.28	22.42	22.44	22.99	22.69	22.82	22.90	22.49
2014..............................	23.06	23.32	23.41	23.50	23.27	23.34	23.18	23.07	22.96	22.89	22.53	22.40	23.07
2015..............................	22.83	23.18	23.19	23.41	22.92	22.89	22.87	22.94	22.97	23.27	23.46	23.89	23.15
Information													
2011..............................	40.67	39.07	39.03	39.11	39.22	39.05	39.09	38.80	39.22	39.99	39.81	40.01	39.43
2012..............................	41.20	41.32	40.64	41.47	41.35	41.03	40.95	40.29	41.23	40.91	40.80	42.22	41.12
2013..............................	42.07	42.16	42.51	42.59	43.06	43.73	42.61	41.86	41.99	41.62	41.72	41.74	42.30
2014..............................	41.21	41.03	41.18	40.55	40.14	42.05	41.04	41.01	41.25	41.10	41.85	40.76	41.10
2015..............................	39.93	40.86	41.20	41.51	40.66	40.61	40.91	41.85	41.07	40.85	41.35	40.40	40.94
Financial Activities													
2011..............................	35.86	34.83	34.75	34.61	35.04	34.62	34.33	34.14	34.75	35.81	35.08	34.84	34.89
2012..............................	36.63	35.97	36.30	37.48	36.36	36.41	36.75	36.65	37.59	37.38	37.15	37.94	36.89
2013..............................	38.18	38.31	38.53	39.09	39.25	40.05	39.22	39.63	40.12	39.83	40.11	40.66	39.43
2014..............................	40.59	41.01	41.25	41.23	41.23	42.85	41.14	40.53	41.19	41.85	43.92	42.58	41.62
2015..............................	43.44	44.02	43.73	43.39	43.12	42.62	42.23	43.28	42.62	42.95	43.98	42.40	43.15
Professional and Business Services													
2011..............................	35.11	34.41	34.32	34.07	34.56	33.74	33.79	33.53	33.97	34.45	33.84	34.06	34.15
2012..............................	35.50	34.83	34.44	34.86	34.19	33.89	34.39	33.72	34.44	34.03	34.31	35.35	34.49
2013..............................	35.29	34.96	34.50	34.57	34.34	34.69	34.27	33.83	34.23	33.83	33.81	34.44	34.39
2014..............................	34.14	34.81	34.94	34.39	34.25	35.00	34.18	34.16	34.51	34.89	35.46	35.17	34.66
2015..............................	35.89	36.45	36.19	35.79	35.64	35.31	35.31	35.89	35.38	35.48	36.30	35.73	35.78
Education and Health Services													
2011..............................	23.19	23.11	23.18	23.23	23.32	23.45	23.83	23.72	23.92	24.17	24.07	24.10	23.61
2012..............................	24.47	24.24	24.29	24.42	24.20	24.30	24.63	24.51	24.78	24.66	24.94	25.33	24.57
2013..............................	25.10	25.08	25.08	25.06	24.98	24.93	25.11	25.08	25.38	25.12	25.17	25.19	25.11
2014..............................	24.79	25.00	24.64	24.60	24.50	24.39	24.54	24.59	24.73	24.76	24.83	24.80	24.68
2015..............................	25.02	25.02	24.83	25.04	24.80	24.74	24.94	24.82	24.88	24.65	24.99	24.95	24.89
Leisure and Hospitality													
2011..............................	17.27	17.24	17.29	17.21	17.31	15.79	15.57	15.78	16.87	17.36	17.33	17.65	16.85
2012..............................	17.15	17.08	16.98	16.89	16.66	16.21	16.19	16.10	16.62	16.84	16.97	17.22	16.72
2013..............................	16.97	16.93	17.00	16.94	16.95	16.65	16.51	16.54	17.13	17.56	17.73	18.10	17.08
2014..............................	17.77	17.93	17.85	17.84	17.84	17.15	16.74	16.66	17.41	17.99	18.22	18.50	17.64
2015..............................	18.16	18.28	18.18	18.24	17.84	17.38	17.25	17.32	17.89	18.17	18.64	18.60	17.98
Other Services													
2011..............................	21.61	21.57	21.68	21.80	22.01	21.73	21.41	21.35	21.89	21.87	22.24	22.60	21.81
2012..............................	22.48	22.38	22.56	23.03	22.50	22.47	22.55	22.73	23.23	23.14	23.42	23.93	22.87
2013..............................	23.63	23.93	23.72	23.78	23.57	24.32	23.80	23.69	24.43	23.90	23.85	24.18	23.90
2014..............................	23.77	24.27	24.51	24.16	24.02	24.31	23.78	23.81	24.79	24.36	25.31	25.35	24.37
2015..............................	25.42	26.15	26.44	26.21	26.36	26.71	26.25	26.56	27.29	26.98	27.23	27.20	26.57

4. Average Weekly Earnings by Selected Industry: New York, 2011–2015

(Dollars, not seasonally adjusted)

Industry and year	January	February	March	April	May	June	July	August	September	October	November	December	Annual average
Total Private													
2011	906.83	891.31	890.69	896.24	908.01	892.96	901.97	895.23	908.35	923.36	911.15	913.14	902.97
2012	933.66	915.64	912.60	930.89	908.54	911.54	927.16	910.18	940.15	914.96	922.06	953.54	924.12
2013	932.31	930.30	931.39	934.08	928.37	953.15	938.01	939.08	956.16	935.51	938.88	952.93	939.98
2014	935.87	950.54	955.19	943.82	938.78	961.52	942.01	943.44	949.10	948.53	973.42	955.06	948.99
2015	961.45	978.31	979.52	966.48	962.14	958.77	961.61	983.25	964.83	969.21	993.82	978.31	970.22
Goods-Producing													
2011	1,010.02	1,017.98	1,039.87	1,047.99	1,058.85	1,055.73	1,077.96	1,072.47	1,079.48	1,089.98	1,113.96	1,110.05	1,065.84
2012	1,078.53	1,090.32	1,101.26	1,096.87	1,091.33	1,108.26	1,107.82	1,101.64	1,117.87	1,110.46	1,108.98	1,122.17	1,104.11
2013	1,105.51	1,087.27	1,092.28	1,103.90	1,094.61	1,090.80	1,110.91	1,113.22	1,114.56	1,104.57	1,103.42	1,105.15	1,102.07
2014	1,108.71	1,073.75	1,091.90	1,116.45	1,126.56	1,118.63	1,131.98	1,145.99	1,157.75	1,147.46	1,153.14	1,160.39	1,127.67
2015	1,147.46	1,116.44	1,159.73	1,152.61	1,164.46	1,161.66	1,168.70	1,163.76	1,147.15	1,181.00	1,186.50	1,202.76	1,162.45
Construction													
2011	1,164.48	1,181.65	1,211.75	1,195.88	1,194.34	1,194.51	1,215.36	1,201.43	1,210.36	1,219.62	1,245.49	1,227.75	1,205.83
2012	1,201.93	1,228.66	1,251.00	1,235.43	1,225.45	1,246.44	1,241.34	1,247.69	1,281.42	1,275.00	1,291.30	1,303.26	1,254.03
2013	1,282.79	1,253.15	1,248.56	1,281.37	1,278.95	1,243.47	1,294.88	1,284.50	1,283.40	1,253.67	1,272.76	1,261.33	1,271.48
2014	1,279.44	1,216.58	1,253.16	1,291.98	1,297.84	1,264.69	1,289.45	1,315.20	1,333.88	1,311.38	1,317.16	1,300.86	1,292.83
2015	1,308.82	1,252.76	1,341.17	1,334.25	1,355.63	1,367.18	1,391.14	1,382.92	1,346.16	1,399.41	1,404.65	1,451.19	1,362.48
Manufacturing													
2011	920.01	927.48	938.11	952.41	971.96	968.33	990.00	991.42	998.98	1,010.52	1,031.81	1,041.76	978.61
2012	1,016.34	1,016.69	1,019.84	1,020.46	1,013.55	1,026.25	1,027.16	1,012.78	1,022.80	1,015.92	1,009.17	1,021.08	1,018.91
2013	1,004.14	992.12	1,001.04	995.11	980.66	994.50	984.92	995.47	1,002.12	1,002.73	993.72	1,015.74	998.22
2014	1,009.95	1,008.54	1,007.65	1,013.97	1,025.20	1,034.98	1,036.39	1,040.00	1,040.38	1,038.93	1,042.56	1,071.43	1,032.21
2015	1,047.81	1,037.12	1,045.38	1,027.83	1,022.67	1,009.17	996.26	987.45	985.30	997.04	1,000.76	1,011.40	1,013.97
Trade, Transportation, and Utilities													
2011	747.66	743.94	749.36	753.23	759.69	753.49	752.38	752.10	771.94	769.04	755.93	763.61	754.97
2012	765.36	753.59	757.39	773.66	755.16	753.49	764.13	743.05	768.42	745.79	751.33	777.31	760.12
2013	762.66	761.46	768.47	773.31	769.65	779.80	780.22	780.91	795.45	776.00	780.44	790.05	775.91
2014	777.12	788.22	800.62	803.70	795.83	802.90	799.71	795.92	794.42	782.84	777.29	775.04	791.30
2015	776.22	792.76	793.10	795.94	781.57	775.97	779.87	789.14	794.76	793.51	809.37	812.26	791.73
Information													
2011	1,399.05	1,344.01	1,334.83	1,353.21	1,384.47	1,362.85	1,364.24	1,354.12	1,372.70	1,411.65	1,405.29	1,400.35	1,376.11
2012	1,470.84	1,442.07	1,422.40	1,463.89	1,438.98	1,415.54	1,449.63	1,410.15	1,463.67	1,435.94	1,448.40	1,515.70	1,447.42
2013	1,485.07	1,479.82	1,483.60	1,499.17	1,498.49	1,565.53	1,487.09	1,465.10	1,482.25	1,452.54	1,451.86	1,460.90	1,484.73
2014	1,425.87	1,419.64	1,428.95	1,390.87	1,384.83	1,459.14	1,391.26	1,406.64	1,410.75	1,401.51	1,452.20	1,381.76	1,413.84
2015	1,381.58	1,430.10	1,433.76	1,423.79	1,398.70	1,392.92	1,423.67	1,481.49	1,433.34	1,433.84	1,467.93	1,405.92	1,424.71
Financial Activities													
2011	1,326.82	1,274.78	1,271.85	1,277.11	1,306.99	1,287.86	1,283.94	1,283.66	1,306.60	1,357.20	1,308.48	1,289.08	1,297.91
2012	1,377.29	1,327.29	1,321.32	1,390.51	1,323.50	1,336.25	1,374.45	1,334.06	1,405.87	1,368.11	1,374.55	1,437.93	1,364.93
2013	1,393.57	1,405.98	1,410.20	1,438.51	1,436.55	1,521.90	1,443.30	1,470.27	1,516.54	1,461.76	1,484.07	1,532.88	1,458.91
2014	1,493.71	1,554.28	1,567.50	1,521.39	1,525.51	1,619.73	1,522.18	1,499.61	1,511.67	1,540.08	1,664.57	1,566.94	1,548.26
2015	1,589.90	1,668.36	1,657.37	1,605.43	1,608.38	1,593.99	1,579.40	1,670.61	1,598.25	1,614.92	1,658.05	1,585.76	1,618.13
Professional and Business Services													
2011	1,239.38	1,204.35	1,194.34	1,195.86	1,223.42	1,180.90	1,182.65	1,170.20	1,182.16	1,222.98	1,184.40	1,195.51	1,198.67
2012	1,256.70	1,212.08	1,201.96	1,241.02	1,189.81	1,192.93	1,231.16	1,190.32	1,253.62	1,187.65	1,200.85	1,262.00	1,217.50
2013	1,213.98	1,216.61	1,200.60	1,199.58	1,191.60	1,241.90	1,199.45	1,184.05	1,225.43	1,177.28	1,176.59	1,212.29	1,203.65
2014	1,181.24	1,225.31	1,226.39	1,189.89	1,185.05	1,242.50	1,196.30	1,202.43	1,207.85	1,214.17	1,265.92	1,223.92	1,213.10
2015	1,245.38	1,293.98	1,281.13	1,234.76	1,236.71	1,228.79	1,214.66	1,266.92	1,217.07	1,234.70	1,292.28	1,243.40	1,248.72
Education and Health Services													
2011	767.59	758.01	760.30	764.27	769.56	769.16	788.77	778.02	782.18	792.78	784.68	785.66	774.41
2012	800.17	787.80	782.14	788.77	779.24	787.32	800.48	794.12	805.35	796.52	803.07	823.23	796.07
2013	813.24	810.08	807.58	804.43	801.86	810.23	816.08	812.59	822.31	811.38	812.99	816.16	811.05
2014	800.72	805.00	795.87	789.66	784.00	787.80	785.28	789.34	793.83	789.84	797.04	786.16	792.23
2015	795.64	795.64	789.59	796.27	791.12	791.68	803.07	801.69	798.65	786.34	799.68	795.91	796.48
Leisure and Hospitality													
2011	464.56	468.93	466.83	469.83	476.03	448.44	451.53	454.46	465.61	480.87	476.58	485.38	466.75
2012	459.62	457.74	458.46	462.79	461.48	449.02	454.94	450.80	460.37	466.47	464.98	476.99	459.80
2013	456.49	455.42	460.70	459.07	464.43	461.21	465.58	473.04	476.21	488.17	491.12	501.37	471.41
2014	479.79	491.28	492.66	497.74	503.09	481.92	475.42	474.81	484.00	503.72	511.98	519.85	492.16
2015	503.03	510.01	505.40	516.19	510.22	491.85	495.08	502.28	502.71	514.21	525.65	524.52	508.83
Other Services													
2011	704.49	703.18	700.26	710.68	721.93	699.71	691.54	685.34	700.48	697.65	705.01	723.20	704.46
2012	717.11	700.49	708.38	732.35	715.50	707.81	719.35	713.72	731.75	703.46	704.94	753.80	718.12
2013	734.89	751.40	747.18	751.45	749.53	783.10	756.84	762.82	796.42	748.07	739.35	764.09	757.63
2014	734.49	774.21	784.32	765.87	759.03	782.78	758.58	764.30	793.28	777.08	814.98	793.46	774.97
2015	793.10	828.96	830.22	817.75	830.34	822.67	824.25	849.92	851.45	839.08	852.30	840.48	831.64

NORTH CAROLINA

At a Glance

Population:
  2005 estimate: 8,705,407
  2010 census: 9,535,483
  2015 estimate: 10,042,802

Percent change in population:
  2005–2015: 15.4%
  2010–2015: 5.3%

Percent change in total nonfarm employment:
  2005–2015: 8.4%

Industry with the largest growth in employment, 2005–2015 (thousands):
  Professional and business services, 140.4

Industry with the largest decline or smallest growth in employment, 2005–2015 (thousands):
  Manufacturing, –104.5

Civilian labor force:
  2005: 4,317,428
  2010: 4,616,691
  2015: 4,769,245

Unemployment rate and rank among states (highest to lowest):
  2005: 5.2%, 18th
  2010: 10.9%, 7th
  2015: 5.7%, 16th

Over-the-year change in unemployment rates:
  2012–2013: –1.4%
  2013–2014: –1.6%
  2014–2015: –0.6%

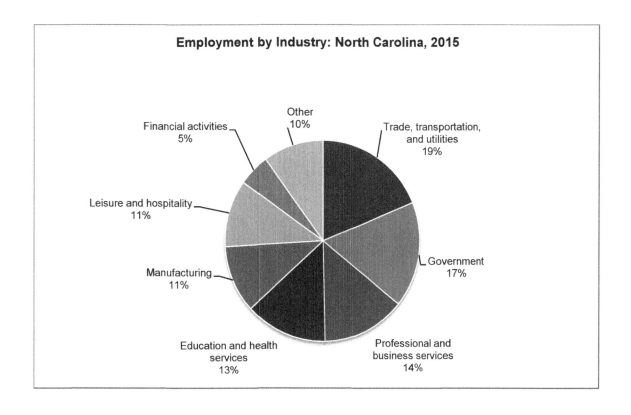

Employment by Industry: North Carolina, 2015

Other 10%
Financial activities 5%
Trade, transportation, and utilities 19%
Leisure and hospitality 11%
Government 17%
Manufacturing 11%
Education and health services 13%
Professional and business services 14%

1. Employment by Industry: North Carolina, 2005–2015

(Numbers in thousands, not seasonally adjusted)

Industry and year	January	February	March	April	May	June	July	August	September	October	November	December	Annual average
Total Nonfarm													
2005	3,829.2	3,845.4	3,876.2	3,902.5	3,922.4	3,906.7	3,850.8	3,922.6	3,958.5	3,965.9	3,980.5	3,983.0	3,912.0
2006	3,918.7	3,933.6	3,969.5	4,016.3	4,048.2	4,045.2	3,988.0	4,060.2	4,085.7	4,107.8	4,134.3	4,139.7	4,037.3
2007	4,050.2	4,073.2	4,113.4	4,122.9	4,160.5	4,164.0	4,077.2	4,155.9	4,182.3	4,185.1	4,203.3	4,206.3	4,141.2
2008	4,109.3	4,128.9	4,149.8	4,152.3	4,177.8	4,159.5	4,067.2	4,135.4	4,154.7	4,131.0	4,112.3	4,089.5	4,130.6
2009	3,947.3	3,936.0	3,929.0	3,921.8	3,937.0	3,909.7	3,818.5	3,879.8	3,902.9	3,889.7	3,893.3	3,882.8	3,904.0
2010	3,792.0	3,797.5	3,833.1	3,866.4	3,907.1	3,886.4	3,810.3	3,877.0	3,893.0	3,921.0	3,930.6	3,920.5	3,869.6
2011	3,825.9	3,861.0	3,891.0	3,922.6	3,942.3	3,928.0	3,852.4	3,925.4	3,946.1	3,960.0	3,974.7	3,969.3	3,916.6
2012	3,899.4	3,923.8	3,957.3	3,982.9	4,014.9	3,988.3	3,910.7	3,993.7	4,016.9	4,037.9	4,056.9	4,052.6	3,986.3
2013	3,964.9	3,994.3	4,023.5	4,049.9	4,076.6	4,056.5	3,983.5	4,064.4	4,091.1	4,114.7	4,131.2	4,130.4	4,056.8
2014	4,039.6	4,040.1	4,087.7	4,131.2	4,166.6	4,151.5	4,075.9	4,152.2	4,172.3	4,207.4	4,223.8	4,227.2	4,139.6
2015	4,141.6	4,165.0	4,183.8	4,227.7	4,266.8	4,257.8	4,184.0	4,249.9	4,271.1	4,298.7	4,318.5	4,310.9	4,239.7
Total Private													
2005	3,155.2	3,165.0	3,191.8	3,218.6	3,236.3	3,257.2	3,263.9	3,277.0	3,273.5	3,276.6	3,288.2	3,292.7	3,241.3
2006	3,233.5	3,242.1	3,272.8	3,317.2	3,345.4	3,371.8	3,386.1	3,398.7	3,388.2	3,401.8	3,417.9	3,425.1	3,350.1
2007	3,348.5	3,364.9	3,399.9	3,409.5	3,443.0	3,474.6	3,461.1	3,475.1	3,463.2	3,465.3	3,476.1	3,480.4	3,438.5
2008	3,392.3	3,404.2	3,419.8	3,420.6	3,441.5	3,451.1	3,437.6	3,439.9	3,414.1	3,388.7	3,365.1	3,344.3	3,409.9
2009	3,214.8	3,199.6	3,187.4	3,176.5	3,192.2	3,196.0	3,184.1	3,182.5	3,165.6	3,157.1	3,157.4	3,149.3	3,180.2
2010	3,068.7	3,068.4	3,097.9	3,125.6	3,148.0	3,168.6	3,180.5	3,187.5	3,172.5	3,188.0	3,192.8	3,186.3	3,148.7
2011	3,102.8	3,131.5	3,157.0	3,187.2	3,207.1	3,228.3	3,232.3	3,243.0	3,233.3	3,233.8	3,242.3	3,242.7	3,203.4
2012	3,180.3	3,196.8	3,226.9	3,251.5	3,280.4	3,299.2	3,299.8	3,309.7	3,298.9	3,303.6	3,316.4	3,318.3	3,273.5
2013	3,240.0	3,260.4	3,286.2	3,313.0	3,340.0	3,365.0	3,367.8	3,380.9	3,370.9	3,377.9	3,392.1	3,394.8	3,340.8
2014	3,316.7	3,312.2	3,356.6	3,395.0	3,428.9	3,451.8	3,457.0	3,469.5	3,455.5	3,473.6	3,484.0	3,494.3	3,424.6
2015	3,413.4	3,431.0	3,447.6	3,487.4	3,526.0	3,549.9	3,555.4	3,562.3	3,548.8	3,559.6	3,573.6	3,572.2	3,518.9
Goods-Producing													
2005	794.6	795.6	798.5	800.7	803.8	807.7	805.9	807.7	808.2	802.8	802.6	800.8	802.4
2006	789.2	788.7	793.6	805.2	807.8	812.8	813.0	815.0	812.8	810.7	808.9	809.8	805.6
2007	797.6	797.8	801.5	796.8	799.6	807.4	801.9	804.1	802.5	799.0	797.5	795.7	800.1
2008	776.2	775.2	775.0	767.5	768.3	766.8	762.7	759.4	755.0	743.9	732.4	720.8	758.6
2009	685.1	673.9	662.2	651.9	646.9	644.8	639.3	636.8	634.5	629.8	625.5	622.7	646.1
2010	606.3	603.0	608.0	612.0	614.6	618.5	620.8	620.4	620.4	618.3	616.0	613.7	614.3
2011	597.4	603.2	608.0	610.5	614.6	617.8	618.6	619.6	619.0	615.1	614.0	613.2	612.6
2012	605.5	608.2	613.6	614.7	618.5	621.1	621.6	621.8	622.3	621.0	621.3	621.5	617.6
2013	609.8	612.4	615.5	617.5	621.2	625.9	626.2	626.1	627.0	626.9	627.0	627.3	621.9
2014	616.7	617.3	624.0	625.4	630.7	636.0	638.0	639.5	641.2	645.0	645.7	647.4	633.9
2015	639.3	642.4	645.8	650.0	655.5	659.9	661.3	662.2	661.9	663.6	658.5	660.2	655.1
Service-Providing													
2005	3,034.6	3,049.8	3,077.7	3,101.8	3,118.6	3,099.0	3,044.9	3,114.9	3,150.3	3,163.1	3,177.9	3,182.2	3,109.6
2006	3,129.5	3,144.9	3,175.9	3,211.1	3,240.4	3,232.4	3,175.0	3,245.2	3,272.9	3,297.1	3,325.4	3,329.9	3,231.6
2007	3,252.6	3,275.4	3,311.9	3,326.1	3,360.9	3,356.6	3,275.3	3,351.8	3,379.8	3,386.1	3,405.8	3,410.6	3,341.1
2008	3,333.1	3,353.7	3,374.8	3,384.8	3,409.5	3,392.7	3,304.5	3,376.0	3,399.7	3,387.1	3,379.9	3,368.7	3,372.0
2009	3,262.2	3,262.1	3,266.8	3,269.9	3,290.1	3,264.9	3,179.2	3,243.0	3,268.4	3,259.9	3,267.8	3,260.1	3,257.9
2010	3,185.7	3,194.5	3,225.1	3,254.4	3,292.5	3,267.9	3,189.5	3,256.6	3,272.6	3,302.7	3,314.6	3,306.8	3,255.2
2011	3,228.5	3,257.8	3,283.0	3,312.1	3,327.7	3,310.2	3,233.8	3,305.8	3,327.1	3,344.9	3,360.7	3,356.1	3,304.0
2012	3,293.9	3,315.6	3,343.7	3,368.2	3,396.4	3,367.2	3,289.1	3,371.9	3,394.6	3,416.9	3,435.6	3,431.1	3,368.7
2013	3,355.1	3,381.9	3,408.0	3,432.4	3,455.4	3,430.6	3,357.3	3,438.3	3,464.1	3,487.8	3,504.2	3,503.1	3,434.9
2014	3,422.9	3,422.8	3,463.7	3,505.8	3,535.9	3,515.5	3,437.9	3,512.7	3,531.1	3,562.4	3,578.1	3,579.8	3,505.7
2015	3,502.3	3,522.6	3,538.0	3,577.7	3,611.3	3,597.9	3,522.7	3,587.7	3,609.2	3,635.1	3,660.0	3,650.7	3,584.6
Mining and Logging													
2005	6.8	6.8	6.8	6.7	6.6	6.7	6.6	6.6	6.6	6.7	6.7	6.6	6.7
2006	6.6	6.6	6.7	6.7	6.7	6.8	6.9	7.0	7.0	6.9	6.9	6.9	6.8
2007	6.9	6.9	7.0	7.1	7.1	7.1	7.0	7.1	7.0	6.9	6.9	6.9	7.0
2008	6.8	6.8	6.7	6.6	6.6	6.6	6.6	6.6	6.6	6.5	6.5	6.4	6.6
2009	6.1	6.0	6.0	5.8	5.8	5.9	5.9	5.9	5.9	5.8	5.7	5.6	5.9
2010	5.6	5.5	5.6	5.6	5.6	5.6	5.8	5.7	5.7	5.7	5.6	5.6	5.6
2011	5.5	5.6	5.6	5.5	5.5	5.6	5.7	5.7	5.7	5.6	5.6	5.6	5.6
2012	5.5	5.5	5.6	5.5	5.5	5.6	5.6	5.6	5.6	5.6	5.6	5.5	5.6
2013	5.4	5.4	5.4	5.5	5.5	5.5	5.5	5.6	5.6	5.6	5.6	5.6	5.5
2014	5.4	5.4	5.5	5.5	5.5	5.6	5.6	5.6	5.6	5.5	5.5	5.5	5.5
2015	5.5	5.5	5.5	5.5	5.5	5.6	5.6	5.6	5.6	5.6	5.6	5.5	5.6

1. Employment by Industry: North Carolina, 2005–2015—*Continued*

(Numbers in thousands, not seasonally adjusted)

Industry and year	January	February	March	April	May	June	July	August	September	October	November	December	Annual average
Construction													
2005	219.3	220.2	223.4	227.2	230.4	233.5	237.2	238.0	238.5	235.6	235.5	234.5	231.1
2006	230.2	231.2	236.4	242.1	244.7	248.7	251.5	253.5	252.5	251.9	252.5	252.7	245.7
2007	246.5	247.0	252.0	253.7	256.0	259.8	258.6	259.2	258.4	256.6	255.0	253.0	254.7
2008	242.1	241.6	242.3	239.9	241.0	240.6	240.2	237.3	234.7	229.9	223.9	218.4	236.0
2009	202.2	199.6	197.5	193.6	193.7	194.1	193.7	191.9	189.8	186.6	183.6	182.1	192.4
2010	171.8	169.7	173.8	177.3	178.5	179.9	180.7	180.2	178.5	177.7	176.2	173.5	176.5
2011	162.5	167.2	170.7	172.9	175.2	176.8	177.7	177.7	177.1	174.8	173.7	172.8	173.3
2012	166.5	167.5	171.2	172.1	173.4	173.5	174.0	174.3	173.6	172.9	172.3	172.1	172.0
2013	165.6	166.6	169.5	172.2	174.3	175.7	176.3	176.8	176.8	176.6	176.8	175.5	173.6
2014	169.7	169.3	173.9	175.5	178.6	180.9	182.7	183.5	183.4	185.2	184.5	184.3	179.3
2015	178.4	180.1	182.3	186.4	190.1	191.9	193.3	193.7	193.4	196.3	192.1	194.4	189.4
Manufacturing													
2005	568.5	568.6	568.3	566.8	566.8	567.5	562.1	563.1	563.1	560.5	560.4	559.7	564.6
2006	552.4	550.9	550.5	556.4	556.4	557.3	554.6	554.5	553.3	551.9	549.5	550.2	553.2
2007	544.2	543.9	542.5	536.0	536.5	540.5	536.3	537.8	537.1	535.5	535.6	535.8	538.5
2008	527.3	526.8	526.0	521.0	520.7	519.6	515.9	515.5	513.7	507.5	502.0	496.0	516.0
2009	476.8	468.3	458.7	452.5	447.4	444.8	439.7	439.0	438.8	437.4	436.2	435.0	447.9
2010	428.9	427.8	428.6	429.1	430.5	433.0	434.3	434.5	436.2	434.9	434.2	434.6	432.2
2011	429.4	430.4	431.7	432.1	433.9	435.4	435.2	436.2	436.2	434.7	434.7	434.8	433.7
2012	433.5	435.2	436.8	437.1	439.6	442.0	442.0	441.9	443.1	442.5	443.4	443.9	440.1
2013	438.8	440.4	440.6	439.8	441.4	444.7	444.4	443.7	444.6	444.7	444.6	446.2	442.8
2014	441.6	442.6	444.6	444.4	446.6	449.5	449.7	450.4	452.2	454.3	455.7	457.6	449.1
2015	455.4	456.8	458.0	458.1	459.9	462.4	462.4	462.9	462.9	461.7	460.8	460.3	460.1
Trade, Transportation, and Utilities													
2005	723.3	723.2	728.0	733.5	736.8	738.9	741.5	742.0	739.8	748.7	761.5	769.5	740.6
2006	739.8	734.7	740.7	750.1	755.3	756.4	761.9	763.7	761.7	768.2	784.8	791.7	759.1
2007	765.9	762.1	770.8	770.7	777.6	780.2	779.3	779.4	776.7	780.3	795.4	802.4	778.4
2008	771.3	768.3	772.9	769.4	772.0	773.6	770.9	769.2	763.3	763.6	767.8	769.2	769.3
2009	729.7	721.3	720.4	715.9	720.7	722.5	719.2	717.9	714.0	716.1	724.1	727.2	720.8
2010	700.2	696.8	703.3	706.8	712.4	715.2	716.0	717.3	712.4	718.0	730.5	736.2	713.8
2011	709.8	710.1	715.2	720.4	724.1	726.8	730.8	731.9	728.7	733.4	746.5	753.0	727.6
2012	729.6	725.6	731.7	735.5	741.9	745.0	745.9	744.8	743.8	747.3	763.9	768.3	743.6
2013	739.3	737.8	742.6	745.6	751.6	756.2	759.0	760.5	758.1	764.6	780.9	789.5	757.1
2014	759.4	752.9	760.6	766.2	771.6	776.4	775.5	778.0	775.3	782.8	799.3	809.3	775.6
2015	776.6	775.3	780.3	787.2	793.3	798.8	798.4	799.5	797.0	800.7	818.9	826.5	796.0
Wholesale Trade													
2005	166.3	166.9	166.8	168.9	169.9	170.2	171.2	171.6	171.8	173.4	174.3	174.8	170.5
2006	171.7	172.1	172.9	175.5	176.3	176.7	177.7	177.7	177.7	177.7	178.6	179.1	176.1
2007	179.1	180.0	181.3	181.7	182.4	183.7	183.6	183.1	182.8	183.0	183.2	183.6	182.3
2008	181.3	182.1	182.8	180.8	181.4	181.3	180.4	179.8	178.4	178.3	176.7	175.2	179.9
2009	170.6	169.9	168.8	167.4	166.9	166.4	165.4	165.0	164.1	164.6	164.2	164.0	166.4
2010	161.7	162.2	163.4	164.1	164.5	164.4	165.0	165.2	164.4	165.5	166.0	166.1	164.4
2011	164.2	165.3	166.0	167.1	167.4	168.0	168.9	168.8	168.7	168.7	169.2	169.4	167.6
2012	167.6	168.5	170.0	170.9	171.9	172.3	172.6	172.7	172.5	172.6	172.8	172.7	171.4
2013	170.2	171.4	172.3	172.1	172.7	173.4	174.0	174.3	174.2	174.5	175.1	175.5	173.3
2014	173.5	173.9	175.0	175.2	175.8	176.4	176.5	177.2	176.6	177.2	177.3	177.7	176.0
2015	175.2	176.1	177.1	177.5	178.4	179.3	179.2	179.4	178.9	178.7	178.4	177.6	178.0
Retail Trade													
2005	430.7	429.7	434.0	437.0	438.9	439.9	442.6	442.3	439.5	445.6	456.5	462.9	441.6
2006	440.1	434.5	438.6	445.3	448.9	448.9	452.3	453.4	450.9	457.0	472.3	478.1	451.7
2007	456.3	452.3	458.7	458.7	464.4	465.7	465.8	466.3	464.1	468.2	482.7	488.0	465.9
2008	463.4	459.7	463.6	462.1	463.4	465.0	464.0	462.7	459.0	459.4	465.3	467.0	462.9
2009	438.4	432.4	433.2	431.8	437.1	439.0	437.9	437.4	434.4	436.5	444.7	447.0	437.5
2010	426.7	423.0	427.4	429.3	433.4	435.7	435.4	436.4	432.0	436.1	447.4	452.2	434.6
2011	430.1	428.9	432.3	435.5	438.8	440.1	442.8	443.5	439.7	444.3	456.4	460.8	441.1
2012	442.9	438.2	441.7	444.9	449.9	452.1	452.8	451.5	449.9	453.0	468.7	470.9	451.4
2013	447.5	446.1	449.0	452.1	456.6	459.8	461.8	462.0	459.4	465.0	479.2	484.8	460.3
2014	460.3	455.3	460.4	465.3	468.8	471.9	471.2	472.2	469.1	475.2	489.8	495.6	471.3
2015	470.8	469.0	472.2	477.2	481.7	485.6	485.6	485.9	483.6	487.3	503.7	508.4	484.3

1. Employment by Industry: North Carolina, 2005–2015—*Continued*

(Numbers in thousands, not seasonally adjusted)

Industry and year	January	February	March	April	May	June	July	August	September	October	November	December	Annual average
Transportation and Utilities													
2005	126.3	126.6	127.2	127.6	128.0	128.8	127.7	128.1	128.5	129.7	130.7	131.8	128.4
2006	128.0	128.1	129.2	129.3	130.1	130.8	131.9	132.6	133.1	133.5	133.9	134.5	131.3
2007	130.5	129.8	130.8	130.3	130.8	130.8	129.9	130.0	129.8	129.1	129.5	130.8	130.2
2008	126.6	126.5	126.5	126.5	127.2	127.3	126.5	126.7	125.9	125.9	125.8	127.0	126.5
2009	120.7	119.0	118.4	116.7	116.7	117.1	115.9	115.5	115.5	115.0	115.2	116.2	116.8
2010	111.8	111.6	112.5	113.4	114.5	115.1	115.6	115.7	116.0	116.4	117.1	117.9	114.8
2011	115.5	115.9	116.9	117.8	117.9	118.7	119.1	119.6	120.3	120.4	120.9	122.8	118.8
2012	119.1	118.9	120.0	119.7	120.1	120.6	120.5	120.6	121.4	121.7	122.4	124.7	120.8
2013	121.6	120.3	121.3	121.4	122.3	123.0	123.2	124.2	124.5	125.1	126.6	129.2	123.6
2014	125.6	123.7	125.2	125.7	127.0	128.1	127.8	128.6	129.6	130.4	132.2	136.0	128.3
2015	130.6	130.2	131.0	132.5	133.2	133.9	133.6	134.2	134.5	134.7	136.8	140.5	133.8
Information													
2005	69.6	69.4	69.6	70.1	70.4	71.0	71.4	72.1	72.5	72.8	73.2	74.5	71.4
2006	74.1	74.0	73.9	72.7	72.9	73.5	72.6	72.7	72.3	72.5	72.5	72.9	73.1
2007	72.2	72.6	72.4	72.5	72.7	73.1	73.0	72.7	72.4	72.7	72.9	72.8	72.7
2008	72.0	72.3	72.2	72.2	72.4	72.6	72.2	72.2	71.5	72.2	72.5	72.4	72.2
2009	71.3	71.1	70.6	70.4	70.3	70.1	69.6	69.1	68.5	68.6	68.8	68.7	69.8
2010	67.7	67.7	67.9	67.8	68.3	68.6	68.7	68.6	68.4	68.3	68.7	68.8	68.3
2011	67.9	67.9	67.9	68.4	68.4	68.9	69.3	69.5	69.2	69.3	69.6	69.5	68.8
2012	69.1	69.2	69.0	69.1	69.0	69.5	69.6	69.3	68.6	68.8	69.1	69.3	69.1
2013	69.2	69.5	69.4	69.2	69.9	70.1	70.6	70.6	70.0	70.7	71.5	71.9	70.2
2014	71.0	71.3	71.4	71.3	72.0	72.8	73.3	73.6	73.2	73.9	74.3	75.0	72.8
2015	74.2	74.7	74.8	74.9	76.2	76.6	76.6	76.4	75.8	76.1	76.4	76.9	75.8
Financial Activities													
2005	192.5	193.3	194.0	196.9	197.7	200.0	201.7	201.9	201.0	200.7	200.1	200.9	198.4
2006	197.7	199.1	200.5	204.6	205.8	208.0	211.7	212.1	210.3	210.5	209.9	210.2	206.7
2007	207.7	208.8	210.2	212.2	213.3	215.6	215.2	215.3	213.6	213.4	212.4	212.9	212.6
2008	210.2	211.4	212.0	213.7	213.8	215.7	214.7	214.7	212.2	211.4	209.6	209.7	212.4
2009	205.3	204.7	203.9	203.3	204.0	204.4	204.5	203.6	201.1	200.1	199.9	200.1	202.9
2010	197.7	197.9	198.7	198.3	198.8	200.6	201.8	202.0	200.8	200.7	200.5	200.7	199.9
2011	198.5	199.0	199.3	199.9	201.3	203.2	203.7	204.1	201.8	201.6	201.1	201.3	201.2
2012	198.7	199.5	201.0	201.6	202.4	204.5	204.5	204.8	203.4	204.3	203.9	204.1	202.7
2013	201.8	202.3	203.0	205.2	206.3	208.7	209.0	209.4	208.0	207.8	207.5	207.9	206.4
2014	206.9	207.0	207.9	208.9	210.8	213.4	214.8	215.7	214.5	214.2	214.3	215.1	212.0
2015	212.7	213.9	214.3	216.3	218.4	221.1	222.4	222.4	221.7	219.8	219.6	217.9	218.4
Professional and Business Services													
2005	435.6	437.4	441.4	446.8	443.5	445.4	450.1	454.4	457.2	460.9	460.0	458.9	449.3
2006	455.4	458.7	463.4	470.3	473.7	479.8	483.4	488.7	489.8	493.9	493.9	492.6	478.6
2007	477.4	484.4	490.1	495.1	498.6	505.6	502.4	507.1	508.7	510.9	508.7	508.7	499.8
2008	497.3	501.1	502.8	505.7	506.8	508.9	504.2	508.4	504.2	502.2	492.4	486.0	501.7
2009	470.5	467.8	463.5	461.3	459.8	460.2	461.5	464.8	466.4	472.6	474.2	473.3	466.3
2010	461.7	464.7	469.7	477.9	477.8	482.6	489.2	493.3	494.4	505.5	503.9	503.1	485.3
2011	490.4	500.2	503.6	509.5	508.6	513.2	516.2	520.6	524.3	526.2	526.1	525.5	513.7
2012	514.6	522.2	526.3	530.5	532.0	535.2	533.0	539.1	538.3	541.2	541.2	540.8	532.9
2013	525.5	534.5	538.3	542.7	544.1	547.5	547.0	555.1	556.0	560.1	560.0	556.7	547.3
2014	544.9	546.1	555.1	566.4	568.2	572.2	575.0	578.5	577.7	583.4	581.2	581.7	569.2
2015	567.9	573.8	574.1	582.8	586.1	589.0	592.3	598.0	598.8	605.0	606.6	601.8	589.7
Education and Health Services													
2005	457.6	461.0	464.6	465.6	467.1	465.5	467.0	471.8	476.1	476.8	479.5	479.3	469.3
2006	479.2	483.3	485.9	487.5	489.5	489.6	489.9	494.6	498.1	502.4	505.8	507.4	492.8
2007	502.4	508.7	512.4	515.0	517.8	517.4	514.7	520.4	523.6	528.1	530.9	531.9	518.6
2008	523.9	528.9	529.4	529.1	531.5	529.3	526.3	530.0	533.3	534.1	537.8	537.9	531.0
2009	532.1	536.6	536.4	537.0	538.7	536.4	532.6	535.9	537.1	539.5	541.0	539.7	536.9
2010	533.8	535.7	537.3	538.0	538.4	533.9	532.7	534.5	533.0	541.0	542.5	540.2	536.8
2011	532.3	538.5	538.7	541.3	540.7	536.6	533.1	536.1	540.6	544.9	546.7	546.0	539.6
2012	541.3	546.1	546.4	546.9	549.0	545.8	543.2	546.3	551.0	555.9	557.3	558.1	548.9
2013	550.6	556.2	557.5	557.8	558.9	555.4	554.1	557.9	562.3	564.4	565.8	565.3	558.9
2014	557.8	560.3	565.4	567.9	569.6	564.6	565.0	569.3	571.0	576.2	577.6	576.6	568.4
2015	566.6	571.8	570.9	572.9	575.1	570.4	568.7	570.9	574.5	580.3	584.3	580.8	573.9

1. Employment by Industry: North Carolina, 2005–2015—*Continued*

(Numbers in thousands, not seasonally adjusted)

Industry and year	January	February	March	April	May	June	July	August	September	October	November	December	Annual average
Leisure and Hospitality													
2005	337.9	339.8	349.4	358.9	368.7	377.4	377.7	378.4	371.3	365.1	362.0	359.3	362.2
2006	349.3	353.1	362.3	377.0	388.3	396.3	401.2	400.9	394.2	390.7	388.8	386.9	382.4
2007	372.8	376.6	386.8	394.6	408.4	417.2	415.6	417.6	409.3	402.6	400.0	397.5	399.9
2008	384.7	389.2	397.6	403.3	415.3	420.7	422.6	423.0	414.3	402.8	395.0	391.7	405.0
2009	374.3	376.8	382.9	390.4	404.7	409.9	410.1	408.9	401.6	389.7	384.2	379.4	392.7
2010	364.3	365.4	374.8	387.3	399.0	408.7	410.7	411.6	404.8	397.0	391.8	385.5	391.7
2011	369.8	375.0	385.9	398.9	410.3	419.9	418.7	420.3	410.6	403.5	399.0	394.8	400.6
2012	383.1	387.1	399.0	412.1	424.6	432.9	436.0	437.8	426.1	419.9	414.2	410.8	415.3
2013	399.1	401.6	412.0	426.7	438.9	450.1	451.6	451.8	441.2	435.7	430.8	429.0	430.7
2014	414.3	411.8	424.8	440.6	456.3	464.6	463.6	463.8	453.3	448.5	442.5	440.3	443.7
2015	428.9	431.4	438.9	453.3	469.3	480.6	480.5	478.8	466.7	460.3	455.8	454.3	458.2
Other Services													
2005	144.1	145.3	146.3	146.1	148.3	151.3	148.6	148.7	147.4	148.8	149.3	149.5	147.8
2006	148.8	150.5	152.5	149.8	152.1	155.4	152.4	151.0	149.0	152.9	153.3	153.6	151.8
2007	152.5	153.9	155.7	152.6	155.0	158.1	159.0	158.5	156.4	158.3	158.3	158.5	156.4
2008	156.7	157.8	157.9	159.7	161.4	163.5	164.0	163.0	160.3	158.5	157.6	156.6	159.8
2009	146.5	147.4	147.5	146.3	147.1	147.7	147.3	145.5	142.4	140.7	139.7	138.2	144.7
2010	137.0	137.2	138.2	137.5	138.7	140.5	140.6	139.8	138.3	139.2	138.9	138.1	138.7
2011	136.7	137.6	138.4	138.3	139.1	141.9	141.9	140.9	139.1	139.8	139.3	139.4	139.4
2012	138.4	138.9	139.9	141.1	143.0	145.2	146.0	145.8	145.4	145.2	145.5	145.4	143.3
2013	144.7	146.1	147.9	148.3	149.1	151.1	150.3	149.5	148.3	147.7	148.6	147.2	148.2
2014	145.7	145.5	147.4	148.3	149.7	151.8	151.8	151.1	149.3	149.6	149.1	148.9	149.0
2015	147.2	147.7	148.5	150.0	152.1	153.5	155.2	154.1	152.4	153.8	153.5	153.8	151.8
Government													
2005	674.0	680.4	684.4	683.9	686.1	649.5	586.9	645.6	685.0	689.3	692.3	690.3	670.6
2006	685.2	691.5	696.7	699.1	702.8	673.4	601.9	661.5	697.5	706.0	716.4	714.6	687.2
2007	701.7	708.3	713.5	713.4	717.5	689.4	616.1	680.8	719.1	719.8	727.2	725.9	702.7
2008	717.0	724.7	730.0	731.7	736.3	708.4	629.6	695.5	740.6	742.3	747.2	745.2	720.7
2009	732.5	736.4	741.6	745.3	744.8	713.7	634.4	697.3	737.3	732.6	735.9	733.5	723.8
2010	723.3	729.1	735.2	740.8	759.1	717.8	629.8	689.5	720.5	733.0	737.8	734.2	720.8
2011	723.1	729.5	734.0	735.4	735.2	699.7	620.1	682.4	712.8	726.2	732.4	726.6	713.1
2012	719.1	727.0	730.4	731.4	734.5	689.1	610.9	684.0	718.0	734.3	740.5	734.3	712.8
2013	724.9	733.9	737.3	736.9	736.6	691.5	615.7	683.5	720.2	736.8	739.1	735.6	716.0
2014	722.9	727.9	731.1	736.2	737.7	699.7	618.9	682.7	716.8	733.8	739.8	732.9	715.0
2015	728.2	734.0	736.2	740.3	740.8	707.9	628.6	687.6	722.3	739.1	744.9	738.7	720.7

2. Average Weekly Hours by Selected Industry: North Carolina, 2011–2015

(Not seasonally adjusted)

Industry and year	January	February	March	April	May	June	July	August	September	October	November	December	Annual average
Total Private													
2011	33.8	34.1	34.1	34.4	34.6	34.3	34.3	34.2	34.2	34.6	34.3	34.4	34.3
2012	34.4	34.3	34.4	34.7	34.3	34.4	34.5	34.3	34.9	34.4	34.5	34.9	34.5
2013	34.0	34.4	34.5	34.4	34.3	34.9	34.2	34.6	35.0	34.4	34.6	34.7	34.5
2014	34.0	33.3	35.2	34.8	34.7	35.2	34.7	34.9	34.7	34.6	35.1	34.7	34.7
2015	34.2	34.5	34.9	34.4	34.5	34.5	34.5	35.0	34.3	34.6	34.6	34.4	34.5
Goods-Producing													
2011	39.2	38.8	39.2	39.8	39.9	40.1	39.8	39.7	39.8	40.0	40.1	40.3	39.7
2012	39.8	39.8	40.2	40.6	40.0	40.0	39.6	39.8	40.3	39.7	40.0	40.2	40.0
2013	39.4	39.5	39.9	39.9	39.9	40.4	39.8	40.7	41.0	40.1	40.8	40.7	40.2
2014	40.0	38.8	42.8	42.3	42.0	42.7	41.7	42.1	41.9	41.6	42.2	41.9	41.7
2015	40.2	40.5	41.3	40.6	41.1	40.9	40.9	41.3	40.3	41.0	40.5	41.2	40.8
Construction													
2011	37.8	38.0	38.2	39.7	39.4	39.4	39.6	39.1	39.0	38.8	38.9	39.1	38.9
2012	37.4	38.0	38.8	39.1	38.8	38.8	38.4	38.5	39.0	38.3	38.6	38.6	38.5
2013	37.8	37.3	38.7	38.9	38.9	39.0	38.7	39.8	40.1	38.9	39.8	38.4	38.9
2014	38.5	35.4	41.2	40.0	40.7	41.3	40.8	40.9	40.0	40.2	40.7	40.6	40.1
2015	37.2	39.0	40.3	39.3	40.9	41.1	41.1	41.4	39.6	40.6	39.4	41.2	40.1
Manufacturing													
2011	40.5	40.3	40.6	40.7	40.9	41.1	40.6	40.5	40.6	40.9	40.9	41.0	40.7
2012	41.0	40.7	40.9	41.3	40.5	40.5	40.0	40.3	40.9	40.4	40.7	41.0	40.7
2013	40.2	40.5	40.5	40.5	40.4	41.1	40.4	41.2	41.5	40.7	41.3	41.8	40.8
2014	40.8	40.3	43.5	43.4	42.7	43.4	42.2	42.8	42.9	42.4	43.0	42.6	42.5
2015	41.7	41.3	41.8	41.3	41.3	40.9	40.8	41.3	40.7	41.1	40.9	41.0	41.2
Trade, Transportation, and Utilities													
2011	34.8	35.3	35.1	35.1	35.1	34.8	34.7	34.6	34.8	34.8	34.2	34.5	34.8
2012	34.3	34.7	34.7	35.1	34.7	34.7	35.0	34.7	35.3	34.8	34.8	34.8	34.8
2013	34.0	34.5	34.7	34.6	34.5	35.0	34.7	34.8	35.1	34.5	34.4	34.7	34.6
2014	33.9	33.1	34.8	34.5	34.4	34.7	34.4	34.3	34.2	34.1	34.2	34.3	34.2
2015	33.8	34.2	34.4	34.3	34.5	34.4	34.6	35.1	34.7	34.6	34.4	34.3	34.4
Information													
2011	36.0	36.0	36.4	35.9	36.7	36.5	36.8	36.5	36.9	37.9	37.0	36.7	36.6
2012	37.5	37.0	36.8	37.0	36.6	36.5	37.2	36.5	37.3	36.6	37.2	37.6	37.0
2013	36.1	36.3	36.1	36.5	37.1	38.9	36.5	36.7	36.8	35.7	36.9	37.2	36.7
2014	36.2	37.0	37.5	36.7	36.4	37.3	35.1	36.5	35.5	35.6	36.9	35.6	36.4
2015	35.4	36.4	36.3	35.7	35.7	36.3	36.1	36.9	36.2	35.9	36.9	35.1	36.1
Financial Activities													
2011	37.4	37.9	37.3	37.4	37.9	37.2	37.4	36.8	37.1	39.0	37.7	37.7	37.6
2012	38.4	37.4	37.4	37.5	36.4	36.7	37.3	36.4	37.8	36.7	36.9	37.9	37.2
2013	36.1	37.0	36.5	36.5	36.6	37.6	36.0	36.1	36.9	36.0	36.2	36.7	36.5
2014	36.4	36.8	36.9	36.2	36.2	37.1	36.2	36.2	36.3	36.8	37.8	36.7	36.6
2015	37.1	38.3	38.5	37.5	37.6	37.6	37.6	38.3	37.5	37.8	38.9	38.1	37.9
Professional and Business Services													
2011	33.5	34.1	34.1	35.3	36.1	35.6	35.3	35.5	35.4	36.1	35.7	35.9	35.2
2012	35.5	35.4	35.5	36.2	35.7	36.2	36.1	36.0	36.5	35.8	36.0	36.9	36.0
2013	35.7	36.2	36.1	36.2	36.4	36.9	35.8	36.6	37.2	36.4	36.5	36.5	36.4
2014	35.4	35.2	36.8	36.4	36.4	37.1	36.4	36.7	36.2	36.4	37.1	36.1	36.4
2015	35.7	36.3	36.7	36.0	36.0	36.2	35.8	36.7	35.4	36.2	36.6	35.7	36.1
Education and Health Services													
2011	32.0	32.3	32.2	32.3	32.7	32.2	32.2	32.1	32.1	32.4	32.2	32.3	32.3
2012	32.8	32.3	32.5	32.8	32.5	32.7	33.1	32.9	33.4	33.0	33.0	33.2	32.8
2013	32.9	33.0	32.8	32.8	32.7	33.4	32.7	32.7	33.2	32.8	32.8	33.0	32.9
2014	32.5	31.9	32.8	32.6	32.6	32.9	32.6	32.8	32.9	32.5	33.0	32.5	32.6
2015	32.5	32.3	32.6	32.2	32.3	32.3	32.1	32.5	32.1	32.2	32.4	32.2	32.3
Leisure and Hospitality													
2011	25.1	26.0	25.9	26.1	25.9	25.7	26.0	25.9	25.2	25.8	25.4	25.1	25.7
2012	25.1	25.5	25.5	25.5	25.6	25.6	25.9	25.7	25.4	25.4	25.1	25.4	25.5
2013	24.5	25.5	25.9	25.8	25.6	25.9	25.8	25.7	25.7	25.7	25.7	25.6	25.6
2014	25.0	24.2	26.0	25.9	25.7	26.2	26.2	26.6	26.0	26.0	26.0	26.0	25.8
2015	25.4	25.8	26.1	26.0	25.9	26.1	26.2	26.5	25.6	25.6	25.7	25.6	25.9
Other Services													
2011	29.6	30.7	30.5	30.6	30.9	30.6	31.3	31.3	31.3	31.1	32.0	31.8	31.0
2012	31.5	31.0	31.1	31.5	31.1	30.8	31.0	30.4	31.3	31.0	31.7	32.1	31.2
2013	30.9	31.1	31.3	30.7	30.3	31.3	30.5	30.8	31.9	30.9	31.4	30.8	31.0
2014	30.2	28.8	30.9	30.9	31.1	31.1	31.3	31.3	30.7	30.9	32.0	31.3	30.9
2015	31.1	31.3	31.9	30.7	31.2	30.8	31.2	31.4	30.8	30.6	30.6	29.9	31.0

3. Average Hourly Earnings by Selected Industry: North Carolina, 2011–2015

(Dollars, not seasonally adjusted)

Industry and year	January	February	March	April	May	June	July	August	September	October	November	December	Annual average
Total Private													
2011	20.86	20.76	20.57	20.68	20.78	20.61	20.79	20.78	21.11	21.39	21.28	21.35	20.91
2012	21.64	21.63	21.53	21.78	21.50	21.67	21.74	21.56	21.90	21.65	21.78	22.10	21.71
2013	21.93	21.85	21.75	21.63	21.55	21.67	21.52	21.51	21.68	21.55	21.65	21.85	21.68
2014	21.81	22.46	22.16	21.69	21.62	21.71	21.60	21.63	21.84	21.77	22.10	21.82	21.85
2015	22.04	22.35	22.03	22.04	22.10	22.03	22.13	22.54	22.35	22.49	22.84	22.65	22.30
Goods-Producing													
2011	20.16	20.33	20.04	20.13	20.28	20.14	20.22	20.09	20.32	20.46	20.52	20.65	20.28
2012	20.68	20.65	20.62	20.58	20.42	20.41	20.66	20.39	20.66	20.58	20.91	21.05	20.63
2013	21.06	20.91	20.96	20.98	20.85	20.79	20.88	20.76	20.81	20.81	20.90	21.15	20.90
2014	20.86	21.34	20.82	20.62	20.72	20.83	21.07	20.95	21.21	21.17	21.24	21.22	21.00
2015	21.56	21.55	21.36	21.50	21.49	21.38	21.26	21.43	21.42	21.46	21.70	21.84	21.50
Construction													
2011	20.17	20.36	20.36	20.31	20.43	20.11	20.14	20.03	20.05	20.55	20.77	20.66	20.33
2012	20.49	20.56	20.46	20.23	20.29	20.25	20.63	20.30	20.53	20.39	20.84	21.10	20.50
2013	21.14	21.05	20.89	20.66	20.70	20.50	20.35	20.59	20.59	20.85	20.64	21.08	20.75
2014	20.66	21.65	20.94	20.81	20.68	20.84	21.13	20.96	21.29	21.38	21.24	21.47	21.09
2015	22.33	21.80	21.71	22.02	21.73	21.90	21.69	21.92	22.23	22.48	22.74	22.77	22.11
Manufacturing													
2011	20.40	20.23	19.83	19.98	20.15	20.08	20.17	20.05	20.38	20.40	20.40	20.62	20.22
2012	20.74	20.65	20.64	20.68	20.43	20.42	20.61	20.36	20.63	20.58	20.86	20.96	20.63
2013	20.97	20.79	20.92	21.04	20.85	20.84	21.03	20.80	20.87	20.79	20.96	21.14	20.92
2014	20.90	21.24	20.81	20.57	20.77	20.85	21.07	20.95	21.22	21.09	21.28	21.13	20.99
2015	21.25	21.44	21.19	21.27	21.35	21.09	21.01	21.15	20.97	20.89	21.14	21.31	21.17
Trade, Transportation, and Utilities													
2011	19.51	19.46	19.14	19.60	19.47	19.46	19.54	19.42	19.67	20.00	19.87	19.71	19.57
2012	20.30	20.47	20.40	20.63	20.36	20.75	20.69	20.70	20.91	20.70	20.70	21.06	20.64
2013	20.92	20.70	20.72	20.70	20.54	20.82	20.82	20.71	21.07	20.90	20.85	20.96	20.81
2014	21.29	21.57	21.96	21.01	20.95	21.07	20.73	20.78	21.13	20.46	20.72	20.43	21.00
2015	20.66	21.08	20.45	20.56	20.36	20.64	20.64	21.03	21.15	21.47	21.28	20.98	20.86
Information													
2011	28.55	29.08	28.19	28.86	28.96	28.53	29.79	29.29	29.82	30.39	30.66	30.29	29.38
2012	31.21	30.52	29.94	31.34	30.95	31.47	31.60	30.72	32.50	30.92	30.50	31.47	31.10
2013	31.20	30.99	31.25	30.93	30.37	31.53	30.73	31.00	31.72	31.29	32.08	31.92	31.26
2014	31.85	33.95	32.05	31.18	31.82	32.15	32.40	32.36	33.26	33.28	34.96	33.91	32.77
2015	34.11	36.40	35.36	35.71	35.55	35.07	34.93	35.93	35.65	36.13	37.15	36.77	35.74
Financial Activities													
2011	26.19	26.34	26.01	25.90	25.75	25.19	25.69	26.50	26.84	26.79	26.83	26.91	26.25
2012	27.41	27.51	27.33	27.96	27.78	27.53	27.83	27.85	28.11	28.05	27.96	27.84	27.76
2013	27.73	28.29	27.77	27.46	28.17	28.19	28.02	28.10	27.62	27.27	27.56	27.75	27.83
2014	27.41	27.99	27.33	26.26	26.56	27.25	26.76	27.34	27.77	28.30	27.68	27.03	27.31
2015	27.14	27.56	28.88	28.23	28.88	28.66	29.24	30.33	29.66	29.93	30.87	30.11	29.14
Professional and Business Services													
2011	27.69	26.88	26.48	26.11	26.56	26.06	26.52	26.27	26.45	26.73	26.33	26.45	26.53
2012	26.67	26.70	26.42	26.89	26.43	26.56	26.85	26.27	26.66	25.76	26.00	26.68	26.49
2013	26.32	26.35	26.30	25.84	25.54	25.90	25.44	25.29	25.68	25.24	25.54	26.01	25.78
2014	25.78	27.25	27.15	26.53	26.01	26.27	26.00	25.78	26.08	26.10	26.74	26.44	26.34
2015	26.54	27.08	26.45	26.43	26.49	26.17	26.72	27.13	26.87	26.58	27.47	27.26	26.77
Education and Health Services													
2011	20.01	19.94	20.40	20.44	20.35	20.52	20.56	20.67	21.08	21.49	21.42	21.47	20.70
2012	21.69	21.71	21.75	22.06	21.89	22.18	22.13	22.11	22.28	22.21	22.34	22.47	22.07
2013	22.08	22.00	21.88	21.89	21.94	21.89	21.88	21.98	21.94	22.05	22.05	22.06	21.97
2014	22.10	22.42	22.12	22.33	22.31	22.02	22.17	22.32	21.66	21.81	22.45	22.22	22.16
2015	22.27	22.50	22.08	22.33	22.77	22.75	22.88	23.25	22.27	22.50	22.74	22.58	22.58
Leisure and Hospitality													
2011	11.24	11.39	11.54	11.64	11.85	11.90	11.96	12.19	12.43	12.61	12.56	12.93	12.03
2012	12.75	12.67	12.75	12.68	12.73	12.85	12.63	12.69	12.97	12.98	13.10	13.21	12.83
2013	13.02	12.96	12.80	12.70	12.68	12.62	12.50	12.54	12.52	12.56	12.57	12.60	12.67
2014	12.56	12.63	12.50	12.40	12.34	12.27	12.18	12.30	12.58	12.55	12.62	12.65	12.46
2015	12.63	12.43	12.33	12.38	12.43	12.34	12.23	12.38	12.44	12.63	12.64	12.88	12.47
Other Services													
2011	16.64	16.30	16.15	16.39	16.95	16.47	16.45	16.53	16.90	16.83	16.58	16.84	16.59
2012	17.09	16.99	17.08	17.44	17.11	17.26	17.14	16.95	17.25	17.63	17.25	17.71	17.25
2013	18.17	17.96	17.90	18.07	17.97	18.03	17.91	18.15	18.10	18.17	17.82	18.12	18.03
2014	17.90	18.49	17.89	17.57	17.76	17.85	17.65	17.75	18.26	18.45	18.56	17.93	18.00
2015	18.52	18.71	18.76	18.52	18.89	18.79	18.75	19.10	19.08	18.88	19.50	19.40	18.91

4. Average Weekly Earnings by Selected Industry: North Carolina, 2011–2015

(Dollars, not seasonally adjusted)

Industry and year	January	February	March	April	May	June	July	August	September	October	November	December	Annual average
Total Private													
2011	705.07	707.92	701.44	711.39	718.99	706.92	713.10	710.68	721.96	740.09	729.90	734.44	717.21
2012	744.42	741.91	740.63	755.77	737.45	745.45	750.03	739.51	764.31	744.76	751.41	771.29	749.00
2013	745.62	751.64	750.38	744.07	739.17	756.28	735.98	744.25	758.80	741.32	749.09	758.20	747.96
2014	741.54	747.92	780.03	754.81	750.21	764.19	749.52	754.89	757.85	753.24	775.71	757.15	758.20
2015	753.77	771.08	768.85	758.18	762.45	760.04	763.49	788.90	766.61	778.15	790.26	779.16	769.35
Goods-Producing													
2011	790.27	788.80	785.57	801.17	809.17	807.61	804.76	797.57	808.74	818.40	822.85	832.20	805.12
2012	823.06	821.87	828.92	835.55	816.80	816.40	818.14	811.52	832.60	817.03	836.40	846.21	825.20
2013	829.76	825.95	836.30	837.10	831.92	839.92	831.02	844.93	853.21	834.48	852.72	860.81	840.18
2014	834.40	827.99	891.10	872.23	870.24	889.44	878.62	882.00	888.70	880.67	896.33	889.12	875.70
2015	866.71	872.78	882.17	872.90	883.24	874.44	869.53	885.06	863.23	879.86	878.85	899.81	877.20
Construction													
2011	762.43	773.68	777.75	806.31	804.94	792.33	797.54	783.17	781.95	797.34	807.95	807.81	790.84
2012	766.33	781.28	793.85	790.99	787.25	785.70	792.19	781.55	800.67	780.94	804.42	814.46	789.25
2013	799.09	785.17	808.44	803.67	805.23	799.50	787.55	819.48	825.66	811.07	821.47	809.47	807.18
2014	795.41	766.41	862.73	832.40	841.68	860.69	862.10	857.26	851.60	859.48	864.47	871.68	845.71
2015	830.68	850.20	874.91	865.39	888.76	900.09	891.46	907.49	880.31	912.69	895.96	938.12	886.61
Manufacturing													
2011	826.20	815.27	805.10	813.19	824.14	825.29	818.90	812.03	827.43	834.36	834.36	845.42	822.95
2012	850.34	840.46	844.18	854.08	827.42	827.01	824.40	820.51	843.77	831.43	849.00	859.36	839.64
2013	842.99	842.00	847.26	852.12	842.34	856.52	849.61	856.96	866.11	846.15	865.65	883.65	853.54
2014	852.72	855.97	905.24	892.74	886.88	904.89	889.15	896.66	910.34	894.22	915.04	900.14	892.08
2015	886.13	885.47	885.74	878.45	881.76	862.58	857.21	873.50	853.48	858.58	864.63	873.71	872.20
Trade, Transportation, and Utilities													
2011	678.95	686.94	671.81	687.96	683.40	677.21	678.04	671.93	684.52	696.00	679.55	680.00	681.04
2012	696.29	710.31	707.88	724.11	706.49	720.03	724.15	718.29	738.12	720.36	720.36	732.89	718.27
2013	711.28	714.15	718.98	716.22	708.63	728.70	722.45	720.71	739.56	721.05	717.24	727.31	720.03
2014	721.73	713.97	764.21	724.85	720.68	731.13	713.11	712.75	722.65	697.69	708.62	700.75	718.20
2015	698.31	720.94	703.48	705.21	702.42	710.02	714.14	738.15	733.91	742.86	732.03	719.61	717.58
Information													
2011	1,027.80	1,046.88	1,026.12	1,036.07	1,062.83	1,041.35	1,096.27	1,069.09	1,100.36	1,151.78	1,134.42	1,111.64	1,075.31
2012	1,170.38	1,129.24	1,101.79	1,159.58	1,132.77	1,148.66	1,175.52	1,121.28	1,212.25	1,131.67	1,134.60	1,183.27	1,150.70
2013	1,126.32	1,124.94	1,128.13	1,128.95	1,126.73	1,226.52	1,121.65	1,137.70	1,167.30	1,117.05	1,183.75	1,187.42	1,147.24
2014	1,152.97	1,256.15	1,201.88	1,144.31	1,158.25	1,199.20	1,137.24	1,181.14	1,180.73	1,184.77	1,290.02	1,207.20	1,192.83
2015	1,207.49	1,324.96	1,283.57	1,274.85	1,269.14	1,273.04	1,260.97	1,325.82	1,290.53	1,297.07	1,370.84	1,290.63	1,290.21
Financial Activities													
2011	979.51	998.29	970.17	968.66	975.93	937.07	960.81	975.20	995.76	1,044.81	1,011.49	1,014.51	987.00
2012	1,052.54	1,028.87	1,022.14	1,048.50	1,011.19	1,010.35	1,038.06	1,013.74	1,062.56	1,029.44	1,031.72	1,055.14	1,032.67
2013	1,001.05	1,046.73	1,013.61	1,002.29	1,031.02	1,059.94	1,008.72	1,014.41	1,019.18	981.72	997.67	1,018.43	1,015.80
2014	997.72	1,030.03	1,008.48	950.61	961.47	1,010.98	968.71	989.71	1,008.05	1,041.44	1,046.30	992.00	999.55
2015	1,006.89	1,055.55	1,111.88	1,058.63	1,085.89	1,077.62	1,099.42	1,161.64	1,112.25	1,131.35	1,200.84	1,147.19	1,104.41
Professional and Business Services													
2011	927.62	916.61	902.97	921.68	958.82	927.74	936.16	932.59	936.33	964.95	939.98	949.56	933.86
2012	946.79	945.18	937.91	973.42	943.55	961.47	969.29	945.72	973.09	922.21	936.00	984.49	953.64
2013	939.62	953.87	949.43	935.41	929.66	955.71	910.75	925.61	955.30	918.74	932.21	949.37	938.39
2014	912.61	959.20	999.12	965.69	946.76	974.62	946.40	946.13	944.10	950.04	992.05	954.48	958.78
2015	947.48	983.00	970.72	951.48	953.64	947.35	956.58	995.67	951.20	962.20	1005.40	973.18	966.40
Education and Health Services													
2011	640.32	644.06	656.88	660.21	665.45	660.74	662.03	663.51	676.67	696.28	689.72	693.48	668.61
2012	711.43	701.23	706.88	723.57	711.43	725.29	732.50	727.42	744.15	732.93	737.22	746.00	723.90
2013	726.43	726.00	717.66	717.99	717.44	731.13	715.48	718.75	728.41	723.24	723.24	727.98	722.81
2014	718.25	715.20	725.54	727.96	727.31	724.46	722.74	732.10	712.61	708.83	740.85	722.15	722.42
2015	723.78	726.75	719.81	719.03	735.47	734.83	734.45	755.63	714.87	724.50	736.78	727.08	729.33
Leisure and Hospitality													
2011	282.12	296.14	298.89	303.80	306.92	305.83	310.96	315.72	313.24	325.34	319.02	324.54	309.17
2012	320.03	323.09	325.13	323.34	325.89	328.96	327.12	326.13	329.44	329.69	328.81	335.53	327.17
2013	318.99	330.48	331.52	327.66	324.61	326.86	322.50	322.28	321.76	322.79	323.05	322.56	324.35
2014	314.00	305.65	325.00	321.16	317.14	321.47	319.12	327.18	327.08	326.30	328.12	328.90	321.47
2015	320.80	320.69	321.81	321.88	321.94	322.07	320.43	328.07	318.46	323.33	324.85	329.73	322.97
Other Services													
2011	492.54	500.41	492.58	501.53	523.76	503.98	514.89	517.39	528.97	523.41	530.56	535.51	514.29
2012	538.34	526.69	531.19	549.36	532.12	531.61	531.34	515.28	539.93	546.53	546.83	568.49	538.20
2013	561.45	558.56	560.27	554.75	544.49	564.34	546.26	559.02	577.39	561.45	559.55	558.10	558.93
2014	540.58	532.51	552.80	542.91	552.34	555.14	552.45	555.58	560.58	570.11	593.92	561.21	556.20
2015	575.97	585.62	598.44	568.56	589.37	578.73	585.00	599.74	587.66	577.73	596.70	580.06	586.21

NORTH DAKOTA
At a Glance

Population:
  2005 estimate: 646,089
  2010 census: 672,591
  2015 estimate: 756,927

Percent change in population:
  2005–2015: 17.2%
  2010–2015: 12.5%

Percent change in total nonfarm employment:
  2005–2015: 31.7%

Industry with the largest growth in employment, 2005–2015 (thousands):
  Transportation and Utilities, 13.1

Industry with the largest decline or smallest growth in employment, 2005–2015 (thousands):
  Manufacturing, –0.4

Civilian labor force:
  2005: 355,545
  2010: 378,342
  2015: 414,344

Unemployment rate and rank among states (highest to lowest):
  2005: 3.4%, 50th
  2010: 3.8%, 51st
  2015: 2.7%, 51st

Over-the-year change in unemployment rates:
  2012–2013: –0.2%
  2013–2014: –0.2%
  2014–2015: 0.0%

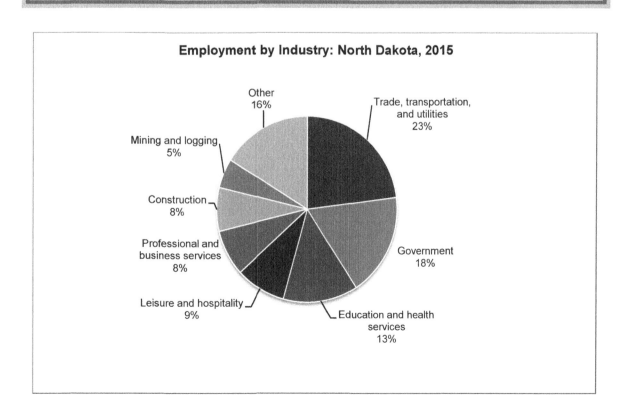

Employment by Industry: North Dakota, 2015

- Other 16%
- Trade, transportation, and utilities 23%
- Mining and logging 5%
- Construction 8%
- Professional and business services 8%
- Government 18%
- Leisure and hospitality 9%
- Education and health services 13%

1. Employment by Industry: North Dakota, 2005–2015

(Numbers in thousands, not seasonally adjusted)

Industry and year	January	February	March	April	May	June	July	August	September	October	November	December	Annual average
Total Nonfarm													
2005	333.4	336.1	338.3	345.7	349.7	348.3	339.5	342.3	351.4	350.7	350.5	350.8	344.7
2006	341.1	343.7	347.0	352.2	357.0	356.2	345.6	349.1	358.6	358.8	358.3	359.0	352.2
2007	348.5	349.6	352.6	356.2	362.7	362.7	352.9	354.2	364.2	365.8	365.8	365.6	358.4
2008	356.9	359.0	361.6	365.9	371.8	371.2	363.0	364.0	373.7	374.9	373.6	372.1	367.3
2009	358.7	359.8	360.5	362.9	370.7	372.0	361.8	362.4	372.6	374.2	372.6	372.1	366.7
2010	360.1	362.6	365.9	374.2	379.0	379.8	371.2	373.1	383.0	388.3	387.4	387.5	376.0
2011	377.5	379.1	382.7	389.2	396.0	397.8	391.8	395.4	408.2	412.1	413.6	415.2	396.6
2012	408.2	411.4	416.3	424.2	432.2	436.0	428.9	430.7	439.3	441.9	439.1	439.2	429.0
2013	428.0	431.1	433.5	436.4	446.7	449.9	441.9	444.4	454.0	456.9	457.2	453.1	444.4
2014	441.3	445.1	447.6	453.9	463.2	466.8	462.0	463.2	470.5	475.1	473.9	471.6	461.2
2015	455.7	455.2	453.6	455.3	459.6	458.6	450.5	448.3	452.9	456.3	453.2	446.6	453.8
Total Private													
2005	257.8	258.4	260.4	267.3	271.6	275.2	275.5	276.2	274.7	273.1	272.8	272.8	269.7
2006	264.9	266.0	268.8	273.7	278.6	282.5	281.4	282.8	281.7	280.3	279.8	280.1	276.7
2007	272.0	271.8	274.6	277.8	284.2	288.0	287.7	287.9	287.2	287.5	287.1	286.8	282.7
2008	279.9	280.6	283.4	287.4	292.5	296.4	296.9	297.0	296.0	295.6	294.3	292.5	291.0
2009	281.2	281.1	281.4	283.2	290.0	294.0	293.5	293.3	293.2	292.9	291.3	290.3	288.8
2010	280.7	281.6	284.0	292.1	296.1	299.8	301.0	302.5	302.5	306.1	305.2	305.1	296.4
2011	297.3	297.7	301.2	307.7	314.2	318.4	322.5	325.7	328.2	330.6	332.3	333.3	317.4
2012	328.5	330.4	335.0	342.7	350.5	356.6	358.6	360.7	358.6	359.5	356.7	356.7	349.5
2013	347.5	349.4	351.8	354.7	364.4	369.5	371.0	373.6	373.1	374.6	374.9	370.4	364.6
2014	361.3	363.3	365.7	372.3	380.9	386.7	388.3	389.9	389.7	393.1	392.0	389.2	381.0
2015	375.8	373.7	371.3	372.6	376.2	377.5	375.8	374.0	371.3	372.0	368.6	361.3	372.5
Goods-Producing													
2005	42.0	42.3	43.2	45.8	48.2	50.1	51.1	51.2	50.4	49.6	48.8	47.3	47.5
2006	44.4	44.4	45.1	48.0	50.1	52.0	52.4	52.7	52.0	50.9	50.1	49.0	49.3
2007	45.9	45.3	46.4	48.2	50.9	52.9	53.7	53.6	53.2	53.1	52.1	50.4	50.5
2008	48.1	48.3	49.6	51.4	54.3	57.0	58.0	58.0	57.7	57.1	55.3	53.0	54.0
2009	47.6	47.7	47.7	48.5	51.2	53.7	54.6	54.9	54.7	54.1	52.4	50.2	51.4
2010	46.6	47.1	48.1	52.0	54.7	56.3	58.0	59.0	59.4	60.2	59.2	58.0	54.9
2011	54.9	55.0	56.5	59.9	63.4	66.0	68.7	70.4	71.6	72.8	72.8	71.4	65.3
2012	69.4	70.5	72.6	76.7	80.4	83.6	85.3	86.0	85.0	84.5	81.3	79.6	79.6
2013	76.2	76.6	77.5	79.2	84.7	87.9	88.9	90.3	89.6	89.6	88.7	84.7	84.5
2014	80.5	81.1	82.1	86.1	90.7	94.5	96.0	97.3	97.1	98.2	96.9	93.6	91.2
2015	88.1	85.3	83.2	83.4	85.0	85.8	85.2	85.0	83.3	81.9	78.2	73.5	83.2
Service-Providing													
2005	291.4	293.8	295.1	299.9	301.5	298.2	288.4	291.1	301.0	301.1	301.7	303.5	297.2
2006	296.7	299.3	301.9	304.2	306.9	304.2	293.2	296.4	306.6	307.9	308.2	310.0	303.0
2007	302.6	304.3	306.2	308.0	311.8	309.8	299.2	300.6	311.0	312.7	313.7	315.2	307.9
2008	308.8	310.7	312.0	314.5	317.5	314.2	305.0	306.0	316.0	317.8	318.3	319.1	313.3
2009	311.1	312.1	312.8	314.4	319.5	318.3	307.2	307.5	317.9	320.1	320.2	321.9	315.3
2010	313.5	315.5	317.8	322.2	324.3	323.5	313.2	314.1	323.6	328.1	328.2	329.5	321.1
2011	322.6	324.1	326.2	329.3	332.6	331.8	323.1	325.0	336.6	339.3	340.8	343.8	331.3
2012	338.8	340.9	343.7	347.5	351.8	352.4	343.6	344.7	354.3	357.4	357.8	359.6	349.4
2013	351.8	354.5	356.0	357.2	362.0	362.0	353.0	354.1	364.4	367.3	368.5	368.4	359.9
2014	360.8	364.0	365.5	367.8	372.5	372.3	366.0	365.9	373.4	376.9	377.0	378.0	370.0
2015	367.6	369.9	370.4	371.9	374.6	372.8	365.3	363.3	369.6	374.4	375.0	373.1	370.7
Mining and Logging													
2005	3.6	3.7	3.7	3.9	4.1	4.2	4.3	4.5	4.4	4.3	4.4	4.4	4.1
2006	4.1	4.3	4.3	4.6	4.8	4.7	4.7	4.9	5.0	5.1	5.1	5.0	4.7
2007	4.8	4.7	4.8	4.9	5.1	5.2	5.3	5.3	5.3	5.3	5.3	5.5	5.1
2008	5.4	5.6	5.9	6.2	6.5	6.8	6.9	7.3	7.5	7.8	8.0	7.9	6.8
2009	7.4	7.2	7.1	6.7	6.8	6.9	6.7	6.7	6.8	6.9	7.1	7.4	7.0
2010	7.6	8.3	8.8	9.4	10.0	10.6	11.2	11.7	12.1	12.5	12.7	13.2	10.7
2011	13.5	14.0	14.5	15.2	15.9	16.3	17.1	17.7	18.3	19.0	20.2	21.0	16.9
2012	21.3	22.2	23.2	23.9	24.6	25.4	26.1	26.1	25.6	25.2	24.9	24.8	24.4
2013	24.6	25.1	25.5	25.5	26.0	26.4	26.3	26.6	26.6	26.9	27.6	27.4	26.2
2014	27.5	28.0	28.3	28.9	29.4	30.0	30.3	30.9	31.2	31.8	32.0	32.0	30.0
2015	30.5	28.6	26.8	24.8	23.6	23.0	22.1	21.7	20.8	19.7	19.5	18.8	23.3

1. Employment by Industry: North Dakota, 2005–2015—*Continued*

(Numbers in thousands, not seasonally adjusted)

Industry and year	January	February	March	April	May	June	July	August	September	October	November	December	Annual average
Construction													
2005	13.6	13.6	14.1	16.3	18.2	19.5	20.4	20.3	19.7	19.0	18.1	16.6	17.5
2006	14.8	14.7	15.2	17.6	19.4	20.9	21.0	21.2	20.6	20.2	18.8	17.6	18.5
2007	15.6	15.3	16.1	17.7	19.9	21.2	21.8	22.0	21.6	21.4	20.4	18.6	19.3
2008	16.7	16.6	17.5	18.9	21.4	23.3	24.3	24.2	23.7	22.7	21.0	19.3	20.8
2009	16.7	16.3	16.5	17.9	20.8	23.2	24.4	24.8	24.6	23.9	22.2	20.0	20.9
2010	17.2	16.9	17.4	20.4	22.4	23.1	24.1	24.6	24.2	24.4	23.2	21.5	21.6
2011	18.5	18.1	18.9	21.1	23.8	25.7	27.6	28.8	29.2	29.4	28.1	25.8	24.6
2012	23.7	23.7	24.5	27.9	30.6	32.6	33.6	34.1	33.7	33.6	31.1	29.8	29.9
2013	27.1	26.9	27.3	28.8	33.1	35.6	36.7	37.8	37.2	36.6	35.3	31.7	32.8
2014	27.7	27.8	28.4	31.5	35.4	38.2	39.3	40.0	39.6	40.1	38.6	35.6	35.2
2015	32.2	31.4	31.1	33.2	35.7	37.1	37.7	37.7	36.9	36.5	33.3	29.7	34.4
Manufacturing													
2005	24.8	25.0	25.4	25.6	25.9	26.4	26.4	26.4	26.3	26.3	26.3	26.3	25.9
2006	25.5	25.4	25.6	25.8	25.9	26.4	26.7	26.6	26.4	25.6	26.2	26.4	26.0
2007	25.5	25.3	25.5	25.6	25.9	26.5	26.6	26.3	26.3	26.4	26.4	26.3	26.1
2008	26.0	26.1	26.2	26.3	26.4	26.9	26.8	26.5	26.5	26.6	26.3	25.8	26.4
2009	23.5	24.2	24.1	23.9	23.6	23.6	23.5	23.4	23.3	23.3	23.1	22.8	23.5
2010	21.8	21.9	21.9	22.2	22.3	22.6	22.7	22.7	23.1	23.3	23.3	23.3	22.6
2011	22.9	22.9	23.1	23.6	23.7	24.0	24.0	23.9	24.1	24.4	24.5	24.6	23.8
2012	24.4	24.6	24.9	24.9	25.2	25.6	25.6	25.8	25.7	25.7	25.3	25.0	25.2
2013	24.5	24.6	24.7	24.9	25.6	25.9	25.9	25.9	25.8	26.1	25.8	25.6	25.4
2014	25.3	25.3	25.4	25.7	25.9	26.3	26.4	26.4	26.3	26.3	26.3	26.0	26.0
2015	25.4	25.3	25.3	25.4	25.7	25.7	25.4	25.6	25.6	25.7	25.4	25.0	25.5
Trade, Transportation, and Utilities													
2005	72.3	72.3	72.8	74.3	75.0	74.9	74.4	74.2	74.4	74.8	75.7	76.5	74.3
2006	74.0	73.9	74.6	76.0	76.9	76.9	76.1	76.3	76.2	76.4	77.4	78.0	76.1
2007	75.4	75.0	75.1	75.9	77.0	76.8	76.7	76.4	76.2	77.1	78.3	78.9	76.6
2008	76.6	76.3	76.7	77.4	78.1	78.0	78.1	77.9	77.9	78.4	79.3	79.7	77.9
2009	77.0	76.5	76.6	76.9	78.5	78.5	78.2	77.8	77.8	78.7	79.8	80.1	78.0
2010	77.7	77.6	77.8	79.7	80.6	80.9	80.9	81.1	81.0	82.4	83.5	84.2	80.6
2011	82.2	82.2	82.6	84.3	85.7	86.2	86.9	87.6	88.0	89.8	91.8	93.2	86.7
2012	91.8	92.0	93.0	95.0	96.8	97.6	97.9	98.2	97.9	99.2	100.3	100.8	96.7
2013	98.3	98.4	98.7	99.5	101.6	101.9	102.1	102.8	102.8	103.5	104.9	105.4	101.7
2014	102.9	103.2	103.6	104.9	106.4	106.5	106.6	106.6	106.6	107.8	108.8	109.6	106.1
2015	106.0	105.7	105.2	105.3	105.2	104.7	104.1	102.7	102.2	103.1	103.1	101.9	104.1
Wholesale Trade													
2005	18.1	18.1	18.3	19.0	19.3	19.3	19.1	19.0	18.8	19.0	18.9	19.0	18.8
2006	18.6	18.6	18.8	19.3	19.6	19.6	19.2	19.2	19.0	19.1	19.0	19.0	19.1
2007	18.8	18.7	18.9	19.4	19.8	19.8	19.5	19.4	19.2	19.5	19.5	19.4	19.3
2008	19.1	19.2	19.4	19.9	20.3	20.2	20.2	20.1	19.9	20.0	20.0	20.0	19.9
2009	19.7	19.7	19.8	20.0	20.7	20.8	20.5	20.4	20.1	20.3	20.4	20.4	20.2
2010	20.1	20.2	20.3	21.1	21.3	21.4	21.4	21.4	21.3	21.5	21.6	21.8	21.1
2011	21.5	21.5	21.8	22.3	22.9	23.1	22.9	22.8	22.7	23.1	23.3	23.6	22.6
2012	23.5	23.7	24.2	24.9	25.5	25.7	25.6	25.6	25.4	25.5	25.7	25.8	25.1
2013	25.4	25.5	25.7	26.1	27.0	27.1	26.8	26.8	26.4	26.6	26.7	26.8	26.4
2014	26.5	26.5	26.7	27.1	27.5	27.7	27.5	27.5	27.3	27.5	27.6	27.7	27.3
2015	27.3	27.1	27.0	27.4	27.4	27.2	26.8	26.7	26.2	26.3	26.1	25.6	26.8
Retail Trade													
2005	41.1	41.0	41.2	41.9	42.3	42.3	42.1	42.0	42.1	42.3	43.3	43.8	42.1
2006	41.9	41.7	42.1	43.0	43.6	43.6	43.3	43.3	43.3	43.4	44.5	44.9	43.2
2007	42.9	42.5	42.4	42.6	43.1	43.1	43.2	42.9	42.7	43.1	44.2	44.8	43.1
2008	43.0	42.5	42.6	42.8	43.0	43.0	43.2	42.9	42.9	43.1	44.0	44.3	43.1
2009	42.4	41.9	41.9	42.0	42.7	42.7	42.8	42.6	42.7	43.2	44.2	44.4	42.8
2010	42.7	42.4	42.4	42.9	43.4	43.5	43.5	43.4	43.2	44.0	44.9	45.2	43.5
2011	43.5	43.3	43.2	43.9	44.3	44.2	44.6	44.7	44.8	45.5	47.0	47.3	44.7
2012	45.7	45.4	45.4	46.2	46.7	47.0	47.2	47.2	47.2	48.1	49.3	49.7	47.1
2013	48.0	47.8	47.7	47.8	48.5	48.6	48.9	49.3	49.5	49.9	51.0	51.4	49.0
2014	49.6	49.7	49.8	50.1	50.7	50.7	50.7	50.3	50.4	51.1	52.2	52.9	50.7
2015	50.5	50.5	50.5	50.6	50.8	50.8	50.9	50.2	50.3	51.0	51.8	52.0	50.8

1. Employment by Industry: North Dakota, 2005–2015—*Continued*

(Numbers in thousands, not seasonally adjusted)

Industry and year	January	February	March	April	May	June	July	August	September	October	November	December	Annual average
Transportation and Utilities													
2005	13.1	13.2	13.3	13.4	13.4	13.3	13.2	13.2	13.5	13.5	13.5	13.7	13.4
2006	13.5	13.6	13.7	13.7	13.7	13.7	13.6	13.8	13.9	13.9	13.9	14.1	13.8
2007	13.7	13.8	13.8	13.9	14.1	13.9	14.0	14.1	14.3	14.5	14.6	14.7	14.1
2008	14.5	14.6	14.7	14.7	14.8	14.8	14.7	14.9	15.1	15.3	15.3	15.4	14.9
2009	14.9	14.9	14.9	14.9	15.1	15.0	14.9	14.8	15.0	15.2	15.2	15.3	15.0
2010	14.9	15.0	15.1	15.7	15.9	16.0	16.0	16.3	16.5	16.9	17.0	17.2	16.0
2011	17.2	17.4	17.6	18.1	18.5	18.9	19.4	20.1	20.5	21.2	21.5	22.3	19.4
2012	22.6	22.9	23.4	23.9	24.6	24.9	25.1	25.4	25.3	25.6	25.3	25.3	24.5
2013	24.9	25.1	25.3	25.6	26.1	26.2	26.4	26.7	26.9	27.0	27.2	27.2	26.2
2014	26.8	27.0	27.1	27.7	28.2	28.1	28.4	28.8	28.9	29.2	29.0	29.0	28.2
2015	28.2	28.1	27.7	27.3	27.0	26.7	26.4	25.8	25.7	25.8	25.2	24.3	26.5
Information													
2005	7.6	7.6	7.5	7.6	7.6	7.6	7.6	7.6	7.6	7.4	7.4	7.5	7.6
2006	7.4	7.4	7.4	7.4	7.4	7.5	7.5	7.6	7.5	7.5	7.6	7.6	7.5
2007	7.6	7.6	7.6	7.6	7.7	7.6	7.6	7.7	7.5	7.5	7.5	7.5	7.6
2008	7.4	7.4	7.4	7.4	7.5	7.6	7.6	7.6	7.6	7.6	7.6	7.6	7.5
2009	7.7	7.7	7.6	7.5	7.5	7.5	7.5	7.5	7.4	7.3	7.3	7.3	7.5
2010	7.3	7.3	7.3	7.3	7.3	7.4	7.3	7.3	7.2	7.2	7.2	7.2	7.3
2011	7.1	7.1	7.1	7.1	7.1	7.2	7.2	7.2	7.1	7.0	7.1	7.1	7.1
2012	7.0	6.9	6.9	6.9	6.9	7.0	7.0	7.0	6.9	6.9	6.9	6.9	6.9
2013	6.9	6.8	6.7	6.7	6.8	6.9	6.9	6.9	6.8	6.8	6.8	6.8	6.8
2014	6.8	6.8	6.8	6.8	6.9	6.8	6.8	6.9	6.8	6.8	6.7	6.7	6.8
2015	6.6	6.6	6.6	6.6	6.6	6.6	6.6	6.6	6.6	6.5	6.5	6.6	6.6
Financial Activities													
2005	18.6	18.6	18.7	18.7	18.8	18.8	18.9	19.1	18.8	18.9	18.8	19.1	18.8
2006	18.9	19.0	19.1	19.0	19.1	19.3	19.4	19.4	19.3	19.2	19.3	19.6	19.2
2007	19.3	19.4	19.5	19.5	19.8	19.9	20.0	20.0	19.9	20.0	19.9	20.2	19.8
2008	19.9	20.0	20.1	20.1	20.2	20.4	20.5	20.5	20.4	20.5	20.5	20.7	20.3
2009	20.2	20.1	20.1	20.1	20.1	20.2	20.3	20.3	20.1	20.2	20.1	20.5	20.2
2010	20.1	20.1	20.1	20.4	20.5	20.7	20.7	20.8	20.7	20.8	20.8	21.2	20.6
2011	20.8	20.8	20.8	21.0	21.2	21.2	21.3	21.3	21.3	21.3	21.4	21.5	21.2
2012	21.2	21.3	21.4	21.6	21.8	22.0	22.1	22.1	22.0	22.2	22.2	22.5	21.9
2013	22.2	22.3	22.5	22.6	22.8	23.0	23.1	23.2	23.1	23.4	23.5	23.6	22.9
2014	23.5	23.6	23.6	23.8	23.9	24.1	24.2	24.4	24.2	24.6	24.6	24.8	24.1
2015	24.4	24.3	24.4	24.1	24.3	24.2	24.3	24.3	24.1	24.1	24.2	23.9	24.2
Professional and Business Services													
2005	24.5	24.7	24.7	26.4	26.6	27.1	27.4	27.7	27.4	27.3	27.2	27.3	26.5
2006	26.8	27.1	27.5	27.8	28.4	29.1	28.9	28.9	29.1	29.0	28.7	28.6	28.3
2007	28.1	28.3	28.8	29.0	29.5	29.9	29.7	29.9	30.0	29.9	29.7	29.8	29.4
2008	29.3	29.5	29.8	30.3	30.6	31.0	30.8	30.9	30.7	30.4	30.0	29.7	30.3
2009	28.8	28.8	28.7	28.7	29.2	29.7	29.3	29.2	29.8	29.0	28.8	28.5	29.0
2010	27.5	27.8	27.9	28.4	28.1	28.8	28.4	28.6	28.6	29.2	28.8	28.7	28.4
2011	28.0	28.1	28.6	29.2	29.2	29.9	30.8	31.2	31.1	31.0	30.4	30.6	29.8
2012	30.3	30.4	31.0	31.7	32.4	33.3	33.5	34.0	33.7	33.8	33.5	33.4	32.6
2013	32.6	33.2	33.3	33.7	34.1	34.7	35.2	35.2	35.1	35.2	34.9	34.2	34.3
2014	33.9	34.1	34.6	35.4	36.0	37.3	37.7	37.5	37.6	37.8	37.2	36.6	36.3
2015	35.4	35.6	35.3	35.8	36.5	37.3	37.4	37.2	36.9	37.1	36.9	36.1	36.5
Education and Health Services													
2005	48.2	48.2	48.2	48.5	48.4	49.1	48.9	49.0	49.0	49.0	49.1	49.4	48.8
2006	49.1	49.3	49.7	49.6	49.4	50.0	49.8	49.9	49.8	50.0	50.0	50.3	49.7
2007	50.0	50.1	50.3	50.3	50.6	51.2	51.0	51.2	51.3	51.4	51.4	51.7	50.9
2008	51.3	51.6	51.6	52.1	52.1	52.2	52.2	52.1	52.2	52.6	52.5	52.8	52.1
2009	52.3	52.7	52.6	52.8	53.1	53.6	53.2	53.2	53.5	54.2	53.8	54.4	53.3
2010	54.1	54.1	54.5	54.8	54.6	55.1	55.2	55.1	55.1	55.7	55.5	55.7	55.0
2011	55.6	55.6	55.8	56.0	56.1	56.1	56.1	56.1	56.6	56.6	56.8	57.1	56.2
2012	56.8	57.1	57.2	57.3	57.6	57.9	57.6	57.9	58.0	58.1	58.1	58.6	57.7
2013	58.1	58.4	58.6	58.7	58.8	58.5	58.4	58.4	58.9	59.5	59.5	59.6	58.8
2014	59.1	59.3	59.1	59.0	59.1	58.9	58.7	58.9	59.3	59.7	60.1	60.0	59.3
2015	59.5	60.0	60.1	60.3	60.5	60.5	60.3	60.5	60.8	61.8	61.9	61.6	60.7

1. Employment by Industry: North Dakota, 2005–2015—*Continued*

(Numbers in thousands, not seasonally adjusted)

Industry and year	January	February	March	April	May	June	July	August	September	October	November	December	Annual average
Leisure and Hospitality													
2005	29.7	29.7	30.1	30.8	31.8	32.5	32.3	32.5	32.2	31.2	30.9	30.7	31.2
2006	29.5	30.0	30.4	30.9	32.2	32.8	32.4	32.9	32.8	32.2	31.4	31.6	31.6
2007	30.7	31.1	31.7	32.1	33.5	34.4	33.9	34.1	33.9	33.3	32.9	33.0	32.9
2008	32.1	32.2	32.7	33.2	34.1	34.7	34.4	34.7	34.2	33.7	33.7	33.6	33.6
2009	32.4	32.4	32.8	33.2	34.8	35.4	35.0	35.2	34.8	34.1	33.8	33.8	34.0
2010	32.3	32.4	33.0	34.1	34.9	35.2	35.1	35.3	35.1	35.0	34.6	34.6	34.3
2011	33.4	33.5	34.2	34.5	35.8	36.3	36.0	36.4	36.8	36.3	36.3	36.7	35.5
2012	36.1	36.3	36.9	37.4	38.5	39.1	39.0	39.4	39.1	38.7	38.2	38.7	38.1
2013	37.3	37.6	38.2	38.0	39.1	40.1	40.1	40.4	40.3	40.1	40.0	39.6	39.2
2014	38.2	38.8	39.3	39.5	41.1	41.8	41.5	41.6	41.4	41.3	40.8	40.9	40.5
2015	39.1	39.4	39.6	40.3	41.2	41.5	41.2	41.1	40.9	40.6	40.6	40.4	40.5
Other Services													
2005	14.9	15.0	15.2	15.2	15.2	15.1	14.9	14.9	14.9	14.9	14.9	15.0	15.0
2006	14.8	14.9	15.0	15.0	15.1	14.9	14.9	15.1	15.0	15.1	15.3	15.4	15.0
2007	15.0	15.0	15.2	15.2	15.2	15.3	15.1	15.0	15.2	15.2	15.3	15.3	15.2
2008	15.2	15.3	15.5	15.5	15.6	15.5	15.3	15.3	15.3	15.3	15.4	15.4	15.4
2009	15.2	15.2	15.3	15.5	15.6	15.4	15.4	15.2	15.1	15.3	15.3	15.5	15.3
2010	15.1	15.2	15.3	15.4	15.4	15.4	15.4	15.3	15.4	15.6	15.6	15.5	15.4
2011	15.3	15.4	15.6	15.7	15.7	15.5	15.5	15.5	15.7	15.8	15.7	15.7	15.6
2012	15.9	15.9	16.0	16.1	16.1	16.1	16.2	16.1	16.0	16.1	16.2	16.2	16.1
2013	15.9	16.1	16.3	16.3	16.5	16.5	16.3	16.4	16.5	16.5	16.6	16.5	16.4
2014	16.4	16.4	16.6	16.8	16.8	16.8	16.8	16.7	16.7	16.9	16.9	17.0	16.7
2015	16.7	16.8	16.9	16.8	16.9	16.9	16.7	16.6	16.5	16.9	17.2	17.3	16.9
Government													
2005	75.6	77.7	77.9	78.4	78.1	73.1	64.0	66.1	76.7	77.6	77.7	78.0	75.1
2006	76.2	77.7	78.2	78.5	78.4	73.7	64.2	66.3	76.9	78.5	78.5	78.9	75.5
2007	76.5	77.8	78.0	78.4	78.5	74.7	65.2	66.3	77.0	78.3	78.7	78.8	75.7
2008	77.0	78.4	78.2	78.5	79.3	74.8	66.1	67.0	77.7	79.3	79.3	79.6	76.3
2009	77.5	78.7	79.1	79.7	80.7	78.0	68.3	69.1	79.4	81.3	81.3	81.8	77.9
2010	79.4	81.0	81.9	82.1	82.9	80.0	70.2	70.6	80.5	82.2	82.2	82.4	79.6
2011	80.2	81.4	81.5	81.5	81.8	79.4	69.3	69.7	80.0	81.5	81.3	81.9	79.1
2012	79.7	81.0	81.3	81.5	81.7	79.4	70.3	70.0	80.7	82.4	82.4	82.5	79.4
2013	80.5	81.7	81.7	81.7	82.3	80.4	70.9	70.8	80.9	82.3	82.3	82.7	79.9
2014	80.0	81.8	81.9	81.6	82.3	80.1	73.7	73.3	80.8	82.0	81.9	82.4	80.2
2015	79.9	81.5	82.3	82.7	83.4	81.1	74.7	74.3	81.6	84.3	84.6	85.3	81.3

2. Average Weekly Hours by Selected Industry: North Dakota, 2011–2015

(Not seasonally adjusted)

Industry and year	January	February	March	April	May	June	July	August	September	October	November	December	Annual average
Total Private													
2011	33.1	33.0	32.8	33.2	34.2	34.4	34.7	35.3	34.5	35.2	34.3	34.1	34.1
2012	34.3	34.1	34.0	34.9	35.0	35.4	35.8	35.4	35.9	35.5	34.7	35.5	35.1
2013	34.3	34.8	34.5	34.6	35.5	37.0	35.8	36.8	36.6	35.6	35.8	35.7	35.6
2014	34.2	35.5	35.2	35.0	35.4	36.7	36.3	36.6	36.2	36.2	36.3	35.4	35.8
2015	34.5	35.0	34.9	34.6	34.7	35.3	35.4	36.0	35.2	35.4	35.3	34.7	35.1
Goods-Producing													
2011	36.5	37.5	37.8	38.3	39.1	39.4	40.2	42.4	42.9	43.2	41.9	41.0	40.2
2012	40.5	41.0	41.1	41.6	42.2	42.5	42.3	42.4	42.3	42.6	40.1	40.8	41.6
2013	38.9	40.0	39.8	40.0	41.2	43.4	41.7	43.9	43.5	42.7	43.2	42.6	41.8
2014	40.3	41.7	42.4	41.8	43.3	44.1	45.0	44.5	45.0	44.8	43.7	43.1	43.4
2015	41.5	40.6	41.8	40.8	40.6	42.3	42.3	43.3	42.2	42.5	42.0	42.2	41.8
Construction													
2011	35.3	36.2	35.6	37.7	39.0	40.4	42.8	45.2	45.6	44.6	42.8	40.7	41.1
2012	39.2	40.2	39.9	41.3	43.3	44.3	44.4	44.0	44.7	43.7	39.7	40.6	42.3
2013	38.3	38.5	38.0	39.1	41.7	44.7	43.2	44.5	42.8	42.1	42.6	43.0	41.8
2014	39.9	39.9	40.8	41.3	45.2	46.2	47.7	46.0	46.8	46.6	42.8	43.2	44.2
2015	41.6	39.0	41.4	41.9	40.9	44.6	44.4	45.3	43.5	44.5	42.1	41.9	42.7
Manufacturing													
2011	38.3	38.8	39.3	39.2	39.1	38.6	37.7	40.1	40.6	41.6	41.3	40.8	39.6
2012	40.8	41.0	41.6	42.0	41.6	40.2	40.1	41.2	39.9	41.5	40.6	40.8	40.9
2013	38.6	40.0	40.9	41.0	40.8	42.3	40.1	43.1	42.5	41.8	41.9	39.3	41.1
2014	38.2	39.4	38.9	38.6	39.3	39.3	39.6	40.7	40.9	39.8	40.5	40.1	39.6
2015	38.2	39.1	39.4	38.6	38.6	38.9	38.9	41.0	40.6	40.5	40.2	41.1	39.6
Trade, Transportation, and Utilities													
2011	33.9	33.2	33.5	33.7	35.4	35.7	35.0	35.2	33.0	34.3	33.7	33.2	34.2
2012	33.5	33.3	33.6	34.6	34.8	35.4	35.3	35.2	36.0	35.8	34.9	36.0	34.9
2013	34.9	35.9	35.4	35.2	36.9	37.5	36.1	36.9	36.8	36.0	36.8	36.8	36.3
2014	35.1	36.5	36.2	35.8	35.7	37.5	36.5	37.1	36.3	36.6	37.0	36.3	36.4
2015	35.5	36.1	35.3	35.4	35.5	35.6	35.9	36.0	35.7	35.8	35.3	34.9	35.6
Financial Activities													
2011	38.1	36.0	35.0	34.3	35.1	35.8	36.2	37.2	37.0	36.6	33.7	35.6	35.9
2012	39.4	35.6	35.2	37.8	35.7	36.5	38.1	36.0	38.5	35.5	35.9	38.3	36.9
2013	36.2	36.3	35.9	36.4	36.2	38.1	36.5	37.1	38.7	36.9	37.3	38.0	37.0
2014	36.9	38.3	37.5	36.9	36.7	38.0	36.4	36.3	36.5	36.1	38.7	36.9	37.1
2015	36.9	37.5	36.5	35.0	34.2	34.3	34.8	36.3	34.9	35.0	37.6	35.0	35.7
Professional and Business Services													
2011	35.4	36.0	35.2	35.0	37.0	36.8	36.4	37.2	37.7	38.3	37.4	37.9	36.7
2012	38.4	38.0	38.1	38.9	38.0	37.9	38.6	37.6	37.8	38.3	37.4	38.9	38.2
2013	37.4	37.5	37.7	37.3	39.0	40.1	39.4	40.1	39.4	38.5	38.0	37.7	38.5
2014	36.0	38.9	37.5	37.6	39.2	39.9	39.0	38.9	39.1	39.3	39.0	38.0	38.5
2015	36.8	38.4	38.1	38.4	38.9	39.1	38.4	39.1	38.1	38.9	37.8	36.8	38.3
Education and Health Services													
2011	33.1	32.8	32.5	32.8	33.2	33.1	34.1	33.3	32.9	33.3	33.4	33.5	33.2
2012	33.9	33.4	33.2	33.7	33.1	33.7	33.6	33.6	33.8	33.1	33.5	33.7	33.5
2013	33.7	33.6	33.0	33.2	33.1	33.8	32.6	33.0	33.1	32.5	32.5	32.6	33.1
2014	32.2	32.3	32.0	32.2	31.6	32.7	31.5	32.1	31.9	31.6	31.8	31.6	32.0
2015	31.7	32.3	32.3	32.7	32.5	32.9	32.6	32.6	32.2	32.3	32.6	32.1	32.4
Leisure and Hospitality													
2011	21.4	21.0	20.7	21.6	22.4	22.6	23.3	23.9	22.2	22.6	21.9	21.9	22.1
2012	21.7	22.1	22.1	22.5	23.3	24.0	24.9	24.5	24.1	23.0	22.6	23.5	23.2
2013	22.0	22.5	22.9	22.8	23.4	25.1	24.6	24.4	24.1	23.2	22.7	23.2	23.4
2014	22.1	23.3	23.7	23.4	23.6	24.7	23.8	24.7	23.8	23.6	24.3	23.4	23.7
2015	22.3	23.9	23.5	22.7	23.9	24.4	24.1	25.2	23.6	23.8	24.3	24.0	23.8
Other Services													
2011	25.1	25.4	24.2	24.9	25.3	26.1	25.7	26.6	26.0	26.7	25.6	25.4	25.6
2012	25.1	25.9	24.5	24.8	26.0	25.1	25.8	25.0	25.2	25.4	25.9	27.0	25.5
2013	25.0	24.9	24.3	25.4	24.3	29.9	28.2	30.5	29.9	26.5	27.1	27.2	26.9
2014	26.4	28.7	26.8	24.4	25.0	27.4	28.7	29.3	25.4	24.7	26.3	25.2	26.6
2015	24.4	25.2	25.8	25.2	26.4	26.6	26.2	27.8	26.8	26.4	27.9	27.5	26.3

3. Average Hourly Earnings by Selected Industry: North Dakota, 2011–2015

(Dollars, not seasonally adjusted)

Industry and year	January	February	March	April	May	June	July	August	September	October	November	December	Annual average
Total Private													
2011	20.85	21.05	20.93	21.35	21.29	21.12	21.25	21.47	21.79	21.90	21.90	22.25	21.45
2012	22.26	22.35	22.54	22.55	22.48	22.49	22.68	22.63	23.39	22.96	23.25	23.53	22.77
2013	23.63	23.64	23.58	23.69	23.51	23.82	23.74	23.69	24.08	24.07	24.35	24.70	23.88
2014	24.89	25.07	24.91	24.95	24.78	24.69	24.76	24.59	24.98	24.94	24.92	24.97	24.87
2015	25.07	24.95	25.13	25.38	25.22	24.85	25.26	25.53	25.44	25.63	25.54	25.39	25.28
Goods-Producing													
2011	22.79	22.61	22.60	23.04	23.27	23.22	23.07	23.20	23.75	23.67	23.44	23.79	23.26
2012	23.98	23.68	24.12	23.88	24.12	24.57	24.48	24.34	24.95	24.74	25.61	26.01	24.56
2013	25.98	25.95	26.17	26.01	25.86	26.46	26.00	26.15	26.19	26.34	27.21	28.20	26.40
2014	27.87	27.98	28.27	27.66	27.38	27.23	27.12	27.04	27.43	27.49	27.43	27.78	27.53
2015	27.45	27.37	27.80	27.60	27.37	27.07	27.41	27.73	27.38	27.85	27.53	27.29	27.49
Construction													
2011	22.13	22.56	22.72	22.88	23.59	23.75	23.71	24.82	24.89	24.48	24.33	24.52	23.91
2012	24.70	24.08	24.95	24.51	25.10	25.24	24.55	25.04	25.73	25.58	26.79	27.09	25.32
2013	26.64	27.23	27.48	27.48	27.25	28.05	26.86	26.92	27.36	27.15	27.80	29.03	27.45
2014	28.80	28.81	29.39	28.91	27.89	27.62	27.86	27.64	28.18	27.98	28.17	29.23	28.28
2015	29.75	28.66	29.18	28.44	28.38	28.14	28.11	28.76	27.87	28.70	27.96	28.31	28.50
Manufacturing													
2011	19.69	19.28	19.29	19.73	19.99	19.93	20.51	19.89	20.29	20.59	20.29	20.86	20.05
2012	21.22	20.84	21.13	21.35	21.42	21.53	22.00	21.46	22.10	21.68	22.06	22.62	21.62
2013	22.97	22.38	22.44	22.27	22.25	22.41	22.17	22.28	22.45	22.55	22.57	23.91	22.55
2014	23.33	23.39	23.57	23.06	23.07	22.90	22.74	22.96	23.04	23.25	22.80	22.55	23.05
2015	21.33	21.46	21.73	22.04	22.11	21.41	22.04	22.13	22.42	22.86	22.95	22.43	22.08
Trade, Transportation, and Utilities													
2011	20.33	20.56	20.57	21.46	20.98	20.73	21.45	21.33	21.04	21.42	21.41	22.05	21.13
2012	22.09	22.09	22.62	22.54	22.04	21.85	22.31	22.11	22.96	22.60	22.54	22.84	22.39
2013	23.13	23.06	22.75	23.54	22.85	23.43	23.13	22.88	23.64	23.46	23.19	23.54	23.22
2014	24.37	25.39	24.88	24.73	24.90	24.86	24.67	24.44	24.95	24.61	24.97	24.58	24.78
2015	25.36	25.01	24.99	25.47	25.09	24.98	25.16	25.34	25.42	25.32	25.07	25.01	25.19
Financial Activities													
2011	18.97	20.52	19.77	19.96	19.80	19.58	19.36	19.45	19.72	19.90	20.64	20.01	19.80
2012	19.26	21.18	20.40	20.04	20.15	20.12	20.62	20.90	22.33	20.79	21.38	21.40	20.72
2013	22.80	22.91	22.74	22.28	22.49	22.29	22.08	22.24	22.67	22.82	23.37	23.84	22.72
2014	24.58	24.65	23.54	24.21	24.00	23.98	24.44	23.95	23.43	23.65	23.22	23.47	23.92
2015	24.06	24.42	25.35	25.91	26.45	26.08	27.55	27.42	25.65	26.99	27.24	26.80	26.14
Professional and Business Services													
2011	23.34	23.72	24.05	23.47	24.25	23.61	24.41	24.41	25.29	25.72	25.92	27.79	24.72
2012	26.35	26.43	26.18	27.25	26.87	26.97	27.15	26.24	27.52	26.95	27.63	28.79	27.04
2013	28.21	28.12	27.95	27.66	27.46	28.18	27.81	27.69	29.35	29.23	29.57	29.91	28.43
2014	29.59	28.94	28.88	28.81	28.37	27.84	27.53	27.94	28.36	28.30	28.26	28.55	28.42
2015	28.00	28.06	28.12	28.68	28.83	28.00	28.82	29.30	29.43	29.17	29.50	29.24	28.77
Education and Health Services													
2011	23.95	24.05	23.43	23.41	23.12	22.91	22.40	23.12	23.06	23.00	22.84	22.68	23.16
2012	23.48	23.36	23.02	22.95	23.17	22.76	23.04	23.56	24.05	23.31	23.22	23.10	23.25
2013	23.39	23.33	23.17	23.06	23.07	22.79	23.66	23.38	23.28	23.40	23.44	23.33	23.27
2014	23.49	23.44	23.50	24.08	23.56	23.58	23.96	23.86	24.29	24.03	24.18	24.41	23.86
2015	24.27	24.41	24.17	24.44	24.46	24.21	24.45	24.90	25.42	25.43	25.59	25.70	24.79
Leisure and Hospitality													
2011	11.21	11.24	11.21	11.29	11.26	11.23	11.20	11.37	11.74	11.82	12.08	12.25	11.50
2012	11.98	11.95	12.01	11.96	12.09	12.25	12.12	11.98	12.40	12.28	12.41	12.77	12.19
2013	12.53	12.81	12.72	12.79	12.88	12.57	12.66	12.62	12.90	12.79	12.85	13.05	12.76
2014	13.10	13.06	13.15	13.36	13.22	13.15	13.34	13.22	13.57	13.77	13.77	13.92	13.39
2015	14.16	14.06	14.15	14.28	14.14	13.99	14.06	14.13	14.35	14.40	14.43	14.50	14.22
Other Services													
2011	16.04	16.08	16.51	17.25	17.49	17.19	17.61	17.96	17.96	17.81	17.61	17.65	17.28
2012	17.26	17.59	18.47	18.04	18.65	18.92	19.77	19.60	19.06	19.85	19.99	19.47	18.90
2013	18.18	20.20	20.53	21.10	20.48	20.92	21.77	21.83	22.75	22.41	22.49	22.63	21.34
2014	23.31	22.06	22.44	23.47	22.57	22.79	22.76	22.23	23.26	23.72	22.81	22.41	22.80
2015	22.88	23.10	23.43	23.04	22.85	22.91	23.37	23.22	22.78	23.03	23.54	23.48	23.14

4. Average Weekly Earnings by Selected Industry: North Dakota, 2011–2015

(Dollars, not seasonally adjusted)

Industry and year	January	February	March	April	May	June	July	August	September	October	November	December	Annual average
Total Private													
2011	690.14	694.65	686.50	708.82	728.12	726.53	737.38	757.89	751.76	770.88	751.17	758.73	731.45
2012	763.52	762.14	766.36	787.00	786.80	796.15	811.94	801.10	839.70	815.08	806.78	835.32	799.23
2013	810.51	822.67	813.51	819.67	834.61	881.34	849.89	871.79	881.33	856.89	871.73	881.79	850.13
2014	851.24	889.99	876.83	873.25	877.21	906.12	898.79	899.99	904.28	902.83	904.60	883.94	890.35
2015	864.92	873.25	877.04	878.15	875.13	877.21	894.20	919.08	895.49	907.30	901.56	881.03	887.33
Goods-Producing													
2011	831.84	847.88	854.28	882.43	909.86	914.87	927.41	983.68	1018.88	1022.54	982.14	975.39	935.05
2012	971.19	970.88	991.33	993.41	1017.86	1044.23	1035.50	1032.02	1055.39	1053.92	1026.96	1061.21	1021.70
2013	1010.62	1038.00	1041.57	1040.40	1065.43	1148.36	1084.20	1147.99	1139.27	1124.72	1175.47	1201.32	1103.52
2014	1123.16	1166.77	1198.65	1156.19	1185.55	1200.84	1220.40	1203.28	1234.35	1231.55	1198.69	1197.32	1194.80
2015	1139.18	1111.22	1162.04	1126.08	1111.22	1145.06	1159.44	1200.71	1155.44	1183.63	1156.26	1151.64	1149.08
Construction													
2011	781.19	816.67	808.83	862.58	920.01	959.50	1014.79	1121.86	1134.98	1091.81	1041.32	997.96	982.70
2012	968.24	968.02	995.51	1012.26	1086.83	1118.13	1090.02	1101.76	1150.13	1117.85	1063.56	1099.85	1071.04
2013	1020.31	1048.36	1044.24	1074.47	1136.33	1253.84	1160.35	1197.94	1171.01	1143.02	1184.28	1248.29	1147.41
2014	1149.12	1149.52	1199.11	1193.98	1260.63	1276.04	1328.92	1271.44	1318.82	1303.87	1205.68	1262.74	1249.98
2015	1237.60	1117.74	1208.05	1191.64	1160.74	1255.04	1248.08	1302.83	1212.35	1277.15	1177.12	1186.19	1216.95
Manufacturing													
2011	754.13	748.06	758.10	773.42	781.61	769.30	773.23	797.59	823.77	856.54	837.98	851.09	793.98
2012	865.78	854.44	879.01	896.70	891.07	865.51	882.20	884.15	881.79	899.72	895.64	922.90	884.26
2013	886.64	895.20	917.80	913.07	907.80	947.94	889.02	960.27	954.13	942.59	945.68	939.66	926.81
2014	891.21	921.57	916.87	890.12	906.65	899.97	900.50	934.47	942.34	925.35	923.40	904.26	912.78
2015	814.81	839.09	856.16	850.74	853.45	832.85	857.36	907.33	910.25	925.83	922.59	921.87	874.37
Trade, Transportation, and Utilities													
2011	689.19	682.59	689.10	723.20	742.69	740.06	750.75	750.82	694.32	734.71	721.52	732.06	722.65
2012	740.02	735.60	760.03	779.88	766.99	773.49	787.54	778.27	826.56	809.08	786.65	822.24	781.41
2013	807.24	827.85	805.35	828.61	843.17	878.63	834.99	844.27	869.95	844.56	853.39	866.27	842.89
2014	855.39	926.74	900.66	885.33	888.93	932.25	900.46	906.72	905.69	900.73	923.89	892.25	901.99
2015	900.28	902.86	882.15	901.64	890.70	889.29	903.24	912.24	907.49	906.46	884.97	872.85	896.76
Financial Activities													
2011	722.76	738.72	691.95	684.63	694.98	700.96	700.83	723.54	729.64	728.34	695.57	712.36	710.82
2012	758.84	754.01	718.08	757.51	719.36	734.38	785.62	752.40	859.71	738.05	767.54	819.62	764.57
2013	825.36	831.63	816.37	810.99	814.14	849.25	805.92	825.10	877.33	842.06	871.70	905.92	840.64
2014	907.00	944.10	882.75	893.35	880.80	911.24	889.62	869.39	855.20	853.77	898.61	866.04	887.43
2015	887.81	915.75	925.28	906.85	904.59	894.54	958.74	995.35	895.19	944.65	1024.22	938.00	933.20
Professional and Business Services													
2011	826.24	853.92	846.56	821.45	897.25	868.85	888.52	908.05	953.43	985.08	969.41	1053.24	907.22
2012	1011.84	1004.34	997.46	1060.03	1021.06	1022.16	1047.99	986.62	1040.26	1032.19	1033.36	1119.93	1032.93
2013	1055.05	1054.50	1053.72	1031.72	1070.94	1130.02	1095.71	1110.37	1156.39	1125.36	1123.66	1127.61	1094.56
2014	1065.24	1125.77	1083.00	1083.26	1112.10	1110.82	1073.67	1086.87	1108.88	1112.19	1102.14	1084.90	1094.17
2015	1030.40	1077.50	1071.37	1101.31	1121.49	1094.80	1106.69	1145.63	1121.28	1134.71	1115.10	1076.03	1101.89
Education and Health Services													
2011	792.75	788.84	761.48	767.85	767.58	758.32	763.84	769.90	758.67	765.90	762.86	759.78	768.91
2012	795.97	780.22	764.26	773.42	766.93	767.01	774.14	791.62	812.89	771.56	777.87	778.47	778.88
2013	788.24	783.89	764.61	765.59	763.62	770.30	771.32	771.54	770.57	760.50	761.80	760.56	770.24
2014	756.38	757.11	752.00	775.38	744.50	771.07	754.74	765.91	774.85	759.35	768.92	771.36	763.52
2015	769.36	788.44	780.69	799.19	794.95	796.51	797.07	811.74	818.52	821.39	834.23	824.97	803.20
Leisure and Hospitality													
2011	239.89	236.04	232.05	243.86	252.22	253.80	260.96	271.74	260.63	267.13	264.55	268.28	254.15
2012	259.97	264.10	265.42	269.10	281.70	294.00	301.79	293.51	298.84	282.44	280.47	300.10	282.81
2013	275.66	288.23	291.29	291.61	301.39	315.51	311.44	307.93	310.89	296.73	291.70	302.76	298.58
2014	289.51	304.30	311.66	312.62	311.99	324.81	317.49	326.53	322.97	324.97	334.61	325.73	317.34
2015	315.77	336.03	332.53	324.16	337.95	341.36	338.85	356.08	338.66	342.72	350.65	348.00	338.44
Other Services													
2011	402.60	408.43	399.54	429.53	442.50	448.66	452.58	477.74	466.96	475.53	450.82	448.31	442.37
2012	433.23	455.58	452.52	447.39	484.90	474.89	510.07	490.00	480.31	504.19	517.74	525.69	481.95
2013	454.50	502.98	498.88	535.94	497.66	625.51	613.91	665.82	680.23	593.87	609.48	615.54	574.05
2014	615.38	633.12	601.39	572.67	564.25	624.45	653.21	651.34	590.80	585.88	599.90	564.73	606.48
2015	558.27	582.12	604.49	580.61	603.24	609.41	612.29	645.52	610.50	607.99	656.77	645.70	608.58

OHIO

At a Glance

Population:
  2005 estimate: 11,463,320
  2010 census: 11,536,504
  2015 estimate: 11,613,423

Percent change in population:
  2005–2015: 1.3%
  2010–2015: 0.7%

Percent change in total nonfarm employment:
  2005–2015: –0.1%

Industry with the largest growth in employment, 2005–2015 (thousands):
  Education and health services, 144.5

Industry with the largest decline or smallest growth in employment, 2005–2015 (thousands):
  Manufacturing, –124.7

Civilian labor force:
  2005: 5,890,046
  2010: 5,846,886
  2015: 5,700,344

Unemployment rate and rank among states (highest to lowest):
  2005: 5.9%, 8th
  2010: 10.3%, 15th
  2015: 4.9%, 30th

Over-the-year change in unemployment rates:
  2012–2013: 0.1%
  2013–2014: –1.7%
  2014–2015: –0.9%

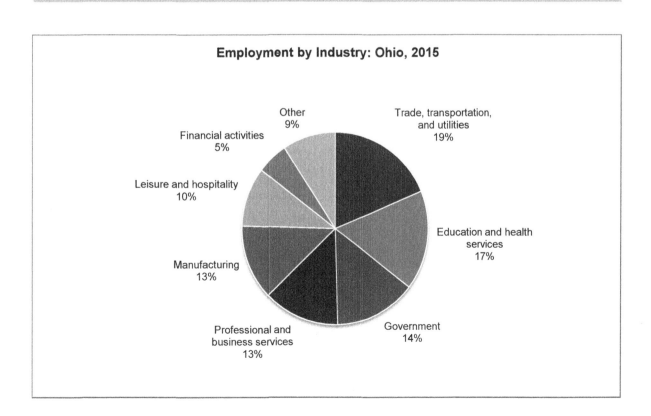

Employment by Industry: Ohio, 2015

Other
9%

Trade, transportation, and utilities
19%

Financial activities
5%

Leisure and hospitality
10%

Manufacturing
13%

Education and health services
17%

Professional and business services
13%

Government
14%

1. Employment by Industry: Ohio, 2005–2015

(Numbers in thousands, not seasonally adjusted)

Industry and year	January	February	March	April	May	June	July	August	September	October	November	December	Annual average
Total Nonfarm													
2005	5,287.2	5,313.9	5,354.0	5,424.3	5,465.4	5,472.4	5,431.2	5,440.1	5,469.1	5,476.8	5,494.6	5,491.3	5,426.7
2006	5,326.3	5,347.0	5,389.7	5,434.7	5,478.4	5,494.0	5,428.5	5,440.8	5,461.0	5,465.7	5,479.2	5,480.0	5,435.4
2007	5,323.1	5,319.8	5,367.8	5,416.3	5,473.8	5,492.6	5,423.3	5,437.6	5,451.3	5,464.4	5,481.8	5,471.6	5,427.0
2008	5,315.9	5,325.1	5,325.0	5,383.9	5,434.5	5,427.8	5,368.1	5,371.8	5,375.6	5,370.1	5,340.8	5,302.7	5,361.8
2009	5,099.5	5,084.2	5,078.1	5,093.5	5,118.7	5,091.4	5,036.3	5,033.6	5,053.6	5,066.7	5,063.3	5,050.6	5,072.5
2010	4,905.0	4,910.5	4,945.2	5,022.8	5,080.9	5,076.8	5,043.6	5,047.4	5,069.5	5,106.4	5,116.5	5,106.8	5,036.0
2011	4,959.3	4,981.4	5,015.2	5,092.5	5,133.1	5,131.6	5,128.2	5,145.4	5,158.9	5,172.8	5,192.5	5,184.4	5,107.9
2012	5,050.8	5,082.5	5,130.1	5,188.9	5,247.3	5,248.8	5,210.5	5,223.8	5,232.8	5,265.5	5,276.1	5,263.9	5,201.8
2013	5,113.7	5,143.0	5,171.7	5,248.6	5,317.3	5,303.6	5,275.8	5,297.0	5,303.7	5,330.9	5,355.1	5,341.1	5,266.8
2014	5,180.4	5,204.0	5,238.5	5,319.0	5,391.3	5,379.0	5,348.3	5,378.9	5,385.1	5,423.6	5,442.3	5,437.9	5,344.0
2015	5,273.5	5,295.5	5,322.3	5,402.8	5,472.1	5,452.9	5,440.4	5,450.2	5,449.4	5,497.2	5,502.7	5,495.7	5,421.2
Total Private													
2005	4,494.9	4,501.5	4,539.6	4,611.7	4,646.7	4,677.6	4,672.1	4,683.9	4,677.7	4,664.1	4,676.8	4,678.1	4,627.1
2006	4,530.8	4,536.0	4,575.6	4,622.6	4,659.6	4,697.6	4,669.5	4,683.9	4,668.3	4,652.8	4,662.2	4,665.7	4,635.4
2007	4,529.3	4,512.1	4,556.4	4,605.3	4,659.0	4,696.0	4,665.7	4,681.7	4,661.0	4,654.0	4,667.3	4,663.5	4,629.3
2008	4,521.6	4,512.8	4,514.2	4,572.1	4,617.8	4,633.4	4,611.5	4,616.4	4,585.5	4,557.5	4,523.2	4,493.8	4,563.3
2009	4,306.2	4,275.9	4,269.3	4,282.3	4,306.4	4,302.7	4,287.3	4,287.8	4,271.2	4,263.2	4,258.3	4,254.8	4,280.5
2010	4,121.7	4,114.9	4,147.2	4,220.4	4,260.8	4,288.5	4,300.7	4,310.1	4,298.3	4,311.2	4,317.8	4,312.0	4,250.3
2011	4,188.0	4,195.4	4,226.6	4,303.9	4,345.2	4,365.9	4,382.6	4,400.9	4,386.1	4,388.1	4,405.5	4,404.2	4,332.7
2012	4,290.1	4,301.4	4,345.0	4,401.0	4,452.5	4,486.2	4,468.5	4,482.7	4,462.3	4,480.2	4,489.4	4,483.1	4,428.5
2013	4,354.0	4,366.5	4,395.6	4,467.2	4,531.8	4,557.3	4,546.5	4,566.2	4,538.8	4,553.6	4,572.0	4,567.2	4,501.4
2014	4,430.6	4,434.3	4,467.5	4,539.7	4,605.3	4,628.5	4,622.4	4,645.9	4,611.0	4,638.7	4,655.2	4,655.9	4,577.9
2015	4,518.4	4,519.1	4,546.0	4,619.7	4,687.2	4,702.6	4,705.9	4,713.9	4,678.0	4,714.6	4,714.9	4,710.7	4,652.6
Goods-Producing													
2005	1,025.7	1,024.2	1,032.4	1,052.7	1,062.5	1,074.1	1,071.5	1,075.6	1,071.7	1,066.2	1,062.3	1,050.5	1,055.8
2006	1,018.1	1,016.0	1,024.1	1,039.4	1,046.3	1,059.4	1,049.0	1,054.1	1,048.8	1,039.3	1,032.4	1,024.5	1,037.6
2007	990.4	982.2	993.7	1,003.5	1,017.5	1,028.9	1,016.4	1,027.0	1,019.7	1,009.6	1,007.2	996.9	1,007.8
2008	962.1	957.8	952.7	964.4	976.3	986.1	978.0	978.8	971.5	960.6	940.5	915.9	962.1
2009	855.4	842.4	832.9	826.4	824.2	819.8	814.9	819.9	816.0	813.1	803.7	797.9	822.2
2010	765.2	760.9	768.4	787.8	801.3	812.6	818.3	821.8	819.6	821.9	819.2	810.1	800.6
2011	785.2	784.1	793.8	810.9	821.5	833.4	843.2	851.5	848.5	848.9	848.9	842.4	826.0
2012	817.8	818.4	828.1	841.0	852.5	864.7	862.5	866.9	862.8	859.9	858.4	851.6	848.7
2013	828.5	828.4	834.6	847.5	863.7	875.7	873.7	881.7	878.1	878.5	878.1	868.1	861.4
2014	844.9	844.2	854.1	870.5	888.1	900.8	900.4	908.7	904.1	906.2	905.4	897.3	885.4
2015	871.5	869.7	875.4	891.2	906.9	914.9	914.6	918.1	911.5	919.1	914.4	904.5	901.0
Service-Providing													
2005	4,261.5	4,289.7	4,321.6	4,371.6	4,402.9	4,398.3	4,359.7	4,364.5	4,397.4	4,410.6	4,432.3	4,440.8	4,370.9
2006	4,308.2	4,331.0	4,365.6	4,395.3	4,432.1	4,434.6	4,379.5	4,386.7	4,412.2	4,426.4	4,446.8	4,455.5	4,397.8
2007	4,332.7	4,337.6	4,374.1	4,412.8	4,456.3	4,463.7	4,406.9	4,410.6	4,431.6	4,454.8	4,474.6	4,474.7	4,419.2
2008	4,353.8	4,367.3	4,372.3	4,419.5	4,458.2	4,441.7	4,390.1	4,393.0	4,404.1	4,409.5	4,400.3	4,386.8	4,399.7
2009	4,244.1	4,241.8	4,245.2	4,267.1	4,294.5	4,271.6	4,221.4	4,213.7	4,237.6	4,253.6	4,259.6	4,252.7	4,250.2
2010	4,139.8	4,149.6	4,176.8	4,235.0	4,279.6	4,264.2	4,225.3	4,225.6	4,249.9	4,284.5	4,297.3	4,296.7	4,235.4
2011	4,174.1	4,197.3	4,221.4	4,281.6	4,311.6	4,298.2	4,285.0	4,293.9	4,310.4	4,323.9	4,343.6	4,342.0	4,281.9
2012	4,233.0	4,264.1	4,302.0	4,347.9	4,394.8	4,384.1	4,348.0	4,356.9	4,370.0	4,405.6	4,417.7	4,412.3	4,353.0
2013	4,285.2	4,314.6	4,337.1	4,401.1	4,453.6	4,427.9	4,402.1	4,415.3	4,425.6	4,452.4	4,477.0	4,473.0	4,405.4
2014	4,335.5	4,359.8	4,384.4	4,448.5	4,503.2	4,478.2	4,447.9	4,470.2	4,481.0	4,517.4	4,536.9	4,540.6	4,458.6
2015	4,402.0	4,425.8	4,446.9	4,511.6	4,565.2	4,538.0	4,525.8	4,532.1	4,537.9	4,578.1	4,588.3	4,591.2	4,520.2
Mining and Logging													
2005	10.8	10.8	10.9	11.3	11.4	11.5	11.7	11.6	11.6	11.7	11.7	11.5	11.4
2006	11.0	11.0	11.2	11.6	11.6	11.8	11.8	11.9	11.7	11.7	11.7	11.6	11.6
2007	11.3	11.0	11.2	11.6	11.8	11.9	12.0	12.1	11.9	11.8	11.9	11.7	11.7
2008	11.3	11.2	11.1	11.5	11.9	12.0	12.4	12.5	12.4	12.5	12.5	12.1	12.0
2009	11.6	11.4	11.5	11.8	12.0	12.0	12.1	12.0	11.8	11.6	11.5	11.3	11.7
2010	10.5	10.5	10.5	11.2	11.4	11.5	11.7	11.6	11.7	11.6	11.5	11.3	11.3
2011	10.7	10.7	10.9	11.2	11.3	11.4	11.6	11.7	11.7	11.7	11.6	11.4	11.3
2012	11.0	10.8	11.0	11.4	11.6	11.7	11.8	11.7	11.6	11.5	11.6	11.4	11.4
2013	11.3	11.3	11.8	12.2	12.5	12.5	12.7	12.9	12.9	13.5	13.5	13.3	12.5
2014	13.1	13.3	13.7	14.2	14.6	14.9	15.4	15.8	15.7	15.8	15.9	15.8	14.9
2015	15.2	14.8	14.7	14.5	14.5	14.1	14.1	14.0	13.5	13.3	13.2	12.7	14.1

1. Employment by Industry: Ohio, 2005–2015—*Continued*

(Numbers in thousands, not seasonally adjusted)

Industry and year	January	February	March	April	May	June	July	August	September	October	November	December	Annual average
Construction													
2005	204.9	203.9	209.5	228.3	237.6	246.0	250.4	250.3	247.3	244.9	241.4	230.0	232.9
2006	208.1	207.5	215.2	227.2	234.9	241.5	243.4	244.0	240.5	237.2	232.4	225.0	229.7
2007	204.3	195.6	206.1	219.2	231.3	238.7	239.7	240.2	237.2	235.9	230.7	218.6	224.8
2008	196.4	192.2	194.6	208.3	218.3	223.7	226.0	225.9	221.3	219.6	210.8	196.8	211.2
2009	173.5	168.9	172.0	175.8	185.9	190.9	193.9	192.1	187.1	185.4	179.3	168.8	181.1
2010	147.4	142.8	149.6	162.8	170.2	176.7	183.1	183.4	181.0	182.5	178.6	167.9	168.8
2011	150.1	147.9	154.2	167.0	175.1	183.0	190.7	193.6	192.6	190.8	187.7	180.8	176.1
2012	162.9	160.3	165.8	176.1	184.0	189.6	191.9	192.4	191.1	191.5	187.3	179.9	181.1
2013	163.0	161.7	166.0	176.2	188.5	195.5	198.7	201.0	199.7	200.2	196.6	185.1	186.0
2014	169.1	166.6	174.9	188.0	199.9	207.3	211.0	211.9	209.5	209.4	205.1	195.6	195.7
2015	175.9	173.9	179.2	192.8	204.4	209.7	213.1	213.9	211.6	215.6	211.3	200.4	200.2
Manufacturing													
2005	810.0	809.5	812.0	813.1	813.5	816.6	809.4	813.7	812.8	809.6	809.2	809.0	811.5
2006	799.0	797.5	797.7	800.6	799.8	806.1	793.8	798.2	796.6	790.4	788.3	787.9	796.3
2007	774.8	775.6	776.4	772.7	774.4	778.3	764.7	774.7	770.6	761.9	764.6	766.6	771.3
2008	754.4	754.4	747.0	744.6	746.1	750.4	739.6	740.4	737.8	728.5	717.2	707.0	739.0
2009	670.3	662.1	649.4	638.8	626.3	616.9	608.9	615.8	617.1	616.1	612.9	617.8	629.4
2010	607.3	607.6	608.3	613.8	619.7	624.4	623.5	626.8	626.9	627.8	629.1	630.9	620.5
2011	624.4	625.5	628.7	632.7	635.1	639.0	640.9	646.2	644.2	646.4	649.6	650.2	638.6
2012	643.9	647.3	651.3	653.5	656.9	663.4	658.8	662.8	660.1	656.9	659.5	660.3	656.2
2013	654.2	655.4	656.8	659.1	662.7	667.7	662.3	667.8	665.5	664.8	668.0	669.7	662.8
2014	662.7	664.3	665.5	668.3	673.6	678.6	674.0	681.0	678.9	681.0	684.4	685.9	674.9
2015	680.4	681.0	681.5	683.9	688.0	691.1	687.4	690.2	686.4	690.2	689.9	691.4	686.8
Trade, Transportation, and Utilities													
2005	1,028.2	1,020.4	1,027.2	1,035.0	1,041.3	1,043.1	1,042.8	1,042.2	1,038.5	1,044.5	1,066.3	1,082.4	1,042.7
2006	1,034.4	1,024.5	1,029.7	1,034.6	1,043.6	1,047.5	1,043.7	1,044.9	1,041.5	1,047.3	1,071.5	1,085.1	1,045.7
2007	1,038.6	1,024.8	1,033.8	1,038.8	1,050.5	1,054.8	1,052.5	1,051.1	1,047.2	1,053.2	1,076.6	1,088.0	1,050.8
2008	1,038.7	1,024.4	1,025.5	1,032.1	1,039.9	1,040.2	1,036.6	1,037.2	1,028.3	1,028.0	1,035.5	1,041.0	1,034.0
2009	985.6	970.0	966.3	963.5	968.6	967.7	962.8	960.1	953.3	957.3	971.6	979.3	967.2
2010	934.4	924.6	929.8	937.6	945.9	950.2	949.1	950.2	944.0	954.4	970.7	980.8	947.6
2011	936.7	931.3	934.4	947.3	953.3	957.7	959.5	962.4	957.6	967.0	987.7	997.8	957.7
2012	956.6	949.7	957.0	962.0	972.1	975.7	971.4	972.3	968.8	979.3	1,001.8	1,007.6	972.9
2013	964.4	956.4	960.5	968.2	980.2	984.9	982.8	984.6	978.8	989.0	1,013.2	1,022.5	982.1
2014	975.2	968.4	971.5	981.8	992.9	997.1	994.6	998.7	993.0	1,006.8	1,029.8	1,041.7	996.0
2015	996.7	989.2	993.2	1,001.8	1,013.1	1,015.6	1,013.7	1,015.8	1,009.0	1,020.5	1,037.3	1,047.9	1,012.8
Wholesale Trade													
2005	232.0	232.1	232.9	234.9	235.7	237.0	238.1	237.6	236.2	235.9	236.6	237.4	235.5
2006	234.7	235.1	235.7	237.0	238.2	239.9	239.5	239.3	237.6	237.5	237.9	238.8	237.6
2007	236.5	236.1	237.1	237.7	239.1	240.3	240.2	239.6	237.8	238.0	237.9	238.5	238.2
2008	235.5	235.2	235.2	236.8	238.2	238.8	238.5	238.0	235.7	235.1	233.1	231.7	236.0
2009	226.8	224.6	223.3	221.7	221.1	220.7	220.2	219.0	217.0	216.9	216.6	216.7	220.4
2010	213.3	213.1	213.6	214.9	215.5	216.5	217.2	216.9	215.1	215.5	215.1	214.8	215.1
2011	212.7	213.1	213.8	216.2	217.6	218.8	220.4	220.8	219.8	220.8	221.0	221.6	218.1
2012	220.0	220.8	221.9	222.7	224.2	225.9	225.7	225.7	224.2	225.1	225.4	225.7	223.9
2013	222.9	223.1	223.9	225.4	227.3	228.2	228.5	228.6	227.2	228.5	229.4	230.0	226.9
2014	227.1	228.3	229.4	230.3	233.0	234.0	234.7	234.6	233.3	234.1	234.8	235.9	232.5
2015	232.3	233.1	234.3	235.3	237.3	238.1	237.7	237.5	235.1	235.7	234.8	235.8	235.6
Retail Trade													
2005	607.0	598.8	603.4	608.7	613.0	613.0	609.7	608.7	604.3	607.2	624.6	637.6	611.3
2006	599.9	589.8	593.6	596.1	602.0	603.4	600.6	600.4	595.9	601.1	621.4	630.8	602.9
2007	594.7	583.3	590.4	592.8	601.0	602.6	601.2	598.7	595.2	599.2	619.1	627.5	600.5
2008	592.2	579.7	581.1	585.5	590.8	592.2	591.2	591.0	584.9	586.0	595.8	603.5	589.5
2009	563.3	552.4	552.2	554.7	561.0	561.6	558.4	557.3	553.5	556.6	570.8	577.6	560.0
2010	543.0	534.9	539.1	544.4	550.4	552.7	552.0	552.5	547.4	555.9	571.2	579.1	551.9
2011	544.0	538.5	540.6	549.2	552.6	555.2	555.1	556.1	550.7	558.5	576.8	583.8	555.1
2012	551.0	543.4	549.0	552.7	559.1	560.0	556.5	556.3	553.8	561.7	581.4	583.9	559.1
2013	552.7	545.5	548.6	554.3	562.3	564.9	563.2	563.8	559.2	566.7	585.9	591.8	563.2
2014	555.1	549.0	550.6	558.9	564.2	566.7	563.8	566.0	560.7	571.4	589.6	594.9	565.9
2015	561.0	555.2	557.7	563.6	570.6	571.9	570.0	570.9	566.0	575.2	590.5	596.4	570.8

1. Employment by Industry: Ohio, 2005–2015—*Continued*

(Numbers in thousands, not seasonally adjusted)

Industry and year	January	February	March	April	May	June	July	August	September	October	November	December	Annual average
Transportation and Utilities													
2005	189.2	189.5	190.9	191.4	192.6	193.1	195.0	195.9	198.0	201.4	205.1	207.4	195.8
2006	199.8	199.6	200.4	201.5	203.4	204.2	203.6	205.2	208.0	208.7	212.2	215.5	205.2
2007	207.4	205.4	206.3	208.3	210.4	211.9	211.1	212.8	214.2	216.0	219.6	222.0	212.1
2008	211.0	209.5	209.2	209.8	210.9	209.2	206.9	208.2	207.7	206.9	206.6	205.8	208.5
2009	195.5	193.0	190.8	187.1	186.5	185.4	184.2	183.8	182.8	183.8	184.2	185.0	186.8
2010	178.1	176.6	177.1	178.3	180.0	181.0	179.9	180.8	181.5	183.0	184.4	186.9	180.6
2011	180.0	179.7	180.0	181.9	183.1	183.7	184.0	185.5	187.1	187.7	189.9	192.4	184.6
2012	185.6	185.5	186.1	186.6	188.8	189.8	189.2	190.3	190.8	192.5	195.0	198.0	189.9
2013	188.8	187.8	188.0	188.5	190.6	191.8	191.1	192.2	192.4	193.8	197.9	200.7	192.0
2014	193.0	191.1	191.5	192.6	195.7	196.4	196.1	198.1	199.0	201.3	205.4	210.9	197.6
2015	203.4	200.9	201.2	202.9	205.2	205.6	206.0	207.4	207.9	209.6	212.0	215.7	206.5
Information													
2005	89.9	89.5	89.5	90.0	90.6	90.8	90.6	90.3	89.7	89.0	89.4	89.8	89.9
2006	88.8	88.6	88.7	88.3	88.6	88.9	88.8	88.6	87.8	87.5	87.8	88.0	88.4
2007	87.3	87.4	87.0	87.8	88.4	88.9	88.8	88.5	87.3	86.9	87.1	87.4	87.7
2008	86.3	86.2	86.1	86.4	86.4	86.4	86.5	86.4	84.8	84.5	84.9	84.8	85.8
2009	83.6	83.1	82.2	81.2	81.3	81.1	80.9	80.4	79.1	78.5	78.7	79.0	80.8
2010	78.5	78.1	77.9	77.4	77.6	77.5	77.9	77.9	77.0	76.8	77.1	77.2	77.6
2011	76.1	75.8	75.3	75.9	76.3	76.4	76.8	76.7	76.2	75.8	76.1	76.0	76.1
2012	75.0	74.8	74.7	74.6	75.0	75.4	75.5	75.0	74.5	74.8	75.1	75.4	75.0
2013	74.9	75.3	75.5	75.5	75.5	75.9	76.0	75.7	74.8	74.5	74.3	74.7	75.2
2014	73.0	73.0	73.0	73.2	73.1	72.8	72.8	72.6	71.3	70.9	71.5	72.1	72.4
2015	70.7	71.1	71.0	71.6	71.6	72.0	72.0	72.0	71.1	71.3	72.2	72.3	71.6
Financial Activities													
2005	305.7	305.8	305.9	306.8	308.0	310.6	310.9	311.2	309.2	309.0	309.1	309.8	308.5
2006	305.6	305.5	306.3	306.1	306.5	307.9	307.3	306.1	304.2	304.5	304.1	303.5	305.6
2007	301.5	301.2	300.0	301.8	302.3	301.7	301.5	301.0	297.9	297.1	295.5	295.8	299.8
2008	292.1	291.6	291.3	291.4	292.1	292.5	291.7	291.2	288.3	287.4	286.9	286.8	290.3
2009	282.9	281.5	280.8	280.4	281.1	281.7	281.5	280.1	277.8	277.2	277.2	277.0	279.9
2010	274.4	273.9	273.6	274.9	275.8	277.3	278.9	278.8	277.1	278.2	278.6	279.3	276.7
2011	277.4	277.5	277.4	277.9	278.6	278.8	278.9	278.7	277.8	277.4	277.5	277.7	278.0
2012	275.7	275.6	276.3	277.9	279.6	281.5	282.5	282.3	280.4	281.6	282.7	282.8	279.9
2013	279.5	280.1	280.1	282.7	284.6	286.7	287.2	287.3	285.2	285.4	286.2	286.3	284.3
2014	283.7	284.5	284.9	285.3	288.1	289.9	290.3	291.2	288.5	289.3	290.6	290.7	288.1
2015	288.4	289.0	289.0	290.0	292.7	294.7	295.7	296.0	292.9	293.2	293.4	292.4	292.3
Professional and Business Services													
2005	615.1	619.0	625.2	639.8	640.5	646.4	649.6	656.4	658.5	659.4	657.1	657.2	643.7
2006	633.4	636.0	644.2	653.4	654.9	663.6	661.2	668.9	666.4	666.0	664.3	664.4	656.4
2007	645.1	646.7	653.4	664.2	667.4	676.8	674.1	677.7	676.0	680.2	680.6	678.8	668.4
2008	660.5	662.1	661.9	673.3	674.0	677.2	678.2	680.1	674.1	668.9	660.4	652.6	668.6
2009	625.8	619.0	614.1	617.0	615.5	614.6	613.7	616.2	613.9	616.0	618.4	614.5	616.6
2010	596.2	598.1	603.0	621.6	622.6	630.1	634.4	639.4	636.6	642.5	643.6	641.8	625.8
2011	624.6	628.1	634.2	649.8	648.6	652.4	659.0	663.6	662.5	664.9	667.1	666.6	651.8
2012	648.8	652.6	658.8	670.5	673.0	677.8	678.2	683.6	680.6	688.9	688.1	683.7	673.7
2013	657.1	662.3	667.1	685.3	690.8	694.8	693.3	700.9	698.8	704.6	707.5	706.4	689.1
2014	683.4	685.5	689.6	705.2	709.2	711.6	714.7	721.4	715.1	722.8	725.8	722.6	708.9
2015	696.0	693.9	696.9	711.0	717.7	720.3	725.4	727.5	719.0	728.4	726.3	722.5	715.4
Education and Health Services													
2005	748.6	757.1	760.2	763.3	759.8	753.3	748.7	750.2	768.6	775.8	780.0	781.4	762.3
2006	766.8	777.6	781.0	782.0	778.5	769.8	763.5	765.6	783.1	789.3	792.3	792.1	778.5
2007	779.9	785.2	789.5	792.5	791.6	785.0	780.7	783.9	801.7	809.2	814.0	814.1	793.9
2008	803.9	811.5	812.6	815.1	813.3	803.7	799.2	802.1	818.9	826.5	829.9	829.9	813.9
2009	818.6	825.7	827.3	829.5	826.8	817.0	815.4	817.0	832.6	841.7	844.5	844.4	828.4
2010	833.6	839.1	842.4	843.2	839.1	827.2	826.6	828.0	845.1	853.7	856.0	853.6	840.6
2011	841.5	849.7	850.6	856.0	857.9	843.6	840.0	841.3	854.9	862.4	864.5	864.9	852.3
2012	856.0	864.2	865.9	869.2	869.2	860.8	851.3	855.3	866.5	876.4	878.2	876.6	865.8
2013	865.4	876.2	875.6	881.7	882.4	872.5	869.7	874.3	880.0	890.4	895.6	893.8	879.8
2014	878.8	886.0	888.1	893.2	893.9	882.5	879.0	883.6	890.7	902.2	905.8	905.5	890.8
2015	891.5	899.2	900.5	908.2	909.7	897.4	896.4	899.4	906.2	921.5	925.8	925.8	906.8

1. Employment by Industry: Ohio, 2005–2015—*Continued*

(Numbers in thousands, not seasonally adjusted)

Industry and year	January	February	March	April	May	June	July	August	September	October	November	December	Annual average
Leisure and Hospitality													
2005	460.6	463.2	475.1	498.4	517.5	531.8	531.7	532.0	517.8	496.6	488.7	483.7	499.8
2006	463.8	467.4	479.5	496.2	517.2	533.9	531.9	532.6	514.9	497.6	489.1	486.8	500.9
2007	468.3	466.4	478.4	495.9	519.4	535.5	529.3	530.9	512.5	498.5	487.6	483.9	500.6
2008	462.6	463.3	467.8	491.8	516.6	527.1	522.3	522.2	503.7	485.8	471.1	469.6	492.0
2009	445.5	445.2	455.9	474.4	497.9	509.7	507.8	505.4	491.8	472.8	458.9	457.0	476.9
2010	436.7	437.3	448.5	472.0	492.3	505.5	506.7	506.1	492.6	476.8	466.2	462.4	475.3
2011	442.6	444.6	455.6	479.5	500.9	514.4	515.0	517.1	500.8	484.0	476.1	471.2	483.5
2012	454.0	459.2	474.2	495.0	518.5	535.0	532.0	533.3	516.4	505.9	492.7	492.7	500.7
2013	474.1	477.2	490.3	512.9	540.1	551.5	550.0	548.6	532.3	521.6	508.2	506.9	517.8
2014	485.8	486.8	499.4	522.0	548.9	560.7	558.2	557.7	538.8	529.3	516.0	514.9	526.5
2015	495.5	498.1	509.7	533.3	561.1	571.6	571.8	570.0	556.0	546.5	531.2	529.8	539.6
Other Services													
2005	221.1	222.3	224.1	225.7	226.5	227.5	226.3	226.0	223.7	223.6	223.9	223.3	224.5
2006	219.9	220.4	222.1	222.6	224.0	226.6	224.1	223.1	221.6	221.3	220.7	221.3	222.3
2007	218.2	218.2	220.6	220.8	221.9	224.4	222.4	221.6	218.7	219.3	218.7	218.6	220.3
2008	215.4	215.9	216.3	217.6	219.2	220.2	219.0	218.4	215.9	215.8	214.0	213.2	216.7
2009	208.8	209.0	209.8	209.9	211.0	211.1	210.3	208.7	206.7	206.6	205.3	205.7	208.6
2010	202.7	202.9	203.6	205.9	206.2	208.1	208.8	207.9	206.3	206.9	206.4	206.8	206.0
2011	203.9	204.3	205.3	206.6	208.1	209.2	210.2	209.6	207.8	207.7	207.6	207.6	207.3
2012	206.2	206.9	210.0	210.8	212.6	215.3	215.1	214.0	212.3	213.4	212.4	212.7	211.8
2013	210.1	210.6	211.9	213.4	214.5	215.3	213.8	213.1	210.8	209.6	208.9	208.5	211.7
2014	205.8	205.9	206.9	208.5	211.1	213.1	212.4	212.0	209.5	211.2	210.3	211.1	209.8
2015	208.1	208.9	210.3	212.6	214.4	216.1	216.3	215.1	212.3	214.1	214.3	215.5	213.2
Government													
2005	792.3	812.4	814.4	812.6	818.7	794.8	759.1	756.2	791.4	812.7	817.8	813.2	799.6
2006	795.5	811.0	814.1	812.1	818.8	796.4	759.0	756.9	792.7	812.9	817.0	814.3	800.1
2007	793.8	807.7	811.4	811.0	814.8	796.6	757.6	755.9	790.3	810.4	814.5	808.1	797.7
2008	794.3	812.3	810.8	811.8	816.7	794.4	756.6	755.4	790.1	812.6	817.6	808.9	798.5
2009	793.3	808.3	808.8	811.2	812.3	788.7	749.0	745.8	782.4	803.5	805.0	795.8	792.0
2010	783.3	795.6	798.0	802.4	820.1	788.3	742.9	737.3	771.2	795.2	798.7	794.8	785.7
2011	771.3	786.0	788.6	788.6	787.9	765.7	745.6	744.5	772.8	784.7	787.0	780.2	775.2
2012	760.7	781.1	785.1	787.9	794.8	762.6	742.0	741.1	770.5	785.3	786.7	780.8	773.2
2013	759.7	776.5	776.1	781.4	785.5	746.3	729.3	730.8	764.9	777.3	783.1	773.9	765.4
2014	749.8	769.7	771.0	779.3	786.0	750.5	725.9	733.0	774.1	784.9	787.1	782.0	766.1
2015	755.1	776.4	776.3	783.1	784.9	750.3	734.5	736.3	771.4	782.6	787.8	785.0	768.6

2. Average Weekly Hours by Selected Industry: Ohio, 2011–2015

(Not seasonally adjusted)

Industry and year	January	February	March	April	May	June	July	August	September	October	November	December	Annual average
Total Private													
2011	33.4	33.4	33.4	33.7	33.9	33.7	33.6	33.6	33.8	34.3	34.0	33.9	33.7
2012	34.0	33.9	33.9	34.4	34.0	34.0	34.2	34.0	34.3	34.1	34.2	34.6	34.1
2013	34.1	34.2	34.2	34.2	34.1	34.4	33.9	34.2	34.5	34.0	34.1	34.3	34.2
2014	33.3	34.1	34.1	34.0	34.6	34.4	34.1	34.3	34.3	34.3	34.6	34.5	34.2
2015	33.8	34.1	34.3	34.0	34.1	34.3	34.1	34.6	34.1	34.4	34.6	34.4	34.2
Goods-Producing													
2011	39.3	39.7	39.7	39.9	39.9	39.9	39.7	40.5	40.3	40.4	40.6	40.5	40.0
2012	40.1	40.2	40.1	40.4	40.3	40.3	40.4	40.2	40.7	40.6	40.5	41.0	40.4
2013	40.3	40.4	40.5	40.4	40.7	40.9	40.0	41.0	41.1	40.9	41.4	41.3	40.7
2014	39.8	40.8	40.8	41.0	40.9	41.3	40.6	41.1	41.3	41.3	41.3	41.4	41.0
2015	40.3	40.3	40.6	40.4	40.6	40.8	40.0	40.7	39.8	41.0	40.5	40.5	40.5
Construction													
2011	37.4	37.6	37.2	38.1	38.4	39.1	40.1	40.4	40.0	39.1	39.8	38.4	38.9
2012	37.4	37.3	36.6	37.5	37.3	38.0	39.2	39.1	39.9	40.1	40.3	39.0	38.5
2013	38.1	38.0	38.1	38.8	39.4	39.6	39.2	40.9	39.9	40.7	40.1	38.8	39.4
2014	37.3	38.4	38.0	39.0	38.5	39.7	39.4	39.4	40.1	39.1	38.3	38.1	38.8
2015	36.9	37.5	37.7	38.4	39.2	39.0	39.2	40.0	37.9	40.3	38.0	38.7	38.6
Manufacturing													
2011	39.5	40.0	40.0	40.1	40.1	40.0	39.4	40.4	40.2	40.6	40.6	40.8	40.1
2012	40.5	40.6	40.7	40.9	40.9	40.6	40.4	40.6	41.1	40.9	40.7	41.7	40.8
2013	41.1	41.2	41.2	41.0	41.3	41.6	40.5	41.3	41.7	41.2	41.9	42.0	41.3
2014	40.5	41.3	41.4	41.4	41.4	41.5	40.7	41.4	41.5	41.8	42.0	42.1	41.4
2015	41.1	40.9	41.2	40.8	40.8	41.1	40.1	40.7	40.5	41.1	41.2	41.0	40.9
Trade, Transportation, and Utilities													
2011	34.6	34.1	34.2	34.6	34.8	34.7	34.6	34.3	34.8	35.3	34.6	35.0	34.6
2012	34.8	34.5	34.4	35.0	34.7	34.7	34.7	34.5	34.9	34.6	34.4	34.5	34.6
2013	34.4	34.6	34.6	34.8	34.9	34.8	34.6	34.8	35.1	34.6	34.3	34.9	34.7
2014	33.9	34.4	34.3	34.1	34.5	34.6	34.7	34.7	34.8	34.6	34.8	34.8	34.5
2015	33.8	34.3	34.4	34.5	34.8	34.7	34.8	35.2	35.1	34.8	35.1	35.2	34.7
Financial Activities													
2011	37.1	36.0	36.1	36.6	37.7	37.1	36.8	36.6	36.9	37.5	36.8	36.9	36.8
2012	38.2	36.7	36.7	37.8	36.2	36.2	38.0	36.4	37.8	36.3	36.3	38.2	37.1
2013	37.1	36.9	37.2	36.8	36.7	37.9	36.2	35.9	37.4	35.8	36.0	37.4	36.8
2014	36.5	37.7	37.3	36.8	36.9	37.4	36.6	37.0	36.8	36.7	38.1	36.4	37.0
2015	36.7	37.8	38.6	37.3	37.3	36.7	36.6	37.4	36.3	36.6	37.2	36.2	37.1
Professional and Business Services													
2011	34.9	34.5	34.6	34.6	34.9	34.1	33.9	34.3	34.1	35.4	34.5	34.3	34.5
2012	34.5	34.5	34.9	36.0	35.1	35.3	35.3	35.3	35.6	35.6	35.9	36.5	35.4
2013	35.6	35.9	36.1	36.4	36.2	36.6	35.9	36.2	36.5	36.0	36.4	36.5	36.2
2014	35.2	36.3	36.4	36.1	35.7	36.5	35.5	35.5	35.8	35.6	35.9	35.7	35.8
2015	34.8	35.7	35.9	35.4	35.3	35.4	35.2	35.8	35.1	35.8	36.3	35.9	35.6
Education and Health Services													
2011	32.4	32.4	32.4	32.6	32.5	32.3	32.7	32.2	32.4	32.6	32.6	32.5	32.5
2012	32.6	32.3	32.2	32.4	32.2	32.1	32.2	32.2	32.5	32.4	32.3	32.4	32.3
2013	32.2	32.1	32.0	31.9	31.5	31.7	31.5	31.6	31.9	31.4	31.4	31.6	31.7
2014	31.1	31.3	31.3	31.2	31.0	30.4	30.6	30.7	30.9	31.1	31.8	31.7	31.1
2015	31.7	31.6	31.8	31.8	32.0	32.2	32.2	32.5	32.5	32.4	32.8	32.5	32.2
Leisure and Hospitality													
2011	22.8	23.5	23.6	23.9	23.8	24.1	24.0	23.9	23.6	24.0	23.9	23.6	23.7
2012	22.8	23.5	23.5	23.7	24.0	24.4	24.5	24.3	23.6	23.7	23.6	24.2	23.8
2013	23.3	24.0	24.0	24.0	24.2	24.3	24.2	24.4	23.7	23.4	23.3	23.1	23.8
2014	22.1	23.3	23.5	23.5	23.9	24.5	24.3	24.6	24.0	24.0	24.0	24.1	23.8
2015	23.1	23.8	24.0	23.7	24.2	24.5	24.8	24.9	24.1	24.4	24.4	24.6	24.2
Other Services													
2011	30.8	30.5	30.5	30.4	30.6	30.4	30.1	29.7	29.9	30.2	29.8	29.8	30.2
2012	29.6	28.6	28.5	28.8	28.4	28.0	28.2	28.0	28.5	28.0	28.4	28.5	28.5
2013	27.8	28.1	28.1	28.6	28.9	29.2	28.8	29.0	29.6	29.4	29.7	30.1	28.9
2014	29.4	30.6	30.7	29.9	30.1	29.9	29.5	29.6	29.8	30.1	30.4	30.1	30.0
2015	30.1	30.3	31.1	30.6	30.5	31.0	30.8	31.8	30.3	30.2	30.8	31.0	30.7

3. Average Hourly Earnings by Selected Industry: Ohio, 2011–2015

(Dollars, not seasonally adjusted)

Industry and year	January	February	March	April	May	June	July	August	September	October	November	December	Annual average
Total Private													
2011	20.85	20.94	20.83	20.85	21.03	20.77	20.93	21.11	21.30	21.43	21.38	21.40	21.07
2012	21.97	21.83	21.86	22.11	21.81	21.69	21.87	21.82	22.32	22.13	22.26	22.48	22.01
2013	22.40	22.32	22.17	22.18	22.01	22.19	22.11	22.08	22.44	22.25	22.34	22.45	22.24
2014	22.40	22.53	22.46	22.35	21.68	21.83	21.79	21.92	22.20	22.14	22.36	22.29	22.16
2015	22.51	22.63	22.67	22.57	22.48	22.37	22.51	22.80	22.90	22.76	22.98	22.93	22.68
Goods-Producing													
2011	22.19	22.43	22.65	22.81	22.85	22.91	22.99	23.21	23.58	23.51	23.57	23.90	23.07
2012	23.92	23.63	23.85	23.95	23.47	23.36	23.55	23.54	23.98	23.94	24.19	24.23	23.80
2013	24.04	23.89	23.80	23.79	23.87	23.86	24.07	24.16	24.28	24.12	24.20	24.66	24.07
2014	24.59	24.68	24.70	24.68	24.41	24.57	24.69	24.70	24.89	24.82	24.74	24.72	24.68
2015	24.56	24.51	24.65	24.67	24.66	24.61	24.90	24.99	25.00	24.75	24.78	25.10	24.77
Construction													
2011	24.95	25.09	25.57	25.14	25.02	25.16	25.10	25.42	25.64	25.61	25.81	26.07	25.40
2012	25.86	26.03	26.68	26.35	26.22	25.81	25.83	25.94	26.66	26.91	26.73	26.76	26.32
2013	26.13	26.18	26.01	25.67	25.43	25.23	25.49	25.66	25.68	25.60	25.45	25.98	25.69
2014	25.50	26.10	26.23	26.12	25.87	26.03	26.31	26.16	26.85	26.43	25.94	26.03	26.15
2015	25.75	25.55	25.97	26.03	26.56	26.33	26.87	26.91	27.05	26.77	26.68	26.94	26.49
Manufacturing													
2011	22.20	22.34	22.51	22.70	22.79	22.73	22.77	22.93	23.23	23.20	23.19	23.38	22.84
2012	23.48	23.27	23.38	23.55	23.04	22.97	23.14	23.09	23.42	23.28	23.64	23.76	23.34
2013	23.70	23.50	23.40	23.46	23.58	23.60	23.81	23.89	24.02	23.84	23.97	24.32	23.76
2014	24.36	24.36	24.36	24.33	24.06	24.21	24.25	24.33	24.34	24.38	24.46	24.43	24.32
2015	24.34	24.30	24.38	24.37	24.18	24.19	24.34	24.44	24.49	24.17	24.31	24.62	24.34
Trade, Transportation, and Utilities													
2011	19.00	19.02	18.91	18.38	18.52	18.55	19.00	19.03	19.09	19.09	19.01	18.69	18.86
2012	19.40	19.24	19.36	19.94	19.59	19.81	20.25	19.94	20.09	20.22	19.95	20.23	19.84
2013	20.48	20.45	20.43	20.51	20.23	20.56	20.39	20.17	20.60	20.16	20.28	20.08	20.36
2014	20.32	20.74	20.91	20.97	20.53	20.60	20.29	20.53	20.79	20.62	20.75	20.64	20.64
2015	21.00	21.19	21.35	21.34	21.16	21.16	21.32	21.56	21.67	21.69	21.76	21.35	21.38
Financial Activities													
2011	24.80	24.53	24.08	24.37	24.66	24.26	24.80	24.56	24.68	25.10	24.92	25.27	24.67
2012	26.84	26.64	26.74	27.78	27.25	27.20	27.18	27.36	27.90	27.36	27.87	27.94	27.34
2013	27.90	27.10	27.00	27.62	27.52	27.45	27.56	27.53	27.79	27.90	27.88	27.64	27.57
2014	27.90	27.41	27.19	27.08	26.75	26.75	27.08	26.92	27.23	27.31	27.47	27.26	27.19
2015	27.39	27.93	27.47	27.15	26.78	26.46	26.55	27.58	27.39	26.87	26.76	26.87	27.10
Professional and Business Services													
2011	24.20	24.11	23.74	24.35	24.33	24.04	24.24	24.02	24.23	24.83	24.69	24.60	24.29
2012	25.41	25.10	25.19	25.64	25.37	25.31	25.52	25.07	25.89	25.37	25.72	26.10	25.48
2013	25.94	25.72	25.46	25.44	25.13	25.58	25.30	25.42	25.89	25.63	25.61	26.00	25.59
2014	25.57	25.80	25.49	25.03	24.81	24.99	24.78	24.76	24.62	24.38	25.14	25.00	25.03
2015	25.39	25.71	25.71	25.44	25.40	25.21	25.40	25.98	25.93	25.81	26.49	26.23	25.73
Education and Health Services													
2011	21.11	21.32	21.30	21.33	21.71	21.23	21.14	21.34	21.34	21.51	21.51	21.47	21.36
2012	21.42	21.66	21.47	21.28	21.44	21.16	21.28	21.15	21.41	21.20	21.27	21.44	21.35
2013	21.19	21.50	21.29	21.34	21.27	21.47	21.38	21.26	21.58	21.65	21.67	21.72	21.44
2014	21.56	21.61	21.57	21.60	21.59	21.69	21.84	22.13	22.54	22.42	22.61	22.69	21.99
2015	23.02	22.88	22.78	22.61	22.57	22.41	22.30	22.43	22.67	22.36	22.46	22.70	22.60
Leisure and Hospitality													
2011	11.78	11.77	11.67	11.72	11.74	11.60	11.56	11.66	11.65	11.66	11.81	11.95	11.71
2012	11.97	12.15	11.96	11.96	11.87	11.74	11.71	11.75	12.03	11.94	12.01	12.07	11.92
2013	12.10	12.20	12.14	12.17	12.11	12.06	12.12	12.09	12.35	12.46	12.57	12.69	12.25
2014	12.80	12.75	12.65	12.63	12.53	12.29	12.29	12.21	12.36	12.39	12.42	12.56	12.48
2015	12.69	12.64	12.61	12.68	12.46	12.41	12.34	12.40	12.51	12.50	12.58	12.79	12.54
Other Services													
2011	16.83	17.03	17.17	17.01	17.42	17.38	17.64	17.76	17.97	17.91	18.03	18.41	17.54
2012	18.66	18.70	18.91	19.25	19.08	18.74	19.18	19.05	19.57	19.36	19.63	19.71	19.15
2013	19.34	19.38	19.36	19.06	19.02	18.95	19.07	19.08	19.17	19.08	19.44	19.49	19.20
2014	19.22	19.43	19.33	18.92	19.15	19.35	19.46	19.52	19.84	20.30	20.28	20.36	19.60
2015	20.25	20.77	20.79	20.71	21.00	20.81	21.15	21.34	21.76	21.03	21.49	21.29	21.04

4. Average Weekly Earnings by Selected Industry: Ohio, 2011–2015

(Dollars, not seasonally adjusted)

Industry and year	January	February	March	April	May	June	July	August	September	October	November	December	Annual average
Total Private													
2011	696.39	699.40	695.72	702.65	712.92	699.95	703.25	709.30	719.94	735.05	726.92	725.46	710.06
2012	746.98	740.04	741.05	760.58	741.54	737.46	747.95	741.88	765.58	754.63	761.29	777.81	750.54
2013	763.84	763.34	758.21	758.56	750.54	763.34	749.53	755.14	774.18	756.50	761.79	770.04	760.61
2014	745.92	768.27	765.89	759.90	750.13	750.95	743.04	751.86	761.46	759.40	773.66	769.01	757.87
2015	760.84	771.68	777.58	767.38	766.57	767.29	767.59	788.88	780.89	782.94	795.11	788.79	775.66
Goods-Producing													
2011	872.07	890.47	899.21	910.12	911.72	914.11	912.70	940.01	950.27	949.80	956.94	967.95	922.80
2012	959.19	949.93	956.39	967.58	945.84	941.41	951.42	946.31	975.99	971.96	979.70	993.43	961.52
2013	968.81	965.16	963.90	961.12	971.51	975.87	962.80	990.56	997.91	986.51	1,001.88	1,018.46	979.65
2014	978.68	1,006.94	1,007.76	1,011.88	998.37	1,014.74	1,002.41	1,015.17	1,027.96	1,025.07	1,021.76	1,023.41	1,011.88
2015	989.77	987.75	1,000.79	996.67	1,001.20	1,004.09	996.00	1,017.09	995.00	1,014.75	1,003.59	1,016.55	1,003.19
Construction													
2011	933.13	943.38	951.20	957.83	960.77	983.76	1,006.51	1,026.97	1,025.60	1,001.35	1,027.24	1,001.09	988.06
2012	967.16	970.92	976.49	988.13	978.01	980.78	1,012.54	1,014.25	1,063.73	1,079.09	1,077.22	1,043.64	1,013.32
2013	995.55	994.84	990.98	996.00	1,001.94	999.11	999.21	1,049.49	1,024.63	1,041.92	1,020.55	1,008.02	1,012.19
2014	951.15	1,002.24	996.74	1,018.68	996.00	1,033.39	1,036.61	1,030.70	1,076.69	1,033.41	993.50	991.74	1,014.62
2015	950.18	958.13	979.07	999.55	1,041.15	1,026.87	1,053.30	1,076.40	1,025.20	1,078.83	1,013.84	1,042.58	1,022.51
Manufacturing													
2011	876.90	893.60	900.40	910.27	913.88	909.20	897.14	926.37	933.85	941.92	941.51	953.90	915.88
2012	950.94	944.76	951.57	963.20	942.34	932.58	934.86	937.45	962.56	952.15	962.15	990.79	952.27
2013	974.07	968.20	964.08	961.86	973.85	981.76	964.31	986.66	1,001.63	982.21	1,004.34	1,021.44	981.29
2014	986.58	1,006.07	1,008.50	1,007.26	996.08	1,004.72	986.98	1,007.26	1,010.11	1,019.08	1,027.32	1,028.50	1,006.85
2015	1,000.37	993.87	1,004.46	994.30	986.54	994.21	976.03	994.71	991.85	993.39	1,001.57	1,009.42	995.51
Trade, Transportation, and Utilities													
2011	657.40	648.58	646.72	635.95	644.50	643.69	657.40	652.73	664.33	673.88	657.75	654.15	652.56
2012	675.12	663.78	665.98	697.90	679.77	687.41	702.68	687.93	701.14	699.61	686.28	697.94	686.46
2013	704.51	707.57	706.88	713.75	706.03	715.49	705.49	701.92	723.06	697.54	695.60	700.79	706.49
2014	688.85	713.46	717.21	715.08	708.29	712.76	704.06	712.39	723.49	713.45	722.10	718.27	712.08
2015	709.80	726.82	734.44	736.23	736.37	734.25	741.94	758.91	760.62	754.81	763.78	751.52	741.89
Financial Activities													
2011	920.08	883.08	869.29	891.94	929.68	900.05	912.64	898.90	910.69	941.25	917.06	932.46	907.86
2012	1,025.29	977.69	981.36	1,050.08	986.45	984.64	1,032.84	995.90	1,054.62	993.17	1,011.68	1,067.31	1,014.31
2013	1,035.09	999.99	1,004.40	1,016.42	1,009.98	1,040.36	997.67	988.33	1,039.35	998.82	1,003.68	1,033.74	1,014.58
2014	1,018.35	1,033.36	1,014.19	996.54	987.08	1,000.45	991.13	996.04	1,002.06	1,002.28	1,046.61	992.26	1,006.03
2015	1,005.21	1,055.75	1,060.34	1,012.70	998.89	971.08	971.73	1,031.49	994.26	983.44	995.47	972.69	1,005.41
Professional and Business Services													
2011	844.58	831.80	821.40	842.51	849.12	819.76	821.74	823.89	826.24	878.98	851.81	843.78	838.01
2012	876.65	865.95	879.13	923.04	890.49	893.44	900.86	884.97	921.68	903.17	923.35	952.65	901.99
2013	923.46	923.35	919.11	926.02	909.71	936.23	908.27	920.20	944.99	922.68	932.20	949.00	926.36
2014	900.06	936.54	927.84	903.58	885.72	912.14	879.69	878.98	881.40	867.93	902.53	892.50	896.07
2015	883.57	917.85	922.99	900.58	896.62	892.43	894.08	930.08	910.14	924.00	961.59	941.66	915.99
Education and Health Services													
2011	683.96	690.77	690.12	695.36	705.58	685.73	691.28	687.15	691.42	701.23	701.23	697.78	694.20
2012	698.29	699.62	691.33	689.47	690.37	679.24	685.22	681.03	695.83	686.88	687.02	694.66	689.61
2013	682.32	690.15	681.28	680.75	670.01	680.60	673.47	671.82	688.40	679.81	680.44	686.35	679.65
2014	670.52	676.39	675.14	673.92	669.29	659.38	668.30	679.39	696.49	697.26	719.00	719.27	683.89
2015	729.73	723.01	724.40	719.00	722.24	721.60	718.06	728.98	736.78	724.46	736.69	737.75	727.72
Leisure and Hospitality													
2011	268.58	276.60	275.41	280.11	279.41	279.56	277.44	278.67	274.94	279.84	282.26	282.02	277.53
2012	272.92	285.53	281.06	283.45	284.88	286.46	286.90	285.53	283.91	282.98	283.44	292.09	283.70
2013	281.93	292.80	291.36	292.08	293.06	293.06	293.30	295.00	292.70	291.56	292.88	293.14	291.55
2014	282.88	297.08	297.28	296.81	299.47	301.11	298.65	300.37	296.64	297.36	298.08	302.70	297.02
2015	293.14	300.83	302.64	300.52	301.53	304.05	306.03	308.76	301.49	305.00	306.95	314.63	303.47
Other Services													
2011	518.36	519.42	523.69	517.10	533.05	528.35	530.96	527.47	537.30	540.88	537.29	548.62	529.71
2012	552.34	534.82	538.94	554.40	541.87	524.72	540.88	533.40	557.75	542.08	557.49	561.74	545.78
2013	537.65	544.58	544.02	545.12	549.68	553.34	549.22	553.32	567.43	560.95	577.37	586.65	554.88
2014	565.07	594.56	593.43	565.71	576.42	578.57	574.07	577.79	591.23	611.03	616.51	612.84	588.00
2015	609.53	629.33	646.57	633.73	640.50	645.11	651.42	678.61	659.33	635.11	661.89	659.99	645.93

OKLAHOMA

At a Glance

Population:
  2005 estimate: 3,548,597
  2010 census: 3,751,351
  2015 estimate: 3,911,338

Percent change in population:
  2005–2015: 10.2%
  2010–2015: 4.3%

Percent change in total nonfarm employment:
  2005–2015: 9.4%

Industry with the largest growth in employment, 2005–2015 (thousands):
  Education and health services, 30.4

Industry with the largest decline or smallest growth in employment, 2005–2015 (thousands):
  Information, –9.3

Civilian labor force:
  2005: 1,703,293
  2010: 1,768,284
  2015: 1,842,049

Unemployment rate and rank among states (highest to lowest):
  2005: 4.5%, 32nd
  2010: 6.8%, 44th
  2015: 4.2%, 37th

Over-the-year change in unemployment rates:
  2012–2013: 0.0%
  2013–2014: –0.8%
  2014–2015: –0.3%

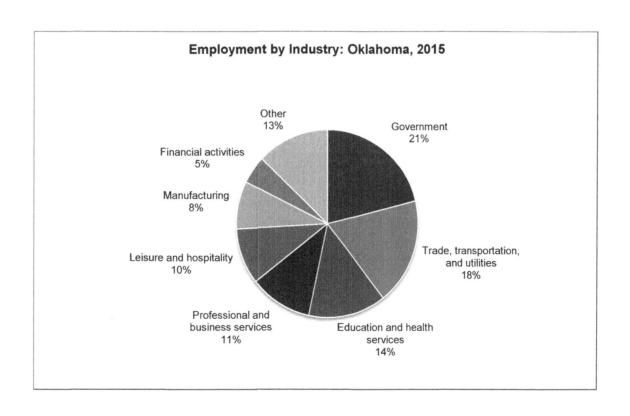

Employment by Industry: Oklahoma, 2015

- Other 13%
- Government 21%
- Financial activities 5%
- Manufacturing 8%
- Leisure and hospitality 10%
- Trade, transportation, and utilities 18%
- Professional and business services 11%
- Education and health services 14%

1. Employment by Industry: Oklahoma, 2005–2015

(Numbers in thousands, not seasonally adjusted)

Industry and year	January	February	March	April	May	June	July	August	September	October	November	December	Annual average
Total Nonfarm													
2005	1,478.3	1,492.8	1,509.7	1,523.6	1,532.2	1,526.0	1,512.0	1,523.3	1,540.1	1,545.7	1,556.9	1,562.2	1,525.2
2006	1,529.0	1,543.2	1,559.8	1,559.5	1,573.2	1,571.1	1,551.2	1,565.2	1,579.9	1,579.7	1,585.6	1,591.4	1,565.7
2007	1,554.5	1,569.5	1,590.6	1,589.0	1,599.8	1,598.9	1,579.0	1,595.0	1,608.0	1,613.8	1,622.5	1,618.0	1,594.9
2008	1,592.1	1,607.0	1,618.3	1,622.3	1,632.2	1,618.0	1,603.8	1,615.2	1,627.0	1,629.3	1,629.2	1,627.3	1,618.5
2009	1,581.3	1,582.1	1,585.2	1,579.8	1,579.8	1,568.1	1,550.4	1,550.8	1,557.5	1,558.1	1,559.8	1,557.8	1,567.6
2010	1,521.6	1,528.6	1,543.7	1,557.2	1,569.6	1,564.0	1,549.9	1,550.8	1,558.3	1,571.7	1,576.1	1,580.2	1,556.0
2011	1,541.9	1,541.5	1,565.1	1,580.8	1,584.5	1,578.2	1,564.9	1,573.1	1,594.6	1,597.8	1,602.3	1,607.3	1,577.7
2012	1,574.9	1,590.0	1,602.8	1,614.6	1,622.8	1,617.4	1,595.9	1,608.4	1,621.0	1,634.2	1,642.3	1,644.5	1,614.1
2013	1,600.7	1,614.5	1,626.3	1,634.4	1,645.9	1,636.7	1,621.1	1,633.5	1,645.6	1,650.7	1,659.9	1,654.4	1,635.3
2014	1,623.0	1,633.5	1,643.4	1,652.8	1,662.5	1,654.4	1,642.2	1,654.1	1,665.0	1,676.1	1,683.6	1,688.4	1,656.6
2015	1,655.7	1,663.6	1,665.6	1,671.4	1,675.3	1,666.4	1,658.9	1,662.9	1,668.1	1,678.5	1,682.0	1,675.4	1,668.7
Total Private													
2005	1,164.6	1,171.7	1,186.4	1,198.6	1,204.7	1,210.7	1,210.7	1,216.2	1,217.2	1,215.3	1,225.1	1,230.4	1,204.3
2006	1,205.7	1,211.8	1,226.9	1,227.3	1,238.0	1,248.0	1,240.6	1,247.6	1,246.9	1,241.2	1,246.6	1,252.8	1,236.1
2007	1,224.0	1,232.3	1,251.6	1,251.4	1,260.2	1,271.1	1,266.6	1,275.2	1,270.9	1,272.2	1,279.8	1,277.1	1,261.0
2008	1,262.5	1,269.9	1,279.5	1,280.7	1,287.3	1,289.8	1,286.9	1,290.9	1,286.8	1,281.5	1,280.4	1,278.4	1,281.2
2009	1,241.1	1,235.0	1,235.1	1,227.6	1,225.5	1,227.1	1,216.3	1,213.1	1,207.1	1,200.5	1,201.9	1,200.7	1,219.3
2010	1,175.3	1,176.7	1,188.9	1,202.2	1,208.7	1,215.5	1,213.5	1,217.1	1,215.4	1,221.5	1,225.5	1,229.2	1,207.5
2011	1,200.6	1,195.3	1,216.9	1,230.9	1,234.5	1,240.1	1,241.1	1,245.8	1,248.3	1,247.3	1,250.9	1,253.9	1,233.8
2012	1,232.1	1,239.6	1,250.8	1,262.5	1,269.9	1,277.6	1,268.5	1,274.4	1,272.7	1,279.9	1,286.2	1,289.1	1,266.9
2013	1,255.2	1,261.0	1,271.6	1,279.2	1,289.3	1,294.6	1,292.0	1,299.0	1,297.5	1,296.7	1,304.1	1,300.5	1,286.7
2014	1,278.4	1,281.5	1,290.4	1,299.7	1,307.2	1,312.6	1,313.1	1,319.0	1,316.6	1,320.2	1,326.9	1,332.9	1,308.2
2015	1,309.0	1,309.3	1,311.0	1,315.3	1,317.6	1,322.2	1,321.7	1,321.0	1,316.2	1,319.7	1,322.0	1,316.0	1,316.8
Goods-Producing													
2005	236.9	238.4	241.8	244.0	244.8	246.4	249.7	250.5	250.6	251.8	252.9	256.0	247.0
2006	253.9	255.5	258.8	256.8	259.8	263.9	263.4	265.7	265.1	264.6	264.5	266.1	261.5
2007	260.8	261.3	265.1	265.0	266.9	271.5	272.1	274.0	271.9	273.4	275.2	274.7	269.3
2008	272.4	273.8	275.7	276.9	279.1	281.0	281.6	281.8	280.2	278.0	275.3	273.3	277.4
2009	263.9	258.3	253.8	246.5	243.3	242.2	238.3	235.5	232.5	230.0	228.4	227.7	241.7
2010	224.2	223.9	226.7	230.3	232.5	235.5	236.9	237.8	237.8	240.9	240.8	242.7	234.2
2011	237.9	237.2	242.3	246.4	247.7	251.4	253.2	254.0	255.3	256.2	256.6	257.8	249.7
2012	254.9	256.3	259.2	260.9	263.3	266.7	266.0	266.7	266.2	269.4	270.2	270.6	264.2
2013	264.3	265.5	267.6	268.0	270.5	273.8	272.9	274.5	273.7	274.7	274.4	273.8	271.1
2014	269.2	270.1	271.6	271.8	274.0	276.2	278.3	280.8	280.3	281.9	282.2	283.4	276.7
2015	279.0	277.7	274.3	270.4	268.3	269.0	268.8	267.2	265.2	262.3	262.5	262.2	268.9
Service-Providing													
2005	1,241.4	1,254.4	1,267.9	1,279.6	1,287.4	1,279.6	1,262.3	1,272.8	1,289.5	1,293.9	1,304.0	1,306.2	1,278.3
2006	1,275.1	1,287.7	1,301.0	1,302.7	1,313.4	1,307.2	1,287.8	1,299.5	1,314.8	1,315.1	1,321.1	1,325.3	1,304.2
2007	1,293.7	1,308.2	1,325.5	1,324.0	1,332.9	1,327.4	1,306.9	1,321.0	1,336.1	1,340.4	1,347.3	1,343.3	1,325.6
2008	1,319.7	1,333.2	1,342.6	1,345.4	1,353.1	1,337.0	1,322.2	1,333.4	1,346.8	1,351.3	1,353.9	1,354.0	1,341.1
2009	1,317.4	1,323.8	1,331.4	1,333.3	1,336.5	1,325.9	1,312.1	1,315.3	1,325.0	1,328.1	1,331.4	1,330.1	1,325.9
2010	1,297.4	1,304.7	1,317.0	1,326.9	1,337.1	1,328.5	1,313.0	1,313.0	1,320.5	1,330.8	1,335.3	1,337.5	1,321.8
2011	1,304.0	1,304.3	1,322.8	1,334.4	1,336.8	1,326.8	1,311.7	1,319.1	1,339.3	1,341.6	1,345.7	1,349.5	1,328.0
2012	1,320.0	1,333.7	1,343.6	1,353.7	1,359.5	1,350.7	1,329.9	1,341.7	1,354.8	1,364.8	1,372.1	1,373.9	1,349.9
2013	1,336.4	1,349.0	1,358.7	1,366.4	1,375.4	1,362.9	1,348.2	1,359.0	1,371.9	1,376.0	1,385.5	1,380.6	1,364.2
2014	1,353.8	1,363.4	1,371.8	1,381.0	1,388.5	1,378.2	1,363.9	1,373.3	1,384.7	1,394.2	1,401.4	1,405.0	1,379.9
2015	1,376.7	1,385.9	1,391.3	1,401.0	1,407.0	1,397.4	1,390.1	1,395.7	1,402.9	1,416.2	1,419.5	1,413.2	1,399.7
Mining and Logging													
2005	34.4	34.5	34.8	34.8	35.3	35.8	36.1	36.5	36.8	37.2	37.5	37.9	36.0
2006	38.4	39.2	40.0	40.7	41.3	42.4	42.5	43.5	43.6	43.4	43.9	44.5	42.0
2007	44.3	44.2	44.8	44.9	45.3	46.4	47.2	47.9	47.6	48.6	49.2	49.3	46.6
2008	49.6	49.9	50.2	50.5	51.4	52.5	52.9	53.5	53.3	53.8	53.3	52.7	52.0
2009	50.4	48.9	47.3	44.7	43.4	42.8	41.9	41.3	40.4	39.8	39.9	40.3	43.4
2010	40.5	40.6	41.3	42.2	42.8	43.9	44.4	45.0	45.1	46.0	46.1	47.1	43.8
2011	47.3	47.8	48.6	49.3	50.0	51.3	52.6	53.0	53.6	54.3	54.8	55.6	51.5
2012	55.4	56.0	56.9	57.2	58.0	59.0	59.4	59.4	58.9	59.3	59.1	58.9	58.1
2013	58.5	58.7	58.8	59.3	59.8	60.5	60.1	60.3	59.9	60.1	60.0	60.3	59.7
2014	59.3	59.2	59.5	59.7	60.3	61.4	62.3	63.2	63.3	63.8	64.3	64.5	61.7
2015	63.0	60.4	58.0	55.2	53.8	53.5	53.2	52.7	51.6	50.2	50.0	50.2	54.3

1. Employment by Industry: Oklahoma, 2005–2015—*Continued*

(Numbers in thousands, not seasonally adjusted)

Industry and year	January	February	March	April	May	June	July	August	September	October	November	December	Annual average
Construction													
2005	61.1	61.4	63.6	65.5	65.3	66.9	68.1	68.1	68.0	68.1	68.0	68.8	66.1
2006	67.7	68.1	69.7	69.6	70.1	72.1	71.1	71.5	71.3	71.0	70.4	70.5	70.3
2007	67.5	67.7	70.2	70.0	70.7	73.0	72.4	73.5	72.4	72.8	73.3	72.2	71.3
2008	71.6	72.3	73.8	74.8	76.2	77.0	78.0	78.0	77.7	76.8	75.7	74.7	75.6
2009	71.4	70.7	70.7	69.4	69.3	70.4	69.8	69.0	68.0	67.0	65.9	65.2	68.9
2010	62.9	62.5	64.2	65.9	66.9	68.0	68.4	68.6	68.6	70.0	69.0	69.1	67.0
2011	65.1	63.7	66.8	68.5	68.6	70.0	69.5	69.6	69.8	69.6	69.0	68.8	68.3
2012	66.6	66.8	67.9	68.8	69.9	71.1	70.6	70.9	70.8	72.8	74.0	74.1	70.4
2013	69.6	70.5	72.2	72.4	74.2	76.0	75.5	77.1	77.2	77.8	77.4	76.3	74.7
2014	73.5	73.6	74.6	74.0	74.7	74.8	75.6	77.2	76.5	77.1	76.4	76.5	75.4
2015	75.1	76.2	76.2	76.5	76.4	78.0	78.9	78.9	78.7	79.3	79.8	79.5	77.8
Manufacturing													
2005	141.4	142.5	143.4	143.7	144.2	143.7	145.5	145.9	145.8	146.5	147.4	149.3	144.9
2006	147.8	148.2	149.1	146.5	148.4	149.4	149.8	150.7	150.2	150.2	150.2	151.1	149.3
2007	149.0	149.4	150.1	150.1	150.9	152.1	152.5	152.6	151.9	152.0	152.7	153.2	151.4
2008	151.2	151.6	151.7	151.6	151.5	151.5	150.7	150.3	149.2	147.4	146.3	145.9	149.9
2009	142.1	138.7	135.8	132.4	130.6	129.0	126.6	125.2	124.1	123.2	122.6	122.2	129.4
2010	120.8	120.8	121.2	122.2	122.8	123.6	124.1	124.2	124.1	124.9	125.7	126.5	123.4
2011	125.5	125.7	126.9	128.6	129.1	130.1	131.1	131.4	131.9	132.3	132.8	133.4	129.9
2012	132.9	133.5	134.4	134.9	135.4	136.6	136.0	136.4	136.5	137.3	137.1	137.6	135.7
2013	136.2	136.3	136.6	136.3	136.5	137.3	137.3	137.1	136.6	136.8	137.0	137.2	136.8
2014	136.4	137.3	137.5	138.1	139.0	140.0	140.4	140.4	140.5	141.0	141.5	142.4	139.5
2015	140.9	141.1	140.1	138.7	138.1	137.5	136.7	135.6	134.9	132.8	132.7	132.5	136.8
Trade, Transportation, and Utilities													
2005	272.0	271.8	274.3	276.7	278.0	278.4	278.9	280.2	280.5	282.2	287.6	290.5	279.3
2006	278.0	278.0	280.3	281.7	284.3	284.8	282.8	283.7	283.6	283.9	288.7	292.8	283.6
2007	282.7	282.5	288.2	285.1	287.2	288.1	286.6	287.3	286.4	287.7	293.1	294.1	287.4
2008	285.8	285.2	287.9	287.8	288.8	289.3	289.3	289.9	289.2	289.9	293.4	295.0	289.3
2009	284.1	282.1	282.7	282.2	282.8	282.4	279.8	279.4	278.4	277.8	281.2	282.5	281.3
2010	272.7	271.3	273.9	275.3	277.2	278.4	277.9	277.8	275.7	278.1	282.8	285.1	277.2
2011	275.8	274.1	278.4	281.2	281.9	282.5	282.5	284.0	283.6	285.0	289.9	292.2	282.6
2012	284.5	283.4	286.2	287.9	289.9	291.2	289.7	289.8	289.7	292.7	298.5	300.9	290.4
2013	287.6	287.7	289.7	291.6	293.8	295.2	295.1	296.3	296.2	297.3	303.5	305.9	295.0
2014	296.8	295.9	297.5	298.2	299.9	301.9	301.0	301.9	301.7	303.8	309.3	313.5	301.8
2015	302.6	302.2	303.4	304.7	306.0	307.8	307.0	307.0	306.1	310.0	312.6	313.9	306.9
Wholesale Trade													
2005	53.7	53.9	54.3	54.7	55.0	55.6	55.7	55.8	55.6	55.9	56.0	56.2	55.2
2006	55.6	56.0	56.5	56.4	57.0	57.5	57.3	57.3	57.2	57.1	57.3	57.5	56.9
2007	57.0	57.2	58.0	57.9	58.2	59.0	58.2	57.9	57.7	58.1	58.4	58.4	58.0
2008	57.9	57.8	58.0	57.8	58.1	58.5	58.3	57.9	57.7	57.8	57.8	57.6	57.9
2009	56.7	56.4	56.1	55.6	55.2	55.0	54.5	53.9	53.5	53.6	53.3	53.3	54.8
2010	52.7	52.8	53.1	53.6	54.0	54.5	54.3	54.2	54.2	54.8	55.0	55.0	54.0
2011	54.4	54.6	55.5	55.7	55.8	56.0	56.3	56.2	56.2	56.6	56.5	56.7	55.9
2012	56.3	56.8	57.4	57.8	58.3	58.7	58.2	58.2	58.1	58.7	58.9	59.3	58.1
2013	58.3	58.5	58.8	58.8	59.2	59.6	59.3	59.2	59.3	59.4	59.7	59.7	59.2
2014	59.8	59.8	60.1	60.2	60.6	61.2	60.8	61.0	61.0	61.5	61.6	61.9	60.8
2015	61.0	61.2	61.0	60.7	60.3	60.7	60.3	59.8	59.4	60.1	59.2	58.9	60.2
Retail Trade													
2005	165.5	164.9	166.7	168.1	169.0	168.5	168.6	169.5	170.0	171.6	176.4	178.5	169.8
2006	167.6	167.2	168.7	169.7	171.1	170.8	168.9	169.3	168.8	169.1	173.5	176.3	170.1
2007	167.8	167.1	171.7	169.5	171.0	170.7	169.9	170.9	170.5	171.6	176.7	177.3	171.2
2008	170.7	170.3	172.6	172.1	172.5	172.3	172.3	173.1	172.5	172.9	176.4	177.7	173.0
2009	169.8	168.4	169.4	169.3	170.6	170.4	168.9	169.4	169.2	168.3	171.9	172.8	169.9
2010	166.0	164.5	166.7	167.4	168.7	169.3	168.9	169.0	166.8	168.7	172.9	174.3	168.6
2011	167.2	165.3	168.2	170.1	170.4	170.1	169.6	170.9	170.4	171.1	175.8	177.0	170.5
2012	170.3	168.6	170.6	171.7	172.7	173.1	172.2	172.1	172.1	174.1	179.4	180.9	173.2
2013	170.0	169.3	170.8	172.3	173.9	174.5	174.6	175.8	175.8	176.9	182.3	184.3	175.0
2014	175.6	174.9	175.4	176.5	177.5	178.5	178.2	178.8	178.7	179.8	184.5	187.4	178.8
2015	178.9	179.0	180.1	181.6	182.9	183.8	183.1	183.6	183.1	185.9	189.4	189.3	183.4

1. Employment by Industry: Oklahoma, 2005–2015—*Continued*

(Numbers in thousands, not seasonally adjusted)

Industry and year	January	February	March	April	May	June	July	August	September	October	November	December	Annual average
Transportation and Utilities													
2005	52.8	53.0	53.3	53.9	54.0	54.3	54.6	54.9	54.9	54.7	55.2	55.8	54.3
2006	54.8	54.8	55.1	55.6	56.2	56.5	56.6	57.1	57.6	57.7	57.9	59.0	56.6
2007	57.9	58.2	58.5	57.7	58.0	58.4	58.5	58.5	58.2	58.0	58.0	58.4	58.2
2008	57.2	57.1	57.3	57.9	58.2	58.5	58.7	58.9	59.0	59.2	59.2	59.7	58.4
2009	57.6	57.3	57.2	57.3	57.0	57.0	56.4	56.1	55.7	55.9	56.0	56.4	56.7
2010	54.0	54.0	54.1	54.3	54.5	54.6	54.7	54.6	54.7	54.6	54.9	55.8	54.6
2011	54.2	54.2	54.7	55.4	55.7	56.4	56.6	56.9	57.0	57.3	57.6	58.5	56.2
2012	57.9	58.0	58.2	58.4	58.9	59.4	59.3	59.5	59.5	59.9	60.2	60.7	59.2
2013	59.3	59.9	60.1	60.5	60.7	61.1	61.2	61.3	61.1	61.0	61.5	61.9	60.8
2014	61.4	61.2	62.0	61.5	61.8	62.2	62.0	62.1	62.0	62.5	63.2	64.2	62.2
2015	62.7	62.0	62.3	62.4	62.8	63.3	63.6	63.6	63.6	64.0	64.0	65.7	63.3
Information													
2005	30.2	30.4	30.1	30.4	30.4	30.4	30.5	30.2	29.9	29.8	30.0	30.3	30.2
2006	30.0	30.0	30.0	29.7	29.8	29.8	29.9	29.8	29.6	29.3	29.3	30.2	29.8
2007	29.2	29.0	28.6	28.6	28.8	28.8	28.8	28.8	28.6	28.8	28.9	29.0	28.8
2008	28.7	28.9	28.8	29.0	29.1	29.0	29.1	28.8	28.4	28.2	28.2	28.2	28.7
2009	27.8	27.8	27.7	27.5	27.4	27.2	27.0	26.5	25.9	25.7	25.6	25.5	26.8
2010	25.1	24.8	24.5	24.7	24.6	24.3	24.4	24.0	23.8	23.6	23.7	23.7	24.3
2011	23.3	23.1	22.9	23.0	23.1	23.1	23.2	23.1	22.8	22.9	23.0	23.0	23.0
2012	22.8	22.7	22.7	22.6	22.6	22.5	22.6	22.3	22.1	22.2	22.2	22.3	22.5
2013	21.8	21.7	21.6	21.9	22.0	22.1	22.0	21.8	21.5	21.7	21.8	21.7	21.8
2014	21.4	21.3	21.3	21.3	21.3	21.3	21.5	21.2	21.1	20.8	20.9	21.2	21.2
2015	20.8	20.9	21.0	20.9	21.2	21.2	21.0	20.8	20.7	20.6	20.9	20.9	20.9
Financial Activities													
2005	79.2	79.2	79.6	79.2	79.7	80.4	80.5	80.6	80.2	79.6	79.8	80.8	79.9
2006	80.2	80.2	80.7	79.8	80.3	80.8	80.2	80.4	80.0	79.8	79.9	80.0	80.2
2007	79.8	80.3	80.6	79.5	79.7	80.2	80.2	80.3	80.0	80.2	80.2	80.4	80.1
2008	80.4	80.4	80.6	80.6	81.1	81.2	81.5	81.1	80.9	80.6	80.6	81.0	80.8
2009	79.6	79.3	79.4	79.9	80.0	80.2	80.1	79.8	79.1	78.9	78.9	79.1	79.5
2010	78.1	78.1	78.1	78.1	78.4	78.6	78.2	78.2	77.7	77.8	77.9	78.3	78.1
2011	77.0	76.8	77.3	77.6	77.5	77.8	77.8	78.1	77.7	77.8	77.8	78.1	77.6
2012	77.2	77.6	77.6	77.8	78.2	78.6	78.5	78.5	78.0	78.3	78.4	79.0	78.1
2013	78.1	78.4	78.4	78.3	78.9	79.1	79.3	79.2	78.9	79.0	79.5	79.6	78.9
2014	78.6	78.8	78.9	79.1	79.4	79.8	80.0	80.0	79.4	79.5	80.0	80.4	79.5
2015	79.5	79.4	79.3	79.4	79.9	80.1	80.4	80.1	79.8	80.3	80.9	80.8	80.0
Professional and Business Services													
2005	165.3	168.1	170.1	172.9	173.4	174.9	174.5	176.4	177.6	175.9	177.8	177.0	173.7
2006	173.4	175.4	178.1	177.9	179.0	181.2	179.7	181.5	182.0	179.6	180.3	179.6	179.0
2007	176.6	179.4	182.6	183.2	184.2	185.8	184.8	187.7	187.3	186.9	187.3	186.8	184.4
2008	184.2	186.5	187.3	187.5	187.1	187.2	185.5	187.0	186.3	184.8	183.6	181.5	185.7
2009	173.1	173.2	172.1	169.9	168.6	169.6	168.0	168.2	168.3	168.7	168.8	169.1	169.8
2010	165.0	166.3	168.1	170.8	171.2	173.3	174.6	175.4	175.3	176.8	176.4	175.9	172.4
2011	171.4	170.6	173.9	176.6	176.2	176.4	177.5	178.2	178.6	178.7	177.3	177.3	176.1
2012	173.1	176.5	177.3	178.8	179.2	181.5	180.3	182.4	181.3	183.1	182.8	180.9	179.8
2013	176.4	177.8	180.3	180.4	181.5	182.3	182.4	183.8	183.1	183.7	184.4	182.1	181.5
2014	179.4	180.5	182.4	184.5	185.3	185.9	186.2	186.8	185.4	187.3	188.0	187.2	184.9
2015	185.5	184.4	185.0	186.0	185.8	186.0	186.5	186.4	184.5	186.6	184.0	182.4	185.3
Education and Health Services													
2005	195.8	196.6	198.3	200.2	200.7	200.6	199.8	201.4	203.2	202.9	204.6	204.9	200.8
2006	201.2	201.9	203.5	204.0	204.9	205.5	203.6	204.9	206.8	206.5	207.8	207.5	204.8
2007	204.0	205.8	207.2	209.7	210.2	210.9	209.5	211.2	212.4	213.5	213.6	213.1	210.1
2008	211.6	213.8	214.4	214.9	215.5	213.7	213.0	214.7	215.6	216.1	216.9	216.9	214.8
2009	215.4	215.7	216.7	217.3	217.8	218.5	218.5	219.5	220.4	220.7	221.3	221.1	218.6
2010	219.0	219.7	220.5	221.8	221.7	221.1	219.9	221.1	222.5	224.1	224.4	224.7	221.7
2011	220.5	219.6	221.6	222.5	222.9	222.7	222.0	223.3	225.2	225.3	225.7	226.1	223.1
2012	223.3	224.4	225.1	226.4	226.6	225.8	223.4	225.8	227.4	228.2	228.8	229.6	226.2
2013	226.3	227.2	227.8	227.9	228.1	226.9	225.5	227.1	228.6	229.0	229.5	228.4	227.7
2014	226.2	226.8	227.3	228.5	228.3	227.5	226.4	227.6	228.7	229.4	229.9	230.4	228.1
2015	228.5	229.1	229.4	230.6	230.8	230.3	230.0	231.0	232.9	234.6	235.1	232.6	231.2

1. Employment by Industry: Oklahoma, 2005–2015—*Continued*

(Numbers in thousands, not seasonally adjusted)

Industry and year	January	February	March	April	May	June	July	August	September	October	November	December	Annual average
Leisure and Hospitality													
2005	124.9	126.5	130.9	134.2	136.5	138.0	135.1	135.6	134.1	132.1	131.4	129.9	132.4
2006	128.7	130.2	134.3	136.2	138.0	139.2	138.7	139.4	137.8	135.6	134.1	134.4	135.6
2007	129.4	131.9	136.6	137.2	139.8	141.3	140.8	142.1	140.6	138.7	138.5	136.3	137.8
2008	136.8	138.2	141.3	140.2	142.7	144.2	142.9	143.6	142.7	140.3	139.4	139.7	141.0
2009	135.3	136.7	140.5	142.4	143.5	144.6	142.6	142.7	141.2	137.9	136.9	135.3	140.0
2010	131.4	132.7	136.7	140.5	142.1	142.8	141.0	142.0	141.9	139.6	139.0	138.4	139.0
2011	135.2	134.5	140.4	144.5	146.1	146.8	146.0	146.8	146.8	143.5	142.7	141.7	142.9
2012	139.1	141.2	145.1	148.6	150.4	151.3	148.6	149.8	149.4	147.6	147.2	147.8	147.2
2013	143.4	145.2	148.5	151.6	154.7	154.8	154.5	156.2	155.8	152.2	151.9	150.1	151.6
2014	148.4	149.6	152.6	156.9	158.7	159.1	158.5	160.0	159.3	156.6	155.8	155.8	155.9
2015	152.4	154.5	156.7	161.3	163.4	165.1	164.5	165.8	164.6	163.1	164.3	161.9	161.5
Other Services													
2005	60.3	60.7	61.3	61.0	61.2	61.6	61.7	61.3	61.1	61.0	61.0	61.0	61.1
2006	60.3	60.6	61.2	61.2	61.9	62.8	62.3	62.2	62.0	61.9	62.0	62.2	61.7
2007	61.5	62.1	62.7	63.1	63.4	64.5	63.8	63.8	63.7	63.0	63.0	62.7	63.1
2008	62.6	63.1	63.5	63.8	63.9	64.2	64.0	64.0	63.5	63.6	63.0	62.8	63.5
2009	61.9	61.9	62.2	61.9	62.1	62.4	62.0	61.5	61.3	60.8	60.8	60.4	61.6
2010	59.8	59.9	60.4	60.7	61.0	61.5	60.6	60.8	60.7	60.6	60.5	60.4	60.6
2011	59.5	59.4	60.1	59.1	59.1	59.4	58.9	58.3	58.3	57.9	57.9	57.7	58.8
2012	57.2	57.5	57.6	59.5	59.7	60.0	59.4	59.1	58.6	58.4	58.1	58.0	58.6
2013	57.3	57.5	57.7	59.5	59.8	60.4	60.3	60.1	59.7	59.1	59.1	58.9	59.1
2014	58.4	58.5	58.8	59.4	60.3	60.9	61.2	60.7	60.7	60.9	60.8	61.0	60.1
2015	60.7	61.1	61.9	62.0	62.2	62.7	63.5	62.7	62.4	62.2	61.7	61.3	62.0
Government													
2005	313.7	321.1	323.3	325.0	327.5	315.3	301.3	307.1	322.9	330.4	331.8	331.8	320.9
2006	323.3	331.4	332.9	332.2	335.2	323.1	310.6	317.6	333.0	338.5	339.0	338.6	329.6
2007	330.5	337.2	339.0	337.6	339.6	327.8	312.4	319.8	337.1	341.6	342.7	340.9	333.9
2008	329.6	337.1	338.8	341.6	344.9	328.2	316.9	324.3	340.2	347.8	348.8	348.9	337.3
2009	340.2	347.1	350.1	352.2	354.3	341.0	334.1	337.7	350.4	357.6	357.9	357.1	348.3
2010	346.3	351.9	354.8	355.0	360.9	348.5	336.4	333.7	342.9	350.2	350.6	351.0	348.5
2011	341.3	346.2	348.2	349.9	350.0	338.1	323.8	327.3	346.3	350.5	351.4	353.4	343.9
2012	342.8	350.4	352.0	352.1	352.9	339.8	327.4	334.0	348.3	354.3	356.1	355.4	347.1
2013	345.5	353.5	354.7	355.2	356.6	342.1	329.1	334.5	348.1	354.0	355.8	353.9	348.6
2014	344.6	352.0	353.0	353.1	355.3	341.8	329.1	335.1	348.4	355.9	356.7	355.5	348.4
2015	346.7	354.3	354.6	356.1	357.7	344.2	337.2	341.9	351.9	358.8	360.0	359.4	351.9

2. Average Weekly Hours by Selected Industry: Oklahoma, 2011–2015

(Not seasonally adjusted)

Industry and year	January	February	March	April	May	June	July	August	September	October	November	December	Annual average
Total Private													
2011	35.5	34.1	35.5	35.6	36.2	35.6	35.4	35.4	35.3	36.0	35.1	35.2	35.4
2012	35.6	35.0	35.4	35.8	35.2	35.3	35.6	35.1	35.9	35.3	35.6	35.6	35.4
2013	34.5	34.7	35.1	34.8	34.8	35.8	34.8	35.1	35.5	34.9	35.0	35.3	35.0
2014	35.0	35.4	35.5	35.2	35.0	35.6	34.9	35.3	35.1	34.8	35.4	35.1	35.2
2015	34.6	35.0	35.1	34.4	34.2	34.8	34.4	35.2	34.3	34.7	35.1	35.0	34.7
Goods-Producing													
2011	40.8	39.8	43.1	43.4	42.6	42.5	41.7	42.0	41.7	41.9	41.1	41.2	41.8
2012	40.8	39.9	41.3	40.8	41.6	41.5	40.9	41.1	40.9	41.2	41.5	41.4	41.1
2013	40.6	40.5	40.7	39.6	39.8	40.8	39.3	40.1	40.9	40.4	40.7	40.8	40.3
2014	40.4	40.2	41.2	41.0	41.1	41.0	40.7	41.9	41.2	40.5	41.1	41.6	41.0
2015	40.7	40.4	40.2	39.9	39.3	40.7	40.0	40.8	39.4	40.9	41.3	41.2	40.4
Construction													
2011	40.0	38.0	44.0	45.1	43.5	43.0	42.9	41.3	41.3	41.0	40.4	40.9	41.8
2012	40.6	38.2	40.2	40.3	40.7	41.3	42.3	42.5	41.2	41.6	41.6	41.5	41.0
2013	40.2	40.7	41.4	39.9	40.8	41.9	39.5	39.7	41.6	41.4	41.3	40.3	40.7
2014	40.4	40.6	42.8	43.0	42.7	42.1	41.8	44.3	42.3	40.1	40.4	40.2	41.7
2015	40.3	40.7	40.6	41.0	39.5	41.3	41.1	41.7	39.8	41.9	42.7	42.2	41.1
Manufacturing													
2011	39.4	40.4	42.2	42.0	42.1	42.2	41.7	42.1	41.9	42.1	41.4	41.7	41.6
2012	40.8	40.8	41.9	40.6	41.8	41.4	41.0	40.9	41.4	41.3	41.8	41.7	41.3
2013	40.6	40.3	40.5	39.1	40.0	40.6	39.8	40.7	40.8	40.5	41.0	41.3	40.4
2014	40.5	40.1	40.8	40.5	40.8	40.8	40.5	40.8	40.4	40.8	41.7	41.9	40.8
2015	40.6	39.8	39.5	38.8	38.8	39.9	38.7	40.0	38.9	40.3	40.4	40.6	39.7
Trade, Transportation, and Utilities													
2011	35.9	34.4	35.2	35.9	36.6	36.3	35.7	35.2	35.2	36.0	35.1	35.2	35.6
2012	35.8	35.8	35.8	36.2	34.9	35.2	35.6	35.5	36.2	35.6	35.7	34.8	35.6
2013	33.7	34.2	34.6	34.3	34.3	35.3	34.8	34.8	35.2	34.7	34.7	34.5	34.6
2014	34.6	35.2	35.1	35.2	35.2	35.6	34.9	35.1	35.3	34.6	35.2	35.2	35.1
2015	34.7	35.3	35.5	34.9	35.1	35.2	35.3	36.1	35.1	34.7	34.8	35.2	35.2
Financial Activities													
2011	36.7	34.9	35.8	36.1	38.2	36.0	36.3	36.1	37.0	38.8	36.9	37.1	36.7
2012	38.9	36.8	37.0	37.7	36.0	35.6	37.7	36.2	38.0	35.7	35.9	38.0	37.0
2013	35.9	36.5	36.5	36.5	36.1	37.1	36.1	36.1	37.3	35.9	36.1	37.2	36.4
2014	36.6	37.4	37.4	36.0	36.0	37.4	36.1	35.7	35.7	35.2	36.6	35.8	36.3
2015	35.7	36.6	37.0	36.1	35.7	36.0	35.5	37.2	36.4	35.9	37.1	36.2	36.3
Professional and Business Services													
2011	37.8	36.5	37.3	37.0	37.9	37.5	37.5	37.7	37.4	37.7	36.6	36.8	37.3
2012	37.4	36.8	37.4	37.8	36.4	36.7	37.3	36.2	38.7	37.0	37.3	36.3	37.1
2013	35.0	35.3	36.2	36.2	36.2	37.6	36.4	36.8	37.7	36.7	36.5	36.8	36.5
2014	36.2	37.0	36.8	36.4	35.8	37.1	35.8	35.7	35.7	35.2	36.2	35.4	36.1
2015	35.0	35.8	35.7	35.3	34.6	35.2	34.4	35.0	33.5	34.8	35.4	35.1	35.0
Education and Health Services													
2011	33.0	31.4	32.6	33.0	33.8	33.0	33.1	33.2	33.5	34.0	33.4	33.4	33.1
2012	33.8	33.1	33.3	34.6	33.5	33.7	34.3	33.5	34.5	33.9	34.0	34.7	33.9
2013	33.8	33.8	33.7	33.6	33.7	34.6	33.7	33.8	34.3	33.5	33.7	33.8	33.8
2014	34.0	34.0	33.6	33.5	33.5	33.9	33.7	33.6	33.3	33.5	33.8	33.3	33.6
2015	33.2	33.4	33.3	32.7	33.2	33.4	33.9	34.4	33.6	33.8	34.4	33.7	33.6
Leisure and Hospitality													
2011	25.9	24.7	26.0	25.9	26.4	26.5	25.6	25.6	25.2	25.9	25.2	25.1	25.7
2012	25.1	25.6	26.1	26.3	26.3	27.1	27.1	26.2	26.4	25.8	26.0	26.9	26.2
2013	25.6	26.3	26.6	26.8	26.4	27.3	26.3	26.5	26.3	26.1	25.9	25.7	26.3
2014	25.7	26.0	26.4	26.0	25.3	26.5	25.6	26.0	25.6	25.9	26.2	26.0	25.9
2015	25.2	26.0	26.3	25.8	25.6	26.5	25.9	26.5	26.4	26.0	26.2	26.3	26.1

3. Average Hourly Earnings by Selected Industry: Oklahoma, 2011–2015

(Dollars, not seasonally adjusted)

Industry and year	January	February	March	April	May	June	July	August	September	October	November	December	Annual average
Total Private													
2011	20.07	20.75	20.40	20.42	20.19	20.12	20.32	20.14	20.31	20.19	20.38	20.96	20.35
2012	21.02	20.80	20.66	20.66	20.61	20.64	20.77	20.95	21.19	21.07	21.05	21.41	20.90
2013	21.19	21.10	21.00	21.09	21.11	21.20	21.09	21.22	21.33	21.39	21.32	21.51	21.21
2014	21.14	21.51	21.36	21.45	21.43	21.49	21.36	21.50	21.61	21.71	22.03	21.63	21.52
2015	21.83	21.93	21.89	21.77	21.78	21.61	21.65	21.81	21.82	21.80	21.98	21.66	21.79
Goods-Producing													
2011	22.56	23.19	22.41	22.00	21.83	21.97	22.17	22.07	21.89	21.97	22.45	22.56	22.24
2012	22.60	22.36	22.25	22.34	22.01	22.32	21.95	22.01	22.17	22.11	22.29	22.51	22.24
2013	22.39	22.56	22.41	22.57	22.97	22.99	22.85	23.16	23.23	23.06	22.85	23.13	22.85
2014	21.95	22.56	22.70	23.14	23.25	23.46	23.16	23.20	23.61	23.51	23.93	23.39	23.16
2015	23.73	23.90	24.13	23.79	23.98	23.77	23.85	23.98	24.21	24.07	24.29	24.13	23.98
Construction													
2011	20.64	21.03	20.27	19.68	19.75	19.43	19.70	19.92	19.76	20.00	19.77	20.08	19.98
2012	20.27	20.44	20.20	20.12	19.69	19.82	19.92	20.11	20.05	20.20	20.42	20.46	20.14
2013	20.54	20.68	20.87	20.79	21.45	20.99	21.09	20.70	21.10	21.01	20.83	21.12	20.94
2014	20.91	21.40	20.99	21.15	21.47	21.35	21.36	20.93	21.32	21.37	21.61	21.30	21.26
2015	21.56	21.61	21.51	21.35	21.77	21.35	21.23	21.36	21.81	21.81	21.79	22.08	21.60
Manufacturing													
2011	18.71	18.89	18.58	18.49	18.19	18.14	18.75	18.85	18.83	18.77	19.13	19.46	18.73
2012	19.55	19.09	19.19	19.54	19.37	19.36	19.53	19.52	19.93	19.78	20.20	20.34	19.62
2013	20.02	20.30	20.19	20.72	20.78	21.04	20.94	21.18	21.25	20.95	21.00	21.42	20.82
2014	21.11	21.39	21.45	21.63	21.53	21.76	21.48	21.85	22.19	22.15	22.49	22.22	21.78
2015	22.51	22.69	23.00	22.89	23.08	23.16	23.53	23.74	23.95	23.76	24.15	23.82	23.35
Trade, Transportation, and Utilities													
2011	18.53	19.45	18.07	18.47	18.43	18.47	18.93	18.66	19.29	18.69	18.81	19.86	18.80
2012	20.67	20.30	19.84	20.30	20.36	20.50	21.31	21.02	21.06	21.01	20.64	21.25	20.69
2013	21.07	20.52	20.37	20.31	20.67	20.55	20.07	20.05	20.10	19.94	19.76	19.41	20.23
2014	19.84	19.68	19.70	19.54	19.25	19.27	19.43	19.72	19.81	19.90	20.17	19.68	19.67
2015	19.90	19.77	19.58	19.60	20.01	19.61	19.82	19.91	19.76	19.96	20.17	19.53	19.80
Financial Activities													
2011	22.24	21.97	20.58	21.45	20.68	20.85	21.57	21.43	21.70	21.43	21.79	21.81	21.46
2012	21.62	22.45	22.34	22.86	22.45	22.51	22.74	22.90	23.71	23.31	23.57	23.90	22.86
2013	23.15	23.59	23.71	23.54	23.71	24.08	23.36	23.56	24.19	23.89	24.00	24.15	23.75
2014	24.13	24.41	24.18	24.20	24.04	24.17	23.82	24.00	23.81	23.92	24.02	23.87	24.05
2015	24.18	24.62	24.34	24.74	24.73	25.02	24.91	25.62	25.14	25.70	25.84	25.86	25.06
Professional and Business Services													
2011	21.49	21.38	21.04	21.29	21.12	20.86	20.64	20.44	20.54	20.94	21.17	22.06	21.08
2012	21.26	20.72	21.05	20.97	21.12	20.96	20.75	20.49	20.81	21.07	21.05	21.55	20.98
2013	21.60	22.10	21.69	21.54	21.27	21.78	21.52	21.88	22.21	22.39	22.71	23.30	22.01
2014	22.89	23.44	23.23	23.09	23.18	23.60	23.37	23.82	23.99	24.32	24.61	24.23	23.65
2015	24.56	24.76	24.66	24.11	23.99	23.89	23.89	24.03	24.15	23.80	24.10	23.80	24.15
Education and Health Services													
2011	18.27	19.18	18.29	18.59	18.51	19.01	19.27	19.38	19.90	19.60	19.78	20.83	19.23
2012	20.85	20.99	20.90	20.29	20.76	21.06	21.21	21.29	21.34	21.23	21.41	21.80	21.10
2013	21.81	21.54	21.63	22.07	21.73	21.75	22.41	22.50	22.34	22.27	22.19	22.55	22.07
2014	22.50	23.10	22.57	22.96	22.86	22.86	23.01	22.85	22.95	23.26	23.67	23.23	22.99
2015	23.05	23.37	23.30	23.67	23.26	23.10	23.14	23.12	23.11	22.85	22.85	22.46	23.10
Leisure and Hospitality													
2011	11.12	11.26	10.87	10.87	10.93	10.59	10.64	10.76	10.87	10.94	10.87	11.02	10.89
2012	11.00	10.91	10.86	11.01	10.99	10.83	11.00	10.95	11.21	11.10	10.98	11.15	11.00
2013	10.73	10.72	10.79	10.85	10.84	10.67	10.69	10.77	10.89	10.81	10.91	11.13	10.82
2014	10.70	11.11	10.99	11.02	11.24	10.94	10.97	11.12	11.18	11.21	11.53	11.54	11.13
2015	11.57	11.65	11.68	11.64	11.69	11.64	11.67	11.78	12.02	12.06	12.18	12.23	11.82

4. Average Weekly Earnings by Selected Industry: Oklahoma, 2011–2015

(Dollars, not seasonally adjusted)

Industry and year	January	February	March	April	May	June	July	August	September	October	November	December	Annual average
Total Private													
2011	712.49	707.58	724.20	726.95	730.88	716.27	719.33	712.96	716.94	726.84	715.34	737.79	720.39
2012	748.31	728.00	731.36	739.63	725.47	728.59	739.41	735.35	760.72	743.77	749.38	762.20	739.86
2013	731.06	732.17	737.10	733.93	734.63	758.96	733.93	744.82	757.22	746.51	746.20	759.30	742.35
2014	739.90	761.45	758.28	755.04	750.05	765.04	745.46	758.95	758.51	755.51	779.86	759.21	757.50
2015	755.32	767.55	768.34	748.89	744.88	752.03	744.76	767.71	748.43	756.46	771.50	758.10	756.11
Goods-Producing													
2011	920.45	922.96	965.87	954.80	929.96	933.73	924.49	926.94	912.81	920.54	922.70	929.47	929.63
2012	922.08	892.16	918.93	911.47	915.62	926.28	897.76	904.61	906.75	910.93	925.04	931.91	914.06
2013	909.03	913.68	912.09	893.77	914.21	937.99	898.01	928.72	950.11	931.62	930.00	943.70	920.86
2014	886.78	906.91	935.24	948.74	955.58	961.86	942.61	972.08	972.73	952.16	983.52	973.02	949.56
2015	965.81	965.56	970.03	949.22	942.41	967.44	954.00	978.38	953.87	984.46	1,003.18	994.16	968.79
Construction													
2011	825.60	799.14	891.88	887.57	859.13	835.49	845.13	822.70	816.09	820.00	798.71	821.27	835.16
2012	822.96	780.81	812.04	810.84	801.38	818.57	842.62	854.68	826.06	840.32	849.47	849.09	825.74
2013	825.71	841.68	864.02	829.52	875.16	879.48	833.06	821.79	877.76	869.81	860.28	851.14	852.26
2014	844.76	868.84	898.37	909.45	916.77	898.84	892.85	927.20	901.84	856.94	873.04	856.26	886.54
2015	868.87	879.53	873.31	875.35	859.92	881.76	872.55	890.71	868.04	913.84	930.43	931.78	887.76
Manufacturing													
2011	737.17	763.16	784.08	776.58	765.80	765.51	781.88	793.59	788.98	790.22	791.98	811.48	779.17
2012	797.64	778.87	804.06	793.32	809.67	801.50	800.73	798.37	825.10	816.91	844.36	848.18	810.31
2013	812.81	818.09	817.70	810.15	831.20	854.22	833.41	862.03	867.00	848.48	861.00	884.65	841.13
2014	854.96	857.74	875.16	876.02	878.42	887.81	869.94	891.48	896.48	903.72	937.83	931.02	888.62
2015	913.91	903.06	908.50	888.13	895.50	924.08	910.61	949.60	931.66	957.53	975.66	967.09	927.00
Trade, Transportation, and Utilities													
2011	665.23	669.08	636.06	663.07	674.54	670.46	675.80	656.83	679.01	672.84	660.23	699.07	669.28
2012	739.99	726.74	710.27	734.86	710.56	721.60	758.64	746.21	762.37	747.96	736.85	739.50	736.56
2013	710.06	701.78	704.80	696.63	708.98	725.42	698.44	697.74	707.52	691.92	685.67	669.65	699.96
2014	686.46	692.74	691.47	687.81	677.60	686.01	678.11	692.17	699.29	688.54	709.98	692.74	690.42
2015	690.53	697.88	695.09	684.04	702.35	690.27	699.65	718.75	693.58	692.61	701.92	687.46	696.96
Financial Activities													
2011	816.21	766.75	736.76	774.35	789.98	750.60	782.99	773.62	802.90	831.48	804.05	809.15	787.58
2012	841.02	826.16	826.58	861.82	808.20	801.36	857.30	828.98	900.98	832.17	846.16	908.20	845.82
2013	831.09	861.04	865.42	859.21	855.93	893.37	843.30	850.52	902.29	857.65	866.40	898.38	864.50
2014	883.16	912.93	904.33	871.20	865.44	903.96	859.90	856.80	850.02	841.98	879.13	854.55	873.02
2015	863.23	901.09	900.58	893.11	882.86	900.72	884.31	953.06	915.10	922.63	958.66	936.13	909.68
Professional and Business Services													
2011	812.32	780.37	784.79	787.73	800.45	782.25	774.00	770.59	768.20	789.44	774.82	811.81	786.28
2012	795.12	762.50	787.27	792.67	768.77	769.23	773.98	741.74	805.35	779.59	785.17	782.27	778.36
2013	756.00	780.13	785.18	779.75	769.97	818.93	783.33	805.18	837.32	821.71	828.92	857.44	803.37
2014	828.62	867.28	854.86	840.48	829.84	875.56	836.65	850.37	856.44	856.06	890.88	857.74	853.77
2015	859.60	886.41	880.36	851.08	830.05	840.93	821.82	841.05	809.03	828.24	853.14	835.38	845.25
Education and Health Services													
2011	602.91	602.25	596.25	613.47	625.64	627.33	637.84	643.42	666.65	666.40	660.65	695.72	636.51
2012	704.73	694.77	695.97	702.03	695.46	709.72	727.50	713.22	736.23	719.70	727.94	756.46	715.29
2013	737.18	728.05	728.93	741.55	732.30	752.55	755.22	760.50	766.26	746.05	747.80	762.19	745.97
2014	765.00	785.40	758.35	769.16	765.81	774.95	775.44	767.76	764.24	779.21	800.05	773.56	772.46
2015	765.26	780.56	775.89	774.01	772.23	771.54	784.45	795.33	776.50	772.33	786.04	756.90	776.16
Leisure and Hospitality													
2011	288.01	278.12	282.62	281.53	288.55	280.64	272.38	275.46	273.92	283.35	273.92	276.60	279.87
2012	276.10	279.30	283.45	289.56	289.04	293.49	298.10	286.89	295.94	286.38	285.48	299.94	288.20
2013	274.69	281.94	287.01	290.78	286.18	291.29	281.15	285.41	286.41	282.14	282.57	286.04	284.57
2014	274.99	288.86	290.14	286.52	284.37	289.91	280.83	289.12	286.21	290.34	302.09	300.04	288.27
2015	291.56	302.90	307.18	300.31	299.26	308.46	302.25	312.17	317.33	313.56	319.12	321.65	308.50

OREGON
At a Glance

Population:
    2005 estimate: 3,613,202
    2010 census: 3,831,074
    2015 estimate: 4,028,977

Percent change in population:
    2005–2015: 11.5%
    2010–2015: 5.2%

Percent change in total nonfarm employment:
    2005–2015: 7.5%

Industry with the largest growth in employment, 2005–2015 (thousands):
    Education and health services, 59.3

Industry with the largest decline or smallest growth in employment, 2005–2015 (thousands):
    Manufacturing, –18.0

Civilian labor force:
    2005: 1,845,761
    2010: 1,984,039
    2015: 1,969,466

Unemployment rate and rank among states (highest to lowest):
    2005: 6.2%, 7th
    2010: 10.6%, 8th
    2015: 5.7%, 16th

Over-the-year change in unemployment rates:
    2012–2013: –0.9%
    2013–2014: –1.1%
    2014–2015: –1.1%

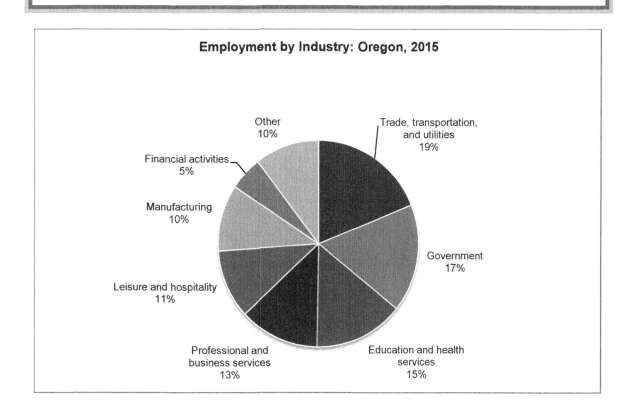

Employment by Industry: Oregon, 2015

Other 10%
Financial activities 5%
Manufacturing 10%
Leisure and hospitality 11%
Professional and business services 13%
Education and health services 15%
Government 17%
Trade, transportation, and utilities 19%

1. Employment by Industry: Oregon, 2005–2015

(Numbers in thousands, not seasonally adjusted)

Industry and year	January	February	March	April	May	June	July	August	September	October	November	December	Annual average
Total Nonfarm													
2005	1,598.6	1,613.5	1,628.1	1,640.0	1,650.9	1,667.7	1,651.0	1,658.3	1,672.7	1,683.3	1,691.4	1,694.5	1,654.2
2006	1,647.9	1,664.9	1,677.8	1,690.3	1,707.0	1,722.4	1,700.1	1,706.8	1,720.4	1,732.0	1,735.2	1,734.0	1,703.2
2007	1,687.9	1,704.2	1,717.4	1,720.7	1,736.0	1,748.6	1,722.9	1,732.1	1,740.5	1,754.7	1,755.6	1,751.4	1,731.0
2008	1,702.6	1,714.5	1,721.4	1,727.9	1,735.3	1,740.2	1,717.9	1,718.5	1,724.3	1,724.3	1,705.9	1,684.2	1,718.1
2009	1,625.6	1,620.9	1,612.8	1,614.8	1,619.9	1,623.3	1,600.5	1,594.9	1,605.6	1,614.7	1,609.9	1,603.5	1,612.2
2010	1,562.5	1,570.5	1,578.9	1,596.4	1,611.2	1,621.0	1,597.4	1,598.3	1,607.1	1,628.9	1,626.6	1,621.0	1,601.7
2011	1,583.2	1,596.2	1,603.0	1,617.9	1,625.0	1,634.9	1,611.1	1,615.1	1,628.5	1,640.9	1,642.3	1,638.7	1,619.7
2012	1,599.4	1,612.5	1,620.2	1,632.0	1,646.1	1,654.3	1,632.1	1,639.6	1,649.3	1,665.7	1,666.4	1,661.2	1,639.9
2013	1,622.2	1,639.5	1,648.1	1,664.5	1,679.9	1,686.8	1,666.3	1,674.6	1,689.5	1,704.2	1,709.3	1,705.4	1,674.2
2014	1,673.3	1,681.2	1,693.8	1,710.1	1,724.8	1,734.4	1,714.0	1,722.6	1,738.2	1,753.4	1,758.4	1,759.1	1,721.9
2015	1,725.6	1,740.9	1,750.7	1,766.9	1,780.6	1,791.8	1,774.8	1,778.7	1,792.7	1,810.1	1,818.0	1,813.9	1,778.7
Total Private													
2005	1,312.5	1,323.1	1,336.7	1,348.1	1,357.4	1,372.3	1,386.8	1,394.6	1,398.4	1,394.8	1,399.2	1,405.3	1,369.1
2006	1,363.4	1,374.3	1,385.7	1,399.1	1,411.9	1,425.9	1,434.8	1,442.1	1,444.3	1,440.6	1,439.9	1,443.2	1,417.1
2007	1,401.3	1,412.1	1,423.2	1,426.4	1,436.8	1,448.1	1,454.1	1,464.0	1,462.0	1,458.1	1,455.6	1,453.3	1,441.3
2008	1,407.8	1,414.4	1,419.4	1,425.5	1,429.6	1,433.4	1,438.1	1,440.2	1,436.0	1,420.0	1,397.9	1,379.0	1,420.1
2009	1,324.6	1,315.0	1,306.1	1,307.1	1,309.7	1,314.4	1,319.6	1,317.2	1,320.8	1,312.1	1,305.0	1,301.2	1,312.7
2010	1,263.8	1,267.1	1,274.0	1,288.9	1,296.3	1,306.6	1,316.0	1,320.6	1,323.5	1,326.1	1,320.4	1,319.5	1,301.9
2011	1,283.6	1,292.6	1,299.2	1,313.4	1,318.1	1,327.7	1,339.2	1,345.5	1,349.5	1,343.7	1,342.4	1,341.7	1,324.7
2012	1,306.9	1,314.8	1,321.8	1,334.2	1,344.6	1,353.1	1,363.5	1,372.3	1,371.2	1,370.2	1,368.2	1,366.3	1,348.9
2013	1,332.5	1,344.0	1,352.5	1,369.0	1,381.1	1,388.9	1,401.8	1,410.7	1,412.5	1,409.9	1,411.5	1,409.3	1,385.3
2014	1,380.7	1,384.3	1,396.1	1,410.8	1,422.2	1,431.3	1,442.7	1,451.6	1,454.9	1,452.0	1,453.7	1,456.0	1,428.0
2015	1,425.9	1,436.6	1,444.9	1,460.5	1,471.2	1,481.4	1,496.8	1,502.4	1,504.0	1,502.7	1,507.9	1,504.4	1,478.2
Goods-Producing													
2005	289.2	291.4	294.4	296.8	300.1	305.9	313.4	315.9	314.8	313.2	309.2	307.9	304.4
2006	302.3	305.4	308.0	311.1	315.0	321.4	328.6	330.2	328.3	325.1	319.5	316.8	317.6
2007	309.7	311.2	312.9	312.1	315.4	319.9	325.6	328.9	325.5	322.1	316.0	311.3	317.6
2008	301.1	300.7	299.7	299.6	300.5	302.4	306.0	306.4	302.2	296.3	284.7	274.7	297.9
2009	259.8	252.2	247.3	245.3	245.0	248.0	253.1	251.9	250.8	246.9	239.6	235.7	248.0
2010	229.2	228.2	229.5	232.3	235.3	239.6	246.4	247.6	247.2	246.2	240.3	236.4	238.2
2011	230.8	232.9	234.5	238.6	241.0	245.2	251.5	255.0	253.6	250.6	246.9	244.3	243.7
2012	238.3	239.3	240.0	242.5	247.1	251.4	257.6	260.9	257.4	255.9	250.1	246.6	248.9
2013	242.1	244.3	246.1	250.2	254.4	258.7	264.9	267.3	266.0	265.4	261.9	259.3	256.7
2014	256.8	256.5	258.9	262.1	265.9	269.5	274.8	277.1	275.7	272.9	269.8	268.4	267.4
2015	265.3	266.7	268.6	271.4	274.8	279.1	284.8	285.5	284.2	281.1	278.4	275.8	276.3
Service-Providing													
2005	1,309.4	1,322.1	1,333.7	1,343.2	1,350.8	1,361.8	1,337.6	1,342.4	1,357.9	1,370.1	1,382.2	1,386.6	1,349.8
2006	1,345.6	1,359.5	1,369.8	1,379.2	1,392.0	1,401.0	1,371.5	1,376.6	1,392.1	1,406.9	1,415.7	1,417.2	1,385.6
2007	1,378.2	1,393.0	1,404.5	1,408.6	1,420.6	1,428.7	1,397.3	1,403.2	1,415.0	1,432.6	1,439.6	1,440.1	1,413.5
2008	1,401.5	1,413.8	1,421.7	1,428.3	1,434.8	1,437.8	1,411.9	1,412.1	1,422.1	1,428.0	1,421.2	1,409.5	1,420.2
2009	1,365.8	1,368.7	1,365.5	1,369.5	1,374.9	1,375.3	1,347.4	1,343.0	1,354.8	1,367.8	1,370.3	1,367.8	1,364.2
2010	1,333.3	1,342.3	1,349.4	1,364.1	1,375.9	1,381.4	1,351.0	1,350.7	1,359.9	1,382.7	1,386.3	1,384.6	1,363.5
2011	1,352.4	1,363.3	1,368.5	1,379.3	1,384.0	1,389.7	1,359.6	1,360.1	1,374.9	1,390.3	1,395.4	1,394.4	1,376.0
2012	1,361.1	1,373.2	1,380.2	1,389.5	1,399.0	1,402.9	1,374.5	1,378.7	1,391.9	1,409.8	1,416.3	1,414.6	1,391.0
2013	1,380.1	1,395.2	1,402.0	1,414.3	1,425.5	1,428.1	1,401.4	1,407.3	1,423.5	1,438.8	1,447.4	1,446.1	1,417.5
2014	1,416.5	1,424.7	1,434.9	1,448.0	1,458.9	1,464.9	1,439.2	1,445.5	1,462.5	1,480.5	1,488.6	1,490.7	1,454.6
2015	1,460.3	1,474.2	1,482.1	1,495.5	1,505.8	1,512.7	1,490.0	1,493.2	1,508.5	1,529.0	1,539.6	1,538.1	1,502.4
Mining and Logging													
2005	9.2	9.4	9.3	9.1	9.2	9.6	10.1	10.1	9.9	9.8	9.6	9.4	9.6
2006	8.8	9.0	8.9	9.0	9.3	9.7	9.9	10.0	9.9	9.8	9.4	9.2	9.4
2007	8.7	8.9	8.9	9.1	9.3	9.6	9.7	9.7	9.6	9.4	9.2	8.8	9.2
2008	8.4	8.4	8.3	8.3	8.5	8.8	9.1	9.3	9.2	9.0	8.7	8.1	8.7
2009	7.1	7.0	6.7	6.7	6.6	6.9	7.0	7.0	7.0	6.9	6.6	6.3	6.8
2010	6.2	6.2	6.3	6.4	6.6	6.9	7.3	7.2	7.2	7.0	6.7	6.5	6.7
2011	6.2	6.5	6.4	6.6	6.8	7.0	7.4	7.5	7.6	7.5	7.4	7.3	7.0
2012	6.7	6.8	6.8	6.8	7.1	7.4	7.5	7.7	7.6	7.6	7.5	7.3	7.2
2013	6.9	7.1	7.1	7.3	7.6	7.8	8.0	8.0	8.0	7.8	7.8	7.6	7.6
2014	7.5	7.5	7.4	7.5	7.6	7.8	8.0	8.1	8.0	7.8	7.8	7.6	7.7
2015	7.5	7.6	7.6	7.5	7.8	7.9	8.0	7.8	7.9	7.8	7.6	7.3	7.7

1. Employment by Industry: Oregon, 2005–2015—*Continued*

(Numbers in thousands, not seasonally adjusted)

Industry and year	January	February	March	April	May	June	July	August	September	October	November	December	Annual average
Construction													
2005	80.8	82.0	84.0	86.1	88.5	91.4	95.2	97.3	98.0	96.9	95.3	95.1	90.9
2006	91.3	93.3	94.7	97.2	100.2	103.2	105.7	107.2	106.9	105.7	103.5	101.9	100.9
2007	97.4	98.9	100.5	101.5	104.2	105.8	109.4	110.8	109.2	107.4	104.5	101.3	104.2
2008	94.4	94.3	94.2	94.7	95.8	96.9	98.7	98.6	96.9	93.1	87.9	83.4	94.1
2009	76.9	74.2	72.6	72.4	73.1	75.0	77.1	77.1	76.3	74.4	70.5	68.1	74.0
2010	63.4	62.7	63.4	65.0	66.6	68.4	71.8	72.6	72.1	71.5	68.1	66.1	67.6
2011	62.1	62.9	63.6	66.4	67.8	70.0	72.4	73.5	73.6	72.2	70.2	68.6	68.6
2012	65.0	65.4	65.4	67.1	69.6	70.9	73.9	75.7	74.0	73.1	70.0	67.9	69.8
2013	64.9	66.2	67.9	70.6	73.6	75.2	78.4	79.8	79.2	79.6	78.2	76.3	74.2
2014	74.9	74.5	76.3	78.2	80.5	81.6	83.9	84.8	84.2	82.2	80.4	79.2	80.1
2015	77.3	77.7	78.7	80.0	81.7	83.5	86.4	87.4	86.8	85.7	84.5	82.4	82.7
Manufacturing													
2005	199.2	200.0	201.1	201.6	202.4	204.9	208.1	208.5	206.9	206.5	204.3	203.4	203.9
2006	202.2	203.1	204.4	204.9	205.5	208.5	213.0	213.0	211.5	209.6	206.6	205.7	207.3
2007	203.6	203.4	203.5	201.5	201.9	204.5	206.5	208.4	206.7	205.3	202.3	201.2	204.1
2008	198.3	198.0	197.2	196.6	196.2	196.7	198.2	198.5	196.1	194.2	188.1	183.2	195.1
2009	175.8	171.0	168.0	166.2	165.3	166.1	169.0	167.8	167.5	165.6	162.5	161.3	167.2
2010	159.6	159.3	159.8	160.9	162.1	164.3	167.3	167.8	167.9	167.7	165.5	163.8	163.8
2011	162.5	163.5	164.5	165.6	166.4	168.2	171.7	174.0	172.4	170.9	169.3	168.4	168.1
2012	166.6	167.1	167.8	168.6	170.4	173.1	176.2	177.5	175.8	175.2	172.6	171.4	171.9
2013	170.3	171.0	171.1	172.3	173.2	175.7	178.5	179.5	178.8	178.0	175.9	175.4	175.0
2014	174.4	174.5	175.2	176.4	177.8	180.1	182.9	184.2	183.5	182.9	181.6	181.6	179.6
2015	180.5	181.4	182.3	183.9	185.3	187.7	190.4	190.3	189.5	187.6	186.3	186.1	185.9
Trade, Transportation, and Utilities													
2005	314.5	313.2	315.9	317.0	318.4	322.3	324.5	326.6	328.1	329.3	336.4	340.7	323.9
2006	323.5	322.0	323.4	324.5	327.7	330.0	330.9	332.2	333.3	334.2	340.5	344.5	330.6
2007	329.2	327.1	328.6	329.1	331.0	333.9	335.0	336.8	338.1	338.6	345.3	347.4	335.0
2008	331.4	329.1	329.5	329.7	329.8	330.5	331.6	331.9	331.5	329.7	329.6	328.8	330.3
2009	311.9	307.1	304.1	303.1	304.6	304.6	304.9	304.9	306.3	305.2	307.9	310.3	306.2
2010	297.1	294.7	295.0	297.6	298.9	300.9	302.7	304.3	305.1	306.9	311.2	314.3	302.4
2011	300.7	298.7	299.0	301.4	303.2	304.9	306.4	307.2	308.4	309.2	314.7	316.7	305.9
2012	304.1	301.8	302.6	304.4	307.5	309.8	309.9	311.6	312.4	313.9	320.1	322.1	310.0
2013	309.8	309.1	309.6	312.2	315.1	316.6	318.6	321.1	322.1	322.6	328.7	330.6	318.0
2014	318.9	316.3	316.9	319.0	322.1	323.9	326.0	328.4	329.1	330.9	336.9	340.7	325.8
2015	327.8	326.2	327.3	329.5	332.2	334.9	336.4	338.6	338.9	339.0	347.6	349.2	335.6
Wholesale Trade													
2005	71.5	72.0	72.3	72.5	72.2	73.0	73.8	73.9	74.3	73.9	74.1	74.1	73.1
2006	73.2	74.0	74.1	74.2	74.8	75.1	75.4	75.3	75.3	75.7	75.7	75.5	74.9
2007	74.9	75.4	75.3	75.1	75.2	75.5	76.1	75.8	75.6	75.9	75.8	75.5	75.5
2008	74.5	75.1	75.2	74.9	75.1	75.1	75.7	75.3	75.2	75.1	74.2	73.3	74.9
2009	71.6	71.1	70.3	69.9	69.9	69.5	69.5	68.9	68.6	68.1	67.6	67.3	69.4
2010	66.1	66.2	66.0	66.8	67.1	67.0	67.6	67.4	67.7	67.9	67.5	67.4	67.1
2011	66.3	66.8	66.9	67.5	67.8	67.9	68.2	68.4	68.2	68.5	68.1	67.9	67.7
2012	66.8	67.4	67.7	68.4	69.1	68.9	69.4	69.7	69.6	69.8	69.6	69.4	68.8
2013	69.9	70.5	70.4	70.9	71.3	71.2	72.1	72.3	72.3	72.2	72.4	72.3	71.5
2014	71.7	71.9	71.9	71.9	72.0	72.3	72.9	73.0	73.1	73.3	73.2	73.4	72.6
2015	72.6	73.0	73.0	73.4	73.6	73.8	74.4	75.0	74.8	74.7	74.3	74.7	73.9
Retail Trade													
2005	186.8	184.8	186.7	187.9	189.6	192.3	194.2	195.7	195.7	197.5	204.3	207.4	193.6
2006	193.2	190.5	191.7	192.7	194.9	196.1	197.7	198.8	198.8	199.3	205.6	208.8	197.3
2007	196.6	193.9	195.3	195.9	197.5	199.3	201.0	202.6	202.9	202.9	209.3	210.9	200.7
2008	198.3	195.2	195.6	195.6	195.4	196.2	197.7	197.9	197.1	195.8	197.9	197.9	196.7
2009	185.1	181.6	180.0	179.9	181.2	181.8	183.0	183.4	183.8	183.8	187.6	189.5	183.4
2010	179.6	177.3	177.8	179.0	180.0	181.6	183.6	184.9	184.4	185.9	190.8	193.1	183.2
2011	182.0	179.6	179.7	181.2	182.3	183.7	185.4	185.8	185.9	186.6	192.1	193.5	184.8
2012	183.9	180.9	181.2	182.5	184.6	186.7	187.6	188.4	188.0	189.5	195.6	196.8	187.1
2013	186.3	184.6	184.9	186.7	189.2	190.4	192.7	194.3	194.2	194.6	200.3	201.3	191.6
2014	191.2	188.4	189.3	191.1	193.7	195.0	197.4	198.8	198.7	199.8	205.4	207.2	196.3
2015	196.7	195.0	195.9	198.5	200.6	201.8	204.3	205.6	204.9	205.3	213.0	213.2	202.9

1. Employment by Industry: Oregon, 2005–2015—*Continued*

(Numbers in thousands, not seasonally adjusted)

Industry and year	January	February	March	April	May	June	July	August	September	October	November	December	Annual average
Transportation and Utilities													
2005	56.2	56.4	56.9	56.6	56.6	57.0	56.5	57.0	58.1	57.9	58.0	59.2	57.2
2006	57.1	57.5	57.6	57.6	58.0	58.8	57.8	58.1	59.2	59.2	59.2	60.2	58.4
2007	57.7	57.8	58.0	58.1	58.3	59.1	57.9	58.4	59.6	59.8	60.2	61.0	58.8
2008	58.6	58.8	58.7	59.2	59.3	59.2	58.2	58.7	59.2	58.8	57.5	57.6	58.7
2009	55.2	54.4	53.8	53.3	53.5	53.3	52.4	52.6	53.9	53.3	52.7	53.5	53.5
2010	51.4	51.2	51.2	51.8	51.8	52.3	51.5	52.0	53.0	53.1	52.9	53.8	52.2
2011	52.4	52.3	52.4	52.7	53.1	53.3	52.8	53.0	54.3	54.1	54.5	55.3	53.4
2012	53.4	53.5	53.7	53.5	53.8	54.2	52.9	53.5	54.8	54.6	54.9	55.9	54.1
2013	53.6	54.0	54.3	54.6	54.6	55.0	53.8	54.5	55.6	55.8	56.0	57.0	54.9
2014	56.0	56.0	55.7	56.0	56.4	56.6	55.7	56.6	57.3	57.8	58.3	60.1	56.9
2015	58.5	58.2	58.4	57.6	58.0	59.3	57.7	58.0	59.2	59.0	60.3	61.3	58.8
Information													
2005	32.3	32.7	32.6	32.9	33.2	33.3	33.4	33.3	33.5	33.8	34.1	34.8	33.3
2006	33.8	34.2	34.2	33.9	34.2	34.5	34.7	34.8	34.8	35.0	35.0	35.6	34.6
2007	34.6	35.0	35.5	35.6	35.9	36.2	35.7	35.9	35.7	35.5	35.9	36.9	35.7
2008	35.8	36.0	36.0	35.6	35.8	36.0	35.3	35.4	35.1	34.5	34.2	33.9	35.3
2009	33.0	33.1	33.0	32.5	32.9	33.9	32.8	32.7	32.2	31.7	32.3	32.5	32.7
2010	31.3	31.4	31.6	31.5	31.9	32.3	31.6	32.0	31.8	31.5	31.9	31.9	31.7
2011	31.5	31.6	32.0	31.8	31.6	31.6	31.8	31.9	31.7	31.5	31.6	31.6	31.7
2012	31.2	31.3	31.9	32.3	32.1	32.5	32.7	32.5	32.1	32.4	32.5	32.3	32.2
2013	32.0	32.1	32.2	32.2	32.0	31.9	32.0	32.3	32.5	32.6	32.7	32.7	32.3
2014	31.7	31.8	32.2	32.3	31.6	31.8	32.2	32.4	32.5	32.5	32.6	32.7	32.2
2015	32.1	32.4	32.5	32.8	32.6	32.9	33.8	34.2	33.8	33.6	34.0	34.3	33.3
Financial Activities													
2005	98.0	98.8	99.5	100.4	101.1	102.0	103.9	104.3	103.9	103.8	104.3	105.1	102.1
2006	103.2	103.8	104.3	105.1	105.8	106.8	107.4	107.9	107.6	107.0	106.9	107.6	106.1
2007	105.8	106.5	107.1	106.4	106.8	107.4	107.9	107.5	105.8	105.6	105.1	105.3	106.4
2008	102.5	102.8	102.6	102.9	102.8	102.5	102.5	102.4	101.2	100.7	99.7	99.5	101.8
2009	96.4	96.2	95.7	95.7	95.5	95.3	96.1	96.0	95.3	95.6	94.9	95.2	95.7
2010	92.4	92.1	92.1	93.1	93.2	93.8	94.2	94.1	93.5	93.4	92.8	93.5	93.2
2011	91.3	91.7	91.4	91.7	91.8	92.4	92.6	92.3	91.5	91.3	90.8	91.3	91.7
2012	89.4	89.6	89.3	89.9	89.9	90.2	91.6	91.7	91.0	91.1	90.9	91.1	90.5
2013	89.7	89.9	90.0	91.0	91.4	91.6	93.0	92.9	92.5	92.4	92.1	92.2	91.6
2014	90.5	90.2	90.3	91.2	92.1	92.7	93.6	93.9	93.6	93.5	93.4	94.0	92.4
2015	92.7	92.8	92.7	93.7	94.5	94.7	96.0	96.3	95.8	96.3	96.3	96.6	94.9
Professional and Business Services													
2005	179.4	182.5	184.6	187.4	187.8	190.8	193.6	195.2	195.4	194.8	195.1	196.8	190.3
2006	189.1	191.9	193.8	196.6	198.0	201.2	202.8	204.6	204.8	204.6	203.1	202.5	199.4
2007	195.7	198.2	200.5	201.4	201.9	204.2	204.5	206.6	205.6	205.9	203.4	202.6	202.5
2008	196.9	199.4	200.8	203.0	203.4	204.1	206.2	207.2	205.3	202.4	197.7	194.3	201.7
2009	187.9	186.6	185.0	186.0	184.9	185.8	187.1	186.1	186.1	185.7	185.2	185.2	186.0
2010	179.7	181.8	183.4	187.4	187.6	189.0	191.7	192.8	192.1	193.4	192.3	192.1	188.6
2011	186.5	188.6	190.2	193.5	193.0	194.7	199.0	199.7	200.0	199.3	198.8	198.9	195.2
2012	194.9	196.8	197.8	200.3	200.6	202.4	204.9	206.4	204.9	205.3	205.3	205.7	202.1
2013	199.0	201.1	203.5	206.7	207.7	209.9	213.8	215.4	214.3	214.0	213.7	214.4	209.5
2014	209.6	211.5	213.9	217.1	218.0	220.5	223.3	225.6	225.3	224.6	224.1	224.1	219.8
2015	218.9	220.8	222.6	225.6	226.3	227.6	231.2	232.2	231.7	233.7	233.5	232.9	228.1
Education and Health Services													
2005	193.9	197.8	199.0	199.7	199.8	196.1	194.0	193.8	199.8	202.7	204.4	204.0	198.8
2006	200.1	204.1	205.5	206.8	206.7	202.7	198.5	199.0	205.2	208.9	210.9	211.0	205.0
2007	206.3	211.3	212.4	212.8	212.7	209.3	205.2	206.2	212.3	217.1	218.0	218.0	211.8
2008	213.7	218.8	219.8	220.8	220.1	217.3	213.8	214.2	220.7	224.7	225.3	225.4	219.6
2009	219.7	223.8	224.1	225.3	224.5	221.2	217.5	217.5	224.3	228.1	228.9	228.2	223.6
2010	225.0	228.4	229.5	230.3	229.4	226.1	222.2	222.3	229.0	234.2	235.4	235.1	228.9
2011	230.8	234.5	235.7	236.2	234.9	231.2	226.9	227.6	234.6	238.6	239.8	239.2	234.2
2012	233.7	238.7	240.0	240.8	239.0	234.0	230.2	231.3	238.2	241.9	243.2	243.0	237.8
2013	238.2	243.6	244.0	245.5	244.4	239.1	234.7	236.0	242.9	247.5	248.6	247.8	242.7
2014	243.9	247.7	249.5	250.2	248.5	244.7	241.0	241.5	249.5	253.8	255.6	255.6	248.5
2015	251.3	257.0	257.4	259.3	257.6	254.2	251.4	252.3	259.7	264.4	266.8	265.9	258.1

1. Employment by Industry: Oregon, 2005–2015—*Continued*

(Numbers in thousands, not seasonally adjusted)

Industry and year	January	February	March	April	May	June	July	August	September	October	November	December	Annual average
Leisure and Hospitality													
2005	149.4	150.1	153.9	156.7	159.5	164.1	166.4	167.9	165.2	159.6	158.2	158.4	159.1
2006	154.6	155.5	158.4	162.5	165.2	169.4	172.6	173.9	170.8	166.2	164.6	165.6	164.9
2007	161.5	163.2	166.2	169.0	172.4	176.1	179.8	181.4	178.4	172.5	171.2	171.1	171.9
2008	166.6	167.2	170.2	172.8	175.5	178.9	181.6	181.7	178.6	171.1	167.0	163.3	172.9
2009	158.1	158.1	159.2	161.4	164.2	167.7	170.0	170.2	168.0	161.7	159.1	157.3	162.9
2010	153.2	154.4	156.5	160.3	163.1	167.4	170.2	170.9	167.9	163.6	160.2	160.0	162.3
2011	156.2	158.3	159.9	163.4	165.6	170.5	173.8	174.6	172.3	166.2	163.0	162.9	165.6
2012	159.1	160.7	163.4	166.7	170.4	174.9	178.7	180.1	177.6	171.9	168.9	168.5	170.1
2013	164.9	166.6	169.5	173.4	177.6	182.7	186.2	187.0	183.8	177.4	175.6	174.5	176.6
2014	171.6	172.5	176.1	180.2	184.5	188.3	192.1	193.0	189.4	184.0	181.7	181.1	182.9
2015	178.9	181.2	184.1	188.1	192.7	197.4	201.8	202.0	198.9	193.4	189.9	188.3	191.4
Other Services													
2005	55.8	56.6	56.8	57.2	57.5	57.8	57.6	57.6	57.7	57.6	57.5	57.6	57.3
2006	56.8	57.4	58.1	58.6	59.3	59.9	59.3	59.5	59.5	59.6	59.4	59.6	58.9
2007	58.5	59.6	60.0	60.0	60.7	61.1	60.4	60.7	60.6	60.8	60.7	60.7	60.3
2008	59.8	60.4	60.8	61.1	61.7	61.7	61.1	61.0	61.4	60.6	59.7	59.1	60.7
2009	57.8	57.9	57.7	57.8	58.1	57.9	58.1	57.9	57.8	57.2	57.1	56.8	57.7
2010	55.9	56.1	56.4	56.4	56.9	57.5	57.0	56.6	56.9	56.9	56.3	56.2	56.6
2011	55.8	56.3	56.5	56.8	57.0	57.2	57.2	57.2	57.4	57.0	56.8	56.8	56.8
2012	56.2	56.6	56.8	57.3	58.0	57.9	57.9	57.8	57.6	57.8	57.2	57.0	57.3
2013	56.8	57.3	57.6	57.8	58.5	58.4	58.6	58.7	58.4	58.0	58.2	57.8	58.0
2014	57.7	57.8	58.3	58.7	59.5	59.9	59.7	59.7	59.8	59.8	59.6	59.4	59.2
2015	58.9	59.5	59.7	60.1	60.5	60.6	61.4	61.3	61.0	61.2	61.4	61.4	60.6
Government													
2005	286.1	290.4	291.4	291.9	293.5	295.4	264.2	263.7	274.3	288.5	292.2	289.2	285.1
2006	284.5	290.6	292.1	291.2	295.1	296.5	265.3	264.7	276.1	291.4	295.3	290.8	286.1
2007	286.6	292.1	294.2	294.3	299.2	300.5	268.8	268.1	278.5	296.6	300.0	298.1	289.8
2008	294.8	300.1	302.0	302.4	305.7	306.8	279.8	278.3	288.3	304.3	308.0	305.2	298.0
2009	301.0	305.9	306.7	307.7	310.2	308.9	280.9	277.7	284.8	302.6	304.9	302.3	299.5
2010	298.7	303.4	304.9	307.5	314.9	314.4	281.4	277.7	283.6	302.8	306.2	301.5	299.8
2011	299.6	303.6	303.8	304.5	306.9	307.2	271.9	269.6	279.0	297.2	299.9	297.0	295.0
2012	292.5	297.7	298.4	297.8	301.5	301.2	268.6	267.3	278.1	295.5	298.2	294.9	291.0
2013	289.7	295.5	295.6	295.5	298.8	297.9	264.5	263.9	277.0	294.3	297.8	296.1	288.9
2014	292.6	296.9	297.7	299.3	302.6	303.1	271.3	271.0	283.3	301.4	304.7	303.1	293.9
2015	299.7	304.3	305.8	306.4	309.4	310.4	278.0	276.3	288.7	307.4	310.1	309.5	300.5

2. Average Weekly Hours by Selected Industry: Oregon, 2011–2015

(Not seasonally adjusted)

Industry and year	January	February	March	April	May	June	July	August	September	October	November	December	Annual average
Total Private													
2011	34.1	33.6	33.3	33.8	34.4	33.6	33.8	33.9	33.9	34.1	33.6	33.6	33.8
2012	33.7	33.3	33.1	34.3	33.3	33.7	34.4	33.8	34.6	33.4	33.2	34.1	33.8
2013	32.8	33.6	33.5	33.6	33.6	34.7	33.4	33.9	34.7	33.6	33.5	34.0	33.7
2014	32.9	33.8	34.3	33.7	33.6	34.7	33.7	34.1	33.9	33.7	34.4	33.5	33.9
2015	33.3	34.6	34.4	33.6	33.7	34.0	34.0	35.0	33.8	33.7	34.5	33.5	34.0
Goods-Producing													
2011	37.0	37.3	37.2	37.6	38.1	37.9	37.7	38.5	38.7	38.8	38.6	38.9	38.0
2012	38.3	38.4	38.3	39.0	38.7	39.1	39.0	38.6	38.8	38.7	38.2	38.4	38.6
2013	37.8	39.0	39.0	39.4	39.1	40.1	38.5	39.5	40.0	39.5	39.3	39.1	39.2
2014	38.2	38.2	39.3	38.8	38.9	39.5	38.7	39.3	39.7	39.5	39.6	39.0	39.1
2015	38.9	39.7	39.4	38.8	38.6	39.2	39.2	39.6	38.1	38.7	38.9	38.5	39.0
Construction													
2011	34.5	34.5	34.1	34.7	35.8	35.3	35.7	36.4	36.8	36.1	36.1	36.3	35.6
2012	36.1	36.0	36.0	37.3	37.0	37.6	37.1	36.9	36.9	36.3	35.0	34.9	36.4
2013	34.2	35.7	36.2	36.7	36.7	37.2	37.3	38.1	38.5	37.8	36.5	36.0	36.8
2014	35.7	34.7	36.2	36.0	36.5	37.1	36.7	38.1	38.0	37.2	36.6	36.2	36.6
2015	36.4	36.9	36.3	36.3	35.7	37.2	37.2	37.5	35.2	36.4	35.7	35.4	36.3
Manufacturing													
2011	38.2	38.6	38.5	38.8	39.1	39.0	38.7	39.5	39.8	40.0	39.9	40.1	39.2
2012	39.2	39.3	39.4	39.7	39.3	39.6	39.7	39.2	39.5	39.6	39.4	39.7	39.5
2013	39.0	39.9	39.9	40.2	39.9	40.8	38.7	39.6	40.2	39.7	40.1	40.2	39.9
2014	38.9	39.4	40.4	39.8	39.8	40.4	39.4	39.6	40.4	40.3	40.8	40.3	40.0
2015	40.0	40.5	40.4	39.5	39.5	39.8	39.7	40.3	39.2	39.3	40.1	39.8	39.8
Trade, Transportation, and Utilities													
2011	35.3	34.5	34.4	35.1	36.0	35.1	35.3	35.5	35.4	35.5	34.8	35.0	35.2
2012	34.2	33.9	33.9	35.0	34.3	34.5	35.2	34.8	35.4	34.1	34.1	34.6	34.5
2013	33.2	33.9	34.2	34.2	34.4	35.4	34.7	35.0	35.3	34.4	34.3	34.7	34.5
2014	33.7	34.6	35.0	34.6	34.8	35.5	35.1	35.2	34.8	34.1	34.7	34.2	34.7
2015	33.5	35.1	35.1	34.4	34.9	34.9	35.0	35.8	35.4	34.7	35.5	34.5	34.9
Financial Activities													
2011	37.8	36.0	35.9	35.8	37.3	35.7	35.5	36.7	36.7	37.8	37.4	37.3	36.7
2012	39.7	37.9	37.8	39.5	37.2	37.7	38.7	37.5	38.9	36.6	36.1	38.4	38.0
2013	36.0	36.3	36.1	36.0	36.1	38.2	36.2	36.3	38.5	35.9	36.6	37.9	36.7
2014	35.7	37.1	36.9	35.1	35.1	37.6	35.6	36.0	36.0	35.5	37.6	35.8	36.2
2015	35.7	37.1	36.5	35.6	35.3	35.4	35.4	36.9	36.2	36.2	37.0	36.4	36.1
Professional and Business Services													
2011	35.6	35.3	34.5	35.3	35.3	34.3	34.6	34.1	34.2	35.0	34.4	34.2	34.7
2012	34.6	34.3	34.2	35.2	34.2	34.6	34.7	34.5	35.4	34.6	34.5	35.5	34.7
2013	33.9	34.8	34.7	35.0	34.6	35.9	34.1	34.6	35.8	34.8	34.9	35.2	34.9
2014	34.2	35.6	35.8	35.0	34.5	36.2	35.2	35.2	35.1	35.1	35.5	34.5	35.2
2015	34.2	35.5	35.3	34.6	34.4	35.2	35.0	36.0	34.4	34.7	35.8	34.4	35.0
Education and Health Services													
2011	31.8	30.8	30.7	31.1	31.6	30.9	31.3	31.1	31.3	31.4	30.9	30.5	31.1
2012	31.2	30.5	30.2	31.6	30.6	30.8	31.5	30.8	32.2	30.9	31.1	32.0	31.1
2013	31.5	32.2	31.5	31.5	31.2	32.2	30.7	31.2	32.0	31.0	31.5	31.8	31.5
2014	31.3	32.5	32.3	31.6	31.4	32.6	31.0	31.7	31.9	31.7	33.0	32.2	31.9
2015	32.1	33.5	33.1	32.4	32.6	32.6	32.4	33.7	32.9	32.9	34.0	33.2	33.0
Leisure and Hospitality													
2011	25.4	25.0	24.9	26.0	26.7	25.6	26.6	26.2	25.7	25.7	24.9	24.4	25.6
2012	24.9	24.6	24.5	26.2	24.7	25.4	27.0	26.3	26.8	24.8	24.1	25.9	25.5
2013	23.9	24.9	24.9	24.9	25.1	26.8	25.5	26.2	26.9	24.5	24.0	25.1	25.3
2014	23.4	24.5	25.8	24.9	24.8	26.4	25.1	26.3	25.2	24.9	25.7	24.2	25.1
2015	24.1	25.8	25.8	24.8	25.1	25.6	26.1	27.4	25.5	25.0	25.5	24.3	25.4
Other Services													
2011	31.3	30.6	29.0	30.3	30.7	29.8	29.8	29.7	29.8	30.0	29.3	29.9	30.0
2012	30.3	30.1	29.2	30.2	28.7	29.4	30.3	29.7	30.3	28.7	28.6	29.8	29.6
2013	28.5	29.3	29.1	28.9	29.3	30.3	29.5	30.0	30.0	29.1	29.0	29.7	29.4
2014	29.1	29.2	30.2	29.8	30.0	30.7	29.6	29.9	29.3	28.7	29.8	27.7	29.5
2015	28.4	30.1	28.9	28.5	28.6	29.1	29.0	29.8	28.2	28.3	28.8	26.7	28.7

3. Average Hourly Earnings by Selected Industry: Oregon, 2011–2015

(Dollars, not seasonally adjusted)

Industry and year	January	February	March	April	May	June	July	August	September	October	November	December	Annual average
Total Private													
2011	21.95	21.75	21.68	21.69	21.57	21.53	21.66	21.52	21.69	21.91	21.90	22.15	21.75
2012	22.40	22.27	22.17	22.30	22.11	22.05	22.09	21.93	22.25	22.23	22.29	22.65	22.23
2013	22.41	22.41	22.31	22.39	22.27	22.37	22.34	22.34	22.65	22.68	22.83	23.21	22.52
2014	23.09	23.05	22.86	22.80	22.84	22.83	22.77	22.61	22.88	22.93	23.10	23.14	22.91
2015	23.37	23.34	23.38	23.32	23.36	23.28	23.32	23.43	23.57	23.78	24.01	24.12	23.53
Goods-Producing													
2011	23.31	23.11	23.14	23.47	23.36	23.41	23.66	23.47	23.69	23.96	23.91	24.30	23.58
2012	24.50	24.17	24.34	24.62	24.35	24.28	24.15	24.00	24.24	23.97	24.09	24.55	24.27
2013	24.05	23.95	23.96	24.08	23.98	23.95	24.03	24.05	24.26	24.28	24.17	24.59	24.12
2014	24.44	24.31	24.14	24.28	24.13	24.28	24.27	24.02	24.18	24.11	24.28	24.27	24.22
2015	24.32	24.17	24.25	24.36	24.21	24.39	24.49	24.49	24.41	24.71	24.78	25.12	24.48
Construction													
2011	26.96	27.02	27.09	27.20	26.96	27.18	27.01	27.08	27.16	27.47	27.29	28.37	27.24
2012	28.89	28.78	29.05	29.37	28.78	28.65	27.84	28.14	28.11	27.68	27.53	28.40	28.42
2013	27.86	27.79	28.30	28.55	28.21	27.91	27.90	28.04	28.00	28.12	27.92	28.76	28.11
2014	28.65	28.67	28.51	28.48	28.35	28.19	28.26	27.91	28.30	28.00	27.95	28.23	28.28
2015	28.29	28.00	28.29	28.23	28.15	28.33	28.67	28.75	28.61	28.78	28.80	29.84	28.57
Manufacturing													
2011	22.14	21.84	21.92	22.30	22.22	22.20	22.61	22.13	22.42	22.65	22.69	22.78	22.33
2012	23.00	22.63	22.76	22.87	22.75	22.65	22.76	22.30	22.71	22.52	22.78	23.19	22.74
2013	22.74	22.54	22.42	22.49	22.49	22.49	22.55	22.46	22.78	22.75	22.75	23.08	22.63
2014	22.86	22.76	22.68	22.73	22.55	22.84	22.84	22.54	22.59	22.69	22.98	22.83	22.74
2015	22.86	22.81	22.78	22.97	22.77	22.81	22.75	22.65	22.68	22.94	23.07	23.10	22.85
Trade, Transportation, and Utilities													
2011	19.91	19.71	19.79	19.53	19.50	19.53	19.70	19.42	19.58	19.78	19.35	19.13	19.57
2012	19.90	19.68	19.61	19.97	19.80	19.79	19.88	19.49	19.88	19.75	19.70	20.06	19.79
2013	20.25	20.23	20.21	20.08	20.03	20.11	20.02	20.01	20.07	19.89	19.92	20.13	20.08
2014	20.28	20.19	19.85	19.82	19.76	19.84	19.80	19.37	19.48	19.64	19.70	19.44	19.76
2015	19.93	19.73	19.82	19.67	19.74	19.71	19.91	19.73	19.69	19.82	19.88	19.78	19.78
Financial Activities													
2011	25.52	25.31	25.20	25.16	24.84	24.41	24.55	24.49	24.67	24.44	24.96	24.72	24.86
2012	24.37	24.59	23.99	24.00	23.83	23.46	23.68	24.16	24.22	24.49	24.54	25.13	24.20
2013	24.36	24.23	23.78	24.42	24.25	24.63	24.60	24.22	24.97	24.86	24.74	25.01	24.51
2014	24.46	24.29	24.21	24.11	24.70	25.40	25.72	26.19	26.00	26.34	26.37	27.44	25.45
2015	27.39	27.90	27.92	27.74	27.87	27.95	27.48	27.98	27.59	27.81	28.00	28.45	27.84
Professional and Business Services													
2011	25.18	25.02	24.71	24.79	24.92	24.60	24.36	24.52	24.36	24.82	24.97	24.98	24.77
2012	25.07	25.18	25.17	25.34	24.82	24.81	25.10	24.77	25.43	25.40	25.53	25.77	25.20
2013	25.23	25.44	25.25	25.38	25.38	25.72	25.36	25.29	25.87	25.75	26.18	26.72	25.64
2014	26.44	26.85	27.03	26.55	26.44	26.78	26.25	26.25	26.36	26.06	26.17	25.96	26.43
2015	26.22	26.18	26.38	26.41	26.64	26.16	26.26	26.37	26.72	26.91	27.56	27.41	26.61
Education and Health Services													
2011	22.31	22.20	22.25	22.49	22.26	22.32	22.75	22.47	22.57	22.54	22.60	22.68	22.45
2012	22.64	22.80	22.54	22.62	22.69	22.86	22.96	22.82	22.98	23.11	23.16	23.35	22.88
2013	23.03	23.00	23.21	23.39	23.24	23.71	24.19	24.44	24.59	24.53	24.86	25.18	23.95
2014	24.84	24.72	24.67	24.86	24.90	24.87	25.30	25.30	25.46	25.65	25.82	25.98	25.20
2015	26.26	26.22	26.19	26.49	26.70	26.76	27.30	27.45	27.66	27.60	27.81	27.76	27.03
Leisure and Hospitality													
2011	13.14	13.27	13.00	13.03	12.92	12.88	13.01	13.00	13.16	13.20	13.26	13.36	13.10
2012	13.46	13.32	13.42	13.23	13.41	13.27	13.20	13.18	13.39	13.42	13.46	13.58	13.36
2013	13.63	13.55	13.43	13.48	13.44	13.31	13.26	13.34	13.46	13.70	13.76	13.96	13.52
2014	14.14	14.10	14.03	13.87	13.98	13.83	13.66	13.68	13.86	13.72	13.79	14.12	13.89
2015	14.03	14.10	14.01	14.27	14.20	13.97	13.93	14.02	14.40	14.58	14.63	14.70	14.23
Other Services													
2011	18.50	18.75	19.00	18.96	19.44	19.45	19.49	19.22	19.29	19.64	19.95	20.25	19.33
2012	20.37	20.73	20.44	20.62	20.50	20.50	20.74	20.51	20.68	20.28	20.40	20.77	20.55
2013	20.16	20.36	20.38	20.40	20.32	20.42	20.19	20.35	20.94	20.73	21.07	21.40	20.56
2014	20.86	20.82	20.34	20.35	20.25	20.14	20.31	20.19	20.53	20.58	21.20	21.80	20.60
2015	21.44	21.27	21.49	21.67	21.61	21.81	21.51	21.98	22.04	22.10	22.20	22.40	21.79

4. Average Weekly Earnings by Selected Industry: Oregon, 2011–2015

(Dollars, not seasonally adjusted)

Industry and year	January	February	March	April	May	June	July	August	September	October	November	December	Annual average
Total Private													
2011	748.50	730.80	721.94	733.12	742.01	723.41	732.11	729.53	735.29	747.13	735.84	744.24	735.15
2012	754.88	741.59	733.83	764.89	736.26	743.09	759.90	741.23	769.85	742.48	740.03	772.37	751.37
2013	735.05	752.98	747.39	752.30	748.27	776.24	746.16	757.33	785.96	762.05	764.81	789.14	758.92
2014	759.66	779.09	784.10	768.36	767.42	792.20	767.35	771.00	775.63	772.74	794.64	775.19	776.65
2015	778.22	807.56	804.27	783.55	787.23	791.52	792.88	820.05	796.67	801.39	828.35	808.02	800.02
Goods-Producing													
2011	862.47	862.00	860.81	882.47	890.02	887.24	891.98	903.60	916.80	929.65	922.93	945.27	896.04
2012	938.35	928.13	932.22	960.18	942.35	949.35	941.85	926.40	940.51	927.64	920.24	942.72	936.82
2013	909.09	934.05	934.44	948.75	937.62	960.40	925.16	949.98	970.40	959.06	949.88	961.47	945.50
2014	933.61	928.64	948.70	942.06	938.66	959.06	939.25	943.99	959.95	952.35	961.49	946.53	947.00
2015	946.05	959.55	955.45	945.17	934.51	956.09	960.01	969.80	930.02	956.28	963.94	967.12	954.72
Construction													
2011	930.12	932.19	923.77	943.84	965.17	959.45	964.26	985.71	999.49	991.67	985.17	1,029.83	969.74
2012	1,042.93	1,036.08	1,045.80	1,095.50	1,064.86	1,077.24	1,032.86	1,038.37	1,037.26	1,004.78	963.55	991.16	1,034.49
2013	952.81	992.10	1,024.46	1,047.79	1,035.31	1,038.25	1,040.67	1,068.32	1,078.00	1,062.94	1,019.08	1,035.36	1,034.45
2014	1,022.81	994.85	1,032.06	1,025.28	1,034.78	1,045.85	1,037.14	1,063.37	1,075.40	1,041.60	1,022.97	1,021.93	1,035.05
2015	1,029.76	1,033.20	1,026.93	1,024.75	1,004.96	1,053.88	1,066.52	1,078.13	1,007.07	1,047.59	1,028.16	1,056.34	1,037.09
Manufacturing													
2011	845.75	843.02	843.92	865.24	868.80	865.80	875.01	874.14	892.32	906.00	905.33	913.48	875.34
2012	901.60	889.36	896.74	907.94	894.08	896.94	903.57	874.16	897.05	891.79	897.53	920.64	898.23
2013	886.86	899.35	894.56	904.10	897.35	917.59	872.69	889.42	915.76	903.18	912.28	927.82	902.94
2014	889.25	896.74	916.27	904.65	897.49	922.74	899.90	892.58	912.64	914.41	937.58	920.05	909.60
2015	914.40	923.81	920.31	907.32	899.42	907.84	903.18	912.80	889.06	901.54	925.11	919.38	909.43
Trade, Transportation, and Utilities													
2011	702.82	680.00	680.78	685.50	702.00	685.50	695.41	689.41	693.13	702.19	673.38	669.55	688.86
2012	680.58	667.15	664.78	698.95	679.14	682.76	699.78	678.25	703.75	673.48	671.77	694.08	682.76
2013	672.30	685.80	691.18	686.74	689.03	711.89	694.69	700.35	708.47	684.22	683.26	698.51	692.76
2014	683.44	698.57	694.75	685.77	687.65	704.32	694.98	681.82	677.90	669.72	683.59	664.85	685.67
2015	667.66	692.52	695.68	676.65	688.93	687.88	696.85	706.33	697.03	687.75	705.74	682.41	690.32
Financial Activities													
2011	964.66	911.16	904.68	900.73	926.53	871.44	871.53	898.78	905.39	923.83	933.50	922.06	912.36
2012	967.49	931.96	906.82	948.00	886.48	884.44	916.42	906.00	942.16	896.33	885.89	964.99	919.60
2013	876.96	879.55	858.46	879.12	875.43	940.87	890.52	879.19	961.35	892.47	905.48	947.88	899.52
2014	873.22	901.16	893.35	846.26	866.97	955.04	915.63	942.84	936.00	935.07	991.51	982.35	921.29
2015	977.82	1,035.09	1,019.08	987.54	983.81	989.43	972.79	1,032.46	998.76	1,006.72	1,036.00	1,035.58	1,005.02
Professional and Business Services													
2011	896.41	883.21	852.50	875.09	879.68	843.78	842.86	836.13	833.11	868.70	858.97	854.32	859.52
2012	867.42	863.67	860.81	891.97	848.84	858.43	870.97	854.57	900.22	878.84	880.79	914.84	874.44
2013	855.30	885.31	876.18	888.30	878.15	923.35	864.78	875.03	926.15	896.10	913.68	940.54	894.84
2014	904.25	955.86	967.67	929.25	912.18	969.44	924.00	924.00	925.24	914.71	929.04	895.62	930.34
2015	896.72	929.39	931.21	913.79	916.42	920.83	919.10	949.32	919.17	933.78	986.65	942.90	931.35
Education and Health Services													
2011	709.46	683.76	683.08	699.44	703.42	689.69	712.08	698.82	706.44	707.76	698.34	691.74	698.20
2012	706.37	695.40	680.71	714.79	694.31	704.09	723.24	702.86	739.96	714.10	720.28	747.20	711.57
2013	725.45	740.60	731.12	736.79	725.09	763.46	742.63	762.53	786.88	760.43	783.09	800.72	754.43
2014	777.49	803.40	796.84	785.58	781.86	810.76	784.30	802.01	812.17	813.11	852.06	836.56	803.88
2015	842.95	878.37	866.89	858.28	870.42	872.38	884.52	925.07	910.01	908.04	945.54	921.63	891.99
Leisure and Hospitality													
2011	333.76	331.75	323.70	338.78	344.96	329.73	346.07	340.60	338.21	339.24	330.17	325.98	335.36
2012	335.15	327.67	328.79	346.63	331.23	337.06	356.40	346.63	358.85	332.82	324.39	351.72	340.68
2013	325.76	337.40	334.41	335.65	337.34	356.71	338.13	349.51	362.07	335.65	330.24	350.40	342.06
2014	330.88	345.45	361.97	345.36	346.70	365.11	342.87	359.78	349.27	341.63	354.40	341.70	348.64
2015	338.12	363.78	361.46	353.90	356.42	357.63	363.57	384.15	367.20	364.50	373.07	357.21	361.44
Other Services													
2011	579.05	573.75	551.00	574.49	596.81	579.61	580.80	570.83	574.84	589.20	584.54	605.48	579.90
2012	617.21	623.97	596.85	622.72	588.35	602.70	628.42	609.15	626.60	582.04	583.44	618.95	608.28
2013	574.56	596.55	593.06	589.56	595.38	618.73	595.61	610.50	628.20	603.24	611.03	635.58	604.46
2014	607.03	607.94	614.27	606.43	607.50	618.30	601.18	603.68	601.53	590.65	631.76	603.86	607.70
2015	608.90	640.23	621.06	617.60	618.05	634.67	623.79	655.00	621.53	625.43	639.36	598.08	625.37

PENNSYLVANIA
At a Glance

Population:
  2005 estimate: 12,449,990
  2010 census: 12,702,379
  2015 estimate: 12,802,503

Percent change in population:
  2005–2015: 2.8%
  2010–2015: 0.8%

Percent change in total nonfarm employment:
  2005–2015: 2.3%

Industry with the largest growth in employment, 2005–2015 (thousands):
  Manufacturing, –111.1

Industry with the largest decline or smallest growth in employment, 2005–2015 (thousands):
  Education and health services, 168.4

Civilian labor force:
  2005: 6,251,402
  2010: 6,380,949
  2015: 6,423,903

Unemployment rate and rank among states (highest to lowest):
  2005: 5.0%, 22nd
  2010: 8.5%, 28th
  2015: 5.1%, 27th

Over-the-year change in unemployment rates:
  2012–2013: –0.4%
  2013–2014: –1.5%
  2014–2015: –0.8%

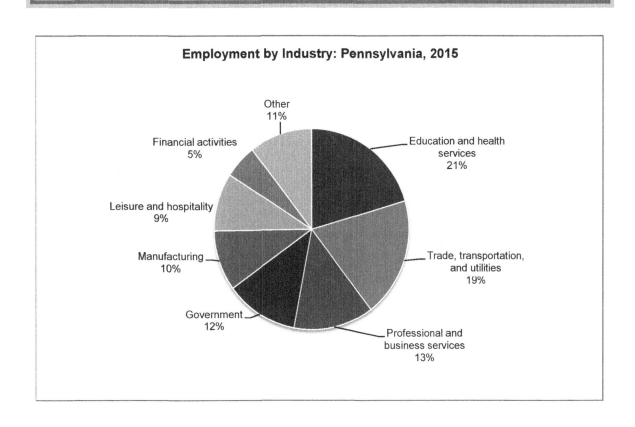

Employment by Industry: Pennsylvania, 2015

- Other 11%
- Financial activities 5%
- Leisure and hospitality 9%
- Manufacturing 10%
- Government 12%
- Education and health services 21%
- Trade, transportation, and utilities 19%
- Professional and business services 13%

1. Employment by Industry: Pennsylvania, 2005–2015

(Numbers in thousands, not seasonally adjusted)

Industry and year	January	February	March	April	May	June	July	August	September	October	November	December	Annual average
Total Nonfarm													
2005	5,569.0	5,598.8	5,629.5	5,708.9	5,740.6	5,748.5	5,693.0	5,685.4	5,742.5	5,765.1	5,782.4	5,772.4	5,703.0
2006	5,622.8	5,656.9	5,701.7	5,761.0	5,796.1	5,801.2	5,732.3	5,730.6	5,788.2	5,822.1	5,836.1	5,835.2	5,757.0
2007	5,680.0	5,691.3	5,742.6	5,793.8	5,838.5	5,854.1	5,785.8	5,777.4	5,819.3	5,861.7	5,875.9	5,866.0	5,798.9
2008	5,712.8	5,733.0	5,761.4	5,827.6	5,862.8	5,856.5	5,784.2	5,778.0	5,820.2	5,846.0	5,823.7	5,795.4	5,800.1
2009	5,601.5	5,605.4	5,604.9	5,635.1	5,661.0	5,642.2	5,568.8	5,550.1	5,598.7	5,646.5	5,651.5	5,633.4	5,616.6
2010	5,472.3	5,483.7	5,540.9	5,622.3	5,677.7	5,673.1	5,605.4	5,601.3	5,650.6	5,703.2	5,722.2	5,711.9	5,622.1
2011	5,555.1	5,587.4	5,630.7	5,700.1	5,730.2	5,729.3	5,654.4	5,648.0	5,713.0	5,748.2	5,772.3	5,758.5	5,685.6
2012	5,600.7	5,647.5	5,701.8	5,741.8	5,774.0	5,759.7	5,687.3	5,687.9	5,748.6	5,780.6	5,798.0	5,781.7	5,725.8
2013	5,619.9	5,664.1	5,702.3	5,745.4	5,784.4	5,771.0	5,706.0	5,710.7	5,765.7	5,797.3	5,819.4	5,801.0	5,740.6
2014	5,648.8	5,669.4	5,717.0	5,788.1	5,830.7	5,825.7	5,757.6	5,765.7	5,824.3	5,869.6	5,888.4	5,879.4	5,788.7
2015	5,709.5	5,737.0	5,761.0	5,834.6	5,878.8	5,867.7	5,810.4	5,810.5	5,867.9	5,922.2	5,916.7	5,915.2	5,836.0
Total Private													
2005	4,817.1	4,827.7	4,854.6	4,930.8	4,971.2	4,997.6	4,996.2	4,995.2	4,992.8	4,996.6	5,008.4	5,004.5	4,949.4
2006	4,873.4	4,886.0	4,927.9	4,985.4	5,022.4	5,049.6	5,036.3	5,036.6	5,035.5	5,051.1	5,057.3	5,062.6	5,002.0
2007	4,928.0	4,920.0	4,968.0	5,018.4	5,067.2	5,102.0	5,087.4	5,082.0	5,069.5	5,091.4	5,100.3	5,094.9	5,044.1
2008	4,959.3	4,960.9	4,986.0	5,049.3	5,091.6	5,101.1	5,086.6	5,077.8	5,057.6	5,063.3	5,036.7	5,015.0	5,040.4
2009	4,840.9	4,824.1	4,821.4	4,844.7	4,880.0	4,877.7	4,855.1	4,842.6	4,830.9	4,858.7	4,857.8	4,846.5	4,848.4
2010	4,711.8	4,701.9	4,753.2	4,828.9	4,875.8	4,893.8	4,890.7	4,892.6	4,886.6	4,919.8	4,932.7	4,929.5	4,851.4
2011	4,792.9	4,808.0	4,849.7	4,918.8	4,959.6	4,977.3	4,965.7	4,964.2	4,972.8	4,992.4	5,009.5	5,000.1	4,934.3
2012	4,870.3	4,893.4	4,946.3	4,986.6	5,021.5	5,036.2	5,014.3	5,013.5	5,018.6	5,036.0	5,049.0	5,036.8	4,993.5
2013	4,897.7	4,922.6	4,960.9	5,003.1	5,040.7	5,060.8	5,044.8	5,045.3	5,048.0	5,065.9	5,081.3	5,067.4	5,019.9
2014	4,936.1	4,941.2	4,988.4	5,057.0	5,106.0	5,119.0	5,101.4	5,107.6	5,112.5	5,144.2	5,159.2	5,155.2	5,077.3
2015	5,009.2	5,017.3	5,040.7	5,110.8	5,161.4	5,171.0	5,159.9	5,156.2	5,161.4	5,200.1	5,189.1	5,189.8	5,130.6
Goods-Producing													
2005	928.9	921.9	928.3	948.9	961.6	973.7	975.6	976.2	969.3	964.4	961.4	947.7	954.8
2006	924.4	921.9	934.4	948.8	958.0	969.8	969.5	971.8	965.6	959.8	952.1	944.1	951.7
2007	921.6	906.3	922.3	936.3	948.6	962.4	962.3	961.6	955.0	953.3	945.3	932.7	942.3
2008	909.8	901.6	909.1	922.8	934.5	942.9	940.6	939.1	929.7	921.8	905.2	885.3	920.2
2009	844.3	827.6	822.3	823.9	824.8	827.5	823.2	820.6	815.5	814.6	806.2	793.0	820.3
2010	765.9	758.3	772.8	796.2	806.9	817.8	822.4	822.5	818.2	817.7	815.1	803.6	801.5
2011	780.4	777.7	792.2	810.4	822.5	834.6	841.1	842.7	839.0	839.6	836.5	826.5	820.3
2012	804.8	804.5	814.9	825.1	832.0	844.2	844.8	844.2	841.0	838.0	829.2	819.1	828.5
2013	797.2	795.9	805.4	818.2	829.2	839.6	841.4	842.5	839.2	837.3	830.6	815.9	824.4
2014	798.3	794.6	807.1	825.9	839.6	850.4	854.4	855.1	850.1	851.1	846.8	836.4	834.2
2015	813.6	808.3	814.3	832.8	845.0	854.3	856.5	854.9	848.4	843.6	834.4	823.2	835.8
Service-Providing													
2005	4,640.1	4,676.9	4,701.2	4,760.0	4,779.0	4,774.8	4,717.4	4,709.2	4,773.2	4,800.7	4,821.0	4,824.7	4,748.2
2006	4,698.4	4,735.0	4,767.3	4,812.2	4,838.1	4,831.4	4,762.8	4,758.8	4,822.6	4,862.3	4,884.0	4,891.1	4,805.3
2007	4,758.4	4,785.0	4,820.3	4,857.5	4,889.9	4,891.7	4,823.5	4,815.8	4,864.3	4,908.4	4,930.6	4,933.3	4,856.6
2008	4,803.0	4,831.4	4,852.3	4,904.8	4,928.3	4,913.6	4,843.6	4,838.9	4,890.5	4,924.2	4,918.5	4,910.1	4,879.9
2009	4,757.2	4,777.8	4,782.6	4,811.2	4,836.2	4,814.7	4,745.6	4,729.5	4,783.2	4,831.9	4,845.3	4,840.4	4,796.3
2010	4,706.4	4,725.4	4,768.1	4,826.1	4,870.8	4,855.3	4,783.0	4,778.8	4,832.4	4,885.5	4,907.1	4,908.3	4,820.6
2011	4,774.7	4,809.7	4,838.5	4,889.7	4,907.7	4,894.7	4,813.3	4,805.3	4,874.0	4,908.6	4,935.8	4,932.0	4,865.3
2012	4,795.9	4,843.0	4,886.9	4,916.7	4,942.0	4,915.5	4,842.5	4,843.7	4,907.6	4,942.6	4,968.8	4,962.6	4,897.3
2013	4,822.7	4,868.2	4,896.9	4,927.2	4,955.2	4,931.4	4,864.6	4,868.2	4,926.5	4,960.0	4,988.8	4,985.1	4,916.2
2014	4,850.5	4,874.8	4,909.9	4,962.2	4,991.1	4,975.3	4,903.2	4,910.6	4,974.2	5,018.5	5,041.6	5,043.0	4,954.6
2015	4,895.9	4,928.7	4,946.7	5,001.8	5,033.8	5,013.4	4,953.9	4,955.6	5,019.5	5,078.6	5,082.3	5,092.0	5,000.2
Mining and Logging													
2005	18.6	18.6	18.6	19.6	19.8	20.3	20.5	20.4	20.4	20.2	20.1	19.6	19.7
2006	19.2	19.3	19.7	20.3	20.6	20.9	21.0	20.9	20.8	20.7	20.7	20.3	20.4
2007	19.9	19.8	20.2	20.8	21.2	21.7	21.9	21.9	21.6	21.5	21.4	21.0	21.1
2008	20.6	20.5	20.9	21.6	22.2	22.8	22.9	23.1	23.1	23.4	23.3	22.5	22.2
2009	21.8	21.5	21.2	21.7	21.9	22.4	22.6	22.6	22.7	22.9	23.1	22.7	22.3
2010	22.4	22.8	23.6	25.3	26.0	26.8	27.5	27.9	28.6	28.9	29.6	29.4	26.6
2011	29.4	30.2	30.8	32.0	32.9	34.0	34.6	35.1	35.5	36.2	37.0	37.3	33.8
2012	36.9	37.7	37.9	37.7	37.8	37.9	37.4	37.0	36.6	36.3	35.9	35.3	37.0
2013	34.7	34.8	35.4	35.8	36.3	36.6	36.6	36.3	36.2	36.5	36.2	36.0	36.0
2014	35.4	35.6	36.0	36.9	37.5	38.0	38.5	38.8	38.8	38.9	39.0	38.9	37.7
2015	38.2	36.8	36.3	35.4	35.0	34.8	34.1	32.9	31.9	31.2	30.6	30.0	33.9

1. Employment by Industry: Pennsylvania, 2005–2015—*Continued*

(Numbers in thousands, not seasonally adjusted)

Industry and year	January	February	March	April	May	June	July	August	September	October	November	December	Annual average
Construction													
2005	229.3	225.4	230.6	250.9	260.8	268.2	272.7	273.7	270.8	267.8	265.3	253.4	255.7
2006	237.2	236.4	245.3	258.1	265.9	272.3	274.8	276.6	274.2	270.4	263.7	256.6	261.0
2007	241.8	232.9	243.9	257.2	267.8	275.8	277.9	278.5	275.8	274.1	266.2	253.6	262.1
2008	238.8	233.7	240.0	254.8	263.9	268.9	269.8	269.3	264.2	260.4	250.0	236.4	254.2
2009	214.9	211.2	215.3	223.9	229.9	233.6	234.7	233.6	230.0	229.2	221.3	209.8	224.0
2010	190.5	184.6	195.4	214.2	221.3	226.4	230.3	230.2	226.9	225.8	222.2	211.0	214.9
2011	193.6	191.3	202.3	216.4	224.7	231.5	236.2	237.1	235.4	236.1	232.3	221.3	221.5
2012	204.7	204.3	212.4	221.6	226.6	233.5	235.1	235.6	236.1	235.1	227.8	218.5	224.3
2013	201.9	201.2	209.2	220.3	228.8	233.8	236.8	238.9	237.7	235.3	228.4	213.7	223.8
2014	201.4	198.3	207.6	225.0	234.8	240.5	244.1	244.5	243.2	243.7	237.9	226.1	228.9
2015	209.3	205.8	211.5	229.9	240.1	246.3	249.2	251.1	249.4	246.7	237.7	225.7	233.6
Manufacturing													
2005	681.0	677.9	679.1	678.4	681.0	685.2	682.4	682.1	678.1	676.4	676.0	674.7	679.4
2006	668.0	666.2	669.4	670.4	671.5	676.6	673.7	674.3	670.6	668.7	667.7	667.2	670.4
2007	659.9	653.6	658.2	658.3	659.6	664.9	662.5	661.2	657.6	657.7	657.7	658.1	659.1
2008	650.4	647.4	648.2	646.4	648.4	651.2	647.9	646.7	642.4	638.0	631.9	626.4	643.8
2009	607.6	594.9	585.8	578.3	573.0	571.5	565.9	564.4	562.8	562.5	561.8	560.5	574.1
2010	553.0	550.9	553.8	556.7	559.6	564.6	564.6	564.4	562.7	563.0	563.3	563.2	560.0
2011	557.4	556.2	559.1	562.0	564.9	569.1	570.3	570.5	568.1	567.3	567.2	567.9	565.0
2012	563.2	562.5	564.6	565.8	567.6	572.8	572.3	571.6	568.3	566.6	565.5	565.3	567.2
2013	560.6	559.9	560.8	562.1	564.1	569.2	568.0	567.3	565.3	565.5	566.0	566.2	564.6
2014	561.5	560.7	563.5	564.0	567.3	571.9	571.8	571.8	568.1	568.5	569.9	571.4	567.5
2015	566.1	565.7	566.5	567.5	569.9	573.2	573.2	570.9	567.1	565.7	566.1	567.5	568.3
Trade, Transportation, and Utilities													
2005	1106.9	1095.6	1099.9	1108.0	1117.1	1119.4	1111.5	1111.7	1116.3	1125.5	1145.3	1160.6	1118.2
2006	1117.3	1100.9	1108.2	1112.8	1120.3	1121.3	1111.1	1112.8	1119.7	1132.5	1154.0	1169.7	1123.4
2007	1128.0	1108.0	1116.4	1120.3	1131.6	1134.6	1123.9	1121.1	1124.8	1134.3	1159.2	1171.6	1131.2
2008	1130.6	1111.3	1115.4	1119.0	1127.8	1127.3	1114.6	1112.4	1116.4	1123.6	1133.2	1143.4	1122.9
2009	1090.4	1074.2	1069.6	1069.1	1079.8	1079.1	1062.9	1061.8	1068.4	1078.8	1097.0	1107.3	1078.2
2010	1065.8	1047.6	1057.7	1064.6	1076.8	1081.5	1068.6	1069.9	1074.9	1088.0	1107.2	1122.6	1077.1
2011	1080.5	1069.7	1072.9	1082.1	1089.6	1089.4	1078.5	1079.2	1085.9	1095.1	1117.2	1130.0	1089.2
2012	1088.1	1076.7	1085.5	1088.4	1097.9	1097.6	1086.9	1087.8	1093.5	1103.3	1129.6	1138.3	1097.8
2013	1092.7	1082.2	1086.6	1089.7	1098.3	1100.2	1087.1	1090.6	1094.8	1104.0	1127.7	1139.7	1099.5
2014	1095.6	1082.5	1089.6	1096.9	1108.5	1113.2	1098.4	1102.0	1108.5	1120.2	1143.4	1158.1	1109.7
2015	1112.2	1098.5	1102.7	1109.6	1122.0	1126.7	1114.5	1116.0	1121.6	1133.3	1150.4	1170.7	1123.2
Wholesale Trade													
2005	229.9	230.0	231.2	233.2	234.6	235.7	236.2	236.2	235.2	235.3	235.5	236.5	234.1
2006	233.3	233.8	235.0	236.7	238.2	239.9	239.7	239.9	238.6	239.0	239.0	239.3	237.7
2007	236.5	235.6	237.2	238.3	239.3	241.2	241.5	240.7	239.2	239.7	240.6	240.8	239.2
2008	237.8	237.7	238.4	239.3	240.5	241.2	241.2	240.3	238.1	237.7	235.6	234.5	238.5
2009	230.0	228.0	227.1	226.3	226.7	226.8	225.5	224.7	223.0	223.1	222.6	222.7	225.5
2010	219.5	218.3	219.7	221.0	222.6	223.7	224.0	224.2	222.6	223.5	223.3	223.5	222.2
2011	221.3	221.2	222.2	223.7	224.5	225.0	225.0	224.7	223.4	223.6	223.3	223.4	223.4
2012	220.8	221.0	222.4	222.9	223.9	225.4	224.4	223.9	222.7	222.5	222.2	222.9	222.9
2013	220.1	220.2	221.3	221.8	222.8	223.6	223.2	223.1	222.3	221.7	221.9	222.4	222.0
2014	219.8	219.6	220.3	221.2	222.9	224.7	225.0	225.1	223.7	224.4	224.9	225.4	223.1
2015	222.8	222.5	222.9	223.9	225.4	226.2	226.8	226.8	225.0	226.6	227.0	227.0	225.2
Retail Trade													
2005	655.1	643.8	645.4	649.7	655.4	657.9	658.0	657.5	650.1	657.6	674.9	686.5	657.7
2006	652.2	636.0	640.3	642.9	646.3	648.9	646.0	646.5	641.7	652.1	672.8	684.2	650.8
2007	651.7	633.7	638.7	640.5	649.0	651.5	650.9	649.0	642.3	651.3	673.8	683.5	651.3
2008	652.3	633.9	637.2	638.1	644.2	645.5	642.5	641.1	634.8	641.8	653.3	662.8	644.0
2009	623.7	611.2	608.8	609.2	618.8	620.9	617.5	617.5	612.2	620.7	638.2	645.7	620.4
2010	616.1	600.1	607.3	611.5	619.8	623.6	621.4	621.9	614.4	624.9	642.7	653.1	621.4
2011	621.3	610.3	611.6	617.9	623.2	624.8	623.6	625.3	618.6	626.7	646.7	655.7	625.5
2012	625.5	613.2	618.8	621.0	627.9	630.6	629.3	630.7	623.6	632.1	656.7	660.7	630.8
2013	626.5	616.2	618.3	620.7	626.8	631.4	629.2	630.7	623.1	631.4	651.7	660.0	630.5
2014	626.0	614.0	618.4	623.2	630.5	635.1	631.5	633.2	625.9	633.9	653.3	662.1	632.3
2015	628.4	616.4	618.9	623.4	632.1	637.4	634.8	635.1	627.7	636.0	648.6	660.8	633.3

1. Employment by Industry: Pennsylvania, 2005–2015—*Continued*

(Numbers in thousands, not seasonally adjusted)

Industry and year	January	February	March	April	May	June	July	August	September	October	November	December	Annual average
Transportation and Utilities													
2005	221.9	221.8	223.3	225.1	227.1	225.8	217.3	218.0	231.0	232.6	234.9	237.6	226.4
2006	231.8	231.1	232.9	233.2	235.8	232.5	225.4	226.4	239.4	241.4	242.2	246.2	234.9
2007	239.8	238.7	240.5	241.5	243.3	241.9	231.5	231.4	243.3	243.3	244.8	247.3	240.6
2008	240.5	239.7	239.8	241.6	243.1	240.6	230.9	231.0	243.5	244.1	244.3	246.1	240.4
2009	236.7	235.0	233.7	233.6	234.3	231.4	219.9	219.6	233.2	235.0	236.2	238.9	232.3
2010	230.2	229.2	230.7	232.1	234.4	234.2	223.2	223.8	237.9	239.6	241.2	246.0	233.5
2011	237.9	238.2	239.1	240.5	241.9	239.6	229.9	229.2	243.9	244.8	247.2	250.9	240.3
2012	241.8	242.5	244.3	244.5	246.1	241.6	233.2	233.2	247.2	248.7	250.7	254.7	244.0
2013	246.1	245.8	247.0	247.2	248.7	245.2	234.7	236.8	249.4	250.9	254.1	257.3	246.9
2014	249.8	248.9	250.9	252.5	255.1	253.4	241.9	243.7	258.9	261.9	265.2	270.6	254.4
2015	261.0	259.6	260.9	262.3	264.5	263.1	252.9	254.1	268.9	270.7	274.8	282.9	264.6
Information													
2005	109.1	108.8	109.0	109.4	110.0	110.5	109.6	109.4	111.6	108.1	108.8	109.1	109.5
2006	107.6	108.0	107.7	108.1	108.7	108.9	108.6	108.4	108.3	108.0	107.5	108.3	108.2
2007	106.8	106.5	106.4	106.6	107.3	109.0	108.1	108.0	108.1	107.0	107.6	108.9	107.5
2008	107.2	106.8	106.5	108.1	108.3	107.8	106.2	105.3	103.9	103.7	103.4	103.2	105.9
2009	101.6	101.0	100.8	100.5	100.3	100.4	99.8	98.7	97.9	98.5	97.8	98.2	99.6
2010	94.1	93.3	93.3	93.3	93.6	94.7	94.7	93.6	93.3	91.5	91.8	92.0	93.3
2011	90.6	90.6	90.7	91.4	92.0	92.5	92.1	87.6	91.2	91.7	92.5	90.6	91.1
2012	89.9	89.4	90.4	89.9	91.1	90.9	90.8	91.2	90.2	89.7	90.6	89.9	90.3
2013	88.8	88.4	88.3	87.8	88.0	88.0	88.1	87.7	86.5	87.7	87.0	87.1	87.8
2014	85.0	84.8	85.0	85.9	85.6	86.0	86.2	85.8	85.1	84.9	85.0	85.6	85.4
2015	83.6	83.9	84.4	84.3	85.0	85.8	85.7	86.0	85.0	86.0	85.8	86.5	85.2
Financial Activities													
2005	332.3	332.4	332.9	333.9	335.5	338.2	339.4	339.9	336.0	335.0	335.6	337.1	335.7
2006	333.9	333.7	334.1	334.9	335.9	339.3	338.9	337.4	333.6	332.7	332.6	333.2	335.0
2007	330.4	330.4	330.6	331.0	332.3	335.9	337.2	336.4	332.5	331.8	332.3	332.3	332.8
2008	328.2	328.7	329.3	329.9	331.1	333.7	334.2	333.6	328.5	327.0	326.5	326.6	329.8
2009	321.5	320.4	319.9	319.3	319.9	321.3	321.0	319.0	315.5	314.8	314.1	313.9	318.4
2010	311.4	310.2	310.9	310.5	311.9	313.3	313.0	312.5	308.8	309.5	309.5	310.0	311.0
2011	308.1	306.9	307.2	307.4	308.3	310.5	311.1	311.1	308.2	307.9	308.1	308.7	308.6
2012	306.7	306.7	307.4	307.3	309.0	312.1	312.6	312.4	309.5	309.4	310.0	310.5	309.5
2013	308.8	309.4	309.9	311.1	312.4	315.8	316.6	316.9	313.6	314.0	314.6	315.1	313.2
2014	312.5	312.8	313.2	313.3	315.3	318.0	318.7	318.6	315.0	314.8	315.1	316.1	315.3
2015	312.8	313.5	313.5	314.1	316.4	319.6	320.7	320.6	316.7	315.7	315.4	316.2	316.3
Professional and Business Services													
2005	634.3	638.1	642.4	657.9	659.1	666.6	668.6	671.3	669.9	672.9	673.0	671.3	660.5
2006	653.8	658.9	666.9	679.1	682.6	692.3	693.0	697.3	696.1	701.4	701.8	700.4	685.3
2007	679.9	681.6	688.1	701.8	706.3	716.3	715.2	717.4	713.7	715.8	716.8	715.8	705.7
2008	695.7	695.5	699.7	713.3	714.8	719.0	720.0	721.0	713.8	713.1	706.8	699.5	709.4
2009	675.9	671.1	669.7	674.4	673.5	675.8	672.8	674.3	670.5	679.5	680.9	679.3	674.8
2010	661.4	662.9	669.3	686.8	689.0	694.8	696.0	698.7	696.4	705.3	709.1	709.0	689.9
2011	690.8	692.7	699.1	714.2	717.4	722.6	721.6	724.9	725.7	730.2	732.6	729.5	716.8
2012	709.5	712.3	721.2	731.8	734.7	739.6	737.6	739.0	738.5	744.5	746.2	742.5	733.1
2013	723.1	729.3	736.3	746.2	749.3	755.5	755.9	757.7	752.0	757.1	760.2	753.8	748.0
2014	734.5	736.8	742.9	758.4	763.7	767.2	765.9	769.5	766.9	774.2	781.1	777.7	761.6
2015	755.4	757.0	759.1	773.2	778.0	780.4	780.6	780.5	779.4	787.8	782.3	778.2	774.3
Education and Health Services													
2005	999.3	1,023.7	1,024.4	1,032.1	1,021.9	1,004.9	1,005.7	1,001.8	1,028.7	1,049.1	1,052.8	1,048.5	1,024.4
2006	1,026.3	1,051.3	1,052.5	1,057.8	1,049.8	1,030.7	1,027.6	1,024.3	1,051.3	1,068.3	1,071.8	1,067.5	1,048.3
2007	1,045.8	1,069.6	1,074.9	1,076.2	1,068.5	1,050.5	1,048.0	1,045.6	1,070.0	1,093.4	1,094.8	1,089.9	1,068.9
2008	1,068.0	1,096.6	1,096.6	1,103.8	1,093.6	1,074.4	1,073.4	1,072.4	1,097.0	1,118.4	1,122.7	1,119.8	1,094.7
2009	1,097.9	1,121.6	1,120.4	1,123.6	1,114.1	1,094.0	1,092.7	1,086.4	1,108.2	1,130.8	1,135.4	1,129.6	1,112.9
2010	1,107.9	1,128.8	1,132.2	1,136.0	1,129.7	1,108.6	1,106.3	1,102.5	1,126.9	1,151.5	1,154.1	1,149.6	1,127.8
2011	1,123.3	1,150.7	1,153.0	1,154.1	1,146.0	1,125.8	1,118.8	1,115.7	1,145.4	1,163.4	1,168.6	1,163.6	1,144.0
2012	1,138.3	1,167.4	1,173.0	1,172.1	1,160.0	1,134.0	1,126.0	1,120.8	1,156.8	1,175.5	1,179.0	1,172.1	1,156.3
2013	1,145.9	1,175.2	1,177.2	1,175.7	1,160.3	1,138.4	1,131.6	1,126.7	1,165.7	1,182.8	1,191.0	1,181.8	1,162.7
2014	1,159.3	1,181.6	1,186.8	1,195.4	1,181.2	1,156.5	1,151.0	1,146.2	1,185.7	1,204.9	1,210.4	1,201.2	1,180.0
2015	1,174.8	1,198.6	1,198.1	1,206.4	1,192.9	1,165.5	1,162.0	1,156.7	1,195.4	1,219.7	1,225.9	1,218.1	1,192.8

1. Employment by Industry: Pennsylvania, 2005–2015—*Continued*

(Numbers in thousands, not seasonally adjusted)

Industry and year	January	February	March	April	May	June	July	August	September	October	November	December	Annual average
Leisure and Hospitality													
2005	446.1	446.5	455.6	477.9	502.4	518.3	519.6	521.4	501.6	483.0	473.1	472.5	484.8
2006	454.4	455.5	466.8	485.0	506.9	524.6	525.0	524.0	503.4	491.4	481.2	483.1	491.8
2007	463.0	464.8	474.9	490.6	515.5	533.5	532.3	533.6	510.5	501.2	489.6	489.4	499.9
2008	468.5	469.5	478.2	498.6	525.8	537.7	538.8	536.7	513.5	501.7	485.9	485.0	503.3
2009	461.4	460.2	469.5	484.8	515.9	525.6	528.7	529.7	506.9	493.4	478.5	477.0	494.3
2010	459.4	456.1	469.6	492.9	516.8	529.2	535.1	538.7	517.5	505.2	494.7	491.9	500.6
2011	471.4	471.2	484.4	506.7	529.9	544.3	544.8	546.4	524.5	511.6	501.4	498.2	511.2
2012	482.6	485.4	500.5	518.0	541.2	558.6	557.2	561.2	535.9	523.1	512.8	512.9	524.1
2013	492.7	493.6	507.3	523.4	549.8	565.9	568.3	567.7	544.1	531.7	518.8	522.6	532.2
2014	501.8	499.2	511.9	529.6	557.7	569.7	568.9	573.0	547.9	540.7	524.3	526.7	537.6
2015	506.2	506.3	515.5	536.7	564.9	578.0	579.2	581.7	559.2	555.7	535.9	538.0	546.4
Other Services													
2005	260.2	260.7	262.1	262.7	263.6	266.0	266.2	263.5	259.4	258.6	258.4	257.7	261.6
2006	255.7	255.8	257.3	258.9	260.2	262.7	262.6	260.6	257.5	257.0	256.3	256.3	258.4
2007	252.5	252.8	254.4	255.6	257.1	259.8	260.4	258.3	254.9	254.6	254.7	254.3	255.8
2008	251.3	250.9	251.2	253.8	255.7	258.3	258.8	257.3	254.8	254.0	253.0	252.2	254.3
2009	247.9	248.0	249.2	249.1	251.7	254.0	254.0	252.1	248.0	248.3	247.9	248.2	249.9
2010	245.9	244.7	247.4	248.6	251.1	253.9	254.6	254.2	250.6	251.1	251.2	250.8	250.3
2011	247.8	248.5	250.2	252.5	253.9	257.6	257.7	256.6	252.9	252.9	252.6	253.0	253.0
2012	250.4	251.0	253.4	254.0	255.6	259.2	258.4	256.9	253.2	252.5	251.6	251.5	254.0
2013	248.5	248.6	249.9	251.0	253.4	257.4	255.8	255.5	252.1	251.3	251.4	251.4	252.2
2014	249.1	248.9	251.9	251.6	254.4	258.0	257.9	257.4	253.3	253.4	253.1	253.4	253.5
2015	250.6	251.2	253.1	253.7	257.2	260.7	260.7	259.8	255.7	258.3	259.0	258.9	256.6
Government													
2005	751.9	771.1	774.9	778.1	769.4	750.9	696.8	690.2	749.7	768.5	774.0	767.9	753.6
2006	749.4	770.9	773.8	775.6	773.7	751.6	696.0	694.0	752.7	771.0	778.8	772.6	755.0
2007	752.0	771.3	774.6	775.4	771.3	752.1	698.4	695.4	749.8	770.3	775.6	771.1	754.8
2008	753.5	772.1	775.4	778.3	771.2	755.4	697.6	700.2	762.6	782.7	787.0	780.4	759.7
2009	760.6	781.3	783.5	790.4	781.0	764.5	713.7	707.5	767.8	787.8	793.7	786.9	768.2
2010	760.5	781.8	787.7	793.4	801.9	779.3	714.7	708.7	764.0	783.4	789.5	782.4	770.6
2011	762.2	779.4	781.0	781.3	770.6	752.0	688.7	683.8	740.2	755.8	762.8	758.4	751.4
2012	730.4	754.1	755.5	755.2	752.5	723.5	673.0	674.4	730.0	744.6	749.0	744.9	732.3
2013	722.2	741.5	741.4	742.3	743.7	710.2	661.2	665.4	717.7	731.4	738.1	733.6	720.7
2014	712.7	728.2	728.6	731.1	724.7	706.7	656.2	658.1	711.8	725.4	729.2	724.2	711.4
2015	700.3	719.7	720.3	723.8	717.4	696.7	650.5	654.3	706.5	722.1	727.6	725.4	705.4

2. Average Weekly Hours by Selected Industry: Pennsylvania, 2011–2015

(Not seasonally adjusted)

Industry and year	January	February	March	April	May	June	July	August	September	October	November	December	Annual average
Total Private													
2011	33.5	33.3	33.4	33.6	33.7	33.5	33.5	33.4	33.4	33.6	33.6	33.6	33.5
2012	33.3	33.1	33.1	33.3	33.1	33.2	33.3	33.0	33.4	33.0	33.0	33.4	33.2
2013	32.9	33.1	33.2	33.3	33.3	33.6	33.6	33.6	33.9	33.6	33.8	33.6	33.5
2014	33.1	33.1	33.8	33.7	33.8	34.0	33.9	33.8	33.8	33.8	34.2	33.8	33.7
2015	33.4	33.7	33.8	33.8	34.0	34.0	34.0	34.3	33.8	34.1	34.3	34.2	34.0
Goods-Producing													
2011	39.0	38.9	38.9	39.2	39.4	39.3	39.3	39.2	39.2	39.5	39.6	39.3	39.2
2012	38.7	38.6	38.2	38.9	38.8	39.3	39.0	38.8	39.2	39.1	38.9	39.2	38.9
2013	38.5	38.7	39.1	39.2	39.2	39.2	39.2	39.3	39.5	39.3	39.5	39.0	39.1
2014	39.0	38.0	39.6	39.6	39.7	40.1	39.7	39.5	39.8	39.9	40.0	39.3	39.5
2015	38.8	39.3	39.6	39.9	40.2	40.7	40.3	40.3	39.6	40.5	40.1	40.3	40.0
Construction													
2011	36.9	37.0	37.0	37.5	38.8	39.3	38.9	38.8	38.1	38.4	38.7	38.1	38.2
2012	36.6	36.8	36.9	37.7	37.6	38.4	38.6	38.6	39.3	39.4	38.5	37.9	38.1
2013	37.4	37.5	38.2	39.1	38.9	38.2	38.7	38.9	39.4	38.6	39.3	37.9	38.5
2014	37.8	37.7	38.8	39.4	39.7	40.2	39.7	38.5	39.6	39.3	39.8	38.0	39.1
2015	37.3	38.3	39.4	40.6	41.7	42.5	42.2	42.0	39.6	41.0	39.4	39.5	40.4
Manufacturing													
2011	39.7	39.8	40.3	40.4	40.1	39.6	39.6	39.6	40.3	40.6	40.7	40.1	40.1
2012	40.0	40.1	39.9	39.8	40.5	40.4	39.8	40.1	40.2	40.3	40.7	41.1	40.2
2013	40.6	40.6	40.8	40.6	40.9	41.0	40.2	40.4	40.5	40.8	40.7	40.5	40.6
2014	40.2	38.8	41.2	40.7	41.2	41.1	40.9	41.6	41.7	41.8	41.7	41.7	41.1
2015	40.9	41.0	40.9	41.0	40.9	41.3	40.5	41.0	40.7	41.4	41.3	41.5	41.0
Trade, Transportation, and Utilities													
2011	33.6	33.8	34.0	34.3	34.3	34.4	34.2	34.1	34.0	34.1	34.0	34.2	34.1
2012	33.7	33.6	33.7	33.8	33.8	34.0	33.9	33.6	33.7	33.1	33.2	33.5	33.6
2013	32.7	33.1	33.4	33.5	33.6	33.7	34.0	34.1	34.3	33.8	34.0	33.8	33.7
2014	33.3	32.8	33.8	33.8	34.0	34.0	34.2	34.1	34.3	34.0	34.3	34.3	33.9
2015	33.5	33.7	33.8	33.8	34.3	34.3	34.2	34.5	34.4	34.2	34.5	34.8	34.2
Information													
2011	33.3	32.5	32.9	33.0	32.0	32.3	32.8	31.6	32.0	31.3	31.7	31.2	32.2
2012	31.9	31.8	31.4	32.0	31.9	32.3	32.2	31.6	32.3	31.7	32.0	32.2	31.9
2013	31.5	30.8	31.7	31.4	31.7	32.6	32.3	32.6	33.3	32.9	34.3	32.2	32.3
2014	30.7	32.9	31.7	30.3	31.3	33.3	32.2	32.3	32.2	32.0	33.5	32.5	32.1
2015	32.4	34.4	34.0	33.5	33.5	33.1	33.5	34.0	33.0	33.6	33.5	32.6	33.4
Financial Activities													
2011	36.5	36.1	36.1	36.5	36.6	36.2	36.2	36.1	36.4	36.8	36.5	36.3	36.4
2012	37.1	36.6	36.8	37.1	36.5	36.7	37.2	36.7	37.2	36.5	36.6	37.2	36.9
2013	36.2	36.7	37.0	36.9	36.6	37.1	36.4	36.4	37.0	36.5	36.5	37.0	36.7
2014	36.2	36.8	36.9	36.8	36.8	37.1	36.6	36.6	36.8	36.9	37.4	36.8	36.8
2015	37.1	37.5	37.7	37.3	37.3	37.2	36.8	37.5	36.9	36.9	37.6	36.9	37.2
Professional and Business Services													
2011	35.8	35.3	35.3	35.4	35.7	35.2	34.9	35.1	35.0	35.6	35.3	35.4	35.3
2012	35.7	35.4	35.4	36.0	35.2	35.1	35.3	34.9	35.8	35.3	35.4	36.4	35.5
2013	35.8	35.8	35.9	36.1	36.1	36.7	36.3	36.2	36.9	36.3	36.4	36.5	36.3
2014	35.5	36.1	36.5	36.3	36.3	36.5	35.7	35.6	35.4	35.6	36.4	35.7	36.0
2015	34.9	35.5	35.7	35.5	35.8	35.8	35.8	36.4	35.2	35.9	36.5	36.0	35.8
Education and Health Services													
2011	32.1	31.9	32.0	32.0	32.1	31.8	31.7	31.6	31.7	31.8	31.7	31.9	31.9
2012	31.4	31.1	31.2	31.2	31.2	31.3	31.4	31.2	31.7	31.5	31.4	31.6	31.4
2013	31.4	31.6	31.4	31.5	31.5	31.9	31.8	31.7	32.1	31.9	32.1	32.1	31.8
2014	31.9	31.8	32.3	32.2	32.2	32.5	32.5	32.4	32.3	32.4	32.8	32.5	32.3
2015	32.7	32.5	32.6	32.5	32.6	32.5	32.7	32.7	32.6	32.6	33.0	32.9	32.7
Leisure and Hospitality													
2011	23.5	23.9	23.9	24.1	24.2	24.5	24.6	24.5	24.2	24.4	24.5	24.2	24.2
2012	23.6	24.0	24.0	23.9	24.1	24.1	24.6	24.6	24.2	23.9	23.8	24.3	24.1
2013	23.6	24.3	24.3	24.4	24.6	25.0	25.2	25.3	25.0	24.9	25.0	24.4	24.7
2014	24.0	24.4	24.9	25.0	25.3	25.3	25.5	25.4	24.8	25.0	24.9	24.6	24.9
2015	24.2	24.6	24.6	24.9	25.1	25.1	25.0	25.6	24.7	25.1	24.8	24.6	24.9
Other Services													
2011	30.5	29.6	30.0	30.2	30.4	30.4	30.4	30.2	30.6	30.8	30.4	30.1	30.3
2012	30.1	29.8	29.6	29.7	29.1	29.2	29.7	28.8	29.0	28.4	28.4	28.7	29.2
2013	28.5	28.6	28.2	28.5	28.0	28.4	28.6	28.8	29.0	28.6	28.4	28.3	28.5
2014	27.9	28.2	29.0	28.8	28.6	28.8	29.4	29.6	29.2	29.1	29.7	29.1	29.0
2015	29.4	29.3	29.4	29.1	29.2	29.1	29.9	30.3	30.0	30.0	30.1	29.6	29.6

3. Average Hourly Earnings by Selected Industry: Pennsylvania, 2011–2015

(Dollars, not seasonally adjusted)

Industry and year	January	February	March	April	May	June	July	August	September	October	November	December	Annual average
Total Private													
2011	21.61	21.61	21.70	21.77	21.81	21.65	21.79	21.79	21.96	22.10	22.13	22.28	21.85
2012	22.43	22.37	22.41	22.57	22.40	22.42	22.61	22.43	22.92	22.84	22.88	23.14	22.62
2013	23.11	23.18	23.19	23.24	23.15	23.21	23.12	23.15	23.43	23.36	23.45	23.73	23.28
2014	23.79	24.10	23.87	23.75	23.57	23.72	23.55	23.55	23.67	23.58	23.80	23.75	23.72
2015	23.94	24.09	24.22	24.10	24.04	24.07	24.11	24.25	24.35	24.31	24.54	24.37	24.20
Goods-Producing													
2011	23.31	23.11	23.14	23.47	23.36	23.41	23.66	23.47	23.69	23.96	23.91	24.30	23.58
2012	24.50	24.17	24.34	24.62	24.35	24.28	24.15	24.00	24.24	23.97	24.09	24.55	24.27
2013	24.05	23.95	23.96	24.08	23.98	23.95	24.03	24.05	24.26	24.28	24.17	24.59	24.12
2014	24.44	24.31	24.14	24.28	24.13	24.28	24.27	24.02	24.18	24.11	24.28	24.27	24.22
2015	24.32	24.17	24.25	24.36	24.21	24.39	24.49	24.49	24.41	24.71	24.78	25.12	24.48
Construction													
2011	25.49	25.57	25.59	25.62	25.62	25.51	25.80	26.19	26.01	25.92	26.02	26.03	25.79
2012	26.21	26.36	26.27	26.09	25.90	26.13	26.37	26.41	26.51	26.46	26.83	27.05	26.39
2013	27.08	27.32	27.37	27.41	27.30	27.27	27.77	27.65	27.84	28.16	27.56	28.11	27.58
2014	27.81	28.48	28.10	27.86	27.24	27.54	27.84	28.28	28.14	27.99	28.30	28.87	28.03
2015	28.83	29.09	29.14	28.76	29.32	28.91	29.20	29.31	29.33	29.52	29.52	29.72	29.23
Manufacturing													
2011	22.30	22.30	22.42	22.56	22.72	22.61	22.63	22.68	22.86	22.97	23.13	23.30	22.71
2012	23.19	23.18	23.42	23.74	23.62	23.55	23.60	23.49	23.78	23.89	23.90	24.13	23.63
2013	23.96	24.20	24.16	24.13	24.20	24.09	23.88	23.97	24.04	23.87	24.10	24.34	24.08
2014	24.15	24.57	24.29	24.31	24.01	24.05	23.81	23.83	23.88	23.88	23.98	23.92	24.05
2015	23.92	23.76	23.91	23.89	23.96	24.03	24.12	24.19	24.23	24.13	24.12	24.03	24.02
Trade, Transportation, and Utilities													
2011	19.01	19.12	19.31	19.12	19.05	18.98	19.06	19.00	19.05	19.14	19.09	19.18	19.09
2012	19.38	19.39	19.47	19.53	19.37	19.50	19.91	19.42	19.95	19.79	19.67	19.76	19.60
2013	19.78	19.86	20.03	20.23	20.21	20.23	20.19	20.19	20.37	20.10	20.13	20.18	20.13
2014	20.54	20.78	20.36	20.33	20.14	20.47	20.40	20.45	20.47	20.38	20.47	20.36	20.43
2015	20.88	20.78	21.36	21.41	21.21	21.09	21.04	21.13	21.11	21.05	21.04	20.75	21.07
Financial Activities													
2011	28.16	28.09	28.15	28.34	28.51	27.98	28.02	27.83	27.89	28.12	28.31	28.54	28.16
2012	29.09	29.08	28.89	29.31	29.56	29.30	29.50	29.50	30.18	29.89	29.58	30.38	29.52
2013	30.20	30.24	30.12	30.54	30.37	30.55	30.50	30.50	30.48	30.20	30.61	30.88	30.43
2014	31.17	31.27	31.14	30.96	30.79	30.93	30.79	30.73	30.99	30.90	31.50	31.33	31.04
2015	31.38	31.86	31.62	31.74	31.50	31.44	31.35	32.25	31.99	32.06	32.79	33.51	31.96
Professional and Business Services													
2011	27.33	27.14	27.25	27.34	27.38	27.03	27.27	27.24	27.49	27.85	28.09	28.34	27.48
2012	28.27	27.90	27.94	28.23	27.97	28.04	28.39	28.20	28.81	28.56	28.74	29.22	28.36
2013	28.83	29.15	28.98	28.77	28.75	29.12	28.49	28.64	29.06	28.89	29.10	29.82	28.97
2014	29.79	30.64	30.66	30.18	30.13	30.44	29.99	30.06	29.99	29.45	29.96	30.26	30.13
2015	30.72	31.16	31.11	30.50	30.53	30.81	30.92	31.13	31.31	31.25	31.92	31.49	31.07
Education and Health Services													
2011	20.23	20.35	20.49	20.82	20.88	21.03	21.37	21.26	21.53	21.52	21.44	21.61	21.04
2012	21.80	21.64	21.71	21.86	21.82	21.78	21.78	21.71	21.97	21.88	22.00	22.19	21.85
2013	22.20	22.06	22.01	22.08	21.90	21.91	22.12	22.13	22.32	22.35	22.34	22.52	22.16
2014	22.58	22.46	22.25	22.37	22.46	22.38	22.44	22.35	22.50	22.54	22.51	22.41	22.44
2015	22.40	22.58	22.48	22.48	22.46	22.57	22.73	22.81	23.15	22.84	23.10	23.10	22.73
Leisure and Hospitality													
2011	12.57	12.62	12.65	12.62	12.59	12.20	12.19	12.25	12.39	12.45	12.45	12.63	12.46
2012	12.53	12.66	12.62	12.70	12.66	12.53	12.50	12.53	12.87	13.03	13.01	13.15	12.73
2013	13.56	13.53	13.63	13.60	13.61	13.50	13.46	13.56	14.06	14.24	14.37	14.85	13.83
2014	14.64	14.71	14.59	14.47	14.34	14.19	14.03	13.98	14.16	14.19	14.16	14.07	14.28
2015	13.92	13.92	13.82	13.91	13.75	13.66	13.47	13.44	13.71	13.79	13.87	13.91	13.76
Other Services													
2011	18.50	18.53	18.30	18.52	18.65	18.64	18.50	18.65	18.84	18.97	19.03	19.27	18.70
2012	19.19	19.14	19.41	19.77	19.19	19.65	19.25	19.57	20.17	20.05	20.23	20.65	19.68
2013	20.15	20.19	20.36	20.10	20.13	19.77	19.48	19.36	20.04	20.05	20.18	20.73	20.04
2014	20.88	21.07	21.06	20.53	20.26	20.26	19.74	19.73	20.26	20.53	20.56	20.67	20.45
2015	20.82	20.73	21.19	21.00	20.80	20.56	20.34	20.28	20.65	20.83	20.74	21.11	20.75

4. Average Weekly Earnings by Selected Industry: Pennsylvania, 2011–2015

(Dollars, not seasonally adjusted)

Industry and year	January	February	March	April	May	June	July	August	September	October	November	December	Annual average
Total Private													
2011	723.94	719.61	724.78	731.47	735.00	725.28	729.97	727.79	733.46	742.56	743.57	748.61	731.98
2012	746.92	740.45	741.77	751.58	741.44	744.34	752.91	740.19	765.53	753.72	755.04	772.88	750.98
2013	760.32	767.26	769.91	773.89	770.90	779.86	776.83	777.84	794.28	784.90	792.61	797.33	779.88
2014	787.45	797.71	806.81	800.38	796.67	806.48	798.35	795.99	800.05	797.00	813.96	802.75	799.36
2015	799.60	811.83	818.64	814.58	817.36	818.38	819.74	831.78	823.03	828.97	841.72	833.45	822.80
Goods-Producing													
2011	904.02	904.81	909.09	919.63	931.81	925.52	929.84	933.35	935.70	943.66	951.59	948.31	927.47
2012	929.96	937.98	930.17	946.83	939.74	950.67	955.89	947.11	965.89	964.21	963.16	978.82	951.11
2013	957.11	970.21	981.02	984.70	987.06	983.92	987.06	989.97	998.56	992.72	996.19	993.72	984.15
2014	983.97	976.60	1,005.84	1,005.84	994.09	1,009.32	997.26	995.80	1,002.96	1,002.69	1,012.40	995.47	998.17
2015	980.09	990.75	1,006.24	1,012.66	1,031.93	1,046.80	1,043.37	1,047.40	1,026.43	1,050.98	1,036.99	1,030.07	1,026.40
Construction													
2011	940.58	946.09	946.83	960.75	994.06	1,002.54	1,003.62	1,016.17	990.98	995.33	1,006.97	991.74	985.18
2012	959.29	970.05	969.36	983.59	973.84	1,003.39	1,017.88	1,019.43	1,041.84	1,042.52	1,032.96	1,025.20	1,005.46
2013	1,012.79	1,024.50	1,045.53	1,071.73	1,061.97	1,041.71	1,074.70	1,075.59	1,096.90	1,086.98	1,083.11	1,065.37	1,061.83
2014	1,051.22	1,073.70	1,090.28	1,097.68	1,081.43	1,107.11	1,105.25	1,088.78	1,114.34	1,100.01	1,126.34	1,097.06	1,095.97
2015	1,075.36	1,114.15	1,148.12	1,167.66	1,222.64	1,228.68	1,232.24	1,231.02	1,161.47	1,210.32	1,163.09	1,173.94	1,180.89
Manufacturing													
2011	878.62	876.39	885.59	893.38	895.17	884.05	887.10	889.06	905.26	914.21	920.57	922.68	897.05
2012	909.05	906.34	915.72	928.23	925.90	925.52	915.68	916.11	934.55	934.10	941.66	967.61	926.30
2013	944.02	955.90	956.74	950.72	955.90	956.37	943.26	949.21	954.39	950.03	959.18	966.30	953.57
2014	956.34	941.03	971.60	967.54	955.60	964.41	947.64	955.58	955.20	962.36	966.39	961.58	959.60
2015	949.62	948.02	954.01	950.82	951.21	961.20	955.15	960.34	961.93	965.20	969.62	970.81	958.40
Trade, Transportation, and Utilities													
2011	638.74	646.26	656.54	655.82	653.42	652.91	651.85	647.90	647.70	652.67	649.06	655.96	650.97
2012	653.11	651.50	656.14	660.11	654.71	663.00	674.95	652.51	672.32	655.05	653.04	661.96	658.56
2013	646.81	657.37	669.00	677.71	679.06	681.75	686.46	688.48	698.69	679.38	684.42	682.08	678.38
2014	683.98	681.58	688.17	687.15	684.76	695.98	697.68	697.35	702.12	692.92	702.12	698.35	692.58
2015	699.48	700.29	721.97	723.66	727.50	723.39	719.57	728.99	726.18	719.91	725.88	722.10	720.59
Information													
2011	770.23	746.20	745.51	733.92	716.16	708.34	712.09	685.72	698.88	680.46	677.75	671.42	711.94
2012	695.74	683.06	676.98	699.20	723.49	743.22	728.69	694.88	728.69	722.13	741.76	751.87	714.88
2013	749.70	742.90	783.31	785.31	791.23	844.01	843.35	857.38	897.10	899.82	965.89	886.79	837.54
2014	839.03	911.66	906.62	856.88	870.45	951.71	903.53	885.02	912.87	902.72	981.22	940.88	905.86
2015	926.64	1,022.37	1,014.90	987.25	993.28	982.74	990.93	1,001.98	966.57	1,001.62	1,012.04	974.41	988.97
Financial Activities													
2011	1,027.84	1,014.05	1,016.22	1,034.41	1,043.47	1,012.88	1,014.32	1,004.66	1,015.20	1,034.82	1,033.32	1,036.00	1,025.02
2012	1,079.24	1,064.33	1,063.15	1,087.40	1,078.94	1,075.31	1,097.40	1,082.65	1,122.70	1,090.99	1,082.63	1,130.14	1,089.29
2013	1,093.24	1,109.81	1,114.44	1,126.93	1,111.54	1,133.41	1,110.20	1,110.20	1,127.76	1,102.30	1,117.27	1,142.56	1,116.78
2014	1,128.35	1,150.74	1,149.07	1,139.33	1,133.07	1,147.50	1,126.91	1,124.72	1,140.43	1,140.21	1,178.10	1,152.94	1,142.27
2015	1,164.20	1,194.75	1,192.07	1,183.90	1,174.95	1,169.57	1,153.68	1,209.38	1,180.43	1,183.01	1,232.90	1,236.52	1,188.91
Professional and Business Services													
2011	978.41	958.04	961.93	967.84	977.47	951.46	951.72	956.12	962.15	991.46	991.58	1,003.24	970.04
2012	1,009.24	987.66	989.08	1,016.28	984.54	984.20	1,002.17	984.18	1,031.40	1,008.17	1,017.40	1,063.61	1,006.78
2013	1,032.11	1,043.57	1,040.38	1,038.60	1,037.88	1,068.70	1,034.19	1,036.77	1,072.31	1,048.71	1,059.24	1,088.43	1,051.61
2014	1,057.55	1,106.10	1,119.09	1,095.53	1,093.72	1,111.06	1,070.64	1,070.14	1,061.65	1,048.42	1,090.54	1,080.28	1,084.68
2015	1,072.13	1,106.18	1,110.63	1,082.75	1,092.97	1,103.00	1,106.94	1,133.13	1,102.11	1,121.88	1,165.08	1,133.64	1,112.31
Education and Health Services													
2011	649.38	649.17	655.68	666.24	670.25	668.75	677.43	671.82	682.50	684.34	679.65	689.36	671.18
2012	684.52	673.00	677.35	682.03	680.78	681.71	683.89	677.35	696.45	689.22	690.80	701.20	686.09
2013	697.08	697.10	691.11	695.52	689.85	698.93	703.42	701.52	716.47	712.97	717.11	722.89	704.69
2014	720.30	714.23	718.68	720.31	723.21	727.35	729.30	724.14	726.75	730.30	738.33	728.33	724.81
2015	732.48	733.85	732.85	730.60	732.20	733.53	743.27	745.89	754.69	744.58	762.30	759.99	743.27
Leisure and Hospitality													
2011	295.40	301.62	302.34	304.14	304.68	298.90	299.87	300.13	299.84	303.78	305.03	305.65	301.53
2012	295.71	303.84	302.88	303.53	305.11	301.97	307.50	308.24	311.45	311.42	309.64	319.55	306.79
2013	320.02	328.78	331.21	331.84	334.81	337.50	339.19	343.07	351.50	354.58	359.25	362.34	341.60
2014	351.36	358.92	363.29	361.75	362.80	359.01	357.77	355.09	351.17	354.75	352.58	346.12	355.57
2015	336.86	342.43	339.97	346.36	345.13	342.87	336.75	344.06	338.64	346.13	343.98	342.19	342.62
Other Services													
2011	564.25	548.49	549.00	559.30	566.96	566.66	562.40	563.23	576.50	584.28	578.51	580.03	566.61
2012	577.62	570.37	574.54	587.17	558.43	573.78	571.73	563.62	584.93	569.42	574.53	592.66	574.66
2013	574.28	577.43	574.15	572.85	563.64	561.47	557.13	557.57	581.16	573.43	573.11	586.66	571.14
2014	582.55	594.17	610.74	591.26	579.44	583.49	580.36	584.01	591.59	597.42	610.63	601.50	593.05
2015	612.11	607.39	622.99	611.10	607.36	598.30	608.17	614.48	619.50	624.90	624.27	624.86	614.20

RHODE ISLAND
At a Glance

Population:
  2005 estimate: 1,067,916
  2010 census: 1,052,567
  2015 estimate: 1,056,298

Percent change in population:
  2005–2015: –1.1%
  2010–2015: 0.4%

Percent change in total nonfarm employment:
  2005–2015: –1.3%

Industry with the largest growth in employment, 2005–2015 (thousands):
  Education and health services, 10.1

Industry with the largest decline or smallest growth in employment, 2005–2015 (thousands):
  Manufacturing, –13.6

Civilian labor force:
  2005: 565,735
  2010: 566,704
  2015: 554,558

Unemployment rate and rank among states (highest to lowest):
  2005: 5.0%, 22nd
  2010: 11.2%, 4th
  2015: 6.0%, 11th

Over-the-year change in unemployment rates:
  2012–2013: –1.1%
  2013–2014: –1.6%
  2014–2015: –1.7%

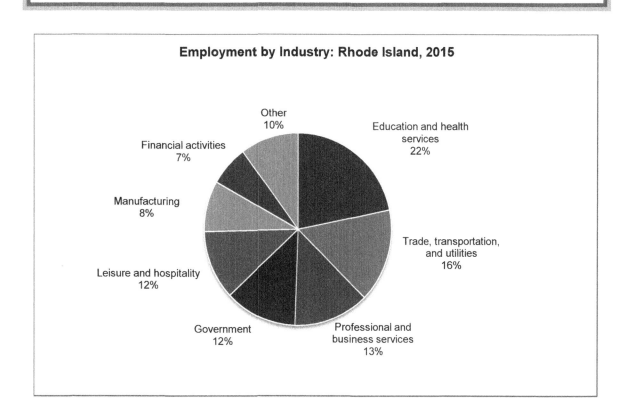

Employment by Industry: Rhode Island, 2015

Other
10%

Financial activities
7%

Manufacturing
8%

Leisure and hospitality
12%

Government
12%

Education and health
services
22%

Trade, transportation,
and utilities
16%

Professional and
business services
13%

1. Employment by Industry: Rhode Island, 2005–2015

(Numbers in thousands, not seasonally adjusted)

Industry and year	January	February	March	April	May	June	July	August	September	October	November	December	Annual average
Total Nonfarm													
2005	475.8	478.6	481.0	491.0	495.7	498.1	491.2	492.8	497.5	496.7	497.8	496.1	491.0
2006	475.5	478.5	482.9	494.0	497.3	500.1	490.6	493.2	500.0	500.7	501.1	500.5	492.9
2007	481.0	482.8	485.2	492.4	498.9	500.7	491.9	492.0	495.3	495.1	494.1	492.5	491.8
2008	473.5	475.5	477.4	484.0	489.2	489.5	479.2	480.2	484.4	482.7	479.9	476.2	481.0
2009	454.3	455.4	454.8	458.7	465.1	465.3	456.2	456.1	461.5	463.2	462.4	460.3	459.4
2010	443.6	445.7	449.1	456.0	463.5	463.6	459.3	460.1	463.9	464.1	464.5	462.3	458.0
2011	444.6	447.8	450.8	460.2	465.8	467.9	461.7	461.1	466.1	467.4	467.2	464.9	460.5
2012	449.0	454.0	457.2	463.4	470.2	472.1	464.4	466.6	472.8	472.1	471.2	471.9	465.4
2013	455.1	457.4	461.3	467.9	475.2	478.9	472.6	473.4	478.3	480.6	479.6	477.1	471.5
2014	460.8	464.0	466.2	476.4	484.4	485.6	480.3	480.6	486.0	487.3	486.9	487.0	478.8
2015	469.9	468.5	472.4	482.8	492.0	491.6	488.3	486.0	490.1	491.6	491.4	489.8	484.5
Total Private													
2005	410.3	412.8	415.1	425.2	429.6	432.2	429.7	432.1	433.4	430.9	431.7	430.2	426.1
2006	410.1	412.6	417.0	428.4	431.5	434.5	429.3	432.2	435.3	435.0	434.7	434.5	427.9
2007	415.8	417.4	419.9	427.1	432.9	435.8	430.4	430.8	431.4	430.4	429.3	427.5	427.4
2008	408.9	411.0	412.5	419.2	423.7	425.0	419.0	420.7	422.0	419.6	415.9	412.5	417.5
2009	391.3	392.1	391.6	395.3	401.4	402.3	398.4	398.6	400.2	400.4	399.4	397.5	397.4
2010	381.3	383.4	386.4	393.3	398.7	400.5	400.8	401.9	403.4	402.5	402.4	400.4	396.3
2011	383.2	386.4	389.0	398.4	403.8	406.3	405.1	404.3	406.2	406.4	406.0	403.7	399.9
2012	388.4	393.1	396.2	402.2	408.4	411.6	408.2	410.0	413.1	411.3	410.1	410.8	405.3
2013	394.6	396.9	400.3	407.1	413.5	418.1	415.5	416.6	418.5	419.5	418.5	415.8	411.2
2014	400.2	403.5	405.4	415.4	422.4	424.3	423.1	423.9	425.7	426.2	425.3	425.8	418.4
2015	409.0	407.6	411.5	421.5	430.0	430.5	431.2	429.3	430.1	430.6	430.2	428.8	424.2
Goods-Producing													
2005	74.8	74.2	74.5	77.1	78.0	79.1	76.4	78.7	78.6	77.6	77.8	76.8	77.0
2006	73.1	72.8	73.4	76.0	76.7	77.8	75.5	77.5	77.3	76.9	76.4	76.0	75.8
2007	72.6	71.6	71.9	73.0	74.2	74.8	72.7	74.3	74.1	73.8	73.1	71.7	73.2
2008	68.4	67.4	67.9	69.3	70.2	70.8	68.4	70.0	69.8	68.5	67.2	65.5	68.6
2009	60.9	59.0	58.5	59.3	59.7	59.9	58.7	59.5	59.2	59.1	58.5	57.5	59.2
2010	54.2	53.7	54.0	55.5	56.8	57.7	57.1	58.2	57.9	57.9	57.8	56.8	56.5
2011	54.0	53.4	53.9	55.6	56.5	57.4	56.9	57.4	57.0	56.9	56.8	56.1	56.0
2012	53.4	53.2	54.0	55.3	55.9	57.1	56.2	57.2	56.9	57.1	56.9	56.6	55.8
2013	53.9	53.2	54.2	55.5	56.6	57.4	56.5	57.8	57.8	57.8	57.9	57.2	56.3
2014	54.8	54.4	54.8	56.9	58.3	59.0	58.5	58.9	58.8	58.9	58.8	58.4	57.5
2015	56.1	55.0	55.5	57.5	58.8	59.4	59.4	59.8	59.7	60.1	60.4	60.5	58.5
Service-Providing													
2005	401.0	404.4	406.5	413.9	417.7	419.0	414.8	414.1	418.9	419.1	420.0	419.3	414.1
2006	402.4	405.7	409.5	418.0	420.6	422.3	415.1	415.7	422.7	423.8	424.7	424.5	417.1
2007	408.4	411.2	413.3	419.4	424.7	425.9	419.2	417.7	421.2	421.3	421.0	420.8	418.7
2008	405.1	408.1	409.5	414.7	419.0	418.7	410.8	410.2	414.6	414.2	412.7	410.7	412.4
2009	393.4	396.4	396.3	399.4	405.4	405.4	397.5	396.6	402.3	404.1	403.9	402.8	400.3
2010	389.4	392.0	395.1	400.5	406.7	405.9	402.2	401.9	406.0	406.2	406.7	405.5	401.5
2011	390.6	394.4	396.9	404.6	409.3	410.5	404.8	403.7	409.1	410.5	410.4	408.8	404.5
2012	395.6	400.8	403.2	408.1	414.3	415.0	408.2	409.4	415.9	415.0	414.3	415.3	409.6
2013	401.2	404.2	407.1	412.4	418.6	421.5	416.1	415.6	420.5	422.8	421.7	419.9	415.1
2014	406.0	409.6	411.4	419.5	426.1	426.6	421.8	421.7	427.2	428.4	428.1	428.6	421.3
2015	413.8	413.5	416.9	425.3	433.2	432.2	428.9	426.2	430.4	431.5	431.0	429.3	426.0
Mining and Logging													
2005	0.2	0.2	0.2	0.3	0.3	0.3	0.3	0.3	0.3	0.3	0.3	0.3	0.3
2006	0.2	0.2	0.2	0.3	0.3	0.3	0.3	0.3	0.3	0.3	0.3	0.3	0.3
2007	0.2	0.2	0.2	0.3	0.3	0.3	0.3	0.3	0.3	0.3	0.3	0.2	0.3
2008	0.2	0.2	0.2	0.2	0.3	0.3	0.3	0.3	0.3	0.3	0.3	0.2	0.3
2009	0.2	0.1	0.2	0.2	0.2	0.2	0.2	0.2	0.2	0.2	0.2	0.2	0.2
2010	0.1	0.1	0.1	0.2	0.2	0.2	0.2	0.2	0.2	0.2	0.2	0.2	0.2
2011	0.1	0.1	0.1	0.2	0.2	0.2	0.2	0.2	0.2	0.2	0.2	0.2	0.2
2012	0.1	0.1	0.2	0.2	0.2	0.2	0.2	0.2	0.2	0.2	0.2	0.2	0.2
2013	0.2	0.1	0.2	0.2	0.2	0.2	0.2	0.2	0.2	0.2	0.2	0.2	0.2
2014	0.1	0.1	0.2	0.2	0.2	0.2	0.3	0.2	0.2	0.2	0.2	0.2	0.2
2015	0.2	0.2	0.2	0.2	0.2	0.2	0.2	0.2	0.2	0.2	0.2	0.2	0.2

1. Employment by Industry: Rhode Island, 2005–2015—*Continued*

(Numbers in thousands, not seasonally adjusted)

Industry and year	January	February	March	April	May	June	July	August	September	October	November	December	Annual average
Construction													
2005	18.8	18.3	18.6	21.3	22.3	23.4	23.5	23.6	23.5	22.8	23.1	22.2	21.8
2006	19.8	19.4	20.0	22.5	23.3	24.3	24.4	24.7	24.4	24.0	23.7	23.3	22.8
2007	21.0	19.9	20.4	21.6	22.8	23.4	23.6	23.4	23.0	22.8	22.5	21.4	22.2
2008	18.8	18.3	18.7	20.3	21.3	21.9	22.0	21.9	21.7	20.9	20.2	19.0	20.4
2009	16.4	15.9	15.9	17.1	17.8	18.0	18.2	18.2	17.8	17.6	17.1	16.3	17.2
2010	13.9	13.5	13.9	15.5	16.4	16.9	17.3	17.5	17.0	16.9	16.7	15.8	15.9
2011	13.6	13.0	13.4	15.0	15.9	16.6	17.2	17.1	16.8	16.8	16.8	16.2	15.7
2012	14.3	13.8	14.5	15.7	16.1	16.9	17.2	17.1	16.8	16.8	16.7	16.3	16.0
2013	14.1	13.7	14.3	15.5	16.5	16.9	17.3	17.4	17.3	17.2	17.0	16.2	16.1
2014	14.4	14.0	14.3	16.0	17.1	17.5	17.8	17.7	17.5	17.5	17.3	16.8	16.5
2015	14.8	14.0	14.4	16.2	17.3	17.8	18.3	18.3	18.2	18.3	18.4	18.4	17.0
Manufacturing													
2005	55.8	55.7	55.7	55.5	55.4	55.4	52.6	54.8	54.8	54.5	54.4	54.3	54.9
2006	53.1	53.2	53.2	53.2	53.1	53.2	50.8	52.5	52.6	52.6	52.4	52.4	52.7
2007	51.4	51.5	51.3	51.1	51.1	51.1	48.8	50.6	50.8	50.7	50.3	50.1	50.7
2008	49.4	48.9	49.0	48.8	48.6	48.6	46.1	47.8	47.8	47.3	46.7	46.3	47.9
2009	44.3	43.0	42.4	42.0	41.7	41.7	40.3	41.1	41.2	41.3	41.2	41.0	41.8
2010	40.2	40.1	40.0	39.8	40.2	40.6	39.6	40.5	40.7	40.8	40.9	40.8	40.4
2011	40.3	40.3	40.4	40.4	40.4	40.6	39.5	40.1	40.0	39.9	39.8	39.7	40.1
2012	39.0	39.3	39.3	39.4	39.6	40.0	38.8	39.9	39.9	40.1	40.0	40.1	39.6
2013	39.6	39.4	39.7	39.8	39.9	40.3	39.0	40.2	40.3	40.4	40.7	40.8	40.0
2014	40.3	40.3	40.3	40.7	41.0	41.3	40.4	41.0	41.1	41.2	41.3	41.4	40.9
2015	41.1	40.8	40.9	41.1	41.3	41.4	40.9	41.3	41.3	41.6	41.8	41.9	41.3
Trade, Transportation, and Utilities													
2005	78.9	78.3	78.3	79.3	79.9	80.7	79.8	80.0	80.1	80.7	82.1	83.1	80.1
2006	78.6	77.7	78.0	79.2	79.5	80.2	79.0	79.0	79.9	80.6	82.1	83.2	79.8
2007	79.1	78.0	78.2	78.9	79.8	80.7	79.8	79.6	79.7	79.8	81.2	82.2	79.8
2008	77.8	76.7	76.6	77.0	77.4	78.3	77.2	77.3	77.3	77.4	77.6	78.0	77.4
2009	73.8	72.8	72.4	71.8	73.1	73.7	72.8	72.6	73.3	73.5	74.4	75.0	73.3
2010	72.0	71.5	71.9	71.4	71.8	72.9	72.3	72.4	73.0	73.5	74.5	75.2	72.7
2011	72.2	71.7	71.9	72.8	73.7	74.4	73.5	73.7	74.5	74.9	76.2	77.1	73.9
2012	73.8	73.1	73.3	73.6	74.6	75.6	74.1	74.2	74.9	75.2	76.4	76.8	74.6
2013	72.7	72.2	72.0	72.7	73.8	74.6	73.9	74.0	74.4	75.1	76.3	77.2	74.1
2014	73.5	73.1	73.0	73.8	74.7	75.7	74.7	75.1	75.5	76.1	77.4	78.8	75.1
2015	75.1	74.2	74.1	75.1	76.1	77.1	76.3	76.2	76.9	76.4	77.5	78.6	76.1
Wholesale Trade													
2005	16.3	16.4	16.5	16.8	16.9	17.0	16.9	17.0	16.9	16.9	16.9	17.0	16.8
2006	16.7	16.7	16.8	17.0	17.0	17.1	17.1	17.1	17.1	17.2	17.2	17.2	17.0
2007	17.0	16.9	16.9	17.2	17.3	17.4	17.4	17.3	17.1	17.2	17.3	17.4	17.2
2008	16.9	16.9	16.9	16.9	17.0	17.1	17.0	16.9	16.9	16.9	16.8	16.7	16.9
2009	16.3	16.2	16.1	16.0	16.0	16.1	15.9	15.9	15.9	16.0	15.9	16.0	16.0
2010	15.6	15.6	15.7	15.6	15.9	16.0	15.9	16.0	16.0	16.0	16.0	16.1	15.9
2011	15.8	15.8	15.9	16.1	16.3	16.5	16.5	16.6	16.7	16.7	16.8	16.9	16.4
2012	16.7	16.8	16.9	16.8	17.0	17.1	17.0	17.0	16.9	16.9	16.9	16.8	16.9
2013	16.5	16.4	16.5	16.5	16.5	16.7	16.7	16.8	16.7	16.8	16.9	16.9	16.7
2014	16.6	16.7	16.7	16.6	16.8	16.9	16.9	17.0	16.9	17.0	17.0	17.1	16.9
2015	16.9	16.9	16.8	16.9	17.0	17.1	17.1	17.0	16.9	16.6	16.7	16.7	16.9
Retail Trade													
2005	52.1	51.4	51.3	51.7	52.0	52.5	52.2	52.2	51.9	52.6	54.0	54.8	52.4
2006	51.3	50.4	50.6	51.3	51.4	51.8	51.4	51.3	51.4	52.1	53.6	54.6	51.8
2007	51.3	50.5	50.7	50.7	51.3	51.9	51.7	51.6	51.1	51.2	52.5	53.2	51.5
2008	50.1	49.1	49.0	49.1	49.3	49.9	49.6	49.6	49.1	49.5	50.0	50.2	49.5
2009	47.3	46.5	46.3	45.9	46.9	47.3	47.3	47.0	46.9	47.2	48.1	48.5	47.1
2010	46.5	46.0	46.3	45.6	45.6	46.3	46.5	46.6	46.2	46.7	47.7	48.0	46.5
2011	46.0	45.5	45.6	46.1	46.6	46.9	46.8	47.1	46.7	47.2	48.4	48.8	46.8
2012	46.4	45.7	45.8	46.1	46.7	47.3	46.9	46.9	46.8	47.2	48.3	48.5	46.9
2013	45.8	45.3	45.0	45.5	46.2	46.8	46.9	46.8	46.5	47.1	48.1	48.6	46.6
2014	46.2	45.8	45.6	46.4	47.0	47.5	47.4	47.5	47.2	47.7	48.8	49.6	47.2
2015	47.0	46.4	46.4	47.0	47.6	48.5	48.4	48.4	48.2	48.0	48.7	49.0	47.8

1. Employment by Industry: Rhode Island, 2005–2015—*Continued*

(Numbers in thousands, not seasonally adjusted)

Industry and year	January	February	March	April	May	June	July	August	September	October	November	December	Annual average
Transportation and Utilities													
2005	10.5	10.5	10.5	10.8	11.0	11.2	10.7	10.8	11.3	11.2	11.2	11.3	10.9
2006	10.6	10.6	10.6	10.9	11.1	11.3	10.5	10.6	11.4	11.3	11.3	11.4	11.0
2007	10.8	10.6	10.6	11.0	11.2	11.4	10.7	10.7	11.5	11.4	11.4	11.6	11.1
2008	10.8	10.7	10.7	11.0	11.1	11.3	10.6	10.8	11.3	11.0	10.8	11.1	10.9
2009	10.2	10.1	10.0	9.9	10.2	10.3	9.6	9.7	10.5	10.3	10.4	10.5	10.1
2010	9.9	9.9	9.9	10.2	10.3	10.6	9.9	9.8	10.8	10.8	10.8	11.1	10.3
2011	10.4	10.4	10.4	10.6	10.8	11.0	10.2	10.0	11.1	11.0	11.0	11.4	10.7
2012	10.7	10.6	10.6	10.7	10.9	11.2	10.2	10.3	11.2	11.1	11.2	11.5	10.9
2013	10.4	10.5	10.5	10.7	10.9	11.1	10.3	10.4	11.2	11.2	11.3	11.7	10.9
2014	10.7	10.6	10.7	10.8	10.9	11.3	10.4	10.6	11.4	11.4	11.6	12.1	11.0
2015	11.2	10.9	10.9	11.2	11.5	11.5	10.8	10.8	11.8	11.8	12.1	12.9	11.5
Information													
2005	10.8	10.8	10.7	10.7	10.7	10.7	10.8	10.8	10.7	10.8	10.9	11.0	10.8
2006	11.0	10.9	11.0	11.3	11.3	11.4	10.8	10.7	10.7	10.6	10.8	10.9	11.0
2007	10.5	10.4	10.5	10.5	10.6	10.6	10.6	10.7	10.6	10.5	10.8	10.8	10.6
2008	10.6	10.9	10.9	10.8	10.6	10.9	10.6	11.0	10.8	10.8	10.5	10.4	10.7
2009	10.4	10.3	10.2	10.3	10.4	10.4	10.0	10.0	9.9	9.7	9.9	9.9	10.1
2010	9.8	9.8	9.9	9.9	9.8	9.8	9.9	10.2	10.3	10.2	10.2	10.2	10.0
2011	9.8	9.8	10.0	10.5	10.7	10.5	10.4	9.5	10.1	10.0	10.0	10.2	10.1
2012	9.9	9.9	10.0	9.8	9.6	9.7	9.5	9.6	9.3	9.2	9.2	9.3	9.6
2013	9.2	9.3	9.1	8.9	9.1	9.1	8.9	9.0	8.9	8.9	9.0	9.0	9.0
2014	9.0	8.8	8.8	8.8	8.9	8.8	8.8	9.0	8.8	8.7	8.7	8.8	8.8
2015	8.5	8.4	8.5	8.6	8.6	8.4	8.7	8.6	8.7	8.7	8.7	8.7	8.6
Financial Activities													
2005	33.7	33.8	33.8	34.3	34.3	34.5	34.7	34.7	34.5	34.2	34.3	34.6	34.3
2006	34.2	34.1	34.4	34.5	34.8	34.9	35.2	35.6	35.7	35.6	35.7	36.1	35.1
2007	35.2	35.3	35.2	35.3	35.4	35.3	35.0	34.7	34.6	34.1	34.1	34.0	34.9
2008	33.6	33.7	33.5	33.4	33.5	33.5	33.3	33.2	33.3	32.4	32.3	32.3	33.2
2009	31.9	31.9	31.6	31.2	31.3	31.5	31.3	30.9	30.7	30.7	30.9	30.8	31.2
2010	30.3	30.4	30.6	30.4	30.5	30.6	30.8	30.7	30.8	31.0	31.0	31.1	30.7
2011	30.5	30.6	30.6	30.7	30.6	31.2	30.8	30.8	30.9	30.8	31.1	31.0	30.8
2012	30.8	31.0	31.2	31.3	31.6	31.8	31.8	31.8	31.8	31.9	31.9	32.0	31.6
2013	31.7	31.9	32.2	32.2	32.3	32.5	32.6	32.4	32.2	32.2	32.2	32.4	32.2
2014	32.1	32.0	32.0	32.4	32.5	32.7	32.8	32.6	32.6	32.5	32.5	32.6	32.4
2015	32.3	32.5	32.7	32.8	32.9	33.3	32.8	32.7	33.0	33.2	32.9	33.1	32.9
Professional and Business Services													
2005	51.8	52.2	52.7	55.2	55.3	55.9	56.2	56.9	57.2	56.2	56.2	55.8	55.1
2006	52.6	53.0	53.6	56.6	56.8	57.9	56.9	57.8	58.7	58.4	57.8	57.3	56.5
2007	54.3	54.0	54.3	56.4	56.9	58.0	56.8	56.8	56.6	56.2	56.0	55.7	56.0
2008	53.2	52.9	53.1	55.2	55.3	56.2	55.4	55.5	55.9	55.5	54.8	53.6	54.7
2009	51.1	51.0	51.1	52.5	52.7	53.5	53.0	53.2	53.4	53.3	53.2	52.5	52.5
2010	50.1	50.2	51.1	54.0	54.2	54.9	54.4	54.5	54.6	54.8	54.6	53.6	53.4
2011	51.5	51.8	52.2	54.2	54.6	55.2	54.9	55.3	55.7	55.9	55.7	54.5	54.3
2012	52.8	53.1	54.1	56.1	56.6	57.5	56.9	57.2	57.2	57.1	57.2	57.1	56.1
2013	55.0	55.6	56.1	58.4	59.0	60.3	59.6	60.2	60.3	60.7	60.3	59.7	58.8
2014	57.0	57.7	57.9	60.5	61.2	61.8	61.7	62.3	62.4	63.0	63.0	62.9	61.0
2015	60.0	59.9	60.7	63.5	64.6	64.7	64.7	64.7	64.4	64.5	64.7	64.2	63.4
Education and Health Services													
2005	92.7	95.2	96.2	96.7	96.6	92.5	92.0	91.7	96.0	97.9	98.5	97.8	95.3
2006	94.0	97.4	98.6	99.2	98.2	93.9	92.6	92.5	96.2	98.9	99.7	99.2	96.7
2007	96.0	99.4	100.3	100.4	100.3	96.1	94.6	94.4	98.2	100.3	101.0	100.4	98.5
2008	97.0	100.5	101.3	101.1	100.8	96.3	94.8	95.0	98.5	101.1	101.5	101.5	99.1
2009	97.8	101.1	101.5	101.3	101.0	97.2	96.0	95.8	99.5	102.4	103.1	102.7	100.0
2010	99.8	102.2	102.9	102.8	102.8	98.1	97.8	97.8	101.6	103.1	103.8	104.1	101.4
2011	99.7	102.8	103.7	104.4	104.3	99.7	98.8	98.3	101.7	104.7	104.9	104.2	102.3
2012	100.7	104.7	104.9	104.1	104.6	100.0	98.7	99.0	104.7	105.8	105.6	106.4	103.3
2013	103.3	105.5	106.3	105.7	105.5	102.2	100.9	100.5	105.0	107.2	107.8	105.8	104.6
2014	103.4	105.9	106.5	107.2	107.0	102.4	101.7	101.6	106.0	108.0	108.1	108.2	105.5
2015	104.4	105.8	106.9	107.5	107.4	102.7	102.9	101.5	104.4	107.3	107.9	106.5	105.4

1. Employment by Industry: Rhode Island, 2005–2015—*Continued*

(Numbers in thousands, not seasonally adjusted)

Industry and year	January	February	March	April	May	June	July	August	September	October	November	December	Annual average
Leisure and Hospitality													
2005	44.7	45.4	45.8	48.8	51.4	55.1	55.8	55.3	53.2	50.5	48.8	48.1	50.2
2006	44.4	44.5	45.6	48.7	51.1	54.8	55.6	55.5	53.7	50.7	48.9	48.6	50.2
2007	45.5	46.0	46.7	49.6	52.4	56.4	57.1	56.7	54.6	52.6	50.0	49.5	51.4
2008	45.9	46.4	46.7	49.7	53.0	55.8	55.9	55.5	53.7	51.2	49.4	48.7	51.0
2009	43.6	44.1	44.4	46.8	51.0	53.6	53.8	54.0	52.3	49.5	47.2	47.0	48.9
2010	43.6	44.0	44.4	47.6	50.8	54.3	55.5	55.2	53.1	50.0	48.3	47.3	49.5
2011	44.0	44.6	45.0	48.1	51.1	55.0	56.1	55.8	53.8	50.9	48.9	48.2	50.1
2012	45.2	46.2	46.8	49.8	53.1	56.9	57.6	57.6	55.4	52.5	50.4	49.9	51.8
2013	46.8	47.2	48.2	51.3	54.6	58.9	59.6	59.5	57.3	55.1	52.5	51.9	53.6
2014	48.4	49.4	50.1	53.3	56.9	60.4	61.0	60.6	58.6	56.3	54.0	53.2	55.2
2015	50.2	49.6	50.6	53.9	58.5	61.4	62.2	61.9	59.9	57.5	55.1	54.3	56.3
Other Services													
2005	22.9	22.9	23.1	23.1	23.4	23.7	24.0	24.0	23.1	23.0	23.1	23.0	23.3
2006	22.2	22.2	22.4	22.9	23.1	23.6	23.7	23.6	23.1	23.3	23.3	23.2	23.1
2007	22.6	22.7	22.8	23.0	23.3	23.9	23.8	23.6	23.0	23.1	23.1	23.2	23.2
2008	22.4	22.5	22.5	22.7	22.9	23.2	23.4	23.2	22.7	22.7	22.6	22.5	22.8
2009	21.8	21.9	21.9	22.1	22.2	22.5	22.8	22.6	21.9	22.2	22.2	22.1	22.2
2010	21.5	21.6	21.6	21.7	22.0	22.2	23.0	22.9	22.1	22.0	22.2	22.1	22.1
2011	21.5	21.7	21.7	22.1	22.3	22.9	23.7	23.5	22.5	22.3	22.4	22.4	22.4
2012	21.8	21.9	21.9	22.2	22.4	23.0	23.4	23.4	22.9	22.5	22.5	22.7	22.6
2013	22.0	22.0	22.2	22.4	22.6	23.1	23.5	23.2	22.6	22.5	22.5	22.6	22.6
2014	22.0	22.2	22.3	22.5	22.9	23.5	23.9	23.8	23.0	22.7	22.8	22.9	22.9
2015	22.4	22.2	22.5	22.6	23.1	23.5	24.2	23.9	23.1	22.9	23.0	22.9	23.0
Government													
2005	65.5	65.8	65.9	65.8	66.1	65.9	61.5	60.7	64.1	65.8	66.1	65.9	64.9
2006	65.4	65.9	65.9	65.6	65.8	65.6	61.3	61.0	64.7	65.7	66.4	66.0	64.9
2007	65.2	65.4	65.3	65.3	66.0	64.9	61.5	61.2	63.9	64.7	64.8	65.0	64.4
2008	64.6	64.5	64.9	64.8	65.5	64.5	60.2	59.5	62.4	63.1	64.0	63.7	63.5
2009	63.0	63.3	63.2	63.4	63.7	63.0	57.8	57.5	61.3	62.8	63.0	62.8	62.1
2010	62.3	62.3	62.7	62.7	64.8	63.1	58.5	58.2	60.5	61.6	62.1	61.9	61.7
2011	61.4	61.4	61.8	61.8	62.0	61.6	56.6	56.8	59.9	61.0	61.2	61.2	60.6
2012	60.6	60.9	61.0	61.2	61.8	60.5	56.2	56.6	59.7	60.8	61.1	61.1	60.1
2013	60.5	60.5	61.0	60.8	61.7	60.8	57.1	56.8	59.8	61.1	61.1	61.3	60.2
2014	60.6	60.5	60.8	61.0	62.0	61.3	57.2	56.7	60.3	61.1	61.6	61.2	60.4
2015	60.9	60.9	60.9	61.3	62.0	61.1	57.1	56.7	60.0	61.0	61.2	61.0	60.3

2. Average Weekly Hours by Selected Industry: Rhode Island, 2011–2015

(Not seasonally adjusted)

Industry and year	January	February	March	April	May	June	July	August	September	October	November	December	Annual average
Total Private													
2011	33.0	33.3	33.2	33.1	33.3	32.9	33.1	32.9	33.0	33.0	32.9	32.9	33.0
2012	33.1	32.9	33.1	33.1	33.2	33.2	33.4	33.1	33.4	32.9	32.7	33.1	33.1
2013	32.7	32.5	32.9	33.0	33.1	33.1	33.2	33.0	33.1	32.7	32.8	32.9	32.9
2014	32.7	32.6	32.8	33.0	33.0	33.3	33.3	33.0	33.0	33.0	33.1	33.1	33.0
2015	32.8	32.5	32.9	32.9	33.1	33.6	33.6	33.5	33.3	32.9	33.1	32.9	33.1
Goods-Producing													
2011	36.6	36.4	36.7	36.9	37.3	37.1	36.8	36.3	36.5	36.5	37.1	38.2	36.9
2012	37.9	38.1	37.8	38.4	38.0	38.6	38.2	37.8	39.4	38.5	38.5	39.9	38.4
2013	38.7	38.3	38.8	39.2	39.3	39.6	39.3	38.7	39.6	38.7	38.6	38.9	39.0
2014	38.7	38.3	38.9	39.4	38.9	39.3	38.2	38.0	38.3	38.6	38.3	39.1	38.7
2015	38.2	37.7	38.7	38.1	37.4	38.0	37.7	37.1	37.7	37.0	37.4	38.9	37.8
Construction													
2011	34.9	35.1	35.4	35.0	35.9	36.0	36.6	35.7	36.3	36.1	37.3	38.5	36.1
2012	35.6	36.8	37.5	37.5	36.8	38.0	38.6	37.3	38.1	35.4	36.6	36.9	37.1
2013	35.2	34.4	36.1	37.0	37.0	36.7	37.1	36.3	37.1	37.4	36.5	36.4	36.5
2014	38.4	36.7	38.0	38.9	38.8	38.8	37.4	36.2	36.5	36.4	36.1	36.6	37.4
2015	36.7	35.6	37.5	36.6	35.5	36.0	35.6	34.6	34.6	33.7	35.4	36.4	35.6
Manufacturing													
2011	38.1	38.4	38.5	38.8	38.9	38.6	37.9	37.5	37.5	38.0	38.3	38.9	38.3
2012	39.2	39.0	38.3	39.0	38.6	39.0	38.3	38.2	39.3	39.0	38.7	40.4	38.9
2013	39.4	39.1	39.1	39.3	39.5	40.1	39.5	39.0	40.0	40.1	40.2	40.5	39.7
2014	39.3	39.3	39.6	39.8	39.1	39.8	38.8	39.0	39.3	39.6	39.3	40.2	39.4
2015	38.9	38.5	39.2	38.8	38.3	38.9	38.6	38.1	39.0	38.4	38.2	39.9	38.7
Trade, Transportation, and Utilities													
2011	34.8	35.2	35.4	34.9	35.2	34.9	34.9	34.7	34.7	33.8	33.4	34.4	34.7
2012	33.5	33.5	34.4	34.4	34.6	35.1	35.0	34.5	34.4	34.1	34.1	34.6	34.3
2013	33.4	33.4	34.6	34.6	34.6	34.2	34.7	34.5	34.1	34.1	34.2	34.4	34.2
2014	33.3	33.1	33.4	34.4	34.3	34.2	34.4	34.4	34.4	33.8	33.7	33.9	34.0
2015	32.4	31.8	32.6	32.4	32.6	32.8	32.9	32.9	33.1	32.7	32.6	32.3	32.6
Professional and Business Services													
2011	35.6	35.9	36.0	35.8	35.7	36.0	36.0	36.1	36.0	35.6	35.2	35.7	35.8
2012	35.4	35.6	35.9	35.0	36.0	35.7	35.6	36.3	36.2	35.8	36.1	36.0	35.8
2013	35.8	35.5	35.5	35.0	35.0	34.6	34.5	34.1	34.5	33.7	33.6	33.3	34.5
2014	33.7	33.7	34.0	34.4	34.1	34.5	34.5	33.8	34.4	34.2	34.6	34.7	34.2
2015	34.8	34.7	35.3	35.3	36.4	36.1	36.1	35.8	35.1	35.3	35.7	34.8	35.5
Education and Health Services													
2011	31.1	31.7	31.5	31.3	31.2	31.1	31.0	30.7	30.5	31.2	31.3	30.7	31.1
2012	30.4	30.4	30.3	30.5	30.4	30.0	30.2	29.9	30.1	30.4	29.7	29.9	30.2
2013	30.3	30.1	30.2	30.4	30.7	30.5	31.0	31.2	30.9	31.1	31.3	31.3	30.7
2014	31.2	31.0	31.2	31.2	31.4	31.7	32.1	31.9	31.9	32.4	32.3	32.1	31.7
2015	32.2	32.0	32.2	32.1	32.1	32.0	32.0	32.5	32.2	31.8	32.1	31.3	32.0
Leisure and Hospitality													
2011	25.3	25.8	25.4	25.9	26.1	25.8	26.8	26.8	25.7	25.6	25.4	25.3	25.9
2012	25.2	25.0	24.3	25.2	25.5	25.8	27.1	26.9	26.4	25.4	24.9	24.8	25.6
2013	24.1	24.1	25.1	25.2	25.5	25.7	26.7	26.7	25.7	25.5	25.6	24.8	25.4
2014	25.2	24.9	25.6	25.4	25.4	25.5	26.7	26.5	25.1	24.3	23.9	23.7	25.2
2015	23.9	23.3	24.0	25.0	25.6	27.1	28.0	27.7	26.7	25.4	25.2	24.6	25.6

3. Average Hourly Earnings by Selected Industry: Rhode Island, 2011–2015

(Dollars, not seasonally adjusted)

Industry and year	January	February	March	April	May	June	July	August	September	October	November	December	Annual average
Total Private													
2011	23.04	22.96	23.13	23.06	23.40	23.41	23.88	24.02	24.12	24.49	24.66	24.46	23.73
2012	25.34	24.99	25.14	25.21	25.01	24.63	24.95	24.62	24.91	24.82	24.89	25.53	25.00
2013	25.66	25.76	25.62	25.56	25.29	25.06	25.13	25.07	25.40	25.37	25.45	25.70	25.42
2014	25.79	25.68	25.53	25.28	24.99	25.00	24.58	24.62	24.74	24.92	25.13	24.98	25.10
2015	25.24	25.59	25.48	25.15	25.02	24.13	24.26	24.31	24.68	25.14	25.36	25.09	24.94
Goods-Producing													
2011	24.42	24.41	24.58	24.55	24.69	24.79	25.64	25.78	25.40	25.42	25.48	25.74	25.09
2012	25.56	25.11	25.16	25.10	25.04	24.68	25.31	25.00	25.06	24.89	25.22	25.08	25.10
2013	25.22	25.35	25.64	25.60	25.51	25.54	26.01	26.28	26.17	27.00	27.25	26.71	26.04
2014	27.51	27.33	27.36	27.13	27.03	27.26	27.42	26.88	26.96	27.20	27.41	27.53	27.25
2015	27.27	27.32	26.89	26.39	26.12	25.33	25.58	25.38	25.33	25.44	25.90	25.39	26.01
Construction													
2011	27.70	27.73	28.33	28.42	28.02	28.02	28.17	28.62	28.03	28.17	28.69	28.77	28.24
2012	28.65	28.89	28.54	28.67	28.56	27.95	28.49	28.13	29.05	28.43	29.07	28.75	28.59
2013	29.26	29.25	28.93	28.96	28.87	29.08	29.24	29.60	29.35	29.66	29.86	30.21	29.37
2014	29.32	29.94	29.38	29.22	29.13	29.75	28.51	28.84	28.78	28.62	28.81	29.48	29.13
2015	29.25	29.70	29.25	28.52	29.11	27.78	27.57	27.72	28.82	28.60	28.89	28.83	28.63
Manufacturing													
2011	22.26	22.20	22.41	22.61	22.94	23.08	23.98	24.14	24.19	24.27	24.16	24.48	23.38
2012	24.63	24.14	24.11	23.84	23.83	23.46	24.00	23.70	23.52	23.65	23.92	24.00	23.90
2013	24.10	24.29	24.68	24.58	24.45	24.42	24.93	25.15	25.08	25.21	25.60	25.27	24.82
2014	26.65	26.24	26.44	26.05	25.94	25.97	26.72	25.81	25.65	26.05	26.33	26.23	26.17
2015	25.94	26.01	25.43	25.20	24.77	24.20	24.59	24.32	23.86	24.12	24.57	23.97	24.74
Trade, Transportation, and Utilities													
2011	19.95	19.96	20.41	20.02	20.23	20.41	20.29	20.72	20.74	21.23	20.99	20.86	20.49
2012	20.74	20.67	20.54	20.64	20.74	20.61	20.82	20.93	20.69	20.59	20.97	21.12	20.76
2013	21.16	21.24	21.50	21.52	21.27	21.23	21.35	21.38	21.19	20.91	21.32	20.92	21.25
2014	21.37	21.32	21.17	20.95	20.40	20.69	20.45	20.68	20.47	20.48	20.67	20.23	20.73
2015	20.48	20.31	20.09	19.66	20.01	19.88	20.02	20.01	20.23	20.66	20.55	19.70	20.13
Professional and Business Services													
2011	27.69	27.64	27.66	27.31	28.08	28.24	29.85	29.48	29.64	29.95	30.65	30.32	28.90
2012	31.28	30.53	30.87	30.68	30.14	29.52	30.29	30.25	30.72	30.33	29.82	30.26	30.38
2013	30.63	30.52	30.42	30.01	30.10	29.15	29.71	29.44	29.42	29.56	29.60	30.32	29.90
2014	30.17	30.23	29.92	29.41	28.86	28.82	27.96	28.65	28.17	28.71	29.47	29.74	29.16
2015	30.40	31.09	30.94	29.84	29.73	29.29	29.50	29.88	29.78	29.91	29.83	29.22	29.93
Education and Health Services													
2011	23.34	23.36	23.37	23.51	23.34	23.16	23.29	23.24	23.51	23.27	23.55	23.51	23.37
2012	23.78	23.51	23.22	23.10	22.95	23.32	23.56	23.58	23.24	23.25	23.42	23.89	23.40
2013	23.55	23.36	23.30	23.16	22.83	23.02	23.18	22.99	23.35	23.04	22.93	23.47	23.18
2014	22.75	22.99	23.13	23.21	23.35	23.38	23.61	23.66	23.67	23.66	23.42	23.22	23.34
2015	23.06	23.65	23.91	24.25	24.65	24.75	25.23	25.03	25.75	26.38	26.86	27.16	25.06
Leisure and Hospitality													
2011	13.92	13.90	13.99	13.97	13.98	13.89	13.62	13.77	13.92	13.96	14.32	14.09	13.94
2012	13.83	13.78	14.01	13.96	13.98	13.62	13.42	13.29	14.14	14.04	13.91	14.03	13.82
2013	13.87	14.19	14.03	14.06	14.14	13.88	13.77	13.67	14.08	14.22	14.03	14.23	14.00
2014	13.83	13.68	13.62	13.67	13.71	13.55	13.65	13.81	13.80	14.10	14.07	14.04	13.79
2015	14.40	14.58	14.66	14.49	14.39	13.99	14.27	14.50	14.84	15.25	15.02	15.42	14.63

4. Average Weekly Earnings by Selected Industry: Rhode Island, 2011–2015

(Dollars, not seasonally adjusted)

Industry and year	January	February	March	April	May	June	July	August	September	October	November	December	Annual average
Total Private													
2011	760.32	764.57	767.92	763.29	779.22	770.19	790.43	790.26	795.96	808.17	811.31	804.73	783.09
2012	838.75	822.17	832.13	834.45	830.33	817.72	833.33	814.92	831.99	816.58	813.90	845.04	827.50
2013	839.08	837.20	842.90	843.48	837.10	829.49	834.32	827.31	840.74	829.60	834.76	845.53	836.32
2014	843.33	837.17	837.38	834.24	824.67	832.50	818.51	812.46	816.42	822.36	831.80	826.84	828.30
2015	827.87	831.68	838.29	827.44	828.16	810.77	815.14	814.39	821.84	827.11	839.42	825.46	825.51
Goods-Producing													
2011	893.77	888.52	902.09	905.90	920.94	919.71	943.55	935.81	927.10	927.83	945.31	983.27	925.82
2012	968.72	956.69	951.05	963.84	951.52	952.65	966.84	945.00	987.36	958.27	970.97	1,000.69	963.84
2013	976.01	970.91	994.83	1,003.52	1,002.54	1,011.38	1,022.19	1,017.04	1,036.33	1,044.90	1,051.85	1,039.02	1,015.56
2014	1,064.64	1,046.74	1,064.30	1,068.92	1,051.47	1,071.32	1,047.44	1,021.44	1,032.57	1,049.92	1,049.80	1,076.42	1,054.58
2015	1,041.71	1,029.96	1,040.64	1,005.46	976.89	962.54	964.37	941.60	954.94	941.28	968.66	987.67	983.18
Construction													
2011	966.73	973.32	1,002.88	994.70	1,005.92	1,008.72	1,031.02	1,021.73	1,017.49	1,016.94	1,070.14	1,107.65	1,019.46
2012	1,019.94	1,063.15	1,070.25	1,075.13	1,051.01	1,062.10	1,099.71	1,049.25	1,106.81	1,006.42	1,063.96	1,060.88	1,060.69
2013	1,029.95	1,006.20	1,044.37	1,071.52	1,068.19	1,067.24	1,084.80	1,074.48	1,088.89	1,109.28	1,089.89	1,099.64	1,072.01
2014	1,125.89	1,098.80	1,116.44	1,136.66	1,130.24	1,154.30	1,066.27	1,044.01	1,050.47	1,041.77	1,040.04	1,078.97	1,089.46
2015	1,073.48	1,057.32	1,096.88	1,043.83	1,033.41	1,000.08	981.49	959.11	997.17	963.82	1,022.71	1,049.41	1,019.23
Manufacturing													
2011	848.11	852.48	862.79	877.27	892.37	890.89	908.84	905.25	907.13	922.26	925.33	952.27	895.45
2012	965.50	941.46	923.41	929.76	919.84	914.94	919.20	905.34	924.34	922.35	925.70	969.60	929.71
2013	949.54	949.74	964.99	965.99	965.78	979.24	984.74	980.85	1,003.20	1,010.92	1,029.12	1,023.44	985.35
2014	1,047.35	1,031.23	1,047.02	1,036.79	1,014.25	1,033.61	1,036.74	1,006.59	1,008.05	1,031.58	1,034.77	1,054.45	1,031.10
2015	1,009.07	1,001.39	996.86	977.76	948.69	941.38	949.17	926.59	930.54	926.21	938.57	956.40	957.44
Trade, Transportation, and Utilities													
2011	694.26	702.59	722.51	698.70	712.10	712.31	708.12	718.98	719.68	717.57	701.07	717.58	711.00
2012	694.79	692.45	706.58	710.02	717.60	723.41	728.70	722.09	711.74	702.12	715.08	730.75	712.07
2013	706.74	709.42	743.90	744.59	735.94	726.07	740.85	737.61	722.58	713.03	729.14	719.65	726.75
2014	711.62	705.69	707.08	720.68	699.72	707.60	703.48	711.39	704.17	692.22	696.58	685.80	704.82
2015	663.55	645.86	654.93	636.98	652.33	652.06	658.66	658.33	669.61	675.58	669.93	636.31	656.24
Professional and Business Services													
2011	985.76	992.28	995.76	977.70	1,002.46	1,016.64	1,074.60	1,064.23	1,067.04	1,066.22	1,078.88	1,082.42	1,034.62
2012	1,107.31	1,086.87	1,108.23	1,073.80	1,085.04	1,053.86	1,078.32	1,098.08	1,112.06	1,085.81	1,076.50	1,089.36	1,087.60
2013	1,096.55	1,083.46	1,064.70	1,050.35	1,053.50	1,008.59	1,025.00	1,003.90	1,014.99	996.17	994.56	1,009.66	1,031.55
2014	1,016.73	1,018.75	1,017.28	1,011.70	984.13	994.29	964.62	968.37	969.05	981.88	1,019.66	1,031.98	997.27
2015	1,057.92	1,078.82	1,092.18	1,053.35	1,082.17	1,057.37	1,064.95	1,069.70	1,045.28	1,055.82	1,064.93	1,016.86	1,062.52
Education and Health Services													
2011	725.87	740.51	736.16	735.86	728.21	720.28	721.99	713.47	717.06	726.02	737.12	721.76	726.81
2012	722.91	714.70	703.57	704.55	697.68	699.60	711.51	705.04	699.52	706.80	695.57	714.31	706.68
2013	713.57	703.14	703.66	704.06	700.88	702.11	718.58	717.29	721.52	716.54	717.71	734.61	711.63
2014	709.80	712.69	721.66	724.15	733.19	741.15	757.88	754.75	755.07	766.58	756.47	745.36	739.88
2015	742.53	756.80	769.90	778.43	791.27	792.00	807.36	813.48	829.15	838.88	862.21	850.11	801.92
Leisure and Hospitality													
2011	352.18	358.62	355.35	361.82	364.88	358.36	365.02	369.04	357.74	357.38	363.73	356.48	361.05
2012	348.52	344.50	340.44	351.79	356.49	351.40	363.68	357.50	373.30	356.62	346.36	347.94	353.79
2013	334.27	341.98	352.15	354.31	360.57	356.72	367.66	364.99	361.86	362.61	359.17	352.90	355.60
2014	348.52	340.63	348.67	347.22	348.23	345.53	364.46	365.97	346.38	342.63	336.27	332.75	347.51
2015	344.16	339.71	351.84	362.25	368.38	379.13	399.56	401.65	396.23	387.35	378.50	379.33	374.53

SOUTH CAROLINA
At a Glance

Population:
  2005 estimate: 4,270,150
  2010 census: 4,625,364
  2015 estimate: 4,896,146

Percent change in population:
  2005–2015: 14.7%
  2010–2015: 5.9%

Percent change in total nonfarm employment:
  2005–2015: 7.6%

Industry with the largest growth in employment, 2005–2015 (thousands):
  Professional and business services, 56.0

Industry with the largest decline or smallest growth in employment, 2005–2015 (thousands):
  Construction, –30.3

Civilian labor force:
  2005: 2,068,599
  2010: 2,155,668
  2015: 2,257,077

Unemployment rate and rank among states (highest to lowest):
  2005: 6.7%, 5th
  2010: 11.2%, 4th
  2015: 6.0%, 11th

Over-the-year change in unemployment rates:
  2012–2013: –1.6%
  2013–2014: –1.2%
  2014–2015: –0.4%

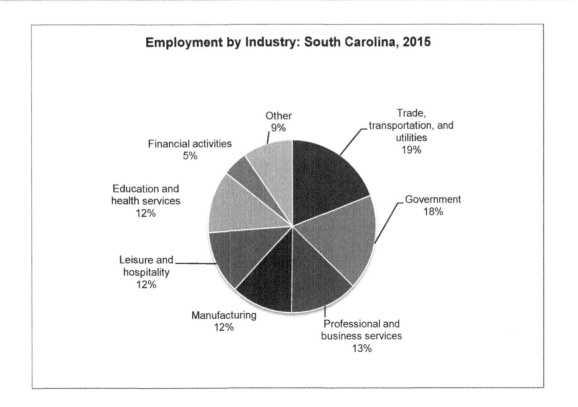

Employment by Industry: South Carolina, 2015

Other 9%
Financial activities 5%
Education and health services 12%
Leisure and hospitality 12%
Manufacturing 12%
Trade, transportation, and utilities 19%
Government 18%
Professional and business services 13%

1. Employment by Industry: South Carolina, 2005–2015

(Numbers in thousands, not seasonally adjusted)

Industry and year	January	February	March	April	May	June	July	August	September	October	November	December	Annual average
Total Nonfarm													
2005	1,815.5	1,830.6	1,843.1	1,863.8	1,874.4	1,862.9	1,863.0	1,874.8	1,874.5	1,881.9	1,890.5	1,879.8	1,862.9
2006	1,856.6	1,875.7	1,896.1	1,913.5	1,922.6	1,902.5	1,890.5	1,899.5	1,908.1	1,929.0	1,933.0	1,940.4	1,905.6
2007	1,903.1	1,914.8	1,938.4	1,946.2	1,959.2	1,966.2	1,939.0	1,948.5	1,955.7	1,953.7	1,958.6	1,956.6	1,945.0
2008	1,916.5	1,927.8	1,942.9	1,946.6	1,960.2	1,953.0	1,918.6	1,919.6	1,923.3	1,912.4	1,904.8	1,888.7	1,926.2
2009	1,826.4	1,822.3	1,826.6	1,830.3	1,834.9	1,825.9	1,802.4	1,803.8	1,801.1	1,800.6	1,802.5	1,795.5	1,814.4
2010	1,760.3	1,771.3	1,789.5	1,816.5	1,837.3	1,832.5	1,816.7	1,820.8	1,817.8	1,822.1	1,826.2	1,825.2	1,811.4
2011	1,779.3	1,799.1	1,819.6	1,842.4	1,851.3	1,850.9	1,833.7	1,839.7	1,841.1	1,840.6	1,847.3	1,846.3	1,832.6
2012	1,813.6	1,830.0	1,851.7	1,865.9	1,877.6	1,882.0	1,859.9	1,866.9	1,870.2	1,874.7	1,891.0	1,887.4	1,864.2
2013	1,844.3	1,860.5	1,878.1	1,897.1	1,911.6	1,917.2	1,899.5	1,906.0	1,912.8	1,919.0	1,932.7	1,933.3	1,901.0
2014	1,891.7	1,898.7	1,928.8	1,951.3	1,966.7	1,967.8	1,945.7	1,953.3	1,960.9	1,972.6	1,987.9	1,989.9	1,951.3
2015	1,944.8	1,960.2	1,979.1	1,996.8	2,015.1	2,017.5	2,007.7	2,012.9	2,016.1	2,027.0	2,034.8	2,038.5	2,004.2
Total Private													
2005	1,482.7	1,493.2	1,504.0	1,524.2	1,535.1	1,530.4	1,546.6	1,551.4	1,535.1	1,539.9	1,546.0	1,535.1	1,527.0
2006	1,518.7	1,532.5	1,549.5	1,567.4	1,576.3	1,569.3	1,571.9	1,574.6	1,568.8	1,583.5	1,586.7	1,592.8	1,566.0
2007	1,559.2	1,568.1	1,589.2	1,598.5	1,610.9	1,623.1	1,612.9	1,614.1	1,606.1	1,599.7	1,601.4	1,600.1	1,598.6
2008	1,563.3	1,570.7	1,584.6	1,587.4	1,598.9	1,598.0	1,583.3	1,582.4	1,565.5	1,549.9	1,539.8	1,524.6	1,570.7
2009	1,469.8	1,463.2	1,466.7	1,468.7	1,473.9	1,472.1	1,463.2	1,460.1	1,448.0	1,442.4	1,442.8	1,436.4	1,458.9
2010	1,405.7	1,413.2	1,429.5	1,455.7	1,466.7	1,474.2	1,475.0	1,476.0	1,466.8	1,468.0	1,471.3	1,471.1	1,456.1
2011	1,430.1	1,446.7	1,466.0	1,488.6	1,498.6	1,503.6	1,501.2	1,504.0	1,492.9	1,489.2	1,494.9	1,494.3	1,484.2
2012	1,466.0	1,477.0	1,497.4	1,511.6	1,523.1	1,531.1	1,523.7	1,529.0	1,518.0	1,517.8	1,529.9	1,528.7	1,512.8
2013	1,492.2	1,504.0	1,520.0	1,538.2	1,553.6	1,565.2	1,562.2	1,567.2	1,560.0	1,561.6	1,573.7	1,575.2	1,547.8
2014	1,538.5	1,541.5	1,570.1	1,591.5	1,606.6	1,613.7	1,606.3	1,610.3	1,603.5	1,610.5	1,624.9	1,626.7	1,595.3
2015	1,587.3	1,598.0	1,616.1	1,633.0	1,651.3	1,659.5	1,663.2	1,664.6	1,654.0	1,660.9	1,666.9	1,671.0	1,643.8
Goods-Producing													
2005	381.6	382.2	383.3	383.6	384.3	382.3	382.1	382.5	379.6	380.2	380.2	377.2	381.6
2006	376.7	378.0	380.0	382.4	384.1	382.3	381.1	380.8	379.4	382.3	381.8	383.6	381.0
2007	377.9	378.8	381.8	380.2	381.5	383.7	380.1	379.4	378.3	374.9	373.9	373.4	378.7
2008	367.3	365.7	366.0	361.1	361.6	360.3	356.2	354.1	351.3	345.8	341.7	336.3	355.6
2009	325.6	320.0	316.0	309.3	306.3	304.8	299.7	297.7	296.2	293.1	292.5	291.6	304.4
2010	286.3	286.1	287.4	290.0	291.4	292.5	292.2	291.6	291.5	291.1	291.6	293.0	290.4
2011	287.3	291.0	294.2	295.9	297.0	298.5	298.0	298.5	298.2	297.9	298.8	299.7	296.3
2012	296.5	298.6	301.0	300.5	302.1	302.8	301.1	302.3	302.0	302.6	303.4	304.2	301.4
2013	301.9	303.5	306.1	306.4	308.1	309.2	308.1	309.3	310.0	310.1	311.5	312.6	308.1
2014	309.9	310.1	313.0	314.6	317.0	318.5	317.5	317.2	318.1	319.8	321.1	322.8	316.6
2015	320.4	322.2	323.5	323.7	325.9	328.3	327.6	327.5	328.6	328.9	329.1	331.3	326.4
Service-Providing													
2005	1,433.9	1,448.4	1,459.8	1,480.2	1,490.1	1,480.6	1,480.9	1,492.3	1,494.9	1,501.7	1,510.3	1,502.6	1,481.3
2006	1,479.9	1,497.7	1,516.1	1,531.1	1,538.5	1,520.2	1,509.4	1,518.7	1,528.7	1,546.7	1,551.2	1,556.8	1,524.6
2007	1,525.2	1,536.0	1,556.6	1,566.0	1,577.7	1,582.5	1,558.9	1,569.1	1,577.4	1,578.8	1,584.7	1,583.2	1,566.3
2008	1,549.2	1,562.1	1,576.9	1,585.5	1,598.6	1,592.7	1,562.4	1,565.5	1,572.0	1,566.6	1,563.1	1,552.4	1,570.6
2009	1,500.8	1,502.3	1,510.6	1,521.0	1,528.6	1,521.1	1,502.7	1,506.1	1,504.9	1,507.5	1,510.0	1,503.9	1,510.0
2010	1,474.0	1,485.2	1,502.1	1,526.5	1,545.9	1,540.0	1,524.5	1,529.2	1,526.3	1,531.0	1,534.6	1,532.2	1,521.0
2011	1,492.0	1,508.1	1,525.4	1,546.5	1,554.3	1,552.4	1,535.7	1,541.2	1,542.9	1,542.7	1,548.5	1,546.6	1,536.4
2012	1,517.1	1,531.4	1,550.7	1,565.4	1,575.5	1,579.2	1,558.8	1,564.6	1,568.2	1,572.1	1,587.6	1,583.2	1,562.8
2013	1,542.4	1,557.0	1,572.0	1,590.7	1,603.5	1,608.0	1,591.4	1,596.7	1,602.8	1,608.9	1,621.2	1,620.7	1,592.9
2014	1,581.8	1,588.6	1,615.8	1,636.7	1,649.7	1,649.3	1,628.2	1,636.1	1,642.8	1,652.8	1,666.8	1,667.1	1,634.6
2015	1,624.4	1,638.0	1,655.6	1,673.1	1,689.2	1,689.2	1,680.1	1,685.4	1,687.5	1,698.1	1,705.7	1,707.2	1,677.8
Mining and Logging													
2005	4.9	4.9	4.9	4.9	4.9	4.9	4.8	4.8	4.7	4.7	4.7	4.7	4.8
2006	4.7	4.7	4.7	4.7	4.7	4.7	4.7	4.7	4.7	4.7	4.7	4.8	4.7
2007	4.7	4.7	4.7	4.6	4.6	4.7	4.6	4.6	4.6	4.6	4.6	4.6	4.6
2008	4.5	4.5	4.5	4.4	4.4	4.3	4.3	4.3	4.3	4.3	4.3	4.3	4.4
2009	4.2	4.1	4.1	4.1	4.1	4.1	4.1	4.1	4.1	4.0	4.0	4.0	4.1
2010	4.0	4.0	4.0	4.0	4.0	4.0	4.0	4.0	4.0	4.0	3.9	3.9	4.0
2011	3.9	3.9	4.0	4.0	4.0	4.0	3.9	3.9	3.9	3.9	3.9	3.9	3.9
2012	3.9	3.9	3.9	3.9	3.9	3.9	3.8	3.8	3.8	3.8	3.8	3.8	3.9
2013	3.8	3.8	3.8	3.8	3.8	3.8	3.8	3.8	3.8	3.8	3.8	3.9	3.8
2014	3.8	3.7	3.8	3.8	3.9	3.9	3.9	3.9	3.9	3.9	3.9	3.9	3.9
2015	3.9	3.9	3.9	3.9	3.9	4.0	4.0	4.1	4.0	4.0	4.1	4.1	4.0

1. Employment by Industry: South Carolina, 2005–2015—*Continued*

(Numbers in thousands, not seasonally adjusted)

Industry and year	January	February	March	April	May	June	July	August	September	October	November	December	Annual average
Construction													
2005...................................	112.5	112.9	114.0	115.1	117.4	116.8	118.7	119.4	118.2	119.5	120.4	118.2	116.9
2006...................................	119.3	120.8	122.5	123.8	125.4	123.9	125.7	126.2	125.8	128.1	127.7	127.6	124.7
2007...................................	124.2	124.4	126.7	125.8	126.6	127.7	126.7	126.7	125.6	122.9	121.8	120.8	125.0
2008...................................	116.3	115.7	116.0	112.5	112.6	112.5	109.9	109.0	107.3	104.4	102.1	99.4	109.8
2009...................................	94.6	92.4	92.5	89.7	89.3	88.9	86.9	85.5	84.2	82.7	81.8	81.3	87.5
2010...................................	77.6	77.1	78.2	80.1	80.6	81.2	81.2	80.3	79.8	79.4	79.1	78.5	79.4
2011...................................	74.0	75.6	76.7	77.2	77.9	78.3	78.0	77.7	77.4	77.3	77.4	76.9	77.0
2012...................................	75.0	76.2	77.5	76.6	77.7	78.4	78.0	78.5	78.2	78.1	78.0	78.0	77.5
2013...................................	77.0	76.9	78.6	79.1	80.0	80.6	80.9	81.0	81.0	80.6	81.1	81.5	79.9
2014...................................	79.8	79.9	81.2	81.8	82.9	83.5	83.2	83.5	83.2	83.7	84.1	84.6	82.6
2015...................................	83.1	83.7	84.9	85.1	86.4	87.7	87.8	87.5	87.9	88.3	87.9	88.4	86.6
Manufacturing													
2005...................................	264.2	264.4	264.4	263.6	262.0	260.6	258.6	258.3	256.7	256.0	255.1	254.3	259.9
2006...................................	252.7	252.5	252.8	253.9	254.0	253.7	250.7	249.9	248.9	249.5	249.4	251.2	251.6
2007...................................	249.0	249.7	250.4	249.8	250.3	251.3	248.8	248.1	248.1	247.4	247.5	248.0	249.0
2008...................................	246.5	245.5	245.5	244.2	244.6	243.5	242.0	240.8	239.7	237.1	235.3	232.6	241.4
2009...................................	226.8	223.5	219.4	215.5	212.9	211.8	208.7	208.1	207.9	206.4	206.7	206.3	212.8
2010...................................	204.7	205.0	205.2	205.9	206.8	207.3	207.0	207.3	207.7	207.7	208.6	210.6	207.0
2011...................................	209.4	211.5	213.5	214.7	215.1	216.2	216.1	216.9	216.9	216.7	217.5	218.9	215.3
2012...................................	217.6	218.5	219.6	220.0	220.5	220.5	219.3	220.0	220.0	220.7	221.6	222.4	220.1
2013...................................	221.1	222.8	223.7	223.5	224.3	224.8	223.4	224.5	225.2	225.7	226.6	227.2	224.4
2014...................................	226.3	226.5	228.0	229.0	230.2	231.1	230.4	229.8	231.0	232.2	233.1	234.3	230.2
2015...................................	233.4	234.6	234.7	234.7	235.6	236.6	235.8	235.9	236.7	236.6	237.1	238.8	235.9
Trade, Transportation, and Utilities													
2005...................................	355.2	355.0	356.5	359.7	363.4	361.1	364.5	365.2	360.7	364.9	370.7	373.1	362.5
2006...................................	361.4	364.7	368.7	368.8	368.9	367.5	367.5	369.0	368.6	374.1	382.0	385.0	370.5
2007...................................	370.1	369.4	374.9	374.8	377.8	380.0	379.5	379.0	378.2	379.5	385.9	388.9	378.2
2008...................................	375.5	374.4	377.1	375.9	375.8	376.0	374.0	373.2	370.5	368.5	370.5	371.2	373.6
2009...................................	353.0	348.4	348.6	349.4	350.9	351.3	348.9	348.3	346.0	345.0	349.1	350.6	349.1
2010...................................	339.0	337.9	341.5	343.6	345.8	347.4	347.2	347.8	345.3	347.7	353.1	355.8	346.0
2011...................................	341.7	342.5	345.0	348.4	349.9	351.9	351.6	351.5	349.0	350.5	355.9	358.4	349.7
2012...................................	347.5	346.4	349.5	351.1	353.8	356.0	355.4	355.3	354.1	356.5	364.6	365.7	354.7
2013...................................	351.4	351.3	354.8	356.9	360.0	363.7	364.7	365.7	363.4	366.6	373.3	377.0	362.4
2014...................................	363.4	361.7	366.1	369.0	372.4	376.0	374.3	374.9	373.3	376.6	384.5	388.5	373.4
2015...................................	373.5	373.3	376.6	380.4	384.0	387.4	389.0	389.1	385.3	386.6	392.1	397.0	384.5
Wholesale Trade													
2005...................................	67.6	68.0	68.0	67.7	68.7	67.9	68.3	68.5	68.2	68.8	68.9	68.6	68.3
2006...................................	69.0	69.5	69.7	70.6	70.7	70.5	69.4	69.8	70.2	71.4	71.6	71.7	70.3
2007...................................	70.7	71.1	71.8	71.9	71.9	72.4	72.1	71.9	71.9	72.2	72.1	72.5	71.9
2008...................................	71.9	72.4	72.6	72.3	72.4	72.5	72.3	72.2	71.9	72.0	71.5	70.8	72.1
2009...................................	68.5	67.8	67.2	67.0	66.8	66.2	65.7	65.6	65.0	65.1	65.0	64.8	66.2
2010...................................	64.0	64.0	64.2	64.5	64.7	64.7	64.7	64.8	64.2	64.4	64.4	64.3	64.4
2011...................................	63.4	64.1	64.2	64.5	64.6	64.7	64.7	64.7	64.5	64.4	64.4	64.7	64.4
2012...................................	64.9	65.3	65.6	65.6	65.8	66.3	65.9	65.9	65.6	65.7	65.7	65.8	65.7
2013...................................	65.5	65.8	66.2	66.4	66.7	67.0	66.6	66.9	66.6	66.6	66.9	67.0	66.5
2014...................................	67.1	67.3	67.6	67.5	68.0	68.5	68.1	68.3	68.3	69.1	69.3	69.3	68.2
2015...................................	69.5	69.8	70.3	70.5	70.8	71.0	70.9	71.0	70.9	70.7	71.1	71.0	70.6
Retail Trade													
2005...................................	225.8	225.0	226.3	229.1	230.9	229.8	232.0	232.2	228.1	231.7	237.1	239.3	230.6
2006...................................	228.5	230.7	234.4	233.7	233.4	231.8	233.3	234.0	233.1	236.8	244.3	246.4	235.0
2007...................................	234.5	232.8	237.3	236.9	239.4	240.7	241.0	240.3	239.5	240.1	246.0	248.0	239.7
2008...................................	237.7	235.8	238.6	237.5	237.5	237.8	236.6	235.7	234.1	231.6	234.3	235.4	236.1
2009...................................	222.4	219.2	220.2	221.9	223.7	224.6	223.9	223.3	221.6	221.0	225.8	226.8	222.9
2010...................................	217.5	216.4	219.1	220.7	222.5	223.6	223.1	223.5	221.6	223.3	228.3	230.5	222.5
2011...................................	219.1	219.2	221.2	224.4	225.2	226.3	226.3	225.7	223.4	224.3	229.1	230.5	224.6
2012...................................	221.2	219.7	222.3	223.7	225.7	226.8	226.9	226.5	225.4	227.0	234.5	234.5	226.2
2013...................................	222.7	222.1	224.8	227.0	229.3	231.9	233.0	233.4	231.5	234.3	240.0	242.2	231.0
2014...................................	230.3	228.9	232.3	233.9	235.8	238.2	237.3	237.1	235.4	237.2	243.7	246.1	236.4
2015...................................	233.3	232.8	235.3	238.3	240.9	244.0	244.5	244.3	241.1	243.3	247.6	249.8	241.3

1. Employment by Industry: South Carolina, 2005–2015—*Continued*

(Numbers in thousands, not seasonally adjusted)

Industry and year	January	February	March	April	May	June	July	August	September	October	November	December	Annual average
Transportation and Utilities													
2005	61.8	62.0	62.2	62.9	63.8	63.4	64.2	64.5	64.4	64.4	64.7	65.2	63.6
2006	63.9	64.5	64.6	64.5	64.8	65.2	64.8	65.2	65.3	65.9	66.1	66.9	65.1
2007	64.9	65.5	65.8	66.0	66.5	66.9	66.4	66.8	66.8	67.2	67.8	68.4	66.6
2008	65.9	66.2	65.9	66.1	65.9	65.7	65.1	65.3	64.5	64.9	64.7	65.0	65.4
2009	62.1	61.4	61.2	60.5	60.4	60.5	59.3	59.4	59.4	58.9	58.3	59.0	60.0
2010	57.5	57.5	58.2	58.4	58.6	59.1	59.4	59.5	59.5	60.0	60.4	61.0	59.1
2011	59.2	59.2	59.6	59.5	60.1	60.9	60.6	61.1	61.1	61.8	62.4	63.2	60.7
2012	61.4	61.4	61.6	61.8	62.3	62.9	62.6	62.9	63.1	63.8	64.4	65.4	62.8
2013	63.2	63.4	63.8	63.5	64.0	64.8	65.1	65.4	65.3	65.7	66.4	67.8	64.9
2014	66.0	65.5	66.2	67.6	68.6	69.3	68.9	69.5	69.6	70.3	71.5	73.1	68.8
2015	70.7	70.7	71.0	71.6	72.3	72.4	73.6	73.8	73.3	72.6	73.4	76.2	72.6
Information													
2005	26.6	26.7	26.6	27.0	27.3	27.2	27.2	27.1	26.9	26.9	27.1	27.4	27.0
2006	27.2	27.6	27.4	27.5	27.6	27.7	27.5	27.4	27.1	27.3	27.8	27.9	27.5
2007	27.1	27.2	27.4	27.6	27.9	28.5	28.7	28.5	28.0	28.1	28.2	28.4	28.0
2008	28.1	28.2	28.2	28.6	28.8	29.0	29.1	28.9	28.4	28.2	28.2	28.4	28.5
2009	27.9	27.7	27.9	27.5	27.4	27.4	27.6	26.9	26.5	26.5	26.4	26.3	27.2
2010	26.3	26.3	26.3	25.5	25.6	26.0	26.3	25.7	25.4	25.5	25.7	26.1	25.9
2011	26.0	25.7	25.9	25.7	25.7	25.8	25.8	25.7	25.3	26.0	26.1	26.1	25.8
2012	25.5	25.8	25.6	25.7	26.0	26.1	25.8	25.6	25.4	25.6	25.9	26.3	25.8
2013	26.1	26.4	26.4	26.7	26.7	26.5	26.6	26.3	26.2	26.2	26.4	26.4	26.4
2014	26.0	26.0	26.1	26.4	26.5	26.5	26.5	26.3	26.1	26.4	27.0	27.0	26.4
2015	26.6	26.6	26.6	26.5	26.8	26.7	27.1	27.0	26.9	27.0	27.0	27.0	26.8
Financial Activities													
2005	90.0	90.3	90.5	91.5	92.7	93.0	94.3	94.4	93.7	93.0	93.1	93.6	92.5
2006	94.0	94.6	94.9	96.6	97.2	97.8	98.6	99.1	98.6	99.1	98.9	99.4	97.4
2007	98.7	98.7	99.6	100.0	100.8	101.8	101.5	101.5	100.8	100.8	100.8	101.2	100.5
2008	99.8	100.6	100.9	100.8	101.3	102.2	101.5	101.3	99.8	99.3	98.7	98.6	100.4
2009	96.3	96.2	96.2	96.0	96.4	96.7	96.8	96.1	94.6	93.5	92.9	92.7	95.4
2010	91.2	91.2	91.6	92.0	92.4	93.1	93.3	92.8	91.4	91.4	91.2	90.9	91.9
2011	89.5	89.5	89.8	90.5	91.3	91.9	92.3	92.3	91.4	91.4	91.7	91.7	91.1
2012	91.0	91.4	91.9	93.1	93.5	94.6	94.5	94.8	94.0	93.7	94.1	94.5	93.4
2013	93.0	93.6	94.4	95.2	96.0	96.9	97.1	97.3	96.2	96.0	96.0	96.1	95.7
2014	94.6	94.7	95.2	96.3	96.7	97.4	97.2	97.4	96.2	95.9	96.0	96.2	96.2
2015	95.1	95.3	95.7	96.6	97.3	98.1	98.3	98.4	97.5	96.7	97.1	97.4	97.0
Professional and Business Services													
2005	196.5	198.6	198.7	204.3	205.1	204.4	206.8	210.3	210.4	213.3	214.6	211.6	206.2
2006	212.6	214.6	216.1	218.9	220.2	218.0	217.3	219.3	220.7	223.7	221.7	224.3	219.0
2007	220.9	223.6	225.2	227.0	228.5	230.0	226.7	229.2	229.2	227.9	227.5	226.5	226.9
2008	220.7	223.3	224.6	225.3	227.5	225.5	221.2	223.5	220.7	218.6	216.6	210.6	221.5
2009	201.0	199.9	200.2	199.2	199.0	198.2	198.5	199.9	199.5	203.8	205.3	203.5	200.7
2010	200.0	202.8	205.5	214.4	216.0	218.0	219.2	221.2	221.0	222.6	223.1	223.0	215.6
2011	217.8	222.0	225.1	230.1	230.4	230.8	231.1	233.1	231.7	230.6	231.4	231.5	228.8
2012	227.4	230.3	234.0	237.2	238.5	239.6	236.7	239.1	236.0	235.6	239.7	240.0	236.2
2013	232.9	234.8	236.2	238.5	241.2	243.4	242.1	243.7	244.1	245.7	251.2	251.7	242.1
2014	242.9	244.0	250.8	252.9	255.3	254.5	253.1	255.0	255.5	257.2	264.0	263.2	254.0
2015	251.6	253.4	255.7	257.5	261.6	261.8	262.9	263.9	263.9	270.1	271.0	272.6	262.2
Education and Health Services													
2005	176.2	178.3	178.8	178.7	179.3	176.6	179.5	180.4	182.3	183.5	183.9	182.7	180.0
2006	183.8	185.7	186.1	187.3	187.5	184.0	185.0	186.2	188.5	192.3	192.5	193.3	187.7
2007	191.3	193.6	194.6	195.2	195.7	195.2	195.1	196.1	198.3	198.9	199.6	199.5	196.1
2008	198.6	200.9	201.8	200.8	202.2	201.0	200.1	201.4	203.3	204.3	204.7	204.2	201.9
2009	201.6	203.3	203.2	203.9	204.6	202.8	202.8	204.3	204.8	206.4	207.5	206.6	204.3
2010	206.4	208.5	208.7	210.4	210.9	208.8	208.8	210.2	210.9	213.5	213.9	213.7	210.4
2011	210.1	213.1	213.7	214.4	214.3	212.2	211.2	212.3	214.2	215.0	215.6	215.2	213.4
2012	213.0	215.2	215.6	214.9	215.3	212.9	212.2	213.7	216.6	218.1	218.7	218.5	215.4
2013	214.9	217.9	217.9	218.5	219.3	217.4	216.6	218.7	220.5	222.6	223.8	223.7	219.3
2014	221.8	223.2	224.9	227.8	227.7	225.6	225.1	227.4	229.2	231.9	232.9	232.9	227.5
2015	229.8	232.3	233.1	234.0	234.9	232.4	232.8	235.2	236.4	240.2	241.7	241.0	235.3

1. Employment by Industry: South Carolina, 2005–2015—*Continued*

(Numbers in thousands, not seasonally adjusted)

Industry and year	January	February	March	April	May	June	July	August	September	October	November	December	Annual average
Leisure and Hospitality													
2005	185.5	189.7	196.5	206.7	209.7	212.9	217.3	215.9	206.1	202.7	200.7	194.6	203.2
2006	191.1	194.7	200.1	209.8	214.5	216.1	218.7	217.0	210.6	210.0	207.7	205.0	207.9
2007	199.8	203.0	211.3	219.4	224.1	229.3	227.9	227.4	220.9	217.9	214.0	210.6	217.1
2008	203.1	207.2	214.7	223.2	229.3	231.5	229.0	228.0	219.9	214.0	208.5	204.8	217.8
2009	195.0	198.1	204.8	213.5	219.1	220.8	219.1	217.7	211.2	205.1	200.5	196.7	208.5
2010	189.1	192.7	200.1	211.0	215.6	219.2	219.3	218.3	212.7	207.5	204.2	200.3	207.5
2011	190.2	195.0	203.7	214.7	221.0	223.5	222.1	222.1	214.8	209.9	207.6	204.1	210.7
2012	197.4	201.4	210.8	220.1	224.4	229.2	228.1	228.5	220.5	216.1	213.7	209.8	216.7
2013	202.6	206.8	213.5	225.1	231.1	236.3	235.6	234.6	227.7	222.8	220.7	216.7	222.8
2014	209.7	211.4	222.1	232.6	238.5	242.4	240.2	239.6	232.8	230.2	226.8	223.7	229.2
2015	218.3	222.5	231.3	240.6	246.6	250.5	251.3	249.4	241.8	238.1	234.8	229.7	237.9
Other Services													
2005	71.1	72.4	73.1	72.7	73.3	72.9	74.9	75.6	75.4	75.4	75.7	74.9	74.0
2006	71.9	72.6	76.2	76.1	76.3	75.9	76.2	75.8	75.3	74.7	74.3	74.3	75.0
2007	73.4	73.8	74.4	74.3	74.6	74.6	73.4	73.0	72.4	71.7	71.5	71.6	73.2
2008	70.2	70.4	71.3	71.7	72.4	72.5	72.2	72.0	71.6	71.2	70.9	70.5	71.4
2009	69.4	69.6	69.8	69.9	70.2	70.1	69.8	69.2	69.2	69.0	68.6	68.4	69.4
2010	67.4	67.7	68.4	68.8	69.0	69.2	68.7	68.4	68.6	68.7	68.5	68.3	68.5
2011	67.5	67.9	68.6	68.9	69.0	69.0	69.1	68.5	68.3	67.9	67.8	67.6	68.3
2012	67.7	67.9	69.0	69.0	69.5	69.9	69.9	69.7	69.4	69.6	69.8	69.7	69.3
2013	69.4	69.7	70.7	70.9	71.2	71.8	71.4	71.6	71.9	71.6	70.8	71.0	71.0
2014	70.2	70.4	71.9	71.9	72.5	72.8	72.4	72.5	72.3	72.5	72.6	72.4	72.0
2015	72.0	72.4	73.6	73.7	74.2	74.3	74.2	74.1	73.6	73.3	74.1	75.0	73.7
Government													
2005	332.8	337.4	339.1	339.6	339.3	332.5	316.4	323.4	339.4	342.0	344.5	344.7	335.9
2006	337.9	343.2	346.6	346.1	346.3	333.2	318.6	324.9	339.3	345.5	346.3	347.6	339.6
2007	343.9	346.7	349.2	347.7	348.3	343.1	326.1	334.4	349.6	354.0	357.2	356.5	346.4
2008	353.2	357.1	358.3	359.2	361.3	355.0	335.3	337.2	357.8	362.5	365.0	364.1	355.5
2009	356.6	359.1	359.9	361.6	361.0	353.8	339.2	343.7	353.1	358.2	359.7	359.1	355.4
2010	354.6	358.1	360.0	360.8	370.6	358.3	341.7	344.8	351.0	354.1	354.9	354.1	355.3
2011	349.2	352.4	353.6	353.8	352.7	347.3	332.5	335.7	348.2	351.4	352.4	352.0	348.4
2012	347.6	353.0	354.3	354.3	354.5	350.9	336.2	337.9	352.2	356.9	361.1	358.7	351.5
2013	352.1	356.5	358.1	358.9	358.0	352.0	337.3	338.8	352.8	357.4	359.0	358.1	353.3
2014	353.2	357.2	358.7	359.8	360.1	354.1	339.4	343.0	357.4	362.1	363.0	363.2	355.9
2015	357.5	362.2	363.0	363.8	363.8	358.0	344.5	348.3	362.1	366.1	367.9	367.5	360.4

2. Average Weekly Hours by Selected Industry: South Carolina, 2011–2015

(Not seasonally adjusted)

Industry and year	January	February	March	April	May	June	July	August	September	October	November	December	Annual average
Total Private													
2011	33.6	34.8	34.8	35.0	35.1	35.1	34.9	34.8	34.7	35.0	34.7	34.8	34.8
2012	34.9	35.1	35.1	35.4	34.9	35.0	35.3	35.1	35.4	35.0	34.9	35.2	35.1
2013	34.5	34.6	35.0	35.0	34.8	35.1	34.6	34.9	35.3	34.8	34.7	35.0	34.9
2014	34.6	33.4	34.7	34.5	34.5	34.9	34.6	34.6	34.5	34.3	34.7	34.6	34.5
2015	34.3	34.6	34.7	34.6	34.7	34.8	34.7	35.2	34.3	34.6	34.8	34.6	34.7
Goods-Producing													
2011	38.2	40.4	40.6	40.8	41.1	41.5	40.7	41.1	41.0	40.9	41.3	41.2	40.7
2012	40.9	41.2	41.4	41.5	41.2	41.7	41.4	41.4	41.7	41.2	40.9	41.8	41.4
2013	40.4	40.3	40.7	41.0	41.1	41.3	39.8	41.2	41.5	41.5	41.4	41.6	41.0
2014	41.3	38.6	39.4	39.2	40.0	40.4	39.7	40.1	40.1	39.7	40.6	40.4	40.0
2015	40.0	40.1	40.4	40.8	41.2	41.1	41.2	41.1	40.7	41.3	41.0	41.3	40.9
Construction													
2011	34.3	36.7	37.1	37.8	39.0	39.2	38.4	39.2	37.7	37.1	40.0	39.2	38.0
2012	38.6	39.1	39.9	39.6	39.7	39.7	39.9	40.3	40.1	40.1	39.5	40.2	39.7
2013	39.8	38.3	40.3	40.1	40.9	40.7	39.3	39.6	40.1	40.2	40.6	40.0	40.0
2014	40.3	35.8	39.3	38.3	39.5	39.6	39.0	39.0	38.6	38.3	39.1	39.3	38.9
2015	38.1	38.5	39.4	38.9	39.7	39.7	39.5	39.7	38.8	40.5	39.7	39.9	39.4
Manufacturing													
2011	39.2	40.9	41.1	41.2	41.2	41.7	40.9	41.3	41.7	41.8	41.5	41.6	41.2
2012	41.3	41.5	41.5	41.7	41.3	42.0	41.6	41.6	42.0	41.4	41.2	42.3	41.6
2013	40.4	40.9	40.7	41.2	41.0	41.4	39.9	41.6	41.9	41.9	41.6	42.1	41.2
2014	41.6	39.5	40.9	40.7	41.3	41.6	40.7	41.2	41.3	40.8	41.6	41.2	41.0
2015	41.2	41.1	41.1	41.9	42.0	41.9	42.1	41.8	41.7	41.6	41.7	42.0	41.7
Trade, Transportation, and Utilities													
2011	34.0	34.9	35.1	35.0	34.9	34.7	34.5	34.7	34.2	34.4	33.7	34.2	34.5
2012	34.2	34.1	34.1	34.6	34.0	34.2	34.5	34.2	34.3	34.1	34.5	34.5	34.3
2013	33.5	33.8	34.2	34.3	34.5	34.5	34.6	34.7	34.5	34.1	34.1	34.8	34.3
2014	34.0	33.0	33.8	33.9	34.1	34.5	34.5	34.3	34.7	34.3	35.0	35.0	34.3
2015	34.4	34.7	35.3	35.0	35.2	35.2	34.9	35.5	34.5	34.6	34.8	34.5	34.9
Financial Activities													
2011	37.8	37.4	37.3	37.9	38.0	37.6	38.2	34.6	35.1	35.8	35.3	36.2	36.8
2012	36.9	36.6	36.3	37.0	36.6	36.0	37.3	36.6	37.5	36.7	36.9	37.7	36.8
2013	37.0	37.5	37.4	37.2	37.2	38.4	37.9	37.7	39.2	38.1	38.0	38.5	37.9
2014	37.6	38.1	38.3	37.2	37.2	38.1	37.1	37.4	37.2	36.8	37.7	36.7	37.5
2015	36.7	37.7	37.4	36.8	36.7	37.0	37.2	38.0	36.9	37.1	38.2	37.0	37.2
Professional and Business Services													
2011	34.0	35.4	35.6	36.8	37.0	36.7	36.8	36.9	36.6	36.6	35.7	35.8	36.2
2012	35.8	36.6	36.4	36.8	36.6	36.8	37.0	36.7	37.4	37.0	37.3	37.9	36.9
2013	36.9	36.7	37.1	37.2	37.1	37.6	36.6	36.7	38.1	36.8	37.2	37.6	37.1
2014	36.9	35.3	38.0	37.8	37.9	38.2	37.6	37.8	37.5	37.5	37.8	37.2	37.5
2015	36.7	37.1	36.6	36.4	36.5	36.5	36.1	36.9	35.8	36.2	37.3	36.9	36.6
Education and Health Services													
2011	32.7	33.6	32.2	32.4	32.5	32.6	32.3	32.8	32.8	33.6	33.8	33.8	32.9
2012	34.4	34.3	34.3	34.6	34.3	34.6	34.7	34.6	35.0	34.4	34.4	34.3	34.5
2013	34.1	34.1	34.3	34.2	33.8	34.0	33.5	33.4	33.6	33.5	33.3	32.9	33.7
2014	32.6	31.9	32.7	32.4	32.3	32.1	32.5	32.6	32.4	32.6	32.9	33.1	32.5
2015	33.2	33.4	33.3	32.8	32.8	32.6	32.7	33.6	32.8	33.0	33.3	33.0	33.0
Leisure and Hospitality													
2011	24.6	25.8	26.1	26.5	26.4	26.6	27.0	27.2	26.4	26.7	26.2	25.6	26.3
2012	25.5	26.4	26.7	27.4	26.3	26.5	26.9	26.9	26.1	25.9	25.2	25.4	26.3
2013	25.0	25.4	26.1	26.2	25.9	26.4	26.6	26.9	25.8	25.5	25.1	25.0	25.8
2014	24.9	24.6	26.1	26.4	25.8	26.3	26.6	26.2	25.2	25.4	24.9	24.9	25.6
2015	24.6	25.1	25.7	26.0	25.8	26.4	26.7	26.6	25.2	25.0	25.0	24.7	25.6
Other Services													
2011	30.6	32.3	32.5	32.9	33.9	34.0	34.0	33.4	33.9	34.5	33.2	32.8	33.2
2012	33.9	33.6	33.3	32.8	32.1	32.5	33.0	31.7	33.1	33.0	32.9	32.9	32.9
2013	34.0	32.6	33.3	33.7	33.1	32.9	31.8	31.6	32.3	31.6	31.3	31.5	32.5
2014	31.2	28.9	31.0	31.4	31.0	30.3	31.1	30.9	31.1	31.2	30.5	30.6	30.8
2015	29.9	30.0	31.3	31.5	31.9	31.5	31.7	31.1	31.1	31.3	31.1	32.4	31.2

3. Average Hourly Earnings by Selected Industry: South Carolina, 2011–2015

(Dollars, not seasonally adjusted)

Industry and year	January	February	March	April	May	June	July	August	September	October	November	December	Annual average
Total Private													
2011	21.00	20.80	20.90	20.90	20.71	20.44	20.54	20.25	20.53	20.37	20.28	20.29	20.58
2012	20.42	20.32	20.17	19.96	19.79	19.78	19.94	19.92	20.22	20.09	20.17	20.37	20.09
2013	20.27	20.57	20.72	20.23	20.15	20.34	20.26	20.40	20.64	20.69	20.92	21.05	20.52
2014	21.06	21.73	21.19	20.80	20.68	20.78	20.64	20.76	21.01	21.07	21.47	21.39	21.05
2015	21.70	21.36	21.75	21.22	21.03	20.99	21.26	21.29	21.50	21.53	21.80	21.67	21.42
Goods-Producing													
2011	21.73	21.22	21.21	21.23	20.98	20.73	20.84	20.74	20.98	20.68	20.64	21.01	20.99
2012	20.76	20.53	20.68	20.77	20.64	20.71	20.95	20.83	21.12	20.89	21.04	21.13	20.84
2013	20.96	20.72	20.85	20.92	20.89	21.14	21.25	21.36	21.69	21.67	21.97	22.24	21.31
2014	22.19	22.97	22.30	22.20	21.87	22.07	22.25	22.19	22.26	22.23	22.48	22.85	22.32
2015	22.67	22.68	22.69	22.52	22.29	22.42	22.69	22.84	22.96	23.13	23.36	23.37	22.80
Construction													
2011	21.77	21.25	21.58	21.65	21.36	21.06	21.01	21.07	21.43	21.44	21.37	21.41	21.36
2012	20.97	20.94	20.57	20.41	20.05	20.25	20.40	20.23	20.27	20.36	20.57	20.16	20.43
2013	19.90	20.38	20.76	20.22	19.99	20.11	19.81	19.90	19.99	19.91	19.86	20.20	20.08
2014	20.14	21.09	20.38	19.98	20.10	20.40	20.55	20.72	20.95	20.97	20.90	20.74	20.57
2015	20.54	20.58	20.81	20.62	20.41	20.55	20.74	20.92	21.05	21.28	21.39	21.65	20.89
Manufacturing													
2011	21.72	21.16	21.04	21.06	20.82	20.56	20.74	20.59	20.78	20.37	20.32	20.83	20.82
2012	20.63	20.34	20.70	20.91	20.84	20.85	21.14	21.03	21.40	21.08	21.21	21.48	20.97
2013	21.37	20.84	21.06	21.33	21.37	21.66	21.95	22.02	22.43	22.43	22.78	23.00	21.86
2014	23.00	23.76	23.16	23.18	22.66	22.82	23.02	22.83	22.82	22.77	23.15	23.75	23.07
2015	23.56	23.57	23.50	23.35	23.11	23.26	23.59	23.75	23.86	24.03	24.34	24.25	23.68
Trade, Transportation, and Utilities													
2011	18.88	18.74	18.48	18.33	18.44	18.21	18.09	18.13	18.61	18.68	18.52	17.90	18.41
2012	18.52	18.53	18.65	17.93	17.86	17.80	18.25	18.50	18.54	18.46	18.63	18.88	18.38
2013	19.01	19.05	19.47	19.06	19.07	19.33	19.34	19.37	19.82	19.80	19.98	19.92	19.44
2014	20.39	20.89	20.87	19.57	19.37	19.60	19.14	19.50	19.73	20.02	20.12	19.57	19.89
2015	20.07	19.59	20.46	19.68	19.66	19.75	19.93	20.04	20.04	20.29	20.60	20.31	20.04
Financial Activities													
2011	24.89	25.30	23.75	23.80	23.40	22.99	22.80	22.49	22.72	22.73	22.76	22.30	23.34
2012	23.11	24.32	22.73	23.00	22.80	22.60	22.73	22.90	23.20	23.18	22.97	23.05	23.05
2013	22.95	22.77	20.16	20.69	20.64	20.69	20.80	21.09	19.87	20.45	20.82	21.32	21.01
2014	21.90	22.68	22.76	22.57	22.52	23.19	23.28	23.25	23.79	23.82	24.66	24.11	23.21
2015	24.95	25.20	25.10	25.01	24.56	24.31	24.84	24.58	24.54	24.31	25.17	25.07	24.80
Professional and Business Services													
2011	22.82	22.42	21.74	22.33	22.05	21.87	22.23	21.90	22.26	22.56	22.09	22.36	22.21
2012	22.54	22.46	22.19	22.09	21.91	22.22	22.32	22.22	23.07	22.63	22.74	23.50	22.50
2013	22.93	23.64	23.42	23.10	22.99	23.41	22.85	22.98	23.23	23.25	23.44	23.54	23.23
2014	23.57	24.64	23.69	23.34	23.45	23.24	23.21	23.17	23.20	23.06	23.17	22.75	23.36
2015	23.75	23.84	23.91	23.66	23.40	23.38	23.92	23.13	23.18	22.86	22.87	22.35	23.34
Education and Health Services													
2011	24.46	24.63	25.50	25.50	25.49	25.34	25.94	25.24	25.02	24.27	24.52	24.02	24.98
2012	23.93	23.87	24.02	23.87	23.42	23.45	23.31	23.02	23.01	23.34	23.25	23.05	23.46
2013	22.80	22.85	22.79	22.81	22.77	23.14	23.33	23.94	23.76	23.73	24.09	24.14	23.34
2014	24.10	24.67	24.19	24.62	24.48	24.79	24.83	24.94	25.40	25.36	25.89	25.94	24.94
2015	25.97	26.01	25.60	25.88	25.54	25.49	25.79	26.10	26.71	26.14	26.48	26.32	26.01
Leisure and Hospitality													
2011	12.13	11.89	11.87	11.93	11.80	11.77	11.91	11.90	11.99	11.93	11.85	12.05	11.91
2012	11.96	11.92	11.84	11.69	11.62	11.63	11.59	11.52	11.55	11.43	11.49	11.35	11.63
2013	11.54	11.75	11.57	11.43	11.56	11.46	11.49	11.36	11.61	11.60	11.70	11.77	11.56
2014	11.64	11.99	11.73	11.86	11.88	11.80	11.80	11.78	11.87	11.97	12.09	11.87	11.86
2015	11.90	12.02	12.09	12.07	12.02	11.89	11.88	12.02	12.05	12.28	12.22	12.40	12.07
Other Services													
2011	17.43	17.63	16.76	17.45	17.59	17.96	18.56	18.29	18.41	18.22	17.77	18.16	17.86
2012	18.16	18.15	18.06	18.21	17.76	17.44	17.64	17.79	17.18	17.23	17.21	17.28	17.67
2013	16.96	17.25	16.85	16.71	16.57	16.63	16.50	16.33	16.21	16.11	16.37	16.25	16.57
2014	16.43	16.75	16.16	15.95	15.69	15.51	14.56	15.04	14.92	14.98	15.46	15.65	15.58
2015	16.09	16.22	16.11	16.22	16.06	16.11	16.23	16.35	16.2	16.37	16.67	16.7	16.28

4. Average Weekly Earnings by Selected Industry: South Carolina, 2011–2015

(Dollars, not seasonally adjusted)

Industry and year	January	February	March	April	May	June	July	August	September	October	November	December	Annual average
Total Private													
2011	705.60	723.84	727.32	731.50	726.92	717.44	716.85	704.70	712.39	712.95	703.72	706.09	716.18
2012	712.66	713.23	707.97	706.58	690.67	692.30	703.88	699.19	715.79	703.15	703.93	717.02	705.16
2013	699.32	711.72	725.20	708.05	701.22	713.93	701.00	711.96	728.59	720.01	725.92	736.75	716.15
2014	728.68	725.78	735.29	717.60	713.46	725.22	714.14	718.30	724.85	722.70	745.01	740.09	726.23
2015	744.31	739.06	754.73	734.21	729.74	730.45	737.72	749.41	737.45	744.94	758.64	749.78	743.27
Goods-Producing													
2011	830.09	857.29	861.13	866.18	862.28	860.30	848.19	852.41	860.18	845.81	852.43	865.61	854.29
2012	849.08	845.84	856.15	861.96	850.37	863.61	867.33	862.36	880.70	860.67	860.54	883.23	862.78
2013	846.78	835.02	848.60	857.72	858.58	873.08	845.75	880.03	900.14	899.31	909.56	925.18	873.71
2014	916.45	886.64	878.62	870.24	874.80	891.63	883.33	889.82	892.63	882.53	912.69	923.14	892.80
2015	906.80	909.47	916.68	918.82	918.35	921.46	934.83	938.72	934.47	955.27	957.76	965.18	932.52
Construction													
2011	746.71	779.88	800.62	818.37	833.04	825.55	806.78	825.94	807.91	795.42	854.80	839.27	811.68
2012	809.44	818.75	820.74	808.24	795.99	803.93	813.96	815.27	812.83	816.44	812.52	810.43	811.07
2013	792.02	780.55	836.63	810.82	817.59	818.48	778.53	788.04	801.60	800.38	806.32	808.00	803.20
2014	811.64	755.02	800.93	765.23	793.95	807.84	801.45	808.08	808.67	803.15	817.19	815.08	800.17
2015	782.57	792.33	819.91	802.12	810.28	815.84	819.23	830.52	816.74	861.84	849.18	863.84	823.07
Manufacturing													
2011	851.42	865.44	864.74	867.67	857.78	857.35	848.27	850.37	866.53	851.47	843.28	866.53	857.78
2012	852.02	844.11	859.05	871.95	860.69	875.70	879.42	874.85	898.80	872.71	873.85	908.60	872.35
2013	863.35	852.36	857.14	878.80	876.17	896.72	875.81	916.03	939.82	939.82	947.65	968.30	900.63
2014	956.80	938.52	947.24	943.43	935.86	949.31	936.91	940.60	942.47	929.02	963.04	978.50	945.87
2015	970.67	968.73	965.85	978.37	970.62	974.59	993.14	992.75	994.96	999.65	1,014.98	1,018.50	987.46
Trade, Transportation, and Utilities													
2011	641.92	654.03	648.65	641.55	643.56	631.89	624.11	629.11	636.46	642.59	624.12	612.18	635.15
2012	633.38	631.87	635.97	620.38	607.24	608.76	629.63	632.70	635.92	629.49	642.74	651.36	630.43
2013	636.84	643.89	665.87	653.76	657.92	666.89	669.16	672.14	683.79	675.18	681.32	693.22	666.79
2014	693.26	689.37	705.41	663.42	660.52	676.20	660.33	668.85	684.63	686.69	704.20	684.95	682.23
2015	690.41	679.77	722.24	688.80	692.03	695.20	695.56	711.42	691.38	702.03	716.88	700.70	699.40
Financial Activities													
2011	940.84	946.22	885.88	902.02	889.20	864.42	870.96	778.15	797.47	813.73	803.43	807.26	858.91
2012	852.76	890.11	825.10	851.00	834.48	813.60	847.83	838.14	870.00	850.71	847.59	868.99	848.24
2013	849.15	853.88	753.98	769.67	767.81	794.50	788.32	795.09	778.90	779.15	791.16	820.82	796.28
2014	823.44	864.11	871.71	839.60	837.74	883.54	863.69	869.55	884.99	876.58	929.68	884.84	870.38
2015	915.67	950.04	938.74	920.37	901.35	899.47	924.05	934.04	905.53	901.90	961.49	927.59	922.56
Professional and Business Services													
2011	775.88	793.67	773.94	821.74	815.85	802.63	818.06	808.11	814.72	825.70	788.61	800.49	804.00
2012	806.93	822.04	807.72	812.91	801.91	817.70	825.84	815.47	862.82	837.31	848.20	890.65	830.25
2013	846.12	867.59	868.88	859.32	852.93	880.22	836.31	843.37	885.06	855.60	871.97	885.10	861.83
2014	869.73	869.79	900.22	882.25	888.76	887.77	872.70	875.83	870.00	864.75	875.83	846.30	876.00
2015	871.63	884.46	875.11	861.22	854.10	853.37	863.51	853.50	829.84	827.53	853.05	824.72	854.24
Education and Health Services													
2011	799.84	827.57	821.10	826.20	828.43	826.08	837.86	827.87	820.66	815.47	828.78	811.88	821.84
2012	823.19	818.74	823.89	825.90	803.31	811.37	808.86	796.49	805.35	802.90	799.80	790.62	809.37
2013	777.48	779.19	781.70	780.10	769.63	786.76	781.56	799.60	798.34	794.96	802.20	794.21	786.56
2014	785.66	786.97	791.01	797.69	790.70	795.76	806.98	813.04	822.96	826.74	851.78	858.61	810.55
2015	862.20	868.73	852.48	848.86	837.71	830.97	843.33	876.96	876.09	862.62	881.78	868.56	858.33
Leisure and Hospitality													
2011	298.40	306.76	309.81	316.15	311.52	313.08	321.57	323.68	316.54	318.53	310.47	308.48	313.23
2012	304.98	314.69	316.13	320.31	305.61	308.20	311.77	309.89	301.46	296.04	289.55	288.29	305.87
2013	288.50	298.45	301.98	299.47	299.40	302.54	305.63	305.58	299.54	295.80	293.67	294.25	298.25
2014	289.84	294.95	306.15	313.10	306.50	310.34	313.88	308.64	299.12	304.04	301.04	295.56	303.62
2015	292.74	301.70	310.71	313.82	310.12	313.90	317.20	319.73	303.66	307.00	305.50	306.28	308.99
Other Services													
2011	533.36	569.45	544.70	574.11	596.30	610.64	631.04	610.89	624.10	628.59	589.96	595.65	592.95
2012	615.62	609.84	601.40	597.29	570.10	566.80	582.12	563.94	568.66	568.59	566.21	568.51	581.34
2013	576.64	562.35	561.11	563.13	548.47	547.13	524.70	516.03	523.58	509.08	512.38	511.88	538.53
2014	512.62	484.08	500.96	500.83	486.39	469.95	452.82	464.74	464.01	467.38	471.53	478.89	479.86
2015	481.09	486.60	504.24	510.93	512.31	507.47	514.49	508.49	503.82	512.38	518.44	541.08	507.94

SOUTH DAKOTA

At a Glance

Population:
2005 estimate: 775,493
2010 census: 814,180
2015 estimate: 858,469

Percent change in population:
2005–2015: 10.7%
2010–2015: 5.4%

Percent change in total nonfarm employment:
2005–2015: 9.7%

Industry with the largest growth in employment, 2005–2015 (thousands):
Education and health services, 11.7

Industry with the largest decline or smallest growth in employment, 2005–2015 (thousands):
Information: –0.9

Civilian labor force:
2005: 430,606
2010: 441,339
2015: 452,300

Unemployment rate and rank among states (highest to lowest):
2005: 3.8%, 43rd
2010: 5.0%, 49th
2015: 3.1%, 49th

Over-the-year change in unemployment rates:
2012–2013: –0.5%
2013–2014: –0.4%
2014–2015: –0.3%

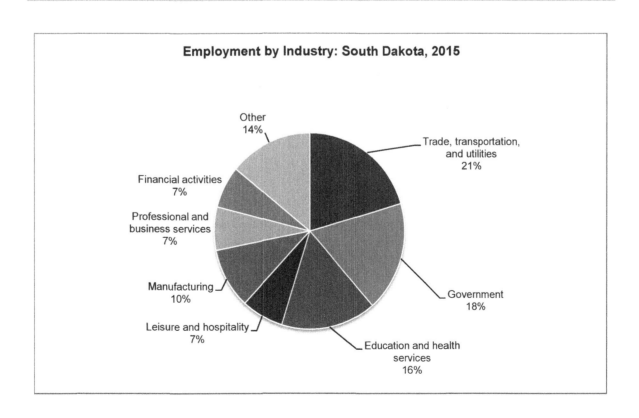

Employment by Industry: South Dakota, 2015

Other 14%
Trade, transportation, and utilities 21%
Financial activities 7%
Professional and business services 7%
Manufacturing 10%
Government 18%
Leisure and hospitality 7%
Education and health services 16%

1. Employment by Industry: South Dakota, 2005–2015

(Numbers in thousands, not seasonally adjusted)

Industry and year	January	February	March	April	May	June	July	August	September	October	November	December	Annual average
Total Nonfarm													
2005	375.3	376.2	379.7	386.9	393.9	399.8	395.7	398.2	395.7	393.6	393.3	393.4	390.1
2006	384.0	385.0	388.1	393.3	402.6	408.8	404.0	407.5	403.5	402.5	401.8	401.9	398.6
2007	392.0	392.8	396.4	401.5	411.6	416.8	413.2	415.8	411.0	410.4	409.1	407.8	406.5
2008	399.6	401.1	403.5	407.1	416.6	420.9	416.6	420.2	415.2	414.7	411.6	409.7	411.4
2009	397.6	397.0	397.2	399.0	409.3	412.9	408.8	409.1	406.3	404.3	402.9	399.9	403.7
2010	388.3	389.1	392.0	399.4	407.4	413.0	409.2	411.6	407.8	408.8	406.8	405.1	403.2
2011	393.0	394.5	396.7	403.3	411.1	417.1	412.6	414.8	412.2	412.9	411.0	411.0	407.5
2012	399.8	400.5	404.6	411.1	418.7	424.4	419.1	420.8	418.5	417.9	417.1	415.4	414.0
2013	404.4	405.6	408.6	411.4	423.0	427.3	422.0	424.2	422.0	422.1	421.7	420.0	417.7
2014	410.1	411.5	413.8	419.1	428.8	433.7	429.3	430.9	428.6	427.8	425.7	425.5	423.7
2015	414.2	416.2	419.5	425.4	433.4	438.2	433.4	434.4	431.9	432.2	429.8	428.5	428.1
Total Private													
2005	300.4	300.8	303.8	310.8	316.6	322.8	323.9	326.7	320.4	317.6	317.1	317.4	314.9
2006	309.6	309.5	312.3	317.4	325.1	331.5	332.1	335.5	328.6	326.4	325.4	325.8	323.3
2007	317.8	317.0	320.6	325.7	334.0	340.0	340.6	343.0	335.7	334.0	332.5	331.5	331.0
2008	324.9	324.6	327.0	330.5	338.2	344.0	344.5	346.9	339.2	337.1	333.9	332.1	335.2
2009	321.5	319.7	319.4	320.4	328.9	334.1	334.0	334.4	328.2	325.2	323.6	321.5	325.9
2010	311.2	310.7	312.6	319.6	326.2	332.7	334.0	336.3	329.1	329.1	327.0	325.7	324.5
2011	315.4	315.5	317.6	323.9	331.3	337.2	338.3	341.3	335.0	334.1	332.3	332.1	329.5
2012	323.0	322.8	326.2	332.4	339.8	345.8	345.6	347.8	341.1	338.9	337.9	336.7	336.5
2013	327.5	327.4	330.2	333.4	344.3	349.8	349.4	351.0	344.2	343.4	342.8	341.5	340.4
2014	333.1	333.3	335.3	340.5	349.4	355.2	355.5	356.8	350.2	348.7	346.4	346.7	345.9
2015	337.5	338.2	341.1	346.6	353.8	359.4	359.4	360.8	353.8	352.5	350.7	349.3	350.3
Goods-Producing													
2005	56.9	56.7	57.8	60.6	62.3	64.3	65.0	64.7	63.7	63.6	63.1	61.4	61.7
2006	59.9	59.6	60.5	62.8	65.0	67.1	67.8	67.7	66.5	65.8	64.9	64.1	64.3
2007	61.6	60.6	61.9	63.6	65.9	67.9	68.3	68.1	67.2	66.9	66.1	64.6	65.2
2008	62.7	62.3	63.2	64.8	67.5	68.8	69.1	68.8	67.6	67.2	65.9	63.4	65.9
2009	59.7	58.5	57.8	57.7	60.4	62.0	62.1	61.2	60.2	59.6	58.5	56.2	59.5
2010	53.2	52.7	53.2	56.2	58.0	60.1	61.3	61.3	60.5	60.7	59.8	58.0	57.9
2011	54.9	54.7	55.3	58.2	60.9	62.8	63.4	63.5	62.9	63.2	62.2	60.7	60.2
2012	58.4	58.2	59.2	61.5	63.3	65.0	65.1	65.0	63.9	63.6	62.9	61.4	62.3
2013	59.0	58.5	59.3	60.7	64.1	66.0	66.0	66.0	64.8	64.6	63.8	62.2	62.9
2014	59.9	59.7	60.5	62.5	65.2	67.3	67.6	67.5	66.7	66.7	65.6	64.7	64.5
2015	62.2	62.0	63.1	65.0	66.8	68.4	68.3	68.0	67.0	67.2	65.7	64.0	65.6
Service-Providing													
2005	318.4	319.5	321.9	326.3	331.6	335.5	330.7	333.5	332.0	330.0	330.2	332.0	328.5
2006	324.1	325.4	327.6	330.5	337.6	341.7	336.2	339.8	337.0	336.7	336.9	337.8	334.3
2007	330.4	332.2	334.5	337.9	345.7	348.9	344.9	347.7	343.8	343.5	343.0	343.2	341.3
2008	336.9	338.8	340.3	342.3	349.1	352.1	347.5	351.4	347.6	347.5	345.7	346.3	345.5
2009	337.9	338.5	339.4	341.3	348.9	350.9	346.7	347.9	346.1	344.7	344.4	343.7	344.2
2010	335.1	336.4	338.8	343.2	349.4	352.9	347.9	350.3	347.3	348.1	347.0	347.1	345.3
2011	338.1	339.8	341.4	345.1	350.2	354.3	349.2	351.3	349.3	349.7	348.8	350.3	347.3
2012	341.4	342.3	345.4	349.6	355.4	359.4	354.0	355.8	354.6	354.3	354.2	354.0	351.7
2013	345.4	347.1	349.3	350.7	358.9	361.3	356.0	358.2	357.2	357.5	357.9	357.8	354.8
2014	350.2	351.8	353.3	356.6	363.6	366.4	361.7	363.4	361.9	361.1	360.1	360.8	359.2
2015	352.0	354.2	356.4	360.4	366.6	369.8	365.1	366.4	364.9	365.0	364.1	364.5	362.5
Mining and Logging													
2005	0.8	0.7	0.8	0.9	0.9	1.0	1.0	1.0	0.9	0.9	0.9	0.8	0.9
2006	0.7	0.8	0.8	0.9	0.9	1.0	1.0	1.0	1.0	0.9	0.9	0.9	0.9
2007	0.8	0.8	0.8	0.9	1.0	1.1	1.1	1.1	1.0	1.0	1.0	0.9	1.0
2008	0.9	0.9	0.9	1.0	1.1	1.2	1.2	1.2	1.1	1.1	1.1	1.0	1.1
2009	0.9	0.9	0.9	0.9	1.0	1.0	1.0	1.0	1.0	0.9	0.9	0.9	0.9
2010	0.8	0.8	0.8	0.9	1.0	1.0	1.1	1.0	1.0	1.0	1.0	0.9	0.9
2011	0.8	0.8	0.8	0.9	1.0	1.1	1.1	1.1	1.1	1.0	1.0	0.9	1.0
2012	0.9	0.8	0.9	0.9	1.0	1.0	1.0	1.1	1.0	1.0	1.0	0.9	1.0
2013	0.8	0.8	0.8	0.9	1.0	1.0	1.0	1.0	1.0	0.9	0.9	0.9	0.9
2014	0.7	0.7	0.8	0.9	1.0	1.0	1.0	1.0	1.0	1.0	0.9	0.9	0.9
2015	0.8	0.8	0.8	0.9	1.0	1.0	1.0	1.0	1.0	0.9	0.9	0.8	0.9

1. Employment by Industry: South Dakota, 2005–2015—*Continued*

(Numbers in thousands, not seasonally adjusted)

Industry and year	January	February	March	April	May	June	July	August	September	October	November	December	Annual average
Construction													
2005	17.3	17.1	17.9	20.2	21.8	23.2	23.8	23.7	22.8	22.5	21.9	20.3	21.0
2006	18.8	18.5	19.0	20.9	22.7	24.1	24.7	24.6	23.5	22.7	21.8	20.9	21.9
2007	19.0	18.2	19.2	20.6	22.9	24.4	24.9	24.9	24.2	23.6	22.9	21.6	22.2
2008	19.7	19.1	19.6	21.2	23.5	24.4	24.7	24.6	23.7	23.2	22.2	20.6	22.2
2009	18.2	17.9	18.0	19.0	21.7	23.3	24.2	23.3	22.3	21.9	21.1	19.1	20.8
2010	16.6	16.0	16.3	19.0	20.3	22.0	22.7	22.9	22.1	22.2	21.3	19.5	20.1
2011	16.6	16.2	16.5	18.8	20.7	22.2	22.7	22.6	22.1	22.1	20.9	19.6	20.1
2012	17.6	17.1	17.9	19.7	21.0	22.2	22.2	22.1	21.3	20.8	20.1	19.1	20.1
2013	17.0	16.6	17.2	18.5	21.4	22.8	23.1	23.2	22.4	22.1	21.5	20.0	20.5
2014	18.1	17.7	18.1	19.8	22.0	23.7	23.9	23.7	23.1	22.8	21.8	20.8	21.3
2015	18.7	18.6	19.7	21.6	23.2	24.5	24.7	24.4	23.5	23.7	22.7	21.5	22.2
Manufacturing													
2005	38.8	38.9	39.1	39.5	39.6	40.1	40.2	40.0	40.0	40.2	40.3	40.3	39.8
2006	40.4	40.3	40.7	41.0	41.4	42.0	42.1	42.1	42.0	42.2	42.2	42.3	41.6
2007	41.8	41.6	41.9	42.1	42.0	42.4	42.3	42.1	42.0	42.3	42.2	42.1	42.1
2008	42.1	42.3	42.7	42.6	42.9	43.2	43.2	43.0	42.8	42.9	42.6	41.8	42.7
2009	40.6	39.7	38.9	37.8	37.7	37.7	36.9	36.9	36.9	36.8	36.5	36.2	37.7
2010	35.8	35.9	36.1	36.3	36.7	37.1	37.5	37.4	37.4	37.5	37.5	37.6	36.9
2011	37.5	37.7	38.0	38.5	39.2	39.5	39.6	39.8	39.7	40.1	40.3	40.2	39.2
2012	39.9	40.3	40.4	40.9	41.3	41.8	41.9	41.8	41.6	41.8	41.8	41.4	41.2
2013	41.2	41.1	41.3	41.3	41.7	42.2	41.9	41.8	41.4	41.6	41.4	41.3	41.5
2014	41.1	41.3	41.6	41.8	42.2	42.6	42.7	42.8	42.6	43.0	42.9	43.0	42.3
2015	42.7	42.6	42.6	42.5	42.6	42.9	42.6	42.6	42.5	42.6	42.1	41.7	42.5
Trade, Transportation, and Utilities													
2005	76.4	76.4	76.9	78.3	79.4	79.6	79.6	80.5	79.2	79.2	80.2	81.0	78.9
2006	78.3	77.7	78.3	79.0	80.4	81.2	80.7	81.6	80.1	80.5	81.4	82.2	80.1
2007	79.5	78.7	79.5	80.2	81.7	82.3	82.3	82.6	81.2	81.6	82.4	82.9	81.2
2008	81.0	80.3	80.6	81.1	82.3	83.0	83.3	83.7	82.2	82.6	82.6	83.1	82.2
2009	80.0	79.2	79.1	79.4	81.1	81.6	81.4	81.8	80.5	80.6	81.5	81.7	80.7
2010	78.8	78.1	78.6	79.7	80.9	81.7	81.6	82.0	80.4	81.2	82.0	82.3	80.6
2011	79.7	79.3	79.6	80.9	82.1	82.7	82.6	83.2	81.7	82.1	83.2	83.7	81.7
2012	81.2	80.4	81.0	82.0	83.5	84.2	83.8	84.3	83.1	83.2	84.4	84.6	83.0
2013	81.7	81.1	81.6	82.2	84.1	84.9	84.8	84.8	83.7	84.2	85.2	85.8	83.7
2014	83.5	83.3	83.6	84.5	85.8	87.0	87.4	87.6	86.0	86.3	87.1	87.8	85.8
2015	85.5	85.2	85.4	86.6	87.9	88.7	88.6	88.8	87.3	88.1	88.8	89.9	87.6
Wholesale Trade													
2005	17.1	17.1	17.1	17.5	17.7	17.7	17.6	17.8	17.6	17.8	17.8	17.8	17.6
2006	18.0	18.0	18.1	18.3	18.6	18.6	18.3	18.3	18.0	18.2	18.1	18.1	18.2
2007	18.0	17.9	18.1	18.3	18.6	18.6	18.5	18.6	18.4	18.5	18.6	18.6	18.4
2008	18.6	18.6	18.7	18.8	19.0	19.0	18.9	18.9	18.6	18.8	18.4	18.6	18.7
2009	18.1	18.1	18.1	18.2	18.6	18.5	18.5	18.5	18.1	18.4	18.4	18.3	18.3
2010	18.1	18.1	18.2	18.6	18.8	18.8	18.8	18.8	18.6	18.8	18.8	18.7	18.6
2011	18.5	18.5	18.7	18.9	19.2	19.3	19.2	19.2	18.9	19.1	19.2	19.2	19.0
2012	19.2	19.1	19.3	19.6	19.8	19.9	19.7	19.6	19.3	19.5	19.5	19.5	19.5
2013	19.4	19.3	19.6	19.8	20.3	20.4	20.3	20.0	19.8	20.0	20.2	20.2	19.9
2014	20.1	20.2	20.4	20.7	21.0	21.2	21.3	21.1	20.7	21.0	21.0	21.0	20.8
2015	20.8	20.8	21.0	21.2	21.4	21.5	21.4	21.2	20.9	21.2	21.4	21.3	21.2
Retail Trade													
2005	47.7	47.7	48.2	49.0	49.7	49.9	49.9	50.5	49.2	49.0	50.0	50.6	49.3
2006	48.0	47.4	47.8	48.2	49.0	49.8	49.7	50.3	49.1	49.3	50.4	51.0	49.2
2007	48.8	48.2	48.8	49.1	50.1	50.7	50.9	51.0	49.6	49.9	50.7	51.2	49.9
2008	49.4	48.7	48.9	49.2	50.0	50.7	51.1	51.5	50.2	50.4	50.9	51.2	50.2
2009	48.9	48.2	48.2	48.5	49.6	50.2	50.3	50.6	49.6	49.5	50.5	50.8	49.6
2010	48.5	47.9	48.2	48.7	49.5	50.2	50.3	50.6	49.1	49.7	50.5	50.9	49.5
2011	48.9	48.5	48.6	49.4	50.2	50.7	50.9	51.3	50.1	50.4	51.4	51.8	50.2
2012	49.8	49.1	49.4	50.2	51.2	51.7	51.6	52.2	51.0	51.0	52.2	52.4	51.0
2013	50.0	49.5	49.7	50.1	51.1	51.8	51.9	52.2	51.2	51.4	52.2	52.6	51.1
2014	50.7	50.3	50.4	50.9	51.6	52.6	53.0	53.2	52.0	51.9	52.8	53.3	51.9
2015	51.6	51.3	51.3	52.1	53.0	53.7	53.8	54.0	52.9	53.3	53.6	54.7	52.9

1. Employment by Industry: South Dakota, 2005–2015—*Continued*

(Numbers in thousands, not seasonally adjusted)

Industry and year	January	February	March	April	May	June	July	August	September	October	November	December	Annual average
Transportation and Utilities													
2005	11.6	11.6	11.6	11.8	12.0	12.0	12.1	12.2	12.4	12.4	12.4	12.6	12.1
2006	12.3	12.3	12.4	12.5	12.8	12.8	12.7	13.0	13.0	13.0	12.9	13.1	12.7
2007	12.7	12.6	12.6	12.8	13.0	13.0	12.9	13.0	13.2	13.2	13.1	13.1	12.9
2008	13.0	13.0	13.0	13.1	13.3	13.3	13.3	13.3	13.4	13.4	13.3	13.3	13.2
2009	13.0	12.9	12.8	12.7	12.9	12.9	12.6	12.7	12.8	12.7	12.6	12.6	12.8
2010	12.2	12.1	12.2	12.4	12.6	12.7	12.5	12.6	12.7	12.7	12.7	12.7	12.5
2011	12.3	12.3	12.3	12.6	12.7	12.7	12.5	12.7	12.7	12.6	12.6	12.7	12.6
2012	12.2	12.2	12.3	12.2	12.5	12.6	12.5	12.5	12.8	12.7	12.7	12.7	12.5
2013	12.3	12.3	12.3	12.3	12.7	12.7	12.6	12.6	12.7	12.8	12.8	13.0	12.6
2014	12.7	12.8	12.8	12.9	13.2	13.2	13.1	13.3	13.3	13.4	13.3	13.5	13.1
2015	13.1	13.1	13.1	13.3	13.5	13.5	13.4	13.6	13.5	13.6	13.8	13.9	13.5
Information													
2005	6.6	6.6	6.5	6.5	6.7	6.8	6.9	6.9	6.9	6.9	6.9	6.9	6.8
2006	6.8	6.9	6.9	6.8	6.9	7.0	7.1	7.1	7.0	6.9	6.9	7.0	6.9
2007	7.0	7.1	7.0	7.3	7.4	7.5	7.1	7.2	7.0	7.0	7.0	7.0	7.1
2008	7.0	7.0	6.9	6.8	6.9	7.0	7.0	7.1	6.9	6.9	6.9	6.9	6.9
2009	6.8	6.8	6.7	6.6	6.8	6.7	6.7	6.7	6.7	6.7	6.7	6.7	6.7
2010	6.6	6.6	6.5	6.5	6.5	6.6	6.6	6.6	6.5	6.4	6.5	6.5	6.5
2011	6.4	6.4	6.4	6.3	6.4	6.5	6.5	6.5	6.4	6.4	6.3	6.3	6.4
2012	6.2	6.3	6.2	6.2	6.3	6.3	6.3	6.3	6.1	6.1	6.1	6.1	6.2
2013	6.0	6.0	6.0	6.0	6.1	6.1	6.1	6.2	6.0	5.9	6.0	6.0	6.0
2014	6.0	6.0	6.0	6.0	6.1	6.2	6.2	6.1	6.0	5.9	5.9	5.9	6.0
2015	5.8	5.8	5.8	5.9	6.0	5.9	5.9	6.0	5.9	5.9	5.9	6.0	5.9
Financial Activities													
2005	28.2	28.0	28.2	27.9	28.2	28.8	28.6	28.6	28.7	28.5	28.6	29.2	28.5
2006	29.0	29.0	29.1	29.0	29.2	29.5	29.7	29.9	29.8	29.8	29.9	30.2	29.5
2007	30.2	30.4	30.7	30.6	30.8	31.3	31.3	31.2	31.1	31.2	31.2	31.2	30.9
2008	31.0	31.0	31.3	30.9	31.2	31.5	31.4	31.1	31.0	30.6	30.6	30.7	31.0
2009	30.7	30.8	30.9	30.7	30.6	30.9	30.6	30.3	30.0	29.9	29.8	29.9	30.4
2010	29.3	29.1	28.9	28.8	28.9	29.0	29.0	28.9	28.5	28.6	28.6	28.7	28.9
2011	28.3	28.3	28.3	28.1	28.1	28.3	28.1	28.1	27.9	27.9	27.9	28.2	28.1
2012	27.9	27.9	28.1	28.3	28.6	29.0	29.0	29.0	28.8	28.8	29.0	29.2	28.6
2013	29.1	29.3	29.4	29.4	29.7	30.1	30.0	30.0	29.8	29.8	30.0	30.1	29.7
2014	29.6	29.6	29.6	29.7	29.9	30.0	30.0	29.9	29.6	29.6	29.6	29.7	29.7
2015	29.4	29.3	29.4	29.4	29.6	29.9	30.1	29.9	29.7	29.3	29.5	29.7	29.6
Professional and Business Services													
2005	23.2	23.7	23.9	24.6	24.4	24.7	25.0	25.2	24.6	24.6	24.8	25.3	24.5
2006	24.6	25.0	25.0	25.5	25.7	26.0	26.1	26.1	25.8	26.1	26.1	26.4	25.7
2007	26.0	26.4	26.6	27.4	28.0	28.5	28.5	28.6	27.9	27.6	27.5	27.8	27.6
2008	27.4	27.6	27.8	28.2	28.2	28.6	28.5	28.8	28.1	27.8	27.7	27.8	28.0
2009	27.1	27.0	26.7	26.7	27.0	27.2	27.2	27.1	26.6	26.5	26.5	26.6	26.9
2010	26.2	26.4	26.6	27.6	27.6	27.9	28.2	28.2	27.7	28.1	27.8	28.0	27.5
2011	27.4	27.6	27.8	28.6	28.8	29.1	29.4	29.3	29.0	29.1	29.0	29.3	28.7
2012	28.3	28.4	28.7	29.1	29.2	29.6	29.9	30.0	29.5	29.3	29.2	29.1	29.2
2013	28.5	28.6	28.8	29.1	29.7	29.9	29.9	29.9	29.4	30.2	30.2	30.2	29.5
2014	29.5	29.5	29.4	30.4	30.8	31.1	31.1	30.9	30.3	30.4	30.3	30.3	30.3
2015	29.7	29.7	30.0	30.5	30.7	31.1	31.4	31.3	30.7	30.5	30.9	31.1	30.6
Education and Health Services													
2005	56.8	57.0	57.3	57.5	57.3	57.2	56.6	57.0	57.6	57.9	58.2	58.4	57.4
2006	57.8	58.0	58.3	58.4	58.4	58.2	57.9	58.2	58.9	59.0	59.5	59.6	58.5
2007	58.9	59.1	59.5	59.8	60.1	59.8	59.6	59.9	60.5	60.9	61.2	61.3	60.1
2008	61.2	61.5	61.7	61.6	62.0	61.9	61.4	61.9	62.2	62.7	63.0	63.4	62.0
2009	62.6	62.7	62.9	63.0	63.2	63.2	62.7	62.6	63.1	63.7	64.1	64.5	63.2
2010	63.5	63.8	64.1	64.2	64.6	64.5	64.3	64.1	64.5	65.0	65.2	65.6	64.5
2011	64.5	64.7	65.0	64.9	65.5	65.4	64.9	65.2	65.3	65.9	66.2	66.5	65.3
2012	65.6	65.9	66.3	67.1	67.5	67.6	66.9	66.9	67.3	67.6	68.0	68.1	67.1
2013	67.2	67.7	68.0	68.0	68.7	68.1	67.6	67.6	67.8	68.1	68.4	68.6	68.0
2014	67.7	68.1	68.3	68.4	68.9	68.6	68.0	67.9	68.1	68.4	68.5	69.0	68.3
2015	67.9	68.5	69.0	69.3	69.7	69.5	68.6	68.6	69.1	69.6	69.6	69.6	69.1

1. Employment by Industry: South Dakota, 2005–2015—*Continued*

(Numbers in thousands, not seasonally adjusted)

Industry and year	January	February	March	April	May	June	July	August	September	October	November	December	Annual average
Leisure and Hospitality													
2005	37.0	37.0	37.8	39.9	42.7	45.7	46.5	48.1	44.1	41.5	39.8	39.7	41.7
2006	37.9	38.0	38.8	40.4	43.8	46.7	46.9	49.0	44.7	42.6	41.0	40.6	42.5
2007	39.0	39.1	39.7	41.1	44.2	46.7	47.5	49.5	45.0	43.1	41.5	41.0	43.1
2008	39.1	39.3	39.9	41.3	44.1	47.1	47.6	49.3	45.2	43.3	41.4	41.0	43.2
2009	39.0	39.1	39.8	40.7	44.0	46.6	47.4	48.9	45.5	42.6	41.0	40.3	42.9
2010	38.2	38.6	39.2	41.0	44.0	47.0	47.1	49.4	45.4	43.5	41.7	41.1	43.0
2011	38.9	39.2	39.8	41.4	43.9	46.5	47.5	49.6	46.2	43.9	42.0	41.7	43.4
2012	39.8	40.2	41.1	42.5	45.5	48.0	48.4	50.2	46.6	44.5	42.6	42.4	44.3
2013	40.4	40.5	41.4	42.1	45.8	48.5	48.8	50.5	46.9	44.9	43.4	42.9	44.7
2014	41.3	41.6	42.3	43.3	46.7	48.9	49.0	50.9	47.8	45.8	43.8	43.6	45.4
2015	41.5	42.1	42.8	44.1	47.2	49.7	50.2	52.0	48.3	46.3	44.3	43.2	46.0
Other Services													
2005	15.3	15.4	15.4	15.5	15.6	15.7	15.7	15.7	15.6	15.4	15.5	15.5	15.5
2006	15.3	15.3	15.4	15.5	15.7	15.8	15.9	15.9	15.8	15.7	15.7	15.7	15.6
2007	15.6	15.6	15.7	15.7	15.9	16.0	16.0	15.9	15.8	15.7	15.6	15.7	15.8
2008	15.5	15.6	15.6	15.8	16.0	16.1	16.2	16.2	16.0	16.0	15.8	15.8	15.9
2009	15.6	15.6	15.5	15.6	15.8	15.9	15.9	15.8	15.6	15.6	15.5	15.6	15.7
2010	15.4	15.4	15.5	15.6	15.7	15.9	15.9	15.8	15.6	15.6	15.4	15.5	15.6
2011	15.3	15.3	15.4	15.5	15.6	15.9	15.9	15.9	15.6	15.6	15.5	15.7	15.6
2012	15.6	15.5	15.6	15.7	15.9	16.1	16.2	16.1	15.8	15.8	15.7	15.8	15.8
2013	15.6	15.7	15.7	15.9	16.1	16.2	16.2	16.0	15.8	15.7	15.8	15.7	15.9
2014	15.6	15.5	15.6	15.7	16.0	16.1	16.2	16.0	15.7	15.6	15.6	15.7	15.8
2015	15.5	15.6	15.6	15.8	15.9	16.2	16.3	16.2	15.8	15.6	16.0	15.8	15.9
Government													
2005	74.9	75.4	75.9	76.1	77.3	77.0	71.8	71.5	75.3	76.0	76.2	76.0	75.3
2006	74.4	75.5	75.8	75.9	77.5	77.3	71.9	72.0	74.9	76.1	76.4	76.1	75.3
2007	74.2	75.8	75.8	75.8	77.6	76.8	72.6	72.8	75.3	76.4	76.6	76.3	75.5
2008	74.7	76.5	76.5	76.6	78.4	76.9	72.1	73.3	76.0	77.6	77.7	77.6	76.2
2009	76.1	77.3	77.8	78.6	80.4	78.8	74.8	74.7	78.1	79.1	79.3	78.4	77.8
2010	77.1	78.4	79.4	79.8	81.2	80.3	75.2	75.3	78.7	79.7	79.8	79.4	78.7
2011	77.6	79.0	79.1	79.4	79.8	79.9	74.3	73.5	77.2	78.8	78.7	78.9	78.0
2012	76.8	77.7	78.4	78.7	78.9	78.6	73.5	73.0	77.4	79.0	79.2	78.7	77.5
2013	76.9	78.2	78.4	78.0	78.7	77.5	72.6	73.2	77.8	78.7	78.9	78.5	77.3
2014	77.0	78.2	78.5	78.6	79.4	78.5	73.8	74.1	78.4	79.1	79.3	78.8	77.8
2015	76.7	78.0	78.4	78.8	79.6	78.8	74.0	73.6	78.1	79.7	79.1	79.2	77.8

2. Average Weekly Hours by Selected Industry: South Dakota, 2011–2015

(Not seasonally adjusted)

Industry and year	January	February	March	April	May	June	July	August	September	October	November	December	Annual average
Total Private													
2011	33.8	33.7	33.8	33.8	34.1	34.1	34.0	33.9	33.9	34.3	34.0	33.8	33.9
2012	34.3	34.1	34.1	34.6	34.6	35.5	35.5	35.1	35.3	34.6	34.3	34.5	34.7
2013	33.9	33.9	34.0	33.2	34.3	35.5	34.6	35.1	35.3	34.4	34.6	34.8	34.5
2014	33.7	34.5	34.5	34.1	34.5	35.1	34.4	34.6	34.2	34.3	34.3	34.0	34.4
2015	33.5	34.2	34.0	33.7	33.7	34.2	34.3	34.7	34.0	34.1	34.4	33.5	34.0
Goods-Producing													
2011	38.2	38.0	39.3	39.5	40.0	39.7	39.7	39.8	40.1	40.5	40.1	39.8	39.6
2012	39.2	39.4	39.6	40.7	41.0	41.2	41.1	41.3	41.2	41.4	40.6	39.9	40.6
2013	38.7	39.5	39.9	38.4	40.3	41.7	41.6	42.1	42.7	41.4	41.8	40.8	40.8
2014	39.8	40.6	40.3	40.8	41.4	40.7	40.4	40.7	40.3	40.9	39.9	39.9	40.5
2015	38.7	39.5	39.5	39.6	40.0	40.1	41.1	41.2	40.2	40.8	40.8	39.7	40.1
Mining, Logging, and Construction													
2011	36.8	36.7	37.7	38.9	38.9	40.1	39.9	40.2	40.0	41.1	41.0	38.6	39.3
2012	37.9	38.2	38.6	39.9	41.9	42.9	42.6	42.7	42.6	42.9	41.2	39.8	41.1
2013	38.0	38.7	37.8	35.8	40.7	42.6	42.1	43.1	43.5	41.0	41.4	37.2	40.4
2014	36.1	38.7	38.1	40.9	41.2	39.8	40.5	39.6	38.5	38.4	37.9	37.4	39.0
2015	36.5	36.9	37.8	38.1	38.3	40.0	41.4	41.3	40.4	41.2	39.6	37.9	39.3
Manufacturing													
2011	38.9	38.7	39.9	39.9	40.6	39.4	39.4	39.5	40.2	40.1	39.7	40.4	39.7
2012	39.8	39.9	40.1	41.2	40.4	40.1	40.2	40.6	40.5	40.6	40.4	40.0	40.3
2013	38.9	39.7	40.8	39.6	40.2	41.3	41.1	41.5	42.2	41.7	42.1	42.6	41.0
2014	41.5	41.5	41.3	40.7	41.4	41.3	40.4	41.3	41.4	42.2	41.1	41.3	41.3
2015	39.6	40.5	40.2	40.3	40.9	40.2	40.9	41.1	40.1	40.5	41.4	40.6	40.5
Trade, Transportation, and Utilities													
2011	33.2	33.1	32.9	33.0	33.6	33.5	33.2	33.0	32.9	33.3	32.7	32.5	33.1
2012	33.2	33.2	33.3	34.1	34.1	34.7	34.5	34.2	33.6	33.5	33.2	33.2	33.7
2013	32.7	33.0	33.0	32.4	34.3	34.9	34.2	34.3	33.9	33.9	33.5	33.2	33.6
2014	32.9	33.0	33.2	33.7	34.6	35.0	34.3	34.5	34.0	34.5	34.5	34.2	34.0
2015	33.6	34.3	34.2	33.9	34.1	34.5	34.3	34.7	34.0	33.8	34.2	33.1	34.1
Professional and Business Services													
2011	37.5	37.2	37.2	37.6	38.7	38.4	37.7	38.3	37.6	39.2	38.1	37.8	38.0
2012	38.3	38.1	37.5	37.7	37.7	38.4	37.0	37.3	37.5	37.9	36.7	37.4	37.6
2013	37.1	37.0	36.8	36.1	36.7	38.1	36.8	37.4	37.3	36.3	37.1	37.0	37.0
2014	35.6	37.1	36.5	35.9	35.8	36.1	34.9	35.2	35.0	34.9	35.7	35.6	35.7
2015	35.8	37.3	36.9	36.9	36.2	37.0	36.3	37.0	36.3	36.3	36.6	35.5	36.5
Education and Health Services													
2011	32.0	31.7	31.3	31.3	30.6	31.2	31.6	30.9	31.5	30.9	31.4	30.6	31.2
2012	30.9	30.6	31.4	31.0	31.6	33.3	32.8	32.4	33.6	31.8	31.9	33.0	32.0
2013	32.8	33.0	33.1	33.0	32.8	33.7	32.2	32.2	32.5	31.6	32.3	32.7	32.7
2014	31.2	32.3	32.9	31.4	31.2	32.8	31.7	32.8	32.3	31.7	32.3	32.2	32.1
2015	32.3	32.7	32.4	32.2	31.7	32.0	31.8	32.7	32.3	32.4	33.1	32.6	32.3
Leisure and Hospitality													
2011	22.9	22.7	23.1	22.7	23.3	23.8	24.5	25.3	23.0	23.4	22.8	22.7	23.4
2012	23.6	23.8	23.6	23.5	23.2	24.8	26.8	26.2	25.2	24.3	24.0	24.2	24.5
2013	23.6	24.0	23.8	22.9	23.9	25.5	25.9	25.6	25.0	23.9	23.3	23.5	24.3
2014	22.5	23.7	24.0	23.0	23.4	25.6	25.3	25.1	24.2	24.0	23.7	23.3	24.0
2015	22.6	24.0	23.9	23.1	23.4	25.0	25.5	26.1	24.5	24.1	24.2	23.5	24.2

3. Average Hourly Earnings by Selected Industry: South Dakota, 2011–2015

(Dollars, not seasonally adjusted)

Industry and year	January	February	March	April	May	June	July	August	September	October	November	December	Annual average
Total Private													
2011	19.20	19.14	19.14	19.21	18.96	18.66	18.72	18.74	18.98	19.19	19.26	19.45	19.05
2012	19.50	19.41	19.34	19.53	19.27	19.14	19.28	19.13	19.63	19.64	19.51	19.74	19.42
2013	19.40	19.61	19.42	19.89	19.56	19.40	19.41	19.52	19.89	19.54	19.75	20.05	19.62
2014	20.00	20.13	20.10	20.17	20.16	19.87	19.89	19.94	20.22	20.45	20.61	20.57	20.17
2015	20.94	20.93	20.88	20.91	20.99	20.72	20.68	20.79	21.04	21.33	21.23	21.39	20.98
Goods-Producing													
2011	19.75	19.68	19.55	19.44	19.12	19.02	18.97	18.99	19.09	19.11	18.80	18.96	19.19
2012	19.25	18.97	19.01	19.01	18.77	18.72	18.96	18.83	19.06	19.08	18.74	19.40	18.98
2013	19.42	19.68	19.34	19.54	19.35	19.13	19.17	19.13	19.61	19.58	19.56	19.95	19.45
2014	19.97	20.29	20.01	20.14	20.42	20.35	20.42	20.59	20.74	21.04	20.88	20.95	20.49
2015	21.85	21.77	21.60	21.63	21.49	21.55	21.31	21.58	21.54	21.97	21.79	22.06	21.67
Mining, Logging, and Construction													
2011	21.15	21.16	21.23	20.71	20.38	19.82	19.68	19.36	19.48	19.39	19.41	19.93	20.04
2012	20.32	20.14	20.05	19.96	19.38	19.10	19.34	19.22	19.39	19.42	19.43	19.96	19.59
2013	20.06	20.27	19.85	20.12	19.65	19.41	19.11	19.44	19.96	20.05	20.02	20.35	19.82
2014	20.99	21.28	21.15	20.98	21.27	20.38	20.90	21.42	21.99	22.52	21.11	22.03	21.34
2015	22.56	22.54	22.65	22.71	22.25	22.55	22.18	22.49	22.40	22.77	22.68	23.18	22.57
Manufacturing													
2011	19.13	19.05	18.83	18.81	18.46	18.54	18.53	18.76	18.87	18.95	18.46	18.49	18.73
2012	18.78	18.47	18.54	18.54	18.44	18.50	18.73	18.60	18.87	18.90	18.38	19.13	18.66
2013	19.15	19.44	19.13	19.29	19.19	18.96	19.21	18.95	19.40	19.32	19.32	19.78	19.26
2014	19.56	19.88	19.53	19.73	19.95	20.33	20.14	20.13	20.09	20.30	20.77	20.46	20.08
2015	21.55	21.45	21.12	21.09	21.09	20.96	20.78	21.04	21.04	21.49	21.31	21.50	21.20
Trade, Transportation, and Utilities													
2011	19.20	19.40	19.43	19.83	19.54	18.70	18.82	18.97	19.00	19.22	19.10	18.96	19.18
2012	19.27	19.55	19.29	19.55	19.11	19.08	19.24	18.96	19.82	19.68	19.64	19.87	19.42
2013	19.60	19.51	19.27	19.75	19.42	19.06	18.69	18.64	18.83	19.01	19.30	19.03	19.17
2014	19.26	19.43	19.32	19.55	19.65	19.32	19.39	19.36	19.42	19.50	19.87	19.91	19.50
2015	19.77	19.56	19.50	19.40	19.91	19.75	19.87	19.91	20.17	20.19	20.04	20.09	19.85
Professional and Business Services													
2011	23.46	22.89	23.01	22.93	22.70	22.34	22.79	22.63	23.54	23.95	24.19	23.98	23.20
2012	23.32	22.42	22.82	23.45	23.13	22.45	23.52	22.95	23.74	23.37	22.97	23.55	23.14
2013	23.15	23.47	23.43	23.74	23.76	23.55	23.65	23.37	24.22	23.84	24.47	24.26	23.75
2014	24.55	24.28	24.61	24.36	24.13	23.65	23.78	23.12	24.02	24.17	24.33	24.47	24.12
2015	24.42	24.43	24.69	24.68	24.23	24.05	24.57	24.73	24.80	24.96	24.98	24.64	24.60
Education and Health Services													
2011	18.65	18.52	18.50	18.44	18.00	17.80	18.28	18.04	18.00	18.09	18.31	18.05	18.22
2012	18.46	18.35	18.17	18.34	18.46	18.93	18.86	18.89	18.87	18.67	18.73	18.85	18.64
2013	18.20	18.51	18.63	19.53	18.94	19.36	19.76	20.52	20.48	20.59	20.43	20.47	19.61
2014	20.60	20.65	20.88	20.75	20.81	20.61	20.74	21.40	21.30	21.54	21.64	21.46	21.03
2015	21.81	22.31	22.08	22.12	22.42	22.04	22.08	22.42	22.73	22.99	22.76	22.81	22.38
Leisure and Hospitality													
2011	11.05	10.99	10.90	10.81	10.74	10.42	10.47	10.91	10.89	10.85	11.18	11.30	10.86
2012	11.46	11.47	11.69	11.72	11.61	11.26	11.21	11.38	11.66	11.80	11.84	12.01	11.58
2013	11.97	12.09	11.89	11.93	11.70	11.41	11.46	11.48	11.80	12.09	12.23	12.44	11.85
2014	12.50	12.39	12.50	12.45	12.26	11.97	11.88	11.98	12.32	12.52	12.56	12.76	12.32
2015	13.10	13.01	13.10	13.15	12.88	12.33	12.52	12.63	12.88	12.99	13.14	13.04	12.87

4. Average Weekly Earnings by Selected Industry: South Dakota, 2011–2015

(Dollars, not seasonally adjusted)

Industry and year	January	February	March	April	May	June	July	August	September	October	November	December	Annual average
Total Private													
2011	648.96	645.02	646.93	649.30	646.54	636.31	636.48	635.29	643.42	658.22	654.84	657.41	645.80
2012	668.85	661.88	659.49	675.74	666.74	679.47	684.44	671.46	692.94	679.54	669.19	681.03	673.87
2013	657.66	664.78	660.28	660.35	670.91	688.70	671.59	685.15	702.12	672.18	683.35	697.74	676.89
2014	674.00	694.49	693.45	687.80	695.52	697.44	684.22	689.92	691.52	701.44	706.92	699.38	693.85
2015	701.49	715.81	709.92	704.67	707.36	708.62	709.32	721.41	715.36	727.35	730.31	716.57	713.32
Goods-Producing													
2011	754.45	747.84	768.32	767.88	764.80	755.09	753.11	755.80	765.51	773.96	753.88	754.61	759.92
2012	754.60	747.42	752.80	773.71	769.57	771.26	779.26	777.68	785.27	789.91	760.84	774.06	770.59
2013	751.55	777.36	771.67	750.34	779.81	797.72	797.47	805.37	837.35	810.61	817.61	813.96	793.56
2014	794.81	823.77	806.40	821.71	845.39	828.25	824.97	838.01	835.82	860.54	833.11	835.91	829.85
2015	845.60	859.92	853.20	856.55	859.60	864.16	875.84	889.10	865.91	896.38	889.03	875.78	868.97
Mining, Logging, and Construction													
2011	778.32	776.57	800.37	805.62	792.78	794.78	785.23	778.27	779.20	796.93	795.81	769.30	787.57
2012	770.13	769.35	773.93	796.40	812.02	819.39	823.88	820.69	826.01	833.12	800.52	794.41	805.15
2013	762.28	784.45	750.33	720.30	799.76	826.87	804.53	837.86	868.26	822.05	828.83	757.02	800.73
2014	757.74	823.54	805.82	858.08	876.32	811.12	846.45	848.23	846.62	864.77	800.07	823.92	832.26
2015	823.44	831.73	856.17	865.25	852.18	902.00	918.25	928.84	904.96	938.12	898.13	878.52	887.00
Manufacturing													
2011	744.16	737.24	751.32	750.52	749.48	730.48	730.08	741.02	758.57	759.90	732.86	747.00	743.58
2012	747.44	736.95	743.45	763.85	744.98	741.85	752.95	755.16	764.24	767.34	742.55	765.20	752.00
2013	744.94	771.77	780.50	763.88	771.44	783.05	789.53	786.43	818.68	805.64	813.37	842.63	789.66
2014	811.74	825.02	806.59	803.01	825.93	839.63	813.66	831.37	831.73	856.66	853.65	845.00	829.30
2015	853.38	868.73	849.02	849.93	862.58	842.59	849.90	864.74	843.70	870.35	882.23	872.90	858.60
Trade, Transportation, and Utilities													
2011	637.44	642.14	639.25	654.39	656.54	626.45	624.82	626.01	625.10	640.03	624.57	616.20	634.86
2012	639.76	649.06	642.36	666.66	651.65	662.08	663.78	648.43	665.95	659.28	652.05	659.68	654.45
2013	640.92	643.83	635.91	639.90	666.11	665.19	639.20	639.35	638.34	644.44	646.55	631.80	644.11
2014	633.65	641.19	641.42	658.84	679.89	676.20	665.08	667.92	660.28	672.75	685.52	680.92	663.00
2015	664.27	670.91	666.90	657.66	678.93	681.38	681.54	690.88	685.78	682.42	685.37	664.98	676.89
Professional and Business Services													
2011	879.75	851.51	855.97	862.17	878.49	857.86	859.18	866.73	885.10	938.84	921.64	906.44	881.60
2012	893.16	854.20	855.75	884.07	872.00	862.08	870.24	856.04	890.25	885.72	843.00	880.77	870.06
2013	858.87	868.39	862.22	857.01	871.99	897.26	870.32	874.04	903.41	865.39	907.84	897.62	878.75
2014	873.98	900.79	898.27	874.52	863.85	853.77	829.92	813.82	840.70	843.53	868.58	871.13	861.08
2015	874.24	911.24	911.06	910.69	877.13	889.85	891.89	915.01	900.24	906.05	914.27	874.72	897.90
Education and Health Services													
2011	596.80	587.08	579.05	577.17	550.80	555.36	577.65	557.44	567.00	558.98	574.93	552.33	568.46
2012	570.41	561.51	570.54	568.54	583.34	630.37	618.61	612.04	634.03	593.71	597.49	622.05	596.48
2013	596.96	610.83	616.65	644.49	621.23	652.43	636.27	660.74	665.60	650.64	659.89	669.37	641.25
2014	642.72	667.00	686.95	651.55	649.27	676.01	657.46	701.92	687.99	682.82	698.97	691.01	675.06
2015	704.46	729.54	715.39	712.26	710.71	705.28	702.14	733.13	734.18	744.88	753.36	743.61	722.87
Leisure and Hospitality													
2011	253.05	249.47	251.79	245.39	250.24	248.00	256.52	276.02	250.47	253.89	254.90	256.51	254.12
2012	270.46	272.99	275.88	275.42	269.35	279.25	300.43	298.16	293.83	286.74	284.16	290.64	283.71
2013	282.49	290.16	282.98	273.20	279.63	290.96	296.81	293.89	295.00	288.95	284.96	292.34	287.96
2014	281.25	293.64	300.00	286.35	286.88	306.43	300.56	300.70	298.14	300.48	297.67	297.31	295.68
2015	296.06	312.24	313.09	303.77	301.39	308.25	319.26	329.64	315.56	313.06	317.99	306.44	311.45

TENNESSEE
At a Glance

Population:
  2005 estimate: 5,991,057
  2010 census: 6,346,105
  2015 estimate: 6,600,299

Percent change in population:
  2005–2014: 10.2%
  2010–2014: 4.0%

Percent change in total nonfarm employment:
  2005–2015: 5.4%

Industry with the largest growth in employment, 2005–2015 (thousands):
  Education and health services, 82.1

Industry with the largest decline or smallest growth in employment, 2005–2015 (thousands):
  Manufacturing, –76.1

Civilian labor force:
  2005: 2,904,794
  2010: 3,090,795
  2015: 3,062,775

Unemployment rate and rank among states (highest to lowest):
  2005: 5.6%, 11th
  2010: 9.7%, 18th
  2015: 5.8%, 15th

Over-the-year change in unemployment rates:
  2012–2013: 0.0%
  2013–2014: –1.3%
  2014–2015: –0.7%

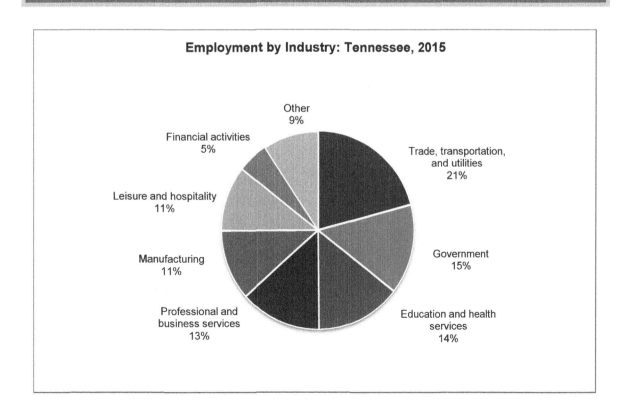

Employment by Industry: Tennessee, 2015

Other 9%
Financial activities 5%
Leisure and hospitality 11%
Manufacturing 11%
Professional and business services 13%
Trade, transportation, and utilities 21%
Government 15%
Education and health services 14%

1. Employment by Industry: Tennessee, 2005–2015

(Numbers in thousands, not seasonally adjusted)

Industry and year	January	February	March	April	May	June	July	August	September	October	November	December	Annual average
Total Nonfarm													
2005	2,671.3	2,696.1	2,718.4	2,739.5	2,746.5	2,743.7	2,731.8	2,753.6	2,776.3	2,767.1	2,784.7	2,788.3	2,743.1
2006	2,727.1	2,734.8	2,765.3	2,781.4	2,791.6	2,791.4	2,769.8	2,796.8	2,810.2	2,793.8	2,811.4	2,818.6	2,782.7
2007	2,744.9	2,753.7	2,784.0	2,787.9	2,799.3	2,798.0	2,782.4	2,811.2	2,821.7	2,815.9	2,833.6	2,836.4	2,797.4
2008	2,762.4	2,771.9	2,790.1	2,797.1	2,805.4	2,784.3	2,758.7	2,779.0	2,779.4	2,766.1	2,758.6	2,745.1	2,774.8
2009	2,647.7	2,636.8	2,634.7	2,629.8	2,630.2	2,599.3	2,582.6	2,600.2	2,609.6	2,616.2	2,629.1	2,621.9	2,619.8
2010	2,556.9	2,562.4	2,585.2	2,614.8	2,638.0	2,613.2	2,600.4	2,619.4	2,635.4	2,645.7	2,657.1	2,655.5	2,615.3
2011	2,587.6	2,609.5	2,632.1	2,660.7	2,669.4	2,646.1	2,643.0	2,670.7	2,688.3	2,697.4	2,716.8	2,715.4	2,661.4
2012	2,648.9	2,667.6	2,699.2	2,715.6	2,725.2	2,705.7	2,687.6	2,714.8	2,734.1	2,745.4	2,766.6	2,769.0	2,715.0
2013	2,690.9	2,710.8	2,733.2	2,757.6	2,767.0	2,744.9	2,729.1	2,758.3	2,778.3	2,796.0	2,825.6	2,827.8	2,760.0
2014	2,752.5	2,764.8	2,791.5	2,815.2	2,824.9	2,800.4	2,792.3	2,825.4	2,847.6	2,863.4	2,890.6	2,897.3	2,822.2
2015	2,820.8	2,831.7	2,845.6	2,878.5	2,889.1	2,871.8	2,871.1	2,895.1	2,922.1	2,938.2	2,962.2	2,976.2	2,891.9
Total Private													
2005	2,263.5	2,280.9	2,301.9	2,325.3	2,333.9	2,346.5	2,342.3	2,354.7	2,360.6	2,349.5	2,365.6	2,370.3	2,332.9
2006	2,317.6	2,319.8	2,347.7	2,361.9	2,373.7	2,389.9	2,374.5	2,389.5	2,390.2	2,372.7	2,387.8	2,396.3	2,368.5
2007	2,329.5	2,333.9	2,361.5	2,367.9	2,378.8	2,395.8	2,384.9	2,399.6	2,396.9	2,387.3	2,403.1	2,408.3	2,379.0
2008	2,340.5	2,344.6	2,360.6	2,366.6	2,374.4	2,381.5	2,355.5	2,362.8	2,351.7	2,330.0	2,321.4	2,309.3	2,349.9
2009	2,222.4	2,206.7	2,202.8	2,196.3	2,197.6	2,198.2	2,180.4	2,185.5	2,180.4	2,178.5	2,190.3	2,186.6	2,193.8
2010	2,128.5	2,129.8	2,150.7	2,176.2	2,190.4	2,201.9	2,193.6	2,200.6	2,199.4	2,207.4	2,218.2	2,219.7	2,184.7
2011	2,158.5	2,175.3	2,196.8	2,225.8	2,236.4	2,246.1	2,246.9	2,256.3	2,258.8	2,263.7	2,282.3	2,283.9	2,235.9
2012	2,226.8	2,237.2	2,265.7	2,282.9	2,298.3	2,310.2	2,295.3	2,310.1	2,309.0	2,314.1	2,333.3	2,336.8	2,293.3
2013	2,272.9	2,283.7	2,304.5	2,320.6	2,335.2	2,346.9	2,335.3	2,351.9	2,351.3	2,361.3	2,390.9	2,393.5	2,337.3
2014	2,329.4	2,333.4	2,358.5	2,381.1	2,395.1	2,404.3	2,398.2	2,417.8	2,418.0	2,427.9	2,451.6	2,459.9	2,397.9
2015	2,395.4	2,399.0	2,412.9	2,445.2	2,463.0	2,477.4	2,478.6	2,488.2	2,491.7	2,502.4	2,523.0	2,538.7	2,468.0
Goods-Producing													
2005	526.0	527.4	531.2	532.4	535.0	538.4	534.3	538.1	539.7	535.6	536.5	533.3	534.0
2006	530.3	529.7	535.0	536.7	538.4	541.8	535.4	538.5	537.7	529.6	527.4	525.2	533.8
2007	517.8	517.4	522.1	520.0	518.2	522.0	517.1	519.4	518.5	515.5	513.6	512.2	517.8
2008	502.0	502.2	503.6	501.9	502.8	503.9	494.7	496.3	491.5	482.8	473.2	464.9	493.3
2009	443.7	435.5	430.9	423.0	418.3	415.0	413.5	413.9	413.2	409.6	408.1	403.8	419.0
2010	393.2	391.5	396.4	402.6	404.6	409.3	408.2	409.8	409.9	408.7	407.8	406.5	404.0
2011	397.2	400.6	404.9	409.6	412.1	416.8	417.8	418.6	419.8	420.7	421.4	417.7	413.1
2012	409.9	412.1	417.3	419.8	422.7	427.0	425.0	428.4	427.4	426.2	426.2	425.1	422.3
2013	417.1	418.9	421.9	422.9	425.7	428.5	426.9	429.8	430.2	431.3	431.9	430.6	426.3
2014	424.6	426.2	429.6	431.9	435.0	436.5	436.4	440.5	440.4	441.2	443.4	444.3	435.8
2015	438.2	439.7	440.0	445.0	449.1	452.3	452.3	454.3	455.9	457.0	459.8	461.2	450.4
Service-Providing													
2005	2,145.3	2,168.7	2,187.2	2,207.1	2,211.5	2,205.3	2,197.5	2,215.5	2,236.6	2,231.5	2,248.2	2,255.0	2,209.1
2006	2,196.8	2,205.1	2,230.3	2,244.7	2,253.2	2,249.6	2,234.4	2,258.3	2,272.5	2,264.2	2,284.0	2,293.4	2,248.9
2007	2,227.1	2,236.3	2,261.9	2,267.9	2,281.1	2,276.0	2,265.3	2,291.8	2,303.2	2,300.4	2,320.0	2,324.2	2,279.6
2008	2,260.4	2,269.7	2,286.5	2,295.2	2,302.6	2,280.4	2,264.0	2,282.7	2,287.9	2,283.3	2,285.4	2,280.2	2,281.5
2009	2,204.0	2,201.3	2,203.8	2,206.8	2,211.9	2,184.3	2,169.1	2,186.3	2,196.4	2,206.6	2,221.0	2,218.1	2,200.8
2010	2,163.7	2,170.9	2,188.8	2,212.2	2,233.4	2,203.9	2,192.2	2,209.6	2,225.5	2,237.0	2,249.3	2,249.0	2,211.3
2011	2,190.4	2,208.9	2,227.2	2,251.1	2,257.3	2,229.3	2,225.2	2,252.1	2,268.5	2,276.7	2,295.4	2,297.7	2,248.3
2012	2,239.0	2,255.5	2,281.9	2,295.8	2,302.5	2,278.7	2,262.6	2,286.4	2,306.7	2,319.2	2,340.4	2,343.9	2,292.7
2013	2,273.8	2,291.9	2,311.3	2,334.7	2,341.3	2,316.4	2,302.2	2,328.5	2,348.1	2,364.7	2,393.7	2,397.2	2,333.7
2014	2,327.9	2,338.6	2,361.9	2,383.3	2,389.9	2,363.9	2,355.9	2,384.9	2,407.2	2,422.2	2,447.2	2,453.0	2,386.3
2015	2,382.6	2,392.0	2,405.6	2,433.5	2,440.0	2,419.5	2,418.8	2,440.8	2,466.2	2,481.2	2,502.4	2,515.0	2,441.5
Mining, Logging and Construction													
2005	117.0	117.6	120.3	121.4	124.2	127.0	128.1	129.4	130.1	129.4	129.2	129.1	125.2
2006	126.4	126.9	131.6	133.3	135.2	138.3	137.4	138.4	138.6	136.5	135.5	134.8	134.4
2007	129.9	130.1	135.0	136.5	138.6	141.5	140.3	141.6	141.5	141.0	139.9	138.5	137.9
2008	132.7	132.6	134.0	134.3	135.6	136.3	134.7	134.7	133.0	130.2	127.1	123.2	132.4
2009	113.2	111.1	111.4	110.3	110.1	111.1	110.7	110.1	110.1	108.2	107.0	104.9	109.9
2010	97.5	96.8	100.1	104.8	105.6	108.2	108.5	108.8	108.9	108.9	107.3	105.9	105.1
2011	97.8	99.8	103.1	107.0	108.3	111.3	112.1	113.1	114.3	113.8	112.8	110.7	108.7
2012	104.3	104.9	107.7	107.8	109.3	110.9	110.5	111.6	111.9	110.4	109.4	107.9	108.9
2013	102.2	103.4	105.1	106.5	108.6	109.9	109.7	110.3	110.4	110.6	109.8	108.0	107.9
2014	103.6	104.2	107.1	109.6	111.8	111.7	112.4	113.4	113.4	114.1	115.0	114.6	110.9
2015	110.0	110.8	111.2	115.2	117.8	119.2	120.1	120.0	121.0	122.1	122.7	122.2	117.7

1. Employment by Industry: Tennessee, 2005–2015—*Continued*

(Numbers in thousands, not seasonally adjusted)

Industry and year	January	February	March	April	May	June	July	August	September	October	November	December	Annual average
Manufacturing													
2005	409.0	409.8	410.9	411.0	410.8	411.4	406.2	408.7	409.6	406.2	407.3	404.2	408.8
2006	403.9	402.8	403.4	403.4	403.2	403.5	398.0	400.1	399.1	393.1	391.9	390.4	399.4
2007	387.9	387.3	387.1	383.5	379.6	380.5	376.8	377.8	377.0	374.5	373.7	373.7	380.0
2008	369.3	369.6	369.6	367.6	367.2	367.6	360.0	361.6	358.5	352.6	346.1	341.7	361.0
2009	330.5	324.4	319.5	312.7	308.2	303.9	302.8	303.8	303.1	301.4	301.1	298.9	309.2
2010	295.7	294.7	296.3	297.8	299.0	301.1	299.7	301.0	301.0	299.8	300.5	300.6	298.9
2011	299.4	300.8	301.8	302.6	303.8	305.5	305.7	305.5	305.5	306.9	308.6	307.0	304.4
2012	305.6	307.2	309.6	312.0	313.4	316.1	314.5	316.8	315.5	315.8	316.8	317.2	313.4
2013	314.9	315.5	316.8	316.4	317.1	318.6	317.2	319.5	319.8	320.7	322.1	322.6	318.4
2014	321.0	322.0	322.5	322.3	323.2	324.8	324.0	327.1	327.0	327.1	328.4	329.7	324.9
2015	328.2	328.9	328.8	329.8	331.3	333.1	332.2	334.3	334.9	334.9	337.1	339.0	332.7
Trade, Transportation, and Utilities													
2005	578.4	585.4	590.5	593.6	595.8	595.8	599.5	600.2	601.7	602.0	613.5	620.0	598.0
2006	598.3	596.2	602.2	603.5	606.1	607.0	604.2	607.7	608.6	607.4	619.4	626.6	607.3
2007	603.8	600.6	607.1	606.3	609.1	609.6	606.8	609.5	610.3	611.2	623.5	628.4	610.5
2008	605.4	602.4	606.1	602.9	602.5	601.5	598.3	599.3	596.7	591.7	596.4	598.1	600.1
2009	571.7	564.4	561.8	557.0	557.7	557.1	553.8	555.1	553.1	554.2	562.0	565.8	559.5
2010	546.5	543.9	547.4	550.4	552.5	554.2	554.7	556.1	554.5	558.8	568.5	573.2	555.1
2011	550.4	550.2	553.9	559.9	561.7	563.4	562.9	564.3	563.9	568.4	579.7	583.7	563.5
2012	564.9	561.5	568.0	570.4	573.3	574.0	572.4	574.2	575.8	578.6	591.7	595.3	575.0
2013	572.5	571.0	572.6	575.3	577.7	579.8	579.4	580.6	579.0	583.5	597.5	603.3	581.0
2014	577.5	575.8	580.1	583.9	585.5	588.0	588.3	590.8	590.8	595.8	608.8	613.2	589.9
2015	589.2	585.8	588.1	594.6	598.4	602.0	604.8	606.7	605.8	608.2	621.0	631.2	603.0
Wholesale Trade													
2005	128.4	128.8	129.7	130.1	130.7	130.4	130.5	130.6	131.0	130.7	131.1	131.4	130.3
2006	130.0	130.6	131.4	131.7	132.3	132.5	132.6	132.9	133.0	132.4	132.5	132.5	132.0
2007	131.0	131.4	132.3	132.7	133.0	133.4	133.1	133.3	133.8	134.0	133.7	133.9	133.0
2008	132.5	132.9	133.1	132.8	133.1	132.5	131.8	131.9	131.7	130.5	129.3	128.2	131.7
2009	124.9	123.9	123.0	122.0	121.4	121.0	119.8	119.3	118.6	118.7	118.3	118.1	120.8
2010	116.6	116.5	117.2	117.2	117.3	117.2	116.9	116.8	116.3	116.6	116.5	116.3	116.8
2011	115.4	116.0	116.5	117.5	118.1	118.4	118.4	118.5	118.6	118.7	119.2	119.2	117.9
2012	118.1	118.9	119.6	120.1	120.8	121.1	120.7	121.1	120.9	121.2	121.2	121.2	120.4
2013	119.4	119.7	120.4	120.7	121.0	121.3	121.0	121.2	121.0	120.8	121.2	121.1	120.7
2014	119.5	119.6	120.1	120.1	120.7	120.8	120.4	120.3	120.7	120.1	120.4	120.8	120.3
2015	119.3	119.5	119.5	119.9	120.6	121.6	121.6	121.9	122.2	123.5	124.6	125.1	121.6
Retail Trade													
2005	311.7	318.1	321.0	322.2	323.5	323.7	324.1	323.7	324.1	324.8	334.9	339.7	324.3
2006	323.2	320.8	324.7	325.9	327.0	327.4	325.7	327.1	326.7	327.6	338.6	343.7	328.2
2007	327.1	323.5	328.3	327.1	329.0	329.1	327.3	328.0	328.3	330.0	342.3	346.5	330.5
2008	328.7	325.9	329.6	326.5	325.5	325.2	323.6	323.6	321.3	320.4	325.9	327.6	325.3
2009	310.6	305.9	305.1	303.7	305.1	305.4	304.5	305.5	304.2	305.1	313.1	316.2	307.0
2010	301.9	299.7	302.2	304.6	306.0	307.0	306.0	306.8	304.0	307.5	316.1	319.0	306.7
2011	303.3	302.1	304.5	307.5	308.1	309.0	308.7	308.9	307.6	309.6	319.1	321.8	309.2
2012	308.2	304.6	309.2	310.7	312.1	312.6	311.7	311.2	310.4	313.4	324.5	325.5	312.8
2013	309.7	307.5	308.8	310.2	312.4	313.7	314.1	314.3	313.3	317.0	327.3	330.9	314.9
2014	314.3	312.5	314.9	317.4	318.5	320.3	320.6	321.0	319.8	322.4	332.6	335.4	320.8
2015	317.8	315.4	317.4	322.0	324.1	325.8	326.0	327.2	325.6	327.6	335.9	339.4	325.4
Transportation and Utilities													
2005	138.3	138.5	139.8	141.3	141.6	141.7	144.9	145.9	146.6	146.5	147.5	148.9	143.5
2006	145.1	144.8	146.1	145.9	146.8	147.1	145.9	147.7	148.9	147.4	148.3	150.4	147.0
2007	145.7	145.7	146.5	146.5	147.1	147.1	146.4	148.2	148.2	147.2	147.5	148.0	147.0
2008	144.2	143.6	143.4	143.6	143.9	143.8	142.9	143.8	143.7	140.8	141.2	142.3	143.1
2009	136.2	134.6	133.7	131.3	131.2	130.7	129.5	130.3	130.3	130.4	130.6	131.5	131.7
2010	128.0	127.7	128.0	128.6	129.2	130.0	131.8	132.5	134.2	134.7	135.9	137.9	131.5
2011	131.7	132.1	132.9	134.9	135.5	136.0	135.8	136.9	137.7	140.1	141.4	142.7	136.5
2012	138.6	138.0	139.2	139.6	140.4	140.3	140.0	141.9	144.5	144.0	146.0	148.6	141.8
2013	143.4	143.8	143.4	144.4	144.3	144.8	144.3	145.1	144.7	145.7	149.0	151.3	145.4
2014	143.7	143.7	145.1	146.4	146.3	146.9	147.3	149.5	150.3	153.3	155.8	157.0	148.8
2015	152.1	150.9	151.2	152.7	153.7	154.6	157.2	157.6	158.0	157.1	160.5	166.7	156.0

1. Employment by Industry: Tennessee, 2005–2015—*Continued*

(Numbers in thousands, not seasonally adjusted)

Industry and year	January	February	March	April	May	June	July	August	September	October	November	December	Annual average
Information													
2005	49.7	49.7	49.6	49.5	49.7	49.9	49.4	49.2	48.8	48.8	49.3	49.3	49.4
2006	49.1	49.2	49.4	49.9	50.1	50.2	49.3	49.2	49.4	49.4	49.8	50.0	49.6
2007	49.1	49.3	49.2	49.6	50.1	50.4	50.7	50.6	50.6	50.6	51.2	51.8	50.3
2008	51.0	51.0	51.2	50.9	51.1	51.2	50.7	50.3	49.9	49.7	49.5	49.7	50.5
2009	49.1	48.8	48.3	47.6	47.3	46.8	46.2	46.1	45.8	45.5	45.9	45.7	46.9
2010	45.4	46.3	45.5	44.8	44.7	44.8	44.7	44.3	44.3	44.9	45.1	45.3	45.0
2011	44.3	44.1	44.1	44.1	44.1	43.9	43.7	43.9	43.3	43.0	43.3	43.2	43.8
2012	42.8	43.1	42.9	43.2	43.9	43.9	42.7	42.9	42.4	43.1	43.4	44.1	43.2
2013	43.5	43.8	44.0	43.8	44.3	44.8	44.2	44.2	43.6	43.8	44.4	44.3	44.1
2014	43.6	43.7	43.8	43.9	43.9	43.9	43.8	43.9	43.5	43.5	43.9	43.9	43.8
2015	43.3	43.5	43.5	43.8	44.0	44.3	44.1	44.2	43.8	43.5	43.9	44.0	43.8
Financial Activities													
2005	141.3	141.7	142.4	142.9	143.4	144.3	143.9	144.1	144.0	143.5	143.7	144.1	143.3
2006	142.5	142.8	143.5	143.1	143.6	144.3	143.7	144.2	143.7	143.2	143.5	144.2	143.5
2007	142.0	142.8	143.8	143.8	145.0	146.1	145.8	146.0	145.5	145.2	145.6	146.3	144.8
2008	144.5	144.9	145.2	145.1	145.6	146.3	145.8	145.7	144.9	144.3	144.1	144.0	145.0
2009	141.8	141.6	141.1	141.1	141.5	141.2	140.3	140.6	139.6	139.1	139.4	139.6	140.6
2010	137.7	137.6	137.5	138.6	138.5	137.9	137.5	137.3	135.9	135.6	135.7	135.6	137.1
2011	134.8	134.7	134.7	136.2	136.9	136.8	137.3	137.6	137.1	137.1	137.6	137.7	136.5
2012	136.4	136.9	137.0	137.0	137.5	137.5	137.5	137.4	136.7	136.8	137.1	137.5	137.1
2013	136.0	135.9	136.2	137.4	138.1	138.8	140.0	140.3	140.0	140.6	141.5	141.9	138.9
2014	141.0	141.6	142.3	143.2	144.0	144.4	145.1	145.3	145.1	145.6	145.8	146.4	144.2
2015	145.4	145.8	145.9	146.5	147.3	148.3	148.8	149.2	148.7	149.7	151.5	150.1	148.1
Professional and Business Services													
2005	300.6	304.4	306.5	309.9	308.7	310.6	308.3	315.1	319.6	319.8	322.6	325.6	312.6
2006	310.9	311.3	314.9	316.2	316.0	319.6	315.4	321.6	324.3	321.9	327.2	329.1	319.0
2007	310.8	312.6	316.0	318.0	319.3	322.6	321.9	326.5	328.6	328.2	332.7	333.7	322.6
2008	318.1	319.3	321.2	325.0	324.1	327.4	317.8	321.2	322.1	321.3	319.4	316.2	321.1
2009	297.9	296.8	294.1	291.0	291.0	290.6	284.5	289.4	291.3	297.2	301.8	300.9	293.9
2010	291.4	293.7	297.1	300.0	307.7	306.3	301.0	304.8	307.6	311.5	313.9	314.7	304.1
2011	304.9	311.7	316.0	319.5	319.2	320.6	320.9	325.9	328.0	331.4	336.4	338.9	322.8
2012	323.3	327.5	331.5	334.9	338.1	340.3	334.7	340.8	342.4	345.7	351.2	351.8	338.5
2013	337.7	341.1	344.8	346.8	349.5	351.7	345.8	355.7	358.4	363.3	376.5	377.1	354.0
2014	360.8	359.7	363.3	370.1	373.6	374.5	369.8	379.4	380.1	384.9	392.9	396.9	375.5
2015	378.1	377.9	381.2	386.7	389.7	392.6	390.9	395.9	397.1	403.0	406.7	411.2	392.6
Education and Health Services													
2005	325.5	327.7	328.4	332.0	332.0	331.7	332.5	334.3	336.6	336.7	337.7	338.5	332.8
2006	335.1	336.9	339.2	341.5	342.3	342.8	342.8	344.7	347.5	348.2	349.3	350.1	343.4
2007	345.4	348.4	350.2	350.1	350.8	350.6	352.2	355.0	357.8	356.7	357.1	358.0	352.7
2008	353.9	356.1	357.3	359.4	360.1	359.7	360.0	362.8	365.3	367.0	368.3	369.0	361.6
2009	363.7	364.9	365.0	368.0	367.3	368.0	367.3	367.7	370.8	372.0	372.9	373.4	368.4
2010	368.6	370.5	372.4	376.2	374.0	372.7	374.2	375.8	379.6	382.8	383.5	383.6	376.2
2011	378.2	382.1	383.0	386.8	386.4	382.7	384.0	385.8	390.6	392.3	393.4	393.0	386.5
2012	389.5	393.4	395.5	395.7	394.4	392.7	391.8	395.0	400.0	401.3	402.2	402.2	396.1
2013	396.9	401.0	402.6	402.7	401.4	397.9	395.4	398.2	403.5	405.5	406.8	406.5	401.5
2014	401.7	404.5	406.6	405.7	403.7	400.8	400.5	403.8	410.0	412.2	412.6	412.9	406.3
2015	408.7	411.4	413.2	413.9	411.6	408.9	409.5	411.4	418.1	422.5	423.5	426.4	414.9
Leisure and Hospitality													
2005	243.0	244.8	252.0	263.6	268.0	273.4	272.9	272.9	269.3	263.1	261.8	259.6	262.0
2006	252.7	254.3	262.7	270.2	275.3	280.2	280.8	280.8	276.1	270.9	269.0	268.6	270.1
2007	258.9	260.5	268.9	276.2	281.2	288.3	285.9	288.2	281.7	276.0	275.5	274.1	276.3
2008	262.4	264.3	270.7	276.6	282.2	285.1	283.1	282.5	277.4	269.3	267.2	264.4	273.8
2009	253.2	253.0	259.1	266.0	271.8	275.5	271.8	270.6	265.4	259.7	258.8	256.9	263.5
2010	247.2	247.4	254.5	263.7	267.7	274.2	270.9	270.3	265.8	262.7	261.3	258.0	262.0
2011	249.0	251.5	259.0	268.2	273.7	278.0	276.8	277.0	273.8	268.8	268.2	267.4	267.6
2012	258.2	260.1	269.6	277.8	283.4	288.5	285.3	286.6	279.9	278.2	277.4	277.0	276.8
2013	266.2	268.3	277.8	285.8	292.0	297.6	296.4	296.7	290.7	287.8	286.7	284.9	285.9
2014	276.0	277.2	286.8	296.3	302.4	308.5	307.0	307.9	302.2	298.8	298.1	296.4	296.5
2015	287.4	289.2	294.8	307.6	314.8	320.0	319.5	318.8	314.7	311.3	308.8	307.3	307.9

1. Employment by Industry: Tennessee, 2005–2015—*Continued*

(Numbers in thousands, not seasonally adjusted)

Industry and year	January	February	March	April	May	June	July	August	September	October	November	December	Annual average
Other Services													
2005	99.0	99.8	101.3	101.4	101.3	102.4	101.5	100.8	100.9	100.0	100.5	99.9	100.7
2006	98.7	99.4	100.8	100.8	101.9	104.0	102.9	102.8	102.9	102.1	102.2	102.5	101.8
2007	101.7	102.3	104.2	103.9	105.1	106.2	104.5	104.4	103.9	103.9	103.9	103.8	104.0
2008	103.2	104.4	105.3	104.8	106.0	106.4	105.1	104.7	103.9	103.9	103.3	103.0	104.5
2009	101.3	101.7	102.5	102.6	102.7	104.0	103.0	102.1	101.2	101.2	101.4	100.5	102.0
2010	98.5	98.9	99.9	99.9	100.7	102.5	102.4	102.2	101.8	102.4	102.4	102.8	101.2
2011	99.7	100.4	101.2	101.5	102.3	103.9	103.5	103.2	102.3	102.0	102.3	102.3	102.1
2012	101.8	102.6	103.9	104.1	105.0	106.3	105.9	104.8	104.4	104.2	104.1	103.8	104.2
2013	103.0	103.7	104.6	105.9	106.5	107.8	107.2	106.4	105.9	105.5	105.6	104.9	105.6
2014	104.2	104.7	106.0	106.1	107.0	107.7	107.3	106.2	105.9	105.9	106.1	105.9	106.1
2015	105.1	105.7	106.2	107.1	108.1	109.0	108.7	107.7	107.6	107.2	107.8	107.3	107.3
Government													
2005	407.8	415.2	416.5	414.2	412.6	397.2	389.5	398.9	415.7	417.6	419.1	418.0	410.2
2006	409.5	415.0	417.6	419.5	417.9	401.5	395.3	407.3	420.0	421.1	423.6	422.3	414.2
2007	415.4	419.8	422.5	420.0	420.5	402.2	397.5	411.6	424.8	428.6	430.5	428.1	418.5
2008	421.9	427.3	429.5	430.5	431.0	402.8	403.2	416.2	427.7	436.1	437.2	435.8	424.9
2009	425.3	430.1	431.9	433.5	432.6	401.1	402.2	414.7	429.2	437.7	438.8	435.3	426.0
2010	428.4	432.6	434.5	438.6	447.6	411.3	406.8	418.8	436.0	438.3	438.9	435.8	430.6
2011	429.1	434.2	435.3	434.9	433.0	400.0	396.1	414.4	429.5	433.7	434.5	431.5	425.5
2012	422.1	430.4	433.5	432.7	426.9	395.5	392.3	404.7	425.1	431.3	433.3	432.2	421.7
2013	418.0	427.1	428.7	437.0	431.8	398.0	393.8	406.4	427.0	434.7	434.7	434.3	422.6
2014	423.1	431.4	433.0	434.1	429.8	396.1	394.1	407.6	429.6	435.5	439.0	437.4	424.2
2015	425.4	432.7	432.7	433.3	426.1	394.4	392.5	406.9	430.4	435.8	439.2	437.5	423.9

2. Average Weekly Hours by Selected Industry: Tennessee, 2011–2015

(Not seasonally adjusted)

Industry and year	January	February	March	April	May	June	July	August	September	October	November	December	Annual average
Total Private													
2011............	34.5	34.8	35.3	35.2	35.5	35.3	35.1	35.3	35.0	35.6	35.0	35.2	35.2
2012............	35.2	35.1	35.0	35.6	35.2	35.4	35.6	35.5	35.8	35.2	35.4	35.6	35.4
2013............	34.7	35.2	35.2	35.2	35.2	35.9	35.2	35.4	35.7	35.3	35.3	35.7	35.3
2014............	34.8	35.0	35.6	35.2	35.3	35.7	35.2	35.4	35.1	34.9	35.6	35.4	35.3
2015............	34.7	34.7	35.2	35.0	35.1	35.3	35.2	35.8	35.0	35.2	35.5	35.6	35.2
Goods-Producing													
2011............	39.7	40.6	41.5	41.0	40.9	41.3	40.3	41.3	41.1	41.4	41.3	41.4	41.0
2012............	41.0	41.2	41.2	41.8	41.3	41.7	40.9	41.3	41.6	40.5	41.3	40.5	41.2
2013............	39.6	40.4	40.6	40.6	40.5	41.0	40.4	41.3	41.4	41.3	41.2	41.1	40.8
2014............	40.2	39.8	41.5	41.1	41.5	41.6	40.8	41.5	41.3	40.3	41.8	41.8	41.1
2015............	40.8	40.1	41.3	41.1	41.2	41.4	41.0	41.6	40.7	41.4	41.8	42.3	41.2
Mining, Logging, and Construction													
2011............	35.1	36.9	37.6	38.6	39.6	39.9	39.4	40.0	39.0	39.4	39.3	38.9	38.7
2012............	37.4	37.7	38.4	39.3	39.2	39.6	38.8	39.8	40.3	38.8	40.2	39.8	39.1
2013............	37.9	39.0	40.0	40.7	40.9	40.9	41.1	41.7	41.0	41.8	41.4	40.0	40.6
2014............	39.1	38.5	41.3	40.4	41.3	41.2	41.7	41.4	40.8	39.2	41.1	40.0	40.5
2015............	37.7	37.5	37.5	38.4	40.2	40.2	40.3	39.8	38.4	40.2	39.7	40.5	39.2
Manufacturing													
2011............	41.2	41.9	42.8	41.8	41.4	41.8	40.6	41.8	41.8	42.2	42.1	42.3	41.8
2012............	42.2	42.4	42.1	42.7	42.1	42.4	41.6	41.9	42.0	41.1	41.7	40.8	41.9
2013............	40.2	40.9	40.8	40.6	40.3	41.1	40.1	41.2	41.6	41.2	41.1	41.5	40.9
2014............	40.6	40.2	41.5	41.4	41.5	41.7	40.5	41.5	41.5	40.7	42.1	42.4	41.3
2015............	41.8	40.9	42.6	42.0	41.5	41.8	41.2	42.3	41.6	41.8	42.6	43.0	41.9
Trade, Transportation, and Utilities													
2011............	34.6	35.1	35.5	35.5	35.8	35.8	35.6	35.7	34.5	34.7	34.2	34.8	35.1
2012............	34.4	34.4	34.2	34.5	34.5	34.7	34.9	34.9	35.3	34.9	35.1	35.1	34.7
2013............	34.2	34.7	34.7	34.6	35.0	35.3	35.3	35.4	35.4	35.1	35.1	35.3	35.0
2014............	33.9	34.2	34.9	34.6	34.7	34.8	34.7	34.7	34.4	34.5	34.8	35.0	34.6
2015............	34.0	33.9	34.8	34.6	34.6	34.8	34.7	34.9	34.7	34.3	34.6	35.0	34.6
Information													
2011............	37.2	37.5	37.0	37.6	38.0	37.5	37.2	37.5	37.4	38.1	37.1	36.9	37.4
2012............	37.9	37.4	37.2	38.5	38.2	38.0	39.6	39.1	40.3	38.0	38.1	38.4	38.4
2013............	37.5	36.7	36.8	36.8	37.4	38.2	37.7	37.1	37.7	36.6	36.5	37.4	37.2
2014............	36.8	38.0	38.5	37.9	37.7	38.0	37.2	37.6	37.4	37.9	38.4	36.5	37.7
2015............	36.6	37.2	37.8	36.8	36.5	36.4	36.0	37.6	36.5	36.4	36.6	35.9	36.7
Financial Activities													
2011............	37.7	36.7	36.4	36.6	37.5	37.0	36.9	37.1	37.0	38.3	37.2	37.1	37.1
2012............	38.1	37.4	37.0	38.0	37.1	37.6	38.4	37.2	38.1	37.3	37.3	38.3	37.7
2013............	37.3	37.2	37.2	36.8	37.2	38.6	37.0	37.0	38.2	37.5	37.0	38.9	37.5
2014............	37.9	39.0	39.6	38.3	38.5	39.8	38.4	38.2	38.4	38.3	39.1	37.8	38.6
2015............	37.4	38.4	38.7	37.8	37.6	37.6	37.6	38.1	37.1	37.0	37.5	37.0	37.6
Professional and Business Services													
2011............	36.0	36.0	36.4	36.4	36.8	36.3	35.9	36.1	36.4	36.5	35.5	35.6	36.2
2012............	36.0	35.8	35.9	36.6	35.8	36.4	36.5	36.5	36.6	36.0	36.5	37.9	36.4
2013............	36.2	37.0	36.5	36.7	36.3	37.4	36.1	36.5	37.0	36.4	36.4	36.9	36.6
2014............	36.0	36.1	36.2	36.2	36.4	36.6	35.9	35.9	35.7	35.2	35.9	35.6	36.0
2015............	35.0	35.7	35.0	35.1	35.6	36.0	35.8	37.3	35.7	36.3	36.9	37.0	36.0
Education and Health Services													
2011............	33.4	33.1	33.5	33.9	34.4	34.0	34.5	34.1	34.2	34.9	34.3	34.5	34.1
2012............	35.1	34.2	34.2	34.9	34.6	34.5	35.4	34.7	35.2	34.7	34.6	35.1	34.8
2013............	34.7	35.1	34.8	34.8	34.9	35.2	34.4	34.3	34.7	34.0	34.5	34.8	34.7
2014............	34.5	34.5	34.7	34.2	34.1	34.5	34.3	34.5	34.4	34.2	34.9	34.7	34.5
2015............	34.6	34.5	34.5	34.4	34.5	34.5	34.7	35.2	34.9	34.7	35.2	34.8	34.7
Leisure and Hospitality													
2011............	24.6	25.8	26.2	26.4	26.1	26.2	26.1	26.3	25.9	27.1	26.2	26.3	26.1
2012............	26.2	26.4	26.9	27.2	26.8	27.2	27.5	27.3	27.1	27.1	26.3	26.1	26.9
2013............	25.2	25.9	26.3	26.5	26.5	27.3	26.9	26.9	26.8	26.8	26.6	26.7	26.6
2014............	26.3	26.7	27.6	27.3	27.0	27.9	27.8	27.5	27.0	27.1	27.2	26.5	27.2
2015............	25.9	25.9	26.6	27.0	26.7	27.3	27.2	27.1	26.5	26.9	26.7	26.6	26.7
Other Services													
2011............	32.2	32.3	32.9	32.4	32.9	32.1	32.4	32.1	31.8	33.6	32.8	33.3	32.6
2012............	33.1	33.1	32.6	34.1	33.1	33.5	33.1	33.5	33.7	33.1	32.7	33.6	33.3
2013............	32.9	33.1	33.2	33.4	33.6	34.6	33.8	33.4	34.4	33.7	32.9	34.1	33.6
2014............	32.4	32.9	32.5	32.3	32.4	33.3	32.8	33.4	32.4	32.5	32.6	32.9	32.7
2015............	32.2	32.8	32.7	32.6	33.0	33.0	33.0	33.8	32.3	32.8	32.7	32.8	32.8

3. Average Hourly Earnings by Selected Industry: Tennessee, 2011–2015

(Dollars, not seasonally adjusted)

Industry and year	January	February	March	April	May	June	July	August	September	October	November	December	Annual average
Total Private													
2011	20.52	20.34	20.15	20.13	20.09	19.92	20.13	20.05	20.23	20.47	20.17	20.22	20.20
2012	20.50	20.34	19.99	20.14	19.90	19.94	20.05	19.93	20.26	20.02	20.20	20.32	20.13
2013	20.15	20.31	20.40	20.22	20.04	20.17	20.24	20.05	20.34	20.28	20.51	20.72	20.29
2014	20.75	20.96	20.80	20.76	20.75	20.79	20.67	20.73	20.73	20.68	20.89	20.46	20.75
2015	20.72	20.97	20.80	20.69	20.63	20.67	20.88	20.92	20.99	21.08	21.23	21.14	20.90
Goods-Producing													
2011	22.33	22.00	21.98	21.45	21.43	21.28	21.14	21.09	20.85	20.74	20.79	20.95	21.32
2012	20.84	20.48	20.50	20.41	20.47	20.64	20.68	20.73	20.82	20.80	20.73	20.91	20.67
2013	20.63	20.60	20.65	20.56	20.54	20.55	20.89	20.83	20.98	20.98	21.14	21.25	20.80
2014	21.19	21.43	20.98	21.02	20.89	21.21	21.35	21.11	21.04	21.06	21.26	21.19	21.14
2015	21.22	21.23	21.35	21.34	21.48	21.54	22.08	21.55	21.97	21.91	22.05	22.37	21.68
Mining, Logging, and Construction													
2011	21.01	20.76	20.63	20.45	20.15	20.34	20.34	20.19	20.23	20.37	20.67	20.84	20.48
2012	20.99	20.79	20.79	20.61	20.74	20.67	21.08	20.87	21.04	20.93	20.96	21.38	20.91
2013	21.24	21.53	21.46	21.04	20.93	20.89	21.02	20.98	21.36	21.53	21.31	22.06	21.27
2014	21.99	22.51	22.08	21.97	21.30	21.58	21.99	21.69	21.66	21.70	21.64	21.72	21.81
2015	21.92	22.10	22.48	22.08	22.01	22.45	22.44	22.19	22.49	22.67	23.16	23.49	22.47
Manufacturing													
2011	22.70	22.36	22.39	21.78	21.87	21.61	21.43	21.41	21.07	20.87	20.83	20.99	21.60
2012	20.79	20.38	20.41	20.34	20.38	20.63	20.55	20.68	20.75	20.76	20.66	20.75	20.59
2013	20.44	20.31	20.38	20.40	20.40	20.43	20.84	20.78	20.85	20.79	21.08	20.99	20.64
2014	20.94	21.09	20.62	20.70	20.75	21.08	21.12	20.91	20.83	20.84	21.13	21.02	20.92
2015	21.01	20.96	21.01	21.11	21.30	21.23	21.95	21.34	21.80	21.64	21.67	21.99	21.42
Trade, Transportation, and Utilities													
2011	18.77	18.28	18.24	18.38	18.22	18.00	18.50	18.30	18.55	18.76	18.20	18.27	18.37
2012	18.61	18.49	18.37	18.51	18.25	18.23	18.42	18.21	18.56	18.43	18.36	18.57	18.42
2013	18.47	18.75	19.15	19.11	18.57	18.84	19.00	18.47	18.82	18.68	18.51	18.82	18.76
2014	19.01	19.17	19.42	19.31	19.07	19.29	18.97	18.96	18.96	18.98	19.00	18.84	19.08
2015	19.37	19.37	19.12	19.41	19.07	19.20	19.25	19.05	19.10	19.11	19.13	18.90	19.17
Information													
2011	24.68	24.31	23.72	23.40	23.61	23.48	23.93	23.23	23.04	23.89	24.11	23.19	23.72
2012	23.75	23.28	22.69	22.55	22.23	23.22	22.76	22.67	23.26	23.27	23.68	24.00	23.11
2013	24.59	25.24	25.49	24.86	25.26	25.10	25.47	25.53	26.10	25.39	25.60	25.88	25.38
2014	25.82	25.16	25.26	24.72	24.64	25.57	25.54	25.70	25.74	26.10	26.44	26.49	25.60
2015	26.99	27.37	26.73	26.16	26.19	26.37	26.84	27.38	27.28	27.93	28.57	28.64	27.20
Financial Activities													
2011	22.88	23.11	22.86	22.91	22.96	22.77	23.37	23.55	23.36	23.67	23.28	23.47	23.19
2012	23.76	23.28	22.65	23.49	22.73	22.93	23.42	22.84	23.26	23.13	23.00	23.52	23.17
2013	23.51	24.23	23.71	24.27	24.01	24.37	23.84	23.46	23.31	23.08	23.66	23.98	23.78
2014	24.51	24.67	24.30	25.62	24.52	24.49	24.31	24.57	24.51	24.12	24.86	24.48	24.58
2015	25.06	25.85	25.30	25.39	25.69	25.63	25.92	27.05	25.82	26.10	26.45	26.27	25.88
Professional and Business Services													
2011	23.36	23.80	23.43	23.96	24.24	24.04	24.23	24.02	24.55	25.38	24.86	24.76	24.23
2012	25.95	25.53	24.83	25.51	25.00	24.91	25.36	24.71	25.53	24.43	25.12	24.31	25.09
2013	24.14	24.13	24.51	23.71	23.75	24.12	24.40	23.83	24.61	24.61	25.60	25.93	24.46
2014	25.64	26.12	25.88	25.46	26.49	26.24	25.90	25.90	25.80	25.40	25.65	23.54	25.66
2015	23.68	24.34	24.55	23.83	23.77	23.69	23.89	24.31	24.53	24.45	24.77	24.28	24.18
Education and Health Services													
2011	21.99	21.90	21.60	21.65	21.31	21.29	21.49	21.36	21.64	21.54	21.15	21.22	21.51
2012	21.08	21.37	20.74	20.71	20.54	20.81	20.57	20.82	20.90	20.81	21.04	21.43	20.90
2013	20.96	21.21	21.21	21.00	20.89	20.90	20.86	21.04	21.06	21.06	21.01	21.04	21.02
2014	21.00	21.23	21.15	21.27	21.27	21.20	21.18	21.38	21.42	21.50	21.45	21.49	21.30
2015	21.70	21.94	21.61	21.64	21.62	21.75	21.87	21.91	21.83	22.25	22.21	22.07	21.87
Leisure and Hospitality													
2011	11.94	11.73	11.56	11.51	11.54	11.44	11.57	11.69	11.80	12.14	12.07	12.04	11.75
2012	12.09	12.27	11.95	11.96	11.95	11.75	11.71	11.77	11.87	11.81	11.90	12.03	11.92
2013	12.03	11.96	11.85	11.81	11.75	11.66	11.59	11.52	11.55	11.62	11.59	11.75	11.72
2014	11.67	11.72	11.63	11.47	11.49	11.41	11.52	11.58	11.59	11.65	11.61	11.76	11.59
2015	11.77	11.94	11.87	11.87	11.89	12.02	12.15	12.13	12.35	12.33	12.36	12.38	12.09
Other Services													
2011	16.99	17.21	17.07	16.99	17.17	17.24	17.05	17.45	17.49	18.47	18.20	18.64	17.50
2012	18.82	18.68	18.64	18.40	18.14	17.60	17.96	17.92	18.15	17.99	18.54	18.62	18.28
2013	18.81	18.92	18.92	19.17	19.26	19.16	19.00	19.21	19.26	19.24	19.63	19.52	19.18
2014	20.00	20.35	20.18	19.67	19.19	19.21	19.52	20.14	19.91	20.02	21.29	20.24	19.97
2015	20.23	20.35	20.11	19.83	19.46	19.28	19.31	19.13	19.37	19.20	19.43	19.64	19.61

4. Average Weekly Earnings by Selected Industry: Tennessee, 2011–2015

(Dollars, not seasonally adjusted)

Industry and year	January	February	March	April	May	June	July	August	September	October	November	December	Annual average
Total Private													
2011	707.94	707.83	711.30	708.58	713.20	703.18	706.56	707.77	708.05	728.73	705.95	711.74	711.04
2012	721.60	713.93	699.65	716.98	700.48	705.88	713.78	707.52	725.31	704.70	715.08	723.39	712.60
2013	699.21	714.91	718.08	711.74	705.41	724.10	712.45	709.77	726.14	715.88	724.00	739.70	716.24
2014	722.10	733.60	740.48	730.75	732.48	742.20	727.58	733.84	727.62	721.73	743.68	724.28	732.48
2015	718.98	727.66	732.16	724.15	724.11	729.65	734.98	748.94	734.65	742.02	753.67	752.58	735.68
Goods-Producing													
2011	886.50	893.20	912.17	879.45	876.49	878.86	851.94	871.02	856.94	858.64	858.63	867.33	874.12
2012	854.44	843.78	844.60	853.14	845.41	860.69	845.81	856.15	866.11	842.40	856.15	846.86	851.60
2013	816.95	832.24	838.39	834.74	831.87	842.55	843.96	860.28	868.57	866.47	870.97	873.38	848.64
2014	851.84	852.91	870.67	863.92	866.94	882.34	871.08	876.07	868.95	848.72	888.67	885.74	868.85
2015	865.78	851.32	881.76	877.07	884.98	891.76	905.28	896.48	894.18	907.07	921.69	946.25	893.22
Mining, Logging, and Construction													
2011	737.45	766.04	775.69	789.37	797.94	811.57	801.40	807.60	788.97	802.58	812.33	810.68	792.58
2012	785.03	783.78	798.34	809.97	813.01	818.53	817.90	830.63	847.91	812.08	842.59	850.92	817.58
2013	805.00	839.67	858.40	856.33	856.04	854.40	863.92	874.87	875.76	899.95	882.23	882.40	863.56
2014	859.81	866.64	911.90	887.59	879.69	889.10	916.98	897.97	883.73	850.64	889.40	868.80	883.31
2015	826.38	828.75	843.00	847.87	884.80	902.49	904.33	883.16	863.62	911.33	919.45	951.35	880.82
Manufacturing													
2011	935.24	936.88	958.29	910.40	905.42	903.30	870.06	894.94	880.73	880.71	876.94	887.88	902.88
2012	877.34	864.11	859.26	868.52	858.00	874.71	854.88	866.49	871.50	853.24	861.52	846.60	862.72
2013	821.69	830.68	831.50	828.24	822.12	839.67	835.68	856.14	867.36	856.55	866.39	871.09	844.18
2014	850.16	847.82	855.73	856.98	861.13	879.04	855.36	867.77	864.45	848.19	889.57	891.25	864.00
2015	878.22	857.26	895.03	886.62	883.95	887.41	904.34	902.68	906.88	904.55	923.14	945.57	897.50
Trade, Transportation, and Utilities													
2011	649.44	641.63	647.52	652.49	652.28	644.40	658.60	653.31	639.98	650.97	622.44	635.80	644.79
2012	640.18	636.06	628.25	638.60	629.63	632.58	642.86	635.53	655.17	643.21	644.44	651.81	639.17
2013	631.67	650.63	664.51	661.21	649.95	665.05	670.70	653.84	666.23	655.67	649.70	664.35	656.60
2014	644.44	655.61	677.76	668.13	661.73	671.29	658.26	657.91	652.22	654.81	661.20	659.40	660.17
2015	658.58	656.64	665.38	671.59	659.82	668.16	667.98	664.85	662.77	655.47	661.90	661.50	663.28
Information													
2011	918.10	911.63	877.64	879.84	897.18	880.50	890.20	871.13	861.70	910.21	894.48	855.71	887.13
2012	900.13	870.67	844.07	868.18	849.19	882.36	901.30	886.40	937.38	884.26	902.21	921.60	887.42
2013	922.13	926.31	938.03	914.85	944.72	958.82	960.22	947.16	983.97	929.27	934.40	967.91	944.14
2014	950.18	956.08	972.51	936.89	928.93	971.66	950.09	966.32	962.68	989.19	1,015.30	966.89	965.12
2015	987.83	1,018.16	1,010.39	962.69	955.94	959.87	966.24	1,029.49	995.72	1,016.65	1,045.66	1,028.18	998.24
Financial Activities													
2011	862.58	848.14	832.10	838.51	861.00	842.49	862.35	873.71	864.32	906.56	866.02	870.74	860.35
2012	905.26	870.67	838.05	892.62	843.28	862.17	899.33	849.65	886.21	862.75	857.90	900.82	873.51
2013	876.92	901.36	882.01	893.14	893.17	940.68	882.08	868.02	890.44	865.50	875.42	932.82	891.75
2014	928.93	962.13	962.28	981.25	944.02	974.70	933.50	938.57	941.18	923.80	972.03	925.34	948.79
2015	937.24	992.64	979.11	959.74	965.94	963.69	974.59	1,030.61	957.92	965.70	991.88	971.99	973.09
Professional and Business Services													
2011	840.96	856.80	852.85	872.14	892.03	872.65	869.86	867.12	893.62	926.37	882.53	881.46	877.13
2012	934.20	913.97	891.40	933.67	895.00	906.72	925.64	901.92	934.40	879.48	916.88	921.35	913.28
2013	873.87	892.81	892.81	870.16	862.13	902.09	880.84	869.80	910.57	895.80	931.84	956.82	895.24
2014	923.04	942.93	936.86	921.65	964.24	960.38	929.81	929.81	921.06	894.08	920.84	838.02	923.76
2015	828.80	868.94	859.25	836.43	846.21	852.84	855.26	906.76	875.72	887.54	914.01	898.36	870.48
Education and Health Services													
2011	734.47	724.89	723.60	733.94	733.06	723.86	741.41	728.38	740.09	751.75	725.45	732.09	733.49
2012	739.91	730.85	709.31	722.78	710.68	717.95	728.18	722.45	735.68	722.11	727.98	752.19	727.32
2013	727.31	744.47	738.11	730.80	729.06	735.68	717.58	721.67	730.78	716.04	724.85	732.19	729.39
2014	724.50	732.44	733.91	727.43	725.31	731.40	726.47	737.61	736.85	735.30	748.61	745.70	734.85
2015	750.82	756.93	745.55	744.42	745.89	750.38	758.89	771.23	761.87	772.08	781.79	768.04	758.89
Leisure and Hospitality													
2011	293.72	302.63	302.87	303.86	301.19	299.73	301.98	307.45	305.62	328.99	316.23	316.65	306.68
2012	316.76	323.93	321.46	325.31	320.26	319.60	322.03	321.32	321.68	320.05	312.97	313.98	320.65
2013	303.16	309.76	311.66	312.97	311.38	318.32	311.77	309.89	309.54	311.42	308.29	313.73	311.75
2014	306.92	312.92	320.99	313.13	310.23	318.34	320.26	318.45	312.93	315.72	315.79	311.64	315.25
2015	304.84	309.25	315.74	320.49	317.46	328.15	330.48	328.72	327.28	331.68	330.01	329.31	322.80
Other Services													
2011	547.08	555.88	561.60	550.48	564.89	553.40	552.42	560.15	556.18	620.59	596.96	620.71	570.50
2012	622.94	618.31	607.66	627.44	600.43	589.60	594.48	600.32	611.66	595.47	606.26	625.63	608.72
2013	618.85	626.25	628.14	640.28	647.14	662.94	642.20	641.61	662.54	648.39	645.83	665.63	644.45
2014	648.00	669.52	655.85	635.34	621.76	639.69	640.26	672.68	645.08	650.65	694.05	665.90	653.02
2015	651.41	667.48	657.60	646.46	642.18	636.24	637.23	646.59	625.65	629.76	635.36	644.19	643.21

TEXAS
At a Glance

Population:
  2005 population: 22,778,123
  2010 census: 25,145,561
  2015 estimate: 27,469,114

Percent change in population:
  2005–2015: 20.6%
  2010–2015: 9.2%

Percent change in total nonfarm employment:
  2005–2015: 21.6%

Industry with the largest growth in employment, 2005–2015 (thousands):
  Professional and Business Services, 429.5

Industry with the largest decline or smallest growth in employment, 2005–2015 (thousands):
  Information, –22.5

Civilian labor force:
  2005: 11,124,240
  2010: 12,241,970
  2015: 13,078,304

Unemployment rate and rank among states (highest to lowest):
  2005: 5.4%, 14th
  2010: 8.1%, 32nd
  2015: 4.5%, 34th

Over-the-year change in unemployment rates:
  2012–2013: –0.5%
  2013–2014: –1.1%
  2014–2015: –0.6%

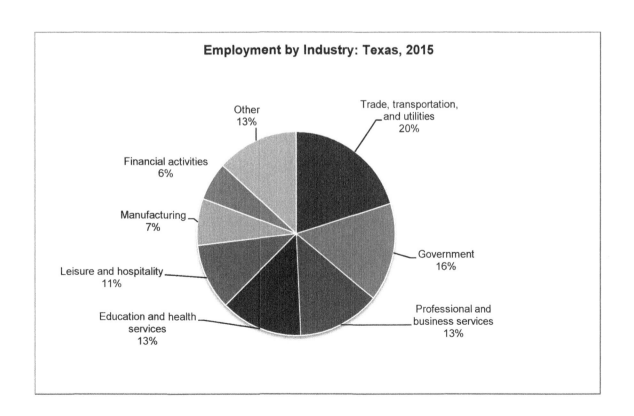

Employment by Industry: Texas, 2015

- Other 13%
- Trade, transportation, and utilities 20%
- Financial activities 6%
- Government 16%
- Manufacturing 7%
- Professional and business services 13%
- Leisure and hospitality 11%
- Education and health services 13%

1. Employment by Industry: Texas, 2005–2015

(Numbers in thousands, not seasonally adjusted)

Industry and year	January	February	March	April	May	June	July	August	September	October	November	December	Annual average
Total Nonfarm													
2005	9,490.4	9,560.5	9,630.4	9,697.3	9,727.6	9,735.1	9,696.1	9,749.6	9,831.1	9,843.5	9,923.2	9,965.6	9,737.5
2006	9,807.4	9,889.4	9,977.8	10,002.5	10,057.9	10,089.1	9,993.0	10,072.5	10,155.9	10,174.9	10,246.6	10,296.4	10,063.6
2007	10,109.4	10,209.8	10,305.1	10,336.9	10,395.4	10,435.4	10,351.9	10,404.0	10,457.4	10,511.9	10,582.4	10,617.0	10,393.1
2008	10,438.4	10,533.3	10,577.8	10,608.4	10,655.3	10,657.8	10,574.3	10,613.2	10,609.1	10,660.8	10,681.6	10,669.9	10,606.7
2009	10,402.3	10,397.6	10,392.8	10,352.6	10,352.9	10,320.8	10,198.4	10,190.2	10,214.7	10,253.6	10,283.8	10,296.4	10,304.7
2010	10,113.8	10,173.3	10,261.4	10,312.0	10,393.1	10,390.7	10,291.5	10,317.1	10,359.7	10,439.0	10,484.6	10,512.6	10,337.4
2011	10,319.7	10,384.6	10,480.1	10,554.0	10,581.4	10,610.1	10,545.2	10,578.0	10,635.0	10,657.8	10,719.1	10,750.3	10,567.9
2012	10,580.3	10,677.8	10,763.5	10,816.7	10,877.1	10,916.0	10,835.3	10,897.4	10,944.4	11,010.3	11,097.3	11,123.7	10,878.3
2013	10,902.1	11,037.7	11,105.8	11,152.9	11,198.7	11,234.4	11,173.8	11,218.2	11,266.1	11,325.3	11,417.2	11,425.6	11,204.8
2014	11,233.2	11,333.8	11,405.4	11,487.6	11,552.8	11,587.7	11,528.3	11,574.2	11,622.6	11,727.9	11,807.0	11,850.2	11,559.2
2015	11,637.6	11,720.2	11,741.3	11,794.4	11,840.4	11,862.9	11,814.0	11,830.9	11,862.7	11,949.1	11,998.1	12,008.2	11,838.3
Total Private													
2005	7,827.0	7,863.5	7,931.2	7,996.0	8,024.4	8,076.8	8,100.9	8,133.5	8,144.3	8,131.7	8,199.6	8,254.1	8,056.9
2006	8,114.1	8,164.3	8,251.8	8,279.7	8,334.7	8,407.2	8,386.2	8,439.9	8,448.4	8,437.9	8,500.8	8,558.0	8,360.3
2007	8,396.7	8,465.6	8,554.7	8,586.9	8,642.9	8,720.3	8,707.9	8,751.1	8,729.6	8,745.2	8,800.8	8,839.7	8,661.8
2008	8,680.3	8,743.8	8,780.2	8,817.0	8,860.0	8,895.7	8,882.3	8,913.7	8,838.7	8,854.2	8,856.0	8,849.5	8,831.0
2009	8,601.8	8,569.1	8,557.5	8,508.0	8,508.8	8,511.2	8,465.0	8,460.9	8,409.9	8,397.9	8,415.4	8,436.1	8,486.8
2010	8,281.2	8,308.4	8,384.0	8,423.0	8,469.6	8,516.6	8,509.8	8,544.6	8,528.1	8,564.3	8,599.2	8,640.4	8,480.8
2011	8,479.1	8,519.5	8,614.4	8,687.4	8,719.5	8,779.9	8,792.5	8,842.1	8,847.1	8,845.1	8,899.2	8,941.0	8,747.2
2012	8,799.5	8,861.4	8,943.5	8,996.8	9,058.8	9,131.6	9,108.6	9,180.5	9,166.5	9,194.7	9,270.7	9,298.4	9,084.3
2013	9,115.8	9,211.9	9,275.1	9,321.1	9,369.6	9,434.8	9,427.6	9,486.1	9,467.8	9,490.4	9,568.4	9,584.4	9,396.1
2014	9,422.4	9,490.7	9,557.1	9,639.3	9,705.2	9,766.3	9,765.0	9,826.0	9,810.1	9,872.0	9,936.7	9,982.9	9,731.1
2015	9,806.6	9,855.5	9,874.2	9,921.9	9,965.0	10,019.3	10,026.3	10,053.8	10,018.8	10,065.2	10,102.3	10,114.6	9,985.3
Goods-Producing													
2005	1,586.6	1,594.7	1,608.3	1,618.7	1,623.8	1,637.9	1,645.3	1,648.2	1,653.8	1,650.7	1,657.8	1,667.0	1,632.7
2006	1,656.8	1,672.9	1,693.0	1,693.2	1,709.5	1,733.6	1,728.4	1,738.0	1,745.1	1,742.1	1,748.0	1,754.4	1,717.9
2007	1,735.5	1,753.2	1,769.6	1,775.0	1,786.4	1,810.1	1,803.0	1,811.5	1,809.9	1,815.9	1,820.6	1,821.8	1,792.7
2008	1,801.1	1,819.3	1,824.3	1,827.5	1,836.5	1,845.0	1,841.9	1,846.9	1,837.4	1,839.4	1,826.3	1,807.2	1,829.4
2009	1,751.7	1,728.0	1,701.3	1,662.3	1,646.5	1,634.3	1,615.7	1,609.4	1,595.6	1,583.1	1,572.9	1,570.0	1,639.2
2010	1,554.3	1,553.9	1,566.4	1,570.5	1,577.3	1,587.5	1,595.6	1,601.4	1,599.2	1,602.7	1,598.8	1,600.3	1,584.0
2011	1,579.7	1,591.6	1,606.8	1,615.3	1,621.5	1,641.3	1,655.1	1,665.1	1,670.3	1,670.8	1,672.6	1,675.9	1,638.8
2012	1,664.6	1,679.8	1,695.1	1,704.2	1,715.3	1,731.8	1,733.9	1,745.1	1,744.1	1,751.2	1,750.4	1,748.7	1,722.0
2013	1,729.4	1,751.6	1,761.0	1,763.9	1,768.4	1,783.0	1,783.7	1,792.4	1,788.3	1,790.0	1,793.1	1,790.9	1,774.6
2014	1,777.8	1,797.4	1,805.8	1,824.3	1,838.9	1,851.4	1,859.8	1,871.7	1,871.8	1,883.9	1,887.9	1,893.2	1,847.0
2015	1,869.9	1,867.9	1,853.9	1,838.0	1,834.8	1,840.5	1,835.6	1,831.3	1,817.4	1,821.9	1,820.1	1,811.5	1,836.9
Service-Providing													
2005	7,903.8	7,965.8	8,022.1	8,078.6	8,103.8	8,097.2	8,050.8	8,101.4	8,177.3	8,192.8	8,265.4	8,298.6	8,104.8
2006	8,150.6	8,216.5	8,284.8	8,309.3	8,348.4	8,355.5	8,264.6	8,334.5	8,410.8	8,432.8	8,498.6	8,542.0	8,345.7
2007	8,373.9	8,456.6	8,535.5	8,561.9	8,609.0	8,625.3	8,548.9	8,592.5	8,647.5	8,696.0	8,761.8	8,795.2	8,600.3
2008	8,637.3	8,714.0	8,753.5	8,780.9	8,818.8	8,812.8	8,732.4	8,766.3	8,771.7	8,821.4	8,855.3	8,862.7	8,777.3
2009	8,650.6	8,669.6	8,691.5	8,690.3	8,706.4	8,686.5	8,582.7	8,580.8	8,619.1	8,670.5	8,710.9	8,726.4	8,665.4
2010	8,559.5	8,619.4	8,695.0	8,741.5	8,815.8	8,803.2	8,695.9	8,715.7	8,760.5	8,836.3	8,885.8	8,912.3	8,753.4
2011	8,740.0	8,793.0	8,873.3	8,938.7	8,959.9	8,968.8	8,890.1	8,912.9	8,964.7	8,987.0	9,046.5	9,074.4	8,929.1
2012	8,915.7	8,998.0	9,068.4	9,112.5	9,161.8	9,184.2	9,101.4	9,152.3	9,200.3	9,259.1	9,346.9	9,375.0	9,156.3
2013	9,172.7	9,286.1	9,344.8	9,389.0	9,430.3	9,451.4	9,390.1	9,425.8	9,477.8	9,535.3	9,624.1	9,634.7	9,430.2
2014	9,455.4	9,536.4	9,599.6	9,663.3	9,713.9	9,736.3	9,668.5	9,702.5	9,750.8	9,844.0	9,919.1	9,957.0	9,712.2
2015	9,767.7	9,852.3	9,887.4	9,956.4	10,005.6	10,022.4	9,978.4	9,999.6	10,045.3	10,127.2	10,178.0	10,196.7	10,001.4
Mining and Logging													
2005	157.1	157.8	158.7	160.2	161.7	164.4	166.5	167.5	168.1	169.3	170.4	172.4	164.5
2006	171.6	173.9	175.8	177.6	179.6	184.0	186.0	188.3	190.4	192.2	193.4	194.9	184.0
2007	195.4	197.1	199.2	200.4	202.1	205.9	207.7	209.7	209.1	211.2	213.0	214.8	205.5
2008	215.7	218.7	219.9	221.5	223.5	227.6	230.2	232.5	232.7	235.5	234.5	232.4	227.1
2009	224.3	218.1	212.0	201.8	196.8	194.1	191.9	190.3	188.7	187.5	188.0	189.7	198.6
2010	189.7	191.9	194.0	197.0	199.6	203.2	204.9	207.2	208.0	210.2	211.4	214.0	202.6
2011	214.6	217.2	220.1	223.9	226.2	231.8	236.8	240.7	242.7	247.0	249.3	252.7	233.6
2012	253.2	256.3	259.6	261.8	265.3	269.1	272.2	273.2	272.6	275.1	275.9	277.5	267.7
2013	276.1	278.4	280.0	282.0	283.5	286.8	288.8	290.4	289.8	290.2	291.2	292.2	285.8
2014	293.1	295.9	297.3	300.4	303.3	307.1	311.4	314.6	314.9	317.6	319.5	320.1	307.9
2015	313.0	301.0	291.5	279.4	273.0	271.0	266.7	263.8	258.2	257.2	255.0	255.1	273.7

1. Employment by Industry: Texas, 2005–2015—*Continued*

(Numbers in thousands, not seasonally adjusted)

Industry and year	January	February	March	April	May	June	July	August	September	October	November	December	Annual average
Construction													
2005	540.1	545.5	555.3	564.6	565.9	570.6	573.6	574.8	579.3	576.6	577.9	581.1	567.1
2006	575.8	586.0	599.5	594.7	602.9	614.8	609.3	613.4	617.4	615.6	617.5	619.8	605.6
2007	609.2	622.2	635.2	637.7	644.9	657.9	652.2	658.7	659.4	665.3	668.5	666.3	648.1
2008	653.8	667.0	672.5	675.3	679.8	681.8	678.0	681.4	676.6	680.2	671.7	661.4	673.3
2009	634.0	627.8	620.5	606.9	603.8	602.1	595.6	591.0	582.0	576.2	569.3	565.0	597.9
2010	554.6	552.4	560.6	563.9	565.0	568.1	572.2	573.6	570.8	569.8	562.7	559.4	564.4
2011	543.5	549.4	557.6	559.0	560.1	567.3	571.6	574.7	576.5	572.2	569.0	565.5	563.9
2012	557.0	564.4	573.1	576.4	584.0	589.7	585.7	594.5	594.8	600.7	597.9	593.2	584.3
2013	583.0	599.1	606.6	607.5	611.4	618.1	617.6	623.7	622.4	623.9	623.7	619.7	613.1
2014	614.6	625.2	632.0	642.5	650.8	654.3	657.6	664.0	665.4	671.5	670.3	670.3	651.5
2015	662.1	673.2	673.1	674.6	680.3	687.0	689.7	692.0	689.3	698.2	697.0	692.9	684.1
Manufacturing													
2005	889.4	891.4	894.3	893.9	896.2	902.9	905.2	905.9	906.4	904.8	909.5	913.5	901.1
2006	909.4	913.0	917.7	920.9	927.0	934.8	933.1	936.3	937.3	934.3	937.1	939.7	928.4
2007	930.9	933.9	935.2	936.9	939.4	946.3	943.1	943.1	941.4	939.4	939.1	940.7	939.1
2008	931.6	933.6	931.9	930.7	933.2	935.6	933.7	933.0	928.1	923.7	920.1	913.4	929.1
2009	893.4	882.1	868.8	853.6	845.9	838.1	828.2	828.1	824.9	819.4	815.6	815.3	842.8
2010	810.0	809.6	811.8	809.6	812.7	816.2	818.5	820.6	820.4	822.7	824.7	826.9	817.0
2011	821.6	825.0	829.1	832.4	835.2	842.2	846.7	849.7	851.1	851.6	854.3	857.7	841.4
2012	854.4	859.1	862.4	866.0	866.0	873.0	876.0	877.4	876.7	875.4	876.6	878.0	870.1
2013	870.3	874.1	874.4	874.4	873.5	878.1	877.3	878.3	876.1	875.9	878.2	879.0	875.8
2014	870.1	876.3	876.5	881.4	884.8	890.0	890.8	893.1	891.5	894.8	898.1	902.8	887.5
2015	894.8	893.7	889.3	884.0	881.5	882.5	879.2	875.5	869.9	866.5	868.1	863.5	879.0
Trade, Transportation, and Utilities													
2005	1,948.6	1,937.1	1,948.9	1,959.1	1,967.7	1,977.8	1,986.9	2,001.2	1,998.4	2,000.9	2,049.1	2,080.3	1,988.0
2006	2,007.9	1,999.0	2,016.2	2,017.3	2,025.9	2,034.6	2,033.6	2,050.4	2,048.4	2,056.7	2,098.2	2,129.6	2,043.2
2007	2,065.8	2,058.2	2,078.6	2,078.5	2,088.8	2,101.1	2,104.4	2,115.2	2,112.3	2,124.3	2,165.3	2,192.3	2,107.1
2008	2,123.5	2,117.9	2,125.8	2,121.3	2,127.0	2,136.0	2,137.8	2,151.0	2,130.7	2,136.2	2,160.1	2,176.5	2,137.0
2009	2,092.2	2,066.7	2,064.6	2,048.8	2,047.1	2,045.4	2,038.1	2,044.0	2,035.6	2,035.3	2,058.2	2,079.8	2,054.7
2010	2,013.6	2,003.0	2,017.5	2,021.5	2,031.7	2,040.7	2,041.8	2,053.7	2,046.3	2,060.9	2,094.8	2,122.8	2,045.7
2011	2,057.2	2,048.4	2,064.8	2,081.2	2,087.1	2,096.3	2,102.0	2,117.6	2,110.1	2,121.8	2,161.5	2,190.1	2,103.2
2012	2,127.0	2,119.3	2,130.7	2,139.4	2,151.9	2,165.9	2,167.8	2,182.9	2,174.1	2,188.4	2,242.1	2,261.2	2,170.9
2013	2,189.9	2,188.4	2,193.8	2,205.7	2,215.7	2,229.5	2,233.2	2,250.5	2,244.5	2,259.4	2,310.2	2,334.8	2,238.0
2014	2,265.7	2,258.7	2,265.0	2,275.8	2,286.4	2,303.5	2,307.1	2,324.2	2,319.2	2,341.0	2,390.8	2,425.3	2,313.6
2015	2,352.2	2,346.4	2,351.4	2,361.5	2,374.5	2,387.7	2,390.9	2,403.8	2,397.4	2,407.6	2,445.3	2,469.9	2,390.7
Wholesale Trade													
2005	459.6	460.5	463.1	467.1	469.2	472.0	475.0	475.9	477.9	477.3	479.2	483.0	471.7
2006	479.6	482.4	486.3	487.0	489.7	494.1	493.2	495.3	497.3	497.2	500.1	503.2	492.1
2007	498.7	502.0	505.3	507.0	509.9	515.2	515.3	517.1	517.1	520.2	521.4	524.4	512.8
2008	519.2	521.7	521.9	523.3	524.8	527.1	526.2	526.8	523.9	523.8	521.9	520.9	523.5
2009	510.5	505.4	502.0	496.7	494.9	493.5	491.3	490.0	487.6	487.2	485.8	486.7	494.3
2010	484.3	484.6	485.9	487.8	490.2	493.1	494.0	495.0	494.7	495.8	496.6	498.7	491.7
2011	495.2	498.4	501.4	505.5	508.9	512.1	513.5	515.6	517.5	519.1	520.4	523.8	511.0
2012	520.9	524.8	528.5	530.1	534.0	538.4	537.9	540.2	539.8	540.9	543.1	545.9	535.4
2013	542.4	546.5	549.0	548.9	551.1	554.7	555.5	557.6	558.9	561.7	565.3	567.3	554.9
2014	561.9	565.4	567.1	568.8	572.7	577.4	579.0	583.0	583.5	587.3	590.5	594.1	577.6
2015	589.9	591.3	591.7	592.0	593.9	596.0	597.9	599.7	598.7	602.0	603.4	609.1	597.1
Retail Trade													
2005	1,088.2	1,077.6	1,085.3	1,090.2	1,094.9	1,102.1	1,106.1	1,115.9	1,109.7	1,111.9	1,154.2	1,176.0	1,109.3
2006	1,118.6	1,106.5	1,117.1	1,116.8	1,120.5	1,122.5	1,122.5	1,134.1	1,127.9	1,135.3	1,172.0	1,191.0	1,132.1
2007	1,142.7	1,130.3	1,143.9	1,142.8	1,148.1	1,152.2	1,156.7	1,162.5	1,158.1	1,167.1	1,206.2	1,224.1	1,161.2
2008	1,170.9	1,160.9	1,168.5	1,161.6	1,162.8	1,168.1	1,170.6	1,180.0	1,164.1	1,171.0	1,196.6	1,209.8	1,173.7
2009	1,151.5	1,135.9	1,137.3	1,132.0	1,133.3	1,133.7	1,131.1	1,138.6	1,132.4	1,132.9	1,156.6	1,171.1	1,140.5
2010	1,118.5	1,107.8	1,118.6	1,119.7	1,125.8	1,129.7	1,128.4	1,137.4	1,128.7	1,141.4	1,172.7	1,192.4	1,135.1
2011	1,138.7	1,125.9	1,136.4	1,146.6	1,148.0	1,152.9	1,154.1	1,165.1	1,153.3	1,164.7	1,200.6	1,217.5	1,158.7
2012	1,167.3	1,153.3	1,157.6	1,164.1	1,170.3	1,176.5	1,179.2	1,188.5	1,179.8	1,193.3	1,240.7	1,250.7	1,185.1
2013	1,191.7	1,186.2	1,187.1	1,197.1	1,203.0	1,210.8	1,215.4	1,228.0	1,220.8	1,232.4	1,275.9	1,292.0	1,220.0
2014	1,236.3	1,228.9	1,231.2	1,236.9	1,239.2	1,249.0	1,250.9	1,259.3	1,251.4	1,263.9	1,305.4	1,323.4	1,256.3
2015	1,265.8	1,262.5	1,266.4	1,275.8	1,284.7	1,294.6	1,296.5	1,304.2	1,298.7	1,308.7	1,339.4	1,348.0	1,295.4

1. Employment by Industry: Texas, 2005–2015—*Continued*

(Numbers in thousands, not seasonally adjusted)

Industry and year	January	February	March	April	May	June	July	August	September	October	November	December	Annual average
Transportation and Utilities													
2005	400.8	399.0	400.5	401.8	403.6	403.7	405.8	409.4	410.8	411.7	415.7	421.3	407.0
2006	409.7	410.1	412.8	413.5	415.7	418.0	417.9	421.0	423.2	424.2	426.1	435.4	419.0
2007	424.4	425.9	429.4	428.7	430.8	433.7	432.4	435.6	437.1	437.0	437.7	443.8	433.0
2008	433.4	435.3	435.4	436.4	439.4	440.8	441.0	444.2	442.7	441.4	441.6	445.8	439.8
2009	430.2	425.4	425.3	420.1	418.9	418.2	415.7	415.4	415.6	415.2	415.8	422.0	419.8
2010	410.8	410.6	413.0	414.0	415.7	417.9	419.4	421.3	422.9	423.7	425.5	431.7	418.9
2011	423.3	424.1	427.0	429.1	430.2	431.3	434.4	436.9	439.3	438.0	440.5	448.8	433.6
2012	438.8	441.2	444.6	445.2	447.6	451.0	450.7	454.2	454.5	454.2	458.3	464.6	450.4
2013	455.8	455.7	457.7	459.7	461.6	464.0	462.3	464.9	464.8	465.3	469.0	475.5	463.0
2014	467.5	464.4	466.7	470.1	474.5	477.1	477.2	481.9	484.3	489.8	494.9	507.8	479.7
2015	496.5	492.6	493.3	493.7	495.9	497.1	496.5	499.9	500.0	496.9	502.5	512.8	498.1
Information													
2005	221.8	222.1	222.5	222.8	223.1	224.6	224.1	223.9	223.9	222.0	223.1	223.7	223.1
2006	221.2	222.1	222.3	221.9	222.7	223.9	221.7	221.4	221.0	219.9	220.6	221.3	221.7
2007	219.4	220.7	220.7	220.0	221.9	222.4	221.9	222.2	220.4	220.0	221.1	221.0	221.0
2008	219.0	219.2	219.2	218.3	219.3	219.3	218.2	217.3	214.4	213.8	214.3	214.3	217.2
2009	211.2	210.2	209.2	207.0	206.1	205.3	203.2	201.5	198.9	198.9	199.3	199.7	204.2
2010	196.8	195.9	196.0	196.5	196.2	197.5	195.6	195.4	193.9	193.8	195.1	195.3	195.7
2011	194.6	194.2	194.6	194.9	195.8	196.5	197.6	196.6	195.3	195.2	196.4	197.1	195.7
2012	196.4	196.1	196.7	196.7	197.3	198.4	198.2	197.6	196.2	196.7	198.9	199.1	197.4
2013	196.9	197.4	198.2	199.5	200.9	202.4	202.8	203.0	200.7	201.7	204.1	204.9	201.0
2014	201.7	201.5	201.4	202.4	202.3	203.5	203.5	202.4	200.1	199.8	201.3	202.6	201.9
2015	198.5	198.1	198.2	200.4	201.7	202.6	203.2	202.8	200.3	200.1	201.3	200.3	200.6
Financial Activities													
2005	597.0	598.7	600.2	602.4	603.7	608.2	613.9	616.1	616.8	617.1	618.7	621.6	609.5
2006	614.2	616.8	620.7	624.0	626.6	631.9	630.5	633.4	633.2	633.5	634.4	638.9	628.2
2007	633.7	636.8	639.8	640.1	643.6	648.1	648.3	649.7	646.4	645.6	646.7	648.4	643.9
2008	641.7	645.2	644.7	647.8	650.6	652.9	652.4	651.7	646.9	644.3	642.4	643.2	647.0
2009	632.9	632.4	630.9	628.8	629.1	629.9	629.1	627.6	624.0	622.9	622.9	624.5	627.9
2010	618.3	619.9	621.4	621.0	623.7	626.6	626.8	627.0	625.0	629.3	631.4	634.1	625.4
2011	629.0	631.4	634.3	636.1	637.4	641.3	644.0	644.9	645.5	647.0	647.8	651.1	640.8
2012	646.9	650.0	652.5	654.3	657.5	663.0	664.3	666.3	665.6	670.4	672.5	675.5	661.6
2013	668.4	673.0	675.6	676.9	679.8	685.3	688.9	690.6	689.0	691.3	693.6	694.1	683.9
2014	686.8	689.4	690.8	692.8	696.0	700.6	703.4	706.2	704.6	709.9	711.2	713.9	700.5
2015	707.7	710.0	711.2	713.6	716.9	722.0	723.9	724.9	723.4	728.3	729.6	730.7	720.2
Professional and Business Services													
2005	1,111.2	1,125.0	1,134.4	1,153.3	1,150.9	1,160.7	1,166.1	1,175.9	1,186.6	1,196.1	1,203.4	1,211.6	1,164.6
2006	1,192.1	1,207.3	1,222.8	1,229.0	1,235.1	1,247.9	1,249.2	1,260.7	1,265.5	1,265.3	1,275.9	1,283.4	1,244.5
2007	1,254.7	1,272.8	1,286.8	1,291.7	1,296.5	1,311.4	1,311.0	1,323.4	1,323.4	1,329.7	1,333.7	1,339.5	1,306.2
2008	1,318.2	1,332.0	1,335.7	1,343.6	1,344.7	1,350.4	1,347.1	1,356.8	1,344.3	1,350.7	1,341.8	1,332.8	1,341.5
2009	1,285.6	1,277.8	1,271.9	1,260.0	1,254.7	1,256.3	1,246.9	1,246.2	1,238.6	1,248.3	1,254.6	1,254.8	1,258.0
2010	1,236.6	1,246.2	1,258.7	1,269.6	1,271.1	1,281.2	1,285.0	1,293.4	1,294.1	1,307.3	1,310.4	1,316.5	1,280.8
2011	1,293.8	1,307.5	1,323.7	1,339.8	1,336.5	1,347.8	1,350.9	1,363.5	1,369.2	1,367.7	1,373.9	1,379.1	1,346.1
2012	1,359.6	1,376.1	1,391.4	1,402.2	1,408.9	1,420.0	1,417.4	1,438.4	1,436.4	1,443.5	1,455.0	1,452.0	1,416.7
2013	1,421.3	1,442.7	1,454.8	1,459.4	1,462.3	1,475.2	1,476.9	1,492.9	1,495.5	1,504.6	1,515.3	1,512.3	1,476.1
2014	1,483.8	1,500.4	1,514.8	1,533.3	1,539.6	1,548.6	1,552.6	1,569.1	1,567.5	1,585.3	1,590.4	1,590.1	1,548.0
2015	1,565.0	1,575.1	1,575.6	1,585.7	1,583.6	1,591.8	1,599.5	1,606.6	1,601.6	1,614.2	1,615.1	1,614.9	1,594.1
Education and Health Services													
2005	1,157.4	1,167.7	1,174.0	1,177.3	1,179.5	1,176.6	1,181.0	1,189.2	1,200.7	1,199.0	1,204.0	1,207.1	1,184.5
2006	1,193.3	1,201.9	1,206.1	1,206.8	1,210.2	1,210.3	1,208.1	1,221.4	1,231.4	1,232.8	1,236.8	1,240.6	1,216.6
2007	1,223.0	1,238.1	1,246.4	1,247.4	1,252.8	1,252.5	1,252.2	1,261.4	1,268.7	1,270.1	1,275.1	1,276.6	1,255.4
2008	1,260.0	1,274.5	1,275.2	1,280.9	1,288.3	1,284.2	1,284.2	1,293.4	1,298.2	1,306.6	1,311.3	1,316.7	1,289.5
2009	1,298.4	1,308.5	1,314.7	1,325.0	1,332.6	1,332.7	1,337.8	1,344.2	1,350.9	1,361.8	1,363.8	1,366.2	1,336.4
2010	1,351.2	1,362.0	1,371.2	1,376.3	1,382.1	1,380.4	1,375.6	1,383.4	1,390.5	1,398.0	1,399.5	1,401.8	1,381.0
2011	1,384.5	1,390.4	1,398.5	1,408.2	1,411.5	1,409.2	1,409.2	1,418.8	1,430.3	1,430.6	1,434.5	1,437.9	1,413.6
2012	1,417.6	1,430.2	1,436.4	1,436.0	1,441.8	1,440.7	1,433.2	1,450.3	1,459.8	1,466.1	1,471.5	1,476.0	1,446.6
2013	1,452.6	1,470.9	1,476.8	1,481.2	1,484.9	1,479.4	1,475.0	1,490.6	1,497.2	1,504.6	1,509.9	1,508.7	1,486.0
2014	1,489.1	1,502.0	1,505.9	1,514.2	1,521.1	1,514.7	1,510.3	1,526.1	1,533.2	1,545.5	1,552.3	1,555.0	1,522.5
2015	1,540.3	1,555.7	1,559.2	1,571.3	1,578.5	1,573.0	1,577.3	1,591.0	1,598.2	1,611.6	1,613.6	1,612.7	1,581.9

1. Employment by Industry: Texas, 2005–2015—*Continued*

(Numbers in thousands, not seasonally adjusted)

Industry and year	January	February	March	April	May	June	July	August	September	October	November	December	Annual average
Leisure and Hospitality													
2005	861.4	874.1	893.6	912.2	925.0	936.6	930.7	928.6	916.1	902.1	899.7	898.7	906.6
2006	887.8	901.8	923.9	938.3	954.4	970.3	964.3	965.5	955.8	940.7	939.2	942.0	940.3
2007	919.8	937.3	960.9	980.6	996.6	1,013.0	1,007.7	1,008.7	991.8	982.7	980.8	982.6	980.2
2008	961.6	977.8	995.7	1,014.8	1,028.8	1,039.2	1,032.4	1,028.8	1,004.9	999.4	996.4	996.3	1,006.3
2009	971.2	984.8	1,003.7	1,014.6	1,029.4	1,040.3	1,029.2	1,025.7	1,008.3	990.2	985.3	983.6	1,005.5
2010	956.3	971.8	994.5	1,007.9	1,025.1	1,036.5	1,025.3	1,027.0	1,018.5	1,011.8	1,009.5	1,009.2	1,007.8
2011	983.4	996.8	1,028.7	1,045.8	1,061.4	1,074.3	1,061.4	1,064.2	1,055.5	1,043.0	1,042.9	1,039.9	1,041.4
2012	1,017.9	1,038.1	1,065.8	1,084.5	1,103.3	1,123.1	1,106.3	1,112.3	1,104.3	1,091.7	1,093.1	1,097.7	1,086.5
2013	1,072.2	1,097.9	1,122.3	1,140.9	1,160.4	1,177.2	1,165.1	1,165.1	1,153.3	1,140.6	1,142.0	1,139.3	1,139.7
2014	1,119.0	1,138.8	1,168.5	1,188.9	1,208.6	1,228.3	1,214.6	1,213.1	1,203.8	1,194.0	1,190.3	1,190.8	1,188.2
2015	1,165.7	1,191.6	1,212.2	1,236.3	1,257.9	1,277.7	1,271.0	1,270.0	1,261.2	1,260.7	1,256.4	1,254.8	1,243.0
Other Services													
2005	343.0	344.1	349.3	350.2	350.7	354.4	352.9	350.4	348.0	343.8	343.8	344.1	347.9
2006	340.8	342.5	346.8	349.2	350.3	354.7	350.4	349.1	348.0	346.9	347.7	347.8	347.9
2007	344.8	348.5	351.9	353.6	356.3	361.7	359.4	359.0	356.7	356.9	357.5	357.5	355.3
2008	355.2	357.9	359.6	362.8	364.8	368.7	368.3	367.8	361.9	363.8	363.4	362.5	363.1
2009	358.6	360.7	361.2	361.5	363.3	367.0	365.0	362.3	358.0	357.4	358.4	357.5	360.9
2010	354.1	355.7	358.3	359.7	362.4	366.2	364.1	363.3	360.6	360.5	359.7	360.4	360.4
2011	356.9	359.2	363.0	366.1	368.3	373.2	372.3	371.4	370.9	369.0	369.6	369.9	367.5
2012	369.5	371.8	374.9	379.5	382.8	388.7	387.5	387.6	386.0	386.7	387.2	388.2	382.5
2013	385.1	390.0	392.6	393.6	397.2	402.8	402.0	401.0	399.3	398.2	400.2	399.4	396.8
2014	398.5	402.5	404.9	407.6	412.3	415.7	413.7	413.2	409.9	412.6	412.5	412.0	409.6
2015	407.3	410.7	412.5	415.1	417.1	424.0	424.9	423.4	419.3	420.8	420.9	419.8	418.0
Government													
2005	1,663.4	1,697.0	1,699.2	1,701.3	1,703.2	1,658.3	1,595.2	1,616.1	1,686.8	1,711.8	1,723.6	1,711.5	1,680.6
2006	1,693.3	1,725.1	1,726.0	1,722.8	1,723.2	1,681.9	1,606.8	1,632.6	1,707.5	1,737.0	1,745.8	1,738.4	1,703.4
2007	1,712.7	1,744.2	1,750.4	1,750.0	1,752.5	1,715.1	1,644.0	1,652.9	1,727.8	1,766.7	1,781.6	1,777.3	1,731.3
2008	1,758.1	1,789.5	1,797.6	1,791.4	1,795.3	1,762.1	1,692.0	1,699.5	1,770.4	1,806.6	1,825.6	1,820.4	1,775.7
2009	1,800.5	1,828.5	1,835.3	1,844.6	1,844.1	1,809.6	1,733.4	1,729.3	1,804.8	1,855.7	1,868.4	1,860.3	1,817.9
2010	1,832.6	1,864.9	1,877.4	1,889.0	1,923.5	1,874.1	1,781.7	1,772.5	1,831.6	1,874.7	1,885.4	1,872.2	1,856.6
2011	1,840.6	1,865.1	1,865.7	1,866.6	1,861.9	1,830.2	1,752.7	1,735.9	1,787.9	1,812.7	1,819.9	1,809.3	1,820.7
2012	1,780.8	1,816.4	1,820.0	1,819.9	1,818.3	1,784.4	1,726.7	1,716.9	1,777.9	1,815.6	1,826.6	1,825.3	1,794.1
2013	1,786.3	1,825.8	1,830.7	1,831.8	1,829.1	1,799.6	1,746.2	1,732.1	1,798.3	1,834.9	1,848.8	1,841.2	1,808.7
2014	1,810.8	1,843.1	1,848.3	1,848.3	1,847.6	1,821.4	1,763.3	1,748.2	1,812.5	1,855.9	1,870.3	1,867.3	1,828.1
2015	1,831.0	1,864.7	1,867.1	1,872.5	1,875.4	1,843.6	1,787.7	1,777.1	1,843.9	1,883.9	1,895.8	1,893.6	1,853.0

2. Average Weekly Hours by Selected Industry: Texas, 2011–2015

(Not seasonally adjusted)

Industry and year	January	February	March	April	May	June	July	August	September	October	November	December	Annual average
Total Private													
2011	36.8	36.1	36.7	36.6	37.0	36.8	36.6	36.7	36.7	37.4	37.0	36.9	36.8
2012	37.3	35.9	36.0	36.4	35.7	36.1	36.6	36.3	36.8	36.3	36.3	37.1	36.4
2013	35.6	36.3	36.4	36.2	36.1	36.9	36.2	36.3	36.7	36.1	36.1	36.5	36.3
2014	36.0	36.7	36.8	36.3	36.2	36.9	36.4	36.7	36.4	36.4	36.9	36.6	36.5
2015	36.1	36.8	36.5	36.0	35.9	36.2	36.2	36.6	35.4	35.7	36.4	35.9	36.1
Goods-Producing													
2011	43.1	42.4	44.0	43.9	43.2	43.7	43.1	43.2	43.1	43.2	43.3	42.7	43.2
2012	42.9	42.5	42.9	43.0	42.7	43.1	42.8	42.8	42.8	42.9	42.9	43.4	42.9
2013	40.5	42.4	42.9	42.4	42.3	43.0	42.8	42.9	43.1	43.2	43.2	42.8	42.6
2014	43.1	43.3	43.5	43.4	43.0	43.5	43.2	43.7	43.4	43.4	43.0	43.4	43.3
2015	42.7	42.7	41.5	41.9	41.4	42.8	42.7	42.8	40.7	42.3	42.4	42.5	42.2
Construction													
2011	43.2	42.7	44.5	44.4	43.2	44.5	43.8	44.1	43.8	43.4	43.5	42.2	43.6
2012	42.6	42.1	43.6	43.4	42.9	44.3	43.1	44.3	43.8	44.7	44.2	44.1	43.6
2013	42.4	44.7	45.6	44.3	43.9	44.8	44.1	44.2	44.0	44.0	43.8	42.4	44.0
2014	43.1	42.3	43.0	43.2	42.1	43.0	43.7	44.3	43.4	43.8	43.2	43.8	43.3
2015	43.1	43.4	40.9	42.2	41.0	43.3	42.9	43.0	39.7	42.1	42.2	42.4	42.2
Manufacturing													
2011	40.9	40.3	40.8	40.9	40.6	40.9	40.5	40.6	40.9	41.3	41.8	41.8	40.9
2012	41.8	41.6	41.4	41.6	41.6	41.6	41.6	40.9	41.3	41.2	41.5	42.4	41.5
2013	40.9	41.9	42.1	42.0	41.7	42.0	42.2	42.4	42.7	42.9	42.9	43.1	42.2
2014	43.1	43.8	43.7	43.3	43.4	43.6	42.5	42.9	42.9	42.6	42.0	42.4	43.0
2015	41.6	41.5	41.4	41.3	41.3	41.4	41.5	41.3	40.6	41.5	41.3	41.6	41.4
Trade, Transportation, and Utilities													
2011	36.7	36.6	36.8	37.1	37.3	36.9	36.9	37.3	37.2	37.6	37.0	37.2	37.1
2012	37.4	37.3	37.3	37.8	37.5	37.8	37.8	37.8	38.4	37.3	37.3	38.2	37.7
2013	37.0	37.4	37.6	37.4	37.2	37.6	37.2	37.2	37.3	36.7	36.6	37.2	37.2
2014	36.2	36.8	37.0	36.3	36.4	36.9	36.6	36.8	36.4	36.5	36.9	36.7	36.6
2015	35.8	36.7	36.6	35.9	36.0	36.0	36.3	36.6	35.9	35.9	36.4	36.2	36.2
Financial Activities													
2011	38.8	38.7	38.8	39.0	40.3	38.7	38.9	38.1	38.6	40.1	39.4	39.5	39.1
2012	40.2	39.7	39.7	40.5	38.8	39.1	40.4	39.1	40.1	39.1	39.1	40.3	39.7
2013	38.5	38.4	38.4	38.4	38.1	39.4	37.7	37.7	39.0	37.5	37.8	38.9	38.3
2014	37.5	38.5	38.3	37.4	37.2	38.6	37.7	37.6	37.7	37.8	39.5	38.0	38.0
2015	38.2	39.7	39.6	38.4	38.3	38.4	38.7	39.9	38.2	38.4	39.8	38.4	38.8
Professional and Business Services													
2011	37.6	37.3	37.9	37.7	38.4	38.6	38.2	38.1	37.9	38.8	38.0	37.6	38.0
2012	38.4	38.0	38.0	39.0	37.9	38.1	38.4	38.0	38.4	37.7	37.9	38.7	38.2
2013	37.2	37.6	37.8	37.7	37.5	38.3	37.2	37.6	37.9	36.9	37.3	37.9	37.6
2014	37.0	38.0	37.8	37.2	37.2	38.1	37.4	37.8	37.4	37.6	38.4	37.7	37.6
2015	36.9	37.9	37.9	37.3	37.2	37.5	37.4	37.6	36.3	36.8	37.6	36.9	37.3
Education and Health Services													
2011	34.6	34.0	34.2	34.1	34.6	33.9	34.0	33.6	33.9	34.4	33.6	33.9	34.1
2012	34.3	33.5	33.4	34.1	33.2	33.7	34.3	33.8	34.4	33.6	33.6	34.2	33.8
2013	33.4	33.7	33.2	33.1	33.3	34.1	33.0	33.2	33.9	32.9	33.0	33.7	33.4
2014	33.0	33.8	33.3	32.8	32.8	33.7	33.1	33.1	33.1	33.0	33.7	32.8	33.2
2015	32.8	33.3	33.0	33.0	32.6	32.6	32.6	33.3	32.5	32.4	33.3	32.5	32.8
Leisure and Hospitality													
2011	27.8	28.0	28.7	27.9	28.8	28.1	28.2	28.1	27.6	28.4	27.7	27.9	28.1
2012	28.0	27.9	28.3	28.3	27.7	28.1	28.5	28.1	27.8	27.5	27.5	28.3	28.0
2013	27.2	28.3	28.7	27.8	28.1	28.8	28.0	28.1	27.7	27.6	27.7	27.8	28.0
2014	27.5	28.2	29.1	28.1	28.1	28.6	28.0	28.5	27.6	27.9	28.3	28.2	28.2
2015	27.6	28.7	29.0	28.2	28.1	28.4	28.4	28.7	27.6	27.8	28.3	28.1	28.2
Other Services													
2011	34.8	34.1	35.5	35.1	35.9	35.1	35.3	35.8	36.0	36.6	35.4	35.9	35.5
2012	36.7	35.9	34.8	35.3	34.5	34.7	35.5	34.9	34.9	34.9	34.8	35.2	35.2
2013	33.8	34.8	34.7	34.2	34.1	34.2	33.1	33.1	33.4	32.7	32.9	33.9	33.7
2014	32.6	33.7	33.5	33.7	33.0	33.5	32.9	33.0	32.7	32.6	33.3	33.5	33.2
2015	32.8	34.1	33.3	32.6	32.7	32.2	32.3	33.6	32.5	32.6	34.0	33.8	33.0

3. Average Hourly Earnings by Selected Industry: Texas, 2011–2015

(Dollars, not seasonally adjusted)

Industry and year	January	February	March	April	May	June	July	August	September	October	November	December	Annual average
Total Private													
2011	21.95	22.00	21.84	21.92	22.02	21.74	21.90	21.86	21.94	22.22	22.15	22.10	21.97
2012	22.36	22.15	21.98	22.28	21.97	21.89	22.18	21.94	22.37	22.25	22.37	22.70	22.21
2013	22.73	22.69	22.60	22.82	22.73	22.88	22.79	22.79	23.15	23.11	23.19	23.43	22.91
2014	23.46	23.76	23.72	23.64	23.74	23.85	23.69	23.69	23.87	24.16	24.40	24.24	23.86
2015	24.46	24.66	24.56	24.39	24.36	24.24	24.21	24.59	24.44	24.56	24.68	24.42	24.46
Goods-Producing													
2011	22.70	22.76	22.33	22.79	22.82	22.48	22.74	22.79	22.99	23.39	23.43	23.64	22.91
2012	23.57	23.60	23.42	23.36	22.97	23.02	23.14	23.08	23.48	23.40	23.59	24.21	23.40
2013	24.44	24.08	23.94	24.13	24.12	24.15	24.31	24.35	24.63	24.61	24.56	24.98	24.36
2014	25.01	25.27	25.25	25.19	25.43	25.63	25.50	25.51	25.84	26.61	26.81	26.99	25.76
2015	26.90	27.16	27.34	27.07	27.10	26.82	26.63	26.96	26.96	26.94	27.16	27.18	27.02
Construction													
2011	19.70	19.74	19.18	19.35	19.86	19.76	19.55	20.03	20.38	20.80	20.99	21.19	20.04
2012	21.07	21.39	21.33	21.38	21.51	21.42	21.73	21.72	22.08	22.21	22.40	22.97	21.78
2013	22.94	22.55	22.13	22.12	22.26	22.22	22.31	22.59	22.80	22.71	22.78	23.41	22.56
2014	23.25	23.63	23.47	23.17	23.41	23.51	23.38	23.52	23.78	24.12	24.56	24.55	23.71
2015	24.75	25.05	25.22	25.02	25.25	24.95	24.43	24.82	24.65	24.80	24.99	25.05	24.91
Manufacturing													
2011	23.69	23.71	23.23	23.87	24.39	23.96	24.36	23.91	23.91	24.15	24.12	24.32	23.97
2012	24.16	24.04	23.78	23.49	22.86	23.09	22.74	23.14	23.47	23.37	23.38	23.97	23.46
2013	24.34	24.17	24.30	24.62	24.55	24.59	24.76	24.62	24.96	25.02	24.94	25.08	24.67
2014	25.29	25.33	25.53	25.58	25.89	26.13	26.05	25.97	26.31	26.37	26.38	26.81	25.97
2015	26.76	27.05	27.19	27.21	26.98	26.97	27.03	27.39	27.52	27.47	27.59	27.70	27.24
Trade, Transportation, and Utilities													
2011	27.84	27.87	27.24	26.50	26.18	25.58	25.22	24.67	24.15	24.40	23.56	23.52	25.53
2012	23.57	22.81	22.68	22.92	22.24	22.18	22.47	21.98	22.12	21.73	21.45	21.39	22.28
2013	21.62	21.35	21.39	21.69	21.25	21.63	21.25	21.26	21.70	21.24	21.10	21.06	21.38
2014	21.16	21.32	21.66	21.65	21.50	21.60	21.35	21.25	21.38	21.56	21.77	21.86	21.51
2015	22.11	22.41	22.34	22.47	22.29	22.29	22.34	22.70	22.62	22.54	22.35	22.26	22.39
Financial Activities													
2011	25.37	25.11	25.14	25.00	25.18	24.68	24.50	24.81	24.61	25.23	24.73	24.41	24.90
2012	25.02	24.83	24.67	25.56	24.87	24.30	24.04	23.61	23.91	23.50	23.76	23.92	24.33
2013	24.24	24.87	24.66	24.93	25.03	25.37	25.35	25.10	25.53	25.44	25.66	26.07	25.19
2014	25.74	26.25	26.62	26.26	26.48	26.95	26.44	26.52	26.61	27.00	27.69	27.10	26.65
2015	27.59	28.17	28.53	28.37	28.27	28.14	28.17	28.87	28.27	28.37	28.96	28.62	28.37
Professional and Business Services													
2011	26.39	26.33	26.00	25.85	26.00	25.15	25.20	25.05	25.34	25.56	25.48	25.74	25.67
2012	25.90	25.59	25.09	25.44	25.19	25.37	25.68	25.33	25.80	25.67	25.79	26.63	25.63
2013	26.39	26.37	26.33	26.24	26.41	26.63	26.30	26.42	26.92	26.60	26.77	27.29	26.56
2014	27.58	28.15	28.10	27.75	28.13	28.34	28.15	28.38	28.40	28.36	28.75	28.19	28.20
2015	28.66	28.98	28.53	28.20	28.21	28.29	28.49	29.27	28.86	28.91	29.29	28.83	28.71
Education and Health Services													
2011	21.91	22.02	21.84	21.77	21.80	21.87	22.36	22.37	22.43	22.48	22.58	22.57	22.17
2012	22.80	23.00	23.04	23.22	23.23	23.00	23.07	22.80	23.11	23.30	23.57	23.62	23.15
2013	23.51	23.79	23.78	23.82	23.70	23.53	23.95	23.77	23.66	24.19	24.31	24.14	23.85
2014	24.18	24.22	24.01	24.07	24.12	23.87	24.16	24.05	24.00	24.40	24.18	24.15	24.12
2015	24.31	24.43	24.51	24.15	24.31	24.15	24.22	24.29	24.26	24.71	24.57	24.58	24.38
Leisure and Hospitality													
2011	11.98	11.95	11.89	11.86	11.82	11.91	11.85	11.91	11.89	11.95	12.08	12.07	11.93
2012	12.02	12.05	11.91	11.93	11.94	11.77	11.88	11.84	11.86	11.92	11.95	12.04	11.92
2013	11.92	11.82	11.77	11.86	11.91	11.78	11.74	11.89	12.06	12.09	12.11	12.42	11.95
2014	12.25	12.40	12.23	12.27	12.38	12.36	12.29	12.32	12.55	12.62	12.65	12.74	12.42
2015	12.68	12.85	12.64	12.74	12.80	12.63	12.51	12.62	12.72	12.80	12.83	12.92	12.73
Other Services													
2011	18.00	17.93	18.40	18.56	19.05	19.16	19.12	20.26	20.21	21.00	20.84	20.87	19.47
2012	21.52	20.71	21.07	20.90	20.96	20.98	20.60	20.53	21.32	21.26	20.76	21.49	21.01
2013	21.43	21.58	21.66	21.65	21.42	21.51	20.62	20.44	20.78	20.84	20.59	20.69	21.10
2014	20.54	20.89	21.04	21.41	20.99	20.91	20.55	20.82	21.22	21.02	21.24	20.94	20.97
2015	21.21	20.86	20.98	20.55	20.40	20.09	19.61	19.62	19.49	19.47	19.40	19.31	20.08

4. Average Weekly Earnings by Selected Industry: Texas, 2011–2015

(Dollars, not seasonally adjusted)

Industry and year	January	February	March	April	May	June	July	August	September	October	November	December	Annual average
Total Private													
2011	807.76	794.20	801.53	802.27	814.74	800.03	801.54	802.26	805.20	831.03	819.55	815.49	808.50
2012	834.03	795.19	791.28	810.99	784.33	790.23	811.79	796.42	823.22	807.68	812.03	842.17	808.44
2013	809.19	823.65	822.64	826.08	820.55	844.27	825.00	827.28	849.61	834.27	837.16	855.20	831.63
2014	844.56	871.99	872.90	858.13	859.39	880.07	862.32	869.42	868.87	879.42	900.36	887.18	870.89
2015	883.01	907.49	896.44	878.04	874.52	877.49	876.40	899.99	865.18	876.79	898.35	876.68	883.01
Goods-Producing													
2011	978.37	965.02	982.52	1,000.48	985.82	982.38	980.09	984.53	990.87	1,010.45	1,014.52	1,009.43	989.71
2012	1,011.15	1,003.00	1,004.72	1,004.48	980.82	992.16	990.39	987.82	1,004.94	1,003.86	1,012.01	1,050.71	1,003.86
2013	989.82	1,020.99	1,027.03	1,023.11	1,020.28	1,038.45	1,040.47	1,044.62	1,061.55	1,063.15	1,060.99	1,069.14	1,037.74
2014	1,077.93	1,094.19	1,098.38	1,093.25	1,093.49	1,114.91	1,101.60	1,114.79	1,121.46	1,154.87	1,152.83	1,171.37	1,115.41
2015	1,148.63	1,159.73	1,134.61	1,134.23	1,121.94	1,147.90	1,137.10	1,153.89	1,097.27	1,139.56	1,151.58	1,155.15	1,140.24
Construction													
2011	851.04	842.90	853.51	859.14	857.95	879.32	856.29	883.32	892.64	902.72	913.07	894.22	873.74
2012	897.58	900.52	929.99	927.89	922.78	948.91	936.56	962.20	967.10	992.79	990.08	1,012.98	949.61
2013	972.66	1,007.99	1,009.13	979.92	977.21	995.46	983.87	998.48	1,003.20	999.24	997.76	992.58	992.64
2014	1,002.08	999.55	1,009.21	1,000.94	985.56	1,010.93	1,021.71	1,041.94	1,032.05	1,056.46	1,060.99	1,075.29	1,026.64
2015	1,066.73	1,087.17	1,031.50	1,055.84	1,035.25	1,080.34	1,048.05	1,067.26	978.61	1,044.08	1,054.58	1,062.12	1,051.20
Manufacturing													
2011	968.92	955.51	947.78	976.28	990.23	979.96	986.58	970.75	977.92	997.40	1,008.22	1,016.58	980.37
2012	1,009.89	1,000.06	984.49	977.18	950.98	960.54	945.98	946.43	969.31	962.84	970.27	1,016.33	973.59
2013	995.51	1,012.72	1,023.03	1,034.04	1,023.74	1,032.78	1,044.87	1,043.89	1,065.79	1,073.36	1,069.93	1,080.95	1,041.07
2014	1,090.00	1,109.45	1,115.66	1,107.61	1,123.63	1,139.27	1,107.13	1,114.11	1,128.70	1,123.36	1,107.96	1,136.74	1,116.71
2015	1,113.22	1,122.58	1,125.67	1,123.77	1,114.27	1,116.56	1,121.75	1,131.21	1,117.31	1,140.01	1,139.47	1,152.32	1,127.74
Trade, Transportation, and Utilities													
2011	1,021.73	1,020.04	1,002.43	983.15	976.51	943.90	930.62	920.19	898.38	917.44	871.72	874.94	947.16
2012	881.52	850.81	845.96	866.38	834.00	838.40	849.37	830.84	849.41	810.53	800.09	817.10	839.96
2013	799.94	798.49	804.26	811.21	790.50	813.29	790.50	790.87	809.41	779.51	772.26	783.43	795.34
2014	765.99	784.58	801.42	785.90	782.60	797.04	781.41	782.00	778.23	786.94	803.31	802.26	787.27
2015	791.54	822.45	817.64	806.67	802.44	802.44	810.94	830.82	812.06	809.19	813.54	805.81	810.52
Financial Activities													
2011	984.36	971.76	975.43	975.00	1,014.75	955.12	953.05	945.26	949.95	1,011.72	974.36	964.20	973.59
2012	1,005.80	985.75	979.40	1,035.18	964.96	950.13	971.22	923.15	958.79	918.85	929.02	963.98	965.90
2013	933.24	955.01	946.94	957.31	953.64	999.58	955.70	946.27	995.67	954.00	969.95	1,014.12	964.78
2014	965.25	1,010.63	1,019.55	982.12	985.06	1,040.27	996.79	997.15	1,003.20	1,020.60	1,093.76	1,029.80	1,012.70
2015	1,053.94	1,118.35	1,129.79	1,089.41	1,082.74	1,080.58	1,090.18	1,151.91	1,079.91	1,089.41	1,152.61	1,099.01	1,100.76
Professional and Business Services													
2011	992.26	982.11	985.40	974.55	998.40	970.79	962.64	954.41	960.39	991.73	968.24	967.82	975.46
2012	994.56	972.42	953.42	992.16	954.70	966.60	986.11	962.54	990.72	967.76	977.44	1,030.58	979.07
2013	981.71	991.51	995.27	989.25	990.38	1,019.93	978.36	993.39	1,020.27	981.54	998.52	1,034.29	998.66
2014	1,020.46	1,069.70	1,062.18	1,032.30	1,046.44	1,079.75	1,052.81	1,072.76	1,062.16	1,066.34	1,104.00	1,062.76	1,060.32
2015	1,057.55	1,098.34	1,081.29	1,051.86	1,049.41	1,060.88	1,065.53	1,100.55	1,047.62	1,063.89	1,101.30	1,063.83	1,070.88
Education and Health Services													
2011	758.09	748.68	746.93	742.36	754.28	741.39	760.24	751.63	760.38	773.31	758.69	765.12	756.00
2012	782.04	770.50	769.54	791.80	771.24	775.10	791.30	770.64	794.98	782.88	791.95	807.80	782.47
2013	785.23	801.72	789.50	788.44	789.21	802.37	790.35	789.16	802.07	795.85	802.23	813.52	796.59
2014	797.94	818.64	799.53	789.50	791.14	804.42	799.70	796.06	794.40	805.20	814.87	792.12	800.78
2015	797.37	813.52	808.83	796.95	792.51	787.29	789.57	808.86	788.45	800.60	818.18	798.85	799.66
Leisure and Hospitality													
2011	333.04	334.60	341.24	330.89	340.42	334.67	334.17	334.67	328.16	339.38	334.62	336.75	335.23
2012	336.56	336.20	337.05	337.62	330.74	330.74	338.58	332.70	329.71	327.80	328.63	340.73	333.76
2013	324.22	334.51	337.80	329.71	334.67	339.26	328.72	334.11	334.06	333.68	335.45	345.28	334.60
2014	336.88	349.68	355.89	344.79	347.88	353.50	344.12	351.12	346.38	352.10	358.00	359.27	350.24
2015	349.97	368.80	366.56	359.27	359.68	358.69	355.28	362.19	351.07	355.84	363.09	363.05	358.99
Other Services													
2011	626.40	611.41	653.20	651.46	683.90	672.52	674.94	725.31	727.56	768.60	737.74	749.23	691.19
2012	789.78	743.49	733.24	737.77	723.12	728.01	731.30	716.50	744.07	741.97	722.45	756.45	739.55
2013	724.33	750.98	751.60	740.43	730.42	735.64	682.52	676.56	694.05	681.47	677.41	701.39	711.07
2014	669.60	703.99	704.84	721.52	692.67	700.49	676.10	687.06	693.89	685.25	707.29	701.49	696.20
2015	695.69	711.33	698.63	669.93	667.08	646.90	633.40	659.23	633.43	634.72	659.60	652.68	662.64

UTAH
At a Glance

Population:
  2005 Population: 2,457,719
  2010 census: 2,763,885
  2015 estimate: 2,995,919

Percent change in population:
  2005–2015: 21.9%
  2010–2015: 8.4%

Percent change in total nonfarm employment:
  2005–2015: 20.0%

Industry with the largest growth in employment, 2005–2015 (thousands):
  Education and health services, 53.6

Industry with the largest decline or smallest growth in employment, 2005–2015 (thousands):
  Information and mining and logging, 2.1

Civilian labor force:
  2005: 1,272,445
  2010: 1,356,097
  2015: 1,464,404

Unemployment rate and rank among states (highest to lowest):
  2005: 4.1%, 37th
  2010: 7.8%, 37th
  2015: 3.5%, 47th

Over-the-year change in unemployment rates:
  2012–2013: –0.8%
  2013–2014: –0.8%
  2014–2015: –0.3%

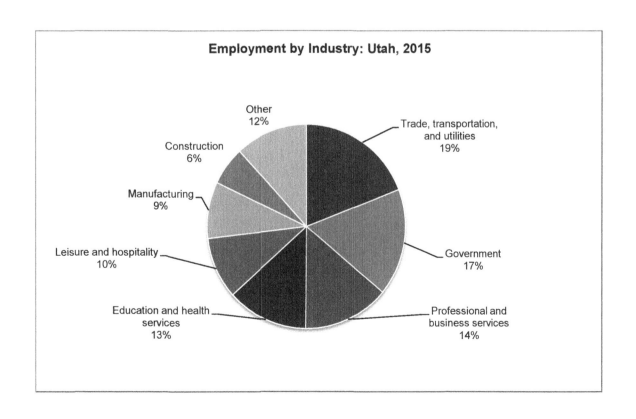

Employment by Industry: Utah, 2015

Other 12%
Construction 6%
Manufacturing 9%
Leisure and hospitality 10%
Education and health services 13%
Trade, transportation, and utilities 19%
Government 17%
Professional and business services 14%

1. Employment by Industry: Utah, 2005–2015

(Numbers in thousands, not seasonally adjusted)

Industry and year	January	February	March	April	May	June	July	August	September	October	November	December	Annual average
Total Nonfarm													
2005	1,110.8	1,118.0	1,126.8	1,138.4	1,139.7	1,149.0	1,140.1	1,152.1	1,168.0	1,170.0	1,177.9	1,185.3	1,148.0
2006	1,162.9	1,171.5	1,182.5	1,192.9	1,196.1	1,211.1	1,196.1	1,208.2	1,222.5	1,222.8	1,234.6	1,243.3	1,203.7
2007	1,219.2	1,226.7	1,238.5	1,247.0	1,250.3	1,261.9	1,244.6	1,256.2	1,266.5	1,270.5	1,276.6	1,281.0	1,253.3
2008	1,244.5	1,248.0	1,253.3	1,259.1	1,256.6	1,261.4	1,242.8	1,252.3	1,261.4	1,254.9	1,249.1	1,246.7	1,252.5
2009	1,203.3	1,197.0	1,195.9	1,194.2	1,189.7	1,190.4	1,168.5	1,174.4	1,187.3	1,187.8	1,187.5	1,190.0	1,188.8
2010	1,159.7	1,159.9	1,168.9	1,182.2	1,183.9	1,187.1	1,171.9	1,179.1	1,193.1	1,198.2	1,201.4	1,204.7	1,182.5
2011	1,177.1	1,182.2	1,190.7	1,204.9	1,203.0	1,209.8	1,197.1	1,207.7	1,224.2	1,227.1	1,231.6	1,236.9	1,207.7
2012	1,212.1	1,218.7	1,229.2	1,246.4	1,251.3	1,257.6	1,237.2	1,249.1	1,265.0	1,272.3	1,281.7	1,283.8	1,250.4
2013	1,257.6	1,265.1	1,274.4	1,286.5	1,287.9	1,291.3	1,279.0	1,287.4	1,301.0	1,312.1	1,320.2	1,323.4	1,290.5
2014	1,293.8	1,301.2	1,309.6	1,320.8	1,323.8	1,327.9	1,311.9	1,324.7	1,342.2	1,352.5	1,358.8	1,364.1	1,327.6
2015	1,340.7	1,350.4	1,361.0	1,369.3	1,373.4	1,379.3	1,369.8	1,376.1	1,394.4	1,401.8	1,405.6	1,407.9	1,377.5
Total Private													
2005	908.5	914.0	922.1	932.4	934.7	944.7	951.3	960.4	964.3	964.5	971.8	979.8	945.7
2006	958.9	965.3	975.6	985.2	989.5	1,004.0	1,004.8	1,014.0	1,016.5	1,015.3	1,026.2	1,035.7	999.3
2007	1,013.2	1,018.7	1,029.8	1,037.0	1,040.8	1,052.3	1,052.3	1,060.2	1,057.9	1,059.5	1,064.7	1,070.0	1,046.4
2008	1,034.4	1,035.9	1,040.3	1,044.7	1,042.3	1,047.8	1,046.5	1,051.3	1,046.7	1,038.0	1,031.6	1,030.1	1,040.8
2009	988.9	980.7	979.4	974.9	971.2	973.8	969.7	971.6	970.7	968.8	968.5	971.8	974.2
2010	943.4	942.2	950.2	961.2	959.2	966.5	969.6	973.1	973.3	975.9	979.2	983.8	964.8
2011	958.1	961.0	968.0	980.6	978.4	987.0	992.4	999.1	1,001.9	1,003.0	1,007.6	1,013.4	987.5
2012	989.6	994.3	1,004.1	1,017.9	1,023.3	1,031.3	1,029.3	1,039.2	1,040.2	1,044.0	1,053.6	1,057.5	1,027.0
2013	1,033.0	1,038.7	1,047.8	1,057.9	1,057.4	1,063.7	1,069.0	1,076.0	1,073.6	1,081.0	1,089.5	1,093.4	1,065.1
2014	1,066.2	1,071.0	1,078.9	1,085.5	1,086.4	1,094.1	1,097.2	1,108.4	1,109.9	1,117.5	1,124.0	1,130.1	1,097.4
2015	1,108.7	1,115.4	1,124.9	1,131.5	1,133.8	1,143.9	1,150.3	1,157.8	1,158.6	1,162.6	1,166.5	1,169.4	1,143.6
Goods-Producing													
2005	194.0	195.4	196.9	202.8	206.4	210.4	213.3	215.6	216.4	215.3	216.4	216.0	208.2
2006	212.0	214.5	218.1	222.0	227.1	232.0	233.0	235.6	236.3	236.1	237.1	237.2	228.4
2007	231.6	232.8	236.7	239.8	243.9	248.6	248.5	250.3	248.2	247.9	244.7	241.6	242.9
2008	231.0	228.9	229.8	230.1	231.7	233.6	233.1	233.0	230.5	226.7	221.5	215.8	228.8
2009	202.1	196.4	194.8	192.3	194.2	195.5	195.3	195.1	193.7	192.9	190.4	187.7	194.2
2010	180.2	178.4	179.6	183.3	186.0	188.3	190.0	191.5	191.6	191.8	190.6	188.4	186.6
2011	181.4	181.2	182.9	186.4	188.3	191.8	195.9	197.5	196.7	196.0	195.3	193.4	190.6
2012	188.6	189.5	191.8	195.0	199.6	202.1	202.6	204.4	203.2	203.0	202.3	201.2	198.6
2013	195.6	195.9	198.7	201.8	204.9	207.1	209.1	210.3	208.8	208.7	208.1	206.2	204.6
2014	201.9	202.7	205.3	208.0	211.9	214.0	214.9	216.2	215.7	216.7	216.1	214.9	211.5
2015	210.3	210.8	213.1	215.6	218.1	221.0	222.5	222.9	222.1	225.1	222.7	219.3	218.6
Service-Providing													
2005	916.8	922.6	929.9	935.6	933.3	938.6	926.8	936.5	951.6	954.7	961.5	969.3	939.8
2006	950.9	957.0	964.4	970.9	969.0	979.1	963.1	972.6	986.2	986.7	997.5	1,006.1	975.3
2007	987.6	993.9	1,001.8	1,007.2	1,006.4	1,013.3	996.1	1,005.9	1,018.3	1,022.6	1,031.9	1,039.4	1,010.4
2008	1,013.5	1,019.1	1,023.5	1,029.0	1,024.9	1,027.8	1,009.7	1,019.3	1,030.9	1,028.2	1,027.6	1,030.9	1,023.7
2009	1,001.2	1,000.6	1,001.1	1,001.9	995.5	994.9	973.2	979.3	993.6	994.9	997.1	1,002.3	994.6
2010	979.5	981.5	989.3	998.9	997.9	998.8	981.9	987.6	1,001.5	1,006.4	1,010.8	1,016.3	995.9
2011	995.7	1,001.0	1,007.8	1,018.5	1,014.7	1,018.0	1,001.2	1,010.2	1,027.5	1,031.1	1,036.3	1,043.5	1,017.1
2012	1,023.5	1,029.2	1,037.4	1,051.4	1,051.7	1,055.5	1,034.6	1,044.7	1,061.8	1,069.3	1,079.4	1,082.6	1,051.8
2013	1,062.0	1,069.2	1,075.7	1,084.7	1,083.0	1,084.2	1,069.9	1,077.1	1,092.2	1,103.4	1,112.1	1,117.2	1,085.9
2014	1,091.9	1,098.5	1,104.3	1,112.8	1,111.9	1,113.9	1,097.0	1,108.5	1,126.5	1,135.8	1,142.7	1,149.2	1,116.1
2015	1,130.4	1,139.6	1,147.9	1,153.7	1,155.3	1,158.3	1,147.3	1,153.2	1,172.3	1,176.7	1,182.9	1,188.6	1,158.9
Mining and Logging													
2005	7.6	7.8	7.8	8.2	8.4	8.6	8.8	8.9	9.0	9.0	9.2	9.2	8.5
2006	9.0	9.2	9.4	9.7	9.9	10.2	10.4	10.5	10.5	10.6	10.7	10.8	10.1
2007	10.6	10.6	10.8	10.9	11.1	11.2	11.3	11.4	11.1	11.4	11.4	11.4	11.1
2008	11.4	11.4	11.5	11.8	12.3	12.6	12.8	13.4	13.5	13.6	13.5	13.2	12.6
2009	12.1	11.8	11.5	10.9	10.6	10.6	10.5	10.3	10.3	10.1	10.1	10.0	10.7
2010	9.8	9.8	10.0	10.2	10.4	10.6	10.6	10.8	10.8	11.0	11.0	11.0	10.5
2011	10.8	10.9	11.1	11.3	11.4	11.7	12.0	12.1	12.3	12.3	12.2	12.2	11.7
2012	12.1	12.3	12.5	12.6	12.8	12.8	12.8	12.9	12.8	12.7	12.6	12.4	12.6
2013	12.1	12.0	12.1	12.2	12.3	12.4	12.4	12.4	12.4	12.2	12.2	12.1	12.2
2014	11.9	11.9	12.0	12.1	12.3	12.4	12.4	12.5	12.4	12.5	12.3	12.1	12.2
2015	11.7	11.1	10.9	10.6	10.6	10.5	10.4	10.3	10.1	10.4	10.2	10.0	10.6

1. Employment by Industry: Utah, 2005–2015—*Continued*

(Numbers in thousands, not seasonally adjusted)

Industry and year	January	February	March	April	May	June	July	August	September	October	November	December	Annual average
Construction													
2005	71.1	72.1	73.7	78.1	80.5	83.3	85.5	86.9	87.5	86.8	86.9	86.0	81.5
2006	83.0	84.5	87.3	90.4	94.6	98.4	99.1	101.1	101.6	100.9	100.9	100.3	95.2
2007	96.0	96.5	99.3	102.1	105.2	108.6	108.3	109.7	108.0	107.2	103.2	99.7	103.7
2008	91.2	89.3	90.3	91.1	92.6	94.0	93.6	93.9	92.0	89.1	85.3	81.7	90.3
2009	72.1	69.3	69.1	68.4	70.9	72.0	72.5	72.6	71.9	71.2	69.2	66.4	70.5
2010	60.5	59.3	60.4	62.6	64.9	66.2	67.4	68.4	68.8	69.1	67.6	65.1	65.0
2011	59.4	58.8	60.0	62.5	64.0	66.5	69.3	70.5	69.7	68.8	68.0	66.0	65.3
2012	62.1	62.6	64.2	66.8	70.2	71.9	72.2	73.6	72.6	72.3	71.6	70.5	69.2
2013	66.2	66.6	68.8	71.3	74.0	75.6	77.3	78.1	77.1	77.0	76.3	74.1	73.5
2014	70.9	71.4	73.7	76.1	78.9	80.4	81.5	82.4	82.0	82.9	82.2	80.8	78.6
2015	76.8	77.7	79.8	82.3	84.1	86.5	87.7	88.3	87.9	89.9	88.3	85.0	84.5
Manufacturing													
2005	115.3	115.5	115.4	116.5	117.5	118.5	119.0	119.8	119.9	119.5	120.3	120.8	118.2
2006	120.0	120.8	121.4	121.9	122.6	123.4	123.5	124.0	124.2	124.6	125.5	126.1	123.2
2007	125.0	125.7	126.6	126.8	127.6	128.8	128.9	129.2	129.1	129.3	130.1	130.5	128.1
2008	128.4	128.2	128.0	127.2	126.8	127.0	126.7	125.7	125.0	124.0	122.7	120.9	125.9
2009	117.9	115.3	114.2	113.0	112.7	112.9	112.3	112.2	111.5	111.6	111.1	111.3	113.0
2010	109.9	109.3	109.2	110.5	110.7	111.5	112.0	112.3	112.0	111.7	112.0	112.3	111.1
2011	111.2	111.5	111.8	112.6	112.9	113.6	114.6	114.9	114.7	114.9	115.1	115.2	113.6
2012	114.4	114.6	115.1	115.6	116.6	117.4	117.6	117.9	117.8	118.0	118.1	118.3	116.8
2013	117.3	117.3	117.8	118.3	118.6	119.1	119.4	119.8	119.3	119.5	119.6	120.0	118.8
2014	119.1	119.4	119.6	119.8	120.7	121.2	121.0	121.3	121.3	121.3	121.6	122.0	120.7
2015	121.8	122.0	122.4	122.7	123.4	124.0	124.4	124.3	124.1	124.8	124.2	124.3	123.5
Trade, Transportation, and Utilities													
2005	219.7	218.8	221.2	221.8	223.0	223.8	225.1	227.5	227.6	229.7	234.2	237.3	225.8
2006	228.6	228.1	229.6	230.0	231.7	234.2	234.8	237.2	237.6	238.3	244.8	248.6	235.3
2007	240.4	239.9	241.8	241.8	243.4	244.3	245.2	246.8	247.0	248.1	253.5	256.4	245.7
2008	246.9	245.5	246.3	247.0	247.8	248.8	248.2	249.1	248.0	247.5	250.1	251.0	248.0
2009	238.6	236.0	235.1	233.2	233.9	233.6	231.6	231.8	231.8	231.8	235.4	237.1	234.2
2010	226.3	225.0	225.9	226.8	227.8	228.5	228.6	229.8	228.9	230.1	234.8	236.7	229.1
2011	227.5	226.5	227.8	230.8	231.6	232.6	233.5	234.7	234.5	235.7	241.3	243.3	233.3
2012	234.9	233.9	235.6	237.8	239.7	241.2	240.9	241.7	242.0	243.5	250.6	251.3	241.1
2013	242.0	241.2	241.6	243.1	244.8	245.5	246.8	247.8	246.4	249.3	254.9	257.0	246.7
2014	246.6	246.0	247.0	248.5	250.4	251.6	251.6	253.6	253.6	256.5	262.7	265.2	252.8
2015	256.8	257.0	258.2	259.0	260.6	261.2	263.1	265.0	264.5	265.1	271.7	275.9	263.2
Wholesale Trade													
2005	41.8	42.0	42.2	42.4	42.9	43.1	43.1	43.3	43.3	43.5	43.7	43.8	42.9
2006	43.3	43.6	43.8	44.1	44.6	45.2	45.1	45.3	45.5	45.7	46.0	46.4	44.9
2007	46.2	46.4	46.6	46.6	47.2	47.5	47.6	47.9	47.8	48.0	48.2	48.5	47.4
2008	47.7	47.8	48.0	48.2	48.5	48.6	48.5	48.6	48.5	48.2	47.9	48.0	48.2
2009	46.6	46.4	46.0	45.3	45.1	45.0	44.7	44.6	44.5	44.5	44.3	44.4	45.1
2010	43.6	43.4	43.6	43.9	44.3	44.3	44.5	44.6	44.5	44.7	44.9	45.3	44.3
2011	44.8	45.1	45.4	45.7	46.0	46.2	46.3	46.5	46.4	46.5	46.7	46.8	46.0
2012	46.4	46.6	46.9	47.1	47.4	47.5	47.4	47.6	47.5	47.6	47.6	47.7	47.3
2013	47.6	47.7	47.7	48.1	48.2	48.2	48.3	48.3	48.1	48.0	48.2	48.3	48.1
2014	47.6	47.8	47.8	48.2	48.5	48.5	48.7	48.9	48.7	49.3	49.5	49.7	48.6
2015	49.0	49.3	49.4	49.8	50.2	50.3	50.5	50.6	50.4	49.8	50.2	50.4	50.0
Retail Trade													
2005	132.4	130.8	132.8	132.4	133.0	133.5	134.6	136.6	136.4	137.9	142.0	144.3	135.6
2006	137.0	135.9	137.1	137.1	138.3	139.9	140.5	142.3	142.2	142.9	148.6	151.2	141.1
2007	144.3	143.4	144.7	144.8	145.6	145.9	146.5	147.5	147.3	147.8	152.7	154.5	147.1
2008	148.3	146.7	147.2	147.5	148.1	149.1	148.6	149.2	148.3	148.2	151.1	151.8	148.7
2009	142.0	140.2	140.2	139.5	140.5	140.7	139.1	139.7	139.8	139.9	143.7	144.9	140.9
2010	136.4	135.2	135.7	136.3	136.9	137.2	136.9	137.6	136.7	137.5	141.4	142.1	137.5
2011	134.8	133.6	134.4	136.8	137.3	137.7	138.5	139.3	139.0	140.3	145.2	146.2	138.6
2012	139.1	138.0	139.1	140.4	141.7	142.9	143.4	143.7	143.6	145.0	151.7	151.5	143.3
2013	143.4	142.6	143.2	145.1	146.4	147.0	147.8	148.7	147.6	149.4	154.2	155.2	147.6
2014	147.3	146.7	147.5	148.6	149.9	150.6	151.3	152.7	152.4	154.1	159.0	160.5	151.7
2015	153.0	152.8	153.5	155.3	156.4	156.8	157.7	159.2	158.8	160.3	165.5	167.5	158.1

1. Employment by Industry: Utah, 2005–2015—*Continued*

(Numbers in thousands, not seasonally adjusted)

Industry and year	January	February	March	April	May	June	July	August	September	October	November	December	Annual average
Transportation and Utilities													
2005	45.5	46.0	46.2	47.0	47.1	47.2	47.4	47.6	47.9	48.3	48.5	49.2	47.3
2006	48.3	48.6	48.7	48.8	48.8	49.1	49.2	49.6	49.9	49.7	50.2	51.0	49.3
2007	49.9	50.1	50.5	50.4	50.6	50.9	51.1	51.4	51.9	52.3	52.6	53.4	51.3
2008	50.9	51.0	51.1	51.3	51.2	51.1	51.1	51.3	51.2	51.1	51.1	51.2	51.1
2009	50.0	49.4	48.9	48.4	48.3	47.9	47.8	47.5	47.5	47.4	47.4	47.8	48.2
2010	46.3	46.4	46.6	46.6	46.6	47.0	47.2	47.6	47.7	47.9	48.5	49.3	47.3
2011	47.9	47.8	48.0	48.3	48.3	48.7	48.7	48.9	49.1	48.9	49.4	50.3	48.7
2012	49.4	49.3	49.6	50.3	50.6	50.8	50.1	50.4	50.9	50.9	51.3	52.1	50.5
2013	51.0	50.9	50.7	49.9	50.2	50.3	50.7	50.8	50.7	51.9	52.5	53.5	51.1
2014	51.7	51.5	51.7	51.7	52.0	52.5	51.6	52.0	52.5	53.1	54.2	55.0	52.5
2015	54.8	54.9	55.3	53.9	54.0	54.1	54.9	55.2	55.3	55.0	56.0	58.0	55.1
Information													
2005	31.0	31.5	31.8	31.6	31.7	31.7	32.4	33.0	32.7	32.2	32.5	32.3	32.0
2006	31.7	31.5	31.5	31.9	32.8	33.0	32.1	32.5	32.2	32.0	32.5	32.0	32.1
2007	32.0	32.0	32.2	30.9	31.1	31.0	30.9	31.0	30.4	30.4	30.5	30.5	31.1
2008	29.8	30.5	30.6	30.9	31.4	31.5	31.1	31.1	30.8	30.5	30.7	30.8	30.8
2009	29.9	30.0	29.9	29.5	29.8	29.9	29.5	29.3	29.0	29.0	29.4	29.7	29.6
2010	28.7	28.9	29.3	29.4	29.3	29.4	29.3	29.0	29.0	29.0	29.8	29.9	29.3
2011	28.9	29.2	29.2	29.2	29.5	29.6	29.6	29.8	29.6	29.8	30.7	30.8	29.7
2012	30.2	30.5	30.6	32.0	32.7	32.7	31.3	31.5	31.1	31.3	32.3	32.5	31.6
2013	33.2	33.3	33.3	32.0	32.3	32.4	32.5	32.8	32.2	32.2	33.2	33.4	32.7
2014	32.6	32.9	33.1	32.8	32.9	33.0	33.1	33.7	33.0	33.1	33.5	33.7	33.1
2015	32.9	33.3	33.5	33.4	33.9	34.3	34.8	35.2	34.8	34.1	34.7	34.8	34.1
Financial Activities													
2005	65.5	66.0	65.5	66.8	66.7	67.2	67.9	68.1	68.1	68.7	69.0	70.3	67.5
2006	69.2	69.9	70.1	70.7	70.9	71.4	71.8	72.1	72.0	72.9	73.5	74.6	71.6
2007	73.7	74.4	74.6	75.0	75.2	75.6	75.6	75.7	75.2	75.7	75.9	76.6	75.3
2008	74.2	74.9	74.6	74.5	74.3	74.2	74.1	74.1	73.4	73.1	72.9	73.8	74.0
2009	72.5	72.5	72.4	71.7	71.4	71.2	70.3	70.3	69.8	69.7	69.6	70.5	71.0
2010	68.5	67.9	68.1	67.8	67.6	67.7	67.6	67.9	67.7	68.2	68.3	68.8	68.0
2011	67.4	67.6	67.7	68.0	67.8	68.2	68.2	68.4	68.0	68.4	68.5	69.3	68.1
2012	67.9	68.2	68.2	68.6	68.6	69.2	69.5	70.3	70.1	70.6	71.0	71.9	69.5
2013	70.6	71.1	71.3	71.8	71.8	72.8	73.6	74.1	73.6	73.7	74.1	74.8	72.8
2014	73.2	73.7	73.3	73.4	73.5	74.2	75.4	76.2	75.7	76.3	76.8	77.4	74.9
2015	76.9	77.4	77.7	78.0	78.2	78.8	79.6	79.9	79.8	80.8	81.5	82.1	79.2
Professional and Business Services													
2005	138.2	139.5	140.9	143.4	145.3	146.1	147.4	149.0	149.1	150.1	150.5	151.1	145.9
2006	147.1	148.5	149.8	152.2	153.8	156.2	156.6	157.5	157.1	156.9	158.1	158.6	154.4
2007	153.5	154.5	156.4	160.0	163.0	164.7	164.1	165.8	165.0	167.0	168.2	167.8	162.5
2008	159.0	159.8	160.6	162.2	164.2	164.4	164.4	165.8	164.6	162.6	160.0	158.9	162.2
2009	150.5	149.6	148.8	149.1	149.5	149.4	149.0	149.0	148.9	149.9	148.9	149.0	149.3
2010	144.2	145.0	147.9	150.9	152.8	154.3	155.4	155.0	154.4	156.1	156.1	156.5	152.4
2011	151.8	153.2	155.0	157.7	158.5	159.3	160.4	161.6	162.2	164.8	165.0	164.9	159.5
2012	158.9	160.7	162.7	165.4	167.4	168.5	168.9	171.5	171.1	173.9	174.2	173.7	168.1
2013	168.0	170.1	172.2	175.5	176.0	176.1	178.0	179.4	179.7	183.8	185.4	184.9	177.4
2014	178.8	178.7	179.8	181.6	183.0	184.0	184.9	187.8	188.3	191.1	191.3	192.3	185.1
2015	185.8	186.6	188.7	191.7	193.5	195.1	196.5	198.1	197.5	198.7	198.4	194.5	193.8
Education and Health Services													
2005	126.8	128.0	128.7	129.0	125.0	125.9	124.5	125.9	130.7	132.0	133.1	133.6	128.6
2006	132.6	133.5	134.6	134.8	131.2	131.6	130.2	131.9	136.5	137.6	138.6	139.1	134.4
2007	137.7	139.1	139.8	140.5	136.7	136.6	135.7	137.7	142.6	144.1	145.2	146.1	140.2
2008	145.0	146.3	146.8	147.2	143.1	142.6	141.7	143.4	148.7	150.4	151.7	152.1	146.6
2009	150.4	150.9	151.7	151.5	147.5	146.8	146.0	147.6	152.6	154.5	155.7	155.7	150.9
2010	154.6	155.3	156.0	156.4	152.1	151.4	150.7	151.7	157.1	158.6	158.9	158.4	155.1
2011	157.6	158.8	159.0	159.7	155.9	155.1	153.5	155.1	160.9	162.5	163.2	163.4	158.7
2012	162.2	163.2	164.0	165.7	161.6	161.0	158.9	161.4	166.8	168.9	170.3	170.4	164.5
2013	169.4	170.9	171.5	172.9	168.1	166.5	164.6	166.8	172.0	174.8	176.0	175.5	170.8
2014	173.2	175.1	176.0	174.4	170.8	169.1	168.0	170.2	175.9	178.4	180.3	179.7	174.3
2015	179.9	181.8	182.4	181.9	179.1	178.2	176.5	178.5	185.2	187.2	187.8	187.9	182.2

1. Employment by Industry: Utah, 2005–2015—*Continued*

(Numbers in thousands, not seasonally adjusted)

Industry and year	January	February	March	April	May	June	July	August	September	October	November	December	Annual average
Leisure and Hospitality													
2005	100.9	102.2	104.0	103.7	103.2	106.0	106.1	106.8	105.8	103.1	102.5	105.4	104.1
2006	104.5	105.8	107.8	109.5	107.4	110.4	110.8	111.6	109.6	106.9	107.0	110.6	108.5
2007	109.9	111.2	113.3	113.8	111.6	115.2	115.7	116.0	113.6	110.6	111.1	115.4	113.1
2008	113.7	114.9	116.3	117.4	114.2	116.8	117.3	117.7	114.9	112.2	109.9	112.9	114.9
2009	111.0	111.3	112.6	113.5	110.7	112.9	113.0	113.6	111.1	107.4	105.7	108.7	111.0
2010	107.8	108.5	109.8	113.1	110.0	113.0	113.4	113.9	111.2	108.7	107.4	111.8	110.7
2011	110.5	111.2	113.0	115.1	112.7	116.0	116.4	116.9	115.4	111.5	109.4	114.1	113.5
2012	113.1	114.3	116.8	118.8	118.7	121.3	121.5	122.6	120.5	117.4	117.5	120.9	118.6
2013	119.0	120.5	123.1	124.2	122.3	126.6	127.2	127.6	124.5	122.1	121.3	125.2	123.6
2014	123.6	125.2	127.3	129.5	126.5	130.2	130.8	132.3	129.9	127.8	125.6	129.2	128.2
2015	128.1	130.1	132.6	133.5	132.0	136.3	137.8	138.7	136.0	134.0	132.3	137.7	134.1
Other Services													
2005	32.4	32.6	33.1	33.3	33.4	33.6	34.6	34.5	33.9	33.4	33.6	33.8	33.5
2006	33.2	33.5	34.1	34.1	34.6	35.2	35.5	35.6	35.2	34.6	34.6	35.0	34.6
2007	34.4	34.8	35.0	35.2	35.9	36.3	36.6	36.9	35.9	35.7	35.6	35.6	35.7
2008	34.8	35.1	35.3	35.4	35.6	35.9	36.6	37.1	35.8	35.0	34.8	34.8	35.5
2009	33.9	34.0	34.1	34.1	34.2	34.5	35.0	34.9	33.8	33.6	33.4	33.4	34.1
2010	33.1	33.2	33.6	33.5	33.6	33.9	34.6	34.3	33.4	33.4	33.3	33.3	33.6
2011	33.0	33.3	33.4	33.7	34.1	34.4	34.9	35.1	34.6	34.3	34.2	34.2	34.1
2012	33.8	34.0	34.4	34.6	35.0	35.3	35.7	35.8	35.4	35.4	35.4	35.6	35.0
2013	35.2	35.7	36.1	36.6	37.2	36.7	37.2	37.2	36.4	36.4	36.5	36.4	36.5
2014	36.3	36.7	37.1	37.3	37.4	38.0	38.5	38.4	37.8	37.6	37.7	37.7	37.5
2015	38.0	38.4	38.7	38.4	38.4	39.0	39.5	39.5	38.7	37.6	37.4	37.2	38.4
Government													
2005	202.3	204.0	204.7	206.0	205.0	204.3	188.8	191.7	203.7	205.5	206.1	205.5	202.3
2006	204.0	206.2	206.9	207.7	206.6	207.1	191.3	194.2	206.0	207.5	208.4	207.6	204.5
2007	206.0	208.0	208.7	210.0	209.5	209.6	192.3	196.0	208.6	211.0	211.9	211.0	206.9
2008	210.1	212.1	213.0	214.4	214.3	213.6	196.3	201.0	214.7	216.9	217.5	216.6	211.7
2009	214.4	216.3	216.5	219.3	218.5	216.6	198.8	202.8	216.6	219.0	219.0	218.2	214.7
2010	216.3	217.7	218.7	221.0	224.7	220.6	202.3	206.0	219.8	222.3	222.2	220.9	217.7
2011	219.0	221.2	222.7	224.3	224.6	222.8	204.7	208.6	222.3	224.1	224.0	223.5	220.2
2012	222.5	224.4	225.1	228.5	228.0	226.3	207.9	209.9	224.8	228.3	228.1	226.3	223.3
2013	224.6	226.4	226.6	228.6	230.5	227.6	210.0	211.4	227.4	231.1	230.7	230.0	225.4
2014	227.6	230.2	230.7	235.3	237.4	233.8	214.7	216.3	232.3	235.0	234.8	234.0	230.2
2015	232.0	235.0	236.1	237.8	239.6	235.4	219.5	218.3	235.8	239.2	239.1	238.5	233.9

2. Average Weekly Hours by Selected Industry: Utah, 2011–2015

(Not seasonally adjusted)

Industry and year	January	February	March	April	May	June	July	August	September	October	November	December	Annual average
Total Private													
2011	35.1	34.8	34.8	34.8	35.3	35.0	34.9	35.0	34.7	35.7	34.9	34.7	35.0
2012	35.1	34.7	34.9	35.2	34.8	35.1	35.7	35.2	35.8	35.3	34.9	35.6	35.2
2013	34.6	34.9	34.8	34.5	35.1	35.7	34.7	35.1	35.5	34.7	34.8	35.3	35.0
2014	34.8	35.5	35.7	34.8	35.1	35.9	35.2	35.4	35.2	35.3	35.6	34.7	35.2
2015	34.4	35.3	35.1	34.2	34.7	34.9	34.8	35.4	34.4	34.8	34.9	34.3	34.8
Goods-Producing													
2011	39.6	39.2	39.2	39.3	39.7	39.4	38.9	39.6	38.9	39.7	40.1	39.5	39.4
2012	39.6	39.7	39.9	39.6	40.4	39.9	40.0	39.7	40.4	40.7	40.1	40.5	40.0
2013	39.2	39.3	39.1	39.4	39.9	39.9	39.6	40.2	40.1	39.7	40.4	40.1	39.7
2014	39.3	39.2	40.0	40.2	39.9	40.3	39.9	39.7	39.6	40.2	39.3	38.8	39.7
2015	37.6	38.4	38.5	38.1	38.5	38.3	37.9	38.4	36.8	38.1	37.7	37.5	38.0
Construction													
2011	36.9	37.4	37.7	38.4	38.4	38.8	38.2	38.5	38.2	38.4	38.7	37.3	38.1
2012	37.2	37.7	38.2	37.3	39.2	39.4	39.7	40.1	40.5	41.3	40.1	39.1	39.2
2013	37.2	38.4	38.0	39.2	39.4	39.5	39.3	40.0	39.8	40.0	39.8	39.1	39.2
2014	38.3	38.1	39.4	40.1	39.7	40.1	39.7	39.9	39.5	40.5	39.1	38.3	39.4
2015	36.6	37.3	37.4	36.8	37.8	38.2	38.3	38.3	36.0	38.9	38.8	37.6	37.7
Manufacturing													
2011	39.5	39.1	39.0	38.9	39.6	39.0	38.7	39.5	38.5	39.7	40.1	39.9	39.3
2012	39.8	39.8	40.0	40.0	40.2	39.4	39.3	39.1	40.0	40.1	39.9	40.8	39.9
2013	39.1	39.8	39.7	39.5	40.2	40.1	39.7	40.2	40.2	39.3	40.4	40.4	39.9
2014	39.4	39.4	39.8	39.8	39.7	40.0	39.8	39.4	39.5	39.6	39.8	39.5	39.6
2015	38.6	39.3	39.4	39.2	39.3	38.6	38.3	39.1	37.9	38.1	37.3	37.6	38.6
Trade, Transportation, and Utilities													
2011	33.6	33.5	34.0	34.1	34.2	34.2	34.1	34.0	33.6	34.4	33.4	33.6	33.9
2012	33.3	33.0	33.4	33.6	33.3	33.8	34.1	33.8	34.1	33.5	33.5	34.4	33.7
2013	32.9	33.3	33.3	33.3	33.5	34.3	33.5	33.6	33.7	32.7	33.0	33.5	33.4
2014	32.9	34.2	34.5	33.6	34.8	34.9	34.3	34.5	34.3	33.9	34.8	34.1	34.2
2015	33.4	34.1	33.8	33.8	34.0	34.0	34.1	34.3	33.0	33.0	33.1	33.1	33.6
Information													
2011	32.6	32.1	32.4	31.8	33.6	32.2	33.1	33.1	33.5	34.8	34.2	34.1	33.1
2012	34.9	33.0	33.4	34.4	33.2	32.8	34.9	32.9	34.6	32.8	32.9	33.2	33.6
2013	31.1	31.7	32.4	32.1	32.6	34.3	31.9	31.4	33.4	32.1	32.7	34.0	32.5
2014	32.0	34.4	34.9	32.9	33.3	35.2	33.1	33.2	33.2	33.6	35.5	34.4	33.8
2015	34.8	36.0	36.0	34.5	34.6	34.5	34.6	36.3	33.6	34.3	35.9	34.5	35.0
Financial Activities													
2011	35.1	34.9	34.8	35.4	36.1	35.3	35.2	35.1	35.3	36.1	35.4	35.7	35.4
2012	35.7	34.7	34.8	35.3	34.2	35.1	35.4	34.8	36.1	35.2	35.5	36.0	35.2
2013	35.1	35.3	35.8	35.5	35.8	36.9	35.8	36.2	37.0	36.0	36.1	37.0	36.0
2014	36.5	36.2	36.9	35.7	35.7	36.9	36.2	36.4	36.3	36.4	37.7	36.1	36.4
2015	36.6	37.1	37.4	36.4	36.4	36.5	37.0	37.5	36.6	37.3	38.4	37.2	37.0
Professional and Business Services													
2011	35.2	35.9	35.8	35.8	36.5	36.2	35.4	35.9	35.8	36.7	35.3	34.7	35.8
2012	35.7	35.1	35.3	36.4	33.7	34.3	35.8	35.5	36.0	35.3	35.0	35.7	35.3
2013	34.5	35.0	35.1	34.7	35.0	36.1	34.3	35.0	35.7	35.0	34.9	35.6	35.1
2014	34.4	36.2	36.2	35.3	34.7	35.2	33.8	34.8	34.9	35.3	35.8	34.9	35.1
2015	34.0	35.2	35.5	34.7	35.0	35.7	35.1	36.2	35.3	35.2	35.7	35.1	35.2
Education and Health Services													
2011	40.2	40.2	39.8	39.5	39.8	39.3	39.3	39.0	38.8	39.4	39.0	39.1	39.4
2012	40.0	39.3	38.3	38.6	38.3	38.6	38.8	38.7	39.1	38.4	38.3	39.3	38.8
2013	39.3	38.9	38.5	37.9	38.4	38.5	37.8	38.1	38.7	37.9	37.9	38.3	38.3
2014	38.5	38.7	38.1	36.9	37.0	37.6	37.4	37.4	37.5	37.2	37.8	37.4	37.6
2015	37.7	38.1	37.1	35.9	36.1	36.8	37.1	37.3	37.4	37.7	38.2	37.7	37.3
Leisure and Hospitality													
2011	26.0	25.9	25.4	25.3	25.5	24.7	25.5	25.2	24.4	26.0	24.2	23.8	25.2
2012	24.4	24.6	24.6	24.8	24.9	25.2	26.3	25.6	26.0	24.9	23.6	24.7	25.0
2013	23.8	25.0	24.8	24.2	24.8	26.5	25.3	25.8	25.8	24.8	23.9	25.5	25.0
2014	25.5	26.2	26.1	24.6	25.0	26.6	26.1	26.6	25.5	25.3	24.7	24.0	25.5
2015	25.4	26.7	26.6	24.4	25.6	26.3	26.3	27.2	25.9	25.9	24.8	24.5	25.8

3. Average Hourly Earnings by Selected Industry: Utah, 2011–2015

(Dollars, not seasonally adjusted)

Industry and year	January	February	March	April	May	June	July	August	September	October	November	December	Annual average
Total Private													
2011	23.90	23.85	24.68	23.31	23.03	22.58	22.75	22.44	22.63	22.70	22.73	22.80	23.11
2012	23.11	23.18	23.00	21.89	21.50	21.47	21.94	21.83	22.19	22.24	22.85	22.21	22.28
2013	22.38	22.47	22.57	23.17	22.82	23.28	22.96	22.85	23.19	23.14	23.70	23.42	23.00
2014	23.40	23.54	23.59	23.66	23.35	23.40	23.47	23.47	23.56	23.59	24.34	23.66	23.59
2015	24.00	24.08	24.13	24.14	23.90	23.81	24.04	24.25	24.36	24.18	24.93	24.19	24.17
Goods-Producing													
2011	23.64	23.47	23.27	23.47	23.41	22.90	23.11	22.91	22.99	23.14	22.99	23.21	23.20
2012	23.46	23.36	22.86	23.11	23.38	23.23	23.76	23.80	23.69	23.65	23.65	23.77	23.48
2013	24.03	23.96	24.02	24.06	23.59	23.59	23.37	23.32	23.46	23.54	23.45	23.99	23.69
2014	23.91	23.86	23.86	24.02	24.24	24.04	24.01	24.10	24.17	24.38	23.84	24.04	24.04
2015	24.16	24.14	24.64	24.66	24.49	24.66	24.86	25.04	25.60	25.86	26.37	26.13	25.06
Construction													
2011	24.37	23.94	23.62	23.50	24.00	23.36	23.30	23.58	23.11	23.27	23.12	23.03	23.50
2012	22.97	23.18	22.44	22.84	24.04	23.75	23.84	24.43	24.41	24.05	24.62	24.85	23.84
2013	24.83	25.33	25.28	25.01	24.50	24.06	24.05	23.71	23.47	23.36	23.30	23.83	24.18
2014	23.99	24.06	24.07	24.01	24.04	23.93	24.04	24.18	24.09	24.30	24.06	24.58	24.12
2015	24.38	24.38	24.70	24.68	24.54	24.52	24.24	24.50	24.91	24.91	24.74	24.88	24.62
Manufacturing													
2011	22.27	21.99	21.84	22.40	21.97	21.53	21.94	21.49	21.88	21.91	21.79	22.21	21.93
2012	22.62	22.45	22.06	22.28	22.12	22.05	22.32	22.17	22.09	22.14	21.93	21.85	22.17
2013	22.29	21.92	22.16	22.50	22.04	22.31	22.00	22.10	22.52	22.67	22.54	23.08	22.35
2014	22.84	22.97	22.83	23.16	23.50	23.18	23.13	23.23	23.50	23.69	23.35	23.39	23.23
2015	23.69	23.69	24.27	24.34	24.16	24.37	24.83	24.83	25.48	25.59	26.10	25.54	24.73
Trade, Transportation, and Utilities													
2011	19.91	20.74	20.66	20.64	20.53	20.32	20.84	20.40	20.65	20.89	20.69	20.58	20.57
2012	21.28	21.06	21.27	22.16	21.84	21.91	22.55	22.12	22.60	22.80	22.23	21.61	21.96
2013	21.19	21.34	21.87	22.98	22.48	22.89	22.53	22.32	22.63	22.34	22.25	22.46	22.28
2014	22.25	23.05	23.32	23.66	22.10	22.59	23.05	23.26	22.79	22.92	23.21	22.81	22.92
2015	23.53	23.84	23.65	23.81	23.01	22.72	23.04	23.47	23.15	23.33	23.19	22.55	23.27
Information													
2011	27.67	26.73	26.70	26.77	25.96	25.65	26.50	26.06	27.42	28.69	28.09	27.94	27.04
2012	27.72	26.85	25.44	25.14	24.84	24.32	25.04	24.78	26.31	25.35	25.80	26.31	25.65
2013	26.75	26.66	28.45	29.70	28.17	32.22	28.63	28.47	29.81	29.23	29.40	29.69	28.96
2014	29.18	29.61	29.48	29.30	29.72	30.22	30.54	29.83	30.39	32.14	32.33	32.18	30.43
2015	32.88	31.90	32.62	32.38	31.37	32.12	32.43	32.69	32.75	33.18	33.78	33.63	32.65
Financial Activities													
2011	24.97	25.11	24.95	24.88	24.66	25.12	25.61	25.90	26.24	25.64	25.98	26.30	25.45
2012	27.23	27.70	27.52	27.36	26.74	26.36	26.17	26.08	26.11	25.94	26.36	26.10	26.63
2013	25.73	26.25	25.85	26.76	26.07	26.81	26.62	26.60	27.11	26.65	27.05	27.66	26.61
2014	28.06	28.02	27.75	27.50	27.81	27.71	27.20	27.38	27.14	26.36	27.31	26.93	27.42
2015	27.24	28.01	27.84	27.86	27.70	27.03	26.99	27.89	27.82	27.61	28.58	28.12	27.73
Professional and Business Services													
2011	27.30	26.43	26.16	26.01	25.82	25.41	25.14	24.67	25.13	25.84	25.60	25.80	25.76
2012	26.71	25.93	26.23	26.72	24.29	24.22	25.59	24.85	25.80	25.06	25.53	26.16	25.59
2013	26.76	26.98	26.82	27.28	27.23	27.79	27.79	27.76	28.77	28.50	28.65	29.38	27.84
2014	28.92	29.28	29.19	29.22	29.31	29.49	29.16	28.82	29.22	28.86	29.68	29.32	29.21
2015	29.32	29.65	29.40	28.51	28.48	28.05	28.13	28.94	28.82	29.16	30.14	30.13	29.06
Education and Health Services													
2011	19.00	20.01	19.65	17.67	17.77	17.47	18.24	18.29	18.39	18.85	18.77	19.49	18.64
2012	19.38	20.90	20.57	20.71	20.45	20.38	20.53	20.78	20.74	21.06	21.78	21.00	20.69
2013	21.29	21.34	21.45	22.05	21.60	22.48	21.74	21.57	21.76	21.76	23.97	21.67	21.89
2014	22.06	21.79	21.56	21.50	20.87	20.86	21.22	21.21	21.44	21.45	23.90	21.65	21.64
2015	22.33	22.28	22.27	22.48	22.62	22.84	23.31	22.91	22.99	22.89	25.22	23.28	22.96
Leisure and Hospitality													
2011	12.83	12.73	12.87	12.25	12.03	11.84	11.75	11.73	11.84	11.68	12.01	12.25	12.15
2012	12.09	12.21	12.23	12.09	12.09	11.95	11.92	12.05	12.07	12.20	12.58	12.66	12.17
2013	12.76	12.94	12.93	12.65	12.44	12.30	12.35	12.44	12.65	12.57	12.72	12.76	12.62
2014	12.88	12.97	13.22	12.55	12.55	12.46	12.60	12.74	12.88	13.09	13.15	13.33	12.86
2015	13.41	13.61	13.58	13.30	13.29	13.15	13.32	13.49	13.48	13.56	13.44	13.70	13.44

4. Average Weekly Earnings by Selected Industry: Utah, 2011–2015

(Dollars, not seasonally adjusted)

Industry and year	January	February	March	April	May	June	July	August	September	October	November	December	Annual average
Total Private													
2011	838.89	829.98	858.86	811.19	812.96	790.30	793.98	785.40	785.26	810.39	793.28	791.16	808.85
2012	811.16	804.35	802.70	770.53	748.20	753.60	783.26	768.42	794.40	785.07	797.47	790.68	784.26
2013	774.35	784.20	785.44	799.37	800.98	831.10	796.71	802.04	823.25	802.96	824.76	826.73	805.00
2014	814.32	835.67	842.16	823.37	819.59	840.06	826.14	830.84	829.31	832.73	866.50	821.00	830.37
2015	825.60	850.02	846.96	825.59	829.33	830.97	836.59	858.45	837.98	841.46	870.06	829.72	841.12
Goods-Producing													
2011	936.14	920.02	912.18	922.37	929.38	902.26	898.98	907.24	894.31	918.66	921.90	916.80	914.08
2012	929.02	927.39	912.11	915.16	944.55	926.88	950.40	944.86	957.08	962.56	948.37	962.69	939.20
2013	941.98	941.63	939.18	947.96	941.24	941.24	925.45	937.46	940.75	934.54	947.38	962.00	940.49
2014	939.66	935.31	954.40	965.60	967.18	968.81	958.00	956.77	957.13	980.08	936.91	932.75	954.39
2015	908.42	926.98	948.64	939.55	942.87	944.48	942.19	961.54	942.08	985.27	994.15	979.88	952.28
Construction													
2011	899.25	895.36	890.47	902.40	921.60	906.37	890.06	907.83	882.80	893.57	894.74	859.02	895.35
2012	854.48	873.89	857.21	851.93	942.37	935.75	946.45	979.64	988.61	993.27	987.26	971.64	934.53
2013	923.68	972.67	960.64	980.39	965.30	950.37	945.17	948.40	934.11	934.40	927.34	931.75	947.86
2014	918.82	916.69	948.36	962.80	954.39	959.59	954.39	964.78	951.56	984.15	940.75	941.41	950.33
2015	892.31	909.37	923.78	908.22	927.61	936.66	928.39	938.35	896.76	969.00	959.91	935.49	928.17
Manufacturing													
2011	879.67	859.81	851.76	871.36	870.01	839.67	849.08	848.86	842.38	869.83	873.78	886.18	861.85
2012	900.28	893.51	882.40	891.20	889.22	868.77	877.18	866.85	883.60	887.81	875.01	891.48	884.58
2013	871.54	872.42	879.75	888.75	886.01	894.63	873.40	888.42	905.30	890.93	910.62	932.43	891.77
2014	899.90	905.02	908.63	921.77	932.95	927.20	920.57	915.26	928.25	938.12	929.33	923.91	919.91
2015	914.43	931.02	956.24	954.13	949.49	940.68	950.99	970.85	965.69	974.98	973.53	960.30	954.58
Trade, Transportation, and Utilities													
2011	668.98	694.79	702.44	703.82	702.13	694.94	710.64	693.60	693.84	718.62	691.05	691.49	697.32
2012	708.62	694.98	710.42	744.58	727.27	740.56	768.96	747.66	770.66	763.80	744.71	743.38	740.05
2013	697.15	710.62	728.27	765.23	753.08	785.13	754.76	749.95	762.63	730.52	734.25	752.41	744.15
2014	732.03	788.31	804.54	794.98	769.08	788.39	790.62	802.47	781.70	776.99	807.71	777.82	783.86
2015	785.90	812.94	799.37	804.78	782.34	772.48	785.66	805.02	763.95	769.89	767.59	746.41	781.87
Information													
2011	902.04	858.03	865.08	851.29	872.26	825.93	877.15	862.59	918.57	998.41	960.68	952.75	895.02
2012	967.43	886.05	849.70	864.82	824.69	797.70	873.90	815.26	910.33	831.48	848.82	873.49	861.84
2013	831.93	845.12	921.78	953.37	918.34	1,105.15	913.30	893.96	995.65	938.28	961.38	1,009.46	941.20
2014	933.76	1,018.58	1,028.85	963.97	989.68	1,063.74	1,010.87	990.36	1,008.95	1,079.90	1,147.72	1,106.99	1,028.53
2015	1,144.22	1,148.40	1,174.32	1,117.11	1,085.40	1,108.14	1,122.08	1,186.65	1,100.40	1,138.07	1,212.70	1,160.24	1,142.75
Financial Activities													
2011	876.45	876.34	868.26	880.75	890.23	886.74	901.47	909.09	926.27	925.60	919.69	938.91	900.93
2012	972.11	961.19	957.70	965.81	914.51	925.24	926.42	907.58	942.57	913.09	935.78	939.60	937.38
2013	903.12	926.63	925.43	949.98	933.31	989.29	953.00	962.92	1,003.07	959.40	976.51	1,023.42	957.96
2014	1,024.19	1,014.32	1,023.98	981.75	992.82	1,022.50	984.64	996.63	985.18	959.50	1,029.59	972.17	998.09
2015	996.98	1,039.17	1,041.22	1,014.10	1,008.28	986.60	998.63	1,045.88	1,018.21	1,029.85	1,097.47	1,046.06	1,026.01
Professional and Business Services													
2011	960.96	948.84	936.53	931.16	942.43	919.84	889.96	885.65	899.65	948.33	903.68	895.26	922.21
2012	953.55	910.14	925.92	972.61	818.57	830.75	916.12	882.18	928.80	884.62	893.55	933.91	903.33
2013	923.22	944.30	941.38	946.62	953.05	1,003.22	953.20	971.60	1,027.09	997.50	999.89	1,045.93	977.18
2014	994.85	1,059.94	1,056.68	1,031.47	1,017.06	1,038.05	985.61	1,002.94	1,019.78	1,018.76	1,062.54	1,023.27	1,025.27
2015	996.88	1,043.68	1,043.70	989.30	996.80	1,001.39	987.36	1,047.63	1,017.35	1,026.43	1,076.00	1,057.56	1,022.91
Education and Health Services													
2011	763.80	804.40	782.07	697.97	707.25	686.57	716.83	713.31	713.53	742.69	732.03	762.06	734.42
2012	775.20	821.37	787.83	799.41	783.24	786.67	796.56	804.19	810.93	808.70	834.17	825.30	802.77
2013	836.70	830.13	825.83	835.70	829.44	865.48	821.77	821.82	842.11	824.70	908.46	829.96	838.39
2014	849.31	843.27	821.44	793.35	772.19	784.34	793.63	793.25	804.00	797.94	903.42	809.71	813.66
2015	841.84	848.87	826.22	807.03	816.58	840.51	864.80	854.54	859.83	862.95	963.40	877.66	856.41
Leisure and Hospitality													
2011	333.58	329.71	326.90	309.93	306.77	292.45	299.63	295.60	288.90	303.68	290.64	291.55	306.18
2012	295.00	300.37	300.86	299.83	301.04	301.14	313.50	308.48	313.82	303.78	296.89	312.70	304.25
2013	303.69	323.50	320.66	306.13	308.51	325.95	312.46	320.95	326.37	311.74	304.01	325.38	315.50
2014	328.44	339.81	345.04	308.73	313.75	331.44	328.86	338.88	328.44	331.18	324.81	319.92	327.93
2015	340.61	363.39	361.23	324.52	340.22	345.85	350.32	366.93	349.13	351.20	333.31	335.65	346.75

VERMONT
At a Glance

Population:
  2005 estimate: 621,215
  2010 census: 625,741
  2015 estimate: 626,042

Percent change in population:
  2005–2015: 0.8%
  2010–2015: 0.05%

Percent change in total nonfarm employment:
  2005–2015: 2.3%

Industry with the largest growth in employment, 2005–2015 (thousands):
  Education and health services, 9.5

Industry with the largest decline or smallest growth in employment, 2005–2015 (thousands):
  Manufacturing, –6.0

Civilian labor force:
  2005: 350,766
  2010: 359,402
  2015: 344,414

Unemployment rate and rank among states (highest to lowest):
  2005: 3.5%, 49th
  2010: 6.1%, 46th
  2015: 3.7%, 43rd

Over-the-year change in unemployment rates:
  2012–2013: –0.6%
  2013–2014: –0.4%
  2014–2015: –0.3%

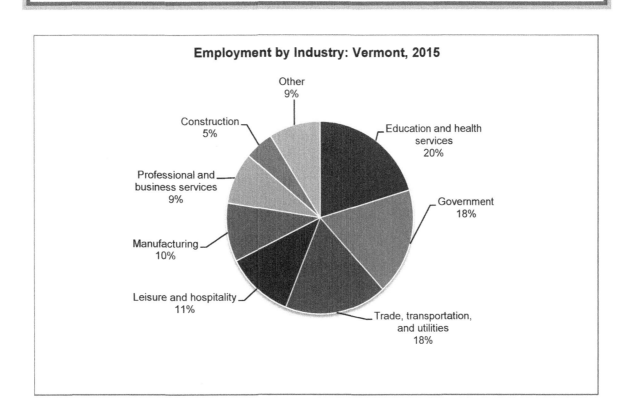

Employment by Industry: Vermont, 2015

Other 9%
Construction 5%
Professional and business services 9%
Manufacturing 10%
Leisure and hospitality 11%
Education and health services 20%
Government 18%
Trade, transportation, and utilities 18%

1. Employment by Industry: Vermont, 2005–2015

(Numbers in thousands, not seasonally adjusted)

Industry and year	January	February	March	April	May	June	July	August	September	October	November	December	Annual average
Total Nonfarm													
2005	302.9	304.0	303.5	302.4	305.1	307.1	300.7	301.1	308.4	309.5	308.1	313.6	305.5
2006	305.3	306.4	306.1	303.5	306.8	310.5	301.9	302.6	310.6	312.6	311.5	314.9	307.7
2007	306.2	307.2	306.8	303.3	308.2	311.6	303.7	303.5	310.8	312.1	311.3	315.5	308.4
2008	307.0	308.4	306.6	304.5	308.6	309.0	301.7	301.5	309.2	311.9	307.9	310.3	307.2
2009	299.0	300.9	297.3	293.8	297.7	297.3	290.1	290.8	297.5	301.6	298.4	302.4	297.2
2010	293.6	296.1	295.2	295.6	297.5	297.5	293.9	294.2	299.7	305.3	301.5	305.6	298.0
2011	297.0	299.9	298.5	295.9	299.1	300.6	294.7	297.8	303.2	306.8	304.5	310.4	300.7
2012	300.8	303.0	303.5	299.1	304.0	304.8	299.9	302.2	307.6	308.3	307.9	312.5	304.5
2013	303.5	304.9	305.6	303.5	304.9	306.9	300.0	304.1	308.2	311.5	311.0	315.1	306.6
2014	306.7	308.4	307.9	304.4	308.3	310.5	304.7	308.4	311.6	313.9	313.3	317.3	309.6
2015	310.5	311.1	310.5	308.2	310.8	312.7	307.8	308.5	313.4	317.9	318.1	320.9	312.5
Total Private													
2005	249.5	248.9	248.3	247.3	250.1	255.2	257.3	256.9	254.3	253.3	251.6	257.3	252.5
2006	250.9	250.4	250.1	247.5	251.1	257.3	258.1	258.6	256.1	255.9	254.5	258.1	254.1
2007	251.4	250.8	250.4	247.3	252.0	257.9	259.4	259.4	256.2	255.6	254.7	258.7	254.5
2008	251.5	252.0	250.3	248.2	252.4	255.6	257.1	256.9	254.3	254.6	250.3	252.9	253.0
2009	244.0	243.9	240.7	236.3	240.0	243.2	245.2	245.8	242.8	243.9	240.8	245.5	242.7
2010	238.3	239.1	237.6	238.1	238.7	242.7	249.4	247.7	245.0	247.8	244.0	248.4	243.1
2011	241.8	242.9	241.5	238.8	241.5	246.4	250.2	250.8	248.0	249.1	246.7	252.3	245.8
2012	245.4	245.6	246.0	241.4	246.0	251.3	254.7	254.9	251.4	250.6	249.8	254.5	249.3
2013	247.3	247.6	248.0	245.6	247.9	253.2	254.9	255.8	252.2	253.2	252.6	256.9	251.3
2014	250.2	250.5	250.1	246.1	250.9	255.9	258.2	259.4	254.7	255.3	254.6	259.2	253.8
2015	253.5	253.0	252.5	250.0	253.5	257.9	260.9	260.0	256.8	258.4	258.6	262.0	256.4
Goods-Producing													
2005	51.6	51.1	51.0	52.9	54.9	56.4	57.1	57.1	56.2	56.1	55.4	54.3	54.5
2006	51.7	51.1	51.1	53.3	54.9	56.2	56.8	56.8	56.0	55.9	55.4	54.6	54.5
2007	51.7	50.8	50.9	51.9	54.6	55.7	55.9	55.7	54.7	54.4	53.6	52.7	53.6
2008	50.0	49.6	49.2	50.1	52.2	53.4	53.9	53.5	52.9	52.7	51.4	49.2	51.5
2009	45.6	44.7	43.7	44.2	45.6	46.4	46.9	47.4	46.8	46.7	45.9	44.8	45.7
2010	41.9	41.7	41.6	43.8	45.5	46.1	47.1	47.0	46.4	46.7	45.9	44.7	44.9
2011	42.4	42.5	42.0	43.4	45.4	47.1	48.1	48.4	48.1	48.7	47.8	47.2	45.9
2012	44.3	44.0	44.4	45.8	47.4	48.4	48.9	48.7	48.3	48.0	47.3	46.7	46.9
2013	44.2	44.2	44.4	45.1	46.9	48.0	48.3	48.2	47.8	47.8	47.5	46.9	46.6
2014	44.3	44.3	44.1	44.6	46.9	48.2	48.9	48.9	48.0	48.0	47.6	47.3	46.8
2015	44.4	44.4	44.2	45.3	47.4	48.3	48.8	48.7	48.2	48.0	48.1	47.0	46.9
Service-Providing													
2005	251.3	252.9	252.5	249.5	250.2	250.7	243.6	244.0	252.2	253.4	252.7	259.3	251.0
2006	253.6	255.3	255.0	250.2	251.9	254.3	245.1	245.8	254.6	256.7	256.1	260.3	253.2
2007	254.5	256.4	255.9	251.4	253.6	255.9	247.8	247.8	256.1	257.7	257.7	262.8	254.8
2008	257.0	258.8	257.4	254.4	256.4	255.6	247.8	248.0	256.3	259.2	256.5	261.1	255.7
2009	253.4	256.2	253.6	249.6	252.1	250.9	243.2	243.4	250.7	254.9	252.5	257.6	251.5
2010	251.7	254.4	253.6	251.8	252.0	251.4	246.8	247.2	253.3	258.6	255.6	260.9	253.1
2011	254.6	257.4	256.5	252.5	253.7	253.5	246.6	249.4	255.1	258.1	256.7	263.2	254.8
2012	256.5	259.0	259.1	253.3	256.6	256.4	251.0	253.5	259.3	260.3	260.6	265.8	257.6
2013	259.3	260.7	261.2	258.4	258.0	258.9	251.7	255.9	260.4	263.7	263.5	268.2	260.0
2014	262.4	264.1	263.8	259.8	261.4	262.3	255.8	259.5	263.6	265.9	265.7	270.0	262.9
2015	266.1	266.7	266.3	262.9	263.4	264.4	259.0	259.8	265.2	269.9	270.0	273.9	265.6
Mining and Logging													
2005	0.7	0.7	0.8	0.8	0.8	0.9	0.9	0.9	0.9	0.9	0.9	0.8	0.8
2006	0.8	0.7	0.8	0.9	0.9	0.9	0.9	0.9	0.9	0.9	0.9	0.9	0.9
2007	0.8	0.8	0.8	0.8	0.9	0.9	0.9	0.9	0.9	0.8	0.8	0.8	0.8
2008	0.8	0.8	0.8	0.8	0.9	0.9	0.9	0.9	0.9	0.9	0.9	0.8	0.9
2009	0.7	0.7	0.7	0.8	0.8	0.8	0.8	0.8	0.8	0.8	0.8	0.7	0.8
2010	0.7	0.7	0.7	0.7	0.8	0.8	0.8	0.8	0.8	0.8	0.8	0.7	0.8
2011	0.7	0.7	0.7	0.7	0.8	0.8	0.8	0.8	0.8	0.8	0.8	0.8	0.8
2012	0.7	0.7	0.7	0.8	0.8	0.8	0.9	0.9	0.9	0.9	0.8	0.8	0.8
2013	0.7	0.7	0.7	0.7	0.8	0.8	0.8	0.8	0.8	0.8	0.8	0.8	0.8
2014	0.7	0.7	0.7	0.7	0.8	0.8	0.9	0.9	0.8	0.8	0.8	0.8	0.8
2015	0.7	0.8	0.8	0.8	0.8	0.9	0.9	0.9	0.9	0.9	0.9	0.8	0.8

1. Employment by Industry: Vermont, 2005–2015—*Continued*

(Numbers in thousands, not seasonally adjusted)

Industry and year	January	February	March	April	May	June	July	August	September	October	November	December	Annual average
Construction													
2005	14.4	13.8	13.8	15.4	17.3	18.3	19.2	19.1	18.5	18.3	17.6	16.6	16.9
2006	14.9	14.5	14.7	16.4	17.8	18.8	19.4	19.4	18.9	18.6	18.0	17.1	17.4
2007	15.1	14.2	14.4	15.3	17.7	18.5	18.8	18.7	18.1	17.8	17.0	16.0	16.8
2008	14.1	13.5	13.3	14.2	16.2	17.1	17.5	17.3	16.9	16.9	15.9	14.3	15.6
2009	12.3	11.6	11.4	12.4	14.0	14.9	15.3	15.6	15.2	15.1	14.4	13.2	13.8
2010	11.4	10.9	10.9	12.8	14.2	14.4	15.2	15.2	14.9	15.0	14.3	13.1	13.5
2011	11.5	11.1	11.0	12.2	13.8	15.0	15.9	16.0	16.0	16.4	15.5	14.5	14.1
2012	12.5	11.9	12.1	13.4	14.6	15.4	15.9	15.8	15.4	15.2	14.6	13.6	14.2
2013	12.1	11.7	12.0	12.7	14.3	15.0	15.4	15.6	15.5	15.5	15.1	14.2	14.1
2014	12.7	12.3	12.4	13.0	14.9	15.9	16.5	16.5	16.2	16.2	15.7	15.0	14.8
2015	13.2	12.8	12.8	13.8	15.6	16.3	16.8	16.7	16.4	16.4	16.5	15.7	15.3
Manufacturing													
2005	36.5	36.6	36.4	36.7	36.8	37.2	37.0	37.1	36.8	36.9	36.9	36.9	36.8
2006	36.0	35.9	35.6	36.0	36.2	36.5	36.5	36.5	36.2	36.4	36.5	36.6	36.2
2007	35.8	35.8	35.7	35.8	36.0	36.3	36.2	36.1	35.7	35.8	35.8	35.9	35.9
2008	35.1	35.3	35.1	35.1	35.1	35.4	35.5	35.3	35.1	34.9	34.6	34.1	35.1
2009	32.6	32.4	31.6	31.0	30.8	30.7	30.8	31.0	30.8	30.8	30.7	30.9	31.2
2010	29.8	30.1	30.0	30.3	30.5	30.9	31.1	31.0	30.7	30.9	30.8	30.9	30.6
2011	30.2	30.7	30.3	30.5	30.8	31.3	31.4	31.6	31.3	31.5	31.5	31.9	31.1
2012	31.1	31.4	31.6	31.6	32.0	32.2	32.1	32.0	32.0	31.9	31.9	32.3	31.8
2013	31.4	31.8	31.7	31.7	31.8	32.2	32.1	31.8	31.5	31.5	31.6	31.9	31.8
2014	30.9	31.3	31.0	30.9	31.2	31.5	31.5	31.5	31.0	31.0	31.1	31.5	31.2
2015	30.5	30.8	30.6	30.7	31.0	31.1	31.1	31.1	30.9	30.7	30.7	30.5	30.8
Trade, Transportation, and Utilities													
2005	59.0	58.6	58.1	58.6	59.1	59.7	59.4	59.4	59.2	59.8	60.6	61.6	59.4
2006	58.9	58.3	58.2	58.4	59.4	59.9	59.4	59.5	59.4	60.1	61.1	61.9	59.5
2007	59.2	58.4	58.0	57.8	58.9	59.7	59.3	59.0	58.9	59.9	61.2	61.8	59.3
2008	59.0	58.7	58.1	58.2	59.1	59.6	58.8	58.9	58.3	58.9	59.3	59.8	58.9
2009	56.5	56.1	55.1	55.0	56.0	56.5	55.8	56.0	55.5	56.3	56.8	57.8	56.1
2010	54.8	54.5	54.0	54.7	54.9	55.7	56.6	56.4	56.0	57.2	57.7	58.4	55.9
2011	55.6	55.3	54.9	54.8	55.3	56.0	55.8	55.9	55.5	56.3	57.0	57.9	55.9
2012	54.7	54.4	54.1	54.4	55.1	56.0	55.8	55.8	55.6	55.8	56.7	57.6	55.5
2013	54.8	54.3	54.3	54.3	55.0	56.0	55.5	55.7	55.4	56.0	56.8	57.7	55.5
2014	54.9	54.4	54.5	54.4	55.5	56.1	55.8	55.9	55.5	56.2	57.3	58.1	55.7
2015	55.4	54.7	54.6	54.4	55.1	56.0	55.4	55.4	54.9	55.5	56.2	57.3	55.4
Wholesale Trade													
2005	9.9	9.9	9.8	10.0	10.0	10.1	10.2	10.3	10.2	10.2	10.3	10.3	10.1
2006	10.2	10.1	10.2	10.2	10.3	10.2	10.4	10.5	10.5	10.5	10.5	10.6	10.4
2007	10.4	10.3	10.3	10.3	10.4	10.4	10.4	10.4	10.4	10.4	10.5	10.5	10.4
2008	10.2	10.2	10.3	10.3	10.3	10.3	10.2	10.2	10.1	10.0	10.0	9.9	10.2
2009	9.8	9.7	9.7	9.7	9.7	9.7	9.6	9.6	9.5	9.5	9.5	9.5	9.6
2010	9.2	9.2	9.2	9.3	9.3	9.4	9.6	9.6	9.5	9.7	9.7	9.6	9.4
2011	9.4	9.4	9.4	9.4	9.4	9.4	9.6	9.6	9.5	9.5	9.5	9.3	9.5
2012	9.1	9.1	9.1	9.2	9.2	9.3	9.3	9.3	9.2	9.2	9.3	9.2	9.2
2013	9.0	9.0	9.0	9.0	9.1	9.3	9.3	9.3	9.2	9.2	9.2	9.3	9.2
2014	9.1	9.0	9.2	9.1	9.3	9.3	9.3	9.4	9.3	9.3	9.4	9.4	9.3
2015	9.3	9.2	9.2	9.2	9.3	9.3	9.4	9.4	9.3	9.4	9.4	9.5	9.3
Retail Trade													
2005	40.1	39.8	39.4	39.8	40.3	40.7	40.8	40.7	40.2	40.6	41.2	42.1	40.5
2006	39.9	39.5	39.3	39.5	40.3	40.9	40.7	40.7	40.1	40.7	41.6	42.2	40.5
2007	40.0	39.4	39.1	39.0	39.7	40.4	40.5	40.2	39.6	40.4	41.5	42.0	40.2
2008	40.1	39.9	39.3	39.4	40.0	40.4	40.2	40.2	39.4	40.1	40.4	40.8	40.0
2009	38.3	38.0	37.2	37.2	38.0	38.5	38.2	38.3	37.6	38.2	38.6	39.3	38.1
2010	37.3	37.0	36.5	37.2	37.2	37.8	38.6	38.4	37.7	38.6	39.1	39.5	37.9
2011	37.5	37.3	36.9	37.0	37.4	37.9	38.0	38.2	37.2	37.8	38.4	39.3	37.7
2012	37.1	36.9	36.6	36.7	37.3	38.0	38.3	38.2	37.6	37.7	38.5	39.1	37.7
2013	37.1	36.8	36.6	36.9	37.4	38.1	38.1	38.2	37.5	37.9	38.5	39.2	37.7
2014	37.3	37.0	36.9	37.0	37.6	38.2	38.4	38.4	37.6	38.2	39.0	39.5	37.9
2015	37.7	37.3	37.2	37.1	37.6	38.3	38.3	38.2	37.3	37.7	38.2	38.8	37.8

1. Employment by Industry: Vermont, 2005–2015—*Continued*

(Numbers in thousands, not seasonally adjusted)

Industry and year	January	February	March	April	May	June	July	August	September	October	November	December	Annual average
Transportation and Utilities													
2005	9.0	8.9	8.9	8.8	8.8	8.9	8.4	8.4	8.8	9.0	9.1	9.2	8.9
2006	8.8	8.7	8.7	8.7	8.8	8.8	8.3	8.3	8.8	8.9	9.0	9.1	8.7
2007	8.8	8.7	8.6	8.5	8.8	8.9	8.4	8.4	8.9	9.1	9.2	9.3	8.8
2008	8.7	8.6	8.5	8.5	8.8	8.9	8.4	8.5	8.8	8.8	8.9	9.1	8.7
2009	8.4	8.4	8.2	8.1	8.3	8.3	8.0	8.1	8.4	8.6	8.7	9.0	8.4
2010	8.3	8.3	8.3	8.2	8.4	8.5	8.4	8.4	8.8	8.9	8.9	9.3	8.6
2011	8.7	8.6	8.6	8.4	8.5	8.7	8.2	8.1	8.8	9.0	9.1	9.3	8.7
2012	8.5	8.4	8.4	8.5	8.6	8.7	8.2	8.3	8.8	8.9	8.9	9.3	8.6
2013	8.7	8.5	8.7	8.4	8.5	8.6	8.1	8.2	8.7	8.9	9.1	9.2	8.6
2014	8.5	8.4	8.4	8.3	8.6	8.6	8.1	8.1	8.6	8.7	8.9	9.2	8.5
2015	8.4	8.2	8.2	8.1	8.2	8.4	7.7	7.8	8.3	8.4	8.6	9.0	8.3
Information													
2005	6.3	6.2	6.2	6.2	6.2	6.2	6.3	6.2	6.2	6.2	6.2	6.3	6.2
2006	6.1	6.1	6.2	6.0	6.0	6.0	6.0	6.0	6.0	5.9	6.0	6.0	6.0
2007	6.0	5.9	5.9	5.9	5.9	5.9	6.0	6.0	5.9	5.8	5.8	5.8	5.9
2008	5.8	5.8	5.8	5.8	5.8	5.7	5.8	5.8	5.8	5.7	5.7	5.7	5.8
2009	5.6	5.6	5.6	5.6	5.5	5.6	5.5	5.5	5.4	5.4	5.4	5.4	5.5
2010	5.4	5.4	5.4	5.4	5.4	5.4	5.3	5.3	5.3	5.3	5.3	5.3	5.4
2011	5.2	5.3	5.2	5.0	4.9	5.0	4.9	4.9	4.8	4.8	4.8	4.8	5.0
2012	4.7	4.7	4.7	4.6	4.7	4.7	4.7	4.7	4.7	4.7	4.7	4.8	4.7
2013	4.7	4.7	4.7	4.7	4.7	4.8	4.7	4.8	4.7	4.7	4.8	4.8	4.7
2014	4.8	4.8	4.9	4.8	4.8	4.9	4.8	4.8	4.8	4.8	4.4	4.4	4.8
2015	4.5	4.5	4.7	4.6	4.7	4.7	4.7	4.6	4.6	4.5	4.5	4.5	4.6
Financial Activities													
2005	13.1	13.1	13.1	13.0	13.1	13.4	13.4	13.4	13.2	13.2	13.1	13.3	13.2
2006	13.2	13.2	13.2	13.1	13.2	13.4	13.4	13.4	13.2	13.1	13.1	13.2	13.2
2007	13.2	13.1	13.2	13.1	13.2	13.4	13.4	13.3	13.1	13.0	13.0	13.0	13.2
2008	12.8	12.8	12.8	12.8	12.9	13.0	13.1	13.0	12.8	12.7	12.6	12.7	12.8
2009	12.5	12.4	12.4	12.2	12.4	12.5	12.6	12.5	12.3	12.3	12.2	12.2	12.4
2010	12.1	12.1	12.0	12.1	12.0	12.3	12.4	12.4	12.1	12.2	12.1	12.2	12.2
2011	12.1	12.0	12.0	11.9	12.0	12.3	12.3	12.3	12.1	12.1	12.0	12.1	12.1
2012	12.0	11.9	12.0	11.8	12.1	12.2	12.3	12.2	12.0	11.9	11.9	12.0	12.0
2013	11.8	11.8	11.8	11.8	12.1	12.3	12.3	12.3	12.1	12.1	12.0	12.1	12.0
2014	12.0	11.9	11.8	11.9	12.1	12.3	12.4	12.4	12.2	12.2	12.1	12.1	12.1
2015	12.0	12.0	11.8	11.9	12.1	12.2	12.3	12.2	12.0	12.3	12.0	12.2	12.1
Professional and Business Services													
2005	20.8	20.9	21.2	21.7	22.0	22.3	22.4	22.4	22.1	22.2	22.1	22.2	21.9
2006	21.5	21.5	21.6	22.0	22.3	22.8	22.8	22.9	22.5	22.4	21.9	22.0	22.2
2007	21.2	21.3	21.6	22.1	22.6	23.1	23.1	23.2	22.9	22.8	22.5	22.7	22.4
2008	21.8	21.9	21.7	22.4	23.3	23.5	23.5	23.3	23.1	23.3	22.7	22.4	22.7
2009	21.3	21.3	21.1	21.8	22.4	22.8	22.9	23.0	22.4	22.9	22.9	22.6	22.3
2010	21.8	21.8	22.0	23.1	23.2	23.6	24.3	24.4	24.1	24.4	24.0	23.6	23.4
2011	23.0	23.2	23.4	24.1	24.9	25.4	25.7	25.9	25.9	25.9	25.6	25.5	24.9
2012	24.6	24.8	25.1	26.0	26.2	26.9	26.9	27.0	26.5	26.4	26.1	26.0	26.0
2013	25.0	25.1	25.5	26.2	26.8	27.2	27.1	27.1	26.8	26.7	26.5	26.3	26.4
2014	25.2	25.4	25.6	26.0	26.9	27.5	27.5	27.4	27.1	27.2	26.9	26.7	26.6
2015	25.8	25.9	25.9	27.0	27.8	28.5	28.2	28.4	27.9	28.0	27.6	26.9	27.3
Education and Health Services													
2005	53.3	53.9	54.2	54.5	54.6	53.7	53.5	53.2	54.7	54.3	54.6	55.2	54.1
2006	54.2	55.1	55.3	55.0	55.1	55.0	55.0	54.8	56.1	56.1	56.3	56.8	55.4
2007	55.7	56.7	56.8	57.1	57.0	57.1	57.1	56.8	58.1	58.0	58.6	58.4	57.3
2008	57.3	58.2	58.6	58.7	59.1	58.0	58.3	58.2	59.3	59.6	59.5	59.6	58.7
2009	58.0	59.5	59.8	59.5	60.0	59.0	59.4	58.8	59.4	59.5	59.1	59.2	59.3
2010	58.1	59.0	59.2	59.7	58.9	58.2	59.5	58.5	59.4	60.0	59.5	59.7	59.1
2011	58.5	59.7	59.8	59.9	59.5	58.5	59.5	59.1	59.8	59.7	59.8	60.1	59.5
2012	59.5	60.2	60.8	60.4	60.2	59.6	61.0	61.0	60.7	61.5	61.4	61.8	60.7
2013	60.7	61.3	61.9	61.6	61.3	60.8	61.9	61.7	61.5	62.3	62.5	62.5	61.7
2014	61.9	61.9	62.3	62.1	62.1	62.0	62.6	62.5	62.2	62.9	63.0	63.3	62.4
2015	62.9	62.8	63.2	63.1	63.2	62.6	64.2	62.8	63.0	64.8	65.2	65.2	63.6

1. Employment by Industry: Vermont, 2005–2015—*Continued*

(Numbers in thousands, not seasonally adjusted)

Industry and year	January	February	March	April	May	June	July	August	September	October	November	December	Annual average
Leisure and Hospitality													
2005	35.6	35.3	34.7	30.4	30.1	33.2	35.0	35.1	32.8	31.7	29.8	34.5	33.2
2006	35.6	35.4	34.8	29.9	30.3	33.9	34.5	35.1	32.9	32.4	30.8	33.7	33.3
2007	34.6	34.8	34.2	29.7	29.9	32.9	34.5	35.3	32.7	31.7	30.1	34.3	32.9
2008	35.1	35.3	34.4	30.4	30.1	32.4	33.8	34.4	32.3	31.9	29.4	33.8	32.8
2009	35.0	34.8	33.6	28.5	28.5	30.6	32.3	32.9	31.3	31.0	28.8	33.7	31.8
2010	34.5	34.9	33.7	29.4	29.0	31.5	34.0	33.6	31.7	32.0	29.7	34.7	32.4
2011	35.3	35.2	34.5	29.8	29.5	32.0	33.7	34.2	31.7	31.5	29.7	34.6	32.6
2012	35.6	35.6	34.8	28.5	30.3	33.4	34.9	35.3	33.5	32.2	31.7	35.6	33.5
2013	36.3	36.4	35.6	31.9	31.1	33.8	34.8	35.7	33.7	33.5	32.5	36.5	34.3
2014	37.2	37.8	36.9	32.3	32.4	34.5	35.7	37.0	34.6	33.8	33.1	37.0	35.2
2015	38.4	38.7	37.9	33.5	33.0	35.2	36.7	37.3	35.8	35.0	34.7	38.4	36.2
Other Services													
2005	9.8	9.8	9.8	10.0	10.1	10.3	10.2	10.1	9.9	9.8	9.8	9.9	10.0
2006	9.7	9.7	9.7	9.8	9.9	10.1	10.2	10.1	10.0	10.0	9.9	9.9	9.9
2007	9.8	9.8	9.8	9.7	9.9	10.1	10.1	10.1	9.9	10.0	9.9	10.0	9.9
2008	9.7	9.7	9.7	9.8	9.9	10.0	9.9	9.8	9.8	9.8	9.7	9.7	9.8
2009	9.5	9.5	9.4	9.5	9.6	9.8	9.8	9.7	9.7	9.8	9.7	9.8	9.7
2010	9.7	9.7	9.7	9.9	9.8	9.9	10.2	10.1	10.0	10.0	9.8	9.8	9.9
2011	9.7	9.7	9.7	9.9	10.0	10.1	10.2	10.1	10.1	10.1	10.0	10.1	10.0
2012	10.0	10.0	10.1	9.9	10.0	10.1	10.2	10.2	10.1	10.1	10.0	10.0	10.1
2013	9.8	9.8	9.8	10.0	10.0	10.3	10.3	10.3	10.2	10.1	10.0	10.1	10.1
2014	9.9	10.0	10.0	10.0	10.2	10.4	10.5	10.5	10.3	10.2	10.2	10.3	10.2
2015	10.1	10.0	10.2	10.2	10.2	10.4	10.6	10.6	10.4	10.3	10.3	10.5	10.3
Government													
2005	53.4	55.1	55.2	55.1	55.0	51.9	43.4	44.2	54.1	56.2	56.5	56.3	53.0
2006	54.4	56.0	56.0	56.0	55.7	53.2	43.8	44.0	54.5	56.7	57.0	56.8	53.7
2007	54.8	56.4	56.4	56.0	56.2	53.7	44.3	44.1	54.6	56.5	56.6	56.8	53.9
2008	55.5	56.4	56.3	56.3	56.2	53.4	44.6	44.6	54.9	57.3	57.6	57.4	54.2
2009	55.0	57.0	56.6	57.5	57.7	54.1	44.9	45.0	54.7	57.7	57.6	56.9	54.6
2010	55.3	57.0	57.6	57.5	58.8	54.8	44.5	46.5	54.7	57.5	57.5	57.2	54.9
2011	55.2	57.0	57.0	57.1	57.6	54.2	44.5	47.0	55.2	57.7	57.8	58.1	54.9
2012	55.4	57.4	57.5	57.7	58.0	53.5	45.2	47.3	56.2	57.7	58.1	58.0	55.2
2013	56.2	57.3	57.6	57.9	57.0	53.7	45.1	48.3	56.0	58.3	58.4	58.2	55.3
2014	56.5	57.9	57.8	58.3	57.4	54.6	46.5	49.0	56.9	58.6	58.7	58.1	55.9
2015	57.0	58.1	58.0	58.2	57.3	54.8	46.9	48.5	56.6	59.5	59.5	58.9	56.1

2. Average Weekly Hours by Selected Industry: Vermont, 2011–2015

(Not seasonally adjusted)

Industry and year	January	February	March	April	May	June	July	August	September	October	November	December	Annual average
Total Private													
2011	33.6	33.5	33.3	33.2	33.9	33.7	34.2	34.0	33.9	34.2	33.8	33.6	33.7
2012	33.5	33.3	33.3	33.9	33.7	33.7	34.2	34.0	34.3	34.1	33.4	33.7	33.8
2013	33.2	33.5	33.5	33.4	34.1	34.1	34.1	34.3	34.2	34.0	33.6	33.6	33.8
2014	33.0	33.0	32.9	33.5	33.7	33.8	33.8	33.6	33.8	33.7	33.5	32.8	33.4
2015	32.9	33.0	33.0	33.2	33.5	33.6	33.8	33.8	33.5	33.6	33.3	33.0	33.3
Goods-Producing													
2011	37.7	38.2	37.6	38.5	38.7	38.2	38.9	38.6	39.0	38.4	38.6	38.6	38.4
2012	38.2	37.8	38.1	38.5	39.0	39.5	39.1	39.5	39.9	39.9	38.6	39.0	39.0
2013	38.0	38.2	38.3	38.4	39.3	39.0	39.0	39.3	39.1	39.1	38.6	38.9	38.8
2014	38.0	37.7	37.4	38.9	39.0	38.7	39.1	38.7	38.8	38.3	38.4	37.5	38.4
2015	37.3	37.0	37.4	37.5	37.9	37.8	37.9	37.9	37.0	37.8	38.0	38.2	37.7
Construction													
2011	38.2	38.1	37.0	38.8	40.3	39.1	40.4	40.2	40.8	39.8	40.1	39.9	39.5
2012	39.5	38.5	38.2	38.8	39.7	40.9	40.2	41.3	41.4	41.5	39.7	38.6	40.0
2013	37.1	37.5	37.1	37.5	39.9	38.7	39.6	39.8	39.5	39.9	38.4	38.1	38.7
2014	36.7	35.8	35.6	37.8	39.8	39.2	40.5	39.7	39.9	38.7	39.2	36.7	38.4
2015	35.9	35.4	36.4	36.5	37.1	37.1	37.9	37.6	36.7	37.7	37.4	38.2	37.1
Manufacturing													
2011	38.4	39.0	38.7	39.1	38.6	38.3	38.5	38.4	38.7	38.2	38.6	38.7	38.6
2012	38.2	38.1	38.7	38.8	39.0	38.9	38.6	38.5	39.0	39.0	38.0	39.3	38.7
2013	38.6	38.6	38.9	38.8	38.9	39.3	38.6	39.0	38.9	38.7	38.8	39.5	38.9
2014	38.8	38.8	38.4	39.5	38.6	38.4	38.2	38.1	38.2	38.2	37.9	38.0	38.4
2015	38.1	37.9	37.9	38.0	38.3	38.1	37.8	38.0	37.1	37.8	38.3	38.1	38.0
Trade, Transportation, and Utilities													
2011	32.5	32.3	32.3	32.4	32.6	32.9	33.6	33.6	33.2	33.6	33.4	33.8	33.0
2012	32.3	32.0	32.6	32.7	32.8	32.4	33.2	33.3	33.3	33.2	32.7	33.5	32.9
2013	32.5	33.0	33.3	33.3	33.8	33.6	33.8	33.8	34.0	33.4	32.8	33.7	33.4
2014	32.9	32.2	32.8	33.1	33.4	33.4	33.2	33.3	33.3	33.5	33.6	33.5	33.2
2015	33.4	33.2	33.6	33.2	33.6	33.6	34.0	33.9	33.9	34.0	34.0	33.6	33.7
Professional and Business Services													
2011	36.0	35.2	35.1	34.9	36.2	36.0	36.5	35.3	35.1	36.4	35.6	35.8	35.7
2012	36.7	35.7	35.4	36.6	35.3	35.2	35.9	35.3	36.3	35.4	35.1	36.0	35.8
2013	35.8	35.5	35.4	35.6	36.1	36.5	35.6	36.0	36.6	35.9	36.4	36.5	36.0
2014	35.3	35.1	35.2	34.9	35.3	35.4	35.3	35.6	35.7	35.3	35.9	35.2	35.4
2015	34.3	35.5	35.2	34.6	34.5	35.4	35.2	35.4	34.9	35.0	35.0	34.5	35.0
Education and Health Services													
2011	33.2	32.8	32.8	32.6	32.9	32.9	33.0	33.4	33.4	33.2	33.1	33.2	33.0
2012	33.2	33.3	33.2	33.0	33.3	33.4	33.4	32.9	33.2	33.2	32.9	32.9	33.2
2013	33.0	33.1	32.7	32.6	32.6	32.9	33.0	33.1	33.3	32.9	32.8	32.9	32.9
2014	33.1	33.0	32.9	32.9	32.8	33.0	33.2	32.9	33.2	33.1	33.2	33.0	33.0
2015	33.2	33.5	33.4	33.1	33.2	33.3	33.5	33.6	33.6	33.4	33.7	33.5	33.4
Leisure and Hospitality													
2011	26.2	26.2	25.1	24.5	25.9	25.8	27.5	27.6	25.7	26.3	24.6	24.4	25.9
2012	25.4	25.7	24.9	25.5	25.1	25.6	27.3	27.6	26.2	26.6	24.8	24.3	25.7
2013	25.7	25.9	26.1	25.0	26.5	26.9	27.6	27.9	26.4	26.7	25.2	24.4	26.2
2014	24.5	25.7	25.0	24.4	25.7	26.1	26.4	26.2	25.6	25.8	23.7	23.4	25.2
2015	24.6	25.4	24.4	24.9	25.7	25.9	26.4	26.5	25.8	25.9	23.3	23.4	25.2

3. Average Hourly Earnings by Selected Industry: Vermont, 2011–2015

(Dollars, not seasonally adjusted)

Industry and year	January	February	March	April	May	June	July	August	September	October	November	December	Annual average
Total Private													
2011	23.65	23.14	23.23	23.53	23.32	22.80	22.57	22.53	22.93	23.07	23.02	22.66	23.03
2012	23.10	22.83	22.97	23.23	22.79	22.47	22.30	22.40	22.59	23.07	22.83	22.99	22.79
2013	22.73	22.68	22.69	22.87	22.72	22.72	22.53	22.58	22.91	23.03	22.91	22.85	22.77
2014	23.08	23.07	23.11	23.15	22.87	23.11	22.85	23.02	23.36	23.43	23.57	23.41	23.17
2015	23.57	23.67	23.88	24.14	24.13	23.96	23.93	23.99	24.12	24.12	24.56	24.67	24.06
Goods-Producing													
2011	22.67	21.91	22.10	21.94	21.90	21.76	21.93	22.00	22.53	22.64	22.35	22.39	22.18
2012	22.77	22.68	22.93	22.81	22.18	22.18	22.04	22.17	22.20	22.22	22.31	22.45	22.40
2013	22.72	22.57	22.51	22.47	21.88	21.95	21.95	21.81	21.88	21.89	21.76	22.02	22.10
2014	22.12	22.23	22.41	22.46	22.20	22.29	22.25	22.32	22.40	22.34	22.43	22.88	22.36
2015	22.83	23.02	23.36	23.53	23.42	23.35	23.49	23.43	23.75	23.56	23.80	24.22	23.49
Construction													
2011	21.65	21.37	21.23	20.92	20.83	20.73	20.69	20.96	21.75	21.61	21.57	22.40	21.31
2012	22.69	23.05	23.36	22.71	21.85	21.96	21.43	21.74	21.70	21.74	21.84	22.42	22.14
2013	22.57	22.75	22.54	22.50	21.57	21.66	21.65	21.57	21.81	21.63	21.82	21.82	21.94
2014	22.29	22.92	22.91	22.98	21.67	22.02	21.80	22.19	22.28	22.45	22.52	23.07	22.38
2015	23.01	23.56	23.59	23.75	23.08	22.93	23.01	22.72	22.80	22.77	22.91	23.03	23.07
Manufacturing													
2011	22.88	22.49	22.80	22.70	22.74	22.57	22.89	22.81	23.04	23.30	22.94	22.60	22.81
2012	22.86	22.54	22.73	22.87	22.39	22.31	22.45	22.49	22.58	22.57	22.61	22.44	22.57
2013	22.81	22.49	22.51	22.47	22.09	22.15	22.18	22.00	21.94	22.08	21.75	22.18	22.22
2014	22.11	21.99	22.28	22.28	22.48	22.43	22.51	22.36	22.45	22.27	22.39	22.81	22.36
2015	22.78	22.78	23.30	23.34	23.56	23.59	23.81	23.88	24.41	24.13	24.44	25.10	23.76
Trade, Transportation, and Utilities													
2011	18.77	18.51	19.04	19.00	18.88	18.52	18.31	18.10	18.38	18.27	18.15	18.00	18.48
2012	18.47	18.41	18.58	18.56	18.24	18.18	18.05	18.08	18.15	18.03	17.88	17.77	18.19
2013	18.41	18.47	18.54	18.56	18.69	18.72	18.78	18.80	19.39	19.27	18.94	18.88	18.79
2014	19.02	18.75	19.04	19.07	18.97	19.07	19.07	19.29	19.40	19.13	19.42	19.59	19.16
2015	19.80	19.62	19.68	19.91	20.04	20.11	20.12	20.12	20.45	20.16	20.38	21.14	20.13
Professional and Business Services													
2011	28.14	27.68	27.70	29.04	29.02	28.71	28.43	29.35	29.54	29.35	29.99	28.99	28.85
2012	29.82	29.96	30.46	30.81	30.46	30.04	30.42	29.91	30.01	30.95	30.28	30.73	30.32
2013	30.50	30.70	30.96	30.44	30.73	30.62	30.11	31.07	30.96	31.07	31.06	31.45	30.81
2014	31.68	31.86	31.28	30.87	30.49	30.38	30.32	30.08	30.35	30.43	30.83	30.68	30.75
2015	30.95	31.45	31.60	31.37	30.93	30.08	31.02	31.02	30.69	30.51	31.02	31.04	30.96
Education and Health Services													
2011	27.16	27.06	26.83	26.69	26.10	25.98	25.78	25.25	25.57	25.82	25.80	25.29	26.11
2012	25.12	24.85	24.61	24.78	24.46	24.24	23.99	24.12	24.16	25.29	24.23	25.09	24.58
2013	23.95	23.98	24.10	24.49	24.43	24.80	24.69	24.55	25.04	25.79	25.24	25.13	24.69
2014	25.30	25.21	25.02	24.94	24.85	25.54	24.99	25.55	26.47	26.95	26.73	26.54	25.68
2015	27.01	27.25	27.50	27.52	27.33	27.19	26.92	26.89	27.03	27.64	28.29	28.76	27.45
Leisure and Hospitality													
2011	14.02	14.14	14.44	14.43	14.35	14.30	14.00	14.08	14.57	15.05	15.04	14.98	14.43
2012	14.63	14.80	14.79	15.25	14.96	14.66	14.41	14.53	14.84	14.98	15.24	14.79	14.81
2013	14.44	14.63	14.37	14.47	14.45	14.35	14.19	14.21	14.80	15.14	15.07	15.09	14.59
2014	15.18	15.18	15.02	15.38	15.23	15.09	15.24	15.37	15.45	15.76	15.59	15.31	15.31
2015	15.25	15.32	15.35	15.94	15.83	15.99	15.78	16.13	16.34	16.40	16.38	16.03	15.89

4. Average Weekly Earnings by Selected Industry: Vermont, 2011–2015

(Dollars, not seasonally adjusted)

Industry and year	January	February	March	April	May	June	July	August	September	October	November	December	Annual average
Total Private													
2011	794.64	775.19	773.56	781.20	790.55	768.36	771.89	766.02	777.33	788.99	778.08	761.38	776.11
2012	773.85	760.24	764.90	787.50	768.02	757.24	762.66	761.60	774.84	786.69	762.52	774.76	770.30
2013	754.64	759.78	760.12	763.86	774.75	774.75	768.27	774.49	783.52	783.02	769.78	767.76	769.63
2014	761.64	761.31	760.32	775.53	770.72	781.12	772.33	773.47	789.57	789.59	789.60	767.85	773.88
2015	775.45	781.11	788.04	801.45	808.36	805.06	808.83	810.86	808.02	810.43	817.85	814.11	801.20
Goods-Producing													
2011	854.66	836.96	830.96	844.69	847.53	831.23	853.08	849.20	878.67	869.38	862.71	864.25	851.71
2012	869.81	857.30	873.63	878.19	865.02	876.11	861.76	875.72	885.78	886.58	861.17	875.55	873.60
2013	863.36	862.17	862.13	862.85	859.88	856.05	856.05	857.13	855.51	855.90	839.94	856.58	857.48
2014	840.56	838.07	838.13	873.69	865.80	862.62	869.98	863.78	869.12	855.62	861.31	858.00	858.62
2015	851.56	851.74	873.66	882.38	887.62	882.63	890.27	888.00	878.75	890.57	904.40	925.20	885.57
Construction													
2011	827.03	814.20	785.51	811.70	839.45	810.54	835.88	842.59	887.40	860.08	864.96	893.76	841.75
2012	896.26	887.43	892.35	881.15	867.45	898.16	861.49	897.86	898.38	902.21	867.05	865.41	885.60
2013	837.35	853.13	836.23	843.75	860.64	838.24	857.34	858.49	861.50	863.04	837.89	831.34	849.08
2014	818.04	820.54	815.60	868.64	862.47	863.18	882.90	880.94	888.97	868.82	882.78	846.67	859.39
2015	826.06	834.02	858.68	866.88	856.27	850.70	872.08	854.27	836.76	858.43	856.83	879.75	855.90
Manufacturing													
2011	878.59	877.11	882.36	887.57	877.76	864.43	881.27	875.90	891.65	890.06	885.48	874.62	880.47
2012	873.25	858.77	879.65	887.36	873.21	867.86	866.57	865.87	880.62	880.23	859.18	881.89	873.46
2013	880.47	868.11	875.64	871.84	859.30	870.50	856.15	858.00	853.47	854.50	843.90	876.11	864.36
2014	857.87	853.21	855.55	880.06	867.73	861.31	859.88	851.92	857.59	850.71	848.58	866.78	858.62
2015	867.92	863.36	883.07	886.92	902.35	898.78	900.02	907.44	905.61	912.11	936.05	956.31	902.88
Trade, Transportation, and Utilities													
2011	610.03	597.87	614.99	615.60	615.49	609.31	615.22	608.16	610.22	613.87	606.21	608.40	609.84
2012	596.58	589.12	605.71	606.91	598.27	589.03	599.26	602.06	604.40	598.60	584.68	595.30	598.45
2013	598.33	609.51	617.38	618.05	631.72	628.99	634.76	635.44	659.26	643.62	621.23	636.26	627.59
2014	625.76	603.75	624.51	631.22	633.60	636.94	633.12	642.36	646.02	640.86	652.51	656.27	636.11
2015	661.32	651.38	661.25	661.01	673.34	675.70	684.08	682.07	693.26	685.44	692.92	710.30	678.38
Professional and Business Services													
2011	1,013.04	974.34	972.27	1,013.50	1,050.52	1,033.56	1,037.70	1,036.06	1,036.85	1,068.34	1,067.64	1,037.84	1,029.95
2012	1,094.39	1,069.57	1,078.28	1,127.65	1,075.24	1,057.41	1,092.08	1,055.82	1,089.36	1,095.63	1,062.83	1,106.28	1,085.46
2013	1,091.90	1,089.85	1,095.98	1,083.66	1,109.35	1,117.63	1,071.92	1,118.52	1,133.14	1,115.41	1,130.58	1,147.93	1,109.16
2014	1,118.30	1,118.29	1,101.06	1,077.36	1,076.30	1,075.45	1,070.30	1,070.85	1,083.50	1,074.18	1,106.80	1,079.94	1,088.55
2015	1,061.59	1,116.48	1,112.32	1,085.40	1,067.09	1,064.83	1,091.90	1,098.11	1,071.08	1,067.85	1,085.70	1,070.88	1,083.60
Education and Health Services													
2011	901.71	887.57	880.02	870.09	858.69	854.74	850.74	843.35	854.04	857.22	853.98	839.63	861.63
2012	833.98	827.51	817.05	817.74	814.52	809.62	801.27	793.55	802.11	839.63	797.17	825.46	816.06
2013	790.35	793.74	788.07	798.37	796.42	815.92	814.77	812.61	833.83	848.49	827.87	826.78	812.30
2014	837.43	831.93	823.16	820.53	815.08	842.82	829.67	840.60	878.80	892.05	887.44	875.82	847.44
2015	896.73	912.88	918.50	910.91	907.36	905.43	901.82	903.50	908.21	923.18	953.37	963.46	916.83
Leisure and Hospitality													
2011	367.32	370.47	362.44	353.54	371.67	368.94	385.00	388.61	374.45	395.82	369.98	365.51	373.74
2012	371.60	380.36	368.27	388.88	375.50	375.30	393.39	401.03	388.81	398.47	377.95	359.40	380.62
2013	371.11	378.92	375.06	361.75	382.93	386.02	391.64	396.46	390.72	404.24	379.76	368.20	382.26
2014	371.91	390.13	375.50	375.27	391.41	393.85	402.34	402.69	395.52	406.61	369.48	358.25	385.81
2015	375.15	389.13	374.54	396.91	406.83	414.14	416.59	427.45	421.57	424.76	381.65	375.10	400.43

VIRGINIA
At a Glance

Population:
  2005 estimate: 7,577,105
  2010 census: 8,001,024
  2015 estimate: 8,382,993

Percent change in population:
  2005–2015: 10.6%
  2010–2015: 4.8%

Percent change in total nonfarm employment:
  2005–2015: 5.0%

Industry with the largest growth in employment, 2005–2015 (thousands):
  Education and health services, 114.5

Industry with the largest decline or smallest growth in employment, 2005–2015 (thousands):
  Construction, –70.3

Civilian labor force:
  2005: 3,897,042
  2010: 4,157,658
  2015: 4,240,470

Unemployment rate and rank among states (highest to lowest):
  2005: 3.6%, 46th
  2010: 7.1%, 41st
  2015: 4.4%, 35th

Over-the-year change in unemployment rates:
  2012–2013: –0.3%
  2013–2014: –0.5%
  2014–2015: –0.8%

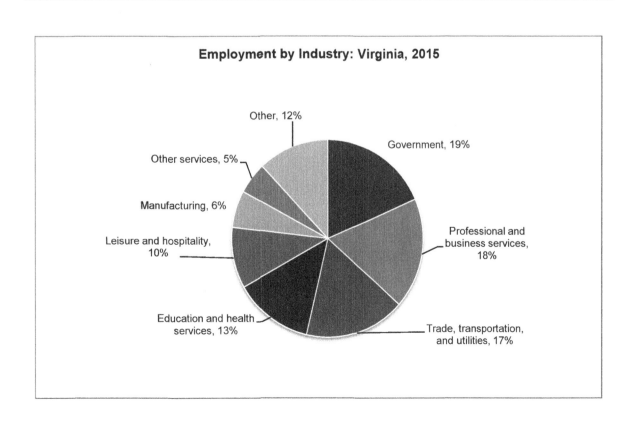

Employment by Industry: Virginia, 2015

Other, 12%
Government, 19%
Other services, 5%
Manufacturing, 6%
Leisure and hospitality, 10%
Professional and business services, 18%
Education and health services, 13%
Trade, transportation, and utilities, 17%

1. Employment by Industry: Virginia, 2005–2015

(Numbers in thousands, not seasonally adjusted)

Industry and year	January	February	March	April	May	June	July	August	September	October	November	December	Annual average
Total Nonfarm													
2005	3,573.1	3,588.4	3,614.0	3,650.6	3,671.2	3,701.0	3,682.5	3,683.3	3,700.3	3,696.8	3,718.8	3,727.6	3,667.3
2006	3,655.9	3,666.5	3,702.5	3,715.8	3,745.1	3,779.4	3,746.3	3,741.8	3,738.6	3,748.4	3,767.2	3,779.1	3,732.2
2007	3,703.7	3,709.7	3,741.1	3,757.2	3,781.9	3,813.0	3,781.7	3,774.1	3,777.4	3,784.3	3,802.7	3,807.0	3,769.5
2008	3,727.1	3,735.7	3,756.6	3,780.6	3,797.9	3,818.8	3,786.3	3,781.0	3,773.7	3,776.9	3,771.2	3,762.6	3,772.4
2009	3,649.5	3,638.3	3,645.0	3,654.9	3,673.3	3,686.1	3,640.8	3,631.6	3,632.0	3,644.9	3,655.6	3,652.9	3,650.4
2010	3,562.7	3,547.9	3,590.4	3,646.3	3,677.6	3,694.9	3,662.8	3,651.8	3,661.3	3,681.7	3,691.7	3,692.2	3,646.8
2011	3,611.5	3,629.5	3,656.2	3,692.3	3,697.4	3,717.1	3,701.1	3,694.1	3,715.7	3,723.7	3,740.5	3,734.4	3,692.8
2012	3,659.2	3,676.4	3,704.0	3,728.1	3,738.5	3,758.9	3,724.6	3,737.8	3,750.9	3,773.0	3,790.2	3,788.3	3,735.8
2013	3,700.5	3,720.2	3,741.0	3,764.0	3,770.3	3,785.3	3,761.6	3,765.5	3,770.5	3,776.8	3,801.9	3,789.9	3,762.3
2014	3,710.5	3,710.6	3,736.8	3,783.8	3,801.7	3,814.6	3,787.4	3,792.5	3,798.9	3,811.2	3,828.7	3,824.6	3,783.4
2015	3,758.3	3,766.5	3,780.0	3,832.7	3,852.2	3,866.7	3,865.6	3,864.0	3,873.1	3,901.0	3,927.6	3,926.6	3,851.2
Total Private													
2005	2,919.2	2,927.1	2,949.9	2,980.2	3,003.0	3,033.5	3,042.3	3,048.2	3,039.0	3,027.1	3,041.9	3,053.9	3,005.4
2006	2,989.9	2,991.7	3,022.2	3,037.7	3,063.4	3,098.2	3,091.6	3,092.5	3,069.4	3,065.8	3,078.8	3,092.0	3,057.4
2007	3,024.5	3,021.7	3,051.6	3,065.3	3,093.0	3,125.6	3,119.3	3,118.7	3,099.6	3,095.7	3,105.3	3,113.0	3,086.1
2008	3,040.0	3,038.1	3,054.7	3,080.2	3,098.3	3,121.4	3,114.9	3,110.6	3,083.0	3,071.0	3,059.0	3,052.3	3,077.0
2009	2,951.9	2,933.0	2,935.3	2,942.9	2,962.8	2,978.0	2,968.4	2,961.0	2,936.8	2,935.9	2,937.8	2,940.4	2,948.7
2010	2,860.6	2,840.8	2,877.3	2,927.6	2,951.6	2,973.7	2,983.1	2,980.2	2,957.8	2,970.1	2,975.8	2,977.9	2,939.7
2011	2,905.2	2,910.9	2,934.2	2,969.2	2,979.8	3,002.1	3,018.1	3,014.9	3,002.4	2,999.9	3,011.4	3,006.3	2,979.5
2012	2,947.8	2,953.6	2,979.5	3,004.3	3,019.5	3,042.9	3,047.2	3,057.5	3,040.2	3,050.8	3,062.6	3,061.5	3,022.3
2013	2,990.7	2,998.0	3,017.6	3,038.6	3,049.2	3,070.3	3,077.1	3,084.5	3,061.3	3,060.4	3,080.0	3,069.6	3,049.8
2014	3,004.1	2,995.8	3,019.5	3,062.7	3,084.2	3,103.2	3,103.0	3,109.7	3,087.4	3,094.7	3,107.1	3,103.3	3,072.9
2015	3,051.9	3,047.8	3,062.7	3,110.2	3,133.0	3,153.4	3,179.9	3,181.3	3,162.2	3,181.9	3,204.0	3,205.4	3,139.5
Goods-Producing													
2005	538.0	537.4	539.8	546.3	549.4	555.3	557.8	560.2	557.3	553.9	553.6	552.8	550.2
2006	543.1	543.0	547.4	549.9	553.7	558.6	554.9	554.9	548.8	543.6	540.4	539.2	548.1
2007	526.8	525.1	529.8	531.2	532.9	537.0	534.0	533.2	529.3	524.1	521.0	518.3	528.6
2008	504.5	500.1	500.4	505.0	504.4	506.5	504.8	503.2	498.7	493.7	486.3	478.9	498.9
2009	456.4	446.7	443.8	441.3	440.0	441.0	440.3	438.5	435.9	434.3	430.7	429.4	439.9
2010	414.1	407.8	415.2	424.5	428.1	429.3	431.6	430.5	429.0	428.0	425.8	423.0	423.9
2011	409.7	410.3	414.1	418.9	421.0	424.4	428.5	427.8	424.7	422.8	421.6	420.2	420.3
2012	411.4	410.8	414.6	416.4	418.3	421.7	424.9	424.5	422.7	421.5	420.3	419.5	418.9
2013	409.4	410.2	412.7	415.6	417.8	422.0	423.2	423.4	421.1	419.2	419.6	417.4	417.6
2014	408.7	407.5	411.6	418.1	421.6	425.1	424.8	425.3	424.2	424.0	423.5	421.4	419.7
2015	413.4	412.6	415.4	424.1	427.6	430.4	433.8	433.1	431.3	429.7	430.3	427.6	425.8
Service-Providing													
2005	3,035.1	3,051.0	3,074.2	3,104.3	3,121.8	3,145.7	3,124.7	3,123.1	3,143.0	3,142.9	3,165.2	3,174.8	3,117.2
2006	3,112.8	3,123.5	3,155.1	3,165.9	3,191.4	3,220.8	3,191.4	3,186.9	3,189.8	3,204.8	3,226.8	3,239.9	3,184.1
2007	3,176.9	3,184.6	3,211.3	3,226.0	3,249.0	3,276.0	3,247.7	3,240.9	3,248.1	3,260.2	3,281.7	3,288.7	3,240.9
2008	3,222.6	3,235.6	3,256.2	3,275.6	3,293.5	3,312.3	3,281.5	3,277.8	3,275.0	3,283.2	3,284.9	3,283.7	3,273.5
2009	3,193.1	3,191.6	3,201.2	3,213.6	3,233.3	3,245.1	3,200.5	3,193.1	3,196.1	3,210.6	3,224.9	3,223.5	3,210.6
2010	3,148.6	3,140.1	3,175.2	3,221.8	3,249.5	3,265.6	3,231.2	3,221.3	3,232.3	3,253.7	3,265.9	3,269.2	3,222.9
2011	3,201.8	3,219.2	3,242.1	3,273.4	3,276.4	3,292.7	3,272.6	3,266.3	3,291.0	3,300.9	3,318.9	3,314.2	3,272.5
2012	3,247.8	3,265.6	3,289.4	3,311.7	3,320.2	3,337.2	3,299.7	3,313.3	3,328.2	3,351.5	3,369.9	3,368.8	3,316.9
2013	3,291.1	3,310.0	3,328.3	3,348.4	3,352.5	3,363.3	3,338.4	3,342.1	3,349.4	3,357.6	3,382.3	3,372.5	3,344.7
2014	3,301.8	3,303.1	3,325.2	3,365.7	3,380.1	3,389.5	3,362.6	3,367.2	3,374.7	3,387.2	3,405.2	3,403.2	3,363.8
2015	3,344.9	3,353.9	3,364.6	3,408.6	3,424.6	3,436.3	3,431.8	3,430.9	3,441.8	3,471.3	3,497.3	3,499.0	3,425.4
Mining and Logging													
2005	10.4	10.4	10.1	10.3	10.4	10.8	10.9	10.9	10.9	10.9	11.0	11.1	10.7
2006	11.0	11.0	11.2	11.0	11.2	11.5	11.5	11.5	11.3	11.2	11.3	11.3	11.3
2007	11.3	11.2	11.4	10.7	10.8	10.8	11.0	11.0	10.6	10.7	10.6	10.8	10.9
2008	10.6	10.9	10.8	10.9	11.0	11.1	11.2	11.2	11.3	11.5	11.5	11.4	11.1
2009	10.8	10.5	10.4	10.2	10.1	10.1	10.0	10.1	10.1	10.2	10.2	10.2	10.2
2010	9.9	9.8	10.0	10.3	10.3	10.4	10.5	10.6	10.6	10.7	10.7	10.6	10.4
2011	10.7	10.6	10.7	10.7	10.8	10.9	11.0	11.1	11.2	11.1	11.2	11.2	10.9
2012	11.1	11.1	11.1	11.0	11.0	11.1	11.0	11.0	10.8	10.3	10.5	10.4	10.9
2013	10.2	10.1	10.1	10.1	10.1	10.2	9.8	9.8	9.7	9.9	9.8	9.9	10.0
2014	9.7	9.7	9.8	9.7	9.6	9.7	9.5	9.4	9.4	9.3	9.3	9.3	9.5
2015	9.4	9.3	9.2	9.1	9.0	8.9	9.1	9.1	8.9	8.9	8.7	8.6	9.0

1. Employment by Industry: Virginia, 2005–2015—*Continued*

(Numbers in thousands, not seasonally adjusted)

Industry and year	January	February	March	April	May	June	July	August	September	October	November	December	Annual average
Construction													
2005	230.5	230.1	232.9	239.6	242.7	247.5	252.5	253.1	250.9	248.5	248.2	247.1	243.6
2006	240.8	241.7	246.8	248.5	252.1	256.0	254.8	254.0	251.1	247.9	246.0	245.3	248.8
2007	236.1	233.3	237.6	240.9	243.3	246.0	244.9	245.2	242.6	238.7	236.1	233.6	239.9
2008	223.7	222.0	223.9	226.2	226.8	228.6	228.3	227.1	223.8	220.4	214.9	209.6	222.9
2009	195.4	190.8	190.2	190.6	191.1	192.4	192.9	192.2	189.9	188.4	185.6	184.0	190.3
2010	173.9	168.6	175.5	184.1	186.4	187.6	190.2	189.4	187.9	186.4	185.0	181.7	183.1
2011	171.7	171.9	174.5	178.1	179.5	181.4	184.3	183.7	180.8	179.7	178.5	177.3	178.5
2012	169.7	169.0	172.3	174.8	177.1	180.4	181.4	181.0	179.2	179.2	177.9	176.9	176.6
2013	169.6	170.3	172.7	175.6	177.4	180.4	181.7	182.1	180.5	178.3	178.4	175.5	176.9
2014	169.4	168.5	171.7	177.3	179.8	182.1	182.5	183.1	182.1	182.3	181.8	179.4	178.3
2015	173.3	172.9	175.2	182.8	185.9	187.5	190.2	189.8	188.3	186.6	186.6	185.2	183.7
Manufacturing													
2005	297.1	296.9	296.8	296.4	296.3	297.0	294.4	296.2	295.5	294.5	294.4	294.6	295.8
2006	291.3	290.3	289.4	290.4	290.4	291.1	288.6	289.4	286.4	284.5	283.1	282.6	288.1
2007	279.4	280.6	280.8	279.6	278.8	280.2	278.1	277.0	276.1	274.7	274.3	273.9	277.8
2008	270.2	267.2	265.7	267.9	266.6	266.8	265.3	264.9	263.6	261.8	259.9	257.9	264.8
2009	250.2	245.4	243.2	240.5	238.8	238.5	237.4	236.2	235.9	235.7	234.9	235.2	239.3
2010	230.3	229.4	229.7	230.1	231.4	231.3	230.9	230.5	230.5	230.9	230.1	230.7	230.5
2011	227.3	227.8	228.9	230.1	230.7	232.1	233.2	233.0	232.7	232.0	231.9	231.7	231.0
2012	230.6	230.7	231.2	230.6	230.2	230.2	232.5	232.5	232.7	232.0	231.9	232.2	231.4
2013	229.6	229.8	229.9	229.9	230.3	231.4	231.7	231.5	230.9	231.0	231.4	232.0	230.8
2014	229.6	229.3	230.1	231.1	232.2	233.3	232.8	232.8	232.7	232.4	232.4	232.7	231.8
2015	230.7	230.4	231.0	232.2	232.7	234.0	234.5	234.2	234.1	234.2	235.0	233.8	233.1
Trade, Transportation, and Utilities													
2005	646.9	640.6	643.6	648.1	651.6	655.1	656.1	657.2	655.6	662.7	678.4	689.4	657.1
2006	659.2	648.1	653.4	652.9	659.0	663.6	660.3	661.0	658.1	665.9	682.0	692.1	663.0
2007	663.5	654.2	658.5	657.6	664.4	668.4	668.2	667.2	665.7	669.1	686.2	694.4	668.1
2008	663.4	653.3	655.3	654.2	658.0	661.5	660.0	659.4	655.7	654.8	663.8	669.7	659.1
2009	633.3	622.3	619.7	618.1	623.6	624.9	620.9	619.8	617.9	620.1	631.9	638.8	624.3
2010	611.2	601.0	607.0	614.2	620.3	623.6	622.6	623.6	618.6	625.9	638.2	647.3	621.1
2011	619.6	614.5	616.8	623.1	626.3	629.1	629.4	630.5	626.6	630.2	644.6	653.1	628.7
2012	626.8	619.9	623.9	625.7	631.5	633.2	631.0	631.2	629.1	636.3	652.4	660.8	633.5
2013	627.8	621.5	623.6	627.5	632.5	636.5	637.3	638.6	635.6	641.0	660.3	667.6	637.5
2014	636.0	626.8	630.2	634.9	640.5	643.7	643.1	643.9	640.6	646.6	665.5	673.8	643.8
2015	643.2	635.1	635.6	641.5	648.0	652.8	656.9	657.7	655.5	665.2	682.4	686.5	655.0
Wholesale Trade													
2005	114.7	115.0	115.6	116.8	117.2	117.4	117.9	118.2	117.8	118.1	118.7	119.1	117.2
2006	117.4	117.8	118.5	119.1	119.7	120.5	119.9	120.1	119.8	120.5	120.8	121.2	119.6
2007	120.0	120.4	121.1	120.7	121.2	121.8	121.2	121.4	120.9	120.7	120.6	121.0	120.9
2008	119.6	119.7	119.7	120.0	120.4	120.6	120.3	120.1	119.2	119.0	118.1	117.6	119.5
2009	115.4	114.7	114.2	113.8	113.6	113.1	112.2	112.0	111.1	110.6	110.2	110.2	112.6
2010	107.9	107.6	108.2	109.5	110.0	110.2	110.7	110.9	110.5	111.2	111.5	111.7	110.0
2011	110.6	110.7	111.1	111.7	111.8	112.1	112.3	112.1	111.2	110.9	111.0	111.2	111.4
2012	110.0	110.3	110.9	111.1	111.7	112.1	112.0	112.2	111.7	111.7	111.8	111.8	111.4
2013	110.6	110.8	111.2	110.9	111.0	111.2	111.0	111.0	110.5	110.5	110.5	110.7	110.8
2014	109.7	109.7	110.2	110.5	111.2	111.3	111.3	111.3	110.7	110.5	110.7	110.9	110.7
2015	109.4	109.3	109.4	109.9	110.3	110.8	111.5	111.4	111.2	111.9	112.5	112.9	110.9
Retail Trade													
2005	412.3	405.9	407.3	410.4	413.3	416.1	416.8	417.7	417.1	422.6	436.5	445.5	418.5
2006	422.2	412.9	416.6	415.8	420.6	423.1	421.2	421.5	418.6	425.3	440.7	447.6	423.8
2007	425.5	416.2	419.2	418.7	424.3	426.4	426.5	425.4	424.4	428.1	444.5	450.3	427.5
2008	425.9	415.8	418.1	415.8	418.5	421.0	420.0	419.2	417.1	417.4	426.7	431.5	420.6
2009	403.5	394.4	392.8	392.4	397.4	399.0	396.2	395.6	394.3	397.3	408.6	414.0	398.8
2010	393.1	383.8	388.5	393.3	398.0	400.0	398.3	398.9	394.4	400.0	410.9	417.9	398.1
2011	396.1	391.4	392.9	397.8	400.3	402.0	401.2	402.2	399.8	403.8	417.4	423.9	402.4
2012	403.4	395.9	399.3	400.0	403.9	404.5	402.4	402.3	400.9	407.6	423.2	429.0	406.0
2013	402.2	396.9	398.1	401.8	405.9	408.8	409.1	410.1	407.8	412.9	430.5	435.0	409.9
2014	409.0	401.5	403.6	407.3	410.8	412.7	411.7	411.7	408.5	414.2	430.4	435.3	413.1
2015	410.8	404.0	404.5	408.6	413.6	416.9	417.5	418.1	416.5	422.7	436.8	437.3	417.3

1. Employment by Industry: Virginia, 2005–2015—*Continued*

(Numbers in thousands, not seasonally adjusted)

Industry and year	January	February	March	April	May	June	July	August	September	October	November	December	Annual average
Transportation and Utilities													
2005	119.9	119.7	120.7	120.9	121.1	121.6	121.4	121.3	120.7	122.0	123.2	124.8	121.4
2006	119.6	117.4	118.3	118.0	118.7	120.0	119.2	119.4	119.7	120.1	120.5	123.3	119.5
2007	118.0	117.6	118.2	118.2	118.9	120.2	120.5	120.4	120.4	120.3	121.1	123.1	119.7
2008	117.9	117.8	117.5	118.4	119.1	119.9	119.7	120.1	119.4	118.4	119.0	120.6	119.0
2009	114.4	113.2	112.7	111.9	112.6	112.8	112.5	112.2	112.5	112.2	113.1	114.6	112.9
2010	110.2	109.6	110.3	111.4	112.3	113.4	113.6	113.8	113.7	114.7	115.8	117.7	113.0
2011	112.9	112.4	112.8	113.6	114.2	115.0	115.9	116.2	115.6	115.5	116.2	118.0	114.9
2012	113.4	113.7	113.7	114.6	115.9	116.6	116.6	116.7	116.5	117.0	117.4	120.0	116.0
2013	115.0	113.8	114.3	114.8	115.6	116.5	117.2	117.5	117.3	117.6	119.3	121.9	116.7
2014	117.3	115.6	116.4	117.1	118.5	119.7	120.1	120.9	121.4	121.9	124.4	127.6	120.1
2015	123.0	121.8	121.7	123.0	124.1	125.1	127.9	128.2	127.8	130.6	133.1	136.3	126.9
Information													
2005	93.5	93.4	93.4	93.0	93.0	93.3	92.9	92.6	91.8	91.6	91.9	92.0	92.7
2006	91.3	91.7	91.8	91.1	93.4	91.8	92.9	91.8	91.3	90.4	90.8	90.8	91.6
2007	91.9	91.3	90.7	90.5	91.0	90.9	90.3	89.8	89.7	89.6	89.7	89.5	90.4
2008	88.7	88.7	88.5	88.1	88.2	88.4	88.0	87.5	86.4	85.6	85.4	84.9	87.4
2009	84.0	83.8	83.1	82.1	81.9	81.8	81.1	80.1	79.1	79.0	78.7	78.5	81.1
2010	77.4	76.7	76.7	75.7	75.7	76.0	75.8	75.8	75.5	75.5	75.5	75.7	76.0
2011	74.7	74.5	74.6	74.0	74.2	74.4	74.8	70.1	73.5	72.7	73.3	74.1	73.7
2012	71.3	72.0	72.6	71.1	71.8	72.8	71.6	72.9	70.3	70.5	72.1	70.9	71.7
2013	70.3	72.1	72.0	71.1	71.2	71.5	71.6	72.8	70.6	71.1	72.6	71.4	71.5
2014	72.2	70.8	71.0	70.9	72.4	71.3	71.5	72.4	70.4	70.8	70.1	70.0	71.2
2015	70.0	69.5	69.2	69.3	70.0	69.8	70.6	69.9	69.1	69.2	69.8	69.6	69.7
Financial Activities													
2005	188.7	189.4	189.9	191.2	192.2	194.5	195.9	195.9	194.2	192.3	192.1	193.5	192.5
2006	191.9	192.6	193.6	193.6	195.0	197.6	197.0	197.1	194.8	194.4	194.3	195.5	194.8
2007	193.7	193.9	194.7	194.0	195.1	196.6	196.0	195.1	193.0	191.3	190.2	190.3	193.7
2008	189.3	189.5	189.6	189.1	189.1	190.5	191.1	190.1	187.7	186.7	185.5	185.6	188.7
2009	182.1	181.1	181.1	181.0	180.6	181.6	181.0	180.8	178.4	177.4	177.0	177.5	180.0
2010	176.3	175.6	176.4	177.4	178.3	180.8	181.7	181.6	179.9	180.1	180.2	180.7	179.1
2011	178.4	178.6	179.0	180.9	182.0	183.7	185.4	185.4	184.2	183.8	184.2	185.3	182.6
2012	183.2	184.0	184.8	186.8	187.3	189.6	190.7	190.8	189.9	190.3	190.7	191.4	188.3
2013	189.2	189.7	190.4	191.4	192.1	193.9	194.8	194.6	193.0	193.4	193.6	193.9	192.5
2014	190.8	191.1	191.7	192.5	193.5	195.6	196.3	196.0	194.5	194.7	195.1	195.7	194.0
2015	194.1	194.8	195.2	195.8	197.1	198.7	200.1	199.7	198.3	199.7	199.0	199.7	197.7
Professional and Business Services													
2005	584.8	590.4	595.1	599.4	600.7	607.0	612.8	615.8	616.5	616.1	616.3	618.7	606.1
2006	610.5	615.0	621.1	622.3	625.4	632.4	633.2	636.0	634.3	636.1	637.2	639.0	628.5
2007	628.4	631.9	638.2	642.1	643.6	650.6	650.9	653.7	649.9	655.0	655.3	656.4	646.3
2008	644.9	647.3	650.3	656.4	657.0	662.5	663.2	665.6	661.1	662.0	658.3	655.8	657.0
2009	640.3	639.0	639.2	638.0	636.7	639.7	639.5	640.8	636.9	642.4	644.6	643.7	640.1
2010	631.2	631.1	636.0	648.7	648.4	652.4	657.5	658.3	655.1	661.7	662.5	661.7	650.4
2011	652.7	655.3	659.5	665.5	663.9	666.2	672.6	674.7	673.7	675.3	677.2	673.1	667.5
2012	664.4	666.9	671.0	675.8	675.7	679.1	681.9	685.4	682.0	687.7	686.6	685.1	678.5
2013	674.2	677.1	679.4	681.5	679.7	682.1	682.1	683.9	677.4	677.8	679.2	674.0	679.0
2014	665.4	667.0	669.7	680.2	681.5	683.9	685.8	687.0	681.3	686.0	686.9	684.4	679.9
2015	678.0	678.8	681.1	692.8	695.6	697.7	703.4	704.0	699.0	709.8	714.7	717.4	697.7
Education and Health Services													
2005	387.0	390.9	392.6	394.9	396.5	395.1	392.2	393.0	403.5	402.4	404.6	404.9	396.5
2006	402.2	405.6	407.9	407.8	409.6	410.3	409.3	408.9	414.5	416.7	419.5	420.6	411.1
2007	415.8	418.7	421.5	424.1	426.6	427.7	425.2	426.8	433.4	437.2	439.7	441.8	428.2
2008	436.9	442.9	444.2	448.8	449.5	448.3	443.9	444.5	450.4	453.9	455.0	455.6	447.8
2009	450.6	452.8	454.1	456.4	458.3	456.1	453.8	453.1	455.4	458.6	460.2	460.8	455.9
2010	454.8	454.6	458.5	462.1	463.2	460.3	462.6	461.4	464.3	471.4	472.8	471.4	463.1
2011	467.2	470.2	472.0	472.0	464.9	462.1	464.0	465.6	473.7	476.6	478.0	469.4	469.6
2012	473.7	477.0	478.8	480.8	473.3	472.1	472.3	478.1	486.2	491.5	493.1	487.5	480.4
2013	488.5	492.9	495.3	494.8	485.9	482.0	482.7	488.0	495.6	498.4	500.6	492.5	491.4
2014	494.1	495.2	497.0	502.3	494.2	491.0	490.7	495.0	501.8	505.6	506.2	499.5	497.7
2015	504.6	506.6	507.7	511.6	503.6	500.8	505.2	508.5	515.4	521.3	523.5	522.8	511.0

1. Employment by Industry: Virginia, 2005–2015—*Continued*

(Numbers in thousands, not seasonally adjusted)

Industry and year	January	February	March	April	May	June	July	August	September	October	November	December	Annual average
Leisure and Hospitality													
2005	302.3	305.9	315.6	326.2	337.6	349.9	350.8	350.6	338.4	328.1	324.9	322.2	329.4
2006	313.2	316.7	326.7	335.3	345.4	360.2	360.4	359.4	345.7	336.8	332.7	332.3	338.7
2007	322.3	323.9	333.7	341.0	353.3	367.0	367.2	366.3	353.1	343.2	337.0	335.4	345.3
2008	327.2	329.7	339.2	349.7	362.1	372.7	372.9	369.6	354.3	344.6	336.2	333.6	349.3
2009	320.2	321.9	328.4	339.7	355.0	364.9	364.0	361.1	348.3	339.0	330.3	327.2	341.7
2010	313.3	312.5	323.8	339.8	351.6	364.2	364.5	363.0	351.2	342.7	336.4	334.0	341.4
2011	319.9	323.5	333.0	346.9	359.2	371.8	372.0	370.7	357.4	350.0	344.0	342.4	349.2
2012	330.2	335.2	344.8	355.2	368.3	379.5	379.3	380.4	367.2	359.4	354.2	353.3	358.9
2013	340.4	342.9	351.7	363.2	375.4	386.1	387.9	387.0	373.6	365.3	360.0	358.9	366.0
2014	345.1	345.4	354.7	368.9	384.2	394.1	392.7	392.1	378.5	371.6	364.8	363.8	371.3
2015	354.7	356.4	363.0	378.5	392.7	403.0	408.4	407.4	394.6	388.4	383.7	381.6	384.4
Other Services													
2005	178.0	179.1	179.9	181.1	182.0	183.3	183.8	182.9	181.7	180.0	180.1	180.4	181.0
2006	178.5	179.0	180.3	180.8	181.9	183.7	183.6	183.4	181.9	181.9	181.9	182.5	181.6
2007	182.1	182.7	184.5	184.8	186.1	187.4	187.5	186.6	185.5	186.2	186.2	186.9	185.5
2008	185.1	186.6	187.2	188.9	190.0	191.0	191.0	190.7	188.7	189.7	188.5	188.2	188.8
2009	185.0	185.4	185.9	186.3	186.7	188.0	187.8	186.8	184.9	185.1	184.4	184.5	185.9
2010	182.3	181.5	183.7	185.2	186.0	187.1	186.8	186.0	184.2	184.8	184.4	184.1	184.7
2011	183.0	184.0	185.2	187.9	188.3	190.4	191.4	190.1	188.6	188.5	188.5	188.7	187.9
2012	186.8	187.8	189.0	192.5	193.3	194.9	195.5	194.2	192.8	193.6	193.2	193.0	192.2
2013	190.9	191.6	192.5	193.5	194.6	196.2	197.5	196.2	194.4	194.2	194.1	193.9	194.1
2014	191.8	192.0	193.6	194.9	196.3	198.5	198.1	198.0	196.1	195.4	195.0	194.7	195.4
2015	193.9	194.0	195.5	196.6	198.4	200.2	201.5	201.0	199.0	198.6	200.6	200.2	198.3
Government													
2005	653.9	661.3	664.1	670.4	668.2	667.5	640.2	635.1	661.3	669.7	676.9	673.7	661.9
2006	666.0	674.8	680.3	682.1	681.7	681.2	654.7	649.3	669.2	682.6	688.4	687.1	674.8
2007	679.2	688.0	689.5	691.9	688.9	687.4	662.4	655.4	677.8	688.6	697.4	694.0	683.4
2008	687.1	697.6	701.9	700.4	699.6	697.4	671.4	670.4	690.7	705.9	712.2	710.3	695.4
2009	697.6	705.3	709.7	712.0	710.5	708.1	672.4	670.6	695.2	709.0	717.8	712.5	701.7
2010	702.1	707.1	713.1	718.7	726.0	721.2	679.7	671.6	703.5	711.6	715.9	714.3	707.1
2011	706.3	718.6	722.0	723.1	717.6	715.0	683.0	679.2	713.3	723.8	729.1	728.1	713.3
2012	711.4	722.8	724.5	723.8	719.0	716.0	677.4	680.3	710.7	722.2	727.6	726.8	713.5
2013	709.8	722.2	723.4	725.4	721.1	715.0	684.5	681.0	709.2	716.4	721.9	720.3	712.5
2014	706.4	714.8	717.3	721.1	717.5	711.4	684.4	682.8	711.5	716.5	721.6	721.3	710.6
2015	706.4	718.7	717.3	722.5	719.2	713.3	685.7	682.7	710.9	719.1	723.6	721.2	711.7

2. Average Weekly Hours by Selected Industry: Virginia, 2011–2015

(Not seasonally adjusted)

Industry and year	January	February	March	April	May	June	July	August	September	October	November	December	Annual average
Total Private													
2011	35.8	35.3	35.2	35.5	35.9	35.5	35.6	35.5	35.3	35.5	34.9	35.0	35.4
2012	35.0	34.8	34.9	35.2	34.7	35.0	35.2	35.1	35.4	34.7	34.8	35.3	35.0
2013	34.1	34.5	34.5	34.7	34.6	34.9	34.5	34.6	34.9	33.9	34.3	34.6	34.5
2014	34.0	33.9	34.7	34.8	34.8	35.2	34.6	34.7	34.8	34.9	35.5	34.9	34.7
2015	34.5	35.1	35.3	35.3	35.3	35.1	35.1	35.6	35.0	34.9	35.4	35.0	35.1
Goods-Producing													
2011	39.0	39.0	39.2	39.9	40.6	40.4	39.5	39.6	39.6	38.6	39.7	39.5	39.6
2012	38.1	38.2	39.2	39.7	39.1	39.5	39.0	39.7	40.2	39.7	39.5	40.0	39.3
2013	38.2	38.5	38.4	39.3	39.3	38.7	39.0	40.1	40.2	38.4	40.3	38.5	39.1
2014	37.5	36.1	39.1	39.7	40.2	40.0	39.6	40.1	39.8	39.6	40.1	39.6	39.3
2015	38.7	38.8	39.3	40.0	40.6	40.6	40.0	40.5	39.8	40.4	40.1	40.4	39.9
Construction													
2011	37.2	37.9	37.1	38.5	39.7	39.5	39.3	39.0	38.9	37.9	39.5	39.1	38.6
2012	37.1	36.8	38.2	39.2	38.3	38.6	38.4	39.1	39.9	39.2	39.0	39.4	38.6
2013	37.2	37.3	37.1	38.9	38.5	38.1	38.1	39.6	39.9	37.1	40.1	37.4	38.3
2014	36.2	34.5	38.2	38.8	39.4	39.2	38.7	38.6	37.5	37.8	38.3	37.4	37.9
2015	35.5	36.6	37.5	38.4	39.7	39.8	38.8	39.1	37.3	38.7	37.8	38.0	38.1
Manufacturing													
2011	40.2	39.6	40.8	40.7	41.0	40.9	39.2	39.7	39.9	39.1	39.7	39.7	40.0
2012	38.9	39.2	39.8	39.8	39.4	40.0	39.2	39.9	40.2	39.9	39.8	40.4	39.7
2013	39.2	39.7	39.8	39.7	40.2	39.5	40.1	40.7	40.9	40.1	40.6	40.8	40.1
2014	40.0	38.8	41.2	41.5	41.7	41.3	41.0	41.6	42.0	41.3	41.9	41.8	41.2
2015	41.7	41.0	41.0	41.6	41.5	41.4	41.1	41.9	42.5	41.7	42.3	42.8	41.7
Trade, Transportation, and Utilities													
2011	33.4	33.1	33.2	34.1	34.3	34.6	34.9	34.7	34.7	34.9	34.4	34.9	34.3
2012	34.1	34.2	34.2	34.7	34.3	34.7	34.8	34.6	35.0	34.2	34.5	34.8	34.5
2013	33.6	34.1	34.1	34.2	34.3	34.5	34.6	34.6	34.9	33.8	33.9	34.3	34.2
2014	33.5	33.4	33.9	34.0	34.0	34.1	33.7	33.8	34.0	33.6	34.2	34.5	33.9
2015	33.7	33.7	33.8	33.9	34.4	34.0	34.3	34.3	34.3	34.0	34.0	34.2	34.1
Financial Activities													
2011	39.7	39.3	38.3	38.7	39.5	37.9	38.5	37.9	38.3	39.4	38.0	38.3	38.6
2012	39.4	38.3	37.8	38.7	38.3	38.6	39.4	38.6	40.0	38.8	38.9	40.2	38.9
2013	38.6	38.6	38.6	38.1	37.7	38.7	37.5	37.4	37.4	36.7	36.8	37.5	37.8
2014	36.8	37.2	36.8	36.5	36.4	37.6	36.6	36.9	37.0	37.3	39.0	37.7	37.2
2015	37.8	39.1	39.1	38.5	38.9	38.6	38.7	40.4	40.0	39.5	40.5	39.4	39.2
Professional and Business Services													
2011	38.1	37.6	37.4	37.7	38.1	37.2	37.1	37.1	37.3	37.2	35.6	36.0	37.2
2012	36.9	36.6	36.6	36.6	35.7	36.0	36.5	36.3	36.9	35.6	35.9	36.7	36.4
2013	35.7	36.3	36.2	36.2	36.2	37.3	36.4	36.3	36.9	35.4	35.9	36.9	36.3
2014	35.9	36.3	36.7	36.5	36.7	37.2	36.2	36.6	36.4	37.0	38.1	36.8	36.7
2015	36.4	37.4	37.7	37.2	37.2	36.9	36.8	37.9	36.6	36.6	37.9	37.3	37.2
Education and Health Services													
2011	35.1	34.3	34.3	34.4	34.8	34.9	35.1	35.1	34.9	35.3	34.8	34.7	34.8
2012	35.0	34.4	34.8	34.9	34.8	35.1	35.1	34.8	35.1	34.7	34.4	34.7	34.8
2013	34.1	34.0	34.0	33.9	33.9	34.2	33.9	33.8	34.1	33.8	33.8	34.1	34.0
2014	33.9	33.7	33.9	34.2	34.1	34.6	34.2	33.9	34.3	34.1	34.5	34.1	34.1
2015	34.2	34.6	34.3	34.2	34.2	34.2	34.1	34.5	34.2	34.3	34.7	33.7	34.3
Leisure and Hospitality													
2011	26.6	26.3	26.2	26.3	26.4	26.1	27.2	26.7	26.1	26.6	26.3	26.0	26.4
2012	25.8	25.7	26.1	26.8	26.7	27.6	27.8	27.6	27.2	27.6	27.6	27.5	27.0
2013	26.6	27.1	27.0	27.5	27.1	27.1	26.7	26.5	26.1	25.9	26.0	25.9	26.6
2014	25.5	25.5	26.5	26.9	26.8	27.0	26.9	26.7	26.5	26.3	26.5	25.9	26.4
2015	25.3	25.4	26.2	26.6	26.6	26.5	26.8	27.1	26.1	26.1	26.2	25.8	26.2
Other Services													
2011	32.1	31.8	32.2	32.1	32.9	32.3	32.3	31.8	32.4	33.8	31.8	31.4	32.2
2012	31.7	31.7	31.5	32.7	32.0	32.0	33.0	32.3	33.3	31.6	31.7	32.4	32.2
2013	31.4	32.1	31.9	32.7	32.4	32.6	32.4	31.5	32.7	31.7	31.4	32.8	32.1
2014	31.8	32.0	32.5	32.4	32.6	32.9	32.2	31.6	32.2	32.3	32.6	32.4	32.3
2015	32.4	32.4	32.5	32.5	31.9	32.7	32.7	32.4	31.8	32.1	32.8	32.4	32.4

3. Average Hourly Earnings by Selected Industry: Virginia, 2011–2015

(Dollars, not seasonally adjusted)

Industry and year	January	February	March	April	May	June	July	August	September	October	November	December	Annual average
Total Private													
2011	24.46	24.54	24.36	24.49	24.53	24.32	24.47	24.38	24.72	25.39	25.10	25.12	24.66
2012	25.17	25.09	25.03	25.29	24.86	24.66	24.99	24.56	25.09	24.79	24.77	25.49	24.98
2013	25.13	25.07	25.25	25.05	25.04	25.28	24.96	24.98	25.50	25.25	25.32	25.90	25.23
2014	25.82	25.29	25.60	25.18	25.04	25.27	25.02	25.18	25.25	25.32	25.64	25.47	25.34
2015	25.79	26.30	26.23	26.04	25.94	25.79	25.81	26.34	26.26	26.36	26.55	26.27	26.14
Goods-Producing													
2011	21.58	21.50	21.47	21.68	21.77	21.66	21.80	21.75	21.79	22.01	22.04	22.11	21.76
2012	22.19	22.01	21.73	21.86	22.03	21.94	22.16	21.85	22.06	22.09	22.42	22.69	22.09
2013	22.34	22.49	22.82	22.60	22.56	22.90	22.79	22.73	22.77	22.84	22.76	23.11	22.73
2014	23.35	23.75	23.06	23.20	23.16	23.22	23.19	23.11	23.19	23.41	23.60	23.47	23.30
2015	23.52	23.61	23.55	23.50	23.39	23.29	23.46	23.36	23.73	23.72	23.75	23.66	23.54
Construction													
2011	22.06	22.00	22.06	22.19	22.04	21.93	22.18	22.13	22.23	22.62	22.53	22.42	22.20
2012	22.29	22.41	22.17	21.99	22.16	22.25	22.48	22.06	22.41	22.48	22.95	23.15	22.40
2013	22.71	23.14	23.56	23.35	23.43	23.55	23.64	23.89	23.88	23.94	23.57	24.39	23.60
2014	24.82	25.23	23.99	24.29	24.25	23.95	23.88	24.08	24.15	24.07	24.04	24.20	24.23
2015	24.30	24.67	24.44	24.14	24.24	24.03	24.27	24.13	24.28	24.66	24.89	24.99	24.42
Manufacturing													
2011	21.17	20.99	20.93	21.19	21.55	21.64	22.31	22.13	22.06	21.99	22.10	22.30	21.70
2012	22.54	22.06	21.64	22.01	22.15	21.84	22.04	21.80	21.85	21.79	21.96	22.32	22.00
2013	22.03	21.87	22.10	21.80	21.63	22.12	21.88	21.44	21.44	21.62	21.77	21.81	21.79
2014	21.90	22.30	22.01	21.98	21.93	22.32	22.34	22.08	22.18	22.37	22.72	22.39	22.21
2015	22.47	22.36	22.40	22.69	22.37	22.36	22.49	22.43	22.60	22.20	22.12	21.92	22.37
Trade, Transportation, and Utilities													
2011	20.56	20.56	20.48	20.73	20.57	20.77	20.85	20.58	20.44	20.70	20.60	20.11	20.58
2012	20.27	19.90	19.72	20.00	19.43	19.90	20.24	19.66	20.31	19.81	19.67	20.13	19.92
2013	20.07	19.76	19.72	19.68	19.76	20.16	19.72	19.92	19.97	19.90	19.82	20.02	19.88
2014	19.76	20.70	20.15	20.15	20.33	20.35	20.36	20.24	20.20	20.01	20.05	19.34	20.13
2015	19.76	20.46	20.21	20.56	20.20	20.36	20.36	20.83	20.29	20.87	20.31	20.00	20.35
Financial Activities													
2011	24.55	25.05	24.91	26.07	25.35	25.59	25.83	25.37	26.56	27.72	27.56	26.90	25.96
2012	25.90	26.01	26.41	26.42	26.18	25.99	26.11	26.09	26.43	26.21	26.36	26.34	26.21
2013	26.15	26.55	26.91	27.21	26.72	26.65	27.22	26.82	27.04	26.54	26.56	27.24	26.80
2014	26.43	26.43	27.07	26.40	26.15	26.78	26.33	26.44	26.41	25.96	25.99	26.03	26.37
2015	25.79	26.29	26.33	26.53	26.69	26.74	26.70	27.10	26.53	26.71	27.13	26.73	26.61
Professional and Business Services													
2011	34.36	34.52	34.19	33.79	34.17	33.45	33.80	33.81	33.58	34.84	34.60	35.08	34.18
2012	35.29	35.53	35.45	36.18	35.31	35.05	35.51	34.96	35.58	35.30	35.08	36.10	35.45
2013	35.29	35.06	35.42	35.20	34.81	34.89	34.12	34.07	34.92	34.49	34.49	35.46	34.85
2014	34.86	35.71	35.33	34.29	33.87	34.33	33.81	33.88	33.65	33.84	34.58	34.28	34.36
2015	35.19	35.87	35.49	34.82	34.81	34.56	34.87	35.55	35.50	36.06	36.36	35.50	35.39
Education and Health Services													
2011	21.42	21.93	21.76	22.10	22.47	22.45	23.00	22.99	23.44	23.82	23.94	23.96	22.78
2012	23.08	23.28	23.48	23.88	23.65	23.49	23.74	23.60	24.22	23.86	23.62	23.86	23.65
2013	23.66	23.84	24.49	24.04	24.47	24.62	24.57	24.59	24.91	24.35	24.52	24.92	24.41
2014	24.32	24.86	24.37	24.23	24.17	24.27	24.36	24.64	24.84	24.56	24.62	25.29	24.54
2015	24.77	25.02	25.40	25.50	25.72	25.85	25.45	25.98	26.22	26.04	26.00	26.94	25.74
Leisure and Hospitality													
2011	13.36	13.34	13.19	13.31	13.04	12.87	12.62	12.62	13.06	13.00	12.99	13.08	13.03
2012	13.02	12.99	12.85	12.76	12.83	12.43	12.37	12.44	12.80	12.76	12.89	13.18	12.76
2013	12.98	12.95	12.84	12.72	12.79	12.78	12.74	12.76	12.90	12.98	13.02	13.22	12.88
2014	13.09	13.35	13.11	13.11	13.08	13.13	12.84	12.88	13.13	13.24	13.21	13.30	13.12
2015	13.32	13.44	13.39	13.34	13.27	13.06	12.93	12.83	13.12	13.27	13.34	13.40	13.22
Other Services													
2011	23.48	23.62	23.39	24.10	24.15	24.07	24.36	24.48	24.38	25.37	24.20	25.35	24.25
2012	24.86	24.89	24.81	25.50	25.01	25.23	25.41	25.35	25.93	25.02	25.27	26.21	25.30
2013	25.43	25.63	26.00	25.24	25.41	25.39	24.95	24.74	25.78	25.51	26.14	25.90	25.51
2014	25.81	25.88	25.89	25.78	25.61	25.68	25.24	25.10	25.12	25.42	25.61	26.17	25.61
2015	26.23	25.79	26.22	25.80	26.37	25.91	25.82	26.21	26.64	26.62	27.15	27.37	26.35

4. Average Weekly Earnings by Selected Industry: Virginia, 2011–2015

(Dollars, not seasonally adjusted)

Industry and year	January	February	March	April	May	June	July	August	September	October	November	December	Annual average
Total Private													
2011	875.67	866.26	857.47	869.40	880.63	863.36	871.13	865.49	872.62	901.35	875.99	879.20	872.96
2012	880.95	873.13	873.55	890.21	862.64	863.10	879.65	862.06	888.19	860.21	862.00	899.80	874.30
2013	856.93	864.92	871.13	869.24	866.38	882.27	861.12	864.31	889.95	855.98	868.48	896.14	870.44
2014	877.88	857.33	888.32	876.26	871.39	889.50	865.69	873.75	878.70	883.67	910.22	888.90	879.30
2015	889.76	923.13	925.92	919.21	915.68	905.23	905.93	937.70	919.10	919.96	939.87	919.45	917.51
Goods-Producing													
2011	841.62	838.50	841.62	865.03	883.86	875.06	861.10	861.30	862.88	849.59	874.99	873.35	861.70
2012	845.44	840.78	851.82	867.84	861.37	866.63	864.24	867.45	886.81	876.97	885.59	907.60	868.14
2013	853.39	865.87	876.29	888.18	886.61	886.23	888.81	911.47	915.35	877.06	917.23	889.74	888.74
2014	875.63	857.38	901.65	921.04	931.03	928.80	918.32	926.71	922.96	927.04	946.36	929.41	915.69
2015	910.22	916.07	925.52	940.00	949.63	945.57	938.40	946.08	944.45	958.29	952.38	955.86	939.25
Construction													
2011	820.63	833.80	818.43	854.32	874.99	866.24	871.67	863.07	864.75	857.30	889.94	876.62	856.92
2012	826.96	824.69	846.89	862.01	848.73	858.85	863.23	862.55	894.16	881.22	895.05	912.11	864.64
2013	844.81	863.12	874.08	908.32	902.06	897.26	900.68	946.04	952.81	888.17	945.16	912.19	903.88
2014	898.48	870.44	916.42	942.45	955.45	938.84	924.16	929.49	905.63	909.85	920.73	905.08	918.32
2015	862.65	902.92	916.50	926.98	962.33	956.39	941.68	943.48	905.64	954.34	940.84	949.62	930.40
Manufacturing													
2011	851.03	831.20	853.94	862.43	883.55	885.08	874.55	878.56	880.19	859.81	877.37	885.31	868.00
2012	876.81	864.75	861.27	876.00	872.71	873.60	863.97	869.82	878.37	869.42	874.01	901.73	873.40
2013	863.58	868.24	879.58	865.46	869.53	873.74	877.39	872.61	876.90	866.96	883.86	889.85	873.78
2014	876.00	865.24	906.81	912.17	914.48	921.82	915.94	918.53	931.56	923.88	951.97	935.90	915.05
2015	937.00	916.76	918.40	943.90	928.36	925.70	924.34	939.82	960.50	925.74	935.68	938.18	932.83
Trade, Transportation, and Utilities													
2011	686.70	680.54	679.94	706.89	705.55	718.64	727.67	714.13	709.27	722.43	708.64	701.84	705.89
2012	691.21	680.58	674.42	694.00	666.45	690.53	704.35	680.24	710.85	677.50	678.62	700.52	687.24
2013	674.35	673.82	672.45	673.06	677.77	695.52	682.31	689.23	696.95	672.62	671.90	686.69	679.90
2014	661.96	691.38	683.09	685.10	691.22	693.94	686.13	684.11	686.80	672.34	685.71	667.23	682.41
2015	665.91	689.50	683.10	696.98	694.88	692.24	698.35	714.47	695.95	709.58	690.54	684.00	693.94
Financial Activities													
2011	974.64	984.47	954.05	1,008.91	1,001.33	969.86	994.46	961.52	1,017.25	1,092.17	1,047.28	1,030.27	1,002.06
2012	1,020.46	996.18	998.30	1,022.45	1,002.69	1,003.21	1,028.73	1,007.07	1,057.20	1,016.95	1,025.40	1,058.87	1,019.57
2013	1,009.39	1,024.83	1,038.73	1,036.70	1,007.34	1,031.36	1,020.75	1,003.07	1,011.30	974.02	977.41	1,021.50	1,013.04
2014	972.62	983.20	996.18	963.60	951.86	1,006.93	963.68	975.64	977.17	968.31	1,013.61	981.33	980.96
2015	974.86	1,027.94	1,029.50	1,021.41	1,038.24	1,032.16	1,033.29	1,094.84	1,061.20	1,055.05	1,098.77	1,053.16	1,043.11
Professional and Business Services													
2011	1,309.12	1,297.95	1,278.71	1,273.88	1,301.88	1,244.34	1,253.98	1,254.35	1,252.53	1,296.05	1,231.76	1,262.88	1,271.50
2012	1,302.20	1,300.40	1,297.47	1,324.19	1,260.57	1,261.80	1,296.12	1,269.05	1,312.90	1,256.68	1,259.37	1,324.87	1,290.38
2013	1,259.85	1,272.68	1,282.20	1,274.24	1,260.12	1,301.40	1,241.97	1,236.74	1,288.55	1,220.95	1,238.19	1,308.47	1,265.06
2014	1,251.47	1,296.27	1,296.61	1,251.59	1,243.03	1,277.08	1,223.92	1,240.01	1,224.86	1,252.08	1,317.50	1,261.50	1,261.01
2015	1,280.92	1,341.54	1,337.97	1,295.30	1,294.93	1,275.26	1,283.22	1,347.35	1,299.30	1,319.80	1,378.04	1,324.15	1,316.51
Education and Health Services													
2011	751.84	752.20	746.37	760.24	781.96	783.51	807.30	806.95	818.06	840.85	833.11	831.41	792.74
2012	807.80	800.83	817.10	833.41	823.02	824.50	833.27	821.28	850.12	827.94	812.53	827.94	823.02
2013	806.81	810.56	832.66	814.96	829.53	842.00	832.92	831.14	849.43	823.03	828.78	849.77	829.94
2014	824.45	837.78	826.14	828.67	824.20	839.74	833.11	835.30	852.01	837.50	849.39	862.39	836.81
2015	847.13	865.69	871.22	872.10	879.62	884.07	867.85	896.31	896.72	893.17	902.20	907.88	882.88
Leisure and Hospitality													
2011	355.38	350.84	345.58	350.05	344.26	335.91	343.26	336.95	340.87	345.80	341.64	340.08	343.99
2012	335.92	333.84	335.39	341.97	342.56	343.07	343.89	343.34	348.16	352.18	355.76	362.45	344.52
2013	345.27	350.95	346.68	349.80	346.61	346.34	340.16	338.14	336.69	336.18	338.52	342.40	342.61
2014	333.80	340.43	347.42	352.66	350.54	354.51	345.40	343.90	347.95	348.21	350.07	344.47	346.37
2015	337.00	341.38	350.82	354.84	352.98	346.09	346.52	347.69	342.43	346.35	349.51	345.72	346.36
Other Services													
2011	753.71	751.12	753.16	773.61	794.54	777.46	786.83	778.46	789.91	857.51	769.56	795.99	780.85
2012	788.06	789.01	781.52	833.85	800.32	807.36	838.53	818.81	863.47	790.63	801.06	849.20	814.66
2013	798.50	822.72	829.40	825.35	823.28	827.71	808.38	779.31	843.01	808.67	820.80	849.52	818.87
2014	820.76	828.16	841.43	835.27	834.89	844.87	812.73	793.16	808.86	821.07	834.89	847.91	827.20
2015	849.85	835.60	852.15	838.50	841.20	847.26	844.31	849.20	847.15	854.50	890.52	886.79	853.74

WASHINGTON
At a Glance

Population:
 2005 estimate: 6,257,305
 2010 census: 6,724,540
 2015 estimate: 7,170,351

Percent change in population:
 2005–2015: 14.6%
 2010–2015: 6.6%

Percent change in total nonfarm employment:
 2005–2015: 12.1%

Industry with the largest growth in employment, 2005–2015 (thousands):
 Education and health services, 95.6

Industry with the largest decline or smallest growth in employment, 2005–2015 (thousands):
 Construction, –4.5

Civilian labor force:
 2005: 3,263,703
 2010: 3,511,326
 2015: 3,544,242

Unemployment rate and rank among states (highest to lowest):
 2005: 5.6%, 11th
 2010: 10.0%, 17th
 2015: 5.7%, 16th

Over-the-year change in unemployment rates:
 2012–2013: –1.1%
 2013–2014: –0.9%
 2014–2015: –0.4%

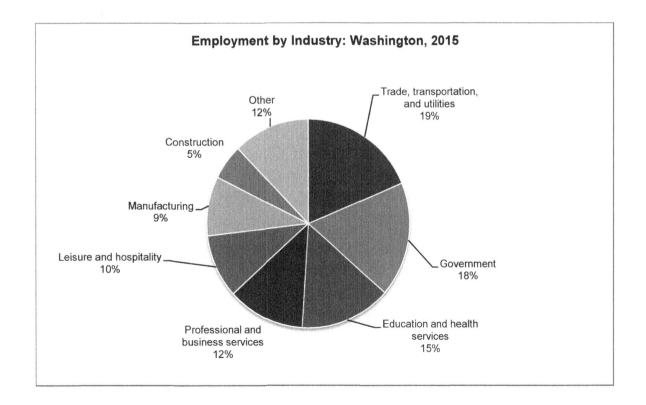

Employment by Industry: Washington, 2015

Other 12%

Construction 5%

Manufacturing 9%

Leisure and hospitality 10%

Professional and business services 12%

Trade, transportation, and utilities 19%

Government 18%

Education and health services 15%

1. Employment by Industry: Washington, 2005–2015

(Numbers in thousands, not seasonally adjusted)

Industry and year	January	February	March	April	May	June	July	August	September	October	November	December	Annual average
Total Nonfarm													
2005	2,724.5	2,740.1	2,765.4	2,790.7	2,815.7	2,836.0	2,822.7	2,822.8	2,835.8	2,856.0	2,869.8	2,870.7	2,812.5
2006	2,811.2	2,831.7	2,852.4	2,867.9	2,897.8	2,928.8	2,898.4	2,902.5	2,929.1	2,931.9	2,941.3	2,937.8	2,894.2
2007	2,878.4	2,908.8	2,926.5	2,944.7	2,974.0	3,000.3	2,978.6	2,979.6	2,995.3	3,005.5	3,019.3	3,009.8	2,968.4
2008	2,951.4	2,971.2	2,983.5	2,994.5	3,015.8	3,028.3	3,013.3	3,009.3	3,014.9	2,989.8	2,993.4	2,960.3	2,993.8
2009	2,886.1	2,879.8	2,871.3	2,867.4	2,880.9	2,880.9	2,857.6	2,836.7	2,850.4	2,859.4	2,849.2	2,832.4	2,862.7
2010	2,777.4	2,785.2	2,802.0	2,827.3	2,853.7	2,859.4	2,847.1	2,829.2	2,848.9	2,871.6	2,870.6	2,859.1	2,836.0
2011	2,807.6	2,820.4	2,832.3	2,862.7	2,880.0	2,893.0	2,888.4	2,877.8	2,895.2	2,905.5	2,908.3	2,894.9	2,872.2
2012	2,840.0	2,854.6	2,876.6	2,897.8	2,926.1	2,945.3	2,931.5	2,928.0	2,942.4	2,963.9	2,968.9	2,955.2	2,919.2
2013	2,907.4	2,925.4	2,940.1	2,961.5	2,991.0	3,003.0	2,995.2	2,997.0	3,014.1	3,030.1	3,037.5	3,028.4	2,985.9
2014	2,990.5	2,998.2	3,016.1	3,032.7	3,058.3	3,076.7	3,081.6	3,084.0	3,101.5	3,109.2	3,116.4	3,117.9	3,065.3
2015	3,072.1	3,084.2	3,106.5	3,130.4	3,156.6	3,178.4	3,169.4	3,165.9	3,183.2	3,196.3	3,205.2	3,198.2	3,153.9
Total Private													
2005	2,198.2	2,209.3	2,231.5	2,256.2	2,279.8	2,298.4	2,314.1	2,328.2	2,321.7	2,324.0	2,330.0	2,338.1	2,285.8
2006	2,281.6	2,295.2	2,314.2	2,331.1	2,358.7	2,386.9	2,389.1	2,405.7	2,411.2	2,396.8	2,398.7	2,401.5	2,364.2
2007	2,347.7	2,371.2	2,389.7	2,405.0	2,432.0	2,458.8	2,461.1	2,475.1	2,473.5	2,464.3	2,469.9	2,467.3	2,434.6
2008	2,410.1	2,421.5	2,434.3	2,444.6	2,463.0	2,475.1	2,482.3	2,489.8	2,481.1	2,433.9	2,429.2	2,405.0	2,447.5
2009	2,334.4	2,323.4	2,312.7	2,302.5	2,316.0	2,325.4	2,325.1	2,322.8	2,320.1	2,303.4	2,289.6	2,282.5	2,313.2
2010	2,226.0	2,230.1	2,245.3	2,266.1	2,281.3	2,298.9	2,311.4	2,313.8	2,318.6	2,317.5	2,312.3	2,310.6	2,286.0
2011	2,258.0	2,267.3	2,278.9	2,307.1	2,322.9	2,343.6	2,359.4	2,367.1	2,371.8	2,357.5	2,357.3	2,353.5	2,328.7
2012	2,297.5	2,308.9	2,328.0	2,346.9	2,373.7	2,398.8	2,405.5	2,419.1	2,417.2	2,414.3	2,415.2	2,411.4	2,378.0
2013	2,361.5	2,375.4	2,389.3	2,408.3	2,436.5	2,455.1	2,469.9	2,485.5	2,485.3	2,479.8	2,483.0	2,482.0	2,442.6
2014	2,441.1	2,445.5	2,460.9	2,474.4	2,498.3	2,522.6	2,546.7	2,562.4	2,560.7	2,548.1	2,553.4	2,561.5	2,514.6
2015	2,512.4	2,520.8	2,539.8	2,560.1	2,584.5	2,612.0	2,622.9	2,632.9	2,631.1	2,626.0	2,629.7	2,630.0	2,591.9
Goods-Producing													
2005	431.1	435.0	442.1	448.8	455.7	462.6	472.4	476.2	464.1	477.3	472.0	470.2	459.0
2006	461.8	467.9	472.7	476.9	485.6	496.5	502.2	506.3	508.3	504.7	498.1	493.6	489.6
2007	484.5	490.4	494.5	499.8	508.0	518.5	522.5	526.8	525.9	521.8	515.4	508.1	509.7
2008	496.9	498.7	500.4	500.6	505.4	509.3	513.6	515.6	511.2	479.7	487.0	471.7	499.2
2009	451.0	444.4	436.5	430.8	431.7	433.8	434.9	434.5	432.0	424.8	412.8	404.5	431.0
2010	393.4	392.5	394.1	397.4	401.4	406.8	414.4	416.7	417.9	415.2	406.9	400.2	404.7
2011	390.4	393.2	395.9	401.6	406.8	413.6	421.6	426.3	428.5	424.4	417.9	412.0	411.0
2012	402.0	403.8	409.2	413.5	420.0	429.2	435.9	441.7	441.4	440.7	435.6	430.1	425.3
2013	422.4	425.9	429.2	431.9	438.5	445.4	452.0	456.9	456.9	453.1	447.4	441.5	441.8
2014	436.3	436.5	440.9	442.8	448.7	456.3	465.5	469.7	469.2	465.8	461.5	460.5	454.5
2015	455.3	456.2	460.5	464.0	468.5	475.6	481.8	482.4	480.5	475.0	470.3	465.2	469.6
Service-Providing													
2005	2,293.4	2,305.1	2,323.3	2,341.9	2,360.0	2,373.4	2,350.3	2,346.6	2,371.7	2,378.7	2,397.8	2,400.5	2,353.6
2006	2,349.4	2,363.8	2,379.7	2,391.0	2,412.2	2,432.3	2,396.2	2,396.2	2,420.8	2,427.2	2,443.2	2,444.2	2,404.7
2007	2,393.9	2,418.4	2,432.0	2,444.9	2,466.0	2,481.8	2,456.1	2,452.8	2,469.4	2,483.7	2,503.9	2,501.7	2,458.7
2008	2,454.5	2,472.5	2,483.1	2,493.9	2,510.4	2,519.0	2,499.7	2,493.7	2,503.7	2,510.1	2,506.4	2,488.6	2,494.6
2009	2,435.1	2,435.4	2,434.8	2,436.6	2,449.2	2,447.1	2,422.7	2,402.2	2,418.4	2,434.6	2,436.4	2,427.9	2,431.7
2010	2,384.0	2,392.7	2,407.9	2,429.9	2,452.3	2,452.6	2,432.7	2,412.5	2,431.0	2,456.4	2,463.7	2,458.9	2,431.2
2011	2,417.2	2,427.2	2,436.4	2,461.1	2,473.2	2,479.4	2,466.8	2,451.5	2,466.7	2,481.1	2,490.4	2,482.9	2,461.2
2012	2,438.0	2,450.8	2,467.4	2,484.3	2,506.1	2,516.1	2,495.6	2,486.3	2,501.0	2,523.2	2,533.3	2,525.1	2,493.9
2013	2,485.0	2,499.5	2,510.9	2,529.6	2,552.5	2,557.6	2,543.2	2,540.1	2,557.2	2,577.0	2,590.1	2,586.9	2,544.1
2014	2,554.2	2,561.7	2,575.2	2,589.9	2,609.6	2,620.4	2,616.1	2,614.3	2,632.3	2,643.4	2,654.9	2,657.4	2,610.8
2015	2,616.8	2,628.0	2,646.0	2,666.4	2,688.1	2,702.8	2,687.6	2,683.5	2,702.7	2,721.3	2,734.9	2,733.0	2,684.3
Mining and Logging													
2005	8.8	8.9	8.8	8.8	9.1	9.2	9.2	9.1	9.1	8.9	8.8	8.8	9.0
2006	8.4	8.5	8.5	8.4	8.8	9.0	9.0	8.9	8.8	8.7	8.6	8.6	8.7
2007	8.4	7.9	7.6	7.9	8.2	8.5	8.5	8.4	8.3	8.3	8.0	7.9	8.2
2008	7.4	7.4	7.3	7.3	7.5	7.6	7.9	7.9	7.8	7.8	7.4	7.2	7.5
2009	6.5	6.4	5.8	5.6	5.8	6.2	6.3	6.3	6.3	6.1	5.7	5.5	6.0
2010	5.4	5.5	5.5	5.6	5.9	6.1	6.2	6.3	6.3	6.2	5.9	5.7	5.9
2011	5.6	5.7	5.7	5.7	5.8	6.1	6.2	6.3	6.2	6.3	6.1	6.0	6.0
2012	5.7	5.6	5.6	5.6	5.7	6.0	6.1	6.2	6.2	6.2	6.0	5.9	5.9
2013	5.7	5.8	5.8	5.8	6.0	6.2	6.3	6.4	6.4	6.4	6.3	6.2	6.1
2014	6.0	6.1	6.1	5.9	6.1	6.2	6.4	6.5	6.4	6.4	6.3	6.3	6.2
2015	6.3	6.3	6.2	6.2	6.3	6.4	6.5	6.3	6.3	6.1	5.9	5.8	6.2

1. Employment by Industry: Washington, 2005–2015—*Continued*

(Numbers in thousands, not seasonally adjusted)

Industry and year	January	February	March	April	May	June	July	August	September	October	November	December	Annual average
Construction													
2005	158.4	162.0	167.0	170.8	175.0	178.7	184.5	188.2	189.3	187.7	184.5	182.8	177.4
2006	175.6	179.5	184.2	187.7	193.8	200.1	203.3	206.9	207.1	204.6	200.0	196.4	194.9
2007	190.3	194.4	199.6	203.5	210.2	215.3	216.5	220.4	218.0	214.6	210.3	205.2	208.2
2008	196.6	197.3	200.3	201.6	204.6	206.9	209.1	210.1	206.5	200.9	190.6	181.1	200.5
2009	168.4	163.7	162.4	159.9	161.8	162.8	162.6	162.3	160.6	156.7	148.9	143.3	159.5
2010	134.7	133.9	135.5	137.2	140.0	142.2	146.8	148.6	147.7	146.2	140.4	135.2	140.7
2011	127.2	127.8	129.3	132.8	136.3	139.3	142.5	144.5	144.5	142.0	137.2	133.4	136.4
2012	125.5	126.9	130.2	133.7	137.6	141.6	144.7	148.1	147.4	147.5	144.2	141.5	139.1
2013	135.2	137.4	139.9	143.0	147.6	150.8	155.2	159.0	158.7	157.1	154.1	149.8	149.0
2014	146.8	146.3	150.4	151.6	155.7	160.0	165.5	169.2	169.5	168.3	166.4	165.8	159.6
2015	162.3	163.3	166.2	169.7	173.2	176.2	179.8	180.5	179.1	176.9	175.2	172.1	172.9
Manufacturing													
2005	263.9	264.1	266.3	269.2	271.6	274.7	278.7	278.9	265.7	280.7	278.7	278.6	272.6
2006	277.8	279.9	280.0	280.8	283.0	287.4	289.9	290.5	292.4	291.4	289.5	288.6	285.9
2007	285.8	288.1	287.3	288.4	289.6	294.7	297.5	298.0	299.6	298.9	297.1	295.0	293.3
2008	292.9	294.0	292.8	291.7	293.3	294.8	296.6	297.6	296.9	271.0	289.0	283.4	291.2
2009	276.1	274.3	268.3	265.3	264.1	264.8	266.0	265.9	265.1	262.0	258.2	255.7	265.5
2010	253.3	253.1	253.1	254.6	255.5	258.5	261.4	261.8	263.9	262.8	260.6	259.3	258.2
2011	257.6	259.7	260.9	263.1	264.7	268.2	272.9	275.5	277.8	276.1	274.6	272.6	268.6
2012	270.8	271.3	273.4	274.2	276.7	281.6	285.1	287.4	287.8	287.0	285.4	282.7	280.3
2013	281.5	282.7	283.5	283.1	284.9	288.4	290.5	291.5	291.8	289.6	287.0	285.5	286.7
2014	283.5	284.1	284.4	285.3	286.9	290.1	293.6	294.0	293.3	291.1	288.8	288.4	288.6
2015	286.7	286.6	288.1	288.1	289.0	293.0	295.5	295.6	295.1	292.0	289.2	287.3	290.5
Trade, Transportation, and Utilities													
2005	517.2	515.2	517.9	520.5	525.8	530.4	531.7	535.3	535.7	536.0	546.3	553.4	530.5
2006	530.4	527.2	530.4	531.4	537.4	543.5	543.0	546.0	546.0	546.2	556.2	561.5	541.6
2007	540.5	539.1	541.9	544.0	549.0	554.2	555.8	557.5	556.2	558.3	570.5	573.5	553.4
2008	552.4	548.2	549.7	549.6	552.6	554.6	557.1	557.5	554.3	553.7	555.1	555.7	553.4
2009	531.2	523.0	518.9	515.6	519.5	520.8	522.8	521.8	521.4	520.8	525.6	527.9	522.4
2010	507.7	504.0	506.3	510.4	514.0	517.6	519.5	519.1	518.6	522.7	529.9	533.8	517.0
2011	512.7	510.0	512.3	515.9	520.4	524.9	530.4	531.3	530.4	531.1	539.9	542.6	525.2
2012	522.1	519.0	521.8	524.0	531.3	537.7	540.8	542.4	541.3	543.8	553.3	555.1	536.1
2013	535.6	533.7	534.5	537.8	545.6	550.1	554.6	557.7	556.7	560.8	571.2	574.7	551.1
2014	555.6	551.9	553.0	555.9	562.2	568.5	574.1	578.1	577.6	578.8	589.2	594.2	569.9
2015	573.5	571.1	574.9	577.0	583.2	589.8	593.3	596.7	596.0	595.5	606.7	613.1	589.2
Wholesale Trade													
2005	119.2	119.8	120.6	120.2	121.2	122.7	122.8	123.3	123.5	124.0	124.5	124.4	122.2
2006	123.7	124.2	125.0	124.8	126.0	127.9	128.1	127.8	127.9	128.3	128.1	127.1	126.6
2007	125.9	126.6	127.3	128.0	128.9	130.3	130.7	130.6	130.2	131.2	131.4	130.9	129.3
2008	129.0	129.6	130.0	130.1	130.7	130.7	131.4	130.8	130.7	131.3	129.4	127.7	130.1
2009	125.6	124.7	123.8	122.7	122.7	122.8	122.9	121.9	121.6	122.5	121.2	120.1	122.7
2010	118.0	118.4	118.9	120.3	120.6	120.8	121.0	120.6	120.4	121.4	121.3	120.1	120.2
2011	119.0	119.4	120.1	120.7	121.9	122.3	123.1	122.8	122.6	123.3	123.1	122.2	121.7
2012	121.0	121.4	122.1	122.8	123.9	124.9	125.1	125.6	125.0	125.8	125.5	124.9	124.0
2013	123.4	124.6	125.0	125.6	126.3	127.2	128.1	128.2	128.2	129.0	128.9	128.0	126.9
2014	127.1	127.5	127.7	128.0	128.9	129.9	131.8	131.8	131.9	131.8	131.7	131.3	130.0
2015	129.7	130.3	130.8	131.5	132.3	133.5	133.8	134.3	134.1	134.3	134.5	134.7	132.8
Retail Trade													
2005	308.7	305.5	307.1	309.1	312.4	314.6	316.5	319.2	318.3	319.1	328.6	334.2	316.1
2006	315.4	311.5	313.3	314.2	317.9	320.4	320.6	323.2	322.0	322.7	333.6	337.8	321.1
2007	321.2	318.9	320.3	321.1	324.4	326.8	328.8	329.7	328.3	329.6	341.9	344.4	328.0
2008	328.7	323.5	324.8	324.3	325.7	327.2	328.8	329.7	326.6	326.3	330.6	332.2	327.4
2009	312.3	307.1	305.0	303.4	306.6	307.7	309.0	309.6	308.7	308.5	315.1	317.6	309.2
2010	303.0	299.4	300.7	302.8	305.4	308.0	308.7	309.2	308.0	311.0	319.0	322.7	308.2
2011	306.3	303.3	303.8	306.0	308.9	312.1	314.1	315.6	314.0	316.3	325.2	327.4	312.8
2012	311.3	307.6	309.2	310.5	315.1	319.1	321.8	322.6	321.7	324.2	334.0	335.3	319.4
2013	320.2	317.0	317.9	320.5	326.2	329.4	332.2	334.4	332.8	336.1	346.0	349.3	330.2
2014	333.1	329.6	330.7	332.4	336.5	340.8	344.1	347.0	345.8	347.5	357.8	360.8	342.2
2015	344.4	342.0	344.9	347.4	351.6	355.6	357.6	360.4	359.4	360.2	370.7	373.9	355.7

1. Employment by Industry: Washington, 2005–2015—*Continued*

(Numbers in thousands, not seasonally adjusted)

Industry and year	January	February	March	April	May	June	July	August	September	October	November	December	Annual average
Transportation and Utilities													
2005	89.3	89.9	90.2	91.2	92.2	93.1	92.4	92.8	93.9	92.9	93.2	94.8	92.2
2006	91.3	91.5	92.1	92.4	93.5	95.2	94.3	95.0	96.1	95.2	94.5	96.6	94.0
2007	93.4	93.6	94.3	94.9	95.7	97.1	96.3	97.2	97.7	97.5	97.2	98.2	96.1
2008	94.7	95.1	94.9	95.2	96.2	96.7	96.9	97.0	97.0	96.1	95.1	95.8	95.9
2009	93.3	91.2	90.1	89.5	90.2	90.3	90.9	90.3	91.1	89.8	89.3	90.2	90.5
2010	86.7	86.2	86.7	87.3	88.0	88.8	89.8	89.3	90.2	90.3	89.6	91.0	88.7
2011	87.4	87.3	88.4	89.2	89.6	90.5	93.2	92.9	93.8	91.5	91.6	93.0	90.7
2012	89.8	90.0	90.5	90.7	92.3	93.7	93.9	94.2	94.6	93.8	93.8	94.9	92.7
2013	92.0	92.1	91.6	91.7	93.1	93.5	94.3	95.1	95.7	95.7	96.3	97.4	94.0
2014	95.4	94.8	94.6	95.5	96.8	97.8	98.2	99.3	99.9	99.5	99.7	102.1	97.8
2015	99.4	98.8	99.2	98.1	99.3	100.7	101.9	102.0	102.5	101.0	101.5	104.5	100.7
Information													
2005	92.7	93.5	93.4	94.1	94.5	94.9	95.7	96.4	95.4	94.6	95.5	96.1	94.7
2006	94.8	95.2	95.9	96.2	96.9	99.5	100.0	100.7	100.6	99.7	100.6	101.1	98.4
2007	100.4	101.3	101.0	101.5	102.4	103.5	103.7	104.0	103.3	102.0	103.1	103.3	102.5
2008	102.7	103.8	104.0	104.2	104.9	106.0	107.2	107.9	106.8	105.9	107.0	107.0	105.6
2009	104.9	105.4	105.0	103.7	104.2	104.5	104.8	104.2	102.9	102.2	102.5	102.4	103.9
2010	102.2	102.4	102.3	101.7	102.5	103.6	103.8	104.2	103.7	102.8	103.3	103.8	103.0
2011	102.8	103.4	103.1	103.3	103.6	104.7	105.7	106.0	104.9	104.0	104.5	104.3	104.2
2012	104.0	104.4	104.0	103.8	104.6	105.9	106.0	106.0	104.5	103.9	104.5	105.0	104.7
2013	104.1	104.8	104.5	104.8	105.7	106.5	107.9	108.4	107.2	106.5	107.3	107.4	106.3
2014	107.0	107.2	107.3	107.8	108.8	110.7	112.4	113.2	112.2	110.3	110.7	110.5	109.8
2015	109.9	110.8	111.0	111.6	112.7	114.6	116.5	117.6	117.0	116.8	116.9	117.6	114.4
Financial Activities													
2005	153.7	154.4	154.6	155.7	156.8	157.8	159.6	160.7	160.2	159.6	159.6	160.5	157.8
2006	158.4	158.5	158.9	159.0	159.6	160.4	160.5	160.3	159.3	158.2	157.7	158.0	159.1
2007	156.4	156.9	157.5	158.0	158.3	159.3	159.2	159.1	157.2	156.5	156.7	156.5	157.6
2008	155.0	155.2	155.1	154.8	155.7	155.4	154.6	154.7	153.1	151.5	150.5	149.6	153.8
2009	146.8	146.4	144.8	144.5	144.5	145.1	144.1	143.5	142.4	140.8	139.8	139.6	143.5
2010	137.4	137.0	137.2	137.7	137.6	138.2	139.1	139.2	138.7	138.4	138.0	138.5	138.1
2011	136.8	136.9	137.0	137.7	137.6	138.7	139.2	139.4	139.2	138.1	138.4	138.5	138.1
2012	137.0	137.7	138.3	139.0	140.1	140.9	142.2	142.1	141.1	140.9	141.0	141.3	140.1
2013	140.8	141.2	141.9	142.4	143.5	144.4	145.7	145.8	144.9	144.6	144.5	145.0	143.7
2014	143.5	143.7	144.1	144.5	144.2	145.2	146.5	147.0	145.9	145.5	145.4	145.9	145.1
2015	145.0	145.3	145.4	146.1	147.1	148.0	149.4	149.5	148.9	148.9	148.5	149.4	147.6
Professional and Business Services													
2005	300.0	304.7	308.3	312.4	314.9	317.0	320.8	323.0	324.8	322.7	322.5	321.8	316.1
2006	313.6	317.4	320.6	325.6	328.5	333.3	335.1	338.8	339.2	338.3	338.6	338.0	330.6
2007	329.4	335.6	339.9	340.8	343.4	347.2	348.5	351.2	350.8	349.3	349.2	349.7	344.6
2008	340.5	344.2	346.9	351.0	352.4	353.6	354.9	355.5	353.6	349.5	342.8	337.7	348.6
2009	330.0	327.5	325.6	323.4	322.8	324.9	324.4	324.1	323.7	323.2	321.5	321.6	324.4
2010	313.2	315.3	319.1	323.3	324.0	326.9	331.6	331.0	332.0	333.8	333.0	333.6	326.4
2011	326.3	329.4	331.9	338.9	338.4	340.8	344.9	345.0	346.3	344.9	344.3	342.7	339.5
2012	335.4	338.6	341.3	346.7	349.0	353.0	352.4	356.6	356.4	358.1	357.4	355.4	350.0
2013	348.9	351.9	354.1	358.1	359.5	362.0	363.5	367.7	368.0	367.7	366.2	365.3	361.1
2014	358.8	360.1	363.0	365.1	366.7	370.6	377.1	380.0	380.6	380.8	381.1	381.7	372.1
2015	373.2	375.1	379.3	383.4	385.5	389.6	392.8	395.5	397.0	397.4	399.6	396.7	388.8
Education and Health Services													
2005	355.2	358.2	360.6	363.4	364.3	360.4	354.9	355.6	363.1	366.8	368.4	367.7	361.6
2006	363.6	367.8	370.2	371.1	372.4	368.4	361.3	362.7	370.0	374.3	375.5	375.1	369.4
2007	371.5	377.4	379.7	380.4	382.9	379.5	373.3	374.7	382.1	388.8	391.0	390.4	381.0
2008	385.8	391.3	392.4	394.3	396.5	393.3	389.2	391.1	397.9	404.6	405.9	405.0	395.6
2009	403.2	408.1	410.6	411.3	413.6	410.4	405.2	405.7	412.9	419.9	421.9	422.4	412.1
2010	418.2	423.1	425.1	426.6	427.5	424.1	417.9	417.0	423.8	431.0	432.2	430.8	424.8
2011	427.7	431.4	432.9	433.1	433.2	430.3	425.3	424.5	430.3	435.2	436.7	436.2	431.4
2012	429.3	434.2	436.5	436.1	437.3	433.5	426.7	426.6	431.8	437.0	438.6	438.0	433.8
2013	432.7	438.8	440.1	440.8	441.7	436.6	432.8	432.7	439.8	447.1	449.1	449.4	440.1
2014	446.7	452.6	452.7	452.9	454.3	449.8	446.8	446.3	452.3	456.3	458.1	459.4	452.4
2015	453.1	457.6	458.2	460.3	460.1	457.1	448.0	447.5	454.4	462.6	463.0	464.2	457.2

1. Employment by Industry: Washington, 2005–2015—*Continued*

(Numbers in thousands, not seasonally adjusted)

Industry and year	January	February	March	April	May	June	July	August	September	October	November	December	Annual average
Leisure and Hospitality													
2005	248.1	247.2	252.4	259.2	265.1	271.2	274.7	276.7	274.9	264.4	263.1	265.4	263.5
2006	257.6	258.9	262.3	267.4	273.9	279.7	281.5	285.4	282.7	271.7	268.4	270.3	271.7
2007	262.9	266.7	270.5	275.9	282.5	289.8	291.5	294.8	292.0	282.1	278.3	280.1	280.6
2008	271.8	274.0	278.5	282.7	287.2	293.7	295.6	297.5	295.2	281.4	274.0	272.3	283.7
2009	261.7	262.5	264.5	266.5	272.7	278.4	281.1	281.6	278.8	266.4	260.9	259.7	269.6
2010	251.2	252.7	257.4	264.6	269.2	275.1	277.5	278.9	277.6	267.4	262.6	263.7	266.5
2011	256.1	257.0	259.5	268.7	274.1	280.3	281.6	283.9	282.7	270.7	267.1	268.3	270.8
2012	260.3	262.8	267.3	273.2	280.0	286.2	288.3	290.8	288.9	278.5	274.0	276.0	277.2
2013	268.9	270.3	275.3	282.1	290.5	297.8	299.9	302.8	299.6	288.0	285.2	287.1	287.3
2014	282.2	282.2	287.3	292.7	299.7	306.4	308.0	311.7	308.1	296.6	293.5	295.0	297.0
2015	290.0	291.9	296.4	302.7	311.4	320.1	323.2	325.9	321.0	312.0	308.7	308.2	309.3
Other Services													
2005	100.2	101.1	102.2	102.1	102.7	104.1	104.3	104.3	103.5	102.6	102.6	103.0	102.7
2006	101.4	102.3	103.2	103.5	104.4	105.6	105.5	105.5	105.1	103.7	103.6	103.9	104.0
2007	102.1	103.8	104.7	104.6	105.5	106.8	106.6	107.0	106.0	105.5	105.7	105.7	105.3
2008	105.0	106.1	107.3	107.4	108.3	109.2	110.1	110.0	109.0	107.6	106.9	106.0	107.7
2009	105.6	106.1	106.8	106.7	107.0	107.5	107.8	107.4	106.0	105.3	104.6	104.4	106.3
2010	102.7	103.1	103.8	104.4	105.1	106.6	107.6	107.7	106.3	106.2	106.4	106.2	105.5
2011	105.2	106.0	106.3	107.9	108.8	110.3	110.7	110.7	109.5	109.1	108.5	108.9	108.5
2012	107.4	108.4	109.6	110.6	111.4	112.4	113.2	112.9	111.8	111.4	110.8	110.5	110.9
2013	108.1	108.8	109.7	110.4	111.5	112.3	113.5	113.5	112.2	112.0	112.1	111.6	111.3
2014	111.0	111.3	112.6	112.7	113.7	115.1	116.3	116.4	114.8	114.0	113.9	114.3	113.8
2015	112.4	112.8	114.1	115.0	116.0	117.2	117.9	117.8	116.3	117.8	116.0	115.6	115.7
Government													
2005	526.3	530.8	533.9	534.5	535.9	537.6	508.6	494.6	514.1	532.0	539.8	532.6	526.7
2006	529.6	536.5	538.2	536.8	539.1	541.9	509.3	496.8	517.9	535.1	542.6	536.3	530.0
2007	530.7	537.6	536.8	539.7	542.0	541.5	517.5	504.5	521.8	541.2	549.4	542.5	533.8
2008	541.3	549.7	549.2	549.9	552.8	553.2	531.0	519.5	533.8	555.9	564.2	555.3	546.3
2009	551.7	556.4	558.6	564.9	564.9	555.5	532.5	513.9	530.3	556.0	559.6	549.9	549.5
2010	551.4	555.1	556.7	561.2	572.4	560.5	535.7	515.4	530.3	554.1	558.3	548.5	550.0
2011	549.6	553.1	553.4	555.6	557.1	549.4	529.0	510.7	523.4	548.0	551.0	541.4	543.5
2012	542.5	545.7	548.6	550.9	552.4	546.5	526.0	508.9	525.2	549.6	553.7	543.8	541.2
2013	545.9	550.0	550.8	553.2	554.5	547.9	525.3	511.5	528.8	550.3	554.5	546.4	543.3
2014	549.4	552.7	555.2	558.3	560.0	554.1	534.9	521.6	540.8	561.1	563.0	556.4	550.6
2015	559.7	563.4	566.7	570.3	572.1	566.4	546.5	533.0	552.1	570.3	575.5	568.2	562.0

2. Average Weekly Hours by Selected Industry: Washington, 2011–2015

(Not seasonally adjusted)

Industry and year	January	February	March	April	May	June	July	August	September	October	November	December	Annual average
Total Private													
2011	34.9	34.1	34.0	34.3	35.1	34.4	34.5	34.5	34.5	35.4	34.2	34.2	34.5
2012	34.4	34.1	34.0	35.0	34.1	34.2	35.2	34.4	35.4	34.2	34.1	35.1	34.5
2013	33.6	34.2	34.1	34.1	34.0	35.1	34.0	34.4	35.1	34.0	34.0	34.7	34.3
2014	33.4	34.7	34.8	33.9	33.9	34.8	34.0	34.3	34.1	33.9	34.9	33.9	34.2
2015	33.6	34.7	34.7	33.9	34.0	34.2	34.3	35.3	34.3	34.3	35.1	33.9	34.4
Goods-Producing													
2011	39.1	39.0	39.2	39.6	40.1	39.7	39.8	40.0	40.0	40.3	40.2	40.0	39.8
2012	39.1	40.0	40.1	40.1	39.9	39.9	39.7	39.9	40.4	40.4	40.1	40.4	40.0
2013	39.6	39.9	40.1	40.0	39.8	40.2	39.5	40.2	40.0	39.9	39.9	39.8	39.9
2014	39.2	39.5	39.7	39.4	39.5	39.9	39.3	39.8	40.0	40.1	40.3	39.9	39.7
2015	39.5	39.8	39.8	39.6	39.8	40.1	39.9	40.3	39.2	40.1	39.9	39.5	39.8
Construction													
2011	32.8	33.4	33.2	34.2	34.8	34.6	35.3	36.5	36.1	35.5	35.3	35.2	34.8
2012	34.2	34.8	35.3	36.0	35.6	35.7	36.4	36.3	36.9	36.4	35.5	36.1	35.8
2013	34.8	35.7	36.3	36.4	36.4	37.4	36.4	38.0	37.7	37.2	36.7	36.2	36.6
2014	36.3	36.1	36.6	36.9	37.0	37.9	37.8	38.3	38.5	38.1	38.2	37.8	37.5
2015	37.8	38.1	37.9	37.9	38.1	38.5	38.3	38.8	36.3	37.9	37.5	36.7	37.8
Manufacturing													
2011	41.5	41.1	41.5	41.6	42.1	41.7	41.6	41.4	41.6	42.1	42.0	41.7	41.7
2012	40.7	41.7	41.6	41.3	41.3	41.2	40.8	41.1	41.6	41.8	41.6	41.8	41.4
2013	41.2	41.3	41.5	41.3	41.0	41.2	40.6	41.0	40.9	41.1	41.3	41.4	41.1
2014	40.4	40.8	40.9	40.4	40.5	40.7	40.0	40.5	40.8	41.1	41.4	41.0	40.7
2015	40.4	40.7	40.8	40.6	40.7	41.0	40.8	41.1	40.7	41.2	41.1	40.9	40.8
Trade, Transportation, and Utilities													
2011	35.9	35.4	35.4	35.8	36.5	36.2	36.3	35.9	36.0	36.5	35.1	35.1	35.8
2012	34.8	34.7	34.5	35.2	34.8	34.9	35.8	35.3	36.2	34.8	34.7	35.7	35.1
2013	34.0	34.7	34.6	34.3	34.6	35.7	34.9	35.1	35.6	34.4	34.3	34.9	34.8
2014	33.5	35.0	35.1	34.5	34.7	35.5	34.9	35.1	35.0	34.4	35.6	34.8	34.8
2015	34.2	35.3	35.3	34.7	35.2	35.2	35.2	36.4	35.9	35.1	36.0	35.0	35.3
Information													
2011	41.3	38.2	38.0	38.3	40.8	38.3	37.9	37.8	37.9	40.8	38.0	37.9	38.8
2012	41.0	38.2	38.0	41.2	38.2	38.3	41.3	38.4	41.5	38.2	38.4	40.7	39.4
2013	37.9	38.3	38.2	38.4	38.3	40.9	37.9	37.6	40.7	39.2	39.2	42.1	39.1
2014	38.8	42.0	41.6	38.6	38.4	41.6	38.4	38.3	39.4	38.4	41.6	38.4	39.6
2015	38.1	41.3	41.3	38.3	38.2	38.2	38.2	41.0	37.9	37.9	41.2	37.7	39.1
Financial Activities													
2011	38.4	36.2	34.9	35.6	36.6	35.2	35.3	35.5	35.6	37.5	34.7	34.8	35.9
2012	37.5	35.2	34.8	36.7	34.5	34.9	36.8	34.9	36.7	34.5	34.2	36.3	35.6
2013	34.8	35.6	35.1	35.0	34.6	36.2	34.5	34.8	35.8	34.2	34.5	35.7	35.1
2014	34.6	36.3	36.2	35.0	35.1	35.9	34.4	34.8	34.8	34.7	36.0	34.9	35.2
2015	35.0	36.6	36.6	35.3	35.1	35.2	35.0	36.7	35.1	35.4	37.1	35.7	35.7
Professional and Business Services													
2011	35.9	35.3	35.2	35.6	36.5	35.8	35.7	35.7	35.5	37.0	35.5	35.6	35.8
2012	36.1	35.5	35.4	37.1	35.8	35.7	36.7	35.7	36.9	35.3	35.2	36.5	36.0
2013	35.1	35.8	35.6	36.0	35.7	37.0	35.3	36.0	36.9	35.6	35.4	36.0	35.9
2014	34.7	36.4	36.6	35.8	35.7	36.7	35.4	35.7	35.7	35.7	36.6	35.3	35.9
2015	35.0	36.4	36.4	35.5	35.3	35.5	35.2	36.5	35.6	35.7	36.5	35.2	35.7
Education and Health Services													
2011	33.3	32.1	32.0	31.9	32.5	31.8	31.7	31.8	32.2	32.8	32.1	32.2	32.2
2012	32.5	32.0	31.9	32.8	31.8	32.0	32.9	31.8	33.2	31.9	32.1	32.9	32.3
2013	31.6	31.8	31.6	31.7	31.6	32.8	31.7	31.8	33.0	31.9	32.1	32.6	32.0
2014	31.7	32.8	32.8	31.8	32.0	32.7	31.7	31.9	32.0	32.0	33.2	32.4	32.3
2015	32.5	33.4	33.1	32.4	32.3	32.5	32.9	33.7	33.1	32.9	33.8	32.5	32.9
Leisure and Hospitality													
2011	24.7	24.9	24.6	25.1	25.8	25.2	25.7	25.9	25.5	26.2	24.8	24.8	25.3
2012	24.8	25.0	25.1	26.2	25.5	25.5	26.8	26.3	26.4	25.3	24.8	26.3	25.7
2013	24.1	25.1	25.0	25.0	25.1	26.3	25.1	26.0	26.2	24.7	24.4	25.4	25.2
2014	24.1	25.3	25.2	24.4	24.2	25.4	25.1	25.7	24.7	23.8	24.7	23.7	24.7
2015	22.8	24.2	24.3	24.0	24.0	24.5	25.0	26.3	24.8	24.6	25.1	24.1	24.5
Other Services													
2011	31.2	30.5	29.7	30.7	31.4	30.3	31.0	30.7	30.5	30.8	29.6	29.7	30.5
2012	30.7	30.3	30.0	31.9	30.2	30.3	32.0	30.9	31.8	30.0	30.4	31.2	30.8
2013	30.0	30.9	30.7	30.5	31.1	32.2	30.8	31.4	32.5	30.7	31.2	32.2	31.2
2014	30.5	31.3	31.7	30.5	30.4	31.3	30.6	30.6	28.2	28.1	29.3	27.6	30.0
2015	28.1	29.8	29.4	28.5	28.6	28.8	29.0	29.7	27.7	27.5	28.8	27.7	28.6

3. Average Hourly Earnings by Selected Industry: Washington, 2011–2015

(Dollars, not seasonally adjusted)

Industry and year	January	February	March	April	May	June	July	August	September	October	November	December	Annual average
Total Private													
2011	27.60	27.48	27.37	27.38	27.32	27.09	27.01	26.69	26.99	27.31	27.25	27.50	27.25
2012	27.85	27.38	27.33	27.48	27.06	27.11	27.18	26.87	27.30	27.26	27.45	27.55	27.32
2013	27.66	27.77	27.75	27.71	27.50	27.65	27.43	27.33	27.79	27.79	27.92	27.99	27.69
2014	28.14	28.24	28.30	28.21	28.13	28.34	28.20	28.18	28.71	28.66	29.11	29.06	28.44
2015	29.49	29.53	29.52	29.38	29.38	29.16	29.12	29.44	29.79	30.00	30.38	30.27	29.63
Goods-Producing													
2011	30.90	30.59	31.23	31.02	30.87	30.92	30.91	30.55	30.65	30.71	30.77	31.16	30.85
2012	31.29	31.10	31.47	31.33	31.27	31.20	31.08	30.79	30.97	31.02	31.25	31.51	31.19
2013	31.58	31.65	31.65	31.66	31.52	31.47	31.38	31.39	31.49	31.72	31.96	32.53	31.67
2014	32.49	32.30	32.70	32.68	32.66	32.69	32.52	32.42	32.53	32.50	32.44	32.66	32.55
2015	32.48	32.61	32.90	32.82	32.80	32.73	32.46	32.58	32.80	32.71	32.80	33.37	32.75
Construction													
2011	31.25	30.90	30.67	30.51	30.06	30.17	29.86	29.78	29.73	29.48	29.36	29.81	30.10
2012	29.92	29.64	29.67	29.52	29.68	29.37	29.52	29.29	29.32	29.39	29.33	29.67	29.52
2013	29.72	30.10	30.17	30.03	30.20	30.11	29.44	29.78	29.50	29.50	30.03	30.09	29.88
2014	30.29	30.42	30.32	30.34	30.60	31.04	30.82	31.11	31.52	31.49	31.60	31.56	30.96
2015	31.32	31.52	31.27	31.41	31.50	31.91	31.60	31.75	31.79	31.55	31.62	32.16	31.62
Manufacturing													
2011	31.00	30.72	31.41	31.35	31.27	31.29	31.27	30.91	31.15	31.25	31.34	31.68	31.22
2012	31.77	31.61	32.08	31.99	31.88	31.89	31.72	31.43	31.64	31.65	31.94	32.16	31.81
2013	32.19	32.19	32.17	32.26	32.04	32.03	32.16	32.08	32.32	32.59	32.74	33.49	32.36
2014	33.40	33.10	33.70	33.67	33.56	33.46	33.32	33.05	33.03	32.97	32.84	33.19	33.27
2015	33.07	33.18	33.71	33.54	33.48	33.17	32.94	33.06	33.30	33.32	33.40	33.83	33.33
Trade, Transportation, and Utilities													
2011	22.26	22.21	22.06	22.28	22.26	22.06	21.98	21.62	21.82	21.85	21.84	22.02	22.02
2012	22.50	21.81	21.62	21.80	21.42	21.63	21.76	21.58	22.09	21.98	22.09	22.03	21.86
2013	22.37	22.55	22.72	22.75	22.56	22.77	22.48	22.37	22.75	22.36	22.32	21.58	22.46
2014	22.72	23.05	23.01	23.10	23.06	23.33	22.99	23.37	23.57	23.52	24.28	23.66	23.32
2015	24.56	24.55	24.50	24.75	24.71	24.69	24.83	25.43	26.31	26.59	26.81	26.36	25.36
Information													
2011	49.20	49.03	48.27	48.38	49.15	47.46	46.81	45.67	48.17	49.21	48.85	49.21	48.29
2012	50.01	49.80	50.20	51.02	50.56	50.68	51.24	50.42	52.03	52.14	52.05	52.42	51.06
2013	52.40	52.51	52.89	52.63	53.13	53.46	52.51	52.62	56.24	54.26	54.05	54.90	53.50
2014	54.65	55.20	55.58	55.47	55.23	55.28	54.61	54.69	59.33	54.28	54.85	54.77	55.34
2015	56.22	55.92	56.27	56.02	56.49	56.09	56.06	57.83	59.80	58.95	60.49	58.79	57.44
Financial Activities													
2011	27.75	28.23	27.77	28.09	28.26	27.70	27.51	27.90	27.64	28.42	28.46	28.58	28.03
2012	28.70	28.56	28.44	29.05	28.56	28.03	28.29	28.36	28.74	28.63	28.91	28.94	28.60
2013	28.70	29.28	29.34	28.77	28.54	28.45	28.88	28.27	28.34	28.54	28.75	28.54	28.70
2014	28.76	28.62	28.90	28.44	28.43	28.64	28.61	28.38	28.60	28.54	29.15	28.54	28.64
2015	29.21	29.15	29.33	29.40	29.82	28.67	29.83	29.37	28.81	29.39	28.97	28.65	29.21
Professional and Business Services													
2011	33.16	33.31	32.84	32.87	32.75	32.65	32.81	32.34	32.94	33.49	33.27	33.45	32.99
2012	33.67	33.03	32.77	32.93	32.07	32.23	32.65	31.82	32.33	32.15	32.42	32.59	32.55
2013	32.42	32.79	32.57	32.48	32.17	32.67	31.87	31.66	32.29	32.48	32.72	32.86	32.41
2014	32.88	32.95	32.70	32.49	32.35	32.56	32.60	32.29	32.51	32.78	33.40	33.23	32.73
2015	33.71	33.92	33.65	33.27	33.38	33.06	32.95	32.83	32.74	33.13	33.69	33.78	33.34
Education and Health Services													
2011	27.02	27.01	26.76	26.92	26.50	26.59	26.63	26.32	26.43	26.52	26.38	26.75	26.65
2012	26.64	26.16	25.95	26.02	25.74	25.86	25.74	25.68	25.56	25.51	25.70	25.72	25.86
2013	25.65	25.41	25.26	25.27	25.06	25.16	25.30	25.50	25.31	25.39	25.74	25.81	25.41
2014	25.25	25.40	25.46	25.58	25.55	25.93	26.56	26.42	26.34	27.12	27.64	28.43	26.31
2015	28.46	28.32	28.13	28.11	28.11	27.81	27.60	27.99	28.26	28.39	28.71	28.72	28.22
Leisure and Hospitality													
2011	13.37	13.30	13.28	13.19	13.31	13.35	13.43	13.38	13.44	13.50	13.71	14.17	13.45
2012	14.23	14.32	14.23	14.15	14.15	14.26	14.15	14.18	14.33	14.44	14.63	14.92	14.33
2013	14.78	14.90	14.85	14.85	14.92	14.92	14.77	14.66	14.94	15.19	15.27	15.54	14.96
2014	15.41	15.58	15.57	15.72	15.44	15.37	15.20	15.27	15.54	15.77	15.73	16.09	15.55
2015	15.95	16.04	16.15	15.98	15.97	15.91	15.80	15.85	16.01	16.12	16.16	16.48	16.03
Other Services													
2011	24.22	23.76	23.27	22.92	22.95	22.36	21.77	21.45	21.36	21.25	21.14	21.23	22.30
2012	21.30	21.35	21.48	21.44	21.17	21.06	20.69	20.83	21.61	21.46	21.52	21.79	21.31
2013	21.70	22.06	21.92	22.08	21.81	21.84	22.59	22.33	22.60	22.56	22.54	23.29	22.28
2014	22.85	21.80	21.71	21.40	21.80	21.50	20.96	21.21	22.50	22.60	23.22	23.67	22.07
2015	23.78	23.42	23.09	23.02	22.81	22.94	23.01	23.45	23.97	24.13	25.35	25.95	23.73

4. Average Weekly Earnings by Selected Industry: Washington, 2011–2015

(Dollars, not seasonally adjusted)

Industry and year	January	February	March	April	May	June	July	August	September	October	November	December	Annual average
Total Private													
2011	963.24	937.07	930.58	939.13	958.93	931.90	931.85	920.81	931.16	966.77	931.95	940.50	940.13
2012	958.04	933.66	929.22	961.80	922.75	927.16	956.74	924.33	966.42	932.29	936.05	967.01	942.54
2013	929.38	949.73	946.28	944.91	935.00	970.52	932.62	940.15	975.43	944.86	949.28	971.25	949.77
2014	939.88	979.93	984.84	956.32	953.61	986.23	958.80	966.57	979.01	971.57	1,015.94	985.13	972.65
2015	990.86	1,024.69	1,024.34	995.98	998.92	997.27	998.82	1,039.23	1,021.80	1,029.00	1,066.34	1,026.15	1,019.27
Goods-Producing													
2011	1,208.19	1,193.01	1,224.22	1,228.39	1,237.89	1,227.52	1,230.22	1,222.00	1,226.00	1,237.61	1,236.95	1,246.40	1,227.83
2012	1,223.44	1,244.00	1,261.95	1,256.33	1,247.67	1,244.88	1,233.88	1,228.52	1,251.19	1,253.21	1,253.13	1,273.00	1,247.60
2013	1,250.57	1,262.84	1,269.17	1,266.40	1,254.50	1,265.09	1,239.51	1,261.88	1,259.60	1,265.63	1,275.20	1,294.69	1,263.63
2014	1,273.61	1,275.85	1,298.19	1,287.59	1,290.07	1,304.33	1,278.04	1,290.32	1,301.20	1,303.25	1,307.33	1,303.13	1,292.24
2015	1,282.96	1,297.88	1,309.42	1,299.67	1,305.44	1,312.47	1,295.15	1,312.97	1,285.76	1,311.67	1,308.72	1,318.12	1,303.45
Construction													
2011	1,025.00	1,032.06	1,018.24	1,043.44	1,046.09	1,043.88	1,054.06	1,086.97	1,073.25	1,046.54	1,036.41	1,049.31	1,047.48
2012	1,023.26	1,031.47	1,047.35	1,062.72	1,056.61	1,048.51	1,074.53	1,063.23	1,081.91	1,069.80	1,041.22	1,071.09	1,056.82
2013	1,034.26	1,074.57	1,095.17	1,093.09	1,099.28	1,126.11	1,071.62	1,131.64	1,112.15	1,097.40	1,102.10	1,089.26	1,093.61
2014	1,099.53	1,098.16	1,109.71	1,119.55	1,132.20	1,176.42	1,165.00	1,191.51	1,213.52	1,199.77	1,207.12	1,192.97	1,161.00
2015	1,183.90	1,200.91	1,185.13	1,190.44	1,200.15	1,228.54	1,210.28	1,231.90	1,153.98	1,195.75	1,185.75	1,180.27	1,195.24
Manufacturing													
2011	1,286.50	1,262.59	1,303.52	1,304.16	1,316.47	1,304.79	1,300.83	1,279.67	1,295.84	1,315.63	1,316.28	1,321.06	1,301.87
2012	1,293.04	1,318.14	1,334.53	1,321.19	1,316.64	1,313.87	1,294.18	1,291.77	1,316.22	1,322.97	1,328.70	1,344.29	1,316.93
2013	1,326.23	1,329.45	1,335.06	1,332.34	1,313.64	1,319.64	1,305.70	1,315.28	1,321.89	1,339.45	1,352.16	1,386.49	1,330.00
2014	1,349.36	1,350.48	1,378.33	1,360.27	1,359.18	1,361.82	1,332.80	1,338.53	1,347.62	1,355.07	1,359.58	1,360.79	1,354.09
2015	1,336.03	1,350.43	1,375.37	1,361.72	1,362.64	1,359.97	1,343.95	1,358.77	1,355.31	1,372.78	1,372.74	1,383.65	1,359.86
Trade, Transportation, and Utilities													
2011	799.13	786.23	780.92	797.62	812.49	798.57	797.87	776.16	785.52	797.53	766.58	772.90	788.32
2012	783.00	756.81	745.89	767.36	745.42	754.89	779.01	761.77	799.66	764.90	766.52	786.47	767.29
2013	760.58	782.49	786.11	780.33	780.58	812.89	784.55	785.19	809.90	769.18	765.58	753.14	781.61
2014	761.12	806.75	807.65	796.95	800.18	828.22	802.35	820.29	824.95	809.09	864.37	823.37	811.54
2015	839.95	866.62	864.85	858.83	869.79	869.09	874.02	925.65	944.53	933.31	965.16	922.60	895.21
Information													
2011	2,031.96	1,872.95	1,834.26	1,852.95	2,005.32	1,817.72	1,774.10	1,726.33	1,825.64	2,007.77	1,856.30	1,865.06	1,873.65
2012	2,050.41	1,902.36	1,907.60	2,102.02	1,931.39	1,941.04	2,116.21	1,936.13	2,159.25	1,991.75	1,998.72	2,133.49	2,011.76
2013	1,985.96	2,011.13	2,020.40	2,020.99	2,034.88	2,186.51	1,990.13	1,978.51	2,288.97	2,126.99	2,118.76	2,311.29	2,091.85
2014	2,120.42	2,318.40	2,312.13	2,141.14	2,120.83	2,299.65	2,097.02	2,094.63	2,337.60	2,084.35	2,281.76	2,103.17	2,191.46
2015	2,141.98	2,309.50	2,323.95	2,145.57	2,157.92	2,142.64	2,141.49	2,371.03	2,266.42	2,234.21	2,492.19	2,216.38	2,245.90
Financial Activities													
2011	1,065.60	1,021.93	969.17	1,000.00	1,034.32	975.04	971.10	990.45	983.98	1,065.75	987.56	994.58	1,006.28
2012	1,076.25	1,005.31	989.71	1,066.14	985.32	978.25	1,041.07	989.76	1,054.76	987.74	988.72	1,050.52	1,018.16
2013	998.76	1,042.37	1,029.83	1,006.95	987.48	1,029.89	996.36	983.80	1,014.57	976.07	991.88	1,018.88	1,007.37
2014	995.10	1,038.91	1,046.18	995.40	997.89	1,028.18	984.18	987.62	995.28	990.34	1,049.40	996.05	1,008.13
2015	1,022.35	1,066.89	1,073.48	1,037.82	1,046.68	1,009.18	1,044.05	1,077.88	1,011.23	1,040.41	1,074.79	1,022.81	1,042.80
Professional and Business Services													
2011	1,190.44	1,175.84	1,155.97	1,170.17	1,195.38	1,168.87	1,171.32	1,154.54	1,169.37	1,239.13	1,181.09	1,190.82	1,181.04
2012	1,215.49	1,172.57	1,160.06	1,221.70	1,148.11	1,150.61	1,198.26	1,135.97	1,192.98	1,134.90	1,141.18	1,189.54	1,171.80
2013	1,137.94	1,173.88	1,159.49	1,169.28	1,148.47	1,208.79	1,125.01	1,139.76	1,191.50	1,156.29	1,158.29	1,182.96	1,163.52
2014	1,140.94	1,199.38	1,196.82	1,163.14	1,154.90	1,194.95	1,154.04	1,152.75	1,160.61	1,170.25	1,222.44	1,173.02	1,175.01
2015	1,179.85	1,234.69	1,224.86	1,181.09	1,178.31	1,173.63	1,159.84	1,198.30	1,165.54	1,182.74	1,229.69	1,189.06	1,190.24
Education and Health Services													
2011	899.77	867.02	856.32	858.75	861.25	845.56	844.17	836.98	851.05	869.86	846.80	861.35	858.13
2012	865.80	837.12	827.81	853.46	818.53	827.52	846.85	816.62	848.59	813.77	824.97	846.19	835.28
2013	810.54	808.04	798.22	801.06	791.90	825.25	802.01	810.90	835.23	809.94	826.25	841.41	813.12
2014	800.43	833.12	835.09	813.44	817.60	847.91	841.95	842.80	842.88	867.84	917.65	921.13	849.81
2015	924.95	945.89	931.10	910.76	907.95	903.83	908.04	943.26	935.41	934.03	970.40	933.40	928.44
Leisure and Hospitality													
2011	330.24	331.17	326.69	331.07	343.40	336.42	345.15	346.54	342.72	353.70	340.01	351.42	340.29
2012	352.90	358.00	357.17	370.73	360.83	363.63	379.22	372.93	378.31	365.33	362.82	392.40	368.28
2013	356.20	373.99	371.25	371.25	374.49	392.40	370.73	381.16	391.43	375.19	372.59	394.72	376.99
2014	371.38	394.17	392.36	383.57	373.65	390.40	381.52	392.44	383.84	375.33	388.53	381.33	384.09
2015	363.66	388.17	392.45	383.52	383.28	389.80	395.00	416.86	397.05	396.55	405.62	397.17	392.74
Other Services													
2011	755.66	724.68	691.12	703.64	720.63	677.51	674.87	658.52	651.48	654.50	625.74	630.53	680.15
2012	653.91	646.91	644.40	683.94	639.33	638.12	662.08	643.65	687.20	643.80	654.21	679.85	656.35
2013	651.00	681.65	672.94	673.44	678.29	703.25	695.77	701.16	734.50	692.59	703.25	749.94	695.14
2014	696.93	682.34	688.21	652.70	662.72	672.95	641.38	649.03	634.50	635.06	680.35	653.29	662.10
2015	668.22	697.92	678.85	656.07	652.37	660.67	667.29	696.47	663.97	663.58	730.08	718.82	678.68

WEST VIRGINIA
At a Glance

Population:
  2005 estimate: 1,820,492
  2010 census: 1,852,994
  2015 estimate: 1,844,128

Percent change in population:
  2005–2015: 1.3%
  2010–2015: –0.5%

Percent change in total nonfarm employment:
  2005–2015: 1.7%

Industry with the largest growth in employment, 2005–2015 (thousands):
  Education and health services, 15.7

Industry with the largest decline or smallest growth in employment, 2005–2015 (thousands):
  Manufacturing, –14.6

Civilian labor force:
  2005: 790,982
  2010: 811,125
  2015: 785,049

Unemployment rate and rank among states (highest to lowest):
  2005: 5.1%, 20th
  2010: 8.7%, 24th
  2015: 6.7%, 2nd

Over-the-year change in unemployment rates:
  2012–2013: –0.8%
  2013–2014: –0.1%
  2014–2015: 0.1%

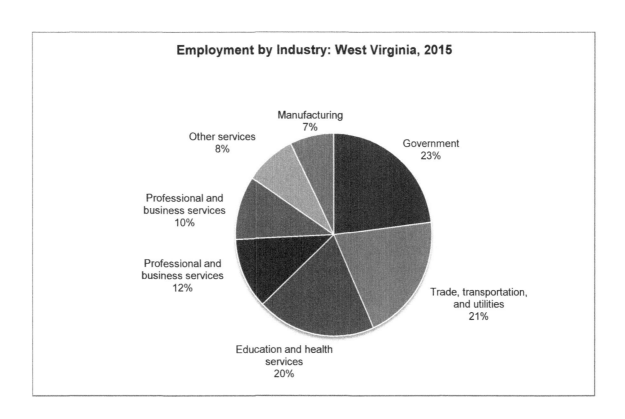

Employment by Industry: West Virginia, 2015

Manufacturing 7%
Other services 8%
Government 23%
Professional and business services 10%
Professional and business services 12%
Trade, transportation, and utilities 21%
Education and health services 20%

1. Employment by Industry: West Virginia, 2005–2015

(Numbers in thousands, not seasonally adjusted)

Industry and year	January	February	March	April	May	June	July	August	September	October	November	December	Annual average
Total Nonfarm													
2005	732.0	734.0	740.4	750.7	757.0	757.7	750.6	752.6	759.4	756.7	762.0	764.2	751.4
2006	743.4	747.1	756.3	760.2	775.9	767.8	755.8	759.7	767.6	768.1	772.5	772.2	762.2
2007	746.0	747.7	758.2	762.1	768.0	769.7	759.3	763.8	770.6	772.3	775.6	775.0	764.0
2008	752.5	757.1	761.4	766.9	783.7	769.3	765.5	767.4	775.4	777.1	776.7	774.5	769.0
2009	746.8	747.7	751.7	754.0	758.9	759.4	747.9	748.9	751.7	754.0	755.5	757.0	752.8
2010	731.7	732.7	745.0	752.6	769.9	760.4	755.0	755.4	762.1	763.8	765.9	762.5	754.8
2011	737.3	743.9	752.6	762.5	766.7	761.3	756.3	761.2	773.8	776.1	779.5	778.9	762.5
2012	756.4	762.2	770.3	775.8	790.1	771.5	763.6	766.5	778.6	779.9	780.5	780.0	773.0
2013	755.3	760.8	767.0	773.7	779.8	773.3	766.0	769.3	775.9	777.8	781.3	778.5	771.6
2014	750.9	753.3	761.8	771.5	786.7	762.4	758.3	763.7	776.0	781.6	782.5	780.5	769.1
2015	755.3	755.6	759.9	767.6	773.2	766.0	756.9	757.5	766.8	771.0	770.3	767.7	764.0
Total Private													
2005	589.5	590.4	595.2	605.1	611.2	614.4	614.1	616.1	616.8	613.2	615.7	617.6	608.3
2006	602.1	602.3	609.8	613.8	618.7	624.2	619.0	621.2	623.5	621.1	624.6	624.2	617.0
2007	603.6	601.9	610.8	614.9	619.9	625.3	621.5	624.8	626.0	625.3	627.7	627.3	619.1
2008	609.2	610.6	613.5	618.8	622.8	624.8	625.2	626.1	628.1	627.3	626.3	624.0	621.4
2009	601.5	598.8	600.7	603.6	606.4	605.4	602.2	602.6	603.2	601.7	602.8	604.1	602.8
2010	582.6	581.0	590.0	598.1	601.0	606.2	608.1	609.0	610.1	610.2	611.3	608.1	601.3
2011	590.5	592.9	599.1	607.7	611.7	614.2	615.6	618.8	619.3	620.2	623.4	622.9	611.4
2012	605.6	607.4	613.7	619.8	623.2	624.1	621.9	623.7	624.8	623.8	623.1	622.8	619.5
2013	604.8	605.9	610.9	617.3	622.0	621.2	620.8	622.8	622.2	621.3	624.4	621.9	618.0
2014	601.0	599.9	606.7	615.1	620.3	621.2	618.9	621.4	622.6	624.9	625.7	624.3	616.8
2015	605.8	602.4	606.2	612.5	617.6	616.5	613.7	613.4	614.4	616.1	614.8	612.1	612.1
Goods-Producing													
2005	118.3	118.8	119.9	123.4	125.6	127.3	127.1	127.9	129.0	128.7	128.1	126.8	125.1
2006	122.7	122.7	125.5	128.1	129.9	131.6	130.1	130.5	130.5	130.2	130.0	129.2	128.4
2007	123.4	121.0	124.3	125.9	127.3	129.4	128.6	128.7	128.2	128.4	127.8	125.5	126.5
2008	120.9	119.8	121.1	124.9	126.3	127.7	128.5	129.4	130.4	132.0	130.4	127.4	126.6
2009	118.9	116.8	116.8	116.3	115.9	114.3	112.7	112.7	112.0	112.7	112.1	111.6	114.4
2010	104.7	104.0	107.5	110.8	111.6	113.6	115.2	115.8	116.3	116.5	115.6	112.2	112.0
2011	107.7	108.4	110.6	114.1	115.8	117.9	118.9	119.7	120.0	120.3	120.5	119.6	116.1
2012	115.8	115.8	117.4	119.0	119.6	121.0	119.8	119.4	119.3	119.1	116.9	115.5	118.2
2013	110.7	110.5	111.7	114.5	116.4	116.2	117.1	117.3	116.7	115.9	114.9	112.0	114.5
2014	106.9	105.9	108.4	111.7	113.6	114.2	113.9	114.4	114.8	114.8	112.5	110.1	111.8
2015	105.4	103.8	105.2	107.5	109.5	108.6	107.6	107.2	106.9	105.4	103.5	101.8	106.0
Service-Providing													
2005	613.7	615.2	620.5	627.3	631.4	630.4	623.5	624.7	630.4	628.0	633.9	637.4	626.4
2006	620.7	624.4	630.8	632.1	646.0	636.2	625.7	629.2	637.1	637.9	642.5	643.0	633.8
2007	622.6	626.7	633.9	636.2	640.7	640.3	630.7	635.1	642.4	643.9	647.8	649.5	637.5
2008	631.6	637.3	640.3	642.0	657.4	641.6	637.0	638.0	645.0	645.1	646.3	647.1	642.4
2009	627.9	630.9	634.9	637.7	643.0	645.1	635.2	636.2	639.7	641.3	643.4	645.4	638.4
2010	627.0	628.7	637.5	641.8	658.3	646.8	639.8	639.6	645.8	647.3	650.3	650.3	642.8
2011	629.6	635.5	642.0	648.4	650.9	643.4	637.4	641.5	653.8	655.8	659.0	659.3	646.4
2012	640.6	646.4	652.9	656.8	670.5	650.5	643.8	647.1	659.3	660.8	663.6	664.5	654.7
2013	644.6	650.3	655.3	659.2	663.4	657.1	648.9	652.0	659.2	661.9	666.4	666.5	657.1
2014	644.0	647.4	653.4	659.8	673.1	648.2	644.4	649.3	661.2	666.8	670.0	670.4	657.3
2015	649.9	651.8	654.7	660.1	663.7	657.4	649.3	650.3	659.9	665.6	666.8	665.9	658.0
Mining and Logging													
2005	24.4	24.7	25.0	25.4	26.0	26.2	26.2	26.4	26.7	26.8	27.2	27.4	26.0
2006	27.2	27.4	27.7	27.8	27.9	28.3	28.3	28.2	28.3	28.0	28.3	28.4	28.0
2007	28.1	27.9	27.9	28.2	28.2	28.9	28.9	29.2	28.9	28.9	29.1	29.1	28.6
2008	28.7	28.8	29.2	29.8	30.5	31.1	31.3	31.7	32.5	33.3	33.4	33.4	31.1
2009	32.7	32.0	31.8	30.9	29.9	29.3	28.5	28.5	28.4	28.5	28.5	28.9	29.8
2010	28.2	28.4	28.8	29.2	29.4	30.1	30.5	30.9	31.1	31.2	31.6	31.6	30.1
2011	31.6	32.0	32.2	32.6	32.9	33.7	33.8	34.4	34.8	35.0	35.3	35.7	33.7
2012	35.2	34.9	34.7	34.0	33.7	33.7	33.1	33.0	32.8	32.6	32.5	32.2	33.5
2013	31.6	31.6	31.7	31.9	32.1	32.3	31.9	32.0	31.6	31.6	31.4	31.1	31.7
2014	30.1	30.2	30.5	30.6	30.5	30.6	30.1	30.2	30.1	30.0	29.8	29.0	30.1
2015	28.5	27.8	27.6	27.3	27.0	26.0	25.5	24.9	24.9	24.1	24.0	23.7	25.9

1. Employment by Industry: West Virginia, 2005–2015—*Continued*

(Numbers in thousands, not seasonally adjusted)

Industry and year	January	February	March	April	May	June	July	August	September	October	November	December	Annual average
Construction													
2005	31.9	32.2	33.0	35.9	37.2	38.3	38.3	38.9	39.6	39.8	39.1	37.5	36.8
2006	34.3	34.0	36.2	39.1	40.8	42.0	40.8	41.3	41.2	41.8	41.3	40.3	39.4
2007	36.2	34.2	37.2	38.7	39.9	40.8	40.2	40.3	40.2	40.9	40.3	38.3	38.9
2008	34.9	34.2	35.3	38.2	39.0	39.6	40.4	41.0	41.6	42.5	41.5	38.7	38.9
2009	32.6	32.6	33.9	33.8	35.1	34.6	34.8	34.5	34.2	34.9	34.4	33.5	34.1
2010	28.3	27.5	30.3	32.8	33.0	34.0	35.0	35.1	35.8	36.0	34.6	31.1	32.8
2011	27.4	27.7	29.2	32.2	33.4	34.2	35.1	35.5	35.6	35.8	35.6	34.3	33.0
2012	31.3	31.6	33.3	35.6	36.4	37.6	37.3	37.9	38.2	37.7	35.9	34.3	35.6
2013	31.0	30.9	32.0	34.5	35.9	35.2	36.3	36.6	36.4	35.9	35.1	32.5	34.4
2014	29.1	28.4	30.3	33.4	35.1	35.4	35.6	36.1	36.8	36.9	35.0	33.2	33.8
2015	29.3	28.5	29.8	32.7	34.7	34.5	34.2	34.6	34.3	34.0	32.3	31.2	32.5
Manufacturing													
2005	62.0	61.9	61.9	62.1	62.4	62.8	62.6	62.6	62.7	62.1	61.8	61.9	62.2
2006	61.2	61.3	61.6	61.2	61.2	61.3	61.0	61.0	61.0	60.4	60.4	60.5	61.0
2007	59.1	58.9	59.2	59.0	59.2	59.7	59.5	59.2	59.1	58.6	58.4	58.1	59.0
2008	57.3	56.8	56.6	56.9	56.8	57.0	56.8	56.7	56.3	56.2	55.5	55.3	56.5
2009	53.6	52.2	51.1	51.6	50.9	50.4	49.4	49.7	49.4	49.3	49.2	49.2	50.5
2010	48.2	48.1	48.4	48.8	49.2	49.5	49.7	49.8	49.4	49.3	49.4	49.5	49.1
2011	48.7	48.7	49.2	49.3	49.5	50.0	50.0	49.8	49.6	49.5	49.6	49.6	49.5
2012	49.3	49.3	49.4	49.4	49.5	49.7	49.4	48.5	48.3	48.8	48.5	49.0	49.1
2013	48.1	48.0	48.0	48.1	48.4	48.7	48.9	48.7	48.7	48.4	48.4	48.4	48.4
2014	47.7	47.3	47.6	47.7	48.0	48.2	48.2	48.1	47.9	47.9	47.7	47.9	47.9
2015	47.6	47.5	47.8	47.5	47.8	48.1	47.9	47.7	47.7	47.3	47.2	46.9	47.6
Trade, Transportation, and Utilities													
2005	136.9	136.1	136.7	138.1	139.6	139.7	139.6	139.8	139.9	140.3	143.2	144.6	139.5
2006	139.0	138.1	139.6	140.3	141.1	142.1	141.2	141.6	142.2	143.2	146.5	147.2	141.8
2007	141.3	140.1	141.6	141.4	142.6	143.3	142.7	143.4	143.6	144.4	147.2	147.8	143.3
2008	141.7	140.8	141.5	140.9	141.4	141.9	141.7	141.5	141.5	141.0	142.6	143.3	141.7
2009	136.5	134.6	134.6	135.0	135.8	136.3	135.5	135.5	135.8	135.6	137.6	138.2	135.9
2010	132.5	131.1	132.5	133.2	134.4	134.8	134.8	134.7	134.1	135.8	138.8	139.1	134.7
2011	133.4	132.5	133.2	134.4	134.8	135.2	135.3	135.8	135.5	136.1	139.1	139.7	135.4
2012	134.4	132.9	132.9	133.8	134.0	134.7	135.0	134.9	135.4	136.4	139.7	140.2	135.6
2013	134.3	133.2	133.4	134.0	134.7	135.4	135.1	135.1	135.1	136.4	140.9	141.1	135.7
2014	133.8	132.5	132.6	133.8	134.5	135.0	134.2	134.8	134.6	136.9	140.9	141.2	135.4
2015	133.7	132.4	132.9	134.1	135.2	135.6	135.0	134.6	135.0	135.4	137.7	138.7	135.0
Wholesale Trade													
2005	23.6	23.6	23.8	24.1	24.3	24.4	24.4	24.3	24.3	24.3	24.4	24.6	24.2
2006	24.3	24.3	24.5	24.7	24.8	25.3	24.9	25.0	25.1	25.2	25.5	25.6	24.9
2007	24.8	24.7	24.9	24.8	24.8	24.9	25.0	25.1	25.2	25.5	25.6	25.7	25.1
2008	24.5	24.5	24.6	24.6	24.8	24.8	24.6	24.6	24.7	24.5	24.4	24.4	24.6
2009	23.8	23.5	23.5	23.4	23.5	23.4	23.3	23.1	23.1	23.0	22.9	22.8	23.3
2010	22.4	22.3	22.5	22.7	22.7	22.8	23.0	22.9	23.0	23.3	23.4	23.3	22.9
2011	22.7	22.6	22.9	23.1	23.2	23.2	23.2	23.3	23.3	23.4	23.6	23.7	23.2
2012	23.1	22.9	23.2	23.1	23.1	23.1	23.0	23.0	23.2	23.4	23.7	23.5	23.2
2013	22.8	22.7	22.6	22.7	22.7	22.8	22.8	22.9	22.9	22.8	22.9	22.9	22.8
2014	22.4	22.4	22.4	22.5	22.6	22.6	22.7	22.7	22.8	22.9	23.0	22.9	22.7
2015	22.4	22.3	22.4	22.4	22.4	22.4	22.2	22.1	22.0	22.2	22.4	22.3	22.3
Retail Trade													
2005	88.0	87.0	87.3	88.3	89.4	89.2	89.2	89.3	89.3	89.7	92.5	93.5	89.4
2006	88.8	87.9	89.0	89.2	89.7	90.0	89.7	89.9	90.4	91.3	94.2	94.6	90.4
2007	90.0	89.0	90.2	89.9	90.8	91.2	90.7	91.2	91.2	91.9	94.5	94.9	91.3
2008	90.4	89.4	90.1	89.1	89.3	89.6	89.6	89.4	89.3	89.1	90.9	91.5	89.8
2009	86.4	84.8	85.0	85.6	86.4	87.0	86.6	86.8	87.1	87.2	89.4	90.0	86.9
2010	85.3	84.0	84.9	85.4	86.3	86.5	86.5	86.5	85.9	87.2	90.1	90.2	86.6
2011	85.7	84.8	85.3	86.5	86.8	87.1	87.1	87.5	87.1	87.6	90.4	90.7	87.2
2012	86.7	85.4	86.1	86.4	87.1	87.3	87.4	87.8	87.6	88.2	91.1	91.4	87.7
2013	86.9	85.9	86.2	86.7	87.3	87.8	87.5	87.2	87.1	87.9	90.5	91.0	87.7
2014	86.2	85.2	85.4	86.4	86.9	87.2	86.4	86.9	86.3	86.5	89.3	89.7	86.9
2015	85.4	84.6	85.0	86.0	86.8	86.9	87.0	86.9	86.9	87.2	89.1	90.1	86.8

1. Employment by Industry: West Virginia, 2005–2015—*Continued*

(Numbers in thousands, not seasonally adjusted)

Industry and year	January	February	March	April	May	June	July	August	September	October	November	December	Annual average
Transportation and Utilities													
2005	25.3	25.5	25.6	25.7	25.9	26.1	26.0	26.2	26.3	26.3	26.3	26.5	26.0
2006	25.9	25.9	26.1	26.4	26.6	26.8	26.6	26.7	26.7	26.7	26.8	27.0	26.5
2007	26.5	26.4	26.5	26.7	27.0	27.2	27.0	27.1	27.2	27.0	27.1	27.2	26.9
2008	26.8	26.9	26.8	27.2	27.3	27.5	27.5	27.5	27.5	27.4	27.3	27.4	27.3
2009	26.3	26.3	26.1	26.0	25.9	25.9	25.6	25.6	25.6	25.4	25.3	25.4	25.8
2010	24.8	24.8	25.1	25.1	25.4	25.5	25.3	25.3	25.2	25.3	25.3	25.6	25.2
2011	25.0	25.1	25.0	24.8	24.8	24.9	25.0	25.0	25.1	25.1	25.1	25.3	25.0
2012	24.6	24.6	24.5	24.5	24.5	24.6	24.5	24.6	24.8	24.8	24.9	25.3	24.7
2013	24.6	24.6	24.6	24.6	24.7	24.8	24.8	25.0	25.1	25.7	27.5	27.2	25.3
2014	25.2	24.9	24.8	24.9	25.0	25.2	25.1	25.2	25.5	27.5	28.6	28.6	25.9
2015	25.9	25.5	25.5	25.7	26.0	26.3	25.8	25.6	26.1	26.0	26.2	26.3	25.9
Information													
2005	11.6	11.4	11.5	11.5	11.7	11.8	11.9	12.0	11.8	11.8	11.9	12.0	11.7
2006	11.7	11.5	11.5	11.4	11.5	11.6	11.5	11.6	11.5	11.5	11.4	11.4	11.5
2007	11.3	11.3	11.2	11.3	11.4	11.5	11.6	11.5	11.5	11.4	11.4	11.5	11.4
2008	11.3	11.3	11.2	11.2	11.2	11.2	11.2	11.2	11.1	11.1	11.0	10.9	11.2
2009	10.9	10.7	10.7	10.6	10.5	10.4	10.3	10.2	10.3	10.2	10.2	10.2	10.4
2010	10.1	10.0	10.0	9.8	10.1	10.3	10.7	10.6	10.5	10.5	10.5	10.6	10.3
2011	10.4	10.4	10.4	10.3	10.2	10.2	10.2	10.2	10.0	10.0	9.9	9.9	10.2
2012	9.5	9.5	9.5	9.6	9.6	9.7	9.6	9.6	9.6	9.6	9.6	9.5	9.6
2013	9.3	9.4	9.5	9.5	9.6	9.6	9.7	9.7	9.7	9.7	9.8	9.8	9.6
2014	9.6	9.6	9.7	9.6	9.6	9.6	9.6	9.6	9.6	9.5	9.6	9.7	9.6
2015	9.6	9.6	9.7	9.7	9.8	9.7	9.3	9.3	9.2	9.1	9.3	9.2	9.5
Financial Activities													
2005	35.1	35.0	35.0	35.3	35.3	35.4	35.5	35.5	35.4	35.3	35.5	35.5	35.3
2006	35.7	35.7	35.9	36.0	36.2	36.6	36.1	36.1	36.0	36.0	36.0	36.1	36.0
2007	35.6	35.7	35.8	36.0	36.2	36.5	36.3	36.4	36.3	36.3	36.3	36.5	36.2
2008	36.2	36.3	36.2	36.4	36.3	36.5	36.5	36.3	36.3	36.3	36.3	36.3	36.3
2009	35.7	35.5	35.5	35.8	35.9	36.0	35.9	35.8	35.6	35.6	35.4	35.4	35.7
2010	35.2	35.2	35.5	35.7	35.7	36.0	35.8	35.7	35.6	35.8	35.9	35.8	35.7
2011	35.3	35.0	35.0	35.1	35.3	35.4	35.5	35.5	35.5	35.7	35.6	35.8	35.4
2012	35.4	35.6	35.7	35.9	36.1	36.3	36.3	36.5	36.5	36.3	36.3	36.6	36.1
2013	36.2	36.4	36.7	36.9	36.9	36.8	36.9	36.9	36.9	37.1	37.1	37.3	36.8
2014	36.9	36.8	37.0	36.7	36.8	36.9	36.8	36.8	36.6	36.6	36.6	36.6	36.8
2015	36.3	36.1	36.3	36.3	36.4	36.5	36.5	36.6	36.3	36.9	36.7	36.8	36.5
Professional and Business Services													
2005	57.6	57.1	57.5	58.6	58.4	59.1	59.2	59.7	59.2	59.3	59.8	60.8	58.9
2006	59.4	59.5	59.7	60.0	59.5	60.6	60.2	60.3	60.2	59.4	59.8	59.6	59.9
2007	59.1	58.8	59.7	60.7	60.7	61.1	60.9	61.4	61.2	61.1	61.4	62.4	60.7
2008	60.2	60.4	60.4	61.4	61.3	61.5	61.4	61.3	60.8	61.1	61.1	61.4	61.0
2009	60.1	60.0	59.7	60.3	60.0	60.1	59.8	60.1	60.0	60.2	60.7	61.7	60.2
2010	59.7	59.5	60.2	61.3	60.4	61.0	61.8	61.7	61.5	61.8	61.9	62.0	61.1
2011	61.3	61.9	62.5	63.4	62.8	63.2	63.7	64.2	64.4	64.6	65.2	65.2	63.5
2012	63.4	63.7	63.9	65.2	65.0	65.1	64.7	65.1	64.8	65.0	64.6	64.7	64.6
2013	63.4	63.9	64.5	65.0	65.1	65.3	65.3	65.9	65.2	64.6	65.0	64.5	64.8
2014	63.6	63.9	64.6	66.1	66.5	67.2	67.7	68.2	67.9	68.8	68.9	69.3	66.9
2015	66.9	66.5	66.5	66.9	66.5	66.9	67.3	67.4	66.7	67.7	67.6	66.7	67.0
Education and Health Services													
2005	110.3	112.1	112.6	113.0	113.1	112.5	112.2	112.6	114.1	113.3	113.9	114.3	112.8
2006	112.1	113.1	113.6	113.4	113.3	111.5	110.5	110.9	113.2	113.6	114.1	114.1	112.8
2007	110.7	112.7	113.5	113.1	113.6	112.9	112.0	112.9	115.5	116.2	116.8	116.4	113.9
2008	114.3	116.6	116.5	116.4	116.4	115.2	114.7	115.0	117.4	117.1	117.6	117.4	116.2
2009	115.0	117.0	117.7	118.5	119.0	118.0	117.7	118.1	120.4	120.7	121.2	121.4	118.7
2010	118.0	119.4	120.4	120.8	120.5	119.8	119.5	119.7	122.2	121.9	122.4	122.4	120.6
2011	119.7	121.5	122.3	123.2	123.5	121.6	121.1	122.0	124.0	124.9	125.6	125.6	122.9
2012	122.5	124.4	125.3	126.2	126.5	124.3	123.7	124.5	127.4	127.2	127.5	127.7	125.6
2013	124.3	126.1	126.5	126.5	126.9	124.4	123.4	124.4	127.1	127.3	127.8	128.2	126.1
2014	124.9	125.6	126.7	127.3	127.6	125.2	124.0	124.9	128.0	128.1	128.6	128.8	126.6
2015	127.9	128.3	128.6	128.7	129.0	126.4	124.9	125.8	129.1	130.8	131.4	130.6	128.5

1. Employment by Industry: West Virginia, 2005–2015—*Continued*

(Numbers in thousands, not seasonally adjusted)

Industry and year	January	February	March	April	May	June	July	August	September	October	November	December	Annual average
Leisure and Hospitality													
2005	65.1	65.3	66.6	68.5	70.6	72.0	72.7	73.0	71.7	69.2	68.1	68.3	69.3
2006	66.9	67.0	68.7	69.3	71.7	74.1	73.8	74.4	73.7	70.9	70.5	70.5	71.0
2007	67.0	66.9	69.0	70.9	72.6	74.6	74.0	75.3	74.3	72.1	71.3	71.9	71.7
2008	69.3	69.9	70.9	72.2	74.1	75.0	75.6	76.0	75.2	73.2	71.6	71.6	72.9
2009	68.8	68.7	70.3	71.3	73.4	74.5	74.8	75.1	73.9	71.4	70.2	70.2	71.9
2010	67.7	67.4	69.3	71.5	73.0	75.0	75.1	75.8	74.8	72.9	71.4	71.2	72.1
2011	68.6	68.9	70.5	72.4	74.3	75.5	75.6	76.3	74.8	73.2	72.1	72.0	72.9
2012	69.9	70.7	72.7	74.0	75.7	76.7	77.1	77.6	76.2	74.6	73.0	73.2	74.3
2013	71.7	71.5	72.9	74.3	76.3	77.4	77.2	77.4	75.6	74.5	73.2	73.6	74.6
2014	70.5	70.8	72.4	73.9	75.8	77.1	76.9	77.1	75.7	74.7	73.3	73.4	74.3
2015	71.3	71.0	72.1	74.1	75.8	77.1	77.4	77.1	76.0	75.5	73.1	73.0	74.5
Other Services													
2005	54.6	54.6	55.4	56.7	56.9	56.6	55.9	55.6	55.7	55.3	55.2	55.3	55.7
2006	54.6	54.7	55.3	55.3	55.5	56.1	55.6	55.8	56.2	56.3	56.3	56.1	55.7
2007	55.2	55.4	55.7	55.6	55.5	56.0	55.4	55.2	55.4	55.4	55.5	55.3	55.5
2008	55.3	55.5	55.7	55.4	55.8	55.8	55.6	55.4	55.4	55.5	55.7	55.7	55.6
2009	55.6	55.5	55.4	55.8	55.9	55.8	55.5	55.1	55.2	55.3	55.4	55.4	55.5
2010	54.7	54.4	54.6	55.0	55.3	55.7	55.2	55.0	55.1	55.0	54.8	54.8	55.0
2011	54.1	54.3	54.6	54.8	55.0	55.2	55.3	55.1	55.1	55.4	55.4	55.1	55.0
2012	54.7	54.8	55.4	55.9	56.0	56.0	55.8	55.6	55.4	55.6	55.5	55.4	55.5
2013	54.9	54.9	55.7	56.6	56.1	56.1	56.1	56.1	55.9	55.8	55.7	55.4	55.8
2014	54.8	54.8	55.3	56.0	55.9	56.0	55.8	55.6	55.4	55.5	55.3	55.2	55.5
2015	54.7	54.7	54.9	55.2	55.4	55.7	55.7	55.4	55.2	55.3	55.5	55.3	55.3
Government													
2005	142.5	143.6	145.2	145.6	145.8	143.3	136.5	136.5	142.6	143.5	146.3	146.6	143.2
2006	141.3	144.8	146.5	146.4	157.2	143.6	136.8	138.5	144.1	147.0	147.9	148.0	145.2
2007	142.4	145.8	147.4	147.2	148.1	144.4	137.8	139.0	144.6	147.0	147.9	147.7	144.9
2008	143.3	146.5	147.9	148.1	160.9	144.5	140.3	141.3	147.3	149.8	150.4	150.5	147.6
2009	145.3	148.9	151.0	150.4	152.5	154.0	145.7	146.3	148.5	152.3	152.7	152.9	150.0
2010	149.1	151.7	155.0	154.5	168.9	154.2	146.9	146.4	152.0	153.6	154.6	154.4	153.4
2011	146.8	151.0	153.5	154.8	155.0	147.1	140.7	142.4	154.5	155.9	156.1	156.0	151.2
2012	150.8	154.8	156.6	156.0	166.9	147.4	141.7	142.8	153.8	156.1	157.4	157.2	153.5
2013	150.5	154.9	156.1	156.4	157.8	152.1	145.2	146.5	153.7	156.5	156.9	156.6	153.6
2014	149.9	153.4	155.1	156.4	166.4	141.2	139.4	142.3	153.4	156.7	156.8	156.2	152.3
2015	149.5	153.2	153.7	155.1	155.6	149.5	143.2	144.1	152.4	154.9	155.5	155.6	151.9

2. Average Weekly Hours by Selected Industry: West Virginia, 2011–2015

(Not seasonally adjusted)

Industry and year	January	February	March	April	May	June	July	August	September	October	November	December	Annual average
Total Private													
2011	34.8	34.5	34.3	34.7	35.0	34.9	34.5	34.4	34.5	34.3	34.2	34.1	34.5
2012	34.0	33.9	34.1	34.4	34.3	34.7	34.8	34.5	34.8	34.4	34.5	34.5	34.4
2013	33.9	34.0	34.3	34.3	34.6	34.9	34.4	34.7	34.9	34.8	34.9	34.5	34.5
2014	33.9	34.0	34.4	34.6	34.6	35.3	35.3	35.3	35.2	35.0	35.2	35.0	34.8
2015	34.3	34.2	34.5	34.6	34.9	34.8	34.9	35.1	34.6	34.9	34.9	34.6	34.7
Goods-Producing													
2011	40.8	40.4	39.9	40.1	40.8	40.6	40.3	40.3	40.1	40.4	40.6	40.5	40.4
2012	40.9	40.1	40.0	40.1	39.7	40.7	39.2	39.5	40.4	39.7	39.7	39.6	40.0
2013	39.2	39.4	39.9	39.7	41.1	40.7	39.9	41.0	41.6	41.6	41.4	39.5	40.4
2014	38.7	39.4	39.8	40.3	39.9	41.8	41.7	41.8	41.6	41.4	40.4	41.4	40.7
2015	39.4	38.9	39.6	39.9	41.3	40.5	39.9	41.1	39.2	41.1	39.8	40.0	40.1
Mining and Logging													
2011	48.7	47.4	46.9	46.3	45.9	45.4	44.0	45.3	44.2	44.0	44.0	44.5	45.5
2012	47.1	42.8	42.9	42.4	42.2	42.9	41.4	42.1	43.6	42.2	39.8	41.5	42.6
2013	41.7	41.0	43.6	42.4	42.6	43.6	42.2	43.1	43.7	45.5	43.9	41.8	42.9
2014	43.7	44.0	44.3	45.6	44.3	47.0	47.0	46.9	46.4	46.3	46.2	48.9	45.9
2015	47.6	44.6	46.3	46.2	45.8	45.3	45.8	46.0	43.2	46.3	46.9	46.0	45.8
Construction													
2011	37.0	36.7	36.7	38.8	40.4	40.3	40.2	40.1	39.2	39.9	40.5	39.2	39.2
2012	37.3	38.0	38.2	39.0	38.7	40.4	39.6	39.7	39.7	39.8	40.1	38.8	39.2
2013	37.9	38.5	38.2	39.6	41.3	40.5	39.9	40.8	41.2	40.0	40.0	38.1	39.7
2014	37.6	37.3	37.7	39.1	38.0	39.7	39.8	40.0	39.3	38.6	37.0	38.0	38.6
2015	36.2	35.7	36.8	37.3	39.2	39.1	38.5	40.1	38.1	40.7	37.4	38.9	38.2
Manufacturing													
2011	37.9	37.9	37.3	36.8	37.6	37.5	38.0	37.0	37.9	38.2	38.2	38.5	37.7
2012	38.8	39.5	39.2	39.4	38.8	39.3	37.3	37.7	38.7	37.9	39.3	38.9	38.7
2013	38.4	38.9	38.5	38.0	39.9	39.0	38.5	39.8	40.6	40.3	40.7	38.9	39.3
2014	36.3	37.7	38.1	37.7	38.6	39.9	39.6	39.9	40.4	40.4	39.4	39.2	38.9
2015	36.5	37.5	37.5	38.1	40.2	39.0	37.9	39.1	37.9	38.8	37.9	37.8	38.2
Trade, Transportation, and Utilities													
2011	35.2	34.7	35.2	35.4	35.8	35.6	35.6	35.4	35.6	35.2	34.7	34.8	35.3
2012	33.8	33.9	34.5	35.1	35.2	34.9	35.5	35.4	35.4	34.8	34.8	35.3	34.9
2013	34.3	34.7	35.0	35.0	34.9	35.3	35.1	35.0	34.9	34.7	34.6	34.5	34.8
2014	33.7	33.3	33.6	34.0	34.4	34.1	34.4	34.9	34.9	34.8	35.0	34.9	34.3
2015	34.2	34.7	35.3	35.5	36.0	35.9	35.7	36.0	35.7	35.8	35.7	35.1	35.5
Financial Activities													
2011	36.3	36.2	36.0	36.5	36.8	36.3	36.0	35.5	36.7	37.4	35.6	35.1	36.2
2012	36.2	36.1	35.4	36.5	35.5	35.5	36.0	34.9	35.9	35.2	35.5	35.8	35.7
2013	34.4	34.4	35.5	36.0	35.9	37.3	35.3	36.7	37.2	37.2	37.4	37.5	36.3
2014	35.3	35.6	35.2	34.5	34.7	35.3	34.7	35.5	35.5	35.5	36.2	34.3	35.2
2015	35.5	35.9	35.8	36.1	36.1	36.6	36.0	37.0	35.6	36.2	36.6	36.1	36.1
Professional and Business Services													
2011	37.0	37.1	37.0	37.6	38.2	37.6	37.0	37.4	37.2	37.5	37.7	36.6	37.3
2012	36.6	35.7	36.1	37.0	36.6	37.0	38.0	36.7	37.5	36.7	37.2	36.6	36.8
2013	35.4	35.4	36.1	36.1	35.9	36.5	35.9	36.1	36.1	36.1	35.4	35.6	35.9
2014	34.5	34.1	34.5	34.9	35.3	36.1	36.7	36.3	36.6	36.2	36.5	35.5	35.6
2015	35.0	34.2	35.2	34.2	34.9	34.6	35.4	35.3	35.4	35.7	36.5	36.5	35.2
Education and Health Services													
2011	34.3	34.3	34.0	34.2	34.4	34.2	34.1	33.8	34.2	33.8	34.1	33.8	34.1
2012	34.1	34.0	33.8	34.0	33.6	34.3	34.3	34.0	34.3	34.1	34.3	34.1	34.1
2013	34.1	33.9	34.1	34.2	34.2	34.3	34.0	33.9	34.5	34.4	35.1	34.8	34.3
2014	34.8	34.7	35.0	34.9	34.9	35.4	35.3	35.0	35.1	34.8	35.3	35.2	35.0
2015	35.0	34.5	34.5	34.7	34.8	34.8	35.1	35.0	34.9	34.5	34.9	34.8	34.8
Leisure and Hospitality													
2011	26.4	27.0	26.7	26.5	26.8	26.9	27.4	27.1	26.4	26.7	26.1	26.0	26.7
2012	25.2	25.9	26.3	26.6	26.9	26.8	27.6	27.3	26.2	26.4	26.1	26.1	26.5
2013	25.3	26.0	26.2	25.8	26.1	26.3	26.5	26.5	26.2	26.0	26.0	25.6	26.1
2014	24.8	25.3	26.1	26.8	26.4	26.9	27.1	26.7	26.2	25.9	25.8	25.7	26.2
2015	25.0	25.2	25.8	26.0	26.3	26.7	27.0	26.8	26.4	26.4	26.5	25.9	26.2
Other Services													
2011	31.2	30.9	30.7	31.1	31.0	31.0	30.9	31.2	30.4	31.4	31.3	31.3	31.0
2012	31.1	32.1	32.0	30.9	31.6	31.8	32.0	32.3	32.5	32.8	32.7	33.1	32.1
2013	32.9	32.3	31.9	32.5	32.0	32.7	31.8	32.9	32.9	31.4	32.0	31.7	32.3
2014	31.4	30.8	32.3	31.4	31.4	32.3	32.7	33.0	31.6	32.7	33.5	32.6	32.1
2015	32.1	32.1	32.1	32.5	31.7	32.1	32.2	32.4	32.0	32.3	32.9	32.4	32.2

3. Average Hourly Earnings by Selected Industry: West Virginia, 2011–2015

(Dollars, not seasonally adjusted)

Industry and year	January	February	March	April	May	June	July	August	September	October	November	December	Annual average
Total Private													
2011	18.80	18.65	18.73	18.85	18.86	18.83	18.95	18.89	19.04	19.11	19.22	19.17	18.93
2012	19.41	19.38	19.32	19.55	19.32	19.35	19.42	19.44	19.84	19.71	19.77	20.04	19.55
2013	20.07	20.25	20.11	20.32	20.28	20.42	20.48	20.38	20.55	20.43	20.40	20.38	20.34
2014	20.59	20.77	20.53	20.57	20.39	20.39	20.54	20.44	20.55	20.58	20.49	20.43	20.52
2015	20.84	20.81	20.73	20.59	20.58	20.53	20.64	20.77	20.82	20.78	20.96	20.78	20.74
Goods-Producing													
2011	22.81	22.60	22.60	22.78	22.82	22.67	22.73	22.82	22.82	23.16	23.31	23.52	22.89
2012	23.51	23.08	23.32	23.25	23.11	23.53	23.53	23.77	24.11	23.87	24.06	24.32	23.62
2013	24.48	24.64	24.95	25.08	25.16	25.32	25.39	25.11	25.37	25.31	25.49	25.38	25.15
2014	25.49	25.18	25.26	25.18	24.94	24.94	25.03	24.78	24.82	24.67	24.66	24.83	24.97
2015	24.96	24.71	24.84	24.90	24.65	24.73	24.56	24.81	25.26	24.97	25.29	25.13	24.90
Mining and Logging													
2011	25.68	25.78	26.05	26.11	26.11	25.60	25.26	25.69	25.80	26.51	26.54	26.86	26.00
2012	27.18	27.06	27.73	27.49	27.21	27.60	27.95	27.94	28.69	27.89	28.49	28.85	27.82
2013	29.40	29.51	30.00	30.41	30.65	31.40	31.73	31.31	31.43	31.80	32.05	32.07	30.99
2014	31.84	31.22	31.04	30.76	30.58	30.32	30.08	30.09	29.78	29.29	29.10	29.22	30.26
2015	29.89	29.86	30.10	29.68	29.78	29.71	29.48	29.31	30.16	29.38	29.47	28.87	29.65
Construction													
2011	23.29	22.69	22.53	22.98	23.14	23.36	23.93	23.75	23.58	23.77	24.42	24.48	23.55
2012	23.52	23.46	23.73	23.10	23.24	23.21	23.27	24.14	23.96	24.33	24.42	24.39	23.74
2013	24.74	24.65	25.12	25.02	25.13	24.90	24.83	24.66	24.91	24.58	24.57	24.58	24.81
2014	24.25	24.00	24.56	24.65	24.35	24.55	24.76	24.57	24.43	24.38	24.55	24.93	24.51
2015	24.26	23.80	24.18	24.90	24.47	25.16	24.30	24.97	25.00	25.36	25.12	25.43	24.78
Manufacturing													
2011	20.16	19.93	19.81	19.88	19.92	19.77	19.85	19.66	19.81	19.96	19.81	20.07	19.89
2012	20.31	19.78	19.66	20.21	19.99	20.76	20.46	20.29	20.74	20.51	20.79	21.09	20.38
2013	20.79	21.24	21.05	21.18	21.30	21.14	21.27	21.04	21.49	21.06	21.57	21.30	21.21
2014	21.44	21.39	21.39	21.24	21.24	21.20	21.50	21.03	21.54	21.57	21.49	21.45	21.37
2015	21.54	21.65	21.50	21.58	21.48	21.29	21.57	21.94	22.52	21.99	22.77	22.62	21.87
Trade, Transportation, and Utilities													
2011	16.52	16.54	16.61	16.88	16.79	16.76	17.02	16.87	17.48	17.11	17.10	16.83	16.88
2012	17.30	17.41	17.59	17.92	17.52	17.59	17.42	17.29	17.80	17.28	17.47	17.20	17.48
2013	17.20	17.29	17.17	17.32	17.40	17.67	17.68	17.59	17.66	17.72	17.77	17.96	17.54
2014	18.17	18.57	18.40	18.75	18.69	18.66	18.56	18.60	18.72	18.82	18.31	17.93	18.51
2015	18.44	18.64	18.39	18.54	18.27	18.53	18.66	18.73	18.88	19.04	18.94	18.72	18.65
Financial Activities													
2011	17.23	17.18	17.33	17.41	17.48	17.14	17.63	17.95	17.80	18.16	18.28	17.86	17.62
2012	17.79	17.96	18.15	18.50	18.01	17.67	18.04	17.99	17.25	17.32	17.11	17.10	17.74
2013	17.39	17.53	17.94	18.49	18.30	18.57	18.88	19.11	19.63	19.23	18.96	20.03	18.70
2014	19.83	19.76	19.85	19.93	20.04	20.61	20.47	20.61	20.44	20.92	20.67	20.34	20.29
2015	20.37	20.39	20.20	20.95	20.60	19.83	21.86	22.73	21.84	21.28	22.27	21.35	21.15
Professional and Business Services													
2011	19.71	19.83	19.90	19.71	19.78	19.81	19.98	20.05	20.23	20.85	20.63	20.72	20.11
2012	21.76	21.52	21.52	22.39	21.91	21.44	22.09	21.90	22.11	21.92	21.77	22.56	21.91
2013	22.08	22.36	22.26	22.58	22.18	22.08	21.38	21.36	21.41	20.73	21.32	21.15	21.74
2014	21.05	21.35	21.15	21.02	20.52	20.48	20.54	20.30	20.38	20.36	20.45	20.07	20.62
2015	20.17	20.18	20.10	20.18	19.94	19.96	20.00	20.28	20.47	20.33	20.85	19.98	20.21
Education and Health Services													
2011	19.42	19.62	19.56	19.50	19.39	19.63	19.94	19.78	19.60	19.50	19.70	19.67	19.61
2012	19.66	20.11	19.81	19.92	20.02	20.00	20.10	20.01	20.41	20.60	20.56	21.12	20.20
2013	21.27	21.61	21.08	21.31	21.26	21.53	21.96	21.79	21.76	21.63	21.15	21.12	21.45
2014	21.70	22.03	21.46	21.57	21.38	21.31	21.83	21.55	21.59	21.52	21.56	21.63	21.59
2015	22.45	22.54	22.49	22.22	22.38	22.23	22.48	22.33	22.20	22.18	22.33	22.34	22.35
Leisure and Hospitality													
2011	10.92	10.85	10.68	10.56	10.61	10.55	10.51	10.54	10.51	10.59	10.64	10.67	10.63
2012	10.71	10.59	10.59	10.45	10.40	10.26	10.31	10.26	10.39	10.42	10.40	10.58	10.44
2013	10.41	10.43	10.31	10.46	10.32	10.37	10.36	10.41	10.50	10.51	10.56	10.71	10.44
2014	10.78	10.69	10.61	10.44	10.61	10.45	10.47	10.54	10.66	10.78	10.76	10.91	10.64
2015	11.24	11.27	11.30	11.17	11.09	11.10	11.07	11.14	11.28	11.36	11.29	11.42	11.22
Other Services													
2011	16.23	16.40	16.21	15.76	15.77	15.74	15.63	15.59	15.67	15.80	15.84	16.14	15.90
2012	16.06	15.77	16.15	16.13	16.05	16.01	15.86	16.17	16.49	16.51	17.01	17.11	16.28
2013	17.06	17.42	17.51	17.56	17.53	17.43	17.48	17.56	18.22	18.63	18.45	18.94	17.81
2014	19.22	20.06	20.25	20.22	20.06	20.20	20.20	20.47	20.71	21.00	20.91	21.02	20.37
2015	21.47	20.91	21.12	20.92	20.60	20.58	20.87	20.89	20.67	20.50	20.31	20.32	20.76

4. Average Weekly Earnings by Selected Industry: West Virginia, 2011–2015

(Dollars, not seasonally adjusted)

Industry and year	January	February	March	April	May	June	July	August	September	October	November	December	Annual average
Total Private													
2011	654.24	643.43	642.44	654.10	660.10	657.17	653.78	649.82	656.88	655.47	657.32	653.70	653.09
2012	659.94	656.98	658.81	672.52	662.68	671.45	675.82	670.68	690.43	678.02	682.07	691.38	672.52
2013	680.37	688.50	689.77	696.98	701.69	712.66	704.51	707.19	717.20	710.96	711.96	703.11	701.73
2014	698.00	706.18	706.23	711.72	705.49	719.77	725.06	721.53	723.36	720.30	721.25	715.05	714.10
2015	714.81	711.70	715.19	712.41	718.24	714.44	720.34	729.03	720.37	725.22	731.50	718.99	719.68
Goods-Producing													
2011	930.65	913.04	901.74	913.48	931.06	920.40	916.02	919.65	915.08	935.66	946.39	952.56	924.76
2012	961.56	925.51	932.80	932.33	917.47	957.67	922.38	938.92	974.04	947.64	955.18	963.07	944.80
2013	959.62	970.82	995.51	995.68	1,034.08	1,030.52	1,013.06	1,029.51	1,055.39	1,052.90	1,055.29	1,002.51	1,016.06
2014	986.46	992.09	1,005.35	1,014.75	995.11	1,042.49	1,043.75	1,035.80	1,032.51	1,021.34	996.26	1,027.96	1,016.28
2015	983.42	961.22	983.66	993.51	1,018.05	1,001.57	979.94	1,019.69	990.19	1,026.27	1,006.54	1,005.20	998.49
Mining and Logging													
2011	1,250.62	1,221.97	1,221.75	1,208.89	1,198.45	1,162.24	1,111.44	1,163.76	1,140.36	1,166.44	1,167.76	1,195.27	1,183.00
2012	1,280.18	1,158.17	1,189.62	1,165.58	1,148.26	1,184.04	1,157.13	1,176.27	1,250.88	1,176.96	1,133.90	1,197.28	1,185.13
2013	1,225.98	1,209.91	1,308.00	1,289.38	1,305.69	1,369.04	1,339.01	1,349.46	1,373.49	1,446.90	1,407.00	1,340.53	1,329.47
2014	1,391.41	1,373.68	1,375.07	1,402.66	1,354.69	1,425.04	1,413.76	1,411.22	1,381.79	1,356.13	1,344.42	1,428.86	1,388.93
2015	1,422.76	1,331.76	1,393.63	1,371.22	1,363.92	1,345.86	1,350.18	1,348.26	1,302.91	1,360.29	1,382.14	1,328.02	1,357.97
Construction													
2011	861.73	832.72	826.85	891.62	934.86	941.41	961.99	952.38	924.34	948.42	989.01	959.62	923.16
2012	877.30	891.48	906.49	900.90	899.39	937.68	921.49	958.36	951.21	968.33	979.24	946.33	930.61
2013	937.65	949.03	959.58	990.79	1,037.87	1,008.45	990.72	1,006.13	1,026.29	983.20	982.80	936.50	984.96
2014	911.80	895.20	925.91	963.82	925.30	974.64	985.45	982.80	960.10	941.07	908.35	947.34	946.09
2015	878.21	849.66	889.82	928.77	959.22	983.76	935.55	1,001.30	952.50	1,032.15	939.49	989.23	946.60
Manufacturing													
2011	764.06	755.35	738.91	731.58	748.99	741.38	754.30	727.42	750.80	762.47	756.74	772.70	749.85
2012	788.03	781.31	770.67	796.27	775.61	815.87	763.16	764.93	802.64	777.33	817.05	820.40	788.71
2013	798.34	826.24	810.43	804.84	849.87	824.46	818.90	837.39	872.49	848.72	877.90	828.57	833.55
2014	778.27	806.40	814.96	800.75	819.86	845.88	851.40	839.10	870.22	871.43	846.71	840.84	831.29
2015	786.21	811.88	806.25	822.20	863.50	830.31	817.50	857.85	853.51	853.21	862.98	855.04	835.43
Trade, Transportation, and Utilities													
2011	581.50	573.94	584.67	597.55	601.08	596.66	605.91	597.20	622.29	602.27	593.37	585.68	595.86
2012	584.74	590.20	606.86	628.99	616.70	613.89	618.41	612.07	630.12	601.34	607.96	607.16	610.05
2013	589.96	599.96	600.95	606.20	607.26	623.75	620.57	615.65	616.33	614.88	614.84	619.62	610.39
2014	612.33	618.38	618.24	637.50	642.94	636.31	638.46	649.14	653.33	654.94	640.85	625.76	634.89
2015	630.65	646.81	649.17	658.17	657.72	665.23	666.16	674.28	674.02	681.63	676.16	657.07	662.08
Financial Activities													
2011	625.45	621.92	623.88	635.47	643.26	622.18	634.68	637.23	653.26	679.18	650.77	626.89	637.84
2012	644.00	648.36	642.51	675.25	639.36	627.29	649.44	627.85	619.28	609.66	607.41	612.18	633.32
2013	598.22	603.03	636.87	665.64	656.97	692.66	666.46	701.34	730.24	715.36	709.10	751.13	678.81
2014	700.00	703.46	698.72	687.59	695.39	727.53	710.31	731.66	725.62	742.66	748.25	697.66	714.21
2015	723.14	732.00	723.16	756.30	743.66	725.78	786.96	841.01	777.50	770.34	815.08	770.74	763.52
Professional and Business Services													
2011	729.27	735.69	736.30	741.10	755.60	744.86	739.26	749.87	752.56	781.88	777.75	758.35	750.10
2012	796.42	768.26	776.87	828.43	801.91	793.28	839.42	803.73	829.13	804.46	809.84	825.70	806.29
2013	781.63	791.54	803.59	815.14	796.26	805.92	767.54	771.10	772.90	748.35	754.73	752.94	780.47
2014	726.23	728.04	729.68	733.60	724.36	739.33	753.82	736.89	745.91	737.03	746.43	712.49	734.07
2015	705.95	690.16	707.52	690.16	695.91	690.62	708.00	715.88	724.64	725.78	761.03	729.27	711.39
Education and Health Services													
2011	666.11	672.97	665.04	666.90	667.02	671.35	679.95	668.56	670.32	659.10	671.77	664.85	668.70
2012	670.41	683.74	669.58	677.28	672.67	686.00	689.43	680.34	700.06	702.46	705.21	720.19	688.82
2013	725.31	732.58	718.83	728.80	727.09	738.48	746.64	738.68	750.72	744.07	742.37	734.98	735.74
2014	755.16	764.44	751.10	752.79	746.16	754.37	770.60	754.25	757.81	748.90	761.07	761.38	755.65
2015	785.75	777.63	775.91	771.03	778.82	773.60	789.05	781.55	774.78	765.21	779.32	777.43	777.78
Leisure and Hospitality													
2011	288.29	292.95	285.16	279.84	284.35	283.80	287.97	285.63	277.46	282.75	277.70	277.42	283.82
2012	269.89	274.28	278.52	277.97	279.76	274.97	284.56	280.10	272.22	275.09	271.44	276.14	276.66
2013	263.37	271.18	270.12	269.87	269.35	272.73	274.54	275.87	275.10	273.26	274.56	274.18	272.48
2014	267.34	270.46	276.92	279.79	280.10	281.11	283.74	281.42	279.29	279.20	277.61	280.39	278.77
2015	281.00	284.00	291.54	290.42	291.67	296.37	298.89	298.55	297.79	299.90	299.19	295.78	293.96
Other Services													
2011	506.38	506.76	497.65	490.14	488.87	487.94	482.97	486.41	476.37	496.12	495.79	505.18	492.90
2012	499.47	506.22	516.80	498.42	507.18	509.12	507.52	522.29	535.93	541.53	556.23	566.34	522.59
2013	561.27	562.67	558.57	570.70	560.96	569.96	555.86	577.72	599.44	584.98	590.40	600.40	575.26
2014	603.51	617.85	654.08	634.91	629.88	652.46	660.54	675.51	654.44	686.70	700.49	685.25	653.88
2015	689.19	671.21	677.95	679.90	653.02	660.62	672.01	676.84	661.44	662.15	668.20	658.37	668.47

WISCONSIN
At a Glance

Population:
  2005 estimate: 5,546,166
  2010 census: 5,686,986
  2015 estimate: 5,771,337

Percent change in population:
  2005–2015: 4.1%
  2010–2015: 1.5%

Percent change in total nonfarm employment:
  2005–2015: 1.9%

Industry with the largest growth in employment, 2005–2015 (thousands):
  Education and health services, 56.0

Industry with the largest decline or smallest growth in employment, 2005–2015 (thousands):
  Manufacturing, –36.3

Civilian labor force:
  2005: 3,021,086
  2010: 3,081,512
  2015: 3,095,376

Unemployment rate and rank among states (highest to lowest):
  2005: 4.7%, 30th
  2010: 8.7%, 24th
  2015: 4.6%, 33rd

Over-the-year change in unemployment rates:
  2012–2013: –0.3%
  2013–2014: –1.3%
  2014–2015: –0.8%

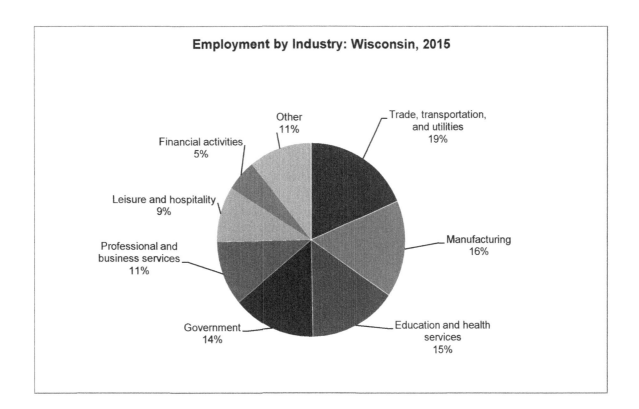

Employment by Industry: Wisconsin, 2015

Other 11%
Financial activities 5%
Leisure and hospitality 9%
Professional and business services 11%
Government 14%
Trade, transportation, and utilities 19%
Manufacturing 16%
Education and health services 15%

1. Employment by Industry: Wisconsin, 2005–2015

(Numbers in thousands, not seasonally adjusted)

Industry and year	January	February	March	April	May	June	July	August	September	October	November	December	Annual average
Total Nonfarm													
2005	2,751.8	2,763.2	2,777.8	2,824.9	2,849.0	2,874.4	2,855.6	2,857.8	2,870.6	2,867.7	2,869.5	2,869.6	2,836.0
2006	2,783.2	2,786.9	2,804.8	2,844.4	2,873.3	2,909.7	2,878.4	2,879.5	2,888.5	2,887.4	2,887.4	2,885.1	2,859.1
2007	2,806.3	2,801.8	2,821.7	2,854.0	2,895.8	2,934.1	2,897.5	2,898.8	2,899.0	2,900.1	2,901.3	2,897.6	2,875.7
2008	2,818.9	2,814.6	2,827.3	2,855.8	2,898.0	2,919.1	2,887.6	2,886.3	2,889.5	2,889.6	2,877.1	2,854.6	2,868.2
2009	2,744.5	2,731.4	2,723.6	2,735.5	2,764.9	2,775.3	2,738.4	2,732.3	2,731.9	2,744.0	2,739.8	2,731.9	2,741.1
2010	2,646.3	2,651.0	2,665.3	2,710.8	2,743.2	2,761.8	2,740.7	2,745.0	2,747.0	2,767.5	2,768.2	2,753.2	2,725.0
2011	2,676.5	2,683.7	2,699.4	2,737.0	2,766.6	2,784.3	2,770.9	2,771.0	2,782.4	2,786.0	2,785.9	2,777.3	2,751.8
2012	2,690.2	2,704.4	2,732.8	2,768.5	2,802.2	2,820.1	2,787.8	2,794.4	2,805.3	2,819.0	2,826.9	2,814.4	2,780.5
2013	2,716.8	2,746.3	2,760.3	2,779.6	2,822.3	2,844.7	2,821.1	2,830.1	2,840.8	2,849.8	2,853.4	2,847.0	2,809.4
2014	2,761.8	2,778.5	2,792.1	2,827.8	2,863.0	2,888.6	2,867.0	2,880.3	2,881.7	2,892.9	2,902.8	2,891.1	2,852.3
2015	2,805.0	2,824.4	2,837.8	2,872.9	2,899.8	2,921.4	2,903.8	2,906.3	2,907.5	2,938.8	2,932.9	2,915.7	2,888.9
Total Private													
2005	2,340.9	2,338.6	2,354.0	2,397.7	2,423.0	2,460.1	2,469.9	2,476.3	2,456.3	2,444.6	2,444.1	2,442.6	2,420.7
2006	2,373.1	2,367.2	2,380.2	2,416.9	2,447.3	2,491.1	2,491.1	2,496.2	2,474.6	2,466.0	2,462.5	2,459.6	2,443.8
2007	2,396.1	2,385.0	2,399.2	2,427.0	2,468.7	2,512.0	2,509.2	2,514.0	2,485.0	2,476.3	2,475.0	2,468.8	2,459.7
2008	2,402.2	2,392.4	2,400.1	2,426.2	2,465.5	2,496.9	2,495.2	2,499.3	2,466.5	2,457.1	2,435.7	2,418.6	2,446.3
2009	2,325.9	2,300.1	2,290.9	2,300.6	2,329.2	2,353.5	2,346.0	2,347.2	2,323.4	2,317.9	2,308.6	2,300.1	2,320.3
2010	2,231.0	2,225.9	2,237.8	2,275.3	2,305.7	2,340.4	2,350.7	2,360.7	2,335.9	2,338.7	2,334.3	2,326.7	2,305.3
2011	2,264.4	2,257.1	2,271.3	2,306.3	2,338.0	2,372.8	2,384.0	2,390.3	2,373.8	2,366.9	2,363.9	2,355.1	2,337.0
2012	2,294.3	2,293.0	2,313.0	2,341.3	2,373.5	2,411.5	2,409.5	2,415.8	2,398.6	2,396.6	2,397.2	2,391.5	2,369.7
2013	2,322.0	2,326.0	2,340.7	2,356.8	2,405.4	2,440.4	2,442.9	2,454.4	2,431.9	2,427.5	2,429.9	2,424.8	2,400.2
2014	2,356.6	2,360.4	2,373.3	2,403.1	2,445.1	2,482.8	2,486.2	2,495.8	2,471.1	2,470.3	2,471.8	2,468.3	2,440.4
2015	2,401.9	2,404.4	2,418.9	2,446.3	2,482.4	2,517.6	2,523.9	2,529.7	2,502.5	2,517.5	2,509.3	2,492.7	2,478.9
Goods-Producing													
2005	612.0	611.3	615.0	628.4	637.1	652.2	656.4	657.0	649.0	644.4	640.5	633.2	636.4
2006	618.8	613.9	617.2	629.7	638.8	656.0	656.7	656.9	648.4	642.9	636.5	630.2	637.2
2007	614.4	607.4	612.2	620.8	633.6	649.2	650.1	650.0	640.9	636.2	632.3	623.2	630.9
2008	606.8	601.7	603.6	610.3	621.3	633.8	633.5	632.1	621.9	616.0	605.5	590.1	614.7
2009	561.4	546.8	538.3	536.2	540.5	546.9	546.2	545.7	541.8	536.5	531.3	521.7	541.1
2010	504.3	500.9	504.7	517.5	526.3	540.1	546.2	548.7	542.8	540.1	536.7	527.8	528.0
2011	515.0	512.5	517.3	529.2	539.9	554.4	561.0	562.0	555.3	551.6	549.2	541.3	540.7
2012	529.3	527.1	533.0	544.3	551.5	566.8	571.5	571.6	563.8	562.1	558.0	552.9	552.7
2013	539.4	537.6	541.0	545.2	559.4	573.0	577.6	579.3	570.8	569.0	566.3	558.0	559.7
2014	546.2	544.5	549.3	559.0	571.5	585.9	593.3	594.2	585.7	583.2	579.9	574.3	572.3
2015	561.8	560.2	563.4	572.8	581.6	594.5	600.3	598.9	590.0	591.4	589.8	583.0	582.3
Service-Providing													
2005	2,139.8	2,151.9	2,162.8	2,196.5	2,211.9	2,222.2	2,199.2	2,200.8	2,221.6	2,223.3	2,229.0	2,236.4	2,199.6
2006	2,164.4	2,173.0	2,187.6	2,214.7	2,234.5	2,253.7	2,221.7	2,222.6	2,240.1	2,244.5	2,250.9	2,254.9	2,221.9
2007	2,191.9	2,194.4	2,209.5	2,233.2	2,262.2	2,284.9	2,247.4	2,248.8	2,258.1	2,263.9	2,269.0	2,274.4	2,244.8
2008	2,212.1	2,212.9	2,223.7	2,245.5	2,276.7	2,285.3	2,254.1	2,254.2	2,267.6	2,273.6	2,271.6	2,264.5	2,253.5
2009	2,183.1	2,184.6	2,185.3	2,199.3	2,224.4	2,228.4	2,192.2	2,186.6	2,190.1	2,207.5	2,208.5	2,210.2	2,200.0
2010	2,142.0	2,150.1	2,160.6	2,193.3	2,216.9	2,221.7	2,194.5	2,196.3	2,204.2	2,227.4	2,231.5	2,225.4	2,197.0
2011	2,161.5	2,171.2	2,182.1	2,207.8	2,226.7	2,229.9	2,209.9	2,209.0	2,227.1	2,234.4	2,236.7	2,236.0	2,211.0
2012	2,160.9	2,177.3	2,199.8	2,224.2	2,250.7	2,253.3	2,216.3	2,222.8	2,241.5	2,256.9	2,268.9	2,261.5	2,227.8
2013	2,177.4	2,208.7	2,219.3	2,234.4	2,262.9	2,271.7	2,243.5	2,250.8	2,270.0	2,280.8	2,287.1	2,289.0	2,249.6
2014	2,215.6	2,234.0	2,242.8	2,268.8	2,291.5	2,302.7	2,273.7	2,286.1	2,296.0	2,309.7	2,322.9	2,316.8	2,280.1
2015	2,243.2	2,264.2	2,274.4	2,300.1	2,318.2	2,326.9	2,303.5	2,307.4	2,317.5	2,347.4	2,343.1	2,332.7	2,306.6
Mining and Logging													
2005	3.3	3.3	3.5	3.8	4.1	4.3	4.4	4.4	4.3	4.2	4.1	3.8	4.0
2006	3.4	3.4	3.5	3.8	4.2	4.3	4.3	4.3	4.2	4.1	3.9	3.7	3.9
2007	3.2	3.2	3.3	3.5	3.9	3.9	4.0	4.0	3.9	3.8	3.7	3.3	3.6
2008	3.0	2.9	3.0	3.1	3.5	3.7	3.7	3.8	3.7	3.6	3.5	3.1	3.4
2009	2.6	2.6	2.6	2.7	3.1	3.2	3.3	3.3	3.3	3.3	3.1	2.8	3.0
2010	2.4	2.4	2.5	2.8	3.1	3.2	3.3	3.3	3.2	3.2	3.1	2.7	2.9
2011	2.5	2.5	2.6	2.7	3.0	3.3	3.3	3.3	3.4	3.4	3.4	3.1	3.0
2012	2.9	2.9	3.1	3.4	3.6	3.7	3.8	3.8	3.8	3.7	3.6	3.4	3.5
2013	3.2	3.2	3.2	3.4	3.8	4.0	4.0	4.1	4.0	4.0	3.9	3.6	3.7
2014	3.4	3.5	3.5	3.8	4.1	4.3	4.4	4.5	4.4	4.5	4.4	4.2	4.1
2015	3.9	4.0	4.0	4.2	4.4	4.4	4.4	4.3	4.2	4.2	4.1	3.8	4.2

1. Employment by Industry: Wisconsin, 2005–2015—*Continued*

(Numbers in thousands, not seasonally adjusted)

Industry and year	January	February	March	April	May	June	July	August	September	October	November	December	Annual average
Construction													
2005	112.1	109.5	111.8	123.2	130.5	136.5	139.5	138.9	136.2	134.6	132.2	125.2	127.5
2006	114.3	111.9	113.4	124.0	131.1	137.8	138.5	138.1	134.9	132.9	129.3	123.6	127.5
2007	112.5	107.9	113.0	120.0	130.2	135.7	137.0	136.9	133.8	132.8	130.0	121.2	125.9
2008	108.0	104.9	106.8	113.8	123.9	127.9	129.4	129.0	125.6	124.1	118.4	108.9	118.4
2009	93.9	91.4	91.0	98.0	105.7	109.5	110.8	109.5	107.6	106.2	102.7	94.3	101.7
2010	82.1	79.9	81.6	92.1	97.1	101.7	103.6	103.9	102.1	102.3	98.5	90.0	94.6
2011	79.2	76.8	79.5	87.7	95.1	100.5	102.8	103.0	101.0	100.3	97.3	89.6	92.7
2012	79.7	78.0	81.5	90.4	95.3	100.6	101.9	102.3	100.5	101.2	98.3	93.1	93.6
2013	83.6	82.9	85.2	89.4	101.0	106.3	108.8	110.2	107.6	107.2	104.4	96.1	98.6
2014	87.1	86.2	89.1	96.2	105.2	111.7	114.1	115.1	113.0	112.5	109.4	103.1	103.6
2015	94.4	93.2	95.5	105.3	112.4	117.3	120.0	119.3	116.7	116.9	115.1	108.9	109.6
Manufacturing													
2005	496.6	498.5	499.7	501.4	502.5	511.4	512.5	513.7	508.5	505.6	504.2	504.2	504.9
2006	501.1	498.6	500.3	501.9	503.5	513.9	513.9	514.5	509.3	505.9	503.3	502.9	505.8
2007	498.7	496.3	495.9	497.3	499.5	509.6	509.1	509.1	503.2	499.6	498.6	498.7	501.3
2008	495.8	493.9	493.8	493.4	493.9	502.2	500.4	499.3	492.6	488.3	483.6	478.1	492.9
2009	464.9	452.8	444.7	435.5	431.7	434.2	432.1	432.9	430.9	427.0	425.5	424.6	436.4
2010	419.8	418.6	420.6	422.6	426.1	435.2	439.3	441.5	437.5	434.6	435.1	435.1	430.5
2011	433.3	433.2	435.2	438.8	441.8	450.6	454.9	455.7	450.9	447.9	448.5	448.6	445.0
2012	446.7	446.2	448.4	450.5	452.6	462.5	465.8	465.5	459.5	457.2	456.1	456.4	455.6
2013	452.6	451.5	452.6	452.4	454.6	462.7	464.8	465.0	459.2	457.8	458.0	458.3	457.5
2014	455.7	454.8	456.7	459.0	462.2	469.9	474.8	474.6	468.3	466.2	466.1	467.0	464.6
2015	463.5	463.0	463.9	463.3	464.8	472.8	475.9	475.3	469.1	470.3	470.6	470.3	468.6
Trade, Transportation, and Utilities													
2005	532.0	526.7	529.0	535.4	541.3	543.8	542.1	543.9	544.1	551.7	561.4	566.8	543.2
2006	536.0	529.6	532.7	536.8	542.9	548.0	542.9	544.3	544.4	549.3	561.4	565.8	544.5
2007	541.3	533.5	536.3	538.3	547.7	552.3	547.5	547.2	546.5	550.0	561.0	563.0	547.1
2008	539.9	531.4	533.2	536.6	543.2	546.3	541.6	542.1	538.8	541.5	546.4	547.7	540.7
2009	520.6	511.9	510.2	512.3	519.0	523.1	515.9	515.7	513.6	517.8	523.2	524.6	517.3
2010	501.3	494.4	496.4	501.7	507.6	512.1	508.0	509.0	507.2	514.7	521.6	524.0	508.2
2011	502.1	495.6	497.8	503.9	508.7	512.1	511.5	512.7	512.2	516.8	525.5	527.8	510.6
2012	505.5	498.6	500.7	503.3	511.2	514.7	511.5	513.2	511.8	517.2	528.9	530.4	512.3
2013	507.6	502.5	504.4	508.5	517.0	522.2	518.8	520.9	517.9	522.6	533.2	537.0	517.7
2014	513.4	509.3	511.9	517.2	524.3	529.2	526.5	527.6	524.4	528.5	539.5	542.9	524.6
2015	519.4	514.3	517.4	520.6	529.1	534.4	534.0	536.5	535.0	543.3	552.6	550.1	532.2
Wholesale Trade													
2005	115.0	114.7	114.9	116.9	117.8	119.3	119.8	119.6	118.4	118.9	119.1	119.8	117.9
2006	118.5	118.1	118.8	119.9	120.6	122.6	122.8	122.5	121.2	121.3	121.4	121.9	120.8
2007	120.0	119.7	120.0	121.1	122.2	124.1	124.3	123.5	122.3	122.2	122.6	122.9	122.1
2008	121.1	120.4	120.9	122.0	123.2	124.3	124.2	123.6	121.5	121.1	120.7	120.1	121.9
2009	117.6	116.5	116.0	115.6	116.2	117.0	116.3	115.3	113.4	113.8	113.5	113.1	115.3
2010	110.6	110.0	110.3	112.0	112.7	114.0	114.7	114.5	112.4	113.3	113.4	113.4	112.6
2011	111.8	111.6	112.1	113.7	114.8	116.2	117.3	116.8	115.5	115.8	115.9	116.0	114.8
2012	114.6	114.4	115.2	116.5	117.2	118.7	118.6	118.0	116.5	116.8	117.0	117.2	116.7
2013	116.8	116.6	116.9	118.1	119.5	120.8	120.8	120.4	118.7	118.8	118.9	119.1	118.8
2014	117.3	117.3	118.1	119.3	120.6	122.0	122.3	122.1	120.1	120.1	120.2	120.5	120.0
2015	119.3	119.0	119.6	121.0	122.4	124.0	124.3	124.0	122.0	123.3	124.6	124.0	122.3
Retail Trade													
2005	311.7	306.2	307.4	310.2	314.0	315.4	315.7	317.7	315.1	321.9	331.5	336.1	316.9
2006	310.4	303.9	305.5	307.6	311.4	314.4	312.5	314.0	311.2	315.5	328.0	331.4	313.8
2007	313.5	305.6	307.6	307.9	314.0	316.1	315.7	315.0	311.9	314.9	325.6	327.4	314.6
2008	310.3	302.5	303.8	305.9	309.9	312.0	311.2	312.0	307.9	310.7	316.8	319.1	310.2
2009	299.4	292.4	291.4	292.5	296.9	299.8	297.8	298.4	294.7	298.5	305.4	307.1	297.9
2010	290.3	283.9	285.3	287.3	291.7	294.5	293.3	294.8	291.6	297.4	304.7	307.0	293.5
2011	290.6	284.6	286.0	289.5	292.2	295.0	295.5	297.1	294.2	298.2	307.0	309.0	294.9
2012	292.0	285.4	286.7	288.1	292.6	295.4	294.5	296.4	293.2	298.0	309.5	310.2	295.2
2013	292.0	287.0	288.2	291.1	296.4	300.8	300.4	301.8	297.8	301.8	311.9	315.0	298.7
2014	296.9	292.6	294.2	297.5	301.6	305.2	305.3	305.7	301.3	304.9	314.7	316.6	303.0
2015	298.9	294.3	296.2	297.4	302.7	306.1	306.9	308.3	305.1	310.6	317.9	315.7	305.0

1. Employment by Industry: Wisconsin, 2005–2015—*Continued*

(Numbers in thousands, not seasonally adjusted)

Industry and year	January	February	March	April	May	June	July	August	September	October	November	December	Annual average
Transportation and Utilities													
2005	105.3	105.8	106.7	108.3	109.5	109.1	106.6	106.6	110.6	110.9	110.8	110.9	108.4
2006	107.1	107.6	108.4	109.3	110.9	111.0	107.6	107.8	112.0	112.5	112.0	112.5	109.9
2007	107.8	108.2	108.7	109.3	111.5	112.1	107.5	108.7	112.3	112.9	112.8	112.7	110.4
2008	108.5	108.5	108.5	108.7	110.1	110.0	106.2	106.5	109.4	109.7	108.9	108.5	108.6
2009	103.6	103.0	102.8	104.2	105.9	106.3	101.8	102.0	105.5	105.5	104.5	104.4	104.1
2010	100.4	100.5	100.8	102.4	103.2	103.6	100.0	99.7	103.2	104.0	103.5	103.6	102.1
2011	99.7	99.4	99.7	100.7	101.7	100.9	98.7	98.8	102.5	102.8	102.6	102.8	100.9
2012	98.9	98.8	98.8	98.7	101.4	100.6	98.4	98.8	102.1	102.4	102.4	103.0	100.4
2013	98.8	98.9	99.3	99.3	101.1	100.6	97.6	98.7	101.4	102.0	102.4	102.9	100.3
2014	99.2	99.4	99.6	100.4	102.1	102.0	98.9	99.8	103.0	103.5	104.6	105.8	101.5
2015	101.2	101.0	101.6	102.2	104.0	104.3	102.8	104.2	107.9	109.4	110.1	110.4	104.9
Information													
2005	49.6	49.4	49.3	49.6	49.7	50.1	49.8	50.0	49.6	49.6	50.0	50.1	49.7
2006	49.6	49.3	49.1	48.9	48.9	49.1	49.2	49.4	48.9	49.3	49.8	50.0	49.3
2007	49.8	49.5	49.4	49.7	49.9	50.4	50.6	50.8	50.3	50.6	50.8	50.9	50.2
2008	50.3	50.0	49.9	50.1	50.9	50.7	50.5	50.5	49.8	49.7	49.9	49.9	50.2
2009	49.1	48.9	48.3	48.0	48.1	48.1	48.1	48.0	47.4	46.9	47.4	47.6	48.0
2010	46.6	46.2	46.1	45.9	46.1	46.7	47.1	47.2	46.8	46.5	47.4	47.4	46.7
2011	46.9	46.6	46.4	46.5	46.5	46.4	47.1	47.2	46.8	46.7	47.2	47.1	46.8
2012	46.4	46.0	45.8	45.9	45.9	46.5	46.8	47.1	46.5	46.6	47.1	46.9	46.5
2013	46.9	46.7	46.5	46.7	47.1	47.2	47.7	47.9	47.1	47.4	47.8	47.9	47.2
2014	47.4	47.3	47.1	47.1	47.5	47.7	48.4	48.8	47.7	48.5	48.7	48.8	47.9
2015	48.5	48.1	47.8	47.9	48.2	48.5	49.6	50.0	49.1	49.0	49.6	49.5	48.8
Financial Activities													
2005	153.1	152.4	152.8	153.5	154.0	155.7	156.4	156.4	155.0	154.6	154.6	155.6	154.5
2006	154.1	153.7	153.8	155.1	156.2	157.6	158.6	158.3	157.0	156.7	156.7	157.6	156.3
2007	156.4	156.1	155.8	156.5	156.9	158.7	158.8	158.3	156.6	157.8	157.7	158.6	157.4
2008	157.4	157.7	157.3	158.1	159.2	160.0	160.7	160.3	157.8	157.3	157.1	157.6	158.4
2009	156.4	155.6	155.1	155.8	156.1	156.9	156.8	156.7	154.1	153.8	153.5	153.8	155.4
2010	152.1	151.7	151.9	152.0	152.2	153.2	153.5	153.2	151.5	151.5	151.3	151.9	152.2
2011	150.2	149.8	149.9	150.3	150.6	151.8	152.3	152.0	151.0	150.6	150.3	150.8	150.8
2012	150.1	149.8	150.0	150.1	150.8	152.2	152.5	152.5	150.8	150.7	150.4	150.9	150.9
2013	149.4	149.2	149.5	149.4	150.3	151.9	152.6	152.4	150.6	150.3	150.0	150.4	150.5
2014	147.9	147.8	148.2	148.9	149.7	151.5	152.0	152.3	150.8	150.0	150.0	150.9	150.0
2015	149.6	149.5	149.7	149.9	151.0	152.6	153.3	152.9	150.9	150.7	151.0	151.3	151.0
Professional and Business Services													
2005	252.6	254.6	257.7	265.3	264.4	268.3	271.5	274.2	273.2	270.7	270.1	270.5	266.1
2006	260.2	263.2	264.6	273.1	273.7	278.5	278.2	280.6	279.7	280.0	278.5	276.7	273.9
2007	268.6	270.4	272.3	279.0	281.3	287.2	286.8	289.8	287.1	287.0	286.6	287.5	282.0
2008	277.4	279.8	278.9	283.5	285.3	288.8	289.6	292.6	289.4	286.5	281.4	278.9	284.3
2009	262.9	258.6	255.6	257.9	258.6	260.4	261.5	263.1	261.5	264.9	265.5	265.8	261.4
2010	256.0	259.5	259.8	269.2	271.0	274.8	279.0	283.2	281.6	285.6	286.0	286.2	274.3
2011	277.2	277.6	280.4	283.9	284.8	290.6	291.3	293.8	294.0	294.0	293.7	291.1	287.7
2012	282.8	284.3	288.2	291.6	292.9	298.2	297.2	298.7	298.8	300.3	301.5	297.6	294.3
2013	287.6	291.3	294.8	294.7	299.6	304.6	306.6	309.1	307.5	307.6	309.0	307.7	301.7
2014	298.0	299.2	299.0	302.3	306.2	309.8	311.2	314.0	312.0	315.4	315.2	311.6	307.8
2015	302.6	303.4	303.9	309.2	311.5	314.5	316.8	319.2	314.3	320.5	315.3	310.8	311.8
Education and Health Services													
2005	373.9	375.8	376.9	379.2	378.8	380.3	378.7	379.0	381.1	382.3	384.4	384.4	379.6
2006	381.5	383.9	384.2	385.3	386.4	387.4	386.3	386.7	388.5	390.8	392.3	392.1	387.1
2007	387.6	389.8	390.7	391.2	392.7	393.5	392.3	393.5	394.7	394.5	395.2	396.2	392.7
2008	392.3	394.3	395.7	396.5	398.1	398.5	397.8	399.5	400.8	405.3	406.5	408.4	399.5
2009	403.7	405.7	407.4	405.9	406.3	406.1	404.4	405.0	405.2	408.9	409.0	409.3	406.4
2010	405.4	407.5	409.3	406.5	407.1	406.1	405.5	406.0	406.2	409.5	410.5	411.0	407.6
2011	405.2	407.5	408.4	410.4	411.6	408.2	406.9	407.4	412.8	415.9	416.7	418.1	410.8
2012	410.1	415.6	418.2	418.4	419.3	416.2	410.6	413.3	420.2	425.1	425.8	427.1	418.3
2013	416.7	423.4	424.8	425.0	425.5	422.0	416.1	419.3	425.4	429.6	430.7	431.0	424.1
2014	422.8	429.3	430.7	431.4	431.5	429.3	423.2	425.7	431.7	435.1	436.9	438.1	430.5
2015	427.6	434.8	436.7	436.3	435.7	433.5	428.1	429.8	435.9	442.5	443.5	443.1	435.6

1. Employment by Industry: Wisconsin, 2005–2015—*Continued*

(Numbers in thousands, not seasonally adjusted)

Industry and year	January	February	March	April	May	June	July	August	September	October	November	December	Annual average
Leisure and Hospitality													
2005	233.8	233.9	237.7	250.3	261.5	271.9	278.0	278.8	267.7	255.2	247.7	245.6	255.2
2006	239.0	239.6	243.4	252.6	264.4	276.5	282.1	283.1	271.0	260.6	251.4	250.2	259.5
2007	242.9	242.8	246.0	254.2	268.6	281.0	284.1	286.1	271.4	261.9	253.6	251.0	262.0
2008	242.2	241.1	244.2	252.7	268.3	277.9	281.2	282.2	268.7	259.6	249.2	246.1	259.5
2009	235.1	235.6	237.9	246.3	262.0	271.9	274.0	274.3	262.2	251.5	241.5	239.6	252.7
2010	230.8	230.7	233.6	245.4	258.1	268.8	273.1	275.4	262.8	253.0	244.1	241.2	251.4
2011	232.7	232.4	235.0	245.1	258.4	270.3	275.1	276.7	264.3	253.8	244.3	241.0	252.4
2012	234.4	235.4	240.4	250.2	263.9	276.5	280.2	280.6	269.0	256.6	247.8	247.6	256.9
2013	238.8	239.6	243.2	250.4	268.6	279.8	284.5	286.6	273.8	262.5	253.6	252.6	261.2
2014	242.5	243.8	246.8	255.8	271.8	284.5	286.3	287.5	273.8	264.4	256.3	255.2	264.1
2015	247.3	248.5	253.1	262.5	277.5	290.3	292.6	293.6	279.9	270.2	258.6	255.9	269.2
Other Services													
2005	133.9	134.5	135.6	136.0	136.2	137.8	137.0	137.0	136.6	136.1	135.4	136.4	136.0
2006	133.9	134.0	135.2	135.4	136.0	138.0	137.1	136.9	136.7	136.4	135.9	137.0	136.0
2007	135.1	135.5	136.5	137.3	138.0	139.7	139.0	138.3	137.5	138.3	137.8	138.4	137.6
2008	135.9	136.4	137.3	138.4	139.2	140.9	140.3	140.0	139.3	141.2	139.7	139.9	139.0
2009	136.7	137.0	138.1	138.2	138.6	140.1	139.1	138.7	137.6	137.6	137.2	137.7	138.1
2010	134.5	135.0	136.0	137.1	137.3	138.6	138.3	138.0	137.0	137.8	136.7	137.2	137.0
2011	135.1	135.1	136.1	137.0	137.5	139.0	138.8	138.5	137.4	137.5	137.0	137.9	137.2
2012	135.7	136.2	136.7	137.5	138.0	140.4	139.2	138.8	137.7	138.0	137.7	138.1	137.8
2013	135.6	135.7	136.5	136.9	137.9	139.7	139.0	138.9	138.8	138.5	139.3	140.2	138.1
2014	138.4	139.2	140.3	141.4	142.6	144.9	145.3	145.7	145.0	145.2	145.3	146.5	143.3
2015	145.1	145.6	146.9	147.1	147.8	149.3	149.2	148.8	147.4	149.9	148.9	149.0	147.9
Government													
2005	410.9	424.6	423.8	427.2	426.0	414.3	385.7	381.5	414.3	423.1	425.4	427.0	415.3
2006	410.1	419.7	424.6	427.5	426.0	418.6	387.3	383.3	413.9	421.4	424.9	425.5	415.2
2007	410.2	416.8	422.5	427.0	427.1	422.1	388.3	384.8	414.0	423.8	426.3	428.8	416.0
2008	416.7	422.2	427.2	429.6	432.5	422.2	392.4	387.0	423.0	432.5	441.4	436.0	421.9
2009	418.6	431.3	432.7	434.9	435.7	421.8	392.4	385.1	408.5	426.1	431.2	431.8	420.8
2010	415.3	425.1	427.5	435.5	437.5	421.4	390.0	384.3	411.1	428.8	433.9	426.5	419.7
2011	412.1	426.6	428.1	430.7	428.6	411.5	386.9	380.7	408.6	419.1	422.0	422.2	414.8
2012	395.9	411.4	419.8	427.2	428.7	408.6	378.3	378.6	406.7	422.4	429.7	422.9	410.9
2013	394.8	420.3	419.6	422.8	416.9	404.3	378.2	375.7	408.9	422.3	423.5	422.2	409.1
2014	405.2	418.1	418.8	424.7	417.9	405.8	380.8	384.5	410.6	422.6	431.0	422.8	411.9
2015	403.1	420.0	418.9	426.6	417.4	403.8	379.9	376.6	405.0	421.3	423.6	423.0	409.9

2. Average Weekly Hours by Selected Industry: Wisconsin, 2011–2015

(Not seasonally adjusted)

Industry and year	January	February	March	April	May	June	July	August	September	October	November	December	Annual average
Total Private													
2011	32.9	32.4	32.8	32.9	33.3	33.1	33.3	33.3	33.3	33.7	33.2	33.3	33.1
2012	33.3	33.2	33.0	33.5	33.1	33.5	33.9	33.6	33.9	33.5	33.3	33.7	33.5
2013	33.2	33.4	33.4	33.3	33.3	33.8	33.6	33.7	33.8	33.5	33.4	33.6	33.5
2014	33.0	33.8	33.9	33.5	33.7	34.2	33.9	34.0	34.1	34.0	34.1	33.8	33.8
2015	33.4	33.7	33.8	33.4	33.6	33.7	33.8	34.1	33.6	33.7	34.0	33.6	33.7
Goods-Producing													
2011	38.8	38.4	39.1	39.3	39.6	39.8	39.6	40.1	40.7	40.3	40.0	40.2	39.7
2012	39.9	39.7	39.4	39.6	39.7	39.8	39.5	39.6	39.6	39.5	38.9	39.4	39.5
2013	39.5	39.4	39.6	39.5	39.5	40.2	39.9	40.1	40.0	40.1	40.0	39.8	39.8
2014	38.9	39.6	40.0	39.8	40.4	40.8	40.6	41.0	41.3	40.9	41.0	40.8	40.4
2015	40.3	39.8	40.0	40.3	40.9	40.7	40.7	41.0	40.6	41.3	41.1	40.6	40.6
Construction													
2011	35.7	34.8	35.5	36.8	37.9	38.0	38.3	38.1	38.1	37.6	35.6	36.6	37.0
2012	35.2	35.1	35.3	36.2	36.9	37.9	37.3	37.9	38.2	38.6	37.2	37.5	37.0
2013	37.1	36.0	37.1	36.2	39.1	40.0	40.0	40.3	39.7	40.0	38.8	37.2	38.6
2014	36.3	36.7	37.5	38.6	40.5	41.1	41.0	41.2	41.0	40.4	39.7	39.0	39.6
2015	37.9	36.0	37.8	38.6	39.7	38.6	39.0	39.7	38.4	40.7	39.0	38.6	38.7
Manufacturing													
2011	39.6	39.2	39.9	39.8	39.9	40.2	39.5	40.3	40.8	40.4	40.6	40.5	40.1
2012	40.4	40.3	39.9	40.1	40.1	40.0	39.8	39.8	39.8	39.5	39.1	39.6	39.9
2013	39.8	40.1	40.1	40.2	39.5	40.1	39.7	39.9	39.9	40.0	40.2	40.3	40.0
2014	39.4	40.1	40.4	39.9	40.3	40.7	40.4	40.8	41.2	40.9	41.2	41.1	40.5
2015	40.7	40.5	40.3	40.6	41.0	41.1	41.0	41.3	40.5	40.7	41.0	40.5	40.8
Trade, Transportation, and Utilities													
2011	32.0	31.6	31.9	32.1	32.6	32.7	32.6	32.5	32.7	32.7	32.5	32.6	32.4
2012	31.6	32.0	31.7	32.0	31.7	32.3	32.4	32.3	32.6	32.7	32.3	32.6	32.2
2013	31.8	32.0	32.7	32.3	32.5	32.8	32.7	32.8	33.0	32.3	32.0	32.5	32.5
2014	31.8	32.8	32.8	32.8	33.1	33.2	33.1	33.3	33.4	33.4	33.5	33.9	33.1
2015	33.2	33.8	33.9	33.4	33.9	33.8	34.0	34.0	33.5	33.4	33.7	33.6	33.7
Financial Activities													
2011	36.8	34.8	34.8	35.3	36.8	35.2	35.8	35.6	36.0	37.1	35.8	35.6	35.8
2012	37.1	36.1	36.3	37.5	35.9	36.4	37.6	36.6	37.8	36.4	36.5	38.0	36.8
2013	36.5	36.9	36.6	36.6	36.4	37.5	36.4	36.6	37.5	36.6	36.6	38.0	36.9
2014	37.1	38.0	38.1	37.0	37.0	38.5	37.2	37.1	36.9	37.1	38.1	37.1	37.4
2015	36.7	37.6	37.9	36.5	36.5	36.3	36.0	37.8	37.1	36.8	37.9	37.2	37.0
Professional and Business Services													
2011	34.2	33.2	33.3	33.6	34.2	33.6	33.2	33.5	33.2	34.1	33.4	33.0	33.5
2012	33.2	33.1	33.3	34.1	33.8	33.8	34.7	33.9	34.6	34.1	33.8	34.2	33.9
2013	33.4	34.5	34.0	33.8	33.7	34.7	34.0	34.6	34.6	34.6	34.5	34.8	34.3
2014	34.1	35.4	35.7	34.9	34.9	35.6	34.8	34.7	34.8	35.0	35.0	34.6	35.0
2015	34.1	34.6	34.8	34.1	34.5	34.6	34.4	34.8	34.0	34.4	35.1	34.3	34.5
Education and Health Services													
2011	30.9	30.7	30.5	30.6	30.8	30.9	31.2	31.0	31.1	31.8	31.5	31.9	31.1
2012	32.0	31.7	31.3	31.6	31.5	31.8	32.3	32.0	32.3	31.9	32.1	32.1	31.9
2013	32.0	31.8	31.7	31.7	31.6	31.8	31.6	31.4	31.7	31.3	31.5	31.7	31.6
2014	31.5	31.7	31.7	31.4	31.5	31.6	31.3	31.3	31.4	31.5	31.8	31.4	31.5
2015	31.2	31.4	31.2	30.9	30.9	30.8	30.9	31.1	31.0	30.8	31.0	30.9	31.0
Leisure and Hospitality													
2011	21.3	22.0	22.1	22.2	22.6	23.7	24.6	23.6	22.7	22.8	22.0	21.9	22.7
2012	21.7	22.1	21.9	22.1	21.9	23.2	24.0	23.4	23.1	22.5	22.1	22.0	22.5
2013	21.5	22.4	22.3	21.9	22.5	23.2	23.4	23.2	22.8	22.6	22.2	22.2	22.5
2014	21.4	22.5	22.5	21.9	22.1	22.9	23.4	23.4	22.8	22.6	22.6	22.0	22.5
2015	21.8	22.5	22.4	22.1	22.0	22.7	22.9	23.2	22.1	22.0	21.8	21.8	22.3
Other Services													
2011	26.7	26.2	27.4	26.9	27.5	26.6	27.6	28.6	26.7	28.3	27.7	27.6	27.3
2012	28.2	28.1	29.1	28.7	28.1	29.6	30.4	29.4	28.2	28.2	28.8	29.7	28.9
2013	29.5	29.6	29.0	29.4	28.9	30.1	29.9	30.5	29.3	29.4	29.4	30.6	29.6
2014	30.6	30.6	30.4	29.6	29.0	30.1	29.2	29.5	29.1	28.7	27.9	28.1	29.4
2015	27.6	27.6	28.1	27.1	27.2	29.0	29.2	29.5	27.8	27.7	28.0	27.8	28.1

3. Average Hourly Earnings by Selected Industry: Wisconsin, 2011–2015

(Dollars, not seasonally adjusted)

Industry and year	January	February	March	April	May	June	July	August	September	October	November	December	Annual average
Total Private													
2011	21.98	22.05	21.78	21.94	21.92	21.50	21.76	21.61	21.75	22.07	21.86	21.94	21.85
2012	22.29	22.14	22.20	22.47	22.18	22.01	22.30	22.04	22.63	22.51	22.66	23.14	22.38
2013	23.10	23.22	23.00	23.26	23.04	22.90	22.92	22.83	23.36	23.10	23.19	23.39	23.11
2014	23.48	23.59	23.45	23.57	23.23	23.11	22.99	22.91	23.11	23.08	23.23	23.21	23.24
2015	23.57	23.60	23.54	23.52	23.40	23.09	23.11	23.25	23.38	23.61	23.69	23.82	23.46
Goods-Producing													
2011	23.04	23.06	22.69	22.96	22.86	22.49	22.89	22.46	22.58	22.78	22.53	22.57	22.74
2012	22.47	22.42	22.63	22.65	22.67	22.58	22.63	22.72	22.86	23.14	23.40	23.53	22.81
2013	23.11	23.21	23.17	23.33	23.37	23.40	23.33	23.23	23.68	23.54	23.55	23.81	23.40
2014	23.87	23.90	23.94	24.11	23.96	23.94	23.85	23.92	24.10	24.23	24.34	24.67	24.07
2015	24.44	24.53	24.61	24.73	24.62	24.38	24.48	24.55	24.48	24.66	24.63	25.08	24.60
Construction													
2011	28.50	29.11	29.01	28.44	27.73	27.27	27.91	27.55	27.79	27.90	27.47	28.21	28.01
2012	26.98	26.81	27.24	26.64	26.68	26.29	26.24	26.51	26.26	26.43	26.31	26.49	26.54
2013	25.96	25.95	26.05	26.40	25.68	25.76	26.06	25.89	26.56	26.47	26.72	27.19	26.22
2014	27.33	26.85	27.08	26.58	25.75	26.03	26.15	26.69	27.08	27.28	26.89	27.39	26.73
2015	27.37	27.26	27.77	27.99	27.91	27.67	27.64	27.82	27.36	27.65	27.72	27.91	27.68
Manufacturing													
2011	21.96	21.93	21.53	21.78	21.68	21.29	21.63	21.23	21.31	21.55	21.43	21.39	21.55
2012	21.60	21.57	21.75	21.85	21.80	21.72	21.79	21.79	22.02	22.30	22.58	22.75	21.96
2013	22.40	22.44	22.36	22.50	22.59	22.59	22.38	22.32	22.72	22.58	22.56	22.91	22.53
2014	23.03	23.18	23.18	23.43	23.36	23.24	23.13	23.10	23.27	23.39	23.66	24.02	23.33
2015	23.79	23.96	23.92	23.94	23.79	23.54	23.64	23.62	23.71	23.81	23.80	24.37	23.82
Trade, Transportation, and Utilities													
2011	19.36	19.11	18.90	19.20	19.05	18.75	19.17	19.07	19.17	19.76	19.22	19.06	19.15
2012	19.84	19.82	19.67	20.19	19.67	19.40	19.92	19.51	20.08	19.62	19.60	20.04	19.78
2013	20.38	20.49	19.82	20.31	20.06	20.03	19.85	19.94	20.31	19.92	19.75	19.58	20.03
2014	19.69	19.89	19.94	20.15	19.99	20.09	20.35	19.97	20.15	20.18	20.25	19.93	20.05
2015	20.68	20.84	20.65	20.96	20.64	20.38	20.57	20.63	20.71	20.57	20.41	20.44	20.62
Financial Activities													
2011	26.23	27.96	27.64	27.30	27.35	27.40	27.73	27.93	27.67	28.52	28.38	28.65	27.73
2012	28.84	29.47	28.95	29.43	28.84	28.54	28.89	28.34	28.78	28.57	28.48	28.83	28.83
2013	29.46	29.09	28.92	29.77	29.04	28.57	28.61	28.28	28.62	28.20	28.37	28.33	28.77
2014	28.61	29.49	28.81	29.00	28.12	28.26	28.00	28.37	28.55	28.22	28.89	29.22	28.63
2015	29.60	29.91	29.75	29.33	29.98	29.31	29.79	29.54	29.21	29.91	29.49	29.38	29.60
Professional and Business Services													
2011	26.31	26.16	26.02	26.04	26.07	25.82	26.01	25.55	25.97	26.05	26.01	26.64	26.05
2012	26.99	26.02	26.26	26.54	26.01	25.87	26.60	26.00	26.75	26.61	26.72	27.77	26.52
2013	27.61	28.58	28.35	28.58	28.79	28.92	29.95	29.66	29.75	29.28	29.49	29.51	29.06
2014	29.69	29.80	29.13	29.54	28.76	28.50	28.05	27.66	27.26	27.11	27.09	26.71	28.26
2015	27.13	26.82	26.86	26.16	25.96	25.80	25.51	25.78	26.04	26.46	26.94	26.96	26.36
Education and Health Services													
2011	21.95	22.27	22.03	22.27	22.40	22.30	22.63	22.57	22.38	22.55	22.48	22.63	22.37
2012	22.82	22.75	22.95	23.19	23.19	23.22	23.40	23.07	23.52	23.34	23.49	23.86	23.24
2013	23.76	23.53	23.50	23.56	23.44	23.18	23.09	23.15	23.90	23.47	23.80	24.39	23.57
2014	24.32	24.16	24.22	24.12	24.06	24.01	23.95	24.06	24.61	24.17	24.28	24.50	24.21
2015	24.93	24.67	24.52	24.57	24.59	24.39	24.29	24.56	24.73	24.86	25.06	25.15	24.70
Leisure and Hospitality													
2011	12.02	12.07	11.94	11.95	11.96	11.70	11.61	11.58	11.82	11.80	11.92	11.94	11.84
2012	11.90	11.92	11.96	11.92	11.80	11.63	11.59	11.59	11.85	11.89	11.89	11.92	11.81
2013	11.86	11.81	11.85	11.93	11.71	11.48	11.49	11.55	11.75	11.98	12.06	12.16	11.79
2014	12.23	12.29	12.25	12.39	12.26	11.96	11.80	12.00	12.09	12.49	12.59	12.59	12.23
2015	12.73	13.03	12.95	13.13	13.01	12.72	12.70	12.69	13.02	13.43	13.52	13.49	13.02
Other Services													
2011	18.95	18.66	18.68	18.53	18.55	18.25	18.41	18.23	18.51	18.42	18.59	19.06	18.57
2012	19.18	19.40	19.39	19.17	18.82	18.55	18.70	18.75	19.44	19.36	19.66	20.00	19.20
2013	19.79	19.95	20.08	19.77	19.71	19.42	19.19	19.11	20.53	20.89	19.77	21.02	19.94
2014	20.80	20.55	20.19	19.99	19.96	19.31	19.10	19.02	19.05	18.81	19.04	18.51	19.53
2015	19.39	19.56	19.47	19.61	19.65	19.20	19.01	19.19	19.48	18.75	19.17	19.27	19.31

4. Average Weekly Earnings by Selected Industry: Wisconsin, 2011–2015

(Dollars, not seasonally adjusted)

Industry and year	January	February	March	April	May	June	July	August	September	October	November	December	Annual average
Total Private													
2011	723.14	714.42	714.38	721.83	729.94	711.65	724.61	719.61	724.28	743.76	725.75	730.60	723.24
2012	742.26	735.05	732.60	752.75	734.16	737.34	755.97	740.54	767.16	754.09	754.58	779.82	749.73
2013	766.92	775.55	768.20	774.56	767.23	774.02	770.11	769.37	789.57	773.85	774.55	785.90	774.19
2014	774.84	797.34	794.96	789.60	782.85	790.36	779.36	778.94	788.05	784.72	792.14	784.50	785.51
2015	787.24	795.32	795.65	785.57	786.24	778.13	781.12	792.83	785.57	795.66	805.46	800.35	790.60
Goods-Producing													
2011	893.95	885.50	887.18	902.33	905.26	895.10	906.44	900.65	919.01	918.03	901.20	907.31	902.78
2012	896.55	890.07	891.62	896.94	900.00	898.68	893.89	899.71	905.26	914.03	910.26	927.08	901.00
2013	912.85	914.47	917.53	921.54	923.12	940.68	930.87	931.52	947.20	943.95	942.00	947.64	931.32
2014	928.54	946.44	957.60	959.58	967.98	976.75	968.31	980.72	995.33	991.01	997.94	1,006.54	972.43
2015	984.93	976.29	984.40	996.62	1,006.96	992.27	996.34	1,006.55	993.89	1,018.46	1,012.29	1,018.25	998.76
Construction													
2011	1,017.45	1,013.03	1,029.86	1,046.59	1,050.97	1,036.26	1,068.95	1,049.66	1,058.80	1,049.04	977.93	1,032.49	1,036.37
2012	949.70	941.03	961.57	964.37	984.49	996.39	978.75	1,004.73	1,003.13	1,020.20	978.73	993.38	981.98
2013	963.12	934.20	966.46	955.68	1,004.09	1,030.40	1,042.40	1,043.37	1,054.43	1,058.80	1,036.74	1,011.47	1,012.09
2014	992.08	985.40	1,015.50	1,025.99	1,042.88	1,069.83	1,072.15	1,099.63	1,110.28	1,102.11	1,067.53	1,068.21	1,058.51
2015	1,037.32	981.36	1,049.71	1,080.41	1,108.03	1,068.06	1,077.96	1,104.45	1,050.62	1,125.36	1,081.08	1,077.33	1,071.22
Manufacturing													
2011	869.62	859.66	859.05	866.84	865.03	855.86	854.39	855.57	869.45	870.62	870.06	866.30	864.16
2012	872.64	869.27	867.83	876.19	874.18	868.80	867.24	867.24	876.40	880.85	882.88	900.90	876.20
2013	891.52	899.84	896.64	904.50	892.31	905.86	888.49	890.57	906.53	903.20	906.91	923.27	901.20
2014	907.38	929.52	936.47	934.86	941.41	945.87	934.45	942.48	958.72	956.65	974.79	987.22	944.87
2015	968.25	970.38	963.98	971.96	975.39	967.49	969.24	975.51	960.26	969.07	975.80	986.99	971.86
Trade, Transportation, and Utilities													
2011	619.52	603.88	602.91	616.32	621.03	613.13	624.94	619.78	626.86	646.15	624.65	621.36	620.46
2012	626.94	634.24	623.54	646.08	623.54	626.62	645.41	630.17	654.61	641.57	633.08	653.30	636.92
2013	648.08	655.68	648.11	656.01	651.95	656.98	649.10	654.03	670.23	643.42	632.00	636.35	650.98
2014	626.14	652.39	654.03	660.92	661.67	666.99	673.59	665.00	673.01	674.01	678.38	675.63	663.66
2015	686.58	704.39	700.04	700.06	699.70	688.84	699.38	701.42	693.79	687.04	687.82	686.78	694.89
Financial Activities													
2011	965.26	973.01	961.87	963.69	1,006.48	964.48	992.73	994.31	996.12	1,058.09	1,016.00	1,019.94	992.73
2012	1,069.96	1,063.87	1,050.89	1,103.63	1,035.36	1,038.86	1,086.26	1,037.24	1,087.88	1,039.95	1,039.52	1,095.54	1,060.94
2013	1,075.29	1,073.42	1,058.47	1,089.58	1,057.06	1,071.38	1,041.40	1,035.05	1,073.25	1,032.12	1,038.34	1,076.54	1,061.61
2014	1,061.43	1,120.62	1,097.66	1,073.00	1,040.44	1,088.01	1,041.60	1,052.53	1,053.50	1,046.96	1,100.71	1,084.06	1,070.76
2015	1,086.32	1,124.62	1,127.53	1,070.55	1,094.27	1,063.95	1,072.44	1,116.61	1,083.69	1,100.69	1,117.67	1,092.94	1,095.20
Professional and Business Services													
2011	899.80	868.51	866.47	874.94	891.59	867.55	863.53	855.93	862.20	888.31	868.73	879.12	872.68
2012	896.07	861.26	874.46	905.01	879.14	874.41	923.02	881.40	925.55	907.40	903.14	949.73	899.03
2013	922.17	986.01	963.90	966.00	970.22	1,003.52	1,018.30	1,026.24	1,029.35	1,013.09	1,017.41	1,026.95	996.76
2014	1,012.43	1,054.92	1,039.94	1,030.95	1,003.72	1,014.60	976.14	959.80	948.65	948.85	948.15	924.17	989.10
2015	925.13	927.97	934.73	892.06	895.62	892.68	877.54	897.14	885.36	910.22	945.59	924.73	909.42
Education and Health Services													
2011	678.26	683.69	671.92	681.46	689.92	689.07	706.06	699.67	696.02	717.09	708.12	721.90	695.71
2012	730.24	721.18	718.34	732.80	730.49	738.40	755.82	738.24	759.70	744.55	754.03	765.91	741.36
2013	760.32	748.25	744.95	746.85	740.70	737.12	729.64	726.91	757.63	734.61	749.70	773.16	744.81
2014	766.08	765.87	767.77	757.37	757.89	758.72	749.64	753.08	772.75	761.36	772.10	769.30	762.62
2015	777.82	774.64	765.02	759.21	759.83	751.21	750.56	763.82	766.63	765.69	776.86	777.14	765.70
Leisure and Hospitality													
2011	256.03	265.54	263.87	265.29	270.30	277.29	285.61	273.29	268.31	269.04	262.24	261.49	268.77
2012	258.23	263.43	261.92	263.43	258.42	269.82	278.16	271.21	273.74	267.53	262.77	262.24	265.73
2013	254.99	264.54	264.26	261.27	263.48	266.34	268.87	267.96	267.90	270.75	267.73	269.95	265.28
2014	261.72	276.53	275.63	271.34	270.95	273.88	276.12	280.80	275.65	282.27	284.53	276.98	275.18
2015	277.51	293.18	290.08	290.17	286.22	288.74	290.83	294.41	287.74	295.46	294.74	294.08	290.35
Other Services													
2011	505.97	488.89	511.83	498.46	510.13	485.45	508.12	521.38	494.22	521.29	514.94	526.06	506.96
2012	540.88	545.14	564.25	550.18	528.84	549.08	568.48	551.25	548.21	545.95	566.21	594.00	554.88
2013	583.81	590.52	582.32	581.24	569.62	584.54	573.78	582.86	601.53	614.17	581.24	643.21	590.22
2014	636.48	628.83	613.78	591.70	578.84	581.23	557.72	561.09	554.36	539.85	531.22	520.13	574.18
2015	535.16	539.86	547.11	531.43	534.48	556.80	555.09	566.11	541.54	519.38	536.76	535.71	542.61

WYOMING
At a Glance

Population:
  2005 estimate: 514,157
  2010 estimate: 563,626
  2015 estimate: 586,107

Percent change in population:
  2005–2015: 14.0%
  2010–2015: 4.0%

Percent change in total nonfarm employment:
  2005–2015: 10.0%

Industry with the largest growth in employment, 2005–2015 (thousands):
  Government, 6.3

Industry with the largest decline or smallest growth in employment, 2005–2015 (thousands):
  Manufacturing, 0.1

Civilian labor force:
  2005: 276,527
  2010: 303,297
  2015: 306,012

Unemployment rate and rank among states (highest to lowest):
  2005: 3.6%, 46th
  2010: 6.4%, 45th
  2015: 4.2%, 37th

Over-the-year change in unemployment rates:
  2012–2013: –0.6%
  2013–2014: –0.6%
  2014–2015: 0.1%

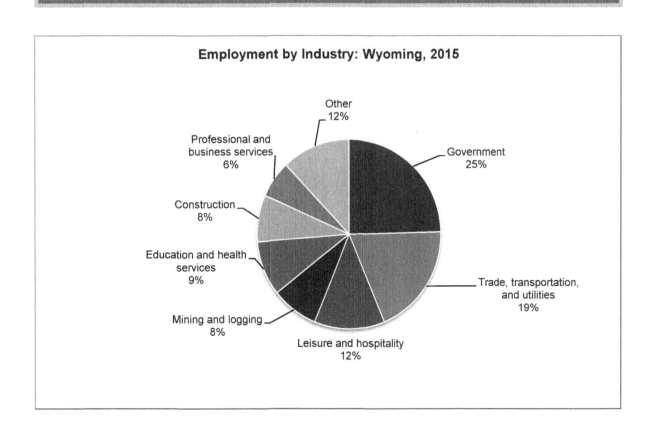

Employment by Industry: Wyoming, 2015

Other 12%
Professional and business services 6%
Construction 8%
Education and health services 9%
Mining and logging 8%
Leisure and hospitality 12%
Government 25%
Trade, transportation, and utilities 19%

1. Employment by Industry: Wyoming, 2005–2015

(Numbers in thousands, not seasonally adjusted)

Industry and year	January	February	March	April	May	June	July	August	September	October	November	December	Annual average
Total Nonfarm													
2005	249.8	251.0	254.3	257.2	264.1	273.1	271.1	271.7	271.7	269.6	266.1	267.5	263.9
2006	262.7	264.6	267.8	269.9	277.9	288.2	283.7	284.1	284.9	282.1	279.4	282.0	277.3
2007	275.4	277.2	280.6	280.7	289.4	298.5	294.8	295.3	296.1	293.9	291.7	292.5	288.8
2008	286.4	288.2	290.0	290.5	299.2	306.5	304.1	303.8	305.4	302.9	297.3	296.0	297.5
2009	286.0	284.1	284.0	281.9	289.2	292.9	287.8	286.8	289.2	283.6	278.8	278.2	285.2
2010	270.4	271.3	273.5	276.1	283.9	290.4	286.4	287.9	290.6	287.8	281.4	281.7	281.8
2011	273.2	274.7	277.1	278.2	285.7	293.6	293.6	294.1	295.8	292.1	286.8	288.1	286.1
2012	279.5	280.9	282.9	284.1	290.3	296.8	295.3	295.2	295.0	291.9	286.8	287.6	288.9
2013	279.4	280.2	282.6	283.1	290.6	298.6	296.9	296.2	295.2	293.2	287.4	288.3	289.3
2014	281.6	282.5	284.4	286.3	294.7	302.1	301.4	300.3	300.0	298.6	290.9	293.0	293.0
2015	285.9	286.1	286.9	286.7	292.2	297.2	297.2	295.9	295.2	291.6	285.4	283.9	290.4
Total Private													
2005	185.1	185.8	188.5	191.4	197.0	206.5	210.1	210.6	206.6	203.1	199.9	201.1	198.8
2006	197.9	199.0	201.6	203.8	210.8	220.8	222.4	223.2	219.4	215.2	212.9	215.0	211.8
2007	209.3	210.3	213.2	213.3	220.6	229.8	232.3	232.8	228.1	224.8	222.6	223.5	221.7
2008	219.0	219.5	220.7	221.0	227.8	236.3	240.3	240.5	235.9	232.3	226.8	225.3	228.8
2009	217.0	213.5	212.8	210.2	216.0	220.8	222.9	222.0	217.8	211.6	207.1	206.4	214.8
2010	200.3	199.8	200.8	203.9	208.9	216.6	220.5	222.2	218.8	215.0	209.1	209.2	210.4
2011	202.6	202.6	204.3	205.5	211.6	220.3	224.4	225.7	223.3	218.8	214.0	215.1	214.0
2012	208.2	207.9	209.5	211.4	216.1	223.7	225.7	226.9	222.4	218.4	213.7	214.3	216.5
2013	207.9	207.4	209.3	210.3	216.7	225.6	228.6	228.3	223.3	220.6	215.2	215.9	217.4
2014	211.0	210.7	211.8	214.3	221.6	230.5	233.1	233.1	228.7	226.5	219.2	221.2	221.8
2015	216.1	215.0	214.9	215.0	219.1	225.3	229.3	227.8	223.0	218.5	212.6	211.2	219.0
Goods-Producing													
2005	47.6	47.8	49.0	50.8	52.6	54.4	55.6	56.2	56.0	56.5	56.1	55.3	53.2
2006	54.6	54.8	55.7	58.2	60.8	62.8	62.8	64.1	63.8	63.9	63.3	62.9	60.6
2007	59.7	59.4	60.6	61.7	63.8	65.8	66.3	67.0	65.9	66.5	66.9	65.6	64.1
2008	63.9	63.6	63.9	64.6	66.9	68.7	70.3	71.1	70.2	70.4	69.0	66.2	67.4
2009	61.6	59.3	58.3	57.7	59.0	58.9	59.4	59.2	58.3	57.6	56.7	55.0	58.4
2010	52.3	51.9	52.5	54.2	55.8	56.9	58.3	59.7	59.3	59.7	57.9	56.1	56.2
2011	52.9	52.7	53.2	54.5	56.5	58.5	59.9	60.7	61.3	61.6	60.7	59.4	57.7
2012	56.1	55.7	56.4	58.3	59.2	59.8	59.9	60.6	60.4	60.1	58.8	57.4	58.6
2013	55.1	54.6	55.2	56.0	58.1	59.6	60.3	60.5	59.5	60.0	59.1	58.5	58.0
2014	56.7	56.6	57.1	58.6	61.4	63.3	63.8	63.7	63.5	63.5	61.7	60.8	60.9
2015	58.3	57.4	56.7	56.9	57.1	57.1	58.2	58.1	57.3	57.4	56.0	53.4	57.0
Service-Providing													
2005	202.2	203.2	205.3	206.4	211.5	218.7	215.5	215.5	215.7	213.1	210.0	212.2	210.8
2006	208.1	209.8	212.1	211.7	217.1	225.4	220.9	220.0	221.1	218.2	216.1	219.1	216.6
2007	215.7	217.8	220.0	219.0	225.6	232.7	228.5	228.3	230.2	227.4	224.8	226.9	224.7
2008	222.5	224.6	226.1	225.9	232.3	237.8	233.8	232.7	235.2	232.5	228.3	229.8	230.1
2009	224.4	224.8	225.7	224.2	230.2	234.0	228.4	227.6	230.9	226.0	222.1	223.2	226.8
2010	218.1	219.4	221.0	221.9	228.1	233.5	228.1	228.2	231.3	228.1	223.5	225.6	225.6
2011	220.3	222.0	223.9	223.7	229.2	235.1	233.7	233.4	234.5	230.5	226.1	228.7	228.4
2012	223.4	225.2	226.5	225.8	231.1	237.0	235.4	234.6	234.6	231.8	228.0	230.2	230.3
2013	224.3	225.6	227.4	227.1	232.5	239.0	236.6	235.7	235.7	233.2	228.3	229.8	231.3
2014	224.9	225.9	227.3	227.7	233.3	238.8	237.6	236.6	236.5	235.1	229.2	232.2	232.1
2015	227.6	228.7	230.2	229.8	235.1	240.1	239.0	237.8	237.9	234.2	229.4	230.5	233.4
Mining and Logging													
2005	21.0	21.3	21.6	21.8	22.1	22.9	23.2	23.4	23.5	23.6	23.9	24.3	22.7
2006	24.6	25.0	25.4	25.8	26.2	27.0	27.3	27.6	27.5	27.5	27.4	27.6	26.6
2007	27.0	26.9	26.8	26.8	27.2	27.7	27.6	27.7	27.5	27.6	27.8	27.9	27.4
2008	28.1	28.1	28.1	28.0	28.6	29.3	29.8	30.2	30.2	30.5	30.5	30.3	29.3
2009	29.2	28.1	27.2	25.8	25.2	24.8	24.6	24.4	24.2	24.1	24.2	24.2	25.5
2010	24.0	24.0	24.1	24.2	24.6	25.1	25.6	25.9	25.8	26.1	26.3	26.5	25.2
2011	26.2	26.2	26.3	26.4	26.7	27.3	27.8	28.1	28.2	28.5	28.6	28.8	27.4
2012	28.3	28.3	28.1	27.8	27.8	28.1	27.8	27.7	27.3	27.3	27.4	27.3	27.8
2013	26.6	26.5	26.5	26.4	26.3	26.6	26.8	26.9	26.7	26.8	26.8	27.0	26.7
2014	26.9	26.8	26.9	26.9	27.0	27.4	27.6	27.8	27.7	27.8	27.9	27.9	27.4
2015	27.4	26.6	25.7	24.5	23.7	23.4	23.3	23.2	22.8	22.9	22.6	22.1	24.0

1. Employment by Industry: Wyoming, 2005–2015—*Continued*

(Numbers in thousands, not seasonally adjusted)

Industry and year	January	February	March	April	May	June	July	August	September	October	November	December	Annual average
Construction													
2005	17.0	17.2	18.0	19.5	21.0	21.8	22.7	23.0	22.7	22.8	22.1	21.0	20.7
2006	20.2	20.1	20.6	22.6	24.6	25.5	25.1	26.2	26.0	25.9	25.4	24.8	23.9
2007	22.4	22.4	23.6	24.9	26.5	28.0	28.6	29.2	28.3	28.6	28.7	27.4	26.6
2008	25.8	25.6	26.2	26.8	28.5	29.4	30.5	30.9	30.1	29.6	28.2	25.9	28.1
2009	22.8	22.0	22.1	23.0	24.9	25.2	25.8	25.8	25.0	24.4	23.5	21.9	23.9
2010	19.7	19.5	19.9	21.6	22.8	23.2	24.0	24.9	24.6	24.5	22.4	20.5	22.3
2011	17.9	17.8	18.3	19.3	20.9	22.1	23.0	23.3	23.8	23.5	22.5	21.0	21.1
2012	18.6	18.2	19.2	21.5	22.3	22.4	22.7	23.6	23.7	23.1	21.8	20.6	21.5
2013	19.1	18.8	19.6	20.5	22.6	23.5	23.9	24.0	23.1	23.2	22.4	21.6	21.9
2014	20.2	20.3	20.6	22.3	24.8	26.1	26.3	26.0	25.9	25.6	23.7	22.8	23.7
2015	21.0	21.0	21.5	22.9	23.7	24.0	25.0	25.2	24.7	24.5	23.5	21.4	23.2
Manufacturing													
2005	9.6	9.3	9.4	9.5	9.5	9.7	9.7	9.8	9.8	10.1	10.1	10.0	9.7
2006	9.8	9.7	9.7	9.8	10.0	10.3	10.4	10.3	10.3	10.5	10.5	10.5	10.2
2007	10.3	10.1	10.2	10.0	10.1	10.1	10.1	10.1	10.1	10.3	10.4	10.3	10.2
2008	10.0	9.9	9.6	9.8	9.8	10.0	10.0	10.0	9.9	10.3	10.3	10.0	10.0
2009	9.6	9.2	9.0	8.9	8.9	8.9	9.0	9.0	9.1	9.1	9.0	8.9	9.1
2010	8.6	8.4	8.5	8.4	8.4	8.6	8.7	8.9	8.9	9.1	9.2	9.1	8.7
2011	8.8	8.7	8.6	8.8	8.9	9.1	9.1	9.3	9.3	9.6	9.6	9.6	9.1
2012	9.2	9.2	9.1	9.0	9.1	9.3	9.4	9.3	9.4	9.7	9.6	9.5	9.3
2013	9.4	9.3	9.1	9.1	9.2	9.5	9.6	9.6	9.7	10.0	9.9	9.9	9.5
2014	9.6	9.5	9.6	9.4	9.6	9.8	9.9	9.9	9.9	10.1	10.1	10.1	9.8
2015	9.9	9.8	9.5	9.5	9.7	9.7	9.9	9.7	9.8	10.0	9.9	9.9	9.8
Trade, Transportation, and Utilities													
2005	48.2	48.2	48.7	49.3	50.4	52.0	52.4	52.5	51.8	51.5	51.5	52.2	50.7
2006	50.7	50.6	51.1	51.0	52.1	53.9	54.2	54.0	53.3	52.8	53.4	54.0	52.6
2007	53.0	53.2	53.8	53.4	54.7	56.3	56.8	56.9	56.1	55.7	56.0	56.7	55.2
2008	55.0	54.7	54.8	54.8	55.8	56.9	57.4	57.3	56.7	56.0	56.0	56.4	56.0
2009	54.1	53.5	53.3	52.8	53.5	54.5	54.5	54.4	53.6	52.5	52.4	52.6	53.5
2010	50.6	50.3	50.3	50.9	51.6	52.9	53.2	53.1	52.5	52.1	52.2	52.7	51.9
2011	50.8	50.7	51.0	51.4	52.3	53.5	54.1	54.1	53.6	52.9	53.2	53.6	52.6
2012	52.1	51.8	52.1	52.5	53.4	54.4	54.7	54.7	53.8	53.5	53.8	54.4	53.4
2013	52.3	52.2	52.5	52.6	54.0	55.2	55.7	55.7	54.5	54.4	54.6	55.1	54.1
2014	53.4	53.1	53.3	53.6	54.7	55.9	56.3	56.5	55.5	55.6	55.7	56.5	55.0
2015	55.1	54.8	55.2	55.1	55.8	56.9	57.5	57.0	56.0	55.6	55.8	56.2	55.9
Wholesale Trade													
2005	7.3	7.4	7.5	7.6	7.8	7.9	7.9	7.9	7.9	7.9	7.9	8.0	7.8
2006	7.8	7.9	8.0	8.0	8.2	8.4	8.3	8.3	8.3	8.3	8.4	8.4	8.2
2007	8.4	8.5	8.6	8.7	8.8	9.0	8.8	8.9	8.8	8.7	8.8	8.9	8.7
2008	8.8	8.8	8.9	9.0	9.2	9.2	9.2	9.2	9.2	9.2	9.2	9.2	9.1
2009	9.0	9.0	8.9	8.8	8.8	8.9	8.7	8.6	8.5	8.4	8.4	8.4	8.7
2010	8.3	8.3	8.4	8.4	8.5	8.6	8.5	8.5	8.5	8.5	8.6	8.6	8.5
2011	8.5	8.6	8.7	8.7	8.8	8.9	8.9	8.9	8.9	8.9	9.0	9.0	8.8
2012	9.0	9.0	9.1	9.3	9.3	9.3	9.2	9.2	9.1	9.1	9.1	9.2	9.2
2013	9.0	9.0	9.1	9.1	9.2	9.2	9.2	9.3	9.2	9.3	9.3	9.4	9.2
2014	9.3	9.3	9.3	9.4	9.5	9.6	9.6	9.6	9.5	9.6	9.6	9.7	9.5
2015	9.6	9.6	9.7	9.6	9.6	9.6	9.6	9.5	9.4	9.1	9.1	9.0	9.5
Retail Trade													
2005	28.9	28.7	29.0	29.2	30.1	31.4	31.7	31.7	31.1	30.7	30.7	31.0	30.4
2006	29.8	29.5	29.8	29.7	30.5	31.8	32.2	32.0	31.3	30.9	31.4	31.7	30.9
2007	30.8	30.8	31.2	30.7	31.7	32.6	33.3	33.1	32.4	32.2	32.4	32.8	32.0
2008	31.6	31.3	31.3	31.2	31.8	32.8	33.3	33.1	32.7	32.2	32.2	32.4	32.2
2009	30.7	30.1	30.1	30.0	30.7	31.4	31.7	31.6	31.0	30.3	30.2	30.3	30.7
2010	28.8	28.7	28.7	28.9	29.5	30.3	30.5	30.2	29.6	29.3	29.3	29.6	29.5
2011	28.2	27.9	28.1	28.4	29.0	29.9	30.4	30.3	29.8	29.3	29.5	29.7	29.2
2012	28.5	28.2	28.3	28.5	29.3	30.3	30.6	30.5	29.8	29.6	29.9	30.1	29.5
2013	28.5	28.3	28.5	28.6	29.7	30.7	31.1	30.9	30.0	29.8	30.0	30.2	29.7
2014	28.7	28.5	28.7	28.9	29.7	30.6	30.9	30.9	30.1	30.1	30.1	30.5	29.8
2015	29.3	29.3	29.6	30.0	30.7	31.5	32.1	31.8	31.1	31.0	31.1	31.2	30.7

1. Employment by Industry: Wyoming, 2005–2015—*Continued*

(Numbers in thousands, not seasonally adjusted)

Industry and year	January	February	March	April	May	June	July	August	September	October	November	December	Annual average
Transportation and Utilities													
2005	12.0	12.1	12.2	12.5	12.5	12.7	12.8	12.9	12.8	12.9	12.9	13.2	12.6
2006	13.1	13.2	13.3	13.3	13.4	13.7	13.7	13.7	13.7	13.6	13.6	13.9	13.5
2007	13.8	13.9	14.0	14.0	14.2	14.7	14.7	14.9	14.9	14.8	14.8	15.0	14.5
2008	14.6	14.6	14.6	14.6	14.8	14.9	14.9	15.0	14.8	14.6	14.6	14.8	14.7
2009	14.4	14.4	14.3	14.0	14.0	14.2	14.1	14.2	14.1	13.8	13.8	13.9	14.1
2010	13.5	13.3	13.2	13.6	13.6	14.0	14.2	14.4	14.4	14.3	14.3	14.5	13.9
2011	14.1	14.2	14.2	14.3	14.5	14.7	14.8	14.9	14.9	14.7	14.7	14.9	14.6
2012	14.6	14.6	14.7	14.7	14.8	14.8	14.9	15.0	14.9	14.8	14.8	15.1	14.8
2013	14.8	14.9	14.9	14.9	15.1	15.3	15.4	15.5	15.3	15.3	15.3	15.5	15.2
2014	15.4	15.3	15.3	15.3	15.5	15.7	15.8	16.0	15.9	15.9	16.0	16.3	15.7
2015	16.2	15.9	15.9	15.5	15.5	15.8	15.8	15.7	15.5	15.5	15.6	16.0	15.7
Information													
2005	4.3	4.3	4.3	4.3	4.3	4.4	4.3	4.3	4.3	4.2	4.3	4.3	4.3
2006	4.3	4.3	4.2	4.1	4.1	4.2	4.1	4.1	4.1	4.0	4.0	4.1	4.1
2007	4.0	4.0	4.0	4.0	4.0	4.1	4.1	4.1	4.0	4.0	4.0	4.1	4.0
2008	4.0	4.0	4.0	4.0	4.0	4.0	4.1	4.1	4.0	4.0	4.0	4.0	4.0
2009	4.0	4.0	4.0	3.9	4.0	4.0	4.0	4.0	3.9	3.9	3.9	3.9	4.0
2010	3.9	3.9	3.9	3.9	3.9	3.9	3.9	3.9	3.9	3.8	3.8	3.8	3.9
2011	3.8	3.8	3.8	3.8	3.9	3.9	3.9	3.9	3.8	3.8	3.8	3.9	3.8
2012	3.9	3.9	3.9	3.9	3.9	4.0	4.0	4.0	3.9	3.8	3.9	3.9	3.9
2013	3.8	3.8	3.8	3.7	3.8	3.8	3.8	3.8	3.8	3.8	3.8	3.8	3.8
2014	3.8	3.7	3.7	3.7	3.8	3.8	3.8	3.8	3.8	3.8	3.8	3.8	3.8
2015	3.8	3.8	3.8	3.8	3.8	3.8	3.8	3.8	3.7	3.7	3.7	3.7	3.8
Financial Activities													
2005	10.5	10.4	10.6	10.6	10.8	11.0	11.0	11.0	10.9	10.8	10.8	11.0	10.8
2006	10.9	10.9	11.0	11.0	11.1	11.3	11.3	11.3	11.2	11.1	11.2	11.3	11.1
2007	11.0	11.0	11.1	11.2	11.3	11.6	11.6	11.6	11.5	11.5	11.4	11.5	11.4
2008	11.4	11.4	11.4	11.5	11.6	11.8	11.9	11.9	11.7	11.7	11.6	11.6	11.6
2009	11.3	11.3	11.2	11.2	11.3	11.4	11.3	11.3	11.1	11.0	10.9	11.0	11.2
2010	10.7	10.7	10.7	10.8	10.9	10.9	10.9	10.8	10.7	10.8	10.7	10.8	10.8
2011	10.7	10.6	10.6	10.7	10.7	10.8	10.8	10.9	10.8	10.7	10.7	10.7	10.7
2012	10.6	10.6	10.7	10.6	10.7	10.9	10.9	11.0	10.8	10.9	10.8	10.8	10.8
2013	10.9	10.9	10.9	11.0	11.1	11.3	11.4	11.4	11.3	11.2	11.2	11.2	11.2
2014	11.0	11.0	11.0	11.0	11.2	11.4	11.4	11.5	11.4	11.4	11.3	11.4	11.3
2015	11.2	11.2	11.1	11.1	11.0	11.1	11.3	11.1	11.1	11.0	11.0	10.9	11.1
Professional and Business Services													
2005	14.5	14.6	14.9	15.5	15.8	16.6	16.8	17.0	16.4	16.3	15.9	15.6	15.8
2006	15.4	15.7	15.9	16.7	17.3	17.9	18.0	18.1	17.8	17.4	17.2	17.3	17.1
2007	16.8	17.1	17.5	17.9	18.8	19.6	19.5	19.5	19.0	18.8	18.0	17.8	18.4
2008	17.3	17.5	17.7	18.2	18.9	19.7	19.8	19.8	19.2	19.0	18.3	18.0	18.6
2009	17.3	17.0	17.0	17.1	17.6	17.9	18.0	18.0	17.5	17.2	16.7	16.3	17.3
2010	16.0	15.8	16.1	16.8	17.2	17.9	18.3	18.6	18.0	17.5	17.0	16.7	17.2
2011	16.4	16.4	16.6	17.1	17.8	18.5	18.8	19.2	18.5	18.2	17.9	17.7	17.8
2012	17.1	17.2	17.3	17.7	18.0	18.9	18.7	19.0	18.4	18.2	17.7	17.6	18.0
2013	16.9	17.0	17.2	17.8	18.3	19.0	19.1	19.0	18.5	18.5	18.3	17.7	18.1
2014	17.1	17.4	17.5	18.1	18.6	19.2	19.5	19.4	18.9	18.9	18.3	18.2	18.4
2015	17.5	17.6	17.6	18.2	18.7	19.0	19.3	19.2	18.6	18.8	18.0	17.4	18.3
Education and Health Services													
2005	21.9	22.0	22.2	21.9	22.0	21.6	21.6	21.7	22.3	22.4	22.6	22.5	22.1
2006	22.4	22.5	22.8	22.4	22.7	22.3	22.1	22.3	22.9	22.9	23.1	22.9	22.6
2007	23.0	23.2	23.3	23.0	23.3	22.9	22.8	23.0	23.7	23.8	24.1	23.9	23.3
2008	24.0	24.4	24.4	24.3	24.3	24.1	24.1	24.2	25.0	25.3	25.2	25.1	24.5
2009	25.5	25.6	25.8	25.5	25.9	25.1	25.1	25.2	25.9	26.1	26.4	26.4	25.7
2010	26.1	26.3	26.4	26.4	26.4	25.8	25.7	25.9	26.7	27.0	27.1	26.9	26.4
2011	26.9	27.2	27.4	27.0	27.1	26.1	25.8	26.1	26.9	26.9	26.6	26.9	26.7
2012	26.5	26.7	26.7	26.6	26.7	26.0	25.8	26.2	26.9	26.9	27.0	27.1	26.6
2013	26.8	26.8	27.2	27.1	27.1	26.5	26.2	26.5	27.1	27.1	27.1	27.1	26.9
2014	27.0	27.0	27.1	27.2	27.3	26.5	26.2	26.4	27.0	27.5	26.9	26.9	26.9
2015	26.9	26.9	27.0	27.0	27.2	26.5	26.3	26.4	27.2	27.6	27.6	27.5	27.0

1. Employment by Industry: Wyoming, 2005–2015—*Continued*

(Numbers in thousands, not seasonally adjusted)

Industry and year	January	February	March	April	May	June	July	August	September	October	November	December	Annual average
Leisure and Hospitality													
2005	28.7	28.9	29.2	29.3	31.3	36.5	38.1	37.6	34.8	31.4	28.7	30.0	32.0
2006	29.3	29.8	30.2	29.6	31.6	37.0	38.4	37.8	35.0	31.8	29.4	31.0	32.6
2007	30.5	31.0	31.3	30.5	32.6	37.4	39.1	38.6	36.0	32.6	30.4	31.9	33.5
2008	31.6	32.0	32.5	31.6	34.1	38.8	40.3	39.7	36.9	33.8	30.6	31.9	34.5
2009	31.1	30.8	31.2	30.1	32.5	36.8	38.5	38.0	35.8	31.8	28.7	29.8	32.9
2010	29.4	29.6	29.6	29.4	31.6	36.7	38.5	38.5	36.1	32.6	28.9	30.8	32.6
2011	29.8	29.8	30.2	29.3	31.7	37.1	39.1	38.9	36.7	33.1	29.6	31.5	33.1
2012	30.6	30.7	31.1	30.4	32.7	38.1	40.1	39.8	36.8	33.9	30.7	32.1	33.9
2013	31.3	31.3	31.7	31.1	33.4	39.0	40.9	40.5	38.0	34.8	31.0	32.5	34.6
2014	32.1	32.1	32.3	31.9	34.3	39.9	41.6	41.5	38.4	35.5	31.4	33.5	35.4
2015	33.2	33.2	33.4	32.8	35.3	40.4	42.4	41.9	39.0	34.2	30.3	31.9	35.7
Other Services													
2005	9.4	9.6	9.6	9.7	9.8	10.0	10.3	10.3	10.1	10.0	10.0	10.2	9.9
2006	10.3	10.4	10.7	10.8	11.1	11.4	11.5	11.5	11.3	11.3	11.3	11.5	11.1
2007	11.3	11.4	11.6	11.6	12.1	12.1	12.1	12.1	11.9	11.9	11.8	12.0	11.8
2008	11.8	11.9	12.0	12.0	12.2	12.3	12.4	12.4	12.2	12.1	12.1	12.1	12.1
2009	12.1	12.0	12.0	11.9	12.2	12.2	12.1	11.9	11.7	11.5	11.4	11.4	11.9
2010	11.3	11.3	11.3	11.5	11.5	11.6	11.7	11.7	11.6	11.5	11.5	11.4	11.5
2011	11.3	11.4	11.5	11.7	11.6	11.9	12.0	11.9	11.7	11.6	11.5	11.4	11.6
2012	11.3	11.3	11.3	11.4	11.5	11.6	11.6	11.6	11.4	11.1	11.0	11.0	11.3
2013	10.8	10.8	10.8	11.0	10.9	11.2	11.2	10.9	10.6	10.8	10.1	10.0	10.8
2014	9.9	9.8	9.8	10.2	10.3	10.5	10.5	10.3	10.2	10.3	10.1	10.1	10.2
2015	10.1	10.1	10.1	10.1	10.2	10.5	10.5	10.3	10.1	10.2	10.2	10.2	10.2
Government													
2005	64.7	65.2	65.8	65.8	67.1	66.6	61.0	61.1	65.1	66.5	66.2	66.4	65.1
2006	64.8	65.6	66.2	66.1	67.1	67.4	61.3	60.9	65.5	66.9	66.5	67.0	65.4
2007	66.1	66.9	67.4	67.4	68.8	68.7	62.5	62.5	68.0	69.1	69.1	69.0	67.1
2008	67.4	68.7	69.3	69.5	71.4	70.2	63.8	63.3	69.5	70.6	70.5	70.7	68.7
2009	69.0	70.6	71.2	71.7	73.2	72.1	64.9	64.8	71.4	72.0	71.7	71.8	70.4
2010	70.1	71.5	72.7	72.2	75.0	73.8	65.9	65.7	71.8	72.8	72.3	72.5	71.4
2011	70.6	72.1	72.8	72.7	74.1	73.3	69.2	68.4	72.5	73.3	72.8	73.0	72.1
2012	71.3	73.0	73.4	72.7	74.2	73.1	69.6	68.3	72.6	73.5	73.1	73.3	72.3
2013	71.5	72.8	73.3	72.8	73.9	73.0	68.3	67.9	71.9	72.6	72.2	72.4	71.9
2014	70.6	71.8	72.6	72.0	73.1	71.6	68.3	67.2	71.3	72.1	71.7	71.8	71.2
2015	69.8	71.1	72.0	71.7	73.1	71.9	67.9	68.1	72.2	73.1	72.8	72.7	71.4

2. Average Weekly Hours by Selected Industry: Wyoming, 2011–2015

(Not seasonally adjusted)

Industry and year	January	February	March	April	May	June	July	August	September	October	November	December	Annual average
Total Private													
2011	35.8	35.3	35.1	36.4	36.3	36.4	36.6	36.5	36.4	37.1	36.0	35.5	36.1
2012	35.9	35.4	35.0	36.3	35.8	36.6	37.1	36.2	37.5	36.6	36.6	37.4	36.4
2013	35.8	36.4	35.7	35.0	36.0	36.8	35.4	36.0	36.5	35.6	36.0	35.8	35.9
2014	35.0	36.3	35.9	35.4	35.3	36.3	35.5	36.2	35.7	35.8	35.6	35.1	35.7
2015	34.8	35.9	35.4	35.0	35.3	35.8	35.6	36.4	34.6	34.5	34.8	33.4	35.1
Goods-Producing													
2011	42.2	41.9	41.9	42.9	42.8	43.4	43.4	43.5	43.2	43.9	43.3	42.2	42.9
2012	41.6	42.4	40.9	42.7	43.2	43.2	42.8	42.3	43.5	43.8	44.1	43.1	42.8
2013	41.7	42.1	41.4	39.8	42.3	42.4	40.8	42.1	41.9	41.1	42.3	41.8	41.6
2014	40.5	41.9	41.7	42.3	41.6	42.2	40.7	42.7	41.5	42.6	40.5	41.6	41.7
2015	40.2	40.6	40.0	40.0	41.4	41.5	41.5	41.9	39.7	41.6	41.3	39.8	40.8
Mining and logging													
2011	46.3	45.4	44.0	45.0	43.9	45.0	45.2	46.1	46.2	48.0	47.1	45.5	45.6
2012	44.2	45.7	44.1	45.0	44.0	44.2	44.7	43.9	44.6	44.7	43.2	43.9	44.3
2013	42.9	42.1	42.9	41.7	42.9	43.9	43.2	44.2	45.3	43.1	45.0	45.0	43.5
2014	45.1	46.2	45.7	45.8	44.9	44.0	43.3	45.0	44.2	45.3	44.5	46.3	45.0
2015	43.8	44.5	44.0	42.9	44.0	42.5	42.8	43.0	41.7	42.6	43.1	42.5	43.2
Construction													
2011	39.9	40.0	41.7	42.8	42.7	44.3	44.3	44.3	43.4	43.3	42.7	41.4	42.7
2012	40.9	41.4	39.6	42.5	44.5	44.7	43.4	42.8	43.8	44.8	45.8	43.8	43.3
2013	42.0	41.8	41.8	38.9	43.5	42.7	41.0	41.8	40.4	40.5	41.2	41.1	41.4
2014	38.3	39.9	39.6	40.7	40.5	42.0	40.0	42.5	41.0	42.3	39.2	40.5	40.6
2015	39.0	39.3	38.8	39.3	40.7	41.6	41.3	41.8	39.9	42.0	41.0	39.2	40.4
Trade, Transportation, and Utilities													
2011	36.4	36.1	35.7	36.7	36.5	36.1	36.5	36.0	35.7	37.0	35.5	35.1	36.1
2012	36.4	35.0	35.1	36.1	35.8	36.4	37.6	36.4	38.0	36.4	36.3	37.8	36.4
2013	36.0	36.9	36.5	35.6	36.6	36.6	35.4	35.6	36.8	36.1	36.2	36.6	36.2
2014	35.4	36.1	36.3	35.3	35.2	35.4	35.1	35.4	35.2	35.0	35.5	34.5	35.4
2015	34.9	36.1	35.7	35.0	35.0	36.0	35.6	35.8	35.2	34.6	34.6	33.8	35.2
Professional and Business Services													
2011	34.2	33.7	32.8	37.3	37.5	36.5	36.8	36.8	36.4	37.9	34.4	34.8	35.8
2012	34.9	35.0	34.6	36.0	34.1	36.1	36.1	34.5	35.8	35.5	35.3	35.4	35.3
2013	34.5	35.3	34.3	34.2	34.2	35.4	33.1	34.1	35.0	34.2	34.8	35.0	34.5
2014	34.0	35.7	34.8	34.5	34.6	36.4	36.1	36.1	35.7	35.7	35.6	35.0	35.4
2015	34.0	35.1	34.9	35.4	35.1	35.4	35.4	36.8	34.9	34.2	34.8	33.4	35.0
Education and Health Services													
2011	35.1	34.3	33.9	35.2	34.9	35.4	35.3	34.9	35.9	35.6	35.4	35.2	35.1
2012	35.8	35.0	35.0	36.2	34.7	35.9	36.2	34.6	36.3	35.1	34.9	36.1	35.5
2013	33.4	34.5	34.2	33.8	33.8	35.5	33.7	34.7	35.3	33.6	34.6	34.3	34.3
2014	33.4	35.1	34.2	33.6	33.7	34.5	33.4	32.9	33.4	33.0	33.5	33.4	33.7
2015	33.4	35.1	34.6	33.8	33.8	34.2	33.3	34.6	33.6	33.6	34.9	33.1	33.9
Leisure and Hospitality													
2011	26.6	25.8	25.8	25.6	25.7	26.8	27.4	27.8	26.5	25.7	24.1	23.5	26.0
2012	24.2	23.6	23.7	24.4	24.0	25.9	27.2	26.4	27.0	24.2	23.7	24.7	25.0
2013	23.9	24.4	24.3	24.3	24.7	27.8	27.7	27.6	27.1	25.6	24.7	24.8	25.7
2014	24.9	26.1	26.4	24.6	25.6	28.7	28.5	28.7	27.4	26.4	26.4	25.7	26.7
2015	26.1	27.4	27.2	25.9	26.7	28.6	29.5	30.2	28.3	25.2	25.0	24.5	27.2
Other Services													
2011	29.8	29.3	30.0	31.4	31.8	33.5	33.1	33.3	33.7	33.8	32.2	33.9	32.2
2012	35.4	34.6	34.0	35.8	34.9	35.1	36.1	36.2	35.7	36.7	36.7	38.0	35.7
2013	36.8	35.4	33.9	34.1	35.0	36.7	34.3	34.5	36.0	36.2	35.4	35.6	35.3
2014	35.4	35.6	35.0	35.6	33.9	35.4	35.0	34.8	34.5	33.3	32.2	30.6	34.3
2015	31.4	32.9	31.8	31.3	30.0	30.3	29.8	30.5	29.3	28.4	28.8	26.7	30.1

3. Average Hourly Earnings by Selected Industry: Wyoming, 2011–2015

(Dollars, not seasonally adjusted)

Industry and year	January	February	March	April	May	June	July	August	September	October	November	December	Annual average
Total Private													
2011	22.00	21.83	21.76	22.69	22.68	21.98	22.05	21.81	22.13	22.36	22.27	22.55	22.18
2012	22.56	22.59	22.66	22.98	22.55	22.17	22.13	22.10	22.65	22.55	22.67	23.06	22.55
2013	22.94	23.01	23.23	23.34	23.05	22.65	22.55	22.53	23.04	22.89	22.98	23.20	22.94
2014	23.36	23.28	23.44	23.42	23.31	22.74	22.66	22.94	23.37	23.30	23.53	23.33	23.22
2015	23.31	23.28	23.34	23.27	23.09	22.65	22.75	23.02	23.26	23.39	23.47	23.30	23.17
Goods-Producing													
2011	26.33	26.05	26.09	26.10	26.52	25.84	25.86	25.48	25.73	25.43	25.42	26.02	25.89
2012	25.79	26.09	26.48	26.64	26.27	25.93	25.90	26.00	26.33	25.97	25.69	26.47	26.13
2013	26.57	26.73	27.24	27.91	27.46	27.21	27.04	27.13	27.59	27.02	27.02	27.47	27.20
2014	28.19	27.71	28.00	27.83	27.83	26.93	27.19	27.26	27.88	27.68	27.89	27.69	27.66
2015	27.85	27.58	27.58	27.69	27.54	27.39	27.56	27.77	27.91	27.77	28.03	28.49	27.76
Mining and logging													
2011	28.58	27.74	27.60	27.50	27.79	27.63	27.99	27.35	27.48	27.84	27.52	28.23	27.77
2012	27.97	28.49	29.18	28.98	29.02	29.13	29.30	29.26	29.55	29.35	28.61	29.76	29.05
2013	29.82	30.01	30.79	31.90	31.80	32.25	32.42	32.69	33.73	33.73	33.50	34.08	32.26
2014	35.13	33.85	33.93	33.72	33.83	33.37	33.82	33.75	34.85	34.04	33.71	34.20	34.02
2015	34.85	34.16	34.36	34.47	34.40	35.04	35.31	36.07	36.34	35.24	35.00	35.69	35.04
Construction													
2011	25.19	25.21	25.35	24.99	25.75	24.48	24.08	23.91	24.61	23.94	23.98	24.63	24.62
2012	24.27	24.55	24.61	25.07	24.31	23.60	23.24	23.34	23.62	23.56	23.76	24.47	23.99
2013	24.43	25.15	24.96	26.18	25.64	24.81	24.54	24.65	25.12	24.56	24.85	25.48	25.02
2014	25.54	25.45	26.19	26.24	26.34	24.96	24.99	24.98	25.30	25.31	25.32	24.99	25.44
2015	25.21	25.14	25.15	25.68	25.50	24.96	25.20	25.28	25.13	25.69	25.92	25.97	25.40
Trade, Transportation, and Utilities													
2011	20.95	20.73	20.77	21.38	20.96	20.63	20.81	20.99	21.05	21.65	21.10	21.71	21.06
2012	22.52	22.14	22.40	23.37	22.45	22.42	22.60	22.36	23.10	22.77	22.84	23.18	22.69
2013	22.82	22.59	22.73	22.95	22.58	22.53	22.12	21.94	22.48	22.16	22.05	22.06	22.41
2014	21.94	22.28	22.33	22.39	21.89	21.68	21.43	21.58	21.79	21.52	21.79	21.55	21.84
2015	21.33	21.51	21.95	21.71	21.30	21.10	21.31	21.60	20.91	20.65	20.75	20.39	21.21
Professional and Business Services													
2011	26.36	26.25	25.87	29.65	28.51	27.02	26.37	26.72	26.68	27.30	27.93	28.02	27.25
2012	27.45	27.10	26.40	26.37	25.46	24.56	24.45	24.16	25.10	25.15	25.33	25.50	25.55
2013	25.23	25.19	25.63	25.52	25.17	25.33	25.84	25.53	25.92	26.05	25.75	26.32	25.63
2014	26.07	25.80	25.92	26.16	26.05	25.68	25.88	26.39	26.67	26.67	26.81	26.98	26.26
2015	27.52	27.27	27.23	27.03	26.63	26.10	26.03	26.12	27.55	27.16	26.39	26.38	26.77
Education and Health Services													
2011	20.03	20.06	19.74	19.83	20.43	19.81	19.87	20.02	20.57	20.32	20.03	20.25	20.08
2012	20.14	20.17	20.28	20.19	20.05	20.08	20.21	20.14	20.52	20.04	20.73	21.15	20.31
2013	21.60	22.00	22.11	21.84	21.49	21.13	21.65	21.56	21.93	21.82	21.60	22.02	21.73
2014	21.91	21.65	21.68	21.30	21.36	21.15	21.34	21.43	21.86	21.45	21.97	22.17	21.61
2015	22.37	22.87	22.83	22.65	22.68	22.65	22.85	22.94	22.82	22.60	22.71	22.42	22.70
Leisure and Hospitality													
2011	12.87	12.75	12.68	12.28	12.40	11.90	11.87	11.77	12.09	11.98	12.00	12.35	12.21
2012	12.41	12.49	12.35	12.28	12.17	11.90	11.85	11.83	12.10	12.10	12.21	12.41	12.14
2013	12.47	12.45	12.43	12.28	12.23	12.09	12.49	12.18	12.49	12.53	12.64	12.72	12.41
2014	13.15	13.25	13.33	12.93	12.93	12.99	13.02	13.33	13.48	13.53	13.84	14.11	13.31
2015	14.06	14.30	14.14	13.91	13.56	13.44	13.36	13.46	13.70	13.68	13.63	13.74	13.72
Other Services													
2011	19.91	19.71	20.61	20.59	20.17	20.47	20.33	21.48	21.28	21.72	22.06	21.52	20.85
2012	21.38	21.50	21.23	20.32	20.71	21.29	21.29	21.18	20.98	20.79	20.79	21.07	21.04
2013	20.47	21.06	21.24	20.29	20.26	19.61	19.39	19.30	18.98	19.30	19.63	19.84	19.94
2014	19.47	19.65	19.57	19.26	20.04	19.78	19.06	19.21	19.39	19.13	19.17	19.26	19.42
2015	19.93	20.89	20.72	20.07	21.27	19.96	20.84	21.65	20.65	20.01	20.53	20.68	20.60

4. Average Weekly Earnings by Selected Industry: Wyoming, 2011–2015

(Dollars, not seasonally adjusted)

Industry and year	January	February	March	April	May	June	July	August	September	October	November	December	Annual average
Total Private													
2011	787.60	770.60	763.78	825.92	823.28	800.07	807.03	796.07	805.53	829.56	801.72	800.53	800.70
2012	809.90	799.69	793.10	834.17	807.29	811.42	821.02	800.02	849.38	825.33	829.72	862.44	820.82
2013	821.25	837.56	829.31	816.90	829.80	833.52	798.27	811.08	840.96	814.88	827.28	830.56	823.55
2014	817.60	845.06	841.50	829.07	822.84	825.46	804.43	830.43	834.31	834.14	837.67	818.88	828.95
2015	811.19	835.75	826.24	814.45	815.08	810.87	809.90	837.93	804.80	806.96	816.76	778.22	813.27
Goods-Producing													
2011	1,111.13	1,091.50	1,093.17	1,119.69	1,135.06	1,121.46	1,122.32	1,108.38	1,111.54	1,116.38	1,100.69	1,098.04	1,110.68
2012	1,072.86	1,106.22	1,083.03	1,137.53	1,134.86	1,120.18	1,108.52	1,099.80	1,145.36	1,137.49	1,132.93	1,140.86	1,118.36
2013	1,107.97	1,125.33	1,127.74	1,110.82	1,161.56	1,153.70	1,103.23	1,142.17	1,156.02	1,110.52	1,142.95	1,148.25	1,131.52
2014	1,141.70	1,161.05	1,167.60	1,177.21	1,157.73	1,136.45	1,106.63	1,164.00	1,157.02	1,179.17	1,129.55	1,151.90	1,153.42
2015	1,119.57	1,119.75	1,103.20	1,107.60	1,140.16	1,136.69	1,143.74	1,163.56	1,108.03	1,155.23	1,157.64	1,133.90	1,132.61
Mining and Logging													
2011	1,323.25	1,259.40	1,214.40	1,237.50	1,219.98	1,243.35	1,265.15	1,260.84	1,269.58	1,336.32	1,296.19	1,284.47	1,266.31
2012	1,236.27	1,301.99	1,286.84	1,304.10	1,276.88	1,287.55	1,309.71	1,284.51	1,317.93	1,311.95	1,235.95	1,306.46	1,286.92
2013	1,279.28	1,263.42	1,320.89	1,330.23	1,364.22	1,415.78	1,400.54	1,444.90	1,527.97	1,453.76	1,507.50	1,533.60	1,403.31
2014	1,584.36	1,563.87	1,550.60	1,544.38	1,518.97	1,468.28	1,464.41	1,518.75	1,540.37	1,542.01	1,500.10	1,583.46	1,530.90
2015	1,526.43	1,520.12	1,511.84	1,478.76	1,513.60	1,489.20	1,511.27	1,551.01	1,515.38	1,501.22	1,508.50	1,516.83	1,513.73
Construction													
2011	1,005.08	1,008.40	1,057.10	1,069.57	1,099.53	1,084.46	1,066.74	1,059.21	1,068.07	1,036.60	1,023.95	1,019.68	1,051.27
2012	992.64	1,016.37	974.56	1,065.48	1,081.80	1,054.92	1,008.62	998.95	1,034.56	1,055.49	1,088.21	1,071.79	1,038.77
2013	1,026.06	1,051.27	1,043.33	1,018.40	1,115.34	1,059.39	1,006.14	1,030.37	1,014.85	994.68	1,023.82	1,047.23	1,035.83
2014	978.18	1,015.46	1,037.12	1,067.97	1,066.77	1,048.32	999.60	1,061.65	1,037.30	1,070.61	992.54	1,012.10	1,032.86
2015	983.19	988.00	975.82	1,009.22	1,037.85	1,038.34	1,040.76	1,056.70	1,002.69	1,078.98	1,062.72	1,018.02	1,026.16
Trade, Transportation, and Utilities													
2011	762.58	748.35	741.49	784.65	765.04	744.74	759.57	755.64	751.49	801.05	749.05	762.02	760.27
2012	819.73	774.90	786.24	843.66	803.71	816.09	849.76	813.90	877.80	828.83	829.09	876.20	825.92
2013	821.52	833.57	829.65	817.02	826.43	824.60	783.05	781.06	827.26	799.98	798.21	807.40	811.24
2014	776.68	804.31	810.58	790.37	770.53	767.47	752.19	763.93	767.01	753.20	773.55	743.48	773.14
2015	744.42	776.51	783.62	759.85	745.50	759.60	758.64	773.28	736.03	714.49	717.95	689.18	746.59
Professional and Business Services													
2011	901.51	884.63	848.54	1,105.95	1,069.13	986.23	970.42	983.30	971.15	1,034.67	960.79	975.10	975.55
2012	958.01	948.50	913.44	949.32	868.19	886.62	882.65	833.52	898.58	892.83	894.15	902.70	901.92
2013	870.44	889.21	879.11	872.78	860.81	896.68	855.30	870.57	907.20	890.91	896.10	921.20	884.24
2014	886.38	921.06	902.02	902.52	901.33	934.75	934.27	952.68	952.12	952.12	954.44	944.30	929.60
2015	935.68	957.18	950.33	956.86	934.71	923.94	921.46	961.22	961.50	928.87	918.37	881.09	936.95
Education and Health Services													
2011	703.05	688.06	669.19	698.02	713.01	701.27	701.41	698.70	738.46	723.39	709.06	712.80	704.81
2012	721.01	705.95	709.80	730.88	695.74	720.87	731.60	696.84	744.88	703.40	723.48	763.52	721.01
2013	721.44	759.00	756.16	738.19	726.36	750.12	729.61	748.13	774.13	733.15	747.36	755.29	745.34
2014	731.79	759.92	741.46	715.68	719.83	729.68	712.76	705.05	730.12	707.85	736.00	740.48	728.26
2015	747.16	802.74	789.92	765.57	766.58	774.63	760.91	793.72	766.75	759.36	792.58	742.10	769.53
Leisure and Hospitality													
2011	342.34	328.95	327.14	314.37	318.68	318.92	325.24	327.21	320.39	307.89	289.20	290.23	317.46
2012	300.32	294.76	292.70	299.63	292.08	308.21	322.32	312.31	326.70	292.82	289.38	306.53	303.50
2013	298.03	303.78	302.05	298.40	302.08	336.10	345.97	336.17	338.48	320.77	312.21	315.46	318.94
2014	327.44	345.83	351.91	318.08	331.01	372.81	371.07	382.57	369.35	357.19	365.38	362.63	355.38
2015	366.97	391.82	384.61	360.27	362.05	384.38	394.12	406.49	387.71	344.74	340.75	336.63	373.18
Other Services													
2011	593.32	577.50	618.30	646.53	641.41	685.75	672.92	715.28	717.14	734.14	710.33	729.53	671.37
2012	756.85	743.90	721.82	727.46	722.78	747.28	768.57	766.72	748.99	762.99	762.99	800.66	751.13
2013	753.30	745.52	720.04	691.89	709.10	719.69	665.08	665.85	683.28	698.66	694.90	706.30	703.88
2014	689.24	699.54	684.95	685.66	679.36	700.21	667.10	668.51	668.96	637.03	617.27	589.36	666.11
2015	625.80	687.28	658.90	628.19	638.10	604.79	621.03	660.33	605.05	568.28	591.26	552.16	620.06

PART B

METROPOLITAN STATISTICAL AREA (MSA) DATA

METROPOLITAN STATISTICAL AREA (MSA) DATA

Part B provides employment data for the 75 largest metropolitan statistical areas (MSAs) and New England city and town areas (NECTAs) in the United States from 2005 through 2015. As mentioned in the technical notes, all employment data are for MSAs unless otherwise noted. NECTAs are similar to MSAs but are defined by cities and towns rather than counties in the New England region.

According to the 2015 estimates from the Census Bureau, New York-Newark-Jersey City, NY-NJ-PA metro area, is the largest MSA in the United States—with a population of 20,182,305. Los Angeles-Long Beach-Anaheim, CA followed with a population of 13,340,068. Although the New York area was the most populated MSA, it was not among the fastest growing among the 75 largest MSAs. The fastest growing MSAs between 2014 and 2015 was Austin–Round Rock–San Marcos, TX with a growth rate of 3.0 percent followed by North Port-Sarasota-Bradenton, FL with a growth rate of 2.7 percent. MSAs in the South and West typically had higher growth rates. Seven MSAs among the 75 largest experienced a decline in growth.

Four of the five fastest growing MSAs in total nonfarm employment were located in Texas. Austin-Round Rock, TX grew the fastest at 37.1 percent, followed by McAllen-Edinburg-Mission, TX at 26.7 percent. Raleigh, NC was the only MSA not located in Texas which ranked in the top five. It grew the fourth fastest at 24.5 percent followed by San Antonio-New Braunfels, TX at 24.4 percent and Dallas-Fort Worth-Arlington at 20.8 percent. Although nonfarm employment increased in most areas during this time period, 8 of the 75 largest MSAs experienced a decline in total nonfarm employment. Detroit-Warren-Dearborn, MI experienced the largest decline dropping 5.3 percent.

According to the 2015 unemployment ratings from the Bureau of Labor Statistics, unemployment rates decreased between 2014 and 2015 in all of the 75 largest MSAs. Detroit-Warren-Dearborn, MI experienced the greatest decline in unemployment from 2014 to 2015 declining 2.1 percent. Unemployment rates ranged from 3.2 percent in Omaha-Council Bluffs, NE-IA, to a high of 10.2 percent in Fresno, CA and Bakersfield, CA. Of the MSAs with population of 1,000,000 or more, Las Vegas-Henderson-Paradise, NV had the highest unemployment rate at 6.8 percent followed by Riverside-San Bernardino-Ontario, CA at 6.6 percent, and Memphis, TN at 6.5 percent.

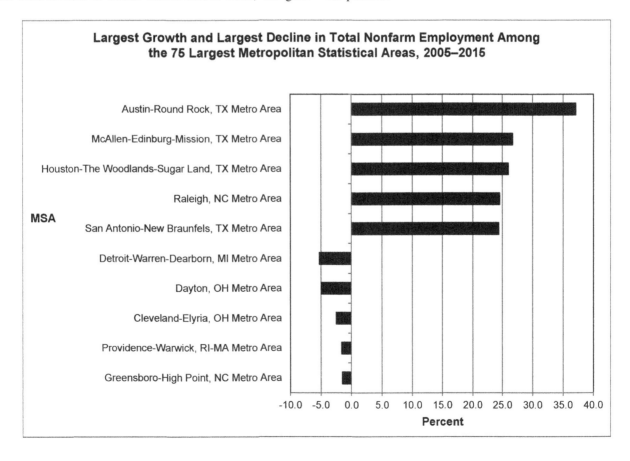

Largest Growth and Largest Decline in Total Nonfarm Employment Among the 75 Largest Metropolitan Statistical Areas, 2005–2015

Metropolitan Statistical Areas: Employment and Unemployment Rates

(Seventy-five largest MSAs; ranked by population)

Rank	Metropolitan statistical area	2015 Census population estimates[1]	Total nonfarm employment		Percent change in total nonfarm employment, 2005–2015	Unemployment rate		
			2005	2015		2010	2014	2015
1	New York-Newark-Jersey City, NY-NJ-PA Metro Area	20,182,305	8,627.9	9,337.2	8.2	8.9	6.4	5.3
2	Los Angeles-Long Beach-Anaheim, CA Metro Area	13,340,068	5,636.7	5,816.9	3.2	11.8	7.6	6.2
3	Chicago-Naperville-Elgin, IL-IN-WI Metro Area	9,551,031	4,458.1	4,585.9	2.9	10.6	7.1	5.8
4	Dallas-Fort Worth-Arlington, TX Metro Area	7,102,796	2,813.9	3,399.3	20.8	8.1	5.0	4.1
5	Houston-The Woodlands-Sugar Land, TX Metro Area	6,656,947	2,372.8	2,988.9	26.0	8.3	4.9	4.6
6	Washington-Arlington-Alexandria, DC-VA-MD-WV Metro Area	6,097,684	2,935.7	3,171.4	8.0	6.3	5.1	4.4
7	Philadelphia-Camden-Wilmington, PA-NJ-DE-MD Metro Area	6,069,875	2,773.6	2,821.0	1.7	8.8	6.2	5.3
8	Miami-Fort Lauderdale-West Palm Beach, FL Metro Area	6,012,331	2,343.1	2,506.6	7.0	10.8	6.4	5.5
9	Atlanta-Sandy Springs-Roswell, GA Metro Area	5,710,795	2,344.8	2,584.9	10.2	10.3	6.7	5.6
10	Boston-Cambridge-Newton, MA-NH Metro Area	4,774,321	1,593.1	1,774.2	11.4	7.6	5.2	4.5
11	San Francisco-Oakland-Hayward, CA Metro Area	4,656,132	2,008.5	2,259.2	12.5	9.9	5.2	4.3
12	Phoenix-Mesa-Scottsdale, AZ Metro Area	4,574,531	1,789.7	1,914.0	6.9	9.6	5.9	5.3
13	Riverside-San Bernardino-Ontario, CA Metro Area	4,489,159	1,239.0	1,347.4	8.7	13.7	8.1	6.6
14	Detroit-Warren-Dearborn, MI Metro Area	4,302,043	2,043.9	1,936.0	-5.3	13.9	8.3	6.2
15	Seattle-Tacoma-Bellevue, WA Metro Area	3,733,580	1,652.4	1,891.6	14.5	9.7	5.3	4.9
16	Minneapolis-St. Paul-Bloomington, MN-WI Metro Area	3,524,583	1,816.6	1,929.9	6.2	7.3	3.9	3.4
17	San Diego-Carlsbad, CA Metro Area	3,299,521	1,294.5	1,386.4	7.1	10.8	6.4	5.2
18	Tampa-St. Petersburg-Clearwater, FL Metro Area	2,975,225	1,207.6	1,249.5	3.5	11.1	6.0	5.1
19	Denver-Aurora-Lakewood, CO Metro Area	2,814,330	1,190.1	1,395.0	17.2	8.7	4.8	3.7
20	St. Louis, MO-IL Metro Area	2,811,588	1,328.1	1,343.7	1.2	9.6	6.3	5.1
21	Baltimore-Columbia-Towson, MD Metro Area	2,797,407	1,284.9	1,364.9	6.2	8.1	6.0	5.4
22	Charlotte-Concord-Gastonia, NC-SC Metro Area	2,426,363	946.9	1,104.6	16.7	11.7	6.1	5.5
23	Portland-Vancouver-Hillsboro, OR-WA Metro Area	2,389,228	991.2	1,111.4	12.1	10.2	6.2	5.3
24	Orlando-Kissimmee-Sanford, FL Metro Area	2,387,138	1,013.1	1,156.5	14.2	11.1	6.0	5.0
25	San Antonio-New Braunfels, TX Metro Area	2,384,075	788.5	980.7	24.4	7.2	4.6	3.8
26	Pittsburgh, PA Metro Area	2,353,045	1,132.8	1,161.7	2.6	8.0	5.7	5.1
27	Sacramento–Roseville–Arden-Arcade, CA Metro Area	2,274,194	895.7	916.1	2.3	12.4	7.1	5.9
28	Cincinnati, OH-KY-IN Metro Area	2,157,719	1,030.8	1,059.8	2.8	9.9	5.5	4.5
29	Las Vegas-Henderson-Paradise, NV Metro Area	2,114,801	871.9	917.0	5.2	13.8	8.0	6.8
30	Kansas City, MO-KS Metro Area	2,087,471	973.0	1,041.9	7.1	8.7	5.6	4.8
31	Cleveland-Elyria, OH Metro Area	2,060,810	1,072.2	1,045.2	-2.5	8.4	6.0	4.8
32	Columbus, OH Metro Area	2,021,632	941.0	1,039.9	10.5	9.0	4.9	4.1
33	Austin-Round Rock, TX Metro Area	2,000,860	699.7	959.3	37.1	7.0	4.2	3.4
34	Indianapolis-Carmel-Anderson, IN Metro Area	1,988,817	928.2	1,016.8	9.5	9.6	5.7	4.5
35	San Jose-Sunnyvale-Santa Clara, CA Metro Area	1,976,836	900.1	1,042.8	15.9	10.5	5.3	4.3
36	Nashville-Davidson—Murfreesboro—Franklin, TN Metro Area	1,830,345	768.6	912.1	18.7	8.6	5.2	4.6
37	Virginia Beach-Norfolk-Newport News, VA-NC Metro Area	1,724,876	761.0	765.4	0.6	7.6	5.7	4.9
38	Providence-Warwick, RI-MA Metro Area	1,613,070	584.4	575.0	-1.6	11.1	7.5	6.0
39	Milwaukee-Waukesha-West Allis, WI Metro Area	1,575,747	844.7	854.2	1.1	8.9	5.9	5.0
40	Jacksonville, FL Metro Area	1,449,481	601.0	647.9	7.8	10.7	6.2	5.2
41	Oklahoma City, OK Metro Area	1,358,452	559.2	629.9	12.6	5.9	4.0	3.7
42	Memphis, TN-MS-AR Metro Area	1,344,127	627.4	625.8	-0.3	9.7	7.4	6.5
43	Louisville/Jefferson County, KY-IN Metro Area	1,278,413	595.6	643.4	8.0	9.9	5.8	4.7
44	Raleigh, NC Metro Area	1,273,568	467.1	581.7	24.5	8.6	5.1	4.8
45	Richmond, VA Metro Area	1,271,334	606.1	651.5	7.5	8.0	5.5	4.6
46	New Orleans-Metairie, LA Metro Area	1,262,888	566.0	573.4	1.3	7.7	6.4	6.0
47	Hartford-West Hartford-East Hartford, CT Metro Area	1,211,324	553.2	568.4	2.7	9.2	6.6	5.7
48	Salt Lake City, UT Metro Area	1,170,266	568.1	676.1	19.0	7.7	3.7	3.4
49	Birmingham-Hoover, AL Metro Area	1,145,647	519.3	515.5	-0.7	9.8	6.0	5.5
50	Buffalo-Cheektowaga-Niagara Falls, NY Metro Area	1,135,230	546.2	555.6	1.7	8.6	6.3	5.6
51	Rochester, NY Metro Area	1,081,954	520.9	526.6	1.1	8.1	5.8	5.2
52	Grand Rapids-Wyoming, MI Metro Area	1,038,583	496.0	527.2	6.3	10.4	5.1	3.7
53	Tucson, AZ Metro Area	1,010,025	367.0	368.1	0.3	9.3	6.0	5.6
54	Urban Honolulu, HI Metro Area	998,714	442.7	468.4	5.8	6.0	4.1	3.4
55	Tulsa, OK Metro Area	981,005	413.9	445.8	7.7	7.3	4.5	4.2
56	Fresno, CA Metro Area	974,861	303.5	324.5	6.9	16.7	11.6	10.2
57	Bridgeport-Stamford-Norwalk, CT Metro Area	948,053	404.0	409.2	1.3	8.7	6.4	5.5
58	Worcester, MA-CT Metro Area	935,536	265.2	278.4	5.0	8.9	6.2	5.3
59	Omaha-Council Bluffs, NE-IA Metro Area	915,312	449.9	491.6	9.3	5.1	3.6	3.2
60	Albuquerque, NM Metro Area	907,301	379.5	380.5	0.3	8.0	6.6	6.2

Metropolitan Statistical Areas: Employment and Unemployment Rates—*Continued*

(Seventy-five largest MSAs; ranked by population)

Rank	Metropolitan statistical area	2015 Census population estimates[1]	Total nonfarm employment		Percent change in total nonfarm employment, 2005–2015	Unemployment rate		
			2005	2015		2010	2014	2015
61	Bakersfield, CA Metro Area	882,176	225.5	258.3	14.5	15.7	10.4	10.2
62	Albany-Schenectady-Troy, NY Metro Area	881,830	443.7	457.7	3.2	7.3	5.1	4.5
63	Greenville-Anderson-Mauldin, SC Metro Area	874,869	364.2	401.3	10.2	10.2	5.7	5.3
64	Knoxville, TN Metro Area	861,424	360.9	386.1	7.0	8.5	6.1	5.4
65	New Haven-Milford, CT Metro Area	859,470	275.1	279.9	1.7	9.3	6.7	5.7
66	Oxnard-Thousand Oaks-Ventura, CA Metro Area	850,536	292.4	294.8	0.8	10.8	6.6	5.7
67	McAllen-Edinburg-Mission, TX Metro Area	842,304	195.9	248.2	26.7	11.8	8.8	7.9
68	El Paso, TX Metro Area	838,972	263.5	302.4	14.8	9.2	6.4	5.2
69	Allentown-Bethlehem-Easton, PA-NJ Metro Area	832,327	225.5	258.3	14.5	9.2	6.2	5.2
70	Baton Rouge, LA Metro Area	830,480	353.3	404.5	14.5	7.8	5.8	5.4
71	Columbia, SC Metro Area	810,068	354.8	384.8	8.5	9.3	5.8	5.5
72	Dayton, OH Metro Area	800,909	399.0	379.1	-5.0	11.0	5.8	4.8
73	North Port-Sarasota-Bradenton, FL Metro Area	768,918	273.6	283.0	3.4	11.5	5.8	5.0
74	Greensboro-High Point, NC Metro Area	752,157	360.5	355.1	-1.5	11.5	6.6	5.9
75	Charleston-North Charleston, SC Metro Area	744,526	282.3	333.3	18.1	9.3	5.5	5.1

[1]Population estimates are as of July 1, 2015.

Employment by Industry: New York-Newark-Jersey City, NY-NJ-PA, 2005–2015

(Numbers in thousands, not seasonally adjusted)

Industry and year	January	February	March	April	May	June	July	August	September	October	November	December	Annual average
Total Nonfarm													
2005	8,429.6	8,452.5	8,506.7	8,601.4	8,650.7	8,728.2	8,650.3	8,616.8	8,649.4	8,684.2	8,756.1	8,808.3	8,627.9
2006	8,521.8	8,543.5	8,624.1	8,665.7	8,742.0	8,820.9	8,727.1	8,686.7	8,721.1	8,797.8	8,866.3	8,926.1	8,720.3
2007	8,649.7	8,668.9	8,733.0	8,777.4	8,859.7	8,945.9	8,853.5	8,803.0	8,820.4	8,920.7	8,980.0	9,025.5	8,836.5
2008	8,752.5	8,774.3	8,825.4	8,874.9	8,921.6	8,977.4	8,886.8	8,830.6	8,831.4	8,877.9	8,893.0	8,892.9	8,861.6
2009	8,551.4	8,540.3	8,550.0	8,555.6	8,613.0	8,641.1	8,565.9	8,506.7	8,493.4	8,573.1	8,612.9	8,648.0	8,571.0
2010	8,359.0	8,378.6	8,447.8	8,558.2	8,638.6	8,678.6	8,562.6	8,517.9	8,544.9	8,650.0	8,695.7	8,725.1	8,563.1
2011	8,452.5	8,491.5	8,554.2	8,656.6	8,700.6	8,759.1	8,702.4	8,652.2	8,694.8	8,766.7	8,825.7	8,854.9	8,675.9
2012	8,589.2	8,648.8	8,723.4	8,765.2	8,847.0	8,908.3	8,800.6	8,774.6	8,822.3	8,910.5	8,916.4	8,992.6	8,808.2
2013	8,700.2	8,750.3	8,826.3	8,915.6	8,976.7	9,034.5	8,975.9	8,934.4	8,969.4	9,085.9	9,158.6	9,174.4	8,958.5
2014	8,862.3	8,908.0	8,982.1	9,084.7	9,169.8	9,226.2	9,172.1	9,135.8	9,161.7	9,275.6	9,348.4	9,380.6	9,142.3
2015	9,072.8	9,114.6	9,182.4	9,285.8	9,377.2	9,433.3	9,373.9	9,332.2	9,347.7	9,467.2	9,522.4	9,537.1	9,337.2
Total Private													
2005	7,106.1	7,118.8	7,170.1	7,258.3	7,304.7	7,372.1	7,323.4	7,318.0	7,346.4	7,351.9	7,410.1	7,458.1	7,294.8
2006	7,192.4	7,204.5	7,280.9	7,321.5	7,395.0	7,467.6	7,408.3	7,396.9	7,418.7	7,458.3	7,514.5	7,568.4	7,385.6
2007	7,311.5	7,318.7	7,378.1	7,425.1	7,501.6	7,580.2	7,525.5	7,501.3	7,508.5	7,572.2	7,619.8	7,658.8	7,491.8
2008	7,408.4	7,418.4	7,464.5	7,508.8	7,554.0	7,603.7	7,538.2	7,516.1	7,509.2	7,518.2	7,516.4	7,512.1	7,505.7
2009	7,200.8	7,177.1	7,181.0	7,181.8	7,237.3	7,268.6	7,191.4	7,161.3	7,182.1	7,217.8	7,246.4	7,279.5	7,210.4
2010	7,020.2	7,026.0	7,088.0	7,188.6	7,234.5	7,293.5	7,243.2	7,237.0	7,251.5	7,315.8	7,355.8	7,390.0	7,220.3
2011	7,148.8	7,170.6	7,229.3	7,324.4	7,375.5	7,433.4	7,400.5	7,373.9	7,418.3	7,452.0	7,503.7	7,538.2	7,364.1
2012	7,310.7	7,345.1	7,411.1	7,454.3	7,537.5	7,598.1	7,526.7	7,529.8	7,560.6	7,607.3	7,613.4	7,685.2	7,515.0
2013	7,427.0	7,450.8	7,522.1	7,608.7	7,670.7	7,733.3	7,704.9	7,694.2	7,714.4	7,783.5	7,848.8	7,868.5	7,668.9
2014	7,597.4	7,618.4	7,684.7	7,777.4	7,865.9	7,927.1	7,899.7	7,889.8	7,898.3	7,974.7	8,036.2	8,071.9	7,853.5
2015	7,806.3	7,822.8	7,883.4	7,978.8	8,070.5	8,129.6	8,096.1	8,078.0	8,076.7	8,151.7	8,197.2	8,213.7	8,042.1
Goods Producing													
2005	817.5	814.9	823.5	838.7	848.3	857.7	852.1	858.7	861.0	852.5	855.0	849.6	844.1
2006	815.6	815.1	825.3	837.7	847.8	857.8	850.0	855.0	856.2	852.8	849.3	845.2	842.3
2007	812.4	805.4	814.7	829.6	841.6	852.4	848.5	850.7	849.4	850.1	846.5	839.0	836.7
2008	806.9	803.8	811.0	820.9	826.6	831.3	828.2	830.0	825.3	818.1	805.9	787.2	816.3
2009	738.2	727.8	726.6	727.6	731.7	733.6	729.0	726.4	720.4	716.9	710.4	702.0	724.2
2010	663.9	658.3	668.3	687.0	691.2	697.4	697.9	699.8	697.3	695.8	694.5	685.3	686.4
2011	650.1	649.2	660.4	675.5	685.6	693.0	697.8	701.3	699.4	698.4	698.1	692.2	683.4
2012	665.1	664.0	672.4	681.0	687.5	694.7	696.3	699.4	698.0	700.0	696.8	700.1	687.9
2013	675.3	673.3	682.7	698.5	705.6	711.8	715.2	720.6	719.0	722.8	722.0	711.9	704.9
2014	682.4	677.1	689.9	708.9	720.3	728.7	735.1	737.5	736.4	739.5	739.6	732.7	719.0
2015	701.9	695.8	707.1	728.7	741.1	749.7	753.0	755.6	751.1	755.9	761.2	753.0	737.8
Service-Providing													
2005	7,612.1	7,637.6	7,683.2	7,762.7	7,802.4	7,870.5	7,798.2	7,758.1	7,788.4	7,831.7	7,901.1	7,958.7	7,783.7
2006	7,706.2	7,728.4	7,798.8	7,828.0	7,894.2	7,963.1	7,877.1	7,831.7	7,864.9	7,945.0	8,017.0	8,080.9	7,877.9
2007	7,837.3	7,863.5	7,918.3	7,947.8	8,018.1	8,093.5	8,005.0	7,952.3	7,971.0	8,070.6	8,133.5	8,186.5	7,999.8
2008	7,945.6	7,970.5	8,014.4	8,054.0	8,095.0	8,146.1	8,058.6	8,000.6	8,006.1	8,059.8	8,087.1	8,105.7	8,045.3
2009	7,813.2	7,812.5	7,823.4	7,828.0	7,881.3	7,907.5	7,836.9	7,780.3	7,773.0	7,856.2	7,902.5	7,946.0	7,846.7
2010	7,695.1	7,720.3	7,779.5	7,871.2	7,947.4	7,981.2	7,864.7	7,818.1	7,847.6	7,954.2	8,001.2	8,039.8	7,876.7
2011	7,802.4	7,842.3	7,893.8	7,981.1	8,015.0	8,066.1	8,004.6	7,950.9	7,995.4	8,068.3	8,127.6	8,162.7	7,992.5
2012	7,924.1	7,984.8	8,051.0	8,084.2	8,159.5	8,213.6	8,104.3	8,075.2	8,124.3	8,210.5	8,219.6	8,292.5	8,120.3
2013	8,024.9	8,077.0	8,143.6	8,217.1	8,271.1	8,322.7	8,260.7	8,213.8	8,250.4	8,363.1	8,436.6	8,462.5	8,253.6
2014	8,179.9	8,230.9	8,292.2	8,375.8	8,449.5	8,497.5	8,437.0	8,398.3	8,425.3	8,536.1	8,608.8	8,647.9	8,423.3
2015	8,370.9	8,418.8	8,475.3	8,557.1	8,636.1	8,683.6	8,620.9	8,576.6	8,596.6	8,711.3	8,761.2	8,784.1	8,599.4
Mining and Logging													
2005	321.4	317.4	324.2	342.2	351.3	358.4	360.1	365.3	366.8	359.8	363.3	357.7	349.0
2006	333.6	333.1	342.5	356.3	364.8	372.7	373.5	378.5	379.2	377.1	375.0	373.1	363.3
2007	348.4	342.0	350.8	367.8	379.2	388.5	389.2	392.4	391.3	392.0	390.0	383.7	376.3
2008	359.1	356.6	363.0	374.7	381.2	384.5	387.5	389.6	385.0	381.8	373.7	360.1	374.7
2009	325.0	320.6	323.1	329.4	334.1	336.2	338.0	337.2	331.4	328.4	324.0	316.1	328.6
2010	286.4	281.0	289.4	306.7	309.9	313.7	317.3	319.3	316.7	314.7	313.4	304.0	306.0
2011	276.4	275.2	285.6	300.2	309.3	314.7	321.7	324.1	321.4	320.8	320.2	314.7	307.0
2012	293.7	291.7	298.3	308.0	312.4	317.4	321.7	324.4	321.7	323.4	322.2	324.8	313.3
2013	307.6	304.5	311.7	326.6	332.4	336.7	342.6	346.9	344.7	348.3	347.3	337.3	332.2
2014	315.2	309.9	321.8	340.9	351.1	357.3	366.0	368.1	367.6	370.6	370.3	363.7	350.2
2015	338.2	331.9	341.9	362.9	373.7	379.5	384.1	386.6	381.6	384.2	390.5	382.2	369.8

Employment by Industry: New York-Newark-Jersey City, NY-NJ-PA, 2005–2015—*Continued*

(Numbers in thousands, not seasonally adjusted)

Industry and year	January	February	March	April	May	June	July	August	September	October	November	December	Annual average
Manufacturing													
2005	496.1	497.5	499.3	496.5	497.0	499.3	492.0	493.4	494.2	492.7	491.7	491.9	495.1
2006	482.0	482.0	482.8	481.4	483.0	485.1	476.5	476.5	477.0	475.7	474.3	472.1	479.0
2007	464.0	463.4	463.9	461.8	462.4	463.9	459.3	458.3	458.1	458.1	456.5	455.3	460.4
2008	447.8	447.2	448.0	446.2	445.4	446.8	440.7	440.4	440.3	436.3	432.2	427.1	441.5
2009	413.2	407.2	403.5	398.2	397.6	397.4	391.0	389.2	389.0	388.5	386.4	385.9	395.6
2010	377.5	377.3	378.9	380.3	381.3	383.7	380.6	380.5	380.6	381.1	381.1	381.3	380.4
2011	373.7	374.0	374.8	375.3	376.3	378.3	376.1	377.2	378.0	377.6	377.9	377.5	376.4
2012	371.4	372.3	374.1	373.0	375.1	377.3	374.6	375.0	376.3	376.6	374.6	375.3	374.6
2013	367.7	368.8	371.0	371.9	373.2	375.1	372.6	373.7	374.3	374.5	374.7	374.6	372.7
2014	367.2	367.2	368.1	368.0	369.2	371.4	369.1	369.4	368.8	368.9	369.3	369.0	368.8
2015	363.7	363.9	365.2	365.8	367.4	370.2	368.9	369.0	369.5	371.7	370.7	370.8	368.1
Trade, Transportation, and Utilities													
2005	1,632.1	1,616.4	1,620.8	1,631.0	1,643.4	1,659.0	1,636.1	1,634.6	1,650.4	1,659.3	1,691.1	1,725.8	1,650.0
2006	1,650.1	1,627.3	1,636.6	1,637.2	1,652.1	1,669.2	1,644.6	1,640.0	1,656.2	1,675.2	1,711.8	1,743.4	1,662.0
2007	1,668.0	1,645.2	1,651.7	1,652.2	1,671.4	1,691.8	1,663.9	1,654.4	1,670.5	1,684.6	1,723.3	1,752.7	1,677.5
2008	1,678.6	1,654.8	1,661.4	1,657.7	1,667.6	1,682.0	1,655.7	1,650.4	1,661.7	1,665.4	1,683.8	1,700.9	1,668.3
2009	1,609.5	1,583.8	1,576.8	1,563.0	1,578.5	1,591.5	1,561.4	1,557.1	1,573.9	1,587.2	1,615.2	1,641.4	1,586.6
2010	1,566.8	1,547.9	1,554.0	1,568.6	1,580.0	1,599.5	1,577.2	1,576.2	1,588.8	1,606.7	1,634.9	1,661.9	1,588.5
2011	1,593.9	1,576.7	1,581.2	1,593.5	1,603.6	1,622.9	1,600.8	1,600.6	1,616.2	1,628.0	1,663.5	1,691.7	1,614.4
2012	1,629.2	1,609.6	1,616.8	1,613.9	1,634.8	1,653.0	1,618.0	1,621.1	1,638.0	1,650.8	1,683.0	1,712.2	1,640.0
2013	1,635.3	1,612.4	1,625.5	1,636.5	1,650.1	1,671.6	1,655.1	1,652.4	1,668.6	1,682.8	1,726.7	1,748.4	1,663.8
2014	1,672.8	1,652.2	1,659.8	1,667.7	1,683.6	1,701.9	1,685.3	1,684.8	1,697.5	1,714.6	1,755.0	1,781.6	1,696.4
2015	1,704.0	1,683.6	1,687.5	1,694.9	1,713.8	1,732.9	1,709.4	1,707.6	1,718.1	1,729.4	1,760.5	1,778.2	1,718.3
Wholesale Trade													
2005	440.3	441.4	442.5	443.2	444.5	446.8	445.1	446.1	446.9	447.2	448.4	451.6	445.3
2006	441.8	442.4	444.6	445.0	447.5	450.1	447.7	447.3	447.0	448.4	449.5	452.5	447.0
2007	444.7	444.7	445.9	446.2	448.0	451.5	449.1	448.4	447.6	450.5	450.0	451.7	448.2
2008	446.1	446.0	447.0	445.3	445.9	447.6	444.7	443.1	441.9	439.6	437.1	435.5	443.3
2009	424.6	420.5	418.2	413.9	413.6	414.3	408.8	407.5	406.5	407.7	407.7	408.7	412.7
2010	400.4	399.4	401.1	401.8	403.5	406.5	406.0	405.3	405.3	406.5	407.6	409.5	404.4
2011	402.8	402.0	403.9	405.4	406.6	409.5	409.1	409.3	407.8	408.4	408.6	411.6	407.1
2012	407.6	408.8	410.5	410.2	411.6	414.7	412.3	411.8	410.6	411.8	411.9	414.4	411.4
2013	407.3	407.7	408.9	411.2	412.7	416.5	416.6	416.2	415.3	415.8	417.2	418.5	413.7
2014	411.5	411.9	413.2	414.8	416.7	419.0	419.5	419.0	418.0	418.9	421.0	422.4	417.2
2015	415.8	415.9	417.4	418.1	420.3	423.8	423.3	423.2	422.1	420.4	423.1	421.1	420.4
Retail Trade													
2005	872.4	855.6	857.3	865.2	873.4	884.2	877.7	877.5	875.7	883.8	911.2	938.2	881.0
2006	882.3	859.4	865.0	866.1	873.7	885.9	880.7	879.1	876.2	892.6	925.5	947.9	886.2
2007	894.0	871.9	875.6	877.2	888.2	902.0	895.8	890.7	887.6	897.0	934.1	956.3	897.5
2008	902.1	878.7	882.0	879.1	886.3	896.8	892.1	889.8	885.3	893.0	912.6	927.2	893.8
2009	863.0	843.0	839.9	834.0	845.9	857.4	850.3	850.6	851.2	862.0	887.1	908.0	857.7
2010	855.7	839.9	843.9	855.3	863.6	877.7	873.5	874.5	869.4	884.5	908.8	928.1	872.9
2011	877.4	862.9	864.0	872.7	879.6	892.9	889.4	890.7	889.2	900.1	930.7	951.5	891.8
2012	905.1	884.7	888.5	890.4	902.3	914.4	906.7	906.7	905.9	917.5	947.5	965.8	911.3
2013	911.1	895.4	900.5	906.6	916.8	932.5	931.2	932.6	929.9	941.4	979.0	994.8	931.0
2014	936.5	919.9	924.0	930.1	939.5	953.2	951.1	953.0	948.8	961.5	993.4	1,011.7	951.9
2015	952.1	934.5	935.9	940.5	952.9	965.3	958.6	958.4	953.6	965.8	986.0	994.7	958.2
Transportation and Utilities													
2005	319.4	319.4	321.0	322.6	325.5	328.0	313.3	311.0	327.8	328.3	331.5	336.0	323.7
2006	326.0	325.5	327.0	326.1	330.9	333.2	316.2	313.6	333.0	334.2	336.8	343.0	328.8
2007	329.3	328.6	330.2	328.8	335.2	338.3	319.0	315.3	335.3	337.1	339.2	344.7	331.8
2008	330.4	330.1	332.4	333.3	335.4	337.6	318.9	317.5	334.5	332.8	334.1	338.2	331.3
2009	321.9	320.3	318.7	315.1	319.0	319.8	302.3	299.0	316.2	317.5	320.4	324.7	316.2
2010	310.7	308.6	309.0	311.5	312.9	315.3	297.7	296.4	314.1	315.7	318.5	324.3	311.2
2011	313.7	311.8	313.3	315.4	317.4	320.5	302.3	300.6	319.2	319.5	324.2	328.6	315.5
2012	316.5	316.1	317.8	313.3	320.9	323.9	299.0	302.6	321.5	321.5	323.6	332.0	317.4
2013	316.9	309.3	316.1	318.7	320.6	322.6	307.3	303.6	323.4	325.6	330.5	335.1	319.1
2014	324.8	320.4	322.6	322.8	327.4	329.7	314.7	312.8	330.7	334.2	340.6	347.5	327.4
2015	336.1	333.2	334.2	336.3	340.6	343.8	327.5	326.0	342.4	343.2	351.4	362.4	339.8

Employment by Industry: New York-Newark-Jersey City, NY-NJ-PA, 2005–2015—*Continued*

(Numbers in thousands, not seasonally adjusted)

Industry and year	January	February	March	April	May	June	July	August	September	October	November	December	Annual average
Information													
2005	284.0	285.5	286.5	285.8	288.0	292.9	290.6	291.9	292.1	292.8	295.1	298.2	290.3
2006	289.8	290.4	292.0	290.0	292.2	295.1	293.2	294.2	293.3	290.1	292.0	293.9	292.2
2007	286.0	288.0	288.2	288.0	290.1	292.6	291.3	291.8	290.8	289.3	291.2	292.7	290.0
2008	287.3	289.5	289.6	287.8	289.2	292.1	288.6	289.2	288.8	287.1	287.3	288.1	288.7
2009	280.3	278.4	279.3	280.0	280.1	279.9	278.4	277.3	276.5	275.4	275.8	276.4	278.2
2010	269.1	269.3	270.4	270.2	271.5	273.5	273.5	274.0	273.6	275.5	275.1	279.2	272.9
2011	270.4	271.5	273.3	275.9	276.3	278.0	279.8	262.9	279.3	277.0	278.3	280.4	275.3
2012	275.5	276.8	278.3	278.6	280.3	282.4	279.8	279.5	277.8	279.5	280.4	280.9	279.2
2013	273.1	275.0	276.5	278.2	280.3	283.1	282.7	285.3	283.2	284.7	288.1	287.3	281.5
2014	279.3	282.2	283.1	281.9	282.8	286.2	284.6	285.8	283.2	285.7	285.4	287.8	284.0
2015	280.9	282.3	282.9	282.4	283.5	285.9	287.4	285.7	285.3	288.8	285.3	289.1	285.0
Financial Activities													
2005	779.5	779.3	781.6	785.8	785.6	795.4	802.4	802.8	795.5	795.0	797.1	802.2	791.9
2006	788.2	790.2	793.4	795.6	798.6	809.4	813.3	814.0	805.7	805.0	807.2	812.0	802.7
2007	800.9	802.2	803.9	803.7	804.3	815.7	819.4	816.4	807.1	809.0	810.6	812.5	808.8
2008	801.3	801.9	802.1	799.8	799.4	806.7	808.2	806.4	792.8	788.1	784.2	783.9	797.9
2009	766.7	761.4	757.5	752.1	749.8	752.0	750.7	746.9	741.3	739.3	738.1	740.3	749.7
2010	728.7	729.6	732.0	732.4	733.7	743.1	745.6	746.4	740.7	739.9	742.1	746.7	738.4
2011	737.2	738.4	739.5	741.6	743.4	753.4	757.0	757.9	749.4	746.5	746.8	749.4	746.7
2012	740.1	742.3	743.3	742.2	743.0	752.2	753.3	751.9	743.2	744.8	744.4	749.9	745.9
2013	736.2	738.4	739.2	739.2	739.5	749.8	753.7	753.1	744.6	746.3	749.0	752.7	745.1
2014	742.0	743.7	745.4	745.6	749.0	760.8	764.3	763.4	754.1	754.7	757.0	762.3	753.5
2015	750.4	752.0	753.4	755.8	759.1	770.7	776.4	777.1	767.4	770.6	770.3	772.2	764.6
Professional and Business Services													
2005	1,237.9	1,239.5	1,249.0	1,275.7	1,277.2	1,294.7	1,291.0	1,294.4	1,293.3	1,292.3	1,299.6	1,304.2	1,279.1
2006	1,252.4	1,260.6	1,278.8	1,289.7	1,298.3	1,318.9	1,316.0	1,320.3	1,314.3	1,319.5	1,328.5	1,335.1	1,302.7
2007	1,289.1	1,294.2	1,309.9	1,323.0	1,332.4	1,353.6	1,356.8	1,361.1	1,350.8	1,363.6	1,369.2	1,373.5	1,339.8
2008	1,327.7	1,333.2	1,342.5	1,356.1	1,357.7	1,370.9	1,369.9	1,367.2	1,355.3	1,350.3	1,345.1	1,338.3	1,351.2
2009	1,279.8	1,273.1	1,271.7	1,273.3	1,273.2	1,281.7	1,274.6	1,269.7	1,264.6	1,268.2	1,272.3	1,275.6	1,273.2
2010	1,233.1	1,239.7	1,251.3	1,277.7	1,281.6	1,299.1	1,295.6	1,297.7	1,292.5	1,304.1	1,309.5	1,312.2	1,282.8
2011	1,276.7	1,281.8	1,294.5	1,316.8	1,320.6	1,339.3	1,343.2	1,344.9	1,342.1	1,347.0	1,356.2	1,355.9	1,326.6
2012	1,311.6	1,320.4	1,336.0	1,351.9	1,361.9	1,380.5	1,376.6	1,386.1	1,383.8	1,393.0	1,400.2	1,407.3	1,367.4
2013	1,354.1	1,360.0	1,373.7	1,387.8	1,395.8	1,414.0	1,419.5	1,422.9	1,414.2	1,422.2	1,428.3	1,430.2	1,401.9
2014	1,379.2	1,387.5	1,394.2	1,421.3	1,431.9	1,447.2	1,454.8	1,456.6	1,446.7	1,459.6	1,468.3	1,470.9	1,434.9
2015	1,426.3	1,434.3	1,445.6	1,472.2	1,482.7	1,499.9	1,500.7	1,501.8	1,494.1	1,512.0	1,516.6	1,516.1	1,483.5
Education and Health Services													
2005	1,398.5	1,420.6	1,431.3	1,437.5	1,435.9	1,416.9	1,397.8	1,388.0	1,421.3	1,451.9	1,461.7	1,465.8	1,427.3
2006	1,430.0	1,450.9	1,463.5	1,465.4	1,468.0	1,449.6	1,423.5	1,414.3	1,449.9	1,484.1	1,493.8	1,502.2	1,457.9
2007	1,463.5	1,485.5	1,497.0	1,492.9	1,494.8	1,476.8	1,450.3	1,439.7	1,475.0	1,513.7	1,519.2	1,526.9	1,486.3
2008	1,491.6	1,515.3	1,524.4	1,526.8	1,526.3	1,509.0	1,476.5	1,470.5	1,505.3	1,538.5	1,550.1	1,557.8	1,516.0
2009	1,522.0	1,545.9	1,552.9	1,552.9	1,553.7	1,537.1	1,504.4	1,498.1	1,531.6	1,570.5	1,581.3	1,589.8	1,545.0
2010	1,553.6	1,575.4	1,588.4	1,592.3	1,589.3	1,565.8	1,535.1	1,527.5	1,562.4	1,601.1	1,613.6	1,616.5	1,576.8
2011	1,579.7	1,605.9	1,617.3	1,622.2	1,620.3	1,589.6	1,560.5	1,552.5	1,595.7	1,624.8	1,635.1	1,642.6	1,603.9
2012	1,603.8	1,634.8	1,648.4	1,648.0	1,654.4	1,625.7	1,592.7	1,585.1	1,633.8	1,661.1	1,656.9	1,671.4	1,634.7
2013	1,633.2	1,663.6	1,677.0	1,689.8	1,687.9	1,653.5	1,626.1	1,617.0	1,661.2	1,706.2	1,720.8	1,723.5	1,671.7
2014	1,675.5	1,702.0	1,719.8	1,729.4	1,733.0	1,705.4	1,680.6	1,675.4	1,715.5	1,759.5	1,776.2	1,782.3	1,721.2
2015	1,736.2	1,764.6	1,779.5	1,788.6	1,789.3	1,758.9	1,733.5	1,724.4	1,759.1	1,805.4	1,823.7	1,828.6	1,774.3
Leisure and Hospitality													
2005	593.9	597.8	610.4	632.6	653.2	678.8	681.1	677.3	663.4	640.9	641.1	640.5	642.6
2006	604.1	606.9	624.3	638.6	666.9	692.2	697.3	691.3	674.4	662.5	660.9	662.5	656.8
2007	623.8	628.7	640.6	661.6	688.5	714.4	719.0	714.1	692.4	685.9	682.0	682.6	677.8
2008	644.9	649.0	660.9	684.6	709.0	730.7	733.4	727.1	706.6	696.4	686.0	682.2	692.6
2009	640.2	641.6	650.5	666.8	700.5	720.2	723.7	718.8	709.5	693.8	685.3	685.1	686.3
2010	645.6	646.7	661.8	694.3	718.0	742.3	747.3	746.1	729.6	721.4	714.7	715.4	706.9
2011	675.2	679.9	693.8	724.1	747.6	774.6	780.7	776.1	759.0	751.2	746.2	744.5	737.7
2012	708.4	719.1	734.6	754.4	786.7	815.0	818.9	817.7	797.1	787.0	762.7	770.8	772.7
2013	735.4	741.8	759.3	787.9	818.3	850.8	855.7	847.3	830.5	822.8	817.0	816.9	807.0
2014	775.2	780.8	797.0	822.3	860.1	887.7	888.3	881.2	861.5	854.6	846.5	844.9	841.7
2015	804.5	807.5	822.7	848.0	887.7	913.7	920.7	912.5	891.2	878.4	866.7	859.0	867.7

Employment by Industry: New York-Newark-Jersey City, NY-NJ-PA, 2005–2015—*Continued*

(Numbers in thousands, not seasonally adjusted)

Industry and year	January	February	March	April	May	June	July	August	September	October	November	December	Annual average
Other Services													
2005	362.7	364.8	367.0	371.2	373.1	376.7	372.3	370.3	369.4	367.2	369.4	371.8	369.7
2006	362.2	363.1	367.0	367.3	371.1	375.4	370.4	367.8	368.7	369.1	371.0	374.1	368.9
2007	367.8	369.5	372.1	374.1	378.5	382.9	376.3	373.1	372.5	376.0	377.8	378.9	375.0
2008	370.1	370.9	372.6	375.1	378.2	381.0	377.7	375.3	373.4	374.3	374.0	373.7	374.7
2009	364.1	365.1	365.8	366.1	369.8	372.6	369.2	367.0	364.3	366.5	368.0	368.9	367.3
2010	359.4	359.1	361.8	366.1	369.2	372.8	371.0	369.3	366.6	371.3	371.4	372.8	367.6
2011	365.6	367.2	369.3	374.8	378.1	382.6	380.7	377.7	377.2	379.1	379.5	381.5	376.1
2012	377.0	378.1	381.3	384.3	388.9	394.6	391.1	389.0	388.9	391.1	389.0	392.6	387.2
2013	384.4	386.3	388.2	390.8	393.2	398.7	396.9	395.6	393.1	395.5	396.9	397.6	393.1
2014	391.0	392.9	395.5	400.3	405.2	409.2	406.7	405.1	403.4	406.5	408.2	409.4	402.8
2015	402.1	402.7	404.7	408.2	413.3	417.9	415.0	413.3	410.4	411.2	412.9	417.5	410.8
Government													
2005	1323.5	1333.7	1336.6	1343.1	1346.0	1356.1	1326.9	1298.8	1303.0	1332.3	1346.0	1350.2	1,333.0
2006	1329.4	1339.0	1343.2	1344.2	1347.0	1353.3	1318.8	1289.8	1302.4	1339.5	1351.8	1357.7	1,334.7
2007	1338.2	1350.2	1354.9	1352.3	1358.1	1365.7	1328.0	1301.7	1311.9	1348.5	1360.2	1366.7	1,344.7
2008	1344.1	1355.9	1360.9	1366.1	1367.6	1373.7	1348.6	1314.5	1322.2	1359.7	1376.6	1380.8	1,355.9
2009	1350.6	1363.2	1368.9	1373.8	1375.7	1372.5	1374.5	1345.4	1311.3	1355.3	1366.5	1368.5	1,360.5
2010	1338.8	1352.6	1359.8	1369.6	1404.1	1385.1	1319.4	1280.9	1293.4	1334.2	1339.9	1335.1	1,342.7
2011	1303.7	1320.9	1324.9	1332.2	1325.1	1325.7	1301.9	1278.3	1276.5	1314.7	1322.0	1316.7	1,311.9
2012	1278.5	1303.7	1312.3	1310.9	1309.5	1310.2	1273.9	1244.8	1261.7	1303.2	1303.0	1307.4	1,293.3
2013	1273.2	1299.5	1304.2	1306.9	1306.0	1301.2	1271.0	1240.2	1255.0	1302.6	1309.8	1305.9	1,289.6
2014	1264.9	1289.6	1297.4	1307.3	1303.9	1299.1	1272.4	1246.0	1263.4	1300.9	1312.2	1308.7	1,288.8
2015	1266.5	1291.8	1299.0	1307.0	1306.7	1303.7	1277.8	1254.2	1271.0	1315.5	1325.2	1323.4	1,295.2

Employment by Industry: Los Angeles-Long Beach-Anaheim, CA, 2005–2015

(Numbers in thousands, not seasonally adjusted)

Industry and year	January	February	March	April	May	June	July	August	September	October	November	December	Annual average
Total Nonfarm													
2005	5,530.0	5,566.3	5,597.5	5,615.9	5,629.0	5,644.8	5,600.6	5,612.8	5,657.9	5,693.9	5,731.8	5,760.2	5,636.7
2006	5,649.4	5,696.9	5,727.7	5,728.0	5,744.8	5,766.3	5,708.6	5,713.8	5,752.9	5,786.7	5,809.7	5,836.3	5,743.4
2007	5,714.7	5,753.1	5,787.9	5,766.2	5,778.5	5,796.7	5,752.7	5,741.3	5,774.7	5,799.7	5,822.9	5,849.5	5,778.2
2008	5,693.5	5,728.9	5,750.5	5,753.5	5,756.1	5,752.7	5,689.5	5,661.5	5,681.0	5,689.6	5,665.8	5,653.0	5,706.3
2009	5,481.8	5,462.1	5,457.3	5,412.5	5,406.1	5,388.7	5,289.8	5,254.2	5,272.0	5,325.1	5,331.3	5,345.1	5,368.8
2010	5,234.8	5,245.4	5,266.7	5,302.0	5,326.0	5,322.8	5,252.3	5,241.0	5,269.0	5,333.2	5,353.8	5,375.5	5,293.5
2011	5,273.9	5,300.4	5,320.0	5,324.6	5,334.3	5,335.8	5,286.2	5,282.5	5,327.0	5,368.8	5,404.6	5,427.0	5,332.1
2012	5,331.0	5,369.5	5,405.1	5,444.3	5,470.8	5,480.0	5,419.9	5,432.9	5,467.7	5,517.4	5,573.0	5,593.0	5,458.7
2013	5,461.0	5,505.3	5,526.0	5,552.7	5,573.6	5,577.6	5,524.0	5,551.9	5,578.6	5,635.6	5,692.4	5,707.3	5,573.8
2014	5,597.1	5,625.1	5,649.3	5,659.5	5,683.1	5,675.5	5,613.0	5,659.9	5,694.8	5,750.3	5,794.0	5,811.8	5,684.5
2015	5,700.9	5,743.7	5,767.2	5,787.7	5,802.3	5,799.2	5,780.7	5,803.7	5,840.9	5,895.1	5,928.5	5,952.5	5,816.9
Total Private													
2005	4,791.7	4,820.8	4,847.3	4,868.1	4,878.8	4,894.7	4,885.5	4,906.8	4,933.3	4,952.1	4,982.1	5,011.8	4,897.8
2006	4,908.0	4,948.2	4,973.0	4,974.0	4,988.3	5,010.0	4,983.9	5,001.8	5,019.5	5,033.7	5,049.4	5,077.8	4,997.3
2007	4,963.1	4,995.3	5,024.0	5,003.4	5,013.5	5,031.5	5,020.1	5,021.5	5,032.8	5,038.0	5,053.3	5,080.7	5,023.1
2008	4,930.8	4,958.2	4,975.1	4,977.3	4,976.1	4,974.4	4,949.4	4,933.3	4,933.8	4,921.1	4,890.9	4,881.5	4,941.8
2009	4,714.7	4,691.4	4,681.3	4,634.9	4,631.0	4,614.7	4,562.1	4,549.8	4,560.4	4,577.0	4,581.1	4,597.8	4,616.4
2010	4,493.7	4,501.6	4,518.0	4,545.1	4,555.2	4,565.7	4,551.4	4,564.2	4,574.7	4,605.7	4,620.2	4,644.8	4,561.7
2011	4,549.1	4,572.6	4,585.6	4,591.4	4,600.1	4,601.2	4,608.1	4,620.0	4,639.3	4,653.0	4,680.4	4,707.4	4,617.4
2012	4,621.5	4,651.0	4,680.8	4,722.4	4,746.3	4,756.8	4,751.8	4,773.1	4,783.2	4,813.9	4,863.1	4,884.7	4,754.1
2013	4,762.8	4,798.0	4,812.1	4,841.6	4,860.2	4,864.5	4,862.3	4,886.8	4,893.4	4,930.4	4,979.7	4,995.3	4,873.9
2014	4,894.8	4,917.8	4,932.1	4,941.2	4,959.7	4,956.9	4,947.4	4,985.7	4,994.6	5,030.8	5,067.0	5,084.7	4,976.1
2015	4,981.9	5,017.0	5,034.7	5,054.4	5,071.3	5,065.7	5,097.5	5,118.4	5,126.9	5,159.6	5,189.7	5,213.2	5,094.2
Goods Producing													
2005	887.2	895.5	900.4	906.5	910.3	914.7	916.3	918.8	920.6	917.5	916.3	915.6	910.0
2006	904.6	912.7	916.6	915.6	917.9	923.4	918.9	920.7	921.8	914.8	911.1	908.2	915.5
2007	892.4	898.1	902.4	898.5	899.9	906.2	902.0	899.7	895.4	889.7	882.7	878.5	895.5
2008	863.2	864.9	864.2	861.8	860.4	859.5	855.6	852.5	847.3	836.9	823.7	812.5	850.2
2009	787.2	773.1	766.3	753.4	749.6	745.1	731.2	725.4	720.2	715.2	711.5	706.2	740.4
2010	697.0	695.4	697.9	699.8	702.8	706.2	704.9	705.2	702.0	702.3	700.6	698.2	701.0
2011	688.8	690.8	694.0	696.6	700.2	702.8	706.7	707.7	706.3	703.1	703.1	701.6	700.1
2012	697.4	699.3	702.8	705.6	709.1	714.5	717.0	717.6	717.2	716.5	718.1	717.2	711.0
2013	710.7	716.4	717.6	718.1	720.8	726.0	728.0	730.6	729.2	730.8	732.3	730.8	724.3
2014	719.5	725.6	726.6	722.9	726.5	728.5	728.9	732.9	731.8	731.4	732.1	730.7	728.1
2015	728.1	729.7	731.8	734.0	736.8	739.8	745.4	747.8	744.8	742.0	742.7	742.5	738.8
Service-Providing													
2005	4,642.8	4,670.8	4,697.1	4,709.4	4,718.7	4,730.1	4,684.3	4,694.0	4,737.3	4,776.4	4,815.5	4,844.6	4,726.8
2006	4,744.8	4,784.2	4,811.1	4,812.4	4,826.9	4,842.9	4,789.7	4,793.1	4,831.1	4,871.9	4,898.6	4,928.1	4,827.9
2007	4,822.3	4,855.0	4,885.5	4,867.7	4,878.6	4,890.5	4,850.7	4,841.6	4,879.3	4,910.0	4,940.2	4,971.0	4,882.7
2008	4,830.3	4,864.0	4,886.3	4,891.7	4,895.7	4,893.2	4,833.9	4,809.0	4,833.7	4,852.7	4,842.1	4,840.5	4,856.1
2009	4,694.6	4,689.0	4,691.0	4,659.1	4,656.5	4,643.6	4,558.6	4,528.8	4,551.8	4,609.9	4,619.8	4,638.9	4,628.5
2010	4,537.8	4,550.0	4,568.8	4,602.2	4,623.2	4,616.6	4,547.4	4,535.8	4,567.0	4,630.9	4,653.2	4,677.3	4,592.5
2011	4,585.1	4,609.6	4,626.0	4,628.0	4,634.1	4,633.0	4,579.5	4,574.8	4,620.7	4,665.7	4,701.5	4,725.4	4,632.0
2012	4,633.6	4,670.2	4,702.3	4,738.7	4,761.7	4,765.5	4,702.9	4,715.3	4,750.5	4,800.9	4,854.9	4,875.8	4,747.7
2013	4,750.3	4,788.9	4,808.4	4,834.6	4,852.8	4,851.6	4,796.0	4,821.3	4,849.4	4,904.8	4,960.1	4,976.5	4,849.6
2014	4,877.6	4,899.5	4,922.7	4,936.6	4,956.6	4,947.0	4,884.1	4,927.0	4,963.0	5,018.9	5,061.9	5,081.1	4,956.3
2015	4,972.8	5,014.0	5,035.4	5,053.7	5,065.5	5,059.4	5,035.3	5,055.9	5,096.1	5,153.1	5,185.8	5,210.0	5,078.1
Mining and Logging													
2005	4.5	4.5	4.5	4.3	4.3	4.3	4.4	4.4	4.4	4.3	4.4	4.4	4.4
2006	4.5	4.5	4.5	4.5	4.6	4.7	4.7	4.7	4.7	4.7	4.7	4.7	4.6
2007	4.9	5.0	5.0	4.9	4.9	5.0	5.0	4.9	5.0	5.0	5.1	5.0	5.0
2008	5.0	5.0	5.0	4.9	4.9	5.0	5.0	5.0	5.0	5.1	5.0	5.0	5.0
2009	4.9	4.8	4.8	4.8	4.8	4.8	4.6	4.5	4.5	4.5	4.5	4.4	4.7
2010	4.7	4.8	4.8	4.7	4.7	4.7	4.7	4.7	4.6	4.7	4.6	4.6	4.7
2011	4.6	4.6	4.6	4.6	4.6	4.7	4.6	4.6	4.6	4.8	4.8	4.8	4.7
2012	4.8	4.8	4.8	4.8	4.8	4.8	4.9	4.9	4.9	4.9	4.9	5.1	4.9
2013	5.1	5.1	5.0	5.1	5.0	5.2	5.2	5.3	5.2	5.1	5.1	5.1	5.1
2014	4.9	5.0	4.9	4.9	5.0	5.0	5.0	5.0	5.0	5.0	4.9	4.9	5.0
2015	4.9	4.2	4.2	4.7	4.7	4.7	4.7	4.6	4.6	4.7	4.6	4.3	4.6

Employment by Industry: Los Angeles-Long Beach-Anaheim, CA, 2005–2015—*Continued*

(Numbers in thousands, not seasonally adjusted)

Industry and year	January	February	March	April	May	June	July	August	September	October	November	December	Annual average
Construction													
2005	226.2	232.9	236.3	241.8	246.4	250.7	254.9	258.5	259.4	259.2	258.8	258.3	248.6
2006	253.9	257.0	259.1	260.0	263.5	267.3	267.9	271.0	272.0	267.9	265.6	264.2	264.1
2007	255.1	257.9	261.6	260.1	261.9	265.8	266.7	266.1	263.8	260.6	255.6	252.7	260.7
2008	242.9	243.3	243.6	241.4	240.6	239.3	237.9	237.9	234.7	230.5	224.9	220.1	236.4
2009	209.1	202.1	201.3	196.0	195.1	193.6	188.3	187.7	185.0	182.8	180.9	176.4	191.5
2010	171.3	169.5	170.9	172.4	173.4	174.1	173.7	174.6	172.8	173.4	173.2	171.2	172.5
2011	167.2	167.8	169.4	171.1	173.5	175.2	178.1	179.8	179.3	177.2	177.4	175.5	174.3
2012	173.9	173.9	175.0	175.0	177.5	181.0	183.6	184.7	184.8	184.9	186.0	185.3	180.5
2013	183.6	185.8	187.4	188.1	190.5	194.0	195.9	197.9	197.0	199.1	199.1	197.3	193.0
2014	193.4	196.3	198.0	197.3	200.2	201.3	202.2	205.8	205.6	206.7	207.5	205.0	201.6
2015	205.7	206.3	209.2	211.0	213.5	216.1	220.5	223.4	222.1	222.8	223.8	223.7	216.5
Manufacturing													
2005	656.5	658.1	659.6	660.4	659.6	659.7	657.0	655.9	656.8	654.0	653.1	652.9	657.0
2006	646.2	651.2	653.0	651.1	649.8	651.4	646.3	645.0	645.1	642.2	640.8	639.3	646.8
2007	632.4	635.2	635.8	633.5	633.1	635.4	630.3	628.7	626.6	624.1	622.0	620.8	629.8
2008	615.3	616.6	615.6	615.5	614.9	615.2	612.7	609.6	607.6	601.3	593.8	587.4	608.8
2009	573.2	566.2	560.2	552.6	549.7	546.7	538.3	533.2	530.7	527.9	526.1	525.4	544.2
2010	521.0	521.1	522.2	522.7	524.7	527.4	526.5	525.9	524.6	524.2	522.8	522.4	523.8
2011	517.0	518.4	520.0	520.9	522.1	522.9	524.0	523.3	522.4	521.1	520.9	521.3	521.2
2012	518.7	520.6	523.0	525.8	526.8	528.7	528.5	528.0	527.5	526.7	527.2	526.8	525.7
2013	522.0	525.5	525.2	524.9	525.3	526.8	526.9	527.4	527.0	526.6	528.1	528.4	526.2
2014	521.2	524.3	523.7	520.7	521.3	522.2	521.7	522.1	521.2	519.7	519.7	520.8	521.6
2015	517.5	519.2	518.4	518.3	518.6	519.0	520.2	519.8	518.1	514.5	514.3	514.5	517.7
Trade, Transportation, and Utilities													
2005	1,053.1	1,046.8	1,046.4	1,046.9	1,050.1	1,055.1	1,058.4	1,061.3	1,065.0	1,074.4	1,094.7	1,115.3	1,064.0
2006	1,073.2	1,068.3	1,072.1	1,069.6	1,072.6	1,078.0	1,078.8	1,083.2	1,087.3	1,094.4	1,116.1	1,133.5	1,085.6
2007	1,092.8	1,083.9	1,081.8	1,081.4	1,083.2	1,087.6	1,093.0	1,092.2	1,093.3	1,101.3	1,122.8	1,142.1	1,096.3
2008	1,094.4	1,085.8	1,081.5	1,077.8	1,077.0	1,077.6	1,074.0	1,068.4	1,064.0	1,065.6	1,069.6	1,074.7	1,075.9
2009	1,028.3	1,011.6	1,003.2	990.0	990.1	986.6	974.9	974.1	977.0	982.3	996.0	1,008.8	993.6
2010	978.6	972.6	971.1	976.6	981.7	983.7	981.5	984.4	982.5	991.1	1,008.6	1,022.2	986.2
2011	989.4	985.8	983.0	987.3	989.9	991.4	993.5	997.5	996.5	1,000.8	1,023.7	1,037.0	998.0
2012	1,006.0	995.4	997.1	1,003.9	1,008.6	1,012.3	1,011.8	1,014.4	1,015.3	1,021.1	1,052.0	1,061.3	1,016.6
2013	1,025.5	1,019.5	1,015.8	1,017.9	1,023.6	1,026.9	1,028.7	1,032.2	1,029.6	1,038.6	1,070.1	1,081.4	1,034.2
2014	1,045.6	1,037.6	1,035.2	1,037.3	1,042.2	1,046.1	1,047.2	1,052.7	1,053.1	1,062.3	1,092.1	1,104.8	1,054.7
2015	1,068.1	1,059.6	1,062.5	1,061.3	1,066.1	1,066.6	1,074.3	1,078.7	1,078.4	1,081.3	1,108.2	1,118.4	1,077.0
Wholesale Trade													
2005	296.5	297.4	298.5	300.3	301.2	302.0	301.1	301.1	301.3	302.4	302.6	305.2	300.8
2006	302.0	304.2	305.5	306.0	307.0	308.4	308.8	308.8	309.9	310.4	310.7	313.0	307.9
2007	311.7	313.2	314.6	314.1	314.0	314.5	314.7	314.2	314.6	315.9	315.6	317.4	314.5
2008	314.5	315.2	315.6	315.2	313.6	313.4	311.3	309.4	308.5	307.3	304.3	303.0	310.9
2009	295.9	293.6	291.2	287.5	285.9	285.1	280.4	279.0	277.9	279.3	278.1	279.2	284.4
2010	277.5	278.0	278.7	280.6	281.8	282.0	281.6	281.7	281.4	283.3	283.2	283.9	281.1
2011	281.0	281.9	281.7	283.1	283.5	283.4	282.9	283.4	283.6	283.7	283.7	285.0	283.1
2012	282.2	283.1	283.9	288.2	289.5	290.2	289.8	291.0	290.7	292.3	293.7	295.5	289.2
2013	293.2	294.6	295.9	296.9	297.6	298.8	298.2	298.7	298.2	299.9	301.3	303.4	298.1
2014	300.0	301.6	301.9	301.0	301.9	302.3	302.6	304.3	304.5	305.3	306.9	307.9	303.4
2015	303.8	305.4	305.5	306.9	307.6	307.6	308.4	309.0	308.7	310.3	311.5	311.2	308.0
Retail Trade													
2005	566.9	559.1	558.7	556.3	559.2	563.4	567.0	570.4	573.5	579.9	600.6	617.6	572.7
2006	580.8	572.9	574.7	572.1	573.7	576.8	576.8	581.0	582.1	588.4	608.8	622.9	584.3
2007	587.5	577.0	576.6	573.5	575.5	579.3	583.1	585.2	583.1	589.2	610.7	626.4	587.3
2008	588.8	577.2	575.8	571.5	570.0	570.9	568.3	564.9	563.8	565.2	573.9	580.0	572.5
2009	547.1	535.1	529.6	523.0	524.4	523.2	518.7	520.0	522.7	525.9	540.7	551.1	530.1
2010	526.1	519.2	517.9	521.0	522.2	523.4	523.1	525.3	523.6	528.4	546.2	557.0	527.8
2011	531.9	525.4	524.1	525.1	527.1	528.8	531.5	533.8	533.5	537.3	559.4	569.3	535.6
2012	544.9	533.9	533.6	533.4	536.3	537.9	538.4	540.5	540.9	545.5	574.3	579.2	544.9
2013	548.5	540.7	538.6	539.7	542.3	544.6	545.3	547.3	545.8	552.5	580.3	588.1	551.1
2014	558.3	548.7	547.8	550.1	551.9	555.0	555.6	558.8	557.7	564.0	590.5	598.8	561.4
2015	570.5	562.3	561.0	559.6	562.5	563.0	567.9	570.8	569.8	572.5	596.1	604.2	571.7

Employment by Industry: Los Angeles-Long Beach-Anaheim, CA, 2005–2015—*Continued*

(Numbers in thousands, not seasonally adjusted)

Industry and year	January	February	March	April	May	June	July	August	September	October	November	December	Annual average
Transportation and Utilities													
2005	189.7	190.3	189.2	190.3	189.7	189.7	190.3	189.8	190.2	192.1	191.5	192.5	190.4
2006	190.4	191.2	191.9	191.5	191.9	192.8	193.2	193.4	195.3	195.6	196.6	197.6	193.5
2007	193.6	193.7	190.6	193.8	193.7	193.8	195.2	192.8	195.6	196.2	196.5	198.3	194.5
2008	191.1	193.4	190.1	191.1	193.4	193.3	194.4	194.1	191.7	193.1	191.4	191.7	192.4
2009	185.3	182.9	182.4	179.5	179.8	178.3	175.8	175.1	176.4	177.1	177.2	178.5	179.0
2010	175.0	175.4	174.5	175.0	177.7	178.3	176.8	177.4	177.5	179.4	179.2	181.3	177.3
2011	176.5	178.5	177.2	179.1	179.3	179.2	179.1	180.3	179.4	179.8	180.6	182.7	179.3
2012	178.9	178.4	179.6	182.3	182.8	184.2	183.6	182.9	183.7	183.3	184.0	186.6	182.5
2013	183.8	184.2	181.3	181.3	183.7	183.5	185.2	186.2	185.6	186.2	188.5	189.9	185.0
2014	187.3	187.3	185.5	186.2	188.4	188.8	189.0	189.6	190.9	193.0	194.7	198.1	189.9
2015	193.8	191.9	196.0	194.8	196.0	196.0	198.0	198.9	199.9	198.5	200.6	203.0	197.3
Information													
2005	238.7	240.4	245.1	238.0	236.8	236.8	234.6	240.6	240.9	241.1	247.9	244.4	240.4
2006	239.0	245.9	245.2	239.1	239.6	241.0	234.6	235.4	232.3	230.5	231.0	236.9	237.5
2007	234.8	241.3	249.0	237.7	241.2	243.5	240.3	244.3	244.6	233.6	238.1	244.7	241.1
2008	226.7	234.9	243.5	242.7	246.7	249.0	240.2	241.5	245.3	240.6	236.6	237.8	240.5
2009	218.5	221.8	225.4	217.9	216.7	219.4	215.4	216.7	221.0	212.4	215.3	222.7	218.6
2010	211.8	212.5	216.1	210.6	211.5	215.3	215.6	220.5	222.4	216.2	218.8	225.0	216.4
2011	219.1	218.5	219.7	215.6	214.4	214.3	213.8	216.1	214.3	215.5	212.9	216.3	215.9
2012	210.3	210.9	213.1	216.9	213.8	211.3	215.1	217.4	214.1	218.2	222.6	225.8	215.8
2013	217.0	218.8	220.4	220.3	219.1	220.7	216.6	220.3	222.3	224.8	228.4	227.3	221.3
2014	222.6	220.7	222.4	224.8	220.5	218.7	217.1	222.8	224.0	226.5	225.0	225.4	222.5
2015	218.8	227.3	230.1	229.0	227.2	227.4	223.9	228.6	230.6	231.4	231.3	233.1	228.2
Financial Activities													
2005	373.2	374.8	376.6	378.3	379.2	380.0	380.9	382.3	383.0	385.2	385.8	388.6	380.7
2006	384.5	385.6	386.6	385.9	386.7	385.7	384.5	384.8	384.1	384.0	383.3	385.1	385.1
2007	380.2	381.3	381.6	377.8	375.5	373.3	371.7	369.6	365.0	363.8	361.2	359.2	371.7
2008	353.9	353.8	352.9	350.8	349.6	348.5	347.0	345.0	341.6	339.5	337.7	337.6	346.5
2009	332.4	330.0	329.2	326.4	324.1	323.6	321.0	319.1	316.2	316.9	315.9	317.1	322.7
2010	312.3	312.6	313.4	313.6	313.6	314.8	315.3	315.2	314.7	315.8	316.0	318.3	314.6
2011	314.3	314.7	315.4	313.1	313.3	314.4	315.1	315.4	314.6	315.6	315.4	317.6	314.9
2012	313.4	314.8	316.2	318.2	319.5	321.2	322.6	323.1	322.7	324.3	325.2	327.4	320.7
2013	323.8	324.9	325.5	326.2	326.6	327.2	327.6	326.9	324.3	326.6	326.8	326.9	326.1
2014	321.6	322.1	321.9	322.6	324.4	325.5	325.0	325.6	324.0	326.2	328.0	329.8	324.7
2015	324.7	326.5	326.7	328.9	330.3	330.5	334.0	334.8	333.3	332.9	333.6	335.8	331.0
Professional and Business Services													
2005	821.9	828.3	830.8	836.1	835.9	839.8	839.4	846.1	850.1	853.6	856.5	860.2	841.6
2006	847.2	857.3	863.1	866.3	867.5	876.8	876.9	883.7	884.6	890.5	890.1	889.9	874.5
2007	867.5	876.9	882.5	872.5	873.0	879.8	877.5	882.1	883.8	886.4	885.8	888.9	879.7
2008	851.9	860.8	863.1	861.0	856.3	855.9	852.8	851.6	847.2	844.0	832.7	827.0	850.4
2009	795.1	790.6	785.1	772.1	768.1	765.3	754.9	756.1	755.1	766.1	766.6	766.2	770.1
2010	752.5	758.2	760.2	766.3	766.1	770.8	767.8	772.9	771.3	791.6	789.9	790.4	771.5
2011	772.2	780.2	782.3	779.7	780.3	784.4	789.7	792.7	798.9	804.5	806.9	811.1	790.2
2012	792.6	806.5	815.1	821.6	825.9	831.9	830.4	836.0	839.4	849.9	858.0	860.6	830.7
2013	832.7	843.4	847.0	851.0	853.5	854.4	858.7	867.8	868.4	877.0	885.9	885.9	860.5
2014	866.3	870.5	873.2	870.5	871.1	870.5	870.2	877.5	876.1	883.9	888.3	890.5	875.7
2015	867.3	874.1	875.6	877.9	877.3	879.6	886.0	889.1	889.8	901.0	903.5	906.9	885.7
Education and Health Services													
2005	706.3	717.0	721.3	726.9	727.4	721.6	711.1	714.8	732.7	740.9	743.7	745.8	725.8
2006	733.3	745.5	748.7	750.6	749.6	742.3	731.2	733.9	751.4	761.0	763.2	765.4	748.0
2007	754.8	767.9	772.7	773.4	773.3	765.0	759.4	759.2	779.0	789.4	793.3	795.2	773.6
2008	785.6	798.4	802.2	806.5	805.8	798.1	794.2	795.5	815.9	826.3	831.5	834.0	807.8
2009	819.0	832.3	837.1	839.1	839.3	830.5	823.3	821.8	837.7	849.2	849.5	850.1	835.7
2010	832.4	840.0	843.5	846.9	842.5	831.5	820.7	822.8	840.3	848.9	852.0	853.8	839.6
2011	841.4	853.3	856.8	854.9	851.9	840.0	829.0	830.6	846.9	857.4	862.2	867.1	849.3
2012	854.9	870.8	874.9	879.6	881.2	870.8	860.3	868.0	879.2	889.1	892.9	896.6	876.5
2013	870.1	882.4	886.1	896.9	894.2	879.3	870.3	877.3	888.4	899.5	903.7	908.6	888.1
2014	894.9	907.5	911.1	912.3	912.2	899.5	890.1	901.9	915.6	928.2	931.7	932.5	911.5
2015	917.5	932.4	934.6	938.2	939.3	924.4	926.3	933.0	946.5	963.3	966.7	969.6	941.0

Employment by Industry: Los Angeles-Long Beach-Anaheim, CA, 2005–2015—*Continued*

(Numbers in thousands, not seasonally adjusted)

Industry and year	January	February	March	April	May	June	July	August	September	October	November	December	Annual average
Leisure and Hospitality													
2005	522.0	526.6	533.5	541.5	544.9	551.2	553.0	551.4	548.0	546.7	544.9	549.3	542.8
2006	536.4	541.3	547.8	554.7	560.5	567.3	567.0	568.1	563.8	564.8	560.8	565.1	558.1
2007	550.4	553.3	560.0	568.0	572.7	579.6	581.7	580.2	575.9	577.4	573.8	576.6	570.8
2008	562.8	566.3	573.2	581.5	585.0	590.6	592.2	588.0	581.1	576.5	569.4	569.3	578.0
2009	550.7	548.8	551.2	554.4	561.1	562.0	562.6	559.4	555.9	554.9	547.6	548.3	554.7
2010	533.3	534.9	539.2	551.8	556.7	562.2	565.4	564.6	561.5	559.1	554.7	558.3	553.5
2011	547.5	551.3	555.7	564.7	569.9	573.4	579.1	579.8	579.7	574.1	574.7	574.5	568.7
2012	566.5	570.9	577.9	591.0	600.7	606.7	607.7	610.2	607.3	605.4	605.6	607.6	596.5
2013	597.0	604.2	610.3	620.0	630.6	637.6	641.0	640.2	638.5	640.0	639.0	641.2	628.3
2014	632.0	639.0	645.8	653.2	664.2	668.3	671.2	674.1	670.7	672.5	670.3	671.8	661.1
2015	661.5	669.6	674.8	685.4	693.1	696.5	705.4	704.8	700.9	706.2	701.2	706.4	692.2
Other Services													
2005	189.3	191.4	193.2	193.9	194.2	195.5	191.8	191.5	193.0	192.7	192.3	192.6	192.6
2006	189.8	191.6	192.9	192.2	193.9	195.5	192.0	192.0	194.2	193.7	193.8	193.7	192.9
2007	190.2	192.6	194.0	194.1	194.7	196.5	194.5	194.2	195.8	196.4	195.6	195.5	194.5
2008	192.3	193.3	194.5	195.2	195.3	195.2	193.4	190.8	191.4	191.7	189.7	188.6	192.6
2009	183.5	183.2	183.8	181.6	182.0	182.2	178.8	177.2	177.3	180.0	178.7	178.4	180.6
2010	175.8	175.4	176.6	179.5	180.3	181.2	180.2	178.6	180.0	180.7	179.6	178.6	178.9
2011	176.4	178.0	178.7	179.5	180.2	180.5	181.2	180.2	182.1	182.0	181.5	182.2	180.2
2012	180.4	182.4	183.7	185.6	187.5	188.1	186.9	186.4	188.0	189.4	188.7	188.2	186.3
2013	186.0	188.4	189.4	191.2	191.8	192.4	191.4	191.5	192.7	193.1	193.5	193.2	191.2
2014	192.3	194.8	195.9	197.6	198.6	199.8	197.7	198.2	199.3	199.8	199.5	199.2	197.7
2015	195.9	197.8	198.6	199.7	201.2	200.9	202.2	201.6	202.6	201.5	202.5	200.5	200.4
Government													
2005	738.3	745.5	750.2	747.8	750.2	750.1	715.1	706.0	724.6	741.8	749.7	748.4	739.0
2006	741.4	748.7	754.7	754.0	756.5	756.3	724.7	712.0	733.4	753.0	760.3	758.5	746.1
2007	751.6	757.8	763.9	762.8	765.0	765.2	732.6	719.8	741.9	761.7	769.6	768.8	755.1
2008	762.7	770.7	775.4	776.2	780.0	778.3	740.1	728.2	747.2	768.5	774.9	771.5	764.5
2009	767.1	770.7	776.0	777.6	775.1	774.0	727.7	704.4	711.6	748.1	750.2	747.3	752.5
2010	741.1	743.8	748.7	756.9	770.8	757.1	700.9	676.8	694.3	727.5	733.6	730.7	731.9
2011	724.8	727.8	734.4	733.2	734.2	734.6	678.1	662.5	687.7	715.8	724.2	719.6	714.7
2012	709.5	718.5	724.3	721.9	724.5	723.2	668.1	659.8	684.5	703.5	709.9	708.3	704.7
2013	698.2	707.3	713.9	711.1	713.4	713.1	661.7	665.1	685.2	705.2	712.7	712.0	699.9
2014	702.3	707.3	717.2	718.3	723.4	718.6	665.6	674.2	700.2	719.5	727.0	727.1	708.4
2015	719.0	726.7	732.5	733.3	731.0	733.5	683.2	685.3	714.0	735.5	738.8	739.3	722.7

Employment by Industry: Chicago-Naperville-Elgin, IL-IN-WI, 2005–2015

(Numbers in thousands, not seasonally adjusted)

Industry and year	January	February	March	April	May	June	July	August	September	October	November	December	Annual average
Total Nonfarm													
2005	4,336.2	4,344.5	4,370.9	4,438.4	4,472.3	4,493.0	4,492.9	4,491.0	4,501.1	4,507.9	4,524.0	4,524.5	4,458.1
2006	4,397.8	4,411.7	4,445.1	4,492.2	4,529.9	4,572.7	4,544.3	4,547.6	4,553.9	4,555.2	4,570.3	4,573.1	4,516.2
2007	4,449.2	4,447.5	4,487.3	4,529.2	4,577.6	4,610.6	4,584.0	4,584.5	4,579.2	4,588.4	4,603.7	4,601.6	4,553.6
2008	4,469.7	4,467.3	4,487.8	4,533.1	4,572.4	4,588.8	4,563.2	4,558.4	4,536.1	4,533.6	4,511.2	4,480.1	4,525.1
2009	4,313.0	4,291.2	4,282.8	4,291.9	4,317.4	4,321.7	4,280.8	4,267.6	4,265.5	4,276.7	4,278.1	4,264.1	4,287.6
2010	4,137.4	4,146.0	4,167.3	4,220.2	4,274.8	4,288.9	4,246.1	4,255.2	4,264.3	4,298.8	4,311.2	4,302.5	4,242.7
2011	4,181.1	4,190.8	4,222.2	4,280.6	4,313.6	4,339.2	4,324.0	4,332.2	4,346.4	4,358.4	4,372.2	4,363.0	4,302.0
2012	4,250.0	4,261.2	4,295.8	4,343.1	4,385.6	4,417.5	4,390.6	4,403.3	4,416.7	4,427.2	4,446.5	4,440.7	4,373.2
2013	4,313.5	4,334.9	4,363.7	4,400.3	4,456.9	4,489.6	4,462.5	4,477.0	4,480.5	4,494.2	4,511.3	4,513.1	4,441.5
2014	4,373.5	4,387.6	4,420.2	4,474.2	4,531.1	4,560.6	4,533.5	4,541.8	4,539.0	4,568.7	4,580.4	4,583.9	4,507.9
2015	4,448.6	4,465.0	4,493.5	4,550.1	4,611.2	4,641.0	4,620.8	4,619.3	4,620.8	4,659.6	4,660.1	4,640.6	4,585.9
Total Private													
2005	3,780.7	3,779.0	3,801.2	3,867.9	3,898.7	3,924.9	3,937.0	3,941.8	3,941.0	3,941.7	3,954.6	3,959.8	3,894.0
2006	3,842.6	3,846.3	3,877.4	3,922.0	3,956.0	4,000.1	3,991.5	3,999.6	3,989.8	3,987.6	3,999.9	4,006.9	3,951.6
2007	3,892.2	3,879.9	3,917.2	3,957.7	4,003.6	4,039.7	4,030.2	4,033.3	4,015.2	4,020.4	4,033.7	4,035.2	3,988.2
2008	3,910.7	3,898.4	3,916.2	3,960.0	3,993.7	4,014.4	4,004.2	4,003.2	3,967.8	3,958.1	3,935.5	3,907.7	3,955.8
2009	3,751.4	3,722.7	3,711.3	3,716.2	3,737.9	3,748.4	3,726.0	3,718.9	3,699.4	3,700.8	3,701.9	3,693.6	3,719.0
2010	3,576.2	3,577.3	3,598.1	3,646.4	3,683.4	3,711.6	3,697.6	3,713.1	3,706.8	3,733.2	3,744.2	3,743.5	3,677.6
2011	3632.3	3634.2	3663.4	3719.7	3749.8	3782.7	3781.0	3796.1	3794.0	3801.7	3813.1	3809.0	3,748.1
2012	3,707.4	3,709.6	3,741.1	3,787.6	3,826.4	3,862.5	3,853.4	3,868.9	3,867.0	3,872.4	3,890.4	3,888.2	3,822.9
2013	3,772.6	3,784.3	3,810.7	3,847.2	3,898.6	3,933.9	3,926.3	3,941.0	3,930.9	3,944.4	3,958.9	3,961.8	3,892.6
2014	3,838.9	3,845.0	3,874.0	3,925.7	3,975.7	4,009.8	3,997.8	4,008.8	3,991.2	4,016.9	4,029.0	4,032.1	3,962.1
2015	3,911.2	3,918.0	3,944.1	3,998.2	4,053.3	4,086.8	4,083.0	4,083.5	4,069.0	4,098.1	4,097.9	4,078.3	4,035.1
Goods Producing													
2005	686.9	686.5	691.8	708.7	715.2	721.8	721.9	723.9	723.7	723.3	721.1	711.4	711.4
2006	688.8	688.7	692.7	709.2	715.2	724.7	720.3	722.0	721.0	719.9	715.5	708.8	710.6
2007	682.3	673.6	686.0	697.8	706.9	716.3	712.8	712.3	710.4	708.9	704.4	696.0	700.6
2008	667.2	660.6	666.3	677.2	685.2	689.9	688.2	688.1	682.1	675.9	662.5	642.7	673.8
2009	601.9	593.3	588.6	586.2	585.4	588.1	582.1	581.4	577.4	573.8	567.1	555.3	581.7
2010	528.0	526.8	533.5	546.6	554.2	560.5	556.0	565.5	563.1	567.3	563.7	553.3	551.5
2011	533.2	531.8	540.5	554.4	563.1	569.9	572.5	574.2	570.5	569.5	566.6	557.5	558.6
2012	538.2	536.8	545.2	555.7	562.8	571.2	573.9	575.0	573.8	571.4	567.4	562.0	561.1
2013	539.9	540.9	546.6	552.9	563.7	571.7	572.4	573.7	570.9	571.6	569.9	560.8	561.3
2014	538.7	540.5	547.9	559.2	569.6	578.6	580.5	581.0	579.1	583.2	581.8	576.1	568.0
2015	555.1	554.4	563.0	574.3	583.2	591.8	593.5	592.2	590.9	593.5	588.9	581.4	580.2
Service-Providing													
2005	3,649.3	3,658.0	3,679.1	3,729.7	3,757.1	3,771.2	3,771.0	3,767.1	3,777.4	3,784.6	3,802.9	3,813.1	3,746.7
2006	3,709.0	3,723.0	3,752.4	3,783.0	3,814.7	3,848.0	3,824.0	3,825.6	3,832.9	3,835.3	3,854.8	3,864.3	3,805.6
2007	3,766.9	3,773.9	3,801.3	3,831.4	3,870.7	3,894.3	3,871.2	3,872.2	3,868.8	3,879.5	3,899.3	3,905.6	3,852.9
2008	3,802.5	3,806.7	3,821.5	3,855.9	3,887.2	3,898.9	3,875.0	3,870.3	3,854.0	3,857.7	3,848.7	3,837.4	3,851.3
2009	3,711.1	3,697.9	3,694.2	3,705.7	3,732.0	3,733.6	3,698.7	3,686.2	3,688.1	3,702.9	3,711.0	3,708.8	3,705.9
2010	3,609.4	3,619.2	3,633.8	3,673.6	3,720.6	3,728.4	3,690.1	3,689.7	3,701.2	3,731.5	3,747.5	3,749.2	3,691.2
2011	3,647.9	3,659.0	3,681.7	3,726.2	3,750.5	3,769.3	3,751.5	3,758.0	3,775.9	3,788.9	3,805.6	3,805.5	3,743.3
2012	3,711.8	3,724.4	3,750.6	3,787.4	3,822.8	3,846.3	3,816.7	3,828.3	3,842.9	3,855.8	3,879.1	3,878.7	3,812.1
2013	3,773.6	3,794.0	3,817.1	3,847.4	3,893.2	3,917.9	3,890.1	3,903.3	3,909.6	3,922.6	3,941.4	3,952.3	3,880.2
2014	3,834.8	3,847.1	3,872.3	3,915.0	3,961.5	3,982.0	3,953.0	3,960.8	3,959.9	3,985.5	3,998.6	4,007.8	3,939.9
2015	3,893.5	3,910.6	3,930.5	3,975.8	4,028.0	4,049.2	4,027.3	4,027.1	4,029.9	4,066.1	4,071.2	4,059.2	4,005.7
Mining and Logging													
2005	2.0	2.0	2.1	2.3	2.3	2.4	2.5	2.4	2.4	2.5	2.4	2.3	2.3
2006	2.0	2.0	2.1	2.4	2.5	2.7	2.7	2.6	2.6	2.5	2.6	2.4	2.4
2007	2.3	2.1	2.4	2.3	2.4	2.4	2.4	2.4	2.3	2.3	2.3	2.1	2.3
2008	1.9	1.8	1.9	2.1	2.1	2.2	2.2	2.2	2.1	2.0	1.9	1.8	2.0
2009	1.5	1.5	1.7	1.8	1.8	1.8	1.8	1.8	1.8	1.7	1.7	1.5	1.7
2010	1.2	1.2	1.3	1.5	1.5	1.6	1.6	1.6	1.7	1.6	1.6	1.5	1.5
2011	1.2	1.2	1.3	1.5	1.5	1.5	1.6	1.5	1.5	1.5	1.5	1.3	1.4
2012	1.2	1.2	1.2	1.3	1.4	1.5	1.5	1.5	1.5	1.5	1.5	1.3	1.4
2013	1.2	1.2	1.2	1.3	1.6	1.6	1.5	1.5	1.5	1.5	1.6	1.3	1.4
2014	1.2	1.2	1.2	1.4	1.5	1.6	1.6	1.6	1.6	1.6	1.6	1.6	1.5
2015	1.3	1.3	1.5	1.6	1.6	1.5	1.5	1.6	1.6	1.6	1.6	1.4	1.5

Employment by Industry: Chicago-Naperville-Elgin, IL-IN-WI, 2005–2015—*Continued*

(Numbers in thousands, not seasonally adjusted)

Industry and year	January	February	March	April	May	June	July	August	September	October	November	December	Annual average
Construction													
2005	189.3	188.7	193.0	209.1	215.2	220.3	224.3	225.5	225.9	226.1	223.8	214.2	213.0
2006	197.9	197.5	203.2	216.7	223.9	229.8	229.1	231.0	228.2	227.7	223.8	216.5	218.8
2007	196.3	188.3	199.4	211.9	220.9	227.1	227.3	227.2	225.5	224.2	221.0	210.7	215.0
2008	188.1	184.6	189.7	201.1	209.3	212.7	215.2	215.9	212.3	209.3	199.9	185.6	202.0
2009	157.4	155.6	157.0	163.4	167.2	170.8	171.0	170.9	167.6	166.2	161.0	149.6	163.1
2010	128.1	126.6	132.3	144.1	149.7	153.7	150.0	157.5	155.4	157.2	152.9	141.9	145.8
2011	125.7	124.2	130.5	142.2	150.1	154.3	157.7	159.5	157.3	155.8	153.2	144.3	146.2
2012	128.6	126.7	133.3	142.7	148.4	154.0	157.4	158.4	158.4	158.0	153.5	146.9	147.2
2013	129.9	130.5	135.5	143.1	152.7	157.4	160.2	160.6	160.0	160.7	157.9	148.7	149.8
2014	130.6	132.1	137.7	148.8	157.7	163.8	167.1	167.6	166.9	169.7	166.9	160.0	155.7
2015	141.9	141.5	148.6	161.1	168.4	172.7	174.6	174.8	174.5	177.1	173.7	165.7	164.6
Manufacturing													
2005	495.6	495.8	496.7	497.3	497.7	499.1	495.1	496.0	495.4	494.7	494.9	494.9	496.1
2006	488.9	489.2	487.4	490.1	488.8	492.2	488.5	488.4	490.2	489.7	489.1	489.9	489.4
2007	483.7	483.2	484.2	483.6	483.6	486.8	483.1	482.7	482.6	482.4	481.1	483.2	483.4
2008	477.2	474.2	474.7	474.0	473.8	475.0	470.8	470.0	467.7	464.6	460.7	455.3	469.8
2009	443.0	436.2	429.9	421.0	416.4	415.5	409.3	408.7	408.0	405.9	404.4	404.2	416.9
2010	398.7	399.0	399.9	401.0	403.0	405.2	404.4	406.4	406.0	408.5	409.2	409.9	404.3
2011	406.3	406.4	408.7	410.7	411.5	414.1	413.2	413.2	411.7	412.2	411.9	411.9	411.0
2012	408.4	408.9	410.7	411.7	413.0	415.7	415.0	415.1	413.9	411.9	412.4	413.8	412.5
2013	408.8	409.2	409.9	408.5	409.4	412.7	410.7	411.6	409.4	409.4	410.4	410.8	410.1
2014	406.9	407.2	409.0	409.0	410.4	413.2	411.8	411.8	410.6	411.9	413.3	414.5	410.8
2015	411.9	411.6	412.9	411.6	413.2	417.6	417.4	415.8	414.8	414.8	413.6	414.3	414.1
Trade, Transportation, and Utilities													
2005	902.1	892.3	895.8	901.8	908.9	913.4	911.2	913.3	914.6	918.4	933.9	949.2	912.9
2006	911.1	902.5	907.8	910.7	917.8	924.8	918.9	919.7	918.7	922.5	941.7	954.3	920.9
2007	923.6	911.6	917.9	916.0	926.5	933.7	928.1	928.0	927.0	931.3	953.6	965.7	930.3
2008	931.2	917.9	920.3	920.5	927.3	930.3	923.3	922.4	917.2	918.5	926.8	931.5	923.9
2009	889.6	875.1	869.8	863.4	868.2	869.3	859.4	859.1	855.2	858.0	868.9	876.4	867.7
2010	842.7	834.9	837.5	843.4	851.0	856.4	853.1	855.3	852.4	861.3	876.8	888.4	854.4
2011	857.1	848.9	851.8	860.3	866.0	872.0	869.2	873.3	873.5	879.6	896.1	907.1	871.2
2012	874.1	864.1	869.1	871.8	879.4	884.5	883.5	885.7	884.9	892.2	913.8	919.8	885.2
2013	884.1	875.9	879.3	883.9	893.3	900.9	898.2	901.5	898.2	903.9	922.1	934.6	898.0
2014	895.1	885.8	891.3	896.0	905.8	913.4	910.1	912.6	910.9	918.0	937.0	948.9	910.4
2015	910.6	904.1	908.3	915.2	925.9	934.4	932.4	934.1	932.6	938.8	951.9	958.1	928.9
Wholesale Trade													
2005	241.1	240.8	241.7	243.4	244.5	246.2	246.4	245.8	246.0	246.3	247.4	249.2	244.9
2006	245.9	246.0	247.2	247.7	248.7	250.8	249.7	249.3	248.5	248.6	248.7	250.1	248.4
2007	247.8	247.7	248.8	248.9	250.2	252.5	252.0	251.3	250.6	251.7	252.0	253.5	250.6
2008	250.4	249.8	250.4	250.8	252.0	252.9	251.0	250.5	249.2	248.6	247.7	247.0	250.0
2009	241.3	239.0	237.7	235.2	234.2	233.8	231.1	230.6	228.6	229.1	228.3	228.8	233.1
2010	225.6	225.0	226.2	227.6	228.9	230.1	230.2	230.4	228.8	229.9	230.1	230.8	228.6
2011	229.0	229.1	229.9	231.5	232.3	234.2	234.3	234.4	233.4	233.6	233.9	235.4	232.6
2012	233.9	233.8	235.1	236.2	237.3	239.4	238.9	238.8	238.1	238.6	239.3	240.0	237.5
2013	237.9	238.0	239.4	240.4	241.5	244.1	243.7	243.2	242.6	242.3	242.9	244.2	241.7
2014	240.2	240.7	241.5	241.1	242.5	243.6	242.9	242.5	241.2	242.5	243.0	244.1	242.2
2015	241.3	241.0	242.1	244.2	246.1	247.9	247.8	246.9	245.5	246.0	246.6	245.2	245.1
Retail Trade													
2005	462.9	453.2	454.8	458.1	463.3	467.2	467.9	469.7	467.5	470.0	483.5	495.2	467.8
2006	466.8	457.6	460.1	461.7	466.0	471.6	469.2	469.9	465.1	469.8	487.8	496.6	470.2
2007	474.5	462.6	466.7	465.6	472.5	478.0	475.8	475.3	471.3	474.2	495.0	502.9	476.2
2008	477.9	465.2	466.3	466.4	470.2	474.2	471.8	469.7	463.5	465.8	475.3	479.7	470.5
2009	452.6	441.8	439.1	437.2	442.1	445.1	441.9	441.5	436.9	439.2	450.9	456.4	443.7
2010	431.7	424.4	425.6	428.2	433.1	437.8	436.9	437.0	432.3	438.6	452.7	460.9	436.6
2011	437.0	428.7	430.2	435.1	438.7	443.3	442.3	444.7	442.0	447.7	463.0	470.5	443.6
2012	444.5	434.9	437.3	437.1	441.7	446.2	445.8	445.8	442.8	449.0	468.7	471.3	447.1
2013	445.6	437.1	438.5	439.7	446.7	453.2	451.6	452.3	448.6	454.4	470.1	478.8	451.4
2014	450.0	440.7	443.7	447.5	453.0	459.6	458.8	458.5	455.5	461.3	476.7	483.1	457.4
2015	455.9	449.6	452.2	455.2	461.1	467.4	466.5	466.4	463.8	470.4	481.8	487.1	464.8

Employment by Industry: Chicago-Naperville-Elgin, IL-IN-WI, 2005–2015—*Continued*

(Numbers in thousands, not seasonally adjusted)

Industry and year	January	February	March	April	May	June	July	August	September	October	November	December	Annual average
Transportation and Utilities													
2005	198.1	198.3	199.3	200.3	201.1	200.0	196.9	197.8	201.1	202.1	203.0	204.8	200.2
2006	198.4	198.9	200.5	201.3	203.1	202.4	200.0	200.5	205.1	204.1	205.2	207.6	202.3
2007	201.3	201.3	202.4	201.5	203.8	203.2	200.3	201.4	205.1	205.4	206.6	209.3	203.5
2008	202.9	202.9	203.6	203.3	205.1	203.2	200.5	202.2	204.5	204.1	203.8	204.8	203.4
2009	195.7	194.3	193.0	191.0	191.9	190.4	186.4	187.0	189.7	189.7	189.7	191.2	190.8
2010	185.4	185.5	185.7	187.6	189.0	188.5	186.0	187.9	191.3	192.8	194.0	196.7	189.2
2011	191.1	191.1	191.7	193.7	195.0	194.5	192.6	194.2	198.1	198.3	199.2	201.2	195.1
2012	195.7	195.4	196.7	198.5	200.4	198.9	198.8	201.1	204.0	204.6	205.8	208.5	200.7
2013	200.6	200.8	201.4	203.8	205.1	203.6	202.9	206.0	207.0	207.2	209.1	211.6	204.9
2014	204.9	204.4	206.1	207.4	210.3	210.2	208.4	211.6	214.2	214.2	217.3	221.7	210.9
2015	213.4	213.5	214.0	215.8	218.7	219.1	218.1	220.8	223.3	222.4	223.5	225.8	219.0
Information													
2005	93.4	93.1	93.1	93.5	93.1	93.4	93.6	92.8	92.0	91.8	91.7	91.7	92.8
2006	91.4	91.2	91.2	91.3	91.6	92.0	91.7	91.4	90.6	90.8	90.7	91.0	91.2
2007	90.4	90.8	90.5	90.5	90.8	91.3	91.6	91.7	91.0	91.0	91.0	91.1	91.0
2008	90.7	90.9	90.9	90.8	91.1	91.0	90.9	90.7	89.0	88.4	88.0	87.9	90.0
2009	86.7	85.8	84.8	84.1	83.9	83.8	83.4	83.2	82.7	82.4	82.1	82.2	83.8
2010	81.5	80.8	80.5	80.4	80.5	80.9	80.8	80.6	79.8	80.2	80.1	79.9	80.5
2011	79.5	79.3	79.1	79.4	79.8	80.5	81.3	81.0	80.1	80.3	80.7	80.6	80.1
2012	80.6	80.4	80.3	80.9	81.5	81.3	81.3	80.9	80.5	81.2	81.2	81.1	80.9
2013	80.0	80.0	79.6	80.2	81.0	81.4	81.2	80.7	79.8	79.5	79.9	80.0	80.3
2014	78.7	78.9	79.5	80.0	80.2	81.2	81.3	81.2	79.8	80.1	80.3	80.7	80.2
2015	80.3	80.4	80.1	80.4	81.9	81.1	82.6	82.7	81.8	82.4	83.4	82.3	81.6
Financial Activities													
2005	323.5	323.1	323.7	325.6	326.7	329.5	331.7	331.8	329.9	330.0	330.3	332.4	328.2
2006	328.0	328.3	329.3	330.2	331.0	334.2	335.1	335.1	333.4	332.5	332.2	333.6	331.9
2007	330.1	329.9	329.7	329.8	330.4	332.6	331.5	330.2	326.1	325.2	324.3	324.5	328.7
2008	319.0	319.0	318.9	318.4	318.8	320.4	318.8	318.1	314.0	312.8	311.0	310.9	316.7
2009	304.7	302.8	301.1	300.1	299.8	300.5	298.9	297.9	294.8	293.9	293.3	293.8	298.5
2010	289.3	288.8	288.8	288.3	288.5	290.5	289.7	289.4	286.4	287.6	287.1	287.6	288.5
2011	283.5	283.1	283.0	283.3	283.9	286.4	287.8	287.9	285.9	286.8	286.6	286.7	285.4
2012	283.6	284.0	284.3	285.2	286.5	289.4	290.3	290.7	288.6	288.2	287.8	288.9	287.3
2013	286.3	286.6	286.3	287.2	288.0	291.6	291.6	291.0	289.3	290.0	289.3	289.9	288.9
2014	286.8	286.1	286.1	286.6	288.6	291.5	292.1	293.2	290.0	290.9	290.3	291.5	289.5
2015	289.1	289.1	289.1	290.1	292.4	295.8	297.2	297.2	293.3	294.2	295.1	295.0	293.1
Professional and Business Services													
2005	672.0	675.2	680.9	698.7	702.5	711.7	714.5	719.4	721.8	728.2	727.7	723.6	706.4
2006	695.2	698.7	708.0	722.3	726.7	738.7	739.0	745.8	744.2	747.8	745.2	740.0	729.3
2007	711.5	714.0	721.1	739.1	744.9	753.2	754.1	760.1	755.0	757.8	755.4	752.9	743.3
2008	723.5	725.1	724.8	739.3	743.2	746.5	744.5	747.7	739.4	736.9	727.3	717.6	734.7
2009	681.8	674.0	666.8	672.2	675.3	677.4	675.4	676.6	672.4	677.2	677.9	674.4	675.1
2010	653.0	655.8	657.0	677.4	681.7	690.9	693.0	698.5	696.7	704.7	704.6	702.8	684.7
2011	677.3	681.3	685.8	704.3	705.0	715.2	719.6	724.9	724.8	728.4	728.9	722.9	709.9
2012	702.9	704.7	711.9	730.2	737.6	749.0	748.0	755.9	757.4	759.2	762.4	757.9	739.8
2013	731.3	737.7	743.6	757.1	769.5	779.6	782.6	790.5	789.0	798.2	800.1	798.0	773.1
2014	763.6	768.7	773.1	788.9	798.7	807.4	805.5	811.0	807.0	815.3	815.3	808.9	797.0
2015	778.6	781.9	783.4	800.1	809.2	817.3	821.8	820.8	817.4	819.9	814.0	802.8	805.6
Education and Health Services													
2005	550.6	555.2	555.9	560.9	561.1	553.5	551.9	549.3	559.3	564.9	568.0	568.5	558.3
2006	560.9	568.9	571.8	571.3	572.5	567.9	564.5	564.5	575.7	577.7	582.3	583.4	571.8
2007	576.9	584.3	587.0	588.0	590.4	585.6	581.4	578.9	589.4	597.5	601.1	601.3	588.5
2008	594.6	601.6	602.7	606.1	606.4	602.5	600.1	599.0	608.5	616.3	620.9	620.5	606.6
2009	611.5	619.1	620.9	620.6	621.0	614.2	611.4	607.8	617.7	626.6	630.3	630.2	619.3
2010	621.5	629.7	632.8	634.5	636.4	629.9	624.2	621.8	633.3	643.4	648.1	648.5	633.7
2011	640.1	648.2	651.1	650.7	650.6	644.8	638.1	637.5	652.5	659.3	662.2	664.5	650.0
2012	652.5	662.7	663.4	665.4	665.0	659.9	651.6	651.3	666.1	671.1	674.4	674.8	663.2
2013	664.0	675.9	677.9	676.1	676.7	668.9	658.9	662.0	674.6	680.8	684.7	685.1	673.8
2014	676.2	684.7	686.5	690.3	691.3	682.7	675.3	677.9	686.1	693.7	697.1	699.3	686.8
2015	688.3	695.9	699.7	700.7	705.0	696.5	688.1	687.8	697.5	713.6	716.4	711.3	700.1

Employment by Industry: Chicago-Naperville-Elgin, IL-IN-WI, 2005–2015—*Continued*

(Numbers in thousands, not seasonally adjusted)

Industry and year	January	February	March	April	May	June	July	August	September	October	November	December	Annual average
Leisure and Hospitality													
2005	360.5	361.5	366.9	384.3	396.5	404.7	408.7	408.0	402.6	389.6	385.5	385.1	387.8
2006	370.8	372.7	379.4	392.3	405.1	418.8	419.6	418.5	409.7	399.9	395.6	397.1	398.3
2007	382.8	381.2	388.0	400.4	415.7	426.2	425.6	426.9	417.8	410.8	405.5	404.3	407.1
2008	388.0	386.2	394.0	409.3	421.8	431.4	430.5	429.5	417.9	409.8	399.9	397.3	409.6
2009	380.8	378.1	383.7	394.9	408.3	416.7	414.3	412.6	405.8	394.6	387.9	386.2	397.0
2010	369.5	369.9	376.4	389.6	403.7	413.2	412.5	413.8	408.0	400.3	395.0	393.7	395.5
2011	375.5	374.8	383.8	398.3	410.6	421.1	420.5	425.9	416.6	408.4	403.2	399.8	403.2
2012	388.1	389.0	397.7	410.0	423.6	434.2	433.3	438.8	426.1	420.4	414.3	414.3	415.8
2013	400.1	399.6	408.6	420.3	435.7	447.1	447.1	447.1	436.6	429.2	422.0	421.5	426.2
2014	409.8	409.4	417.1	431.8	446.5	457.2	455.4	456.6	445.3	442.1	433.9	433.0	436.5
2015	418.2	420.4	427.4	444.0	461.3	472.9	471.1	472.9	461.6	459.9	451.9	452.2	451.2
Other Services													
2005	191.7	192.1	193.1	194.4	194.7	196.9	203.5	203.3	197.1	195.5	196.4	197.9	196.4
2006	196.4	195.3	197.2	194.7	196.1	199.0	202.4	202.6	196.5	196.5	196.7	198.7	197.7
2007	194.6	194.5	197.0	196.1	198.0	200.8	205.1	205.2	198.5	197.9	198.4	199.4	198.8
2008	196.5	197.1	198.3	198.4	199.9	202.4	207.9	207.7	199.7	199.5	199.1	199.3	200.5
2009	194.4	194.5	195.6	194.7	196.0	198.4	201.1	200.3	193.4	194.3	194.4	195.1	196.0
2010	190.7	190.6	191.6	186.2	187.4	189.3	188.3	188.2	187.1	188.4	188.8	189.3	188.8
2011	186.1	186.8	188.3	189.0	190.8	192.8	192.0	191.4	190.1	189.4	188.8	189.9	189.6
2012	187.4	187.9	189.2	188.4	190.0	193.0	191.5	190.6	189.6	188.7	189.1	189.4	189.6
2013	186.9	187.7	188.8	189.5	190.7	192.7	194.3	194.5	192.5	191.2	190.9	191.9	191.0
2014	190.0	190.9	192.5	192.9	195.0	197.8	197.6	195.3	193.0	193.6	193.3	193.7	193.8
2015	191.0	191.8	193.1	193.4	194.4	197.0	196.3	195.8	193.9	195.8	196.3	195.2	194.5
Government													
2005	555.5	565.5	569.7	570.5	573.6	568.1	555.9	549.2	560.1	566.2	569.4	564.7	564.0
2006	555.2	565.4	567.7	570.2	573.9	572.6	552.8	548.0	564.1	567.6	570.4	566.2	564.5
2007	557.0	567.6	570.1	571.5	574.0	570.9	553.8	551.2	564.0	568.0	570.0	566.4	565.4
2008	559.0	568.9	571.6	573.1	578.7	574.4	559.0	555.2	568.3	575.5	575.7	572.4	569.3
2009	561.6	568.5	571.5	575.7	579.5	573.3	554.8	548.7	566.1	575.9	576.2	570.5	568.5
2010	561.2	568.7	569.2	573.8	591.4	577.3	548.5	542.1	557.5	565.6	567.0	559.0	565.1
2011	548.8	556.6	558.8	560.9	563.8	556.5	543.0	536.1	552.4	556.7	559.1	554.0	553.9
2012	542.6	551.6	554.7	555.5	559.2	555.0	537.2	534.4	549.7	554.8	556.1	552.5	550.3
2013	540.9	550.6	553.0	553.1	558.3	555.7	536.2	536.0	549.6	549.8	552.4	551.3	548.9
2014	534.6	542.6	546.2	548.5	555.4	550.8	535.7	533.0	547.8	551.8	551.4	551.8	545.8
2015	537.4	547.0	549.4	551.9	557.9	554.2	537.8	535.8	551.8	561.5	562.2	562.3	550.8

Employment by Industry: Dallas-Fort Worth-Arlington, TX, 2005–2015

(Numbers in thousands, not seasonally adjusted)

Industry and year	January	February	March	April	May	June	July	August	September	October	November	December	Annual average
Total Nonfarm													
2005	2,734.4	2,752.6	2,771.5	2,797.4	2,806.7	2,813.2	2,811.7	2,827.0	2,844.8	2,854.0	2,873.8	2,879.5	2,813.9
2006	2,830.3	2,850.2	2,872.2	2,888.3	2,904.1	2,917.8	2,895.4	2,920.0	2,934.8	2,940.1	2,964.2	2,978.0	2,908.0
2007	2,912.6	2,942.0	2,970.6	2,977.2	2,992.7	3,006.6	2,981.2	3,001.9	3,012.7	3,028.1	3,048.2	3,057.9	2,994.3
2008	2,998.7	3,021.4	3,032.6	3,038.5	3,056.0	3,054.4	3,030.5	3,037.7	3,034.4	3,035.8	3,030.5	3,028.1	3,033.2
2009	2,946.0	2,940.3	2,938.1	2,932.6	2,935.2	2,926.1	2,897.5	2,899.9	2,895.8	2,907.1	2,911.9	2,916.8	2,920.6
2010	2,858.4	2,869.4	2,892.9	2,906.0	2,929.3	2,936.9	2,913.5	2,921.9	2,926.2	2,952.0	2,961.7	2,973.1	2,920.1
2011	2,918.0	2,931.8	2,959.7	2,983.5	2,994.1	3,007.1	2,993.9	3,006.3	3,018.5	3,024.2	3,038.6	3,046.8	2,993.5
2012	2,994.5	3,017.6	3,040.5	3,056.5	3,072.2	3,086.7	3,059.9	3,081.5	3,090.8	3,105.0	3,130.6	3,138.9	3,072.9
2013	3,068.7	3,098.1	3,118.1	3,134.7	3,155.0	3,173.0	3,157.7	3,179.0	3,191.2	3,203.2	3,232.6	3,235.7	3,162.3
2014	3,174.7	3,199.3	3,220.9	3,246.1	3,267.5	3,285.2	3,267.6	3,287.4	3,297.2	3,323.9	3,349.8	3,367.0	3,273.9
2015	3,309.6	3,331.0	3,336.7	3,367.6	3,389.8	3,409.3	3,401.6	3,415.1	3,420.4	3,451.7	3,475.3	3,483.6	3,399.3
Total Private													
2005	2,380.0	2,390.9	2,410.7	2,435.6	2,443.8	2,459.1	2,473.7	2,480.4	2,481.9	2,487.4	2,503.9	2,515.7	2,455.3
2006	2,468.7	2,481.5	2,504.8	2,520.0	2,534.9	2,556.8	2,547.8	2,565.5	2,567.4	2,566.5	2,588.2	2,604.7	2,542.2
2007	2,543.3	2,565.8	2,593.6	2,602.0	2,615.5	2,637.0	2,628.8	2,645.2	2,639.5	2,646.5	2,663.4	2,674.4	2,621.3
2008	2,619.8	2,635.0	2,644.9	2,651.1	2,666.7	2,672.5	2,662.8	2,667.8	2,650.5	2,642.9	2,634.1	2,631.5	2,648.3
2009	2,556.8	2,544.0	2,541.0	2,535.0	2,536.9	2,536.6	2,523.8	2,526.0	2,509.5	2,509.3	2,511.7	2,520.2	2,529.2
2010	2,466.3	2,470.0	2,492.1	2,505.3	2,517.8	2,532.9	2,530.0	2,541.7	2,537.0	2,552.1	2,559.9	2,572.1	2,523.1
2011	2,522.4	2,531.8	2,559.2	2,581.1	2,591.1	2,609.1	2,613.2	2,627.3	2,628.7	2,630.7	2,643.8	2,653.6	2,599.3
2012	2,607.3	2,625.0	2,647.5	2,663.5	2,677.7	2,699.6	2,688.2	2,708.9	2,703.3	2,711.3	2,735.3	2,742.2	2,684.2
2013	2,679.6	2,702.4	2,721.0	2,737.0	2,756.8	2,779.4	2,777.9	2,798.3	2,798.7	2,804.1	2,830.2	2,833.1	2,768.2
2014	2,779.8	2,796.9	2,816.5	2,841.6	2,861.4	2,885.0	2,883.6	2,901.3	2,898.7	2,917.6	2,940.2	2,956.5	2,873.3
2015	2,906.2	2,920.6	2,926.3	2,956.1	2,975.8	2,999.3	3,008.5	3,020.8	3,012.9	3,035.0	3,055.8	3,062.5	2,990.0
Goods Producing													
2005	446.7	450.5	454.1	457.7	460.3	465.8	469.7	470.1	469.5	468.9	468.7	469.6	462.6
2006	463.4	467.6	472.3	473.7	478.6	485.4	482.6	485.4	487.1	483.8	485.7	486.6	479.4
2007	479.0	484.3	489.5	487.9	489.8	496.1	492.6	494.8	495.5	492.3	492.8	493.5	490.7
2008	486.6	491.4	493.1	490.7	492.9	495.3	493.0	493.7	491.2	487.0	480.9	477.2	489.4
2009	462.4	457.3	452.4	445.1	440.8	437.1	430.4	431.2	425.9	418.5	415.4	414.0	435.9
2010	408.7	406.1	409.8	411.5	413.6	417.9	418.6	419.7	417.9	416.8	416.0	416.4	414.4
2011	409.1	411.2	415.3	417.5	419.1	424.4	427.3	428.6	427.7	425.9	426.4	426.9	421.6
2012	423.1	426.7	429.6	430.9	431.2	436.5	439.1	440.5	439.4	438.2	439.2	439.4	434.5
2013	433.3	436.2	439.6	439.7	442.2	446.6	448.0	449.4	448.4	445.5	446.2	444.2	443.3
2014	440.3	445.3	447.3	451.8	455.4	458.9	460.8	461.7	460.9	461.9	462.9	464.7	456.0
2015	460.2	461.3	458.9	460.6	461.2	464.6	466.6	465.7	462.5	462.6	464.0	461.2	462.5
Service-Providing													
2005	2,287.7	2,302.1	2,317.4	2,339.7	2,346.4	2,347.4	2,342.0	2,356.9	2,375.3	2,385.1	2,405.1	2,409.9	2,351.3
2006	2,366.9	2,382.6	2,399.9	2,414.6	2,425.5	2,432.4	2,412.8	2,434.6	2,447.7	2,456.3	2,478.5	2,491.4	2,428.6
2007	2,433.6	2,457.7	2,481.1	2,489.3	2,502.9	2,510.5	2,488.6	2,507.1	2,517.2	2,535.8	2,555.4	2,564.4	2,503.6
2008	2,512.1	2,530.0	2,539.5	2,547.8	2,563.1	2,559.1	2,537.5	2,544.0	2,543.2	2,548.8	2,549.6	2,550.9	2,543.8
2009	2,483.6	2,483.0	2,485.7	2,487.5	2,494.4	2,489.0	2,467.1	2,468.7	2,469.9	2,488.6	2,496.5	2,502.8	2,484.7
2010	2,449.7	2,463.3	2,483.1	2,494.5	2,515.7	2,519.0	2,494.9	2,502.2	2,508.3	2,535.2	2,545.7	2,556.7	2,505.7
2011	2,508.9	2,520.6	2,544.4	2,566.0	2,575.0	2,582.7	2,566.6	2,577.7	2,590.8	2,598.3	2,612.2	2,619.9	2,571.9
2012	2,571.4	2,590.9	2,610.9	2,625.6	2,641.0	2,650.2	2,620.8	2,641.0	2,651.4	2,666.8	2,691.4	2,699.5	2,638.4
2013	2,635.4	2,661.9	2,678.5	2,695.0	2,712.8	2,726.4	2,709.7	2,729.6	2,742.8	2,757.7	2,786.4	2,791.5	2,719.0
2014	2,734.4	2,754.0	2,773.6	2,794.3	2,812.1	2,826.3	2,806.8	2,825.7	2,836.3	2,862.0	2,886.9	2,902.3	2,817.9
2015	2,849.4	2,869.7	2,877.8	2,907.0	2,928.6	2,944.7	2,935.0	2,949.4	2,957.9	2,989.1	3,011.3	3,022.4	2,936.9
Mining and Logging													
2005	158.1	159.7	162.5	165.6	167.5	170.9	172.3	172.5	173.2	172.6	171.7	172.0	168.2
2006	168.4	170.7	174.2	174.5	177.9	182.2	180.5	182.3	183.9	182.9	184.1	185.4	178.9
2007	181.0	184.5	189.1	189.1	190.5	195.1	193.0	196.1	197.4	196.6	197.8	197.9	192.3
2008	194.1	198.5	201.2	200.3	202.0	204.6	202.8	203.5	202.2	199.6	195.7	193.4	199.8
2009	184.6	182.7	180.8	176.9	175.3	175.3	172.9	171.1	166.9	161.6	160.0	159.2	172.3
2010	155.1	154.1	157.4	158.8	159.8	162.4	163.4	164.1	162.8	161.9	160.8	160.6	160.1
2011	156.1	157.2	160.0	161.2	162.1	165.1	167.1	168.1	167.0	165.3	165.5	165.9	163.4
2012	163.7	166.0	168.3	169.5	172.4	175.6	175.6	176.9	176.1	175.7	176.6	176.3	172.7
2013	172.6	174.9	177.6	178.2	180.4	183.3	185.4	187.0	186.7	184.7	185.2	183.5	181.6
2014	183.6	184.9	187.2	190.3	193.1	195.6	197.2	197.9	197.9	198.7	199.1	199.4	193.7
2015	197.0	197.7	196.1	197.6	198.1	200.6	202.0	201.7	200.1	200.2	201.7	200.8	199.5

Employment by Industry: Dallas-Fort Worth-Arlington, TX, 2005–2015—*Continued*

(Numbers in thousands, not seasonally adjusted)

Industry and year	January	February	March	April	May	June	July	August	September	October	November	December	Annual average
Manufacturing													
2005	288.6	290.8	291.6	292.1	292.8	294.9	297.4	297.6	296.3	296.3	297.0	297.6	294.4
2006	295.0	296.9	298.1	299.2	300.7	303.2	302.1	303.1	303.2	300.9	301.6	301.2	300.4
2007	298.0	299.8	300.4	298.8	299.3	301.0	299.6	298.7	298.1	295.7	295.0	295.6	298.3
2008	292.5	292.9	291.9	290.4	290.9	290.7	290.2	290.2	289.0	287.4	285.2	283.8	289.6
2009	277.8	274.6	271.6	268.2	265.5	261.8	257.5	260.1	259.0	256.9	255.4	254.8	263.6
2010	253.6	252.0	252.4	252.7	253.8	255.5	255.2	255.6	255.1	254.9	255.2	255.8	254.3
2011	253.0	254.0	255.3	256.3	257.0	259.3	260.2	260.5	260.7	260.6	260.9	261.0	258.2
2012	259.4	260.7	261.3	261.4	258.8	260.9	263.5	263.6	263.3	262.5	262.6	263.1	261.8
2013	260.7	261.3	262.0	261.5	261.8	263.3	262.6	262.4	261.7	260.8	261.0	260.7	261.7
2014	256.7	260.4	260.1	261.5	262.3	263.3	263.6	263.8	263.0	263.2	263.8	265.3	262.3
2015	263.2	263.6	262.8	263.0	263.1	264.0	264.6	264.0	262.4	262.4	262.3	260.4	263.0
Trade, Transportation, and Utilities													
2005	608.6	603.4	607.6	608.6	610.8	614.2	617.5	621.8	621.6	622.5	636.7	644.5	618.2
2006	622.0	618.8	623.1	623.9	626.6	628.6	627.4	631.9	629.3	631.4	644.5	653.4	630.1
2007	631.9	629.9	635.3	634.4	636.4	640.1	640.3	642.5	641.3	646.3	658.8	665.9	641.9
2008	645.6	643.1	645.2	642.6	644.4	645.7	644.9	648.1	643.0	642.5	647.0	651.4	645.3
2009	627.5	619.5	618.1	612.3	611.7	609.8	608.0	608.6	605.9	606.7	612.8	619.3	613.4
2010	599.8	596.3	600.9	601.8	605.3	607.6	607.3	610.2	607.8	612.8	623.0	629.6	608.5
2011	610.2	608.0	612.6	617.6	619.1	621.4	623.0	627.6	626.3	629.6	640.4	647.6	623.6
2012	628.5	626.8	630.4	631.5	635.6	639.7	639.8	644.3	642.0	645.5	661.3	666.7	641.0
2013	643.5	642.7	644.0	646.9	650.7	655.5	655.8	661.9	661.8	667.7	685.2	691.8	659.0
2014	667.3	664.1	667.5	669.8	674.7	681.2	682.6	688.3	688.1	696.3	713.2	725.5	684.9
2015	704.4	702.2	703.9	708.9	714.7	721.2	724.1	729.1	728.4	736.3	749.7	758.9	723.5
Wholesale Trade													
2005	167.0	167.3	168.0	169.3	169.7	170.2	171.7	172.0	172.4	171.7	172.5	173.5	170.4
2006	172.2	172.9	173.8	174.2	175.1	176.1	176.1	177.1	177.5	177.7	178.7	179.5	175.9
2007	177.0	178.4	179.3	179.3	180.0	181.5	181.4	181.8	181.8	183.9	184.9	185.3	181.2
2008	183.3	184.0	183.9	183.6	183.8	183.8	183.0	183.0	182.0	181.4	180.8	180.2	182.7
2009	176.8	175.8	174.2	172.2	171.6	170.5	169.7	169.1	168.3	167.8	166.9	167.4	170.9
2010	165.5	165.4	166.1	165.7	166.6	167.0	167.6	167.9	167.5	168.2	168.4	169.1	167.1
2011	167.3	168.6	169.1	169.9	170.9	171.5	171.4	172.0	172.2	172.6	172.9	173.9	171.0
2012	172.2	173.5	174.5	175.2	176.5	177.0	177.6	178.3	178.1	177.7	178.6	179.4	176.6
2013	177.8	178.8	179.4	179.8	180.6	181.7	181.6	182.4	183.5	185.2	187.5	188.5	182.2
2014	184.6	185.2	186.2	186.6	187.7	189.1	190.1	191.3	191.4	192.9	194.3	195.6	189.6
2015	194.8	195.4	195.8	196.8	198.5	200.1	201.9	203.0	203.1	206.8	208.4	213.1	201.5
Retail Trade													
2005	305.6	301.8	303.7	304.9	306.1	308.8	309.7	312.5	311.0	312.6	325.0	331.1	311.1
2006	313.2	309.0	311.7	311.7	312.7	313.1	311.6	314.0	310.3	311.6	323.0	328.5	314.2
2007	312.7	308.8	312.4	311.7	312.3	313.6	314.8	315.6	313.7	316.7	328.0	333.4	316.1
2008	318.2	314.9	317.1	314.2	315.2	316.6	317.2	318.9	314.6	315.8	321.0	324.9	317.4
2009	308.3	303.2	303.5	301.3	301.9	301.6	301.1	302.6	300.6	302.3	309.0	313.9	304.1
2010	300.0	296.8	300.1	301.8	304.0	305.1	304.0	306.1	303.6	307.6	316.5	321.6	305.6
2011	305.9	301.8	305.0	308.7	309.1	310.7	312.2	315.7	313.0	316.7	326.4	331.3	313.0
2012	316.3	312.3	314.0	314.4	316.1	318.1	318.0	320.7	317.8	322.0	335.5	337.6	320.2
2013	321.1	319.1	319.3	321.4	323.4	326.2	326.6	331.2	329.5	333.4	346.9	350.6	329.1
2014	333.4	330.5	332.1	333.2	334.7	338.3	338.5	341.6	339.2	343.9	356.9	362.9	340.4
2015	346.7	345.1	345.6	348.8	351.1	354.6	355.8	357.8	355.9	361.0	370.9	373.1	355.5
Transportation and Utilities													
2005	136.0	134.3	135.9	134.4	135.0	135.2	136.1	137.3	138.2	138.2	139.2	139.9	136.6
2006	136.6	136.9	137.6	138.0	138.8	139.4	139.7	140.8	141.5	142.1	142.8	145.4	140.0
2007	142.2	142.7	143.6	143.4	144.1	145.0	144.1	145.1	145.8	145.7	145.9	147.2	144.6
2008	144.1	144.2	144.2	144.8	145.4	145.3	144.7	146.2	146.4	145.3	145.2	146.3	145.2
2009	142.4	140.5	140.4	138.8	138.2	137.7	137.2	136.9	137.0	136.6	136.9	138.0	138.4
2010	134.3	134.1	134.7	134.3	134.7	135.5	135.7	136.2	136.7	137.0	138.1	138.9	135.9
2011	137.0	137.6	138.5	139.0	139.1	139.2	139.4	139.9	141.1	140.3	141.1	142.4	139.6
2012	140.0	141.0	141.9	141.9	143.0	144.0	144.2	145.3	146.1	145.8	147.2	149.7	144.2
2013	144.6	144.8	145.3	145.7	146.7	147.6	147.6	148.3	148.8	149.1	150.8	152.7	147.7
2014	149.3	148.4	149.2	150.0	152.3	153.8	154.0	155.4	157.5	159.5	162.0	167.0	154.9
2015	162.9	161.7	162.5	163.3	165.1	166.5	166.4	168.3	169.4	168.5	170.4	172.7	166.5

Employment by Industry: Dallas-Fort Worth-Arlington, TX, 2005–2015—*Continued*

(Numbers in thousands, not seasonally adjusted)

Industry and year	January	February	March	April	May	June	July	August	September	October	November	December	Annual average
Information													
2005	94.1	94.0	94.3	94.0	93.7	94.1	94.3	94.0	94.3	93.6	93.9	93.6	94.0
2006	92.9	93.8	93.8	92.4	91.7	91.7	90.7	89.9	89.4	88.0	87.6	87.4	90.8
2007	89.3	89.9	90.1	89.6	90.2	90.3	90.8	91.6	91.1	91.3	91.8	91.6	90.6
2008	90.5	90.6	90.7	90.3	90.2	90.0	89.7	89.3	88.0	87.4	87.7	87.7	89.3
2009	86.8	86.2	85.6	85.0	84.8	84.6	83.7	83.0	82.2	82.3	82.4	82.7	84.1
2010	81.2	80.7	80.8	81.3	81.0	81.6	81.0	81.0	80.3	80.0	80.3	80.3	80.8
2011	80.4	80.2	80.2	80.0	80.3	80.5	80.8	80.4	79.9	80.2	80.5	80.7	80.3
2012	79.5	79.4	79.3	79.5	79.5	79.9	79.3	79.0	78.6	79.1	80.1	80.0	79.4
2013	79.6	79.9	79.8	80.2	80.9	81.2	81.5	81.7	80.7	81.2	81.8	82.2	80.9
2014	81.8	81.6	81.3	81.5	81.9	82.4	82.2	81.8	80.8	80.1	80.5	80.7	81.4
2015	79.5	79.3	79.5	79.9	80.0	80.1	81.1	81.3	80.4	79.9	80.9	80.6	80.2
Financial Activities													
2005	220.8	221.3	221.7	222.7	223.2	224.8	226.8	228.0	228.6	228.8	229.8	230.9	225.6
2006	229.0	230.0	232.1	233.7	234.3	235.6	234.5	235.6	235.3	235.5	236.2	237.6	234.1
2007	234.2	235.2	236.8	237.5	238.4	240.4	239.6	240.7	239.7	239.0	239.2	239.7	238.4
2008	237.0	237.9	238.1	239.6	240.7	241.3	239.8	239.6	237.6	236.5	235.2	234.8	238.2
2009	231.9	231.7	231.4	233.9	234.5	234.6	234.0	234.0	232.5	232.5	232.9	233.8	233.1
2010	231.7	232.3	232.8	232.9	233.5	234.4	235.1	235.2	234.9	236.5	236.7	238.0	234.5
2011	237.0	237.8	239.0	238.9	238.9	240.6	241.8	242.4	242.7	243.4	244.0	245.6	241.0
2012	243.8	245.4	246.5	247.2	248.4	250.6	250.5	250.8	250.9	252.5	253.8	255.2	249.6
2013	253.2	255.0	256.9	257.0	258.6	260.9	262.8	263.2	262.7	263.0	263.8	264.3	260.1
2014	260.9	261.8	262.3	264.1	264.0	265.9	267.8	268.4	267.7	269.9	270.5	271.5	266.2
2015	269.9	271.1	271.7	273.3	274.5	276.6	277.3	278.0	278.3	280.4	281.4	283.0	276.3
Professional and Business Services													
2005	380.1	384.6	387.8	397.0	396.4	399.5	404.3	406.8	410.1	415.6	418.1	420.6	401.7
2006	410.1	414.2	418.9	424.2	426.2	430.4	431.3	437.1	439.8	442.3	447.5	449.9	431.0
2007	437.4	443.9	448.7	451.0	451.9	457.4	456.2	462.5	463.4	468.1	470.3	473.2	457.0
2008	460.0	462.7	464.6	466.2	468.3	470.2	468.0	470.3	466.6	465.7	461.7	456.3	465.1
2009	437.9	433.8	431.2	428.7	429.1	430.6	430.0	431.0	427.8	432.7	434.6	434.0	431.8
2010	424.3	427.1	430.6	436.0	436.8	440.1	442.0	446.5	448.5	453.1	454.7	456.4	441.3
2011	447.5	451.4	456.4	462.1	461.9	465.6	467.1	471.7	474.3	474.7	477.1	476.3	465.5
2012	468.0	473.5	478.7	483.3	486.9	489.8	484.9	493.8	492.9	497.7	502.6	498.1	487.5
2013	485.8	492.0	495.3	497.3	500.6	505.8	506.4	513.9	517.0	520.6	524.9	522.3	506.8
2014	512.8	518.4	522.7	529.4	532.6	536.2	537.8	543.6	544.1	549.5	552.8	552.0	536.0
2015	545.3	548.7	548.9	554.2	556.5	559.5	563.8	567.5	565.7	572.6	573.4	575.6	561.0
Education and Health Services													
2005	279.1	282.3	283.4	286.5	287.0	286.3	290.3	290.7	292.6	295.4	296.0	296.4	288.8
2006	294.6	296.9	297.5	298.4	299.0	300.0	299.9	304.2	306.8	308.4	309.7	312.1	302.3
2007	305.4	310.6	313.7	314.8	316.3	316.1	315.8	319.0	321.3	322.9	324.6	325.1	317.1
2008	321.2	326.2	327.0	327.5	330.3	328.1	329.0	331.1	333.2	334.6	336.0	338.4	330.2
2009	333.6	336.4	339.3	341.3	343.3	342.8	344.8	347.0	349.7	353.3	353.5	355.1	345.0
2010	347.7	350.7	354.2	356.5	358.0	356.9	356.2	358.6	360.3	363.7	363.9	365.7	357.7
2011	360.8	361.8	365.7	368.2	369.8	369.7	369.6	371.6	375.2	375.4	376.0	378.0	370.2
2012	372.4	375.9	378.2	378.2	378.4	377.5	376.1	379.3	381.0	381.8	382.6	384.0	378.8
2013	376.8	381.5	383.0	385.6	387.1	385.6	384.2	388.7	391.0	392.6	394.6	395.0	387.1
2014	390.1	394.0	395.7	396.3	398.3	397.5	395.7	400.7	403.0	405.7	408.1	409.7	399.6
2015	403.5	407.7	408.6	413.2	416.5	415.6	416.2	419.9	421.1	425.5	428.1	423.5	416.6
Leisure and Hospitality													
2005	247.3	250.4	254.4	261.3	263.8	265.2	264.4	263.1	260.0	259.2	257.0	255.9	258.5
2006	253.0	255.7	260.1	265.2	269.9	274.8	271.5	271.8	270.1	268.6	267.6	267.8	266.3
2007	261.6	265.7	271.8	280.0	284.6	286.8	286.1	286.8	281.0	282.1	281.4	281.1	279.1
2008	275.0	278.5	281.7	289.0	293.6	294.6	292.6	289.9	285.5	285.2	281.7	281.8	285.8
2009	274.3	276.2	280.0	285.3	288.9	292.2	289.4	288.0	283.5	281.5	277.6	278.9	283.0
2010	271.5	275.0	280.4	283.1	287.1	290.6	287.0	287.8	285.3	287.1	283.3	283.4	283.5
2011	276.1	279.3	286.7	292.4	297.1	300.7	297.3	298.6	295.7	295.6	293.3	292.1	292.1
2012	285.8	290.5	297.1	304.5	308.6	314.8	308.5	311.1	309.1	306.6	305.5	308.0	304.2
2013	298.2	304.7	311.1	318.4	323.9	329.5	325.5	325.4	323.0	320.8	320.4	319.7	318.4
2014	313.0	317.7	324.7	332.5	337.5	344.3	339.0	339.0	337.4	337.1	334.8	334.7	332.6
2015	327.5	333.5	337.1	347.4	353.2	360.1	357.9	358.3	356.8	359.0	360.5	361.4	351.1

Employment by Industry: Dallas-Fort Worth-Arlington, TX, 2005–2015—*Continued*

(Numbers in thousands, not seasonally adjusted)

Industry and year	January	February	March	April	May	June	July	August	September	October	November	December	Annual average
Other Services													
2005	103.3	104.4	107.4	107.8	108.6	109.2	106.4	105.9	105.2	103.4	103.7	104.2	105.8
2006	103.7	104.5	107.0	108.5	108.6	110.3	109.9	109.6	109.6	108.5	109.4	109.9	108.3
2007	104.5	106.3	107.7	106.8	107.9	109.8	107.4	107.3	106.2	104.5	104.5	104.3	106.4
2008	103.9	104.6	104.5	105.2	106.3	107.3	105.8	105.8	105.4	104.0	103.9	103.9	105.1
2009	102.4	102.9	103.0	103.4	103.8	104.9	103.5	103.2	102.0	101.8	102.5	102.4	103.0
2010	101.4	101.8	102.6	102.2	102.5	103.8	102.8	102.7	102.0	102.1	102.0	102.3	102.4
2011	101.3	102.1	103.3	104.4	104.9	106.2	106.3	106.4	106.9	105.9	106.1	106.4	105.0
2012	106.2	106.8	107.7	108.4	109.1	110.8	110.0	110.1	109.4	109.9	110.2	110.8	109.1
2013	109.2	110.4	111.3	111.9	112.8	114.3	113.7	114.1	114.1	112.7	113.3	113.6	112.6
2014	113.6	114.0	115.0	116.2	117.0	118.6	117.7	117.8	116.7	117.1	117.4	117.7	116.6
2015	115.9	116.8	117.7	118.6	119.2	121.6	121.5	121.0	119.7	118.7	117.8	118.3	118.9
Government													
2005	354.4	361.7	360.8	361.8	362.9	354.1	338.0	346.6	362.9	366.6	369.9	363.8	358.6
2006	361.6	368.7	367.4	368.3	369.2	361.0	347.6	354.5	367.4	373.6	376.0	373.3	365.7
2007	369.3	376.2	377.0	375.2	377.2	369.6	352.4	356.7	373.2	381.6	384.8	383.5	373.1
2008	378.9	386.4	387.7	387.4	389.3	381.9	367.7	369.9	383.9	392.9	396.4	396.6	384.9
2009	389.2	396.3	397.1	397.6	398.3	389.5	373.7	373.9	386.3	397.8	400.2	396.6	391.4
2010	392.1	399.4	400.8	400.7	411.5	404.0	383.5	380.2	389.2	399.9	401.8	401.0	397.0
2011	395.6	400.0	400.5	402.4	403.0	398.0	380.7	379.0	389.8	393.5	394.8	393.2	394.2
2012	387.2	392.6	393.0	393.0	394.5	387.1	371.7	372.6	387.5	393.7	395.3	396.7	388.7
2013	389.1	395.7	397.1	397.7	398.2	393.6	379.8	380.7	392.5	399.1	402.4	402.6	394.0
2014	394.9	402.4	404.4	404.5	406.1	400.2	384.0	386.1	398.5	406.3	409.6	410.5	400.6
2015	403.4	410.4	410.4	411.5	414.0	410.0	393.1	394.3	407.5	416.7	419.5	421.1	409.3

Employment by Industry: Houston-The Woodlands-Sugar Land, TX, 2005–2015

(Numbers in thousands, not seasonally adjusted)

Industry and year	January	February	March	April	May	June	July	August	September	October	November	December	Annual average
Total Nonfarm													
2005	2,314.3	2,327.4	2,346.4	2,357.1	2,364.6	2,369.1	2,364.3	2,377.4	2,392.8	2,400.0	2,421.6	2,438.2	2,372.8
2006	2,398.3	2,419.6	2,444.0	2,443.7	2,461.6	2,473.5	2,463.8	2,481.2	2,498.9	2,505.9	2,526.5	2,545.2	2,471.9
2007	2,499.2	2,523.3	2,547.7	2,553.4	2,572.3	2,589.1	2,571.4	2,580.3	2,588.3	2,603.1	2,622.4	2,635.9	2,573.9
2008	2,583.6	2,606.3	2,617.4	2,623.5	2,635.7	2,643.2	2,631.5	2,639.4	2,620.5	2,640.9	2,656.0	2,657.5	2,629.6
2009	2,591.9	2,592.4	2,588.4	2,572.2	2,572.8	2,566.7	2,536.8	2,529.6	2,533.2	2,536.7	2,541.0	2,546.9	2,559.1
2010	2,501.1	2,515.7	2,533.5	2,546.5	2,565.7	2,566.0	2,550.6	2,554.0	2,561.7	2,576.2	2,587.3	2,596.7	2,554.6
2011	2,554.1	2,569.9	2,593.6	2,612.7	2,618.3	2,630.9	2,618.8	2,625.9	2,642.8	2,648.6	2,664.6	2,679.9	2,621.7
2012	2,638.1	2,663.2	2,689.5	2,700.4	2,721.2	2,735.5	2,721.1	2,736.9	2,752.0	2,768.3	2,788.5	2,798.5	2,726.1
2013	2,748.2	2,785.6	2,803.2	2,812.1	2,825.1	2,835.1	2,824.6	2,830.2	2,842.5	2,861.7	2,879.9	2,888.3	2,828.0
2014	2,840.3	2,870.1	2,888.9	2,904.5	2,923.6	2,931.8	2,922.7	2,932.8	2,947.3	2,975.0	2,991.5	3,006.1	2,927.9
2015	2,954.1	2,974.6	2,980.1	2,983.5	2,990.0	2,993.5	2,980.0	2,979.2	2,986.1	3,009.4	3,015.4	3,021.3	2,988.9
Total Private													
2005	1,979.9	1,987.0	2,004.8	2,014.9	2,022.5	2,038.3	2,040.9	2,051.0	2,052.9	2,055.1	2,073.5	2,091.0	2,034.3
2006	2,055.8	2,071.0	2,094.7	2,097.2	2,114.7	2,136.4	2,139.0	2,151.3	2,153.1	2,154.3	2,173.1	2,193.1	2,127.8
2007	2,153.5	2,170.3	2,193.2	2,197.6	2,216.3	2,243.3	2,238.5	2,245.4	2,236.9	2,243.5	2,259.0	2,272.8	2,222.5
2008	2,223.3	2,241.6	2,251.1	2,258.3	2,270.9	2,287.6	2,285.0	2,293.9	2,258.8	2,275.6	2,285.8	2,288.2	2,268.3
2009	2,226.4	2,221.4	2,215.9	2,196.7	2,198.5	2,200.9	2,185.3	2,181.7	2,166.2	2,157.8	2,159.9	2,167.1	2,189.8
2010	2,129.5	2,135.4	2,151.0	2,161.8	2,172.6	2,186.5	2,187.5	2,194.4	2,187.9	2,194.4	2,203.9	2,216.2	2,176.8
2011	2,177.3	2,189.1	2,211.6	2,230.7	2,239.2	2,260.9	2,263.4	2,277.1	2,278.9	2,279.1	2,295.2	2,312.2	2,251.2
2012	2,278.1	2,295.7	2,320.6	2,331.8	2,352.6	2,376.9	2,373.8	2,392.4	2,390.4	2,399.0	2,417.5	2,427.7	2,363.0
2013	2,387.6	2,415.0	2,431.3	2,439.7	2,452.5	2,471.4	2,472.9	2,485.1	2,474.3	2,484.8	2,501.1	2,510.4	2,460.5
2014	2,472.1	2,492.0	2,509.4	2,525.6	2,544.6	2,558.4	2,563.7	2,579.7	2,573.7	2,592.0	2,605.9	2,621.9	2,553.3
2015	2,579.1	2,590.5	2,594.1	2,597.9	2,604.2	2,614.1	2,614.5	2,618.5	2,605.2	2,619.8	2,623.2	2,629.7	2,607.6
Goods Producing													
2005	442.4	444.9	449.2	449.8	449.2	453.4	454.4	456.1	458.4	458.8	461.5	464.6	453.6
2006	464.0	470.1	475.8	474.8	480.6	487.4	487.0	490.4	493.5	496.7	500.1	502.7	485.3
2007	500.6	506.7	510.6	510.1	515.7	522.7	521.0	521.1	520.4	526.9	529.9	530.8	518.0
2008	520.1	527.0	527.8	530.7	533.7	536.1	535.9	537.8	534.7	541.1	540.3	535.7	533.4
2009	521.6	516.8	507.3	494.6	491.1	487.1	481.2	478.2	474.3	470.9	466.0	464.8	487.8
2010	461.7	461.8	463.1	464.5	466.5	468.8	470.5	472.0	471.8	473.3	471.7	471.9	468.1
2011	466.3	472.2	475.3	478.0	478.8	486.7	491.0	494.8	498.4	500.6	501.0	503.2	487.2
2012	498.1	504.4	510.6	512.5	517.8	523.3	523.3	527.5	529.8	535.9	534.9	535.3	521.1
2013	530.5	540.1	542.0	543.6	544.5	549.4	548.5	550.3	548.5	551.3	550.9	552.0	546.0
2014	548.7	556.4	558.2	562.1	566.4	568.7	571.3	575.5	577.3	581.9	583.5	586.3	569.7
2015	578.7	578.8	574.8	567.5	565.5	565.7	562.7	560.0	555.9	561.3	558.7	557.4	565.6
Service-Providing													
2005	1,871.9	1,882.5	1,897.2	1,907.3	1,915.4	1,915.7	1,909.9	1,921.3	1,934.4	1,941.2	1,960.1	1,973.6	1,919.2
2006	1,934.3	1,949.5	1,968.2	1,968.9	1,981.0	1,986.1	1,976.8	1,990.8	2,005.4	2,009.2	2,026.4	2,042.5	1,986.6
2007	1,998.6	2,016.6	2,037.1	2,043.3	2,056.6	2,066.4	2,050.4	2,059.2	2,067.9	2,076.2	2,092.5	2,105.1	2,055.8
2008	2,063.5	2,079.3	2,089.6	2,092.8	2,102.0	2,107.1	2,095.6	2,101.6	2,085.8	2,099.8	2,115.7	2,121.8	2,096.2
2009	2,070.3	2,075.6	2,081.1	2,077.6	2,081.7	2,079.6	2,055.6	2,051.4	2,058.9	2,065.8	2,075.0	2,082.1	2,071.2
2010	2,039.4	2,053.9	2,070.4	2,082.0	2,099.2	2,097.2	2,080.1	2,082.0	2,089.9	2,102.9	2,115.6	2,124.8	2,086.5
2011	2,087.8	2,097.7	2,118.3	2,134.7	2,139.5	2,144.2	2,127.8	2,131.1	2,144.4	2,148.0	2,163.6	2,176.7	2,134.5
2012	2,140.0	2,158.8	2,178.9	2,187.9	2,203.4	2,212.2	2,197.8	2,209.4	2,222.2	2,232.4	2,253.6	2,263.2	2,205.0
2013	2,217.7	2,245.5	2,261.2	2,268.5	2,280.6	2,285.7	2,276.1	2,279.9	2,294.0	2,310.4	2,329.0	2,336.3	2,282.1
2014	2,291.6	2,313.7	2,330.7	2,342.4	2,357.2	2,363.1	2,351.4	2,357.3	2,370.0	2,393.1	2,408.0	2,419.8	2,358.2
2015	2,375.4	2,395.8	2,405.3	2,416.0	2,424.5	2,427.8	2,417.3	2,419.2	2,430.2	2,448.1	2,456.7	2,463.9	2,423.4
Mining and Logging													
2005	65.3	65.7	66.1	65.1	65.5	66.8	67.3	67.5	67.7	68.4	68.6	68.5	66.9
2006	69.2	69.8	69.8	70.8	71.3	72.8	74.1	74.9	75.6	76.9	77.2	78.0	73.4
2007	78.0	78.4	78.7	78.3	79.0	80.1	80.5	80.5	79.8	80.9	81.4	81.6	79.8
2008	80.9	81.9	82.0	82.6	83.4	85.3	86.0	86.5	86.2	87.4	87.3	86.9	84.7
2009	85.2	83.6	82.3	79.4	78.3	77.9	77.9	77.3	76.6	76.0	75.5	75.7	78.8
2010	75.5	75.8	76.0	77.4	78.2	79.7	80.0	80.6	80.4	81.0	81.5	81.9	79.0
2011	81.7	82.6	83.1	84.1	84.4	87.1	88.8	90.2	90.4	91.8	92.5	93.8	87.5
2012	92.6	93.3	94.4	95.0	96.3	97.5	99.2	99.2	99.3	100.1	100.4	101.2	97.4
2013	101.0	101.6	102.1	103.1	103.6	104.9	106.1	106.4	105.8	106.7	107.2	107.6	104.7
2014	106.7	107.7	107.5	107.8	108.6	109.3	110.6	110.8	110.8	110.5	111.6	112.0	109.5
2015	110.5	107.0	104.6	102.3	100.7	100.3	99.9	98.6	97.1	94.8	95.1	94.3	100.4

Employment by Industry: Houston-The Woodlands-Sugar Land, TX, 2005–2015—*Continued*

(Numbers in thousands, not seasonally adjusted)

Industry and year	January	February	March	April	May	June	July	August	September	October	November	December	Annual average
Construction													
2005	170.4	172.0	175.0	175.8	173.9	174.2	174.3	175.5	177.4	177.6	178.6	180.7	175.5
2006	179.9	184.7	188.9	184.7	187.6	190.5	188.9	190.3	192.8	194.4	195.7	196.3	189.6
2007	195.4	200.7	203.0	202.6	205.6	209.1	206.7	206.8	207.0	211.2	212.2	211.9	206.0
2008	203.3	208.5	208.9	209.4	209.9	208.4	206.7	208.1	205.8	210.8	209.3	205.3	207.9
2009	197.9	196.6	193.0	187.6	187.3	185.4	182.1	181.2	179.2	179.0	175.6	173.9	184.9
2010	172.2	171.5	172.4	173.2	173.9	173.9	174.5	175.0	174.9	175.2	172.4	171.0	173.3
2011	165.9	169.6	170.8	170.9	170.7	173.3	174.5	175.9	178.0	177.7	176.1	174.5	173.2
2012	171.7	175.3	178.2	178.0	180.6	181.8	179.5	183.8	184.9	190.2	188.1	186.7	181.6
2013	183.6	190.8	191.6	192.0	192.3	193.9	192.0	193.4	192.5	194.2	192.5	192.1	191.7
2014	191.5	196.9	198.3	202.2	204.4	203.7	204.0	207.5	209.4	212.4	211.1	211.8	204.4
2015	208.8	214.4	214.9	214.4	216.3	217.9	217.5	218.6	218.4	227.6	225.8	224.4	218.3
Manufacturing													
2005	206.7	207.2	208.1	208.9	209.8	212.4	212.8	213.1	213.3	212.8	214.3	215.4	211.2
2006	214.9	215.6	217.1	219.3	221.7	224.1	224.0	225.2	225.1	225.4	227.2	228.4	222.3
2007	227.2	227.6	228.9	229.2	231.1	233.5	233.8	233.8	233.6	234.8	236.3	237.3	232.3
2008	235.9	236.6	236.9	238.7	240.4	242.4	243.2	243.2	242.7	242.9	243.7	243.5	240.8
2009	238.5	236.6	232.0	227.6	225.5	223.8	221.2	219.7	218.5	215.9	214.9	215.2	224.1
2010	214.0	214.5	214.7	213.9	214.4	215.2	216.0	216.4	216.5	217.1	217.8	219.0	215.8
2011	218.7	220.0	221.4	223.0	223.7	226.3	227.7	228.7	230.0	231.1	232.4	234.9	226.5
2012	233.8	235.8	238.0	239.5	240.9	244.0	244.6	244.5	245.6	245.6	246.4	247.4	242.2
2013	245.9	247.7	248.3	248.5	248.6	250.6	250.4	250.5	250.2	250.4	251.2	252.3	249.6
2014	250.5	251.8	252.4	252.1	253.4	255.7	256.7	257.2	257.1	259.0	260.8	262.5	255.8
2015	259.4	257.4	255.3	250.8	248.5	247.5	245.3	242.8	240.4	238.9	237.8	238.7	246.9
Trade, Transportation, and Utilities													
2005	481.5	478.5	480.3	484.3	486.6	489.8	491.8	495.4	493.7	496.0	508.2	519.4	492.1
2006	499.0	497.2	501.6	501.4	502.9	506.4	507.2	510.7	510.0	512.3	521.4	531.2	508.4
2007	514.1	512.5	517.9	518.4	522.0	528.0	529.0	532.0	531.4	534.4	544.5	553.3	528.1
2008	534.7	534.4	537.1	535.9	537.8	542.0	543.0	546.3	538.7	540.2	550.4	557.9	541.5
2009	535.1	530.7	530.5	526.9	526.4	527.0	524.0	525.5	523.0	522.2	527.2	535.4	527.8
2010	518.7	516.3	519.4	519.7	521.6	525.1	525.6	528.7	526.3	529.5	538.4	547.7	526.4
2011	530.7	528.4	532.6	536.6	537.6	541.6	541.9	546.1	543.2	546.4	557.6	567.7	542.5
2012	549.3	547.3	550.5	552.4	555.6	559.6	560.1	564.5	561.3	565.2	579.1	584.7	560.8
2013	567.5	566.8	568.7	571.2	573.4	577.3	578.8	583.5	579.8	582.3	594.5	602.4	578.9
2014	587.6	585.5	586.7	588.2	590.6	594.7	596.3	601.4	598.0	602.5	614.7	624.3	597.5
2015	606.3	604.6	604.8	606.3	609.2	611.2	611.9	615.0	611.5	612.5	619.5	627.5	611.7
Wholesale Trade													
2005	125.4	125.6	126.3	127.4	127.8	128.8	128.9	129.2	129.9	130.2	130.5	131.6	128.5
2006	130.9	132.2	133.5	133.1	133.7	135.0	134.9	135.5	136.2	136.4	136.7	137.3	134.6
2007	135.6	137.1	138.1	138.4	139.2	140.8	141.0	141.7	141.9	142.4	142.6	143.4	140.2
2008	142.4	143.8	144.2	144.5	145.3	146.3	146.0	146.4	145.7	145.7	145.6	145.6	145.1
2009	142.1	142.1	141.3	139.6	139.0	138.8	137.5	137.3	136.9	136.7	136.5	137.1	138.7
2010	136.3	136.5	137.1	137.1	137.7	138.6	138.9	139.1	139.1	138.9	139.1	139.6	138.2
2011	139.5	140.3	141.2	142.3	143.1	144.2	144.9	145.7	146.4	146.8	147.6	148.8	144.2
2012	148.1	149.3	150.3	150.5	151.8	153.5	153.5	154.5	154.4	155.0	155.7	156.3	152.7
2013	155.3	156.9	157.8	157.9	158.9	160.3	161.0	162.1	162.4	162.8	163.8	164.2	160.3
2014	163.3	164.8	165.6	165.6	167.0	168.7	169.0	170.8	171.2	172.0	172.8	174.0	168.7
2015	172.9	173.9	173.8	173.2	173.0	173.0	172.8	173.4	172.6	172.3	172.2	172.8	173.0
Retail Trade													
2005	242.4	238.6	239.9	242.4	243.6	245.7	246.8	249.2	247.4	248.7	259.0	265.5	247.4
2006	250.6	247.5	249.7	250.1	250.3	251.6	252.4	254.6	252.9	254.2	262.8	267.6	253.7
2007	257.0	253.2	256.8	257.0	259.2	262.3	262.9	264.3	263.1	265.6	275.2	279.8	263.0
2008	265.8	263.4	265.8	264.5	264.8	266.8	267.3	269.8	264.3	265.6	275.4	280.2	267.8
2009	266.5	262.8	263.4	262.4	262.9	263.8	263.0	264.9	263.3	263.2	268.6	273.0	264.8
2010	260.5	258.1	260.2	260.0	261.2	263.1	262.5	264.9	262.3	265.7	274.1	279.4	264.3
2011	266.7	263.6	266.3	268.8	269.1	271.5	270.2	273.3	269.4	272.7	282.3	287.0	271.7
2012	274.2	270.6	271.6	272.8	274.6	276.4	276.8	279.6	276.9	280.4	292.0	295.4	278.4
2013	280.4	278.5	279.1	281.4	282.6	284.7	285.8	288.4	284.9	287.0	297.4	302.6	286.1
2014	290.4	288.2	288.2	288.9	289.2	291.2	292.1	294.1	290.8	292.9	302.7	307.3	293.0
2015	293.6	292.1	292.8	294.4	297.4	299.9	300.8	302.8	300.8	302.6	307.5	311.6	299.7

Employment by Industry: Houston-The Woodlands-Sugar Land, TX, 2005–2015—*Continued*

(Numbers in thousands, not seasonally adjusted)

Industry and year	January	February	March	April	May	June	July	August	September	October	November	December	Annual average
Transportation and Utilities													
2005	113.7	114.3	114.1	114.5	115.2	115.3	116.1	117.0	116.4	117.1	118.7	122.3	116.2
2006	117.5	117.5	118.4	118.2	118.9	119.8	119.9	120.6	120.9	121.7	121.9	126.3	120.1
2007	121.5	122.2	123.0	123.0	123.6	124.9	125.1	126.0	126.4	126.4	126.7	130.1	124.9
2008	126.5	127.2	127.1	126.9	127.7	128.9	129.7	130.1	128.7	128.9	129.4	132.1	128.6
2009	126.5	125.8	125.8	124.9	124.5	124.4	123.5	123.3	122.8	122.3	122.1	125.3	124.3
2010	121.9	121.7	122.1	122.6	122.7	123.4	124.2	124.7	124.9	124.9	125.2	128.7	123.9
2011	124.5	124.5	125.1	125.5	125.4	125.9	126.8	127.1	127.4	126.9	127.7	131.9	126.6
2012	127.0	127.4	128.6	129.1	129.2	129.7	129.8	130.4	130.0	129.8	131.4	133.0	129.6
2013	131.8	131.4	131.8	131.9	131.9	132.3	132.0	133.0	132.5	132.5	133.3	135.6	132.5
2014	133.9	132.5	132.9	133.7	134.4	134.8	135.2	136.5	136.0	137.6	139.2	143.0	135.8
2015	139.8	138.6	138.2	138.7	138.8	138.3	138.3	138.8	138.1	137.6	139.8	143.1	139.0
Information													
2005	37.4	37.4	37.6	36.7	36.7	37.0	36.6	36.6	36.3	35.8	36.1	36.1	36.7
2006	35.8	36.0	36.0	36.4	36.7	37.0	37.0	37.0	36.7	36.8	37.0	37.1	36.6
2007	37.1	37.3	37.3	37.0	37.4	37.7	37.6	37.7	37.4	37.2	37.3	37.4	37.4
2008	37.1	37.3	37.2	37.0	37.2	37.2	37.3	37.0	36.4	36.3	36.3	36.4	36.9
2009	35.7	35.7	35.6	35.1	35.0	35.0	34.6	34.3	33.8	34.0	34.0	34.0	34.7
2010	33.2	32.9	32.7	32.6	32.5	33.1	32.5	32.5	32.1	32.2	32.4	32.5	32.6
2011	32.5	32.4	32.2	32.2	32.4	32.5	32.3	32.2	32.0	31.8	31.8	31.9	32.2
2012	31.7	31.7	31.7	31.7	31.9	32.4	32.7	32.9	32.8	32.3	32.6	32.7	32.3
2013	32.2	32.4	32.7	32.7	32.9	33.4	33.4	33.4	33.0	33.5	33.6	33.7	33.1
2014	33.0	32.9	32.9	32.9	32.8	33.0	32.8	32.5	31.9	31.9	32.0	32.2	32.6
2015	32.0	32.0	32.0	32.4	32.5	32.7	32.9	32.7	32.1	31.7	31.5	31.5	32.2
Financial Activities													
2005	137.6	138.0	138.4	138.5	138.7	139.7	141.1	141.7	141.6	140.9	141.3	141.3	139.9
2006	139.8	140.1	140.9	140.6	141.1	142.3	142.7	143.3	143.1	143.3	143.1	144.0	142.0
2007	142.9	143.8	144.6	143.9	144.7	146.2	146.6	147.1	146.4	146.7	146.8	146.9	145.6
2008	145.0	146.2	145.9	145.7	146.3	146.9	147.0	147.1	145.6	144.8	144.7	144.8	145.8
2009	142.2	142.1	141.7	141.3	141.3	141.6	141.3	140.8	139.9	138.6	138.5	138.6	140.7
2010	137.2	137.4	137.8	137.5	137.6	138.3	138.3	138.4	137.6	138.3	138.5	139.0	138.0
2011	137.9	138.0	138.5	138.6	138.8	139.4	139.9	140.0	140.6	140.9	140.6	140.6	139.5
2012	139.5	140.2	140.6	141.1	141.9	142.9	143.0	143.1	142.5	143.8	143.9	144.4	142.2
2013	142.2	143.4	143.1	143.7	144.2	145.5	146.3	146.5	146.1	146.8	146.7	146.8	145.1
2014	145.1	145.9	145.8	146.5	147.6	148.3	148.9	149.6	149.1	150.2	150.0	150.7	148.1
2015	149.1	149.7	150.1	150.5	151.1	151.6	152.1	152.3	151.8	152.9	153.3	152.1	151.4
Professional and Business Services													
2005	332.9	337.3	340.7	343.1	343.7	346.3	348.5	350.6	353.9	358.6	360.0	361.5	348.1
2006	355.2	359.8	364.9	364.3	367.7	373.1	374.7	377.0	377.8	377.9	381.8	384.2	371.5
2007	376.4	380.7	384.9	388.4	390.7	396.1	396.7	397.0	394.8	395.3	395.3	396.3	391.1
2008	390.1	395.4	397.2	398.6	399.2	403.2	402.6	404.2	397.3	403.7	401.1	398.0	399.2
2009	384.3	382.2	380.2	375.9	374.5	374.7	372.8	371.2	368.8	368.6	369.5	369.4	374.3
2010	362.0	364.8	367.9	373.0	374.5	378.6	380.8	381.9	380.9	382.3	383.0	384.9	376.2
2011	379.5	383.8	388.8	395.2	395.6	401.0	403.4	406.5	406.8	405.3	406.6	410.1	398.6
2012	407.3	412.1	417.5	420.8	423.8	430.3	431.7	436.1	435.4	434.4	437.5	439.2	427.2
2013	432.2	438.2	443.5	443.6	444.5	449.6	450.5	452.8	451.0	453.8	454.8	454.8	447.4
2014	446.2	450.3	455.4	459.5	462.8	466.2	468.2	472.7	471.2	474.8	474.3	475.2	464.7
2015	467.9	470.3	469.7	471.7	470.3	473.3	473.7	474.2	471.1	471.5	469.3	468.6	471.0
Education and Health Services													
2005	256.9	258.3	260.0	260.4	261.4	260.7	261.0	263.8	265.7	265.8	267.2	268.1	262.4
2006	265.1	267.2	268.3	269.7	270.9	270.4	270.1	272.4	274.3	274.6	275.2	276.8	271.3
2007	275.0	277.4	278.9	280.0	281.4	281.0	280.4	282.3	283.3	284.3	284.9	285.4	281.2
2008	281.0	282.9	282.2	284.3	285.4	286.0	285.7	288.5	285.9	289.4	291.0	292.1	286.2
2009	288.9	291.5	292.6	294.4	296.4	297.5	298.0	300.1	300.6	302.6	303.2	303.6	297.5
2010	302.5	304.6	306.2	308.0	309.5	308.7	308.7	310.4	311.6	313.1	313.6	313.7	309.2
2011	309.8	310.9	312.3	314.1	315.0	314.6	314.4	316.2	318.4	318.5	320.6	321.5	315.5
2012	318.0	320.8	322.6	323.6	325.5	325.9	325.1	328.8	330.8	332.7	333.5	334.5	326.8
2013	330.4	334.3	335.1	336.4	338.0	337.1	337.0	341.2	342.1	345.2	346.7	345.9	339.1
2014	341.7	344.5	345.1	347.8	349.2	347.3	348.8	352.7	354.0	358.5	359.7	360.3	350.8
2015	358.0	361.6	362.8	364.9	366.1	364.4	366.8	370.0	372.1	375.8	376.1	377.5	368.0

Employment by Industry: Houston-The Woodlands-Sugar Land, TX, 2005-2015—*Continued*

(Numbers in thousands, not seasonally adjusted)

Industry and year	January	February	March	April	May	June	July	August	September	October	November	December	Annual average
Leisure and Hospitality													
2005	199.2	200.3	205.2	208.5	212.5	216.3	214.2	214.4	211.4	208.6	208.4	209.2	209.0
2006	206.8	209.8	215.6	217.0	221.1	224.1	225.2	225.6	223.0	218.3	219.7	221.6	219.0
2007	215.8	219.3	225.2	227.3	231.2	236.9	234.1	235.2	230.9	227.3	228.7	230.8	228.6
2008	224.8	227.4	232.5	234.3	238.6	242.1	239.5	238.9	228.9	227.7	229.4	231.0	232.9
2009	226.7	230.0	235.4	235.9	240.8	244.1	240.3	239.7	234.9	230.1	230.5	230.4	234.9
2010	224.0	226.8	232.6	235.9	238.8	241.7	238.8	239.1	236.8	234.9	235.4	235.6	235.0
2011	230.5	232.8	240.5	243.9	247.7	250.6	246.5	247.9	246.4	242.6	244.0	244.0	243.1
2012	241.4	245.7	253.1	254.8	259.9	265.1	260.7	262.3	260.7	257.5	259.1	259.7	256.7
2013	255.8	262.1	267.7	270.1	275.4	278.1	277.3	277.5	273.6	271.2	272.7	273.9	271.3
2014	269.1	274.4	282.2	285.0	290.6	294.8	292.3	290.9	287.9	286.2	286.0	287.3	285.6
2015	282.8	288.3	294.0	298.3	302.8	307.0	305.8	306.3	303.5	305.8	307.7	309.0	300.9
Other Services													
2005	92.0	92.3	93.4	93.6	93.7	95.1	93.3	92.4	91.9	90.6	90.8	90.8	92.5
2006	90.1	90.8	91.6	93.0	93.7	95.7	95.1	94.9	94.7	94.4	94.8	95.5	93.7
2007	91.6	92.6	93.8	92.5	93.2	94.7	93.1	93.0	92.3	91.4	91.6	91.9	92.6
2008	90.5	91.0	91.2	91.8	92.7	94.1	94.0	94.1	91.3	92.4	92.6	92.3	92.3
2009	91.9	92.4	92.6	92.6	93.0	93.9	93.1	91.9	90.9	90.8	91.0	90.9	92.1
2010	90.2	90.8	91.3	90.6	91.6	92.2	92.3	91.4	90.8	90.8	90.9	90.9	91.2
2011	90.1	90.6	91.4	92.1	93.3	94.5	94.0	93.4	93.1	93.0	93.0	93.2	92.6
2012	92.8	93.5	94.0	94.9	96.2	97.4	97.2	97.2	97.1	97.2	96.9	97.2	96.0
2013	96.8	97.7	98.5	98.4	99.6	101.0	101.1	99.9	100.2	100.7	101.2	100.9	99.7
2014	100.7	102.1	103.1	103.6	104.6	105.4	105.1	104.4	104.3	106.0	105.7	105.6	104.2
2015	104.3	105.2	105.9	106.3	106.7	108.2	108.6	108.0	107.2	108.3	107.1	106.1	106.8
Government													
2005	334.4	340.4	341.6	342.2	342.1	330.8	323.4	326.4	339.9	344.9	348.1	347.2	338.5
2006	342.5	348.6	349.3	346.5	346.9	337.1	324.8	329.9	345.8	351.6	353.4	352.1	344.0
2007	345.7	353.0	354.5	355.8	356.0	345.8	332.9	334.9	351.4	359.6	363.4	363.1	351.3
2008	360.3	364.7	366.3	365.2	364.8	355.6	346.5	345.5	361.7	365.3	370.2	369.3	361.3
2009	365.5	371.0	372.5	375.5	374.3	365.8	351.5	347.9	367.0	378.9	381.1	379.8	369.2
2010	371.6	380.3	382.5	384.7	393.1	379.5	363.1	359.6	373.8	381.8	383.4	380.5	377.8
2011	376.8	380.8	382.0	382.0	379.1	370.0	355.4	348.8	363.9	369.5	369.4	367.7	370.5
2012	360.0	367.5	368.9	368.6	368.6	358.6	347.3	344.5	361.6	369.3	371.0	370.8	363.1
2013	360.6	370.6	371.9	372.4	372.6	363.7	351.7	345.1	368.2	376.9	378.8	377.9	367.5
2014	368.2	378.1	379.5	378.9	379.0	373.4	359.0	353.1	373.6	383.0	385.6	384.2	374.6
2015	375.0	384.1	386.0	385.6	385.8	379.4	365.5	360.7	380.9	389.6	392.2	391.6	381.4

Employment by Industry: Washington-Arlington-Alexandria, DC-VA-MD-WV, 2005–2015

(Numbers in thousands, not seasonally adjusted)

Industry and year	January	February	March	April	May	June	July	August	September	October	November	December	Annual average
Total Nonfarm													
2005	2,866.0	2,878.3	2,896.8	2,919.2	2,937.7	2,956.3	2,954.8	2,948.1	2,954.2	2,954.3	2,975.6	2,986.8	2,935.7
2006	2,927.1	2,938.1	2,965.7	2,972.8	2,991.1	3,015.7	2,998.4	2,991.1	2,993.0	2,999.9	3,011.6	3,025.9	2,985.9
2007	2,960.9	2,967.1	2,991.1	2,997.2	3,015.4	3,032.6	3,020.8	3,010.2	3,006.9	3,024.8	3,037.7	3,048.1	3,009.4
2008	2,978.1	2,987.0	3,005.2	3,024.1	3,041.1	3,048.7	3,046.6	3,034.8	3,023.7	3,026.4	3,027.2	3,025.4	3,022.4
2009	2,956.5	2,954.2	2,962.8	2,963.5	2,979.1	2,990.1	2,986.9	2,967.3	2,952.2	2,973.7	2,986.4	2,988.7	2,971.8
2010	2,919.3	2,895.9	2,942.1	2,979.2	3,003.9	3,017.1	3,014.9	2,982.1	2,987.0	3,008.3	3,019.4	3,025.1	2,982.9
2011	2,966.3	2,975.5	2,997.6	3,023.7	3,024.7	3,042.7	3,049.7	3,023.6	3,040.6	3,046.7	3,057.0	3,061.4	3,025.8
2012	2,998.1	3,012.0	3,039.1	3,054.3	3,068.6	3,085.7	3,075.4	3,063.7	3,074.6	3,095.8	3,109.1	3,107.6	3,065.3
2013	3,047.4	3,060.0	3,076.0	3,091.6	3,103.9	3,109.1	3,104.8	3,089.6	3,097.9	3,102.3	3,122.9	3,115.3	3,093.4
2014	3,051.7	3,058.6	3,076.3	3,103.6	3,126.3	3,137.5	3,120.4	3,107.5	3,123.6	3,138.3	3,150.9	3,149.5	3,112.0
2015	3,100.9	3,111.7	3,119.9	3,160.6	3,185.4	3,195.0	3,184.9	3,168.8	3,180.9	3,206.6	3,219.5	3,222.2	3,171.4
Total Private													
2005	2,236.9	2,247.0	2,263.3	2,285.2	2,300.3	2,321.3	2,323.5	2,319.8	2,319.7	2,313.7	2,329.0	2,340.7	2,300.0
2006	2,290.8	2,296.4	2,320.3	2,328.9	2,343.7	2,372.2	2,360.6	2,357.0	2,350.3	2,349.3	2,359.6	2,371.9	2,341.8
2007	2,321.1	2,321.3	2,342.3	2,349.1	2,363.2	2,384.4	2,375.2	2,368.6	2,358.6	2,366.0	2,375.1	2,383.7	2,359.1
2008	2,325.1	2,326.2	2,340.4	2,363.9	2,377.3	2,387.2	2,384.0	2,375.1	2,363.6	2,357.1	2,353.8	2,350.5	2,358.7
2009	2,289.8	2,279.7	2,284.3	2,287.0	2,299.8	2,312.6	2,303.2	2,294.6	2,278.3	2,289.8	2,297.6	2,300.5	2,293.1
2010	2,240.0	2,214.0	2,253.7	2,289.4	2,302.8	2,320.0	2,313.5	2,309.1	2,298.7	2,311.3	2,318.6	2,326.4	2,291.5
2011	2,279.4	2,281.2	2,299.5	2,328.0	2,327.6	2,347.5	2,361.3	2,352.8	2,346.6	2,350.8	2,361.4	2,365.3	2,333.5
2012	2,314.4	2,320.1	2,341.9	2,359.8	2,373.3	2,392.7	2,393.5	2,395.6	2,384.8	2,397.1	2,409.0	2,408.2	2,374.2
2013	2,360.6	2,365.4	2,379.3	2,394.6	2,405.1	2,414.8	2,425.0	2,423.7	2,410.3	2,408.7	2,425.6	2,420.7	2,402.8
2014	2,374.9	2,373.2	2,389.7	2,416.8	2,435.4	2,447.5	2,446.5	2,444.6	2,435.0	2,444.4	2,454.3	2,455.1	2,426.5
2015	2,419.1	2,418.7	2,426.4	2,465.1	2,487.0	2,497.9	2,505.1	2,501.1	2,487.4	2,505.5	2,516.1	2,520.0	2,479.1
Goods Producing													
2005	243.9	243.7	246.1	252.4	255.2	259.4	261.3	262.4	262.3	258.9	259.9	259.2	255.4
2006	252.4	252.5	256.9	258.6	260.7	264.6	264.7	264.0	261.6	257.8	255.8	255.3	258.7
2007	247.5	244.5	248.5	250.7	252.5	255.8	255.1	255.3	252.6	249.9	247.5	244.8	250.4
2008	237.6	236.5	237.8	238.6	238.8	240.4	239.7	239.4	237.2	233.9	229.5	225.0	236.2
2009	213.6	210.5	209.2	208.9	208.7	208.7	208.5	207.4	204.8	201.9	199.8	197.8	206.7
2010	188.6	181.0	188.8	194.8	196.5	197.9	199.8	199.7	198.2	197.0	196.0	194.1	194.4
2011	187.5	187.2	189.2	193.7	195.1	197.7	201.1	200.4	197.6	196.1	195.5	195.0	194.7
2012	188.9	188.8	191.6	193.9	195.0	198.9	200.6	200.1	198.7	199.0	197.7	196.3	195.8
2013	190.7	190.5	192.2	194.8	197.3	199.8	201.1	202.0	199.7	198.1	198.6	195.8	196.7
2014	191.6	190.4	193.0	198.2	200.7	203.4	202.9	203.9	202.3	202.9	202.3	200.1	199.3
2015	193.6	193.4	194.6	200.7	203.5	205.8	207.7	208.4	207.2	208.4	209.6	207.3	203.4
Service-Providing													
2005	2,622.1	2,634.6	2,650.7	2,666.8	2,682.5	2,696.9	2,693.5	2,685.7	2,691.9	2,695.4	2,715.7	2,727.6	2,680.3
2006	2,674.7	2,685.6	2,708.8	2,714.2	2,730.4	2,751.1	2,733.7	2,727.1	2,731.4	2,742.1	2,755.8	2,770.6	2,727.1
2007	2,713.4	2,722.6	2,742.6	2,746.5	2,762.9	2,776.8	2,765.7	2,754.9	2,754.3	2,774.9	2,790.2	2,803.3	2,759.0
2008	2,740.5	2,750.5	2,767.4	2,785.5	2,802.3	2,808.3	2,806.9	2,795.4	2,786.5	2,792.5	2,797.7	2,800.4	2,786.2
2009	2,742.9	2,743.7	2,753.6	2,754.6	2,770.4	2,781.4	2,778.4	2,759.9	2,747.4	2,771.8	2,786.6	2,790.9	2,765.1
2010	2,730.7	2,714.9	2,753.3	2,784.4	2,807.4	2,819.2	2,815.1	2,782.4	2,788.8	2,811.3	2,823.4	2,831.0	2,788.5
2011	2,778.8	2,788.3	2,808.4	2,830.0	2,829.6	2,845.0	2,848.6	2,823.2	2,843.0	2,850.6	2,861.5	2,866.4	2,831.1
2012	2,809.2	2,823.2	2,847.5	2,860.4	2,873.6	2,886.8	2,874.8	2,863.6	2,875.9	2,896.8	2,911.4	2,911.3	2,869.5
2013	2,856.7	2,869.5	2,883.8	2,896.8	2,906.6	2,909.3	2,903.7	2,887.6	2,898.2	2,904.2	2,924.3	2,919.5	2,896.7
2014	2,860.1	2,868.2	2,883.3	2,905.4	2,925.6	2,934.1	2,917.5	2,903.6	2,921.3	2,935.4	2,948.6	2,949.4	2,912.7
2015	2,907.3	2,918.3	2,925.3	2,959.9	2,981.9	2,989.2	2,977.2	2,960.4	2,973.7	2,998.2	3,009.9	3,014.9	2,968.0
Mining, Logging, and Construction													
2005	177.1	177.0	179.2	185.3	187.9	191.8	193.9	194.9	194.9	192.4	193.0	192.2	188.3
2006	187.1	187.3	191.4	192.8	195.0	198.3	198.1	197.8	195.9	192.9	191.2	190.3	193.2
2007	183.7	180.5	184.5	187.0	188.7	191.2	190.6	190.9	188.6	186.2	184.0	181.2	186.4
2008	174.8	173.7	175.0	175.9	176.1	177.4	176.9	176.6	174.9	172.0	168.0	163.8	173.8
2009	154.4	152.1	151.2	151.4	151.4	151.8	152.1	151.1	149.2	146.4	144.4	142.5	149.8
2010	135.0	128.0	135.3	141.0	142.6	143.8	146.2	146.4	145.3	143.9	143.1	141.3	141.0
2011	135.4	135.2	137.0	141.5	143.0	145.4	148.9	148.5	146.2	144.8	144.3	143.8	142.8
2012	138.1	138.6	141.1	143.3	144.5	147.9	149.5	149.1	148.1	148.6	147.3	146.4	145.2
2013	141.1	141.0	142.7	145.1	147.4	149.7	151.0	151.9	150.2	148.3	148.8	145.9	146.9
2014	142.0	140.8	143.2	146.9	149.2	151.6	151.2	152.1	150.7	151.0	150.3	148.2	148.1
2015	142.1	141.8	142.7	148.1	150.7	152.6	154.7	155.1	154.1	154.9	155.5	153.8	150.5

Employment by Industry: Washington-Arlington-Alexandria, DC-VA-MD-WV, 2005–2015—*Continued*

(Numbers in thousands, not seasonally adjusted)

Industry and year	January	February	March	April	May	June	July	August	September	October	November	December	Annual average
Manufacturing													
2005	66.8	66.7	66.9	67.1	67.3	67.6	67.4	67.5	67.4	66.5	66.9	67.0	67.1
2006	65.3	65.2	65.5	65.8	65.7	66.3	66.6	66.2	65.7	64.9	64.6	65.0	65.6
2007	63.8	64.0	64.0	63.7	63.8	64.6	64.5	64.4	64.0	63.7	63.5	63.6	64.0
2008	62.8	62.8	62.8	62.7	62.7	63.0	62.8	62.8	62.3	61.9	61.5	61.2	62.4
2009	59.2	58.4	58.0	57.5	57.3	56.9	56.4	56.3	55.6	55.5	55.4	55.3	56.8
2010	53.6	53.0	53.5	53.8	53.9	54.1	53.6	53.3	52.9	53.1	52.9	52.8	53.4
2011	52.1	52.0	52.2	52.2	52.1	52.3	52.2	51.9	51.4	51.3	51.2	51.2	51.8
2012	50.8	50.2	50.5	50.6	50.5	51.0	51.1	51.0	50.6	50.4	50.4	49.9	50.6
2013	49.6	49.5	49.5	49.7	49.9	50.1	50.1	50.1	49.5	49.8	49.8	49.9	49.8
2014	49.6	49.6	49.8	51.3	51.5	51.8	51.7	51.8	51.6	51.9	52.0	51.9	51.2
2015	51.5	51.6	51.9	52.6	52.8	53.2	53.0	53.3	53.1	53.5	54.1	53.5	52.8
Trade, Transportation, and Utilities													
2005	404.5	401.4	403.1	403.6	406.4	409.6	410.4	409.6	407.0	409.7	418.4	429.2	409.4
2006	408.1	399.6	401.7	400.4	404.9	408.8	406.5	406.2	405.0	407.5	417.3	425.7	407.6
2007	407.2	399.6	401.9	402.5	405.9	409.6	408.1	406.1	404.0	406.1	416.7	424.8	407.7
2008	404.9	398.0	398.5	398.4	400.5	403.1	401.7	399.9	396.9	396.4	401.7	406.8	400.6
2009	385.2	377.9	376.9	374.7	378.2	380.1	377.8	377.3	376.3	378.8	387.5	393.3	380.3
2010	375.7	366.0	372.3	375.4	379.2	383.0	381.2	381.5	379.0	384.5	393.0	400.6	381.0
2011	382.2	377.3	378.9	382.4	383.9	386.7	387.1	387.1	385.0	389.1	398.0	405.0	386.9
2012	387.1	382.5	384.7	384.4	388.2	390.8	388.9	388.7	387.2	390.6	401.8	407.0	390.2
2013	388.0	382.7	384.6	385.6	388.5	391.4	391.7	391.9	389.7	393.2	404.0	410.6	391.8
2014	391.8	386.2	388.7	391.0	394.4	397.7	397.5	397.2	394.9	398.7	408.6	416.1	396.9
2015	397.9	391.7	392.4	396.1	400.9	403.9	404.6	404.4	403.0	404.5	412.6	420.0	402.7
Wholesale Trade													
2005	70.7	71.1	71.4	71.8	71.9	71.8	72.2	72.2	71.6	70.8	70.9	71.2	71.5
2006	69.7	70.0	70.4	70.4	70.9	71.0	70.7	70.6	70.2	70.4	70.4	70.8	70.5
2007	70.5	70.6	70.9	70.9	71.1	71.5	70.8	70.7	70.4	70.5	70.6	70.7	70.8
2008	70.0	70.3	70.3	70.0	70.0	70.1	69.8	69.5	68.9	68.7	68.0	67.6	69.4
2009	66.9	66.6	66.2	65.7	65.5	65.3	64.9	64.8	64.2	64.1	63.9	64.1	65.2
2010	63.1	62.8	63.1	62.8	63.0	63.1	63.0	63.0	62.6	63.0	62.8	63.1	63.0
2011	62.8	62.8	63.0	62.9	62.9	62.8	63.0	63.0	62.5	62.8	62.6	62.7	62.8
2012	62.3	62.6	62.9	62.0	62.8	63.0	63.0	63.3	63.0	63.2	63.3	63.2	62.9
2013	63.0	63.1	63.2	62.9	62.9	63.0	62.8	62.7	62.2	62.6	62.7	62.8	62.8
2014	62.0	62.0	62.3	62.0	62.4	62.4	62.4	62.4	61.9	61.6	61.6	61.6	62.1
2015	61.1	60.9	61.0	61.2	61.6	61.8	62.2	62.0	61.9	62.5	62.5	63.4	61.8
Retail Trade													
2005	267.5	263.6	264.8	265.3	267.7	270.4	271.2	270.6	269.0	271.5	279.5	288.2	270.8
2006	272.7	265.9	267.1	266.1	269.5	272.5	271.3	271.4	270.1	272.9	282.4	287.8	272.5
2007	273.7	266.0	267.6	268.5	271.2	273.6	273.1	271.1	269.4	271.7	281.7	287.2	272.9
2008	272.1	264.8	265.6	265.9	267.5	269.3	268.5	266.8	264.8	264.8	269.8	273.5	267.8
2009	256.4	250.3	249.7	248.4	251.2	252.9	251.6	251.5	250.9	254.1	262.2	266.2	253.8
2010	252.9	244.1	249.4	252.5	255.5	258.2	257.1	257.4	255.4	260.6	268.1	273.1	257.0
2011	258.4	254.2	255.2	258.5	259.8	261.9	261.5	261.7	260.7	264.2	272.8	277.7	262.2
2012	263.6	258.6	260.7	260.5	263.0	264.7	263.4	262.9	262.1	265.1	275.4	278.1	264.8
2013	263.7	259.6	260.8	262.3	264.7	266.8	267.4	267.5	266.2	269.7	278.8	282.7	267.5
2014	268.3	264.0	265.7	267.9	270.2	272.8	272.8	272.5	270.7	274.6	282.8	287.4	272.5
2015	273.8	269.5	270.3	273.0	276.5	279.2	279.0	278.9	278.1	279.3	286.1	290.2	277.8
Transportation and Utilities													
2005	66.3	66.7	66.9	66.5	66.8	67.4	67.0	66.8	66.4	67.4	68.0	69.8	67.2
2006	65.7	63.7	64.2	63.9	64.5	65.3	64.5	64.2	64.7	64.2	64.5	67.1	64.7
2007	63.0	63.0	63.4	63.1	63.6	64.5	64.2	64.3	64.2	63.9	64.4	66.9	64.0
2008	62.8	62.9	62.6	62.5	63.0	63.7	63.4	63.6	63.2	62.9	63.9	65.7	63.4
2009	61.9	61.0	61.0	60.6	61.5	61.9	61.3	61.0	61.2	60.6	61.4	63.0	61.4
2010	59.7	59.1	59.8	60.1	60.7	61.7	61.1	61.1	61.0	60.9	62.1	64.4	61.0
2011	61.0	60.3	60.7	61.0	61.2	62.0	62.6	62.4	61.8	62.1	62.6	64.6	61.9
2012	61.2	61.3	61.1	61.9	62.4	63.1	62.5	62.5	62.1	62.3	63.1	65.7	62.4
2013	61.3	60.0	60.6	60.4	60.9	61.6	61.5	61.7	61.3	60.9	62.5	65.1	61.5
2014	61.5	60.2	60.7	61.1	61.8	62.5	62.3	62.3	62.3	62.5	64.2	67.1	62.4
2015	63.0	61.3	61.1	61.9	62.8	62.9	63.4	63.5	63.0	62.7	64.0	66.4	63.0

Employment by Industry: Washington-Arlington-Alexandria, DC-VA-MD-WV, 2005–2015—*Continued*

(Numbers in thousands, not seasonally adjusted)

Industry and year	January	February	March	April	May	June	July	August	September	October	November	December	Annual average
Information													
2005	100.6	101.0	100.9	100.2	100.3	100.8	101.0	100.3	100.1	100.0	99.9	100.0	100.4
2006	98.9	99.3	100.0	98.6	98.5	98.5	97.9	97.2	96.4	95.1	95.1	94.8	97.5
2007	95.1	95.2	95.0	94.0	94.3	94.9	95.1	94.8	93.9	93.4	93.7	94.0	94.5
2008	92.6	93.0	92.9	92.7	92.5	92.4	92.1	91.6	90.8	89.7	90.0	89.2	91.6
2009	87.0	87.0	86.4	84.7	84.4	84.9	83.8	83.2	82.0	81.7	81.6	81.6	84.0
2010	80.5	80.0	80.2	79.7	79.6	80.6	80.9	80.8	81.9	81.8	81.3	83.1	80.9
2011	80.1	80.7	81.0	82.0	80.0	81.8	81.6	76.2	80.2	77.3	78.5	79.8	79.9
2012	76.1	77.3	78.1	76.3	77.1	78.8	77.9	79.1	77.0	76.8	78.4	77.3	77.5
2013	76.5	78.0	77.9	76.5	77.2	77.2	77.6	78.7	76.6	76.7	78.5	77.3	77.4
2014	79.1	77.8	77.8	77.9	79.3	78.5	78.5	79.3	77.3	78.1	77.4	77.4	78.2
2015	77.7	77.0	76.6	77.2	77.6	77.1	77.5	76.8	75.8	75.3	76.3	75.6	76.7
Financial Activities													
2005	158.8	159.2	159.0	160.7	161.5	162.4	162.6	162.2	161.5	160.7	160.5	161.3	160.9
2006	159.9	160.7	161.5	161.2	162.2	163.9	163.3	163.1	162.3	161.6	161.6	162.7	162.0
2007	160.7	161.1	161.3	160.2	160.7	161.7	161.4	160.2	158.9	157.9	157.3	157.4	159.9
2008	155.1	155.1	155.0	155.6	155.5	156.3	156.4	155.7	154.2	153.2	152.6	152.4	154.8
2009	149.6	148.8	148.2	148.0	148.3	149.4	149.1	148.7	147.5	148.1	147.9	148.5	148.5
2010	146.3	145.6	146.6	146.4	147.1	148.5	148.6	148.0	146.4	147.5	147.7	148.0	147.2
2011	145.4	145.5	145.7	147.1	147.2	147.9	148.2	147.8	147.1	147.4	147.1	147.8	147.0
2012	146.3	146.7	147.1	147.8	148.2	149.6	149.8	149.4	148.9	149.7	149.8	150.3	148.6
2013	149.2	149.5	150.2	150.6	150.9	152.3	152.8	152.4	151.1	151.9	152.1	152.5	151.3
2014	150.4	150.2	150.7	150.8	151.3	152.8	153.3	152.8	151.8	152.2	152.3	152.6	151.8
2015	152.1	152.3	152.6	152.6	153.7	155.3	155.5	155.1	153.9	155.7	154.6	155.2	154.1
Professional and Business Services													
2005	624.8	630.4	636.2	642.9	645.0	652.2	657.2	657.1	657.8	655.5	656.6	658.0	647.8
2006	647.0	652.6	659.0	663.3	665.4	674.9	674.2	674.4	670.8	669.4	670.1	671.6	666.1
2007	661.4	666.4	671.8	675.2	677.3	684.2	681.7	681.8	675.3	680.9	681.3	682.6	676.7
2008	671.2	674.4	678.0	685.7	686.0	690.3	690.7	689.6	684.7	685.4	683.7	681.8	683.5
2009	672.8	672.2	673.7	673.3	673.3	678.7	679.2	677.2	670.0	678.0	678.8	679.0	675.5
2010	666.2	665.8	673.1	683.7	684.3	690.3	687.9	686.2	680.6	687.5	687.7	688.4	681.8
2011	682.0	684.5	689.6	693.0	691.7	696.8	704.2	703.6	698.0	701.9	702.2	700.6	695.7
2012	690.3	693.2	699.4	706.7	707.1	713.4	715.8	717.1	708.9	714.7	715.5	712.4	707.9
2013	702.8	706.4	708.6	708.7	706.6	709.6	713.6	713.1	704.6	703.6	705.0	701.1	707.0
2014	691.9	694.5	696.4	702.8	705.2	709.6	713.4	711.8	705.1	709.6	710.1	708.3	704.9
2015	705.1	706.9	707.7	718.8	721.8	726.4	729.2	727.5	720.2	730.7	732.6	729.9	721.4
Education and Health Services													
2005	309.3	314.1	315.0	314.8	313.2	308.7	303.6	302.5	312.5	317.3	321.2	320.7	312.7
2006	315.3	320.8	323.1	323.5	320.8	317.5	311.6	310.6	321.3	327.7	331.5	332.1	321.3
2007	328.3	333.3	336.0	334.7	332.1	328.0	322.5	321.2	332.2	339.5	341.3	342.1	332.6
2008	335.5	339.1	340.7	343.1	344.4	339.6	337.0	336.6	345.6	349.6	351.4	352.5	342.9
2009	349.2	352.1	353.5	355.8	356.1	350.8	347.1	345.3	351.5	360.3	362.6	362.9	353.9
2010	358.1	355.8	361.2	366.0	366.1	359.4	356.7	356.1	363.7	366.0	367.9	367.5	362.0
2011	369.0	370.8	372.6	375.7	369.7	366.4	368.5	367.4	377.5	380.4	381.9	379.7	373.3
2012	378.1	380.9	382.5	385.1	382.9	376.1	374.2	376.0	388.1	393.8	395.0	393.7	383.9
2013	390.6	394.3	396.0	399.4	396.3	386.2	388.9	388.8	400.8	403.7	405.5	403.0	396.1
2014	399.8	402.8	404.7	407.1	405.1	395.4	392.3	393.2	407.2	410.2	412.2	411.4	403.5
2015	409.6	413.2	413.2	417.6	416.0	405.3	404.8	404.4	414.0	417.5	419.4	419.9	412.9
Leisure and Hospitality													
2005	230.6	232.0	236.5	243.7	251.3	259.8	258.9	257.6	251.4	245.5	245.7	244.7	246.5
2006	236.0	237.1	243.1	247.1	254.1	264.6	262.5	262.3	255.0	250.0	248.2	248.5	250.7
2007	240.9	240.2	245.9	251.6	258.9	266.9	268.2	267.5	260.7	256.7	255.0	254.7	255.6
2008	246.8	247.8	253.8	264.3	272.2	276.6	277.4	274.8	267.7	263.0	259.0	256.5	263.3
2009	247.5	246.8	251.4	257.1	265.5	272.5	271.5	269.7	262.2	258.6	256.7	253.8	259.4
2010	243.9	240.4	249.7	260.5	265.9	274.8	273.5	272.9	266.8	264.0	261.9	261.1	261.3
2011	251.5	252.7	259.4	268.8	274.3	282.8	282.2	283.2	275.5	272.8	271.4	269.8	270.4
2012	262.0	264.3	271.3	278.6	287.0	295.9	295.1	295.2	287.1	283.7	281.4	280.7	281.9
2013	274.6	275.8	281.3	289.4	297.7	306.5	306.4	304.7	296.5	290.6	289.8	288.4	291.8
2014	280.1	280.6	286.6	296.3	305.6	314.1	312.6	311.1	302.4	299.0	297.1	295.0	298.4
2015	290.4	291.2	295.6	305.8	315.6	324.5	325.6	324.6	314.4	315.3	311.5	312.1	310.6

Employment by Industry: Washington-Arlington-Alexandria, DC-VA-MD-WV, 2005–2015—*Continued*

(Numbers in thousands, not seasonally adjusted)

Industry and year	January	February	March	April	May	June	July	August	September	October	November	December	Annual average
Other Services													
2005	164.4	165.2	166.5	166.9	167.4	168.4	168.5	168.1	167.1	166.1	166.8	167.6	166.9
2006	173.2	173.8	175.0	176.2	177.1	179.4	179.9	179.2	177.9	180.2	180.0	181.2	177.8
2007	180.0	181.0	181.9	180.2	181.5	183.3	183.1	181.7	181.0	181.6	182.3	183.3	181.7
2008	181.4	182.3	183.7	185.5	187.4	188.5	189.0	187.5	186.5	185.9	185.9	186.3	185.8
2009	184.9	184.4	185.0	184.5	185.3	187.5	186.2	185.8	184.0	182.4	182.7	183.6	184.7
2010	180.7	179.4	181.8	182.9	184.1	185.5	184.9	183.9	182.1	183.0	183.1	183.6	182.9
2011	181.7	182.5	183.1	185.3	185.7	187.4	188.4	187.1	185.7	185.8	186.8	187.6	185.6
2012	185.6	186.4	187.2	187.0	187.8	189.2	191.2	190.0	188.9	188.8	189.4	190.5	188.5
2013	188.2	188.2	188.5	189.6	190.6	191.8	192.9	192.1	191.3	190.9	192.1	192.0	190.7
2014	190.2	190.7	191.8	192.7	193.8	196.0	196.0	195.3	194.0	193.7	194.3	194.2	193.6
2015	192.7	193.0	193.7	196.3	197.9	199.6	200.2	199.9	198.9	198.1	199.5	200.0	197.5
Government													
2005	629.1	631.3	633.5	634.0	637.4	635.0	631.3	628.3	634.5	640.6	646.6	646.1	635.6
2006	636.3	641.7	645.4	643.9	647.4	643.5	637.8	634.1	642.7	650.6	652.0	654.0	644.1
2007	639.8	645.8	648.8	648.1	652.2	648.2	645.6	641.6	648.3	658.8	662.6	664.4	650.4
2008	653.0	660.8	664.8	660.2	663.8	661.5	662.6	659.7	660.1	669.3	673.4	674.9	663.7
2009	666.7	674.5	678.5	676.5	679.3	677.5	683.7	672.7	673.9	683.9	688.8	688.2	678.7
2010	679.3	681.9	688.4	689.8	701.1	697.1	701.4	673.0	688.3	697.0	700.8	698.7	691.4
2011	686.9	694.3	698.1	695.7	697.1	695.2	688.4	670.8	694.0	695.9	695.6	696.1	692.3
2012	683.7	691.9	697.2	694.5	695.3	693.0	681.9	668.1	689.8	698.7	700.1	699.4	691.1
2013	686.8	694.6	696.7	697.0	698.8	694.3	679.8	665.9	687.6	693.6	697.3	694.6	690.6
2014	676.8	685.4	686.6	686.8	690.9	690.0	673.9	662.9	688.6	693.9	696.6	694.4	685.6
2015	681.8	693.0	693.5	695.5	698.4	697.1	679.8	667.7	693.5	701.1	703.4	702.2	692.3

Employment by Industry: Philadelphia-Camden-Wilmington, PA-NJ-DE-MD, 2005–2015

(Numbers in thousands, not seasonally adjusted)

Industry and year	January	February	March	April	May	June	July	August	September	October	November	December	Annual average
Total Nonfarm													
2005	2,716.2	2,728.7	2,741.2	2,777.6	2,789.9	2,790.0	2,765.9	2,755.3	2,781.5	2,800.1	2,816.9	2,819.7	2,773.6
2006	2,747.1	2,760.3	2,777.9	2,805.4	2,818.4	2,818.8	2,784.4	2,776.9	2,797.2	2,819.7	2,832.5	2,836.7	2,797.9
2007	2,764.7	2,770.4	2,789.4	2,810.7	2,824.4	2,831.9	2,801.8	2,792.0	2,805.7	2,835.8	2,851.2	2,851.1	2,810.8
2008	2,778.7	2,788.5	2,801.5	2,830.2	2,833.8	2,833.8	2,793.0	2,783.5	2,799.5	2,820.1	2,815.2	2,807.6	2,807.1
2009	2,718.4	2,718.4	2,714.6	2,725.7	2,731.1	2,725.2	2,685.3	2,669.5	2,686.0	2,720.7	2,723.9	2,719.0	2,711.5
2010	2,648.9	2,647.6	2,667.8	2,702.1	2,725.4	2,723.0	2,684.8	2,674.1	2,692.7	2,724.2	2,736.7	2,738.8	2,697.2
2011	2,663.1	2,675.0	2,696.1	2,725.7	2,726.6	2,725.2	2,686.7	2,676.5	2,705.7	2,726.6	2,740.5	2,741.4	2,707.4
2012	2,669.6	2,685.6	2,711.4	2,725.3	2,736.4	2,738.4	2,699.5	2,697.6	2,725.0	2,751.9	2,768.4	2,768.4	2,723.1
2013	2,690.8	2,709.7	2,729.7	2,751.1	2,759.9	2,763.0	2,720.6	2,718.4	2,747.9	2,771.8	2,792.6	2,785.2	2,745.1
2014	2,713.6	2,718.9	2,742.7	2,776.9	2,790.9	2,795.6	2,755.6	2,753.7	2,788.9	2,817.6	2,836.0	2,836.7	2,777.3
2015	2,754.5	2,766.9	2,782.2	2,818.6	2,838.3	2,841.8	2,804.5	2,799.9	2,830.3	2,860.8	2,875.4	2,879.2	2,821.0
Total Private													
2005	2,358.1	2,364.4	2,374.7	2,410.4	2,425.4	2,430.5	2,428.1	2,422.4	2,430.0	2,438.4	2,453.9	2,457.4	2,416.1
2006	2,389.9	2,396.3	2,412.2	2,439.7	2,453.1	2,460.3	2,449.5	2,445.0	2,446.3	2,459.2	2,469.4	2,475.1	2,441.3
2007	2,410.8	2,409.4	2,426.6	2,447.9	2,463.2	2,474.2	2,468.0	2,462.4	2,457.0	2,475.0	2,488.4	2,490.1	2,456.1
2008	2,423.9	2,428.0	2,439.1	2,466.4	2,472.4	2,474.9	2,463.7	2,454.8	2,447.1	2,455.1	2,448.9	2,441.6	2,451.3
2009	2,359.6	2,354.0	2,347.8	2,357.8	2,367.1	2,364.0	2,350.8	2,338.2	2,330.7	2,354.5	2,355.8	2,352.3	2,352.7
2010	2,290.7	2,283.4	2,301.6	2,333.9	2,351.5	2,355.0	2,349.3	2,344.5	2,343.6	2,365.7	2,374.8	2,376.9	2,339.2
2011	2,310.2	2,317.3	2,336.5	2,365.2	2,370.7	2,373.3	2,364.3	2,357.9	2,366.1	2,377.5	2,389.5	2,390.4	2,359.9
2012	2,328.8	2,337.6	2,362.2	2,376.1	2,389.8	2,396.7	2,384.0	2,383.8	2,390.3	2,406.4	2,421.2	2,421.1	2,383.2
2013	2,352.7	2,364.5	2,382.6	2,404.7	2,413.9	2,422.5	2,408.0	2,408.5	2,415.6	2,429.5	2,447.9	2,442.1	2,407.7
2014	2,378.6	2,377.1	2,399.6	2,432.7	2,448.3	2,456.3	2,443.5	2,444.4	2,455.9	2,476.2	2,492.9	2,495.4	2,441.7
2015	2,420.8	2,427.4	2,440.1	2,476.7	2,497.1	2,504.2	2,494.9	2,490.3	2,497.4	2,518.6	2,530.5	2,534.8	2,486.1
Goods Producing													
2005	345.9	344.7	348.2	355.9	360.2	362.4	363.2	364.3	362.8	361.4	364.5	359.3	357.7
2006	351.9	350.6	354.4	359.6	362.8	364.6	362.6	362.6	359.9	358.3	354.5	352.5	357.9
2007	343.2	338.6	342.8	346.9	350.4	354.2	354.4	354.8	352.3	351.9	351.3	347.7	349.0
2008	338.1	337.2	340.0	343.8	344.0	347.4	345.5	344.3	339.5	335.6	332.1	324.7	339.4
2009	309.1	303.2	301.7	301.3	300.8	301.2	299.3	298.0	294.3	294.5	291.1	288.9	298.6
2010	279.7	275.4	279.8	286.5	289.1	291.9	292.6	292.4	290.2	290.8	289.6	286.7	287.1
2011	276.2	275.0	281.0	286.8	287.6	290.1	291.2	291.4	289.5	289.6	288.1	284.6	285.9
2012	276.3	276.0	278.9	280.8	281.6	285.1	285.3	285.8	285.0	284.3	282.2	280.9	281.9
2013	273.7	273.4	277.2	281.2	282.5	285.5	286.1	288.1	286.6	286.7	285.8	280.4	282.3
2014	274.7	273.3	278.9	283.6	286.7	289.4	290.7	290.8	289.6	289.9	289.7	287.4	285.4
2015	279.5	279.5	282.1	289.8	293.4	296.0	296.7	297.3	295.9	296.6	295.6	294.6	291.4
Service-Providing													
2005	2,370.3	2,384.0	2,393.0	2,421.7	2,429.7	2,427.6	2,402.7	2,391.0	2,418.7	2,438.7	2,452.4	2,460.4	2,415.9
2006	2,395.2	2,409.7	2,423.5	2,445.8	2,455.6	2,454.2	2,421.8	2,414.3	2,437.3	2,461.4	2,478.0	2,484.2	2,440.1
2007	2,421.5	2,431.8	2,446.6	2,463.8	2,474.0	2,477.7	2,447.4	2,437.2	2,453.4	2,483.9	2,499.9	2,503.4	2,461.7
2008	2,440.6	2,451.3	2,461.5	2,486.4	2,489.8	2,486.4	2,447.5	2,439.2	2,460.0	2,484.5	2,483.1	2,482.9	2,467.8
2009	2,409.3	2,415.2	2,412.9	2,424.4	2,430.3	2,424.0	2,386.0	2,371.5	2,391.7	2,426.2	2,432.8	2,430.1	2,412.9
2010	2,369.2	2,372.2	2,388.0	2,415.6	2,436.3	2,431.1	2,392.2	2,381.7	2,402.5	2,433.4	2,447.1	2,452.1	2,410.1
2011	2,386.9	2,400.0	2,415.1	2,438.9	2,439.0	2,435.1	2,395.5	2,385.1	2,416.2	2,437.0	2,452.4	2,456.8	2,421.5
2012	2,393.3	2,409.6	2,432.5	2,444.5	2,454.8	2,453.3	2,414.2	2,411.8	2,440.0	2,467.6	2,486.2	2,487.5	2,441.3
2013	2,417.1	2,436.3	2,452.5	2,469.9	2,477.4	2,477.5	2,434.5	2,430.3	2,461.3	2,485.1	2,506.8	2,504.8	2,462.8
2014	2,438.9	2,445.6	2,463.8	2,493.3	2,504.2	2,506.2	2,464.9	2,462.9	2,499.3	2,527.7	2,546.3	2,549.3	2,491.9
2015	2,475.0	2,487.4	2,500.1	2,528.8	2,544.9	2,545.8	2,507.8	2,502.6	2,534.4	2,564.2	2,579.8	2,584.6	2,529.6
Mining, Logging, and Construction													
2005	116.6	114.7	117.6	125.3	129.1	131.5	133.4	133.4	132.7	133.0	134.3	130.1	127.6
2006	122.8	122.2	126.3	131.6	134.8	136.0	135.8	135.8	134.1	133.1	130.5	128.8	131.0
2007	121.7	117.9	121.7	126.1	128.9	131.3	132.5	133.3	132.4	131.8	129.9	125.9	127.8
2008	120.4	118.6	121.2	126.0	127.2	128.5	128.6	128.2	125.3	123.1	120.1	114.9	123.5
2009	104.6	101.9	103.2	104.3	105.1	106.2	106.8	106.3	103.7	103.7	101.0	98.6	103.8
2010	92.0	89.1	93.5	99.4	101.6	103.1	104.6	104.6	103.1	103.7	102.7	99.3	99.7
2011	90.6	90.0	95.2	100.8	101.5	103.2	104.9	105.2	104.4	104.6	103.3	99.9	100.3
2012	93.4	93.5	96.0	98.2	98.9	101.4	102.2	102.9	103.0	102.6	101.3	99.8	99.4
2013	94.3	94.1	98.1	101.5	102.4	104.3	105.4	106.9	105.8	106.0	104.7	99.3	101.9
2014	95.3	94.0	99.1	104.2	106.0	107.9	109.5	109.3	108.8	109.1	108.4	105.5	104.8
2015	99.1	99.3	101.4	109.0	111.6	113.5	114.7	115.5	114.9	115.5	114.4	112.6	110.1

Employment by Industry: Philadelphia-Camden-Wilmington, PA-NJ-DE-MD, 2005–2015—*Continued*

(Numbers in thousands, not seasonally adjusted)

Industry and year	January	February	March	April	May	June	July	August	September	October	November	December	Annual average
Manufacturing													
2005	229.3	230.0	230.6	230.6	231.1	230.9	229.8	230.9	230.1	228.4	230.2	229.2	230.1
2006	229.1	228.4	228.1	228.0	228.0	228.6	226.8	226.8	225.8	225.2	224.0	223.7	226.9
2007	221.5	220.7	221.1	220.8	221.5	222.9	221.9	221.5	219.9	220.1	221.4	221.8	221.3
2008	217.7	218.6	218.8	217.8	216.8	218.9	216.9	216.1	214.2	212.5	212.0	209.8	215.8
2009	204.5	201.3	198.5	197.0	195.7	195.0	192.5	191.7	190.6	190.8	190.1	190.3	194.8
2010	187.7	186.3	186.3	187.1	187.5	188.8	188.0	187.8	187.1	187.1	186.9	187.4	187.3
2011	185.6	185.0	185.8	186.0	186.1	186.9	186.3	186.2	185.1	185.0	184.8	184.7	185.6
2012	182.9	182.5	182.9	182.6	182.7	183.7	183.1	182.9	182.0	181.7	180.9	181.1	182.4
2013	179.4	179.3	179.1	179.7	180.1	181.2	180.7	181.2	180.8	180.7	181.1	181.1	180.4
2014	179.4	179.3	179.8	179.4	180.7	181.5	181.2	181.5	180.8	180.8	181.3	181.9	180.6
2015	180.4	180.2	180.7	180.8	181.8	182.5	182.0	181.8	181.0	181.1	181.2	182.0	181.3
Trade, Transportation, and Utilities													
2005	529.0	523.3	525.0	527.4	531.1	532.1	529.8	528.9	529.8	534.3	544.8	554.6	532.5
2006	531.2	523.3	527.2	527.7	531.0	532.5	527.7	526.3	527.1	533.0	544.4	551.9	531.9
2007	530.8	521.3	523.3	524.2	529.2	532.5	529.3	527.2	527.0	531.5	544.0	551.8	531.0
2008	532.0	522.2	523.9	525.3	528.5	529.1	523.5	521.8	522.4	526.6	530.0	536.0	526.8
2009	509.8	501.5	498.5	496.3	500.6	502.9	495.6	494.3	496.5	502.4	511.7	517.1	502.3
2010	497.4	488.3	491.7	494.8	499.9	502.6	496.3	495.1	496.2	501.6	511.4	520.1	499.6
2011	498.9	493.8	494.8	498.6	500.4	501.7	496.3	495.8	497.9	501.8	513.4	520.9	501.2
2012	500.6	495.5	499.0	498.6	504.3	505.0	500.4	500.4	501.7	507.0	521.1	525.5	504.9
2013	503.9	498.8	500.7	502.3	505.9	508.5	503.8	504.3	506.1	511.0	524.1	531.2	508.4
2014	508.4	502.6	506.1	508.4	512.5	515.7	509.4	509.9	510.9	516.2	529.6	536.9	513.9
2015	511.1	505.4	507.4	511.7	516.7	520.8	516.0	516.7	518.1	522.8	531.6	539.6	518.2
Wholesale Trade													
2005	129.8	129.1	129.7	130.1	130.4	130.6	130.5	130.5	129.8	129.9	130.1	130.7	130.1
2006	128.6	128.7	129.6	129.9	130.3	131.3	131.3	131.2	130.3	129.9	129.8	130.1	130.1
2007	128.7	128.2	129.0	130.0	130.2	131.4	131.8	131.3	130.4	130.5	131.0	131.4	130.3
2008	130.0	129.8	130.2	130.4	131.0	131.4	131.5	131.0	130.0	130.1	129.1	128.8	130.3
2009	127.2	126.2	125.8	124.9	124.7	124.6	123.5	122.8	121.8	122.0	121.7	121.8	123.9
2010	120.5	119.8	120.2	120.8	121.4	121.7	121.6	121.5	120.9	121.1	121.1	121.3	121.0
2011	120.3	120.4	121.1	121.9	122.1	122.7	123.0	123.0	122.4	122.6	122.6	123.0	122.1
2012	121.0	121.3	122.1	122.2	122.5	123.2	122.8	122.5	121.7	121.9	121.8	122.1	122.1
2013	120.5	120.6	121.2	121.5	122.1	122.6	122.0	121.5	121.7	121.2	121.5	121.9	121.5
2014	120.3	120.5	120.9	121.0	121.5	122.3	121.6	121.2	120.3	119.9	120.3	120.8	120.9
2015	118.1	117.9	118.0	118.7	119.6	120.3	120.4	120.8	120.2	119.8	120.0	120.1	119.5
Retail Trade													
2005	308.4	303.4	304.0	305.5	308.5	309.0	309.0	308.7	306.6	310.6	319.7	327.5	310.1
2006	309.4	301.1	303.3	303.6	305.1	306.1	304.2	302.8	301.3	307.0	317.7	323.1	307.1
2007	307.5	299.0	299.8	300.2	304.1	305.9	305.1	304.2	302.0	307.3	318.4	324.3	306.5
2008	308.0	298.7	300.0	300.4	302.7	303.9	301.0	300.6	298.8	302.6	307.2	312.0	303.0
2009	291.7	285.0	282.9	281.7	286.0	287.8	285.7	285.6	284.2	289.1	298.0	302.2	288.3
2010	287.0	278.9	282.1	284.0	288.1	290.1	288.3	288.0	285.0	289.8	299.1	305.1	288.8
2011	288.5	283.4	283.4	286.0	287.0	287.8	285.8	286.2	284.3	288.1	298.8	304.1	288.6
2012	289.8	284.0	286.4	287.0	291.0	291.6	290.6	291.3	288.9	292.9	305.9	308.4	292.3
2013	292.0	286.9	287.8	288.6	291.0	293.3	292.5	293.4	291.0	295.3	306.6	311.4	294.2
2014	294.0	288.7	291.1	292.6	295.4	297.7	296.5	297.2	294.5	298.8	310.0	314.4	297.6
2015	296.4	291.0	292.6	295.5	299.1	302.2	299.6	299.7	297.0	301.3	308.6	314.0	299.8
Transportation and Utilities													
2005	90.8	90.8	91.3	91.8	92.2	92.5	90.3	89.7	93.4	93.8	95.0	96.4	92.3
2006	93.2	93.5	94.3	94.2	95.6	95.1	92.2	92.3	95.5	96.1	96.9	98.7	94.8
2007	94.6	94.1	94.5	94.0	94.9	95.2	92.4	91.7	94.6	93.7	94.6	96.1	94.2
2008	94.0	93.7	93.7	94.5	94.8	93.8	91.0	90.2	93.6	93.9	93.7	95.2	93.5
2009	90.9	90.3	89.8	89.7	89.9	90.5	86.4	85.9	90.5	91.3	92.0	93.1	90.0
2010	89.9	89.6	89.4	90.0	90.4	90.8	86.4	85.6	90.3	90.7	91.2	93.7	89.8
2011	90.1	90.0	90.3	90.7	91.3	91.2	87.5	86.6	91.2	91.1	92.0	93.8	90.5
2012	89.8	90.2	90.5	89.4	90.8	90.2	87.0	86.6	91.1	92.2	93.4	95.0	90.5
2013	91.4	91.3	91.7	92.2	92.8	92.6	89.3	89.4	93.4	94.5	96.0	97.9	92.7
2014	94.1	93.4	94.1	94.8	95.6	95.7	91.3	91.5	96.1	97.5	99.3	101.7	95.4
2015	96.6	96.5	96.8	97.5	98.0	98.3	96.0	96.2	100.9	101.7	103.0	105.5	98.9

Employment by Industry: Philadelphia-Camden-Wilmington, PA-NJ-DE-MD, 2005–2015—*Continued*

(Numbers in thousands, not seasonally adjusted)

Industry and year	January	February	March	April	May	June	July	August	September	October	November	December	Annual average
Information													
2005	54.7	54.7	54.9	55.4	55.5	56.1	55.7	55.7	58.6	55.7	56.0	56.3	55.8
2006	55.4	56.1	55.4	55.4	55.7	55.9	55.8	55.9	56.4	56.4	56.3	56.8	56.0
2007	56.4	56.4	56.5	57.1	57.3	58.1	57.8	58.1	58.9	58.2	58.3	58.8	57.7
2008	57.8	57.8	57.6	57.9	57.9	57.6	57.3	57.1	56.5	56.3	56.2	56.1	57.2
2009	55.4	55.1	54.8	54.5	54.3	54.3	54.0	53.6	53.2	53.3	52.7	52.9	54.0
2010	51.8	51.4	51.7	51.9	51.8	52.4	52.2	51.8	51.9	51.1	51.0	51.3	51.7
2011	50.2	50.2	50.0	50.6	50.4	50.8	50.7	47.7	50.9	50.3	50.7	50.1	50.2
2012	49.7	49.5	49.9	49.5	49.4	49.8	49.8	50.4	49.6	49.2	50.1	49.5	49.7
2013	49.2	49.3	49.1	48.3	48.2	48.0	48.0	48.1	47.2	47.2	47.2	47.4	48.1
2014	46.5	46.4	46.2	46.4	46.3	46.6	46.6	46.6	46.3	46.4	46.4	46.8	46.5
2015	45.9	46.1	46.4	46.1	46.2	46.9	46.7	46.8	46.5	46.7	46.5	46.9	46.5
Financial Activities													
2005	217.9	218.0	218.1	218.4	219.3	221.1	221.9	222.1	220.2	219.8	220.3	221.3	219.9
2006	219.6	219.2	219.2	220.2	220.4	222.0	222.6	222.3	220.5	220.4	220.6	221.1	220.7
2007	219.6	219.6	219.6	219.9	220.0	221.7	222.8	222.1	219.7	220.0	220.0	220.4	220.5
2008	217.8	218.0	218.2	218.1	217.9	218.9	219.4	218.2	215.3	214.1	213.6	212.7	216.9
2009	210.2	209.2	208.4	208.2	208.1	208.3	207.9	206.1	204.0	203.4	202.6	202.1	206.5
2010	200.4	199.8	199.7	199.6	200.3	201.0	201.6	201.4	200.0	200.3	200.5	201.5	200.5
2011	199.6	198.9	198.9	198.9	198.8	199.7	200.6	200.1	199.2	198.7	198.4	199.3	199.3
2012	198.1	198.0	198.5	198.6	199.5	201.1	202.0	202.1	200.8	200.9	201.5	202.4	200.3
2013	201.7	202.5	202.5	202.8	202.9	204.7	205.0	204.7	202.8	202.5	202.7	203.2	203.2
2014	201.6	201.5	201.6	202.2	203.2	205.3	205.8	206.0	204.6	205.1	205.7	207.0	204.1
2015	205.3	205.9	206.3	206.9	207.9	209.9	210.9	210.5	208.9	209.4	209.2	210.4	208.5
Professional and Business Services													
2005	395.7	396.8	399.1	410.7	410.8	413.2	414.7	413.2	413.0	415.3	416.4	417.2	409.7
2006	404.3	407.0	411.8	420.2	421.4	424.6	424.5	425.3	425.2	428.5	430.9	432.2	421.3
2007	417.6	418.3	422.6	430.6	432.6	435.8	434.2	434.7	431.8	435.5	438.5	438.2	430.9
2008	425.4	424.7	428.7	435.4	435.7	437.0	434.4	434.0	430.8	430.9	428.3	425.2	430.9
2009	411.5	408.9	408.3	412.0	410.5	410.2	407.5	406.7	403.1	409.5	409.9	407.3	408.8
2010	396.4	397.3	399.4	408.0	409.8	411.8	411.0	411.3	409.9	414.1	415.5	415.0	408.3
2011	406.5	406.4	410.3	418.8	417.9	420.5	418.2	418.2	419.3	422.0	423.2	422.0	416.9
2012	410.0	411.3	416.5	421.4	422.6	425.9	424.2	425.4	427.3	431.8	433.6	430.9	423.4
2013	417.4	419.8	424.7	430.7	432.4	436.0	431.2	432.3	432.3	437.0	440.9	436.9	431.0
2014	424.6	423.5	427.3	437.8	440.3	442.7	437.6	438.7	443.0	448.1	452.0	451.0	438.9
2015	435.4	435.3	437.4	446.5	451.3	452.1	449.4	448.0	450.1	454.8	460.2	459.3	448.3
Education and Health Services													
2005	488.5	501.6	498.7	503.3	500.7	490.2	489.6	487.3	499.9	511.2	513.0	510.3	499.5
2006	499.6	512.0	509.5	514.5	512.5	503.4	501.8	499.2	511.0	519.5	521.7	519.2	510.3
2007	511.8	523.9	525.0	525.1	522.0	513.3	513.5	511.2	520.2	532.9	533.2	531.0	521.9
2008	521.3	536.6	534.3	539.6	535.0	525.4	524.4	523.8	534.6	545.7	548.5	548.5	534.8
2009	538.9	551.4	547.5	549.9	545.9	535.8	534.3	530.8	539.8	551.5	553.9	551.3	544.3
2010	542.2	551.5	551.3	553.7	551.7	540.7	539.9	537.2	546.7	560.7	561.9	559.4	549.7
2011	547.1	560.8	561.2	561.8	558.2	547.4	545.8	543.8	556.6	565.0	567.9	567.7	556.9
2012	556.7	569.3	571.8	572.7	568.5	557.2	552.8	550.1	565.8	576.3	577.7	575.8	566.2
2013	564.6	577.4	578.9	579.1	573.4	563.6	560.4	558.5	576.5	585.6	590.4	586.1	574.5
2014	576.8	586.7	588.3	594.0	588.6	578.5	576.8	575.6	592.9	602.8	606.6	602.8	589.2
2015	593.1	604.6	603.3	608.9	603.9	593.5	590.7	587.7	603.8	615.5	619.4	616.8	603.4
Leisure and Hospitality													
2005	203.2	201.8	206.3	215.1	222.9	229.3	228.2	226.5	222.2	217.6	215.7	215.0	217.0
2006	205.9	205.9	211.4	219.0	225.5	232.4	230.5	230.2	224.4	221.3	219.3	219.7	220.5
2007	211.0	210.6	215.5	222.1	228.9	234.3	232.6	231.9	225.5	223.4	221.3	220.4	223.1
2008	210.7	210.8	215.8	225.8	231.9	237.3	237.5	234.5	227.7	226.2	220.9	219.2	224.9
2009	207.2	207.1	210.6	217.7	227.8	231.5	233.0	230.3	222.7	222.6	216.7	215.4	220.2
2010	206.3	204.1	211.0	221.4	229.8	234.4	236.4	236.1	230.4	228.4	226.1	224.0	224.0
2011	213.9	214.2	221.5	230.0	237.2	241.4	240.9	240.9	233.7	231.2	229.0	226.9	230.1
2012	219.0	219.7	228.6	234.8	243.1	250.1	248.3	248.6	240.3	237.2	235.4	236.1	236.8
2013	223.6	224.5	230.2	240.2	247.8	253.8	254.0	253.4	246.7	242.2	239.9	240.5	241.4
2014	231.2	229.1	236.1	244.1	253.0	258.6	258.2	259.0	252.0	250.6	245.9	246.7	247.0
2015	235.1	235.0	240.8	249.8	259.3	264.9	265.2	264.5	256.8	254.9	249.7	248.5	252.0

Employment by Industry: Philadelphia-Camden-Wilmington, PA-NJ-DE-MD, 2005–2015—*Continued*

(Numbers in thousands, not seasonally adjusted)

Industry and year	January	February	March	April	May	June	July	August	September	October	November	December	Annual average
Other Services													
2005	123.2	123.5	124.4	124.2	124.9	126.1	125.0	124.4	123.5	123.1	123.2	123.4	124.1
2006	122.0	122.2	123.3	123.1	123.8	124.9	124.0	123.2	121.8	121.8	121.7	121.7	122.8
2007	120.4	120.7	121.3	122.0	122.8	124.3	123.4	122.4	121.6	121.6	121.8	121.8	122.0
2008	120.8	120.7	120.6	120.5	121.5	122.2	121.7	121.1	120.3	119.7	119.3	119.2	120.6
2009	117.5	117.6	118.0	117.9	119.1	119.8	119.2	118.4	117.1	117.3	117.2	117.3	118.0
2010	116.5	115.6	117.0	118.0	119.1	120.2	119.3	119.2	118.3	118.7	118.8	118.9	118.3
2011	117.8	118.0	118.8	119.7	120.2	121.7	120.6	120.0	119.0	118.9	118.8	118.9	119.4
2012	118.4	118.3	119.0	119.7	120.8	122.5	121.2	121.0	119.8	119.7	119.6	120.0	120.0
2013	118.6	118.8	119.3	120.1	120.8	122.4	119.5	119.1	117.4	117.3	116.9	116.4	118.9
2014	114.8	114.0	115.1	116.2	117.7	119.5	118.4	117.8	116.6	117.1	117.0	116.8	116.8
2015	115.4	115.6	116.4	117.0	118.4	120.1	119.3	118.8	117.3	117.9	118.3	118.7	117.8
Government													
2005	358.1	364.3	366.5	367.2	364.5	359.5	337.8	332.9	351.5	361.7	363.0	362.3	357.4
2006	357.2	364.0	365.7	365.7	365.3	358.5	334.9	331.9	350.9	360.5	363.1	361.6	356.6
2007	353.9	361.0	362.8	362.8	361.2	357.7	333.8	329.6	348.7	360.8	362.8	361.0	354.7
2008	354.8	360.5	362.4	363.8	361.4	358.9	329.3	328.7	352.4	365.0	366.3	366.0	355.8
2009	358.8	364.4	366.8	367.9	364.0	361.2	334.5	331.3	355.3	366.2	368.1	366.7	358.8
2010	358.2	364.2	366.2	368.2	373.9	368.0	335.5	329.6	349.1	358.5	361.9	361.9	357.9
2011	352.9	357.7	359.6	360.5	355.9	351.9	322.4	318.6	339.6	349.1	351.0	351.0	347.5
2012	340.8	348.0	349.2	349.2	346.6	341.7	315.5	313.8	334.7	345.5	347.2	347.3	340.0
2013	338.1	345.2	347.1	346.4	346.0	340.5	312.6	309.9	332.3	342.3	344.7	343.1	337.4
2014	335.0	341.8	343.1	344.2	342.6	339.3	312.1	309.3	333.0	341.4	343.1	341.3	335.5
2015	333.7	339.5	342.1	341.9	341.2	337.6	309.6	309.6	332.9	342.2	344.9	344.4	335.0

Employment by Industry: Miami-Fort Lauderdale-West Palm Beach, 2005–2015

(Numbers in thousands, not seasonally adjusted)

Industry and year	January	February	March	April	May	June	July	August	September	October	November	December	Annual average
Total Nonfarm													
2005	2,295.6	2,319.4	2,330.1	2,345.2	2,347.5	2,320.2	2,306.8	2,346.5	2,362.3	2,357.5	2,376.4	2,409.4	2,343.1
2006	2,365.7	2,389.1	2,409.9	2,396.4	2,406.9	2,383.5	2,352.4	2,391.8	2,401.6	2,405.2	2,436.8	2,462.9	2,400.2
2007	2,415.3	2,433.8	2,449.6	2,428.6	2,436.7	2,408.3	2,366.6	2,406.4	2,414.4	2,410.4	2,441.4	2,463.0	2,422.9
2008	2,406.3	2,420.3	2,426.5	2,397.4	2,391.5	2,347.7	2,300.5	2,325.9	2,321.7	2,315.0	2,327.2	2,335.6	2,359.6
2009	2,265.1	2,259.6	2,254.4	2,232.2	2,223.8	2,186.1	2,152.8	2,175.9	2,178.0	2,190.7	2,213.7	2,226.6	2,213.2
2010	2,180.7	2,192.5	2,200.2	2,199.3	2,207.6	2,172.4	2,150.5	2,178.9	2,181.5	2,203.3	2,229.3	2,247.2	2,195.3
2011	2,211.8	2,224.4	2,230.5	2,243.2	2,237.2	2,202.2	2,186.7	2,217.6	2,231.4	2,249.5	2,278.0	2,297.2	2,234.1
2012	2,261.3	2,274.6	2,287.1	2,288.8	2,290.3	2,259.3	2,237.5	2,267.8	2,279.6	2,306.7	2,338.3	2,350.7	2,286.8
2013	2,313.7	2,333.2	2,344.7	2,345.7	2,348.2	2,320.0	2,303.7	2,336.4	2,346.2	2,367.8	2,407.5	2,423.0	2,349.2
2014	2,383.5	2,401.5	2,413.3	2,421.1	2,424.9	2,395.6	2,380.0	2,416.2	2,429.3	2,459.7	2,497.7	2,513.7	2,428.0
2015	2,472.0	2,487.0	2,498.3	2,502.1	2,505.0	2,474.9	2,465.1	2,499.0	2,507.1	2,532.3	2,564.1	2,572.7	2,506.6
Total Private													
2005	1,975.4	1,998.0	2,007.6	2,020.5	2,022.1	2,023.2	2,013.9	2,025.7	2,038.4	2,031.5	2,051.1	2,083.7	2,024.3
2006	2,041.4	2,063.6	2,082.9	2,071.0	2,081.0	2,085.8	2,058.9	2,069.7	2,075.8	2,078.0	2,106.5	2,133.3	2,079.0
2007	2,088.8	2,105.9	2,119.4	2,098.2	2,105.5	2,106.2	2,068.8	2,078.6	2,082.8	2,080.2	2,108.8	2,129.5	2,097.7
2008	2,075.5	2,087.0	2,093.5	2,065.8	2,058.9	2,044.6	2,001.9	2,000.5	1,994.5	1,988.4	1,998.6	2,005.8	2,034.6
2009	1,937.2	1,933.2	1,927.8	1,905.2	1,898.3	1,888.7	1,858.1	1,859.4	1,859.0	1,869.7	1,891.8	1,904.9	1,894.4
2010	1,862.4	1,873.6	1,881.4	1,879.4	1,878.6	1,876.8	1,861.4	1,868.7	1,870.1	1,889.6	1,915.2	1,933.7	1,882.6
2011	1,899.8	1,910.8	1,918.4	1,931.0	1,927.1	1,918.8	1,906.3	1,914.0	1,924.9	1,939.7	1,969.7	1,988.4	1,929.1
2012	1,956.0	1,968.0	1,981.5	1,983.2	1,985.7	1,980.0	1,960.9	1,969.5	1,977.3	2,001.0	2,032.7	2,045.4	1,986.8
2013	2,010.5	2,027.1	2,038.3	2,039.5	2,042.1	2,039.7	2,025.7	2,037.8	2,042.8	2,062.5	2,100.4	2,117.5	2,048.7
2014	2,079.5	2,095.6	2,106.7	2,114.3	2,118.9	2,115.1	2,102.3	2,118.2	2,127.5	2,154.8	2,191.0	2,208.7	2,127.7
2015	2,169.0	2,181.8	2,192.0	2,194.8	2,199.1	2,193.5	2,185.8	2,199.1	2,203.1	2,224.6	2,255.6	2,266.1	2,205.4
Goods Producing													
2005	238.9	241.0	242.7	244.7	247.1	249.7	250.8	253.1	256.1	256.3	257.6	260.0	249.8
2006	256.1	259.6	262.2	263.6	266.7	269.6	267.3	268.8	270.6	269.1	270.0	270.7	266.2
2007	265.0	266.3	267.4	262.0	263.0	266.0	258.8	259.5	259.4	255.3	254.6	253.8	260.9
2008	244.4	243.3	241.9	234.8	233.4	232.4	225.3	223.9	222.0	217.6	214.1	210.9	228.7
2009	199.1	196.3	193.5	187.4	185.8	184.2	179.5	178.1	177.0	174.7	173.1	172.0	183.4
2010	164.5	165.0	164.9	164.4	165.0	165.7	165.3	165.8	165.6	165.1	164.6	164.3	165.0
2011	160.1	160.7	160.8	161.3	161.4	162.0	161.3	162.2	163.1	163.3	163.8	163.8	162.0
2012	160.9	161.5	162.5	161.5	162.7	164.1	163.1	165.5	166.2	166.6	167.7	167.6	164.2
2013	163.8	165.7	167.0	166.9	169.5	170.9	171.9	174.5	174.9	175.6	177.1	177.5	171.3
2014	174.8	177.2	178.7	179.6	181.7	183.6	184.3	186.5	187.6	189.4	189.8	190.3	183.6
2015	188.3	190.5	192.2	193.2	195.5	197.3	197.5	199.4	200.5	201.5	204.0	204.7	197.1
Service-Providing													
2005	2,056.7	2,078.4	2,087.4	2,100.5	2,100.4	2,070.5	2,056.0	2,093.4	2,106.2	2,101.2	2,118.8	2,149.4	2,093.2
2006	2,109.6	2,129.5	2,147.7	2,132.8	2,140.2	2,113.9	2,085.1	2,123.0	2,131.0	2,136.1	2,166.8	2,192.2	2,134.0
2007	2,150.3	2,167.5	2,182.2	2,166.6	2,173.7	2,142.3	2,107.8	2,146.9	2,155.0	2,155.1	2,186.8	2,209.2	2,162.0
2008	2,161.9	2,177.0	2,184.6	2,162.6	2,158.1	2,115.3	2,075.2	2,102.0	2,099.7	2,097.4	2,113.1	2,124.7	2,131.0
2009	2,066.0	2,063.3	2,060.9	2,044.8	2,038.0	2,001.9	1,973.3	1,997.8	2,001.0	2,016.0	2,040.6	2,054.6	2,029.9
2010	2,016.2	2,027.5	2,035.3	2,034.9	2,042.6	2,006.7	1,985.2	2,013.1	2,015.9	2,038.2	2,064.7	2,082.9	2,030.3
2011	2,051.7	2,063.7	2,069.7	2,081.9	2,075.8	2,040.2	2,025.4	2,055.4	2,068.3	2,086.2	2,114.2	2,133.4	2,072.2
2012	2,100.4	2,113.1	2,124.6	2,127.3	2,127.6	2,095.2	2,074.4	2,102.3	2,113.4	2,140.1	2,170.6	2,183.1	2,122.7
2013	2,149.9	2,167.5	2,177.7	2,178.8	2,178.7	2,149.1	2,131.8	2,161.9	2,171.3	2,192.2	2,230.4	2,245.5	2,177.9
2014	2,208.7	2,224.3	2,234.6	2,241.5	2,243.2	2,212.0	2,195.7	2,229.7	2,241.7	2,270.3	2,307.9	2,323.4	2,244.4
2015	2,283.7	2,296.5	2,306.1	2,308.9	2,309.5	2,277.6	2,267.6	2,299.6	2,306.6	2,330.8	2,360.1	2,368.0	2,309.6
Mining and Logging													
2005	0.5	0.6	0.6	0.6	0.7	0.7	0.7	0.7	0.6	0.6	0.6	0.5	0.6
2006	0.5	0.6	0.6	0.6	0.6	0.7	0.7	0.7	0.7	0.7	0.8	0.8	0.7
2007	0.8	0.8	0.8	0.8	0.8	0.8	0.8	0.8	0.8	0.9	0.9	0.9	0.8
2008	0.7	0.7	0.8	0.8	0.8	0.7	0.6	0.6	0.6	0.6	0.6	0.6	0.7
2009	0.6	0.6	0.5	0.5	0.5	0.5	0.5	0.5	0.5	0.5	0.5	0.5	0.5
2010	0.5	0.5	0.5	0.5	0.5	0.5	0.5	0.5	0.5	0.5	0.5	0.6	0.5
2011	0.6	0.6	0.6	0.7	0.6	0.6	0.6	0.6	0.5	0.6	0.6	0.6	0.6
2012	0.6	0.6	0.6	0.5	0.6	0.6	0.6	0.6	0.6	0.6	0.6	0.6	0.6
2013	0.6	0.6	0.6	0.6	0.6	0.5	0.6	0.6	0.6	0.6	0.6	0.6	0.6
2014	0.6	0.6	0.6	0.6	0.6	0.6	0.6	0.6	0.6	0.6	0.6	0.6	0.6
2015	0.6	0.6	0.6	0.6	0.6	0.6	0.6	0.6	0.6	0.6	0.6	0.6	0.6

Employment by Industry: Miami-Fort Lauderdale-West Palm Beach, 2005–2015—*Continued*

(Numbers in thousands, not seasonally adjusted)

Industry and year	January	February	March	April	May	June	July	August	September	October	November	December	Annual average
Construction													
2005	138.2	139.6	140.7	142.6	144.2	146.3	148.2	149.8	152.3	153.5	154.6	156.1	147.2
2006	153.7	156.7	159.5	161.7	164.4	166.8	165.9	167.0	168.3	168.0	168.4	168.1	164.0
2007	163.6	164.4	165.4	161.4	162.1	164.6	160.1	160.3	160.1	156.3	155.1	154.1	160.6
2008	146.4	145.2	144.5	138.8	137.8	137.2	132.5	131.3	129.6	126.5	123.8	121.5	134.6
2009	112.3	110.5	109.3	105.1	104.3	103.2	100.6	99.2	98.5	96.5	94.7	93.8	102.3
2010	88.0	88.4	88.3	88.2	88.6	88.9	89.3	89.4	89.4	88.6	87.8	87.1	88.5
2011	84.1	84.5	84.7	84.7	84.4	84.7	84.7	85.1	86.1	85.8	86.0	85.8	85.1
2012	83.5	83.6	84.3	84.3	85.1	86.5	86.3	88.1	88.8	88.9	89.5	89.4	86.5
2013	87.4	88.5	89.4	89.6	91.6	92.5	93.5	95.6	96.1	96.3	96.9	97.0	92.9
2014	94.7	96.5	98.0	99.0	100.7	102.2	102.9	104.5	105.2	106.4	106.4	106.7	101.9
2015	105.2	107.0	108.1	109.1	110.7	112.0	112.5	113.9	114.8	116.4	118.1	119.1	112.2
Manufacturing													
2005	100.2	100.8	101.4	101.5	102.2	102.7	101.9	102.6	103.2	102.2	102.4	103.4	102.0
2006	101.9	102.3	102.1	101.3	101.7	102.1	100.7	101.1	101.6	100.4	100.8	101.8	101.5
2007	100.6	101.1	101.2	99.8	100.1	100.6	97.9	98.4	98.5	98.1	98.6	98.8	99.5
2008	97.3	97.4	96.6	95.2	94.8	94.5	92.2	92.0	91.8	90.5	89.7	88.8	93.4
2009	86.2	85.2	83.7	81.8	81.0	80.5	78.4	78.4	78.0	77.7	77.9	77.7	80.5
2010	76.0	76.1	76.1	75.7	75.9	76.3	75.5	75.9	75.7	76.0	76.3	76.6	76.0
2011	75.4	75.6	75.5	75.9	76.4	76.7	76.0	76.5	76.5	76.9	77.2	77.4	76.3
2012	76.8	77.3	77.6	76.7	77.0	77.0	76.2	76.8	76.8	77.1	77.6	77.6	77.0
2013	75.8	76.6	77.0	76.7	77.3	77.9	77.8	78.3	78.2	78.7	79.6	79.9	77.8
2014	79.5	80.1	80.1	80.0	80.4	80.8	80.8	81.4	81.8	82.4	82.8	83.0	81.1
2015	82.5	82.9	83.5	83.5	84.2	84.7	84.4	84.9	85.1	84.5	85.3	85.0	84.2
Trade, Transportation, and Utilities													
2005	523.4	523.4	523.9	526.7	528.0	527.4	528.4	530.7	531.6	533.2	539.5	552.2	530.7
2006	538.5	539.1	541.8	540.2	542.3	542.7	538.0	540.2	540.4	543.4	555.1	565.4	543.9
2007	547.6	546.8	549.0	545.7	549.2	549.4	543.5	545.4	545.8	547.4	561.8	570.9	550.2
2008	551.5	550.5	550.5	544.6	544.5	541.6	534.6	534.4	532.8	531.2	537.1	542.6	541.3
2009	519.9	515.8	512.6	505.0	504.3	501.8	495.7	495.8	495.0	499.1	510.4	517.7	506.1
2010	500.4	499.1	500.0	501.1	502.7	502.7	498.9	500.8	500.3	507.3	519.8	528.1	505.1
2011	511.8	511.1	512.1	515.5	515.4	515.5	515.3	517.5	519.5	525.5	538.9	546.7	520.4
2012	532.8	531.7	533.0	533.5	535.3	533.7	530.5	531.1	533.0	538.2	553.4	558.6	537.1
2013	543.9	542.7	543.9	544.2	545.7	546.9	543.6	545.7	546.7	552.8	570.4	579.3	550.5
2014	558.4	558.3	558.7	560.0	561.1	561.4	559.4	563.6	564.3	572.4	590.3	599.3	567.3
2015	581.1	578.9	580.3	580.6	581.0	582.3	579.6	582.2	580.9	586.2	598.0	605.3	584.7
Wholesale Trade													
2005	140.3	141.3	141.4	142.2	142.8	142.4	141.7	141.9	142.1	142.0	142.1	143.5	142.0
2006	142.3	143.7	144.4	144.3	144.9	145.5	145.0	145.9	146.1	146.5	147.5	149.0	145.4
2007	147.6	149.2	149.8	148.7	149.4	149.2	147.0	147.3	147.5	147.4	148.2	149.3	148.4
2008	146.7	147.6	147.7	146.7	147.1	146.1	144.0	143.8	143.8	143.0	142.8	143.0	145.2
2009	139.5	139.4	138.1	136.7	136.6	135.1	133.2	133.1	132.5	133.2	134.2	135.0	135.6
2010	132.1	132.7	132.8	132.7	133.4	132.7	131.6	131.8	131.7	132.7	133.5	134.5	132.7
2011	132.3	133.3	133.5	134.5	134.1	133.9	133.4	133.8	134.3	135.7	136.7	138.3	134.5
2012	137.0	138.1	139.0	139.4	139.8	139.1	138.3	138.3	138.7	139.5	140.5	141.6	139.1
2013	139.6	140.6	140.9	140.4	141.0	140.7	139.6	140.0	140.3	140.7	141.9	142.8	140.7
2014	141.3	142.4	142.1	142.3	142.8	142.1	141.3	142.3	142.6	143.9	145.4	146.2	142.9
2015	144.9	145.3	145.4	145.3	145.6	145.2	144.5	144.7	145.0	144.9	146.0	146.3	145.3
Retail Trade													
2005	288.8	287.6	288.0	289.6	290.0	290.7	292.4	295.0	295.4	297.3	302.5	312.2	294.1
2006	300.8	299.8	301.5	300.6	302.7	302.2	299.5	300.0	299.9	302.9	312.7	319.1	303.5
2007	305.1	302.8	303.9	302.0	304.9	304.8	301.7	303.0	303.0	304.1	315.9	321.6	306.1
2008	307.6	305.2	305.1	301.8	301.7	300.8	297.0	296.8	295.8	294.7	300.0	303.8	300.9
2009	288.0	284.6	282.9	278.5	278.7	278.1	274.9	275.3	275.8	278.6	287.7	292.9	281.3
2010	280.1	278.1	278.7	279.9	281.4	282.2	279.9	281.6	281.1	286.4	296.5	302.2	284.0
2011	290.1	287.7	288.2	290.3	290.8	290.9	291.3	293.1	294.4	298.5	309.5	314.0	294.9
2012	303.0	299.9	300.1	300.3	301.7	300.9	298.8	299.5	300.6	303.9	316.8	319.1	303.7
2013	308.7	306.1	306.7	307.4	308.5	309.6	308.4	310.1	310.3	315.1	330.1	336.1	313.1
2014	319.2	317.5	317.9	318.9	319.6	320.5	319.5	322.3	322.3	328.5	342.7	348.8	324.8
2015	334.0	331.6	332.3	332.8	333.4	334.9	332.7	335.0	333.0	337.1	346.9	350.9	336.2

Employment by Industry: Miami-Fort Lauderdale-West Palm Beach, 2005–2015—*Continued*

(Numbers in thousands, not seasonally adjusted)

Industry and year	January	February	March	April	May	June	July	August	September	October	November	December	Annual average
Transportation and Utilities													
2005	94.3	94.5	94.5	94.9	95.2	94.3	94.3	93.8	94.1	93.9	94.9	96.5	94.6
2006	95.4	95.6	95.9	95.3	94.7	95.0	93.5	94.3	94.4	94.0	94.9	97.3	95.0
2007	94.9	94.8	95.3	95.0	94.9	95.4	94.8	95.1	95.3	95.9	97.7	100.0	95.8
2008	97.2	97.7	97.7	96.1	95.7	94.7	93.6	93.8	93.2	93.5	94.3	95.8	95.3
2009	92.4	91.8	91.6	89.8	89.0	88.6	87.6	87.4	86.7	87.3	88.5	89.8	89.2
2010	88.2	88.3	88.5	88.5	87.9	87.8	87.4	87.4	87.5	88.2	89.8	91.4	88.4
2011	89.4	90.1	90.4	90.7	90.5	90.7	90.6	90.6	90.8	91.3	92.7	94.4	91.0
2012	92.8	93.7	93.9	93.8	93.8	93.7	93.4	93.3	93.7	94.8	96.1	97.9	94.2
2013	95.6	96.0	96.3	96.4	96.2	96.6	95.6	95.6	96.1	97.0	98.4	100.4	96.7
2014	97.9	98.4	98.7	98.8	98.7	98.8	98.6	99.0	99.4	100.0	102.2	104.3	99.6
2015	102.2	102.0	102.6	102.5	102.0	102.2	102.4	102.5	102.9	104.2	105.1	108.1	103.2
Information													
2005	55.7	56.1	56.2	55.7	55.6	55.7	55.1	54.9	54.8	53.7	54.0	54.1	55.1
2006	53.0	53.4	53.5	52.7	53.1	53.0	52.5	52.3	51.7	51.3	51.3	51.4	52.4
2007	50.7	51.1	51.4	51.2	51.4	51.7	51.3	51.3	50.7	51.0	51.1	51.3	51.2
2008	50.7	50.7	50.7	50.3	50.4	50.3	49.6	49.3	48.9	48.6	48.7	48.4	49.7
2009	47.1	46.9	46.6	45.8	45.7	45.2	44.3	44.2	43.4	43.5	43.5	43.5	45.0
2010	43.1	43.1	43.5	43.4	43.6	43.7	43.6	43.8	43.5	43.9	44.0	44.1	43.6
2011	43.9	43.9	44.0	43.9	43.9	43.9	43.8	44.2	44.2	44.3	44.6	44.7	44.1
2012	44.7	44.7	45.1	45.1	45.1	44.9	45.0	45.1	44.8	45.9	45.9	46.1	45.2
2013	45.5	45.6	46.2	45.9	46.1	46.2	46.4	46.6	46.6	47.2	47.3	47.6	46.4
2014	47.3	47.5	47.2	47.5	47.5	48.2	48.1	47.7	47.6	47.8	48.5	48.5	47.8
2015	47.6	47.5	47.9	47.6	48.2	48.2	48.2	48.6	48.4	48.6	48.7	48.5	48.2
Financial Activities													
2005	174.3	175.8	176.5	177.8	178.3	179.4	179.8	180.9	181.1	181.3	182.3	184.3	179.3
2006	180.9	183.0	184.2	184.2	184.9	185.6	184.3	185.0	184.2	185.0	185.7	187.7	184.6
2007	183.3	184.3	184.4	183.2	183.0	183.3	182.0	181.7	180.7	179.9	180.9	182.2	182.4
2008	177.5	177.6	177.7	175.2	174.5	173.3	170.7	169.4	167.9	166.6	165.9	166.0	171.9
2009	160.2	159.7	159.1	157.4	157.2	156.8	154.7	154.3	153.2	154.0	154.4	155.2	156.4
2010	151.8	152.3	152.8	152.4	152.6	153.5	153.3	153.3	152.7	154.1	155.1	156.2	153.3
2011	153.4	153.9	154.3	155.6	156.0	155.7	156.2	156.7	157.0	158.3	159.0	160.3	156.4
2012	158.4	159.1	159.7	160.7	161.3	161.6	161.4	161.7	161.1	163.1	163.8	164.9	161.4
2013	162.4	162.7	163.3	163.7	163.9	164.7	164.4	164.5	164.5	166.0	166.7	167.8	164.6
2014	165.5	166.2	166.6	167.4	168.2	168.4	168.5	168.6	168.8	171.3	172.4	173.4	168.8
2015	171.5	172.4	172.6	173.2	173.9	174.6	175.3	175.9	175.4	177.5	178.0	177.6	174.8
Professional and Business Services													
2005	338.4	346.0	348.7	352.4	352.1	352.6	351.4	353.7	358.5	354.1	359.3	365.5	352.7
2006	353.1	358.7	363.7	361.1	364.4	367.1	362.4	363.9	366.4	365.8	369.7	376.4	364.4
2007	366.6	371.6	373.9	368.7	369.5	369.4	361.9	363.7	363.6	361.8	363.4	365.9	366.7
2008	354.1	358.9	360.8	356.2	353.2	350.9	344.5	344.3	343.3	343.8	343.6	344.3	349.8
2009	327.8	327.8	325.5	321.7	320.0	320.1	316.6	317.9	318.1	321.2	325.2	326.9	322.4
2010	319.6	324.2	325.9	323.8	322.1	323.1	322.8	324.7	325.1	329.3	332.4	336.8	325.8
2011	331.4	336.2	337.7	340.6	338.5	337.3	336.1	336.8	338.7	342.6	346.5	350.0	339.4
2012	341.3	345.8	348.9	350.6	350.4	351.2	349.4	350.7	352.6	361.1	366.0	368.2	353.0
2013	360.7	366.5	368.5	369.0	369.1	368.4	368.3	370.6	370.7	376.2	382.0	383.7	371.1
2014	377.1	380.7	382.6	386.3	388.1	386.7	386.6	389.9	391.5	398.5	403.5	407.0	389.9
2015	395.1	399.4	399.7	401.2	402.8	400.5	403.3	405.8	406.6	410.7	418.7	417.3	405.1
Education and Health Services													
2005	294.2	298.4	298.9	302.0	302.0	300.3	299.4	302.5	305.1	304.1	304.5	306.4	301.5
2006	300.7	303.7	306.1	306.0	307.9	307.3	304.5	307.9	310.4	311.3	313.3	315.6	307.9
2007	312.0	315.4	316.9	317.2	319.0	318.6	314.5	317.8	321.2	322.1	324.0	326.5	318.8
2008	322.6	326.1	328.0	326.3	328.0	326.6	320.9	324.0	326.1	327.3	329.0	330.0	326.2
2009	325.4	327.2	328.7	329.4	331.5	330.2	326.3	329.0	332.2	335.6	337.0	337.0	330.8
2010	332.6	334.8	335.3	335.5	337.0	335.4	331.6	332.8	335.2	338.2	340.1	340.7	335.8
2011	338.6	341.4	341.7	344.3	343.7	340.6	334.7	336.4	340.6	342.1	343.7	343.8	341.0
2012	339.2	342.3	343.8	343.2	343.1	340.4	334.6	338.6	342.0	343.7	345.3	344.8	341.8
2013	341.9	345.5	346.5	347.9	348.1	345.8	339.8	344.1	346.9	348.7	351.2	352.1	346.5
2014	349.0	352.4	353.0	355.2	355.7	353.6	349.4	354.9	358.9	361.2	362.9	364.1	355.9
2015	360.6	363.7	364.9	366.4	368.5	365.5	361.8	364.9	369.9	373.3	373.3	376.5	367.4

Employment by Industry: Miami-Fort Lauderdale-West Palm Beach, 2005–2015—*Continued*

(Numbers in thousands, not seasonally adjusted)

Industry and year	January	February	March	April	May	June	July	August	September	October	November	December	Annual average
Leisure and Hospitality													
2005	244.0	249.8	253.3	253.5	251.4	250.8	242.9	243.6	244.5	243.2	247.7	253.8	248.2
2006	251.6	257.3	261.4	256.0	254.3	252.4	244.1	245.6	245.9	246.2	254.6	258.4	252.3
2007	255.8	261.3	265.9	262.6	262.3	259.3	250.0	252.0	253.5	252.9	261.4	265.7	258.6
2008	262.6	267.1	270.3	266.4	263.7	259.1	248.0	247.7	247.1	247.6	254.9	258.2	257.7
2009	254.4	256.3	258.6	255.5	251.4	248.3	240.1	239.5	239.5	240.5	246.4	250.2	248.4
2010	248.9	252.8	256.4	256.0	253.4	250.8	245.4	246.9	247.4	250.5	257.2	261.2	252.2
2011	259.1	261.6	265.2	266.3	264.4	260.9	255.6	256.5	257.5	258.4	266.7	272.0	262.0
2012	271.9	275.2	280.0	279.4	278.6	275.0	268.9	269.3	269.7	273.5	281.0	285.2	275.6
2013	282.9	287.8	291.7	290.2	288.2	285.2	280.2	280.7	280.8	283.2	291.8	294.8	286.5
2014	292.8	297.3	303.0	301.4	299.6	296.6	289.6	290.4	291.8	295.9	303.9	306.0	297.4
2015	305.3	308.9	313.3	311.4	308.3	304.1	299.8	302.3	301.1	304.8	311.7	313.5	307.0
Other Services													
2005	106.5	107.5	107.4	107.7	107.6	107.3	106.1	106.3	106.7	105.6	106.2	107.4	106.9
2006	107.5	108.8	110.0	107.2	107.4	108.1	105.8	106.0	106.2	105.9	106.8	107.7	107.3
2007	107.8	109.1	110.5	107.6	108.1	108.5	106.8	107.2	107.9	109.8	111.6	113.2	109.0
2008	112.1	112.8	113.6	112.0	111.2	110.4	108.3	107.5	106.4	105.7	105.3	105.4	109.2
2009	103.3	103.2	103.2	103.0	102.4	102.1	100.9	100.6	100.6	101.1	101.8	102.4	102.1
2010	101.5	102.3	102.6	102.8	102.2	101.9	100.5	100.6	100.3	101.2	102.0	102.3	101.7
2011	101.5	102.0	102.6	103.5	103.8	102.9	103.3	103.7	104.3	105.2	106.5	107.1	103.9
2012	106.8	107.7	108.5	109.2	109.2	109.1	108.0	107.5	107.9	108.9	109.6	110.0	108.5
2013	109.4	110.6	111.2	111.7	111.5	111.6	111.1	111.1	111.7	112.8	113.9	114.7	111.8
2014	114.6	116.0	116.9	116.9	117.0	116.6	116.4	116.6	117.0	118.3	119.7	120.1	117.2
2015	119.5	120.5	121.1	121.2	120.9	121.0	120.3	120.0	120.3	122.0	123.2	122.7	121.1
Government													
2005	320.2	321.4	322.5	324.7	325.4	297.0	292.9	320.8	323.9	326.0	325.3	325.7	318.8
2006	324.3	325.5	327.0	325.4	325.9	297.7	293.5	322.1	325.8	327.2	330.3	329.6	321.2
2007	326.5	327.9	330.2	330.4	331.2	302.1	297.8	327.8	331.6	330.2	332.6	333.5	325.2
2008	330.8	333.3	333.0	331.6	332.6	303.1	298.6	325.4	327.2	326.6	328.6	329.8	325.1
2009	327.9	326.4	326.6	327.0	325.5	297.4	294.7	316.5	319.0	321.0	321.9	321.7	318.8
2010	318.3	318.9	318.8	319.9	329.0	295.6	289.1	310.2	311.4	313.7	314.1	313.5	312.7
2011	312.0	313.6	312.1	312.2	310.1	283.4	280.4	303.6	306.5	309.8	308.3	308.8	305.1
2012	305.3	306.6	305.6	305.6	304.6	279.3	276.6	298.3	302.3	305.7	305.6	305.3	300.1
2013	303.2	306.1	306.4	306.2	306.1	280.3	278.0	298.6	303.4	305.3	307.1	305.5	300.5
2014	304.0	305.9	306.6	306.8	306.0	280.5	277.7	298.0	301.8	304.9	306.7	305.0	300.3
2015	303.0	305.2	306.3	307.3	305.9	281.4	279.3	299.9	304.0	307.7	308.5	306.6	301.3

Employment by Industry: Atlanta-Sandy Springs-Roswell, GA, 2005–2015

(Numbers in thousands, not seasonally adjusted)

Industry and year	January	February	March	April	May	June	July	August	September	October	November	December	Annual average
Total Nonfarm													
2005	2,286.3	2,297.8	2,305.0	2,335.7	2,347.6	2,338.2	2,336.6	2,361.3	2,362.3	2,375.6	2,393.1	2,398.0	2,344.8
2006	2,361.0	2,370.6	2,384.0	2,395.8	2,408.1	2,409.3	2,394.7	2,417.7	2,420.6	2,444.8	2,459.2	2,465.9	2,411.0
2007	2,427.6	2,439.9	2,451.9	2,449.9	2,461.6	2,455.4	2,451.1	2,474.2	2,469.9	2,470.0	2,482.6	2,484.4	2,459.9
2008	2,439.5	2,450.7	2,452.2	2,452.5	2,460.1	2,445.0	2,421.3	2,434.9	2,419.6	2,415.4	2,408.8	2,396.6	2,433.1
2009	2,337.3	2,331.3	2,321.5	2,315.3	2,312.6	2,293.9	2,271.1	2,274.3	2,267.9	2,274.0	2,280.5	2,278.4	2,296.5
2010	2,236.0	2,243.0	2,255.4	2,272.4	2,290.8	2,281.8	2,274.4	2,280.2	2,272.5	2,295.4	2,304.7	2,301.1	2,275.6
2011	2,248.0	2,283.0	2,298.9	2,313.9	2,322.2	2,310.8	2,305.3	2,318.0	2,317.5	2,330.7	2,343.2	2,342.8	2,311.2
2012	2,304.4	2,316.4	2,331.5	2,349.2	2,362.2	2,359.7	2,342.6	2,360.4	2,353.1	2,375.6	2,396.6	2,391.8	2,353.6
2013	2,356.6	2,372.3	2,381.2	2,400.4	2,410.1	2,408.6	2,401.0	2,423.7	2,423.2	2,447.3	2,467.7	2,469.9	2,413.5
2014	2,427.5	2,430.5	2,462.2	2,482.7	2,502.2	2,500.6	2,498.9	2,525.0	2,519.2	2,541.8	2,565.4	2,574.1	2,502.5
2015	2,519.2	2,534.0	2,545.5	2,563.4	2,585.2	2,589.5	2,581.4	2,596.8	2,592.6	2,623.2	2,643.7	2,643.8	2,584.9
Total Private													
2005	1,975.1	1,982.4	1,988.9	2,018.9	2,031.3	2,032.6	2,039.6	2,047.2	2,045.0	2,055.2	2,071.8	2,077.4	2,030.5
2006	2,041.1	2,047.0	2,058.8	2,072.3	2,085.4	2,091.9	2,089.9	2,096.6	2,093.2	2,114.5	2,126.5	2,133.7	2,087.6
2007	2,097.3	2,105.5	2,116.3	2,115.4	2,127.9	2,130.1	2,132.0	2,141.2	2,131.9	2,132.7	2,143.5	2,145.5	2,126.6
2008	2,100.5	2,106.4	2,106.3	2,107.3	2,115.5	2,107.9	2,096.0	2,096.3	2,080.2	2,069.2	2,059.4	2,049.8	2,091.2
2009	1,990.7	1,981.4	1,970.8	1,965.5	1,966.8	1,957.8	1,948.1	1,942.9	1,928.2	1,934.8	1,941.2	1,940.5	1,955.7
2010	1,899.2	1,904.2	1,915.5	1,931.9	1,945.0	1,944.7	1,951.5	1,955.1	1,945.2	1,966.8	1,972.1	1,972.8	1,942.0
2011	1,923.5	1,955.0	1,969.3	1,986.3	1,994.4	1,989.8	1,994.0	2,001.2	1,995.8	2,007.3	2,016.9	2,018.2	1,987.6
2012	1,982.5	1,992.2	2,003.8	2,022.7	2,037.1	2,038.5	2,035.3	2,045.1	2,033.9	2,054.0	2,070.2	2,069.6	2,032.1
2013	2,036.3	2,049.9	2,058.5	2,075.8	2,088.0	2,093.2	2,096.9	2,111.1	2,105.4	2,125.7	2,142.8	2,146.4	2,094.2
2014	2,110.3	2,111.1	2,140.0	2,159.8	2,178.4	2,183.6	2,192.0	2,206.8	2,197.8	2,218.3	2,237.6	2,249.6	2,182.1
2015	2,197.1	2,209.2	2,220.3	2,238.3	2,261.2	2,270.2	2,272.7	2,279.4	2,271.3	2,295.8	2,314.8	2,317.6	2,262.3
Goods Producing													
2005	305.6	307.1	306.9	311.6	313.9	314.2	314.1	315.2	316.9	315.1	317.4	316.7	312.9
2006	313.5	315.1	315.5	315.7	317.9	320.5	320.3	323.1	322.4	323.6	320.4	319.0	318.9
2007	317.2	318.8	319.5	318.0	318.9	319.6	318.2	319.1	316.7	316.0	315.2	313.3	317.5
2008	307.7	308.0	306.5	303.1	303.0	301.9	299.0	296.7	293.5	289.9	284.9	279.2	297.8
2009	267.5	264.3	260.0	255.7	253.5	250.5	245.0	243.0	241.1	239.9	238.7	236.8	249.7
2010	234.1	234.0	234.3	235.0	236.6	237.1	238.7	238.5	237.7	238.7	237.9	236.2	236.6
2011	228.6	234.8	236.6	239.0	239.7	240.4	241.4	240.7	239.1	239.6	238.6	237.1	238.0
2012	233.7	234.5	235.0	236.1	237.0	237.4	238.2	238.3	238.2	239.5	240.1	238.8	237.2
2013	236.3	237.5	239.2	239.0	241.2	242.7	244.8	245.5	246.2	247.0	248.5	247.8	243.0
2014	245.7	246.8	249.3	251.4	253.6	255.6	257.2	258.7	259.0	261.4	261.1	261.9	255.1
2015	259.3	261.5	261.8	263.8	265.5	267.4	268.1	268.9	269.5	271.8	273.3	274.5	267.1
Service-Providing													
2005	1,980.7	1,990.7	1,998.1	2,024.1	2,033.7	2,024.0	2,022.5	2,046.1	2,045.4	2,060.5	2,075.7	2,081.3	2,031.9
2006	2,047.5	2,055.5	2,068.5	2,080.1	2,090.2	2,088.8	2,074.4	2,094.6	2,098.2	2,121.2	2,138.8	2,146.9	2,092.1
2007	2,110.4	2,121.1	2,132.4	2,131.9	2,142.7	2,135.8	2,132.9	2,155.1	2,153.2	2,154.0	2,167.4	2,171.1	2,142.3
2008	2,131.8	2,142.7	2,145.7	2,149.4	2,157.1	2,143.1	2,122.3	2,138.2	2,126.1	2,125.5	2,123.9	2,117.4	2,135.3
2009	2,069.8	2,067.0	2,061.5	2,059.6	2,059.1	2,043.4	2,026.1	2,031.3	2,026.8	2,034.1	2,041.8	2,041.6	2,046.8
2010	2,001.9	2,009.0	2,021.1	2,037.4	2,054.2	2,044.7	2,035.7	2,041.7	2,034.8	2,056.7	2,066.8	2,064.9	2,039.1
2011	2,019.4	2,048.2	2,062.3	2,074.9	2,082.5	2,070.4	2,063.9	2,077.3	2,078.4	2,091.1	2,104.6	2,105.7	2,073.2
2012	2,070.7	2,081.9	2,096.5	2,113.1	2,125.2	2,122.3	2,104.4	2,122.1	2,114.9	2,136.1	2,156.5	2,153.0	2,116.4
2013	2,120.3	2,134.8	2,142.0	2,161.4	2,168.9	2,165.9	2,156.2	2,178.2	2,177.0	2,200.3	2,219.2	2,222.1	2,170.5
2014	2,181.8	2,183.7	2,212.9	2,231.3	2,248.6	2,245.0	2,241.7	2,266.3	2,260.2	2,280.4	2,304.3	2,312.2	2,247.4
2015	2,259.9	2,272.5	2,283.7	2,299.6	2,319.7	2,322.1	2,313.3	2,327.9	2,323.1	2,351.4	2,370.4	2,369.3	2,317.7
Mining and Logging													
2005	1.9	1.9	1.9	2.2	2.2	2.2	2.1	2.1	2.1	2.1	2.1	2.1	2.1
2006	2.2	2.1	2.1	2.1	2.1	2.1	2.1	2.1	2.0	2.1	2.1	2.1	2.1
2007	2.1	2.0	2.1	2.0	2.0	2.0	2.0	2.0	2.0	2.0	2.0	1.9	2.0
2008	1.8	1.8	1.8	1.7	1.6	1.6	1.5	1.5	1.5	1.5	1.5	1.5	1.6
2009	1.4	1.4	1.4	1.4	1.3	1.3	1.4	1.4	1.3	1.3	1.3	1.3	1.4
2010	1.4	1.3	1.4	1.3	1.4	1.4	1.3	1.3	1.4	1.4	1.4	1.4	1.4
2011	1.3	1.3	1.3	1.3	1.3	1.3	1.4	1.4	1.4	1.4	1.3	1.3	1.3
2012	1.2	1.2	1.3	1.2	1.2	1.2	1.2	1.2	1.2	1.2	1.2	1.1	1.2
2013	1.1	1.1	1.2	1.2	1.2	1.2	1.3	1.3	1.3	1.3	1.3	1.3	1.2
2014	1.3	1.3	1.3	1.4	1.4	1.4	1.3	1.3	1.3	1.4	1.4	1.4	1.4
2015	1.4	1.4	1.4	1.4	1.5	1.4	1.4	1.5	1.5	1.5	1.5	1.5	1.5

Employment by Industry: Atlanta-Sandy Springs-Roswell, GA, 2005–2015—*Continued*

(Numbers in thousands, not seasonally adjusted)

Industry and year	January	February	March	April	May	June	July	August	September	October	November	December	Annual average
Construction													
2005	126.2	127.4	127.3	130.4	132.4	132.8	133.6	134.4	135.3	134.8	135.3	134.1	132.0
2006	131.5	133.1	133.8	135.0	136.8	138.7	140.8	141.7	141.5	142.0	141.5	140.1	138.0
2007	137.3	139.0	139.9	139.4	140.2	140.7	140.2	140.9	139.5	139.4	138.7	137.0	139.4
2008	133.0	133.6	132.5	130.7	130.9	130.3	129.2	127.8	126.0	123.6	120.4	117.1	127.9
2009	110.7	109.5	107.1	105.1	104.4	102.9	99.9	98.0	96.8	96.2	95.6	93.9	101.7
2010	91.2	91.6	91.4	92.4	92.9	92.8	93.4	93.2	92.7	92.8	92.0	89.8	92.2
2011	84.3	88.4	90.0	91.7	91.6	92.0	92.3	91.9	91.3	91.4	90.1	88.6	90.3
2012	85.6	86.4	86.5	87.3	87.1	87.4	88.0	88.2	87.9	88.9	89.4	88.0	87.6
2013	85.9	87.0	88.6	88.7	90.5	91.7	93.4	94.3	94.8	95.6	96.7	95.7	91.9
2014	94.5	95.7	97.5	98.6	99.9	101.3	102.9	103.8	104.2	105.8	105.1	105.1	101.2
2015	102.9	104.5	104.4	106.7	107.4	108.7	109.0	109.5	109.8	110.4	111.0	111.7	108.0
Manufacturing													
2005	177.5	177.8	177.7	179.0	179.3	179.2	178.4	178.7	179.5	178.2	180.0	180.5	178.8
2006	179.8	179.9	179.6	178.6	179.0	179.7	177.4	179.3	178.9	179.5	176.8	176.8	178.8
2007	177.8	177.8	177.5	176.6	176.7	176.9	176.0	176.0	175.2	174.6	174.5	174.4	176.2
2008	172.9	172.6	172.2	170.7	170.5	170.0	168.3	167.4	166.0	164.8	163.0	160.6	168.3
2009	155.4	153.4	151.5	149.2	147.8	146.3	143.7	143.6	143.0	142.4	141.8	141.6	146.6
2010	141.5	141.1	141.5	141.3	142.3	142.9	144.0	144.0	143.6	144.5	144.5	145.0	143.0
2011	143.0	145.1	145.3	146.0	146.8	147.1	147.7	147.4	146.4	146.8	147.2	147.2	146.3
2012	146.9	146.9	147.2	147.6	148.7	148.8	149.0	148.9	149.1	149.4	149.5	149.7	148.5
2013	149.3	149.4	149.4	149.1	149.5	149.8	150.1	149.9	150.1	150.1	150.5	150.8	149.8
2014	149.9	149.8	150.5	151.4	152.3	152.9	153.0	153.6	153.5	154.2	154.6	155.4	152.6
2015	155.0	155.6	156.0	155.7	156.6	157.3	157.7	157.9	158.2	159.9	160.8	161.3	157.7
Trade, Transportation, and Utilities													
2005	528.1	527.0	528.8	535.8	538.5	538.9	544.6	543.4	541.5	547.5	559.5	566.3	541.7
2006	547.2	544.6	547.7	552.1	555.4	556.5	554.6	555.8	557.5	566.7	579.4	587.1	558.7
2007	567.5	563.5	564.2	564.5	567.9	568.1	568.6	568.3	568.4	570.6	581.1	585.6	569.9
2008	567.4	565.0	565.3	561.7	562.9	560.8	560.4	559.3	556.9	554.1	557.2	558.8	560.8
2009	535.7	529.7	526.3	521.7	522.1	520.7	518.9	519.1	516.8	516.1	523.7	527.5	523.2
2010	513.1	511.0	512.3	513.0	516.2	517.0	518.0	519.1	515.5	524.1	531.6	536.1	518.9
2011	515.7	519.4	521.7	525.0	527.0	526.6	527.6	528.4	526.1	531.6	540.3	543.5	527.7
2012	528.2	526.0	528.0	530.8	533.9	533.5	533.8	533.9	531.6	536.4	549.2	550.7	534.7
2013	534.0	532.5	532.3	534.0	537.0	538.1	540.9	543.3	541.5	546.6	558.6	564.6	542.0
2014	547.5	543.7	547.9	552.6	555.1	555.7	558.9	560.0	558.2	567.4	581.6	588.8	559.8
2015	569.5	567.0	568.8	571.9	575.3	577.0	577.8	579.4	577.8	586.2	601.0	604.5	579.7
Wholesale Trade													
2005	153.7	154.5	155.0	155.8	155.7	155.7	156.3	156.7	156.4	155.8	156.0	156.6	155.7
2006	155.1	155.8	156.1	157.8	158.6	158.9	159.8	159.7	159.8	161.1	160.4	161.6	158.7
2007	159.7	160.1	160.1	160.6	160.4	160.2	161.1	161.1	160.6	160.6	160.5	160.9	160.5
2008	160.2	160.7	160.4	160.1	160.2	159.6	159.9	159.7	159.1	158.1	156.7	155.5	159.2
2009	152.8	151.3	149.5	148.2	147.1	146.0	145.5	145.0	144.5	144.5	144.3	144.3	146.9
2010	143.6	143.9	143.9	144.5	145.0	144.8	144.9	144.9	143.7	145.3	145.0	144.6	144.5
2011	143.4	144.5	144.6	145.4	146.0	145.4	146.5	146.7	145.9	146.8	147.0	146.7	145.7
2012	145.7	146.5	146.6	147.2	148.0	147.7	148.6	148.6	147.2	148.3	148.5	148.4	147.6
2013	146.7	147.4	147.0	147.7	148.1	148.1	148.4	148.7	147.9	149.5	150.4	150.9	148.4
2014	150.5	151.0	151.2	151.6	152.1	152.2	153.1	153.6	153.4	154.4	155.7	156.4	152.9
2015	155.3	156.0	156.4	157.1	158.1	158.2	157.8	158.4	158.0	159.2	160.7	159.1	157.9
Retail Trade													
2005	254.6	251.5	252.6	259.2	261.6	262.3	264.9	263.8	261.9	268.1	277.8	283.0	263.4
2006	269.2	265.8	267.7	269.8	271.5	271.8	268.4	269.2	269.6	277.6	290.2	294.4	273.8
2007	281.6	276.8	277.0	276.7	278.0	277.2	278.0	277.4	277.4	279.8	289.9	292.8	280.2
2008	278.1	274.8	275.2	272.2	272.7	271.3	271.2	270.4	269.0	268.2	273.0	274.4	272.5
2009	257.1	253.8	252.4	251.1	252.2	251.8	250.5	251.2	249.4	249.0	256.4	259.1	252.8
2010	247.2	245.0	246.0	247.1	248.8	249.3	249.7	250.1	247.8	253.0	260.1	263.1	250.6
2011	248.8	250.0	251.2	253.7	254.3	254.2	254.2	254.6	253.1	257.4	265.3	267.4	255.4
2012	256.3	253.9	255.3	256.4	258.2	258.0	257.6	257.5	256.8	260.2	271.6	271.7	259.5
2013	259.3	258.2	258.7	259.8	261.8	262.9	264.6	266.4	265.7	269.3	278.8	282.6	265.7
2014	268.2	264.6	266.8	268.3	269.6	270.5	271.3	271.6	270.4	275.5	287.5	291.0	272.9
2015	274.8	273.5	275.4	277.8	279.3	280.5	280.7	281.1	280.3	286.1	298.9	301.2	282.4

Employment by Industry: Atlanta-Sandy Springs-Roswell, GA, 2005–2015—*Continued*

(Numbers in thousands, not seasonally adjusted)

Industry and year	January	February	March	April	May	June	July	August	September	October	November	December	Annual average
Transportation and Utilities													
2005	119.8	121.0	121.2	120.8	121.2	120.9	123.4	122.9	123.2	123.6	125.7	126.7	122.5
2006	122.9	123.0	123.9	124.5	125.3	125.8	126.4	126.9	128.1	128.0	128.8	131.1	126.2
2007	126.2	126.6	127.1	127.2	129.5	130.7	129.5	129.8	130.4	130.2	130.7	131.9	129.2
2008	129.1	129.5	129.7	129.4	130.0	129.9	129.3	129.2	128.8	127.8	127.5	128.9	129.1
2009	125.8	124.6	124.4	122.4	122.8	122.9	122.9	122.9	122.9	122.6	123.0	124.1	123.4
2010	122.3	122.1	122.4	121.4	122.4	122.9	123.4	124.1	124.0	125.8	126.5	128.4	123.8
2011	123.5	124.9	125.9	125.9	126.7	127.0	126.9	127.1	127.1	127.4	128.0	129.4	126.7
2012	126.2	125.6	126.1	127.2	127.7	127.8	127.6	127.8	127.6	127.9	129.1	130.6	127.6
2013	128.0	126.9	126.6	126.5	127.1	127.1	127.9	128.2	127.9	127.8	129.4	131.1	127.9
2014	128.8	128.1	129.9	132.7	133.4	133.0	134.5	134.8	134.4	137.5	138.4	141.4	133.9
2015	139.4	137.5	137.0	137.0	137.9	138.3	139.7	139.9	139.5	140.9	141.4	144.2	139.4
Information													
2005	81.4	81.4	81.9	81.9	80.9	82.4	81.8	80.5	81.0	81.4	82.1	82.5	81.6
2006	80.6	81.0	81.4	80.8	81.3	80.9	80.3	80.0	79.9	80.0	80.8	81.0	80.7
2007	81.4	81.2	81.2	80.4	80.9	80.9	80.6	80.7	80.8	79.7	80.1	80.2	80.7
2008	78.3	78.8	79.1	79.1	79.6	79.8	78.9	78.7	78.1	77.3	77.4	77.3	78.5
2009	78.7	78.5	78.1	77.9	77.6	77.1	76.2	75.8	75.3	74.6	74.6	75.0	76.6
2010	73.9	73.9	74.2	74.8	75.3	74.9	75.1	74.9	74.3	74.4	74.9	75.1	74.6
2011	76.5	76.6	77.0	77.2	77.0	76.3	77.1	77.3	77.0	77.5	79.0	77.2	77.1
2012	76.9	78.1	77.9	77.5	78.4	78.1	78.7	79.1	78.9	80.3	80.6	80.6	78.8
2013	79.1	80.0	80.1	80.8	81.3	80.5	81.6	81.9	81.9	84.1	83.8	83.7	81.6
2014	84.1	84.5	85.4	85.8	86.0	86.6	86.9	86.9	86.3	88.3	88.9	88.9	86.6
2015	86.0	86.7	87.4	88.0	90.5	90.0	94.5	90.6	88.1	88.4	88.0	87.4	88.8
Financial Activities													
2005	161.9	162.3	162.3	163.0	163.9	164.2	163.6	164.6	164.6	166.8	167.0	168.3	164.4
2006	165.1	166.0	166.5	168.4	169.0	169.4	169.3	170.1	170.0	171.5	171.3	172.0	169.1
2007	169.0	170.5	170.8	170.1	170.0	169.8	169.9	169.8	168.5	168.3	168.2	167.9	169.4
2008	164.2	164.7	164.2	163.9	163.8	163.1	163.1	162.1	160.3	160.9	159.3	158.6	162.4
2009	156.2	155.4	154.4	153.7	153.9	153.6	152.9	152.0	150.7	150.4	150.2	150.2	152.8
2010	148.4	148.3	148.1	147.9	148.3	148.2	148.1	148.6	147.9	149.4	149.6	149.9	148.6
2011	149.2	149.8	150.1	150.5	150.7	150.8	151.0	151.5	151.4	152.2	152.4	152.6	151.0
2012	152.5	153.0	153.3	153.3	153.1	153.4	153.7	153.7	152.8	154.2	155.3	155.3	153.6
2013	153.3	154.0	154.5	155.3	155.8	156.2	156.4	156.9	155.9	157.2	158.4	158.2	156.0
2014	156.3	156.6	157.1	157.5	158.1	158.7	159.0	159.6	158.6	160.3	160.4	160.6	158.6
2015	159.6	160.0	160.4	161.6	161.9	162.6	163.0	162.8	162.0	164.0	164.5	163.4	162.2
Professional and Business Services													
2005	378.1	381.6	382.3	385.9	386.4	387.0	391.7	395.0	396.3	398.2	399.3	397.7	390.0
2006	393.3	394.7	397.1	399.8	400.1	403.1	403.6	403.3	402.2	406.1	406.4	407.5	401.4
2007	401.7	405.2	408.9	405.6	407.8	409.3	413.1	416.5	415.7	415.9	417.2	418.1	411.3
2008	409.8	410.6	408.3	412.8	411.9	412.8	407.6	408.6	405.3	405.3	401.2	398.7	407.7
2009	381.2	378.7	375.6	374.3	373.1	374.1	375.9	373.0	370.6	379.6	381.4	382.0	376.6
2010	371.6	374.3	377.5	384.4	385.5	387.0	389.3	388.8	387.1	393.8	393.5	393.6	385.5
2011	387.1	397.5	400.7	400.7	400.1	400.4	401.5	404.7	405.4	408.0	409.0	410.7	402.2
2012	400.6	404.7	407.5	412.2	415.3	419.5	416.4	419.7	416.8	423.5	426.6	426.4	415.8
2013	419.7	427.0	428.7	432.0	432.7	436.7	435.5	439.4	439.6	446.3	449.3	448.0	436.2
2014	441.5	443.4	454.1	454.2	458.7	461.8	465.3	469.4	468.2	472.0	475.1	475.8	461.6
2015	462.9	467.6	470.3	471.2	478.6	482.0	480.3	482.8	482.6	489.5	489.5	489.6	478.9
Education and Health Services													
2005	219.8	221.0	218.9	223.8	225.2	222.4	223.7	226.4	227.2	229.8	230.4	230.6	224.9
2006	230.9	232.4	232.4	232.9	233.6	230.9	231.8	234.1	235.7	240.5	241.1	241.1	234.8
2007	239.0	241.2	241.4	242.8	242.8	240.6	241.5	245.4	246.7	249.3	250.2	250.3	244.3
2008	247.2	250.4	250.5	251.4	252.8	248.2	248.9	253.3	253.4	255.3	256.3	256.7	252.0
2009	254.7	256.1	255.1	255.8	257.2	252.5	251.5	254.9	254.3	258.5	259.4	259.2	255.8
2010	256.9	259.4	260.5	261.2	262.8	259.4	261.0	264.4	264.4	268.6	268.6	268.2	263.0
2011	263.7	267.7	268.6	273.6	273.3	268.9	269.3	273.4	275.0	278.9	279.0	279.9	272.6
2012	278.0	280.9	282.2	284.3	285.1	281.0	280.0	285.6	286.7	289.8	290.0	290.4	284.5
2013	289.7	292.4	293.0	295.4	296.0	292.2	290.6	296.4	297.7	300.8	303.0	303.3	295.9
2014	300.2	300.9	303.7	305.4	307.0	303.3	302.6	309.4	310.4	311.7	313.2	314.6	306.9
2015	312.9	314.7	315.2	316.8	318.5	315.4	314.8	320.2	321.3	323.0	323.3	323.7	318.3

Employment by Industry: Atlanta-Sandy Springs-Roswell, GA, 2005–2015—*Continued*

(Numbers in thousands, not seasonally adjusted)

Industry and year	January	February	March	April	May	June	July	August	September	October	November	December	Annual average
Leisure and Hospitality													
2005	206.7	207.8	213.2	221.2	226.2	227.3	223.5	224.3	221.6	220.8	220.5	219.6	219.4
2006	215.0	217.5	222.4	225.4	230.2	232.4	231.4	232.2	228.7	229.3	230.3	229.7	227.0
2007	225.1	228.4	233.2	235.8	240.7	242.5	240.6	242.0	237.3	234.8	233.7	232.9	235.6
2008	228.4	230.4	234.0	237.0	242.1	242.0	239.4	238.9	235.1	229.5	226.7	224.8	234.0
2009	217.9	219.6	222.9	227.1	230.3	230.8	229.0	227.9	224.3	220.6	219.0	216.8	223.9
2010	209.4	211.1	216.3	222.2	226.2	227.6	227.0	226.9	224.8	223.4	221.6	220.5	221.4
2011	211.2	216.1	221.4	227.8	233.4	233.3	232.9	232.4	229.4	227.2	226.3	225.7	226.4
2012	221.7	223.5	228.4	235.7	241.0	241.8	240.5	241.2	236.0	236.6	234.7	234.7	234.7
2013	231.8	233.7	238.1	245.6	249.9	252.5	253.0	253.8	249.3	250.3	247.9	248.1	246.2
2014	243.0	242.9	249.9	258.7	265.1	266.6	266.6	267.3	262.4	262.9	262.7	264.3	259.4
2015	253.3	257.2	261.6	268.7	273.9	278.1	276.0	277.2	273.2	275.6	277.2	275.8	270.7
Other Services													
2005	93.5	94.2	94.6	95.7	96.3	96.2	96.6	97.8	95.9	95.6	95.6	95.7	95.6
2006	95.5	95.7	95.8	97.2	97.9	98.2	98.6	98.0	96.8	96.8	96.8	96.3	97.0
2007	96.4	96.7	97.1	98.2	98.9	99.3	99.5	99.4	97.8	98.1	97.8	97.2	98.0
2008	97.5	98.5	98.4	98.3	99.4	99.3	98.7	98.7	97.6	96.9	96.4	95.7	98.0
2009	98.8	99.1	98.4	99.3	99.1	98.5	98.7	97.2	95.1	95.1	94.2	93.0	97.2
2010	91.8	92.2	92.3	93.4	94.1	93.5	94.3	93.9	93.5	94.4	94.4	93.2	93.4
2011	91.5	93.1	93.2	92.5	93.2	93.1	93.2	92.8	92.4	92.3	92.3	91.5	92.6
2012	90.9	91.5	91.5	92.8	93.3	93.8	94.0	93.6	92.9	93.7	93.7	92.7	92.9
2013	92.4	92.8	92.6	93.7	94.1	94.3	94.1	93.9	93.3	93.4	93.3	92.7	93.4
2014	92.0	92.3	92.6	94.2	94.8	95.3	95.5	95.5	94.7	94.3	94.6	94.7	94.2
2015	93.6	94.5	94.8	96.3	97.0	97.7	98.2	97.5	96.8	97.3	98.0	98.7	96.7
Government													
2005	311.2	315.4	316.1	316.8	316.3	305.6	297.0	314.1	317.3	320.4	321.3	320.6	314.3
2006	319.9	323.6	325.2	323.5	322.7	317.4	304.8	321.1	327.4	330.3	332.7	332.2	323.4
2007	330.3	334.4	335.6	334.5	333.7	325.3	319.1	333.0	338.0	337.3	339.1	338.9	333.3
2008	339.0	344.3	345.9	345.2	344.6	337.1	325.3	338.6	339.4	346.2	349.4	346.8	341.8
2009	346.6	349.9	350.7	349.8	345.8	336.1	323.0	331.4	339.7	339.2	339.3	337.9	340.8
2010	336.8	338.8	339.9	340.5	345.8	337.1	322.9	325.1	327.3	328.6	332.6	328.3	333.6
2011	324.5	328.0	329.6	327.6	327.8	321.0	311.3	316.8	321.7	323.4	326.3	324.6	323.6
2012	321.9	324.2	327.7	326.5	325.1	321.2	307.3	315.3	319.2	321.6	326.4	322.2	321.6
2013	320.3	322.4	322.7	324.6	322.1	315.4	304.1	312.6	317.8	321.6	324.9	323.5	319.3
2014	317.2	319.4	322.2	322.9	323.8	317.0	306.9	318.2	321.4	323.5	327.8	324.5	320.4
2015	322.1	324.8	325.2	325.1	324.0	319.3	308.7	317.4	321.3	327.4	328.9	326.2	322.5

Employment by Industry: Boston-Cambridge-Newton, MA NECTA, 2005–2015

(Numbers in thousands, not seasonally adjusted)

Industry and year	January	February	March	April	May	June	July	August	September	October	November	December	Annual average
Total Nonfarm													
2005	1,556.2	1,566.2	1,570.7	1,590.6	1,594.7	1,601.1	1,595.9	1,592.2	1,601.9	1,608.7	1,617.8	1,621.7	1,593.1
2006	1,577.4	1,584.0	1,592.6	1,608.0	1,613.2	1,627.9	1,618.8	1,616.9	1,628.2	1,639.1	1,647.1	1,649.6	1,616.9
2007	1,610.3	1,615.5	1,622.0	1,640.6	1,648.4	1,660.5	1,649.9	1,647.5	1,653.6	1,668.0	1,676.0	1,676.9	1,647.4
2008	1,635.2	1,642.7	1,648.4	1,664.3	1,668.7	1,677.0	1,666.5	1,662.0	1,666.8	1,676.3	1,671.4	1,663.9	1,661.9
2009	1,607.3	1,605.8	1,603.3	1,614.1	1,615.3	1,614.9	1,603.8	1,596.0	1,606.8	1,619.6	1,621.1	1,622.0	1,610.8
2010	1,589.1	1,593.1	1,598.6	1,617.5	1,626.8	1,624.7	1,618.7	1,612.8	1,620.4	1,639.3	1,643.0	1,644.8	1,619.1
2011	1,602.6	1,608.7	1,616.7	1,640.8	1,643.6	1,647.7	1,650.6	1,644.6	1,656.6	1,668.4	1,672.6	1,673.6	1,643.9
2012	1,632.3	1,637.6	1,648.6	1,663.2	1,671.0	1,684.1	1,678.1	1,674.6	1,683.2	1,696.7	1,704.0	1,702.0	1,673.0
2013	1,660.7	1,665.4	1,677.5	1,702.3	1,711.3	1,722.5	1,708.3	1,706.8	1,712.7	1,730.2	1,738.1	1,735.5	1,705.9
2014	1,688.6	1,698.7	1,708.3	1,733.1	1,743.9	1,752.7	1,747.8	1,740.2	1,748.4	1,768.5	1,777.2	1,778.3	1,740.5
2015	1,727.9	1,728.7	1,744.5	1,769.4	1,783.7	1,793.4	1,791.7	1,783.2	1,780.0	1,795.7	1,797.9	1,794.4	1,774.2
Total Private													
2005	1,367.9	1,375.7	1,379.9	1,399.1	1,403.2	1,410.1	1,414.4	1,413.2	1,413.1	1,418.9	1,427.0	1,431.5	1,404.5
2006	1,388.3	1,392.7	1,401.1	1,415.9	1,420.7	1,435.0	1,436.4	1,436.7	1,438.7	1,447.6	1,455.0	1,458.0	1,427.2
2007	1,418.6	1,422.5	1,428.5	1,446.4	1,453.9	1,466.3	1,467.6	1,467.5	1,462.8	1,474.8	1,481.7	1,482.8	1,456.1
2008	1,441.8	1,447.5	1,452.9	1,468.3	1,472.6	1,480.7	1,480.3	1,477.8	1,472.7	1,480.6	1,475.0	1,467.9	1,468.2
2009	1,413.1	1,410.1	1,407.6	1,415.3	1,417.5	1,418.5	1,418.8	1,413.8	1,414.0	1,424.9	1,426.3	1,426.4	1,417.2
2010	1,395.2	1,398.1	1,403.1	1,420.8	1,425.4	1,426.9	1,432.8	1,429.5	1,427.8	1,444.1	1,446.3	1,448.5	1,424.9
2011	1,409.2	1,413.4	1,421.4	1,446.0	1,448.4	1,453.2	1,466.6	1,463.1	1,464.1	1,475.0	1,478.9	1,478.7	1,451.5
2012	1,439.8	1,443.2	1,453.4	1,469.5	1,477.1	1,490.3	1,494.0	1,492.3	1,491.1	1,503.6	1,508.8	1,507.8	1,480.9
2013	1,470.2	1,471.8	1,483.7	1,507.2	1,515.7	1,527.5	1,525.2	1,525.6	1,520.1	1,533.7	1,539.9	1,537.9	1,513.2
2014	1,494.2	1,501.1	1,510.4	1,533.1	1,544.2	1,553.8	1,560.6	1,555.1	1,552.2	1,569.7	1,575.8	1,578.2	1,544.0
2015	1,532.3	1,531.2	1,545.3	1,569.9	1,584.7	1,594.7	1,604.5	1,600.1	1,585.6	1,599.1	1,599.3	1,596.6	1,578.6
Goods Producing													
2005	156.3	154.7	155.3	159.3	161.8	164.1	164.9	165.4	164.2	162.1	162.0	160.4	160.9
2006	155.4	153.9	154.3	157.9	159.9	162.2	162.5	163.3	161.7	159.8	158.9	157.1	158.9
2007	152.2	150.1	151.1	153.0	156.3	159.3	159.7	160.0	158.8	157.9	157.3	155.2	155.9
2008	149.6	147.8	148.4	150.7	153.1	154.7	154.9	154.6	152.9	151.1	148.6	145.2	151.0
2009	137.1	134.2	132.8	134.1	134.6	135.4	135.6	135.5	134.0	133.1	132.4	130.7	134.1
2010	125.7	124.2	124.7	127.6	130.0	132.3	134.1	133.9	132.8	132.8	132.5	131.3	130.2
2011	126.0	125.0	126.0	129.4	131.3	133.5	135.3	135.3	133.1	132.4	131.6	130.6	130.8
2012	127.2	125.9	127.0	130.1	132.0	135.1	137.1	137.1	136.0	136.5	136.4	135.7	133.0
2013	131.3	130.1	131.4	134.5	137.9	140.3	141.2	141.5	140.2	139.6	138.9	138.1	137.1
2014	133.8	132.8	133.5	136.1	139.3	141.8	143.8	143.8	142.3	142.3	142.8	142.4	139.6
2015	138.6	137.2	138.4	142.4	145.7	148.1	149.1	149.2	146.8	148.3	149.5	147.6	145.1
Service-Providing													
2005	1,399.9	1,411.5	1,415.4	1,431.3	1,432.9	1,437.0	1,431.0	1,426.8	1,437.7	1,446.6	1,455.8	1,461.3	1,432.3
2006	1,422.0	1,430.1	1,438.3	1,450.1	1,453.3	1,465.7	1,456.3	1,453.6	1,466.5	1,479.3	1,488.2	1,492.5	1,458.0
2007	1,458.1	1,465.4	1,470.9	1,487.6	1,492.1	1,501.2	1,490.2	1,487.5	1,494.8	1,510.1	1,518.7	1,521.7	1,491.5
2008	1,485.6	1,494.9	1,500.0	1,513.6	1,515.6	1,522.3	1,511.6	1,507.4	1,513.9	1,525.2	1,522.8	1,518.7	1,511.0
2009	1,470.2	1,471.6	1,470.5	1,480.0	1,480.7	1,479.5	1,468.2	1,460.5	1,472.8	1,486.5	1,488.7	1,491.3	1,476.7
2010	1,463.4	1,468.9	1,473.9	1,489.9	1,496.8	1,492.4	1,484.6	1,478.9	1,487.6	1,506.5	1,510.5	1,513.5	1,488.9
2011	1,476.6	1,483.7	1,490.7	1,511.4	1,512.3	1,514.2	1,515.3	1,509.3	1,523.5	1,536.0	1,541.0	1,543.0	1,513.1
2012	1,505.1	1,511.7	1,521.6	1,533.1	1,539.0	1,549.0	1,541.0	1,537.5	1,547.2	1,560.2	1,567.6	1,566.3	1,539.9
2013	1,529.4	1,535.3	1,546.1	1,567.8	1,573.4	1,582.2	1,567.1	1,565.3	1,572.5	1,590.6	1,599.2	1,597.4	1,568.9
2014	1,554.8	1,565.9	1,574.8	1,597.0	1,604.6	1,610.9	1,604.0	1,596.4	1,606.1	1,626.2	1,634.4	1,635.9	1,600.9
2015	1,589.3	1,591.5	1,606.1	1,627.0	1,638.0	1,645.3	1,642.6	1,634.0	1,633.2	1,647.4	1,648.4	1,646.8	1,629.1
Mining, Logging, and Construction													
2005	56.7	55.2	55.9	60.2	62.8	64.7	66.3	66.7	66.0	64.5	64.8	63.2	62.3
2006	58.8	57.8	58.4	62.0	63.6	65.2	66.1	66.5	65.2	64.2	63.4	61.4	62.7
2007	57.2	55.1	56.3	58.8	61.7	64.1	65.3	65.5	64.9	64.2	63.6	61.3	61.5
2008	56.8	55.5	56.6	59.0	61.3	62.5	63.8	63.4	62.2	60.7	58.9	56.4	59.8
2009	50.3	48.4	47.9	49.7	50.8	51.6	52.4	52.2	50.9	50.2	49.1	47.3	50.1
2010	43.8	42.5	43.2	46.0	47.9	49.4	51.0	50.8	49.9	49.3	48.8	47.5	47.5
2011	43.5	42.6	43.4	46.7	48.8	50.5	52.2	52.4	51.1	50.3	49.7	48.7	48.3
2012	45.2	44.1	45.1	47.9	49.5	51.7	53.9	54.1	53.4	53.8	53.5	52.4	50.4
2013	49.1	48.3	49.3	52.2	55.1	56.8	58.3	58.5	57.6	57.1	56.3	55.2	54.5
2014	52.0	51.2	51.7	54.6	57.7	59.6	61.5	61.6	60.6	60.9	61.0	60.4	57.7
2015	57.3	55.6	56.7	60.6	63.5	65.1	66.5	66.8	65.5	66.8	67.5	65.5	63.1

Employment by Industry: Boston-Cambridge-Newton, MA NECTA, 2005–2015—*Continued*

(Numbers in thousands, not seasonally adjusted)

Industry and year	January	February	March	April	May	June	July	August	September	October	November	December	Annual average
Manufacturing													
2005	99.6	99.5	99.4	99.1	99.0	99.4	98.6	98.7	98.2	97.6	97.2	97.2	98.6
2006	96.6	96.1	95.9	95.9	96.3	97.0	96.4	96.8	96.5	95.6	95.5	95.7	96.2
2007	95.0	95.0	94.8	94.2	94.6	95.2	94.4	94.5	93.9	93.7	93.7	93.9	94.4
2008	92.8	92.3	91.8	91.7	91.8	92.2	91.1	91.2	90.7	90.4	89.7	88.8	91.2
2009	86.8	85.8	84.9	84.4	83.8	83.8	83.2	83.3	83.1	82.9	83.3	83.4	84.1
2010	81.9	81.7	81.5	81.6	82.1	82.9	83.1	83.1	82.9	83.5	83.7	83.8	82.7
2011	82.5	82.4	82.6	82.7	82.5	83.0	83.1	82.9	82.0	82.1	81.9	81.9	82.5
2012	82.0	81.8	81.9	82.2	82.5	83.4	83.2	83.0	82.6	82.7	82.9	83.3	82.6
2013	82.2	81.8	82.1	82.3	82.8	83.5	82.9	83.0	82.6	82.5	82.6	82.9	82.6
2014	81.8	81.6	81.8	81.5	81.6	82.2	82.3	82.2	81.7	81.4	81.8	82.0	81.8
2015	81.3	81.6	81.7	81.8	82.2	83.0	82.6	82.4	81.3	81.5	82.0	82.1	82.0
Trade, Transportation, and Utilities													
2005	240.4	238.3	237.7	239.2	240.3	242.3	239.4	239.0	238.5	240.3	244.5	249.5	240.8
2006	239.5	235.1	235.8	236.8	238.0	240.8	237.7	237.6	239.1	241.9	246.3	250.3	239.9
2007	240.1	236.0	236.3	236.1	238.5	241.8	238.7	238.0	238.1	241.3	246.5	249.2	240.1
2008	241.2	236.7	236.7	238.1	239.5	242.2	239.1	238.7	238.6	240.1	241.0	243.2	239.6
2009	231.1	226.6	224.7	223.9	225.8	228.3	225.2	224.1	226.0	229.1	231.7	234.2	227.6
2010	226.8	223.4	223.5	225.7	227.7	229.6	227.8	227.1	226.6	230.0	233.0	237.0	228.2
2011	228.3	225.4	225.5	228.7	229.6	232.3	231.7	231.4	231.7	233.8	236.9	240.0	231.3
2012	231.1	226.8	227.6	228.0	230.7	233.9	231.6	231.2	231.3	234.7	239.4	241.4	232.3
2013	233.8	230.0	230.8	232.7	234.9	238.7	236.6	236.8	237.0	238.7	242.7	246.4	236.6
2014	239.0	235.7	236.1	237.5	240.0	243.1	240.3	237.5	241.0	244.4	248.8	252.3	241.3
2015	243.9	238.3	240.1	242.3	245.2	248.9	247.6	247.2	246.1	247.2	248.7	250.2	245.5
Wholesale Trade													
2005	59.2	59.2	58.9	59.1	59.4	59.6	60.1	60.1	59.8	60.3	60.6	61.1	59.8
2006	60.3	60.2	60.1	60.3	60.4	61.0	61.5	61.7	61.4	62.0	62.2	62.3	61.1
2007	61.4	61.3	61.4	61.0	61.1	61.7	61.5	61.5	60.8	61.2	61.2	61.4	61.3
2008	60.7	60.3	60.4	60.6	60.4	60.8	60.8	60.4	59.8	59.6	59.3	59.2	60.2
2009	57.6	56.7	56.3	55.8	55.5	55.7	55.4	55.0	54.4	54.8	54.5	54.3	55.5
2010	53.6	53.5	53.5	53.3	53.7	54.0	54.3	54.1	53.6	53.8	53.8	53.9	53.8
2011	53.2	53.1	53.3	53.9	53.8	53.9	54.5	54.3	53.7	53.9	53.8	53.7	53.8
2012	53.2	53.0	53.2	53.5	53.7	54.1	54.4	54.5	53.9	54.7	55.4	55.4	54.1
2013	55.1	55.0	55.2	55.6	55.5	56.0	56.6	56.6	56.2	56.5	56.5	56.5	55.9
2014	56.2	56.1	56.1	56.5	56.7	57.2	57.3	57.2	56.8	57.0	57.3	57.3	56.8
2015	56.8	56.4	56.5	57.1	57.4	58.0	58.9	58.8	58.2	58.8	58.9	57.9	57.8
Retail Trade													
2005	141.3	139.4	139.3	140.0	140.6	142.2	139.9	139.8	138.9	141.3	145.3	149.4	141.5
2006	141.4	137.2	137.9	138.6	138.9	140.6	138.0	138.0	137.6	140.0	144.4	148.0	140.1
2007	139.5	135.7	135.7	135.8	137.5	139.4	138.1	137.6	136.6	139.5	145.0	147.5	139.0
2008	141.0	137.1	136.9	137.7	138.7	140.4	139.0	139.4	138.0	140.2	142.2	144.2	139.6
2009	135.3	131.9	130.4	129.9	131.7	133.7	132.5	132.6	132.7	135.4	138.6	140.8	133.8
2010	135.2	132.1	132.2	134.0	135.0	136.3	136.0	136.2	134.5	137.7	141.0	144.2	136.2
2011	137.4	134.6	134.3	135.8	136.4	138.1	138.2	138.8	137.7	140.1	143.6	146.4	138.5
2012	139.1	135.1	135.5	135.5	137.5	139.6	138.4	138.6	137.2	140.0	144.6	145.9	138.9
2013	140.0	136.3	136.7	137.7	139.2	141.4	140.5	141.3	139.8	141.3	145.5	148.6	140.7
2014	142.4	139.3	139.3	140.3	141.8	143.8	142.6	140.7	142.1	145.5	149.6	152.1	143.3
2015	146.0	141.2	142.3	143.2	145.0	147.2	146.4	146.5	143.9	145.0	147.2	148.8	145.2
Transportation and Utilities													
2005	39.9	39.7	39.5	40.1	40.3	40.5	39.4	39.1	39.8	38.7	38.6	39.0	39.6
2006	37.8	37.7	37.8	37.9	38.7	39.2	38.2	37.9	40.1	39.9	39.7	40.0	38.7
2007	39.2	39.0	39.2	39.3	39.9	40.7	39.1	38.9	40.7	40.6	40.3	40.3	39.8
2008	39.5	39.3	39.4	39.8	40.4	41.0	39.3	38.9	40.8	40.3	39.5	39.8	39.8
2009	38.2	38.0	38.0	38.2	38.6	38.9	37.3	36.5	38.9	38.9	38.6	39.1	38.3
2010	38.0	37.8	37.8	38.4	39.0	39.3	37.5	36.8	38.5	38.5	38.2	38.9	38.2
2011	37.7	37.7	37.9	39.0	39.4	40.3	39.0	38.3	40.3	39.8	39.5	39.9	39.1
2012	38.8	38.7	38.9	39.0	39.5	40.2	38.8	38.1	40.2	40.0	39.4	40.1	39.3
2013	38.7	38.7	38.9	39.4	40.2	41.3	39.5	38.9	41.0	40.9	40.7	41.3	40.0
2014	40.4	40.3	40.7	40.7	41.5	42.1	40.4	39.6	42.1	41.9	41.9	42.9	41.2
2015	41.1	40.7	41.3	42.0	42.8	43.7	42.3	41.9	44.0	43.4	42.6	43.5	42.4

Employment by Industry: Boston-Cambridge-Newton, MA NECTA, 2005–2015—*Continued*

(Numbers in thousands, not seasonally adjusted)

Industry and year	January	February	March	April	May	June	July	August	September	October	November	December	Annual average
Information													
2005	50.3	50.4	50.7	50.4	50.5	51.0	51.5	51.4	51.0	51.2	51.3	51.7	51.0
2006	51.6	51.7	51.9	51.5	51.5	51.9	51.4	51.5	51.0	51.9	52.0	52.1	51.7
2007	51.1	51.2	51.5	51.4	51.8	52.4	52.7	52.4	52.2	52.1	52.5	52.7	52.0
2008	52.9	53.3	53.5	53.3	53.2	53.9	54.1	54.1	53.7	53.5	53.4	53.4	53.5
2009	53.5	52.4	52.1	51.7	51.7	51.9	52.2	52.3	52.1	52.4	52.8	53.1	52.4
2010	53.6	53.4	53.5	53.8	53.9	54.5	54.1	53.9	53.3	52.9	53.0	53.3	53.6
2011	52.9	53.0	53.1	53.3	53.7	54.5	55.7	54.1	55.2	55.6	55.7	56.0	54.4
2012	53.9	53.8	53.9	54.3	54.3	55.7	56.6	55.8	54.1	54.3	54.2	54.0	54.6
2013	53.7	53.6	53.5	54.3	54.4	55.6	55.8	55.7	55.1	54.8	56.1	55.1	54.8
2014	54.3	54.4	54.5	54.8	55.1	56.0	56.2	56.1	55.5	55.7	55.8	56.1	55.4
2015	56.0	55.7	56.1	56.2	56.4	57.5	57.9	57.7	57.2	56.7	56.5	57.0	56.7
Financial Activities													
2005	150.7	150.6	150.8	150.8	151.4	153.5	155.6	155.6	154.5	153.4	154.0	155.2	153.0
2006	152.6	152.6	152.9	153.3	153.7	155.8	158.0	157.8	156.6	155.9	156.8	158.0	155.3
2007	157.0	157.1	157.1	157.1	157.3	159.0	159.6	159.6	157.2	156.5	156.3	157.1	157.6
2008	155.5	155.3	155.5	155.5	155.6	157.2	158.3	158.2	156.2	155.5	155.1	155.3	156.1
2009	153.4	152.5	152.1	151.2	151.0	151.7	151.4	150.9	148.7	148.5	148.6	148.7	150.7
2010	147.0	146.7	146.4	146.2	146.6	147.6	148.6	148.3	146.6	146.3	146.0	147.0	146.9
2011	144.9	144.8	144.8	145.1	145.3	146.6	148.1	148.3	146.4	145.8	145.5	145.8	146.0
2012	144.5	144.8	144.7	144.7	145.3	147.2	147.6	147.8	145.7	145.6	145.5	146.0	145.8
2013	144.3	144.8	145.0	144.9	145.4	147.1	147.8	148.4	146.1	146.1	146.3	146.9	146.1
2014	145.3	145.3	145.3	145.7	146.5	148.5	149.1	149.2	147.1	147.7	148.1	148.8	147.2
2015	147.4	147.4	147.3	147.8	148.5	150.6	153.0	153.6	150.9	151.7	152.1	152.5	150.2
Professional and Business Services													
2005	274.7	274.9	275.9	281.0	282.0	286.2	288.4	288.9	287.3	287.0	288.5	289.0	283.7
2006	281.6	282.4	283.8	287.5	289.3	295.1	296.5	297.2	295.6	297.7	299.5	299.6	292.2
2007	291.7	293.4	295.2	301.1	303.1	307.8	307.5	308.4	305.7	307.5	308.4	309.1	303.2
2008	302.6	304.2	305.2	308.0	308.9	312.2	312.3	311.3	309.0	308.7	306.3	303.3	307.7
2009	293.1	290.1	288.5	289.8	288.6	290.0	289.3	288.0	285.2	286.2	285.6	286.3	288.4
2010	282.8	283.3	284.1	289.0	289.0	291.4	293.3	293.0	289.8	292.9	293.0	293.2	289.6
2011	288.8	289.0	289.8	297.5	297.6	300.4	304.1	302.8	301.2	303.8	304.5	305.2	298.7
2012	297.4	297.8	300.3	306.4	307.7	312.9	314.7	314.8	313.0	315.9	316.8	316.6	309.5
2013	309.7	311.5	313.2	320.2	321.7	325.9	327.6	327.5	324.3	327.4	329.0	328.2	322.2
2014	320.3	320.4	321.0	327.5	329.5	333.6	336.1	336.1	332.9	335.3	335.9	335.7	330.4
2015	328.9	328.4	330.6	337.6	340.1	344.6	347.5	347.0	342.0	345.0	345.0	342.6	339.9
Education and Health Services													
2005	312.2	322.6	323.4	325.7	319.9	310.0	311.3	310.0	319.0	328.2	331.4	331.0	320.4
2006	321.7	331.0	333.5	334.2	328.9	322.5	321.9	320.5	330.9	338.5	341.2	341.3	330.5
2007	334.8	342.6	343.1	348.4	342.6	333.3	335.3	333.7	341.1	351.5	354.1	354.3	342.9
2008	343.6	353.1	354.7	357.5	351.5	342.9	344.7	342.9	350.4	360.7	363.3	362.9	352.4
2009	352.6	361.3	362.7	364.3	358.0	348.6	353.2	351.8	361.2	369.5	372.3	372.1	360.6
2010	362.9	372.0	373.5	371.0	364.6	352.2	355.4	353.7	364.9	373.5	376.1	375.2	366.3
2011	365.2	374.4	376.2	376.1	370.3	358.4	361.7	360.6	371.6	380.2	383.4	382.7	371.7
2012	373.4	382.4	384.1	382.5	377.2	367.0	368.1	366.9	377.6	386.0	389.0	388.5	378.6
2013	379.1	385.6	388.0	391.0	385.5	376.1	374.5	371.8	379.9	388.9	391.6	390.9	383.6
2014	378.6	390.4	392.5	397.6	392.5	382.0	385.4	382.9	390.6	401.3	404.8	404.0	391.9
2015	388.3	399.4	402.5	405.7	402.4	391.5	393.3	390.5	396.8	406.3	407.1	407.3	399.3
Leisure and Hospitality													
2005	126.7	127.3	129.0	135.0	139.4	144.4	144.4	144.4	140.7	138.8	137.2	136.0	136.9
2006	128.0	128.5	130.7	136.1	140.4	146.2	147.8	148.1	144.8	142.8	141.3	140.5	139.6
2007	133.7	133.5	135.2	140.0	144.1	150.5	151.5	152.7	148.8	147.3	145.4	143.9	143.9
2008	136.7	137.2	138.8	144.6	149.7	154.5	153.6	154.8	150.6	149.6	146.1	143.6	146.7
2009	132.9	133.5	134.8	140.2	147.2	150.2	149.8	149.6	147.1	146.1	142.9	141.3	143.0
2010	137.2	136.0	137.9	146.3	151.5	155.6	155.3	155.6	151.9	153.7	150.4	149.1	148.4
2011	141.7	139.9	143.2	151.9	156.2	161.3	163.1	163.1	160.5	159.0	156.5	153.9	154.3
2012	149.1	148.1	151.1	158.2	163.8	170.3	170.1	171.0	167.2	164.5	161.5	159.8	161.2
2013	153.8	151.7	156.1	163.4	169.4	175.9	173.7	176.1	171.7	172.5	169.5	166.7	166.7
2014	158.7	157.8	162.3	167.9	174.5	180.0	180.6	180.8	176.2	176.2	172.9	172.2	171.7
2015	164.3	160.7	164.6	171.6	179.3	184.4	186.1	185.4	178.6	175.9	172.5	170.3	174.5

Employment by Industry: Boston-Cambridge-Newton, MA NECTA, 2005–2015—*Continued*

(Numbers in thousands, not seasonally adjusted)

Industry and year	January	February	March	April	May	June	July	August	September	October	November	December	Annual average
Other Services													
2005	56.6	56.9	57.1	57.7	57.9	58.6	58.9	58.5	57.9	57.9	58.1	58.7	57.9
2006	57.9	57.5	58.2	58.6	59.0	60.5	60.6	60.7	59.0	59.1	59.0	59.1	59.1
2007	58.0	58.6	59.0	59.3	60.2	62.2	62.6	62.7	60.9	60.7	61.2	61.3	60.6
2008	59.7	59.9	60.1	60.6	61.1	63.1	63.3	63.2	61.3	61.3	61.2	61.0	61.3
2009	59.4	59.5	59.9	60.1	60.6	62.4	62.1	61.6	59.7	60.0	60.0	60.0	60.4
2010	59.2	59.1	59.5	61.2	62.1	63.7	64.2	64.0	61.9	62.0	62.3	62.4	61.8
2011	61.4	61.9	62.8	64.0	64.4	66.2	66.9	66.7	64.4	64.4	64.8	64.5	64.4
2012	63.2	63.6	64.7	65.3	66.1	68.2	68.2	67.7	66.2	66.1	66.0	65.8	65.9
2013	64.5	64.5	65.7	66.2	66.5	67.9	68.0	67.8	65.8	65.7	65.8	65.6	66.2
2014	64.2	64.3	65.2	66.0	66.8	68.8	69.1	68.7	66.6	66.8	66.7	66.7	66.7
2015	64.9	64.1	65.7	66.3	67.1	69.1	70.0	69.5	67.2	68.0	67.9	69.1	67.4
Government													
2005	188.3	190.5	190.8	191.5	191.5	191.0	181.5	179.0	188.8	189.8	190.8	190.2	188.6
2006	189.1	191.3	191.5	192.1	192.5	192.9	182.4	180.2	189.5	191.5	192.1	191.6	189.7
2007	191.7	193.0	193.5	194.1	194.5	194.2	182.3	180.0	190.8	193.2	194.3	194.1	191.3
2008	193.4	195.2	195.5	196.0	196.1	196.3	186.2	184.2	194.1	195.7	196.4	196.0	193.8
2009	194.2	195.7	195.7	198.8	197.8	196.4	185.0	182.2	192.8	194.7	194.8	195.6	193.6
2010	193.9	195.0	195.5	196.7	201.4	197.8	185.9	183.3	192.6	195.2	196.7	196.3	194.2
2011	193.4	195.3	195.3	194.8	195.2	194.5	184.0	181.5	192.5	193.4	193.7	194.9	192.4
2012	192.5	194.4	195.2	193.7	193.9	193.8	184.1	182.3	192.1	193.1	195.2	194.2	192.0
2013	190.5	193.6	193.8	195.1	195.6	195.0	183.1	181.2	192.6	196.5	198.2	197.6	192.7
2014	194.4	197.6	197.9	200.0	199.7	198.9	187.2	185.1	196.2	198.8	201.4	200.1	196.4
2015	195.6	197.5	199.2	199.5	199.0	198.7	187.2	183.1	194.4	196.6	198.6	197.8	195.6

Employment by Industry: San Francisco-Oakland-Hayward, CA, 2005–2015

(Numbers in thousands, not seasonally adjusted)

Industry and year	January	February	March	April	May	June	July	August	September	October	November	December	Annual average
Total Nonfarm													
2005	1,974.0	1,987.1	1,994.8	2,001.8	2,006.4	2,014.7	2,002.6	2,003.1	2,016.1	2,022.5	2,035.2	2,043.2	2,008.5
2006	2,001.4	2,017.8	2,026.5	2,027.7	2,045.0	2,055.3	2,039.0	2,043.1	2,053.4	2,061.7	2,072.5	2,076.0	2,043.3
2007	2,031.8	2,048.2	2,059.6	2,053.5	2,069.6	2,078.1	2,069.2	2,071.9	2,078.0	2,084.2	2,097.6	2,103.6	2,070.4
2008	2,054.0	2,067.5	2,070.6	2,074.2	2,079.1	2,083.8	2,073.9	2,067.9	2,066.2	2,067.9	2,060.8	2,056.7	2,068.6
2009	1,996.6	1,987.0	1,979.3	1,972.5	1,969.1	1,965.6	1,940.6	1,923.7	1,929.6	1,947.6	1,949.2	1,948.1	1,959.1
2010	1,905.3	1,907.5	1,915.0	1,929.6	1,941.4	1,943.4	1,923.6	1,917.2	1,933.1	1,946.0	1,949.1	1,953.9	1,930.4
2011	1,921.9	1,929.8	1,934.9	1,953.6	1,961.9	1,964.5	1,962.6	1,966.8	1,977.5	1,990.2	1,998.9	2,004.1	1,963.9
2012	1,971.3	1,984.6	1,996.3	2,020.3	2,035.8	2,047.7	2,040.9	2,048.1	2,053.2	2,070.8	2,085.2	2,092.9	2,037.3
2013	2,050.3	2,068.3	2,080.4	2,093.8	2,105.3	2,106.8	2,102.4	2,113.1	2,114.8	2,134.4	2,153.4	2,156.8	2,106.7
2014	2,118.1	2,135.1	2,145.8	2,160.7	2,174.1	2,180.1	2,174.7	2,184.7	2,188.1	2,205.8	2,222.2	2,230.0	2,176.6
2015	2,196.2	2,209.2	2,224.4	2,238.9	2,251.0	2,257.2	2,266.4	2,275.6	2,277.7	2,296.7	2,304.1	2,313.1	2,259.2
Total Private													
2005	1,663.6	1,673.1	1,679.6	1,685.3	1,689.1	1,698.5	1,697.4	1,702.3	1,705.8	1,706.8	1,717.1	1,727.5	1,695.5
2006	1,687.1	1,700.1	1,706.5	1,708.3	1,724.9	1,736.8	1,729.8	1,736.2	1,738.5	1,740.0	1,747.8	1,754.9	1,725.9
2007	1,712.8	1,724.8	1,734.4	1,728.4	1,741.9	1,751.6	1,755.1	1,758.7	1,756.3	1,767.4	1,778.2	1,784.9	1,749.5
2008	1,739.1	1,749.8	1,751.6	1,754.6	1,760.2	1,763.0	1,763.5	1,761.2	1,754.8	1,752.5	1,743.9	1,741.7	1,753.0
2009	1,683.6	1,671.5	1,662.4	1,654.4	1,653.0	1,649.3	1,640.2	1,635.6	1,629.9	1,641.5	1,643.1	1,645.9	1,650.9
2010	1,605.3	1,605.5	1,611.5	1,620.6	1,626.1	1,632.6	1,637.3	1,634.5	1,634.3	1,643.8	1,643.8	1,650.3	1,628.8
2011	1,620.9	1,626.1	1,628.8	1,646.9	1,655.0	1,659.3	1,672.2	1,676.5	1,684.5	1,690.5	1,698.1	1,705.4	1,663.7
2012	1,675.1	1,685.5	1,694.5	1,718.3	1,733.5	1,746.6	1,750.2	1,759.3	1,760.8	1,774.0	1,783.7	1,792.9	1,739.5
2013	1,754.6	1,770.5	1,778.7	1,791.2	1,802.7	1,808.8	1,814.9	1,824.5	1,820.8	1,834.4	1,850.5	1,858.1	1,809.1
2014	1,819.2	1,834.0	1,843.5	1,855.1	1,867.3	1,875.4	1,879.6	1,891.0	1,889.0	1,900.1	1,912.7	1,921.4	1,874.0
2015	1,890.4	1,902.2	1,914.0	1,926.6	1,938.5	1,946.6	1,966.8	1,974.0	1,972.2	1,984.8	1,990.2	2,000.4	1,950.6
Goods Producing													
2005	245.0	246.8	248.6	249.1	249.6	253.0	255.3	256.6	256.7	256.3	255.8	254.1	252.2
2006	248.4	250.6	250.7	248.8	254.9	258.9	259.5	262.3	261.7	260.1	258.4	255.1	255.8
2007	249.7	250.2	252.7	252.1	254.0	256.8	257.6	259.5	258.1	257.6	256.9	255.0	255.0
2008	247.5	248.5	247.3	246.1	246.5	247.4	247.7	246.9	244.8	241.6	236.0	232.1	244.4
2009	222.9	215.9	213.8	209.8	208.8	209.0	207.7	207.5	206.1	205.9	205.4	202.5	209.6
2010	197.0	195.3	197.0	193.1	195.3	196.8	199.1	199.5	197.9	198.4	196.9	195.6	196.8
2011	193.3	193.1	191.3	193.9	195.8	197.7	202.8	203.8	202.9	202.6	201.7	200.6	198.3
2012	197.0	197.2	197.2	198.8	203.0	206.3	209.5	209.8	210.6	210.8	209.8	208.8	204.9
2013	205.3	207.2	208.1	208.8	210.8	213.3	216.1	218.4	217.8	218.5	218.9	216.9	213.3
2014	213.9	215.8	216.9	218.6	221.0	223.9	226.2	228.3	228.8	229.6	230.4	228.6	223.5
2015	228.1	229.4	231.9	231.4	234.1	237.0	241.9	243.5	243.7	244.3	243.2	244.1	237.7
Service-Providing													
2005	1,729.0	1,740.3	1,746.2	1,752.7	1,756.8	1,761.7	1,747.3	1,746.5	1,759.4	1,766.2	1,779.4	1,789.1	1,756.2
2006	1,753.0	1,767.2	1,775.8	1,778.9	1,790.1	1,796.4	1,779.5	1,780.8	1,791.7	1,801.6	1,814.1	1,820.9	1,787.5
2007	1,782.1	1,798.0	1,806.9	1,801.4	1,815.6	1,821.3	1,811.6	1,812.4	1,819.9	1,826.6	1,840.7	1,848.6	1,815.4
2008	1,806.5	1,819.0	1,823.3	1,828.1	1,832.6	1,836.4	1,826.2	1,821.0	1,821.4	1,826.3	1,824.8	1,824.6	1,824.2
2009	1,773.7	1,771.1	1,765.5	1,762.7	1,760.3	1,756.6	1,732.9	1,716.2	1,723.5	1,741.7	1,743.8	1,745.6	1,749.5
2010	1,708.3	1,712.2	1,718.0	1,736.5	1,746.1	1,746.6	1,724.5	1,717.7	1,735.2	1,747.6	1,752.2	1,758.3	1,733.6
2011	1,728.6	1,736.7	1,743.6	1,759.7	1,766.1	1,766.8	1,759.8	1,763.0	1,774.6	1,787.6	1,797.2	1,803.5	1,765.6
2012	1,774.3	1,787.4	1,799.1	1,821.5	1,832.8	1,841.4	1,831.4	1,838.3	1,842.6	1,860.0	1,875.4	1,884.1	1,832.4
2013	1,845.0	1,861.1	1,872.3	1,885.0	1,894.5	1,893.5	1,886.3	1,894.7	1,897.0	1,915.9	1,934.5	1,939.9	1,893.3
2014	1,904.2	1,919.3	1,928.9	1,942.1	1,953.1	1,956.2	1,948.5	1,956.4	1,959.3	1,976.2	1,991.8	2,001.4	1,953.1
2015	1,968.1	1,979.8	1,992.5	2,007.5	2,016.9	2,020.2	2,024.5	2,032.1	2,034.0	2,052.4	2,060.9	2,069.0	2,021.5
Mining and Logging													
2005	1.3	1.4	1.3	1.3	1.3	1.3	1.4	1.3	1.3	1.3	1.3	1.3	1.3
2006	1.3	1.3	1.3	1.3	1.4	1.4	1.4	1.5	1.5	1.5	1.5	1.5	1.4
2007	1.4	1.5	1.4	1.5	1.5	1.5	1.4	1.5	1.4	1.4	1.4	1.4	1.4
2008	1.4	1.4	1.4	1.4	1.4	1.4	1.4	1.4	1.4	1.4	1.4	1.4	1.4
2009	1.4	1.4	1.4	1.4	1.4	1.4	1.4	1.4	1.3	1.3	1.3	1.3	1.4
2010	1.3	1.3	1.3	1.3	1.3	1.3	1.3	1.4	1.4	1.3	1.2	1.2	1.3
2011	1.2	1.2	1.2	1.2	1.2	1.2	1.1	1.1	1.0	1.0	1.0	1.0	1.1
2012	1.0	1.0	1.0	1.0	1.0	1.0	1.1	1.1	1.1	1.1	1.0	1.0	1.0
2013	1.0	1.0	1.0	1.0	1.0	1.0	1.0	1.0	0.9	0.9	0.8	0.8	1.0
2014	0.9	0.9	0.9	0.9	0.9	0.9	0.9	0.9	0.9	0.9	0.9	0.9	0.9
2015	1.0	1.0	1.0	1.0	1.0	1.0	1.0	1.0	1.0	1.0	1.0	1.0	1.0

Employment by Industry: San Francisco-Oakland-Hayward, CA, 2005–2015—*Continued*

(Numbers in thousands, not seasonally adjusted)

Industry and year	January	February	March	April	May	June	July	August	September	October	November	December	Annual average
Construction													
2005	106.3	108.0	110.1	111.4	112.4	115.3	117.3	118.5	118.5	118.5	117.6	115.8	114.1
2006	110.1	112.0	111.0	109.7	115.5	118.4	120.0	122.3	122.1	121.2	118.8	116.2	116.4
2007	112.3	112.3	114.7	114.8	116.5	118.8	120.5	121.7	120.3	119.3	117.7	115.9	117.1
2008	110.3	110.8	109.8	109.5	110.2	110.9	111.6	111.3	109.9	108.9	104.7	102.0	109.2
2009	95.5	90.7	90.2	88.4	88.5	89.0	88.6	88.5	87.1	86.7	86.3	83.5	88.6
2010	78.4	76.6	78.0	78.2	79.7	80.7	82.3	82.6	81.1	81.7	79.9	78.5	79.8
2011	76.3	76.1	74.0	76.4	78.0	79.7	84.0	85.3	85.7	85.7	84.9	83.9	80.8
2012	81.3	81.5	81.0	81.8	85.6	88.4	91.0	91.6	92.1	92.7	92.2	91.2	87.5
2013	88.8	90.4	90.7	91.4	92.8	94.7	97.0	98.3	97.9	98.9	98.6	96.6	94.7
2014	94.4	96.2	96.6	97.7	99.5	101.6	103.0	104.4	104.5	104.4	104.5	102.2	100.8
2015	102.9	104.0	105.7	106.2	108.2	110.0	113.3	114.7	114.9	115.4	114.4	114.7	110.4
Manufacturing													
2005	137.4	137.4	137.2	136.4	135.9	136.4	136.6	136.8	136.9	136.5	136.9	137.0	136.8
2006	137.0	137.3	138.4	137.8	138.0	139.1	138.1	138.5	138.1	137.4	138.1	137.4	137.9
2007	136.0	136.4	136.6	135.8	136.0	136.5	135.7	136.3	136.4	136.9	137.8	137.7	136.5
2008	135.8	136.3	136.1	135.2	134.9	135.1	134.7	134.2	133.5	131.3	129.9	128.7	133.8
2009	126.0	123.8	122.2	120.0	118.9	118.6	117.7	117.6	117.7	117.9	117.8	117.7	119.7
2010	117.3	117.4	117.7	113.6	114.3	114.8	115.5	115.5	115.4	115.4	115.8	115.9	115.7
2011	115.8	115.8	116.1	116.3	116.6	116.8	117.7	117.4	116.2	115.9	115.8	115.7	116.3
2012	114.7	114.7	115.2	116.0	116.4	116.9	117.4	117.1	117.4	117.0	116.6	116.6	116.3
2013	115.5	115.8	116.4	116.4	117.0	117.6	118.1	119.1	119.0	118.7	119.5	119.5	117.7
2014	118.6	118.7	119.4	120.0	120.6	121.4	122.3	123.0	123.4	124.3	125.0	125.5	121.9
2015	124.2	124.4	125.2	124.2	124.9	126.0	127.6	127.8	127.8	127.9	127.8	128.4	126.4
Trade, Transportation, and Utilities													
2005	359.9	356.1	355.2	355.3	356.0	358.0	357.3	358.0	358.8	357.8	365.2	372.9	359.2
2006	359.7	356.2	356.5	355.0	357.1	359.5	358.5	359.1	359.4	360.6	368.3	374.8	360.4
2007	363.2	359.8	359.6	356.5	358.1	359.6	360.0	360.7	360.3	361.3	370.1	376.0	362.1
2008	361.6	357.3	356.5	353.1	353.7	353.9	353.1	351.9	349.0	348.3	351.5	353.5	353.6
2009	340.2	334.7	331.3	328.1	327.7	326.6	323.5	323.4	322.8	324.3	330.7	335.6	329.1
2010	321.8	318.2	317.3	317.8	318.9	320.1	318.7	319.2	318.3	320.2	326.4	332.2	320.8
2011	319.6	317.0	316.4	318.9	320.2	321.0	322.7	323.9	323.4	325.1	333.5	338.5	323.4
2012	328.1	324.0	324.1	327.5	329.6	331.4	332.7	334.3	333.7	336.9	347.6	352.5	333.5
2013	340.9	338.1	337.7	338.0	340.1	341.9	343.4	344.8	344.4	348.4	358.1	364.5	345.0
2014	351.2	347.9	348.4	348.6	350.4	352.3	354.0	356.2	354.1	357.0	366.3	372.7	354.9
2015	361.4	358.0	357.9	358.8	360.9	362.6	366.1	367.5	366.6	371.0	380.5	386.7	366.5
Wholesale Trade													
2005	74.7	74.4	74.3	75.0	74.8	75.4	74.8	74.7	74.7	74.6	74.7	74.9	74.8
2006	74.2	74.6	75.0	75.3	75.7	76.1	75.5	75.7	75.9	76.2	76.2	76.7	75.6
2007	75.8	76.2	76.7	75.6	76.1	76.3	75.7	75.7	75.5	75.8	75.6	75.7	75.9
2008	75.2	75.4	75.4	75.2	75.3	75.0	74.6	74.2	74.0	73.7	73.1	72.7	74.5
2009	70.8	70.3	69.5	69.1	68.8	68.4	67.7	67.4	66.7	66.9	66.8	66.6	68.3
2010	65.4	65.4	65.3	65.8	66.1	66.3	66.0	65.9	65.7	66.2	66.1	65.9	65.8
2011	65.3	65.4	65.5	66.2	66.6	66.7	67.2	67.4	67.6	67.8	68.2	68.3	66.9
2012	67.5	67.7	67.9	69.1	69.6	69.9	70.6	70.8	70.5	71.0	71.2	71.5	69.8
2013	71.2	71.2	71.3	71.7	72.1	72.5	73.0	73.2	73.2	73.4	73.8	74.5	72.6
2014	73.5	73.7	73.7	73.7	74.0	74.4	74.8	75.1	74.9	75.4	75.8	76.2	74.6
2015	76.1	76.4	76.5	76.7	77.1	77.4	78.4	78.6	78.4	78.8	79.0	78.9	77.7
Retail Trade													
2005	206.4	202.7	202.0	201.9	202.3	203.4	203.6	204.9	205.2	205.6	212.5	219.2	205.8
2006	208.2	203.8	203.6	202.5	203.5	204.8	205.5	206.1	205.2	206.5	214.0	218.8	206.9
2007	210.1	206.0	205.8	203.6	204.5	205.4	206.8	207.2	206.6	207.2	215.9	220.8	208.3
2008	209.6	204.9	204.2	202.6	202.2	203.1	203.1	202.3	200.0	199.8	203.5	205.4	203.4
2009	197.0	192.3	190.2	187.9	187.5	187.0	185.6	185.9	185.9	187.0	193.6	198.1	189.8
2010	188.0	184.3	183.8	184.4	185.3	185.8	185.6	186.2	185.1	186.6	192.7	197.1	187.1
2011	187.2	184.6	184.1	185.0	185.6	186.1	187.2	187.9	187.2	188.8	196.3	199.7	188.3
2012	191.8	187.7	187.3	188.8	190.2	190.9	192.0	192.9	192.4	194.6	204.1	207.4	193.3
2013	197.7	195.0	194.6	194.0	195.3	196.7	197.4	198.5	197.7	200.4	208.9	212.7	199.1
2014	203.1	199.3	199.6	199.8	200.5	201.8	202.7	204.0	202.0	204.2	212.4	216.0	203.8
2015	207.1	203.8	203.6	203.9	204.8	205.6	207.4	208.2	207.5	211.1	219.2	222.9	208.8

Employment by Industry: San Francisco-Oakland-Hayward, CA, 2005–2015—*Continued*

(Numbers in thousands, not seasonally adjusted)

Industry and year	January	February	March	April	May	June	July	August	September	October	November	December	Annual average
Transportation and Utilities													
2005	78.8	79.0	78.9	78.4	78.9	79.2	78.9	78.4	78.9	77.6	78.0	78.8	78.7
2006	77.3	77.8	77.9	77.2	77.9	78.6	77.5	77.3	78.3	77.9	78.1	79.3	77.9
2007	77.3	77.6	77.1	77.3	77.5	77.9	77.5	77.8	78.2	78.3	78.6	79.5	77.9
2008	76.8	77.0	76.9	75.3	76.2	75.8	75.4	75.4	75.0	74.8	74.9	75.4	75.7
2009	72.4	72.1	71.6	71.1	71.4	71.2	70.2	70.1	70.2	70.4	70.3	70.9	71.0
2010	68.4	68.5	68.2	67.6	67.5	68.0	67.1	67.1	67.5	67.4	67.6	69.2	67.8
2011	67.1	67.0	66.8	67.7	68.0	68.2	68.3	68.6	68.6	68.5	69.0	70.5	68.2
2012	68.8	68.6	68.9	69.6	69.8	70.6	70.1	70.6	70.8	71.3	72.3	73.6	70.4
2013	72.0	71.9	71.8	72.3	72.7	72.7	73.0	73.1	73.5	74.6	75.4	77.3	73.4
2014	74.6	74.9	75.1	75.1	75.9	76.1	76.5	77.1	77.2	77.4	78.1	80.5	76.5
2015	78.2	77.8	77.8	78.2	79.0	79.6	80.3	80.7	80.7	81.1	82.3	84.9	80.1
Information													
2005	73.1	73.5	72.5	71.8	71.7	71.7	71.3	71.3	70.6	70.1	70.2	69.9	71.5
2006	69.4	69.6	69.3	68.7	68.8	68.9	68.7	69.1	68.7	68.9	69.3	69.5	69.1
2007	68.2	68.4	68.4	68.3	68.7	68.7	69.0	69.0	68.5	68.2	68.1	68.1	68.5
2008	67.9	68.3	68.0	68.5	68.7	68.7	69.7	69.5	68.8	68.6	68.4	68.2	68.6
2009	67.3	66.6	66.3	64.9	64.7	64.7	65.0	64.5	63.8	63.8	63.7	63.7	64.9
2010	63.0	62.6	62.7	62.3	62.4	62.9	63.0	62.7	62.2	62.3	62.7	63.0	62.7
2011	63.2	63.6	64.1	64.4	65.0	65.8	66.5	67.0	66.8	67.4	67.9	68.1	65.8
2012	68.7	69.1	69.3	70.2	70.7	71.6	72.0	72.3	72.1	72.1	72.9	73.4	71.2
2013	71.6	72.3	72.0	72.7	73.1	74.1	74.7	74.7	74.0	74.5	76.1	75.8	73.8
2014	75.0	75.6	76.3	76.6	77.4	78.5	79.7	80.3	79.6	80.2	80.7	81.6	78.5
2015	81.3	82.0	82.5	83.0	83.9	85.4	86.5	86.8	86.2	86.9	86.5	86.4	84.8
Financial Activities													
2005	151.1	151.4	151.8	151.8	152.4	153.4	153.0	152.8	152.5	151.9	151.9	152.5	152.2
2006	150.9	151.4	151.7	151.7	152.3	152.1	150.6	150.6	150.2	149.5	148.8	148.3	150.7
2007	146.2	146.8	146.9	145.8	146.2	146.0	145.4	145.2	144.0	142.2	142.3	141.6	144.9
2008	139.1	139.0	138.8	138.0	137.9	138.2	137.2	137.0	135.7	135.4	134.2	134.1	137.1
2009	129.4	128.8	128.0	126.5	125.7	125.2	123.5	122.8	121.8	122.5	121.9	121.8	124.8
2010	121.8	122.1	122.0	122.1	122.4	122.2	122.6	122.5	122.3	122.0	121.5	122.2	122.1
2011	120.2	120.5	120.4	120.3	120.6	121.1	121.6	121.8	122.0	121.6	121.6	122.2	121.2
2012	121.3	122.1	122.4	123.0	123.5	124.4	124.5	124.8	124.2	124.8	124.5	125.3	123.7
2013	124.9	125.6	125.6	126.0	126.4	126.8	127.4	127.5	126.8	127.0	127.1	127.5	126.6
2014	125.7	126.2	126.1	126.0	126.5	126.9	127.8	128.1	127.3	127.6	127.8	128.1	127.0
2015	127.3	127.7	127.9	128.1	129.1	129.9	131.7	131.7	130.5	130.2	129.5	129.8	129.5
Professional and Business Services													
2005	328.7	332.0	334.1	334.8	333.9	336.3	337.5	339.4	339.7	341.5	344.4	347.6	337.5
2006	341.2	345.2	347.8	348.3	349.7	353.6	353.0	355.1	355.2	356.4	357.9	360.4	352.0
2007	351.3	354.9	357.0	355.7	358.2	361.7	364.8	367.0	366.0	376.7	377.9	379.0	364.2
2008	372.8	375.1	376.0	375.9	374.9	377.0	378.3	379.0	377.0	377.1	373.9	372.4	375.8
2009	361.7	359.0	356.2	352.6	349.5	350.0	349.4	348.7	345.7	351.3	350.9	350.5	352.1
2010	343.6	345.4	347.5	349.9	349.4	352.9	356.3	356.3	356.0	358.0	358.2	358.4	352.7
2011	356.9	359.0	360.8	365.2	366.1	368.9	374.4	376.4	378.8	380.8	382.4	383.6	371.1
2012	380.8	383.6	386.6	393.8	395.9	401.0	402.4	405.9	405.8	411.2	411.8	412.6	399.3
2013	406.8	409.9	412.3	416.2	416.3	418.6	422.9	426.2	423.4	427.2	429.6	431.4	420.1
2014	427.4	430.8	433.6	435.6	438.8	440.2	442.4	446.7	445.3	447.9	449.4	451.8	440.8
2015	446.2	449.5	452.7	457.8	457.8	459.7	467.9	471.9	469.4	471.6	473.1	475.0	462.7
Education and Health Services													
2005	245.5	251.1	251.8	251.7	252.2	249.6	248.2	248.4	251.4	254.0	255.3	255.9	251.3
2006	251.5	256.7	258.1	260.3	261.0	259.1	256.4	256.4	260.1	262.6	264.0	265.2	259.3
2007	260.0	266.9	269.1	267.4	268.5	267.9	264.8	263.7	267.2	271.1	273.2	274.0	267.8
2008	269.5	276.6	278.4	282.2	283.9	280.3	280.1	280.3	284.8	288.9	290.4	292.1	282.3
2009	286.2	290.4	291.5	293.2	293.3	290.0	287.2	285.4	288.9	292.3	292.8	293.9	290.4
2010	289.4	292.0	293.8	294.7	295.1	291.5	290.1	286.8	291.7	294.8	294.7	295.4	292.5
2011	291.2	294.1	294.7	295.9	295.4	290.5	288.2	287.2	293.3	296.5	297.3	298.3	293.6
2012	292.9	300.0	302.6	304.2	305.0	302.3	300.5	300.6	304.2	307.0	308.7	310.5	303.2
2013	303.7	311.5	314.0	314.9	316.4	312.9	309.6	309.9	312.2	316.6	318.6	319.1	313.3
2014	310.9	318.1	319.4	320.9	320.9	317.6	314.3	314.1	317.6	322.1	324.4	324.3	318.7
2015	320.1	325.4	326.8	328.1	328.7	326.9	326.0	324.9	330.2	334.5	335.3	335.3	328.5

Employment by Industry: San Francisco-Oakland-Hayward, CA, 2005–2015—*Continued*

(Numbers in thousands, not seasonally adjusted)

Industry and year	January	February	March	April	May	June	July	August	September	October	November	December	Annual average
Leisure and Hospitality													
2005	189.3	190.6	193.1	197.7	200.1	202.6	201.9	203.7	204.0	202.7	202.2	202.0	199.2
2006	195.1	198.6	200.0	202.6	207.1	210.0	209.0	209.9	209.5	208.5	207.9	208.0	205.5
2007	202.0	204.4	206.6	208.5	213.2	215.7	217.8	218.1	216.9	214.8	214.2	215.3	212.3
2008	207.1	210.3	211.5	215.1	218.4	221.1	220.9	220.9	219.4	216.7	214.3	214.2	215.8
2009	203.1	203.5	202.8	206.0	210.0	210.7	211.0	210.9	209.2	208.7	205.3	205.8	207.3
2010	197.9	198.7	199.7	208.0	209.2	212.3	213.6	214.4	213.3	214.2	210.4	210.5	208.5
2011	204.3	206.3	208.3	213.8	217.4	219.5	220.4	221.3	222.1	220.7	218.0	218.4	215.9
2012	212.4	214.8	216.8	224.3	228.1	231.2	230.8	233.9	232.3	232.9	230.2	231.2	226.6
2013	224.6	227.8	230.5	234.9	239.7	240.8	240.5	242.6	241.8	241.5	241.3	242.0	237.3
2014	235.1	238.6	241.4	245.9	249.2	252.8	252.4	254.5	253.6	252.8	251.0	251.9	248.3
2015	244.4	247.8	251.5	256.0	259.9	261.1	262.1	263.9	262.0	262.2	258.5	259.9	257.4
Other Services													
2005	71.0	71.6	72.5	73.1	73.2	73.9	72.9	72.1	72.1	72.5	72.1	72.6	72.5
2006	70.9	71.8	72.4	72.9	74.0	74.7	74.1	73.7	73.7	73.4	73.2	73.6	73.2
2007	72.2	73.4	74.1	74.1	75.0	75.2	75.7	75.5	75.3	75.5	75.5	75.9	74.8
2008	73.6	74.7	75.1	75.7	76.2	76.4	76.5	75.7	75.3	75.9	75.2	75.1	75.5
2009	72.8	72.6	72.5	73.3	73.3	73.1	72.9	72.4	71.6	72.7	72.4	72.1	72.6
2010	70.8	71.2	71.5	72.7	73.4	73.9	73.9	73.1	72.6	73.9	73.0	73.0	72.8
2011	72.2	72.5	72.8	74.5	74.5	74.8	75.6	75.1	75.2	75.8	75.7	75.7	74.5
2012	73.9	74.7	75.5	76.5	77.7	78.4	77.8	77.7	77.9	78.3	78.2	78.6	77.1
2013	76.8	78.1	78.5	79.7	79.9	80.4	80.3	80.4	80.4	80.7	80.8	80.9	79.7
2014	80.0	81.0	81.4	82.9	83.1	83.2	82.8	82.8	82.7	82.9	82.7	82.4	82.3
2015	81.6	82.4	82.8	83.4	84.1	84.0	84.6	83.8	83.6	84.1	83.6	83.2	83.4
Government													
2005	310.4	314.0	315.2	316.5	317.3	316.2	305.2	300.8	310.3	315.7	318.1	315.7	313.0
2006	314.3	317.7	320.0	319.4	320.1	318.5	309.2	306.9	314.9	321.7	324.7	321.1	317.4
2007	319.0	323.4	325.2	325.1	327.7	326.5	314.1	313.2	321.7	316.8	319.4	318.7	320.9
2008	314.9	317.7	319.0	319.6	318.9	320.8	310.4	306.7	311.4	315.4	316.9	315.0	315.6
2009	313.0	315.5	316.9	318.1	316.1	316.3	300.4	288.1	299.7	306.1	306.1	302.2	308.2
2010	300.0	302.0	303.5	309.0	315.3	310.8	286.3	282.7	298.8	302.2	305.3	303.6	301.6
2011	301.0	303.7	306.1	306.7	306.9	305.2	290.4	290.3	293.0	299.7	300.8	298.7	300.2
2012	296.2	299.1	301.8	302.0	302.3	301.1	290.7	288.8	292.4	296.8	301.5	300.0	297.7
2013	295.7	297.8	301.7	302.6	302.6	298.0	287.5	288.6	294.0	300.0	302.9	298.7	297.5
2014	298.9	301.1	302.3	305.6	306.8	304.7	295.1	293.7	299.1	305.7	309.5	308.6	302.6
2015	305.8	307.0	310.4	312.3	312.5	310.6	299.6	301.6	305.5	311.9	313.9	312.7	308.7

Employment by Industry: Phoenix-Mesa-Scottsdale, AZ, 2005–2015

(Numbers in thousands, not seasonally adjusted)

Industry and year	January	February	March	April	May	June	July	August	September	October	November	December	Annual average
Total Nonfarm													
2005	1,716.5	1,744.5	1,760.4	1,785.1	1,787.2	1,770.4	1,763.7	1,789.9	1,818.6	1,827.3	1,849.9	1,862.4	1,789.7
2006	1,831.3	1,863.9	1,881.1	1,885.2	1,893.3	1,873.5	1,856.8	1,881.8	1,902.7	1,910.2	1,924.5	1,932.1	1,886.4
2007	1,884.8	1,911.4	1,924.1	1,917.9	1,922.4	1,902.0	1,885.2	1,914.1	1,925.7	1,935.2	1,946.5	1,947.7	1,918.1
2008	1,900.9	1,912.9	1,909.6	1,900.5	1,893.9	1,855.1	1,822.0	1,853.1	1,858.0	1,852.4	1,849.7	1,837.3	1,870.5
2009	1,776.8	1,772.3	1,765.2	1,751.1	1,739.1	1,694.5	1,671.1	1,683.7	1,696.0	1,703.8	1,716.0	1,716.0	1,723.8
2010	1,677.0	1,689.3	1,699.4	1,704.3	1,708.9	1,664.9	1,647.2	1,670.0	1,681.5	1,705.8	1,723.0	1,728.1	1,691.6
2011	1,694.2	1,708.2	1,718.6	1,727.2	1,724.5	1,680.2	1,665.8	1,702.9	1,725.2	1,738.8	1,758.6	1,762.2	1,717.2
2012	1,732.1	1,746.5	1,759.3	1,760.5	1,758.1	1,727.4	1,707.3	1,749.4	1,768.9	1,786.1	1,809.9	1,817.6	1,760.3
2013	1,779.0	1,797.5	1,807.1	1,812.9	1,811.1	1,777.1	1,761.6	1,801.2	1,817.1	1,838.3	1,865.1	1,870.0	1,811.5
2014	1,827.9	1,842.4	1,849.5	1,855.0	1,843.5	1,814.6	1,798.6	1,840.6	1,855.2	1,882.7	1,908.3	1,918.6	1,853.1
2015	1,879.7	1,897.8	1,903.1	1,909.3	1,902.1	1,868.9	1,866.6	1,903.2	1,920.8	1,952.5	1,979.0	1,984.7	1,914.0
Total Private													
2005	1,495.4	1,512.7	1,530.3	1,554.1	1,557.9	1,561.4	1,562.3	1,573.1	1,586.8	1,593.7	1,614.7	1,627.5	1,564.2
2006	1,607.7	1,629.7	1,646.9	1,651.1	1,657.4	1,663.2	1,650.8	1,661.3	1,667.3	1,670.9	1,684.7	1,694.8	1,657.2
2007	1,654.0	1,670.9	1,682.2	1,676.3	1,680.0	1,682.5	1,668.8	1,678.4	1,679.6	1,686.9	1,695.8	1,697.1	1,679.4
2008	1,651.7	1,659.3	1,656.1	1,647.1	1,641.7	1,630.7	1,609.3	1,613.8	1,606.5	1,598.9	1,594.8	1,584.0	1,624.5
2009	1,531.4	1,520.6	1,514.4	1,500.2	1,492.1	1,477.7	1,461.3	1,460.1	1,454.3	1,459.1	1,470.8	1,473.4	1,484.6
2010	1,438.7	1,444.7	1,456.1	1,460.2	1,458.1	1,450.3	1,440.2	1,446.8	1,445.5	1,467.2	1,483.0	1,490.9	1,456.8
2011	1,460.5	1,469.4	1,480.0	1,488.0	1,485.6	1,476.8	1,472.9	1,483.4	1,490.4	1,501.0	1,519.9	1,527.8	1,488.0
2012	1,500.5	1,508.4	1,520.9	1,521.6	1,524.2	1,520.4	1,510.4	1,525.3	1,531.0	1,546.7	1,569.1	1,577.7	1,529.7
2013	1,543.9	1,557.2	1,567.6	1,572.6	1,573.9	1,569.3	1,563.1	1,577.1	1,578.8	1,597.0	1,623.7	1,630.9	1,579.6
2014	1,592.3	1,601.7	1,609.3	1,613.8	1,612.0	1,605.2	1,598.5	1,613.9	1,615.3	1,639.0	1,663.8	1,676.4	1,620.1
2015	1,644.6	1,654.5	1,660.3	1,666.9	1,666.5	1,660.8	1,665.0	1,677.4	1,680.8	1,709.9	1,734.9	1,745.2	1,680.6
Goods Producing													
2005	283.8	287.2	291.4	297.0	299.9	304.9	306.4	308.3	309.9	310.4	313.3	316.1	302.4
2006	312.5	317.6	321.6	323.8	326.0	329.2	328.0	327.6	325.5	321.3	318.6	316.7	322.4
2007	309.9	311.6	312.1	310.5	311.6	314.8	313.8	314.5	310.8	307.3	301.2	296.9	309.6
2008	288.7	286.3	283.7	280.8	279.6	277.8	274.2	272.6	267.8	261.2	253.2	246.1	272.7
2009	234.7	227.6	223.3	218.5	215.7	214.5	211.2	208.9	205.9	203.8	201.6	199.2	213.7
2010	194.2	194.2	194.7	196.1	196.0	196.9	197.0	196.8	196.0	197.5	197.0	196.5	196.1
2011	193.4	193.1	194.4	196.4	198.1	199.8	201.8	202.2	202.3	202.1	202.0	202.3	199.0
2012	200.7	201.6	204.0	205.1	206.6	209.6	210.3	212.1	212.3	212.7	212.3	211.4	208.2
2013	207.9	209.6	211.0	211.7	213.6	216.4	216.6	217.0	216.0	216.8	216.5	215.8	214.1
2014	214.5	215.9	215.9	217.4	217.9	218.2	217.9	217.8	216.5	217.8	218.3	218.6	217.2
2015	216.0	217.7	218.2	219.4	220.4	221.8	223.7	224.2	223.6	223.9	227.2	225.7	221.8
Service-Providing													
2005	1,432.7	1,457.3	1,469.0	1,488.1	1,487.3	1,465.5	1,457.3	1,481.6	1,508.7	1,516.9	1,536.6	1,546.3	1,487.3
2006	1,518.8	1,546.3	1,559.5	1,561.4	1,567.3	1,544.3	1,528.8	1,554.2	1,577.2	1,588.9	1,605.9	1,615.4	1,564.0
2007	1,574.9	1,599.8	1,612.0	1,607.4	1,610.8	1,587.2	1,571.4	1,599.6	1,614.9	1,627.9	1,645.3	1,650.8	1,608.5
2008	1,612.2	1,626.6	1,625.9	1,619.7	1,614.3	1,577.3	1,547.8	1,580.5	1,590.2	1,591.2	1,596.5	1,591.2	1,597.8
2009	1,542.1	1,544.7	1,541.9	1,532.6	1,523.4	1,480.0	1,459.9	1,474.8	1,490.1	1,500.0	1,514.4	1,516.8	1,510.1
2010	1,482.8	1,495.1	1,504.7	1,508.2	1,512.9	1,468.0	1,450.2	1,473.2	1,485.5	1,508.3	1,526.0	1,531.6	1,495.5
2011	1,500.8	1,515.1	1,524.2	1,530.8	1,526.4	1,480.4	1,464.0	1,500.7	1,522.9	1,536.7	1,556.6	1,559.9	1,518.2
2012	1,531.4	1,544.9	1,555.3	1,555.4	1,551.5	1,517.8	1,497.0	1,537.3	1,556.6	1,573.4	1,597.6	1,606.2	1,552.0
2013	1,571.1	1,587.9	1,596.1	1,601.2	1,597.5	1,560.7	1,545.0	1,584.2	1,601.1	1,621.5	1,648.6	1,654.2	1,597.4
2014	1,613.4	1,626.5	1,633.6	1,637.6	1,625.6	1,596.4	1,580.7	1,622.8	1,638.7	1,664.9	1,690.0	1,700.0	1,635.9
2015	1,663.7	1,680.1	1,684.9	1,689.9	1,681.7	1,647.1	1,642.9	1,679.0	1,697.2	1,728.6	1,751.8	1,759.0	1,692.2
Mining and Logging													
2005	2.2	2.2	2.2	2.3	2.4	2.4	2.0	1.9	1.9	1.9	2.1	2.4	2.2
2006	2.5	2.4	2.5	2.6	2.6	2.8	2.8	2.9	2.9	2.8	2.9	2.9	2.7
2007	2.9	3.0	3.1	3.0	3.0	3.1	3.4	3.4	3.4	3.5	3.5	3.5	3.2
2008	3.5	3.5	3.6	3.6	3.7	3.9	3.9	4.0	3.9	3.9	3.9	3.8	3.8
2009	3.3	3.3	3.3	3.2	3.0	3.0	2.9	2.9	2.9	3.0	3.0	3.0	3.1
2010	3.0	3.0	3.0	3.0	3.1	3.0	3.0	3.0	3.0	3.0	3.1	3.1	3.0
2011	3.2	3.2	3.2	3.1	3.2	3.2	3.2	3.2	3.2	3.4	3.4	3.4	3.2
2012	3.4	3.4	3.4	3.4	3.4	3.5	3.6	3.6	3.7	3.6	3.6	3.6	3.5
2013	3.6	3.6	3.6	3.6	3.6	3.8	3.8	3.7	3.6	3.5	3.5	3.5	3.6
2014	3.4	3.4	3.4	3.4	3.4	3.4	3.4	3.4	3.4	3.4	3.4	3.4	3.4
2015	3.4	3.4	3.4	3.3	3.4	3.4	3.5	3.4	3.3	3.3	3.3	3.3	3.4

Employment by Industry: Phoenix-Mesa-Scottsdale, AZ, 2005–2015—*Continued*

(Numbers in thousands, not seasonally adjusted)

Industry and year	January	February	March	April	May	June	July	August	September	October	November	December	Annual average
Construction													
2005	148.9	151.7	155.3	159.6	161.3	165.0	166.7	168.3	170.1	170.6	173.1	174.6	163.8
2006	172.0	175.9	179.3	180.9	182.9	185.4	184.1	183.8	182.4	179.2	177.4	175.3	179.9
2007	169.6	170.8	171.2	170.2	171.1	174.2	172.1	172.9	170.9	167.3	162.1	158.1	169.2
2008	151.5	149.8	148.6	145.9	144.9	143.3	140.4	139.0	135.3	130.0	123.9	118.6	139.3
2009	110.0	105.1	102.7	99.4	97.8	97.6	95.1	93.1	90.6	88.5	86.3	84.1	95.9
2010	81.1	81.3	81.8	82.7	82.2	83.1	83.2	83.1	82.3	83.4	82.6	81.5	82.4
2011	79.2	78.9	80.0	81.5	82.4	83.9	85.3	85.6	85.8	85.2	84.5	83.9	83.0
2012	82.5	83.0	84.8	85.5	86.5	88.5	89.4	90.9	91.3	91.9	91.5	90.2	88.0
2013	87.8	89.1	90.6	91.4	92.9	95.1	95.3	96.2	95.6	96.2	95.8	94.9	93.4
2014	93.8	94.4	94.4	95.7	96.0	96.1	95.9	95.6	94.7	95.9	96.0	95.8	95.4
2015	94.8	96.0	96.7	97.4	98.0	98.6	99.6	100.0	99.9	100.0	102.5	101.2	98.7
Manufacturing													
2005	132.7	133.3	133.9	135.1	136.2	137.5	137.7	138.1	137.9	137.9	138.1	139.1	136.5
2006	138.0	139.3	139.8	140.3	140.5	141.0	141.1	140.9	140.2	139.3	138.3	138.5	139.8
2007	137.4	137.8	137.8	137.3	137.5	137.5	138.3	138.2	136.5	136.5	135.6	135.3	137.1
2008	133.7	133.0	131.5	131.3	131.0	130.6	129.9	129.6	128.6	127.3	125.4	123.7	129.6
2009	121.4	119.2	117.3	115.9	114.9	113.9	113.2	112.9	112.4	112.3	112.3	112.1	114.8
2010	110.1	109.9	109.9	110.4	110.7	110.8	110.8	110.7	110.7	111.1	111.3	111.9	110.7
2011	111.0	111.0	111.2	111.8	112.5	112.7	113.3	113.4	113.3	113.5	114.1	115.0	112.7
2012	114.8	115.2	115.8	116.2	116.7	117.4	117.3	117.6	117.3	117.2	117.2	117.6	116.7
2013	116.5	116.9	116.8	116.7	117.1	117.5	117.5	117.1	116.8	117.1	117.2	117.4	117.1
2014	117.3	118.1	118.1	118.3	118.5	118.7	118.6	118.8	118.4	118.5	118.9	119.4	118.5
2015	117.8	118.3	118.1	118.7	119.0	119.8	120.6	120.8	120.4	120.6	121.4	121.2	119.7
Trade, Transportation, and Utilities													
2005	351.7	352.9	354.5	357.0	357.6	357.6	360.5	361.5	363.6	366.2	375.7	380.8	361.6
2006	370.7	370.5	373.4	374.5	374.9	374.9	376.5	377.8	377.9	383.4	392.5	398.5	378.8
2007	385.7	385.1	386.1	386.5	387.5	387.6	388.6	389.8	391.1	393.4	402.5	407.5	391.0
2008	390.9	389.2	387.7	385.4	385.5	384.3	378.3	379.0	376.4	377.0	381.3	381.3	383.0
2009	366.3	360.3	358.4	355.0	353.6	351.1	348.7	347.9	346.5	347.1	354.1	356.8	353.8
2010	345.8	345.2	345.5	345.6	345.8	343.5	341.5	341.4	339.2	343.8	351.8	356.1	345.4
2011	345.4	345.2	345.9	347.9	347.6	346.5	346.1	346.8	346.6	351.2	360.7	362.8	349.4
2012	351.3	349.0	350.2	350.5	351.2	350.0	349.0	348.8	349.7	353.9	365.1	367.7	353.0
2013	351.5	350.6	350.3	351.1	352.1	351.7	352.1	353.6	354.5	359.1	370.0	375.3	356.0
2014	361.2	360.0	360.0	360.5	360.3	360.5	360.4	362.2	362.3	367.5	378.2	383.9	364.8
2015	369.9	369.5	370.4	370.7	371.2	372.2	373.8	375.9	377.5	384.5	395.4	398.7	377.5
Wholesale Trade													
2005	80.2	81.1	81.6	82.3	82.4	82.5	83.0	83.0	83.2	83.6	84.3	84.9	82.7
2006	84.2	84.9	85.2	85.8	86.0	86.5	86.9	87.1	87.4	88.0	88.0	88.6	86.6
2007	87.5	88.0	88.4	88.6	88.8	89.4	89.9	89.8	89.7	90.0	90.1	90.2	89.2
2008	88.6	89.2	89.0	88.8	89.1	88.7	88.3	88.4	88.2	88.2	87.6	87.0	88.4
2009	85.5	84.8	84.0	83.2	82.4	81.8	81.6	81.3	80.6	80.7	80.5	80.3	82.2
2010	79.0	79.3	79.5	79.3	79.3	79.1	78.9	78.7	78.1	78.3	78.3	78.4	78.9
2011	77.6	78.2	78.2	78.6	78.6	78.5	78.3	78.1	77.8	77.9	77.9	77.9	78.1
2012	77.4	77.7	78.1	78.0	77.9	78.1	78.2	78.1	78.1	78.3	78.3	78.3	78.0
2013	77.1	77.8	77.7	77.9	77.7	77.8	77.7	77.8	77.5	78.1	78.1	78.4	77.8
2014	77.1	77.3	77.5	77.2	77.4	77.2	77.3	77.4	77.2	77.2	77.1	77.7	77.3
2015	76.3	76.4	76.5	76.8	77.0	77.3	77.3	77.6	77.8	78.6	79.2	79.1	77.5
Retail Trade													
2005	210.4	210.4	211.7	213.4	213.2	213.1	215.3	215.6	216.9	219.3	227.1	230.8	216.4
2006	223.1	222.2	224.6	224.5	224.5	224.2	224.9	225.3	224.6	229.6	238.3	242.4	227.4
2007	231.7	230.4	231.1	231.0	231.3	230.7	231.6	232.5	233.6	235.6	244.5	247.9	234.3
2008	235.2	232.5	231.4	229.2	229.1	228.6	223.5	223.9	221.8	222.8	227.1	227.5	227.7
2009	215.8	211.1	210.3	208.8	208.4	206.7	204.9	204.5	204.2	205.2	212.3	214.5	208.9
2010	206.3	205.4	205.7	206.6	206.6	204.6	203.2	203.0	201.2	205.1	212.7	215.2	206.3
2011	206.9	206.0	206.5	207.5	207.0	205.8	205.9	206.6	206.6	210.2	219.0	220.0	209.0
2012	210.5	207.9	208.4	209.2	209.9	208.7	207.3	207.2	208.0	211.8	222.7	224.0	211.3
2013	210.2	208.6	208.9	210.0	210.6	210.3	211.1	212.3	213.5	216.7	226.9	230.5	214.1
2014	219.1	217.9	217.5	218.8	218.2	218.4	218.5	219.5	219.7	223.9	233.7	237.0	221.9
2015	225.6	224.7	225.2	226.1	226.2	226.9	228.2	229.8	231.0	236.3	244.9	246.7	231.0

Employment by Industry: Phoenix-Mesa-Scottsdale, AZ, 2005–2015—*Continued*

(Numbers in thousands, not seasonally adjusted)

Industry and year	January	February	March	April	May	June	July	August	September	October	November	December	Annual average
Transportation and Utilities													
2005	61.1	61.4	61.2	61.3	62.0	62.0	62.2	62.9	63.5	63.3	64.3	65.1	62.5
2006	63.4	63.4	63.6	64.2	64.4	64.2	64.7	65.4	65.9	65.8	66.2	67.5	64.9
2007	66.5	66.7	66.6	66.9	67.4	67.5	67.1	67.5	67.8	67.8	67.9	69.4	67.4
2008	67.1	67.5	67.3	67.4	67.3	67.0	66.5	66.7	66.4	66.0	66.6	66.8	66.9
2009	65.0	64.4	64.1	63.0	62.8	62.6	62.2	62.1	61.7	61.2	61.3	62.0	62.7
2010	60.5	60.5	60.3	59.7	59.9	59.8	59.4	59.7	59.9	60.4	60.8	62.5	60.3
2011	60.9	61.0	61.2	61.8	62.0	62.2	61.9	62.1	62.2	63.1	63.8	64.9	62.3
2012	63.4	63.4	63.7	63.3	63.4	63.2	63.5	63.5	63.6	63.8	64.1	65.4	63.7
2013	64.2	64.2	63.7	63.2	63.8	63.6	63.3	63.5	63.5	64.3	65.0	66.4	64.1
2014	65.0	64.8	65.0	64.5	64.7	64.9	64.6	65.3	65.4	66.4	67.4	69.2	65.6
2015	68.0	68.4	68.7	67.8	68.0	68.0	68.3	68.5	68.7	69.6	71.3	72.9	69.0
Information													
2005	32.1	32.8	33.1	33.9	34.0	33.6	33.2	32.9	32.5	32.8	33.4	33.9	33.2
2006	33.0	33.1	33.2	32.7	32.8	32.6	32.0	32.0	31.2	31.0	31.6	32.0	32.3
2007	30.0	30.9	30.8	31.1	31.7	31.7	31.5	31.1	30.9	30.5	31.4	31.0	31.1
2008	30.5	31.5	31.9	31.2	32.2	32.0	30.8	30.5	31.0	30.2	30.6	30.5	31.1
2009	29.6	29.9	29.6	29.5	29.9	29.2	28.8	28.5	28.0	27.5	28.0	27.8	28.9
2010	27.2	27.5	27.7	27.8	27.6	28.0	27.2	27.1	26.9	26.7	27.2	27.6	27.4
2011	27.4	27.4	27.8	28.0	28.1	28.3	28.6	28.7	28.6	28.9	29.7	29.8	28.4
2012	29.8	30.1	30.4	30.7	31.2	31.2	31.4	31.6	31.2	31.2	32.2	32.5	31.1
2013	32.1	32.7	33.0	32.9	33.6	33.3	33.4	33.5	33.0	33.3	34.0	33.9	33.2
2014	33.8	33.8	34.3	34.6	35.0	35.4	35.7	35.6	34.8	35.2	35.4	35.7	34.9
2015	35.4	36.5	35.8	36.4	36.9	36.8	36.8	36.2	35.7	37.0	37.6	38.3	36.6
Financial Activities													
2005	143.3	144.7	144.9	147.1	147.3	147.7	149.0	150.1	150.8	152.2	152.8	153.8	148.6
2006	152.4	153.7	154.5	154.2	154.8	155.2	155.2	155.9	156.1	156.7	157.0	158.2	155.3
2007	156.1	157.3	157.8	158.0	157.7	157.2	156.3	155.5	154.7	153.5	153.4	153.7	155.9
2008	150.7	151.8	151.6	151.1	150.8	150.5	149.7	149.2	148.9	149.1	148.1	147.8	149.9
2009	144.6	144.5	144.2	143.4	143.6	143.0	142.3	142.1	141.1	140.9	140.7	141.6	142.7
2010	139.4	139.9	140.7	139.7	139.7	139.7	140.2	140.7	140.2	142.3	142.9	144.0	140.8
2011	142.2	143.0	143.6	144.3	144.2	144.6	145.2	145.8	145.9	146.3	147.1	148.7	145.1
2012	147.3	149.0	149.2	148.9	149.1	149.1	149.2	150.1	150.4	152.3	153.6	154.4	150.2
2013	153.3	155.8	155.9	156.9	157.5	157.9	158.0	158.6	158.7	160.8	162.1	162.4	158.2
2014	160.6	161.5	161.0	160.4	160.7	160.6	160.5	161.0	161.0	162.8	164.0	164.3	161.5
2015	163.1	164.3	164.5	165.0	165.6	165.9	167.0	168.0	168.1	169.3	169.6	171.8	166.9
Professional and Business Services													
2005	279.3	283.7	287.9	293.8	293.4	296.1	297.4	300.3	304.0	303.6	306.6	308.0	296.2
2006	302.1	309.3	312.4	314.7	317.1	320.7	318.4	322.0	325.0	325.8	326.6	328.0	318.5
2007	317.2	321.7	325.5	323.5	324.0	325.9	324.2	326.3	325.2	327.7	328.6	326.7	324.7
2008	315.9	318.8	316.0	314.0	311.8	308.6	305.8	307.5	305.0	303.8	301.3	298.4	308.9
2009	285.2	282.8	280.0	277.4	274.4	272.0	270.2	268.0	267.4	271.2	273.7	273.9	274.7
2010	264.8	265.8	269.5	271.9	271.0	270.3	268.4	269.2	268.6	275.0	276.6	280.3	271.0
2011	272.0	274.8	276.5	278.0	275.0	274.2	274.3	276.1	276.6	279.8	282.5	286.7	277.2
2012	277.9	279.2	281.2	282.1	282.5	284.5	283.8	286.7	286.7	291.0	296.3	299.8	286.0
2013	294.3	293.6	296.5	298.5	298.7	301.3	300.3	301.8	300.5	306.4	314.5	316.2	301.9
2014	301.3	301.0	303.0	305.7	306.0	306.8	306.7	309.6	309.4	316.6	323.5	327.3	309.7
2015	316.4	315.7	315.6	318.3	317.8	318.6	320.4	321.3	321.6	330.2	336.8	342.2	322.9
Education and Health Services													
2005	178.1	179.9	182.8	185.8	186.8	185.5	183.6	186.9	188.5	189.7	190.9	191.7	185.9
2006	191.2	193.9	196.0	196.9	197.6	197.1	196.8	200.4	201.8	202.5	203.8	206.0	198.7
2007	202.6	206.0	207.3	206.0	206.5	207.7	205.6	209.4	211.2	214.8	215.3	216.5	209.1
2008	213.9	217.4	218.2	219.5	220.5	219.5	218.5	221.8	223.8	225.0	226.3	228.1	221.0
2009	223.2	225.1	225.7	226.3	227.1	225.6	224.4	228.4	229.9	233.3	235.3	236.7	228.4
2010	234.2	235.2	236.4	236.4	237.4	235.4	234.7	239.4	241.0	245.4	246.9	245.9	239.0
2011	242.7	244.4	245.3	246.2	247.2	242.7	242.1	247.3	250.5	252.1	253.8	254.6	247.4
2012	251.8	254.2	254.8	255.0	255.2	251.8	249.0	255.2	257.3	259.2	260.8	262.2	255.5
2013	257.3	259.9	261.8	261.9	261.0	256.6	254.7	260.8	262.8	263.3	265.7	265.8	261.0
2014	263.7	265.7	266.2	267.1	266.9	263.6	262.9	269.4	271.2	274.4	276.5	278.0	268.8
2015	274.6	277.9	278.2	279.5	279.3	275.8	276.6	282.6	283.7	288.8	290.7	291.9	281.6

Employment by Industry: Phoenix-Mesa-Scottsdale, AZ, 2005–2015—*Continued*

(Numbers in thousands, not seasonally adjusted)

Industry and year	January	February	March	April	May	June	July	August	September	October	November	December	Annual average
Leisure and Hospitality													
2005	163.5	167.3	170.6	174.0	173.0	169.9	166.2	167.1	170.8	172.0	174.8	175.6	170.4
2006	175.5	179.6	182.6	183.4	182.3	180.2	175.0	176.1	179.3	181.1	184.6	185.1	180.4
2007	182.7	186.8	190.4	189.8	189.0	184.5	177.8	181.0	183.4	187.4	190.2	191.1	186.2
2008	188.0	190.4	192.6	191.5	187.7	184.2	178.6	180.0	180.5	180.5	181.6	180.0	184.6
2009	177.9	179.9	182.9	181.5	179.0	173.5	168.1	168.9	168.6	169.5	171.6	171.8	174.4
2010	169.2	172.4	176.9	179.0	176.5	172.2	167.8	169.2	170.8	173.2	176.7	176.4	173.4
2011	173.7	176.9	181.7	182.4	180.4	175.9	171.1	173.3	176.8	177.8	181.4	180.7	177.7
2012	180.1	183.5	188.9	187.2	185.7	181.2	175.7	179.2	181.4	184.1	185.9	186.7	183.3
2013	185.1	190.7	195.2	195.6	193.2	188.1	184.6	188.7	190.1	193.4	196.7	197.3	191.6
2014	194.2	200.0	204.7	204.1	201.1	196.1	191.0	195.1	196.4	200.1	203.1	203.8	199.1
2015	204.8	207.7	212.2	212.4	209.9	204.3	201.7	204.6	205.8	210.0	211.7	210.9	208.0
Other Services													
2005	63.6	64.2	65.1	65.5	65.9	66.1	66.0	66.0	66.7	66.8	67.2	67.6	65.9
2006	70.3	72.0	73.2	70.9	71.9	73.3	68.9	69.5	70.5	69.1	70.0	70.3	70.8
2007	69.8	71.5	72.2	70.9	72.0	73.1	71.0	70.8	72.3	72.3	73.2	73.7	71.9
2008	73.1	73.9	74.4	73.6	73.6	73.8	73.4	73.2	73.1	72.1	72.4	71.8	73.2
2009	69.9	70.5	70.3	68.6	68.8	68.8	67.6	67.4	66.9	65.8	65.8	65.6	68.0
2010	63.9	64.5	64.7	63.7	64.1	64.3	63.4	63.0	62.8	63.3	63.9	64.1	63.8
2011	63.7	64.6	64.8	64.8	65.0	64.8	63.7	63.2	63.1	62.8	62.7	62.2	63.8
2012	61.6	61.8	62.2	62.1	62.7	63.0	62.0	61.6	62.0	62.3	62.9	63.0	62.3
2013	62.4	64.3	63.9	64.0	64.2	64.0	63.4	63.1	63.2	63.9	64.2	64.2	63.7
2014	63.0	63.8	64.2	64.0	64.1	64.0	63.4	63.2	63.7	64.6	64.8	64.8	64.0
2015	64.4	65.2	65.4	65.2	65.4	65.4	65.0	64.6	64.8	66.2	65.9	65.7	65.3
Government													
2005	221.1	231.8	230.1	231.0	229.3	209.0	201.4	216.8	231.8	233.6	235.2	234.9	225.5
2006	223.6	234.2	234.2	234.1	235.9	210.3	206.0	220.5	235.4	239.3	239.8	237.3	229.2
2007	230.8	240.5	241.9	241.6	242.4	219.5	216.4	235.7	246.1	248.3	250.7	250.6	238.7
2008	249.2	253.6	253.5	253.4	252.2	224.4	212.7	239.3	251.5	253.5	254.9	253.3	246.0
2009	245.4	251.7	250.8	250.9	247.0	216.8	209.8	223.6	241.7	244.7	245.2	242.6	239.2
2010	238.3	244.6	243.3	244.1	250.8	214.6	207.0	223.2	236.0	238.6	240.0	237.2	234.8
2011	233.7	238.8	238.6	239.2	238.9	203.4	192.9	219.5	234.8	237.8	238.7	234.4	229.2
2012	231.6	238.1	238.4	238.9	233.9	207.0	196.9	224.1	237.9	239.4	240.8	239.9	230.6
2013	235.1	240.3	239.5	240.3	237.2	207.8	198.5	224.1	238.3	241.3	241.4	239.1	231.9
2014	235.6	240.7	240.2	241.2	231.5	209.4	200.1	226.7	239.9	243.7	244.5	242.2	233.0
2015	235.1	243.3	242.8	242.4	235.6	208.1	201.6	225.8	240.0	242.6	244.1	239.5	233.4

Employment by Industry: Riverside-San Bernardino-Ontario, CA, 2005–2015

(Numbers in thousands, not seasonally adjusted)

Industry and year	January	February	March	April	May	June	July	August	September	October	November	December	Annual average
Total Nonfarm													
2005	1,201.1	1,212.3	1,224.3	1,236.6	1,237.6	1,238.6	1,226.9	1,230.9	1,247.6	1,258.0	1,271.7	1,282.2	1,239.0
2006	1,264.2	1,272.3	1,282.4	1,286.6	1,291.3	1,296.1	1,281.0	1,277.6	1,286.3	1,289.9	1,298.8	1,301.1	1,285.6
2007	1,280.8	1,285.7	1,293.6	1,291.6	1,297.8	1,297.4	1,283.5	1,278.5	1,282.9	1,289.1	1,297.9	1,300.3	1,289.9
2008	1,267.9	1,267.0	1,267.4	1,265.8	1,260.8	1,257.1	1,232.7	1,229.8	1,227.8	1,232.3	1,233.2	1,227.9	1,247.5
2009	1,198.6	1,188.7	1,187.9	1,182.3	1,179.1	1,172.9	1,146.3	1,145.1	1,141.2	1,154.5	1,163.3	1,163.3	1,168.6
2010	1,142.2	1,143.1	1,149.7	1,157.4	1,161.3	1,158.2	1,131.1	1,138.1	1,139.2	1,152.9	1,166.4	1,168.6	1,150.7
2011	1,144.6	1,148.8	1,153.8	1,157.3	1,157.1	1,151.3	1,135.3	1,143.1	1,149.2	1,160.8	1,176.2	1,176.3	1,154.5
2012	1,165.1	1,167.5	1,173.2	1,183.1	1,186.6	1,185.5	1,166.4	1,176.8	1,182.0	1,201.1	1,218.9	1,216.5	1,185.2
2013	1,207.8	1,214.6	1,220.8	1,226.3	1,230.1	1,229.4	1,210.1	1,225.2	1,234.0	1,252.5	1,273.6	1,275.0	1,233.3
2014	1,257.2	1,263.5	1,271.2	1,279.9	1,282.0	1,281.3	1,265.7	1,281.4	1,292.0	1,312.6	1,340.2	1,344.4	1,289.3
2015	1,323.0	1,325.0	1,332.3	1,337.1	1,340.9	1,338.3	1,332.5	1,345.0	1,349.7	1,369.6	1,384.9	1,389.9	1,347.4
Total Private													
2005	981.1	990.8	1,001.1	1,012.1	1,013.1	1,018.4	1,016.1	1,020.3	1,030.1	1,035.5	1,047.4	1,056.7	1,018.6
2006	1,043.2	1,051.0	1,059.0	1,060.5	1,064.4	1,068.8	1,064.9	1,065.5	1,067.7	1,065.0	1,072.5	1,075.5	1,063.2
2007	1,056.1	1,060.5	1,066.0	1,063.2	1,068.6	1,068.4	1,066.2	1,065.3	1,063.7	1,060.9	1,067.5	1,068.8	1,064.6
2008	1,037.1	1,035.4	1,033.9	1,031.2	1,025.8	1,023.3	1,010.7	1,007.6	1,004.1	998.7	997.8	991.9	1,016.5
2009	963.0	953.2	950.2	941.5	938.1	933.5	920.5	916.4	914.6	918.5	925.3	925.8	933.4
2010	905.4	905.7	910.0	915.6	916.6	916.6	909.6	912.1	913.5	919.8	932.7	938.6	916.4
2011	913.3	917.2	920.4	923.9	923.5	920.5	921.3	925.3	929.2	932.9	947.1	949.5	927.0
2012	937.0	939.4	943.6	953.3	956.5	959.4	957.2	961.8	965.3	974.6	989.9	989.5	960.6
2013	980.9	987.4	992.2	997.8	1,000.5	1,001.6	999.1	1,008.6	1,013.0	1,024.9	1,044.0	1,047.5	1,008.1
2014	1,028.8	1,034.9	1,039.6	1,047.1	1,049.3	1,049.9	1,050.6	1,061.1	1,067.2	1,080.4	1,106.1	1,111.4	1,060.5
2015	1,090.6	1,091.7	1,096.2	1,100.7	1,104.0	1,103.7	1,113.5	1,119.8	1,120.2	1,132.3	1,145.5	1,149.8	1,114.0
Goods Producing													
2005	230.7	235.3	238.3	242.3	243.2	247.0	248.6	250.7	252.7	253.3	253.1	253.1	245.7
2006	250.4	253.4	254.4	253.7	256.5	259.4	257.1	256.7	255.3	247.7	242.2	240.3	252.3
2007	234.2	234.6	235.8	235.0	236.4	237.8	237.2	236.7	233.1	226.6	222.3	218.5	232.4
2008	208.9	207.2	206.8	205.0	203.8	203.5	200.5	199.4	196.0	190.2	184.9	179.5	198.8
2009	170.0	164.2	163.3	160.4	160.9	159.9	157.1	155.6	153.3	151.7	150.4	147.6	157.9
2010	144.5	143.9	144.9	146.5	147.5	147.9	146.7	147.4	146.3	145.3	145.2	144.2	145.9
2011	140.4	141.9	142.8	144.5	145.5	146.2	147.5	147.9	147.9	146.7	146.3	145.0	145.2
2012	144.0	144.7	146.0	147.1	149.6	152.1	152.9	154.4	154.2	154.6	153.8	153.1	150.5
2013	151.8	153.9	155.2	155.3	156.4	157.5	159.6	161.4	161.7	163.3	163.6	163.1	158.6
2014	163.2	164.6	165.7	166.4	168.3	169.7	172.0	174.6	174.8	174.4	174.9	173.7	170.2
2015	173.8	176.0	177.7	178.6	180.3	182.2	185.0	186.8	185.5	188.8	186.0	184.8	182.1
Service-Providing													
2005	970.4	977.0	986.0	994.3	994.4	991.6	978.3	980.2	994.9	1,004.7	1,018.6	1,029.1	993.3
2006	1,013.8	1,018.9	1,028.0	1,032.9	1,034.8	1,036.7	1,023.9	1,020.9	1,031.0	1,042.2	1,056.6	1,060.8	1,033.4
2007	1,046.6	1,051.1	1,057.8	1,056.6	1,061.4	1,059.6	1,046.3	1,041.8	1,049.8	1,062.5	1,075.6	1,081.8	1,057.6
2008	1,059.0	1,059.8	1,060.6	1,060.8	1,057.0	1,053.6	1,032.2	1,030.4	1,031.8	1,042.1	1,048.3	1,048.4	1,048.7
2009	1,028.6	1,024.5	1,024.6	1,021.9	1,018.2	1,013.0	989.2	989.5	987.9	1,002.8	1,012.9	1,015.7	1,010.7
2010	997.7	999.2	1,004.8	1,010.9	1,013.8	1,010.3	984.4	990.7	992.9	1,007.6	1,021.2	1,024.4	1,004.8
2011	1,004.2	1,006.9	1,011.0	1,012.8	1,011.6	1,005.1	987.8	995.2	1,001.3	1,014.1	1,029.9	1,031.3	1,009.3
2012	1,021.1	1,022.8	1,027.2	1,036.0	1,037.0	1,033.4	1,013.5	1,022.4	1,027.8	1,046.5	1,065.1	1,063.4	1,034.7
2013	1,056.0	1,060.7	1,065.6	1,071.0	1,073.7	1,071.9	1,050.5	1,063.8	1,072.3	1,089.2	1,110.0	1,111.9	1,074.7
2014	1,094.0	1,098.9	1,105.5	1,113.5	1,113.7	1,111.6	1,093.7	1,106.8	1,117.2	1,138.2	1,165.3	1,170.7	1,119.1
2015	1,149.2	1,149.0	1,154.6	1,158.5	1,160.6	1,156.1	1,147.5	1,158.2	1,164.2	1,180.8	1,198.9	1,205.1	1,165.2
Mining and Logging													
2005	1.3	1.3	1.3	1.3	1.3	1.3	1.4	1.4	1.4	1.4	1.4	1.4	1.4
2006	1.4	1.4	1.4	1.4	1.4	1.4	1.5	1.4	1.4	1.4	1.4	1.4	1.4
2007	1.4	1.3	1.3	1.3	1.3	1.3	1.4	1.4	1.4	1.3	1.3	1.2	1.3
2008	1.3	1.3	1.3	1.2	1.2	1.2	1.2	1.2	1.2	1.2	1.1	1.2	1.2
2009	1.2	1.2	1.2	1.2	1.2	1.2	1.1	1.1	1.1	1.1	1.1	1.0	1.1
2010	1.0	1.0	1.0	1.0	1.0	1.0	1.0	1.0	1.0	1.0	1.0	1.0	1.0
2011	1.0	1.0	1.0	1.0	1.0	1.0	1.0	1.1	1.1	1.1	1.1	1.1	1.0
2012	1.1	1.2	1.2	1.2	1.2	1.2	1.2	1.2	1.2	1.2	1.2	1.2	1.2
2013	1.2	1.2	1.2	1.2	1.2	1.2	1.2	1.2	1.2	1.2	1.2	1.2	1.2
2014	1.2	1.3	1.3	1.3	1.3	1.3	1.3	1.3	1.3	1.3	1.3	1.3	1.3
2015	1.3	1.3	1.4	1.4	1.4	1.4	1.4	1.3	1.3	1.3	1.3	1.2	1.3

Employment by Industry: Riverside-San Bernardino-Ontario, CA, 2005–2015—*Continued*

(Numbers in thousands, not seasonally adjusted)

Industry and year	January	February	March	April	May	June	July	August	September	October	November	December	Annual average
Construction													
2005	109.9	113.8	116.1	120.5	121.7	124.9	125.7	127.6	129.3	130.2	130.2	129.9	123.3
2006	126.7	128.6	128.9	128.3	130.2	132.6	131.6	131.5	130.2	123.9	119.6	117.7	127.5
2007	112.2	112.9	114.2	114.4	115.3	116.6	116.5	116.4	113.6	108.8	105.8	103.2	112.5
2008	95.8	94.8	95.3	94.0	93.6	93.8	92.3	92.0	89.5	85.7	82.5	79.5	90.7
2009	73.7	70.0	70.5	68.9	70.0	69.8	68.4	67.9	66.1	64.6	63.9	61.6	68.0
2010	59.0	58.5	59.8	60.5	61.2	61.3	60.4	60.7	59.7	58.8	58.8	57.7	59.7
2011	55.6	56.9	57.3	58.6	59.1	59.4	60.8	61.0	61.0	60.5	60.0	58.7	59.1
2012	58.0	58.0	58.8	59.3	61.1	63.5	64.4	65.7	65.8	66.1	65.7	65.2	62.6
2013	64.7	66.4	67.1	67.5	68.1	68.9	70.9	72.4	72.7	74.0	74.1	73.5	70.0
2014	72.9	73.6	74.5	75.1	76.3	77.2	79.3	81.4	81.2	80.4	80.3	78.8	77.6
2015	78.7	80.3	81.4	81.9	83.2	84.8	87.7	89.5	88.6	91.2	88.2	87.2	85.2
Manufacturing													
2005	119.5	120.2	120.9	120.5	120.2	120.8	121.5	121.7	122.0	121.7	121.5	121.8	121.0
2006	122.3	123.4	124.1	124.0	124.9	125.4	124.0	123.8	123.7	122.4	121.2	121.2	123.4
2007	120.6	120.4	120.3	119.3	119.8	119.9	119.3	118.9	118.1	116.5	115.2	114.1	118.5
2008	111.8	111.1	110.2	109.8	109.0	108.5	107.0	106.2	105.3	103.3	101.3	98.8	106.9
2009	95.1	93.0	91.6	90.3	89.7	88.9	87.6	86.6	86.1	86.0	85.4	85.0	88.8
2010	84.5	84.4	84.1	85.0	85.3	85.6	85.3	85.7	85.6	85.5	85.4	85.5	85.2
2011	83.8	84.0	84.5	84.9	85.4	85.8	85.7	85.8	85.8	85.1	85.2	85.2	85.1
2012	84.9	85.5	86.0	86.6	87.3	87.4	87.3	87.5	87.2	87.3	86.9	86.7	86.7
2013	85.9	86.3	86.9	86.6	87.1	87.4	87.5	87.8	87.8	88.1	88.3	88.4	87.3
2014	89.1	89.7	89.9	90.0	90.7	91.2	91.4	91.9	92.3	92.7	93.3	93.6	91.3
2015	93.8	94.4	94.9	95.3	95.7	96.0	95.9	96.0	95.6	96.3	96.5	96.4	95.6
Trade, Transportation, and Utilities													
2005	269.0	267.3	268.7	270.3	271.7	273.1	274.1	275.8	278.9	280.6	289.3	296.3	276.3
2006	284.6	282.9	285.5	286.2	288.0	290.0	290.7	291.2	292.3	296.1	304.3	308.6	291.7
2007	298.3	295.9	297.1	296.7	298.1	298.2	299.6	299.9	301.1	302.3	310.8	314.8	301.1
2008	301.3	296.5	295.2	294.0	293.7	292.5	289.3	288.5	287.9	286.3	289.7	290.3	292.1
2009	279.5	274.8	272.2	269.0	269.5	269.3	266.3	265.7	267.2	268.1	274.0	277.5	271.1
2010	268.2	265.9	266.2	266.7	267.9	268.4	267.1	267.2	268.2	271.2	279.8	283.1	270.0
2011	272.7	270.6	270.5	271.3	272.3	272.3	272.9	274.1	275.1	277.3	287.6	290.0	275.6
2012	281.8	278.4	279.0	282.3	283.9	284.5	284.8	286.6	288.1	291.7	304.6	305.3	287.6
2013	293.4	291.9	292.2	292.8	294.8	295.6	295.6	298.1	298.6	304.1	317.8	321.1	299.7
2014	306.8	304.9	305.0	307.1	308.9	309.8	309.8	313.9	316.4	321.7	335.4	339.0	314.9
2015	325.0	322.6	323.3	322.9	325.6	325.7	330.9	334.2	335.0	338.4	351.4	354.9	332.5
Wholesale Trade													
2005	48.0	48.1	48.6	49.4	49.7	50.0	50.3	50.5	50.9	51.2	51.5	52.2	50.0
2006	52.7	53.2	53.6	54.1	54.1	54.3	54.7	54.7	54.9	54.7	54.9	55.1	54.3
2007	55.4	56.0	56.3	56.4	56.6	57.0	57.2	57.3	57.5	57.6	57.7	57.8	56.9
2008	56.4	56.1	55.7	55.3	55.2	55.1	53.9	53.7	53.2	52.8	52.0	51.3	54.2
2009	50.5	49.9	49.2	48.9	48.8	48.9	48.7	48.5	48.3	48.5	48.6	48.6	49.0
2010	48.4	48.4	48.5	48.7	48.9	49.0	48.9	48.7	48.7	48.9	48.8	48.9	48.7
2011	48.5	48.8	49.0	49.0	49.1	49.1	49.3	49.3	49.4	49.5	49.5	49.5	49.2
2012	49.4	49.6	50.0	51.7	52.1	52.5	52.7	53.2	53.5	54.0	54.0	54.1	52.2
2013	54.6	55.0	55.6	55.6	56.0	56.3	56.6	57.1	57.1	57.2	57.7	58.0	56.4
2014	57.4	57.8	58.1	58.6	59.0	58.9	59.2	59.0	59.2	59.7	60.0	60.2	58.9
2015	59.7	60.0	60.1	60.6	61.1	60.8	62.2	62.7	62.9	63.1	63.2	63.8	61.7
Retail Trade													
2005	162.3	160.1	160.4	161.0	161.7	162.7	163.4	164.6	166.0	166.9	174.3	179.8	165.3
2006	168.9	166.8	168.1	168.6	169.7	171.0	171.5	171.8	171.7	175.0	182.2	185.1	172.5
2007	176.7	173.2	174.2	173.1	174.1	173.3	173.2	173.5	173.4	174.4	182.4	185.3	175.6
2008	175.2	170.8	170.3	169.2	168.7	168.1	166.7	165.8	165.3	164.7	168.7	169.6	168.6
2009	161.1	157.6	156.0	154.4	154.6	154.1	153.3	153.0	153.5	154.4	160.0	162.7	156.2
2010	154.9	153.1	153.3	153.8	154.1	154.0	153.2	153.1	153.0	155.5	163.0	165.2	155.5
2011	157.3	155.0	154.6	155.5	155.8	155.7	156.4	157.2	157.1	159.0	168.4	170.2	158.5
2012	162.6	158.9	158.5	159.8	160.1	159.3	159.6	160.0	160.1	162.3	173.8	173.3	162.4
2013	163.3	161.2	160.6	161.0	162.1	162.4	162.3	162.8	162.3	165.4	176.1	178.4	164.8
2014	167.7	165.4	165.5	166.4	166.3	166.5	166.8	167.9	167.6	170.2	180.2	182.4	169.4
2015	172.2	169.8	169.7	169.9	171.1	170.9	171.9	172.5	172.0	174.0	183.3	184.4	173.5

Employment by Industry: Riverside-San Bernardino-Ontario, CA, 2005–2015—*Continued*

(Numbers in thousands, not seasonally adjusted)

Industry and year	January	February	March	April	May	June	July	August	September	October	November	December	Annual average
Transportation and Utilities													
2005	58.7	59.1	59.7	59.9	60.3	60.4	60.4	60.7	62.0	62.5	63.5	64.3	61.0
2006	63.0	62.9	63.8	63.5	64.2	64.7	64.5	64.7	65.7	66.4	67.2	68.4	64.9
2007	66.2	66.7	66.6	67.2	67.4	67.9	69.2	69.1	70.2	70.3	70.7	71.7	68.6
2008	69.7	69.6	69.2	69.5	69.8	69.3	68.7	69.0	69.4	68.8	69.0	69.4	69.3
2009	67.9	67.3	67.0	65.7	66.1	66.3	64.3	64.2	65.4	65.2	65.4	66.2	65.9
2010	64.9	64.4	64.4	64.2	64.9	65.4	65.0	65.4	66.5	66.8	68.0	69.0	65.7
2011	66.9	66.8	66.9	66.8	67.4	67.5	67.2	67.6	68.6	68.8	69.7	70.3	67.9
2012	69.8	69.9	70.5	70.8	71.7	72.7	72.5	73.4	74.5	75.4	76.8	77.9	73.0
2013	75.5	75.7	76.0	76.2	76.7	76.9	76.7	78.2	79.2	81.5	84.0	84.7	78.4
2014	81.7	81.7	81.4	82.1	83.6	84.4	83.8	87.0	89.6	91.8	95.2	96.4	86.6
2015	93.1	92.8	93.5	92.4	93.4	94.0	96.8	99.0	100.1	101.3	104.9	106.7	97.3
Information													
2005	14.3	14.5	14.5	14.6	14.7	14.6	14.5	14.2	14.4	14.4	14.6	14.7	14.5
2006	14.6	14.9	14.9	15.1	15.2	15.4	15.5	15.5	15.5	15.4	15.6	15.7	15.3
2007	15.7	15.6	15.3	15.3	15.5	15.5	15.5	15.4	15.2	15.1	15.3	15.3	15.4
2008	15.3	15.4	15.2	15.1	15.1	14.8	14.7	14.6	14.3	14.2	14.3	14.1	14.8
2009	13.9	13.9	14.0	14.0	14.1	14.3	14.4	14.5	14.4	14.0	14.0	13.9	14.1
2010	14.2	14.2	14.3	14.2	14.2	14.3	14.2	14.1	13.8	13.6	13.6	13.5	14.0
2011	12.9	12.7	12.5	12.4	12.3	12.3	12.4	12.2	11.8	11.7	11.6	11.6	12.2
2012	12.0	11.9	11.8	11.7	11.7	11.8	11.8	11.6	11.5	11.5	11.6	11.7	11.7
2013	11.6	11.6	11.5	11.5	11.6	11.6	11.6	11.5	11.4	11.5	11.5	11.5	11.5
2014	11.5	11.4	11.3	11.3	11.3	11.4	11.2	11.1	11.0	11.1	11.2	11.3	11.3
2015	11.3	11.3	11.3	11.3	11.4	11.2	11.4	11.4	11.3	11.2	11.2	11.3	11.3
Financial Activities													
2005	47.3	47.6	47.8	48.2	48.2	48.2	48.7	49.0	49.3	49.6	49.9	50.1	48.7
2006	50.9	51.0	51.3	51.6	51.9	51.8	51.0	51.1	50.9	50.7	51.0	50.9	51.2
2007	50.7	50.9	51.0	50.2	49.9	49.8	49.2	49.0	48.7	47.9	47.8	47.9	49.4
2008	46.6	46.6	46.5	46.3	46.0	46.1	45.3	45.2	44.9	44.9	44.9	44.6	45.7
2009	44.3	44.1	43.7	43.0	42.1	41.9	41.3	41.1	40.8	41.2	41.1	41.2	42.2
2010	40.6	40.7	40.9	40.8	40.5	40.5	40.3	40.1	40.4	40.6	40.4	40.6	40.5
2011	39.7	39.9	39.7	39.7	39.5	39.5	39.2	39.2	39.1	39.3	39.3	39.3	39.5
2012	39.0	39.3	39.6	40.2	40.2	40.2	40.3	40.4	40.5	40.8	41.0	41.2	40.2
2013	40.7	41.0	40.9	41.2	41.5	41.5	41.4	41.5	41.4	41.6	41.7	41.7	41.3
2014	41.5	41.5	41.5	42.5	42.5	42.5	42.4	42.4	42.2	42.5	42.7	42.8	42.3
2015	42.7	42.9	42.9	43.3	43.4	43.1	43.3	43.3	43.1	43.8	43.8	43.2	43.2
Professional and Business Services													
2005	125.6	128.6	130.6	132.9	131.6	132.9	133.8	135.3	136.6	137.3	137.9	137.2	133.4
2006	138.4	139.6	140.6	141.4	140.7	141.9	143.2	143.3	145.1	145.4	146.1	144.5	142.5
2007	142.5	144.5	146.1	144.4	145.7	145.6	146.3	146.4	146.7	147.0	146.1	144.8	145.5
2008	140.0	140.8	139.6	138.1	136.5	138.8	138.5	138.5	138.3	138.2	137.5	135.3	138.3
2009	131.1	129.8	129.4	127.8	125.4	124.8	122.9	122.5	122.1	123.4	123.4	121.4	125.3
2010	118.7	119.7	120.5	121.8	122.1	123.1	123.6	125.0	125.1	127.5	127.7	128.3	123.6
2011	123.1	125.2	125.7	125.8	124.4	123.6	124.9	127.6	128.2	128.4	128.3	127.0	126.0
2012	125.0	126.9	126.1	128.4	127.2	128.4	127.5	127.9	127.5	130.2	128.7	126.2	127.5
2013	126.8	129.9	129.2	132.0	130.8	131.4	132.3	134.7	135.6	136.2	135.8	134.2	132.4
2014	131.1	133.6	134.4	136.8	134.8	135.6	136.9	138.5	140.3	144.8	151.9	153.3	139.3
2015	145.9	143.3	142.5	144.0	142.9	143.7	144.4	144.4	144.1	145.9	146.0	145.8	144.4
Education and Health Services													
2005	135.4	136.7	137.4	138.1	138.1	138.1	135.5	135.3	137.0	139.4	139.7	140.1	137.6
2006	138.9	141.1	141.5	141.4	141.2	140.5	138.8	139.4	140.4	142.1	142.7	143.0	140.9
2007	142.8	144.5	145.4	145.4	145.7	145.7	144.6	147.1	148.1	150.8	151.6	151.9	147.1
2008	150.5	153.5	154.1	155.7	155.1	154.1	152.8	153.1	154.8	158.0	158.8	159.4	155.0
2009	157.8	160.2	161.0	162.4	162.1	161.7	160.7	161.4	161.9	163.4	163.7	163.5	161.7
2010	159.7	160.9	161.1	161.6	161.3	160.3	159.1	160.0	161.1	162.4	164.2	164.5	161.4
2011	162.1	164.4	164.8	165.9	165.1	163.6	163.1	163.6	166.3	167.8	169.0	169.7	165.4
2012	169.6	171.4	172.5	172.7	172.8	172.4	170.9	171.8	174.4	177.3	178.3	179.2	173.6
2013	183.6	185.1	186.5	186.9	187.3	187.2	184.3	186.3	188.5	190.8	192.5	192.5	187.6
2014	190.4	192.4	193.3	194.5	194.1	193.2	192.2	194.4	196.0	198.3	199.2	199.7	194.8
2015	200.4	202.2	202.6	203.7	203.6	202.6	204.1	205.4	207.1	209.8	209.0	209.0	205.0

Employment by Industry: Riverside-San Bernardino-Ontario, CA, 2005–2015—*Continued*

(Numbers in thousands, not seasonally adjusted)

Industry and year	January	February	March	April	May	June	July	August	September	October	November	December	Annual average
Leisure and Hospitality													
2005	119.2	120.9	123.4	125.1	125.0	124.3	121.4	120.8	121.2	121.4	123.4	125.4	122.6
2006	125.3	127.2	129.4	130.0	129.4	128.4	127.0	126.6	126.4	126.4	129.5	131.5	128.1
2007	131.7	133.6	134.6	134.6	135.4	133.8	130.7	129.7	129.4	130.2	132.5	134.7	132.6
2008	133.8	134.4	134.9	134.6	133.0	131.3	128.8	127.5	127.5	127.4	128.8	130.2	131.0
2009	129.2	129.1	129.2	127.5	126.5	124.1	120.3	118.7	118.1	119.0	121.0	123.3	123.8
2010	122.4	122.9	124.1	125.2	124.2	122.9	120.2	120.1	120.6	121.1	123.6	126.1	122.8
2011	124.4	124.0	125.8	125.2	125.0	123.6	122.2	121.4	121.5	122.2	125.6	127.5	124.0
2012	126.8	127.6	129.1	130.6	130.5	129.2	128.5	128.4	128.3	128.6	131.9	133.1	129.4
2013	133.2	133.8	135.7	137.0	137.0	135.5	133.4	133.7	134.3	135.7	139.2	141.7	135.9
2014	142.2	143.9	145.3	144.8	145.8	144.3	143.2	143.0	143.4	144.9	147.8	148.8	144.8
2015	148.8	150.1	152.2	152.7	152.7	151.2	149.6	149.8	149.7	150.9	153.9	156.2	151.5
Other Services													
2005	39.6	39.9	40.4	40.6	40.6	40.2	39.5	39.2	40.0	39.5	39.5	39.8	39.9
2006	40.1	40.9	41.4	41.1	41.5	41.4	41.6	41.7	41.8	41.2	41.1	41.0	41.2
2007	40.2	40.9	40.7	41.6	41.9	42.0	41.1	41.1	41.4	41.0	41.1	40.9	41.2
2008	40.7	41.0	41.6	42.4	42.6	42.2	40.8	40.8	40.4	39.5	38.9	38.5	40.8
2009	37.2	37.1	37.4	37.4	37.5	37.5	37.5	36.9	36.8	37.7	37.7	37.4	37.3
2010	37.1	37.5	38.0	38.8	38.9	39.2	38.4	38.2	38.0	38.1	38.2	38.3	38.2
2011	38.0	38.5	38.6	39.1	39.4	39.4	39.1	39.4	39.3	39.5	39.4	39.4	39.1
2012	38.8	39.2	39.5	40.3	40.6	40.8	40.5	40.7	40.8	39.9	40.0	39.7	40.1
2013	39.8	40.2	41.0	41.1	41.1	41.3	40.9	41.4	41.5	41.7	41.9	41.7	41.1
2014	42.1	42.6	43.1	43.7	43.6	43.4	42.9	43.2	43.1	42.7	43.0	42.8	43.0
2015	42.7	43.3	43.7	44.2	44.1	44.0	44.8	44.5	44.4	43.5	44.2	44.6	44.0
Government													
2005	220.0	221.5	223.2	224.5	224.5	220.2	210.8	210.6	217.5	222.5	224.3	225.5	220.4
2006	221.0	221.3	223.4	226.1	226.9	227.3	216.1	212.1	218.6	224.9	226.3	225.6	222.5
2007	224.7	225.2	227.6	228.4	229.2	229.0	217.3	213.2	219.2	228.2	230.4	231.5	225.3
2008	230.8	231.6	233.5	234.6	235.0	233.8	222.0	222.2	223.7	233.6	235.4	236.0	231.0
2009	235.6	235.5	237.7	240.8	241.0	239.4	225.8	228.7	226.6	236.0	238.0	237.5	235.2
2010	236.8	237.4	239.7	241.8	244.7	241.6	221.5	226.0	225.7	233.1	233.7	230.0	234.3
2011	231.3	231.6	233.4	233.4	233.6	230.8	214.0	217.8	220.0	227.9	229.1	226.8	227.5
2012	228.1	228.1	229.6	229.8	230.1	226.1	209.2	215.0	216.7	226.5	229.0	227.0	224.6
2013	226.9	227.2	228.6	228.5	229.6	227.8	211.0	216.6	221.0	227.6	229.6	227.5	225.2
2014	228.4	228.6	231.6	232.8	232.7	231.4	215.1	220.3	224.8	232.2	234.1	233.0	228.8
2015	232.4	233.3	236.1	236.4	236.9	234.6	219.0	225.2	229.5	237.3	239.4	240.1	233.4

Employment by Industry: Detroit-Warren-Dearborn, MI, 2005–2015

(Numbers in thousands, not seasonally adjusted)

Industry and year	January	February	March	April	May	June	July	August	September	October	November	December	Annual average
Total Nonfarm													
2005	2,005.4	2,020.5	2,021.1	2,046.9	2,071.5	2,072.9	2,000.6	2,029.8	2,060.2	2,059.0	2,072.7	2,066.6	2,043.9
2006	1,988.1	1,991.5	1,999.4	2,011.5	2,029.8	2,035.4	1,953.5	1,982.0	2,001.2	1,994.9	2,010.1	2,007.0	2,000.4
2007	1,936.1	1,948.5	1,952.4	1,965.4	1,990.4	1,994.0	1,928.4	1,957.0	1,966.9	1,960.2	1,977.5	1,970.3	1,962.3
2008	1,907.7	1,909.3	1,905.0	1,908.7	1,928.9	1,937.3	1,866.8	1,887.1	1,894.2	1,893.9	1,885.7	1,866.4	1,899.3
2009	1,751.9	1,760.8	1,757.5	1,757.5	1,749.3	1,738.8	1,706.0	1,716.4	1,734.0	1,744.2	1,743.5	1,739.3	1,741.6
2010	1,694.4	1,698.5	1,701.8	1,725.9	1,750.1	1,757.9	1,723.5	1,727.3	1,750.2	1,767.1	1,770.6	1,767.5	1,736.2
2011	1,731.0	1,739.4	1,751.2	1,775.2	1,793.4	1,800.1	1,770.2	1,786.0	1,805.8	1,820.4	1,827.4	1,822.0	1,785.2
2012	1,790.8	1,797.7	1,812.0	1,817.9	1,840.6	1,849.3	1,822.0	1,835.1	1,843.0	1,855.8	1,863.9	1,863.2	1,832.6
2013	1,825.9	1,834.9	1,845.2	1,851.8	1,880.1	1,889.7	1,845.2	1,867.0	1,878.3	1,894.0	1,898.9	1,892.2	1,866.9
2014	1,848.0	1,862.6	1,871.8	1,873.7	1,905.0	1,925.0	1,893.1	1,902.8	1,904.7	1,922.0	1,933.0	1,935.0	1,898.1
2015	1,894.2	1,897.0	1,905.0	1,919.7	1,952.4	1,962.0	1,930.9	1,940.2	1,946.0	1,955.4	1,965.1	1,964.4	1,936.0
Total Private													
2005	1,770.4	1,779.6	1,780.1	1,805.4	1,828.2	1,834.9	1,793.5	1,824.2	1,826.9	1,820.9	1,832.1	1,829.1	1,810.4
2006	1,756.8	1,754.6	1,761.3	1,773.9	1,791.1	1,801.1	1,746.1	1,778.3	1,774.4	1,761.2	1,774.6	1,774.3	1,770.6
2007	1,707.6	1,716.7	1,718.3	1,732.7	1,755.0	1,762.8	1,723.5	1,753.3	1,746.7	1,734.2	1,751.0	1,745.2	1,737.3
2008	1,687.8	1,685.4	1,680.6	1,684.7	1,703.2	1,714.6	1,664.4	1,683.6	1,676.8	1,670.7	1,661.6	1,645.4	1,679.9
2009	1,535.3	1,540.4	1,536.1	1,534.5	1,527.9	1,519.8	1,508.4	1,519.1	1,522.4	1,527.4	1,526.4	1,524.6	1,526.9
2010	1,484.8	1,484.8	1,487.5	1,510.0	1,531.2	1,544.2	1,529.5	1,538.2	1,547.3	1,559.8	1,563.9	1,562.4	1,528.6
2011	1,531.8	1,535.9	1,547.6	1,571.6	1,592.4	1,600.5	1,586.9	1,603.8	1,608.3	1,619.8	1,625.8	1,622.6	1,587.3
2012	1,596.4	1,599.5	1,613.5	1,619.9	1,644.4	1,653.5	1,643.3	1,656.6	1,649.8	1,661.3	1,668.3	1,669.4	1,639.7
2013	1,637.3	1,642.8	1,653.2	1,660.3	1,690.9	1,700.7	1,672.4	1,695.7	1,691.9	1,704.6	1,709.2	1,704.3	1,680.3
2014	1,664.3	1,674.8	1,683.5	1,684.7	1,718.2	1,738.6	1,722.2	1,733.2	1,721.5	1,734.0	1,743.4	1,748.4	1,713.9
2015	1,712.2	1,711.2	1,718.3	1,732.4	1,765.7	1,778.0	1,762.5	1,772.7	1,763.7	1,770.4	1,778.5	1,779.9	1,753.8
Goods Producing													
2005	352.6	358.7	353.8	358.2	369.0	370.5	342.0	363.6	367.5	365.0	367.5	359.7	360.7
2006	333.8	334.3	337.8	343.5	349.6	349.4	315.0	339.7	338.9	331.0	336.2	329.8	336.6
2007	305.5	316.9	317.1	319.9	325.0	327.3	306.5	326.5	323.9	311.3	317.7	312.4	317.5
2008	295.3	296.7	290.7	287.6	291.4	302.9	272.7	289.8	289.1	286.0	283.3	272.0	288.1
2009	223.9	233.4	233.7	231.2	219.1	216.6	217.6	226.4	230.0	231.8	227.0	223.7	226.2
2010	217.3	215.2	215.2	222.7	228.8	234.2	232.9	231.7	240.9	242.0	240.7	237.8	230.0
2011	232.4	233.9	236.2	244.6	251.2	257.0	253.9	260.4	261.7	262.4	263.2	261.6	251.5
2012	256.4	255.4	258.4	259.2	266.6	270.6	270.3	273.1	273.3	274.1	273.3	271.3	266.8
2013	266.3	266.7	268.4	270.6	279.1	282.9	275.5	284.5	285.3	286.8	286.1	278.9	277.6
2014	273.1	278.5	280.1	276.6	288.0	299.6	295.7	300.7	296.8	299.3	301.6	301.3	290.9
2015	292.3	291.8	292.8	297.0	305.7	310.7	307.4	310.6	309.9	306.0	308.4	303.6	303.0
Service-Providing													
2005	1,652.8	1,661.8	1,667.3	1,688.7	1,702.5	1,702.4	1,658.6	1,666.2	1,692.7	1,694.0	1,705.2	1,706.9	1,683.3
2006	1,654.3	1,657.2	1,661.6	1,668.0	1,680.2	1,686.0	1,638.5	1,642.3	1,662.3	1,663.9	1,673.9	1,677.2	1,663.8
2007	1,630.6	1,631.6	1,635.3	1,645.5	1,665.4	1,666.7	1,621.9	1,630.5	1,643.0	1,648.9	1,659.8	1,657.9	1,644.8
2008	1,612.4	1,612.6	1,614.3	1,621.1	1,637.5	1,634.4	1,594.1	1,597.3	1,605.1	1,607.9	1,602.4	1,594.4	1,611.1
2009	1,528.0	1,527.4	1,523.8	1,526.3	1,530.2	1,522.2	1,488.4	1,490.0	1,504.0	1,512.4	1,516.5	1,515.6	1,515.4
2010	1,477.1	1,483.3	1,486.6	1,503.2	1,521.3	1,523.7	1,490.6	1,495.6	1,509.3	1,525.1	1,529.9	1,529.7	1,506.3
2011	1,498.6	1,505.5	1,515.0	1,530.6	1,542.2	1,543.1	1,516.3	1,525.6	1,544.1	1,558.0	1,564.2	1,560.4	1,533.6
2012	1,534.4	1,542.3	1,553.6	1,558.7	1,574.0	1,578.7	1,551.7	1,562.0	1,569.7	1,581.7	1,590.6	1,591.9	1,565.8
2013	1,559.6	1,568.2	1,576.8	1,581.2	1,601.0	1,606.8	1,569.7	1,582.5	1,593.0	1,607.2	1,612.8	1,613.3	1,589.3
2014	1,574.9	1,584.1	1,591.7	1,597.1	1,617.0	1,625.4	1,597.4	1,602.1	1,607.9	1,622.7	1,631.4	1,633.7	1,607.1
2015	1,601.9	1,605.2	1,612.2	1,622.7	1,646.7	1,651.3	1,623.5	1,629.6	1,636.1	1,649.4	1,656.7	1,660.8	1,633.0
Mining, Logging, and Construction													
2005	76.6	74.8	75.8	81.2	86.5	89.9	92.0	90.4	88.9	87.6	85.9	80.7	84.2
2006	71.5	70.1	70.9	74.6	80.0	82.6	82.8	81.8	79.8	78.5	76.8	72.8	76.9
2007	64.9	62.4	64.4	67.1	72.7	75.5	77.9	77.7	76.4	74.0	71.8	68.1	71.1
2008	61.0	58.6	58.6	61.6	66.8	68.9	69.2	68.9	67.4	66.5	63.3	57.8	64.1
2009	50.0	48.4	48.3	49.8	53.9	55.1	55.5	55.0	54.0	54.4	52.6	49.4	52.2
2010	43.9	42.6	44.3	47.9	51.6	53.7	56.2	56.8	56.2	56.6	55.3	52.3	51.5
2011	47.4	46.2	47.3	50.3	54.7	58.6	60.4	60.6	59.7	59.0	57.8	55.2	54.8
2012	51.0	49.1	50.3	52.9	56.4	59.1	59.9	60.0	60.0	59.7	58.4	55.8	56.1
2013	52.2	50.7	51.8	53.3	59.6	61.1	62.7	62.6	61.6	61.9	60.7	57.9	58.0
2014	53.1	52.6	52.9	55.3	62.2	65.5	66.3	67.9	68.0	67.7	66.1	63.4	61.8
2015	58.0	56.9	58.3	62.0	67.2	70.0	70.0	70.2	69.4	69.0	68.5	63.7	65.3

Employment by Industry: Detroit-Warren-Dearborn, MI, 2005–2015—*Continued*

(Numbers in thousands, not seasonally adjusted)

Industry and year	January	February	March	April	May	June	July	August	September	October	November	December	Annual average
Manufacturing													
2005	276.0	283.9	278.0	277.0	282.5	280.6	250.0	273.2	278.6	277.4	281.6	279.0	276.5
2006	262.3	264.2	266.9	268.9	269.6	266.8	232.2	257.9	259.1	252.5	259.4	257.0	259.7
2007	240.6	254.5	252.7	252.8	252.3	251.8	228.6	248.8	247.5	237.3	245.9	244.3	246.4
2008	234.3	238.1	232.1	226.0	224.6	234.0	203.5	220.9	221.7	219.5	220.0	214.2	224.1
2009	173.9	185.0	185.4	181.4	165.2	161.5	162.1	171.4	176.0	177.4	174.4	174.3	174.0
2010	173.4	172.6	170.9	174.8	177.2	180.5	176.7	174.9	184.7	185.4	185.4	185.5	178.5
2011	185.0	187.7	188.9	194.3	196.5	198.4	193.5	199.8	202.0	203.4	205.4	206.4	196.8
2012	205.4	206.3	208.1	206.3	210.2	211.5	210.4	213.1	213.3	214.4	214.9	215.5	210.8
2013	214.1	216.0	216.6	217.3	219.5	221.8	212.8	221.9	223.7	224.9	225.4	221.0	219.6
2014	220.0	225.9	227.2	221.3	225.8	234.1	229.4	232.8	228.8	231.6	235.5	237.9	229.2
2015	234.3	234.9	234.5	235.0	238.5	240.7	237.4	240.4	240.5	237.0	239.9	239.9	237.8
Trade, Transportation, and Utilities													
2005	376.0	373.5	374.8	376.4	380.0	380.8	378.2	379.5	376.9	379.3	387.1	391.1	379.5
2006	371.8	367.6	368.7	369.7	372.8	374.4	368.8	370.9	369.4	371.5	379.6	384.1	372.4
2007	366.2	361.7	361.5	362.2	366.6	366.8	362.1	365.2	364.4	366.5	375.2	378.7	366.4
2008	363.3	358.3	358.9	357.0	359.7	360.5	356.2	356.4	355.5	354.4	357.2	358.3	358.0
2009	336.6	332.7	330.1	326.0	328.2	327.4	323.4	323.8	323.8	326.0	331.5	334.8	328.7
2010	320.6	317.6	319.0	322.1	326.1	328.1	326.2	327.8	326.1	332.4	338.1	341.7	327.2
2011	328.3	325.4	326.3	329.1	333.0	334.6	333.7	335.0	334.7	338.0	345.9	349.0	334.4
2012	337.8	334.5	336.1	335.1	339.9	341.4	339.3	340.5	339.4	343.2	353.1	354.7	341.3
2013	341.2	338.6	339.3	339.5	344.8	347.7	345.9	347.8	346.3	349.6	357.2	361.9	346.7
2014	348.3	346.5	347.2	349.5	353.9	356.2	353.9	355.0	353.0	357.5	365.6	370.2	354.7
2015	355.6	352.5	353.3	355.7	360.6	362.7	359.6	360.7	358.3	359.3	364.4	368.6	359.3
Wholesale Trade													
2005	93.2	93.2	93.5	93.7	94.2	94.1	93.8	93.5	93.0	93.7	93.4	93.7	93.6
2006	92.4	92.5	92.7	93.0	93.3	93.8	93.0	92.7	91.9	91.8	91.7	91.9	92.6
2007	90.5	90.0	89.8	89.9	90.5	90.4	90.2	89.9	89.4	89.9	89.3	89.7	90.0
2008	89.2	88.8	88.9	89.0	89.3	89.2	88.7	88.5	88.2	87.7	86.7	86.0	88.4
2009	84.1	83.1	81.9	80.8	80.2	78.7	77.7	77.9	77.5	77.6	77.5	77.8	79.6
2010	76.3	76.6	76.8	77.4	78.1	78.6	78.5	79.1	78.7	79.6	79.8	80.2	78.3
2011	79.2	79.3	79.6	80.5	81.0	81.1	81.5	81.7	81.3	81.6	82.1	82.1	80.9
2012	81.8	82.1	82.4	82.5	83.4	83.7	83.7	83.9	83.5	83.8	84.0	84.3	83.3
2013	83.9	83.9	84.2	84.1	84.8	85.1	84.8	84.8	84.5	84.3	84.2	84.7	84.4
2014	84.0	84.0	84.2	84.3	85.2	85.8	85.1	85.4	84.8	84.8	85.1	85.6	84.9
2015	84.5	84.7	84.9	85.5	86.2	86.8	86.3	86.5	85.7	85.9	86.4	87.6	85.9
Retail Trade													
2005	218.7	215.5	216.3	218.7	221.3	222.1	219.8	219.7	218.2	219.9	227.2	230.8	220.7
2006	215.1	210.9	211.5	212.3	214.7	215.7	213.8	214.4	213.5	216.2	223.8	226.6	215.7
2007	212.2	207.0	207.3	207.7	210.7	210.6	209.1	210.2	209.9	212.2	220.7	223.0	211.7
2008	211.3	206.4	206.6	205.6	208.0	207.8	206.6	206.7	205.7	206.3	210.0	211.4	207.7
2009	197.5	193.4	192.3	190.9	194.5	195.9	193.2	192.7	192.1	194.3	199.8	201.7	194.9
2010	190.6	187.5	188.2	191.0	193.9	194.8	193.7	194.2	192.3	196.7	201.8	204.1	194.1
2011	192.9	190.1	190.6	192.6	194.9	195.5	195.1	195.8	195.3	198.4	205.2	207.5	196.2
2012	197.2	193.5	194.6	194.1	197.2	198.0	196.7	197.3	196.0	199.0	208.3	208.8	198.4
2013	197.3	194.4	194.9	195.4	199.2	201.3	200.9	201.9	200.4	203.0	210.0	212.7	201.0
2014	201.0	199.1	199.7	201.7	204.8	206.2	204.9	205.5	204.0	208.3	215.7	217.6	205.7
2015	205.0	203.0	203.8	204.7	208.2	209.3	207.5	208.5	206.4	208.1	212.1	214.1	207.6
Transportation and Utilities													
2005	64.1	64.8	65.0	64.0	64.5	64.6	64.6	66.3	65.7	65.7	66.5	66.6	65.2
2006	64.3	64.2	64.5	64.4	64.8	64.9	62.0	63.8	64.0	63.5	64.1	65.6	64.2
2007	63.5	64.7	64.4	64.6	65.4	65.8	62.8	65.1	65.1	64.4	65.2	66.0	64.8
2008	62.8	63.1	63.4	62.4	62.4	63.5	60.9	61.2	61.6	60.4	60.5	60.9	61.9
2009	55.0	56.2	55.9	54.3	53.5	52.8	52.5	53.2	54.2	54.1	54.2	55.3	54.3
2010	53.7	53.5	54.0	53.7	54.1	54.7	54.0	54.5	55.1	56.1	56.5	57.4	54.8
2011	56.2	56.0	56.1	56.0	57.1	58.0	57.1	57.5	58.1	58.0	58.6	59.4	57.3
2012	58.8	58.9	59.1	58.5	59.3	59.7	58.9	59.3	59.9	60.4	60.8	61.6	59.6
2013	60.0	60.3	60.2	60.0	60.8	61.3	60.2	61.1	61.4	62.3	63.0	64.5	61.3
2014	63.3	63.4	63.3	63.5	63.9	64.2	63.9	64.1	64.2	64.4	64.8	67.0	64.2
2015	66.1	64.8	64.6	65.5	66.2	66.6	65.8	65.7	66.2	65.3	65.9	66.9	65.8

Employment by Industry: Detroit-Warren-Dearborn, MI, 2005–2015—*Continued*

(Numbers in thousands, not seasonally adjusted)

Industry and year	January	February	March	April	May	June	July	August	September	October	November	December	Annual average
Information													
2005	31.9	31.5	31.5	31.4	31.6	31.6	31.5	31.3	30.9	30.5	30.8	30.9	31.3
2006	30.5	30.7	30.3	30.1	30.4	30.4	30.2	30.1	29.6	29.7	29.8	29.9	30.1
2007	30.1	29.9	29.7	30.0	30.3	30.2	30.0	29.9	29.6	29.6	29.7	29.6	29.9
2008	29.7	29.7	29.3	29.2	29.4	29.5	29.2	29.5	29.8	29.0	29.2	28.8	29.4
2009	28.2	28.3	27.7	27.5	27.6	27.7	27.5	27.2	27.0	27.1	27.5	27.7	27.6
2010	26.9	26.8	26.7	26.8	27.0	27.2	26.8	28.6	28.4	26.4	26.3	26.5	27.0
2011	26.4	26.1	26.1	25.8	26.0	26.0	26.1	26.2	26.0	26.7	26.7	26.6	26.2
2012	26.8	26.6	26.7	26.3	26.5	26.3	26.6	27.0	26.2	26.4	26.6	26.6	26.6
2013	26.7	26.7	26.8	27.4	27.6	27.9	27.6	27.6	27.1	27.0	27.2	27.2	27.2
2014	27.5	27.2	27.4	27.8	27.8	28.3	28.8	28.6	27.6	28.2	28.2	27.9	27.9
2015	27.2	27.0	26.9	26.7	27.3	27.5	28.1	27.5	27.5	27.6	27.6	27.6	27.4
Financial Activities													
2005	116.1	116.2	116.2	116.7	116.9	118.1	117.4	117.4	116.1	115.7	115.7	115.7	116.5
2006	114.0	113.9	113.4	113.2	113.9	114.8	114.1	114.0	112.4	111.7	111.5	112.2	113.3
2007	111.0	110.8	110.5	111.1	111.4	112.2	112.1	111.1	109.0	108.0	107.6	107.5	110.2
2008	106.8	106.7	106.2	105.8	106.7	106.7	105.9	105.0	103.5	102.7	101.9	101.6	105.0
2009	99.9	99.4	98.8	98.8	99.2	99.2	98.8	98.3	97.0	96.0	95.6	95.6	98.1
2010	95.1	94.9	94.2	93.8	95.0	96.1	96.4	96.8	95.7	96.0	96.3	96.9	95.6
2011	96.5	96.7	97.3	98.0	98.1	98.8	99.2	99.5	98.1	97.6	97.6	97.8	97.9
2012	97.3	97.6	98.1	98.1	98.9	100.3	101.5	101.9	100.1	100.4	100.8	101.7	99.7
2013	101.6	102.1	102.5	102.7	103.6	105.7	106.4	106.5	104.2	104.1	104.3	104.3	104.0
2014	103.5	103.5	103.4	103.2	104.6	106.1	106.0	106.4	104.6	104.6	104.6	105.1	104.6
2015	104.6	104.7	105.0	105.7	107.0	108.9	109.0	109.3	107.9	108.7	108.7	109.6	107.4
Professional and Business Services													
2005	373.5	374.0	373.4	381.2	383.8	386.1	380.9	386.6	388.5	384.9	385.3	384.7	381.9
2006	372.3	368.8	367.7	370.5	371.7	376.2	368.6	374.1	372.7	371.7	373.4	372.6	371.7
2007	359.1	359.1	356.5	363.2	365.0	367.2	361.6	367.7	365.7	366.2	369.1	365.1	363.8
2008	353.2	352.9	351.6	356.5	358.4	356.6	346.6	347.8	345.1	347.6	342.4	337.7	349.7
2009	316.0	314.6	310.9	309.9	305.9	301.8	299.8	301.9	305.8	307.8	308.1	307.1	307.5
2010	301.9	304.6	304.0	310.7	313.7	316.0	310.6	315.1	320.4	325.7	326.8	324.1	314.5
2011	323.0	325.4	329.3	335.3	339.0	337.0	330.5	337.8	343.5	350.0	350.4	345.0	337.2
2012	343.4	347.1	350.0	354.8	359.8	357.5	353.0	358.8	359.8	365.3	364.6	363.2	356.4
2013	359.0	362.3	366.0	367.2	374.8	374.5	360.1	370.2	373.4	378.2	377.8	375.4	369.9
2014	366.4	369.8	371.5	370.2	377.7	378.9	372.3	375.7	376.8	380.0	380.1	379.4	374.9
2015	378.6	380.1	380.8	385.7	392.5	392.3	383.5	387.1	389.0	394.7	393.8	393.1	387.6
Education and Health Services													
2005	259.5	262.7	263.8	265.5	265.5	263.4	262.2	262.9	267.1	270.8	272.7	273.3	265.8
2006	269.0	271.0	272.8	270.7	272.0	271.0	268.2	267.9	273.1	272.7	274.2	275.2	271.5
2007	272.5	275.2	276.4	275.9	277.3	277.8	273.4	273.3	277.4	278.9	280.7	280.8	276.6
2008	277.8	279.9	280.2	280.5	282.2	280.8	278.3	278.1	281.0	283.3	284.1	284.1	280.9
2009	279.8	283.0	283.9	283.3	284.7	284.2	280.2	280.5	281.6	284.6	286.4	285.6	283.2
2010	281.3	283.9	284.7	283.9	284.8	283.7	282.2	282.2	283.5	288.4	289.4	289.3	284.8
2011	285.8	287.8	288.8	291.4	291.9	290.3	289.5	289.9	291.8	294.7	295.7	296.4	291.2
2012	292.2	295.5	296.7	295.3	296.1	295.5	293.8	294.4	294.6	297.9	298.8	299.9	295.9
2013	295.4	298.2	298.8	298.3	298.8	297.9	295.2	296.0	297.7	300.3	301.2	301.2	298.3
2014	296.2	299.8	300.7	299.2	300.0	299.0	296.7	297.2	298.3	301.8	303.3	304.2	299.7
2015	299.2	301.4	302.6	301.2	302.9	302.6	301.4	303.8	302.1	307.5	310.3	310.3	303.8
Leisure and Hospitality													
2005	173.1	174.6	177.6	185.3	191.0	192.7	189.8	191.3	188.5	183.6	181.7	181.8	184.3
2006	175.9	178.6	180.4	186.0	190.0	193.6	191.2	191.5	188.6	184.0	180.9	181.3	185.2
2007	175.9	175.5	178.6	182.8	191.0	192.3	189.5	191.0	188.6	185.9	183.4	183.2	184.8
2008	175.9	175.2	177.5	181.5	187.9	189.9	187.8	189.4	185.7	181.3	178.0	177.8	182.3
2009	167.8	166.1	168.4	175.2	180.1	179.7	178.7	179.0	176.5	173.2	169.7	169.4	173.7
2010	162.8	163.0	164.9	171.8	177.1	179.9	176.6	178.8	176.0	173.2	171.1	171.0	172.2
2011	165.5	166.9	169.7	173.4	178.6	181.5	179.2	180.0	177.9	175.7	172.0	171.5	174.3
2012	168.6	168.7	172.5	175.3	180.2	184.3	181.7	183.1	179.1	177.1	174.6	175.6	176.7
2013	171.1	171.7	174.2	177.8	184.8	186.1	184.2	185.3	180.7	181.5	178.3	178.3	179.5
2014	172.9	173.0	176.5	181.5	188.9	192.7	190.8	191.7	187.1	185.2	183.1	183.5	183.9
2015	179.7	178.6	181.7	185.3	193.7	196.5	196.2	196.1	192.0	189.4	188.5	189.0	188.9

Employment by Industry: Detroit-Warren-Dearborn, MI, 2005–2015—*Continued*

(Numbers in thousands, not seasonally adjusted)

Industry and year	January	February	March	April	May	June	July	August	September	October	November	December	Annual average
Other Services													
2005	87.7	88.4	89.0	90.7	90.4	91.7	91.5	91.6	91.4	91.1	91.3	91.9	90.6
2006	89.5	89.7	90.2	90.2	90.7	91.3	90.0	90.1	89.7	88.9	89.0	89.2	89.9
2007	87.3	87.6	88.0	87.6	88.4	89.0	88.3	88.6	88.1	87.8	87.6	87.9	88.0
2008	85.8	86.0	86.2	86.6	87.5	87.7	87.7	87.6	87.1	86.4	85.5	85.1	86.6
2009	83.1	82.9	82.6	82.6	83.1	83.2	82.4	82.0	80.7	80.9	80.6	80.7	82.1
2010	78.9	78.8	78.8	78.2	78.7	79.0	77.8	77.2	76.3	75.7	75.2	75.1	77.5
2011	73.9	73.7	73.9	74.0	74.6	75.3	74.8	75.0	74.6	74.7	74.3	74.7	74.5
2012	73.9	74.1	75.0	75.8	76.4	77.6	77.1	77.8	77.3	76.9	76.5	76.4	76.2
2013	76.0	76.5	77.2	76.8	77.4	78.0	77.5	77.8	77.2	77.1	77.1	77.1	77.1
2014	76.4	76.5	76.7	76.7	77.3	77.8	78.0	77.9	77.3	77.4	76.9	76.8	77.1
2015	75.0	75.1	75.2	75.1	76.0	76.8	77.3	77.6	77.0	77.2	76.8	78.1	76.4
Government													
2005	235.0	240.9	241.0	241.5	243.3	238.0	207.1	205.6	233.3	238.1	240.6	237.5	233.5
2006	231.3	236.9	238.1	237.6	238.7	234.3	207.4	203.7	226.8	233.7	235.5	232.7	229.7
2007	228.5	231.8	234.1	232.7	235.4	231.2	204.9	203.7	220.2	226.0	226.5	225.1	225.0
2008	219.9	223.9	224.4	224.0	225.7	222.7	202.4	203.5	217.4	223.2	224.1	221.0	219.4
2009	216.6	220.4	221.4	223.0	221.4	219.0	197.6	197.3	211.6	216.8	217.1	214.7	214.7
2010	209.6	213.7	214.3	215.9	218.9	213.7	194.0	189.1	202.9	207.3	206.7	205.1	207.6
2011	199.2	203.5	203.6	203.6	201.0	199.6	183.3	182.2	197.5	200.6	201.6	199.4	197.9
2012	194.4	198.2	198.5	198.0	196.2	195.8	178.7	178.5	193.2	194.5	195.6	193.8	193.0
2013	188.6	192.1	192.0	191.5	189.2	189.0	172.8	171.3	186.4	189.4	189.7	187.9	186.7
2014	183.7	187.8	188.3	189.0	186.8	186.4	170.9	169.6	183.2	188.0	189.6	186.6	184.2
2015	182.0	185.8	186.7	187.3	186.7	184.0	168.4	167.5	182.3	185.0	186.6	184.5	182.2

Employment by Industry: Seattle-Tacoma-Bellevue, WA, 2005–2015

(Numbers in thousands, not seasonally adjusted)

Industry and year	January	February	March	April	May	June	July	August	September	October	November	December	Annual average
Total Nonfarm													
2005	1,605.6	1,612.9	1,624.5	1,635.1	1,649.6	1,660.7	1,658.8	1,659.6	1,661.6	1,675.5	1,690.2	1,695.2	1,652.4
2006	1,660.3	1,671.5	1,680.1	1,687.3	1,703.8	1,719.6	1,706.9	1,711.0	1,726.4	1,724.7	1,737.5	1,740.0	1,705.8
2007	1,707.4	1,727.4	1,735.1	1,740.4	1,757.1	1,772.2	1,764.9	1,766.7	1,770.4	1,776.1	1,790.6	1,790.8	1,758.3
2008	1,756.8	1,769.2	1,769.9	1,775.2	1,785.4	1,793.7	1,788.0	1,787.6	1,786.5	1,757.4	1,774.8	1,759.6	1,775.3
2009	1,716.6	1,710.3	1,700.4	1,691.5	1,695.3	1,696.3	1,682.7	1,668.3	1,677.0	1,674.6	1,673.0	1,669.6	1,688.0
2010	1,636.6	1,639.2	1,646.3	1,658.4	1,671.2	1,678.2	1,675.1	1,664.3	1,675.1	1,683.6	1,688.1	1,687.5	1,667.0
2011	1,656.3	1,664.2	1,669.1	1,683.9	1,693.0	1,703.3	1,705.2	1,698.1	1,706.4	1,711.5	1,719.3	1,718.9	1,694.1
2012	1,688.5	1,697.1	1,707.9	1,717.6	1,734.1	1,746.6	1,742.6	1,739.1	1,747.1	1,755.8	1,765.9	1,764.0	1,733.9
2013	1,737.9	1,747.6	1,754.3	1,765.1	1,781.5	1,791.4	1,791.4	1,791.5	1,798.5	1,805.0	1,815.2	1,816.8	1,783.0
2014	1,794.8	1,798.4	1,806.3	1,812.6	1,827.6	1,839.7	1,848.1	1,849.3	1,854.7	1,857.4	1,866.3	1,872.0	1,835.6
2015	1,846.4	1,851.5	1,863.0	1,872.4	1,886.4	1,904.3	1,903.8	1,903.6	1,910.5	1,913.2	1,922.1	1,922.2	1,891.6
Total Private													
2005	1,353.8	1,359.1	1,369.5	1,380.4	1,394.0	1,404.2	1,414.0	1,422.6	1,412.5	1,422.5	1,431.1	1,440.7	1,400.4
2006	1,407.3	1,414.7	1,423.1	1,431.4	1,446.7	1,462.0	1,461.1	1,473.5	1,477.2	1,470.8	1,477.7	1,485.2	1,452.6
2007	1,454.3	1,470.4	1,478.0	1,483.6	1,499.2	1,513.2	1,515.2	1,523.2	1,522.5	1,519.2	1,527.7	1,531.9	1,503.2
2008	1,498.9	1,506.1	1,508.6	1,513.6	1,522.2	1,529.1	1,531.8	1,536.5	1,530.5	1,492.7	1,503.5	1,493.8	1,513.9
2009	1,451.1	1,443.6	1,433.3	1,421.3	1,425.1	1,429.2	1,424.1	1,420.8	1,419.0	1,408.9	1,405.5	1,406.3	1,424.0
2010	1,371.9	1,373.0	1,380.0	1,390.0	1,397.0	1,407.6	1,414.8	1,415.9	1,417.3	1,418.9	1,421.0	1,425.8	1,402.8
2011	1,393.4	1,399.8	1,404.8	1,419.4	1,427.3	1,440.4	1,449.1	1,453.2	1,456.0	1,449.7	1,456.3	1,460.0	1,434.1
2012	1,428.1	1,435.6	1,444.8	1,454.0	1,469.9	1,484.9	1,486.8	1,494.7	1,494.4	1,493.0	1,501.1	1,503.9	1,474.3
2013	1,476.2	1,483.9	1,490.4	1,500.6	1,516.3	1,528.3	1,536.0	1,545.1	1,543.7	1,540.9	1,549.4	1,554.5	1,522.1
2014	1,530.6	1,533.2	1,539.9	1,545.0	1,559.2	1,573.0	1,587.5	1,597.6	1,594.4	1,589.0	1,596.5	1,605.3	1,570.9
2015	1,577.7	1,581.2	1,591.1	1,598.9	1,612.9	1,630.8	1,638.4	1,645.7	1,644.2	1,639.7	1,645.4	1,649.7	1,621.3
Goods Producing													
2005	261.4	263.7	267.6	270.3	273.5	277.3	282.7	285.3	271.6	286.1	285.5	286.3	275.9
2006	283.1	286.9	288.5	290.5	294.3	299.0	301.5	303.9	305.3	304.5	303.1	302.4	296.9
2007	299.3	304.6	305.7	307.4	311.9	317.4	319.8	322.3	322.0	320.0	318.9	316.0	313.8
2008	310.9	312.8	311.8	311.0	312.8	314.0	315.7	316.7	313.4	285.4	301.3	294.5	308.4
2009	283.7	280.8	274.1	269.7	268.4	268.1	267.2	266.0	263.9	259.8	255.5	251.8	267.4
2010	247.5	246.5	246.2	247.2	248.2	250.7	254.5	255.5	255.1	254.1	251.2	249.1	250.5
2011	244.8	245.9	246.9	249.3	251.6	255.6	260.1	262.0	263.5	262.0	260.4	259.9	255.2
2012	255.6	256.8	258.6	260.5	263.8	268.9	272.0	275.2	275.6	274.9	273.9	272.5	267.4
2013	269.8	271.4	272.8	273.5	276.1	279.8	282.6	285.5	284.7	282.6	280.9	279.9	278.3
2014	276.7	277.1	278.6	278.7	281.7	285.1	289.8	291.8	291.3	290.8	289.9	290.3	285.2
2015	288.2	288.8	291.1	291.5	293.4	296.8	300.7	300.7	300.1	295.8	294.1	294.0	294.6
Service-Providing													
2005	1,344.2	1,349.2	1,356.9	1,364.8	1,376.1	1,383.4	1,376.1	1,374.3	1,390.0	1,389.4	1,404.7	1,408.9	1,376.5
2006	1,377.2	1,384.6	1,391.6	1,396.8	1,409.5	1,420.6	1,405.4	1,407.1	1,421.1	1,420.2	1,434.4	1,437.6	1,408.8
2007	1,408.1	1,422.8	1,429.4	1,433.0	1,445.2	1,454.8	1,445.1	1,444.4	1,448.4	1,456.1	1,471.7	1,474.8	1,444.5
2008	1,445.9	1,456.4	1,458.1	1,464.2	1,472.6	1,479.7	1,472.3	1,470.9	1,473.1	1,472.0	1,473.5	1,465.1	1,467.0
2009	1,432.9	1,429.5	1,426.3	1,421.8	1,426.9	1,428.2	1,415.5	1,402.3	1,413.1	1,414.8	1,417.5	1,417.8	1,420.6
2010	1,389.1	1,392.7	1,400.1	1,411.2	1,423.0	1,427.5	1,420.6	1,408.8	1,420.0	1,429.5	1,436.9	1,438.4	1,416.5
2011	1,411.5	1,418.3	1,422.2	1,434.6	1,441.4	1,447.7	1,445.1	1,436.1	1,442.9	1,449.5	1,458.9	1,459.0	1,438.9
2012	1,432.9	1,440.3	1,449.3	1,457.1	1,470.3	1,477.7	1,470.6	1,463.9	1,471.5	1,480.9	1,492.0	1,491.5	1,466.5
2013	1,468.1	1,476.2	1,481.5	1,491.6	1,505.4	1,511.6	1,508.8	1,506.0	1,513.8	1,522.4	1,534.3	1,536.9	1,504.7
2014	1,518.1	1,521.3	1,527.7	1,533.9	1,545.9	1,554.6	1,558.3	1,557.5	1,563.4	1,566.6	1,576.4	1,581.7	1,550.5
2015	1,558.2	1,562.7	1,571.9	1,580.9	1,593.0	1,607.5	1,603.1	1,602.9	1,610.4	1,617.4	1,628.0	1,628.2	1,597.0
Mining and Logging													
2005	1.5	1.5	1.5	1.5	1.5	1.5	1.5	1.5	1.5	1.5	1.5	1.5	1.5
2006	1.4	1.5	1.5	1.5	1.5	1.5	1.5	1.5	1.5	1.5	1.5	1.5	1.5
2007	1.4	1.5	1.4	1.6	1.6	1.6	1.7	1.6	1.5	1.6	1.5	1.5	1.5
2008	1.3	1.4	1.4	1.4	1.4	1.4	1.4	1.4	1.4	1.4	1.3	1.3	1.4
2009	1.3	1.3	1.2	1.1	1.1	1.1	1.1	1.1	1.1	1.1	1.1	1.0	1.1
2010	1.0	1.1	1.0	1.0	1.1	1.1	1.1	1.1	1.1	1.1	1.0	1.0	1.1
2011	1.0	1.0	1.0	1.0	1.0	1.0	1.0	1.0	1.0	1.1	1.1	1.0	1.0
2012	1.0	1.0	1.0	1.0	1.0	1.0	1.0	1.1	1.0	1.1	1.0	1.0	1.0
2013	1.0	1.0	1.0	1.0	1.0	1.0	1.0	1.1	1.1	1.0	1.0	1.0	1.0
2014	1.0	1.0	1.0	1.0	1.0	1.0	1.0	1.0	1.0	1.1	1.1	1.1	1.0
2015	1.1	1.1	1.0	1.1	1.1	1.1	1.1	1.1	1.1	1.1	1.1	1.1	1.1

Employment by Industry: Seattle-Tacoma-Bellevue, WA, 2005–2015—*Continued*

(Numbers in thousands, not seasonally adjusted)

Industry and year	January	February	March	April	May	June	July	August	September	October	November	December	Annual average
Construction													
2005	93.1	94.9	97.1	98.9	101.1	103.2	106.5	108.7	109.9	108.9	107.9	107.9	103.2
2006	104.3	106.8	108.8	110.6	113.4	116.4	117.9	120.1	120.5	119.8	117.6	116.5	114.4
2007	114.4	117.5	119.7	121.6	124.9	128.2	128.8	131.1	130.3	128.3	126.4	124.5	124.6
2008	120.0	120.2	120.7	120.7	121.7	122.5	123.7	124.1	122.2	119.0	113.3	108.4	119.7
2009	101.2	98.8	97.0	94.8	94.8	94.9	94.7	94.0	93.1	90.6	87.0	84.3	93.8
2010	80.4	79.6	79.8	80.6	81.9	82.9	85.6	86.6	85.9	85.1	81.8	79.7	82.5
2011	75.5	75.3	75.5	76.6	78.2	80.1	82.1	83.2	83.4	82.1	79.9	79.0	79.2
2012	75.0	76.1	76.8	78.4	80.6	83.2	85.1	87.2	87.4	87.3	85.9	85.1	82.3
2013	82.4	83.8	84.5	85.7	88.0	89.9	92.6	95.0	94.5	93.7	92.5	91.1	89.5
2014	89.4	89.6	91.2	91.3	93.8	96.1	99.1	101.3	101.7	102.0	101.4	101.6	96.5
2015	99.8	100.5	102.0	103.4	105.0	107.2	109.5	109.8	109.3	107.4	106.2	106.3	105.5
Manufacturing													
2005	166.8	167.3	169.0	169.9	170.9	172.6	174.7	175.1	160.2	175.7	176.1	176.9	171.3
2006	177.4	178.6	178.2	178.4	179.4	181.1	182.1	182.3	183.3	183.2	184.0	184.4	181.0
2007	183.5	185.6	184.6	184.2	185.4	187.6	189.3	189.6	190.2	190.1	191.0	190.0	187.6
2008	189.6	191.2	189.7	188.9	189.7	190.1	190.6	191.2	189.8	165.0	186.7	184.8	187.3
2009	181.2	180.7	175.9	173.8	172.5	172.1	171.4	170.9	169.7	168.1	167.4	166.5	172.5
2010	166.1	165.8	165.4	165.6	165.2	166.7	167.8	167.8	168.1	167.9	168.4	168.4	166.9
2011	168.3	169.6	170.4	171.7	172.4	174.5	177.0	177.8	179.1	178.8	179.4	179.8	174.9
2012	179.6	179.7	180.8	181.1	182.2	184.7	185.9	186.9	187.2	186.5	187.0	186.4	184.0
2013	186.4	186.6	187.3	186.8	187.1	188.8	189.0	189.4	189.1	187.9	187.4	187.8	187.8
2014	186.3	186.5	186.4	186.4	186.9	188.0	189.7	189.5	188.6	187.7	187.4	187.6	187.6
2015	187.3	187.2	188.1	187.0	187.3	188.5	190.1	189.8	189.7	187.3	186.8	186.6	188.0
Trade, Transportation, and Utilities													
2005	307.0	305.6	306.6	307.2	310.4	312.3	313.6	315.3	315.0	315.7	322.0	327.7	313.2
2006	313.8	311.4	312.5	312.5	315.6	318.9	318.9	320.6	319.8	319.2	326.1	331.3	318.4
2007	319.5	319.0	319.5	320.1	322.9	325.3	326.8	327.4	325.8	326.7	334.3	338.2	325.5
2008	326.5	324.4	324.2	323.7	324.6	326.0	327.4	328.5	325.3	323.9	325.4	327.6	325.6
2009	312.9	307.5	304.8	301.8	303.4	303.8	304.3	303.9	303.4	301.6	304.9	308.4	305.1
2010	297.1	295.2	295.5	297.0	298.8	301.2	302.4	303.1	302.0	304.1	308.9	314.1	301.6
2011	301.7	300.5	301.4	302.7	305.1	308.0	310.5	311.5	310.2	310.3	316.2	319.8	308.2
2012	308.6	306.6	308.0	308.8	313.0	317.1	319.5	320.2	319.1	320.0	326.9	329.3	316.4
2013	319.3	317.3	317.8	319.0	323.6	326.5	329.5	331.5	330.3	332.0	339.5	343.2	327.5
2014	333.5	331.5	331.4	332.3	336.3	340.4	344.0	346.3	345.5	346.0	352.9	357.3	341.5
2015	346.8	344.8	346.4	346.2	350.1	354.6	357.0	358.9	358.7	359.2	365.5	369.4	354.8
Wholesale Trade													
2005	76.6	76.9	77.4	77.6	78.0	78.4	78.9	79.3	79.4	79.4	79.6	80.2	78.5
2006	80.2	80.4	80.9	80.7	81.3	81.8	82.1	82.2	82.2	81.8	82.1	82.2	81.5
2007	81.6	82.0	82.3	82.4	83.0	83.5	83.7	83.8	83.5	83.6	84.0	84.4	83.2
2008	83.5	83.9	84.0	84.0	84.4	84.6	84.4	84.6	84.1	83.5	83.0	82.6	83.9
2009	81.8	80.8	80.2	79.4	79.1	79.0	78.9	78.3	78.0	77.5	77.2	77.2	79.0
2010	76.1	76.4	76.5	76.8	76.9	76.9	77.0	77.0	76.7	76.8	77.0	77.0	76.8
2011	76.4	76.7	76.9	77.3	77.6	77.8	78.1	78.0	77.8	77.6	77.5	77.8	77.5
2012	77.2	77.3	77.7	78.1	78.4	78.8	79.3	79.7	79.3	79.0	79.2	79.5	78.6
2013	78.9	79.5	79.8	79.8	80.1	80.6	81.0	81.2	81.1	80.7	81.1	81.2	80.4
2014	80.9	81.2	81.0	80.7	81.2	81.7	82.6	82.7	82.9	82.2	82.5	82.8	81.9
2015	82.0	82.2	82.6	82.6	83.1	83.7	83.9	84.3	84.2	83.9	84.0	84.7	83.4
Retail Trade													
2005	170.3	168.0	168.3	169.1	171.3	172.3	173.4	174.8	173.9	175.1	180.8	184.8	173.5
2006	172.9	170.3	170.6	170.5	172.3	174.3	174.2	175.6	174.5	175.2	181.8	185.5	174.8
2007	176.2	175.1	175.0	174.9	176.7	177.8	179.3	179.6	178.5	179.4	186.7	189.3	179.0
2008	180.8	177.9	177.8	177.3	177.2	178.1	179.5	180.6	178.5	178.7	181.1	183.0	179.2
2009	170.6	167.7	166.1	164.0	165.6	166.3	166.8	167.2	166.9	166.5	170.5	173.1	167.6
2010	165.0	163.0	163.1	164.2	165.5	167.1	167.6	168.3	167.5	169.6	174.3	177.8	167.8
2011	168.3	166.6	166.5	167.0	168.9	171.0	172.2	173.3	172.0	173.4	178.9	181.3	171.6
2012	172.7	170.4	171.0	171.3	174.1	176.9	178.7	178.9	178.5	180.3	186.6	188.1	177.3
2013	180.4	178.2	178.3	179.4	182.8	184.9	187.2	188.7	187.5	189.8	196.2	199.0	186.0
2014	190.3	188.3	188.5	188.7	191.3	194.3	196.7	198.4	197.3	198.6	204.9	207.5	195.4
2015	199.6	197.7	198.8	199.2	201.6	204.7	206.1	207.6	207.3	208.7	214.1	216.2	205.1

Employment by Industry: Seattle-Tacoma-Bellevue, WA, 2005–2015—*Continued*

(Numbers in thousands, not seasonally adjusted)

Industry and year	January	February	March	April	May	June	July	August	September	October	November	December	Annual average
Transportation and Utilities													
2005	60.1	60.7	60.9	60.5	61.1	61.6	61.3	61.2	61.7	61.2	61.6	62.7	61.2
2006	60.7	60.7	61.0	61.3	62.0	62.8	62.6	62.8	63.1	62.2	62.2	63.6	62.1
2007	61.7	61.9	62.2	62.8	63.2	64.0	63.8	64.0	63.8	63.7	63.6	64.5	63.3
2008	62.2	62.6	62.4	62.4	63.0	63.3	63.5	63.3	62.7	61.7	61.3	62.0	62.5
2009	60.5	59.0	58.5	58.4	58.7	58.5	58.6	58.4	58.5	57.6	57.2	58.1	58.5
2010	56.0	55.8	55.9	56.0	56.4	57.2	57.8	57.8	57.8	57.7	57.6	59.3	57.1
2011	57.0	57.2	58.0	58.4	58.6	59.2	60.2	60.2	60.4	59.3	59.8	60.7	59.1
2012	58.7	58.9	59.3	59.4	60.5	61.4	61.5	61.6	61.3	60.7	61.1	61.7	60.5
2013	60.0	59.6	59.7	59.8	60.7	61.0	61.3	61.6	61.7	61.5	62.2	63.0	61.0
2014	62.3	62.0	61.9	62.9	63.8	64.4	64.7	65.2	65.3	65.2	65.5	67.0	64.2
2015	65.2	64.9	65.0	64.4	65.4	66.2	67.0	67.0	67.2	66.6	67.4	68.5	66.2
Information													
2005	76.2	76.8	76.6	76.8	77.1	77.3	78.1	78.8	78.1	77.6	78.4	78.9	77.6
2006	77.9	78.1	78.7	79.2	79.8	82.1	82.5	83.3	83.4	82.8	83.6	84.0	81.3
2007	83.3	84.3	83.9	84.3	85.1	85.9	86.1	86.4	86.0	85.1	86.2	86.4	85.3
2008	85.9	87.0	87.2	87.5	88.0	89.1	90.4	91.2	90.2	89.6	90.6	90.7	89.0
2009	88.9	89.4	89.1	87.8	88.4	88.6	88.9	88.4	87.6	87.0	87.3	87.1	88.2
2010	86.6	86.9	86.8	86.5	87.0	88.1	88.3	88.8	88.7	87.9	88.3	88.6	87.7
2011	87.2	88.0	87.7	87.8	88.0	89.1	90.1	90.4	89.6	88.9	89.2	88.9	88.7
2012	88.8	89.3	89.0	88.8	89.6	90.7	90.7	91.0	89.7	89.1	89.6	89.5	89.7
2013	89.0	89.8	89.3	89.6	90.3	91.2	92.5	93.1	92.2	91.6	92.3	92.4	91.1
2014	92.1	92.3	92.5	92.9	93.3	95.0	96.8	97.7	96.9	95.2	95.6	95.3	94.6
2015	93.8	94.7	94.8	95.2	96.1	97.9	99.9	100.9	100.3	100.3	100.7	101.1	98.0
Financial Activities													
2005	104.3	104.7	104.8	105.1	105.7	106.2	107.7	108.4	108.1	108.3	108.5	108.9	106.7
2006	107.6	108.0	107.8	107.9	108.1	108.3	108.6	108.5	107.8	107.5	107.3	107.6	107.9
2007	106.4	106.7	107.2	107.3	107.3	107.6	107.9	107.9	106.7	106.8	107.2	107.1	107.2
2008	106.0	106.0	105.8	105.4	106.0	105.8	105.3	105.3	104.3	102.9	102.6	102.0	104.8
2009	100.0	99.9	98.7	98.1	97.9	97.8	96.9	96.1	95.5	94.4	93.8	93.6	96.9
2010	91.9	91.7	91.7	92.4	92.2	92.3	92.9	92.3	92.0	91.9	91.6	91.9	92.1
2011	90.7	90.9	90.7	91.1	90.7	91.0	91.1	90.9	90.6	90.2	90.4	90.2	90.7
2012	89.0	89.3	89.5	89.7	90.3	90.7	91.5	91.3	90.9	91.0	91.3	91.5	90.5
2013	91.3	91.7	92.2	92.7	93.3	93.5	94.3	94.3	93.8	93.7	93.7	94.2	93.2
2014	93.1	93.3	93.6	93.7	94.0	94.5	95.2	95.5	94.9	94.7	94.7	95.0	94.4
2015	94.3	94.5	94.4	94.7	95.3	95.7	96.5	96.8	96.4	96.5	96.5	97.5	95.8
Professional and Business Services													
2005	203.6	206.2	207.4	210.1	212.0	213.8	216.8	218.9	220.6	220.4	221.3	221.2	214.4
2006	215.2	217.4	219.6	222.6	225.2	228.3	229.9	232.7	233.3	233.6	234.5	234.6	227.2
2007	228.0	232.3	234.7	235.2	237.1	239.7	240.6	242.6	243.0	242.4	243.2	244.1	238.6
2008	237.5	239.5	240.5	243.2	244.4	244.9	245.7	245.5	244.9	242.8	238.3	234.5	241.8
2009	228.3	226.3	224.4	221.4	220.0	221.1	219.9	219.5	219.7	218.8	218.4	219.2	221.4
2010	212.1	213.2	216.1	218.6	219.2	220.8	223.8	223.0	223.9	225.1	225.1	225.8	220.6
2011	220.3	222.5	223.9	228.0	227.9	229.3	232.5	233.1	233.9	234.3	234.7	234.6	229.6
2012	228.9	231.3	232.6	236.4	238.6	240.8	239.8	242.6	242.7	244.1	244.8	244.6	238.9
2013	240.2	242.3	242.8	245.2	247.0	249.1	249.5	251.9	252.2	252.8	253.5	253.2	248.3
2014	248.8	249.4	251.0	251.8	252.9	254.9	258.5	261.0	260.7	261.8	262.6	263.8	256.4
2015	258.4	259.1	261.5	264.0	265.5	268.3	270.5	272.7	273.3	273.3	275.5	273.4	268.0
Education and Health Services													
2005	195.7	197.2	198.5	199.6	200.4	198.1	194.2	194.7	198.5	200.8	201.8	201.0	198.4
2006	199.4	201.4	202.5	202.7	203.7	201.3	196.4	197.3	200.9	203.9	204.7	204.3	201.5
2007	203.1	205.6	207.2	207.5	208.9	206.2	202.4	203.0	206.5	211.6	212.9	212.5	207.3
2008	210.1	213.1	213.3	214.3	215.6	214.4	211.3	211.9	215.2	220.1	220.8	220.8	215.1
2009	220.5	222.8	223.8	223.8	225.3	224.2	220.4	220.5	224.1	229.7	230.6	230.7	224.7
2010	228.0	230.0	231.1	231.6	232.4	230.9	227.2	226.8	230.6	235.8	237.3	236.0	231.5
2011	235.0	237.5	238.2	238.6	238.6	237.4	234.2	233.6	236.8	240.0	242.0	240.9	237.7
2012	238.2	240.9	242.5	241.8	242.8	240.9	236.2	235.9	238.8	242.4	244.0	244.0	240.7
2013	240.1	244.0	244.8	245.7	245.9	243.4	240.8	240.9	244.7	248.7	250.5	250.7	245.0
2014	249.0	252.4	252.4	252.3	253.2	250.8	249.3	249.1	251.9	254.1	255.3	256.2	252.2
2015	252.8	254.9	255.4	256.5	256.6	255.3	249.9	249.9	253.3	256.9	257.6	259.0	254.8

Employment by Industry: Seattle-Tacoma-Bellevue, WA, 2005–2015—*Continued*

(Numbers in thousands, not seasonally adjusted)

Industry and year	January	February	March	April	May	June	July	August	September	October	November	December	Annual average
Leisure and Hospitality													
2005	145.1	144.0	146.5	149.9	153.1	156.7	158.2	158.5	158.5	152.1	152.1	154.7	152.5
2006	149.3	150.0	151.6	154.0	157.5	160.8	161.3	164.0	163.7	157.5	156.5	158.7	157.1
2007	153.7	155.9	157.3	159.5	163.0	167.4	168.0	169.6	169.1	163.7	161.9	164.3	162.8
2008	159.3	160.0	161.9	164.3	165.9	169.6	170.2	171.5	171.6	163.6	160.1	159.9	164.8
2009	153.3	153.3	154.4	154.9	157.8	161.3	162.0	162.1	161.5	154.8	152.6	152.9	156.7
2010	147.4	148.0	150.8	154.5	156.4	159.9	161.2	161.8	161.5	156.1	154.5	156.4	155.7
2011	150.7	151.2	152.4	157.5	160.3	164.0	163.9	165.2	165.6	158.7	158.1	160.1	159.0
2012	154.4	156.1	158.7	161.8	165.2	168.4	169.0	170.7	170.2	164.5	163.5	165.6	164.0
2013	161.2	161.6	164.5	168.3	172.8	177.0	178.1	179.5	178.1	171.7	171.1	173.2	171.4
2014	170.1	169.7	172.3	175.2	178.8	182.5	183.3	185.5	183.6	177.1	175.9	177.5	177.6
2015	174.8	175.5	177.8	181.0	185.4	190.9	192.2	194.0	191.1	187.2	185.9	185.8	185.1
Other Services													
2005	60.5	60.9	61.5	61.4	61.8	62.5	62.7	62.7	62.1	61.5	61.5	62.0	61.8
2006	61.0	61.5	61.9	62.0	62.5	63.3	63.0	63.2	63.0	61.8	61.9	62.3	62.3
2007	61.0	62.0	62.5	62.3	63.0	63.7	63.6	64.0	63.4	62.9	63.1	63.3	62.9
2008	62.7	63.3	63.9	64.2	64.9	65.3	65.8	65.9	65.6	64.4	64.4	63.8	64.5
2009	63.5	63.6	64.0	63.8	63.9	64.3	64.5	64.3	63.3	62.8	62.4	62.6	63.6
2010	61.3	61.5	61.8	62.2	62.8	63.7	64.5	64.6	63.5	63.9	64.1	63.9	63.2
2011	63.0	63.3	63.6	64.4	65.1	66.0	66.7	66.5	65.8	65.3	65.3	65.6	65.1
2012	64.6	65.3	65.9	66.2	66.6	67.4	68.1	67.8	67.4	67.0	67.1	66.9	66.7
2013	65.3	65.8	66.2	66.6	67.3	67.8	68.7	68.4	67.7	67.8	67.9	67.7	67.3
2014	67.3	67.5	68.1	68.1	69.0	69.8	70.6	70.7	69.6	69.3	69.6	69.9	69.1
2015	68.6	68.9	69.7	69.8	70.5	71.3	71.7	71.8	71.0	70.5	69.6	69.5	70.2
Government													
2005	251.8	253.8	255.0	254.7	255.6	256.5	244.8	237.0	249.1	253.0	259.1	254.5	252.1
2006	253.0	256.8	257.0	255.9	257.1	257.6	244.8	237.5	249.2	253.9	259.8	254.8	253.1
2007	253.1	257.0	257.1	256.8	257.9	259.0	249.7	243.5	247.9	256.9	262.9	258.9	255.1
2008	257.9	263.1	261.3	261.6	263.2	264.6	256.2	251.1	256.0	264.7	271.3	265.8	261.4
2009	265.5	266.7	267.1	270.2	270.2	267.1	258.6	247.5	258.0	265.7	267.5	263.3	264.0
2010	264.7	266.2	266.3	268.4	274.2	270.6	260.3	248.4	257.8	264.7	267.1	261.7	264.2
2011	262.9	264.4	264.3	264.5	265.7	262.9	256.1	244.9	250.4	261.8	263.0	258.9	260.0
2012	260.4	261.5	263.1	263.6	264.2	261.7	255.8	244.4	252.7	262.8	264.8	260.1	259.6
2013	261.7	263.7	263.9	264.5	265.2	263.1	255.4	246.4	254.8	264.1	265.8	262.3	260.9
2014	264.2	265.2	266.4	267.6	268.4	266.7	260.6	251.7	260.3	268.4	269.8	266.7	264.7
2015	268.7	270.3	271.9	273.5	273.5	273.5	265.4	257.9	266.3	273.5	276.7	272.5	270.3

Employment by Industry: Minneapolis-St. Paul-Bloomington, MN-WI, 2005–2015

(Numbers in thousands, not seasonally adjusted)

Industry and year	January	February	March	April	May	June	July	August	September	October	November	December	Annual average
Total Nonfarm													
2005	1,763.1	1,764.8	1,773.2	1,804.4	1,827.1	1,839.6	1,819.0	1,822.3	1,836.9	1,846.2	1,850.7	1,851.8	1,816.6
2006	1,807.0	1,804.0	1,813.7	1,830.5	1,851.9	1,870.0	1,840.0	1,839.5	1,847.4	1,852.9	1,861.5	1,859.0	1,839.8
2007	1,815.5	1,816.7	1,820.9	1,834.0	1,860.1	1,874.3	1,850.0	1,850.2	1,855.0	1,864.9	1,868.7	1,863.0	1,847.8
2008	1,817.6	1,820.2	1,824.2	1,834.9	1,858.1	1,868.7	1,848.5	1,847.5	1,848.0	1,850.8	1,840.5	1,825.3	1,840.4
2009	1,765.7	1,755.2	1,747.4	1,759.5	1,776.2	1,775.9	1,756.5	1,749.9	1,745.6	1,759.9	1,759.4	1,754.1	1,758.8
2010	1,705.3	1,705.2	1,710.3	1,744.9	1,765.7	1,773.6	1,752.9	1,754.1	1,759.9	1,778.7	1,780.6	1,774.9	1,750.5
2011	1,739.7	1,744.4	1,750.9	1,783.3	1,804.4	1,811.1	1,781.5	1,801.3	1,817.2	1,823.6	1,825.5	1,822.6	1,792.1
2012	1,779.3	1,783.8	1,792.8	1,815.2	1,832.5	1,842.5	1,816.0	1,824.8	1,840.5	1,851.3	1,854.4	1,847.3	1,823.4
2013	1,813.1	1,821.3	1,824.4	1,842.3	1,868.9	1,881.3	1,852.8	1,864.8	1,880.6	1,892.8	1,894.0	1,889.0	1,860.4
2014	1,843.0	1,848.1	1,850.1	1,875.3	1,903.0	1,919.0	1,901.9	1,907.4	1,908.0	1,920.6	1,924.4	1,920.7	1,893.5
2015	1,876.0	1,883.0	1,887.5	1,921.1	1,944.6	1,959.9	1,942.3	1,946.3	1,942.4	1,955.7	1,953.9	1,946.6	1,929.9
Total Private													
2005	1,513.3	1,512.0	1,520.4	1,551.6	1,574.1	1,589.9	1,587.1	1,595.2	1,590.8	1,593.8	1,599.3	1,599.2	1,568.9
2006	1,558.2	1,553.3	1,562.6	1,579.5	1,599.8	1,620.9	1,607.9	1,612.9	1,600.7	1,600.5	1,607.5	1,604.9	1,592.4
2007	1,568.9	1,567.0	1,571.8	1,585.2	1,608.6	1,626.5	1,621.3	1,626.7	1,611.8	1,616.1	1,618.4	1,613.8	1,603.0
2008	1,571.4	1,568.3	1,572.9	1,583.8	1,603.8	1,616.9	1,614.0	1,616.0	1,599.2	1,598.8	1,586.9	1,572.9	1,592.1
2009	1,520.5	1,504.3	1,497.0	1,509.6	1,524.8	1,527.3	1,520.3	1,519.5	1,505.1	1,513.0	1,511.1	1,506.8	1,513.3
2010	1,462.8	1,458.0	1,463.0	1,495.0	1,512.0	1,524.5	1,528.1	1,532.3	1,521.1	1,531.9	1,532.1	1,527.5	1,507.4
2011	1,497.9	1,496.8	1,504.5	1,536.1	1,556.1	1,567.8	1,572.4	1,582.0	1,581.2	1,580.3	1,581.7	1,579.4	1,553.0
2012	1,541.6	1,541.5	1,550.1	1,570.0	1,587.1	1,599.4	1,598.4	1,605.0	1,600.2	1,605.1	1,606.3	1,600.6	1,583.8
2013	1,572.1	1,574.3	1,578.4	1,593.0	1,620.0	1,636.0	1,635.4	1,645.1	1,636.6	1,641.6	1,641.0	1,638.3	1,617.7
2014	1,598.4	1,597.5	1,600.1	1,623.6	1,651.4	1,669.0	1,670.9	1,678.2	1,663.7	1,667.8	1,670.1	1,668.6	1,646.6
2015	1,629.9	1,631.8	1,637.8	1,668.7	1,692.8	1,708.0	1,708.9	1,715.3	1,697.3	1,702.5	1,698.8	1,692.2	1,682.0
Goods Producing													
2005	283.9	282.4	284.1	293.0	300.7	308.1	307.8	310.1	306.8	302.5	300.2	294.4	297.8
2006	285.0	282.5	284.1	290.8	297.0	304.3	303.2	304.3	299.7	298.0	294.0	287.8	294.2
2007	278.9	275.9	276.7	279.9	288.4	294.8	294.6	295.8	290.7	289.4	286.1	279.6	285.9
2008	269.8	267.1	267.0	269.6	277.7	283.4	283.5	283.9	278.8	276.6	268.8	259.6	273.8
2009	246.6	239.7	235.8	237.7	241.8	245.1	244.7	243.9	241.0	239.7	236.3	231.0	240.3
2010	220.9	217.5	217.8	226.7	232.2	237.7	241.4	241.5	239.4	239.3	236.5	231.8	231.9
2011	225.7	224.6	226.2	232.7	239.7	245.7	248.8	250.7	248.4	248.1	244.9	240.1	239.6
2012	231.7	231.0	234.2	240.5	245.8	252.0	254.3	255.6	252.7	252.3	248.8	244.3	245.3
2013	238.0	237.8	239.6	243.7	252.6	258.5	260.6	263.1	260.9	260.5	258.0	252.9	252.2
2014	245.7	244.9	247.0	252.3	261.6	268.7	271.0	272.7	269.3	269.7	266.4	263.3	261.1
2015	255.6	255.7	257.8	267.0	273.3	279.5	282.2	282.6	277.9	276.9	273.8	265.9	270.7
Service-Providing													
2005	1,479.2	1,482.4	1,489.1	1,511.4	1,526.4	1,531.5	1,511.2	1,512.2	1,530.1	1,543.7	1,550.5	1,557.4	1,518.8
2006	1,522.0	1,521.5	1,529.6	1,539.7	1,554.9	1,565.7	1,536.8	1,535.2	1,547.7	1,554.9	1,567.5	1,571.2	1,545.6
2007	1,536.6	1,540.8	1,544.2	1,554.1	1,571.7	1,579.5	1,555.4	1,554.4	1,564.3	1,575.5	1,582.6	1,583.4	1,561.9
2008	1,547.8	1,553.1	1,557.2	1,565.3	1,580.4	1,585.3	1,565.0	1,563.6	1,569.2	1,574.2	1,571.7	1,565.7	1,566.5
2009	1,519.1	1,515.5	1,511.6	1,521.8	1,534.4	1,530.8	1,511.8	1,506.0	1,504.6	1,520.2	1,523.1	1,523.1	1,518.5
2010	1,484.4	1,487.7	1,492.5	1,518.2	1,533.5	1,535.9	1,511.5	1,512.6	1,520.5	1,539.4	1,544.1	1,543.1	1,518.6
2011	1,514.0	1,519.8	1,524.7	1,550.6	1,564.7	1,565.4	1,532.7	1,550.6	1,568.8	1,575.5	1,580.6	1,582.5	1,552.5
2012	1,547.6	1,552.8	1,558.6	1,574.7	1,586.7	1,590.5	1,561.7	1,569.2	1,587.8	1,599.0	1,605.6	1,603.0	1,578.1
2013	1,575.1	1,583.5	1,584.8	1,598.6	1,616.3	1,622.8	1,592.2	1,601.7	1,619.7	1,632.3	1,636.0	1,636.1	1,608.3
2014	1,597.3	1,603.2	1,603.1	1,623.0	1,641.4	1,650.3	1,630.9	1,634.7	1,638.7	1,650.9	1,658.0	1,657.4	1,632.4
2015	1,620.4	1,627.3	1,629.7	1,654.1	1,671.3	1,680.4	1,660.1	1,663.7	1,664.5	1,678.8	1,680.1	1,680.7	1,659.3
Mining, Logging, and Construction													
2005	76.9	75.9	77.2	84.6	90.1	95.4	97.7	98.0	95.9	93.1	91.3	86.4	88.5
2006	78.4	77.5	78.4	83.2	88.7	93.0	93.2	92.8	91.5	89.0	85.6	80.3	86.0
2007	73.7	71.5	72.7	75.2	82.5	86.6	86.9	87.2	84.8	83.5	80.4	74.3	79.9
2008	67.7	66.3	66.7	68.6	75.6	79.3	80.2	80.1	77.6	75.4	70.0	63.9	72.6
2009	54.8	53.1	52.9	56.5	62.4	64.3	64.8	64.3	64.0	63.0	60.5	56.4	59.8
2010	48.3	45.7	45.8	52.4	56.2	59.5	61.7	61.9	60.8	60.6	58.0	53.0	55.3
2011	48.5	47.8	49.1	53.8	59.1	62.8	64.4	65.7	64.7	64.0	61.2	56.7	58.2
2012	50.4	50.0	52.3	57.7	61.7	65.4	67.1	68.0	66.6	66.0	62.8	58.7	60.6
2013	53.7	53.9	55.3	59.1	66.8	70.4	72.7	74.8	74.0	73.2	70.4	65.1	65.8
2014	59.3	58.7	60.1	64.7	72.4	76.6	78.4	79.4	77.7	77.2	73.6	70.0	70.7
2015	64.1	64.2	65.7	74.0	79.5	83.2	85.3	85.8	83.2	82.3	79.3	71.1	76.5

Employment by Industry: Minneapolis-St. Paul-Bloomington, MN-WI, 2005–2015—*Continued*

(Numbers in thousands, not seasonally adjusted)

Industry and year	January	February	March	April	May	June	July	August	September	October	November	December	Annual average
Manufacturing													
2005	207.0	206.5	206.9	208.4	210.6	212.7	210.1	212.1	210.9	209.4	208.9	208.0	209.3
2006	206.6	205.0	205.7	207.6	208.3	211.3	210.0	211.5	208.2	209.0	208.4	207.5	208.3
2007	205.2	204.4	204.0	204.7	205.9	208.2	207.7	208.6	205.9	205.9	205.7	205.3	206.0
2008	202.1	200.8	200.3	201.0	202.1	204.1	203.3	203.8	201.2	201.2	198.8	195.7	201.2
2009	191.8	186.6	182.9	181.2	179.4	180.8	179.9	179.6	177.0	176.7	175.8	174.6	180.5
2010	172.6	171.8	172.0	174.3	176.0	178.2	179.7	179.6	178.6	178.7	178.5	178.8	176.6
2011	177.2	176.8	177.1	178.9	180.6	182.9	184.4	185.0	183.7	184.1	183.7	183.4	181.5
2012	181.3	181.0	181.9	182.8	184.1	186.6	187.2	187.6	186.1	186.3	186.0	185.6	184.7
2013	184.3	183.9	184.3	184.6	185.8	188.1	187.9	188.3	186.9	187.3	187.6	187.8	186.4
2014	186.4	186.2	186.9	187.6	189.2	192.1	192.6	193.3	191.6	192.5	192.8	193.3	190.4
2015	191.5	191.5	192.1	193.0	193.8	196.3	196.9	196.8	194.7	194.6	194.5	194.8	194.2
Trade, Transportation, and Utilities													
2005	350.0	346.4	347.4	352.6	356.3	356.3	354.8	355.1	353.8	358.3	364.9	368.3	355.4
2006	354.2	349.4	349.6	350.8	353.9	356.7	352.4	352.5	351.5	353.6	361.8	364.3	354.2
2007	352.7	349.6	348.6	351.1	354.9	357.2	354.6	354.7	353.2	356.2	362.1	365.2	355.0
2008	352.0	346.8	347.7	347.5	350.7	350.9	347.8	347.2	344.5	345.4	348.6	348.8	348.2
2009	334.4	328.2	326.3	325.9	328.3	329.2	325.1	324.5	321.8	323.5	328.8	330.0	327.2
2010	318.7	314.7	315.5	319.8	323.0	325.9	323.6	322.8	321.7	324.6	330.3	332.9	322.8
2011	321.1	317.9	319.1	325.6	328.5	329.7	330.1	330.3	330.5	331.8	337.6	340.9	328.6
2012	329.6	324.6	326.1	329.9	333.7	335.6	332.8	333.1	331.6	334.9	342.3	343.2	333.1
2013	333.4	329.6	329.7	331.8	336.9	340.1	338.0	340.3	338.2	340.6	346.9	350.2	338.0
2014	337.8	334.5	334.7	339.2	343.2	346.2	345.1	345.9	341.8	345.2	351.5	356.2	343.4
2015	342.9	339.6	340.4	345.0	349.5	353.7	351.1	352.0	348.5	350.2	353.4	355.8	348.5
Wholesale Trade													
2005	95.2	95.3	95.2	97.7	98.6	98.9	98.7	98.8	98.0	98.7	98.7	99.0	97.7
2006	97.7	97.9	98.4	98.1	98.7	99.7	99.6	99.7	98.6	98.6	98.6	98.7	98.7
2007	97.6	97.8	97.9	98.4	99.2	100.0	100.5	100.5	98.9	98.9	98.9	99.1	99.0
2008	98.4	98.2	98.5	98.4	98.8	99.4	99.5	99.3	97.8	97.4	96.7	96.2	98.2
2009	94.5	93.4	92.6	92.6	92.4	92.8	92.7	92.0	90.1	90.2	90.3	90.2	92.0
2010	88.6	88.4	88.6	89.4	90.0	91.0	91.3	91.0	89.7	90.3	90.3	90.3	89.9
2011	89.9	89.9	90.2	91.7	92.2	92.6	93.6	93.7	92.7	92.6	92.6	92.7	92.0
2012	92.3	92.2	92.6	93.8	94.5	95.6	95.6	95.1	94.0	94.1	94.1	94.3	94.0
2013	93.8	93.8	93.9	94.2	95.0	95.9	96.1	96.0	95.0	95.0	95.2	95.2	94.9
2014	94.6	94.8	94.9	95.4	96.3	97.3	97.5	97.3	96.1	96.3	96.5	96.7	96.1
2015	95.5	95.4	95.6	96.4	96.9	98.0	98.5	98.1	96.6	97.5	96.9	97.3	96.9
Retail Trade													
2005	186.4	182.5	183.1	186.8	189.0	189.2	187.8	188.7	187.8	191.5	197.9	201.2	189.3
2006	189.7	185.3	185.0	186.8	188.8	191.0	188.5	188.7	186.3	188.6	195.5	198.4	189.4
2007	189.5	185.5	185.4	186.5	189.1	190.9	189.2	189.3	187.0	189.5	195.5	197.4	189.6
2008	187.3	182.2	182.5	182.7	185.0	185.5	184.1	183.9	180.7	181.9	185.7	185.8	183.9
2009	176.4	171.9	170.4	170.7	173.4	174.8	172.7	173.3	169.8	171.3	175.9	177.1	173.1
2010	169.0	165.6	165.9	169.1	171.3	173.3	172.1	172.6	169.8	171.6	176.4	178.3	171.3
2011	169.2	166.0	166.4	170.6	172.8	174.3	174.5	175.3	173.6	174.7	180.4	182.7	173.4
2012	174.0	169.4	170.3	172.6	175.1	176.9	175.6	176.1	173.9	176.6	183.5	183.9	175.7
2013	176.3	172.4	172.6	174.3	177.6	180.6	179.8	181.1	178.2	179.4	185.0	187.6	178.7
2014	178.2	175.1	175.2	178.1	180.8	183.4	183.4	183.9	179.5	181.9	187.6	190.6	181.5
2015	181.3	178.1	178.5	181.3	185.1	188.8	187.5	188.6	184.5	185.5	188.8	189.4	184.8
Transportation and Utilities													
2005	68.4	68.6	69.1	68.1	68.7	68.2	68.3	67.6	68.0	68.1	68.3	68.1	68.3
2006	66.8	66.2	66.2	65.9	66.4	66.0	64.3	64.1	66.6	66.4	67.7	67.2	66.2
2007	65.6	66.3	65.3	66.2	66.6	66.3	64.9	64.9	67.3	67.8	67.7	68.7	66.5
2008	66.3	66.4	66.7	66.4	66.9	66.0	64.2	64.0	66.0	66.1	66.2	66.8	66.0
2009	63.5	62.9	63.3	62.6	62.5	61.6	59.7	59.2	61.9	62.0	62.6	62.7	62.0
2010	61.1	60.7	61.0	61.3	61.7	61.6	60.2	59.2	62.2	62.7	63.6	64.3	61.6
2011	62.0	62.0	62.5	63.3	63.5	62.8	62.0	61.3	64.2	64.5	64.6	65.5	63.2
2012	63.3	63.0	63.2	63.5	64.1	63.1	61.6	61.9	63.7	64.2	64.7	65.0	63.4
2013	63.3	63.4	63.2	63.3	64.3	63.6	62.1	63.2	65.0	66.2	66.7	67.4	64.3
2014	65.0	64.6	64.6	65.7	66.1	65.5	64.2	64.7	66.2	67.0	67.4	68.9	65.8
2015	66.1	66.1	66.3	67.3	67.5	66.9	65.1	65.3	67.4	67.2	67.7	69.1	66.8

Employment by Industry: Minneapolis-St. Paul-Bloomington, MN-WI, 2005–2015—*Continued*

(Numbers in thousands, not seasonally adjusted)

Industry and year	January	February	March	April	May	June	July	August	September	October	November	December	Annual average
Information													
2005	43.0	43.0	43.1	44.6	44.6	44.8	44.1	43.5	43.2	43.0	43.2	43.4	43.6
2006	43.0	42.8	43.1	42.5	42.9	43.1	42.8	43.1	42.5	42.4	42.7	43.0	42.8
2007	43.1	43.2	43.3	43.4	43.5	43.7	43.6	43.7	43.2	43.2	43.1	43.4	43.4
2008	43.0	42.8	43.0	43.1	43.0	43.1	43.4	43.3	43.2	42.8	43.0	42.3	43.0
2009	41.8	41.7	41.6	41.2	41.2	41.1	41.3	41.2	40.7	40.5	40.6	40.3	41.1
2010	40.3	40.3	40.3	40.4	40.1	40.2	40.7	40.7	40.3	40.4	40.3	40.2	40.4
2011	40.6	40.2	40.0	40.7	40.6	40.8	41.3	41.6	41.2	41.1	41.0	41.1	40.9
2012	40.0	40.1	40.2	40.6	40.9	40.8	40.9	40.9	40.7	40.9	40.8	40.9	40.6
2013	40.2	40.2	40.2	40.3	40.2	40.3	40.8	40.5	40.0	39.9	40.0	40.2	40.2
2014	39.6	39.6	39.3	39.3	39.4	39.8	40.0	39.9	39.2	39.4	39.3	39.6	39.5
2015	38.7	38.5	38.5	38.6	38.9	39.4	39.2	40.0	39.2	39.2	39.2	39.4	39.1
Financial Activities													
2005	143.1	143.2	143.5	144.7	145.4	147.6	147.4	148.0	147.0	146.5	146.8	147.5	145.9
2006	147.0	147.1	147.3	146.0	146.6	147.8	147.0	146.6	145.5	145.3	145.4	145.8	146.5
2007	144.8	145.3	145.2	144.4	144.7	146.3	145.8	145.8	144.6	144.6	144.7	145.1	145.1
2008	142.8	143.1	143.1	143.0	143.0	143.8	144.5	144.0	142.4	141.9	141.5	142.1	142.9
2009	140.2	139.8	139.3	138.9	139.4	139.9	140.1	139.7	138.9	139.0	138.9	139.4	139.5
2010	137.6	137.5	137.3	137.8	138.2	139.6	140.2	140.5	139.7	140.6	141.0	141.4	139.3
2011	140.7	140.9	140.9	140.5	140.8	141.3	142.2	142.5	141.5	141.3	141.4	141.7	141.3
2012	142.0	142.4	142.5	144.2	144.8	144.6	144.5	144.4	143.4	144.1	144.1	144.3	143.8
2013	144.0	144.0	143.9	143.9	144.4	146.0	146.4	146.4	145.0	145.2	145.1	145.4	145.0
2014	144.3	144.1	144.1	143.4	144.0	145.5	145.8	145.6	144.0	144.4	144.6	145.0	144.6
2015	145.7	145.8	145.8	146.9	147.9	149.3	150.4	150.5	148.3	147.5	147.5	148.8	147.9
Professional and Business Services													
2005	247.1	247.6	250.2	256.6	258.7	261.8	261.8	264.1	265.4	269.5	269.4	269.3	260.1
2006	263.1	263.7	265.0	268.9	272.0	276.8	273.7	275.5	274.2	275.3	276.5	276.4	271.8
2007	268.6	269.9	271.4	271.9	274.1	278.1	278.9	281.6	278.3	280.7	280.8	279.4	276.1
2008	271.9	272.8	272.5	274.6	276.7	279.2	280.5	280.5	279.0	279.3	276.2	273.6	276.4
2009	260.8	256.8	254.7	257.5	258.4	259.1	258.6	260.0	256.6	261.8	262.4	262.5	259.1
2010	253.7	254.6	254.3	261.7	263.8	266.7	270.5	272.0	268.8	272.5	273.5	272.9	265.4
2011	266.7	267.1	268.8	276.3	277.5	280.5	285.5	288.0	288.0	289.5	289.8	289.7	280.6
2012	280.7	281.0	281.6	283.7	285.3	287.8	289.6	291.6	290.2	292.8	292.3	291.7	287.4
2013	284.7	287.2	287.2	288.7	290.7	294.4	295.6	297.3	295.6	299.6	298.2	297.8	293.1
2014	289.2	289.5	288.9	292.7	296.3	299.4	302.2	303.5	301.1	304.3	306.6	302.9	298.1
2015	295.2	296.1	295.5	302.3	304.7	305.1	306.7	306.9	302.3	308.2	308.2	305.1	303.0
Education and Health Services													
2005	220.0	223.8	224.9	226.1	227.5	225.5	225.5	226.6	229.4	232.2	234.5	235.6	227.6
2006	233.4	235.4	237.7	240.8	242.0	240.8	240.9	241.0	242.3	245.3	248.1	248.7	241.4
2007	248.3	250.5	251.8	254.6	255.8	254.2	252.5	253.2	254.0	258.2	260.4	259.8	254.4
2008	257.1	260.0	261.5	264.2	263.6	261.7	260.9	261.0	263.3	268.5	269.5	268.9	263.4
2009	266.1	268.7	269.5	272.4	272.3	267.3	266.4	265.5	267.0	271.9	273.0	273.2	269.4
2010	267.7	270.4	272.2	274.8	275.4	271.8	268.8	270.2	272.3	277.5	278.9	277.9	273.2
2011	276.8	279.9	280.5	284.3	284.7	280.7	276.5	278.5	283.1	286.4	287.7	288.1	282.3
2012	285.2	289.2	289.6	289.3	289.3	285.0	283.2	284.5	290.8	294.5	295.7	295.1	289.3
2013	294.3	298.0	297.9	300.6	301.9	297.4	295.1	296.9	300.9	304.5	306.2	305.6	299.9
2014	301.4	304.6	304.8	307.4	308.2	304.5	303.1	304.8	308.5	311.2	312.3	312.6	307.0
2015	307.5	311.6	312.6	314.9	315.9	311.8	311.4	313.5	317.7	320.6	320.8	321.1	315.0
Leisure and Hospitality													
2005	150.6	150.0	151.3	156.2	161.9	167.5	167.5	169.1	166.9	163.6	162.2	161.9	160.7
2006	156.9	156.8	158.8	162.2	167.5	172.4	169.5	171.2	167.2	162.5	160.3	160.2	163.8
2007	156.6	156.9	157.7	163.1	169.8	174.1	172.9	173.6	170.6	166.3	162.9	162.7	165.6
2008	157.4	157.1	158.9	162.1	169.4	173.8	172.9	174.9	169.0	165.1	160.6	159.1	165.0
2009	154.1	152.8	153.1	158.4	165.6	167.1	166.3	167.1	162.7	159.4	154.3	153.7	159.6
2010	148.5	147.4	149.3	157.2	162.7	164.8	165.0	166.5	162.6	159.7	155.0	153.9	157.7
2011	150.5	150.1	152.5	158.7	166.7	170.6	168.8	170.8	169.7	163.9	161.0	159.6	161.9
2012	155.2	155.8	158.3	163.7	168.9	173.6	173.6	175.3	172.5	167.1	164.0	162.9	165.9
2013	160.0	159.8	161.7	165.9	174.1	179.2	179.2	180.5	176.7	172.9	168.4	168.0	170.5
2014	163.1	163.1	163.8	170.6	179.2	184.2	183.0	185.0	180.2	174.0	170.0	170.1	173.9
2015	167.1	167.1	169.2	175.0	183.4	188.8	187.8	189.4	184.6	179.2	175.1	174.9	178.5

Employment by Industry: Minneapolis-St. Paul-Bloomington, MN-WI, 2005–2015—*Continued*

(Numbers in thousands, not seasonally adjusted)

Industry and year	January	February	March	April	May	June	July	August	September	October	November	December	Annual average
Other Services													
2005............	75.6	75.6	75.9	77.8	79.0	78.3	78.2	78.7	78.3	78.2	78.1	78.8	77.7
2006............	75.6	75.6	77.0	77.5	77.9	79.0	78.4	78.7	77.8	78.1	78.7	78.7	77.8
2007............	75.9	75.7	77.1	76.8	77.4	78.1	78.4	78.3	77.2	77.5	78.3	78.6	77.4
2008............	77.4	78.6	79.2	79.7	79.7	81.0	80.5	81.2	79.0	79.2	78.7	78.5	79.4
2009............	76.5	76.6	76.7	77.6	77.8	78.5	77.8	77.6	76.4	77.2	76.8	76.7	77.2
2010............	75.4	75.6	76.3	76.6	76.6	77.8	77.9	78.1	76.3	77.3	76.6	76.5	76.8
2011............	75.8	76.1	76.5	77.3	77.6	78.5	79.2	79.6	78.8	78.2	78.3	78.2	77.8
2012............	77.2	77.4	77.6	78.1	78.4	80.0	79.5	79.6	78.3	78.5	78.3	78.2	78.4
2013............	77.5	77.7	78.2	78.1	79.2	80.1	79.7	80.1	79.3	78.4	78.2	78.2	78.7
2014............	77.3	77.2	77.5	78.7	79.5	80.7	80.7	80.8	79.6	79.6	79.4	78.9	79.2
2015............	77.2	77.4	78.0	79.0	79.2	80.4	80.1	80.4	78.8	80.7	80.8	81.2	79.4
Government													
2005............	249.8	252.8	252.8	252.8	253.0	249.7	231.9	227.1	246.1	252.4	251.4	252.6	247.7
2006............	248.8	250.7	251.1	251.0	252.1	249.1	232.1	226.6	246.7	252.4	254.0	254.1	247.4
2007............	246.6	249.7	249.1	248.8	251.5	247.8	228.7	223.5	243.2	248.8	250.3	249.2	244.8
2008............	246.2	251.9	251.3	251.1	254.3	251.8	234.5	231.5	248.8	252.0	253.6	252.4	248.3
2009............	245.2	250.9	250.4	249.9	251.4	248.6	236.2	230.4	240.5	246.9	248.3	247.3	245.5
2010............	242.5	247.2	247.3	249.9	253.7	249.1	224.8	221.8	238.8	246.8	248.5	247.4	243.2
2011............	241.8	247.6	246.4	247.2	248.3	243.3	209.1	219.3	236.0	243.3	243.8	243.2	239.1
2012............	237.7	242.3	242.7	245.2	245.4	243.1	217.6	219.8	240.3	246.2	248.1	246.7	239.6
2013............	241.0	247.0	246.0	249.3	248.9	245.3	217.4	219.7	244.0	251.2	253.0	250.7	242.8
2014............	244.6	250.6	250.0	251.7	251.6	250.0	231.0	229.2	244.3	252.8	254.3	252.1	246.9
2015............	246.1	251.2	249.7	252.4	251.8	251.9	233.4	231.0	245.1	253.2	255.1	254.4	247.9

Employment by Industry: San Diego-Carlsbad, CA, 2005–2015

(Numbers in thousands, not seasonally adjusted)

Industry and year	January	February	March	April	May	June	July	August	September	October	November	December	Annual average
Total Nonfarm													
2005	1,268.1	1,276.4	1,283.3	1,292.7	1,297.7	1,303.1	1,291.8	1,295.0	1,300.0	1,299.9	1,309.1	1,317.0	1,294.5
2006	1,290.9	1,300.5	1,307.3	1,308.4	1,316.9	1,325.9	1,311.2	1,315.5	1,320.1	1,320.8	1,331.0	1,333.8	1,315.2
2007	1,303.2	1,311.7	1,319.5	1,317.8	1,326.4	1,335.0	1,325.8	1,326.4	1,325.8	1,324.9	1,331.5	1,337.7	1,323.8
2008	1,307.0	1,315.5	1,320.5	1,320.1	1,324.4	1,328.5	1,316.8	1,316.5	1,312.5	1,311.7	1,310.9	1,307.5	1,316.0
2009	1,270.8	1,266.3	1,264.0	1,256.2	1,257.7	1,257.0	1,234.1	1,234.4	1,229.9	1,240.4	1,246.4	1,248.0	1,250.4
2010	1,218.8	1,222.6	1,227.3	1,240.7	1,251.8	1,253.5	1,242.1	1,245.1	1,243.1	1,248.5	1,253.3	1,257.3	1,242.0
2011	1,234.9	1,242.4	1,246.3	1,249.0	1,252.1	1,255.8	1,245.7	1,248.7	1,252.9	1,258.5	1,267.7	1,270.4	1,252.0
2012	1,246.5	1,255.4	1,262.3	1,280.0	1,289.5	1,297.1	1,282.4	1,288.4	1,288.4	1,299.5	1,310.8	1,314.0	1,284.5
2013	1,289.8	1,298.3	1,305.4	1,311.1	1,316.3	1,322.5	1,311.5	1,316.3	1,317.4	1,332.9	1,344.5	1,346.7	1,317.7
2014	1,316.9	1,326.0	1,333.3	1,337.0	1,343.7	1,351.4	1,340.0	1,348.6	1,348.2	1,361.1	1,374.5	1,377.2	1,346.5
2015	1,354.3	1,360.6	1,367.2	1,375.1	1,384.9	1,389.2	1,390.1	1,395.0	1,392.1	1,402.2	1,414.2	1,412.4	1,386.4
Total Private													
2005	1,053.1	1,059.6	1,065.7	1,074.7	1,079.0	1,084.0	1,083.9	1,089.7	1,088.5	1,083.9	1,091.2	1,099.5	1,079.4
2006	1,074.7	1,081.7	1,087.6	1,088.5	1,096.9	1,104.7	1,100.6	1,107.3	1,105.6	1,100.6	1,108.1	1,110.7	1,097.3
2007	1,081.7	1,088.0	1,094.5	1,092.7	1,101.4	1,109.3	1,110.9	1,114.2	1,107.7	1,100.5	1,105.6	1,110.6	1,101.4
2008	1,082.8	1,088.0	1,091.8	1,092.3	1,095.6	1,098.4	1,100.1	1,101.2	1,092.4	1,084.9	1,082.9	1,080.1	1,090.9
2009	1,044.6	1,039.4	1,035.4	1,026.4	1,028.2	1,027.0	1,019.6	1,022.2	1,013.8	1,014.1	1,018.8	1,021.4	1,025.9
2010	994.2	996.9	999.9	1,005.9	1,011.1	1,015.5	1,016.5	1,021.3	1,015.5	1,016.6	1,020.0	1,025.1	1,011.5
2011	1,004.8	1,009.5	1,012.5	1,015.2	1,019.4	1,022.2	1,026.0	1,031.5	1,029.7	1,028.9	1,036.6	1,040.6	1,023.1
2012	1,019.8	1,026.0	1,031.4	1,049.2	1,058.2	1,065.0	1,064.3	1,069.4	1,065.4	1,070.1	1,078.7	1,082.8	1,056.7
2013	1,062.2	1,068.3	1,073.0	1,079.2	1,084.0	1,088.5	1,091.0	1,095.4	1,091.5	1,101.6	1,110.6	1,113.6	1,088.2
2014	1,087.6	1,093.6	1,098.9	1,102.3	1,108.5	1,113.7	1,117.7	1,125.3	1,121.1	1,127.2	1,137.9	1,141.1	1,114.6
2015	1,119.8	1,124.8	1,129.6	1,137.5	1,146.5	1,149.4	1,162.5	1,167.6	1,160.3	1,163.3	1,173.5	1,171.8	1,150.6
Goods Producing													
2005	189.1	191.8	193.7	195.1	196.9	198.0	198.9	199.0	198.1	196.3	195.9	196.7	195.8
2006	194.3	196.2	197.5	196.7	198.9	200.4	198.5	198.9	198.2	196.1	195.7	194.7	197.2
2007	189.9	190.5	191.5	190.0	191.7	193.2	192.3	191.7	189.6	187.1	186.0	185.4	189.9
2008	181.1	181.1	181.4	180.4	181.0	181.7	181.3	180.7	179.1	177.2	174.7	172.3	179.3
2009	168.3	165.5	164.2	160.6	159.5	158.6	156.7	156.1	154.0	153.0	152.5	152.1	158.4
2010	150.5	149.5	150.3	151.8	152.2	152.0	151.9	152.3	151.0	150.3	150.4	150.5	151.1
2011	149.5	150.0	150.3	150.5	151.3	152.1	152.4	153.3	152.8	152.8	152.4	152.3	151.6
2012	150.2	150.5	151.5	153.3	154.8	156.1	156.8	157.5	157.0	157.4	158.4	158.1	155.1
2013	156.6	157.5	158.1	158.9	159.1	160.2	161.2	162.0	161.6	162.1	163.1	163.1	160.3
2014	161.3	161.8	162.2	163.1	164.3	165.0	166.8	167.9	168.0	169.4	170.1	170.1	165.8
2015	168.9	169.8	171.3	172.5	174.0	175.1	178.0	179.4	178.4	177.8	179.0	178.5	175.2
Service-Providing													
2005	1,079.0	1,084.6	1,089.6	1,097.6	1,100.8	1,105.1	1,092.9	1,096.0	1,101.9	1,103.6	1,113.2	1,120.3	1,098.7
2006	1,096.6	1,104.3	1,109.8	1,111.7	1,118.0	1,125.5	1,112.7	1,116.6	1,121.9	1,124.7	1,135.3	1,139.1	1,118.0
2007	1,113.3	1,121.2	1,128.0	1,127.8	1,134.7	1,141.8	1,133.5	1,134.7	1,136.2	1,137.8	1,145.5	1,152.3	1,133.9
2008	1,125.9	1,134.4	1,139.1	1,139.7	1,143.4	1,146.8	1,135.5	1,135.8	1,133.4	1,134.5	1,136.2	1,135.2	1,136.7
2009	1,102.5	1,100.8	1,099.8	1,095.6	1,098.2	1,098.4	1,077.4	1,078.3	1,075.9	1,087.4	1,093.9	1,095.9	1,092.0
2010	1,068.3	1,073.1	1,077.0	1,088.9	1,099.6	1,101.5	1,090.2	1,092.8	1,092.1	1,098.2	1,102.9	1,106.8	1,091.0
2011	1,085.4	1,092.4	1,096.0	1,098.5	1,100.8	1,103.7	1,093.3	1,095.4	1,100.1	1,105.7	1,115.3	1,118.1	1,100.4
2012	1,096.3	1,104.9	1,110.8	1,126.7	1,134.7	1,141.0	1,125.6	1,130.9	1,131.4	1,142.1	1,152.4	1,155.9	1,129.4
2013	1,133.2	1,140.8	1,147.3	1,152.2	1,157.2	1,162.3	1,150.3	1,154.3	1,155.8	1,170.8	1,181.4	1,183.6	1,157.4
2014	1,155.6	1,164.2	1,171.1	1,173.9	1,179.4	1,186.4	1,173.2	1,180.7	1,180.2	1,191.7	1,204.4	1,207.1	1,180.7
2015	1,185.4	1,190.8	1,195.9	1,202.6	1,210.9	1,214.1	1,212.1	1,215.6	1,213.7	1,224.4	1,235.2	1,233.9	1,211.2
Mining and Logging													
2005	0.4	0.4	0.4	0.4	0.4	0.4	0.4	0.4	0.4	0.4	0.4	0.4	0.4
2006	0.5	0.4	0.4	0.4	0.5	0.5	0.5	0.5	0.5	0.5	0.5	0.5	0.5
2007	0.4	0.4	0.4	0.4	0.4	0.4	0.4	0.4	0.4	0.4	0.4	0.4	0.4
2008	0.4	0.4	0.4	0.4	0.4	0.4	0.4	0.4	0.4	0.4	0.4	0.4	0.4
2009	0.4	0.4	0.4	0.4	0.4	0.4	0.4	0.4	0.4	0.3	0.3	0.3	0.4
2010	0.4	0.4	0.4	0.4	0.4	0.4	0.4	0.4	0.4	0.4	0.4	0.4	0.4
2011	0.4	0.4	0.4	0.4	0.5	0.4	0.5	0.5	0.5	0.4	0.4	0.4	0.4
2012	0.4	0.4	0.4	0.4	0.4	0.4	0.4	0.4	0.4	0.4	0.4	0.4	0.4
2013	0.4	0.4	0.4	0.4	0.4	0.4	0.4	0.4	0.4	0.4	0.4	0.4	0.4
2014	0.4	0.4	0.4	0.4	0.4	0.4	0.4	0.4	0.5	0.5	0.4	0.4	0.4
2015	0.4	0.4	0.4	0.4	0.4	0.4	0.4	0.4	0.4	0.4	0.4	0.4	0.4

Employment by Industry: San Diego-Carlsbad, CA, 2005–2015—*Continued*

(Numbers in thousands, not seasonally adjusted)

Industry and year	January	February	March	April	May	June	July	August	September	October	November	December	Annual average
Construction													
2005	84.1	86.6	88.5	89.9	91.5	92.7	93.4	93.7	93.5	91.9	91.6	92.4	90.8
2006	90.5	91.8	92.5	92.1	94.1	95.1	93.4	94.2	93.7	92.2	91.6	90.7	92.7
2007	86.8	87.6	88.3	87.9	89.5	90.9	89.1	88.8	87.0	83.9	82.4	81.3	87.0
2008	78.0	78.0	77.9	77.0	77.5	77.9	77.7	76.9	75.7	73.8	72.0	70.2	76.1
2009	66.0	64.2	64.0	62.1	62.1	61.7	60.5	60.4	58.8	58.3	58.0	57.5	61.1
2010	55.7	54.8	55.1	55.7	56.2	56.1	56.2	56.3	55.3	54.5	54.5	54.1	55.4
2011	53.6	54.2	54.3	54.6	55.1	55.4	55.8	56.6	56.0	56.1	55.6	55.1	55.2
2012	54.1	54.1	55.1	56.0	57.0	58.1	57.7	58.2	57.9	58.2	58.9	58.3	57.0
2013	57.9	58.5	58.9	59.8	60.2	61.4	61.9	62.7	62.2	62.3	62.9	62.6	60.9
2014	61.4	61.6	61.8	62.1	63.0	63.2	64.4	65.3	65.3	66.0	66.2	65.8	63.8
2015	65.0	65.6	66.4	67.5	68.6	69.5	71.4	72.5	72.1	71.9	72.2	71.4	69.5
Manufacturing													
2005	104.6	104.8	104.8	104.8	105.0	104.9	105.1	104.9	104.2	104.0	103.9	103.9	104.6
2006	103.3	104.0	104.6	104.2	104.3	104.8	104.6	104.2	104.0	103.4	103.6	103.5	104.0
2007	102.7	102.5	102.8	101.7	101.8	101.9	102.8	102.5	102.2	102.8	103.2	103.7	102.6
2008	102.7	102.7	103.1	103.0	103.1	103.4	103.2	103.4	103.0	103.0	102.3	101.7	102.9
2009	101.9	100.9	99.8	98.1	97.0	96.5	95.8	95.3	94.8	94.4	94.2	94.3	96.9
2010	94.4	94.3	94.8	95.7	95.6	95.5	95.3	95.6	95.3	95.4	95.5	96.0	95.3
2011	95.5	95.4	95.6	95.5	95.7	96.3	96.1	96.2	96.3	96.3	96.4	96.8	96.0
2012	95.7	96.0	96.0	96.9	97.4	97.6	98.7	98.9	98.7	98.8	99.1	99.4	97.8
2013	98.3	98.6	98.8	98.7	98.5	98.4	98.9	98.9	99.0	99.4	99.8	100.1	99.0
2014	99.5	99.8	100.0	100.6	100.9	101.4	102.0	102.2	102.3	102.9	103.4	103.9	101.6
2015	103.5	103.8	104.5	104.6	105.0	105.2	106.2	106.5	105.9	105.5	106.4	106.7	105.3
Trade, Transportation, and Utilities													
2005	217.8	216.3	215.8	215.6	216.7	216.9	217.9	219.0	220.2	220.5	226.4	231.5	219.6
2006	220.9	219.5	219.1	218.5	219.7	220.2	220.3	221.5	221.6	222.6	229.6	233.0	222.2
2007	222.4	220.5	220.0	219.0	220.4	220.9	222.0	223.2	221.7	221.1	226.9	230.6	222.4
2008	219.6	217.0	216.0	216.0	215.0	215.1	216.4	215.4	214.4	213.5	215.9	217.2	216.0
2009	204.3	201.0	199.1	197.4	198.5	198.2	197.0	197.1	196.6	197.9	202.7	205.3	199.6
2010	195.0	193.5	192.7	194.0	195.1	196.0	196.9	197.7	197.0	198.6	204.3	207.7	197.4
2011	198.4	196.2	195.9	197.2	197.9	198.8	200.3	201.3	201.6	202.6	209.1	212.2	201.0
2012	204.5	202.2	201.9	204.3	205.9	206.7	207.0	207.4	207.7	209.6	218.6	220.3	208.0
2013	210.4	208.7	208.6	208.9	210.1	210.6	211.0	211.6	210.4	213.3	221.2	223.6	212.4
2014	213.6	212.2	211.0	210.8	211.8	213.1	213.5	214.4	213.9	215.6	223.4	226.2	215.0
2015	216.7	215.4	214.5	214.9	216.5	216.5	219.1	219.8	218.2	221.0	226.8	228.8	219.0
Wholesale Trade													
2005	42.4	42.9	42.8	43.4	43.7	43.8	43.9	44.0	44.3	44.3	44.6	44.6	43.7
2006	44.4	45.0	44.9	45.1	45.5	45.4	45.2	45.3	45.2	45.1	45.3	45.4	45.2
2007	44.8	45.3	45.4	45.3	45.8	45.8	46.1	46.0	45.8	45.5	45.7	45.6	45.6
2008	44.9	45.3	45.1	45.6	45.0	44.8	45.4	45.3	44.9	44.7	44.4	44.3	45.0
2009	42.2	42.1	41.5	41.0	41.0	40.5	40.0	39.9	39.6	40.0	39.9	39.9	40.6
2010	38.8	39.0	38.8	39.4	39.8	40.0	40.3	40.5	40.5	41.3	41.7	42.0	40.2
2011	40.7	41.0	41.0	41.3	41.4	41.4	41.4	41.6	41.6	41.9	42.0	42.1	41.5
2012	41.8	42.4	42.3	43.2	43.7	43.4	43.8	44.0	43.8	44.3	44.6	44.4	43.5
2013	44.0	44.6	44.4	43.9	44.2	43.7	43.4	43.4	43.1	44.1	44.2	44.0	43.9
2014	43.3	44.0	43.7	43.5	43.6	43.8	43.5	43.8	43.6	43.4	43.7	44.0	43.7
2015	42.9	43.8	43.4	43.7	44.0	43.8	44.6	44.6	44.5	44.8	44.2	44.0	44.0
Retail Trade													
2005	146.9	144.9	144.5	144.0	144.6	144.9	145.6	146.7	147.5	148.2	153.7	158.2	147.5
2006	148.3	146.3	145.9	145.1	145.8	146.1	146.3	147.4	147.4	148.7	155.2	157.8	148.4
2007	149.5	146.9	146.6	145.8	146.4	146.4	146.7	147.9	146.6	146.7	151.9	155.2	148.1
2008	145.7	142.3	141.7	141.5	141.0	141.3	141.9	141.1	140.5	140.2	143.0	144.2	142.0
2009	134.2	131.6	130.3	129.2	130.3	130.1	129.7	129.9	129.8	130.9	136.0	138.2	131.7
2010	130.0	128.4	127.8	128.3	128.7	129.3	129.8	130.4	129.8	130.9	136.1	138.7	130.7
2011	131.6	129.5	129.1	130.1	130.7	131.4	132.8	133.4	133.6	134.7	141.0	143.3	133.4
2012	136.4	133.4	133.0	134.2	135.0	135.6	135.5	135.8	136.2	137.9	146.3	147.4	137.2
2013	139.2	137.0	137.0	137.5	138.4	139.4	140.1	140.9	140.4	142.6	150.1	152.4	141.3
2014	143.6	141.5	140.9	140.9	141.4	142.2	142.8	143.7	143.2	145.0	152.3	154.1	143.3
2015	146.2	144.1	143.6	143.8	144.8	144.7	146.0	146.8	145.4	147.7	153.5	155.3	146.8

Employment by Industry: San Diego-Carlsbad, CA, 2005–2015—*Continued*

(Numbers in thousands, not seasonally adjusted)

Industry and year	January	February	March	April	May	June	July	August	September	October	November	December	Annual average
Transportation and Utilities													
2005	28.5	28.5	28.5	28.2	28.4	28.2	28.4	28.3	28.4	28.0	28.1	28.7	28.4
2006	28.2	28.2	28.3	28.3	28.4	28.7	28.8	28.8	29.0	28.8	29.1	29.8	28.7
2007	28.1	28.3	28.0	27.9	28.2	28.7	29.2	29.3	29.3	28.9	29.3	29.8	28.8
2008	29.0	29.4	29.2	28.9	29.0	29.0	29.1	29.0	29.0	28.6	28.5	28.7	29.0
2009	27.9	27.3	27.3	27.2	27.2	27.6	27.3	27.3	27.2	27.0	26.8	27.2	27.3
2010	26.2	26.1	26.1	26.3	26.6	26.7	26.8	26.8	26.7	26.4	26.5	27.0	26.5
2011	26.1	25.7	25.8	25.8	25.8	26.0	26.1	26.3	26.4	26.0	26.1	26.8	26.1
2012	26.3	26.4	26.6	26.9	27.2	27.7	27.7	27.6	27.7	27.4	27.7	28.5	27.3
2013	27.2	27.1	27.2	27.5	27.5	27.5	27.5	27.3	26.9	26.6	26.9	27.2	27.2
2014	26.7	26.7	26.4	26.4	26.8	27.1	27.2	26.9	27.1	27.2	27.4	28.1	27.0
2015	27.6	27.5	27.5	27.4	27.7	28.0	28.5	28.4	28.3	28.5	29.1	29.5	28.2
Information													
2005	32.8	32.9	32.7	32.7	32.8	32.7	32.7	32.5	32.2	32.1	32.3	32.3	32.6
2006	31.9	31.8	31.5	31.2	31.3	31.6	32.1	32.0	31.4	31.8	31.7	31.9	31.7
2007	31.5	31.6	31.4	31.3	31.1	31.1	31.2	31.2	30.9	31.1	31.3	31.5	31.3
2008	31.3	31.4	31.2	31.0	31.3	31.6	31.9	31.9	31.4	31.2	31.3	31.3	31.4
2009	30.5	30.3	29.9	29.2	28.8	28.5	28.2	27.6	26.8	26.5	26.2	26.0	28.2
2010	25.7	25.5	25.3	25.2	25.2	25.3	25.1	25.1	24.7	24.6	24.6	24.6	25.1
2011	24.4	24.3	24.3	24.1	24.2	24.0	24.2	24.2	24.2	24.2	24.1	24.3	24.2
2012	24.5	24.4	24.3	24.6	24.6	24.7	24.6	24.5	24.3	24.4	24.5	24.6	24.5
2013	24.3	24.1	24.1	24.1	24.3	24.4	24.3	24.4	24.4	24.4	24.6	24.7	24.3
2014	24.4	24.6	24.5	24.4	24.5	24.4	24.5	24.5	24.4	24.4	24.2	24.2	24.4
2015	23.7	23.7	23.6	23.9	24.0	23.9	24.2	24.1	23.8	23.7	23.8	23.8	23.9
Financial Activities													
2005	81.7	82.1	82.3	82.8	82.9	83.2	83.6	83.8	83.5	84.1	84.2	84.4	83.2
2006	83.9	84.4	84.4	84.2	84.7	84.5	83.5	83.6	83.2	82.8	82.6	82.6	83.7
2007	80.9	81.9	81.9	81.2	81.5	81.6	80.7	80.2	79.3	78.6	77.9	77.8	80.3
2008	76.3	76.7	76.6	76.6	76.3	75.9	75.4	75.0	74.1	73.7	73.2	72.9	75.2
2009	71.6	71.9	71.6	70.5	70.2	70.0	69.5	69.0	68.1	68.4	68.2	67.9	69.7
2010	66.9	67.2	67.1	67.0	66.8	66.9	67.2	67.0	66.7	67.6	67.5	67.6	67.1
2011	66.8	67.1	66.8	66.8	67.0	67.2	67.8	67.5	67.6	68.0	67.9	68.5	67.4
2012	68.0	68.1	68.5	69.3	69.5	69.8	70.7	70.5	70.0	70.5	70.8	71.2	69.7
2013	70.3	70.8	70.8	70.9	71.1	71.1	71.3	71.0	70.5	70.8	70.2	70.3	70.8
2014	69.3	69.2	69.2	68.8	69.1	69.3	70.1	69.9	69.2	69.5	69.7	69.7	69.4
2015	69.8	69.9	69.9	70.7	71.0	71.1	72.3	72.0	71.6	72.6	72.6	72.9	71.4
Professional and Business Services													
2005	210.7	212.7	213.7	216.5	215.5	217.1	215.3	216.2	216.7	216.6	217.1	217.8	215.5
2006	214.5	217.1	218.3	218.5	219.2	221.1	220.1	221.7	222.1	220.2	220.4	220.1	219.4
2007	218.2	220.6	221.6	221.9	222.2	224.2	224.9	225.9	225.3	225.3	225.1	225.2	223.4
2008	222.2	224.6	225.4	225.3	224.2	223.8	222.6	223.8	222.1	220.2	218.0	217.2	222.5
2009	211.3	209.9	207.5	205.4	204.6	204.0	203.7	204.0	201.9	203.8	204.9	206.0	205.6
2010	200.1	201.9	201.4	203.4	204.0	205.8	207.3	209.2	208.8	209.4	208.4	209.7	205.8
2011	205.9	207.4	207.9	207.2	206.0	206.4	207.7	209.4	207.9	208.3	208.9	209.6	207.7
2012	205.3	208.5	209.1	214.2	214.8	216.3	214.8	216.1	214.7	217.4	216.9	218.6	213.9
2013	216.2	218.5	218.9	218.4	219.2	219.9	221.3	222.1	222.3	227.0	227.4	227.7	221.6
2014	221.0	223.8	224.7	222.1	222.6	223.4	224.0	225.9	225.0	228.1	229.0	229.4	224.9
2015	225.8	227.3	227.3	228.6	229.2	230.0	233.2	234.5	232.2	234.0	234.9	234.0	230.9
Education and Health Services													
2005	132.5	133.0	133.9	135.3	135.3	134.5	132.1	132.4	134.7	135.2	136.9	137.2	134.4
2006	135.3	136.3	137.8	138.0	138.2	138.1	136.4	136.8	139.0	140.1	141.3	141.4	138.2
2007	139.4	140.9	142.9	143.1	144.2	143.4	142.4	143.7	145.7	146.8	147.7	149.2	144.1
2008	148.3	150.6	151.6	152.0	153.1	152.7	152.4	153.9	155.3	158.6	160.2	161.2	154.2
2009	159.6	161.3	162.7	161.9	162.8	162.3	159.2	160.9	162.7	165.2	166.8	167.9	162.8
2010	163.1	164.8	165.6	164.8	165.3	164.5	161.9	162.4	163.9	165.4	166.0	166.5	164.5
2011	165.8	167.7	168.4	167.7	168.2	167.4	165.3	165.6	167.9	168.8	170.7	170.9	167.9
2012	168.8	170.7	172.3	174.5	175.9	175.1	172.9	173.6	175.6	177.8	178.2	178.9	174.5
2013	179.1	180.6	181.9	182.6	182.2	180.3	177.2	178.2	180.0	183.3	183.7	183.4	181.0
2014	181.7	183.0	184.6	187.3	186.6	185.4	182.6	183.9	186.8	189.2	190.5	190.9	186.0
2015	189.2	189.8	191.5	192.2	192.6	191.3	190.6	191.7	193.8	197.4	198.8	199.2	193.2

Employment by Industry: San Diego-Carlsbad, CA, 2005–2015—*Continued*

(Numbers in thousands, not seasonally adjusted)

Industry and year	January	February	March	April	May	June	July	August	September	October	November	December	Annual average
Leisure and Hospitality													
2005	141.0	142.5	144.9	147.7	149.7	152.2	154.2	157.5	154.4	150.5	149.7	150.7	149.6
2006	147.0	148.7	151.3	153.0	155.9	159.4	161.7	164.8	161.3	158.3	158.0	158.1	156.5
2007	152.1	154.2	157.0	158.5	161.9	165.7	168.5	169.7	166.5	162.5	162.4	162.4	161.8
2008	156.6	158.7	161.1	162.9	166.1	168.2	171.0	171.4	167.7	162.4	161.5	159.9	164.0
2009	152.7	152.5	153.1	154.3	156.5	157.9	158.6	160.4	157.5	152.9	151.2	149.9	154.8
2010	147.4	148.4	150.8	154.3	156.4	158.4	159.7	161.2	157.6	154.4	152.9	152.7	154.5
2011	148.3	150.0	152.0	153.9	156.3	158.0	160.2	162.2	159.5	155.9	155.7	155.4	155.6
2012	151.3	153.3	155.1	159.7	162.8	165.9	167.9	170.5	166.7	163.2	162.2	162.2	161.7
2013	157.6	159.8	162.4	166.7	168.9	172.1	174.7	176.1	172.4	170.8	170.3	170.9	168.6
2014	166.3	168.3	171.7	174.4	177.5	180.9	183.5	186.1	180.8	178.1	178.4	178.2	177.0
2015	174.3	176.8	179.3	181.9	185.9	187.9	190.7	191.7	188.2	183.7	184.7	182.4	184.0
Other Services													
2005	47.5	48.3	48.7	49.0	49.2	49.4	49.2	49.3	48.7	48.6	48.7	48.9	48.8
2006	46.9	47.7	47.7	48.4	49.0	49.4	48.0	48.0	48.8	48.7	48.8	48.9	48.4
2007	47.3	47.8	48.2	48.7	48.4	49.2	48.9	48.6	48.7	48.0	48.3	48.5	48.3
2008	47.4	47.9	48.5	48.1	48.6	49.4	49.1	49.1	48.3	48.1	48.1	48.1	48.4
2009	46.3	47.0	47.3	47.1	47.3	47.5	46.7	47.1	46.2	46.4	46.3	46.3	46.8
2010	45.5	46.1	46.7	45.4	46.1	46.6	46.5	46.4	45.8	46.3	45.9	45.8	46.1
2011	45.7	46.8	46.9	47.8	48.5	48.3	48.1	48.0	48.2	48.3	47.8	47.4	47.7
2012	47.2	48.3	48.7	49.3	49.9	50.4	49.6	49.3	49.4	49.8	49.1	48.9	49.2
2013	47.7	48.3	48.2	48.7	49.1	49.9	50.0	50.0	49.9	49.9	50.1	49.9	49.3
2014	50.0	50.7	51.0	51.4	52.1	52.2	52.7	52.7	53.0	52.9	52.6	52.4	52.0
2015	51.4	52.1	52.2	52.8	53.3	53.6	54.4	54.4	54.1	53.1	52.9	52.2	53.0
Government													
2005	215.0	216.8	217.6	218.0	218.7	219.1	207.9	205.3	211.5	216.0	217.9	217.5	215.1
2006	216.2	218.8	219.7	219.9	220.0	221.2	210.6	208.2	214.5	220.2	222.9	223.1	217.9
2007	221.5	223.7	225.0	225.1	225.0	225.7	214.9	212.2	218.1	224.4	225.9	227.1	222.4
2008	224.2	227.5	228.7	227.8	228.8	230.1	216.7	215.3	220.1	226.8	228.0	227.4	225.1
2009	226.2	226.9	228.6	229.8	229.5	230.0	214.5	212.2	216.1	226.3	227.6	226.6	224.5
2010	224.6	225.7	227.4	234.8	240.7	238.0	225.6	223.8	227.6	231.9	233.3	232.2	230.5
2011	230.1	232.9	233.8	233.8	232.7	233.6	219.7	217.2	223.2	229.6	231.1	229.8	229.0
2012	226.7	229.4	230.9	230.8	231.3	232.1	218.1	219.0	223.0	229.4	232.1	231.2	227.8
2013	227.6	230.0	232.4	231.9	232.3	234.0	220.5	220.9	225.9	231.3	233.9	233.1	229.5
2014	229.3	232.4	234.4	234.7	235.2	237.7	222.3	223.3	227.1	233.9	236.6	236.1	231.9
2015	234.5	235.8	237.6	237.6	238.4	239.8	227.6	227.4	231.8	238.9	240.7	240.6	235.9

Employment by Industry: Tampa-St. Petersburg-Clearwater, FL, 2005–2015

(Numbers in thousands, not seasonally adjusted)

Industry and year	January	February	March	April	May	June	July	August	September	October	November	December	Annual average
Total Nonfarm													
2005	1,185.7	1,199.8	1,206.2	1,211.4	1,213.6	1,200.0	1,194.7	1,207.2	1,212.2	1,211.3	1,220.8	1,228.5	1,207.6
2006	1,212.2	1,221.9	1,237.0	1,236.2	1,238.7	1,228.0	1,216.6	1,233.6	1,236.5	1,233.5	1,241.2	1,249.8	1,232.2
2007	1,228.5	1,236.9	1,248.6	1,243.0	1,239.8	1,230.5	1,212.7	1,225.3	1,222.1	1,219.9	1,227.8	1,232.3	1,230.6
2008	1,207.0	1,214.9	1,219.6	1,206.3	1,201.2	1,185.3	1,168.1	1,178.5	1,173.4	1,168.1	1,167.4	1,169.2	1,188.3
2009	1,139.3	1,139.7	1,140.2	1,132.8	1,125.2	1,109.3	1,095.6	1,105.0	1,102.9	1,104.2	1,106.9	1,109.7	1,117.6
2010	1,089.8	1,098.8	1,107.3	1,106.8	1,113.0	1,100.1	1,093.0	1,103.6	1,102.0	1,113.8	1,118.7	1,123.8	1,105.9
2011	1,106.6	1,115.1	1,123.1	1,127.2	1,123.1	1,110.5	1,107.5	1,121.2	1,128.3	1,132.3	1,139.8	1,145.2	1,123.3
2012	1,132.2	1,140.7	1,148.3	1,153.0	1,152.0	1,139.9	1,132.3	1,146.7	1,146.9	1,155.2	1,165.8	1,172.0	1,148.8
2013	1,154.9	1,165.4	1,173.8	1,177.4	1,178.4	1,166.5	1,162.9	1,176.9	1,176.9	1,185.5	1,198.6	1,200.6	1,176.5
2014	1,181.9	1,190.4	1,200.2	1,208.0	1,210.8	1,198.6	1,195.2	1,209.7	1,211.7	1,221.5	1,234.2	1,239.1	1,208.4
2015	1,222.1	1,234.3	1,241.8	1,247.7	1,248.8	1,238.9	1,236.6	1,249.4	1,251.6	1,264.0	1,276.2	1,282.4	1,249.5
Total Private													
2005	1,037.2	1,048.7	1,055.9	1,061.9	1,063.7	1,061.9	1,057.4	1,059.4	1,062.4	1,060.2	1,069.3	1,077.8	1,059.7
2006	1,062.6	1,071.5	1,087.6	1,085.4	1,088.4	1,089.5	1,079.2	1,084.4	1,084.4	1,079.7	1,087.7	1,096.9	1,083.1
2007	1,076.2	1,083.5	1,094.5	1,089.2	1,087.6	1,088.2	1,071.4	1,074.1	1,068.0	1,064.5	1,072.4	1,077.3	1,078.9
2008	1,053.6	1,059.1	1,064.4	1,051.5	1,048.0	1,042.6	1,026.7	1,026.0	1,017.7	1,011.7	1,010.4	1,011.2	1,035.2
2009	983.7	981.6	982.7	974.3	969.6	963.8	950.9	950.6	947.7	947.7	950.8	954.1	963.1
2010	935.3	941.4	950.3	950.5	951.7	952.2	946.4	949.7	946.3	957.4	962.1	968.7	951.0
2011	951.7	957.7	966.0	970.9	968.6	966.2	964.9	969.5	973.2	976.9	984.7	990.1	970.0
2012	977.5	985.5	993.5	997.3	997.3	995.8	989.5	995.8	994.1	1,002.0	1,011.6	1,018.2	996.5
2013	1,000.6	1,009.9	1,018.4	1,021.9	1,025.0	1,023.4	1,020.9	1,026.0	1,024.2	1,030.8	1,043.5	1,046.2	1,024.2
2014	1,028.9	1,037.0	1,044.5	1,051.9	1,055.3	1,054.0	1,051.8	1,058.5	1,058.1	1,066.1	1,079.0	1,083.9	1,055.8
2015	1,068.3	1,078.7	1,086.5	1,092.1	1,094.5	1,094.9	1,093.4	1,098.1	1,099.0	1,109.9	1,121.3	1,127.3	1,097.0
Goods Producing													
2005	160.1	161.6	162.7	163.7	164.9	166.1	167.8	168.5	169.4	169.7	171.0	171.5	166.4
2006	170.2	171.4	173.2	173.4	174.4	175.4	173.6	174.4	173.8	172.4	171.4	171.2	172.9
2007	168.9	169.1	169.8	166.2	166.2	166.3	162.8	162.0	161.1	158.4	157.1	156.7	163.7
2008	153.3	154.0	153.8	151.3	151.0	151.0	148.4	147.2	145.4	142.3	139.8	137.4	147.9
2009	131.1	129.3	127.6	125.3	123.9	123.2	120.6	119.8	118.4	116.8	115.2	114.0	122.1
2010	110.6	110.6	110.7	110.4	111.5	111.6	111.9	111.8	110.9	110.8	110.3	110.2	110.9
2011	108.3	108.9	110.1	111.0	111.6	111.9	112.4	112.3	113.0	112.6	112.3	112.5	111.4
2012	110.7	111.7	112.5	112.8	113.6	114.6	114.2	114.9	114.1	114.6	114.9	115.0	113.6
2013	112.6	113.3	114.5	116.0	116.6	117.4	117.5	118.2	118.3	119.0	120.1	119.7	116.9
2014	117.5	118.8	119.8	120.9	122.4	123.2	123.1	123.6	123.6	123.9	123.6	123.7	122.0
2015	122.2	123.1	124.3	125.1	125.8	127.0	127.5	128.2	128.6	127.7	127.8	127.2	126.2
Service-Providing													
2005	1,025.6	1,038.2	1,043.5	1,047.7	1,048.7	1,033.9	1,026.9	1,038.7	1,042.8	1,041.6	1,049.8	1,057.0	1,041.2
2006	1,042.0	1,050.5	1,064.7	1,062.8	1,064.3	1,052.6	1,043.0	1,059.2	1,062.7	1,061.1	1,069.8	1,078.6	1,059.3
2007	1,059.6	1,067.8	1,078.8	1,076.8	1,073.6	1,064.2	1,049.9	1,063.3	1,061.0	1,061.5	1,070.7	1,075.6	1,066.9
2008	1,053.7	1,060.9	1,065.8	1,055.0	1,050.2	1,034.3	1,019.7	1,031.3	1,028.0	1,025.8	1,027.6	1,031.8	1,040.3
2009	1,008.2	1,010.4	1,012.6	1,007.5	1,001.3	986.1	975.0	985.2	984.5	987.4	991.7	995.7	995.5
2010	979.2	988.2	996.6	996.4	1,001.5	988.5	981.1	991.8	991.1	1,003.0	1,008.4	1,013.6	995.0
2011	998.3	1,006.2	1,013.0	1,016.2	1,011.5	998.6	995.1	1,008.9	1,015.3	1,019.7	1,027.5	1,032.7	1,011.9
2012	1,021.5	1,029.0	1,035.8	1,040.2	1,038.4	1,025.3	1,018.1	1,031.8	1,032.8	1,040.6	1,050.9	1,057.0	1,035.1
2013	1,042.3	1,052.1	1,059.3	1,061.4	1,061.8	1,049.1	1,045.4	1,058.7	1,058.6	1,066.5	1,078.5	1,080.9	1,059.6
2014	1,064.4	1,071.6	1,080.4	1,087.1	1,088.4	1,075.4	1,072.1	1,086.1	1,088.1	1,097.6	1,110.6	1,115.4	1,086.4
2015	1,099.9	1,111.2	1,117.5	1,122.6	1,123.0	1,111.9	1,109.1	1,121.2	1,123.0	1,136.3	1,148.4	1,155.2	1,123.3
Mining and Logging													
2005	0.6	0.6	0.6	0.6	0.7	0.7	0.7	0.8	0.8	0.8	0.8	0.8	0.7
2006	0.9	0.9	0.9	0.9	0.9	0.8	0.7	0.6	0.6	0.6	0.6	0.7	0.8
2007	0.6	0.6	0.6	0.7	0.7	0.7	0.7	0.7	0.7	0.7	0.7	0.7	0.7
2008	0.7	0.6	0.7	0.7	0.7	0.7	0.6	0.6	0.6	0.5	0.5	0.5	0.6
2009	0.5	0.5	0.5	0.5	0.5	0.5	0.5	0.5	0.5	0.5	0.5	0.5	0.5
2010	0.5	0.5	0.4	0.4	0.4	0.4	0.4	0.4	0.4	0.4	0.4	0.4	0.4
2011	0.4	0.4	0.4	0.4	0.4	0.4	0.4	0.4	0.4	0.4	0.5	0.5	0.4
2012	0.5	0.5	0.5	0.5	0.5	0.5	0.5	0.5	0.4	0.5	0.5	0.5	0.5
2013	0.4	0.4	0.5	0.5	0.4	0.4	0.5	0.4	0.4	0.4	0.4	0.4	0.4
2014	0.4	0.4	0.4	0.4	0.4	0.4	0.4	0.4	0.4	0.4	0.4	0.4	0.4
2015	0.3	0.3	0.4	0.4	0.4	0.4	0.4	0.4	0.3	0.3	0.3	0.3	0.4

Employment by Industry: Tampa-St. Petersburg-Clearwater, FL, 2005–2015—*Continued*

(Numbers in thousands, not seasonally adjusted)

Industry and year	January	February	March	April	May	June	July	August	September	October	November	December	Annual average
Construction													
2005	83.1	84.4	85.4	86.0	87.0	87.8	89.4	89.7	90.2	90.5	91.7	92.2	88.1
2006	91.0	92.1	93.3	94.0	94.7	95.3	94.5	95.0	94.6	93.7	92.9	92.7	93.7
2007	91.3	91.3	92.2	88.9	88.8	89.0	86.3	85.6	84.9	83.1	82.4	82.2	87.2
2008	79.2	80.0	79.8	78.0	77.8	77.9	75.8	75.1	74.1	72.1	70.5	69.1	75.8
2009	64.4	63.2	62.3	61.2	60.4	60.2	59.2	58.8	58.2	57.0	55.9	55.2	59.7
2010	52.4	52.4	52.6	52.2	52.7	52.7	53.0	52.7	52.2	52.4	51.6	51.4	52.4
2011	50.1	50.5	51.3	52.0	52.5	52.5	52.8	52.6	53.3	53.2	52.8	52.9	52.2
2012	51.3	52.0	52.6	52.8	53.5	54.4	54.0	54.5	54.5	54.7	55.0	55.1	53.7
2013	53.4	54.0	54.8	55.5	56.2	56.8	56.8	57.4	57.6	58.0	58.8	58.5	56.5
2014	56.8	57.8	58.5	59.6	60.5	61.4	61.5	61.8	61.8	61.9	61.7	61.8	60.4
2015	60.9	61.6	62.4	63.2	63.8	64.6	64.8	65.4	65.8	65.5	65.1	64.7	64.0
Manufacturing													
2005	76.4	76.6	76.7	77.1	77.2	77.6	77.7	78.0	78.4	78.4	78.5	78.5	77.6
2006	78.3	78.4	79.0	78.5	78.8	79.3	78.4	78.8	78.6	78.1	77.9	77.8	78.5
2007	77.0	77.2	77.0	76.6	76.7	76.6	75.8	75.7	75.5	74.6	74.0	73.8	75.9
2008	73.4	73.4	73.3	72.6	72.5	72.4	72.0	71.5	70.7	69.7	68.8	67.8	71.5
2009	66.2	65.6	64.8	63.6	63.0	62.5	60.9	60.5	59.7	59.3	58.8	58.3	61.9
2010	57.7	57.7	57.7	57.8	58.4	58.5	58.5	58.7	58.3	58.0	58.3	58.4	58.2
2011	57.8	58.0	58.4	58.6	58.7	59.0	59.2	59.3	59.3	59.0	59.0	59.1	58.8
2012	58.9	59.2	59.4	59.5	59.6	59.7	59.7	59.9	59.2	59.4	59.4	59.4	59.4
2013	58.8	58.9	59.2	60.0	60.0	60.2	60.2	60.4	60.3	60.6	60.9	60.8	60.0
2014	60.3	60.6	60.9	60.9	61.5	61.4	61.2	61.4	61.4	61.6	61.5	61.5	61.2
2015	61.0	61.2	61.5	61.5	61.6	62.0	62.3	62.4	62.5	61.9	62.4	62.2	61.9
Trade, Transportation, and Utilities													
2005	231.0	231.1	232.1	233.9	234.6	234.0	232.9	233.0	232.9	234.3	238.9	243.4	234.3
2006	236.9	236.3	238.3	236.1	236.5	235.6	234.0	234.3	234.1	234.3	239.2	243.3	236.6
2007	235.6	234.4	235.6	234.4	235.1	234.6	232.2	232.9	232.9	232.8	238.8	241.3	235.1
2008	233.5	232.6	232.6	229.3	229.1	227.2	224.4	223.9	222.2	222.1	224.6	226.5	227.3
2009	217.2	214.6	213.2	210.8	210.7	209.0	206.7	206.7	206.3	207.2	210.9	213.4	210.6
2010	206.6	206.5	207.3	207.6	208.7	208.7	207.5	208.1	207.9	210.5	214.7	218.7	209.4
2011	210.9	210.3	211.3	211.9	212.1	211.2	211.6	212.6	212.9	214.1	219.4	222.6	213.4
2012	217.7	217.3	216.8	217.4	218.3	217.2	216.7	217.4	217.4	218.9	225.0	227.5	219.0
2013	220.8	220.7	220.4	220.3	221.2	221.2	220.5	221.4	221.3	223.6	230.4	233.2	222.9
2014	226.8	227.5	228.0	229.4	230.1	229.9	229.3	230.4	231.3	233.6	241.8	245.8	232.0
2015	237.1	236.7	237.5	238.2	238.7	239.0	237.8	238.4	238.1	240.1	243.7	247.7	239.4
Wholesale Trade													
2005	52.1	52.1	52.6	52.9	53.3	53.1	52.6	52.6	52.6	52.8	52.9	53.6	52.8
2006	53.3	53.5	53.8	53.8	54.2	54.0	53.7	54.0	54.0	54.1	54.6	55.0	54.0
2007	54.4	54.5	54.6	54.3	54.6	54.5	53.8	54.0	53.8	54.0	54.6	54.8	54.3
2008	54.3	54.3	54.2	53.8	54.0	53.4	52.5	52.2	51.8	51.5	51.4	51.2	52.9
2009	50.0	49.4	49.1	48.4	48.3	47.5	46.7	46.6	46.4	46.6	46.5	46.7	47.7
2010	45.7	45.8	46.2	46.1	46.5	46.2	45.6	45.6	45.5	45.9	45.8	46.3	45.9
2011	45.5	45.5	45.7	45.8	46.1	45.8	46.1	46.3	46.6	46.8	47.2	47.8	46.3
2012	48.2	48.5	48.3	48.4	48.7	48.4	47.9	48.2	48.3	48.4	49.1	49.0	48.5
2013	48.9	49.0	49.1	48.7	48.9	48.6	48.4	48.7	48.6	48.9	49.5	49.6	48.9
2014	49.4	49.8	50.0	50.2	50.5	50.3	50.2	50.5	50.5	50.7	51.2	51.6	50.4
2015	50.9	50.9	51.2	51.1	51.4	51.0	51.2	51.3	51.4	51.5	51.9	52.4	51.4
Retail Trade													
2005	147.1	147.0	147.4	148.8	149.3	149.2	148.9	149.1	149.1	150.4	154.7	157.6	149.9
2006	152.4	151.6	153.2	151.2	151.2	150.7	149.6	149.7	149.8	150.5	154.8	157.4	151.8
2007	151.9	150.9	151.8	151.1	151.7	151.2	149.5	149.9	150.2	150.0	155.2	156.7	151.7
2008	151.0	150.0	150.1	147.3	146.9	145.8	144.5	144.5	143.3	143.4	146.0	147.1	146.7
2009	140.3	138.7	137.9	136.4	136.5	135.8	134.5	134.8	134.7	135.8	139.5	140.8	137.1
2010	136.1	135.9	136.4	136.6	137.1	137.6	136.9	137.5	137.4	139.3	143.4	145.8	138.3
2011	140.0	139.5	140.1	140.7	140.4	139.8	139.7	140.5	140.4	141.4	146.0	147.5	141.3
2012	143.2	142.4	142.1	142.5	143.0	142.2	142.2	142.9	142.7	144.1	149.2	150.9	144.0
2013	145.1	144.6	144.2	144.4	145.1	145.2	145.0	145.6	145.6	147.5	153.1	155.0	146.7
2014	149.5	149.6	149.7	150.8	151.0	151.0	150.5	151.3	152.1	154.0	161.2	163.5	152.9
2015	156.9	156.7	157.1	157.9	157.9	158.5	157.0	157.4	157.0	158.1	161.9	163.6	158.3

Employment by Industry: Tampa-St. Petersburg-Clearwater, FL, 2005–2015—*Continued*

(Numbers in thousands, not seasonally adjusted)

Industry and year	January	February	March	April	May	June	July	August	September	October	November	December	Annual average
Transportation and Utilities													
2005	31.8	32.0	32.1	32.2	32.0	31.7	31.4	31.3	31.2	31.1	31.3	32.2	31.7
2006	31.2	31.2	31.3	31.1	31.1	30.9	30.7	30.6	30.3	29.7	29.8	30.9	30.7
2007	29.3	29.0	29.2	29.0	28.8	28.9	28.9	29.0	28.9	28.8	29.0	29.8	29.1
2008	28.2	28.3	28.3	28.2	28.2	28.0	27.4	27.2	27.1	27.2	27.2	28.2	27.8
2009	26.9	26.5	26.2	26.0	25.9	25.7	25.5	25.3	25.2	24.8	24.9	25.9	25.7
2010	24.8	24.8	24.7	24.9	25.1	24.9	25.0	25.0	25.0	25.3	25.5	26.6	25.1
2011	25.4	25.3	25.5	25.4	25.6	25.6	25.8	25.8	25.9	25.9	26.2	27.3	25.8
2012	26.3	26.4	26.4	26.5	26.6	26.6	26.6	26.3	26.4	26.4	26.7	27.6	26.6
2013	26.8	27.1	27.1	27.2	27.2	27.4	27.1	27.1	27.1	27.2	27.8	28.6	27.3
2014	27.9	28.1	28.3	28.4	28.6	28.6	28.6	28.6	28.7	28.9	29.4	30.7	28.7
2015	29.3	29.1	29.2	29.2	29.4	29.5	29.6	29.7	29.7	30.5	29.9	31.7	29.7
Information													
2005	31.6	31.6	31.8	31.5	31.6	31.6	31.8	32.0	32.4	32.2	32.3	32.2	31.9
2006	32.1	32.2	32.0	31.8	31.9	32.0	31.8	31.7	31.6	31.5	31.6	31.7	31.8
2007	31.6	31.8	31.9	32.1	32.2	32.4	31.9	31.9	31.7	31.4	31.4	31.3	31.8
2008	30.9	31.1	31.0	31.0	30.9	30.7	30.3	30.0	29.5	29.6	29.3	29.0	30.3
2009	28.7	28.6	28.5	28.1	27.8	27.7	27.6	27.3	26.9	26.5	26.5	26.5	27.6
2010	26.0	26.0	26.0	25.8	25.8	25.7	25.7	25.6	25.5	25.5	25.6	25.6	25.7
2011	25.8	25.9	25.7	25.6	25.7	25.8	26.0	25.9	25.9	26.0	26.1	26.2	25.9
2012	25.8	25.7	25.7	25.7	25.6	25.8	25.7	25.6	25.6	25.9	25.9	25.9	25.7
2013	26.1	26.1	26.2	26.2	26.3	26.4	26.1	26.1	25.9	25.9	26.0	26.0	26.1
2014	25.5	25.6	25.4	25.5	25.5	25.6	25.6	25.5	25.4	25.7	25.7	25.6	25.6
2015	25.5	25.6	25.4	25.5	25.6	25.6	25.9	25.7	25.7	25.8	25.9	25.8	25.7
Financial Activities													
2005	98.2	98.9	98.9	100.1	100.5	101.3	101.6	101.0	101.5	102.3	102.8	104.2	100.9
2006	103.2	104.0	104.6	104.8	105.0	104.9	104.1	104.1	103.7	103.8	103.6	104.3	104.2
2007	103.2	104.2	104.3	104.4	104.2	104.0	103.7	102.8	102.4	102.1	102.0	101.8	103.3
2008	100.5	100.5	100.2	99.3	99.1	98.6	98.3	98.0	97.4	97.2	97.0	96.9	98.6
2009	96.0	95.3	95.0	94.4	94.2	93.7	93.0	92.6	91.8	91.1	90.7	90.8	93.2
2010	89.3	89.2	89.4	89.1	89.1	89.2	89.0	89.5	89.0	89.6	89.7	90.5	89.4
2011	89.7	89.9	90.3	90.5	90.4	90.9	91.2	92.1	93.0	93.5	93.4	94.2	91.6
2012	93.3	93.8	94.4	94.5	94.8	95.5	95.5	96.0	96.1	96.9	97.6	98.1	95.5
2013	97.6	98.4	99.0	98.8	99.2	99.8	100.2	100.5	100.1	100.3	100.9	101.3	99.7
2014	100.3	100.5	101.0	101.0	101.3	101.6	102.3	102.4	102.5	102.3	102.8	103.0	101.8
2015	102.3	102.5	102.6	103.0	103.4	103.6	104.3	104.7	104.4	105.3	106.1	106.5	104.1
Professional and Business Services													
2005	184.2	189.3	190.2	192.0	191.2	189.7	188.7	190.1	191.9	187.9	189.6	190.4	189.6
2006	188.5	191.1	197.5	198.0	198.7	199.9	199.1	201.4	200.8	197.5	198.9	200.6	197.7
2007	196.9	198.2	201.1	201.3	199.1	200.9	196.9	198.2	193.7	192.4	192.8	193.3	197.1
2008	188.0	189.1	190.6	185.9	184.0	184.4	181.9	182.1	179.7	177.0	176.2	177.2	183.0
2009	172.6	172.8	173.0	171.2	169.4	170.1	168.0	168.4	168.2	167.6	168.6	169.6	170.0
2010	167.0	169.8	172.2	172.1	172.1	174.2	173.8	175.9	174.5	178.8	179.2	180.6	174.2
2011	177.6	179.8	180.6	182.1	180.7	181.5	182.4	183.8	183.7	184.2	186.2	188.0	182.6
2012	185.8	188.4	190.3	190.9	190.3	190.0	189.8	191.6	190.2	192.9	194.7	196.3	190.9
2013	192.1	195.6	196.9	197.6	199.0	198.1	198.8	199.9	198.7	199.7	201.3	201.2	198.2
2014	198.0	200.1	200.2	201.5	202.8	202.7	203.7	206.6	205.0	208.6	211.0	211.5	204.3
2015	210.1	213.5	214.0	215.8	216.6	217.1	218.4	219.9	219.1	224.2	226.2	228.5	218.6
Education and Health Services													
2005	155.9	156.8	157.4	158.5	158.1	157.5	156.5	157.4	157.6	158.3	158.8	159.6	157.7
2006	158.0	159.5	160.7	161.0	161.3	160.6	159.2	160.4	162.1	163.2	164.7	166.1	161.4
2007	164.2	166.0	167.9	168.2	168.4	168.2	166.1	168.2	169.2	171.0	172.6	173.4	168.6
2008	171.6	172.9	174.0	173.6	173.9	172.1	170.4	171.7	172.3	173.5	174.9	175.6	173.0
2009	172.1	172.9	174.3	174.2	174.6	173.4	172.2	173.0	174.3	176.5	177.8	178.6	174.5
2010	176.4	177.3	179.3	178.5	178.1	177.2	175.8	176.1	176.8	179.5	180.4	180.6	178.0
2011	179.0	180.1	181.1	182.5	181.6	179.7	178.6	179.8	181.0	182.0	182.9	182.8	180.9
2012	180.7	182.0	182.9	183.5	183.1	182.0	179.2	181.1	182.1	183.1	183.7	184.2	182.3
2013	182.2	183.6	185.0	185.4	185.2	183.4	181.7	183.6	184.5	186.5	187.6	187.1	184.7
2014	185.1	186.3	187.6	188.4	188.5	186.8	185.5	188.0	188.8	191.0	192.1	192.4	188.4
2015	190.2	192.4	192.8	194.3	194.5	193.6	191.7	193.5	195.3	198.6	202.3	202.1	195.1

Employment by Industry: Tampa-St. Petersburg-Clearwater, FL, 2005–2015—*Continued*

(Numbers in thousands, not seasonally adjusted)

Industry and year	January	February	March	April	May	June	July	August	September	October	November	December	Annual average
Leisure and Hospitality													
2005	126.4	129.1	132.3	132.0	132.5	131.4	129.0	129.0	128.5	128.1	128.7	129.5	129.7
2006	128.2	130.9	134.7	134.0	133.6	133.4	130.6	131.6	131.6	130.3	131.5	132.5	131.9
2007	129.4	132.6	136.0	136.1	135.2	133.9	131.1	131.4	130.4	129.1	129.8	130.9	132.2
2008	128.0	130.6	133.7	133.5	132.0	130.5	126.1	126.4	125.2	124.8	123.8	124.1	128.2
2009	122.2	124.4	127.2	126.8	125.4	123.3	120.1	120.1	119.3	119.3	118.6	118.8	122.1
2010	117.8	120.0	123.3	124.8	124.1	123.1	120.7	121.0	120.3	120.6	120.5	120.7	121.4
2011	119.1	121.2	124.8	125.2	124.5	123.7	121.5	122.1	123.0	123.8	123.8	123.2	123.0
2012	123.1	125.9	129.8	131.3	130.4	129.5	127.5	128.3	127.5	128.5	128.4	129.7	128.3
2013	128.1	130.8	134.7	135.3	135.0	134.3	133.6	133.6	132.7	133.0	134.0	134.4	133.3
2014	132.7	134.7	138.7	141.6	141.2	140.6	138.9	138.7	138.3	137.8	138.9	138.7	138.4
2015	138.2	142.0	146.7	147.0	146.6	145.5	144.8	144.5	144.5	144.5	145.7	146.5	144.7
Other Services													
2005	49.8	50.3	50.5	50.2	50.3	50.3	49.1	48.4	48.2	47.4	47.2	47.0	49.1
2006	45.5	46.1	46.6	46.3	47.0	47.7	46.8	46.5	46.7	46.7	46.8	47.2	46.7
2007	46.4	47.2	47.9	47.2	47.2	47.9	46.7	46.7	46.6	47.3	47.9	48.6	47.2
2008	47.8	48.3	48.5	47.6	48.0	48.1	46.9	46.7	46.0	45.2	44.8	44.5	46.9
2009	43.8	43.7	43.9	43.5	43.6	43.4	42.7	42.7	42.5	42.7	42.5	42.4	43.1
2010	41.6	42.0	42.1	42.2	42.3	42.5	42.0	41.7	41.4	42.1	41.7	41.8	42.0
2011	41.3	41.6	42.1	42.0	42.0	41.5	41.2	40.9	40.7	40.7	40.6	40.6	41.3
2012	40.4	40.7	41.1	41.2	41.2	41.2	40.9	40.9	41.1	41.2	41.4	41.5	41.1
2013	41.1	41.4	41.7	42.3	42.5	42.8	42.5	42.7	42.7	42.8	43.2	43.3	42.4
2014	43.0	43.5	43.8	43.6	43.5	43.6	43.4	43.3	43.2	43.2	43.1	43.2	43.4
2015	42.7	42.9	43.2	43.2	43.3	43.5	43.0	43.2	43.3	43.7	43.6	43.0	43.2
Government													
2005	148.5	151.1	150.3	149.5	149.9	138.1	137.3	147.8	149.8	151.1	151.5	150.7	148.0
2006	149.6	150.4	150.3	150.8	150.3	138.5	137.4	149.2	152.1	153.8	153.5	152.9	149.1
2007	152.3	153.4	154.1	153.8	152.2	142.3	141.3	151.2	154.1	155.4	155.4	155.0	151.7
2008	153.4	155.8	155.2	154.8	153.2	142.7	141.4	152.5	155.7	156.4	157.0	158.0	153.0
2009	155.6	158.1	157.5	158.5	155.6	145.5	144.7	154.4	155.2	156.5	156.1	155.6	154.4
2010	154.5	157.4	157.0	156.3	161.3	147.9	146.6	153.9	155.7	156.4	156.6	155.1	154.9
2011	154.9	157.4	157.1	156.3	154.5	144.3	142.6	151.7	155.1	155.4	155.1	155.1	153.3
2012	154.7	155.2	154.8	155.7	154.7	144.1	142.8	150.9	152.8	153.2	154.2	153.8	152.2
2013	154.3	155.5	155.4	155.5	153.4	143.1	142.0	150.9	152.7	154.7	155.1	154.4	152.3
2014	153.0	153.4	155.7	156.1	155.5	144.6	143.4	151.2	153.6	155.4	155.2	155.2	152.7
2015	153.8	155.6	155.3	155.6	154.3	144.0	143.2	151.3	152.6	154.1	154.9	155.1	152.5

Employment by Industry: Denver-Aurora-Lakewood, CO, 2005–2015

(Numbers in thousands, not seasonally adjusted)

Industry and year	January	February	March	April	May	June	July	August	September	October	November	December	Annual average
Total Nonfarm													
2005	1,154.5	1,161.8	1,170.6	1,180.2	1,190.2	1,201.5	1,198.9	1,199.0	1,203.6	1,202.6	1,206.2	1,212.1	1,190.1
2006	1,182.1	1,187.7	1,196.4	1,204.2	1,217.1	1,231.8	1,222.3	1,225.8	1,225.3	1,225.3	1,229.6	1,234.1	1,215.1
2007	1,202.6	1,209.0	1,221.4	1,230.3	1,244.0	1,257.7	1,249.5	1,252.7	1,252.9	1,254.2	1,258.6	1,261.1	1,241.2
2008	1,231.3	1,237.3	1,244.5	1,252.3	1,261.9	1,271.6	1,261.8	1,265.9	1,259.4	1,256.2	1,251.2	1,244.5	1,253.2
2009	1,206.6	1,198.4	1,197.4	1,199.1	1,206.8	1,210.6	1,199.9	1,197.9	1,194.7	1,197.1	1,195.7	1,193.8	1,199.8
2010	1,162.1	1,167.2	1,174.6	1,185.9	1,199.7	1,206.8	1,202.5	1,203.1	1,199.7	1,206.4	1,207.9	1,207.3	1,193.6
2011	1,180.6	1,184.1	1,191.7	1,208.0	1,217.6	1,226.8	1,219.2	1,224.1	1,224.8	1,226.3	1,231.2	1,233.0	1,214.0
2012	1,207.6	1,213.0	1,224.6	1,236.4	1,248.8	1,262.6	1,256.4	1,258.6	1,259.6	1,269.5	1,275.9	1,276.7	1,249.1
2013	1,250.7	1,259.7	1,269.9	1,281.9	1,294.3	1,306.7	1,302.7	1,310.2	1,308.9	1,318.2	1,323.6	1,323.6	1,295.9
2014	1,299.2	1,305.1	1,314.0	1,330.2	1,344.0	1,354.9	1,350.8	1,363.0	1,362.5	1,373.1	1,374.4	1,379.5	1,345.9
2015	1,356.4	1,364.5	1,369.9	1,383.7	1,395.0	1,407.3	1,404.2	1,409.6	1,409.2	1,410.3	1,414.8	1,415.5	1,395.0
Total Private													
2005	994.1	997.3	1,005.7	1,013.7	1,023.0	1,035.9	1,039.3	1,040.3	1,037.4	1,035.9	1,039.1	1,045.1	1,025.6
2006	1,019.5	1,021.2	1,028.8	1,037.1	1,048.4	1,063.5	1,061.2	1,063.9	1,057.5	1,057.3	1,060.7	1,064.9	1,048.7
2007	1,038.7	1,040.0	1,051.1	1,059.6	1,072.2	1,086.9	1,086.1	1,088.4	1,081.2	1,081.7	1,085.2	1,088.1	1,071.6
2008	1,063.4	1,065.0	1,070.9	1,078.1	1,085.6	1,097.1	1,094.1	1,095.4	1,084.0	1,078.8	1,072.9	1,067.2	1,079.4
2009	1,033.8	1,022.5	1,020.1	1,020.8	1,026.5	1,032.8	1,030.9	1,027.8	1,017.5	1,017.5	1,016.8	1,016.1	1,023.6
2010	990.2	989.6	995.8	1,006.1	1,014.5	1,026.6	1,029.7	1,031.7	1,021.1	1,025.3	1,026.4	1,027.8	1,015.4
2011	1,006.7	1,004.8	1,011.7	1,026.6	1,034.7	1,046.3	1,047.6	1,052.7	1,046.2	1,046.1	1,050.7	1,053.5	1,035.6
2012	1,033.7	1,033.8	1,043.7	1,054.6	1,065.4	1,080.1	1,083.0	1,086.2	1,079.7	1,088.0	1,092.7	1,095.1	1,069.7
2013	1,074.5	1,077.7	1,086.7	1,097.3	1,108.7	1,122.6	1,126.9	1,133.1	1,123.4	1,129.5	1,135.2	1,137.2	1,112.7
2014	1,118.0	1,120.1	1,127.9	1,143.3	1,155.8	1,168.3	1,175.3	1,183.1	1,174.9	1,181.6	1,182.0	1,189.6	1,160.0
2015	1,170.9	1,174.8	1,179.4	1,191.4	1,201.0	1,215.3	1,221.8	1,223.8	1,215.0	1,215.4	1,218.8	1,221.2	1,204.1
Goods Producing													
2005	154.3	155.7	158.1	158.9	160.8	164.6	166.8	167.3	166.8	166.2	165.6	164.3	162.5
2006	161.4	162.6	164.8	165.8	167.9	171.0	170.1	169.8	169.0	167.6	165.8	163.9	166.6
2007	157.3	158.0	161.1	162.5	164.7	168.0	168.6	168.7	167.2	167.6	166.2	163.3	164.4
2008	159.7	159.7	160.9	161.5	163.0	165.6	164.9	165.0	162.8	161.7	158.1	153.9	161.4
2009	146.7	143.2	141.4	140.0	140.0	141.5	141.3	139.7	137.9	136.9	135.6	132.7	139.7
2010	127.8	127.2	128.0	129.9	131.1	133.3	134.4	133.8	132.2	132.3	131.1	130.2	130.9
2011	126.1	125.4	127.4	130.6	131.0	133.9	134.9	135.5	134.8	134.7	134.1	132.8	131.8
2012	130.0	130.0	131.7	133.5	135.5	138.6	139.4	139.9	139.5	140.7	140.2	139.3	136.5
2013	136.6	137.3	139.2	140.3	143.4	146.4	147.4	148.7	147.7	149.0	149.2	148.5	144.5
2014	146.6	147.3	149.3	152.3	154.9	157.6	159.4	160.3	160.0	160.5	160.1	160.5	155.7
2015	157.8	158.6	159.5	160.7	162.1	164.5	165.5	165.1	164.4	166.0	166.2	165.4	163.0
Service-Providing													
2005	1,000.2	1,006.1	1,012.5	1,021.3	1,029.4	1,036.9	1,032.1	1,031.7	1,036.8	1,036.4	1,040.6	1,047.8	1,027.7
2006	1,020.7	1,025.1	1,031.6	1,038.4	1,049.2	1,060.8	1,052.2	1,056.0	1,056.3	1,057.7	1,063.8	1,070.2	1,048.5
2007	1,045.3	1,051.0	1,060.3	1,067.8	1,079.3	1,089.7	1,080.9	1,084.0	1,085.7	1,086.6	1,092.4	1,097.8	1,076.7
2008	1,071.6	1,077.6	1,083.6	1,090.8	1,098.9	1,106.0	1,096.9	1,100.9	1,096.6	1,094.5	1,093.1	1,090.6	1,091.8
2009	1,059.9	1,055.2	1,056.0	1,059.1	1,066.8	1,069.1	1,058.6	1,058.2	1,056.8	1,060.2	1,060.1	1,061.1	1,060.1
2010	1,034.3	1,040.0	1,046.6	1,056.0	1,068.6	1,073.5	1,068.1	1,069.3	1,067.5	1,074.1	1,076.8	1,077.1	1,062.7
2011	1,054.5	1,058.7	1,064.3	1,077.4	1,086.6	1,092.9	1,084.3	1,088.6	1,090.0	1,091.6	1,097.1	1,100.2	1,082.2
2012	1,077.6	1,083.0	1,092.9	1,102.9	1,113.3	1,124.0	1,117.0	1,118.7	1,120.1	1,128.8	1,135.7	1,137.4	1,112.6
2013	1,114.1	1,122.4	1,130.7	1,141.6	1,150.9	1,160.3	1,155.3	1,161.5	1,161.2	1,169.2	1,174.4	1,175.1	1,151.4
2014	1,152.6	1,157.8	1,164.7	1,177.9	1,189.1	1,197.3	1,191.4	1,202.7	1,202.5	1,212.6	1,214.3	1,219.0	1,190.2
2015	1,198.6	1,205.9	1,210.4	1,223.0	1,232.9	1,242.8	1,238.7	1,244.5	1,244.8	1,244.3	1,248.6	1,250.1	1,232.1
Mining, Logging, and Construction													
2005	82.8	83.9	86.1	87.0	88.8	92.3	94.1	94.7	94.4	93.6	93.2	91.9	90.2
2006	89.7	90.8	92.7	93.7	95.7	98.4	97.4	97.1	96.5	95.3	93.6	92.0	94.4
2007	86.1	87.1	90.1	91.7	93.4	96.1	96.7	96.8	95.4	95.7	94.3	91.5	92.9
2008	88.7	89.3	90.5	91.4	92.9	95.1	94.5	94.8	93.0	92.3	89.7	86.2	91.5
2009	80.7	78.5	77.3	76.4	76.9	78.5	78.4	77.2	76.0	75.1	73.8	71.2	76.7
2010	67.5	66.9	67.6	69.4	70.0	71.7	72.7	72.1	70.7	70.8	69.6	68.7	69.8
2011	64.9	64.3	66.0	68.8	68.9	71.4	72.3	72.7	72.0	72.3	71.6	70.4	69.6
2012	68.1	67.9	69.2	70.8	72.5	75.0	75.5	76.1	75.7	76.8	76.3	75.5	73.3
2013	73.3	73.9	75.4	76.7	79.6	82.1	83.2	84.4	83.6	85.0	85.1	84.3	80.6
2014	83.0	83.5	85.3	87.7	89.9	92.1	93.5	94.2	93.9	94.2	93.4	93.5	90.4
2015	91.2	91.8	92.4	93.5	94.5	96.0	96.7	96.3	95.8	97.2	96.9	95.9	94.9

Employment by Industry: Denver-Aurora-Lakewood, CO, 2005–2015—*Continued*

(Numbers in thousands, not seasonally adjusted)

Industry and year	January	February	March	April	May	June	July	August	September	October	November	December	Annual average
Manufacturing													
2005	71.5	71.8	72.0	71.9	72.0	72.3	72.7	72.6	72.4	72.6	72.4	72.4	72.2
2006	71.7	71.8	72.1	72.1	72.2	72.6	72.7	72.7	72.5	72.3	72.2	71.9	72.2
2007	71.2	70.9	71.0	70.8	71.3	71.9	71.9	71.9	71.8	71.9	71.9	71.8	71.5
2008	71.0	70.4	70.4	70.1	70.1	70.5	70.4	70.2	69.8	69.4	68.4	67.7	69.9
2009	66.0	64.7	64.1	63.6	63.1	63.0	62.9	62.5	61.9	61.8	61.8	61.5	63.1
2010	60.3	60.3	60.4	60.5	61.1	61.6	61.7	61.7	61.5	61.5	61.5	61.5	61.1
2011	61.2	61.1	61.4	61.8	62.1	62.5	62.6	62.8	62.8	62.4	62.5	62.4	62.1
2012	61.9	62.1	62.5	62.7	63.0	63.6	63.9	63.8	63.8	63.9	63.9	63.8	63.2
2013	63.3	63.4	63.8	63.6	63.8	64.3	64.2	64.3	64.1	64.0	64.1	64.2	63.9
2014	63.6	63.8	64.0	64.6	65.0	65.5	65.9	66.1	66.1	66.3	66.7	67.0	65.4
2015	66.6	66.8	67.1	67.2	67.6	68.5	68.8	68.8	68.6	68.8	69.3	69.5	68.1
Trade, Transportation, and Utilities													
2005	232.4	231.3	232.2	232.5	234.3	236.1	236.6	236.3	237.8	239.6	244.2	247.2	236.7
2006	236.6	233.5	234.3	235.3	236.8	238.8	238.4	239.0	238.6	241.4	246.8	250.8	239.2
2007	242.2	239.4	240.1	241.0	242.8	244.3	244.5	244.5	243.8	245.6	251.2	253.8	244.4
2008	245.8	243.0	244.1	244.3	245.0	246.2	245.9	245.5	243.5	243.0	244.7	246.3	244.8
2009	235.7	231.7	229.8	229.1	229.9	230.7	229.5	229.1	227.9	229.3	231.7	234.1	230.7
2010	225.0	223.9	224.0	224.9	226.5	228.2	228.8	229.2	227.7	229.6	232.9	235.3	228.0
2011	226.4	224.6	225.4	227.5	228.8	230.1	230.8	231.2	230.0	231.8	236.1	238.1	230.1
2012	231.0	229.0	229.9	231.1	232.8	235.0	235.7	235.8	235.5	238.3	243.9	246.5	235.4
2013	238.2	236.9	237.7	238.6	240.5	242.2	243.1	244.5	243.3	245.1	250.3	253.2	242.8
2014	245.3	244.3	244.9	246.4	248.2	250.8	250.8	251.9	250.4	252.7	257.7	261.6	250.4
2015	253.7	252.5	252.9	254.1	255.2	257.8	259.2	259.5	257.9	258.0	261.6	263.4	257.2
Wholesale Trade													
2005	61.6	61.9	62.2	62.4	62.6	63.0	63.1	63.2	63.3	63.3	63.5	63.8	62.8
2006	63.3	63.6	64.0	64.3	64.7	65.4	65.3	65.5	65.3	65.6	65.9	66.4	64.9
2007	65.0	65.4	65.8	65.8	66.3	66.7	66.6	66.7	66.4	66.8	66.9	66.8	66.3
2008	66.5	66.7	66.8	67.0	67.2	67.4	67.4	67.1	66.8	66.4	66.1	66.0	66.8
2009	64.8	64.2	63.5	62.8	62.6	62.5	62.1	61.8	61.3	61.4	61.2	61.4	62.5
2010	60.9	60.7	60.8	60.9	61.1	61.5	61.7	61.7	61.5	61.7	61.7	61.8	61.3
2011	61.3	61.4	61.7	62.0	62.2	62.4	62.6	62.7	62.5	62.4	62.4	62.4	62.2
2012	62.0	62.2	62.6	63.0	63.2	63.7	64.0	64.1	64.0	64.3	64.3	64.7	63.5
2013	63.9	64.3	64.6	64.7	65.0	65.5	65.5	65.7	65.5	65.7	65.9	66.0	65.2
2014	65.7	66.1	66.4	66.9	67.2	67.6	68.0	68.5	68.2	68.7	69.0	69.4	67.6
2015	68.8	69.2	69.3	69.3	69.6	69.9	70.2	70.3	70.1	69.9	69.9	69.9	69.7
Retail Trade													
2005	121.9	120.3	121.0	121.2	122.9	123.9	124.1	123.7	125.2	126.7	131.0	133.2	124.6
2006	124.4	121.1	121.3	122.3	123.2	123.9	123.9	124.3	124.0	126.4	131.3	133.4	125.0
2007	127.0	124.2	124.5	125.1	126.3	127.2	127.5	127.2	126.8	127.7	132.4	134.0	127.5
2008	127.7	125.3	126.2	126.3	126.7	127.6	127.3	127.7	126.7	127.1	128.8	129.6	127.3
2009	122.5	119.8	118.9	118.3	119.6	120.5	119.8	119.8	119.4	120.6	123.5	124.7	120.6
2010	118.3	117.1	117.4	118.6	120.0	121.2	121.8	122.1	120.8	122.1	125.1	126.3	120.9
2011	119.8	118.4	118.8	120.3	121.4	122.3	122.6	123.1	122.3	123.7	127.6	128.9	122.4
2012	123.2	120.9	121.6	122.3	123.8	125.1	125.2	125.2	125.0	126.2	131.1	132.4	125.2
2013	125.8	124.2	124.6	125.3	126.9	128.1	128.9	129.8	128.8	129.9	134.2	136.0	128.5
2014	129.4	128.0	128.6	129.3	130.4	132.3	132.1	132.4	131.3	132.9	136.8	139.1	131.9
2015	132.5	131.3	132.1	133.0	134.1	136.1	136.5	137.0	135.7	135.8	139.2	139.9	135.3
Transportation and Utilities													
2005	48.9	49.1	49.0	48.9	48.8	49.2	49.4	49.4	49.3	49.6	49.7	50.2	49.3
2006	48.9	48.8	49.0	48.7	48.9	49.5	49.2	49.2	49.3	49.4	49.6	51.0	49.3
2007	50.2	49.8	49.8	50.2	50.1	50.2	50.4	50.6	50.6	51.1	51.9	53.0	50.7
2008	51.6	51.0	51.1	51.0	51.1	51.2	51.2	50.7	50.0	49.5	49.8	50.7	50.7
2009	48.4	47.7	47.4	48.0	47.7	47.7	47.6	47.5	47.2	47.3	47.0	48.0	47.6
2010	45.8	46.1	45.8	45.4	45.4	45.5	45.3	45.4	45.4	45.8	46.1	47.2	45.8
2011	45.3	44.8	44.9	45.2	45.2	45.4	45.6	45.4	45.2	45.7	46.1	46.8	45.5
2012	45.8	45.9	45.7	45.8	45.8	46.2	46.5	46.5	46.5	47.8	48.5	49.4	46.7
2013	48.5	48.4	48.5	48.6	48.6	48.6	48.7	49.0	49.0	49.5	50.2	51.2	49.1
2014	50.2	50.2	49.9	50.2	50.6	50.9	50.7	51.0	50.9	51.1	51.9	53.1	50.9
2015	52.4	52.0	51.5	51.8	51.5	51.8	52.5	52.2	52.1	52.3	52.5	53.6	52.2

Employment by Industry: Denver-Aurora-Lakewood, CO, 2005–2015—*Continued*

(Numbers in thousands, not seasonally adjusted)

Industry and year	January	February	March	April	May	June	July	August	September	October	November	December	Annual average
Information													
2005	49.2	49.0	48.9	48.4	48.4	48.2	47.9	47.7	47.5	47.4	47.7	47.9	48.2
2006	47.7	47.8	48.0	47.7	47.9	48.0	47.8	47.4	47.1	47.2	47.5	47.4	47.6
2007	47.0	47.2	47.2	47.9	48.1	48.5	48.3	48.0	47.5	47.5	47.7	47.6	47.7
2008	47.0	47.1	47.0	47.0	46.8	46.9	47.0	46.8	46.3	46.3	46.4	46.5	46.8
2009	45.8	45.6	45.5	45.1	44.9	44.8	44.7	44.3	44.0	43.8	43.9	43.9	44.7
2010	43.6	43.3	43.4	43.1	43.2	43.5	43.4	43.5	43.4	43.5	43.9	43.9	43.5
2011	43.6	43.6	43.3	43.5	43.5	43.5	43.3	43.3	43.1	43.1	43.2	43.1	43.3
2012	42.9	43.1	43.0	42.8	43.0	43.1	43.0	43.0	42.9	43.0	43.2	43.3	43.0
2013	43.4	43.8	43.9	43.9	44.0	44.5	44.6	44.5	44.1	44.0	44.3	44.3	44.1
2014	44.4	44.6	44.5	44.5	44.6	45.3	45.8	45.8	44.8	44.8	44.8	45.1	44.9
2015	45.2	45.4	45.5	45.4	45.6	45.9	46.3	46.3	45.7	45.7	46.1	46.5	45.8
Financial Activities													
2005	97.3	97.9	98.5	98.8	99.2	99.7	100.3	100.5	100.7	100.6	101.0	101.8	99.7
2006	99.6	99.8	100.0	100.1	100.8	101.4	101.3	101.3	100.9	100.5	100.5	101.1	100.6
2007	99.4	99.9	99.9	100.0	100.1	100.5	100.4	100.0	99.1	98.8	98.7	98.8	99.6
2008	97.5	97.7	98.1	97.8	97.6	98.0	97.9	97.3	96.4	96.0	95.5	95.6	97.1
2009	93.7	93.5	93.0	93.2	93.3	93.0	92.9	92.6	92.0	92.0	91.7	92.1	92.8
2010	90.5	90.4	90.4	90.5	90.5	90.9	91.2	91.2	90.8	91.0	90.9	91.4	90.8
2011	90.2	90.1	90.1	90.2	90.3	90.9	90.9	91.1	90.8	90.6	91.1	91.7	90.7
2012	90.7	90.8	91.3	91.5	92.0	92.8	93.0	93.4	93.2	94.1	94.1	94.9	92.7
2013	93.9	94.5	94.9	95.3	95.6	96.4	96.7	96.8	96.6	96.7	96.9	97.1	96.0
2014	95.7	96.0	96.2	96.8	97.5	97.9	98.6	99.0	98.7	99.5	99.9	100.7	98.0
2015	99.6	100.2	100.6	101.2	101.9	102.7	103.5	103.8	103.3	104.3	104.6	104.7	102.5
Professional and Business Services													
2005	184.3	184.8	186.7	191.1	191.8	194.5	195.9	196.5	195.8	195.1	194.8	196.9	192.4
2006	190.2	192.2	193.8	197.0	199.6	203.5	203.4	204.7	203.9	203.8	203.3	204.6	200.0
2007	201.6	202.7	205.5	208.3	211.1	215.3	215.3	216.9	217.0	216.1	215.3	216.8	211.8
2008	211.2	213.2	213.9	218.0	218.0	220.5	219.8	221.5	219.5	217.9	216.0	214.5	217.0
2009	207.4	204.5	204.2	204.9	205.0	205.7	204.9	204.1	202.5	202.8	203.0	202.8	204.3
2010	197.1	198.0	199.9	203.4	205.0	207.3	208.2	208.6	205.5	207.3	207.3	206.5	204.5
2011	204.2	204.4	205.1	210.5	212.4	213.8	214.3	215.9	214.8	215.1	216.7	217.0	212.0
2012	212.5	213.3	216.2	220.0	222.1	225.3	226.3	227.8	226.5	229.3	229.1	228.3	223.1
2013	223.8	225.4	227.5	230.8	232.4	235.2	236.0	237.9	235.5	237.7	237.4	237.2	233.1
2014	232.2	233.0	234.5	238.7	240.5	243.2	245.0	248.6	247.0	249.4	246.8	247.7	242.2
2015	243.4	244.7	245.6	249.2	251.0	253.3	254.6	255.6	253.9	254.9	255.5	255.2	251.4
Education and Health Services													
2005	117.0	118.6	119.1	119.2	119.8	119.6	118.8	119.3	119.7	119.9	120.6	120.9	119.4
2006	120.3	121.7	122.0	122.7	123.1	123.0	122.3	122.9	123.5	124.7	125.1	125.5	123.1
2007	124.5	126.0	126.8	127.2	127.9	127.8	127.3	127.9	128.5	129.6	130.7	131.5	128.0
2008	130.0	131.8	132.0	132.5	133.4	133.3	132.8	133.8	134.5	136.1	137.1	136.8	133.7
2009	135.7	136.8	136.9	137.3	137.7	137.7	137.5	137.9	138.1	139.5	140.3	140.7	138.0
2010	139.6	140.8	141.7	142.1	142.7	142.7	142.1	143.0	143.4	144.5	145.4	145.7	142.8
2011	144.8	145.9	146.4	147.0	147.5	147.4	146.9	148.4	148.8	150.0	150.5	151.9	148.0
2012	150.5	152.0	152.4	152.8	153.0	152.8	152.7	153.2	153.7	155.2	156.0	156.9	153.4
2013	155.8	157.2	157.7	159.1	159.1	158.8	159.2	160.4	161.1	162.8	164.1	164.6	160.0
2014	163.1	164.7	165.4	167.4	167.8	167.0	167.1	168.5	169.2	171.4	172.1	172.7	168.0
2015	172.6	174.3	174.6	176.0	176.2	175.5	176.0	176.8	177.0	176.5	177.6	178.1	175.9
Leisure and Hospitality													
2005	114.2	114.9	116.9	119.5	123.3	127.3	127.4	127.1	123.9	122.1	120.5	121.1	121.5
2006	118.0	118.1	120.0	122.4	126.0	130.7	131.2	132.0	128.1	125.9	125.5	125.2	125.3
2007	120.4	120.5	123.7	125.8	130.4	134.8	134.3	134.9	130.9	129.2	128.2	128.8	128.5
2008	124.4	124.6	126.7	129.1	133.5	137.9	136.8	136.4	132.1	129.1	126.8	125.8	130.3
2009	120.9	119.9	121.9	124.2	128.2	131.6	132.2	132.3	127.8	125.9	123.5	122.7	125.9
2010	119.5	119.1	121.4	125.3	128.2	132.9	133.6	134.3	130.6	129.8	127.4	127.4	127.5
2011	124.0	123.5	126.4	129.2	132.7	137.7	137.6	138.1	135.2	132.4	130.6	130.3	131.5
2012	127.5	127.0	130.2	133.7	137.6	142.3	142.7	142.8	138.4	137.2	136.2	136.0	136.0
2013	132.7	132.9	135.7	139.0	142.7	147.9	148.6	149.0	144.3	143.4	142.1	141.5	141.7
2014	139.2	139.0	141.8	145.4	150.1	153.7	155.1	155.4	152.0	149.9	147.5	148.5	148.1
2015	145.6	146.3	147.7	151.7	155.7	161.4	162.4	162.3	158.8	156.2	153.5	153.8	154.6

Employment by Industry: Denver-Aurora-Lakewood, CO, 2005–2015—*Continued*

(Numbers in thousands, not seasonally adjusted)

Industry and year	January	February	March	April	May	June	July	August	September	October	November	December	Annual average
Other Services													
2005	45.4	45.1	45.3	45.3	45.4	45.9	45.6	45.6	45.2	45.0	44.7	45.0	45.3
2006	45.7	45.5	45.9	46.1	46.3	47.1	46.7	46.8	46.4	46.2	46.2	46.4	46.3
2007	46.3	46.3	46.8	46.9	47.1	47.7	47.4	47.5	47.2	47.3	47.2	47.5	47.1
2008	47.8	47.9	48.2	47.9	48.3	48.7	49.0	49.1	48.9	48.7	48.3	47.8	48.4
2009	47.9	47.3	47.4	47.0	47.5	47.8	47.9	47.8	47.3	47.3	47.1	47.1	47.5
2010	47.1	46.9	47.0	46.9	47.3	47.8	48.0	48.1	47.5	47.3	47.5	47.4	47.4
2011	47.4	47.3	47.6	48.1	48.5	49.0	48.9	49.2	48.7	48.4	48.4	48.6	48.3
2012	48.6	48.6	49.0	49.2	49.4	50.2	50.2	50.3	50.0	50.2	50.0	49.9	49.6
2013	50.1	49.7	50.1	50.3	51.0	51.2	51.3	51.3	50.8	50.8	50.9	50.8	50.7
2014	51.5	51.2	51.3	51.8	52.2	52.8	53.5	53.6	52.8	53.4	53.1	52.8	52.5
2015	53.0	52.8	53.0	53.1	53.3	54.2	54.3	54.4	54.0	53.8	53.7	54.1	53.6
Government													
2005	160.4	164.5	164.9	166.5	167.2	165.6	159.6	158.7	166.2	166.7	167.1	167.0	164.5
2006	162.6	166.5	167.6	167.1	168.7	168.3	161.1	161.9	167.8	168.0	168.9	169.2	166.5
2007	163.9	169.0	170.3	170.7	171.8	170.8	163.4	164.3	171.7	172.5	173.4	173.0	169.6
2008	167.9	172.3	173.6	174.2	176.3	174.5	167.7	170.5	175.4	177.4	178.3	177.3	173.8
2009	172.8	175.9	177.3	178.3	180.3	177.8	169.0	170.1	177.2	179.6	178.9	177.7	176.2
2010	171.9	177.6	178.8	179.8	185.2	180.2	172.8	171.4	178.6	181.1	181.5	179.5	178.2
2011	173.9	179.3	180.0	181.4	182.9	180.5	171.6	171.4	178.6	180.2	180.5	179.5	178.3
2012	173.9	179.2	180.9	181.8	183.4	182.5	173.4	172.4	179.9	181.5	183.2	181.6	179.5
2013	176.2	182.0	183.2	184.6	185.6	184.1	175.8	177.1	185.5	188.7	188.4	186.4	183.1
2014	181.2	185.0	186.1	186.9	188.2	186.6	175.5	179.9	187.6	191.5	192.4	189.9	185.9
2015	185.5	189.7	190.5	192.3	194.0	192.0	182.4	185.8	194.2	194.9	196.0	194.3	191.0

Employment by Industry: St. Louis, MO-IL, 2005–2015

(Numbers in thousands, not seasonally adjusted)

Industry and year	January	February	March	April	May	June	July	August	September	October	November	December	Annual average
Total Nonfarm													
2005	1,296.9	1,302.7	1,314.4	1,333.6	1,337.5	1,341.7	1,318.8	1,329.8	1,339.7	1,338.1	1,340.8	1,343.5	1,328.1
2006	1,312.2	1,316.9	1,327.9	1,343.4	1,350.1	1,357.6	1,335.1	1,337.8	1,352.5	1,354.4	1,354.3	1,359.6	1,341.8
2007	1,320.9	1,324.6	1,341.3	1,353.3	1,366.1	1,366.7	1,338.1	1,346.1	1,359.3	1,361.8	1,365.7	1,367.1	1,350.9
2008	1,334.0	1,340.1	1,343.5	1,355.0	1,367.8	1,371.0	1,337.7	1,345.8	1,353.0	1,347.3	1,339.6	1,333.2	1,347.3
2009	1,293.3	1,292.1	1,293.9	1,302.3	1,307.3	1,303.9	1,274.7	1,280.6	1,286.8	1,285.7	1,283.5	1,284.3	1,290.7
2010	1,256.4	1,262.0	1,273.1	1,286.1	1,294.5	1,291.4	1,268.1	1,280.4	1,286.2	1,293.9	1,292.9	1,290.8	1,281.3
2011	1,266.7	1,269.5	1,282.6	1,303.5	1,308.9	1,304.5	1,285.5	1,293.8	1,302.0	1,303.1	1,301.4	1,302.2	1,293.6
2012	1,270.0	1,275.5	1,287.9	1,300.3	1,308.5	1,304.8	1,280.7	1,290.0	1,297.6	1,304.6	1,304.9	1,306.9	1,294.3
2013	1,276.1	1,282.9	1,289.8	1,307.2	1,317.3	1,313.6	1,293.0	1,302.3	1,310.9	1,317.0	1,317.5	1,319.3	1,303.9
2014	1,281.9	1,292.0	1,301.2	1,325.7	1,333.5	1,328.9	1,309.0	1,319.5	1,325.7	1,340.3	1,339.0	1,340.2	1,319.7
2015	1,309.1	1,314.6	1,321.1	1,344.7	1,356.6	1,355.3	1,338.0	1,346.6	1,355.1	1,365.9	1,359.1	1,358.5	1,343.7
Total Private													
2005	1,132.4	1,135.1	1,147.0	1,164.3	1,167.3	1,175.5	1,170.5	1,176.1	1,172.8	1,170.3	1,171.6	1,174.7	1,163.1
2006	1,147.0	1,148.9	1,159.6	1,173.9	1,179.6	1,192.9	1,186.6	1,185.4	1,184.6	1,184.9	1,183.7	1,188.9	1,176.3
2007	1,154.1	1,154.7	1,171.3	1,182.9	1,194.6	1,201.2	1,194.1	1,195.3	1,191.0	1,190.6	1,193.3	1,195.0	1,184.8
2008	1,165.8	1,167.5	1,171.8	1,183.0	1,193.8	1,203.3	1,190.7	1,191.4	1,181.9	1,173.4	1,165.6	1,159.8	1,179.0
2009	1,122.9	1,119.4	1,120.6	1,125.1	1,129.9	1,131.5	1,125.5	1,123.3	1,113.5	1,111.4	1,109.6	1,110.5	1,120.3
2010	1,086.9	1,089.7	1,100.7	1,111.5	1,116.0	1,123.8	1,123.0	1,124.2	1,117.9	1,123.8	1,122.6	1,121.2	1,113.4
2011	1,100.3	1,101.4	1,113.8	1,133.5	1,138.2	1,142.5	1,143.6	1,143.4	1,135.0	1,135.8	1,134.1	1,134.8	1,129.7
2012	1,107.1	1,109.8	1,121.3	1,132.7	1,140.0	1,144.8	1,141.2	1,142.0	1,134.1	1,140.0	1,140.4	1,142.1	1,133.0
2013	1,115.7	1,119.5	1,125.7	1,138.5	1,148.0	1,152.8	1,153.4	1,154.2	1,147.0	1,152.0	1,152.0	1,153.6	1,142.7
2014	1,120.8	1,127.6	1,136.2	1,161.7	1,168.8	1,172.6	1,173.3	1,175.5	1,166.4	1,177.5	1,177.0	1,177.9	1,161.3
2015	1,151.8	1,153.7	1,160.0	1,182.8	1,193.8	1,197.4	1,201.2	1,201.2	1,194.2	1,201.9	1,195.4	1,194.6	1,185.7
Goods Producing													
2005	216.6	217.0	220.5	223.0	224.6	226.6	221.6	226.8	226.2	225.5	224.5	223.0	223.0
2006	217.3	217.4	219.8	221.5	222.0	226.3	225.4	222.8	224.3	222.4	221.1	219.8	221.7
2007	211.4	211.4	216.7	218.1	221.2	222.6	219.6	221.0	220.3	219.6	218.4	216.1	218.0
2008	206.7	207.5	206.3	209.1	212.4	216.5	211.7	211.6	210.8	207.3	202.3	197.8	208.3
2009	185.5	183.9	183.1	179.8	179.1	178.9	179.6	176.7	174.7	173.3	170.2	167.7	177.7
2010	161.3	160.4	163.9	166.2	166.9	170.7	170.8	170.6	170.1	171.0	169.7	168.2	167.5
2011	165.2	165.3	169.3	172.6	173.8	176.1	177.0	176.2	173.9	171.7	169.3	168.2	171.6
2012	162.0	161.7	164.3	166.6	168.6	170.8	171.4	171.3	169.4	169.2	167.4	167.0	167.5
2013	162.2	162.9	163.7	166.5	169.4	173.0	173.4	173.0	171.8	171.5	169.9	168.0	168.8
2014	161.5	163.3	166.7	170.1	172.5	175.4	176.6	176.5	176.1	176.0	174.0	173.3	171.8
2015	168.3	168.2	170.5	174.4	177.3	179.4	180.9	180.9	180.4	180.4	176.8	176.1	176.1
Service-Providing													
2005	1,080.3	1,085.7	1,093.9	1,110.6	1,112.9	1,115.1	1,097.2	1,103.0	1,113.5	1,112.6	1,116.3	1,120.5	1,105.1
2006	1,094.9	1,099.5	1,108.1	1,121.9	1,128.1	1,131.3	1,109.7	1,115.0	1,128.2	1,132.0	1,133.2	1,139.8	1,120.1
2007	1,109.5	1,113.2	1,124.6	1,135.2	1,144.9	1,144.1	1,118.5	1,125.1	1,139.0	1,142.2	1,147.3	1,151.0	1,132.9
2008	1,127.3	1,132.6	1,137.2	1,145.9	1,155.4	1,154.5	1,126.0	1,134.2	1,142.2	1,140.0	1,137.3	1,135.4	1,139.0
2009	1,107.8	1,108.2	1,110.8	1,122.5	1,128.2	1,125.0	1,095.1	1,103.9	1,112.1	1,112.4	1,113.3	1,116.6	1,113.0
2010	1,095.1	1,101.6	1,109.2	1,119.9	1,127.6	1,120.7	1,097.3	1,109.8	1,116.1	1,122.9	1,123.2	1,122.6	1,113.8
2011	1,101.5	1,104.2	1,113.3	1,130.9	1,135.1	1,128.4	1,108.5	1,117.6	1,128.1	1,131.4	1,132.1	1,134.0	1,122.1
2012	1,108.0	1,113.8	1,123.6	1,133.7	1,139.9	1,134.0	1,109.3	1,118.7	1,128.2	1,135.4	1,137.5	1,139.9	1,126.8
2013	1,113.9	1,120.0	1,126.1	1,140.7	1,147.9	1,140.6	1,119.6	1,129.3	1,139.1	1,145.5	1,147.6	1,151.3	1,135.1
2014	1,120.4	1,128.7	1,134.5	1,155.6	1,161.0	1,153.5	1,132.4	1,143.0	1,149.6	1,164.3	1,165.0	1,166.9	1,147.9
2015	1,140.8	1,146.4	1,150.6	1,170.3	1,179.3	1,175.9	1,157.1	1,165.7	1,174.7	1,185.5	1,182.3	1,182.4	1,167.6
Mining, Logging, and Construction													
2005	73.7	74.2	77.5	79.9	81.6	83.1	84.6	84.6	84.0	83.2	82.2	80.6	80.8
2006	77.7	77.5	79.3	81.9	82.4	85.4	85.5	85.4	84.5	83.2	81.9	80.2	82.1
2007	76.9	73.9	79.3	80.8	83.7	86.6	86.1	86.0	84.1	83.6	82.5	79.9	82.0
2008	75.7	73.6	76.0	77.9	79.9	82.0	82.2	82.1	80.6	77.9	74.9	71.5	77.9
2009	63.8	62.9	64.4	64.6	65.5	66.6	67.7	66.6	65.6	64.5	62.1	59.9	64.5
2010	54.9	53.9	57.1	59.2	59.5	62.2	62.5	62.2	61.8	61.8	60.4	58.4	59.5
2011	56.5	56.5	59.8	62.9	63.9	65.2	65.4	64.7	62.7	60.5	58.6	57.0	61.1
2012	51.9	51.4	53.5	55.7	57.3	58.8	59.6	60.0	59.5	58.9	57.5	56.9	56.8
2013	52.3	52.4	53.6	56.4	59.0	61.7	62.9	62.2	61.3	60.6	59.1	57.1	58.2
2014	52.9	52.1	55.8	58.3	59.8	61.4	62.5	62.5	62.4	62.2	60.5	59.6	59.2
2015	55.5	55.3	57.4	60.8	63.0	63.9	64.8	65.7	65.5	67.1	63.9	63.1	62.2

Employment by Industry: St. Louis, MO-IL, 2005–2015—*Continued*

(Numbers in thousands, not seasonally adjusted)

Industry and year	January	February	March	April	May	June	July	August	September	October	November	December	Annual average
Manufacturing													
2005	142.9	142.8	143.0	143.1	143.0	143.5	137.0	142.2	142.2	142.3	142.3	142.4	142.2
2006	139.6	139.9	140.5	139.6	139.6	140.9	139.9	137.4	139.8	139.2	139.2	139.6	139.6
2007	134.5	137.5	137.4	137.3	137.5	136.0	133.5	135.0	136.2	136.0	135.9	136.2	136.1
2008	131.0	133.9	130.3	131.2	132.5	134.5	129.5	129.5	130.2	129.4	127.4	126.3	130.5
2009	121.7	121.0	118.7	115.2	113.6	112.3	111.9	110.1	109.1	108.8	108.1	107.8	113.2
2010	106.4	106.5	106.8	107.0	107.4	108.5	108.3	108.4	108.3	109.2	109.3	109.8	108.0
2011	108.7	108.8	109.5	109.7	109.9	110.9	111.6	111.5	111.2	111.2	110.7	111.2	110.4
2012	110.1	110.3	110.8	110.9	111.3	112.0	111.8	111.3	109.9	110.3	109.9	110.1	110.7
2013	109.9	110.5	110.1	110.1	110.4	111.3	110.5	110.8	110.5	110.9	110.8	110.9	110.6
2014	108.6	111.2	110.9	111.8	112.7	114.0	114.1	114.0	113.7	113.8	113.5	113.7	112.7
2015	112.8	112.9	113.1	113.6	114.3	115.5	116.1	115.2	114.9	113.3	112.9	113.0	114.0
Trade, Transportation, and Utilities													
2005	251.8	248.7	250.1	251.6	252.6	252.9	253.0	253.5	252.1	252.9	257.8	261.1	253.2
2006	251.2	248.1	249.4	250.5	252.2	253.6	252.5	253.2	253.1	254.9	259.6	263.3	253.5
2007	254.4	251.3	254.4	255.6	257.9	258.5	257.1	256.3	256.7	257.7	263.8	266.5	257.5
2008	258.5	255.0	256.1	256.3	257.8	258.9	256.6	257.0	255.6	255.1	257.7	259.0	257.0
2009	248.7	245.4	244.8	244.8	245.6	245.2	242.6	243.5	242.9	242.4	246.0	247.4	244.9
2010	239.1	236.7	238.3	239.0	240.5	240.7	239.3	240.7	239.4	240.4	243.9	246.8	240.4
2011	239.9	238.2	239.5	242.2	243.3	243.2	242.4	243.2	242.1	242.5	247.1	249.3	242.7
2012	241.1	239.0	240.5	242.4	244.1	243.8	242.9	244.2	243.8	245.7	251.2	253.0	244.3
2013	242.9	240.2	240.6	243.0	244.7	245.1	244.4	245.9	245.1	247.3	252.5	255.9	245.6
2014	245.2	243.2	244.7	247.1	248.7	250.2	248.6	250.0	249.0	251.6	257.2	260.2	249.6
2015	249.7	247.2	248.5	251.0	253.1	253.6	252.6	254.3	253.4	255.6	259.2	260.9	253.3
Wholesale Trade													
2005	59.6	59.0	59.2	59.6	59.6	60.0	60.4	60.6	59.8	59.5	59.6	59.9	59.7
2006	59.3	59.2	59.5	60.3	60.6	61.3	61.4	61.5	61.3	61.3	61.3	61.8	60.7
2007	61.2	61.4	61.8	61.6	62.0	62.5	62.8	62.7	62.5	62.6	62.7	62.9	62.2
2008	62.6	62.6	62.7	63.0	63.2	63.6	63.5	63.5	63.1	62.5	62.0	61.9	62.9
2009	60.7	60.4	60.1	59.8	59.5	59.7	59.5	59.3	58.8	59.2	58.9	59.2	59.6
2010	58.5	58.4	58.8	60.6	60.6	60.5	60.2	59.8	59.5	59.5	59.3	59.5	59.6
2011	59.1	59.1	59.3	59.5	59.6	60.0	60.4	60.2	59.9	59.9	60.0	60.0	59.8
2012	59.7	59.7	60.0	60.6	61.0	61.3	61.1	61.4	60.9	61.0	61.0	61.2	60.7
2013	60.0	59.9	60.0	60.3	60.8	61.2	61.2	61.3	61.0	61.5	61.7	61.9	60.9
2014	61.0	61.1	61.4	61.7	62.0	62.5	62.6	62.7	62.1	62.2	62.4	62.5	62.0
2015	61.4	61.2	61.3	61.5	62.1	62.3	62.4	62.4	62.0	62.9	63.5	63.4	62.2
Retail Trade													
2005	144.7	142.2	142.9	143.9	144.8	145.3	145.8	145.8	144.1	145.6	150.1	152.2	145.6
2006	144.2	141.2	142.1	142.9	143.9	144.9	144.3	144.2	143.5	145.5	150.2	152.6	145.0
2007	145.1	142.1	144.3	145.5	146.8	147.7	146.3	145.2	144.8	145.7	151.4	153.3	146.5
2008	146.8	143.4	144.2	144.3	145.2	146.2	144.5	144.2	142.6	142.9	145.8	147.0	144.8
2009	139.0	136.5	136.4	137.2	138.1	138.8	137.4	137.6	136.9	137.0	140.9	141.8	138.1
2010	135.3	133.2	134.3	134.9	136.2	137.5	136.8	136.8	135.4	136.3	139.9	142.1	136.6
2011	136.6	134.8	135.6	137.6	138.3	138.9	138.6	138.4	137.0	137.5	141.9	143.4	138.2
2012	137.1	134.9	136.0	136.8	137.6	138.2	137.8	137.2	136.8	138.6	143.7	144.5	138.3
2013	137.6	135.2	135.3	137.0	138.1	139.3	138.7	138.7	137.8	139.6	144.1	146.4	139.0
2014	138.2	136.2	137.3	138.9	139.8	141.6	140.7	140.6	139.3	141.3	146.2	147.8	140.7
2015	140.2	138.2	139.3	141.0	142.1	143.6	142.8	143.4	142.2	143.3	145.5	146.1	142.3
Transportation and Utilities													
2005	47.5	47.5	48.0	48.1	48.2	47.6	46.8	47.1	48.2	47.8	48.1	49.0	47.8
2006	47.7	47.7	47.8	47.3	47.7	47.4	46.8	47.5	48.3	48.1	48.1	48.9	47.8
2007	48.1	47.8	48.3	48.5	49.1	48.3	48.0	48.4	49.4	49.4	49.7	50.3	48.8
2008	49.1	49.0	49.2	49.0	49.4	49.1	48.6	49.3	49.9	49.7	49.9	50.1	49.4
2009	49.0	48.5	48.3	47.8	48.0	46.7	45.7	46.6	47.2	46.2	46.2	46.4	47.2
2010	45.3	45.1	45.2	43.5	43.7	42.7	42.3	44.1	44.5	44.6	44.7	45.2	44.2
2011	44.2	44.3	44.6	45.1	45.4	44.3	43.4	44.6	45.2	45.1	45.2	45.9	44.8
2012	44.3	44.4	44.5	45.0	45.5	44.3	44.0	45.6	46.1	46.1	46.5	47.3	45.3
2013	45.3	45.1	45.3	45.7	45.8	44.6	44.5	45.9	46.3	46.2	46.7	47.6	45.8
2014	46.0	45.9	46.0	46.5	46.9	46.1	45.3	46.7	47.6	48.1	48.6	49.9	47.0
2015	48.1	47.8	47.9	48.5	48.9	47.7	47.4	48.5	49.2	49.4	50.2	51.4	48.8

Employment by Industry: St. Louis, MO-IL, 2005–2015—*Continued*

(Numbers in thousands, not seasonally adjusted)

Industry and year	January	February	March	April	May	June	July	August	September	October	November	December	Annual average
Information													
2005	29.0	29.0	29.0	29.3	29.3	29.6	29.9	29.8	29.8	30.0	30.0	30.2	29.6
2006	30.0	29.8	29.8	29.8	29.9	30.1	30.3	30.2	30.0	30.4	30.4	30.6	30.1
2007	29.7	29.6	29.7	30.0	30.3	30.5	30.3	30.3	30.2	30.6	30.8	30.8	30.2
2008	30.3	30.1	30.2	30.7	31.1	31.2	31.1	30.9	30.7	30.8	30.9	31.0	30.8
2009	30.7	30.6	30.5	30.2	30.2	30.4	30.4	30.4	30.1	29.8	29.8	30.1	30.3
2010	29.8	29.6	29.6	31.6	31.3	31.8	31.4	31.4	31.1	30.9	30.8	31.0	30.9
2011	30.4	30.3	30.1	30.9	31.1	31.3	31.6	31.5	31.3	30.9	30.8	30.8	30.9
2012	30.6	30.5	30.4	30.0	30.2	30.2	30.3	30.1	29.7	29.3	29.2	29.2	30.0
2013	29.1	29.2	29.2	29.1	29.4	29.4	29.2	29.2	28.9	28.8	28.7	28.9	29.1
2014	28.2	28.1	28.3	28.6	28.9	29.1	29.3	29.2	28.9	28.6	28.7	28.7	28.7
2015	28.6	28.6	28.6	28.7	28.9	29.2	29.2	29.1	28.8	28.3	28.1	28.0	28.7
Financial Activities													
2005	76.1	76.5	76.6	77.7	77.6	78.2	78.9	78.8	78.5	78.0	77.8	78.1	77.7
2006	77.1	77.3	77.5	78.2	78.8	79.2	79.1	79.3	78.8	78.6	78.7	78.9	78.5
2007	78.3	78.4	78.6	78.8	79.5	80.0	80.2	80.0	79.4	79.5	79.1	79.4	79.3
2008	79.8	80.0	80.1	79.6	79.6	79.7	79.2	79.5	78.7	78.1	77.9	77.8	79.2
2009	77.9	78.1	78.2	78.7	78.8	79.1	79.0	78.9	78.2	78.6	78.2	78.2	78.5
2010	78.1	78.1	78.2	79.5	79.6	80.1	81.0	80.9	80.5	81.5	81.3	81.4	80.0
2011	80.4	80.3	80.5	81.8	82.0	81.9	82.8	82.9	82.5	83.0	83.2	83.3	82.1
2012	82.7	83.0	83.6	84.2	84.4	84.8	85.0	85.1	84.8	85.7	86.0	85.9	84.6
2013	83.9	84.1	84.3	84.5	85.3	85.8	85.9	85.8	85.3	85.7	85.8	85.5	85.2
2014	84.5	84.6	84.5	84.9	85.3	85.4	85.8	85.7	85.0	85.4	85.6	85.6	85.2
2015	84.6	84.6	84.7	85.0	85.6	86.1	86.6	86.4	85.5	85.8	85.8	86.3	85.6
Professional and Business Services													
2005	180.0	181.1	183.8	188.1	186.6	188.6	187.4	188.2	188.2	187.7	187.9	188.2	186.3
2006	185.0	185.9	188.5	191.7	191.3	194.5	192.8	193.9	194.0	195.0	193.8	195.3	191.8
2007	188.4	189.0	191.6	194.1	194.2	195.0	194.3	195.0	194.6	194.6	194.2	194.5	193.3
2008	193.2	194.7	196.3	199.8	198.6	199.9	198.2	198.2	195.4	193.6	191.0	189.1	195.7
2009	183.5	183.2	181.9	184.0	183.0	183.2	181.9	181.9	180.7	180.6	180.8	181.3	182.2
2010	178.6	180.6	182.0	187.5	186.7	187.7	188.7	189.0	187.9	189.6	189.4	188.5	186.4
2011	186.7	187.5	189.5	193.7	192.3	192.4	192.2	191.6	191.0	191.3	190.9	190.4	190.8
2012	185.9	186.6	188.7	192.8	192.4	193.4	191.1	191.0	190.2	191.9	192.4	192.5	190.7
2013	189.1	190.8	193.7	197.4	197.8	198.6	199.6	200.6	199.9	201.2	201.4	202.2	197.7
2014	196.6	198.4	200.5	205.6	204.6	205.1	203.0	204.1	203.8	205.8	205.1	205.6	203.2
2015	200.2	201.5	203.0	206.8	207.8	207.2	208.8	209.4	208.9	212.7	208.6	208.2	206.9
Education and Health Services													
2005	193.9	196.5	196.8	197.4	196.7	196.2	196.0	195.6	198.4	199.5	200.3	200.8	197.3
2006	198.2	201.1	202.3	202.3	202.0	201.8	200.4	200.2	203.1	205.3	205.9	206.4	202.4
2007	202.7	205.4	206.5	207.3	207.4	206.8	206.6	206.4	209.0	210.6	211.6	212.1	207.7
2008	207.1	210.3	210.1	210.8	210.7	209.9	209.6	209.9	212.5	213.9	214.6	215.0	211.2
2009	211.7	214.0	214.2	213.6	214.1	213.0	212.6	212.9	215.4	216.9	218.7	220.7	214.8
2010	218.8	221.8	222.2	223.2	223.1	222.1	220.5	220.6	223.6	227.3	228.0	227.6	223.2
2011	225.6	228.2	228.6	230.0	229.6	227.9	227.9	228.0	231.1	233.3	234.8	234.8	230.0
2012	232.5	235.6	235.9	232.3	231.2	229.0	228.8	228.6	231.7	233.8	233.8	234.1	232.3
2013	231.3	235.0	234.1	231.0	229.0	225.7	226.1	225.8	228.0	230.5	231.0	230.1	229.8
2014	227.3	232.0	229.6	234.6	232.2	228.6	230.9	230.7	232.6	237.6	238.3	236.2	232.6
2015	236.1	238.4	236.5	241.9	240.1	237.4	239.8	238.5	239.9	246.4	244.7	243.9	240.3
Leisure and Hospitality													
2005	128.5	129.3	132.8	139.9	142.8	145.6	146.4	146.3	143.3	139.9	136.7	136.4	139.0
2006	132.1	133.1	135.7	142.8	146.3	149.5	148.5	148.2	144.0	141.3	137.3	137.5	141.4
2007	133.1	133.2	137.0	142.0	146.8	150.2	148.8	149.1	144.3	141.2	138.5	138.9	141.9
2008	134.0	133.7	136.1	139.8	146.1	149.4	146.8	147.0	141.5	137.6	134.7	134.0	140.1
2009	129.9	129.2	132.6	138.5	143.5	146.3	144.5	144.5	137.6	135.2	131.5	130.5	137.0
2010	127.3	128.5	131.9	139.1	142.5	145.0	145.7	145.4	140.5	138.0	134.3	132.5	137.6
2011	127.7	127.2	131.3	136.4	140.0	143.0	142.9	143.5	137.0	137.3	132.3	132.2	135.9
2012	127.4	128.3	132.4	139.0	143.2	146.5	145.5	145.7	139.2	139.1	135.2	135.3	138.1
2013	131.8	131.9	134.5	141.5	146.4	148.4	148.3	147.3	142.3	140.9	136.6	136.8	140.6
2014	131.7	131.9	135.2	143.5	148.9	150.4	150.6	151.2	143.9	145.5	141.4	141.4	143.0
2015	137.7	138.3	140.9	147.0	152.9	155.5	154.6	154.4	150.0	144.7	144.9	143.1	147.0

Employment by Industry: St. Louis, MO-IL, 2005–2015—*Continued*

(Numbers in thousands, not seasonally adjusted)

Industry and year	January	February	March	April	May	June	July	August	September	October	November	December	Annual average
Other Services													
2005	56.5	57.0	57.4	57.3	57.1	57.8	57.3	57.1	56.3	56.8	56.6	56.9	57.0
2006	56.1	56.2	56.6	57.1	57.1	57.9	57.6	57.6	57.3	57.0	56.9	57.1	57.0
2007	56.1	56.4	56.8	57.0	57.3	57.6	57.2	57.2	56.5	56.8	56.9	56.7	56.9
2008	56.2	56.2	56.6	56.9	57.5	57.8	57.5	57.3	56.7	57.0	56.5	56.1	56.9
2009	55.0	55.0	55.3	55.5	55.6	55.4	54.9	54.5	53.9	54.6	54.4	54.6	54.9
2010	53.9	54.0	54.6	45.4	45.4	45.7	45.6	45.6	44.8	45.1	45.2	45.2	47.5
2011	44.4	44.4	45.0	45.9	46.1	46.7	46.8	46.5	46.1	45.8	45.7	45.8	45.8
2012	44.9	45.1	45.5	45.4	45.9	46.3	46.2	46.0	45.3	45.3	45.2	45.1	45.5
2013	45.4	45.4	45.6	45.5	46.0	46.8	46.5	46.6	45.7	46.1	46.1	46.2	46.0
2014	45.8	46.1	46.7	47.3	47.7	48.4	48.5	48.1	47.1	47.0	46.7	46.9	47.2
2015	46.6	46.9	47.3	48.0	48.1	49.0	48.7	48.2	47.3	48.0	47.3	48.1	47.8
Government													
2005	164.5	167.6	167.4	169.3	170.2	166.2	148.3	153.7	166.9	167.8	169.2	168.8	165.0
2006	165.2	168.0	168.3	169.5	170.5	164.7	148.5	152.4	167.9	169.5	170.6	170.7	165.5
2007	166.8	169.9	170.0	170.4	171.5	165.5	144.0	150.8	168.3	171.2	172.4	172.1	166.1
2008	168.2	172.6	171.7	172.0	174.0	167.7	147.0	154.4	171.1	173.9	174.0	173.4	168.3
2009	170.4	172.7	173.3	177.2	177.4	172.4	149.2	157.3	173.3	174.3	173.9	173.8	170.4
2010	169.5	172.3	172.4	174.6	178.5	167.6	145.1	156.2	168.3	170.1	170.3	169.6	167.9
2011	166.4	168.1	168.8	170.0	170.7	162.0	141.9	150.4	167.0	167.3	167.3	167.4	163.9
2012	162.9	165.7	166.6	167.6	168.5	160.0	139.5	148.0	163.5	164.6	164.5	164.8	161.4
2013	160.4	163.4	164.1	168.7	169.3	160.8	139.6	148.1	163.9	165.0	165.5	165.7	161.2
2014	161.1	164.4	165.0	164.0	164.7	156.3	135.7	144.0	159.3	162.8	162.0	162.3	158.5
2015	157.3	160.9	161.1	161.9	162.8	157.9	136.8	145.4	160.9	164.0	163.7	163.9	158.1

Employment by Industry: Baltimore-Columbia-Towson, MD, 2005–2015

(Numbers in thousands, not seasonally adjusted)

Industry and year	January	February	March	April	May	June	July	August	September	October	November	December	Annual average
Total Nonfarm													
2005	1,247.7	1,255.1	1,263.3	1,278.6	1,286.7	1,293.2	1,290.8	1,286.0	1,299.1	1,300.4	1,306.6	1,311.5	1,284.9
2006	1,274.0	1,280.2	1,295.2	1,304.0	1,311.5	1,316.7	1,305.5	1,304.0	1,308.6	1,317.0	1,323.2	1,330.3	1,305.9
2007	1,291.2	1,292.8	1,309.0	1,315.2	1,324.3	1,328.2	1,318.2	1,317.9	1,319.2	1,323.9	1,330.3	1,334.2	1,317.0
2008	1,297.0	1,301.6	1,311.4	1,320.6	1,325.2	1,325.0	1,316.2	1,313.2	1,311.2	1,316.8	1,313.1	1,311.7	1,313.6
2009	1,264.3	1,263.5	1,268.4	1,276.9	1,282.2	1,284.5	1,269.1	1,263.9	1,268.6	1,277.2	1,278.0	1,278.6	1,272.9
2010	1,240.8	1,229.6	1,259.4	1,278.4	1,284.8	1,288.0	1,274.4	1,272.0	1,273.6	1,287.8	1,290.7	1,291.9	1,272.6
2011	1,257.6	1,264.7	1,279.2	1,294.7	1,298.4	1,300.5	1,292.6	1,290.9	1,297.4	1,307.1	1,312.3	1,315.5	1,292.6
2012	1,284.6	1,290.9	1,304.0	1,312.5	1,319.6	1,321.9	1,311.2	1,311.7	1,320.2	1,328.4	1,334.0	1,337.0	1,314.7
2013	1,301.8	1,309.8	1,321.8	1,330.7	1,338.2	1,341.4	1,330.2	1,329.1	1,335.3	1,343.0	1,350.9	1,348.1	1,331.7
2014	1,305.5	1,311.6	1,324.2	1,346.1	1,353.5	1,355.2	1,341.8	1,345.7	1,352.8	1,363.7	1,369.6	1,370.7	1,345.0
2015	1,327.4	1,335.7	1,343.6	1,362.1	1,375.8	1,373.9	1,370.2	1,369.1	1,370.6	1,382.9	1,382.6	1,385.3	1,364.9
Total Private													
2005	1,034.1	1,037.0	1,045.2	1,058.7	1,065.9	1,075.1	1,080.7	1,080.2	1,082.0	1,078.4	1,082.6	1,088.1	1,067.3
2006	1,058.8	1,060.1	1,073.1	1,080.6	1,087.9	1,097.3	1,092.2	1,091.5	1,089.9	1,092.2	1,096.5	1,103.2	1,085.3
2007	1,072.1	1,068.9	1,082.6	1,089.9	1,098.3	1,106.7	1,103.6	1,103.6	1,099.8	1,098.6	1,103.2	1,107.6	1,094.6
2008	1,077.7	1,076.7	1,084.9	1,092.1	1,096.5	1,101.0	1,097.4	1,095.5	1,088.2	1,086.8	1,082.5	1,081.1	1,088.4
2009	1,041.1	1,035.1	1,038.2	1,044.8	1,050.3	1,056.5	1,047.2	1,044.7	1,043.8	1,042.6	1,043.6	1,044.8	1,044.4
2010	1,014.0	998.1	1,024.0	1,040.8	1,046.0	1,052.7	1,047.9	1,047.0	1,044.9	1,051.6	1,052.8	1,056.4	1,039.7
2011	1,028.1	1,029.6	1,040.0	1,055.2	1,061.1	1,066.9	1,068.6	1,066.8	1,067.0	1,069.1	1,075.5	1,078.8	1,058.9
2012	1,054.7	1,055.1	1,065.0	1,074.8	1,083.4	1,091.9	1,088.1	1,090.0	1,090.1	1,091.5	1,097.0	1,100.6	1,081.9
2013	1,073.2	1,075.6	1,085.5	1,094.6	1,102.5	1,110.9	1,109.5	1,109.4	1,107.7	1,110.3	1,116.2	1,115.0	1,100.9
2014	1,081.2	1,080.6	1,091.5	1,110.2	1,120.5	1,126.2	1,124.2	1,127.2	1,125.2	1,129.8	1,134.7	1,137.8	1,115.8
2015	1,103.9	1,106.4	1,112.1	1,129.9	1,144.0	1,147.4	1,152.8	1,152.2	1,147.0	1,153.7	1,153.0	1,156.8	1,138.3
Goods Producing													
2005	154.2	153.6	154.9	158.0	159.1	160.9	161.1	161.7	161.7	160.3	160.8	160.9	158.9
2006	157.0	156.5	158.6	159.3	159.9	161.9	161.8	161.8	160.9	159.1	158.4	158.1	159.4
2007	154.4	152.5	155.0	155.9	157.4	159.3	159.8	159.9	158.5	156.8	156.2	155.3	156.8
2008	152.4	151.3	151.9	151.8	151.9	153.3	153.8	153.5	151.7	149.6	147.8	145.6	151.2
2009	138.7	136.6	135.9	135.3	135.8	137.1	136.7	136.1	134.8	133.8	132.8	132.1	135.5
2010	127.6	123.1	126.7	130.1	131.0	132.6	132.5	132.5	131.5	130.9	130.4	130.0	129.9
2011	126.8	126.2	127.5	130.2	130.9	132.3	133.0	132.6	131.1	130.6	130.0	129.7	130.1
2012	126.5	125.4	126.4	127.3	127.6	129.4	129.9	129.9	128.2	127.6	127.8	127.5	127.8
2013	124.2	123.2	124.0	126.0	126.7	128.2	129.2	129.3	128.3	127.7	127.3	125.7	126.7
2014	122.3	121.2	122.9	125.9	127.4	128.8	129.1	129.5	128.8	128.2	128.0	127.3	126.6
2015	123.5	122.8	123.8	126.7	128.3	130.1	131.2	132.0	131.1	132.2	132.1	132.5	128.9
Service-Providing													
2005	1,093.5	1,101.5	1,108.4	1,120.6	1,127.6	1,132.3	1,129.7	1,124.3	1,137.4	1,140.1	1,145.8	1,150.6	1,126.0
2006	1,117.0	1,123.7	1,136.6	1,144.7	1,151.6	1,154.8	1,143.7	1,142.2	1,147.7	1,157.9	1,164.8	1,172.2	1,146.4
2007	1,136.8	1,140.3	1,154.0	1,159.3	1,166.9	1,168.9	1,158.4	1,158.0	1,160.7	1,167.1	1,174.1	1,178.9	1,160.3
2008	1,144.6	1,150.3	1,159.5	1,168.8	1,173.3	1,171.7	1,162.4	1,159.7	1,159.5	1,167.2	1,165.3	1,166.1	1,162.4
2009	1,125.6	1,126.9	1,132.5	1,141.6	1,146.4	1,147.4	1,132.4	1,127.8	1,133.8	1,143.4	1,145.2	1,146.5	1,137.5
2010	1,113.2	1,106.5	1,132.7	1,148.3	1,153.8	1,155.4	1,141.9	1,139.5	1,142.1	1,156.9	1,160.3	1,161.9	1,142.7
2011	1,130.8	1,138.5	1,151.7	1,164.5	1,167.5	1,168.2	1,159.6	1,158.3	1,166.3	1,176.5	1,182.3	1,185.8	1,162.5
2012	1,158.1	1,165.5	1,177.6	1,185.2	1,192.0	1,192.5	1,181.3	1,181.8	1,192.0	1,200.8	1,206.2	1,209.5	1,186.9
2013	1,177.6	1,186.6	1,197.8	1,204.7	1,211.5	1,213.2	1,201.0	1,199.8	1,207.0	1,215.3	1,223.6	1,222.4	1,205.0
2014	1,183.2	1,190.4	1,201.3	1,220.2	1,226.1	1,226.4	1,212.7	1,216.2	1,224.0	1,235.5	1,241.6	1,243.4	1,218.4
2015	1,203.9	1,212.9	1,219.8	1,235.4	1,247.5	1,243.8	1,239.0	1,237.1	1,239.5	1,250.7	1,250.5	1,252.8	1,236.1
Mining, Logging, and Construction													
2005	78.9	78.1	79.4	82.3	83.6	85.3	85.9	86.3	86.3	85.6	86.0	85.9	83.6
2006	83.2	82.9	84.7	85.8	86.7	88.4	88.4	88.6	88.0	87.1	86.6	86.3	86.4
2007	83.2	81.5	83.9	84.9	86.2	87.7	88.2	88.4	87.4	86.0	85.5	84.3	85.6
2008	82.1	81.1	81.9	82.4	82.5	83.6	84.4	84.2	83.0	81.8	80.5	78.5	82.2
2009	73.2	72.0	71.6	71.7	72.2	73.4	73.5	72.9	71.7	70.8	70.0	69.2	71.9
2010	65.2	61.7	64.9	68.1	68.9	70.1	69.9	69.9	69.4	69.2	69.1	68.5	67.9
2011	64.8	64.2	65.4	67.6	68.5	69.8	70.7	70.5	69.8	69.8	69.5	69.2	68.3
2012	66.4	65.6	66.7	67.7	68.1	69.4	69.8	70.0	69.9	69.6	69.8	69.4	68.5
2013	66.9	66.1	67.1	69.3	70.2	71.4	72.3	72.5	72.1	71.9	71.9	70.4	70.2
2014	68.0	67.1	68.7	71.4	72.9	74.1	74.6	74.9	74.5	74.0	73.7	73.2	72.3
2015	69.8	69.2	70.3	73.2	74.6	76.0	76.9	77.5	77.2	78.0	77.4	76.8	74.7

Employment by Industry: Baltimore-Columbia-Towson, MD, 2005–2015—*Continued*

(Numbers in thousands, not seasonally adjusted)

Industry and year	January	February	March	April	May	June	July	August	September	October	November	December	Annual average
Manufacturing													
2005	75.3	75.5	75.5	75.7	75.5	75.6	75.2	75.4	75.4	74.7	74.8	75.0	75.3
2006	73.8	73.6	73.9	73.5	73.2	73.5	73.4	73.2	72.9	72.0	71.8	71.8	73.1
2007	71.2	71.0	71.1	71.0	71.2	71.6	71.6	71.5	71.1	70.8	70.7	71.0	71.2
2008	70.3	70.2	70.0	69.4	69.4	69.7	69.4	69.3	68.7	67.8	67.3	67.1	69.1
2009	65.5	64.6	64.3	63.6	63.6	63.7	63.2	63.2	63.1	63.0	62.8	62.9	63.6
2010	62.4	61.4	61.8	62.0	62.1	62.5	62.6	62.6	62.1	61.7	61.3	61.5	62.0
2011	62.0	62.0	62.1	62.6	62.4	62.5	62.3	62.1	61.3	60.8	60.5	60.5	61.8
2012	60.1	59.8	59.7	59.6	59.5	60.0	60.1	59.9	58.3	58.0	58.0	58.1	59.3
2013	57.3	57.1	56.9	56.7	56.5	56.8	56.9	56.8	56.2	55.8	55.4	55.3	56.5
2014	54.3	54.1	54.2	54.5	54.5	54.7	54.5	54.6	54.3	54.2	54.3	54.1	54.4
2015	53.7	53.6	53.5	53.5	53.7	54.1	54.3	54.5	53.9	54.2	54.7	55.7	54.1
Trade, Transportation, and Utilities													
2005	239.1	237.1	238.1	239.2	240.9	242.7	242.8	242.2	243.4	244.4	248.4	253.1	242.6
2006	243.7	241.4	243.3	243.6	245.2	246.8	244.2	244.0	243.8	246.6	251.9	256.5	245.9
2007	246.3	242.3	244.4	243.7	246.9	247.9	246.2	245.3	244.8	246.1	251.2	255.7	246.7
2008	244.1	240.4	241.4	240.2	241.2	242.4	240.5	239.9	238.6	238.8	240.4	242.7	240.9
2009	231.5	227.5	226.8	226.5	227.4	229.0	225.0	224.8	225.6	226.2	230.3	231.8	227.7
2010	221.5	216.1	220.9	224.7	225.7	226.4	224.8	224.8	224.4	228.1	231.7	235.0	225.3
2011	226.1	224.2	225.7	228.4	229.7	230.5	229.4	230.0	230.0	231.4	236.7	240.4	230.2
2012	230.6	228.1	230.0	231.2	232.8	233.3	231.4	231.5	232.7	233.8	239.5	242.3	233.1
2013	234.3	231.6	232.7	233.2	235.2	235.9	234.7	234.5	234.7	235.7	241.1	244.4	235.7
2014	233.1	229.2	231.2	233.4	235.1	236.8	235.6	236.2	236.2	238.8	245.5	249.4	236.7
2015	237.8	235.5	235.9	239.4	241.6	244.0	244.2	244.0	244.5	244.9	248.0	249.4	242.4
Wholesale Trade													
2005	54.3	54.4	54.5	54.8	55.1	55.6	55.9	55.7	55.8	56.0	56.1	56.5	55.4
2006	56.0	56.3	56.4	56.7	56.7	57.0	56.8	56.8	56.7	56.7	56.6	56.9	56.6
2007	55.9	56.0	56.0	56.2	56.4	56.5	56.4	56.3	56.1	55.8	55.8	56.1	56.1
2008	55.5	55.3	55.7	55.7	55.9	56.0	55.5	55.3	55.0	54.8	54.4	54.2	55.3
2009	53.6	53.3	52.9	52.7	52.5	52.4	51.8	51.7	51.6	51.6	51.4	51.3	52.2
2010	50.3	50.1	50.5	51.0	51.2	51.1	51.2	51.0	50.6	51.1	51.2	51.3	50.9
2011	50.9	51.1	51.3	51.7	51.9	52.0	52.0	51.9	51.6	51.4	51.4	51.5	51.6
2012	51.0	51.1	51.5	52.2	52.6	52.8	52.6	52.6	52.3	52.4	52.4	52.6	52.2
2013	51.9	52.1	52.2	52.5	52.6	52.7	52.6	52.4	52.2	51.7	51.8	51.9	52.2
2014	51.1	51.0	50.9	51.5	51.8	52.0	52.1	52.0	51.7	52.4	52.4	53.1	51.8
2015	52.3	52.3	52.2	52.7	52.9	53.1	53.7	53.6	53.4	53.4	53.6	53.3	53.0
Retail Trade													
2005	140.7	138.7	139.3	140.6	141.6	142.5	143.2	143.2	142.9	143.7	147.7	151.2	142.9
2006	143.6	140.6	142.1	141.9	143.1	144.0	142.8	142.6	141.6	144.4	149.8	153.1	144.1
2007	145.1	141.2	142.8	142.1	144.4	144.9	144.4	144.1	143.0	144.6	149.7	153.2	145.0
2008	143.8	140.3	141.1	140.6	141.0	141.8	141.0	140.7	139.0	139.6	141.7	143.4	141.2
2009	135.0	131.8	131.7	131.8	132.9	133.7	132.4	132.3	131.8	132.7	136.5	138.2	133.4
2010	130.1	125.7	129.0	130.5	131.7	132.3	131.9	132.1	130.9	133.4	137.1	139.7	132.0
2011	132.4	130.5	131.6	132.5	133.5	134.2	133.4	134.0	133.3	135.4	140.0	143.0	134.5
2012	135.1	132.5	133.9	133.9	134.9	135.1	134.4	134.5	134.4	135.6	140.4	142.2	135.6
2013	136.9	134.7	135.3	135.5	136.7	137.4	137.4	137.6	136.4	137.6	142.3	144.3	137.7
2014	136.4	133.7	134.9	136.1	136.8	138.1	138.0	138.4	137.1	138.6	143.2	145.7	138.1
2015	137.5	135.1	135.8	137.2	138.3	139.6	139.3	139.2	138.0	139.0	141.8	143.7	138.7
Transportation and Utilities													
2005	44.1	44.0	44.3	43.8	44.2	44.6	43.7	43.3	44.7	44.7	44.6	45.4	44.3
2006	44.1	44.5	44.8	45.0	45.4	45.8	44.6	44.6	45.5	45.5	45.5	46.5	45.2
2007	45.3	45.1	45.6	45.4	46.1	46.5	45.4	44.9	45.7	45.7	45.7	46.4	45.7
2008	44.8	44.8	44.6	43.9	44.3	44.6	44.0	43.9	44.6	44.4	44.3	45.1	44.4
2009	42.9	42.4	42.2	42.0	42.0	42.9	40.8	40.8	42.2	41.9	42.4	42.3	42.1
2010	41.1	40.3	41.4	43.2	42.8	43.0	41.7	41.7	42.9	43.6	43.4	44.0	42.4
2011	42.8	42.6	42.8	44.2	44.3	44.3	44.0	44.1	45.1	44.6	45.3	45.9	44.2
2012	44.5	44.5	44.6	45.1	45.3	45.4	44.4	44.4	46.0	45.8	46.7	47.5	45.4
2013	45.5	44.8	45.2	45.2	45.9	45.8	44.7	44.5	46.1	46.4	47.0	48.2	45.8
2014	45.6	44.5	45.4	45.8	46.5	46.7	45.5	45.8	47.4	47.8	49.9	50.6	46.8
2015	48.0	48.1	47.9	49.5	50.4	51.3	51.2	51.2	53.1	52.5	52.6	52.4	50.7

Employment by Industry: Baltimore-Columbia-Towson, MD, 2005–2015—*Continued*

(Numbers in thousands, not seasonally adjusted)

Industry and year	January	February	March	April	May	June	July	August	September	October	November	December	Annual average
Information													
2005	20.8	20.9	21.0	21.2	21.3	21.6	22.2	22.6	22.2	22.2	22.2	22.2	21.7
2006	21.6	21.8	21.9	21.9	22.1	22.3	22.1	22.2	22.3	22.2	22.7	22.9	22.2
2007	22.4	22.6	23.1	23.1	23.3	24.0	23.7	24.1	24.1	23.1	23.6	23.6	23.4
2008	23.1	23.1	23.4	23.2	23.3	22.9	22.7	23.0	22.8	22.1	22.4	22.3	22.9
2009	21.3	21.3	21.5	20.6	20.5	20.8	20.1	20.3	19.9	19.5	19.7	19.6	20.4
2010	19.4	19.8	21.1	20.8	20.9	21.3	20.0	19.3	19.3	18.9	18.5	19.3	19.9
2011	17.7	18.1	18.2	17.7	17.8	17.5	17.5	16.6	17.1	17.2	17.6	17.3	17.5
2012	17.1	17.1	17.1	16.7	16.7	17.2	17.2	17.2	17.1	16.8	16.9	17.6	17.1
2013	17.0	16.9	16.9	16.6	16.7	16.8	17.0	17.0	16.8	16.9	17.0	17.0	16.9
2014	16.8	16.3	16.4	16.2	16.5	16.2	16.5	16.8	16.2	16.6	16.4	16.4	16.4
2015	16.1	16.0	16.2	16.3	16.5	16.3	16.6	16.5	16.2	16.5	16.6	16.6	16.4
Financial Activities													
2005	81.0	81.7	81.7	82.3	82.4	83.0	83.7	84.1	83.7	83.0	83.2	83.6	82.8
2006	82.8	82.9	83.2	82.9	82.7	83.3	83.1	82.8	82.4	82.0	81.8	82.4	82.7
2007	81.6	81.6	81.7	81.7	81.8	82.2	82.1	81.7	80.8	80.4	80.2	80.5	81.4
2008	79.2	79.5	79.7	79.2	79.3	79.7	79.1	78.8	78.1	78.2	77.5	77.7	78.8
2009	75.9	75.7	75.4	75.3	75.2	75.5	74.8	74.8	74.4	74.5	74.6	74.6	75.1
2010	73.4	72.9	73.3	73.2	73.4	74.0	74.2	74.3	74.0	74.4	74.5	75.0	73.9
2011	73.9	74.0	74.5	74.6	74.6	74.9	74.8	74.5	74.1	74.2	74.1	74.0	74.4
2012	74.0	73.9	73.7	73.7	74.1	74.6	75.1	75.4	75.2	75.2	75.7	75.9	74.7
2013	75.4	75.5	75.5	76.0	76.1	76.9	77.2	77.2	76.9	76.6	76.8	76.9	76.4
2014	76.0	76.1	75.8	76.8	77.1	77.7	78.0	78.1	77.6	77.8	77.9	78.1	77.3
2015	77.4	77.6	77.4	78.1	78.5	79.2	79.9	79.8	79.0	79.3	79.1	77.9	78.6
Professional and Business Services													
2005	177.3	178.5	181.2	183.0	184.6	185.7	189.8	190.4	190.5	189.5	188.8	188.3	185.6
2006	182.0	183.5	186.6	188.9	190.1	191.5	191.6	192.0	191.4	191.3	190.8	191.3	189.3
2007	185.5	185.5	188.1	191.1	191.7	193.5	193.1	194.9	194.5	194.6	195.1	195.1	191.9
2008	190.4	190.6	192.4	194.7	195.6	195.9	196.1	196.8	194.7	193.5	191.0	188.9	193.4
2009	182.0	180.0	180.4	183.1	182.9	184.7	184.8	185.4	184.2	184.6	183.7	183.3	183.3
2010	177.9	175.6	180.7	184.6	185.0	188.0	186.9	188.0	187.0	189.7	189.1	189.0	185.1
2011	184.2	184.2	186.7	192.4	193.7	196.5	198.5	200.2	201.0	202.4	203.9	204.3	195.7
2012	200.1	199.8	202.0	204.2	206.8	208.6	208.2	211.6	211.9	212.0	213.7	212.7	207.6
2013	207.7	208.9	211.8	212.7	214.5	217.8	216.6	219.1	219.1	218.4	220.0	217.6	215.4
2014	212.3	213.2	215.3	219.9	221.7	223.4	223.4	224.6	223.3	223.6	223.5	223.0	220.6
2015	216.7	217.4	218.8	222.8	224.4	225.7	228.5	229.9	226.6	228.1	226.4	227.6	224.4
Education and Health Services													
2005	203.5	206.7	207.0	208.5	208.1	206.7	206.7	206.0	209.8	213.6	215.0	216.2	209.0
2006	211.3	214.3	215.8	216.3	215.7	213.8	212.1	211.6	215.4	220.1	221.2	222.5	215.8
2007	217.1	220.4	222.1	222.9	221.7	219.9	218.9	218.0	221.4	225.3	225.8	226.8	221.7
2008	222.7	226.0	227.4	229.2	227.6	225.7	224.8	224.2	228.6	232.8	234.0	235.2	228.2
2009	230.2	233.2	234.3	235.9	234.0	232.1	229.6	228.3	232.5	236.9	238.0	239.2	233.7
2010	234.9	234.4	238.7	239.9	237.9	235.3	234.4	232.7	236.4	241.4	242.5	243.0	237.6
2011	240.3	243.2	243.4	242.8	240.5	237.8	237.4	236.0	240.2	244.8	245.5	245.8	241.5
2012	242.1	245.7	246.8	248.0	245.7	244.0	242.6	241.4	245.3	249.9	250.2	252.0	246.1
2013	245.9	250.2	251.6	252.5	250.3	247.9	246.9	245.8	249.8	255.6	256.7	257.3	250.9
2014	250.2	254.0	255.4	256.5	254.2	252.1	250.6	250.0	254.3	258.9	260.2	261.3	254.8
2015	254.8	259.0	259.2	260.9	261.5	256.6	255.8	254.3	258.6	262.6	262.5	264.5	259.2
Leisure and Hospitality													
2005	104.4	104.3	106.6	111.4	114.2	118.6	118.9	117.9	115.8	110.8	109.5	108.8	111.8
2006	105.9	105.0	108.5	111.7	115.8	120.8	120.5	120.4	117.1	114.6	113.2	112.9	113.9
2007	108.7	108.0	111.5	115.4	119.0	122.7	122.4	123.0	119.3	115.9	114.5	113.9	116.2
2008	110.0	109.7	112.2	117.1	120.8	123.7	123.4	122.6	117.3	115.5	113.2	112.7	116.5
2009	106.4	105.8	108.5	112.7	118.7	121.2	120.2	119.2	116.9	111.5	108.9	108.5	113.2
2010	104.8	102.5	107.4	112.1	116.3	119.1	119.0	119.6	116.7	112.8	110.6	109.8	112.6
2011	104.5	105.0	108.8	113.4	118.1	121.1	121.9	121.1	118.5	113.7	113.0	112.4	114.3
2012	110.1	111.0	114.5	118.6	124.6	129.1	128.2	128.1	125.2	122.0	119.3	118.6	120.8
2013	115.4	115.7	119.1	123.5	128.9	132.9	133.4	132.9	128.5	126.4	124.2	123.3	125.4
2014	118.5	118.7	122.2	127.9	134.7	136.8	136.7	138.1	134.7	132.3	129.6	128.6	129.9
2015	124.7	125.1	127.6	132.2	139.3	141.1	142.0	141.4	137.0	136.2	133.7	134.0	134.5

Employment by Industry: Baltimore-Columbia-Towson, MD, 2005–2015—*Continued*

(Numbers in thousands, not seasonally adjusted)

Industry and year	January	February	March	April	May	June	July	August	September	October	November	December	Annual average
Other Services													
2005	53.8	54.2	54.7	55.1	55.3	55.9	55.5	55.3	54.9	54.6	54.7	55.0	54.9
2006	54.5	54.7	55.2	56.0	56.4	56.9	56.8	56.7	56.6	56.3	56.5	56.6	56.1
2007	56.1	56.0	56.7	56.1	56.5	57.2	57.4	56.7	56.4	56.4	56.6	56.7	56.6
2008	55.8	56.1	56.5	56.7	56.8	57.4	57.0	56.7	56.4	56.3	56.2	56.0	56.5
2009	55.1	55.0	55.4	55.4	55.8	56.1	56.0	55.8	55.5	55.6	55.6	55.7	55.6
2010	54.5	53.7	55.2	55.4	55.8	56.0	56.1	55.8	55.6	55.4	55.5	55.3	55.4
2011	54.6	54.7	55.2	55.7	55.8	56.3	56.1	55.8	55.0	54.8	54.7	54.9	55.3
2012	54.2	54.1	54.5	55.1	55.1	55.7	55.5	54.9	54.5	54.2	53.9	54.0	54.6
2013	53.3	53.6	53.9	54.1	54.1	54.5	54.5	53.6	53.6	53.0	53.1	52.8	53.7
2014	52.0	51.9	52.3	53.6	53.8	54.4	54.3	53.9	54.1	53.6	53.6	53.7	53.4
2015	52.9	53.0	53.2	53.5	53.9	54.4	54.6	54.3	54.0	53.9	54.6	54.3	53.9
Government													
2005	213.6	218.1	218.1	219.9	220.8	218.1	210.1	205.8	217.1	222.0	224.0	223.4	217.6
2006	215.2	220.1	222.1	223.4	223.6	219.4	213.3	212.5	218.7	224.8	226.7	227.1	220.6
2007	219.1	223.9	226.4	225.3	226.0	221.5	214.6	214.3	219.4	225.3	227.1	226.6	222.5
2008	219.3	224.9	226.5	228.5	228.7	224.0	218.8	217.7	223.0	230.0	230.6	230.6	225.2
2009	223.2	228.4	230.2	232.1	231.9	228.0	221.9	219.2	224.8	234.6	234.4	233.8	228.5
2010	226.8	231.5	235.4	237.6	238.8	235.3	226.5	225.0	228.7	236.2	237.9	235.5	232.9
2011	229.5	235.1	239.2	239.5	237.3	233.6	224.0	224.1	230.4	238.0	236.8	236.7	233.7
2012	229.9	235.8	239.0	237.7	236.2	230.0	223.1	221.7	230.1	236.9	237.0	236.4	232.8
2013	228.6	234.2	236.3	236.1	235.7	230.5	220.7	219.7	227.6	232.7	234.7	233.1	230.8
2014	224.3	231.0	232.7	235.9	233.0	229.0	217.6	218.5	227.6	233.9	234.9	232.9	229.3
2015	223.5	229.3	231.5	232.2	231.8	226.5	217.4	216.9	223.6	229.2	229.6	228.5	226.7

Employment by Industry: Charlotte-Concord-Gastonia, NC-SC, 2005–2015

(Numbers in thousands, not seasonally adjusted)

Industry and year	January	February	March	April	May	June	July	August	September	October	November	December	Annual average
Total Nonfarm													
2005	924.1	928.7	935.8	942.7	948.1	945.0	928.6	947.1	957.4	966.9	969.0	969.6	946.9
2006	959.3	962.7	972.4	983.2	990.2	984.6	968.3	990.5	1,000.7	1,009.9	1,017.0	1,018.3	988.1
2007	999.5	1,005.3	1,016.4	1,017.2	1,025.6	1,021.9	999.6	1,024.1	1,030.5	1,038.6	1,042.7	1,044.4	1,022.2
2008	1,016.5	1,022.9	1,029.0	1,026.0	1,031.4	1,024.0	997.7	1,019.4	1,023.8	1,020.6	1,014.0	1,010.9	1,019.7
2009	973.7	971.8	970.1	962.9	964.7	955.8	930.1	950.3	951.5	950.8	952.2	951.8	957.1
2010	933.2	935.9	945.4	952.6	962.8	954.5	931.9	953.9	957.3	968.7	972.7	973.7	953.6
2011	951.3	961.6	969.8	975.9	979.5	975.1	954.3	978.9	982.9	988.3	995.5	996.2	975.8
2012	981.0	986.2	997.4	1,000.7	1,010.2	999.5	982.1	1,003.3	1,008.6	1,018.9	1,025.2	1,026.5	1,003.3
2013	1,005.1	1,012.0	1,020.3	1,025.7	1,032.9	1,023.8	1,007.3	1,027.7	1,031.9	1,046.0	1,053.4	1,057.0	1,028.6
2014	1,039.3	1,038.4	1,052.2	1,061.0	1,070.7	1,064.6	1,046.6	1,065.5	1,071.0	1,087.1	1,093.1	1,098.3	1,065.7
2015	1,078.0	1,085.2	1,091.2	1,097.5	1,109.9	1,109.3	1,091.4	1,104.5	1,108.4	1,121.6	1,128.0	1,130.1	1,104.6
Total Private													
2005	801.0	804.5	811.0	817.1	822.6	824.8	829.0	831.4	831.5	838.2	840.1	841.1	824.4
2006	832.0	834.7	843.7	854.3	861.1	864.9	867.7	871.9	871.1	878.5	883.6	884.7	862.4
2007	867.5	871.7	882.3	884.2	891.6	898.1	894.7	897.9	896.3	901.9	904.4	905.8	891.4
2008	878.8	883.7	889.1	886.1	890.9	891.5	885.4	885.9	880.7	877.7	869.6	865.9	882.1
2009	830.8	828.2	825.8	818.2	820.5	817.7	814.1	812.7	809.0	807.7	808.2	807.8	816.7
2010	788.5	789.9	798.2	805.0	811.3	814.9	815.0	817.7	817.5	823.0	826.3	827.1	811.2
2011	807.9	817.0	824.3	829.8	833.4	838.3	838.2	841.2	842.5	843.7	848.0	849.1	834.5
2012	836.1	840.0	849.8	852.5	861.1	865.8	864.3	865.7	864.9	868.9	873.8	875.5	859.9
2013	856.3	862.2	869.2	874.5	881.2	887.4	886.9	890.3	888.5	894.3	900.6	904.6	883.0
2014	889.9	888.5	901.3	908.8	917.9	923.9	923.8	926.8	926.6	934.6	939.4	945.1	918.9
2015	927.8	933.8	939.0	944.9	957.1	964.2	965.6	965.9	964.6	969.8	974.7	977.5	957.1
Goods Producing													
2005	182.7	183.7	184.5	184.5	185.7	187.1	187.5	187.3	187.4	186.5	186.6	186.4	185.8
2006	185.0	185.3	187.2	189.0	189.6	190.3	190.7	191.4	190.7	190.7	190.3	190.9	189.3
2007	188.5	188.8	189.4	186.5	186.4	189.4	187.8	188.5	188.0	186.9	186.9	186.3	187.8
2008	181.1	181.5	181.3	179.4	179.3	178.9	177.2	176.3	175.2	172.0	168.7	165.4	176.4
2009	155.0	154.2	151.9	148.0	147.0	145.9	144.9	143.6	142.8	141.3	140.7	140.4	146.3
2010	136.1	135.8	136.4	137.3	137.5	138.1	138.2	137.8	137.2	137.0	137.2	136.7	137.1
2011	132.5	134.5	135.3	136.6	137.4	138.5	139.9	140.3	140.7	140.4	140.7	140.6	138.1
2012	140.4	141.3	142.8	143.3	144.5	145.6	145.6	145.6	145.3	144.1	145.6	146.1	144.2
2013	144.6	145.8	147.3	146.9	147.1	148.4	148.6	148.7	148.4	148.3	148.7	148.9	147.6
2014	147.3	147.4	149.4	150.1	151.7	152.9	153.4	154.0	154.2	155.0	155.8	156.6	152.3
2015	155.4	156.3	157.0	158.2	159.8	161.2	162.1	162.4	162.9	162.6	161.4	162.0	160.1
Service-Providing													
2005	741.4	745.0	751.3	758.2	762.4	757.9	741.1	759.8	770.0	780.4	782.4	783.2	761.1
2006	774.3	777.4	785.2	794.2	800.6	794.3	777.6	799.1	810.0	819.2	826.7	827.4	798.8
2007	811.0	816.5	827.0	830.7	839.2	832.5	811.8	835.6	842.5	851.7	855.8	858.1	834.4
2008	835.4	841.4	847.7	846.6	852.1	845.1	820.5	843.1	848.6	848.6	845.3	845.5	843.3
2009	818.7	817.6	818.2	814.9	817.7	809.9	785.2	806.7	808.7	809.5	811.5	811.4	810.8
2010	797.1	800.1	809.0	815.3	825.3	816.4	793.7	816.1	820.1	831.7	835.5	837.0	816.4
2011	818.8	827.1	834.5	839.3	842.1	836.6	814.4	838.6	842.2	847.9	854.8	855.6	837.7
2012	840.6	844.9	854.6	857.4	865.7	853.9	836.5	857.7	863.3	874.8	879.6	880.4	859.1
2013	860.5	866.2	873.0	878.8	885.8	875.4	858.7	879.0	883.5	897.7	904.7	908.1	881.0
2014	892.0	891.0	902.8	910.9	919.0	911.7	893.2	911.5	916.8	932.1	937.3	941.7	913.3
2015	922.6	928.9	934.2	939.3	950.1	948.1	929.3	942.1	945.5	959.0	966.6	968.1	944.5
Mining, Logging, and Construction													
2005	60.3	60.6	61.2	61.2	61.8	62.9	64.4	64.8	64.9	64.3	64.5	64.4	62.9
2006	63.2	63.6	65.1	66.5	67.1	68.2	68.9	69.6	69.3	69.6	69.6	69.8	67.5
2007	68.6	69.1	70.2	70.9	71.1	72.2	72.5	72.7	72.3	71.8	71.1	70.5	71.1
2008	67.6	67.4	67.2	66.8	67.0	66.7	66.2	65.5	64.6	63.0	61.2	59.8	65.3
2009	55.3	54.5	53.8	52.3	52.2	52.1	51.8	51.0	50.3	49.1	48.6	48.2	51.6
2010	45.1	44.7	45.3	46.0	46.0	46.6	46.4	46.1	45.7	45.6	45.7	45.2	45.7
2011	41.7	43.4	43.8	44.7	45.1	45.5	46.1	46.0	45.9	45.6	45.5	45.2	44.9
2012	44.7	45.0	46.0	46.2	46.7	47.4	47.2	47.1	46.9	46.9	47.1	47.2	46.5
2013	46.2	46.8	48.0	48.6	48.8	49.3	49.7	50.0	50.1	50.5	50.7	50.5	49.1
2014	49.4	49.5	50.9	51.2	52.1	52.6	53.0	53.3	53.4	54.0	54.2	54.3	52.3
2015	53.1	53.4	53.8	54.6	55.8	56.4	57.0	57.0	57.6	58.6	57.5	57.5	56.0

Employment by Industry: Charlotte-Concord-Gastonia, NC-SC, 2005–2015—*Continued*

(Numbers in thousands, not seasonally adjusted)

Industry and year	January	February	March	April	May	June	July	August	September	October	November	December	Annual average
Manufacturing													
2005	122.4	123.1	123.3	123.3	123.9	124.2	123.1	122.5	122.5	122.2	122.1	122.0	122.9
2006	121.8	121.7	122.1	122.5	122.5	122.1	121.8	121.8	121.4	121.1	120.7	121.1	121.7
2007	119.9	119.7	119.2	115.6	115.3	117.2	115.3	115.8	115.7	115.1	115.8	115.8	116.7
2008	113.5	114.1	114.1	112.6	112.3	112.2	111.0	110.8	110.6	109.0	107.5	105.6	111.1
2009	99.7	99.7	98.1	95.7	94.8	93.8	93.1	92.6	92.5	92.2	92.1	92.2	94.7
2010	91.0	91.1	91.1	91.3	91.5	91.5	91.8	91.7	91.5	91.4	91.5	91.5	91.4
2011	90.8	91.1	91.5	91.9	92.3	93.0	93.8	94.3	94.8	94.8	95.2	95.4	93.2
2012	95.7	96.3	96.8	97.1	97.8	98.2	98.4	98.5	98.4	97.2	98.5	98.9	97.7
2013	98.4	99.0	99.3	98.3	98.3	99.1	98.9	98.7	98.3	97.8	98.0	98.4	98.5
2014	97.9	97.9	98.5	98.9	99.6	100.3	100.4	100.7	100.8	101.0	101.6	102.3	100.0
2015	102.3	102.9	103.2	103.6	104.0	104.8	105.1	105.4	105.3	104.0	103.9	104.5	104.1
Trade, Transportation, and Utilities													
2005	198.0	198.5	199.7	200.2	200.5	200.0	199.9	200.1	199.0	202.8	205.7	208.1	201.0
2006	201.8	200.4	202.0	204.3	205.6	205.2	205.5	206.0	205.6	208.4	213.2	214.9	206.1
2007	209.3	208.4	210.8	211.4	212.8	213.1	213.5	213.7	213.9	215.8	220.0	221.7	213.7
2008	214.2	213.1	214.5	213.0	213.3	213.1	211.5	211.2	209.9	210.2	211.5	212.0	212.3
2009	204.7	202.3	201.8	199.1	200.0	199.5	198.4	198.4	197.4	197.8	199.8	200.5	200.0
2010	194.1	193.1	194.8	195.0	196.5	196.7	196.8	197.5	196.6	198.3	201.8	203.6	197.1
2011	196.8	196.8	198.2	198.7	199.3	199.4	200.4	200.8	200.1	202.0	205.9	207.5	200.5
2012	202.1	201.1	202.8	203.6	205.0	206.0	206.3	206.4	206.4	208.0	212.9	214.3	206.2
2013	206.8	206.4	207.5	207.7	209.0	209.9	210.7	211.6	211.1	213.2	218.5	221.7	211.2
2014	214.3	212.6	214.8	214.9	216.4	217.9	217.3	217.9	218.4	221.4	226.9	229.9	218.6
2015	221.3	220.8	222.0	223.9	225.3	226.8	226.5	227.1	226.3	230.4	234.4	236.7	226.8
Wholesale Trade													
2005	52.3	52.3	52.5	53.2	53.6	53.2	53.3	53.3	53.2	53.8	54.0	54.0	53.2
2006	54.1	54.2	54.4	54.8	54.9	54.9	54.2	54.2	54.0	54.1	54.2	54.3	54.4
2007	54.4	54.8	55.3	55.6	55.7	55.9	56.2	56.1	56.0	56.8	56.7	56.8	55.9
2008	56.4	56.7	57.3	56.5	56.5	56.3	55.5	55.6	55.3	55.4	55.0	55.0	56.0
2009	54.0	53.9	53.3	51.9	51.5	51.1	50.7	50.4	50.0	50.2	49.9	49.8	51.4
2010	49.2	49.4	49.7	49.5	49.6	49.4	49.6	49.7	49.5	49.9	49.9	50.1	49.6
2011	49.6	49.9	50.0	49.7	49.8	49.8	50.2	50.2	50.2	50.6	50.7	50.9	50.1
2012	50.5	50.6	50.9	51.0	51.3	51.4	51.5	51.5	51.4	51.4	51.5	51.7	51.2
2013	51.0	51.4	51.6	51.6	51.7	51.8	52.1	52.4	52.3	52.7	53.1	53.4	52.1
2014	53.1	53.2	53.5	53.4	53.6	53.8	53.9	54.2	54.1	54.3	54.7	54.9	53.9
2015	54.3	54.6	55.1	55.2	55.5	55.9	55.9	56.0	55.9	56.9	57.1	57.2	55.8
Retail Trade													
2005	101.8	102.2	103.0	102.9	102.8	102.4	102.9	103.1	102.3	105.1	107.6	109.3	103.8
2006	104.0	102.6	103.6	105.4	106.5	106.0	106.8	106.9	106.9	109.5	113.9	115.2	107.3
2007	110.7	109.7	111.3	111.5	112.8	112.9	113.0	113.4	113.6	114.9	119.2	120.5	113.6
2008	114.1	112.9	113.9	112.6	112.7	112.8	112.2	111.8	111.1	111.4	113.1	113.3	112.7
2009	108.7	107.0	107.0	106.2	107.6	107.4	107.0	107.4	106.7	107.3	109.6	110.2	107.7
2010	105.5	104.4	105.5	105.8	106.8	107.1	107.0	107.7	106.9	108.1	111.2	112.6	107.4
2011	106.9	106.5	107.4	107.9	108.3	108.4	109.0	109.2	108.5	109.9	113.3	114.4	109.1
2012	110.4	109.3	110.3	111.0	112.1	112.6	112.8	112.8	112.7	114.3	118.7	119.3	113.0
2013	113.4	112.8	113.3	113.6	114.5	115.1	115.5	115.8	115.3	116.8	120.9	122.9	115.8
2014	116.6	115.2	116.5	116.7	117.4	118.1	117.8	118.0	117.7	120.2	124.5	126.2	118.7
2015	119.9	119.3	119.7	120.9	121.6	122.5	122.1	122.6	121.9	124.3	127.6	128.8	122.6
Transportation and Utilities													
2005	43.9	44.0	44.2	44.1	44.1	44.4	43.7	43.7	43.5	43.9	44.1	44.8	44.0
2006	43.7	43.6	44.0	44.1	44.2	44.3	44.5	44.9	44.7	44.8	45.1	45.4	44.4
2007	44.2	43.9	44.2	44.3	44.3	44.3	44.3	44.2	44.3	44.1	44.1	44.4	44.2
2008	43.7	43.5	43.3	43.9	44.1	44.0	43.8	43.8	43.5	43.4	43.4	43.7	43.7
2009	42.0	41.4	41.5	41.0	40.9	41.0	40.7	40.6	40.7	40.3	40.3	40.5	40.9
2010	39.4	39.3	39.6	39.7	40.1	40.2	40.2	40.1	40.2	40.3	40.7	40.9	40.1
2011	40.3	40.4	40.8	41.1	41.2	41.2	41.2	41.4	41.4	41.5	41.9	42.2	41.2
2012	41.2	41.2	41.6	41.6	41.6	42.0	42.0	42.1	42.3	42.3	42.7	43.3	42.0
2013	42.4	42.2	42.6	42.5	42.8	43.0	43.1	43.4	43.5	43.7	44.5	45.4	43.3
2014	44.6	44.2	44.8	44.8	45.4	46.0	45.6	45.7	46.6	46.9	47.7	48.8	45.9
2015	47.1	46.9	47.2	47.8	48.2	48.4	48.5	48.5	48.5	49.2	49.7	50.7	48.4

Employment by Industry: Charlotte-Concord-Gastonia, NC-SC, 2005–2015—*Continued*

(Numbers in thousands, not seasonally adjusted)

Industry and year	January	February	March	April	May	June	July	August	September	October	November	December	Annual average
Information													
2005	21.6	21.5	21.6	21.9	22.1	22.2	22.3	22.3	22.3	22.3	22.7	23.2	22.2
2006	23.2	23.2	23.2	23.0	23.1	23.2	22.8	23.2	23.1	23.0	23.2	23.4	23.1
2007	23.1	23.1	23.0	23.0	23.1	23.5	23.4	23.4	23.3	23.2	23.5	23.6	23.3
2008	23.0	23.2	23.3	23.2	23.3	23.4	23.3	23.3	23.2	23.5	23.5	23.6	23.3
2009	22.9	22.7	22.7	22.8	22.7	22.6	22.5	22.3	22.2	22.1	22.2	22.3	22.5
2010	22.2	22.1	22.3	22.2	22.3	22.5	22.4	22.5	22.6	22.6	22.8	22.8	22.4
2011	22.6	22.6	22.6	22.7	22.5	22.8	22.9	23.0	23.2	23.1	23.2	23.1	22.9
2012	23.0	23.1	23.2	23.1	23.1	23.3	23.4	23.3	23.2	23.1	23.2	23.2	23.2
2013	23.3	23.3	23.3	23.3	23.7	23.8	23.9	24.0	23.9	24.1	24.2	24.5	23.8
2014	24.2	24.3	24.3	24.1	24.4	24.6	24.7	24.7	24.7	25.1	25.3	25.5	24.7
2015	25.6	25.7	25.8	25.7	26.0	26.2	26.5	26.5	26.2	26.4	26.5	26.7	26.2
Financial Activities													
2005	72.6	73.0	73.1	73.3	74.0	74.7	75.6	75.4	75.4	76.0	76.2	76.9	74.7
2006	77.9	78.8	79.2	81.5	81.8	82.4	82.7	82.8	82.5	84.5	84.6	84.9	82.0
2007	81.2	81.8	82.0	82.3	82.6	82.7	82.4	82.3	81.8	82.3	82.2	82.3	82.2
2008	79.9	80.1	80.2	80.9	80.2	80.4	79.3	79.3	78.5	78.4	77.9	78.3	79.5
2009	76.6	76.4	76.1	75.4	75.5	75.0	74.7	74.2	73.2	73.2	73.2	73.4	74.7
2010	72.9	73.5	73.6	73.3	73.5	73.9	73.7	73.9	74.5	74.9	75.3	75.4	74
2011	75.5	75.9	75.9	75.1	75.5	75.9	75.1	75.2	74.8	75.5	75.8	76.0	75.5
2012	75.6	76.0	76.2	75.8	76.0	76.4	76.3	76.4	76.3	76.6	77.0	77.2	76.3
2013	76.9	77.2	76.9	77.8	78.0	78.3	78.6	78.4	78.3	78.6	78.6	78.7	78.0
2014	79.0	78.9	79.2	79.4	79.7	80.4	80.9	81.1	81.1	81.5	81.9	82.2	80.4
2015	81.9	82.2	82.5	82.8	83.3	84.0	84.7	84.5	84.5	84.2	86.0	86.2	83.9
Professional and Business Services													
2005	124.2	124.7	125.5	128.4	128.9	128.5	130.9	131.7	133.8	135.7	134.9	133.1	130.0
2006	130.9	132.2	133.7	136.3	137.9	138.8	140.8	142.5	143.8	145.2	145.2	142.9	139.2
2007	139.9	141.8	144.8	147.1	149.0	150.0	149.8	151.7	152.1	154.2	153.6	152.8	148.9
2008	148.3	151.0	151.9	151.7	153.2	153.5	152.0	152.5	151.8	150.6	147.1	145.3	150.7
2009	140.5	140.3	139.4	138.3	137.4	136.8	137.2	137.5	138.2	140.0	140.5	140.9	138.9
2010	137.6	138.7	141.5	143.8	144.4	145.3	146.3	147.7	148.5	151.3	151.2	151.5	145.7
2011	148.0	152.3	153.8	155.7	155.0	155.9	155.5	156.1	158.1	157.8	158.0	157.6	155.3
2012	154.8	156.4	158.3	159.0	159.9	160.6	158.5	159.5	160.3	162.5	161.3	160.7	159.3
2013	155.8	157.9	159.3	162.1	162.7	163.9	164.4	166.2	166.8	169.9	170.5	170.0	164.1
2014	168.5	169.4	172.3	175.8	176.4	177.5	177.9	178.5	179.1	181.5	181.1	182.3	176.7
2015	178.4	181.1	181.5	182.1	183.8	184.5	185.1	186.3	187.8	189.8	189.4	189.0	184.9
Education and Health Services													
2005	82.4	82.7	83.5	84.1	83.8	83.6	84.1	84.9	85.4	86.4	86.5	86.6	84.5
2006	87.6	88.3	88.6	88.2	88.4	89.2	89.3	90.0	90.9	92.1	92.6	93.1	89.9
2007	92.3	93.4	94.0	94.4	94.6	95.0	94.8	95.4	95.9	97.3	97.1	97.7	95.2
2008	95.4	96.4	96.8	96.4	96.6	96.5	96.2	97.3	97.8	99.9	100.6	101.1	97.6
2009	98.9	99.5	99.3	99.6	99.8	99.4	98.8	99.7	99.8	100.7	101.2	101.1	99.8
2010	99.7	100.4	100.4	101.7	101.8	100.9	101.1	101.7	101.8	103.5	104.0	104.1	101.8
2011	103.2	104.3	104.4	104.2	103.8	103.0	102.8	103.6	104.9	105.6	106.1	106.6	104.4
2012	105.3	106.5	106.3	105.4	105.8	105.2	104.6	105.1	106.0	108.1	108.3	108.9	106.3
2013	106.2	107.7	107.2	107.3	107.8	107.2	106.2	107.1	108.3	108.5	109.4	110.0	107.7
2014	108.3	108.8	109.5	109.3	109.9	109.1	109.1	110.1	111.1	112.4	113.1	113.4	110.3
2015	112.4	113.4	113.6	113.5	114.3	113.1	112.8	112.4	113.5	114.0	115.7	114.6	113.6
Leisure and Hospitality													
2005	84.3	85.2	87.6	89.3	91.6	92.4	92.6	93.7	92.2	92.4	91.5	90.8	90.3
2006	89.5	90.0	92.9	95.7	97.8	98.3	99.3	99.4	98.1	98.0	97.8	97.7	96.2
2007	96.5	97.4	100.6	102.9	106.1	107.0	105.7	105.6	104.2	104.3	103.1	103.3	103.1
2008	100.3	101.8	104.5	105.7	108.5	109.3	109.6	109.8	108.8	107.9	105.5	105.6	106.4
2009	98.8	99.3	101.2	102.2	105.2	105.7	104.9	104.5	103.5	101.1	99.1	98.2	102.0
2010	95.2	95.5	98.1	100.7	104.0	105.8	104.7	104.6	104.1	103.0	101.5	100.3	101.5
2011	96.8	97.7	101.0	103.5	106.4	109.0	107.9	108.4	107.2	105.7	104.7	104.0	104.4
2012	101.5	102.1	106.3	108.2	112.3	114.1	114.5	114.2	112.1	111.2	110.0	109.4	109.7
2013	107.0	107.7	110.6	112.3	116.2	119.2	117.8	117.6	115.1	115.2	113.4	114.3	113.9
2014	112.2	111.1	115.0	118.0	122.2	124.2	123.0	122.9	120.6	120.2	117.9	117.6	118.7
2015	115.8	117.0	119.2	121.1	126.4	130.1	129.3	128.1	125.2	124.1	123.0	124.1	123.6

Employment by Industry: Charlotte-Concord-Gastonia, NC-SC, 2005–2015—*Continued*

(Numbers in thousands, not seasonally adjusted)

Industry and year	January	February	March	April	May	June	July	August	September	October	November	December	Annual average
Other Services													
2005	35.2	35.2	35.5	35.4	36.0	36.3	36.1	36.0	36.0	36.1	36.0	36.0	35.8
2006	36.1	36.5	36.9	36.3	36.9	37.5	36.6	36.6	36.4	36.6	36.7	36.9	36.7
2007	36.7	37.0	37.7	36.6	37.0	37.4	37.3	37.3	37.1	37.9	38.0	38.1	37.3
2008	36.6	36.6	36.6	35.8	36.5	36.4	36.3	36.2	35.5	35.2	34.8	34.6	35.9
2009	33.4	33.5	33.4	32.8	32.9	32.8	32.7	32.5	31.9	31.5	31.5	31.0	32.5
2010	30.7	30.8	31.1	31.0	31.3	31.7	31.8	32.0	32.2	32.4	32.5	32.7	31.7
2011	32.5	32.9	33.1	33.3	33.5	33.8	33.7	33.8	33.5	33.6	33.6	33.7	33.4
2012	33.4	33.5	33.9	34.1	34.5	34.6	35.1	35.2	35.3	35.3	35.5	35.7	34.7
2013	35.7	36.2	37.1	37.1	36.7	36.7	36.7	36.7	36.6	36.5	37.3	36.5	36.7
2014	36.1	36.0	36.8	37.2	37.2	37.3	37.5	37.6	37.4	37.5	37.4	37.6	37.1
2015	37.0	37.3	37.4	37.6	38.2	38.3	38.6	38.6	38.2	38.3	38.3	38.2	38.0
Government													
2005	123.1	124.2	124.8	125.6	125.5	120.2	99.6	115.7	125.9	128.7	128.9	128.5	122.6
2006	127.3	128.0	128.7	128.9	129.1	119.7	100.6	118.6	129.6	131.4	133.4	133.6	125.7
2007	132.0	133.6	134.1	133.0	134.0	123.8	104.9	126.2	134.2	136.7	138.3	138.6	130.8
2008	137.7	139.2	139.9	139.9	140.5	132.5	112.3	133.5	143.1	142.9	144.4	145.0	137.6
2009	142.9	143.6	144.3	144.7	144.2	138.1	116.0	137.6	142.5	143.1	144.0	144.0	140.4
2010	144.7	146.0	147.2	147.6	151.5	139.6	116.9	136.2	139.8	145.7	146.4	146.6	142.4
2011	143.4	144.6	145.5	146.1	146.1	136.8	116.1	137.7	140.4	144.6	147.5	147.1	141.3
2012	144.9	146.2	147.6	148.2	149.1	133.7	117.8	137.6	143.7	150.0	151.4	151.0	143.4
2013	148.8	149.8	151.1	151.2	151.7	136.4	120.4	137.4	143.4	151.7	152.8	152.4	145.6
2014	149.4	149.9	150.9	152.2	152.8	140.7	122.8	138.7	144.4	152.5	153.7	153.2	146.8
2015	150.2	151.4	152.2	152.6	152.8	145.1	125.8	138.6	143.8	151.8	153.3	152.6	147.5

Employment by Industry: Portland-Vancouver-Hillsboro, OR-WA, 2005–2015

(Numbers in thousands, not seasonally adjusted)

Industry and year	January	February	March	April	May	June	July	August	September	October	November	December	Annual average
Total Nonfarm													
2005	961.5	970.0	976.1	982.9	988.5	993.3	987.7	991.4	998.5	1,008.6	1,015.9	1,020.0	991.2
2006	993.7	1,003.0	1,009.8	1,016.9	1,024.3	1,029.5	1,020.0	1,021.6	1,030.9	1,039.7	1,045.3	1,045.9	1,023.4
2007	1,020.9	1,030.7	1,037.5	1,038.1	1,045.3	1,046.7	1,038.8	1,040.1	1,046.8	1,056.7	1,061.3	1,060.2	1,043.6
2008	1,035.0	1,041.9	1,045.6	1,049.7	1,052.5	1,050.6	1,044.3	1,041.7	1,046.8	1,045.7	1,039.5	1,027.4	1,043.6
2009	997.7	994.5	989.0	988.0	988.3	984.0	973.0	969.4	973.9	981.7	981.9	979.4	983.4
2010	958.6	962.9	967.5	975.8	981.9	983.9	973.5	974.2	981.0	995.7	997.7	997.2	979.2
2011	976.9	983.6	987.5	997.8	999.7	1,000.8	994.7	995.4	1,001.6	1,011.6	1,015.9	1,016.4	998.5
2012	998.0	1,004.6	1,009.7	1,016.2	1,022.5	1,024.5	1,016.3	1,018.4	1,022.5	1,034.4	1,037.6	1,036.2	1,020.1
2013	1,013.9	1,023.8	1,028.4	1,038.5	1,045.6	1,047.8	1,040.1	1,045.6	1,051.5	1,062.6	1,068.6	1,067.1	1,044.5
2014	1,050.1	1,053.6	1,061.6	1,069.4	1,075.5	1,078.9	1,071.5	1,076.1	1,083.3	1,092.6	1,097.9	1,101.0	1,076.0
2015	1,082.8	1,091.6	1,096.8	1,104.9	1,110.2	1,113.0	1,109.8	1,112.9	1,118.3	1,127.8	1,133.0	1,135.2	1,111.4
Total Private													
2005	823.2	829.7	835.5	842.6	847.4	851.9	858.8	864.1	866.6	869.3	874.5	879.3	853.6
2006	855.4	862.6	868.3	875.4	880.9	886.5	889.4	893.5	897.3	898.6	901.7	903.7	884.4
2007	879.8	887.8	893.4	893.8	898.8	900.2	904.1	908.5	910.7	911.4	914.3	913.3	901.3
2008	889.3	894.8	897.3	901.1	902.4	900.8	903.2	903.4	904.0	896.2	887.7	876.6	896.4
2009	848.7	843.5	837.2	836.1	835.6	832.9	832.0	831.2	833.6	832.4	831.0	829.5	835.3
2010	810.0	812.9	817.1	826.2	828.5	830.6	833.9	836.9	841.5	847.3	847.3	849.3	831.8
2011	828.6	834.3	838.3	846.9	848.3	851.9	857.6	860.6	864.5	864.8	867.5	869.7	852.8
2012	851.5	856.6	861.7	868.3	873.3	876.1	879.5	883.7	885.3	888.1	889.8	889.9	875.3
2013	868.8	876.5	881.3	891.0	897.2	899.2	905.3	911.6	914.9	916.9	921.0	920.3	900.3
2014	903.8	906.1	913.5	920.3	925.1	929.7	934.4	938.8	942.7	943.1	946.4	950.2	929.5
2015	932.4	939.6	944.5	952.1	956.2	960.8	969.2	972.8	975.3	974.9	978.4	981.1	961.4
Goods Producing													
2005	176.5	177.5	179.0	180.2	181.9	184.4	188.2	189.5	188.6	189.2	187.6	187.9	184.2
2006	184.6	185.9	187.4	188.7	190.3	193.9	196.5	197.7	197.5	195.7	193.4	192.7	192.0
2007	189.4	190.5	191.7	190.8	193.0	193.9	197.3	198.6	197.4	196.3	193.9	191.8	193.7
2008	187.3	187.5	187.4	187.0	187.9	188.7	190.3	189.8	188.7	184.3	180.3	174.9	186.2
2009	169.3	165.3	162.3	160.1	159.5	159.8	160.8	160.5	159.7	158.4	154.5	153.0	160.3
2010	149.3	148.8	149.7	150.7	151.9	153.5	156.8	157.6	157.7	158.3	155.8	155.0	153.8
2011	151.7	153.0	154.4	156.4	157.9	160.3	162.9	164.1	163.7	163.4	161.9	161.5	159.3
2012	158.9	159.4	160.2	161.1	163.5	165.4	168.3	169.3	168.0	167.3	165.0	163.3	164.1
2013	161.2	162.1	163.2	165.5	167.7	169.9	172.2	173.7	173.4	173.7	172.5	171.1	168.9
2014	170.4	170.1	172.1	172.7	174.2	176.0	178.2	178.7	178.0	176.7	175.4	175.2	174.8
2015	174.0	174.6	175.6	176.6	177.9	180.1	182.7	183.1	182.2	180.7	179.6	179.1	178.9
Service-Providing													
2005	785.0	792.5	797.1	802.7	806.6	808.9	799.5	801.9	809.9	819.4	828.3	832.1	807.0
2006	809.1	817.1	822.4	828.2	834.0	835.6	823.5	823.9	833.4	844.0	851.9	853.2	831.4
2007	831.5	840.2	845.8	847.3	852.3	852.8	841.5	841.5	849.4	860.4	867.4	868.4	849.9
2008	847.7	854.4	858.2	862.7	864.6	861.9	854.0	851.9	858.1	861.4	859.2	852.5	857.2
2009	828.4	829.2	826.7	827.9	828.8	824.2	812.2	808.9	814.2	823.3	827.4	826.4	823.1
2010	809.3	814.1	817.8	825.1	830.0	830.4	816.7	816.6	823.3	837.4	841.9	842.2	825.4
2011	825.2	830.6	833.1	841.4	841.8	840.5	831.8	831.3	837.9	848.2	854.0	854.9	839.2
2012	839.1	845.2	849.5	855.1	859.0	859.1	848.0	849.1	854.5	867.1	872.6	872.9	855.9
2013	852.7	861.7	865.2	873.0	877.9	877.9	867.9	871.9	878.1	888.9	896.1	896.0	875.6
2014	879.7	883.5	889.5	896.7	901.3	902.9	893.3	897.4	905.3	915.9	922.5	925.8	901.2
2015	908.8	917.0	921.2	928.3	932.3	932.9	927.1	929.8	936.1	947.1	953.4	956.1	932.5
Mining and Logging													
2005	1.7	1.7	1.7	1.7	1.8	1.8	1.9	1.9	1.8	1.8	1.8	1.7	1.8
2006	1.6	1.6	1.6	1.6	1.7	1.8	1.8	1.8	1.8	1.7	1.6	1.6	1.7
2007	1.5	1.6	1.6	1.6	1.7	1.7	1.7	1.7	1.7	1.7	1.6	1.5	1.6
2008	1.5	1.5	1.5	1.5	1.6	1.6	1.6	1.7	1.6	1.6	1.5	1.4	1.6
2009	1.2	1.2	1.2	1.1	1.2	1.2	1.3	1.3	1.3	1.3	1.2	1.1	1.2
2010	1.0	1.0	1.1	1.0	1.1	1.1	1.1	1.1	1.1	1.1	1.1	1.0	1.1
2011	0.9	1.0	1.0	1.0	1.1	1.1	1.1	1.1	1.1	1.1	1.1	1.0	1.1
2012	0.9	0.9	0.9	0.9	1.0	1.0	1.0	1.0	1.0	1.0	1.0	1.0	1.0
2013	1.0	1.0	1.0	1.0	1.0	1.1	1.1	1.1	1.1	1.2	1.2	1.1	1.1
2014	1.1	1.1	1.1	1.2	1.2	1.2	1.2	1.3	1.3	1.2	1.2	1.2	1.2
2015	1.2	1.2	1.2	1.2	1.2	1.3	1.3	1.3	1.3	1.3	1.2	1.2	1.2

Employment by Industry: Portland-Vancouver-Hillsboro, OR-WA, 2005–2015—*Continued*

(Numbers in thousands, not seasonally adjusted)

Industry and year	January	February	March	April	May	June	July	August	September	October	November	December	Annual average
Construction													
2005	53.7	54.3	55.5	56.2	57.6	58.9	61.4	62.8	62.8	62.4	61.2	61.3	59.0
2006	58.8	59.9	60.7	61.5	62.6	64.8	66.0	67.1	67.1	66.3	64.9	64.1	63.7
2007	61.9	62.7	63.7	64.0	66.1	66.2	68.6	69.7	69.1	68.1	66.6	64.9	66.0
2008	61.4	61.5	61.5	61.5	62.5	63.2	63.8	63.9	63.3	61.0	57.8	54.9	61.4
2009	52.4	50.9	49.9	49.4	49.6	50.6	51.4	51.4	50.8	49.7	47.1	46.1	49.9
2010	43.2	42.8	43.4	44.1	44.8	45.6	47.8	48.4	48.3	48.1	45.8	45.3	45.6
2011	42.8	43.3	44.2	45.6	46.4	47.7	49.4	50.1	50.0	49.6	48.2	48.0	47.1
2012	46.2	46.3	46.7	47.3	49.0	49.7	51.3	52.5	51.4	50.8	48.8	47.7	49.0
2013	46.4	47.0	48.1	49.8	51.8	52.8	54.7	55.6	55.5	55.7	55.0	54.0	52.2
2014	53.6	53.2	54.7	54.9	55.8	56.7	57.7	58.0	57.2	55.8	54.8	54.3	55.6
2015	53.3	53.5	53.8	54.2	55.0	56.1	57.7	58.5	57.9	57.6	56.8	55.0	55.8
Manufacturing													
2005	121.1	121.5	121.8	122.3	122.5	123.7	124.9	124.8	124.0	125.0	124.6	124.9	123.4
2006	124.2	124.4	125.1	125.6	126.0	127.3	128.7	128.8	128.6	127.7	126.9	127.0	126.7
2007	126.0	126.2	126.4	125.2	125.2	126.0	127.0	127.2	126.6	126.5	125.7	125.4	126.1
2008	124.4	124.5	124.4	124.0	123.8	123.9	124.9	124.2	123.8	121.7	121.0	118.6	123.3
2009	115.7	113.2	111.2	109.6	108.7	108.0	108.1	107.8	107.6	107.4	106.2	105.8	109.1
2010	105.1	105.0	105.2	105.6	106.0	106.8	107.9	108.1	108.3	109.1	108.9	108.7	107.1
2011	108.0	108.7	109.2	109.8	110.4	111.5	112.4	112.9	112.6	112.7	112.6	112.5	111.1
2012	111.8	112.2	112.6	112.9	113.5	114.7	116.0	115.8	115.6	115.5	115.2	114.6	114.2
2013	113.8	114.1	114.1	114.7	114.9	116.0	116.4	117.0	116.8	116.8	116.3	116.0	115.6
2014	115.7	115.8	116.3	116.6	117.2	118.1	119.3	119.4	119.5	119.7	119.4	119.7	118.1
2015	119.5	119.9	120.6	121.2	121.7	122.7	123.7	123.3	123.0	121.8	121.6	122.9	121.8
Trade, Transportation, and Utilities													
2005	192.3	191.3	191.9	192.6	193.5	195.2	196.5	197.3	197.5	198.3	202.9	206.1	196.3
2006	197.1	196.1	196.6	197.4	199.1	200.3	201.1	201.5	201.2	201.4	206.2	209.1	200.6
2007	200.7	199.7	200.1	200.3	201.8	203.0	203.7	204.0	204.3	204.4	209.3	211.2	203.5
2008	202.8	201.4	201.1	201.1	201.3	201.2	202.4	202.3	201.7	200.6	201.0	200.9	201.5
2009	192.1	189.1	186.6	185.6	186.3	186.0	185.7	185.5	185.4	184.9	187.1	189.2	187.0
2010	182.3	180.9	181.0	182.2	182.8	183.7	184.8	185.1	185.2	186.5	189.8	192.2	184.7
2011	185.0	183.7	183.6	185.1	186.2	187.0	188.2	188.0	188.2	188.7	192.5	194.4	187.6
2012	187.4	186.0	186.4	187.7	189.6	191.1	190.9	191.4	191.0	192.2	197.1	199.1	190.8
2013	191.4	191.2	191.3	192.5	194.1	194.6	196.0	197.0	196.9	197.5	201.9	203.7	195.7
2014	197.5	195.9	196.1	197.0	198.7	200.1	201.5	202.7	202.8	203.6	207.8	210.6	201.2
2015	203.7	202.6	202.9	203.5	205.1	206.6	207.6	208.8	209.1	208.6	212.8	215.0	207.2
Wholesale Trade													
2005	53.4	53.8	53.9	53.9	54.1	54.5	54.8	54.7	54.8	54.6	54.7	55.0	54.4
2006	54.1	54.6	54.6	55.2	55.6	55.6	55.9	56.0	55.5	55.5	55.6	55.7	55.3
2007	55.2	55.7	55.6	55.7	56.0	56.0	56.3	55.9	55.5	55.7	55.6	55.6	55.7
2008	55.0	55.3	55.1	55.0	55.4	55.4	56.0	55.6	55.3	55.2	54.9	54.2	55.2
2009	53.2	53.0	52.2	52.1	52.1	51.6	51.6	51.2	50.7	50.2	49.9	49.8	51.5
2010	48.9	49.1	49.0	49.7	50.1	50.1	50.7	50.6	50.3	50.6	50.7	50.8	50.1
2011	49.9	50.3	50.1	51.1	51.6	51.5	52.0	52.0	51.6	51.8	51.7	51.7	51.3
2012	51.1	51.5	51.6	52.6	53.1	53.0	53.3	53.4	53.0	53.2	53.3	53.5	52.7
2013	52.5	53.2	53.1	53.5	53.9	53.7	54.4	54.5	54.2	54.0	54.4	54.4	53.8
2014	53.6	53.8	53.7	53.7	53.9	54.2	54.5	54.6	54.5	54.4	54.6	54.8	54.2
2015	54.2	54.7	54.6	54.8	55.2	55.3	55.6	55.9	55.7	55.2	55.2	56.4	55.2
Retail Trade													
2005	102.5	100.9	101.2	101.8	102.7	103.8	105.1	105.9	105.5	106.5	110.7	112.8	105.0
2006	106.0	104.2	104.6	105.1	106.2	106.9	107.9	108.2	107.9	108.0	112.5	114.7	107.7
2007	108.2	106.6	106.8	107.0	107.9	109.0	110.2	110.7	110.5	110.4	114.9	116.3	109.9
2008	110.2	108.4	108.3	107.9	107.7	107.9	109.2	109.1	108.5	107.5	109.1	109.5	108.6
2009	102.9	100.9	99.7	99.2	99.9	100.2	100.8	101.0	100.6	100.9	103.5	105.1	101.2
2010	100.2	98.9	99.1	99.2	99.5	100.2	101.3	101.7	101.2	102.1	105.3	106.8	101.3
2011	101.5	100.1	100.1	100.5	100.9	101.8	102.8	102.7	102.3	103.0	106.5	108.0	102.5
2012	102.8	101.0	101.0	101.6	102.7	104.0	104.5	104.7	104.1	105.0	109.3	110.5	104.3
2013	105.2	104.2	104.3	104.9	106.1	106.8	108.1	108.8	108.3	109.0	112.6	113.8	107.7
2014	109.0	107.3	107.7	108.4	109.7	110.6	112.3	112.9	112.5	113.0	116.5	118.0	111.5
2015	112.6	111.3	111.7	112.7	113.6	114.2	115.8	116.3	115.9	116.2	119.3	120.0	115.0

Employment by Industry: Portland-Vancouver-Hillsboro, OR-WA, 2005–2015—*Continued*

(Numbers in thousands, not seasonally adjusted)

Industry and year	January	February	March	April	May	June	July	August	September	October	November	December	Annual average
Transportation and Utilities													
2005	36.4	36.6	36.8	36.9	36.7	36.9	36.6	36.7	37.2	37.2	37.5	38.3	37.0
2006	37.0	37.3	37.4	37.1	37.3	37.8	37.3	37.3	37.8	37.9	38.1	38.7	37.6
2007	37.3	37.4	37.7	37.6	37.9	38.0	37.2	37.4	38.3	38.3	38.8	39.3	37.9
2008	37.6	37.7	37.7	38.2	38.2	37.9	37.2	37.6	37.9	37.9	37.0	37.2	37.7
2009	36.0	35.2	34.7	34.3	34.3	34.2	33.3	33.3	34.1	33.8	33.7	34.3	34.3
2010	33.2	32.9	32.9	33.3	33.2	33.4	32.8	32.8	33.7	33.8	33.8	34.6	33.4
2011	33.6	33.3	33.4	33.5	33.7	33.7	33.4	33.3	34.3	33.9	34.3	34.7	33.8
2012	33.5	33.5	33.8	33.5	33.8	34.1	33.1	33.3	33.9	34.0	34.5	35.1	33.8
2013	33.7	33.8	33.9	34.1	34.1	34.1	33.5	33.7	34.4	34.5	34.9	35.5	34.2
2014	34.9	34.8	34.7	34.9	35.1	35.3	34.7	35.2	35.8	36.2	36.7	37.8	35.5
2015	36.9	36.6	36.6	36.0	36.3	37.1	36.2	36.6	37.5	37.2	38.3	38.6	37.0
Information													
2005	22.5	22.6	22.6	22.8	23.1	23.2	23.3	23.4	23.3	23.5	23.7	23.9	23.2
2006	23.6	23.9	23.9	23.6	23.8	24.0	24.5	24.5	24.7	24.6	24.3	24.6	24.2
2007	24.3	24.7	25.0	24.9	25.2	25.0	24.9	25.2	25.0	25.0	25.2	25.3	25.0
2008	25.1	25.2	25.2	25.0	25.2	25.2	24.8	24.9	24.7	24.2	24.1	23.9	24.8
2009	23.5	23.5	23.4	23.2	23.3	24.1	23.0	23.1	22.8	22.6	22.9	22.9	23.2
2010	22.4	22.5	22.6	22.6	23.0	23.0	22.5	22.8	22.7	22.4	22.7	22.7	22.7
2011	22.7	22.7	23.0	22.8	22.6	22.5	22.7	22.9	22.6	22.5	22.7	22.7	22.7
2012	22.4	22.6	23.1	23.2	23.1	23.4	23.6	23.4	23.2	23.7	23.7	23.5	23.2
2013	23.1	23.1	23.2	23.2	23.1	23.0	23.1	23.3	23.4	23.5	23.5	23.6	23.3
2014	22.8	22.9	23.2	23.3	23.2	23.4	23.8	23.9	23.8	23.8	23.9	24.0	23.5
2015	23.4	23.7	23.8	23.8	24.0	24.2	24.9	25.3	24.9	24.8	25.2	25.7	24.5
Financial Activities													
2005	66.7	66.9	67.0	67.5	68.0	68.5	69.1	69.4	69.4	69.6	70.0	70.3	68.5
2006	69.6	69.8	70.0	70.4	70.6	71.1	71.6	71.8	71.7	71.5	71.6	71.7	71.0
2007	71.0	71.2	71.3	71.1	71.1	71.1	71.2	70.9	70.0	69.8	69.8	69.6	70.7
2008	68.9	69.0	68.7	68.8	68.8	68.4	68.4	68.2	67.5	67.2	66.7	66.2	68.1
2009	65.5	65.0	64.5	64.5	64.4	64.1	64.1	64.0	63.4	63.4	63.1	63.0	64.1
2010	62.2	61.9	61.9	62.3	62.1	62.4	62.4	62.4	62.2	62.2	62.0	62.2	62.2
2011	61.6	61.6	61.4	61.4	61.5	61.8	62.0	61.9	61.7	61.6	61.7	61.9	61.7
2012	61.6	61.7	61.7	61.9	62.0	62.1	62.8	62.9	62.6	62.7	62.7	62.9	62.3
2013	62.2	62.2	62.3	62.9	63.3	63.4	64.4	64.3	64.0	64.1	64.0	64.0	63.4
2014	63.1	62.9	62.9	63.3	63.5	64.0	64.5	64.9	64.7	65.0	65.0	65.2	64.1
2015	64.9	65.1	64.9	65.6	66.0	66.2	67.0	67.2	66.9	67.7	67.2	67.7	66.4
Professional and Business Services													
2005	127.8	129.6	131.0	133.2	133.5	135.2	136.9	138.1	138.2	138.5	138.8	138.9	135.0
2006	134.8	136.8	137.9	139.6	140.6	142.7	143.0	144.1	144.6	145.3	145.1	143.5	141.5
2007	139.4	140.8	142.4	142.8	142.6	143.9	144.2	145.8	145.7	146.1	145.2	144.4	143.6
2008	141.0	142.7	143.9	145.4	145.1	145.5	146.8	147.6	146.2	144.8	141.8	139.4	144.2
2009	134.9	133.7	132.7	133.2	131.9	132.0	132.5	132.3	131.4	132.4	132.4	132.1	132.6
2010	129.7	131.0	132.5	135.2	134.9	135.8	137.3	138.6	138.5	140.0	139.6	139.7	136.1
2011	136.1	137.6	138.8	141.0	140.9	141.9	144.3	144.9	145.4	145.4	145.5	145.9	142.3
2012	143.8	144.5	145.6	147.0	147.4	148.6	149.9	151.0	150.6	151.8	151.1	151.1	148.5
2013	147.9	149.4	151.3	153.6	154.4	155.6	158.0	159.6	159.4	160.2	160.2	160.1	155.8
2014	157.2	158.2	159.9	162.0	162.8	164.4	165.9	167.3	167.6	167.8	167.4	167.8	164.0
2015	164.4	165.9	167.6	169.3	169.9	170.8	173.2	174.0	173.7	174.4	173.7	174.0	170.9
Education and Health Services													
2005	118.2	121.4	122.1	122.6	122.0	118.6	117.2	117.8	122.4	124.9	125.7	125.9	121.6
2006	121.9	125.4	126.2	126.9	126.0	122.5	119.9	120.4	124.9	128.7	129.7	130.0	125.2
2007	126.1	130.1	131.0	131.2	130.5	127.3	125.1	125.2	130.1	133.9	134.8	134.4	130.0
2008	131.1	135.0	135.7	136.5	135.4	132.5	130.4	130.4	135.7	138.8	139.4	139.2	135.0
2009	135.1	138.4	138.7	139.6	139.0	135.5	133.6	133.5	139.4	142.0	142.9	142.2	138.3
2010	140.1	142.9	143.8	144.7	143.6	140.3	137.9	137.7	143.0	146.9	147.9	147.9	143.1
2011	145.2	147.9	148.5	148.8	147.1	144.1	141.6	142.0	147.0	150.0	150.9	150.5	147.0
2012	147.1	150.8	151.5	152.2	150.1	146.6	143.7	144.3	149.3	152.0	153.0	152.6	149.4
2013	148.5	152.6	152.7	154.1	153.0	149.1	146.3	147.4	152.5	156.1	157.1	156.5	152.2
2014	153.4	156.2	157.0	157.6	156.0	153.6	150.9	150.7	156.1	159.0	160.4	160.4	155.9
2015	157.1	161.1	161.4	163.0	160.8	158.4	156.7	156.7	162.1	164.5	166.4	165.7	161.2

Employment by Industry: Portland-Vancouver-Hillsboro, OR-WA, 2005–2015—*Continued*

(Numbers in thousands, not seasonally adjusted)

Industry and year	January	February	March	April	May	June	July	August	September	October	November	December	Annual average
Leisure and Hospitality													
2005	85.5	86.2	87.6	89.2	90.7	92.1	92.7	93.7	92.4	90.5	90.9	91.4	90.2
2006	89.4	89.8	91.1	93.3	94.5	95.7	96.6	97.5	96.7	95.3	95.3	95.8	94.3
2007	93.2	94.4	95.4	96.3	97.9	99.0	101.1	102.0	101.2	98.8	98.9	99.4	98.1
2008	96.3	97.0	98.1	99.8	101.0	101.5	102.5	102.7	101.7	99.0	97.6	95.8	99.4
2009	92.6	92.7	93.3	94.4	95.5	95.9	96.9	97.0	96.6	94.0	93.4	92.5	94.6
2010	90.1	90.8	91.3	94.0	95.3	96.4	97.1	97.7	97.2	95.7	94.8	94.8	94.6
2011	91.9	93.0	93.7	96.2	96.8	98.8	100.1	100.8	100.0	97.3	96.5	97.0	96.8
2012	94.6	95.5	97.0	98.6	100.4	101.9	103.3	104.4	103.8	101.5	100.6	101.0	100.2
2013	98.3	99.4	100.7	102.5	104.4	106.6	107.8	108.8	108.2	104.9	104.6	104.4	104.2
2014	102.5	102.9	104.9	106.9	108.5	109.6	111.0	112.0	111.1	108.7	108.1	108.6	107.9
2015	106.9	108.2	109.8	111.5	113.5	115.5	117.4	117.9	116.9	114.2	113.5	114.1	113.3
Other Services													
2005	33.7	34.2	34.3	34.5	34.7	34.7	34.9	34.9	34.8	34.8	34.9	34.9	34.6
2006	34.4	34.9	35.2	35.5	36.0	36.3	36.2	36.0	36.0	36.1	36.1	36.3	35.8
2007	35.7	36.4	36.5	36.4	36.7	37.0	36.6	36.8	37.0	37.1	37.2	37.2	36.7
2008	36.8	37.0	37.2	37.5	37.7	37.8	37.6	37.5	37.8	37.3	36.8	36.3	37.3
2009	35.7	35.8	35.7	35.5	35.7	35.5	35.4	35.3	34.9	34.7	34.7	34.6	35.3
2010	33.9	34.1	34.3	34.5	34.9	35.5	35.1	35.0	35.0	35.3	34.7	34.8	34.8
2011	34.4	34.8	34.9	35.2	35.3	35.5	35.8	36.0	35.9	35.9	35.8	35.8	35.4
2012	35.7	36.1	36.2	36.6	37.2	37.0	37.0	37.0	36.8	36.9	36.6	36.4	36.6
2013	36.2	36.5	36.6	36.7	37.2	37.0	37.5	37.5	37.1	36.9	37.2	36.9	36.9
2014	36.9	37.0	37.4	37.5	38.2	38.6	38.6	38.6	38.6	38.5	38.4	38.4	38.1
2015	38.0	38.4	38.5	38.8	39.0	39.0	39.7	39.8	39.5	40.0	40.0	39.8	39.2
Government													
2005	138.3	140.3	140.6	140.3	141.1	141.4	128.9	127.3	131.9	139.3	141.4	140.7	137.6
2006	138.3	140.4	141.5	141.5	143.4	143.0	130.6	128.1	133.6	141.1	143.6	142.2	138.9
2007	141.1	142.9	144.1	144.3	146.5	146.5	134.7	131.6	136.1	145.3	147.0	146.9	142.3
2008	145.7	147.1	148.3	148.6	150.1	149.8	141.1	138.3	142.8	149.5	151.8	150.8	147.0
2009	149.0	151.0	151.8	151.9	152.7	151.1	141.0	138.2	140.3	149.3	150.9	149.9	148.1
2010	148.6	150.0	150.4	149.6	153.4	153.3	139.6	137.3	139.5	148.4	150.4	147.9	147.4
2011	148.3	149.3	149.2	150.9	151.4	148.9	137.1	134.8	137.1	146.8	148.4	146.7	145.7
2012	146.5	148.0	148.0	147.9	149.2	148.4	136.8	134.7	137.2	146.3	147.8	146.3	144.8
2013	145.1	147.3	147.1	147.5	148.4	148.6	134.8	134.0	136.6	145.7	147.6	146.8	144.1
2014	146.3	147.5	148.1	149.1	150.4	149.2	137.1	137.3	140.6	149.5	151.5	150.8	146.5
2015	150.4	152.0	152.3	152.8	154.0	152.2	140.6	140.1	143.0	152.9	154.6	154.1	149.9

Employment by Industry: Orlando-Kissimmee-Sanford, FL, 2005–2015

(Numbers in thousands, not seasonally adjusted)

Industry and year	January	February	March	April	May	June	July	August	September	October	November	December	Annual average
Total Nonfarm													
2005	985.0	992.7	1,000.1	1,007.2	1,013.9	1,003.6	1,003.5	1,018.7	1,023.9	1,026.5	1,037.3	1,044.4	1,013.1
2006	1,034.4	1,041.4	1,050.2	1,055.5	1,059.8	1,050.5	1,041.5	1,059.3	1,064.2	1,064.7	1,076.7	1,084.4	1,056.9
2007	1,072.1	1,082.0	1,087.6	1,087.7	1,089.1	1,076.0	1,067.9	1,081.1	1,080.3	1,084.3	1,095.5	1,096.4	1,083.3
2008	1,077.6	1,087.8	1,091.3	1,080.1	1,077.6	1,060.6	1,051.2	1,059.1	1,052.5	1,048.5	1,046.4	1,044.5	1,064.8
2009	1,018.0	1,017.9	1,015.5	1,009.5	1,005.5	988.6	977.7	985.9	984.6	986.6	992.9	993.6	998.0
2010	976.2	982.4	989.9	995.9	1,000.9	989.0	984.3	994.2	989.9	998.1	1,004.3	1,005.7	992.6
2011	989.5	996.1	1,002.5	1,007.5	1,006.9	995.4	993.8	1,004.3	1,009.7	1,012.3	1,022.9	1,025.1	1,005.5
2012	1,011.2	1,021.2	1,031.0	1,030.6	1,031.2	1,021.2	1,018.0	1,029.0	1,031.5	1,043.5	1,056.3	1,057.0	1,031.8
2013	1,037.1	1,051.3	1,058.9	1,059.7	1,063.8	1,056.8	1,054.2	1,069.4	1,069.5	1,079.0	1,092.7	1,094.9	1,065.6
2014	1,082.5	1,091.6	1,100.7	1,103.3	1,109.2	1,101.0	1,098.9	1,114.6	1,114.4	1,122.6	1,134.6	1,138.4	1,109.3
2015	1,122.9	1,135.9	1,143.1	1,150.1	1,155.8	1,147.8	1,148.5	1,161.2	1,162.9	1,173.7	1,185.4	1,190.6	1,156.5
Total Private													
2005													
2006	874.9	881.6	888.6	895.7	901.4	903.4	905.4	908.9	911.4	913.3	923.5	930.8	903.2
2007	921.2	926.8	935.7	940.0	944.5	946.1	939.4	944.7	948.1	948.0	959.3	967.8	943.5
2008	955.0	963.4	968.6	968.0	969.7	967.9	962.0	961.9	960.4	965.2	976.3	978.3	966.4
2009	959.9	969.2	971.6	960.3	957.6	952.8	945.6	941.4	933.7	929.7	926.9	925.1	947.8
2010	899.7	898.6	896.1	890.2	887.9	881.9	872.4	870.4	868.3	869.5	875.2	877.0	882.3
2011	859.6	865.6	872.9	878.0	880.2	881.1	877.8	877.5	873.6	880.4	886.6	889.2	876.9
2012	873.2	878.1	884.3	891.0	890.4	889.8	889.1	889.4	893.4	894.7	904.7	907.8	890.4
2013	893.6	901.8	911.1	912.4	914.0	914.7	912.0	911.9	914.3	924.9	936.9	938.5	915.5
2014	919.5	931.9	939.1	939.8	944.8	948.9	947.0	951.1	951.5	960.5	973.6	976.3	948.7
2015	963.7	972.5	981.3	983.0	989.8	992.4	990.9	995.5	995.5	1,001.8	1,013.6	1,017.5	991.5
	1,002.3	1,014.5	1,021.1	1,028.0	1,035.1	1,038.1	1,038.8	1,040.6	1,042.7	1,051.7	1,062.6	1,068.2	1,037.0
Goods Producing													
2005	124.4	125.5	126.8	128.5	129.6	130.7	131.9	132.4	133.0	132.6	133.5	134.1	130.3
2006	133.0	134.2	136.0	136.3	137.4	138.1	137.1	137.2	136.9	136.4	135.5	135.6	136.1
2007	132.2	131.9	132.4	130.9	130.9	131.1	129.6	129.9	129.4	127.9	127.5	126.0	130.0
2008	121.8	121.8	121.2	118.4	117.7	116.9	115.3	114.2	113.5	110.7	108.3	106.2	115.5
2009	102.8	100.8	99.4	95.4	94.3	93.7	91.3	90.2	88.9	88.0	87.4	86.5	93.2
2010	84.7	85.1	85.7	86.1	86.2	86.9	87.0	86.4	86.0	85.4	84.6	84.3	85.7
2011	83.1	83.2	83.0	83.0	83.0	82.9	83.2	83.4	83.7	83.3	83.4	83.4	83.2
2012	82.6	83.1	83.6	82.3	83.0	83.3	84.1	84.8	85.2	85.9	86.4	85.8	84.2
2013	85.0	86.1	86.9	87.9	88.7	89.3	90.1	90.9	91.4	91.7	92.2	92.3	89.4
2014	92.0	93.1	93.3	94.1	94.8	95.5	96.1	96.9	97.3	97.8	98.0	97.5	95.5
2015	97.0	98.1	98.7	99.6	100.8	102.0	102.8	103.2	103.8	104.2	106.1	106.8	101.9
Service-Providing													
2005	860.6	867.2	873.3	878.7	884.3	872.9	871.6	886.3	890.9	893.9	903.8	910.3	882.8
2006	901.4	907.2	914.2	919.2	922.4	912.4	904.4	922.1	927.3	928.3	941.2	948.8	920.7
2007	939.9	950.1	955.2	956.8	958.2	944.9	938.3	951.2	950.9	956.4	968.0	970.4	953.4
2008	955.8	966.0	970.1	961.7	959.9	943.7	935.9	944.9	939.0	937.8	938.1	938.3	949.3
2009	915.2	917.1	916.1	914.1	911.2	894.9	886.4	895.7	895.7	898.6	905.5	907.1	904.8
2010	891.5	897.3	904.2	909.8	914.7	902.1	897.3	907.8	903.9	912.7	919.7	921.4	906.9
2011	906.4	912.9	919.5	924.5	923.9	912.5	910.6	920.9	926.0	929.0	939.5	941.7	922.3
2012	928.6	938.1	947.4	948.3	948.2	937.9	933.9	944.2	946.3	957.6	969.9	971.2	947.6
2013	952.1	965.2	972.0	971.8	975.1	967.5	964.1	978.5	978.1	987.3	1,000.5	1,002.6	976.2
2014	990.5	998.5	1,007.4	1,009.2	1,014.4	1,005.5	1,002.8	1,017.7	1,017.1	1,024.8	1,036.6	1,040.9	1,013.8
2015	1,025.9	1,037.8	1,044.4	1,050.5	1,055.0	1,045.8	1,045.7	1,058.0	1,059.1	1,069.5	1,079.3	1,083.8	1,054.6
Mining and Logging													
2005	0.3	0.3	0.3	0.4	0.4	0.4	0.3	0.3	0.3	0.3	0.3	0.3	0.3
2006	0.3	0.3	0.3	0.3	0.3	0.3	0.3	0.3	0.3	0.3	0.3	0.4	0.3
2007	0.3	0.4	0.4	0.4	0.4	0.4	0.3	0.3	0.3	0.4	0.4	0.4	0.4
2008	0.4	0.4	0.4	0.4	0.4	0.3	0.3	0.3	0.3	0.3	0.2	0.2	0.3
2009	0.2	0.2	0.2	0.2	0.3	0.3	0.3	0.2	0.2	0.2	0.2	0.2	0.2
2010	0.2	0.2	0.2	0.2	0.2	0.2	0.2	0.2	0.2	0.2	0.2	0.2	0.2
2011	0.2	0.2	0.2	0.2	0.2	0.2	0.2	0.2	0.2	0.2	0.2	0.2	0.2
2012	0.2	0.2	0.2	0.2	0.2	0.2	0.2	0.2	0.2	0.2	0.2	0.2	0.2
2013	0.2	0.2	0.2	0.2	0.2	0.2	0.3	0.3	0.3	0.3	0.3	0.3	0.3
2014	0.3	0.3	0.3	0.3	0.3	0.3	0.3	0.3	0.3	0.3	0.3	0.3	0.3
2015	0.3	0.3	0.3	0.3	0.3	0.3	0.3	0.3	0.3	0.3	0.3	0.3	0.3

Employment by Industry: Orlando-Kissimmee-Sanford, FL, 2005–2015—*Continued*

(Numbers in thousands, not seasonally adjusted)

Industry and year	January	February	March	April	May	June	July	August	September	October	November	December	Annual average
Construction													
2005	78.4	79.4	80.5	81.7	83.0	84.0	85.4	86.2	87.0	86.9	87.9	88.8	84.1
2006	88.1	89.3	90.6	91.1	92.0	92.4	91.7	91.9	91.7	91.1	90.3	90.2	90.9
2007	87.4	86.9	87.2	85.6	85.7	85.8	84.6	85.0	84.6	83.3	82.7	81.2	85.0
2008	77.7	77.7	77.2	74.5	74.0	73.3	72.1	71.5	70.9	68.4	66.5	64.8	72.4
2009	62.3	60.7	59.6	56.3	55.2	54.5	52.7	51.8	50.7	49.9	49.2	48.6	54.3
2010	47.2	47.7	48.0	48.3	47.9	48.5	48.2	47.9	47.5	47.0	46.1	45.6	47.5
2011	44.7	44.7	44.6	44.5	44.6	44.7	45.1	45.3	45.6	45.4	45.4	45.4	45.0
2012	44.4	44.8	45.1	43.9	44.6	44.9	45.8	46.8	47.4	48.0	48.4	47.9	46.0
2013	47.4	48.3	49.1	49.6	50.3	50.8	51.5	52.4	52.6	52.9	53.2	53.3	51.0
2014	53.0	53.9	54.2	54.5	55.0	55.5	55.9	56.6	57.0	57.4	57.7	57.0	55.6
2015	56.7	57.6	58.0	58.5	59.5	60.4	61.2	61.6	62.0	61.9	63.4	63.6	60.4
Manufacturing													
2005	45.7	45.8	46.0	46.4	46.2	46.3	46.2	45.9	45.7	45.4	45.3	45.0	45.8
2006	44.6	44.6	45.1	44.9	45.1	45.4	45.1	45.0	44.9	45.0	44.9	45.0	45.0
2007	44.5	44.6	44.8	44.9	44.8	44.9	44.7	44.6	44.5	44.2	44.4	44.4	44.6
2008	43.7	43.7	43.6	43.5	43.3	43.3	42.9	42.4	42.3	42.0	41.6	41.2	42.8
2009	40.3	39.9	39.6	38.9	38.8	38.9	38.3	38.2	38.0	37.9	38.0	37.7	38.7
2010	37.3	37.2	37.5	37.6	38.1	38.2	38.6	38.3	38.3	38.2	38.3	38.5	38.0
2011	38.2	38.3	38.2	38.3	38.2	38.0	37.9	37.9	37.9	37.7	37.8	37.8	38.0
2012	38.0	38.1	38.3	38.2	38.2	38.2	38.1	37.8	37.6	37.7	37.8	37.7	38.0
2013	37.4	37.6	37.6	38.1	38.2	38.3	38.3	38.2	38.5	38.5	38.7	38.7	38.2
2014	38.7	38.9	38.8	39.3	39.5	39.7	39.9	40.0	40.0	40.1	40.0	40.2	39.6
2015	40.0	40.2	40.4	40.8	41.0	41.3	41.3	41.3	41.5	42.0	42.4	42.9	41.3
Trade, Transportation, and Utilities													
2005	187.7	187.9	189.2	190.8	191.7	191.8	192.8	193.3	193.2	194.4	198.4	201.8	192.8
2006	196.8	196.3	196.7	197.3	198.3	198.1	197.4	198.0	197.8	198.4	203.5	207.1	198.8
2007	200.7	201.2	200.9	201.2	203.1	202.9	202.4	203.5	204.1	205.1	210.1	212.6	204.0
2008	205.7	205.1	204.7	201.9	201.3	200.4	199.0	198.6	197.5	196.3	198.6	199.9	200.8
2009	191.9	190.1	188.4	186.4	185.7	184.6	183.1	183.2	182.6	182.3	186.4	188.0	186.1
2010	182.6	182.9	182.7	183.9	184.6	185.1	185.0	185.8	185.1	187.2	192.7	195.5	186.1
2011	188.8	188.4	188.7	189.3	189.7	189.6	190.5	191.5	191.4	193.5	199.9	202.0	191.9
2012	195.9	194.9	196.1	195.7	196.4	196.3	196.6	196.9	196.5	198.4	205.8	207.5	198.1
2013	200.2	199.6	200.0	200.1	201.3	202.3	203.2	204.2	204.5	206.2	214.1	216.8	204.4
2014	209.6	209.7	210.5	209.7	210.1	210.5	210.8	211.8	211.6	213.5	221.4	224.4	212.8
2015	216.3	216.3	216.7	217.3	218.1	219.4	219.6	221.1	220.7	222.2	229.1	231.2	220.7
Wholesale Trade													
2005	43.3	43.7	43.7	44.3	44.6	44.8	45.0	45.1	45.3	45.2	45.5	45.9	44.7
2006	45.7	46.1	46.2	46.2	46.8	46.5	46.4	46.0	46.2	46.1	46.1	46.3	46.2
2007	46.6	47.2	47.1	47.1	47.3	47.2	47.2	47.1	47.2	47.6	47.6	47.8	47.3
2008	47.3	48.0	47.5	46.4	46.2	46.0	45.5	45.3	45.0	44.4	44.2	43.9	45.8
2009	42.4	42.5	41.6	41.0	40.7	40.5	39.9	39.7	39.5	39.2	39.0	39.0	40.4
2010	38.4	38.9	38.7	38.7	38.8	38.5	38.1	38.1	38.0	38.2	38.1	38.1	38.4
2011	38.5	38.6	38.6	38.4	38.5	38.4	38.4	38.3	38.3	38.3	38.4	38.6	38.4
2012	38.5	38.5	38.7	38.9	38.8	38.9	39.1	39.3	39.2	39.4	39.6	39.6	39.0
2013	39.2	39.6	39.7	39.8	39.9	39.9	39.9	40.0	40.3	40.6	41.0	41.1	40.1
2014	40.7	41.1	41.3	41.4	41.7	41.8	42.1	42.3	42.4	42.6	42.7	42.9	41.9
2015	42.8	43.0	43.1	43.2	43.6	43.7	43.8	43.9	44.0	43.6	44.4	43.9	43.6
Retail Trade													
2005	117.5	117.4	118.3	119.0	119.2	119.2	120.0	120.1	119.5	120.7	124.0	126.3	120.1
2006	122.1	121.2	121.3	121.6	121.6	121.6	121.0	121.3	120.6	121.3	126.1	128.4	122.3
2007	122.6	121.8	121.7	121.5	123.0	123.2	122.6	123.3	123.2	123.8	128.4	129.8	123.7
2008	124.5	123.2	123.3	121.6	121.3	121.1	120.6	120.7	120.2	120.0	122.6	123.4	121.9
2009	117.8	116.4	115.8	114.9	114.7	114.3	113.7	114.2	113.8	113.9	118.1	119.1	115.6
2010	114.9	114.3	114.3	115.5	116.0	117.0	117.3	118.1	117.5	119.4	124.6	126.7	118.0
2011	120.8	120.3	120.2	120.9	121.2	121.2	122.1	123.1	122.9	124.6	130.5	131.7	123.3
2012	126.6	125.5	126.3	125.9	126.7	126.5	126.7	126.9	126.8	128.2	135.1	136.3	128.1
2013	130.4	129.4	129.5	129.4	130.1	130.9	132.1	132.8	132.6	134.1	141.0	143.4	133.0
2014	137.3	136.8	137.1	136.5	136.6	136.9	136.7	137.3	137.1	138.5	145.5	147.2	138.6
2015	140.3	140.1	140.4	140.6	140.7	141.4	141.3	142.5	142.1	143.8	149.2	150.0	142.7

Employment by Industry: Orlando-Kissimmee-Sanford, FL, 2005–2015—*Continued*

(Numbers in thousands, not seasonally adjusted)

Industry and year	January	February	March	April	May	June	July	August	September	October	November	December	Annual average
Transportation and Utilities													
2005	26.9	26.8	27.2	27.5	27.9	27.8	27.8	28.1	28.4	28.5	28.9	29.6	28.0
2006	29.0	29.0	29.2	29.5	29.9	30.0	30.0	30.7	31.0	31.0	31.3	32.4	30.3
2007	31.5	32.2	32.1	32.6	32.8	32.5	32.6	33.1	33.7	33.7	34.1	35.0	33.0
2008	33.9	33.9	33.9	33.9	33.8	33.3	32.9	32.6	32.3	31.9	31.8	32.6	33.1
2009	31.7	31.2	31.0	30.5	30.3	29.8	29.5	29.3	29.3	29.2	29.3	29.9	30.1
2010	29.3	29.7	29.7	29.7	29.8	29.6	29.6	29.6	29.6	29.6	30.0	30.7	29.7
2011	29.5	29.5	29.9	30.0	30.0	30.0	30.0	30.1	30.2	30.6	31.0	31.7	30.2
2012	30.8	30.9	31.1	30.9	30.9	30.9	30.8	30.7	30.5	30.8	31.1	31.6	30.9
2013	30.6	30.6	30.8	30.9	31.3	31.5	31.2	31.4	31.6	31.5	32.1	32.3	31.3
2014	31.6	31.8	32.1	31.8	31.8	31.8	32.0	32.2	32.1	32.4	33.2	34.3	32.3
2015	33.2	33.2	33.2	33.5	33.8	34.3	34.5	34.7	34.6	34.8	35.5	37.3	34.4
Information													
2005	23.7	24.1	24.0	24.1	25.0	24.8	24.7	24.8	24.8	24.8	25.1	25.3	24.6
2006	25.2	25.4	25.7	25.8	25.9	25.9	25.8	25.6	25.8	25.8	25.9	25.9	25.7
2007	26.1	26.3	26.8	27.1	27.3	27.2	26.9	26.7	26.5	26.5	26.4	26.5	26.7
2008	26.5	26.7	26.7	26.4	26.4	26.4	26.3	26.2	25.5	25.9	25.9	25.8	26.2
2009	25.8	25.9	25.7	25.1	25.1	25.0	24.7	24.4	24.1	23.9	23.9	23.9	24.8
2010	23.9	23.8	23.9	23.8	23.6	23.7	23.7	23.9	23.7	23.7	23.9	23.9	23.8
2011	23.8	23.9	23.9	23.9	24.0	24.0	24.2	24.1	24.1	23.9	24.2	24.1	24.0
2012	23.9	23.9	23.8	23.6	23.5	23.5	23.6	23.5	23.3	23.6	23.5	23.5	23.6
2013	23.2	23.5	23.4	23.4	23.5	23.7	23.7	23.7	23.6	23.6	23.7	23.7	23.6
2014	23.7	23.6	23.8	23.7	23.9	24.1	23.9	23.8	23.7	23.8	24.2	24.2	23.9
2015	24.3	24.3	24.2	24.3	24.4	24.4	24.1	23.9	23.7	23.7	23.8	23.7	24.1
Financial Activities													
2005	63.7	64.5	64.9	65.6	66.0	66.4	67.5	67.8	67.9	68.3	68.6	69.2	66.7
2006	68.6	69.1	69.4	69.7	69.9	70.1	69.8	70.2	70.1	70.6	71.1	71.5	70.0
2007	70.3	70.9	71.1	70.6	70.8	71.4	70.9	70.8	70.5	70.5	70.6	70.9	70.8
2008	69.9	70.2	70.3	69.7	70.2	69.8	69.6	69.6	69.0	68.6	68.5	68.6	69.5
2009	67.3	67.1	66.8	66.4	66.2	66.1	65.4	65.3	64.6	64.9	65.2	65.2	65.9
2010	64.1	64.4	64.7	64.6	65.0	65.5	65.5	65.6	65.0	65.7	65.6	65.9	65.1
2011	65.5	65.8	66.1	65.7	65.7	65.5	65.9	65.9	66.1	65.8	66.0	66.2	65.9
2012	65.9	66.3	66.7	66.7	67.0	67.2	67.4	67.4	67.3	68.0	68.4	68.5	67.2
2013	68.0	68.5	68.8	69.1	69.3	69.9	69.8	70.2	70.1	70.8	71.1	71.1	69.7
2014	70.2	70.6	70.8	70.6	71.0	71.0	71.0	71.2	71.1	71.5	71.6	71.7	71.0
2015	71.3	71.6	72.0	72.1	72.5	72.6	72.8	73.0	73.0	72.4	71.7	72.0	72.3
Professional and Business Services													
2005	154.0	155.4	156.3	158.8	159.7	159.9	159.5	161.0	162.2	163.2	165.4	166.1	160.1
2006	165.4	165.6	168.2	171.1	172.1	172.9	170.2	172.7	175.5	175.1	178.2	180.2	172.3
2007	179.2	181.7	182.3	182.5	182.4	179.3	178.6	178.0	178.3	180.5	182.3	180.8	180.5
2008	178.4	182.5	181.4	179.3	177.9	175.6	174.3	174.2	174.4	175.1	173.1	171.6	176.5
2009	166.7	166.5	165.3	164.0	165.6	163.1	160.3	161.0	163.0	165.0	165.1	164.3	164.2
2010	161.3	161.6	163.0	163.7	163.4	162.2	159.9	160.0	159.7	159.9	159.6	159.0	161.1
2011	157.4	158.8	159.4	161.7	161.8	161.5	160.5	161.4	163.6	164.0	166.1	165.8	161.8
2012	164.7	167.8	169.8	169.7	170.3	168.8	166.1	166.9	168.1	172.0	173.6	173.2	169.3
2013	169.5	173.1	174.3	174.7	176.2	176.3	173.9	175.3	175.7	178.2	180.4	179.7	175.6
2014	179.5	180.7	182.1	182.0	184.6	184.1	183.0	184.6	183.8	185.3	186.7	185.6	183.5
2015	185.3	187.7	189.7	193.3	195.3	195.3	196.0	195.3	195.3	201.0	201.2	201.8	194.8
Education and Health Services													
2005	99.6	100.1	100.6	100.8	101.7	100.9	101.3	102.8	103.6	104.2	105.0	105.3	102.2
2006	104.8	105.8	106.3	106.4	107.0	106.8	106.3	107.9	108.9	109.3	109.9	110.3	107.5
2007	109.5	110.6	111.0	111.7	112.5	112.3	111.5	112.7	113.7	114.8	115.8	116.1	112.7
2008	115.5	116.3	116.6	116.6	117.2	116.3	115.3	116.0	116.2	116.9	117.0	117.4	116.4
2009	116.0	116.8	117.8	117.7	118.1	117.9	118.0	118.3	118.8	120.2	121.1	121.4	118.5
2010	120.0	120.2	120.7	121.3	121.7	120.8	120.2	120.7	120.3	121.5	122.0	121.1	120.9
2011	121.1	121.9	122.2	123.4	123.6	122.6	122.9	123.6	124.6	124.9	125.6	125.9	123.5
2012	124.3	125.1	125.8	128.4	128.5	127.9	127.6	128.3	129.3	130.5	130.9	131.1	128.1
2013	129.7	130.9	131.4	131.4	131.6	130.6	129.2	131.3	131.6	132.6	133.4	133.3	131.4
2014	132.3	133.5	134.2	135.1	136.0	134.7	133.5	135.8	136.8	138.2	139.2	139.8	135.8
2015	139.1	140.6	141.4	142.5	143.7	142.6	141.2	143.2	144.5	144.8	145.3	145.3	142.9

Employment by Industry: Orlando-Kissimmee-Sanford, FL, 2005–2015—*Continued*

(Numbers in thousands, not seasonally adjusted)

Industry and year	January	February	March	April	May	June	July	August	September	October	November	December	Annual average
Leisure and Hospitality													
2005	180.0	182.1	184.8	184.7	184.7	185.8	184.4	183.4	182.8	182.0	183.6	184.8	183.6
2006	183.0	185.5	188.4	188.5	188.5	188.3	187.0	186.8	185.9	184.7	187.0	188.6	186.9
2007	188.0	191.1	193.9	194.7	193.5	194.8	194.2	193.0	190.8	193.1	197.1	199.3	193.6
2008	196.9	201.2	205.0	203.4	202.5	203.6	202.6	200.3	195.4	194.6	194.6	195.0	199.6
2009	189.1	191.3	192.3	194.7	192.8	191.9	190.4	189.1	187.4	186.4	187.7	189.3	190.2
2010	184.7	189.2	193.6	195.7	196.8	198.0	197.7	196.6	195.5	198.6	199.9	201.4	195.6
2011	195.7	198.2	202.8	205.1	204.9	206.5	205.4	203.7	204.5	204.2	204.8	206.1	203.5
2012	202.2	206.4	210.7	211.2	210.5	212.6	211.7	209.3	209.8	211.3	213.1	213.5	210.2
2013	208.7	214.9	218.8	217.4	218.3	220.7	221.1	219.5	218.5	221.1	222.1	222.6	218.6
2014	219.2	223.9	229.0	230.1	231.4	234.6	234.9	233.5	233.0	233.2	233.8	235.4	231.0
2015	229.8	236.3	238.6	238.6	239.7	241.5	241.9	240.3	241.1	242.4	243.2	245.2	239.9
Other Services													
2005	41.8	42.0	42.0	42.4	43.0	43.1	43.3	43.4	43.9	43.8	43.9	44.2	43.1
2006	44.4	44.9	45.0	44.9	45.4	45.9	45.8	46.3	47.2	47.7	48.2	48.6	46.2
2007	49.0	49.7	50.2	49.3	49.2	48.9	47.9	47.3	47.1	46.8	46.5	46.1	48.2
2008	45.2	45.4	45.7	44.6	44.4	43.8	43.2	42.3	42.2	41.6	40.9	40.6	43.3
2009	40.1	40.1	40.4	40.5	40.1	39.6	39.2	38.9	38.9	38.8	38.4	38.4	39.5
2010	38.3	38.4	38.6	38.9	38.9	38.9	38.8	38.5	38.3	38.4	38.3	38.1	38.5
2011	37.8	37.9	38.2	38.0	37.7	37.2	36.5	35.8	35.4	35.1	34.7	34.3	36.6
2012	34.1	34.3	34.6	34.8	34.8	35.1	34.9	34.8	34.8	35.2	35.2	35.4	34.8
2013	35.2	35.3	35.5	35.8	35.9	36.1	36.0	36.0	36.1	36.3	36.6	36.8	36.0
2014	37.2	37.4	37.6	37.7	38.0	37.9	37.7	37.9	38.2	38.5	38.7	38.9	38.0
2015	39.2	39.6	39.8	40.3	40.6	40.3	40.4	40.6	40.6	41.0	42.2	42.2	40.6
Government													
2005	110.1	111.1	111.5	111.5	112.5	100.2	98.1	109.8	112.5	113.2	113.8	113.6	109.8
2006	113.2	114.6	114.5	115.5	115.3	104.4	102.1	114.6	116.1	116.7	117.4	116.6	113.4
2007	117.1	118.6	119.0	119.7	119.4	108.1	105.9	119.2	119.9	119.1	119.2	118.1	116.9
2008	117.7	118.6	119.7	119.8	120.0	107.8	105.6	117.7	118.8	118.8	119.5	119.4	117.0
2009	118.3	119.3	119.4	119.3	117.6	106.7	105.3	115.5	116.3	117.1	117.7	116.6	115.8
2010	116.6	116.8	117.0	117.9	120.7	107.9	106.5	116.7	116.3	117.7	117.7	116.5	115.7
2011	116.3	118.0	118.2	117.4	116.5	105.6	104.7	114.9	116.3	117.6	118.2	117.3	115.1
2012	117.6	119.4	119.9	118.2	117.2	106.5	106.0	117.1	117.2	118.6	119.4	118.5	116.3
2013	117.6	119.4	119.8	119.9	119.0	107.9	107.2	118.3	118.0	118.5	119.1	118.6	116.9
2014	118.8	119.1	119.4	120.3	119.4	108.6	108.0	119.1	118.9	120.8	121.0	120.9	117.9
2015	120.6	121.4	122.0	122.1	120.7	109.7	109.7	120.6	120.2	122.0	122.8	122.4	119.5

Employment by Industry: San Antonio-New Braunfels, TX, 2005–2015

(Numbers in thousands, not seasonally adjusted)

Industry and year	January	February	March	April	May	June	July	August	September	October	November	December	Annual average
Total Nonfarm													
2005................	762.8	772.3	778.2	784.8	789.6	792.2	787.3	791.4	796.4	798.0	802.9	806.0	788.5
2006................	793.1	801.4	810.4	816.2	821.2	824.4	816.7	821.2	825.6	826.9	830.3	832.9	818.4
2007................	816.1	827.2	833.5	836.9	844.5	847.3	841.0	844.0	847.5	848.1	855.4	859.7	841.8
2008................	843.4	853.5	858.5	863.0	867.3	868.4	859.3	860.7	860.9	862.2	864.3	863.0	860.4
2009................	840.1	844.8	845.8	846.8	848.5	850.0	839.2	838.6	839.6	843.4	848.1	849.5	844.5
2010................	833.9	842.0	848.6	852.5	859.6	859.6	847.7	849.4	849.9	856.8	859.4	861.5	851.7
2011................	847.2	854.4	862.5	867.8	870.9	872.5	867.7	869.6	872.4	873.3	877.1	879.8	867.9
2012................	865.3	873.7	880.7	885.2	890.4	895.6	887.8	894.5	896.0	899.6	905.6	908.7	890.3
2013................	892.0	903.1	909.0	913.9	918.5	924.7	919.8	921.8	924.3	926.9	933.9	934.6	918.5
2014................	919.8	928.7	936.1	943.7	950.1	955.8	950.2	952.4	953.9	963.2	969.1	970.6	949.5
2015................	957.5	966.9	970.7	976.3	981.8	985.2	979.6	980.8	984.3	993.4	996.9	995.2	980.7
Total Private													
2005................	620.3	627.0	633.0	639.2	644.0	649.2	650.2	652.6	652.7	652.1	656.0	659.1	644.6
2006................	647.7	653.6	662.8	666.8	672.1	677.6	677.3	680.6	679.3	677.5	680.0	682.9	671.5
2007................	667.4	676.1	682.0	685.7	693.1	698.6	697.5	700.0	697.0	697.1	702.3	705.6	691.9
2008................	690.4	698.0	702.6	707.5	711.6	713.5	711.2	711.9	708.2	704.9	705.7	704.8	705.9
2009................	683.0	685.1	685.9	685.5	688.2	690.8	686.9	686.6	682.1	682.2	685.7	687.6	685.8
2010................	674.7	679.7	685.5	688.9	693.5	696.5	693.7	693.7	689.3	692.7	694.6	697.3	690.0
2011................	685.6	690.2	698.9	704.6	707.7	710.7	712.8	715.4	713.5	712.2	715.6	718.2	707.1
2012................	705.8	712.1	719.2	723.7	729.5	737.1	735.5	740.4	736.4	738.2	743.4	746.5	730.7
2013................	731.8	740.4	746.5	751.2	756.3	763.6	763.7	766.1	763.7	763.8	769.8	770.9	757.3
2014................	758.1	764.7	772.1	780.0	787.0	793.9	794.1	796.2	792.0	797.9	802.5	804.5	786.9
2015................	792.4	799.9	804.0	809.1	814.8	820.7	820.4	821.4	818.1	824.0	826.3	824.8	814.7
Goods Producing													
2005................	90.9	91.5	92.8	94.2	94.4	95.1	95.5	95.3	96.0	95.9	96.2	97.2	94.6
2006................	96.4	97.8	99.3	98.6	99.4	101.0	100.7	100.8	101.3	100.5	100.6	100.8	99.8
2007................	99.3	100.7	101.1	101.2	102.4	104.1	103.8	104.2	103.9	104.6	104.6	105.2	102.9
2008................	103.7	104.5	104.9	105.1	105.6	106.2	104.9	105.0	104.1	103.4	102.5	101.1	104.3
2009................	98.1	97.1	96.3	95.8	95.5	95.1	94.9	94.3	93.3	92.7	92.1	92.1	94.8
2010................	91.2	90.6	90.9	91.6	91.6	91.7	91.9	91.5	90.7	91.0	90.5	90.5	91.1
2011................	89.0	89.2	90.0	90.7	90.8	91.6	92.1	91.9	91.4	91.0	90.8	90.4	90.7
2012................	90.0	90.4	90.7	91.4	91.8	93.0	93.4	93.8	93.4	93.7	94.0	93.9	92.5
2013................	93.0	93.3	94.2	95.2	95.7	96.9	97.5	97.7	97.4	97.2	97.7	97.4	96.1
2014................	96.8	97.6	98.2	99.2	100.1	101.3	101.8	102.5	102.5	104.0	104.4	104.8	101.1
2015................	103.7	104.4	104.0	104.6	104.9	105.8	105.9	105.9	104.9	105.8	105.5	105.8	105.1
Service-Providing													
2005................	671.9	680.8	685.4	690.6	695.2	697.1	691.8	696.1	700.4	702.1	706.7	708.8	693.9
2006................	696.7	703.6	711.1	717.6	721.8	723.4	716.0	720.4	724.3	726.4	729.7	732.1	718.6
2007................	716.8	726.5	732.4	735.7	742.1	743.2	737.2	739.8	743.6	743.5	750.8	754.5	738.8
2008................	739.7	749.0	753.6	757.9	761.7	762.2	754.4	755.7	756.8	758.8	761.8	761.9	756.1
2009................	742.0	747.7	749.5	751.0	753.0	754.9	744.3	744.3	746.3	750.7	756.0	757.4	749.8
2010................	742.7	751.4	757.7	760.9	768.0	767.9	755.8	757.9	759.2	765.8	768.9	771.0	760.6
2011................	758.2	765.2	772.5	777.1	780.1	780.9	775.6	777.7	781.0	782.3	786.3	789.4	777.2
2012................	775.3	783.3	790.0	793.8	798.6	802.6	794.4	800.7	802.6	805.9	811.6	814.8	797.8
2013................	799.0	809.8	814.8	818.7	822.8	827.8	822.3	824.1	826.9	829.7	836.2	837.2	822.4
2014................	823.0	831.1	837.9	844.5	850.0	854.5	848.4	849.9	851.4	859.2	864.7	865.8	848.4
2015................	853.8	862.5	866.7	871.7	876.9	879.4	873.7	874.9	879.4	887.6	891.4	889.4	875.6
Mining and Logging													
2005................	2.3	2.4	2.4	2.4	2.4	2.5	2.6	2.6	2.6	2.8	2.8	2.8	2.6
2006................	2.9	3.0	3.0	3.0	3.1	3.1	3.1	3.2	3.2	3.1	3.1	3.1	3.1
2007................	3.0	3.1	3.1	3.1	3.2	3.2	3.3	3.4	3.4	3.5	3.5	3.6	3.3
2008................	3.4	3.4	3.4	3.5	3.6	3.7	3.7	3.7	3.6	3.6	3.5	3.4	3.5
2009................	3.3	3.3	3.2	3.1	3.1	3.0	3.1	3.0	3.0	3.0	3.0	3.0	3.1
2010................	3.0	3.0	2.9	3.0	3.0	3.1	3.0	3.0	3.0	3.0	2.9	2.9	3.0
2011................	2.9	2.9	2.9	3.0	3.0	3.1	3.3	3.3	3.3	3.4	3.4	3.5	3.2
2012................	3.5	3.6	3.7	4.0	4.0	4.2	4.4	4.5	4.6	4.7	4.8	4.9	4.2
2013................	5.0	5.1	5.2	5.5	5.7	5.8	6.3	6.3	6.3	6.8	6.8	6.9	6.0
2014................	7.5	7.7	7.9	8.2	8.4	8.7	8.6	8.8	8.9	9.3	9.4	9.5	8.6
2015................	9.3	9.2	8.8	8.6	8.3	8.3	8.2	8.0	7.6	7.5	7.4	7.3	8.2

Employment by Industry: San Antonio-New Braunfels, TX, 2005–2015—*Continued*

(Numbers in thousands, not seasonally adjusted)

Industry and year	January	February	March	April	May	June	July	August	September	October	November	December	Annual average
Construction													
2005	43.3	43.6	44.8	46.0	46.3	46.8	46.7	46.7	47.1	46.6	46.6	47.0	46.0
2006	46.3	47.1	48.1	47.8	48.1	49.2	48.8	48.8	48.7	48.1	48.0	47.9	48.1
2007	47.1	48.3	49.2	49.1	50.0	51.3	51.2	51.6	51.4	51.9	52.0	52.6	50.5
2008	52.1	53.2	53.7	54.1	54.5	55.0	54.3	54.6	54.2	53.8	53.1	52.1	53.7
2009	50.1	49.5	49.1	49.0	48.9	49.0	48.8	48.5	47.6	46.7	46.0	45.6	48.2
2010	45.0	44.3	44.8	45.0	44.7	44.3	44.5	44.0	43.1	43.0	42.4	42.3	44.0
2011	40.8	41.0	41.9	42.2	42.2	42.5	42.7	42.5	41.9	41.4	41.1	40.5	41.7
2012	40.3	40.5	40.7	40.6	41.1	41.9	42.2	42.6	42.2	42.3	42.3	42.1	41.6
2013	41.6	41.9	42.9	43.4	43.8	44.7	44.8	45.0	44.7	44.5	44.6	44.2	43.8
2014	43.6	44.1	44.6	45.1	45.5	46.1	46.8	47.1	47.1	47.8	48.1	48.3	46.2
2015	47.8	48.4	48.5	49.1	49.7	50.2	50.9	51.3	50.7	51.4	50.9	51.3	50.0
Manufacturing													
2005	45.3	45.5	45.6	45.8	45.7	45.8	46.2	46.0	46.3	46.5	46.8	47.4	46.1
2006	47.2	47.7	48.2	47.8	48.2	48.7	48.8	48.8	49.4	49.3	49.5	49.8	48.6
2007	49.2	49.3	48.8	49.0	49.2	49.6	49.3	49.2	49.1	49.2	49.1	49.0	49.2
2008	48.2	47.9	47.8	47.5	47.5	47.5	46.9	46.7	46.3	46.0	45.9	45.6	47.0
2009	44.7	44.3	44.0	43.7	43.5	43.1	43.0	42.8	42.7	43.0	43.1	43.5	43.5
2010	43.2	43.3	43.2	43.6	43.9	44.3	44.4	44.5	44.6	45.0	45.2	45.3	44.2
2011	45.3	45.3	45.2	45.5	45.6	46.0	46.1	46.1	46.2	46.2	46.3	46.4	45.9
2012	46.2	46.3	46.3	46.8	46.7	46.9	46.8	46.7	46.6	46.7	46.9	46.9	46.7
2013	46.4	46.3	46.1	46.3	46.2	46.4	46.4	46.4	46.4	45.9	46.3	46.3	46.3
2014	45.7	45.8	45.7	45.9	46.2	46.5	46.4	46.6	46.5	46.9	46.9	47.0	46.3
2015	46.6	46.8	46.7	46.9	46.9	47.3	46.8	46.6	46.6	46.9	47.2	47.2	46.9
Trade, Transportation, and Utilities													
2005	138.3	137.9	138.9	139.6	140.1	140.6	141.5	142.3	141.8	142.6	145.8	147.4	141.4
2006	142.7	142.1	143.8	143.7	144.2	144.5	144.9	146.3	146.3	148.6	152.5	154.6	146.2
2007	149.4	148.3	149.3	149.3	149.9	150.1	151.4	152.3	151.5	152.1	155.7	157.6	151.4
2008	151.8	151.4	152.2	151.4	151.4	151.6	152.3	153.5	152.0	152.4	154.1	154.6	152.4
2009	148.1	146.6	145.7	145.3	145.2	145.6	145.1	146.0	145.2	145.4	147.5	148.5	146.2
2010	143.5	142.4	142.9	143.5	143.9	144.1	143.8	145.1	144.0	145.5	147.7	149.4	144.7
2011	145.3	144.1	144.9	145.8	146.0	146.5	147.0	148.2	147.7	149.1	152.0	153.7	147.5
2012	149.3	148.4	148.9	149.6	150.2	151.2	151.2	152.3	152.1	153.9	158.1	159.0	152.0
2013	154.0	153.8	153.8	154.7	155.5	156.2	156.7	158.3	158.3	160.0	163.6	165.6	157.5
2014	160.7	160.3	160.5	161.7	162.0	163.4	163.7	164.7	164.9	167.2	170.7	172.8	164.4
2015	167.4	166.5	166.8	167.7	168.7	169.8	170.2	170.9	171.5	173.2	175.3	176.3	170.4
Wholesale Trade													
2005	27.2	27.3	27.4	27.6	27.8	28.0	28.1	28.2	28.2	28.0	28.3	28.4	27.9
2006	28.3	28.4	28.5	28.6	28.8	29.2	29.2	29.3	29.4	29.6	30.0	30.0	29.1
2007	29.7	29.9	30.1	30.3	30.4	30.5	30.5	30.6	30.5	30.6	30.6	30.8	30.4
2008	30.2	30.4	30.4	30.3	30.4	30.5	30.5	30.7	30.5	30.4	30.3	30.1	30.4
2009	29.8	29.7	29.5	29.5	29.5	29.5	29.0	29.0	28.9	29.2	29.2	29.1	29.3
2010	29.0	29.0	28.4	29.3	29.4	29.5	29.4	29.5	29.5	29.8	29.7	29.7	29.4
2011	29.3	29.4	29.7	29.9	30.0	30.2	30.3	30.3	30.3	30.5	30.6	30.5	30.1
2012	30.6	30.7	30.9	31.0	31.1	31.4	31.4	31.6	31.3	31.6	31.5	31.5	31.2
2013	31.8	32.1	31.8	31.7	31.9	32.1	32.0	32.2	32.3	32.2	32.4	32.4	32.1
2014	32.2	32.6	32.7	32.7	32.8	33.1	33.2	33.3	33.5	33.8	34.1	34.1	33.2
2015	34.2	34.4	34.5	34.3	34.6	34.8	34.8	34.8	34.8	35.8	35.5	35.3	34.8
Retail Trade													
2005	90.7	90.1	90.9	91.3	91.3	91.4	92.0	92.5	91.8	92.9	95.4	96.7	92.3
2006	92.7	91.9	93.2	93.0	93.2	93.0	93.5	94.7	94.6	96.7	100.0	101.6	94.8
2007	97.3	95.8	96.4	96.1	96.7	96.7	98.1	98.8	98.2	98.9	102.5	104.1	98.3
2008	99.6	99.0	99.7	99.1	98.9	99.1	99.6	100.7	99.5	100.1	101.9	102.5	100.0
2009	97.0	95.9	95.2	95.3	95.3	95.7	95.9	96.9	96.2	96.1	98.1	99.3	96.4
2010	94.7	93.8	94.6	94.3	94.6	94.7	94.5	95.7	94.5	95.6	97.8	99.3	95.3
2011	95.6	94.3	94.7	95.3	95.3	95.5	95.8	96.8	96.0	97.2	99.9	101.2	96.5
2012	97.4	96.3	96.4	96.9	97.2	97.6	97.6	98.3	98.3	99.8	103.8	104.2	98.7
2013	99.3	99.0	99.2	100.1	100.6	100.9	101.6	102.8	102.7	104.5	107.3	108.8	102.2
2014	104.4	104.0	103.9	104.7	104.7	105.7	105.8	106.5	106.6	108.1	110.9	112.1	106.5
2015	107.4	106.8	106.9	108.1	108.7	109.4	109.7	110.4	110.9	111.5	114.1	114.6	109.9

Employment by Industry: San Antonio-New Braunfels, TX, 2005–2015—*Continued*

(Numbers in thousands, not seasonally adjusted)

Industry and year	January	February	March	April	May	June	July	August	September	October	November	December	Annual average
Transportation and Utilities													
2005	20.4	20.5	20.6	20.7	21.0	21.2	21.4	21.6	21.8	21.7	22.1	22.3	21.3
2006	21.7	21.8	22.1	22.1	22.2	22.3	22.2	22.3	22.3	22.3	22.5	23.0	22.2
2007	22.4	22.6	22.8	22.9	22.8	22.9	22.8	22.9	22.8	22.6	22.6	22.7	22.7
2008	22.0	22.0	22.1	22.0	22.1	22.0	22.2	22.1	22.0	21.9	21.9	22.0	22.0
2009	21.3	21.0	21.0	20.5	20.4	20.4	20.2	20.1	20.1	20.1	20.2	20.1	20.5
2010	19.8	19.6	19.9	19.9	19.9	19.9	19.9	19.9	20.0	20.1	20.2	20.4	20.0
2011	20.4	20.4	20.5	20.6	20.7	20.8	20.9	21.1	21.4	21.4	21.5	22.0	21.0
2012	21.3	21.4	21.6	21.7	21.9	22.2	22.2	22.4	22.5	22.5	22.8	23.3	22.2
2013	22.9	22.7	22.8	22.9	23.0	23.2	23.1	23.3	23.3	23.3	23.9	24.4	23.2
2014	24.1	23.7	23.9	24.3	24.5	24.6	24.7	24.9	24.8	25.3	25.7	26.6	24.8
2015	25.8	25.3	25.4	25.3	25.4	25.6	25.7	25.7	25.8	25.9	25.7	26.4	25.7
Information													
2005	20.9	21.0	20.8	20.5	20.7	21.1	21.0	21.0	21.0	21.0	21.4	21.3	21.0
2006	20.9	20.7	20.8	20.8	21.2	21.5	21.4	21.5	21.3	21.6	22.0	22.2	21.3
2007	22.0	22.2	22.0	21.8	22.0	22.0	22.0	21.8	21.6	21.6	21.8	21.8	21.9
2008	21.7	21.8	22.0	21.7	21.9	21.7	21.3	21.2	21.0	21.2	21.2	21.0	21.5
2009	20.8	20.8	20.9	20.5	20.2	19.8	19.4	19.2	18.8	18.8	18.8	18.6	19.7
2010	18.5	18.6	18.9	19.5	19.3	19.0	18.7	18.5	18.3	18.1	18.3	18.4	18.7
2011	18.6	18.6	19.0	19.3	19.3	19.8	19.7	19.5	19.3	19.3	19.5	19.7	19.2
2012	19.7	19.7	20.1	20.3	20.3	20.3	20.3	20.4	20.3	20.2	20.6	20.5	20.2
2013	20.4	20.6	20.9	21.5	21.6	21.6	21.6	21.5	21.2	21.2	21.7	21.5	21.3
2014	20.8	20.8	21.0	21.6	21.7	21.5	21.6	21.4	21.4	21.4	21.5	21.8	21.4
2015	21.0	21.0	21.1	21.6	22.1	22.2	21.8	21.6	21.3	21.2	21.4	21.4	21.5
Financial Activities													
2005	61.9	62.1	62.0	62.2	62.5	63.0	64.0	64.1	64.0	64.2	64.1	64.4	63.2
2006	63.7	63.8	63.9	64.4	64.7	65.0	65.2	65.1	65.2	65.3	65.4	65.7	64.8
2007	65.1	65.7	65.5	66.3	66.8	66.7	66.7	66.5	66.2	66.4	66.5	66.7	66.3
2008	66.0	66.3	66.1	67.9	68.2	68.0	68.4	67.8	67.5	67.2	66.8	67.4	67.3
2009	65.9	66.0	65.4	65.6	65.9	66.4	66.8	66.8	66.7	66.8	66.9	67.1	66.4
2010	66.8	67.4	67.6	67.5	68.2	68.8	68.6	68.5	68.1	69.0	69.4	69.8	68.3
2011	69.2	70.0	70.4	70.6	70.8	71.2	71.9	71.5	71.2	71.5	71.5	71.9	71.0
2012	71.9	72.3	72.5	72.8	73.2	73.8	74.4	74.6	74.6	75.2	75.7	76.3	73.9
2013	75.7	76.6	77.0	77.2	77.4	78.0	78.4	78.3	78.1	78.1	78.6	78.6	77.7
2014	78.4	78.7	78.8	79.5	80.0	81.0	81.1	81.3	81.2	81.6	82.1	82.4	80.5
2015	82.5	82.7	82.7	82.9	83.3	83.9	84.1	84.0	83.6	84.1	84.8	84.5	83.6
Professional and Business Services													
2005	94.9	96.6	96.9	99.6	100.4	101.0	99.7	100.8	102.4	103.0	103.1	104.2	100.2
2006	101.7	103.2	104.9	106.8	107.7	108.0	108.2	109.0	108.9	107.1	106.6	107.3	106.6
2007	104.6	105.9	106.6	108.1	109.1	109.6	108.7	109.4	109.5	110.2	110.8	110.8	108.6
2008	110.1	111.8	111.9	112.6	112.2	112.0	109.5	109.6	110.1	108.7	108.5	107.8	110.4
2009	104.1	103.7	103.8	102.8	102.4	103.1	100.9	102.0	101.5	102.9	104.5	105.8	103.1
2010	104.3	105.2	105.5	104.5	104.0	104.5	103.0	103.4	103.1	104.2	104.3	104.3	104.2
2011	103.6	104.7	105.8	106.1	105.4	105.7	105.3	106.8	107.8	107.1	107.3	108.2	106.2
2012	106.0	107.4	108.3	108.7	109.0	109.8	110.0	112.3	112.3	112.1	112.9	114.1	110.2
2013	111.4	113.0	113.8	113.5	113.0	114.4	114.6	115.3	116.3	116.4	117.3	117.3	114.7
2014	115.3	117.3	118.1	120.4	120.5	121.2	121.4	122.5	122.1	123.6	123.9	122.8	120.8
2015	122.9	124.3	124.9	125.5	124.7	124.8	123.7	123.7	124.2	124.7	125.4	125.2	124.5
Education and Health Services													
2005	103.9	105.8	106.2	105.7	105.7	105.4	105.6	106.9	108.8	109.3	109.9	110.3	107.0
2006	108.6	109.9	110.6	109.6	110.1	109.7	108.7	110.5	112.4	112.3	112.4	112.3	110.6
2007	110.3	112.7	113.4	113.1	113.9	113.7	113.1	114.3	115.6	116.2	117.0	117.4	114.2
2008	114.4	116.5	116.5	117.2	118.2	117.1	117.0	118.1	120.4	121.6	122.1	122.9	118.5
2009	119.9	121.8	122.1	122.8	123.7	123.1	123.3	123.4	125.0	126.4	126.8	127.1	123.8
2010	125.5	127.5	128.1	128.5	129.1	129.3	128.8	129.1	130.2	131.4	131.6	131.9	129.3
2011	130.1	131.1	131.9	133.1	133.4	132.7	132.7	134.2	136.1	136.2	136.5	137.1	133.8
2012	134.7	136.3	137.1	136.8	137.6	137.7	135.3	137.0	137.2	137.7	138.2	138.7	137.0
2013	135.8	137.5	138.2	138.8	139.5	139.4	138.2	139.9	140.8	141.0	141.5	142.2	139.4
2014	140.5	142.0	142.9	143.1	144.4	144.5	144.3	145.4	145.9	146.9	147.1	147.4	144.5
2015	146.1	148.0	148.7	148.6	149.0	148.6	148.4	150.1	150.5	153.0	153.5	153.1	149.8

Employment by Industry: San Antonio-New Braunfels, TX, 2005–2015—*Continued*

(Numbers in thousands, not seasonally adjusted)

Industry and year	January	February	March	April	May	June	July	August	September	October	November	December	Annual average
Leisure and Hospitality													
2005	83.0	85.6	88.6	90.2	93.0	95.4	95.3	94.7	91.2	89.2	88.5	87.4	90.2
2006	87.0	89.1	92.2	94.8	96.4	99.1	99.5	98.7	95.1	93.6	91.7	91.5	94.1
2007	89.2	92.6	95.9	97.5	100.2	102.9	102.5	102.0	98.9	96.3	95.6	95.9	97.5
2008	92.8	95.4	98.3	100.6	102.9	105.4	106.2	105.2	101.9	99.7	99.6	99.3	100.6
2009	95.7	98.4	101.0	101.9	104.1	106.2	105.3	103.8	100.9	98.6	97.9	97.5	100.9
2010	94.3	97.1	100.5	102.4	105.7	107.3	107.3	106.0	103.3	102.0	101.3	101.2	102.4
2011	98.9	101.3	105.6	107.3	110.2	112.2	112.1	111.3	108.1	106.4	106.0	105.6	107.1
2012	102.4	105.6	109.2	111.6	114.8	118.0	117.7	116.9	113.3	112.3	110.5	110.8	111.9
2013	108.4	112.0	114.8	116.4	119.3	122.5	122.0	120.6	117.2	115.6	114.8	114.2	116.5
2014	111.6	113.8	118.3	120.0	123.4	125.7	125.1	123.3	119.1	118.4	117.6	117.7	119.5
2015	114.1	117.9	120.6	122.7	126.2	129.2	129.8	128.7	125.7	124.8	123.8	121.3	123.7
Other Services													
2005	26.5	26.5	26.8	27.2	27.2	27.6	27.6	27.5	27.5	26.9	27.0	26.9	27.1
2006	26.7	27.0	27.3	28.1	28.4	28.8	28.7	28.7	28.8	28.5	28.8	28.5	28.2
2007	27.5	28.0	28.2	28.4	28.8	29.5	29.3	29.5	29.8	29.7	30.3	30.2	29.1
2008	29.9	30.3	30.7	31.0	31.2	31.5	31.6	31.5	31.2	30.7	30.9	30.7	30.9
2009	30.4	30.7	30.7	30.8	31.2	31.5	31.2	31.1	30.7	30.6	31.2	30.9	30.9
2010	30.6	30.9	31.1	31.4	31.7	31.8	31.6	31.6	31.6	31.5	31.5	31.8	31.4
2011	30.9	31.2	31.3	31.7	31.8	31.9	32.0	32.0	31.9	31.6	32.0	31.6	31.7
2012	31.8	32.0	32.4	32.5	32.6	33.3	33.2	33.1	33.2	33.1	33.4	33.2	32.8
2013	33.1	33.6	33.8	33.9	34.3	34.6	34.7	34.5	34.4	34.3	34.6	34.1	34.2
2014	34.0	34.2	34.3	34.5	34.9	35.3	35.1	35.1	34.9	34.8	35.2	34.8	34.8
2015	34.7	35.1	35.2	35.5	35.9	36.4	36.5	36.5	36.4	37.2	36.6	37.2	36.1
Government													
2005	142.5	145.3	145.2	145.6	145.6	143.0	137.1	138.8	143.7	145.9	146.9	146.9	143.9
2006	145.4	147.8	147.6	149.4	149.1	146.8	139.4	140.6	146.3	149.4	150.3	150.0	146.8
2007	148.7	151.1	151.5	151.2	151.4	148.7	143.5	144.0	150.5	151.0	153.1	154.1	149.9
2008	153.0	155.5	155.9	155.5	155.7	154.9	148.1	148.8	152.7	157.3	158.6	158.2	154.5
2009	157.1	159.7	159.9	161.3	160.3	159.2	152.3	152.0	157.5	161.2	162.4	161.9	158.7
2010	159.2	162.3	163.1	163.6	166.1	163.1	154.0	155.7	160.6	164.1	164.8	164.2	161.7
2011	161.6	164.2	163.6	163.2	163.2	161.8	154.9	154.2	158.9	161.1	161.5	161.6	160.8
2012	159.5	161.6	161.5	161.5	160.9	158.5	152.3	154.1	159.6	161.4	162.2	162.2	159.6
2013	160.2	162.7	162.5	162.7	162.2	161.1	156.1	155.7	160.6	163.1	164.1	163.7	161.2
2014	161.7	164.0	164.0	163.7	163.1	161.9	156.1	156.2	161.9	165.3	166.6	166.1	162.6
2015	165.1	167.0	166.7	167.2	167.0	164.5	159.2	159.4	166.2	169.4	170.6	170.4	166.1

Employment by Industry: Pittsburgh, PA, 2005–2015

(Numbers in thousands, not seasonally adjusted)

Industry and year	January	February	March	April	May	June	July	August	September	October	November	December	Annual average
Total Nonfarm													
2005	1,110.9	1,110.8	1,118.2	1,134.7	1,142.6	1,147.7	1,133.6	1,129.6	1,138.9	1,141.0	1,144.3	1,141.2	1,132.8
2006	1,110.3	1,115.0	1,124.9	1,135.7	1,145.4	1,151.5	1,136.1	1,130.9	1,144.3	1,149.1	1,151.1	1,150.7	1,137.1
2007	1,120.3	1,119.9	1,132.3	1,142.0	1,156.1	1,164.4	1,147.4	1,145.0	1,151.8	1,157.8	1,159.7	1,156.7	1,146.1
2008	1,125.9	1,128.0	1,135.5	1,150.2	1,161.9	1,165.3	1,151.1	1,147.6	1,154.7	1,160.1	1,157.0	1,149.6	1,148.9
2009	1,112.5	1,111.4	1,114.3	1,123.2	1,131.4	1,132.6	1,115.9	1,111.6	1,119.3	1,124.8	1,126.8	1,124.8	1,120.7
2010	1,090.6	1,088.4	1,102.7	1,122.2	1,134.1	1,142.1	1,130.0	1,127.4	1,135.5	1,143.1	1,144.6	1,143.3	1,125.3
2011	1,116.1	1,118.0	1,128.3	1,142.7	1,152.9	1,160.3	1,144.1	1,140.1	1,153.3	1,160.4	1,162.9	1,159.8	1,144.9
2012	1,130.3	1,137.4	1,151.0	1,160.7	1,168.4	1,170.9	1,154.5	1,150.3	1,160.0	1,169.2	1,170.8	1,165.6	1,157.4
2013	1,133.7	1,140.8	1,148.1	1,158.3	1,167.8	1,169.9	1,157.1	1,152.8	1,161.7	1,167.5	1,168.1	1,164.5	1,157.5
2014	1,134.3	1,135.2	1,144.4	1,160.3	1,171.4	1,173.1	1,158.5	1,156.3	1,166.1	1,172.5	1,172.3	1,170.5	1,159.6
2015	1,139.7	1,139.8	1,145.8	1,162.0	1,173.9	1,172.7	1,162.6	1,160.7	1,167.7	1,175.4	1,171.3	1,169.0	1,161.7
Total Private													
2005	983.1	980.8	987.3	1,003.7	1,012.3	1,018.3	1,017.6	1,017.6	1,013.2	1,011.7	1,013.1	1,011.1	1,005.8
2006	983.4	984.9	994.2	1,005.1	1,015.0	1,022.3	1,018.9	1,017.3	1,017.6	1,019.7	1,020.4	1,020.7	1,010.0
2007	993.6	990.4	1,002.0	1,012.2	1,027.5	1,037.1	1,029.8	1,028.8	1,026.4	1,029.4	1,030.2	1,027.6	1,019.6
2008	1,000.5	999.3	1,006.2	1,021.1	1,033.6	1,038.7	1,032.7	1,030.5	1,028.3	1,030.3	1,026.8	1,020.6	1,022.4
2009	987.3	982.6	985.1	992.9	1,002.2	1,004.9	996.5	993.7	992.4	994.7	995.2	993.9	993.5
2010	964.9	958.8	972.1	990.8	1,000.8	1,011.0	1,009.8	1,009.6	1,008.3	1,012.9	1,014.1	1,013.2	997.2
2011	989.5	988.7	998.3	1,013.2	1,025.1	1,034.4	1,028.7	1,026.8	1,031.7	1,035.8	1,037.2	1,034.3	1,020.3
2012	1,010.8	1,013.2	1,026.5	1,036.4	1,044.2	1,049.7	1,041.9	1,038.6	1,040.0	1,046.6	1,047.1	1,042.3	1,036.4
2013	1,015.3	1,018.0	1,025.2	1,035.3	1,044.2	1,050.8	1,046.6	1,042.7	1,042.7	1,046.6	1,045.9	1,042.8	1,038.0
2014	1,016.3	1,014.9	1,023.9	1,039.2	1,050.1	1,055.2	1,049.1	1,047.7	1,048.5	1,052.5	1,051.4	1,049.8	1,041.6
2015	1,023.6	1,020.6	1,026.4	1,041.8	1,053.8	1,055.6	1,053.1	1,052.2	1,050.9	1,057.5	1,052.6	1,049.9	1,044.8
Goods Producing													
2005	151.9	150.8	152.6	158.3	160.7	162.0	163.0	164.0	163.5	162.4	161.1	157.3	159.0
2006	152.1	152.5	155.8	159.5	161.5	163.0	164.2	164.9	164.8	163.7	162.7	160.5	160.4
2007	155.7	153.3	157.5	161.1	164.8	166.8	166.3	166.0	165.4	164.9	163.1	159.2	162.0
2008	154.2	152.6	155.3	160.3	163.6	165.3	165.7	165.8	165.0	164.6	160.7	156.1	160.8
2009	148.2	146.2	146.7	148.2	148.8	149.5	148.1	147.0	146.5	146.9	145.0	141.0	146.8
2010	134.0	131.9	136.5	142.8	145.3	147.2	149.0	148.8	147.8	147.6	146.9	143.3	143.4
2011	137.7	137.7	141.7	145.9	149.2	151.9	153.6	154.0	154.3	154.7	153.3	150.4	148.7
2012	145.5	145.6	148.3	153.1	155.4	157.6	158.0	157.8	157.7	158.5	155.5	151.9	153.7
2013	146.2	146.3	148.7	152.4	155.2	156.9	157.5	157.4	156.7	156.5	153.8	150.1	153.1
2014	146.0	144.9	148.1	153.2	156.1	159.0	159.4	159.5	158.9	158.4	155.9	152.8	154.4
2015	147.4	145.8	147.7	152.5	155.2	157.5	158.8	158.5	157.1	154.9	153.2	149.1	153.1
Service-Providing													
2005	959.0	960.0	965.6	976.4	981.9	985.7	970.6	965.6	975.4	978.6	983.2	983.9	973.8
2006	958.2	962.5	969.1	976.2	983.9	988.5	971.9	966.0	979.5	985.4	988.4	990.2	976.7
2007	964.6	966.6	974.8	980.9	991.3	997.6	981.1	979.0	986.4	992.9	996.6	997.5	984.1
2008	971.7	975.4	980.2	989.9	998.3	1,000.0	985.4	981.8	989.7	995.5	996.3	993.5	988.1
2009	964.3	965.2	967.6	975.0	982.6	983.1	967.8	964.6	972.8	977.9	981.8	983.8	973.9
2010	956.6	956.5	966.2	979.4	988.8	994.9	981.0	978.6	987.7	995.5	997.7	1,000.0	981.9
2011	978.4	980.3	986.6	996.8	1,003.7	1,008.4	990.5	986.1	999.0	1,005.7	1,009.6	1,009.4	996.2
2012	984.8	991.8	1,002.7	1,007.6	1,013.0	1,013.3	996.5	992.5	1,002.3	1,010.7	1,015.3	1,013.7	1,003.7
2013	987.5	994.5	999.4	1,005.9	1,012.6	1,013.0	999.6	995.4	1,005.0	1,011.0	1,014.3	1,014.4	1,004.4
2014	988.3	990.3	996.3	1,007.1	1,015.3	1,014.1	999.1	996.8	1,007.2	1,014.1	1,016.4	1,017.7	1,005.2
2015	992.3	994.0	998.1	1,009.5	1,018.7	1,015.2	1,003.8	1,002.2	1,010.6	1,020.5	1,018.1	1,019.9	1,008.6
Mining and Logging													
2005	5.1	5.1	4.7	5.1	5.0	5.0	5.0	5.0	5.0	4.9	5.0	5.0	5.0
2006	4.9	4.9	4.9	4.9	4.9	4.9	4.9	4.9	4.8	4.8	4.8	4.8	4.9
2007	4.8	4.7	4.7	4.7	4.8	4.9	5.0	5.0	4.9	4.9	5.0	5.0	4.9
2008	5.0	5.0	5.0	5.1	5.3	5.5	5.5	5.6	5.6	5.7	5.7	5.7	5.4
2009	5.6	5.5	5.3	5.4	5.4	5.5	5.6	5.6	5.7	5.8	5.9	5.9	5.6
2010	5.9	6.0	6.2	6.4	6.5	6.7	6.9	7.1	7.3	7.2	7.3	7.4	6.7
2011	7.5	7.7	7.9	8.2	8.4	8.6	8.9	9.0	9.1	9.2	9.4	9.5	8.6
2012	9.6	9.6	9.7	9.8	9.9	10.0	10.0	10.1	10.1	10.1	10.1	10.1	9.9
2013	10.1	10.2	10.4	10.7	10.7	10.8	10.8	10.9	10.9	11.0	10.9	11.1	10.7
2014	11.2	11.1	11.3	11.5	11.7	11.9	12.0	12.1	12.1	12.2	12.3	12.3	11.8
2015	12.1	12.0	11.9	11.5	11.4	11.3	11.3	11.0	10.7	10.7	10.7	10.8	11.3

Employment by Industry: Pittsburgh, PA, 2005–2015—*Continued*

(Numbers in thousands, not seasonally adjusted)

Industry and year	January	February	March	April	May	June	July	August	September	October	November	December	Annual average
Construction													
2005	46.0	45.3	47.0	52.3	54.8	55.6	57.0	57.9	57.9	57.3	56.0	52.1	53.3
2006	48.1	48.6	51.4	54.7	56.3	57.2	58.4	59.1	59.6	58.5	57.1	54.7	55.3
2007	50.6	48.7	52.5	55.8	59.2	60.5	60.5	60.6	60.8	60.4	58.3	54.4	56.9
2008	50.6	49.2	51.6	56.7	59.4	60.4	61.0	61.4	61.1	60.9	57.8	53.9	57.0
2009	48.7	48.9	50.8	53.1	54.8	55.6	54.9	54.4	54.2	54.0	51.8	47.4	52.4
2010	41.7	40.0	44.0	49.7	51.9	52.6	53.9	53.6	52.7	52.4	51.2	47.5	49.3
2011	42.6	42.3	45.7	49.3	52.2	54.1	55.1	55.6	55.8	56.2	54.5	51.4	51.2
2012	47.1	47.2	49.6	54.1	55.8	57.1	57.4	57.0	57.4	58.3	55.1	51.8	54.0
2013	46.6	46.9	49.0	52.4	55.1	56.1	56.9	56.9	56.6	56.3	53.7	49.6	53.0
2014	46.5	45.6	48.1	53.2	55.9	58.0	58.5	58.2	58.2	57.9	55.1	51.7	53.9
2015	47.2	46.0	47.9	52.8	55.7	57.3	58.8	59.4	59.1	58.4	56.4	52.6	54.3
Manufacturing													
2005	100.8	100.4	100.9	100.9	100.9	101.4	101.0	101.1	100.6	100.2	100.1	100.2	100.7
2006	99.1	99.0	99.5	99.9	100.3	100.9	100.9	100.9	100.4	100.4	100.8	101.0	100.3
2007	100.3	99.9	100.3	100.6	100.8	101.4	100.8	100.4	99.7	99.6	99.8	99.8	100.3
2008	98.6	98.4	98.7	98.5	98.9	99.4	99.2	98.8	98.3	98.0	97.2	96.5	98.4
2009	93.9	91.8	90.6	89.7	88.6	88.4	87.6	87.0	86.6	87.1	87.3	87.7	88.9
2010	86.4	85.9	86.3	86.7	86.9	87.9	88.2	88.1	87.8	88.0	88.4	88.4	87.4
2011	87.6	87.7	88.1	88.4	88.6	89.2	89.6	89.4	89.4	89.3	89.4	89.5	88.9
2012	88.8	88.8	89.0	89.2	89.7	90.5	90.6	90.7	90.2	90.1	90.3	90.0	89.8
2013	89.5	89.2	89.3	89.3	89.4	90.0	89.8	89.6	89.2	89.2	89.2	89.4	89.4
2014	88.3	88.2	88.7	88.5	88.5	89.1	88.9	89.2	88.6	88.3	88.5	88.8	88.6
2015	88.1	87.8	87.9	88.2	88.1	88.9	88.7	88.1	87.3	85.8	86.1	85.7	87.6
Trade, Transportation, and Utilities													
2005	226.6	224.0	224.8	225.9	227.6	227.9	225.5	225.9	225.7	227.8	231.9	235.3	227.4
2006	226.3	223.2	224.4	224.5	226.3	226.2	222.7	223.0	224.5	226.9	230.7	233.9	226.1
2007	225.9	221.5	223.3	223.4	225.9	226.2	222.8	222.1	222.6	224.2	228.8	231.3	224.8
2008	223.6	220.0	220.9	221.1	223.3	223.2	219.4	218.7	220.3	222.6	225.0	227.6	222.1
2009	217.2	213.8	213.0	213.5	215.3	214.5	210.2	210.1	211.3	213.0	217.3	219.4	214.1
2010	211.6	208.0	210.1	211.6	214.0	215.3	212.2	212.5	213.8	217.0	220.8	224.2	214.3
2011	215.3	213.1	213.8	215.6	217.5	217.1	214.4	214.4	216.2	218.1	222.5	225.3	216.9
2012	217.0	214.9	216.7	216.8	218.0	217.2	213.8	212.9	214.5	216.5	221.7	223.3	216.9
2013	214.2	211.6	212.2	212.3	214.6	214.7	212.1	212.7	213.6	215.4	220.4	223.4	214.8
2014	213.7	211.0	212.0	213.5	216.3	217.4	213.2	213.4	214.8	217.0	221.6	225.2	215.8
2015	216.2	212.6	212.8	214.0	217.0	217.3	214.1	213.8	214.1	217.7	220.8	224.7	216.3
Wholesale Trade													
2005	46.4	46.6	46.7	47.0	47.4	47.7	47.7	47.8	47.6	47.8	48.0	48.1	47.4
2006	48.0	48.0	48.1	48.3	48.7	49.1	49.1	49.2	48.9	49.2	49.1	49.4	48.8
2007	49.1	48.9	49.2	49.1	49.2	49.5	49.5	49.6	49.1	49.0	49.1	49.1	49.2
2008	48.9	48.8	48.9	49.2	49.5	49.7	49.5	49.4	49.0	49.0	48.7	48.6	49.1
2009	47.8	47.4	47.1	46.9	46.9	46.7	46.3	46.1	45.8	45.6	45.5	45.5	46.5
2010	45.3	44.9	45.4	46.0	46.2	46.4	46.7	46.9	46.6	47.1	46.9	47.1	46.3
2011	46.6	46.6	46.9	47.3	47.6	47.3	47.2	47.3	46.9	47.0	46.9	46.9	47.0
2012	46.4	46.6	47.0	47.1	46.8	46.9	46.6	46.3	45.9	45.8	45.7	45.7	46.4
2013	45.0	44.8	45.0	45.0	45.2	45.4	45.4	45.4	45.1	45.1	45.0	45.3	45.1
2014	44.8	44.7	44.8	44.7	45.1	45.5	45.5	45.2	45.0	45.2	45.3	45.4	45.1
2015	44.8	44.6	44.4	44.6	44.9	45.0	45.0	44.8	44.4	44.7	45.0	45.1	44.8
Retail Trade													
2005	133.9	131.5	132.0	132.8	134.0	134.7	135.0	135.0	132.0	133.8	137.5	140.3	134.4
2006	132.6	129.8	130.6	130.6	131.8	132.4	131.2	131.5	129.8	131.8	135.9	138.3	132.2
2007	131.6	127.7	129.0	129.0	131.2	131.9	131.4	130.9	128.7	130.6	135.3	137.4	131.2
2008	130.9	127.6	128.5	128.0	129.3	129.8	129.2	128.7	127.5	129.0	131.6	133.8	129.5
2009	126.1	123.3	123.2	123.8	125.6	126.2	125.3	125.4	123.7	125.2	129.3	130.8	125.7
2010	124.7	121.8	123.1	123.7	125.6	126.6	126.5	126.6	124.6	126.7	130.4	132.6	126.1
2011	126.0	123.7	124.1	125.2	126.7	127.3	127.5	127.9	126.1	127.5	131.6	133.5	127.3
2012	127.2	124.9	126.0	126.2	127.4	128.1	127.4	127.0	125.3	127.0	132.0	132.8	127.6
2013	125.9	123.7	124.0	124.2	125.9	127.0	126.6	126.9	124.9	126.5	130.7	132.7	126.6
2014	125.2	122.9	123.7	124.6	126.5	127.7	126.7	127.1	125.0	126.5	130.3	132.7	126.6
2015	125.9	123.0	123.4	124.1	126.1	127.0	126.7	126.7	124.3	127.0	129.1	131.2	126.2

Employment by Industry: Pittsburgh, PA, 2005–2015—*Continued*

(Numbers in thousands, not seasonally adjusted)

Industry and year	January	February	March	April	May	June	July	August	September	October	November	December	Annual average
Transportation and Utilities													
2005	46.3	45.9	46.1	46.1	46.2	45.5	42.8	43.1	46.1	46.2	46.4	46.9	45.6
2006	45.7	45.4	45.7	45.6	45.8	44.7	42.4	42.3	45.8	45.9	45.7	46.2	45.1
2007	45.2	44.9	45.1	45.3	45.5	44.8	41.9	41.6	44.8	44.6	44.4	44.8	44.4
2008	43.8	43.6	43.5	43.9	44.5	43.7	40.7	40.6	43.8	44.6	44.7	45.2	43.6
2009	43.3	43.1	42.7	42.8	42.8	41.6	38.6	38.6	41.8	42.2	42.5	43.1	41.9
2010	41.6	41.3	41.6	41.9	42.2	42.3	39.0	39.0	42.6	43.2	43.5	44.5	41.9
2011	42.7	42.8	42.8	43.1	43.2	42.5	39.7	39.2	43.2	43.6	44.0	44.9	42.6
2012	43.4	43.4	43.7	43.5	43.8	42.2	39.8	39.6	43.3	43.7	44.0	44.8	42.9
2013	43.3	43.1	43.2	43.1	43.5	42.3	40.1	40.4	43.6	43.8	44.7	45.4	43.0
2014	43.7	43.4	43.5	44.2	44.7	44.2	41.0	41.1	44.8	45.3	46.0	47.1	44.1
2015	45.5	45.0	45.0	45.3	46.0	45.3	42.4	42.3	45.4	46.0	46.7	48.4	45.3
Information													
2005	23.2	23.0	23.0	23.0	23.3	23.5	23.3	23.2	22.9	23.0	23.2	23.3	23.2
2006	22.9	22.9	23.0	23.0	23.0	23.1	23.0	22.9	22.6	22.6	22.4	22.7	22.8
2007	22.0	21.9	22.1	21.8	21.9	22.2	21.9	21.8	21.4	21.2	21.2	21.6	21.8
2008	21.3	21.2	21.1	21.3	21.4	21.3	20.8	20.5	20.2	20.1	20.1	20.2	20.8
2009	19.9	19.8	19.8	19.9	19.8	20.0	19.8	19.5	19.3	19.7	19.6	20.3	19.8
2010	18.6	18.5	18.2	18.4	18.4	18.9	18.8	18.5	18.7	18.1	18.2	18.3	18.5
2011	18.2	18.2	18.3	18.5	18.7	18.9	18.8	17.3	18.5	18.6	18.9	18.3	18.4
2012	18.2	18.2	18.5	18.5	19.5	19.0	18.8	18.9	18.7	18.6	18.7	18.5	18.7
2013	18.6	18.2	18.2	18.1	18.3	18.3	18.7	18.6	18.6	19.7	19.0	19.1	18.6
2014	18.0	18.1	18.1	18.9	18.4	18.4	18.4	18.4	18.3	18.1	18.1	18.2	18.3
2015	17.8	18.0	18.0	18.0	18.2	18.4	18.4	18.5	18.1	18.1	18.1	18.2	18.2
Financial Activities													
2005	68.7	68.6	68.9	69.0	69.3	69.5	70.1	70.0	69.2	69.1	69.2	69.2	69.2
2006	68.1	68.3	68.4	68.7	69.0	69.6	69.0	68.8	67.9	67.7	67.7	67.9	68.4
2007	67.6	67.8	68.0	67.8	68.2	68.8	68.9	68.8	68.0	67.7	67.8	67.6	68.1
2008	66.8	67.1	67.5	67.7	68.3	69.0	68.9	68.8	67.6	67.4	67.4	67.4	67.8
2009	66.9	66.9	66.8	67.0	67.4	68.1	68.1	68.0	67.4	67.7	67.9	68.1	67.5
2010	67.6	67.4	67.7	68.0	68.4	68.9	69.0	69.0	68.2	68.3	68.3	68.5	68.3
2011	68.6	68.4	68.5	68.8	69.3	70.1	70.4	70.4	69.7	69.9	70.1	70.3	69.5
2012	69.9	70.0	70.3	70.3	70.7	71.7	71.8	71.8	71.0	71.1	71.3	71.3	70.9
2013	70.8	70.9	71.0	71.1	71.2	71.9	71.8	71.9	70.9	71.0	71.1	70.8	71.2
2014	70.9	70.7	70.5	70.3	70.8	71.2	71.3	71.0	69.9	70.0	70.1	70.1	70.6
2015	69.3	69.5	69.5	69.7	70.4	71.1	71.3	71.3	70.5	68.8	69.4	69.8	70.1
Professional and Business Services													
2005	141.4	141.3	142.5	145.8	145.8	146.8	147.4	147.7	146.1	145.9	145.9	145.5	145.2
2006	141.5	142.5	144.2	146.4	147.4	149.7	151.1	151.2	150.7	151.4	151.6	150.8	148.2
2007	148.2	149.4	151.1	154.2	155.7	159.1	158.7	159.7	158.0	158.3	159.2	159.4	155.9
2008	156.2	156.8	157.2	160.6	161.1	162.8	163.2	163.0	161.0	160.7	160.3	158.6	160.1
2009	154.3	153.7	153.3	153.9	154.7	155.3	154.3	154.3	153.4	153.9	153.8	153.9	154.1
2010	151.0	151.1	152.7	156.6	157.5	159.6	160.6	160.9	159.7	161.1	162.0	161.4	157.9
2011	159.7	160.0	161.1	164.2	165.8	167.0	167.3	167.4	167.4	169.4	169.2	168.1	165.6
2012	167.0	167.6	170.0	172.0	172.9	174.3	173.6	173.0	171.9	174.0	173.8	173.0	171.9
2013	170.6	172.2	173.7	175.4	176.5	177.4	177.5	176.7	175.1	175.7	175.1	173.9	175.0
2014	170.9	171.6	172.8	176.0	177.5	178.3	178.7	179.0	177.8	179.0	179.5	178.5	176.6
2015	176.0	176.4	177.4	180.0	181.1	181.6	182.2	181.7	180.7	180.9	179.2	177.8	179.6
Education and Health Services													
2005	217.0	218.8	219.3	219.9	217.2	217.1	217.2	215.4	220.1	222.9	224.1	224.6	219.5
2006	221.0	223.6	223.9	223.8	222.0	220.3	219.5	217.9	223.6	226.0	227.3	227.1	223.0
2007	222.6	225.4	226.5	226.4	225.2	224.0	223.3	221.9	226.9	230.7	231.2	230.4	226.2
2008	226.3	229.9	230.1	231.0	229.4	227.4	226.5	225.8	231.1	234.1	235.3	234.0	230.1
2009	231.1	232.7	233.0	234.1	232.8	231.2	230.7	228.4	233.2	235.9	236.9	236.6	233.1
2010	234.2	234.6	235.9	236.4	234.8	234.7	233.7	231.6	236.6	240.0	239.8	239.5	236.0
2011	238.2	240.0	240.6	240.5	238.6	239.1	235.9	234.4	240.3	243.1	244.1	243.2	239.8
2012	240.1	243.5	245.1	244.1	240.7	237.8	235.6	233.0	239.7	243.7	244.5	242.4	240.9
2013	239.6	243.4	243.3	243.3	238.5	237.1	235.1	231.9	239.4	242.7	244.0	242.7	240.1
2014	240.3	242.2	243.2	243.9	240.1	237.1	235.5	232.2	240.3	243.7	244.5	242.6	240.5
2015	239.6	240.9	241.2	242.6	239.7	234.1	233.5	232.5	239.9	244.3	244.6	242.7	239.6

Employment by Industry: Pittsburgh, PA, 2005–2015—*Continued*

(Numbers in thousands, not seasonally adjusted)

Industry and year	January	February	March	April	May	June	July	August	September	October	November	December	Annual average
Leisure and Hospitality													
2005	96.3	96.3	98.0	103.7	110.4	113.4	113.4	114.7	110.9	106.2	103.7	102.7	105.8
2006	97.2	97.9	100.2	104.4	110.7	114.6	113.6	113.5	109.1	107.5	104.2	104.1	106.4
2007	98.7	98.4	100.2	104.2	112.3	116.0	113.8	114.9	111.2	109.5	105.9	105.4	107.5
2008	100.0	99.9	102.0	106.4	113.4	116.1	114.6	114.9	110.7	108.4	105.7	104.2	108.0
2009	98.2	98.1	100.7	104.5	111.1	113.3	112.3	114.0	110.0	106.3	103.6	103.5	106.3
2010	97.6	97.3	100.3	106.2	111.0	114.2	114.1	115.9	112.5	109.7	107.1	106.9	107.7
2011	101.5	100.8	103.4	108.6	114.3	117.8	115.9	116.7	114.0	110.8	107.9	107.4	109.9
2012	102.4	102.5	106.1	109.9	115.0	119.0	117.4	118.9	114.8	112.9	110.5	110.8	111.7
2013	105.2	105.2	107.6	111.8	118.5	122.1	121.4	121.4	117.0	114.7	111.7	111.9	114.0
2014	106.3	106.1	108.5	112.8	119.8	121.9	120.0	121.8	117.2	115.2	110.9	111.4	114.3
2015	106.9	106.9	108.8	114.2	120.2	122.9	121.9	123.2	119.0	120.6	115.6	115.8	116.3
Other Services													
2005	58.0	58.0	58.2	58.1	58.0	58.1	57.7	56.7	54.8	54.4	54.0	53.2	56.6
2006	54.3	54.0	54.3	54.8	55.1	55.8	55.8	55.1	54.4	53.9	53.8	53.7	54.6
2007	52.9	52.7	53.3	53.5	53.5	54.0	54.1	53.6	52.9	52.9	53.0	52.7	53.2
2008	52.1	51.8	52.1	52.7	53.1	53.6	53.6	53.0	52.4	52.4	52.3	52.5	52.6
2009	51.5	51.4	51.8	51.8	52.3	53.0	53.0	52.4	51.3	51.3	51.1	51.1	51.8
2010	50.3	50.0	50.7	50.8	51.4	52.2	52.4	52.4	51.0	51.1	51.0	51.1	51.2
2011	50.3	50.5	50.9	51.4	51.7	52.5	52.4	52.2	51.3	51.2	51.2	51.3	51.4
2012	50.7	50.9	51.5	51.7	52.0	53.1	52.9	52.3	51.7	51.3	51.1	51.1	51.7
2013	50.1	50.2	50.5	50.9	51.4	52.4	52.5	52.1	51.4	50.9	50.8	50.9	51.2
2014	50.2	50.3	50.7	50.6	51.1	51.9	52.6	52.4	51.3	51.1	50.8	51.0	51.2
2015	50.4	50.5	51.0	50.8	52.0	52.7	52.9	52.7	51.5	52.2	51.7	51.8	51.7
Government													
2005	127.8	130.0	130.9	131.0	130.3	129.4	116.0	112.0	125.7	129.3	131.2	130.1	127.0
2006	126.9	130.1	130.7	130.6	130.4	129.2	117.2	113.6	126.7	129.4	130.7	130.0	127.1
2007	126.7	129.5	130.3	129.8	128.6	127.3	117.6	116.2	125.4	128.4	129.5	129.1	126.5
2008	125.4	128.7	129.3	129.1	128.3	126.6	118.4	117.1	126.4	129.8	130.2	129.0	126.5
2009	125.2	128.8	129.2	130.3	129.2	127.7	119.4	117.9	126.9	130.1	131.6	130.9	127.3
2010	125.7	129.6	130.6	131.4	133.3	131.1	120.2	117.8	127.2	130.2	130.5	130.1	128.1
2011	126.6	129.3	130.0	129.5	127.8	125.9	115.4	113.3	121.6	124.6	125.7	125.5	124.6
2012	119.5	124.2	124.5	124.3	124.2	121.2	112.6	111.7	120.0	122.6	123.7	123.3	121.0
2013	118.4	122.8	122.9	123.0	123.6	119.1	110.5	110.1	119.0	120.9	122.2	121.7	119.5
2014	118.0	120.3	120.5	121.1	121.3	117.9	109.4	108.6	117.6	120.0	120.9	120.7	118.0
2015	116.1	119.2	119.4	120.2	120.1	117.1	109.5	108.5	116.8	117.9	118.7	119.1	116.9

Employment by Industry: Sacramento—Roseville—Arden-Arcade, CA, 2005–2015

(Numbers in thousands, not seasonally adjusted)

Industry and year	January	February	March	April	May	June	July	August	September	October	November	December	Annual average
Total Nonfarm													
2005	875.9	879.4	884.8	889.2	893.6	898.2	897.5	898.1	903.1	904.7	910.1	914.2	895.7
2006	903.7	907.7	909.3	906.2	916.1	924.0	917.0	918.0	920.5	918.2	921.0	922.8	915.4
2007	909.7	913.0	920.0	917.8	924.5	928.7	923.1	923.9	923.7	920.5	923.7	924.3	921.1
2008	904.0	907.7	909.6	908.3	911.1	912.1	903.8	899.2	897.0	893.5	892.1	890.3	902.4
2009	871.3	866.2	864.8	862.3	863.3	861.1	844.0	839.0	837.4	845.2	846.0	844.1	853.7
2010	826.9	826.4	829.7	834.1	839.7	841.1	828.4	825.7	827.1	832.6	833.3	831.2	831.4
2011	819.7	822.2	823.9	827.7	829.3	831.0	822.2	826.9	831.1	835.3	839.6	837.4	828.9
2012	825.8	831.3	835.2	845.5	850.8	858.5	844.6	848.2	848.1	854.1	860.6	857.9	846.7
2013	854.1	860.1	863.7	866.0	869.7	872.9	863.3	868.4	870.4	875.9	883.8	882.7	869.3
2014	872.1	875.5	880.0	884.8	890.8	897.5	884.7	890.6	892.0	898.8	905.7	902.9	889.6
2015	896.5	898.8	905.0	909.9	914.7	920.4	918.7	920.9	921.5	927.7	930.0	929.2	916.1
Total Private													
2005	654.1	656.6	660.8	664.1	667.4	672.1	676.5	678.4	679.1	679.3	683.8	688.1	671.7
2006	678.6	680.4	680.7	677.2	686.4	693.2	691.4	694.9	693.3	688.5	689.3	690.1	687.0
2007	678.3	680.1	684.0	681.7	686.9	689.9	691.8	693.1	689.7	684.1	686.2	686.6	686.0
2008	667.0	668.8	668.8	668.3	669.1	670.2	667.7	666.9	662.5	656.0	653.2	651.4	664.2
2009	632.6	625.8	622.6	619.7	620.5	620.4	618.5	616.8	611.5	610.6	611.0	610.9	618.4
2010	595.9	594.4	596.1	597.7	599.6	604.0	605.7	606.4	603.0	602.6	602.5	605.2	601.1
2011	592.4	593.1	593.6	596.8	599.8	602.7	608.1	611.9	611.9	610.1	614.4	616.4	604.3
2012	604.1	607.4	609.0	619.0	624.2	630.8	632.2	635.3	632.1	631.9	637.5	639.1	625.2
2013	633.4	637.6	639.0	641.2	643.7	646.5	648.5	652.3	651.0	651.8	656.5	659.0	646.7
2014	646.8	648.0	651.4	653.9	659.3	664.4	666.1	670.3	668.5	667.1	672.2	674.4	661.9
2015	665.6	667.2	671.6	675.8	680.9	685.2	694.0	695.0	692.5	692.6	692.9	696.6	684.2
Goods Producing													
2005	110.8	112.0	113.7	114.5	116.1	118.0	119.8	121.7	122.0	121.0	119.1	117.4	117.2
2006	113.0	113.1	111.3	109.3	114.4	117.2	116.8	119.0	119.0	115.1	112.2	109.6	114.2
2007	107.2	107.4	108.5	108.1	110.7	112.0	111.1	112.3	110.5	107.2	104.6	101.6	108.4
2008	95.0	94.9	95.2	95.3	96.9	98.3	98.7	99.4	97.9	95.1	91.4	88.8	95.6
2009	83.2	79.8	79.2	78.3	79.2	79.9	79.0	79.0	77.8	77.2	75.3	72.9	78.4
2010	69.8	68.6	69.5	70.3	71.4	73.1	73.9	74.8	73.9	73.0	71.4	69.7	71.6
2011	67.1	67.0	66.6	68.2	69.5	70.9	72.6	74.1	74.5	74.0	72.3	70.4	70.6
2012	68.3	68.1	67.4	69.2	71.7	73.8	75.6	77.0	76.9	76.1	74.8	73.8	72.7
2013	72.4	73.5	74.2	75.6	77.1	78.5	80.0	81.9	81.8	80.9	79.6	78.6	77.8
2014	76.8	77.0	77.4	78.4	80.8	82.2	83.7	85.1	85.0	84.1	83.6	81.4	81.3
2015	80.8	81.1	82.4	83.8	85.7	87.7	89.5	90.6	90.4	90.0	89.4	89.4	86.7
Service-Providing													
2005	765.1	767.4	771.1	774.7	777.5	780.2	777.7	776.4	781.1	783.7	791.0	796.8	778.6
2006	790.7	794.6	798.0	796.9	801.7	806.8	800.2	799.0	801.5	803.1	808.8	813.2	801.2
2007	802.5	805.6	811.5	809.7	813.8	816.7	812.0	811.6	813.2	813.3	819.1	822.7	812.6
2008	809.0	812.8	814.4	813.0	814.2	813.8	805.1	799.8	799.1	798.4	800.7	801.5	806.8
2009	788.1	786.4	785.6	784.0	784.1	781.2	765.0	760.0	759.6	768.0	770.7	771.2	775.3
2010	757.1	757.8	760.2	763.8	768.3	768.0	754.5	750.9	753.2	759.6	761.9	761.5	759.7
2011	752.6	755.2	757.3	759.5	759.8	760.1	749.6	752.8	756.6	761.3	767.3	767.0	758.3
2012	757.5	763.2	767.8	776.3	779.1	784.7	769.0	771.2	771.2	778.0	785.8	784.1	774.0
2013	781.7	786.6	789.5	790.4	792.6	794.4	783.3	786.5	788.6	795.0	804.2	804.1	791.4
2014	795.3	798.5	802.6	806.4	810.0	815.3	801.0	805.5	807.0	814.7	822.1	821.5	808.3
2015	815.7	817.7	822.6	826.1	829.0	832.7	829.2	830.3	831.1	837.7	840.6	839.8	829.4
Mining and Logging													
2005	0.7	0.7	0.7	0.7	0.7	0.7	0.8	0.8	0.7	0.7	0.7	0.7	0.7
2006	0.7	0.7	0.7	0.6	0.6	0.8	0.7	0.8	0.8	0.7	0.7	0.7	0.7
2007	0.6	0.6	0.6	0.6	0.7	0.7	0.7	0.7	0.7	0.8	0.7	0.7	0.7
2008	0.6	0.6	0.6	0.7	0.7	0.7	0.7	0.7	0.7	0.7	0.6	0.6	0.7
2009	0.4	0.4	0.4	0.4	0.4	0.4	0.5	0.5	0.5	0.5	0.5	0.4	0.4
2010	0.3	0.3	0.4	0.4	0.4	0.5	0.5	0.5	0.5	0.5	0.5	0.5	0.4
2011	0.4	0.4	0.4	0.4	0.4	0.4	0.5	0.5	0.5	0.5	0.5	0.5	0.5
2012	0.4	0.4	0.4	0.3	0.4	0.4	0.4	0.4	0.4	0.5	0.5	0.4	0.4
2013	0.4	0.3	0.4	0.4	0.4	0.5	0.5	0.5	0.5	0.5	0.5	0.5	0.5
2014	0.4	0.4	0.4	0.4	0.5	0.5	0.5	0.6	0.5	0.6	0.6	0.6	0.5
2015	0.5	0.5	0.5	0.5	0.5	0.6	0.6	0.6	0.6	0.6	0.6	0.6	0.6

Employment by Industry: Sacramento—Roseville—Arden-Arcade, CA, 2005–2015—*Continued*

(Numbers in thousands, not seasonally adjusted)

Industry and year	January	February	March	April	May	June	July	August	September	October	November	December	Annual average
Construction													
2005	67.8	68.9	70.4	71.8	73.1	74.8	76.0	76.5	76.6	76.5	75.2	73.2	73.4
2006	69.5	69.6	67.9	66.1	71.1	73.3	73.4	74.6	74.3	71.4	69.7	67.1	70.7
2007	65.7	65.7	67.0	66.8	69.0	70.0	69.6	69.8	68.2	66.1	63.9	61.1	66.9
2008	55.2	55.3	55.5	55.7	57.2	58.5	59.2	59.0	57.6	56.2	53.6	51.2	56.2
2009	47.0	44.2	44.0	43.5	44.4	45.0	44.3	43.9	42.7	42.4	41.5	39.4	43.5
2010	37.1	36.1	36.8	37.6	38.6	40.0	40.5	40.5	39.5	39.2	38.2	36.4	38.4
2011	34.4	34.2	33.6	35.1	36.2	37.3	39.2	39.6	39.6	39.2	38.5	36.4	36.9
2012	34.8	34.6	34.0	35.5	37.7	39.4	40.7	41.4	41.2	41.4	40.6	39.8	38.4
2013	38.7	39.7	40.5	41.5	42.9	44.1	45.3	46.3	46.0	45.9	44.7	43.5	43.3
2014	42.2	42.1	42.5	43.3	45.4	46.5	47.4	47.9	47.8	47.7	47.2	45.0	45.4
2015	44.8	45.1	46.1	47.3	49.0	50.5	51.8	52.9	52.8	53.3	52.9	52.3	49.9
Manufacturing													
2005	42.3	42.4	42.6	42.0	42.3	42.5	43.0	44.4	44.7	43.8	43.2	43.5	43.1
2006	42.8	42.8	42.7	42.6	42.7	43.1	42.7	43.6	43.9	43.0	41.8	41.8	42.8
2007	40.9	41.1	40.9	40.7	41.0	41.3	40.8	41.8	41.6	40.3	40.0	39.8	40.9
2008	39.2	39.0	39.1	38.9	39.0	39.1	38.8	39.7	39.6	38.2	37.2	37.0	38.7
2009	35.8	35.2	34.8	34.4	34.4	34.5	34.2	34.6	34.6	34.3	33.3	33.1	34.4
2010	32.4	32.2	32.3	32.3	32.4	32.6	32.9	33.8	33.9	33.3	32.7	32.8	32.8
2011	32.3	32.4	32.6	32.7	32.9	33.2	32.9	34.0	34.4	34.3	33.3	33.5	33.2
2012	33.1	33.1	33.0	33.4	33.6	34.0	34.5	35.2	35.3	34.2	33.7	33.6	33.9
2013	33.3	33.5	33.3	33.7	33.8	33.9	34.2	35.1	35.3	34.5	34.4	34.6	34.1
2014	34.2	34.5	34.5	34.7	34.9	35.2	35.8	36.6	36.7	35.8	35.8	35.8	35.4
2015	35.5	35.5	35.8	36.0	36.2	36.6	37.1	37.1	37.0	36.1	35.9	36.5	36.3
Trade, Transportation, and Utilities													
2005	147.1	146.0	146.3	146.3	146.8	147.3	148.5	148.8	149.2	150.2	154.2	157.6	149.0
2006	151.3	150.0	150.9	150.5	151.9	153.2	154.4	155.2	154.5	154.7	157.9	160.0	153.7
2007	153.9	152.2	152.0	151.2	151.7	152.2	152.8	152.7	152.2	152.3	156.3	158.2	153.1
2008	150.5	148.5	148.2	147.3	147.0	147.1	146.4	145.7	144.3	143.7	145.2	145.8	146.6
2009	138.2	135.4	134.1	133.6	134.6	134.7	133.8	133.2	133.4	133.7	136.9	137.8	135.0
2010	132.4	130.3	130.3	130.9	131.5	131.6	131.9	132.5	132.1	133.4	136.1	138.1	132.6
2011	132.5	131.0	131.0	131.2	132.0	132.7	133.4	134.0	134.2	135.8	140.0	141.8	134.1
2012	135.9	134.2	134.6	136.7	137.7	138.7	138.8	139.4	139.6	140.4	145.0	146.3	138.9
2013	140.3	139.2	139.3	139.4	140.1	140.6	141.1	141.0	140.8	142.4	147.3	148.6	141.7
2014	142.1	140.7	140.9	140.7	141.3	142.1	142.7	143.5	143.0	144.0	148.6	150.6	143.4
2015	144.4	142.9	143.3	144.1	145.5	145.4	146.7	147.5	147.5	147.9	152.2	153.6	146.8
Wholesale Trade													
2005	26.5	26.6	26.6	26.8	26.8	26.8	27.0	27.1	27.2	27.5	27.6	27.7	27.0
2006	27.8	28.1	28.4	28.2	28.6	28.8	28.9	28.9	28.7	28.8	28.7	28.5	28.5
2007	28.4	28.2	28.5	28.1	28.0	28.1	27.8	27.7	27.5	27.4	27.3	27.5	27.9
2008	27.0	27.0	26.8	26.8	26.9	26.8	26.6	26.3	26.2	26.0	25.7	25.4	26.5
2009	25.0	24.7	24.5	24.4	24.6	24.6	24.1	23.7	23.5	23.6	23.5	23.1	24.1
2010	23.0	22.8	22.6	22.9	23.0	22.8	22.7	22.7	22.6	22.8	22.8	22.9	22.8
2011	22.8	22.7	22.8	23.3	23.5	23.7	23.7	23.7	23.9	24.3	24.6	24.8	23.7
2012	24.6	24.8	25.2	25.5	25.6	25.6	25.3	25.2	25.1	25.2	25.2	25.2	25.2
2013	24.9	24.9	25.0	25.0	25.0	25.1	25.1	24.8	24.8	25.1	25.1	25.0	25.0
2014	24.8	24.9	24.8	24.5	24.5	24.5	24.4	24.3	24.3	24.2	24.3	24.3	24.5
2015	24.3	24.2	24.2	24.4	24.6	24.5	24.9	24.9	24.9	24.8	24.7	25.1	24.6
Retail Trade													
2005	97.3	96.3	96.4	96.5	96.8	97.2	98.3	98.3	98.5	99.3	103.1	105.8	98.7
2006	100.1	98.7	99.1	98.9	99.7	100.3	100.9	101.0	100.3	100.6	103.7	105.2	100.7
2007	100.4	98.9	98.4	98.2	98.6	98.7	99.5	99.3	98.9	99.3	103.3	104.4	99.8
2008	98.4	96.3	96.1	95.5	95.2	95.2	94.5	94.1	92.9	92.8	94.8	95.4	95.1
2009	89.4	87.0	86.1	85.9	86.9	87.0	86.9	86.5	86.8	87.3	90.4	91.6	87.7
2010	87.2	85.6	85.7	86.4	86.9	87.1	87.6	88.1	88.0	89.0	91.7	93.2	88.0
2011	89.0	87.6	87.3	87.1	87.5	87.9	88.6	89.0	89.1	90.2	94.0	95.3	89.4
2012	90.7	88.7	88.8	89.7	90.3	90.9	91.2	91.8	91.9	92.6	97.0	97.8	91.8
2013	92.8	91.7	91.7	91.8	92.4	92.6	93.2	93.3	93.0	94.3	98.8	99.7	93.8
2014	94.5	93.1	93.4	93.3	93.6	94.2	94.7	95.2	94.7	95.8	99.8	101.1	95.3
2015	96.2	94.9	95.2	95.7	96.7	96.6	97.0	97.6	97.6	98.3	101.9	102.6	97.5

Employment by Industry: Sacramento—Roseville—Arden-Arcade, CA, 2005–2015—*Continued*

(Numbers in thousands, not seasonally adjusted)

Industry and year	January	February	March	April	May	June	July	August	September	October	November	December	Annual average
Transportation and Utilities													
2005	23.3	23.1	23.3	23.0	23.2	23.3	23.2	23.4	23.5	23.4	23.5	24.1	23.4
2006	23.4	23.2	23.4	23.4	23.6	24.1	24.6	25.3	25.5	25.3	25.5	26.3	24.5
2007	25.1	25.1	25.1	24.9	25.1	25.4	25.5	25.7	25.8	25.6	25.7	26.3	25.4
2008	25.1	25.2	25.3	25.0	24.9	25.1	25.3	25.3	25.2	24.9	24.7	25.0	25.1
2009	23.8	23.7	23.5	23.3	23.1	23.1	22.8	23.0	23.1	22.8	23.0	23.1	23.2
2010	22.2	21.9	22.0	21.6	21.6	21.7	21.6	21.7	21.5	21.6	21.6	22.0	21.8
2011	20.7	20.7	20.9	20.8	21.0	21.1	21.1	21.3	21.2	21.3	21.4	21.7	21.1
2012	20.6	20.7	20.6	21.5	21.8	22.2	22.3	22.4	22.6	22.6	22.8	23.3	22.0
2013	22.6	22.6	22.6	22.6	22.7	22.9	22.8	22.9	23.0	23.0	23.4	23.9	22.9
2014	22.8	22.7	22.7	22.9	23.2	23.4	23.6	24.0	24.0	24.0	24.5	25.2	23.6
2015	23.9	23.8	23.9	24.0	24.2	24.3	24.8	25.0	25.0	24.8	25.6	25.9	24.6
Information													
2005	20.5	20.6	20.2	20.3	20.1	19.9	19.8	19.8	19.5	19.2	19.4	19.5	19.9
2006	19.6	19.8	19.7	19.9	19.9	19.8	20.4	20.3	20.1	20.0	20.1	20.4	20.0
2007	20.4	20.7	20.4	20.1	20.3	20.0	20.0	20.0	19.8	19.7	19.7	19.7	20.1
2008	19.5	19.7	19.5	19.4	19.4	19.4	19.3	19.3	19.1	18.6	18.8	18.8	19.2
2009	18.9	18.8	18.6	18.1	18.3	18.2	18.4	18.3	18.1	18.0	18.0	18.0	18.3
2010	17.8	17.7	17.4	17.3	17.2	17.6	17.1	16.9	16.7	16.7	17.0	17.0	17.2
2011	16.9	16.8	16.8	16.7	16.6	16.5	16.4	16.2	15.9	15.9	15.7	15.6	16.3
2012	15.6	15.6	15.6	15.7	15.7	15.8	15.7	15.5	15.3	15.3	15.5	15.6	15.6
2013	15.3	15.3	15.0	15.1	15.0	15.0	14.9	14.7	14.4	14.2	14.2	14.1	14.8
2014	13.8	13.7	13.6	13.7	13.8	13.9	14.0	14.0	13.8	13.9	14.0	14.2	13.9
2015	14.2	14.2	14.1	14.2	14.2	14.3	14.3	14.2	14.1	14.1	14.0	14.1	14.2
Financial Activities													
2005	61.6	61.9	62.3	62.6	63.1	63.1	63.5	63.7	63.8	63.9	64.1	64.4	63.2
2006	64.9	65.0	65.0	64.8	64.7	64.9	64.5	64.3	64.1	63.2	63.4	63.2	64.3
2007	62.7	62.9	62.5	62.5	62.3	62.1	61.9	61.4	60.7	60.2	59.6	59.6	61.5
2008	58.6	58.6	58.2	58.0	57.7	57.5	57.4	56.9	56.5	55.8	55.6	55.4	57.2
2009	55.5	55.3	55.1	53.9	53.5	53.1	52.8	52.4	51.3	51.0	50.6	50.6	52.9
2010	49.8	49.5	49.5	49.0	48.7	48.8	48.3	48.1	47.8	47.5	46.5	46.5	48.3
2011	46.3	46.0	46.2	46.5	46.7	46.7	47.0	47.3	47.1	46.8	46.6	46.7	46.7
2012	47.0	47.1	47.3	47.7	47.8	48.2	48.7	48.8	48.6	48.9	48.8	49.2	48.2
2013	49.0	49.2	49.1	49.5	49.6	49.7	50.2	50.0	49.5	49.1	48.8	49.0	49.4
2014	48.6	48.4	48.2	48.1	48.4	48.8	49.0	49.1	49.1	49.6	49.6	49.9	48.9
2015	49.8	50.1	50.3	50.3	50.6	51.0	51.8	51.5	51.0	51.7	51.4	51.8	50.9
Professional and Business Services													
2005	103.8	105.2	106.5	107.9	108.1	109.9	109.9	109.9	109.9	110.7	111.5	112.2	108.8
2006	111.2	112.2	112.5	111.9	112.6	113.7	113.1	113.5	112.9	113.3	113.2	112.8	112.7
2007	108.7	110.1	110.9	111.5	111.5	112.5	113.5	113.9	113.4	113.7	113.6	114.1	112.3
2008	110.1	111.3	111.0	111.4	110.9	110.3	110.1	110.0	109.5	110.0	108.9	108.4	110.2
2009	104.0	103.3	102.4	101.4	100.1	100.1	101.4	101.2	99.7	100.8	100.4	100.3	101.3
2010	98.9	100.5	100.9	101.6	101.7	103.0	103.8	103.8	103.3	104.0	103.2	102.8	102.3
2011	100.5	102.3	101.5	102.7	102.9	103.3	105.4	106.7	106.3	106.9	107.2	107.2	104.4
2012	104.0	106.4	105.8	109.9	111.6	113.1	114.1	114.8	112.5	114.3	114.0	113.1	111.1
2013	112.2	113.8	113.0	112.7	113.0	114.1	113.8	115.6	116.2	117.2	117.1	116.6	114.6
2014	114.4	116.6	117.1	117.7	118.3	118.7	118.6	119.8	119.7	118.9	119.3	119.3	118.2
2015	116.6	117.5	117.8	118.5	118.6	119.3	121.8	122.5	121.6	121.1	119.9	120.6	119.7
Education and Health Services													
2005	101.4	101.0	101.4	102.4	103.1	102.8	102.8	102.2	103.9	104.8	105.4	105.3	103.0
2006	106.9	106.7	107.3	107.4	108.7	108.8	107.8	107.5	109.0	110.7	110.3	110.4	108.5
2007	112.1	112.4	114.0	113.9	115.2	114.3	114.6	114.5	116.2	116.5	118.3	117.9	115.0
2008	117.8	119.2	119.3	120.1	120.4	119.5	118.5	119.1	120.4	120.8	122.1	121.7	119.9
2009	121.3	121.8	121.9	122.1	122.9	121.6	120.3	120.6	121.1	122.7	122.7	122.4	121.8
2010	120.1	120.0	120.1	121.2	121.8	120.7	119.6	119.6	120.2	121.2	121.8	121.8	120.7
2011	121.1	121.2	121.7	122.5	123.0	122.0	121.2	121.8	123.0	123.2	124.3	124.4	122.5
2012	124.5	125.3	126.6	126.3	127.0	126.1	123.8	124.1	125.6	125.1	126.7	126.2	125.6
2013	129.0	130.1	130.8	131.3	132.1	129.8	128.7	129.6	130.5	131.6	132.2	132.3	130.7
2014	132.3	131.8	132.9	133.5	135.1	133.8	132.8	134.0	135.2	136.1	136.7	137.0	134.3
2015	136.9	137.4	138.6	139.7	140.5	139.5	140.2	140.5	141.5	143.5	142.5	142.5	140.3

Employment by Industry: Sacramento—Roseville—Arden-Arcade, CA, 2005–2015—*Continued*

(Numbers in thousands, not seasonally adjusted)

Industry and year	January	February	March	April	May	June	July	August	September	October	November	December	Annual average
Leisure and Hospitality													
2005	80.6	81.3	81.4	81.0	81.1	82.3	83.7	83.9	82.4	81.4	82.2	84.0	82.1
2006	83.8	85.2	85.5	85.2	85.5	86.9	86.5	87.0	85.2	83.2	83.9	85.6	85.3
2007	85.5	86.2	87.2	85.8	86.1	87.6	88.6	88.8	87.4	85.1	85.0	86.2	86.6
2008	87.0	87.7	88.4	87.1	86.7	88.1	87.1	86.3	84.6	82.2	81.8	83.3	85.9
2009	82.6	82.4	82.5	82.9	82.4	83.6	83.7	83.3	81.4	78.7	78.8	81.0	81.9
2010	79.5	80.2	80.6	79.3	78.9	80.7	82.4	82.1	80.4	78.5	78.6	81.7	80.2
2011	80.5	81.2	82.2	80.9	80.9	82.3	83.6	83.4	82.4	79.7	80.6	82.5	81.7
2012	80.9	82.7	83.3	84.9	83.7	85.7	86.9	86.9	85.1	83.3	84.2	86.5	84.5
2013	87.0	87.9	88.8	88.7	87.7	89.6	90.7	90.3	88.6	87.1	88.0	90.5	88.7
2014	89.8	90.4	91.6	91.6	91.0	93.9	94.5	94.2	92.1	90.1	90.1	92.0	91.8
2015	93.1	94.0	94.8	94.2	94.6	96.7	98.1	96.8	95.2	93.6	93.0	94.6	94.9
Other Services													
2005	28.3	28.6	29.0	29.1	29.0	28.8	28.5	28.4	28.4	28.1	27.9	27.7	28.5
2006	27.9	28.4	28.5	28.2	28.7	28.7	27.9	28.1	28.5	28.3	28.3	28.1	28.3
2007	27.8	28.2	28.5	28.6	29.1	29.2	29.3	29.5	29.5	29.4	29.1	29.3	29.0
2008	28.5	28.9	29.0	29.7	30.1	30.0	30.2	30.2	30.2	29.8	29.4	29.2	29.6
2009	28.9	29.0	28.8	29.4	29.5	29.2	29.1	28.8	28.7	28.5	28.3	27.9	28.8
2010	27.6	27.6	27.8	28.1	28.4	28.5	28.7	28.6	28.6	28.3	27.9	27.6	28.1
2011	27.5	27.6	27.6	28.1	28.2	28.3	28.5	28.4	28.5	27.8	27.7	27.8	28.0
2012	27.9	28.0	28.4	28.6	29.0	29.4	28.6	28.8	28.5	28.5	28.5	28.4	28.6
2013	28.2	28.6	28.8	28.9	29.1	29.2	29.1	29.2	29.2	29.3	29.3	29.3	29.0
2014	29.0	29.4	29.7	30.2	30.6	31.0	30.8	30.6	30.6	30.4	30.3	30.0	30.2
2015	29.8	30.0	30.3	31.0	31.2	31.3	31.6	31.4	31.2	30.7	30.5	30.0	30.8
Government													
2005	221.8	222.8	224.0	225.1	226.2	226.1	221.0	219.7	224.0	225.4	226.3	226.1	224.0
2006	225.1	227.3	228.6	229.0	229.7	230.8	225.6	223.1	227.2	229.7	231.7	232.7	228.4
2007	231.4	232.9	236.0	236.1	237.6	238.8	231.3	230.8	234.0	236.4	237.5	237.7	235.0
2008	237.0	238.9	240.8	240.0	242.0	241.9	236.1	232.3	234.5	237.5	238.9	238.9	238.2
2009	238.7	240.4	242.2	242.6	242.8	240.7	225.5	222.2	225.9	234.6	235.0	233.2	235.3
2010	231.0	232.0	233.6	236.4	240.1	237.1	222.7	219.3	224.1	230.0	230.8	226.0	230.3
2011	227.3	229.1	230.3	230.9	229.5	228.3	214.1	215.0	219.2	225.2	225.2	221.0	224.6
2012	221.7	223.9	226.2	226.5	226.6	227.7	212.4	212.9	216.0	222.2	223.1	218.8	221.5
2013	220.7	222.5	224.7	224.8	226.0	226.4	214.8	216.1	219.4	224.1	227.3	223.7	222.5
2014	225.3	227.5	228.6	230.9	231.5	233.1	218.6	220.3	223.5	231.7	233.5	228.5	227.8
2015	230.9	231.6	233.4	234.1	233.8	235.2	224.7	225.9	229.0	235.1	237.1	232.6	232.0

Employment by Industry: Cincinnati, OH-KY-IN, 2005–2015

(Numbers in thousands, not seasonally adjusted)

Industry and year	January	February	March	April	May	June	July	August	September	October	November	December	Annual average
Total Nonfarm													
2005	1,001.6	1,006.6	1,017.4	1,029.9	1,037.9	1,040.9	1,033.6	1,035.8	1,040.8	1,037.5	1,042.2	1,045.1	1,030.8
2006	1,014.5	1,017.9	1,025.2	1,033.3	1,040.5	1,043.5	1,033.2	1,038.5	1,039.7	1,037.2	1,041.1	1,043.7	1,034.0
2007	1,019.5	1,020.0	1,033.0	1,042.5	1,053.9	1,052.6	1,041.0	1,047.3	1,048.3	1,052.8	1,056.0	1,058.1	1,043.8
2008	1,030.9	1,032.6	1,035.3	1,049.4	1,056.7	1,049.2	1,043.2	1,046.8	1,040.4	1,040.9	1,036.3	1,033.8	1,041.3
2009	996.6	993.3	992.7	994.9	1,000.5	992.9	982.3	988.4	987.1	988.3	989.7	989.8	991.4
2010	959.8	960.4	970.9	985.4	995.6	989.2	978.2	983.1	983.8	990.3	992.3	990.7	981.6
2011	964.9	968.3	978.1	993.4	999.9	994.6	992.3	1,000.7	1,001.6	1,003.0	1,005.6	1,004.8	992.3
2012	979.6	986.8	996.6	1,008.4	1,019.4	1,016.5	1,006.5	1,012.9	1,017.0	1,021.9	1,021.1	1,018.0	1,008.7
2013	990.9	1,000.1	1,006.9	1,026.3	1,036.5	1,031.5	1,021.4	1,031.8	1,035.2	1,038.6	1,041.5	1,036.9	1,024.8
2014	1,009.1	1,015.2	1,027.6	1,041.8	1,054.7	1,047.7	1,040.6	1,049.1	1,048.6	1,053.5	1,057.5	1,058.9	1,042.0
2015	1,030.2	1,032.1	1,041.7	1,057.6	1,070.5	1,068.0	1,064.2	1,068.8	1,069.1	1,070.1	1,073.2	1,072.3	1,059.8
Total Private													
2005	870.9	873.1	882.9	895.0	902.5	909.6	910.7	911.1	909.7	903.1	907.3	910.9	898.9
2006	883.6	883.9	889.8	897.8	904.3	912.7	910.7	913.9	908.4	902.7	906.3	909.1	901.9
2007	887.7	885.2	896.8	906.6	917.9	924.0	919.1	921.3	916.6	918.0	919.0	921.9	911.2
2008	898.7	896.1	898.8	912.7	919.7	921.1	920.0	919.5	907.6	904.6	898.0	896.3	907.8
2009	862.4	856.4	856.0	857.2	863.5	864.3	861.6	861.9	854.4	852.6	853.6	854.5	858.2
2010	827.0	825.2	834.7	848.1	855.8	860.1	858.9	859.2	853.8	857.5	857.8	856.5	849.6
2011	834.4	835.4	844.3	859.3	867.0	870.6	874.0	875.6	871.3	870.1	873.1	875.2	862.5
2012	853.7	854.7	863.3	874.8	885.3	891.8	888.4	890.7	887.3	889.5	888.2	889.2	879.7
2013	864.5	867.7	874.9	891.1	902.2	907.3	905.0	906.6	903.2	905.3	907.9	908.0	895.3
2014	882.8	883.3	895.4	908.0	920.1	923.3	922.0	924.9	917.4	921.0	925.0	927.3	912.5
2015	902.4	901.2	909.7	924.7	936.5	942.6	943.7	943.3	938.3	937.5	939.9	940.9	930.1
Goods Producing													
2005	169.0	169.4	171.6	173.9	176.1	177.3	177.8	177.9	177.9	176.8	176.5	175.1	174.9
2006	169.8	169.9	168.8	172.7	174.2	175.9	175.1	176.1	174.6	172.3	171.7	171.5	172.7
2007	167.1	166.1	169.3	171.5	173.4	174.2	173.4	173.7	172.6	171.7	170.6	169.3	171.1
2008	164.9	164.1	164.4	167.3	168.6	169.3	168.7	168.4	166.2	164.9	162.3	159.5	165.7
2009	151.2	148.9	147.7	145.9	146.4	146.2	145.2	145.7	144.2	143.7	142.8	141.4	145.8
2010	135.0	133.6	135.7	138.5	139.7	140.5	141.6	141.7	141.5	142.2	141.6	139.4	139.3
2011	135.5	135.6	137.3	140.1	141.8	143.1	144.5	144.8	144.6	144.6	144.1	143.7	141.6
2012	139.7	139.3	140.7	142.6	144.1	146.0	146.1	146.0	145.3	144.8	144.3	143.5	143.5
2013	139.4	138.9	139.3	142.3	144.8	146.5	147.3	147.1	147.4	148.0	148.1	146.8	144.7
2014	143.5	143.6	146.5	149.3	152.1	153.4	153.6	154.2	153.6	154.4	154.4	153.7	151.0
2015	149.7	149.6	150.9	153.8	156.2	158.1	158.3	159.0	157.9	158.9	160.0	158.6	155.9
Service-Providing													
2005	832.6	837.2	845.8	856.0	861.8	863.6	855.8	857.9	862.9	860.7	865.7	870.0	855.8
2006	844.7	848.0	856.4	860.6	866.3	867.6	858.1	862.4	865.1	864.9	869.4	872.2	861.3
2007	852.4	853.9	863.7	871.0	880.5	878.4	867.6	873.6	875.7	881.1	885.4	888.8	872.7
2008	866.0	868.5	870.9	882.1	888.1	879.9	874.5	878.4	874.2	876.0	874.0	874.3	875.6
2009	845.4	844.4	845.0	849.0	854.1	846.7	837.1	842.7	842.9	844.6	846.9	848.4	845.6
2010	824.8	826.8	835.2	846.9	855.9	848.7	836.6	841.4	842.3	848.1	850.7	851.3	842.4
2011	829.4	832.7	840.8	853.3	858.1	851.5	847.8	855.9	857.0	858.4	861.5	861.1	850.6
2012	839.9	847.5	855.9	865.8	875.3	870.5	860.4	866.9	871.7	877.1	876.8	874.5	865.2
2013	851.5	861.2	867.6	884.0	891.7	885.0	874.1	884.7	887.8	890.6	893.4	890.1	880.1
2014	865.6	871.6	881.1	892.5	902.6	894.3	887.0	894.9	895.0	899.1	903.1	905.2	891.0
2015	880.5	882.5	890.8	903.8	914.3	909.9	905.9	909.8	911.2	911.2	913.2	913.7	903.9
Mining, Logging, and Construction													
2005	47.2	47.9	49.4	51.4	53.0	54.1	54.9	54.9	54.7	53.9	53.5	51.9	52.2
2006	48.3	48.6	49.7	51.8	52.8	53.9	54.0	54.6	53.4	51.9	51.2	50.3	51.7
2007	47.1	45.6	47.8	50.2	51.8	52.5	52.8	52.8	52.2	52.0	51.0	49.4	50.4
2008	45.2	44.4	44.9	47.1	48.5	49.2	49.5	49.3	48.0	47.7	46.4	44.5	47.1
2009	39.8	39.0	39.2	39.0	40.5	40.7	40.8	40.9	40.0	39.7	38.9	37.7	39.7
2010	32.9	31.8	33.3	35.8	36.6	37.3	38.1	38.3	37.9	38.8	38.1	36.4	36.3
2011	33.3	33.3	34.6	36.8	37.9	38.7	39.8	40.1	39.8	39.8	39.0	38.4	37.6
2012	35.4	34.9	36.1	37.9	38.8	39.6	39.7	39.9	39.8	39.4	39.0	38.0	38.2
2013	35.2	34.8	35.4	37.3	38.7	39.7	40.2	40.5	41.0	41.1	40.6	39.1	38.6
2014	36.5	36.0	38.0	40.2	42.0	42.5	42.8	43.3	43.1	43.2	42.9	41.8	41.0
2015	38.6	38.5	39.3	41.5	43.3	44.3	44.4	44.8	44.4	44.8	44.8	43.0	42.6

Employment by Industry: Cincinnati, OH-KY-IN, 2005–2015—*Continued*

(Numbers in thousands, not seasonally adjusted)

Industry and year	January	February	March	April	May	June	July	August	September	October	November	December	Annual average
Manufacturing													
2005	121.8	121.5	122.2	122.5	123.1	123.2	122.9	123.0	123.2	122.9	123.0	123.2	122.7
2006	121.5	121.3	119.1	120.9	121.4	122.0	121.1	121.5	121.2	120.4	120.5	121.2	121.0
2007	120.0	120.5	121.5	121.3	121.6	121.7	120.6	120.9	120.4	119.7	119.6	119.9	120.6
2008	119.7	119.7	119.5	120.2	120.1	120.1	119.2	119.1	118.2	117.2	115.9	115.0	118.7
2009	111.4	109.9	108.5	106.9	105.9	105.5	104.4	104.8	104.2	104.0	103.9	103.7	106.1
2010	102.1	101.8	102.4	102.7	103.1	103.2	103.5	103.4	103.6	103.4	103.5	103.0	103.0
2011	102.2	102.3	102.7	103.3	103.9	104.4	104.7	104.7	104.8	104.8	105.1	105.3	104.0
2012	104.3	104.4	104.6	104.7	105.3	106.4	106.4	106.1	105.5	105.4	105.3	105.5	105.3
2013	104.2	104.1	103.9	105.0	106.1	106.8	107.1	106.6	106.4	106.9	107.5	107.7	106.0
2014	107.0	107.6	108.5	109.1	110.1	110.9	110.8	110.9	110.5	111.2	111.5	111.9	110.0
2015	111.1	111.1	111.6	112.3	112.9	113.8	113.9	114.2	113.5	114.1	115.2	115.6	113.3
Trade, Transportation, and Utilities													
2005	208.1	206.6	208.0	208.9	210.2	210.3	211.3	210.4	210.7	209.7	213.3	216.8	210.4
2006	208.4	206.1	206.8	206.8	208.5	209.0	208.2	208.7	209.1	210.0	214.4	217.0	209.4
2007	209.8	207.9	209.6	210.1	212.4	212.8	212.3	212.1	212.4	213.8	218.0	220.7	212.7
2008	211.7	209.4	209.7	210.4	211.9	211.3	210.4	210.8	209.0	208.9	210.7	212.3	210.5
2009	201.8	199.0	197.6	195.6	196.8	196.2	195.2	196.2	195.4	197.3	200.2	201.9	197.8
2010	192.8	192.1	193.1	194.1	195.7	195.8	194.2	194.2	193.3	195.8	199.8	200.9	195.2
2011	192.5	191.4	192.4	194.2	195.1	195.5	196.3	197.3	197.4	199.2	204.1	205.6	196.8
2012	196.5	195.4	196.8	197.7	200.1	200.0	199.0	199.8	199.7	201.4	205.1	205.9	199.8
2013	198.1	196.9	198.0	199.4	201.2	201.6	200.2	201.0	199.8	202.0	206.8	208.2	201.1
2014	199.5	198.7	199.6	201.0	202.5	203.3	202.4	204.0	202.4	206.0	209.7	211.7	203.4
2015	203.4	202.4	203.5	205.3	207.2	207.7	207.3	207.9	207.0	210.1	215.0	217.1	207.8
Wholesale Trade													
2005	56.7	56.6	56.8	57.2	57.5	58.0	58.6	58.9	59.4	58.6	58.9	59.2	58.0
2006	58.9	58.9	59.0	59.1	59.3	59.8	59.6	59.8	59.5	59.4	59.5	59.9	59.4
2007	60.5	60.4	60.6	60.7	60.8	61.3	61.1	61.1	61.2	61.3	61.3	61.7	61.0
2008	61.3	61.4	61.5	61.3	61.5	61.8	61.6	61.3	60.7	60.8	60.6	60.4	61.2
2009	59.1	58.6	58.0	56.4	56.3	55.8	55.7	55.4	55.0	55.2	55.2	55.4	56.3
2010	54.8	54.8	54.8	54.7	54.8	55.2	54.9	54.7	54.3	54.5	54.6	54.5	54.7
2011	54.5	54.6	54.9	55.4	55.6	55.7	56.0	56.1	56.3	56.1	56.2	56.1	55.6
2012	56.2	56.4	56.7	57.2	57.6	58.2	57.9	58.1	57.9	58.2	58.1	58.5	57.6
2013	58.6	58.8	59.1	59.2	59.5	59.7	59.6	59.5	59.4	59.1	59.4	59.4	59.3
2014	58.4	58.9	58.9	59.2	59.4	59.7	59.7	59.9	59.6	59.7	59.8	60.1	59.4
2015	59.6	59.8	60.0	60.4	61.0	61.3	60.9	61.0	60.5	60.7	61.1	61.1	60.6
Retail Trade													
2005	108.7	106.9	107.8	108.3	109.1	108.9	109.5	108.4	107.9	108.2	111.4	114.7	109.2
2006	107.9	106.0	106.7	107.0	108.2	108.3	108.1	108.3	107.9	108.7	112.3	113.9	108.6
2007	107.6	106.0	107.5	108.1	109.5	109.4	109.4	108.8	108.2	109.0	112.5	114.0	109.2
2008	108.0	105.9	106.2	107.1	108.1	107.9	107.7	107.8	106.6	106.5	108.4	109.8	107.5
2009	102.9	101.3	101.0	101.0	102.3	102.4	101.4	101.6	101.2	102.4	104.9	106.0	102.4
2010	99.5	98.9	99.9	100.8	102.0	101.5	101.4	101.2	100.4	102.2	105.4	106.1	101.6
2011	100.0	99.0	99.4	100.5	101.0	101.4	101.5	101.5	100.4	102.0	105.5	106.6	101.6
2012	100.3	99.0	100.1	100.9	102.3	102.2	101.8	101.7	101.5	103.3	107.0	107.3	102.3
2013	101.3	100.1	100.9	102.1	103.4	103.8	103.1	103.5	102.1	104.0	107.4	108.4	103.3
2014	102.2	101.1	101.6	103.0	103.9	104.4	103.9	104.5	103.2	105.9	109.0	110.0	104.4
2015	103.6	102.8	103.4	104.4	105.2	105.6	105.3	105.5	105.0	107.5	111.7	112.8	106.1
Transportation and Utilities													
2005	42.7	43.1	43.4	43.4	43.6	43.4	43.2	43.1	43.4	42.9	43.0	42.9	43.2
2006	41.6	41.2	41.1	40.7	41.0	40.9	40.5	40.6	41.7	41.9	42.6	43.2	41.4
2007	41.7	41.5	41.5	41.3	42.1	42.1	41.8	42.2	43.0	43.5	44.2	45.0	42.5
2008	42.4	42.1	42.0	42.0	42.3	41.6	41.1	41.7	41.7	41.6	41.7	42.1	41.9
2009	39.8	39.1	38.6	38.2	38.2	38.0	38.1	39.2	39.2	39.7	40.1	40.5	39.1
2010	38.5	38.4	38.4	38.6	38.9	39.1	37.9	38.3	38.6	39.1	39.8	40.3	38.8
2011	38.0	37.8	38.1	38.3	38.5	38.4	38.8	39.7	40.7	41.1	42.4	42.9	39.6
2012	40.0	40.0	40.0	39.6	40.2	39.6	39.3	40.0	40.3	39.9	40.0	40.1	39.9
2013	38.2	38.0	38.0	38.1	38.3	38.1	37.5	38.0	38.3	38.9	40.0	40.4	38.5
2014	38.9	38.7	39.1	38.8	39.2	39.2	38.8	39.6	39.6	40.4	40.9	41.6	39.6
2015	40.2	39.8	40.1	40.5	41.0	40.8	41.1	41.4	41.5	41.9	42.2	43.2	41.1

Employment by Industry: Cincinnati, OH-KY-IN, 2005–2015—*Continued*

(Numbers in thousands, not seasonally adjusted)

Industry and year	January	February	March	April	May	June	July	August	September	October	November	December	Annual average
Information													
2005	15.9	15.9	15.9	15.8	16.0	15.9	15.9	15.8	15.7	15.8	15.9	16.1	15.9
2006	15.7	15.6	15.7	15.8	15.7	15.8	15.8	15.8	15.5	15.5	15.6	15.6	15.7
2007	15.3	15.4	15.3	15.5	15.6	15.7	15.7	15.7	15.3	15.2	15.2	15.2	15.4
2008	15.1	15.1	15.2	15.1	15.1	15.2	15.3	15.3	15.1	15.2	15.1	15.1	15.2
2009	15.0	14.9	14.9	14.8	14.8	14.8	14.8	14.6	14.4	14.3	14.4	14.3	14.7
2010	14.2	14.0	14.0	13.9	14.0	14.0	14.2	14.2	14.1	14.0	14.1	14.0	14.1
2011	13.9	13.9	13.8	13.8	13.9	14.0	14.0	14.1	14.0	13.8	14.0	13.9	13.9
2012	13.9	13.9	13.8	13.7	13.8	13.9	13.9	13.8	13.7	14.0	14.1	14.2	13.9
2013	14.1	14.2	14.1	14.1	14.1	14.1	14.0	13.9	13.6	13.5	13.5	13.5	13.9
2014	13.3	13.3	13.4	13.6	13.7	13.5	13.6	13.7	13.4	13.3	13.5	13.7	13.5
2015	13.5	13.5	13.6	13.6	13.5	13.6	13.6	13.8	13.5	13.5	13.8	13.8	13.6
Financial Activities													
2005	64.6	64.0	64.0	64.2	64.4	65.0	64.8	64.8	64.2	64.1	64.2	64.7	64.4
2006	63.9	64.0	64.2	64.5	64.8	65.0	64.7	64.7	64.2	64.2	64.2	64.5	64.4
2007	64.3	64.5	64.6	64.7	65.1	65.4	65.7	65.4	64.9	64.7	64.5	65.0	64.9
2008	64.6	64.5	64.6	65.1	65.3	65.5	65.6	65.5	64.8	64.6	64.6	64.4	64.9
2009	63.6	63.3	63.2	63.0	63.4	63.3	63.3	62.7	62.1	62.1	62.1	61.9	62.8
2010	61.5	61.3	61.3	62.0	62.3	62.6	63.3	63.2	63.1	63.1	63.2	63.5	62.5
2011	63.3	63.3	63.3	63.2	63.4	63.5	63.2	63.2	63.0	62.9	63.1	63.4	63.2
2012	63.4	63.3	63.4	63.6	64.0	64.5	64.6	64.5	64.5	64.5	64.7	65.1	64.2
2013	64.4	64.6	64.9	65.2	65.6	66.2	66.5	66.6	66.2	66.0	66.2	66.2	65.7
2014	65.6	65.7	65.8	66.1	66.8	67.4	67.8	67.8	67.2	67.2	67.9	67.8	66.9
2015	67.3	67.4	67.5	67.7	68.4	68.9	69.1	69.4	68.8	68.8	68.9	69.5	68.5
Professional and Business Services													
2005	144.5	145.8	147.7	149.9	150.3	152.9	153.4	155.2	156.6	156.3	156.7	157.4	152.2
2006	151.2	151.6	153.6	154.1	153.4	154.5	155.8	156.5	156.2	154.7	154.7	154.5	154.2
2007	150.6	150.9	153.6	155.4	155.6	157.5	156.4	157.5	157.5	160.3	161.0	161.1	156.5
2008	157.6	157.0	157.0	159.1	158.3	159.0	160.1	160.3	158.8	159.3	157.3	156.2	158.3
2009	149.7	148.6	147.8	147.0	146.0	145.9	145.8	146.6	145.5	145.8	147.0	147.7	147.0
2010	143.6	143.6	145.2	148.2	147.9	149.4	149.4	150.1	149.6	151.4	151.3	150.8	148.4
2011	148.9	149.2	151.1	154.0	153.0	153.5	156.0	156.8	156.8	157.4	158.6	158.6	154.5
2012	156.1	155.9	157.4	160.1	160.2	161.2	161.3	163.0	163.1	163.8	162.6	162.3	160.6
2013	156.8	157.6	159.0	162.6	162.6	163.7	163.6	165.2	165.7	166.0	166.6	167.5	163.1
2014	161.7	161.4	163.4	166.1	166.2	166.0	167.0	168.4	167.9	168.2	169.9	169.9	166.3
2015	164.6	163.6	164.3	166.9	166.9	168.5	170.0	170.1	169.1	170.2	169.9	170.0	167.8
Education and Health Services													
2005	131.2	132.4	132.9	134.8	134.5	133.9	133.0	133.8	134.6	135.3	135.9	136.1	134.0
2006	134.8	135.9	136.7	137.7	137.7	137.4	136.3	137.3	138.6	139.8	140.5	140.7	137.8
2007	139.0	139.6	140.6	141.3	141.9	140.7	139.3	139.9	142.5	143.6	144.6	144.5	141.5
2008	142.9	143.8	144.5	145.7	146.1	143.6	144.0	144.2	144.9	145.8	146.4	146.2	144.8
2009	143.8	144.3	144.9	146.5	146.7	144.9	145.2	144.9	145.5	146.9	147.9	147.4	145.7
2010	144.7	145.6	146.6	148.3	148.6	146.7	146.1	146.1	147.2	148.7	149.2	149.2	147.3
2011	146.4	147.6	148.2	150.1	151.2	149.4	148.6	148.8	150.0	150.7	151.0	151.2	149.4
2012	149.4	151.0	151.6	152.5	153.3	152.0	150.3	150.8	152.8	154.1	154.7	154.5	152.3
2013	152.4	154.1	154.7	156.3	157.5	156.1	155.2	155.5	157.1	158.0	159.6	158.9	156.3
2014	157.3	158.1	159.2	159.3	160.5	158.9	158.0	158.6	159.9	160.3	161.7	161.8	159.5
2015	159.4	159.7	160.9	161.9	162.8	160.9	159.8	160.2	162.0	163.6	164.5	165.1	161.7
Leisure and Hospitality													
2005	95.7	96.8	100.2	104.4	107.8	111.0	111.4	110.3	107.4	102.5	102.3	102.1	104.3
2006	98.1	99.1	101.9	104.0	107.4	112.1	111.7	111.7	107.3	103.6	102.7	102.6	105.2
2007	99.4	98.6	100.9	105.0	110.4	113.5	112.5	113.0	108.2	105.1	101.5	102.5	105.9
2008	98.7	99.0	99.9	106.3	110.5	112.9	112.0	111.3	105.9	102.7	98.7	99.6	104.8
2009	95.0	95.1	97.3	102.0	106.7	110.2	109.2	108.6	105.1	100.2	97.3	97.7	102.0
2010	93.9	93.9	97.2	102.3	106.9	110.1	109.0	108.7	104.5	101.8	98.3	98.5	102.1
2011	94.1	94.8	98.2	103.7	108.1	111.3	111.3	110.8	106.2	102.7	99.7	100.4	103.4
2012	96.9	98.3	101.7	106.1	110.9	114.6	113.7	113.3	109.0	107.5	103.3	104.1	106.6
2013	100.1	102.0	105.2	111.3	116.4	118.9	118.2	117.5	113.9	112.5	108.1	107.9	111.0
2014	103.6	104.2	108.8	113.6	119.0	121.3	120.3	119.0	114.6	112.8	109.2	109.9	113.0
2015	106.6	107.2	110.8	117.0	122.6	125.8	126.4	123.8	121.6	113.7	109.2	108.2	116.1

Employment by Industry: Cincinnati, OH-KY-IN, 2005–2015—*Continued*

(Numbers in thousands, not seasonally adjusted)

Industry and year	January	February	March	April	May	June	July	August	September	October	November	December	Annual average
Other Services													
2005	41.9	42.2	42.6	43.1	43.2	43.3	43.1	42.9	42.6	42.6	42.5	42.6	42.7
2006	41.7	41.7	42.1	42.2	42.6	43.0	43.1	43.1	42.9	42.6	42.5	42.7	42.5
2007	42.2	42.2	42.9	43.1	43.5	44.2	43.8	44.0	43.2	43.6	43.6	43.6	43.3
2008	43.2	43.2	43.5	43.7	43.9	44.3	43.9	43.7	42.9	43.2	42.9	43.0	43.5
2009	42.3	42.3	42.6	42.4	42.7	42.8	42.9	42.6	42.2	42.3	41.9	42.2	42.4
2010	41.3	41.1	41.6	40.8	40.7	41.0	41.1	41.0	40.5	40.5	40.3	40.2	40.8
2011	39.8	39.6	40.0	40.2	40.5	40.3	40.1	39.8	39.3	38.8	38.5	38.4	39.6
2012	37.8	37.6	37.9	38.5	38.9	39.6	39.5	39.5	39.2	39.4	39.4	39.6	38.9
2013	39.2	39.4	39.7	39.9	40.0	40.2	40.0	39.8	39.5	39.3	39.0	39.0	39.6
2014	38.3	38.3	38.7	39.0	39.3	39.5	39.3	39.2	38.4	38.8	38.7	38.8	38.9
2015	37.9	37.8	38.2	38.5	38.9	39.1	39.2	39.1	38.4	38.7	38.6	38.6	38.6
Government													
2005	130.7	133.5	134.5	134.9	135.4	131.3	122.9	124.7	131.1	134.4	134.9	134.2	131.9
2006	130.9	134.0	135.4	135.5	136.2	130.8	122.5	124.6	131.3	134.5	134.8	134.6	132.1
2007	131.8	134.8	136.2	135.9	136.0	128.6	121.9	126.0	131.7	134.8	137.0	136.2	132.6
2008	132.2	136.5	136.5	136.7	137.0	128.1	123.2	127.3	132.8	136.3	138.3	137.5	133.5
2009	134.2	136.9	136.7	137.7	137.0	128.6	120.7	126.5	132.7	135.7	136.1	135.3	133.2
2010	132.8	135.2	136.2	137.3	139.8	129.1	119.3	123.9	130.0	132.8	134.5	134.2	132.1
2011	130.5	132.9	133.8	134.1	132.9	124.0	118.3	125.1	130.3	132.9	132.5	129.6	129.7
2012	125.9	132.1	133.3	133.6	134.1	124.7	118.1	122.2	129.7	132.4	132.9	128.8	129.0
2013	126.4	132.4	132.0	135.2	134.3	124.2	116.4	125.2	132.0	133.3	133.6	128.9	129.5
2014	126.3	131.9	132.2	133.8	134.6	124.4	118.6	124.2	131.2	132.5	132.5	131.6	129.5
2015	127.8	130.9	132.0	132.9	134.0	125.4	120.5	125.5	130.8	132.6	133.3	131.4	129.8

Employment by Industry: Las Vegas-Henderson-Paradise, 2005–2015

(Numbers in thousands, not seasonally adjusted)

Industry and year	January	February	March	April	May	June	July	August	September	October	November	December	Annual average
Total Nonfarm													
2005	832.6	841.0	850.8	867.6	870.2	872.7	870.6	873.6	887.6	892.8	899.5	903.6	871.9
2006	891.6	901.1	910.8	916.1	922.4	923.9	915.8	917.6	925.4	926.9	929.4	928.1	917.4
2007	913.3	924.0	928.0	930.5	936.8	933.4	921.3	921.2	924.7	932.3	935.4	936.4	928.1
2008	919.6	921.5	923.6	926.3	929.7	923.1	910.3	906.8	910.1	903.6	893.6	880.7	912.4
2009	855.8	850.3	842.8	836.3	832.3	824.3	811.2	807.4	815.6	815.7	815.7	816.9	827.0
2010	798.2	798.6	799.5	808.2	811.7	807.9	800.5	799.5	799.8	806.4	808.0	805.5	803.7
2011	797.3	797.4	803.5	810.3	811.2	807.3	804.6	803.7	811.6	817.6	818.3	816.5	808.3
2012	808.6	810.6	815.7	822.2	827.8	826.8	818.8	822.6	830.6	837.7	842.4	838.5	825.2
2013	831.0	832.2	839.5	846.4	850.3	850.9	844.8	849.2	853.9	861.6	867.9	865.5	849.4
2014	858.4	863.3	871.6	878.2	884.9	881.3	874.6	885.5	893.5	903.5	906.0	906.1	883.9
2015	898.5	901.1	908.7	915.5	919.1	915.0	909.9	918.0	923.8	934.3	932.0	928.0	917.0
Total Private													
2005	748.6	753.9	762.2	778.8	781.1	787.2	788.8	792.8	800.1	801.5	807.2	811.0	784.4
2006	803.0	809.2	818.5	822.6	828.7	833.9	829.9	832.2	833.2	830.4	831.9	830.6	825.3
2007	819.5	826.2	829.7	830.6	836.7	837.4	829.7	831.1	827.6	831.1	833.4	834.0	830.6
2008	821.0	819.2	820.6	822.2	825.7	823.7	814.4	812.2	808.4	798.0	787.9	775.1	810.7
2009	755.2	747.8	740.4	734.5	731.5	727.8	718.1	715.7	717.4	716.6	717.2	718.8	728.4
2010	702.6	700.4	701.1	709.5	710.8	712.6	707.3	708.3	704.0	709.6	711.1	708.7	707.2
2011	702.1	700.6	706.6	713.6	714.9	717.2	715.6	714.6	718.3	723.0	723.7	721.0	714.3
2012	716.0	716.1	720.0	726.6	732.0	735.4	729.5	733.9	736.2	742.3	746.1	741.3	731.3
2013	736.6	736.8	743.3	749.9	753.9	758.2	755.3	758.1	758.7	764.7	770.1	766.8	754.4
2014	762.6	766.0	773.2	780.3	786.7	788.7	783.7	793.6	796.6	805.3	807.3	806.6	787.6
2015	801.5	802.9	809.3	816.1	819.9	819.4	817.3	824.1	824.7	833.7	830.6	826.3	818.8
Goods Producing													
2005	117.7	120.5	122.3	124.6	124.6	126.0	128.4	129.9	131.9	131.6	131.8	132.9	126.9
2006	130.8	133.6	135.8	137.3	138.5	139.9	138.8	139.3	138.2	135.6	133.7	132.3	136.2
2007	128.1	129.6	131.9	131.0	132.7	132.1	131.5	132.0	129.5	127.9	126.5	125.5	129.9
2008	121.3	121.4	120.9	120.7	121.7	122.0	121.9	120.6	118.0	114.7	109.7	104.8	118.1
2009	99.3	96.8	94.0	90.8	86.5	84.8	82.9	82.2	81.2	79.8	77.2	73.7	85.8
2010	66.8	65.3	64.6	66.8	66.7	66.3	65.2	65.0	63.6	63.0	61.7	60.1	64.6
2011	57.7	57.5	57.2	57.6	57.1	57.2	57.9	58.5	58.0	58.0	57.2	57.0	57.6
2012	54.8	54.7	55.1	55.6	56.6	57.8	58.0	59.5	60.0	60.5	61.0	61.0	57.9
2013	59.3	59.8	60.4	61.2	61.1	61.9	62.0	63.4	63.3	64.2	64.4	64.1	62.1
2014	63.7	64.2	64.4	65.3	65.8	66.0	66.9	68.6	68.9	69.6	69.4	69.6	66.9
2015	69.8	70.3	70.3	70.8	72.1	72.6	72.6	74.2	74.5	74.9	76.0	75.5	72.8
Service-Providing													
2005	714.9	720.5	728.5	743.0	745.6	746.7	742.2	743.7	755.7	761.2	767.7	770.7	745.0
2006	760.8	767.5	775.0	778.8	783.9	784.0	777.0	778.3	787.2	791.3	795.7	795.8	781.3
2007	785.2	794.4	796.1	799.5	804.1	801.3	789.8	789.2	795.2	804.4	808.9	810.9	798.3
2008	798.3	800.1	802.7	805.6	808.0	801.1	788.4	786.2	792.1	788.9	783.9	775.9	794.3
2009	756.5	753.5	748.8	745.5	745.8	739.5	728.3	725.2	734.4	735.9	738.5	743.2	741.3
2010	731.4	733.3	734.9	741.4	745.0	741.6	735.3	734.5	736.2	743.4	746.3	745.4	739.1
2011	739.6	739.9	746.3	752.7	754.1	750.1	746.7	745.2	753.6	759.6	761.1	759.5	750.7
2012	753.8	755.9	760.6	766.6	771.2	769.0	760.8	763.1	770.6	777.2	781.4	777.5	767.3
2013	771.7	772.4	779.1	785.2	789.2	789.0	782.8	785.8	790.6	797.4	803.5	801.4	787.3
2014	794.7	799.1	807.2	812.9	819.1	815.3	807.7	816.9	824.6	833.9	836.6	836.5	817.0
2015	828.7	830.8	838.4	844.7	847.0	842.4	837.3	843.8	849.3	859.4	856.0	852.5	844.2
Mining, Logging, and Construction													
2005	93.6	96.4	97.9	99.9	99.8	101.0	103.3	104.7	106.3	106.0	106.1	107.2	101.9
2006	105.0	107.5	109.3	110.4	111.3	112.5	111.3	111.8	110.5	108.2	106.4	104.9	109.1
2007	101.4	102.9	105.0	104.1	105.7	104.9	104.5	105.1	102.8	101.6	100.2	99.4	103.1
2008	95.4	95.6	95.1	94.9	95.8	96.0	96.1	95.0	92.7	89.8	85.5	81.1	92.8
2009	76.5	74.5	72.1	69.3	65.5	64.1	62.3	61.5	60.5	59.4	57.0	53.6	64.7
2010	47.1	45.8	45.2	47.1	47.1	46.7	45.7	45.7	44.2	43.6	42.2	40.7	45.1
2011	38.3	38.1	37.7	38.0	37.6	37.5	38.2	38.5	38.0	37.9	37.2	36.9	37.8
2012	35.1	35.1	35.3	35.6	36.5	37.3	37.6	39.0	39.6	40.1	40.5	40.5	37.7
2013	39.1	39.5	40.0	40.6	40.3	41.0	41.1	42.5	42.5	43.3	43.4	42.9	41.4
2014	42.7	43.3	43.5	44.3	44.7	44.9	45.8	47.4	47.7	48.2	48.0	48.2	45.7
2015	48.5	49.0	48.8	49.4	50.5	50.9	51.0	52.6	52.9	53.2	54.3	53.7	51.2

Employment by Industry: Las Vegas-Henderson-Paradise, 2005–2015—*Continued*

(Numbers in thousands, not seasonally adjusted)

Industry and year	January	February	March	April	May	June	July	August	September	October	November	December	Annual average
Construction													
2005................	93.2	96.0	97.5	99.5	99.4	100.6	102.9	104.3	105.9	105.6	105.7	106.8	101.5
2006................	104.6	107.1	108.9	110.0	110.9	112.0	110.8	111.3	110.0	107.7	105.9	104.4	108.6
2007................	100.9	102.4	104.5	103.6	105.2	104.4	104.0	104.6	102.3	101.1	99.8	99.0	102.7
2008................	95.0	95.2	94.7	94.5	95.4	95.6	95.7	94.6	92.3	89.5	85.2	80.8	92.4
2009................	76.2	74.2	71.8	69.0	65.2	63.8	62.0	61.2	60.2	59.1	56.7	53.3	64.4
2010................	46.8	45.5	45.0	46.8	46.8	46.4	45.4	45.4	43.9	43.3	41.9	40.5	44.8
2011................	38.1	37.9	37.5	37.8	37.4	37.3	38.0	38.2	37.7	37.6	36.9	36.6	37.6
2012................	34.8	34.8	35.0	35.3	36.2	37.0	37.3	38.7	39.3	39.8	40.2	40.2	37.4
2013................	38.8	39.2	39.7	40.3	40.0	40.7	40.8	42.2	42.2	43.0	43.1	42.6	41.1
2014................	42.4	43.0	43.2	43.9	44.3	44.5	45.4	47.0	47.3	47.8	47.6	47.8	45.4
2015................	48.2	48.7	48.5	49.0	50.2	50.5	50.6	52.2	52.5	52.8	53.9	53.4	50.9
Manufacturing													
2005................	24.1	24.1	24.4	24.7	24.8	25.0	25.1	25.2	25.6	25.6	25.7	25.7	25.0
2006................	25.8	26.1	26.5	26.9	27.2	27.4	27.5	27.5	27.7	27.4	27.3	27.4	27.1
2007................	26.7	26.7	26.9	26.9	27.0	27.2	27.0	26.9	26.7	26.3	26.3	26.1	26.7
2008................	25.9	25.8	25.8	25.8	25.9	26.0	25.8	25.6	25.3	24.9	24.2	23.7	25.4
2009................	22.8	22.3	21.9	21.5	21.0	20.7	20.6	20.7	20.7	20.4	20.2	20.1	21.1
2010................	19.7	19.5	19.4	19.7	19.6	19.6	19.5	19.3	19.4	19.4	19.5	19.4	19.5
2011................	19.4	19.4	19.5	19.6	19.5	19.7	19.7	20.0	20.0	20.1	20.0	20.1	19.8
2012................	19.7	19.6	19.8	20.0	20.1	20.5	20.4	20.5	20.4	20.4	20.5	20.5	20.2
2013................	20.2	20.3	20.4	20.6	20.8	20.9	20.9	20.9	20.8	20.9	21.0	21.2	20.7
2014................	21.0	20.9	20.9	21.0	21.1	21.1	21.1	21.2	21.2	21.4	21.4	21.4	21.1
2015................	21.3	21.3	21.5	21.4	21.6	21.7	21.6	21.6	21.6	21.7	21.7	21.8	21.6
Trade, Transportation, and Utilities													
2005................	143.7	143.2	144.0	145.6	146.2	147.3	148.2	149.0	150.6	151.8	155.2	157.2	148.5
2006................	152.6	152.1	153.7	153.8	154.8	155.3	155.3	155.9	156.8	158.0	161.4	163.3	156.1
2007................	158.4	157.7	158.4	158.8	160.0	160.7	160.0	161.0	161.0	162.1	166.6	168.9	161.1
2008................	163.2	161.2	161.6	161.0	160.9	160.9	161.1	161.1	160.3	159.5	160.4	160.0	160.9
2009................	152.8	150.1	149.1	147.6	147.4	147.5	146.6	146.5	147.1	148.0	151.2	152.2	148.8
2010................	146.5	144.7	144.8	145.1	145.8	146.6	146.8	147.3	146.9	148.4	151.8	152.9	147.3
2011................	147.1	145.7	146.1	147.5	147.8	148.4	149.1	149.6	149.8	151.9	156.2	156.7	149.7
2012................	152.2	150.3	151.2	152.0	152.8	153.4	153.2	153.4	153.9	154.5	160.1	159.8	153.9
2013................	154.5	152.4	151.7	152.4	154.7	155.5	156.1	156.7	157.4	158.9	164.1	165.3	156.6
2014................	159.1	158.0	158.6	159.1	160.0	160.7	161.0	162.1	162.8	165.5	170.4	171.8	162.4
2015................	166.0	164.6	165.7	166.6	167.5	167.8	167.9	168.6	168.9	171.9	174.7	176.8	168.9
Wholesale Trade													
2005................	21.2	21.4	21.6	21.9	22.0	22.2	22.4	22.5	22.7	22.6	22.7	22.9	22.2
2006................	22.8	23.0	23.2	23.4	23.6	23.6	23.7	23.8	24.0	23.9	23.9	24.1	23.6
2007................	23.8	23.9	24.0	24.0	24.2	24.3	24.2	24.3	24.3	24.2	24.2	24.2	24.1
2008................	24.0	24.0	24.1	23.9	24.0	24.0	24.1	24.1	24.0	23.7	23.4	23.1	23.9
2009................	22.5	22.3	22.0	21.6	21.3	21.2	21.1	21.0	20.9	20.9	20.8	20.8	21.4
2010................	20.4	20.3	20.4	20.4	20.5	20.6	20.5	20.5	20.4	20.6	20.5	20.5	20.5
2011................	20.2	20.1	20.2	20.3	20.2	20.3	20.3	20.2	20.1	20.1	20.1	20.1	20.2
2012................	19.9	19.9	20.0	20.0	20.1	20.2	20.2	20.2	20.2	20.2	20.2	20.3	20.1
2013................	20.0	20.0	20.1	20.2	20.3	20.4	20.5	20.7	20.7	20.7	20.8	20.9	20.4
2014................	20.7	20.9	20.9	20.8	20.9	20.9	21.1	21.1	21.1	21.2	21.2	21.3	21.0
2015................	21.2	21.2	21.2	21.2	21.3	21.3	21.5	21.5	21.6	21.7	21.7	21.6	21.4
Retail Trade													
2005................	91.6	90.7	91.1	91.7	91.9	92.6	93.5	93.9	94.9	96.1	99.0	100.5	94.0
2006................	96.1	95.4	96.3	96.1	96.6	97.0	96.7	97.1	97.4	98.7	101.6	103.1	97.7
2007................	98.7	97.8	98.1	98.5	99.2	99.5	99.4	99.9	99.6	100.2	104.1	106.2	100.1
2008................	101.6	99.9	100.0	99.6	99.2	99.4	99.4	99.3	98.8	98.5	99.8	100.0	99.6
2009................	94.5	92.2	91.6	90.7	90.8	91.0	90.6	90.7	91.6	92.6	95.6	96.7	92.4
2010................	91.6	90.1	90.2	90.6	91.1	91.6	92.0	92.5	92.2	93.5	96.8	97.6	92.5
2011................	92.7	91.3	91.5	92.2	92.7	93.0	93.4	94.0	94.2	95.9	100.1	100.6	94.3
2012................	96.5	94.8	95.5	96.0	96.4	96.8	96.5	96.7	97.2	98.1	103.6	103.0	97.6
2013................	98.0	96.3	96.4	96.7	97.9	98.4	98.9	99.4	99.7	101.0	105.8	106.8	99.6
2014................	101.2	99.8	100.2	100.5	101.1	101.5	101.6	102.5	103.0	105.4	110.0	110.9	103.1
2015................	105.2	104.0	104.7	105.5	105.9	106.1	105.9	106.5	106.3	108.7	111.3	112.5	106.9

Employment by Industry: Las Vegas-Henderson-Paradise, 2005–2015—*Continued*

(Numbers in thousands, not seasonally adjusted)

Industry and year	January	February	March	April	May	June	July	August	September	October	November	December	Annual average
Transportation and Utilities													
2005	30.9	31.1	31.3	32.0	32.3	32.5	32.3	32.6	33.0	33.1	33.5	33.8	32.4
2006	33.7	33.7	34.2	34.3	34.6	34.7	34.9	35.0	35.4	35.4	35.9	36.1	34.8
2007	35.9	36.0	36.3	36.3	36.6	36.9	36.4	36.8	37.1	37.7	38.3	38.5	36.9
2008	37.6	37.3	37.5	37.5	37.7	37.5	37.6	37.7	37.5	37.3	37.2	36.9	37.4
2009	35.8	35.6	35.5	35.3	35.3	35.3	34.9	34.8	34.6	34.5	34.8	34.7	35.1
2010	34.5	34.3	34.2	34.1	34.2	34.4	34.3	34.3	34.3	34.3	34.5	34.8	34.4
2011	34.2	34.3	34.4	35.0	34.9	35.1	35.4	35.4	35.5	35.9	36.0	36.0	35.2
2012	35.8	35.6	35.7	36.0	36.3	36.4	36.5	36.5	36.5	36.2	36.3	36.5	36.2
2013	36.5	36.1	35.2	35.5	36.5	36.7	36.7	36.6	37.0	37.2	37.5	37.6	36.6
2014	37.2	37.3	37.5	37.8	38.0	38.3	38.3	38.5	38.7	38.9	39.2	39.6	38.3
2015	39.6	39.4	39.8	39.9	40.3	40.4	40.5	40.6	41.0	41.5	41.7	42.7	40.6
Information													
2005	10.5	10.1	10.1	10.6	11.0	10.4	10.1	10.2	10.2	10.6	10.5	10.3	10.4
2006	10.8	10.8	10.5	10.9	10.9	11.0	11.5	11.5	11.1	11.1	11.0	10.8	11.0
2007	11.3	11.6	11.3	11.4	11.6	11.5	10.9	11.3	10.9	11.4	11.4	11.1	11.3
2008	11.0	11.1	11.1	11.3	11.8	11.2	10.8	10.8	10.7	11.0	10.6	10.2	11.0
2009	9.8	9.9	10.0	9.5	9.5	9.6	9.5	9.7	9.4	9.4	9.4	9.4	9.6
2010	9.0	9.0	8.9	9.3	9.1	9.1	9.4	9.2	9.0	9.1	9.3	9.3	9.1
2011	9.2	9.0	9.1	9.4	9.4	9.4	9.2	9.1	9.5	9.8	9.1	9.6	9.3
2012	9.1	9.2	9.4	9.4	9.5	9.5	9.2	9.5	9.6	10.2	11.3	9.9	9.7
2013	9.1	9.3	9.5	9.7	9.8	10.8	10.1	9.8	9.8	9.9	10.1	10.1	9.8
2014	9.8	9.9	9.7	10.9	11.7	12.2	10.3	10.1	10.4	10.5	10.9	10.7	10.6
2015	10.3	10.7	10.6	10.5	10.5	10.8	10.2	10.4	10.2	10.8	10.9	10.8	10.6
Financial Activities													
2005	47.7	47.7	48.3	48.2	48.4	48.9	48.9	49.1	49.7	49.4	49.6	49.9	48.8
2006	49.0	49.0	49.6	49.6	50.0	50.4	50.5	50.6	50.9	50.6	50.8	51.3	50.2
2007	50.4	50.4	50.7	50.2	50.5	50.6	50.0	49.8	49.7	49.4	48.9	49.0	50.0
2008	48.0	48.1	48.2	48.0	47.9	48.0	47.5	47.1	47.0	46.9	46.4	45.9	47.4
2009	44.1	43.9	43.5	43.1	42.9	42.9	41.7	41.7	41.3	41.4	41.0	40.9	42.4
2010	40.3	39.9	40.0	40.5	40.3	40.1	40.2	39.9	39.8	40.3	40.2	40.3	40.2
2011	39.8	39.6	39.8	40.0	39.9	40.0	39.9	39.7	40.0	40.2	40.2	40.5	40.0
2012	40.2	40.3	40.6	41.4	41.7	41.9	41.8	42.0	42.2	42.8	42.8	42.9	41.7
2013	42.5	42.9	43.6	43.3	43.7	43.5	43.0	43.0	42.9	43.4	43.6	43.8	43.3
2014	42.8	42.9	43.0	43.0	43.5	43.4	43.1	43.6	43.7	44.4	44.5	44.7	43.6
2015	44.3	44.8	45.0	45.2	45.7	45.3	45.6	45.6	45.6	45.9	45.4	44.7	45.3
Professional and Business Services													
2005	101.7	102.7	103.9	105.2	104.9	105.3	104.7	106.5	107.2	109.9	112.5	112.4	106.4
2006	113.2	114.4	115.4	115.6	116.4	116.7	114.5	115.7	115.3	115.8	116.3	114.2	115.3
2007	117.0	119.6	117.6	118.0	118.0	117.0	113.7	115.4	113.9	116.4	115.4	113.2	116.3
2008	116.0	115.2	115.0	115.1	116.1	113.7	109.9	110.1	110.9	108.0	106.8	103.1	111.7
2009	105.6	103.8	101.5	99.3	99.6	98.4	94.8	95.5	97.6	97.6	99.0	98.5	99.3
2010	100.3	99.1	98.6	99.7	99.7	100.4	98.2	100.4	98.4	100.9	100.7	99.3	99.6
2011	102.7	101.1	101.5	101.9	101.6	101.8	101.1	101.2	102.8	104.2	103.8	102.7	102.2
2012	107.2	106.6	105.0	106.1	106.2	106.7	103.4	106.8	107.8	109.7	108.5	106.9	106.7
2013	111.6	110.2	111.4	112.4	112.7	111.6	108.9	111.2	110.3	113.4	113.6	111.7	111.6
2014	115.5	115.6	116.5	116.6	116.9	116.9	113.6	117.5	118.3	122.9	121.7	120.5	117.7
2015	124.7	123.1	124.3	126.4	126.1	124.4	123.5	127.1	127.0	131.0	127.8	124.8	125.9
Education and Health Services													
2005	55.8	56.4	57.0	57.7	57.9	58.1	57.6	57.7	58.1	58.0	58.4	59.0	57.6
2006	58.5	59.1	59.8	59.4	59.6	60.2	59.3	59.8	60.7	61.2	61.7	62.1	60.1
2007	61.5	62.4	62.7	62.6	63.2	63.4	63.3	63.5	64.0	64.6	64.9	64.7	63.4
2008	64.6	65.3	65.6	66.3	66.5	66.6	66.2	66.5	67.0	67.2	67.5	67.6	66.4
2009	66.4	66.9	66.9	66.9	67.3	67.5	67.4	67.7	67.7	68.8	68.9	69.0	67.6
2010	68.3	68.6	69.1	69.7	69.8	69.7	69.1	69.3	69.6	70.7	71.1	71.3	69.7
2011	70.8	71.4	71.9	72.5	72.5	72.7	72.3	72.7	73.0	73.7	74.0	74.4	72.7
2012	73.9	74.6	74.6	75.2	75.8	75.4	74.9	76.0	75.9	76.8	76.8	77.2	75.6
2013	76.7	77.8	78.3	78.8	78.9	79.0	78.9	79.5	80.0	80.6	81.0	81.0	79.2
2014	80.4	81.2	81.7	81.8	82.2	82.5	82.3	83.1	83.5	84.6	84.8	85.0	82.8
2015	84.4	85.2	85.7	86.2	86.5	87.1	87.3	88.2	88.7	90.2	91.2	91.9	87.7

Employment by Industry: Las Vegas-Henderson-Paradise, 2005–2015—*Continued*

(Numbers in thousands, not seasonally adjusted)

Industry and year	January	February	March	April	May	June	July	August	September	October	November	December	Annual average
Leisure and Hospitality													
2005	249.2	250.7	253.7	263.9	264.8	267.5	267.2	266.6	268.3	266.2	265.0	264.8	262.3
2006	264.4	266.3	269.4	271.7	273.8	275.3	274.9	274.1	274.7	272.8	271.8	271.5	271.7
2007	268.3	270.4	272.1	273.4	275.1	276.1	274.4	272.1	272.6	273.5	273.8	275.4	273.1
2008	271.1	271.3	272.4	274.1	274.7	275.1	271.1	269.9	268.4	265.0	261.4	258.9	269.5
2009	253.7	253.0	251.9	253.6	254.4	253.2	251.6	248.7	249.4	248.3	247.5	252.1	251.5
2010	248.8	251.1	252.1	255.1	256.0	257.0	254.9	253.6	253.2	253.6	253.2	252.6	253.4
2011	252.1	253.3	257.8	261.4	263.1	264.1	262.4	260.2	261.8	261.9	260.0	256.9	259.6
2012	255.5	257.3	260.6	263.1	265.2	266.2	264.6	262.2	262.2	262.8	261.6	259.9	261.8
2013	259.3	260.6	264.3	267.7	268.4	271.1	271.6	269.9	270.5	269.9	268.9	266.4	267.4
2014	267.1	269.8	274.6	278.4	281.0	281.3	280.7	282.9	283.2	281.6	280.0	279.0	278.3
2015	276.9	278.9	282.1	284.7	285.6	285.3	284.1	283.9	283.9	283.1	279.0	276.3	282.0
Other Services													
2005	22.3	22.6	22.9	23.0	23.3	23.7	23.7	23.8	24.1	24.0	24.2	24.5	23.5
2006	23.7	23.9	24.3	24.3	24.7	25.1	25.1	25.3	25.5	25.3	25.2	25.1	24.8
2007	24.5	24.5	25.0	25.2	25.6	26.0	25.9	26.0	26.0	25.8	25.9	26.2	25.6
2008	25.8	25.6	25.8	25.7	26.1	26.2	25.9	26.1	26.1	25.7	25.1	24.6	25.7
2009	23.5	23.4	23.5	23.7	23.9	23.9	23.6	23.7	23.7	23.3	23.0	23.0	23.5
2010	22.6	22.7	23.0	23.3	23.4	23.4	23.5	23.6	23.5	23.6	23.1	22.9	23.2
2011	22.7	23.0	23.2	23.3	23.5	23.6	23.7	23.6	23.4	23.3	23.2	23.2	23.3
2012	23.1	23.1	23.5	23.8	24.2	24.5	24.4	24.5	24.6	25.0	24.0	23.7	24.0
2013	23.6	23.8	24.1	24.4	24.6	24.8	24.7	24.6	24.5	24.4	24.4	24.4	24.4
2014	24.2	24.4	24.7	25.2	25.6	25.7	25.8	25.7	25.8	26.2	25.6	25.3	25.4
2015	25.1	25.3	25.6	25.7	25.9	26.1	26.1	26.1	25.9	25.9	25.6	25.5	25.7
Government													
2005	84.0	87.1	88.6	88.8	89.1	85.5	81.8	80.8	87.5	91.3	92.3	92.6	87.5
2006	88.6	91.9	92.3	93.5	93.7	90.0	85.9	85.4	92.2	96.5	97.5	97.5	92.1
2007	93.8	97.8	98.3	99.9	100.1	96.0	91.6	90.1	97.1	101.2	102.0	102.4	97.5
2008	98.6	102.3	103.0	104.1	104.0	99.4	95.9	94.6	101.7	105.6	105.7	105.6	101.7
2009	100.6	102.5	102.4	101.8	100.8	96.5	93.1	91.7	98.2	99.1	98.5	98.1	98.6
2010	95.6	98.2	98.4	98.7	100.9	95.3	93.2	91.2	95.8	96.8	96.9	96.8	96.5
2011	95.2	96.8	96.9	96.7	96.3	90.1	89.0	89.1	93.3	94.6	94.6	95.5	94.0
2012	92.6	94.5	95.7	95.6	95.8	91.4	89.3	88.7	94.4	95.4	96.3	97.2	93.9
2013	94.4	95.4	96.2	96.5	96.4	92.7	89.5	91.1	95.2	96.9	97.8	98.7	95.1
2014	95.8	97.3	98.4	97.9	98.2	92.6	90.9	91.9	96.9	98.2	98.7	99.5	96.4
2015	97.0	98.2	99.4	99.4	99.2	95.6	92.6	93.9	99.1	100.6	101.4	101.7	98.2

Employment by Industry: Kansas City, MO-KS, 2005–2015

(Numbers in thousands, not seasonally adjusted)

Industry and year	January	February	March	April	May	June	July	August	September	October	November	December	Annual average
Total Nonfarm													
2005	949.0	954.7	966.6	976.7	979.9	984.5	967.0	968.2	978.3	980.5	984.5	986.5	973.0
2006	965.4	970.3	979.6	989.2	994.0	998.9	980.9	985.1	996.5	996.3	1,001.6	1,005.4	988.6
2007	982.6	986.2	1,001.3	1,007.0	1,013.2	1,017.6	1,008.4	1,012.1	1,014.9	1,013.1	1,018.6	1,015.5	1,007.5
2008	996.1	998.9	1,008.4	1,019.9	1,019.5	1,022.5	1,011.3	1,010.1	1,012.7	1,014.0	1,008.5	1,003.5	1,010.5
2009	976.9	974.3	976.9	982.9	983.7	984.3	970.3	968.7	970.2	969.7	968.4	965.9	974.4
2010	940.7	943.8	951.9	971.1	977.8	978.8	958.9	959.8	970.6	975.8	975.6	975.4	965.0
2011	949.1	952.1	964.7	975.2	980.6	980.8	970.6	970.2	979.6	984.3	988.7	987.9	973.7
2012	967.2	972.4	983.0	991.5	997.4	999.4	983.1	990.7	992.5	998.7	1,001.2	997.6	989.6
2013	976.4	980.2	986.7	998.9	1,005.7	1,010.0	994.5	1,001.1	1,008.5	1,013.3	1,013.3	1,013.1	1,000.1
2014	987.9	993.8	1,004.5	1,018.2	1,026.6	1,030.4	1,016.6	1,021.9	1,025.2	1,034.0	1,036.5	1,037.7	1,019.4
2015	1,014.9	1,021.6	1,029.9	1,040.0	1,048.9	1,053.1	1,043.0	1,042.9	1,048.7	1,053.8	1,055.0	1,051.5	1,041.9
Total Private													
2005	807.6	810.4	820.7	829.5	834.5	841.1	833.5	837.4	835.7	837.0	840.0	842.0	830.8
2006	823.1	823.6	831.9	842.2	846.5	853.9	847.7	853.5	850.6	849.6	854.0	858.8	844.6
2007	837.2	837.1	850.7	854.9	861.8	867.5	865.4	870.0	866.2	863.3	867.4	866.0	859.0
2008	847.9	847.4	855.1	865.7	865.0	869.3	868.6	866.5	861.3	861.2	855.6	850.7	859.5
2009	826.1	819.5	821.9	826.3	826.4	829.6	826.9	826.0	817.8	816.5	815.5	813.5	822.2
2010	791.0	790.9	797.5	814.7	818.8	822.8	821.5	823.5	820.3	825.4	825.0	825.5	814.7
2011	800.9	801.6	811.6	821.4	827.4	829.8	832.0	833.4	831.8	835.8	839.9	839.1	825.4
2012	821.6	823.1	832.5	840.3	845.8	851.7	847.5	851.5	845.2	849.9	852.4	849.2	842.6
2013	831.8	832.0	837.8	847.7	855.0	862.4	860.5	866.0	861.0	866.6	866.7	866.7	854.5
2014	844.4	847.2	856.9	870.2	877.5	883.4	881.9	887.7	878.3	886.6	889.2	891.4	874.6
2015	869.1	873.5	880.4	890.0	899.1	905.8	907.7	906.6	900.2	905.2	905.8	903.4	895.6
Goods Producing													
2005	127.2	128.4	132.0	133.7	135.2	136.9	133.2	136.5	135.6	135.4	135.4	134.3	133.7
2006	131.1	131.4	134.4	135.5	136.4	139.3	134.9	138.2	135.2	134.2	135.7	135.5	135.2
2007	130.3	127.8	132.4	132.6	133.9	135.2	133.1	135.2	134.7	131.8	132.8	130.2	132.5
2008	126.2	125.4	128.3	129.7	128.0	129.9	130.9	129.7	128.9	128.3	126.3	123.0	127.9
2009	116.4	113.7	114.8	115.3	114.2	115.8	115.6	114.3	112.7	112.4	110.9	107.7	113.7
2010	103.3	102.9	105.1	108.5	108.9	110.6	109.7	111.7	111.3	111.4	110.2	108.8	108.5
2011	102.4	101.6	104.6	107.0	107.9	109.2	109.2	107.3	108.9	108.6	108.6	107.7	106.9
2012	104.5	104.0	106.4	107.5	107.7	109.6	109.0	109.8	109.7	109.2	108.8	106.5	107.7
2013	105.1	104.6	106.7	108.3	110.5	112.4	110.2	112.3	112.9	112.9	112.7	111.1	110.0
2014	106.5	109.1	111.7	114.3	114.9	117.1	116.2	117.9	117.0	117.7	118.0	118.1	114.9
2015	113.0	115.5	117.9	116.9	120.3	121.6	120.9	120.6	121.5	122.5	122.3	122.4	119.6
Service-Providing													
2005	821.8	826.3	834.6	843.0	844.7	847.6	833.8	831.7	842.7	845.1	849.1	852.2	839.4
2006	834.3	838.9	845.2	853.7	857.6	859.6	846.0	846.9	861.3	862.1	865.9	869.9	853.5
2007	852.3	858.4	868.9	874.4	879.3	882.4	875.3	876.9	880.2	881.3	885.8	885.3	875.0
2008	869.9	873.5	880.1	890.2	891.5	892.6	880.4	880.4	883.8	885.7	882.2	880.5	882.6
2009	860.5	860.6	862.1	867.6	869.5	868.5	854.7	854.4	857.5	857.3	857.5	858.2	860.7
2010	837.4	840.9	846.8	862.6	868.9	868.2	849.2	848.1	859.3	864.4	865.4	866.6	856.5
2011	846.7	850.5	860.1	868.2	872.7	871.6	861.4	862.9	870.7	875.7	880.1	880.2	866.7
2012	862.7	868.4	876.6	884.0	889.7	889.8	874.1	880.9	882.8	889.5	892.4	891.1	881.8
2013	871.3	875.6	880.0	890.6	895.2	897.6	884.3	888.8	895.6	900.4	900.6	902.0	890.2
2014	881.4	884.7	892.8	903.9	911.7	913.3	900.4	904.0	908.2	916.3	918.5	919.6	904.6
2015	901.9	906.1	912.0	923.1	928.6	931.5	922.1	922.3	927.2	931.3	932.7	929.1	922.3
Mining, Logging, and Construction													
2005	45.8	46.9	49.9	51.6	53.2	54.7	55.5	55.3	54.7	54.4	53.8	52.6	52.4
2006	50.9	51.4	53.0	54.1	54.7	56.5	55.6	55.6	55.3	54.1	53.5	52.9	54.0
2007	49.9	47.5	51.5	52.2	53.5	54.6	55.2	54.7	54.5	53.7	53.2	50.9	52.6
2008	47.4	46.6	49.1	50.3	51.6	52.2	52.1	51.8	50.8	50.7	49.5	46.8	49.9
2009	42.6	42.3	43.1	43.6	44.8	45.1	45.2	43.7	42.4	41.9	41.0	38.4	42.8
2010	33.8	33.5	35.7	38.8	38.8	40.1	40.8	40.8	40.2	40.4	39.5	37.9	38.4
2011	33.1	32.4	35.1	37.4	38.1	38.9	39.4	39.2	38.9	38.7	38.6	37.6	37.3
2012	35.3	34.8	36.7	38.0	39.4	40.4	40.5	40.5	40.2	40.0	39.6	39.1	38.7
2013	36.6	37.2	37.9	39.7	41.6	42.8	43.7	43.4	43.0	43.2	42.6	41.0	41.1
2014	39.0	38.4	41.0	42.6	43.9	44.7	45.9	45.1	44.3	44.5	44.4	44.4	43.2
2015	42.1	42.3	43.5	45.3	45.6	46.3	47.1	47.0	46.5	47.2	46.4	46.2	45.5

Employment by Industry: Kansas City, MO-KS, 2005–2015—*Continued*

(Numbers in thousands, not seasonally adjusted)

Industry and year	January	February	March	April	May	June	July	August	September	October	November	December	Annual average
Manufacturing													
2005	81.4	81.5	82.1	82.1	82.0	82.2	77.7	81.2	80.9	81.0	81.6	81.7	81.3
2006	80.2	80.0	81.4	81.4	81.7	82.8	79.3	82.6	79.9	80.1	82.2	82.6	81.2
2007	80.4	80.3	80.9	80.4	80.4	80.6	77.9	80.5	80.2	78.1	79.6	79.3	79.9
2008	78.8	78.8	79.2	79.4	76.4	77.7	78.8	77.9	78.1	77.6	76.8	76.2	78.0
2009	73.8	71.4	71.7	71.7	69.4	70.7	70.4	70.6	70.3	70.5	69.9	69.3	70.8
2010	69.5	69.4	69.4	69.7	70.1	70.5	68.9	70.9	71.1	71.0	70.7	70.9	70.2
2011	69.3	69.2	69.5	69.6	69.8	70.3	69.8	68.1	70.0	69.9	70.0	70.1	69.6
2012	69.2	69.2	69.7	69.5	68.3	69.2	68.5	69.3	69.5	69.2	69.2	67.4	69.0
2013	68.5	67.4	68.8	68.6	68.9	69.6	66.5	68.9	69.9	69.7	70.1	70.1	68.9
2014	67.5	70.7	70.7	71.7	71.0	72.4	70.3	72.8	72.7	73.2	73.6	73.7	71.7
2015	70.9	73.2	74.4	71.6	74.7	75.3	73.8	73.6	75.0	75.3	75.9	76.2	74.2
Trade, Transportation, and Utilities													
2005	199.7	198.2	199.4	199.6	200.7	200.6	198.5	198.8	199.3	201.3	205.2	207.5	200.7
2006	200.5	199.0	200.1	200.5	201.4	201.4	199.6	200.8	201.9	202.6	206.3	209.1	201.9
2007	201.8	200.9	202.9	203.0	203.9	203.8	203.6	204.3	204.7	205.3	209.4	210.9	204.5
2008	202.9	201.3	201.5	202.6	203.0	202.5	202.1	201.5	201.0	203.4	204.6	204.9	202.6
2009	196.7	194.0	193.4	193.0	192.9	192.9	191.7	191.8	190.7	191.8	194.3	194.3	193.1
2010	187.5	186.0	186.7	189.2	190.7	191.3	190.8	191.2	190.6	192.8	195.8	196.9	190.8
2011	190.0	188.9	190.3	192.3	193.4	192.9	193.0	193.8	193.3	194.8	198.6	199.7	193.4
2012	194.0	192.0	193.1	194.0	195.6	195.9	194.4	194.9	194.4	195.7	199.6	200.0	195.3
2013	193.5	192.2	192.7	194.5	195.4	196.5	196.7	197.5	196.7	199.2	203.2	204.5	196.9
2014	198.1	196.0	198.5	200.0	201.5	202.3	202.1	203.0	201.3	203.5	207.1	209.0	201.9
2015	203.0	201.6	202.2	204.1	206.3	207.6	207.1	206.8	205.9	208.0	210.9	211.8	206.3
Wholesale Trade													
2005	47.9	48.0	48.3	49.1	49.2	49.4	49.1	49.2	49.0	48.8	49.1	49.2	48.9
2006	48.6	48.6	48.9	48.5	48.9	49.2	49.0	49.3	49.3	49.7	49.8	50.5	49.2
2007	50.0	50.2	50.9	50.5	50.5	50.9	51.1	51.3	51.3	51.6	51.6	51.7	51.0
2008	51.3	51.3	51.1	51.5	51.4	51.4	51.7	51.5	51.1	52.2	51.8	51.5	51.5
2009	50.7	50.2	49.8	49.2	48.6	48.4	48.1	47.6	47.2	47.3	47.1	46.8	48.4
2010	46.4	46.4	46.5	47.8	47.9	48.0	47.9	47.7	47.4	47.6	47.5	47.4	47.4
2011	46.8	46.9	47.0	47.4	47.9	47.8	48.0	48.0	47.9	47.6	47.7	48.0	47.6
2012	47.9	47.9	48.0	48.2	48.4	48.7	48.5	48.6	48.3	48.2	48.2	48.3	48.3
2013	47.7	48.0	47.8	48.0	48.1	48.3	49.3	49.3	49.0	49.4	49.5	49.6	48.7
2014	49.2	49.1	50.0	49.9	50.2	50.5	50.5	50.4	50.1	50.4	50.2	50.4	50.1
2015	50.3	50.3	50.2	50.6	50.9	51.3	51.2	51.1	50.7	51.0	51.3	50.7	50.8
Retail Trade													
2005	109.2	107.4	108.0	107.7	108.2	108.3	107.8	107.1	106.9	108.5	111.9	113.5	108.7
2006	107.7	106.4	107.1	107.4	107.8	108.0	107.1	107.0	107.1	107.3	110.7	112.1	108.0
2007	106.3	105.4	106.5	106.9	107.6	107.8	107.4	107.2	106.6	107.5	111.1	112.4	107.7
2008	106.5	104.4	105.1	105.4	105.9	106.2	105.8	105.3	104.4	105.4	107.0	107.6	105.8
2009	102.3	100.5	100.9	101.0	101.6	102.2	101.9	102.0	101.3	102.2	104.9	105.2	102.2
2010	100.0	98.7	99.2	100.8	101.9	102.4	102.0	102.1	101.2	102.6	105.5	106.4	101.9
2011	101.3	100.0	101.1	102.5	103.1	103.3	103.3	103.5	102.6	103.9	107.4	107.8	103.3
2012	103.0	101.4	102.4	102.8	104.0	104.0	103.8	103.3	103.1	103.9	107.6	107.9	103.9
2013	102.7	101.2	101.9	103.2	103.8	104.8	104.7	104.6	104.0	105.5	108.7	110.0	104.6
2014	104.8	102.9	104.1	105.4	106.2	107.0	107.2	107.0	105.8	107.2	110.6	111.7	106.7
2015	106.4	105.1	105.8	107.2	108.7	110.0	109.8	109.2	108.0	109.8	112.0	112.5	108.7
Transportation and Utilities													
2005	42.6	42.8	43.1	42.8	43.3	42.9	41.6	42.5	43.4	44.0	44.2	44.8	43.2
2006	44.2	44.0	44.1	44.6	44.7	44.2	43.5	44.5	45.5	45.6	45.8	46.5	44.8
2007	45.5	45.3	45.5	45.6	45.8	45.1	45.1	45.8	46.8	46.2	46.7	46.8	45.9
2008	45.1	45.6	45.3	45.7	45.7	44.9	44.6	44.7	45.5	45.8	45.8	45.8	45.4
2009	43.7	43.3	42.7	42.8	42.7	42.3	41.7	42.2	42.2	42.3	42.3	42.3	42.5
2010	41.1	40.9	41.0	40.6	40.9	40.9	40.9	41.4	42.0	42.6	42.8	43.1	41.5
2011	41.9	42.0	42.2	42.4	42.4	41.8	41.7	42.3	42.8	43.3	43.5	43.9	42.5
2012	43.1	42.7	42.7	43.0	43.2	43.2	42.1	43.0	43.0	43.6	43.8	43.8	43.1
2013	43.1	43.0	43.0	43.3	43.5	43.4	42.7	43.6	43.7	44.3	45.0	44.9	43.6
2014	44.1	44.0	44.4	44.7	45.1	44.8	44.4	45.6	45.4	45.9	46.3	46.9	45.1
2015	46.3	46.2	46.2	46.3	46.7	46.3	46.1	46.5	47.2	47.2	47.6	48.6	46.8

Employment by Industry: Kansas City, MO-KS, 2005–2015—*Continued*

(Numbers in thousands, not seasonally adjusted)

Industry and year	January	February	March	April	May	June	July	August	September	October	November	December	Annual average
Information													
2005	42.1	41.9	41.9	41.7	41.6	41.8	41.4	40.9	40.5	39.6	39.4	39.2	41.0
2006	39.3	39.1	39.4	40.6	40.6	41.0	40.7	40.7	40.6	39.6	39.7	40.1	40.1
2007	40.0	39.9	39.8	39.7	40.0	40.0	40.4	40.2	39.9	40.3	40.3	40.4	40.1
2008	40.4	40.0	40.0	39.2	39.3	39.2	39.1	38.8	38.0	37.5	37.0	36.7	38.8
2009	36.5	36.1	35.8	35.8	35.3	34.9	34.6	34.0	33.2	30.8	30.3	30.3	34.0
2010	28.4	27.9	27.9	28.7	28.5	28.0	27.4	27.0	26.6	26.4	26.2	25.8	27.4
2011	24.7	24.6	24.5	24.6	24.6	24.6	24.6	24.6	24.6	24.5	24.6	24.8	24.6
2012	24.7	24.6	24.6	24.7	24.7	24.8	24.6	24.8	24.4	24.7	24.7	24.8	24.7
2013	24.4	24.5	24.3	24.3	24.4	24.6	24.7	24.7	24.3	24.3	24.4	24.2	24.4
2014	24.2	24.1	23.9	23.3	23.1	23.1	22.8	22.4	21.8	21.5	21.4	21.3	22.7
2015	21.0	20.8	20.9	20.7	20.7	20.7	20.8	20.4	20.0	19.8	19.7	19.5	20.4
Financial Activities													
2005	69.8	69.9	70.0	70.5	70.7	71.1	71.5	71.3	71.1	71.3	71.4	71.9	70.9
2006	71.8	72.0	72.0	72.3	72.8	73.2	73.9	73.7	73.4	72.9	73.2	73.7	72.9
2007	73.3	73.6	74.3	73.5	73.6	74.2	74.9	74.7	74.1	73.8	73.8	74.0	74.0
2008	73.0	73.3	73.2	73.6	73.6	73.3	73.5	73.1	72.1	71.7	71.1	70.7	72.7
2009	70.1	69.8	70.1	70.8	70.8	71.2	71.8	71.8	70.6	70.7	70.8	70.7	70.8
2010	70.7	70.9	70.9	71.6	71.8	71.9	71.7	71.3	70.7	71.0	70.9	71.0	71.2
2011	70.3	70.5	70.5	70.9	71.5	71.6	71.5	71.5	71.1	72.7	72.7	72.6	71.5
2012	73.0	73.5	73.8	73.9	73.8	74.1	74.4	74.4	73.6	73.9	73.9	73.7	73.8
2013	74.1	74.3	73.9	73.6	73.7	74.3	74.6	74.2	73.5	73.0	73.1	72.9	73.8
2014	72.0	72.2	72.5	73.1	73.5	73.8	74.1	74.4	73.8	74.1	74.2	74.4	73.5
2015	74.1	74.4	74.7	74.8	75.1	75.7	76.4	76.5	75.7	75.2	75.4	74.9	75.2
Professional and Business Services													
2005	132.3	134.2	136.6	138.8	138.6	140.5	140.6	141.5	141.8	142.1	143.2	144.4	139.6
2006	138.4	140.2	141.8	143.8	143.2	144.8	144.6	145.6	146.1	148.0	148.6	149.6	144.6
2007	146.0	147.1	149.2	149.6	151.0	152.5	152.5	154.0	154.0	154.4	155.4	155.6	151.8
2008	151.8	152.5	154.1	156.6	154.3	155.7	155.6	155.4	155.5	153.7	153.2	152.7	154.3
2009	149.7	148.8	148.6	148.8	147.5	147.5	146.8	146.5	145.3	145.4	146.4	147.6	147.4
2010	145.1	145.2	146.7	153.0	152.3	152.7	153.3	153.3	152.6	154.7	154.8	156.1	151.7
2011	152.8	154.0	155.9	158.2	158.1	158.5	159.2	160.0	160.2	160.8	162.3	161.8	158.5
2012	158.7	160.1	162.2	164.7	165.0	166.9	166.8	167.2	167.5	170.5	170.3	169.7	165.8
2013	164.9	166.3	168.0	170.6	170.2	172.3	172.1	173.6	172.8	174.3	174.4	175.1	171.2
2014	169.4	170.7	171.7	174.9	174.8	177.3	178.5	180.1	178.4	181.3	182.9	183.8	177.0
2015	176.6	178.0	179.2	182.1	182.6	184.6	185.7	185.7	185.1	185.4	186.3	183.3	182.9
Education and Health Services													
2005	108.8	109.5	109.6	110.6	111.1	110.8	110.0	109.9	111.0	112.1	112.3	112.4	110.7
2006	110.8	111.9	111.9	113.3	113.5	113.3	113.4	113.4	115.0	115.6	116.0	116.4	113.7
2007	114.6	115.9	116.5	117.3	117.5	117.5	117.8	118.0	118.7	119.8	120.1	119.9	117.8
2008	119.7	121.2	121.4	123.1	123.1	123.2	123.1	122.9	123.3	125.3	125.6	125.6	123.1
2009	123.5	124.3	124.6	125.9	126.0	125.9	126.8	126.5	127.4	128.8	129.2	129.3	126.5
2010	127.7	128.8	128.9	127.9	128.3	128.2	128.8	128.8	129.9	131.3	131.7	132.2	129.4
2011	130.1	131.5	132.0	131.6	131.8	130.8	131.2	132.4	133.4	135.1	135.7	135.9	132.6
2012	132.9	134.1	134.4	134.4	135.1	134.6	133.4	134.5	134.2	135.8	136.5	137.1	134.8
2013	135.0	135.8	135.1	136.9	137.9	136.7	136.5	137.4	137.3	140.2	140.4	140.3	137.5
2014	138.3	139.3	138.9	141.9	142.8	142.1	141.8	142.1	142.4	144.3	144.8	144.7	142.0
2015	143.6	144.9	144.3	146.2	146.3	145.6	146.9	146.6	146.5	148.8	148.1	149.7	146.5
Leisure and Hospitality													
2005	85.7	86.0	88.6	92.5	94.6	96.9	95.5	95.8	94.0	93.2	91.2	90.4	92.0
2006	88.0	88.0	90.3	94.0	96.1	98.1	97.8	98.4	96.1	94.5	92.3	92.1	93.8
2007	89.1	89.5	93.0	95.3	97.8	99.6	98.1	98.8	95.9	94.0	91.9	91.4	94.5
2008	89.8	89.5	92.2	96.4	99.0	100.6	99.4	100.4	97.9	96.7	93.3	92.9	95.7
2009	89.0	88.6	90.6	92.4	95.3	96.8	95.1	96.9	94.2	92.6	89.9	90.0	92.6
2010	85.0	85.8	88.0	92.1	94.5	96.1	95.6	96.2	95.0	93.9	91.5	90.8	92.0
2011	86.9	86.9	89.9	92.7	95.9	97.8	98.8	99.4	96.2	95.0	93.2	92.4	93.8
2012	90.2	91.1	94.1	97.2	100.0	102.1	101.4	102.6	98.5	97.4	96.1	94.9	97.1
2013	92.7	92.3	95.0	97.7	100.9	103.4	103.5	103.9	101.4	100.8	96.7	96.7	98.8
2014	94.7	94.5	97.9	101.7	105.5	106.5	105.1	106.7	102.7	103.1	100.0	99.3	101.5
2015	97.1	97.6	100.3	103.9	106.4	108.5	108.2	108.3	104.2	104.2	102.0	100.6	103.4

Employment by Industry: Kansas City, MO-KS, 2005–2015—*Continued*

(Numbers in thousands, not seasonally adjusted)

Industry and year	January	February	March	April	May	June	July	August	September	October	November	December	Annual average
Other Services													
2005	42.0	42.3	42.6	42.1	42.0	42.5	42.8	42.7	42.4	42.0	41.9	41.9	42.3
2006	43.2	42.0	42.0	42.2	42.5	42.8	42.8	42.7	42.3	42.2	42.2	42.3	42.4
2007	42.1	42.4	42.6	43.9	44.1	44.7	45.0	44.8	44.2	43.9	43.7	43.6	43.8
2008	44.1	44.2	44.4	44.5	44.7	44.9	44.9	44.7	44.6	44.6	44.5	44.2	44.5
2009	44.2	44.2	44.0	44.3	44.4	44.6	44.5	44.2	43.7	44.0	43.7	43.6	44.1
2010	43.3	43.4	43.3	43.7	43.8	44.0	44.2	44.0	43.6	43.9	43.9	43.9	43.8
2011	43.7	43.6	43.9	44.1	44.2	44.4	44.5	44.4	44.1	44.3	44.2	44.2	44.1
2012	43.6	43.7	43.9	43.9	43.9	43.7	43.5	43.3	42.9	42.7	42.5	42.5	43.3
2013	42.1	42.0	42.1	41.8	42.0	42.2	42.2	42.4	42.1	41.9	41.8	41.9	42.0
2014	41.2	41.3	41.8	41.0	41.4	41.2	41.3	41.1	40.9	41.1	40.8	40.8	41.2
2015	40.7	40.7	40.9	41.3	41.4	41.5	41.7	41.7	41.3	41.3	41.1	41.2	41.2
Government													
2005	141.4	144.3	145.9	147.2	145.4	143.4	133.5	130.8	142.6	143.5	144.5	144.5	142.3
2006	142.3	146.7	147.7	147.0	147.5	145.0	133.2	131.6	145.9	146.7	147.6	146.6	144.0
2007	145.4	149.1	150.6	152.1	151.4	150.1	143.0	142.1	148.7	149.8	151.2	149.5	148.6
2008	148.2	151.5	153.3	154.2	154.5	153.2	142.7	143.6	151.4	152.8	152.9	152.8	150.9
2009	150.8	154.8	155.0	156.6	157.3	154.7	143.4	142.7	152.4	153.2	152.9	152.4	152.2
2010	149.7	152.9	154.4	156.4	159.0	156.0	137.4	136.3	150.3	150.4	150.6	149.9	150.3
2011	148.2	150.5	153.1	153.8	153.2	151.0	138.6	136.8	147.8	148.5	148.8	148.8	148.3
2012	145.6	149.3	150.5	151.2	151.6	147.7	135.6	139.2	147.3	148.8	148.8	148.4	147.0
2013	144.6	148.2	148.9	151.2	150.7	147.6	134.0	135.1	147.5	146.7	146.6	146.4	145.6
2014	143.5	146.6	147.6	148.0	149.1	147.0	134.7	134.2	146.9	147.4	147.3	146.3	144.9
2015	145.8	148.1	149.5	150.0	149.8	147.3	135.3	136.3	148.5	148.6	149.2	148.1	146.4

Employment by Industry: Cleveland-Elyria, OH, 2005–2015

(Numbers in thousands, not seasonally adjusted)

Industry and year	January	February	March	April	May	June	July	August	September	October	November	December	Annual average
Total Nonfarm													
2005	1,044.9	1,051.2	1,058.1	1,068.6	1,075.5	1,082.0	1,075.4	1,077.2	1,079.8	1,082.7	1,085.3	1,085.3	1,072.2
2006	1,053.6	1,057.6	1,065.4	1,074.8	1,082.1	1,088.9	1,076.9	1,078.4	1,079.1	1,080.2	1,081.1	1,081.3	1,075.0
2007	1,052.8	1,052.6	1,061.5	1,070.4	1,080.2	1,090.2	1,075.6	1,076.9	1,073.8	1,076.6	1,079.4	1,077.4	1,072.3
2008	1,049.9	1,050.4	1,048.2	1,060.9	1,072.8	1,075.8	1,064.3	1,062.6	1,060.8	1,058.9	1,052.6	1,044.9	1,058.5
2009	1,009.3	1,006.1	1,003.4	1,004.9	1,008.6	1,006.7	995.9	992.4	994.1	995.8	997.2	994.7	1,000.8
2010	969.1	969.8	973.0	986.3	998.5	1,000.1	996.2	995.7	995.4	1,002.2	1,003.4	1,001.4	990.9
2011	971.5	977.4	981.9	998.7	1,006.2	1,008.0	1,009.0	1,011.7	1,007.2	1,009.9	1,016.6	1,015.2	1,001.1
2012	987.1	994.4	1,002.9	1,016.3	1,027.3	1,033.1	1,025.9	1,025.4	1,023.7	1,031.3	1,034.8	1,032.0	1,019.5
2013	1,002.2	1,004.8	1,009.9	1,024.0	1,037.2	1,042.7	1,033.4	1,039.9	1,032.8	1,040.5	1,044.6	1,043.5	1,029.6
2014	1,010.9	1,012.1	1,017.6	1,031.5	1,044.9	1,048.9	1,039.7	1,044.6	1,039.3	1,048.0	1,050.5	1,051.3	1,036.6
2015	1,018.6	1,022.1	1,024.5	1,040.5	1,055.5	1,058.1	1,052.0	1,053.9	1,044.4	1,056.9	1,058.0	1,058.1	1,045.2
Total Private													
2005	905.8	908.4	914.7	924.9	931.1	938.8	940.7	943.7	940.9	940.5	943.0	942.7	931.3
2006	914.8	915.8	922.3	931.7	938.1	946.6	943.0	945.3	940.3	938.2	937.9	938.2	934.4
2007	913.0	909.3	916.8	925.2	934.3	942.9	936.1	938.6	933.7	932.9	935.1	934.1	929.3
2008	908.6	906.2	904.8	916.9	926.3	928.6	924.8	924.7	920.6	915.3	909.0	902.6	915.7
2009	868.9	863.4	860.8	861.8	864.5	863.9	860.0	857.9	855.9	854.7	855.9	854.8	860.2
2010	831.4	829.4	833.1	845.8	853.9	859.1	861.7	863.6	860.4	863.3	864.4	863.3	852.5
2011	838.9	840.4	844.4	862.0	868.1	870.7	877.5	881.6	873.9	875.1	880.4	879.3	865.9
2012	855.2	858.6	866.5	879.6	889.4	896.4	894.3	895.2	889.6	895.8	899.3	897.3	884.8
2013	868.9	870.7	876.2	889.4	900.8	908.1	904.8	909.6	900.4	906.2	909.6	908.8	896.1
2014	878.9	878.6	884.1	897.1	908.4	913.8	910.3	913.6	906.0	912.4	914.8	916.2	902.9
2015	885.8	888.0	891.8	905.3	918.0	921.5	921.9	921.5	910.7	921.3	921.0	921.2	910.7
Goods Producing													
2005	185.8	185.4	187.1	191.6	193.4	195.9	195.3	195.8	195.4	194.7	194.1	191.2	192.1
2006	185.5	184.3	185.3	189.0	190.1	193.0	192.6	192.8	191.9	190.9	188.7	184.7	189.1
2007	180.8	178.8	181.1	182.9	186.4	188.5	184.2	186.8	185.5	184.8	184.4	181.9	183.8
2008	176.1	175.3	174.9	177.8	180.3	181.7	181.5	179.6	179.4	178.1	173.4	167.8	177.2
2009	158.6	156.9	154.6	152.9	151.9	151.5	149.8	149.5	149.4	148.6	149.1	147.1	151.7
2010	142.1	141.6	143.1	145.1	148.4	150.9	150.6	151.8	151.2	151.9	151.1	149.0	148.1
2011	145.2	145.2	146.4	149.7	152.0	152.9	156.3	158.4	156.2	156.8	158.4	157.3	152.9
2012	150.4	151.6	153.4	156.1	158.1	160.2	159.4	160.0	159.4	158.5	159.5	158.5	157.1
2013	153.6	153.4	154.3	156.4	158.8	160.6	158.4	161.6	160.8	160.9	161.6	158.7	158.3
2014	154.1	153.6	155.1	157.6	160.2	162.4	161.0	163.2	162.6	163.0	162.9	161.6	159.8
2015	156.3	156.2	157.3	160.1	162.1	163.5	163.3	163.0	161.2	162.3	162.1	159.0	160.5
Service-Providing													
2005	859.1	865.8	871.0	877.0	882.1	886.1	880.1	881.4	884.4	888.0	891.2	894.1	880.0
2006	868.1	873.3	880.1	885.8	892.0	895.9	884.3	885.6	887.2	889.3	892.4	896.6	885.9
2007	872.0	873.8	880.4	887.5	893.8	901.7	891.4	890.1	888.3	891.8	895.0	895.5	888.4
2008	873.8	875.1	873.3	883.1	892.5	894.1	882.8	883.0	881.4	880.8	879.2	877.1	881.4
2009	850.7	849.2	848.8	852.0	856.7	855.2	846.1	842.9	844.7	847.2	848.1	847.6	849.1
2010	827.0	828.2	829.9	841.2	850.1	849.2	845.6	843.9	844.2	850.3	852.3	852.4	842.9
2011	826.3	832.2	835.5	849.0	854.2	855.1	852.7	853.3	851.0	853.1	858.2	857.9	848.2
2012	836.7	842.8	849.5	860.2	869.2	872.9	866.5	865.4	864.3	872.8	875.3	873.5	862.4
2013	848.6	851.4	855.6	867.6	878.4	882.1	875.0	878.3	872.0	879.6	883.0	884.8	871.4
2014	856.8	858.5	862.5	873.9	884.7	886.5	878.7	881.4	876.7	885.0	887.6	889.7	876.8
2015	862.3	865.9	867.2	880.4	893.4	894.6	888.9	890.9	883.2	894.6	895.9	899.1	884.7
Mining, Logging, and Construction													
2005	37.1	37.0	37.8	42.2	44.0	45.9	46.4	46.5	45.9	45.7	44.5	41.5	42.9
2006	37.0	36.5	37.5	40.7	42.5	43.7	44.7	44.8	44.3	44.0	43.0	40.7	41.6
2007	36.6	34.9	36.6	39.6	43.0	44.4	43.9	44.2	43.5	43.3	42.4	39.9	41.0
2008	35.1	34.4	34.5	37.1	39.7	40.9	42.0	41.9	40.9	40.6	38.5	35.6	38.4
2009	30.6	29.9	30.6	31.9	34.0	35.2	35.8	35.5	34.9	34.9	33.6	31.6	33.2
2010	27.3	26.6	27.9	30.2	31.9	33.4	34.7	34.6	34.1	34.2	33.3	30.8	31.6
2011	27.6	27.2	28.1	30.3	32.1	33.6	35.8	36.3	36.2	36.1	35.7	34.4	32.8
2012	30.0	29.3	30.4	32.6	34.4	35.4	36.1	35.7	35.0	35.5	35.2	33.9	33.6
2013	30.0	29.7	30.4	32.4	34.7	35.8	36.2	36.9	36.9	38.0	37.2	34.1	34.4
2014	30.3	30.2	31.5	33.9	36.1	37.4	38.0	38.4	38.1	38.4	37.7	35.9	35.5
2015	31.7	31.3	32.3	35.2	36.9	37.8	38.3	38.3	37.6	37.8	37.7	34.8	35.8

Employment by Industry: Cleveland-Elyria, OH, 2005–2015—*Continued*

(Numbers in thousands, not seasonally adjusted)

Industry and year	January	February	March	April	May	June	July	August	September	October	November	December	Annual average
Manufacturing													
2005	148.7	148.4	149.3	149.4	149.4	150.0	148.9	149.3	149.5	149.0	149.6	149.7	149.3
2006	148.5	147.8	147.8	148.3	147.6	149.3	147.9	148.0	147.6	146.9	145.7	144.0	147.5
2007	144.2	143.9	144.5	143.3	143.4	144.1	140.3	142.6	142.0	141.5	142.0	142.0	142.8
2008	141.0	140.9	140.4	140.7	140.6	140.8	139.5	137.7	138.5	137.5	134.9	132.2	138.7
2009	128.0	127.0	124.0	121.0	117.9	116.3	114.0	114.0	114.5	113.7	115.5	115.5	118.5
2010	114.8	115.0	115.2	114.9	116.5	117.5	115.9	117.2	117.1	117.7	117.8	118.2	116.5
2011	117.6	118.0	118.3	119.4	119.9	119.3	120.5	122.1	120.0	120.7	122.7	122.9	120.1
2012	120.4	122.3	123.0	123.5	123.7	124.8	123.3	124.3	124.4	123.0	124.3	124.6	123.5
2013	123.6	123.7	123.9	124.0	124.1	124.8	122.2	124.7	123.9	122.9	124.4	124.6	123.9
2014	123.8	123.4	123.6	123.7	124.1	125.0	123.0	124.8	124.5	124.6	125.2	125.7	124.3
2015	124.6	124.9	125.0	124.9	125.2	125.7	125.0	124.7	123.6	124.5	124.4	124.2	124.7
Trade, Transportation, and Utilities													
2005	197.0	195.5	196.3	196.5	198.0	198.8	199.1	199.0	197.7	198.7	202.0	205.2	198.7
2006	197.6	196.0	197.1	198.5	199.6	200.4	198.9	199.3	198.2	199.3	203.1	206.5	199.5
2007	198.2	195.4	196.8	197.4	198.6	199.8	199.0	198.1	196.6	197.6	201.3	204.0	198.6
2008	196.5	193.2	192.6	193.9	195.4	195.4	194.9	195.2	192.9	192.7	193.9	195.7	194.4
2009	185.7	182.9	182.2	180.7	181.3	181.4	179.9	179.0	177.1	177.6	179.6	181.5	180.7
2010	174.3	172.3	172.6	173.6	175.0	176.4	176.8	177.3	175.5	176.9	179.5	182.1	176.0
2011	174.0	172.9	173.5	175.7	176.7	177.7	177.7	178.3	176.4	178.3	182.0	184.6	177.3
2012	177.8	176.4	177.8	179.0	181.2	181.8	181.2	180.7	179.7	181.5	185.4	187.1	180.8
2013	179.1	177.2	177.8	179.5	181.9	182.8	181.7	182.0	180.4	182.1	186.5	188.5	181.6
2014	180.3	178.8	178.8	180.7	183.1	183.9	182.4	182.9	180.7	182.7	186.8	189.2	182.5
2015	181.7	179.6	180.3	181.7	184.0	184.8	184.3	184.7	182.6	184.1	187.6	187.8	183.6
Wholesale Trade													
2005	54.6	54.6	54.8	54.9	55.0	55.5	55.7	55.8	55.6	55.3	55.4	55.8	55.3
2006	55.5	55.6	55.9	56.2	56.3	56.6	56.5	56.3	56.1	55.8	55.9	56.2	56.1
2007	55.4	55.4	55.5	55.3	55.3	55.4	55.2	54.8	54.1	53.9	53.8	53.8	54.8
2008	53.7	53.5	53.3	53.7	53.9	53.8	53.5	53.3	52.7	52.5	52.0	51.5	53.1
2009	50.6	50.0	49.5	48.9	48.7	48.4	48.0	47.7	47.2	47.1	46.9	46.6	48.3
2010	46.2	46.1	46.0	46.2	46.3	46.5	47.1	47.1	46.8	46.8	46.7	46.8	46.6
2011	47.1	47.1	47.2	47.6	47.8	48.1	48.4	48.4	47.9	48.3	48.5	48.8	47.9
2012	48.6	48.6	48.8	49.1	49.5	49.8	49.8	49.6	49.3	49.5	49.6	49.7	49.3
2013	48.9	48.8	49.0	49.2	49.5	49.8	49.5	49.5	49.2	49.9	50.1	50.3	49.5
2014	49.6	49.6	49.7	49.8	50.4	50.7	50.7	50.8	50.4	50.7	50.9	51.2	50.4
2015	50.4	50.4	50.7	50.6	51.0	51.3	51.5	51.5	50.9	51.2	51.7	52.0	51.1
Retail Trade													
2005	110.2	108.5	108.9	109.2	110.3	110.7	110.5	110.3	109.2	110.1	113.1	115.5	110.5
2006	109.0	107.4	108.0	108.7	109.6	109.9	108.9	109.1	107.8	109.3	112.8	115.4	109.7
2007	108.9	106.3	107.3	107.5	109.0	110.0	109.8	109.2	108.1	109.1	112.8	115.2	109.4
2008	108.9	106.1	105.9	106.4	107.4	107.9	107.8	108.1	106.6	106.8	108.7	110.6	107.6
2009	103.1	100.9	101.1	100.9	101.9	102.4	101.8	101.4	100.1	100.7	103.2	105.0	101.9
2010	99.1	97.3	97.7	98.4	99.6	100.5	100.4	100.7	99.3	100.6	103.4	105.5	100.2
2011	98.3	97.3	97.7	99.2	99.8	100.4	100.3	100.6	99.1	100.4	103.9	105.6	100.2
2012	100.2	98.7	99.8	100.4	101.8	102.0	101.4	100.8	100.1	101.6	104.9	106.0	101.5
2013	100.4	98.7	99.2	100.2	101.9	102.4	102.1	102.1	100.7	101.7	105.3	106.5	101.8
2014	100.3	99.0	99.1	100.4	101.8	102.3	101.4	101.6	99.9	101.4	104.7	105.9	101.5
2015	100.5	98.9	99.4	100.5	102.0	102.5	101.9	102.1	100.6	101.8	104.5	104.8	101.6
Transportation and Utilities													
2005	32.2	32.4	32.6	32.4	32.7	32.6	32.9	32.9	32.9	33.3	33.5	33.9	32.9
2006	33.1	33.0	33.2	33.6	33.7	33.9	33.5	33.9	34.3	34.2	34.4	34.9	33.8
2007	33.9	33.7	34.0	34.6	34.3	34.4	34.0	34.1	34.4	34.6	34.7	35.0	34.3
2008	33.9	33.6	33.4	33.8	34.1	33.7	33.6	33.8	33.6	33.4	33.2	33.6	33.6
2009	32.0	32.0	31.6	30.9	30.7	30.6	30.1	29.9	29.8	29.8	29.5	29.9	30.6
2010	29.0	28.9	28.9	29.0	29.1	29.4	29.3	29.5	29.4	29.5	29.4	29.8	29.3
2011	28.6	28.5	28.6	28.9	29.1	29.2	29.1	29.3	29.4	29.6	29.6	30.2	29.2
2012	29.0	29.1	29.2	29.5	29.9	30.0	30.0	30.3	30.3	30.4	30.9	31.4	30.0
2013	29.8	29.7	29.6	30.1	30.5	30.6	30.1	30.4	30.5	30.5	31.1	31.7	30.4
2014	30.4	30.2	30.0	30.5	30.9	30.9	30.3	30.5	30.4	30.6	31.2	32.1	30.7
2015	30.8	30.3	30.2	30.6	31.0	31.0	30.9	31.1	31.1	31.1	31.4	31.0	30.9

Employment by Industry: Cleveland-Elyria, OH, 2005–2015—*Continued*

(Numbers in thousands, not seasonally adjusted)

Industry and year	January	February	March	April	May	June	July	August	September	October	November	December	Annual average
Information													
2005	19.5	19.5	19.4	19.7	19.7	19.6	19.5	19.5	19.2	19.2	19.3	19.2	19.4
2006	19.2	19.1	19.1	18.8	18.9	18.9	18.9	18.9	18.7	18.6	18.7	18.7	18.9
2007	18.4	18.5	18.3	18.5	18.6	18.6	18.7	18.5	18.4	18.3	18.4	18.4	18.5
2008	18.2	18.0	18.0	18.0	18.0	17.9	17.8	17.7	17.2	17.2	17.3	17.3	17.7
2009	17.1	17.0	16.7	16.5	16.5	16.6	16.5	16.4	16.1	16.1	16.2	16.2	16.5
2010	16.0	15.9	15.8	15.8	15.9	15.8	15.8	15.9	15.5	15.6	15.6	15.7	15.8
2011	15.4	15.3	15.2	15.3	15.4	15.4	15.5	15.5	15.5	15.4	15.5	15.5	15.4
2012	15.5	15.3	15.3	15.3	15.3	15.4	15.5	15.4	15.2	15.2	15.3	15.2	15.3
2013	14.9	15.0	15.0	15.0	15.1	15.3	15.4	15.3	15.2	15.1	15.0	15.3	15.1
2014	14.7	14.6	14.6	14.6	14.6	14.6	14.7	14.6	14.5	14.5	14.4	14.6	14.6
2015	14.3	14.3	14.3	14.4	14.3	14.3	14.4	14.3	14.2	14.2	14.2	14.3	14.3
Financial Activities													
2005	75.5	75.4	75.2	74.4	74.3	75.3	75.1	75.0	74.2	74.9	74.7	74.6	74.9
2006	73.6	73.7	73.8	73.5	73.5	74.0	74.4	74.2	73.7	73.5	73.7	73.8	73.8
2007	73.1	73.0	72.9	72.8	72.9	72.8	72.7	72.3	71.3	71.0	70.7	70.5	72.2
2008	69.7	69.3	69.3	69.1	69.2	69.2	69.4	69.2	68.2	67.9	67.9	67.7	68.8
2009	66.9	66.5	66.2	65.9	65.9	66.1	66.1	65.8	65.3	64.9	64.9	64.9	65.8
2010	64.4	64.3	64.1	64.5	64.6	64.8	65.1	65.0	64.3	64.7	64.6	64.6	64.6
2011	64.4	64.3	64.0	64.1	63.9	63.7	63.5	63.2	62.7	62.5	62.4	62.2	63.4
2012	61.8	61.8	61.9	62.2	62.4	62.7	63.1	63.1	62.6	62.8	63.0	63.0	62.5
2013	62.4	62.5	62.4	63.1	63.2	63.9	64.3	64.7	64.2	64.6	64.8	64.9	63.8
2014	63.9	64.3	64.5	64.5	64.7	65.2	64.9	64.9	64.2	64.5	64.8	64.9	64.6
2015	64.3	64.5	64.5	64.7	64.9	65.5	65.7	65.5	64.9	65.5	65.3	65.2	65.0
Professional and Business Services													
2005	133.2	134.9	136.2	139.4	139.5	141.3	143.0	144.3	144.2	144.6	144.3	143.1	140.7
2006	138.6	139.4	140.8	143.4	143.8	145.8	145.8	147.2	146.4	146.1	145.3	145.3	144.0
2007	140.2	140.4	141.0	143.3	144.1	146.4	146.2	147.0	146.0	146.1	146.0	145.3	144.3
2008	142.1	142.2	141.5	144.3	145.6	146.5	146.6	147.5	145.9	143.3	141.7	139.0	143.9
2009	134.1	132.3	131.3	131.4	131.5	132.0	131.5	131.7	131.1	131.7	131.6	129.9	131.7
2010	126.4	126.1	126.5	131.3	132.1	133.9	134.7	135.0	134.4	134.8	135.0	134.7	132.1
2011	131.2	132.5	133.6	138.5	139.2	140.5	143.1	144.3	142.9	143.2	143.0	141.9	139.5
2012	137.5	138.6	140.1	142.3	143.6	145.0	145.9	146.4	144.1	147.1	147.0	144.3	143.5
2013	138.2	139.6	141.3	145.3	147.3	149.1	148.7	150.2	146.9	149.5	149.2	148.4	146.1
2014	142.8	143.5	144.3	148.2	149.6	150.4	150.8	152.1	149.7	151.1	150.9	149.3	148.6
2015	143.5	144.3	144.5	147.1	150.5	151.1	151.9	152.0	148.1	150.3	149.0	148.3	148.4
Education and Health Services													
2005	164.9	167.5	167.8	166.6	166.2	165.4	164.6	164.9	169.2	170.1	171.3	172.0	167.5
2006	168.5	171.7	172.2	171.3	170.7	169.9	168.0	167.7	170.8	172.5	173.4	173.3	170.8
2007	171.3	172.8	173.9	174.7	174.0	173.2	172.1	172.3	176.6	178.4	179.2	179.5	174.8
2008	176.9	179.2	179.0	179.8	179.0	177.3	174.7	175.4	180.6	183.4	184.1	184.3	179.5
2009	182.1	184.1	184.5	184.8	183.7	181.4	180.8	181.0	185.6	187.6	188.2	188.1	184.3
2010	186.9	188.3	188.4	188.1	187.1	184.3	184.7	184.2	188.8	190.5	191.0	190.3	187.7
2011	187.0	188.7	188.6	189.9	190.2	187.5	186.7	186.6	189.2	191.0	191.6	191.4	189.0
2012	189.3	192.4	192.5	194.2	194.7	193.3	191.2	191.4	195.0	197.7	197.7	196.8	193.9
2013	193.5	195.9	195.9	195.9	195.3	194.7	194.2	194.6	195.9	198.1	199.0	198.9	196.0
2014	193.7	194.9	195.6	196.3	196.0	194.7	194.1	193.7	196.0	199.3	199.8	199.8	196.2
2015	195.4	197.8	198.0	199.5	199.3	197.6	197.2	197.2	198.9	202.7	203.7	204.1	199.3
Leisure and Hospitality													
2005	86.3	86.4	88.6	92.3	95.6	97.8	99.3	100.6	96.8	94.2	93.1	93.0	93.7
2006	88.1	87.9	90.2	93.5	97.4	99.7	99.8	101.0	96.7	93.5	91.3	91.8	94.2
2007	87.6	87.0	89.0	91.6	95.5	98.7	98.3	99.0	95.2	92.8	91.2	90.5	93.0
2008	85.7	85.4	86.0	90.6	95.1	96.7	96.2	96.5	93.2	89.7	87.8	87.8	90.9
2009	82.1	81.4	82.9	87.1	91.1	92.4	92.8	92.2	89.4	86.3	84.6	85.2	87.3
2010	80.2	80.0	81.4	86.0	89.5	91.4	92.3	92.9	89.5	87.5	86.3	85.4	86.9
2011	80.8	80.7	82.3	86.3	89.9	92.2	93.4	94.3	90.6	87.4	87.2	86.3	87.6
2012	83.2	82.7	85.4	90.4	93.8	97.2	97.3	97.7	93.7	93.2	91.7	92.6	91.6
2013	87.9	88.0	90.3	94.5	99.3	101.7	102.2	101.2	97.6	96.3	93.9	94.5	95.6
2014	90.2	89.7	91.9	95.7	100.2	102.6	102.5	102.3	99.0	97.6	95.6	96.9	97.0
2015	91.4	92.2	93.8	98.2	103.0	104.6	105.1	104.9	101.5	102.4	99.6	101.8	99.9

Employment by Industry: Cleveland-Elyria, OH, 2005–2015—*Continued*

(Numbers in thousands, not seasonally adjusted)

Industry and year	January	February	March	April	May	June	July	August	September	October	November	December	Annual average
Other Services													
2005	43.6	43.8	44.1	44.4	44.4	44.7	44.8	44.6	44.2	44.1	44.2	44.4	44.3
2006	43.7	43.7	43.8	43.7	44.1	44.9	44.6	44.2	43.9	43.8	43.7	44.1	44.0
2007	43.4	43.4	43.8	44.0	44.2	44.9	44.9	44.6	44.1	43.9	43.9	44.0	44.1
2008	43.4	43.6	43.5	43.4	43.7	43.9	43.7	43.6	43.2	43.0	42.9	43.0	43.4
2009	42.3	42.3	42.4	42.5	42.6	42.5	42.6	42.3	41.9	41.9	41.7	41.9	42.2
2010	41.1	40.9	41.2	41.4	41.3	41.6	41.7	41.5	41.2	41.4	41.3	41.5	41.3
2011	40.9	40.8	40.8	40.8	40.8	40.8	41.2	41.0	40.4	40.5	40.3	40.1	40.7
2012	39.7	39.8	40.1	40.1	40.3	40.8	40.7	40.5	39.9	39.8	39.7	39.8	40.1
2013	39.3	39.1	39.2	39.7	39.9	40.0	39.9	40.0	39.4	39.6	39.6	39.6	39.6
2014	39.2	39.2	39.3	39.5	40.0	40.0	39.9	39.9	39.3	39.7	39.6	39.9	39.6
2015	38.9	39.1	39.1	39.6	39.9	40.1	40.0	39.9	39.3	39.8	39.5	40.7	39.7
Government													
2005	139.1	142.8	143.4	143.7	144.4	143.2	134.7	133.5	138.9	142.2	142.3	142.6	140.9
2006	138.8	141.8	143.1	143.1	144.0	142.3	133.9	133.1	138.8	142.0	143.2	143.1	140.6
2007	139.8	143.3	144.7	145.2	145.9	147.3	139.5	138.3	140.1	143.7	144.3	143.3	143.0
2008	141.3	144.2	143.4	144.0	146.5	147.2	139.5	137.9	140.2	143.6	143.6	142.3	142.8
2009	140.4	142.7	142.6	143.1	144.1	142.8	135.9	134.5	138.2	141.1	141.3	139.9	140.6
2010	137.7	140.4	139.9	140.5	144.6	141.0	134.5	132.1	135.0	138.9	139.0	138.1	138.5
2011	132.6	137.0	137.5	138.4	138.1	137.3	131.5	130.1	133.3	134.8	136.2	135.9	135.2
2012	131.9	135.8	136.4	136.7	137.9	136.7	131.6	130.2	134.1	135.5	135.5	134.7	134.8
2013	133.3	134.1	133.7	134.6	136.4	134.6	128.6	130.3	132.4	134.3	135.0	134.7	133.5
2014	132.0	133.5	133.5	134.4	136.5	135.1	129.4	131.0	133.3	135.6	135.7	135.1	133.8
2015	132.8	134.1	132.7	135.2	137.5	136.6	130.3	132.4	133.7	135.6	137.0	136.9	134.6

Employment by Industry: Columbus, OH, 2005–2015

(Numbers in thousands, not seasonally adjusted)

Industry and year	January	February	March	April	May	June	July	August	September	October	November	December	Annual average
Total Nonfarm													
2005	920.2	922.6	929.4	938.9	944.9	941.4	937.1	938.5	945.3	953.3	959.8	960.0	941.0
2006	929.1	934.1	941.5	948.6	954.7	951.7	945.2	946.5	951.7	959.9	966.6	969.1	949.9
2007	944.3	941.9	949.9	959.2	967.7	966.2	957.6	957.5	962.5	970.1	976.8	975.7	960.8
2008	948.8	950.1	950.0	960.2	966.3	960.3	955.2	955.1	956.9	963.5	961.8	957.6	957.2
2009	926.9	923.2	923.5	927.3	931.4	922.7	913.8	913.3	916.8	925.0	926.7	923.6	922.9
2010	900.0	901.5	906.8	919.3	927.3	921.3	916.0	918.7	923.3	933.8	938.1	937.8	920.3
2011	912.3	917.0	922.4	939.2	945.9	939.6	938.7	942.7	951.9	958.0	965.0	964.0	941.4
2012	941.0	947.7	952.9	961.9	971.7	969.0	960.4	963.6	973.0	987.3	994.8	993.2	968.0
2013	966.4	968.5	972.1	986.6	996.9	989.8	986.4	991.9	997.2	1,007.1	1,018.1	1,018.0	991.6
2014	987.8	990.2	993.5	1,009.9	1,021.2	1,013.9	1,012.6	1,020.2	1,025.6	1,034.9	1,044.9	1,045.6	1,016.7
2015	1,015.1	1,016.9	1,019.7	1,034.0	1,045.1	1,039.1	1,040.0	1,044.8	1,045.9	1,057.0	1,060.0	1,060.6	1,039.9
Total Private													
2005	758.2	757.4	763.0	771.7	776.6	779.7	780.0	781.9	783.4	787.1	792.0	793.0	777.0
2006	765.8	767.8	773.9	780.7	785.9	790.5	788.2	789.6	789.5	793.0	798.6	801.0	785.4
2007	778.9	774.5	781.3	790.1	797.9	802.5	800.3	801.4	797.9	801.3	806.7	806.2	794.9
2008	782.9	781.2	780.9	790.6	795.2	796.2	797.0	797.5	792.6	793.9	792.0	789.0	790.8
2009	761.9	755.5	755.0	757.3	761.1	760.2	757.9	758.3	752.8	755.5	756.8	755.5	757.3
2010	735.1	734.1	738.9	749.4	753.9	757.2	760.5	763.4	759.3	764.7	768.5	767.9	754.4
2011	748.6	751.1	755.4	769.4	775.2	776.9	782.6	785.8	786.0	790.6	796.3	796.7	776.2
2012	777.0	780.9	786.4	795.6	803.1	808.9	807.5	809.9	808.2	818.2	824.6	824.3	803.7
2013	803.2	803.2	807.0	819.5	828.6	832.0	832.3	836.0	832.7	839.7	848.6	849.1	827.7
2014	824.5	824.3	827.9	841.9	851.8	855.8	856.9	863.2	857.8	865.7	875.4	877.0	851.9
2015	849.3	848.8	851.9	865.0	874.8	879.7	882.1	885.4	878.0	886.6	888.6	888.8	873.3
Goods Producing													
2005	118.2	117.6	118.4	121.4	123.0	124.9	125.6	125.7	125.6	124.7	124.4	123.1	122.7
2006	117.9	118.0	119.0	121.1	122.0	123.6	123.3	123.8	123.3	122.1	120.8	120.2	121.3
2007	116.5	114.3	115.8	117.4	119.2	121.1	120.8	121.0	120.3	118.7	118.1	116.6	118.3
2008	112.7	111.8	111.3	112.8	114.3	115.4	115.2	115.0	114.3	112.7	110.9	108.4	112.9
2009	102.6	100.1	99.3	99.3	99.6	100.1	98.9	98.8	97.5	96.2	95.3	93.9	98.5
2010	89.8	88.9	89.8	92.1	93.6	94.8	95.6	95.8	95.5	96.0	95.6	94.2	93.5
2011	90.8	90.8	91.7	94.4	95.6	97.0	98.6	98.9	98.3	98.5	98.2	97.1	95.8
2012	94.3	94.7	95.6	97.5	99.0	100.3	101.2	101.3	100.7	100.6	100.5	99.5	98.8
2013	97.2	97.3	98.3	100.3	102.4	104.1	104.3	104.5	104.1	104.3	104.3	103.0	102.0
2014	99.5	99.3	100.7	102.9	104.9	106.0	106.8	107.0	106.3	106.4	107.1	105.2	104.3
2015	102.5	102.8	103.4	105.8	108.4	109.1	109.8	110.0	109.2	110.1	108.9	108.8	107.4
Service-Providing													
2005	802.0	805.0	811.0	817.5	821.9	816.5	811.5	812.8	819.7	828.6	835.4	836.9	818.2
2006	811.2	816.1	822.5	827.5	832.7	828.1	821.9	822.7	828.4	837.8	845.8	848.9	828.6
2007	827.8	827.6	834.1	841.8	848.5	845.1	836.8	836.5	842.2	851.4	858.7	859.1	842.5
2008	836.1	838.3	838.7	847.4	852.0	844.9	840.0	840.1	842.6	850.8	850.9	849.2	844.3
2009	824.3	823.1	824.2	828.0	831.8	822.6	814.9	814.5	819.3	828.8	831.4	829.7	824.4
2010	810.2	812.6	817.0	827.2	833.7	826.5	820.4	822.9	827.8	837.8	842.5	843.6	826.9
2011	821.5	826.2	830.7	844.8	850.3	842.6	840.1	843.8	853.6	859.5	866.8	866.9	845.6
2012	846.7	853.0	857.3	864.4	872.7	868.7	859.2	862.3	872.3	886.7	894.3	893.7	869.3
2013	869.2	871.2	873.8	886.3	894.5	885.7	882.1	887.4	893.1	902.8	913.8	915.0	889.6
2014	888.3	890.9	892.8	907.0	916.3	907.9	905.8	913.2	919.3	928.5	937.8	940.4	912.4
2015	912.6	914.1	916.3	928.2	936.7	930.0	930.2	934.8	936.7	946.9	951.1	951.8	932.5
Mining, Logging, and Construction													
2005	37.1	36.6	37.5	40.5	42.1	43.2	44.4	44.5	44.1	43.4	43.0	41.6	41.5
2006	38.0	37.9	38.8	40.8	41.8	42.7	43.1	43.2	42.8	42.2	41.3	40.4	41.1
2007	37.3	35.6	37.1	38.5	40.2	41.7	41.9	41.8	41.3	40.7	39.8	38.1	39.5
2008	35.1	34.2	34.2	36.5	37.9	38.6	38.2	38.1	37.5	37.0	35.5	33.5	36.4
2009	30.0	29.2	29.6	30.2	31.3	32.4	32.8	32.6	31.6	30.3	29.6	28.2	30.7
2010	25.5	24.6	25.4	27.5	28.8	29.7	30.5	30.6	30.5	30.7	30.1	28.6	28.5
2011	26.0	25.9	26.7	28.6	29.7	30.7	32.2	32.4	32.0	31.7	31.1	30.0	29.8
2012	27.8	27.8	28.6	30.0	31.2	32.0	32.7	32.8	32.4	32.3	31.5	30.5	30.8
2013	28.6	28.6	29.4	31.2	33.1	34.3	34.6	35.0	34.6	34.7	34.4	32.7	32.6
2014	30.5	30.2	31.7	33.5	35.1	36.3	36.5	36.6	36.2	36.1	35.6	34.3	34.4
2015	31.6	31.8	32.6	34.4	36.5	37.2	37.6	37.8	37.5	38.6	37.7	37.0	35.9

Employment by Industry: Columbus, OH, 2005–2015—*Continued*

(Numbers in thousands, not seasonally adjusted)

Industry and year	January	February	March	April	May	June	July	August	September	October	November	December	Annual average
Manufacturing													
2005	81.1	81.0	80.9	80.9	80.9	81.7	81.2	81.2	81.5	81.3	81.4	81.5	81.2
2006	79.9	80.1	80.2	80.3	80.2	80.9	80.2	80.6	80.5	79.9	79.5	79.8	80.2
2007	79.2	78.7	78.7	78.9	79.0	79.4	78.9	79.2	79.0	78.0	78.3	78.5	78.8
2008	77.6	77.6	77.1	76.3	76.4	76.8	77.0	76.9	76.8	75.7	75.4	74.9	76.5
2009	72.6	70.9	69.7	69.1	68.3	67.7	66.1	66.2	65.9	65.9	65.7	65.7	67.8
2010	64.3	64.3	64.4	64.6	64.8	65.1	65.1	65.2	65.0	65.3	65.5	65.6	64.9
2011	64.8	64.9	65.0	65.8	65.9	66.3	66.4	66.5	66.3	66.8	67.1	67.1	66.1
2012	66.5	66.9	67.0	67.5	67.8	68.3	68.5	68.5	68.3	68.3	69.0	69.0	68.0
2013	68.6	68.7	68.9	69.1	69.3	69.8	69.7	69.5	69.5	69.6	69.9	70.3	69.4
2014	69.0	69.1	69.0	69.4	69.8	69.7	70.3	70.4	70.1	70.3	71.5	70.9	70.0
2015	70.9	71.0	70.8	71.4	71.9	71.9	72.2	72.2	71.7	71.5	71.2	71.8	71.5
Trade, Transportation, and Utilities													
2005	187.9	185.3	186.3	186.4	187.0	186.5	186.3	186.4	186.9	189.9	195.5	199.4	188.7
2006	187.9	185.9	186.2	186.5	188.2	188.1	188.1	187.8	187.9	191.2	198.2	201.4	189.8
2007	191.3	188.0	189.2	189.7	191.8	192.0	192.5	192.6	192.8	195.6	201.6	203.6	193.4
2008	192.7	189.4	189.2	190.7	191.7	191.1	192.0	192.6	191.7	193.3	196.0	197.8	192.4
2009	185.2	181.4	180.3	180.5	181.2	180.3	179.9	180.2	179.1	180.6	184.6	186.5	181.7
2010	176.9	174.8	174.9	175.7	177.3	177.6	176.7	177.5	176.7	179.7	183.2	185.6	178.1
2011	177.9	177.5	177.4	179.9	180.6	180.7	181.5	182.2	181.5	184.4	188.7	191.4	182.0
2012	183.0	181.4	181.6	182.3	183.9	184.3	184.0	184.1	183.9	187.3	192.3	193.9	185.2
2013	184.6	182.7	182.6	183.9	185.4	186.4	187.0	187.1	186.6	189.9	195.6	197.6	187.5
2014	187.4	185.4	185.2	187.5	189.4	190.5	191.1	192.4	192.2	196.1	202.4	205.5	192.1
2015	194.9	193.1	193.1	194.3	195.5	196.0	196.6	197.2	196.3	198.7	202.1	205.7	197.0
Wholesale Trade													
2005	37.2	37.2	37.2	37.5	37.5	37.4	37.9	37.7	37.7	37.6	37.9	37.9	37.6
2006	37.6	37.8	37.7	37.8	38.0	38.0	38.0	37.9	37.8	37.9	38.3	38.3	37.9
2007	38.0	38.0	38.2	38.3	38.9	39.0	39.0	39.0	38.9	39.0	38.9	38.9	38.7
2008	39.0	39.0	39.0	39.4	39.6	39.6	39.7	39.8	39.5	39.1	38.9	38.7	39.3
2009	38.5	38.3	38.4	37.8	37.7	37.6	37.5	37.4	36.9	36.7	36.7	36.7	37.5
2010	37.0	37.2	37.1	37.4	37.6	37.7	37.5	37.6	37.3	37.4	37.4	37.2	37.4
2011	37.3	37.3	37.3	37.6	37.8	37.7	37.8	37.9	37.6	37.8	37.8	37.8	37.6
2012	38.0	38.2	38.1	38.4	38.5	38.6	38.8	38.8	38.6	38.6	38.7	38.6	38.5
2013	38.4	38.6	38.6	38.9	39.1	39.0	39.3	39.5	39.3	39.6	39.9	39.9	39.2
2014	40.3	40.7	40.9	41.1	41.5	41.5	41.7	41.7	41.6	41.5	41.8	42.0	41.4
2015	41.3	41.5	41.6	41.8	42.0	42.0	42.1	42.2	41.9	42.3	42.5	42.4	42.0
Retail Trade													
2005	110.1	107.8	108.6	108.4	108.8	108.3	107.2	107.2	107.2	108.4	112.3	116.1	109.2
2006	106.4	104.4	104.7	104.5	105.6	105.2	104.9	104.3	103.5	105.1	110.0	112.4	105.9
2007	103.9	101.6	102.6	102.9	103.8	103.5	104.0	103.8	103.4	104.6	108.8	110.5	104.5
2008	103.0	100.7	100.4	101.8	103.0	102.9	104.1	104.5	103.4	104.9	107.1	109.3	103.8
2009	100.4	98.1	97.4	98.3	99.1	98.7	98.3	98.5	97.9	99.2	102.5	104.4	99.4
2010	96.4	94.7	95.1	96.1	97.0	97.3	97.2	97.8	97.1	99.5	102.2	104.1	97.9
2011	97.4	96.9	96.9	98.6	98.8	98.9	99.7	100.2	99.4	101.4	104.7	106.9	100.0
2012	99.8	98.4	98.6	99.3	100.3	100.2	99.7	99.8	99.5	101.8	105.7	106.5	100.8
2013	100.1	98.5	98.4	99.6	100.6	101.0	101.5	101.5	101.0	103.5	107.5	108.6	101.8
2014	100.6	99.2	98.7	100.7	101.1	101.8	102.0	102.8	101.9	104.6	108.6	109.8	102.7
2015	102.2	100.9	101.0	101.6	102.4	102.5	102.9	103.1	102.1	103.5	106.2	107.8	103.0
Transportation and Utilities													
2005	40.6	40.3	40.5	40.5	40.7	40.8	41.2	41.5	42.0	43.9	45.3	45.4	41.9
2006	43.9	43.7	43.8	44.2	44.6	44.9	45.2	45.6	46.6	48.2	49.9	50.7	45.9
2007	49.4	48.4	48.4	48.5	49.1	49.5	49.5	49.8	50.5	52.0	53.9	54.2	50.3
2008	50.7	49.7	49.8	49.5	49.1	48.6	48.2	48.3	48.8	49.3	50.0	49.8	49.3
2009	46.3	45.0	44.5	44.4	44.4	44.0	44.1	44.3	44.3	44.7	45.4	45.4	44.7
2010	43.5	42.9	42.7	42.2	42.7	42.6	42.0	42.1	42.3	42.8	43.6	44.3	42.8
2011	43.2	43.3	43.2	43.7	44.0	44.1	44.0	44.1	44.5	45.2	46.2	46.7	44.4
2012	45.2	44.8	44.9	44.6	45.1	45.5	45.5	45.5	45.8	46.9	47.9	48.8	45.9
2013	46.1	45.6	45.6	45.4	45.7	46.4	46.2	46.1	46.3	46.8	48.2	49.1	46.5
2014	46.5	45.5	45.6	45.7	46.8	47.2	47.4	47.9	48.7	50.0	52.0	53.7	48.1
2015	51.4	50.7	50.5	50.9	51.1	51.5	51.6	51.9	52.3	52.9	53.4	55.5	52.0

Employment by Industry: Columbus, OH, 2005–2015—*Continued*

(Numbers in thousands, not seasonally adjusted)

Industry and year	January	February	March	April	May	June	July	August	September	October	November	December	Annual average
Information													
2005	19.5	19.3	19.4	19.4	19.5	19.5	19.5	19.6	19.7	19.3	19.3	19.3	19.4
2006	19.2	19.1	19.1	18.9	19.0	19.0	18.9	18.8	18.6	18.5	18.6	18.6	18.9
2007	18.8	18.9	18.8	18.9	18.9	18.9	18.9	18.7	18.4	18.1	18.1	18.1	18.6
2008	17.7	17.8	17.8	17.9	17.8	17.8	17.8	17.8	17.6	17.6	17.7	17.7	17.8
2009	17.7	17.6	17.4	17.2	17.2	17.1	17.2	17.0	16.7	16.6	16.6	16.8	17.1
2010	16.9	16.9	16.8	16.6	16.7	16.7	16.8	16.8	16.7	16.6	16.9	16.9	16.8
2011	16.7	16.7	16.6	16.9	17.0	17.0	17.1	17.1	16.8	16.8	16.9	17.0	16.9
2012	16.7	16.8	16.8	16.9	17.0	17.3	17.4	17.3	17.3	17.4	17.6	17.8	17.2
2013	18.0	18.3	18.5	18.7	18.6	18.7	18.7	18.8	18.6	18.5	18.5	18.5	18.5
2014	18.2	18.2	18.1	18.1	17.8	17.7	17.5	17.3	16.8	16.6	16.9	17.0	17.5
2015	16.6	16.8	16.8	17.1	17.0	17.1	17.0	16.9	16.7	16.7	16.8	16.8	16.9
Financial Activities													
2005	72.8	72.8	72.8	72.8	73.0	73.3	73.6	73.7	73.8	73.8	74.0	74.3	73.4
2006	73.6	73.5	73.6	73.7	73.8	74.3	74.8	74.4	74.5	75.1	75.2	75.0	74.3
2007	74.6	74.5	73.9	74.7	74.2	73.5	73.4	73.4	72.7	72.7	72.3	72.3	73.5
2008	71.7	71.9	71.7	71.5	71.6	71.5	71.1	71.2	70.8	71.0	70.6	70.7	71.3
2009	70.1	69.9	69.9	69.5	69.6	69.4	69.6	69.4	69.0	69.1	69.5	69.4	69.5
2010	68.6	68.6	68.5	69.2	69.2	69.4	69.8	69.6	69.3	69.8	69.9	70.0	69.3
2011	70.1	70.1	70.2	70.0	70.5	70.7	70.9	71.4	71.9	72.1	72.1	72.0	71.0
2012	72.3	72.5	72.9	72.9	73.5	74.0	74.2	74.3	74.0	74.3	74.8	74.9	73.7
2013	74.8	75.1	75.3	75.3	75.7	76.0	75.9	75.9	75.2	74.9	75.1	75.0	75.4
2014	75.2	75.3	75.1	75.3	76.0	76.5	76.9	77.4	77.0	77.6	78.0	78.1	76.5
2015	77.9	78.2	78.2	78.6	79.2	79.7	80.4	80.7	79.9	81.1	81.1	81.3	79.7
Professional and Business Services													
2005	134.8	135.5	136.6	137.5	137.5	138.0	138.4	140.1	141.0	142.6	142.1	142.3	138.9
2006	138.0	138.9	140.4	142.7	142.7	144.5	144.1	145.6	145.6	146.5	147.1	148.1	143.7
2007	144.3	144.5	146.3	148.9	149.5	151.4	151.4	152.0	151.6	153.3	154.1	154.6	150.2
2008	151.7	152.0	152.2	154.7	154.0	154.3	155.7	155.4	154.0	154.3	153.3	152.5	153.7
2009	149.4	147.4	146.5	146.8	146.3	145.5	145.3	146.0	144.0	145.5	145.2	143.6	146.0
2010	141.7	142.0	142.8	146.4	145.7	147.0	148.6	149.9	147.9	149.5	150.2	150.3	146.8
2011	146.2	146.6	148.0	150.4	149.9	150.7	152.8	153.7	154.2	155.5	157.2	157.5	151.9
2012	153.3	154.3	155.6	157.4	157.4	158.8	158.9	160.1	159.8	163.4	165.5	165.8	159.2
2013	160.0	159.3	159.7	163.0	164.1	165.3	166.3	167.4	167.3	170.1	173.0	174.3	165.8
2014	169.3	168.9	169.5	172.7	173.1	174.6	175.7	177.9	177.3	179.8	182.7	183.8	175.4
2015	173.7	171.8	172.3	175.4	176.0	178.0	180.5	181.4	179.2	181.6	182.2	179.7	177.7
Education and Health Services													
2005	103.3	104.7	105.2	106.7	106.1	104.8	104.8	104.8	106.8	108.5	109.2	109.0	106.2
2006	107.0	108.9	109.7	110.1	109.4	107.7	106.7	106.9	109.8	110.9	111.4	111.1	109.1
2007	109.8	110.7	111.5	112.5	112.7	111.8	111.1	111.4	113.0	114.3	115.2	114.9	112.4
2008	113.9	115.6	115.5	115.9	115.7	114.5	114.2	114.5	116.3	117.7	118.6	118.6	115.9
2009	117.7	119.2	119.4	120.0	120.1	119.3	119.4	120.0	122.2	123.9	124.4	124.8	120.9
2010	124.0	125.1	126.3	126.6	126.4	124.4	125.3	126.4	128.0	129.0	129.5	128.9	126.7
2011	128.0	129.6	129.8	132.2	132.7	129.8	130.6	131.3	134.6	135.6	136.3	136.2	132.2
2012	135.0	137.3	137.4	139.2	138.9	137.3	135.1	136.0	137.1	139.5	140.0	139.4	137.7
2013	138.6	139.7	139.1	141.4	141.6	138.8	138.0	140.1	140.7	143.3	144.4	144.4	140.8
2014	142.8	144.9	145.0	147.8	147.7	145.3	144.2	145.7	146.4	148.4	149.1	148.8	146.3
2015	148.2	149.7	149.6	151.9	152.5	150.9	149.8	150.7	150.9	153.2	153.3	152.7	151.1
Leisure and Hospitality													
2005	84.1	84.3	86.1	89.4	92.2	94.3	93.8	93.4	91.9	90.2	88.9	87.9	89.7
2006	84.7	85.8	87.9	89.6	92.6	94.5	93.9	93.9	91.8	90.6	89.3	88.8	90.3
2007	86.1	86.0	88.0	90.5	93.7	95.7	94.3	94.6	92.1	91.4	90.2	89.2	91.0
2008	86.1	86.2	86.6	90.2	93.0	94.2	93.4	93.3	90.6	89.3	87.6	86.8	89.8
2009	83.2	83.5	85.7	87.5	90.2	91.7	91.1	90.6	88.6	87.7	85.5	84.8	87.5
2010	81.6	82.1	83.9	87.0	89.2	91.2	91.2	91.1	89.3	88.0	87.3	86.1	87.3
2011	83.7	84.5	86.4	89.9	93.0	94.9	94.6	94.8	92.8	91.4	90.8	89.7	90.5
2012	86.6	87.9	90.3	92.7	96.4	99.1	98.4	99.0	97.6	96.7	95.6	94.8	94.6
2013	92.6	93.2	95.7	98.7	102.3	104.1	103.5	103.8	102.0	100.5	99.3	98.1	99.5
2014	93.9	93.9	95.7	98.8	103.6	105.3	104.5	105.2	101.8	100.7	99.3	98.8	100.1
2015	95.9	96.6	98.3	101.3	105.4	107.7	106.4	106.8	104.5	103.4	102.4	101.8	102.5

Employment by Industry: Columbus, OH, 2005–2015—*Continued*

(Numbers in thousands, not seasonally adjusted)

Industry and year	January	February	March	April	May	June	July	August	September	October	November	December	Annual average
Other Services													
2005	37.6	37.9	38.2	38.1	38.3	38.4	38.0	38.2	37.7	38.1	38.6	37.7	38.1
2006	37.5	37.7	38.0	38.1	38.2	38.8	38.4	38.4	38.0	38.1	38.0	37.8	38.1
2007	37.5	37.6	37.8	37.5	37.9	38.1	37.9	37.7	37.0	37.2	37.1	36.9	37.5
2008	36.4	36.5	36.6	36.9	37.1	37.4	37.6	37.7	37.3	38.0	37.3	36.5	37.1
2009	36.0	36.4	36.5	36.5	36.9	36.8	36.5	36.3	35.7	35.9	35.7	35.7	36.2
2010	35.6	35.7	35.9	35.8	35.8	36.1	36.5	36.3	35.9	36.1	35.9	35.9	36.0
2011	35.2	35.3	35.3	35.7	35.9	36.1	36.5	36.4	35.9	36.3	36.1	35.8	35.9
2012	35.8	36.0	36.2	36.7	37.0	37.8	38.3	37.8	37.8	39.0	38.3	38.2	37.4
2013	37.4	37.6	37.8	38.2	38.5	38.6	38.6	38.4	38.2	38.2	38.4	38.2	38.2
2014	38.2	38.4	38.6	38.8	39.3	39.9	40.2	40.3	40.0	40.1	39.9	39.8	39.5
2015	39.6	39.8	40.2	40.6	40.8	41.2	41.6	41.7	41.3	41.8	41.8	42.0	41.0
Government													
2005	162.0	165.2	166.4	167.2	168.3	161.7	157.1	156.6	161.9	166.2	167.8	167.0	164.0
2006	163.3	166.3	167.6	167.9	168.8	161.2	157.0	156.9	162.2	166.9	168.0	168.1	164.5
2007	165.4	167.4	168.6	169.1	169.8	163.7	157.3	156.1	164.6	168.8	170.1	169.5	165.9
2008	165.9	168.9	169.1	169.6	171.1	164.1	158.2	157.6	164.3	169.6	169.8	168.6	166.4
2009	165.0	167.7	168.5	170.0	170.3	162.5	155.9	155.0	164.0	169.5	169.9	168.1	165.5
2010	164.9	167.4	167.9	169.9	173.4	164.1	155.5	155.3	164.0	169.1	169.6	169.9	165.9
2011	163.7	165.9	167.0	169.8	170.7	162.7	156.1	156.9	165.9	167.4	168.7	167.3	165.2
2012	164.0	166.8	166.5	166.3	168.6	160.1	152.9	153.7	164.8	169.1	170.2	168.9	164.3
2013	163.2	165.3	165.1	167.1	168.3	157.8	154.1	155.9	164.5	167.4	169.5	168.9	163.9
2014	163.3	165.9	165.6	168.0	169.4	158.1	155.7	157.0	167.8	169.2	169.5	168.6	164.8
2015	165.8	168.1	167.8	169.0	170.3	159.4	157.9	159.4	167.9	170.4	171.4	171.8	166.6

Employment by Industry: Austin-Round Rock, TX, 2005–2015

(Numbers in thousands, not seasonally adjusted)

Industry and year	January	February	March	April	May	June	July	August	September	October	November	December	Annual average
Total Nonfarm													
2005	679.4	686.5	691.8	697.7	700.2	700.8	697.8	701.4	706.0	707.0	713.4	714.8	699.7
2006	704.1	711.9	718.6	724.8	728.7	731.6	723.8	732.4	743.1	746.2	753.4	757.4	731.3
2007	740.7	752.6	760.7	764.0	768.2	770.9	763.0	767.4	772.1	777.4	782.7	783.3	766.9
2008	773.3	781.5	783.8	786.2	789.0	788.4	779.7	784.0	788.2	790.6	793.4	789.2	785.6
2009	769.6	770.1	770.2	772.0	773.4	770.6	760.2	762.0	763.6	768.2	772.3	770.8	768.6
2010	759.8	765.3	773.9	777.3	781.8	783.4	774.7	778.3	780.1	791.3	796.9	795.6	779.9
2011	783.4	791.3	798.3	806.8	807.4	808.4	801.3	806.8	811.2	815.6	822.0	822.5	806.3
2012	813.2	819.7	826.6	831.5	835.8	839.6	832.3	838.8	844.9	853.7	864.4	862.6	838.6
2013	849.2	858.4	865.1	872.4	876.7	881.0	874.8	878.9	884.7	892.5	902.6	900.7	878.1
2014	889.2	899.5	906.9	912.3	916.3	920.8	914.4	917.3	921.4	931.7	939.7	940.1	917.5
2015	928.2	938.2	944.6	951.0	956.7	962.4	958.2	960.8	964.4	977.1	985.5	984.6	959.3
Total Private													
2005	532.5	535.8	540.9	546.0	548.5	553.2	554.6	557.0	558.2	556.5	561.2	565.1	550.8
2006	554.7	558.8	564.9	570.4	574.8	581.4	581.8	586.5	588.5	590.1	597.4	603.0	579.4
2007	586.7	595.2	602.1	605.1	609.4	615.3	613.9	616.5	616.0	617.3	621.5	624.4	610.3
2008	613.3	618.1	618.0	623.0	626.0	627.3	625.2	628.2	625.5	626.3	626.8	624.6	623.5
2009	604.9	602.2	601.4	601.8	603.4	603.0	600.9	602.1	597.5	599.4	601.0	601.8	601.6
2010	591.1	594.4	599.9	603.9	607.2	610.6	611.4	614.6	613.6	619.9	624.0	625.8	609.7
2011	615.1	619.7	626.3	634.1	635.7	638.4	640.3	645.9	646.6	648.6	653.5	656.6	638.4
2012	646.7	651.3	657.7	661.9	666.8	672.7	672.1	679.2	680.1	685.3	693.4	694.7	671.8
2013	680.9	687.8	693.6	700.5	705.3	711.0	711.1	717.1	717.7	722.6	730.4	731.5	709.1
2014	719.7	727.9	734.3	740.0	744.2	750.4	750.1	754.8	753.8	759.6	766.6	768.1	747.5
2015	756.5	765.3	770.9	777.0	783.2	790.3	792.1	796.4	794.8	803.2	810.3	810.5	787.5
Goods Producing													
2005	101.0	101.4	102.1	102.6	102.9	104.2	105.2	105.1	104.8	104.4	105.0	105.4	103.7
2006	104.8	105.8	107.3	107.6	108.7	110.9	111.6	112.1	111.8	111.8	112.3	113.5	109.9
2007	111.5	112.9	114.0	115.0	115.8	117.4	117.0	117.3	116.2	116.4	115.9	115.5	115.4
2008	113.3	113.8	113.4	112.9	112.9	112.9	111.9	111.1	109.5	107.4	105.6	104.0	110.7
2009	99.0	97.3	95.2	95.8	95.4	95.5	95.0	94.4	93.5	92.9	92.2	92.5	94.9
2010	90.7	90.7	91.4	92.4	92.3	93.4	94.2	95.1	94.6	95.0	94.8	94.6	93.3
2011	93.3	93.6	94.3	94.3	94.5	95.5	96.0	96.2	95.9	96.0	95.9	96.0	95.1
2012	95.3	96.3	97.1	97.5	98.3	100.1	100.6	101.5	101.2	101.2	100.8	100.7	99.2
2013	99.7	100.3	101.1	102.2	103.0	103.9	104.1	104.6	104.4	104.7	105.2	105.6	103.2
2014	104.5	105.7	106.4	106.8	108.0	109.4	110.0	110.5	109.8	109.6	110.0	110.3	108.4
2015	110.1	111.1	111.5	111.2	111.7	113.4	114.2	114.5	113.7	115.3	115.6	116.0	113.2
Service-Providing													
2005	578.4	585.1	589.7	595.1	597.3	596.6	592.6	596.3	601.2	602.6	608.4	609.4	596.1
2006	599.3	606.1	611.3	617.2	620.0	620.7	612.2	620.3	631.3	634.4	641.1	643.9	621.5
2007	629.2	639.7	646.7	649.0	652.4	653.5	646.0	650.1	655.9	661.0	666.8	667.8	651.5
2008	660.0	667.7	670.4	673.3	676.1	675.5	667.8	672.9	678.7	683.2	687.8	685.2	674.9
2009	670.6	672.8	675.0	676.2	678.0	675.1	665.2	667.6	670.1	675.3	680.1	678.3	673.7
2010	669.1	674.6	682.5	684.9	689.5	690.0	680.5	683.2	685.5	696.3	702.1	701.0	686.6
2011	690.1	697.7	704.0	712.5	712.9	712.9	705.3	710.6	715.3	719.6	726.1	726.5	711.1
2012	717.9	723.4	729.5	734.0	737.5	739.5	731.7	737.3	743.7	752.5	763.6	761.9	739.4
2013	749.5	758.1	764.0	770.2	773.7	777.1	770.7	774.3	780.3	787.8	797.4	795.1	774.9
2014	784.7	793.8	800.5	805.5	808.3	811.4	804.4	806.8	811.6	822.1	829.7	829.8	809.1
2015	818.1	827.1	833.1	839.8	845.0	849.0	844.0	846.3	850.7	861.8	869.9	868.6	846.1
Mining, Logging, and Construction													
2005	38.1	38.5	39.2	39.7	40.2	40.8	41.7	41.5	41.7	41.5	41.8	41.9	40.6
2006	41.6	42.3	43.3	43.9	44.5	45.7	46.1	46.4	46.5	46.2	46.6	47.3	45.0
2007	46.2	47.2	48.0	48.7	49.4	50.4	50.2	50.7	50.4	50.8	51.2	50.4	49.5
2008	48.5	48.9	48.8	48.8	49.0	49.1	48.5	48.4	47.7	46.5	45.4	44.5	47.8
2009	42.8	42.4	41.8	41.1	41.2	41.8	41.6	41.0	40.6	40.1	40.1	40.2	41.2
2010	38.6	38.4	39.1	40.2	40.0	40.7	41.5	42.0	41.4	41.5	41.1	40.8	40.4
2011	39.8	39.8	40.1	39.7	39.6	40.2	40.3	40.4	40.4	40.1	40.0	40.1	40.0
2012	40.0	40.5	41.2	41.6	42.1	43.2	43.4	44.0	44.0	44.0	43.8	44.0	42.7
2013	43.4	44.1	44.9	45.4	46.1	46.3	46.4	46.8	46.9	47.0	47.2	47.4	46.0
2014	46.9	47.8	48.5	49.3	50.3	51.2	51.9	52.4	52.3	52.4	52.7	52.9	50.7
2015	52.9	53.8	54.1	54.0	54.5	55.3	55.9	56.2	56.0	57.6	58.0	59.1	55.6

Employment by Industry: Austin-Round Rock, TX, 2005–2015—*Continued*

(Numbers in thousands, not seasonally adjusted)

Industry and year	January	February	March	April	May	June	July	August	September	October	November	December	Annual average
Manufacturing													
2005	62.9	62.9	62.9	62.9	62.7	63.4	63.5	63.6	63.1	62.9	63.2	63.5	63.1
2006	63.2	63.5	64.0	63.7	64.2	65.2	65.5	65.7	65.3	65.6	65.7	66.2	64.8
2007	65.3	65.7	66.0	66.3	66.4	67.0	66.8	66.6	65.8	65.6	64.7	65.1	65.9
2008	64.8	64.9	64.6	64.1	63.9	63.8	63.4	62.7	61.8	60.9	60.2	59.5	62.9
2009	56.2	54.9	53.4	54.7	54.2	53.7	53.4	53.4	52.9	52.8	52.1	52.3	53.7
2010	52.1	52.3	52.3	52.2	52.3	52.7	52.7	53.1	53.2	53.5	53.7	53.8	52.8
2011	53.5	53.8	54.2	54.6	54.9	55.3	55.7	55.8	55.5	55.9	55.9	55.9	55.1
2012	55.3	55.8	55.9	55.9	56.2	56.9	57.2	57.5	57.2	57.2	57.0	56.7	56.6
2013	56.3	56.2	56.2	56.8	56.9	57.6	57.7	57.8	57.5	57.7	58.0	58.2	57.2
2014	57.6	57.9	57.9	57.5	57.7	58.2	58.1	58.1	57.5	57.2	57.3	57.4	57.7
2015	57.2	57.3	57.4	57.2	57.2	58.1	58.3	58.3	57.7	57.7	57.6	56.9	57.6
Trade, Transportation, and Utilities													
2005	114.7	114.5	115.4	115.9	117.0	118.1	119.0	120.0	119.7	119.9	122.7	125.1	118.5
2006	120.0	119.5	120.2	121.4	122.0	123.3	124.0	125.2	125.0	126.2	130.4	133.3	124.2
2007	128.6	128.8	129.9	130.6	131.0	132.4	132.8	133.0	133.0	134.5	137.3	140.1	132.7
2008	135.5	135.0	134.7	135.1	135.1	135.8	136.2	137.4	136.7	137.8	139.5	140.3	136.6
2009	134.6	130.8	130.9	129.0	129.2	129.1	129.2	130.2	129.3	130.2	132.5	134.1	130.8
2010	131.1	130.1	130.7	131.6	132.1	132.5	132.7	133.8	133.5	135.0	138.4	140.6	133.5
2011	136.0	135.6	136.6	137.4	137.7	137.6	137.6	140.2	139.8	141.3	144.4	146.9	139.3
2012	142.0	141.3	141.9	142.7	143.4	144.1	144.2	145.9	145.3	146.7	151.4	153.0	145.2
2013	148.0	147.8	147.8	149.1	149.9	151.4	151.8	153.4	153.0	154.9	159.2	161.4	152.3
2014	156.3	155.8	155.6	156.2	156.5	157.5	157.5	158.5	158.2	159.9	163.9	165.9	158.5
2015	160.5	160.2	160.8	161.1	162.2	163.7	164.3	165.8	165.8	167.8	172.3	173.4	164.8
Wholesale Trade													
2005	32.7	32.9	32.9	33.1	33.4	33.5	33.9	34.0	33.9	33.7	33.3	33.4	33.4
2006	33.2	33.4	33.6	33.9	33.9	34.4	34.6	34.7	34.9	35.2	36.2	36.8	34.6
2007	36.4	36.6	36.8	36.9	37.2	38.0	37.8	37.5	37.3	37.5	37.0	38.0	37.3
2008	37.7	37.8	37.7	37.7	37.8	38.3	38.5	38.6	38.6	38.7	38.7	38.6	38.2
2009	38.2	35.3	35.4	34.5	34.4	34.3	34.8	34.6	34.4	34.4	34.5	34.6	35.0
2010	36.4	36.4	36.6	37.0	37.1	37.3	37.4	37.5	37.4	37.9	38.2	38.3	37.3
2011	38.3	38.7	38.9	39.2	39.4	39.6	39.9	40.1	40.4	41.0	41.2	41.5	39.9
2012	41.0	41.2	41.4	41.6	41.9	42.1	42.0	42.2	42.0	41.9	42.1	42.4	41.8
2013	42.6	42.9	43.1	43.2	43.0	43.7	43.8	44.1	43.9	44.4	44.5	44.7	43.7
2014	44.5	44.6	44.4	44.6	44.8	45.1	45.3	45.5	45.6	46.0	46.4	46.5	45.3
2015	46.8	47.0	47.2	47.2	47.5	47.8	48.4	49.0	48.9	50.2	50.8	51.8	48.6
Retail Trade													
2005	70.5	70.1	70.8	71.2	71.9	72.9	73.5	74.2	73.8	74.3	77.3	79.2	73.3
2006	74.8	74.0	74.3	75.1	75.5	76.4	76.8	77.7	77.1	77.9	81.0	82.9	77.0
2007	79.2	79.1	79.7	80.5	80.5	81.1	81.8	82.0	82.1	83.3	86.5	88.1	82.0
2008	84.3	83.6	83.4	84.0	83.9	84.1	84.6	85.4	84.6	85.7	87.3	88.1	84.9
2009	83.4	82.6	82.7	81.7	82.0	82.0	81.8	82.8	82.0	82.7	84.8	85.9	82.9
2010	81.9	80.9	81.2	81.8	82.1	82.4	82.7	83.5	83.0	84.1	87.0	88.6	83.3
2011	84.2	83.5	84.2	84.7	84.7	84.9	85.4	86.3	85.5	86.6	89.4	91.0	85.9
2012	87.1	86.2	86.5	87.2	87.6	88.2	88.5	89.6	89.0	90.6	94.9	95.7	89.3
2013	91.1	90.8	90.7	91.5	92.2	92.9	93.5	94.3	94.0	95.3	99.1	100.6	93.8
2014	96.3	95.9	95.9	96.1	96.2	96.8	97.1	97.6	96.9	98.1	101.5	102.6	97.6
2015	97.7	97.6	97.9	98.0	98.7	99.8	100.0	100.6	100.7	101.4	105.2	104.9	100.2
Transportation and Utilities													
2005	11.5	11.5	11.7	11.6	11.7	11.7	11.6	11.8	12.0	11.9	12.1	12.5	11.8
2006	12.0	12.1	12.3	12.4	12.6	12.5	12.6	12.8	13.0	13.1	13.2	13.6	12.7
2007	13.0	13.1	13.4	13.2	13.3	13.3	13.2	13.5	13.6	13.7	13.8	14.0	13.4
2008	13.5	13.6	13.6	13.4	13.4	13.4	13.1	13.4	13.5	13.4	13.5	13.6	13.5
2009	13.0	12.9	12.8	12.8	12.8	12.8	12.6	12.8	12.9	13.1	13.2	13.6	12.9
2010	12.8	12.8	12.9	12.8	12.9	12.8	12.6	12.8	13.1	13.0	13.2	13.7	13.0
2011	13.5	13.4	13.5	13.5	13.6	13.1	13.3	13.8	13.9	13.7	13.8	14.4	13.6
2012	13.9	13.9	14.0	13.9	13.9	13.8	13.7	14.1	14.3	14.2	14.4	14.9	14.1
2013	14.3	14.1	14.0	14.4	14.7	14.8	14.5	15.0	15.1	15.2	15.6	16.1	14.8
2014	15.5	15.3	15.3	15.5	15.5	15.6	15.1	15.4	15.7	15.8	16.0	16.8	15.6
2015	16.0	15.6	15.7	15.9	16.0	16.1	15.9	16.2	16.2	16.2	16.3	16.7	16.1

Employment by Industry: Austin-Round Rock, TX, 2005–2015—*Continued*

(Numbers in thousands, not seasonally adjusted)

Industry and year	January	February	March	April	May	June	July	August	September	October	November	December	Annual average
Information													
2005	21.3	21.4	21.6	21.5	21.7	21.9	22.0	21.8	22.4	21.8	22.0	22.2	21.8
2006	22.1	22.1	22.1	22.1	22.0	22.0	21.8	21.9	21.9	22.1	22.5	22.6	22.1
2007	22.3	22.5	22.5	22.6	22.7	22.6	22.0	22.0	22.0	21.9	22.2	22.1	22.3
2008	21.6	21.4	21.3	21.1	21.3	21.4	21.4	21.5	21.2	21.1	21.4	21.4	21.3
2009	20.7	20.6	20.5	20.3	20.2	19.9	19.9	19.9	19.7	19.6	19.7	19.9	20.1
2010	19.5	19.5	19.6	19.6	19.7	19.8	19.9	20.0	20.0	20.1	20.3	20.5	19.9
2011	20.1	20.2	20.3	20.4	20.6	20.8	21.2	21.3	21.4	21.4	21.8	21.9	21.0
2012	21.9	21.9	22.1	22.1	22.3	22.6	23.0	23.0	22.9	23.2	23.6	23.8	22.7
2013	23.1	23.2	23.6	23.4	23.4	23.8	24.1	24.2	24.1	24.1	24.6	24.9	23.9
2014	24.3	24.3	24.4	24.9	24.4	25.1	25.4	25.5	25.4	25.7	26.2	26.7	25.2
2015	26.2	26.2	26.3	26.9	27.0	27.4	27.1	27.2	27.2	27.1	27.3	27.4	26.9
Financial Activities													
2005	40.7	41.0	41.2	41.3	41.5	41.8	42.1	42.4	42.4	42.6	42.6	43.1	41.9
2006	42.6	42.9	43.2	43.4	43.7	44.1	44.2	44.5	44.7	44.9	44.9	45.4	44.0
2007	44.6	44.9	45.3	45.4	45.8	46.0	45.9	45.9	45.7	45.5	45.8	46.1	45.6
2008	45.3	45.7	45.7	45.9	46.0	46.2	46.2	46.2	46.0	45.7	45.8	46.0	45.9
2009	44.6	44.6	44.5	44.6	44.6	44.7	44.5	44.4	44.1	44.1	44.0	44.1	44.4
2010	43.1	43.2	43.3	43.2	43.4	43.4	43.4	43.4	43.1	43.5	43.6	43.7	43.4
2011	43.5	43.7	44.1	44.5	44.7	44.9	45.2	45.3	45.2	45.4	45.6	46.0	44.8
2012	45.7	45.9	46.2	46.3	46.7	47.1	47.0	47.4	47.4	48.0	48.1	48.3	47.0
2013	47.9	48.2	48.3	48.7	49.0	49.3	49.7	49.8	49.8	50.3	50.4	50.7	49.3
2014	50.7	51.1	51.3	51.4	51.7	52.1	52.0	52.2	51.9	52.4	52.5	53.0	51.9
2015	52.4	52.9	52.9	53.2	53.5	53.9	54.1	54.3	53.9	54.6	55.0	54.2	53.7
Professional and Business Services													
2005	93.2	94.2	95.1	96.0	96.1	97.4	98.2	98.8	98.8	98.5	99.2	99.7	97.1
2006	97.7	98.6	100.0	100.5	101.7	102.9	103.4	104.3	104.7	105.6	107.1	107.3	102.8
2007	104.1	106.3	107.8	107.3	108.3	109.8	110.1	111.4	111.4	111.8	112.3	112.3	109.4
2008	112.2	113.2	112.7	114.7	115.6	115.7	115.0	115.9	115.3	116.0	115.4	114.4	114.7
2009	111.5	111.3	111.1	111.0	111.1	111.2	109.8	110.1	108.9	110.4	110.5	109.8	110.6
2010	108.5	109.6	111.2	111.4	112.1	113.3	113.4	113.8	113.9	116.3	116.4	116.8	113.1
2011	115.8	117.4	118.8	120.3	120.0	121.2	121.6	123.0	123.8	124.1	124.7	125.5	121.4
2012	123.9	125.0	126.8	126.8	127.5	128.8	129.8	131.8	132.2	133.6	134.9	134.2	129.6
2013	131.3	133.4	135.0	137.0	137.8	139.0	140.0	142.1	142.7	143.9	145.1	144.6	139.3
2014	142.5	145.2	147.7	149.0	149.5	150.3	151.0	152.4	152.3	154.6	155.2	154.9	150.4
2015	153.3	155.6	157.5	158.5	159.4	161.0	162.6	163.5	163.1	166.5	167.3	167.1	161.3
Education and Health Services													
2005	69.5	70.4	70.9	71.3	71.4	70.6	70.1	70.6	72.3	72.3	72.4	72.7	71.2
2006	71.7	72.7	73.0	73.5	73.6	73.2	73.0	74.0	75.2	76.0	75.9	75.8	74.0
2007	73.8	75.7	76.5	76.4	77.1	76.7	77.0	77.5	78.9	79.4	79.8	80.0	77.4
2008	79.0	80.4	80.3	80.9	81.3	80.3	80.0	80.9	81.8	82.5	82.8	83.1	81.1
2009	81.0	82.3	82.9	83.5	84.0	83.1	83.3	83.9	84.0	84.9	85.2	85.3	83.6
2010	84.5	86.0	86.4	87.4	87.8	87.3	87.8	88.2	88.6	89.8	90.1	89.7	87.8
2011	88.7	89.8	90.1	92.2	92.5	91.9	92.6	94.3	95.0	95.4	96.1	95.9	92.9
2012	95.0	96.4	97.0	97.2	97.7	97.5	96.8	98.3	99.4	100.1	100.7	100.6	98.1
2013	99.7	101.3	101.3	102.4	102.6	102.0	101.3	102.7	103.4	104.3	104.9	104.4	102.5
2014	102.9	104.6	104.9	106.2	106.7	106.1	105.3	106.5	107.0	108.5	109.5	109.1	106.4
2015	107.7	109.7	109.9	111.6	112.3	111.7	111.0	112.5	113.0	113.1	112.5	113.4	111.5
Leisure and Hospitality													
2005	66.0	66.7	68.2	70.5	71.1	71.9	71.1	71.3	70.8	70.6	70.8	70.3	69.9
2006	69.5	70.6	72.2	74.2	75.1	76.6	75.4	76.1	76.6	75.3	75.9	76.5	74.5
2007	74.5	76.1	77.8	79.4	80.0	81.3	80.6	81.0	80.4	79.4	79.5	79.5	79.1
2008	78.0	79.5	80.7	82.4	83.3	84.0	83.0	83.3	82.8	83.5	83.7	82.5	82.2
2009	80.6	81.7	82.7	83.9	85.0	85.1	85.3	85.5	84.7	84.0	83.7	82.9	83.8
2010	80.7	82.1	83.9	85.3	86.6	87.4	86.4	86.6	86.5	86.8	87.2	86.9	85.5
2011	84.8	86.2	88.6	91.3	91.9	92.2	90.9	91.5	91.7	91.0	91.1	90.6	90.2
2012	88.8	90.2	92.2	94.1	95.3	96.3	94.4	94.9	95.3	95.9	97.1	97.2	94.3
2013	94.5	96.5	99.2	100.1	101.6	103.1	101.7	101.9	102.3	102.1	102.4	101.6	100.6
2014	100.3	102.6	105.1	106.4	107.8	109.6	108.6	108.9	109.3	108.8	109.3	108.6	107.1
2015	106.8	109.7	112.2	114.5	116.8	118.2	117.2	117.1	117.1	117.6	119.0	117.9	115.3

Employment by Industry: Austin-Round Rock, TX, 2005–2015—*Continued*

(Numbers in thousands, not seasonally adjusted)

Industry and year	January	February	March	April	May	June	July	August	September	October	November	December	Annual average
Other Services													
2005	26.1	26.2	26.4	26.9	26.8	27.3	26.9	27.0	27.0	26.4	26.5	26.6	26.7
2006	26.3	26.6	26.9	27.7	28.0	28.4	28.4	28.4	28.6	28.2	28.4	28.6	27.9
2007	27.3	28.0	28.3	28.4	28.7	29.1	28.5	28.4	28.4	28.4	28.7	28.8	28.4
2008	28.4	29.1	29.2	30.0	30.5	31.0	31.5	31.9	32.2	32.3	32.6	32.9	31.0
2009	32.9	33.6	33.6	33.7	33.9	34.4	33.9	33.7	33.3	33.3	33.2	33.2	33.6
2010	33.0	33.2	33.4	33.0	33.2	33.5	33.6	33.7	33.4	33.4	33.2	33.0	33.3
2011	32.9	33.2	33.5	33.7	33.8	34.3	34.2	34.1	33.8	34.0	33.9	33.8	33.8
2012	34.1	34.3	34.4	35.2	35.6	36.2	36.3	36.4	36.4	36.6	36.8	36.9	35.8
2013	36.7	37.1	37.3	37.6	38.0	38.5	38.4	38.4	38.0	38.3	38.6	38.3	37.9
2014	38.2	38.6	38.9	39.1	39.6	40.3	40.3	40.3	39.9	40.1	40.0	39.6	39.6
2015	39.5	39.9	39.8	40.0	40.3	41.0	41.6	41.5	41.0	41.2	41.3	41.1	40.7
Government													
2005	146.9	150.7	150.9	151.7	151.7	147.6	143.2	144.4	147.8	150.5	152.2	149.7	148.9
2006	149.4	153.1	153.7	154.4	153.9	150.2	142.0	145.9	154.6	156.1	156.0	154.4	152.0
2007	154.0	157.4	158.6	158.9	158.8	155.6	149.1	150.9	156.1	160.1	161.2	158.9	156.6
2008	160.0	163.4	165.8	163.2	163.0	161.1	154.5	155.8	162.7	164.3	166.6	164.6	162.1
2009	164.7	167.9	168.8	170.2	170.0	167.6	159.3	159.9	166.1	168.8	171.3	169.0	167.0
2010	168.7	170.9	174.0	173.4	174.6	172.8	163.3	163.7	166.5	171.4	172.9	169.8	170.2
2011	168.3	171.6	172.0	172.7	171.7	170.0	161.0	160.9	164.6	167.0	168.5	165.9	167.9
2012	166.5	168.4	168.9	169.6	169.0	166.9	160.2	159.6	164.8	168.4	171.0	167.9	166.8
2013	168.3	170.6	171.5	171.9	171.4	170.0	163.7	161.8	167.0	169.9	172.2	169.2	169.0
2014	169.5	171.6	172.6	172.3	172.1	170.4	164.3	162.5	167.6	172.1	173.1	172.0	170.0
2015	171.7	172.9	173.7	174.0	173.5	172.1	166.1	164.4	169.6	173.9	175.2	174.1	171.8

Employment by Industry: Indianapolis-Carmel-Anderson, 2005–2015

(Numbers in thousands, not seasonally adjusted)

Industry and year	January	February	March	April	May	June	July	August	September	October	November	December	Annual average
Total Nonfarm													
2005	902.7	909.3	917.1	928.4	935.1	931.1	922.3	930.4	939.6	939.1	942.7	940.4	928.2
2006	914.4	921.0	930.5	939.5	948.4	944.7	930.2	941.5	949.7	952.0	956.2	955.8	940.3
2007	926.2	925.4	940.9	948.5	960.7	957.4	942.8	956.8	962.3	965.4	968.8	967.0	951.9
2008	934.3	939.9	946.6	953.1	967.2	960.1	951.3	963.4	962.0	961.6	956.4	947.7	953.6
2009	912.3	910.5	911.4	912.4	917.8	910.2	898.9	910.0	913.4	914.2	917.2	914.6	911.9
2010	888.2	888.3	897.5	912.3	921.2	915.2	906.6	917.9	916.1	924.8	926.3	923.5	911.5
2011	900.1	901.5	912.3	924.9	933.0	923.8	924.0	935.3	942.3	945.1	947.5	949.7	928.3
2012	926.0	936.2	941.9	948.5	958.7	955.1	946.8	962.6	967.5	968.6	972.1	971.0	954.6
2013	943.7	950.9	958.4	966.2	974.8	972.1	963.9	983.7	986.2	989.3	1,002.1	999.6	974.2
2014	962.4	965.7	976.6	987.0	999.8	995.4	984.2	1,001.5	1,000.7	1,004.3	1,016.8	1,018.1	992.7
2015	986.2	989.9	999.5	1,011.5	1,023.2	1,019.8	1,014.1	1,028.3	1,027.1	1,029.2	1,034.9	1,038.1	1,016.8
Total Private													
2005	779.9	783.3	791.7	804.6	811.1	815.8	814.9	818.6	816.0	816.0	819.3	817.2	807.4
2006	792.2	795.1	804.2	813.3	821.0	827.6	820.7	826.8	823.8	824.2	828.2	827.2	817.0
2007	801.7	797.3	811.8	820.2	830.9	835.4	829.4	835.2	832.2	834.4	837.0	835.0	825.0
2008	806.3	807.2	812.9	820.6	833.0	833.4	829.6	833.9	828.7	827.2	821.7	813.1	822.3
2009	780.9	776.3	776.7	779.7	784.1	786.8	780.2	783.4	782.1	781.7	785.0	782.1	781.6
2010	757.2	755.3	764.3	779.1	784.4	788.5	787.7	792.5	787.1	793.8	795.0	793.1	781.5
2011	770.7	771.3	781.7	794.3	802.0	801.9	807.0	811.9	814.2	816.0	818.3	820.1	800.8
2012	798.7	806.4	812.9	820.2	829.3	834.9	832.0	837.6	838.6	839.9	843.3	842.5	828.0
2013	818.8	822.2	829.2	837.5	845.8	852.2	851.8	857.6	857.8	860.7	872.3	870.0	848.0
2014	835.9	836.2	846.3	857.2	869.3	870.9	868.2	873.7	871.6	875.5	886.8	887.4	864.9
2015	857.3	859.9	869.1	881.2	892.0	896.4	895.8	900.2	896.7	901.0	903.3	905.8	888.2
Goods Producing													
2005	156.0	155.8	157.5	160.3	161.5	163.4	162.6	164.1	163.7	162.9	162.4	160.9	160.9
2006	156.5	156.4	158.2	161.3	162.4	165.3	163.1	164.9	163.3	162.5	161.5	160.0	161.3
2007	153.8	150.7	154.1	156.3	158.2	160.1	159.7	160.9	159.9	157.8	156.8	155.3	157.0
2008	150.7	150.5	151.3	151.9	154.0	155.0	154.2	153.7	151.0	149.5	146.6	142.4	150.9
2009	135.3	132.4	131.2	130.9	130.5	131.1	130.8	131.3	130.1	128.8	127.6	125.6	130.5
2010	121.4	120.3	122.4	125.4	126.7	128.5	129.1	128.9	127.7	127.2	125.8	123.5	125.6
2011	119.1	118.4	120.9	123.5	125.4	128.1	129.0	129.9	129.9	130.1	128.6	127.7	125.9
2012	125.1	124.8	126.8	129.2	131.0	133.7	134.1	134.6	133.0	132.5	130.8	129.7	130.4
2013	127.1	127.3	127.7	129.9	131.8	134.4	134.6	134.9	134.3	134.9	134.3	132.6	132.0
2014	127.7	127.1	129.5	131.6	133.2	135.8	136.8	136.9	136.2	135.6	135.4	134.5	133.4
2015	130.2	130.3	131.8	134.3	136.3	138.7	139.3	139.7	138.9	138.5	137.4	136.2	136.0
Service-Providing													
2005	746.7	753.5	759.6	768.1	773.6	767.7	759.7	766.3	775.9	776.2	780.3	779.5	767.3
2006	757.9	764.6	772.3	778.2	786.0	779.4	767.1	776.6	786.4	789.5	794.7	795.8	779.0
2007	772.4	774.7	786.8	792.2	802.5	797.3	783.1	795.9	802.4	807.6	812.0	811.7	794.9
2008	783.6	789.4	795.3	801.2	813.2	805.1	797.1	809.7	811.0	812.1	809.8	805.3	802.7
2009	777.0	778.1	780.2	781.5	787.3	779.1	768.1	778.7	783.3	785.4	789.6	789.0	781.4
2010	766.8	768.0	775.1	786.9	794.5	786.7	777.5	789.0	788.4	797.6	800.5	800.0	785.9
2011	781.0	783.1	791.4	801.4	807.6	795.7	795.0	805.4	812.4	815.0	818.9	822.0	802.4
2012	800.9	811.4	815.1	819.3	827.7	821.4	812.7	828.0	834.5	836.1	841.3	841.3	824.1
2013	816.6	823.6	830.7	836.3	843.0	837.7	829.3	848.8	851.9	854.4	867.8	867.0	842.3
2014	834.7	838.6	847.1	855.4	866.6	859.6	847.4	864.6	864.5	868.7	881.4	883.6	859.4
2015	856.0	859.6	867.7	877.2	886.9	881.1	874.8	888.6	888.2	890.7	897.5	901.9	880.9
Mining and Logging													
2005	0.8	0.8	0.8	0.8	0.8	0.8	0.8	0.8	0.8	0.8	0.8	0.8	0.8
2006	0.8	0.8	0.8	0.8	0.8	0.8	0.8	0.8	0.8	0.8	0.8	0.8	0.8
2007	0.8	0.7	0.8	0.8	0.8	0.8	0.8	0.8	0.8	0.8	0.8	0.8	0.8
2008	0.7	0.7	0.8	0.8	0.8	0.8	0.8	0.8	0.8	0.8	0.8	0.8	0.8
2009	0.7	0.7	0.7	0.8	0.8	0.8	0.8	0.8	0.8	0.7	0.7	0.7	0.8
2010	0.7	0.7	0.7	0.7	0.7	0.7	0.7	0.7	0.7	0.7	0.7	0.7	0.7
2011	0.5	0.5	0.6	0.6	0.7	0.7	0.7	0.7	0.6	0.6	0.6	0.6	0.6
2012	0.6	0.6	0.6	0.6	0.6	0.6	0.6	0.6	0.6	0.6	0.6	0.6	0.6
2013	0.6	0.6	0.6	0.6	0.6	0.6	0.6	0.6	0.6	0.6	0.6	0.6	0.6
2014	0.5	0.5	0.6	0.6	0.6	0.6	0.7	0.6	0.6	0.6	0.6	0.6	0.6
2015	0.6	0.6	0.6	0.6	0.6	0.7	0.6	0.6	0.6	0.6	0.6	0.6	0.6

Employment by Industry: Indianapolis-Carmel-Anderson, 2005–2015—*Continued*

(Numbers in thousands, not seasonally adjusted)

Industry and year	January	February	March	April	May	June	July	August	September	October	November	December	Annual average
Construction													
2005.................	47.8	47.6	49.3	51.8	52.8	54.3	55.0	55.2	54.9	55.0	54.7	53.1	52.6
2006.................	49.2	49.5	51.0	53.7	54.9	56.7	56.6	56.8	56.2	56.0	55.3	54.3	54.2
2007.................	50.2	48.0	51.0	53.6	55.6	57.0	57.3	57.7	56.8	56.3	55.5	53.1	54.3
2008.................	49.2	48.9	49.8	51.4	52.8	53.1	53.7	52.8	51.7	50.4	49.2	46.3	50.8
2009.................	41.4	40.6	41.0	41.8	42.3	43.0	43.4	43.0	42.4	41.7	41.0	38.8	41.7
2010.................	35.3	34.3	36.2	39.1	40.3	41.6	42.3	42.0	41.0	41.0	40.2	37.9	39.3
2011.................	35.0	34.6	36.4	38.7	40.3	42.3	43.3	43.9	43.9	44.0	43.3	42.1	40.7
2012.................	39.4	39.2	40.5	42.5	43.8	45.1	45.5	45.5	44.6	44.4	43.6	42.6	43.1
2013.................	39.4	39.5	39.9	41.9	43.7	45.5	45.9	45.8	45.7	46.4	46.1	44.1	43.7
2014.................	39.7	39.1	40.8	42.7	43.8	45.6	46.2	46.1	45.7	45.1	45.0	43.6	43.6
2015.................	40.0	39.8	41.1	43.7	45.6	47.0	47.6	47.9	47.6	47.7	46.9	45.4	45.0
Manufacturing													
2005.................	107.4	107.4	107.4	107.7	107.9	108.3	106.8	108.1	108.0	107.1	106.9	107.0	107.5
2006.................	106.5	106.1	106.4	106.8	106.7	107.8	105.7	107.3	106.3	105.7	105.4	104.9	106.3
2007.................	102.8	102.0	102.3	101.9	101.8	102.3	101.6	102.4	102.3	100.7	100.5	101.4	101.8
2008.................	100.8	100.9	100.7	99.7	100.4	101.1	99.7	100.1	98.5	98.3	96.6	95.3	99.3
2009.................	93.2	91.1	89.5	88.3	87.4	87.3	86.6	87.5	86.9	86.4	85.9	86.1	88.0
2010.................	85.4	85.3	85.5	85.6	85.7	86.2	86.1	86.2	86.0	85.5	84.9	84.9	85.6
2011.................	83.6	83.3	83.9	84.2	84.4	85.1	85.0	85.3	85.4	85.5	84.7	85.0	84.6
2012.................	85.1	85.0	85.7	86.1	86.6	88.0	88.0	88.5	87.8	87.5	86.6	86.5	86.8
2013.................	87.1	87.2	87.2	87.4	87.5	88.3	88.1	88.5	88.0	87.9	87.6	87.9	87.7
2014.................	87.5	87.5	88.1	88.3	88.8	89.6	89.9	90.2	89.9	89.9	89.8	90.3	89.2
2015.................	89.6	89.9	90.1	90.0	90.1	91.0	91.1	91.2	90.7	90.2	89.9	90.2	90.3
Trade, Transportation, and Utilities													
2005.................	197.5	197.4	198.9	200.9	202.3	202.6	203.2	203.9	203.3	205.1	208.8	210.0	202.8
2006.................	201.3	199.9	201.5	201.4	203.0	203.9	203.5	203.4	202.9	204.4	209.1	211.1	203.8
2007.................	202.2	199.5	202.6	202.5	205.0	206.5	205.3	204.6	204.3	204.9	209.6	211.3	204.9
2008.................	201.8	200.5	201.7	201.9	204.9	205.3	204.4	204.8	203.6	204.5	205.7	206.1	203.8
2009.................	196.1	193.5	193.1	192.5	194.4	194.8	193.5	193.3	192.0	193.3	196.1	196.7	194.1
2010.................	189.6	187.5	189.2	190.9	192.7	193.5	193.7	194.2	192.4	195.1	198.4	199.7	193.1
2011.................	192.5	191.6	192.4	194.7	196.7	197.2	197.6	198.0	196.8	199.1	202.8	203.9	196.9
2012.................	196.8	195.8	197.1	198.3	200.9	202.2	201.6	201.5	201.6	203.9	208.5	209.8	201.5
2013.................	201.3	201.1	202.0	203.7	206.0	207.6	206.5	207.2	207.4	209.1	213.9	215.1	206.7
2014.................	205.7	205.1	205.9	206.7	209.1	210.2	210.2	210.5	210.2	211.0	215.0	216.8	209.7
2015.................	208.7	208.1	209.2	210.5	213.1	214.6	215.3	216.3	215.2	217.2	221.4	226.6	214.7
Wholesale Trade													
2005.................	47.5	47.7	48.0	48.2	48.2	48.4	48.6	48.6	48.4	48.5	48.5	48.7	48.3
2006.................	48.3	48.3	48.4	48.5	48.8	49.1	48.9	48.7	48.5	48.9	48.8	49.0	48.7
2007.................	48.6	48.6	49.0	48.9	49.1	49.5	49.9	49.4	49.2	49.2	49.5	49.6	49.2
2008.................	49.1	49.3	49.6	49.6	49.9	49.9	49.9	49.6	49.4	49.4	49.4	49.2	49.5
2009.................	47.9	47.5	47.2	46.6	46.6	46.4	46.5	46.0	45.5	45.7	45.6	45.6	46.4
2010.................	45.2	45.0	45.3	45.4	45.4	45.5	46.0	45.9	45.6	45.7	45.6	45.5	45.5
2011.................	45.7	45.9	46.0	46.4	46.8	46.8	47.0	47.0	46.8	46.9	47.0	46.9	46.6
2012.................	46.4	46.4	46.5	46.8	47.1	47.3	47.4	47.1	47.0	47.1	46.9	47.0	46.9
2013.................	46.4	46.7	47.0	47.2	47.4	47.7	47.9	47.5	47.3	47.3	47.4	47.4	47.3
2014.................	46.9	46.9	47.0	47.1	47.4	47.7	47.8	47.7	47.4	47.4	47.4	47.5	47.4
2015.................	47.2	47.3	47.4	47.6	47.8	48.0	48.3	48.3	48.0	47.0	46.2	46.3	47.5
Retail Trade													
2005.................	100.7	100.0	100.9	102.0	103.3	103.1	103.2	103.1	102.5	103.8	106.8	108.3	103.1
2006.................	101.6	100.2	101.3	101.0	101.8	102.1	102.1	101.8	101.1	101.9	105.8	107.4	102.3
2007.................	100.9	98.6	100.2	100.1	101.8	102.5	101.6	101.0	100.5	101.0	104.4	105.8	101.5
2008.................	99.0	97.5	97.8	97.8	100.0	100.2	100.2	100.3	99.6	100.3	101.4	101.8	99.7
2009.................	95.4	93.7	93.8	94.3	95.8	96.4	95.4	95.2	94.1	94.9	97.6	98.0	95.4
2010.................	93.5	91.9	92.8	93.6	95.0	95.5	95.3	95.3	93.6	95.6	98.4	99.2	95.0
2011.................	94.4	93.1	93.8	95.1	96.3	96.6	96.8	97.1	96.2	98.2	101.1	101.9	96.7
2012.................	97.2	96.2	97.2	97.8	99.4	99.7	99.0	98.7	98.7	100.4	104.2	104.3	99.4
2013.................	98.5	97.7	97.9	99.2	100.7	101.6	100.8	101.2	101.2	102.5	106.1	106.7	101.2
2014.................	100.1	99.8	100.4	101.4	103.1	103.8	103.6	103.7	103.6	104.2	107.4	108.3	103.3
2015.................	102.6	102.0	102.8	103.8	105.4	106.1	106.5	107.4	106.6	108.7	111.2	112.2	106.3

Employment by Industry: Indianapolis-Carmel-Anderson, 2005–2015—*Continued*

(Numbers in thousands, not seasonally adjusted)

Industry and year	January	February	March	April	May	June	July	August	September	October	November	December	Annual average
Transportation and Utilities													
2005	49.3	49.7	50.0	50.7	50.8	51.1	51.4	52.2	52.4	52.8	53.5	53.0	51.4
2006	51.4	51.4	51.8	51.9	52.4	52.7	52.5	52.9	53.3	53.6	54.5	54.7	52.8
2007	52.7	52.3	53.4	53.5	54.1	54.5	53.8	54.2	54.6	54.7	55.7	55.9	54.1
2008	53.7	53.7	54.3	54.5	55.0	55.2	54.3	54.9	54.6	54.8	54.9	55.1	54.6
2009	52.8	52.3	52.1	51.6	52.0	52.0	51.6	52.1	52.4	52.7	52.9	53.1	52.3
2010	50.9	50.6	51.1	51.9	52.3	52.5	52.4	53.0	53.2	53.8	54.4	55.0	52.6
2011	52.4	52.6	52.6	53.2	53.6	53.8	53.8	53.9	53.8	54.0	54.7	55.1	53.6
2012	53.2	53.2	53.4	53.7	54.4	55.2	55.2	55.7	55.9	56.4	57.4	58.5	55.2
2013	56.4	56.7	57.1	57.3	57.9	58.3	57.8	58.5	58.9	59.3	60.4	61.0	58.3
2014	58.7	58.4	58.5	58.2	58.6	58.7	58.8	59.1	59.2	59.4	60.2	61.0	59.1
2015	58.9	58.8	59.0	59.1	59.9	60.5	60.5	60.6	60.6	61.5	64.0	68.1	61.0
Information													
2005	16.7	16.9	16.9	16.9	17.1	17.3	17.2	17.2	16.8	16.7	16.8	17.0	17.0
2006	16.4	16.6	16.6	16.8	16.9	17.0	17.0	16.9	16.7	16.6	16.7	16.7	16.7
2007	16.7	16.8	16.7	16.8	17.0	17.2	17.3	17.3	17.2	17.1	17.1	17.3	17.0
2008	17.3	17.3	17.3	17.3	17.5	17.6	17.6	17.5	17.2	17.0	16.9	16.9	17.3
2009	16.7	16.7	16.4	16.3	16.4	16.6	16.4	16.3	16.1	15.9	15.8	15.9	16.3
2010	15.6	15.6	15.5	15.6	15.8	16.0	15.8	15.7	15.4	15.2	15.3	15.2	15.6
2011	14.9	14.8	14.9	14.8	15.1	15.3	15.2	15.3	15.3	15.3	15.4	15.4	15.1
2012	15.8	15.9	16.0	15.9	16.1	16.3	16.2	16.2	16.1	16.4	16.4	16.4	16.1
2013	16.4	16.4	16.5	16.6	16.5	16.9	17.0	16.8	16.6	16.7	16.7	16.7	16.7
2014	16.6	16.6	16.8	16.8	17.0	17.2	17.3	17.1	16.8	16.6	16.5	16.6	16.8
2015	16.6	16.7	16.6	16.5	16.5	16.7	16.6	16.4	16.1	16.0	16.0	16.1	16.4
Financial Activities													
2005	64.4	64.5	64.4	64.8	64.8	65.3	65.7	65.7	65.3	65.2	65.1	65.3	65.0
2006	64.4	64.5	64.5	64.6	64.9	65.3	65.2	65.3	64.7	64.5	64.3	64.5	64.7
2007	63.3	63.6	63.7	64.0	64.1	64.7	65.0	64.8	64.4	64.0	63.8	63.9	64.1
2008	62.2	62.3	62.2	62.1	62.3	62.7	62.9	62.4	61.6	61.5	60.8	61.0	62.0
2009	60.4	60.3	60.2	60.1	60.1	60.2	60.2	60.0	59.3	59.2	59.0	59.2	59.9
2010	59.1	58.9	59.0	59.1	59.3	59.8	60.3	60.2	59.7	60.1	60.1	60.2	59.7
2011	59.8	59.9	60.1	60.0	60.3	60.7	60.8	60.5	60.2	60.3	60.2	60.4	60.3
2012	60.0	60.0	60.1	60.1	60.4	60.8	60.8	60.6	60.1	60.1	60.0	60.2	60.3
2013	59.7	59.6	59.6	59.9	60.4	61.1	61.1	61.0	60.6	60.7	60.8	61.0	60.5
2014	59.8	59.9	60.2	60.4	60.9	61.3	61.5	61.6	61.4	61.7	61.9	62.0	61.1
2015	61.6	61.9	62.2	62.3	62.9	63.4	63.7	63.9	63.6	63.0	62.9	63.2	62.9
Professional and Business Services													
2005	118.5	118.8	120.4	122.1	122.7	123.2	125.0	124.4	124.3	125.2	125.1	123.3	122.8
2006	119.6	120.5	122.4	125.1	127.0	127.9	127.6	129.9	129.3	129.3	130.3	128.9	126.5
2007	126.7	125.9	129.2	131.9	133.8	133.3	132.9	134.5	134.6	137.0	136.7	134.6	132.6
2008	129.7	129.0	130.1	132.5	133.3	133.7	133.0	135.0	133.8	135.3	132.8	129.1	132.3
2009	121.5	120.3	120.0	120.7	120.2	121.8	119.6	121.6	122.4	124.8	127.0	126.7	122.2
2010	118.4	117.7	119.5	124.7	124.3	125.8	126.3	128.2	126.0	129.6	130.0	130.8	125.1
2011	125.7	125.1	127.6	131.2	131.3	130.3	132.9	135.0	135.7	136.8	137.4	139.1	132.3
2012	131.8	135.6	135.7	137.3	138.8	141.7	141.0	143.5	143.4	143.8	145.0	143.8	140.1
2013	138.2	137.6	139.8	142.2	143.0	144.9	146.8	149.9	150.1	151.0	159.0	157.3	146.7
2014	148.2	145.5	148.1	152.7	155.3	154.3	152.8	156.6	156.7	160.2	167.8	166.9	155.4
2015	154.9	154.2	157.0	161.5	163.8	164.1	163.3	164.1	163.0	164.2	166.3	165.2	161.8
Education and Health Services													
2005	106.1	108.1	108.8	109.7	108.7	107.3	105.9	106.3	110.2	110.7	111.3	111.5	108.7
2006	108.9	111.0	111.8	111.5	110.4	109.4	107.6	108.5	112.1	113.7	113.9	113.9	111.1
2007	111.3	113.4	114.5	115.5	114.8	113.1	112.1	114.0	117.2	118.8	119.4	120.0	115.3
2008	116.4	118.9	119.4	120.4	120.6	118.1	117.9	118.9	123.0	124.5	125.1	125.6	120.7
2009	123.4	125.5	125.6	126.8	126.0	124.2	123.4	124.8	128.9	129.6	130.4	130.4	126.6
2010	128.9	131.0	131.5	132.5	131.4	128.8	127.5	128.9	133.1	134.5	134.8	134.5	131.5
2011	132.9	135.1	135.5	136.8	136.2	132.6	133.3	134.3	140.2	139.5	139.6	139.8	136.3
2012	138.1	141.3	141.7	141.3	140.2	136.7	135.9	137.6	143.6	143.4	143.7	144.0	140.6
2013	141.2	144.6	145.0	144.5	143.0	140.2	139.7	141.1	144.6	145.1	145.3	145.2	143.3
2014	141.5	144.2	144.7	144.7	144.2	140.9	140.0	140.6	143.8	144.2	144.7	145.0	143.2
2015	143.3	145.6	145.9	146.8	145.8	143.6	144.1	145.0	148.2	149.9	149.9	150.2	146.5

Employment by Industry: Indianapolis-Carmel-Anderson, 2005–2015—*Continued*

(Numbers in thousands, not seasonally adjusted)

Industry and year	January	February	March	April	May	June	July	August	September	October	November	December	Annual average
Leisure and Hospitality													
2005	83.6	84.3	86.9	91.8	95.4	97.8	96.3	97.9	94.0	92.0	91.7	90.9	91.9
2006	87.3	88.1	90.7	93.7	97.1	98.7	97.0	98.3	95.6	94.2	93.5	93.1	93.9
2007	88.9	88.5	91.7	93.5	97.8	99.7	96.3	98.8	94.8	95.0	93.9	92.9	94.3
2008	89.1	89.2	91.3	94.3	99.6	99.9	98.3	100.6	98.0	94.7	93.6	92.2	95.1
2009	88.2	88.4	90.8	93.0	96.6	97.8	96.2	96.6	94.4	91.2	90.3	88.8	92.7
2010	85.6	85.8	88.1	91.7	94.7	96.0	94.9	96.6	93.3	92.5	91.0	89.8	91.7
2011	86.7	87.2	90.5	93.4	96.8	97.0	97.1	97.9	95.6	94.6	93.9	93.5	93.7
2012	91.0	92.5	94.8	97.3	100.7	101.6	100.5	101.8	99.6	98.4	97.5	97.3	97.8
2013	93.8	94.1	96.5	99.2	103.1	103.9	103.0	103.8	101.7	100.5	99.3	98.8	99.8
2014	93.8	94.7	97.4	100.7	105.4	106.2	104.8	106.1	102.7	102.6	101.7	101.9	101.5
2015	98.5	99.4	102.3	105.0	108.8	109.8	107.9	109.6	107.0	107.7	104.9	104.0	105.4
Other Services													
2005	37.1	37.5	37.9	38.1	38.6	38.9	39.0	39.1	38.4	38.2	38.1	38.3	38.3
2006	37.8	38.1	38.5	38.9	39.3	40.1	39.7	39.6	39.2	39.0	38.9	39.0	39.0
2007	38.8	38.9	39.3	39.7	40.2	40.8	40.8	40.3	39.8	39.8	39.7	39.7	39.8
2008	39.1	39.5	39.6	40.2	40.8	41.1	41.3	41.0	40.5	40.2	40.2	39.8	40.3
2009	39.3	39.2	39.4	39.4	39.9	40.3	40.1	39.5	38.9	38.9	38.8	38.8	39.4
2010	38.6	38.5	39.1	39.2	39.5	40.1	40.1	39.8	39.5	39.6	39.6	39.4	39.4
2011	39.1	39.2	39.8	39.9	40.2	40.7	41.1	41.0	40.5	40.3	40.4	40.3	40.2
2012	40.1	40.5	40.7	40.8	41.2	41.9	41.9	41.8	41.2	41.4	41.4	41.3	41.2
2013	41.1	41.5	42.1	41.5	42.0	43.2	43.1	42.9	42.5	42.7	43.0	43.3	42.4
2014	42.6	43.1	43.7	43.6	44.2	45.0	44.8	44.3	43.8	43.6	43.8	43.7	43.9
2015	43.5	43.7	44.1	44.3	44.8	45.5	45.6	45.2	44.7	44.5	44.5	44.3	44.6
Government													
2005	122.8	126.0	125.4	123.8	124.0	115.3	107.4	111.8	123.6	123.1	123.4	123.2	120.8
2006	122.2	125.9	126.3	126.2	127.4	117.1	109.5	114.7	125.9	127.8	128.0	128.6	123.3
2007	124.5	128.1	129.1	128.3	129.8	122.0	113.4	121.6	130.1	131.0	131.8	132.0	126.8
2008	128.0	132.7	133.7	132.5	134.2	126.7	121.7	129.5	133.3	134.4	134.7	134.6	131.3
2009	131.4	134.2	134.7	132.7	133.7	123.4	118.7	126.6	131.3	132.5	132.2	132.5	130.3
2010	131.0	133.0	133.2	133.2	136.8	126.7	118.9	125.4	129.0	131.0	131.3	130.4	130.0
2011	129.4	130.2	130.6	130.6	131.0	121.9	117.0	123.4	128.1	129.1	129.2	129.6	127.5
2012	127.3	129.8	129.0	128.3	129.4	120.2	114.8	125.0	128.9	128.7	128.8	128.5	126.6
2013	124.9	128.7	129.2	128.7	129.0	119.9	112.1	126.1	128.4	128.6	129.8	129.6	126.3
2014	126.5	129.5	130.3	129.8	130.5	124.5	116.0	127.8	129.1	128.8	130.0	130.7	127.8
2015	128.9	130.0	130.4	130.3	131.2	123.4	118.3	128.1	130.4	128.2	131.6	132.3	128.6

Employment by Industry: San Jose-Sunnyvale-Santa Clara, CA, 2005–2015

(Numbers in thousands, not seasonally adjusted)

Industry and year	January	February	March	April	May	June	July	August	September	October	November	December	Annual average
Total Nonfarm													
2005	863.8	867.2	870.8	871.4	875.0	881.0	878.2	880.0	879.6	885.8	889.2	895.6	878.1
2006	880.9	888.7	892.1	892.1	899.2	905.1	902.2	904.3	904.5	906.4	910.1	916.0	900.1
2007	901.7	908.0	914.1	911.3	918.8	926.9	926.1	924.8	923.7	929.6	933.5	935.2	921.1
2008	922.4	926.2	930.0	927.9	931.6	934.3	928.5	932.5	931.0	926.6	922.5	918.7	927.7
2009	893.2	885.0	881.0	875.1	875.4	875.6	852.2	855.8	858.5	865.6	868.4	868.3	871.2
2010	853.3	855.0	859.3	866.4	873.1	874.9	863.3	864.1	868.2	879.3	883.6	885.7	868.9
2011	871.7	877.2	880.7	884.5	888.0	893.6	883.8	887.5	893.7	902.4	905.2	908.2	889.7
2012	895.5	902.0	908.5	917.2	922.8	931.4	920.7	926.2	930.2	940.0	945.6	948.7	924.1
2013	934.6	943.1	947.3	952.5	958.7	964.6	953.5	963.1	966.7	974.4	984.2	987.2	960.8
2014	975.3	983.0	988.3	993.0	999.0	1,004.7	995.8	1,005.2	1,009.3	1,018.1	1,022.9	1,026.1	1,001.7
2015	1,014.6	1,020.6	1,025.3	1,031.4	1,038.8	1,044.6	1,044.8	1,049.6	1,049.0	1,059.6	1,066.5	1,068.7	1,042.8
Total Private													
2005	768.3	771.0	773.9	774.4	777.6	784.0	783.9	786.3	785.8	789.6	792.6	799.4	782.2
2006	785.2	792.2	795.4	794.8	801.4	807.7	807.1	810.6	810.2	808.7	812.5	818.5	803.7
2007	804.0	811.0	815.8	813.2	820.5	829.1	831.0	830.9	828.8	831.3	834.9	836.9	824.0
2008	823.4	828.0	830.9	829.5	832.6	835.7	834.5	838.0	833.0	827.9	824.2	820.9	829.9
2009	795.8	788.2	783.4	775.6	775.2	775.3	767.1	767.0	762.5	767.1	769.1	770.2	774.7
2010	757.3	758.8	761.7	767.0	772.2	778.3	778.3	780.6	778.3	783.9	786.6	789.6	774.4
2011	777.1	781.9	785.0	788.0	791.2	797.4	802.5	805.1	802.8	808.6	810.8	813.8	797.0
2012	803.8	809.1	814.5	823.0	828.6	836.5	839.6	843.1	840.0	846.5	851.5	855.4	832.6
2013	842.0	849.1	854.2	858.2	863.0	870.2	874.9	879.7	875.4	880.3	888.8	893.0	869.1
2014	880.8	887.4	892.5	896.1	902.0	910.5	913.5	919.1	917.1	922.9	927.0	930.9	908.3
2015	920.8	926.0	931.2	936.6	943.5	949.8	961.0	962.2	957.2	965.8	971.9	974.7	950.1
Goods Producing													
2005	205.5	205.2	205.2	207.5	207.6	209.9	211.6	212.0	211.2	210.9	209.4	209.9	208.8
2006	207.7	208.5	208.3	207.3	209.7	210.7	212.6	213.4	212.5	210.8	208.7	208.9	209.9
2007	207.1	208.7	209.5	209.5	211.3	215.1	217.7	218.3	217.5	216.0	214.1	212.8	213.1
2008	210.7	211.0	210.6	210.4	212.2	213.4	214.9	215.2	213.3	210.5	207.0	205.1	211.2
2009	198.5	194.8	192.6	190.0	188.5	188.0	187.0	186.9	185.9	184.1	183.4	182.1	188.5
2010	180.5	180.0	180.9	180.9	181.9	184.5	186.1	187.5	187.0	186.7	185.2	185.1	183.9
2011	183.0	183.6	184.2	185.2	186.2	188.5	190.7	191.6	190.1	188.2	187.0	186.8	187.1
2012	186.1	186.4	186.7	188.3	190.3	193.6	194.3	195.1	193.6	192.1	191.5	191.2	190.8
2013	188.2	188.6	189.4	190.2	191.1	194.1	196.8	198.1	197.2	194.8	195.1	195.2	193.2
2014	193.1	193.9	194.7	195.1	196.9	199.4	200.5	203.0	202.5	200.0	200.2	200.6	198.3
2015	198.3	199.7	200.9	202.1	203.7	206.4	208.9	209.9	208.5	208.2	207.2	206.5	205.0
Service-Providing													
2005	658.3	662.0	665.6	663.9	667.4	671.1	666.6	668.0	668.4	674.9	679.8	685.7	669.3
2006	673.2	680.2	683.8	684.8	689.5	694.4	689.6	690.9	692.0	695.6	701.4	707.1	690.2
2007	694.6	699.3	704.6	701.8	707.5	711.8	708.4	706.5	706.2	713.6	719.4	722.4	708.0
2008	711.7	715.2	719.4	717.5	719.4	720.9	713.6	717.3	717.7	716.1	715.5	713.6	716.5
2009	694.7	690.2	688.4	685.1	686.9	687.6	665.2	668.9	672.6	681.5	685.0	686.2	682.7
2010	672.8	675.0	678.4	685.5	691.2	690.4	677.2	676.6	681.2	692.6	698.4	700.6	685.0
2011	688.7	693.6	696.5	699.3	701.8	705.1	693.1	695.9	703.6	714.2	718.2	721.4	702.6
2012	709.4	715.6	721.8	728.9	732.5	737.8	726.4	731.1	736.6	747.9	754.1	757.5	733.3
2013	746.4	754.5	757.9	762.3	767.6	770.5	756.7	765.0	769.5	779.6	789.1	792.0	767.6
2014	782.2	789.1	793.6	797.9	802.1	805.3	795.3	802.2	806.8	818.1	822.7	825.5	803.4
2015	816.3	820.9	824.4	829.3	835.1	838.2	835.9	839.7	840.5	851.4	859.3	862.2	837.8
Mining and Logging													
2005	0.1	0.1	0.1	0.2	0.2	0.2	0.2	0.2	0.2	0.3	0.3	0.2	0.2
2006	0.3	0.3	0.2	0.2	0.2	0.3	0.3	0.3	0.3	0.3	0.3	0.3	0.3
2007	0.3	0.3	0.3	0.3	0.3	0.3	0.3	0.3	0.3	0.3	0.3	0.3	0.3
2008	0.3	0.3	0.3	0.3	0.3	0.3	0.3	0.3	0.3	0.3	0.3	0.3	0.3
2009	0.3	0.2	0.2	0.2	0.2	0.2	0.2	0.2	0.2	0.3	0.2	0.2	0.2
2010	0.2	0.2	0.2	0.2	0.2	0.2	0.2	0.2	0.2	0.2	0.2	0.2	0.2
2011	0.2	0.2	0.2	0.2	0.2	0.2	0.2	0.2	0.2	0.2	0.2	0.2	0.2
2012	0.2	0.2	0.2	0.2	0.2	0.2	0.2	0.3	0.3	0.3	0.3	0.2	0.2
2013	0.2	0.2	0.2	0.2	0.3	0.3	0.3	0.3	0.3	0.3	0.3	0.3	0.3
2014	0.3	0.3	0.3	0.3	0.3	0.3	0.3	0.3	0.3	0.3	0.3	0.3	0.3
2015	0.2	0.2	0.2	0.2	0.2	0.2	0.3	0.3	0.3	0.3	0.3	0.2	0.2

Employment by Industry: San Jose-Sunnyvale-Santa Clara, CA, 2005–2015—*Continued*

(Numbers in thousands, not seasonally adjusted)

Industry and year	January	February	March	April	May	June	July	August	September	October	November	December	Annual average
Construction													
2005	41.6	41.7	42.3	43.0	43.6	45.0	45.7	46.4	46.7	46.3	46.0	45.9	44.5
2006	44.9	45.4	45.1	44.3	46.2	47.4	47.9	48.7	48.9	48.2	47.6	46.9	46.8
2007	45.0	45.5	46.3	46.0	47.0	47.9	48.6	49.2	49.2	48.3	47.3	46.6	47.2
2008	44.3	44.6	44.2	44.0	44.6	45.1	45.5	45.9	45.1	43.7	41.9	40.9	44.2
2009	37.8	36.2	35.9	34.9	34.2	34.2	33.8	33.8	33.4	33.2	33.1	32.3	34.4
2010	31.2	30.8	31.2	31.8	32.1	32.9	33.4	33.2	33.1	32.9	32.0	31.7	32.2
2011	29.8	29.8	30.2	30.2	30.5	31.2	32.8	33.1	33.4	32.9	32.8	32.6	31.6
2012	31.9	32.1	32.4	33.2	34.7	35.6	35.8	35.9	35.7	35.9	36.0	36.0	34.6
2013	34.9	35.3	35.6	35.9	36.3	37.2	38.7	39.1	38.5	38.4	38.3	38.5	37.2
2014	37.2	37.4	37.6	37.8	38.3	39.3	40.5	41.1	41.0	40.8	40.8	40.4	39.4
2015	40.0	40.6	41.4	42.2	42.6	43.4	44.6	45.2	44.8	44.8	44.3	44.5	43.2
Manufacturing													
2005	163.8	163.4	162.8	164.3	163.8	164.7	165.7	165.4	164.3	164.3	163.1	163.8	164.1
2006	162.5	162.8	163.0	162.8	163.3	163.0	164.4	164.4	163.3	162.3	160.8	161.7	162.9
2007	161.8	162.9	162.9	163.2	164.0	166.9	168.8	168.8	168.0	167.4	166.5	165.9	165.6
2008	166.1	166.1	166.1	166.1	167.3	168.0	169.1	169.0	167.9	166.5	164.8	163.9	166.7
2009	160.4	158.4	156.5	154.9	154.1	153.6	153.0	152.9	152.2	150.7	150.1	149.6	153.9
2010	149.1	149.0	149.5	148.9	149.6	151.4	152.5	154.1	153.7	153.6	153.0	153.2	151.5
2011	153.0	153.6	153.8	154.8	155.5	157.1	157.7	158.3	156.5	155.1	154.0	154.0	155.3
2012	154.0	154.1	154.1	154.9	155.4	157.8	158.3	158.9	157.6	155.9	155.2	155.0	155.9
2013	153.1	153.1	153.6	154.1	154.5	156.6	157.8	158.7	158.4	156.1	156.5	156.4	155.7
2014	155.6	156.2	156.8	157.0	158.3	159.8	159.7	161.6	161.2	158.9	159.1	159.9	158.7
2015	158.1	158.9	159.3	159.7	160.9	162.8	164.0	164.4	163.4	163.1	162.6	161.8	161.6
Trade, Transportation, and Utilities													
2005	131.4	130.3	130.4	130.3	130.8	131.3	132.2	132.9	133.6	134.3	137.2	140.1	132.9
2006	135.4	133.9	133.9	133.8	134.5	135.3	136.5	137.7	138.2	138.7	142.7	145.2	137.2
2007	139.4	137.7	137.9	137.3	137.9	138.9	140.1	140.0	139.7	140.0	143.3	145.3	139.8
2008	140.3	138.8	139.0	137.2	137.3	136.9	137.4	137.6	136.3	136.0	137.4	138.1	137.7
2009	130.9	128.5	126.9	125.4	126.0	125.5	124.4	124.4	124.3	124.7	127.8	129.2	126.5
2010	124.7	123.5	123.1	123.8	124.5	125.2	125.6	126.2	125.8	126.2	129.9	131.3	125.8
2011	125.8	124.7	124.2	125.4	125.8	126.7	127.5	128.2	128.1	129.6	133.2	135.3	127.9
2012	129.7	128.1	128.0	129.4	130.1	131.0	132.2	132.4	132.0	133.3	138.4	140.1	132.1
2013	134.1	133.1	132.6	132.9	133.2	134.3	135.3	135.5	134.7	135.7	140.3	142.3	135.3
2014	136.6	135.2	135.4	135.8	135.9	136.8	137.5	137.8	137.3	137.8	142.3	144.5	137.7
2015	139.2	137.3	137.0	137.1	137.3	138.1	138.9	139.3	138.7	139.0	143.8	145.9	139.3
Wholesale Trade													
2005	34.9	35.2	35.2	35.3	35.6	35.9	36.2	36.4	36.6	36.6	36.5	36.8	35.9
2006	37.1	37.4	37.5	37.9	38.0	38.3	38.8	38.9	39.1	39.1	39.2	39.4	38.4
2007	39.0	39.4	39.4	39.1	39.3	39.9	40.1	40.1	40.2	40.4	40.5	40.8	39.9
2008	40.6	40.5	41.0	40.3	40.4	40.1	39.7	39.5	39.3	39.2	38.8	38.4	39.8
2009	37.2	36.7	36.3	36.2	36.0	35.7	35.1	35.1	34.8	35.0	34.9	34.9	35.7
2010	34.6	34.7	34.7	34.8	34.9	35.1	35.3	35.2	35.3	35.0	34.9	34.9	35.0
2011	34.5	34.5	34.3	33.9	33.9	33.8	33.9	33.8	33.6	33.8	33.6	33.9	34.0
2012	34.0	34.3	34.0	34.4	34.6	34.7	35.3	35.4	35.2	36.0	35.9	36.0	35.0
2013	36.0	36.1	36.1	36.3	36.2	36.3	36.7	36.6	36.4	36.2	36.5	36.5	36.3
2014	36.4	36.4	36.5	36.4	36.3	36.4	36.6	36.5	36.4	36.4	36.6	36.6	36.5
2015	36.0	36.1	36.0	36.1	36.3	36.5	36.7	36.6	36.4	36.3	36.6	36.6	36.4
Retail Trade													
2005	83.4	82.0	82.1	81.9	82.1	82.3	82.9	83.5	83.9	84.8	87.8	90.3	83.9
2006	85.8	83.9	83.8	83.4	83.7	84.0	84.8	85.6	85.8	86.5	90.1	92.3	85.8
2007	87.5	85.3	85.4	84.8	85.1	85.2	86.2	86.1	85.6	85.9	89.1	90.6	86.4
2008	86.5	84.9	84.6	83.6	83.3	83.1	84.3	84.6	83.5	83.4	85.2	86.0	84.4
2009	81.0	79.3	78.5	77.3	77.8	77.8	77.5	77.5	77.5	77.8	81.1	82.3	78.8
2010	78.3	77.1	76.7	77.3	77.6	78.0	78.2	78.8	78.2	79.1	82.9	84.0	78.9
2011	79.5	78.3	78.0	79.5	79.8	80.7	81.4	82.3	82.3	83.7	87.4	88.8	81.8
2012	83.4	81.5	81.7	82.5	82.9	83.4	83.8	83.8	83.4	83.9	89.0	90.1	84.1
2013	84.7	83.3	82.9	83.0	83.3	84.1	84.4	84.7	84.0	84.8	88.8	90.2	84.9
2014	85.6	84.4	84.3	84.9	84.9	85.5	85.9	86.4	86.0	86.4	90.5	91.9	86.4
2015	87.6	86.4	86.2	86.0	86.0	86.5	86.9	87.4	87.0	86.8	91.0	92.2	87.5

Employment by Industry: San Jose-Sunnyvale-Santa Clara, CA, 2005–2015—*Continued*

(Numbers in thousands, not seasonally adjusted)

Industry and year	January	February	March	April	May	June	July	August	September	October	November	December	Annual average
Transportation and Utilities													
2005............	13.1	13.1	13.1	13.1	13.1	13.1	13.1	13.0	13.1	12.9	12.9	13.0	13.1
2006............	12.5	12.6	12.6	12.5	12.8	13.0	12.9	13.2	13.3	13.1	13.4	13.5	13.0
2007............	12.9	13.0	13.1	13.4	13.5	13.8	13.8	13.8	13.9	13.7	13.7	13.9	13.5
2008............	13.2	13.4	13.4	13.3	13.6	13.7	13.4	13.5	13.5	13.4	13.4	13.7	13.5
2009............	12.7	12.5	12.1	11.9	12.2	12.0	11.8	11.8	12.0	11.9	11.8	12.0	12.1
2010............	11.8	11.7	11.7	11.7	12.0	12.1	12.1	12.2	12.3	12.1	12.1	12.4	12.0
2011............	11.8	11.9	11.9	12.0	12.1	12.2	12.2	12.1	12.2	12.1	12.2	12.6	12.1
2012............	12.3	12.3	12.3	12.5	12.6	12.9	13.1	13.2	13.4	13.4	13.5	14.0	13.0
2013............	13.4	13.7	13.6	13.6	13.7	13.9	14.2	14.2	14.3	14.7	15.0	15.6	14.2
2014............	14.6	14.4	14.6	14.5	14.7	14.9	15.0	14.9	14.9	15.0	15.2	16.0	14.9
2015............	15.6	14.8	14.8	15.0	15.0	15.1	15.3	15.3	15.3	15.9	16.2	17.1	15.5
Information													
2005............	34.6	34.9	35.2	34.8	35.2	35.9	36.3	36.7	36.6	37.1	37.8	38.2	36.1
2006............	38.0	38.2	38.3	38.2	38.4	38.6	38.9	38.9	38.5	38.1	38.3	38.6	38.4
2007............	38.8	39.4	39.7	39.3	40.1	40.9	41.4	41.7	41.5	41.7	42.3	42.6	40.8
2008............	42.5	42.5	42.3	42.8	43.4	43.8	45.0	44.9	44.3	44.0	44.3	44.0	43.7
2009............	44.7	43.6	43.3	42.8	43.0	43.4	44.5	44.3	43.9	44.0	44.3	44.4	43.9
2010............	44.1	44.5	44.2	44.8	45.4	46.6	47.6	47.8	47.5	47.9	48.5	48.6	46.5
2011............	49.2	49.7	49.8	50.0	50.4	51.9	52.7	52.7	52.1	52.2	52.2	52.5	51.3
2012............	52.1	52.6	52.8	53.3	53.5	54.5	55.5	55.5	54.9	55.1	55.2	55.6	54.2
2013............	56.4	56.6	57.1	57.0	57.2	58.9	60.2	60.0	59.3	60.0	60.7	61.3	58.7
2014............	61.4	62.4	63.3	63.6	64.2	66.5	68.9	68.7	68.3	69.0	69.5	70.2	66.3
2015............	71.1	71.4	72.0	72.5	73.1	75.9	78.0	77.3	76.9	76.6	76.1	77.2	74.8
Financial Activities													
2005............	35.7	35.6	35.8	35.7	35.8	36.0	36.1	36.4	36.2	36.5	36.5	36.8	36.1
2006............	36.5	36.6	36.8	36.9	37.3	37.0	37.1	37.0	36.9	36.9	36.9	36.9	36.9
2007............	37.0	37.1	37.1	37.0	37.2	37.0	37.1	36.9	36.8	36.6	36.2	36.3	36.9
2008............	35.3	35.5	35.1	34.9	34.8	34.5	34.3	34.0	33.8	33.4	32.7	32.8	34.3
2009............	32.2	31.9	31.9	31.8	31.7	31.5	31.3	31.2	30.9	31.2	31.2	31.3	31.5
2010............	30.8	30.9	31.5	30.2	30.6	30.8	31.0	31.1	30.9	31.4	31.7	31.8	31.1
2011............	31.6	31.8	31.8	31.9	32.0	32.3	32.6	32.5	32.6	32.9	33.2	33.3	32.4
2012............	32.8	32.7	33.0	33.0	33.2	33.5	33.6	33.5	33.4	33.7	33.9	33.7	33.3
2013............	32.8	33.1	33.4	33.7	34.0	34.0	34.1	34.2	34.0	34.4	34.5	34.5	33.9
2014............	34.0	34.2	34.4	34.4	34.7	35.1	34.9	34.8	34.8	34.9	34.9	34.9	34.7
2015............	34.7	34.8	34.7	34.9	35.3	35.5	35.9	35.8	35.5	35.6	35.8	35.6	35.3
Professional and Business Services													
2005............	164.4	166.0	166.8	165.0	165.1	165.9	164.3	165.2	165.7	166.1	166.4	168.3	165.8
2006............	166.1	168.5	169.2	169.4	169.6	171.4	172.4	173.7	174.6	174.1	174.9	177.6	171.8
2007............	176.0	177.5	177.5	176.9	177.3	177.9	178.4	178.0	177.8	178.5	179.4	180.1	177.9
2008............	176.9	178.0	179.2	179.3	178.4	179.6	179.5	180.0	179.3	177.6	176.5	175.3	178.3
2009............	167.8	165.9	164.5	160.7	159.3	159.7	158.3	158.1	157.4	158.0	158.4	158.9	160.6
2010............	156.3	157.4	158.1	159.5	159.9	161.6	162.2	162.7	162.0	163.3	163.6	164.3	160.9
2011............	162.5	163.6	164.7	165.1	164.6	166.1	168.7	169.4	168.7	169.0	168.8	169.3	166.7
2012............	168.4	170.4	172.2	175.2	175.6	178.0	181.0	182.3	181.5	183.1	184.1	186.2	178.2
2013............	184.0	186.3	187.6	187.2	187.5	189.9	193.2	195.3	193.7	194.4	196.6	198.2	191.2
2014............	196.4	197.8	198.5	198.8	199.0	201.9	204.2	206.2	205.7	207.9	209.0	210.0	203.0
2015............	208.0	209.2	210.3	211.9	212.8	214.0	219.3	220.3	218.6	221.0	223.0	223.4	216.0
Education and Health Services													
2005............	103.8	104.6	104.7	104.2	104.4	104.8	103.5	103.6	103.6	106.9	108.4	108.7	105.1
2006............	107.0	109.6	110.4	109.7	110.4	111.0	107.9	107.6	107.9	110.2	111.5	111.3	109.5
2007............	109.2	112.0	113.4	111.7	113.5	114.5	112.6	112.2	112.4	116.1	117.7	117.7	113.6
2008............	118.7	121.4	121.9	121.5	121.3	121.0	117.6	121.0	121.0	122.6	124.1	124.1	121.4
2009............	123.4	124.9	125.1	125.0	125.7	125.2	121.7	122.1	121.1	126.1	126.3	126.6	124.4
2010............	124.8	125.9	126.0	128.2	128.8	128.4	125.6	125.4	124.8	128.3	129.0	129.6	127.1
2011............	128.5	130.3	130.7	129.5	130.0	129.1	125.9	126.4	126.7	131.8	133.5	133.8	129.7
2012............	133.5	136.7	137.3	137.3	137.7	136.8	133.2	134.6	134.4	139.2	140.5	140.7	136.8
2013............	140.4	142.7	143.5	144.1	145.1	143.8	140.5	141.9	141.8	146.1	147.9	147.6	143.8
2014............	147.9	149.6	150.1	150.8	151.4	150.2	147.0	147.7	148.0	152.7	152.3	152.0	150.0
2015............	153.1	154.7	155.5	156.1	157.2	155.9	154.9	155.3	155.2	160.3	161.1	161.4	156.7

Employment by Industry: San Jose-Sunnyvale-Santa Clara, CA, 2005–2015—*Continued*

(Numbers in thousands, not seasonally adjusted)

Industry and year	January	February	March	April	May	June	July	August	September	October	November	December	Annual average
Leisure and Hospitality													
2005	68.4	69.5	70.9	72.1	73.7	74.8	75.2	75.3	74.5	73.5	72.7	73.1	72.8
2006	70.5	72.4	73.8	74.7	76.2	77.9	76.9	77.4	76.6	75.4	74.9	75.3	75.2
2007	72.6	74.0	75.9	76.7	78.0	79.2	78.6	78.7	77.7	76.9	76.5	76.7	76.8
2008	74.3	75.6	77.3	77.9	79.3	80.6	80.5	80.2	79.5	78.3	76.9	76.3	78.1
2009	73.8	74.0	74.4	75.1	76.1	77.1	75.9	76.2	74.8	74.7	73.1	73.2	74.9
2010	71.5	71.7	72.7	75.5	76.9	76.7	76.4	76.2	76.3	75.9	74.4	74.8	74.9
2011	72.4	73.9	75.3	76.4	77.5	78.1	79.5	79.7	79.9	80.2	78.0	78.1	77.4
2012	77.1	78.0	80.1	81.7	83.2	83.9	84.6	85.0	85.4	85.1	83.1	83.2	82.5
2013	81.4	83.6	85.5	87.7	89.2	89.5	89.2	89.3	89.2	89.3	88.0	88.3	87.5
2014	85.9	88.5	90.1	91.1	93.2	93.7	93.9	94.3	94.0	93.9	92.1	92.3	91.9
2015	90.2	92.5	94.2	95.2	96.9	97.0	97.7	97.0	96.7	97.3	97.1	96.9	95.7
Other Services													
2005	24.5	24.9	24.9	24.8	25.0	25.4	24.7	24.2	24.4	24.3	24.2	24.3	24.6
2006	24.0	24.5	24.7	24.8	25.3	25.8	24.8	24.9	25.0	24.5	24.6	24.7	24.8
2007	23.9	24.6	24.8	24.8	25.2	25.6	25.1	25.1	25.4	25.5	25.4	25.4	25.1
2008	24.7	25.2	25.5	25.5	25.9	25.9	25.3	25.1	25.5	25.5	25.3	25.2	25.4
2009	24.5	24.6	24.7	24.8	24.9	24.9	24.0	23.8	24.2	24.3	24.6	24.5	24.5
2010	24.6	24.9	25.2	24.1	24.2	24.5	23.8	23.7	24.0	24.2	24.3	24.1	24.3
2011	24.1	24.3	24.3	24.5	24.7	24.7	24.9	24.6	24.6	24.7	24.9	24.7	24.6
2012	24.1	24.2	24.4	24.8	25.0	25.2	25.2	24.9	24.8	24.9	24.8	24.7	24.8
2013	24.7	25.1	25.1	25.4	25.7	25.7	25.6	25.4	25.5	25.6	25.7	25.6	25.4
2014	25.5	25.8	26.0	26.5	26.7	26.9	26.6	26.6	26.5	26.7	26.7	26.4	26.4
2015	26.2	26.4	26.6	26.8	27.2	27.0	27.4	27.3	27.1	27.8	27.8	27.8	27.1
Government													
2005	95.5	96.2	96.9	97.0	97.4	97.0	94.3	93.7	93.8	96.2	96.6	96.2	95.9
2006	95.7	96.5	96.7	97.3	97.8	97.4	95.1	93.7	94.3	97.7	97.6	97.5	96.4
2007	97.7	97.0	98.3	98.1	98.3	97.8	95.1	93.9	94.9	98.3	98.6	98.3	97.2
2008	99.0	98.2	99.1	98.4	99.0	98.6	94.0	94.5	98.0	98.7	98.3	97.8	97.8
2009	97.4	96.8	97.6	99.5	100.2	100.3	85.1	88.8	96.0	98.5	99.3	98.1	96.5
2010	96.0	96.2	97.6	99.4	100.9	96.6	85.0	83.5	89.9	95.4	97.0	96.1	94.5
2011	94.6	95.3	95.7	96.5	96.8	96.2	81.3	82.4	90.9	93.8	94.4	94.4	92.7
2012	91.7	92.9	94.0	94.2	94.2	94.9	81.1	83.1	90.2	93.5	94.1	93.3	91.4
2013	92.6	94.0	93.1	94.3	95.7	94.4	79.1	83.4	91.3	94.1	95.4	94.2	91.8
2014	94.5	95.6	95.8	96.9	97.0	94.2	82.3	86.1	92.2	95.2	95.9	95.2	93.4
2015	93.8	94.6	94.1	94.8	95.3	94.8	83.8	87.4	91.8	93.8	94.6	94.0	92.7

Employment by Industry: Nashville-Davidson—Murfreesboro—Franklin, TN, 2005–2015

(Numbers in thousands, not seasonally adjusted)

Industry and year	January	February	March	April	May	June	July	August	September	October	November	December	Annual average
Total Nonfarm													
2005	746.2	752.2	757.4	766.0	767.7	764.6	766.0	773.7	778.2	779.2	785.1	787.0	768.6
2006	770.1	772.9	780.2	781.9	783.6	783.6	782.2	791.2	793.9	789.3	795.1	797.6	785.1
2007	776.2	780.5	788.7	787.6	789.4	792.1	788.9	802.6	806.7	800.8	811.2	811.7	794.7
2008	786.2	792.2	795.7	796.2	801.3	794.3	785.7	793.4	797.3	793.8	793.4	791.9	793.5
2009	762.2	761.5	759.2	757.8	758.1	745.7	742.0	749.9	754.7	758.3	764.0	762.5	756.3
2010	742.4	745.0	751.5	760.2	766.7	758.3	752.5	761.1	770.6	777.3	781.9	782.2	762.5
2011	759.9	765.7	773.1	781.7	785.5	779.4	780.8	790.3	796.4	801.4	808.6	810.5	786.1
2012	791.4	798.0	808.8	811.4	815.0	810.9	806.9	818.5	824.8	830.9	839.5	841.2	816.4
2013	817.7	827.1	833.1	841.0	845.2	840.9	837.1	849.7	855.0	863.1	871.3	872.4	846.1
2014	850.9	857.7	862.3	874.6	879.6	873.3	870.5	885.4	891.5	899.8	907.1	909.8	880.2
2015	885.1	890.7	895.4	905.5	911.4	907.8	904.8	915.4	923.0	929.8	936.3	940.4	912.1
Total Private													
2005	644.3	648.1	653.3	661.5	664.2	667.3	669.0	672.4	673.8	674.9	680.6	682.4	666.0
2006	666.2	667.2	674.2	676.2	678.8	685.6	683.5	688.3	687.9	683.3	688.3	690.4	680.8
2007	670.7	673.6	681.6	682.6	686.0	694.5	690.2	697.8	696.0	691.9	700.2	702.3	689.0
2008	678.0	682.0	685.4	686.5	690.3	693.7	685.3	687.7	685.7	681.4	680.2	677.8	684.5
2009	651.5	647.9	646.1	644.2	645.2	645.1	640.5	643.3	642.5	644.6	649.8	648.7	645.8
2010	630.9	631.6	637.7	645.7	650.4	654.2	651.1	654.0	655.5	661.7	666.7	667.4	650.6
2011	648.1	653.6	660.4	668.4	672.4	676.0	677.3	681.1	683.6	688.3	695.2	697.4	675.2
2012	680.5	685.2	695.2	698.8	704.0	709.6	706.5	711.6	714.0	719.1	726.8	728.6	706.7
2013	707.9	714.9	720.7	727.1	732.5	738.5	735.3	741.4	742.5	749.0	757.2	758.5	735.5
2014	739.5	743.7	748.2	760.6	765.5	770.0	767.8	776.1	777.8	784.7	790.1	794.3	768.2
2015	774.0	776.6	781.3	791.6	798.0	804.8	802.3	806.3	809.0	813.7	818.5	823.2	799.9
Goods Producing													
2005	125.7	126.5	127.3	129.2	129.9	131.0	130.0	131.2	131.1	131.2	131.5	131.8	129.7
2006	130.4	130.3	131.0	131.7	131.7	133.6	132.8	133.9	133.5	132.0	132.2	132.2	132.1
2007	128.6	128.5	129.7	129.1	127.4	130.4	126.9	129.4	129.6	126.1	128.2	127.9	128.5
2008	122.5	124.2	123.9	123.3	123.9	124.2	121.6	121.1	119.1	115.7	113.3	111.4	120.4
2009	105.7	104.4	103.0	101.4	100.2	97.9	99.0	99.0	98.6	97.9	97.6	95.3	100.0
2010	92.0	91.4	92.3	94.2	94.5	95.8	95.6	96.3	96.4	96.8	96.3	96.1	94.8
2011	93.4	94.2	95.7	97.7	97.8	98.8	99.0	99.3	99.9	100.5	100.5	100.9	98.1
2012	98.6	100.0	101.7	102.1	102.7	103.9	104.2	105.0	105.8	105.3	105.6	105.7	103.4
2013	104.1	105.0	105.9	106.3	107.5	108.6	108.7	109.5	109.8	110.5	110.4	110.7	108.1
2014	109.5	110.0	110.9	111.6	112.8	113.1	112.8	114.5	114.1	114.8	115.7	116.4	113.0
2015	114.6	115.5	115.5	117.3	118.6	119.5	118.9	119.7	120.4	120.6	120.6	121.5	118.6
Service-Providing													
2005	620.5	625.7	630.1	636.8	637.8	633.6	636.0	642.5	647.1	648.0	653.6	655.2	638.9
2006	639.7	642.6	649.2	650.2	651.9	650.0	649.4	657.3	660.4	657.3	662.9	665.4	653.0
2007	647.6	652.0	659.0	658.5	662.0	661.7	662.0	673.2	677.1	674.7	683.0	683.8	666.2
2008	663.7	668.0	671.8	672.9	677.4	670.1	664.1	672.3	678.2	678.1	680.1	680.5	673.1
2009	656.5	657.1	656.2	656.4	657.9	647.8	643.0	650.9	656.1	660.4	666.4	667.2	656.3
2010	650.4	653.6	659.2	666.0	672.2	662.5	656.9	664.8	674.2	680.5	685.6	686.1	667.7
2011	666.5	671.5	677.4	684.0	687.7	680.6	681.8	691.0	696.5	700.9	708.1	709.6	688.0
2012	692.8	698.0	707.1	709.3	712.3	707.0	702.7	713.5	719.0	725.6	733.9	735.5	713.1
2013	713.6	722.1	727.2	734.7	737.7	732.3	728.4	740.2	745.2	752.6	760.9	761.7	738.1
2014	741.4	747.7	751.4	763.0	766.8	760.2	757.7	770.9	777.4	785.0	791.4	793.4	767.2
2015	770.5	775.2	779.9	788.2	792.8	788.3	785.9	795.7	802.6	809.2	815.7	818.9	793.6
Mining, Logging, and Construction													
2005	34.0	34.3	35.2	36.5	37.4	38.5	38.6	38.9	38.9	38.7	38.6	38.7	37.4
2006	38.4	38.6	39.6	40.0	40.5	41.7	41.5	41.8	41.7	41.0	40.9	41.0	40.6
2007	40.2	40.7	42.3	42.6	43.3	44.5	44.3	44.7	44.7	44.3	44.0	43.5	43.3
2008	41.9	41.7	41.8	41.7	42.0	42.2	41.4	41.4	40.7	39.4	38.1	37.0	40.8
2009	34.5	33.7	33.4	32.8	32.7	32.9	32.9	32.7	32.4	31.9	31.6	31.2	32.7
2010	29.0	28.7	29.6	31.5	31.7	32.7	32.8	33.1	33.0	33.4	32.5	32.1	31.7
2011	29.5	30.1	31.3	32.8	32.9	33.8	33.7	33.9	34.2	33.8	33.5	33.1	32.7
2012	31.9	32.3	33.6	33.2	33.4	33.6	33.4	33.7	34.0	33.1	32.6	32.3	33.1
2013	31.0	31.8	32.5	33.0	33.7	34.3	34.2	34.2	34.2	34.2	33.4	33.3	33.3
2014	32.5	32.8	34.1	34.8	35.6	35.4	35.8	36.2	35.9	36.4	36.8	37.1	35.3
2015	36.2	36.8	37.2	38.8	39.9	40.4	40.7	40.4	40.8	41.0	40.3	40.5	39.4

Employment by Industry: Nashville-Davidson—Murfreesboro—Franklin, TN, 2005–2015—*Continued*

(Numbers in thousands, not seasonally adjusted)

Industry and year	January	February	March	April	May	June	July	August	September	October	November	December	Annual average
Manufacturing													
2005	91.7	92.2	92.1	92.7	92.5	92.5	91.4	92.3	92.2	92.5	92.9	93.1	92.3
2006	92.0	91.7	91.4	91.7	91.2	91.9	91.3	92.1	91.8	91.0	91.3	91.2	91.6
2007	88.4	87.8	87.4	86.5	84.1	85.9	82.6	84.7	84.9	81.8	84.2	84.4	85.2
2008	80.6	82.5	82.1	81.6	81.9	82.0	80.2	79.7	78.4	76.3	75.2	74.4	79.6
2009	71.2	70.7	69.6	68.6	67.5	65.0	66.1	66.3	66.2	66.0	66.0	64.1	67.3
2010	63.0	62.7	62.7	62.7	62.8	63.1	62.8	63.2	63.4	63.4	63.8	64.0	63.1
2011	63.9	64.1	64.4	64.9	64.9	65.0	65.3	65.4	65.7	66.7	67.0	67.8	65.4
2012	66.7	67.7	68.1	68.9	69.3	70.3	70.8	71.3	71.8	72.2	73.0	73.4	70.3
2013	73.1	73.2	73.4	73.3	73.8	74.3	74.5	75.3	75.6	76.3	77.0	77.4	74.8
2014	77.0	77.2	76.8	76.8	77.2	77.7	77.0	78.3	78.2	78.4	78.9	79.3	77.7
2015	78.4	78.7	78.3	78.5	78.7	79.1	78.2	79.3	79.6	79.6	80.3	81.0	79.1
Trade, Transportation, and Utilities													
2005	151.7	151.4	152.6	153.9	154.6	154.5	155.9	156.3	157.5	158.7	162.3	164.1	156.1
2006	157.3	156.9	158.4	158.0	158.5	159.3	158.1	159.2	159.5	158.7	161.9	164.1	159.2
2007	158.0	157.4	159.1	158.2	159.0	159.1	158.8	159.5	160.0	160.3	164.2	166.2	160.0
2008	159.7	159.5	160.6	159.6	159.7	159.7	159.9	160.2	160.1	159.9	161.9	163.4	160.4
2009	156.1	153.7	152.6	151.3	151.7	151.8	151.5	152.3	151.5	152.7	155.4	156.9	153.1
2010	150.7	149.7	150.5	151.2	151.5	152.5	152.2	153.1	152.6	154.9	158.0	159.8	153.1
2011	153.2	153.3	154.5	156.0	156.6	157.0	157.2	157.5	157.9	160.0	163.8	165.3	157.7
2012	159.3	158.4	160.3	161.0	161.9	161.9	161.7	162.4	163.1	165.2	170.1	171.1	163.0
2013	162.9	162.7	163.4	165.3	166.2	167.2	166.6	167.6	167.3	169.5	174.7	177.4	167.6
2014	167.6	167.1	168.0	170.9	171.6	172.4	172.2	173.2	173.4	176.3	180.1	182.1	172.9
2015	173.4	172.0	172.3	174.1	175.3	176.6	175.0	176.2	176.4	177.6	179.9	183.5	176.0
Wholesale Trade													
2005	36.6	36.9	36.9	37.3	37.5	37.3	37.4	37.5	37.8	37.9	38.2	38.0	37.4
2006	37.6	37.7	37.7	37.6	37.7	37.9	37.7	37.9	38.2	37.5	37.4	37.5	37.7
2007	37.0	37.2	37.6	37.6	37.8	38.0	38.0	38.1	38.5	38.5	38.7	38.7	38.0
2008	38.4	38.6	38.5	38.6	39.0	39.2	39.3	39.5	39.8	39.7	39.7	39.5	39.2
2009	38.4	38.1	37.7	37.6	37.4	37.2	37.0	37.1	37.0	37.2	37.1	37.1	37.4
2010	36.5	36.4	36.6	36.7	36.8	36.8	36.9	37.1	37.0	37.5	37.5	37.7	37.0
2011	37.4	37.6	37.9	37.9	38.1	38.3	38.3	38.4	38.7	38.9	39.2	39.4	38.3
2012	38.9	39.1	39.3	39.4	39.7	39.8	40.0	40.3	40.3	40.5	40.7	40.7	39.9
2013	40.1	40.4	40.8	41.0	41.1	41.3	41.3	41.4	41.3	41.4	41.6	41.4	41.1
2014	40.5	40.4	40.6	40.6	40.7	40.8	40.7	40.7	40.8	40.9	40.8	40.9	40.7
2015	40.0	40.1	40.0	40.0	40.1	40.6	40.6	40.8	41.0	42.3	42.2	42.1	40.8
Retail Trade													
2005	86.6	86.0	87.0	87.3	87.7	87.5	87.7	87.7	88.3	88.9	91.9	93.3	88.3
2006	88.2	87.8	88.8	89.0	89.4	89.6	88.8	89.4	89.1	89.3	92.7	94.2	89.7
2007	89.9	89.1	90.3	89.6	90.2	90.0	89.6	90.0	90.1	90.8	94.3	96.1	90.8
2008	91.1	90.8	92.0	90.7	90.3	90.0	89.9	90.1	89.6	89.4	91.6	92.5	90.7
2009	87.6	86.2	85.7	85.2	85.7	85.8	85.6	86.1	85.2	86.0	88.3	89.6	86.4
2010	85.4	84.7	85.1	85.8	85.9	86.5	86.0	86.5	85.6	86.8	89.3	90.5	86.5
2011	86.5	86.5	87.1	88.1	88.2	88.5	88.5	88.5	88.3	89.1	91.8	93.0	88.7
2012	88.9	87.7	89.0	89.1	89.3	89.2	88.7	88.5	88.2	89.2	92.5	92.8	89.4
2013	88.0	87.1	87.4	88.7	89.4	89.7	89.4	89.8	89.4	90.7	93.4	94.6	89.8
2014	90.0	89.6	90.1	92.8	93.4	93.8	93.6	93.8	93.6	94.7	97.5	98.7	93.5
2015	93.9	93.0	93.3	94.4	95.3	95.8	94.1	94.3	93.9	94.3	97.0	98.0	94.8
Transportation and Utilities													
2005	28.5	28.5	28.7	29.3	29.4	29.7	30.8	31.1	31.4	31.9	32.2	32.8	30.4
2006	31.5	31.4	31.9	31.4	31.4	31.8	31.6	31.9	32.2	31.9	31.8	32.4	31.8
2007	31.1	31.1	31.2	31.0	31.0	31.1	31.2	31.4	31.4	31.0	31.2	31.4	31.2
2008	30.2	30.1	30.1	30.3	30.4	30.5	30.7	30.6	30.7	30.8	30.6	31.4	30.5
2009	30.1	29.4	29.2	28.5	28.6	28.8	28.9	29.1	29.3	29.5	30.0	30.2	29.3
2010	28.8	28.6	28.8	28.7	28.8	29.2	29.3	29.5	30.0	30.6	31.2	31.6	29.6
2011	29.3	29.2	29.5	30.0	30.3	30.2	30.4	30.6	30.9	32.0	32.8	32.9	30.7
2012	31.5	31.6	32.0	32.5	32.9	32.9	33.0	33.6	34.6	35.5	36.9	37.6	33.7
2013	34.8	35.2	35.2	35.6	35.7	36.2	35.7	36.4	36.6	37.4	39.7	41.4	36.7
2014	37.1	37.1	37.3	37.5	37.5	37.8	37.9	38.7	39.0	40.7	41.8	42.5	38.7
2015	39.5	38.9	39.0	39.7	39.9	40.2	40.3	41.1	41.5	41.0	40.7	43.4	40.4

Employment by Industry: Nashville-Davidson—Murfreesboro—Franklin, TN, 2005–2015—*Continued*

(Numbers in thousands, not seasonally adjusted)

Industry and year	January	February	March	April	May	June	July	August	September	October	November	December	Annual average
Information													
2005	20.4	20.5	20.4	20.1	20.1	20.3	20.3	20.2	20.2	20.3	20.4	20.4	20.3
2006	20.2	20.2	20.3	20.2	20.3	20.3	19.6	19.5	19.6	19.6	19.7	19.8	19.9
2007	19.6	19.6	19.6	19.9	20.3	20.4	20.6	20.7	20.8	20.9	21.0	21.4	20.4
2008	21.7	21.7	21.8	21.8	21.9	21.9	21.6	21.6	21.5	21.8	21.7	21.8	21.7
2009	21.4	21.3	21.1	20.8	20.7	20.5	20.4	20.5	20.3	20.0	20.0	19.9	20.6
2010	19.9	19.9	20.0	19.9	19.8	19.9	19.8	19.5	19.5	19.8	19.8	19.8	19.8
2011	19.4	19.3	19.3	19.4	19.6	19.7	19.7	20.1	19.8	20.1	20.4	20.5	19.8
2012	20.3	20.5	20.4	20.5	21.3	21.5	20.4	20.6	20.4	20.6	20.6	20.7	20.7
2013	20.4	20.7	20.8	20.6	21.0	21.6	20.9	21.0	20.7	20.8	21.2	21.1	20.9
2014	20.5	20.5	20.6	20.6	20.7	20.7	20.6	20.5	20.4	20.6	20.6	20.5	20.6
2015	20.4	20.5	20.5	20.5	20.8	21.3	21.1	21.4	21.1	21.1	21.2	21.2	20.9
Financial Activities													
2005	46.9	46.9	47.2	47.6	47.8	47.9	47.9	48.1	48.1	47.9	48.1	48.2	47.7
2006	47.8	47.7	48.0	48.2	48.4	48.5	48.5	48.5	48.2	48.3	48.2	48.4	48.2
2007	47.7	48.1	48.3	48.5	49.0	49.2	49.0	49.0	48.7	48.7	48.6	48.8	48.6
2008	48.3	48.6	48.5	48.5	48.6	48.9	48.8	48.6	48.2	47.8	47.7	47.7	48.4
2009	47.1	47.0	46.9	47.0	47.2	47.3	47.1	47.6	47.4	47.6	47.8	48.1	47.3
2010	47.6	47.7	47.6	48.1	48.4	48.4	48.5	48.8	48.5	48.9	49.1	49.2	48.4
2011	48.4	48.5	48.5	49.3	49.8	49.5	49.7	50.0	50.0	50.2	50.5	50.4	49.6
2012	49.8	50.2	50.2	50.3	50.6	51.0	51.1	51.5	51.5	51.6	51.9	52.4	51.0
2013	52.1	52.4	52.8	53.4	53.7	53.7	54.4	54.2	54.0	54.4	54.7	54.7	53.7
2014	54.7	55.0	55.2	55.8	56.3	56.6	57.0	57.4	57.5	57.8	57.9	58.3	56.6
2015	57.9	58.3	58.6	58.9	59.3	59.7	59.9	60.1	60.0	60.5	61.5	60.7	59.6
Professional and Business Services													
2005	94.3	95.5	96.0	97.4	97.4	98.0	98.3	100.0	101.5	101.9	102.8	103.3	98.9
2006	97.6	97.7	98.6	98.9	99.3	101.7	100.9	103.4	104.7	103.1	104.4	104.4	101.2
2007	98.6	99.5	101.1	101.3	102.3	104.9	105.4	107.0	106.4	106.5	108.3	108.0	104.1
2008	101.2	101.0	101.5	102.5	103.4	105.8	100.9	102.6	104.2	104.5	104.5	102.4	102.9
2009	95.3	95.0	94.3	93.3	94.0	95.6	92.0	94.0	94.9	96.6	98.5	97.8	95.1
2010	93.9	94.7	96.0	97.9	102.3	102.2	100.6	101.3	103.1	103.1	104.9	105.1	100.4
2011	101.1	103.3	104.8	106.0	106.8	109.1	109.2	110.7	111.6	112.3	113.8	113.7	108.5
2012	109.7	111.4	114.4	114.7	116.0	118.3	117.8	119.6	120.7	122.2	123.9	123.6	117.7
2013	118.6	120.6	121.7	121.5	122.7	125.1	124.4	127.7	128.9	131.4	133.6	132.5	125.7
2014	129.1	130.1	129.7	133.3	134.5	136.9	135.3	139.6	140.1	142.3	142.7	144.2	136.5
2015	138.3	139.0	141.2	143.3	144.2	147.5	148.4	149.8	150.2	152.5	153.2	154.1	146.8
Education and Health Services													
2005	102.2	103.0	103.0	104.9	105.4	105.2	106.1	106.1	105.9	105.9	106.0	106.2	105.0
2006	105.9	106.5	107.3	107.9	108.1	108.4	108.7	108.9	109.0	109.1	109.6	109.5	108.2
2007	108.8	109.7	110.2	110.9	111.3	111.7	112.7	113.6	114.4	113.6	113.8	114.1	112.1
2008	113.0	113.8	113.8	115.4	115.6	115.8	116.3	117.0	117.8	117.8	118.2	118.7	116.1
2009	117.5	118.0	117.9	119.1	118.6	118.1	118.5	118.2	119.6	119.9	120.4	120.6	118.9
2010	119.7	120.5	121.0	122.6	121.4	120.9	122.5	122.6	124.5	125.3	125.6	125.3	122.7
2011	123.9	125.3	125.4	126.2	125.6	124.4	125.0	125.3	126.9	127.6	128.2	128.4	126.0
2012	127.6	128.8	129.3	129.6	128.5	128.3	127.9	128.8	130.9	131.1	131.7	131.4	129.5
2013	130.2	131.8	132.3	133.2	132.4	131.8	131.0	132.0	134.2	134.0	133.9	133.9	132.6
2014	133.2	134.2	134.8	136.0	135.3	134.4	134.5	135.4	137.7	138.5	138.5	138.8	135.9
2015	138.1	139.1	139.4	140.2	139.5	138.3	138.9	139.2	142.0	143.9	144.1	145.7	140.7
Leisure and Hospitality													
2005	72.8	73.8	75.2	77.2	78.0	78.9	79.3	79.4	78.1	77.8	77.9	77.2	77.1
2006	75.8	76.5	78.5	79.7	80.5	81.5	83.0	83.0	81.6	80.7	80.7	80.7	80.2
2007	78.5	79.5	81.7	83.0	84.7	86.7	85.2	86.7	84.4	83.8	84.1	84.0	83.5
2008	79.8	80.9	82.4	83.2	84.6	84.9	83.7	84.3	82.9	81.3	80.7	80.3	82.4
2009	77.2	77.0	78.4	79.9	81.2	82.0	80.4	80.5	79.5	78.7	78.9	79.1	79.4
2010	76.5	76.8	79.1	80.7	81.1	82.4	79.9	80.3	78.9	80.5	80.4	79.2	79.7
2011	75.9	76.4	78.6	80.5	82.5	83.0	83.2	84.1	83.7	83.8	83.9	84.1	81.6
2012	81.3	81.7	84.3	85.9	88.0	88.9	87.8	88.5	86.6	87.9	87.7	88.2	86.4
2013	84.3	85.9	87.7	90.4	92.3	93.3	92.4	92.7	91.2	92.0	92.1	91.9	90.5
2014	88.8	90.4	92.3	95.4	97.1	98.4	97.9	98.6	97.8	97.4	97.4	97.0	95.7
2015	94.5	95.4	96.8	100.1	102.5	103.7	102.2	102.6	101.6	100.7	100.4	98.8	99.9

Employment by Industry: Nashville-Davidson—Murfreesboro—Franklin, TN, 2005–2015—*Continued*

(Numbers in thousands, not seasonally adjusted)

Industry and year	January	February	March	April	May	June	July	August	September	October	November	December	Annual average
Other Services													
2005	30.3	30.5	31.6	31.2	31.0	31.5	31.2	31.1	31.4	31.2	31.6	31.2	31.2
2006	31.2	31.4	32.1	31.6	32.0	32.3	31.9	31.9	31.8	31.8	31.6	31.3	31.7
2007	30.9	31.3	31.9	31.7	32.0	32.1	31.6	31.9	31.7	32.0	32.0	31.9	31.8
2008	31.8	32.3	32.9	32.2	32.6	32.5	32.5	32.3	31.9	32.6	32.2	32.1	32.3
2009	31.2	31.5	31.9	31.4	31.6	31.9	31.6	31.2	30.7	31.2	31.2	31.0	31.4
2010	30.6	30.9	31.2	31.1	31.4	32.1	32.0	32.1	32.0	32.4	32.6	32.9	31.8
2011	32.8	33.3	33.6	33.3	33.7	34.5	34.3	34.1	33.8	33.8	34.1	34.1	33.8
2012	33.9	34.2	34.6	34.7	35.0	35.8	35.6	35.2	35.0	35.2	35.3	35.5	35.0
2013	35.3	35.8	36.1	36.4	36.7	37.2	36.9	36.7	36.4	36.4	36.6	36.3	36.4
2014	36.1	36.4	36.7	37.0	37.2	37.5	37.5	36.9	36.8	37.0	37.2	37.0	36.9
2015	36.8	36.8	37.0	37.2	37.8	38.2	37.9	37.3	37.3	36.8	37.6	37.7	37.4
Government													
2005	101.9	104.1	104.1	104.5	103.5	97.3	97.0	101.3	104.4	104.3	104.5	104.6	102.6
2006	103.9	105.7	106.0	105.7	104.8	98.0	98.7	102.9	106.0	106.0	106.8	107.2	104.3
2007	105.5	106.9	107.1	105.0	103.4	97.6	98.7	104.8	110.7	108.9	111.0	109.4	105.8
2008	108.2	110.2	110.3	109.7	111.0	100.6	100.4	105.7	111.6	112.4	113.2	114.1	109.0
2009	110.7	113.6	113.1	113.6	112.9	100.6	101.5	106.6	112.2	113.7	114.2	113.8	110.5
2010	111.5	113.4	113.8	114.5	116.3	104.1	101.4	107.1	115.1	115.6	115.2	114.8	111.9
2011	111.8	112.1	112.7	113.3	113.1	103.4	103.5	109.2	112.8	113.1	113.4	113.1	111.0
2012	110.9	112.8	113.6	112.6	111.0	101.3	100.4	106.9	110.8	111.8	112.7	112.6	109.8
2013	109.8	112.2	112.4	113.9	112.7	102.4	101.8	108.3	112.5	114.1	114.1	113.9	110.7
2014	111.4	114.0	114.1	114.0	114.1	103.3	102.7	109.3	113.7	115.1	117.0	115.5	112.0
2015	111.1	114.1	114.1	113.9	113.4	103.0	102.5	109.1	114.0	116.1	117.8	117.2	112.2

Employment by Industry: Virginia Beach-Norfolk-Newport News, VA-NC, 2005–2015

(Numbers in thousands, not seasonally adjusted)

Industry and year	January	February	March	April	May	June	July	August	September	October	November	December	Annual average
Total Nonfarm													
2005	738.3	741.5	749.4	759.4	764.6	774.3	770.0	773.5	771.1	760.4	764.8	765.1	761.0
2006	748.0	750.2	759.2	765.9	770.7	780.7	773.9	775.0	768.1	768.8	773.1	775.0	767.4
2007	758.1	759.5	767.6	773.0	778.6	786.7	788.4	787.2	782.1	772.8	776.4	775.6	775.5
2008	754.0	757.3	763.7	767.5	774.3	781.8	777.8	777.8	769.5	763.5	761.1	757.6	767.2
2009	737.5	736.3	739.4	742.6	747.9	753.1	744.9	745.3	740.1	741.0	739.4	739.0	742.2
2010	720.6	720.0	727.5	738.1	743.7	748.4	744.4	744.5	739.8	740.0	739.3	738.9	737.1
2011	720.9	722.5	730.6	739.8	743.1	751.1	749.4	749.1	745.5	742.8	743.5	743.5	740.2
2012	728.5	731.7	738.1	744.7	747.0	754.4	751.3	753.0	748.8	753.6	755.3	755.6	746.8
2013	740.2	742.6	748.7	755.1	758.4	765.2	763.7	765.5	758.7	758.9	760.4	760.4	756.5
2014	742.8	742.4	748.9	758.3	762.8	768.2	764.9	767.5	761.0	760.5	761.6	761.7	758.4
2015	748.1	748.7	752.3	763.4	767.6	773.9	774.0	774.3	768.6	769.7	772.0	772.0	765.4
Total Private													
2005	588.5	590.2	597.6	606.8	611.5	620.1	620.6	623.7	619.6	609.1	611.8	613.1	609.4
2006	597.2	598.3	606.7	611.7	616.4	625.5	622.6	624.1	616.9	614.7	617.3	619.5	614.2
2007	604.1	603.9	611.6	617.3	623.0	630.1	635.1	633.8	626.8	616.8	618.0	618.1	619.9
2008	598.1	599.2	605.1	610.1	616.3	622.5	622.3	622.1	612.1	604.1	599.4	597.4	609.1
2009	578.3	576.3	578.5	581.6	587.3	591.6	590.4	589.1	582.0	579.5	576.1	577.2	582.3
2010	559.9	558.4	565.2	575.2	578.6	584.1	586.9	586.5	579.0	577.9	576.8	576.8	575.4
2011	559.9	560.7	567.9	576.9	580.5	588.1	590.1	589.2	583.2	578.9	577.8	578.0	577.6
2012	565.5	567.6	574.5	581.0	583.6	590.7	592.4	593.8	587.5	590.2	590.4	591.5	584.1
2013	578.8	579.6	585.6	592.1	596.0	603.1	605.3	606.7	598.3	597.0	597.6	597.3	594.8
2014	582.8	581.6	587.7	596.8	602.2	608.2	608.1	609.8	602.0	600.9	600.8	600.7	598.5
2015	589.2	588.2	592.4	602.1	607.3	613.4	617.4	617.9	611.2	610.5	611.7	611.9	606.1
Goods Producing													
2005	108.3	108.3	109.0	110.4	110.6	111.4	110.0	112.0	111.2	109.2	109.0	109.3	109.9
2006	107.3	107.3	108.6	109.1	109.5	110.4	107.9	109.8	107.2	106.7	106.6	108.0	108.2
2007	105.8	104.7	105.6	106.7	106.9	107.5	107.4	107.4	106.9	105.1	104.9	104.4	106.1
2008	102.1	101.8	101.9	102.1	102.5	103.0	102.8	102.7	101.4	100.4	99.5	98.2	101.5
2009	94.2	93.2	92.9	92.1	91.9	92.1	92.1	91.8	91.2	91.1	90.2	90.4	91.9
2010	87.8	87.5	88.2	89.2	89.6	89.1	89.3	89.2	88.9	88.4	88.3	87.7	88.6
2011	85.6	85.6	86.5	86.4	87.0	87.5	88.1	88.2	87.7	86.7	86.7	86.5	86.9
2012	86.5	86.7	87.2	86.6	86.2	86.5	89.4	89.3	89.6	89.4	89.3	89.2	88.0
2013	87.9	88.3	88.6	88.6	88.8	89.4	90.0	90.0	89.7	89.1	89.3	89.4	89.1
2014	88.0	87.9	88.3	89.0	89.3	89.9	90.0	89.8	89.3	89.2	89.2	89.2	89.1
2015	87.9	87.7	88.0	89.1	89.4	90.0	90.5	90.1	89.8	89.0	90.1	89.1	89.2
Service-Providing													
2005	630.0	633.2	640.4	649.0	654.0	662.9	660.0	661.5	659.9	651.2	655.8	655.8	651.1
2006	640.7	642.9	650.6	656.8	661.2	670.3	666.0	665.2	660.9	662.1	666.5	667.0	659.2
2007	652.3	654.8	662.0	666.3	671.7	679.2	681.0	679.8	675.2	667.7	671.5	671.2	669.4
2008	651.9	655.5	661.8	665.4	671.8	678.8	675.0	675.1	668.1	663.1	661.6	659.4	665.6
2009	643.3	643.1	646.5	650.5	656.0	661.0	652.8	653.5	648.9	649.9	649.2	648.6	650.3
2010	632.8	632.5	639.3	648.9	654.1	659.3	655.1	655.3	650.9	651.6	651.0	651.2	648.5
2011	635.3	636.9	644.1	653.4	656.1	663.6	661.3	660.9	657.8	656.1	656.8	657.0	653.3
2012	642.0	645.0	650.9	658.1	660.8	667.9	661.9	663.7	659.2	664.2	666.0	666.4	658.8
2013	652.3	654.3	660.1	666.5	669.6	675.8	673.7	675.5	669.0	669.8	671.1	671.0	667.4
2014	654.8	654.5	660.6	669.3	673.5	678.3	674.9	677.7	671.7	671.3	672.4	672.5	669.3
2015	660.2	661.0	664.3	674.3	678.2	683.9	683.5	684.2	678.8	680.7	681.9	682.9	676.2
Mining, Logging, and Construction													
2005	48.0	48.0	48.6	49.9	50.2	50.7	51.4	51.3	51.1	49.6	49.7	50.1	49.9
2006	48.6	48.6	49.7	50.4	50.5	51.1	50.5	50.2	49.7	49.3	49.3	49.3	49.8
2007	47.9	47.8	48.5	48.6	48.7	49.1	49.6	49.6	49.1	47.7	47.4	46.8	48.4
2008	45.4	45.3	45.6	45.8	46.1	46.4	46.3	46.2	45.1	44.5	43.7	42.5	45.2
2009	39.9	39.2	39.0	38.6	38.4	38.5	38.6	38.4	37.9	37.6	36.9	37.0	38.3
2010	35.8	35.5	36.2	37.1	37.5	37.4	37.8	37.7	37.3	36.9	36.8	36.3	36.9
2011	34.8	34.9	35.1	35.5	35.6	35.7	35.6	35.5	35.0	34.6	34.5	34.4	35.1
2012	33.4	33.5	33.8	34.2	34.7	35.4	35.5	35.3	34.6	34.9	34.6	34.5	34.5
2013	33.9	34.1	34.4	34.4	34.7	35.2	35.4	35.4	35.1	34.6	34.7	34.5	34.7
2014	33.6	33.3	33.6	34.1	34.4	34.9	35.1	35.2	34.9	34.8	34.8	34.8	34.5
2015	34.1	34.1	34.4	35.4	35.9	36.3	36.8	36.7	36.4	35.7	36.8	36.5	35.8

Employment by Industry: Virginia Beach-Norfolk-Newport News, VA-NC, 2005–2015—*Continued*

(Numbers in thousands, not seasonally adjusted)

Industry and year	January	February	March	April	May	June	July	August	September	October	November	December	Annual average
Manufacturing													
2005	60.3	60.3	60.4	60.5	60.4	60.7	58.6	60.7	60.1	59.6	59.3	59.2	60.0
2006	58.7	58.7	58.9	58.7	59.0	59.3	57.4	59.6	57.5	57.4	57.3	58.7	58.4
2007	57.9	56.9	57.1	58.1	58.2	58.4	57.8	57.8	57.8	57.4	57.5	57.6	57.7
2008	56.7	56.5	56.3	56.3	56.4	56.6	56.5	56.5	56.3	55.9	55.8	55.7	56.3
2009	54.3	54.0	53.9	53.5	53.5	53.6	53.5	53.4	53.3	53.5	53.3	53.4	53.6
2010	52.0	52.0	52.0	52.1	52.1	51.7	51.5	51.5	51.6	51.5	51.5	51.4	51.7
2011	50.8	50.7	51.4	50.9	51.4	51.8	52.5	52.7	52.7	52.1	52.2	52.1	51.8
2012	53.1	53.2	53.4	52.4	51.5	51.1	53.9	54.0	55.0	54.5	54.7	54.7	53.5
2013	54.0	54.2	54.2	54.2	54.1	54.2	54.6	54.6	54.6	54.5	54.6	54.9	54.4
2014	54.4	54.6	54.7	54.9	54.9	55.0	54.9	54.6	54.4	54.4	54.4	54.4	54.6
2015	53.8	53.6	53.6	53.7	53.5	53.7	53.7	53.4	53.4	53.3	53.3	52.6	53.5
Trade, Transportation, and Utilities													
2005	137.2	135.8	136.8	138.6	139.4	140.2	141.3	141.5	141.4	141.6	145.5	146.1	140.5
2006	139.1	137.5	138.9	139.6	140.8	141.8	141.6	141.1	140.0	142.4	147.1	147.6	141.5
2007	141.5	139.7	140.5	140.0	141.3	142.5	144.5	143.8	142.1	142.3	146.8	147.0	142.7
2008	139.1	137.1	137.4	137.3	138.0	139.0	138.7	138.5	137.1	135.6	138.2	138.9	137.9
2009	130.0	127.3	127.0	127.5	129.0	129.4	128.9	128.7	127.4	128.1	130.5	131.7	128.8
2010	125.9	124.3	125.4	126.8	128.2	128.6	128.7	128.8	127.3	128.7	131.0	132.5	128.0
2011	126.4	125.3	125.8	127.2	127.6	128.5	128.0	128.1	126.7	127.3	130.1	131.6	127.7
2012	125.6	124.4	125.3	126.2	127.4	128.2	127.7	127.2	125.9	127.7	130.9	131.9	127.4
2013	125.9	124.7	125.2	126.0	127.2	128.4	129.0	129.4	128.3	129.1	132.4	133.7	128.3
2014	127.0	125.8	126.2	127.2	128.3	129.4	129.6	130.2	129.5	130.6	134.4	135.5	129.5
2015	129.3	128.3	128.5	129.3	130.8	131.9	132.4	132.3	131.1	132.7	134.3	134.4	131.3
Wholesale Trade													
2005	23.5	23.6	23.6	23.9	24.0	24.1	24.1	24.2	24.1	24.0	24.1	24.3	24.0
2006	23.9	23.9	24.0	24.1	24.1	24.2	24.3	24.1	24.1	24.1	24.2	24.2	24.1
2007	24.1	24.2	24.3	24.2	24.3	24.3	24.4	24.2	24.1	23.7	23.7	23.7	24.1
2008	23.5	23.4	23.4	23.5	23.5	23.5	23.4	23.4	23.1	22.9	22.7	22.6	23.2
2009	22.4	22.1	22.1	22.0	22.0	22.0	21.9	21.9	21.6	21.6	21.6	21.5	21.9
2010	20.9	20.7	20.8	21.1	21.1	21.1	21.1	21.2	21.1	21.1	21.1	21.1	21.0
2011	20.8	20.6	20.7	20.8	20.8	20.9	20.8	20.7	20.4	20.3	20.3	20.5	20.6
2012	20.2	20.2	20.2	20.2	20.2	20.3	20.3	20.3	20.1	20.2	20.2	20.2	20.2
2013	19.7	19.7	19.7	19.8	19.8	19.9	20.0	20.1	20.0	20.1	20.1	20.2	19.9
2014	20.0	20.0	20.0	20.0	20.2	20.0	20.0	20.1	20.0	20.0	20.2	20.3	20.1
2015	20.0	20.0	19.9	19.9	20.0	20.1	20.2	20.1	20.1	20.1	20.2	20.3	20.1
Retail Trade													
2005	88.8	87.3	87.5	89.2	89.9	90.5	91.6	91.8	92.0	92.2	95.5	96.0	91.0
2006	90.7	89.0	90.0	90.6	91.6	92.3	92.2	91.8	90.8	92.9	97.2	97.9	92.3
2007	93.1	91.2	91.7	91.3	92.4	93.2	94.7	94.6	93.2	93.6	97.9	98.2	93.8
2008	92.1	90.1	90.5	89.7	90.3	90.9	90.7	90.5	89.6	88.4	90.9	91.6	90.4
2009	84.8	82.8	82.6	83.0	84.4	84.9	84.3	84.3	83.3	83.7	85.7	86.9	84.2
2010	82.8	81.6	82.5	83.4	84.4	84.7	84.4	84.5	83.0	83.8	86.0	87.4	84.0
2011	82.6	81.9	82.3	83.4	84.2	84.9	84.6	84.7	83.5	84.1	86.7	88.0	84.2
2012	83.3	81.9	82.8	83.4	84.3	84.8	84.4	84.0	82.9	84.3	87.6	88.4	84.3
2013	83.8	83.0	83.5	84.0	84.9	85.7	85.9	86.2	85.2	85.8	88.7	89.9	85.6
2014	84.1	83.1	83.4	84.4	85.1	86.1	86.2	86.7	86.0	87.2	90.1	90.8	86.1
2015	86.0	84.9	85.3	86.1	87.2	87.9	87.8	87.9	86.8	87.5	89.3	89.0	87.1
Transportation and Utilities													
2005	24.9	24.9	25.7	25.5	25.5	25.6	25.6	25.5	25.3	25.4	25.9	25.8	25.5
2006	24.5	24.6	24.9	24.9	25.1	25.3	25.1	25.2	25.1	25.4	25.7	25.5	25.1
2007	24.3	24.3	24.5	24.5	24.6	25.0	25.4	25.0	24.8	25.0	25.2	25.1	24.8
2008	23.5	23.6	23.5	24.1	24.2	24.6	24.6	24.6	24.4	24.3	24.6	24.7	24.2
2009	22.8	22.4	22.3	22.5	22.6	22.5	22.7	22.5	22.5	22.8	23.2	23.3	22.7
2010	22.2	22.0	22.1	22.3	22.7	22.8	23.2	23.1	23.2	23.8	23.9	24.0	22.9
2011	23.0	22.8	22.8	23.0	22.6	22.7	22.6	22.7	22.8	22.9	23.1	23.1	22.8
2012	22.1	22.3	22.3	22.6	22.9	23.1	23.0	22.9	22.9	23.2	23.1	23.3	22.8
2013	22.4	22.0	22.0	22.2	22.5	22.8	23.1	23.1	23.1	23.2	23.6	23.6	22.8
2014	22.9	22.7	22.8	22.8	23.0	23.3	23.4	23.4	23.5	23.4	24.1	24.4	23.3
2015	23.3	23.4	23.3	23.3	23.6	23.9	24.4	24.3	24.2	25.1	24.8	25.1	24.1

Employment by Industry: Virginia Beach-Norfolk-Newport News, VA-NC, 2005–2015—*Continued*

(Numbers in thousands, not seasonally adjusted)

Industry and year	January	February	March	April	May	June	July	August	September	October	November	December	Annual average
Information													
2005	15.0	14.8	14.7	14.9	15.0	15.1	15.3	15.4	15.3	15.2	15.3	15.5	15.1
2006	15.5	15.5	15.5	15.4	15.5	15.6	15.6	15.5	15.3	15.2	15.3	15.4	15.4
2007	15.5	15.6	15.6	15.6	15.7	15.8	15.6	15.6	15.4	15.2	15.2	15.3	15.5
2008	15.3	15.2	15.1	15.0	15.2	15.2	15.0	14.9	14.5	14.2	14.0	13.9	14.8
2009	13.7	13.7	13.6	13.5	13.6	13.5	13.3	13.2	12.9	12.9	12.8	12.8	13.3
2010	12.6	12.4	12.5	12.3	12.4	12.4	12.2	12.2	12.0	11.8	11.8	11.7	12.2
2011	11.6	11.5	11.6	11.6	11.7	11.8	11.9	10.9	11.6	11.4	11.4	11.6	11.6
2012	11.6	11.6	11.7	11.7	11.8	11.8	11.5	11.7	11.3	11.4	11.6	11.6	11.6
2013	11.5	11.6	11.6	11.4	11.6	11.6	11.6	11.6	11.3	11.3	11.4	11.2	11.5
2014	11.2	10.9	10.9	10.8	11.2	11.0	11.0	11.1	10.8	10.8	10.8	10.8	10.9
2015	10.8	10.7	10.7	10.7	10.9	10.9	11.1	10.9	10.7	10.7	10.7	10.7	10.8
Financial Activities													
2005	38.4	38.6	38.7	39.9	40.2	41.4	41.5	41.4	40.7	39.3	39.3	39.8	39.9
2006	39.1	39.3	39.5	40.2	40.6	41.7	41.9	41.9	41.2	40.9	40.9	41.1	40.7
2007	40.9	41.1	41.3	41.6	41.8	42.3	42.5	42.5	41.8	41.1	40.8	40.8	41.5
2008	40.3	40.5	40.5	40.3	40.3	41.0	41.3	41.0	40.2	39.3	38.8	38.7	40.2
2009	38.2	38.1	38.0	37.9	37.9	38.4	38.1	38.0	37.1	36.3	35.9	36.0	37.5
2010	36.1	35.9	35.9	36.2	36.2	37.1	37.3	37.4	36.8	36.2	36.2	36.1	36.5
2011	36.0	36.1	36.1	36.9	37.0	37.6	37.9	37.6	37.0	36.6	36.5	36.9	36.9
2012	36.4	36.7	36.8	37.3	37.1	37.9	38.3	38.2	37.8	37.7	37.6	37.7	37.5
2013	37.1	37.1	37.2	37.8	38.0	38.6	38.7	38.5	38.0	37.7	37.7	37.8	37.9
2014	36.9	37.0	37.2	37.5	37.9	38.4	38.6	38.5	38.2	37.7	37.6	37.8	37.8
2015	37.6	37.8	37.8	38.1	38.4	39.0	39.0	38.9	38.5	38.3	37.3	37.8	38.2
Professional and Business Services													
2005	99.2	100.2	101.3	101.4	101.4	102.6	102.3	102.6	102.8	100.9	101.2	101.2	101.4
2006	99.6	100.3	101.3	101.2	101.7	102.4	101.9	102.1	102.4	102.5	102.5	102.9	101.7
2007	99.9	100.3	101.5	101.9	102.4	102.9	103.3	104.0	104.0	103.0	103.8	104.8	102.7
2008	101.7	102.5	103.6	105.0	105.1	106.4	106.1	107.0	106.3	105.1	104.0	103.8	104.7
2009	100.6	100.4	100.1	99.6	98.9	99.4	98.8	99.2	98.8	98.9	99.4	99.5	99.5
2010	96.8	96.3	96.5	97.8	96.6	97.5	98.9	99.0	98.7	98.7	98.9	99.0	97.9
2011	96.5	96.5	96.9	98.0	97.7	98.6	99.5	100.4	100.7	99.5	99.3	99.0	98.6
2012	97.6	98.2	98.6	99.3	98.7	99.7	99.6	100.4	99.9	101.5	101.4	101.7	99.7
2013	101.3	101.7	102.2	102.7	102.3	103.1	103.2	103.8	102.1	102.6	102.9	102.3	102.5
2014	101.6	102.1	103.1	104.9	104.5	105.5	105.5	106.1	104.9	105.5	104.9	104.3	104.4
2015	102.8	103.0	103.3	104.7	104.6	105.3	105.6	106.0	104.9	105.8	105.1	104.5	104.6
Education and Health Services													
2005	84.3	84.6	84.9	85.0	84.3	84.4	84.1	85.2	87.3	87.2	87.6	88.1	85.6
2006	86.7	87.4	87.8	87.6	86.9	86.9	86.6	87.0	89.3	89.6	89.8	90.4	88.0
2007	89.2	89.6	90.2	90.5	89.6	89.4	89.8	90.4	92.0	92.1	92.2	92.8	90.7
2008	90.1	90.9	91.4	91.7	90.8	90.7	90.8	91.5	92.4	93.3	93.3	93.7	91.7
2009	93.3	93.5	93.8	93.6	92.6	92.2	92.5	93.0	94.5	95.1	94.9	95.3	93.7
2010	93.4	93.8	94.7	95.0	93.9	93.3	93.7	94.1	94.7	96.5	96.8	96.9	94.7
2011	96.3	97.1	97.7	98.4	97.3	97.0	97.3	97.6	99.1	99.5	99.7	98.4	98.0
2012	98.8	99.6	99.9	100.4	99.1	99.2	98.6	99.6	101.2	102.9	103.3	102.5	100.4
2013	102.9	103.6	103.8	104.7	103.0	103.0	102.4	103.9	105.2	106.0	106.6	105.3	104.2
2014	105.1	105.3	105.3	106.2	104.7	104.1	103.8	105.0	106.0	106.4	106.4	105.3	105.3
2015	106.6	106.9	107.0	108.1	106.6	106.1	107.5	108.2	109.2	110.5	111.6	111.2	108.3
Leisure and Hospitality													
2005	72.1	73.6	77.7	81.7	85.4	89.7	90.8	90.2	85.3	80.5	78.7	77.9	82.0
2006	75.9	76.8	80.5	84.7	87.3	92.4	93.0	92.5	87.3	83.5	81.1	79.9	84.6
2007	77.2	78.5	82.3	85.2	88.7	93.5	95.9	94.7	89.7	84.4	81.0	80.2	85.9
2008	78.1	79.6	83.4	86.4	90.9	94.2	94.7	93.7	87.9	84.1	79.4	78.1	85.9
2009	74.3	75.9	78.8	83.0	88.8	91.8	91.9	90.7	86.0	82.9	78.4	77.5	83.3
2010	74.0	74.9	78.2	83.7	87.2	91.5	92.0	91.1	86.3	83.2	79.6	79.1	83.4
2011	74.0	74.9	79.1	83.6	87.2	91.8	92.0	91.0	85.3	82.9	79.3	79.3	83.4
2012	75.0	76.1	80.3	83.7	87.4	91.2	91.3	91.3	86.2	83.6	80.4	81.1	84.0
2013	76.8	77.0	81.2	84.7	88.7	92.3	93.6	93.0	87.6	85.3	81.5	81.9	85.3
2014	77.9	77.4	81.1	85.3	90.0	93.3	93.0	92.5	87.0	84.9	81.9	82.3	85.6
2015	78.9	78.5	81.5	86.2	90.3	93.6	94.7	94.8	90.7	87.7	86.9	88.1	87.7

Employment by Industry: Virginia Beach-Norfolk-Newport News, VA-NC, 2005–2015—*Continued*

(Numbers in thousands, not seasonally adjusted)

Industry and year	January	February	March	April	May	June	July	August	September	October	November	December	Annual average
Other Services													
2005	34.0	34.3	34.5	34.9	35.2	35.3	35.3	35.4	35.6	35.2	35.2	35.2	35.0
2006	34.0	34.2	34.6	33.9	34.1	34.3	34.1	34.2	34.2	33.9	34.0	34.2	34.1
2007	34.1	34.4	34.6	35.8	36.6	36.2	36.1	35.4	34.9	33.6	33.3	32.8	34.8
2008	31.4	31.6	31.8	32.3	33.5	33.0	32.9	32.8	32.3	32.1	32.2	32.1	32.3
2009	34.0	34.2	34.3	34.4	34.6	34.8	34.8	34.5	34.1	34.2	34.0	34.0	34.3
2010	33.3	33.3	33.8	34.2	34.5	34.6	34.8	34.7	34.3	34.4	34.2	33.8	34.2
2011	33.5	33.7	34.2	34.8	35.0	35.3	35.4	35.4	35.1	35.0	34.8	34.7	34.7
2012	34.0	34.3	34.7	35.8	35.9	36.2	36.0	36.1	35.6	36.0	35.9	35.8	35.5
2013	35.4	35.6	35.8	36.2	36.4	36.7	36.8	36.5	36.1	35.9	35.8	35.7	36.1
2014	35.1	35.2	35.6	35.9	36.3	36.6	36.6	36.6	36.3	35.8	35.6	35.5	35.9
2015	35.3	35.3	35.6	35.9	36.3	36.6	36.6	36.7	36.3	35.8	35.7	36.1	36.0
Government													
2005	149.8	151.3	151.8	152.6	153.1	154.2	149.4	149.8	151.5	151.3	153.0	152.0	151.7
2006	150.8	151.9	152.5	154.2	154.3	155.2	151.3	150.9	151.2	154.1	155.8	155.5	153.1
2007	154.0	155.6	156.0	155.7	155.6	156.6	153.3	153.4	155.3	156.0	158.4	157.5	155.6
2008	155.9	158.1	158.6	157.4	158.0	159.3	155.5	155.7	157.4	159.4	161.7	160.2	158.1
2009	159.2	160.0	160.9	161.0	160.6	161.5	154.5	156.2	158.1	161.5	163.3	161.8	159.9
2010	160.7	161.6	162.3	162.9	165.1	164.3	157.5	158.0	160.8	162.1	162.5	162.1	161.7
2011	161.0	161.8	162.7	162.9	162.6	163.0	159.3	159.9	162.3	163.9	165.7	165.5	162.6
2012	163.0	164.1	163.6	163.7	163.4	163.7	158.9	159.2	161.3	163.4	164.9	164.1	162.8
2013	161.4	163.0	163.1	163.0	162.4	162.1	158.4	158.8	160.4	161.9	162.8	163.1	161.7
2014	160.0	160.8	161.2	161.5	160.6	160.0	156.8	157.7	159.0	159.6	160.8	161.0	159.9
2015	158.9	160.5	159.9	161.3	160.3	160.5	156.6	156.4	157.4	159.2	160.3	160.1	159.3

Employment by Industry: Providence-Warwick, RI-MA NECTA, 2005–2015

(Numbers in thousands, not seasonally adjusted)

Industry and year	January	February	March	April	May	June	July	August	September	October	November	December	Annual average
Total Nonfarm													
2005	570.0	571.7	573.4	585.4	589.9	592.7	581.4	583.2	590.5	590.3	592.6	591.1	584.4
2006	567.0	569.8	574.4	587.4	591.2	593.6	580.0	583.4	591.8	593.9	595.7	594.4	585.2
2007	572.5	573.1	575.8	583.8	590.7	592.7	580.7	581.6	586.1	585.8	585.9	584.9	582.8
2008	562.5	563.8	566.2	573.8	579.6	579.4	565.9	566.5	572.4	571.1	567.9	563.9	569.4
2009	538.4	538.7	537.6	542.2	548.5	548.4	536.0	536.0	543.4	545.1	545.0	543.3	541.9
2010	524.2	526.4	530.7	538.8	547.1	547.4	540.2	541.3	546.8	549.0	550.6	548.1	540.9
2011	527.7	531.0	533.5	544.9	550.7	552.5	543.4	542.7	550.0	552.8	553.2	550.5	544.4
2012	533.0	537.1	541.0	548.4	555.7	557.0	546.9	549.4	557.0	558.2	558.4	558.7	550.1
2013	539.9	541.2	545.5	555.0	563.3	566.9	557.0	557.8	565.2	568.9	568.8	566.7	558.0
2014	548.4	550.8	554.1	565.1	574.0	574.7	566.1	567.1	575.3	578.8	579.8	579.5	567.8
2015	558.5	556.2	561.0	573.5	583.2	583.6	577.3	575.0	580.9	583.5	584.5	583.1	575.0
Total Private													
2005	495.1	496.6	498.5	510.3	514.3	517.3	512.6	515.1	517.4	515.3	517.3	515.8	510.5
2006	492.4	494.7	499.4	512.6	516.1	518.8	511.1	514.8	518.0	518.9	519.7	518.8	511.3
2007	497.8	498.2	500.8	508.9	515.2	518.0	511.0	512.2	513.0	511.7	511.6	510.3	509.1
2008	488.6	489.6	491.8	499.4	504.3	505.1	498.0	499.3	501.0	498.6	494.6	490.8	496.8
2009	466.2	466.4	465.4	469.6	475.6	476.1	470.3	470.8	473.2	473.2	472.8	471.2	470.9
2010	452.7	454.9	458.5	466.6	472.9	474.9	473.9	475.2	477.2	477.7	478.5	476.3	469.9
2011	456.7	459.9	461.8	473.3	478.9	481.1	478.4	477.6	480.7	482.1	482.3	479.5	474.4
2012	462.8	466.5	470.3	477.5	484.0	486.8	482.2	484.4	487.8	487.5	487.1	487.5	480.4
2013	469.3	471.0	474.8	484.2	491.5	496.0	491.3	492.9	495.6	497.6	497.3	494.8	488.0
2014	477.6	479.8	482.9	493.6	501.5	503.1	500.4	502.0	505.0	507.3	507.6	507.7	497.4
2015	487.3	485.1	489.8	501.7	510.9	512.1	511.6	509.9	511.2	512.3	512.9	511.3	504.7
Goods Producing													
2005	97.3	96.5	96.3	99.5	100.8	102.2	98.8	101.3	101.0	99.8	100.1	98.7	99.4
2006	93.7	93.6	94.2	97.6	98.4	99.7	96.5	99.0	98.5	98.0	96.8	96.1	96.8
2007	92.3	90.9	91.3	92.5	94.1	95.1	92.7	94.9	94.6	93.0	92.1	90.6	92.8
2008	86.2	85.1	85.6	87.4	88.6	89.1	86.5	88.1	87.5	86.0	84.1	82.1	86.4
2009	76.2	74.1	73.0	73.8	74.3	74.5	72.9	73.5	73.2	72.7	72.1	71.0	73.4
2010	67.0	66.5	67.0	69.0	70.6	71.7	71.3	72.5	72.1	72.1	72.0	70.9	70.2
2011	67.2	66.6	67.1	69.5	70.7	71.8	71.3	72.1	71.7	71.7	71.4	70.4	70.1
2012	67.3	66.9	67.7	69.4	70.2	71.5	70.6	71.7	71.4	71.5	71.2	70.9	70.0
2013	67.5	66.7	67.9	69.6	71.2	72.2	71.1	72.6	72.6	72.5	72.6	71.7	70.7
2014	68.9	68.1	68.6	71.1	72.9	73.9	73.0	74.0	73.9	73.9	73.9	73.4	72.1
2015	70.3	69.0	69.7	72.3	73.9	74.9	74.8	75.4	75.3	75.8	76.4	75.9	73.6
Service-Providing													
2005	472.7	475.2	477.1	485.9	489.1	490.5	482.6	481.9	489.5	490.5	492.5	492.4	485.0
2006	473.3	476.2	480.2	489.8	492.8	493.9	483.5	484.4	493.3	495.9	498.9	498.3	488.4
2007	480.2	482.2	484.5	491.3	496.6	497.6	488.0	486.7	491.5	492.8	493.8	494.3	490.0
2008	476.3	478.7	480.6	486.4	491.0	490.3	479.4	478.4	484.9	485.1	483.8	481.8	483.1
2009	462.2	464.6	464.6	468.4	474.2	473.9	463.1	462.5	470.2	472.4	472.9	472.3	468.4
2010	457.2	459.9	463.7	469.8	476.5	475.7	468.9	468.8	474.7	476.9	478.6	477.2	470.7
2011	460.5	464.4	466.4	475.4	480.0	480.7	472.1	470.6	478.3	481.1	481.8	480.1	474.3
2012	465.7	470.2	473.3	479.0	485.5	485.5	476.3	477.7	485.6	486.7	487.2	487.8	480.0
2013	472.4	474.5	477.6	485.4	492.1	494.7	485.9	485.2	492.6	496.4	496.2	495.0	487.3
2014	479.5	482.7	485.5	494.0	501.1	500.8	493.1	493.1	501.4	504.9	505.9	506.1	495.7
2015	488.2	487.2	491.3	501.2	509.3	508.7	502.5	499.6	505.6	507.7	508.1	507.2	501.4
Mining and Logging													
2005	0.3	0.2	0.2	0.3	0.3	0.3	0.3	0.3	0.3	0.3	0.3	0.3	0.3
2006	0.2	0.2	0.2	0.3	0.3	0.3	0.3	0.3	0.3	0.3	0.3	0.3	0.3
2007	0.3	0.2	0.2	0.3	0.3	0.3	0.3	0.3	0.3	0.3	0.3	0.3	0.3
2008	0.2	0.2	0.2	0.2	0.3	0.3	0.3	0.3	0.3	0.3	0.3	0.3	0.3
2009	0.2	0.2	0.2	0.2	0.2	0.2	0.2	0.2	0.2	0.2	0.2	0.2	0.2
2010	0.1	0.1	0.1	0.2	0.2	0.2	0.2	0.2	0.2	0.2	0.2	0.2	0.2
2011	0.1	0.1	0.1	0.2	0.2	0.2	0.2	0.2	0.2	0.2	0.2	0.2	0.2
2012	0.1	0.1	0.1	0.2	0.2	0.2	0.2	0.2	0.2	0.2	0.2	0.2	0.2
2013	0.1	0.1	0.1	0.2	0.2	0.2	0.2	0.2	0.2	0.2	0.2	0.2	0.2
2014	0.1	0.1	0.1	0.2	0.2	0.2	0.2	0.2	0.2	0.2	0.2	0.2	0.2
2015	0.2	0.2	0.2	0.2	0.2	0.2	0.2	0.2	0.2	0.2	0.2	0.2	0.2

Employment by Industry: Providence-Warwick, RI-MA NECTA, 2005–2015—*Continued*

(Numbers in thousands, not seasonally adjusted)

Industry and year	January	February	March	April	May	June	July	August	September	October	November	December	Annual average
Construction													
2005	23.3	22.7	23.1	26.5	27.8	28.9	29.2	29.4	29.2	28.6	29.1	27.9	27.1
2006	24.8	24.3	25.2	28.4	29.3	30.4	30.4	30.7	30.4	30.0	29.4	28.8	28.5
2007	26.0	24.6	25.2	26.7	28.3	29.1	29.6	29.5	29.0	28.4	27.9	26.6	27.6
2008	23.2	22.6	23.1	25.1	26.2	26.9	27.2	27.1	26.8	25.8	24.9	23.4	25.2
2009	20.2	19.6	19.4	20.9	21.8	21.9	22.2	22.1	21.7	21.4	20.8	19.8	21.0
2010	16.8	16.3	16.8	18.8	20.1	20.7	21.4	21.6	21.0	20.8	20.6	19.5	19.5
2011	16.6	16.0	16.4	18.5	19.7	20.5	21.2	21.1	20.8	20.8	20.7	19.8	19.3
2012	17.6	17.0	17.8	19.3	19.9	20.8	21.2	21.1	20.8	20.8	20.5	20.1	19.7
2013	17.4	16.9	17.6	19.2	20.6	21.2	21.8	21.9	21.8	21.7	21.4	20.3	20.2
2014	18.2	17.5	17.9	20.0	21.4	22.0	22.4	22.3	22.2	22.2	22.0	21.3	20.8
2015	18.7	17.7	18.2	20.5	22.0	22.6	23.3	23.3	23.2	23.4	23.7	23.1	21.6
Manufacturing													
2005	73.7	73.6	73.0	72.7	72.7	73.0	69.3	71.6	71.5	70.9	70.7	70.5	71.9
2006	68.7	69.1	68.8	68.9	68.8	69.0	65.8	68.0	67.8	67.7	67.1	67.0	68.1
2007	66.0	66.1	65.9	65.5	65.5	65.7	62.8	65.1	65.3	64.3	63.9	63.7	65.0
2008	62.8	62.3	62.3	62.1	62.1	61.9	59.0	60.7	60.4	59.9	58.9	58.4	60.9
2009	55.8	54.3	53.4	52.7	52.3	52.4	50.5	51.2	51.3	51.1	51.1	51.0	52.3
2010	50.1	50.1	50.1	50.0	50.3	50.8	49.7	50.7	50.9	51.1	51.2	51.2	50.5
2011	50.5	50.5	50.6	50.8	50.8	51.1	49.9	50.8	50.7	50.7	50.5	50.4	50.6
2012	49.6	49.8	49.8	49.9	50.1	50.5	49.2	50.4	50.4	50.5	50.5	50.6	50.1
2013	50.0	49.7	50.2	50.2	50.4	50.8	49.1	50.5	50.6	50.6	51.0	51.2	50.4
2014	50.6	50.5	50.6	50.9	51.3	51.7	50.4	51.5	51.5	51.5	51.7	51.9	51.2
2015	51.4	51.1	51.3	51.6	51.7	52.1	51.3	51.9	51.9	52.2	52.5	52.6	51.8
Trade, Transportation, and Utilities													
2005	102.2	101.3	101.2	102.4	103.0	103.9	102.5	102.9	103.4	104.4	106.6	108.4	103.5
2006	102.3	100.6	101.1	102.5	102.9	103.7	101.8	102.0	102.9	104.0	106.4	107.9	103.2
2007	102.6	100.7	101.0	101.7	102.6	103.6	102.0	101.7	102.2	102.5	104.8	106.3	102.6
2008	100.5	98.8	98.7	99.1	100.0	100.7	99.1	99.2	99.5	99.7	100.4	100.8	99.7
2009	95.4	93.9	93.4	92.6	94.2	95.1	93.2	93.2	94.4	95.0	96.5	97.3	94.5
2010	93.5	92.6	93.1	92.5	93.2	94.4	93.2	93.4	94.3	95.2	96.9	97.8	94.2
2011	93.6	93.0	92.8	94.0	95.0	95.6	94.2	94.4	95.5	96.6	98.5	99.7	95.2
2012	95.5	94.3	94.5	94.9	96.2	97.0	94.9	95.2	96.3	97.0	99.0	99.5	96.2
2013	94.6	93.7	93.7	94.6	95.7	96.6	95.0	95.3	96.2	97.2	99.1	100.3	96.0
2014	95.8	95.1	94.9	95.8	96.9	97.8	96.1	96.3	97.5	99.0	101.2	102.7	97.4
2015	98.1	96.8	96.7	97.7	98.9	99.9	98.5	98.5	99.4	99.3	100.8	102.2	98.9
Wholesale Trade													
2005	20.7	20.7	20.8	21.2	21.2	21.4	21.3	21.4	21.3	21.3	21.4	21.7	21.2
2006	21.1	21.1	21.2	21.4	21.5	21.6	21.5	21.5	21.5	21.6	21.5	21.5	21.4
2007	21.4	21.2	21.2	21.5	21.5	21.6	21.6	21.5	21.3	21.3	21.4	21.5	21.4
2008	20.9	20.9	20.9	21.0	21.1	21.2	21.1	21.0	21.0	21.0	20.9	20.6	21.0
2009	20.2	20.0	20.0	19.9	20.0	20.1	19.8	19.8	19.9	20.0	19.9	19.9	20.0
2010	19.4	19.4	19.5	19.4	19.7	19.8	19.8	19.9	19.8	19.8	19.9	19.9	19.7
2011	19.5	19.6	19.2	19.3	19.5	19.6	19.7	19.7	19.7	19.8	19.8	20.0	19.6
2012	19.9	19.9	20.0	20.0	20.2	20.3	20.2	20.2	20.1	20.1	20.1	20.0	20.1
2013	19.8	19.7	19.9	19.9	20.0	20.1	20.0	20.1	20.0	20.1	20.2	20.1	20.0
2014	19.9	19.9	19.9	19.8	20.0	20.0	20.1	20.2	20.1	20.2	20.3	20.3	20.1
2015	20.1	20.1	20.1	20.2	20.3	20.3	20.3	20.3	20.2	20.0	20.0	20.2	20.2
Retail Trade													
2005	69.0	68.1	68.0	68.4	68.8	69.3	68.8	69.0	68.9	69.9	72.0	73.4	69.5
2006	68.6	67.0	67.3	68.2	68.3	68.8	68.1	68.1	68.0	69.0	71.5	72.9	68.8
2007	68.4	67.0	67.2	67.3	68.0	68.6	68.0	67.8	67.4	67.9	70.1	71.2	68.2
2008	66.9	65.3	65.2	65.2	65.7	66.2	65.5	65.5	64.9	65.5	66.5	66.9	65.8
2009	62.9	61.7	61.3	60.7	61.9	62.5	62.1	62.0	61.9	62.6	64.1	64.8	62.4
2010	62.2	61.2	61.6	60.8	61.0	61.8	61.8	62.0	61.6	62.4	64.0	64.7	62.1
2011	61.6	60.9	61.1	61.8	62.4	62.7	62.4	62.8	62.4	63.4	65.3	65.9	62.7
2012	62.6	61.5	61.6	61.9	62.7	63.2	62.6	62.7	62.7	63.4	65.4	65.7	63.0
2013	62.1	61.2	61.0	61.6	62.4	63.0	62.7	62.8	62.6	63.5	65.2	66.0	62.8
2014	62.8	62.1	61.9	62.7	63.4	63.9	63.4	63.3	63.3	64.7	66.6	67.6	63.8
2015	64.2	63.0	63.1	63.6	64.4	65.3	65.0	65.1	64.8	64.9	66.0	66.5	64.7

Employment by Industry: Providence-Warwick, RI-MA NECTA, 2005–2015—*Continued*

(Numbers in thousands, not seasonally adjusted)

Industry and year	January	February	March	April	May	June	July	August	September	October	November	December	Annual average
Transportation and Utilities													
2005	12.5	12.5	12.4	12.8	13.0	13.2	12.4	12.5	13.2	13.2	13.2	13.3	12.9
2006	12.6	12.5	12.6	12.9	13.1	13.3	12.2	12.4	13.4	13.4	13.4	13.5	12.9
2007	12.8	12.5	12.6	12.9	13.1	13.4	12.4	12.4	13.5	13.3	13.3	13.6	13.0
2008	12.7	12.6	12.6	12.9	13.2	13.3	12.5	12.7	13.6	13.2	13.0	13.3	13.0
2009	12.3	12.2	12.1	12.0	12.3	12.5	11.3	11.4	12.6	12.4	12.5	12.6	12.2
2010	11.9	12.0	12.0	12.3	12.5	12.8	11.6	11.5	12.9	13.0	13.0	13.2	12.4
2011	12.5	12.5	12.5	12.9	13.1	13.3	12.1	11.9	13.4	13.4	13.4	13.8	12.9
2012	13.0	12.9	12.9	13.0	13.3	13.5	12.1	12.3	13.5	13.5	13.5	13.8	13.1
2013	12.7	12.8	12.8	13.1	13.3	13.5	12.3	12.4	13.6	13.6	13.7	14.2	13.2
2014	13.1	13.1	13.1	13.3	13.5	13.9	12.6	12.8	14.1	14.1	14.3	14.8	13.6
2015	13.8	13.7	13.5	13.9	14.2	14.3	13.2	13.1	14.4	14.4	14.8	15.5	14.1
Information													
2005	11.7	11.7	11.6	11.6	11.5	11.6	11.6	11.6	11.5	11.6	11.8	11.8	11.6
2006	11.9	11.8	11.8	12.2	12.1	12.2	11.6	11.5	11.5	11.4	11.7	11.7	11.8
2007	11.3	11.2	11.2	11.3	11.4	11.5	11.5	11.6	11.5	11.5	11.7	11.7	11.5
2008	11.6	11.9	11.9	11.7	11.8	12.0	11.8	12.2	11.9	11.9	11.7	11.6	11.8
2009	11.6	11.5	11.4	11.6	11.6	11.6	11.2	11.2	11.1	10.9	11.1	11.1	11.3
2010	11.0	11.1	11.2	11.1	11.1	11.2	11.2	11.5	11.6	11.4	11.5	11.4	11.3
2011	11.0	11.0	11.1	11.6	11.8	11.7	11.5	10.6	11.3	11.1	11.2	11.4	11.3
2012	11.1	11.1	11.1	10.9	10.8	10.9	10.7	10.7	10.5	10.5	10.5	10.5	10.8
2013	10.5	10.5	10.3	10.1	10.3	10.3	10.2	10.2	10.1	10.0	10.2	10.2	10.2
2014	10.3	10.0	10.0	10.0	10.1	10.0	10.1	10.2	10.0	9.9	9.9	10.0	10.0
2015	9.7	9.5	9.7	9.8	9.8	9.7	10.0	9.9	9.9	9.9	10.0	10.0	9.8
Financial Activities													
2005	37.0	37.2	37.2	37.7	37.6	37.9	38.0	38.0	37.8	37.5	37.6	37.9	37.6
2006	37.4	37.4	37.6	37.8	38.0	38.2	38.4	38.8	38.9	38.8	39.0	39.4	38.3
2007	38.5	38.6	38.5	38.6	38.7	38.5	38.2	37.8	37.7	37.3	37.2	37.2	38.1
2008	36.8	36.9	36.7	36.5	36.6	36.5	36.3	36.1	36.2	35.4	35.2	35.2	36.2
2009	34.7	34.6	34.3	34.0	34.1	34.2	33.9	33.5	33.2	33.3	33.5	33.4	33.9
2010	32.9	32.9	33.1	32.9	33.1	33.2	33.3	33.2	33.3	33.5	33.5	33.6	33.2
2011	32.9	33.0	33.1	33.2	33.1	33.6	33.3	33.3	33.3	33.3	33.7	33.5	33.3
2012	33.4	33.6	33.8	33.9	34.1	34.3	34.3	34.3	34.4	34.5	34.5	34.5	34.1
2013	34.2	34.5	34.7	34.7	34.8	34.9	35.0	34.7	34.6	34.7	34.6	34.9	34.7
2014	34.5	34.4	34.4	34.9	35.0	35.2	35.3	35.0	35.0	35.0	35.0	35.1	34.9
2015	34.8	34.9	35.1	35.2	35.4	35.7	35.3	35.2	35.5	35.8	35.6	35.9	35.4
Professional and Business Services													
2005	59.2	59.1	59.7	62.4	62.3	63.0	62.9	63.6	63.8	62.7	62.6	62.0	61.9
2006	58.9	59.2	59.9	63.1	63.1	64.3	63.2	64.4	65.1	65.1	64.5	63.8	62.9
2007	60.6	60.3	60.7	63.0	63.5	64.6	63.4	63.4	63.1	62.7	62.5	62.2	62.5
2008	59.5	59.0	59.3	61.6	61.4	62.5	61.7	61.9	62.3	61.8	60.8	59.6	61.0
2009	56.9	56.8	56.8	58.2	58.1	58.8	58.1	58.5	58.7	58.5	58.3	57.5	57.9
2010	54.9	55.3	56.2	59.5	59.5	60.4	60.2	60.1	60.2	60.4	60.3	59.2	58.9
2011	56.9	57.3	57.5	59.7	59.9	60.4	60.2	60.7	61.3	61.3	61.2	59.7	59.7
2012	57.8	58.1	59.2	61.3	61.7	62.5	62.1	62.5	62.3	62.3	62.4	62.1	61.2
2013	59.9	60.4	60.8	63.6	64.3	65.8	64.9	65.7	65.8	66.7	66.3	65.5	64.1
2014	62.6	63.5	63.9	66.7	67.3	68.0	67.9	68.7	68.9	69.8	69.9	69.4	67.2
2015	64.9	65.1	65.6	69.0	70.2	70.4	70.5	70.4	70.2	70.6	70.9	70.5	69.0
Education and Health Services													
2005	107.5	110.1	111.1	111.6	111.3	107.4	106.7	106.3	110.8	113.0	113.6	112.8	110.2
2006	108.9	112.6	113.9	114.5	113.6	109.4	107.8	107.7	111.7	114.5	115.7	114.8	112.1
2007	111.5	115.1	115.7	116.0	115.9	111.6	110.0	109.9	113.7	116.2	117.1	116.4	114.1
2008	113.0	116.4	117.4	117.6	116.9	112.5	111.0	110.9	114.7	117.3	117.9	117.7	115.3
2009	113.8	117.3	117.9	117.7	117.4	113.6	112.3	112.4	116.0	118.6	119.2	119.1	116.3
2010	116.0	118.6	119.6	119.4	119.6	114.9	114.2	114.4	118.3	120.3	121.0	121.1	118.1
2011	116.9	120.2	120.7	121.8	121.8	117.2	116.0	115.2	119.0	122.1	122.1	121.4	119.5
2012	118.0	121.8	122.4	121.5	122.0	117.6	116.0	116.3	122.0	123.3	123.2	124.0	120.7
2013	120.9	123.2	123.8	123.9	123.6	120.4	119.1	118.8	123.3	125.7	126.2	124.4	122.8
2014	121.9	124.1	125.1	125.6	125.4	120.8	120.2	120.1	124.5	126.9	127.0	127.2	124.1
2015	123.4	124.6	126.0	126.6	126.5	122.0	121.9	120.5	123.7	126.5	126.9	125.4	124.5

Employment by Industry: Providence-Warwick, RI-MA NECTA, 2005–2015—*Continued*

(Numbers in thousands, not seasonally adjusted)

Industry and year	January	February	March	April	May	June	July	August	September	October	November	December	Annual average
Leisure and Hospitality													
2005	54.0	54.5	55.0	58.6	61.1	64.2	64.7	64.0	62.6	59.9	58.5	57.7	59.6
2006	53.7	53.8	55.0	58.5	61.3	64.0	64.4	64.2	62.9	60.3	58.9	58.4	59.6
2007	54.9	55.3	56.1	59.4	62.3	65.6	65.7	65.6	63.8	62.0	59.7	59.2	60.8
2008	55.1	55.6	56.1	59.3	62.6	65.0	64.5	64.1	62.8	60.3	58.5	57.8	60.1
2009	52.4	53.0	53.3	56.2	60.2	62.4	62.4	62.5	61.4	58.6	56.6	56.2	57.9
2010	52.6	52.9	53.3	57.1	60.3	63.3	64.0	63.7	62.0	59.5	57.9	56.9	58.6
2011	53.4	53.9	54.4	58.1	60.9	64.4	64.7	64.3	62.8	60.5	58.5	57.6	59.5
2012	54.6	55.5	56.3	59.7	62.9	66.2	66.4	66.4	64.4	62.3	60.1	59.6	61.2
2013	56.1	56.4	57.7	61.2	64.8	68.3	68.1	68.0	66.2	64.3	61.7	61.1	62.8
2014	57.6	58.4	59.5	62.9	66.8	69.5	69.4	69.4	68.0	65.9	63.7	62.8	64.5
2015	59.6	58.9	60.2	64.2	68.8	71.4	71.7	71.4	69.8	67.1	64.8	64.0	66.0
Other Services													
2005	26.2	26.2	26.4	26.5	26.7	27.1	27.4	27.4	26.5	26.4	26.5	26.5	26.7
2006	25.6	25.7	25.9	26.4	26.7	27.3	27.4	27.2	26.5	26.8	26.7	26.7	26.6
2007	26.1	26.1	26.3	26.4	26.7	27.5	27.5	27.3	26.4	26.5	26.5	26.7	26.7
2008	25.9	25.9	26.1	26.2	26.4	26.8	27.1	26.8	26.1	26.2	26.0	26.0	26.3
2009	25.2	25.2	25.3	25.5	25.7	25.9	26.3	26.0	25.2	25.6	25.5	25.6	25.6
2010	24.8	25.0	25.0	25.1	25.5	25.8	26.5	26.4	25.4	25.3	25.4	25.4	25.5
2011	24.8	24.9	25.1	25.4	25.7	26.4	27.2	27.0	25.8	25.5	25.7	25.8	25.8
2012	25.1	25.2	25.3	25.9	26.1	26.8	27.2	27.3	26.5	26.1	26.2	26.4	26.2
2013	25.6	25.6	25.9	26.5	26.8	27.5	27.9	27.6	26.8	26.5	26.6	26.7	26.7
2014	26.0	26.2	26.5	26.6	27.1	27.9	28.4	28.3	27.2	26.9	27.0	27.1	27.1
2015	26.5	26.3	26.8	26.9	27.4	28.1	28.9	28.6	27.4	27.3	27.5	27.4	27.4
Government													
2005	74.9	75.1	74.9	75.1	75.6	75.4	68.8	68.1	73.1	75.0	75.3	75.3	73.9
2006	74.6	75.1	75.0	74.8	75.1	74.8	68.9	68.6	73.8	75.0	76.0	75.6	73.9
2007	74.7	74.9	75.0	74.9	75.5	74.7	69.7	69.4	73.1	74.1	74.3	74.6	73.7
2008	73.9	74.2	74.4	74.4	75.3	74.3	67.9	67.2	71.4	72.5	73.3	73.1	72.7
2009	72.2	72.3	72.2	72.6	72.9	72.3	65.7	65.2	70.2	71.9	72.2	72.1	71.0
2010	71.5	71.5	72.2	72.2	74.2	72.5	66.3	66.1	69.6	71.3	72.1	71.8	70.9
2011	71.0	71.1	71.7	71.6	71.8	71.4	65.0	65.1	69.3	70.7	70.9	71.0	70.1
2012	70.2	70.6	70.7	70.9	71.7	70.2	64.7	65.0	69.2	70.7	71.3	71.2	69.7
2013	70.6	70.2	70.7	70.8	71.8	70.9	64.9	65.1	69.6	71.3	71.5	71.9	70.0
2014	70.8	71.0	71.2	71.5	72.5	71.6	65.7	65.1	70.3	71.5	72.2	71.8	70.4
2015	71.2	71.1	71.2	71.8	72.3	71.5	65.7	65.1	69.7	71.2	71.6	71.8	70.4

Employment by Industry: Milwaukee-Waukesha-West Allis, WI, 2005–2015

(Numbers in thousands, not seasonally adjusted)

Industry and year	January	February	March	April	May	June	July	August	September	October	November	December	Annual average
Total Nonfarm													
2005	826.3	828.9	831.6	843.6	846.0	853.5	847.2	848.6	851.4	851.0	853.3	854.6	844.7
2006	833.6	836.6	840.0	850.0	854.7	863.4	855.8	858.9	862.2	865.3	867.5	867.3	854.6
2007	846.9	846.6	849.6	856.7	865.6	874.9	862.9	865.7	864.2	866.4	867.4	867.5	861.2
2008	847.6	846.9	850.0	857.0	864.0	869.0	859.1	858.9	859.9	860.7	856.8	851.6	856.8
2009	824.2	818.9	814.0	816.9	820.6	822.9	809.9	809.3	814.0	814.9	813.1	811.4	815.8
2010	793.3	792.8	795.5	804.2	812.0	813.5	810.9	812.7	810.9	817.9	820.1	817.5	808.4
2011	798.6	800.5	804.1	811.8	816.2	820.0	817.4	818.9	818.6	819.2	822.2	818.6	813.8
2012	799.6	802.9	809.7	815.6	825.2	828.2	821.7	824.6	826.1	830.8	835.1	832.2	821.0
2013	808.9	816.5	820.5	826.2	835.8	840.0	835.5	837.4	842.0	842.9	846.1	846.0	833.2
2014	822.0	829.0	830.7	837.0	843.7	851.6	846.1	853.6	852.4	853.5	859.4	858.0	844.8
2015	831.0	839.1	842.3	850.1	857.1	862.5	855.5	860.8	858.1	867.9	866.2	860.3	854.2
Total Private													
2005	734.7	734.1	738.0	749.9	752.6	760.0	762.1	763.2	759.1	758.0	759.8	761.8	752.8
2006	743.4	743.7	746.6	756.3	761.2	769.5	770.3	773.0	770.0	771.7	773.9	774.1	762.8
2007	756.8	754.9	757.6	764.1	772.6	781.3	777.9	780.8	772.7	774.2	775.2	774.5	770.2
2008	756.4	755.6	756.3	763.7	769.7	774.8	773.2	774.3	766.4	765.6	759.9	756.0	764.3
2009	731.0	723.9	719.1	721.6	726.0	729.3	726.3	726.7	722.5	721.9	720.0	718.2	723.9
2010	701.6	701.2	703.5	712.6	718.0	722.2	726.0	728.7	722.9	727.6	728.3	727.4	718.3
2011	709.7	707.7	711.8	720.2	725.2	729.3	730.2	732.3	730.7	732.7	733.7	729.8	724.4
2012	713.8	715.7	720.9	725.5	734.2	738.9	738.4	739.6	739.3	742.2	743.9	743.3	733.0
2013	724.2	728.4	732.4	738.2	748.1	752.7	753.7	754.0	754.6	755.2	758.2	758.4	746.5
2014	737.0	741.8	743.1	749.6	756.5	763.8	764.1	767.5	764.9	766.1	770.6	770.7	758.0
2015	747.9	751.6	755.0	761.8	769.5	775.9	773.8	777.7	772.2	779.6	777.7	771.6	767.9
Goods Producing													
2005	164.3	164.0	164.6	167.1	168.5	171.0	171.3	171.2	169.7	168.5	168.0	167.0	167.9
2006	164.3	163.2	163.7	166.6	168.4	171.4	171.2	172.1	170.6	170.6	170.0	169.4	168.5
2007	166.1	163.9	165.1	167.5	170.2	172.7	172.3	172.9	170.9	170.7	169.8	168.1	169.2
2008	164.5	163.4	163.9	165.4	167.3	168.9	167.8	168.0	165.3	164.5	162.5	159.4	165.1
2009	153.5	149.7	146.5	145.7	145.4	145.7	144.1	144.3	143.3	142.4	140.8	138.6	145.0
2010	135.2	133.6	134.0	136.7	137.9	140.4	142.2	142.9	141.5	141.7	140.8	139.1	138.8
2011	136.6	135.9	137.0	140.1	141.7	144.8	145.8	146.2	144.6	144.4	144.1	142.4	142.0
2012	139.7	139.1	140.1	142.3	143.6	146.6	147.4	147.0	145.4	145.3	144.6	143.7	143.7
2013	141.5	141.0	141.6	143.2	145.7	148.3	148.8	149.4	147.5	147.6	147.1	145.1	145.6
2014	142.6	142.4	143.5	145.4	147.6	149.9	151.9	152.3	150.8	149.9	149.9	148.6	147.9
2015	146.2	145.7	146.7	148.3	150.1	152.3	153.2	153.2	151.4	152.0	152.0	151.3	150.2
Service-Providing													
2005	662.0	664.9	667.0	676.5	677.5	682.5	675.9	677.4	681.7	682.5	685.3	687.6	676.7
2006	669.3	673.4	676.3	683.4	686.3	692.0	684.6	686.8	691.6	694.7	697.5	697.9	686.2
2007	680.8	682.7	684.5	689.2	695.4	702.2	690.6	692.8	693.3	695.7	697.6	699.4	692.0
2008	683.1	683.5	686.1	691.6	696.7	700.1	691.3	690.9	694.6	696.2	694.3	692.2	691.7
2009	670.7	669.2	667.5	671.2	675.2	677.2	665.8	665.0	670.7	672.5	672.3	672.8	670.8
2010	658.1	659.2	661.5	667.5	674.1	673.1	668.7	669.8	669.4	676.2	679.3	678.4	669.6
2011	662.0	664.6	667.1	671.7	674.5	675.2	671.6	672.7	674.0	674.8	678.1	676.2	671.9
2012	659.9	663.8	669.6	673.3	681.6	681.6	674.3	677.6	680.7	685.5	690.5	688.5	677.2
2013	667.4	675.5	678.9	683.0	690.1	691.7	686.7	688.0	694.5	695.3	699.0	700.9	687.6
2014	679.4	686.6	687.2	691.6	696.1	701.7	694.2	701.3	701.6	703.6	709.5	709.4	696.9
2015	684.8	693.4	695.6	701.8	707.0	710.2	702.3	707.6	706.7	715.9	714.2	709.0	704.0
Mining and Logging													
2005	0.4	0.4	0.4	0.5	0.5	0.5	0.5	0.5	0.5	0.5	0.5	0.5	0.5
2006	0.5	0.5	0.5	0.5	0.5	0.5	0.5	0.5	0.5	0.5	0.5	0.5	0.5
2007	0.5	0.4	0.5	0.5	0.5	0.5	0.5	0.5	0.5	0.5	0.5	0.5	0.5
2008	0.4	0.4	0.4	0.4	0.4	0.4	0.4	0.4	0.4	0.4	0.4	0.4	0.4
2009	0.3	0.3	0.3	0.4	0.4	0.4	0.4	0.4	0.4	0.4	0.4	0.3	0.4
2010	0.3	0.3	0.3	0.4	0.4	0.4	0.4	0.4	0.4	0.4	0.3	0.3	0.4
2011	0.3	0.3	0.3	0.3	0.3	0.4	0.4	0.4	0.4	0.4	0.4	0.3	0.4
2012	0.3	0.3	0.3	0.4	0.4	0.4	0.4	0.4	0.4	0.4	0.4	0.3	0.4
2013	0.3	0.3	0.3	0.4	0.4	0.4	0.4	0.4	0.4	0.4	0.4	0.4	0.4
2014	0.3	0.3	0.3	0.4	0.4	0.4	0.5	0.4	0.4	0.4	0.4	0.4	0.4
2015	0.4	0.4	0.4	0.4	0.5	0.5	0.5	0.5	0.5	0.5	0.5	0.4	0.5

Employment by Industry: Milwaukee-Waukesha-West Allis, WI, 2005–2015—*Continued*

(Numbers in thousands, not seasonally adjusted)

Industry and year	January	February	March	April	May	June	July	August	September	October	November	December	Annual average
Construction													
2005	30.5	30.1	30.6	32.9	34.6	35.9	36.3	36.3	35.8	35.4	35.1	33.7	33.9
2006	31.4	30.7	31.2	33.8	35.3	36.7	37.0	37.0	36.6	36.4	35.8	34.7	34.7
2007	32.2	30.8	32.6	34.1	36.4	37.8	38.2	38.2	37.4	37.1	36.5	34.3	35.5
2008	31.3	30.5	31.2	32.9	35.3	36.2	36.4	36.2	35.1	35.3	33.9	31.7	33.8
2009	27.9	27.2	27.0	28.7	30.0	30.8	31.1	30.9	30.0	29.5	28.5	26.2	29.0
2010	23.3	22.5	22.8	25.2	26.2	27.4	27.9	28.2	27.5	27.2	26.2	24.2	25.7
2011	21.6	21.0	21.6	23.8	25.2	26.4	26.7	26.8	26.4	26.2	25.6	23.6	24.6
2012	20.8	20.5	21.2	23.1	24.2	25.4	25.8	25.7	25.3	25.2	24.7	23.4	23.8
2013	21.6	21.6	22.1	23.1	25.8	26.9	27.8	28.3	27.7	27.7	27.2	25.2	25.4
2014	23.2	23.0	23.8	25.6	27.6	28.8	29.7	30.2	29.8	29.4	29.0	27.5	27.3
2015	25.3	25.0	25.7	27.6	29.2	30.3	30.8	30.9	30.2	30.6	30.2	29.4	28.8
Manufacturing													
2005	133.4	133.5	133.6	133.7	133.4	134.6	134.5	134.4	133.4	132.6	132.4	132.8	133.5
2006	132.4	132.0	132.0	132.3	132.6	134.2	133.7	134.6	133.5	133.7	133.7	134.2	133.2
2007	133.4	132.7	132.0	132.9	133.3	134.4	133.6	134.2	133.0	133.1	132.8	133.3	133.2
2008	132.8	132.5	132.3	132.1	131.6	132.3	131.0	131.4	129.8	128.8	128.2	127.3	130.8
2009	125.3	122.2	119.2	116.6	115.0	114.5	112.6	113.0	112.9	112.5	111.9	112.1	115.7
2010	111.6	110.8	110.9	111.1	111.3	112.6	113.9	114.3	113.6	114.1	114.3	114.6	112.8
2011	114.7	114.6	115.1	116.0	116.2	118.0	118.7	119.0	117.8	117.8	118.1	118.5	117.0
2012	118.6	118.3	118.6	118.8	119.0	120.8	121.2	120.9	119.7	119.7	119.5	120.0	119.6
2013	119.6	119.1	119.2	119.7	119.5	121.0	120.6	120.7	119.4	119.5	119.5	119.5	119.8
2014	119.1	119.1	119.4	119.4	119.6	120.7	121.7	121.7	120.6	120.1	120.5	120.7	120.2
2015	120.5	120.3	120.6	120.3	120.4	121.5	121.9	121.8	120.7	120.9	121.3	121.5	121.0
Trade, Transportation, and Utilities													
2005	154.6	153.2	153.7	154.3	155.5	156.1	155.5	156.4	156.7	157.3	160.0	161.5	156.2
2006	155.7	154.0	154.9	155.4	156.6	157.4	155.5	156.0	156.5	157.6	160.7	162.2	156.9
2007	156.6	154.5	154.5	154.4	156.4	157.1	155.2	155.3	154.9	155.7	158.5	159.4	156.0
2008	154.3	152.0	152.0	153.0	153.7	154.2	153.2	153.2	152.3	152.7	153.5	153.8	153.2
2009	147.4	145.0	144.2	143.4	145.0	145.9	143.3	142.9	143.4	145.2	145.8	146.2	144.8
2010	140.9	138.6	138.8	139.1	140.5	141.2	139.8	140.3	140.6	143.9	145.0	145.8	141.2
2011	140.7	139.2	139.9	140.8	141.5	141.8	141.3	141.7	142.4	144.6	145.9	146.2	142.2
2012	141.9	140.2	140.5	139.6	142.2	142.8	141.7	142.2	142.5	144.1	146.8	147.3	142.7
2013	141.7	140.6	140.8	141.6	143.5	144.3	143.1	143.2	143.3	144.2	146.6	148.0	143.4
2014	142.1	141.3	141.9	142.8	143.9	145.4	143.8	144.3	143.4	144.2	147.2	148.2	144.0
2015	142.8	141.4	141.7	142.3	143.8	145.1	144.4	145.4	144.6	147.3	148.6	147.9	144.6
Wholesale Trade													
2005	42.0	42.0	41.9	42.5	42.6	43.0	43.3	43.1	42.8	42.9	43.0	43.2	42.7
2006	42.5	42.7	42.8	43.0	43.0	43.5	43.7	43.6	43.4	43.5	43.6	43.8	43.3
2007	43.0	43.1	43.1	43.2	43.4	44.0	44.0	43.9	43.5	43.5	43.4	43.5	43.5
2008	42.8	42.9	42.9	43.0	43.0	43.1	43.2	43.1	42.5	42.1	42.2	41.8	42.7
2009	41.1	40.8	40.3	39.8	39.7	39.7	39.4	39.0	38.6	38.6	38.4	38.3	39.5
2010	37.5	37.4	37.3	37.2	37.4	37.6	37.9	37.9	37.5	37.9	37.8	37.8	37.6
2011	37.3	37.3	37.5	37.7	37.8	38.0	38.6	38.5	38.2	38.7	38.6	38.4	38.1
2012	38.1	38.2	38.4	38.5	38.7	39.0	39.0	38.9	38.5	38.7	38.7	38.8	38.6
2013	38.2	38.1	38.1	38.2	38.4	38.6	38.6	38.6	38.3	38.1	38.0	38.2	38.3
2014	37.7	37.7	37.9	38.1	38.2	38.6	38.5	38.5	38.1	38.1	38.2	38.4	38.2
2015	38.1	38.0	38.2	38.3	38.5	38.8	38.9	38.9	38.4	39.4	39.5	39.8	38.7
Retail Trade													
2005	82.3	80.9	81.4	81.9	82.6	83.1	82.9	83.8	83.0	83.6	85.7	86.9	83.2
2006	82.7	80.8	81.3	81.6	82.6	83.2	82.9	82.9	82.1	83.1	86.1	87.1	83.0
2007	83.5	81.3	81.3	80.7	82.1	82.2	81.9	81.7	80.3	81.0	83.6	84.4	82.0
2008	81.4	79.1	79.3	79.8	80.4	80.8	80.9	80.8	79.4	80.1	81.2	81.8	80.4
2009	77.7	75.7	75.6	75.4	76.5	77.4	76.8	76.8	76.2	77.8	78.6	78.9	77.0
2010	75.6	73.7	74.1	74.5	75.5	75.8	75.5	75.8	75.4	77.7	78.7	79.3	76.0
2011	75.8	74.2	74.7	75.3	75.7	76.2	76.1	76.6	76.1	77.8	79.1	79.7	76.4
2012	76.4	74.6	74.8	74.8	75.9	76.6	76.5	77.0	76.6	77.9	80.5	80.7	76.9
2013	76.8	75.8	76.0	76.7	78.0	78.8	78.7	78.8	78.2	79.2	81.4	82.4	78.4
2014	78.3	77.3	77.8	78.3	79.0	80.0	79.7	79.9	78.4	79.0	81.6	82.1	79.3
2015	78.3	77.1	77.2	77.4	78.3	79.4	79.7	80.4	79.2	80.6	81.6	80.5	79.1

Employment by Industry: Milwaukee-Waukesha-West Allis, WI, 2005–2015—*Continued*

(Numbers in thousands, not seasonally adjusted)

Industry and year	January	February	March	April	May	June	July	August	September	October	November	December	Annual average
Transportation and Utilities													
2005	30.3	30.3	30.4	29.9	30.3	30.0	29.3	29.5	30.9	30.8	31.3	31.4	30.4
2006	30.5	30.5	30.8	30.8	31.0	30.7	29.5	29.5	31.0	31.0	31.0	31.3	30.6
2007	30.1	30.1	30.1	30.5	30.9	30.9	29.3	29.7	31.1	31.2	31.5	31.5	30.6
2008	30.1	30.0	29.8	30.2	30.3	30.3	29.1	29.3	30.4	30.5	30.1	30.2	30.0
2009	28.6	28.5	28.3	28.2	28.8	28.8	27.1	27.1	28.6	28.8	28.8	29.0	28.4
2010	27.8	27.5	27.4	27.4	27.6	27.8	26.4	26.6	27.7	28.3	28.5	28.7	27.6
2011	27.6	27.7	27.7	27.8	28.0	27.6	26.6	26.6	28.1	28.1	28.2	28.1	27.7
2012	27.4	27.4	27.3	26.3	27.6	27.2	26.2	26.3	27.4	27.5	27.6	27.8	27.2
2013	26.7	26.7	26.7	26.7	27.1	26.9	25.8	25.8	26.8	26.9	27.2	27.4	26.7
2014	26.1	26.3	26.2	26.4	26.7	26.8	25.6	25.9	26.9	27.1	27.4	27.7	26.6
2015	26.4	26.3	26.3	26.6	27.0	26.9	25.8	26.1	27.0	27.3	27.5	27.6	26.7
Information													
2005	18.3	18.2	18.2	18.3	18.3	18.4	18.2	18.3	18.2	18.2	18.3	18.4	18.3
2006	18.1	18.2	18.1	18.0	18.0	17.8	17.8	17.8	17.6	17.6	17.7	17.6	17.9
2007	17.6	17.6	17.6	17.6	17.6	17.8	17.7	17.7	17.5	17.5	17.7	17.6	17.6
2008	17.2	17.3	17.2	17.6	17.6	17.9	17.7	17.6	17.5	17.4	17.4	17.5	17.5
2009	17.1	17.1	16.9	16.8	16.7	16.7	16.6	16.6	16.4	16.3	16.4	16.3	16.7
2010	15.8	15.7	15.7	15.7	15.6	15.8	16.0	15.9	15.7	15.4	15.9	15.8	15.8
2011	15.7	15.7	15.6	15.6	15.6	15.6	15.5	15.6	15.5	15.4	15.4	15.3	15.5
2012	15.1	15.0	14.9	14.9	14.8	15.0	15.0	15.0	14.9	15.0	15.0	14.8	15.0
2013	14.8	14.7	14.6	14.9	15.0	15.0	15.0	15.0	14.9	14.7	14.8	14.6	14.8
2014	14.4	14.5	14.5	14.5	14.5	14.5	14.7	14.6	14.4	14.5	14.6	14.6	14.5
2015	14.4	14.3	14.2	14.1	14.2	14.2	14.1	14.1	14.0	14.0	14.1	14.0	14.1
Financial Activities													
2005	55.8	55.5	55.8	56.0	55.9	56.1	56.6	56.4	55.8	55.8	55.8	56.0	56.0
2006	55.7	55.5	55.4	55.9	56.2	56.6	57.1	57.0	56.7	56.7	56.7	56.8	56.4
2007	56.4	56.5	56.2	56.6	56.8	57.3	57.3	57.0	56.3	56.7	56.9	57.1	56.8
2008	56.5	56.7	56.3	56.6	57.0	57.0	57.5	57.4	56.3	56.7	56.6	56.6	56.8
2009	56.0	55.8	55.5	56.0	55.9	55.9	56.1	56.0	54.9	55.2	55.1	54.8	55.6
2010	54.0	54.0	54.2	54.1	54.0	54.1	54.3	54.2	53.7	53.8	53.7	54.0	54.0
2011	52.9	52.8	52.9	52.9	52.9	53.3	53.2	52.9	52.7	52.5	52.5	51.9	52.8
2012	51.9	51.8	51.9	51.8	52.0	52.4	52.5	52.4	51.7	51.9	51.7	51.9	52.0
2013	51.4	51.3	51.4	51.8	51.9	52.4	53.0	52.5	52.1	52.1	51.9	52.1	52.0
2014	51.1	51.1	51.3	51.3	51.5	52.1	52.3	52.4	51.9	51.7	51.8	52.1	51.7
2015	51.7	51.5	51.7	51.8	52.1	52.7	53.1	52.8	51.8	51.4	50.8	50.8	51.9
Professional and Business Services													
2005	105.1	105.6	106.5	109.6	108.7	110.5	112.3	112.7	113.0	112.5	112.5	113.3	110.2
2006	108.1	109.0	109.6	112.4	112.0	113.7	114.5	115.6	115.8	116.3	116.1	115.7	113.2
2007	112.4	113.1	113.8	115.2	115.8	118.4	117.9	119.7	118.3	118.1	118.3	118.5	116.6
2008	115.2	116.0	114.9	116.5	116.8	118.2	118.2	119.0	118.3	116.8	114.8	113.6	116.5
2009	107.8	105.6	103.9	104.3	104.4	104.9	105.4	105.1	104.4	105.7	105.9	106.2	105.3
2010	102.5	103.8	102.8	106.4	107.0	108.5	111.0	112.5	112.0	113.4	114.4	114.6	109.1
2011	111.5	111.7	113.0	113.0	112.6	115.2	115.1	116.5	116.4	115.9	116.7	115.6	114.4
2012	113.9	114.7	116.3	116.6	117.5	119.7	119.1	120.0	121.0	121.4	121.9	120.9	118.6
2013	117.3	119.0	121.1	120.4	121.5	123.1	123.9	124.0	124.9	124.0	125.0	125.4	122.5
2014	120.6	121.8	121.2	121.4	122.9	124.2	124.3	126.2	126.0	126.7	127.3	126.3	124.1
2015	120.8	121.6	120.8	122.7	124.1	125.6	125.3	126.9	125.5	128.5	127.6	125.4	124.6
Education and Health Services													
2005	131.3	132.4	132.7	134.1	133.6	133.6	131.9	132.2	133.4	135.0	135.7	136.0	133.5
2006	134.5	136.3	136.0	137.0	137.1	136.7	136.3	136.5	138.4	140.2	140.7	140.1	137.5
2007	137.6	139.0	139.2	139.5	139.9	139.4	138.7	139.6	141.0	141.7	142.1	142.2	140.0
2008	140.1	141.5	142.1	142.5	142.8	141.7	140.8	141.6	142.5	144.8	144.9	145.3	142.6
2009	142.6	144.0	144.4	145.3	145.6	145.2	144.5	145.1	146.1	147.8	148.0	148.0	145.6
2010	146.2	147.9	148.9	148.4	148.3	146.4	146.0	145.6	145.7	147.5	147.8	147.7	147.2
2011	144.1	144.9	145.2	146.1	146.6	143.3	142.1	141.6	145.4	147.3	147.9	148.0	145.2
2012	143.1	146.4	147.9	148.8	149.1	145.8	144.3	145.2	149.0	151.8	152.0	152.4	148.0
2013	147.8	151.7	151.9	153.0	152.9	150.2	148.8	149.7	154.0	156.8	157.3	157.4	152.6
2014	153.2	157.1	157.4	158.0	157.5	155.3	154.1	155.2	159.0	161.0	162.2	162.6	157.7
2015	156.8	161.5	162.5	162.7	162.1	159.8	158.0	158.8	162.5	164.7	166.0	165.2	161.7

Employment by Industry: Milwaukee-Waukesha-West Allis, WI, 2005–2015—*Continued*

(Numbers in thousands, not seasonally adjusted)

Industry and year	January	February	March	April	May	June	July	August	September	October	November	December	Annual average
Leisure and Hospitality													
2005	64.0	63.8	65.0	68.7	70.4	72.1	74.2	73.9	71.0	69.5	68.5	68.5	69.1
2006	66.4	66.8	68.1	69.8	71.6	74.0	75.9	76.2	72.8	71.2	70.5	70.5	71.2
2007	69.0	69.0	69.8	71.1	74.0	76.0	76.6	76.7	72.5	71.4	69.7	69.3	72.1
2008	66.9	66.7	67.8	69.5	71.8	73.7	74.8	74.5	71.8	69.8	67.6	67.2	70.2
2009	65.2	65.3	66.1	67.8	70.3	71.6	72.6	72.7	70.1	67.4	65.8	65.6	68.4
2010	63.3	63.4	64.4	67.1	69.9	70.7	71.7	72.4	69.6	68.0	67.0	66.7	67.9
2011	65.0	64.5	65.1	68.2	70.7	71.6	73.3	74.0	70.7	69.4	68.3	67.4	69.0
2012	66.2	66.6	67.4	69.6	72.9	73.8	75.8	75.4	72.8	70.6	69.8	70.1	70.9
2013	68.2	68.6	69.3	71.1	75.2	76.5	78.1	77.4	75.2	73.4	73.0	73.1	73.3
2014	71.1	71.6	71.2	73.3	75.6	78.4	78.7	78.0	75.2	73.8	73.2	73.6	74.5
2015	70.8	71.0	72.3	74.8	77.8	80.5	79.6	80.5	76.9	75.8	72.7	71.0	75.3
Other Services													
2005	41.3	41.4	41.5	41.8	41.7	42.2	42.1	42.1	41.3	41.2	41.0	41.1	41.6
2006	40.6	40.7	40.8	41.2	41.3	41.9	42.0	41.8	41.6	41.5	41.5	41.8	41.4
2007	41.1	41.3	41.4	42.2	41.9	42.6	42.2	41.9	41.3	42.4	42.2	42.3	41.9
2008	41.7	42.0	42.1	42.6	42.7	43.2	43.2	43.0	42.4	42.9	42.6	42.6	42.6
2009	41.4	41.4	41.6	42.3	42.7	43.4	43.7	44.0	43.9	41.9	42.2	42.5	42.6
2010	43.7	44.2	44.7	45.1	44.8	45.1	45.0	44.9	44.1	43.9	43.7	43.7	44.4
2011	43.2	43.0	43.1	43.5	43.6	43.7	43.9	43.8	43.0	43.2	42.9	43.0	43.3
2012	42.0	41.9	41.9	41.9	42.1	42.8	42.6	42.4	42.0	42.2	42.1	42.2	42.2
2013	41.5	41.5	41.7	42.2	42.4	42.9	43.0	42.8	42.7	42.4	42.5	42.7	42.4
2014	41.9	42.0	42.1	42.9	43.0	44.0	44.3	44.5	44.2	44.3	44.4	44.7	43.5
2015	44.4	44.6	45.1	45.1	45.3	45.7	46.1	46.0	45.5	45.9	45.9	46.0	45.5
Government													
2005	91.6	94.8	93.6	93.7	93.4	93.5	85.1	85.4	92.3	93.0	93.5	92.8	91.9
2006	90.2	92.9	93.4	93.7	93.5	93.9	85.5	85.9	92.2	93.6	93.6	93.2	91.8
2007	90.1	91.7	92.0	92.6	93.0	93.6	85.0	84.9	91.5	92.2	92.2	93.0	91.0
2008	91.2	91.3	93.7	93.3	94.3	94.2	85.9	84.6	93.5	95.1	96.9	95.6	92.5
2009	93.2	95.0	94.9	95.3	94.6	93.6	83.6	82.6	91.5	93.0	93.1	93.2	92.0
2010	91.7	91.6	92.0	91.6	94.0	91.3	84.9	84.0	88.0	90.3	91.8	90.1	90.1
2011	88.9	92.8	92.3	91.6	91.0	90.7	87.2	86.6	87.9	86.5	88.5	88.8	89.4
2012	85.8	87.2	88.8	90.1	91.0	89.3	83.3	85.0	86.8	88.6	91.2	88.9	88.0
2013	84.7	88.1	88.1	88.0	87.7	87.3	81.8	83.4	87.4	87.7	87.9	87.6	86.6
2014	85.0	87.2	87.6	87.4	87.2	87.8	82.0	86.1	87.5	87.4	88.8	87.3	86.8
2015	83.1	87.5	87.3	88.3	87.6	86.6	81.7	83.1	85.9	88.3	88.5	88.7	86.4

Employment by Industry: Jacksonville, FL, 2005–2015

(Numbers in thousands, not seasonally adjusted)

Industry and year	January	February	March	April	May	June	July	August	September	October	November	December	Annual average
Total Nonfarm													
2005	587.2	592.2	595.3	596.9	599.3	595.7	595.4	605.2	607.4	606.6	613.7	617.6	601.0
2006	609.2	614.9	620.9	618.7	622.8	618.0	615.1	623.3	624.4	626.9	634.2	636.2	622.1
2007	625.5	628.8	634.7	634.0	636.2	631.0	623.5	629.9	628.9	629.7	634.7	634.9	631.0
2008	623.6	626.7	628.0	627.3	627.8	619.1	610.9	613.4	612.7	611.4	612.8	610.2	618.7
2009	592.6	592.3	591.7	588.2	587.6	580.0	574.3	576.6	575.8	579.1	582.9	582.7	583.7
2010	571.1	573.7	577.0	579.0	583.2	576.4	575.1	578.2	580.0	585.5	589.5	590.9	580.0
2011	580.4	584.0	588.6	589.7	590.0	583.0	578.7	583.2	584.9	587.7	591.3	592.8	586.2
2012	584.4	589.0	593.4	595.8	597.9	592.9	588.3	593.6	594.1	598.4	602.7	604.3	594.6
2013	592.2	599.3	603.8	605.9	607.8	604.1	603.8	609.7	610.7	614.7	620.3	623.1	608.0
2014	608.9	613.7	617.7	621.6	624.1	619.4	617.8	624.7	624.2	634.2	639.0	643.6	624.1
2015	630.5	637.5	642.1	645.4	647.7	643.0	643.7	649.8	650.9	655.3	662.7	666.7	647.9
Total Private													
2005	512.2	516.3	519.2	521.5	523.5	524.7	526.3	530.5	532.3	531.7	538.6	542.4	526.6
2006	534.8	539.7	545.6	544.3	548.6	548.2	546.8	549.7	550.1	551.5	557.8	559.7	548.1
2007	549.9	552.2	557.9	557.0	559.0	558.0	552.8	553.4	552.0	552.3	556.5	556.8	554.8
2008	546.6	548.8	550.0	549.8	550.1	546.1	539.3	537.5	535.7	534.0	534.1	532.1	542.0
2009	516.3	514.9	514.2	510.6	509.7	506.9	502.0	500.7	499.1	501.8	505.4	505.7	507.3
2010	494.1	496.2	499.5	501.1	502.7	502.2	501.5	502.2	503.1	507.8	511.3	513.0	502.9
2011	502.6	505.7	510.3	511.6	512.0	509.6	506.5	507.6	509.0	511.1	514.5	516.1	509.7
2012	509.0	512.5	516.8	520.3	522.5	521.9	517.8	519.9	519.4	522.8	527.0	528.9	519.9
2013	518.1	523.9	528.4	530.5	532.6	533.7	534.3	536.8	537.0	540.4	545.4	548.1	534.1
2014	536.1	539.1	542.8	546.3	549.2	549.2	548.0	551.5	550.0	559.4	564.0	568.2	550.3
2015	556.9	561.6	565.8	569.0	571.5	571.9	572.3	575.0	575.2	578.0	585.5	588.6	572.6
Goods Producing													
2005	77.3	77.6	78.4	78.8	79.1	80.1	80.6	81.1	81.7	81.1	82.0	82.6	80.0
2006	81.8	83.0	83.9	84.2	85.0	86.0	85.2	85.6	85.4	84.5	84.5	84.3	84.5
2007	82.7	82.6	83.5	82.5	83.6	84.5	83.9	84.0	83.1	81.6	81.5	81.2	82.9
2008	78.8	79.1	78.9	77.4	77.4	77.3	75.9	75.3	75.1	73.5	72.4	71.2	76.0
2009	68.3	67.3	66.4	63.9	62.8	62.6	61.6	61.1	60.5	59.2	58.9	58.6	62.6
2010	56.3	56.1	56.6	56.7	56.7	56.8	57.1	56.7	56.9	56.7	56.5	56.1	56.6
2011	54.2	54.1	54.7	54.9	54.8	54.9	55.4	55.6	55.3	54.9	55.2	54.9	54.9
2012	54.2	54.3	54.7	55.4	55.4	56.0	55.9	56.1	56.3	56.5	56.7	56.5	55.7
2013	56.0	56.7	57.6	57.5	57.6	58.1	58.3	58.4	58.6	58.6	59.1	59.0	58.0
2014	58.5	58.9	59.2	59.6	60.2	60.7	61.0	61.2	61.4	62.1	62.5	62.6	60.7
2015	62.5	63.2	63.9	64.3	64.8	65.3	65.7	65.7	65.7	65.0	66.6	66.6	64.9
Service-Providing													
2005	509.9	514.6	516.9	518.1	520.2	515.6	514.8	524.1	525.7	525.5	531.7	535.0	521.0
2006	527.4	531.9	537.0	534.5	537.8	532.0	529.9	537.7	539.0	542.4	549.7	551.9	537.6
2007	542.8	546.2	551.2	551.5	552.6	546.5	539.6	545.9	545.8	548.1	553.2	553.7	548.1
2008	544.8	547.6	549.1	549.9	550.4	541.8	535.0	538.1	537.6	537.9	540.4	539.0	542.6
2009	524.3	525.0	525.3	524.3	524.8	517.4	512.7	515.5	515.3	519.9	524.0	524.1	521.1
2010	514.8	517.6	520.4	522.3	526.5	519.6	518.0	521.5	523.1	528.8	533.0	534.8	523.4
2011	526.2	529.9	533.9	534.8	535.2	528.1	523.3	527.6	529.6	532.8	536.1	537.9	531.3
2012	530.2	534.7	538.7	540.4	542.5	536.9	532.4	537.5	537.8	541.9	546.0	547.8	538.9
2013	536.2	542.6	546.2	548.4	550.2	546.0	545.5	551.3	552.1	556.1	561.2	564.1	550.0
2014	550.4	554.8	558.5	562.0	563.9	558.7	556.8	563.5	562.8	572.1	576.5	581.0	563.4
2015	568.0	574.3	578.2	581.1	582.9	577.7	578.0	584.1	585.2	590.3	596.1	600.1	583.0
Mining and Logging													
2005	0.4	0.4	0.4	0.4	0.4	0.4	0.4	0.4	0.4	0.4	0.4	0.4	0.4
2006	0.4	0.4	0.4	0.4	0.4	0.4	0.4	0.4	0.4	0.4	0.4	0.4	0.4
2007	0.4	0.4	0.4	0.4	0.4	0.4	0.4	0.4	0.4	0.4	0.4	0.4	0.4
2008	0.4	0.4	0.4	0.4	0.4	0.4	0.4	0.4	0.4	0.4	0.4	0.4	0.4
2009	0.4	0.4	0.4	0.4	0.4	0.4	0.3	0.4	0.4	0.3	0.3	0.3	0.4
2010	0.3	0.3	0.3	0.3	0.3	0.4	0.3	0.3	0.3	0.4	0.4	0.4	0.3
2011	0.3	0.3	0.3	0.3	0.3	0.3	0.3	0.3	0.3	0.3	0.3	0.3	0.3
2012	0.3	0.3	0.3	0.3	0.3	0.3	0.3	0.3	0.3	0.4	0.4	0.4	0.3
2013	0.4	0.4	0.4	0.4	0.4	0.4	0.4	0.4	0.4	0.4	0.4	0.4	0.4
2014	0.4	0.4	0.4	0.4	0.4	0.4	0.4	0.4	0.4	0.4	0.4	0.4	0.4
2015	0.4	0.4	0.4	0.4	0.4	0.4	0.4	0.4	0.4	0.4	0.4	0.4	0.4

Employment by Industry: Jacksonville, FL, 2005–2015—*Continued*

(Numbers in thousands, not seasonally adjusted)

Industry and year	January	February	March	April	May	June	July	August	September	October	November	December	Annual average
Construction													
2005	43.1	43.1	43.8	44.4	44.8	45.6	46.0	46.6	47.1	46.8	47.6	48.1	45.6
2006	47.5	48.7	49.5	50.1	50.7	51.5	50.9	51.4	51.2	50.6	50.7	50.5	50.3
2007	49.0	48.8	49.7	49.4	50.4	51.1	50.5	50.5	49.6	48.3	48.2	47.8	49.4
2008	45.5	45.8	45.7	44.3	44.3	44.3	43.0	42.6	42.4	41.2	40.2	39.1	43.2
2009	36.6	36.3	35.7	33.9	33.3	33.2	32.5	32.0	31.6	30.6	30.3	30.1	33.0
2010	28.3	28.4	29.0	29.2	29.2	29.2	29.4	29.1	29.1	28.6	28.4	27.9	28.8
2011	26.5	26.5	27.1	27.2	27.1	27.2	27.6	27.8	27.7	27.3	27.4	27.1	27.2
2012	26.2	26.3	26.7	27.2	27.1	27.6	27.6	28.0	28.1	28.2	28.4	28.4	27.5
2013	27.7	28.4	29.2	29.2	29.3	29.7	30.1	30.3	30.6	30.7	31.1	31.0	29.8
2014	30.5	31.1	31.5	31.7	32.0	32.3	32.6	32.7	32.8	33.1	33.3	33.4	32.3
2015	33.2	33.8	34.4	34.6	34.9	35.3	35.6	35.6	35.6	34.9	36.4	36.3	35.1
Manufacturing													
2005	33.8	34.1	34.2	34.0	33.9	34.1	34.2	34.1	34.2	33.9	34.0	34.1	34.1
2006	33.9	33.9	34.0	33.7	33.9	34.1	33.9	33.8	33.8	33.5	33.4	33.4	33.8
2007	33.3	33.4	33.4	32.7	32.8	33.0	33.0	33.1	33.1	32.9	32.9	33.0	33.1
2008	32.9	32.9	32.8	32.7	32.7	32.6	32.5	32.3	32.3	31.9	31.8	31.7	32.4
2009	31.3	30.6	30.3	29.6	29.1	29.0	28.8	28.7	28.5	28.3	28.3	28.2	29.2
2010	27.7	27.4	27.3	27.2	27.2	27.2	27.4	27.3	27.5	27.7	27.7	27.8	27.5
2011	27.4	27.3	27.3	27.4	27.4	27.4	27.5	27.5	27.3	27.3	27.5	27.5	27.4
2012	27.7	27.7	27.7	27.9	28.0	28.1	28.0	27.8	27.9	27.9	27.9	27.7	27.9
2013	27.9	27.9	28.0	27.9	27.9	28.0	27.8	27.7	27.6	27.5	27.6	27.6	27.8
2014	27.6	27.4	27.3	27.5	27.8	28.0	28.0	28.1	28.2	28.6	28.8	28.8	28.0
2015	28.9	29.0	29.1	29.3	29.5	29.6	29.7	29.7	29.7	29.7	29.8	29.9	29.5
Trade, Transportation, and Utilities													
2005	130.0	130.6	131.5	131.8	132.3	131.8	132.0	132.8	132.9	133.0	135.9	138.0	132.7
2006	133.8	133.6	135.1	135.1	135.8	135.8	135.8	137.1	137.4	138.7	141.2	143.1	136.9
2007	138.0	137.6	139.1	138.9	139.3	138.7	137.9	138.1	138.1	139.1	142.4	143.3	139.2
2008	138.5	138.0	138.3	137.2	137.1	136.0	135.3	135.5	134.2	134.2	135.5	136.0	136.3
2009	130.3	128.9	128.3	126.8	126.8	126.2	125.3	125.0	124.9	125.2	127.1	128.2	126.9
2010	124.3	123.4	123.7	123.7	123.7	123.7	123.1	123.9	123.3	124.5	126.7	128.2	124.4
2011	123.0	123.2	123.9	124.2	123.6	123.7	123.7	123.9	123.4	123.4	125.9	126.7	124.1
2012	124.5	124.5	125.0	124.9	125.3	125.2	124.0	124.8	125.0	125.2	128.0	129.1	125.5
2013	125.4	125.4	126.1	127.0	127.1	127.0	127.1	127.5	127.2	128.7	131.5	133.5	127.8
2014	128.0	128.1	128.0	128.5	128.9	128.8	129.1	130.4	130.2	133.1	136.6	138.5	130.7
2015	133.4	133.5	133.4	134.3	134.8	134.9	134.8	136.2	136.2	136.5	138.8	140.5	135.6
Wholesale Trade													
2005	27.0	27.3	27.2	27.3	27.5	27.7	27.9	28.0	28.1	28.3	28.4	28.7	27.8
2006	29.0	29.1	29.3	29.4	29.6	29.9	29.8	30.1	30.3	30.6	30.7	30.9	29.9
2007	30.2	30.4	30.6	30.4	30.3	30.4	30.3	30.2	30.0	30.1	29.8	29.7	30.2
2008	29.0	29.0	29.0	28.8	28.7	28.8	28.8	28.7	28.5	28.2	28.0	27.9	28.6
2009	27.7	27.4	27.1	27.0	26.8	26.8	26.6	26.4	26.2	26.2	26.1	26.0	26.7
2010	25.7	25.5	25.4	25.5	25.6	25.7	25.8	25.9	25.7	25.6	25.5	25.5	25.6
2011	24.8	25.0	25.1	24.9	24.9	24.8	24.8	24.8	24.6	24.6	24.6	24.5	24.8
2012	24.5	24.6	24.8	24.7	24.8	24.7	24.9	24.8	24.7	24.7	24.7	24.8	24.7
2013	24.6	24.7	24.8	25.0	25.0	25.1	24.8	24.6	24.5	24.5	24.5	24.3	24.7
2014	24.0	24.1	24.1	23.8	24.0	24.0	24.0	24.0	23.9	24.2	24.2	24.2	24.0
2015	24.2	24.3	24.2	24.2	24.3	24.5	24.5	24.6	24.7	24.7	24.8	24.9	24.5
Retail Trade													
2005	72.2	72.4	73.3	73.4	73.6	73.8	73.9	73.9	73.7	73.6	75.8	77.0	73.9
2006	72.9	72.8	73.7	73.7	74.0	74.6	74.7	74.9	74.7	75.5	77.7	78.6	74.8
2007	75.5	75.0	76.2	75.7	76.2	76.0	75.7	76.0	75.7	76.2	79.2	80.2	76.5
2008	77.1	76.5	76.8	75.9	76.0	75.5	74.7	74.5	74.0	73.8	75.2	75.3	75.4
2009	70.8	70.0	70.0	69.1	69.4	69.3	68.8	68.7	68.4	68.6	70.4	71.0	69.5
2010	68.8	68.2	68.5	68.5	68.4	68.3	67.9	68.1	67.7	68.6	70.7	71.3	68.8
2011	67.9	67.8	68.3	68.4	68.5	68.8	68.7	68.9	68.7	69.0	71.3	71.8	69.0
2012	69.6	69.5	69.9	69.9	70.3	70.2	69.1	69.5	69.6	69.8	72.2	72.6	70.2
2013	70.1	69.8	70.2	70.5	70.8	71.1	71.5	71.4	71.0	72.2	75.0	75.5	71.6
2014	71.9	71.7	71.6	71.9	72.1	72.1	72.5	73.1	73.2	75.3	78.7	79.5	73.6
2015	75.4	75.3	75.3	75.7	76.1	76.4	76.4	77.0	76.6	76.7	78.7	79.7	76.6

Employment by Industry: Jacksonville, FL, 2005–2015—*Continued*

(Numbers in thousands, not seasonally adjusted)

Industry and year	January	February	March	April	May	June	July	August	September	October	November	December	Annual average
Transportation and Utilities													
2005	30.8	30.9	31.0	31.1	31.2	30.3	30.2	30.9	31.1	31.1	31.7	32.3	31.1
2006	31.9	31.7	32.1	32.0	32.2	31.3	31.3	32.1	32.4	32.6	32.8	33.6	32.2
2007	32.3	32.2	32.3	32.8	32.8	32.3	31.9	31.9	32.4	32.8	33.4	33.4	32.5
2008	32.4	32.5	32.5	32.5	32.4	31.7	31.8	32.3	31.7	32.2	32.3	32.8	32.3
2009	31.8	31.5	31.2	30.7	30.6	30.1	29.9	29.9	30.3	30.4	30.6	31.2	30.7
2010	29.8	29.7	29.8	29.7	29.7	29.7	29.4	29.9	29.9	30.3	30.5	31.4	30.0
2011	30.3	30.4	30.5	30.9	30.2	30.1	30.2	30.2	30.1	29.8	30.0	30.4	30.3
2012	30.4	30.4	30.3	30.3	30.2	30.3	30.0	30.5	30.7	30.7	31.1	31.7	30.6
2013	30.7	30.9	31.1	31.5	31.3	30.8	30.8	31.5	31.7	32.0	32.0	33.7	31.5
2014	32.1	32.3	32.3	32.8	32.8	32.7	32.6	33.3	33.1	33.6	33.7	34.8	33.0
2015	33.8	33.9	33.9	34.4	34.4	34.0	33.9	34.6	34.9	35.1	35.3	35.9	34.5
Information													
2005	12.0	12.0	11.9	11.8	12.0	12.0	12.1	12.2	12.0	11.7	11.8	11.4	11.9
2006	11.5	11.5	11.5	11.4	11.3	11.4	11.4	11.1	10.6	10.5	10.4	10.5	11.1
2007	10.1	10.1	10.2	10.2	10.2	10.3	10.2	10.2	10.2	10.1	10.0	10.0	10.2
2008	9.9	9.9	10.0	10.1	10.1	10.2	10.4	10.3	10.4	10.4	10.5	10.5	10.2
2009	10.4	10.4	10.4	10.5	10.5	10.5	10.4	10.4	10.2	10.1	10.2	10.2	10.4
2010	10.2	10.2	10.4	10.4	10.3	10.2	10.2	10.2	10.1	10.0	10.0	9.9	10.2
2011	9.7	9.6	9.6	9.7	9.7	9.6	9.6	9.6	9.5	9.5	9.6	9.5	9.6
2012	9.4	9.3	9.2	9.3	9.3	9.3	9.3	9.1	9.0	9.1	9.1	9.2	9.2
2013	9.1	9.1	9.1	9.0	9.1	9.1	9.2	9.2	9.2	9.2	9.3	9.3	9.2
2014	9.3	9.2	9.3	9.2	9.3	9.3	9.3	9.2	9.1	9.1	9.2	9.1	9.2
2015	9.1	9.2	9.2	9.2	9.2	9.2	9.3	9.4	9.3	9.2	9.2	9.2	9.2
Financial Activities													
2005	58.8	58.9	59.2	59.1	59.0	59.0	58.9	59.0	58.9	59.5	60.1	60.9	59.3
2006	59.7	60.1	60.3	60.4	60.4	60.2	59.9	59.6	59.4	59.1	59.3	59.6	59.8
2007	58.9	59.1	59.4	59.5	59.8	60.1	60.5	60.8	60.7	60.7	61.1	61.1	60.1
2008	60.7	60.7	60.8	60.7	60.5	60.3	60.0	59.6	59.1	58.6	58.0	57.9	59.7
2009	56.9	56.7	56.5	55.7	55.8	55.7	55.8	55.5	55.0	55.1	55.1	55.2	55.8
2010	54.9	55.0	55.0	54.8	55.1	55.4	55.9	55.9	55.9	56.4	56.9	57.3	55.7
2011	57.0	57.3	57.8	57.8	57.7	58.0	57.9	58.0	58.5	58.4	58.3	59.0	58.0
2012	58.6	59.2	59.5	59.5	59.8	60.0	60.1	60.1	60.2	60.8	61.2	61.4	60.0
2013	60.8	61.1	61.1	61.2	61.2	61.6	61.7	61.7	61.6	61.7	61.9	62.0	61.5
2014	61.0	60.9	61.2	61.1	61.0	60.8	61.0	60.7	60.3	60.7	60.9	60.9	60.9
2015	61.2	61.2	61.3	60.7	60.8	61.0	61.3	61.5	61.8	62.5	62.8	62.8	61.6
Professional and Business Services													
2005	80.1	81.8	81.3	81.9	82.2	82.9	84.3	85.8	86.7	87.4	88.7	89.3	84.4
2006	88.6	90.4	91.8	90.4	91.7	90.3	90.4	91.1	91.7	93.2	95.5	95.3	91.7
2007	93.8	94.0	94.6	94.2	92.7	91.0	88.8	87.9	87.4	88.2	87.6	86.8	90.6
2008	85.0	86.2	86.6	87.0	87.6	85.8	82.0	81.9	82.7	82.6	82.3	82.1	84.3
2009	79.4	80.1	79.7	79.6	79.5	79.0	77.2	77.3	78.1	80.4	81.4	82.0	79.5
2010	79.2	80.5	81.1	81.0	81.5	81.5	81.2	81.8	83.3	85.6	85.9	85.9	82.4
2011	85.3	87.2	88.0	88.0	88.7	87.5	84.8	85.2	87.3	88.8	89.7	90.0	87.5
2012	89.0	90.1	90.7	92.3	93.1	92.1	89.6	90.4	90.0	91.4	91.7	91.5	91.0
2013	89.0	90.6	92.0	92.4	93.7	93.8	94.1	95.0	95.5	97.3	97.4	97.5	94.0
2014	94.9	95.2	95.6	96.9	98.0	97.6	97.2	98.5	98.8	101.1	102.1	102.9	98.2
2015	99.3	100.3	100.6	101.7	101.8	100.9	101.0	100.3	100.5	101.7	103.1	103.6	101.2
Education and Health Services													
2005	70.1	70.4	70.6	70.7	71.2	70.8	70.8	71.3	72.3	72.1	72.3	72.7	71.3
2006	72.9	73.5	73.9	73.8	74.0	73.6	73.6	74.5	75.1	76.0	76.4	76.4	74.5
2007	76.2	77.1	77.5	77.4	77.6	77.3	77.0	77.6	78.6	78.9	79.4	79.9	77.9
2008	80.6	81.0	80.9	81.8	81.5	80.9	80.8	80.9	81.5	82.8	83.9	83.8	81.7
2009	82.5	83.2	83.5	83.3	83.4	82.9	82.6	82.9	83.7	85.2	85.9	85.6	83.7
2010	84.5	85.0	85.2	85.4	85.5	84.9	84.6	84.8	85.5	87.5	87.9	88.0	85.7
2011	87.1	87.6	87.7	87.4	87.4	86.4	86.3	86.8	88.1	89.2	89.5	89.8	87.8
2012	87.6	88.4	88.7	88.7	89.0	88.6	88.2	88.9	90.0	90.5	90.8	91.3	89.2
2013	90.0	91.4	91.4	90.8	91.0	90.7	90.0	90.6	91.3	92.1	92.7	93.0	91.3
2014	91.4	92.5	92.8	93.4	93.3	92.4	92.2	93.2	93.7	95.1	95.3	96.0	93.4
2015	95.0	95.7	96.4	96.6	96.8	96.1	96.0	97.2	98.1	99.3	100.5	100.4	97.3

Employment by Industry: Jacksonville, FL, 2005–2015—*Continued*

(Numbers in thousands, not seasonally adjusted)

Industry and year	January	February	March	April	May	June	July	August	September	October	November	December	Annual average
Leisure and Hospitality													
2005	58.4	59.3	60.5	61.3	61.5	61.6	61.1	62.0	61.4	61.0	61.8	61.6	61.0
2006	60.6	61.3	62.5	62.5	63.6	63.8	63.3	63.6	63.3	62.3	63.1	62.9	62.7
2007	62.6	64.0	65.5	66.7	68.1	68.1	67.0	67.6	67.0	66.7	67.4	67.4	66.5
2008	66.2	66.8	67.4	68.8	69.2	69.1	69.1	68.5	67.8	67.4	67.4	67.0	67.9
2009	65.3	65.1	66.1	67.4	67.6	66.7	66.1	65.4	63.8	63.5	63.6	62.8	65.3
2010	61.8	63.0	64.4	66.0	66.8	66.5	66.4	66.0	65.4	64.2	64.5	64.9	65.0
2011	63.8	64.1	65.8	67.1	68.0	67.7	67.1	67.2	66.0	66.3	66.1	66.3	66.3
2012	65.7	66.6	68.7	69.7	70.1	70.2	70.3	70.1	68.6	69.0	69.3	69.7	69.0
2013	67.8	69.5	70.9	72.2	72.4	72.7	73.1	73.5	72.9	71.9	72.4	72.7	71.8
2014	71.9	73.0	75.2	75.8	76.6	77.7	76.5	76.5	74.7	76.2	75.5	76.3	75.5
2015	74.5	76.4	78.7	79.9	80.7	81.7	81.3	81.7	80.7	80.8	81.4	82.5	80.0
Other Services													
2005	25.5	25.7	25.8	26.1	26.2	26.5	26.5	26.3	26.4	25.9	26.0	25.9	26.1
2006	25.9	26.3	26.6	26.5	26.8	27.1	27.2	27.1	27.2	27.2	27.4	27.6	26.9
2007	27.6	27.7	28.1	27.6	27.7	28.0	27.5	27.2	26.9	27.0	27.1	27.1	27.5
2008	26.9	27.1	27.1	26.8	26.7	26.5	25.8	25.5	24.9	24.5	24.1	23.6	25.8
2009	23.2	23.2	23.3	23.4	23.3	23.3	23.0	23.1	22.9	23.1	23.2	23.1	23.2
2010	22.9	23.0	23.1	23.1	23.1	23.2	23.0	22.9	22.7	22.9	22.9	22.7	23.0
2011	22.5	22.6	22.8	22.5	22.1	21.8	21.7	21.3	20.9	20.6	20.2	19.9	21.6
2012	20.0	20.1	20.3	20.5	20.5	20.5	20.4	20.4	20.3	20.3	20.2	20.2	20.3
2013	20.0	20.1	20.2	20.4	20.5	20.7	20.8	20.9	20.7	20.9	21.1	21.1	20.6
2014	21.1	21.3	21.5	21.8	21.9	21.9	21.7	21.8	21.8	22.0	21.9	21.9	21.7
2015	21.9	22.1	22.3	22.3	22.6	22.8	22.9	23.0	22.9	23.0	23.1	23.0	22.7
Government													
2005	75.0	75.9	76.1	75.4	75.8	71.0	69.1	74.7	75.1	74.9	75.1	75.2	74.4
2006	74.4	75.2	75.3	74.4	74.2	69.8	68.3	73.6	74.3	75.4	76.4	76.5	74.0
2007	75.6	76.6	76.8	77.0	77.2	73.0	70.7	76.5	76.9	77.4	78.2	78.1	76.2
2008	77.0	77.9	78.0	77.5	77.7	73.0	71.6	75.9	77.0	77.4	78.7	78.1	76.7
2009	76.3	77.4	77.5	77.6	77.9	73.1	72.3	75.9	76.7	77.3	77.5	77.0	76.4
2010	77.0	77.5	77.5	77.9	80.5	74.2	73.6	76.0	76.9	77.7	78.2	77.9	77.1
2011	77.8	78.3	78.3	78.1	78.0	73.4	72.2	75.6	75.9	76.6	76.8	76.7	76.5
2012	75.4	76.5	76.6	75.5	75.4	71.0	70.5	73.7	74.7	75.6	75.7	75.4	74.7
2013	74.1	75.4	75.4	75.4	75.2	70.4	69.5	72.9	73.7	74.3	74.9	75.0	73.9
2014	72.8	74.6	74.9	75.3	74.9	70.2	69.8	73.2	74.2	74.8	75.0	75.4	73.8
2015	73.6	75.9	76.3	76.4	76.2	71.1	71.4	74.8	75.7	77.3	77.2	78.1	75.3

Employment by Industry: Oklahoma City, OK, 2005–2015

(Numbers in thousands, not seasonally adjusted)

Industry and year	January	February	March	April	May	June	July	August	September	October	November	December	Annual average
Total Nonfarm													
2005	541.1	547.8	553.6	559.8	561.3	558.7	553.8	558.0	566.3	566.1	570.7	572.9	559.2
2006	557.8	563.1	568.5	569.4	572.0	571.0	561.1	566.1	573.7	572.6	574.2	576.9	568.9
2007	563.2	568.8	576.1	575.7	578.3	578.3	568.2	574.4	581.1	583.5	588.5	586.8	576.9
2008	573.5	579.7	583.6	585.6	588.3	583.8	575.9	580.8	589.2	589.6	591.5	590.3	584.3
2009	575.5	573.6	575.3	572.3	570.7	566.8	559.4	560.0	565.5	565.2	566.8	566.5	568.1
2010	552.5	555.3	561.7	565.9	569.5	566.5	560.3	564.4	571.3	575.7	578.3	580.7	566.8
2011	564.7	567.6	575.5	582.0	582.2	579.1	574.1	577.8	586.6	587.4	590.8	593.6	580.1
2012	579.5	586.1	591.9	595.4	597.3	595.1	584.3	589.9	596.6	602.4	605.6	606.3	594.2
2013	592.7	599.6	604.2	607.0	611.1	607.7	601.5	606.4	611.4	615.1	620.6	618.1	608.0
2014	603.8	609.0	614.1	617.7	621.0	617.8	612.8	618.3	625.2	628.8	632.3	634.3	619.6
2015	620.9	626.0	627.2	629.4	631.0	628.7	624.2	627.8	631.7	636.5	640.0	635.5	629.9
Total Private													
2005	428.3	432.7	438.1	443.7	444.8	446.4	448.4	450.4	451.1	449.0	452.9	455.3	445.1
2006	443.4	445.8	450.9	451.7	454.0	457.2	454.7	456.9	457.9	453.5	454.8	457.8	453.2
2007	446.5	449.9	456.5	456.3	458.6	462.1	459.3	462.8	462.9	462.5	466.9	466.1	459.2
2008	457.7	459.9	463.0	465.1	467.2	468.7	467.2	467.9	469.1	467.6	468.5	468.0	465.8
2009	454.9	452.8	453.2	449.9	448.0	448.9	446.4	445.2	444.3	441.0	441.9	441.8	447.4
2010	432.6	432.5	437.7	441.5	443.3	445.6	445.2	447.8	449.0	452.0	454.2	456.2	444.8
2011	445.6	444.8	451.9	458.1	458.2	459.9	459.7	462.6	463.5	462.7	465.6	467.9	458.4
2012	459.4	462.6	467.4	470.4	472.4	475.2	470.8	473.8	473.5	476.1	478.7	480.2	471.7
2013	471.2	473.6	477.6	479.9	483.2	485.0	484.0	486.7	486.9	488.1	492.7	491.1	483.3
2014	482.3	483.1	487.8	491.3	493.6	495.4	495.7	498.8	499.5	500.7	503.8	506.4	494.9
2015	497.4	498.0	498.8	500.8	501.6	504.3	504.6	505.8	504.1	506.3	509.3	505.0	503.0
Goods Producing													
2005	70.5	72.0	73.2	73.5	73.7	73.1	75.4	75.6	75.5	76.0	76.3	77.3	74.3
2006	76.3	76.7	77.5	77.1	77.5	78.4	77.5	77.9	77.7	77.7	77.3	77.9	77.5
2007	75.4	75.5	76.9	77.1	77.4	78.8	78.6	79.4	79.0	79.2	79.8	79.3	78.0
2008	78.5	79.0	79.6	80.3	81.0	82.1	82.0	82.1	81.6	81.4	80.7	79.7	80.7
2009	77.6	75.9	74.6	72.6	71.8	72.0	71.3	70.6	69.6	68.8	68.7	68.6	71.8
2010	67.6	67.1	68.1	69.1	69.7	70.6	70.9	71.4	71.6	73.1	72.8	73.6	70.5
2011	72.3	72.2	73.4	74.9	75.2	76.3	76.9	77.0	77.1	77.3	77.6	78.6	75.7
2012	77.9	78.5	79.5	80.4	81.0	82.5	81.9	82.3	81.9	82.5	82.5	82.6	81.1
2013	82.1	82.3	82.7	83.0	83.6	84.6	84.4	84.4	84.1	84.6	84.8	84.7	83.8
2014	83.2	83.4	84.6	84.8	85.8	86.9	87.4	88.2	88.4	88.8	88.9	89.4	86.7
2015	88.8	88.2	87.1	85.7	85.4	85.4	86.3	86.0	85.1	84.7	85.9	85.1	86.1
Service-Providing													
2005	470.6	475.8	480.4	486.3	487.6	485.6	478.4	482.4	490.8	490.1	494.4	495.6	484.8
2006	481.5	486.4	491.0	492.3	494.5	492.6	483.6	488.2	496.0	494.9	496.9	499.0	491.4
2007	487.8	493.3	499.2	498.6	500.9	499.5	489.6	495.0	502.1	504.3	508.7	507.5	498.9
2008	495.0	500.7	504.0	505.3	507.3	501.7	493.9	498.7	507.6	508.2	510.8	510.6	503.7
2009	497.9	497.7	500.7	499.7	498.9	494.8	488.1	489.4	495.9	496.4	498.1	497.9	496.3
2010	484.9	488.2	493.6	496.8	499.8	495.9	489.4	493.0	499.7	502.6	505.5	507.1	496.4
2011	492.4	495.4	502.1	507.1	507.0	502.8	497.2	500.8	509.5	510.1	513.2	515.0	504.4
2012	501.6	507.6	512.4	515.0	516.3	512.6	502.4	507.6	514.7	519.9	523.1	523.7	513.1
2013	510.6	517.3	521.5	524.0	527.5	523.1	517.1	522.0	527.3	530.5	535.8	533.4	524.2
2014	520.6	525.6	529.5	532.9	535.2	530.9	525.4	530.1	536.8	540.0	543.4	544.9	532.9
2015	532.1	537.8	540.1	543.7	545.6	543.3	537.9	541.8	546.6	551.8	554.1	550.4	543.8
Mining and Logging													
2005	9.7	9.8	10.0	10.1	10.2	10.3	10.6	10.7	10.9	11.0	11.3	11.7	10.5
2006	11.7	12.0	12.2	12.4	12.6	12.8	12.7	13.0	13.1	13.3	13.5	13.8	12.8
2007	13.7	13.7	13.7	13.9	14.0	14.2	14.6	14.9	14.9	15.1	15.3	15.3	14.4
2008	14.9	15.1	15.2	15.6	15.9	16.3	16.4	16.6	16.5	16.8	16.7	16.3	16.0
2009	15.9	15.2	14.5	13.6	13.3	13.2	12.9	12.8	12.6	12.6	12.8	13.1	13.5
2010	13.1	13.2	13.5	13.7	13.9	14.2	14.4	14.6	14.7	15.3	15.1	15.5	14.3
2011	15.6	15.9	16.0	16.4	16.7	17.0	17.3	17.4	17.6	17.8	17.9	18.2	17.0
2012	18.3	18.6	19.0	19.4	19.7	20.3	20.2	20.2	19.9	19.9	19.8	19.7	19.6
2013	20.4	20.2	20.1	20.3	20.4	20.6	20.1	20.1	20.0	20.0	20.0	20.1	20.2
2014	19.5	19.6	19.8	19.8	20.1	20.6	21.0	21.2	21.5	21.9	22.1	22.2	20.8
2015	22.1	21.1	20.3	19.4	19.0	18.6	19.0	18.7	18.4	17.9	17.9	18.0	19.2

Employment by Industry: Oklahoma City, OK, 2005–2015—*Continued*

(Numbers in thousands, not seasonally adjusted)

Industry and year	January	February	March	April	May	June	July	August	September	October	November	December	Annual average
Construction													
2005	23.1	23.2	24.1	24.6	24.9	25.7	26.0	26.1	26.0	26.1	26.2	26.4	25.2
2006	25.8	25.9	26.6	26.2	26.5	27.2	26.7	26.9	26.7	26.3	26.1	26.2	26.4
2007	25.3	25.2	26.2	26.3	26.3	27.3	26.9	27.2	27.0	26.9	27.2	26.8	26.6
2008	26.6	26.9	27.4	27.5	27.9	28.4	28.5	28.3	28.1	27.7	27.4	27.1	27.7
2009	26.1	25.8	26.1	25.7	25.8	26.5	26.4	26.3	25.9	25.1	25.0	24.7	25.8
2010	23.9	23.4	24.1	24.7	25.0	25.5	25.7	25.8	25.7	26.3	26.0	26.2	25.2
2011	25.3	24.7	25.5	26.0	25.9	26.5	26.5	26.2	26.0	25.8	25.8	26.1	25.9
2012	25.4	25.5	25.9	26.3	26.5	27.1	26.7	26.9	26.7	26.9	26.8	26.9	26.5
2013	25.9	26.2	26.6	26.5	26.8	27.4	27.6	27.6	27.6	27.7	27.7	27.5	27.1
2014	27.0	26.7	27.7	27.9	28.4	28.7	28.9	29.3	29.1	28.9	28.7	28.8	28.3
2015	28.2	28.6	28.6	28.5	28.7	29.3	29.8	29.9	29.6	30.2	31.0	30.2	29.4
Manufacturing													
2005	37.7	39.0	39.1	38.8	38.6	37.1	38.8	38.8	38.6	38.9	38.8	39.2	38.6
2006	38.8	38.8	38.7	38.5	38.4	38.4	38.1	38.0	37.9	38.1	37.7	37.9	38.3
2007	36.4	36.6	37.0	36.9	37.1	37.3	37.1	37.3	37.1	37.2	37.3	37.2	37.0
2008	37.0	37.0	37.0	37.2	37.2	37.4	37.1	37.2	37.0	36.9	36.6	36.3	37.0
2009	35.6	34.9	34.0	33.3	32.7	32.3	32.0	31.5	31.1	31.1	30.9	30.8	32.5
2010	30.6	30.5	30.5	30.7	30.8	30.9	30.8	31.0	31.2	31.5	31.7	31.9	31.0
2011	31.4	31.6	31.9	32.5	32.6	32.8	33.1	33.4	33.5	33.7	33.9	34.3	32.9
2012	34.2	34.4	34.6	34.7	34.8	35.1	35.0	35.2	35.3	35.7	35.9	36.0	35.1
2013	35.8	35.9	36.0	36.2	36.4	36.6	36.7	36.7	36.5	36.9	37.1	37.1	36.5
2014	36.7	37.1	37.1	37.1	37.3	37.6	37.5	37.7	37.8	38.0	38.1	38.4	37.5
2015	38.5	38.5	38.2	37.8	37.7	37.5	37.5	37.4	37.1	36.6	37.0	36.9	37.6
Trade, Transportation, and Utilities													
2005	96.4	96.4	97.1	97.8	98.0	98.0	98.6	99.3	99.5	100.0	102.6	104.2	99.0
2006	99.1	99.0	99.5	99.3	99.7	100.1	99.4	100.1	100.4	100.4	102.5	104.0	100.3
2007	100.3	100.3	102.0	100.9	101.3	101.2	100.4	100.7	100.3	100.7	102.9	103.3	101.2
2008	100.4	99.8	100.5	99.8	99.9	100.1	100.5	100.4	100.8	100.9	102.5	102.9	100.7
2009	98.9	97.9	98.2	97.6	97.4	97.6	96.8	96.7	96.4	96.5	97.9	98.4	97.5
2010	94.8	94.4	95.5	95.8	96.5	97.2	97.4	97.6	97.1	98.3	100.2	101.6	97.2
2011	97.9	97.5	98.8	99.2	99.1	99.5	99.6	100.6	100.5	100.7	102.8	103.8	100.0
2012	100.4	100.2	101.0	101.5	102.3	102.5	102.4	102.7	103.1	104.2	106.7	107.9	102.9
2013	103.7	104.0	104.9	105.4	106.3	106.7	106.8	107.4	107.5	108.3	111.0	112.0	107.0
2014	108.3	107.5	107.9	107.8	108.3	109.0	108.8	109.4	109.8	110.4	112.7	114.5	109.5
2015	110.0	109.8	110.0	110.6	111.0	111.8	111.8	111.9	111.4	112.3	113.9	113.9	111.5
Wholesale Trade													
2005	20.0	20.0	20.1	20.1	20.2	20.4	20.7	20.7	20.5	20.7	20.8	21.0	20.4
2006	20.7	20.9	21.0	21.1	21.3	21.5	21.4	21.5	21.5	21.6	21.7	21.8	21.3
2007	21.5	21.6	21.7	21.7	21.8	21.9	21.7	21.4	21.3	21.6	21.6	21.8	21.6
2008	21.6	21.5	21.6	21.5	21.6	21.8	21.8	21.6	21.7	21.7	21.7	21.6	21.6
2009	21.2	21.1	20.9	20.7	20.4	20.4	20.4	20.3	20.2	20.4	20.2	20.2	20.5
2010	20.1	20.1	20.1	20.2	20.4	20.5	20.6	20.7	20.7	21.0	21.1	21.2	20.6
2011	21.1	21.1	21.3	21.5	21.5	21.7	21.6	21.6	21.7	21.8	21.8	21.9	21.6
2012	22.1	22.3	22.4	22.3	22.6	22.7	22.8	22.9	22.8	23.1	23.3	23.6	22.7
2013	23.6	23.7	23.8	23.7	23.9	24.1	23.9	23.9	23.9	24.0	24.2	24.2	23.9
2014	24.2	24.1	24.1	24.2	24.3	24.5	24.3	24.5	24.7	24.9	24.9	25.1	24.5
2015	24.9	24.9	24.7	24.5	24.5	24.5	24.5	24.4	24.3	24.1	24.0	23.9	24.4
Retail Trade													
2005	60.0	59.8	60.3	60.7	60.8	60.7	60.6	61.2	61.4	61.9	64.2	65.4	61.4
2006	61.1	60.8	61.1	61.1	61.2	61.4	60.8	61.3	61.3	61.1	63.1	64.2	61.5
2007	61.1	60.9	62.2	61.3	61.7	61.6	61.6	61.2	61.7	61.5	61.9	64.3	64.4	62.0
2008	62.5	62.0	62.4	61.5	61.5	61.4	61.8	61.9	62.2	62.3	63.8	64.1	62.3
2009	60.8	60.0	60.2	59.9	60.1	60.2	59.6	59.7	59.6	59.4	61.0	61.4	60.2
2010	58.6	58.2	59.1	59.2	59.7	60.1	60.1	60.2	59.6	60.6	62.3	63.0	60.1
2011	60.1	59.6	60.5	60.8	60.6	60.5	60.7	61.6	61.3	61.3	63.3	63.9	61.2
2012	60.9	60.5	61.2	61.7	61.9	62.0	61.6	61.8	62.2	63.0	65.2	65.9	62.3
2013	62.0	61.7	62.4	63.0	63.6	63.6	63.9	64.4	64.6	65.2	67.5	68.4	64.2
2014	65.0	64.6	64.7	64.9	65.0	65.4	65.5	65.8	66.0	66.3	68.4	69.4	65.9
2015	65.8	65.8	66.2	66.9	67.0	67.6	67.5	67.8	67.4	68.3	70.0	69.5	67.5

Employment by Industry: Oklahoma City, OK, 2005–2015—*Continued*

(Numbers in thousands, not seasonally adjusted)

Industry and year	January	February	March	April	May	June	July	August	September	October	November	December	Annual average
Transportation and Utilities													
2005	16.4	16.6	16.7	17.0	17.0	16.9	17.3	17.4	17.6	17.4	17.6	17.8	17.1
2006	17.3	17.3	17.4	17.1	17.2	17.2	17.2	17.3	17.6	17.7	17.7	18.0	17.4
2007	17.7	17.8	18.1	17.9	17.8	17.7	17.5	17.6	17.5	17.2	17.0	17.1	17.6
2008	16.3	16.3	16.5	16.8	16.8	16.9	16.9	16.9	16.9	16.9	17.0	17.2	16.8
2009	16.9	16.8	17.1	17.0	16.9	17.0	16.8	16.7	16.6	16.7	16.7	16.8	16.8
2010	16.1	16.1	16.3	16.4	16.4	16.6	16.7	16.7	16.8	16.7	16.8	17.4	16.6
2011	16.7	16.8	17.0	16.9	17.0	17.3	17.3	17.4	17.5	17.6	17.7	18.0	17.3
2012	17.4	17.4	17.4	17.5	17.8	17.8	18.0	18.0	18.1	18.1	18.2	18.4	17.8
2013	18.1	18.6	18.7	18.7	18.8	19.0	19.0	19.1	19.0	19.1	19.3	19.4	18.9
2014	19.1	18.8	19.1	18.7	19.0	19.1	19.0	19.1	19.1	19.2	19.4	20.0	19.1
2015	19.3	19.1	19.1	19.2	19.5	19.7	19.8	19.7	19.7	19.9	19.9	20.5	19.6
Information													
2005	13.6	13.7	13.6	13.7	13.7	13.5	13.6	13.3	13.0	12.9	13.0	13.0	13.4
2006	12.4	12.5	12.6	13.5	13.4	13.3	13.5	13.5	13.4	13.2	13.2	13.6	13.2
2007	13.0	12.6	12.3	12.3	12.2	12.3	12.2	12.2	12.2	12.1	12.2	12.2	12.3
2008	12.2	12.3	12.1	12.3	12.3	12.3	12.4	12.2	12.0	11.9	12.0	11.9	12.2
2009	11.8	11.6	11.6	11.5	11.4	11.3	11.1	10.9	10.6	10.4	10.3	10.2	11.1
2010	10.2	10.1	9.9	9.8	9.7	9.6	9.5	9.3	9.2	9.1	9.2	9.1	9.6
2011	9.2	9.1	8.9	9.0	9.0	9.0	9.0	8.9	8.9	9.0	9.0	9.0	9.0
2012	8.9	8.9	8.8	8.7	8.7	8.6	8.7	8.5	8.3	8.4	8.4	8.3	8.6
2013	8.1	8.1	8.0	8.2	8.2	8.2	8.2	8.2	8.2	8.2	8.4	8.3	8.2
2014	8.1	8.1	8.1	8.1	8.1	8.1	8.2	8.2	8.2	8.1	8.2	8.1	8.1
2015	8.1	8.0	8.1	8.1	8.2	8.2	8.2	8.1	8.1	8.1	8.1	8.1	8.1
Financial Activities													
2005	31.0	30.9	31.1	31.1	31.2	31.5	31.6	31.6	31.5	31.0	31.1	31.8	31.3
2006	31.3	31.2	31.3	31.0	31.2	31.2	31.3	31.5	31.4	31.4	31.4	31.4	31.3
2007	31.7	32.1	32.0	31.5	31.6	31.6	31.5	31.5	31.2	31.2	31.2	31.3	31.5
2008	31.6	31.5	31.6	31.7	32.1	32.1	32.2	32.0	31.9	31.7	31.8	31.9	31.8
2009	31.2	31.1	31.2	31.2	31.3	31.4	31.4	31.4	31.2	31.3	31.3	31.5	31.3
2010	31.1	31.1	31.2	30.9	31.0	31.0	30.9	30.9	30.7	30.9	30.9	31.2	31.0
2011	30.3	30.3	30.5	30.6	30.7	30.7	30.8	31.0	30.9	31.1	31.3	31.4	30.8
2012	31.2	31.4	31.5	31.6	31.8	32.0	31.8	31.8	31.7	31.9	32.0	32.3	31.8
2013	32.1	32.2	32.2	32.1	32.2	32.3	32.4	32.5	32.4	32.5	32.7	32.8	32.4
2014	32.5	32.7	32.8	32.9	33.1	33.2	33.3	33.3	33.2	33.3	33.5	33.9	33.1
2015	33.4	33.4	33.3	33.4	33.5	33.6	33.7	33.7	33.5	33.6	33.6	33.3	33.5
Professional and Business Services													
2005	68.4	69.7	70.7	73.2	73.2	74.5	74.4	75.4	75.4	74.1	74.8	74.2	73.2
2006	72.9	73.4	74.6	74.6	75.3	76.6	76.2	76.7	77.4	75.2	75.5	75.8	75.4
2007	74.3	75.6	76.6	76.9	77.5	78.8	77.4	78.5	79.1	78.3	79.4	79.5	77.7
2008	77.2	77.9	78.0	77.9	77.8	77.9	76.5	77.0	77.5	76.9	76.8	76.9	77.4
2009	73.6	73.7	73.5	72.4	71.1	71.4	71.2	71.0	71.9	71.0	70.7	70.8	71.9
2010	69.7	70.3	71.0	71.8	71.7	72.7	73.5	74.6	74.9	75.6	75.8	75.7	73.1
2011	73.9	73.7	74.8	76.4	76.2	75.8	76.0	76.8	76.2	76.4	76.3	76.9	75.8
2012	75.4	76.5	77.0	76.9	76.4	77.5	76.3	77.3	76.3	77.5	77.3	76.7	76.8
2013	75.7	76.2	77.5	77.4	77.4	78.0	77.5	78.0	77.6	78.4	79.2	78.0	77.6
2014	76.8	77.0	77.8	78.2	78.1	78.3	79.0	79.9	79.3	80.3	81.0	80.6	78.9
2015	79.6	79.6	79.7	80.3	80.1	80.8	81.0	81.5	81.1	82.1	81.5	80.4	80.6
Education and Health Services													
2005	73.2	73.9	74.5	75.4	75.1	74.9	75.3	76.2	77.2	77.1	77.3	77.7	75.7
2006	75.1	75.9	76.2	76.6	76.8	77.3	76.7	77.2	77.8	77.5	77.3	77.5	76.8
2007	77.1	77.8	78.4	78.8	79.0	78.7	78.7	79.4	80.3	80.9	81.2	81.1	79.3
2008	80.0	80.9	81.0	82.0	82.3	81.7	81.9	82.6	83.1	83.4	83.6	83.6	82.2
2009	83.0	82.9	83.0	82.8	82.8	82.8	82.6	82.8	83.4	82.9	83.0	82.9	82.9
2010	82.0	82.4	82.7	83.3	83.2	83.0	82.2	82.8	83.8	84.3	84.4	84.3	83.2
2011	82.6	82.6	83.5	84.1	84.2	84.3	83.8	84.5	85.5	85.4	86.0	86.0	84.4
2012	84.5	85.2	85.8	86.4	86.6	86.5	85.4	86.5	87.3	87.4	87.7	88.0	86.4
2013	86.9	87.3	87.7	87.9	88.1	87.7	86.9	87.7	88.3	88.9	89.3	88.7	88.0
2014	87.7	88.1	88.6	89.4	89.3	88.8	88.2	88.5	89.1	89.5	89.6	89.9	88.9
2015	89.2	89.7	89.9	90.3	90.3	90.1	89.4	89.8	90.6	91.9	92.1	90.9	90.4

Employment by Industry: Oklahoma City, OK, 2005–2015—*Continued*

(Numbers in thousands, not seasonally adjusted)

Industry and year	January	February	March	April	May	June	July	August	September	October	November	December	Annual average
Leisure and Hospitality													
2005	52.3	53.1	54.8	55.9	56.8	57.6	56.0	55.7	55.7	54.7	54.6	53.9	55.1
2006	53.5	54.2	56.0	56.7	56.9	56.8	56.9	57.0	56.8	55.3	54.9	54.8	55.8
2007	52.1	53.3	55.4	55.5	56.1	56.5	57.0	57.7	57.5	56.9	57.0	56.4	56.0
2008	54.7	55.1	56.6	57.2	57.8	58.3	57.6	57.5	58.1	57.4	57.2	57.3	57.1
2009	55.2	56.1	57.4	58.3	58.7	58.7	58.6	58.7	58.2	57.2	57.0	56.6	57.6
2010	54.7	54.6	56.6	58.0	58.7	58.6	58.2	58.6	59.1	58.0	58.1	57.9	57.6
2011	57.0	57.0	59.5	61.2	60.8	61.3	60.8	61.1	61.6	60.1	59.9	59.6	60.0
2012	58.6	59.3	61.2	62.1	62.8	62.7	61.7	62.4	62.8	62.4	62.3	62.6	61.7
2013	60.9	61.7	62.8	64.0	65.3	65.1	65.2	65.9	66.3	64.6	64.6	63.8	64.2
2014	63.0	63.5	64.8	66.6	67.1	67.0	66.6	67.3	67.4	66.2	65.8	65.8	65.9
2015	64.2	65.0	66.0	67.6	68.2	69.3	69.2	69.9	69.4	68.8	69.4	68.6	68.0
Other Services													
2005	22.9	23.0	23.1	23.1	23.1	23.3	23.5	23.3	23.3	23.2	23.2	23.2	23.2
2006	22.8	22.9	23.2	22.9	23.2	23.5	23.2	23.0	23.0	22.8	22.7	22.8	23.0
2007	22.6	22.7	22.9	23.3	23.5	23.8	23.5	23.4	23.3	23.2	23.2	23.0	23.2
2008	23.1	23.4	23.6	23.9	24.0	24.2	24.1	24.1	24.1	24.0	23.9	23.8	23.9
2009	23.6	23.6	23.7	23.5	23.5	23.7	23.4	23.1	23.0	22.9	23.0	22.8	23.3
2010	22.5	22.5	22.7	22.8	22.8	22.9	22.6	22.6	22.6	22.7	22.8	22.8	22.7
2011	22.4	22.4	22.5	22.7	23.0	23.0	22.8	22.7	22.8	22.7	22.7	22.6	22.7
2012	22.5	22.6	22.6	22.8	22.8	22.9	22.6	22.3	22.1	21.8	21.8	21.8	22.4
2013	21.7	21.8	21.8	21.9	22.1	22.4	22.6	22.6	22.5	22.6	22.7	22.8	22.3
2014	22.7	22.8	23.2	23.5	23.8	24.1	24.2	24.0	24.1	24.1	24.1	24.2	23.7
2015	24.1	24.3	24.7	24.8	24.9	25.1	25.0	24.9	24.9	24.8	24.8	24.7	24.8
Government													
2005	112.8	115.1	115.5	116.1	116.5	112.3	105.4	107.6	115.2	117.1	117.8	117.6	114.1
2006	114.4	117.3	117.6	117.7	118.0	113.8	106.4	109.2	115.8	119.1	119.4	119.1	115.7
2007	116.7	118.9	119.6	119.4	119.7	116.2	108.9	111.6	118.2	121.0	121.6	120.7	117.7
2008	115.8	119.8	120.6	120.5	121.1	115.1	108.7	112.9	120.1	122.0	123.0	122.3	118.5
2009	120.6	120.8	122.1	122.4	122.7	117.9	113.0	114.8	121.2	124.2	124.9	124.7	120.8
2010	119.9	122.8	124.0	124.4	126.2	120.9	115.1	116.6	122.3	123.7	124.1	124.5	122.0
2011	119.1	122.8	123.6	123.9	124.0	119.2	114.4	115.2	123.1	124.7	125.2	125.7	121.7
2012	120.1	123.5	124.5	125.0	124.9	119.9	113.5	116.1	123.1	126.3	126.9	126.1	122.5
2013	121.5	126.0	126.6	127.1	127.9	122.7	117.5	119.7	124.5	127.0	127.9	127.0	124.6
2014	121.5	125.9	126.3	126.4	127.4	122.4	117.1	119.5	125.7	128.1	128.5	127.9	124.7
2015	123.5	128.0	128.4	128.6	129.4	124.4	119.6	122.0	127.6	130.2	130.7	130.5	126.9

Employment by Industry: Memphis, TN-MS-AR, 2005–2015

(Numbers in thousands, not seasonally adjusted)

Industry and year	January	February	March	April	May	June	July	August	September	October	November	December	Annual average
Total Nonfarm													
2005	611.2	615.0	619.2	625.5	627.1	623.8	627.7	632.5	637.3	632.7	638.1	639.2	627.4
2006	628.1	628.0	632.8	634.6	636.1	634.6	637.2	642.1	644.3	641.9	649.8	650.4	638.3
2007	631.3	632.7	639.0	640.8	642.4	641.4	639.5	644.5	646.3	645.0	650.1	651.1	642.0
2008	633.6	632.4	635.1	637.9	638.7	633.5	633.7	636.2	633.7	632.2	632.5	628.7	634.0
2009	609.1	608.5	607.2	606.3	605.2	602.3	599.0	599.5	598.0	599.2	603.4	601.0	603.2
2010	584.4	586.2	591.0	591.9	597.8	592.5	588.5	591.8	589.8	596.3	599.3	598.4	592.3
2011	584.3	586.4	589.8	595.8	596.3	591.8	592.8	596.8	597.8	600.5	606.7	607.2	595.5
2012	590.6	595.1	598.4	600.5	603.1	600.8	598.7	603.9	605.7	609.6	618.0	618.9	603.6
2013	599.6	604.4	606.3	610.5	611.7	606.8	600.9	605.4	607.4	609.1	620.6	622.3	608.8
2014	604.0	605.5	609.0	617.5	617.7	613.8	609.8	617.0	617.8	622.3	630.4	633.1	616.5
2015	614.1	617.5	618.3	622.1	624.0	621.5	626.1	629.2	629.8	630.7	635.1	641.6	625.8
Total Private													
2005	524.8	527.4	531.2	537.2	539.8	541.4	546.1	547.3	550.8	545.6	550.8	552.7	541.3
2006	542.7	542.0	546.6	548.8	551.6	554.3	556.3	558.4	558.3	553.9	561.7	562.8	553.1
2007	545.0	545.6	551.9	554.2	556.7	560.2	558.5	560.1	559.9	556.6	561.4	562.7	556.1
2008	546.3	543.9	546.5	549.0	551.0	550.9	550.3	549.8	546.2	543.5	543.9	541.2	546.9
2009	523.2	521.2	519.7	518.8	517.8	518.4	514.9	514.8	511.8	511.5	515.3	513.5	516.7
2010	499.6	499.2	503.7	504.4	508.4	509.6	506.0	507.2	503.8	508.7	511.7	512.3	506.2
2011	498.9	499.5	503.1	508.9	510.6	512.2	513.5	513.8	513.0	515.2	521.0	522.5	511.0
2012	506.4	509.3	512.5	514.2	518.2	520.6	518.0	520.9	520.4	523.9	531.8	533.7	519.2
2013	515.7	518.2	520.4	523.7	527.2	528.0	522.8	524.5	524.3	525.6	536.5	539.8	525.6
2014	522.0	522.2	525.5	533.4	535.7	536.6	532.7	536.8	535.2	539.1	546.9	550.4	534.7
2015	532.4	533.3	534.2	539.1	543.3	545.4	549.9	550.0	547.9	548.9	553.2	560.9	544.9
Goods Producing													
2005	76.7	77.7	78.7	79.9	80.9	81.8	82.1	80.7	83.0	82.0	81.9	79.5	80.4
2006	80.2	80.8	81.7	81.8	82.4	83.4	83.1	83.0	83.0	81.0	80.4	78.0	81.6
2007	78.0	78.4	80.0	79.8	80.2	81.0	80.4	79.8	79.3	78.8	78.3	77.3	79.3
2008	75.9	75.4	76.2	76.8	77.3	77.4	76.7	76.8	76.2	74.7	73.7	72.5	75.8
2009	70.9	69.5	69.1	68.4	68.3	68.6	68.0	68.1	67.9	66.4	66.8	64.8	68.1
2010	62.7	63.0	64.0	64.1	64.6	65.1	65.2	65.1	64.8	63.8	64.1	63.8	64.2
2011	63.0	62.6	62.9	63.6	64.3	65.3	65.8	65.5	65.1	64.0	64.8	64.4	64.3
2012	63.4	63.5	64.1	64.8	65.5	66.3	66.2	66.5	65.3	64.7	65.4	65.0	65.1
2013	64.3	64.3	64.7	65.0	65.5	65.9	65.6	65.1	64.9	64.5	64.7	64.5	64.9
2014	64.6	64.5	64.4	65.4	66.1	65.9	66.3	66.4	66.0	66.1	66.2	66.5	65.7
2015	65.3	65.4	65.7	66.4	67.0	67.8	68.7	67.8	67.6	67.2	67.1	67.0	66.9
Service-Providing													
2005	534.5	537.3	540.5	545.6	546.2	542.0	545.6	551.8	554.3	550.7	556.2	559.7	547.0
2006	547.9	547.2	551.1	552.8	553.7	551.2	554.1	559.1	561.3	560.9	569.4	572.4	556.8
2007	553.3	554.3	559.0	561.0	562.2	560.4	559.1	564.7	567.0	566.2	571.8	573.8	562.7
2008	557.7	557.0	558.9	561.1	561.4	556.1	557.0	559.4	557.5	557.5	558.8	556.2	558.2
2009	538.2	539.0	538.1	537.9	536.9	533.7	531.0	531.4	530.1	532.8	536.6	536.2	535.2
2010	521.7	523.2	527.0	527.8	533.2	527.4	523.3	526.7	525.0	532.5	535.2	534.6	528.1
2011	521.3	523.8	526.9	532.2	532.0	526.5	527.0	531.3	532.7	536.5	541.9	542.8	531.2
2012	527.2	531.6	534.3	535.7	537.6	534.5	532.5	537.4	540.4	544.9	552.6	553.9	538.6
2013	535.3	540.1	541.6	545.5	546.2	540.9	535.3	540.3	542.5	544.6	555.9	557.8	543.8
2014	539.4	541.0	544.6	552.1	551.6	547.9	543.5	550.6	551.8	556.2	564.2	566.6	550.8
2015	548.8	552.1	552.6	555.7	557.0	553.7	557.4	561.4	562.2	563.5	568.0	574.6	558.9
Mining, Logging, and Construction													
2005	23.7	24.1	24.7	25.4	26.1	26.8	27.0	27.3	27.7	27.0	26.9	26.8	26.1
2006	25.9	26.1	26.8	27.2	27.8	28.3	28.4	28.3	28.1	27.1	26.6	26.4	27.3
2007	25.6	25.6	26.0	26.3	26.8	27.3	26.9	27.0	26.8	26.5	26.3	26.2	26.4
2008	24.5	24.5	25.0	25.5	25.7	25.8	25.2	25.1	24.7	23.8	23.4	22.9	24.7
2009	21.8	21.5	21.5	21.5	21.5	22.0	21.7	21.7	21.4	20.5	20.6	20.1	21.3
2010	19.0	18.7	19.3	19.2	19.4	19.8	19.8	19.8	19.7	19.4	19.1	18.9	19.3
2011	18.1	18.2	18.5	19.0	19.4	20.2	20.7	20.8	20.8	20.8	20.7	20.6	19.8
2012	19.5	19.5	20.0	20.4	20.9	21.4	21.3	21.5	21.3	20.8	20.6	20.5	20.6
2013	19.8	19.8	20.0	20.2	20.7	20.9	20.8	20.8	20.7	20.5	20.7	20.5	20.5
2014	20.5	20.3	19.9	21.0	21.4	21.1	21.1	21.2	21.1	21.4	21.5	21.4	21.0
2015	20.6	20.6	20.5	21.1	21.3	21.7	22.6	22.5	22.5	22.5	22.2	22.1	21.7

Employment by Industry: Memphis, TN-MS-AR, 2005–2015—*Continued*

(Numbers in thousands, not seasonally adjusted)

Industry and year	January	February	March	April	May	June	July	August	September	October	November	December	Annual average
Manufacturing													
2005	53.0	53.6	54.0	54.5	54.8	55.0	55.1	53.4	55.3	55.0	55.0	52.7	54.3
2006	54.3	54.7	54.9	54.6	54.6	55.1	54.7	54.7	54.9	53.9	53.8	51.6	54.3
2007	52.4	52.8	54.0	53.5	53.4	53.7	53.5	52.8	52.5	52.3	52.0	51.1	52.8
2008	51.4	50.9	51.2	51.3	51.6	51.6	51.5	51.7	51.5	50.9	50.3	49.6	51.1
2009	49.1	48.0	47.6	46.9	46.8	46.6	46.3	46.4	46.5	45.9	46.2	44.7	46.8
2010	43.7	44.3	44.7	44.9	45.2	45.3	45.4	45.3	45.1	44.4	45.0	44.9	44.9
2011	44.9	44.4	44.4	44.6	44.9	45.1	45.1	44.7	44.3	43.2	44.1	43.8	44.5
2012	43.9	44.0	44.1	44.4	44.6	44.9	44.9	45.0	44.0	43.9	44.8	44.5	44.4
2013	44.5	44.5	44.7	44.8	44.8	45.0	44.8	44.3	44.2	44.0	44.0	44.0	44.5
2014	44.1	44.2	44.5	44.4	44.7	44.8	45.2	45.2	44.9	44.7	44.7	45.1	44.7
2015	44.7	44.8	45.2	45.3	45.7	46.1	46.1	45.3	45.1	44.7	44.9	44.9	45.2
Trade, Transportation, and Utilities													
2005	170.1	169.0	170.0	170.3	170.8	170.9	173.8	173.5	173.8	173.2	176.5	178.7	172.6
2006	173.9	172.7	173.3	173.6	174.3	174.0	175.0	175.4	175.2	175.0	178.5	180.2	175.1
2007	173.6	172.8	174.1	175.0	175.8	175.9	175.6	175.6	175.9	175.1	178.3	179.4	175.6
2008	173.1	171.7	172.0	172.0	172.0	171.6	171.1	170.5	169.6	168.6	170.2	170.7	171.1
2009	164.7	163.3	162.6	161.3	161.3	160.8	160.2	159.7	159.0	158.6	160.0	161.1	161.1
2010	157.5	156.6	157.1	158.2	158.4	158.6	158.8	158.8	157.3	158.9	161.3	162.5	158.7
2011	157.2	156.6	156.9	158.6	159.1	159.4	160.1	159.7	159.9	161.8	164.4	165.5	159.9
2012	160.4	159.6	160.3	160.3	161.4	161.7	161.6	161.6	162.0	162.7	166.4	167.7	162.1
2013	162.1	161.7	161.1	162.0	162.0	162.3	162.6	161.8	161.1	162.0	165.7	167.1	162.6
2014	161.1	161.1	162.0	163.5	163.4	164.1	163.9	164.2	164.5	166.5	170.1	170.9	164.6
2015	165.1	164.0	164.2	165.8	166.9	168.0	170.8	169.5	169.1	169.3	173.2	176.1	168.5
Wholesale Trade													
2005	36.7	36.8	37.1	37.3	37.4	37.5	37.9	38.0	37.7	37.6	37.6	37.7	37.4
2006	37.3	37.4	37.5	37.5	37.7	37.8	37.8	37.9	37.7	37.3	37.5	37.4	37.6
2007	37.0	37.2	37.3	37.5	37.6	37.6	37.5	37.5	37.6	37.3	37.1	37.0	37.4
2008	36.2	36.0	35.9	36.3	36.1	35.8	35.2	35.2	35.0	34.9	34.7	34.3	35.5
2009	33.6	33.6	33.3	33.4	33.3	33.2	32.8	32.7	32.4	32.3	32.2	32.2	32.9
2010	32.0	32.0	32.0	32.8	32.7	32.8	32.7	32.8	32.5	32.6	32.8	32.8	32.5
2011	32.6	32.7	32.6	32.9	33.0	33.0	33.1	33.2	33.1	33.2	33.2	33.1	33.0
2012	33.1	33.3	33.3	33.4	33.7	33.8	33.8	33.8	33.8	33.8	33.9	33.9	33.6
2013	33.4	33.5	33.5	33.8	33.8	33.9	33.8	33.9	33.9	33.6	33.6	33.7	33.7
2014	33.2	33.4	33.6	33.6	33.7	33.8	33.6	33.6	33.7	33.5	33.7	33.9	33.6
2015	33.7	33.7	33.7	34.1	34.4	34.5	35.0	35.2	35.3	35.4	35.8	36.4	34.8
Retail Trade													
2005	70.6	69.7	69.9	69.9	70.1	70.3	71.6	71.1	71.5	71.5	74.3	75.9	71.4
2006	72.5	71.3	71.9	71.7	72.0	71.9	73.0	72.8	72.7	72.6	75.4	76.4	72.9
2007	72.1	71.1	72.0	72.3	72.6	73.0	72.8	71.9	71.9	71.8	74.9	75.7	72.7
2008	71.7	70.7	71.2	70.6	70.6	70.5	70.6	69.6	68.9	68.5	69.7	70.0	70.2
2009	66.9	66.0	65.9	65.3	65.6	65.8	65.9	65.3	64.9	65.1	67.0	67.8	66.0
2010	64.6	64.0	64.5	64.4	64.6	64.5	64.7	64.1	63.0	63.9	65.8	66.5	64.6
2011	62.5	61.8	61.9	62.6	62.7	62.6	62.8	62.2	61.9	62.7	65.3	66.0	62.9
2012	62.7	62.0	62.6	62.7	63.2	63.3	63.2	62.6	62.3	63.1	66.0	66.3	63.3
2013	63.6	63.1	63.2	63.3	63.6	63.8	64.3	64.0	63.8	64.4	67.0	68.1	64.4
2014	64.4	63.9	64.2	65.2	65.4	65.6	65.5	65.2	65.0	65.6	68.0	68.7	65.6
2015	65.0	64.3	64.6	65.4	66.0	66.6	66.7	66.2	65.5	65.9	67.3	67.5	65.9
Transportation and Utilities													
2005	62.8	62.5	63.0	63.1	63.3	63.1	64.3	64.4	64.6	64.1	64.6	65.1	63.7
2006	64.1	64.0	63.9	64.4	64.6	64.3	64.2	64.7	64.8	65.1	65.6	66.4	64.7
2007	64.5	64.5	64.8	65.2	65.6	65.3	65.3	66.2	66.4	66.0	66.3	66.7	65.6
2008	65.2	65.0	64.9	65.1	65.3	65.3	65.3	65.7	65.7	65.2	65.8	66.4	65.4
2009	64.2	63.7	63.4	62.6	62.4	61.8	61.5	61.7	61.7	61.2	60.8	61.1	62.2
2010	60.9	60.6	60.6	61.0	61.1	61.3	61.4	61.9	61.8	62.4	62.7	63.2	61.6
2011	62.1	62.1	62.4	63.1	63.4	63.8	64.2	64.3	64.9	65.9	65.9	66.4	64.0
2012	64.6	64.3	64.4	64.2	64.5	64.6	64.6	65.2	65.9	65.8	66.5	67.5	65.2
2013	65.1	65.1	64.4	64.9	64.6	64.6	64.5	63.9	63.4	64.0	65.1	65.3	64.6
2014	63.5	63.8	64.2	64.7	64.3	64.7	64.8	65.4	65.8	67.4	68.4	68.3	65.4
2015	66.4	66.0	65.9	66.3	66.5	66.9	69.1	68.1	68.3	68.0	70.1	72.2	67.8

Employment by Industry: Memphis, TN-MS-AR, 2005–2015—*Continued*

(Numbers in thousands, not seasonally adjusted)

Industry and year	January	February	March	April	May	June	July	August	September	October	November	December	Annual average
Information													
2005	8.2	8.1	8.2	8.2	8.2	8.0	7.8	7.7	7.6	7.7	7.6	7.4	7.9
2006	7.3	7.3	7.3	7.4	7.5	7.5	7.5	7.5	7.8	7.7	7.8	7.9	7.5
2007	7.4	7.4	7.3	7.4	7.4	7.5	7.5	7.4	7.3	7.3	7.4	7.4	7.4
2008	7.4	7.4	7.4	7.4	7.4	7.4	7.2	7.2	7.2	7.3	7.2	7.3	7.3
2009	7.2	7.1	7.0	6.9	6.9	6.8	6.8	6.7	6.7	6.6	6.6	6.6	6.8
2010	6.4	6.3	6.3	6.2	6.3	6.3	6.2	6.2	6.2	6.2	6.2	6.3	6.3
2011	6.2	6.1	6.1	6.1	6.2	6.1	6.1	6.1	6.0	6.0	6.0	6.0	6.1
2012	6.1	6.1	6.1	6.1	6.1	6.0	6.1	6.1	6.0	6.0	6.0	6.0	6.1
2013	5.9	5.9	5.9	5.9	6.0	6.1	6.0	6.0	6.0	6.0	6.1	6.1	6.0
2014	6.0	6.0	6.0	6.0	6.0	6.0	5.9	6.0	5.9	5.8	6.0	6.0	6.0
2015	5.8	5.8	5.8	5.9	5.9	5.9	5.8	5.8	5.7	5.8	5.8	5.8	5.8
Financial Activities													
2005	32.8	32.7	32.9	32.9	32.9	32.9	32.9	33.0	32.9	32.7	32.8	32.8	32.9
2006	32.7	32.8	32.9	32.7	32.8	33.2	33.1	33.1	33.0	32.5	33.0	33.1	32.9
2007	32.4	32.8	33.0	33.0	33.3	33.6	33.5	33.7	33.5	33.1	33.2	33.2	33.2
2008	32.8	32.7	33.0	32.9	33.0	32.9	32.6	32.5	32.1	32.0	31.9	31.4	32.5
2009	31.3	31.2	31.1	31.2	31.2	31.1	30.9	30.7	30.5	30.2	30.4	30.3	30.8
2010	29.7	29.6	29.5	29.2	29.1	29.0	28.9	28.8	28.5	28.2	28.0	28.1	28.9
2011	27.6	27.3	27.2	27.5	27.6	27.6	27.7	27.7	27.6	27.5	27.5	27.6	27.5
2012	27.4	27.4	27.4	27.3	27.5	27.3	27.5	27.4	27.1	27.3	27.4	27.4	27.4
2013	27.2	27.0	27.0	27.0	27.0	27.2	27.4	27.3	27.3	27.3	27.4	27.5	27.2
2014	27.1	27.1	27.1	27.4	27.6	27.6	27.6	27.6	27.4	27.5	27.5	27.5	27.4
2015	27.3	27.2	27.1	27.2	27.3	27.6	27.7	27.7	27.5	27.8	28.1	28.1	27.6
Professional and Business Services													
2005	73.8	75.5	75.2	77.1	77.3	77.2	78.3	80.2	81.3	80.3	81.2	83.8	78.4
2006	79.2	78.9	79.3	79.6	80.0	80.2	81.9	83.5	84.1	83.4	87.2	88.8	82.2
2007	80.4	80.5	81.3	82.0	81.9	81.7	82.7	84.0	85.3	85.4	87.0	87.5	83.3
2008	81.5	81.1	81.0	81.9	81.6	81.5	83.6	84.0	84.1	85.1	85.1	84.0	82.9
2009	77.9	77.9	76.9	76.1	75.0	74.5	73.7	74.8	74.6	76.7	78.0	77.7	76.2
2010	74.0	73.4	74.1	73.2	76.0	75.8	73.0	74.7	75.7	79.8	80.8	81.0	76.0
2011	77.0	78.2	79.3	80.3	80.2	79.9	80.4	81.5	81.7	84.8	86.9	87.7	81.5
2012	80.2	82.1	81.7	82.0	82.9	83.5	82.0	83.3	85.0	87.7	91.3	91.6	84.4
2013	83.6	85.1	86.1	86.5	87.9	87.6	84.0	86.9	88.1	88.7	94.9	97.3	88.1
2014	88.6	87.3	88.2	92.0	92.9	92.1	91.2	93.5	93.7	95.7	100.1	102.1	93.1
2015	94.5	94.6	94.9	95.1	96.1	95.9	96.2	97.9	98.0	98.3	99.5	102.7	97.0
Education and Health Services													
2005	75.0	75.7	76.0	76.2	76.5	76.1	76.0	77.2	77.9	77.1	77.7	77.5	76.6
2006	77.7	77.5	78.3	78.2	78.0	78.2	78.0	78.5	79.1	79.0	79.0	79.2	78.4
2007	78.9	79.2	80.1	79.8	80.3	80.2	79.9	80.8	81.2	81.2	81.4	82.2	80.4
2008	81.5	81.8	82.3	82.1	82.6	82.2	81.4	81.7	82.2	82.6	82.8	82.8	82.2
2009	81.3	82.1	82.4	83.0	82.6	82.3	81.6	81.9	82.6	83.7	84.3	84.2	82.7
2010	82.4	83.1	83.8	83.5	83.3	82.8	82.6	83.0	83.0	83.6	83.9	83.8	83.2
2011	82.5	83.0	83.5	84.3	84.1	83.6	83.8	84.5	85.6	85.8	86.2	86.1	84.4
2012	85.7	86.6	87.3	86.2	86.3	85.8	85.6	87.2	88.1	88.3	88.9	89.4	87.1
2013	88.1	89.3	89.5	89.3	89.4	88.4	87.4	88.1	89.2	89.6	90.1	90.1	89.0
2014	88.8	89.4	89.4	89.6	89.0	87.8	87.6	88.9	89.5	89.6	89.6	89.6	89.1
2015	88.3	89.5	89.6	89.5	89.1	88.1	88.5	89.8	90.5	91.4	91.4	91.8	89.8
Leisure and Hospitality													
2005	63.9	64.2	65.5	67.8	68.4	69.4	70.4	70.3	69.6	68.1	68.6	68.6	67.9
2006	67.5	67.7	69.3	71.0	72.1	72.8	72.9	72.7	71.5	71.2	71.7	71.6	71.0
2007	70.5	70.7	71.9	72.8	73.2	75.3	74.3	74.3	73.1	71.5	71.7	71.7	72.6
2008	70.1	69.8	70.5	71.7	72.5	72.8	72.7	72.1	69.9	68.3	68.1	67.5	70.5
2009	65.1	65.2	65.7	66.9	67.4	69.0	68.5	68.0	65.7	64.6	64.7	64.4	66.3
2010	62.5	62.8	64.3	65.2	66.0	67.3	66.9	66.5	64.6	64.3	63.8	63.4	64.8
2011	62.3	62.6	63.9	65.1	65.7	66.6	65.7	64.9	63.3	61.7	61.6	61.6	63.8
2012	59.7	60.4	61.7	63.4	64.2	65.4	64.6	64.6	62.8	62.4	62.6	62.6	62.9
2013	60.8	61.1	62.1	63.7	65.0	65.8	65.2	65.0	63.5	63.5	63.6	63.3	63.6
2014	62.1	62.9	64.4	65.5	66.6	68.6	65.9	66.1	64.1	63.9	63.6	63.9	64.8
2015	62.2	62.7	62.8	65.0	66.7	67.5	67.5	67.1	65.1	64.8	63.9	65.3	65.1

Employment by Industry: Memphis, TN-MS-AR, 2005–2015—*Continued*

(Numbers in thousands, not seasonally adjusted)

Industry and year	January	February	March	April	May	June	July	August	September	October	November	December	Annual average
Other Services													
2005	24.3	24.5	24.7	24.8	24.8	25.1	24.8	24.7	24.7	24.5	24.5	24.4	24.7
2006	24.2	24.3	24.5	24.5	24.5	25.0	24.8	24.7	24.6	24.1	24.1	24.0	24.4
2007	23.8	23.8	24.2	24.4	24.6	25.0	24.6	24.5	24.3	24.2	24.1	24.0	24.3
2008	24.0	24.0	24.1	24.2	24.6	25.1	25.0	25.0	24.9	24.9	24.9	25.0	24.6
2009	24.8	24.9	24.9	25.0	25.1	25.3	25.2	24.9	24.8	24.7	24.5	24.4	24.9
2010	24.4	24.4	24.6	24.8	24.7	24.7	24.4	24.1	23.7	23.9	23.6	23.4	24.2
2011	23.1	23.1	23.3	23.4	23.4	23.7	23.9	23.9	23.8	23.6	23.6	23.6	23.5
2012	23.5	23.6	23.9	24.1	24.3	24.6	24.4	24.2	24.1	24.1	24.0	24.0	24.1
2013	23.7	23.8	24.0	24.3	24.4	24.7	24.6	24.3	24.2	24.0	24.0	23.9	24.2
2014	23.7	23.9	24.0	24.0	24.1	24.5	24.3	24.1	24.1	24.0	23.8	23.9	24.0
2015	23.9	24.1	24.1	24.2	24.3	24.6	24.7	24.4	24.4	24.3	24.2	24.1	24.3
Government													
2005	86.4	87.6	88.0	88.3	87.3	82.4	81.6	85.2	86.5	87.1	87.3	86.5	86.2
2006	85.4	86.0	86.2	85.8	84.5	80.3	80.9	83.7	86.0	88.0	88.1	87.6	85.2
2007	86.3	87.1	87.1	86.6	85.7	81.2	81.0	84.4	86.4	88.4	88.7	88.4	85.9
2008	87.3	88.5	88.6	88.9	87.7	82.6	83.4	86.4	87.5	88.7	88.6	87.5	87.1
2009	85.9	87.3	87.5	87.5	87.4	83.9	84.1	84.7	86.2	87.7	88.1	87.5	86.5
2010	84.8	87.0	87.3	87.5	89.4	82.9	82.5	84.6	86.0	87.6	87.6	86.1	86.1
2011	85.4	86.9	86.7	86.9	85.7	79.6	79.3	83.0	84.8	85.3	85.7	84.7	84.5
2012	84.2	85.8	85.9	86.3	84.9	80.2	80.7	83.0	85.3	85.7	86.2	85.2	84.5
2013	83.9	86.2	85.9	86.8	84.5	78.8	78.1	80.9	83.1	83.5	84.1	82.5	83.2
2014	82.0	83.3	83.5	84.1	82.0	77.2	77.1	80.2	82.6	83.2	83.5	82.7	81.8
2015	81.7	84.2	84.1	83.0	80.7	76.1	76.2	79.2	81.9	81.8	81.9	80.7	81.0

Employment by Industry: Louisville/Jefferson County, KY-IN, 2005–2015

(Numbers in thousands, not seasonally adjusted)

Industry and year	January	February	March	April	May	June	July	August	September	October	November	December	Annual average
Total Nonfarm													
2005	581.0	583.7	587.5	593.2	597.4	602.2	591.1	598.4	601.4	602.1	605.5	604.2	595.6
2006	589.4	591.9	599.7	603.5	609.9	613.2	599.4	608.2	610.7	604.5	607.6	614.3	604.4
2007	599.7	600.0	603.0	611.3	619.6	623.6	611.0	614.2	616.6	615.1	620.7	618.2	612.8
2008	603.2	603.5	605.4	610.5	620.6	619.4	607.2	612.1	606.9	605.7	608.7	602.8	608.8
2009	580.0	579.1	580.8	584.6	587.1	586.4	580.1	582.3	582.5	583.7	584.9	582.6	582.8
2010	567.0	561.3	572.3	579.3	586.1	586.7	578.4	581.2	582.6	586.3	590.2	591.9	580.3
2011	572.0	574.1	579.2	584.9	587.2	589.4	580.3	587.2	588.8	589.8	594.8	593.1	585.1
2012	580.7	580.0	588.2	594.0	602.3	604.5	597.9	603.1	605.5	607.6	614.7	615.8	599.5
2013	599.9	600.4	605.2	611.7	615.4	616.4	608.8	619.7	619.1	619.5	625.5	625.9	614.0
2014	608.4	607.8	614.0	622.8	627.0	629.9	627.3	633.1	633.4	634.7	640.1	642.9	626.8
2015	628.1	627.3	631.5	635.9	645.6	647.5	639.1	646.6	647.8	650.7	658.8	661.6	643.4
Total Private													
2005	508.4	510.3	513.7	519.2	522.9	528.1	521.0	526.4	526.8	527.4	530.7	529.6	522.0
2006	515.7	517.1	524.8	528.2	534.2	538.0	527.9	534.2	533.7	528.6	531.5	538.6	529.4
2007	525.4	524.9	527.5	534.4	542.4	546.8	538.5	539.4	540.1	539.2	544.5	541.9	537.1
2008	527.2	526.6	528.2	533.4	543.0	542.3	534.6	537.4	530.2	528.5	531.4	525.9	532.4
2009	504.1	503.1	504.3	507.3	509.2	509.4	506.3	506.2	503.8	504.2	505.8	504.6	505.7
2010	489.7	483.8	493.0	498.9	504.0	506.4	502.8	504.8	504.9	508.1	512.2	514.6	501.9
2011	495.2	496.5	501.3	506.7	508.7	511.9	506.3	510.7	509.8	510.7	515.3	514.0	507.3
2012	502.2	501.1	508.7	514.5	522.7	525.8	523.3	526.1	526.3	528.0	535.0	536.4	520.8
2013	521.1	520.6	524.9	531.0	534.6	536.4	532.2	540.0	538.3	539.1	544.6	545.3	534.0
2014	529.1	528.3	533.9	542.7	547.0	550.5	550.6	553.7	552.5	554.3	559.7	563.1	547.1
2015	549.0	548.2	552.1	556.7	566.2	569.4	564.8	571.1	570.7	573.8	581.8	584.9	565.7
Goods Producing													
2005	109.7	109.6	110.5	111.5	111.8	113.4	108.0	112.5	112.2	111.9	112.2	110.9	111.2
2006	108.6	108.3	108.9	109.5	110.4	111.7	105.5	111.2	110.7	105.8	105.5	109.4	108.8
2007	106.6	105.9	104.0	108.3	109.8	111.3	105.4	106.5	109.5	105.2	108.7	105.7	107.2
2008	104.2	104.4	104.5	104.0	107.3	106.3	101.7	104.2	101.9	100.9	103.1	98.6	103.4
2009	93.3	93.4	92.2	93.1	91.9	91.7	90.2	91.2	90.6	90.2	89.4	88.4	91.3
2010	85.2	80.5	85.2	85.5	86.5	87.0	84.8	87.1	87.5	87.5	87.3	86.7	85.9
2011	83.2	83.4	84.1	85.6	86.0	87.4	84.6	88.0	88.3	88.1	88.7	87.9	86.3
2012	87.0	85.9	89.5	91.3	92.9	94.5	94.8	95.5	95.8	95.8	96.5	96.6	93.0
2013	94.4	94.3	94.8	95.8	96.5	97.5	95.0	98.6	98.4	98.1	98.4	98.2	96.7
2014	96.2	96.3	97.5	99.5	100.9	102.2	102.6	102.8	102.5	102.8	103.8	103.6	100.9
2015	102.1	101.9	102.3	100.9	105.2	106.4	104.0	107.5	107.5	107.6	108.2	108.5	105.2
Service-Providing													
2005	471.3	474.1	477.0	481.7	485.6	488.8	483.1	485.9	489.2	490.2	493.3	493.3	484.5
2006	480.8	483.6	490.8	494.0	499.5	501.5	493.9	497.0	500.0	498.7	502.1	504.9	495.6
2007	493.1	494.1	499.0	503.0	509.8	512.3	505.6	507.7	507.1	509.9	512.0	512.5	505.5
2008	499.0	499.1	500.9	506.5	513.3	513.1	505.5	507.9	505.0	504.8	505.6	504.2	505.4
2009	486.7	485.7	488.6	491.5	495.2	494.7	489.9	491.1	491.9	493.5	495.5	494.2	491.5
2010	481.8	480.8	487.1	493.8	499.6	499.7	493.6	494.1	495.1	498.8	502.9	505.2	494.4
2011	488.8	490.7	495.1	499.3	501.2	502.0	495.7	499.2	500.5	501.7	506.1	505.2	498.8
2012	493.7	494.1	498.7	502.7	509.4	510.0	503.1	507.6	509.7	511.8	518.2	519.2	506.5
2013	505.5	506.1	510.4	515.9	518.9	518.9	513.8	521.1	520.7	521.4	527.1	527.7	517.3
2014	512.2	511.5	516.5	523.3	526.1	527.7	524.7	530.3	530.9	531.9	536.3	539.3	525.9
2015	526.0	525.4	529.2	535.0	540.4	541.1	535.1	539.1	540.3	543.1	550.6	553.1	538.2
Mining, Logging, and Construction													
2005	29.9	30.4	31.1	32.2	32.8	34.2	35.2	34.3	34.0	34.0	33.6	32.9	32.9
2006	30.8	30.5	31.1	31.4	32.1	32.6	32.6	32.3	32.0	31.7	31.3	31.1	31.6
2007	29.0	28.5	30.0	31.4	32.4	33.2	33.7	33.5	33.4	33.2	33.0	32.4	32.0
2008	30.5	30.3	30.7	32.2	33.2	33.8	33.8	33.9	33.5	33.4	32.7	32.0	32.5
2009	29.7	29.0	29.0	29.3	29.2	29.3	29.4	29.3	29.1	29.2	28.4	27.3	29.0
2010	24.7	23.8	24.5	25.3	25.3	25.7	26.3	25.8	25.4	25.2	24.7	23.8	25.0
2011	21.9	21.9	22.9	23.9	24.2	25.1	25.5	25.4	25.2	24.8	24.7	24.2	24.1
2012	22.7	22.6	23.6	24.2	24.7	25.3	25.2	25.0	24.8	24.5	24.7	24.4	24.3
2013	22.7	22.5	23.2	24.1	24.7	25.4	26.1	26.1	26.0	25.7	25.7	25.4	24.8
2014	23.9	23.9	25.2	26.2	27.0	28.1	28.4	28.2	28.2	28.2	28.3	27.8	27.0
2015	26.3	26.4	26.6	27.6	28.6	29.2	30.5	29.8	29.6	29.4	29.9	30.0	28.7

Employment by Industry: Louisville/Jefferson County, KY-IN, 2005–2015—*Continued*

(Numbers in thousands, not seasonally adjusted)

Industry and year	January	February	March	April	May	June	July	August	September	October	November	December	Annual average
Manufacturing													
2005	79.8	79.2	79.4	79.3	79.0	79.2	72.8	78.2	78.2	77.9	78.6	78.0	78.3
2006	77.8	77.8	77.8	78.1	78.3	79.1	72.9	78.9	78.7	74.1	74.2	78.3	77.2
2007	77.6	77.4	74.0	76.9	77.4	78.1	71.7	73.0	76.1	72.0	75.7	73.3	75.3
2008	73.7	74.1	73.8	71.8	74.1	72.5	67.9	70.3	68.4	67.5	70.4	66.6	70.9
2009	63.6	64.4	63.2	63.8	62.7	62.4	60.8	61.9	61.5	61.0	61.0	61.1	62.3
2010	60.5	56.7	60.7	60.2	61.2	61.3	58.5	61.3	62.1	62.3	62.6	62.9	60.9
2011	61.3	61.5	61.2	61.7	61.8	62.3	59.1	62.6	63.1	63.3	64.0	63.7	62.1
2012	64.3	63.3	65.9	67.1	68.2	69.2	69.6	70.5	71.0	71.3	71.8	72.2	68.7
2013	71.7	71.8	71.6	71.7	71.8	72.1	68.9	72.5	72.4	72.4	72.7	72.8	71.9
2014	72.3	72.4	72.3	73.3	73.9	74.1	74.2	74.6	74.3	74.6	75.5	75.8	73.9
2015	75.8	75.5	75.7	73.3	76.6	77.2	73.5	77.7	77.9	78.2	78.3	78.5	76.5
Trade, Transportation, and Utilities													
2005	129.0	128.0	128.9	129.6	130.3	130.7	130.8	130.9	131.4	132.4	135.5	137.2	131.2
2006	131.8	130.9	132.9	133.3	134.9	135.8	134.3	134.8	134.9	135.1	138.4	140.6	134.8
2007	135.9	134.7	135.6	135.7	137.0	138.4	137.1	137.4	137.6	139.3	141.3	143.0	137.8
2008	136.3	134.4	134.2	134.6	136.1	135.8	134.6	135.1	133.1	133.0	135.3	137.5	135.0
2009	129.0	127.1	127.2	126.5	127.2	127.4	126.0	125.8	125.4	126.1	128.7	130.4	127.2
2010	124.1	122.9	124.0	125.5	126.4	127.1	127.3	127.9	127.9	129.8	132.9	136.2	127.7
2011	128.4	127.7	128.8	129.4	129.5	130.2	129.4	129.6	129.1	129.6	133.0	134.4	129.9
2012	128.2	128.0	128.6	128.7	130.1	130.8	130.4	130.5	130.7	131.5	135.0	137.3	130.8
2013	130.9	130.4	131.2	131.1	131.8	132.5	132.3	133.4	133.7	133.8	137.4	140.3	133.2
2014	133.0	132.5	133.0	133.2	134.6	135.3	135.3	136.6	137.0	138.5	141.9	145.8	136.4
2015	139.0	138.0	138.6	138.9	140.3	141.3	140.9	142.7	142.5	144.4	147.3	150.2	142.0
Wholesale Trade													
2005	29.0	29.0	29.1	29.0	29.1	29.2	29.4	29.3	29.3	29.2	29.3	29.4	29.2
2006	29.6	29.6	29.8	29.7	29.9	30.1	29.8	29.9	29.8	29.8	30.0	30.0	29.8
2007	30.0	30.1	30.2	30.0	30.0	30.1	29.9	29.9	29.9	30.0	29.8	29.9	30.0
2008	29.6	29.7	29.6	29.7	29.8	29.8	29.7	29.7	29.6	29.5	29.3	29.2	29.6
2009	28.4	28.2	28.0	27.9	27.9	27.7	27.5	27.6	27.7	27.6	27.6	27.5	27.8
2010	27.2	27.1	27.3	27.3	27.4	27.5	27.7	27.7	27.7	27.7	27.8	27.7	27.5
2011	27.5	27.6	27.8	27.7	27.7	27.8	27.9	28.0	28.0	28.0	28.0	28.1	27.8
2012	27.7	27.8	27.9	27.9	28.2	28.2	28.4	28.5	28.6	28.6	28.6	28.6	28.3
2013	28.7	28.8	28.9	28.8	28.7	28.8	28.9	29.0	29.0	28.9	29.0	29.1	28.9
2014	28.8	28.9	28.9	28.8	28.9	28.8	28.9	28.9	28.9	28.8	28.8	28.8	28.9
2015	28.7	28.7	28.8	28.8	29.1	29.1	29.1	29.4	29.4	29.9	30.0	29.4	29.2
Retail Trade													
2005	63.8	62.7	63.2	63.6	64.1	64.3	64.0	63.7	63.6	64.3	66.5	67.9	64.3
2006	63.9	63.0	63.9	63.9	64.3	64.0	63.4	63.0	62.5	63.0	65.3	66.3	63.9
2007	63.3	62.3	63.0	62.9	63.7	64.2	64.2	63.9	63.6	63.8	65.9	66.5	63.9
2008	63.2	62.3	62.8	62.3	63.1	63.1	62.9	62.9	61.8	62.0	63.5	64.1	62.8
2009	60.2	59.0	59.4	59.4	59.9	60.1	59.6	59.3	58.8	59.6	61.3	62.0	59.9
2010	58.5	57.8	58.5	58.6	59.0	59.2	59.2	59.3	58.7	59.9	61.5	62.1	59.4
2011	58.9	58.2	58.9	59.5	59.6	59.6	59.3	59.3	58.7	59.6	61.6	62.2	59.6
2012	59.6	59.1	59.6	59.8	60.5	61.0	60.8	60.7	60.5	61.5	64.2	64.3	61.0
2013	61.0	60.5	60.9	61.1	61.7	62.0	61.9	62.2	62.0	62.4	64.8	65.5	62.2
2014	61.2	61.1	61.3	61.8	62.4	62.7	62.6	63.2	62.7	63.6	65.7	67.0	62.9
2015	63.7	63.1	63.5	63.9	64.8	65.5	65.4	66.0	65.4	66.6	68.3	68.9	65.4
Transportation and Utilities													
2005	36.2	36.3	36.6	37.0	37.1	37.2	37.4	37.9	38.5	38.9	39.7	39.9	37.7
2006	38.3	38.3	39.2	39.7	40.7	41.7	41.1	41.9	42.6	42.3	43.1	44.3	41.1
2007	42.6	42.3	42.4	42.8	43.3	44.1	43.0	43.6	44.1	45.5	45.6	46.6	43.8
2008	43.5	42.4	41.8	42.6	43.2	42.9	42.0	42.5	41.7	41.5	42.5	44.2	42.6
2009	40.4	39.9	39.8	39.2	39.4	39.6	38.9	38.9	38.9	38.9	39.8	40.9	39.6
2010	38.4	38.0	38.2	39.6	40.0	40.4	40.4	40.9	41.5	42.2	43.6	46.4	40.8
2011	42.0	41.9	42.1	42.2	42.2	42.8	42.2	42.3	42.4	42.0	43.4	44.1	42.5
2012	40.9	41.1	41.1	41.0	41.4	41.6	41.2	41.3	41.6	41.4	42.2	44.4	41.6
2013	41.2	41.1	41.4	41.2	41.4	41.7	41.5	42.2	42.7	42.5	43.6	45.7	42.2
2014	43.0	42.5	42.8	42.6	43.3	43.8	43.8	44.5	45.4	46.1	47.4	50.0	44.6
2015	46.6	46.2	46.3	46.2	46.4	46.7	46.4	47.3	47.7	47.9	49.0	51.9	47.4

Employment by Industry: Louisville/Jefferson County, KY-IN, 2005–2015—*Continued*

(Numbers in thousands, not seasonally adjusted)

Industry and year	January	February	March	April	May	June	July	August	September	October	November	December	Annual average
Information													
2005	9.6	9.6	9.6	9.7	9.8	9.9	10.0	10.0	9.9	9.8	9.9	10.0	9.8
2006	9.7	9.8	9.8	9.8	9.9	10.0	10.0	10.0	9.9	10.1	10.1	10.3	10.0
2007	10.3	10.3	10.3	10.3	10.4	10.4	10.5	10.4	10.3	10.2	10.2	10.2	10.3
2008	10.2	10.1	10.2	10.2	10.4	10.7	10.6	10.5	10.3	10.1	10.1	10.0	10.3
2009	9.9	9.8	9.7	9.6	9.6	9.6	9.7	9.6	9.5	9.4	9.5	9.5	9.6
2010	9.3	9.2	9.3	9.3	9.3	9.3	9.3	9.3	9.2	9.1	9.2	9.3	9.3
2011	9.2	9.1	9.1	9.2	9.2	9.1	9.2	9.1	9.1	9.1	9.3	9.3	9.2
2012	9.2	9.2	9.5	9.6	9.6	9.6	9.5	9.5	9.3	9.2	9.3	9.3	9.4
2013	9.4	9.4	9.4	9.4	9.5	9.5	9.5	9.6	9.4	9.3	9.3	9.3	9.4
2014	9.4	9.4	9.5	9.4	9.4	9.4	9.3	9.3	9.1	9.2	9.3	9.2	9.3
2015	9.1	9.1	9.0	9.0	9.1	9.1	9.2	9.2	9.0	9.0	9.1	9.1	9.1
Financial Activities													
2005	38.8	38.8	38.7	38.9	38.9	39.6	39.4	39.8	39.8	40.0	40.1	40.3	39.4
2006	40.5	40.8	41.1	41.2	41.5	41.9	41.6	41.7	41.9	41.8	42.2	42.8	41.6
2007	42.7	42.7	42.8	43.0	43.0	43.3	43.4	43.3	43.0	43.2	43.2	43.1	43.1
2008	42.9	43.1	43.0	43.0	43.2	43.0	43.2	43.3	43.1	42.8	42.9	42.8	43.0
2009	42.5	42.4	42.2	42.2	42.3	42.3	42.4	42.0	41.7	41.6	41.4	41.6	42.1
2010	41.1	40.9	40.8	40.4	40.4	40.5	40.4	40.1	39.7	39.9	40.1	40.3	40.4
2011	40.1	40.2	40.3	39.7	39.8	40.0	40.0	40.2	40.5	40.4	40.5	40.7	40.2
2012	40.4	40.3	40.5	40.2	40.6	41.1	41.4	41.5	41.6	41.7	41.9	42.3	41.1
2013	42.1	42.1	42.3	42.3	42.6	42.9	43.1	43.4	43.4	43.6	43.8	44.0	43.0
2014	43.9	43.8	43.9	44.0	44.3	44.6	44.8	44.9	45.1	45.5	45.7	45.9	44.7
2015	45.6	45.6	45.7	45.3	45.6	46.0	46.0	45.9	45.8	46.8	47.0	47.9	46.1
Professional and Business Services													
2005	64.2	64.8	65.6	66.6	67.0	67.8	67.3	68.1	69.1	69.8	70.8	70.2	67.6
2006	66.9	67.6	70.5	70.1	70.6	71.3	70.5	71.2	72.1	72.1	72.1	72.3	70.6
2007	69.4	70.1	71.5	71.5	73.4	73.7	72.9	73.2	72.9	74.2	74.8	74.2	72.7
2008	70.9	71.1	71.4	72.8	74.3	75.1	73.9	73.9	73.7	73.8	73.5	71.9	73.0
2009	67.4	68.1	68.1	68.4	68.3	68.2	68.9	69.0	69.3	70.6	71.4	70.5	69.0
2010	68.6	68.6	69.4	71.2	71.7	72.3	71.8	71.6	72.7	72.7	73.6	74.2	71.5
2011	69.9	70.8	71.5	72.0	72.4	72.8	72.5	73.4	73.5	75.3	75.3	75.4	72.9
2012	72.0	71.3	72.0	73.5	74.7	74.6	73.9	75.4	76.3	77.5	79.0	78.8	74.9
2013	74.4	73.7	74.9	76.9	77.0	77.4	76.7	79.3	78.8	80.6	81.4	80.9	77.7
2014	77.4	76.2	77.8	79.9	80.8	81.0	81.2	82.7	82.2	83.3	84.3	84.9	81.0
2015	81.7	80.9	81.7	83.7	85.1	84.9	84.3	84.7	85.4	86.6	89.0	91.1	84.9
Education and Health Services													
2005	74.6	76.0	75.4	75.4	75.7	75.7	75.7	75.7	75.8	76.0	75.6	75.6	75.6
2006	74.9	75.2	75.5	76.1	75.9	76.0	75.9	75.6	75.8	76.0	75.8	76.3	75.8
2007	75.7	76.1	76.4	76.7	77.3	77.6	78.2	77.8	77.8	78.6	78.4	78.6	77.4
2008	78.2	78.1	78.2	79.3	79.4	79.4	79.3	79.5	79.3	79.8	79.7	79.8	79.2
2009	79.6	79.4	80.0	80.4	80.6	80.8	80.4	81.4	81.7	82.2	82.0	82.3	80.9
2010	81.6	81.7	82.3	82.3	82.8	82.5	82.6	82.7	83.0	83.5	83.8	83.8	82.7
2011	83.2	83.2	83.5	82.9	83.0	83.0	83.1	83.2	83.6	83.4	83.4	82.6	83.2
2012	83.3	83.4	83.6	84.0	84.2	84.4	84.0	84.3	84.6	85.1	85.5	85.7	84.3
2013	84.5	84.7	85.0	85.2	84.7	84.3	84.3	84.3	84.6	85.3	85.5	85.2	84.8
2014	84.2	84.4	84.8	85.1	84.5	84.1	84.1	84.7	85.6	86.1	85.2	86.0	84.9
2015	85.1	85.5	86.2	86.5	86.4	85.6	85.6	87.3	88.4	88.8	89.7	88.8	87.0
Leisure and Hospitality													
2005	54.0	54.8	56.1	59.0	60.5	61.9	61.2	60.8	60.1	58.9	58.0	56.7	58.5
2006	55.1	56.1	57.4	59.8	62.4	62.3	61.5	61.4	60.3	59.6	59.4	58.6	59.5
2007	56.8	57.1	58.7	60.5	62.8	63.1	62.6	62.4	60.8	60.4	59.9	58.8	60.3
2008	56.9	57.7	58.9	61.5	63.9	63.5	63.4	63.0	61.5	60.5	59.4	58.1	60.7
2009	55.8	56.3	58.3	60.6	62.8	62.7	62.3	60.9	59.7	58.7	58.0	56.5	59.4
2010	54.7	54.9	56.5	59.1	61.2	61.6	60.7	60.3	59.4	59.9	59.7	58.3	58.9
2011	55.8	56.5	58.2	62.1	63.0	63.3	61.3	61.3	60.0	59.3	59.6	58.0	59.9
2012	56.6	57.4	59.2	61.4	64.9	64.7	63.4	63.9	62.7	61.8	62.4	60.9	61.6
2013	59.8	60.3	61.5	64.4	66.6	66.3	65.5	65.6	64.5	63.2	63.7	62.3	63.6
2014	60.4	61.1	62.6	66.6	67.5	68.8	68.2	67.7	66.1	64.3	64.5	63.1	65.1
2015	62.0	62.6	63.8	67.7	69.5	70.7	69.7	68.7	67.3	65.8	66.4	64.3	66.5

Employment by Industry: Louisville/Jefferson County, KY-IN, 2005–2015—*Continued*

(Numbers in thousands, not seasonally adjusted)

Industry and year	January	February	March	April	May	June	July	August	September	October	November	December	Annual average
Other Services													
2005	28.5	28.7	28.9	28.5	28.9	29.1	28.6	28.6	28.5	28.6	28.6	28.7	28.7
2006	28.2	28.4	28.7	28.4	28.6	29.0	28.6	28.3	28.1	28.1	28.0	28.3	28.4
2007	28.0	28.0	28.2	28.4	28.7	29.0	28.4	28.4	28.2	28.1	28.0	28.3	28.3
2008	27.6	27.7	27.8	28.0	28.4	28.5	27.9	27.9	27.3	27.6	27.4	27.2	27.8
2009	26.6	26.6	26.6	26.5	26.5	26.7	26.4	26.3	25.9	25.4	25.4	25.4	26.2
2010	25.1	25.1	25.5	25.6	25.7	26.1	25.9	25.8	25.5	25.7	25.6	25.8	25.6
2011	25.4	25.6	25.8	25.8	25.8	26.1	26.2	25.9	25.7	25.5	25.5	25.7	25.8
2012	25.5	25.6	25.8	25.8	25.7	26.1	25.9	25.5	25.3	25.4	25.4	25.5	25.6
2013	25.6	25.7	25.8	25.9	25.9	26.0	25.8	25.8	25.5	25.2	25.1	25.1	25.6
2014	24.6	24.6	24.8	25.0	25.0	25.1	25.1	25.0	24.9	24.6	25.0	24.6	24.9
2015	24.4	24.6	24.8	24.7	25.0	25.4	25.1	25.1	24.8	24.8	25.1	25.0	24.9
Government													
2005	72.6	73.4	73.8	74.0	74.5	74.1	70.1	72.0	74.6	74.7	74.8	74.6	73.6
2006	73.7	74.8	74.9	75.3	75.7	75.2	71.5	74.0	77.0	75.9	76.1	75.7	75.0
2007	74.3	75.1	75.5	76.9	77.2	76.8	72.5	74.8	76.5	75.9	76.2	76.3	75.7
2008	76.0	76.9	77.2	77.1	77.6	77.1	72.6	74.7	76.7	77.2	77.3	76.9	76.4
2009	75.9	76.0	76.5	77.3	77.9	77.0	73.8	76.1	78.7	79.5	79.1	78.0	77.2
2010	77.3	77.5	79.3	80.4	82.1	80.3	75.6	76.4	77.7	78.2	78.0	77.3	78.3
2011	76.8	77.6	77.9	78.2	78.5	77.5	74.0	76.5	79.0	79.1	79.5	79.1	77.8
2012	78.5	78.9	79.5	79.5	79.6	78.7	74.6	77.0	79.2	79.6	79.7	79.4	78.7
2013	78.8	79.8	80.3	80.7	80.8	80.0	76.6	79.7	80.8	80.4	80.9	80.6	80.0
2014	79.3	79.5	80.1	80.1	80.0	79.4	76.7	79.4	80.9	80.4	80.4	79.8	79.7
2015	79.1	79.1	79.4	79.2	79.4	78.1	74.3	75.5	77.1	76.9	77.0	76.7	77.7

Employment by Industry: Raleigh, NC, 2005–2015

(Numbers in thousands, not seasonally adjusted)

Industry and year	January	February	March	April	May	June	July	August	September	October	November	December	Annual average
Total Nonfarm													
2005	451.5	453.4	456.9	461.9	465.6	467.0	466.9	472.6	475.4	474.6	479.3	479.8	467.1
2006	472.3	474.2	478.1	485.9	490.3	493.2	490.5	496.8	498.7	502.5	508.0	509.5	491.7
2007	501.5	504.9	509.5	510.7	517.2	520.1	514.4	520.7	520.7	525.1	528.2	528.5	516.8
2008	518.3	520.4	521.6	521.6	525.8	523.6	520.3	524.1	523.9	524.9	522.9	520.1	522.3
2009	503.8	501.9	501.0	501.4	504.0	500.7	496.7	497.9	497.4	498.0	499.8	499.3	500.2
2010	487.7	487.9	492.2	497.6	502.3	502.2	500.7	503.2	502.8	506.8	509.1	508.2	500.1
2011	499.0	502.6	505.6	508.3	509.8	509.2	507.6	511.4	512.2	515.2	517.7	516.8	509.6
2012	512.2	514.6	518.4	522.7	525.9	526.2	524.8	529.8	528.8	531.9	535.5	534.7	525.5
2013	525.5	530.3	533.6	535.4	537.9	537.6	536.5	545.1	547.7	550.0	553.9	553.8	540.6
2014	544.2	544.1	550.1	555.1	559.5	562.2	557.5	563.8	564.7	571.6	574.9	575.0	560.2
2015	563.8	567.2	570.2	576.5	580.1	583.2	580.3	586.9	587.8	590.1	595.9	598.0	581.7
Total Private													
2005	368.7	369.9	372.9	377.9	381.4	384.1	386.6	387.9	389.3	390.6	393.6	396.4	383.3
2006	387.7	388.7	392.0	398.5	402.3	406.0	406.7	408.7	409.5	412.5	417.4	419.4	404.1
2007	411.7	414.2	418.2	419.1	424.9	429.3	427.0	430.0	428.0	432.1	434.8	435.4	425.4
2008	425.7	427.0	427.7	427.4	431.3	430.8	429.8	431.2	428.4	427.3	426.2	423.8	428.1
2009	410.3	408.2	406.6	405.3	407.9	406.8	406.8	406.7	404.1	403.8	405.6	405.7	406.5
2010	395.6	395.0	398.7	402.6	405.4	407.6	410.3	411.0	408.8	412.3	415.1	414.5	406.4
2011	406.3	409.1	411.8	414.9	416.5	419.1	421.3	422.0	420.6	422.3	425.0	426.1	417.9
2012	420.9	422.1	425.9	430.6	434.4	436.4	438.8	440.0	437.0	439.0	442.5	443.4	434.3
2013	434.0	437.4	440.4	442.7	446.5	449.5	450.8	454.9	454.3	455.0	458.7	460.3	448.7
2014	451.1	450.5	456.0	460.2	465.5	469.6	469.9	472.6	470.0	474.5	477.5	479.5	466.4
2015	469.1	471.2	474.3	479.6	485.2	489.4	491.3	494.2	491.4	492.5	497.9	501.8	486.5
Goods Producing													
2005	65.7	66.1	66.7	68.0	68.8	69.9	70.4	70.5	70.8	70.7	70.9	70.9	69.1
2006	70.0	70.2	71.4	72.2	73.3	74.3	74.8	75.1	75.0	75.1	75.3	75.5	73.5
2007	74.3	74.5	75.3	75.2	75.8	76.4	76.6	77.2	76.6	76.0	75.8	75.3	75.8
2008	73.6	73.5	73.6	72.6	72.8	72.7	72.6	72.0	71.4	69.9	68.7	67.1	71.7
2009	64.1	63.0	62.4	61.1	60.7	60.7	60.5	60.2	59.6	59.1	58.7	58.6	60.7
2010	56.8	56.5	57.1	57.3	57.9	58.3	59.1	59.2	59.0	59.0	58.9	58.4	58.1
2011	57.4	58.0	58.6	58.6	58.8	59.3	59.8	59.6	59.3	59.0	59.0	59.0	58.9
2012	58.7	59.0	59.5	59.7	60.2	60.8	61.4	61.4	61.2	61.0	61.0	61.0	60.4
2013	59.6	60.0	60.3	60.4	60.8	61.4	61.7	62.1	62.0	62.4	62.5	62.7	61.3
2014	61.8	61.9	62.9	62.7	63.6	64.5	65.3	65.6	65.5	65.5	65.5	65.4	64.2
2015	65.1	65.5	65.8	66.5	67.3	68.1	68.5	68.4	68.0	67.4	67.5	68.2	67.2
Service-Providing													
2005	385.8	387.3	390.2	393.9	396.8	397.1	396.5	402.1	404.6	403.9	408.4	408.9	398.0
2006	402.3	404.0	406.7	413.7	417.0	418.9	415.7	421.7	423.7	427.4	432.7	434.0	418.2
2007	427.2	430.4	434.2	435.5	441.4	443.7	437.8	443.5	444.1	449.1	452.4	453.2	441.0
2008	444.7	446.9	448.0	449.0	453.0	450.9	447.7	452.1	452.5	455.0	454.2	453.0	450.6
2009	439.7	438.9	438.6	440.3	443.3	440.0	436.2	437.7	437.8	438.9	441.1	440.7	439.4
2010	430.9	431.4	435.1	440.3	444.4	443.9	441.6	444.0	443.8	447.8	450.2	449.8	441.9
2011	441.6	444.6	447.0	449.7	451.0	449.9	447.8	451.8	452.9	456.2	458.7	457.8	450.8
2012	453.5	455.6	458.9	463.0	465.7	465.4	463.4	468.4	467.6	470.9	474.5	473.7	465.1
2013	465.9	470.3	473.3	475.0	477.1	476.2	474.8	483.0	485.7	487.6	491.4	491.1	479.3
2014	482.4	482.2	487.2	492.4	495.9	497.7	492.2	498.2	499.2	506.1	509.4	509.6	496.0
2015	498.7	501.7	504.4	510.0	512.8	515.1	511.8	518.5	519.8	522.7	528.4	529.8	514.5
Mining, Logging, and Construction													
2005	32.3	32.5	33.0	33.8	34.6	35.3	35.7	35.8	36.0	36.1	36.1	35.9	34.8
2006	35.2	35.4	36.1	37.2	38.0	38.8	39.5	39.7	39.6	39.5	39.6	39.7	38.2
2007	39.2	39.4	40.1	40.3	40.8	41.3	41.5	41.8	41.5	41.1	40.9	40.4	40.7
2008	39.2	39.2	39.3	38.3	38.6	38.5	38.4	38.0	37.6	36.4	35.3	34.2	37.8
2009	31.7	31.1	30.7	29.9	30.0	30.1	30.0	29.8	29.4	28.8	28.5	28.3	29.9
2010	27.0	26.8	27.3	27.7	28.1	28.4	29.0	29.1	28.9	28.9	28.6	28.1	28.2
2011	27.2	27.8	28.2	28.0	28.3	28.8	29.3	29.1	28.9	28.7	28.6	28.6	28.5
2012	28.4	28.6	29.1	29.2	29.6	30.0	30.5	30.5	30.4	30.3	30.2	30.2	29.8
2013	29.0	29.3	29.6	29.6	30.1	30.4	30.4	30.6	30.5	30.9	30.9	30.8	30.2
2014	30.1	30.0	30.9	30.9	31.5	31.9	32.5	32.6	32.4	32.3	32.0	31.8	31.6
2015	31.6	31.8	32.1	32.7	33.4	33.8	34.4	34.2	33.9	33.6	33.7	34.2	33.3

Employment by Industry: Raleigh, NC, 2005–2015—*Continued*

(Numbers in thousands, not seasonally adjusted)

Industry and year	January	February	March	April	May	June	July	August	September	October	November	December	Annual average
Manufacturing													
2005	33.4	33.6	33.7	34.2	34.2	34.6	34.7	34.7	34.8	34.6	34.8	35.0	34.4
2006	34.8	34.8	35.3	35.0	35.3	35.5	35.3	35.4	35.4	35.6	35.7	35.8	35.3
2007	35.1	35.1	35.2	34.9	35.0	35.1	35.1	35.4	35.1	34.9	34.9	34.9	35.1
2008	34.4	34.3	34.3	34.3	34.2	34.2	34.2	34.0	33.8	33.5	33.4	32.9	34.0
2009	32.4	31.9	31.7	31.2	30.7	30.6	30.5	30.4	30.2	30.3	30.2	30.3	30.9
2010	29.8	29.7	29.8	29.6	29.8	29.9	30.1	30.1	30.1	30.1	30.3	30.3	30.0
2011	30.2	30.2	30.4	30.6	30.5	30.5	30.5	30.5	30.4	30.3	30.4	30.4	30.4
2012	30.3	30.4	30.4	30.5	30.6	30.8	30.9	30.9	30.8	30.7	30.8	30.8	30.7
2013	30.6	30.7	30.7	30.8	30.7	31.0	31.3	31.5	31.5	31.5	31.6	31.9	31.2
2014	31.7	31.9	32.0	31.8	32.1	32.6	32.8	33.0	33.1	33.2	33.5	33.6	32.6
2015	33.5	33.7	33.7	33.8	33.9	34.3	34.1	34.2	34.1	33.8	33.8	34.0	33.9
Trade, Transportation, and Utilities													
2005	82.5	81.8	82.3	82.9	83.5	83.6	84.2	84.3	84.4	85.7	87.3	88.9	84.3
2006	85.0	84.2	84.4	85.1	85.5	85.9	87.0	87.9	87.8	89.0	92.0	93.3	87.3
2007	90.0	89.2	90.2	90.2	91.2	91.4	91.3	91.2	91.1	92.1	95.0	96.3	91.6
2008	91.9	91.5	91.9	91.8	91.8	92.0	91.6	91.7	90.9	91.5	92.3	92.8	91.8
2009	88.1	87.1	87.1	86.5	87.0	86.9	87.0	86.8	86.4	87.1	88.7	89.5	87.4
2010	86.0	85.3	85.5	86.0	86.7	86.9	87.2	87.3	86.2	87.6	89.7	91.1	87.1
2011	87.5	87.3	87.8	88.6	88.9	89.2	89.5	89.7	89.6	90.0	92.5	93.5	89.5
2012	91.4	90.6	91.3	91.0	92.0	92.2	92.4	92.1	92.0	92.6	95.1	95.7	92.4
2013	91.9	91.3	92.0	91.7	92.6	93.2	93.5	94.1	94.0	95.3	98.0	99.3	93.9
2014	96.1	95.6	96.5	97.2	98.0	98.4	98.5	99.2	98.9	100.3	103.4	105.1	98.9
2015	100.7	100.6	101.3	102.4	103.0	103.6	103.4	103.9	103.6	103.9	106.2	107.1	103.3
Wholesale Trade													
2005	19.8	19.8	19.8	19.9	20.1	20.2	20.1	20.3	20.4	20.6	20.5	20.7	20.2
2006	20.4	20.4	20.4	20.5	20.6	20.9	21.1	21.3	21.5	21.4	21.6	21.7	21.0
2007	21.9	22.0	22.2	22.1	22.2	22.2	22.3	22.2	22.2	22.1	22.2	22.2	22.2
2008	22.0	22.2	22.2	22.1	22.2	22.3	22.3	22.4	22.2	22.3	22.0	21.9	22.2
2009	21.4	21.4	21.2	21.0	20.9	20.8	20.7	20.7	20.5	20.5	20.4	20.4	20.8
2010	20.0	20.0	19.9	20.1	20.2	20.2	20.4	20.5	20.3	20.5	20.5	20.5	20.3
2011	20.7	20.7	20.7	21.1	21.3	21.4	21.8	21.9	22.1	21.8	22.1	22.1	21.5
2012	22.5	22.7	22.8	22.7	22.9	22.9	23.3	23.3	23.2	23.0	22.9	22.8	22.9
2013	22.5	22.5	22.5	22.1	22.3	22.5	22.7	22.8	22.7	22.7	22.8	22.8	22.6
2014	22.6	22.7	22.8	22.9	23.1	23.1	23.3	23.7	23.6	23.8	24.0	24.1	23.3
2015	23.9	24.0	24.1	24.2	24.2	24.3	24.2	24.3	24.2	24.1	23.6	23.7	24.1
Retail Trade													
2005	53.3	52.7	53.0	53.5	53.9	53.8	54.3	54.2	54.2	54.8	56.4	57.8	54.3
2006	54.4	53.6	53.7	54.2	54.5	54.5	55.1	55.7	55.4	56.8	59.3	60.4	55.6
2007	57.1	56.3	57.0	57.0	57.8	58.0	57.9	57.9	57.8	59.1	61.9	62.8	58.4
2008	59.3	58.8	59.1	58.9	58.8	58.9	58.6	58.5	58.0	58.5	59.7	59.9	58.9
2009	56.2	55.4	55.7	55.4	56.1	56.2	56.4	56.3	56.0	56.7	58.3	59.0	56.5
2010	56.2	55.5	55.8	55.9	56.5	56.6	56.7	56.7	56.0	57.1	59.2	60.4	56.9
2011	57.2	57.0	57.4	57.5	57.6	57.7	57.6	57.7	57.3	58.2	60.4	61.1	58.1
2012	58.8	57.9	58.4	58.3	58.9	59.0	58.9	58.7	58.7	59.5	62.0	62.4	59.3
2013	59.2	58.8	59.4	59.5	60.1	60.4	60.5	60.9	60.8	61.9	64.3	65.2	60.9
2014	61.9	61.5	62.1	62.8	63.2	63.6	63.6	63.8	63.5	64.8	67.4	68.4	63.9
2015	65.0	64.7	65.3	66.2	66.7	67.1	67.1	67.3	67.1	67.5	70.2	70.8	67.1
Transportation and Utilities													
2005	9.4	9.3	9.5	9.5	9.5	9.6	9.8	9.8	9.8	10.3	10.4	10.4	9.8
2006	10.2	10.2	10.3	10.4	10.4	10.5	10.8	10.9	10.9	10.8	11.1	11.2	10.6
2007	11.0	10.9	11.0	11.1	11.2	11.2	11.1	11.1	11.1	10.9	10.9	11.3	11.1
2008	10.6	10.5	10.6	10.8	10.8	10.8	10.7	10.8	10.7	10.7	10.6	11.0	10.7
2009	10.5	10.3	10.2	10.1	10.0	9.9	9.9	9.8	9.9	9.9	10.0	10.1	10.1
2010	9.8	9.8	9.8	10.0	10.0	10.1	10.1	10.1	9.9	10.0	10.0	10.2	10.0
2011	9.6	9.6	9.7	10.0	10.0	10.1	10.1	10.1	10.2	10.0	10.0	10.3	10.0
2012	10.1	10.0	10.1	10.0	10.2	10.3	10.2	10.1	10.1	10.1	10.2	10.5	10.2
2013	10.2	10.0	10.1	10.1	10.2	10.3	10.3	10.4	10.5	10.7	10.9	11.3	10.4
2014	11.6	11.4	11.6	11.5	11.7	11.7	11.6	11.7	11.8	11.7	12.0	12.6	11.7
2015	11.8	11.9	11.9	12.0	12.1	12.2	12.1	12.3	12.3	12.3	12.4	12.6	12.2

Employment by Industry: Raleigh, NC, 2005–2015—*Continued*

(Numbers in thousands, not seasonally adjusted)

Industry and year	January	February	March	April	May	June	July	August	September	October	November	December	Annual average
Information													
2005	16.7	16.7	16.9	17.1	17.2	17.3	17.3	17.4	17.2	17.0	17.1	17.2	17.1
2006	17.0	16.9	16.6	16.8	16.8	16.8	16.7	16.6	16.5	16.4	16.4	16.4	16.7
2007	16.3	16.6	16.5	16.4	16.5	16.8	16.9	16.9	16.7	16.9	16.8	16.8	16.7
2008	16.7	16.8	16.7	17.0	17.1	17.2	17.1	17.2	17.1	17.2	17.2	17.3	17.1
2009	17.1	17.0	16.9	17.0	16.8	16.9	16.9	16.8	16.7	16.8	16.8	16.8	16.9
2010	16.5	16.5	16.6	16.6	16.5	16.7	16.8	16.8	16.7	16.7	16.9	16.9	16.7
2011	16.9	17.0	17.0	17.1	17.1	17.4	17.5	17.7	17.5	17.6	17.8	17.8	17.4
2012	17.7	17.7	17.7	17.5	17.5	17.7	17.7	17.7	17.5	17.6	17.6	17.7	17.6
2013	17.7	17.8	17.8	17.8	17.9	18.0	18.2	18.2	18.0	17.9	18.1	18.2	18.0
2014	18.2	18.2	18.3	18.3	18.5	18.8	19.0	19.3	19.1	19.1	19.1	19.3	18.8
2015	19.2	19.2	19.3	19.3	19.3	19.6	19.8	19.9	19.8	19.9	20.0	20.1	19.6
Financial Activities													
2005	23.4	23.4	23.4	23.4	23.5	23.6	23.8	24.0	24.1	24.4	24.5	24.8	23.9
2006	24.4	24.4	24.6	24.9	25.0	25.2	25.3	25.4	25.4	25.6	25.8	25.9	25.2
2007	25.6	25.7	25.8	26.3	26.6	26.9	27.1	27.3	27.1	27.5	27.4	27.7	26.8
2008	26.8	27.0	27.0	27.1	27.2	27.4	27.4	27.5	27.4	27.5	27.3	27.3	27.2
2009	26.9	26.9	26.7	26.8	26.7	26.8	26.9	26.8	26.4	26.5	26.6	26.8	26.7
2010	26.4	26.4	26.4	26.3	26.4	26.4	26.6	26.6	26.8	26.7	26.9	27.0	26.6
2011	26.4	26.4	26.4	26.3	26.3	26.3	26.3	26.4	26.2	26.2	26.1	26.2	26.3
2012	25.8	26.1	26.2	26.4	26.4	26.5	26.4	26.3	26.2	26.7	26.6	26.7	26.4
2013	26.5	26.4	26.6	26.9	27.0	27.1	27.1	27.2	27.1	27.4	27.5	27.7	27.0
2014	27.2	27.3	27.3	27.5	27.7	27.9	27.9	28.0	27.9	28.2	28.2	28.5	27.8
2015	28.2	28.5	28.7	29.2	29.8	30.1	30.0	30.1	30.0	29.7	30.1	29.5	29.5
Professional and Business Services													
2005	76.0	76.5	77.0	79.1	78.6	79.1	80.8	81.1	81.5	81.2	81.5	81.8	79.5
2006	80.9	81.2	82.0	83.9	83.9	84.9	85.7	86.1	87.3	88.5	88.8	88.8	85.2
2007	87.3	88.3	89.0	89.4	89.7	91.6	89.2	89.7	89.5	92.2	90.8	90.0	89.7
2008	88.5	88.5	88.6	89.1	89.2	88.9	88.1	89.1	88.1	88.3	87.3	86.0	88.3
2009	84.1	83.3	81.9	81.8	81.8	81.7	81.7	81.8	82.1	82.8	83.5	83.4	82.5
2010	81.8	81.9	82.7	84.3	84.7	85.7	86.2	86.3	86.4	89.2	89.3	89.3	85.7
2011	87.7	88.5	88.4	89.7	90.0	91.0	91.6	91.4	92.1	92.5	92.7	92.9	90.7
2012	91.9	92.0	92.6	95.5	95.7	96.8	98.3	98.6	97.8	98.5	99.3	99.2	96.4
2013	98.0	100.5	100.9	101.0	102.0	102.0	103.0	105.2	105.3	104.8	105.2	104.5	102.7
2014	102.7	102.2	103.5	105.0	106.1	107.2	107.3	108.1	107.3	108.9	108.6	108.5	106.3
2015	105.0	105.5	106.0	107.0	108.2	109.3	110.3	111.8	111.4	111.9	113.0	115.0	109.5
Education and Health Services													
2005	49.4	49.9	50.2	50.1	50.3	49.9	50.0	50.3	51.4	52.0	52.4	52.3	50.7
2006	51.6	52.2	52.6	53.4	53.9	53.5	53.0	53.3	54.0	54.8	55.6	55.7	53.6
2007	54.9	55.8	56.2	56.6	57.0	56.5	56.1	56.9	57.5	58.5	58.7	58.8	57.0
2008	58.1	58.9	58.9	58.9	59.3	58.4	57.9	58.4	59.1	59.9	60.5	60.2	59.0
2009	59.2	59.8	59.9	60.2	60.8	59.7	59.2	60.0	60.0	60.3	60.4	60.3	60.0
2010	59.6	60.1	60.5	61.3	61.4	60.3	60.3	60.7	60.6	61.0	61.2	60.7	60.6
2011	60.7	61.5	61.6	61.1	61.3	60.6	60.5	60.8	61.0	62.2	62.3	62.1	61.3
2012	62.1	62.8	63.4	63.2	63.8	62.9	62.7	63.3	63.7	64.5	64.7	64.8	63.5
2013	63.5	64.2	64.4	64.6	64.9	64.1	64.2	65.1	65.6	65.7	65.9	65.9	64.8
2014	64.9	65.5	66.0	66.1	66.7	65.8	66.0	66.8	66.9	67.9	68.3	68.2	66.6
2015	67.5	68.1	68.3	68.8	69.3	68.6	69.0	70.0	70.0	70.4	71.4	71.2	69.4
Leisure and Hospitality													
2005	38.6	39.0	40.0	40.5	42.0	43.0	42.6	42.7	42.8	42.1	42.3	42.8	41.5
2006	41.3	41.8	42.6	44.0	45.4	46.2	45.6	45.9	45.9	45.1	45.2	45.3	44.5
2007	44.7	45.2	45.8	45.5	48.1	49.1	48.8	49.7	49.0	47.5	48.6	48.8	47.6
2008	47.6	48.0	48.5	48.5	50.9	50.9	51.3	51.5	50.8	49.4	49.5	50.1	49.8
2009	48.5	48.6	49.1	49.3	51.4	51.5	51.6	51.5	50.6	49.4	49.4	49.2	50.0
2010	47.4	47.3	48.6	49.7	50.6	51.9	52.7	52.9	52.4	50.9	51.4	50.7	50.5
2011	49.5	50.2	51.5	53.1	53.6	54.3	55.1	55.4	54.2	53.8	53.7	53.9	53.2
2012	52.5	53.0	54.2	55.9	56.9	57.5	57.7	58.1	56.1	55.8	55.9	56.5	55.8
2013	55.1	55.2	56.1	57.8	58.5	60.5	60.4	60.5	59.9	59.1	59.2	59.8	58.5
2014	58.0	57.6	58.9	60.7	61.7	63.5	62.5	62.3	61.4	61.5	61.3	61.8	60.9
2015	61.0	61.3	62.2	63.5	65.1	66.8	66.8	66.8	65.5	65.7	65.9	66.7	64.8

Employment by Industry: Raleigh, NC, 2005–2015—*Continued*

(Numbers in thousands, not seasonally adjusted)

Industry and year	January	February	March	April	May	June	July	August	September	October	November	December	Annual average
Other Services													
2005	16.4	16.5	16.4	16.8	17.5	17.7	17.5	17.6	17.1	17.5	17.6	17.7	17.2
2006	17.5	17.8	17.8	18.2	18.5	19.2	18.6	18.4	17.6	18.0	18.3	18.5	18.2
2007	18.6	18.9	19.4	19.5	20.0	20.6	21.0	21.1	20.5	21.4	21.7	21.7	20.4
2008	22.5	22.8	22.5	22.4	23.0	23.3	23.8	23.8	23.6	23.6	23.4	23.0	23.1
2009	22.3	22.5	22.6	22.6	22.7	22.6	23.0	22.8	22.3	21.8	21.5	21.1	22.3
2010	21.1	21.0	21.3	21.1	21.2	21.4	21.4	21.2	20.7	21.2	20.8	20.4	21.1
2011	20.2	20.2	20.5	20.4	20.5	21.0	21.0	21.0	20.7	21.0	20.9	20.7	20.7
2012	20.8	20.9	21.0	21.4	21.9	22.0	22.2	22.5	22.5	22.3	22.3	21.8	21.8
2013	21.7	22.0	22.3	22.5	22.8	23.2	22.7	22.5	22.4	22.4	22.3	22.2	22.4
2014	22.2	22.2	22.6	22.7	23.2	23.5	23.4	23.3	23.0	23.1	23.1	22.7	22.9
2015	22.4	22.5	22.7	22.9	23.2	23.3	23.5	23.3	23.1	23.6	23.8	24.0	23.2
Government													
2005	82.8	83.5	84.0	84.0	84.2	82.9	80.3	84.7	86.1	84.0	85.7	83.4	83.8
2006	84.6	85.5	86.1	87.4	88.0	87.2	83.8	88.1	89.2	90.0	90.6	90.1	87.6
2007	89.8	90.7	91.3	91.6	92.3	90.8	87.4	90.7	92.7	93.0	93.4	93.1	91.4
2008	92.6	93.4	93.9	94.2	94.5	92.8	90.5	92.9	95.5	97.6	96.7	96.3	94.2
2009	93.5	93.7	94.4	96.1	96.1	93.9	89.9	91.2	93.3	94.2	94.2	93.6	93.7
2010	92.1	92.9	93.5	95.0	96.9	94.6	90.4	92.2	94.0	94.5	94.0	93.7	93.7
2011	92.7	93.5	93.8	93.4	93.3	90.1	86.3	89.4	91.6	92.9	92.7	90.7	91.7
2012	91.3	92.5	92.5	92.1	91.5	89.8	86.0	89.8	91.8	92.9	93.0	91.3	91.2
2013	91.5	92.9	93.2	92.7	91.4	88.1	85.7	90.2	93.4	95.0	95.2	93.5	91.9
2014	93.1	93.6	94.1	94.9	94.0	92.6	87.6	91.2	94.7	97.1	97.4	95.5	93.8
2015	94.7	96.0	95.9	96.9	94.9	93.8	89.0	92.7	96.4	97.6	98.0	96.2	95.2

Employment by Industry: Richmond, VA, 2005–2015

(Numbers in thousands, not seasonally adjusted)

Industry and year	January	February	March	April	May	June	July	August	September	October	November	December	Annual average
Total Nonfarm													
2005	593.7	596.4	600.3	608.2	610.7	614.2	605.0	601.4	608.0	609.3	613.0	613.2	606.1
2006	602.7	602.9	610.2	611.9	617.6	619.6	616.5	614.8	613.7	621.4	625.3	626.5	615.3
2007	614.2	617.5	619.2	620.3	625.6	631.6	622.4	622.6	622.9	624.4	625.5	626.8	622.8
2008	615.9	616.9	619.3	622.8	622.5	626.0	618.4	617.5	618.5	622.3	620.9	618.5	620.0
2009	603.0	598.5	598.7	598.9	600.1	601.4	588.8	586.3	589.5	592.9	594.0	592.9	595.4
2010	581.8	579.0	585.4	593.5	599.2	600.7	593.3	590.7	591.1	595.5	596.5	596.5	591.9
2011	587.2	589.3	593.8	600.6	601.0	602.8	601.7	599.1	601.6	607.9	611.5	610.0	600.5
2012	598.3	600.4	605.4	611.2	613.6	617.9	611.5	614.4	615.3	619.9	622.9	624.6	613.0
2013	609.5	612.3	616.6	621.5	622.2	625.2	622.8	623.6	623.7	626.0	635.1	632.7	622.6
2014	620.9	618.9	624.4	631.8	636.4	638.5	634.0	635.2	634.1	637.7	644.0	644.4	633.4
2015	633.8	634.1	636.7	643.9	648.6	651.7	652.2	652.9	655.1	666.9	671.3	670.5	651.5
Total Private													
2005	482.1	482.9	486.3	493.2	496.6	500.5	496.9	496.2	497.9	499.5	501.9	502.0	494.7
2006	491.0	490.3	497.4	499.7	505.2	507.5	508.6	507.4	504.6	509.6	512.2	513.2	503.9
2007	501.1	503.2	505.9	507.1	512.9	519.7	515.4	516.7	516.5	515.6	516.3	518.4	512.4
2008	508.0	508.0	510.5	511.8	512.5	515.7	513.5	513.3	510.6	511.1	508.8	508.1	511.0
2009	491.9	486.9	486.7	486.3	488.4	489.7	484.2	481.5	481.2	481.4	481.4	481.6	485.1
2010	470.5	467.2	473.3	480.0	485.0	487.4	485.8	483.9	482.4	484.7	484.7	485.3	480.9
2011	475.8	477.1	481.4	488.0	489.8	492.1	494.6	493.1	492.3	496.2	499.1	498.1	489.8
2012	486.7	487.6	492.3	499.3	502.8	507.3	505.9	508.7	507.3	510.0	511.5	513.4	502.7
2013	499.3	501.4	505.7	509.7	512.2	515.0	516.9	518.4	515.7	516.3	524.7	522.3	513.1
2014	510.8	508.6	513.6	521.1	526.4	528.5	527.5	528.3	524.8	527.2	532.8	533.2	523.6
2015	523.3	523.2	526.2	533.4	539.1	542.1	545.9	547.0	546.7	556.6	560.4	559.7	542.0
Goods Producing													
2005	86.1	85.4	85.3	86.0	86.2	86.9	87.7	87.7	87.2	86.8	87.1	87.0	86.6
2006	85.2	85.6	86.2	86.0	86.5	87.2	86.9	86.9	86.1	85.7	85.2	85.4	86.1
2007	84.3	83.9	84.5	85.3	86.1	87.2	86.7	87.0	86.6	85.8	85.1	85.0	85.6
2008	82.5	82.1	81.8	81.7	81.2	80.9	80.5	80.3	79.2	78.8	76.7	75.5	80.1
2009	71.9	69.0	68.8	68.3	67.5	67.6	67.0	66.5	66.2	65.9	65.5	65.0	67.4
2010	62.8	61.7	62.7	64.1	64.3	64.6	65.2	64.5	64.2	64.5	64.2	63.6	63.9
2011	61.3	61.5	62.0	62.4	62.6	62.6	63.0	62.8	62.6	63.2	63.1	63.0	62.5
2012	61.1	60.6	61.6	62.7	63.2	63.7	63.7	64.2	63.9	63.7	63.6	63.5	63.0
2013	61.9	62.5	63.3	64.0	64.3	65.1	65.2	65.2	64.7	64.2	64.1	63.6	64.0
2014	62.5	62.3	63.1	64.1	64.9	65.3	65.9	66.1	65.8	65.7	65.6	65.6	64.7
2015	64.2	64.3	65.1	66.7	67.3	67.6	68.2	68.4	68.2	68.6	68.2	67.8	67.1
Service-Providing													
2005	507.6	511.0	515.0	522.2	524.5	527.3	517.3	513.7	520.8	522.5	525.9	526.2	519.5
2006	517.5	517.3	524.0	525.9	531.1	532.4	529.6	527.9	527.6	535.7	540.1	541.1	529.2
2007	529.9	533.6	534.7	535.0	539.5	544.4	535.7	535.6	536.3	538.6	540.4	541.8	537.1
2008	533.4	534.8	537.5	541.1	541.3	545.1	537.9	537.2	539.3	543.5	544.2	543.0	539.9
2009	531.1	529.5	529.9	530.6	532.6	533.8	521.8	519.8	523.3	527.0	528.5	527.9	528.0
2010	519.0	517.3	522.7	529.4	534.9	536.1	528.1	526.2	526.9	531.0	532.3	532.9	528.1
2011	525.9	527.8	531.8	538.2	538.4	540.2	538.7	536.3	539.0	544.7	548.4	547.0	538.0
2012	537.2	539.8	543.8	548.5	550.4	554.2	547.8	550.2	551.4	556.2	559.3	561.1	550.0
2013	547.6	549.8	553.3	557.5	557.9	560.1	557.6	558.4	559.0	561.8	571.0	569.1	558.6
2014	558.4	556.6	561.3	567.7	571.5	573.2	568.1	569.1	568.3	572.0	578.4	578.8	568.6
2015	569.6	569.8	571.6	577.2	581.3	584.1	584.0	584.5	586.9	598.3	603.1	602.7	584.4
Mining, Logging, and Construction													
2005	41.7	41.5	41.8	42.5	42.8	43.4	44.6	44.4	43.8	43.6	43.7	43.4	43.1
2006	42.3	42.8	43.6	43.4	44.2	44.9	45.1	45.0	44.5	44.5	44.2	44.3	44.1
2007	43.4	43.2	43.7	44.6	45.4	46.2	46.1	46.4	46.3	45.5	44.8	44.5	45.0
2008	42.4	42.1	42.2	42.2	41.9	41.9	41.9	42.0	41.0	40.8	39.4	38.6	41.4
2009	36.3	35.2	35.1	35.2	35.0	34.9	34.7	34.4	33.9	33.9	33.5	33.0	34.6
2010	31.2	30.3	31.3	32.6	32.8	32.9	33.5	33.0	32.7	33.1	33.0	32.4	32.4
2011	30.7	30.7	31.2	31.7	31.9	31.8	32.3	32.1	31.9	32.4	32.4	32.3	31.8
2012	31.0	30.6	31.4	32.3	32.7	33.0	33.2	33.6	33.4	33.2	33.2	32.9	32.5
2013	31.6	31.9	32.7	33.3	33.4	34.0	34.1	34.2	33.8	33.3	33.2	32.7	33.2
2014	31.7	31.7	32.5	33.4	34.0	34.3	34.9	34.9	34.7	34.8	34.7	34.6	33.9
2015	33.6	33.8	34.5	36.1	36.6	36.6	37.3	37.5	37.4	37.8	37.4	37.0	36.3

Employment by Industry: Richmond, VA, 2005–2015—*Continued*

(Numbers in thousands, not seasonally adjusted)

Industry and year	January	February	March	April	May	June	July	August	September	October	November	December	Annual average
Manufacturing													
2005	44.4	43.9	43.5	43.5	43.4	43.5	43.1	43.3	43.4	43.2	43.4	43.6	43.5
2006	42.9	42.8	42.6	42.6	42.3	42.3	41.8	41.9	41.6	41.2	41.0	41.1	42.0
2007	40.9	40.7	40.8	40.7	40.7	41.0	40.6	40.6	40.3	40.3	40.3	40.5	40.6
2008	40.1	40.0	39.6	39.5	39.3	39.0	38.6	38.3	38.2	38.0	37.3	36.9	38.7
2009	35.6	33.8	33.7	33.1	32.5	32.7	32.3	32.1	32.3	32.0	32.0	32.0	32.8
2010	31.6	31.4	31.4	31.5	31.5	31.7	31.7	31.5	31.5	31.4	31.2	31.2	31.5
2011	30.6	30.8	30.8	30.7	30.7	30.8	30.7	30.7	30.7	30.8	30.7	30.7	30.7
2012	30.1	30.0	30.2	30.4	30.5	30.7	30.5	30.6	30.5	30.5	30.4	30.6	30.4
2013	30.3	30.6	30.6	30.7	30.9	31.1	31.1	31.0	30.9	30.9	30.9	30.9	30.8
2014	30.8	30.6	30.6	30.7	30.9	31.0	31.0	31.2	31.1	30.9	30.9	31.0	30.9
2015	30.6	30.5	30.6	30.6	30.7	31.0	30.9	30.9	30.8	30.8	30.8	30.8	30.8
Trade, Transportation, and Utilities													
2005	108.6	107.7	108.5	109.1	109.6	110.1	110.3	110.6	110.3	111.0	113.5	115.4	110.4
2006	111.5	110.2	111.1	110.9	112.0	112.2	112.1	112.3	111.7	113.5	115.9	118.0	112.6
2007	113.9	112.9	113.6	113.2	114.4	115.2	115.0	115.2	115.2	115.7	118.2	119.6	115.2
2008	114.7	113.1	113.3	112.9	113.3	113.9	113.6	113.6	113.6	114.3	115.9	116.9	114.1
2009	111.2	109.3	108.6	107.6	108.0	107.9	106.9	106.7	106.1	107.3	108.9	110.2	108.2
2010	106.0	104.5	105.3	106.6	107.9	108.2	107.7	107.6	106.4	107.7	109.6	111.2	107.4
2011	107.4	106.6	107.0	108.6	108.9	109.3	109.4	109.7	108.7	110.2	112.7	114.3	109.4
2012	109.8	108.7	109.5	110.1	111.2	111.2	110.3	110.7	111.0	113.9	117.2	120.8	112.0
2013	114.0	112.5	112.6	113.5	114.7	115.1	115.7	116.4	116.3	118.1	125.2	126.3	116.7
2014	119.0	116.4	116.8	117.6	119.2	119.3	119.0	119.2	118.2	119.6	125.8	127.0	119.8
2015	120.1	117.5	116.9	117.7	119.0	120.4	121.7	121.3	122.1	125.1	130.6	132.0	122.0
Wholesale Trade													
2005	25.6	25.6	25.7	26.0	26.0	26.1	26.3	26.4	26.3	26.3	26.4	26.5	26.1
2006	26.6	26.7	26.8	26.9	27.1	27.3	27.5	27.6	27.5	27.7	27.8	27.8	27.3
2007	27.8	28.0	28.2	28.2	28.3	28.5	28.5	28.5	28.4	28.6	28.4	28.4	28.3
2008	28.2	28.3	28.3	28.3	28.2	28.3	28.4	28.3	28.1	28.0	27.8	27.6	28.2
2009	27.2	26.9	26.7	26.4	26.3	26.1	25.9	25.9	25.6	25.8	25.7	25.6	26.2
2010	25.3	25.3	25.4	25.9	26.1	26.1	26.2	26.3	26.0	26.5	26.6	26.6	26.0
2011	26.7	26.7	26.9	27.0	27.0	27.2	27.4	27.4	27.1	27.1	27.1	27.1	27.1
2012	26.9	27.0	27.3	27.7	27.9	28.1	27.9	28.1	28.0	28.0	28.1	28.1	27.8
2013	28.1	28.2	28.3	28.2	28.3	28.4	28.4	28.4	28.3	28.3	28.2	28.2	28.3
2014	27.8	27.7	27.8	28.0	28.2	28.3	28.4	28.5	28.3	28.1	28.2	28.2	28.1
2015	28.3	28.3	28.4	28.6	28.8	28.9	28.8	28.8	28.9	29.2	29.7	29.9	28.9
Retail Trade													
2005	65.0	64.1	64.5	64.8	65.3	65.6	65.4	65.6	65.3	65.8	68.1	69.6	65.8
2006	66.4	65.2	65.8	65.7	66.5	66.4	66.1	66.0	65.4	66.8	69.0	70.5	66.7
2007	67.2	66.1	66.5	66.2	67.3	67.7	67.6	67.6	67.6	68.2	70.6	71.5	67.8
2008	68.0	66.4	66.6	66.1	66.5	66.9	66.6	66.7	67.0	67.9	69.5	70.2	67.4
2009	66.0	64.6	64.2	63.8	64.2	64.4	63.6	63.5	63.3	64.2	65.7	66.7	64.5
2010	63.5	62.1	62.6	63.2	64.4	64.6	64.0	63.8	62.9	63.7	65.4	66.4	63.9
2011	63.3	62.5	62.6	63.4	63.6	63.6	63.3	63.6	62.9	64.3	66.6	67.8	64.0
2012	64.4	63.3	63.6	63.7	64.5	64.2	63.6	63.8	64.1	67.1	70.1	73.0	65.5
2013	66.6	65.1	64.9	65.8	66.8	66.9	67.4	67.9	67.8	69.6	76.3	76.5	68.5
2014	70.2	68.0	68.1	68.4	69.4	69.0	68.5	68.3	67.4	68.8	74.4	74.8	69.6
2015	68.5	66.0	65.2	65.4	66.4	67.4	67.2	66.6	67.1	69.4	73.6	74.2	68.1
Transportation and Utilities													
2005	18.0	18.0	18.3	18.3	18.3	18.4	18.6	18.6	18.7	18.9	19.0	19.3	18.5
2006	18.5	18.3	18.5	18.3	18.4	18.5	18.5	18.7	18.8	19.0	19.1	19.7	18.7
2007	18.9	18.8	18.9	18.8	18.8	19.0	18.9	19.1	19.2	18.9	19.2	19.7	19.0
2008	18.5	18.4	18.4	18.5	18.6	18.7	18.6	18.6	18.5	18.4	18.6	19.1	18.6
2009	18.0	17.8	17.7	17.4	17.5	17.4	17.4	17.3	17.2	17.3	17.5	17.9	17.5
2010	17.2	17.1	17.3	17.5	17.4	17.5	17.5	17.5	17.5	17.5	17.6	18.2	17.5
2011	17.4	17.4	17.5	18.2	18.3	18.5	18.7	18.7	18.7	18.8	19.0	19.4	18.4
2012	18.5	18.4	18.6	18.7	18.8	18.9	18.8	18.8	18.9	18.8	19.0	19.7	18.8
2013	19.3	19.2	19.4	19.5	19.6	19.8	19.9	20.1	20.2	20.2	20.7	21.6	20.0
2014	21.0	20.7	20.9	21.2	21.6	22.0	22.1	22.4	22.5	22.7	23.2	24.0	22.0
2015	23.3	23.2	23.3	23.7	23.8	24.1	25.7	25.9	26.1	26.5	27.3	27.9	25.1

Employment by Industry: Richmond, VA, 2005–2015—*Continued*

(Numbers in thousands, not seasonally adjusted)

Industry and year	January	February	March	April	May	June	July	August	September	October	November	December	Annual average
Information													
2005	11.0	11.0	11.1	11.1	11.1	11.1	11.1	11.1	11.1	11.0	11.1	11.1	11.1
2006	11.0	11.0	11.0	10.8	12.9	10.8	11.8	11.2	11.1	11.1	11.2	11.2	11.3
2007	11.6	11.6	11.5	11.7	11.9	11.6	11.3	11.2	11.0	10.8	10.7	10.6	11.3
2008	10.5	10.4	10.5	10.4	10.3	10.4	10.2	10.1	10.1	10.3	10.4	10.4	10.3
2009	10.4	10.4	10.3	10.3	10.3	10.3	10.1	9.8	9.7	9.6	9.6	9.6	10.0
2010	9.5	9.4	9.4	9.3	9.4	9.4	9.4	9.4	9.4	9.5	9.4	9.4	9.4
2011	9.2	9.1	9.1	8.8	8.8	8.8	8.9	7.6	8.5	9.2	9.3	9.4	8.9
2012	8.0	8.1	8.2	8.0	8.0	8.1	8.0	8.2	7.7	7.6	7.9	7.9	8.0
2013	7.7	8.0	8.0	8.4	7.9	8.0	7.8	7.9	7.7	7.7	7.9	7.9	7.9
2014	8.3	7.9	7.9	7.8	8.0	7.6	7.9	8.0	7.7	7.8	7.6	7.6	7.8
2015	7.5	7.5	7.4	7.5	7.6	7.5	7.5	7.4	7.4	7.5	7.5	7.5	7.5
Financial Activities													
2005	46.4	46.5	46.6	46.3	46.4	46.5	47.1	47.0	46.5	46.2	46.1	46.3	46.5
2006	46.2	46.3	46.6	46.3	46.5	46.7	46.8	46.8	46.2	46.0	45.8	45.9	46.3
2007	45.5	45.4	45.7	45.7	45.8	46.1	46.0	46.2	45.5	45.1	44.9	44.8	45.6
2008	44.4	44.3	44.3	43.8	43.6	43.8	44.1	44.1	43.5	43.9	43.8	43.9	44.0
2009	43.5	43.3	43.4	43.3	42.9	42.9	42.9	42.9	42.4	42.4	42.3	42.4	42.9
2010	42.0	41.9	42.2	42.3	42.5	42.8	42.6	42.7	42.3	42.6	42.6	42.8	42.4
2011	42.5	42.6	43.0	43.2	43.4	43.8	44.3	44.5	44.3	44.7	45.4	45.8	44.0
2012	45.1	45.4	45.6	46.1	46.4	46.9	47.0	47.2	47.0	47.0	47.3	47.3	46.5
2013	46.9	47.0	47.2	47.4	47.6	47.9	48.4	48.4	48.1	48.2	48.3	48.1	47.8
2014	47.9	48.2	48.2	48.4	48.5	48.8	49.0	49.1	48.7	48.9	49.4	49.6	48.7
2015	49.6	50.1	50.1	50.1	50.2	50.4	50.3	50.3	49.9	51.0	51.5	51.3	50.4
Professional and Business Services													
2005	89.3	89.9	90.4	91.9	92.3	93.0	93.4	93.1	93.2	94.6	94.5	94.6	92.5
2006	92.7	92.9	93.3	93.2	94.1	94.8	94.7	95.3	95.8	97.9	98.2	98.7	95.1
2007	96.4	97.0	97.7	97.7	97.6	99.1	98.7	98.9	99.0	99.6	99.3	99.7	98.4
2008	98.9	99.4	99.7	99.6	99.4	100.0	99.1	99.2	98.0	98.6	97.7	96.9	98.9
2009	94.7	94.2	94.0	92.4	92.1	91.6	91.3	91.0	90.7	91.3	91.6	91.8	92.2
2010	89.9	89.9	90.6	91.9	92.1	92.4	93.4	93.5	93.7	94.5	94.5	94.7	92.6
2011	94.1	94.7	95.8	96.7	96.4	96.0	96.6	96.5	96.9	97.4	98.3	96.4	96.3
2012	95.9	96.8	96.9	98.2	98.5	99.4	99.5	100.0	100.4	101.0	100.0	99.7	98.9
2013	97.4	98.2	98.8	97.9	98.1	98.0	98.0	98.6	98.1	98.2	98.8	97.7	98.2
2014	97.3	97.6	98.6	100.3	101.0	101.4	100.4	100.5	100.7	101.6	102.3	102.3	100.3
2015	101.8	102.2	103.4	104.9	106.4	106.5	107.2	108.1	108.8	111.4	111.8	112.7	107.1
Education and Health Services													
2005	67.2	68.0	68.0	68.6	69.0	68.5	64.8	64.7	69.6	71.2	71.7	70.9	68.5
2006	69.3	68.6	71.1	73.1	71.5	71.1	70.9	70.0	71.1	73.1	73.4	72.3	71.3
2007	71.8	74.2	72.8	71.5	72.9	73.5	70.9	71.4	75.5	76.8	77.7	78.5	74.0
2008	78.2	79.2	79.5	80.6	80.7	80.6	78.3	78.6	81.3	82.3	82.9	83.0	80.4
2009	81.9	82.2	82.1	82.7	83.7	83.5	80.5	80.5	83.3	84.5	85.3	85.1	82.9
2010	84.4	84.3	85.0	85.0	85.7	84.9	82.4	82.1	84.2	85.5	85.7	85.3	84.5
2011	84.7	85.2	85.3	86.1	85.1	84.7	85.6	85.8	87.0	88.0	88.4	87.1	86.1
2012	87.0	87.5	87.7	88.9	87.7	87.7	87.8	88.7	90.2	90.7	90.9	90.0	88.7
2013	89.6	90.5	90.7	91.1	90.1	89.2	89.9	90.7	92.0	92.8	93.3	92.0	91.0
2014	92.0	92.4	92.8	94.1	93.0	92.5	92.4	93.0	93.6	94.7	94.8	93.6	93.2
2015	94.3	94.8	94.9	95.4	94.3	93.8	94.3	95.0	95.9	98.3	97.5	97.3	95.5
Leisure and Hospitality													
2005	44.5	45.0	47.1	48.9	50.5	52.5	52.5	52.0	50.5	49.0	48.3	47.4	49.0
2006	46.5	47.0	49.2	50.5	52.4	55.0	54.4	54.0	51.4	52.0	50.7	50.5	51.1
2007	48.2	48.7	50.2	51.2	53.4	55.8	55.6	55.2	53.1	51.6	50.2	49.9	51.9
2008	48.6	48.9	50.7	52.7	54.8	56.6	56.2	55.4	52.6	51.5	50.0	50.1	52.3
2009	48.3	48.4	49.4	51.6	53.9	55.7	55.2	54.2	52.3	50.7	48.6	48.3	51.4
2010	46.7	46.2	48.2	51.2	53.4	55.2	55.2	54.3	52.7	50.9	49.2	48.9	51.0
2011	47.4	48.1	49.8	52.4	54.9	56.9	56.9	56.4	54.9	54.0	52.4	52.5	53.1
2012	50.6	51.3	53.3	55.2	57.4	59.7	59.1	59.0	56.7	55.5	54.0	54.1	55.5
2013	52.3	53.0	55.1	57.1	58.9	60.8	60.8	60.1	58.0	56.3	56.4	56.1	57.1
2014	53.5	53.5	55.7	58.0	60.7	62.1	61.5	61.0	59.0	58.0	56.4	56.7	58.0
2015	55.2	56.0	57.4	59.9	62.7	64.1	64.7	64.4	62.7	62.2	60.9	59.3	60.8

Employment by Industry: Richmond, VA, 2005–2015—*Continued*

(Numbers in thousands, not seasonally adjusted)

Industry and year	January	February	March	April	May	June	July	August	September	October	November	December	Annual average
Other Services													
2005	29.0	29.4	29.3	31.3	31.5	31.9	30.0	30.0	29.5	29.7	29.6	29.3	30.0
2006	28.6	28.7	28.9	28.9	29.3	29.6	31.0	30.9	31.2	30.3	31.8	31.2	30.0
2007	29.4	29.5	29.9	30.8	30.8	31.2	31.2	31.6	30.6	30.2	30.2	30.3	30.5
2008	30.2	30.6	30.7	30.1	29.2	29.5	31.5	32.0	32.3	31.4	31.4	31.4	30.9
2009	30.0	30.1	30.1	30.1	30.0	30.2	30.3	29.9	30.5	29.7	29.6	29.2	30.0
2010	29.2	29.3	29.9	29.6	29.7	29.9	29.9	29.8	29.5	29.5	29.5	29.4	29.6
2011	29.2	29.3	29.4	29.8	29.7	30.0	29.9	29.8	29.4	29.5	29.5	29.6	29.6
2012	29.2	29.2	29.5	30.1	30.4	30.6	30.5	30.7	30.4	30.6	30.6	30.1	30.2
2013	29.5	29.7	30.0	30.3	30.6	30.9	31.1	31.1	30.8	30.8	30.7	30.6	30.5
2014	30.3	30.3	30.5	30.8	31.1	31.5	31.4	31.4	31.1	30.9	30.9	30.8	30.9
2015	30.6	30.8	31.0	31.2	31.6	31.8	32.0	32.1	31.7	32.5	32.4	31.8	31.6
Government													
2005	111.6	113.5	114.0	115.0	114.1	113.7	108.1	105.2	110.1	109.8	111.1	111.2	111.5
2006	111.7	112.6	112.8	112.2	112.4	112.1	107.9	107.4	109.1	111.8	113.1	113.3	111.4
2007	113.1	114.3	113.3	113.2	112.7	111.9	107.0	105.9	106.4	108.8	109.2	108.4	110.4
2008	107.9	108.9	108.8	111.0	110.0	110.3	104.9	104.2	107.9	111.2	112.1	110.4	109.0
2009	111.1	111.6	112.0	112.6	111.7	111.7	104.6	104.8	108.3	111.5	112.6	111.3	110.3
2010	111.3	111.8	112.1	113.5	114.2	113.3	107.5	106.8	108.7	110.8	111.8	111.2	111.1
2011	111.4	112.2	112.4	112.6	111.2	110.7	107.1	106.0	109.3	111.7	112.4	111.9	110.7
2012	111.6	112.8	113.1	111.9	110.8	110.6	105.6	105.7	108.0	109.9	111.4	111.2	110.2
2013	110.2	110.9	110.9	111.8	110.0	110.2	105.9	105.2	108.0	109.7	110.4	110.4	109.5
2014	110.1	110.3	110.8	110.7	110.0	110.0	106.5	106.9	109.3	110.5	111.2	111.2	109.8
2015	110.5	110.9	110.5	110.5	109.5	109.6	106.3	105.9	108.4	110.3	110.9	110.8	109.5

Employment by Industry: New Orleans-Metairie, LA, 2005–2015

(Numbers in thousands, not seasonally adjusted)

Industry and year	January	February	March	April	May	June	July	August	September	October	November	December	Annual average
Total Nonfarm													
2005	616.9	617.6	623.5	623.4	622.9	627.1	615.3	614.5	484.0	436.3	449.5	461.4	566.0
2006	456.6	466.7	479.4	482.8	488.5	495.6	491.9	496.2	500.6	507.1	514.4	519.0	491.6
2007	515.2	519.9	526.5	519.9	521.5	524.1	518.3	523.1	524.2	534.3	539.4	543.3	525.8
2008	533.2	537.1	541.0	540.1	539.6	538.9	531.9	539.2	532.2	540.7	543.4	545.5	538.6
2009	532.7	535.1	535.1	536.8	538.3	533.4	528.7	532.8	530.6	533.2	535.2	535.2	533.9
2010	525.9	528.4	532.8	535.4	535.2	534.5	527.4	528.8	532.0	535.2	539.1	541.3	533.0
2011	533.3	536.6	539.6	541.1	541.7	536.9	533.2	536.9	538.8	542.1	546.3	548.1	539.6
2012	537.2	540.5	542.9	549.4	550.8	545.1	541.0	543.6	539.7	547.0	552.1	554.2	545.3
2013	550.4	554.4	553.5	553.5	554.6	553.5	546.8	555.6	553.1	560.8	565.7	565.1	555.6
2014	555.8	560.8	564.2	563.8	565.9	567.6	562.8	566.8	564.4	570.7	577.5	577.4	566.5
2015	568.4	571.1	572.3	577.1	578.2	574.8	571.0	571.1	569.7	575.3	575.0	576.7	573.4
Total Private													
2005	510.1	509.7	515.0	516.7	516.7	520.5	512.2	510.6	380.5	354.4	367.8	380.1	466.2
2006	382.3	392.3	404.3	407.8	413.1	420.5	418.3	422.0	423.0	429.4	435.6	439.4	415.7
2007	437.2	440.9	446.8	445.5	446.7	448.9	445.2	448.9	446.7	454.5	458.9	462.5	448.6
2008	453.6	456.7	460.7	457.7	457.1	457.7	451.7	456.8	448.8	456.5	458.7	461.0	456.4
2009	449.2	451.1	451.5	451.7	453.5	451.0	445.5	447.8	446.0	447.4	449.6	450.0	449.5
2010	442.0	444.0	447.7	450.5	448.7	450.0	445.5	446.1	448.9	451.7	455.3	458.0	449.0
2011	450.9	454.2	457.5	458.8	459.6	456.8	454.8	457.1	457.5	461.3	465.4	467.6	458.5
2012	458.7	461.2	464.0	469.2	470.7	466.2	464.5	465.8	461.0	467.9	472.8	474.9	466.4
2013	472.8	476.3	475.4	475.7	476.5	476.5	473.0	482.1	478.6	486.0	490.6	489.8	479.4
2014	482.2	485.9	489.0	489.2	491.6	491.4	489.9	493.9	490.1	495.9	502.5	503.2	492.1
2015	495.1	496.7	498.4	503.0	504.1	501.9	500.4	499.8	496.6	501.4	500.7	503.1	500.1
Goods Producing													
2005	78.0	78.7	79.5	79.3	79.7	80.5	80.0	80.1	63.4	68.6	71.7	74.0	76.1
2006	74.2	75.3	76.6	77.3	77.5	79.2	77.7	78.8	78.7	79.4	79.6	79.8	77.8
2007	77.9	78.4	78.6	78.7	79.0	79.6	79.5	79.8	79.9	80.0	80.0	80.3	79.3
2008	80.1	79.6	79.5	79.9	80.3	80.6	81.2	81.5	80.9	81.8	81.0	81.3	80.6
2009	79.4	79.1	78.4	78.2	78.4	78.1	77.0	76.3	75.8	76.1	75.6	74.6	77.3
2010	72.7	72.8	73.2	73.3	73.7	74.2	73.9	73.7	73.5	74.3	73.6	73.7	73.6
2011	72.7	72.9	73.1	73.3	73.2	72.8	73.0	72.8	72.2	72.3	72.3	72.2	72.7
2012	71.2	71.3	71.5	71.0	71.6	72.0	72.2	72.2	71.9	72.2	72.2	71.6	71.7
2013	70.2	70.0	70.4	70.1	70.8	71.5	71.7	72.0	71.9	71.8	71.1	70.6	71.0
2014	70.2	70.4	70.6	70.1	70.9	70.6	70.6	70.2	69.8	70.2	70.3	70.6	70.4
2015	70.7	70.3	69.4	70.1	70.1	70.4	70.4	70.3	70.2	70.6	69.3	69.1	70.1
Service-Providing													
2005	538.9	538.9	544.0	544.1	543.2	546.6	535.3	534.4	420.6	367.7	377.8	387.4	489.9
2006	382.4	391.4	402.8	405.5	411.0	416.4	414.2	417.4	421.9	427.7	434.8	439.2	413.7
2007	437.3	441.5	447.9	441.2	442.5	444.5	438.8	443.3	444.3	454.3	459.4	463.0	446.5
2008	453.1	457.5	461.5	460.2	459.3	458.3	450.7	457.7	451.3	458.9	462.4	464.2	457.9
2009	453.3	456.0	456.7	458.6	459.9	455.3	451.7	456.5	454.8	457.1	459.6	460.6	456.7
2010	453.2	455.6	459.6	462.1	461.5	460.3	453.5	455.1	458.5	460.9	465.5	467.6	459.5
2011	460.6	463.7	466.5	467.8	468.5	464.1	460.2	464.1	466.6	469.8	474.0	475.9	466.8
2012	466.0	469.2	471.4	478.4	479.2	473.1	468.8	471.4	467.8	474.8	479.9	482.6	473.6
2013	480.2	484.4	483.1	483.4	483.8	482.0	475.1	483.6	481.2	489.0	494.6	494.5	484.6
2014	485.6	490.4	493.6	493.7	495.0	497.0	492.2	496.6	494.6	500.5	507.2	506.8	496.1
2015	497.7	500.8	502.9	507.0	508.1	504.4	500.6	500.8	499.5	504.7	505.7	507.6	503.3
Mining and Logging													
2005	8.3	8.4	8.6	8.3	8.4	8.6	8.4	8.5	8.1	8.3	8.3	8.4	8.4
2006	7.9	8.0	8.1	8.0	8.0	8.1	8.4	8.5	8.7	8.7	8.5	8.3	8.3
2007	7.8	8.0	8.1	8.3	8.3	8.4	8.4	8.3	8.3	8.6	8.6	8.6	8.3
2008	8.9	8.4	8.4	8.5	8.4	8.4	8.6	8.7	8.8	8.9	8.8	8.7	8.6
2009	8.6	8.6	8.5	8.3	8.3	8.3	7.8	7.8	7.7	7.8	7.7	7.8	8.1
2010	7.5	7.6	7.6	7.6	7.7	7.8	7.7	7.6	7.5	7.6	7.5	7.4	7.6
2011	7.4	7.5	7.5	7.4	7.4	7.5	7.6	7.6	7.5	7.6	7.6	7.7	7.5
2012	7.8	7.7	7.7	7.5	7.6	7.6	7.8	7.7	7.7	7.7	7.7	7.5	7.7
2013	7.4	7.5	7.5	7.5	7.6	7.7	7.8	7.9	7.9	7.9	7.9	7.9	7.7
2014	7.9	8.0	8.0	8.0	8.0	8.1	8.2	8.2	8.1	8.1	8.0	8.1	8.1
2015	7.9	7.7	7.5	7.3	7.3	7.2	7.1	7.1	7.0	6.9	6.7	6.7	7.2

Employment by Industry: New Orleans-Metairie, LA, 2005–2015—*Continued*

(Numbers in thousands, not seasonally adjusted)

Industry and year	January	February	March	April	May	June	July	August	September	October	November	December	Annual average
Construction													
2005	29.6	29.4	30.0	30.2	30.4	30.4	30.2	30.1	22.2	26.2	28.8	29.8	28.9
2006	30.9	31.5	32.5	33.1	33.2	34.0	31.8	32.4	32.2	32.8	32.7	32.7	32.5
2007	32.0	32.0	32.3	32.1	32.3	32.5	32.4	32.8	32.6	32.6	32.4	32.3	32.4
2008	32.3	32.4	32.3	32.9	33.0	33.1	33.5	33.8	33.7	34.2	33.6	33.7	33.2
2009	32.5	32.5	32.3	32.3	32.6	32.6	32.3	31.9	31.8	32.4	32.1	31.1	32.2
2010	30.1	30.3	30.6	30.3	30.5	31.0	31.2	31.3	31.4	32.3	32.1	32.1	31.1
2011	31.4	31.4	31.8	32.7	32.4	32.1	31.9	31.8	31.5	31.5	31.5	31.3	31.8
2012	30.6	31.0	31.4	31.3	31.6	31.9	31.8	32.0	32.1	32.4	32.3	31.9	31.7
2013	30.9	30.9	31.3	31.1	31.3	31.6	31.7	31.9	32.0	31.9	31.3	31.0	31.4
2014	30.8	31.0	31.2	31.0	31.4	31.2	31.2	30.9	30.9	31.3	31.7	31.8	31.2
2015	32.1	32.0	32.1	32.2	32.3	32.4	32.5	32.4	32.5	32.6	32.2	32.1	32.3
Manufacturing													
2005	40.1	40.9	40.9	40.8	40.9	41.5	41.4	41.5	33.1	34.1	34.6	35.8	38.8
2006	35.4	35.8	36.0	36.2	36.3	37.1	37.5	37.9	37.8	37.9	38.4	38.8	37.1
2007	38.1	38.4	38.2	38.3	38.4	38.7	38.7	38.7	39.0	38.8	39.0	39.4	38.6
2008	38.9	38.8	38.8	38.5	38.9	39.1	39.1	39.0	38.4	38.7	38.6	38.9	38.8
2009	38.3	38.0	37.6	37.6	37.5	37.2	36.9	36.6	36.3	35.9	35.8	35.7	37.0
2010	35.1	34.9	35.0	35.4	35.5	35.4	35.0	34.8	34.6	34.4	34.0	34.2	34.9
2011	33.9	34.0	33.8	33.2	33.4	33.2	33.5	33.4	33.2	33.2	33.2	33.2	33.4
2012	32.8	32.6	32.4	32.2	32.4	32.5	32.6	32.5	32.1	32.1	32.2	32.2	32.4
2013	31.9	31.6	31.6	31.5	31.9	32.2	32.2	32.2	32.0	32.0	31.9	31.7	31.9
2014	31.5	31.4	31.4	31.1	31.5	31.3	31.2	31.1	30.8	30.8	30.6	30.7	31.1
2015	30.7	30.6	29.8	30.6	30.5	30.8	30.8	30.8	30.7	31.1	30.4	30.3	30.6
Trade, Transportation, and Utilities													
2005	122.7	121.9	122.9	122.5	122.9	123.3	122.3	121.8	89.9	85.3	91.1	95.5	111.8
2006	95.9	97.9	100.5	102.3	103.5	105.2	105.2	105.7	105.6	107.4	109.2	111.5	104.2
2007	109.0	108.6	109.7	108.9	109.1	109.4	109.1	109.3	108.6	111.3	113.8	115.5	110.2
2008	111.6	110.7	111.2	110.3	110.5	110.3	109.8	110.2	107.9	110.0	111.9	113.0	110.6
2009	108.3	107.4	107.2	106.7	106.4	106.9	105.7	105.8	105.3	104.9	106.4	107.0	106.5
2010	103.7	103.2	104.0	104.4	104.5	104.6	104.9	104.7	104.6	106.3	108.3	109.6	105.2
2011	107.9	107.4	107.5	107.7	107.9	107.7	107.8	107.6	107.3	107.9	109.9	110.7	108.1
2012	108.1	107.4	107.7	108.1	108.3	108.2	107.8	107.8	107.3	109.3	112.3	113.2	108.8
2013	111.4	110.4	111.3	110.5	110.5	110.6	110.8	111.6	111.5	112.5	114.4	116.0	111.8
2014	112.6	112.1	112.7	112.8	113.6	114.2	114.7	115.2	114.8	115.5	118.0	120.2	114.7
2015	116.2	115.3	115.8	116.0	116.3	116.5	116.5	116.5	116.0	116.8	117.7	118.6	116.5
Wholesale Trade													
2005	25.5	25.5	25.6	26.0	26.1	26.2	26.4	26.3	22.0	22.1	22.4	22.7	24.7
2006	22.0	22.4	22.6	22.8	23.0	23.2	23.2	23.3	23.3	23.3	23.4	23.6	23.0
2007	23.8	23.9	24.2	24.0	24.2	24.4	24.8	25.0	24.7	25.1	25.1	25.2	24.5
2008	24.7	24.8	24.9	24.2	24.2	24.2	24.1	24.1	23.9	24.0	24.1	24.1	24.3
2009	23.6	23.6	23.5	23.8	23.7	23.7	23.1	23.1	22.9	22.9	22.9	22.8	23.3
2010	22.2	22.3	22.3	22.3	22.4	22.5	22.4	22.4	22.3	22.5	22.6	22.6	22.4
2011	23.1	23.2	23.1	22.6	22.8	22.9	22.8	22.8	22.7	22.8	22.8	22.8	22.9
2012	22.5	22.5	22.5	22.8	22.7	22.7	22.6	22.6	22.5	22.5	22.5	22.6	22.6
2013	23.1	23.2	23.3	23.1	23.1	23.2	23.2	23.4	23.3	23.4	23.4	23.5	23.3
2014	23.4	23.5	23.5	23.4	23.4	23.5	23.6	23.6	23.6	23.6	23.7	23.8	23.6
2015	23.3	23.3	23.4	23.5	23.5	23.5	23.5	23.5	23.3	23.6	23.2	24.0	23.5
Retail Trade													
2005	68.2	67.4	68.0	68.1	68.5	68.7	67.8	67.5	44.7	41.6	46.3	49.4	60.5
2006	50.9	52.2	53.8	55.0	55.8	56.8	57.4	57.5	57.5	59.4	60.8	62.0	56.6
2007	60.1	59.6	60.3	59.7	60.0	60.0	60.0	59.6	59.5	61.1	63.4	64.7	60.7
2008	62.1	60.9	61.3	60.8	60.8	60.7	60.4	60.6	58.9	60.1	61.6	62.6	60.9
2009	59.1	58.7	58.6	58.3	58.4	58.7	58.2	58.3	58.0	57.5	58.9	59.4	58.5
2010	57.1	56.6	57.3	57.0	56.9	56.9	56.9	56.6	56.7	57.9	59.8	60.7	57.5
2011	58.7	58.4	58.6	58.9	58.8	58.6	58.7	58.4	58.0	58.8	60.6	61.1	59.0
2012	59.2	58.4	58.5	58.5	58.7	58.6	58.6	58.3	57.9	59.5	62.1	62.6	59.2
2013	60.4	59.4	59.9	59.8	60.0	60.1	60.4	60.7	60.8	61.3	63.1	64.0	60.8
2014	61.3	60.9	61.1	61.2	61.7	62.4	62.8	62.9	62.4	63.0	65.1	66.5	62.6
2015	63.5	63.0	63.4	63.4	63.7	64.2	64.2	64.2	63.7	64.3	64.9	64.8	63.9

Employment by Industry: New Orleans-Metairie, LA, 2005–2015—*Continued*

(Numbers in thousands, not seasonally adjusted)

Industry and year	January	February	March	April	May	June	July	August	September	October	November	December	Annual average
Transportation and Utilities													
2005	29.0	29.0	29.3	28.4	28.3	28.4	28.1	28.0	23.2	21.6	22.4	23.4	26.6
2006	23.0	23.3	24.1	24.5	24.7	25.2	24.6	24.9	24.8	24.7	25.0	25.9	24.6
2007	25.1	25.1	25.2	25.2	24.9	25.0	24.3	24.7	24.4	25.1	25.3	25.6	25.0
2008	24.8	25.0	25.0	25.3	25.5	25.4	25.3	25.5	25.1	25.9	26.2	26.3	25.4
2009	25.6	25.1	25.1	24.6	24.3	24.5	24.4	24.4	24.4	24.5	24.6	24.8	24.7
2010	24.4	24.3	24.4	25.1	25.2	25.2	25.6	25.7	25.6	25.9	25.9	26.3	25.3
2011	26.1	25.8	25.8	26.2	26.3	26.2	26.3	26.4	26.6	26.3	26.5	26.8	26.3
2012	26.4	26.5	26.7	26.8	26.9	26.9	26.6	26.9	26.9	27.3	27.7	28.0	27.0
2013	27.9	27.8	28.1	27.6	27.4	27.3	27.2	27.5	27.4	27.8	27.9	28.5	27.7
2014	27.9	27.7	28.1	28.2	28.5	28.3	28.3	28.7	28.8	28.9	29.2	29.9	28.5
2015	29.4	29.0	29.0	29.1	29.1	28.8	28.8	28.8	29.0	28.9	29.6	29.8	29.1
Information													
2005	10.8	10.6	10.5	9.5	9.6	9.8	10.1	10.5	9.0	7.3	7.4	7.7	9.4
2006	7.1	7.3	8.8	8.1	8.4	7.5	6.7	6.8	6.9	6.9	7.4	7.5	7.5
2007	7.4	8.2	10.1	9.5	9.2	9.8	8.7	8.3	7.3	7.1	7.4	7.3	8.4
2008	8.0	9.2	11.2	9.8	10.6	11.2	7.2	8.6	8.9	6.9	7.4	7.9	8.9
2009	6.0	6.4	6.6	6.3	6.7	7.1	6.4	6.4	6.4	6.0	6.4	6.2	6.4
2010	6.8	7.3	7.2	6.9	7.5	8.3	6.0	6.3	8.7	6.5	6.9	7.1	7.1
2011	6.9	6.8	8.4	7.6	8.5	8.0	6.9	6.9	7.1	7.4	7.4	8.0	7.5
2012	7.2	7.8	8.0	10.5	11.9	9.2	8.6	8.7	7.9	7.7	8.6	8.9	8.8
2013	9.1	10.1	9.2	9.6	10.2	10.5	7.6	8.3	8.0	9.6	10.6	9.1	9.3
2014	7.4	8.4	9.0	8.5	8.7	8.2	8.2	8.0	7.6	7.7	9.6	9.0	8.4
2015	6.8	8.4	8.5	8.8	9.8	9.0	7.4	6.5	6.3	6.1	6.7	6.5	7.6
Financial Activities													
2005	33.5	33.5	33.5	33.1	33.0	33.1	33.2	33.3	27.9	26.5	26.4	26.2	31.1
2006	26.0	26.1	26.4	26.0	26.3	26.6	26.7	26.7	26.7	26.9	27.0	27.1	26.5
2007	27.7	27.8	27.6	27.4	27.5	27.7	27.9	27.8	27.6	27.9	27.8	27.8	27.7
2008	27.3	27.5	27.5	27.2	27.2	27.2	26.9	26.7	26.3	26.5	26.4	26.4	26.9
2009	26.0	26.1	26.1	26.5	26.5	26.6	26.5	26.4	26.3	26.1	26.2	26.3	26.3
2010	26.0	26.0	26.1	26.1	26.4	26.3	26.3	26.2	26.1	26.4	26.5	26.5	26.2
2011	26.7	26.7	26.7	26.4	26.6	26.5	26.8	26.8	26.7	26.9	27.0	27.0	26.7
2012	26.7	26.8	26.8	26.8	26.9	27.0	26.9	26.9	26.8	27.0	27.1	27.1	26.9
2013	27.0	27.1	27.1	27.3	27.5	27.6	27.8	28.0	27.9	28.2	28.1	28.1	27.6
2014	28.0	28.2	28.3	28.5	28.6	28.6	28.7	28.8	28.5	28.6	28.7	28.6	28.5
2015	28.6	28.6	28.7	28.9	28.8	28.9	28.9	28.8	28.7	28.2	28.6	28.2	28.7
Professional and Business Services													
2005	73.6	73.8	74.7	77.3	76.2	75.7	74.6	74.3	54.5	56.0	59.5	61.5	69.3
2006	61.1	63.2	64.8	65.0	65.6	66.8	66.1	67.1	66.7	67.1	67.5	67.9	65.7
2007	67.7	68.8	69.4	68.8	69.5	69.2	67.3	68.4	68.3	70.3	70.5	70.7	69.1
2008	67.5	69.1	69.5	69.9	69.7	69.1	68.7	69.5	68.2	69.2	69.3	69.4	69.1
2009	67.2	67.9	67.7	67.9	68.2	67.7	66.5	66.3	66.2	67.8	68.0	68.5	67.5
2010	66.2	67.1	67.8	69.7	69.5	69.8	69.5	69.0	68.0	68.6	68.8	68.7	68.6
2011	67.1	68.6	68.3	68.8	68.5	68.1	67.4	68.0	68.0	69.7	69.8	69.9	68.5
2012	67.8	69.0	69.5	71.4	71.0	69.4	69.8	69.1	68.1	70.5	70.4	70.0	69.7
2013	70.3	73.6	71.7	72.0	71.7	71.6	72.1	72.5	71.8	73.9	74.0	74.3	72.5
2014	72.9	73.9	74.7	75.2	74.5	74.8	74.0	74.0	73.2	75.1	75.4	75.5	74.4
2015	73.8	74.1	75.0	76.4	75.7	74.9	75.1	75.4	74.1	75.5	75.0	75.7	75.1
Education and Health Services													
2005	84.4	84.0	84.6	84.8	84.0	85.4	82.0	81.0	67.0	53.7	52.8	53.5	74.8
2006	55.5	55.4	56.8	58.1	58.6	58.2	58.1	58.3	60.4	61.6	63.7	62.8	59.0
2007	64.3	65.0	65.6	65.9	64.7	64.5	64.4	66.2	67.4	69.2	69.8	70.0	66.4
2008	69.6	70.4	70.9	71.0	68.9	68.8	68.9	70.6	70.7	73.0	73.5	73.7	70.8
2009	74.1	74.9	75.3	75.8	76.1	73.4	73.6	75.5	75.7	77.3	77.6	77.6	75.6
2010	77.5	77.8	78.3	79.2	76.4	75.3	75.2	76.0	77.1	78.4	78.8	78.8	77.4
2011	77.5	78.6	79.1	79.8	79.1	77.4	77.5	78.6	80.2	81.4	82.1	81.7	79.4
2012	80.0	81.0	81.8	81.7	81.7	81.0	80.4	81.9	81.9	82.7	82.9	83.0	81.7
2013	84.4	84.9	84.5	84.0	83.6	82.2	81.5	85.9	86.6	88.3	88.4	88.2	85.2
2014	87.7	88.3	88.4	88.7	88.9	88.0	88.1	91.0	91.8	92.3	92.7	92.3	89.9
2015	92.3	92.7	92.9	94.1	94.3	93.1	93.1	94.0	94.4	95.0	94.6	95.5	93.8

Employment by Industry: New Orleans-Metairie, LA, 2005–2015—*Continued*

(Numbers in thousands, not seasonally adjusted)

Industry and year	January	February	March	April	May	June	July	August	September	October	November	December	Annual average
Leisure and Hospitality													
2005	84.0	84.0	85.9	86.6	87.6	89.0	86.2	86.0	52.1	42.5	44.4	46.6	72.9
2006	47.6	51.5	54.4	54.7	56.5	60.0	60.6	61.1	60.3	61.9	63.0	64.5	58.0
2007	63.8	64.3	65.7	65.4	66.6	67.4	66.3	66.9	65.3	66.0	66.9	68.0	66.1
2008	67.5	68.0	68.6	69.3	69.4	69.9	68.8	69.4	65.8	67.5	67.4	67.6	68.3
2009	66.6	67.5	68.3	68.2	69.0	69.1	67.6	68.7	67.8	67.3	67.4	67.7	67.9
2010	67.8	68.4	69.6	70.2	70.0	70.6	69.1	69.6	70.4	70.2	71.3	72.4	70.0
2011	70.9	71.9	73.0	73.6	74.2	74.5	73.6	74.6	74.3	73.8	74.9	76.1	73.8
2012	75.8	75.9	76.5	77.4	76.9	76.9	76.3	76.8	74.8	76.1	76.9	78.6	76.6
2013	77.9	77.6	78.5	79.3	79.3	79.5	78.4	80.7	78.0	78.8	81.1	80.6	79.1
2014	80.4	81.7	82.3	82.5	83.3	83.9	82.6	83.7	81.6	83.5	84.9	84.0	82.9
2015	83.8	84.3	85.2	85.5	85.8	85.7	85.3	84.7	83.5	85.6	85.2	85.9	85.0
Other Services													
2005	23.1	23.2	23.4	23.6	23.7	23.7	23.8	23.6	16.7	14.5	14.5	15.1	20.7
2006	14.9	15.6	16.0	16.3	16.7	17.0	17.2	17.5	17.7	18.2	18.2	18.3	17.0
2007	19.4	19.8	20.1	20.9	21.1	21.3	22.0	22.2	22.3	22.7	22.7	22.9	21.5
2008	22.0	22.2	22.3	20.3	20.5	20.6	20.2	20.3	20.1	21.6	21.8	21.7	21.1
2009	21.6	21.8	21.9	22.1	22.2	22.1	22.2	22.4	22.5	21.9	22.0	22.1	22.1
2010	21.3	21.4	21.5	20.7	20.7	20.9	20.6	20.6	20.5	21.0	21.1	21.2	21.0
2011	21.2	21.3	21.4	21.6	21.6	21.8	21.8	21.8	21.7	21.9	22.0	22.0	21.7
2012	21.9	22.0	22.2	22.3	22.4	22.5	22.5	22.4	22.3	22.4	22.4	22.5	22.3
2013	22.5	22.6	22.7	22.9	22.9	23.0	23.1	23.1	22.9	22.9	22.9	22.9	22.9
2014	23.0	22.9	23.0	22.9	23.1	23.1	23.0	23.0	22.8	23.0	22.9	23.0	23.0
2015	22.9	23.0	22.9	23.2	23.3	23.4	23.7	23.6	23.4	23.6	23.6	23.6	23.4
Government													
2005	106.8	107.9	108.5	106.7	106.2	106.6	103.1	103.9	103.5	81.9	81.7	81.3	99.8
2006	74.3	74.4	75.1	75.0	75.4	75.1	73.6	74.2	77.6	77.7	78.8	79.6	75.9
2007	78.0	79.0	79.7	74.4	74.8	75.2	73.1	74.2	77.5	79.8	80.5	80.8	77.3
2008	79.6	80.4	80.3	82.4	82.5	81.2	80.2	82.4	83.4	84.2	84.7	84.5	82.2
2009	83.5	84.0	83.6	85.1	84.8	82.4	83.2	85.0	84.6	85.8	85.6	85.2	84.4
2010	83.9	84.4	85.1	84.9	86.5	84.5	81.9	82.7	83.1	83.5	83.8	83.3	84.0
2011	82.4	82.4	82.1	82.3	82.1	80.1	78.4	79.8	81.3	80.8	80.9	80.5	81.1
2012	78.5	79.3	78.9	80.2	80.1	78.9	76.5	77.8	78.7	79.1	79.3	79.3	78.9
2013	77.6	78.1	78.1	77.8	78.1	77.0	73.8	73.5	74.5	74.8	75.1	75.3	76.1
2014	73.6	74.9	75.2	74.6	74.3	76.2	72.9	72.9	74.3	74.8	75.0	74.2	74.4
2015	73.3	74.4	73.9	74.1	74.1	72.9	70.6	71.3	73.1	73.9	74.3	73.6	73.3

Employment by Industry: Hartford-West Hartford-East Hartford, CT NECTA, 2005–2015

(Numbers in thousands, not seasonally adjusted)

Industry and year	January	February	March	April	May	June	July	August	September	October	November	December	Annual average
Total Nonfarm													
2005	544.3	545.6	546.7	554.2	556.1	558.3	548.8	547.2	556.2	557.2	561.4	562.4	553.2
2006	550.6	551.3	553.3	559.7	561.9	563.2	557.3	555.5	562.7	567.3	569.4	570.4	560.2
2007	556.4	558.8	560.2	565.0	568.5	571.7	562.8	560.6	568.7	571.9	576.0	575.4	566.3
2008	562.0	565.7	567.5	571.4	572.6	574.9	565.6	562.0	570.5	572.6	571.1	567.5	568.6
2009	551.1	553.7	551.2	552.3	553.5	552.3	543.0	539.9	549.3	552.1	552.7	551.6	550.2
2010	530.9	534.3	536.6	544.3	546.2	545.1	538.6	536.3	548.0	552.7	554.8	554.7	543.5
2011	539.9	543.6	544.4	551.9	550.6	549.9	544.2	539.7	551.6	553.2	553.6	555.6	548.2
2012	541.4	546.5	548.6	551.4	551.8	554.2	547.6	545.3	556.7	561.8	564.8	563.7	552.8
2013	549.0	550.4	553.3	558.7	559.9	563.3	554.4	551.2	560.5	562.5	565.9	565.2	557.9
2014	552.8	554.1	556.6	563.9	565.7	568.1	559.2	556.6	567.1	571.4	573.4	573.3	563.5
2015	559.5	560.5	562.9	568.4	570.8	574.1	564.4	560.9	570.7	574.5	578.3	576.1	568.4
Total Private													
2005	457.0	455.5	457.0	463.1	465.8	470.5	466.7	466.0	466.5	465.8	468.3	471.0	464.4
2006	461.9	460.1	462.2	467.0	469.8	474.2	473.1	472.2	471.6	473.3	474.1	476.7	469.7
2007	465.9	464.8	466.3	470.4	476.9	482.7	478.8	477.6	477.3	477.4	480.6	482.0	475.1
2008	472.3	471.4	473.2	476.3	480.6	485.4	480.8	478.2	478.8	478.1	476.7	475.3	477.3
2009	462.6	459.3	457.2	456.9	461.5	463.3	459.8	457.7	457.7	457.1	457.4	457.5	459.0
2010	443.4	442.9	444.8	452.0	456.1	459.2	457.4	456.4	458.4	460.3	462.2	463.1	454.7
2011	452.0	452.3	453.3	460.1	463.0	465.8	464.1	461.3	462.3	461.6	462.1	464.7	460.2
2012	455.5	456.0	458.4	461.9	464.4	470.2	467.6	466.5	467.3	470.0	472.3	472.2	465.4
2013	461.3	460.3	463.0	468.3	472.7	476.4	472.4	471.6	471.9	471.9	475.0	474.8	470.0
2014	464.0	463.7	465.6	473.1	477.7	480.9	477.1	476.1	477.1	478.9	480.7	481.5	474.7
2015	470.6	470.0	472.2	477.8	483.2	487.7	482.7	481.1	481.5	483.0	486.6	485.0	480.1
Goods Producing													
2005	83.9	83.2	83.6	85.4	86.2	87.6	86.9	86.8	86.5	86.2	86.3	85.9	85.7
2006	84.0	83.7	84.1	86.0	86.7	88.0	88.4	88.5	88.0	87.8	87.6	87.4	86.7
2007	85.0	84.3	84.7	86.3	87.7	88.8	88.7	88.8	87.9	87.7	87.6	86.8	87.0
2008	84.3	83.9	83.7	85.5	86.0	87.0	86.6	86.4	86.0	85.2	83.9	82.4	85.1
2009	79.8	78.2	77.2	77.2	77.5	77.7	77.3	76.8	76.9	75.7	75.2	74.6	77.0
2010	71.3	70.5	70.7	72.7	73.7	74.7	74.6	74.7	75.0	75.2	75.1	74.9	73.6
2011	72.2	72.0	72.5	73.7	74.7	76.0	76.1	75.9	75.8	75.4	75.5	75.0	74.6
2012	73.1	72.7	73.0	74.0	74.6	75.7	76.1	75.9	75.3	75.5	75.3	75.1	74.7
2013	73.0	72.6	72.7	74.1	75.4	76.1	76.6	75.9	75.5	75.0	74.8	74.3	74.7
2014	71.9	71.6	71.6	73.5	74.4	75.3	75.9	75.9	75.5	75.6	75.4	74.9	74.3
2015	72.8	72.6	73.1	75.2	76.3	77.3	76.8	77.0	76.5	76.4	76.7	75.1	75.5
Service-Providing													
2005	460.4	462.4	463.1	468.8	469.9	470.7	461.9	460.4	469.7	471.0	475.1	476.5	467.5
2006	466.6	467.6	469.2	473.7	475.2	475.2	468.9	467.0	474.7	479.5	481.8	483.0	473.5
2007	471.4	474.5	475.5	478.7	480.8	482.9	474.1	471.8	480.8	484.2	488.4	488.6	479.3
2008	477.7	481.8	483.8	485.9	486.6	487.9	479.0	475.6	484.5	487.4	487.2	485.1	483.5
2009	471.3	475.5	474.0	475.1	476.0	474.6	465.7	463.1	472.4	476.4	477.5	477.0	473.2
2010	459.6	463.8	465.9	471.6	472.5	470.4	464.0	461.6	473.0	477.5	479.7	479.8	470.0
2011	467.7	471.6	471.9	478.2	475.9	473.9	468.1	463.8	475.8	477.8	478.1	480.6	473.6
2012	468.3	473.8	475.6	477.4	477.2	478.5	471.5	469.4	481.4	486.3	489.5	488.6	478.1
2013	476.0	477.8	480.6	484.6	484.5	487.2	477.8	475.3	485.0	487.5	491.1	490.9	483.2
2014	480.9	482.5	485.0	490.4	491.3	492.8	483.3	480.7	491.6	495.8	498.0	498.4	489.2
2015	486.7	487.9	489.8	493.2	494.5	496.8	487.6	483.9	494.2	498.1	501.6	501.0	492.9
Mining, Logging, and Construction													
2005	20.0	19.4	19.7	21.1	21.8	22.8	22.9	23.0	22.6	22.2	22.2	21.6	21.6
2006	20.1	19.7	20.0	21.4	22.1	22.7	23.3	23.6	23.1	22.9	22.7	22.2	22.0
2007	20.5	19.8	20.2	21.8	23.1	23.6	23.8	23.9	23.5	23.3	23.0	22.1	22.4
2008	20.2	19.9	19.9	21.2	21.7	22.1	22.3	22.1	21.7	21.2	20.4	19.4	21.0
2009	17.6	17.0	17.0	17.8	18.5	18.9	19.2	19.2	19.0	18.5	18.3	17.7	18.2
2010	15.2	14.5	14.6	16.6	17.3	17.8	18.0	18.2	18.0	18.1	17.9	17.3	17.0
2011	15.4	15.1	15.3	16.5	17.3	18.1	18.4	18.4	18.2	18.0	18.1	17.4	17.2
2012	15.8	15.3	15.7	16.7	17.1	17.7	18.2	18.3	18.1	18.2	18.0	17.6	17.2
2013	16.0	15.8	16.0	17.3	18.5	18.9	19.4	19.4	19.3	19.3	19.1	18.4	18.1
2014	16.8	16.5	16.5	18.3	19.3	19.7	20.4	20.5	20.3	20.2	20.0	19.3	19.0
2015	17.7	17.4	17.6	19.6	20.6	21.1	21.1	21.3	21.0	21.0	20.8	19.5	19.9

Employment by Industry: Hartford-West Hartford-East Hartford, CT NECTA, 2005–2015—*Continued*

(Numbers in thousands, not seasonally adjusted)

Industry and year	January	February	March	April	May	June	July	August	September	October	November	December	Annual average
Manufacturing													
2005	63.9	63.8	63.9	64.3	64.4	64.8	64.0	63.8	63.9	64.0	64.1	64.3	64.1
2006	63.9	64.0	64.1	64.6	64.6	65.3	65.1	64.9	64.9	64.9	64.9	65.2	64.7
2007	64.5	64.5	64.5	64.5	64.6	65.2	64.9	64.9	64.4	64.4	64.6	64.7	64.6
2008	64.1	64.0	63.8	64.3	64.3	64.9	64.3	64.3	64.3	64.0	63.5	63.0	64.1
2009	62.2	61.2	60.2	59.4	59.0	58.8	58.1	57.6	57.9	57.2	56.9	56.9	58.8
2010	56.1	56.0	56.1	56.1	56.4	56.9	56.6	56.5	57.0	57.1	57.2	57.6	56.6
2011	56.8	56.9	57.2	57.2	57.4	57.9	57.7	57.5	57.6	57.4	57.4	57.6	57.4
2012	57.3	57.4	57.3	57.3	57.5	58.0	57.9	57.6	57.2	57.3	57.3	57.5	57.5
2013	57.0	56.8	56.7	56.8	56.9	57.2	57.2	56.5	56.2	55.7	55.7	55.9	56.6
2014	55.1	55.1	55.1	55.2	55.1	55.6	55.5	55.4	55.2	55.4	55.4	55.6	55.3
2015	55.1	55.2	55.5	55.6	55.7	56.2	55.7	55.7	55.5	55.4	55.9	55.6	55.6
Trade, Transportation, and Utilities													
2005	90.6	89.5	89.6	90.5	90.8	91.4	89.0	88.8	90.4	90.3	92.5	94.2	90.6
2006	90.6	88.6	89.1	89.9	90.2	90.5	88.3	88.2	89.7	90.3	92.0	93.7	90.1
2007	89.6	88.2	88.6	88.4	90.1	91.1	89.2	88.7	90.3	91.3	93.6	95.3	90.4
2008	91.4	90.0	90.2	90.2	90.9	91.5	89.2	88.8	90.1	90.4	91.3	92.3	90.5
2009	88.0	86.4	85.7	84.4	85.8	86.3	84.3	84.2	85.3	85.9	87.3	88.2	86.0
2010	85.0	83.8	83.8	84.1	85.4	86.3	84.8	84.4	85.0	86.1	87.8	89.3	85.5
2011	85.8	84.9	85.0	86.2	86.5	87.1	85.4	85.0	85.7	86.0	87.7	89.4	86.2
2012	86.2	85.1	85.6	85.7	87.0	87.3	85.4	85.2	86.5	87.4	89.5	90.3	86.8
2013	87.7	86.2	87.0	87.9	88.6	89.4	87.3	87.3	88.8	89.8	91.9	92.9	88.7
2014	89.2	88.0	88.2	89.1	89.7	90.3	87.9	87.4	89.3	90.1	91.7	92.7	89.5
2015	89.5	88.2	88.2	88.7	89.8	90.5	87.8	87.6	89.9	89.8	91.0	92.1	89.4
Wholesale Trade													
2005	19.3	19.2	19.3	19.7	19.8	20.0	19.8	19.8	19.9	19.8	19.8	19.8	19.7
2006	19.8	19.7	19.8	20.0	19.9	20.1	19.9	19.9	19.8	19.8	19.7	19.7	19.8
2007	19.7	19.7	19.8	19.8	20.0	20.1	20.2	20.1	20.1	20.1	20.1	20.3	20.0
2008	20.1	20.1	20.3	20.2	20.4	20.5	20.3	20.2	20.1	20.0	19.8	19.6	20.1
2009	19.4	19.2	19.1	18.9	18.8	18.9	18.8	18.8	18.6	18.5	18.4	18.5	18.8
2010	18.0	18.0	18.0	18.2	18.3	18.5	18.5	18.5	18.3	18.3	18.4	18.4	18.3
2011	18.0	18.0	18.1	18.3	18.4	18.5	18.4	18.4	18.2	18.1	18.0	18.0	18.2
2012	17.8	17.8	17.8	17.9	18.1	18.1	18.2	18.1	18.0	18.2	18.0	18.1	18.0
2013	17.9	17.9	17.9	18.0	18.1	18.2	18.1	18.1	18.0	18.1	18.0	18.1	18.0
2014	17.9	17.8	17.9	18.0	18.0	18.1	18.1	18.0	18.0	17.9	17.8	17.9	18.0
2015	17.8	17.7	17.8	17.9	18.0	18.1	18.0	18.1	18.1	17.8	17.6	17.8	17.9
Retail Trade													
2005	58.0	57.2	57.1	57.5	57.6	57.8	56.8	56.9	57.1	57.1	59.0	60.4	57.7
2006	57.7	55.9	56.4	57.0	57.2	57.2	56.4	56.3	56.5	57.0	58.8	60.0	57.2
2007	56.7	55.3	55.7	55.8	57.1	57.8	56.9	57.0	56.9	57.7	59.9	61.1	57.3
2008	58.2	56.7	56.8	56.8	57.2	57.6	56.5	56.7	56.4	56.6	57.6	58.5	57.1
2009	55.1	53.8	53.4	53.0	53.8	54.3	53.6	53.7	53.7	54.2	55.6	56.4	54.2
2010	53.7	52.5	52.6	53.0	53.6	54.4	54.1	53.9	53.4	54.4	55.8	57.2	54.1
2011	54.6	53.6	53.5	54.4	54.5	54.9	54.3	54.3	53.8	54.3	56.0	57.4	54.6
2012	55.1	54.0	54.3	54.4	55.1	55.3	54.6	54.6	54.2	54.9	57.1	57.5	55.1
2013	55.6	54.4	54.8	55.3	55.7	56.2	55.7	56.0	55.6	56.4	58.2	58.8	56.1
2014	56.3	55.2	55.3	55.9	56.4	56.8	55.9	55.7	55.6	56.3	58.0	58.5	56.3
2015	56.2	55.1	55.1	55.3	56.0	56.5	55.5	55.5	55.3	55.4	56.7	57.1	55.8
Transportation and Utilities													
2005	13.3	13.1	13.2	13.3	13.4	13.6	12.4	12.1	13.4	13.4	13.7	14.0	13.2
2006	13.1	13.0	12.9	12.9	13.1	13.2	12.0	12.0	13.4	13.5	13.5	14.0	13.1
2007	13.2	13.2	13.1	12.8	13.0	13.2	12.1	11.6	13.3	13.5	13.6	13.9	13.0
2008	13.1	13.2	13.1	13.2	13.3	13.4	12.4	11.9	13.6	13.8	13.9	14.2	13.3
2009	13.5	13.4	13.2	12.5	13.2	13.1	11.9	11.7	13.0	13.2	13.3	13.3	12.9
2010	13.3	13.3	13.2	12.9	13.5	13.4	12.2	12.0	13.3	13.4	13.6	13.7	13.2
2011	13.2	13.3	13.4	13.5	13.6	13.7	12.7	12.3	13.7	13.6	13.7	14.0	13.4
2012	13.3	13.3	13.5	13.4	13.8	13.9	12.6	12.5	14.3	14.3	14.4	14.7	13.7
2013	14.2	13.9	14.3	14.6	14.8	15.0	13.5	13.2	15.2	15.3	15.7	16.0	14.6
2014	15.0	15.0	15.0	15.2	15.3	15.4	13.9	13.7	15.7	15.9	15.9	16.3	15.2
2015	15.5	15.4	15.3	15.5	15.8	15.9	14.3	14.0	16.5	16.6	16.7	17.2	15.7

Employment by Industry: Hartford-West Hartford-East Hartford, CT NECTA, 2005–2015—*Continued*

(Numbers in thousands, not seasonally adjusted)

Industry and year	January	February	March	April	May	June	July	August	September	October	November	December	Annual average
Information													
2005	11.8	11.7	11.7	11.7	11.8	11.9	11.9	11.9	11.8	11.9	12.0	12.1	11.9
2006	12.3	12.3	12.3	12.2	12.2	12.4	12.4	12.3	12.1	12.2	12.1	12.1	12.2
2007	12.1	12.2	12.2	12.3	12.3	12.5	12.6	12.6	12.5	12.4	12.5	12.6	12.4
2008	12.6	12.6	12.6	12.6	12.6	12.8	12.9	12.7	12.4	12.3	12.4	12.3	12.6
2009	12.2	12.2	12.0	12.0	11.9	11.9	11.9	11.8	11.7	11.5	11.4	11.4	11.8
2010	11.3	11.2	11.2	11.2	11.2	11.2	11.3	11.4	11.4	11.4	11.5	11.5	11.3
2011	11.5	11.4	11.4	11.3	11.3	11.3	11.3	11.3	11.2	11.1	11.1	11.0	11.3
2012	11.0	11.1	10.9	11.1	11.2	11.2	11.2	11.3	11.3	11.3	11.6	11.3	11.2
2013	11.5	11.7	11.7	11.4	11.5	11.5	11.5	11.6	11.2	11.2	11.3	11.3	11.5
2014	11.2	11.3	11.5	11.5	11.4	11.5	11.6	11.7	11.5	11.3	11.6	11.7	11.5
2015	11.5	11.6	11.6	11.8	11.8	11.9	11.9	11.9	11.9	11.9	11.9	11.9	11.8
Financial Activities													
2005	68.3	68.0	67.2	68.1	67.8	68.6	68.6	68.6	68.0	67.7	67.6	67.9	68.0
2006	68.0	67.8	67.7	67.3	67.4	68.1	68.4	68.2	67.6	67.5	67.6	67.8	67.8
2007	67.8	67.3	67.1	66.8	66.9	67.7	67.4	67.3	66.6	66.3	66.3	66.4	67.0
2008	66.1	66.2	66.8	66.1	66.2	67.0	67.0	66.9	65.9	65.5	65.6	65.4	66.2
2009	64.9	64.6	64.6	64.0	64.0	64.3	63.9	63.6	62.8	62.4	62.3	62.1	63.6
2010	61.8	61.8	62.2	61.4	61.5	62.4	62.4	62.6	62.0	62.2	62.2	62.3	62.1
2011	62.2	62.0	62.2	61.8	61.8	62.3	62.5	62.3	61.7	61.6	61.4	61.5	61.9
2012	61.1	61.1	61.3	60.7	60.7	61.6	61.6	61.1	60.5	60.3	60.1	60.1	60.9
2013	60.0	59.5	59.4	59.1	58.8	59.6	59.4	58.7	57.6	56.9	56.7	56.7	58.5
2014	57.0	56.6	56.4	56.3	56.5	57.1	57.4	57.1	56.6	56.7	56.7	56.8	56.8
2015	56.7	56.6	56.7	56.7	56.9	57.8	58.0	57.8	57.1	57.1	57.5	57.4	57.2
Professional and Business Services													
2005	59.0	59.0	59.7	60.3	60.2	61.4	61.6	61.6	61.7	61.1	61.4	61.7	60.7
2006	60.4	60.7	61.0	62.1	61.9	62.8	62.8	62.8	62.6	62.7	62.5	62.6	62.1
2007	60.8	61.1	61.4	63.0	63.4	64.5	63.8	64.0	63.4	63.2	63.6	64.3	63.0
2008	63.7	64.0	64.2	64.5	65.0	65.9	65.5	65.2	64.7	64.2	63.9	63.1	64.5
2009	62.0	61.2	60.7	61.2	61.5	61.6	60.8	61.1	60.5	60.8	60.8	60.7	61.1
2010	58.3	59.1	59.0	61.4	61.6	62.0	61.8	61.6	61.5	61.9	61.8	61.6	61.0
2011	60.6	60.9	60.5	62.4	62.5	63.2	63.4	63.1	63.2	63.7	63.5	64.1	62.6
2012	62.8	63.3	63.9	65.0	65.5	66.2	66.1	66.3	66.0	66.4	66.4	66.0	65.3
2013	63.6	64.4	64.3	65.9	66.5	67.4	67.5	68.1	68.4	68.4	68.9	68.9	66.9
2014	67.6	68.5	68.7	70.3	71.5	71.9	71.2	71.2	71.0	71.7	71.9	72.0	70.6
2015	70.7	71.5	71.9	72.7	73.6	74.9	74.1	73.6	73.4	73.4	73.8	73.4	73.1
Education and Health Services													
2005	85.9	86.4	86.6	86.9	87.1	86.2	85.6	85.4	86.8	88.3	88.3	88.6	86.8
2006	87.6	88.0	88.0	88.6	88.8	88.1	88.5	88.2	89.2	90.6	91.0	91.2	89.0
2007	90.7	91.5	92.0	92.1	92.3	92.0	91.4	90.6	92.7	93.4	94.3	94.1	92.3
2008	93.7	94.1	94.5	94.9	94.8	94.9	94.5	93.7	95.8	96.9	97.5	97.6	95.2
2009	96.4	97.1	97.4	97.7	97.3	97.0	97.8	97.1	98.2	99.1	99.3	99.4	97.8
2010	98.1	98.5	99.2	99.9	99.3	98.5	97.7	97.2	99.4	100.4	101.0	101.1	99.2
2011	100.4	101.0	101.5	102.0	101.4	100.0	99.2	98.4	100.2	100.0	99.8	100.3	100.4
2012	99.4	100.4	100.8	100.7	100.4	99.6	99.2	98.8	101.2	102.3	103.0	103.5	100.8
2013	101.5	102.1	103.0	103.1	102.5	102.0	100.6	100.8	103.2	103.5	104.3	103.9	102.5
2014	102.1	102.9	103.4	104.8	104.3	103.9	102.4	103.0	105.0	105.3	105.8	105.9	104.1
2015	103.8	104.2	104.4	104.9	104.6	104.5	103.5	103.0	104.3	104.9	105.9	106.0	104.5
Leisure and Hospitality													
2005	36.8	37.0	37.8	39.2	41.0	42.1	42.0	42.0	40.6	39.5	39.4	39.7	39.8
2006	38.3	38.3	39.1	39.9	41.5	43.0	43.0	42.9	41.4	41.1	40.3	40.9	40.8
2007	39.0	39.3	39.4	40.4	43.1	44.6	44.5	44.5	42.9	41.9	41.7	41.5	41.9
2008	39.7	39.7	40.2	41.4	43.9	44.9	44.3	43.8	43.0	42.7	41.2	41.5	42.2
2009	38.7	39.2	39.2	39.9	42.9	43.9	43.5	42.8	42.0	41.3	40.8	40.7	41.2
2010	37.5	38.0	38.6	41.1	43.0	43.5	44.3	44.0	43.6	42.6	42.2	41.9	41.7
2011	39.1	39.9	39.9	42.2	44.1	44.8	45.5	44.8	44.2	43.5	42.7	43.0	42.8
2012	41.4	41.8	42.6	44.2	46.2	47.4	46.8	46.6	45.3	45.2	44.6	44.8	44.7
2013	43.0	42.7	43.7	45.9	48.3	48.9	48.3	48.2	46.4	46.4	46.3	45.9	46.2
2014	44.2	44.0	44.9	46.5	48.6	49.3	49.1	48.4	46.8	46.7	46.1	46.1	46.7
2015	44.3	44.0	44.8	46.3	48.4	48.9	48.7	47.9	46.8	47.8	48.0	47.3	46.9

Employment by Industry: Hartford-West Hartford-East Hartford, CT NECTA, 2005–2015—*Continued*

(Numbers in thousands, not seasonally adjusted)

Industry and year	January	February	March	April	May	June	July	August	September	October	November	December	Annual average
Other Services													
2005	20.7	20.7	20.8	21.0	20.9	21.3	21.1	20.9	20.7	20.8	20.8	20.9	20.9
2006	20.7	20.7	20.9	21.0	21.1	21.3	21.3	21.1	21.0	21.1	21.0	21.0	21.0
2007	20.9	20.9	20.9	21.1	21.1	21.5	21.2	21.1	21.0	21.2	21.0	21.0	21.1
2008	20.8	20.9	21.0	21.1	21.2	21.4	20.8	20.7	20.9	20.9	20.9	20.7	20.9
2009	20.6	20.4	20.4	20.5	20.6	20.6	20.3	20.3	20.3	20.4	20.3	20.4	20.4
2010	20.1	20.0	20.1	20.2	20.4	20.6	20.5	20.5	20.5	20.5	20.6	20.5	20.4
2011	20.2	20.2	20.3	20.5	20.7	21.1	20.7	20.5	20.3	20.3	20.4	20.4	20.5
2012	20.5	20.5	20.3	20.5	20.8	21.2	21.2	21.3	21.2	21.6	21.8	21.1	21.0
2013	21.0	21.1	21.2	20.9	21.1	21.5	21.2	21.0	20.8	20.7	20.8	20.9	21.0
2014	20.8	20.8	20.9	21.1	21.3	21.6	21.6	21.4	21.4	21.5	21.5	21.4	21.3
2015	21.3	21.3	21.5	21.5	21.8	21.9	21.9	22.3	21.6	21.7	21.8	21.8	21.7
Government													
2005	87.3	90.1	89.7	91.1	90.3	87.8	82.1	81.2	89.7	91.4	93.1	91.4	88.8
2006	88.7	91.2	91.1	92.7	92.1	89.0	84.2	83.3	91.1	94.0	95.3	93.7	90.5
2007	90.5	94.0	93.9	94.6	91.6	89.0	84.0	83.0	91.4	94.5	95.4	93.4	91.3
2008	89.7	94.3	94.3	95.1	92.0	89.5	84.8	83.8	91.7	94.5	94.4	92.2	91.4
2009	88.5	94.4	94.0	95.4	92.0	89.0	83.2	82.2	91.6	95.0	95.3	94.1	91.2
2010	87.5	91.4	91.8	92.3	90.1	85.9	81.2	79.9	89.6	92.4	92.6	91.6	88.9
2011	87.9	91.3	91.1	91.8	87.6	84.1	80.1	78.4	89.3	91.6	91.5	90.9	88.0
2012	85.9	90.5	90.2	89.5	85.4	84.0	80.0	78.8	89.4	91.8	92.5	91.5	87.5
2013	87.7	90.1	90.3	90.4	87.2	86.9	82.0	79.6	88.6	90.6	90.9	90.4	87.9
2014	88.8	90.4	91.0	90.8	88.0	87.2	82.1	80.5	90.0	92.5	92.7	91.8	88.8
2015	88.9	90.5	90.7	90.6	87.6	86.4	81.7	79.8	89.2	91.5	91.7	91.1	88.3

Employment by Industry: Salt Lake City, UT, 2005–2015

(Numbers in thousands, not seasonally adjusted)

Industry and year	January	February	March	April	May	June	July	August	September	October	November	December	Annual average
Total Nonfarm													
2005	550.8	553.5	555.4	563.0	563.9	567.4	568.4	572.7	575.7	577.2	582.3	586.4	568.1
2006	574.3	578.2	582.6	586.4	590.2	595.8	592.8	598.1	600.5	601.2	607.7	612.3	593.3
2007	601.1	603.8	608.2	610.6	614.4	618.9	614.6	619.0	619.1	620.3	625.2	627.8	615.3
2008	613.8	615.1	617.1	619.4	619.8	621.8	617.4	621.2	620.8	618.8	616.9	616.4	618.2
2009	595.6	592.3	590.9	588.4	588.9	588.6	582.0	583.9	586.2	587.6	588.8	591.1	588.7
2010	576.9	576.6	580.7	583.9	586.8	588.4	586.6	587.7	590.4	594.7	597.4	598.5	587.4
2011	585.5	586.9	589.9	594.7	595.1	597.8	596.2	600.2	603.8	604.7	609.2	610.6	597.9
2012	600.9	603.9	607.4	617.2	621.8	624.4	616.2	620.8	625.0	629.2	636.0	636.3	619.9
2013	625.0	628.7	632.2	636.6	637.9	639.5	634.7	638.3	641.1	648.9	654.5	655.9	639.4
2014	641.7	644.2	646.7	650.7	652.1	655.6	647.5	652.7	658.0	663.0	668.6	671.1	654.3
2015	660.3	663.6	668.3	670.5	674.2	676.1	674.7	677.5	682.1	686.0	688.9	690.5	676.1
Total Private													
2005	462.5	465.0	467.2	474.2	475.6	479.0	482.4	486.5	486.9	488.1	492.9	496.7	479.8
2006	485.2	488.5	493.1	496.7	501.0	505.9	505.8	511.1	510.9	511.1	517.6	521.8	504.1
2007	511.2	513.7	518.1	520.1	524.2	528.1	527.3	531.2	528.6	529.2	533.8	536.1	525.1
2008	522.4	523.4	525.0	527.2	527.6	529.0	528.4	531.1	527.2	524.9	522.7	522.1	525.9
2009	502.2	498.4	497.2	494.0	494.8	494.3	491.7	492.8	491.8	492.8	494.2	496.3	495.0
2010	482.6	482.4	486.5	489.0	490.2	492.8	494.6	495.3	494.3	497.8	500.5	502.4	492.4
2011	490.3	491.6	494.5	498.4	498.7	501.3	503.5	507.0	507.4	508.6	512.5	513.7	502.3
2012	504.1	506.7	510.1	518.6	523.6	526.2	522.6	527.3	527.3	530.2	537.2	538.2	522.7
2013	527.4	530.7	534.4	537.0	537.8	539.0	539.2	543.1	540.7	546.1	552.1	553.5	540.1
2014	539.5	541.2	543.5	546.2	547.2	550.4	549.5	555.4	555.4	559.4	564.9	567.2	551.7
2015	557.2	559.7	563.7	565.3	568.5	571.3	574.7	578.9	577.7	580.0	582.9	584.2	572.0
Goods Producing													
2005	84.3	84.6	85.2	87.5	89.0	90.6	91.8	92.8	92.9	92.2	92.4	92.3	89.6
2006	90.5	91.5	93.0	94.5	97.1	99.3	99.6	100.8	101.4	101.4	101.5	101.1	97.6
2007	98.9	99.1	100.6	101.7	103.6	105.7	105.6	106.7	105.5	104.5	103.7	102.3	103.2
2008	99.3	98.3	99.0	99.5	100.1	101.2	101.4	101.6	100.4	99.2	96.7	94.7	99.3
2009	88.7	86.4	86.0	85.0	86.3	86.9	87.3	87.5	87.1	86.8	86.0	85.0	86.6
2010	82.2	81.6	82.1	83.4	84.5	85.3	85.9	86.6	86.6	86.8	86.0	85.1	84.7
2011	82.9	82.6	83.2	84.2	85.2	86.4	88.5	89.3	88.8	88.6	88.3	87.3	86.3
2012	85.3	85.9	86.5	88.0	89.9	90.7	90.6	91.2	90.8	90.7	90.1	89.6	89.1
2013	87.4	87.2	88.0	89.1	89.7	90.1	89.9	90.8	90.1	89.6	89.2	88.4	89.1
2014	86.5	86.9	87.6	88.6	89.4	90.2	90.4	91.1	91.1	91.5	91.0	90.3	89.6
2015	88.5	88.8	89.9	90.8	91.8	92.8	93.5	93.7	93.4	95.0	93.9	92.4	92.0
Service-Providing													
2005	466.5	468.9	470.2	475.5	474.9	476.8	476.6	479.9	482.8	485.0	489.9	494.1	478.4
2006	483.8	486.7	489.6	491.9	493.1	496.5	493.2	497.3	499.1	499.8	506.2	511.2	495.7
2007	502.2	504.7	507.6	508.9	510.8	513.2	509.0	512.3	513.6	515.8	521.5	525.5	512.1
2008	514.5	516.8	518.1	519.9	519.7	520.6	516.0	519.6	520.4	519.6	520.2	521.7	518.9
2009	506.9	505.9	504.9	503.4	502.6	501.7	494.7	496.4	499.1	500.8	502.8	506.1	502.1
2010	494.7	495.0	498.6	500.5	502.3	503.1	500.7	501.1	503.8	507.9	511.4	513.4	502.7
2011	502.6	504.3	506.7	510.5	509.9	511.4	507.7	510.9	515.0	516.1	520.9	523.3	511.6
2012	515.6	518.0	520.9	529.2	531.9	533.7	525.6	529.6	534.2	538.5	545.9	546.7	530.8
2013	537.6	541.5	544.2	547.5	548.2	549.4	544.8	547.5	551.0	559.3	565.3	567.5	550.3
2014	555.2	557.3	559.1	562.1	562.7	565.4	557.1	561.6	566.9	571.5	577.6	580.8	564.8
2015	571.8	574.8	578.4	579.7	582.4	583.3	581.2	583.8	588.7	591.0	595.0	598.1	584.0
Mining, Logging, and Construction													
2005	32.6	32.7	33.7	35.4	36.4	37.4	38.5	39.2	39.2	39.0	39.0	38.7	36.8
2006	37.2	37.8	39.1	40.4	42.4	44.0	44.3	45.1	45.6	45.5	45.2	44.8	42.6
2007	43.1	43.0	44.1	45.1	46.7	48.1	48.0	48.7	47.8	46.8	45.8	44.4	46.0
2008	41.4	40.5	41.2	42.1	42.8	43.8	44.0	44.5	43.6	42.6	40.8	39.3	42.2
2009	34.8	33.8	33.8	33.4	34.7	35.1	35.5	35.8	35.6	35.3	34.6	33.3	34.6
2010	31.1	30.6	31.1	31.9	33.1	33.5	33.8	34.3	34.6	35.0	34.2	33.3	33.0
2011	31.1	30.8	31.4	32.1	32.8	33.8	35.2	35.7	35.3	35.1	34.8	33.7	33.5
2012	32.0	32.6	32.9	34.2	35.7	36.1	35.9	36.5	36.2	35.9	35.6	34.9	34.9
2013	33.1	33.0	33.7	34.8	35.3	35.6	35.5	36.3	35.8	35.3	35.1	34.1	34.8
2014	32.5	32.8	33.5	34.5	35.3	35.9	36.4	36.9	37.1	37.4	36.9	36.0	35.4
2015	34.3	34.6	35.4	36.1	36.7	37.4	38.0	38.1	38.1	39.4	38.6	37.2	37.0

Employment by Industry: Salt Lake City, UT, 2005–2015—*Continued*

(Numbers in thousands, not seasonally adjusted)

Industry and year	January	February	March	April	May	June	July	August	September	October	November	December	Annual average
Manufacturing													
2005	51.7	51.9	51.5	52.1	52.6	53.2	53.3	53.6	53.7	53.2	53.4	53.6	52.8
2006	53.3	53.7	53.9	54.1	54.7	55.3	55.3	55.7	55.8	55.9	56.3	56.3	55.0
2007	55.8	56.1	56.5	56.6	56.9	57.6	57.6	58.0	57.7	57.7	57.9	57.9	57.2
2008	57.9	57.8	57.8	57.4	57.3	57.4	57.4	57.1	56.8	56.6	55.9	55.4	57.1
2009	53.9	52.6	52.2	51.6	51.6	51.8	51.8	51.7	51.5	51.5	51.4	51.7	51.9
2010	51.1	51.0	51.0	51.5	51.4	51.8	52.1	52.3	52.0	51.8	51.8	51.8	51.6
2011	51.8	51.8	51.8	52.1	52.4	52.6	53.3	53.6	53.5	53.5	53.5	53.6	52.8
2012	53.3	53.3	53.6	53.8	54.2	54.6	54.7	54.7	54.6	54.8	54.5	54.7	54.2
2013	54.3	54.2	54.3	54.3	54.4	54.5	54.4	54.5	54.3	54.3	54.1	54.3	54.3
2014	54.0	54.1	54.1	54.1	54.1	54.3	54.0	54.2	54.0	54.1	54.1	54.3	54.1
2015	54.2	54.2	54.5	54.7	55.1	55.4	55.5	55.6	55.3	55.6	55.3	55.2	55.1
Trade, Transportation, and Utilities													
2005	116.5	116.3	116.7	117.6	118.3	118.4	119.3	120.1	119.8	121.0	123.3	124.8	119.3
2006	120.6	120.3	120.7	120.8	121.6	122.7	122.7	124.0	124.0	124.3	127.5	130.0	123.3
2007	126.0	125.4	126.3	126.1	127.1	127.7	128.0	128.9	128.7	129.2	132.1	133.9	128.3
2008	129.0	128.0	128.1	128.7	129.0	129.7	129.1	129.6	128.7	128.8	129.8	130.3	129.1
2009	124.2	122.6	121.7	120.6	120.6	120.1	119.4	119.4	119.4	119.5	121.5	122.4	121.0
2010	117.7	117.1	117.4	117.4	118.0	118.4	118.5	119.2	118.7	119.7	121.8	122.9	118.9
2011	118.6	118.2	118.8	119.9	120.0	120.7	121.1	121.7	121.8	122.1	124.9	126.1	121.2
2012	122.9	122.5	123.5	124.6	125.5	126.3	125.6	126.2	126.7	127.3	130.4	130.9	126.0
2013	127.1	126.8	126.9	126.7	127.5	127.8	128.2	128.6	127.9	129.7	132.3	133.3	128.6
2014	128.6	128.1	128.4	128.7	129.4	130.0	129.6	130.4	130.9	132.6	135.5	136.7	130.7
2015	133.2	133.2	133.6	133.5	134.3	134.3	135.2	136.4	136.2	137.2	139.7	142.2	135.8
Wholesale Trade													
2005	28.0	28.1	28.3	28.4	28.6	28.5	28.5	28.5	28.4	28.5	28.6	28.6	28.4
2006	28.4	28.7	28.8	28.9	29.2	29.5	29.4	29.5	29.5	29.7	29.7	30.2	29.3
2007	29.8	29.9	30.0	30.0	30.3	30.5	30.6	30.8	30.7	30.7	30.8	31.0	30.4
2008	30.7	30.7	30.7	31.1	31.2	31.3	31.2	31.3	31.1	30.9	30.8	30.8	31.0
2009	30.0	29.9	29.6	29.3	29.2	29.1	29.0	28.9	28.8	28.7	28.6	28.7	29.2
2010	28.2	28.1	28.3	28.4	28.7	28.7	28.9	29.0	28.8	29.0	29.1	29.3	28.7
2011	29.2	29.4	29.7	29.9	29.9	30.2	30.3	30.4	30.5	30.4	30.6	30.7	30.1
2012	30.5	30.7	30.8	30.8	31.0	31.0	30.8	30.9	30.7	30.6	30.5	30.6	30.7
2013	30.7	30.7	30.7	30.7	30.8	30.8	30.8	30.9	30.6	30.6	30.7	30.7	30.7
2014	30.2	30.3	30.2	30.3	30.5	30.6	30.7	30.7	30.7	31.0	31.1	31.3	30.6
2015	30.9	31.1	31.3	31.5	31.7	31.8	31.9	32.0	31.8	31.6	31.6	31.5	31.6
Retail Trade													
2005	61.6	60.7	60.7	61.0	61.4	61.6	62.4	63.2	62.9	63.8	65.7	66.9	62.7
2006	63.3	62.7	63.0	63.0	63.4	64.0	64.2	64.9	64.8	65.0	67.8	69.0	64.6
2007	66.0	65.3	65.9	65.8	66.3	66.5	66.7	67.2	66.8	67.0	69.5	70.7	67.0
2008	67.6	66.6	66.8	67.0	67.2	67.9	67.4	67.8	67.2	67.5	68.7	69.3	67.6
2009	64.7	63.6	63.4	63.0	63.3	63.3	62.6	63.0	63.2	63.5	65.6	66.2	63.8
2010	62.7	62.1	62.1	62.0	62.3	62.4	62.3	62.6	62.2	62.7	64.4	64.9	62.7
2011	61.4	60.8	61.0	61.6	61.8	62.0	62.2	62.6	62.6	63.3	65.5	66.2	62.6
2012	63.5	62.8	63.5	64.1	64.7	65.3	65.6	65.8	66.2	66.9	69.8	69.9	65.7
2013	66.4	66.1	66.3	66.9	67.5	67.8	68.0	68.4	68.1	68.9	71.0	71.4	68.1
2014	67.5	67.2	67.5	67.7	68.2	68.3	68.7	69.3	69.4	70.4	72.5	73.3	69.2
2015	69.9	69.6	69.5	69.9	70.4	70.3	70.6	71.4	71.2	72.3	75.0	76.3	71.4
Transportation and Utilities													
2005	26.9	27.5	27.7	28.2	28.3	28.3	28.4	28.4	28.5	28.7	29.0	29.3	28.3
2006	28.9	28.9	28.9	28.9	29.0	29.2	29.1	29.6	29.7	29.6	30.0	30.8	29.4
2007	30.2	30.2	30.4	30.3	30.5	30.7	30.7	30.9	31.2	31.5	31.8	32.2	30.9
2008	30.7	30.7	30.6	30.6	30.6	30.5	30.5	30.5	30.4	30.4	30.3	30.2	30.5
2009	29.5	29.1	28.7	28.3	28.1	27.7	27.8	27.5	27.4	27.3	27.3	27.5	28.0
2010	26.8	26.9	27.0	27.0	27.0	27.3	27.3	27.6	27.7	28.0	28.3	28.7	27.5
2011	28.0	28.0	28.1	28.4	28.3	28.5	28.6	28.7	28.7	28.4	28.8	29.2	28.5
2012	28.9	29.0	29.2	29.7	29.8	30.0	29.2	29.5	29.8	29.8	30.1	30.4	29.6
2013	30.0	30.0	29.9	29.1	29.2	29.2	29.4	29.3	29.2	30.2	30.6	31.2	29.8
2014	30.9	30.6	30.7	30.7	30.7	31.1	30.2	30.4	30.8	31.2	31.9	32.1	30.9
2015	32.4	32.5	32.8	32.1	32.2	32.2	32.7	33.0	33.2	33.3	33.1	34.4	32.8

Employment by Industry: Salt Lake City, UT, 2005–2015—*Continued*

(Numbers in thousands, not seasonally adjusted)

Industry and year	January	February	March	April	May	June	July	August	September	October	November	December	Annual average
Information													
2005	17.6	18.0	18.4	18.0	17.9	17.8	18.3	18.7	18.5	18.2	18.5	18.3	18.2
2006	17.9	18.1	18.0	18.3	19.1	19.2	18.3	18.6	18.5	18.3	18.6	18.4	18.4
2007	18.4	18.4	18.6	17.3	17.5	17.3	17.2	17.4	17.1	17.0	17.1	17.2	17.5
2008	16.8	17.4	17.5	17.8	18.1	18.0	17.7	17.8	17.6	17.3	17.5	17.5	17.6
2009	17.0	17.1	17.0	16.6	16.8	16.9	16.6	16.5	16.3	16.4	16.5	16.7	16.7
2010	16.0	16.2	16.6	16.7	16.5	16.5	16.6	16.2	16.4	16.4	16.9	16.9	16.5
2011	16.0	16.2	16.3	16.0	16.1	16.1	16.1	16.2	16.1	16.0	16.5	16.5	16.2
2012	15.9	16.1	16.1	18.4	19.1	19.0	17.6	17.8	17.5	17.8	18.6	18.5	17.7
2013	19.2	19.3	19.3	17.9	18.1	18.0	18.0	18.2	17.8	17.8	18.5	18.6	18.4
2014	17.9	18.2	18.3	18.0	18.1	18.2	18.1	18.6	18.1	17.8	18.0	18.1	18.1
2015	17.5	17.7	17.8	17.5	17.7	17.7	18.2	18.5	18.3	17.6	18.0	18.4	17.9
Financial Activities													
2005	43.4	43.8	43.2	44.4	44.4	44.6	45.2	45.3	45.4	45.5	45.8	46.4	44.8
2006	45.8	46.4	46.5	46.9	47.1	47.4	47.8	48.0	47.9	48.5	48.8	49.3	47.5
2007	49.1	49.8	50.0	50.2	50.5	50.6	50.6	50.5	50.2	50.4	50.5	50.8	50.3
2008	49.6	50.1	50.0	50.2	49.9	49.8	49.9	49.9	49.4	49.3	49.0	49.4	49.7
2009	48.7	48.8	48.6	48.3	48.0	47.9	47.2	47.3	46.9	46.8	46.7	47.0	47.7
2010	45.8	45.4	45.5	45.2	45.2	45.3	45.4	45.6	45.7	46.1	46.2	46.4	45.7
2011	45.5	45.7	45.8	46.0	45.9	46.2	46.2	46.4	46.3	46.3	46.4	46.6	46.1
2012	45.9	46.0	46.1	46.4	46.5	46.8	47.0	47.6	47.4	47.5	47.9	48.4	47.0
2013	47.4	47.8	47.8	48.2	48.5	49.2	49.7	50.1	49.9	50.1	50.4	50.6	49.1
2014	49.4	49.7	49.5	49.6	49.9	50.4	50.8	51.4	51.0	51.5	51.9	52.1	50.6
2015	51.9	52.3	52.4	52.5	52.9	53.3	53.8	54.0	54.1	55.2	55.2	55.3	53.6
Professional and Business Services													
2005	84.7	85.1	85.7	87.8	88.7	89.7	90.3	91.6	91.9	92.6	93.5	94.0	89.6
2006	91.3	92.1	93.3	94.9	95.6	96.1	96.8	97.2	96.9	96.4	97.5	97.6	95.5
2007	94.8	95.6	96.1	98.3	99.6	100.2	99.8	100.5	99.9	101.5	102.3	102.1	99.2
2008	98.8	99.1	99.1	99.6	100.0	99.7	99.9	100.6	99.9	99.1	97.8	97.3	99.2
2009	93.1	92.8	92.0	91.9	92.1	91.9	91.7	91.8	91.7	92.4	92.2	92.5	92.2
2010	90.0	90.5	92.4	93.2	94.2	95.1	95.9	95.1	94.5	95.6	96.0	96.7	94.1
2011	94.4	95.1	95.9	96.9	97.3	97.7	98.4	99.3	99.8	101.4	101.8	101.7	98.3
2012	99.1	100.1	100.9	101.1	102.1	103.1	103.3	104.6	104.7	106.5	107.5	107.0	103.3
2013	102.9	104.6	105.8	108.5	107.8	108.3	108.8	110.0	109.9	113.0	114.1	113.9	109.0
2014	110.6	110.5	110.9	111.9	112.3	113.3	112.8	114.4	115.0	116.4	117.0	117.7	113.6
2015	113.9	113.9	115.1	116.4	117.5	118.9	119.5	120.6	120.2	120.3	121.5	118.1	118.0
Education and Health Services													
2005	53.1	53.7	53.7	54.2	54.3	54.3	53.8	53.9	54.7	55.0	55.5	55.6	54.3
2006	54.7	55.2	55.5	55.4	55.7	55.9	55.0	56.0	56.6	57.3	57.6	57.5	56.0
2007	57.0	57.6	58.0	58.4	58.5	58.4	58.0	59.1	60.0	60.2	60.7	60.9	58.9
2008	60.5	61.5	61.6	61.6	61.6	61.4	61.1	61.7	62.6	63.7	64.4	64.5	62.2
2009	63.5	63.8	64.3	64.4	64.3	63.8	63.0	63.7	65.0	66.1	66.5	66.7	64.6
2010	65.9	66.1	66.3	66.6	66.3	66.0	65.3	65.5	66.8	67.8	67.8	67.6	66.5
2011	67.1	67.6	67.6	68.0	67.4	66.9	65.6	66.0	67.6	68.2	68.3	68.0	67.4
2012	67.7	68.1	68.1	70.7	70.6	70.3	68.4	69.2	70.3	71.2	71.9	71.9	69.9
2013	72.3	73.0	73.3	72.7	72.7	72.0	70.5	71.3	72.2	73.3	74.0	73.7	72.6
2014	72.3	72.9	73.3	73.1	73.4	72.5	71.8	73.0	73.6	74.3	75.3	75.2	73.4
2015	75.6	76.3	76.5	76.3	76.6	76.1	75.2	76.0	77.0	77.7	78.0	78.9	76.7
Leisure and Hospitality													
2005	45.2	45.7	46.3	46.6	45.0	45.5	45.1	45.6	45.4	45.6	46.0	47.2	45.8
2006	46.6	47.0	47.9	47.6	46.3	46.5	46.7	47.6	46.8	46.5	47.7	49.2	47.2
2007	48.6	49.3	49.8	49.4	48.4	49.0	48.6	48.5	48.1	47.5	48.5	49.9	48.8
2008	49.7	50.1	50.7	50.8	49.8	50.0	49.7	49.8	49.2	48.8	48.9	49.7	49.8
2009	48.7	48.6	49.2	48.9	48.2	48.2	47.7	47.8	47.3	46.7	46.9	48.0	48.0
2010	47.1	47.5	47.9	48.5	47.4	48.1	48.6	48.7	47.7	47.4	47.9	49.0	48.0
2011	48.2	48.4	49.0	49.4	48.5	48.9	48.9	49.3	48.6	47.7	48.1	49.3	48.7
2012	49.2	49.7	50.4	50.9	51.1	51.2	50.9	51.4	50.9	50.2	51.8	52.8	50.9
2013	52.1	52.7	53.6	53.8	53.1	53.8	53.8	53.8	53.2	53.0	53.9	55.2	53.5
2014	54.5	54.9	55.3	55.9	54.3	55.1	54.9	55.4	55.0	54.8	55.6	56.6	55.2
2015	55.6	56.2	57.0	57.3	56.7	57.1	57.7	58.2	57.4	56.8	56.2	58.4	57.1

Employment by Industry: Salt Lake City, UT, 2005–2015—*Continued*

(Numbers in thousands, not seasonally adjusted)

Industry and year	January	February	March	April	May	June	July	August	September	October	November	December	Annual average
Other Services													
2005	17.7	17.8	18.0	18.1	18.0	18.1	18.6	18.5	18.3	18.0	17.9	18.1	18.1
2006	17.8	17.9	18.2	18.3	18.5	18.8	18.9	18.9	18.8	18.4	18.4	18.7	18.5
2007	18.4	18.5	18.7	18.7	19.0	19.2	19.5	19.6	19.1	18.9	18.9	19.0	19.0
2008	18.7	18.9	19.0	19.0	19.1	19.2	19.6	20.1	19.4	18.7	18.6	18.7	19.1
2009	18.3	18.3	18.4	18.3	18.5	18.6	18.8	18.8	18.1	18.1	17.9	18.0	18.3
2010	17.9	18.0	18.3	18.0	18.1	18.1	18.4	18.4	17.9	18.0	17.9	17.8	18.1
2011	17.6	17.8	17.9	18.0	18.3	18.4	18.7	18.8	18.4	18.3	18.2	18.2	18.2
2012	18.1	18.3	18.5	18.5	18.8	18.8	19.2	19.3	19.0	19.0	19.0	19.1	18.8
2013	19.0	19.3	19.7	20.1	20.4	19.8	20.3	20.3	19.7	19.6	19.7	19.8	19.8
2014	19.7	20.0	20.2	20.4	20.4	20.7	21.1	21.1	20.7	20.5	20.6	20.5	20.5
2015	21.0	21.3	21.4	21.0	21.0	21.1	21.6	21.5	21.1	20.2	20.4	20.5	21.0
Government													
2005	88.3	88.5	88.2	88.8	88.3	88.4	86.0	86.2	88.8	89.1	89.4	89.7	88.3
2006	89.1	89.7	89.5	89.7	89.2	89.9	87.0	87.0	89.6	90.1	90.1	90.5	89.3
2007	89.9	90.1	90.1	90.5	90.2	90.8	87.3	87.8	90.5	91.1	91.4	91.7	90.1
2008	91.4	91.7	92.1	92.2	92.2	92.8	89.0	90.1	93.6	93.9	94.2	94.3	92.3
2009	93.4	93.9	93.7	94.4	94.1	94.3	90.3	91.1	94.4	94.8	94.6	94.8	93.7
2010	94.3	94.2	94.2	94.9	96.6	95.6	92.0	92.4	96.1	96.9	96.9	96.1	95.0
2011	95.2	95.3	95.4	96.3	96.4	96.5	92.7	93.2	96.4	96.1	96.7	96.9	95.6
2012	96.8	97.2	97.3	98.6	98.2	98.2	93.6	93.5	97.7	99.0	98.8	98.1	97.3
2013	97.6	98.0	97.8	99.6	100.1	100.5	95.5	95.2	100.4	102.8	102.4	102.4	99.4
2014	102.2	103.0	103.2	104.5	104.9	105.2	98.0	97.3	102.6	103.6	103.7	103.9	102.7
2015	103.1	103.9	104.6	105.2	105.7	104.8	100.0	98.6	104.4	106.0	106.0	106.3	104.1

Employment by Industry: Birmingham-Hoover, AL, 2005–2015

(Numbers in thousands, not seasonally adjusted)

Industry and year	January	February	March	April	May	June	July	August	September	October	November	December	Annual average
Total Nonfarm													
2005	510.2	512.2	515.2	518.9	519.5	520.3	518.9	519.5	521.6	522.8	525.7	526.6	519.3
2006	519.1	521.4	524.5	527.0	529.0	533.2	528.4	529.8	531.8	531.7	534.6	535.6	528.8
2007	528.0	530.5	533.8	530.7	533.7	536.2	531.2	532.9	533.9	534.2	537.3	538.7	533.4
2008	527.2	528.7	529.5	531.3	533.7	534.9	529.4	529.4	528.0	527.7	526.2	525.3	529.3
2009	507.7	506.0	504.4	502.7	503.0	501.5	496.0	494.0	494.4	494.7	496.8	496.3	499.8
2010	487.3	488.0	489.4	492.2	495.7	495.1	491.4	490.0	489.4	492.9	495.3	495.4	491.8
2011	484.9	487.2	490.1	492.4	493.9	496.1	493.2	493.4	496.2	495.8	499.2	500.3	493.6
2012	493.4	495.5	499.9	502.8	503.7	505.3	499.5	500.7	502.7	503.3	506.9	506.5	501.7
2013	497.7	501.0	503.1	506.8	508.7	510.1	505.9	506.6	508.5	509.2	512.8	514.4	507.1
2014	502.5	503.3	507.4	510.4	511.7	513.4	509.3	511.2	512.7	512.9	515.5	516.9	510.6
2015	506.8	509.4	510.7	514.2	517.5	518.5	516.5	516.9	515.9	517.1	522.0	520.6	515.5
Total Private													
2005	431.4	432.9	435.7	439.1	439.6	440.9	442.0	442.0	441.9	442.1	444.8	445.9	439.9
2006	437.7	439.8	442.8	444.8	446.6	450.9	449.3	450.2	449.5	448.7	451.4	452.3	447.0
2007	445.1	447.2	450.3	447.2	449.9	452.6	451.2	452.2	450.6	450.3	453.2	454.7	450.4
2008	443.6	444.7	445.3	446.9	449.0	450.2	448.3	447.8	444.4	442.7	441.3	440.1	445.4
2009	423.2	421.4	419.8	417.7	418.2	416.7	415.4	413.1	411.3	410.8	412.5	412.1	416.0
2010	403.4	403.9	404.8	407.2	408.4	409.1	409.5	408.8	406.4	409.0	411.4	411.4	407.8
2011	401.2	403.4	406.2	408.4	409.7	412.2	412.6	413.3	413.8	413.8	417.1	418.1	410.8
2012	411.8	413.3	417.3	420.3	421.2	423.4	421.1	422.1	422.2	421.7	425.0	424.5	420.3
2013	416.2	419.2	421.3	425.0	427.3	429.0	427.4	428.2	428.3	428.2	431.6	433.0	426.2
2014	421.7	422.4	426.2	428.9	429.8	431.7	430.0	431.4	431.4	431.3	433.6	434.8	429.4
2015	425.8	428.1	429.2	432.4	435.5	436.6	436.5	436.3	434.4	435.1	439.6	438.2	434.0
Goods Producing													
2005	78.4	78.4	78.7	79.7	79.4	79.3	80.1	80.4	80.5	80.9	81.1	80.6	79.8
2006	79.7	79.9	80.6	81.3	82.0	82.9	82.8	82.5	82.9	82.5	82.1	81.8	81.8
2007	81.1	81.7	82.2	81.4	81.5	82.2	81.5	81.8	81.7	81.2	80.7	80.5	81.5
2008	79.0	79.0	78.6	78.9	79.2	79.3	79.4	78.6	78.2	76.6	75.5	74.5	78.1
2009	70.4	69.3	68.6	67.0	66.9	66.0	65.9	65.3	64.9	64.0	63.9	63.9	66.3
2010	62.2	61.8	61.6	62.1	62.0	61.9	62.3	62.3	61.7	61.3	61.5	61.4	61.8
2011	60.3	60.8	61.8	61.9	62.6	63.3	62.9	63.3	63.8	63.9	64.3	64.7	62.8
2012	63.9	63.8	64.5	64.9	65.3	65.5	65.6	65.5	65.5	65.7	65.6	65.7	65.1
2013	65.2	64.8	65.6	66.0	66.3	66.5	66.4	66.6	66.4	66.4	66.3	66.9	66.1
2014	65.3	65.2	66.2	66.1	66.3	66.6	66.4	66.5	66.6	66.5	66.7	66.7	66.3
2015	66.1	66.4	66.1	65.6	65.9	66.3	66.5	66.5	66.3	66.4	66.7	66.3	66.3
Service-Providing													
2005	431.8	433.8	436.5	439.2	440.1	441.0	438.8	439.1	441.1	441.9	444.6	446.0	439.5
2006	439.4	441.5	443.9	445.7	447.0	450.3	445.6	447.3	448.9	449.2	452.5	453.8	447.1
2007	446.9	448.8	451.6	449.3	452.2	454.0	449.7	451.1	452.2	453.0	456.6	458.2	452.0
2008	448.2	449.7	450.9	452.4	454.5	455.6	450.0	450.8	449.8	451.1	450.7	450.8	451.2
2009	437.3	436.7	435.8	435.7	436.1	435.5	430.1	428.7	429.5	430.7	432.9	432.4	433.5
2010	425.1	426.2	427.8	430.1	433.7	433.2	429.1	427.7	427.7	431.6	433.8	434.0	430.0
2011	424.6	426.4	428.3	430.5	431.3	432.8	430.3	430.1	432.4	431.9	434.9	435.6	430.8
2012	429.5	431.7	435.4	437.9	438.4	439.8	433.9	435.2	437.2	437.6	441.3	440.8	436.6
2013	432.5	436.2	437.5	440.8	442.4	443.6	439.5	440.0	442.1	442.8	446.5	447.5	441.0
2014	437.2	438.1	441.2	444.3	445.4	446.8	442.9	444.7	446.1	446.4	448.8	450.2	444.3
2015	440.7	443.0	444.6	448.6	451.6	452.2	450.0	450.4	449.6	450.7	455.3	454.3	449.3
Mining and Logging													
2005	3.0	3.0	3.1	3.1	3.2	3.2	3.3	3.3	3.3	3.3	3.3	3.3	3.2
2006	3.1	3.1	3.1	3.0	3.1	3.1	3.2	3.1	3.2	3.1	3.1	3.2	3.1
2007	3.1	3.1	3.1	3.0	3.0	2.9	2.9	3.0	3.0	3.0	3.0	3.1	3.0
2008	3.0	3.0	3.0	3.0	3.0	3.0	3.1	3.1	3.1	3.1	3.1	3.1	3.1
2009	2.9	2.9	2.9	2.9	2.9	2.8	2.8	2.7	2.8	2.8	2.8	2.8	2.8
2010	2.8	2.8	2.8	2.9	2.9	3.0	3.0	3.1	2.9	3.1	3.1	3.1	3.0
2011	3.1	3.1	3.2	3.4	3.4	3.5	3.4	3.5	3.6	3.6	3.7	3.7	3.4
2012	3.6	3.6	3.6	3.6	3.6	3.5	3.5	3.5	3.5	3.4	3.4	3.4	3.5
2013	3.4	3.2	3.3	3.2	3.2	3.2	3.3	3.2	3.2	3.1	3.1	3.1	3.2
2014	3.0	2.9	3.0	3.0	3.0	2.9	3.0	3.0	3.0	3.0	2.9	2.9	3.0
2015	2.9	2.9	2.9	2.9	2.9	2.8	2.8	2.8	2.8	2.8	2.8	2.9	2.9

Employment by Industry: Birmingham-Hoover, AL, 2005–2015—*Continued*

(Numbers in thousands, not seasonally adjusted)

Industry and year	January	February	March	April	May	June	July	August	September	October	November	December	Annual average
Construction													
2005	32.4	32.6	32.6	33.6	32.9	32.7	33.3	33.3	33.3	34.1	34.0	33.4	33.2
2006	33.0	33.0	33.7	34.3	34.6	35.2	34.8	34.9	35.0	34.9	34.7	34.2	34.4
2007	33.8	34.3	34.8	34.1	34.1	34.4	34.2	34.4	34.7	34.7	34.2	33.9	34.3
2008	33.2	33.0	32.9	33.4	33.8	33.5	33.7	33.2	32.8	31.7	31.0	30.6	32.7
2009	28.5	28.0	28.0	27.1	27.2	27.3	27.1	26.7	26.4	25.2	25.1	25.0	26.8
2010	24.1	23.9	24.0	24.2	24.3	24.4	24.6	24.7	24.3	23.9	23.7	23.7	24.2
2011	22.8	23.2	23.9	23.9	24.3	24.6	24.5	24.5	24.9	24.7	24.8	25.0	24.3
2012	24.2	24.1	24.4	24.5	24.7	24.7	24.9	24.7	24.5	24.9	24.7	24.6	24.6
2013	24.2	23.9	24.6	24.8	25.0	25.0	25.0	25.2	24.8	24.9	24.6	25.0	24.8
2014	23.9	23.8	24.4	24.3	24.5	24.7	24.7	24.8	24.8	24.9	24.9	24.9	24.6
2015	24.3	24.6	24.4	24.6	25.0	25.4	25.6	25.8	25.7	25.8	26.2	26.1	25.3
Manufacturing													
2005	43.0	42.8	43.0	43.0	43.3	43.4	43.5	43.8	43.9	43.5	43.8	43.9	43.4
2006	43.6	43.8	43.8	44.0	44.3	44.6	44.8	44.5	44.7	44.5	44.3	44.4	44.3
2007	44.2	44.3	44.3	44.3	44.4	44.9	44.4	44.4	44.0	43.5	43.5	43.5	44.1
2008	42.8	43.0	42.7	42.5	42.4	42.8	42.6	42.3	42.3	41.8	41.4	40.8	42.3
2009	39.0	38.4	37.7	37.0	36.8	35.9	36.0	35.9	35.7	36.0	36.0	36.1	36.7
2010	35.3	35.1	34.8	35.0	34.8	34.5	34.7	34.5	34.5	34.3	34.7	34.6	34.7
2011	34.4	34.5	34.7	34.6	34.9	35.2	35.0	35.3	35.3	35.6	35.8	36.0	35.1
2012	36.1	36.1	36.5	36.8	37.0	37.3	37.2	37.3	37.5	37.4	37.5	37.7	37.0
2013	37.6	37.7	37.7	38.0	38.1	38.3	38.1	38.2	38.4	38.4	38.6	38.8	38.2
2014	38.4	38.5	38.8	38.8	38.8	39.0	38.7	38.7	38.8	38.6	38.9	38.9	38.7
2015	38.9	38.9	38.8	38.1	38.0	38.1	38.1	37.9	37.8	37.8	37.7	37.3	38.1
Trade, Transportation, and Utilities													
2005	110.5	110.2	110.6	111.0	111.3	111.7	111.4	111.8	111.6	112.2	114.0	115.7	111.8
2006	112.4	112.1	112.9	112.9	113.3	114.0	113.5	114.0	113.8	115.0	117.2	118.7	114.2
2007	114.7	114.4	115.5	114.5	115.5	116.4	116.2	115.8	115.9	116.1	118.4	119.7	116.1
2008	115.7	115.1	115.5	115.2	115.2	115.3	114.9	115.0	114.4	114.2	115.2	115.9	115.1
2009	110.4	109.4	108.8	107.9	107.9	107.3	106.8	106.3	106.0	106.1	107.0	107.8	107.6
2010	104.3	104.1	104.6	104.5	105.1	105.2	105.2	105.3	105.0	106.3	107.9	108.8	105.5
2011	104.9	104.9	105.1	104.9	105.1	105.3	105.4	105.7	105.7	106.3	108.1	109.3	105.9
2012	106.4	106.2	107.2	106.9	107.6	107.5	107.1	106.9	106.8	107.3	109.8	110.5	107.5
2013	106.8	107.0	107.6	107.4	107.9	108.2	108.5	108.5	108.4	108.9	111.3	112.7	108.6
2014	108.5	107.9	108.8	108.4	108.6	109.0	108.7	108.7	108.8	109.0	111.7	112.7	109.2
2015	108.5	108.4	109.0	109.7	110.5	110.7	110.4	110.4	110.0	110.7	113.3	113.6	110.4
Wholesale Trade													
2005	30.1	30.2	30.2	30.3	30.2	30.3	30.4	30.5	30.6	30.4	30.4	30.6	30.4
2006	30.6	30.8	31.0	31.1	31.2	31.5	31.5	31.6	31.5	31.5	31.6	31.7	31.3
2007	31.4	31.6	31.8	31.4	31.4	31.7	31.5	31.5	31.6	31.6	31.7	31.8	31.6
2008	31.5	31.6	31.6	31.6	31.6	31.5	31.4	31.5	31.5	31.5	31.2	31.2	31.5
2009	30.4	30.2	30.0	29.7	29.6	29.4	29.4	29.3	29.2	29.3	28.9	28.9	29.5
2010	28.3	28.3	28.3	28.3	28.4	28.3	28.3	28.4	28.2	28.5	28.4	28.4	28.3
2011	27.9	28.1	28.0	28.2	28.2	28.1	28.4	28.4	28.5	28.7	28.7	28.9	28.3
2012	28.5	28.8	29.0	28.8	29.1	29.1	29.0	29.0	29.0	29.1	29.1	29.3	29.0
2013	29.1	29.3	29.3	29.2	29.2	29.1	29.3	29.3	29.3	29.5	29.6	29.6	29.3
2014	29.0	29.0	29.1	28.9	29.0	29.1	29.2	29.2	29.3	29.4	29.4	29.5	29.2
2015	28.8	28.9	29.0	29.0	29.1	29.0	29.1	29.1	28.9	28.9	28.7	28.9	29.0
Retail Trade													
2005	61.5	61.0	61.2	61.5	61.8	62.0	61.7	62.0	61.6	62.2	64.1	65.5	62.2
2006	62.3	61.8	62.3	62.0	62.2	62.3	61.7	62.0	61.8	62.7	64.8	66.0	62.7
2007	62.8	62.2	62.9	62.4	63.2	63.6	63.4	62.9	62.8	63.1	65.2	66.2	63.4
2008	63.0	62.4	62.8	62.3	62.3	62.5	62.1	61.9	61.4	61.5	62.9	63.6	62.4
2009	59.3	58.6	58.4	58.0	58.1	57.8	57.4	56.9	56.7	56.7	58.0	58.5	57.9
2010	55.9	55.6	56.1	56.0	56.2	56.3	55.9	55.9	55.7	56.7	58.4	59.2	56.5
2011	56.1	55.7	55.9	56.1	56.2	56.5	56.2	56.5	56.3	56.7	58.5	59.3	56.7
2012	56.5	55.8	56.2	56.2	56.7	56.6	56.3	56.1	55.9	56.5	59.0	59.4	56.8
2013	55.5	55.4	55.8	55.9	56.3	56.6	56.7	56.6	56.4	57.1	59.4	60.5	56.9
2014	57.0	56.4	57.1	57.1	57.2	57.4	57.1	57.1	57.0	57.3	59.8	60.5	57.6
2015	57.1	57.1	57.5	58.1	58.8	59.0	58.5	58.4	58.3	59.1	61.8	61.7	58.8

Employment by Industry: Birmingham-Hoover, AL, 2005–2015—*Continued*

(Numbers in thousands, not seasonally adjusted)

Industry and year	January	February	March	April	May	June	July	August	September	October	November	December	Annual average
Transportation and Utilities													
2005	18.9	19.0	19.2	19.2	19.3	19.4	19.3	19.3	19.4	19.6	19.5	19.6	19.3
2006	19.5	19.5	19.6	19.8	19.9	20.2	20.3	20.4	20.5	20.8	20.8	21.0	20.2
2007	20.5	20.6	20.8	20.7	20.9	21.1	21.3	21.4	21.5	21.4	21.5	21.7	21.1
2008	21.2	21.1	21.1	21.3	21.3	21.3	21.4	21.6	21.5	21.2	21.1	21.1	21.3
2009	20.7	20.6	20.4	20.2	20.2	20.1	20.0	20.1	20.1	20.1	20.1	20.4	20.3
2010	20.1	20.2	20.2	20.2	20.5	20.6	21.0	21.0	21.1	21.1	21.1	21.2	20.7
2011	20.9	21.1	21.2	20.6	20.7	20.7	20.8	20.8	20.9	20.9	20.9	21.1	20.9
2012	21.4	21.6	22.0	21.9	21.8	21.8	21.8	21.8	21.9	21.7	21.7	21.8	21.8
2013	22.2	22.3	22.5	22.3	22.4	22.5	22.5	22.6	22.7	22.3	22.3	22.6	22.4
2014	22.5	22.5	22.6	22.4	22.4	22.5	22.4	22.4	22.5	22.3	22.5	22.7	22.5
2015	22.6	22.4	22.5	22.6	22.6	22.7	22.8	22.9	22.8	22.7	22.8	23.0	22.7
Information													
2005	12.9	12.8	12.8	12.8	12.7	12.7	12.7	12.6	12.7	12.6	12.5	12.5	12.7
2006	12.2	12.1	12.2	12.0	12.0	12.0	11.9	11.8	11.7	11.7	11.7	11.7	11.9
2007	11.6	11.6	11.6	11.5	11.5	11.5	11.4	11.5	11.4	11.3	11.4	11.4	11.5
2008	11.1	11.1	11.2	11.2	11.2	11.1	11.0	11.1	10.9	10.9	10.8	10.8	11.0
2009	10.5	10.4	10.4	10.3	10.2	10.2	10.1	10.0	9.9	9.9	9.8	9.9	10.1
2010	9.8	9.7	9.7	9.5	9.5	9.6	9.4	9.4	9.3	9.3	9.3	9.3	9.5
2011	9.2	9.1	9.1	9.0	9.0	9.0	9.0	9.0	9.0	8.9	8.9	8.9	9.0
2012	8.9	8.9	9.0	8.8	8.8	8.9	8.9	8.9	8.9	8.8	8.8	8.9	8.9
2013	8.9	8.9	8.8	8.9	9.0	9.0	9.1	9.0	8.9	8.9	8.9	9.0	8.9
2014	8.8	8.7	8.7	8.6	8.6	8.5	8.3	8.3	8.2	8.3	8.4	8.4	8.5
2015	8.3	8.4	8.4	8.3	8.3	8.3	8.3	8.2	8.1	8.1	8.2	8.2	8.3
Financial Activities													
2005	41.0	41.2	41.5	41.6	41.5	41.6	41.6	41.5	41.5	41.7	41.8	42.0	41.5
2006	41.2	41.4	41.4	41.4	41.4	41.5	41.6	41.5	41.3	41.5	41.7	41.9	41.5
2007	41.7	41.8	42.0	41.0	41.2	41.5	41.4	41.4	41.5	41.5	41.7	41.9	41.6
2008	41.3	41.4	41.5	41.5	41.5	41.5	41.7	41.8	41.3	41.3	41.2	41.2	41.4
2009	40.8	40.9	40.7	40.6	40.5	40.5	40.3	40.1	39.9	39.8	39.6	39.5	40.3
2010	39.1	39.1	39.2	39.2	39.3	39.3	39.3	39.3	39.3	40.0	40.2	40.4	39.5
2011	40.0	40.1	40.0	40.2	40.1	39.7	40.1	39.9	39.8	39.8	39.9	40.0	40.0
2012	39.9	40.0	40.2	40.4	40.6	40.6	40.7	40.7	40.7	41.0	41.1	41.1	40.6
2013	40.6	40.8	40.8	41.0	41.3	41.5	41.8	42.1	42.1	42.4	42.8	42.9	41.7
2014	42.0	42.2	42.2	42.3	42.4	42.4	42.4	42.4	42.0	42.1	42.2	42.2	42.2
2015	42.1	42.1	42.2	42.2	42.3	42.3	42.5	42.5	42.2	42.0	42.3	42.2	42.2
Professional and Business Services													
2005	63.7	64.5	64.8	65.2	65.2	65.4	66.4	66.2	66.7	67.1	67.5	67.5	65.9
2006	66.8	67.2	67.7	67.9	67.7	69.0	68.6	69.1	69.2	68.9	69.0	69.1	68.4
2007	68.1	68.8	68.7	68.0	68.1	68.3	67.5	67.9	67.7	67.8	68.5	68.1	68.1
2008	66.3	66.6	66.2	66.5	66.7	67.0	65.9	65.9	65.6	65.6	65.4	64.9	66.1
2009	62.0	61.6	61.0	60.5	60.1	59.8	59.3	59.0	58.6	59.4	59.6	59.1	60.0
2010	58.9	59.1	59.2	60.0	59.8	59.4	60.2	60.0	59.3	59.9	59.7	59.5	59.6
2011	58.6	59.2	59.4	60.3	60.3	61.0	61.2	61.3	61.9	61.5	61.6	62.0	60.7
2012	61.1	61.8	62.4	63.3	62.9	63.7	63.4	64.0	63.6	63.3	63.0	62.4	62.9
2013	61.0	62.4	62.5	62.9	62.4	62.9	62.8	62.8	62.4	62.8	62.8	62.8	62.5
2014	60.9	61.5	61.8	62.8	62.8	63.0	63.0	63.9	63.8	64.2	63.6	63.6	62.9
2015	62.4	63.1	63.7	64.3	64.7	64.9	64.9	64.7	64.6	65.1	65.6	65.0	64.4
Education and Health Services													
2005	60.9	61.4	61.7	62.0	62.1	61.9	62.2	62.1	62.1	62.4	62.5	62.5	62.0
2006	61.2	61.9	61.9	62.2	62.2	62.1	62.1	62.3	62.5	62.8	63.5	63.0	62.3
2007	62.2	62.7	62.8	63.3	63.6	63.7	64.0	64.5	64.3	64.6	64.7	64.9	63.8
2008	64.0	64.5	64.7	64.6	65.1	65.0	65.0	65.1	65.2	65.8	65.2	65.1	64.9
2009	63.9	64.1	64.1	64.5	64.6	64.2	65.1	65.0	65.1	65.4	66.3	65.6	64.8
2010	65.0	65.6	65.3	65.6	65.7	65.6	65.7	65.6	65.6	65.9	66.2	65.6	65.6
2011	64.6	64.9	65.5	65.4	65.5	65.2	65.4	65.6	66.2	66.0	66.7	66.1	65.6
2012	65.9	66.2	66.5	67.0	66.6	66.8	66.3	67.1	67.9	67.5	68.4	68.3	67.0
2013	67.3	68.5	68.0	68.5	68.9	68.6	67.7	68.4	68.9	68.6	69.3	69.4	68.5
2014	67.8	68.4	68.5	69.1	68.7	68.7	68.3	68.9	69.5	69.9	69.4	69.7	68.9
2015	68.7	69.5	69.0	69.7	69.8	69.8	70.0	70.4	70.7	70.5	71.1	70.9	70.0

Employment by Industry: Birmingham-Hoover, AL, 2005–2015—*Continued*

(Numbers in thousands, not seasonally adjusted)

Industry and year	January	February	March	April	May	June	July	August	September	October	November	December	Annual average
Leisure and Hospitality													
2005	40.5	40.9	42.1	43.2	43.8	44.5	43.8	43.8	43.5	42.0	42.2	42.0	42.7
2006	41.2	42.1	42.9	43.8	44.7	45.5	45.1	45.4	44.7	43.2	42.9	42.8	43.7
2007	42.4	42.9	43.9	43.8	44.7	45.1	45.1	45.3	44.4	44.0	43.9	44.2	44.1
2008	42.2	42.8	43.4	44.7	45.8	46.3	45.6	45.7	44.6	44.2	44.0	43.8	44.4
2009	41.4	41.9	42.4	43.2	44.1	44.3	43.5	43.3	43.4	42.7	42.8	42.8	43.0
2010	40.7	41.0	41.6	42.7	43.3	43.8	43.0	42.8	42.7	42.5	43.0	43.0	42.5
2011	40.7	41.3	42.1	43.3	43.7	45.0	44.8	45.0	44.1	44.0	44.1	43.8	43.5
2012	42.3	42.9	43.7	45.3	45.6	46.1	44.9	45.0	45.2	44.4	44.8	44.2	44.5
2013	43.1	43.5	44.5	46.7	47.8	48.2	47.1	46.8	47.3	46.6	46.7	45.8	46.2
2014	45.0	45.1	46.3	47.9	48.5	49.5	48.8	48.8	48.7	47.7	48.0	48.0	47.7
2015	46.3	46.7	47.3	48.8	50.0	50.2	49.9	49.7	48.6	48.5	48.6	48.2	48.6
Other Services													
2005	23.5	23.5	23.5	23.6	23.6	23.8	23.8	23.6	23.3	23.2	23.2	23.1	23.5
2006	23.0	23.1	23.2	23.3	23.3	23.9	23.7	23.6	23.4	23.1	23.3	23.3	23.4
2007	23.3	23.3	23.6	23.7	23.8	23.9	24.1	24.0	23.7	23.8	23.9	24.0	23.8
2008	24.0	24.2	24.2	24.3	24.3	24.7	24.8	24.6	24.2	24.1	24.0	23.9	24.3
2009	23.8	23.8	23.8	23.7	23.9	24.4	24.4	24.1	23.5	23.5	23.5	23.5	23.8
2010	23.4	23.5	23.6	23.6	23.7	24.3	24.4	24.1	23.5	23.8	23.6	23.4	23.7
2011	22.9	23.1	23.2	23.4	23.4	23.7	23.8	23.5	23.3	23.4	23.5	23.3	23.4
2012	23.4	23.5	23.8	23.7	23.8	24.3	24.2	24.0	23.6	23.7	23.5	23.4	23.7
2013	23.3	23.3	23.5	23.6	23.7	24.1	24.0	24.0	23.9	23.6	23.5	23.5	23.7
2014	23.4	23.4	23.7	23.7	23.9	24.0	24.1	23.9	23.8	23.6	23.6	23.5	23.7
2015	23.4	23.5	23.5	23.8	24.0	24.1	24.0	23.9	23.9	23.8	23.8	23.8	23.8
Government													
2005	78.8	79.3	79.5	79.8	79.9	79.4	76.9	77.5	79.7	80.7	80.9	80.7	79.4
2006	81.4	81.6	81.7	82.2	82.4	82.3	79.1	79.6	82.3	83.0	83.2	83.3	81.8
2007	82.9	83.3	83.5	83.5	83.8	83.6	80.0	80.7	83.3	83.9	84.1	84.0	83.1
2008	83.6	84.0	84.2	84.4	84.7	84.7	81.1	81.6	83.6	85.0	84.9	85.2	83.9
2009	84.5	84.6	84.6	85.0	84.8	84.8	80.6	80.9	83.1	83.9	84.3	84.2	83.8
2010	83.9	84.1	84.6	85.0	87.3	86.0	81.9	81.2	83.0	83.9	83.9	84.0	84.1
2011	83.7	83.8	83.9	84.0	84.2	83.9	80.6	80.1	82.4	82.0	82.1	82.2	82.7
2012	81.6	82.2	82.6	82.5	82.5	81.9	78.4	78.6	80.5	81.6	81.9	82.0	81.4
2013	81.5	81.8	81.8	81.8	81.4	81.1	78.5	78.4	80.2	81.0	81.2	81.4	80.8
2014	80.8	80.9	81.2	81.5	81.9	81.7	79.3	79.8	81.3	81.6	81.9	82.1	81.2
2015	81.0	81.3	81.5	81.8	82.0	81.9	80.0	80.6	81.5	82.0	82.4	82.4	81.5

Employment by Industry: Buffalo-Cheektowaga-Niagara Falls, NY, 2005–2015

(Numbers in thousands, not seasonally adjusted)

Industry and year	January	February	March	April	May	June	July	August	September	October	November	December	Annual average
Total Nonfarm													
2005..............	534.3	537.3	538.2	544.5	549.4	550.4	540.1	543.3	551.4	554.9	555.5	554.8	546.2
2006..............	533.6	536.8	539.6	544.1	550.3	551.5	540.9	544.1	547.4	548.0	554.2	555.7	545.5
2007..............	534.0	536.9	540.6	540.2	550.2	551.4	541.9	544.8	549.8	556.7	558.2	558.3	546.9
2008..............	538.4	540.7	542.2	548.8	555.7	558.4	550.4	551.7	555.6	561.4	558.4	555.5	551.4
2009..............	531.1	531.5	532.4	534.3	539.5	540.1	535.2	535.7	538.5	544.3	544.4	542.3	537.4
2010..............	523.9	525.9	528.7	536.3	542.3	541.7	532.4	534.9	539.8	547.6	548.4	547.7	537.5
2011..............	529.6	532.1	533.0	541.0	545.3	547.5	539.4	540.5	549.4	551.3	552.0	551.8	542.7
2012..............	533.1	537.8	539.7	542.2	549.1	550.7	542.0	544.6	548.5	554.2	554.1	554.2	545.9
2013..............	534.8	538.3	540.8	544.4	550.9	552.2	545.7	547.7	553.2	559.9	559.7	558.9	548.9
2014..............	537.9	541.8	543.7	550.1	555.3	557.5	551.1	552.3	556.5	562.6	561.2	562.3	552.7
2015..............	540.6	544.1	545.8	552.1	560.1	561.9	556.3	557.0	560.4	564.5	563.0	561.6	555.6
Total Private													
2005..............	439.7	440.6	442.8	449.2	453.7	457.1	452.1	455.5	458.8	459.6	459.8	459.3	452.4
2006..............	441.0	442.3	445.2	449.5	455.3	457.5	452.1	455.5	455.2	453.2	458.8	460.1	452.1
2007..............	440.4	441.7	445.1	445.3	454.6	456.6	453.1	454.7	456.8	460.5	461.5	461.7	452.7
2008..............	444.6	444.8	446.0	452.2	459.0	462.4	459.7	460.5	461.3	463.7	460.5	458.0	456.1
2009..............	436.3	435.3	435.9	437.6	442.2	444.4	443.3	443.8	444.6	447.1	446.8	445.2	441.9
2010..............	428.7	429.1	431.4	439.2	443.3	445.1	444.3	446.4	448.3	451.4	451.5	451.0	442.5
2011..............	435.1	436.5	437.8	445.3	450.0	453.9	450.5	451.5	458.0	457.2	457.7	457.5	449.3
2012..............	441.4	443.8	445.8	448.9	455.5	458.8	454.9	457.9	459.3	461.8	461.3	461.4	454.2
2013..............	444.7	446.0	448.4	452.8	459.5	462.1	460.0	461.8	464.9	468.2	468.0	467.5	458.7
2014..............	449.6	451.3	452.8	459.3	465.1	468.6	466.2	467.3	469.0	472.3	470.6	472.2	463.7
2015..............	452.1	454.1	455.7	462.4	470.0	473.0	471.1	471.6	472.2	473.3	471.5	470.2	466.4
Goods Producing													
2005..............	81.8	80.9	81.0	82.3	83.9	84.8	83.8	85.4	84.8	84.5	84.3	82.3	83.3
2006..............	79.8	79.0	79.5	81.5	83.1	84.3	83.3	84.3	83.5	82.1	82.2	80.8	82.0
2007..............	77.7	76.5	77.3	78.2	81.0	82.4	81.6	82.3	81.6	81.1	80.5	79.0	79.9
2008..............	75.2	74.7	74.3	76.4	79.3	80.8	80.9	81.6	80.8	80.3	78.3	76.1	78.2
2009..............	70.6	69.0	68.4	69.6	70.7	70.5	70.8	71.2	70.9	70.4	69.7	67.9	70.0
2010..............	64.5	63.8	64.2	66.9	68.7	69.8	70.8	71.3	71.1	71.2	70.6	69.0	68.5
2011..............	66.7	66.4	67.0	69.4	71.2	72.9	73.4	74.1	73.5	73.1	72.4	70.5	70.9
2012..............	68.0	67.5	68.3	69.8	71.6	72.9	73.1	73.4	72.6	72.3	71.3	70.2	70.9
2013..............	67.3	66.7	67.3	68.6	71.2	72.4	72.2	73.5	73.0	73.0	72.1	70.9	70.7
2014..............	68.3	68.3	68.7	70.8	73.2	74.7	74.3	75.6	75.0	74.7	73.1	72.2	72.4
2015..............	68.6	68.2	69.0	71.0	73.7	74.9	75.3	75.3	74.9	75.3	74.1	72.3	72.7
Service-Providing													
2005..............	452.5	456.4	457.2	462.2	465.5	465.6	456.3	457.9	466.6	470.4	471.2	472.5	462.9
2006..............	453.8	457.8	460.1	462.6	467.2	467.2	457.6	459.8	463.9	465.9	472.0	474.9	463.6
2007..............	456.3	460.4	463.3	462.0	469.2	469.0	460.3	462.5	468.2	475.6	477.7	479.3	467.0
2008..............	463.2	466.0	467.9	472.4	476.4	477.6	469.5	470.1	474.8	481.1	480.1	479.4	473.2
2009..............	460.5	462.5	464.0	464.7	468.8	469.6	464.4	464.5	467.6	473.9	474.7	474.4	467.5
2010..............	459.4	462.1	464.5	469.4	473.6	471.9	461.6	463.6	468.7	476.4	477.8	478.7	469.0
2011..............	462.9	465.7	466.0	471.6	474.1	474.6	466.0	466.4	475.9	478.2	479.6	481.3	471.9
2012..............	465.1	470.3	471.4	472.4	477.5	477.8	468.9	471.2	475.9	481.9	482.8	484.0	474.9
2013..............	467.5	471.6	473.5	475.8	479.7	479.8	473.5	474.2	480.2	486.9	487.6	488.0	478.2
2014..............	469.6	473.5	475.0	479.3	482.1	482.8	476.8	476.7	481.5	487.9	488.1	490.1	480.3
2015..............	472.0	475.9	476.8	481.1	486.4	487.0	481.0	481.7	485.5	489.2	488.9	489.3	482.9
Mining, Logging, and Construction													
2005..............	17.4	17.0	16.7	18.7	20.2	21.2	21.7	22.3	21.7	21.6	21.3	19.6	20.0
2006..............	17.2	16.7	17.1	19.2	20.8	21.8	21.9	22.3	21.7	21.3	21.1	19.9	20.1
2007..............	17.6	16.3	17.2	18.3	20.8	21.9	22.1	22.4	21.7	21.6	20.8	19.6	20.0
2008..............	17.3	16.5	16.9	19.0	21.4	22.3	23.5	23.8	23.3	23.1	21.6	20.0	20.7
2009..............	17.1	16.6	17.0	18.3	19.9	20.5	21.2	21.5	20.8	20.5	19.8	17.9	19.3
2010..............	15.5	15.0	15.3	18.1	19.5	20.2	21.1	21.3	20.9	21.0	20.5	18.5	18.9
2011..............	16.5	16.1	16.7	18.6	20.3	21.4	22.2	22.5	22.2	21.8	21.0	19.1	19.9
2012..............	17.1	16.6	17.4	18.9	20.3	21.3	21.5	21.7	21.1	20.8	19.9	18.7	19.6
2013..............	16.6	16.2	16.5	17.6	20.0	20.8	21.3	21.6	21.1	21.0	20.2	18.7	19.3
2014..............	16.5	16.3	16.8	18.6	20.9	22.1	22.6	23.0	22.7	22.4	20.8	19.6	20.2
2015..............	17.2	16.6	17.1	19.1	21.6	22.3	23.0	23.1	22.9	23.1	22.1	20.2	20.7

Employment by Industry: Buffalo-Cheektowaga-Niagara Falls, NY, 2005–2015—*Continued*

(Numbers in thousands, not seasonally adjusted)

Industry and year	January	February	March	April	May	June	July	August	September	October	November	December	Annual average
Manufacturing													
2005	64.4	63.9	64.3	63.6	63.7	63.6	62.1	63.1	63.1	62.9	63.0	62.7	63.4
2006	62.6	62.3	62.4	62.3	62.3	62.5	61.4	62.0	61.8	60.8	61.1	60.9	61.9
2007	60.1	60.2	60.1	59.9	60.2	60.5	59.5	59.9	59.9	59.5	59.7	59.4	59.9
2008	57.9	58.2	57.4	57.4	57.9	58.5	57.4	57.8	57.5	57.2	56.7	56.1	57.5
2009	53.5	52.4	51.4	51.3	50.8	50.0	49.6	49.7	50.1	49.9	49.9	50.0	50.7
2010	49.0	48.8	48.9	48.8	49.2	49.6	49.7	50.0	50.2	50.2	50.1	50.5	49.6
2011	50.2	50.3	50.3	50.8	50.9	51.5	51.2	51.6	51.3	51.3	51.4	51.4	51.0
2012	50.9	50.9	50.9	50.9	51.3	51.6	51.6	51.7	51.5	51.5	51.4	51.5	51.3
2013	50.7	50.5	50.8	51.0	51.2	51.6	50.9	51.9	51.9	52.0	51.9	52.2	51.4
2014	51.8	52.0	51.9	52.2	52.3	52.6	51.7	52.6	52.3	52.3	52.3	52.6	52.2
2015	51.4	51.6	51.9	51.9	52.1	52.6	52.3	52.2	52.0	52.2	52.0	52.1	52.0
Trade, Transportation, and Utilities													
2005	102.0	100.7	101.8	102.4	103.3	104.3	103.1	103.3	103.6	103.9	105.2	107.1	103.4
2006	102.1	99.5	100.0	100.9	102.2	103.7	102.2	102.7	102.8	103.7	106.1	107.5	102.8
2007	102.7	100.9	101.2	100.8	102.9	104.1	102.9	103.0	104.3	104.9	107.0	108.9	103.6
2008	103.4	101.1	101.2	101.8	103.1	104.4	102.5	102.5	103.3	103.7	104.3	105.0	103.0
2009	98.4	96.9	96.6	96.1	97.6	98.4	97.7	97.7	98.2	98.8	100.4	101.2	98.2
2010	96.4	95.0	95.1	96.1	97.4	98.4	96.9	97.3	98.3	99.3	101.3	101.9	97.8
2011	97.3	95.8	96.0	97.1	98.2	99.6	98.3	99.1	99.9	100.8	103.2	104.0	99.1
2012	99.5	97.5	98.1	98.1	100.1	101.3	99.9	100.4	101.2	101.5	103.3	104.4	100.4
2013	99.2	97.5	98.0	98.2	99.8	101.0	99.9	99.9	100.9	101.5	104.0	105.6	100.5
2014	100.7	99.4	99.9	100.7	101.7	103.4	101.8	101.7	102.3	103.2	105.8	107.2	102.3
2015	102.0	100.9	100.8	101.7	103.2	104.5	103.1	103.2	103.6	104.2	106.4	107.9	103.5
Wholesale Trade													
2005	23.4	23.4	23.5	23.6	23.6	23.7	23.8	23.6	23.5	23.3	23.5	23.5	23.5
2006	23.3	23.2	23.3	23.3	23.4	23.6	23.3	23.3	23.1	23.3	23.4	23.6	23.3
2007	23.6	23.5	23.5	23.5	23.6	23.9	23.9	23.8	23.7	23.8	23.8	24.0	23.7
2008	23.4	23.2	23.2	23.1	23.1	23.2	23.2	23.0	22.7	22.6	22.5	22.4	23.0
2009	22.1	21.8	21.7	21.5	21.5	21.5	21.4	21.2	21.2	21.1	21.1	21.1	21.4
2010	20.9	20.8	20.8	21.0	21.1	21.2	21.3	21.3	21.2	21.3	21.4	21.4	21.1
2011	21.2	21.0	21.1	21.3	21.5	21.7	21.8	21.8	21.7	21.7	21.9	21.9	21.6
2012	21.6	21.6	21.6	21.6	21.7	22.0	21.9	22.1	21.9	21.9	21.8	22.0	21.8
2013	21.7	21.6	21.7	21.6	21.7	21.8	21.9	22.0	21.9	22.1	22.1	22.3	21.9
2014	22.2	22.0	22.0	22.2	22.4	22.5	22.3	22.3	22.3	22.4	22.4	22.5	22.3
2015	22.3	22.2	22.1	22.3	22.3	22.5	22.6	22.5	22.3	22.2	22.3	22.4	22.3
Retail Trade													
2005	61.4	60.2	61.1	61.5	62.0	62.7	62.3	62.6	62.4	62.8	64.2	65.8	62.4
2006	61.8	59.6	59.8	60.5	61.2	62.1	61.6	61.9	61.2	62.0	64.3	65.2	61.8
2007	61.2	59.6	59.8	59.2	60.8	61.5	61.3	61.6	61.7	62.3	64.5	65.9	61.6
2008	62.0	60.1	60.2	60.4	61.4	62.3	62.1	62.2	62.1	62.8	63.6	64.3	62.0
2009	59.7	58.6	58.6	58.4	59.6	60.4	60.2	60.6	60.7	61.3	62.9	63.5	60.4
2010	59.8	58.7	58.8	59.4	60.3	60.9	60.4	60.8	60.8	61.8	63.5	64.0	60.8
2011	60.4	59.3	59.5	60.3	60.8	61.7	61.4	62.3	62.0	62.9	65.0	65.5	61.8
2012	62.1	60.5	61.0	61.1	62.3	62.9	62.8	63.1	63.0	63.4	65.3	65.8	62.8
2013	61.7	60.3	60.6	60.9	61.9	62.8	62.5	62.5	62.3	62.7	65.0	66.1	62.4
2014	62.0	61.0	61.5	61.9	62.3	63.6	63.1	63.1	62.4	63.1	65.3	66.2	63.0
2015	62.5	61.7	61.7	62.4	63.2	63.9	63.5	63.9	63.4	64.0	65.6	66.7	63.5
Transportation and Utilities													
2005	17.2	17.1	17.2	17.3	17.7	17.9	17.0	17.1	17.7	17.8	17.5	17.8	17.4
2006	17.0	16.7	16.9	17.1	17.6	18.0	17.3	17.5	18.5	18.4	18.4	18.7	17.7
2007	17.9	17.8	17.9	18.1	18.5	18.7	17.7	17.6	18.9	18.8	18.7	19.0	18.3
2008	18.0	17.8	17.8	18.3	18.6	18.9	17.2	17.3	18.5	18.3	18.2	18.3	18.1
2009	16.6	16.5	16.3	16.2	16.5	16.5	16.1	15.9	16.3	16.4	16.4	16.6	16.4
2010	15.7	15.5	15.5	15.7	16.0	16.3	15.2	15.2	16.3	16.2	16.4	16.5	15.9
2011	15.7	15.5	15.4	15.5	15.9	16.2	15.1	15.0	16.2	16.2	16.3	16.6	15.8
2012	15.8	15.4	15.5	15.4	16.1	16.4	15.2	15.2	16.3	16.2	16.2	16.6	15.9
2013	15.8	15.6	15.7	15.7	16.2	16.4	15.5	15.4	16.7	16.7	16.9	17.2	16.2
2014	16.5	16.4	16.4	16.6	17.0	17.3	16.4	16.3	17.6	17.7	18.1	18.5	17.1
2015	17.2	17.0	17.0	17.0	17.7	18.1	17.0	16.8	17.9	18.0	18.5	18.8	17.6

Employment by Industry: Buffalo-Cheektowaga-Niagara Falls, NY, 2005–2015—*Continued*
(Numbers in thousands, not seasonally adjusted)

Industry and year	January	February	March	April	May	June	July	August	September	October	November	December	Annual average
Information													
2005	9.5	9.4	9.4	9.5	9.5	9.5	9.7	9.7	9.6	9.6	9.6	9.7	9.6
2006	9.4	9.3	9.3	9.2	9.3	9.3	9.2	9.1	8.9	8.6	8.6	8.6	9.1
2007	8.5	8.5	8.5	8.4	8.6	8.6	8.6	8.5	8.4	8.3	8.4	8.4	8.5
2008	8.3	8.3	8.3	8.3	8.6	8.6	8.6	8.7	8.5	8.4	8.4	8.5	8.5
2009	8.3	8.2	8.3	8.4	8.4	8.5	8.4	8.3	8.1	8.2	8.1	8.1	8.3
2010	7.9	7.8	7.9	7.7	7.7	7.8	7.9	7.9	7.8	7.8	7.8	7.7	7.8
2011	7.6	7.6	7.6	7.7	7.7	7.8	7.8	6.9	7.7	7.6	7.6	7.7	7.6
2012	7.6	7.6	7.6	7.6	7.7	7.8	7.7	7.6	7.6	7.5	7.6	7.6	7.6
2013	7.5	7.5	7.5	7.5	7.5	7.6	7.6	7.6	7.6	7.6	7.6	7.6	7.6
2014	7.6	7.6	7.6	7.6	7.6	7.7	7.6	7.6	7.6	7.6	7.6	7.6	7.6
2015	7.3	7.2	7.3	7.4	7.4	7.4	7.4	7.4	7.3	7.3	7.4	7.4	7.4
Financial Activities													
2005	33.4	33.3	33.3	34.0	34.1	34.7	34.8	34.9	34.8	34.8	35.0	35.2	34.4
2006	35.0	35.1	35.2	34.9	35.1	35.2	35.1	35.0	34.5	34.0	34.0	34.3	34.8
2007	33.3	33.4	33.6	32.9	33.0	33.5	33.5	33.4	33.0	33.3	33.4	33.9	33.4
2008	32.8	32.7	32.6	32.7	32.9	33.1	33.0	32.9	32.5	32.5	32.5	32.8	32.8
2009	31.4	31.3	31.3	31.4	31.5	31.7	31.7	31.4	31.0	31.0	30.9	31.1	31.3
2010	30.3	30.3	30.4	30.4	30.4	30.6	30.7	30.5	30.2	30.5	30.6	31.1	30.5
2011	31.1	31.1	31.2	31.5	31.1	31.4	31.4	31.7	31.5	31.4	31.5	32.2	31.4
2012	31.5	31.6	31.5	31.8	31.8	32.3	32.3	32.3	31.9	32.2	32.3	32.4	32.0
2013	31.9	31.9	32.0	31.9	31.9	32.2	32.8	32.1	31.7	32.0	32.1	32.6	32.1
2014	31.9	31.9	32.0	32.2	32.5	33.0	33.1	33.0	32.9	33.0	33.1	33.5	32.7
2015	32.9	32.9	33.0	33.1	33.6	33.9	34.3	34.4	34.0	33.4	33.9	34.5	33.7
Professional and Business Services													
2005	63.4	63.7	63.8	65.7	66.0	67.8	67.5	68.2	68.9	68.8	68.1	67.8	66.6
2006	65.7	66.1	66.4	67.9	68.2	69.4	68.8	69.9	68.9	69.1	70.5	70.4	68.4
2007	67.1	67.6	68.3	68.9	69.6	70.9	70.8	71.5	71.0	71.4	71.5	71.3	70.0
2008	69.4	70.0	70.4	72.9	73.3	74.6	74.8	74.6	73.7	73.2	72.4	71.6	72.6
2009	69.4	69.3	69.7	69.9	70.4	72.1	72.2	72.0	71.2	71.5	71.2	70.5	70.8
2010	69.2	68.9	69.4	71.6	71.7	72.5	73.5	73.5	72.8	72.6	71.5	71.5	71.6
2011	70.1	70.3	70.1	72.0	72.5	73.7	74.4	73.9	73.8	73.7	72.8	72.6	72.5
2012	71.0	71.2	71.3	72.4	72.9	74.3	74.6	74.8	73.6	74.4	73.9	73.2	73.1
2013	71.2	71.6	71.9	73.1	73.7	74.9	75.0	74.9	74.8	74.0	73.4	72.6	73.4
2014	69.9	69.7	69.2	71.0	71.9	73.4	73.7	73.3	72.7	72.9	72.1	72.3	71.8
2015	69.4	69.8	69.4	71.2	72.7	73.7	73.8	73.7	73.0	71.8	70.3	70.0	71.6
Education and Health Services													
2005	82.7	85.5	85.4	85.9	85.4	83.2	80.9	80.5	84.7	86.1	86.5	86.1	84.4
2006	82.2	85.3	85.8	85.5	85.4	83.0	81.5	81.6	85.1	86.1	86.7	86.8	84.6
2007	82.9	85.4	86.2	85.8	85.7	83.1	81.5	81.3	85.2	87.3	87.4	87.4	84.9
2008	85.1	87.0	87.6	87.9	86.9	85.0	83.9	83.6	87.2	89.5	89.8	89.9	87.0
2009	87.3	89.5	90.0	89.2	88.8	86.8	85.3	85.0	88.6	91.2	91.6	91.8	88.8
2010	88.9	91.1	91.5	91.9	91.3	88.9	86.7	86.7	90.3	92.4	92.9	92.6	90.4
2011	89.8	92.1	92.2	92.6	91.9	89.2	87.1	87.0	91.1	92.3	92.9	92.9	90.9
2012	90.4	93.2	93.0	92.9	92.5	89.2	87.5	87.7	91.9	93.9	94.0	94.4	91.7
2013	91.5	93.8	94.3	94.7	93.8	91.0	89.8	90.0	94.3	96.3	96.5	96.5	93.5
2014	93.2	96.1	96.3	96.0	94.9	92.6	91.0	90.8	94.2	96.4	96.4	96.6	94.5
2015	93.3	95.7	96.0	96.1	95.2	92.9	91.3	91.6	94.4	97.3	97.9	97.5	94.9
Leisure and Hospitality													
2005	44.2	44.4	44.8	46.4	48.3	49.7	49.5	50.7	49.6	49.0	48.2	48.0	47.7
2006	44.5	45.6	46.1	46.8	48.9	49.6	49.2	49.9	48.6	46.6	47.6	48.3	47.6
2007	45.6	46.5	46.8	47.2	50.5	50.6	50.8	51.2	50.1	50.6	49.8	49.2	49.1
2008	47.1	47.6	47.9	48.5	51.0	52.0	51.9	52.4	51.5	51.8	50.8	50.1	50.2
2009	47.5	47.5	47.8	49.0	50.8	52.4	53.2	54.2	52.9	52.0	51.0	51.0	50.8
2010	48.6	49.2	49.8	51.4	52.9	53.8	53.6	54.7	54.7	54.3	53.5	53.8	52.5
2011	49.7	50.2	50.7	51.8	54.1	55.8	54.8	55.5	57.1	55.2	54.2	54.3	53.6
2012	50.4	52.2	52.8	53.1	55.4	57.3	56.3	58.2	57.2	56.5	55.4	55.6	55.0
2013	52.5	53.4	53.7	55.1	57.6	59.0	58.7	59.6	58.6	59.3	57.8	56.9	56.9
2014	53.7	53.9	54.4	56.5	58.6	59.2	59.9	60.5	60.0	59.8	57.9	58.1	57.7
2015	54.3	55.1	55.6	57.1	59.3	60.8	60.8	61.0	60.4	59.4	57.3	56.5	58.1

Employment by Industry: Buffalo-Cheektowaga-Niagara Falls, NY, 2005–2015—*Continued*

(Numbers in thousands, not seasonally adjusted)

Industry and year	January	February	March	April	May	June	July	August	September	October	November	December	Annual average
Other Services													
2005	22.7	22.7	23.3	23.0	23.2	23.1	22.8	22.8	22.8	22.9	22.9	23.1	22.9
2006	22.3	22.4	22.9	22.8	23.1	23.0	22.8	23.0	22.9	23.0	23.1	23.4	22.9
2007	22.6	22.9	23.2	23.1	23.3	23.4	23.4	23.5	23.2	23.6	23.5	23.6	23.3
2008	23.3	23.4	23.7	23.7	23.9	23.9	24.1	24.2	23.8	24.3	24.0	24.0	23.9
2009	23.4	23.6	23.8	24.0	24.0	24.0	24.0	24.0	23.7	24.0	23.9	23.6	23.8
2010	22.9	23.0	23.1	23.2	23.2	23.3	24.2	24.5	23.1	23.3	23.3	23.4	23.4
2011	22.8	23.0	23.0	23.2	23.3	23.5	23.3	23.3	23.4	23.1	23.1	23.3	23.2
2012	23.0	23.0	23.2	23.2	23.5	23.7	23.5	23.5	23.3	23.5	23.5	23.6	23.4
2013	23.6	23.6	23.7	23.7	24.0	24.0	24.0	24.2	24.0	24.5	24.5	24.8	24.1
2014	24.3	24.4	24.7	24.5	24.7	24.6	24.8	24.8	24.3	24.7	24.6	24.7	24.6
2015	24.3	24.3	24.6	24.8	24.9	24.9	25.1	25.0	24.6	24.6	24.2	24.1	24.6
Government													
2005	94.6	96.7	95.4	95.3	95.7	93.3	88.0	87.8	92.6	95.3	95.7	95.5	93.8
2006	92.6	94.5	94.4	94.6	95.0	94.0	88.8	88.6	92.2	94.8	95.4	95.6	93.4
2007	93.6	95.2	95.5	94.9	95.6	94.8	88.8	90.1	93.0	96.2	96.7	96.6	94.3
2008	93.8	95.9	96.2	96.6	96.7	96.0	90.7	91.2	94.3	97.7	97.9	97.5	95.4
2009	94.8	96.2	96.5	96.7	97.3	95.7	91.9	91.9	93.9	97.2	97.6	97.1	95.6
2010	95.2	96.8	97.3	97.1	99.0	96.6	88.1	88.5	91.5	96.2	96.9	96.7	95.0
2011	94.5	95.6	95.2	95.7	95.3	93.6	88.9	89.0	91.4	94.1	94.3	94.3	93.5
2012	91.7	94.0	93.9	93.3	93.6	91.9	87.1	86.7	89.2	92.4	92.8	92.8	91.6
2013	90.1	92.3	92.4	91.6	91.4	90.1	85.7	85.9	88.3	91.7	91.7	91.4	90.2
2014	88.3	90.5	90.9	90.8	90.2	88.9	84.9	85.0	87.5	90.3	90.6	90.1	89.0
2015	88.5	90.0	90.1	89.7	90.1	88.9	85.2	85.4	88.2	91.2	91.5	91.4	89.2

Employment by Industry: Rochester, NY, 2005–2015

(Numbers in thousands, not seasonally adjusted)

Industry and year	January	February	March	April	May	June	July	August	September	October	November	December	Annual average
Total Nonfarm													
2005	509.0	512.9	515.2	521.8	526.4	526.3	517.3	517.4	520.9	526.7	528.2	529.1	520.9
2006	509.0	511.8	514.2	517.9	522.2	523.6	513.4	513.3	520.2	526.0	526.7	526.8	518.8
2007	510.6	513.7	515.2	517.3	525.6	527.1	517.3	516.3	521.4	527.9	528.3	528.2	520.7
2008	510.4	515.1	516.0	522.0	528.6	528.7	519.9	519.1	524.1	529.8	527.1	525.5	522.2
2009	505.3	507.2	506.6	507.0	511.8	510.0	505.6	503.7	506.5	513.8	513.0	512.8	508.6
2010	496.2	500.1	502.4	508.5	513.5	513.3	505.1	505.2	510.3	519.4	519.7	517.5	509.3
2011	500.5	505.2	507.1	516.5	519.0	520.2	512.2	513.0	520.3	526.2	526.5	526.7	516.1
2012	506.7	512.9	515.8	517.9	524.4	524.2	514.7	513.5	520.6	528.5	528.6	529.0	519.7
2013	508.5	516.0	517.3	521.5	527.0	524.8	515.2	515.5	523.1	530.1	531.3	531.4	521.8
2014	511.0	518.4	520.1	523.2	528.2	528.1	518.5	519.1	525.5	533.2	533.7	533.9	524.4
2015	514.3	520.5	521.6	527.0	532.3	532.6	523.5	523.5	528.3	534.1	531.3	530.4	526.6
Total Private													
2005	427.5	428.5	430.5	437.0	441.3	442.0	440.8	441.2	440.5	443.2	443.7	443.6	438.3
2006	428.7	429.1	430.9	435.1	439.4	442.3	439.8	439.9	440.7	444.1	443.9	443.8	438.1
2007	430.4	431.2	432.5	434.4	442.2	444.4	442.6	442.2	441.4	445.2	444.9	444.0	439.6
2008	429.7	432.2	432.8	438.2	444.5	445.3	443.9	443.8	443.1	446.0	442.9	441.0	440.3
2009	424.2	423.6	423.0	422.8	427.6	427.1	426.8	426.9	426.9	429.8	428.4	427.9	426.3
2010	413.9	415.8	418.1	424.0	427.5	428.4	429.4	430.6	430.6	435.4	435.0	432.5	426.8
2011	419.4	421.4	423.3	432.3	435.1	437.0	437.5	438.3	440.4	443.2	442.8	442.4	434.4
2012	426.7	429.8	432.6	435.4	441.1	442.0	440.8	440.4	441.8	446.6	446.3	445.7	439.1
2013	429.1	433.8	434.8	439.1	444.1	443.3	442.1	442.7	444.7	449.3	449.8	449.4	441.9
2014	432.9	437.6	439.4	442.3	447.5	448.0	446.3	446.9	447.7	453.2	452.6	452.1	445.5
2015	436.3	439.9	441.1	446.4	450.7	451.9	451.3	451.6	450.9	454.4	450.6	448.9	447.8
Goods Producing													
2005	95.4	94.5	94.5	96.4	97.9	99.2	100.6	101.0	100.0	99.4	98.7	97.0	97.9
2006	94.3	93.5	93.3	95.0	96.5	98.5	98.6	98.9	97.6	97.3	96.6	95.3	96.3
2007	92.4	91.3	91.7	92.7	94.3	95.5	95.4	95.5	94.2	93.6	92.7	91.6	93.4
2008	89.1	88.0	87.7	88.6	90.8	92.2	93.2	93.1	92.1	91.4	89.4	87.4	90.3
2009	83.7	81.9	80.8	80.6	81.7	82.2	82.9	83.5	82.0	81.5	80.2	78.5	81.6
2010	75.9	75.0	75.3	77.0	78.2	79.6	80.8	81.3	80.4	80.6	80.0	77.9	78.5
2011	76.2	75.5	75.9	77.5	79.4	81.5	82.5	82.8	81.9	81.7	80.6	79.3	79.6
2012	77.2	76.5	76.7	78.0	79.6	81.6	82.2	82.1	80.9	80.6	79.4	78.7	79.5
2013	76.3	75.3	75.4	76.8	78.6	79.8	80.5	81.0	80.0	80.0	79.2	78.0	78.4
2014	75.7	74.9	75.4	76.3	78.5	80.2	81.3	81.5	80.5	80.7	79.5	78.2	78.6
2015	76.0	75.1	75.6	77.2	79.4	80.8	81.5	81.7	80.8	80.8	79.7	78.5	78.9
Service-Providing													
2005	413.6	418.4	420.7	425.4	428.5	427.1	416.7	416.4	420.9	427.3	429.5	432.1	423.1
2006	414.7	418.3	420.9	422.9	425.7	425.1	414.8	414.4	422.6	428.7	430.1	431.5	422.5
2007	418.2	422.4	423.5	424.6	431.3	431.6	421.9	420.8	427.2	434.3	435.6	436.6	427.3
2008	421.3	427.1	428.3	433.4	437.8	436.5	426.7	426.0	432.0	438.4	437.7	438.1	431.9
2009	421.6	425.3	425.8	426.4	430.1	427.8	422.7	420.2	424.5	432.3	432.8	434.3	427.0
2010	420.3	425.1	427.1	431.5	435.3	433.7	424.3	423.9	429.9	438.8	439.7	439.6	430.8
2011	424.3	429.7	431.2	439.0	439.6	438.7	429.7	430.2	438.4	444.5	445.9	447.4	436.6
2012	429.5	436.4	439.1	439.9	444.8	442.6	432.5	431.4	439.7	447.9	449.2	450.3	440.3
2013	432.2	440.7	441.9	444.7	448.4	445.0	434.7	434.5	443.1	450.1	452.1	453.4	443.4
2014	435.3	443.5	444.7	446.9	449.7	447.9	437.2	437.6	445.0	452.5	454.2	455.7	445.9
2015	438.3	445.4	446.0	449.8	452.9	451.8	442.0	441.8	447.5	453.3	451.6	451.9	447.7
Mining and Logging													
2005	0.5	0.5	0.5	0.6	0.6	0.7	0.7	0.7	0.7	0.6	0.6	0.6	0.6
2006	0.5	0.5	0.5	0.6	0.6	0.7	0.7	0.7	0.6	0.6	0.6	0.4	0.6
2007	0.4	0.5	0.5	0.6	0.6	0.6	0.6	0.6	0.6	0.6	0.6	0.6	0.6
2008	0.6	0.5	0.5	0.5	0.6	0.6	0.6	0.6	0.6	0.6	0.6	0.6	0.6
2009	0.5	0.5	0.5	0.5	0.6	0.6	0.6	0.6	0.6	0.6	0.6	0.6	0.6
2010	0.5	0.5	0.5	0.6	0.6	0.6	0.6	0.6	0.6	0.5	0.6	0.5	0.6
2011	0.5	0.5	0.5	0.6	0.6	0.6	0.6	0.6	0.6	0.6	0.6	0.6	0.6
2012	0.4	0.5	0.5	0.5	0.5	0.5	0.5	0.5	0.5	0.6	0.6	0.5	0.5
2013	0.5	0.5	0.5	0.5	0.5	0.5	0.6	0.5	0.6	0.6	0.6	0.6	0.5
2014	0.5	0.5	0.6	0.6	0.6	0.6	0.6	0.6	0.7	0.7	0.7	0.6	0.6
2015	0.6	0.6	0.6	0.6	0.7	0.7	0.7	0.6	0.7	0.7	0.7	0.7	0.7

Employment by Industry: Rochester, NY, 2005–2015—*Continued*

(Numbers in thousands, not seasonally adjusted)

Industry and year	January	February	March	April	May	June	July	August	September	October	November	December	Annual average
Construction													
2005	16.3	15.7	15.6	17.2	19.0	19.5	20.0	20.4	19.9	19.5	19.1	17.8	18.3
2006	16.2	15.5	15.4	16.8	18.3	19.3	19.7	19.9	19.3	19.2	18.6	18.0	18.0
2007	16.5	15.4	15.9	17.2	19.0	20.0	20.3	20.5	20.0	19.9	19.4	18.4	18.5
2008	17.1	16.3	16.4	17.7	19.4	20.3	21.1	21.3	20.9	20.6	19.4	18.2	19.1
2009	15.8	15.1	15.0	16.1	17.7	18.7	19.5	19.8	19.0	18.6	17.8	16.5	17.5
2010	14.8	14.2	14.5	16.2	17.2	18.3	19.1	19.5	18.7	18.6	18.1	16.4	17.1
2011	15.0	14.5	14.8	16.0	17.6	18.9	19.6	19.9	19.5	19.3	18.5	17.5	17.6
2012	16.0	15.5	15.9	17.2	18.5	19.8	20.4	20.5	19.9	19.5	18.7	18.0	18.3
2013	16.4	16.0	16.1	17.1	19.1	20.0	20.5	20.7	20.0	20.0	19.2	18.2	18.6
2014	16.5	16.1	16.3	17.4	19.4	20.5	21.1	21.2	20.5	20.7	19.9	18.7	19.0
2015	16.9	16.2	16.5	18.0	19.8	20.6	20.9	21.3	20.8	20.8	20.0	18.8	19.2
Manufacturing													
2005	78.6	78.3	78.4	78.6	78.3	79.0	79.9	79.9	79.4	79.3	79.0	78.6	78.9
2006	77.6	77.5	77.4	77.6	78.5	78.5	78.2	78.3	77.7	77.5	77.4	76.9	77.7
2007	75.5	75.4	75.3	74.9	74.7	74.9	74.5	74.4	73.6	73.1	72.7	72.6	74.3
2008	71.4	71.2	70.8	70.4	70.8	71.3	71.5	71.2	70.6	70.2	69.4	68.6	70.6
2009	67.4	66.3	65.3	64.0	63.4	62.9	62.8	63.1	62.4	62.3	61.8	61.4	63.6
2010	60.6	60.3	60.3	60.2	60.4	60.7	61.1	61.2	61.1	61.5	61.3	61.0	60.8
2011	60.7	60.5	60.6	60.9	61.2	62.0	62.3	62.3	61.8	61.8	61.5	61.2	61.4
2012	60.8	60.5	60.3	60.3	60.6	61.3	61.3	61.1	60.5	60.5	60.1	60.2	60.6
2013	59.4	58.8	58.8	59.2	59.0	59.3	59.4	59.8	59.4	59.4	59.4	59.2	59.3
2014	58.7	58.3	58.5	58.3	58.5	59.1	59.6	59.7	59.3	59.3	58.9	58.9	58.9
2015	58.5	58.3	58.5	58.6	58.9	59.5	59.9	59.8	59.3	59.3	59.0	59.0	59.1
Trade, Transportation, and Utilities													
2005	85.2	83.7	83.8	84.4	85.5	86.9	86.1	86.5	85.3	86.1	87.3	89.1	85.8
2006	85.1	82.9	83.1	83.1	84.5	86.2	85.1	85.5	84.8	85.9	87.2	88.4	85.2
2007	85.3	83.1	83.5	83.1	86.1	87.2	86.5	86.1	85.4	86.5	87.9	88.9	85.8
2008	85.7	83.8	83.7	84.3	85.8	86.5	85.4	85.2	84.3	85.3	85.6	86.3	85.2
2009	82.2	80.4	80.0	79.9	81.6	82.5	82.0	82.0	80.7	81.7	82.5	83.5	81.6
2010	80.5	79.3	79.6	80.6	81.9	83.2	82.2	82.5	81.6	83.1	83.7	84.6	81.9
2011	81.5	80.3	80.3	81.4	82.3	83.4	82.5	82.6	81.8	83.3	84.3	85.6	82.4
2012	82.2	80.3	80.7	80.8	83.1	84.3	83.4	83.2	82.6	83.9	85.0	85.7	82.9
2013	82.2	80.7	80.7	81.2	82.6	83.6	82.6	82.2	81.8	82.9	84.1	84.8	82.5
2014	81.8	80.8	80.5	81.3	82.7	83.7	82.6	82.7	82.2	83.1	84.2	85.1	82.6
2015	81.8	80.6	80.8	81.2	83.0	84.3	83.4	83.4	82.9	83.2	83.4	84.0	82.7
Wholesale Trade													
2005	17.3	17.4	17.4	17.4	17.5	17.7	17.8	17.8	17.4	17.1	17.4	17.3	17.5
2006	17.3	17.3	17.3	17.3	17.4	17.8	17.9	18.1	17.7	17.5	17.5	17.6	17.6
2007	17.5	17.5	17.5	17.5	17.7	17.9	18.2	18.1	17.8	17.9	17.7	17.8	17.8
2008	17.3	17.3	17.2	17.5	17.7	17.8	17.9	17.8	17.6	17.9	17.7	17.6	17.6
2009	17.2	17.0	16.8	16.7	16.9	16.9	16.9	16.8	16.6	16.6	16.4	16.5	16.8
2010	16.1	16.1	16.1	16.3	16.4	16.6	16.6	16.6	16.4	16.6	16.5	16.6	16.4
2011	16.2	16.2	16.3	16.5	16.6	16.8	16.8	16.7	16.6	17.0	16.9	16.9	16.6
2012	16.5	16.5	16.6	17.0	17.2	17.3	17.3	17.2	17.0	17.3	17.3	17.3	17.0
2013	17.2	17.1	17.1	17.2	17.3	17.4	17.4	17.3	17.3	17.2	17.1	17.2	17.2
2014	17.0	17.1	17.0	17.2	17.4	17.6	17.6	17.5	17.3	17.4	17.3	17.3	17.3
2015	17.1	17.0	17.1	17.1	17.2	17.4	17.3	17.3	17.1	17.0	17.0	17.0	17.1
Retail Trade													
2005	57.7	56.1	56.1	56.6	57.5	58.6	58.3	58.6	57.2	58.1	59.0	60.7	57.9
2006	57.2	55.0	55.2	55.1	56.3	57.4	56.8	57.0	56.2	57.5	58.8	59.8	56.9
2007	57.2	55.1	55.5	55.2	57.7	58.6	58.1	57.8	56.8	57.7	59.2	60.0	57.4
2008	57.7	55.8	55.8	56.0	57.1	57.7	57.1	57.1	56.2	56.9	57.4	58.0	56.9
2009	55.0	53.4	53.4	53.2	54.6	55.4	55.0	55.1	54.0	54.8	55.9	56.5	54.7
2010	54.4	53.3	53.6	54.3	55.3	56.3	56.0	56.3	55.1	56.3	57.0	57.7	55.5
2011	55.5	54.3	54.2	54.9	55.5	56.4	56.1	56.3	55.0	56.1	57.2	58.3	55.8
2012	55.8	54.0	54.3	54.1	55.8	56.7	56.5	56.4	55.4	56.4	57.6	57.9	55.9
2013	55.1	53.7	53.8	54.1	55.2	56.0	55.6	55.5	54.2	55.3	56.4	56.9	55.2
2014	54.5	53.5	53.3	53.9	54.9	55.7	55.2	55.5	54.5	55.2	56.3	57.0	55.0
2015	54.5	53.5	53.6	54.1	55.4	56.3	56.0	56.1	55.1	55.6	55.6	56.0	55.2

Employment by Industry: Rochester, NY, 2005–2015—*Continued*

(Numbers in thousands, not seasonally adjusted)

Industry and year	January	February	March	April	May	June	July	August	September	October	November	December	Annual average
Transportation and Utilities													
2005	10.2	10.2	10.3	10.4	10.5	10.6	10.0	10.1	10.7	10.9	10.9	11.1	10.5
2006	10.6	10.6	10.6	10.7	10.8	11.0	10.4	10.4	10.9	10.9	10.9	11.0	10.7
2007	10.6	10.5	10.5	10.4	10.7	10.7	10.2	10.2	10.8	10.9	11.0	11.1	10.6
2008	10.7	10.7	10.7	10.8	11.0	11.0	10.4	10.3	10.5	10.5	10.5	10.7	10.7
2009	10.0	10.0	9.8	10.0	10.1	10.2	10.1	10.1	10.1	10.3	10.2	10.5	10.1
2010	10.0	9.9	9.9	10.0	10.2	10.3	9.6	9.6	10.1	10.2	10.2	10.3	10.0
2011	9.8	9.8	9.8	10.0	10.2	10.2	9.6	9.6	10.2	10.2	10.2	10.4	10.0
2012	9.9	9.8	9.8	9.7	10.1	10.3	9.6	9.6	10.2	10.2	10.1	10.5	10.0
2013	9.9	9.9	9.8	9.9	10.1	10.2	9.6	9.4	10.3	10.4	10.6	10.7	10.1
2014	10.3	10.2	10.2	10.2	10.4	10.4	9.8	9.7	10.4	10.5	10.6	10.8	10.3
2015	10.2	10.1	10.1	10.0	10.4	10.6	10.1	10.0	10.7	10.6	10.8	11.0	10.4
Information													
2005	11.9	11.7	11.7	11.7	11.8	11.8	11.7	11.7	11.7	11.9	11.8	11.9	11.8
2006	11.8	11.7	11.6	11.2	11.2	11.2	11.0	10.8	10.6	10.7	10.7	10.6	11.1
2007	10.7	10.6	10.6	10.7	10.8	10.8	10.8	10.8	10.7	10.7	10.7	10.8	10.7
2008	10.6	10.6	10.6	10.5	10.5	10.5	10.5	10.5	10.3	10.4	10.5	10.5	10.5
2009	10.2	10.1	10.1	10.2	10.2	10.1	10.1	9.9	9.7	9.8	9.8	9.8	10.0
2010	9.6	9.5	9.5	9.4	9.5	9.5	9.6	9.6	9.4	9.4	9.4	9.3	9.5
2011	9.3	9.2	9.1	9.1	9.1	9.1	9.2	9.2	9.1	9.1	9.0	9.0	9.1
2012	8.6	8.5	8.6	8.6	8.8	8.8	9.0	9.0	8.9	8.9	9.1	9.1	8.8
2013	8.9	8.8	8.7	8.8	8.7	8.7	8.8	8.9	8.6	8.6	8.7	8.8	8.8
2014	8.7	8.7	8.8	8.7	8.8	8.9	9.0	9.0	8.9	9.1	9.1	9.2	8.9
2015	9.1	9.1	9.0	9.1	9.0	9.0	9.0	9.0	8.9	8.9	9.0	9.0	9.0
Financial Activities													
2005	21.9	21.7	21.8	21.7	22.0	22.2	22.4	22.4	21.9	21.9	22.1	22.2	22.0
2006	21.9	21.7	21.7	21.7	21.9	22.3	22.7	22.7	21.8	22.0	21.8	21.8	22.0
2007	21.8	21.7	21.7	21.7	21.7	22.2	22.6	22.6	21.6	21.6	21.6	21.7	21.9
2008	21.2	21.2	21.2	21.3	21.7	22.1	22.3	22.3	21.6	21.5	21.4	21.4	21.6
2009	20.6	20.3	20.3	20.4	20.9	21.4	21.4	21.5	21.1	20.8	20.7	20.8	20.9
2010	20.4	20.2	20.4	20.3	20.6	21.2	21.3	21.1	20.3	20.4	20.3	20.3	20.6
2011	20.3	20.3	20.4	20.7	20.9	21.6	21.9	22.0	21.3	21.3	21.2	21.4	21.1
2012	21.3	21.3	21.2	21.3	21.5	22.2	22.3	22.4	21.6	21.6	21.5	21.7	21.7
2013	21.2	21.2	21.1	21.2	21.5	22.0	22.3	22.2	21.6	21.2	21.2	21.4	21.5
2014	21.0	20.9	21.1	21.0	21.4	22.0	22.2	22.2	21.7	21.7	21.6	21.9	21.6
2015	21.6	21.6	21.7	21.7	21.8	22.1	22.1	22.1	21.1	21.1	21.0	21.1	21.6
Professional and Business Services													
2005	57.3	57.5	58.2	60.3	60.6	61.2	61.7	61.2	60.9	61.3	61.6	61.8	60.3
2006	59.4	58.8	59.5	60.8	60.6	62.0	61.7	61.6	62.4	62.5	61.9	62.4	61.1
2007	60.9	61.4	61.3	61.3	62.0	63.3	62.8	62.9	62.0	62.9	62.5	62.4	62.1
2008	61.3	61.6	61.8	63.4	63.6	64.8	64.5	65.1	64.0	64.4	63.8	63.3	63.5
2009	61.2	60.9	60.6	59.8	59.8	60.7	60.5	60.6	60.3	61.0	60.9	60.8	60.6
2010	58.9	59.3	59.5	60.3	60.3	61.8	62.6	63.1	62.1	63.3	63.2	62.4	61.4
2011	60.4	60.4	61.1	63.5	63.5	65.2	65.7	66.1	66.3	65.5	65.9	65.8	64.1
2012	64.3	64.5	64.8	66.1	66.3	67.4	67.0	66.7	65.8	66.6	66.8	66.0	66.0
2013	64.8	64.8	64.9	65.7	66.1	67.6	67.5	67.6	66.8	67.1	67.6	67.2	66.5
2014	65.0	65.6	66.0	65.8	66.2	66.9	66.9	66.7	66.1	66.4	67.3	67.1	66.3
2015	65.7	66.3	65.9	67.0	67.5	69.1	69.4	69.4	68.2	67.8	67.4	65.8	67.5
Education and Health Services													
2005	99.5	102.9	103.4	103.5	101.9	97.3	95.5	95.5	100.9	103.7	104.5	103.9	101.0
2006	101.0	104.8	105.0	105.1	104.1	99.6	97.4	97.4	103.3	106.2	106.9	106.3	103.1
2007	102.8	106.4	106.7	107.0	105.4	101.0	99.7	100.0	106.2	109.2	109.6	109.2	105.3
2008	104.9	109.5	110.0	110.3	108.7	104.4	102.9	102.7	109.4	112.0	112.7	112.6	108.3
2009	108.8	112.8	113.3	112.8	110.6	105.8	104.7	104.5	110.7	113.9	114.5	114.6	110.6
2010	110.6	114.7	115.2	115.6	113.3	108.2	107.1	106.9	114.0	116.8	117.4	117.5	113.1
2011	112.3	116.2	116.5	117.9	115.3	109.9	108.7	108.6	115.6	118.4	118.9	118.8	114.8
2012	112.6	118.0	118.7	118.4	115.9	110.1	109.0	109.2	117.0	120.2	120.8	121.2	115.9
2013	114.4	120.9	121.4	121.3	119.1	112.4	110.8	111.4	119.6	123.1	123.9	123.9	118.5
2014	118.7	124.2	124.8	124.8	121.8	116.9	114.8	115.7	121.8	125.6	125.8	125.7	121.7
2015	120.0	124.8	125.1	125.4	121.7	117.2	116.3	116.6	122.0	125.5	125.7	125.7	122.2

Employment by Industry: Rochester, NY, 2005–2015—*Continued*

(Numbers in thousands, not seasonally adjusted)

Industry and year	January	February	March	April	May	June	July	August	September	October	November	December	Annual average
Leisure and Hospitality													
2005	37.1	37.2	37.6	39.2	41.8	43.6	43.3	43.5	40.7	39.6	38.4	38.3	40.0
2006	36.0	36.4	37.3	38.8	41.1	43.2	43.8	43.8	41.2	40.3	39.4	39.3	40.1
2007	37.0	37.2	37.5	38.4	42.1	44.6	45.1	44.6	41.9	41.0	40.2	39.6	40.8
2008	37.3	37.9	38.2	39.8	43.2	44.6	44.8	44.8	41.8	41.1	39.6	39.6	41.1
2009	37.7	37.4	38.0	39.2	42.7	44.3	44.9	44.8	42.6	41.2	39.8	39.8	41.0
2010	38.2	38.2	38.9	40.9	43.7	44.8	45.5	45.7	43.0	41.7	40.7	40.1	41.8
2011	39.2	39.3	39.6	41.4	43.8	45.6	46.2	46.2	43.7	43.1	42.1	41.4	42.6
2012	39.5	39.8	40.6	41.0	44.4	46.0	46.8	46.8	44.3	43.9	42.8	42.3	43.2
2013	40.5	41.2	41.7	43.1	46.2	47.7	48.1	47.8	45.5	45.4	44.0	44.0	44.6
2014	41.0	41.6	41.8	43.2	46.7	47.8	48.2	48.0	45.7	45.5	44.0	43.7	44.8
2015	41.2	41.6	42.0	43.6	46.9	47.9	48.4	48.1	46.1	46.0	43.3	43.6	44.9
Other Services													
2005	19.2	19.3	19.5	19.8	19.8	19.8	19.5	19.4	19.1	19.3	19.3	19.4	19.5
2006	19.2	19.3	19.4	19.4	19.5	19.3	19.5	19.2	19.0	19.2	19.4	19.7	19.3
2007	19.5	19.5	19.5	19.5	19.8	19.8	19.7	19.7	19.4	19.7	19.7	19.8	19.6
2008	19.6	19.6	19.6	20.0	20.2	20.2	20.3	20.1	19.6	19.9	19.9	19.9	19.9
2009	19.8	19.8	19.9	19.9	20.1	20.1	20.3	20.1	19.8	19.9	20.0	20.1	20.0
2010	19.8	19.6	19.7	19.9	20.0	20.1	20.3	20.4	19.8	20.1	20.3	20.4	20.0
2011	20.2	20.2	20.4	20.8	20.8	20.7	20.8	20.8	20.7	20.8	20.8	21.1	20.7
2012	21.0	20.9	21.3	21.2	21.5	21.6	21.1	21.0	20.7	20.9	20.9	21.0	21.1
2013	20.8	20.9	20.9	21.0	21.3	21.5	21.5	21.6	20.8	21.0	21.1	21.3	21.1
2014	21.0	20.9	21.0	21.2	21.4	21.6	21.3	21.1	20.8	21.1	21.1	21.2	21.1
2015	20.9	20.8	21.0	21.2	21.4	21.5	21.2	21.3	20.9	21.1	21.1	21.2	21.1
Government													
2005	81.5	84.4	84.7	84.8	85.1	84.3	76.5	76.2	80.4	83.5	84.5	85.5	82.6
2006	80.3	82.7	83.3	82.8	82.8	81.3	73.6	73.4	79.5	81.9	82.8	83.0	80.6
2007	80.2	82.5	82.7	82.9	83.4	82.7	74.7	74.1	80.0	82.7	83.4	84.2	81.1
2008	80.7	82.9	83.2	83.8	84.1	83.4	76.0	75.3	81.0	83.8	84.2	84.5	81.9
2009	81.1	83.6	83.6	84.2	84.2	82.9	78.8	76.8	79.6	84.0	84.6	84.9	82.4
2010	82.3	84.3	84.3	84.5	86.0	84.9	75.7	74.6	79.7	84.0	84.7	85.0	82.5
2011	81.1	83.8	83.8	84.2	83.9	83.2	74.7	74.7	79.9	83.0	83.7	84.3	81.7
2012	80.0	83.1	83.2	82.5	83.3	82.2	73.9	73.1	78.8	81.9	82.3	83.3	80.6
2013	79.4	82.2	82.5	82.4	82.9	81.5	73.1	72.8	78.4	80.8	81.5	82.0	80.0
2014	78.1	80.8	80.7	80.9	80.7	80.1	72.2	72.2	77.8	80.0	81.1	81.8	78.9
2015	78.0	80.6	80.5	80.6	81.6	80.7	72.2	71.9	77.4	79.7	80.7	81.5	78.8

Employment by Industry: Grand Rapids-Wyoming, MI, 2005–2015

(Numbers in thousands, not seasonally adjusted)

Industry and year	January	February	March	April	May	June	July	August	September	October	November	December	Annual average
Total Nonfarm													
2005........	482.8	485.6	489.6	495.4	501.0	498.4	492.2	494.9	502.9	502.6	503.3	503.1	496.0
2006........	483.1	485.4	488.4	493.4	498.2	496.8	484.4	488.3	496.7	495.2	496.9	496.8	492.0
2007........	480.1	482.8	485.2	489.0	494.2	495.1	484.1	488.8	493.5	492.9	494.7	493.8	489.5
2008........	481.0	481.5	482.0	484.9	491.1	490.8	477.2	481.7	483.6	482.6	480.2	475.4	482.7
2009........	446.2	447.8	446.1	451.8	454.3	450.1	437.7	441.4	450.6	454.5	455.1	453.0	449.1
2010........	437.8	442.0	443.2	450.7	457.5	458.6	451.2	454.0	462.8	464.0	465.6	463.4	454.2
2011........	452.4	454.5	457.3	465.4	470.0	470.1	466.6	468.3	476.4	476.3	479.0	479.1	468.0
2012........	471.2	472.8	476.5	483.4	488.1	488.0	481.6	484.1	491.9	494.2	496.1	495.0	485.2
2013........	486.7	489.7	492.2	494.5	501.3	502.8	496.9	501.5	507.7	508.9	511.1	512.6	500.5
2014........	502.1	504.1	506.5	510.0	518.9	520.5	507.8	510.4	516.9	520.1	522.5	524.4	513.7
2015........	513.8	516.1	518.7	522.5	529.8	531.0	523.7	523.1	532.6	538.7	538.9	537.8	527.2
Total Private													
2005........	431.4	432.2	436.1	442.5	447.4	447.8	448.4	451.2	452.5	450.1	450.7	451.0	445.1
2006........	432.4	433.0	435.6	441.3	446.7	448.0	442.1	445.6	447.1	443.6	445.4	445.3	442.2
2007........	431.2	432.1	434.4	438.5	445.2	447.2	441.7	445.4	444.7	443.0	445.0	445.5	441.2
2008........	432.0	431.4	431.7	434.7	442.1	442.5	434.7	437.6	434.7	432.3	430.2	425.5	434.1
2009........	398.0	397.9	396.0	401.1	405.0	402.7	395.3	398.9	401.4	404.0	404.8	404.0	400.8
2010........	390.0	392.2	393.6	400.9	408.3	410.9	408.4	411.7	414.2	414.0	415.2	414.3	406.1
2011........	404.3	405.6	407.9	415.7	422.7	423.6	424.1	426.5	429.0	427.9	430.0	431.0	420.7
2012........	423.1	424.3	427.9	435.2	441.1	443.5	440.3	442.7	444.3	445.7	447.3	447.4	438.6
2013........	439.7	441.6	444.4	447.1	454.9	458.0	456.9	461.0	461.1	461.4	464.0	465.6	454.6
2014........	455.4	456.6	458.9	462.8	473.0	475.6	467.8	470.1	470.4	472.1	474.4	477.0	467.8
2015........	467.0	468.4	471.1	475.0	483.8	486.6	483.1	482.9	486.2	490.6	491.0	490.0	481.3
Goods Producing													
2005........	131.6	130.6	131.5	131.9	133.0	134.2	133.1	134.0	133.2	133.1	132.5	132.0	132.6
2006........	128.1	127.1	127.6	128.7	129.7	131.0	128.5	130.0	128.8	127.3	126.2	125.8	128.2
2007........	122.3	121.4	121.3	123.2	124.4	125.6	123.6	125.4	124.5	123.6	123.7	123.2	123.5
2008........	120.1	118.8	118.4	118.5	120.3	122.1	118.3	120.3	118.9	116.9	114.8	112.1	118.3
2009........	101.3	100.5	99.2	99.4	99.3	99.5	98.5	100.9	101.0	100.1	99.2	98.6	99.8
2010........	95.3	95.3	96.3	98.5	100.8	102.5	103.1	103.9	103.5	102.1	101.9	102.0	100.4
2011........	100.8	101.0	101.7	103.9	106.0	107.9	108.2	109.0	108.6	108.6	108.9	109.1	106.1
2012........	107.6	107.5	108.3	110.0	111.6	113.7	114.1	114.8	114.1	113.8	113.5	113.7	111.9
2013........	112.5	112.6	113.5	114.6	116.9	118.9	119.4	120.1	119.5	119.4	119.8	119.8	117.3
2014........	118.4	118.9	119.6	121.0	123.4	125.7	125.9	125.8	125.3	125.1	125.3	125.5	123.3
2015........	123.6	124.0	124.7	126.1	128.1	130.4	131.2	131.2	130.6	130.7	131.2	131.1	128.6
Service-Providing													
2005........	351.2	355.0	358.1	363.5	368.0	364.2	359.1	360.9	369.7	369.5	370.8	371.1	363.4
2006........	355.0	358.3	360.8	364.7	368.5	365.8	355.9	358.3	367.9	367.9	370.7	371.0	363.7
2007........	357.8	361.4	363.9	365.8	369.8	369.5	360.5	363.4	369.0	369.3	371.0	370.6	366.0
2008........	360.9	362.7	363.6	366.4	370.8	368.7	358.9	361.4	364.7	365.7	365.4	363.3	364.4
2009........	344.9	347.3	346.9	352.4	355.0	350.6	339.2	340.5	349.6	354.4	355.9	354.4	349.3
2010........	342.5	346.7	346.9	352.2	356.7	356.1	348.1	350.1	359.3	361.9	363.7	361.4	353.8
2011........	351.6	353.5	355.6	361.5	364.0	362.2	358.4	359.3	367.8	367.7	370.1	370.0	361.8
2012........	363.6	365.3	368.2	373.4	376.5	374.3	367.5	369.3	377.8	380.4	382.6	381.3	373.4
2013........	374.2	377.1	378.7	379.9	384.4	383.9	377.5	381.4	388.2	389.5	391.3	392.8	383.2
2014........	383.7	385.2	386.9	389.0	395.5	394.8	381.9	384.6	391.6	395.0	397.2	398.9	390.4
2015........	390.2	392.1	394.0	396.4	401.7	400.6	392.5	391.9	402.0	408.0	407.7	406.7	398.7
Mining, Logging, and Construction													
2005........	22.5	22.0	22.4	24.2	25.1	25.8	25.9	25.9	25.5	25.1	24.5	23.6	24.4
2006........	21.5	21.1	21.5	23.2	24.3	25.1	24.7	24.7	24.2	23.6	23.0	22.3	23.3
2007........	20.5	19.9	20.1	21.5	22.6	23.2	23.4	23.3	23.0	22.4	22.0	21.4	21.9
2008........	19.8	19.4	19.7	20.6	21.9	22.4	22.3	22.3	21.9	21.1	20.1	19.1	20.9
2009........	16.7	16.4	16.3	17.4	18.2	18.4	18.7	18.5	18.1	17.8	17.1	16.4	17.5
2010........	14.8	14.6	15.0	16.1	16.9	17.5	17.8	17.8	17.4	17.0	16.5	16.0	16.5
2011........	14.7	14.5	14.8	15.9	17.0	17.7	18.3	18.2	17.9	17.6	17.3	16.8	16.7
2012........	15.6	15.3	15.8	16.8	17.5	18.1	18.5	18.7	18.4	18.2	17.7	17.5	17.3
2013........	16.6	16.4	16.7	17.3	18.7	19.5	20.0	20.2	19.9	19.8	19.5	18.9	18.6
2014........	17.9	17.9	18.2	19.0	20.3	21.2	21.4	21.5	21.3	20.8	20.5	20.0	20.0
2015........	18.7	18.6	19.0	20.1	21.1	21.9	22.1	22.1	21.8	21.4	20.7	20.3	20.7

Employment by Industry: Grand Rapids-Wyoming, MI, 2005–2015—*Continued*

(Numbers in thousands, not seasonally adjusted)

Industry and year	January	February	March	April	May	June	July	August	September	October	November	December	Annual average
Manufacturing													
2005	109.1	108.6	109.1	107.7	107.9	108.4	107.2	108.1	107.7	108.0	108.0	108.4	108.2
2006	106.6	106.0	106.1	105.5	105.4	105.9	103.8	105.3	104.6	103.7	103.2	103.5	105.0
2007	101.8	101.5	101.2	101.7	101.8	102.4	100.2	102.1	101.5	101.2	101.7	101.8	101.6
2008	100.3	99.4	98.7	97.9	98.4	99.7	96.0	98.0	97.0	95.8	94.7	93.0	97.4
2009	84.6	84.1	82.9	82.0	81.1	81.1	79.8	82.4	82.9	82.3	82.1	82.2	82.3
2010	80.5	80.7	81.3	82.4	83.9	85.0	85.3	86.1	86.1	85.1	85.4	86.0	84.0
2011	86.1	86.5	86.9	88.0	89.0	90.2	89.9	90.8	90.7	91.0	91.6	92.3	89.4
2012	92.0	92.2	92.5	93.2	94.1	95.6	95.6	96.1	95.7	95.6	95.8	96.2	94.6
2013	95.9	96.2	96.8	97.3	98.2	99.4	99.4	99.9	99.6	99.6	100.3	100.9	98.6
2014	100.5	101.0	101.4	102.0	103.1	104.5	104.5	104.3	104.0	104.3	104.8	105.5	103.3
2015	104.9	105.4	105.7	106.0	107.0	108.5	109.1	109.1	108.8	109.3	110.5	110.8	107.9
Trade, Transportation, and Utilities													
2005	89.3	88.9	89.4	91.0	92.1	92.2	92.3	92.3	91.8	91.8	92.9	93.5	91.5
2006	89.0	88.3	88.6	89.4	89.9	90.1	89.8	89.6	89.4	89.7	91.2	91.8	89.7
2007	88.7	87.7	87.9	88.8	89.9	90.4	90.2	90.0	89.7	90.0	91.2	91.5	89.7
2008	88.3	87.4	87.7	87.5	88.7	89.0	87.7	87.7	86.7	86.4	86.9	86.8	87.6
2009	82.8	81.7	81.2	82.3	83.3	83.3	82.0	81.8	81.4	82.1	82.6	82.8	82.3
2010	80.0	79.3	79.3	80.2	81.1	81.7	81.2	81.3	80.5	81.6	82.8	82.9	81.0
2011	79.8	79.4	79.5	81.3	82.1	82.5	82.5	82.6	82.2	82.5	83.7	84.1	81.9
2012	81.1	80.5	81.1	82.7	83.9	84.1	84.0	84.2	83.8	84.7	86.3	86.6	83.6
2013	84.0	83.9	84.4	85.7	87.0	87.9	87.9	88.5	87.9	88.5	89.7	90.4	87.2
2014	86.5	86.3	86.7	88.1	89.5	90.4	90.5	90.5	90.1	91.1	92.9	93.6	89.7
2015	91.4	91.0	91.4	92.7	94.1	94.9	94.8	94.4	93.8	94.4	96.1	96.2	93.8
Wholesale Trade													
2005	25.8	25.9	26.1	26.3	26.7	26.7	26.7	26.8	26.6	26.7	26.6	26.7	26.5
2006	26.2	26.2	26.2	26.5	26.7	26.8	26.9	26.7	26.7	26.8	26.7	26.7	26.6
2007	26.4	26.3	26.4	26.9	27.0	27.1	27.2	27.1	27.0	27.0	27.0	27.0	26.9
2008	26.6	26.6	26.7	26.8	27.0	27.1	26.8	26.9	26.7	26.4	26.2	26.0	26.7
2009	25.2	25.0	24.8	24.9	25.2	25.0	24.7	24.7	24.6	24.7	24.7	24.8	24.9
2010	24.3	24.3	24.4	24.6	24.8	24.9	25.0	25.0	24.6	24.6	24.7	24.8	24.7
2011	24.3	24.3	24.4	24.9	25.2	25.4	25.5	25.6	25.4	25.4	25.4	25.4	25.1
2012	25.1	25.1	25.3	25.8	26.2	26.3	26.5	26.4	26.3	26.6	26.6	26.7	26.1
2013	26.3	26.3	26.4	26.9	27.2	27.6	27.8	28.0	28.0	28.1	28.2	28.6	27.5
2014	27.2	27.4	27.5	28.3	28.7	29.0	29.1	29.0	28.7	28.7	29.0	29.1	28.5
2015	28.9	29.0	29.2	29.7	30.1	30.4	30.5	30.6	30.3	30.6	30.8	30.9	30.1
Retail Trade													
2005	50.8	50.3	50.5	51.6	52.1	52.0	52.1	51.9	51.6	51.6	52.7	53.1	51.7
2006	49.5	48.9	49.2	49.6	49.8	49.8	49.4	49.4	49.2	49.4	51.0	51.5	49.7
2007	49.2	48.3	48.3	48.6	49.4	49.6	49.4	49.4	49.2	49.6	50.7	51.1	49.4
2008	48.8	48.0	48.2	47.7	48.5	48.6	47.9	47.8	47.2	47.1	48.1	48.2	48.0
2009	45.6	44.9	44.7	45.4	45.9	46.0	45.4	45.2	45.0	45.5	46.2	46.3	45.5
2010	44.1	43.5	43.4	44.0	44.6	44.9	44.4	44.6	44.0	45.0	46.0	46.1	44.6
2011	43.8	43.4	43.3	44.3	44.8	44.9	44.8	44.8	44.5	44.8	46.0	46.3	44.6
2012	44.0	43.3	43.7	44.5	45.2	45.2	45.0	45.2	44.9	45.4	46.9	46.8	45.0
2013	44.8	44.6	45.0	45.1	46.0	46.4	46.5	46.7	46.3	46.7	47.8	48.2	46.2
2014	45.8	45.5	45.7	46.2	47.1	47.5	47.5	47.6	47.3	48.3	49.6	49.8	47.3
2015	48.0	47.6	47.8	48.3	49.2	49.5	49.1	48.9	48.4	48.8	50.2	50.2	48.8
Transportation and Utilities													
2005	12.7	12.7	12.8	13.1	13.3	13.5	13.5	13.6	13.6	13.5	13.6	13.7	13.3
2006	13.3	13.2	13.2	13.3	13.4	13.5	13.5	13.5	13.5	13.5	13.5	13.6	13.4
2007	13.1	13.1	13.2	13.3	13.5	13.7	13.6	13.5	13.5	13.4	13.5	13.4	13.4
2008	12.9	12.8	12.8	13.0	13.2	13.3	13.0	13.0	12.8	12.9	12.6	12.6	12.9
2009	12.0	11.8	11.7	12.0	12.2	12.3	11.9	11.9	11.8	11.9	11.7	11.7	11.9
2010	11.6	11.5	11.5	11.6	11.7	11.9	11.8	11.7	11.9	12.0	12.1	12.0	11.8
2011	11.7	11.7	11.8	12.1	12.1	12.2	12.3	12.2	12.3	12.3	12.3	12.4	12.1
2012	12.0	12.1	12.1	12.4	12.5	12.6	12.5	12.6	12.6	12.7	12.8	13.1	12.5
2013	12.9	13.0	13.0	13.7	13.8	13.9	13.6	13.8	13.6	13.7	13.7	13.6	13.5
2014	13.5	13.4	13.5	13.6	13.7	13.9	13.9	13.9	14.1	14.1	14.3	14.7	13.9
2015	14.5	14.4	14.4	14.7	14.8	15.0	15.2	14.9	15.1	15.0	15.1	15.1	14.9

Employment by Industry: Grand Rapids-Wyoming, MI, 2005–2015—*Continued*

(Numbers in thousands, not seasonally adjusted)

Industry and year	January	February	March	April	May	June	July	August	September	October	November	December	Annual average
Information													
2005	6.7	6.8	6.8	6.8	6.7	6.8	6.8	6.7	6.6	6.8	7.0	7.0	6.8
2006	6.8	6.8	6.8	6.7	6.7	6.8	6.6	6.6	6.5	6.5	6.5	6.4	6.6
2007	6.4	6.4	6.3	6.3	6.4	6.4	6.2	6.2	6.0	5.9	6.0	6.0	6.2
2008	6.0	5.9	5.7	5.8	5.9	5.9	5.9	5.9	5.8	5.8	5.8	5.8	5.9
2009	5.6	5.6	5.5	5.4	5.5	5.5	5.4	5.3	5.2	5.2	5.2	5.2	5.4
2010	5.2	5.1	5.1	5.2	5.3	5.4	5.3	5.4	5.3	5.1	5.1	5.1	5.2
2011	5.1	5.1	5.1	5.0	5.1	5.1	5.1	5.1	5.0	5.1	5.1	5.1	5.1
2012	5.1	5.0	5.0	5.0	5.1	5.1	5.2	5.2	5.1	5.1	5.1	5.1	5.1
2013	5.2	5.2	5.2	5.2	5.3	5.3	5.3	5.3	5.2	5.2	5.2	5.3	5.2
2014	5.3	5.2	5.3	5.4	5.4	5.5	5.6	5.5	5.4	5.4	5.4	5.4	5.4
2015	5.2	5.2	5.2	5.2	5.2	5.2	5.3	5.2	5.1	5.1	5.1	5.2	5.2
Financial Activities													
2005	22.9	23.1	22.9	23.1	23.2	23.3	23.5	23.5	23.4	23.4	23.4	23.5	23.3
2006	23.6	23.6	23.5	23.6	23.6	23.7	23.6	23.6	23.4	23.1	23.1	23.0	23.5
2007	22.6	22.6	22.6	23.0	23.2	23.1	23.1	22.6	22.4	22.7	22.5	22.5	22.7
2008	22.5	22.6	22.4	22.6	22.7	22.3	22.0	22.1	21.8	21.9	21.8	21.6	22.2
2009	21.1	21.2	20.9	21.4	21.4	21.4	21.2	21.3	20.7	20.9	20.8	20.7	21.1
2010	20.7	20.8	20.6	20.7	21.1	21.1	21.4	21.4	21.6	21.8	21.9	22.2	21.3
2011	21.7	21.9	21.7	22.1	22.2	22.3	22.6	22.8	22.8	22.8	23.1	23.3	22.4
2012	22.8	22.9	23.0	23.2	23.4	23.4	23.6	23.3	23.3	23.7	23.8	23.7	23.3
2013	24.0	24.2	24.2	24.3	24.5	24.6	24.4	24.4	24.4	24.3	24.4	24.3	24.3
2014	24.6	24.3	24.3	24.5	24.7	24.8	24.9	25.1	25.0	24.7	24.8	24.9	24.7
2015	24.8	24.4	24.4	24.2	24.7	24.5	24.8	24.9	24.7	24.8	25.2	25.1	24.7
Professional and Business Services													
2005	58.6	58.4	59.8	62.0	63.2	64.2	66.7	68.2	68.6	66.9	66.7	65.9	64.1
2006	61.5	62.1	61.7	64.2	66.0	67.8	67.0	68.9	69.2	67.7	68.6	69.1	66.2
2007	64.6	65.7	67.0	66.9	68.7	70.0	68.8	70.9	70.0	68.7	69.3	69.6	68.4
2008	67.1	67.3	67.1	67.3	68.4	68.0	67.6	68.3	67.6	67.9	67.4	66.1	67.5
2009	58.6	58.7	58.7	58.7	59.6	58.4	55.0	56.4	58.7	60.6	61.9	62.0	58.9
2010	57.5	59.4	59.2	62.0	63.9	64.8	62.8	64.9	68.3	68.7	69.3	68.2	64.1
2011	65.2	66.2	67.1	69.2	71.1	70.6	70.6	71.5	73.3	71.8	71.9	72.2	70.1
2012	71.8	72.2	72.8	74.7	75.6	75.6	72.8	73.5	74.5	74.8	74.7	74.1	73.9
2013	73.2	73.8	73.8	74.4	75.7	75.3	74.1	75.8	76.6	77.1	77.8	78.5	75.5
2014	76.1	76.1	75.8	77.7	80.6	79.4	72.7	74.0	74.4	76.1	76.1	76.5	76.3
2015	74.0	74.2	74.2	75.1	77.2	76.6	74.8	74.9	76.9	78.1	76.7	74.8	75.6
Education and Health Services													
2005	64.0	65.8	66.3	67.3	66.9	64.1	64.0	64.0	66.6	67.3	67.7	67.6	66.0
2006	65.0	66.0	67.4	67.8	67.8	65.1	63.8	64.1	67.5	68.2	69.3	69.0	66.8
2007	67.8	69.2	69.5	69.9	69.8	68.2	67.0	67.4	69.6	70.5	71.3	71.3	69.3
2008	69.6	70.9	71.3	71.9	72.3	70.8	69.9	69.9	71.5	72.8	73.9	73.2	71.5
2009	71.2	72.5	72.4	73.9	73.7	71.6	70.8	71.1	72.8	74.7	75.4	75.0	72.9
2010	73.2	74.2	74.3	74.2	74.1	72.6	72.5	72.6	73.3	74.5	75.1	74.5	73.8
2011	73.8	74.3	74.7	75.0	74.8	73.3	73.5	73.6	75.8	77.0	77.7	77.3	75.1
2012	75.8	77.1	77.7	78.1	78.1	76.9	76.5	77.1	79.1	80.1	80.9	80.8	78.2
2013	78.6	79.9	80.7	79.9	79.6	79.0	78.8	79.6	81.2	81.5	82.7	82.5	80.3
2014	81.4	82.7	83.2	82.1	82.4	81.6	80.6	81.3	83.3	83.4	84.3	84.9	82.6
2015	83.5	84.7	85.4	85.2	85.3	84.5	82.7	82.9	86.0	87.8	88.3	88.5	85.4
Leisure and Hospitality													
2005	37.3	37.4	38.0	39.9	41.6	42.1	41.3	41.8	41.7	40.5	40.1	41.0	40.2
2006	38.2	38.7	39.4	39.9	41.9	42.2	41.8	41.9	41.6	40.4	39.9	39.5	40.5
2007	38.4	38.8	39.2	39.7	41.9	42.4	41.7	41.9	41.7	40.8	40.1	40.3	40.6
2008	37.8	37.9	38.4	39.8	42.4	42.7	41.8	41.9	41.0	39.1	38.1	38.3	39.9
2009	36.2	36.4	36.7	38.0	40.3	40.9	40.4	40.3	40.0	38.8	38.2	38.2	38.7
2010	36.9	37.0	37.6	38.9	40.9	41.5	41.0	41.2	41.0	39.4	38.4	38.6	39.4
2011	37.5	37.5	37.9	39.1	41.1	41.7	41.4	41.6	41.3	40.2	39.8	40.0	39.9
2012	39.6	39.7	40.4	41.5	43.2	44.1	43.6	44.1	43.9	43.0	42.4	42.6	42.3
2013	41.3	41.2	41.7	42.3	45.0	45.9	45.7	46.0	45.1	44.3	43.3	43.6	43.8
2014	41.9	41.8	42.6	42.9	45.6	46.6	46.2	46.7	45.7	45.0	44.4	44.9	44.5
2015	43.4	43.8	44.5	45.1	47.7	48.7	47.8	47.9	47.5	48.0	46.8	47.3	46.5

Employment by Industry: Grand Rapids-Wyoming, MI, 2005–2015—*Continued*

(Numbers in thousands, not seasonally adjusted)

Industry and year	January	February	March	April	May	June	July	August	September	October	November	December	Annual average
Other Services													
2005..	21.0	21.2	21.4	20.5	20.7	20.9	20.7	20.7	20.6	20.3	20.4	20.5	20.7
2006..	20.2	20.4	20.6	21.0	21.1	21.3	21.0	20.9	20.7	20.7	20.6	20.7	20.8
2007..	20.4	20.3	20.6	20.7	20.9	21.1	21.1	21.0	20.8	20.8	20.9	21.1	20.8
2008..	20.6	20.6	20.7	21.3	21.4	21.7	21.5	21.5	21.4	21.5	21.5	21.6	21.3
2009..	21.2	21.3	21.4	22.0	21.9	22.1	22.0	21.8	21.6	21.6	21.5	21.5	21.7
2010..	21.2	21.1	21.2	21.2	21.1	21.3	21.1	21.0	20.7	20.8	20.7	20.8	21.0
2011..	20.4	20.2	20.2	20.1	20.3	20.2	20.1	20.3	20.0	19.9	19.8	19.9	20.1
2012..	19.3	19.4	19.6	20.0	20.2	20.6	20.5	20.5	20.5	20.5	20.6	20.8	20.2
2013..	20.9	20.8	20.9	20.7	20.9	21.1	21.3	21.3	21.2	21.1	21.1	21.2	21.0
2014..	21.2	21.3	21.4	21.1	21.4	21.6	21.4	21.2	21.2	21.3	21.2	21.3	21.3
2015..	21.1	21.1	21.3	21.4	21.5	21.8	21.7	21.5	21.6	21.7	21.6	21.8	21.5
Government													
2005..	51.4	53.4	53.5	52.9	53.6	50.6	43.8	43.7	50.4	52.5	52.6	52.1	50.9
2006..	50.7	52.4	52.8	52.1	51.5	48.8	42.3	42.7	49.6	51.6	51.5	51.5	49.8
2007..	48.9	50.7	50.8	50.5	49.0	47.9	42.4	43.4	48.8	49.9	49.7	48.3	48.4
2008..	49.0	50.1	50.3	50.2	49.0	48.3	42.5	44.1	48.9	50.3	50.0	49.9	48.6
2009..	48.2	49.9	50.1	50.7	49.3	47.4	42.4	42.5	49.2	50.5	50.3	49.0	48.3
2010..	47.8	49.8	49.6	49.8	49.2	47.7	42.8	42.3	48.6	50.0	50.4	49.1	48.1
2011..	48.1	48.9	49.4	49.7	47.3	46.5	42.5	41.8	47.4	48.4	49.0	48.1	47.3
2012..	48.1	48.5	48.6	48.2	47.0	44.5	41.3	41.4	47.6	48.5	48.8	47.6	46.7
2013..	47.0	48.1	47.8	47.4	46.4	44.8	40.0	40.5	46.6	47.5	47.1	47.0	45.9
2014..	46.7	47.5	47.6	47.2	45.9	44.9	40.0	40.3	46.5	48.0	48.1	47.4	45.8
2015..	46.8	47.7	47.6	47.5	46.0	44.4	40.6	40.2	46.4	48.1	47.9	47.8	45.9

Employment by Industry: Tucson, AZ, 2005–2015

(Numbers in thousands, not seasonally adjusted)

Industry and year	January	February	March	April	May	June	July	August	September	October	November	December	Annual average
Total Nonfarm													
2005	356.4	362.4	364.4	368.7	368.6	361.3	359.0	365.1	371.2	372.0	375.4	379.2	367.0
2006	371.8	378.7	379.4	380.6	380.4	373.8	369.8	376.2	382.0	386.4	388.6	392.3	380.0
2007	381.1	387.9	389.1	387.4	387.5	379.3	376.1	379.6	386.6	388.7	391.7	392.0	385.6
2008	379.2	385.2	385.1	385.6	384.5	376.1	375.1	379.6	382.4	381.6	381.3	380.6	381.4
2009	369.5	369.6	367.1	365.4	363.1	353.3	351.1	355.6	359.2	359.2	361.0	361.9	361.3
2010	352.4	356.3	355.7	357.9	358.3	346.1	342.4	348.6	351.4	354.2	357.3	359.2	353.3
2011	351.3	355.4	355.9	357.1	356.8	344.7	340.2	351.6	356.0	359.1	362.9	362.2	354.4
2012	357.4	361.2	362.6	362.7	362.2	352.3	344.4	355.3	360.9	363.6	367.2	368.1	359.8
2013	360.4	364.4	365.8	367.4	366.5	353.0	350.4	357.9	365.1	366.2	370.1	370.6	363.2
2014	364.0	367.1	367.1	368.4	366.5	356.8	353.6	357.6	365.9	369.3	372.7	373.6	365.2
2015	366.7	369.5	369.9	370.4	368.0	356.1	351.4	361.5	369.6	373.6	379.4	380.9	368.1
Total Private													
2005	280.2	282.9	284.5	289.0	289.0	288.4	288.6	291.7	293.6	293.7	296.5	300.5	289.9
2006	296.1	300.3	301.2	302.0	302.5	302.5	301.3	303.8	306.3	307.2	309.0	312.4	303.7
2007	304.3	307.8	309.3	307.8	308.8	307.8	305.2	306.2	306.0	308.0	310.4	310.9	307.7
2008	302.5	303.8	304.4	303.9	302.7	301.3	300.1	301.6	301.2	299.6	298.7	298.4	301.5
2009	289.9	288.0	286.1	283.6	282.2	280.1	278.5	279.5	279.1	278.5	280.1	281.3	282.2
2010	274.3	275.6	276.3	277.1	276.0	274.5	272.1	273.2	272.1	274.7	276.4	279.0	275.1
2011	274.3	275.6	276.5	277.5	277.7	276.2	274.3	276.7	277.2	279.3	282.6	283.9	277.7
2012	279.9	281.2	282.7	282.6	282.2	281.0	277.8	280.1	280.9	283.2	286.5	287.7	282.2
2013	282.5	284.0	285.5	286.8	286.6	284.1	282.6	285.4	286.1	286.6	290.3	290.9	286.0
2014	285.6	287.2	287.6	288.9	288.1	286.2	283.6	286.4	287.5	290.0	292.9	294.5	288.2
2015	289.1	290.4	290.7	291.1	290.0	288.3	287.5	290.2	290.7	294.0	298.8	300.4	291.8
Goods Producing													
2005	53.0	53.8	54.2	54.8	55.1	55.8	55.8	56.4	56.5	56.0	56.3	56.9	55.4
2006	56.3	57.3	57.0	57.5	57.8	58.5	58.8	58.6	58.4	58.1	56.6	56.3	57.6
2007	54.9	56.4	56.0	55.5	55.9	56.5	56.4	56.5	55.9	55.2	54.9	54.3	55.7
2008	53.6	53.3	53.2	52.5	52.4	52.8	52.6	52.4	51.6	50.4	49.3	48.3	51.9
2009	46.2	45.1	44.2	43.5	43.4	43.6	43.4	42.9	42.5	42.0	41.7	41.6	43.3
2010	40.6	40.5	40.6	40.9	41.0	41.1	41.0	41.1	40.6	40.6	40.3	40.4	40.7
2011	39.9	39.7	39.9	39.7	39.8	40.0	39.9	39.9	39.7	39.5	39.4	39.2	39.7
2012	38.9	38.8	39.1	39.1	39.3	40.0	40.1	40.2	40.0	40.2	40.5	40.7	39.7
2013	40.0	40.1	40.4	40.7	40.8	41.3	41.5	41.4	40.9	40.4	40.2	40.0	40.6
2014	39.6	39.5	39.5	39.4	39.4	39.6	39.8	40.2	39.9	39.8	39.4	39.3	39.6
2015	38.7	38.8	38.8	39.2	39.2	39.6	39.9	40.0	39.4	39.7	39.9	39.7	39.4
Service-Providing													
2005	303.4	308.6	310.2	313.9	313.5	305.5	303.2	308.7	314.7	316.0	319.1	322.3	311.6
2006	315.5	321.4	322.4	323.1	322.6	315.3	311.0	317.6	323.6	328.3	332.0	336.0	322.4
2007	326.2	331.5	333.1	331.9	331.6	322.8	319.7	323.1	330.7	333.5	336.8	337.7	329.9
2008	325.6	331.9	331.9	333.1	332.1	323.3	322.5	327.2	330.8	331.2	332.0	332.3	329.5
2009	323.3	324.5	322.9	321.9	319.7	309.7	307.7	312.7	316.7	317.2	319.3	320.3	318.0
2010	311.8	315.8	315.1	317.0	317.3	305.0	301.4	307.5	310.8	313.6	317.0	318.8	312.6
2011	311.4	315.7	316.0	317.4	317.0	304.7	300.3	311.7	316.3	319.6	323.5	323.0	314.7
2012	318.5	322.4	323.5	323.6	322.9	312.3	304.3	315.1	320.9	323.4	326.7	327.4	320.1
2013	320.4	324.3	325.4	326.7	325.7	311.7	308.9	316.5	324.2	325.8	329.9	330.6	322.5
2014	324.4	327.6	327.6	329.0	327.1	317.2	313.8	317.4	326.0	329.5	333.3	334.3	325.6
2015	328.0	330.7	331.1	331.2	328.8	316.5	311.5	321.5	330.2	333.9	339.5	341.2	328.7
Mining and Logging													
2005	1.4	1.4	1.5	1.5	1.5	1.5	1.2	1.2	1.2	1.2	1.4	1.5	1.4
2006	1.4	1.5	1.5	1.5	1.5	1.6	1.6	1.6	1.6	1.6	1.7	1.7	1.6
2007	1.7	1.7	1.7	1.7	1.8	1.8	1.8	1.8	1.8	1.8	1.8	1.9	1.8
2008	1.9	1.9	1.9	1.9	1.9	2.0	2.0	2.0	2.0	1.9	1.9	1.9	1.9
2009	1.8	1.8	1.7	1.7	1.7	1.7	1.7	1.7	1.7	1.7	1.7	1.8	1.7
2010	1.7	1.8	1.8	1.8	1.8	1.8	1.8	1.9	1.8	1.9	1.9	1.9	1.8
2011	1.9	1.9	1.9	1.9	1.9	1.9	1.9	1.9	1.9	2.0	2.0	2.0	1.9
2012	2.0	2.0	2.0	2.1	2.1	2.1	2.1	2.2	2.1	2.2	2.2	2.2	2.1
2013	2.2	2.2	2.2	2.3	2.3	2.3	2.3	2.3	2.3	2.3	2.2	2.3	2.3
2014	2.3	2.3	2.3	2.3	2.3	2.4	2.4	2.3	2.3	2.3	2.3	2.3	2.3
2015	2.3	2.3	2.3	2.3	2.3	2.3	2.3	2.3	2.2	2.2	2.2	2.2	2.3

Employment by Industry: Tucson, AZ, 2005–2015—*Continued*

(Numbers in thousands, not seasonally adjusted)

Industry and year	January	February	March	April	May	June	July	August	September	October	November	December	Annual average
Construction													
2005	23.7	24.3	24.7	25.4	25.6	26.1	26.3	26.6	26.9	26.5	26.7	26.9	25.8
2006	26.4	26.8	27.0	27.6	28.0	28.5	28.8	28.8	28.8	28.8	28.6	28.4	28.0
2007	27.2	27.0	27.0	26.6	26.9	27.2	27.0	27.0	26.4	25.9	25.5	24.9	26.6
2008	24.1	23.9	23.9	23.4	23.3	23.4	23.4	23.3	22.7	21.9	20.9	20.1	22.9
2009	18.8	17.9	17.4	16.7	16.7	16.8	16.6	16.3	16.1	15.8	15.6	15.4	16.7
2010	14.7	14.5	14.7	15.0	15.1	15.4	15.3	15.4	15.2	15.3	15.1	15.1	15.1
2011	14.7	14.6	14.8	14.6	14.6	14.8	14.7	14.6	14.4	14.3	14.2	14.0	14.5
2012	13.7	13.5	13.8	13.8	14.0	14.6	14.7	14.7	14.7	14.8	15.1	15.3	14.4
2013	14.9	14.9	15.3	15.4	15.5	15.9	15.9	15.8	15.5	15.2	15.2	15.1	15.4
2014	14.7	14.7	14.7	14.7	14.6	14.6	14.7	15.3	15.1	15.2	14.8	14.5	14.8
2015	14.1	14.2	14.2	14.6	14.6	14.7	14.9	14.9	14.6	14.7	14.8	14.3	14.6
Manufacturing													
2005	27.9	28.1	28.0	27.9	28.0	28.2	28.3	28.6	28.4	28.3	28.2	28.5	28.2
2006	28.5	29.0	28.5	28.4	28.3	28.4	28.4	28.2	28.0	27.7	26.3	26.2	28.0
2007	26.0	27.7	27.3	27.2	27.2	27.5	27.6	27.7	27.7	27.5	27.6	27.5	27.4
2008	27.6	27.5	27.4	27.2	27.2	27.4	27.2	27.1	26.9	26.6	26.5	26.3	27.1
2009	25.6	25.4	25.1	25.1	25.0	25.1	25.1	24.9	24.7	24.5	24.4	24.4	24.9
2010	24.2	24.2	24.1	24.1	24.1	23.9	23.9	23.8	23.6	23.4	23.3	23.4	23.8
2011	23.3	23.2	23.2	23.2	23.3	23.3	23.3	23.4	23.4	23.2	23.2	23.2	23.3
2012	23.2	23.3	23.3	23.2	23.2	23.3	23.3	23.3	23.2	23.2	23.2	23.2	23.2
2013	22.9	23.0	22.9	23.0	23.0	23.1	23.3	23.3	23.1	22.9	22.8	22.6	23.0
2014	22.6	22.5	22.5	22.4	22.5	22.6	22.7	22.6	22.5	22.3	22.3	22.5	22.5
2015	22.3	22.3	22.3	22.3	22.3	22.6	22.7	22.8	22.6	22.8	22.9	23.2	22.6
Trade, Transportation, and Utilities													
2005	58.1	58.1	58.3	58.4	58.4	58.4	59.1	59.7	60.1	61.1	62.9	64.4	59.8
2006	61.4	61.3	61.5	61.6	62.0	61.8	62.3	63.0	63.5	64.2	65.9	67.5	63.0
2007	64.4	63.7	64.5	64.2	64.6	64.2	64.1	64.5	64.4	64.9	66.5	67.1	64.8
2008	64.0	63.3	63.4	62.6	62.8	62.8	62.5	63.1	62.7	62.9	63.3	63.5	63.1
2009	60.9	59.6	59.0	58.4	58.2	57.7	57.6	58.0	57.8	57.6	58.5	59.4	58.6
2010	57.3	57.0	56.9	56.9	57.0	56.9	56.7	57.0	56.4	56.7	58.3	59.0	57.2
2011	57.5	57.1	57.1	57.3	57.6	57.5	57.2	58.1	57.4	58.1	60.0	60.5	58.0
2012	58.4	57.5	57.5	57.4	57.4	57.4	56.9	57.5	57.7	58.0	59.9	60.6	58.0
2013	58.5	57.9	58.1	58.2	58.6	58.4	58.5	59.5	59.5	59.6	61.5	62.6	59.2
2014	60.3	59.9	60.1	60.1	60.1	59.9	59.6	60.3	60.2	60.6	62.4	63.3	60.6
2015	60.7	59.8	59.8	59.7	59.7	59.6	59.4	60.3	60.3	61.1	63.0	63.3	60.6
Wholesale Trade													
2005	8.1	8.2	8.3	8.4	8.5	8.6	8.8	8.9	9.1	9.2	9.2	9.4	8.7
2006	9.2	9.3	9.4	9.4	9.5	9.6	9.8	9.9	10.1	10.0	10.1	10.2	9.7
2007	9.9	9.9	10.1	10.0	10.1	10.2	10.1	10.2	10.2	10.2	10.2	10.2	10.1
2008	10.0	10.0	10.1	10.0	10.0	10.0	9.9	10.0	10.0	9.9	9.7	9.6	9.9
2009	9.3	9.1	8.8	8.8	8.7	8.7	8.7	8.7	8.7	8.7	8.6	8.6	8.8
2010	8.3	8.3	8.2	8.3	8.3	8.2	8.2	8.1	8.0	7.9	8.0	8.0	8.2
2011	7.9	8.0	8.0	7.9	8.0	7.9	8.0	7.9	8.0	8.0	8.0	8.0	8.0
2012	7.8	7.8	7.9	7.9	8.0	8.0	8.0	8.0	8.1	8.0	8.0	8.1	8.0
2013	7.9	7.9	7.9	7.9	7.9	7.9	7.8	7.9	8.0	8.0	7.9	8.0	7.9
2014	7.8	7.8	7.9	7.9	7.9	7.9	7.9	7.8	7.9	7.8	7.8	7.8	7.9
2015	7.7	7.7	7.7	7.7	7.8	7.8	7.9	7.8	7.8	7.9	7.9	7.9	7.8
Retail Trade													
2005	41.2	41.0	41.0	41.1	41.0	40.8	41.4	41.9	42.1	42.9	44.7	45.9	42.1
2006	43.2	43.0	43.1	43.1	43.3	43.0	43.2	43.8	44.0	44.8	46.3	47.4	44.0
2007	45.2	44.7	45.1	45.0	45.0	44.7	44.7	44.8	44.8	45.4	46.9	47.2	45.3
2008	44.7	44.0	44.1	43.5	43.7	43.7	43.5	43.8	43.4	43.7	44.3	44.3	43.9
2009	42.3	41.2	40.9	40.6	40.6	40.2	40.2	40.5	40.3	40.0	41.1	41.7	40.8
2010	40.1	39.7	39.6	39.6	39.6	39.6	39.3	39.7	39.2	39.5	41.0	41.4	39.9
2011	39.9	39.4	39.4	39.6	39.7	39.7	39.4	40.2	39.4	40.1	41.9	42.2	40.1
2012	40.7	39.7	39.7	39.6	39.6	39.6	39.2	39.8	39.9	40.5	42.4	42.7	40.3
2013	41.2	40.6	40.9	41.1	41.3	41.2	41.2	41.9	41.8	41.9	43.8	44.5	41.8
2014	42.8	42.3	42.4	42.5	42.4	42.2	42.0	42.7	42.4	42.8	44.5	45.1	42.8
2015	42.8	41.9	41.9	41.9	41.8	41.7	41.5	42.3	42.2	42.8	44.6	44.7	42.5

Employment by Industry: Tucson, AZ, 2005–2015—*Continued*

(Numbers in thousands, not seasonally adjusted)

Industry and year	January	February	March	April	May	June	July	August	September	October	November	December	Annual average
Transportation and Utilities													
2005	8.8	8.9	9.0	8.9	8.9	9.0	8.9	8.9	8.9	9.0	9.0	9.1	8.9
2006	9.0	9.0	9.0	9.1	9.2	9.2	9.3	9.3	9.4	9.4	9.5	9.9	9.3
2007	9.3	9.1	9.3	9.2	9.5	9.3	9.3	9.5	9.4	9.3	9.4	9.7	9.4
2008	9.3	9.3	9.2	9.1	9.1	9.1	9.1	9.3	9.3	9.3	9.3	9.6	9.3
2009	9.3	9.3	9.3	9.0	8.9	8.8	8.7	8.8	8.8	8.9	8.8	9.1	9.0
2010	8.9	9.0	9.1	9.0	9.1	9.1	9.2	9.2	9.2	9.3	9.3	9.6	9.2
2011	9.7	9.7	9.7	9.8	9.9	9.9	9.8	10.0	10.0	10.0	10.1	10.3	9.9
2012	9.9	10.0	9.9	9.9	9.8	9.8	9.7	9.7	9.7	9.5	9.5	9.8	9.8
2013	9.4	9.4	9.3	9.2	9.4	9.3	9.5	9.7	9.7	9.7	9.8	10.1	9.5
2014	9.7	9.8	9.8	9.7	9.8	9.8	9.7	9.8	9.9	10.0	10.1	10.4	9.9
2015	10.2	10.2	10.2	10.1	10.1	10.1	10.0	10.2	10.3	10.4	10.5	10.7	10.3
Information													
2005	7.4	7.3	7.3	7.3	7.3	7.3	7.3	7.3	7.3	7.4	7.4	7.5	7.3
2006	7.7	7.7	7.6	7.1	7.1	7.1	6.9	6.7	6.7	6.5	6.4	6.2	7.0
2007	6.5	6.4	6.4	6.3	6.3	6.0	5.9	5.9	5.9	6.0	6.0	5.9	6.1
2008	5.9	5.7	5.6	5.5	5.5	5.4	5.4	5.3	5.3	5.2	5.3	5.4	5.5
2009	5.2	5.3	5.1	5.1	5.0	4.8	4.8	4.7	4.7	4.6	4.6	4.7	4.9
2010	4.7	4.7	4.7	4.6	4.6	4.5	4.5	4.4	4.4	4.4	4.4	4.4	4.5
2011	4.3	4.5	4.3	4.3	4.4	4.3	4.4	4.5	4.4	4.4	4.5	4.5	4.4
2012	4.4	4.6	4.5	4.5	4.6	4.4	4.4	4.5	4.3	4.4	4.5	4.4	4.5
2013	4.5	4.6	4.4	4.5	4.8	4.5	4.5	4.7	4.4	4.4	4.6	4.5	4.5
2014	4.5	4.6	4.4	4.4	4.5	4.4	4.4	4.4	4.3	4.4	4.5	4.5	4.4
2015	4.4	4.6	4.4	4.5	4.5	4.4	4.4	4.6	4.4	4.6	4.6	4.7	4.5
Financial Activities													
2005	15.3	15.5	15.5	15.8	16.0	16.2	16.4	16.8	16.9	17.0	17.0	17.3	16.3
2006	16.5	16.7	16.8	17.1	17.2	17.3	17.4	17.6	17.8	18.1	18.2	18.5	17.4
2007	18.2	18.3	18.4	18.5	18.6	18.6	18.6	17.5	17.2	17.2	17.2	17.5	18.0
2008	16.6	16.7	16.8	17.0	16.9	17.1	17.1	17.1	17.0	16.6	16.6	16.9	16.9
2009	16.6	16.7	16.7	16.9	17.0	17.0	17.5	17.5	17.3	17.4	17.4	17.6	17.1
2010	17.5	17.6	17.3	17.1	17.2	17.3	17.2	17.2	17.0	17.1	17.1	17.3	17.2
2011	17.0	17.0	17.0	16.9	16.8	16.8	16.9	16.8	16.8	16.8	16.8	17.0	16.9
2012	16.8	16.9	16.6	16.6	16.7	16.8	16.8	16.9	16.9	17.1	17.1	17.3	16.9
2013	17.0	17.1	17.2	17.0	17.1	17.3	17.2	17.2	17.2	17.5	17.5	17.7	17.3
2014	17.4	17.4	17.5	17.5	17.5	17.5	17.6	17.4	17.3	17.5	17.6	17.8	17.5
2015	17.3	17.4	17.4	17.4	17.5	17.5	17.4	17.4	17.4	18.3	17.9	18.7	17.6
Professional and Business Services													
2005	44.5	44.9	44.9	46.2	45.9	45.9	46.7	47.5	47.5	47.0	47.1	48.1	46.4
2006	47.8	48.9	49.0	49.1	49.1	49.6	50.0	50.5	51.4	51.4	52.6	53.7	50.3
2007	52.1	52.7	52.9	52.6	52.5	53.1	52.5	53.5	53.5	54.2	54.5	54.2	53.2
2008	52.4	52.6	52.9	52.9	52.0	51.7	52.2	52.5	52.2	51.2	50.6	50.8	52.0
2009	49.6	48.9	48.6	47.7	47.1	47.0	46.9	46.9	46.8	46.8	47.3	47.5	47.6
2010	46.3	46.6	46.9	46.7	45.7	45.7	45.6	45.4	45.2	46.3	46.3	47.3	46.2
2011	46.0	46.4	46.7	46.7	46.4	46.6	46.3	46.5	47.5	48.4	48.8	49.4	47.1
2012	48.2	48.7	49.3	49.1	48.7	48.7	48.4	48.4	48.6	49.4	49.8	49.8	48.9
2013	49.5	49.9	50.3	50.8	50.3	49.2	48.9	49.1	49.6	49.7	50.7	50.6	49.9
2014	49.6	49.6	49.4	49.7	49.7	49.6	48.9	49.4	50.4	50.9	51.5	51.7	50.0
2015	50.9	51.1	50.7	50.5	49.8	49.4	49.9	50.1	50.9	51.5	52.8	52.3	50.8
Education and Health Services													
2005	49.2	49.6	49.8	50.3	50.6	49.9	50.0	50.9	51.5	51.7	51.8	52.3	50.6
2006	51.7	52.2	52.6	52.1	52.4	52.1	51.8	52.7	53.1	53.4	53.7	54.3	52.7
2007	53.6	54.1	54.4	54.1	54.8	54.2	54.1	54.7	55.0	56.0	56.0	56.3	54.8
2008	55.1	55.7	56.1	57.1	57.2	56.7	56.8	57.7	58.2	58.5	58.9	58.9	57.2
2009	58.5	58.8	58.8	58.4	58.6	58.1	57.9	58.5	58.7	58.8	59.0	59.2	58.6
2010	58.0	58.3	58.4	58.6	58.6	58.0	57.4	58.2	58.3	58.8	58.8	59.2	58.4
2011	58.7	59.2	59.1	59.8	59.9	59.4	59.2	60.1	60.4	60.5	60.9	61.2	59.9
2012	61.1	61.2	61.5	61.3	61.2	60.7	59.7	60.4	60.8	61.2	61.4	61.7	61.0
2013	60.6	61.1	61.3	61.5	61.4	60.8	61.0	61.9	62.1	62.2	62.6	62.6	61.6
2014	60.9	61.2	61.4	61.7	61.6	61.0	60.3	61.1	61.3	62.1	62.2	62.7	61.5
2015	61.9	62.0	62.3	62.7	62.9	62.3	62.1	63.0	63.1	63.7	64.4	65.3	63.0

Employment by Industry: Tucson, AZ, 2005–2015—*Continued*

(Numbers in thousands, not seasonally adjusted)

Industry and year	January	February	March	April	May	June	July	August	September	October	November	December	Annual average
Leisure and Hospitality													
2005	38.7	39.6	40.2	41.6	41.1	40.4	39.0	38.9	39.6	39.1	39.4	39.6	39.8
2006	39.7	40.9	41.2	41.9	41.1	40.2	39.3	39.9	40.8	40.5	40.7	40.9	40.6
2007	39.8	41.1	41.5	41.5	41.0	39.9	38.6	38.7	39.3	39.6	40.3	40.7	40.2
2008	40.3	41.7	41.6	41.3	41.0	39.9	38.8	39.0	39.7	40.4	40.4	40.6	40.4
2009	39.2	39.9	39.9	40.0	39.5	38.5	37.0	37.7	38.1	38.1	38.5	38.2	38.7
2010	37.4	38.4	38.9	39.5	39.1	38.0	36.8	37.1	37.5	38.0	38.4	38.7	38.2
2011	38.4	39.0	39.7	40.1	40.1	39.0	37.8	38.4	38.7	39.1	39.6	39.6	39.1
2012	39.7	40.9	41.4	41.8	41.4	40.0	38.6	39.3	39.8	40.0	40.4	40.4	40.3
2013	39.9	40.7	41.0	41.2	40.7	39.7	38.2	38.9	39.8	40.1	40.4	40.3	40.1
2014	40.6	42.1	42.3	43.1	42.4	41.1	40.0	40.6	41.3	41.7	42.3	42.1	41.6
2015	42.6	43.9	44.3	44.2	43.4	42.4	41.5	42.0	42.4	42.2	43.5	43.7	43.0
Other Services													
2005	14.0	14.1	14.3	14.6	14.6	14.5	14.3	14.2	14.2	14.4	14.6	14.4	14.4
2006	15.0	15.3	15.5	15.6	15.8	15.9	14.8	14.8	14.6	15.0	14.9	15.0	15.2
2007	14.8	15.1	15.2	15.1	15.1	15.3	15.0	14.9	14.8	14.9	15.0	14.9	15.0
2008	14.6	14.8	14.8	15.0	14.9	14.9	14.7	14.5	14.5	14.4	14.3	14.0	14.6
2009	13.7	13.7	13.8	13.6	13.4	13.4	13.4	13.3	13.2	13.2	13.1	13.1	13.4
2010	12.5	12.5	12.6	12.8	12.8	13.0	12.9	12.8	12.7	12.8	12.8	12.7	12.7
2011	12.5	12.7	12.7	12.7	12.7	12.6	12.6	12.4	12.3	12.5	12.6	12.5	12.6
2012	12.4	12.6	12.8	12.8	12.9	13.0	12.9	12.9	12.8	12.9	12.9	12.8	12.8
2013	12.5	12.6	12.8	12.9	12.9	12.9	12.8	12.7	12.6	12.7	12.8	12.6	12.7
2014	12.7	12.9	13.0	13.0	12.9	13.1	13.0	13.0	12.8	13.0	13.0	13.1	13.0
2015	12.6	12.8	13.0	12.9	13.0	13.1	12.9	12.8	12.8	12.9	12.7	12.7	12.9
Government													
2005	76.2	79.5	79.9	79.7	79.6	72.9	70.4	73.4	77.6	78.3	78.9	78.7	77.1
2006	75.7	78.4	78.2	78.6	77.9	71.3	68.5	72.4	75.7	79.2	79.6	79.9	76.3
2007	76.8	80.1	79.8	79.6	78.7	71.5	70.9	73.4	80.6	80.7	81.3	81.1	77.9
2008	76.7	81.4	80.7	81.7	81.8	74.8	75.0	78.0	81.2	82.0	82.6	82.2	79.8
2009	79.6	81.6	81.0	81.8	80.9	73.2	72.6	76.1	80.1	80.7	80.9	80.6	79.1
2010	78.1	80.7	79.4	80.8	82.3	71.6	70.3	75.4	79.3	79.5	80.9	80.2	78.2
2011	77.0	79.8	79.4	79.6	79.1	68.5	65.9	74.9	78.8	79.8	80.3	78.3	76.8
2012	77.5	80.0	79.9	80.1	80.0	71.3	66.6	75.2	80.0	80.4	80.7	80.4	77.7
2013	77.9	80.4	80.3	80.6	79.9	68.9	67.8	72.5	79.0	79.6	79.8	79.7	77.2
2014	78.4	79.9	79.5	79.5	78.4	70.6	70.0	71.2	78.4	79.3	79.8	79.1	77.0
2015	77.6	79.1	79.2	79.3	78.0	67.8	63.9	71.3	78.9	79.6	80.6	80.5	76.3

Employment by Industry: Urban Honolulu, HI, 2005–2015

(Numbers in thousands, not seasonally adjusted)

Industry and year	January	February	March	April	May	June	July	August	September	October	November	December	Annual average
Total Nonfarm													
2005	429.9	437.3	440.0	440.4	443.5	444.3	437.6	441.0	444.2	446.2	451.1	456.3	442.7
2006	440.0	449.6	452.7	448.9	453.5	454.9	445.5	448.7	453.9	451.8	460.1	461.4	451.8
2007	447.2	454.2	457.2	449.9	457.3	458.9	448.3	449.7	456.2	458.0	462.3	465.8	455.4
2008	450.9	456.6	459.0	451.6	457.3	455.5	445.7	447.2	449.4	450.1	455.7	454.3	452.8
2009	440.4	443.5	444.6	439.3	440.4	439.0	429.1	427.6	432.0	435.2	436.4	439.7	437.3
2010	427.9	432.9	434.8	434.1	437.0	433.2	428.8	425.0	433.2	438.0	442.9	445.4	434.4
2011	429.2	439.3	442.0	439.1	439.8	437.7	433.4	430.8	440.2	443.4	448.8	451.9	439.6
2012	430.7	444.7	446.8	447.5	450.3	448.3	441.2	446.1	449.3	453.4	461.3	461.2	448.4
2013	440.6	455.4	457.4	454.2	459.0	455.8	451.8	449.4	457.1	461.5	467.4	469.5	456.6
2014	456.3	460.6	463.4	461.5	464.1	460.7	454.5	456.0	462.3	465.6	471.9	470.6	462.3
2015	462.1	466.9	469.3	467.2	468.9	467.1	460.6	464.2	466.7	473.8	475.5	479.0	468.4
Total Private													
2005	337.8	340.5	342.4	343.6	345.4	347.6	348.0	349.8	351.7	350.7	354.1	358.3	347.5
2006	348.8	352.5	354.7	351.8	354.6	357.5	355.7	357.6	358.7	354.6	358.7	361.7	355.6
2007	352.6	355.4	357.7	355.4	357.7	360.9	358.2	359.8	360.6	360.2	362.9	365.5	358.9
2008	355.4	357.4	358.6	356.1	356.2	356.2	353.6	353.4	352.4	349.8	351.3	352.5	354.4
2009	342.1	343.2	342.8	337.9	337.7	338.3	335.7	335.5	336.3	336.7	336.9	339.6	338.6
2010	332.1	333.9	334.5	333.4	334.6	334.3	334.7	335.1	337.2	338.9	340.4	344.5	336.1
2011	335.2	338.8	341.0	338.4	338.4	338.7	339.8	341.3	343.9	344.2	347.9	350.5	341.5
2012	341.7	343.8	345.2	345.9	348.1	348.8	348.9	351.4	352.1	353.6	357.8	359.5	349.7
2013	351.5	354.2	355.9	355.8	356.9	357.6	359.6	359.7	360.1	361.7	366.5	368.1	359.0
2014	358.4	359.3	361.8	360.6	361.8	361.7	362.2	363.6	365.0	366.1	369.5	372.3	363.5
2015	364.6	366.2	368.2	366.3	367.2	368.2	369.0	369.7	369.4	373.4	374.2	376.8	369.4
Goods Producing													
2005	33.1	33.5	34.0	34.4	34.8	35.2	35.4	35.9	36.3	36.1	36.2	36.5	35.1
2006	35.5	35.7	35.7	35.5	36.2	36.7	36.9	37.3	37.7	37.3	37.8	38.1	36.7
2007	37.0	37.3	37.4	37.4	37.9	38.6	38.7	39.0	39.2	39.0	39.3	39.3	38.3
2008	38.4	38.6	38.7	38.2	38.0	37.8	38.0	37.9	37.7	36.9	36.9	36.5	37.8
2009	34.8	34.5	34.3	33.6	33.6	33.6	33.5	33.2	33.0	32.7	32.3	32.5	33.5
2010	32.0	31.8	31.8	31.7	31.7	31.5	31.8	31.7	31.9	32.4	32.4	32.6	31.9
2011	31.5	31.9	32.1	32.2	32.2	32.8	33.1	33.3	33.6	33.3	33.1	33.1	32.7
2012	32.4	32.3	32.3	32.2	32.2	32.6	32.8	33.0	33.4	33.5	33.7	33.5	32.8
2013	32.9	33.2	33.5	33.5	34.0	33.8	34.2	34.4	34.3	34.3	34.5	34.6	33.9
2014	33.7	34.0	34.2	34.0	34.4	34.9	35.4	35.7	35.7	36.0	35.9	35.8	35.0
2015	34.9	35.0	35.6	35.5	35.9	36.6	37.3	37.3	37.4	39.0	39.0	39.4	36.9
Service-Providing													
2005	396.8	403.8	406.0	406.0	408.7	409.1	402.2	405.1	407.9	410.1	414.9	419.8	407.5
2006	404.5	413.9	417.0	413.4	417.3	418.2	408.6	411.4	416.2	414.5	422.3	423.3	415.1
2007	410.2	416.9	419.8	412.5	419.4	420.3	409.6	410.7	417.0	419.0	423.0	426.5	417.1
2008	412.5	418.0	420.3	413.4	419.3	417.7	407.7	409.3	411.7	413.2	418.8	417.8	415.0
2009	405.6	409.0	410.3	405.7	406.8	405.4	395.6	394.4	399.0	402.5	404.1	407.2	403.8
2010	395.9	401.1	403.0	402.4	405.3	401.7	397.0	393.3	401.3	405.6	410.5	412.8	402.5
2011	397.7	407.4	409.9	406.9	407.6	404.9	400.3	397.5	406.6	410.1	415.7	418.8	407.0
2012	398.3	412.4	414.5	415.3	418.1	415.7	408.4	413.1	415.9	419.9	427.6	427.7	415.6
2013	407.7	422.2	423.9	420.7	425.0	422.0	417.6	415.0	422.8	427.2	432.9	434.9	422.7
2014	422.6	426.6	429.2	427.5	429.7	425.8	419.1	420.3	426.6	429.6	436.0	434.8	427.3
2015	427.2	431.9	433.7	431.7	433.0	430.5	423.3	426.9	429.3	434.8	436.5	439.6	431.5
Mining, Logging, and Construction													
2005	21.4	21.6	22.1	22.6	23.0	23.4	23.7	24.0	24.4	24.3	24.4	24.6	23.3
2006	23.9	24.0	24.0	23.9	24.5	24.8	25.0	25.3	25.7	25.5	25.8	26.1	24.9
2007	25.2	25.4	25.6	25.7	26.1	26.7	26.9	27.1	27.3	27.3	27.4	27.3	26.5
2008	26.6	26.8	26.8	26.4	26.1	26.0	26.2	26.1	26.0	25.5	25.4	25.0	26.1
2009	23.7	23.4	23.2	22.7	22.7	22.7	22.8	22.4	22.2	22.0	21.6	21.7	22.6
2010	21.4	21.3	21.3	21.3	21.3	21.2	21.5	21.3	21.4	21.9	21.8	21.9	21.5
2011	20.9	21.2	21.3	21.5	21.5	22.1	22.4	22.5	22.7	22.4	22.1	22.2	21.9
2012	21.6	21.5	21.6	21.6	21.7	22.0	22.2	22.3	22.6	22.7	22.8	22.6	22.1
2013	22.2	22.4	22.7	22.8	23.2	23.0	23.4	23.5	23.3	23.3	23.5	23.6	23.1
2014	22.9	23.2	23.3	23.2	23.6	23.9	24.2	24.4	24.6	24.7	24.7	24.5	23.9
2015	23.7	23.8	24.4	24.4	24.8	25.4	26.1	26.1	26.3	27.8	27.9	28.4	25.8

Employment by Industry: Urban Honolulu, HI, 2005–2015—*Continued*

(Numbers in thousands, not seasonally adjusted)

Industry and year	January	February	March	April	May	June	July	August	September	October	November	December	Annual average
Manufacturing													
2005	11.7	11.9	11.9	11.8	11.8	11.8	11.7	11.9	11.9	11.8	11.8	11.9	11.8
2006	11.6	11.7	11.7	11.6	11.7	11.9	11.9	12.0	12.0	11.8	12.0	12.0	11.8
2007	11.8	11.9	11.8	11.7	11.8	11.9	11.8	11.9	11.9	11.7	11.9	12.0	11.8
2008	11.8	11.8	11.9	11.8	11.9	11.8	11.8	11.8	11.7	11.4	11.5	11.5	11.7
2009	11.1	11.1	11.1	10.9	10.9	10.9	10.7	10.8	10.8	10.7	10.7	10.8	10.9
2010	10.6	10.5	10.5	10.4	10.4	10.3	10.3	10.4	10.5	10.5	10.6	10.7	10.5
2011	10.6	10.7	10.8	10.7	10.7	10.7	10.7	10.8	10.9	10.9	11.0	10.9	10.8
2012	10.8	10.8	10.7	10.6	10.5	10.6	10.6	10.7	10.8	10.8	10.9	10.9	10.7
2013	10.7	10.8	10.8	10.7	10.8	10.8	10.8	10.9	11.0	11.0	11.0	11.0	10.9
2014	10.8	10.8	10.9	10.8	10.8	11.0	11.2	11.3	11.1	11.3	11.2	11.3	11.0
2015	11.2	11.2	11.2	11.1	11.1	11.2	11.2	11.2	11.1	11.2	11.1	11.0	11.2
Trade, Transportation, and Utilities													
2005	81.8	81.7	81.9	82.3	83.1	83.9	84.6	85.1	85.4	85.3	86.7	88.1	84.2
2006	85.3	85.0	85.7	85.2	85.5	86.4	86.0	86.7	86.7	85.7	87.7	88.9	86.2
2007	86.3	85.3	85.8	85.0	85.3	85.5	85.5	85.6	85.4	85.9	88.0	89.7	86.1
2008	86.2	84.9	84.9	83.7	83.7	83.4	82.7	82.9	82.4	81.7	82.6	83.2	83.5
2009	80.6	80.0	79.4	78.3	78.3	78.5	78.2	78.1	78.3	78.4	79.7	80.9	79.1
2010	78.3	77.6	77.4	77.7	77.3	77.9	78.3	78.5	78.2	78.7	80.3	81.6	78.5
2011	79.2	78.7	78.7	78.3	78.4	78.6	78.9	79.1	79.4	80.2	82.0	83.0	79.5
2012	80.9	80.4	80.6	80.4	81.1	81.5	81.8	81.9	82.2	82.7	85.2	86.1	82.1
2013	82.8	82.6	82.9	82.6	82.7	83.2	83.3	83.5	83.2	83.5	85.6	86.7	83.6
2014	83.5	82.6	82.9	82.6	82.7	83.0	83.3	83.0	83.2	83.7	85.8	87.6	83.7
2015	84.6	84.2	84.2	83.7	83.7	84.2	84.2	84.1	83.9	84.0	84.2	85.2	84.2
Wholesale Trade													
2005	13.8	13.9	14.0	14.0	14.1	14.1	14.2	14.3	14.4	14.4	14.4	14.5	14.2
2006	14.2	14.2	14.2	14.3	14.3	14.5	14.4	14.6	14.5	14.6	14.7	14.9	14.5
2007	14.6	14.6	14.7	14.7	14.8	14.9	14.9	15.0	15.0	15.0	15.1	15.3	14.9
2008	15.0	15.0	15.1	15.1	15.1	15.1	15.1	15.1	15.1	15.0	15.0	15.0	15.1
2009	14.7	14.6	14.5	14.4	14.4	14.3	14.3	14.3	14.3	14.2	14.2	14.3	14.4
2010	14.1	14.1	14.1	14.2	14.2	14.2	14.3	14.3	14.2	14.3	14.3	14.4	14.2
2011	14.1	14.0	14.0	14.0	14.1	14.1	14.1	14.2	14.2	14.2	14.2	14.3	14.1
2012	14.1	14.1	14.1	14.0	14.1	14.2	14.2	14.3	14.3	14.3	14.3	14.4	14.2
2013	14.2	14.2	14.3	14.2	14.2	14.2	14.2	14.2	14.2	14.1	14.2	14.2	14.2
2014	14.1	14.0	14.1	14.0	14.0	14.1	14.0	14.0	14.1	14.2	14.2	14.5	14.1
2015	14.2	14.2	14.3	14.2	14.2	14.3	14.3	14.3	14.3	14.3	14.2	14.4	14.3
Retail Trade													
2005	46.3	45.9	45.9	45.7	45.8	46.1	46.7	46.9	46.9	47.3	48.6	49.9	46.8
2006	47.5	47.1	47.2	46.6	46.5	46.9	46.6	46.7	46.5	46.5	48.2	49.0	47.1
2007	47.0	46.3	46.5	45.9	46.0	46.2	46.1	46.1	46.0	46.3	48.2	49.3	46.7
2008	46.7	46.3	46.9	46.1	46.0	46.3	46.4	46.5	46.3	45.9	46.8	47.5	46.5
2009	45.7	45.2	44.8	44.1	44.0	44.3	44.2	44.1	44.5	44.8	46.0	46.9	44.9
2010	44.8	44.2	44.1	44.1	43.8	44.2	44.5	44.6	44.5	44.8	46.3	47.3	44.8
2011	45.5	45.0	45.0	44.8	44.8	44.8	45.1	45.2	45.5	46.1	47.8	48.6	45.7
2012	46.8	46.4	46.4	46.3	46.8	46.9	47.0	46.9	47.1	47.4	49.8	50.4	47.4
2013	47.8	47.4	47.5	47.2	47.2	47.4	47.5	47.6	47.3	47.5	49.5	50.3	47.9
2014	47.5	46.7	46.8	46.7	46.7	47.1	47.4	47.2	47.4	47.6	49.4	50.6	47.6
2015	48.2	47.8	47.7	47.4	47.3	47.5	47.5	47.5	47.4	47.6	47.8	48.4	47.7
Transportation and Utilities													
2005	21.7	21.9	22.0	22.6	23.2	23.7	23.7	23.9	24.1	23.6	23.7	23.7	23.2
2006	23.6	23.7	24.3	24.3	24.7	25.0	25.0	25.4	25.7	24.6	24.8	25.0	24.7
2007	24.7	24.4	24.6	24.4	24.5	24.4	24.5	24.5	24.4	24.6	24.7	25.1	24.6
2008	24.5	23.6	22.9	22.5	22.6	22.0	21.2	21.3	21.0	20.8	20.8	20.7	22.0
2009	20.2	20.2	20.1	19.8	19.9	19.9	19.7	19.7	19.5	19.4	19.5	19.7	19.8
2010	19.4	19.3	19.2	19.4	19.3	19.5	19.5	19.6	19.5	19.6	19.7	19.9	19.5
2011	19.6	19.7	19.7	19.5	19.5	19.7	19.7	19.7	19.7	19.9	20.0	20.1	19.7
2012	20.0	19.9	20.1	20.1	20.2	20.4	20.6	20.7	20.8	21.0	21.1	21.3	20.5
2013	20.8	21.0	21.1	21.2	21.3	21.6	21.6	21.7	21.7	21.9	21.9	22.2	21.5
2014	21.9	21.9	22.0	21.9	22.0	21.8	21.9	21.8	21.7	21.9	22.2	22.5	22.0
2015	22.2	22.2	22.2	22.1	22.2	22.4	22.4	22.3	22.2	22.1	22.2	22.4	22.2

Employment by Industry: Urban Honolulu, HI, 2005–2015—*Continued*

(Numbers in thousands, not seasonally adjusted)

Industry and year	January	February	March	April	May	June	July	August	September	October	November	December	Annual average
Information													
2005	8.6	8.8	8.6	8.9	9.0	8.7	8.7	9.1	9.1	9.1	9.3	9.8	9.0
2006	9.0	9.3	9.2	8.4	9.2	8.9	8.5	8.7	9.2	8.4	8.8	9.0	8.9
2007	8.4	8.9	8.9	8.6	9.3	9.2	8.5	9.0	8.6	8.4	8.5	8.6	8.7
2008	7.8	8.3	8.6	8.7	9.0	9.4	8.0	7.8	7.8	7.6	8.1	8.3	8.3
2009	7.4	7.9	7.7	7.7	7.3	7.4	7.0	7.2	7.3	7.6	7.3	7.3	7.4
2010	7.3	8.1	8.3	7.7	8.9	8.3	7.0	7.5	9.4	8.3	7.9	8.8	8.1
2011	6.9	7.9	8.7	6.6	6.5	6.3	6.8	6.8	6.7	6.8	7.1	7.2	7.0
2012	6.8	7.0	7.1	7.0	7.0	6.3	6.7	6.9	6.9	7.2	7.7	7.5	7.0
2013	6.9	7.0	7.1	7.0	6.6	6.5	8.2	7.0	7.3	8.0	8.3	8.5	7.4
2014	6.9	7.0	7.1	6.9	7.4	6.7	6.8	7.3	7.3	7.1	7.3	7.4	7.1
2015	7.1	7.2	7.2	7.0	6.9	6.8	7.2	7.2	7.1	7.2	7.2	7.3	7.1
Financial Activities													
2005	22.1	22.3	22.3	22.2	22.4	22.5	22.5	22.6	22.7	22.6	22.8	22.9	22.5
2006	22.5	22.7	22.9	22.8	22.9	23.2	23.0	23.0	22.8	22.9	22.9	23.0	22.9
2007	22.8	22.7	23.0	22.8	22.9	23.1	23.1	23.0	22.9	23.1	23.0	23.1	23.0
2008	22.6	22.7	22.9	22.9	22.9	22.8	22.7	22.7	22.5	22.3	22.3	22.3	22.6
2009	21.7	21.6	21.5	21.4	21.5	21.4	21.3	21.1	21.1	21.1	21.0	21.0	21.3
2010	20.6	20.7	20.7	20.6	20.6	20.5	20.7	20.6	20.6	20.6	20.5	20.7	20.6
2011	20.3	20.3	20.3	20.3	20.3	20.2	20.4	20.3	20.2	20.3	20.5	20.4	20.3
2012	20.0	20.1	20.1	20.1	20.2	20.4	20.4	20.4	20.4	20.4	20.5	20.4	20.3
2013	20.1	20.2	20.4	20.4	20.5	20.6	20.6	20.5	20.6	20.5	20.5	20.7	20.5
2014	20.5	20.5	20.8	20.7	20.7	20.8	21.0	20.9	20.8	20.9	20.9	21.1	20.8
2015	20.8	20.9	21.1	21.0	21.2	21.3	21.3	21.2	21.1	21.1	21.3	21.4	21.1
Professional and Business Services													
2005	58.0	58.5	59.0	59.2	58.7	59.4	59.9	60.4	60.3	60.9	61.7	62.5	59.9
2006	61.0	62.5	62.8	62.0	61.7	62.5	62.2	62.3	61.6	60.2	60.4	61.1	61.7
2007	59.3	59.8	60.2	59.4	59.4	60.9	60.5	60.8	61.1	61.3	61.2	61.8	60.5
2008	60.2	60.6	60.8	60.6	60.1	60.2	60.4	60.6	60.2	60.1	60.0	60.9	60.4
2009	59.3	59.3	59.4	57.9	57.5	57.6	57.1	57.0	57.0	57.8	57.4	58.1	58.0
2010	57.0	57.3	57.4	57.5	57.5	57.6	58.1	58.0	58.1	58.6	58.7	59.3	57.9
2011	59.0	60.0	60.5	60.4	60.0	60.2	60.0	60.8	61.1	60.9	61.4	62.6	60.6
2012	60.6	61.0	61.5	62.1	62.5	62.7	62.2	62.9	62.5	63.0	63.5	63.8	62.4
2013	62.9	63.6	63.9	63.8	63.6	63.6	64.3	64.5	64.5	65.3	66.1	66.2	64.4
2014	65.6	65.8	66.2	66.3	65.9	66.2	66.0	66.6	66.7	66.6	67.2	67.6	66.4
2015	66.9	67.2	67.6	67.4	67.3	67.4	67.6	67.4	67.1	68.2	67.8	68.5	67.5
Education and Health Services													
2005	54.4	55.1	55.5	55.3	55.7	55.5	54.9	54.6	55.5	55.3	55.7	56.1	55.3
2006	54.4	55.2	55.7	55.7	56.3	56.6	55.8	55.9	56.7	56.7	57.2	57.6	56.2
2007	56.3	57.3	57.6	57.6	57.8	58.2	57.2	57.0	57.8	57.8	58.1	58.1	57.6
2008	56.9	57.9	58.2	58.0	58.3	58.5	58.0	57.8	58.3	58.5	59.0	59.3	58.2
2009	58.0	58.7	59.0	58.4	58.5	58.6	57.8	57.7	58.3	58.5	58.7	59.2	58.5
2010	58.1	58.8	59.0	58.7	59.1	58.7	58.6	58.3	58.3	59.5	59.7	60.1	58.9
2011	58.1	59.5	59.6	59.5	59.8	59.1	59.2	58.9	60.0	60.1	60.8	61.0	59.6
2012	59.0	60.1	60.1	60.4	60.8	60.4	60.0	60.8	61.2	61.3	61.6	62.2	60.7
2013	60.7	61.7	62.0	62.0	62.2	62.1	61.3	61.6	62.1	61.8	62.9	62.6	61.9
2014	61.1	61.8	62.2	62.2	62.2	61.6	61.4	61.4	62.3	62.7	63.1	63.5	62.1
2015	62.5	63.5	63.9	63.8	63.7	63.3	62.7	63.0	63.8	64.9	65.2	65.2	63.8
Leisure and Hospitality													
2005	60.8	61.5	61.9	61.8	61.9	62.7	62.4	62.4	62.6	61.7	61.8	62.3	62.0
2006	61.2	62.0	62.4	62.0	62.4	62.8	63.0	63.2	63.5	62.9	63.2	63.4	62.7
2007	62.5	63.7	64.2	64.2	64.6	64.9	64.2	64.8	64.8	63.8	63.9	64.0	64.1
2008	62.8	63.4	63.3	62.8	62.9	63.1	63.0	62.9	62.5	61.7	61.4	61.1	62.6
2009	60.2	60.8	61.1	60.4	60.8	61.1	60.7	60.9	60.9	60.2	60.1	60.2	60.6
2010	58.9	59.4	59.6	59.5	59.5	59.9	60.2	60.4	60.7	60.7	60.9	61.4	60.1
2011	60.5	60.6	61.2	61.1	61.1	61.4	61.3	61.9	62.4	62.1	62.5	62.6	61.6
2012	62.0	62.6	63.1	63.3	63.7	64.4	64.6	64.9	64.9	64.9	65.0	65.5	64.1
2013	64.6	65.2	65.4	65.6	66.4	66.8	66.8	67.2	67.0	67.2	67.5	67.7	66.5
2014	66.4	66.8	67.4	67.2	67.7	67.7	67.6	67.8	68.0	68.1	68.2	68.1	67.6
2015	67.0	67.3	67.5	67.1	67.6	67.6	67.9	68.7	68.1	68.1	68.5	68.8	67.9

Employment by Industry: Urban Honolulu, HI, 2005–2015—*Continued*

(Numbers in thousands, not seasonally adjusted)

Industry and year	January	February	March	April	May	June	July	August	September	October	November	December	Annual average
Other Services													
2005	19.0	19.1	19.2	19.5	19.8	19.7	19.6	19.7	19.8	19.7	19.9	20.1	19.6
2006	19.9	20.1	20.3	20.2	20.4	20.4	20.3	20.5	20.5	20.5	20.7	20.6	20.4
2007	20.0	20.4	20.6	20.4	20.5	20.5	20.5	20.6	20.8	20.9	20.9	20.9	20.6
2008	20.5	21.0	21.2	21.2	21.3	21.0	20.8	20.8	21.0	21.0	21.0	20.9	21.0
2009	20.1	20.4	20.4	20.2	20.2	20.1	20.1	20.3	20.4	20.4	20.4	20.4	20.3
2010	19.9	20.2	20.3	20.0	20.0	19.9	20.0	20.1	20.0	20.1	20.0	20.0	20.0
2011	19.7	19.9	19.9	20.0	20.1	20.1	20.1	20.2	20.5	20.5	20.5	20.6	20.2
2012	20.0	20.3	20.4	20.4	20.6	20.5	20.4	20.6	20.6	20.6	20.6	20.5	20.5
2013	20.6	20.7	20.7	20.9	20.9	20.8	20.9	21.0	21.1	21.1	21.1	21.1	20.9
2014	20.7	20.8	21.0	20.7	20.8	20.8	20.7	20.9	21.0	21.0	21.1	21.2	20.9
2015	20.8	20.9	21.1	20.8	20.9	21.0	20.8	20.8	20.9	20.9	21.0	21.0	20.9
Government													
2005	92.1	96.8	97.6	96.8	98.1	96.7	89.6	91.2	92.5	95.5	97.0	98.0	95.2
2006	91.2	97.1	98.0	97.1	98.9	97.4	89.8	91.1	95.2	97.2	101.4	99.7	96.2
2007	94.6	98.8	99.5	94.5	99.6	98.0	90.1	89.9	95.6	97.8	99.4	100.3	96.5
2008	95.5	99.2	100.4	95.5	101.1	99.3	92.1	93.8	97.0	100.3	104.4	101.8	98.4
2009	98.3	100.3	101.8	101.4	102.7	100.7	93.4	92.1	95.7	98.5	99.5	100.1	98.7
2010	95.8	99.0	100.3	100.7	102.4	98.9	94.1	89.9	96.0	99.1	102.5	100.9	98.3
2011	94.0	100.5	101.0	100.7	101.4	99.0	93.6	89.5	96.3	99.2	100.9	101.4	98.1
2012	89.0	100.9	101.6	101.6	102.2	99.5	92.3	94.7	97.2	99.8	103.5	101.7	98.7
2013	89.1	101.2	101.5	98.4	102.1	98.2	92.2	89.7	97.0	99.8	100.9	101.4	97.6
2014	97.9	101.3	101.6	100.9	102.3	99.0	92.3	92.4	97.3	99.5	102.4	98.3	98.8
2015	97.5	100.7	101.1	100.9	101.7	98.9	91.6	94.5	97.3	100.4	101.3	102.2	99.0

Employment by Industry: Tulsa, OK, 2005–2015

(Numbers in thousands, not seasonally adjusted)

Industry and year	January	February	March	April	May	June	July	August	September	October	November	December	Annual average
Total Nonfarm													
2005	401.8	404.5	407.8	410.8	414.1	415.8	412.6	415.7	418.7	418.9	421.7	424.0	413.9
2006	418.2	420.4	425.0	424.4	429.2	430.4	423.2	426.1	428.8	430.3	431.7	433.9	426.8
2007	424.2	428.2	433.8	434.4	437.5	437.7	433.2	435.0	436.5	439.9	441.2	439.3	435.1
2008	435.1	438.6	441.5	441.5	444.5	442.1	438.1	439.7	442.2	441.9	441.5	441.0	440.6
2009	428.1	427.1	427.3	424.3	424.4	421.5	413.5	413.8	414.8	417.2	417.9	416.7	420.6
2010	406.5	408.0	411.2	414.9	417.7	416.3	410.1	409.2	411.9	417.2	418.8	419.4	413.4
2011	407.6	405.1	411.6	414.5	415.8	415.6	414.2	414.1	417.9	421.7	422.6	423.7	415.4
2012	414.0	417.7	420.4	424.3	426.9	426.6	421.5	422.5	425.7	431.3	434.2	434.7	425.0
2013	422.9	425.5	428.4	430.9	433.3	433.4	430.6	432.0	434.1	437.0	438.3	437.9	432.0
2014	431.4	433.9	436.1	438.2	440.9	440.4	438.2	438.8	441.2	446.6	448.4	449.4	440.3
2015	442.2	443.9	444.7	447.0	447.5	446.6	444.7	442.4	444.2	448.2	449.6	449.1	445.8
Total Private													
2005	349.3	351.1	354.2	357.1	359.6	361.8	363.0	364.7	365.2	363.5	366.4	368.5	360.4
2006	363.4	364.8	369.0	369.3	373.3	376.3	374.0	376.2	375.0	374.7	376.5	378.8	372.6
2007	370.7	373.3	378.4	378.9	381.6	384.7	384.0	385.3	382.2	383.8	385.3	383.7	381.0
2008	380.8	382.9	385.6	385.1	387.5	388.3	387.6	388.5	385.7	383.2	382.9	382.4	385.0
2009	372.3	369.8	369.4	365.7	365.3	366.5	363.0	361.1	357.0	357.0	357.6	356.8	363.5
2010	349.5	349.9	352.3	355.4	356.6	358.3	358.8	358.3	356.0	358.6	360.0	360.7	356.2
2011	351.5	348.3	354.4	357.3	358.9	360.7	362.5	362.4	362.8	363.9	364.7	365.7	359.4
2012	358.5	360.6	362.7	366.9	369.2	371.8	370.8	371.5	369.8	373.2	375.8	376.4	368.9
2013	366.7	367.7	370.3	372.8	375.3	377.4	377.7	379.2	377.5	378.0	378.8	378.5	375.0
2014	374.1	374.8	376.7	379.1	381.5	383.9	384.9	385.1	383.8	386.6	388.0	389.4	382.3
2015	384.5	384.5	385.4	387.2	387.8	389.7	390.7	388.5	386.1	387.4	388.6	388.1	387.4
Goods Producing													
2005	68.9	69.0	69.9	70.6	71.2	72.0	72.7	73.1	73.3	73.2	73.7	75.0	71.9
2006	74.5	75.0	76.2	75.0	76.3	77.5	77.7	78.4	78.2	78.3	78.7	79.0	77.1
2007	77.8	77.8	79.1	78.6	79.4	80.6	81.4	81.9	81.0	81.8	82.1	81.8	80.3
2008	81.9	82.2	82.9	82.8	83.8	84.2	84.5	84.5	84.0	82.9	82.6	82.9	83.3
2009	81.0	79.1	77.8	75.7	74.4	74.6	73.0	72.2	71.1	70.2	69.6	69.3	74.0
2010	68.0	68.1	68.5	68.9	69.4	70.5	71.2	70.9	70.7	71.6	72.0	72.6	70.2
2011	70.7	70.0	71.7	72.5	72.8	73.7	74.1	73.9	74.3	75.0	75.3	75.5	73.3
2012	74.4	74.8	75.4	76.4	77.2	77.7	77.9	78.3	78.2	80.4	80.8	80.6	77.7
2013	78.4	78.6	79.1	79.4	79.8	80.5	80.4	80.9	80.2	80.6	80.0	79.9	79.8
2014	79.6	80.1	80.0	79.9	80.4	80.9	81.8	82.0	81.9	82.9	82.8	82.9	81.3
2015	81.7	82.1	81.4	80.7	80.1	80.1	80.1	79.2	78.6	77.6	77.7	77.6	79.7
Service-Providing													
2005	332.9	335.5	337.9	340.2	342.9	343.8	339.9	342.6	345.4	345.7	348.0	349.0	342.0
2006	343.7	345.4	348.8	349.4	352.9	352.9	345.5	347.7	350.6	352.0	353.0	354.9	349.7
2007	346.4	350.4	354.7	355.8	358.1	357.1	351.8	353.1	355.5	358.1	359.1	357.5	354.8
2008	353.2	356.4	358.6	358.7	360.7	357.9	353.6	355.2	358.2	359.0	358.9	358.1	357.4
2009	347.1	348.0	349.5	348.6	350.0	346.9	340.5	341.6	343.7	347.0	348.3	347.4	346.6
2010	338.5	339.9	342.7	346.0	348.3	345.8	338.9	338.3	341.2	345.6	346.8	346.8	343.2
2011	336.9	335.1	339.9	342.0	343.0	341.9	340.1	340.2	343.6	346.7	347.3	348.2	342.1
2012	339.6	342.9	345.0	347.9	349.7	348.9	343.6	344.2	347.5	350.9	353.4	354.1	347.3
2013	344.5	346.9	349.3	351.5	353.5	352.9	350.2	351.1	353.9	356.4	358.3	358.0	352.2
2014	351.8	353.8	356.1	358.3	360.5	359.5	356.4	356.8	359.3	363.7	365.6	366.5	359.0
2015	360.5	361.8	363.3	366.3	367.4	366.5	364.6	363.2	365.6	370.6	371.9	371.5	366.1
Mining and Logging													
2005	4.8	4.8	4.8	4.9	5.0	5.1	5.3	5.3	5.4	5.3	5.4	5.5	5.1
2006	5.6	5.7	5.8	6.2	6.1	6.2	6.3	6.3	6.3	6.2	6.3	6.3	6.1
2007	6.4	6.4	6.5	6.4	6.5	6.7	6.9	6.9	6.8	7.0	7.0	7.1	6.7
2008	7.0	7.1	7.1	7.0	7.1	7.4	7.5	7.5	7.4	7.2	7.1	7.1	7.2
2009	7.3	7.1	6.9	6.8	6.7	6.8	6.8	6.9	6.8	6.6	6.6	6.6	6.8
2010	6.7	6.6	6.6	6.7	6.8	7.0	7.1	7.1	7.1	7.2	7.3	7.3	7.0
2011	7.2	7.2	7.3	7.3	7.4	7.5	7.6	7.7	7.7	7.8	7.9	7.9	7.5
2012	7.4	7.4	7.5	7.5	7.6	7.6	7.8	7.9	7.8	8.3	8.2	8.0	7.8
2013	7.7	7.8	7.8	7.8	7.9	7.9	7.9	7.9	7.8	7.9	7.9	7.9	7.9
2014	7.9	7.8	7.8	7.6	7.7	7.7	7.8	7.8	7.8	7.8	7.8	7.8	7.8
2015	7.6	7.6	7.2	7.1	7.0	7.0	7.0	6.9	6.7	6.7	6.7	6.8	7.0

Employment by Industry: Tulsa, OK, 2005–2015—*Continued*

(Numbers in thousands, not seasonally adjusted)

Industry and year	January	February	March	April	May	June	July	August	September	October	November	December	Annual average
Construction													
2005	18.4	18.4	18.9	19.3	19.7	20.1	20.7	20.8	20.8	20.6	20.5	20.9	19.9
2006	20.7	20.7	21.2	21.1	21.3	21.9	21.8	21.9	21.9	22.1	22.0	22.1	21.6
2007	20.6	20.6	21.5	21.3	21.5	22.2	22.2	22.5	22.1	22.4	22.5	22.1	21.8
2008	22.1	22.2	22.7	22.9	23.2	23.3	23.6	23.5	23.3	23.0	22.8	22.7	22.9
2009	21.7	21.5	21.5	21.0	20.7	21.0	20.8	20.5	20.1	19.9	19.5	19.4	20.6
2010	18.6	18.8	19.1	19.2	19.4	19.8	20.1	19.9	19.9	20.3	20.3	20.5	19.7
2011	19.0	18.4	19.4	19.7	19.7	19.9	19.7	19.5	19.6	19.8	19.6	19.5	19.5
2012	19.0	19.0	19.2	19.6	19.9	20.0	20.1	20.2	20.3	21.4	22.1	21.7	20.2
2013	20.0	20.1	20.7	21.2	21.6	22.1	21.9	22.5	22.2	22.8	22.2	21.9	21.6
2014	21.5	21.8	21.6	21.2	21.3	21.4	21.9	22.1	22.1	22.8	22.5	22.4	21.9
2015	21.9	22.4	22.5	22.7	22.7	23.0	23.3	23.1	23.1	23.1	23.5	23.3	22.9
Manufacturing													
2005	45.7	45.8	46.2	46.4	46.5	46.8	46.7	47.0	47.1	47.3	47.8	48.6	46.8
2006	48.2	48.6	49.2	47.7	48.9	49.4	49.6	50.2	50.0	50.0	50.4	50.6	49.4
2007	50.8	50.8	51.1	50.9	51.4	51.7	52.3	52.5	52.1	52.4	52.6	52.6	51.8
2008	52.8	52.9	53.1	52.9	53.5	53.5	53.4	53.5	53.3	52.7	52.7	53.1	53.1
2009	52.0	50.5	49.4	47.9	47.0	46.8	45.4	44.8	44.2	43.7	43.5	43.3	46.5
2010	42.7	42.7	42.8	43.0	43.2	43.7	44.0	43.9	43.7	44.1	44.4	44.8	43.6
2011	44.5	44.4	45.0	45.5	45.7	46.3	46.8	46.7	47.0	47.4	47.8	48.1	46.3
2012	48.0	48.4	48.7	49.3	49.7	50.1	50.0	50.2	50.1	50.7	50.5	50.9	49.7
2013	50.7	50.7	50.6	50.4	50.3	50.5	50.6	50.5	50.2	49.9	49.9	50.1	50.4
2014	50.2	50.5	50.6	51.1	51.4	51.8	52.1	52.1	52.0	52.3	52.5	52.7	51.6
2015	52.2	52.1	51.7	50.9	50.4	50.1	49.8	49.2	48.8	47.8	47.5	47.5	49.8
Trade, Transportation, and Utilities													
2005	79.9	79.3	79.4	79.7	80.1	80.2	80.8	81.3	81.4	81.7	83.2	84.2	80.9
2006	81.3	80.8	81.7	83.2	84.0	83.9	83.4	83.5	83.6	83.8	85.5	86.7	83.5
2007	83.8	83.9	85.2	84.7	85.0	85.3	84.9	84.3	84.2	85.1	86.7	86.7	85.0
2008	83.6	83.9	84.8	85.3	85.6	85.6	86.2	86.4	85.8	85.7	86.9	87.3	85.6
2009	83.6	82.8	83.1	83.6	84.0	83.9	83.0	82.8	82.2	82.6	83.8	84.3	83.3
2010	80.5	79.9	80.3	80.4	80.9	81.0	81.1	80.9	80.0	80.5	82.1	82.7	80.9
2011	79.7	78.7	79.8	80.7	81.0	81.2	81.4	81.5	81.5	81.9	83.7	84.4	81.3
2012	81.7	81.3	81.8	82.1	82.5	83.1	82.5	82.2	81.9	82.9	84.9	85.3	82.7
2013	81.1	80.7	81.2	82.0	82.5	82.8	83.0	83.3	83.2	83.6	85.4	86.4	82.9
2014	84.0	83.7	83.9	84.3	85.0	85.8	85.9	86.1	85.9	86.6	88.3	89.4	85.7
2015	86.6	86.6	86.8	86.9	87.2	88.1	87.7	87.8	87.4	88.6	89.5	90.2	87.8
Wholesale Trade													
2005	16.7	16.7	16.8	16.9	17.0	17.2	17.5	17.5	17.5	17.5	17.6	17.7	17.2
2006	17.4	17.3	17.4	17.7	17.8	17.9	17.7	17.7	17.7	17.7	17.7	17.7	17.6
2007	17.8	18.0	18.2	18.3	18.2	18.3	18.2	18.0	17.9	18.0	18.0	17.9	18.1
2008	17.7	17.7	17.7	17.5	17.4	17.4	17.5	17.4	17.3	17.1	17.1	17.0	17.4
2009	16.6	16.5	16.4	16.3	16.2	16.0	15.8	15.6	15.4	15.4	15.2	15.2	15.9
2010	15.1	15.1	15.1	15.1	15.2	15.3	15.3	15.3	15.3	15.2	15.3	15.3	15.2
2011	15.0	15.0	15.1	15.1	15.1	15.1	15.4	15.3	15.3	15.2	15.2	15.2	15.2
2012	15.0	15.1	15.2	15.3	15.4	15.5	15.3	15.4	15.5	15.6	15.5	15.5	15.4
2013	15.3	15.3	15.3	15.5	15.5	15.5	15.6	15.7	15.7	15.7	15.7	15.7	15.5
2014	15.8	15.9	15.9	15.9	15.9	16.1	16.3	16.4	16.4	16.4	16.5	16.5	16.2
2015	16.4	16.6	16.5	16.5	16.4	16.5	16.5	16.4	16.2	16.7	16.7	16.7	16.5
Retail Trade													
2005	43.2	42.6	42.6	42.8	43.0	42.8	43.2	43.5	43.8	44.2	45.5	46.3	43.6
2006	43.4	43.4	43.9	44.4	44.9	44.6	44.4	44.2	44.2	44.6	46.1	47.0	44.6
2007	44.1	43.8	44.9	44.7	45.0	45.1	44.5	44.4	44.3	44.9	46.4	46.5	44.9
2008	43.9	44.2	45.1	45.7	45.9	45.8	46.0	46.2	45.6	45.5	46.6	46.9	45.6
2009	44.8	44.3	44.8	44.9	45.5	45.6	45.1	45.2	45.0	45.3	46.7	47.0	45.4
2010	44.8	44.1	44.5	44.9	45.2	45.3	45.3	45.2	44.4	45.0	46.5	46.8	45.2
2011	44.7	43.7	44.5	45.2	45.4	45.3	45.1	45.3	45.3	45.7	47.4	47.7	45.4
2012	45.5	44.8	45.3	45.5	45.8	46.2	45.9	45.6	45.4	46.3	48.4	48.7	46.1
2013	45.5	45.1	45.6	46.0	46.5	46.8	46.8	47.0	46.9	47.4	49.1	49.9	46.9
2014	47.4	47.0	47.2	47.5	48.1	48.6	48.4	48.5	48.3	48.9	50.2	51.2	48.4
2015	48.7	48.7	48.9	49.2	49.5	50.0	49.4	49.6	49.4	50.0	51.1	51.4	49.7

Employment by Industry: Tulsa, OK, 2005–2015—*Continued*

(Numbers in thousands, not seasonally adjusted)

Industry and year	January	February	March	April	May	June	July	August	September	October	November	December	Annual average
Transportation and Utilities													
2005	20.0	20.0	20.0	20.0	20.1	20.2	20.1	20.3	20.1	20.0	20.1	20.2	20.1
2006	20.5	20.1	20.4	21.1	21.3	21.4	21.3	21.6	21.7	21.5	21.7	22.0	21.2
2007	21.9	22.1	22.1	21.7	21.8	21.9	22.2	21.9	22.0	22.2	22.3	22.3	22.0
2008	22.0	22.0	22.0	22.1	22.3	22.4	22.7	22.8	22.9	23.1	23.2	23.4	22.6
2009	22.2	22.0	21.9	22.4	22.3	22.3	22.1	22.0	21.8	21.9	21.9	22.1	22.1
2010	20.6	20.7	20.7	20.4	20.5	20.4	20.5	20.4	20.3	20.3	20.3	20.6	20.5
2011	20.0	20.0	20.2	20.4	20.5	20.8	20.9	20.9	20.9	21.0	21.1	21.5	20.7
2012	21.2	21.4	21.3	21.3	21.3	21.4	21.3	21.2	21.0	21.0	21.0	21.1	21.2
2013	20.3	20.3	20.3	20.5	20.5	20.5	20.6	20.6	20.6	20.5	20.6	20.8	20.5
2014	20.8	20.8	20.8	20.9	21.0	21.1	21.2	21.2	21.2	21.3	21.6	21.7	21.1
2015	21.5	21.3	21.4	21.2	21.3	21.6	21.8	21.8	21.8	21.9	21.7	22.1	21.6
Information													
2005	10.8	10.7	10.5	10.6	10.6	10.7	10.7	10.7	10.8	10.8	11.0	11.0	10.7
2006	10.5	10.3	10.3	10.0	10.1	10.1	10.0	10.0	9.7	9.8	9.8	10.2	10.1
2007	9.9	10.1	10.0	9.9	10.0	9.9	10.0	9.9	9.9	10.0	10.0	10.0	10.0
2008	9.8	9.9	9.8	10.0	10.0	10.0	10.0	9.8	9.7	9.6	9.7	9.7	9.8
2009	9.4	9.4	9.2	9.1	9.0	8.9	8.9	8.8	8.5	8.5	8.5	8.5	8.9
2010	8.4	8.3	8.3	8.7	8.7	8.5	8.7	8.5	8.4	8.3	8.3	8.4	8.5
2011	8.3	8.2	8.2	8.1	8.2	8.2	8.3	8.3	8.2	8.2	8.1	8.2	8.2
2012	8.1	8.0	8.0	7.9	7.9	7.9	8.0	7.9	7.9	7.9	7.9	7.9	7.9
2013	7.8	7.8	7.8	7.9	7.9	7.9	7.9	7.8	7.7	7.7	7.6	7.6	7.8
2014	7.5	7.4	7.5	7.4	7.3	7.4	7.4	7.3	7.1	6.9	7.0	7.2	7.3
2015	7.1	7.1	7.1	7.1	7.1	7.1	7.1	7.0	7.0	6.9	7.0	7.0	7.1
Financial Activities													
2005	25.1	25.2	25.2	24.9	24.9	25.1	25.2	25.2	25.0	24.9	25.1	25.1	25.1
2006	25.3	25.4	25.5	25.3	25.4	25.7	25.3	25.4	25.3	25.4	25.5	25.7	25.4
2007	24.9	25.1	25.3	25.0	25.0	25.1	25.2	25.1	24.9	25.0	24.8	24.8	25.0
2008	24.6	24.6	24.6	24.6	24.6	24.6	24.9	24.8	24.5	24.5	24.4	24.5	24.6
2009	24.0	23.9	23.9	24.0	24.1	24.0	24.2	23.9	23.6	23.5	23.5	23.4	23.8
2010	23.2	23.2	23.2	23.3	23.3	23.2	23.2	23.2	23.0	23.0	22.9	23.0	23.1
2011	22.7	22.6	22.6	22.6	22.5	22.6	22.6	22.6	22.5	22.6	22.6	22.7	22.6
2012	22.4	22.5	22.4	22.2	22.3	22.4	22.5	22.5	22.4	22.6	22.6	22.7	22.5
2013	22.6	22.6	22.6	22.7	22.8	22.9	23.0	23.0	22.9	23.1	23.2	23.1	22.9
2014	22.8	22.8	22.8	22.9	22.8	22.8	22.9	22.9	22.8	22.9	23.0	23.0	22.9
2015	22.9	22.9	23.0	23.0	23.1	23.2	23.5	23.4	23.3	23.4	23.8	23.5	23.3
Professional and Business Services													
2005	56.2	57.7	58.3	59.3	59.8	59.8	59.9	60.3	61.2	60.5	61.1	61.0	59.6
2006	59.8	60.7	61.1	61.1	61.7	61.8	61.2	62.1	61.9	61.4	61.4	60.5	61.2
2007	60.2	61.0	61.7	62.1	62.8	62.7	62.4	63.6	62.8	63.1	63.0	62.5	62.3
2008	63.3	64.0	64.4	64.2	64.1	63.9	63.3	63.8	63.5	62.7	62.0	60.6	63.3
2009	57.2	57.0	56.4	55.1	55.0	55.1	54.4	54.4	53.7	54.5	54.7	54.6	55.2
2010	53.6	54.0	54.4	55.3	55.1	55.3	55.2	55.1	54.9	55.7	55.1	54.6	54.9
2011	53.0	52.8	53.7	53.7	53.8	53.9	54.6	54.8	55.4	55.6	55.1	55.1	54.3
2012	53.3	54.6	54.8	55.9	56.1	56.8	56.9	57.4	57.0	57.3	57.4	56.9	56.2
2013	55.7	56.0	56.8	56.9	57.4	57.8	58.4	58.5	58.2	58.5	58.1	57.3	57.5
2014	56.8	56.9	57.6	58.3	58.8	59.2	59.0	58.7	58.4	59.9	59.6	59.3	58.5
2015	59.4	58.6	58.9	59.7	59.8	59.7	60.2	59.6	58.4	59.1	57.7	58.3	59.1
Education and Health Services													
2005	58.5	58.9	59.3	59.6	59.8	59.8	59.7	60.0	60.2	60.2	60.4	60.5	59.7
2006	60.1	60.5	60.7	60.8	61.2	61.8	61.3	61.6	62.3	62.5	62.6	62.9	61.5
2007	61.9	62.5	63.0	63.4	63.6	63.4	63.7	63.9	64.0	64.0	63.9	63.6	63.5
2008	63.8	64.2	64.4	63.4	63.7	63.6	62.8	63.0	63.2	63.1	63.2	63.2	63.5
2009	63.4	63.7	64.0	63.5	63.6	64.2	64.2	64.2	63.9	64.8	64.8	64.7	64.1
2010	64.6	64.8	65.0	65.2	65.2	65.2	65.3	65.7	65.6	66.4	66.6	66.7	65.5
2011	66.0	65.4	66.1	66.3	66.7	66.6	66.8	66.8	66.7	67.0	66.6	66.6	66.5
2012	66.1	66.1	65.9	66.6	66.8	66.8	66.5	66.9	67.1	67.4	67.6	68.0	66.8
2013	67.6	68.0	68.1	67.9	67.8	67.7	67.4	67.7	68.0	68.3	68.5	68.4	68.0
2014	67.8	68.0	68.2	68.4	68.4	68.3	68.1	68.5	68.8	69.1	69.2	69.4	68.5
2015	68.8	68.7	68.9	68.9	68.9	68.9	69.6	69.8	70.1	70.8	71.1	70.2	69.6

Employment by Industry: Tulsa, OK, 2005–2015—*Continued*

(Numbers in thousands, not seasonally adjusted)

Industry and year	January	February	March	April	May	June	July	August	September	October	November	December	Annual average
Leisure and Hospitality													
2005	33.1	33.4	34.5	35.5	36.2	36.9	36.4	36.8	36.1	35.2	34.9	34.6	35.3
2006	34.8	35.0	36.2	36.5	37.2	37.6	37.4	37.6	36.5	36.2	35.6	36.3	36.4
2007	35.0	35.6	36.6	36.9	37.4	37.8	37.6	37.7	36.8	36.4	36.4	36.0	36.7
2008	35.5	35.8	36.4	36.8	37.6	38.0	37.4	37.9	37.0	36.7	36.3	36.4	36.8
2009	36.1	36.4	37.4	37.6	38.0	38.3	37.7	37.4	36.8	35.8	35.6	35.0	36.8
2010	34.3	34.7	35.6	36.7	37.1	37.3	37.1	37.2	36.7	36.4	36.3	36.1	36.3
2011	34.8	34.3	35.8	36.9	37.3	37.6	37.8	37.9	37.6	37.0	36.6	36.5	36.7
2012	36.0	36.7	37.7	38.6	39.1	39.6	39.1	39.1	38.4	37.8	37.7	38.1	38.2
2013	36.9	37.3	38.1	39.0	40.0	40.2	40.1	40.6	40.1	39.2	39.0	38.9	39.1
2014	38.7	38.9	39.7	40.7	41.4	41.7	41.9	41.9	41.3	40.6	40.4	40.4	40.6
2015	40.2	40.6	41.2	42.8	43.4	44.2	43.5	43.4	43.2	43.0	43.8	43.3	42.7
Other Services													
2005	16.8	16.9	17.1	16.9	17.0	17.3	17.6	17.3	17.2	17.0	17.0	17.1	17.1
2006	17.1	17.1	17.3	17.4	17.4	17.9	17.7	17.6	17.5	17.3	17.4	17.5	17.4
2007	17.2	17.3	17.5	18.3	18.4	19.1	18.8	18.9	18.6	18.4	18.4	18.3	18.3
2008	18.3	18.3	18.3	18.0	18.1	18.4	18.5	18.3	18.0	18.0	17.8	17.8	18.2
2009	17.6	17.5	17.6	17.1	17.2	17.5	17.6	17.4	17.2	17.1	17.1	17.0	17.3
2010	16.9	16.9	17.0	16.9	16.9	17.3	17.0	16.8	16.7	16.7	16.7	16.6	16.9
2011	16.3	16.3	16.5	16.5	16.6	16.9	16.9	16.6	16.6	16.6	16.7	16.7	16.6
2012	16.5	16.6	16.7	17.2	17.3	17.5	17.4	17.2	16.9	16.9	16.9	16.9	17.0
2013	16.6	16.7	16.6	17.0	17.1	17.6	17.5	17.4	17.2	17.0	17.0	16.9	17.1
2014	16.9	17.0	17.0	17.2	17.4	17.8	17.9	17.7	17.6	17.7	17.7	17.8	17.5
2015	17.8	17.9	18.1	18.1	18.2	18.4	19.0	18.3	18.1	18.0	18.0	18.0	18.2
Government													
2005	52.5	53.4	53.6	53.7	54.5	54.0	49.6	51.0	53.5	55.4	55.3	55.5	53.5
2006	54.8	55.6	56.0	55.1	55.9	54.1	49.2	49.9	53.8	55.6	55.2	55.1	54.2
2007	53.5	54.9	55.4	55.5	55.9	53.0	49.2	49.7	54.3	56.1	55.9	55.6	54.1
2008	54.3	55.7	55.9	56.4	57.0	53.8	50.5	51.2	56.5	58.7	58.6	58.6	55.6
2009	55.8	57.3	57.9	58.6	59.1	55.0	50.5	52.7	57.8	60.2	60.3	59.9	57.1
2010	57.0	58.1	58.9	59.5	61.1	58.0	51.3	50.9	55.9	58.6	58.8	58.7	57.2
2011	56.1	56.8	57.2	57.2	56.9	54.9	51.7	51.7	55.1	57.8	57.9	58.0	55.9
2012	55.5	57.1	57.7	57.4	57.7	54.8	50.7	51.0	55.9	58.1	58.4	58.3	56.1
2013	56.2	57.8	58.1	58.1	58.0	56.0	52.9	52.8	56.6	59.0	59.5	59.4	57.0
2014	57.3	59.1	59.4	59.1	59.4	56.5	53.3	53.7	57.4	60.0	60.4	60.0	58.0
2015	57.7	59.4	59.3	59.8	59.7	56.9	54.0	53.9	58.1	60.8	61.0	61.0	58.5

Employment by Industry: Fresno, CA, 2005–2015

(Numbers in thousands, not seasonally adjusted)

Industry and year	January	February	March	April	May	June	July	August	September	October	November	December	Annual average
Total Nonfarm													
2005	293.5	296.6	298.6	303.1	304.3	304.4	302.4	304.8	305.9	308.6	309.2	310.9	303.5
2006	302.9	306.9	310.2	310.8	313.9	312.9	310.0	312.2	315.5	315.4	315.8	315.7	311.9
2007	308.9	312.4	315.6	317.7	318.6	318.3	316.6	318.2	318.3	316.8	316.1	315.3	316.1
2008	308.4	312.1	313.7	315.9	318.6	317.2	311.0	312.2	314.1	314.5	312.3	310.2	313.4
2009	300.1	301.1	301.9	302.2	303.1	299.3	293.5	292.8	294.7	295.5	294.8	292.5	297.6
2010	284.7	287.9	290.0	291.7	295.0	294.1	286.2	287.8	290.5	294.7	292.9	291.2	290.6
2011	285.3	289.6	292.1	293.8	294.7	292.7	289.4	289.4	292.7	293.3	292.2	290.3	291.3
2012	285.3	287.9	290.9	292.1	295.8	297.0	292.9	293.6	294.9	298.1	298.5	296.6	293.6
2013	292.7	297.2	299.9	300.8	303.0	303.8	299.9	302.4	305.1	307.1	307.8	307.2	302.2
2014	301.6	306.2	308.6	310.8	312.6	313.5	312.0	313.3	315.7	320.2	319.1	318.7	312.7
2015	313.7	317.2	320.1	322.1	324.3	326.0	323.3	324.0	327.8	332.7	332.4	330.5	324.5
Total Private													
2005	227.0	228.6	229.5	233.7	235.0	236.1	238.5	241.3	240.9	241.5	241.9	244.2	236.5
2006	236.4	238.7	240.2	240.9	243.6	245.1	246.3	248.6	249.5	246.9	247.3	247.8	244.3
2007	241.3	242.6	244.4	245.7	247.1	248.3	250.8	252.7	251.0	247.0	246.2	245.8	246.9
2008	239.4	240.4	241.0	242.6	246.0	245.5	246.0	246.9	246.0	244.2	242.0	240.8	243.4
2009	231.9	230.8	230.6	229.6	231.3	230.1	227.7	228.6	227.7	226.5	226.7	225.3	228.9
2010	218.3	218.3	219.3	221.3	224.5	225.3	224.1	226.0	226.2	227.2	226.2	225.2	223.5
2011	219.9	221.5	223.0	224.1	225.7	226.1	226.6	228.4	230.0	228.0	227.0	226.4	225.6
2012	221.8	222.6	224.7	225.7	229.4	231.3	231.3	234.0	233.3	233.3	234.1	233.0	229.5
2013	229.6	231.6	233.5	234.3	236.7	237.9	239.7	242.6	242.8	242.9	242.6	242.7	238.1
2014	237.1	239.4	240.9	242.9	244.1	245.3	248.1	251.5	251.5	253.1	251.7	251.6	246.4
2015	246.4	247.7	250.5	252.0	253.6	255.3	258.3	260.4	260.2	262.6	261.8	260.3	255.8
Goods Producing													
2005	45.3	46.0	46.1	47.1	47.6	48.4	51.5	52.7	51.6	50.7	50.0	50.5	49.0
2006	48.7	49.3	49.3	49.3	50.6	51.2	52.6	53.8	53.6	51.6	50.4	49.8	50.9
2007	48.2	48.1	48.6	48.7	49.3	49.7	52.9	53.6	51.7	48.3	46.7	45.9	49.3
2008	44.1	44.2	44.3	44.7	46.4	46.2	47.2	47.3	46.7	45.0	42.9	41.9	45.1
2009	39.8	38.8	38.8	38.5	40.0	39.2	40.2	40.9	40.0	38.0	37.2	36.3	39.0
2010	34.8	34.3	34.6	35.2	36.9	37.4	37.5	38.2	38.2	37.7	36.0	35.2	36.3
2011	33.9	34.0	34.1	34.4	35.5	36.3	36.9	37.4	37.8	36.5	34.8	34.5	35.5
2012	33.9	33.6	34.0	34.1	36.5	37.7	38.3	39.0	37.6	37.0	35.7	35.4	36.1
2013	34.6	34.5	34.8	34.9	36.0	36.9	38.1	39.0	38.6	37.7	36.4	36.3	36.5
2014	35.7	35.6	35.8	36.3	36.9	38.3	39.6	40.7	40.7	40.2	38.9	38.3	38.1
2015	37.9	38.1	39.0	39.4	39.8	41.3	42.8	43.3	43.2	42.5	40.4	40.0	40.6
Service-Providing													
2005	248.2	250.6	252.5	256.0	256.7	256.0	250.9	252.1	254.3	257.9	259.2	260.4	254.6
2006	254.2	257.6	260.9	261.5	263.3	261.7	257.4	258.4	261.9	263.8	265.4	265.9	261.0
2007	260.7	264.3	267.0	269.0	269.3	268.6	263.7	264.6	266.6	268.5	269.4	269.4	266.8
2008	264.3	267.9	269.4	271.2	272.2	271.0	263.8	264.9	267.4	269.5	269.4	268.3	268.3
2009	260.3	262.3	263.1	263.7	263.1	260.1	253.3	251.9	254.7	257.5	257.6	256.2	258.7
2010	249.9	253.6	255.4	256.5	258.1	256.7	248.7	249.6	252.3	257.0	256.9	256.0	254.2
2011	251.4	255.6	258.0	259.4	259.2	256.4	252.5	252.0	254.9	256.8	257.4	255.8	255.8
2012	251.4	254.3	256.9	258.0	259.3	259.3	254.6	254.6	257.3	261.1	262.8	261.2	257.6
2013	258.1	262.7	265.1	265.9	267.0	266.9	261.8	263.4	266.5	269.4	271.4	270.9	265.8
2014	265.9	270.6	272.8	274.5	275.7	275.2	272.4	272.6	275.0	280.0	280.2	280.4	274.6
2015	275.8	279.1	281.1	282.7	284.5	284.7	280.5	280.7	284.6	290.2	292.0	290.5	283.9
Mining and Logging													
2005	0.2	0.2	0.2	0.2	0.2	0.2	0.2	0.2	0.2	0.2	0.2	0.2	0.2
2006	0.2	0.2	0.2	0.2	0.2	0.2	0.2	0.2	0.2	0.2	0.2	0.1	0.2
2007	0.1	0.1	0.1	0.1	0.1	0.1	0.2	0.2	0.2	0.2	0.2	0.1	0.1
2008	0.1	0.1	0.1	0.1	0.1	0.1	0.2	0.1	0.1	0.2	0.2	0.1	0.1
2009	0.2	0.2	0.2	0.2	0.2	0.2	0.2	0.2	0.2	0.3	0.3	0.2	0.2
2010	0.2	0.2	0.2	0.2	0.2	0.2	0.2	0.2	0.2	0.2	0.2	0.2	0.2
2011	0.2	0.2	0.2	0.2	0.2	0.2	0.2	0.2	0.2	0.2	0.2	0.2	0.2
2012	0.2	0.2	0.2	0.2	0.2	0.3	0.3	0.3	0.3	0.3	0.3	0.2	0.3
2013	0.2	0.2	0.3	0.2	0.3	0.3	0.3	0.3	0.3	0.3	0.3	0.3	0.3
2014	0.3	0.3	0.3	0.3	0.3	0.3	0.3	0.3	0.3	0.3	0.3	0.3	0.3
2015	0.3	0.3	0.3	0.3	0.3	0.3	0.3	0.3	0.3	0.3	0.3	0.3	0.3

Employment by Industry: Fresno, CA, 2005–2015—*Continued*

(Numbers in thousands, not seasonally adjusted)

Industry and year	January	February	March	April	May	June	July	August	September	October	November	December	Annual average
Construction													
2005	19.3	19.8	20.2	20.7	20.9	21.6	22.4	22.7	22.7	22.7	22.9	23.1	21.6
2006	22.3	22.6	22.6	22.8	23.4	23.7	23.8	24.0	23.6	23.3	23.0	22.9	23.2
2007	21.7	21.5	21.9	21.8	21.7	21.9	21.7	21.4	20.4	20.0	19.7	19.0	21.1
2008	17.9	18.1	18.1	18.6	18.6	18.4	18.6	18.3	17.7	17.4	16.7	16.1	17.9
2009	14.6	14.1	14.3	14.1	14.2	14.1	14.1	13.9	13.5	12.8	12.6	12.0	13.7
2010	11.7	11.5	11.7	11.9	12.3	12.4	12.5	12.4	12.2	12.1	11.8	11.6	12.0
2011	11.0	11.1	11.4	11.4	11.5	11.7	12.1	12.1	12.0	11.6	11.2	11.3	11.5
2012	11.2	11.1	11.4	11.5	12.0	12.6	12.9	13.0	12.5	12.7	12.5	12.5	12.2
2013	12.2	12.2	12.5	12.8	13.2	13.5	13.8	13.9	13.7	13.4	13.3	13.2	13.1
2014	12.9	13.0	13.1	13.4	13.6	14.0	14.3	14.5	14.4	14.6	14.4	14.0	13.9
2015	13.7	13.8	14.3	14.8	15.0	15.5	15.7	15.6	15.3	15.3	14.8	14.5	14.9
Manufacturing													
2005	25.8	26.0	25.7	26.2	26.5	26.6	28.9	29.8	28.7	27.8	26.9	27.2	27.2
2006	26.2	26.5	26.5	26.3	27.0	27.3	28.6	29.6	29.8	28.1	27.2	26.8	27.5
2007	26.4	26.5	26.6	26.8	27.5	27.7	31.0	32.0	31.1	28.1	26.8	26.8	28.1
2008	26.1	26.0	26.1	26.0	27.7	27.7	28.4	28.9	28.9	27.4	26.0	25.7	27.1
2009	25.0	24.5	24.3	24.2	25.6	24.9	25.9	26.8	26.3	24.9	24.3	24.1	25.1
2010	22.9	22.6	22.7	23.1	24.4	24.8	24.8	25.6	25.8	25.4	24.0	23.4	24.1
2011	22.7	22.7	22.5	22.8	23.8	24.4	24.6	25.1	25.6	24.7	23.4	23.0	23.8
2012	22.5	22.3	22.4	22.4	24.3	24.8	25.1	25.7	24.8	24.0	22.9	22.7	23.7
2013	22.2	22.1	22.0	21.9	22.5	23.1	24.0	24.8	24.6	24.0	22.8	22.8	23.1
2014	22.5	22.3	22.4	22.6	23.0	24.0	25.0	25.9	26.0	25.3	24.2	24.0	23.9
2015	23.9	24.0	24.4	24.3	24.5	25.5	26.8	27.4	27.6	26.9	25.3	25.2	25.5
Trade, Transportation, and Utilities													
2005	55.7	55.1	55.3	55.8	56.2	56.9	57.3	57.9	58.0	58.4	59.1	60.0	57.1
2006	56.8	56.4	57.0	56.9	57.5	58.4	58.7	59.0	59.5	59.6	60.8	60.9	58.5
2007	58.8	58.3	58.9	59.1	59.9	60.6	61.1	61.4	61.3	61.1	62.0	62.6	60.4
2008	58.8	58.0	58.0	57.8	59.2	59.4	59.4	59.6	59.9	59.9	60.1	60.0	59.2
2009	56.4	55.6	55.1	54.7	55.3	55.4	54.6	55.0	55.9	55.8	56.8	56.9	55.6
2010	53.7	53.3	53.3	53.8	54.1	54.8	54.8	55.6	56.1	56.7	57.8	58.0	55.2
2011	55.6	55.5	55.2	55.9	56.2	56.4	57.3	58.0	58.8	59.2	60.1	60.0	57.4
2012	56.3	55.6	55.9	56.3	57.1	57.8	58.1	58.7	59.5	59.9	61.3	61.2	58.1
2013	58.2	58.7	59.1	59.2	60.3	60.1	60.8	61.8	61.9	61.9	63.1	63.2	60.7
2014	60.3	60.3	60.6	61.0	61.2	61.5	61.8	62.2	62.6	63.2	64.1	64.7	62.0
2015	61.5	61.4	61.5	61.5	61.9	62.2	63.1	63.9	64.5	65.2	67.2	67.5	63.5
Wholesale Trade													
2005	12.0	12.0	12.1	12.3	12.4	12.8	13.0	13.1	13.2	13.1	13.0	12.9	12.7
2006	12.7	12.8	12.9	12.9	13.1	13.7	13.6	13.6	13.6	13.6	13.3	13.0	13.2
2007	12.9	13.0	13.3	13.3	13.6	14.0	14.0	14.0	13.8	13.5	13.3	13.0	13.5
2008	12.5	12.5	12.6	12.9	13.1	13.4	13.3	13.2	13.1	12.8	12.6	12.3	12.9
2009	11.9	11.8	11.7	11.7	11.8	12.1	11.9	11.9	12.0	11.9	11.9	11.6	11.9
2010	11.1	11.1	11.1	11.2	11.2	11.6	11.8	11.8	11.7	12.0	11.9	11.6	11.5
2011	12.1	12.2	12.2	12.2	12.3	12.4	12.7	12.8	12.9	12.9	12.8	12.6	12.5
2012	12.2	12.3	12.4	12.4	12.6	12.9	13.1	13.2	13.2	13.2	13.1	13.0	12.8
2013	12.9	13.1	13.2	13.4	13.8	13.8	13.8	14.0	13.8	13.8	13.7	13.6	13.6
2014	13.7	13.7	13.8	13.5	13.6	13.8	13.9	13.9	13.8	13.9	13.7	13.6	13.7
2015	13.3	13.4	13.3	13.3	13.4	13.7	14.0	14.0	14.0	14.1	14.3	14.3	13.8
Retail Trade													
2005	34.6	34.0	34.0	34.4	34.5	34.6	34.7	35.1	35.1	35.6	36.6	37.7	35.1
2006	35.0	34.5	34.8	34.6	34.7	34.7	34.8	35.1	35.2	35.5	36.7	37.3	35.2
2007	35.7	35.1	35.3	35.5	35.9	36.0	36.2	36.4	36.4	36.6	37.7	38.5	36.3
2008	35.8	35.1	35.0	35.0	35.0	34.8	34.9	35.0	35.2	35.6	36.3	36.6	35.4
2009	33.8	33.2	32.9	32.5	32.8	32.6	32.3	32.5	33.0	33.1	34.2	34.8	33.1
2010	32.4	32.0	32.0	32.2	32.3	32.4	32.2	32.6	33.1	33.4	34.4	35.0	32.8
2011	32.7	32.5	32.2	32.7	32.8	32.8	33.0	33.3	33.8	34.1	35.3	35.7	33.4
2012	33.0	32.3	32.4	32.7	33.0	33.2	33.3	33.6	34.3	34.8	36.5	36.4	33.8
2013	34.0	34.0	34.2	34.2	34.5	34.5	34.7	35.3	35.5	35.8	37.4	37.6	35.1
2014	35.2	35.0	35.3	35.9	35.9	35.9	35.8	36.0	36.4	37.0	38.3	39.0	36.3
2015	36.5	36.3	36.5	36.4	36.6	36.5	36.8	37.4	37.8	38.4	40.3	40.6	37.5

Employment by Industry: Fresno, CA, 2005–2015—*Continued*

(Numbers in thousands, not seasonally adjusted)

Industry and year	January	February	March	April	May	June	July	August	September	October	November	December	Annual average
Transportation and Utilities													
2005	9.1	9.1	9.2	9.1	9.3	9.5	9.6	9.7	9.7	9.7	9.5	9.4	9.4
2006	9.1	9.1	9.3	9.4	9.7	10.0	10.3	10.3	10.7	10.5	10.8	10.6	10.0
2007	10.2	10.2	10.3	10.3	10.4	10.6	10.9	11.0	11.1	11.0	11.0	11.1	10.7
2008	10.5	10.4	10.4	9.9	11.1	11.2	11.2	11.4	11.6	11.5	11.2	11.1	11.0
2009	10.7	10.6	10.5	10.5	10.7	10.7	10.4	10.6	10.9	10.8	10.7	10.5	10.6
2010	10.2	10.2	10.2	10.4	10.6	10.8	10.8	11.2	11.3	11.3	11.5	11.4	10.8
2011	10.8	10.8	10.8	11.0	11.1	11.2	11.6	11.9	12.1	12.2	12.0	11.7	11.4
2012	11.1	11.0	11.1	11.2	11.5	11.7	11.7	11.9	12.0	11.9	11.7	11.8	11.6
2013	11.3	11.6	11.7	11.6	12.0	11.8	12.3	12.5	12.6	12.3	12.0	12.0	12.0
2014	11.4	11.6	11.5	11.6	11.7	11.8	12.1	12.3	12.4	12.3	12.1	12.1	11.9
2015	11.7	11.7	11.7	11.8	11.9	12.0	12.3	12.5	12.7	12.7	12.6	12.6	12.2
Information													
2005	4.4	4.5	4.4	4.4	4.4	4.4	4.3	4.3	4.3	4.2	4.3	4.2	4.3
2006	4.2	4.2	4.2	4.2	4.2	4.2	4.2	4.2	4.2	4.2	4.2	4.2	4.2
2007	4.1	4.2	4.1	4.1	4.2	4.2	4.2	4.2	4.2	4.2	4.2	4.2	4.2
2008	4.5	4.5	4.4	4.8	4.8	4.8	4.9	4.9	4.8	4.8	4.8	4.8	4.7
2009	4.6	4.6	4.5	4.3	4.2	4.3	4.0	4.0	3.9	3.9	3.9	3.8	4.2
2010	3.8	3.7	3.7	3.5	3.5	3.5	3.6	3.5	3.5	3.5	3.5	3.5	3.6
2011	3.4	3.4	3.4	3.4	3.5	3.5	3.5	3.5	3.6	3.6	3.7	3.6	3.5
2012	3.8	3.7	3.7	3.8	3.8	3.9	3.8	3.8	3.8	3.8	3.8	3.8	3.8
2013	3.8	3.8	3.8	3.8	3.8	3.8	3.8	3.8	3.8	3.8	3.8	3.8	3.8
2014	3.8	3.8	3.8	3.8	3.8	3.8	3.9	3.9	3.9	3.9	3.9	4.0	3.9
2015	3.9	3.9	3.9	3.9	3.9	4.0	3.9	4.0	3.9	3.9	3.9	3.9	3.9
Financial Activities													
2005	14.3	14.2	14.3	14.5	14.5	14.6	14.8	14.8	15.0	15.1	15.2	15.3	14.7
2006	15.2	15.3	15.3	15.5	15.6	15.6	15.7	15.7	15.7	15.5	15.5	15.6	15.5
2007	15.3	15.4	15.4	15.5	15.5	15.6	15.4	15.3	15.3	14.9	15.0	15.0	15.3
2008	14.9	14.9	14.9	14.8	14.9	14.9	14.7	14.8	14.6	14.6	14.6	14.5	14.8
2009	14.3	14.2	14.1	14.1	13.9	13.8	13.7	13.6	13.5	13.6	13.5	13.5	13.8
2010	13.5	13.4	13.3	13.4	13.4	13.4	13.4	13.4	13.3	13.4	13.3	13.3	13.4
2011	13.2	13.2	13.2	13.2	13.1	13.1	13.0	13.0	12.8	12.6	12.6	12.6	13.0
2012	12.6	12.6	12.6	12.8	12.9	12.9	13.0	13.0	13.0	12.9	12.9	13.0	12.9
2013	12.9	12.9	12.9	13.0	12.9	12.9	13.0	12.9	12.9	12.8	12.8	12.7	12.9
2014	12.7	12.7	12.7	12.7	12.7	12.7	12.8	12.7	12.7	12.9	12.9	12.9	12.8
2015	12.8	12.8	12.9	12.9	13.0	13.0	13.2	13.2	13.1	13.1	13.1	13.2	13.0
Professional and Business Services													
2005	27.7	28.4	28.6	29.2	29.3	29.0	28.6	28.9	28.6	29.0	29.0	29.3	28.8
2006	28.7	29.1	29.4	29.8	29.5	29.4	29.3	29.9	29.8	29.9	29.7	29.7	29.5
2007	29.3	29.6	29.9	30.0	29.8	30.0	30.2	30.2	30.3	30.6	30.1	29.9	30.0
2008	30.3	30.6	30.4	30.8	30.4	30.3	31.2	31.2	31.1	30.7	30.3	30.5	30.7
2009	29.6	29.4	29.3	28.8	28.3	28.0	28.0	27.5	27.2	27.5	27.3	27.0	28.2
2010	26.1	26.3	26.6	27.3	27.3	27.2	26.8	26.8	26.4	26.7	26.7	26.4	26.7
2011	26.7	27.4	27.4	27.4	27.5	26.9	26.7	26.8	27.1	26.9	26.4	26.5	27.0
2012	26.5	26.8	27.2	26.8	26.3	26.2	26.2	26.5	26.7	27.4	28.5	27.2	26.9
2013	27.8	28.1	27.9	28.3	28.0	28.6	29.2	29.6	30.1	30.5	30.3	30.2	29.1
2014	29.1	30.3	30.4	30.0	30.4	30.2	31.4	32.2	32.4	33.1	31.9	31.7	31.1
2015	30.9	31.1	31.3	31.6	31.5	31.6	31.7	31.5	31.2	32.1	31.4	31.2	31.4
Education and Health Services													
2005	44.9	45.1	45.2	45.9	45.7	45.5	45.3	45.5	46.4	46.8	46.8	46.8	45.8
2006	45.9	46.5	46.5	46.4	46.4	46.4	46.3	46.3	47.0	47.2	47.8	48.1	46.7
2007	47.5	48.2	48.3	48.6	48.2	48.2	47.9	48.3	48.9	49.4	49.5	49.6	48.6
2008	49.0	49.8	50.2	50.9	50.8	50.5	49.8	50.1	50.2	51.0	51.3	51.5	50.4
2009	50.8	51.4	51.8	52.0	51.6	51.4	50.3	50.4	50.9	51.7	52.1	51.9	51.4
2010	51.0	51.3	51.4	51.9	51.8	51.5	50.9	51.1	51.7	52.0	52.1	52.2	51.6
2011	51.4	51.5	52.5	52.7	52.3	51.9	51.2	51.4	52.2	52.0	52.5	52.6	52.0
2012	52.1	53.1	53.5	53.5	53.4	53.1	52.4	53.0	53.5	53.5	53.5	53.9	53.2
2013	54.1	55.1	55.6	55.6	55.5	55.2	54.1	54.6	55.2	56.0	56.1	56.2	55.3
2014	55.3	55.8	56.6	57.4	56.7	56.4	56.0	56.8	57.2	58.0	58.1	58.4	56.9
2015	58.1	58.5	59.5	59.9	59.7	59.6	59.9	60.6	61.1	62.5	62.7	62.6	60.4

Employment by Industry: Fresno, CA, 2005–2015—*Continued*

(Numbers in thousands, not seasonally adjusted)

Industry and year	January	February	March	April	May	June	July	August	September	October	November	December	Annual average
Leisure and Hospitality													
2005	24.4	24.8	25.1	25.8	26.3	26.3	26.1	26.1	26.0	26.3	26.5	27.0	25.9
2006	26.5	27.1	27.5	27.8	28.5	28.9	28.7	28.7	28.7	28.1	28.2	28.6	28.1
2007	27.5	27.9	28.3	28.6	28.9	29.1	28.3	28.5	28.2	27.6	27.7	27.7	28.2
2008	27.3	27.7	28.0	28.0	28.7	28.6	28.4	28.4	28.1	27.6	27.5	27.1	28.0
2009	26.2	26.5	26.6	26.9	27.5	27.5	27.2	27.1	26.3	26.0	25.9	25.9	26.6
2010	25.5	25.9	26.3	26.2	27.4	27.4	27.4	27.5	27.1	27.2	26.8	26.7	26.8
2011	26.0	26.6	27.3	27.1	27.6	27.9	27.9	28.0	27.3	26.8	26.5	26.3	27.1
2012	26.5	27.0	27.5	27.8	28.6	28.8	29.0	29.2	28.5	28.0	27.6	27.7	28.0
2013	27.5	27.6	28.4	28.5	29.2	29.6	30.0	29.9	29.3	29.3	29.1	29.3	29.0
2014	29.2	29.8	29.8	30.5	31.1	31.3	31.6	31.6	30.7	30.5	30.5	30.3	30.6
2015	30.1	30.5	31.0	31.3	32.2	32.2	32.3	32.3	31.6	31.6	31.5	30.5	31.4
Other Services													
2005	10.3	10.5	10.5	11.0	11.0	11.0	10.6	11.1	11.0	11.0	11.0	11.1	10.8
2006	10.4	10.8	11.0	11.0	11.3	11.0	10.8	11.0	11.0	10.8	10.7	10.9	10.9
2007	10.6	10.9	10.9	11.1	11.3	10.9	10.8	11.2	11.1	10.9	11.0	10.9	11.0
2008	10.5	10.7	10.8	10.8	10.8	10.8	10.4	10.6	10.6	10.6	10.5	10.5	10.6
2009	10.2	10.3	10.4	10.3	10.5	10.5	9.7	10.1	10.0	10.0	10.0	10.0	10.2
2010	9.9	10.1	10.1	10.0	10.1	10.1	9.7	9.9	9.9	10.0	10.0	9.9	10.0
2011	9.7	9.9	9.9	10.0	10.0	10.1	10.1	10.3	10.4	10.4	10.4	10.3	10.1
2012	10.1	10.2	10.3	10.6	10.8	10.9	10.5	10.8	10.7	10.8	10.8	10.8	10.6
2013	10.7	10.9	11.0	11.0	11.0	10.8	10.7	11.0	11.0	10.9	11.0	11.0	10.9
2014	11.0	11.1	11.2	11.2	11.3	11.1	11.0	11.4	11.3	11.3	11.4	11.3	11.2
2015	11.2	11.4	11.4	11.5	11.6	11.4	11.4	11.6	11.6	11.7	11.6	11.4	11.5
Government													
2005	66.5	68.0	69.1	69.4	69.3	68.3	63.9	63.5	65.0	67.1	67.3	66.7	67.0
2006	66.5	68.2	70.0	69.9	70.3	67.8	63.7	63.6	66.0	68.5	68.5	67.9	67.6
2007	67.6	69.8	71.2	72.0	71.5	70.0	65.8	65.5	67.3	69.8	69.9	69.5	69.2
2008	69.0	71.7	72.7	73.3	72.6	71.7	65.0	65.3	68.1	70.3	70.3	69.4	70.0
2009	68.2	70.3	71.3	72.6	71.8	69.2	65.8	64.2	67.0	69.0	68.1	67.2	68.7
2010	66.4	69.6	70.7	70.4	70.5	68.8	62.1	61.8	64.3	67.5	66.7	66.0	67.1
2011	65.4	68.1	69.1	69.7	69.0	66.6	62.8	61.0	62.7	65.3	65.2	63.9	65.7
2012	63.5	65.3	66.2	66.4	66.4	65.7	61.6	59.6	61.6	64.8	64.4	63.6	64.1
2013	63.1	65.6	66.4	66.5	65.9	65.9	60.2	59.8	62.3	64.2	65.2	64.5	64.2
2014	64.5	66.8	67.7	67.9	68.5	68.2	63.9	61.8	64.2	67.1	67.4	67.1	66.3
2015	67.3	69.5	69.6	70.1	70.7	70.7	65.0	63.6	67.6	70.1	70.6	70.2	68.8

Employment by Industry: Bridgeport-Stamford-Norwalk, CT NECTA, 2005–2015

(Numbers in thousands, not seasonally adjusted)

Industry and year	January	February	March	April	May	June	July	August	September	October	November	December	Annual average
Total Nonfarm													
2005	394.9	395.7	397.4	403.7	406.5	409.8	407.0	403.1	404.6	405.9	408.5	411.1	404.0
2006	401.1	401.7	401.7	408.3	411.4	414.5	410.5	407.1	408.6	410.6	413.8	417.6	408.9
2007	404.5	404.1	405.7	409.6	414.3	417.5	416.2	411.8	411.3	413.6	416.1	418.8	412.0
2008	406.6	405.5	407.8	410.1	413.3	416.4	411.1	407.0	407.5	408.4	409.0	408.9	409.3
2009	394.2	391.6	391.4	389.0	393.2	395.2	390.5	387.1	388.9	389.3	390.8	392.3	391.1
2010	378.0	376.7	379.2	385.3	393.3	396.0	395.7	391.8	390.9	392.3	393.6	396.0	389.1
2011	384.0	384.8	386.5	392.0	395.1	397.5	397.4	393.4	394.4	395.3	397.0	399.2	393.1
2012	389.9	389.0	392.4	395.2	399.4	403.7	402.1	398.5	398.3	399.4	401.4	404.1	397.8
2013	392.6	390.6	394.3	400.1	404.3	409.8	407.3	404.1	403.8	404.4	406.7	407.1	402.1
2014	395.8	394.0	397.2	403.1	407.6	412.0	407.0	403.9	406.9	408.4	411.5	413.0	405.0
2015	401.1	399.1	400.6	406.0	411.4	416.9	413.2	409.9	409.1	412.0	415.5	415.3	409.2
Total Private													
2005	349.4	349.8	351.4	356.8	359.3	362.6	362.5	360.2	358.8	359.6	362.1	364.4	358.1
2006	354.9	355.1	354.8	361.6	364.6	368.8	367.2	365.3	363.2	364.5	367.3	371.2	363.2
2007	358.9	357.8	359.4	363.3	367.1	371.6	371.1	368.5	365.8	367.0	369.1	372.1	366.0
2008	360.2	358.3	360.8	363.5	365.9	370.0	367.6	364.9	361.7	361.6	361.3	361.8	363.1
2009	348.0	345.1	344.6	343.4	346.0	348.5	347.1	344.8	343.2	343.2	344.3	346.3	345.4
2010	332.8	331.5	333.9	340.8	345.7	350.1	351.6	349.6	346.7	347.8	348.7	350.8	344.2
2011	339.7	339.9	341.6	346.7	349.5	353.3	355.9	353.2	350.4	350.7	352.2	354.3	349.0
2012	345.8	344.8	347.9	350.7	354.4	359.7	359.6	357.2	354.2	355.0	356.4	359.2	353.7
2013	348.1	346.0	349.5	355.4	359.3	364.6	364.3	362.3	359.5	359.9	361.6	362.2	357.7
2014	352.0	349.9	352.7	358.0	361.9	366.1	366.7	364.3	361.9	363.5	365.9	367.7	360.9
2015	357.1	354.9	356.1	361.0	366.5	371.2	370.1	367.4	364.2	366.6	369.5	369.5	364.5
Goods Producing													
2005	54.4	54.1	54.1	55.5	55.9	56.4	56.3	55.9	55.5	55.6	55.6	55.1	55.4
2006	54.1	54.3	51.5	55.6	55.8	56.4	56.4	56.3	56.0	55.9	55.7	55.5	55.3
2007	54.2	53.9	54.3	54.9	55.3	56.0	56.1	55.9	55.7	55.3	55.1	54.9	55.1
2008	53.3	52.7	53.2	53.8	54.4	54.7	54.4	54.1	53.9	53.3	52.8	52.0	53.6
2009	50.0	49.0	48.7	48.8	48.7	49.0	48.4	48.0	47.7	47.3	47.0	46.7	48.3
2010	44.6	44.2	44.5	45.7	46.2	47.1	47.3	47.2	46.8	46.6	46.1	45.8	46.0
2011	44.6	44.6	44.9	45.8	46.3	46.8	46.8	46.7	46.3	46.0	46.0	45.9	45.9
2012	44.6	44.6	44.4	44.7	45.0	45.8	45.7	45.5	44.9	44.9	44.9	44.9	45.0
2013	43.6	43.4	43.4	44.4	44.9	45.6	45.3	45.4	45.1	45.0	45.0	44.7	44.7
2014	43.3	43.1	43.2	44.0	44.4	44.8	44.8	44.7	44.3	44.6	44.4	44.1	44.1
2015	42.6	42.2	42.2	43.2	44.0	44.7	44.5	44.5	44.2	44.2	44.0	43.8	43.7
Service-Providing													
2005	340.5	341.6	343.3	348.2	350.6	353.4	350.7	347.2	349.1	350.3	352.9	356.0	348.7
2006	347.0	347.4	350.2	352.7	355.6	358.1	354.1	350.8	352.6	354.7	358.1	362.1	353.6
2007	350.3	350.2	351.4	354.7	359.0	361.5	360.1	355.9	355.6	358.3	361.0	363.9	356.8
2008	353.3	352.8	354.6	356.3	358.9	361.7	356.7	352.9	353.6	355.1	356.2	356.9	355.8
2009	344.2	342.6	342.7	340.2	344.5	346.2	342.1	339.1	341.2	342.0	343.8	345.6	342.9
2010	333.4	332.5	334.7	339.6	347.1	348.9	348.4	344.6	344.1	345.7	347.5	350.2	343.1
2011	339.4	340.2	341.6	346.2	348.8	350.7	350.6	346.7	348.1	349.3	351.0	353.3	347.2
2012	345.3	344.4	348.0	350.5	354.4	357.9	356.4	353.0	353.4	354.5	356.5	359.2	352.8
2013	349.0	347.2	350.9	355.7	359.4	364.2	362.0	358.7	358.7	359.4	361.7	362.4	357.4
2014	352.5	350.9	354.0	359.1	363.2	367.2	362.2	359.2	362.6	363.8	367.1	368.9	360.9
2015	358.5	356.9	358.4	362.8	367.4	372.2	368.7	365.4	364.9	367.8	371.5	371.5	365.5
Mining, Logging, and Construction													
2005	13.2	13.0	13.1	14.7	15.1	15.3	15.6	15.5	15.2	15.2	15.2	14.6	14.6
2006	13.9	13.8	14.2	15.1	15.4	15.6	16.0	15.9	15.7	15.6	15.4	15.1	15.1
2007	14.2	13.7	14.0	15.2	15.6	15.9	16.1	16.1	15.9	15.8	15.6	15.3	15.3
2008	13.9	13.7	13.9	14.8	15.2	15.3	15.3	15.3	15.1	14.6	14.2	13.6	14.6
2009	12.2	11.8	11.6	11.9	12.1	12.2	12.2	12.0	11.8	11.7	11.5	11.2	11.9
2010	9.4	9.2	9.5	10.7	11.0	11.4	11.6	11.7	11.5	11.4	11.2	10.8	10.8
2011	9.6	9.6	9.8	10.8	11.3	11.6	11.8	11.8	11.7	11.6	11.6	11.4	11.1
2012	10.4	10.3	10.5	11.2	11.5	11.8	12.0	11.9	11.7	11.6	11.6	11.5	11.3
2013	10.5	10.2	10.3	11.3	11.7	12.0	12.2	12.3	12.2	12.1	12.1	11.6	11.5
2014	10.4	10.2	10.4	11.5	12.2	12.5	12.6	12.7	12.6	12.7	12.6	12.2	11.9
2015	11.0	10.6	10.7	11.9	12.5	12.8	12.7	12.9	12.8	12.8	12.8	12.5	12.2

Employment by Industry: Bridgeport-Stamford-Norwalk, CT NECTA, 2005–2015—*Continued*

(Numbers in thousands, not seasonally adjusted)

Industry and year	January	February	March	April	May	June	July	August	September	October	November	December	Annual average
Manufacturing													
2005	41.2	41.1	41.0	40.8	40.8	41.1	40.7	40.4	40.3	40.4	40.4	40.5	40.7
2006	40.2	40.5	37.3	40.5	40.4	40.8	40.4	40.4	40.3	40.3	40.3	40.4	40.2
2007	40.0	40.2	40.3	39.7	39.7	40.1	40.0	39.8	39.8	39.5	39.5	39.6	39.9
2008	39.4	39.0	39.3	39.0	39.2	39.4	39.1	38.8	38.8	38.7	38.6	38.4	39.0
2009	37.8	37.2	37.1	36.9	36.6	36.8	36.2	36.0	35.9	35.6	35.5	35.5	36.4
2010	35.2	35.0	35.0	35.0	35.2	35.7	35.7	35.5	35.3	35.2	34.9	35.0	35.2
2011	35.0	35.0	35.1	35.0	35.0	35.2	35.0	34.9	34.6	34.4	34.4	34.5	34.8
2012	34.2	34.3	33.9	33.5	33.5	34.0	33.7	33.6	33.2	33.3	33.3	33.4	33.7
2013	33.1	33.2	33.1	33.1	33.2	33.6	33.1	33.1	32.9	32.9	32.9	33.1	33.1
2014	32.9	32.9	32.8	32.5	32.2	32.3	32.2	32.0	31.7	31.9	31.8	31.9	32.3
2015	31.6	31.6	31.5	31.3	31.5	31.9	31.8	31.6	31.4	31.4	31.2	31.3	31.5
Trade, Transportation, and Utilities													
2005	73.4	72.2	72.3	72.3	72.8	73.4	72.2	72.0	72.8	73.6	75.5	77.6	73.3
2006	74.5	73.3	73.5	73.4	73.8	74.7	73.2	72.7	73.0	73.8	76.1	77.9	74.2
2007	74.1	72.3	72.7	72.6	73.8	75.0	73.7	73.4	73.6	74.1	76.6	78.7	74.2
2008	75.2	73.4	73.5	73.2	73.8	74.5	73.0	72.7	73.0	72.8	74.0	75.3	73.7
2009	71.2	69.4	69.1	67.9	68.7	69.4	67.8	67.5	67.7	68.3	70.1	71.6	69.1
2010	67.7	66.5	66.7	66.9	68.5	69.6	68.6	68.4	68.4	69.3	71.1	72.8	68.7
2011	69.2	68.1	68.1	68.9	69.4	70.2	69.3	68.8	68.7	69.2	71.0	72.9	69.5
2012	70.1	68.5	68.9	68.8	69.7	70.6	69.3	69.0	69.1	69.8	71.6	72.9	69.9
2013	70.3	68.7	69.3	69.6	70.2	71.0	69.9	69.9	70.0	70.6	72.4	73.9	70.5
2014	71.0	69.6	69.8	69.9	70.5	71.3	70.1	69.8	70.1	71.0	72.9	74.3	70.9
2015	71.2	69.7	69.8	69.8	70.8	71.8	70.3	70.1	70.5	70.7	72.6	74.4	71.0
Wholesale Trade													
2005	14.5	14.5	14.5	14.4	14.5	14.6	14.5	14.5	14.4	14.5	14.4	14.6	14.5
2006	14.4	14.5	14.5	14.4	14.4	14.4	14.4	14.2	14.2	14.3	14.3	14.4	14.4
2007	14.2	14.2	14.3	14.2	14.2	14.4	14.4	14.5	14.4	14.4	14.5	14.7	14.4
2008	14.6	14.5	14.6	14.6	14.6	14.7	14.6	14.6	14.5	14.5	14.5	14.6	14.6
2009	14.2	14.1	14.0	13.7	13.6	13.7	13.6	13.5	13.4	13.4	13.2	13.3	13.6
2010	12.9	12.9	13.0	13.1	13.2	13.4	13.3	13.3	13.2	13.2	13.3	13.4	13.2
2011	13.2	13.2	13.3	13.4	13.4	13.6	13.6	13.5	13.4	13.3	13.3	13.4	13.4
2012	13.2	13.2	13.2	13.2	13.2	13.4	13.4	13.3	13.3	13.4	13.3	13.3	13.3
2013	13.3	13.2	13.3	13.3	13.4	13.5	13.5	13.5	13.4	13.5	13.5	13.6	13.4
2014	13.4	13.5	13.5	13.5	13.5	13.6	13.5	13.5	13.4	13.4	13.4	13.4	13.5
2015	13.3	13.3	13.3	13.4	13.5	13.7	13.6	13.6	13.6	13.6	13.7	13.8	13.5
Retail Trade													
2005	49.3	48.2	48.2	48.3	48.7	49.2	48.8	48.8	48.8	49.3	51.2	52.9	49.3
2006	50.3	48.9	49.1	49.1	49.3	50.1	49.4	49.2	48.6	49.2	51.4	52.7	49.8
2007	49.5	47.8	48.0	48.0	49.1	49.9	49.4	49.2	48.8	49.3	51.5	53.1	49.5
2008	50.2	48.5	48.6	48.1	48.6	49.2	48.6	48.6	48.3	48.3	49.4	50.4	48.9
2009	47.0	45.4	45.2	44.8	45.5	46.1	45.3	45.3	44.9	45.5	47.4	48.4	45.9
2010	45.6	44.4	44.5	44.8	45.9	46.6	46.4	46.2	45.6	46.5	48.0	49.2	46.1
2011	46.4	45.3	45.2	45.8	46.2	46.7	46.4	46.2	45.6	46.2	47.9	49.3	46.4
2012	47.1	45.5	45.9	45.8	46.5	47.2	46.7	46.6	46.1	46.6	48.4	49.3	46.8
2013	47.3	46.0	46.3	46.5	47.0	47.6	47.2	47.3	46.6	47.2	48.9	50.0	47.3
2014	47.7	46.3	46.5	46.7	47.2	47.9	47.5	47.3	46.9	47.7	49.3	50.3	47.6
2015	47.9	46.7	46.8	46.7	47.4	48.1	47.4	47.5	47.1	47.2	48.9	50.0	47.6
Transportation and Utilities													
2005	9.6	9.5	9.6	9.6	9.6	9.6	8.9	8.7	9.6	9.8	9.9	10.1	9.5
2006	9.8	9.9	9.9	9.9	10.1	10.2	9.4	9.3	10.2	10.3	10.4	10.8	10.0
2007	10.4	10.3	10.4	10.4	10.5	10.7	9.9	9.7	10.4	10.4	10.6	10.9	10.4
2008	10.4	10.4	10.3	10.5	10.6	10.6	9.8	9.5	10.2	10.0	10.1	10.3	10.2
2009	10.0	9.9	9.9	9.4	9.6	9.6	8.9	8.7	9.4	9.4	9.5	9.9	9.5
2010	9.2	9.2	9.2	9.0	9.4	9.6	8.9	8.9	9.6	9.6	9.8	10.2	9.4
2011	9.6	9.6	9.6	9.7	9.8	9.9	9.3	9.1	9.7	9.7	9.8	10.2	9.7
2012	9.8	9.8	9.8	9.8	10.0	10.0	9.2	9.1	9.7	9.8	9.9	10.3	9.8
2013	9.7	9.5	9.7	9.8	9.8	9.9	9.2	9.1	10.0	9.9	10.0	10.3	9.7
2014	9.9	9.8	9.8	9.7	9.8	9.8	9.1	9.0	9.8	9.9	10.2	10.6	9.8
2015	10.0	9.7	9.7	9.7	9.9	10.0	9.3	9.0	9.8	9.9	10.0	10.6	9.8

Employment by Industry: Bridgeport-Stamford-Norwalk, CT NECTA, 2005–2015—*Continued*

(Numbers in thousands, not seasonally adjusted)

Industry and year	January	February	March	April	May	June	July	August	September	October	November	December	Annual average
Information													
2005	10.9	10.9	10.9	11.0	11.0	10.9	10.8	10.9	10.7	10.8	10.7	10.7	10.9
2006	10.6	10.6	10.8	10.7	10.8	10.8	10.7	10.6	10.6	10.5	10.6	10.8	10.7
2007	10.7	10.8	10.9	10.7	10.9	10.8	11.1	11.2	11.4	11.1	10.5	10.6	10.9
2008	10.6	10.6	10.7	10.6	10.6	10.8	10.8	10.9	10.8	10.8	10.9	11.0	10.8
2009	11.1	11.1	11.0	10.8	10.8	10.7	10.7	10.6	10.5	10.3	10.4	10.4	10.7
2010	10.2	10.2	10.2	10.3	10.4	10.3	10.2	10.2	10.2	10.1	10.2	10.3	10.2
2011	10.2	10.2	10.2	10.2	10.2	10.3	10.5	10.5	10.3	10.3	10.4	10.6	10.3
2012	10.6	10.5	10.5	10.5	10.5	10.5	10.6	10.7	10.6	10.6	10.7	10.8	10.6
2013	10.8	11.1	11.1	11.0	11.3	11.4	11.6	11.4	11.4	11.4	11.4	11.5	11.3
2014	11.3	11.4	11.4	11.4	11.4	11.4	11.5	11.5	11.4	11.4	12.0	12.1	11.5
2015	12.0	11.9	12.0	12.1	12.0	12.1	12.1	12.1	12.0	12.1	12.1	12.3	12.1
Financial Activities													
2005	41.9	42.1	42.4	42.5	42.5	42.9	43.2	43.1	42.6	42.7	42.8	43.0	42.6
2006	42.9	42.9	43.2	43.0	43.4	43.9	44.1	44.5	44.1	44.3	44.7	44.9	43.8
2007	44.7	44.7	44.8	44.7	45.0	45.6	46.0	45.8	45.1	45.3	45.3	45.6	45.2
2008	44.9	45.1	45.3	45.1	45.1	45.7	45.5	45.6	44.8	44.7	44.6	44.7	45.1
2009	43.7	43.7	43.8	42.7	42.6	43.0	43.2	43.1	42.7	42.7	42.7	42.9	43.1
2010	42.0	42.0	42.1	42.1	42.2	42.9	43.1	43.2	42.5	42.4	42.4	42.7	42.5
2011	42.4	42.4	42.4	42.4	42.3	42.3	43.2	43.0	42.1	42.1	42.1	42.1	42.4
2012	41.7	41.6	41.6	41.6	41.6	42.2	42.3	42.0	41.4	41.5	41.4	41.5	41.7
2013	41.4	41.2	41.2	41.1	41.3	41.9	42.1	41.9	41.4	41.3	41.4	41.5	41.5
2014	40.3	40.2	40.3	40.2	40.4	41.1	41.4	41.3	40.8	40.9	41.0	41.3	40.8
2015	40.9	40.9	41.0	41.0	41.1	41.6	41.6	41.4	40.7	40.8	40.9	41.0	41.1
Professional and Business Services													
2005	65.9	66.4	67.1	68.6	68.8	69.6	69.4	69.5	70.2	69.9	70.4	70.6	68.9
2006	67.8	68.5	69.7	70.7	70.9	71.7	70.2	70.4	70.4	70.0	70.3	71.2	70.2
2007	67.8	67.7	67.9	69.8	70.2	70.8	69.5	69.3	69.1	69.6	69.5	69.6	69.2
2008	66.8	66.1	66.6	68.0	67.9	68.4	67.7	67.4	66.5	66.3	65.7	65.3	66.9
2009	62.9	62.2	62.2	62.5	62.3	62.8	62.2	62.2	61.8	62.0	61.7	61.8	62.2
2010	59.2	59.6	60.5	63.0	63.3	64.0	64.5	64.4	64.2	64.5	64.0	63.8	62.9
2011	61.7	62.4	62.9	64.3	64.7	65.2	65.8	65.4	65.1	65.3	65.3	65.0	64.4
2012	63.5	63.6	64.9	66.3	66.5	67.1	67.3	67.1	66.7	66.1	66.0	65.7	65.9
2013	63.0	63.2	63.7	65.7	66.2	67.1	67.2	67.4	66.6	66.5	66.1	65.5	65.7
2014	63.2	63.2	63.6	65.8	66.3	66.8	67.1	67.1	66.4	66.2	66.4	66.0	65.7
2015	63.9	64.0	63.9	65.8	66.5	66.9	67.2	67.2	66.4	67.1	67.3	66.0	66.0
Education and Health Services													
2005	57.5	58.7	58.5	58.8	58.8	57.8	58.2	57.4	58.1	59.0	59.4	59.4	58.5
2006	58.7	59.4	59.3	59.7	59.8	58.9	59.2	58.3	59.0	60.3	60.8	61.2	59.6
2007	59.7	61.1	60.9	61.4	60.9	60.5	60.4	59.5	60.5	61.8	62.3	62.7	61.0
2008	61.3	62.6	63.0	63.0	62.5	62.5	62.2	61.2	62.4	63.7	64.2	64.4	62.8
2009	62.8	63.6	63.5	63.4	63.6	62.7	62.8	62.2	63.3	64.2	64.6	64.9	63.5
2010	63.7	64.0	64.2	65.0	65.1	64.3	64.7	63.8	64.7	65.6	66.1	66.3	64.8
2011	65.2	65.7	65.9	66.2	66.1	65.6	65.6	64.9	65.9	66.3	66.9	67.1	66.0
2012	66.5	67.1	67.5	67.5	67.5	67.2	67.0	66.4	67.5	68.2	68.6	69.3	67.5
2013	67.6	67.7	68.4	69.3	69.3	69.0	68.4	67.5	68.6	69.4	69.9	69.4	68.7
2014	69.4	69.4	69.9	70.5	70.9	70.2	70.4	69.4	70.6	71.3	71.6	72.0	70.5
2015	71.3	71.3	71.5	71.5	72.1	71.8	71.2	70.4	71.0	71.8	73.1	72.1	71.6
Leisure and Hospitality													
2005	29.4	29.3	29.8	31.6	32.9	34.8	35.3	34.7	32.6	31.7	31.3	31.4	32.1
2006	29.9	29.8	30.4	32.0	33.5	35.6	36.0	35.5	33.6	33.0	32.4	32.9	32.9
2007	31.0	30.7	31.2	32.5	34.2	35.9	36.8	36.3	33.8	33.4	33.4	33.6	33.6
2008	31.8	31.7	32.3	33.5	35.2	36.6	36.9	36.1	34.1	33.7	32.8	32.8	34.0
2009	30.5	30.3	30.5	31.6	33.4	34.7	35.5	34.9	33.7	32.6	31.9	32.1	32.6
2010	29.9	29.6	30.2	32.1	34.0	35.5	36.5	35.7	34.0	33.4	32.8	33.1	33.1
2011	30.7	30.8	31.4	33.0	34.4	36.6	37.9	37.3	36.0	35.6	34.6	34.7	34.4
2012	32.8	32.9	34.0	35.2	37.2	39.5	40.3	39.6	37.7	37.5	36.8	37.6	36.8
2013	35.3	34.7	36.2	37.9	39.5	41.7	42.6	41.7	39.8	39.1	38.8	39.1	38.9
2014	37.1	36.7	38.0	39.6	41.2	43.4	44.0	43.2	41.5	41.2	40.6	40.8	40.6
2015	38.3	38.0	38.8	40.5	42.6	44.6	45.5	44.1	42.0	42.5	42.1	42.3	41.8

Employment by Industry: Bridgeport-Stamford-Norwalk, CT NECTA, 2005–2015—*Continued*

(Numbers in thousands, not seasonally adjusted)

Industry and year	January	February	March	April	May	June	July	August	September	October	November	December	Annual average
Other Services													
2005	16.0	16.1	16.3	16.5	16.6	16.8	17.1	16.7	16.3	16.3	16.4	16.6	16.5
2006	16.4	16.3	16.4	16.5	16.6	16.8	17.4	17.0	16.5	16.7	16.7	16.8	16.7
2007	16.7	16.6	16.7	16.7	16.8	17.0	17.5	17.1	16.6	16.4	16.4	16.4	16.7
2008	16.3	16.1	16.2	16.3	16.4	16.8	17.1	16.9	16.2	16.3	16.3	16.3	16.4
2009	15.8	15.8	15.8	15.7	15.9	16.2	16.5	16.3	15.8	15.8	15.9	15.9	16.0
2010	15.5	15.4	15.5	15.7	16.0	16.4	16.7	16.7	15.9	15.9	16.0	16.0	16.0
2011	15.7	15.7	15.8	15.9	16.1	16.3	16.8	16.6	16.0	15.9	15.9	16.0	16.1
2012	16.0	16.0	16.1	16.2	16.4	16.8	17.1	16.9	16.3	16.4	16.4	16.5	16.4
2013	16.1	16.0	16.2	16.4	16.6	16.9	17.2	17.1	16.6	16.6	16.6	16.6	16.6
2014	16.4	16.3	16.5	16.6	16.8	17.1	17.4	17.3	16.8	16.9	17.0	17.1	16.9
2015	16.9	16.9	16.9	17.1	17.4	17.7	17.7	17.6	17.4	17.4	17.4	17.6	17.3
Government													
2005	45.5	45.9	46.0	46.9	47.2	47.2	44.5	42.9	45.8	46.3	46.4	46.7	45.9
2006	46.2	46.6	46.9	46.7	46.8	45.7	43.3	41.8	45.4	46.1	46.5	46.4	45.7
2007	45.6	46.3	46.3	46.3	47.2	45.9	45.1	43.3	45.5	46.6	47.0	46.7	46.0
2008	46.4	47.2	47.0	46.6	47.4	46.4	43.5	42.1	45.8	46.8	47.7	47.1	46.2
2009	46.2	46.5	46.8	45.6	47.2	46.7	43.4	42.3	45.7	46.1	46.5	46.0	45.8
2010	45.2	45.2	45.3	44.5	47.6	45.9	44.1	42.2	44.2	44.5	44.9	45.2	44.9
2011	44.3	44.9	44.9	45.3	45.6	44.2	41.5	40.2	44.0	44.6	44.8	44.9	44.1
2012	44.1	44.2	44.5	44.5	45.0	44.0	42.5	41.3	44.1	44.4	45.0	44.9	44.0
2013	44.5	44.6	44.8	44.7	45.0	45.2	43.0	41.8	44.3	44.5	45.1	44.9	44.4
2014	43.8	44.1	44.5	45.1	45.7	45.9	40.3	39.6	45.0	44.9	45.6	45.3	44.2
2015	44.0	44.2	44.5	45.0	44.9	45.7	43.1	42.5	44.9	45.4	46.0	45.8	44.7

Employment by Industry: Worcester, MA-CT, 2005–2015

(Numbers in thousands, not seasonally adjusted)

Industry and year	January	February	March	April	May	June	July	August	September	October	November	December	Annual average
Total Nonfarm													
2005	259.9	261.0	261.7	265.4	267.5	268.3	263.4	262.6	267.1	267.5	269.2	269.3	265.2
2006	263.9	263.1	264.9	268.3	270.0	271.4	266.9	267.0	270.5	272.4	272.2	272.5	268.6
2007	265.2	266.2	267.1	269.2	272.2	274.0	266.9	266.8	270.3	273.1	274.4	273.0	269.9
2008	266.1	267.3	267.9	269.4	271.1	271.2	265.6	265.2	269.1	270.7	268.8	267.2	268.3
2009	259.5	259.3	258.5	260.4	261.4	260.4	255.6	255.4	258.7	261.2	260.8	262.4	259.5
2010	255.4	255.4	255.9	259.4	262.7	262.7	258.0	258.1	261.0	264.1	264.6	265.7	260.3
2011	259.3	260.1	261.0	263.9	265.2	264.5	262.3	261.0	266.0	268.2	269.0	269.0	264.1
2012	261.8	262.1	264.4	265.4	266.6	268.7	264.9	264.7	268.5	270.6	271.1	270.4	266.6
2013	264.7	265.5	267.3	270.8	273.1	273.8	267.4	268.6	271.7	273.8	274.9	274.9	270.5
2014	268.4	270.1	271.7	276.1	277.7	277.5	272.9	273.1	277.1	280.5	281.6	281.4	275.7
2015	272.6	273.4	275.3	278.9	281.6	281.8	276.2	276.2	279.0	281.7	281.7	282.3	278.4
Total Private													
2005	220.5	220.9	221.9	225.6	227.4	228.3	227.1	227.2	228.1	227.3	228.8	228.9	226.0
2006	223.7	222.9	224.5	227.6	228.9	230.9	230.0	230.2	230.3	231.3	230.7	231.1	228.5
2007	224.5	224.9	225.8	227.7	230.3	232.4	229.3	229.6	229.5	231.6	232.3	231.0	229.1
2008	225.2	225.7	226.1	227.7	229.1	230.1	227.7	228.0	228.4	228.9	227.0	225.7	227.5
2009	218.5	217.5	216.6	218.4	219.4	218.9	217.4	217.3	217.7	219.2	218.8	219.2	218.2
2010	213.9	213.6	214.0	217.3	219.7	220.7	220.0	220.3	220.0	222.4	222.5	223.4	219.0
2011	218.4	218.5	219.2	222.1	223.2	223.4	224.4	223.8	225.3	226.7	227.5	227.4	223.3
2012	221.2	220.7	222.5	224.0	225.1	227.4	227.0	226.9	227.1	228.7	228.7	227.9	225.6
2013	223.6	223.0	224.7	227.0	229.5	232.1	229.5	230.3	229.5	230.5	231.0	230.7	228.5
2014	226.4	226.2	227.7	231.4	233.4	235.3	234.4	234.5	234.1	236.5	236.7	236.7	232.8
2015	230.6	229.5	230.9	234.2	237.0	238.5	237.6	238.0	236.5	238.1	237.4	238.0	235.5
Goods Producing													
2005	43.9	43.3	43.4	44.5	45.2	45.7	45.6	45.6	45.3	45.1	45.3	45.2	44.8
2006	44.2	43.7	43.6	44.6	45.2	45.9	45.8	45.8	45.2	45.0	44.7	44.6	44.9
2007	43.1	42.4	42.5	43.0	43.8	44.7	44.5	44.4	44.2	44.4	44.4	43.9	43.8
2008	42.6	41.9	41.9	42.3	42.8	43.4	43.0	42.8	42.6	42.5	41.9	41.0	42.4
2009	38.8	37.7	37.0	37.3	37.6	38.0	37.7	37.7	37.6	37.5	37.4	37.1	37.6
2010	35.8	35.2	35.3	36.2	36.7	37.3	37.1	37.2	37.0	37.3	37.3	37.1	36.6
2011	35.7	35.2	35.3	36.2	37.0	37.6	38.4	38.4	38.3	38.3	38.2	38.0	37.2
2012	36.0	35.6	35.9	36.4	36.5	37.0	37.1	36.9	36.9	36.9	36.6	35.9	36.5
2013	35.0	34.8	35.0	35.5	36.2	36.9	37.1	37.1	36.9	36.6	36.4	36.1	36.1
2014	35.4	35.1	35.2	35.9	36.5	37.1	37.5	37.4	37.2	37.7	37.6	37.1	36.6
2015	36.3	35.8	36.0	36.9	37.7	38.2	38.3	38.2	37.8	38.1	37.7	38.1	37.4
Service-Providing													
2005	216.0	217.7	218.3	220.9	222.3	222.6	217.8	217.0	221.8	222.4	223.9	224.1	220.4
2006	219.7	219.4	221.3	223.7	224.8	225.5	221.1	221.2	225.3	227.4	227.5	227.9	223.7
2007	222.1	223.8	224.6	226.2	228.4	229.3	222.4	222.4	226.1	228.7	230.0	229.1	226.1
2008	223.5	225.4	226.0	227.1	228.3	227.8	222.6	222.4	226.5	228.2	226.9	226.2	225.9
2009	220.7	221.6	221.5	223.1	223.8	222.4	217.9	217.7	221.1	223.7	223.4	225.3	221.9
2010	219.6	220.2	220.6	223.2	226.0	225.4	220.9	220.9	224.0	226.8	227.3	228.6	223.6
2011	223.6	224.9	225.7	227.7	228.2	226.9	223.9	222.6	227.7	229.9	230.8	231.0	226.9
2012	225.8	226.5	228.5	229.0	230.1	231.7	227.8	227.8	231.6	233.7	234.5	234.5	230.1
2013	229.7	230.7	232.3	235.3	236.9	236.9	230.3	231.5	234.8	237.2	238.5	238.8	234.4
2014	233.0	235.0	236.5	240.2	241.2	240.4	235.4	235.7	239.9	242.8	244.0	244.3	239.0
2015	236.3	237.6	239.3	242.0	243.9	243.6	237.9	238.0	241.2	243.6	244.0	244.2	241.0
Mining, Logging, and Construction													
2005	10.0	9.6	9.7	10.8	11.5	11.8	12.4	12.4	12.2	11.9	12.0	11.6	11.3
2006	10.7	10.4	10.5	11.4	11.9	12.2	12.5	12.5	12.2	12.0	11.5	11.1	11.6
2007	9.9	9.4	9.5	10.1	10.9	11.4	11.6	11.6	11.5	11.3	11.2	10.6	10.8
2008	9.5	9.2	9.4	9.9	10.4	10.8	10.8	10.9	10.7	10.5	10.2	9.5	10.2
2009	8.3	7.9	7.7	8.4	8.8	9.1	9.2	9.3	9.2	9.1	8.9	8.5	8.7
2010	7.5	7.1	7.2	7.9	8.3	8.7	8.9	8.9	8.7	8.9	8.8	8.5	8.3
2011	7.5	7.1	7.1	8.0	8.6	9.0	9.5	9.6	9.5	9.5	9.4	9.0	8.7
2012	8.2	7.8	8.1	8.7	8.9	9.2	9.5	9.5	9.4	9.3	9.2	8.9	8.9
2013	8.2	8.0	8.1	8.7	9.3	9.8	10.0	10.0	9.8	9.6	9.4	9.0	9.2
2014	8.3	8.1	8.2	8.9	9.5	10.0	10.3	10.3	10.2	10.3	10.2	9.7	9.5
2015	8.9	8.5	8.6	9.3	10.1	10.4	10.6	10.5	10.2	10.5	10.2	10.4	9.9

Employment by Industry: Worcester, MA-CT, 2005–2015—*Continued*

(Numbers in thousands, not seasonally adjusted)

Industry and year	January	February	March	April	May	June	July	August	September	October	November	December	Annual average
Manufacturing													
2005	33.9	33.7	33.7	33.7	33.7	33.9	33.2	33.2	33.1	33.2	33.3	33.6	33.5
2006	33.5	33.3	33.1	33.2	33.3	33.7	33.3	33.3	33.0	33.0	33.2	33.5	33.3
2007	33.2	33.0	33.0	32.9	32.9	33.3	32.9	32.8	32.7	33.1	33.2	33.3	33.0
2008	33.1	32.7	32.5	32.4	32.4	32.6	32.2	31.9	31.9	32.0	31.7	31.5	32.2
2009	30.5	29.8	29.3	28.9	28.8	28.9	28.5	28.4	28.4	28.4	28.5	28.6	28.9
2010	28.3	28.1	28.1	28.3	28.4	28.6	28.2	28.3	28.3	28.4	28.5	28.6	28.3
2011	28.2	28.1	28.2	28.2	28.4	28.6	28.9	28.8	28.8	28.8	28.8	29.0	28.6
2012	27.8	27.8	27.8	27.7	27.6	27.8	27.6	27.4	27.5	27.6	27.4	27.0	27.6
2013	26.8	26.8	26.9	26.8	26.9	27.1	27.1	27.1	27.1	27.0	27.0	27.1	27.0
2014	27.1	27.0	27.0	27.0	27.0	27.1	27.2	27.1	27.0	27.4	27.4	27.4	27.1
2015	27.4	27.3	27.4	27.6	27.6	27.8	27.7	27.7	27.6	27.6	27.5	27.7	27.6
Trade, Transportation, and Utilities													
2005	49.8	49.3	49.6	50.0	50.4	50.6	49.9	50.1	50.3	50.4	51.3	51.7	50.3
2006	50.3	49.5	49.9	50.1	50.5	50.5	50.2	50.5	51.1	51.4	51.9	52.3	50.7
2007	50.9	50.4	50.8	50.8	51.3	51.8	50.8	50.5	50.8	51.7	52.6	52.8	51.3
2008	51.5	50.5	50.8	50.8	51.1	51.2	50.4	50.4	50.8	51.3	51.4	51.6	51.0
2009	49.2	48.2	48.1	48.1	48.4	48.7	47.5	47.3	47.6	48.2	48.7	49.2	48.3
2010	47.9	47.3	47.9	48.7	49.4	49.8	49.0	49.0	49.0	49.7	50.4	51.1	49.1
2011	49.3	48.7	48.8	49.1	49.4	49.4	48.8	48.8	49.5	50.5	51.2	51.9	49.6
2012	50.0	49.3	49.5	49.9	50.4	50.7	50.2	50.3	50.9	51.5	52.2	52.2	50.6
2013	50.5	49.9	50.2	51.0	51.8	52.5	51.4	51.5	51.8	52.3	53.4	53.8	51.7
2014	52.2	51.6	51.8	52.4	52.9	53.2	52.8	52.6	53.1	53.5	54.4	55.2	53.0
2015	52.3	51.4	51.7	52.2	52.6	53.1	52.4	52.6	52.6	53.0	53.9	54.0	52.7
Wholesale Trade													
2005	10.2	10.1	10.3	10.5	10.5	10.6	10.5	10.7	10.6	10.7	10.8	10.8	10.5
2006	10.6	10.7	10.8	10.8	10.8	10.8	10.9	11.0	11.0	11.0	11.0	11.0	10.9
2007	10.8	10.8	10.9	10.9	11.0	11.0	11.0	11.0	10.9	11.3	11.4	11.3	11.0
2008	11.3	11.3	11.5	11.5	11.7	11.7	11.7	11.8	11.7	11.9	11.8	11.8	11.6
2009	11.2	11.0	11.0	11.1	11.0	10.9	10.9	10.8	10.7	10.7	10.6	10.5	10.9
2010	10.4	10.3	10.4	10.4	10.4	10.4	10.2	10.1	9.9	10.2	10.1	10.0	10.2
2011	9.8	9.6	9.6	9.8	9.9	9.9	9.8	9.8	9.8	9.9	9.9	9.9	9.8
2012	9.9	9.9	9.9	10.1	10.1	10.2	10.3	10.3	10.3	10.5	10.5	10.3	10.2
2013	10.2	10.2	10.3	10.3	10.4	10.5	10.5	10.5	10.5	10.6	10.6	10.6	10.4
2014	10.5	10.4	10.4	10.6	10.7	10.7	10.8	10.7	10.6	10.6	10.6	10.6	10.6
2015	10.4	10.3	10.4	10.5	10.5	10.5	10.5	10.5	10.4	10.5	10.4	10.4	10.4
Retail Trade													
2005	30.6	30.0	29.9	30.1	30.4	30.4	30.1	30.2	29.9	30.0	30.6	30.8	30.3
2006	30.0	29.2	29.4	29.5	29.5	29.7	29.7	30.0	29.9	30.1	30.6	30.9	29.9
2007	29.9	29.3	29.6	29.6	29.9	30.3	29.9	29.7	29.5	30.1	30.7	30.9	30.0
2008	29.8	28.9	29.0	29.0	29.2	29.4	29.3	29.3	29.1	29.4	29.7	29.8	29.3
2009	28.5	27.8	27.7	27.7	27.9	28.3	27.7	27.7	27.5	27.9	28.4	28.9	28.0
2010	28.0	27.5	28.0	28.5	28.8	29.1	28.9	29.0	28.5	28.9	29.5	30.0	28.7
2011	29.0	28.5	28.5	28.8	28.9	29.0	28.9	28.9	29.1	29.8	30.4	30.9	29.2
2012	29.6	28.9	29.0	29.1	29.5	29.7	29.6	29.7	29.7	30.0	30.7	30.7	29.7
2013	29.5	28.9	29.0	29.6	30.2	30.5	30.0	30.1	29.9	30.3	31.1	31.3	30.0
2014	30.4	29.7	29.8	30.2	30.4	30.5	30.4	30.3	30.4	30.7	31.3	31.5	30.5
2015	30.2	29.4	29.5	29.9	30.3	30.6	30.3	30.5	30.0	30.3	31.0	30.7	30.2
Transportation and Utilities													
2005	9.0	9.2	9.4	9.4	9.5	9.6	9.3	9.2	9.8	9.7	9.9	10.1	9.5
2006	9.7	9.6	9.7	9.8	9.8	10.0	9.6	9.5	10.2	10.3	10.3	10.4	9.9
2007	10.2	10.3	10.3	10.3	10.4	10.5	9.9	9.8	10.4	10.3	10.5	10.6	10.3
2008	10.4	10.3	10.3	10.3	10.2	10.1	9.4	9.3	10.0	10.0	9.9	10.0	10.0
2009	9.5	9.4	9.4	9.3	9.5	9.5	8.9	8.8	9.4	9.6	9.7	9.8	9.4
2010	9.5	9.5	9.5	9.8	10.2	10.3	9.9	9.9	10.6	10.6	10.8	11.1	10.1
2011	10.5	10.6	10.7	10.5	10.6	10.5	10.1	10.1	10.6	10.8	10.9	11.1	10.6
2012	10.5	10.5	10.6	10.7	10.8	10.8	10.3	10.3	10.9	11.0	11.0	11.2	10.7
2013	10.8	10.8	10.9	11.1	11.2	11.5	10.9	10.9	11.4	11.4	11.7	11.9	11.2
2014	11.3	11.5	11.6	11.6	11.8	12.0	11.6	11.6	12.1	12.2	12.5	13.1	11.9
2015	11.7	11.7	11.8	11.8	11.8	12.0	11.6	11.6	12.2	12.2	12.5	12.9	12.0

Employment by Industry: Worcester, MA-CT, 2005–2015—*Continued*

(Numbers in thousands, not seasonally adjusted)

Industry and year	January	February	March	April	May	June	July	August	September	October	November	December	Annual average
Information													
2005	4.0	4.0	4.0	3.8	3.8	3.7	3.7	3.7	3.7	3.7	3.7	3.7	3.8
2006	3.7	3.7	3.7	3.7	3.7	3.8	3.8	3.8	3.8	3.8	3.8	3.8	3.8
2007	4.0	4.0	4.0	4.0	4.1	4.1	4.1	4.1	4.0	4.1	4.1	4.0	4.1
2008	4.1	4.1	4.1	4.2	4.2	4.2	4.1	4.1	4.0	3.7	3.7	3.7	4.0
2009	3.6	3.5	3.5	3.5	3.5	3.5	3.5	3.5	3.4	3.4	3.4	3.4	3.5
2010	3.4	3.6	3.6	3.6	3.6	3.7	3.6	3.6	3.5	3.5	3.6	3.6	3.6
2011	3.6	3.6	3.6	3.5	3.6	3.6	3.6	3.4	3.6	3.6	3.6	3.6	3.6
2012	3.6	3.6	3.6	3.6	3.6	3.7	3.7	3.7	3.6	3.6	3.6	3.6	3.6
2013	3.6	3.6	3.6	3.6	3.6	3.7	3.6	3.6	3.5	3.4	3.6	3.6	3.6
2014	3.6	3.5	3.5	3.4	3.5	3.6	3.6	3.6	3.5	3.5	3.5	3.5	3.5
2015	3.5	3.5	3.5	3.5	3.5	3.6	3.6	3.6	3.5	3.5	3.5	3.5	3.5
Financial Activities													
2005	15.0	15.0	15.1	15.2	15.2	15.4	15.5	15.5	15.4	15.3	15.4	15.5	15.3
2006	15.4	15.4	15.4	15.6	15.6	15.7	15.6	15.5	15.3	15.4	15.3	15.3	15.5
2007	15.2	15.1	15.1	15.1	15.0	15.0	15.1	15.1	14.9	14.9	14.9	14.9	15.0
2008	14.7	14.8	14.7	14.8	14.8	14.9	15.0	14.9	14.8	14.7	14.8	14.7	14.8
2009	14.8	14.8	14.8	14.7	14.7	14.9	14.8	14.8	14.7	14.7	14.7	14.7	14.8
2010	14.6	14.6	14.6	14.6	14.6	14.7	14.7	14.7	14.6	14.9	14.8	14.9	14.7
2011	14.7	14.7	14.7	14.7	14.7	14.7	14.9	14.9	15.0	15.0	15.0	15.0	14.8
2012	15.0	15.0	14.9	15.0	15.1	15.1	15.2	15.2	15.0	15.1	15.0	15.1	15.1
2013	15.0	15.0	15.0	15.0	15.0	15.2	15.1	15.2	15.0	15.0	15.1	15.0	15.1
2014	15.0	15.0	15.0	15.1	15.3	15.4	15.5	15.5	15.3	15.3	15.3	15.3	15.3
2015	15.1	15.1	15.1	15.3	15.3	15.4	15.6	15.6	15.3	15.0	15.1	15.5	15.3
Professional and Business Services													
2005	28.5	28.7	29.1	30.0	30.4	30.6	30.5	30.6	30.9	30.7	31.0	30.8	30.2
2006	29.6	29.3	29.9	30.3	30.8	31.1	31.4	31.5	31.0	31.1	30.7	30.5	30.6
2007	28.9	28.9	28.9	29.8	30.2	30.6	29.7	29.7	29.3	29.4	29.5	29.4	29.5
2008	27.9	28.0	27.9	28.4	28.6	28.9	28.6	28.8	28.6	28.3	28.0	27.9	28.3
2009	26.9	26.5	26.3	26.4	26.4	26.0	25.9	26.0	25.8	26.2	26.0	25.8	26.2
2010	25.3	24.9	25.2	25.7	26.1	26.4	26.5	26.5	26.3	26.4	26.1	26.6	26.0
2011	26.9	27.0	26.7	27.9	27.6	27.6	27.7	27.4	27.3	27.2	27.9	26.9	27.3
2012	25.8	25.5	25.9	26.2	26.0	26.6	26.4	26.6	26.0	26.3	26.3	26.0	26.1
2013	25.3	25.4	25.6	26.2	26.4	26.6	26.3	26.5	26.1	26.2	26.0	25.6	26.0
2014	25.5	25.6	25.6	26.6	26.7	27.0	26.5	26.7	26.6	26.7	26.7	26.4	26.4
2015	26.1	26.1	25.8	26.4	26.5	26.8	27.0	27.2	27.1	26.3	26.2	26.1	26.5
Education and Health Services													
2005	48.3	49.5	49.4	49.7	49.4	49.0	48.3	48.4	49.7	50.2	50.6	50.2	49.4
2006	49.4	50.5	50.7	51.0	50.6	49.8	49.4	49.2	50.8	52.0	52.0	52.0	50.6
2007	50.7	52.3	52.4	52.7	52.5	51.7	51.2	51.6	53.3	54.3	54.4	54.2	52.6
2008	53.0	54.9	55.0	54.9	54.2	53.7	53.3	53.5	55.1	56.2	56.2	56.1	54.7
2009	55.4	56.7	56.7	57.1	56.4	55.3	55.6	55.9	57.1	57.9	58.3	58.4	56.7
2010	57.3	58.6	58.4	58.2	57.8	56.8	56.9	57.1	58.6	59.4	59.8	59.7	58.2
2011	58.5	59.5	59.9	59.4	59.0	57.9	58.4	58.4	59.8	60.4	60.6	60.7	59.4
2012	60.0	61.0	61.6	61.4	61.1	60.6	60.7	60.6	61.9	62.7	63.0	63.0	61.5
2013	62.3	62.9	63.4	62.7	62.6	62.1	61.3	61.5	62.2	62.9	63.1	63.4	62.5
2014	61.9	62.9	63.6	64.1	63.8	63.2	62.8	62.9	63.8	64.8	65.0	65.0	63.7
2015	63.6	64.5	65.0	65.4	65.7	65.0	64.3	64.2	65.3	66.8	66.8	67.1	65.3
Leisure and Hospitality													
2005	21.5	21.5	21.7	22.7	23.4	23.6	23.5	23.3	23.0	22.2	21.8	22.0	22.5
2006	21.4	21.2	21.6	22.6	23.2	24.2	23.8	23.9	23.4	23.1	22.7	22.9	22.8
2007	22.1	22.2	22.5	22.7	23.7	24.5	23.8	24.1	23.3	23.2	22.7	22.2	23.1
2008	21.9	22.0	22.1	22.9	23.9	24.3	23.7	24.1	23.4	23.1	22.0	21.8	22.9
2009	21.1	21.3	21.4	22.3	23.4	23.4	23.2	23.0	22.8	22.7	21.8	22.0	22.4
2010	21.2	20.9	20.6	21.7	22.8	23.1	23.0	23.1	22.4	22.6	21.8	21.8	22.1
2011	21.2	21.2	21.4	22.4	23.0	23.5	23.4	23.4	23.0	22.9	22.2	22.4	22.5
2012	22.0	21.9	22.3	22.5	23.3	24.3	24.1	24.0	23.5	23.1	22.4	22.4	23.0
2013	22.2	21.9	22.2	23.1	23.9	24.7	24.0	24.3	23.9	24.0	23.3	23.0	23.4
2014	22.8	22.5	22.9	23.6	24.3	25.1	24.8	24.9	24.3	24.7	23.9	23.8	24.0
2015	23.4	23.0	23.5	24.1	25.2	25.5	25.2	25.4	24.4	24.8	23.7	23.1	24.3

Employment by Industry: Worcester, MA-CT, 2005–2015—*Continued*

(Numbers in thousands, not seasonally adjusted)

Industry and year	January	February	March	April	May	June	July	August	September	October	November	December	Annual average
Other Services													
2005	9.5	9.6	9.6	9.7	9.6	9.7	10.1	10.0	9.8	9.7	9.7	9.8	9.7
2006	9.7	9.6	9.7	9.7	9.7	9.9	10.0	10.0	9.7	9.5	9.6	9.7	9.7
2007	9.6	9.6	9.6	9.6	9.7	10.0	10.1	10.1	9.7	9.6	9.7	9.6	9.7
2008	9.5	9.5	9.6	9.4	9.5	9.5	9.6	9.4	9.1	9.1	9.0	8.9	9.3
2009	8.7	8.8	8.8	9.0	9.0	9.1	9.2	9.1	8.7	8.6	8.5	8.6	8.8
2010	8.4	8.5	8.4	8.6	8.7	8.9	9.2	9.1	8.6	8.6	8.7	8.6	8.7
2011	8.5	8.6	8.8	8.9	8.9	9.1	9.2	9.1	8.8	8.8	8.8	8.9	8.9
2012	8.8	8.8	8.8	9.0	9.1	9.4	9.6	9.6	9.3	9.5	9.6	9.7	9.3
2013	9.7	9.5	9.7	9.9	10.0	10.4	10.7	10.6	10.1	10.1	10.1	10.2	10.1
2014	10.0	10.0	10.1	10.3	10.4	10.7	10.9	10.9	10.3	10.3	10.3	10.4	10.4
2015	10.3	10.1	10.3	10.4	10.5	10.9	11.2	11.2	10.5	10.6	10.5	10.6	10.6
Government													
2005	39.4	40.1	39.8	39.8	40.1	40.0	36.3	35.4	39.0	40.2	40.4	40.4	39.2
2006	40.2	40.2	40.4	40.7	41.1	40.5	36.9	36.8	40.2	41.1	41.5	41.4	40.1
2007	40.7	41.3	41.3	41.5	41.9	41.6	37.6	37.2	40.8	41.5	42.1	42.0	40.8
2008	40.9	41.6	41.8	41.7	42.0	41.1	37.9	37.2	40.7	41.8	41.8	41.5	40.8
2009	41.0	41.8	41.9	42.0	42.0	41.5	38.2	38.1	41.0	42.0	42.0	43.2	41.2
2010	41.5	41.8	41.9	42.1	43.0	42.0	38.0	37.8	41.0	41.7	42.1	42.3	41.3
2011	40.9	41.6	41.8	41.8	42.0	41.1	37.9	37.2	40.7	41.5	41.5	41.6	40.8
2012	40.6	41.4	41.9	41.4	41.5	41.3	37.9	37.8	41.4	41.9	42.4	42.5	41.0
2013	41.1	42.5	42.6	43.8	43.6	41.7	37.9	38.3	42.2	43.3	43.9	44.2	42.1
2014	42.0	43.9	44.0	44.7	44.3	42.2	38.5	38.6	43.0	44.0	44.9	44.7	42.9
2015	42.0	43.9	44.4	44.7	44.6	43.3	38.6	38.2	42.5	43.6	44.3	44.3	42.9

Employment by Industry: Omaha-Council Bluffs, NE-IA, 2005–2015

(Numbers in thousands, not seasonally adjusted)

Industry and year	January	February	March	April	May	June	July	August	September	October	November	December	Annual average
Total Nonfarm													
2005	438.4	439.2	442.9	448.2	451.4	455.0	450.9	451.3	452.5	453.9	457.4	457.3	449.9
2006	445.9	448.0	451.7	455.4	460.3	463.8	458.4	458.8	461.5	462.0	465.0	464.5	457.9
2007	452.9	453.7	456.2	461.8	466.8	469.7	464.3	467.0	468.1	470.7	473.4	472.5	464.8
2008	462.5	462.9	465.3	470.2	476.0	475.7	470.5	472.5	472.3	475.5	475.3	472.7	471.0
2009	458.9	457.7	457.9	461.5	464.9	464.1	461.8	461.4	459.6	461.2	462.2	459.0	460.9
2010	448.0	447.5	451.1	458.6	463.4	464.7	461.0	462.0	458.7	464.4	465.0	464.9	459.1
2011	453.3	453.9	455.9	463.9	467.4	467.8	464.8	465.8	464.5	467.6	469.8	469.3	463.7
2012	459.6	459.7	463.5	468.7	473.2	472.6	471.3	471.2	470.2	474.0	476.7	475.9	469.7
2013	465.7	466.2	468.3	473.9	480.3	480.6	478.6	480.4	480.0	483.4	486.1	485.6	477.4
2014	474.7	476.3	478.4	482.8	487.9	487.3	484.2	486.2	485.5	489.3	491.1	492.2	484.7
2015	480.0	481.2	484.4	490.9	494.8	495.9	493.0	493.9	492.0	497.5	498.3	497.3	491.6
Total Private													
2005	378.8	379.1	382.9	388.1	390.7	394.5	393.5	394.2	392.9	392.8	396.1	396.4	390.0
2006	385.2	387.0	390.7	393.8	398.3	402.1	400.8	401.1	400.7	400.3	403.1	403.2	397.2
2007	391.7	392.1	394.7	399.6	404.2	407.7	407.6	409.3	407.2	408.3	411.0	410.9	403.7
2008	400.8	400.9	403.6	407.2	412.6	413.8	412.4	413.4	410.3	411.4	411.0	409.2	408.9
2009	395.4	393.8	394.1	396.3	399.0	399.9	398.5	398.6	395.5	395.5	396.4	394.5	396.5
2010	383.5	382.7	385.3	392.1	396.1	398.2	398.4	399.0	395.0	398.0	398.6	399.2	393.8
2011	387.9	387.9	390.5	397.1	400.4	402.6	401.7	402.0	399.9	401.1	403.1	403.4	398.1
2012	393.8	393.5	397.8	402.7	406.7	405.9	408.7	408.1	405.9	408.2	410.8	410.9	404.7
2013	400.9	400.8	403.2	408.2	413.9	415.8	415.5	417.0	415.6	417.7	420.2	420.6	412.5
2014	409.4	410.3	412.9	416.7	421.1	422.9	421.2	422.4	420.1	422.5	424.3	426.2	419.2
2015	414.3	415.1	418.6	423.8	427.5	430.4	429.3	429.7	427.0	430.8	431.5	431.2	425.8
Goods Producing													
2005	56.0	55.6	57.1	58.5	58.7	60.0	60.3	60.1	59.6	59.4	59.2	58.2	58.6
2006	56.4	56.8	57.7	59.2	60.2	61.4	61.6	61.6	61.7	61.1	60.2	59.2	59.8
2007	56.6	55.7	56.2	57.6	58.7	59.8	60.2	60.6	59.9	60.5	60.2	59.1	58.8
2008	57.5	57.3	57.9	59.4	60.6	61.2	60.9	60.9	60.4	60.2	59.4	58.1	59.5
2009	55.0	54.5	54.5	55.8	56.2	56.6	56.5	56.3	55.7	55.0	54.7	53.1	55.3
2010	50.4	49.9	50.4	52.4	52.9	53.3	53.5	53.2	52.5	52.3	52.2	51.3	52.0
2011	49.0	49.0	49.8	51.0	51.6	52.6	52.7	52.4	51.8	52.1	52.1	52.0	51.3
2012	49.9	49.5	50.6	51.7	52.5	53.3	53.6	53.5	53.4	53.6	53.7	53.5	52.4
2013	51.6	52.0	52.4	54.0	55.4	56.0	56.9	56.9	56.7	56.5	56.3	55.0	55.0
2014	53.3	53.4	53.9	56.2	56.9	57.9	58.3	58.5	58.3	58.4	58.1	57.8	56.8
2015	55.8	56.0	56.9	58.5	58.9	59.3	59.4	59.2	58.9	59.7	59.1	57.1	58.2
Service-Providing													
2005	382.4	383.6	385.8	389.7	392.7	395.0	390.6	391.2	392.9	394.5	398.2	399.1	391.3
2006	389.5	391.2	394.0	396.2	400.1	402.4	396.8	397.2	399.8	400.9	404.8	405.3	398.2
2007	396.3	398.0	400.0	404.2	408.1	409.9	404.1	406.4	408.2	410.2	413.2	413.4	406.0
2008	405.0	405.6	407.4	410.8	415.4	414.5	409.6	411.6	411.9	415.3	415.9	414.6	411.5
2009	403.9	403.2	403.4	405.7	408.7	407.5	405.3	405.1	403.9	406.2	407.5	405.9	405.5
2010	397.6	397.6	400.7	406.2	410.5	411.4	407.5	408.8	406.2	412.1	412.8	413.6	407.1
2011	404.3	404.9	406.1	412.9	415.8	415.2	412.1	413.4	412.7	415.5	417.7	417.3	412.3
2012	409.7	410.2	412.9	417.0	420.7	419.3	417.7	417.7	416.8	420.4	423.0	422.4	417.3
2013	414.1	414.2	415.9	419.9	424.9	424.6	421.7	423.5	423.3	426.9	429.8	430.6	422.5
2014	421.4	422.9	424.5	426.6	431.0	429.4	425.9	427.7	427.2	430.9	433.0	434.4	427.9
2015	424.2	425.2	427.5	432.4	435.9	436.6	433.6	434.7	433.1	437.8	439.2	440.2	433.4
Mining, Logging, and Construction													
2005	23.1	23.0	24.3	25.5	25.9	27.0	27.2	27.3	26.8	26.7	26.4	25.3	25.7
2006	24.1	24.4	25.2	26.4	27.3	28.3	28.4	28.5	28.7	27.8	26.8	25.8	26.8
2007	23.7	22.7	23.1	24.4	25.3	26.2	26.3	26.6	26.1	26.5	26.2	25.2	25.2
2008	23.6	23.4	24.0	25.5	26.5	27.0	27.0	27.1	26.8	26.5	25.9	25.1	25.7
2009	22.6	22.4	22.8	24.4	24.8	25.2	25.3	25.1	24.5	23.8	23.3	21.8	23.8
2010	19.4	19.0	19.4	21.4	21.7	22.0	22.1	22.0	21.4	21.1	21.0	20.0	20.9
2011	18.2	18.0	18.7	19.7	20.3	21.2	21.3	21.3	21.0	21.0	20.8	20.1	20.1
2012	19.0	18.6	19.5	20.6	21.3	21.8	22.0	22.1	22.0	22.0	22.2	21.9	21.1
2013	20.3	20.4	20.8	22.2	23.2	23.6	24.3	24.3	24.1	24.0	23.6	22.4	22.8
2014	21.1	21.0	21.6	23.7	24.4	25.3	25.5	25.8	25.7	25.8	25.4	25.0	24.2
2015	23.4	23.5	24.4	26.0	26.3	26.5	26.6	26.5	26.3	26.8	26.1	24.4	25.6

Employment by Industry: Omaha-Council Bluffs, NE-IA, 2005-2015—*Continued*

(Numbers in thousands, not seasonally adjusted)

Industry and year	January	February	March	April	May	June	July	August	September	October	November	December	Annual average
Manufacturing													
2005...............	32.9	32.6	32.8	33.0	32.8	33.0	33.1	32.8	32.8	32.7	32.8	32.9	32.9
2006...............	32.3	32.4	32.5	32.8	32.9	33.1	33.2	33.1	33.0	33.3	33.4	33.4	33.0
2007...............	32.9	33.0	33.1	33.2	33.4	33.6	33.9	34.0	33.8	34.0	34.0	33.9	33.6
2008...............	33.9	33.9	33.9	33.9	34.1	34.2	33.9	33.8	33.6	33.7	33.5	33.0	33.8
2009...............	32.4	32.1	31.7	31.4	31.4	31.4	31.2	31.2	31.2	31.2	31.4	31.3	31.5
2010...............	31.0	30.9	31.0	31.0	31.2	31.3	31.4	31.2	31.1	31.2	31.2	31.3	31.2
2011...............	30.8	31.0	31.1	31.3	31.3	31.4	31.4	31.1	30.8	31.1	31.3	31.9	31.2
2012...............	30.9	30.9	31.1	31.1	31.2	31.5	31.6	31.4	31.4	31.2	31.5	31.6	31.3
2013...............	31.3	31.6	31.6	31.8	32.2	32.4	32.6	32.6	32.6	32.5	32.7	32.6	32.2
2014...............	32.2	32.4	32.3	32.5	32.5	32.6	32.8	32.7	32.6	32.6	32.7	32.8	32.6
2015...............	32.4	32.5	32.5	32.5	32.6	32.8	32.8	32.7	32.6	32.9	33.0	32.7	32.7
Trade, Transportation, and Utilities													
2005...............	98.2	97.9	98.3	98.2	99.5	99.5	98.9	99.3	99.4	99.9	101.9	102.8	99.5
2006...............	97.0	96.6	97.4	97.4	98.5	98.7	98.6	98.9	99.1	100.0	102.7	103.7	99.1
2007...............	98.6	98.1	98.7	99.2	100.0	100.1	99.8	100.3	100.4	100.6	103.2	103.9	100.2
2008...............	99.4	98.5	99.0	98.7	99.9	99.6	99.0	99.4	98.9	100.1	101.8	102.6	99.7
2009...............	96.7	95.3	95.1	94.3	95.1	94.6	94.0	94.3	94.0	94.9	96.6	97.1	95.2
2010...............	92.1	91.4	92.0	93.0	94.2	93.9	93.4	93.5	92.9	94.3	96.4	98.1	93.8
2011...............	92.7	92.0	92.4	93.1	93.7	93.3	93.0	93.5	93.6	93.9	96.6	97.5	93.8
2012...............	92.9	91.8	92.4	93.0	94.0	94.2	93.5	93.3	93.4	94.6	97.5	98.6	94.1
2013...............	93.8	92.5	92.9	93.1	94.4	94.7	94.4	95.1	95.0	95.9	99.0	100.9	95.1
2014...............	95.9	95.0	95.2	95.6	96.3	96.3	95.7	96.6	96.1	97.1	99.9	102.1	96.8
2015...............	95.8	95.2	95.6	96.5	97.3	98.0	97.4	97.8	97.3	98.5	100.1	101.2	97.6
Wholesale Trade													
2005...............	18.7	18.7	18.9	18.7	18.7	18.7	18.8	18.6	18.4	18.5	18.4	18.4	18.6
2006...............	18.1	18.2	18.3	18.2	18.3	18.3	18.4	18.2	18.1	18.1	18.1	18.2	18.2
2007...............	17.7	17.7	17.8	18.0	18.0	18.3	18.3	18.3	18.4	18.4	18.5	18.6	18.2
2008...............	18.4	18.4	18.5	18.4	18.6	18.6	18.6	18.5	18.4	18.4	18.4	18.3	18.5
2009...............	18.0	17.9	17.8	17.9	17.9	18.0	18.0	17.9	17.8	17.9	17.9	17.9	17.9
2010...............	17.5	17.5	17.5	17.6	17.7	17.7	17.6	17.4	17.2	17.3	17.3	17.2	17.5
2011...............	17.0	17.0	17.0	17.0	17.1	17.1	17.1	17.0	17.2	17.1	17.2	17.1	17.1
2012...............	16.7	16.7	16.8	16.9	16.9	17.0	16.9	16.8	16.7	16.8	16.9	16.8	16.8
2013...............	16.6	16.6	16.7	16.8	17.0	17.1	17.0	16.9	16.8	16.9	17.0	17.1	16.9
2014...............	16.9	16.9	17.0	17.1	17.1	17.2	17.2	17.1	17.0	16.9	17.0	17.0	17.0
2015...............	16.4	16.4	16.5	16.7	16.8	16.9	16.8	16.7	16.6	16.5	16.6	16.5	16.6
Retail Trade													
2005...............	50.8	50.1	50.2	50.6	51.2	51.0	50.8	51.0	50.9	51.8	53.6	54.4	51.4
2006...............	50.5	49.6	50.1	50.3	50.8	50.9	50.7	50.7	50.7	51.7	54.0	54.8	51.2
2007...............	50.9	50.2	50.6	51.1	51.9	51.9	51.7	51.7	51.5	52.4	54.5	55.3	52.0
2008...............	52.1	51.1	51.2	50.9	51.3	51.2	50.8	50.7	50.2	51.0	52.6	53.6	51.4
2009...............	50.1	49.1	49.0	49.1	49.9	49.8	49.5	49.5	49.2	50.0	51.5	51.6	49.9
2010...............	48.9	48.3	48.7	49.3	50.1	50.2	49.6	49.6	49.1	50.2	51.8	52.7	49.9
2011...............	49.3	48.7	49.0	49.6	50.1	49.9	49.7	49.9	49.6	50.3	52.7	53.4	50.2
2012...............	50.0	49.0	49.4	49.8	50.5	50.6	50.2	50.0	49.9	51.1	53.3	53.8	50.6
2013...............	50.2	49.4	49.7	50.1	50.7	50.9	51.0	51.0	51.0	52.0	54.6	55.5	51.3
2014...............	52.3	51.5	51.5	52.1	52.5	52.7	52.5	52.8	52.4	53.3	55.2	56.0	52.9
2015...............	52.7	52.3	52.5	52.9	53.3	53.9	53.5	53.6	53.2	54.4	55.5	55.7	53.6
Transportation and Utilities													
2005...............	28.7	29.1	29.2	28.9	29.6	29.8	29.3	29.7	30.1	29.6	29.9	30.0	29.5
2006...............	28.4	28.8	29.0	28.9	29.4	29.5	29.5	30.0	30.3	30.2	30.6	30.7	29.6
2007...............	30.0	30.2	30.2	30.1	30.1	29.9	29.8	30.3	30.5	29.8	30.2	30.0	30.1
2008...............	28.9	29.0	29.3	29.4	30.0	29.8	29.6	30.2	30.3	30.7	30.8	30.7	29.9
2009...............	28.6	28.3	28.3	27.3	27.3	26.8	26.5	26.9	27.0	27.0	27.2	27.6	27.4
2010...............	25.7	25.6	25.8	26.1	26.4	26.0	26.2	26.5	26.6	26.8	27.3	28.2	26.4
2011...............	26.4	26.3	26.4	26.5	26.5	26.3	26.2	26.6	26.8	26.5	26.7	27.0	26.5
2012...............	26.2	26.1	26.2	26.3	26.6	26.6	26.4	26.5	26.8	26.7	27.3	28.0	26.6
2013...............	27.0	26.5	26.5	26.2	26.7	26.7	26.4	27.2	27.2	27.0	27.4	28.3	26.9
2014...............	26.7	26.6	26.7	26.4	26.7	26.4	26.0	26.7	26.7	26.9	27.7	29.1	26.9
2015...............	26.7	26.5	26.6	26.9	27.2	27.2	27.1	27.5	27.5	27.6	28.0	29.0	27.3

Employment by Industry: Omaha-Council Bluffs, NE-IA, 2005–2015—*Continued*

(Numbers in thousands, not seasonally adjusted)

Industry and year	January	February	March	April	May	June	July	August	September	October	November	December	Annual average
Information													
2005	13.3	13.3	13.3	13.2	13.1	13.3	13.3	13.4	13.2	13.3	13.4	13.4	13.3
2006	13.1	13.0	13.0	13.0	13.1	13.1	13.0	12.8	12.7	12.5	12.6	12.6	12.9
2007	12.3	12.4	12.4	12.5	12.6	12.7	12.7	12.7	12.6	12.6	12.6	12.6	12.6
2008	12.3	12.3	12.3	12.4	12.4	12.3	12.3	12.1	12.0	12.0	12.0	11.9	12.2
2009	11.6	11.6	11.6	11.5	11.4	11.5	11.5	11.5	11.4	11.3	11.5	11.5	11.5
2010	11.3	11.3	11.2	11.2	11.3	11.3	11.2	11.2	11.1	11.1	11.1	11.2	11.2
2011	11.2	11.2	11.1	11.1	11.1	11.2	11.4	11.4	11.3	11.3	11.4	11.4	11.3
2012	11.3	11.4	11.4	11.4	11.3	11.3	11.3	11.2	11.2	11.1	11.1	11.1	11.3
2013	11.0	11.0	11.0	11.0	11.1	11.1	11.1	11.1	11.1	11.1	11.1	11.1	11.1
2014	11.1	11.0	11.0	11.0	11.1	11.1	11.2	11.2	11.2	11.2	11.3	11.4	11.2
2015	11.3	11.4	11.4	11.5	11.5	11.6	11.6	11.6	11.5	11.5	11.6	11.6	11.5
Financial Activities													
2005	37.3	37.3	37.3	37.3	37.5	37.6	37.6	37.8	37.7	37.6	37.7	38.0	37.6
2006	37.8	38.1	38.2	38.3	38.6	39.1	39.2	39.4	39.1	39.1	39.3	39.6	38.8
2007	39.3	39.5	39.7	39.8	40.1	40.3	40.2	40.0	39.9	39.9	39.9	40.1	39.9
2008	40.2	40.5	40.7	40.5	40.8	41.0	40.9	40.7	40.6	40.7	40.6	40.8	40.7
2009	40.1	40.4	40.4	40.0	40.1	40.1	40.0	40.0	39.7	39.8	40.0	40.1	40.1
2010	40.0	40.1	40.3	40.1	40.3	40.5	40.7	40.8	40.5	40.9	40.8	40.9	40.5
2011	40.9	40.9	41.0	41.2	41.4	41.4	41.4	41.3	41.3	41.3	41.5	41.7	41.3
2012	41.3	41.2	41.3	41.5	41.6	41.6	41.8	41.8	41.7	41.8	42.0	42.1	41.6
2013	41.8	41.9	41.9	42.0	42.1	42.2	42.2	42.1	42.0	42.1	42.2	42.2	42.1
2014	42.0	42.1	42.0	41.8	41.9	42.1	42.2	42.0	41.9	42.0	42.0	42.0	42.0
2015	41.5	41.6	41.5	41.7	42.0	42.3	42.4	42.3	42.3	42.5	43.0	43.1	42.2
Professional and Business Services													
2005	59.4	59.7	60.5	61.5	61.7	62.1	61.7	62.0	62.2	62.6	62.9	63.6	61.7
2006	61.8	62.3	63.1	63.4	63.7	64.6	64.4	64.1	63.9	63.3	63.1	63.2	63.4
2007	62.0	62.7	63.2	63.9	64.3	65.1	65.4	65.3	65.3	65.4	65.9	66.6	64.6
2008	64.8	64.8	65.1	66.1	66.3	66.4	65.8	66.1	65.5	65.5	65.2	64.7	65.5
2009	63.1	62.9	62.5	63.1	63.1	63.4	63.1	63.0	62.1	62.3	62.2	62.3	62.8
2010	61.3	60.9	61.1	62.8	63.2	63.8	64.4	64.8	64.4	65.1	65.0	65.2	63.5
2011	63.3	63.4	63.7	65.3	65.3	66.0	66.8	67.0	67.0	66.6	66.6	66.3	65.6
2012	65.5	65.8	65.7	67.0	67.3	68.5	68.6	68.2	67.8	68.6	68.9	68.7	67.6
2013	67.6	67.7	67.8	69.3	69.8	70.5	70.4	70.5	70.7	72.1	72.4	73.0	70.2
2014	70.4	71.0	71.5	71.9	72.4	72.8	72.1	72.0	71.8	72.2	72.4	72.2	71.9
2015	71.7	71.9	72.5	73.8	73.8	74.6	74.3	74.0	73.7	75.3	75.5	74.6	73.8
Education and Health Services													
2005	59.5	60.1	60.3	61.3	60.9	61.0	60.9	60.8	61.5	61.8	63.0	62.9	61.2
2006	62.0	62.8	63.1	62.8	63.0	63.0	62.4	62.9	63.9	63.7	65.0	64.4	63.3
2007	63.8	64.7	64.9	65.1	65.4	65.6	65.5	66.3	66.6	67.1	67.6	67.6	65.9
2008	66.9	67.9	68.1	68.4	68.8	68.5	68.6	69.5	69.9	70.1	70.6	70.5	69.0
2009	69.8	70.2	70.1	70.3	70.2	69.7	69.7	69.9	70.5	71.1	71.4	71.2	70.3
2010	70.5	71.1	71.2	71.4	71.6	71.5	71.5	71.8	71.5	72.2	72.2	72.4	71.6
2011	72.0	72.6	72.6	73.2	73.4	73.0	72.3	72.8	73.0	74.1	74.3	74.4	73.1
2012	73.4	73.9	74.6	74.5	74.7	74.3	74.1	74.8	74.9	75.4	75.7	75.5	74.7
2013	74.5	75.1	75.1	75.1	75.3	74.8	74.3	74.7	75.0	75.4	75.6	75.5	75.0
2014	74.5	75.3	75.8	75.3	75.6	74.7	74.3	75.0	75.3	76.3	76.5	76.8	75.5
2015	75.5	75.7	76.1	76.0	76.2	75.5	75.6	76.1	76.5	77.9	77.6	78.7	76.5
Leisure and Hospitality													
2005	39.2	39.2	40.1	42.1	43.2	44.7	44.4	44.5	43.3	42.1	41.9	41.5	42.2
2006	40.9	41.2	42.0	43.3	44.7	45.6	45.0	44.9	43.9	44.0	43.7	43.9	43.6
2007	42.7	42.6	43.1	44.9	46.5	47.4	47.2	47.6	46.1	45.7	45.0	44.4	45.3
2008	43.2	43.1	43.9	45.1	46.9	48.0	48.1	48.0	46.4	45.8	44.4	43.7	45.6
2009	42.4	42.2	43.2	44.4	45.9	46.8	46.4	46.4	44.9	43.8	42.6	41.7	44.2
2010	40.7	40.8	41.8	43.7	45.0	46.1	45.9	46.0	44.6	44.7	43.5	42.7	43.8
2011	41.5	41.6	42.6	44.8	46.5	47.5	46.6	46.3	44.7	44.6	43.5	43.0	44.4
2012	42.4	42.8	44.5	46.1	47.6	48.4	48.0	47.6	45.9	45.7	44.6	44.1	45.6
2013	43.4	43.5	44.8	46.3	48.4	49.0	48.7	49.0	47.6	47.3	46.3	45.6	46.7
2014	44.9	45.2	46.0	47.2	49.1	49.9	49.5	49.3	47.7	47.6	46.3	46.2	47.4
2015	45.1	45.6	46.9	48.1	50.0	51.2	50.5	50.7	49.1	47.6	46.8	47.2	48.2

Employment by Industry: Omaha-Council Bluffs, NE-IA, 2005–2015—*Continued*

(Numbers in thousands, not seasonally adjusted)

Industry and year	January	February	March	April	May	June	July	August	September	October	November	December	Annual average
Other Services													
2005	15.9	16.0	16.0	16.0	16.1	16.3	16.4	16.3	16.0	16.1	16.1	16.0	16.1
2006	16.2	16.2	16.2	16.4	16.5	16.6	16.6	16.5	16.4	16.6	16.5	16.6	16.4
2007	16.4	16.4	16.5	16.6	16.6	16.7	16.6	16.5	16.4	16.5	16.6	16.6	16.5
2008	16.5	16.5	16.6	16.6	16.9	16.8	16.8	16.7	16.6	17.0	17.0	16.9	16.7
2009	16.7	16.7	16.7	16.9	17.0	17.2	17.3	17.2	17.2	17.3	17.4	17.5	17.1
2010	17.2	17.2	17.3	17.5	17.6	17.8	17.8	17.7	17.5	17.4	17.4	17.4	17.5
2011	17.3	17.2	17.3	17.4	17.4	17.6	17.5	17.3	17.2	17.2	17.1	17.1	17.3
2012	17.1	17.1	17.3	17.5	17.7	17.9	17.8	17.7	17.6	17.4	17.3	17.3	17.5
2013	17.2	17.1	17.3	17.4	17.4	17.5	17.5	17.6	17.5	17.3	17.3	17.3	17.4
2014	17.3	17.3	17.5	17.7	17.8	18.1	17.9	17.8	17.8	17.7	17.8	17.7	17.7
2015	17.6	17.7	17.7	17.7	17.8	17.9	18.1	18.0	17.7	17.8	17.8	17.7	17.8
Government													
2005	59.6	60.1	60.0	60.1	60.7	60.5	57.4	57.1	59.6	61.1	61.3	60.9	59.9
2006	60.7	61.0	61.0	61.6	62.0	61.7	57.6	57.7	60.8	61.7	61.9	61.3	60.8
2007	61.2	61.6	61.5	62.2	62.6	62.0	56.7	57.7	60.9	62.4	62.4	61.6	61.1
2008	61.7	62.0	61.7	63.0	63.4	61.9	58.1	59.1	62.0	64.1	64.3	63.5	62.1
2009	63.5	63.9	63.8	65.2	65.9	64.2	63.3	62.8	64.1	65.7	65.8	64.5	64.4
2010	64.5	64.8	65.8	66.5	67.3	66.5	62.6	63.0	63.7	66.4	66.4	65.7	65.3
2011	65.4	66.0	65.4	66.8	67.0	65.2	63.1	63.8	64.6	66.5	66.7	65.9	65.5
2012	65.8	66.2	65.7	66.0	66.5	63.1	62.6	63.1	64.3	65.8	65.9	65.0	65.0
2013	64.8	65.4	65.1	65.7	66.4	64.8	63.1	63.4	64.4	65.7	65.9	65.0	65.0
2014	65.3	66.0	65.5	66.1	66.8	64.4	63.0	63.8	65.4	66.8	66.8	66.0	65.5
2015	65.7	66.1	65.8	67.1	67.3	65.5	63.7	64.2	65.0	66.7	66.8	66.1	65.8

Employment by Industry: Albuquerque, NM, 2005–2015

(Numbers in thousands, not seasonally adjusted)

Industry and year	January	February	March	April	May	June	July	August	September	October	November	December	Annual average
Total Nonfarm													
2005	369.0	372.0	374.6	377.8	379.5	379.9	378.2	380.1	383.5	383.9	386.7	388.9	379.5
2006	383.3	387.2	391.6	391.7	393.8	396.0	392.0	393.5	397.6	397.3	399.2	399.8	393.6
2007	389.9	393.6	398.0	397.6	399.8	399.8	395.9	398.1	399.2	400.0	401.2	401.5	397.9
2008	391.9	394.7	396.4	398.4	399.8	398.1	395.9	398.6	400.4	399.1	395.1	392.5	396.7
2009	382.4	381.1	380.8	381.4	381.4	378.7	375.7	378.3	379.9	379.7	378.3	378.3	379.7
2010	369.3	370.3	371.8	375.4	376.0	374.8	370.9	372.0	373.4	375.8	375.6	376.3	373.5
2011	367.5	371.5	372.1	375.6	375.1	373.0	370.1	370.3	373.4	373.6	372.7	371.6	372.2
2012	363.8	366.8	369.5	370.8	371.4	368.0	366.4	368.6	372.4	377.6	377.4	376.3	370.8
2013	368.7	371.8	372.4	376.1	377.0	373.5	372.2	374.0	374.9	377.6	378.6	378.6	374.6
2014	370.9	372.7	373.8	376.3	379.3	375.2	375.4	377.8	377.7	381.3	381.7	381.3	377.0
2015	373.3	376.3	376.9	380.8	381.6	378.3	379.2	380.6	382.0	383.5	387.2	385.9	380.5
Total Private													
2005	295.2	295.6	298.0	301.4	303.3	304.2	304.5	306.1	306.7	306.1	308.8	310.4	303.4
2006	306.9	308.7	312.7	313.1	315.3	318.2	316.1	316.4	318.2	317.5	319.1	319.4	315.1
2007	312.5	314.1	317.5	317.9	320.2	321.3	319.4	320.3	318.8	318.9	319.7	320.0	318.4
2008	313.2	313.7	314.9	316.9	317.7	317.7	317.4	318.8	318.0	316.0	312.1	309.5	315.5
2009	301.2	297.9	297.1	297.6	298.2	297.2	296.7	298.0	297.1	295.6	294.3	294.0	297.1
2010	287.8	286.7	287.6	290.4	290.6	291.8	290.9	291.4	290.4	291.4	291.2	291.7	290.2
2011	285.6	287.5	287.5	291.1	291.3	290.4	290.0	289.7	290.0	289.1	288.2	286.8	288.9
2012	282.8	283.5	285.7	287.8	288.6	289.5	288.4	289.0	289.7	293.6	293.2	291.9	288.6
2013	287.6	288.4	288.8	292.7	294.1	292.2	293.0	293.8	292.0	294.3	294.8	295.1	292.2
2014	290.2	289.9	290.4	294.3	296.6	295.2	296.4	298.0	295.9	298.9	299.0	298.5	295.3
2015	293.4	294.4	294.9	298.9	299.8	299.0	300.5	301.0	300.2	300.8	304.0	302.6	299.1
Goods Producing													
2005	49.1	49.3	49.8	50.7	51.2	51.6	52.4	52.5	52.7	53.0	53.5	53.8	51.6
2006	53.7	54.6	55.3	55.2	55.8	56.7	56.6	56.7	56.5	56.5	55.6	55.7	55.7
2007	53.8	54.2	54.8	54.8	55.3	55.6	55.1	55.0	54.1	53.8	53.3	52.4	54.4
2008	51.1	51.1	51.3	51.5	51.6	52.0	51.5	51.1	50.6	49.3	48.2	47.0	50.5
2009	44.7	43.4	42.6	42.5	42.3	42.4	42.3	42.4	41.7	41.4	40.7	39.9	42.2
2010	38.9	38.4	38.3	38.8	39.1	39.4	40.0	39.8	39.6	39.3	38.9	38.5	39.1
2011	37.6	37.3	38.0	38.4	38.5	38.8	39.0	38.6	37.9	37.7	37.1	36.6	38.0
2012	36.2	36.2	36.5	36.6	37.0	37.5	37.3	37.2	36.9	37.7	37.4	37.1	37.0
2013	36.3	36.4	36.7	37.2	37.6	37.9	38.0	37.8	37.4	37.8	37.2	36.8	37.3
2014	36.3	35.9	36.0	36.3	36.8	37.0	37.4	37.5	36.9	37.4	37.1	36.9	36.8
2015	36.4	36.2	36.2	36.8	36.8	37.2	37.5	37.2	36.9	37.0	36.7	36.3	36.8
Service-Providing													
2005	319.9	322.7	324.8	327.1	328.3	328.3	325.8	327.6	330.8	330.9	333.2	335.1	327.9
2006	329.6	332.6	336.3	336.5	338.0	339.3	335.4	336.8	341.1	340.8	343.6	344.1	337.8
2007	336.1	339.4	343.2	342.8	344.5	344.2	340.8	343.1	345.1	346.2	347.9	349.1	343.5
2008	340.8	343.6	345.1	346.9	348.2	346.1	344.4	347.5	349.8	349.8	346.9	345.5	346.2
2009	337.7	337.7	338.2	338.9	339.1	336.3	333.4	335.9	338.2	338.3	337.6	338.4	337.5
2010	330.4	331.9	333.5	336.6	336.9	335.4	330.9	332.2	333.8	336.5	336.7	337.8	334.4
2011	329.9	334.2	334.1	337.2	336.6	334.2	331.1	331.7	335.5	335.9	335.6	335.0	334.3
2012	327.6	330.6	333.0	334.2	334.4	330.5	329.1	331.4	335.5	339.9	340.0	339.2	333.8
2013	332.4	335.4	335.7	338.9	339.4	335.6	334.2	336.2	337.5	339.8	341.4	341.8	337.4
2014	334.6	336.8	337.8	340.0	342.5	338.2	338.0	340.3	340.8	343.9	344.6	344.4	340.2
2015	336.9	340.1	340.7	344.0	344.8	341.1	341.7	343.4	345.1	346.5	350.5	349.6	343.7
Mining, Logging, and Construction													
2005	26.5	26.8	27.3	28.0	28.4	28.9	29.7	29.7	29.8	29.8	30.2	30.4	28.8
2006	30.4	30.8	31.5	31.3	31.9	32.5	32.2	32.3	32.0	32.0	31.5	31.6	31.7
2007	30.0	30.1	30.8	31.0	31.4	31.6	31.1	31.0	30.5	30.7	30.3	29.6	30.7
2008	28.8	28.8	29.0	29.2	29.2	29.5	29.1	28.6	28.2	27.9	27.2	26.3	28.5
2009	24.8	24.1	23.9	24.1	24.1	24.3	24.3	24.6	24.2	24.0	23.4	22.5	24.0
2010	21.6	21.1	21.0	21.3	21.4	21.7	22.2	22.1	21.8	21.6	21.3	20.9	21.5
2011	20.1	19.9	20.5	20.7	20.8	21.0	21.1	20.6	20.1	19.8	19.4	18.9	20.2
2012	18.6	18.6	18.8	18.9	19.2	19.6	19.3	19.3	19.1	19.8	19.7	19.5	19.2
2013	18.8	19.0	19.4	19.8	20.2	20.4	20.5	20.3	20.1	20.5	20.2	19.8	19.9
2014	19.5	19.4	19.5	19.8	20.2	20.4	20.8	20.8	20.4	20.9	20.8	20.6	20.3
2015	20.1	19.8	19.8	20.5	20.4	20.7	20.9	20.6	20.5	20.6	20.6	20.1	20.4

Employment by Industry: Albuquerque, NM, 2005–2015—*Continued*

(Numbers in thousands, not seasonally adjusted)

Industry and year	January	February	March	April	May	June	July	August	September	October	November	December	Annual average
Manufacturing													
2005	22.6	22.5	22.5	22.7	22.8	22.7	22.7	22.8	22.9	23.2	23.3	23.4	22.8
2006	23.3	23.8	23.8	23.9	23.9	24.2	24.4	24.4	24.5	24.5	24.1	24.1	24.1
2007	23.8	24.1	24.0	23.8	23.9	24.0	24.0	24.0	23.6	23.1	23.0	22.8	23.7
2008	22.3	22.3	22.3	22.3	22.4	22.5	22.4	22.5	22.4	21.4	21.0	20.7	22.0
2009	19.9	19.3	18.7	18.4	18.2	18.1	18.0	17.8	17.5	17.4	17.3	17.4	18.2
2010	17.3	17.3	17.3	17.5	17.7	17.7	17.8	17.7	17.8	17.7	17.6	17.6	17.6
2011	17.5	17.4	17.5	17.7	17.7	17.8	17.9	18.0	17.8	17.9	17.7	17.7	17.7
2012	17.6	17.6	17.7	17.7	17.8	17.9	18.0	17.9	17.8	17.9	17.7	17.6	17.8
2013	17.5	17.4	17.3	17.4	17.4	17.5	17.5	17.5	17.3	17.3	17.0	17.0	17.3
2014	16.8	16.5	16.5	16.5	16.6	16.6	16.6	16.7	16.5	16.5	16.3	16.3	16.5
2015	16.3	16.4	16.4	16.3	16.4	16.5	16.6	16.6	16.4	16.4	16.1	16.2	16.4
Trade, Transportation, and Utilities													
2005	66.6	66.3	66.3	66.4	67.0	66.4	66.8	67.5	67.3	67.7	69.1	70.2	67.3
2006	67.1	66.5	67.0	67.1	67.7	67.4	67.6	68.0	68.1	68.3	70.0	70.7	68.0
2007	68.7	68.2	68.4	68.2	69.0	68.9	68.9	69.3	69.2	69.7	71.4	72.4	69.4
2008	69.9	69.0	69.0	68.8	68.7	68.3	68.4	68.6	68.4	68.2	68.3	68.6	68.7
2009	65.3	63.8	63.6	62.8	63.2	63.0	63.1	63.2	63.3	63.6	64.3	65.0	63.7
2010	62.3	61.6	61.7	61.6	61.9	61.9	61.9	62.4	61.9	62.5	63.6	64.3	62.3
2011	61.9	61.5	61.4	62.1	62.3	61.7	62.1	61.4	61.4	61.9	63.2	63.6	62.0
2012	61.9	61.4	61.6	61.6	61.8	61.6	61.5	61.8	61.9	62.8	64.0	64.0	62.2
2013	62.0	61.5	61.4	62.0	62.1	62.0	62.6	62.9	62.4	63.2	64.7	65.3	62.7
2014	62.8	62.3	62.4	62.9	62.9	62.6	63.0	63.1	63.1	63.8	65.1	65.5	63.3
2015	63.5	63.1	63.0	63.3	63.5	63.2	63.5	63.6	63.6	64.1	66.8	66.5	64.0
Wholesale Trade													
2005	13.0	13.2	13.2	13.2	13.3	13.2	13.3	13.3	13.3	13.3	13.4	13.5	13.3
2006	13.2	13.4	13.5	13.6	13.7	13.7	13.7	13.7	13.8	13.8	13.7	13.8	13.6
2007	13.7	13.6	13.6	13.6	13.6	13.7	13.8	13.8	13.8	13.9	13.8	13.9	13.7
2008	13.8	13.6	13.5	13.5	13.5	13.4	13.5	13.4	13.2	13.1	12.9	12.8	13.4
2009	12.5	12.4	12.3	12.1	12.1	12.1	12.3	12.3	12.3	12.4	12.4	12.4	12.3
2010	12.1	12.1	12.0	12.1	12.1	12.1	12.0	12.0	11.9	11.9	11.8	11.8	12.0
2011	11.7	11.7	11.7	11.8	11.8	11.7	11.7	11.7	11.6	11.6	11.6	11.7	11.7
2012	11.6	11.7	11.8	11.8	11.9	11.9	11.9	11.9	11.8	11.9	11.9	11.9	11.8
2013	11.7	11.7	11.6	11.7	11.7	11.7	11.7	11.7	11.6	11.6	11.7	11.7	11.7
2014	11.8	11.8	11.8	12.0	12.0	11.9	12.0	11.9	11.9	11.9	11.9	11.9	11.9
2015	11.8	11.8	11.9	11.9	11.9	11.9	11.9	11.8	11.8	11.8	11.8	11.8	11.8
Retail Trade													
2005	43.1	42.6	42.6	42.8	43.2	43.2	43.4	43.7	43.4	43.9	45.3	45.9	43.6
2006	43.3	42.6	43.0	43.0	43.4	43.3	43.5	43.6	43.6	43.8	45.5	45.8	43.7
2007	44.1	43.6	43.9	43.7	44.4	44.5	44.5	44.5	44.3	44.6	46.4	47.0	44.6
2008	44.9	44.3	44.5	44.3	44.2	44.4	44.4	44.4	44.4	44.6	44.9	45.2	44.5
2009	42.4	41.2	41.2	41.0	41.2	41.4	41.5	41.5	41.6	41.6	42.4	42.9	41.7
2010	40.7	40.0	40.3	40.1	40.4	40.5	40.6	41.0	40.5	41.0	42.1	42.6	40.8
2011	40.6	40.2	40.3	40.8	41.0	40.6	40.2	40.4	40.3	40.7	42.0	42.1	40.8
2012	40.7	40.1	40.2	40.3	40.4	40.4	40.2	40.3	40.5	41.1	42.3	42.2	40.7
2013	40.5	40.1	40.1	40.6	40.7	40.7	41.2	41.4	41.0	41.8	43.2	43.5	41.2
2014	41.3	40.8	41.0	41.3	41.2	41.1	41.3	41.4	41.3	42.0	43.2	43.4	41.6
2015	41.6	41.2	41.1	41.5	41.7	41.5	41.9	42.1	42.1	42.5	45.2	44.6	42.3
Transportation and Utilities													
2005	10.5	10.5	10.5	10.4	10.5	10.0	10.1	10.5	10.6	10.5	10.4	10.8	10.4
2006	10.6	10.5	10.5	10.5	10.6	10.4	10.4	10.7	10.7	10.7	10.8	11.1	10.6
2007	10.9	11.0	10.9	10.9	11.0	10.7	10.6	11.0	11.1	11.2	11.2	11.5	11.0
2008	11.2	11.1	11.0	11.0	11.0	10.5	10.5	10.8	10.8	10.5	10.5	10.6	10.8
2009	10.4	10.2	10.1	9.7	9.9	9.5	9.3	9.4	9.4	9.6	9.5	9.7	9.7
2010	9.5	9.5	9.4	9.4	9.4	9.3	9.3	9.4	9.5	9.6	9.7	9.9	9.5
2011	9.6	9.6	9.4	9.5	9.5	9.4	9.3	9.3	9.5	9.6	9.6	9.8	9.5
2012	9.6	9.6	9.6	9.5	9.5	9.3	9.4	9.6	9.6	9.8	9.8	9.9	9.6
2013	9.8	9.7	9.7	9.7	9.7	9.6	9.7	9.8	9.8	9.8	9.8	10.1	9.8
2014	9.7	9.7	9.6	9.6	9.7	9.6	9.7	9.8	9.9	9.9	10.0	10.2	9.8
2015	10.1	10.1	10.0	9.9	9.9	9.8	9.7	9.7	9.7	9.8	9.8	10.1	9.9

Employment by Industry: Albuquerque, NM, 2005–2015—*Continued*

(Numbers in thousands, not seasonally adjusted)

Industry and year	January	February	March	April	May	June	July	August	September	October	November	December	Annual average
Information													
2005	8.6	8.6	8.7	8.7	8.9	8.8	8.8	8.8	8.6	8.8	8.9	9.1	8.8
2006	8.8	9.4	9.6	9.2	9.4	10.2	9.3	9.6	10.5	9.5	10.0	10.1	9.6
2007	8.8	9.1	9.4	9.4	9.5	10.2	9.3	9.3	9.3	9.5	9.5	9.5	9.4
2008	9.4	9.5	9.4	9.1	9.1	9.1	9.8	9.8	9.9	9.7	9.6	9.5	9.5
2009	8.9	8.8	8.7	9.0	8.9	9.1	9.2	9.4	9.6	9.2	9.3	9.4	9.1
2010	9.0	8.7	8.4	9.4	8.9	9.4	8.8	8.9	8.4	8.4	8.7	8.8	8.8
2011	8.6	8.6	8.6	9.2	9.5	9.2	8.7	8.1	7.8	7.9	8.0	7.8	8.5
2012	8.1	8.4	8.8	8.8	8.1	8.0	8.3	8.4	8.6	8.4	8.5	8.4	8.4
2013	8.1	8.8	8.4	8.5	8.6	8.0	7.9	7.8	7.6	7.9	8.0	7.8	8.1
2014	7.4	7.7	7.9	7.7	8.2	8.1	8.0	8.2	7.5	7.8	8.2	8.1	7.9
2015	7.4	8.0	8.2	8.0	8.4	8.0	8.3	8.6	8.4	8.4	8.7	8.3	8.2
Financial Activities													
2005	19.2	19.2	19.4	19.3	19.5	19.7	19.7	19.6	19.5	19.6	19.6	19.8	19.5
2006	19.5	19.5	19.5	19.4	19.4	19.6	19.5	19.4	19.3	19.3	19.3	19.4	19.4
2007	19.2	19.3	19.4	19.4	19.4	19.5	19.4	19.5	19.3	19.4	19.2	19.2	19.4
2008	18.9	18.9	18.8	18.9	18.8	18.8	19.0	19.0	19.0	18.8	18.5	18.5	18.8
2009	18.2	18.1	18.0	18.2	18.3	18.4	18.5	18.4	18.4	18.7	18.4	18.5	18.3
2010	18.3	18.1	18.3	18.0	17.9	18.0	18.0	17.9	17.7	17.8	17.7	17.7	18.0
2011	17.4	17.4	17.4	17.6	17.5	17.6	17.7	17.7	17.7	17.7	17.6	17.7	17.6
2012	17.5	17.6	17.7	17.6	17.7	17.7	17.8	17.8	17.7	17.8	17.8	17.8	17.7
2013	17.8	17.7	17.6	17.7	17.9	17.8	17.9	18.0	17.9	18.0	18.2	18.2	17.9
2014	17.7	17.8	17.8	17.7	17.8	17.7	18.0	17.9	17.8	18.0	17.9	17.9	17.8
2015	17.7	17.8	17.9	18.0	18.1	18.0	18.2	18.1	17.9	17.8	18.2	18.1	18.0
Professional and Business Services													
2005	60.0	60.0	60.2	61.2	60.9	61.8	61.8	62.1	62.4	61.6	62.3	62.2	61.4
2006	62.5	63.0	63.5	63.7	63.6	64.6	63.6	63.7	63.8	64.2	64.2	64.5	63.7
2007	63.6	64.4	64.9	64.7	65.1	65.7	65.8	66.5	65.6	65.2	65.2	65.4	65.2
2008	64.5	64.9	64.7	64.9	65.2	65.4	65.8	67.1	66.4	66.2	64.6	64.1	65.3
2009	62.8	62.1	61.5	61.4	61.0	60.9	60.9	61.4	60.6	59.8	59.2	59.0	60.9
2010	57.8	57.8	57.5	58.1	57.6	58.4	58.2	58.5	58.6	59.0	58.6	58.6	58.2
2011	57.3	59.3	57.7	58.0	57.8	58.1	58.2	58.3	58.7	57.7	57.3	56.7	57.9
2012	55.2	55.2	55.6	55.9	56.0	56.8	56.4	56.4	56.5	57.2	57.3	56.6	56.3
2013	56.6	56.9	56.6	57.5	57.5	57.0	57.7	57.7	57.0	57.5	57.1	57.4	57.2
2014	56.7	56.8	56.3	57.7	57.7	57.1	57.8	58.0	56.8	57.5	57.2	57.3	57.2
2015	56.3	56.4	56.3	56.9	56.7	57.0	57.7	57.7	57.4	57.5	58.0	57.7	57.1
Education and Health Services													
2005	45.7	45.9	46.5	46.6	46.8	45.9	45.3	45.7	46.8	47.0	47.2	47.2	46.4
2006	47.3	47.3	48.5	48.1	48.4	47.7	47.3	47.1	48.6	48.4	48.6	48.5	48.0
2007	48.6	48.9	49.6	49.7	49.8	48.6	48.2	48.0	48.9	49.5	49.8	49.9	49.1
2008	49.5	50.1	50.8	51.6	51.9	51.1	50.4	50.7	51.8	52.4	52.6	52.7	51.3
2009	53.1	53.5	54.1	54.1	54.3	53.0	52.5	52.9	53.9	54.0	54.2	54.2	53.7
2010	54.3	54.5	55.0	55.1	55.2	54.3	53.8	53.7	55.0	55.4	55.6	55.8	54.8
2011	55.5	55.6	55.8	55.9	55.8	54.4	54.8	54.9	56.3	56.5	56.2	56.0	55.6
2012	56.1	56.3	56.3	56.7	56.6	55.7	55.4	55.3	56.9	57.7	57.7	57.8	56.5
2013	57.5	57.7	58.0	58.3	58.3	57.1	56.1	56.8	58.0	58.4	58.6	58.6	57.8
2014	58.7	58.8	59.0	59.5	59.7	58.8	58.2	58.8	60.2	60.8	60.8	60.5	59.5
2015	60.7	61.2	61.4	61.8	61.9	60.8	60.2	60.7	62.2	63.0	63.0	63.4	61.7
Leisure and Hospitality													
2005	34.4	34.7	35.4	36.8	37.2	37.8	37.4	37.7	37.5	36.6	36.4	36.3	36.5
2006	36.3	36.6	37.4	38.3	38.9	39.5	39.7	39.6	39.3	39.0	39.2	38.6	38.5
2007	37.9	38.0	38.8	39.6	39.9	40.3	40.2	40.5	40.3	39.6	39.1	39.0	39.4
2008	37.8	37.9	38.6	39.8	40.0	40.1	39.7	39.9	39.4	38.7	37.8	37.1	38.9
2009	36.2	36.1	36.6	37.6	38.2	38.1	38.1	38.3	37.9	37.2	36.5	36.2	37.3
2010	35.5	35.9	36.7	37.7	38.3	38.1	38.0	37.9	37.4	37.1	36.5	36.4	37.1
2011	35.8	36.1	36.8	38.1	38.2	38.4	38.2	38.6	38.5	38.1	37.3	36.9	37.6
2012	36.3	36.6	37.3	38.7	39.6	39.9	39.7	40.0	39.4	39.8	38.8	38.4	38.7
2013	37.8	37.8	38.5	39.8	40.5	40.6	40.9	41.0	40.2	39.9	39.4	39.4	39.7
2014	39.1	38.9	39.3	40.8	41.8	41.9	42.0	42.4	41.8	41.8	41.0	40.7	41.0
2015	40.1	40.2	40.4	42.6	43.0	43.0	43.1	43.1	42.2	41.3	41.0	40.7	41.7

Employment by Industry: Albuquerque, NM, 2005–2015—*Continued*

(Numbers in thousands, not seasonally adjusted)

Industry and year	January	February	March	April	May	June	July	August	September	October	November	December	Annual average
Other Services													
2005	11.6	11.6	11.7	11.7	11.8	12.2	12.3	12.2	11.9	11.8	11.8	11.8	11.9
2006	11.7	11.8	11.9	12.1	12.1	12.5	12.5	12.3	12.1	12.3	12.2	11.9	12.1
2007	11.9	12.0	12.2	12.1	12.2	12.5	12.5	12.2	12.1	12.2	12.2	12.2	12.2
2008	12.1	12.3	12.3	12.3	12.4	12.9	12.8	12.6	12.5	12.7	12.5	12.0	12.5
2009	12.0	12.1	12.0	12.0	12.0	12.3	12.1	12.0	11.7	11.7	11.7	11.8	12.0
2010	11.7	11.7	11.7	11.7	11.7	12.3	12.2	12.3	11.8	11.9	11.6	11.6	11.9
2011	11.5	11.7	11.8	11.8	11.7	12.2	12.2	12.1	11.7	11.6	11.5	11.5	11.8
2012	11.5	11.8	11.9	11.9	11.8	12.3	12.0	12.1	11.8	12.1	11.7	11.8	11.9
2013	11.5	11.6	11.6	11.7	11.6	11.8	11.9	11.8	11.5	11.6	11.6	11.6	11.7
2014	11.5	11.7	11.7	11.7	11.7	12.0	12.0	12.1	11.8	11.8	11.7	11.6	11.8
2015	11.3	11.5	11.5	11.5	11.4	11.8	12.0	12.0	11.6	11.7	11.6	11.6	11.6
Government													
2005	73.8	76.4	76.6	76.4	76.2	75.7	73.7	74.0	76.8	77.8	77.9	78.5	76.2
2006	76.4	78.5	78.9	78.6	78.5	77.8	75.9	77.1	79.4	79.8	80.1	80.4	78.5
2007	77.4	79.5	80.5	79.7	79.6	78.5	76.5	77.8	80.4	81.1	81.5	81.5	79.5
2008	78.7	81.0	81.5	81.5	82.1	80.4	78.5	79.8	82.4	83.1	83.0	83.0	81.3
2009	81.2	83.2	83.7	83.8	83.2	81.5	79.0	80.3	82.8	84.1	84.0	84.3	82.6
2010	81.5	83.6	84.2	85.0	85.4	83.0	80.0	80.6	83.0	84.4	84.4	84.6	83.3
2011	81.9	84.0	84.6	84.5	83.8	82.6	80.1	80.6	83.4	84.5	84.5	84.8	83.3
2012	81.0	83.3	83.8	83.0	82.8	78.5	78.0	79.6	82.7	84.0	84.2	84.4	82.1
2013	81.1	83.4	83.6	83.4	82.9	81.3	79.2	80.2	82.9	83.3	83.8	83.5	82.4
2014	80.7	82.8	83.4	82.0	82.7	80.0	79.0	79.8	81.8	82.4	82.7	82.8	81.7
2015	79.9	81.9	82.0	81.9	81.8	79.3	78.7	79.6	81.8	82.7	83.2	83.3	81.3

Employment by Industry: Bakersfield, CA, 2005–2015

(Numbers in thousands, not seasonally adjusted)

Industry and year	January	February	March	April	May	June	July	August	September	October	November	December	Annual average
Total Nonfarm													
2005..................	217.9	219.1	220.6	223.5	225.7	227.2	224.0	225.2	228.1	230.0	231.6	232.7	225.5
2006..................	230.9	232.4	233.6	234.6	237.3	238.7	234.4	236.7	239.1	241.4	242.3	242.6	237.0
2007..................	239.2	240.3	241.6	243.9	244.4	244.7	238.8	240.6	243.1	243.9	244.7	245.2	242.5
2008..................	239.9	241.5	242.4	243.9	244.8	245.6	239.9	239.5	241.4	243.6	244.4	243.1	242.5
2009..................	237.5	236.8	236.4	236.0	235.8	236.0	224.7	227.9	229.4	228.9	229.7	229.0	232.3
2010..................	226.0	226.2	229.1	233.6	233.6	233.9	224.2	227.2	230.3	232.1	233.0	234.4	230.3
2011..................	230.5	232.0	233.7	236.4	238.3	238.1	235.6	238.0	238.6	239.5	240.6	241.1	236.9
2012..................	238.5	240.6	243.5	245.5	247.9	249.0	243.6	245.1	247.1	249.6	250.6	250.5	246.0
2013..................	245.5	247.4	248.8	250.7	252.3	250.0	247.0	249.4	251.2	253.6	254.5	254.8	250.4
2014..................	250.7	252.1	254.3	256.3	258.0	255.7	252.0	255.9	258.7	259.2	261.6	261.5	256.3
2015..................	257.1	256.6	257.9	257.8	259.2	256.7	252.5	256.5	257.3	261.0	263.1	264.3	258.3
Total Private													
2005..................	162.6	163.1	164.3	167.3	169.3	170.5	172.0	171.9	173.5	172.6	174.1	175.4	169.7
2006..................	173.4	174.7	175.7	176.6	179.5	180.6	180.5	181.6	182.1	181.7	182.5	183.0	179.3
2007..................	179.7	180.7	181.9	182.1	182.8	183.0	183.3	184.2	184.5	182.6	182.9	183.3	182.6
2008..................	178.4	179.3	179.9	181.5	182.5	182.9	181.7	182.2	181.8	180.9	180.8	180.2	181.0
2009..................	175.2	173.9	173.2	172.9	173.2	173.0	170.5	171.5	170.0	168.8	168.6	168.0	171.6
2010..................	165.8	165.3	166.6	169.4	169.5	170.4	170.8	171.4	171.5	171.1	171.5	172.7	169.7
2011..................	170.0	170.9	171.9	174.7	176.5	176.5	178.8	180.3	180.5	179.5	180.2	180.8	176.7
2012..................	179.4	180.8	183.1	185.9	188.1	189.1	189.1	189.9	189.6	189.8	190.7	190.6	187.2
2013..................	187.0	188.1	189.0	191.0	193.0	192.6	192.6	194.1	193.4	194.0	194.5	194.6	192.0
2014..................	191.6	192.3	193.6	195.5	197.1	197.1	196.7	199.2	199.0	198.2	199.6	199.8	196.6
2015..................	195.9	195.3	195.8	195.4	196.4	195.6	196.4	197.6	196.2	197.9	199.7	201.0	196.9
Goods Producing													
2005..................	36.6	37.0	37.4	38.1	38.5	39.2	40.0	39.7	40.7	40.5	40.6	40.7	39.1
2006..................	40.6	41.2	41.5	41.5	42.3	42.8	43.2	43.2	43.5	43.1	42.6	42.5	42.3
2007..................	41.0	41.3	41.6	41.0	41.2	41.4	42.0	42.3	42.2	41.7	41.2	40.9	41.5
2008..................	40.0	40.0	39.9	40.5	40.7	41.4	41.5	41.5	41.7	41.5	41.1	41.2	40.9
2009..................	39.1	37.8	37.5	36.6	36.1	36.1	35.5	35.4	35.3	34.7	34.6	34.4	36.1
2010..................	34.3	33.7	34.3	35.1	35.7	36.0	36.5	36.7	37.1	37.1	36.9	37.4	35.9
2011..................	36.9	37.2	37.3	38.3	38.6	39.4	39.8	40.2	40.4	40.1	39.9	40.5	39.1
2012..................	40.8	41.4	42.1	42.9	43.2	43.9	44.5	44.8	44.9	44.5	44.4	43.8	43.4
2013..................	42.7	42.8	43.2	43.6	43.9	44.3	44.5	45.1	45.3	45.5	45.2	45.1	44.3
2014..................	44.8	44.9	45.1	45.7	46.0	46.4	46.6	47.2	47.2	46.8	46.6	46.2	46.1
2015..................	45.1	44.3	43.7	43.0	42.5	42.4	42.7	43.1	42.5	42.1	42.0	42.0	43.0
Service-Providing													
2005..................	181.3	182.1	183.2	185.4	187.2	188.0	184.0	185.5	187.4	189.5	191.0	192.0	186.4
2006..................	190.3	191.2	192.1	193.1	195.0	195.9	191.2	193.5	195.6	198.3	199.7	200.1	194.7
2007..................	198.2	199.0	200.0	202.9	203.2	203.3	196.8	198.3	200.9	202.2	203.5	204.3	201.1
2008..................	199.9	201.5	202.5	203.4	204.1	204.2	198.4	198.0	199.7	202.1	203.3	201.9	201.6
2009..................	198.4	199.0	198.9	199.4	199.7	199.9	189.2	192.5	194.1	194.2	195.1	194.6	196.3
2010..................	191.7	192.5	194.8	198.5	197.9	197.9	187.7	190.5	193.2	195.0	196.1	197.0	194.4
2011..................	193.6	194.8	196.4	198.1	199.7	198.7	195.8	197.8	198.2	199.4	200.7	200.6	197.8
2012..................	197.7	199.2	201.4	202.6	204.7	205.1	199.1	200.3	202.2	205.1	206.2	206.7	202.5
2013..................	202.8	204.6	205.6	207.1	208.4	205.7	202.5	204.3	205.9	208.1	209.3	209.7	206.2
2014..................	205.9	207.2	209.2	210.6	212.0	209.3	205.4	208.7	211.5	212.4	215.0	215.3	210.2
2015..................	212.0	212.3	214.2	214.8	216.7	214.3	209.8	213.4	214.8	218.9	221.1	222.3	215.4
Mining and Logging													
2005..................	8.1	8.2	8.3	8.4	8.4	8.4	8.5	8.6	8.7	8.7	8.7	8.8	8.5
2006..................	8.9	8.9	9.0	9.1	9.2	9.4	9.4	9.6	9.6	9.7	9.7	9.7	9.4
2007..................	9.5	9.6	9.6	9.6	9.6	9.6	9.9	10.0	9.9	9.9	9.9	10.0	9.8
2008..................	10.1	10.2	10.3	10.3	10.4	10.5	10.9	10.9	10.9	11.2	11.3	11.2	10.7
2009..................	10.7	10.4	10.2	10.0	9.9	10.0	9.7	9.5	9.5	9.3	9.3	9.5	9.8
2010..................	9.5	9.1	9.2	9.6	10.2	10.3	10.6	10.7	10.8	10.7	10.8	11.1	10.2
2011..................	11.1	11.3	11.4	11.7	11.9	12.0	12.2	12.3	12.4	12.5	12.6	12.7	12.0
2012..................	12.8	12.9	13.0	13.0	13.1	13.4	13.6	13.7	13.6	13.5	13.5	13.4	13.3
2013..................	12.8	13.0	13.0	13.2	13.2	13.4	13.0	13.0	12.9	12.8	12.9	12.9	13.0
2014..................	12.9	13.0	13.0	13.1	13.2	13.4	13.6	13.7	13.7	13.7	13.8	13.7	13.4
2015..................	13.2	12.8	12.5	12.1	11.8	11.7	11.7	11.5	11.3	11.3	11.2	11.1	11.9

Employment by Industry: Bakersfield, CA, 2005–2015—*Continued*

(Numbers in thousands, not seasonally adjusted)

Industry and year	January	February	March	April	May	June	July	August	September	October	November	December	Annual average
Construction													
2005	15.9	16.3	16.8	17.4	17.8	18.5	19.0	18.7	19.2	19.3	19.5	19.5	18.2
2006	19.0	19.5	19.7	19.8	20.4	20.7	20.8	20.4	20.4	20.0	19.8	19.7	20.0
2007	18.8	18.9	19.1	18.5	18.7	18.7	18.5	18.6	18.2	18.2	17.7	17.4	18.4
2008	16.5	16.4	16.2	16.6	16.6	16.9	16.9	16.8	16.7	16.5	16.0	16.1	16.5
2009	14.8	14.0	14.0	13.4	13.1	13.1	12.7	12.6	12.4	12.3	12.4	12.2	13.1
2010	12.1	12.0	12.4	12.6	12.7	12.9	12.9	13.0	12.8	12.9	12.9	13.1	12.7
2011	12.8	13.0	13.0	13.6	13.8	14.2	14.5	14.6	14.4	14.4	14.3	14.7	13.9
2012	15.2	15.6	16.1	16.8	17.0	17.1	17.2	17.3	17.1	17.1	17.1	16.7	16.7
2013	16.5	16.4	16.6	16.7	16.9	16.9	17.4	17.8	17.7	18.1	17.9	17.8	17.2
2014	17.7	17.7	17.8	18.0	18.3	18.3	18.5	18.6	18.4	18.3	18.3	18.1	18.2
2015	17.7	17.4	17.1	16.8	16.8	16.5	17.0	16.9	16.6	16.7	16.9	17.0	17.0
Manufacturing													
2005	12.6	12.5	12.3	12.3	12.3	12.3	12.5	12.4	12.8	12.5	12.4	12.4	12.4
2006	12.7	12.8	12.8	12.6	12.7	12.7	13.0	13.2	13.5	13.4	13.1	13.1	13.0
2007	12.7	12.8	12.9	12.9	12.9	13.1	13.6	13.7	14.1	13.6	13.6	13.5	13.3
2008	13.4	13.4	13.4	13.6	13.7	14.0	13.7	13.8	14.1	13.8	13.8	13.9	13.7
2009	13.6	13.4	13.3	13.2	13.1	13.0	13.1	13.3	13.4	13.1	12.9	12.7	13.2
2010	12.7	12.6	12.7	12.9	12.8	12.8	13.0	13.0	13.5	13.5	13.2	13.2	13.0
2011	13.0	12.9	12.9	13.0	12.9	13.2	13.1	13.3	13.6	13.2	13.0	13.1	13.1
2012	12.8	12.9	13.0	13.1	13.1	13.4	13.7	13.8	14.2	13.9	13.8	13.7	13.5
2013	13.4	13.4	13.6	13.7	13.8	14.0	14.1	14.3	14.7	14.6	14.4	14.4	14.0
2014	14.2	14.2	14.3	14.6	14.5	14.7	14.5	14.9	15.1	14.8	14.5	14.4	14.6
2015	14.2	14.1	14.1	14.1	13.9	14.2	14.0	14.7	14.6	14.1	13.9	13.9	14.2
Trade, Transportation, and Utilities													
2005	41.9	41.9	42.2	42.8	43.6	43.5	43.8	44.0	44.4	44.7	45.7	46.8	43.8
2006	45.5	45.2	45.5	45.4	46.5	46.5	46.4	46.7	46.8	46.7	47.9	48.3	46.5
2007	46.3	46.0	46.4	46.6	47.1	46.9	46.7	46.8	46.8	46.7	47.5	47.9	46.8
2008	45.8	45.4	45.6	45.6	46.3	45.9	45.2	45.2	45.1	44.6	45.0	45.0	45.4
2009	43.3	43.2	42.6	43.0	43.5	43.0	43.2	43.8	42.7	42.5	42.6	42.7	43.0
2010	41.7	41.5	41.4	41.9	42.0	42.0	42.8	43.2	43.1	42.2	42.8	43.7	42.4
2011	42.4	42.2	42.2	43.1	43.9	43.6	44.5	44.8	44.7	44.3	44.8	45.1	43.8
2012	43.7	43.4	43.6	44.8	45.3	45.8	45.9	45.8	45.7	46.0	47.3	47.9	45.4
2013	46.1	46.0	46.1	47.0	47.4	47.5	47.8	48.0	47.8	47.9	49.2	49.8	47.6
2014	47.8	47.7	48.0	48.8	49.4	49.3	49.4	50.5	50.3	49.8	51.0	51.6	49.5
2015	49.7	49.5	49.7	50.1	50.5	50.5	51.1	51.4	51.1	51.6	52.8	53.7	51.0
Wholesale Trade													
2005	6.6	6.6	6.6	6.8	6.8	6.9	6.9	6.9	6.9	7.0	7.0	7.1	6.8
2006	7.2	7.3	7.4	7.4	7.6	7.7	7.7	7.7	7.8	7.8	7.9	7.9	7.6
2007	7.8	7.8	7.9	8.0	8.0	8.2	8.2	8.1	8.2	8.2	8.1	8.1	8.1
2008	8.0	8.0	8.1	8.1	8.2	8.3	8.3	8.3	8.4	8.2	8.2	8.0	8.2
2009	8.1	8.4	8.0	8.1	8.3	8.1	9.0	9.5	8.3	7.9	7.6	7.2	8.2
2010	7.4	7.4	7.1	7.6	7.6	8.0	8.9	9.1	9.1	7.8	7.7	7.8	8.0
2011	7.7	7.6	7.4	7.8	7.9	8.0	8.9	8.9	8.9	8.5	8.0	7.9	8.1
2012	8.0	7.8	7.8	8.4	8.5	8.8	8.7	8.6	8.6	8.7	8.7	8.8	8.5
2013	8.9	9.0	9.0	9.0	9.1	9.2	9.2	9.2	9.2	9.2	9.2	9.2	9.1
2014	9.2	9.3	9.3	9.5	9.5	9.5	9.4	9.6	9.4	9.4	9.5	9.5	9.4
2015	9.4	9.4	9.3	9.1	9.1	9.2	9.3	9.3	9.2	9.3	9.3	9.3	9.3
Retail Trade													
2005	26.7	26.5	26.8	27.2	27.3	27.4	27.6	27.8	28.1	28.2	29.4	30.4	27.8
2006	29.3	28.8	29.0	28.9	29.2	29.3	29.2	29.5	29.5	29.5	30.6	30.9	29.5
2007	29.4	29.0	29.1	29.2	29.2	29.0	28.8	28.9	28.8	28.6	29.7	30.1	29.2
2008	28.5	28.1	28.2	28.0	28.1	27.9	27.4	27.3	27.0	26.7	27.2	27.5	27.7
2009	26.0	25.7	25.6	25.9	26.0	25.8	25.2	25.3	25.4	25.9	26.5	27.0	25.9
2010	26.0	25.8	26.0	26.0	25.8	25.6	25.4	25.6	25.5	25.8	26.6	27.6	26.0
2011	26.5	26.3	26.5	26.8	27.1	27.0	26.9	27.0	26.8	26.9	28.0	28.4	27.0
2012	27.3	27.0	27.2	27.7	27.8	27.8	27.7	27.7	27.6	27.8	29.2	29.6	27.9
2013	28.1	27.9	28.0	28.6	28.8	28.7	28.9	29.0	28.8	29.0	30.3	30.7	28.9
2014	29.2	29.0	29.2	29.8	30.2	30.0	30.0	30.7	30.7	30.6	31.7	32.0	30.3
2015	30.6	30.5	30.8	31.1	31.4	31.4	31.5	31.7	31.5	31.9	33.2	34.1	31.6

Employment by Industry: Bakersfield, CA, 2005–2015—*Continued*

(Numbers in thousands, not seasonally adjusted)

Industry and year	January	February	March	April	May	June	July	August	September	October	November	December	Annual average
Transportation and Utilities													
2005	8.6	8.8	8.8	8.8	9.5	9.2	9.3	9.3	9.4	9.5	9.3	9.3	9.2
2006	9.0	9.1	9.1	9.1	9.7	9.5	9.5	9.5	9.5	9.4	9.4	9.5	9.4
2007	9.1	9.2	9.4	9.4	9.9	9.7	9.7	9.8	9.8	9.9	9.7	9.7	9.6
2008	9.3	9.3	9.3	9.5	10.0	9.7	9.5	9.6	9.7	9.7	9.6	9.5	9.6
2009	9.2	9.1	9.0	9.0	9.2	9.1	9.0	9.0	9.0	8.7	8.5	8.5	8.9
2010	8.3	8.3	8.3	8.3	8.6	8.4	8.5	8.5	8.5	8.6	8.5	8.3	8.4
2011	8.2	8.3	8.3	8.5	8.9	8.6	8.7	8.9	9.0	8.9	8.8	8.8	8.7
2012	8.4	8.6	8.6	8.7	9.0	9.2	9.5	9.5	9.5	9.5	9.4	9.5	9.1
2013	9.1	9.1	9.1	9.4	9.5	9.6	9.7	9.8	9.8	9.7	9.7	9.9	9.5
2014	9.4	9.4	9.5	9.5	9.7	9.8	10.0	10.2	10.2	9.8	9.8	10.1	9.8
2015	9.7	9.6	9.6	9.9	10.0	9.9	10.3	10.4	10.4	10.4	10.3	10.3	10.1
Information													
2005	2.5	2.5	2.5	2.5	2.5	2.5	2.6	2.5	2.6	2.5	2.6	2.6	2.5
2006	2.6	2.7	2.6	2.6	2.7	2.7	2.7	2.7	2.6	2.6	2.7	2.7	2.7
2007	2.8	2.8	2.7	2.8	2.8	2.9	2.8	2.9	2.8	2.8	2.9	2.9	2.8
2008	2.9	3.0	3.0	3.1	3.1	3.1	3.0	3.0	3.0	3.0	3.0	2.9	3.0
2009	2.8	2.8	2.8	2.8	2.8	2.8	2.8	2.7	2.7	2.7	2.7	2.7	2.8
2010	2.7	2.6	2.6	2.6	2.6	2.6	2.9	2.8	2.7	2.7	2.7	2.8	2.7
2011	2.7	2.6	2.6	2.6	2.6	2.6	2.7	2.6	2.6	2.6	2.6	2.6	2.6
2012	2.7	2.7	2.7	2.7	2.7	2.8	2.6	2.6	2.6	2.6	2.7	2.7	2.7
2013	2.7	2.6	2.6	2.6	2.6	2.6	2.5	2.5	2.5	2.4	2.5	2.4	2.5
2014	2.4	2.4	2.4	2.4	2.4	2.4	2.3	2.4	2.3	2.4	2.4	2.4	2.4
2015	2.4	2.4	2.4	2.4	2.4	2.8	2.9	3.0	3.0	3.0	3.0	3.0	2.7
Financial Activities													
2005	8.6	8.5	8.6	8.6	8.7	8.8	8.9	8.9	8.8	8.7	8.8	8.8	8.7
2006	8.9	8.9	8.9	8.9	9.1	9.1	9.0	9.0	8.9	9.0	9.0	9.0	9.0
2007	9.1	9.2	9.2	9.1	9.1	9.2	9.1	9.1	9.0	9.0	8.9	8.9	9.1
2008	8.8	8.8	8.9	9.0	9.0	8.9	8.9	8.9	8.9	8.8	8.8	8.8	8.9
2009	8.7	8.7	8.5	8.5	8.5	8.5	8.5	8.5	8.4	8.4	8.2	8.3	8.5
2010	8.2	8.3	8.3	8.3	8.4	8.3	8.2	8.1	8.1	8.0	7.9	7.9	8.2
2011	7.8	8.0	8.0	8.2	8.3	8.2	8.5	8.6	8.5	8.5	8.5	8.4	8.3
2012	8.4	8.5	8.5	8.8	9.0	8.9	8.9	8.9	8.8	8.8	8.7	8.7	8.7
2013	8.8	8.8	8.8	8.9	9.0	8.9	8.9	8.9	8.7	8.9	8.8	8.7	8.8
2014	8.7	8.6	8.7	8.7	8.8	8.7	8.7	8.6	8.6	8.8	8.6	8.7	8.7
2015	8.6	8.5	8.6	8.5	8.6	8.4	8.5	8.5	8.5	8.5	8.5	8.5	8.5
Professional and Business Services													
2005	22.1	22.1	22.0	22.8	22.8	23.0	23.4	23.6	23.9	23.4	23.8	23.6	23.0
2006	23.7	24.0	24.1	24.3	24.8	25.0	25.3	25.6	25.9	26.0	25.8	25.7	25.0
2007	26.0	26.3	26.2	26.5	26.5	26.3	26.2	26.5	26.7	25.3	25.3	25.4	26.1
2008	24.7	25.2	25.2	25.4	25.1	25.1	25.0	25.1	25.1	25.0	24.9	24.5	25.0
2009	24.6	24.0	24.0	23.8	23.8	23.9	23.3	23.6	23.6	23.2	23.7	23.3	23.7
2010	23.3	23.1	23.5	24.4	24.0	24.3	23.6	23.6	23.6	24.2	24.5	24.4	23.9
2011	24.4	24.7	25.1	25.2	25.1	24.9	25.5	25.7	26.0	25.7	26.0	25.6	25.3
2012	25.6	26.1	26.8	26.5	27.0	26.9	27.0	27.0	26.8	26.7	26.4	26.3	26.6
2013	25.9	26.5	26.4	26.3	26.7	26.5	26.3	26.5	26.3	26.2	25.7	25.6	26.2
2014	25.5	25.7	25.8	25.6	25.9	26.0	25.7	25.9	26.0	26.2	26.6	26.4	25.9
2015	25.8	25.8	25.9	25.5	26.0	25.6	25.4	25.3	25.0	25.0	25.3	25.7	25.5
Education and Health Services													
2005	24.6	24.8	24.9	25.2	25.4	25.4	25.7	25.7	25.6	25.7	25.7	25.8	25.4
2006	25.8	26.0	26.0	26.0	26.1	26.4	26.2	26.5	26.6	27.0	27.2	27.4	26.4
2007	27.5	27.9	27.9	27.8	27.6	27.7	28.1	28.1	28.3	28.4	28.5	28.7	28.0
2008	28.6	28.8	29.0	29.1	29.1	29.2	29.3	29.6	29.5	29.6	29.7	29.8	29.3
2009	29.4	29.7	29.9	29.9	30.0	30.3	29.7	30.0	29.8	30.0	29.7	29.7	29.8
2010	29.2	29.3	29.4	29.5	29.3	29.4	29.6	29.8	29.6	29.9	29.8	29.9	29.6
2011	29.5	29.6	29.7	29.9	30.1	29.9	30.1	30.4	30.6	30.5	30.5	30.8	30.1
2012	30.6	30.8	31.1	31.4	31.6	31.4	31.2	31.6	31.8	32.0	31.9	32.0	31.5
2013	31.6	32.0	32.1	32.4	32.6	32.1	32.1	32.4	32.3	32.5	32.6	32.5	32.3
2014	32.2	32.4	32.5	32.6	32.7	32.5	32.3	32.7	32.7	32.7	32.8	32.8	32.6
2015	32.5	32.7	32.9	33.2	33.4	33.3	33.2	33.6	33.5	34.2	34.5	34.7	33.5

Employment by Industry: Bakersfield, CA, 2005–2015—*Continued*

(Numbers in thousands, not seasonally adjusted)

Industry and year	January	February	March	April	May	June	July	August	September	October	November	December	Annual average
Leisure and Hospitality													
2005	19.3	19.3	19.6	20.1	20.5	20.9	20.6	20.5	20.3	20.0	20.1	20.3	20.1
2006	19.6	19.9	20.2	20.9	21.0	21.3	21.0	20.9	20.9	20.6	20.7	20.9	20.7
2007	20.5	20.7	21.2	21.7	21.9	22.1	21.7	21.7	21.8	21.7	21.6	21.6	21.5
2008	20.9	21.2	21.4	21.8	22.0	22.1	22.0	21.9	21.5	21.2	21.2	21.0	21.5
2009	20.6	20.9	21.2	21.5	21.7	21.7	21.0	20.8	20.8	20.5	20.4	20.3	21.0
2010	19.8	20.1	20.3	20.8	20.8	21.1	20.8	20.6	20.7	20.4	20.4	20.1	20.5
2011	19.8	20.1	20.4	20.7	21.1	21.2	21.0	21.0	20.7	20.9	20.9	20.8	20.7
2012	20.6	20.8	21.2	21.6	22.0	22.2	22.0	21.9	21.7	21.8	21.9	21.9	21.6
2013	21.9	22.0	22.3	22.6	23.1	23.4	23.2	23.1	23.0	23.1	22.9	23.0	22.8
2014	22.6	22.9	23.4	23.8	24.0	24.1	24.1	24.0	24.0	23.6	23.8	24.0	23.7
2015	24.0	24.3	24.8	24.9	25.3	25.2	25.1	25.2	25.1	26.0	26.1	26.0	25.2
Other Services													
2005	7.0	7.0	7.1	7.2	7.3	7.2	7.0	7.0	7.2	7.1	6.8	6.8	7.1
2006	6.7	6.8	6.9	7.0	7.0	6.8	6.7	7.0	6.9	6.7	6.6	6.5	6.8
2007	6.5	6.5	6.7	6.6	6.6	6.5	6.7	6.8	6.9	7.0	7.0	7.0	6.7
2008	6.7	6.9	6.9	7.0	7.2	7.2	6.8	7.0	7.0	7.2	7.1	7.0	7.0
2009	6.7	6.8	6.7	6.8	6.8	6.7	6.5	6.7	6.7	6.8	6.7	6.6	6.7
2010	6.6	6.7	6.8	6.8	6.7	6.7	6.4	6.6	6.6	6.6	6.5	6.5	6.6
2011	6.5	6.5	6.6	6.7	6.8	6.7	6.7	7.0	7.0	6.9	7.0	7.0	6.8
2012	7.0	7.1	7.1	7.2	7.3	7.2	7.0	7.3	7.3	7.4	7.4	7.3	7.2
2013	7.3	7.4	7.5	7.6	7.7	7.3	7.3	7.6	7.5	7.5	7.6	7.5	7.5
2014	7.6	7.7	7.7	7.9	7.9	7.7	7.6	7.9	7.9	7.9	7.8	7.7	7.8
2015	7.8	7.8	7.8	7.8	7.7	7.4	7.5	7.5	7.5	7.5	7.5	7.4	7.6
Government													
2005	55.3	56.0	56.3	56.2	56.4	56.7	52.0	53.3	54.6	57.4	57.5	57.3	55.8
2006	57.5	57.7	57.9	58.0	57.8	58.1	53.9	55.1	57.0	59.7	59.8	59.6	57.7
2007	59.5	59.6	59.7	61.8	61.6	61.7	55.5	56.4	58.6	61.3	61.8	61.9	60.0
2008	61.5	62.2	62.5	62.4	62.3	62.7	58.2	57.3	59.6	62.7	63.6	62.9	61.5
2009	62.3	62.9	63.2	63.1	62.6	63.0	54.2	56.4	59.4	60.1	61.1	61.0	60.8
2010	60.2	60.9	62.5	64.2	64.1	63.5	53.4	55.8	58.8	61.0	61.5	61.7	60.6
2011	60.5	61.1	61.8	61.7	61.8	61.6	56.8	57.7	58.1	60.0	60.4	60.3	60.2
2012	59.1	59.8	60.4	59.6	59.8	59.9	54.5	55.2	57.5	59.8	59.9	59.9	58.8
2013	58.5	59.3	59.8	59.7	59.3	57.4	54.4	55.3	57.8	59.6	60.0	60.2	58.4
2014	59.1	59.8	60.7	60.8	60.9	58.6	55.3	56.7	59.7	61.0	62.0	61.7	59.7
2015	61.2	61.3	62.1	62.4	62.8	61.1	56.1	58.9	61.1	63.1	63.4	63.3	61.4

Employment by Industry: Albany-Schenectady-Troy, NY, 2005–2015

(Numbers in thousands, not seasonally adjusted)

Industry and year	January	February	March	April	May	June	July	August	September	October	November	December	Annual average
Total Nonfarm													
2005	434.3	437.1	437.5	444.4	445.8	447.1	442.6	443.6	445.3	448.0	449.7	449.1	443.7
2006	434.1	438.4	441.5	445.6	447.8	448.7	441.9	442.5	444.8	449.8	451.9	453.0	445.0
2007	436.9	439.7	442.2	443.6	449.5	451.9	443.9	445.0	447.9	453.0	455.2	455.4	447.0
2008	440.2	443.9	444.8	450.1	455.4	456.5	449.6	449.5	450.3	454.8	455.1	452.8	450.3
2009	435.9	440.1	440.1	442.7	445.3	445.0	437.2	436.3	438.2	442.8	444.0	441.9	440.8
2010	426.5	430.9	432.2	438.5	441.9	440.9	433.0	431.7	434.6	438.6	440.9	439.0	435.7
2011	423.3	429.7	430.3	437.8	439.5	439.4	435.0	434.1	438.3	443.0	445.3	443.3	436.6
2012	430.2	436.5	437.7	444.0	447.6	447.7	439.7	440.0	444.0	450.0	452.9	450.0	443.4
2013	435.2	442.5	443.8	448.9	452.8	453.0	445.9	445.0	449.0	455.3	457.7	455.5	448.7
2014	438.1	445.9	447.3	452.4	456.0	456.6	449.8	449.6	452.7	461.8	462.5	460.3	452.8
2015	447.8	453.0	453.6	458.2	462.4	462.9	456.0	455.1	455.8	462.5	463.6	461.3	457.7
Total Private													
2005	327.1	328.6	328.9	335.3	336.7	338.7	339.8	341.5	339.4	339.7	341.2	340.5	336.5
2006	328.0	330.3	333.4	337.0	339.3	341.1	339.6	341.2	339.9	341.9	343.4	343.8	338.2
2007	330.0	330.8	333.6	334.8	340.1	342.7	341.4	342.3	341.8	343.6	345.4	344.5	339.3
2008	333.1	334.7	335.8	339.6	344.1	345.7	344.4	345.4	343.1	344.4	344.6	341.8	341.4
2009	328.6	330.0	330.5	331.6	334.3	334.8	332.9	333.5	332.4	333.7	334.3	332.0	332.4
2010	319.3	322.0	323.7	329.4	331.0	330.7	331.7	332.6	332.4	334.4	336.1	334.4	329.8
2011	322.6	326.4	327.2	333.5	334.9	335.3	336.3	336.9	338.8	340.1	342.0	339.9	334.5
2012	329.5	333.5	335.4	340.8	343.8	345.0	343.3	344.2	345.0	348.0	349.9	347.5	342.2
2013	334.5	339.0	340.7	345.9	349.2	349.9	348.7	349.0	350.6	353.7	354.9	353.2	347.4
2014	338.9	343.6	345.1	349.9	353.5	354.7	353.5	354.4	354.2	359.9	360.3	357.9	352.2
2015	347.6	350.9	351.5	356.2	359.8	361.2	360.2	360.4	357.7	361.0	361.6	359.3	357.3
Goods Producing													
2005	38.8	38.1	38.3	40.5	41.8	42.6	43.3	43.4	42.8	42.4	42.3	40.9	41.3
2006	39.1	38.5	39.1	40.9	42.1	42.9	43.0	43.3	42.7	42.7	42.0	40.8	41.4
2007	38.8	37.8	38.6	39.9	41.9	42.8	43.4	43.4	42.9	43.0	42.2	40.9	41.3
2008	38.7	37.8	38.1	39.5	41.3	42.3	42.7	42.9	42.4	42.3	41.3	39.6	40.7
2009	36.7	35.8	35.7	36.8	37.8	38.8	39.3	39.5	38.9	38.7	38.3	36.9	37.8
2010	34.7	34.0	34.4	36.1	37.0	37.9	38.0	38.2	38.5	38.1	37.7	36.8	36.8
2011	35.2	34.8	35.1	37.1	38.2	39.4	40.4	40.8	40.4	40.2	39.9	38.5	38.3
2012	37.0	36.4	37.0	39.0	40.1	41.3	41.8	42.0	41.6	41.3	40.9	40.3	39.9
2013	38.7	38.5	38.9	40.2	42.0	42.8	43.4	43.5	42.9	42.8	42.4	41.3	41.5
2014	39.5	39.0	39.3	40.9	43.2	44.4	44.8	45.3	44.7	44.7	44.4	43.6	42.8
2015	42.6	42.2	42.4	43.9	45.6	46.7	47.3	47.3	46.3	46.2	45.9	44.9	45.1
Service-Providing													
2005	395.5	399.0	399.2	403.9	404.0	404.5	399.3	400.2	402.5	405.6	407.4	408.2	402.4
2006	395.0	399.9	402.4	404.7	405.7	405.8	398.9	399.2	402.1	407.1	409.9	412.2	403.6
2007	398.1	401.9	403.6	403.7	407.6	409.1	400.5	401.6	405.0	410.0	413.0	414.5	405.7
2008	401.5	406.1	406.7	410.6	414.1	414.2	406.9	406.6	407.9	412.5	413.8	413.2	409.5
2009	399.2	404.3	404.4	405.9	407.5	406.2	397.9	396.8	399.3	404.1	405.7	405.0	403.0
2010	391.8	396.9	397.8	402.4	404.9	403.0	395.0	393.5	396.1	400.5	403.2	402.2	398.9
2011	388.1	394.9	395.2	400.7	401.3	400.0	394.6	393.3	397.9	402.8	405.4	404.8	398.3
2012	393.2	400.1	400.7	405.0	407.5	406.4	397.9	398.0	402.4	408.7	412.0	409.7	403.5
2013	396.5	404.0	404.9	408.7	410.8	410.2	402.5	401.5	406.1	412.5	415.3	414.2	407.3
2014	398.6	406.9	408.0	411.5	412.8	412.2	405.0	404.3	408.0	417.1	418.1	416.7	409.9
2015	405.2	410.8	411.2	414.3	416.8	416.2	408.7	407.8	409.5	416.3	417.7	416.4	412.6
Mining, Logging, and Construction													
2005	16.0	15.4	15.5	17.4	18.6	19.3	20.0	20.0	19.6	19.4	19.2	17.9	18.2
2006	16.1	15.6	16.1	17.6	18.7	19.4	19.6	19.8	19.4	19.4	18.6	17.6	18.2
2007	16.0	15.1	15.7	16.8	18.8	19.4	20.0	20.1	19.8	19.9	19.2	17.9	18.2
2008	16.1	15.5	15.7	17.2	18.7	19.4	20.0	20.2	19.9	19.9	19.0	17.5	18.3
2009	15.3	14.7	14.9	16.1	17.2	18.0	18.7	18.9	18.3	18.1	17.7	16.4	17.0
2010	14.5	14.0	14.3	15.9	16.7	17.4	18.1	18.4	18.1	17.6	17.0	16.2	16.5
2011	14.7	14.2	14.4	15.9	16.9	17.8	18.6	19.0	18.6	18.2	17.8	16.5	16.9
2012	15.2	14.5	14.8	16.7	17.6	18.5	18.8	18.9	18.5	18.2	17.7	17.1	17.2
2013	15.2	14.9	15.2	16.4	18.0	18.4	19.2	19.4	19.0	18.9	18.4	17.4	17.5
2014	15.9	15.6	15.8	17.2	19.3	20.0	20.3	20.7	20.3	20.3	19.9	19.0	18.7
2015	18.1	17.6	17.7	19.0	20.5	21.1	21.3	21.3	20.5	20.4	20.0	19.1	19.7

Employment by Industry: Albany-Schenectady-Troy, NY, 2005–2015—*Continued*

(Numbers in thousands, not seasonally adjusted)

Industry and year	January	February	March	April	May	June	July	August	September	October	November	December	Annual average
Manufacturing													
2005	22.8	22.7	22.8	23.1	23.2	23.3	23.3	23.4	23.2	23.0	23.1	23.0	23.1
2006	23.0	22.9	23.0	23.3	23.4	23.5	23.4	23.5	23.3	23.3	23.4	23.2	23.3
2007	22.8	22.7	22.9	23.1	23.1	23.4	23.4	23.3	23.1	23.1	23.0	23.0	23.1
2008	22.6	22.3	22.4	22.3	22.6	22.9	22.7	22.7	22.5	22.4	22.3	22.1	22.5
2009	21.4	21.1	20.8	20.7	20.6	20.8	20.6	20.6	20.6	20.6	20.6	20.5	20.7
2010	20.2	20.0	20.1	20.2	20.3	20.5	19.9	19.8	20.4	20.5	20.7	20.6	20.3
2011	20.5	20.6	20.7	21.2	21.3	21.6	21.8	21.8	21.8	22.0	22.1	22.0	21.5
2012	21.8	21.9	22.2	22.3	22.5	22.8	23.0	23.1	23.1	23.1	23.2	23.2	22.7
2013	23.5	23.6	23.7	23.8	24.0	24.4	24.2	24.1	23.9	23.9	24.0	23.9	23.9
2014	23.6	23.4	23.5	23.7	23.9	24.4	24.5	24.6	24.4	24.4	24.5	24.6	24.1
2015	24.5	24.6	24.7	24.9	25.1	25.6	26.0	26.0	25.8	25.8	25.9	25.8	25.4
Trade, Transportation, and Utilities													
2005	79.4	78.0	77.9	78.6	79.1	79.7	79.8	80.1	79.6	80.2	82.0	83.5	79.8
2006	78.8	77.4	77.7	78.0	79.0	79.6	78.4	78.5	77.8	78.9	81.1	82.4	79.0
2007	77.9	76.1	76.8	75.9	77.2	77.8	77.1	76.8	76.7	77.6	79.4	80.3	77.5
2008	76.4	74.9	75.0	75.2	76.1	76.8	76.1	76.2	75.8	76.5	77.4	78.5	76.2
2009	74.1	72.9	72.5	72.4	73.3	74.1	73.0	73.1	72.6	73.1	74.6	75.6	73.4
2010	71.7	70.2	70.7	71.3	71.8	72.6	72.0	72.5	71.8	72.4	73.9	75.0	72.2
2011	71.3	70.2	70.4	71.3	71.8	72.5	72.0	72.6	72.2	72.7	74.5	75.9	72.3
2012	72.6	71.4	71.5	72.2	73.3	74.0	73.5	73.6	73.1	73.9	75.7	76.3	73.4
2013	72.4	71.4	71.6	72.3	73.2	74.4	74.0	74.0	73.7	74.9	76.5	77.2	73.8
2014	73.2	72.4	72.7	73.1	73.9	74.6	74.1	74.4	74.2	76.0	76.7	77.2	74.4
2015	73.9	72.7	72.9	73.4	74.2	75.2	74.7	74.9	74.7	74.9	76.2	77.0	74.6
Wholesale Trade													
2005	15.9	15.7	15.7	15.7	15.6	15.6	15.9	15.8	15.6	15.6	15.7	15.7	15.7
2006	15.3	15.2	15.2	14.9	14.9	15.0	14.9	14.9	14.7	14.7	14.6	14.8	14.9
2007	14.7	14.6	14.8	14.7	14.7	14.8	14.6	14.5	14.2	14.2	14.1	14.1	14.5
2008	13.7	13.7	13.7	13.7	13.8	13.9	14.0	14.0	13.9	13.9	13.9	14.0	13.9
2009	13.6	13.6	13.5	13.5	13.4	13.4	13.4	13.4	13.2	13.1	13.1	13.2	13.4
2010	12.7	12.7	12.7	12.9	13.0	13.0	13.0	13.1	13.1	13.2	13.3	13.2	13.0
2011	13.1	13.1	13.1	13.3	13.3	13.3	13.3	13.4	13.2	13.1	13.2	13.2	13.2
2012	13.1	13.1	13.2	13.4	13.6	13.7	13.8	13.7	13.6	13.6	13.6	13.6	13.5
2013	13.5	13.4	13.5	13.5	13.6	13.7	13.8	13.8	13.6	13.6	13.6	13.5	13.6
2014	13.5	13.5	13.5	13.7	13.8	13.9	13.9	14.0	13.9	13.9	13.9	13.9	13.8
2015	13.9	13.9	13.9	13.9	13.9	14.0	14.1	14.1	13.9	13.8	13.9	13.9	13.9
Retail Trade													
2005	50.6	49.3	49.2	49.5	49.9	50.3	50.3	50.5	49.8	50.5	52.0	53.5	50.5
2006	49.8	48.5	48.7	49.4	50.2	50.7	50.1	50.0	49.2	50.2	52.6	53.6	50.3
2007	50.0	48.4	48.7	48.1	49.1	49.6	49.3	49.2	49.0	49.8	51.6	52.4	49.6
2008	49.6	48.2	48.2	48.3	48.8	49.3	48.8	48.9	48.3	48.8	49.7	50.6	49.0
2009	47.3	46.2	45.9	45.8	46.6	47.4	46.7	46.8	46.2	46.8	48.2	49.0	46.9
2010	46.2	44.8	45.1	45.5	45.9	46.7	46.2	46.6	45.9	46.5	47.8	48.9	46.3
2011	46.1	45.0	45.3	45.9	46.2	46.9	46.5	46.9	46.5	47.1	48.7	49.8	46.7
2012	47.3	46.2	46.2	46.7	47.5	48.0	47.5	47.7	47.1	47.9	49.7	50.0	47.7
2013	47.0	45.9	46.1	46.6	47.2	48.1	47.8	47.8	47.5	48.5	49.8	50.3	47.7
2014	47.2	46.3	46.4	46.8	47.4	48.0	47.6	47.8	47.5	49.2	49.6	49.8	47.8
2015	47.1	46.0	46.1	46.5	47.2	48.0	47.7	47.9	47.7	48.0	49.0	49.7	47.6
Transportation and Utilities													
2005	12.9	13.0	13.0	13.4	13.6	13.8	13.6	13.8	14.2	14.1	14.3	14.3	13.7
2006	13.7	13.7	13.8	13.7	13.9	13.9	13.4	13.6	13.9	14.0	13.9	14.0	13.8
2007	13.2	13.1	13.3	13.1	13.4	13.4	13.2	13.1	13.5	13.6	13.7	13.8	13.4
2008	13.1	13.0	13.1	13.2	13.5	13.6	13.3	13.3	13.6	13.8	13.8	13.9	13.4
2009	13.2	13.1	13.1	13.1	13.3	13.3	12.9	12.9	13.2	13.2	13.3	13.4	13.2
2010	12.8	12.7	12.9	12.9	12.9	12.9	12.8	12.8	12.8	12.7	12.8	12.9	12.8
2011	12.1	12.1	12.0	12.1	12.3	12.3	12.2	12.3	12.5	12.5	12.6	12.9	12.3
2012	12.2	12.1	12.1	12.1	12.2	12.3	12.2	12.2	12.4	12.4	12.4	12.7	12.3
2013	11.9	12.1	12.0	12.2	12.4	12.6	12.4	12.4	12.6	12.8	13.1	13.4	12.5
2014	12.5	12.6	12.8	12.6	12.7	12.7	12.6	12.6	12.8	12.9	13.2	13.5	12.8
2015	12.9	12.8	12.9	13.0	13.1	13.2	12.9	12.9	13.1	13.1	13.3	13.4	13.1

Employment by Industry: Albany-Schenectady-Troy, NY, 2005–2015—*Continued*

(Numbers in thousands, not seasonally adjusted)

Industry and year	January	February	March	April	May	June	July	August	September	October	November	December	Annual average
Information													
2005................	10.5	10.6	10.8	11.1	11.0	11.1	11.0	11.1	10.9	10.9	10.8	10.9	10.9
2006................	10.8	10.7	10.7	10.6	10.6	10.6	10.5	10.4	10.1	10.2	10.2	10.2	10.5
2007................	10.1	10.0	10.0	9.9	10.0	10.0	10.0	10.0	9.8	9.7	9.7	9.8	9.9
2008................	9.4	9.4	9.4	9.5	9.8	9.9	9.9	9.9	9.7	9.8	9.8	9.8	9.7
2009................	9.8	9.7	9.6	9.6	9.6	9.7	9.6	9.6	9.4	9.2	9.3	9.3	9.5
2010................	9.0	9.0	9.0	8.8	8.9	8.9	9.0	9.0	8.8	8.8	8.8	8.8	8.9
2011................	8.8	8.7	8.7	8.8	8.8	8.9	9.0	8.2	8.8	8.8	8.8	8.8	8.8
2012................	8.7	8.7	8.7	8.7	8.7	8.7	8.7	8.6	8.5	8.6	8.6	8.5	8.6
2013................	8.5	8.5	8.5	8.6	8.5	8.5	8.5	8.6	8.5	8.5	8.6	8.7	8.5
2014................	8.6	8.7	8.7	8.7	8.7	8.8	8.5	8.5	8.4	8.4	8.4	8.4	8.6
2015................	8.3	8.2	8.2	8.2	8.2	8.2	8.4	8.3	8.2	8.3	8.4	8.4	8.3
Financial Activities													
2005................	25.9	25.9	26.0	26.1	26.2	26.6	26.8	26.8	26.5	26.5	26.4	26.6	26.4
2006................	26.2	26.3	26.5	26.7	26.6	27.0	27.1	27.0	26.6	26.7	26.7	26.7	26.7
2007................	26.3	26.0	26.0	26.1	26.2	26.7	26.5	26.4	26.0	26.0	26.1	26.1	26.2
2008................	25.9	25.8	25.9	25.9	26.0	26.4	26.4	26.3	25.8	25.6	25.5	25.4	25.9
2009................	25.3	25.2	25.2	24.9	25.0	25.3	25.1	25.1	24.6	24.5	24.4	24.4	24.9
2010................	24.3	24.2	24.3	24.3	24.3	24.7	24.8	24.7	24.3	24.5	24.4	24.6	24.5
2011................	24.3	24.3	24.3	24.4	24.4	24.8	25.0	25.1	24.7	24.6	24.6	24.7	24.6
2012................	24.7	24.7	24.8	24.9	24.9	25.5	25.6	25.5	25.2	25.3	25.4	25.5	25.2
2013................	25.0	25.0	25.1	25.2	25.3	25.7	25.7	25.6	25.2	25.3	25.2	25.3	25.3
2014................	25.2	25.1	25.1	25.0	25.2	25.7	25.9	25.7	25.4	25.5	25.4	25.5	25.4
2015................	25.5	25.5	25.5	25.7	25.8	26.2	26.2	26.2	25.8	25.9	26.2	26.2	25.9
Professional and Business Services													
2005................	49.5	49.7	49.6	50.7	50.5	51.7	52.2	51.9	52.0	51.3	51.5	50.8	51.0
2006................	50.6	50.8	51.4	52.3	51.7	52.5	53.0	53.0	52.8	52.4	52.9	53.0	52.2
2007................	51.3	51.8	52.1	52.4	52.5	54.0	54.2	54.2	53.6	53.5	53.9	54.0	53.1
2008................	54.0	54.1	54.4	55.1	54.9	56.0	55.8	56.0	55.0	54.8	54.5	54.1	54.9
2009................	52.9	52.3	52.6	52.3	51.7	51.8	51.6	51.2	50.9	51.2	50.8	50.5	51.7
2010................	49.1	49.2	49.5	50.5	50.6	51.0	51.9	51.5	50.7	51.1	51.2	50.9	50.6
2011................	50.0	50.2	50.3	51.4	51.2	51.8	52.1	51.8	51.7	51.8	52.4	51.6	51.4
2012................	51.4	51.4	51.8	52.7	52.8	53.3	53.2	53.2	52.3	52.6	53.2	52.0	52.5
2013................	51.8	51.8	51.9	52.9	53.0	53.6	53.5	53.2	52.8	52.3	52.3	51.8	52.6
2014................	51.1	51.2	51.4	52.4	53.0	53.5	53.9	53.8	53.1	53.3	53.7	53.1	52.8
2015................	53.3	53.2	53.0	53.9	54.4	55.1	54.9	54.9	53.9	53.2	53.1	52.9	53.8
Education and Health Services													
2005................	75.6	78.5	78.1	78.8	77.5	75.2	74.9	74.3	76.7	78.3	78.5	78.1	77.0
2006................	75.6	78.7	78.8	79.2	78.3	76.0	75.2	74.9	78.7	80.1	80.4	80.5	78.0
2007................	77.2	80.3	80.4	80.5	79.9	77.7	76.6	76.3	80.4	81.7	82.7	82.5	79.7
2008................	79.6	83.0	82.6	82.9	82.6	80.1	78.4	77.8	81.5	82.8	84.2	83.5	81.6
2009................	80.8	84.6	84.8	84.8	83.7	81.1	79.7	79.4	83.3	85	85.7	84.5	83.1
2010................	82.2	86.3	86.4	87.1	85.6	82.4	81.3	81	85.4	87	88	86.7	85
2011................	83.6	88.1	88	88.5	87.2	83.8	82.5	81.9	86.6	88.8	89.3	88.1	86.4
2012................	85.1	89.8	90.1	90.3	89.2	85.9	83.8	83.2	88.7	91.2	91.7	91.1	88.3
2013................	87.3	92.0	92.0	92.9	91.2	87.0	85.7	85.2	91.0	93.7	94.4	93.8	90.5
2014................	89.0	94.3	94.5	94.9	92.7	89.5	88.1	87.7	92.1	95.5	95.8	94.6	92.4
2015................	90.4	95.1	95.3	95.5	93.5	90.9	89.0	88.5	91.3	94.2	94.5	93.4	92.6
Leisure and Hospitality													
2005................	29.1	29.3	29.8	31.1	32.3	33.6	33.8	35.9	32.9	31.9	31.4	31.5	31.9
2006................	29.2	29.9	30.9	31.1	32.7	34.2	34.2	36.0	33.1	32.5	31.7	31.7	32.3
2007................	30.2	30.4	31.2	31.8	33.9	35.2	35.6	37.2	34.4	33.8	33.0	32.4	33.3
2008................	30.7	31.2	31.9	33.1	34.9	35.7	36.5	37.7	34.6	33.9	33.1	32.2	33.8
2009................	30.4	30.7	31.2	32.2	34.4	35.3	36.0	37.3	34.6	33.7	33.0	32.6	33.5
2010................	30.7	31.4	31.7	33.5	34.9	35.5	36.8	37.7	35.3	34.8	34.4	33.7	34.2
2011................	31.8	32.4	32.7	34.1	35.3	36.4	37.3	38.5	36.4	35.5	34.8	34.5	35.0
2012................	32.5	33.5	33.6	35.1	36.9	38.3	38.7	40.2	37.8	37.2	36.5	36.0	36.4
2013................	33.3	34.1	34.8	36.0	38.1	39.8	39.8	40.9	38.8	38.1	37.3	36.8	37.3
2014................	34.3	34.8	35.2	36.6	38.6	40.2	39.9	40.7	38.2	38.2	37.4	37.0	37.6
2015................	35.3	35.6	35.8	37.1	39.5	40.2	40.9	41.7	39.5	40.1	39.0	38.2	38.6

Employment by Industry: Albany-Schenectady-Troy, NY, 2005–2015—*Continued*

(Numbers in thousands, not seasonally adjusted)

Industry and year	January	February	March	April	May	June	July	August	September	October	November	December	Annual average
Other Services													
2005	18.3	18.5	18.4	18.4	18.3	18.2	18.0	18.0	18.0	18.2	18.3	18.2	18.2
2006	17.7	18.0	18.3	18.2	18.3	18.3	18.2	18.1	18.1	18.4	18.4	18.5	18.2
2007	18.2	18.4	18.5	18.3	18.5	18.5	18.0	18.0	18.0	18.3	18.4	18.5	18.3
2008	18.4	18.5	18.5	18.4	18.5	18.5	18.6	18.6	18.3	18.7	18.8	18.7	18.5
2009	18.6	18.8	18.9	18.6	18.8	18.7	18.6	18.3	18.1	18.3	18.2	18.2	18.5
2010	17.6	17.7	17.7	17.8	17.9	17.7	17.9	18.0	17.6	17.7	17.7	17.9	17.8
2011	17.6	17.7	17.7	17.9	18.0	17.7	18.0	18.0	18.0	17.7	17.7	17.8	17.8
2012	17.5	17.6	17.9	17.9	17.9	18.0	18.0	17.9	17.8	17.9	17.9	17.8	17.8
2013	17.5	17.7	17.9	17.8	17.9	18.1	18.1	18.0	17.7	18.1	18.2	18.3	17.9
2014	18.0	18.1	18.2	18.3	18.2	18.0	18.3	18.3	18.1	18.3	18.5	18.5	18.2
2015	18.3	18.4	18.4	18.5	18.6	18.7	18.8	18.6	18.0	18.2	18.3	18.3	18.4
Government													
2005	107.2	108.5	108.6	109.1	109.1	108.4	102.8	102.1	105.9	108.3	108.5	108.6	107.3
2006	106.1	108.1	108.1	108.6	108.5	107.6	102.3	101.3	104.9	107.9	108.5	109.2	106.8
2007	106.9	108.9	108.6	108.8	109.4	109.2	102.5	102.7	106.1	109.4	109.8	110.9	107.8
2008	107.1	109.2	109.0	110.5	111.3	110.8	105.2	104.1	107.2	110.4	110.5	111.0	108.9
2009	107.3	110.1	109.6	111.1	111.0	110.2	104.3	102.8	105.8	109.1	109.7	109.9	108.4
2010	107.2	108.9	108.5	109.1	110.9	110.2	101.3	99.1	102.2	104.2	104.8	104.6	105.9
2011	100.7	103.3	103.1	104.3	104.6	104.1	98.7	97.2	99.5	102.9	103.3	103.4	102.1
2012	100.7	103.0	102.3	103.2	103.8	102.7	96.4	95.8	99.0	102.0	103.0	102.5	101.2
2013	100.7	103.5	103.1	103.0	103.6	103.1	97.2	96.0	98.4	101.6	102.8	102.3	101.3
2014	99.2	102.3	102.2	102.5	102.5	101.9	96.3	95.2	98.5	101.9	102.2	102.4	100.6
2015	100.2	102.1	102.1	102.0	102.6	101.7	95.8	94.7	98.1	101.5	102.0	102.0	100.4

Employment by Industry: Greenville-Anderson-Mauldin, SC, 2005–2015

(Numbers in thousands, not seasonally adjusted)

Industry and year	January	February	March	April	May	June	July	August	September	October	November	December	Annual average
Total Nonfarm													
2005	358.1	360.4	361.0	364.1	365.8	362.8	361.2	363.6	366.4	368.1	371.1	368.0	364.2
2006	364.3	367.0	368.0	370.0	371.8	369.8	365.9	368.9	372.0	375.9	377.6	378.4	370.8
2007	371.7	374.6	378.1	379.6	381.8	381.8	377.3	378.5	381.3	380.9	384.9	385.2	379.6
2008	378.9	380.9	382.4	381.6	384.5	381.1	375.2	376.0	378.4	376.9	376.6	372.4	378.7
2009	358.8	358.3	358.1	355.1	356.2	351.7	348.8	348.8	349.9	351.4	353.2	352.4	353.6
2010	345.0	347.1	350.0	353.6	357.9	355.9	353.3	354.7	356.3	358.6	360.5	361.1	354.5
2011	351.0	357.2	360.8	363.6	364.5	362.2	360.6	363.0	365.1	365.6	367.8	367.5	362.4
2012	360.8	363.6	366.8	367.5	370.8	369.8	364.9	367.5	370.3	370.6	374.7	375.1	368.5
2013	368.3	371.2	373.9	375.3	379.0	381.3	376.7	379.9	383.9	386.3	388.0	388.7	379.4
2014	378.6	380.3	385.2	386.8	389.5	389.4	384.3	387.7	390.7	393.8	397.1	398.6	388.5
2015	390.8	393.1	395.2	397.7	401.4	402.0	400.3	402.8	404.0	408.7	408.5	410.7	401.3
Total Private													
2005	305.3	307.1	307.4	310.6	312.2	309.7	310.9	312.8	312.7	314.0	316.5	313.5	311.1
2006	310.5	312.2	313.3	315.5	317.2	316.0	314.8	317.2	317.7	319.9	321.9	322.4	316.6
2007	316.5	319.0	322.1	323.7	325.7	326.2	324.3	325.7	325.2	324.0	327.0	327.7	323.9
2008	321.8	323.3	324.3	323.9	325.9	323.3	320.2	321.4	320.6	318.2	317.2	313.8	321.2
2009	301.2	300.4	300.0	296.8	297.9	294.3	294.1	293.8	293.0	293.6	295.1	294.4	296.2
2010	288.4	290.3	293.1	296.4	299.3	298.7	299.4	301.1	300.8	302.4	304.2	305.0	298.3
2011	295.7	301.6	305.2	307.7	308.5	307.1	307.0	309.8	309.8	309.6	311.6	311.4	307.1
2012	304.8	307.2	310.3	311.0	313.8	313.7	311.0	313.2	313.7	313.2	317.0	317.5	312.2
2013	311.0	313.7	316.0	317.2	321.1	323.7	321.7	324.5	326.4	327.9	329.7	330.3	321.9
2014	320.8	322.1	326.8	328.4	330.7	331.4	328.7	331.4	332.4	334.6	337.7	339.1	330.3
2015	332.1	333.8	335.6	338.1	341.6	342.9	343.6	345.4	344.6	348.4	348.2	350.3	342.1
Goods Producing													
2005	78.6	78.9	79.2	79.3	79.3	78.5	78.0	77.9	77.3	77.6	77.3	76.6	78.2
2006	76.3	76.3	76.1	76.4	77.0	76.7	76.1	76.4	76.5	76.5	76.9	76.8	76.5
2007	76.2	76.6	77.1	77.1	77.4	77.8	77.4	77.7	77.5	77.0	77.1	77.0	77.2
2008	76.7	76.9	76.7	76.5	76.6	76.6	75.4	75.0	74.6	73.8	72.9	72.0	75.3
2009	70.6	69.5	68.4	67.1	66.8	66.5	65.6	64.9	64.4	64.1	63.8	63.7	66.3
2010	62.0	61.6	61.8	62.2	62.7	62.9	63.0	63.0	62.9	62.8	63.0	63.4	62.6
2011	61.5	63.1	63.4	63.9	64.0	64.3	64.4	64.7	64.3	64.4	64.6	64.5	63.9
2012	64.0	64.3	64.8	64.9	65.4	65.3	65.1	65.6	65.6	66.0	66.2	66.4	65.3
2013	66.2	66.9	67.5	67.5	68.1	68.5	68.2	68.7	68.9	69.2	69.5	69.6	68.2
2014	68.8	69.0	69.7	69.9	70.5	70.9	70.3	70.7	70.6	70.6	70.9	71.2	70.3
2015	70.7	70.7	71.0	71.1	72.0	72.7	72.8	72.8	72.7	72.9	72.2	72.5	72.0
Service-Providing													
2005	279.5	281.5	281.8	284.8	286.5	284.3	283.2	285.7	289.1	290.5	293.8	291.4	286.0
2006	288.0	290.7	291.9	293.6	294.8	293.1	289.8	292.5	295.5	299.4	300.7	301.6	294.3
2007	295.5	298.0	301.0	302.5	304.4	304.0	299.9	300.8	303.8	303.9	307.8	308.2	302.5
2008	302.2	304.0	305.7	305.1	307.9	304.5	299.8	301.0	303.8	303.1	303.7	300.4	303.4
2009	288.2	288.8	289.7	288.0	289.4	285.2	283.2	283.9	285.5	287.3	289.4	288.7	287.3
2010	283.0	285.5	288.2	291.4	295.2	293.0	290.3	291.7	293.4	295.8	297.5	297.7	291.9
2011	289.5	294.1	297.4	299.7	300.5	297.9	296.2	298.3	300.8	301.2	303.2	303.0	298.5
2012	296.8	299.3	302.0	302.6	305.4	304.5	299.8	301.9	304.7	304.6	308.5	308.7	303.2
2013	302.1	304.3	306.4	307.8	310.9	312.8	308.5	311.2	315.0	317.1	318.5	319.1	311.1
2014	309.8	311.3	315.5	316.9	319.0	318.5	314.0	317.0	320.1	323.2	326.2	327.4	318.2
2015	320.1	322.4	324.2	326.6	329.4	329.3	327.5	330.0	331.3	335.8	336.3	338.2	329.3
Mining, Logging, and Construction													
2005	20.5	20.5	20.7	21.0	21.3	21.3	21.9	21.8	21.8	21.7	21.9	21.5	21.3
2006	21.4	21.2	21.1	21.5	21.7	21.5	21.8	22.1	22.3	22.0	22.4	22.2	21.8
2007	21.8	21.8	22.4	22.6	22.8	23.1	23.1	23.1	22.8	22.3	22.2	22.0	22.5
2008	21.5	21.6	21.6	21.3	21.5	21.6	20.9	20.7	20.4	20.0	19.7	19.3	20.8
2009	18.1	17.8	17.5	17.0	17.0	16.9	16.5	16.1	15.7	15.3	15.2	15.3	16.5
2010	14.5	14.3	14.4	14.7	14.9	15.0	15.0	14.8	14.7	14.6	14.6	14.7	14.7
2011	13.4	14.2	14.3	14.4	14.6	14.6	14.5	14.5	14.3	14.2	14.4	14.3	14.3
2012	14.1	14.3	14.6	14.4	14.7	14.7	14.6	14.7	14.6	14.8	14.9	14.9	14.6
2013	14.7	14.8	15.1	15.2	15.5	15.7	15.8	15.9	15.9	16.0	16.2	16.3	15.6
2014	15.7	15.7	16.1	16.1	16.3	16.5	16.1	16.4	16.3	16.3	16.5	16.6	16.2
2015	16.1	16.1	16.2	16.2	16.7	17.1	17.1	17.1	17.0	17.2	17.4	17.4	16.8

Employment by Industry: Greenville-Anderson-Mauldin, SC, 2005–2015—*Continued*

(Numbers in thousands, not seasonally adjusted)

Industry and year	January	February	March	April	May	June	July	August	September	October	November	December	Annual average
Manufacturing													
2005	58.1	58.4	58.5	58.3	58.0	57.2	56.1	56.1	55.5	55.9	55.4	55.1	56.9
2006	54.9	55.1	55.0	54.9	55.3	55.2	54.3	54.3	54.2	54.5	54.5	54.6	54.7
2007	54.4	54.8	54.7	54.5	54.6	54.7	54.3	54.6	54.7	54.7	54.9	55.0	54.7
2008	55.2	55.3	55.1	55.2	55.1	55.0	54.5	54.3	54.2	53.8	53.2	52.7	54.5
2009	52.5	51.7	50.9	50.1	49.8	49.6	49.1	48.8	48.7	48.8	48.6	48.4	49.8
2010	47.5	47.3	47.4	47.5	47.8	47.9	48.0	48.2	48.2	48.2	48.4	48.7	47.9
2011	48.1	48.9	49.1	49.5	49.4	49.7	49.9	50.2	50.0	50.2	50.2	50.2	49.6
2012	49.9	50.0	50.2	50.5	50.7	50.6	50.5	50.9	51.0	51.2	51.3	51.5	50.7
2013	51.5	52.1	52.4	52.3	52.6	52.8	52.4	52.8	53.0	53.2	53.3	53.3	52.6
2014	53.1	53.3	53.6	53.8	54.2	54.4	54.2	54.3	54.3	54.3	54.4	54.6	54.0
2015	54.6	54.6	54.8	54.9	55.3	55.6	55.7	55.7	55.7	55.7	54.8	55.1	55.2
Trade, Transportation, and Utilities													
2005	73.1	73.2	73.5	74.3	74.8	73.7	74.6	75.1	74.4	75.3	77.3	78.1	74.8
2006	75.7	75.7	76.3	76.2	76.3	76.3	76.0	76.6	76.2	77.2	78.8	79.5	76.7
2007	76.6	76.8	77.3	77.5	78.1	78.2	77.7	77.1	76.9	76.8	78.8	79.5	77.6
2008	77.4	77.1	77.3	75.4	75.6	75.3	75.5	75.4	75.1	74.2	74.9	75.0	75.7
2009	70.5	69.4	69.0	68.8	68.9	68.2	68.0	67.9	67.6	67.4	68.1	68.4	68.5
2010	66.2	66.2	66.6	67.4	67.9	67.9	67.8	68.0	67.7	68.7	70.0	70.5	67.9
2011	67.6	68.3	68.8	69.0	69.2	69.3	69.3	69.4	69.0	69.2	70.4	70.9	69.2
2012	68.8	68.6	69.1	69.3	69.6	69.6	69.5	69.5	69.3	69.6	71.3	71.4	69.6
2013	68.5	68.5	69.3	69.6	70.2	70.8	70.6	71.2	70.8	71.5	72.9	73.6	70.6
2014	70.2	70.1	70.5	70.8	71.3	71.9	71.5	71.9	71.7	72.8	74.3	75.3	71.9
2015	73.1	72.9	73.5	74.2	74.6	74.8	75.1	75.3	74.8	75.9	76.7	77.7	74.9
Wholesale Trade													
2005	15.6	15.9	15.9	16.4	16.6	16.4	16.5	16.5	16.5	16.8	16.9	17.1	16.4
2006	17.0	17.1	17.1	17.4	17.3	17.3	17.0	17.1	17.1	17.5	17.6	17.7	17.3
2007	17.6	17.9	17.7	17.8	17.9	18.1	18.0	17.8	17.7	17.9	18.1	18.1	17.9
2008	18.0	18.2	18.2	18.0	18.0	17.9	17.9	17.8	17.6	17.4	17.3	17.1	17.8
2009	16.7	16.4	16.3	16.2	16.1	15.9	15.9	15.9	15.8	15.9	15.8	15.7	16.1
2010	15.7	15.9	15.9	16.4	16.6	16.6	16.6	16.7	16.6	16.9	16.9	16.9	16.5
2011	16.8	17.0	17.1	17.0	17.0	17.1	17.2	17.2	17.2	17.2	17.2	17.3	17.1
2012	17.1	17.1	17.2	17.3	17.3	17.4	17.4	17.5	17.2	17.3	17.3	17.4	17.3
2013	17.1	17.2	17.2	17.3	17.5	17.6	17.5	17.7	17.5	17.6	17.7	17.7	17.5
2014	17.1	17.1	17.1	17.2	17.4	17.6	17.6	17.7	17.7	18.2	18.3	18.4	17.6
2015	18.7	18.7	18.9	19.0	19.1	19.2	19.3	19.3	19.3	19.4	19.5	19.5	19.2
Retail Trade													
2005	45.3	44.9	45.1	45.7	45.8	45.0	45.6	46.0	45.3	46.1	47.8	48.5	45.9
2006	46.1	45.9	46.4	46.0	46.1	46.0	46.1	46.4	45.9	46.8	48.4	49.0	46.6
2007	46.2	45.8	46.4	46.7	47.1	46.9	46.7	46.4	46.3	46.0	47.5	48.1	46.7
2008	46.3	45.7	45.9	44.2	44.4	44.2	44.3	44.5	44.5	44.0	44.8	45.0	44.8
2009	41.5	41.0	40.7	40.8	40.9	40.5	40.4	40.4	40.2	40.2	41.1	41.5	40.8
2010	39.7	39.5	39.9	40.1	40.4	40.4	40.3	40.4	40.2	40.8	42.0	42.5	40.5
2011	40.0	40.3	40.7	40.9	40.9	40.8	40.9	41.0	40.7	40.9	42.0	42.4	41.0
2012	40.7	40.6	40.8	40.7	41.0	40.9	40.8	40.8	40.8	40.9	42.6	42.6	41.1
2013	40.4	40.2	41.0	41.2	41.5	41.9	41.9	42.2	42.1	42.6	43.9	44.3	41.9
2014	42.0	42.0	42.3	42.2	42.4	42.8	42.5	42.7	42.5	43.1	44.5	45.1	42.8
2015	43.2	43.0	43.3	43.9	44.1	44.2	44.3	44.6	44.2	45.2	45.9	46.6	44.4
Transportation and Utilities													
2005	12.2	12.4	12.5	12.2	12.4	12.3	12.5	12.6	12.6	12.4	12.6	12.5	12.4
2006	12.6	12.7	12.8	12.8	12.9	13.0	12.9	13.1	13.2	12.9	12.8	12.8	12.9
2007	12.8	13.1	13.2	13.0	13.1	13.2	13.0	12.9	12.9	12.9	13.2	13.3	13.1
2008	13.1	13.2	13.2	13.2	13.2	13.2	13.3	13.1	13.0	12.8	12.8	12.9	13.1
2009	12.3	12.0	12.0	11.8	11.9	11.8	11.7	11.6	11.6	11.3	11.2	11.2	11.7
2010	10.8	10.8	10.8	10.9	10.9	10.9	10.9	10.9	10.9	11.0	11.1	11.1	10.9
2011	10.8	11.0	11.0	11.1	11.3	11.4	11.2	11.2	11.1	11.1	11.2	11.2	11.1
2012	11.0	10.9	11.1	11.3	11.3	11.3	11.3	11.2	11.3	11.4	11.4	11.4	11.2
2013	11.0	11.1	11.1	11.1	11.2	11.3	11.2	11.3	11.2	11.3	11.3	11.6	11.2
2014	11.1	11.0	11.1	11.4	11.5	11.5	11.4	11.5	11.5	11.5	11.5	11.8	11.4
2015	11.2	11.2	11.3	11.3	11.4	11.4	11.5	11.4	11.3	11.3	11.3	11.6	11.4

Employment by Industry: Greenville-Anderson-Mauldin, SC, 2005–2015—*Continued*

(Numbers in thousands, not seasonally adjusted)

Industry and year	January	February	March	April	May	June	July	August	September	October	November	December	Annual average
Information													
2005	7.1	7.2	7.2	7.3	7.3	7.3	7.2	7.2	7.1	7.1	7.0	7.2	7.2
2006	7.1	7.3	7.2	7.3	7.3	7.2	7.2	7.2	6.9	7.0	7.0	7.0	7.1
2007	6.9	7.0	7.0	7.0	7.1	7.2	7.5	7.4	7.1	7.1	7.2	7.2	7.1
2008	7.1	7.3	7.3	7.7	7.8	7.7	7.8	7.7	7.6	7.6	7.5	7.6	7.6
2009	7.2	7.4	7.5	7.3	7.3	7.3	7.5	7.1	6.9	6.8	6.8	6.8	7.2
2010	6.9	7.1	7.1	6.6	6.7	7.1	7.2	6.6	6.6	6.6	6.6	7.0	6.8
2011	7.1	7.0	7.3	7.1	6.9	7.0	6.8	6.8	6.7	7.5	7.5	7.5	7.1
2012	7.3	7.6	7.5	7.6	7.8	7.8	7.2	7.1	7.1	7.0	7.1	7.3	7.4
2013	7.3	7.4	7.3	7.3	7.4	7.3	7.4	7.2	7.2	7.2	7.1	7.1	7.3
2014	7.0	6.9	6.9	6.9	7.1	7.1	7.2	7.1	7.1	7.1	7.3	7.3	7.1
2015	7.4	7.4	7.4	7.3	7.4	7.4	7.4	7.4	7.4	7.4	7.4	7.5	7.4
Financial Activities													
2005	16.1	16.2	16.5	16.4	16.3	16.3	16.4	16.4	16.4	16.0	16.1	15.8	16.2
2006	15.7	15.4	15.5	15.4	15.3	15.2	15.2	15.2	15.1	14.5	14.4	14.3	15.1
2007	14.5	14.5	14.6	14.6	14.9	14.9	15.0	15.3	15.4	15.7	15.8	16.0	15.1
2008	16.0	16.1	16.2	16.0	16.0	15.9	15.7	16.0	15.8	15.7	15.8	15.7	15.9
2009	15.5	15.5	15.4	15.1	15.3	15.0	15.2	15.2	15.2	15.3	15.4	15.4	15.3
2010	15.1	15.2	15.2	15.2	15.3	15.2	15.1	15.1	14.9	15.2	15.3	15.2	15.2
2011	15.0	15.0	15.0	15.1	15.1	14.9	15.1	15.1	15.1	15.1	15.1	15.1	15.1
2012	14.8	14.8	15.0	14.9	15.0	15.1	15.2	15.1	15.2	15.2	15.3	15.5	15.1
2013	15.5	15.6	15.7	15.9	16.0	16.1	16.0	16.0	16.0	16.1	16.2	16.2	15.9
2014	15.7	15.7	15.9	15.9	16.0	16.2	16.3	16.4	16.3	16.3	16.4	16.6	16.1
2015	16.2	16.2	16.3	16.4	16.5	16.7	16.8	16.7	16.7	16.6	16.7	16.8	16.6
Professional and Business Services													
2005	49.2	49.2	48.3	50.1	50.9	50.3	50.8	51.7	52.8	53.5	53.7	51.9	51.0
2006	51.7	52.6	53.1	54.0	54.4	54.8	53.8	54.9	55.9	56.7	56.6	56.5	54.6
2007	55.5	56.5	57.7	58.1	58.8	59.0	58.2	58.7	58.6	58.1	58.8	58.8	58.1
2008	57.3	57.7	57.8	58.8	59.8	58.9	57.4	58.1	57.9	57.1	56.3	54.4	57.6
2009	50.8	51.0	51.2	49.3	49.4	48.6	49.8	50.0	50.4	51.8	52.9	52.2	50.6
2010	51.4	52.5	53.6	54.8	55.4	55.4	56.3	57.3	57.3	57.9	58.3	58.3	55.7
2011	56.4	58.2	59.3	60.4	60.5	60.4	61.0	62.6	63.1	62.4	62.5	62.4	60.8
2012	60.6	61.1	62.3	62.5	62.9	63.4	62.7	63.8	63.2	62.6	63.6	63.6	62.7
2013	62.0	62.8	63.3	62.9	64.1	65.4	64.4	65.3	66.4	66.7	66.9	66.6	64.7
2014	64.1	65.0	66.4	67.0	67.0	66.6	65.9	66.9	67.7	68.7	69.1	69.0	67.0
2015	67.0	67.6	67.4	68.4	69.5	69.7	70.5	71.1	71.4	73.0	72.5	72.5	70.1
Education and Health Services													
2005	35.7	36.1	36.0	36.2	36.1	36.2	35.9	36.2	36.6	36.7	36.9	36.4	36.3
2006	36.8	37.0	36.9	37.1	37.1	36.5	36.6	36.8	37.2	37.7	37.6	37.5	37.1
2007	37.3	37.5	37.6	38.1	38.1	38.0	38.2	38.6	38.7	38.2	38.2	38.1	38.1
2008	38.3	38.8	38.8	38.7	39.0	38.6	38.8	39.0	39.2	39.2	39.4	39.2	38.9
2009	38.6	38.9	39.1	39.4	39.8	39.6	39.4	39.6	39.4	39.6	39.7	39.7	39.4
2010	40.4	40.9	41.1	41.6	42.1	41.8	41.5	41.9	41.8	42.4	42.5	42.3	41.7
2011	41.5	42.3	42.5	42.0	42.1	41.9	41.5	41.6	41.6	41.4	41.6	41.6	41.8
2012	40.8	41.4	41.6	41.4	41.9	40.9	40.4	40.7	42.1	42.0	42.3	42.3	41.5
2013	41.5	42.0	42.2	42.3	42.9	42.6	42.3	42.9	43.5	43.9	44.2	44.5	42.9
2014	43.6	44.1	44.4	44.3	44.5	44.4	44.1	44.8	45.2	45.8	45.9	46.1	44.8
2015	45.1	45.8	46.1	46.2	46.4	46.3	45.8	46.9	46.9	47.4	47.6	47.6	46.5
Leisure and Hospitality													
2005	32.7	33.3	33.6	34.2	34.6	34.6	35.0	35.1	34.8	35.1	35.4	34.8	34.4
2006	34.6	35.1	35.3	36.0	36.5	36.1	36.6	36.7	36.4	36.8	37.0	37.2	36.2
2007	35.8	36.3	36.7	37.4	37.3	37.2	36.7	37.4	37.4	37.8	37.8	37.7	37.1
2008	36.3	36.5	37.1	37.6	37.7	37.1	36.7	37.2	37.2	37.6	37.3	36.9	37.1
2009	35.4	35.9	36.6	37.1	37.6	36.5	36.2	36.8	36.5	36.1	36.0	35.8	36.4
2010	34.5	34.8	35.6	36.4	36.9	36.2	36.6	37.3	37.3	36.6	36.3	36.1	36.2
2011	34.6	35.5	36.5	37.4	37.8	36.7	36.3	37.0	37.0	36.6	36.8	36.4	36.6
2012	35.1	35.6	36.4	36.6	37.4	37.8	37.2	37.8	37.6	37.1	37.4	37.2	36.9
2013	36.4	36.9	37.0	37.9	38.5	39.0	39.0	39.3	39.1	38.8	39.1	39.0	38.3
2014	38.0	37.9	39.3	39.9	40.5	40.5	39.8	40.1	40.3	39.8	40.2	40.1	39.7
2015	39.2	39.7	40.2	40.8	41.3	41.4	41.5	41.5	41.1	41.6	41.4	42.1	41.0

Employment by Industry: Greenville-Anderson-Mauldin, SC, 2005–2015—*Continued*

(Numbers in thousands, not seasonally adjusted)

Industry and year	January	February	March	April	May	June	July	August	September	October	November	December	Annual average
Other Services													
2005	12.8	13.0	13.1	12.8	12.9	12.8	13.0	13.2	13.3	12.7	12.8	12.7	12.9
2006	12.6	12.8	12.9	13.1	13.3	13.2	13.3	13.4	13.5	13.5	13.6	13.6	13.2
2007	13.7	13.8	14.1	13.9	14.0	13.9	13.6	13.5	13.6	13.3	13.3	13.4	13.7
2008	12.7	12.9	13.1	13.2	13.4	13.2	12.9	13.0	13.2	13.0	13.1	13.0	13.1
2009	12.6	12.8	12.8	12.7	12.8	12.6	12.4	12.3	12.6	12.5	12.4	12.4	12.6
2010	11.9	12.0	12.1	12.2	12.3	12.2	11.9	11.9	12.3	12.2	12.2	12.2	12.1
2011	12.0	12.2	12.4	12.8	12.9	12.6	12.6	12.6	13.0	13.0	13.1	13.0	12.7
2012	13.4	13.8	13.6	13.8	13.8	13.8	13.7	13.6	13.6	13.7	13.8	13.8	13.7
2013	13.6	13.6	13.7	13.8	13.9	14.0	13.8	13.9	14.5	14.5	13.8	13.7	13.9
2014	13.4	13.4	13.7	13.7	13.8	13.8	13.6	13.5	13.5	13.5	13.6	13.5	13.6
2015	13.4	13.5	13.7	13.7	13.9	13.9	13.7	13.7	13.6	13.6	13.7	13.6	13.7
Government													
2005	52.8	53.3	53.6	53.5	53.6	53.1	50.3	50.8	53.7	54.1	54.6	54.5	53.2
2006	53.8	54.8	54.7	54.5	54.6	53.8	51.1	51.7	54.3	56.0	55.7	56.0	54.3
2007	55.2	55.6	56.0	55.9	56.1	55.6	53.0	52.8	56.1	56.9	57.9	57.5	55.7
2008	57.1	57.6	58.1	57.7	58.6	57.8	55.0	54.6	57.8	58.7	59.4	58.6	57.6
2009	57.6	57.9	58.1	58.3	58.3	57.4	54.7	55.0	56.9	57.8	58.1	58.0	57.3
2010	56.6	56.8	56.9	57.2	58.6	57.2	53.9	53.6	55.5	56.2	56.3	56.1	56.2
2011	55.3	55.6	55.6	55.9	56.0	55.1	53.6	53.2	55.3	56.0	56.2	56.1	55.3
2012	56.0	56.4	56.5	56.5	57.0	56.1	53.9	54.3	56.6	57.4	57.7	57.6	56.3
2013	57.3	57.5	57.9	58.1	57.9	57.6	55.0	55.4	57.5	58.4	58.3	58.4	57.4
2014	57.8	58.2	58.4	58.4	58.8	58.0	55.6	56.3	58.3	59.2	59.4	59.5	58.2
2015	58.7	59.3	59.6	59.6	59.8	59.1	56.7	57.4	59.4	60.3	60.3	60.4	59.2

Employment by Industry: Knoxville, TN, 2005–2015

(Numbers in thousands, not seasonally adjusted)

Industry and year	January	February	March	April	May	June	July	August	September	October	November	December	Annual average
Total Nonfarm													
2005	354.5	355.0	357.6	359.6	361.5	362.6	360.1	362.8	364.5	362.9	364.3	365.3	360.9
2006	359.1	360.3	363.9	365.8	367.5	367.7	366.0	370.6	372.9	369.6	370.4	372.2	367.2
2007	364.9	365.2	368.6	370.2	371.5	371.3	369.9	374.6	374.9	373.6	376.0	376.1	371.4
2008	369.2	370.8	372.2	373.6	376.0	374.6	370.6	375.0	375.5	374.6	373.7	372.4	373.2
2009	359.6	357.7	356.5	356.6	357.4	354.9	352.4	355.2	356.9	357.6	358.7	357.9	356.8
2010	349.6	350.3	352.6	357.9	361.3	357.9	357.8	360.5	362.2	361.7	363.5	363.2	358.2
2011	355.5	358.5	361.1	364.2	365.0	363.6	361.6	366.6	368.4	367.8	369.6	368.2	364.2
2012	361.2	362.7	365.9	367.6	368.8	366.7	364.7	368.6	369.7	370.4	372.3	371.9	367.5
2013	362.5	364.6	366.7	368.9	370.0	366.1	365.1	370.2	371.5	374.6	376.1	375.9	369.4
2014	367.8	369.3	372.0	374.6	376.7	372.1	372.3	377.6	380.9	382.6	386.3	385.1	376.4
2015	378.1	378.2	380.0	384.2	386.0	381.7	382.8	387.5	390.7	392.4	395.3	395.7	386.1
Total Private													
2005	296.4	296.4	299.3	300.3	302.2	303.6	303.2	304.9	305.7	303.5	304.9	305.9	302.2
2006	301.1	301.9	305.3	306.9	308.4	310.1	309.0	311.6	313.0	309.8	310.8	312.4	308.4
2007	306.6	306.5	309.9	311.0	312.6	313.8	313.0	315.6	315.3	313.4	315.8	315.9	312.5
2008	310.1	311.1	312.6	313.8	316.3	316.9	313.3	315.1	314.4	313.2	312.4	311.0	313.4
2009	300.5	298.1	296.8	296.2	296.7	296.6	295.1	296.2	296.4	296.3	297.3	296.7	296.9
2010	289.7	289.9	292.1	296.3	298.2	299.0	299.9	301.0	301.3	300.2	301.9	301.9	297.6
2011	296.3	299.0	301.6	304.4	305.2	306.6	306.5	308.0	308.6	308.0	309.2	308.2	305.1
2012	301.7	303.1	305.9	307.5	308.6	309.2	308.3	310.6	310.6	310.1	311.7	311.4	308.2
2013	303.5	305.2	307.3	308.1	309.4	309.5	309.3	312.2	312.1	312.5	314.9	314.4	309.9
2014	308.2	308.6	311.3	313.5	315.5	315.1	315.9	319.1	320.7	321.1	323.7	324.1	316.4
2015	316.7	316.7	318.8	322.3	324.4	324.2	326.0	328.3	329.6	330.2	332.1	334.0	325.3
Goods Producing													
2005	61.9	61.5	61.9	61.7	61.8	62.0	62.4	62.7	62.7	62.1	62.2	62.3	62.1
2006	62.3	62.2	63.0	63.2	63.3	63.9	63.4	63.9	64.3	62.9	62.6	62.4	63.1
2007	61.8	61.3	62.0	62.1	62.3	62.6	62.2	62.7	62.9	62.3	62.2	61.7	62.2
2008	60.1	60.2	60.5	60.4	60.9	61.3	60.1	60.3	59.7	59.1	57.7	56.2	59.7
2009	54.0	53.1	52.5	50.8	50.7	50.4	50.0	49.9	50.2	50.4	50.1	49.5	51.0
2010	48.1	48.3	48.9	50.0	50.3	50.8	51.3	51.3	51.5	51.5	51.4	51.4	50.4
2011	50.2	50.9	51.5	51.7	51.8	52.5	52.8	53.1	53.6	54.1	53.7	52.8	52.4
2012	51.2	51.5	51.6	51.7	52.0	52.5	52.6	52.9	53.0	52.9	52.7	52.3	52.2
2013	51.1	51.7	51.8	51.6	51.7	51.8	51.8	52.1	52.0	53.0	53.0	51.8	52.0
2014	50.7	51.1	51.5	51.6	51.5	51.6	52.0	52.5	52.9	53.2	53.7	53.3	52.1
2015	51.8	51.7	51.8	52.1	52.3	52.5	53.1	53.4	54.4	54.7	54.4	54.9	53.1
Service-Providing													
2005	292.6	293.5	295.7	297.9	299.7	300.6	297.7	300.1	301.8	300.8	302.1	303.0	298.8
2006	296.8	298.1	300.9	302.6	304.2	303.8	302.6	306.7	308.6	306.7	307.8	309.8	304.1
2007	303.1	303.9	306.6	308.1	309.2	308.7	307.7	311.9	312.0	311.3	313.8	314.4	309.2
2008	309.1	310.6	311.7	313.2	315.1	313.3	310.5	314.7	315.8	315.5	316.0	316.2	313.5
2009	305.6	304.6	304.0	305.8	306.7	304.5	302.4	305.3	306.7	307.2	308.6	308.4	305.8
2010	301.5	302.0	303.7	307.9	311.0	307.1	306.5	309.2	310.7	310.2	312.1	311.8	307.8
2011	305.3	307.6	309.6	312.5	313.2	311.1	308.8	313.5	314.8	313.7	315.9	315.4	311.8
2012	310.0	311.2	314.3	315.9	316.8	314.2	312.1	315.7	316.7	317.5	319.6	319.6	315.3
2013	311.4	312.9	314.9	317.3	318.3	314.3	313.3	318.1	319.5	321.6	323.1	324.1	317.4
2014	317.1	318.2	320.5	323.0	325.2	320.5	320.3	325.1	328.0	329.4	332.6	331.8	324.3
2015	326.3	326.5	328.2	332.1	333.7	329.2	329.7	334.1	336.3	337.7	340.9	340.8	333.0
Mining, Logging, and Construction													
2005	17.8	17.6	17.8	17.8	17.8	18.0	18.2	18.4	18.5	18.2	18.2	18.0	18.0
2006	17.9	18.0	18.8	19.1	19.3	19.9	19.8	20.2	20.7	20.4	20.2	19.8	19.5
2007	19.3	19.3	19.9	20.2	20.4	20.6	20.5	20.9	21.0	20.8	20.6	20.2	20.3
2008	19.0	19.2	19.7	19.9	20.4	20.6	20.2	20.4	20.3	20.3	19.9	18.9	19.9
2009	17.4	17.2	17.3	17.0	17.3	17.5	17.5	17.4	17.5	17.6	17.4	16.8	17.3
2010	15.6	15.7	16.3	16.9	16.9	17.2	17.7	17.7	17.8	17.8	17.7	17.6	17.1
2011	16.1	16.5	17.0	17.2	17.1	17.5	17.8	18.1	18.7	19.0	18.4	17.4	17.6
2012	15.9	16.1	16.4	16.3	16.6	17.0	17.0	17.4	17.5	17.4	17.2	16.9	16.8
2013	16.0	16.5	16.6	16.6	16.8	16.8	16.8	17.1	17.2	17.9	17.8	16.9	16.9
2014	15.9	16.2	16.5	16.7	16.7	16.7	17.0	17.3	17.6	17.9	18.2	17.8	17.0
2015	16.6	16.5	16.7	17.0	17.3	17.2	17.3	17.6	18.3	18.3	18.3	18.5	17.5

Employment by Industry: Knoxville, TN, 2005–2015—*Continued*

(Numbers in thousands, not seasonally adjusted)

Industry and year	January	February	March	April	May	June	July	August	September	October	November	December	Annual average
Manufacturing													
2005	44.1	43.9	44.1	43.9	44.0	44.0	44.2	44.3	44.2	43.9	44.0	44.3	44.1
2006	44.4	44.2	44.2	44.1	44.0	44.0	43.6	43.7	43.6	42.5	42.4	42.6	43.6
2007	42.5	42.0	42.1	41.9	41.9	42.0	41.7	41.8	41.9	41.5	41.6	41.5	41.9
2008	41.1	41.0	40.8	40.5	40.5	40.7	39.9	39.9	39.4	38.8	37.8	37.3	39.8
2009	36.6	35.9	35.2	33.8	33.4	32.9	32.5	32.5	32.7	32.8	32.7	32.7	33.6
2010	32.5	32.6	32.6	33.1	33.4	33.6	33.6	33.6	33.7	33.7	33.7	33.8	33.3
2011	34.1	34.4	34.5	34.5	34.7	35.0	35.0	35.0	34.9	35.1	35.3	35.4	34.8
2012	35.3	35.4	35.2	35.4	35.4	35.5	35.6	35.5	35.5	35.5	35.5	35.4	35.4
2013	35.1	35.2	35.2	35.0	34.9	35.0	35.0	35.0	34.8	35.1	35.2	34.9	35.0
2014	34.8	34.9	35.0	34.9	34.8	34.9	35.0	35.2	35.3	35.3	35.5	35.5	35.1
2015	35.2	35.2	35.1	35.1	35.0	35.3	35.8	35.8	36.1	36.4	36.1	36.4	35.6
Trade, Transportation, and Utilities													
2005	74.6	74.4	75.0	74.4	75.0	74.9	75.0	75.4	75.3	74.8	76.1	77.0	75.2
2006	75.0	74.9	75.8	75.8	76.3	76.5	76.3	77.1	77.7	77.2	78.5	79.9	76.8
2007	77.6	77.1	77.9	78.3	78.7	78.5	78.1	78.7	78.7	78.8	80.6	80.9	78.7
2008	78.8	78.2	78.4	78.2	78.0	77.9	77.4	77.8	77.4	78.1	78.5	78.4	78.1
2009	74.7	73.2	72.4	72.1	71.9	72.0	71.6	71.8	71.6	71.9	72.8	73.6	72.5
2010	71.3	70.6	70.9	71.1	71.4	71.4	71.9	72.1	72.0	72.3	73.7	74.0	71.9
2011	71.5	71.3	71.8	72.4	72.7	72.9	72.9	72.9	72.9	73.3	74.9	75.5	72.9
2012	73.0	72.9	73.5	73.8	74.1	74.1	74.4	74.5	74.4	75.0	76.7	77.1	74.5
2013	74.1	74.1	74.4	74.4	74.5	74.5	74.7	74.9	74.6	75.1	76.8	77.4	75.0
2014	74.6	74.5	75.1	75.1	75.3	75.7	76.2	76.5	76.5	76.9	78.5	79.3	76.2
2015	76.4	75.6	76.2	77.0	77.2	77.5	78.2	78.7	78.8	79.4	81.5	82.4	78.2
Wholesale Trade													
2005	16.7	16.8	16.8	16.6	16.5	16.6	16.6	16.6	16.5	16.3	16.2	16.2	16.5
2006	16.3	16.4	16.5	16.6	16.7	16.7	16.9	16.8	17.0	17.0	16.9	17.1	16.7
2007	17.2	17.1	17.1	17.1	17.3	17.3	17.3	17.5	17.4	17.5	17.5	17.5	17.3
2008	17.3	17.4	17.4	17.6	17.9	17.9	17.8	17.9	18.0	18.1	17.9	17.9	17.8
2009	17.6	17.3	17.1	17.0	16.9	16.8	16.8	16.7	16.6	16.8	16.7	16.8	16.9
2010	16.7	16.6	16.7	16.5	16.5	16.5	16.4	16.2	16.2	16.1	16.0	15.9	16.4
2011	15.9	15.9	16.0	16.3	16.4	16.5	16.5	16.5	16.5	16.5	16.6	16.7	16.4
2012	16.6	16.7	16.7	16.7	16.8	16.8	16.7	16.8	16.9	16.8	16.8	16.7	16.8
2013	16.6	16.7	16.7	16.5	16.5	16.5	16.4	16.5	16.4	16.4	16.4	16.4	16.5
2014	16.3	16.4	16.4	16.3	16.4	16.3	16.2	16.4	16.5	16.4	16.5	16.6	16.4
2015	16.4	16.4	16.5	16.6	16.6	16.6	16.7	16.7	16.8	16.8	17.1	17.0	16.7
Retail Trade													
2005	46.7	46.4	46.9	46.8	47.3	47.2	47.0	47.1	47.0	46.9	48.2	48.9	47.2
2006	47.1	46.9	47.4	47.5	47.7	47.9	47.7	48.3	48.6	48.3	49.6	50.5	48.1
2007	48.7	48.2	48.9	49.4	49.5	49.3	49.1	49.3	49.4	49.5	51.1	51.4	49.5
2008	49.7	49.0	49.3	48.8	48.3	48.2	47.9	48.0	47.5	48.1	48.6	48.5	48.5
2009	46.0	45.0	44.6	44.6	44.5	44.6	44.3	44.3	44.2	44.3	45.3	45.6	44.8
2010	43.9	43.4	43.5	43.7	43.9	43.9	44.0	44.3	44.1	44.5	45.8	45.9	44.2
2011	44.0	43.6	43.9	44.1	44.2	44.4	44.4	44.3	44.2	44.7	46.1	46.4	44.5
2012	44.5	44.2	44.8	45.1	45.1	45.3	45.7	45.5	45.2	45.7	47.2	47.3	45.5
2013	45.0	44.8	45.0	45.0	45.0	45.0	45.4	45.2	44.9	45.4	47.0	47.3	45.4
2014	45.1	44.8	45.1	45.2	45.2	45.7	46.2	46.0	45.8	46.1	47.5	47.9	45.9
2015	45.6	45.0	45.4	46.0	46.0	46.4	46.9	47.1	47.0	47.6	49.2	49.9	46.8
Transportation and Utilities													
2005	11.2	11.2	11.3	11.0	11.2	11.1	11.4	11.7	11.8	11.6	11.7	11.9	11.4
2006	11.6	11.6	11.9	11.7	11.9	11.9	11.7	12.0	12.1	11.9	12.0	12.3	11.9
2007	11.7	11.8	11.9	11.8	11.9	11.9	11.7	11.9	11.9	11.8	12.0	12.0	11.9
2008	11.8	11.8	11.7	11.8	11.8	11.8	11.7	11.9	11.9	11.9	12.0	12.0	11.8
2009	11.1	10.9	10.7	10.5	10.5	10.6	10.5	10.8	10.8	10.8	10.8	11.2	10.8
2010	10.7	10.6	10.7	10.9	11.0	11.0	11.5	11.6	11.7	11.7	11.9	12.2	11.3
2011	11.6	11.8	11.9	12.0	12.1	12.0	12.0	12.1	12.2	12.1	12.2	12.4	12.0
2012	11.9	12.0	12.0	12.0	12.2	12.0	12.0	12.2	12.3	12.5	12.7	13.1	12.2
2013	12.5	12.6	12.7	12.9	13.0	13.0	12.9	13.2	13.3	13.3	13.4	13.7	13.0
2014	13.2	13.3	13.6	13.6	13.7	13.7	13.8	14.1	14.2	14.4	14.5	14.8	13.9
2015	14.4	14.2	14.3	14.4	14.6	14.5	14.6	14.9	15.0	15.0	15.2	15.5	14.7

Employment by Industry: Knoxville, TN, 2005–2015—*Continued*

(Numbers in thousands, not seasonally adjusted)

Industry and year	January	February	March	April	May	June	July	August	September	October	November	December	Annual average
Information													
2005	6.0	6.0	6.1	6.1	6.1	6.1	6.2	6.1	6.1	6.1	6.1	6.1	6.1
2006	6.2	6.3	6.3	6.3	6.2	6.2	6.2	6.1	6.0	6.0	6.1	6.0	6.2
2007	5.8	5.8	5.8	5.8	5.9	5.9	5.9	5.9	5.8	5.7	5.8	5.8	5.8
2008	5.8	5.8	5.8	5.8	5.9	5.9	5.8	5.7	5.7	5.8	5.8	5.8	5.8
2009	5.8	5.7	5.7	5.7	5.7	5.7	5.7	5.6	5.6	5.6	5.6	5.6	5.7
2010	5.6	5.6	5.6	5.6	5.6	5.7	5.7	5.6	5.6	5.8	5.7	5.8	5.7
2011	5.9	5.9	5.8	5.8	5.8	5.8	5.8	5.8	5.7	5.6	5.7	5.6	5.8
2012	5.6	5.7	5.6	5.7	5.7	5.7	5.8	5.7	5.6	5.7	5.7	5.7	5.7
2013	5.8	5.8	5.7	5.8	5.8	5.9	5.8	5.8	5.7	5.7	5.8	5.8	5.8
2014	5.8	5.8	5.8	5.8	5.8	5.8	5.8	5.9	5.8	5.7	5.8	5.7	5.8
2015	5.8	5.8	5.8	5.8	5.7	5.7	5.7	5.7	5.7	5.7	5.7	5.7	5.7
Financial Activities													
2005	17.8	17.8	17.9	18.0	18.1	18.3	18.1	18.2	18.1	18.1	18.1	18.3	18.1
2006	18.1	18.1	18.2	18.1	18.2	18.3	18.4	18.6	18.5	18.3	18.4	18.5	18.3
2007	18.2	18.2	18.3	18.3	18.4	18.6	18.6	18.6	18.6	18.6	18.7	18.7	18.5
2008	18.4	18.5	18.6	18.6	18.7	18.9	18.9	19.0	18.9	18.9	18.9	19.0	18.8
2009	18.4	18.5	18.3	18.3	18.3	18.1	18.0	18.0	17.9	17.8	17.8	17.8	18.1
2010	17.8	17.8	17.8	18.0	18.0	18.0	17.9	17.8	17.7	17.6	17.7	17.7	17.8
2011	17.5	17.5	17.5	17.6	17.6	17.8	17.7	17.8	17.7	17.8	17.8	17.9	17.7
2012	17.8	17.9	18.0	18.0	18.1	18.1	18.0	18.0	17.9	17.9	17.9	18.0	18.0
2013	17.7	17.6	17.9	17.9	18.0	18.1	18.1	18.1	18.1	18.0	18.0	18.1	18.0
2014	17.9	18.0	18.0	18.1	18.1	18.2	18.3	18.3	18.3	18.4	18.5	18.6	18.2
2015	18.5	18.6	18.6	18.6	18.6	18.8	18.9	18.9	18.8	18.7	18.8	18.5	18.7
Professional and Business Services													
2005	44.4	44.7	45.3	45.8	45.8	45.9	45.5	46.3	47.0	46.6	46.4	46.4	45.8
2006	45.7	46.0	46.4	47.0	47.1	46.8	46.6	47.3	47.9	47.7	47.6	47.8	47.0
2007	46.8	47.3	47.6	48.0	47.7	47.5	47.5	48.4	48.3	48.2	48.4	48.7	47.9
2008	48.3	48.7	48.6	49.4	49.4	49.3	49.3	50.2	50.8	50.9	51.1	51.3	49.8
2009	49.9	49.5	48.9	48.8	48.7	48.4	48.6	49.5	50.0	50.4	50.9	50.7	49.5
2010	50.0	50.1	50.3	52.1	52.4	51.9	52.7	53.9	53.9	54.2	54.5	54.7	52.6
2011	54.5	55.6	56.1	56.2	56.0	55.4	55.6	56.3	56.4	56.4	56.5	56.2	55.9
2012	54.9	55.1	55.7	55.7	55.8	55.4	54.7	56.1	56.1	55.4	55.6	55.4	55.5
2013	54.5	55.0	55.3	55.4	55.7	55.5	55.4	57.0	57.2	57.1	57.6	57.8	56.1
2014	57.5	57.6	58.2	59.1	59.4	58.6	58.2	59.9	60.6	60.6	60.9	61.1	59.3
2015	59.9	59.9	60.3	61.3	62.2	61.2	61.2	62.5	62.5	63.0	63.2	63.9	61.8
Education and Health Services													
2005	42.3	42.2	42.5	42.8	43.1	43.3	43.4	43.6	43.7	44.2	44.2	44.4	43.3
2006	43.8	43.8	44.3	44.2	44.4	44.8	44.8	45.1	45.0	45.2	45.2	45.4	44.7
2007	44.9	44.9	45.2	45.3	45.5	45.8	46.0	46.3	46.6	46.7	46.8	47.0	45.9
2008	46.9	47.1	47.1	47.6	47.9	47.9	47.4	47.6	47.5	47.9	48.1	48.3	47.6
2009	47.4	47.4	47.4	48.0	48.4	48.4	48.5	48.7	48.7	48.4	48.2	48.5	48.2
2010	47.9	48.1	48.4	48.6	48.7	48.8	48.6	48.8	49.2	49.0	49.2	49.2	48.7
2011	48.7	49.1	49.4	50.1	50.1	50.3	50.3	50.5	50.8	50.2	50.0	49.9	50.0
2012	49.5	49.7	49.9	49.9	50.1	50.1	50.1	50.5	50.7	50.8	50.6	50.8	50.2
2013	49.6	50.0	50.2	50.2	50.2	49.6	49.5	49.8	50.1	50.1	50.4	50.6	50.0
2014	49.7	49.8	50.0	50.0	50.6	50.4	50.4	50.9	51.4	51.7	51.7	51.9	50.7
2015	51.4	51.6	52.0	51.9	52.2	52.1	52.0	52.2	52.4	52.3	52.4	52.6	52.1
Leisure and Hospitality													
2005	34.9	35.3	36.0	36.8	37.6	38.2	37.7	37.8	38.0	36.9	37.1	36.6	36.9
2006	35.4	35.9	36.5	37.5	38.0	38.4	38.1	38.5	38.5	37.6	37.4	37.4	37.4
2007	36.4	36.7	37.8	38.1	38.8	39.3	39.2	39.6	39.0	37.7	37.9	37.7	38.2
2008	36.5	37.0	37.9	38.2	39.3	39.7	38.7	38.8	38.7	37.0	36.9	36.6	37.9
2009	35.0	35.4	36.1	36.6	37.6	37.9	37.1	37.2	37.0	36.1	36.0	35.7	36.5
2010	34.0	34.3	35.0	36.0	37.0	37.5	37.2	37.1	37.3	35.9	35.9	35.4	36.1
2011	34.6	35.2	35.9	36.9	37.5	37.8	37.4	37.6	37.8	36.9	36.7	36.4	36.7
2012	35.8	36.4	37.6	38.4	38.5	38.8	38.3	38.6	38.6	38.3	38.5	38.2	38.0
2013	36.9	37.1	37.9	38.5	39.1	39.5	39.5	39.9	39.9	39.1	38.9	38.5	38.7
2014	37.8	37.5	38.2	39.5	40.4	40.4	40.6	40.7	40.8	40.4	40.2	39.8	39.7
2015	38.6	39.1	39.7	41.1	41.5	41.7	42.1	42.1	42.3	41.8	41.5	41.5	41.1

Employment by Industry: Knoxville, TN, 2005–2015—*Continued*

(Numbers in thousands, not seasonally adjusted)

Industry and year	January	February	March	April	May	June	July	August	September	October	November	December	Annual average
Other Services													
2005	14.5	14.5	14.6	14.7	14.7	14.9	14.9	14.8	14.8	14.7	14.7	14.8	14.7
2006	14.6	14.7	14.8	14.8	14.9	15.2	15.2	15.0	15.1	14.9	15.0	15.0	14.9
2007	15.1	15.2	15.3	15.1	15.3	15.6	15.5	15.4	15.4	15.4	15.4	15.4	15.3
2008	15.3	15.6	15.7	15.6	16.2	16.0	15.7	15.7	15.7	15.5	15.4	15.4	15.7
2009	15.3	15.3	15.5	15.9	15.4	15.7	15.6	15.5	15.4	15.7	15.9	15.3	15.5
2010	15.0	15.1	15.2	14.9	14.8	14.9	14.6	14.4	14.1	13.9	13.8	13.7	14.5
2011	13.4	13.5	13.6	13.7	13.7	14.1	14.0	14.0	13.7	13.7	13.9	13.9	13.8
2012	13.9	13.9	14.0	14.3	14.3	14.5	14.4	14.3	14.3	14.1	14.0	13.9	14.2
2013	13.8	13.9	14.1	14.3	14.4	14.6	14.5	14.6	14.5	14.4	14.4	14.4	14.3
2014	14.2	14.3	14.5	14.3	14.4	14.4	14.4	14.4	14.4	14.2	14.4	14.4	14.4
2015	14.3	14.4	14.4	14.5	14.7	14.7	14.8	14.8	14.7	14.6	14.6	14.5	14.6
Government													
2005	58.1	58.6	58.3	59.3	59.3	59.0	56.9	57.9	58.8	59.4	59.4	59.4	58.7
2006	58.0	58.4	58.6	58.9	59.1	57.6	57.0	59.0	59.9	59.8	59.6	59.8	58.8
2007	58.3	58.7	58.7	59.2	58.9	57.5	56.9	59.0	59.6	60.2	60.2	60.2	59.0
2008	59.1	59.7	59.6	59.8	59.7	57.7	57.3	59.9	61.1	61.4	61.3	61.4	59.8
2009	59.1	59.6	59.7	60.4	60.7	58.3	57.3	59.0	60.5	61.3	61.4	61.2	59.9
2010	59.9	60.4	60.5	61.6	63.1	58.9	57.9	59.5	60.9	61.5	61.6	61.3	60.6
2011	59.2	59.5	59.5	59.8	59.8	57.0	55.1	58.6	59.8	59.8	60.4	60.0	59.0
2012	59.5	59.6	60.0	60.1	60.2	57.5	56.4	58.0	59.1	60.3	60.6	60.5	59.3
2013	59.0	59.4	59.4	60.8	60.6	56.6	55.8	58.0	59.4	62.1	61.2	61.5	59.5
2014	59.6	60.7	60.7	61.1	61.2	57.0	56.4	58.5	60.2	61.5	62.6	61.0	60.0
2015	61.4	61.5	61.2	61.9	61.6	57.5	56.8	59.2	61.1	62.2	63.2	61.7	60.8

Employment by Industry: New Haven, CT NECTA, 2005–2015

(Numbers in thousands, not seasonally adjusted)

Industry and year	January	February	March	April	May	June	July	August	September	October	November	December	Annual average
Total Nonfarm													
2005.................	270.1	272.5	270.9	276.8	277.4	279.4	271.9	269.7	276.1	276.5	279.4	280.6	275.1
2006.................	272.2	275.7	275.4	278.7	280.7	282.3	274.2	272.4	278.5	280.7	282.5	283.9	278.1
2007.................	274.2	276.8	275.7	279.7	281.8	284.0	275.9	274.6	280.4	282.8	284.5	285.4	279.7
2008.................	277.9	280.3	278.8	280.4	282.6	282.4	273.6	271.7	277.9	279.1	281.0	280.2	278.8
2009.................	269.9	270.7	267.4	268.2	270.7	270.0	261.3	259.8	267.4	268.0	269.8	270.5	267.8
2010.................	260.4	262.4	260.8	265.1	268.9	268.3	263.8	261.4	267.3	269.1	269.5	269.3	265.5
2011.................	263.2	264.8	263.0	269.4	270.9	271.1	264.2	262.8	268.8	270.4	271.4	271.7	267.6
2012.................	266.5	269.6	268.9	273.4	275.7	276.0	268.4	266.8	273.1	274.9	276.5	277.9	272.3
2013.................	269.2	269.7	270.9	276.9	277.3	279.0	272.6	271.1	277.0	279.0	281.1	279.8	275.3
2014.................	273.6	273.9	273.4	279.1	279.3	280.6	274.8	273.0	280.3	281.1	283.4	283.7	278.0
2015.................	275.8	276.1	275.9	280.6	282.1	284.0	276.1	274.2	281.2	282.8	285.0	285.0	279.9
Total Private													
2005.................	234.0	235.5	234.0	239.3	240.2	241.8	239.8	238.2	240.7	240.0	242.2	243.3	239.1
2006.................	235.1	238.4	238.2	241.6	243.2	244.5	241.7	240.3	242.9	244.0	245.3	246.6	241.8
2007.................	237.4	239.7	238.6	242.7	244.6	246.0	243.5	242.5	244.6	245.8	246.9	247.9	243.4
2008.................	240.8	242.7	241.5	243.6	245.0	245.3	241.4	240.0	241.8	242.0	243.3	242.7	242.5
2009.................	232.9	233.5	230.3	231.4	233.2	233.5	229.8	228.9	231.6	232.3	233.2	234.4	232.1
2010.................	224.2	225.9	224.9	229.0	230.8	231.2	231.3	230.1	231.8	233.6	233.6	233.6	230.0
2011.................	227.5	228.8	227.9	233.0	234.5	235.0	232.9	232.4	234.3	235.3	236.0	236.2	232.8
2012.................	231.8	233.8	233.3	237.5	240.0	240.6	237.7	237.1	239.2	240.2	241.3	242.2	237.9
2013.................	233.9	234.5	235.5	240.3	241.1	241.8	241.0	240.7	241.8	244.1	245.3	244.6	240.4
2014.................	237.9	238.0	237.5	242.6	243.4	243.9	243.1	241.8	244.0	245.7	247.2	247.9	242.8
2015.................	240.3	239.9	239.6	244.1	245.7	246.8	244.0	242.8	245.0	247.0	248.5	248.6	244.4
Goods Producing													
2005.................	44.4	43.9	44.2	44.8	45.1	45.9	45.9	45.7	45.1	44.8	44.7	44.4	44.9
2006.................	43.9	43.7	43.9	44.5	44.9	45.5	45.5	45.3	44.7	44.6	44.5	44.3	44.6
2007.................	43.5	43.1	43.3	44.0	44.2	44.8	44.5	44.7	44.4	44.2	44.3	43.9	44.1
2008.................	43.1	42.6	42.6	42.7	43.2	43.4	43.1	42.9	42.5	42.2	42.0	41.1	42.6
2009.................	38.3	37.4	37.1	37.6	38.1	38.4	37.5	37.3	37.0	36.4	36.2	36.0	37.3
2010.................	34.2	33.7	34.0	34.7	35.4	35.7	35.8	35.9	35.8	35.3	35.1	34.9	35.0
2011.................	33.8	33.9	34.0	34.6	35.2	35.7	35.5	35.7	35.4	35.3	35.2	34.9	34.9
2012.................	34.1	34.1	34.1	34.5	35.0	35.4	35.4	35.4	35.2	34.9	34.8	34.6	34.8
2013.................	33.6	33.3	33.6	34.1	34.6	35.0	35.5	35.5	35.2	35.3	34.8	34.6	34.6
2014.................	33.5	33.3	33.4	34.3	34.8	35.2	35.7	35.6	35.4	35.2	34.8	34.6	34.7
2015.................	33.9	33.4	33.5	34.6	35.1	35.6	35.5	35.6	35.3	35.1	34.8	34.7	34.8
Service-Providing													
2005.................	225.7	228.6	226.7	232.0	232.3	233.5	226.0	224.0	231.0	231.7	234.7	236.2	230.2
2006.................	228.3	232.0	231.5	234.2	235.8	236.8	228.7	227.1	233.8	236.1	238.0	239.6	233.5
2007.................	230.7	233.7	232.4	235.7	237.6	239.2	231.4	229.9	236.0	238.6	240.2	241.5	235.6
2008.................	234.8	237.7	236.2	237.7	239.4	239.0	230.5	228.8	235.4	236.9	239.0	239.1	236.2
2009.................	231.6	233.3	230.3	230.6	232.6	231.6	223.8	222.5	230.4	231.6	233.6	234.5	230.5
2010.................	226.2	228.7	226.8	230.4	233.5	232.6	228.0	225.5	231.5	233.8	234.4	234.4	230.5
2011.................	229.4	230.9	229.0	234.8	235.7	235.4	228.7	227.1	233.4	235.1	236.2	236.8	232.7
2012.................	232.4	235.5	234.8	238.9	240.7	240.6	233.0	231.4	237.9	240.0	241.7	243.3	237.5
2013.................	235.6	236.4	237.3	242.8	242.7	244.0	237.1	235.6	241.8	243.7	246.3	245.2	240.7
2014.................	240.1	240.6	240.0	244.8	244.5	245.4	239.1	237.4	244.9	245.9	248.6	249.1	243.4
2015.................	241.9	242.7	242.4	246.0	247.0	248.4	240.6	238.6	245.9	247.7	250.2	250.3	245.1
Mining, Logging, and Construction													
2005.................	10.2	9.9	10.1	10.9	11.3	11.7	12.0	12.1	11.7	11.6	11.5	11.2	11.2
2006.................	10.4	10.4	10.6	11.4	11.8	12.2	12.5	12.5	12.4	12.1	12.0	11.8	11.7
2007.................	11.1	10.8	11.1	11.7	12.1	12.5	12.8	12.9	12.7	12.6	12.7	12.3	12.1
2008.................	11.4	11.2	11.3	11.4	11.9	12.0	12.0	12.0	11.7	11.5	11.4	10.8	11.6
2009.................	9.5	9.1	9.1	9.6	10.1	10.3	10.2	10.2	10.1	9.7	9.6	9.3	9.7
2010.................	7.9	7.6	7.8	8.6	9.1	9.1	9.3	9.4	9.4	9.3	9.2	8.9	8.8
2011.................	8.2	8.3	8.3	8.9	9.4	9.7	9.7	9.8	9.6	9.6	9.4	9.2	9.2
2012.................	8.5	8.5	8.5	8.9	9.3	9.5	9.7	9.8	9.7	9.5	9.5	9.2	9.2
2013.................	8.4	8.1	8.4	9.1	9.5	9.8	10.2	10.3	10.2	10.0	9.8	9.5	9.4
2014.................	8.6	8.5	8.7	9.6	10.1	10.3	10.6	10.7	10.6	10.4	10.3	10.1	9.9
2015.................	9.4	9.1	9.2	10.2	10.7	11.0	11.1	11.2	11.0	10.9	10.7	10.6	10.4

Employment by Industry: New Haven, CT NECTA, 2005–2015—*Continued*

(Numbers in thousands, not seasonally adjusted)

Industry and year	January	February	March	April	May	June	July	August	September	October	November	December	Annual average
Manufacturing													
2005	34.2	34.0	34.1	33.9	33.8	34.2	33.9	33.6	33.4	33.2	33.2	33.2	33.7
2006	33.5	33.3	33.3	33.1	33.1	33.3	33.0	32.8	32.3	32.5	32.5	32.5	32.9
2007	32.4	32.3	32.2	32.3	32.1	32.3	31.7	31.8	31.7	31.6	31.6	31.6	32.0
2008	31.7	31.4	31.3	31.3	31.3	31.4	31.1	30.9	30.8	30.7	30.6	30.3	31.1
2009	28.8	28.3	28.0	28.0	28.0	28.1	27.3	27.1	26.9	26.7	26.6	26.7	27.5
2010	26.3	26.1	26.2	26.1	26.3	26.6	26.5	26.5	26.4	26.0	25.9	26.0	26.2
2011	25.6	25.6	25.7	25.7	25.8	26.0	25.8	25.9	25.8	25.7	25.8	25.7	25.8
2012	25.6	25.6	25.6	25.6	25.7	25.9	25.7	25.6	25.5	25.4	25.3	25.4	25.6
2013	25.2	25.2	25.2	25.0	25.1	25.2	25.3	25.2	25.0	25.3	25.0	25.1	25.2
2014	24.9	24.8	24.7	24.7	24.7	24.9	25.1	24.9	24.8	24.8	24.5	24.5	24.8
2015	24.5	24.3	24.3	24.4	24.4	24.6	24.4	24.4	24.3	24.2	24.1	24.1	24.3
Trade, Transportation, and Utilities													
2005	49.5	48.8	48.7	49.3	49.8	50.1	49.1	48.9	49.6	49.8	50.9	51.6	49.7
2006	49.9	48.9	49.3	49.7	50.3	50.7	49.4	49.1	49.6	50.0	51.1	51.9	50.0
2007	50.1	49.5	49.5	49.4	50.3	50.9	49.6	49.2	49.6	50.0	50.8	51.3	50.0
2008	50.2	49.1	49.1	49.0	49.4	49.8	48.9	48.3	48.7	48.6	49.3	49.7	49.2
2009	47.7	46.8	46.4	45.9	46.9	47.1	46.2	46.0	46.5	47.0	48.0	48.5	46.9
2010	46.1	45.3	45.4	45.2	46.3	46.7	46.2	46.3	46.1	46.7	47.6	48.3	46.4
2011	46.1	45.4	45.5	46.4	46.8	47.1	46.3	46.4	46.6	47.0	47.8	48.6	46.7
2012	47.2	46.5	46.7	46.9	47.8	48.4	47.6	47.5	47.7	48.4	49.8	50.1	47.9
2013	48.2	47.1	47.6	48.5	48.9	49.3	48.4	48.7	48.9	49.4	50.6	51.3	48.9
2014	48.8	48.2	48.4	49.0	49.6	49.8	49.3	49.3	49.5	50.1	51.5	52.1	49.6
2015	49.8	48.6	49.1	49.2	50.1	50.6	49.6	49.3	49.9	50.4	51.3	52.3	50.0
Wholesale Trade													
2005	11.5	11.4	11.4	11.5	11.5	11.5	11.5	11.5	11.5	11.6	11.7	11.7	11.5
2006	11.6	11.6	11.6	11.7	11.8	11.9	11.8	11.8	11.7	11.6	11.6	11.6	11.7
2007	11.7	11.7	11.6	11.5	11.6	11.7	11.7	11.7	11.7	11.6	11.6	11.7	11.7
2008	12.0	11.9	11.9	12.0	12.0	12.1	12.1	12.1	12.2	12.1	12.2	12.2	12.1
2009	12.0	11.9	11.7	11.6	11.6	11.6	11.6	11.5	11.6	11.5	11.5	11.5	11.6
2010	11.3	11.3	11.3	11.3	11.4	11.4	11.5	11.5	11.4	11.3	11.4	11.4	11.4
2011	11.3	11.2	11.2	11.3	11.3	11.4	11.4	11.4	11.3	11.3	11.2	11.3	11.3
2012	11.1	11.1	11.1	11.3	11.3	11.4	11.3	11.2	11.2	11.2	11.2	11.2	11.2
2013	11.0	10.9	11.0	11.2	11.2	11.2	11.2	11.2	11.1	11.1	11.1	11.1	11.1
2014	10.9	10.9	10.9	11.1	11.2	11.2	11.2	11.2	11.1	11.1	11.1	11.1	11.1
2015	11.1	11.0	11.0	11.2	11.3	11.3	11.3	11.2	11.1	11.0	11.1	11.3	11.2
Retail Trade													
2005	30.5	29.8	29.6	30.0	30.3	30.6	30.3	30.2	30.2	30.5	31.4	32.1	30.5
2006	30.7	29.8	30.1	30.4	30.9	31.3	30.9	30.8	30.6	31.2	32.3	32.9	31.0
2007	31.2	30.6	30.7	30.7	31.3	31.7	31.0	30.9	30.5	30.8	31.7	32.0	31.1
2008	30.9	29.9	29.9	29.6	30.0	30.2	29.7	29.5	29.1	29.1	29.8	30.2	29.8
2009	28.8	28.0	27.8	27.6	28.3	28.5	28.1	28.2	28.0	28.6	29.6	30.0	28.5
2010	28.2	27.4	27.5	27.4	28.0	28.3	28.2	28.3	27.8	28.4	29.2	29.7	28.2
2011	28.2	27.6	27.6	28.2	28.5	28.6	28.3	28.5	28.3	28.6	29.5	30.1	28.5
2012	29.1	28.4	28.5	28.4	29.1	29.4	28.9	28.9	28.5	29.0	30.4	30.6	29.1
2013	29.0	28.2	28.3	28.8	29.1	29.4	29.1	29.4	29.1	29.7	30.9	31.5	29.4
2014	29.5	28.9	29.0	29.2	29.6	29.8	29.8	29.8	29.5	30.0	31.3	31.8	29.9
2015	30.0	29.0	29.3	29.1	29.7	30.1	29.6	29.6	29.6	30.1	30.9	31.3	29.9
Transportation and Utilities													
2005	7.5	7.6	7.7	7.8	8.0	8.0	7.3	7.2	7.9	7.7	7.8	7.8	7.7
2006	7.6	7.5	7.6	7.6	7.6	7.5	6.7	6.5	7.3	7.2	7.2	7.4	7.3
2007	7.2	7.2	7.2	7.2	7.4	7.5	6.9	6.6	7.4	7.6	7.5	7.6	7.3
2008	7.3	7.3	7.3	7.4	7.4	7.5	7.1	6.7	7.4	7.4	7.3	7.3	7.3
2009	6.9	6.9	6.9	6.7	7.0	7.0	6.5	6.3	6.9	6.9	6.9	7.0	6.8
2010	6.6	6.6	6.6	6.5	6.9	7.0	6.5	6.5	6.9	7.0	7.0	7.2	6.8
2011	6.6	6.6	6.7	6.9	7.0	7.1	6.6	6.5	7.0	7.1	7.1	7.2	6.9
2012	7.0	7.0	7.1	7.2	7.4	7.6	7.4	7.4	8.0	8.2	8.2	8.3	7.6
2013	8.2	8.0	8.3	8.5	8.6	8.7	8.1	8.1	8.7	8.6	8.6	8.7	8.4
2014	8.4	8.4	8.5	8.7	8.8	8.8	8.3	8.3	8.9	9.0	9.1	9.2	8.7
2015	8.7	8.6	8.8	8.9	9.1	9.2	8.7	8.5	9.2	9.3	9.3	9.7	9.0

Employment by Industry: New Haven, CT NECTA, 2005–2015—*Continued*

(Numbers in thousands, not seasonally adjusted)

Industry and year	January	February	March	April	May	June	July	August	September	October	November	December	Annual average
Information													
2005..........	8.6	8.8	8.5	8.4	8.4	8.5	8.4	8.3	8.3	8.2	8.3	8.2	8.4
2006..........	8.3	8.3	8.2	8.2	8.2	8.2	8.1	8.1	8.0	8.1	8.1	8.2	8.2
2007..........	8.1	8.2	8.1	8.2	8.2	8.1	8.1	8.1	8.1	8.1	8.1	8.2	8.1
2008..........	8.1	8.3	8.0	7.9	7.8	7.8	7.7	7.8	7.6	7.6	7.6	7.5	7.8
2009..........	7.3	7.3	7.0	6.8	6.7	6.6	6.6	6.4	6.3	6.2	6.1	5.9	6.6
2010..........	5.7	5.6	5.5	5.3	5.3	5.2	5.1	5.1	5.0	4.9	4.9	4.9	5.2
2011..........	4.8	4.8	4.8	4.7	4.7	4.7	4.6	4.5	4.5	4.6	4.6	4.6	4.7
2012..........	4.5	4.5	4.4	4.3	4.3	4.3	4.3	4.3	4.3	4.3	4.3	4.3	4.3
2013..........	4.3	4.3	4.3	4.2	4.2	4.2	4.2	4.2	4.1	4.2	4.2	4.3	4.2
2014..........	4.3	4.2	4.1	4.1	4.1	4.1	4.2	4.1	4.0	3.7	3.7	3.7	4.0
2015..........	3.6	3.6	3.6	3.6	3.6	3.6	3.5	3.5	3.5	3.5	3.5	3.5	3.6
Financial Activities													
2005..........	13.8	13.8	13.8	13.9	14.1	14.3	14.3	14.3	14.1	14.0	14.1	14.1	14.1
2006..........	14.0	14.0	13.9	14.0	14.0	14.1	14.1	14.1	13.9	13.9	14.0	14.0	14.0
2007..........	13.8	13.8	13.7	13.7	13.8	13.9	13.8	13.7	13.4	13.4	13.3	13.4	13.6
2008..........	13.3	13.3	13.3	13.0	13.1	13.2	13.1	13.1	12.9	12.7	12.7	12.7	13.0
2009..........	12.6	12.5	12.5	12.5	12.5	12.6	12.4	12.3	12.2	12.2	12.3	12.4	12.4
2010..........	12.1	12.1	12.2	12.1	12.2	12.3	12.6	12.5	12.2	12.2	12.2	12.2	12.2
2011..........	12.3	12.3	12.3	12.2	12.2	12.3	12.3	12.3	12.0	12.0	11.8	12.0	12.2
2012..........	12.1	12.0	12.1	12.1	12.1	12.3	12.3	12.2	12.1	12.0	12.0	12.1	12.1
2013..........	12.1	12.0	12.0	12.0	12.0	12.2	12.3	12.3	12.3	12.3	12.3	12.4	12.2
2014..........	12.3	12.3	12.3	12.4	12.5	12.6	12.7	12.7	12.6	12.5	12.5	12.6	12.5
2015..........	12.5	12.4	12.4	12.5	12.6	12.7	12.7	12.8	12.6	12.6	12.7	12.7	12.6
Professional and Business Services													
2005..........	25.1	25.2	25.3	26.2	26.0	27.0	26.7	26.6	26.4	26.0	26.1	26.4	26.1
2006..........	25.5	26.2	26.4	26.7	27.0	27.8	26.5	26.7	26.8	26.6	26.8	27.0	26.7
2007..........	26.0	26.2	26.4	26.7	27.0	27.5	27.1	27.4	27.4	27.3	27.3	27.8	27.0
2008..........	27.1	27.5	27.3	27.8	27.8	28.2	26.8	26.9	26.9	26.1	25.9	26.1	27.0
2009..........	25.2	24.7	24.5	24.6	24.6	24.7	24.2	24.8	24.7	25.0	25.2	25.9	24.8
2010..........	24.8	25.4	25.2	25.9	25.8	26.4	26.5	26.5	26.2	26.3	26.3	26.4	26.0
2011..........	25.8	26.1	25.8	26.8	26.7	27.2	27.2	27.2	27.1	27.1	27.4	27.6	26.8
2012..........	27.6	27.6	27.9	28.8	28.8	28.9	28.5	28.5	28.9	28.9	29.0	29.4	28.6
2013..........	28.8	29.0	29.0	29.2	29.4	29.8	29.9	29.8	29.3	29.6	29.9	29.9	29.5
2014..........	29.0	29.2	29.1	29.6	29.8	29.9	30.0	29.7	29.5	29.9	30.2	30.5	29.7
2015..........	29.7	30.0	29.9	30.5	30.6	30.9	30.5	30.4	30.4	30.6	30.4	30.6	30.4
Education and Health Services													
2005..........	63.0	65.1	63.6	65.6	64.5	62.4	61.8	60.9	64.9	65.6	66.7	66.9	64.3
2006..........	62.9	66.9	65.3	67.1	66.1	64.2	64.1	63.2	67.3	68.6	69.1	69.0	66.2
2007..........	65.1	68.5	66.7	68.9	68.0	66.4	66.0	65.1	68.7	70.1	70.6	70.7	67.9
2008..........	68.2	71.0	69.6	71.1	70.3	68.6	67.9	67.2	70.3	72.4	73.6	73.2	70.3
2009..........	71.2	74.1	71.4	72.2	71.4	70.1	69.1	68.6	71.9	73.6	73.9	74.0	71.8
2010..........	72.1	74.0	72.5	74.6	73.6	71.8	71.7	70.7	74.1	76.2	75.8	75.0	73.5
2011..........	74.8	75.9	74.7	76.0	75.6	73.6	72.8	72.2	75.4	76.5	76.8	75.7	75.0
2012..........	74.9	77.5	76.0	77.3	77.6	75.7	74.4	74.0	76.7	78.0	77.8	77.9	76.5
2013..........	75.4	77.7	76.7	78.5	77.2	75.4	75.1	74.8	77.6	79.3	79.7	78.6	77.2
2014..........	77.6	78.4	77.1	79.4	77.8	76.4	75.5	75.1	78.4	79.9	80.3	80.1	78.0
2015..........	78.0	79.2	77.7	79.5	78.3	76.8	76.3	75.6	78.4	80.7	81.6	80.5	78.6
Leisure and Hospitality													
2005..........	18.8	19.1	19.1	20.3	21.3	22.3	22.4	22.4	21.4	20.7	20.4	20.5	20.7
2006..........	19.8	19.7	20.4	20.5	21.6	22.8	22.8	22.6	21.6	21.0	20.5	20.9	21.2
2007..........	19.8	19.7	20.1	20.9	22.1	23.1	23.2	23.1	22.0	21.7	21.5	21.4	21.6
2008..........	20.0	20.1	20.6	21.2	22.4	23.1	22.9	22.8	22.1	21.6	21.4	21.4	21.6
2009..........	19.9	20.0	20.6	21.1	22.3	23.1	23.1	22.9	22.3	21.5	21.1	21.2	21.6
2010..........	19.0	19.6	19.8	20.8	21.9	22.5	22.8	22.6	21.9	21.6	21.4	21.5	21.3
2011..........	19.9	20.3	20.7	21.9	23.0	23.7	23.7	23.6	23.0	22.6	22.2	22.4	22.3
2012..........	21.0	21.2	21.7	22.9	23.8	24.9	24.5	24.5	23.8	23.1	23.0	23.2	23.1
2013..........	21.2	20.8	21.8	23.2	24.1	25.1	24.9	24.8	24.0	23.6	23.3	23.0	23.3
2014..........	22.0	22.0	22.6	23.2	24.1	25.0	24.8	24.5	24.0	23.6	23.5	23.5	23.6
2015..........	22.3	22.2	22.7	23.4	24.5	25.5	25.1	24.8	24.2	23.4	23.5	23.5	23.8

Employment by Industry: New Haven, CT NECTA, 2005–2015—*Continued*

(Numbers in thousands, not seasonally adjusted)

Industry and year	January	February	March	April	May	June	July	August	September	October	November	December	Annual average
Other Services													
2005	10.8	10.8	10.8	10.8	11.0	11.3	11.2	11.1	10.9	10.9	11.0	11.2	11.0
2006	10.8	10.7	10.8	10.9	11.1	11.2	11.2	11.2	11.0	11.2	11.2	11.3	11.1
2007	11.0	10.7	10.8	10.9	11.0	11.3	11.2	11.2	11.0	11.0	11.0	11.2	11.0
2008	10.8	10.8	11.0	10.9	11.0	11.2	11.0	11.0	10.8	10.8	10.8	11.0	10.9
2009	10.7	10.7	10.8	10.7	10.7	10.9	10.7	10.6	10.7	10.4	10.4	10.5	10.7
2010	10.2	10.2	10.3	10.4	10.3	10.6	10.6	10.5	10.5	10.4	10.3	10.4	10.4
2011	10.0	10.1	10.1	10.4	10.3	10.7	10.5	10.5	10.3	10.2	10.2	10.4	10.3
2012	10.4	10.4	10.4	10.7	10.6	10.7	10.7	10.7	10.5	10.6	10.6	10.6	10.6
2013	10.3	10.3	10.5	10.6	10.7	10.8	10.7	10.6	10.4	10.4	10.5	10.5	10.5
2014	10.4	10.4	10.5	10.6	10.7	10.9	10.9	10.8	10.6	10.8	10.7	10.8	10.7
2015	10.5	10.5	10.7	10.8	10.9	11.1	10.8	10.8	10.7	10.7	10.7	10.8	10.8
Government													
2005	36.1	37.0	36.9	37.5	37.2	37.6	32.1	31.5	35.4	36.5	37.2	37.3	36.0
2006	37.1	37.3	37.2	37.1	37.5	37.8	32.5	32.1	35.6	36.7	37.2	37.3	36.3
2007	36.8	37.1	37.1	37.0	37.2	38.0	32.4	32.1	35.8	37.0	37.6	37.5	36.3
2008	37.1	37.6	37.3	36.8	37.6	37.1	32.2	31.7	36.1	37.1	37.7	37.5	36.3
2009	37.0	37.2	37.1	36.8	37.5	36.5	31.5	30.9	35.8	35.7	36.6	36.1	35.7
2010	36.2	36.5	35.9	36.1	38.1	37.1	32.5	31.3	35.5	35.5	35.9	35.7	35.5
2011	35.7	36.0	35.1	36.4	36.4	36.1	31.3	30.4	34.5	35.1	35.4	35.5	34.8
2012	34.7	35.8	35.6	35.9	35.7	35.4	30.7	29.7	33.9	34.7	35.2	35.7	34.4
2013	35.3	35.2	35.4	36.6	36.2	37.2	31.6	30.4	35.2	34.9	35.8	35.2	34.9
2014	35.7	35.9	35.9	36.5	35.9	36.7	31.7	31.2	36.3	35.4	36.2	35.8	35.3
2015	35.5	36.2	36.3	36.5	36.4	37.2	32.1	31.4	36.2	35.8	36.5	36.4	35.5

Employment by Industry: Oxnard-Thousand Oaks-Ventura, CA, 2005–2015

(Numbers in thousands, not seasonally adjusted)

Industry and year	January	February	March	April	May	June	July	August	September	October	November	December	Annual average
Total Nonfarm													
2005	286.7	289.4	291.3	292.6	293.2	294.4	290.4	290.3	292.5	293.7	296.0	298.2	292.4
2006	293.7	296.4	298.0	299.0	301.6	302.7	298.2	298.0	299.8	299.8	301.6	303.0	299.3
2007	295.4	297.1	299.0	297.3	299.8	301.3	297.2	297.2	297.5	298.2	299.7	300.9	298.4
2008	292.6	294.5	294.6	295.1	295.9	295.9	290.6	289.8	291.7	291.9	291.1	291.9	293.0
2009	283.7	281.5	280.2	279.7	280.0	279.3	271.4	272.4	273.3	274.9	276.9	277.6	277.6
2010	270.7	271.7	272.2	276.8	279.8	276.7	272.7	273.4	274.4	277.1	279.6	280.5	275.5
2011	274.5	275.4	275.6	277.2	277.6	277.8	274.4	275.4	276.9	279.1	282.5	282.0	277.4
2012	278.0	279.5	280.2	281.0	282.9	283.7	278.4	279.5	280.8	285.1	288.5	289.3	282.2
2013	284.4	286.6	287.1	286.8	288.8	288.2	284.7	286.7	287.8	291.5	295.3	297.0	288.7
2014	289.8	290.9	292.1	293.0	293.8	293.6	289.2	290.6	291.5	295.3	297.4	297.7	292.9
2015	291.5	293.3	293.8	294.3	295.7	294.6	291.1	292.9	294.0	297.4	299.5	299.6	294.8
Total Private													
2005	244.5	246.7	248.5	249.9	250.1	251.5	250.2	250.4	250.7	251.5	253.1	255.4	250.2
2006	251.2	253.6	255.0	256.0	258.7	259.5	257.3	257.6	257.2	257.3	258.4	259.9	256.8
2007	252.7	254.0	255.7	253.8	256.1	257.5	255.7	256.1	254.5	255.1	255.9	257.1	255.4
2008	249.1	250.6	250.6	251.3	251.8	251.5	249.5	249.6	250.0	248.7	247.4	248.1	249.9
2009	240.5	237.9	236.6	235.5	235.6	234.8	231.4	231.7	231.7	232.1	233.6	234.5	234.7
2010	228.1	228.5	228.9	230.9	232.3	231.7	231.4	231.0	231.1	232.3	233.9	235.0	231.3
2011	229.7	230.1	230.1	231.8	232.4	232.1	233.3	233.5	233.6	234.4	236.9	237.7	233.0
2012	234.1	234.9	235.6	236.5	238.0	239.0	237.9	238.6	238.4	241.3	244.0	245.1	238.6
2013	240.6	242.2	242.5	242.4	243.9	243.5	244.2	245.6	245.3	247.6	251.0	252.7	245.1
2014	246.1	246.6	247.7	248.4	249.2	249.0	248.7	248.7	248.2	250.2	251.8	252.3	248.9
2015	246.4	247.2	247.8	248.2	248.9	248.1	249.9	250.3	249.6	251.4	252.9	253.2	249.5
Goods Producing													
2005	55.6	56.6	57.3	57.4	57.4	58.1	57.6	57.5	57.5	57.5	57.2	57.5	57.3
2006	57.7	58.8	59.1	59.3	60.2	61.2	61.1	61.2	61.1	60.2	59.8	59.2	59.9
2007	58.0	58.2	58.6	57.9	58.7	59.0	58.3	58.3	57.5	57.3	56.7	56.1	57.9
2008	54.0	54.3	54.2	54.3	54.2	54.3	54.2	53.9	53.8	53.5	52.5	52.0	53.8
2009	50.3	48.9	48.9	48.3	47.7	47.8	46.6	46.3	45.8	45.1	44.7	44.2	47.1
2010	43.7	43.6	43.7	43.7	44.3	44.5	44.7	44.1	44.1	44.1	44.0	43.5	44.0
2011	43.1	43.1	43.1	43.2	43.2	43.2	43.4	43.4	43.3	43.2	43.3	42.8	43.2
2012	42.3	42.3	42.6	42.5	42.7	43.1	43.2	43.4	43.3	43.3	43.2	43.4	42.9
2013	43.2	43.2	43.2	43.0	43.2	43.4	43.8	44.0	44.1	44.5	44.7	44.7	43.8
2014	44.6	44.9	45.5	45.0	45.5	45.5	46.1	46.3	46.3	46.1	45.8	45.5	45.6
2015	45.2	44.9	45.6	45.2	45.4	45.5	46.1	46.4	46.0	45.5	45.7	45.6	45.6
Service-Providing													
2005	231.1	232.8	234.0	235.2	235.8	236.3	232.8	232.8	235.0	236.2	238.8	240.7	235.1
2006	236.0	237.6	238.9	239.7	241.4	241.5	237.1	236.8	238.7	239.6	241.8	243.8	239.4
2007	237.4	238.9	240.4	239.4	241.1	242.3	238.9	238.9	240.0	240.9	243.0	244.8	240.5
2008	238.6	240.2	240.4	240.8	241.7	241.6	236.4	235.9	237.9	238.4	238.6	239.9	239.2
2009	233.4	232.6	231.3	231.4	232.3	231.5	224.8	226.1	227.5	229.8	232.2	233.4	230.5
2010	227.0	228.1	228.5	233.1	235.5	232.2	228.0	229.3	230.3	233.0	235.6	237.0	231.5
2011	231.4	232.3	232.5	234.0	234.4	234.6	231.0	232.0	233.6	235.9	239.2	239.2	234.2
2012	235.7	237.2	237.6	238.5	240.2	240.6	235.2	236.1	237.5	241.8	245.3	245.9	239.3
2013	241.2	243.4	243.9	243.8	245.6	244.8	240.9	242.7	243.7	247.0	250.6	252.3	245.0
2014	245.2	246.0	246.6	248.0	248.3	248.1	243.1	244.3	245.2	249.2	251.6	252.2	247.3
2015	246.3	248.4	248.2	249.1	250.3	249.1	245.0	246.5	248.0	251.9	253.8	254.0	249.2
Mining and Logging													
2005	0.7	0.6	0.7	0.7	0.7	0.8	0.8	0.8	0.8	0.9	0.9	0.9	0.8
2006	1.0	1.0	1.0	1.0	1.0	1.0	1.1	1.1	1.1	1.1	1.1	1.1	1.1
2007	1.1	1.1	1.1	1.1	1.1	1.1	1.0	1.0	1.0	1.1	1.1	1.1	1.1
2008	1.0	1.1	1.1	1.1	1.1	1.1	1.2	1.2	1.2	1.3	1.3	1.3	1.2
2009	1.3	1.3	1.3	1.3	1.2	1.3	1.2	1.2	1.2	1.2	1.2	1.2	1.2
2010	1.1	1.1	1.1	1.1	1.2	1.2	1.2	1.2	1.3	1.3	1.3	1.3	1.2
2011	1.3	1.3	1.3	1.2	1.2	1.2	1.2	1.3	1.3	1.3	1.3	1.3	1.3
2012	1.3	1.3	1.3	1.3	1.3	1.3	1.3	1.3	1.2	1.2	1.2	1.2	1.3
2013	1.2	1.2	1.2	1.2	1.2	1.2	1.2	1.2	1.2	1.2	1.3	1.3	1.2
2014	1.3	1.3	1.3	1.3	1.3	1.3	1.3	1.3	1.3	1.3	1.3	1.3	1.3
2015	1.2	1.1	1.1	1.1	1.0	1.0	1.0	1.0	1.0	0.9	0.9	0.9	1.0

Employment by Industry: Oxnard-Thousand Oaks-Ventura, CA, 2005–2015—*Continued*

(Numbers in thousands, not seasonally adjusted)

Industry and year	January	February	March	April	May	June	July	August	September	October	November	December	Annual average
Construction													
2005	16.6	17.4	18.0	18.5	18.7	19.2	19.2	19.4	19.5	19.7	19.5	19.8	18.8
2006	19.8	20.4	20.4	20.4	21.0	21.4	21.2	21.2	21.0	20.2	19.6	19.2	20.5
2007	18.3	18.5	18.7	18.5	19.1	19.7	19.5	19.7	19.1	18.8	18.3	17.9	18.8
2008	16.9	17.1	17.0	17.2	17.1	17.2	17.0	16.7	16.6	16.2	15.7	15.4	16.7
2009	14.2	13.6	13.9	13.7	13.6	13.6	13.2	13.2	12.8	12.4	12.3	11.9	13.2
2010	11.2	11.2	11.3	11.2	11.5	11.5	11.5	11.4	11.2	11.3	11.3	11.1	11.3
2011	11.1	11.0	11.0	11.3	11.3	11.3	11.5	11.5	11.3	11.5	11.5	11.3	11.3
2012	11.2	11.3	11.5	11.4	11.6	11.8	11.8	11.9	12.1	12.1	12.3	12.4	11.8
2013	12.2	12.3	12.2	12.1	12.3	12.4	12.6	12.7	12.8	13.1	13.3	13.2	12.6
2014	13.1	13.3	13.6	13.4	13.7	13.7	13.9	14.1	14.1	14.0	13.9	13.7	13.7
2015	13.8	13.7	13.8	13.9	14.1	14.2	14.6	14.8	14.3	14.1	14.4	14.3	14.2
Manufacturing													
2005	38.3	38.6	38.6	38.2	38.0	38.1	37.6	37.3	37.2	36.9	36.8	36.8	37.7
2006	36.9	37.4	37.7	37.9	38.2	38.8	38.8	38.9	39.0	38.9	39.1	38.9	38.4
2007	38.6	38.6	38.8	38.3	38.5	38.2	37.8	37.6	37.4	37.4	37.3	37.1	38.0
2008	36.1	36.1	36.1	36.0	36.0	36.0	36.0	36.0	36.0	36.0	35.5	35.3	35.9
2009	34.8	34.0	33.7	33.3	32.9	32.9	32.2	31.9	31.8	31.5	31.2	31.1	32.6
2010	31.4	31.3	31.3	31.4	31.6	31.8	32.0	31.5	31.6	31.5	31.4	31.1	31.5
2011	30.7	30.8	30.8	30.7	30.7	30.7	30.7	30.6	30.7	30.4	30.5	30.2	30.6
2012	29.8	29.7	29.8	29.8	29.8	30.0	30.1	30.2	30.0	30.0	29.7	29.8	29.9
2013	29.8	29.7	29.8	29.7	29.7	29.8	30.0	30.1	30.1	30.2	30.1	30.2	29.9
2014	30.2	30.3	30.6	30.3	30.5	30.5	30.9	30.9	30.9	30.8	30.6	30.5	30.6
2015	30.2	30.1	30.7	30.2	30.3	30.3	30.5	30.6	30.7	30.5	30.4	30.4	30.4
Trade, Transportation, and Utilities													
2005	53.7	53.5	53.6	54.0	54.2	54.6	54.5	54.7	55.0	55.3	56.8	58.1	54.8
2006	55.4	55.1	55.2	55.8	56.3	56.5	56.4	56.4	56.1	56.6	58.1	59.1	56.4
2007	56.4	55.8	55.9	55.5	55.8	56.5	56.7	57.1	56.7	56.6	58.3	59.8	56.8
2008	56.5	56.4	56.4	56.1	56.1	56.1	55.7	55.5	55.7	55.6	56.2	57.1	56.1
2009	54.1	53.0	52.1	51.8	52.0	51.8	51.7	51.7	51.8	52.2	53.5	54.9	52.6
2010	52.2	51.8	51.8	53.0	53.2	52.9	52.9	52.8	52.7	53.4	54.9	56.0	53.1
2011	53.5	53.0	53.0	53.7	53.7	53.9	54.2	54.3	54.0	54.4	56.6	57.4	54.3
2012	55.3	54.3	54.1	54.6	55.1	55.2	55.3	55.1	55.1	55.8	58.7	59.4	55.7
2013	56.6	56.4	56.0	56.0	56.5	56.7	56.8	56.9	56.6	57.1	60.1	61.0	57.2
2014	57.9	57.2	56.9	57.1	57.3	57.3	57.6	57.6	57.4	58.1	60.2	61.0	58.0
2015	58.2	57.8	57.4	57.3	57.6	57.7	58.3	58.3	58.1	58.5	59.5	60.1	58.2
Wholesale Trade													
2005	12.3	12.4	12.4	12.5	12.5	12.6	12.6	12.7	12.7	12.6	12.5	12.6	12.5
2006	12.4	12.6	12.7	12.8	12.9	12.9	12.8	12.6	12.5	12.6	12.4	12.5	12.6
2007	12.6	12.9	13.0	13.1	13.1	13.2	13.1	13.2	13.1	13.0	13.0	13.0	13.0
2008	12.7	12.9	12.8	12.8	12.9	12.9	12.9	12.9	12.9	12.9	12.7	12.8	12.8
2009	12.6	12.5	12.4	12.2	12.2	12.1	11.9	11.8	11.8	11.8	11.8	11.8	12.1
2010	11.8	12.0	12.1	13.0	13.0	12.7	12.5	12.3	12.0	12.1	12.3	12.2	12.3
2011	12.1	12.2	12.4	12.7	12.6	12.6	12.8	12.7	12.7	12.4	12.4	12.3	12.5
2012	12.4	12.4	12.4	12.6	12.7	12.8	12.7	12.7	12.7	12.5	12.6	12.7	12.6
2013	12.5	12.7	12.8	12.8	12.9	13.0	12.9	12.9	12.8	12.8	13.0	13.1	12.9
2014	12.9	12.9	12.9	12.9	12.9	12.8	12.7	12.7	12.6	12.7	12.7	12.8	12.8
2015	12.5	12.5	12.5	12.5	12.5	12.6	12.6	12.7	12.6	12.6	12.6	12.7	12.6
Retail Trade													
2005	35.7	35.5	35.4	35.6	35.8	36.1	36.2	36.3	36.5	36.9	38.4	39.5	36.5
2006	37.1	36.5	36.5	36.9	37.2	37.3	37.3	37.6	37.4	37.9	39.5	40.3	37.6
2007	37.9	37.0	36.9	36.6	36.7	37.1	37.4	37.7	37.4	37.4	38.9	40.2	37.6
2008	37.5	37.1	37.0	37.0	36.9	37.1	37.0	36.9	37.0	37.1	38.0	38.7	37.3
2009	35.9	35.1	34.4	34.4	34.5	34.4	34.5	34.6	34.6	35.1	36.4	37.6	35.1
2010	35.2	34.6	34.5	34.8	35.0	34.9	35.0	35.1	35.3	36.0	37.3	38.3	35.5
2011	36.1	35.5	35.3	35.6	35.6	35.8	35.8	36.0	35.8	36.5	38.5	39.3	36.3
2012	37.3	36.3	36.0	36.4	36.7	36.7	36.8	36.6	36.6	37.5	40.3	40.7	37.3
2013	38.4	37.9	37.5	37.4	37.8	37.9	38.0	38.1	37.9	38.4	41.1	41.7	38.5
2014	39.0	38.3	38.1	38.3	38.4	38.5	38.9	38.9	38.8	39.4	41.5	42.2	39.2
2015	39.8	39.3	39.0	38.8	39.1	39.1	39.6	39.6	39.5	39.9	40.9	41.4	39.7

Employment by Industry: Oxnard-Thousand Oaks-Ventura, CA, 2005–2015—*Continued*

(Numbers in thousands, not seasonally adjusted)

Industry and year	January	February	March	April	May	June	July	August	September	October	November	December	Annual average
Transportation and Utilities													
2005	5.7	5.6	5.8	5.9	5.9	5.9	5.7	5.7	5.8	5.8	5.9	6.0	5.8
2006	5.9	6.0	6.0	6.1	6.2	6.3	6.1	6.2	6.2	6.1	6.2	6.3	6.1
2007	5.9	5.9	6.0	5.8	6.0	6.2	6.2	6.2	6.2	6.2	6.4	6.6	6.1
2008	6.3	6.4	6.6	6.3	6.3	6.1	5.8	5.7	5.8	5.6	5.5	5.6	6.0
2009	5.6	5.4	5.3	5.2	5.3	5.3	5.3	5.3	5.4	5.3	5.3	5.5	5.4
2010	5.2	5.2	5.2	5.2	5.2	5.3	5.4	5.4	5.4	5.3	5.3	5.5	5.3
2011	5.3	5.3	5.3	5.4	5.5	5.5	5.6	5.6	5.5	5.5	5.7	5.8	5.5
2012	5.6	5.6	5.7	5.6	5.7	5.7	5.8	5.8	5.8	5.8	5.8	6.0	5.7
2013	5.7	5.8	5.7	5.8	5.8	5.8	5.9	5.9	5.9	5.9	6.0	6.2	5.9
2014	6.0	6.0	5.9	5.9	6.0	6.0	6.0	6.0	6.0	6.0	6.0	6.0	6.0
2015	5.9	6.0	5.9	6.0	6.0	6.0	6.1	6.0	6.0	6.0	6.0	6.0	6.0
Information													
2005	6.1	6.2	6.1	6.2	6.2	6.2	6.1	6.2	6.2	6.1	6.1	6.2	6.2
2006	6.1	6.1	6.1	6.0	6.1	6.0	6.0	5.9	5.8	5.8	5.7	5.8	6.0
2007	5.7	5.9	5.9	5.8	5.9	5.9	5.8	5.8	5.8	5.7	5.8	5.7	5.8
2008	5.7	5.7	5.7	5.7	5.7	5.7	5.6	5.6	5.5	5.5	5.5	5.4	5.6
2009	5.4	5.4	5.4	5.3	5.3	5.3	5.3	5.2	5.2	5.2	5.3	5.3	5.3
2010	5.2	5.2	5.2	5.2	5.2	5.2	5.2	5.2	5.1	5.0	5.0	5.0	5.1
2011	4.9	4.8	4.8	4.8	4.9	4.9	4.9	4.9	4.8	4.8	4.9	5.0	4.9
2012	5.0	5.0	5.1	5.0	5.1	5.2	5.2	5.2	5.1	5.3	5.3	5.3	5.2
2013	5.1	5.1	5.1	5.1	5.1	5.2	5.3	5.3	5.2	5.3	5.3	5.4	5.2
2014	5.4	5.4	5.4	5.4	5.4	5.5	5.4	5.3	5.2	5.2	5.2	5.3	5.3
2015	5.1	5.1	5.1	5.1	5.1	5.1	5.1	5.1	5.0	5.0	5.0	5.0	5.1
Financial Activities													
2005	24.1	24.2	24.3	24.1	24.3	24.5	24.4	24.6	24.6	24.7	24.8	25.1	24.5
2006	25.0	24.8	24.9	24.6	24.5	24.4	23.9	23.6	23.3	23.2	22.9	23.3	24.0
2007	22.7	22.7	22.8	22.8	22.9	23.1	23.0	22.8	22.6	22.7	22.1	22.1	22.7
2008	21.5	21.5	21.3	21.4	21.4	21.4	21.1	20.9	20.8	20.7	20.5	20.5	21.1
2009	20.7	20.7	20.6	20.6	20.5	20.4	20.4	20.4	20.5	20.2	20.4	20.5	20.5
2010	20.2	20.3	20.3	20.1	20.1	20.1	20.3	20.4	20.3	20.5	20.6	20.8	20.3
2011	20.6	20.6	20.8	20.7	20.7	20.7	20.7	20.3	20.1	20.0	19.6	19.9	20.4
2012	19.9	20.1	20.0	19.7	19.6	19.6	19.5	19.4	19.2	19.4	19.4	19.4	19.6
2013	19.1	19.1	19.2	18.8	18.8	18.7	18.8	18.9	18.9	18.9	18.9	18.9	18.9
2014	19.0	18.9	19.0	18.9	18.8	18.9	18.8	18.7	18.4	18.5	18.4	18.4	18.7
2015	18.0	17.8	17.8	17.8	18.1	17.7	17.8	17.6	17.6	17.6	17.6	17.6	17.8
Professional and Business Services													
2005	37.6	38.1	38.3	39.0	38.7	38.7	38.4	38.4	38.0	38.1	38.3	38.4	38.3
2006	38.0	38.8	39.2	39.4	40.0	39.9	39.1	39.6	39.5	39.5	39.4	39.7	39.3
2007	38.8	39.1	39.4	38.5	38.5	38.6	38.0	37.8	37.3	37.2	37.3	37.4	38.2
2008	37.2	37.6	37.6	37.5	37.7	37.8	37.8	38.2	38.4	37.8	37.6	37.8	37.8
2009	36.6	36.1	36.1	35.4	35.1	34.9	34.6	34.6	34.4	34.6	35.0	34.6	35.2
2010	33.6	33.6	33.9	33.6	33.6	33.8	33.7	33.7	33.6	33.7	33.6	33.8	33.7
2011	32.7	32.8	32.8	33.0	33.0	33.1	33.8	33.6	33.4	33.5	33.6	33.8	33.3
2012	33.5	34.0	34.4	34.4	34.4	34.9	34.9	35.2	35.2	35.9	36.0	36.0	34.9
2013	35.5	35.8	36.2	36.0	36.0	36.0	36.4	36.4	36.3	36.7	36.7	37.0	36.3
2014	35.4	35.0	35.4	35.4	35.0	35.0	35.1	34.8	34.7	35.0	34.9	34.9	35.1
2015	34.0	34.3	34.5	35.1	34.4	34.4	34.6	34.6	34.4	35.8	35.1	34.6	34.7
Education and Health Services													
2005	28.7	29.1	29.4	29.6	29.6	29.7	29.4	29.2	29.7	30.0	30.1	30.2	29.6
2006	29.7	30.2	30.2	30.4	30.6	30.5	29.9	29.9	30.4	31.2	31.3	31.6	30.5
2007	31.0	31.6	31.9	31.7	31.9	31.9	31.5	32.0	32.4	33.2	33.3	33.4	32.2
2008	32.8	33.6	33.4	34.0	34.2	33.7	33.1	33.7	34.5	35.0	34.9	35.2	34.0
2009	34.6	35.1	34.9	35.3	35.4	34.9	33.6	34.2	34.8	35.6	35.7	35.9	35.0
2010	34.6	35.3	35.1	36.0	36.0	35.6	34.8	35.0	35.3	35.9	36.1	36.2	35.5
2011	35.6	36.2	35.9	36.3	36.3	35.6	35.3	35.8	36.7	37.2	37.5	37.6	36.3
2012	37.3	38.0	38.0	38.3	38.4	38.0	37.1	37.6	38.1	39.0	38.9	39.4	38.2
2013	39.3	40.2	40.3	40.5	40.6	39.8	39.1	39.9	40.3	41.2	41.5	41.6	40.4
2014	40.6	41.6	41.4	42.1	42.1	41.4	40.4	40.8	41.4	42.5	42.6	42.6	41.6
2015	41.8	42.7	42.6	42.7	42.9	42.2	42.2	42.3	42.7	42.9	43.4	44.1	42.7

Employment by Industry: Oxnard-Thousand Oaks-Ventura, CA, 2005–2015—*Continued*

(Numbers in thousands, not seasonally adjusted)

Industry and year	January	February	March	April	May	June	July	August	September	October	November	December	Annual average
Leisure and Hospitality													
2005	28.2	28.4	28.8	29.0	29.2	29.3	29.5	29.6	29.4	29.6	29.6	29.7	29.2
2006	29.2	29.6	30.0	30.2	30.6	30.6	30.9	31.0	30.9	30.8	31.1	31.2	30.5
2007	30.6	31.1	31.4	31.7	32.3	32.5	32.5	32.5	32.2	32.0	32.3	32.5	32.0
2008	31.4	31.4	31.8	32.1	32.3	32.3	31.9	31.8	31.3	30.9	30.7	30.6	31.5
2009	29.5	29.4	29.3	29.5	30.2	30.4	30.2	30.1	30.0	29.9	29.7	29.8	29.8
2010	29.5	29.6	29.7	30.1	30.6	30.4	30.7	30.7	30.7	30.5	30.5	30.6	30.3
2011	30.3	30.5	30.6	31.0	31.4	31.6	31.8	32.1	32.0	31.9	31.9	31.8	31.4
2012	31.6	31.8	32.1	32.6	33.1	33.3	33.2	33.3	33.0	33.1	33.2	32.9	32.8
2013	32.4	32.9	33.0	33.4	34.1	34.1	34.2	34.4	34.1	34.1	34.0	34.3	33.8
2014	33.5	33.8	34.2	34.6	35.1	35.5	35.5	35.5	35.2	35.0	34.9	34.9	34.8
2015	34.5	35.0	35.2	35.4	35.7	35.8	36.1	36.4	36.2	36.5	37.0	36.6	35.9
Other Services													
2005	10.5	10.6	10.7	10.6	10.5	10.4	10.3	10.2	10.3	10.2	10.2	10.2	10.4
2006	10.1	10.2	10.3	10.3	10.4	10.4	10.0	10.0	10.1	10.0	10.1	10.0	10.2
2007	9.5	9.6	9.8	9.9	10.1	10.0	9.9	9.8	10.0	10.4	10.1	10.1	9.9
2008	10.0	10.1	10.2	10.2	10.2	10.2	10.1	10.0	10.0	9.7	9.5	9.5	10.0
2009	9.3	9.3	9.3	9.3	9.4	9.3	9.0	9.2	9.2	9.3	9.3	9.3	9.3
2010	9.1	9.1	9.2	9.2	9.3	9.2	9.1	9.1	9.3	9.2	9.2	9.1	9.2
2011	9.0	9.1	9.1	9.1	9.2	9.1	9.2	9.1	9.3	9.4	9.5	9.4	9.2
2012	9.2	9.4	9.3	9.4	9.6	9.7	9.5	9.4	9.4	9.5	9.3	9.3	9.4
2013	9.4	9.5	9.5	9.6	9.6	9.6	9.8	9.8	9.8	9.8	9.8	9.8	9.7
2014	9.7	9.8	9.9	9.9	10.0	9.9	9.8	9.7	9.6	9.8	9.8	9.7	9.8
2015	9.6	9.6	9.6	9.6	9.7	9.7	9.7	9.6	9.6	9.6	9.6	9.6	9.6
Government													
2005	42.2	42.7	42.8	42.7	43.1	42.9	40.2	39.9	41.8	42.2	42.9	42.8	42.2
2006	42.5	42.8	43.0	43.0	42.9	43.2	40.9	40.4	42.6	42.5	43.2	43.1	42.5
2007	42.7	43.1	43.3	43.5	43.7	43.8	41.5	41.1	43.0	43.1	43.8	43.8	43.0
2008	43.5	43.9	44.0	43.8	44.1	44.4	41.1	40.2	41.7	43.2	43.7	43.8	43.1
2009	43.2	43.6	43.6	44.2	44.4	44.5	40.0	40.7	41.6	42.8	43.3	43.1	42.9
2010	42.6	43.2	43.3	45.9	47.5	45.0	41.3	42.4	43.3	44.8	45.7	45.5	44.2
2011	44.8	45.3	45.5	45.4	45.2	45.7	41.1	41.9	43.3	44.7	45.6	44.3	44.4
2012	43.9	44.6	44.6	44.5	44.9	44.7	40.5	40.9	42.4	43.8	44.5	44.2	43.6
2013	43.8	44.4	44.6	44.4	44.9	44.7	40.5	41.1	42.5	43.9	44.3	44.3	43.6
2014	43.7	44.3	44.4	44.6	44.6	44.6	40.5	41.9	43.3	45.1	45.6	45.4	44.0
2015	45.1	46.1	46.0	46.1	46.8	46.5	41.2	42.6	44.4	46.0	46.6	46.4	45.3

Employment by Industry: McAllen-Edinburg-Mission, TX, 2005–2015

(Numbers in thousands, not seasonally adjusted)

Industry and year	January	February	March	April	May	June	July	August	September	October	November	December	Annual average
Total Nonfarm													
2005	190.9	193.1	194.5	197.2	196.6	196.0	188.8	193.6	196.4	199.2	201.1	203.0	195.9
2006	202.0	202.9	204.0	203.5	202.9	202.9	194.2	199.6	202.8	206.8	209.7	211.1	203.5
2007	209.3	209.9	211.2	213.1	212.9	212.0	207.6	211.6	213.3	217.1	219.3	220.7	213.2
2008	220.2	221.3	221.6	222.5	222.2	219.7	214.1	216.8	217.6	222.8	223.5	224.3	220.6
2009	220.1	219.2	219.3	220.5	220.7	217.9	213.0	215.0	216.6	220.5	222.0	222.3	218.9
2010	219.8	220.4	221.5	221.3	223.2	221.2	212.2	215.5	219.2	222.9	225.0	226.9	220.8
2011	224.2	224.9	226.4	227.5	228.1	226.8	220.7	224.1	226.0	226.5	230.1	231.1	226.4
2012	228.4	229.3	231.4	231.5	231.5	230.3	223.4	226.7	228.7	231.9	235.3	237.2	230.5
2013	232.3	234.4	236.2	236.5	237.4	236.6	229.5	233.8	235.5	238.3	241.8	243.9	236.4
2014	238.6	239.7	240.9	242.3	244.1	243.0	236.3	239.8	241.2	244.9	247.4	249.9	242.3
2015	245.7	247.2	248.2	248.4	250.2	249.1	243.4	245.6	247.1	249.5	250.7	253.1	248.2
Total Private													
2005	143.2	144.5	145.8	148.5	147.9	147.9	147.8	148.3	148.8	149.9	151.4	153.3	148.1
2006	152.0	152.2	153.4	153.8	153.3	153.2	153.1	153.8	154.8	156.3	158.7	160.2	154.6
2007	159.1	159.1	160.1	162.5	162.2	161.6	162.6	163.8	163.3	165.2	166.8	167.9	162.9
2008	167.9	168.4	168.4	169.4	168.4	167.2	166.9	167.6	165.7	168.8	168.6	169.2	168.0
2009	165.8	164.4	164.4	165.8	165.6	164.1	164.4	164.1	163.5	165.6	166.5	166.7	165.1
2010	164.8	164.7	165.5	164.9	166.6	165.5	163.9	165.4	166.6	167.9	169.5	171.6	166.4
2011	168.8	169.1	170.7	172.1	172.3	172.1	171.6	173.1	173.2	172.8	175.5	176.6	172.3
2012	174.3	174.7	176.4	176.7	176.6	176.1	174.5	176.2	175.9	177.3	180.0	181.8	176.7
2013	177.7	179.2	180.5	181.2	181.4	181.4	179.8	182.3	181.8	182.7	185.7	187.7	181.8
2014	182.6	183.4	184.3	186.1	186.7	186.6	185.6	187.5	187.1	188.6	190.6	192.8	186.8
2015	189.5	190.4	191.1	191.7	192.3	191.9	191.7	192.1	191.5	192.4	193.3	195.5	192.0
Goods Producing													
2005	18.9	19.0	19.1	18.9	19.0	19.1	18.7	18.7	18.9	19.0	19.1	19.2	19.0
2006	19.0	19.1	19.3	19.1	19.0	19.0	18.7	18.9	19.0	18.7	19.1	19.3	19.0
2007	19.1	19.0	19.1	19.4	19.4	19.3	19.0	19.6	19.6	19.5	19.5	19.5	19.3
2008	19.4	19.2	19.1	18.8	18.5	18.3	17.7	17.9	17.5	18.0	17.6	17.7	18.3
2009	17.0	16.7	16.4	15.8	15.7	15.5	15.3	15.3	15.1	15.3	15.1	15.1	15.7
2010	15.1	14.8	15.1	14.8	15.0	14.5	14.2	14.4	14.5	14.5	14.6	14.7	14.7
2011	14.7	14.7	14.8	14.5	14.6	14.7	14.7	14.9	15.0	15.1	15.4	15.3	14.9
2012	15.2	15.2	15.5	15.3	15.3	15.3	15.1	15.4	15.3	15.6	15.7	15.9	15.4
2013	15.6	15.8	15.9	16.0	16.0	16.1	15.9	16.2	16.0	16.2	16.3	16.4	16.0
2014	16.0	16.4	16.2	16.6	16.4	16.5	16.3	16.6	16.5	16.8	16.7	16.9	16.5
2015	16.5	16.7	16.4	16.4	16.2	16.2	15.9	15.6	15.4	15.6	15.7	15.7	16.0
Service-Providing													
2005	172.0	174.1	175.4	178.3	177.6	176.9	170.1	174.9	177.5	180.2	182.0	183.8	176.9
2006	183.0	183.8	184.7	184.4	183.9	183.9	175.5	180.7	183.8	188.1	190.6	191.8	184.5
2007	190.2	190.9	192.1	193.7	193.5	192.7	188.6	192.0	193.7	197.6	199.8	201.2	193.8
2008	200.8	202.1	202.5	203.7	203.7	201.4	196.4	198.9	200.1	204.8	205.9	206.6	202.2
2009	203.1	202.5	202.9	204.7	205.0	202.4	197.7	199.7	201.5	205.2	206.9	207.2	203.2
2010	204.7	205.6	206.4	206.5	208.2	206.7	198.0	201.1	204.7	208.4	210.4	212.2	206.1
2011	209.5	210.2	211.6	213.0	213.5	212.1	206.0	209.2	211.0	211.4	214.7	215.8	211.5
2012	213.2	214.1	215.9	216.2	216.2	215.0	208.3	211.3	213.4	216.3	219.6	221.3	215.1
2013	216.7	218.6	220.3	220.5	221.4	220.5	213.6	217.6	219.5	222.1	225.5	227.5	220.3
2014	222.6	223.3	224.7	225.7	227.7	226.5	220.0	223.2	224.7	228.1	230.7	233.0	225.9
2015	229.2	230.5	231.8	232.0	234.0	232.9	227.5	230.0	231.7	233.9	235.0	237.4	232.2
Mining, Logging, and Construction													
2005	10.4	10.6	10.6	10.7	10.8	11.0	10.7	10.7	10.8	10.6	10.7	10.7	10.7
2006	10.5	10.7	11.0	10.8	10.9	11.0	11.1	11.2	11.1	11.0	11.0	11.1	11.0
2007	11.0	11.0	11.1	11.2	11.2	11.4	11.5	11.8	11.7	11.4	11.4	11.4	11.3
2008	11.4	11.3	11.2	11.2	11.0	10.9	10.8	10.9	10.7	10.8	10.6	10.6	11.0
2009	10.3	10.1	9.8	9.7	9.5	9.3	9.3	9.1	8.9	8.9	8.8	8.8	9.4
2010	8.7	8.6	8.7	8.6	8.8	8.7	8.6	8.6	8.7	8.5	8.5	8.5	8.6
2011	8.5	8.6	8.7	8.6	8.7	8.8	8.9	9.1	9.1	9.0	9.1	9.0	8.8
2012	8.9	9.0	9.2	9.1	9.2	9.2	9.2	9.3	9.2	9.3	9.3	9.4	9.2
2013	9.0	9.1	9.3	9.5	9.6	9.8	9.7	9.9	9.8	9.8	9.8	9.9	9.6
2014	9.8	9.9	9.9	10.0	10.0	10.1	10.1	10.3	10.2	10.4	10.3	10.4	10.1
2015	10.0	9.8	9.7	9.6	9.6	9.6	9.3	9.1	9.0	9.0	9.1	9.1	9.4

Employment by Industry: McAllen-Edinburg-Mission, TX, 2005–2015—*Continued*

(Numbers in thousands, not seasonally adjusted)

Industry and year	January	February	March	April	May	June	July	August	September	October	November	December	Annual average
Manufacturing													
2005	8.5	8.4	8.5	8.2	8.2	8.1	8.0	8.0	8.1	8.4	8.4	8.5	8.3
2006	8.5	8.4	8.3	8.3	8.1	8.0	7.6	7.7	7.9	7.7	8.1	8.2	8.1
2007	8.1	8.0	8.0	8.2	8.2	7.9	7.5	7.8	7.9	8.1	8.1	8.1	8.0
2008	8.0	7.9	7.9	7.6	7.5	7.4	6.9	7.0	6.8	7.2	7.0	7.1	7.4
2009	6.7	6.6	6.6	6.1	6.2	6.2	6.0	6.2	6.2	6.4	6.3	6.3	6.3
2010	6.4	6.2	6.4	6.2	6.2	5.8	5.6	5.8	5.8	6.0	6.1	6.2	6.1
2011	6.2	6.1	6.1	5.9	5.9	5.9	5.8	5.8	5.9	6.1	6.3	6.3	6.0
2012	6.3	6.2	6.3	6.2	6.1	6.1	5.9	6.1	6.1	6.3	6.4	6.5	6.2
2013	6.6	6.7	6.6	6.5	6.4	6.3	6.2	6.3	6.2	6.4	6.5	6.5	6.4
2014	6.2	6.5	6.3	6.6	6.4	6.4	6.2	6.3	6.3	6.4	6.4	6.5	6.4
2015	6.5	6.9	6.7	6.8	6.6	6.6	6.6	6.5	6.4	6.6	6.6	6.6	6.6
Trade, Transportation, and Utilities													
2005	40.0	39.8	40.2	41.4	41.2	41.2	41.3	41.4	41.1	41.4	42.6	43.5	41.3
2006	42.4	42.0	42.5	43.0	42.9	42.7	43.0	43.4	43.8	44.5	45.9	46.6	43.6
2007	45.2	44.8	45.6	46.1	45.8	45.4	46.1	46.4	46.1	46.6	47.9	48.5	46.2
2008	47.6	46.8	47.1	47.3	47.0	46.8	46.9	47.2	46.5	47.2	47.6	48.2	47.2
2009	46.0	45.1	45.2	46.0	45.8	45.6	45.6	46.0	45.8	46.0	46.7	47.3	45.9
2010	45.2	44.8	45.1	45.5	45.9	45.8	45.4	46.0	45.8	46.5	47.6	48.8	46.0
2011	46.8	46.3	46.7	47.4	47.5	47.4	47.3	47.9	47.4	47.7	49.4	50.2	47.7
2012	48.6	48.2	48.8	49.0	49.0	49.3	49.4	50.1	49.5	49.8	52.0	52.6	49.7
2013	50.7	50.3	50.5	50.8	50.9	51.1	50.7	51.1	50.8	51.0	53.1	54.2	51.3
2014	51.5	51.0	51.3	52.2	52.1	52.6	52.8	52.9	52.4	52.9	54.9	55.8	52.7
2015	53.7	53.4	53.8	54.1	54.3	54.2	54.3	54.7	54.2	54.6	55.4	56.4	54.4
Wholesale Trade													
2005	7.1	7.0	7.0	7.2	7.0	7.0	6.9	6.7	6.8	6.9	7.0	7.1	7.0
2006	7.1	7.2	7.3	7.3	7.2	7.1	7.0	6.9	6.9	6.7	6.6	6.7	7.0
2007	6.5	6.6	6.9	7.2	7.1	6.9	7.0	6.9	7.0	7.3	7.3	7.3	7.0
2008	7.4	7.1	7.2	7.5	7.4	7.2	7.0	6.7	6.6	7.1	6.9	7.0	7.1
2009	6.8	6.7	6.6	7.0	6.8	6.6	6.5	6.4	6.4	6.6	6.4	6.4	6.6
2010	6.3	6.4	6.3	6.5	6.6	6.6	6.4	6.4	6.5	6.6	6.6	6.8	6.5
2011	6.6	6.6	6.8	6.9	6.9	6.8	6.7	6.7	6.8	6.7	6.8	6.9	6.8
2012	6.9	6.9	7.1	7.3	7.2	7.2	7.0	7.1	7.2	7.3	7.3	7.5	7.2
2013	7.5	7.5	7.7	7.9	7.9	7.7	7.5	7.4	7.5	7.5	7.6	7.7	7.6
2014	7.6	7.6	7.8	8.2	8.1	8.0	7.8	7.8	7.8	7.9	7.9	8.0	7.9
2015	8.1	8.1	8.2	8.4	8.4	8.4	8.2	8.3	8.3	8.2	8.3	8.3	8.3
Retail Trade													
2005	27.3	27.2	27.5	28.4	28.3	28.2	28.3	28.6	28.2	28.6	29.6	30.3	28.4
2006	29.0	28.5	28.7	29.2	29.1	28.8	29.3	29.7	30.1	30.9	32.3	32.8	29.9
2007	31.8	31.2	31.7	31.9	31.6	31.3	31.9	32.3	31.8	32.3	33.7	34.2	32.1
2008	33.2	32.7	32.8	32.6	32.3	32.3	32.7	33.3	32.7	33.2	33.8	34.2	33.0
2009	32.3	31.6	31.7	32.1	32.0	31.9	32.1	32.5	32.4	32.3	33.2	33.7	32.3
2010	32.0	31.5	31.9	32.0	32.1	32.0	32.0	32.5	32.2	32.8	33.9	34.7	32.5
2011	33.3	32.7	32.8	33.3	33.3	33.3	33.3	33.8	33.3	33.6	35.2	35.8	33.6
2012	34.2	33.6	33.9	34.0	34.0	34.2	34.5	35.0	34.6	34.8	36.9	37.2	34.7
2013	35.4	35.0	35.0	35.0	35.0	35.3	35.2	35.6	35.2	35.4	37.4	38.3	35.7
2014	35.8	35.4	35.5	35.9	35.9	36.5	36.8	36.9	36.4	36.7	38.6	39.2	36.6
2015	37.0	36.8	37.0	37.3	37.3	37.3	37.4	37.7	37.2	37.7	38.4	39.1	37.5
Transportation and Utilities													
2005	5.6	5.6	5.7	5.8	5.9	6.0	6.1	6.1	6.1	5.9	6.0	6.1	5.9
2006	6.3	6.3	6.5	6.5	6.6	6.8	6.7	6.8	6.8	6.9	7.0	7.1	6.7
2007	6.9	7.0	7.0	7.0	7.1	7.2	7.2	7.2	7.3	7.0	6.9	7.0	7.1
2008	7.0	7.0	7.1	7.2	7.3	7.3	7.2	7.2	7.2	6.9	6.9	7.0	7.1
2009	6.9	6.8	6.9	6.9	7.0	7.1	7.0	7.1	7.0	7.1	7.1	7.2	7.0
2010	6.9	6.9	6.9	7.0	7.2	7.2	7.0	7.1	7.1	7.1	7.1	7.3	7.1
2011	6.9	7.0	7.1	7.2	7.3	7.3	7.3	7.4	7.3	7.4	7.4	7.5	7.3
2012	7.5	7.7	7.8	7.7	7.8	7.9	7.9	8.0	7.7	7.7	7.8	7.9	7.8
2013	7.8	7.8	7.8	7.9	8.0	8.1	8.0	8.1	8.1	8.1	8.1	8.2	8.0
2014	8.1	8.0	8.0	8.1	8.1	8.1	8.2	8.2	8.2	8.3	8.4	8.6	8.2
2015	8.6	8.5	8.6	8.4	8.6	8.5	8.7	8.7	8.7	8.7	8.7	9.0	8.6

Employment by Industry: McAllen-Edinburg-Mission, TX, 2005–2015—*Continued*

(Numbers in thousands, not seasonally adjusted)

Industry and year	January	February	March	April	May	June	July	August	September	October	November	December	Annual average
Information													
2005	2.0	2.0	2.0	2.1	2.1	2.2	2.2	2.2	2.3	2.3	2.3	2.3	2.2
2006	2.2	2.2	2.3	2.2	2.2	2.2	2.1	2.1	2.1	2.3	2.3	2.2	2.2
2007	2.2	2.2	2.2	2.3	2.3	2.3	2.2	2.2	2.1	2.1	2.1	2.2	2.2
2008	2.2	2.2	2.2	2.2	2.2	2.3	2.3	2.3	2.2	2.2	2.3	2.3	2.2
2009	2.3	2.2	2.2	2.2	2.2	2.2	2.2	2.2	2.1	2.1	2.1	2.1	2.2
2010	2.1	2.0	2.0	2.0	2.1	2.0	2.0	1.9	1.9	2.0	2.0	2.0	2.0
2011	2.1	2.1	2.1	2.1	2.1	2.1	2.1	2.1	2.0	2.0	2.1	2.1	2.1
2012	2.1	2.0	2.0	2.0	2.0	2.0	2.0	2.0	1.9	2.1	2.1	2.2	2.0
2013	2.1	2.1	2.1	2.1	2.2	2.2	2.2	2.2	2.1	2.2	2.3	2.3	2.2
2014	2.2	2.2	2.2	2.2	2.2	2.2	2.2	2.2	2.1	2.2	2.3	2.3	2.2
2015	2.3	2.2	2.2	2.2	2.2	2.3	2.3	2.3	2.3	2.3	2.4	2.4	2.3
Financial Activities													
2005	8.0	8.0	8.1	8.2	8.1	8.2	8.3	8.3	8.3	8.4	8.4	8.4	8.2
2006	8.4	8.4	8.5	8.3	8.3	8.4	8.5	8.5	8.5	8.7	8.7	8.8	8.5
2007	8.8	8.8	8.8	8.9	8.9	8.9	8.9	8.9	8.9	8.9	9.0	8.9	8.9
2008	9.0	9.0	8.9	9.0	8.9	8.9	8.9	8.8	8.7	8.6	8.6	8.5	8.8
2009	8.4	8.2	8.2	8.1	8.1	8.0	8.1	8.0	7.9	8.1	8.1	8.1	8.1
2010	8.0	8.0	8.0	8.0	8.1	8.1	8.1	8.1	8.2	8.3	8.4	8.5	8.2
2011	8.4	8.4	8.5	8.5	8.5	8.6	8.6	8.6	8.6	8.6	8.6	8.7	8.6
2012	8.8	8.8	8.8	8.8	8.8	8.8	8.8	8.8	8.8	8.9	8.9	9.0	8.8
2013	8.8	8.8	8.8	8.8	8.9	8.9	8.9	9.0	8.9	9.0	9.0	9.0	8.9
2014	9.0	9.0	9.0	9.0	9.1	9.1	9.0	9.0	9.0	9.0	9.1	9.2	9.0
2015	9.0	9.0	9.0	8.9	9.0	9.1	9.0	9.0	9.0	9.1	9.1	9.1	9.0
Professional and Business Services													
2005	12.7	13.2	13.5	13.8	13.6	13.7	13.7	13.9	13.9	13.9	14.0	14.2	13.7
2006	14.2	14.5	14.7	14.4	14.3	14.5	14.2	14.2	14.3	14.4	14.6	15.0	14.4
2007	14.9	15.0	15.2	15.1	15.2	15.2	15.0	15.0	15.2	15.1	15.2	15.4	15.1
2008	15.6	15.9	15.6	15.2	15.1	15.0	15.0	15.0	14.8	15.3	15.3	15.2	15.3
2009	15.0	14.9	14.7	14.8	14.8	14.6	14.5	13.9	13.8	13.9	14.1	13.8	14.4
2010	14.0	14.2	14.0	14.0	14.0	14.1	13.9	14.0	14.1	14.3	14.4	14.7	14.1
2011	14.5	14.7	14.8	15.6	15.5	15.3	15.0	15.2	15.0	14.9	15.0	15.0	15.0
2012	15.3	15.4	15.3	15.7	15.5	15.0	15.0	15.0	15.1	15.2	14.8	14.9	15.2
2013	15.1	15.6	15.8	15.9	15.6	15.5	15.1	15.5	15.5	15.5	15.7	16.2	15.6
2014	15.5	15.7	16.0	16.1	15.9	15.7	15.3	15.7	15.6	16.1	15.5	15.8	15.7
2015	16.1	16.3	16.3	16.3	15.9	15.8	15.7	15.6	15.6	15.8	15.8	15.9	15.9
Education and Health Services													
2005	40.4	41.0	41.2	41.6	41.7	41.6	42.0	42.4	43.0	43.3	43.5	44.0	42.1
2006	43.6	43.9	43.9	44.0	44.1	44.1	44.1	44.6	45.0	45.1	45.4	45.6	44.5
2007	46.1	46.4	46.4	47.2	47.4	47.2	47.4	47.9	48.3	48.5	49.0	49.1	47.6
2008	49.3	50.2	50.2	50.9	51.1	50.6	50.9	51.1	51.4	52.3	52.6	53.0	51.1
2009	52.5	52.7	52.9	53.8	54.1	53.6	54.1	54.3	54.6	55.6	55.9	55.9	54.2
2010	55.7	55.9	56.1	55.8	56.4	56.1	55.8	56.3	57.2	57.4	57.6	57.9	56.5
2011	57.4	57.7	58.0	58.3	58.5	58.2	58.6	59.2	60.0	59.6	59.9	60.2	58.8
2012	59.4	59.9	60.1	59.9	60.0	59.6	58.6	59.2	59.5	59.8	60.2	60.4	59.7
2013	59.0	59.6	59.8	60.2	60.4	60.2	60.1	61.0	61.3	61.8	62.1	62.3	60.7
2014	61.2	61.6	61.6	61.9	62.5	62.0	62.0	62.8	63.1	63.4	63.9	64.2	62.5
2015	63.9	64.3	64.4	64.7	65.3	64.8	65.0	65.7	66.0	65.9	65.7	66.5	65.2
Leisure and Hospitality													
2005	16.6	16.9	17.0	17.6	17.3	17.0	16.9	16.7	16.6	16.8	16.7	17.0	16.9
2006	17.6	17.5	17.5	17.9	17.6	17.4	17.4	17.1	16.9	17.4	17.4	17.4	17.4
2007	17.9	17.9	17.7	18.3	18.0	18.0	18.6	18.4	17.8	18.9	18.6	18.7	18.2
2008	19.0	19.2	19.3	19.9	19.7	19.4	19.2	19.3	18.8	19.3	18.8	18.7	19.2
2009	19.0	19.0	19.1	19.3	19.1	18.8	18.9	18.8	18.6	18.9	18.8	18.8	18.9
2010	19.0	19.3	19.5	19.1	19.4	19.2	18.9	19.2	19.3	19.2	19.2	19.4	19.2
2011	19.2	19.5	20.0	20.0	19.9	20.1	19.6	19.6	19.5	19.2	19.4	19.4	19.6
2012	19.2	19.6	20.2	20.2	20.1	20.2	19.8	20.0	20.0	19.9	20.3	20.8	20.0
2013	20.5	21.0	21.5	21.4	21.3	21.3	20.9	21.3	21.2	20.9	21.1	21.2	21.1
2014	21.1	21.3	21.8	21.9	22.2	22.2	21.7	22.1	22.2	22.0	22.0	22.4	21.9
2015	21.9	22.3	22.8	22.9	23.1	23.2	23.2	22.9	22.8	22.8	22.8	23.1	22.8

Employment by Industry: McAllen-Edinburg-Mission, TX, 2005–2015—*Continued*

(Numbers in thousands, not seasonally adjusted)

Industry and year	January	February	March	April	May	June	July	August	September	October	November	December	Annual average
Other Services													
2005	4.6	4.6	4.7	4.9	4.9	4.9	4.7	4.7	4.7	4.8	4.8	4.7	4.8
2006	4.6	4.6	4.7	4.9	4.9	4.9	5.1	5.0	5.2	5.2	5.3	5.3	5.0
2007	4.9	5.0	5.1	5.2	5.2	5.3	5.4	5.4	5.3	5.6	5.5	5.6	5.3
2008	5.8	5.9	6.0	6.1	5.9	5.9	6.0	6.0	5.8	5.9	5.8	5.6	5.9
2009	5.6	5.6	5.7	5.8	5.8	5.8	5.7	5.6	5.6	5.7	5.7	5.6	5.7
2010	5.7	5.7	5.7	5.7	5.7	5.7	5.6	5.5	5.6	5.7	5.7	5.6	5.7
2011	5.7	5.7	5.8	5.7	5.7	5.7	5.7	5.6	5.7	5.7	5.7	5.7	5.7
2012	5.7	5.6	5.7	5.8	5.9	5.9	5.8	5.7	5.8	6.0	6.0	6.0	5.8
2013	5.9	6.0	6.1	6.0	6.1	6.1	6.0	6.0	6.0	6.1	6.1	6.1	6.0
2014	6.1	6.2	6.2	6.2	6.3	6.3	6.3	6.2	6.2	6.2	6.2	6.2	6.2
2015	6.1	6.2	6.2	6.2	6.3	6.3	6.3	6.3	6.2	6.3	6.4	6.4	6.3
Government													
2005	47.7	48.6	48.7	48.7	48.7	48.1	41.0	45.3	47.6	49.3	49.7	49.7	47.8
2006	50.0	50.7	50.6	49.7	49.6	49.7	41.1	45.8	48.0	50.5	51.0	50.9	49.0
2007	50.2	50.8	51.1	50.6	50.7	50.4	45.0	47.8	50.0	51.9	52.5	52.8	50.3
2008	52.3	52.9	53.2	53.1	53.8	52.5	47.2	49.2	51.9	54.0	54.9	55.1	52.5
2009	54.3	54.8	54.9	54.7	55.1	53.8	48.6	50.9	53.1	54.9	55.5	55.6	53.9
2010	55.0	55.7	56.0	56.4	56.6	55.7	48.3	50.1	52.6	55.0	55.5	55.3	54.4
2011	55.4	55.8	55.7	55.4	55.8	54.7	49.1	51.0	52.8	53.7	54.6	54.5	54.0
2012	54.1	54.6	55.0	54.8	54.9	54.2	48.9	50.5	52.8	54.6	55.3	55.4	53.8
2013	54.6	55.2	55.7	55.3	56.0	55.2	49.7	51.5	53.7	55.6	56.1	56.2	54.6
2014	56.0	56.3	56.6	56.2	57.4	56.4	50.7	52.3	54.1	56.3	56.8	57.1	55.5
2015	56.2	56.8	57.1	56.7	57.9	57.2	51.7	53.5	55.6	57.1	57.4	57.6	56.2

Employment by Industry: El Paso, TX, 2005–2015

(Numbers in thousands, not seasonally adjusted)

Industry and year	January	February	March	April	May	June	July	August	September	October	November	December	Annual average
Total Nonfarm													
2005	257.9	259.4	261.0	262.9	263.7	263.3	260.2	262.4	267.1	267.0	268.3	268.9	263.5
2006	264.2	265.9	268.3	266.9	267.8	266.5	262.7	265.6	270.7	270.6	272.4	274.4	268.0
2007	268.3	269.8	271.8	273.0	274.5	272.6	269.7	271.9	277.4	280.5	282.0	284.2	274.6
2008	280.4	282.2	282.8	281.4	282.8	279.8	275.5	278.2	280.8	283.7	283.7	283.4	281.2
2009	277.7	277.1	276.9	277.8	276.9	276.3	271.3	272.6	276.1	278.1	279.4	280.3	276.7
2010	276.2	277.6	280.8	281.5	283.5	282.4	275.3	277.3	281.4	282.0	283.8	284.8	280.6
2011	280.9	281.2	282.5	284.1	284.5	283.2	280.4	281.7	285.3	282.8	284.9	286.3	283.2
2012	282.5	284.5	286.1	287.7	288.9	286.3	283.9	286.1	288.3	289.8	291.8	292.2	287.3
2013	286.7	288.9	289.9	291.1	292.4	289.5	287.2	290.4	293.0	294.3	297.0	297.2	291.5
2014	292.7	294.4	295.4	296.6	297.6	295.6	290.9	293.2	294.4	296.3	298.5	299.7	295.4
2015	296.3	298.2	298.9	301.1	303.0	302.2	299.2	301.4	303.8	306.6	308.5	309.1	302.4
Total Private													
2005	196.3	197.0	198.6	200.7	201.4	203.6	203.3	205.0	206.1	204.9	206.4	207.8	202.6
2006	202.7	203.4	205.7	204.7	205.5	207.6	206.2	208.6	208.8	207.3	208.9	210.8	206.7
2007	204.7	205.6	207.5	207.6	208.9	210.0	209.7	211.8	212.0	213.6	214.9	217.2	210.3
2008	213.9	214.2	214.9	215.6	216.2	215.8	215.6	218.2	215.9	216.3	216.3	216.0	215.7
2009	210.1	209.0	208.9	208.3	207.8	208.8	208.6	209.8	208.2	207.7	208.9	210.0	208.8
2010	206.1	206.7	209.9	210.1	211.4	212.7	210.5	212.0	211.4	211.6	213.2	214.3	210.8
2011	210.9	211.1	212.5	213.6	214.1	213.8	214.5	215.6	215.1	213.0	214.8	216.5	213.8
2012	212.4	214.3	216.0	217.4	218.4	218.7	218.1	220.0	219.3	219.4	221.1	221.8	218.1
2013	216.4	218.1	219.2	220.4	221.8	222.1	221.5	223.9	223.6	224.6	226.9	227.4	222.2
2014	223.8	225.0	226.2	226.5	227.4	227.5	225.6	227.4	225.9	226.4	228.3	229.7	226.6
2015	226.4	227.8	228.7	230.7	232.4	233.6	233.3	234.9	234.5	236.1	237.7	238.5	232.9
Goods Producing													
2005	34.3	34.4	34.7	34.8	35.3	35.4	34.8	35.1	35.7	34.9	34.9	34.8	34.9
2006	34.4	34.3	34.5	34.5	34.8	35.6	34.9	34.9	34.8	34.4	34.2	34.5	34.7
2007	33.8	34.0	34.3	34.5	34.6	34.9	34.8	35.5	35.6	35.8	36.0	36.0	35.0
2008	35.5	35.5	35.4	35.8	35.8	35.6	35.5	35.8	35.6	35.2	35.0	34.5	35.4
2009	33.9	33.4	32.8	32.9	32.8	32.3	32.5	33.1	32.7	32.8	32.4	32.5	32.8
2010	32.1	32.1	32.3	32.3	32.4	32.3	32.5	33.3	32.9	32.1	31.9	31.6	32.3
2011	31.2	31.1	31.3	31.3	31.4	31.2	31.1	31.9	31.6	30.7	30.7	30.5	31.2
2012	30.1	30.3	30.4	30.6	30.8	31.0	30.9	31.6	31.5	31.4	31.3	31.0	30.9
2013	30.4	30.9	30.8	30.9	31.0	31.0	30.9	31.6	31.5	31.3	31.1	30.9	31.0
2014	30.7	31.0	31.0	30.9	31.0	30.9	29.9	30.8	30.4	30.0	29.8	29.9	30.5
2015	29.7	30.2	30.3	30.6	31.1	31.1	31.2	31.5	31.6	31.4	31.5	31.4	31.0
Service-Providing													
2005	223.6	225.0	226.3	228.1	228.4	227.9	225.4	227.3	231.4	232.1	233.4	234.1	228.6
2006	229.8	231.6	233.8	232.4	233.0	230.9	227.8	230.7	235.9	236.2	238.2	239.9	233.4
2007	234.5	235.8	237.5	238.5	239.9	237.7	234.9	236.4	241.8	244.7	246.0	248.2	239.7
2008	244.9	246.7	247.4	245.6	247.0	244.2	240.0	242.4	245.2	248.5	248.7	248.9	245.8
2009	243.8	243.7	244.1	244.9	244.1	244.0	238.8	239.5	243.4	245.3	247.0	247.8	243.9
2010	244.1	245.5	248.5	249.2	251.1	250.1	242.8	244.0	248.5	249.9	251.9	253.2	248.2
2011	249.7	250.1	251.2	252.8	253.1	252.0	249.3	249.8	253.7	252.1	254.2	255.8	252.0
2012	252.4	254.2	255.7	257.1	258.1	255.3	253.0	254.5	256.8	258.4	260.5	261.2	256.4
2013	256.3	258.0	259.1	260.2	261.4	258.5	256.3	258.8	261.5	263.0	265.9	266.3	260.4
2014	262.0	263.4	264.4	265.7	266.6	264.7	261.0	262.4	264.0	266.3	268.7	269.8	264.9
2015	266.6	268.0	268.6	270.5	271.9	271.1	268.0	269.9	272.2	275.2	277.0	277.7	271.4
Mining, Logging, and Construction													
2005	11.6	11.7	11.7	11.8	12.1	12.2	12.1	12.2	12.6	12.4	12.4	12.3	12.1
2006	12.3	12.3	12.5	12.6	12.7	13.0	12.9	12.9	13.0	13.0	13.1	13.3	12.8
2007	13.4	13.7	14.1	14.3	14.4	14.7	14.6	15.1	15.2	15.6	15.8	15.8	14.7
2008	15.4	15.4	15.5	15.9	15.9	15.7	15.8	16.1	16.1	16.0	15.9	15.8	15.8
2009	15.5	15.4	15.6	15.4	15.6	15.2	15.6	15.8	15.5	15.9	15.7	15.8	15.6
2010	15.7	15.8	15.9	15.9	15.9	15.7	15.7	15.8	15.4	14.8	14.7	14.4	15.5
2011	14.2	14.0	14.1	14.0	14.0	13.7	13.8	14.1	13.9	13.2	13.2	13.0	13.8
2012	12.8	12.8	12.8	12.8	12.9	13.1	13.1	13.3	13.2	13.2	13.2	13.0	13.0
2013	12.5	12.8	12.7	12.7	12.9	13.0	13.1	13.4	13.4	13.5	13.4	13.3	13.1
2014	13.4	13.8	13.9	13.8	13.9	13.8	12.9	13.2	12.9	12.8	12.8	12.9	13.3
2015	12.8	13.1	13.2	13.5	14.0	14.0	14.2	14.4	14.5	14.5	14.5	14.4	13.9

Employment by Industry: El Paso, TX, 2005–2015—*Continued*

(Numbers in thousands, not seasonally adjusted)

Industry and year	January	February	March	April	May	June	July	August	September	October	November	December	Annual average
Manufacturing													
2005	22.7	22.7	23.0	23.0	23.2	23.2	22.7	22.9	23.1	22.5	22.5	22.5	22.8
2006	22.1	22.0	22.0	21.9	22.1	22.6	22.0	22.0	21.8	21.4	21.1	21.2	21.9
2007	20.4	20.3	20.2	20.2	20.2	20.2	20.2	20.4	20.4	20.2	20.2	20.2	20.3
2008	20.1	20.1	19.9	19.9	19.9	19.9	19.7	19.7	19.5	19.2	19.1	18.7	19.6
2009	18.4	18.0	17.2	17.5	17.2	17.1	16.9	17.3	17.2	16.9	16.7	16.7	17.3
2010	16.4	16.3	16.4	16.4	16.5	16.6	16.8	17.5	17.5	17.3	17.2	17.2	16.8
2011	17.0	17.1	17.2	17.3	17.4	17.5	17.3	17.8	17.7	17.5	17.5	17.5	17.4
2012	17.3	17.5	17.6	17.8	17.9	17.9	17.8	18.3	18.3	18.2	18.1	18.0	17.9
2013	17.9	18.1	18.1	18.2	18.1	18.0	17.8	18.2	18.1	17.8	17.7	17.6	18.0
2014	17.3	17.2	17.1	17.1	17.1	17.1	17.0	17.6	17.5	17.2	17.0	17.0	17.2
2015	16.9	17.1	17.1	17.1	17.1	17.1	17.0	17.1	17.1	16.9	17.0	17.0	17.0
Trade, Transportation, and Utilities													
2005	55.9	55.5	55.9	56.4	56.5	56.9	57.2	57.8	58.0	58.0	59.8	60.3	57.4
2006	58.0	57.9	58.7	58.4	58.6	58.8	58.8	59.5	59.6	59.3	60.7	61.5	59.2
2007	59.0	58.6	59.2	59.5	59.7	59.8	59.7	60.3	60.7	61.4	62.5	63.3	60.3
2008	61.0	60.2	60.3	60.0	59.9	59.9	60.0	60.6	59.8	60.1	60.5	60.7	60.3
2009	57.4	56.4	56.4	55.6	55.4	55.7	55.5	55.8	55.9	55.7	56.7	57.4	56.2
2010	55.2	55.1	55.8	56.1	56.3	56.3	56.6	56.9	56.8	57.4	58.8	59.8	56.8
2011	57.3	56.7	57.1	57.7	57.9	57.8	58.2	58.6	58.2	58.3	59.9	60.9	58.2
2012	58.7	58.3	58.6	59.4	60.0	60.2	59.7	60.1	59.7	60.0	61.9	62.4	59.9
2013	59.9	59.8	60.3	61.1	61.6	61.8	61.6	62.2	61.8	62.8	64.7	65.5	61.9
2014	63.4	62.9	63.4	63.2	63.5	63.7	63.6	63.8	63.3	63.9	65.6	66.7	63.9
2015	64.1	63.8	64.3	64.5	65.0	65.1	65.1	65.4	65.1	65.8	66.8	67.5	65.2
Wholesale Trade													
2005	10.6	10.6	10.7	10.7	10.8	10.8	10.8	10.9	11.0	10.8	11.0	11.1	10.8
2006	11.0	11.0	11.1	11.0	11.1	11.1	11.1	11.1	11.1	10.9	10.9	11.0	11.0
2007	11.0	11.0	11.1	11.3	11.3	11.4	11.3	11.4	11.4	11.5	11.5	11.6	11.3
2008	11.3	11.3	11.1	11.4	11.2	11.1	11.3	11.3	11.1	11.1	10.7	10.6	11.1
2009	10.2	10.1	10.1	9.9	9.8	9.8	9.8	9.8	9.8	9.8	9.8	9.8	9.9
2010	9.8	9.8	10.0	10.1	10.0	10.1	10.2	10.2	10.1	10.1	10.1	10.1	10.1
2011	10.0	10.0	10.1	10.1	10.2	10.2	10.4	10.4	10.4	10.3	10.2	10.3	10.2
2012	10.2	10.3	10.4	10.4	10.4	10.4	10.3	10.3	10.3	10.3	10.4	10.4	10.3
2013	10.3	10.3	10.4	10.4	10.5	10.6	10.6	10.7	10.7	10.7	10.8	10.8	10.6
2014	10.6	10.8	10.8	10.8	10.9	11.0	11.0	11.0	10.9	11.0	10.9	11.0	10.9
2015	10.9	10.9	11.0	11.1	11.2	11.2	11.2	11.3	11.3	11.3	11.2	11.3	11.2
Retail Trade													
2005	32.2	31.7	31.9	32.3	32.3	32.6	32.8	33.2	33.2	33.6	35.0	35.5	33.0
2006	33.5	33.3	33.9	33.8	33.8	33.8	33.8	34.4	34.5	34.4	35.8	36.4	34.3
2007	34.3	33.8	34.3	34.3	34.5	34.5	34.5	35.0	35.4	36.2	37.2	37.8	35.2
2008	36.1	35.3	35.6	35.0	35.0	35.2	35.2	35.6	35.3	35.5	36.3	36.6	35.6
2009	34.2	33.4	33.4	33.0	32.9	33.2	32.9	33.3	33.4	33.3	34.3	34.8	33.5
2010	33.0	32.9	33.3	33.5	33.7	33.6	33.8	34.1	34.2	34.7	36.1	37.0	34.2
2011	34.7	34.1	34.3	35.0	35.1	35.1	35.0	35.3	34.9	35.2	36.8	37.5	35.3
2012	35.7	35.1	35.2	35.9	36.3	36.4	36.0	36.3	35.9	36.2	37.9	38.4	36.3
2013	36.2	36.1	36.2	36.9	37.2	37.2	37.2	37.6	37.3	38.2	40.0	40.7	37.6
2014	38.7	38.1	38.3	38.4	38.5	38.5	38.5	38.6	38.3	38.7	40.5	41.2	38.9
2015	38.8	38.5	38.6	38.7	39.0	39.1	38.9	39.1	38.8	39.6	40.7	41.2	39.3
Transportation and Utilities													
2005	13.1	13.2	13.3	13.4	13.4	13.5	13.6	13.7	13.8	13.6	13.8	13.7	13.5
2006	13.5	13.6	13.7	13.6	13.7	13.9	13.9	14.0	14.0	14.0	14.0	14.1	13.8
2007	13.7	13.8	13.8	13.9	13.9	13.9	13.9	13.9	13.9	13.7	13.8	13.9	13.8
2008	13.6	13.6	13.6	13.6	13.7	13.6	13.5	13.7	13.4	13.5	13.5	13.5	13.6
2009	13.0	12.9	12.9	12.7	12.7	12.7	12.8	12.7	12.7	12.6	12.6	12.8	12.8
2010	12.4	12.4	12.5	12.5	12.6	12.6	12.6	12.6	12.5	12.6	12.6	12.7	12.6
2011	12.6	12.6	12.7	12.6	12.6	12.5	12.8	12.9	12.9	12.8	12.9	13.1	12.8
2012	12.8	12.9	13.0	13.1	13.3	13.4	13.4	13.5	13.5	13.5	13.6	13.6	13.3
2013	13.4	13.4	13.7	13.8	13.9	14.0	13.8	13.9	13.8	13.9	13.9	14.0	13.8
2014	14.1	14.0	14.3	14.0	14.1	14.2	14.1	14.2	14.1	14.2	14.2	14.5	14.2
2015	14.4	14.4	14.7	14.7	14.8	14.8	15.0	15.0	15.0	14.9	14.9	15.0	14.8

Employment by Industry: El Paso, TX, 2005–2015—*Continued*

(Numbers in thousands, not seasonally adjusted)

Industry and year	January	February	March	April	May	June	July	August	September	October	November	December	Annual average
Information													
2005	4.8	4.8	4.8	4.9	4.9	5.0	4.9	4.9	4.8	4.8	4.9	4.8	4.9
2006	4.8	4.8	5.0	4.7	4.8	5.0	4.7	4.7	4.8	4.9	4.9	5.1	4.9
2007	5.0	5.1	5.1	5.1	5.1	5.1	5.4	5.4	5.3	5.6	5.6	5.6	5.3
2008	5.8	5.8	5.8	5.7	5.9	5.9	5.6	5.6	5.5	5.5	5.5	5.5	5.7
2009	5.4	5.5	5.4	5.4	5.3	5.3	5.2	5.1	5.0	5.0	5.0	5.0	5.2
2010	5.2	5.2	5.2	5.3	5.4	5.6	5.5	5.4	5.4	5.4	5.5	5.4	5.4
2011	5.4	5.4	5.4	5.4	5.4	5.5	5.5	5.5	5.5	5.5	5.5	5.6	5.5
2012	5.7	5.7	5.8	5.7	5.8	5.8	5.9	5.9	5.9	6.0	6.0	6.1	5.9
2013	6.1	6.0	6.1	5.9	5.9	5.9	5.8	5.8	5.8	5.8	5.9	5.9	5.9
2014	5.8	5.8	5.7	5.7	5.7	5.7	5.6	5.6	5.6	5.8	5.9	6.0	5.7
2015	5.9	5.9	5.8	5.8	5.8	5.9	5.9	5.9	5.9	5.8	5.9	5.9	5.9
Financial Activities													
2005	11.3	11.3	11.4	11.5	11.5	11.5	11.6	11.6	11.6	11.6	11.5	11.6	11.5
2006	11.3	11.4	11.4	11.1	11.1	11.2	11.2	11.3	11.4	11.4	11.5	11.6	11.3
2007	11.4	11.4	11.5	11.6	11.7	11.7	11.7	11.8	11.8	11.8	11.9	12.2	11.7
2008	12.2	12.3	12.3	12.0	12.1	12.2	12.3	12.5	12.4	12.4	12.3	12.3	12.3
2009	12.2	12.2	12.2	12.2	12.1	12.0	12.0	12.0	12.0	12.0	12.0	12.0	12.1
2010	11.6	11.6	11.7	11.7	11.8	11.8	11.9	11.9	11.9	12.0	12.1	12.2	11.9
2011	12.1	12.1	12.2	12.3	12.4	12.5	12.5	12.4	12.4	12.5	12.4	12.6	12.4
2012	12.4	12.6	12.6	12.6	12.6	12.7	12.7	12.7	12.6	12.6	12.5	12.5	12.6
2013	12.3	12.3	12.3	12.4	12.4	12.4	12.1	12.1	12.1	12.1	12.1	12.1	12.2
2014	11.9	12.0	12.0	12.1	12.1	12.2	11.6	11.6	11.7	11.7	11.7	11.7	11.9
2015	11.9	12.0	12.0	12.1	12.2	12.2	12.2	12.2	12.2	12.1	12.1	12.5	12.1
Professional and Business Services													
2005	26.6	26.9	26.9	27.2	26.8	27.4	27.9	28.4	28.9	29.0	29.2	29.8	27.9
2006	29.3	29.4	29.6	29.7	29.8	30.3	30.3	31.8	32.0	32.1	32.6	32.8	30.8
2007	31.5	31.9	31.8	31.1	31.0	30.8	30.8	31.3	31.2	32.0	31.8	32.4	31.5
2008	31.7	32.0	32.0	32.1	31.8	31.7	32.2	33.5	32.7	33.2	32.9	32.8	32.4
2009	32.1	31.6	31.6	31.7	30.7	30.8	30.7	31.1	31.0	31.4	31.7	31.7	31.3
2010	31.4	31.4	32.3	31.5	31.3	30.9	31.0	31.1	31.0	31.5	31.5	31.5	31.4
2011	31.0	31.3	31.0	31.0	30.5	29.9	30.2	30.1	30.4	29.7	29.9	30.4	30.5
2012	29.9	30.1	30.5	30.5	30.1	29.8	30.0	30.3	30.3	30.5	30.4	30.6	30.3
2013	30.2	30.7	30.6	30.2	29.9	29.9	30.2	30.8	31.3	31.6	31.9	32.0	30.8
2014	31.4	31.5	31.5	31.6	31.4	31.1	31.3	31.5	31.1	31.7	31.7	31.5	31.4
2015	31.9	31.8	31.5	31.8	31.5	32.1	32.0	32.6	32.6	32.6	33.2	33.2	32.2
Education and Health Services													
2005	31.8	32.1	32.3	32.4	32.5	32.9	33.0	33.1	33.2	33.2	33.3	33.5	32.8
2006	33.3	33.5	33.6	32.9	32.4	32.2	32.0	32.4	32.0	31.3	31.5	31.4	32.4
2007	31.0	31.3	31.5	31.5	31.8	32.2	32.1	32.4	32.3	32.1	32.3	32.7	31.9
2008	32.3	32.7	32.9	32.6	32.9	32.9	32.7	33.0	33.1	33.2	33.5	33.7	33.0
2009	33.5	33.9	34.0	34.0	34.2	35.4	36.0	35.9	35.2	35.2	35.2	35.3	34.8
2010	35.2	35.2	35.7	35.9	36.1	37.7	35.8	36.0	36.2	36.3	36.4	36.7	36.1
2011	36.6	36.8	36.9	37.3	37.4	37.4	37.5	37.6	37.8	37.7	37.8	37.8	37.4
2012	37.5	38.3	38.6	38.4	38.5	38.5	38.3	38.7	38.8	39.3	39.4	39.4	38.6
2013	38.6	39.0	39.1	39.5	39.6	39.5	39.8	40.1	40.3	40.7	40.7	40.5	39.8
2014	40.3	40.9	40.9	40.9	41.1	41.0	41.0	41.2	41.1	41.5	41.8	42.0	41.1
2015	41.8	42.2	42.3	42.7	42.9	42.9	43.0	43.2	43.4	43.9	43.9	44.0	43.0
Leisure and Hospitality													
2005	24.2	24.6	25.0	25.7	26.0	26.5	26.2	26.3	26.1	25.6	25.2	25.5	25.6
2006	24.5	24.9	25.6	25.8	26.3	26.7	26.4	26.2	26.4	25.9	25.6	26.0	25.9
2007	25.6	25.8	26.5	26.6	27.1	27.4	27.1	26.9	26.8	26.6	26.4	26.5	26.6
2008	26.8	26.8	27.2	27.9	28.2	28.0	27.8	27.7	27.3	27.3	27.2	27.1	27.4
2009	26.4	26.7	27.1	27.1	28.0	27.9	27.4	27.5	27.2	26.3	26.6	26.9	27.1
2010	26.3	26.8	27.6	28.1	28.8	28.8	28.0	28.1	28.0	27.6	27.7	27.8	27.8
2011	28.0	28.3	29.1	29.1	29.6	29.9	29.9	29.8	29.5	28.9	29.0	29.1	29.2
2012	28.6	29.4	29.8	30.4	30.8	30.8	30.7	30.8	30.7	29.9	30.0	30.2	30.2
2013	29.5	29.9	30.5	30.9	31.7	31.8	31.4	31.5	31.0	30.8	30.9	31.0	30.9
2014	30.8	31.3	32.1	32.5	33.0	33.2	32.9	33.3	33.0	32.2	32.2	32.3	32.4
2015	31.5	32.2	32.7	33.4	34.1	34.4	33.9	34.1	33.8	34.6	34.4	34.1	33.6

Employment by Industry: El Paso, TX, 2005–2015—*Continued*

(Numbers in thousands, not seasonally adjusted)

Industry and year	January	February	March	April	May	June	July	August	September	October	November	December	Annual average
Other Services													
2005	7.4	7.4	7.6	7.8	7.9	8.0	7.7	7.8	7.8	7.8	7.6	7.5	7.7
2006	7.1	7.2	7.3	7.6	7.7	7.8	7.9	7.8	7.8	8.0	7.9	7.9	7.7
2007	7.4	7.5	7.6	7.7	7.9	8.1	8.1	8.2	8.3	8.3	8.4	8.5	8.0
2008	8.6	8.9	9.0	9.5	9.6	9.6	9.5	9.5	9.5	9.4	9.4	9.4	9.3
2009	9.2	9.3	9.4	9.4	9.3	9.4	9.3	9.3	9.2	9.3	9.3	9.2	9.3
2010	9.1	9.3	9.3	9.2	9.3	9.3	9.2	9.3	9.2	9.3	9.3	9.3	9.3
2011	9.3	9.4	9.5	9.5	9.5	9.6	9.6	9.7	9.7	9.7	9.6	9.6	9.6
2012	9.5	9.6	9.7	9.8	9.8	9.9	9.9	9.9	9.8	9.7	9.6	9.6	9.7
2013	9.4	9.5	9.5	9.5	9.7	9.8	9.7	9.8	9.8	9.5	9.6	9.5	9.6
2014	9.5	9.6	9.6	9.6	9.6	9.7	9.7	9.6	9.7	9.6	9.6	9.6	9.6
2015	9.6	9.7	9.8	9.8	9.8	9.9	10.0	10.0	9.9	9.9	9.9	9.9	9.9
Government													
2005	61.6	62.4	62.4	62.2	62.3	59.7	56.9	57.4	61.0	62.1	61.9	61.1	60.9
2006	61.5	62.5	62.6	62.2	62.3	58.9	56.5	57.0	61.9	63.3	63.5	63.6	61.3
2007	63.6	64.2	64.3	65.4	65.6	62.6	60.0	60.1	65.4	66.9	67.1	67.0	64.4
2008	66.5	68.0	67.9	65.8	66.6	64.0	59.9	60.0	64.9	67.4	67.4	67.4	65.5
2009	67.6	68.1	68.0	69.5	69.1	67.5	62.7	62.8	67.9	70.4	70.5	70.3	67.9
2010	70.1	70.9	70.9	71.4	72.1	69.7	64.8	65.3	70.0	70.4	70.6	70.5	69.7
2011	70.0	70.1	70.0	70.5	70.4	69.4	65.9	66.1	70.2	69.8	70.1	69.8	69.4
2012	70.1	70.2	70.1	70.3	70.5	67.6	65.8	66.1	69.0	70.4	70.7	70.4	69.3
2013	70.3	70.8	70.7	70.7	70.6	67.4	65.7	66.5	69.4	69.7	70.1	69.8	69.3
2014	68.9	69.4	69.2	70.1	70.2	68.1	65.3	65.8	68.5	69.9	70.2	70.0	68.8
2015	69.9	70.4	70.2	70.4	70.6	68.6	65.9	66.5	69.3	70.5	70.8	70.6	69.5

Employment by Industry: Allentown-Bethlehem-Easton, PA-NJ, 2005–2015

(Numbers in thousands, not seasonally adjusted)

Industry and year	January	February	March	April	May	June	July	August	September	October	November	December	Annual average
Total Nonfarm													
2005	325.8	328.1	331.1	336.7	339.5	340.7	334.9	334.1	339.1	340.6	341.4	341.1	336.1
2006	332.7	334.4	339.3	341.6	344.2	346.0	338.4	340.2	344.9	347.0	346.4	346.7	341.8
2007	336.7	337.0	341.8	343.3	348.0	350.2	342.5	342.4	346.5	350.0	349.5	349.4	344.8
2008	338.6	339.3	342.5	344.8	348.7	349.7	342.6	342.4	344.8	346.7	343.7	343.6	344.0
2009	331.0	331.0	332.5	333.4	337.9	337.4	330.3	330.1	332.9	335.5	335.8	335.2	333.6
2010	324.7	325.9	329.9	334.2	338.4	338.6	330.4	330.8	335.2	337.9	339.1	341.2	333.9
2011	328.9	331.1	334.9	340.0	343.7	345.1	338.0	338.2	343.0	344.4	345.3	346.7	339.9
2012	337.1	339.9	343.1	346.3	349.0	349.2	340.7	341.0	346.6	347.9	349.3	349.1	344.9
2013	340.5	341.4	344.1	347.9	351.3	352.4	345.0	345.8	350.4	351.8	354.1	352.8	348.1
2014	343.6	342.9	346.3	352.0	356.8	357.3	349.1	350.1	355.2	358.7	360.4	361.1	352.8
2015	349.2	349.0	351.1	355.9	361.2	360.9	354.6	355.3	360.5	361.9	360.7	360.6	356.7
Total Private													
2005	285.5	286.3	289.2	293.9	297.0	299.2	299.2	299.2	298.5	299.0	299.4	299.0	295.5
2006	291.5	292.3	296.9	299.2	301.5	304.1	302.6	304.1	303.8	304.8	303.5	303.9	300.7
2007	295.2	294.3	298.9	300.3	304.3	307.0	305.2	305.3	304.4	306.8	305.8	305.6	302.8
2008	296.6	296.0	299.0	301.3	304.9	305.6	304.2	304.0	302.2	302.7	299.3	299.3	301.3
2009	288.8	287.1	288.2	288.7	293.0	293.3	291.7	291.5	290.3	291.4	291.2	290.7	290.5
2010	282.0	281.9	285.6	289.5	292.6	293.7	292.3	293.4	293.5	295.5	296.2	298.5	291.2
2011	287.7	288.6	292.1	297.1	300.7	302.2	301.1	302.0	302.5	302.7	303.1	304.5	298.7
2012	296.1	298.1	301.3	304.2	306.4	308.0	305.3	305.9	306.5	306.5	307.8	307.3	304.5
2013	299.7	300.1	302.5	306.4	309.4	311.5	309.7	310.3	310.4	311.0	312.6	311.8	308.0
2014	303.3	302.2	305.4	310.9	315.4	316.6	314.3	314.9	315.5	318.1	319.4	320.0	313.0
2015	309.9	308.9	311.0	315.6	320.5	321.5	319.6	320.1	321.0	321.9	320.3	320.3	317.6
Goods Producing													
2005	56.8	56.4	56.8	58.1	58.7	59.6	59.2	59.3	59.0	58.6	58.4	57.8	58.2
2006	56.1	56.1	56.8	57.2	57.2	58.4	57.6	58.2	57.5	57.4	56.8	56.6	57.2
2007	55.5	54.9	55.7	56.2	57.0	57.8	57.4	57.5	57.3	57.0	56.6	55.7	56.6
2008	54.4	54.1	54.8	55.4	56.2	56.8	56.1	56.2	55.9	55.4	54.1	53.0	55.2
2009	50.9	49.8	49.6	49.6	49.7	49.7	49.6	49.2	48.7	48.2	48.1	47.4	49.2
2010	45.7	45.0	45.7	46.7	47.4	48.2	48.2	48.2	48.1	48.0	47.8	47.3	47.2
2011	45.7	45.3	46.3	47.1	47.8	48.7	48.5	48.9	48.5	47.9	47.5	47.0	47.4
2012	45.8	45.8	46.5	47.0	47.2	48.0	48.0	47.8	47.7	47.5	47.3	46.9	47.1
2013	45.8	45.5	46.0	46.8	47.5	48.0	48.1	48.2	48.1	48.3	48.1	47.6	47.3
2014	46.3	45.8	46.6	48.1	49.0	49.7	49.6	49.6	49.2	49.2	49.1	48.7	48.4
2015	47.3	46.8	47.4	48.5	49.5	49.9	50.0	50.1	49.6	49.8	49.4	48.8	48.9
Service-Providing													
2005	269.0	271.7	274.3	278.6	280.8	281.1	275.7	274.8	280.1	282.0	283.0	283.3	277.9
2006	276.6	278.3	282.5	284.4	287.0	287.6	280.8	282.0	287.4	289.6	289.6	290.1	284.7
2007	281.2	282.1	286.1	287.1	291.0	292.4	285.1	284.9	289.2	293.0	292.9	293.7	288.2
2008	284.2	285.2	287.7	289.4	292.5	292.9	286.5	286.2	288.9	291.3	289.6	290.6	288.8
2009	280.1	281.2	282.9	283.8	288.2	287.7	280.7	280.9	284.2	287.3	287.7	287.8	284.4
2010	279.0	280.9	284.2	287.5	291.0	290.4	282.2	282.6	287.1	289.9	291.3	293.9	286.7
2011	283.2	285.8	288.6	292.9	295.9	296.4	289.5	289.3	294.5	296.5	297.8	299.7	292.5
2012	291.3	294.1	296.6	299.3	301.8	301.2	292.7	293.2	298.9	300.4	302.0	302.2	297.8
2013	294.7	295.9	298.1	301.1	303.8	304.4	296.9	297.6	302.3	303.5	306.0	305.2	300.8
2014	297.3	297.1	299.7	303.9	307.8	307.6	299.5	300.5	306.0	309.5	311.3	312.4	304.4
2015	301.9	302.2	303.7	307.4	311.7	311.0	304.6	305.2	310.9	312.1	311.3	311.8	307.8
Mining, Logging, and Construction													
2005	15.3	15.1	15.3	16.6	17.1	17.8	18.0	17.9	17.6	17.3	17.4	16.9	16.9
2006	15.8	15.8	16.2	16.9	17.1	17.7	17.7	17.9	17.5	17.3	16.9	16.7	17.0
2007	15.6	14.9	15.4	16.2	17.0	17.5	17.7	17.8	17.4	17.0	16.6	15.8	16.6
2008	14.9	14.6	15.0	15.6	16.4	16.9	16.8	16.5	16.2	15.9	15.1	14.3	15.7
2009	13.0	12.6	12.8	13.3	13.6	13.6	13.6	13.4	13.1	13.0	12.7	12.1	13.1
2010	10.8	10.5	11.0	12.0	12.5	12.9	13.0	13.1	13.1	13.0	12.7	12.1	12.2
2011	10.9	10.7	11.4	12.2	12.8	13.1	13.2	13.2	13.2	13.0	12.8	12.2	12.4
2012	11.3	11.3	11.7	12.2	12.4	12.8	12.7	12.6	12.6	12.6	12.4	11.9	12.2
2013	11.1	10.9	11.4	12.1	12.7	12.9	13.0	13.1	13.3	13.4	13.1	12.5	12.5
2014	11.6	11.3	11.7	13.0	13.6	13.8	13.7	13.9	13.7	13.6	13.3	12.7	13.0
2015	11.6	11.1	11.5	12.6	13.3	13.4	13.5	13.6	13.5	13.4	13.0	12.3	12.7

Employment by Industry: Allentown-Bethlehem-Easton, PA-NJ, 2005–2015—*Continued*

(Numbers in thousands, not seasonally adjusted)

Industry and year	January	February	March	April	May	June	July	August	September	October	November	December	Annual average
Manufacturing													
2005	41.5	41.3	41.5	41.5	41.6	41.8	41.2	41.4	41.4	41.3	41.0	40.9	41.4
2006	40.3	40.3	40.6	40.3	40.1	40.7	39.9	40.3	40.0	40.1	39.9	39.9	40.2
2007	39.9	40.0	40.3	40.0	40.0	40.3	39.7	39.7	39.9	40.0	40.0	39.9	40.0
2008	39.5	39.5	39.8	39.8	39.8	39.9	39.3	39.7	39.7	39.5	39.0	38.7	39.5
2009	37.9	37.2	36.8	36.3	36.1	36.1	36.0	35.8	35.6	35.2	35.4	35.3	36.1
2010	34.9	34.5	34.7	34.7	34.9	35.3	35.2	35.1	35.0	35.0	35.1	35.2	35.0
2011	34.8	34.6	34.9	34.9	35.0	35.6	35.3	35.7	35.3	34.9	34.7	34.8	35.0
2012	34.5	34.5	34.8	34.8	34.8	35.2	35.3	35.2	35.1	34.9	34.9	35.0	34.9
2013	34.7	34.6	34.6	34.7	34.8	35.1	35.1	35.1	34.8	34.9	35.0	35.1	34.9
2014	34.7	34.5	34.9	35.1	35.4	35.9	35.9	35.7	35.5	35.6	35.8	36.0	35.4
2015	35.7	35.7	35.9	35.9	36.2	36.5	36.5	36.5	36.1	36.4	36.4	36.5	36.2
Trade, Transportation, and Utilities													
2005	66.1	65.5	65.9	66.7	67.5	68.0	67.6	67.7	67.6	68.3	70.0	70.9	67.7
2006	68.9	68.0	68.5	69.3	69.7	70.3	69.9	70.3	70.5	71.1	72.4	73.2	70.2
2007	70.3	68.9	69.3	69.3	70.2	70.7	70.2	70.1	69.9	71.0	72.8	73.5	70.5
2008	70.9	69.3	69.5	69.4	70.1	70.4	69.6	69.5	69.5	70.0	70.7	71.2	70.0
2009	67.9	66.8	66.5	65.9	67.0	67.3	66.6	66.4	66.4	67.3	68.2	68.7	67.1
2010	66.1	64.9	65.6	65.9	66.4	67.0	67.1	67.5	67.7	68.7	69.9	71.0	67.3
2011	68.1	67.3	67.7	68.1	68.9	69.8	69.8	70.1	70.5	71.6	73.1	74.4	70.0
2012	71.9	71.3	71.9	72.0	72.2	72.6	72.0	72.1	72.2	72.9	74.6	75.3	72.6
2013	72.5	71.6	71.7	71.9	72.5	72.8	71.8	72.3	72.3	72.9	74.4	75.3	72.7
2014	72.8	71.7	72.5	73.1	73.8	74.4	74.2	74.5	74.8	75.5	77.3	78.6	74.4
2015	75.7	74.6	75.2	75.6	77.0	77.6	77.5	77.7	77.7	78.8	80.6	81.8	77.5
Wholesale Trade													
2005	12.1	12.1	12.3	12.6	12.6	12.6	12.6	12.5	12.3	12.3	12.3	12.3	12.4
2006	12.5	12.7	12.9	13.3	13.5	13.7	13.7	13.8	13.7	13.8	13.8	13.9	13.4
2007	13.4	13.4	13.5	13.6	13.8	14.0	14.1	14.0	13.9	14.1	14.1	14.1	13.8
2008	13.8	13.8	13.8	14.0	14.1	14.2	14.3	14.2	14.0	14.0	13.9	13.8	14.0
2009	13.4	13.3	13.3	13.4	13.4	13.5	13.4	13.3	13.3	13.5	13.4	13.4	13.4
2010	13.0	12.9	13.0	13.3	13.3	13.5	13.5	13.5	13.5	13.6	13.6	13.6	13.4
2011	13.2	13.2	13.4	13.4	13.5	13.6	13.8	13.8	13.7	13.9	13.8	13.8	13.6
2012	13.7	13.7	13.8	13.9	13.8	14.0	13.8	13.7	13.7	13.6	13.5	13.5	13.7
2013	13.2	13.2	13.2	13.2	13.3	13.4	13.3	13.3	13.3	13.2	13.2	13.2	13.3
2014	13.2	13.2	13.4	13.5	13.6	13.7	13.8	13.8	13.7	13.8	13.7	13.7	13.6
2015	13.5	13.5	13.5	13.6	13.8	13.8	13.9	13.8	13.7	13.8	13.9	13.9	13.7
Retail Trade													
2005	41.2	40.6	40.6	40.8	41.4	41.8	41.6	41.6	40.9	41.2	42.5	43.3	41.5
2006	41.3	40.1	40.4	40.5	40.8	41.3	41.3	41.5	41.2	41.7	43.0	43.7	41.4
2007	41.5	40.2	40.4	40.2	40.8	41.2	41.1	41.1	40.5	41.2	42.9	43.6	41.2
2008	41.8	40.4	40.5	40.3	40.8	41.0	40.5	40.4	40.1	40.5	41.3	42.0	40.8
2009	39.5	38.8	38.6	38.2	38.9	39.3	39.1	39.1	38.5	38.9	40.0	40.5	39.1
2010	38.9	37.9	38.3	38.3	38.7	39.1	39.0	39.0	38.6	39.3	40.4	41.4	39.1
2011	39.3	38.5	38.7	38.9	39.3	39.7	39.4	39.6	39.0	39.5	40.8	41.9	39.6
2012	39.9	39.1	39.3	39.4	39.7	39.9	39.8	40.0	39.3	40.0	41.6	42.0	40.0
2013	40.1	39.3	39.3	39.4	39.8	40.1	39.7	39.9	39.5	40.0	41.2	42.0	40.0
2014	39.9	38.9	39.3	39.8	40.3	40.6	40.4	40.4	40.0	40.3	41.8	42.6	40.4
2015	40.4	39.3	39.5	39.8	40.6	41.0	40.8	40.9	40.4	41.0	42.4	43.0	40.8
Transportation and Utilities													
2005	12.8	12.8	13.0	13.3	13.5	13.6	13.4	13.6	14.4	14.8	15.2	15.3	13.8
2006	15.1	15.2	15.2	15.5	15.4	15.3	14.9	15.0	15.6	15.6	15.6	15.6	15.3
2007	15.4	15.3	15.4	15.5	15.6	15.5	15.0	15.0	15.5	15.7	15.8	15.8	15.5
2008	15.3	15.1	15.2	15.1	15.2	15.2	14.8	14.9	15.4	15.5	15.5	15.4	15.2
2009	15.0	14.7	14.6	14.3	14.7	14.5	14.1	14.0	14.6	14.9	14.8	14.8	14.6
2010	14.2	14.1	14.3	14.3	14.4	14.4	14.6	15.0	15.6	15.8	15.9	16.0	14.9
2011	15.6	15.6	15.6	15.8	16.1	16.5	16.6	16.7	17.8	18.2	18.5	18.7	16.8
2012	18.3	18.5	18.8	18.7	18.7	18.7	18.4	18.4	19.2	19.3	19.5	19.8	18.9
2013	19.2	19.1	19.2	19.3	19.4	19.3	18.8	19.1	19.5	19.7	20.0	20.1	19.4
2014	19.7	19.6	19.8	19.8	19.9	20.1	20.0	20.3	21.1	21.4	21.8	22.3	20.5
2015	21.8	21.8	22.2	22.2	22.6	22.8	22.8	23.0	23.6	24.0	24.3	24.9	23.0

Employment by Industry: Allentown-Bethlehem-Easton, PA-NJ, 2005–2015—*Continued*

(Numbers in thousands, not seasonally adjusted)

Industry and year	January	February	March	April	May	June	July	August	September	October	November	December	Annual average
Information													
2005	7.6	7.6	7.6	7.6	7.6	7.6	7.6	7.6	7.4	7.4	7.4	7.4	7.5
2006	7.4	7.4	7.4	7.4	7.5	7.6	7.5	7.5	7.5	7.4	7.4	7.5	7.5
2007	7.4	7.3	7.3	7.3	7.4	7.5	7.5	7.5	7.4	7.4	7.4	7.5	7.4
2008	7.4	7.4	7.4	7.5	7.6	7.5	7.5	7.4	7.3	7.3	7.1	7.2	7.4
2009	7.1	7.0	6.9	6.7	6.7	6.6	6.5	6.3	6.2	6.1	5.9	5.9	6.5
2010	5.6	5.5	5.5	5.6	5.6	5.7	5.7	5.7	5.7	5.6	5.6	5.6	5.6
2011	5.5	5.6	5.6	5.7	5.8	5.8	5.9	5.7	5.8	5.8	5.9	5.8	5.7
2012	5.7	5.8	5.9	6.0	6.0	6.1	6.0	6.1	6.1	6.0	6.1	6.1	6.0
2013	6.1	6.1	6.2	6.1	6.2	6.2	6.2	6.2	6.1	6.1	6.1	6.1	6.1
2014	6.1	6.1	6.2	6.2	6.3	6.3	6.3	6.3	6.2	6.1	6.0	6.1	6.2
2015	6.0	6.1	6.1	6.1	6.3	6.3	6.2	6.2	6.1	6.1	6.1	6.1	6.1
Financial Activities													
2005	16.3	16.3	16.3	16.5	16.6	16.7	16.7	16.8	16.6	16.5	16.6	16.6	16.5
2006	16.4	16.5	16.6	16.6	16.6	16.8	16.7	16.7	16.6	16.4	16.4	16.5	16.6
2007	16.3	16.4	16.4	16.2	16.2	16.3	16.2	16.2	16.0	16.0	15.9	15.8	16.2
2008	15.7	15.8	15.8	15.9	15.9	15.9	16.0	15.9	15.7	15.6	15.7	15.7	15.8
2009	15.5	15.6	15.5	15.6	15.7	15.8	15.8	15.7	15.6	15.6	15.6	15.6	15.6
2010	15.6	15.6	15.5	15.4	15.4	15.4	15.4	15.4	15.2	15.3	15.3	15.4	15.4
2011	15.2	15.2	15.2	15.2	15.2	15.3	15.1	15.0	15.0	15.0	15.0	15.1	15.1
2012	15.2	15.2	15.2	15.1	15.1	15.1	15.1	15.1	14.9	14.8	14.8	14.9	15.0
2013	14.9	15.0	15.0	15.1	15.1	15.2	15.2	15.1	14.9	14.8	14.8	14.8	15.0
2014	14.5	14.6	14.6	14.7	14.9	15.1	15.2	15.1	14.9	14.9	14.9	15.0	14.9
2015	15.0	14.9	15.0	14.9	15.1	15.2	15.2	15.3	15.1	15.0	15.1	14.9	15.1
Professional and Business Services													
2005	40.0	40.4	40.4	41.3	41.4	42.0	42.5	42.7	42.6	43.3	43.5	43.1	41.9
2006	41.4	41.6	42.3	42.6	43.0	43.7	44.0	44.5	44.3	44.9	44.4	44.1	43.4
2007	42.7	42.6	43.1	43.6	43.7	44.3	44.0	43.6	43.8	44.6	44.2	44.0	43.7
2008	42.2	41.5	41.9	42.6	42.7	42.7	43.2	43.2	42.7	42.9	42.4	42.7	42.6
2009	40.5	39.9	40.0	40.1	40.3	41.0	40.4	41.2	41.2	41.6	42.3	42.5	40.9
2010	41.1	40.9	41.7	42.7	42.8	43.0	42.4	42.6	42.9	44.2	45.5	47.0	43.1
2011	43.8	44.0	44.8	46.1	46.4	46.0	45.8	46.5	46.8	46.2	46.5	47.6	45.9
2012	45.3	45.2	45.4	46.1	46.1	46.4	45.8	46.0	46.5	46.7	47.1	47.5	46.2
2013	46.1	45.4	45.8	46.6	46.5	47.3	47.8	48.5	47.9	48.7	50.0	50.0	47.6
2014	48.1	47.2	47.1	48.3	48.7	49.0	48.2	48.8	49.0	49.6	51.0	51.1	48.8
2015	48.6	47.8	47.5	47.9	48.0	48.1	47.7	48.3	48.5	49.0	47.9	47.4	48.1
Education and Health Services													
2005	57.4	58.1	59.3	59.6	59.2	57.8	58.1	57.7	59.5	60.8	60.9	60.5	59.1
2006	59.2	60.2	61.8	61.5	60.9	59.2	59.2	59.3	61.4	62.9	62.6	62.3	60.9
2007	60.6	61.6	63.3	63.2	63.0	61.3	61.2	62.0	63.5	65.0	64.7	64.5	62.8
2008	62.6	64.3	65.3	65.3	64.0	62.9	62.9	63.4	64.6	65.8	66.1	65.9	64.4
2009	64.6	65.6	66.6	66.4	65.6	64.0	64.0	64.3	65.8	67.3	67.6	67.2	65.8
2010	65.0	67.5	68.2	67.8	67.8	65.9	65.4	66.0	67.3	68.2	68.4	68.2	67.1
2011	66.6	68.0	68.6	68.5	68.6	67.1	66.6	66.4	68.4	69.7	70.1	69.4	68.2
2012	67.9	70.2	71.1	71.1	70.6	69.1	68.2	68.0	70.7	71.5	71.6	71.0	70.1
2013	69.0	71.3	71.8	72.0	71.6	70.0	69.4	69.2	71.9	72.3	73.1	71.7	71.1
2014	69.9	71.6	72.2	72.8	72.5	70.6	69.8	69.4	72.3	73.9	74.2	73.7	71.9
2015	71.3	72.9	73.3	74.3	73.7	72.0	71.1	70.7	73.4	74.1	74.9	74.7	73.0
Leisure and Hospitality													
2005	26.2	26.7	27.5	28.9	30.6	31.9	31.9	32.0	30.6	29.2	27.7	27.7	29.2
2006	27.4	27.7	28.6	29.5	31.3	32.7	32.3	32.3	30.9	29.8	28.6	28.6	30.0
2007	27.6	27.8	28.7	29.4	31.5	33.7	33.2	33.0	31.3	30.8	29.2	29.4	30.5
2008	28.5	28.6	29.3	30.1	33.2	33.9	33.5	33.2	31.5	30.8	28.4	28.7	30.8
2009	27.8	27.8	28.5	29.7	33.2	34.0	34.0	33.7	32.1	31.0	29.2	29.1	30.8
2010	28.9	28.6	29.3	31.2	33.0	34.1	33.8	33.7	32.6	31.5	29.7	29.9	31.4
2011	29.0	29.4	30.0	32.3	33.8	35.0	34.9	35.1	33.5	32.5	30.9	31.0	32.3
2012	30.2	30.5	31.1	32.8	34.9	36.3	36.0	36.6	34.5	33.2	32.5	31.7	33.4
2013	31.7	31.6	32.3	34.1	36.1	37.9	37.2	36.9	35.6	34.3	32.5	32.7	34.4
2014	32.2	31.9	32.7	34.1	36.5	37.6	37.2	37.4	35.7	35.4	33.3	33.1	34.8
2015	32.5	32.4	33.0	34.7	37.1	38.5	38.1	38.1	37.1	35.5	32.7	33.0	35.2

Employment by Industry: Allentown-Bethlehem-Easton, PA-NJ, 2005–2015—*Continued*

(Numbers in thousands, not seasonally adjusted)

Industry and year	January	February	March	April	May	June	July	August	September	October	November	December	Annual average
Other Services													
2005	15.1	15.3	15.4	15.2	15.4	15.6	15.6	15.4	15.2	14.9	14.9	15.0	15.3
2006	14.7	14.8	14.9	15.1	15.3	15.4	15.4	15.3	15.1	14.9	14.9	15.1	15.1
2007	14.8	14.8	15.1	15.1	15.3	15.4	15.5	15.4	15.2	15.0	15.0	15.2	15.2
2008	14.9	15.0	15.0	15.1	15.2	15.5	15.4	15.2	15.0	14.9	14.8	14.9	15.1
2009	14.5	14.6	14.6	14.7	14.8	14.9	14.8	14.7	14.3	14.3	14.3	14.3	14.6
2010	14.0	13.9	14.1	14.2	14.2	14.4	14.3	14.3	14.0	14.0	14.0	14.1	14.1
2011	13.8	13.8	13.9	14.1	14.2	14.5	14.5	14.3	14.0	14.0	14.1	14.2	14.1
2012	14.1	14.1	14.2	14.1	14.3	14.4	14.2	14.2	13.9	13.9	13.8	13.9	14.1
2013	13.6	13.6	13.7	13.8	13.9	14.1	14.0	13.9	13.6	13.6	13.6	13.6	13.8
2014	13.4	13.3	13.5	13.6	13.7	13.9	13.8	13.8	13.4	13.5	13.6	13.7	13.6
2015	13.5	13.4	13.5	13.6	13.8	13.9	13.8	13.7	13.5	13.6	13.6	13.6	13.6
Government													
2005	40.3	41.8	41.9	42.8	42.5	41.5	35.7	34.9	40.6	41.6	42.0	42.1	40.6
2006	41.2	42.1	42.4	42.4	42.7	41.9	35.8	36.1	41.1	42.2	42.9	42.8	41.1
2007	41.5	42.7	42.9	43.0	43.7	43.2	37.3	37.1	42.1	43.2	43.7	43.8	42.0
2008	42.0	43.3	43.5	43.5	43.8	44.1	38.4	38.4	42.6	44.0	44.4	44.3	42.7
2009	42.2	43.9	44.3	44.7	44.9	44.1	38.6	38.6	42.6	44.1	44.6	44.5	43.1
2010	42.7	44.0	44.3	44.7	45.8	44.9	38.1	37.4	41.7	42.4	42.9	42.7	42.6
2011	41.2	42.5	42.8	42.9	43.0	42.9	36.9	36.2	40.5	41.7	42.2	42.2	41.3
2012	41.0	41.8	41.8	42.1	42.6	41.2	35.4	35.1	40.1	41.4	41.5	41.8	40.5
2013	40.8	41.3	41.6	41.5	41.9	40.9	35.3	35.5	40.0	40.8	41.5	41.0	40.2
2014	40.3	40.7	40.9	41.1	41.4	40.7	34.8	35.2	39.7	40.6	41.0	41.1	39.8
2015	39.3	40.1	40.1	40.3	40.7	39.4	35.0	35.2	39.5	40.0	40.4	40.3	39.2

Employment by Industry: Baton Rouge, LA, 2005–2015

(Numbers in thousands, not seasonally adjusted)

Industry and year	January	February	March	April	May	June	July	August	September	October	November	December	Annual average
Total Nonfarm													
2005	338.5	343.8	346.9	353.4	351.7	351.3	351.1	352.6	359.0	361.1	365.6	364.9	353.3
2006	357.0	362.4	365.7	364.1	364.2	359.9	350.9	357.6	362.5	363.3	365.0	367.4	361.7
2007	361.3	366.7	370.7	371.9	372.8	373.6	372.0	375.3	379.6	380.2	382.2	383.6	374.2
2008	371.1	376.1	377.5	375.6	375.5	376.1	371.3	374.1	371.1	378.9	381.9	382.5	376.0
2009	370.2	373.8	375.1	374.9	374.4	371.1	369.2	370.0	373.3	371.0	372.3	370.2	372.1
2010	359.9	362.0	364.9	364.9	366.1	365.6	361.3	364.1	365.4	368.3	368.9	368.5	365.0
2011	364.6	368.5	370.4	372.0	371.4	368.0	365.8	366.4	371.9	374.5	374.5	373.8	370.2
2012	369.0	373.9	376.1	376.8	376.7	374.5	368.2	374.2	377.6	380.1	382.2	380.7	375.8
2013	375.0	381.1	383.8	385.6	386.6	384.7	381.7	386.3	389.3	392.4	393.3	389.4	385.8
2014	383.7	388.6	391.7	393.3	396.5	393.9	392.5	397.1	401.3	405.8	403.9	402.3	395.9
2015	397.8	401.1	401.9	402.4	405.4	403.3	402.4	404.8	406.2	407.4	410.3	410.8	404.5
Total Private													
2005	265.9	268.6	271.5	278.1	278.0	277.8	279.6	280.0	283.5	284.2	288.2	288.8	278.7
2006	284.5	287.2	290.3	290.2	290.8	291.5	284.2	285.9	288.5	289.1	290.4	293.8	288.9
2007	288.8	291.5	294.8	295.1	296.8	298.0	298.8	299.4	300.4	301.8	303.2	305.2	297.8
2008	295.6	297.6	299.3	297.5	298.3	299.5	296.4	298.8	295.1	299.7	302.2	303.7	298.6
2009	293.9	294.7	295.9	296.0	296.6	294.3	294.4	295.4	294.5	291.9	293.0	291.8	294.4
2010	283.6	284.2	286.8	287.1	288.0	289.2	288.3	288.6	287.8	290.2	290.7	291.1	288.0
2011	289.7	291.5	293.7	295.0	294.6	292.9	292.8	293.9	295.1	296.9	296.7	296.6	294.1
2012	294.1	297.9	300.5	301.5	301.8	301.3	298.1	301.7	303.0	305.7	307.6	306.7	301.7
2013	303.1	307.5	310.2	312.1	313.4	312.9	313.0	315.1	315.4	318.8	319.2	316.3	313.1
2014	312.4	315.8	318.8	320.8	324.3	322.9	323.8	326.2	328.0	332.6	330.2	329.3	323.8
2015	326.6	328.3	329.0	329.9	333.3	332.6	334.1	334.3	333.5	334.6	337.2	338.2	332.6
Goods Producing													
2005	58.4	60.5	61.5	65.1	65.1	64.3	63.7	63.8	64.2	63.5	64.8	64.5	63.3
2006	65.6	66.1	67.0	67.4	66.9	66.7	62.6	63.2	64.4	65.4	65.4	66.8	65.6
2007	65.5	66.7	67.5	68.3	69.2	69.2	69.2	68.6	68.8	70.6	70.7	71.3	68.8
2008	66.2	67.0	67.5	67.3	67.7	68.2	67.1	68.3	67.8	69.0	69.5	69.9	68.0
2009	67.5	68.0	68.4	68.2	68.6	67.4	68.4	68.6	68.3	66.1	65.7	64.0	67.4
2010	63.5	63.4	63.5	62.8	62.6	63.8	64.5	64.7	64.6	64.8	64.0	64.0	63.9
2011	64.5	65.7	66.5	66.4	65.6	64.8	64.8	64.6	65.6	66.5	65.1	64.4	65.4
2012	65.1	67.1	67.8	67.5	67.4	67.1	66.4	67.8	68.8	70.1	70.4	69.3	67.9
2013	68.9	71.3	72.4	72.2	72.7	72.9	72.6	73.2	74.0	76.8	75.7	73.7	73.0
2014	73.7	75.9	77.0	76.3	77.6	77.2	78.8	80.2	82.2	84.1	80.2	78.5	78.5
2015	77.5	78.4	79.0	78.1	78.8	80.1	81.6	81.7	82.0	83.1	83.7	84.2	80.7
Service-Providing													
2005	280.1	283.3	285.4	288.3	286.6	287.0	287.4	288.8	294.8	297.6	300.8	300.4	290.0
2006	291.4	296.3	298.7	296.7	297.3	293.2	288.3	294.4	298.1	297.9	299.6	300.6	296.0
2007	295.8	300.0	303.2	303.6	303.6	304.4	302.8	306.7	310.8	309.6	311.5	312.3	305.4
2008	304.9	309.1	310.0	308.3	307.8	307.9	304.2	305.8	303.3	309.9	312.4	312.6	308.0
2009	302.7	305.8	306.7	306.7	305.8	303.7	300.8	301.4	305.0	304.9	306.6	306.2	304.7
2010	296.4	298.6	301.4	302.1	303.5	301.8	296.8	299.4	300.8	303.5	304.9	304.5	301.1
2011	300.1	302.8	303.9	305.6	305.8	303.2	301.0	301.8	306.3	308.0	309.4	309.4	304.8
2012	303.9	306.8	308.3	309.3	309.3	307.4	301.8	306.4	308.8	310.0	311.8	311.4	307.9
2013	306.1	309.8	311.4	313.4	313.9	311.8	309.1	313.1	315.3	315.6	317.6	315.7	312.7
2014	310.0	312.7	314.7	317.0	318.9	316.7	313.7	316.9	319.1	321.7	323.7	323.8	317.4
2015	320.3	322.7	322.9	324.3	326.6	323.2	320.8	323.1	324.2	324.3	326.6	326.6	323.8
Mining and Logging													
2005	1.5	1.5	1.5	1.6	1.5	1.6	1.5	1.5	1.6	1.8	1.8	1.8	1.6
2006	1.6	1.6	1.6	1.5	1.5	1.5	1.5	1.4	1.5	1.4	1.4	1.4	1.5
2007	1.6	1.7	1.7	1.8	1.9	1.9	1.8	1.9	1.9	1.9	1.9	1.9	1.8
2008	1.6	1.6	1.7	1.7	1.7	1.7	1.6	1.6	1.6	1.6	1.6	1.6	1.6
2009	1.5	1.5	1.5	1.5	1.5	1.5	1.4	1.4	1.5	1.4	1.4	1.5	1.5
2010	1.5	1.7	1.7	1.9	1.7	1.7	1.7	1.7	1.8	1.8	1.7	1.6	1.7
2011	1.7	1.8	1.9	1.7	1.4	1.5	1.4	1.4	1.4	1.5	1.3	1.3	1.5
2012	1.3	1.4	1.3	1.2	1.4	1.1	1.0	1.1	1.1	1.1	1.1	1.0	1.2
2013	0.9	0.9	0.9	0.9	0.9	0.9	1.0	0.9	0.9	1.0	1.0	0.9	0.9
2014	1.1	1.1	1.2	1.2	1.4	1.2	1.2	1.1	1.1	1.1	1.2	1.2	1.2
2015	1.2	1.1	1.0	0.9	1.1	1.0	1.0	1.0	1.0	1.0	1.0	1.0	1.0

Employment by Industry: Baton Rouge, LA, 2005–2015—*Continued*

(Numbers in thousands, not seasonally adjusted)

Industry and year	January	February	March	April	May	June	July	August	September	October	November	December	Annual average
Construction													
2005	31.4	33.4	34.2	37.5	37.6	36.9	36.2	36.4	36.8	36.0	37.3	36.9	35.9
2006	38.5	39.0	39.7	40.4	39.9	39.5	36.0	36.6	37.5	38.5	38.4	39.7	38.6
2007	38.1	39.1	39.8	40.4	41.0	40.6	40.6	40.6	40.8	42.1	42.0	42.5	40.6
2008	38.8	39.4	39.8	39.6	39.9	40.4	39.5	40.7	40.4	41.3	41.8	42.0	40.3
2009	40.4	40.9	41.4	41.1	41.5	40.5	42.0	42.3	42.1	40.1	39.8	38.0	40.8
2010	37.4	37.0	37.1	36.3	36.1	37.2	37.9	38.1	37.9	37.9	37.2	37.2	37.3
2011	37.6	38.7	39.4	39.5	38.8	37.9	37.5	37.0	37.8	38.5	37.4	36.6	38.1
2012	37.6	39.5	40.0	39.8	39.3	39.0	38.5	39.8	40.8	42.1	42.3	41.3	40.0
2013	41.2	43.6	44.6	44.4	44.7	44.6	44.1	44.5	45.1	47.7	46.6	44.7	44.7
2014	44.1	46.4	47.4	46.6	47.6	47.2	48.7	50.2	51.9	53.7	49.7	48.0	48.5
2015	47.5	48.3	49.0	48.1	48.5	49.6	51.0	51.0	51.4	52.4	53.0	53.6	50.3
Manufacturing													
2005	25.5	25.6	25.8	26.0	26.0	25.8	26.0	25.9	25.8	25.7	25.7	25.8	25.8
2006	25.5	25.5	25.7	25.5	25.5	25.7	25.1	25.2	25.4	25.5	25.6	25.7	25.5
2007	25.8	25.9	26.0	26.1	26.3	26.7	26.8	26.1	26.1	26.6	26.8	26.9	26.3
2008	25.8	26.0	26.0	26.0	26.1	26.1	26.0	26.0	25.8	26.1	26.1	26.3	26.0
2009	25.6	25.6	25.5	25.6	25.6	25.4	25.0	24.9	24.7	24.6	24.5	24.5	25.1
2010	24.6	24.7	24.7	24.6	24.8	24.9	24.9	24.9	24.9	25.1	25.1	25.2	24.9
2011	25.2	25.2	25.2	25.2	25.4	25.4	25.9	26.2	26.4	26.5	26.4	26.5	25.8
2012	26.2	26.2	26.5	26.5	26.7	27.0	26.9	26.9	26.9	26.9	27.0	27.0	26.7
2013	26.8	26.8	26.9	26.9	27.1	27.4	27.5	27.8	28.0	28.1	28.1	28.1	27.5
2014	28.5	28.4	28.4	28.5	28.6	28.8	28.9	28.9	29.2	29.3	29.3	29.3	28.8
2015	28.8	29.0	29.0	29.1	29.2	29.5	29.6	29.7	29.6	29.7	29.7	29.6	29.4
Trade, Transportation, and Utilities													
2005	62.3	62.3	62.8	63.1	63.6	63.7	64.7	64.9	65.7	66.5	68.6	69.4	64.8
2006	66.4	66.2	67.0	66.1	66.5	66.3	65.6	65.6	65.8	65.9	67.2	68.2	66.4
2007	65.7	65.5	66.3	65.4	65.9	66.1	66.7	67.2	67.6	67.7	69.4	70.2	67.0
2008	67.7	67.1	67.7	66.7	66.8	66.9	66.8	67.3	66.4	66.8	67.9	68.8	67.2
2009	66.1	65.5	65.6	65.8	65.7	65.3	65.3	65.3	65.3	64.9	66.0	66.6	65.6
2010	64.0	63.9	64.5	64.9	65.0	64.9	64.4	64.5	64.3	65.2	66.5	67.2	64.9
2011	65.0	64.8	65.0	65.5	65.6	65.4	65.0	65.2	65.0	65.7	66.8	67.7	65.6
2012	65.8	65.8	66.4	66.5	66.7	66.4	66.0	66.3	65.8	66.8	68.7	69.1	66.7
2013	66.5	66.4	66.8	67.2	67.2	67.1	66.9	67.4	67.4	67.6	69.0	69.8	67.4
2014	67.7	67.2	67.7	67.7	67.8	67.8	67.7	67.9	67.8	68.5	70.3	71.3	68.3
2015	69.5	69.1	69.4	69.6	69.6	69.5	69.5	69.9	69.8	69.7	71.1	71.4	69.8
Wholesale Trade													
2005	12.6	12.5	12.6	12.7	12.8	12.8	13.1	13.1	13.1	12.9	12.9	13.0	12.8
2006	12.7	12.7	12.8	12.8	12.9	13.0	12.9	12.8	12.9	12.9	13.0	13.0	12.9
2007	13.2	13.2	13.3	13.2	13.3	13.5	13.7	13.8	13.8	13.8	13.9	14.0	13.6
2008	13.6	13.6	13.7	13.4	13.5	13.4	13.4	13.4	13.5	13.5	13.4	13.4	13.5
2009	13.2	13.2	13.1	13.3	13.2	13.1	12.7	12.6	12.7	12.6	12.7	12.7	12.9
2010	12.4	12.4	12.4	12.5	12.5	12.4	12.4	12.5	12.4	12.7	12.6	12.6	12.5
2011	12.7	12.7	12.7	12.8	12.9	12.9	12.9	12.9	12.9	13.0	13.0	13.0	12.9
2012	13.1	13.1	13.2	13.2	13.2	13.2	13.1	13.1	13.1	13.3	13.4	13.4	13.2
2013	13.6	13.7	13.8	13.9	13.8	13.7	13.6	13.6	13.6	13.6	13.6	13.5	13.7
2014	13.4	13.3	13.4	13.3	13.3	13.3	13.2	13.2	13.2	13.1	13.1	13.1	13.2
2015	13.2	13.2	13.3	13.3	13.3	13.3	13.2	13.2	13.2	13.1	13.1	13.2	13.2
Retail Trade													
2005	37.5	37.5	37.9	37.9	38.2	38.4	39.1	39.3	40.1	41.1	43.0	43.6	39.5
2006	41.5	41.2	41.9	41.1	41.2	40.9	40.2	40.3	40.3	40.5	41.6	42.4	41.1
2007	40.3	40.0	40.8	40.0	40.3	40.3	40.6	40.7	41.0	41.4	42.9	43.6	41.0
2008	41.5	40.9	41.4	40.8	40.7	41.0	40.9	41.1	40.2	40.9	42.1	42.9	41.2
2009	40.6	40.3	40.5	40.8	40.8	40.8	41.1	41.0	40.9	40.4	41.5	41.9	40.9
2010	40.0	39.9	40.4	40.5	40.6	40.6	40.2	40.1	40.0	40.5	41.9	42.3	40.6
2011	40.2	39.9	40.2	40.6	40.6	40.4	40.2	40.0	39.9	40.3	41.6	42.2	40.5
2012	40.5	40.5	40.9	41.0	41.0	41.0	40.9	40.8	40.5	41.3	43.0	43.2	41.2
2013	40.5	40.2	40.4	40.6	40.5	40.8	40.7	40.8	41.0	41.1	42.4	43.0	41.0
2014	40.9	40.6	40.8	40.9	40.9	41.2	41.2	41.0	41.0	41.7	43.5	44.1	41.5
2015	42.4	42.1	42.4	42.5	42.4	42.5	42.5	42.7	42.5	42.4	43.8	43.5	42.6

Employment by Industry: Baton Rouge, LA, 2005–2015—*Continued*

(Numbers in thousands, not seasonally adjusted)

Industry and year	January	February	March	April	May	June	July	August	September	October	November	December	Annual average
Transportation and Utilities													
2005	12.2	12.3	12.3	12.5	12.6	12.5	12.5	12.5	12.5	12.5	12.7	12.8	12.5
2006	12.2	12.3	12.3	12.2	12.4	12.4	12.5	12.5	12.6	12.5	12.6	12.8	12.4
2007	12.2	12.3	12.2	12.2	12.3	12.3	12.4	12.7	12.8	12.5	12.6	12.6	12.4
2008	12.6	12.6	12.6	12.5	12.6	12.5	12.5	12.8	12.7	12.4	12.4	12.5	12.6
2009	12.3	12.0	12.0	11.7	11.7	11.4	11.5	11.7	11.7	11.9	11.8	12.0	11.8
2010	11.6	11.6	11.7	11.9	11.9	11.9	11.8	11.9	11.9	12.0	12.0	12.3	11.9
2011	12.1	12.2	12.1	12.1	12.1	12.1	11.9	12.3	12.2	12.4	12.2	12.5	12.2
2012	12.2	12.2	12.3	12.3	12.5	12.2	12.0	12.4	12.2	12.2	12.3	12.5	12.3
2013	12.4	12.5	12.6	12.7	12.9	12.6	12.6	13.0	12.8	12.9	13.0	13.3	12.8
2014	13.4	13.3	13.5	13.5	13.6	13.3	13.3	13.7	13.6	13.7	13.7	14.1	13.6
2015	13.9	13.8	13.7	13.8	13.9	13.7	13.8	14.0	14.1	14.2	14.2	14.7	14.0
Information													
2005	5.8	5.7	5.7	5.9	5.6	5.5	5.6	5.5	5.4	5.4	5.6	5.5	5.6
2006	5.6	5.6	5.7	5.7	5.6	5.5	5.4	5.3	5.2	5.4	5.5	5.4	5.5
2007	5.5	5.5	5.5	5.7	5.8	5.6	6.0	5.9	5.8	6.6	5.9	5.8	5.8
2008	5.6	6.0	5.8	6.4	6.2	6.4	5.8	5.8	5.6	5.6	6.0	6.0	5.9
2009	5.5	5.4	5.2	5.1	5.0	4.9	4.7	4.8	4.6	4.7	4.7	4.7	4.9
2010	4.6	4.6	4.6	4.8	4.8	4.8	4.7	4.6	4.4	4.7	4.7	5.0	4.7
2011	4.8	4.9	4.8	4.9	4.8	4.8	4.8	4.9	4.8	5.0	4.9	5.0	4.9
2012	4.8	5.0	4.9	5.4	4.8	5.0	4.9	4.7	5.3	4.7	4.9	5.2	5.0
2013	5.5	5.9	6.3	6.7	6.7	6.7	7.2	6.4	5.8	5.9	6.1	5.6	6.2
2014	5.3	5.6	6.1	6.9	8.3	8.0	7.6	6.5	6.0	6.6	6.6	6.5	6.7
2015	7.0	7.2	6.1	6.9	8.0	7.6	7.9	7.0	6.1	6.0	6.2	6.1	6.8
Financial Activities													
2005	17.9	18.0	18.0	18.1	18.2	18.2	18.5	18.5	18.5	18.5	18.6	18.7	18.3
2006	18.5	18.5	18.6	18.6	18.6	18.6	18.4	18.5	18.5	18.7	18.7	18.8	18.6
2007	19.1	19.2	18.9	18.9	18.8	18.8	18.7	18.7	18.4	18.3	18.4	18.5	18.7
2008	18.2	18.2	18.3	18.1	18.1	18.2	18.0	18.0	17.8	17.9	17.8	17.8	18.0
2009	17.4	17.3	17.3	17.5	17.6	17.5	17.3	17.3	17.1	17.1	17.3	17.4	17.3
2010	17.2	17.2	17.3	17.2	17.2	17.2	16.9	16.9	16.7	16.9	16.9	17.0	17.1
2011	17.0	17.0	17.0	16.9	16.9	16.8	16.9	16.8	16.8	16.9	16.9	17.0	16.9
2012	16.9	16.9	17.0	17.0	17.0	17.0	16.9	17.1	16.9	17.1	17.3	17.3	17.0
2013	17.0	17.1	17.1	17.1	17.3	17.6	17.6	17.8	17.9	18.3	18.3	18.1	17.6
2014	17.5	17.4	17.4	17.5	17.6	17.7	18.0	18.2	18.3	18.5	18.5	18.5	17.9
2015	18.2	18.3	18.2	18.2	18.3	18.4	18.4	18.6	18.4	18.4	18.5	18.5	18.4
Professional and Business Services													
2005	37.6	37.7	38.1	39.7	38.5	38.4	38.8	39.1	40.5	41.3	42.0	42.4	39.5
2006	41.1	41.8	42.3	42.7	42.7	43.0	42.5	42.6	43.1	43.4	43.0	43.8	42.7
2007	43.8	44.2	44.9	45.1	44.4	45.0	45.4	45.8	46.3	46.7	47.0	47.3	45.5
2008	47.0	46.7	46.7	45.9	45.8	45.8	44.9	45.2	45.6	46.3	46.3	46.4	46.1
2009	44.8	44.7	44.7	44.6	44.5	44.1	43.0	43.3	42.7	42.3	42.3	42.4	43.6
2010	41.0	41.1	41.5	41.7	41.8	41.9	41.8	41.9	41.5	41.9	41.6	41.7	41.6
2011	41.6	41.9	42.3	42.8	42.6	42.4	42.2	42.8	43.3	43.0	42.7	42.8	42.5
2012	42.9	43.4	43.9	44.8	45.0	44.7	43.6	43.9	44.4	44.8	44.3	44.0	44.1
2013	44.0	44.8	45.0	45.3	44.9	44.5	44.7	45.3	45.3	45.5	45.3	44.8	45.0
2014	44.8	45.4	45.7	46.2	46.1	45.6	45.8	46.0	46.3	47.2	47.9	48.0	46.3
2015	48.2	48.7	49.0	49.1	49.3	48.5	48.8	49.1	48.6	49.3	49.7	49.5	49.0
Education and Health Services													
2005	39.4	39.6	39.7	40.1	40.4	40.4	41.3	41.2	41.6	42.4	42.4	42.0	40.9
2006	41.7	42.1	42.4	42.8	43.0	43.2	42.8	43.3	43.7	43.9	43.8	43.7	43.0
2007	42.9	43.3	43.5	44.0	44.6	44.5	44.3	44.8	44.7	44.3	44.4	44.8	44.2
2008	44.2	44.8	45.0	45.2	45.3	45.6	45.6	46.2	45.3	46.0	46.1	46.3	45.5
2009	45.7	46.2	46.4	46.7	46.6	46.3	47.4	47.5	47.8	48.5	48.6	48.6	47.2
2010	47.7	47.9	48.4	48.9	49.2	48.8	48.8	48.8	49.2	49.6	49.8	49.5	48.9
2011	49.6	49.9	50.0	49.4	49.4	49.2	49.7	49.6	50.0	50.2	50.5	50.4	49.8
2012	49.9	50.6	50.8	50.3	50.3	50.4	49.9	50.6	50.5	51.1	51.1	51.2	50.6
2013	50.9	51.3	51.3	51.5	51.7	51.3	51.3	52.3	52.3	52.5	52.8	52.5	51.8
2014	52.4	52.6	52.8	52.8	52.8	52.4	52.1	53.3	53.6	54.0	53.8	53.7	53.0
2015	53.5	53.6	53.7	53.9	53.9	53.2	52.9	53.3	53.7	53.3	54.2	54.7	53.7

Employment by Industry: Baton Rouge, LA, 2005–2015—*Continued*

(Numbers in thousands, not seasonally adjusted)

Industry and year	January	February	March	April	May	June	July	August	September	October	November	December	Annual average
Leisure and Hospitality													
2005	30.2	30.5	31.1	31.5	31.9	32.4	32.0	32.0	32.6	32.0	31.7	31.7	31.6
2006	31.3	32.4	32.7	32.3	32.8	33.2	32.1	32.5	32.7	31.7	32.0	32.1	32.3
2007	31.3	32.0	33.0	32.5	33.0	33.4	32.9	32.8	33.2	32.3	32.3	32.1	32.6
2008	31.7	32.5	32.9	33.3	33.6	33.5	33.2	33.3	32.1	32.9	33.4	33.4	33.0
2009	32.0	32.6	33.3	33.0	33.5	33.4	32.8	33.2	33.0	32.4	32.5	32.1	32.8
2010	31.0	31.3	32.2	32.4	32.9	33.1	32.7	32.8	32.8	32.4	32.6	32.1	32.4
2011	32.5	32.6	33.3	34.1	34.8	34.4	34.1	34.6	34.3	34.4	34.5	34.2	34.0
2012	33.7	33.9	34.5	34.7	35.3	35.2	35.2	36.1	36.0	35.8	35.6	35.5	35.1
2013	35.1	35.3	35.7	36.6	37.3	37.1	37.2	37.1	37.1	36.7	36.5	36.3	36.5
2014	35.5	36.0	36.4	37.6	38.2	38.3	37.8	38.1	37.8	37.4	36.8	36.9	37.2
2015	36.7	37.0	37.5	38.1	39.1	39.1	38.7	38.6	38.7	38.5	37.5	37.6	38.1
Other Services													
2005	14.3	14.3	14.6	14.6	14.7	14.9	15.0	15.0	15.0	14.6	14.5	14.6	14.7
2006	14.3	14.5	14.6	14.6	14.7	15.0	14.8	14.9	15.1	14.7	14.8	15.0	14.8
2007	15.0	15.1	15.2	15.2	15.1	15.4	15.6	15.6	15.6	15.3	15.1	15.2	15.3
2008	15.0	15.3	15.4	14.6	14.8	14.9	15.0	14.7	14.5	15.2	15.2	15.1	15.0
2009	14.9	15.0	15.0	15.1	15.1	15.4	15.5	15.4	15.7	15.9	15.9	16.0	15.4
2010	14.6	14.8	14.8	14.4	14.5	14.7	14.5	14.4	14.3	14.7	14.6	14.6	14.6
2011	14.7	14.7	14.8	15.0	14.9	15.1	15.3	15.4	15.3	15.2	15.3	15.1	15.1
2012	15.0	15.2	15.2	15.3	15.3	15.5	15.2	15.2	15.3	15.3	15.3	15.1	15.2
2013	15.2	15.4	15.6	15.5	15.6	15.7	15.5	15.6	15.6	15.5	15.5	15.5	15.5
2014	15.5	15.7	15.7	15.8	15.9	15.9	16.0	16.0	16.0	16.3	16.1	15.9	15.9
2015	16.0	16.0	16.1	16.0	16.3	16.2	16.3	16.1	16.2	16.3	16.3	16.2	16.2
Government													
2005	72.6	75.2	75.4	75.3	73.7	73.5	71.5	72.6	75.5	76.9	77.4	76.1	74.6
2006	72.5	75.2	75.4	73.9	73.4	68.4	66.7	71.7	74.0	74.2	74.6	73.6	72.8
2007	72.5	75.2	75.9	76.8	76.0	75.6	73.2	75.9	79.2	78.4	79.0	78.4	76.3
2008	75.5	78.5	78.2	78.1	77.2	76.6	74.9	75.3	76.0	79.2	79.7	78.8	77.3
2009	76.3	79.1	79.2	78.9	77.8	76.8	74.8	74.6	78.8	79.1	79.3	78.4	77.8
2010	76.3	77.8	78.1	77.8	78.1	76.4	73.0	75.5	77.6	78.1	78.2	77.4	77.0
2011	74.9	77.0	76.7	77.0	76.8	75.1	73.0	72.5	76.8	77.6	77.8	77.2	76.0
2012	74.9	76.0	75.6	75.3	74.9	73.2	70.1	72.5	74.6	74.4	74.6	74.0	74.2
2013	71.9	73.6	73.6	73.5	73.2	71.8	68.7	71.2	73.9	73.6	74.1	73.1	72.7
2014	71.3	72.8	72.9	72.5	72.2	71.0	68.7	70.9	73.3	73.2	73.7	73.0	72.1
2015	71.2	72.8	72.9	72.5	72.1	70.7	68.3	70.5	72.7	72.8	73.1	72.6	71.9

Employment by Industry: Columbia, SC, 2005–2015

(Numbers in thousands, not seasonally adjusted)

Industry and year	January	February	March	April	May	June	July	August	September	October	November	December	Annual average
Total Nonfarm													
2005	349.9	352.6	352.9	354.1	354.0	351.1	351.4	356.1	355.7	358.1	360.8	361.4	354.8
2006	356.9	359.1	360.3	361.9	363.8	360.0	356.4	360.9	362.8	363.6	366.0	368.5	361.7
2007	362.0	363.7	365.6	367.5	370.3	370.8	366.4	368.2	370.1	370.9	371.4	372.1	368.3
2008	366.6	368.1	368.6	369.0	370.6	368.0	363.0	366.0	365.5	364.2	364.5	363.5	366.5
2009	352.0	351.1	351.3	350.1	350.4	348.0	344.6	344.7	345.4	347.1	347.9	347.0	348.3
2010	342.3	344.0	345.5	347.3	349.3	347.9	343.5	344.0	345.1	348.2	349.5	348.2	346.2
2011	339.8	343.8	345.8	349.1	349.7	348.3	344.6	347.5	349.1	351.4	354.8	355.6	348.3
2012	349.7	351.7	353.8	353.9	355.8	354.6	352.5	355.0	356.5	359.3	366.4	366.3	356.3
2013	355.6	358.2	359.6	362.7	364.2	362.2	360.4	361.4	365.8	368.2	375.3	376.2	364.2
2014	367.3	366.9	371.7	373.6	375.1	372.1	369.9	373.6	375.8	380.1	385.7	386.7	374.9
2015	377.1	379.7	380.8	382.3	384.6	382.9	381.8	384.0	386.8	389.8	393.7	393.9	384.8
Total Private													
2005	271.6	273.7	273.6	274.4	274.5	273.8	276.5	278.0	276.1	278.1	280.4	281.1	276.0
2006	277.4	278.8	279.8	282.0	283.9	282.3	281.2	283.4	283.6	284.4	286.3	288.6	282.6
2007	282.2	283.7	285.3	287.5	290.0	291.7	289.3	290.0	289.9	289.7	289.5	290.2	288.3
2008	284.5	285.6	286.0	285.9	287.4	286.7	284.6	285.4	282.4	280.8	280.4	279.6	284.1
2009	269.2	267.7	267.9	266.5	267.1	266.6	264.7	264.3	263.7	264.6	265.0	264.1	266.0
2010	260.2	261.3	262.4	264.0	264.8	265.2	264.0	264.7	264.5	266.7	267.8	266.9	264.4
2011	259.3	262.6	264.3	268.1	269.3	269.1	267.9	269.5	268.9	270.7	273.9	274.9	268.2
2012	269.5	270.3	272.3	272.5	274.2	274.0	273.8	275.7	275.8	277.4	283.8	283.8	275.3
2013	274.4	275.7	276.9	280.4	282.1	282.1	282.6	284.7	285.0	286.4	292.8	294.1	283.1
2014	285.1	283.7	288.1	289.8	291.3	289.9	289.6	292.3	292.1	295.7	301.0	302.1	291.7
2015	293.0	294.7	295.6	296.9	299.3	299.5	299.8	300.9	301.5	304.1	307.4	307.6	300.0
Goods Producing													
2005	52.1	52.2	52.1	52.3	52.9	52.2	52.2	52.2	51.7	51.8	52.0	51.7	52.1
2006	51.7	52.0	52.2	53.3	53.7	53.9	53.4	53.5	53.2	52.9	53.0	52.6	53.0
2007	52.1	52.4	52.6	52.9	53.4	53.8	53.7	53.8	53.2	52.9	52.8	52.7	53.0
2008	51.6	51.2	51.0	50.4	50.4	50.8	50.5	50.4	49.8	49.0	48.8	48.3	50.2
2009	46.4	45.6	45.0	44.5	44.5	44.4	44.0	43.5	43.1	42.9	42.8	42.6	44.1
2010	42.1	42.1	42.0	41.8	41.9	42.3	42.3	41.9	42.0	42.1	42.2	42.0	42.1
2011	41.1	41.6	42.0	42.2	42.4	42.5	42.7	42.8	42.4	42.4	42.4	42.6	42.3
2012	41.9	42.1	42.4	41.9	42.1	42.5	42.7	42.7	42.6	42.8	42.8	42.7	42.4
2013	41.9	42.0	42.3	42.4	42.5	42.8	43.0	43.0	43.1	43.2	43.5	43.6	42.8
2014	43.5	43.4	44.0	44.4	44.5	44.4	44.8	45.0	45.0	45.3	45.5	45.8	44.6
2015	45.7	45.9	45.9	46.0	46.3	46.5	46.6	46.6	47.1	47.3	48.1	48.1	46.7
Service-Providing													
2005	297.8	300.4	300.8	301.8	301.1	298.9	299.2	303.9	304.0	306.3	308.8	309.7	302.7
2006	305.2	307.1	308.1	308.6	310.1	306.1	303.0	307.4	309.6	310.7	313.0	315.9	308.7
2007	309.9	311.3	313.0	314.6	316.9	317.0	312.7	314.4	316.9	318.0	318.6	319.4	315.2
2008	315.0	316.9	317.6	318.6	320.2	317.2	312.5	315.6	315.7	315.2	315.7	315.2	316.3
2009	305.6	305.5	306.3	305.6	305.9	303.6	300.6	301.2	302.3	304.2	305.1	304.4	304.2
2010	300.2	301.9	303.5	305.5	307.4	305.6	301.2	302.1	303.1	306.1	307.3	306.2	304.2
2011	298.7	302.2	303.8	306.9	307.3	305.8	301.9	304.7	306.7	309.0	312.4	313.0	306.0
2012	307.8	309.6	311.4	312.0	313.7	312.1	309.8	312.3	313.9	316.5	323.6	323.6	313.9
2013	313.7	316.2	317.3	320.3	321.7	319.4	317.4	318.4	322.7	325.0	331.8	332.6	321.4
2014	323.8	323.5	327.7	329.2	330.6	327.7	325.1	328.6	330.8	334.8	340.2	340.9	330.2
2015	331.4	333.8	334.9	336.3	338.3	336.4	335.2	337.4	339.7	342.5	345.6	345.8	338.1
Mining, Logging, and Construction													
2005	20.2	20.2	20.0	20.6	21.1	20.5	20.7	20.7	20.4	20.6	20.8	20.6	20.5
2006	20.7	20.9	21.1	22.1	22.4	22.4	22.4	22.5	22.3	22.1	22.2	21.7	21.9
2007	21.0	21.2	21.4	21.6	21.9	22.1	22.1	22.0	21.7	21.4	21.3	21.2	21.6
2008	20.3	20.3	20.2	19.6	19.6	19.9	19.7	19.7	19.4	18.9	18.7	18.4	19.6
2009	17.6	17.2	17.1	17.1	17.1	17.0	16.7	16.4	16.0	15.9	15.8	15.6	16.6
2010	15.3	15.2	15.3	15.1	15.0	15.2	15.2	14.9	14.8	14.8	14.7	14.6	15.0
2011	13.9	14.2	14.5	14.5	14.5	14.6	14.8	14.8	14.6	14.8	14.8	14.8	14.6
2012	14.2	14.2	14.4	14.0	14.2	14.4	14.6	14.5	14.5	14.5	14.5	14.6	14.4
2013	14.3	14.3	14.5	14.6	14.7	14.9	15.1	15.0	14.9	14.9	14.9	14.9	14.8
2014	14.9	14.7	14.9	14.9	14.9	14.9	15.0	15.0	14.8	14.9	14.9	14.9	14.9
2015	14.7	14.6	14.6	14.7	14.9	15.1	15.1	15.1	15.3	15.4	15.5	15.5	15.0

Employment by Industry: Columbia, SC, 2005–2015—*Continued*

(Numbers in thousands, not seasonally adjusted)

Industry and year	January	February	March	April	May	June	July	August	September	October	November	December	Annual average
Manufacturing													
2005	31.9	32.0	32.1	31.7	31.8	31.7	31.5	31.5	31.3	31.2	31.2	31.1	31.6
2006	31.0	31.1	31.1	31.2	31.3	31.5	31.0	31.0	30.9	30.8	30.8	30.9	31.1
2007	31.1	31.2	31.2	31.3	31.5	31.7	31.6	31.8	31.5	31.5	31.5	31.5	31.5
2008	31.3	30.9	30.8	30.8	30.8	30.9	30.8	30.7	30.4	30.1	30.1	29.9	30.6
2009	28.8	28.4	27.9	27.4	27.4	27.4	27.3	27.1	27.1	27.0	27.0	27.0	27.5
2010	26.8	26.9	26.7	26.7	26.9	27.1	27.1	27.0	27.2	27.3	27.5	27.4	27.1
2011	27.2	27.4	27.5	27.7	27.9	27.9	27.9	28.0	27.8	27.6	27.6	27.8	27.7
2012	27.7	27.9	28.0	27.9	27.9	28.1	28.1	28.2	28.1	28.3	28.3	28.1	28.1
2013	27.6	27.7	27.8	27.8	27.8	27.9	27.9	28.0	28.2	28.3	28.6	28.7	28.0
2014	28.6	28.7	29.1	29.5	29.6	29.5	29.8	30.0	30.2	30.4	30.6	30.9	29.7
2015	31.0	31.3	31.3	31.3	31.4	31.4	31.5	31.5	31.8	31.9	32.6	32.6	31.6
Trade, Transportation, and Utilities													
2005	65.4	65.2	65.5	65.9	65.8	65.4	66.1	66.2	65.7	66.8	68.2	69.1	66.3
2006	66.8	66.8	67.4	67.1	67.5	67.1	66.8	67.2	67.6	68.2	69.8	71.2	67.8
2007	68.8	68.9	69.1	69.3	69.8	69.9	69.5	69.6	69.4	69.8	70.8	71.4	69.7
2008	69.6	69.6	69.6	69.7	69.5	69.4	69.0	68.6	68.0	66.8	67.3	68.1	68.8
2009	64.6	63.6	63.2	63.1	63.4	63.3	63.2	63.1	63.0	62.9	63.7	64.5	63.5
2010	62.5	62.1	62.3	62.4	62.4	62.4	62.2	62.5	61.8	62.3	63.2	64.0	62.5
2011	61.4	61.7	61.8	62.3	62.4	62.8	62.3	62.5	62.5	62.9	64.3	64.9	62.7
2012	63.1	62.5	62.9	62.7	63.2	63.0	63.2	63.9	63.9	64.5	66.3	66.7	63.8
2013	63.9	64.0	64.3	64.5	64.9	65.2	65.7	66.1	66.2	66.9	68.1	69.1	65.7
2014	67.0	66.8	67.4	67.2	67.6	67.7	67.8	68.3	68.2	68.8	70.2	71.4	68.2
2015	68.4	68.8	68.8	69.1	69.7	70.4	70.9	71.4	71.0	71.5	72.5	73.4	70.5
Wholesale Trade													
2005	16.0	15.9	16.0	15.9	16.0	15.9	16.2	16.2	16.1	16.2	16.2	16.3	16.1
2006	16.5	16.6	16.8	16.9	16.9	16.8	16.9	16.9	17.1	17.0	17.0	17.1	16.9
2007	17.4	17.9	17.7	17.3	17.1	17.1	16.9	16.8	16.7	16.7	16.6	16.6	17.1
2008	16.8	16.9	16.7	16.8	16.9	16.8	16.7	16.3	16.0	15.9	15.8	15.9	16.5
2009	15.2	15.0	14.9	14.8	14.8	14.7	14.5	14.4	14.4	14.4	14.3	14.3	14.6
2010	14.0	14.0	14.0	14.0	13.9	13.9	13.8	13.7	13.5	13.7	13.7	13.7	13.8
2011	13.5	13.6	13.6	13.7	13.7	13.7	13.6	13.6	13.6	13.5	13.6	13.6	13.6
2012	13.7	13.8	13.8	13.7	13.9	13.9	14.1	14.1	14.0	14.0	14.0	14.0	13.9
2013	13.8	13.9	14.0	14.1	14.2	14.3	14.3	14.4	14.4	14.5	14.6	14.7	14.3
2014	14.8	14.9	15.0	14.9	14.9	14.9	15.0	15.0	15.0	14.9	14.9	15.0	14.9
2015	14.8	14.9	14.9	14.9	15.0	15.1	15.0	15.1	15.1	15.1	15.1	15.1	15.0
Retail Trade													
2005	38.2	38.1	38.1	38.7	38.4	38.1	38.4	38.4	38.0	38.8	40.0	40.6	38.7
2006	38.7	38.5	38.8	38.5	38.8	38.5	38.2	38.4	38.5	39.5	40.8	41.7	39.1
2007	39.7	39.3	39.7	40.2	40.7	40.6	40.5	40.7	40.5	40.9	41.8	42.1	40.6
2008	41.2	41.0	41.2	41.2	40.9	40.9	40.5	40.7	40.6	39.8	40.3	40.7	40.8
2009	38.7	37.9	37.8	37.9	38.1	38.1	38.1	38.2	38.1	38.0	39.0	39.5	38.3
2010	38.0	37.6	37.8	38.2	38.3	38.2	37.9	38.3	37.9	38.1	39.0	39.7	38.3
2011	37.5	37.6	37.7	38.0	38.1	38.3	38.2	38.3	38.2	38.3	39.3	39.8	38.3
2012	38.2	37.6	38.0	37.8	38.0	37.7	37.7	38.0	37.9	38.2	39.6	39.8	38.2
2013	37.8	37.7	37.9	38.2	38.4	38.4	38.6	38.9	38.8	39.4	40.2	40.7	38.8
2014	38.9	38.5	38.8	38.7	38.9	38.9	38.9	39.2	39.0	39.5	40.6	41.2	39.3
2015	39.2	39.1	39.3	39.5	39.7	40.1	40.0	40.3	39.9	40.5	41.4	41.8	40.1
Transportation and Utilities													
2005	11.2	11.2	11.4	11.3	11.4	11.4	11.5	11.6	11.6	11.8	12.0	12.2	11.6
2006	11.6	11.7	11.8	11.7	11.8	11.8	11.7	11.9	12.0	11.7	12.0	12.4	11.8
2007	11.7	11.7	11.7	11.8	12.0	12.2	12.1	12.1	12.2	12.2	12.4	12.7	12.1
2008	11.6	11.7	11.7	11.7	11.7	11.7	11.8	11.6	11.4	11.1	11.2	11.5	11.6
2009	10.7	10.7	10.5	10.4	10.5	10.5	10.6	10.5	10.5	10.5	10.4	10.7	10.5
2010	10.5	10.5	10.5	10.2	10.2	10.3	10.5	10.5	10.4	10.5	10.5	10.6	10.4
2011	10.4	10.5	10.5	10.6	10.6	10.8	10.5	10.6	10.7	11.1	11.4	11.5	10.8
2012	11.2	11.1	11.1	11.2	11.3	11.4	11.4	11.8	12.0	12.3	12.7	12.9	11.7
2013	12.3	12.4	12.4	12.2	12.3	12.5	12.8	12.8	13.0	13.0	13.3	13.7	12.7
2014	13.3	13.4	13.6	13.6	13.8	13.9	13.9	14.1	14.2	14.4	14.7	15.2	14.0
2015	14.4	14.8	14.6	14.7	15.0	15.2	15.9	16.0	16.0	15.9	16.0	16.5	15.4

Employment by Industry: Columbia, SC, 2005–2015—*Continued*

(Numbers in thousands, not seasonally adjusted)

Industry and year	January	February	March	April	May	June	July	August	September	October	November	December	Annual average
Information													
2005	6.0	6.1	6.0	6.1	6.1	6.2	6.2	6.1	6.0	6.1	6.1	6.1	6.1
2006	6.2	6.2	6.2	6.2	6.2	6.2	6.2	6.1	6.1	6.1	6.3	6.4	6.2
2007	6.1	6.1	6.1	6.1	6.2	6.2	6.1	6.0	6.0	6.2	6.1	6.2	6.1
2008	5.8	5.9	5.9	5.9	5.9	6.0	6.0	6.0	5.9	5.9	5.9	5.9	5.9
2009	5.9	5.8	5.9	5.8	5.8	5.8	5.7	5.7	5.7	5.7	5.7	5.6	5.8
2010	5.6	5.6	5.6	5.6	5.6	5.5	5.6	5.7	5.6	5.6	5.7	5.6	5.6
2011	5.4	5.4	5.4	5.3	5.4	5.4	5.4	5.4	5.3	5.3	5.4	5.4	5.4
2012	5.4	5.4	5.4	5.2	5.2	5.2	5.2	5.2	5.2	5.3	5.4	5.4	5.3
2013	5.5	5.8	5.8	5.9	5.6	5.4	5.5	5.5	5.5	5.6	5.7	5.7	5.6
2014	5.6	5.5	5.4	5.6	5.4	5.5	5.4	5.4	5.4	5.5	5.7	5.4	5.5
2015	5.5	5.5	5.4	5.5	5.5	5.3	5.5	5.4	5.5	5.5	5.5	5.5	5.5
Financial Activities													
2005	28.5	28.9	28.7	28.5	28.9	29.0	29.2	29.2	29.2	29.1	29.3	29.7	29.0
2006	29.4	29.5	29.5	29.3	29.6	29.6	29.7	29.7	29.8	29.9	30.0	30.5	29.7
2007	30.4	30.4	30.3	30.4	30.5	30.6	30.2	29.8	30.0	30.0	30.2	30.3	30.3
2008	30.0	30.1	30.2	30.1	30.1	30.2	29.8	29.8	29.7	29.8	29.9	30.0	30.0
2009	29.3	29.5	29.5	29.0	29.1	28.9	28.8	28.6	28.3	27.9	27.8	27.6	28.7
2010	27.4	27.4	27.3	27.0	27.0	27.0	26.7	26.7	26.5	26.7	26.7	26.7	26.9
2011	26.6	26.6	26.7	26.7	26.9	27.1	27.0	27.2	27.2	27.5	27.7	27.9	27.1
2012	27.9	28.0	28.1	28.1	28.3	28.4	28.5	28.6	28.7	28.7	28.9	28.9	28.4
2013	28.8	29.0	29.3	29.4	29.6	29.8	29.9	30.1	30.2	29.9	30.0	30.1	29.7
2014	29.7	29.7	29.7	29.7	29.8	29.8	29.7	29.8	29.8	29.7	29.7	29.8	29.7
2015	29.6	29.7	29.7	29.7	29.8	29.8	29.7	29.8	29.8	29.4	29.4	29.8	29.7
Professional and Business Services													
2005	39.5	40.2	39.5	40.0	39.3	40.5	40.9	42.1	42.3	42.5	43.2	43.3	41.1
2006	42.6	42.4	42.2	43.4	43.9	42.8	43.0	44.3	43.9	43.0	43.0	43.4	43.2
2007	42.5	42.8	43.0	43.2	43.4	43.8	43.4	44.1	44.4	44.2	43.5	43.4	43.5
2008	41.9	42.3	41.9	41.6	42.8	41.4	41.2	42.5	41.0	41.3	41.2	40.2	41.6
2009	38.3	37.7	37.9	37.6	37.4	37.4	37.0	37.3	37.1	38.8	38.9	38.4	37.8
2010	38.1	38.8	39.1	39.8	40.0	40.4	40.2	40.6	40.9	41.5	41.2	40.9	40.1
2011	40.1	41.1	41.3	42.4	42.3	42.2	42.0	42.5	42.1	42.5	43.3	44.1	42.2
2012	42.8	43.0	43.3	44.0	44.5	44.5	44.4	44.4	43.9	44.4	47.8	48.3	44.6
2013	45.0	44.0	43.8	44.8	45.2	45.2	45.2	45.6	45.7	45.9	49.9	50.8	45.9
2014	46.4	44.8	46.1	45.9	46.5	45.6	45.5	46.1	46.1	47.5	51.5	51.8	47.0
2015	47.7	47.4	47.3	47.2	47.5	47.8	47.5	47.3	47.8	49.8	50.6	50.3	48.2
Education and Health Services													
2005	39.0	39.3	39.6	38.8	38.8	37.9	38.7	38.7	38.6	39.3	39.4	39.3	39.0
2006	39.2	39.9	39.8	39.5	39.5	39.3	39.3	39.4	39.7	41.0	41.0	41.1	39.9
2007	40.4	40.8	41.0	41.7	42.1	42.5	42.1	41.9	42.4	42.2	42.2	42.1	41.8
2008	42.7	43.1	43.3	43.2	43.3	43.3	43.1	43.0	43.3	43.2	43.3	43.3	43.2
2009	42.1	42.4	42.5	42.3	42.4	42.1	42.2	42.3	42.7	42.6	42.8	42.6	42.4
2010	42.3	42.6	42.6	42.8	43.0	42.9	42.8	42.8	42.9	43.5	43.5	43.3	42.9
2011	42.5	43.1	43.1	44.2	44.2	43.8	43.6	43.3	43.7	43.9	44.0	43.8	43.6
2012	43.3	43.6	43.7	43.6	43.6	42.9	42.8	43.0	43.7	43.9	44.1	43.9	43.5
2013	42.9	43.6	43.6	44.1	44.4	44.1	44.2	44.5	44.7	45.2	45.4	45.4	44.3
2014	44.8	45.0	45.8	46.3	46.4	45.8	46.1	46.3	46.6	46.8	46.9	46.9	46.1
2015	46.3	46.8	47.0	47.1	47.6	47.4	47.4	47.3	47.4	49.0	48.9	49.0	47.6
Leisure and Hospitality													
2005	28.8	29.2	29.4	30.1	30.0	29.8	30.2	30.3	29.6	30.0	29.6	29.3	29.7
2006	28.8	29.2	29.8	30.4	30.5	30.4	30.2	30.4	30.3	30.7	30.5	30.7	30.2
2007	29.3	29.7	30.3	31.2	31.7	32.0	31.5	31.9	31.8	31.7	31.2	31.1	31.1
2008	30.0	30.5	31.0	31.9	32.3	32.6	31.9	32.0	31.8	31.8	31.1	31.0	31.5
2009	29.8	30.4	31.1	31.5	31.8	32.0	31.1	31.2	31.3	31.3	30.8	30.4	31.1
2010	29.7	30.2	30.8	31.9	32.1	31.8	31.5	31.9	32.1	32.1	32.6	31.7	31.5
2011	29.8	30.7	31.5	32.3	32.8	32.2	31.7	32.6	32.5	33.1	33.6	32.8	32.1
2012	31.4	31.9	32.5	33.0	33.2	33.1	32.7	33.6	33.5	33.5	34.1	33.4	33.0
2013	31.9	32.8	33.1	34.5	35.0	34.7	34.2	34.9	34.7	34.7	35.2	34.3	34.2
2014	33.2	33.5	34.6	35.4	35.7	35.6	35.0	35.9	35.7	36.7	36.1	35.6	35.3
2015	34.4	35.1	35.8	36.7	37.1	36.6	36.5	37.2	37.1	35.8	36.6	35.7	36.2

Employment by Industry: Columbia, SC, 2005–2015—*Continued*

(Numbers in thousands, not seasonally adjusted)

Industry and year	January	February	March	April	May	June	July	August	September	October	November	December	Annual average
Other Services													
2005	12.3	12.6	12.8	12.7	12.7	12.8	13.0	13.2	13.0	12.5	12.6	12.6	12.7
2006	12.7	12.8	12.7	12.8	13.0	13.0	12.6	12.8	13.0	12.6	12.7	12.7	12.8
2007	12.6	12.6	12.9	12.7	12.9	12.9	12.8	12.9	12.7	12.7	12.7	13.0	12.8
2008	12.9	12.9	13.1	13.1	13.1	13.0	13.1	13.1	12.9	13.0	12.9	12.8	13.0
2009	12.8	12.7	12.8	12.7	12.7	12.7	12.7	12.6	12.5	12.5	12.5	12.4	12.6
2010	12.5	12.5	12.7	12.7	12.8	12.9	12.7	12.6	12.7	12.9	12.7	12.7	12.7
2011	12.4	12.4	12.5	12.7	12.9	13.1	13.2	13.2	13.2	13.1	13.2	13.4	12.9
2012	13.7	13.8	14.0	14.0	14.1	14.4	14.3	14.3	14.3	14.3	14.4	14.5	14.2
2013	14.5	14.5	14.7	14.8	14.9	14.9	14.9	15.0	14.9	15.0	15.0	15.1	14.9
2014	14.9	15.0	15.1	15.3	15.4	15.5	15.3	15.5	15.3	15.4	15.4	15.4	15.3
2015	15.4	15.5	15.7	15.6	15.8	15.7	15.7	15.9	15.8	15.8	15.8	15.8	15.7
Government													
2005	78.3	78.9	79.3	79.7	79.5	77.3	74.9	78.1	79.6	80.0	80.4	80.3	78.9
2006	79.5	80.3	80.5	79.9	79.9	77.7	75.2	77.5	79.2	79.2	79.7	79.9	79.0
2007	79.8	80.0	80.3	80.0	80.3	79.1	77.1	78.2	80.2	81.2	81.9	81.9	80.0
2008	82.1	82.5	82.6	83.1	83.2	81.3	78.4	80.6	83.1	83.4	84.1	83.9	82.4
2009	82.8	83.4	83.4	83.6	83.3	81.4	79.9	80.4	81.7	82.5	82.9	82.9	82.4
2010	82.1	82.7	83.1	83.3	84.5	82.7	79.5	79.3	80.6	81.5	81.7	81.3	81.9
2011	80.5	81.2	81.5	81.0	80.4	79.2	76.7	78.0	80.2	80.7	80.9	80.7	80.1
2012	80.2	81.4	81.5	81.4	81.6	80.6	78.7	79.3	80.7	81.9	82.6	82.5	81.0
2013	81.2	82.5	82.7	82.3	82.1	80.1	77.8	76.7	80.8	81.8	82.5	82.1	81.1
2014	82.2	83.2	83.6	83.8	83.8	82.2	80.3	81.3	83.7	84.4	84.7	84.6	83.2
2015	84.1	85.0	85.2	85.4	85.3	83.4	82.0	83.1	85.3	85.7	86.3	86.3	84.8

Employment by Industry: Dayton, OH, 2005–2015

(Numbers in thousands, not seasonally adjusted)

Industry and year	January	February	March	April	May	June	July	August	September	October	November	December	Annual average
Total Nonfarm													
2005	393.4	394.6	397.0	400.9	401.1	400.4	396.0	398.0	401.7	401.4	402.0	402.0	399.0
2006	391.1	393.5	396.8	399.0	401.1	400.9	393.5	395.2	397.4	397.8	399.3	400.4	397.2
2007	386.4	388.9	392.0	394.5	395.6	396.3	389.7	391.4	394.2	395.1	395.5	394.1	392.8
2008	384.4	385.0	383.2	385.1	386.6	387.3	382.1	383.8	384.8	383.6	381.6	379.7	383.9
2009	365.9	364.7	364.7	363.2	364.5	362.1	357.9	358.4	362.3	363.1	363.6	362.8	362.8
2010	353.7	354.3	357.2	361.1	363.2	362.1	357.7	359.1	362.5	364.8	366.4	366.3	360.7
2011	358.0	359.4	362.3	366.7	367.8	366.3	362.3	363.2	368.0	369.4	371.3	370.5	365.4
2012	363.2	365.4	367.7	369.8	371.0	372.0	365.8	367.0	369.1	369.9	372.1	372.1	368.8
2013	360.9	363.7	365.2	367.9	371.3	370.4	366.1	367.9	369.1	370.5	374.1	373.1	368.4
2014	363.3	365.2	368.2	370.9	372.9	373.7	370.8	373.4	375.0	377.4	379.5	380.3	372.6
2015	370.3	371.9	373.5	377.9	380.5	379.6	379.5	380.2	379.6	383.7	385.4	386.9	379.1
Total Private													
2005	331.2	331.0	333.6	337.5	337.0	337.8	335.4	337.6	339.1	338.3	338.8	339.5	336.4
2006	329.1	330.1	333.4	335.6	336.7	337.1	332.5	334.4	335.5	334.3	335.9	337.0	334.3
2007	324.2	326.1	328.9	331.6	332.0	333.4	329.9	331.6	332.2	332.1	333.4	333.0	330.7
2008	323.5	322.5	320.6	322.4	322.9	325.1	322.4	324.1	322.6	320.3	318.0	317.1	321.8
2009	303.2	301.5	301.1	299.5	299.3	298.1	297.3	297.7	298.7	298.2	298.9	299.4	299.4
2010	290.2	290.0	292.4	296.0	296.4	297.0	296.7	297.7	298.8	299.7	301.4	301.4	296.5
2011	294.0	294.5	297.0	301.3	301.6	301.7	300.6	301.8	304.1	304.6	306.3	307.4	301.2
2012	300.7	301.3	303.4	305.4	306.3	308.1	305.9	306.3	305.8	306.0	308.0	308.2	305.5
2013	299.4	300.3	301.7	304.6	307.4	308.4	306.6	307.8	306.3	307.5	310.7	310.3	305.9
2014	302.5	302.4	305.1	308.7	310.7	312.6	312.2	313.8	312.2	314.1	315.9	317.0	310.6
2015	309.0	308.9	310.8	314.5	318.2	318.0	318.2	318.6	316.9	320.5	321.6	323.2	316.5
Goods Producing													
2005	67.6	67.3	67.5	68.9	69.1	70.3	69.6	70.4	70.1	69.5	68.8	68.1	68.9
2006	65.7	66.0	66.7	67.3	67.6	68.5	66.3	67.2	66.7	66.0	65.5	65.6	66.6
2007	60.3	62.1	62.7	63.4	63.6	64.6	63.3	64.3	63.8	62.9	63.0	62.3	63.0
2008	60.0	59.4	57.0	57.0	57.5	60.3	59.7	60.5	59.0	58.3	56.6	55.1	58.4
2009	50.0	49.1	48.6	47.8	47.6	47.1	47.0	47.4	47.0	47.0	46.5	46.4	47.6
2010	44.4	44.1	44.7	45.8	46.5	47.3	47.7	48.1	48.0	47.7	47.8	47.5	46.6
2011	46.4	46.4	47.2	47.7	48.5	49.0	49.4	49.6	49.6	49.6	49.7	49.6	48.6
2012	48.5	48.4	48.8	49.2	49.7	50.4	50.1	50.1	50.0	49.8	49.8	49.8	49.6
2013	48.4	48.5	48.9	48.9	49.8	50.3	50.0	49.9	49.6	49.7	49.9	49.7	49.5
2014	48.5	48.7	49.3	49.7	50.6	51.4	51.4	51.8	51.6	51.6	51.6	51.5	50.6
2015	50.5	50.6	50.7	51.4	52.1	52.4	52.7	52.8	52.5	53.0	52.9	52.8	52.0
Service-Providing													
2005	325.8	327.3	329.5	332.0	332.0	330.1	326.4	327.6	331.6	331.9	333.2	333.9	330.1
2006	325.4	327.5	330.1	331.7	333.5	332.4	327.2	328.0	330.7	331.8	333.8	334.8	330.6
2007	326.1	326.8	329.3	331.1	332.0	331.7	326.4	327.1	330.4	332.2	332.5	331.8	329.8
2008	324.4	325.6	326.2	328.1	329.1	327.0	322.4	323.3	325.8	325.3	325.0	324.6	325.6
2009	315.9	315.6	316.1	315.4	316.9	315.0	310.9	311.0	315.3	316.1	317.1	316.4	315.1
2010	309.3	310.2	312.5	315.3	316.7	314.8	310.0	311.0	314.5	317.1	318.6	318.8	314.1
2011	311.6	313.0	315.1	319.0	319.3	317.3	312.9	313.6	318.4	319.8	321.6	320.9	316.9
2012	314.7	317.0	318.9	320.6	321.3	321.6	315.7	316.9	319.1	320.1	322.3	322.3	319.2
2013	312.5	315.2	316.3	319.0	321.5	320.1	316.1	318.0	319.5	320.8	324.2	323.4	318.9
2014	314.8	316.5	318.9	321.2	322.3	322.3	319.4	321.6	323.4	325.8	327.9	328.8	321.9
2015	319.8	321.3	322.8	326.5	328.4	327.2	326.8	327.4	327.1	330.7	332.5	334.1	327.1
Mining, Logging, and Construction													
2005	13.5	13.2	13.7	14.7	15.2	15.8	16.1	15.8	15.6	15.2	15.1	14.5	14.9
2006	13.6	13.5	13.9	14.5	14.9	15.6	15.7	15.7	15.2	14.6	14.3	14.0	14.6
2007	13.0	12.4	13.1	14.1	14.7	15.4	15.4	15.2	14.7	14.4	14.5	13.8	14.2
2008	12.6	12.4	12.5	13.2	13.8	14.0	14.2	14.1	13.6	13.3	12.7	12.1	13.2
2009	10.9	10.7	10.9	11.0	11.6	11.8	12.1	11.8	11.4	11.4	11.2	10.8	11.3
2010	9.7	9.3	9.8	10.5	10.7	11.2	11.5	11.4	11.2	11.0	10.9	10.4	10.6
2011	9.5	9.5	9.8	10.4	11.1	11.5	11.8	11.8	11.7	11.4	11.4	11.0	10.9
2012	10.5	10.3	10.5	10.9	11.4	11.6	11.5	11.4	11.3	11.2	11.1	10.9	11.1
2013	10.1	10.2	10.6	10.8	11.5	11.8	11.7	11.7	11.6	11.6	11.6	11.2	11.2
2014	10.4	10.4	10.9	11.2	11.9	12.3	12.5	12.5	12.3	12.2	12.0	11.8	11.7
2015	11.1	11.0	11.2	11.9	12.3	12.5	12.7	12.6	12.5	12.4	12.3	12.0	12.0

Employment by Industry: Dayton, OH, 2005–2015—*Continued*

(Numbers in thousands, not seasonally adjusted)

Industry and year	January	February	March	April	May	June	July	August	September	October	November	December	Annual average
Manufacturing													
2005	54.1	54.1	53.8	54.2	53.9	54.5	53.5	54.6	54.5	54.3	53.7	53.6	54.1
2006	52.1	52.5	52.8	52.8	52.7	52.9	50.6	51.5	51.5	51.4	51.2	51.6	52.0
2007	47.3	49.7	49.6	49.3	48.9	49.2	47.9	49.1	49.1	48.5	48.5	48.5	48.8
2008	47.4	47.0	44.5	43.8	43.7	46.3	45.5	46.4	45.4	45.0	43.9	43.0	45.2
2009	39.1	38.4	37.7	36.8	36.0	35.3	34.9	35.6	35.6	35.6	35.3	35.6	36.3
2010	34.7	34.8	34.9	35.3	35.8	36.1	36.2	36.7	36.8	36.7	36.9	37.1	36.0
2011	36.9	36.9	37.4	37.3	37.4	37.5	37.6	37.8	37.9	38.2	38.3	38.6	37.7
2012	38.0	38.1	38.3	38.3	38.3	38.8	38.6	38.7	38.7	38.6	38.7	38.9	38.5
2013	38.3	38.3	38.3	38.1	38.3	38.5	38.3	38.2	38.0	38.1	38.3	38.5	38.3
2014	38.1	38.3	38.4	38.5	38.7	39.1	38.9	39.3	39.3	39.4	39.6	39.7	38.9
2015	39.4	39.6	39.5	39.5	39.8	39.9	40.0	40.2	40.0	40.6	40.6	40.8	40.0
Trade, Transportation, and Utilities													
2005	68.6	68.2	68.8	69.4	69.4	69.5	69.0	69.0	68.7	68.8	70.1	71.1	69.2
2006	67.7	67.2	67.9	67.9	68.6	68.4	67.8	68.0	67.2	67.4	68.8	69.6	68.0
2007	66.3	65.5	66.3	66.9	67.1	67.2	67.0	66.6	66.5	66.7	68.1	68.7	66.9
2008	65.5	64.6	64.8	65.1	65.4	65.7	64.9	65.1	64.7	64.1	64.7	65.6	65.0
2009	62.2	61.3	61.3	61.3	61.6	61.4	60.9	60.7	60.4	60.7	61.7	62.5	61.3
2010	59.4	58.7	59.2	59.6	59.9	60.2	59.7	59.8	59.4	60.3	61.9	62.9	60.1
2011	60.1	59.3	59.7	60.5	60.9	61.1	60.9	61.1	61.1	62.1	63.7	64.7	61.3
2012	61.9	61.3	62.0	62.2	62.7	62.7	62.3	62.5	62.4	63.1	64.8	65.3	62.8
2013	62.2	61.8	62.0	62.5	63.1	63.1	63.1	63.2	62.9	63.7	65.8	66.5	63.3
2014	63.5	62.9	63.3	63.8	64.0	64.2	64.0	64.1	63.9	64.7	66.5	67.3	64.4
2015	64.7	64.4	64.5	65.1	66.0	65.8	65.7	65.7	65.3	65.8	67.5	68.5	65.8
Wholesale Trade													
2005	13.7	13.8	13.8	13.9	13.9	14.0	14.0	13.9	13.8	13.8	13.7	13.8	13.8
2006	13.5	13.5	13.6	13.6	13.8	13.8	13.8	13.7	13.7	13.7	13.7	13.8	13.7
2007	13.6	13.6	13.7	13.7	13.7	13.8	13.9	13.8	13.7	13.8	13.7	13.8	13.7
2008	13.7	13.6	13.7	13.7	13.7	13.6	13.5	13.4	13.3	13.0	12.9	12.9	13.4
2009	12.8	12.7	12.6	12.5	12.3	12.3	12.2	12.1	11.9	11.7	11.7	11.8	12.2
2010	11.7	11.7	11.7	11.7	11.7	11.8	11.8	11.8	11.7	11.8	11.7	11.8	11.7
2011	12.0	11.9	12.0	12.1	12.2	12.3	12.4	12.4	12.4	12.6	12.5	12.6	12.3
2012	12.7	12.8	12.9	12.6	12.7	12.8	12.9	12.9	12.8	12.9	12.8	12.9	12.8
2013	12.7	12.6	12.6	12.6	12.7	12.7	12.7	12.6	12.5	12.6	12.6	12.6	12.6
2014	12.6	12.6	12.6	12.7	12.8	12.9	12.8	12.8	12.8	12.8	12.9	12.9	12.8
2015	13.1	13.1	13.1	13.2	13.3	13.2	13.3	13.3	13.1	13.2	13.1	13.2	13.2
Retail Trade													
2005	42.9	42.3	42.8	43.4	43.3	43.2	42.5	42.5	42.3	42.5	43.8	44.6	43.0
2006	41.9	41.2	41.7	41.6	42.0	41.7	41.3	41.5	41.5	41.8	43.2	43.8	41.9
2007	41.3	40.5	41.1	41.7	41.8	41.7	41.4	41.1	41.1	41.3	42.8	43.2	41.6
2008	40.7	39.9	40.2	40.5	40.6	40.7	40.1	40.2	40.0	39.8	40.5	41.3	40.4
2009	38.7	37.9	38.1	38.5	39.0	38.8	38.3	38.2	38.0	38.3	39.3	39.8	38.6
2010	37.5	36.8	37.2	37.6	37.9	37.9	37.5	37.5	37.2	37.8	39.2	39.8	37.8
2011	37.4	36.8	37.1	37.7	37.9	38.0	37.7	37.8	37.7	38.6	40.2	40.8	38.1
2012	38.3	37.6	38.2	38.5	38.8	38.6	38.2	38.3	38.2	38.7	40.3	40.5	38.7
2013	38.2	37.8	38.1	38.6	39.0	38.9	38.8	38.9	38.6	39.2	40.9	41.3	39.0
2014	38.5	38.1	38.5	38.9	38.9	39.0	38.7	38.8	38.7	39.5	41.0	41.4	39.2
2015	38.7	38.5	38.6	39.0	39.5	39.6	39.3	39.3	39.0	39.3	41.0	41.6	39.5
Transportation and Utilities													
2005	12.0	12.1	12.2	12.1	12.2	12.3	12.5	12.6	12.6	12.5	12.6	12.7	12.4
2006	12.3	12.5	12.6	12.7	12.8	12.9	12.7	12.8	12.0	11.9	11.9	12.0	12.4
2007	11.4	11.4	11.5	11.5	11.6	11.7	11.7	11.7	11.7	11.6	11.6	11.7	11.6
2008	11.1	11.1	10.9	10.9	11.1	11.4	11.3	11.5	11.4	11.3	11.3	11.4	11.2
2009	10.7	10.7	10.6	10.3	10.3	10.3	10.4	10.4	10.5	10.7	10.7	10.9	10.5
2010	10.2	10.2	10.3	10.3	10.3	10.5	10.4	10.5	10.5	10.7	11.0	11.3	10.5
2011	10.7	10.6	10.6	10.7	10.8	10.8	10.8	10.9	11.0	10.9	11.0	11.3	10.8
2012	10.9	10.9	10.9	11.1	11.2	11.3	11.2	11.3	11.4	11.5	11.7	11.9	11.3
2013	11.3	11.4	11.3	11.3	11.4	11.5	11.6	11.7	11.8	11.9	12.3	12.6	11.7
2014	12.4	12.2	12.2	12.2	12.3	12.3	12.5	12.5	12.4	12.4	12.6	13.0	12.4
2015	12.9	12.8	12.8	12.9	13.2	13.0	13.1	13.1	13.2	13.3	13.4	13.7	13.1

Employment by Industry: Dayton, OH, 2005–2015—*Continued*

(Numbers in thousands, not seasonally adjusted)

Industry and year	January	February	March	April	May	June	July	August	September	October	November	December	Annual average
Information													
2005	12.2	12.1	12.1	12.1	12.1	12.2	12.1	11.9	11.7	11.6	11.6	11.7	12.0
2006	11.6	11.6	11.6	11.6	11.6	11.7	11.8	11.9	11.8	12.0	12.0	12.1	11.8
2007	12.1	12.1	12.0	12.1	12.2	12.2	12.1	12.1	12.0	12.0	12.1	12.1	12.1
2008	12.2	12.1	12.1	12.1	12.0	11.9	12.2	12.1	11.7	11.6	11.6	11.5	11.9
2009	11.4	11.4	11.2	10.9	10.9	10.9	10.8	10.8	10.7	10.6	10.7	10.7	10.9
2010	10.7	10.7	10.7	10.5	10.4	10.4	10.3	10.2	10.1	10.0	9.9	9.9	10.3
2011	9.8	9.8	9.8	9.8	9.7	9.8	9.8	9.7	9.7	9.5	9.4	9.3	9.7
2012	9.2	9.1	9.0	9.0	8.9	8.9	9.0	8.8	8.8	8.7	8.7	8.7	8.9
2013	8.7	8.7	8.7	8.7	8.7	8.8	8.8	8.7	8.6	8.5	8.5	8.5	8.7
2014	8.4	8.4	8.4	8.5	8.5	8.6	8.6	8.5	8.4	8.4	8.4	8.5	8.5
2015	8.4	8.4	8.4	8.5	8.5	8.5	8.5	8.5	8.4	8.3	8.4	8.4	8.4
Financial Activities													
2005	18.5	18.6	18.5	18.8	18.9	19.1	19.2	19.3	19.3	19.4	19.4	19.5	19.0
2006	19.4	19.6	19.7	19.8	19.8	19.9	19.9	19.9	19.8	19.9	19.9	19.9	19.8
2007	19.6	19.7	19.7	19.8	19.8	19.6	19.5	19.4	19.1	19.0	18.9	18.8	19.4
2008	18.7	18.4	18.3	18.2	18.1	18.0	17.8	17.7	17.4	17.2	17.1	17.1	17.8
2009	17.0	16.8	16.6	16.6	16.6	16.6	16.6	16.5	16.3	16.4	16.4	16.3	16.6
2010	16.3	16.3	16.3	16.5	16.6	16.5	16.6	16.5	16.4	16.6	16.6	16.6	16.5
2011	16.3	16.3	16.3	16.4	16.4	16.5	16.5	16.5	16.4	16.4	16.5	16.6	16.4
2012	16.4	16.4	16.5	16.7	16.7	16.8	17.0	17.0	17.0	17.0	17.1	17.1	16.8
2013	16.8	16.9	16.8	16.9	17.1	17.1	17.1	17.1	17.0	17.0	17.1	17.1	17.0
2014	16.9	17.0	17.1	17.1	17.3	17.4	17.4	17.7	17.5	17.6	17.6	17.6	17.4
2015	17.3	17.2	17.3	17.3	17.5	17.6	17.7	17.7	17.4	17.9	17.8	18.0	17.6
Professional and Business Services													
2005	51.4	51.0	51.4	51.6	51.5	51.4	51.2	51.7	51.7	52.4	52.1	52.3	51.6
2006	50.5	50.4	50.9	51.6	52.0	52.4	52.0	52.1	51.8	51.7	51.8	52.0	51.6
2007	51.0	51.2	51.3	51.5	51.4	52.1	51.7	51.8	51.8	52.3	52.0	52.0	51.7
2008	50.6	50.9	51.0	51.1	51.0	51.2	50.5	50.4	49.8	49.4	48.3	48.3	50.2
2009	46.4	45.6	45.2	45.0	44.7	45.0	45.2	45.3	45.1	44.9	45.0	45.1	45.2
2010	43.6	43.9	44.1	45.4	45.4	45.9	45.8	46.5	46.1	46.2	46.3	46.1	45.4
2011	45.6	45.7	46.2	46.9	46.6	46.9	47.0	47.5	47.4	47.3	47.3	47.7	46.8
2012	46.9	47.1	47.1	47.4	47.4	47.7	47.8	47.8	47.3	47.7	47.4	47.4	47.4
2013	46.3	46.3	46.1	47.2	47.3	47.6	47.5	48.0	47.8	48.1	48.5	48.0	47.4
2014	47.2	47.0	47.4	48.5	48.6	49.2	49.6	49.8	49.2	49.9	50.0	49.9	48.9
2015	48.3	48.1	48.7	49.8	50.5	50.7	50.9	50.9	50.4	51.3	51.2	50.8	50.1
Education and Health Services													
2005	62.5	63.2	63.6	63.9	62.4	61.0	60.8	61.0	64.3	64.8	65.2	65.2	63.2
2006	63.8	64.6	64.9	64.8	63.6	61.8	61.0	61.6	64.8	65.6	66.1	65.9	64.0
2007	64.6	65.3	65.6	65.6	64.7	63.8	63.1	63.9	66.6	67.5	67.8	68.0	65.5
2008	66.9	67.6	67.6	67.5	66.5	65.4	65.0	65.7	68.3	68.8	69.1	69.2	67.3
2009	67.6	68.6	68.7	67.9	66.9	65.7	65.4	65.6	68.5	69.1	69.2	69.1	67.7
2010	67.9	68.5	68.7	68.2	67.0	65.5	65.3	65.4	68.3	69.4	69.6	69.6	67.8
2011	68.4	69.3	69.5	69.9	68.6	66.7	65.8	66.1	69.6	70.2	70.2	70.4	68.7
2012	69.2	70.2	70.1	69.9	68.9	68.6	67.3	67.7	69.1	69.5	69.9	69.6	69.2
2013	68.0	68.9	69.1	69.3	69.0	68.3	67.8	68.4	69.1	70.0	70.5	70.0	69.0
2014	68.6	69.2	69.6	69.9	69.6	68.7	68.4	69.1	70.3	70.9	71.1	71.5	69.7
2015	70.2	70.6	70.9	70.9	70.8	69.8	69.7	70.3	71.4	72.6	72.3	72.7	71.0
Leisure and Hospitality													
2005	34.4	34.6	35.5	36.5	37.2	37.8	37.3	37.6	37.1	35.9	35.8	35.8	36.3
2006	34.8	35.0	35.9	36.5	37.4	38.1	37.7	37.8	37.4	36.0	36.1	36.2	36.6
2007	34.9	34.8	35.6	36.6	37.5	38.0	37.6	37.9	36.9	36.2	36.0	35.7	36.5
2008	34.5	34.4	34.7	36.3	37.2	37.5	37.2	37.5	36.7	36.0	35.7	35.4	36.1
2009	34.1	34.1	35.0	35.5	36.4	36.9	36.8	36.8	36.1	35.0	34.8	34.6	35.5
2010	33.4	33.3	34.0	35.3	35.9	36.5	36.6	36.6	36.0	35.1	34.9	34.6	35.2
2011	33.3	33.5	34.1	35.7	36.4	37.1	36.7	36.9	36.0	35.4	35.3	35.0	35.5
2012	34.4	34.6	35.6	36.5	37.3	38.1	37.8	37.8	36.8	35.8	35.8	35.8	36.4
2013	34.7	34.7	35.5	36.3	37.5	38.3	37.7	37.9	36.9	36.2	36.2	36.3	36.5
2014	35.5	35.3	36.0	37.2	38.2	39.1	38.9	38.9	37.6	37.3	37.1	37.1	37.4
2015	36.0	36.0	36.7	37.7	38.8	39.2	38.9	38.8	37.8	37.9	37.8	38.3	37.8

Employment by Industry: Dayton, OH, 2005–2015—*Continued*

(Numbers in thousands, not seasonally adjusted)

Industry and year	January	February	March	April	May	June	July	August	September	October	November	December	Annual average
Other Services													
2005	16.0	16.0	16.2	16.3	16.4	16.5	16.2	16.7	16.2	15.9	15.8	15.8	16.2
2006	15.6	15.7	15.8	16.1	16.1	16.3	16.0	15.9	16.0	15.7	15.7	15.7	15.9
2007	15.4	15.4	15.7	15.7	15.7	15.9	15.6	15.6	15.5	15.5	15.5	15.4	15.6
2008	15.1	15.1	15.1	15.1	15.2	15.1	15.1	15.1	15.0	14.9	14.9	14.9	15.1
2009	14.5	14.6	14.5	14.5	14.6	14.5	14.6	14.6	14.6	14.5	14.6	14.7	14.6
2010	14.5	14.5	14.7	14.7	14.7	14.7	14.7	14.6	14.5	14.4	14.4	14.2	14.6
2011	14.1	14.2	14.2	14.4	14.5	14.6	14.5	14.4	14.3	14.1	14.2	14.1	14.3
2012	14.2	14.2	14.3	14.5	14.7	14.9	14.6	14.6	14.4	14.4	14.5	14.5	14.5
2013	14.3	14.5	14.6	14.8	14.9	14.9	14.6	14.6	14.4	14.3	14.2	14.2	14.5
2014	13.9	13.9	14.0	14.0	13.9	14.0	13.9	13.9	13.7	13.7	13.6	13.6	13.8
2015	13.6	13.6	13.6	13.8	14.0	14.0	14.1	13.9	13.7	13.7	13.7	13.7	13.8
Government													
2005	62.2	63.6	63.4	63.4	64.1	62.6	60.6	60.4	62.6	63.1	63.2	62.5	62.6
2006	62.0	63.4	63.4	63.4	64.4	63.8	61.0	60.8	61.9	63.5	63.4	63.4	62.9
2007	62.2	62.8	63.1	62.9	63.6	62.9	59.8	59.8	62.0	63.0	62.1	61.1	62.1
2008	60.9	62.5	62.6	62.7	63.7	62.2	59.7	59.7	62.2	63.3	63.6	62.6	62.1
2009	62.7	63.2	63.6	63.7	65.2	64.0	60.6	60.7	63.6	64.9	64.7	63.4	63.4
2010	63.5	64.3	64.8	65.1	66.8	65.1	61.0	61.4	63.7	65.1	65.0	64.9	64.2
2011	64.0	64.9	65.3	65.4	66.2	64.6	61.7	61.4	63.9	64.8	65.0	63.1	64.2
2012	62.5	64.1	64.3	64.4	64.7	63.9	59.9	60.7	63.3	63.9	64.1	63.9	63.3
2013	61.5	63.4	63.5	63.3	63.9	62.0	59.5	60.1	62.8	63.0	63.4	62.8	62.4
2014	60.8	62.8	63.1	62.2	62.2	61.1	58.6	59.6	62.8	63.3	63.6	63.3	62.0
2015	61.3	63.0	62.7	63.4	62.3	61.6	61.3	61.6	62.7	63.2	63.8	63.7	62.6

Employment by Industry: North Port-Sarasota-Bradenton, 2005–2015

(Numbers in thousands, not seasonally adjusted)

Industry and year	January	February	March	April	May	June	July	August	September	October	November	December	Annual average
Total Nonfarm													
2005	268.3	271.7	273.8	273.1	274.1	271.0	269.5	273.0	273.8	274.8	278.1	281.5	273.6
2006	275.8	279.5	283.5	282.0	282.8	280.7	276.3	279.4	279.7	277.8	280.9	282.9	280.1
2007	276.9	278.9	281.1	277.1	276.4	272.5	266.6	270.0	268.6	267.6	270.9	273.6	273.4
2008	268.5	271.0	272.3	266.2	264.8	259.6	254.7	256.9	255.9	253.7	254.1	255.0	261.1
2009	248.3	247.8	248.3	245.5	243.9	239.3	234.7	236.4	235.4	237.8	240.3	241.8	241.6
2010	236.2	238.0	240.0	240.1	241.7	236.5	233.1	235.0	233.6	235.1	238.4	240.5	237.4
2011	236.5	239.6	241.2	243.1	241.1	236.9	235.1	238.4	238.3	239.5	243.9	246.1	240.0
2012	243.2	245.0	248.2	247.7	247.0	242.8	240.0	242.5	243.4	246.8	252.2	253.8	246.1
2013	250.6	254.4	256.1	256.3	256.4	252.3	251.2	254.0	254.4	258.6	265.0	267.0	256.4
2014	263.1	266.4	268.9	269.0	268.7	265.2	263.9	267.5	268.3	273.8	278.6	282.0	269.6
2015	278.7	281.4	284.4	284.3	284.4	280.9	278.7	281.6	281.6	284.0	287.6	288.4	283.0
Total Private													
2005	241.4	244.6	246.7	245.8	246.7	246.5	245.1	246.0	246.6	247.0	250.1	253.6	246.7
2006	248.0	251.6	255.4	253.6	254.3	255.1	251.0	251.2	251.1	249.2	251.6	253.6	252.1
2007	248.1	249.8	251.9	247.9	247.3	246.4	240.7	241.2	239.7	238.8	241.8	244.5	244.8
2008	239.5	241.8	242.8	236.7	235.3	233.1	228.4	227.7	226.7	224.7	225.3	226.2	232.4
2009	219.7	219.1	219.4	216.2	215.0	213.5	209.1	208.8	207.6	209.8	212.1	213.7	213.7
2010	208.4	210.1	212.0	212.1	212.2	211.0	207.9	208.3	206.5	207.6	210.8	212.9	210.0
2011	209.1	212.0	213.5	215.4	213.9	212.6	211.1	211.3	211.3	212.3	216.5	218.8	213.2
2012	216.0	217.7	220.7	220.4	219.7	218.7	216.0	216.6	216.7	219.6	224.9	226.6	219.5
2013	223.5	227.1	228.7	229.0	229.4	228.3	227.2	228.1	227.9	231.3	237.4	239.5	229.8
2014	236.2	239.2	241.5	241.7	241.5	241.0	239.7	241.6	241.6	246.2	250.7	254.3	242.9
2015	251.2	253.7	256.4	256.6	256.8	256.3	254.1	255.2	254.5	255.9	259.2	260.3	255.9
Goods Producing													
2005	46.4	47.1	47.4	47.3	48.0	48.2	48.7	49.0	49.6	49.7	50.1	50.6	48.5
2006	50.3	50.9	51.3	51.1	51.6	51.9	51.5	51.5	51.3	50.7	50.2	50.1	51.0
2007	48.6	48.2	48.1	46.7	46.5	46.1	45.0	44.8	43.9	43.0	42.6	42.3	45.5
2008	41.0	40.9	40.4	39.3	39.1	39.0	38.0	37.7	37.4	36.0	35.4	35.2	38.3
2009	32.8	31.9	31.6	30.9	30.8	30.5	29.8	29.6	29.3	29.1	28.9	28.9	30.3
2010	27.8	27.8	27.7	28.0	28.3	28.6	28.6	28.7	28.6	28.4	28.3	28.4	28.3
2011	27.5	27.7	27.9	28.3	28.6	29.0	29.1	29.2	29.4	29.3	29.5	29.6	28.8
2012	29.3	29.4	29.6	29.6	29.9	30.0	29.9	30.2	30.3	30.5	30.8	30.8	30.0
2013	30.4	30.7	30.8	30.8	31.2	31.4	31.5	31.8	31.9	32.2	32.7	32.9	31.5
2014	32.8	33.0	33.2	33.6	34.1	34.3	34.5	34.8	35.3	35.4	35.5	35.8	34.4
2015	35.3	35.6	35.7	36.0	36.3	36.5	36.6	36.8	37.1	37.2	37.4	37.4	36.5
Service-Providing													
2005	221.9	224.6	226.4	225.8	226.1	222.8	220.8	224.0	224.2	225.1	228.0	230.9	225.1
2006	225.5	228.6	232.2	230.9	231.2	228.8	224.8	227.9	228.4	227.1	230.7	232.8	229.1
2007	228.3	230.7	233.0	230.4	229.9	226.4	221.6	225.2	224.7	224.6	228.3	231.3	227.9
2008	227.5	230.1	231.9	226.9	225.7	220.6	216.7	219.2	218.5	217.7	218.7	219.8	222.8
2009	215.5	215.9	216.7	214.6	213.1	208.8	204.9	206.8	206.1	208.7	211.4	212.9	211.3
2010	208.4	210.2	212.3	212.1	213.4	207.9	204.5	206.3	205.0	206.7	210.1	212.1	209.1
2011	209.0	211.9	213.3	214.8	212.5	207.9	206.0	209.2	208.9	210.2	214.4	216.5	211.2
2012	213.9	215.6	218.6	218.1	217.1	212.8	210.1	212.3	213.1	216.3	221.4	223.0	216.0
2013	220.2	223.7	225.3	225.5	225.2	220.9	219.7	222.2	222.5	226.4	232.3	234.1	224.8
2014	230.3	233.4	235.7	235.4	234.6	230.9	229.4	232.7	233.0	238.4	243.1	246.2	235.3
2015	243.4	245.8	248.7	248.3	248.1	244.4	242.1	244.8	244.5	246.8	250.2	251.0	246.5
Mining, Logging, and Construction													
2005	27.5	28.1	28.4	28.4	28.9	29.0	29.4	29.6	30.1	30.2	30.6	31.0	29.3
2006	30.9	31.5	31.9	31.8	32.2	32.4	32.2	32.4	32.4	32.0	31.6	31.4	31.9
2007	30.2	30.0	29.9	28.7	28.5	28.1	27.0	26.9	26.1	25.3	24.9	24.6	27.5
2008	23.4	23.3	23.0	22.2	22.0	22.0	21.4	21.3	21.2	20.2	19.7	19.6	21.6
2009	18.0	17.6	17.4	17.0	17.0	16.8	16.5	16.4	16.1	16.0	15.8	15.7	16.7
2010	14.9	14.9	14.9	15.0	15.2	15.5	15.5	15.6	15.5	15.3	15.2	15.1	15.2
2011	14.5	14.6	14.8	14.9	14.9	15.1	15.1	15.1	15.4	15.3	15.4	15.4	15.0
2012	14.9	15.0	15.1	15.2	15.3	15.5	15.5	15.7	15.7	16.0	16.1	16.1	15.5
2013	15.8	16.0	16.1	16.2	16.4	16.6	16.8	17.1	17.1	17.4	17.6	17.8	16.7
2014	17.7	17.8	18.1	18.4	18.7	18.9	19.1	19.3	19.6	19.7	19.6	19.7	18.9
2015	19.5	19.6	19.7	19.9	20.1	20.2	20.2	20.4	20.6	20.8	20.9	20.8	20.2

Employment by Industry: North Port-Sarasota-Bradenton, 2005–2015—*Continued*

(Numbers in thousands, not seasonally adjusted)

Industry and year	January	February	March	April	May	June	July	August	September	October	November	December	Annual average
Manufacturing													
2005.........	18.9	19.0	19.0	18.9	19.1	19.2	19.3	19.4	19.5	19.5	19.5	19.6	19.2
2006.........	19.4	19.4	19.4	19.3	19.4	19.5	19.3	19.1	18.9	18.7	18.6	18.7	19.1
2007.........	18.4	18.2	18.2	18.0	18.0	18.0	18.0	17.9	17.8	17.7	17.7	17.7	18.0
2008.........	17.6	17.6	17.4	17.1	17.1	17.0	16.6	16.4	16.2	15.8	15.7	15.6	16.7
2009.........	14.8	14.3	14.2	13.9	13.8	13.7	13.3	13.2	13.2	13.1	13.1	13.2	13.7
2010.........	12.9	12.9	12.8	13.0	13.1	13.1	13.1	13.1	13.1	13.1	13.1	13.3	13.1
2011.........	13.0	13.1	13.1	13.4	13.7	13.9	14.0	14.1	14.0	14.0	14.1	14.2	13.7
2012.........	14.4	14.4	14.5	14.4	14.6	14.5	14.4	14.5	14.6	14.5	14.7	14.7	14.5
2013.........	14.6	14.7	14.7	14.6	14.8	14.8	14.7	14.7	14.8	14.8	15.1	15.1	14.8
2014.........	15.1	15.2	15.1	15.2	15.4	15.4	15.4	15.5	15.7	15.7	15.9	16.1	15.5
2015.........	15.8	16.0	16.0	16.1	16.2	16.3	16.4	16.4	16.5	16.4	16.5	16.6	16.3
Trade, Transportation, and Utilities													
2005.........	52.1	52.5	52.8	52.9	52.8	52.4	51.9	51.8	51.8	51.9	53.0	53.8	52.5
2006.........	52.0	52.1	52.6	52.7	52.7	52.5	51.4	51.4	51.4	51.4	52.7	53.8	52.2
2007.........	53.0	52.6	52.9	52.1	52.1	51.7	51.1	50.8	50.5	50.8	52.0	53.4	51.9
2008.........	51.9	51.7	51.9	50.7	50.4	49.7	48.9	48.6	48.5	48.3	48.8	49.5	49.9
2009.........	47.5	47.3	46.9	46.2	45.9	45.4	44.6	44.4	44.4	44.7	45.9	46.6	45.8
2010.........	45.2	45.4	45.6	45.7	45.5	45.2	44.5	44.7	44.5	45.1	46.4	47.4	45.4
2011.........	46.3	46.2	46.4	46.8	46.4	46.0	45.8	46.0	46.2	46.6	48.4	49.1	46.7
2012.........	48.1	48.1	48.5	48.6	48.8	48.5	47.9	47.9	48.3	49.1	50.6	51.5	48.8
2013.........	49.8	50.2	50.1	50.4	50.4	50.4	50.3	50.3	50.3	51.3	53.2	54.0	50.9
2014.........	52.0	52.3	52.5	52.7	52.6	52.5	51.8	52.3	52.3	53.1	55.1	56.2	53.0
2015.........	54.5	54.5	54.8	54.4	54.3	54.2	54.0	54.4	54.2	54.6	55.9	56.4	54.7
Wholesale Trade													
2005.........	7.8	8.0	8.0	8.2	8.3	8.2	8.1	8.2	8.3	8.3	8.4	8.6	8.2
2006.........	8.4	8.5	8.6	8.6	8.7	8.8	8.6	8.6	8.7	8.5	8.4	8.6	8.6
2007.........	8.7	8.7	8.7	8.8	8.9	8.9	8.8	8.8	8.7	8.7	8.7	8.8	8.8
2008.........	8.5	8.5	8.5	8.4	8.3	8.2	8.1	8.0	8.0	8.0	7.8	7.7	8.2
2009.........	7.4	7.4	7.3	7.3	7.2	7.3	7.2	7.2	7.2	7.2	7.1	7.2	7.3
2010.........	7.1	7.1	7.2	7.2	7.2	7.2	7.1	7.1	7.1	7.2	7.2	7.2	7.2
2011.........	7.3	7.3	7.4	7.3	7.2	7.2	7.2	7.3	7.3	7.2	7.3	7.3	7.3
2012.........	7.3	7.3	7.4	7.5	7.5	7.5	7.4	7.3	7.4	7.5	7.5	7.5	7.4
2013.........	7.4	7.5	7.6	7.6	7.6	7.7	7.6	7.6	7.6	7.8	7.8	7.8	7.6
2014.........	7.6	7.7	7.7	7.8	7.9	7.9	7.9	8.0	8.0	8.1	8.2	8.3	7.9
2015.........	8.2	8.2	8.3	8.3	8.3	8.3	8.4	8.5	8.5	8.5	8.6	8.6	8.4
Retail Trade													
2005.........	39.6	39.8	40.0	39.9	39.7	39.4	39.0	38.8	38.7	38.8	39.5	40.0	39.4
2006.........	38.8	38.8	39.2	39.2	39.1	38.9	38.1	38.1	37.9	38.1	39.4	39.9	38.8
2007.........	39.4	39.2	39.4	38.6	38.6	38.2	37.8	37.6	37.4	37.7	38.8	39.8	38.5
2008.........	39.1	38.9	39.0	38.0	37.8	37.3	36.6	36.4	36.3	36.1	36.7	37.2	37.5
2009.........	35.9	35.7	35.5	34.7	34.5	34.0	33.4	33.2	33.2	33.5	34.7	35.1	34.5
2010.........	34.1	34.2	34.3	34.4	34.2	33.9	33.4	33.5	33.3	33.9	35.0	35.7	34.2
2011.........	34.7	34.7	34.8	35.2	35.0	34.6	34.4	34.5	34.7	35.2	36.8	37.3	35.2
2012.........	36.4	36.4	36.7	36.9	37.0	36.7	36.3	36.4	36.7	37.3	38.6	39.2	37.1
2013.........	37.9	38.1	37.9	38.2	38.2	38.2	38.1	38.1	38.1	38.8	40.5	41.2	38.6
2014.........	39.7	39.9	40.1	40.2	40.0	39.8	39.2	39.5	39.5	40.2	41.9	42.6	40.2
2015.........	41.4	41.4	41.5	41.3	41.1	41.1	40.8	41.1	40.9	41.2	42.2	42.5	41.4
Transportation and Utilities													
2005.........	4.7	4.7	4.8	4.8	4.8	4.8	4.8	4.8	4.8	4.8	5.1	5.2	4.8
2006.........	4.8	4.8	4.8	4.9	4.9	4.8	4.7	4.7	4.8	4.8	4.9	5.3	4.9
2007.........	4.9	4.7	4.8	4.7	4.6	4.6	4.5	4.4	4.4	4.4	4.5	4.8	4.6
2008.........	4.3	4.3	4.4	4.3	4.3	4.2	4.2	4.2	4.2	4.2	4.3	4.6	4.3
2009.........	4.2	4.2	4.1	4.2	4.2	4.1	4.0	4.0	4.0	4.0	4.1	4.3	4.1
2010.........	4.0	4.1	4.1	4.1	4.1	4.1	4.0	4.1	4.1	4.0	4.2	4.5	4.1
2011.........	4.3	4.2	4.2	4.3	4.2	4.2	4.2	4.2	4.2	4.2	4.3	4.5	4.3
2012.........	4.4	4.4	4.4	4.2	4.3	4.3	4.2	4.2	4.2	4.3	4.5	4.8	4.4
2013.........	4.5	4.6	4.6	4.6	4.6	4.5	4.6	4.6	4.6	4.7	4.9	5.0	4.7
2014.........	4.7	4.7	4.7	4.7	4.7	4.8	4.7	4.8	4.8	4.8	5.0	5.3	4.8
2015.........	4.9	4.9	5.0	4.8	4.9	4.8	4.8	4.8	4.8	4.9	5.1	5.3	4.9

Employment by Industry: North Port-Sarasota-Bradenton, 2005–2015—*Continued*

(Numbers in thousands, not seasonally adjusted)

Industry and year	January	February	March	April	May	June	July	August	September	October	November	December	Annual average
Information													
2005	4.1	4.2	4.2	4.3	4.3	4.4	4.4	4.4	4.3	4.3	4.4	4.4	4.3
2006	4.2	4.3	4.3	4.3	4.3	4.3	4.4	4.5	4.4	4.6	4.6	4.6	4.4
2007	4.4	4.3	4.3	4.3	4.2	4.2	4.1	4.1	4.1	4.1	4.1	4.0	4.2
2008	4.0	4.0	4.0	3.9	3.9	3.9	3.8	3.8	3.8	3.7	3.6	3.6	3.8
2009	3.6	3.6	3.5	3.5	3.4	3.5	3.4	3.4	3.4	3.4	3.4	3.4	3.5
2010	3.4	3.4	3.3	3.3	3.4	3.4	3.4	3.4	3.4	3.4	3.5	3.5	3.4
2011	3.4	3.5	3.5	3.5	3.4	3.4	3.4	3.4	3.4	3.4	3.4	3.4	3.4
2012	3.5	3.4	3.4	3.4	3.4	3.3	3.3	3.3	3.3	3.3	3.3	3.4	3.4
2013	3.3	3.3	3.4	3.4	3.4	3.4	3.4	3.4	3.3	3.3	3.3	3.3	3.4
2014	3.3	3.3	3.3	3.4	3.4	3.4	3.4	3.4	3.4	3.4	3.4	3.5	3.4
2015	3.4	3.5	3.5	3.5	3.6	3.5	3.6	3.6	3.6	3.6	3.6	3.6	3.6
Financial Activities													
2005	15.4	15.5	15.4	15.6	15.6	15.7	15.7	15.9	15.9	16.2	16.3	16.5	15.8
2006	16.1	16.2	16.3	16.2	16.2	16.3	16.2	16.1	16.1	16.3	16.3	16.5	16.2
2007	16.0	16.0	16.1	16.4	16.4	16.3	16.2	16.2	16.3	16.5	16.4	16.5	16.3
2008	16.3	16.3	16.2	15.8	15.7	15.7	15.4	15.3	15.2	15.1	15.0	15.0	15.6
2009	14.5	14.4	14.3	14.2	14.2	14.2	14.0	13.9	13.9	13.9	13.9	13.8	14.1
2010	13.6	13.6	13.6	13.7	13.6	13.6	13.7	13.7	13.6	13.7	13.8	13.9	13.7
2011	13.8	13.9	14.0	13.9	14.0	14.0	14.1	14.1	14.0	14.1	14.2	14.3	14.0
2012	14.1	14.1	14.2	14.4	14.4	14.4	14.4	14.4	14.3	14.4	14.5	14.5	14.3
2013	14.3	14.3	14.3	14.5	14.4	14.4	14.5	14.5	14.5	14.5	14.6	14.7	14.5
2014	14.3	14.4	14.4	14.4	14.4	14.4	14.5	14.5	14.5	14.7	14.7	14.7	14.5
2015	14.5	14.5	14.7	14.7	14.7	14.7	14.8	14.8	14.7	14.8	14.9	15.0	14.7
Professional and Business Services													
2005	35.7	36.8	37.3	37.1	37.8	38.3	38.5	38.7	38.7	38.3	38.4	39.6	37.9
2006	37.5	38.8	40.3	39.0	39.4	40.3	39.3	39.1	39.4	37.5	37.4	37.0	38.8
2007	35.3	36.1	36.7	35.4	35.9	36.5	34.6	35.3	35.1	33.8	34.6	35.2	35.4
2008	33.2	34.4	35.0	33.5	33.8	33.9	33.5	33.7	33.7	32.9	32.9	32.5	33.6
2009	30.8	30.9	31.3	30.4	30.6	31.2	30.2	30.3	30.3	30.6	30.6	30.8	30.7
2010	29.0	29.2	29.6	29.6	31.0	31.1	29.9	30.1	29.2	29.0	29.7	30.1	29.8
2011	28.5	29.8	29.9	31.0	30.9	31.0	30.6	30.6	30.3	30.3	31.0	31.4	30.4
2012	30.4	30.7	31.4	31.3	31.1	31.4	31.0	31.0	31.0	32.1	33.6	33.7	31.6
2013	33.1	33.9	34.5	34.6	35.2	35.2	35.0	35.3	35.4	36.1	37.1	37.4	35.2
2014	36.2	36.7	37.1	37.2	38.0	38.2	37.9	38.4	38.5	39.7	40.2	41.0	38.3
2015	39.7	40.5	40.9	41.5	42.4	43.1	41.8	41.9	41.8	41.6	41.5	41.7	41.5
Education and Health Services													
2005	39.1	39.4	39.6	39.3	39.5	39.4	39.1	39.3	39.5	39.6	39.9	40.3	39.5
2006	39.5	40.0	40.3	40.2	40.4	40.4	40.0	40.3	40.5	40.3	40.7	41.1	40.3
2007	40.8	41.6	41.5	41.3	41.3	41.3	41.0	41.3	41.6	41.7	42.0	42.2	41.5
2008	42.5	43.0	43.2	42.7	42.7	42.4	41.9	42.1	42.4	42.7	43.1	43.3	42.7
2009	43.3	43.3	43.4	43.2	43.1	42.8	42.3	42.7	42.4	43.3	43.6	43.9	43.1
2010	43.3	43.7	44.0	44.1	43.8	43.5	43.3	43.5	43.5	43.8	44.0	44.2	43.7
2011	44.1	44.5	44.7	44.8	44.7	44.3	44.1	44.3	44.4	44.7	44.9	45.3	44.6
2012	44.7	45.1	45.4	45.2	45.2	44.8	44.3	44.7	45.1	45.4	45.9	45.9	45.1
2013	45.6	46.1	46.1	46.2	46.2	45.6	45.4	45.8	46.0	46.6	47.0	47.2	46.2
2014	47.1	47.7	48.0	48.0	48.1	47.8	47.4	48.0	48.0	48.7	49.0	49.5	48.1
2015	49.3	49.6	49.8	49.9	50.1	49.8	49.6	50.0	50.1	50.3	50.7	50.5	50.0
Leisure and Hospitality													
2005	35.2	35.7	36.5	36.1	35.5	34.9	33.8	33.9	33.6	33.9	34.9	35.2	34.9
2006	35.0	35.7	36.5	36.4	35.9	35.5	34.7	34.6	34.1	34.5	35.5	36.3	35.4
2007	36.1	37.1	38.2	37.8	37.1	36.2	35.0	34.9	34.3	34.7	35.6	36.2	36.1
2008	36.0	36.7	37.2	36.5	35.5	34.6	33.4	33.2	32.6	33.1	33.9	34.6	34.8
2009	34.9	35.4	36.1	35.6	34.8	33.7	32.9	32.6	32.0	32.9	33.8	34.3	34.1
2010	34.3	35.1	36.1	35.7	34.8	34.0	33.0	32.8	32.4	32.9	33.8	34.0	34.1
2011	34.4	35.2	35.9	35.8	34.7	33.8	33.1	32.9	32.7	33.2	34.4	35.0	34.3
2012	35.4	36.3	37.5	37.1	36.2	35.6	34.7	34.6	33.8	34.3	35.6	36.0	35.6
2013	36.3	37.8	38.6	38.1	37.6	36.9	36.3	36.1	35.5	36.1	38.0	38.5	37.2
2014	38.8	39.9	41.0	40.4	39.0	38.6	38.5	38.4	37.8	39.2	40.6	41.4	39.5
2015	42.3	43.1	44.4	44.0	42.8	42.1	41.4	41.4	40.7	41.5	42.7	43.2	42.5

Employment by Industry: North Port-Sarasota-Bradenton, 2005–2015—*Continued*

(Numbers in thousands, not seasonally adjusted)

Industry and year	January	February	March	April	May	June	July	August	September	October	November	December	Annual average
Other Services													
2005	13.4	13.4	13.5	13.2	13.2	13.2	13.0	13.0	13.2	13.1	13.1	13.2	13.2
2006	13.4	13.6	13.8	13.7	13.8	13.9	13.5	13.7	13.9	13.9	14.2	14.2	13.8
2007	13.9	13.9	14.1	13.9	13.8	14.1	13.7	13.8	13.9	14.2	14.5	14.7	14.0
2008	14.6	14.8	14.9	14.3	14.2	13.9	13.5	13.3	13.1	12.9	12.6	12.5	13.7
2009	12.3	12.3	12.3	12.2	12.2	12.2	11.9	11.9	11.9	11.9	12.0	12.0	12.1
2010	11.8	11.9	12.1	12.0	11.8	11.6	11.5	11.4	11.3	11.3	11.3	11.4	11.6
2011	11.1	11.2	11.2	11.3	11.2	11.1	10.9	10.8	10.9	10.7	10.7	10.7	11.0
2012	10.5	10.6	10.7	10.8	10.7	10.7	10.5	10.5	10.6	10.5	10.6	10.8	10.6
2013	10.7	10.8	10.9	11.0	11.0	11.0	10.8	10.9	11.0	11.2	11.5	11.5	11.0
2014	11.7	11.9	12.0	12.0	11.9	11.8	11.7	11.8	11.8	12.0	12.2	12.2	11.9
2015	12.2	12.4	12.6	12.6	12.6	12.4	12.3	12.3	12.3	12.3	12.5	12.5	12.4
Government													
2005	26.9	27.1	27.1	27.3	27.4	24.5	24.4	27.0	27.2	27.8	28.0	27.9	26.9
2006	27.8	27.9	28.1	28.4	28.5	25.6	25.3	28.2	28.6	28.6	29.3	29.3	28.0
2007	28.8	29.1	29.2	29.2	29.1	26.1	25.9	28.8	28.9	28.8	29.1	29.1	28.5
2008	29.0	29.2	29.5	29.5	29.5	26.5	26.3	29.2	29.2	29.0	28.8	28.8	28.7
2009	28.6	28.7	28.9	29.3	28.9	25.8	25.6	27.6	27.8	28.0	28.2	28.1	28.0
2010	27.8	27.9	28.0	28.0	29.5	25.5	25.2	26.7	27.1	27.5	27.6	27.6	27.4
2011	27.4	27.6	27.7	27.7	27.2	24.3	24.0	27.1	27.0	27.2	27.4	27.3	26.8
2012	27.2	27.3	27.5	27.3	27.3	24.1	24.0	25.9	26.7	27.2	27.3	27.2	26.6
2013	27.1	27.3	27.4	27.3	27.0	24.0	24.0	25.9	26.5	27.3	27.6	27.5	26.6
2014	26.9	27.2	27.4	27.3	27.2	24.2	24.2	25.9	26.7	27.6	27.9	27.7	26.7
2015	27.5	27.7	28.0	27.7	27.6	24.6	24.6	26.4	27.1	28.1	28.4	28.1	27.2

Employment by Industry: Greensboro-High Point, NC, 2005–2015

(Numbers in thousands, not seasonally adjusted)

Industry and year	January	February	March	April	May	June	July	August	September	October	November	December	Annual average
Total Nonfarm													
2005	354.8	357.3	360.0	362.2	362.1	361.5	355.1	360.3	361.5	362.9	363.8	364.4	360.5
2006	359.6	361.0	364.2	367.9	370.7	367.8	362.2	367.7	368.1	371.8	373.6	375.0	367.5
2007	365.3	366.5	370.1	370.8	372.3	370.8	363.7	369.4	370.4	373.2	373.5	373.9	370.0
2008	367.1	367.6	369.0	367.5	367.7	364.9	358.0	364.0	365.9	366.0	364.2	359.2	365.1
2009	347.6	346.5	343.4	342.6	341.7	339.8	333.0	337.5	340.1	339.5	339.2	338.2	340.8
2010	331.5	331.7	334.5	336.0	337.8	337.7	333.5	337.3	337.8	341.8	340.0	340.0	336.6
2011	333.0	335.7	337.7	340.7	341.3	338.8	333.8	338.6	341.5	342.6	343.1	342.5	339.1
2012	337.2	339.5	341.2	342.6	343.8	339.1	330.7	340.7	342.7	345.7	347.5	347.9	341.6
2013	341.0	343.1	344.4	346.4	346.8	343.7	336.5	345.6	347.6	349.8	350.3	350.5	345.5
2014	342.6	342.6	345.7	349.2	350.6	346.3	339.9	347.6	350.1	353.6	354.6	354.8	348.1
2015	348.7	350.4	351.2	356.4	357.5	354.7	347.5	355.0	356.9	359.9	362.4	360.6	355.1
Total Private													
2005	311.3	313.4	315.8	317.8	317.5	318.7	317.9	318.8	317.8	317.5	318.9	319.3	317.1
2006	315.4	316.4	319.0	322.3	324.9	324.5	324.2	325.5	323.7	326.2	327.5	328.5	323.2
2007	320.2	321.2	324.3	324.8	326.1	327.0	325.0	326.5	325.3	326.7	326.6	327.4	325.1
2008	320.6	320.7	321.7	320.0	319.8	319.6	318.0	319.9	318.4	318.2	316.2	311.7	318.7
2009	300.4	298.9	295.5	294.2	293.5	292.9	292.1	292.7	291.6	291.9	291.5	290.9	293.8
2010	284.3	284.4	286.7	287.6	288.2	290.2	291.9	292.9	291.1	294.1	292.7	293.0	289.8
2011	286.6	289.0	290.7	293.7	294.4	295.5	295.1	296.1	295.8	295.9	296.1	295.7	293.7
2012	291.7	293.5	294.8	296.0	296.8	297.1	297.1	298.1	297.4	299.0	300.5	301.4	297.0
2013	295.0	296.8	297.6	299.9	300.2	301.0	300.9	303.0	302.4	303.9	304.0	304.4	300.8
2014	297.1	297.0	299.7	302.8	303.7	303.4	304.0	305.4	305.3	308.1	308.7	309.3	303.7
2015	303.8	305.3	306.1	310.9	311.8	312.1	311.8	313.5	312.7	314.9	317.0	315.7	311.3
Goods Producing													
2005	84.7	84.8	84.9	85.4	85.5	85.8	84.9	84.7	84.2	83.4	83.3	83.4	84.6
2006	82.1	82.3	82.6	83.2	83.3	83.1	82.4	82.9	82.5	82.6	82.5	82.7	82.7
2007	81.7	81.4	81.8	81.9	81.6	81.9	81.2	81.2	80.8	81.1	80.9	81.3	81.4
2008	79.8	79.6	79.6	78.4	78.5	78.2	77.6	77.5	77.2	76.2	75.5	74.0	77.7
2009	70.6	69.4	67.7	67.2	66.2	65.9	65.4	65.3	65.1	64.4	64.0	64.1	66.3
2010	62.4	62.3	62.8	63.2	63.2	63.8	64.0	64.1	63.9	63.8	63.4	63.6	63.4
2011	62.6	63.1	63.5	64.4	64.7	65.2	65.3	65.6	65.3	64.9	64.6	64.6	64.5
2012	64.6	64.9	64.9	64.5	64.7	64.9	64.9	64.8	65.1	65.1	65.2	65.7	64.9
2013	64.7	64.4	64.8	65.3	65.5	66.2	66.2	66.2	66.4	66.6	66.4	66.5	65.8
2014	65.6	65.6	66.1	66.2	66.5	67.0	66.8	66.8	67.0	66.9	67.0	67.4	66.6
2015	66.7	67.3	67.7	68.3	68.5	68.8	69.0	69.3	69.1	69.1	69.0	69.1	68.5
Service-Providing													
2005	270.1	272.5	275.1	276.8	276.6	275.7	270.2	275.6	277.3	279.5	280.5	281.0	275.9
2006	277.5	278.7	281.6	284.7	287.4	284.7	279.8	284.8	285.6	289.2	291.1	292.3	284.8
2007	283.6	285.1	288.3	288.9	290.7	288.9	282.5	288.2	289.6	292.1	292.6	292.6	288.6
2008	287.3	288.0	289.4	289.1	289.2	286.7	280.4	286.5	288.7	289.8	288.7	285.2	287.4
2009	277.0	277.1	275.7	275.4	275.5	273.9	267.6	272.2	275.0	275.1	275.2	274.1	274.5
2010	269.1	269.4	271.7	272.8	274.6	273.9	269.5	273.2	273.9	278.0	276.6	276.4	273.3
2011	270.4	272.6	274.2	276.3	276.6	273.6	268.5	273.0	276.2	277.7	278.5	277.9	274.6
2012	272.6	274.6	276.3	278.1	279.1	274.2	265.8	275.9	277.6	280.6	282.3	282.2	276.6
2013	276.3	278.7	279.6	281.1	281.3	277.5	270.3	279.4	281.2	283.2	283.9	284.0	279.7
2014	277.0	277.0	279.6	283.0	284.1	279.3	273.1	280.8	283.1	286.7	287.6	287.4	281.6
2015	282.0	283.1	283.5	288.1	289.0	285.9	278.5	285.7	287.8	290.8	293.4	291.5	286.6
Mining, Logging, and Construction													
2005	18.0	17.9	18.0	18.5	18.7	18.9	18.8	18.8	18.8	18.5	18.5	18.4	18.5
2006	17.9	17.9	18.2	18.5	18.6	18.8	18.9	19.0	18.9	18.8	18.8	18.8	18.6
2007	18.3	18.2	18.6	18.6	18.6	18.8	18.8	18.7	18.5	18.6	18.5	18.5	18.6
2008	17.7	17.7	17.9	17.5	17.5	17.5	17.5	17.3	17.3	17.1	16.9	16.3	17.4
2009	15.1	14.8	14.5	14.4	14.1	14.1	14.0	13.9	13.7	13.3	13.1	13.1	14.0
2010	12.1	12.0	12.3	12.6	12.5	12.7	12.6	12.6	12.5	12.7	12.6	12.5	12.5
2011	11.7	12.1	12.4	12.8	12.9	13.1	13.1	13.1	13.1	12.9	12.7	12.7	12.7
2012	12.5	12.4	12.5	12.2	12.2	12.3	12.4	12.4	12.3	12.3	12.2	12.2	12.3
2013	11.9	11.9	12.2	12.4	12.5	12.7	12.8	13.0	13.0	13.0	13.0	12.9	12.6
2014	12.6	12.6	12.9	12.9	13.1	13.3	13.3	13.3	13.4	13.4	13.4	13.4	13.1
2015	12.9	13.1	13.3	13.8	13.9	14.0	14.1	14.2	14.1	14.3	14.2	14.3	13.9

Employment by Industry: Greensboro-High Point, NC, 2005–2015—*Continued*

(Numbers in thousands, not seasonally adjusted)

Industry and year	January	February	March	April	May	June	July	August	September	October	November	December	Annual average
Manufacturing													
2005	66.7	66.9	66.9	66.9	66.8	66.9	66.1	65.9	65.4	64.9	64.8	65.0	66.1
2006	64.2	64.4	64.4	64.7	64.7	64.3	63.5	63.9	63.6	63.8	63.7	63.9	64.1
2007	63.4	63.2	63.2	63.3	63.0	63.1	62.4	62.5	62.3	62.5	62.4	62.8	62.8
2008	62.1	61.9	61.7	60.9	61.0	60.7	60.1	60.2	59.9	59.1	58.6	57.7	60.3
2009	55.5	54.6	53.2	52.8	52.1	51.8	51.4	51.4	51.4	51.1	50.9	51.0	52.3
2010	50.3	50.3	50.5	50.6	50.7	51.1	51.4	51.5	51.4	51.1	50.8	51.1	50.9
2011	50.9	51.0	51.1	51.6	51.8	52.1	52.2	52.5	52.2	52.0	51.9	51.9	51.8
2012	52.1	52.5	52.4	52.3	52.5	52.6	52.5	52.4	52.8	52.8	53.0	53.5	52.6
2013	52.8	52.5	52.6	52.9	53.0	53.5	53.4	53.2	53.4	53.6	53.4	53.6	53.2
2014	53.0	53.0	53.2	53.3	53.4	53.7	53.5	53.5	53.6	53.5	53.6	54.0	53.4
2015	53.8	54.2	54.4	54.5	54.6	54.8	54.9	55.1	55.0	54.8	54.8	54.8	54.6
Trade, Transportation, and Utilities													
2005	72.1	72.2	72.6	73.0	73.1	73.2	73.5	73.7	73.3	74.8	76.1	76.9	73.7
2006	75.4	75.0	75.1	75.8	76.2	75.4	75.6	75.7	75.7	76.3	78.1	78.9	76.1
2007	76.1	75.7	76.5	76.3	76.8	76.6	76.5	76.9	76.7	77.0	78.0	78.9	76.8
2008	75.3	74.8	74.8	74.6	74.8	74.7	73.8	73.8	73.7	74.0	74.2	74.4	74.4
2009	70.9	70.2	70.0	69.1	69.2	68.9	68.5	68.6	68.6	68.5	69.3	69.6	69.3
2010	67.4	67.2	67.5	67.9	68.1	68.1	68.1	68.2	68.1	68.8	69.5	70.3	68.3
2011	67.9	68.1	68.3	68.7	68.9	68.8	68.8	68.8	68.7	69.0	69.9	70.5	68.9
2012	69.0	68.9	69.0	69.8	70.2	69.8	69.8	69.8	69.9	70.3	71.7	72.2	70.0
2013	69.9	70.0	70.1	70.7	70.8	70.6	70.8	71.0	70.9	72.1	72.8	73.6	71.1
2014	70.9	70.5	71.2	72.1	72.3	72.2	71.9	72.2	71.9	72.4	73.7	74.3	72.1
2015	71.8	71.7	71.9	72.7	72.6	72.7	72.6	72.9	73.0	73.6	75.0	75.6	73.0
Wholesale Trade													
2005	18.5	18.5	18.5	18.5	18.6	18.5	18.8	18.9	18.8	18.8	18.8	18.8	18.7
2006	18.9	19.1	19.1	19.4	19.6	19.5	19.5	19.6	19.7	19.8	19.9	20.0	19.5
2007	20.1	20.1	20.3	20.3	20.4	20.5	20.6	20.6	20.6	20.6	20.6	20.7	20.5
2008	20.4	20.4	20.4	20.2	20.3	20.2	20.0	19.9	19.9	19.8	19.6	19.3	20.0
2009	18.8	18.7	18.5	18.5	18.5	18.3	18.2	18.4	18.2	18.2	18.2	18.2	18.4
2010	18.0	18.0	18.2	18.2	18.2	18.1	18.1	18.2	18.0	18.0	18.0	18.0	18.1
2011	17.8	18.0	18.0	18.0	18.0	17.9	17.9	17.8	17.7	17.5	17.4	17.4	17.8
2012	17.5	17.6	17.8	18.0	18.0	18.0	18.0	18.0	18.1	18.1	18.2	18.4	18.0
2013	18.2	18.4	18.5	18.6	18.6	18.6	18.6	18.7	18.7	18.7	18.7	18.7	18.6
2014	18.5	18.5	18.7	19.1	19.2	19.0	19.0	19.0	18.9	18.7	18.7	18.8	18.8
2015	18.6	18.7	18.7	18.9	19.0	18.9	19.1	19.2	19.0	19.0	19.1	19.1	18.9
Retail Trade													
2005	36.6	36.7	37.0	37.3	37.2	37.3	37.4	37.3	36.9	38.4	39.5	40.4	37.7
2006	39.4	38.9	38.9	39.2	39.4	38.8	38.9	39.1	38.9	39.5	41.2	41.8	39.5
2007	39.6	39.3	39.7	39.6	39.9	39.7	39.5	39.6	39.4	39.7	40.6	40.9	39.8
2008	38.7	38.2	38.1	38.1	38.0	37.9	37.7	37.7	37.5	37.9	38.2	38.5	38.0
2009	36.5	36.1	36.2	35.6	35.8	35.7	35.6	35.5	35.6	35.6	36.2	36.4	35.9
2010	34.8	34.6	34.7	34.9	35.0	34.9	34.8	34.8	34.7	35.1	35.9	36.3	35.0
2011	34.6	34.5	34.7	34.9	35.1	35.1	35.1	35.2	35.0	35.4	36.4	36.8	35.2
2012	35.6	35.4	35.2	35.7	36.1	35.8	35.9	35.8	35.8	36.0	37.4	37.5	36.0
2013	35.8	35.8	35.9	36.2	36.4	36.2	36.4	36.3	36.2	37.1	38.0	38.5	36.6
2014	36.5	36.2	36.5	36.8	36.9	36.9	36.7	36.9	36.6	37.1	38.2	38.3	37.0
2015	36.7	36.5	36.6	36.9	37.0	37.2	37.0	37.2	37.2	37.8	39.0	39.4	37.4
Transportation and Utilities													
2005	17.0	17.0	17.1	17.2	17.3	17.4	17.3	17.5	17.6	17.6	17.8	17.7	17.4
2006	17.1	17.0	17.1	17.2	17.2	17.1	17.2	17.0	17.1	17.0	17.0	17.1	17.1
2007	16.4	16.3	16.5	16.4	16.5	16.4	16.4	16.7	16.7	16.7	16.8	17.3	16.6
2008	16.2	16.2	16.3	16.3	16.5	16.6	16.1	16.2	16.3	16.3	16.4	16.6	16.3
2009	15.6	15.4	15.3	15.0	14.9	14.9	14.7	14.7	14.8	14.7	14.9	15.0	15.0
2010	14.6	14.6	14.6	14.8	14.9	15.1	15.2	15.2	15.4	15.7	15.6	16.0	15.1
2011	15.5	15.6	15.6	15.8	15.8	15.8	15.8	15.8	16.0	16.1	16.1	16.3	15.9
2012	15.9	15.9	16.0	16.1	16.1	16.0	15.9	16.0	16.0	16.2	16.1	16.3	16.0
2013	15.9	15.8	15.7	15.9	15.8	15.8	15.8	16.0	16.0	16.3	16.1	16.4	16.0
2014	15.9	15.8	16.0	16.2	16.2	16.3	16.2	16.3	16.4	16.6	16.8	17.2	16.3
2015	16.5	16.5	16.6	16.9	16.6	16.6	16.5	16.5	16.8	16.8	16.9	17.1	16.7

Employment by Industry: Greensboro-High Point, NC, 2005–2015—*Continued*

(Numbers in thousands, not seasonally adjusted)

Industry and year	January	February	March	April	May	June	July	August	September	October	November	December	Annual average
Information													
2005	6.5	6.4	6.5	6.6	6.6	6.6	6.6	6.6	6.6	6.5	6.5	6.6	6.6
2006	6.6	6.5	6.5	6.3	6.4	6.3	6.3	6.3	6.3	6.4	6.4	6.5	6.4
2007	6.3	6.3	6.2	6.3	6.2	6.2	6.2	6.2	6.2	6.2	6.3	6.3	6.2
2008	6.2	6.1	6.2	6.2	6.2	6.3	6.2	6.1	6.0	6.0	6.2	6.2	6.2
2009	5.9	5.8	5.8	5.8	5.8	5.7	5.6	5.6	5.5	5.5	5.5	5.6	5.7
2010	5.6	5.5	5.5	5.5	5.5	5.5	5.6	5.6	5.5	5.5	5.5	5.6	5.5
2011	5.5	5.5	5.5	5.5	5.5	5.5	5.5	5.5	5.5	5.5	5.4	5.4	5.5
2012	5.4	5.5	5.4	5.4	5.4	5.4	5.4	5.3	5.3	5.3	5.3	5.3	5.4
2013	5.2	5.2	5.1	5.0	5.0	5.0	5.0	4.9	4.9	4.9	4.9	5.0	5.0
2014	4.9	4.9	4.9	4.9	4.9	5.0	5.0	5.0	5.0	5.1	5.1	5.1	5.0
2015	5.1	5.1	5.1	5.0	5.1	5.1	5.1	5.0	4.9	4.9	5.0	5.0	5.0
Financial Activities													
2005	20.9	21.0	21.1	21.2	21.2	21.3	21.5	21.5	21.5	21.2	21.3	21.3	21.3
2006	21.3	21.4	21.6	21.6	21.8	21.9	22.1	22.2	22.2	22.3	22.3	22.4	21.9
2007	22.1	22.3	22.3	22.3	22.2	22.4	22.2	22.1	22.2	22.2	22.2	22.0	22.2
2008	21.7	21.8	21.8	21.9	22.0	22.1	22.0	22.0	21.9	21.9	22.0	21.9	21.9
2009	21.5	21.4	21.2	21.2	21.2	21.2	21.0	21.0	20.9	20.9	20.8	20.6	21.1
2010	20.3	20.2	20.2	20.0	19.8	19.8	19.9	19.9	19.9	19.9	19.8	19.9	20.0
2011	19.6	19.6	19.7	19.7	19.6	19.6	19.6	19.5	19.4	19.0	18.9	18.8	19.4
2012	18.3	18.4	18.4	18.4	18.3	18.4	18.4	18.5	18.5	18.7	18.7	18.8	18.5
2013	18.3	18.4	18.4	18.4	18.4	18.5	18.3	18.4	18.1	18.1	18.2	18.2	18.3
2014	18.2	18.1	18.1	17.8	17.8	17.7	17.8	17.7	17.6	17.6	17.6	17.6	17.8
2015	17.6	17.5	17.5	17.7	17.8	18.0	18.1	18.0	18.0	17.9	17.9	17.9	17.8
Professional and Business Services													
2005	43.7	44.7	45.1	44.8	43.9	44.0	44.1	44.5	44.9	44.2	44.3	44.1	44.4
2006	43.1	43.4	44.5	46.3	47.1	46.8	47.0	47.4	46.7	47.9	47.6	47.2	46.3
2007	44.2	45.1	45.9	45.9	46.1	46.3	45.9	47.1	47.4	47.6	47.0	46.7	46.3
2008	46.1	46.2	46.6	46.5	45.7	45.4	46.0	47.5	47.5	48.0	46.0	43.8	46.3
2009	41.7	41.5	40.5	40.1	39.6	40.1	40.6	41.5	42.0	43.4	42.6	42.3	41.3
2010	42.0	42.3	42.9	42.9	42.8	43.6	44.9	45.4	45.3	46.5	45.5	45.1	44.1
2011	44.2	45.1	45.7	46.1	45.9	46.1	46.4	46.7	47.3	47.6	47.6	47.1	46.3
2012	46.6	47.0	47.7	47.5	47.1	47.1	46.6	47.2	46.8	47.4	47.6	47.6	47.2
2013	46.2	47.0	46.9	47.4	47.0	47.0	47.0	48.1	48.5	49.0	48.6	48.3	47.6
2014	47.0	47.0	47.7	48.4	48.0	47.7	48.7	49.4	50.0	51.7	51.1	51.0	49.0
2015	49.5	49.7	49.4	50.8	50.5	50.4	50.7	51.6	51.5	53.5	54.7	53.2	51.3
Education and Health Services													
2005	42.9	43.4	43.8	44.0	44.0	43.9	44.1	44.4	44.7	44.9	45.1	45.0	44.2
2006	45.2	45.5	45.6	45.5	45.4	45.4	45.3	45.6	45.6	45.9	46.0	46.1	45.6
2007	46.1	46.5	46.6	46.3	46.5	46.2	45.8	45.9	45.6	46.4	46.2	46.2	46.2
2008	45.8	46.0	46.0	46.5	46.4	46.4	46.0	46.5	46.5	47.4	47.9	47.5	46.6
2009	47.2	47.6	47.0	47.3	47.2	46.8	46.6	46.7	46.1	47.0	47.2	47.0	47.0
2010	46.4	46.3	46.5	46.5	46.5	46.3	46.3	46.5	45.9	47.1	47.0	46.9	46.5
2011	46.1	46.4	46.2	46.7	46.6	46.4	45.9	46.2	46.7	47.4	47.5	47.3	46.6
2012	46.5	47.1	47.0	47.2	47.1	46.6	47.0	47.4	48.0	48.2	48.5	48.4	47.4
2013	47.9	48.5	48.5	48.5	48.4	47.8	47.7	48.2	48.7	48.5	48.5	48.4	48.3
2014	47.3	47.7	47.6	48.0	48.0	47.4	47.3	47.5	48.2	48.6	48.8	48.6	47.9
2015	48.9	49.4	49.3	50.0	49.9	49.5	49.0	49.3	49.9	50.7	50.8	50.9	49.8
Leisure and Hospitality													
2005	27.7	27.9	28.8	29.7	30.2	30.8	30.2	30.5	29.8	29.6	29.4	29.0	29.5
2006	28.9	29.4	30.0	30.8	31.6	32.6	32.8	32.9	32.3	32.0	31.9	31.9	31.4
2007	31.0	31.2	32.1	32.6	33.4	34.0	33.6	33.7	33.1	32.6	32.6	32.5	32.7
2008	32.3	32.7	33.2	32.5	33.0	33.2	32.9	33.1	32.4	31.5	31.2	30.7	32.4
2009	29.6	29.9	30.2	30.5	31.4	31.5	31.6	31.3	30.8	29.7	29.7	29.3	30.5
2010	28.1	28.4	29.1	29.5	30.2	30.9	30.9	31.1	30.6	30.5	30.1	29.8	29.9
2011	28.8	29.3	30.0	30.7	31.3	31.8	31.5	31.8	31.0	30.6	30.3	30.0	30.6
2012	29.4	29.8	30.5	31.1	31.7	32.3	32.5	32.7	31.6	31.7	31.2	31.0	31.3
2013	30.5	30.9	31.4	32.3	32.7	33.2	33.2	33.6	32.5	32.3	32.1	32.0	32.2
2014	30.9	30.9	31.7	32.8	33.5	33.5	33.6	34.0	33.1	33.2	32.9	32.8	32.7
2015	31.8	32.2	32.8	33.9	34.8	34.9	34.3	34.7	33.8	32.6	32.0	31.4	33.3

Employment by Industry: Greensboro-High Point, NC, 2005–2015—*Continued*

(Numbers in thousands, not seasonally adjusted)

Industry and year	January	February	March	April	May	June	July	August	September	October	November	December	Annual average
Other Services													
2005	12.8	13.0	13.0	13.1	13.0	13.1	13.0	12.9	12.8	12.9	12.9	13.0	13.0
2006	12.8	12.9	13.1	12.8	13.1	13.0	12.7	12.5	12.4	12.8	12.7	12.8	12.8
2007	12.7	12.7	12.9	13.2	13.3	13.4	13.6	13.4	13.3	13.6	13.4	13.5	13.3
2008	13.4	13.5	13.5	13.4	13.2	13.3	13.5	13.4	13.2	13.2	13.2	13.2	13.3
2009	13.0	13.1	13.1	13.0	12.9	12.8	12.8	12.7	12.6	12.5	12.4	12.4	12.8
2010	12.1	12.2	12.2	12.1	12.1	12.2	12.2	12.1	11.9	12.0	11.9	11.8	12.1
2011	11.9	11.9	11.8	11.9	11.9	12.1	12.1	12.0	11.9	11.9	11.9	12.0	11.9
2012	11.9	11.9	11.9	12.1	12.3	12.6	12.5	12.4	12.2	12.3	12.3	12.4	12.2
2013	12.3	12.4	12.4	12.3	12.4	12.7	12.7	12.6	12.4	12.4	12.5	12.4	12.5
2014	12.3	12.3	12.4	12.6	12.7	12.9	12.9	12.8	12.5	12.6	12.5	12.5	12.6
2015	12.4	12.4	12.4	12.5	12.6	12.7	13.0	12.7	12.5	12.6	12.6	12.6	12.6
Government													
2005	43.5	43.9	44.2	44.4	44.6	42.8	37.2	41.5	43.7	45.4	44.9	45.1	43.4
2006	44.2	44.6	45.2	45.6	45.8	43.3	38.0	42.2	44.4	45.6	46.1	46.5	44.3
2007	45.1	45.3	45.8	46.0	46.2	43.8	38.7	42.9	45.1	46.5	46.9	46.5	44.9
2008	46.5	46.9	47.3	47.5	47.9	45.3	40.0	44.1	47.5	47.8	48.0	47.5	46.4
2009	47.2	47.6	47.9	48.4	48.2	46.9	40.9	44.8	48.5	47.6	47.7	47.3	46.9
2010	47.2	47.3	47.8	48.4	49.6	47.5	41.6	44.4	46.7	47.7	47.3	47.0	46.9
2011	46.4	46.7	47.0	47.0	46.9	43.3	38.7	42.5	45.7	46.7	47.0	46.8	45.4
2012	45.5	46.0	46.4	46.6	47.0	42.0	33.6	42.6	45.3	46.7	47.0	46.5	44.6
2013	46.0	46.3	46.8	46.5	46.6	42.7	35.6	42.6	45.2	45.9	46.3	46.1	44.7
2014	45.5	45.6	46.0	46.4	46.9	42.9	35.9	42.2	44.8	45.5	45.9	45.5	44.4
2015	44.9	45.1	45.1	45.5	45.7	42.6	35.7	41.5	44.2	45.0	45.4	44.9	43.8

Employment by Industry: Charleston-North Charleston, SC, 2005–2015

(Numbers in thousands, not seasonally adjusted)

Industry and year	January	February	March	April	May	June	July	August	September	October	November	December	Annual average
Total Nonfarm													
2005	274.0	276.9	278.6	282.5	284.9	282.7	283.2	285.0	284.2	284.8	286.3	284.0	282.3
2006	280.5	283.7	284.3	288.5	290.9	288.0	288.1	290.5	291.7	292.2	294.3	295.6	289.0
2007	292.1	294.6	298.3	301.2	303.5	304.4	302.0	302.5	303.3	304.7	304.5	304.5	301.3
2008	299.5	300.6	302.4	304.8	306.7	306.4	301.7	301.5	301.1	300.2	300.1	297.8	301.9
2009	287.4	286.1	287.5	288.6	289.3	289.4	284.5	284.4	284.1	284.4	284.6	283.5	286.2
2010	278.5	279.8	283.4	286.6	290.5	290.7	288.2	288.1	287.7	290.7	292.3	292.3	287.4
2011	287.9	289.5	292.2	296.5	298.7	298.5	296.7	296.3	296.9	298.0	299.3	299.5	295.8
2012	295.6	298.9	302.1	306.2	307.6	308.1	305.2	306.6	306.4	307.5	311.2	309.8	305.4
2013	303.1	305.5	307.9	311.2	313.0	314.3	313.2	314.0	313.8	315.4	317.0	317.3	312.1
2014	310.9	313.7	316.6	322.2	325.1	325.3	322.5	324.0	324.0	326.2	328.3	328.4	322.3
2015	322.5	325.5	328.9	332.1	335.3	335.4	335.2	336.3	335.2	336.2	338.9	338.0	333.3
Total Private													
2005	218.8	220.7	222.1	225.9	228.1	226.9	229.1	229.3	227.7	228.3	229.6	227.2	226.1
2006	224.7	227.3	227.7	231.7	233.9	233.1	234.7	235.2	234.9	234.9	236.8	238.0	232.7
2007	234.8	236.9	240.5	243.0	245.3	246.4	245.6	246.0	244.6	245.5	245.0	245.0	243.2
2008	240.4	241.1	242.5	244.4	246.0	246.1	243.0	242.4	240.4	239.2	238.7	236.5	241.7
2009	227.4	225.8	227.1	228.3	229.2	229.7	226.5	226.2	224.0	223.8	223.9	222.9	226.2
2010	218.2	219.1	222.3	225.0	227.3	229.8	228.3	228.3	226.8	229.0	230.3	230.5	226.2
2011	226.8	228.1	230.7	234.5	236.7	237.4	236.8	237.0	235.6	236.7	237.8	237.9	234.7
2012	234.5	237.3	240.1	243.8	245.2	246.2	244.4	245.3	243.5	244.4	245.9	246.3	243.1
2013	240.8	242.7	244.9	247.7	249.9	251.7	251.8	252.7	250.8	253.0	254.2	254.7	249.6
2014	249.3	251.3	254.1	258.7	261.6	263.3	262.0	262.3	260.7	262.4	264.1	264.4	259.5
2015	259.7	261.7	264.8	267.9	271.2	272.4	272.7	273.4	270.7	271.1	273.4	272.7	269.3
Goods Producing													
2005	41.5	41.6	41.3	41.2	41.5	41.3	41.9	42.0	41.9	41.8	42.1	41.5	41.6
2006	41.6	41.7	41.6	42.5	42.9	42.7	43.2	43.2	43.1	43.6	43.5	43.5	42.8
2007	43.3	43.6	43.9	44.3	44.5	44.7	44.7	44.6	44.4	44.8	44.6	44.5	44.3
2008	43.7	43.2	43.1	42.5	42.2	42.0	41.7	41.4	41.0	40.8	40.2	39.6	41.8
2009	37.7	37.0	37.2	36.7	36.3	36.6	35.7	36.1	36.1	35.4	35.4	35.1	36.3
2010	34.5	34.5	34.9	34.8	35.0	35.2	35.1	35.1	35.0	34.7	34.9	35.2	34.9
2011	35.0	35.1	35.4	35.7	36.2	36.6	36.6	36.6	36.6	36.5	36.7	36.7	36.1
2012	36.4	36.5	36.9	37.1	37.3	37.5	37.5	37.5	37.4	37.4	37.6	37.8	37.2
2013	37.7	38.0	38.1	38.3	38.8	39.1	39.5	39.5	39.6	39.5	39.7	40.1	39.0
2014	39.8	39.9	40.1	40.4	40.9	41.5	41.4	41.4	41.3	41.7	41.9	42.1	41.0
2015	42.1	42.7	42.5	42.3	42.8	43.4	43.5	43.5	43.4	43.2	43.4	43.9	43.1
Service-Providing													
2005	232.5	235.3	237.3	241.3	243.4	241.4	241.3	243.0	242.3	243.0	244.2	242.5	240.6
2006	238.9	242.0	242.7	246.0	248.0	245.3	244.9	247.3	248.6	248.6	250.8	252.1	246.3
2007	248.8	251.0	254.4	256.9	259.0	259.7	257.3	257.9	258.9	259.9	259.9	260.0	257.0
2008	255.8	257.4	259.3	262.3	264.5	264.4	260.0	260.1	260.1	259.4	259.9	258.2	260.1
2009	249.7	249.1	250.3	251.9	253.0	252.8	248.8	248.3	248.0	249.0	249.2	248.4	249.9
2010	244.0	245.3	248.5	251.8	255.5	255.5	253.1	253.0	252.7	256.0	257.4	257.1	252.5
2011	252.9	254.4	256.8	260.8	262.5	261.9	260.1	259.7	260.3	261.5	262.6	262.8	259.7
2012	259.2	262.4	265.2	269.1	270.3	270.6	267.7	269.1	269.0	270.1	273.6	272.0	268.2
2013	265.4	267.5	269.8	272.9	274.2	275.2	273.7	274.5	274.2	275.9	277.3	277.2	273.2
2014	271.1	273.8	276.5	281.8	284.2	283.8	281.1	282.6	282.7	284.5	286.4	286.3	281.2
2015	280.4	282.8	286.4	289.8	292.5	292.0	291.7	292.8	291.8	293.0	295.5	294.1	290.2
Mining, Logging, and Construction													
2005	20.0	20.2	19.9	20.0	20.2	20.1	20.7	20.7	20.5	20.7	20.9	20.3	20.4
2006	20.5	20.6	20.8	21.3	21.6	21.5	22.0	22.0	21.8	22.1	21.9	21.7	21.5
2007	21.6	21.8	21.8	21.9	22.0	22.1	21.9	22.2	21.9	21.7	21.5	21.2	21.8
2008	20.7	20.4	20.2	19.7	19.4	19.3	18.8	18.6	18.2	18.0	17.7	17.4	19.0
2009	16.2	15.9	16.1	15.6	15.5	15.6	15.4	15.2	15.0	14.7	14.6	14.4	15.4
2010	13.9	13.9	14.2	14.3	14.4	14.5	14.4	14.3	14.2	14.0	14.0	14.0	14.2
2011	13.8	13.8	13.9	13.9	14.2	14.3	14.1	13.9	13.8	13.6	13.6	13.4	13.9
2012	13.0	13.1	13.3	13.5	13.7	13.9	14.0	14.0	13.9	13.7	13.8	13.9	13.7
2013	14.1	14.0	14.2	14.5	14.9	15.2	15.4	15.5	15.5	15.4	15.6	15.8	15.0
2014	15.5	15.6	15.7	15.9	16.3	16.7	16.5	16.5	16.4	16.7	16.8	16.9	16.3
2015	16.7	17.0	17.2	17.1	17.4	17.7	17.7	17.6	17.5	17.5	17.6	17.7	17.4

Employment by Industry: Charleston-North Charleston, SC, 2005–2015—*Continued*

(Numbers in thousands, not seasonally adjusted)

Industry and year	January	February	March	April	May	June	July	August	September	October	November	December	Annual average
Manufacturing													
2005	21.5	21.4	21.4	21.2	21.3	21.2	21.2	21.3	21.4	21.1	21.2	21.2	21.3
2006	21.1	21.1	20.8	21.2	21.3	21.2	21.2	21.2	21.3	21.5	21.6	21.8	21.3
2007	21.7	21.8	22.1	22.4	22.5	22.6	22.8	22.4	22.5	23.1	23.1	23.3	22.5
2008	23.0	22.8	22.9	22.8	22.8	22.7	22.9	22.8	22.8	22.8	22.5	22.2	22.8
2009	21.5	21.1	21.1	21.1	20.8	21.0	20.3	20.9	21.1	20.7	20.8	20.7	20.9
2010	20.6	20.6	20.7	20.5	20.6	20.7	20.7	20.8	20.8	20.7	20.9	21.2	20.7
2011	21.2	21.3	21.5	21.8	22.0	22.3	22.5	22.7	22.8	22.9	23.1	23.3	22.3
2012	23.4	23.4	23.6	23.6	23.6	23.6	23.5	23.5	23.5	23.7	23.8	23.9	23.6
2013	23.6	24.0	23.9	23.8	23.9	23.9	24.1	24.0	24.1	24.1	24.1	24.3	24.0
2014	24.3	24.3	24.4	24.5	24.6	24.8	24.9	24.9	24.9	25.0	25.1	25.2	24.7
2015	25.4	25.7	25.3	25.2	25.4	25.7	25.8	25.9	25.9	25.7	25.8	26.2	25.7
Trade, Transportation, and Utilities													
2005	55.5	55.4	55.6	55.8	56.7	56.3	57.6	57.7	57.4	58.0	58.6	59.0	57.0
2006	56.7	57.4	57.7	57.0	57.8	57.6	58.0	58.0	57.8	57.7	59.7	60.2	58.0
2007	57.4	57.8	58.6	58.7	59.2	59.4	59.2	59.4	59.1	59.1	59.8	60.2	59.0
2008	57.8	57.4	57.5	57.7	57.9	57.9	57.4	57.3	56.6	57.5	58.0	57.8	57.6
2009	54.6	53.7	53.6	53.7	53.7	53.6	53.2	52.7	52.2	52.2	52.9	53.4	53.3
2010	51.6	51.6	52.4	52.5	53.1	53.8	53.8	53.7	53.4	54.3	55.3	55.9	53.5
2011	54.0	53.9	54.1	54.5	54.8	55.0	55.4	55.3	55.0	55.7	56.3	56.7	55.1
2012	55.3	55.5	56.0	56.5	56.9	57.1	57.1	57.1	56.7	57.4	58.9	59.3	57.0
2013	56.6	56.6	56.9	57.6	58.0	58.5	58.7	58.8	58.6	59.6	60.2	61.0	58.4
2014	58.6	58.5	58.6	59.4	59.9	60.8	60.2	60.2	59.8	60.2	61.5	61.9	60.0
2015	59.8	59.5	60.2	61.0	61.4	62.0	62.3	62.3	61.9	61.9	63.8	64.0	61.7
Wholesale Trade													
2005	8.3	8.4	8.5	8.4	8.5	8.3	8.5	8.5	8.4	8.6	8.6	8.5	8.5
2006	8.6	8.5	8.5	8.5	8.6	8.5	8.6	8.6	8.7	8.9	9.0	9.0	8.7
2007	9.0	9.2	9.2	9.2	9.2	9.2	9.4	9.4	9.3	9.3	9.3	9.3	9.3
2008	9.2	9.0	8.9	8.8	8.9	9.0	9.0	8.9	8.8	8.7	8.9	8.7	8.9
2009	8.3	8.2	8.2	8.2	8.2	8.0	8.1	8.1	7.9	7.9	7.9	8.0	8.1
2010	8.1	8.0	8.1	8.2	8.3	8.3	8.3	8.4	8.2	8.1	8.1	8.1	8.2
2011	8.0	8.0	8.0	8.1	8.1	8.0	8.1	8.0	7.9	7.9	7.9	7.9	8.0
2012	7.8	7.9	7.9	8.0	8.0	8.0	7.9	7.9	7.8	7.9	7.9	7.9	7.9
2013	7.7	7.7	7.8	7.9	7.9	8.0	8.0	8.0	8.0	8.0	7.9	8.0	7.9
2014	7.8	7.9	7.9	7.9	7.9	8.1	8.1	8.2	8.2	8.2	8.2	8.2	8.1
2015	8.2	8.3	8.3	8.4	8.4	8.4	8.4	8.4	8.4	8.4	8.4	8.4	8.4
Retail Trade													
2005	35.6	35.6	35.9	35.7	36.4	36.5	37.7	37.8	37.8	38.0	38.8	39.0	37.1
2006	37.1	37.5	37.8	37.4	37.9	37.8	38.2	38.1	38.0	37.5	38.9	39.0	37.9
2007	37.2	37.1	37.7	37.4	37.7	37.9	37.8	37.7	37.6	37.5	38.3	38.8	37.7
2008	36.6	36.2	36.5	36.5	36.6	36.7	36.4	36.0	35.7	35.7	36.1	36.2	36.3
2009	34.2	33.5	33.6	33.9	34.1	34.3	34.3	33.9	33.7	33.9	34.8	34.9	34.1
2010	33.4	33.3	33.7	33.7	34.2	34.6	34.5	34.3	33.9	34.6	35.6	35.9	34.3
2011	34.3	34.1	34.4	34.9	35.2	35.3	35.6	35.3	35.2	35.8	36.4	36.6	35.3
2012	34.9	34.9	35.3	35.5	35.8	36.0	36.1	36.1	35.8	36.2	37.6	37.7	36.0
2013	35.6	35.5	35.6	36.1	36.4	36.8	37.0	37.2	37.0	37.7	38.7	39.1	36.9
2014	37.0	36.9	37.3	37.7	38.0	38.5	38.4	38.2	37.9	38.1	39.4	39.8	38.1
2015	37.7	37.5	37.9	38.4	38.8	39.6	39.8	39.9	39.6	39.7	41.6	41.5	39.3
Transportation and Utilities													
2005	11.6	11.4	11.2	11.7	11.8	11.5	11.4	11.4	11.2	11.4	11.2	11.5	11.4
2006	11.0	11.4	11.4	11.1	11.3	11.3	11.2	11.3	11.1	11.3	11.8	12.2	11.4
2007	11.2	11.5	11.7	12.1	12.3	12.3	12.0	12.3	12.2	12.3	12.2	12.1	12.0
2008	12.0	12.2	12.1	12.4	12.4	12.2	12.0	12.4	12.1	13.1	13.0	12.9	12.4
2009	12.1	12.0	11.8	11.6	11.4	11.3	10.8	10.7	10.6	10.4	10.2	10.5	11.1
2010	10.1	10.3	10.6	10.6	10.6	10.9	11.0	11.0	11.3	11.6	11.6	11.9	11.0
2011	11.7	11.8	11.7	11.5	11.5	11.7	11.7	12.0	11.9	12.0	12.0	12.2	11.8
2012	12.6	12.7	12.8	13.0	13.1	13.1	13.1	13.1	13.1	13.3	13.4	13.7	13.1
2013	13.3	13.4	13.5	13.6	13.7	13.7	13.7	13.6	13.6	13.9	13.6	13.9	13.6
2014	13.8	13.7	13.4	13.8	14.0	14.2	13.7	13.8	13.7	13.9	13.9	13.9	13.8
2015	13.9	13.7	14.0	14.2	14.2	14.0	14.1	14.0	13.9	13.8	13.8	14.1	14.0

Employment by Industry: Charleston-North Charleston, SC, 2005–2015—*Continued*

(Numbers in thousands, not seasonally adjusted)

Industry and year	January	February	March	April	May	June	July	August	September	October	November	December	Annual average
Information													
2005...........	5.0	5.0	4.9	5.0	5.1	5.2	5.1	5.0	5.0	5.1	5.1	5.1	5.1
2006...........	5.3	5.4	5.4	5.4	5.4	5.4	5.4	5.4	5.4	5.4	5.5	5.5	5.4
2007...........	5.4	5.5	5.5	5.5	5.5	5.6	5.7	5.7	5.7	5.8	5.8	5.9	5.6
2008...........	5.6	5.6	5.6	5.5	5.6	5.7	5.7	5.7	5.6	5.4	5.4	5.5	5.6
2009...........	5.6	5.4	5.4	5.4	5.3	5.4	5.5	5.2	5.2	5.3	5.1	5.2	5.3
2010...........	5.3	5.3	5.3	5.0	4.9	5.0	4.9	5.0	4.9	4.9	4.9	5.0	5.0
2011...........	5.0	4.9	4.9	5.0	5.0	5.0	5.0	5.0	4.9	4.8	4.8	4.8	4.9
2012...........	4.8	4.9	4.8	4.8	4.8	4.9	5.0	5.0	4.9	5.0	5.1	5.2	4.9
2013...........	5.0	5.0	5.0	5.1	5.0	5.1	5.1	5.0	5.0	5.0	5.0	5.1	5.0
2014...........	5.0	5.0	5.1	5.2	5.2	5.3	5.3	5.2	5.2	5.2	5.4	5.4	5.2
2015...........	5.3	5.3	5.3	5.3	5.3	5.4	5.4	5.4	5.3	5.4	5.3	5.4	5.3
Financial Activities													
2005...........	11.5	11.6	11.6	11.9	12.1	11.9	12.1	12.0	11.9	11.9	11.9	11.8	11.9
2006...........	12.0	12.1	11.8	12.3	12.4	12.5	12.2	12.2	12.1	12.3	11.9	12.2	12.2
2007...........	12.6	12.6	12.7	12.8	12.9	13.1	13.1	13.1	12.9	12.9	12.9	13.0	12.9
2008...........	13.1	13.1	13.1	12.8	12.9	13.0	12.8	12.8	12.7	12.5	12.4	12.5	12.8
2009...........	12.1	12.0	12.0	11.9	11.8	11.9	11.7	11.7	11.5	11.6	11.5	11.5	11.8
2010...........	11.2	11.1	11.2	11.3	11.4	11.5	11.6	11.6	11.4	11.7	11.7	11.7	11.5
2011...........	11.7	11.6	11.7	11.7	11.8	11.8	11.8	11.9	12.0	12.3	12.5	12.5	11.9
2012...........	12.4	12.6	12.5	12.4	12.4	12.6	12.4	12.6	12.5	12.6	12.7	12.9	12.6
2013...........	12.5	12.7	12.7	12.7	12.9	12.8	12.9	13.1	13.0	13.2	13.3	13.3	12.9
2014...........	12.9	13.2	13.1	13.1	13.3	13.3	13.3	13.4	13.5	13.7	13.7	13.9	13.4
2015...........	14.0	14.0	14.1	14.1	14.2	14.3	14.1	14.2	14.1	14.1	14.2	14.2	14.1
Professional and Business Services													
2005...........	34.0	34.4	34.5	36.2	36.0	35.4	35.8	36.0	36.1	36.7	36.8	36.6	35.7
2006...........	35.9	36.2	36.3	37.0	36.8	37.3	38.1	38.7	39.1	39.8	40.4	41.1	38.1
2007...........	41.1	41.5	42.3	41.8	41.9	42.0	41.7	42.1	42.3	42.7	42.3	42.6	42.0
2008...........	42.5	43.3	43.8	43.7	43.8	44.0	42.6	43.1	43.2	42.5	42.5	41.7	43.1
2009...........	40.4	40.1	40.1	40.6	40.8	40.6	39.8	40.2	39.9	40.3	40.7	40.2	40.3
2010...........	39.8	40.2	40.4	41.7	41.8	42.4	41.8	42.2	41.9	42.9	43.1	42.9	41.8
2011...........	42.9	43.4	43.9	44.7	44.8	44.3	44.1	44.6	44.2	44.9	44.9	44.8	44.3
2012...........	44.6	45.6	46.1	46.9	46.8	46.6	45.3	45.8	45.9	45.8	45.7	45.8	45.9
2013...........	45.2	45.9	46.3	46.3	46.3	46.2	45.9	46.3	46.4	47.2	47.4	47.3	46.4
2014...........	46.0	47.4	48.1	48.5	48.7	48.2	48.0	48.2	48.6	48.9	49.1	49.1	48.2
2015...........	47.7	48.6	49.1	49.8	50.2	50.2	49.7	50.3	50.0	50.0	50.0	49.2	49.6
Education and Health Services													
2005...........	28.5	29.2	29.3	29.3	29.2	28.4	28.2	28.5	28.9	29.2	29.3	29.0	28.9
2006...........	28.9	29.4	29.4	30.0	30.1	29.1	29.3	29.6	30.3	29.9	29.9	30.1	29.7
2007...........	29.8	30.2	30.5	30.8	31.0	30.6	30.6	30.8	31.3	31.5	31.6	31.5	30.9
2008...........	31.5	31.8	31.8	32.3	32.5	32.2	32.3	32.2	32.8	32.9	33.0	32.9	32.4
2009...........	32.5	32.7	32.6	32.7	32.7	32.8	32.6	32.9	32.8	33.3	33.3	33.3	32.9
2010...........	33.0	33.1	33.5	33.4	33.4	33.4	33.3	33.5	33.9	34.4	34.7	34.9	33.7
2011...........	34.5	35.1	35.2	35.1	35.0	34.7	34.4	34.5	34.8	34.6	34.7	34.6	34.8
2012...........	34.1	34.6	34.7	34.6	34.7	34.3	34.2	34.4	34.7	35.2	35.3	35.2	34.7
2013...........	34.8	35.2	35.2	35.0	35.1	34.9	35.0	35.3	35.1	35.7	35.9	35.8	35.3
2014...........	35.8	36.0	36.2	36.5	36.6	36.6	36.4	36.7	36.7	37.3	37.4	37.4	36.6
2015...........	37.1	37.4	37.5	37.6	37.9	37.3	37.7	38.1	38.2	38.5	39.1	39.2	38.0
Leisure and Hospitality													
2005...........	31.7	32.0	33.4	35.0	35.9	36.7	36.4	35.9	34.5	34.1	34.2	32.7	34.4
2006...........	32.5	33.2	33.8	35.5	36.5	36.6	37.0	36.6	35.3	34.6	34.3	33.6	35.0
2007...........	33.5	33.7	34.8	37.1	38.4	39.1	39.0	38.8	37.6	37.5	36.9	36.2	36.9
2008...........	35.0	35.4	36.2	38.4	39.6	39.6	38.8	38.3	37.1	36.3	35.9	35.3	37.2
2009...........	33.8	34.2	35.4	36.4	37.6	37.7	37.0	36.5	35.4	34.8	34.3	33.5	35.6
2010...........	32.3	32.8	34.0	35.7	37.1	37.7	37.1	36.7	35.9	35.7	35.3	34.6	35.4
2011...........	33.4	33.7	35.1	37.2	38.3	38.9	38.2	37.9	36.8	36.6	36.4	36.2	36.6
2012...........	35.2	35.7	37.0	39.0	39.6	40.3	39.9	40.0	38.7	38.3	37.8	37.3	38.2
2013...........	36.3	36.6	37.7	39.7	40.8	41.8	41.4	41.5	40.0	39.8	39.7	39.1	39.5
2014...........	38.2	38.3	39.8	42.3	43.5	43.9	43.6	43.5	42.0	41.8	41.5	41.0	41.6
2015...........	40.2	40.7	42.5	44.1	45.5	45.7	45.9	45.6	44.0	44.3	43.8	43.0	43.8

Employment by Industry: Charleston-North Charleston, SC, 2005–2015—*Continued*

(Numbers in thousands, not seasonally adjusted)

Industry and year	January	February	March	April	May	June	July	August	September	October	November	December	Annual average
Other Services													
2005	11.1	11.5	11.5	11.5	11.6	11.7	12.0	12.2	12.0	11.5	11.6	11.5	11.6
2006	11.8	11.9	11.7	12.0	12.0	11.9	11.5	11.5	11.8	11.6	11.6	11.8	11.8
2007	11.7	12.0	12.2	12.0	11.9	11.9	11.6	11.5	11.3	11.2	11.1	11.1	11.6
2008	11.2	11.3	11.4	11.5	11.5	11.7	11.7	11.6	11.4	11.3	11.3	11.2	11.4
2009	10.7	10.7	10.8	10.9	11.0	11.1	11.0	10.9	10.9	10.9	10.7	10.7	10.9
2010	10.5	10.5	10.6	10.6	10.6	10.8	10.7	10.5	10.4	10.4	10.4	10.3	10.5
2011	10.3	10.4	10.4	10.6	10.8	11.1	11.3	11.2	11.3	11.3	11.5	11.6	11.0
2012	11.7	11.9	12.1	12.5	12.7	12.9	13.0	12.9	12.7	12.7	12.8	12.8	12.6
2013	12.7	12.7	13.0	13.0	13.0	13.3	13.3	13.2	13.1	13.0	13.0	13.0	13.0
2014	13.0	13.0	13.1	13.3	13.5	13.7	13.8	13.7	13.6	13.6	13.6	13.6	13.5
2015	13.5	13.5	13.6	13.7	13.9	14.1	14.1	14.0	13.8	13.7	13.8	13.8	13.8
Government													
2005	55.2	56.2	56.5	56.6	56.8	55.8	54.1	55.7	56.5	56.5	56.7	56.8	56.1
2006	55.8	56.4	56.6	56.8	57.0	54.9	53.4	55.3	56.8	57.3	57.5	57.6	56.3
2007	57.3	57.7	57.8	58.2	58.2	58.0	56.4	56.5	58.7	59.2	59.5	59.5	58.1
2008	59.1	59.5	59.9	60.4	60.7	60.3	58.7	59.1	60.7	61.0	61.4	61.3	60.2
2009	60.0	60.3	60.4	60.3	60.1	59.7	58.0	58.2	60.1	60.6	60.7	60.6	59.9
2010	60.3	60.7	61.1	61.6	63.2	60.9	59.9	59.8	60.9	61.7	62.0	61.8	61.2
2011	61.1	61.4	61.5	62.0	62.0	61.1	59.9	59.3	61.3	61.3	61.5	61.6	61.2
2012	61.1	61.6	62.0	62.4	62.4	61.9	60.8	61.3	62.9	63.1	65.3	63.5	62.4
2013	62.3	62.8	63.0	63.5	63.1	62.6	61.4	61.3	63.0	62.4	62.8	62.6	62.6
2014	61.6	62.4	62.5	63.5	63.5	62.0	60.5	61.7	63.3	63.8	64.2	64.0	62.8
2015	62.8	63.8	64.1	64.2	64.1	63.0	62.5	62.9	64.5	65.1	65.5	65.3	64.0

APPENDIX

SEVENTY-FIVE LARGEST MSAs AND COMPONENTS
(as defined February 2013)

Core based statistical area	State/ County FIPS code	Title and Geographic Components
35620		**New York-Newark-Jersey City, NY-NJ-PA Metro area**
35620		Dutchess County-Putnam County, NY Metro Div 20524
	36027	Dutchess County, NY
	36079	Putnam County, NY
35620		Nassau County-Suffolk County, NY Metro Div 35004
	36059	Nassau County, NY
	36103	Suffolk County, NY
35620		Newark, NJ-PA Metro Div 35084
	34013	Essex County, NJ
	34019	Hunterdon County, NJ
	34027	Morris County, NJ
	34035	Somerset County, NJ
	34037	Sussex County, NJ
	34039	Union County, NJ
	42103	Pike County, PA
35620		New York-Jersey City-White Plains, NY-NJ Metro Div 35614
	34003	Bergen County, NJ
	34017	Hudson County, NJ
	34023	Middlesex County, NJ
	34025	Monmouth County, NJ
	34029	Ocean County, NJ
	34031	Passaic County, NJ
	36005	Bronx County, NY
	36047	Kings County, NY
	36061	New York County, NY
	36071	Orange County, NY
	36081	Queens County, NY
	36085	Richmond County, NY
	36087	Rockland County, NY
	36119	Westchester County, NY
31080		**Los Angeles-Long Beach-Anaheim, CA Metro area**
31080		Anaheim-Santa Ana-Irvine, CA Metro Div 11244
	06059	Orange County, CA
31080		Los Angeles-Long Beach-Glendale, CA Metro Div 31084
	06037	Los Angeles County, CA
16980		**Chicago-Naperville-Elgin, IL-IN-WI Metro area**
16980		Chicago-Naperville-Arlington Heights, IL Metro Div 16974
	17031	Cook County, IL
	17043	DuPage County, IL
	17063	Grundy County, IL
	17093	Kendall County, IL
	17111	McHenry County, IL
	17197	Will County, IL
16980		Elgin, IL Metro Div 20994
	17037	DeKalb County, IL
	17089	Kane County, IL
16980		Gary, IN Metro Div 23844
	18073	Jasper County, IN
	18089	Lake County, IN
	18111	Newton County, IN
	18127	Porter County, IN
16980		Lake County-Kenosha County, IL-WI Metro Div 29404
	17097	Lake County, IL
	55059	Kenosha County, WI
19100		**Dallas-Fort Worth-Arlington, TX Metro area**
19100		Dallas-Plano-Irving, TX Metro Div 19124
	48085	Collin County, TX
	48113	Dallas County, TX
	48121	Denton County, TX
	48139	Ellis County, TX

Core based statistical area	State/ County FIPS code	Title and Geographic Components
	48231	Hunt County, TX
	48257	Kaufman County, TX
	48397	Rockwall County, TX
19100		Fort Worth-Arlington, TX Metro Div 23104
	48221	Hood County, TX
	48251	Johnson County, TX
	48367	Parker County, TX
	48425	Somervell County, TX
	48439	Tarrant County, TX
	48497	Wise County, TX
26420		**Houston-The Woodlands-Sugar Land, TX Metro area**
	48015	Austin County, TX
	48039	Brazoria County, TX
	48071	Chambers County, TX
	48157	Fort Bend County, TX
	48167	Galveston County, TX
	48201	Harris County, TX
	48291	Liberty County, TX
	48339	Montgomery County, TX
	48473	Waller County, TX
47900		**Washington-Arlington-Alexandria, DC-VA-MD-WV Metro area**
47900		Silver Spring-Frederick-Rockville, MD Metro Div 43524
	24021	Frederick County, MD
	24031	Montgomery County, MD
47900		Washington-Arlington-Alexandria, DC-VA-MD-WV Metro Div 47894
	11001	District of Columbia, DC
	24009	Calvert County, MD
	24017	Charles County, MD
	24033	Prince George's County, MD
	51013	Arlington County, VA
	51043	Clarke County, VA
	51047	Culpeper County, VA
	51059	Fairfax County, VA
	51061	Fauquier County, VA
	51107	Loudoun County, VA
	51153	Prince William County, VA
	51157	Rappahannock County, VA
	51177	Spotsylvania County, VA
	51179	Stafford County, VA
	51187	Warren County, VA
	51510	Alexandria city, VA
	51600	Fairfax city, VA
	51610	Falls Church city, VA
	51630	Fredericksburg city, VA
	51683	Manassas city, VA
	51685	Manassas Park city, VA
	54037	Jefferson County, WV
37980		**Philadelphia-Camden-Wilmington, PA-NJ-DE-MD Metro area**
37980		Camden, NJ Metro Div 15804
	34005	Burlington County, NJ
	34007	Camden County, NJ
	34015	Gloucester County, NJ
37980		Montgomery County-Bucks County-Chester County, PA Metro Div 33874
	42017	Bucks County, PA
	42029	Chester County, PA
	42091	Montgomery County, PA
37980		Philadelphia, PA Metro Div 37964

Core based statistical area	State/ County FIPS code	Title and Geographic Components	Core based statistical area	State/ County FIPS code	Title and Geographic Components
	42045	Delaware County, PA		04021	Pinal County, AZ
	42101	Philadelphia County, PA			
37980		Wilmington, DE-MD-NJ Metro Div 48864	40140		**Riverside-San Bernardino-Ontario, CA**
	10003	New Castle County, Delaware		06065	Riverside County, CA
	24015	Cecil County, MD		06071	San Bernardino County, CA
	34033	Salem County, NJ			
			19820		**Detroit-Warren-Dearborn, MI Metro area**
33100		**Miami-Fort Lauderdale-West Palm Beach, FL Metro area**	19820		Detroit-Dearborn-Livonia, MI Metro Div 19804
33100		Fort Lauderdale-Pompano Beach-Deerfield Beach, FL Metro Div 22744		26163	Wayne County, MI
	12011	Broward County, FL	19820		Warren-Troy-Farmington Hills, MI Metro Div 47664
33100		Miami-Miami Beach-Kendall, FL Metro Div 33124		26087	Lapeer County, MI
	12086	Miami-Dade County, FL		26093	Livingston County, MI
33100		West Palm Beach-Boca Raton-Delray Beach, FL Metro Div 48424		26099	Macomb County, MI
	12099	Palm Beach County, FL		26125	Oakland County, MI
				26147	St. Clair County, MI
12060		**Atlanta-Sandy Springs-Roswell, GA Metro area**			
	13013	Barrow County, GA	42660		**Seattle-Tacoma-Bellevue, WA Metro area**
	13015	Bartow County, GA	42660		Seattle-Bellevue-Everett, WA Metro Div 42644
	13035	Butts County, GA		53033	King County, WA
	13045	Carroll County, GA		53061	Snohomish County, WA
	13057	Cherokee County, GA	42660		Tacoma-Lakewood, WA Metro Div 45104
	13063	Clayton County, GA		53053	Pierce County, WA
	13067	Cobb County, GA			
	13077	Coweta County, GA	33460		**Minneapolis-St. Paul-Bloomington, MN Metro area**
	13085	Dawson County, GA		27003	Anoka County, MN
	13089	DeKalb County, GA		27019	Carver County, MN
	13097	Douglas County, GA		27025	Chisago County, MN
	13113	Fayette County, GA		27037	Dakota County, MN
	13117	Forsyth County, GA		27053	Hennepin County, MN
	13121	Fulton County, GA		27059	Isanti County, MN
	13135	Gwinnett County, GA		27079	Le Sueur County, MN
	13143	Haralson County, GA		27095	Mille Lacs County, MN
	13149	Heard County, GA		27123	Ramsey County, MN
	13151	Henry County, GA		27139	Scott County, MN
	13159	Jasper County, GA		27141	Sherburne County, MN
	13171	Lamar County, GA		27143	Sibley County, MN
	13199	Meriwether County, GA		27163	Washington County, MN
	13211	Morgan County, GA		27171	Wright County, MN
	13217	Newton County, GA		55093	Pierce County, WI
	13223	Paulding County, GA		55109	St. Croix County, WI
	13227	Pickens County, GA			
	13231	Pike County, GA	41740		**San Diego-Carlsbad, CA Metro area**
	13247	Rockdale County, GA		06073	San Diego County, CA
	13255	Spalding County, GA			
	13297	Walton County, GA	45300		**Tampa-St. Petersburg-Clearwater, FL Metro area**
				12053	Hernando County, FL
14460		**Boston-Cambridge Newton, MA-NH Metro area**		12057	Hillsborough County, FL
14460		Boston, MA Metro Div 14454		12101	Pasco County, FL
	25021	Norfolk County, MA		12103	Pinellas County, FL
	25023	Plymouth County, MA			
	25025	Suffolk County, MA	19740		**Denver-Aurora-Lakewood, CO Metro area**
14460		Cambridge-Newton-Framingham, MA Metro Div 15764		08001	Adams County, CO
	25009	Essex County, MA		08005	Arapahoe County, CO
	25017	Middlesex County, MA		08014	Broomfield County, CO
14460		Rockingham County-Strafford County-NH Metro Div 40484		08019	Clear Creek County, CO
	33015	Rockingham County, NH		08031	Denver County, CO
	33017	Strafford County, NH		08035	Douglas County, CO
				08039	Elbert County, CO
41860		**San Francisco-Oakland-Hayward, CA Metro area**		08047	Gilpin County, CO
41860		Oakland-Hayward-Berkeley, CA Metro Div 36084		08059	Jefferson County, CO
	06001	Alameda County, CA		08093	Park County, CO
	06013	Contra Costa County, CA			
41860		San Francisco-Redwood City-South San Francisco, CA Metro Div 41884	41180		**St. Louis, MO-IL Metro area**
	06075	San Francisco County, CA		17005	Bond County, IL
	06081	San Mateo County, CA		17013	Calhoun County, IL
41860		San Rafael, CA Metropolitan Div 42034		17027	Clinton County, IL
	06041	Marin County, CA		17083	Jersey County, IL
				17117	Macoupin County, IL
38060		**Phoenix-Mesa-Scottsdale, AZ Metro area**		17119	Madison County, IL
	04013	Maricopa County, AZ		17133	Monroe County, IL
				17163	St. Clair County, IL
				29071	Franklin County, MO
				29099	Jefferson County, MO

Core based statistical area	State/County FIPS code	Title and Geographic Components	Core based statistical area	State/County FIPS code	Title and Geographic Components
	29113	Lincoln County, MO		21037	Campbell County, KY
	29183	St. Charles County, MO		21077	Gallatin County, KY
	29189	St. Louis County, MO		21081	Grant County, KY
	29219	Warren County, MO		21117	Kenton County, KY
	29510	St. Louis city, MO		21191	Pendleton County, KY
				39015	Brown County, OH
12580		**Baltimore-Columbia-Towson, MD Metro area**		39017	Butler County, OH
	24003	Anne Arundel County, MD		39025	Clermont County, OH
	24005	Baltimore County, MD		39061	Hamilton County, OH
	24013	Carroll County, MD		39165	Warren County, OH
	24025	Harford County, MD			
	24027	Howard County, MD	29820		**Las Vegas-Henderson-Paradise, NV Metro area**
	24035	Queen Anne's County, MD		32003	Clark County, NV
	24510	Baltimore city, MD			
			28140		**Kansas City, MO-KS Metro area**
16740		**Charlotte-Concord-Gastonia, NC-SC Metro area**		20091	Johnson County, KS
	37025	Cabarrus County, NC		20103	Leavenworth County, KS
	37071	Gaston County, NC		20107	Linn County, KS
	37097	Iredell County, NC		20121	Miami County, KS
	37109	Lincoln County, NC		20209	Wyandotte County, KS
	37119	Mecklenburg County, NC		29013	Bates County, MO
	37159	Rowan County, NC		29025	Caldwell County, MO
	37179	Union County, NC		29037	Cass County, MO
	45023	Chester County, SC		29047	Clay County, MO
	45057	Lancaster County, SC		29049	Clinton County, MO
	45091	York County, SC		29095	Jackson County, MO
				29107	Lafayette County, MO
38900		**Portland-Vancouver-Hillsboro, OR-WA Metro area**		29165	Platte County, MO
	41005	Clackamas County, OR		29177	Ray County, MO
	41009	Columbia County, OR			
	41051	Multnomah County, OR			
	41067	Washington County, OR	17460		**Cleveland-Elyria, OH Metro area**
	41071	Yamhill County, OR		39035	Cuyahoga County, OH
	53011	Clark County, WA		39055	Geauga County, OH
	53059	Skamania County, WA		39085	Lake County, OH
				39093	Lorain County, OH
36740		**Orlando-Kissimmee-Sanford, FL Metro**		39103	Medina County, OH
	12069	Lake County, FL			
	12095	Orange County, FL	18140		**Columbus, OH Metro area**
	12097	Osceola County, FL		39041	Delaware County, OH
	12117	Seminole County, FL		39045	Fairfield County, OH
				39049	Franklin County, OH
41700		**San Antonio-New Braunfels, TX Metro**		39073	Hocking County, OH
	48013	Atascosa County, TX		39089	Licking County, OH
	48019	Bandera County, TX		39097	Madison County, OH
	48029	Bexar County, TX		39117	Morrow County, OH
	48091	Comal County, TX		39127	Perry County, OH
	48187	Guadalupe County, TX		39129	Pickaway County, OH
	48259	Kendall County, TX		39159	Union County, OH
	48325	Medina County, TX			
	48493	Wilson County, TX	12420		**Austin-Round Rock, TX Metro area**
				48021	Bastrop County, TX
38300		**Pittsburgh, PA Metro area**		48055	Caldwell County, TX
	42003	Allegheny County, PA		48209	Hays County, TX
	42005	Armstrong County, PA		48453	Travis County, TX
	42007	Beaver County, PA		48491	Williamson County, TX
	42019	Butler County, PA			
	42051	Fayette County, PA	26900		**Indianapolis-Carmel-Anderson, IN Metro area**
	42125	Washington County, PA		18011	Boone County, IN
	42129	Westmoreland County, PA		18013	Brown County, IN
				18057	Hamilton County, IN
40900		**Sacramento**		18059	Hancock County, IN
	06017	El Dorado County, CA		18063	Hendricks County, IN
	06061	Placer County, CA		18081	Johnson County, IN
	06067	Sacramento County, CA		18095	Madison County, IN
	06113	Yolo County, CA		18097	Marion County, IN
				18109	Morgan County, IN
17140		**Cincinnati, OH-KY-IN Metro area**		18133	Putnam County, IN
	18029	Dearborn County, IN		18145	Shelby County, IN
	18115	Ohio County, IN			
	18161	Union County, IN	41940		**San Jose-Sunnyvale-Santa Clara, CA Metro area**
	21015	Boone County, KY		06069	San Benito County, CA
	21023	Bracken County, KY		06085	Santa Clara County, CA

Core based statistical area	State/ County FIPS code	Title and Geographic Components
34980		Nashville-Davidson–Murfreesboro–Franklin, TN Metro area
	47015	Cannon County, TN
	47021	Cheatham County, TN
	47037	Davidson County, TN
	47043	Dickson County, TN
	47081	Hickman County, TN
	47111	Macon County, TN
	47119	Maury County, TN
	47147	Robertson County, TN
	47149	Rutherford County, TN
	47159	Smith County, TN
	47165	Sumner County, TN
	47169	Trousdale County, TN
	47187	Williamson County, TN
	47189	Wilson County, TN
47260		Virginia Beach-Norfolk-Newport News, VA-NC Metro area
	37053	Currituck County, NC
	37073	Gates County, NC
	51073	Gloucester County, VA
	51093	Isle of Wight County, VA
	51095	James City County, VA
	51115	Mathews County, VA
	51199	York County, VA
	51550	Chesapeake city, VA
	51650	Hampton city, VA
	51700	Newport News city, VA
	51710	Norfolk city, VA
	51735	Poquoson city, VA
	51740	Portsmouth city, VA
	51800	Suffolk city, VA
	51810	Virginia Beach city, VA
	51830	Williamsburg city, VA
39300		Providence-Warwick, RI-MA Metro area
	25005	Bristol County, MA
	44001	Bristol County, RI
	44003	Kent County, RI
	44005	Newport County, RI
	44007	Providence County, RI
	44009	Washington County, RI
33340		Milwaukee-Waukesha-West Allis, WI Metro area
	55079	Milwaukee County, WI
	55089	Ozaukee County, WI
	55131	Washington County, WI
	55133	Waukesha County, WI
27260		Jacksonville, FL Metro area
	12003	Baker County, FL
	12019	Clay County, FL
	12031	Duval County, FL
	12089	Nassau County, FL
	12109	St. Johns County, FL
36420		Oklahoma City, OK Metro area
	40017	Canadian County, OK
	40027	Cleveland County, OK
	40051	Grady County, OK
	40081	Lincoln County, OK
	40083	Logan County, OK
	40087	McClain County, OK
	40109	Oklahoma County, OK
32820		Memphis, TN-MS-AR Metro area
	05035	Crittenden County, AR
	28009	Benton County, MS
	28033	DeSoto County, MS
	28093	Marshall County, MS
	28137	Tate County, MS
	28143	Tunica County, MS
	47047	Fayette County, TN
	47157	Shelby County, TN
	47167	Tipton County, TN
31140		Louisville/Jefferson County, KY-IN Metro area
	18019	Clark County, IN
	18043	Floyd County, IN
	18061	Harrison County, IN
	18143	Scott County, IN
	18175	Washington County, IN
	21029	Bullitt County, KY
	21103	Henry County, KY
	21111	Jefferson County, KY
	21185	Oldham County, KY
	21211	Shelby County, KY
	21215	Spencer County, KY
	21223	Trimble County, KY
39580		Raleigh, NC Metro area
	37069	Franklin County, NC
	37101	Johnston County, NC
	37183	Wake County, NC
40060		Richmond, VA Metro area
	51007	Amelia County, VA
	51033	Caroline County, VA
	51036	Charles City County, VA
	51041	Chesterfield County, VA
	51053	Dinwiddie County, VA
	51075	Goochland County, VA
	51085	Hanover County, VA
	51087	Henrico County, VA
	51101	King William County, VA
	51127	New Kent County, VA
	51145	Powhatan County, VA
	51149	Prince George County, VA
	51183	Sussex County, VA
	51570	Colonial Heights city, VA
	51670	Hopewell city, VA
	51730	Petersburg city, VA
	51760	Richmond city, VA
35380		New Orleans-Metairie, LA Metro area
	22051	Jefferson Parish, LA
	22071	Orleans Parish, LA
	22075	Plaquemines Parish, LA
	22087	St. Bernard Parish, LA
	22089	St. Charles Parish, LA
	22093	St. James Parish, LA
	22095	St. John the Baptist Parish, LA
	22103	St. Tammany Parish, LA
25540		Hartford-West Hartford-East Hartford, CT Metro area
	09003	Hartford County, CT
	09007	Middlesex County, CT
	09013	Tolland County, CT
41620		Salt Lake City, UT Metro area
	49035	Salt Lake County, UT
	49045	Tooele County, UT
13820		Birmingham-Hoover, AL Metro area
	01007	Bibb County, AL
	01009	Blount County, AL
	01021	Chilton County, AL
	01073	Jefferson County, AL
	01115	St. Clair County, AL
	01117	Shelby County, AL
	01127	Walker County, AL
15380		Buffalo-Cheektowaga-Niagara Falls, NY Metro area
	36029	Erie County, NY
	36063	Niagara County, NY

Core based statistical area	State/ County FIPS code	Title and Geographic Components	Core based statistical area	State/ County FIPS code	Title and Geographic Components
				45059	Laurens County, SC
40380		**Rochester, NY Metro area**		45077	Pickens County, SC
	36051	Livingston County, NY			
	36055	Monroe County, NY	28940		**Knoxville, TN Metro area**
	36069	Ontario County, NY		47001	Anderson County, TN
	36073	Orleans County, NY		47009	Blount County, TN
	36117	Wayne County, NY		47013	Campbell County, TN
	36123	Yates County, NY		47057	Grainger County, TN
				47093	Knox County, TN
24340		**Grand Rapids-Wyoming, MI Metro area**		47105	Loudon County, TN
	26015	Barry County, MI		47129	Morgan County, TN
	26081	Kent County, MI		47145	Roane County, TN
	26117	Montcalm County, MI		47173	Union County, TN
	26139	Ottawa County, MI			
			35300		**New Haven-Milford, CT Metro area**
46060		**Tucson, AZ Metro area**		09009	New Haven County, CT
	04019	Pima County, AZ			
			37100		**Oxnard-Thousand Oaks-Ventura, CA Metro area**
46520		**Urban Honolulu, HI Metro area**		06111	Ventura County, CA
	15003	Honolulu County, HI			
			32580		**McAllen-Edinburg-Mission, TX Metro area**
46140		**Tulsa, OK Metro area**		48215	Hidalgo County, TX
	40037	Creek County, OK			
	40111	Okmulgee County, OK	21340		**El Paso, TX Metro area**
	40113	Osage County, OK		48141	El Paso County, TX
	40117	Pawnee County, OK		48229	Hudspeth County, TX
	40131	Rogers County, OK			
	40143	Tulsa County, OK	10900		**Allentown-Bethlehem-Easton, PA-NJ Metro area**
	40145	Wagoner County, OK		34041	Warren County, NJ
				42025	Carbon County, PA
23420		**Fresno, CA Metro area**		42077	Lehigh County, PA
	06019	Fresno County, CA		42095	Northampton County, PA
14860		**Bridgeport-Stamford-Norwalk, CT Metro area**	12940		**Baton Rouge, LA Metro area**
	09001	Fairfield County, CT		22005	Ascension Parish, LA
				22033	East Baton Rouge Parish, LA
49340		**Worcester, MA-CT Metro area**		22037	East Feliciana Parish, LA
	09015	Windham County, CT		22047	Iberville Parish, LA
	25027	Worcester County, MA		22063	Livingston Parish, LA
				22077	Pointe Coupee Parish, LA
36540		**Omaha-Council Bluffs, NE-IA Metro area**		22091	St. Helena Parish, LA
	19085	Harrison County, IA		22121	West Baton Rouge Parish, LA
	19129	Mills County, IA		22125	West Feliciana Parish, LA
	19155	Pottawattamie County, IA			
	31025	Cass County, NE	17900		**Columbia, SC Metro area**
	31055	Douglas County, NE		45017	Calhoun County, SC
	31153	Sarpy County, NE		45039	Fairfield County, SC
	31155	Saunders County, NE		45055	Kershaw County, SC
	31177	Washington County, NE		45063	Lexington County, SC
				45079	Richland County, SC
10740		**Albuquerque, NM Metro area**		45081	Saluda County, SC
	35001	Bernalillo County, NM			
	35043	Sandoval County, NM	19380		**Dayton, OH Metro area**
	35057	Torrance County, NM		39057	Greene County, OH
	35061	Valencia County, NM		39109	Miami County, OH
				39113	Montgomery County, OH
12540		**Bakersfield, CA Metro area**			
	06029	Kern County, CA	35840		**North Port-Sarasota-Bradenton, FL Metro area**
				12081	Manatee County, FL
				12115	Sarasota County, FL
10580		**Albany-Schenectady-Troy, NY Metro area**			
	36001	Albany County, NY	24660		**Greensboro-High Point, NC Metro area**
	36083	Rensselaer County, NY		37081	Guilford County, NC
	36091	Saratoga County, NY		37151	Randolph County, NC
	36093	Schenectady County, NY		37157	Rockingham County, NC
	36095	Schoharie County, NY			
			16700		**Charleston-North Charleston, SC Metro area**
24860		**Greenville-Anderson-Mauldin, SC Metro area**		45015	Berkeley County, SC
	45007	Anderson County, SC		45019	Charleston County, SC
	45045	Greenville County, SC		45035	Dorchester County, SC